Literature & Composition
Reading · Writing · Thinking

Carol Jago
Santa Monica High School, California

Renée H. Shea
Bowie State University, Maryland

Lawrence Scanlon
Brewster High School, New York

Robin Dissin Aufses
Lycée Français de New York

Bedford/St. Martin's　　　　　　　　Boston · New York

For Bedford/St. Martin's

Developmental Editor: Nathan Odell
Senior Production Editor: Bill Imbornoni
Production Supervisor: Jennifer Peterson
Marketing Manager: Daniel McDonough
Art Director: Lucy Krikorian
Text Design: Linda M. Robertson
Copy Editor: Jamie Thaman
Indexer: Kirsten Kite
Photo Research: Helane Prottas
Cover Design: Donna Dennison
Cover Art: The Phillips Collection, Washington, D.C.
Composition: Glyph International
Printing and Binding: Worldcolor/Taunton

President: Joan E. Feinberg
Editorial Director: Denise B. Wydra
Editor in Chief: Karen S. Henry
Director of Development: Erica T. Appel
Director of Marketing: Karen R. Soeltz
Director of Editing, Design, and Production: Susan W. Brown
Assistant Director of Editing, Design, and Production: Elise S. Kaiser
Managing Editor: Shuli Traub

Library of Congress Control Number: 2010925397

Manufactured in the United States of America.

7   15   14   13

For information, write: Bedford/St. Martin's, 75 Arlington Street, Boston, MA 02116
(617-399-4000)

ISBN-10: 0-312-38806-3
ISBN-13: 978-0-312-38806-5

Acknowledgments
Acknowledgments and copyrights appear at the back of the book on pages 1510–1517, which constitute an extension of the copyright page.

To Michael and James Jago

Bertha Vogelsang Bahn

Kate and Michael Aufses

Alison, Lindsay, Maura, & Kaitlin, and to Mary-Grace

Regency Era 1811-1820
Romantic Era 1800-1850
Victorian 1837-1901

Medieval 500-1500
Renaissance 1500-1670

Enlightenment 1700-1800
Romanticism 1798-1870 Ltranscendentalism 1830-1860
Victorian 1937-1901
Realism 1820-1920
Naturalism 1870-1920
Existentialism 1850-Today
Modernism 1910-1965
Beat Generation 1945-1965
Post-Modernism 1965-Today

About the Authors

Carol Jago taught AP Literature and was department chair at Santa Monica High School for thirty-two years. She has served on the AP Literature Development Committee and as a content advisor on AP Central. She is the author of many books, including *With Rigor for All: Teaching the Classics to Contemporary Students; Beyond Standards: Excellence in the High School English Classroom;* and four titles in the NCTE High School Literature series. In 2010, Carol is the president of NCTE and an advisor for the Common Core State Standards Initiative.

Renée H. Shea is professor of English and Modern Languages at Bowie State University and former Director of Composition. She is coauthor of *The Language of Composition: Reading • Writing • Rhetoric* and two titles in the NCTE High School Literature series on Amy Tan and Zora Neale Hurston. She has been a reader and question leader for both AP Literature and Language readings.

Lawrence Scanlon taught at Brewster High School for more than thirty years. Over the last fifteen years he has been a reader and question leader for the AP Language exam. As a College Board consultant in the U.S. and abroad, he has conducted AP workshops in both Language and Literature, as well as serving on the AP Language Development Committee. Larry is coauthor of *The Language of Composition: Reading • Writing • Rhetoric* and has published articles for the College Board and elsewhere on composition and curriculum.

Robin Dissin Aufses is director of English Studies at Lycée Français de New York. She is coauthor of *The Language of Composition: Reading • Writing • Rhetoric.* Robin also has published articles for the College Board on the novelist Chang Rae Lee and the novel *All the King's Men.*

Preface

Why read literature? To many of us, that question seems as strange as asking "why breathe?" Literature has been part of our life, family, school, and community for as long as we can remember. Of course, there are those who argue that what today's students need is preparation for the "real world," but in the push for practical university and workplace preparedness we sometimes overlook the importance of educating students' imaginations. Literature offers windows to worlds outside students' experience as well as mirrors onto the world they already know. Literature also prepares students for the personal challenges and moral dilemmas they are likely to face. How better to reflect on the demands of contemporary life than to study William Wordsworth's "The World Is Too Much with Us" alongside Nathalie Handal's "Caribe in Nueva York"? And does not the proffered wisdom of William Shakespeare, Emily Dickinson, Seamus Heaney, and Rita Dove provide important preparation for surviving and thriving in this complex world?

Literary analysis is an intellectual discipline that hones students' thinking by requiring them to probe a text deeply and analyze the means that writers employ to achieve their effects. Along with preparing students for the rigors of an Advanced Placement* exam, learning how to analyze text and articulate a perspective prepares students for life, both in academia and in the workplace. This preparation and exploration are what we hope to achieve in *Literature & Composition* by specifically targeting the skills and habits of mind that are the keys to success in an Advanced Placement Literature course.

Features of the Book

The opening chapters introduce strategies and scaffolding that guide students toward deep reading of difficult texts while fostering an understanding of key literary terms and analytical techniques.

We understand that high school teachers are in the classroom every single day, and with that in mind we designed these opening chapters to be highly instructional and activity-oriented.

---

*AP and Advanced Placement Program are registered trademarks of the College Entrance Examination Board, which was not involved in the publication of and does not endorse this product.

- Chapter 1, "Thinking about Literature," introduces the study of literature and the approaches and habits of mind that lead to both insightful analysis and enjoyment.
- Chapter 2, "Close Reading: Analyzing Poetry and Passages of Fiction," introduces students to close reading strategies that reveal how the elements of style create meaning in fiction and poetry. Students are also introduced to the process of writing a close analysis, and a comparison and contrast of two poems.
- Chapter 3, "The Big Picture: Analyzing Fiction and Drama," teaches students to analyze the major elements of fiction and drama and then discuss them thoughtfully in an interpretive essay.
- Chapter 4, "Entering the Conversation," guides students through the process of using multiple texts to write about literary, cultural, and historical issues.

These approaches to reading and writing are revisited repeatedly in the subsequent thematic chapters through the discussion and close reading questions that follow each piece of literature, as well as in the Conversation, Student Writing, and Writer's Craft sections at the end of each thematic chapter.

The literature in this book is organized thematically to foster classroom conversation and promote connections between and among texts.

The themes in this book—Home and Family, Identity and Culture, Love and Relationships, Conformity and Rebellion, Art and the Artist, Tradition and Progress, and War and Peace—are those our students have found engaging, and they can easily be adapted for use with longer works of literature. We know from our own experience, as well as from research such as the National Endowment for the Humanities "Reading at Risk" report, that many students today are not reading poetry, fiction, and drama with the same enthusiasm as previous generations; however, students remain interested in big questions—social, political, economic, aesthetic, and literary. The thematic arrangement of this book offers them the opportunity to consider such questions through the eyes of William Shakespeare and Naomi Shihab Nye, Homer and Walt Whitman, Franz Kafka and Gwendolyn Brooks, whose literary texts offer compelling perspectives on complex human issues. As students grapple with these issues, they read the literature closely and even reread one text in light of another.

Each thematic chapter includes a wide variety of classic and contemporary fiction, poetry, drama, nonfiction, and visual texts that are rich, rigorous, and appealing to sixteen- to eighteen-year-olds.

A Classic Text and a Modern Text of significant literary merit begin and anchor each thematic chapter. These works invite students to delve deeply into the theme, forming a foundation for interpreting the stories and poems in the rest of the chapter. The Classic Texts challenge students to read literature from an earlier time, written for a very different audience, with syntax and vocabulary that may be unfamiliar. These Classic Texts, which include such works as *Heart of Darkness*, *Hamlet*, and *The Importance of Being Earnest*, enlarge students' background knowledge by offering windows into other times and other worlds. The Modern Texts range from selections written by late twentieth-century writers, such as James Baldwin and Flannery O'Connor, to pieces written by celebrated contemporary authors such as Edwidge Danticat and Jhumpa Lahiri.

The Classic and Modern Texts are followed by a collection of short stories and poems that span the ages, drawing from diverse authors who offer varying interpretations of the chapter's theme. Bridging the old and new emphasizes that many questions and issues — about the nature of war, or the role of the artist, for example — have captivated and puzzled humanity through the ages and across cultures. Contemporary literary voices such as Billy Collins, Sandra Cisneros, and Sherman Alexie are living proof that these issues continue to be vital.

Probing questions after each selection guide students' reading and scaffold their emerging interpretation of the works.

The Classic and Modern Texts are followed by these types of questions:

- **Questions for Discussion** invite students to investigate the text, probing the work for meaning, and direct students' attention to important ideas in the story, poem, or play.
- **Questions on Style and Structure** get students to focus on the technical and artistic aspects of the work. Responding to these questions will help students begin to analyze the tools writers employ to achieve an effect and prepare them for the kinds of essay and multiple-choice questions they will face on exams.
- **Suggestions for Writing** offer students multiple opportunities to use writing to explore their developing understanding of a text. In every set of writing suggestions, students are offered one or more questions resembling those on the AP exam, and in some cases students are asked to try their hand at the techniques the author has used.

Other selections in the book are accompanied by **Exploring the Text** questions that call for close careful reading and ask students to discuss and interpret the work. These questions allow students to practice what they have learned in the opening chapters and to broaden their experience of literature. **Suggestions for Writing** at the end of each chapter are prompts for longer writing projects. Most require the use of multiple literary sources — an important skill in college classes.

One pair of poems in each thematic chapter provides practice in comparison and contrast, a key Advanced Placement Literature skill.

The paired poems encourage students to explore different types of connections, whether the poems have similar topics, rely on similar allusions, represent different perspectives on the same subject, or even express similar emotions through different styles. These pairs help students go beyond surface similarities in order to understand both poems in greater depth.

Visual texts in each thematic chapter help students develop visual literacy and expand their analytical vocabulary.

Every chapter features a painting or photograph related to the chapter's theme with supporting Exploring the Text questions that invite students to analyze the images with the same analytical tools that they use for literary texts. In addition to exposing students to fine art and photography, these pieces give visual learners and students gifted with an artistic eye a chance to shine. In some chapters, we have even paired a visual text with a poem; for example, in the chapter on Love and Relationships, we have paired Gustav Klimt's painting *The Kiss* with Lawrence Ferlinghetti's poem "Short Story on a Painting of Gustav Klimt." Such pairings offer students the opportunity to compare treatments of a theme across different media.

The Conversation sections in each thematic chapter ask students to apply high-level thinking skills to a collection of fiction, poetry, nonfiction, and visual texts.

Synthesizing ideas is one of the highest levels of cognition. Some students may have been introduced to this skill in an Advanced Placement English Language and Composition class in preparation for the synthesis essay question. Here, we ask students to use that same skill to explore a variety of literary, cultural, and historical issues. The topics and texts range in difficulty from familiar and high-interest topics such as "Courtship: The Rules of Engagement" and "The Lure and Language of Food" to more academic inquiries such as "Seamus Heaney: The Responsibility of the Artist" and "The Legacy of Colonialism." Through a series of questions and writing prompts, students are invited to enter the conversation and express their viewpoints on the subject in light of the readings.

Writer on Writing interviews in each thematic chapter were conducted *exclusively* for *Literature & Composition*, giving students a unique look into an author's world.

The author interviews offer students a glimpse of who the authors are and why they wrote what they wrote. For instance, in the Love and Relationships chapter, students can read how Annie Finch wrote her poem "Coy Mistress" in an attempt to "channel the coy mistress herself and write in a way she would have written had she responded to [Andrew] Marvell." Hearing professional writers discuss their composing processes helps students put their own trials at the keyboard in perspective. Fine writing doesn't happen magically; it is the product of conscious effort and constant practice. Learning that published authors grapple with unwieldy ideas, rethink organizational structures, and revise their work repeatedly can be eye-opening for young writers.

Student Writing in each thematic chapter is accompanied by questions to help guide revision.

Students often find it difficult to figure out how to improve their writing. They are told to revise, but how? Revision entails much more than correcting mechanical errors; it requires a careful examination of whether the words clearly communicate the ideas, the syntax creates the right emphasis, and the tone is appropriate for the audience. One method for assisting students in this process is to provide them with sample student essays that require revision and to ask them to reflect on the changes needed for improvement. Each chapter in *Literature & Composition* offers students a work-in-progress essay written by a high school or first-year college student, with accompanying questions that direct their attention to the kinds of alterations that can turn a C or B paper into an A.

The Writer's Craft—Close Reading section in each thematic chapter breaks down the close reading process to explore how a writer uses elements of style to create meaning.

Focusing on particular aspects of writing—connotation; specialized, archaic, and unfamiliar diction; irony; tone; figurative language; syntax; and imagery—this section offers students explanations of these elements using examples taken from the readings in the chapter. For instance, scrutinizing how Henry James, Salman Rushdie, and Gerard Manley Hopkins employ syntax to convey meaning deepens students' understanding of how literary texts work. The exercises that follow give students firsthand experience with the concepts and practice in analyzing works for a specific element of style, before inviting them to try out the technique in their own writing.

Ancillaries

The *Literature & Composition* TEACHER'S MANUAL

This helpful manual offers a wealth of resources for teachers of all levels. It includes insightful responses to the questions following each reading, suggested approaches to each thematic chapter and to the Classic and Modern Texts, teaching strategies for each feature in the thematic chapters, as well as sample multiple-choice and AP-style essay prompts. Written by leaders in the AP Literature and Composition community—including the *Literature & Composition* author team along with Lance Balla, Shirley Counsil, Ellen Greenblatt, Minaz Jooma, Skip Nicholson, and Ed Schmieder—this Teacher's Manual is an in-depth and indispensable guide for teaching a successful AP Literature course.

ISBN-10: 0-312-61726-7; ISBN-13: 978-0-312-61726-4

Student Center for Literature & Composition

This resource includes connections to online audio and video related to the readings in *Literature & Composition*, as well as access to *Re:Writing for Literature*, which gathers in one place Bedford/St. Martin's most popular **free** Web resources for literature. Thousands of students and instructors already rely on these resources: illustrated tutorials for the close reading of stories, poems, and plays; links to information on literary authors; quizzes on literary works; a glossary of literary terms; MLA-style sample papers; and tools for finding and citing sources. *Re:Writing for Literature* is completely free and open (no codes required) to ensure access for all students.

bedfordstmartins.com/literatureandcomp

Acknowledgments

We would like to thank the talented team at Bedford/St. Martin's. We've relied upon their expertise, enjoyed their enthusiasm, and appreciated their encouragement more than we can say. Their support started at the top with the vision of president Joan Feinberg and her exceptional team of editorial director Denise Wydra, editor in chief Karen Henry, director of marketing Karen Soeltz, director of development Erica Appel, and senior executive editor Steve Scipione. We are grateful that Nancy Perry has stayed with us even though her responsibilities as editorial director of custom publishing have pulled her in other directions. We salute Bill Imbornoni, senior project editor, and freelance editors Jan Weber and Anne Stameshkin for their patience and keen editorial eyes. To say a simple thanks to Dan McDonough, senior marketing manager, is to deal in understatement. His unflagging determination and creativity sustained us throughout the project. We also send a heartfelt thanks to Lisa Kozempel, high school marketing manager, for all the many ways she has gone above and beyond to guide this project. And to our editor Nathan Odell, we give thanks for being a cheerleader, taskmaster, diplomat, advocate and chief skeptic at once, perfectionist, and best of friends—as well as our "dear reader." We are grateful to the reviewers who always kept us anchored in the world of the classroom reality and generously shared their amazing experience and expertise: Lance Balla, Barbara Bloy, Barbra A. Brooks-Barker, Caryl Catzlaff, Jolinda Collins, Shirley Counsil, Cathy A. D'Agostino, Peter Drewniany, Carol Elsen, Michael Feuer, Kelly E. Guilfoil, David Herring, Erica Jacobs, Marie Leone Meyer, Skip Nicholson, Frazier L. O'Leary Jr., Linda A. Pavich, Bill Pell, Catherine Pfaff, Sally P. Pfeifer, Amy Regis, Linda Rood, Edward Schmieder, Conni Shelnut, Deborah Shepard, Pat Sherbert, Doranna Tindle, Luke Wiseman, Carol Yoakley-Terrell, and David Youngblood. We are deeply grateful for spouses, children, friends, and family who have supported our efforts, given up their weekends and evenings to advise us, and kept the faith that this project was absolutely worthwhile and would eventually be finished!

Finally, we would like to thank our students over the years, including more than a few who have become admirable teachers themselves, for honoring the tradition of reading and writing that gives meaning to our lives.

This is the book we committed ourselves to developing for you and your students. We've brought to the task our many years of working with high school and college students as well as our deep love of literature, reading, and writing. We hope *Literature & Composition* helps you and your students, and that you enjoy using it as much as we enjoyed writing it.

Best Wishes,

CAROL JAGO
RENÉE H. SHEA
LAWRENCE SCANLON
ROBIN DISSIN AUFSES

Contents

3   THE BIG PICTURE   Analyzing Fiction and Drama   59

7 LOVE AND RELATIONSHIPS 573

Ay me! for aught that I could ever read,
Could ever hear by tale or history,
The course of true love never did run smooth.
—WILLIAM SHAKESPEARE, *A Midsummer Night's Dream*

All.

8 CONFORMITY AND REBELLION 719

Not all those who wander are lost. — J. R. R. TOLKIEN, *The Lord of the Rings*

9 ART AND THE ARTIST   1031

Art for art's sake? I should think so, and more so than ever at the present time. It is the one orderly product which our middling race has produced. It is the cry of a thousand sentinels, the echo from a thousand labyrinths, it is the lighthouse which cannot be hidden . . . it is the best evidence we can have of our dignity.   — E. M. FORSTER

10   **TRADITION AND PROGRESS**   1165   *[handwritten: 1837–1901 Victorian Unit (?)]*

The world owes all its onward impulses to men ill at ease. The happy man inevitably confines himself within ancient limits.
—NATHANIEL HAWTHORNE

[handwritten: Start with, and then launch unit]

[handwritten: End with A Doll's House – Ibsen 1879]

11   WAR AND PEACE   1325   Macbeth   Slaughterhouse Five–Vonnegut

*Do dreams offer lessons? Do nightmares have themes, do we awaken and
analyze them and live our lives and advise others as a result? Can the
foot soldier teach anything important about war, merely for having been
there? I think not. He can tell war stories.*

— Tim O'Brien, *If I Die in a Combat Zone*

War is kind—
Stephen Crane

Intro to Course: Critical Thinking, Close Reading, Discussion Formats/Expectations

- War & Peace

(52) - Identity & Culture

- Tradition & Progress (Victorian Unit

Contents by Genre

Fiction

Poetry

Drama

Nonfiction

Visual Texts

Thinking about Literature

In the past, most people curled up with a book, whether on a sofa on a rainy day, under a tree on a sunny one, or under the covers with a flashlight. Today, those scenes may sound downright quaint, when the very idea of "the book" is open to debate. With more and more books being digitized, people are starting to click on a screen as often as they flip a page. In fact, some believe that e-readers will supplant the physical book, and the ads make a convincing argument: "Simple to use: no computer, no cables, no syncing. Buy a book and it is auto-delivered wirelessly in less than one minute. More than 250,000 books available" (amazon.com). Plus, there's no denying that having a text online, whether on a laptop or e-reader, could make for efficient reading, with hyperlinks, access to search engines, built-in dictionaries, and other bells and whistles. Literature has also moved from the page to the stage as spoken-word poetry has become a global phenomenon, with large audiences of all ages, lively competitions, and stars with enthusiastic followings.

Yet amid stories that "the book" will become a cultural artifact, literature lives on. Leo Tolstoy's *Anna Karenina*, written in the late 1800s, topped the best-seller list in 2004, thanks to Oprah Winfrey and her book club. More recently, sales of the final installment of the Harry Potter series exceeded four hundred million copies. So whether you have a paperback, an audiobook, an e-text, or the author right in front of you performing the work, what still seems to matter is, does the work hold your interest? give you a break from your day-to-day life? inform you? challenge or provoke you? or even entertain you?

There are stories or poems that don't go beyond entertaining—they're fun—and there's nothing wrong with that. But many of those works are probably not what we would call "literature." Of course, not everyone agrees on precisely what defines literature, but what we mean is a work that rewards the time, concentration, and creativity put into reading, rereading, exploring, analyzing, discussing, and interpreting it. Literary texts are ones we're likely to remember—ones that may, in fact, influence who we are, how we experience our world, and what truths guide our lives.

Many writers believe that the truth of human experience is too complex, too dazzling, to be reduced to simple facts. The poet Emily Dickinson suggests that anyone attempting to understand or explain the nature of life would do well to adopt a roundabout approach. From her perspective, "Success in Circuit lies."

Literary Merit

1

Tell all the Truth but tell it slant—
Success in Circuit lies
Too bright for our infirm Delight
The Truth's superb surprise

As Lightning to the Children eased   5
With explanation kind
The Truth must dazzle gradually
Or every man be blind—

                                    [c. 1868]

Dickinson suggests that indirection is the way toward "truth"—which might "dazzle" but does so "gradually," more like a process of discovery than steps in an instruction manual. But why in a poem about "truth" do we find the word "lies"? Why must truth reveal itself (or be revealed) "with explanation kind"—the way we explain lightning to children while trying not to frighten them? In this short, somewhat enigmatic poem, Dickinson may be getting at the heart of what literature is: works that ask more questions than they answer, that draw us in to explore them. These texts often ask us to go beyond the obvious or literal level and to think metaphorically.

The poet Robert Frost once wrote, "Unless you are at home in the metaphor, you are not safe anywhere." Although he makes his point somewhat playfully, he reminds us that making sense of our lives and world requires going beyond a surface understanding. We must be able to infer meanings that may only be suggested, to understand the significance of symbolic gestures, to comprehend not just what has happened but what it means.

• ACTIVITY •

Select one of the poems that follow, and discuss how the poet "tell[s] all the Truth but tell[s] it slant," or how he is "at home in the metaphor."

The Sacred
STEPHEN DUNN

After the teacher asked if anyone had
    a sacred place
and the students fidgeted and shrank

in their chairs, the most serious of them all
    said it was his car,   5
being in it alone, his tape deck playing

things he'd chosen, and others knew the truth
    had been spoken
and began speaking about their rooms,

their hiding places, but the car kept coming up,   10
  the car in motion,
music filling it, and sometimes one other person

who understood the bright altar of the dashboard
  and how far away
a car could take him from the need   15

to speak, or to answer, the key
  in having a key
and putting it in, and going.

[1989]

When my love swears that she is made of truth
WILLIAM SHAKESPEARE

When my love swears that she is made of truth,
I do believe her though I know she lies,
That she might think me some untutored youth,
Unlearnèd in the world's false subtleties.

Thus vainly thinking that she thinks me young,   5
Although she knows my days are past the best,
Simply I credit her false-speaking tongue.
On both sides thus is simple truth suppressed.

But wherefore says she not she is unjust?
And wherefore say not I that I am old?   10
O, love's best habit is in seeming trust,
And age in love loves not to have years told.

  Therefore I lie with her and she with me,
  And in our faults by lies we flattered be.

[1599]

Vegetarian Physics
DAVID CLEWELL

The tofu that's shown up overnight in this house is
  frightening
proof of the Law of Conservation: matter that simply
  cannot be
created or destroyed. Matter older than Newton,
who knew better than to taste it. Older than Lao-tzu,
who thought about it but finally chose harmonious non-   5
  interference.
I'd like to be philosophical too, see it as some kind of pale

inscrutable wisdom among the hot dogs, the cold chicken,
the leftover deviled eggs, but I'm talking curdled
soybean milk. And I don't have that kind of energy.

I'd rather not be part of the precariously metaphorical   10
wedding of modern physics and the ancient Eastern
    mysteries.
But still: whoever stashed the tofu in my Frigidaire
had better come back for it soon. I'm not Einstein
but I'm smart enough to know a bad idea when I see it
taking up space, biding its time.   15
Like so much that demands our imperfect attention
amid the particle roar of the world: going nowhere, fast.

                                                                  [1994]

Why Study Literature?

Why is reading and studying literature worth the effort? This is a reasonable question to ask as you embark on the study of poetry, fiction, and drama. If it's factual information you want, there are better places to search than within the pages of a novel or play or the lines of a poem. Writers of imaginative literature often stretch facts, play with historical events and characters, and even alter geography, but they do so in order to tell us something about ourselves and the world we live in. Studying a play by William Shakespeare (p. 720), a poem by early American poet Anne Bradstreet (p. 298), or a story by contemporary Nigerian writer Chimamanda Ngozi Adichie (p. 903) holds the promise of helping us to understand ourselves a little better. As we explore the motivations, actions, thoughts, and ideas of an author or the characters he or she created, we consider the issues at hand, weigh right and wrong, and contemplate how we would react. In the process, we learn something about ourselves. As individuals, we sometimes turn to literary texts to escape, to take a break from our current life or situation, to be entertained for a while. Such departures from daily reality help put things in perspective. Many find comfort in reading about the motivation and thoughts of others—how they respond to disappointment or confusion, come of age, deal with the joys and challenges of family life, or cope with conflict and change. In this way, we learn to empathize with people in situations similar to our own, as well as those in entirely different cultures, circumstances, and even time periods. Literature brings people together; it builds community.

Sometimes we look to our poets on state occasions to give us this sense of community. Several United States presidents have had poems written for their inauguration, including President Barack Obama, who invited Elizabeth Alexander to write and read a poem for his inauguration in 2009. The result was "Praise Song for the Day":

Each day we go about our business,
walking past each other, catching each other's
eyes or not, about to speak or speaking.

All about us is noise. All about us is
noise and bramble, thorn and din, each   5
one of our ancestors on our tongues.

Someone is stitching up a hem, darning
a hole in a uniform, patching a tire,
repairing the things in need of repair.

Someone is trying to make music somewhere,   10
with a pair of wooden spoons on an oil drum,
with cello, boom box, harmonica, voice.

A woman and her son wait for the bus.
A farmer considers the changing sky.
A teacher says, *Take out your pencils. Begin.*   15

We encounter each other in words, words
spiny or smooth, whispered or declaimed,
words to consider, reconsider.

We cross dirt roads and highways that mark
the will of some one and then others, who said   20
I need to see what's on the other side.

I know there's something better down the road.
We need to find a place where we are safe.
We walk into that which we cannot yet see.

Say it plain: that many have died for this day.   25
Sing the names of the dead who brought us here,
who laid the train tracks, raised the bridges,

picked the cotton and the lettuce, built
brick by brick the glittering edifices
they would then keep clean and work inside of.   30

Praise song for struggle, praise song for the day.
Praise song for every hand-lettered sign,
the figuring-it-out at kitchen tables.

Some live by *love thy neighbor as thyself,*
others by *first do no harm* or *take no more*   35
than you need. What if the mightiest word is love?

Love beyond marital, filial, national,
love that casts a widening pool of light,
love with no need to pre-empt grievance.

In today's sharp sparkle, this winter air,   40
any thing can be made, any sentence begun.
On the brink, on the brim, on the cusp,

praise song for walking forward in that light.

How does Alexander ask us to think about the inaugural day? She emphasizes the common person (the woman and her son waiting for a bus, the farmer, the teacher) and alludes to the unsung heroes who built the nation, not only those who died for it but those who "laid the train tracks, raised the bridges, / picked the cotton and the lettuce" (ll. 27–28). She calls for optimism and hope in "walking forward in that light" (l. 43), but she also reminds us that we are writing history or that we have an opportunity to do so at a time when "any thing can be made, any sentence begun" (l. 41). An inaugural ceremony is what its name suggests—a beginning, an ushering in of a new era, a time of promise—and in this poem, politics and literature join to remind the nation that despite all differences of history, origin, and interest, we have a common purpose.

In short, literature reminds us that we're not alone. We're part of a community, an ongoing conversation that some call "cultural literacy." These days, in a heterogeneous population amid a global culture, the very concept is controversial, yet there are certain authors, works, allusions, and even phrases that contribute to our collective identity. Even those who haven't read *Hamlet* recognize "To be, or not to be" as a phrase suggesting indecisiveness. Even those who have not read the Bible or had a Judeo-Christian upbringing are likely to recognize references to the Garden of Eden.

Granted, our schools do not have a formalized reading list, nor would most of us want one. We pride ourselves on a fluid and open society that welcomes the new and incorporates it into our traditions. Yet familiarity with certain works gives us a kind of common vocabulary to explore our day-to-day world. Let's use *The Great Gatsby* as an example. This seminal novel, written by F. Scott Fitzgerald in 1925, captures both the promise and the illusion of the American Dream. It's inspired other novels, such as *Bodega Dreams*, whose author, Ernesto Quiñonez, says that he used the plot of *The Great Gatsby* as a model for his story, set in Spanish Harlem and told in a mixture of urban **dialects** and Spanglish: "When I see Gatsby, I see a poor guy who would do anything to become rich. When rich people see Gatsby they think that he belongs to them, but Gatsby does not belong to the rich. Gatsby belongs to the poor." The 2005 film *G* is billed as a modern-day hip-hop version of Fitzgerald's novel, though not one that critics thought would give the original novel a run for its money. Charles Schulz references *The Great Gatsby* in a number of his classic *Peanuts* cartoons, such as the following one, which alludes to the symbolic green light at the end of a dock in the novel and Gatsby's studied use of the expression "old sport."

PEANUTS: © United Feature Syndicate, Inc.

In 2002, *Book* magazine named Jay Gatsby the number one literary figure of our time, "the cynical idealist, who embodies America in all of its messy glory." In 2009, *The Great Gatsby* is still around. Writing an article with the provocative title "The End of White America?" Hua Hsu begins:

> "Civilization's going to pieces," he remarks. He is in polite company, gathered with friends around a bottle of wine in the late-afternoon sun, chatting and gossiping. "I've gotten to be a terrible pessimist about things. Have you read *The Rise of the Colored Empires* by this man Goddard?" They hadn't. "Well, it's a fine book, and everybody ought to read it. The idea is if we don't look out the white race will be—will be utterly submerged. It's all scientific stuff; it's been proved."
>
> He is Tom Buchanan, a character in F. Scott Fitzgerald's *The Great Gatsby*, a book that nearly everyone who passes through the American education system is compelled to read at least once. Although *Gatsby* doesn't gloss as a book on racial anxiety—it's too busy exploring a different set of anxieties entirely—Buchanan was hardly alone in feeling besieged.

Hsu continues on to discuss the actual book Tom Buchanan referenced and then launches into an analysis of where the changing demographic and popular culture are leading the United States in the twenty-first century. But his **hook**, his choice of an opening that will catch his audience's attention, relies on the assumption that "nearly everyone who passes through the American education system" has read *The Great Gatsby*. So if you haven't read the novel, can you still read *Bodega Dreams*, see G, be amused by a *Peanuts* cartoon, understand Hua Hsu's article? Probably. Yet being familiar with Fitzgerald's characters and themes deepens your understanding, lets you approach the texts critically, and gives you confidence to join the conversation.

• ACTIVITY •

Research a modern retelling of a classic work such as Jane Austen's novel *Pride and Prejudice* or Shakespeare's play *Hamlet*. What assumptions are made about the modern reader's familiarity with the work? How is the work updated?

Discussing a work of literature might be even more important than the solitary act of reading. As we share an interpretation with others, we learn how to communicate, how to agree and disagree. Perhaps more important, we share an experience. While reading across cultural, socioeconomic, political, age, religious, and racial lines, we find that a book or poem can be a neutral space for us to learn about different ways of seeing the world and to discover similarities. Book clubs and community reading projects are cropping up these days on every level, from a national book selection to a novel chosen by a group of friends. Many schools select one book to develop common ground among students, as they explore this shared text with teachers and administrators—and sometimes even parents. Certainly, the primary goal is to encourage people to read, but the real benefit is in the conversations that the book sparks among friends, neighbors, and classmates. And sometimes these conversations will even include the author of the work itself.

Some of the largest literary communities are online. Oprah's famous book club has over two million members from all over the globe, who meet online to discuss the latest selection. And then there's goodreads.com, a book-lovers' social network that founder Otis Chandler describes as "a website where I could see my friends' bookshelves and learn about what they thought of all their books." The site claims over 2,300,000 members—an impressive community of readers.

• ACTIVITY •

Choose a book that you think would be appropriate for establishing common ground through discussion in your school or class. What issues would this book enable the community to explore? Why are those issues important to your school community?

What Makes an Effective Reader?

It is probably safe to say that no one ever wrote a poem, play, short story, or novel with the express purpose of having students puzzle over it to find the "right" interpretation. Writers write because they have something to say, or want to evoke an emotion. Keeping that in mind, it's usually best to start out reading without an analytic agenda and meet the work on its own terms. Enjoy it, listen to it, connect with it. And sometimes that's all you want or need to do. Poet and longtime literature professor Billy Collins began a project called Poetry 180 with the idea that every school day would begin with the reading of a poem—no analysis, no discussion, no quiz to take or paper to write. Here's one of the poems from his Web site:

The Bagel
DAVID IGNATOW

> I stopped to pick up the bagel
> rolling away in the wind,
> annoyed with myself
> for having dropped it
> as if it were a portent.   5
> Faster and faster it rolled,
> with me running after it
> bent low, gritting my teeth,
> and I found myself doubled over
> and rolling down the street   10

head over heels, one complete somersault
after another like a bagel
and strangely happy with myself.

[1993]

Do we need to say more? We could probably find a way (Why use such a formal word as "portent"? Is the bagel a metaphor?), but do we always need to? "The Bagel" is a delightful poem likely to bring on a smile. You might even think it's a bit silly, and maybe that's the point. Sometimes it's important simply to enjoy.

Yet there are times when reading and rereading, examining closely and carefully, and thinking critically about literature adds to our understanding and appreciation of it. Reading literature is neither a treasure hunt for metaphors nor an interrogation to figure out what the author's hiding. It is a meeting of reader, writer, and text; it involves participation and engagement. Some describe it as a transaction, some a conversation, and some an act of imagination. English novelist Virginia Woolf advised readers to become the author's "fellow-worker and accomplice" and "open [their] mind as widely as possible." Toni Morrison, the first African American woman to win the Nobel Prize for Literature, describes "the reader as artist" who must bring both "willing acceptance" and "intense inquiry" to the text. She points out, "I don't need to 'like' the work: I want instead to 'think' it."

As you read literary texts, many of them complex and challenging, find a comfortable middle ground where you can appreciate and understand the work and also analyze it in a way that deepens your appreciation of it. Writers worth their salt are bound to puzzle readers, spark a debate, invite diverse interpretations—and inspire rereading.

• ACTIVITY •

In each of the following poems, the speaker comments on readers. In what ways are the two speakers' expectations about readers similar? What can you infer about each speaker's beliefs about the value of literature? Consider how each speaker uses playful humor to make a serious point.

Shawl
ALBERT GOLDBARTH

Eight hours by bus, and night
was on them. He could see himself now
in the window, see his head there with the country
running through it like a long thought made of steel and wheat.
Darkness outside; darkness in the bus—as if the sea   5
were dark and the belly of the whale were dark to match it.
He was twenty: of course his eyes returned, repeatedly,

to the knee of the woman two rows up: positioned so
occasional headlights struck it into life.
But more reliable was the book; he was discovering himself   10
to be among the tribe that reads. Now his, the only
overhead turned on. Now nothing else existed:
only him, and the book, and the light thrown over his shoulders
as luxuriously as a cashmere shawl.

                                                                    [2007]

Introduction to Poetry
BILLY COLLINS

I ask them to take a poem
and hold it up to the light
like a color slide

or press an ear against its hive.

I say drop a mouse into a poem   5
and watch him probe his way out,

or walk inside the poem's room
and feel the walls for a light switch.

I want them to water-ski
across the surface of a poem   10
waving at the author's name on the shore.

But all they want to do
is tie the poem to a chair with rope
and torture a confession out of it.

They begin beating it with a hose   15
to find out what it really means.

                                                                    [1988]

To get the most out of a literary text, try to cultivate certain habits of mind. Start with the pleasure of enjoying the text and then move on to a more critical understanding. At all times, remain open to possibilities, to accepting the text on its own terms. The following list of qualities describes an effective reader — and rereader!

- *Fearlessness*: Be daring and plunge into the text, allowing it to surprise, shock, annoy, or delight you. Take risks with interpretation. Don't be afraid to get it "wrong." Changing your mind and revising your analysis is the smart thing to do when a better idea presents itself.

- *Patience*: Hold off on passing judgment on a text. Liking or disliking a story isn't immediately important. There is no reason to suppose that your initial reaction is the most reliable measure of the worth of a literary work.

- *Many-mindedness*: Literature rarely offers simple answers to simple questions. Trust yourself to become comfortable with ambiguity and contradiction. Listen to what others say about a text, particularly when the interpretation differs from your own.

- *Attentiveness*: Pay attention to your own reading—where you got confused, where you grew bored, where you became frustrated with a character or the author. Awareness of what is going on inside your head is an important step toward becoming an astute reader.

- *Stamina*: Concentrate when you read, think hard, and keep thinking hard. Literary analysis can be exhausting work.

• ACTIVITY •

Following are two views on being a reader. What are their similarities and differences? Discuss your own experience.

From *Superman and Me*
SHERMAN ALEXIE

My father, who is one of the few Indians who went to Catholic school on purpose, was an avid reader of westerns, spy thrillers, murder mysteries, gangster epics, basketball-player biographies, and anything else he could find. He bought his books by the pound at Dutch's Pawn Shop, Goodwill, Salvation Army, and Value Village. When he had extra money, he bought new novels at supermarkets, convenience stores, and hospital gift shops. Our house was filled with books. They were stacked in crazy piles in the bathroom, bedrooms, and living room. In a fit of unemployment-inspired creative energy, my father built a set of bookshelves and soon filled them with a random assortment of books about the Kennedy assassination, Watergate, the Vietnam War, and the entire twenty-three-book series of the Apache westerns. My father loved books, and since I loved my father with an aching devotion, I decided to love books as well.

I can remember picking up my father's books before I could read. The words themselves were mostly foreign, but I still remember the exact moment when I first understood, with a sudden clarity, the purpose of a paragraph. I didn't have the vocabulary to say "paragraph," but I realized that a paragraph was a fence that held words. The words inside a paragraph worked together for a common purpose. They had some specific reason for being inside the same fence. This knowledge delighted me. I began to think of everything in terms of paragraphs. Our reservation was a small paragraph within the United States. My family's house was a paragraph, distinct from the other paragraphs of the LeBrets to the north, the Fords to our south, and the Tribal School to the west. Inside our house, each family member existed as a separate paragraph, but still had genetics and common experiences to link us. Now, using this logic, I can see my changed family as an essay of seven paragraphs: mother, father, older brother, the deceased sister, my younger twin sisters, and our adopted little brother.

[1997]

Learning to Read
FRANZ WRIGHT

If I had to look up every fifth or sixth word,
so what. I looked them up.
I had nowhere important to be.

My father was unavailable, and my mother
looked like she was about to break,   5
and not into blossom, every time I spoke.

My favorite was the Iliad. True,
I had trouble pronouncing the names,
but when was I going to pronounce them, and

to whom?   10
My stepfather maybe?
Number one, he could barely speak English;

two, he had sufficient intent
to smirk or knock me down
without any prompting from me.   15

Loneliness, boredom and terror
my motivation
fiercely fuelled.

I get down on my knees and thank God for them.

Du Fu, the Psalms, Whitman, Rilke.   20
Life has taught me
to understand books.

[2009]

Approaching Literature

There are many specific strategies to approaching a literary text and writing about it. Some of these strategies we'll discuss in detail in the next three chapters; others, your teachers will recommend. We want to start, though, by suggesting a straightforward three-step approach that will give you a way into any written text: *experience, analysis,* and *extension*.

Let's try these steps with the following poem, "'Out, Out—,'" by Robert Frost.

> The buzz-saw snarled and rattled in the yard
> And made dust and dropped stove-length sticks of wood,
> Sweet-scented stuff when the breeze drew across it.
> And from there those that lifted eyes could count
> Five mountain ranges one behind the other   5
> Under the sunset far into Vermont.
> And the saw snarled and rattled, snarled and rattled,
> As it ran light, or had to bear a load.
> And nothing happened: day was all but done.
> Call it a day, I wish they might have said   10
> To please the boy by giving him the half hour
> That a boy counts so much when saved from work.
> His sister stood beside them in her apron
> To tell them "Supper." At the word, the saw,
> As if to prove saws knew what supper meant,   15
> Leaped out at the boy's hand, or seemed to leap—
> He must have given the hand. However it was,
> Neither refused the meeting. But the hand!
> The boy's first outcry was a rueful laugh,
> As he swung toward them holding up the hand   20
> Half in appeal, but half as if to keep
> The life from spilling. Then the boy saw all—
> Since he was old enough to know, big boy
> Doing a man's work, though a child at heart—
> He saw all spoiled. "Don't let him cut my hand off—   25
> The doctor, when he comes. Don't let him, sister!"
> So. But the hand was gone already.
> The doctor put him in the dark of ether.
> He lay and puffed his lips out with his breath.
> And then—the watcher at his pulse took fright.   30
> No one believed. They listened at his heart.
> Little—less—nothing!—and that ended it.
> No more to build on there. And they, since they
> Were not the one dead, turned to their affairs.

[1916]

Experience

When we experience literature, we respond to it subjectively, personally, emotionally. This poem presents a fairly grisly scene: A boy is at work cutting wood, the saw slips, and he cuts his hand. Despite the doctor's efforts, the boy dies. Then everyone goes back to work—end of story. You might find this a distasteful scene, you might find it sad, you might think that the people in the poem are heartless and cold, it might remind you of something you read about or even experienced. Maybe you came away thinking that most people aren't really as callous as the ones in this poem. If you live in the city, you might feel removed from the rural Vermont setting; if you've spent time on a farm, the poem might have a more familiar ring to it. Any or all of these responses are perfectly legitimate; in fact, at this early stage, there truly are no wrong answers, or any answers at all. Even at this first step, however, you cannot help but notice the language and details—such as the pretty sunset next to the sound of the buzz saw or the fact that the boy appeals to his sister while the parents are absent from the scene.

Analysis

But you're just getting started. You might think that you haven't done very productive work by merely responding, but you have: you've entered the world of the poem. The next step is to move from feeling to thinking—to analyze the work. Here's where you begin to ask questions, to think about the way language is used, to draw inferences. The key is observation: no detail is unimportant, so notice, notice, notice. In the next chapters, we'll talk more about what to look for, and give you strategies for paying close attention to the work. For now, we'll keep it simple. What do you notice about the language and structure of this poem? What connections or patterns emerge? What inferences might you draw from those connections? If you notice something unusual, something that stands out from the rest of the poem, you probably want to ask why. At this stage, you're basically reading between the lines as you consider what is directly expressed along with what is indirectly expressed through figurative language (language that's not literal) and other poetic techniques.

In the first line of "'Out, Out—'" you probably noted that the buzz saw is depicted as an animal that "snarled and rattled," a description repeated three times before the saw "leaped out at the boy's hand, or seemed to leap" (l. 16). This **personification** suggests that this wasn't an accident; the saw is a predator that intended to hurt the boy. Frost then gives us a description of the natural beauty of the landscape, the "five mountain ranges one behind the other / under the sunset far into Vermont" (ll. 5–6). Why would Frost turn a saw into a vicious animal and then show us the beautiful Vermont countryside? Maybe he's saying that nature has two sides, violent and peaceful, predatory and nourishing? What do you think?

Notice that the poem is told from the third-person **point of view**, except in line 10, when the speaker comments that he wishes they would have "Call[ed] it a day" and given the boy a half hour away from his work. Why shift perspective here? Perhaps it was Frost's way of anticipating the accident to come. Maybe lines 10–12 are put in there to give the poem a bit of soul, to express some regret, to temper the cold practicality of the final lines. Perhaps you have another interpretation of this choice.

Titles can be a clue to larger issues in a poem, and the quotation marks that surround this one signal that it's taken from another source. The phrase "Out, out" is from act V, scene v, of Shakespeare's tragedy *Macbeth*. The exact lines are:

> Out, out, brief candle!
> Life's but a walking shadow, a poor player
> That struts and frets his hour upon the stage
> And then is heard no more. It is a tale
> Told by an idiot, full of sound and fury,
> Signifying nothing.

Macbeth himself utters this speech at the end of the play after being informed of Lady Macbeth's death, recognizing the brevity of life and the futility of all his worldly ambitions. You might ask why Frost would connect this rural scene with a Shakespearean **tragedy**. Is Frost saying that death is tragic? Is it a reminder that life is fleeting? Is it a recognition that the forces of nature (those "mountain ranges one behind the other / Under the sunset") are uncaring, indifferent to human beings? Is the speaker denouncing those who "were not the one dead" for their lack of feeling, acknowledging the necessity to carry on—or perhaps both? Is Frost arguing for a **carpe diem** (seize the day) belief system, in which the best we can do is appreciate the mountains and sunset because anything can happen? The answers to such analytical questions will lead to your interpretation of the poem.

Extension

At this point, you have analyzed a text and drawn inferences to arrive at an interpretation. For many assignments, that's all you will need to do. But sometimes you'll be asked to extend your interpretation from the world of the poem to the real world. This type of extension may involve examination of the background of the author, research into the historical context of the work, or application of the ideas in the piece to life in general.

For instance, biographical research on Frost and "'Out, Out—'" reveals that Frost based the poem on an actual incident in 1915, when his neighbor's son lost his hand to a buzz saw. The boy went into shock from blood loss, and the efforts of the physician called to the scene could not save him. Obviously, Frost did not write the poem to report this specific incident, but he must have seen something in it that had meaning beyond the actual event. The poem might be seen as his way of immortalizing the boy and thus giving his young life meaning. Or perhaps Frost—who was over forty at the time the poem was written—was recognizing his own mortality and reflecting on the fleeting nature of all human life.

If you research the time period when this poem was written, you'll find that young children often worked long hours in unsafe conditions to help support their families. Child labor laws adopted in 1924 ended this practice. Using this information, you might build the case that Frost was making a political statement by illustrating the dangers of expecting a boy, "a child at heart," to do "a man's work." Also, the poem offers an entrance into understanding the social conditions of this time period, when everyone in the family had to contribute in order to survive. When the boy "saw all spoiled," he may have been thinking of the hardship of losing a hand, but he may also have been thinking that his loss of productivity would be a real hardship for a family struggling to make it in the face of harsh economic realities.

The poem also asks how we should grieve. Is the best way to honor the dead to return to the activities of the living? In an extension paper you might argue that getting right back to work instead of grieving is an economic reality of the working class, regardless of time and place. You might also consider the language of the poem as a way to extend its meaning. Frost's personification of the predatory saw within the idyllic natural beauty could be read as the intrusion of the machine into the garden, the negative or dangerous impact of technology (or, in Frost's day, mechanization) on the unspoiled beauty of nature. Can the two coexist? If you pursue this line of thinking, imagine how you might tie it to earlier works of American literature or to contemporary warnings of the dangers of technology on the natural world.

• ACTIVITY •

Read the following story—"Snow" by Julia Alvarez—and then discuss your experience of it, your analysis of it, and how you might extend your analysis beyond the story. Keep in mind that these are not entirely separate steps. Simply go through the three steps by talking with your classmates about the story.

Snow
JULIA ALVAREZ

Our first year in New York we rented a small apartment with a Catholic school nearby, taught by the Sisters of Charity, hefty women in long black gowns and bonnets that made them look peculiar, like dolls in mourning. I liked them a lot, especially my grandmotherly fourth grade teacher, Sister Zoe. I had a lovely name, she said, and she had me teach the whole class how to pronounce it. *Yo-lan-da.* As the only immigrant in my class, I was put in a special seat in the first row by the window, apart from the other children so that Sister Zoe could tutor me without disturbing them. Slowly, she enunciated the new words I was to repeat: *laundromat, corn flakes, subway, snow.*

Soon I picked up enough English to understand holocaust was in the air. Sister Zoe explained to a wide-eyed classroom what was happening in Cuba. Russian missiles were being assembled, trained supposedly on New York City. President Kennedy, looking worried too, was on the television at home, explaining we might have to go to war against the Communists. At school, we had air-raid drills: an ominous bell would go off and we'd file into the hall, fall to the floor, cover our heads with our coats, and imagine our hair falling out, the bones in our arms going soft. At home, Mami and my sisters and I said a rosary for world peace. I heard new vocabulary: *nuclear bomb, radioactive fallout, bomb shelter.* Sister Zoe explained how it would happen.

She drew a picture of a mushroom on the blackboard and dotted a flurry of chalkmarks for the dusty fallout that would kill us all.

The months grew cold, November, December. It was dark when I got up in the morning, frosty when I followed my breath to school. One morning as I sat at my desk daydreaming out the window, I saw dots in the air like the ones Sister Zoe had drawn—random at first, then lots and lots. I shrieked, "Bomb! Bomb!" Sister Zoe jerked around, her full black skirt ballooning as she hurried to my side. A few girls began to cry.

But then Sister Zoe's shocked look faded. "Why, Yolanda dear, that's snow!" She laughed. "Snow."

"Snow," I repeated. I looked out the window warily. All my life I had heard about the white crystals that fell out of American skies in the winter. From my desk I watched the fine powder dust the sidewalk and parked cars below. Each flake was different, Sister Zoe had said, like a person, irreplaceable and beautiful.

[1984]

2

Close Reading: Analyzing Poetry and Passages of Fiction

What Is Close Reading?

Close reading, sometimes called explication of text, means developing an understanding of a text that is based on its small details and the larger ideas those details evoke or suggest. Although you might worry that taking a work apart somehow lessens its power or the pleasure of reading it, the opposite is usually true. By looking at the various parts of a poem or passage of fiction, you come to appreciate the writer's artistry and understand how a writer uses various techniques to make a statement, suggest an emotion, or convey an idea. John Ciardi's classic book on analyzing poetry is entitled *How Does a Poem Mean?*—and that's the purpose of close reading: to analyze not just *what* a piece of literature means but *how* that meaning comes about. When you write a close analysis essay, you start with the larger ideas you've discovered and use the small details—the words themselves and how they're arranged—to support your interpretation of the meaning of the piece.

The key to close reading is, of course, observation—taking note of what you read and what you think about it, and asking questions. The good news is that the texts you are asked to read closely are usually not that long, which means you can read them several times. Each time you read a text, you will notice more and more. Later in the chapter we'll suggest specific strategies—such as annotating and using a graphic organizer—that will help you organize what you notice, pose questions about your observations, and even answer the questions you've posed. Let's start with what you notice when you first read a poem or passage of fiction.

First-Impression Questions

Take a look at this excerpt from *My Antonia* by Willa Cather, a novel about early settlers in the American West, narrated by a young boy who moves from Virginia to Nebraska to be brought up by his grandparents. As you read, jot down some questions that arise from your first impressions.

> I sat down in the middle of the garden, where snakes could scarcely approach unseen, and leaned my back against a warm yellow pumpkin. There were some

ground-cherry bushes growing along the furrows, full of fruit. I turned back the papery triangular sheaths that protected the berries and ate a few. All about me giant grasshoppers, twice as big as any I had ever seen, were doing acrobatic feats among the dried vines. The gophers scurried up and down the ploughed ground. There in the sheltered draw-bottom the wind did not blow very hard, but I could hear it singing its humming tune up on the level, and I could see the tall grasses wave. The earth was warm under me, and warm as I crumbled it through my fingers. Queer little red bugs came out and moved in slow squadrons around me. Their backs were polished vermilion, with black spots. I kept as still as I could. Nothing happened. I did not expect anything to happen. I was something that lay under the sun and felt it, like the pumpkins, and I did not want to be anything more. I was entirely happy. Perhaps we feel like that when we die and become a part of something entire, whether it is sun and air, or goodness and knowledge. At any rate, that is happiness; to be dissolved into something complete and great. When it comes to one, it comes as naturally as sleep.

[1918]

After just one reading, you can probably get a sense of the **tone** of this passage and the **mood** it creates; you might even be able to imagine a few things about its **narrator**, its **setting**, and even its **themes**. You will surely have questions about how and why Cather's style is so distinct, and that is the first step in reading closely.

Here are some questions that a first reading may raise. Your questions may be similar to the ones here, or you may have come up with completely different ones.

- What part do the snakes play in this passage about happiness?
- What might it mean that the passage is set in a garden?
- How big is that pumpkin? How big are the grasshoppers, really?
- What makes the objects in the passage so vivid?
- Why does the narrator connect happiness and death?
- How does the narrator fit—literally and figuratively—into the landscape?
- How does the passage change from beginning to end?

What's important at this point is not necessarily answering the questions but simply asking them. By posing questions, you're engaging with the text—you're reading actively.

• ACTIVITY •

Read the following poem by A. E. Housman. Then create your own first-impression questions.

To an Athlete Dying Young
A. E. HOUSMAN

The time you won your town the race
We chaired you through the market-place;
Man and boy stood cheering by,
And home we brought you shoulder-high.

To-day, the road all runners come,   5
Shoulder-high we bring you home,
And set you at your threshold down,
Townsman of a stiller town.

Smart lad, to slip betimes away
From fields where glory does not stay   10
And early though the laurel grows
It withers quicker than the rose.

Eyes the shady night has shut
Cannot see the record cut,
And silence sounds no worse than cheers   15
After earth has stopped the ears:

Now you will not swell the rout
Of lads that wore their honours out,
Runners whom renown outran
And the name died before the man.   20

So set, before its echoes fade,
The fleet foot on the sill of shade,
And hold to the low lintel up
The still-defended challenge-cup.

And round that early-laurelled head   25
Will flock to gaze the strengthless dead,
And find unwithered on its curls
The garland briefer than a girl's.

[1896]

The Elements of Style

The point of close reading is to go beyond merely summarizing a work to figuring out how a writer's stylistic choices convey the work's message or meaning. Once you begin to analyze literature closely, you will see how all of the parts of a piece of literature work together, from the structure of the piece down to individual word choices. The following is a brief introduction to the essential elements of style. Understanding these terms and concepts will give you things to be on the lookout for as you close-read, as well as vocabulary to help you describe what you see. Examples for all of these concepts, and more, are available in the glossary at the back of the book.

Diction

Authors choose their words carefully to convey precise meanings. We call these word choices the author's **diction**. A word can have more than one dictionary definition, or **denotation**, so when you analyze diction, you must consider all of a word's possible meanings. If the words have meanings or associations beyond the dictionary definitions, their **connotations**, you should ask how those relate to the meaning of the piece. Sometimes a word's connotations will reveal another layer of meaning; sometimes they will affect the tone, as in the case of **formal** or **informal** diction, which is sometimes called **slang**, or **colloquial**, language. Diction can also be **abstract** or **concrete**. Let's look at an example of diction from the third stanza of Housman's poem:

> Smart lad, to slip betimes away
> From fields where glory does not stay
> And early though the laurel grows
> It withers quicker than the rose.

In the third line, Housman plays with the multiple denotations of the word *laurel*, which is both a small evergreen tree, and an honor or accolade. Housman is using these multiple denotations to establish a paradox. Though the laurel that represents fame is evergreen, fame itself is fleeting, even more fleeting than the rosy bloom of youth.

Figurative Language

Language that is not literal is called figurative, as in a **figure of speech**. Sometimes this kind of language is called *metaphorical* because it explains or expands on an idea by comparing it to something else. The comparison can be explicit, as in the case of a **simile**, which makes a comparison using *like* or *as*; or it can be an implied comparison, as in the case of a **metaphor**. **Personification** is a figure of speech in which an object or animal is given human characteristics. An **analogy** is a figure of speech that usually helps explain something unfamiliar or complicated by comparing it to something familiar or simple.

When a metaphor is extended over several lines in a work, it's called an **extended metaphor**. Other forms of figurative language include **overstatement** (or **hyperbole**), **understatement**, **paradox** (a statement that seems contradictory but actually reveals a surprising truth), and **irony**. There are a few different types of **irony**, but **verbal irony** is the most common. It occurs when a speaker says one thing but really means something else, or when there is a noticeable incongruity between what is expected and what is said.

Imagery

Imagery is the verbal expression of a sensory experience and can appeal to any of the five senses. Sometimes imagery depends on very concrete language—that is, descriptions of how things look, feel, sound, smell, or taste. In considering imagery, look carefully at how the sense impressions are created. Also pay attention to patterns of images that are repeated throughout a work. Often writers use figurative language to make their descriptions even more vivid. Look at this description from the Cather passage:

> Queer little red bugs came out and moved in slow squadrons around me. Their backs were polished vermilion, with black spots.

The imagery tells us that these are little red bugs with black spots, but consider what is added with the words "squadrons" and "vermilion," both figurative descriptions.

Syntax

Syntax is the arrangement of words into phrases, clauses, and sentences. When we read closely, we consider whether the sentences in a work are long or short, **simple** or **complex**. The sentence might also be **cumulative**, beginning with an independent clause and followed by subordinate clauses or phrases that add detail; or **periodic**, beginning with subordinate clauses or phrases that build toward the main clause. The word order can be the traditional subject-verb-object order or **inverted** (e.g., verb-subject-object or object-subject-verb). You might also look at syntactic patterns, such as several long sentences followed by a short sentence. Housman uses inversion in several places, perhaps to ensure the rhyme scheme but also to emphasize a point. When he writes, "And home we brought you shoulder-high" (l. 4), the shift in expected word order ("We brought you home") emphasizes "home," which is further emphasized by being repeated two lines later.

Tone and Mood

Tone reflects the speaker's attitude toward the subject of the work. **Mood** is the feeling the reader experiences as a result of the tone. Tone and mood provide the emotional coloring of a work and are created by the writer's stylistic choices. When you describe the tone and mood of a work, try to use at least two precise words, rather than words that are vague and general, such as *happy*, *sad*, or *different*. In describing the tone of the Cather passage, you might say that it is contented and joyful. What is most important is that you consider the style elements that went into creating the tone.

Now that you have some familiarity with the elements of style, you can use them as a starting point for close reading. Here are some questions you can ask of any text:

Diction

- Which of the important words (verbs, nouns, adjectives, and adverbs) in the poem or passage are general and abstract, and which are specific and concrete?
- Are the important words formal, informal, colloquial, or slang?
- Are there words with strong connotations, words we might refer to as "loaded"?

Figurative Language

• Are some words not literal but figurative, creating figures of speech such as metaphors, similes, and personification?

Imagery

• Are the images—the parts of the passage we experience with our five senses—concrete, or do they depend on figurative language to come alive?

Syntax

• What is the order of the words in the sentences? Are they in the usual subject-verb-object order, or are they inverted?

• Which is more prevalent in the passage, nouns or verbs?

• What are the sentences like? Do their meanings build periodically or cumulatively?

• How do the sentences connect their words, phrases, and clauses?

• How is the poem or passage organized? Is it chronological? Does it move from concrete to abstract or vice versa? Or does it follow some other pattern?

• ACTIVITY •

Reread Housman's "To an Athlete Dying Young" (p. 21), and use it to answer the preceding questions on style.

A Sample Close Analysis

Let's look at a passage from Eudora Welty's short story "Old Mr. Marblehall."

> There is Mr. Marblehall's ancestral home. It's not so wonderfully large—it has only four columns—but you always look toward it, the way you always glance into tunnels and see nothing. The river is after it now, and the little back garden has assuredly crumbled away, but the box maze is there on the edge like a trap, to confound the Mississippi River. Deep in the red wall waits the front door—it weighs such a lot, it is perfectly solid, all one piece, black mahogany. . . . And you see—one of *them* is always going in it. There is a knocker shaped like a gasping fish on the door. You have every reason in the world to imagine the inside is dark, with old things about. There's many a big, deathly-looking tapestry, wrinkling and thin, many a sofa shaped like an S. Brocades as tall as the wicked queens in Italian tales stand gathered before the windows. Everything is draped and hooded and shaded, of course, unaffectionate but close. Such rosy lamps! The only sound would be a breath against the prisms, a stirring of the chandelier. It's like old eyelids, the house with one of its shutters, in careful working order, slowly opening outward.
>
> *[1937]*

The passage begins with an incongruity: the house is an "ancestral home," yet "it's not so wonderfully large." This sets up a discrepancy between what we might expect and what the speaker describes. The concrete details in the passage—columns, box maze, front door, knocker, tapestry, sofa, brocades, lamps—suggest formality and elegance, yet adjectives such as "wrinkling and thin," "draped," "hooded," and "shaded" create images of decay, deception, even death. The S-shaped sofas are so snake-like that they practically hiss. The speaker's description creates a sense of decay and menace, from this house that does not live up to the grand description of "ancestral home."

Figurative language emphasizes these incongruities. The speaker uses a simile (in this simile, "like" is implied rather than explicit) to describe the way observers look at the house without actually seeing anything, "the way you always glance into tunnels and see nothing." The box maze is not fun or beautiful but "like a trap," a door knocker is not welcoming but "shaped like a gasping fish," brocades are not elegant but "tall as the wicked queens in Italian tales." Personification deepens this sense of mystery. The river "is after it now," as if in pursuit of the house. The front door "waits," prepared to swallow up any visitors. The furniture is "draped and hooded and shaded," calling to mind both ghosts and executioners. The final simile personifies the house as being "like old eyelids." This image literally refers to the shutters opening slowly but also emphasizes age and decrepitude while suggesting that this house is alive, and watching you. In fact, all of these figures of speech suggest that something sinister is afoot.

Apart from the one short sentence fragment—"Such rosy lamps!"—the sentences are fairly long and build through accumulation of detail. Most are in normal word order with clauses and phrases added one after another to characterize the house and add description and qualification. One exception is an example of inverted syntax—"Deep in the red wall waits the front door"—a phrase that underscores the menace of the entranceway. These sentences acquaint the reader with the house—and suggest something about the character of its owner, Mr. Marblehall. Through the eye of the speaker, we become wary of this place and its occupant.

• ACTIVITY •

Below is the conclusion to F. Scott Fitzgerald's novel *The Great Gatsby*. At the end of the novel, its narrator, Nick Carraway, remembers Jay Gatsby as a person with a great "capacity for wonder." Read the passage carefully. Then analyze how the style conveys this sense of Gatsby.

From *The Great Gatsby*
F. Scott Fitzgerald

Most of the big shore places were closed now and there were hardly any lights except the shadowy, moving glow of a ferryboat across the Sound. And as the moon rose higher the inessential houses began to melt away until gradually I became aware of the old island here that flowered once for Dutch sailors' eyes—a fresh, green breast of the new world. Its vanished trees, the trees that had made way for Gatsby's house, had once pandered in whispers to the last and greatest of all human dreams; for a transitory enchanted moment man must have held his breath in the presence of this continent, compelled into an aesthetic contemplation he neither understood nor desired, face to face for the last time in history with something commensurate to his capacity for wonder.

And as I sat there brooding on the old, unknown world, I thought of Gatsby's wonder when he first picked out the green light at the end of Daisy's dock. He had come a long way to this blue lawn, and his dream must have seemed so close that he could hardly fail to grasp it. He did not know that it was already behind him, somewhere back in that vast obscurity beyond the city, where the dark fields of the republic rolled on under the night.

Gatsby believed in the green light, the orgastic future that year by year recedes before us. It eluded us then, but that's no matter—tomorrow we will run faster, stretch out our arms farther. . . . And one fine morning——

So we beat on, boats against the current, borne back ceaselessly into the past.

[1925]

Special Considerations for Reading Poetry Closely

Reading poetry and fiction closely requires the same careful attention to language, but when you read poetry closely, you will look at some additional elements of style and structure.

Rhyme

As you know, some poems **rhyme** and some—those written in **free verse**—do not. Rhyme at the end of a line is called **end rhyme**, while rhyme within a line of poetry is called **internal rhyme**. Eye (or **sight**) **rhymes** should be considered in addition to the rhymes you can hear. When an author uses poetic license to rhyme words that do not sound quite the same, it is called **near rhyme**. Rhyme is usually notated using letters of the alphabet. For instance, a simple **quatrain** or four-line stanza might rhyme *abab*, or be arranged as **couplets** that rhyme *aabb*. The pattern of rhyme for an entire poem is called its rhyme scheme. It can be useful to consider the effects of rhyme in a poem by charting its rhyme scheme; reading a rhyming poem out loud is also helpful.

Meter

The lines in structured poems often follow a regular pattern of **rhythm** called a **meter**. Literally, meter counts the measure of a line, referring to the pattern of stressed or unstressed syllables, combinations of which we call **feet**. **Iambic** meter is by far the most common in English. An iamb is a poetic foot of two syllables with the stress, or accent, on the second, as in the word "again," or the phrase "by far." The two most common metric patterns are **iambic pentameter**, in which a line consists of five iambic feet, and **iambic tetrameter**, which measures four iambic feet. Notice how "To an Athlete Dying Young," the Housman poem that you read, is in iambic tetrameter. Each of its lines follows a rhythm of four beats, each one an iambic foot with the emphasis on the second syllable:

> The time | you won | your town | the race
> We chaired | you through | the mar | ket-place.

Notice how odd it would sound if you were to emphasize the first syllable.

> The time | you won | your town | the race.

Shakespeare often uses **blank verse** — that is, unrhymed iambic pentameter. For example, in *Hamlet* (p. 720) the ghost speaks chiefly in blank verse. The same blank verse may be spoken in ten words of one syllable each, as in "To prick and sting her. Fare thee well at once," or in as few as three words: "Unhouseled, disappointed, unanealed."

Form

Poetry is sometimes written in conventional forms that can give you hints about how the structure relates to the meaning of the poem. When you recognize a traditional form, consider whether it maintains the conventions or defies them. When you look at the structure of a poem that is not in a traditional form, try to figure out how it is organized. Is it a narrative, in which the action dictates the structure? Are the stanzas chronological, cause and effect, or question and answer? Look for word or sentence patterns or patterns of imagery that might reveal the relationships among the stanzas. Ultimately, what you should be on the lookout for is how the structure reinforces the meaning of the poem.

Although poems have many specialized forms, the most common is the **sonnet**. Traditionally written as love poems, the sonnet form has been used for a wide variety of purposes, including war poems, protest poems, and parodies. Sonnets generally consist of fourteen lines, usually in iambic pentameter, as you may observe in the opening lines of the Shakespearean sonnet you will read in this chapter (p. 36):

> When, in | dis- grace | with For- | tune and | men's eyes
> I all | a- lone | be- weep | my out- | cast state.

There are two classic types of sonnet. The **Italian**, or **Petrarchan**, **sonnet** is divided into an octave (eight lines) rhyming *abba*, *abba* and a sestet (six lines) with a variety of different rhyme schemes: *cdcdcd*, *cdecde*, or *cddcdd*. Traditionally, the octave raises an issue or expresses a doubt, and the sestet resolves the issue or doubt. The shift from the first to the second section is called the "turn." The **English**, or **Shakespearean**, **sonnet** consists of three four-line stanzas and a couplet at the end. This type of sonnet rhymes *abab*, *cdcd*, *efef*, *gg*. The third stanza usually provides the turn, and the last two lines often close the sonnet with a witty remark.

Other common traditional forms include:

- **Elegy.** A contemplative poem, usually for someone who has died.
- **Lyric.** A short poem expressing the personal thoughts or feelings of a first-person speaker.
- **Ode.** A form of poetry used to meditate on or address a single object or condition. It originally followed strict rules of rhythm and rhyme, but by the Romantic period it was more flexible.
- **Villanelle.** A form of poetry in which five **tercets,** or three-line stanzas (rhyme scheme *aba*), are followed by a quatrain (rhyme scheme *abaa*). At the end of tercets two and four, the first line of tercet one is repeated. At the end of tercets three and five, the last line of tercet one is repeated. These two repeated lines, called *refrain lines*, are repeated again to conclude the quatrain. Much of the power of this form lies in its repeated lines and their subtly shifting sense or meaning over the course of the poem.

Poetic Syntax

In addition to looking at the principles of syntax already discussed, when analyzing poetry you will want to be on the lookout for **enjambment** (also called a run-on line, when one line ends without a pause and must continue into the next line to complete its meaning) and **caesura** (a pause within a line of poetry, sometimes punctuated, sometimes not). Consider also line length: are the poem's lines long or short? Do the poem's lines create a visual pattern?

Sound

Sound is the musical quality of poetry. It can be created through some of the techniques we've already mentioned, such as rhyme, enjambment, and caesura. It can also be created by word choice, especially through **alliteration** (the repetition of initial consonant sounds in a sequence of words), **assonance** (the repetition of vowel sounds in a sequence of words), and **onomatopoeia** (use of a word that refers to a noise and whose pronunciation mimics that noise). Sound can also be created by rhythm and **cadence** (similar to rhythm, but related to the rise and fall of the voice). Like all of the elements of style, the key to analysis is to connect the sound of the poem to its meaning.

Let's consider form in "The Red Wheelbarrow," a famous short poem by William Carlos Williams.

> so much depends
> upon
>
> a red wheel
> barrow

glazed with rain   5
water

beside the white
chickens.

[1923]

In only sixteen words, this poem demonstrates how form and sound can not only reinforce an image but can actually create meaning. In this piece, Williams creates a visual image, analogous to a still-life painting. Instead of treating the text as a sentence, he breaks it up into four couplets that guide the way we experience the language, and thus the ideas.

The poem is written in <u>free verse</u> with no capitalization or internal punctuation, so we approach it word by word. <u>The use of enjambment stops us at each interval</u> as if Williams is asking us to consider carefully as we go along. He begins, "so much depends," stressing the verb and reinforcing how much is at stake by pausing there before continuing to the next line. By giving the preposition "upon" its own line, he seems to be withholding the central image of the poem, thus making it even starker when, in the second stanza, we encounter "a red wheel / barrow." The monosyllables in the third line give us a closer perspective and break the image down into its parts. Even the word "wheelbarrow" is divided, perhaps to remind us that it is a compound—and crafted—word, just as the wheelbarrow itself is a well-crafted tool (a wheel + a barrow).

In the next stanza, Williams vividly develops the image: the red wheelbarrow is "glazed with rain / water," giving us a clearer sense of its texture and appearance. The fourth couplet adds a contrast of color and movement when the position of the wheelbarrow is described as "beside the white / chickens"—static red juxtaposed with moving white.

The sounds reinforce the sensuous image being created. Williams unifies the first and second stanzas with the long *o* sounds present in the words "so" and "barrow." The alliteration of *r* in "red" and "rain" links the second and third stanzas, as does the assonance of "glazed" with "rain" and "beside" with "white." The *ch* of "much" in the opening line echoes in the final line's "chickens," bringing the poem full circle.

Thus, even a modern poem—one that does not have the formality or strict rules of a villanelle or sonnet—illustrates the importance of form and sound. By arranging a series of very simple words, carefully chosen and placed, Williams turns a straightforward declarative sentence into a vivid image full of subtle shades of meaning.

Now that you have some familiarity with the elements of style specific to poetry, you can use them when reading poetry closely. Here are some questions you can ask of any text:

Rhyme

- Does the poem have a regular rhyme scheme? If so, what is it?
- What other types of rhymes does the poem include, such as internal rhymes, sight rhymes, or near rhymes?
- How does the rhyme scheme affect the poem's sound, tone, or meaning?

Meter

- Does the poem have a regular meter? If so, what is it?
- Read the poem aloud. How does the meter affect the tone of the poem? For instance, does the meter make the poem seem formal, informal, singsongy, celebratory, somber?

Form

- Does the poem follow a traditional form? If so, which?
- If the poem follows a traditional form, but has untraditional content, what might be the poet's purpose in subverting the traditional form?
- If the poem does not follow a traditional form, what sort of logic structures the poem? For instance, why are the stanzas broken as they are? What is the relationship among the stanzas?

Poetic Syntax

- What examples of enjambment can you find? How does the enjambment affect the sound and meaning of the line?
- What examples of caesura can you find? What is the impact of the caesura?
- If the poem has sentences, are they long or short or a combination of the two? How does the length of the sentences relate to the meaning of the poem?

Sound

- How does the poem use rhyme, meter, form, and poetic syntax to create sound?
- How does the poem use repetition, such as alliteration and assonance, to create sound?
- How do the sounds created in the poem connect to the meaning of the poem?

• ACTIVITY •

Use the following sonnet by John Keats to answer the questions above.

Bright Star, would I were stedfast as thou art—
JOHN KEATS

Bright Star, would I were stedfast as thou art—
  Not in lone splendor hung aloft the night,
And watching, with eternal lids apart,
  Like nature's patient, sleepless Eremite,[1]
The moving waters at their priestlike task   5
  Of pure ablution round earth's human shores,
Or gazing on the new soft-fallen masque
  Of snow upon the mountains and the moors—

---

[1]Hermit, particularly one under a religious vow.—EDS.

No—yet still stedfast, still unchangeable
   Pillow'd upon my fair love's ripening breast,   10
To feel for ever its soft swell and fall,
   Awake for ever in a sweet unrest,
Still, still to hear her tender-taken breath,
And so live ever—or else swoon to death—

                                   [1820]

A Sample Close Analysis

Now that we've considered some of the specific techniques poets use to convey their message, let's look at a poem by Robert Herrick, "Delight in Disorder," in which he describes the appeal of dressing in a way that is careless—or seemingly so.

A sweet disorder in the dress
Kindles in clothes a wantonness.
A lawn[1] about the shoulders thrown
Into a fine distraction;
An erring lace, which here and there   5
Enthralls the crimson stomacher,[2]
A cuff neglectful, and thereby
Ribbons to flow confusedly;
A winning wave, deserving note,
In the tempestuous petticoat;   10
A careless shoestring, in whose tie
I see a wild civility;
Do more bewitch me than when art
Is too precise in every part.

                                   [1648]

This is a great poem for practicing close reading. Written over 350 years ago, it may seem difficult at first; after a few readings, though, its meaning becomes clear, and it offers some obvious examples of how style and structure create deeper meaning and nuance.

First, be sure you understand what Herrick is talking about. The speaker describes in detail a woman's clothing—style, color, and fabric. Some of the vocabulary is unfamiliar to readers today, such as *lawn* and *stomacher*. Other words, such as *petticoat*, may be **archaic**, but you have probably come across them before. As always, if you don't know what something means, you should look it up.

As you read the poem, you might have noticed the personification. The speaker notes the "fine distraction" of the scarf thrown over the woman's shoulders, a "cuff"

---

[1] Linen scarf.—EDS.
[2] A piece of stiff, embroidered cloth worn over the stomach.—EDS.

that is "neglectful," ribbons that "flow confusedly," and a "tempestuous petticoat." The personification suggests that the clothes reflect qualities of the person wearing them. Similarly, the "erring lace" "[e]nthralls the crimson stomacher," as if a mere decoration could take such deliberate action. Two **oxymorons** (paradoxes made up of two seemingly contradictory words) support the possibility that something is going on other than the literal description of clothing. The opening line refers to a "sweet disorder," but most would consider disorder unsettling, hardly "sweet"; later, the speaker sees a "wild civility," another seeming contradiction, because how can "civility"—or courteous behavior—be "wild"? Now that you're aware of the personification and the oxymorons in this poem, reread it to see if you can pick up on what they suggest.

Note the words suggesting passion: *Kindles, wantonness, crimson, tempestuous,* and *bewitch*. Is this poem actually about seduction? If so, its indirect manner is not overtly sexual or vulgar but flirtatious, sly, even mischievous. Alliteration adds a teasing singsong quality: "Delight . . . Disorder," "winning wave," and "precise . . . part." Further, the symmetry of the alliteration brings a bit of order into the description of disorder—but only a bit.

We might look to the structure of the poem for further evidence of the playful tone. The structure seems regular and predictable. The fourteen lines are presented in seven rhymed pairs, or couplets, most having eight syllables. The opening and closing couplets have exactly rhyming final syllables ("dress" / "wantonness" and "art" / "part"). Notice the neatly repeating **parallel structure** of lines 3, 5, 7, 9, and 11. However, there are inconsistencies within the poem. Some of the rhymes are only near rhymes (e.g., ll. 11 and 12: "tie" does not rhyme with "civility"). The poem's lines are in iambic tetrameter, but the rhythm is not always even. The evenness of the opening line, for instance ("A sweet disorder in the dress") is violated by line 10 ("In the tempestuous petticoat"). It seems Herrick's contention that "disorder" can be "sweet" is reflected in the structure of the poem.

Or, put in more thematic terms, Herrick might be reminding us that appearances can be deceiving, that perfection may not be as appealing as charming imperfections. Or, given the cultural mores of his time dictating strict outward propriety, he might be telling his readers that passion lurks just beneath the veneer of polite society.

• ACTIVITY •

Spend some time reading the following poem by Simon Ortiz closely. Analyze how the poem's style and structure help the reader understand why the speaker needs his father's song and what that song might be.

My Father's Song
SIMON ORTIZ

Wanting to say things,
I miss my father tonight.
His voice, the slight catch,

the depth from his thin chest,
the tremble of emotion   5
in something he has just said
to his son, his song:

    We planted corn one Spring at Acu—
    we planted several times
    but this one particular time   10
    I remember the soft damp sand
    in my hand.

    My father had stopped at one point
    to show me an overturned furrow;
    the plowshare had unearthed   15
    the burrow nest of a mouse
    in the soft moist sand.

    Very gently, he scooped tiny pink animals
    into the palm of his hand
    and told me to touch them.   20
    We took them to the edge
    of the field and put them in the shade
    of a sand moist clod.

    I remember the very softness
    of cool and warm sand and tiny alive mice   25
    and my father saying things.

[1977]

Talking with the Text

To become a more careful reader, the most important and helpful thing you can do is read, read, and reread, but there are some techniques that can make your reading more active. The most important point to keep in mind is that your goal is not simply to identify and list **literary elements**—although that's a first step—but to analyze their effect. In other words, how do the choices the writer makes help to deliver the work's message or meaning? We'll discuss several strategies to help you become a more active reader, a reader who goes beyond summary to analysis and interpretation.

Think Aloud

As we mentioned at the beginning of this chapter, the first step to close reading is to start asking questions. These can be simple ones (such as the meaning of unfamiliar vocabulary) or more complex ones (such as the meaning suggested by figurative language). Since the goal is to "talk with the text," a good place to start is by talking to one another.

Pair up with a classmate and take turns reading and thinking out loud; that is, read a line or a sentence, then stop and comment. See what your partner has to say. Then let him or her read the next line or sentence, and repeat the process until you've finished the text. Although your comments can go in a number of directions, here are a few suggestions:

- Pose questions about something that confuses you or about a possible interpretation
- Identify unfamiliar vocabulary or allusions
- Note specific stylistic elements and their effect
- Rephrase inverted lines
- Make connections within the poem, or passage of fiction, noting any repetitions, patterns, or contrasts

Once you've gone through the text carefully by reading, talking, questioning, and analyzing, you have a strong foundation to either contribute to a discussion in a larger group or prepare to write about the piece.

• ACTIVITY •

Think aloud with a partner on the following poem by Christina Georgina Rossetti. Keep in mind that the title reflects an old English proverb: "Promises are like pie-crust, made to be broken."

Promises like Pie-Crust
CHRISTINA GEORGINA ROSSETTI

Promise me no promises,
    So will I not promise you;
Keep we both our liberties,
    Never false and never true:
Let us hold the die uncast,   5
    Free to come as free to go;
For I cannot know your past,
    And of mine what can you know?

You, so warm, may once have been
    Warmer towards another one;   10
I, so cold, may once have seen
    Sunlight, once have felt the sun:
Who shall show us if it was
    Thus indeed in time of old?
Fades the image from the glass   15
    And the fortune is not told.

If you promised, you might grieve
   For lost liberty again;
If I promised, I believe
   I should fret to break the chain: 20
Let us be the friends we were,
   Nothing more but nothing less;
Many thrive on frugal fare
   Who would perish of excess.

[1861]

Annotation

Annotation is simply noting on the page words that strike you, phrases that confuse or thrill you, or places where you want to talk back to the speaker or narrator. Your goal is to record ideas and impressions for later analysis. If you are not allowed to write in your book, make your annotations on sticky notes attached to the outside margins of the pages. Why bother to do this? Here's what well-known scholar and avid reader Mortimer Adler says:

> Why is marking up a book indispensable to reading? First, it keeps you awake. (And I don't mean merely conscious; I mean awake.) In the second place, reading, if it is active, is thinking, and thinking tends to express itself in words, spoken or written. The marked book is usually the thought-through book. Finally, writing helps you remember the thought you had, or the thoughts the author expressed. (*How to Read a Book*)

So whether you use sticky notes, highlight passages, or write comments directly in the margins, annotation helps you become a better reader. There are no hard-and-fast rules for annotating properly, but the following approach is a good way to get started.

On your first reading, circle or highlight words or phrases that are interesting or unfamiliar, as well as any elements of style. Note in the margins or on a sticky note why you are circling or highlighting these words. If you just circle, or just highlight, you will soon forget why you did so. Don't worry if you can't remember the literary term for what you find; just describe it. Note words that stand out for their beauty or oddity as well as words you need to look up. Don't hesitate to make an educated guess at their meaning.

On your second reading, move from investigating individual words and phrases to making larger-scale observations. If you see patterns, words, or ideas that seem to connect to one another or are repeated, circle those words or ideas and use lines to connect them. Note shifts in tone or viewpoint. Underline lines or passages that you think are important for understanding the meaning of the poem or passage. Look for themes in the piece. Pose questions. You might want to use colored pencils to differentiate your first-reading annotations from your second-reading annotations. Think of this as a work in progress, an emerging interpretation. You may change your mind later, but annotating will record how your thinking develops.

After the third reading, write for three to five minutes about the work. Paraphrase it, and then react to it as a whole and to its parts. Respond to the work in any way you like. Informal, exploratory writing can help you begin to understand what you read.

Here is an example of annotation, using William Shakespeare's Sonnet 29:

First Reading

> When, in disgrace with Fortune and men's eyes,   *Personification*
> I all alone beweep my outcast state,
> And trouble deaf heaven with my bootless cries,   *? Look up*
> And look upon myself and curse my fate,
> Wishing me like to one more rich in hope,   5
> Featured like him, like him with friends possessed,
> Desiring this man's art, and that man's scope,   *? odd use of this word*
> With what I most enjoy contented least,
> Yet in these thoughts myself almost despising,
> Haply I think on thee, and then my state,   10
> Like to the lark at break of day arising   *Long simile!*
> From sullen earth, sings hymns at heaven's gate;
>   For thy sweet love remembered such wealth brings
>   That then I scorn to change my state with kings.

More personification (on line 3)

Multiple meanings (on line 7)

Sounds like "Happily" (on line 10)

More personification (on line 12)

[1609]

Second Reading

> When, in disgrace with Fortune and men's eyes,   *Personification*
> I all alone beweep my outcast state,
> And trouble deaf heaven with my bootless cries,   *? Look up*
> And look upon myself and curse my fate,   *Contrast: cries vs. sings*
> Wishing me like to one more rich in hope,   *Repeated references to wealth . . . but of hope of friends*
> Featured like him, like him with friends possessed,
> Desiring this man's art, and that man's scope,   *? odd use of this word*
> With what I most enjoy contented least,
> Yet in these thoughts myself almost despising,   *Shift in tone*
> Haply I think on thee, and then my state,
> Like to the lark at break of day arising   *Long simile!*
> From sullen earth, sings hymns at heaven's gate
>   For thy sweet love remembered such wealth brings
>   That then I scorn to change my state with kings.

More personification (on line 3)

Multiple meanings (on line 7)

Sounds like "Happily" (on line 10)

More personification (on line 12)

Key! They're poor, but they have each other

Juxtaposing heaven & earth. Earthly things (wealth) not as important as love.

Repetition of "state" Dual meaning?

[1609]

Exploratory Writing

In this Shakespearean sonnet, the speaker seems miserable at first. He's crying about being an outcast. I'm not sure about those "bootless cries." He says he's jealous of people who have it better than he has it. He envies people with hope, with talent, with friends, and with scope (not sure what that means, but maybe more open-minded?). He seems to also just wish he had more money. He uses words related to fortune and wealth a few times in the poem, once in the first line, again in line 5, and finally in the second-to-last line, but the meaning is a little different each time. Something happens around line 9, with the word "Yet." Just when he hates himself the most ("almost despising"), he thinks of someone (his beloved?) and the whole tone of the poem changes. Suddenly birds are singing "hymns at heaven's gate." And they're larks — morning birds, if I remember from *Romeo & Juliet* — which suggests they're pretty optimistic. By the last line the speaker has decided that he wouldn't trade places with a king. It seems as though the speaker is reflecting on how we often get down on ourselves when we are criticized or when things don't go our way. When the speaker is most depressed, he has only to think of how he is loved, and his optimism returns. He no longer wishes to trade places with those who seem more fortunate (like kings) because somebody loves him. Lucky guy.

Graphic Organizer

Another approach to close reading is to use a graphic organizer, which helps break the poem or passage of fiction down into specific areas for commentary. Your teacher may divide the text for you, or you may discover the divisions as you begin your analysis. For poetry, you can always use the line or stanza divisions as natural breaking points. The graphic organizer on pages 38–39 asks you first to paraphrase what the poem is saying, then to identify a literary element by name or description, and finally to consider its effect. Setting up the close reading in such a structured way guides you through an analysis that does not stop with simple restatement or even identification of elements of style but links them to effect and meaning.

LINES	PARAPHRASE (PUT IN YOUR OWN WORDS OR SUMMARIZE)
When, in disgrace with Fortune and men's eyes,	When things are bad, he cries about it by himself.
I all alone beweep my outcast state,	
And trouble deaf heaven with my bootless cries,	God doesn't listen to speaker; he is miserable and self-pitying.
And look upon myself and curse my fate,	
Wishing me like to one more rich in hope,	List of anonymous people the speaker envies.
Featured like him, like him with friends possessed,	
Desiring this man's art, and that man's scope,	
With what I most enjoy contented least,	
Yet in these thoughts myself almost despising,	When he's just about hating himself, by chance he thinks of his beloved.
Haply I think on thee, and then my state,	
Like to the lark at break of day arising	Compares state of mind to lark, singing heavenly music.
From sullen earth, sings hymns at heaven's gate;	
For thy sweet love remembered such wealth brings	His beloved makes him feel so wealthy that he wouldn't trade places with a king.
That then I scorn to change my state with kings.	

ELEMENT OF STYLE	EFFECT OR FUNCTION
"Fortune" refers to both wealth and luck. Inversion "all alone" before "beweep" "outcast state."	First reference to words connected to money or riches. Inversion sounds more formal, mournful, sadder. First appearance of three "states."
Figures of speech "bootless cries" "deaf heaven."	"Bootless" means "useless" but more pathetic — suggests bare feet. He's so pathetic that heaven offers no comfort; he can only look inward.
The word "like" is repeated. Second word related to wealth: "rich." Quatrain ends with "contented least"; line also has unconventional word order.	The speaker wants so badly to be someone else that he says it twice; there is no "I" in these lines, just those more fortunate than he is. A person with hope seems "rich" to the speaker. Quatrain ends on a negative note.
Shift — "Yet" Diction — "Haply" Repetition — second "state"	Tone shifts with "Yet." "Haply" means "by chance" but sounds like *happily*. "State" a little better this time.
Simile — his state is like a lark. "hymns" and "heaven"	The lark — associated with morning — suggests awakening. Word choices change the sonnet's mood and tone.
Repetition — third "state"; third reference to wealth. Word order is straightforward in last line.	The poem ends with a direct, clear state-ment of what makes the speaker feel fortunate, rich, and wealthy — and it's not money. He's content with the "state" he's in. Word order is traditional: subject, verb, object. Order is restored.

• ACTIVITY •

The following passage is from the opening of Nathaniel Hawthorne's novel *The Scarlet Letter.* Annotate the passage using the three-step process we have described.

From *The Scarlet Letter*
NATHANIEL HAWTHORNE

A throng of bearded men, in sad-colored garments and gray, steeple-crowned hats, intermixed with women, some wearing hoods, and others bareheaded, was assembled in front of a wooden edifice, the door of which was heavily timbered with oak, and studded with iron spikes.

The founders of a new colony, whatever Utopia of human virtue and happiness they might originally project, have invariably recognized it among their earliest practical necessities to allot a portion of the virgin soil as a cemetery, and another portion as the site of a prison. In accordance with this rule, it may safely be assumed that the forefathers of Boston had built the first prison-house, somewhere in the vicinity of Cornhill, almost as seasonably as they marked out the first burial-ground, on Isaac Johnson's lot, and round about his grave, which subsequently became the nucleus of all the congregated sepulchres in the old church-yard of King's Chapel. Certain it is, that, some fifteen or twenty years after the settlement of the town, the wooden jail was already marked with weather-stains and other indications of age, which gave a yet darker aspect to its beetle-browed and gloomy front. The rust on the ponderous iron-work of its oaken door looked more antique than any thing else in the new world. Like all that pertains to crime, it seemed never to have known a youthful era. Before this ugly edifice, and between it and the wheel-track of the street, was a grass-plot, much overgrown with burdock, pig-weed, apple-peru, and such unsightly vegetation, which evidently found something congenial in the soil that had so early borne the black flower of civilized society, a prison. But, on one side of the portal, and rooted almost at the threshold, was a wild rose-bush, covered, in this month of June, with its delicate gems, which might be imagined to offer their fragrance and fragile beauty to the prisoner as he went in, and to the condemned criminal as he came forth to his doom, in token that the deep heart of Nature could pity and be kind to him.

This rose-bush, by a strange chance, has been kept alive in history; but whether it had merely survived out of the stern old wilderness, so long after the fall of the gigantic pines and oaks that originally overshadowed it,—or whether, as there is fair authority for believing, it had sprung up under the footsteps of the sainted Ann Hutchinson, as she entered the prison-door,—we shall not take upon us to determine. Finding it so directly on the threshold of our narrative, which is now about to issue from that inauspicious portal, we could hardly do otherwise than pluck one of its flowers and present it to the reader. It may serve, let us hope, to symbolize some sweet moral blossom, that may be found along the track, or relieve the darkening close of a tale of human frailty and sorrow.

[1850]

From Analysis to Essay: Writing a Close Analysis Essay

It should be clear by now that the closer we examine a piece of writing on the word and sentence level, the closer we come to understanding its deeper level of meaning. When we write about literature, it is those deeper levels that we are interested in; otherwise, we run the risk of summarizing a work rather than analyzing it.

Let's do a close reading of "Slam, Dunk, & Hook" by Yusef Komunyakaa. Begin by reading the piece and formulating some first-impression questions and observations.

Fast breaks. Lay ups. With Mercury's
Insignia on our sneakers,
We outmaneuvered the footwork
Of bad angels. Nothing but a hot
Swish of strings like silk   5
Ten feet out. In the roundhouse
Labyrinth our bodies
Created, we could almost
Last forever, poised in midair
Like storybook sea monsters.   10
A high note hung there
A long second. Off
The rim. We'd corkscrew
Up & dunk balls that exploded
The skullcap of hope & good   15
Intention. Bug-eyed, lanky,
All hands & feet . . . sprung rhythm.
We were metaphysical when girls
Cheered on the sidelines.
Tangled up in a falling,   20
Muscles were a bright motor
Double-flashing to the metal hoop
Nailed to our oak.
When Sonny Boy's mama died
He played nonstop all day, so hard   25
Our backboard splintered.
Glistening with sweat, we jibed
& rolled the ball off our
Fingertips. Trouble
Was there slapping a blackjack   30
Against an open palm.
Dribble, drive to the inside, feint,
& glide like a sparrow hawk.
Lay ups. Fast breaks.
We had moves we didn't know   35
We had. Our bodies spun
On swivels of bone & faith,
Through a lyric slipknot

> Of joy, & we knew we were
> Beautiful & dangerous.   40

[1992]

Analyzing

Sometimes it's helpful to start by summarizing the work in one sentence, just so you're sure what's going on.

> In "Slam, Dunk, & Hook," the speaker expresses how basketball provided an escape from his life's troubles.

Clearly, even this initial statement engages in a certain level of interpretation—not only does it state that the poem is about basketball, but it also draws the inference that the speaker's life was troubled and that basketball was his means of escape. The next step is examining what makes the poem more complex than this brief summary. How does Komunyakaa convey a sense of exuberance? of joy? of danger? How does he make the situation something we feel rather than just read about?

Let's begin our analysis by thinking a bit about the poem's title. It's all about action, about moves. But a "slam dunk" is just one move, so why is there a comma between "Slam" and "Dunk"? Does this construction anticipate the rhythm in the poem itself? Our next consideration could be the speaker, who is evidently reflecting on a time in his youth when he played basketball with his friends. The speaker describes the "metal hoop" that was "Nailed to [their] oak" and a backboard "splintered" by hard use. We're not in the world of professional sports or even in the school gym. You will probably notice some things about the poem as a whole, such as its short lines, strong verbs, and vivid images. Keep those things in mind as you take a look at the following annotation, where we examine the way specific elements of style and structure add layers of meaning to Komunyakaa's poem. We'll use the three-step annotation process introduced on pages 35–37.

Slam, Dunk, & Hook
YUSEF KOMUNYAKAA

Begins with matter-of-fact tone	Fast breaks. Lay ups. With Mercury's	— Allusion: Greek god
	Insignia on our sneakers,	
	We outmaneuvered the footwork	
Oxymoron. Refers to opponents. Symbolic?	Of bad angels. Nothing but a hot	*Strong visual and tactile imagery.*
	Swish of strings like silk 5	*Alliteration*
Great metaphor!	Ten feet out. In the roundhouse	
Another allusion	Labyrinth our bodies	
	Created, we could almost	
Interesting contrast with fast pace of the poem	Last forever, poised in midair	*Another allusion. All*
	Like storybook sea monsters. 10	*to things that are mythical, and possibly*
	A high note hung there	*dangerous*
	A long second. Off	
	The rim. We'd corkscrew	

Powerful image —— Up & dunk balls that (exploded)
The skullcap of hope & good   15
Intention. (Bug-eyed, lanky,)
All hands & feet . . . sprung rhythm. ——
We were metaphysical when girls
Cheered on the sidelines.
Tangled up in a falling,   20
Muscles were a bright motor
Double-flashing to the metal hoop
Nailed to our oak. ——
When Sonny Boy's mama died
He played nonstop all day, so hard   25
Our backboard splintered.
Glistening with sweat, we jibed ——
& rolled the ball off our
Fingertips. Trouble ——
Was there slapping a blackjack ——   30 —— Look up
Against an open palm.
Dribble, drive to the inside, feint,
& glide like a sparrow hawk.
(Lay ups. Fast breaks.)
We had moves we didn't know ——   35
We had. Our bodies spun
On swivels of bone & faith, ——
Through a lyric slipknot
Of joy, & we knew we were
Beautiful & dangerous.   40

[1992]

Margin annotations:
- Contrast between their powerful play and awkward bodies
- Good description
- Shift in tone. Not about their power, but power of the game.
- Refers to tree, but oak is strong. Is basketball the player's "oak"?
- Returns to vivid description, but tone is reverent, not boastful
- Personification
- Inversion of first line
- Realizing potential
- Interesting. Game is more than physical
- Key idea.

Exploratory Writing

A "slam dunk" is a type of shot in basketball—a skillful play, and a little victory in itself, so you say about something you did really well, "It was a slam dunk." But Komunyakaa separates the two words as if "slam" and "dunk"—and "hook"—are separate. Maybe there are connoisseurs of the game who know the difference between a slam and a dunk? But the commas create a sense of jerky movement, abruptness. The title is fragmented, just like the images in the poem—lines break up sentences, some sentences aren't full sentences, lots of strong verbs are used ("outmaneuvered," "poised," "corkscrew," "exploded," "tangled up," "rolled," "dribble," "glide"). Maybe the poet has pent-up emotion or maybe he is signifying that the players do. All the motion and movement gets played out in the game, but even the basketball court can't contain it. There's energy but also anger. The speaker (Komunyakaa?) is remembering, so the images might be fragmented the way memory is often thought to be. Still, even with the fragmentation, these guys are beautiful, almost majestic in the way they fly and spin in the air and take control of the ball.

Playing basketball's a release for some, like the way Sonny Boy tries to forget the pain of his mother's death when he's on the court. He plays until the "backboard splintered," just like his emotions are splintered. I think these young black men — their race isn't actually mentioned, but you get a sense that they're African American like Komunyakaa — are overflowing with potential to defy their hard lives and racial oppression. They take out their anger on the basketball court. Those references to "Mercury" and "sea monsters" are about gods, mythical creatures who are superhuman. That's how the players feel on the court, where being young and strong means everything. But off the court — it's a different world.

There is no denying that doing a detailed annotation like this one takes time. But understanding a text with layers of meaning requires time and attention to detail, especially if you are preparing to write about it. Plus, once you have examined the work so closely, you'll have already found ideas and evidence to use in your essay.

Developing a Thesis Statement

When it comes time to write a close analysis essay, the first thing to do is formulate a **thesis statement**. You may end up changing it as you go, but having some idea of your argument will help you stay focused. Your teacher will likely have provided you with a prompt or an assignment, and if you've done a thorough job of reading and taking notes in the form of annotation or a graphic organizer, you will probably have more ideas than you can actually use in the essay. For example, your reading may have revealed the intense and vivid imagery that Komunyakaa develops. You may have also noticed mythic allusions to Mercury and sea monsters, and underlying themes — like the transformative power of the game. You might also have noticed the feeling that trouble always seems to be looming nearby, but never seems to touch the players while they're playing. You may have noted the poem's syntax, with lines that alternate between sentences and fragments. Does this pattern suggest the quick movements of the game? There are several ways to approach this poem and many possible interpretations.

Let's say your teacher has assigned you the following prompt:

> Write an essay in which you discuss how the style and structure of Yusef Komunyakaa's "Slam, Dunk, & Hook" convey the speaker's attitude toward the game of basketball.

Remember, your thesis must be an interpretation: an argument about the meaning of the poem that you will support with evidence from the text. You should avoid creating a thesis statement that is so broad that it just restates the prompt or assignment, such as the following:

> Yusef Komunyakaa uses style and structure to convey the speaker's attitude toward the game of basketball in his poem "Slam, Dunk, & Hook."

Not only does this thesis fail to mention which specific elements the writer plans to discuss, but it also fails to identify the speaker's attitude. The thesis needs to focus on specific characteristics of the poem's style and structure, so that in the body of the essay you can analyze how they help convey your interpretation of the speaker's attitude toward the game of basketball.

On the other hand, it is important not to narrow your thesis so much that there is nothing to say about it, such as the following:

> In "Slam, Dunk, & Hook," Yusef Komunyakaa uses classical allusions.

Although this thesis isolates a style element—classical allusions—it does not interpret the speaker's attitude, nor does it recognize the complexity of the poem. You could not discuss a thesis like this for long before running out of things to say. A good thesis should be expressed clearly and should inform the reader of the essay's purpose. It is the backbone of your essay, and everything in the essay will connect to it.

Working with the prompt above, let's consider the poem's style and structure. Looking back at what we've noted about "Slam, Dunk, & Hook" in the annotations, we see many vivid images of action, grace, beauty, and the players' "sprung rhythm." We also find danger: the danger of a "roundhouse / Labyrinth," and "Trouble . . . slapping a blackjack / Against an open palm." The players are also "Beautiful & dangerous," and when they are on the court they are able to outmaneuver the "bad angels" in their lives. The game seems to help the players both escape the world, and transcend it. They are not just playing basketball with a rickety hoop nailed to an oak tree; they are gods like "Mercury," they are "sea monsters," they are "metaphysical." Remembering that it is always important to address a work's complexity, we might develop the following thesis—though this is only one possibility—for an essay that examines the way the style and structure of "Slam, Dunk, & Hook" conveys the speaker's attitude.

> In "Slam, Dunk, & Hook," Yusef Komunyakaa uses vivid images, classical allusions, and metaphors to characterize the game that offers both escape and transcendence for its players.

Organizing a Close Analysis Essay

Once you have an idea for a thesis statement—and, remember, it can change as you plan and write—think about the way you will support it. Look back at the text and at your notes. Think about the ideas that inspired your thesis. Your essay might be organized around the style elements, with a paragraph each on vivid images, classical allusions, and metaphor, in the case of our sample thesis statement. Or you could approach it a different way: you might group your ideas according to the different attitudes the speaker has about basketball, with one paragraph on the beauty of the game, another on how it serves as escape from the troubles of everyday life, and another on how basketball helps the players transcend themselves, becoming mythical, metaphysical.

You've probably noticed that the thesis we developed is likely to lead to a five-paragraph essay. Perhaps you've been warned to stay away from this organization because it is formulaic or prescriptive. We agree: stay away from the formulaic or prescriptive. However, the five-paragraph essay may or may not fall into that category. There's no rule that says that every question or topic will fit neatly into an introduction, three body (or developmental) paragraphs, and a conclusion. Yet if you happen to have three points to make, you'll end up with five paragraphs that could form a cogent and insightful essay.

Integrating Quotations

The following essay uses brief quotes from the poem as textual evidence, a word or two woven into the writer's own sentence. For longer quotations, a forward slash mark indicates a line break. You will notice that each of the examples is explained. In fact, it's a good idea to aim for a sentence or two of explanation, sometimes called commentary or analysis, for each of your examples. If you need more help with integrating quotations smoothly into your own sentences, see page 152 in Chapter 4.

Documenting Sources

In a close analysis essay, you are likely only writing about one text, so you won't need a formal Works Cited page. Your teacher may ask you to use line numbers to identify where your quotations can be found, but with a short poem or passage of fiction it may be unnecessary. If you do add line numbers, they should go in parentheses after the quotation mark and before your punctuation, like this:

> Described as a "roundhouse / Labyrinth" (ll. 6–7), the activity on the court . . .

A Sample Close Analysis Essay

Read the sample essay here, and respond to the questions at the end.

The Beauty and Danger of Basketball

Carlton Curtis

In "Slam, Dunk, & Hook," African American poet Yusef Komunyakaa moves from a description of the physicality of basketball to a philosophical reflection on the lives of the players. Written in terse lines, this poem embodies the energy of young athletes on the court, set against the stark backdrop of the society they live in. Vivid images, classical allusions, and metaphors characterize the game that is both escape and transcendence for its players.

[handwritten margin note: 3 sentences]

"Slam, Dunk, & Hook" is an exaltation of the sport of basketball and the force of the rhythm, power, and grace it inspires in its players. The beginning lines describe the motion of shots in basketball as swift and beautiful, ballet-like maneuvers, yet the short lines pulse with their own energy, conveying the steady beat of a basketball being dribbled down the court or maybe even a drum beat. By using a fragment such as "Nothing but a hot / Swish of strings like silk / Ten feet out," Komunyakaa lets an image replace the measured thought of a full sentence. That image captures the quick movement and vitality of the players as they take their best shots. Enjambment, such as "A high note hung there / A long second," suspends the moment in time, making the reader part of the "long second." In fact, Komunyakaa ends several lines in midair, as it were, giving a feeling of the players being in flight. They "could almost / Last forever, poised in midair," they "corkscrew / Up," and they "feint, / & glide." Even the ampersand that replaces the word "and" suggests motion and speed.

The poem flows with exuberant motion, captured in verbs such as "corkscrew," "exploded," "tangled," "splintered," and "Double-flashing." Komunyakaa emphasizes the sheer physicality with images such as "the roundhouse / Labyrinth our bodies / Created." These players are "All hands & feet . . . sprung rhythm"; they sweat and dribble. The comparisons created by similes and metaphors emphasize their power. They "glide like a sparrow hawk," their "Muscles were a bright motor / Double-flashing," and their "bodies spun / On swivels of bone & faith." That last image, combining both concrete and abstract words, is a reminder that this game is more than just basketball to them.

The classical allusions to Mercury, a labyrinth, and sea monsters suggest that these players become more than just kids on the street. Although the reference to Mercury — the Roman messenger of the gods — starts as an actual insignia on a player's sneakers, the symbol also associates the players' movement with speed, flight, and purpose. They are imbued with a mythical power, an epic sensibility, and are frozen in time with their youthful beauty intact: "we could almost / Last forever, poised in midair / Like storybook sea monsters." They become so swift that they can "outmaneuver[ed] the footwork / Of bad angels." The speaker sums up the mythical power of the players on the court when he says, "We were metaphysical when girls / Cheered on the sidelines." They transcend their physical and perceived limitations and play as the chorus of fans lifts them to a higher state of being. They may not be gods, but they have mythic possibilities.

Yet they are not all grace and beauty. The struggle on the basketball court develops as a metaphor for the lives of these players, trying to "outmaneuver[ed] the footwork / Of bad angels." The description of muscle and movement gives way in the second half of the poem to a passage about the death of Sonny Boy's mother, a loss he copes with by escaping to the court: "He played nonstop all day, so hard / Our backboard splintered." Sonny Boy's crisis, the speaker seems to be saying, is not the exception because "Trouble / Was there slapping a blackjack / Against an open palm." Trouble is part of the lives of these young men, who play with a powerful intent in their hearts, the intent to defy the limitations of their bodies and the limitations of their fortunes as young black men in America. They vent their frustrations on the steel rims and backboards of street ball courts and dream of breaking whatever boundaries that personified "Trouble" brings.

The game of basketball is a release for the players in the poem, whether from the perceived limitations of their youth or perhaps racial or economic barriers. The young men lose themselves on the court, wishing to manipulate their lives as effortlessly as they do the ball. They know they must fight to soar and excel beyond their station of second-class citizens. In the end, the game is not just an escape but an exercise in transcendence, where the stakes are control, freedom, and possibility. The intensity and concentration of losing themselves in basketball becomes a "lyric slipknot / Of joy." These young men are not only confident but also menacing in the knowledge that they are both "Beautiful & dangerous."

Questions

1. Examine the relationship between the thesis and the topic sentences. Do you think the basic structure of the essay is effective or ineffective? Why?
2. Paragraphs 2 and 3 discuss vivid imagery, but the second paragraph focuses on how syntax conveys those images. Should syntax have been specified in the thesis? Explain.
3. How does the essay support its argument with evidence from the text? Cite a paragraph that you find especially effective and explain why.
4. The student writer argues that the basketball players are using the sport to overcome racial and economic challenges. To what extent do you think that the textual evidence supports this interpretation?
5. What is another argument you might make based on a close reading of "Slam, Dunk, & Hook"? It does not have to contradict this student's interpretation entirely but rather offer another way to read the poem or a different conclusion than the one drawn in this sample essay.

· ACTIVITY ·

Read the following poem by Edward Hirsch. Then use one of the close reading techniques you've learned to generate ideas for a thesis statement and several topic sentences for a close analysis essay.

Fast Break

EDWARD HIRSCH

(In Memory of Dennis Turner, 1946–1984)

A hook shot kisses the rim and
hangs there, helplessly, but doesn't drop

and for once our gangly starting center
boxes out his man and times his jump

perfectly, gathering the orange leather   5
from the air like a cherished possession

and spinning around to throw a strike
to the outlet who is already shoveling

an underhand pass toward the other guard
scissoring past a flat-footed defender   10

who looks stunned and nailed to the floor
in the wrong direction, turning to catch sight

of a high, gliding dribble and a man
letting the play develop in front of him

in slow motion, almost exactly   15
like a coach's drawing on the blackboard,

both forwards racing down the court
the way that forwards should, fanning out

and filling the lanes in tandem, moving
together as brothers passing the ball   20

between them without a dribble, without
a single bounce hitting the hardwood

until the guard finally lunges out
and commits to the wrong man

while the power-forward explodes past them   25
in a fury, taking the ball into the air

by himself now and laying it gently
against the glass for a layup,

but losing his balance in the process,
inexplicably falling, hitting the floor   30

with a wild, headlong motion
for the game he loved like a country

and swiveling back to see an orange blur
floating perfectly through the net.

                                                [1985]

Working with Two Texts:
The Comparison and Contrast Essay

You have probably written comparison and contrast essays in English or other classes. Essay questions that ask you to compare and contrast two poems or prose passages are common in the classroom as well as on standardized tests. They require close reading, of course, but as you read you will also be looking for elements that the two works have in common—or that set them apart. The prompt will frequently give you an idea of what connects the two texts on the surface—often the subjects are the same—but your task is to develop an argument that goes beyond those surface similarities or differences.

Since you have already worked with two poems that are about basketball, let's consider what else "Slam, Dunk, & Hook" and "Fast Break" have in common and what makes them different. As you plan a comparison and contrast essay, you might want to make a graphic organizer, such as the one below, that will help you generate ideas about the similarities and differences in situation, speaker, imagery, or tone, to name a few.

TITLE	"Slam, Dunk, & Hook"	"Fast Break"
SITUATION	Playing pick-up basketball outdoors	Playing organized basketball in a gym
SPEAKER (POINT OF VIEW)	First person. The speaker recollects a time when he played basketball with friends.	Also first person, as indicated by "our," line 3. The speaker describes a particular play, a "fast break" in a game.
IMAGERY	Vivid and powerful: "hot / Swish of strings like silk," "the roundhouse / Labyrinth," "corkscrew / Up & dunk balls that exploded," "All hands & feet . . . sprung rhythm," "so hard / Our backboard splintered," "slapping a blackjack / Against an open palm," "feint, / & glide like a sparrow hawk"	Graceful and picturesque: "A hook shot kisses the rim," "gathering the orange leather / from the air," "who looks stunned and nailed to the floor," "fanning out / and filling the lanes in tandem," "for the game he loved like a country," "an orange blur / floating perfectly through the net"
SYNTAX	Combination of fragments ("Fast breaks. Lay ups," "Nothing but a hot / Swish of strings like silk / Ten feet out") with the enjambment of complete sentences throughout ("We were metaphysical when girls / Cheered on the sidelines," "We had moves we didn't know / We had")	The entire poem is one long sentence broken up by enjambment. It feels run-on but actually is not. The syntax evokes the graceful flow of a fast break. The poem describes, in its seventeen couplets, one play, the "fast break" of the title.

> • ACTIVITY •
>
> After rereading "Slam, Dunk, & Hook" and "Fast Break," continue to fill in the chart with your own observations about some of the poems' other similarities and differences. In continuing to fill out this graphic organizer, you might add rows for theme, rhythm, allusion, figurative language, or other characteristics that you find significant.

Developing a Thesis Statement

Developing your thesis depends in large measure on the question you're asked. If your assignment is simply to compare and contrast these two poems, it's up to you to determine if you want to focus primarily on differences or similarities and then decide which areas or literary elements you will analyze. Keep in mind that the purpose of putting two works (or ideas) next to each other is usually to emphasize something that is not immediately obvious. For instance, the fact that both of these poems are about basketball is pretty obvious; there's probably not much point in contrasting a dunk with a fast break. However, if you examine how the game affects the players in these poems, you'll discover more interesting issues, such as how one poem recalls past experience while the other presents the action as if it's happening now. One presents memories and reflections; the other observes and reports. One is jerky, with a "sprung rhythm," while the other is more fluid.

If you are given a prompt, you'll have clearer direction, but it is still up to you to determine the specifics of your analysis. Suppose you are given the following prompt:

> Basketball figures prominently in both Yusef Komunyakaa's "Slam, Dunk, & Hook" and Edward Hirsch's "Fast Break." In an essay, compare and contrast the two poems, analyzing the literary devices each writer uses to explore the speaker's attitude toward the game of basketball.

Even though this prompt is pretty specific, it leaves many questions and decisions up to you. First, it directs you to analyze the literary devices, but it does not indicate which ones. Whether the prompt asks for "literary devices," "stylistic devices," "literary techniques," "resources of language," "literary elements," or "formal elements," you're being asked to consider the writer's language. Second, it asks that you "explore the speaker's attitude toward the game of basketball," but it doesn't indicate what that attitude is. So before you can craft a thesis, you need to analyze the poems carefully and think about the themes. How is the relationship between the game and the players in each poem similar or different? Usually you want to begin by finding the common ground, and then note the differences. For instance, you could claim that in both of these poems the speaker attempts to communicate the beauty and excitement of playing basketball. The presentations are, however, quite different. In the Komunyakaa poem, the speaker reflects, identifying memories through imagery, while the speaker in the Hirsch poem observes and reports.

Remember that your thesis should not be too broad:

> Basketball is central to both poems, but the poets use it in different ways.

Your thesis should not focus too narrowly on the meaning of the poem without specifying which resources of language you intend to discuss:

> In both poems, the game of basketball is the means the poets use to dramatize the way the speaker is involved with the sport; however, each speaker's involvement is different.

Nor should your thesis focus too narrowly on the resources of language and ignore the theme:

> In these two poems, the point of view, images, and rhythmic structure of the two poems are different.

If we balance the two components—attention to the resources of language and attention to meaning—we'll come up with a working thesis:

> In both poems, the game of basketball is the means the poets use to dramatize an intense experience; however, the point of view, imagery, and rhythm of the two poems convey very different experiences.

This is only a working thesis, a draft to be used as a starting point—you can tell by the awkward language and repetition. It identifies the specific resources of language the writer will discuss and begins to develop an interpretation of how the poets are using those resources. The following revised thesis statement attempts, in a succinct fashion, to narrow our scope of interpretation while maintaining focus on the resources of language that the poems share:

> In these two poems, the point of view, imagery, and rhythm reveal the relationship between the players and the sport they love, but a world of difference separates the experience of basketball for each of the speakers.

Organizing a Comparison and Contrast Essay

After you have created a thesis statement for your comparison and contrast essay, you need to consider how to organize your essay. In general, you have two alternatives:

Text-by-Text Organization

One way to organize a comparison and contrast essay about two literary works is to divide it into a discussion of the works one by one. In the first developmental paragraphs, you could, for instance, discuss literary elements in "Slam, Dunk, & Hook," and then in the next paragraphs, discuss how those same elements are used similarly or differently in "Fast Break." If you are under time constraints, you might write only one paragraph for each poem, but be careful that you don't try to include too much in a single paragraph. Instead, be sure that your paragraphs are clearly focused and supported and that you draw connections between the two texts.

Let's consider an outline for an essay responding to the prompt about "Slam, Dunk, & Hook" and "Fast Break."

Thesis

> Although both Komunyakaa and Hirsch depict basketball as a transformative experience, the rhythm and imagery in the poems show just how different those experiences are.

Topic Sentence 1

> In "Slam, Dunk, & Hook," the prevalent images of struggle alongside the fragmented rhythm of the verse suggest that life is a battleground both on and off the court for the players.

Topic Sentence 2

> In "Fast Break," the fluid structure and positive connotations of the words in the poem suggest that the players are achieving a singular moment of grace on the court, which is intended to be appreciated as fine art.

If you are faced with time constraints or a restricted length, you might find this text-by-text approach especially useful. An essay developed from this outline, for instance, addresses the prompt and, with the inclusion of strong textual support, could result in an insightful reading of the two poems. Its structure is essentially two sections—one poem, then the next. This logical pattern can be effective as long as the introduction and conclusion emphasize the connections between the two poems that are analyzed in the body paragraphs.

Element-by-Element Organization

The alternative is to organize the paragraphs around the literary elements you want to discuss. In the case of the thesis we're working with here, you could analyze the speaker in both poems, then the imagery in both poems, then the rhythmic structure in both poems. Should each paragraph refer to both works? In most instances, yes, but there are no hard and fast rules. If you have a lot to say about one of the literary elements you're analyzing, then break the discussion into two paragraphs, one on each poem. As always, form follows function when you are organizing an essay. Rather than a template, your own ideas and the material should guide your decisions about the best way to present an analysis.

The chief advantage of this element-by-element organization is that you are comparing and contrasting as you go, rather than waiting until the end. After a topic sentence that focuses on the point you want to make, you would offer evidence from both poems, reminding the reader of the impact of the difference or similarity.

Consider this outline for an essay organized according to literary elements:

Thesis

> In these two poems, the point of view, images, and rhythmic structure reveal the relationship between the players and the sport they love, but a world of difference separates the experience of basketball for each of the speakers.

Topic Sentence 1

> Though both poems are told from a first-person point of view, the speakers are connected to the game in different ways.

Topic Sentence 2

> While the two poets use syntax in a different manner, in both cases it establishes a rhythm that reflects the pace of the game.

Topic Sentence 3

> The diction and imagery reflect the meaning of the game of basketball to each speaker.

Transitions

Because you must juggle two works in a comparison and contrast essay, it is especially important that your transitions are effective. Here are some words and phrases you might use to help keep your work and its intentions clear:

COMPARISON TRANSITIONS	CONTRAST TRANSITIONS
in comparison	in contrast
compared to	on the one hand . . . on the other hand
like	conversely
similar to	on the contrary
likewise	unlike
also	however
similarly	although
in the same way	yet
as in . . . , so in the other	still
moreover	but
	even though
	nevertheless
	regardless
	despite
	while

Documenting Sources

In a comparison and contrast essay, you will have two sources, so while you probably won't need a formal Works Cited page, you might be asked to use parenthetical citations in which you identify the work by the writer's name and line number:

> Described as a "roundhouse / Labyrinth" (Komunyakaa ll. 6–7), the basketball court . . .

> Described as an "orange blur" (Hirsch l. 33), the descending basketball . . .

If the author of the work is introduced in the sentence, just use the line number:

> Komunyakaa describes the players' movement as "spun . . . Through a lyric slipknot / Of joy" (ll. 38–39) . . .

A Sample Comparison and Contrast Essay

Following is a sample essay that follows the element-by-element form of comparison. Read it, and then discuss the questions that follow.

One Game, Two Lives

Talat Rubin

There are many different types of streets in our world, some paved with gold and others with potholes. In the poems "Fast Break" by Edward Hirsch and "Slam, Dunk, & Hook" by Yusef Komunyakaa, each poet captures the essence of the game of basketball and its meaning to the players they depict. While the only piece of equipment needed is a hoop and a ball, the manner and tone of each game differs from community to community. Indeed, the manner of playing in the community of each poet is quite different. I fear that the players in Komunyakaa's "Slam, Dunk, & Hook" would make mincemeat out of Hirsch's players in "Fast Break." In these two poems, the point of view, images, and rhythmic structure reveal the relationship between the players and the sport they love, but a world of difference separates the experience of basketball for each of the speakers.

Though both poems are told from a first-person point of view, the speakers are connected to the game in different ways. Hirsch's speaker seems to be observing as a reporter, a member of the audience. Yet the description of "our gangly starting center" makes it sound as if the speaker is on the team himself and right in the action. Told in the present tense and described moment-by-moment, this perspective adds excitement to the poem because we feel that we're with the speaker, watching the action unfold. In contrast, Komunyakaa's poem is written as the memory of past events. "We outmaneuvered," he recalls; "we could almost / Last forever," he reflects, and "we knew we were / Beautiful & dangerous." The speaker's tone indicates an experience that he has considered and examined. The fact that he remembers so vividly and intensely emphasizes the lasting importance the game had (or has) for him.

While the two poets use syntax in a different manner, in both cases it establishes a rhythm that reflects the pace of the game. In Komunyakaa's poem, sentence fragments along with the abundant use of periods and commas within sentences emphasize the poem's truncated beat, which could be the beat of a basketball bouncing off the court, or the heartbeat of the players in excited motion. The abrupt and short lines suggest a combative and harsh pace. In contrast, Hirsch's poem is one long sentence divided into couplets through enjambment, creating a fluid rhythm to express the grace in this one continuous play. The long sentence, consisting of multiple clauses and descriptive phrases, suggests that this poem, like the play, is a team effort dependent on many small parts. The different syntax of these poems defines the rhythm of two different games.

The diction and imagery reflect the meaning of the game of basketball to each speaker. Hirsch's words have positive connotations: "kisses," "cherished possession," and "together" demonstrate his sense of companionship that is fostered in the sport. They are not mere fellow team members, but "brothers" who share a common purpose. This point is made explicit when the speaker refers to the forward who is playing "the game he loved like a country." Komunyakaa's word choice reflects the energy and anger expended during the game. The players are not merely young men — they are almost god-like, with "Mercury's / Insignia on [their] sneakers." Komunyakaa evokes the shattering of a young man's emotional core when the "backboard splintered" in his attempt to forget about the loss of his mother. The language expresses the aggressive manner in which they play, as well as the society they come from. It is an aggressive game where even their graceful motions have violent undertones — they "glide" not like sparrows, but like "sparrow hawk[s]". Yet while Komunyakaa's basketball is a more physical demonstration of the game than Hirsch's, the same vitality of spirit can be found in each poem. Like Komunyakaa's players who "rolled the ball off [their] / Fingertips," Hirsch's lay the ball "gently / against the glass."

These two poets create different visions of their world and game by the imagery they employ. Hirsch creates a gentler, more tender image as a "hook shot kisses the rim." In contrast, Komunyakaa uses imagery of war, power, and brute force: the players are alternately "storybook sea monsters," birds of prey, and boys with god-like speed. Basketball was not merely a game to the speaker in "Slam, Dunk, & Hook," but a battle, similar, we can assume, to the one he waged outside the court.

In their poems, Edward Hirsch and Yusef Komunyakaa describe the physical dimensions of the sport of basketball. In doing so, they not only articulate the meaning of a moment of time in their players' lives, but also expose the world in which they live. Komunyakaa's game has its origin on the streets, and his diction demonstrates the roughness of those streets, while Hirsch's graceful depiction of the sport demonstrates a more benign view of the world. For Hirsch, the game is a beautiful complement to life. For Komunyakaa, it is the battle that is life. It is clear that the poets come from different neighborhoods, different communities, and most likely different time periods. But what is even clearer is the manner in which this simple game, with a round ball, touched and shaped their lives.

Questions

1. Is the introduction effective? Explain why or why not. If you believe it is not effective, how could it be improved?
2. Why are there two separate paragraphs for the analysis of imagery? Explain whether you think that dividing the analysis into two paragraphs was a good decision.
3. In what ways are transitions used within this essay to emphasize the similarities and differences between the poems?
4. Do you agree with the essay's argument? Explain why or why not. Which parts of the interpretation do you find most persuasive? questionable?
5. What other literary elements might you have used to make a similar argument?
6. What suggestions can you offer for polishing the essay?

• ACTIVITY •

Read "Traveling through the Dark" by William Stafford and "Woodchucks" by Maxine Kumin, two poems in which a speaker considers the death of animals. Plan and write a comparison and contrast essay in which you analyze the resources of language Stafford and Kumin use to reveal the relationship between the speakers and the animals.

Traveling through the Dark
WILLIAM STAFFORD

Traveling through the dark I found a deer
dead on the edge of the Wilson River road.
It is usually best to roll them into the canyon:
that road is narrow; to swerve might make more dead.

By glow of the tail-light I stumbled back of the car   5
and stood by the heap, a doe, a recent killing;
she had stiffened already, almost cold.
I dragged her off; she was large in the belly.

My fingers touching her side brought me the reason—
her side was warm; her fawn lay there waiting,   10
alive, still, never to be born.
Beside that mountain road I hesitated.

The car aimed ahead its lowered parking lights;
under the hood purred the steady engine.

I stood in the glare of the warm exhaust turning red;   15
around our group I could hear the wilderness listen.

I thought hard for us all—my only swerving—,
then pushed her over the edge into the river.

                                                    [1962]

Woodchucks
MAXINE KUMIN

Gassing the woodchucks didn't turn out right.
The knockout bomb from the Feed and Grain Exchange
was featured as merciful, quick at the bone
and the case we had against them was airtight,
both exits shoehorned shut with puddingstone,   5
but they had a sub-sub-basement out of range.

Next morning they turned up again, no worse
for the cyanide than we for our cigarettes
and state-store Scotch, all of us up to scratch.
They brought down the marigolds as a matter of course   10
and then took over the vegetable patch
nipping the broccoli shoots, beheading the carrots.

The food from our mouths, I said, righteously thrilling
to the feel of the .22, the bullets' neat noses.
I, a lapsed pacifist fallen from grace   15
puffed with Darwinian pieties for killing,
now drew a bead on the littlest woodchuck's face.
He died down in the everbearing roses.

Ten minutes later I dropped the mother. She
flipflopped in the air and fell, her needle teeth   20
still hooked in a leaf of early Swiss chard.
Another baby next. O one-two-three
the murderer inside me rose up hard,
the hawkeye killer came on stage forthwith.

There's one chuck left. Old wily fellow, he keeps   25
me cocked and ready day after day after day.
All night I hunt his humped-up form. I dream
I sight along the barrel in my sleep.
If only they'd all consented to die unseen
gassed underground the quiet Nazi way.   30

                                                    [1972]

The Big Picture: Analyzing Fiction and Drama

 n Chapter 2, we talked about close reading—a way to look at texts as if
 through a microscope, examining writers' choices on the word and sentence
levels and how those choices affect the meaning of a poem or passage of fiction. In
this chapter, we will take a step back and look at the bigger picture.

When someone asks us about a novel, play, or short story, we usually respond by
describing what happened, retelling the plot in our own words. After all, who doesn't
enjoy a good page-turner? But in literary fiction and drama, the way the story is told
and the ideas the piece explores may be just as important as the events of the plot. In
these pieces, plots may be built on conflicts within a character or between characters,
which play out in a particular setting. The story is told to us from a certain point of
view. Sometimes there are symbols that carry more than a literal meaning. An author
uses these elements to deliver a message or theme. By studying how all of these literary elements work and work together, we can begin to understand how they produce
the meaning of the work as a whole.

Elements of Fiction

Plot

Essentially, **plot** is what happens in a **narrative**. Yet plot is more than a series of
events; authors must arrange **conflicts**, complications, and resolutions to create
logical cause-and-effect relationships. Readers must understand not just *what* is
happening but also *why* it's happening. A plot must be believable, though it doesn't
have to be realistic.

A conventional narrative—whether in a short story, novel, or play—typically involves five main stages:

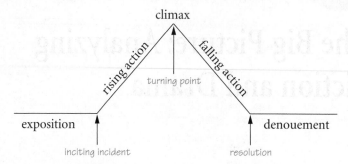

- **Exposition:** This opening section provides background information about the characters, setting, and situation, describing the nature of the conflict, which is generally an unstable situation.
- **Rising action:** After an inciting incident, the conflict and complications for the main character begin to build.
- **Climax:** The climax occurs when the emotional tension or **suspense** of the plot reaches its peak. The climax may include a turning point where the fortunes of the protagonist improve (in **comedy**) or worsen (in **tragedy**). Building to the climax usually occupies most of a story, and what follows is comparatively brief.
- **Falling action:** This section details the result (or fallout) of the climax or turning point. In this phase, the conflict gets resolved.
- **Denouement** (pronounced *day-noo-mah*): This French word means "untying the knot." In this often very brief phase, the conflict has been resolved, and balance is restored to the world of the story. In fairy tales, this phase is often represented by a single sentence: "And they lived happily ever after." The denouement was traditionally used to tell "the moral of the story," but writers in the twentieth and twenty-first centuries frequently close without this final **resolution**, leaving readers to ponder the possible meanings of what came before.

It bears repeating that this is a structure for traditional narratives and was originally used to describe Greek and Shakespearean plays. Most modern stories do not follow this model exactly, and it can be interesting to investigate how and where they depart from it.

Plot may follow a chronological sequence, particularly in realistic fiction and drama, but sometimes writers deliberately present events in a manner that requires readers to assemble them into a cohesive pattern. A story may begin **in medias res**, a Latin term meaning "in the middle of the action"—that is, just as an important event is about to take place. Homer's *Iliad*, for example, opens not in the first year of the Trojan War but after nine years of fighting. Writers may also employ **flashback** to describe events that have taken place before the story begins, or **foreshadowing** to hint at things that might happen later in the story.

Let's look at a short story, "One of These Days" by Gabriel García Márquez, a Nobel Prize–winning author from Colombia.

> Monday dawned warm and rainless. Aurelio Escovar, a dentist without a degree, and a very early riser, opened his office at six. He took some false teeth, still mounted in their plaster mold, out of the glass case and put on the table a fistful of instruments which he arranged in size order, as if they were on display. He wore a collarless striped shirt, closed at the neck with a golden stud, and pants held up by suspenders. He was erect and skinny, with a look that rarely corresponded to the situation, the way deaf people have of looking.
>
> When he had things arranged on the table, he pulled the drill toward the dental chair and sat down to polish the false teeth. He seemed not to be thinking about what he was doing, but worked steadily, pumping the drill with his feet, even when he didn't need it.
>
> After eight he stopped for a while to look at the sky through the window, and he saw two pensive buzzards who were drying themselves in the sun on the ridgepole of the house next door. He went on working with the idea that before lunch it would rain again. The shrill voice of his eleven-year-old son interrupted his concentration.
>
> "Papa."
>
> "What?"   5
>
> "The Mayor wants to know if you'll pull his tooth."
>
> "Tell him I'm not here."
>
> He was polishing a gold tooth. He held it at arm's length, and examined it with his eyes half closed. His son shouted again from the little waiting room.
>
> "He says you are, too, because he can hear you."
>
> The dentist kept examining the tooth. Only when he had put it on the table   10 with the finished work did he say:
>
> "So much the better."
>
> He operated the drill again. He took several pieces of a bridge out of a cardboard box where he kept the things he still had to do and began to polish the gold.
>
> "Papa."
>
> "What?"
>
> He still hadn't changed his expression.   15
>
> "He says if you don't take out his tooth, he'll shoot you."
>
> Without hurrying, with an extremely tranquil movement, he stopped pedaling the drill, pushed it away from the chair, and pulled the lower drawer of the table all the way out. There was a revolver. "OK," he said. "Tell him to come and shoot me."
>
> He rolled the chair over opposite the door, his hand resting on the edge of the drawer. The Mayor appeared at the door. He had shaved the left side of his face, but the other side, swollen and in pain, had a five-day-old beard. The dentist saw many nights of desperation in his dull eyes. He closed the drawer with his fingertips and said softly:

"Sit down."

"Good morning," said the Mayor. 20

"Morning," said the dentist.

While the instruments were boiling, the Mayor leaned his skull on the headrest of the chair and felt better. His breath was icy. It was a poor office: an old wooden chair, the pedal drill, a glass case with ceramic bottles. Opposite the chair was a window with a shoulder-high cloth curtain. When he felt the dentist approach, the Mayor braced his heels and opened his mouth.

Aurelio Escovar turned his head toward the light. After inspecting the infected tooth, he closed the Mayor's jaw with a cautious pressure of his fingers.

"It has to be without anesthesia," he said.

"Why?" 25

"Because you have an abscess."

The Mayor looked him in the eye. "All right," he said, and tried to smile. The dentist did not return the smile. He brought the basin of sterilized instruments to the worktable and took them out of the water with a pair of cold tweezers, still without hurrying. Then he pushed the spittoon with the tip of his shoe, and went to wash his hands in the washbasin. He did all this without looking at the Mayor. But the Mayor didn't take his eyes off him.

It was a lower wisdom tooth. The dentist spread his feet and grasped the tooth with the hot forceps. The Mayor seized the arms of the chair, braced his feet with all his strength, and felt an icy void in his kidneys, but didn't make a sound. The dentist moved only his wrist. Without rancor, rather with a bitter tenderness, he said:

"Now you'll pay for our twenty dead men."

The Mayor felt the crunch of bones in his jaw, and his eyes filled with tears. 30 But he didn't breathe until he felt the tooth come out. Then he saw it through his tears. It seemed so foreign to his pain that he failed to understand his torture of the five previous nights.

Bent over the spittoon, sweating, panting, he unbuttoned his tunic and reached for the handkerchief in his pants pocket. The dentist gave him a clean cloth.

"Dry your tears," he said.

The Mayor did. He was trembling. While the dentist washed his hands, he saw the crumbling ceiling and a dusty spider web with spider's eggs and dead insects. The dentist returned, drying his hands. "Go to bed," he said, "and gargle with salt water." The Mayor stood up, said goodbye with a casual military salute, and walked toward the door, stretching his legs, without buttoning up his tunic.

"Send the bill," he said.

"To you or the town?" 35

The Mayor didn't look at him. He closed the door and said through the screen:

"It's the same damn thing."

[1962]

This very short story takes place over a few hours, and the plot seems quite simple: a poor dentist pulls the wisdom tooth of the mayor. Yet even this brief story more or less follows the conventional narrative structure. Márquez opens with two paragraphs of exposition that introduce Aurelio Escovar and his dental office. When Escovar tells his son to lie to the mayor and say he is not in, we recognize conflict—something's amiss. The dentist goes about his work until his son tells him that the mayor has threatened to shoot him if he does not pull the tooth. The dentist makes his revolver available and agrees to attend to the mayor. Suspense is mounting by this point because of the potentially volatile situation. In less than a page, a visit to the dentist has become a matter of life and death. The action rises as the dentist prepares for the extraction and denies the mayor anesthesia, and reaches a climax when the dentist tells the mayor that he will "pay for our twenty dead men" (para. 29) as he pulls the tooth. Experiencing such acute pain that he tears up, the mayor seems to have been defanged, literally and figuratively, and the dentist emerges victorious. However, the story does not end at this climactic moment. The falling action occurs when the dentist asks if the bill should go to the mayor or the town, and the mayor replies that they are the same thing. This plot unfolds and ends without a denouement; in fact, the ending suggests that the conflict is not entirely over. Nonetheless, in the world of this story, a shootout was averted, and order has been restored.

The following questions will help guide your analysis of plot:

- Is the plot arranged in chronological order, or does it begin in medias res?
- Does the plot involve a flashback? If so, what is its purpose?
- What is the nature of the conflict?
- What conditions at the outset make the situation unstable?
- Is the conflict external or internal?
- What is the high point, or climax?
- How is the conflict resolved? If there is no resolution, why not?
- Is there a denouement? If not, why is the story inconclusive?
- What patterns do you find in the plot's structure?

• ACTIVITY •

Choose a fairy tale, legend, or folktale and analyze its plot. Identify specific parts of the plot, such as exposition, rising action, climax, falling action, and denouement, and examine whether the plot employs flashbacks or begins in medias res.

Character

Character and plot go hand-in-hand because the conflict that structures a plot usually arises between two or more characters, as we saw in "One of These Days." In a plot with an external conflict, the story usually has a **protagonist**, or main character, who is in conflict with another person, called the **antagonist**. A conflict may also be internal, such as those in which a character struggles with temptation or tries to reconcile two incompatible traits. The main characters in a literary work grow or change over the course of the story or play; in fact, that change often structures the plot. The clearest example of character change structuring a plot is seen in a **coming-of-age story**, also called a **bildungsroman**, which chronicles how a young character grows from innocence to experience. For a character's growth to be believable, it must be clearly motivated by the circumstances of the story. Sometimes the change is gradual and sometimes it is sudden, as with an **epiphany**, a term Irish author James Joyce used to describe when a character suddenly realizes something significant about life.

Characters commonly fall into two categories: round (also called dynamic) or flat (also called static). The protagonist is typically a **round character**, one who exhibits a range of emotions and changes over the course of the story. Round characters have multiple personality traits and thus resemble real people. **Flat characters** embody only one or two traits and provide a background for the protagonist's actions. A common type of flat character is the **foil**, a contrasting character who allows the protagonist to stand out more distinctly. **Stock characters** may represent stereotypes, such as the absent-minded professor or the town drunk, occasionally providing comic relief.

Developing Character

Authors can reveal character either directly or indirectly. **Direct characterization** occurs when a narrator explicitly describes the background, motivation, temperament, or appearance of a character. In Jane Austen's *Pride and Prejudice*, for instance, we are told directly that Mrs. Bennet "was a woman of mean understanding, little information, and uncertain temper. When she was discontented, she fancied herself nervous. The business of her life was to get her daughters married." **Indirect characterization** occurs when an author shows rather than tells us what a character is like through what he or she says, does, or thinks, or what others say about the character.

Let's take a look at another excerpt from *Pride and Prejudice* by Jane Austen. Notice the way Austen directly and indirectly characterizes Mr. Darcy.

> Mr. Bingley was good looking and gentlemanlike; he had a pleasant countenance, and easy, unaffected manners. His sisters were fine women, with an air of decided fashion. His brother-in-law, Mr. Hurst, merely looked the gentleman; but his friend Mr. Darcy soon drew the attention of the room by his fine, tall person, handsome features, noble mien; and the report which was in general circulation within five minutes after his entrance, of his having ten thousand a year. The gentlemen pronounced him to be a fine figure of a man, the ladies declared he was much handsomer than Mr. Bingley, and he was looked at with great admiration for about half the evening, till his manners gave a disgust which turned the tide of his popularity; for he was discovered to be proud, to be above his company,

and above being pleased; and not all his large estate in Derbyshire could then save him from having a most forbidding, disagreeable countenance, and being unworthy to be compared with his friend.

Mr. Bingley had soon made himself acquainted with all the principal people in the room; he was lively and unreserved, danced every dance, was angry that the ball closed so early, and talked of giving one himself at Netherfield. Such amiable qualities must speak for themselves. What a contrast between him and his friend! Mr. Darcy danced only once with Mrs. Hurst and once with Miss Bingley, declined being introduced to any other lady, and spent the rest of the evening in walking about the room, speaking occasionally to one of his own party. His character was decided. He was the proudest, most disagreeable man in the world, and every body hoped that he would never come there again. Amongst the most violent against him was Mrs. Bennet, whose dislike of his general behaviour was sharpened into particular resentment by his having slighted one of her daughters.

Elizabeth Bennet had been obliged, by the scarcity of gentlemen, to sit down for two dances; and during part of that time, Mr. Darcy had been standing near enough for her to overhear a conversation between him and Mr. Bingley, who came from the dance for a few minutes to press his friend to join it.

"Come, Darcy," said he, "I must have you dance. I hate to see you standing about by yourself in this stupid manner. You had much better dance."

"I certainly shall not. You know how I detest it, unless I am particularly   5 acquainted with my partner. At such an assembly as this, it would be insupportable. Your sisters are engaged, and there is not another woman in the room whom it would not be a punishment to me to stand up with."

"I would not be so fastidious as you are," cried Bingley, "for a kingdom! Upon my honour, I never met with so many pleasant girls in my life, as I have this evening; and there are several of them, you see, uncommonly pretty."

"*You* are dancing with the only handsome girl in the room," said Mr. Darcy, looking at the eldest Miss Bennet.

"Oh! she is the most beautiful creature I ever beheld! But there is one of her sisters sitting down just behind you, who is very pretty, and I dare say, very agreeable. Do let me ask my partner to introduce you."

"Which do you mean?" and turning round, he looked for a moment at Elizabeth, till catching her eye, he withdrew his own and coldly said, "She is tolerable; but not handsome enough to tempt *me*; and I am in no humour at present to give consequence to young ladies who are slighted by other men. You had better return to your partner and enjoy her smiles, for you are wasting your time with me."

[1813]

Austen's narrator offers direct commentary on the physical appearance of Mr. Darcy, noting his "fine, tall person, handsome features, noble mien," and points out that he is quite wealthy. The narrator also explains that Darcy's "manners gave a disgust which turned the tide of his popularity" (para. 1). But much of the characterization is indirect: we see Darcy in action. Bingley acts as a foil, or contrasting character, with Bingley's warmth emphasizing Darcy's cool, aloof nature. The dialogue between Bingley and Darcy allows the latter to speak for himself, and what he says further characterizes him as arrogant. His meeting Elizabeth's eye, then turning away with a judgmental comment, suggests his inflated sense of self-importance.

The following questions will help guide your analysis of character:

- Who are the main characters in this story? Who is the protagonist? Who is the antagonist?
- What do we know about them? What is their relationship to each other?
- How do they change from beginning to end?
- What is the function of the minor characters?
- Do some characters see themselves differently from the way readers see them? If so, how?

· ACTIVITY ·

Nineteenth-century English novelist Charles Dickens opens his novel *Hard Times* with a description of the central character, Mr. Gradgrind. Even before his rather appropriate name is revealed, Dickens makes sure the reader understands what Mr. Gradgrind is like. Discuss the direct and indirect methods used to characterize him in the following passage.

From *Hard Times*
CHARLES DICKENS

'Now, what I want is, Facts. Teach these boys and girls nothing but Facts. Facts alone are wanted in life. Plant nothing else, and root out everything else. You can only form the minds of reasoning animals upon Facts: nothing else will ever be of any service to them. This is the principle on which I bring up my own children, and this is the principle on which I bring up these children. Stick to Facts, sir!'

The scene was a plain, bare, monotonous vault of a school-room, and the speaker's square forefinger emphasized his observations by underscoring every sentence with a line on the schoolmaster's sleeve. The emphasis was helped by the speaker's square wall of a forehead, which had his eyebrows for its base, while his eyes found commodious cellarage in two dark caves, overshadowed by the wall. The emphasis was helped by the speaker's mouth, which was wide, thin, and hard set. The emphasis was helped by the speaker's voice, which was inflexible, dry, and dictatorial. The emphasis was helped by the speaker's hair, which bristled on the skirts of his bald head, a plantation of firs to keep the wind from its shining surface, all covered with knobs, like the crust of a plum pie, as if the head had scarcely warehouse-room for the hard facts stored inside. The speaker's obstinate carriage, square coat, square legs, square shoulders—nay, his very neckcloth, trained to take him by the throat with an unaccommodating grasp, like a stubborn fact, as it was—all helped the emphasis.

'In this life, we want nothing but Facts, sir; nothing but Facts!'

The speaker, and the schoolmaster, and the third grown person present, all backed a little, and swept with their eyes the inclined plane of little vessels, then and there arranged in order, ready to have imperial gallons of facts poured into them until they were full to the brim.

[1854]

Setting

Setting indicates the time and place, the when and where, of a literary text. Author Eudora Welty described it as "the named, identified, concrete, exact and exacting, and therefore credible, gathering spot of all that has been felt, is about to be experienced." It includes such objective facts as the nation or town, date and time, weather and season in which the story occurs. If events occur on a dark and stormy night, we can reasonably expect a dark and stormy tale. If the action opens on a spring morning in a sunlit glade, it is likely that the author is preparing us for a lighter tale, establishing a contrast between different settings in the story, or being ironic. In order to understand how setting relates to the meaning of the work as a whole, you will have to consider the thematic significance of things that might at first seem merely physical and objective. The most important thing is that you pay attention to the details—the sights and sounds, textures and tones, colors and shapes.

In the following passage from Edgar Allan Poe's "The Masque of the Red Death," Poe describes the castle where Prince Prospero and his friends seclude themselves in an attempt to escape the plague that is threatening the community. Notice how the physical details of the description create a sinister and foreboding atmosphere.

It was a voluptuous scene, that masquerade. But first let me tell of the rooms in which it was held. There were seven—an imperial suite. In many palaces, however, such suites form a long and straight vista, while the folding doors slide back nearly to the walls on either hand, so that the view of the whole extent is scarcely impeded. Here the case was very different; as might have been expected from the duke's love of the *bizarre*. The apartments were so irregularly disposed that the vision embraced but little more than one at a time. There was a sharp turn at every twenty or thirty yards, and at each turn a novel effect. To the right and left, in the middle of each wall, a tall and narrow Gothic window looked out upon a closed corridor which pursued the windings of the suite. These windows were of stained glass whose color varied in accordance with the prevailing hue of the decorations of the chamber into which it opened. That at the eastern extremity was hung, for example, in blue—and vividly blue were its windows. The second chamber was purple in its ornaments and tapestries, and here the panes were purple. The third was green throughout, and so were the casements. The fourth was furnished and lighted with orange—the fifth with white—the sixth with violet. The seventh apartment was closely shrouded in black velvet tapestries that hung all over the ceiling and down the walls, falling in heavy folds upon a carpet of the same material and hue. But in this chamber only, the color of the windows failed to correspond with the decorations. The panes here were scarlet—a deep blood color. Now in no one of the seven apartments was there any lamp or candelabrum, amid the profusion of golden ornaments that lay scattered to and fro or depended from the roof. There was no light of any kind emanating from lamp or candle within the suite of chambers. But in the corridors that followed the suite, there stood, opposite to each window, a heavy tripod, bearing a brazier of fire that projected its rays through the tinted glass and so glaringly illumined the room. And thus were produced a multitude of gaudy and fantastic appearances. But in the western or black chamber the effect of the fire-light that streamed upon the dark hangings through the blood-tinted panes was ghastly in the extreme, and produced so wild a look upon the countenances of those who entered, that there were few of the company bold enough to set foot within its precincts at all.

It was in this apartment, also, that there stood against the western wall, a gigantic clock of ebony. Its pendulum swung to and fro with a dull, heavy, monotonous clang; and when the minute-hand made the circuit of the face, and the hour was to be stricken, there came from the brazen lungs of the clock a sound which was clear and loud and deep and exceedingly musical, but of so peculiar a note and emphasis that, at each lapse of an hour, the musicians of the orchestra were constrained to pause, momentarily, in their performance, to hearken to the sound; and thus the waltzers perforce ceased their evolutions; and there was a brief disconcert of the whole gay company; and, while the chimes of the clock yet rang, it was observed that the giddiest grew pale, and the more aged and sedate passed their hands over their brows as if in confused revery or meditation. But when the echoes had fully ceased, a light laughter at once pervaded the assembly; the musicians looked at each other and smiled as if at their own nervousness and folly, and made whispering vows, each to the other, that the next chiming of the clock should produce in them no similar emotion; and then, after the lapse of sixty minutes (which embrace three thousand and six hundred seconds of the Time that flies), there came yet another chiming of the clock, and then were the same disconcert and tremulousness and meditation as before.

[1845]

The first paragraph takes us on a detailed tour of the suite, telling us what is on our right and left, how many yards of space are between various apartments, what is on the walls, where the windows are, what colors the curtains are, and the like. As we realize the difficulty of navigating from apartment to apartment and note the colors, culminating in "scarlet—a deep blood color," we recognize that the setting is opulent yet oppressive; it is filled with the trappings of wealth yet seems to entrap its residents. Poe deepens the atmosphere of foreboding by telling us what is *not* there—no gentle light "from lamp or candle"; instead, illumination is by fire, a hellish glow that was "ghastly in the extreme."

After he has given us a view of this odd suite, Poe zeroes in on one particular part of the furnishings: a large black pendulum clock, whose sound rang with "so peculiar a note and emphasis" that it reminded the residents every hour of their own mortality. Poe's description of the setting is literal, but when we analyze those details, an atmosphere of menace, even doom, is revealed.

Historical Context

A novel, short story, or play may be set in a historical era—a time and place that has its own political, economic, or social upheavals. In many cases, historical context goes unstated; it is part of the knowledge that the author expects the reader to bring to the book. For instance, in John Steinbeck's novel *The Grapes of Wrath*, we follow the Joad family as they migrate from middle America to California, along the legendary Route 66, on a search for work, prosperity, and stability:

> Highway 66 is the main migrant road. 66—the long concrete path across the country, waving gently up and down on the map, from Mississippi to Bakersfield—over the red lands and the gray lands, twisting up into the mountains, crossing the Divide and down into the bright and terrible desert, and across the desert to the mountains again, and into the rich California valleys.
>
> 66 is the path of a people in flight, refugees from dust and shrinking land, from the thunder of tractors and shrinking ownership, from the desert's slow northward invasion, from the twisting winds that howl up out of Texas, from the floods that bring no richness to the land and steal what little richness is there. From all of these the people are in flight, and they come into 66 from the tributary side roads, from the wagon tracks and the rutted country roads. 66 is the mother road, the road of flight.
>
> Clarksville and Ozark and Van Buren and Fort Smith on 64, and there's an end of Arkansas. And all the roads into Oklahoma City, 66 down from Tulsa, 270 up from McAlester. 81 from Wichita Falls south, from Enid north. Edmond, McLoud, Purcell. 66 out of Oklahoma City; El Reno and Clinton, going west on 66. Hydro, Elk City, and Texola; and there's an end to Oklahoma. 66 across the Panhandle of Texas. Shamrock and McLean, Conway and Amarillo, the yellow. Wildorado and Vega and Boise, and there's an end of Texas. Tucumcari and Santa Rosa and into the New Mexican mountains to Albuquerque, where the road comes down from Santa Fe. Then down the gorged Rio Grande to Los Lunas and west again on 66 to Gallup, and there's the border of New Mexico.
>
> *[1939]*

In this description, we get a good sense of the physical setting. The first paragraph, one long sentence that rambles along like the road itself, describes Highway 66— it goes from Mississippi to Bakersfield, California—and sets a mood with the sensory images of the "long concrete path." In the second paragraph, the narrator introduces the people who follow this road in the hope of finding something better than the desolation of the drought that has worsened their economic hardship. The word *flight* appears three times, so we get a clear sense of movement from one thing to another, though what that thing is, we're not sure. The third paragraph consists almost entirely of names of places along Highway 66. Even if we do not know these towns, we still get a clear sense of movement, of going from one stop to the next.

What is unstated is the reason for the migration, though it is implied when the narrator describes the migrating families as "refugees from dust and shrinking land" (para. 2). This passage refers to the great migration of families to California as a result of the Dust Bowl, a historic drought combined with severe storms that destroyed much of the farmland in middle America during the Great Depression of the 1930s. This historical setting, not just Route 66 but the context of the Dust Bowl and the Great Depression, makes the story of the Joad family emblematic of an entire era in American history.

Sometimes historical settings are not implicit but explicit—with dates and places clearly identified. In the following passage from *Call It Sleep* by Henry Roth, the setting is essential to the novel's exploration of the Jewish American experience in early twentieth-century America.

> The small white steamer, *Peter Stuyvesant*, that delivered the immigrants from the stench and throb of the steerage to the stench and the throb of New York tenements, rolled slightly on the water beside the stone quay in the lee of the weathered barracks and new brick buildings of Ellis Island. Her skipper was waiting for the last of the officials, laborers and guards to embark upon her before he cast off and started for Manhattan. Since this was Saturday afternoon and this the last trip she would make for the week-end, those left behind might have to stay over till Monday. Her whistle bellowed its hoarse warning. A few figures in overalls sauntered from the high doors of the immigration quarters and down the grey pavement that led to the dock.
>
> It was May of the year 1907, the year that was destined to bring the greatest number of immigrants to the shores of the United States. All that day, as on all the days since spring began, her decks had been thronged by hundreds upon hundreds of foreigners, natives from almost every land in the world. . . .
>
> *[1934]*

From the first sentence, we are placed in New York City, arriving via a steamer filled with immigrants. The entrance to the United States through Ellis Island where the "immigration quarters" are is also our entrance into the novel. Roth opens the next paragraph with a specific date—1907, which marked the high point of immigration during that era. As the paragraph continues, the narrator of this autobiographical novel describes the crowds of immigrants aboard the ship, then focuses on a woman and her child. Thus, the historical setting provides a particular context for the life that is beginning as these two step onto a new land.

Cultural Environment

Setting may also establish the cultural environment of a work—the manners, mores, customs, rituals, and codes of conduct. In some instances, this cultural environment is based on an actual period, culture, or community. In other instances, an author has to invent a new culture, as in the case of George Orwell's novel *1984*:

It was a bright cold day in April, and the clocks were striking thirteen. Winston Smith, his chin nuzzled into his breast in an effort to escape the vile wind, slipped quickly through the glass doors of Victory Mansions, though not quickly enough to prevent a swirl of gritty dust from entering along with him.

The hallway smelt of boiled cabbage and old rag mats. At one end of it a colored poster, too large for indoor display, had been tacked to the wall. It depicted simply an enormous face, more than a meter wide: the face of a man of about forty-five, with a heavy black mustache and ruggedly handsome features. Winston made for the stairs. It was no use trying the lift. Even at the best of times it was seldom working, and at present the electric current was cut off during daylight hours. It was part of the economy drive in preparation for Hate Week. The flat was seven flights up, and Winston, who was thirty-nine, and had a varicose ulcer above his right ankle, went slowly, resting several times on the way. On each landing, opposite the lift shaft, the poster with the enormous face gazed from the wall. It was one of those pictures which are so contrived that the eyes follow you about when you move. BIG BROTHER IS WATCHING YOU, the caption beneath it ran.

Inside the flat a fruity voice was reading out a list of figures which had something to do with the production of pig iron. The voice came from an oblong metal plaque like a dulled mirror which formed part of the surface of the right-hand wall. Winston turned a switch and the voice sank somewhat, though the words were still distinguishable. The instrument (the telescreen, it was called) could be dimmed, but there was no way of shutting it off completely. He moved over to the window: a smallish, frail figure, the meagerness of his body merely emphasized by the blue overalls which were the uniform of the Party. His hair was very fair, his face naturally sanguine, his skin roughened by coarse soap and blunt razor blades and the cold of the winter that had just ended.

Outside, even through the shut window pane, the world looked cold. Down in the street little eddies of wind were whirling dust and torn paper into spirals, and though the sun was shining and the sky a harsh blue, there seemed to be no color in anything except the posters that were plastered everywhere. The black-mustachio'd face gazed down from every commanding corner. There was one on the house front immediately opposite. BIG BROTHER IS WATCHING YOU, the caption said, while the dark eyes looked deep into Winston's own. Down at street level another poster, torn at one corner, flapped fitfully in the wind, alternately covering and uncovering the single word INGSOC. In the far distance a helicopter skimmed down between the roofs, hovered for an instant like a bluebottle, and darted away again with a curving flight. It was the Police Patrol, snooping into people's windows. The patrols did not matter, however. Only the Thought Police mattered.

[1949]

From the very beginning of this novel, when the clocks strike thirteen, we know we're in a different world. For *1984*, Orwell created a social environment in which the values we take for granted are dispensed with. In their place is a society built on surveillance and **propaganda**, with odd customs and institutions such as Hate Week and the Thought Police. It's an environment where the "telescreen" broadcasting Big

Brother's voice can be "dimmed" but cannot be silenced; the omnipresent drone of the voice is part of the setting. Posters of Big Brother are everywhere, and the sound of a helicopter is a reminder of the constant surveillance. Of course, Orwell's point was to warn us of one possible future for our world, and the shocking comparisons between the society of his novel and our own society is one of the main reasons that *1984* continues to be so powerful and so disturbing.

The following questions will help guide your analysis of setting:

- What is the geographical setting? The time, place, weather, season? Why is it important?
- What historical context or social environment is being depicted, and what background information is required to understand the situation?
- What details of the setting does the author use to create atmosphere or mood?
- How does the setting seem to relate to the themes?

• ACTIVITY •

Authors often use setting as another means of developing a character. Discuss the interaction between setting and character in the following passage from *Tess of the D'Urbervilles* by Thomas Hardy. The context is that Tess, who lives in a traditional nineteenth-century village in rural England, has had a child out of wedlock. Pay close attention to the way the narrator uses setting to comment on Tess's situation.

From *Tess of the D'Urbervilles*
THOMAS HARDY

The bedroom which she shared with some of the children formed her retreat more continually than ever. Here, under her few square yards of thatch, she watched winds, and snows, and rains, gorgeous sunsets, and successive moons at their full. So close kept she that at length almost everybody thought she had gone away.

The only exercise that Tess took at this time was after dark; and it was then, when out in the woods, that she seemed least solitary. She knew how to hit to a hair's-breadth that moment of evening when the light and the darkness are so evenly balanced that the constraint of day and the suspense of night neutralize each other, leaving absolute mental liberty. It is then that the plight of being alive becomes attenuated to its least possible dimensions. She had no fear of the shadows; her sole idea seemed to be to shun mankind—or rather that cold accretion called the world, which, so terrible in the mass, is so unformidable, even pitiable, in its units.

On these lonely hills and dales her quiescent glide was of a piece with the element she moved in. Her flexuous and stealthy figure became an integral part of the scene. At times her whimsical fancy would intensify natural processes around her till they seemed a part of her own story. Rather they became a part of it; for the world is only a psychological phenomenon, and what they seemed they were. The midnight airs and gusts, moaning amongst the tightly-wrapped buds and bark of the winter twigs, were formulae of bitter reproach. A wet day was the expression of irremediable grief at her weakness in the mind of some vague ethical being whom she could not class definitely as the God of her childhood, and could not comprehend as any other.

But this encompassment of her own characterization, based on shreds of convention, peopled by phantoms and voices antipathetic to her, was a sorry and mistaken creation of Tess's fancy—a cloud of moral hobgoblins by which she was terrified without reason. It was they that were out of harmony with the actual world, not she. Walking among the sleeping birds in the hedges, watching the skipping rabbits on a moonlit warren, or standing under a pheasant-laden bough, she looked upon herself as a figure of Guilt intruding into the haunts of Innocence. But all the while she was making a distinction where there was no difference. Feeling herself in antagonism she was quite in accord. She had been made to break an accepted social law, but no law known to the environment in which she fancied herself such an anomaly.

[1891]

Point of View

Point of view is the perspective through which a story is told. This perspective determines what the reader knows as well as the manner in which the story is told. Writers of fiction most commonly use first- and third-person narrators. Second-person narrators are rare but not unheard of, as in Jay McInerney's novel *Bright Lights, Big City*, which begins as follows:

> You are not the kind of guy who would be at a place like this at this time of the morning. But here you are, and you cannot say that the terrain is entirely unfamiliar, although the details are fuzzy.

Second-person point of view puts the reader right in the story, but it is rarely used and viewed as a gimmick, perhaps because it makes the reading experience too literal—you are not just asked to imagine a character, you are told that you *are* the character.

First-Person Point of View

A first-person narrator tells a story using first-person pronouns such as *I* and *we*. From this point of view, we see the world from a single character's perspective (usually the main character's, though it can be a minor character's). The first-person narrator gives us a vivid on-the-spot view of what is happening. Just be careful not to confuse a first-person narrator with the author. In most cases, a first-person narrator is every bit as much a creation of the writer's imagination as any other character.

Let's examine a passage from *The Beautiful Things That Heaven Bears*, the first novel by Ethiopian-born Dinaw Mengestu, in which the main character is preparing to have dinner with his neighbor and her daughter.

> I went home early and changed into a neatly pressed button-down white shirt and a pair of slightly worn gray wool slacks Kenneth had handed down to me. The cuff links, a holdover from my father's days in the Ethiopian government, had the old Ethiopian flag with the Lion of Judah and his crooked crown on it. They were the only things of my father I had left. He used to keep them in a small gray jewelry box with the lid open on top of the dresser in his bedroom, although I can't remember ever having seen him wear them. What I can remember is him holding them out to me and saying with a slight, sarcastic lilt to his voice, "Someday all this will be yours." I don't think he ever actually intended for them to become heirlooms. They were just cheap cuff links from an old, decaying regime, but you hold on to what you can and hope the meaning comes later.
>
> Before leaving the house I stood in front of my bathroom mirror and practiced my introduction. I brushed forward the edges of my thinning hair and patted down the sides of my small Afro. My reflection stared back disapprovingly. I had aged, but there was nothing distinguished about me. The laugh lines around my mouth had burrowed in, and there was more of my forehead than I cared to show. I smiled and tried to find a hint of a younger and better version of myself, but there was no doing. He was gone.
>
> *[2007]*

Notice how the first-person viewpoint helps reveal the speaker's character. We see the world through his eyes. The first paragraph shows us how meticulous he is as he chooses what to wear; he is not wealthy, yet he takes care to choose clothes that are ironed and to wear cuff links that belonged to his father. The way he remembers his father adds to our understanding of this character, who is living a long way from Ethiopia, where he grew up. The second paragraph continues the studied concern with how he looks, though it adds more self-criticism. He stands before the mirror and assesses himself, as though he's looking at another person entirely. He worries about his aging and searches to find traces of his younger self. These details and his admission that he is practicing the way he will introduce himself betray his insecurity.

Imagine how different the story would be if it had been told in the third person with a narrator explaining how Sepha (the main character's name) is feeling. Let's just change the pronouns in one section:

> Sepha's reflection stared back disapprovingly. He had aged, but there was nothing distinguished about him. . . . He smiled and tried to find a hint of a younger and better version of himself, but there was no doing.

It's essentially the same information, yet note the difference in authority. The third-person narrator's observations are more convincing, because they seem like objective observations. With first-person narration, we don't know if the narrator's perceptions of his own looks are accurate or if they just reflect his lack of confidence, because his perceptions are obviously subjective. The first-person viewpoint in this passage makes the character seem more vulnerable — a guy going on a first date and worried about the impression he'll make.

One quirk of first-person narration (and occasionally third-person narration) is that the author might choose to tell the story from the perspective of someone who is naive, mentally ill, biased, corrupt, or downright immoral. A narrator of this sort is called an **unreliable narrator**. An author might use an unreliable narrator to distinguish the character's point of view from his or her own, or to make an ironic point. In the *Adventures of Huckleberry Finn*, Huck tells the story from a perspective that is sometimes naive, sometimes mischievous, and certainly ironic, as demonstrated in the following passage.

> The Widow Douglas, she took me for her son, and allowed she would sivilize me; but it was rough living in the house all the time, considering how dismal regular and decent the widow was in all her ways; and so when I couldn't stand it no longer, I lit out. I got into my old rags, and my sugar-hogshead again, and was free and satisfied. But Tom Sawyer, he hunted me up and said he was going to start a band of robbers, and I might join if I would go back to the widow and be respectable. So I went back.
>
> The widow she cried over me, and called me a poor lost lamb, and she called me a lot of other names, too, but she never meant no harm by it. She put me in them new clothes again, and I couldn't do nothing but sweat and sweat, and feel all cramped up. Well, then, the old thing commenced again. The widow rung a bell for supper, and you had to come to time. When you got to the table you couldn't go right to eating, but you had to wait for the widow to tuck down her head and grumble a little over the victuals, though there warn't really anything the matter with them. That is, nothing only everything was cooked by itself. In a barrel of odds and ends it is different; things get mixed up, and the juice kind of swaps around, and the things go better.
>
> [1885]

In this passage, Huck tells us about his time with the Widow Douglas, particularly her efforts to "sivilize" him. Huck's point of view gives us a skewed version of what it means to be "respectable." He calls the widow "regular and decent" but thinks that is "dismal." Later in the passage, instead of telling us that the widow says grace over dinner, Huck tells us that the widow would "tuck down her head and grumble a little over the victuals, though there warn't really anything the matter with them." The reason Huck tolerates all of this civilizing is so he'll be respectable enough to join Tom Sawyer's band of robbers. What irony! Twain is using Huck's naive perspective to satirize the ways of "regular and decent" folk. Twain's point seems to be that the trappings of respectability are not what make you a good person; indeed, that's just about enough to qualify you for membership in a band of robbers. The thing to remember is that we are seeing this world through the eyes of the naive and mischievous Huckleberry Finn, who is a tool of the great satirist Mark Twain — which means that as readers we need to stay alert or will miss the ironic complexity of this story.

Third-Person Point of View

A third-person narrator tells the story using the third-person pronouns *he*, *she*, and *it*. This type of narrator views all events in a story from a distance and does not play a role in the actual plot. When the narrator is **omniscient**, readers have access to what all the characters are thinking and feeling. A **limited omniscient narrator** tells us what just one major or minor character is thinking and feeling. This perspective both conceals and reveals. While it restricts how much readers know, it can also give readers insight into who a character is and how that character sees the world. In "Miss Brill" by Katherine Mansfield, we see through the eyes of an aging woman sitting in a park in a vacation town in France, observing others around her. We experience all of the action and characters through her perspective.

> Oh, how fascinating it was! How she enjoyed it! How she loved sitting here, watching it all! It was like a play. It was exactly like a play. Who could believe the sky at the back wasn't painted? But it wasn't till a little brown dog trotted on solemn and then slowly trotted off, like a little "theatre" dog, a little dog that had been drugged, that Miss Brill discovered what it was that made it so exciting. They were all on the stage. They weren't only the audience, not only looking on; they were acting. Even she had a part and came every Sunday. No doubt somebody would have noticed if she hadn't been there; she was part of the performance after all. How strange she'd never thought of it like that before! And yet it explained why she made such a point of starting from home at just the same time each week — so as not to be late for the performance — and it also explained why she had quite a queer, shy feeling at telling her English pupils how she spent her Sunday afternoons. No wonder! Miss Brill nearly laughed out loud. She was on the stage. She thought of the old invalid gentleman to whom she read the newspaper four afternoons a week while he slept in the garden. She had got quite used to the frail head on the cotton pillow, the hollowed eyes, the open mouth, and the high pinched nose. If he'd been dead she mightn't have noticed for weeks; she wouldn't have minded. But suddenly he knew he was having the paper read to him by an actress! "An actress!" The old head lifted; two points of light quivered in the old eyes. "An actress — are ye?" And Miss Brill smoothed the newspaper as though it were the manuscript of her part and said gently: "Yes, I have been an actress for a long time."
>
> *[1920]*

In this passage, Miss Brill (whose first name is never revealed) feels like part of the world she is observing. Priding herself on her ability to notice the rich details all around her, she does not see herself as a solitary or pitiful figure. We get to know her as a vibrant, joyful, appreciative, perhaps even contemplative person. Soon after, however, she overhears a young couple laughing at her, a slight that causes her to question whether she really has a part in this world that belongs to the young. We never know the motivation or level of awareness of any other character because the limited omniscient third-person viewpoint is that of Miss Brill.

Another variation on the third-person perspective involves an **objective narrator** (also called a neutral narrator), who recounts only what characters say and do, offering no insight into their thinking or analysis of events; all interpretation is left to the reader. In the short story "The Lottery," author Shirley Jackson uses this perspective to stand back and suspend judgment on an incident that turns ugly and violent: individuals are participating in a lottery to determine which member of the community will be stoned to death. Notice that the objectivity emphasizes the community's willingness to go along with this "tradition."

> The lottery was conducted—as were the square dances, the teen-age club, the Halloween program—by Mr. Summers, who had time and energy to devote to civic activities. He was a round-faced, jovial man and he ran the coal business, and people were sorry for him, because he had no children and his wife was a scold. When he arrived in the square, carrying the black wooden box, there was a murmur of conversation among the villagers, and he waved and called, "Little late today, folks." The postmaster, Mr. Graves, followed him, carrying a three-legged stool, and the stool was put in the center of the square and Mr. Summers set the black box down on it. The villagers kept their distance, leaving a space between themselves and the stool, and when Mr. Summers said, "Some of you fellows want to give me a hand?" there was a hesitation before two men, Mr. Martin and his oldest son, Baxter, came forward to hold the box steady on the stool while Mr. Summers stirred up the papers inside it.
>
> *[1948]*

The characters' actions are described straightforwardly but without any commentary on why they do what they do or how they feel about it. There is no tone of approval or disapproval. Somehow, the detached reporting makes the horror of what is being reported even more striking because the failure to express an opinion suggests the narrator's acceptance.

Stream of Consciousness

Stream of consciousness is a narrative technique characteristic of such twentieth-century writers as William Faulkner, James Joyce, and Virginia Woolf. It takes readers inside the mind of a narrator, recounting thoughts, impressions, and feelings, from either a first-person or a third-person limited omniscient perspective. The reader is privy to exactly what the character is thinking, without the filters of causality or logic. Such interior monologues are often characterized by fragments, swift transitions, and a free association of ideas. In the following passage from *Mrs. Dalloway*, Woolf takes us into the mind of Clarissa Dalloway as she walks through the streets of London.

> For having lived in Westminster—how many years now? over twenty,—one feels even in the midst of the traffic, or waking at night, Clarissa was positive, a particular hush, or solemnity; an indescribable pause; a suspense (but that might be her heart, affected, they said, by influenza) before Big Ben strikes. There! Out it boomed. First a warning, musical; then the hour, irrevocable. The leaden circles dissolved in the air. Such fools we are, she thought, crossing Victoria Street. For Heaven only knows why one loves it so, how one sees it so, making it up, building

it round one, tumbling it, creating it every moment afresh; but the veriest frumps, the most dejected of miseries sitting on doorsteps (drink their downfall) do the same; can't be dealt with, she felt positive, by Acts of Parliament for that very reason: they love life. In people's eyes, in the swing, tramp, and trudge; in the bellow and the uproar; the carriages, motor cars, omnibuses, vans, sandwich men shuffling and swinging; brass bands; barrel organs; in the triumph and the jingle and the strange high singing of some aeroplane overhead was what she loved; life; London; this moment of June.

[1925]

While this narrative technique gives us access to an intimate perspective, it also requires us to sort through information. Random observations such as the sound of Big Ben and the traffic on Victoria Street are interwoven with philosophical musings on why Clarissa loves to be part of the "moment of June" in London. We hear and see what she does as she hears and sees it. The momentum picks up as the passage goes on, and we feel her joy in being part of the world increase moment by moment. Yet the narrator offers no causality or other connections among the perceptions and ideas. Woolf actually describes this technique perfectly in the title of another of her works called *Moments of Being*. Stream of consciousness can be challenging to read in that making order out of what seems to be chaos is largely left to the reader.

• ACTIVITY •

Read "Seeing Eye," a short story by Brad Watson. What is the point of view from which the story is told? Discuss the effect this viewpoint has on the overall story.

Seeing Eye
BRAD WATSON

The dog came to the curb's edge and stopped. The man holding on to his halter stopped beside him. Across the street, the signal flashed the words "Don't Walk." The dog saw the signal but paid little notice. He was trained to see what mattered: the absence of moving traffic. The signal kept blinking. The cars kept driving through the intersection. He watched the cars, listened to the intensity of their engines, the arid whine of their tires. He listened for something he'd become accustomed to hearing, the buzz and tumbling of switches from the box on the pole next to them. The dog associated it with the imminent stopping of the cars. He looked back over his right shoulder at the man, who stood with his head cocked, listening to the traffic.

A woman behind them spoke up.

"Huh," she said. "The light's stuck."

The dog looked at her, then turned back to watch the traffic, which continued to rush through the intersection without pause.

"I'm going down a block," the woman said. She spoke to the man. "Would you like me to show you a detour? No telling how long this light will be."

"No, thank you," the man said. "We'll just wait a little bit. Right, Buck?" The dog looked back over his shoulder at the man, then watched the woman walk away.

"Good luck," the woman said. The dog's ears stood up and he stiffened for just a second.

"She said 'luck,' not 'Buck,'" the man said, laughing easily and reaching down to scratch the dog's ears. He gripped the loose skin on Buck's neck with his right hand and gave it an affectionate shake. He continued to hold the halter guide loosely with his left.

The dog watched the traffic rush by.

"We'll just wait here, Buck," the man said. "By the time we go a block out of our way, the light will've fixed itself." He cleared his throat and cocked his head, as if listening for something. The dog dipped his head and shifted his shoulders in the halter.

The man laughed softly.

"If we went down a block, I'll bet that light would get stuck, too. We'd be following some kind of traveling glitch across town. We could go for miles, and then end up in some field, and a voice saying, 'I suppose you're wondering why I've summoned you here.'"

It was the longest they'd ever stood waiting for traffic to stop. The dog saw people across the street wait momentarily, glance around, then leave. He watched the traffic. It began to have a hypnotic effect upon him: the traffic, the blinking crossing signal. His focus on the next move, the crossing, on the implied courses of the pedestrians around them and those still waiting at the opposite curb, on the potential obstructions ahead, dissolved into the rare luxury of wandering attention.

The sounds of the traffic grinding through the intersection were diminished to a small aural dot in the back of his mind, and he became aware of the regular bleat of a slow-turning box fan in an open window of the building behind them. Odd scents distinguished themselves in his nostrils and blended into a rich funk that swirled about the pedestrians who stopped next to them, a secret aromatic history that eddied about him even as the pedestrians muttered among themselves and moved on.

The hard clean smell of new shoe leather seeped from the air-conditioned stores, overlaying the drift of worn leather and grime that eased from tiny musty pores in the sidewalk. He snuffled at them and sneezed. In a trembling confusion he was aware of all that was carried in the breeze, the strong odor of tobacco and the sharp rake of its smoke, the gasoline and exhaust fumes and the stench of aging rubber, the fetid waves that rolled through it all from garbage bins in the alleys and on the backstreet curbs.

He lowered his head and shifted his shoulders in the harness like a boxer. "Easy, Buck," the man said.

Sometimes in their room the man paced the floor and seemed to say his words in time with his steps until he became like a lulling clock to Buck as he lay resting beneath the dining table. He dozed to the man's mumbling and the sifting sound of his fingers as they grazed the pages of his book. At times in their dark room the man sat on the edge of his cot and scratched Buck's ears and spoke to him. "Panorama, Buck," he would say. "That's the most difficult to recall. I can see the details, with my hands, with my nose, my tongue. It brings them back. But the big picture. I feel like I must be replacing it with something phony, like a Disney movie or something." Buck looked up at the man's shadowed face in the dark room, at his small eyes in their sallow depressions.

On the farm where he'd been raised before his training at the school, Buck's name had been Pete. The children and the old man and the woman had tussled with him, thrown sticks, said, "Pete! Good old Pete." They called out to him, mumbled the name into his fur. But now the man always said "Buck" in the same tone of voice, soft and gentle. As if the man were speaking to himself. As if Buck were not really there.

"I miss colors, Buck," the man would say. "It's getting harder to remember them. The blue planet. I remember that. Pictures from space. From out in the blackness."

Looking up from the intersection, Buck saw birds dart through the sky between buildings as quickly as they slipped past the open window at dawn. He heard their high-pitched cries so clearly that he saw their beady eyes, their barbed tongues flicking between parted beaks. He salivated at the dusky taste of a dove once he'd held in his mouth. And in his most delicate bones he felt the murmur of some incessant activity, the low hum beyond the visible world. His hackles rose and his muscles tingled with electricity.

There was a metallic whirring, like a big fat June bug stuck on its back, followed by the dull clunk of the switch in the traffic control box. Cars stopped. The lane opened up before them, and for a moment no one moved, as if the empty-eyed vehicles were not to be trusted, restrained only by some fragile miracle of faith. He felt the man carefully regrip the leather harness. He felt the activity of the world spool down into the tight and rifled tunnel of their path.

"Forward, Buck," said the man.

He leaned into the harness and moved them into the world.

[1996]

Layered Points of View

Not every story has a straightforward first- or third-person point of view. Often a novel is told through multiple layered perspectives. In her novel *A Crime in the Neighborhood*, Suzanne Berne tells the story from the viewpoint of a woman, Marsha,

who recalls a violent crime that occurred when she was an adolescent. In the following passage, Marsha is remembering an encounter between a suspicious neighbor
and her mother, who is waiting for guests to arrive for a barbecue.

> "I think I would like a little more wine, thank you," [my mother] added after a
> moment, and held out her cup.
>
> As he bent to refill her cup, their eyes met and she smiled up at him. "It's still
> early," she told him. "They might still come."
>
> "Yes," he said.
>
> Two stories above them, I propped my chin on the back of a hand, leaning
> on the windowsill. Had she remembered to turn off the burner from under the pan
> of hamburger meat? Had she noticed, on her way out, if the freezer door was
> ajar?
>
> When I look back I don't have trouble understanding how my mother got   5
> herself into Mr. Green's yard that night. All the time she had been preparing
> dinner she must have been glancing out the kitchen window, watching him as
> he sat alone in his unsteady chair, stiff khaki shirt fading into the early evening.
> I suppose it was the cumulative effect of that vision that finally made her fumble
> toward the door as if the hamburger meat had already burned, as if the whole
> house were filled with smoke. Because as I recall it now there *was* something
> dire in the sight of Mr. Green that evening. Something powerful enough to send
> my mother rushing from the house, barefoot half-dressed. . . . What must have
> made my mother's eyes sting that summer evening, what must have made her
> almost run to the kitchen door, had to be the fury of mortal fear—the fear that
> comes from understanding all at once that you are by yourself in a vast world,
> and that one day something worse than anything that has ever happened before
> will happen.
>
> *[1998]*

The narrator begins recounting the story through dialogue between her mother
and Mr. Green, dialogue that the narrator reconstructs from memory but presents as
though it were just occurring. Her narrative voice intrudes from "[t]wo stories above
them," as she remembers herself as a young girl looking down from an upstairs window, where she watched the encounter and wondered if her mother "remembered to
turn off the burner from under the pan of hamburger meat." In the next paragraph,
the narrator reminds us that an older, more mature person is telling the story as a
flashback: "When I look back . . ." What follows is hardly the consciousness of the
young girl at the windowsill but that of an adult who is remembering the story and
reflecting on how it influenced her.

Another layered technique is to introduce a story using another story, called
a **narrative frame** or frame story. A narrative frame establishes who is telling the
main story and under what circumstances. Narrative frames usually create a shift in
perspective. If the frame story is told in first-person present tense, perhaps the main
story will be told as a flashback, or in third person as something that happened to

someone else. When a frame is used to pass on a secondhand story, the reader is left to wonder if the narrator is getting everything right, or if he or she is misremembering or embellishing the tale. Mary Shelley uses a narrative frame for her novel *Frankenstein*. The primary narrator is Captain Robert Walton, who is on a scientific mission above the Arctic Circle to "tread a land never before imprinted by the foot of man." In letters written to his sister, he retells the story being told to him by "the stranger" his crew found stranded on the ice, one Victor Frankenstein.

August 19th, 17—.

Yesterday the stranger said to me, "You may easily perceive, Captain Walton, that I have suffered great and unparalleled misfortunes. I had determined, at one time, that the memory of these evils should die with me; but you have won me to alter my determination. You seek for knowledge and wisdom, as I once did; and I ardently hope that the gratification of your wishes may not be a serpent to sting you, as mine has been. I do not know that the relation of my disasters will be useful to you; yet, when I reflect that you are pursuing the same course, exposing yourself to the same dangers which have rendered me what I am, I imagine that you may deduce an apt moral from my tale; one that may direct you if you succeed in your undertaking, and console you in case of failure. Prepare to hear of occurrences which are usually deemed marvellous. Were we among the tamer scenes of nature, I might fear to encounter your unbelief, perhaps your ridicule; but many things will appear possible in these wild and mysterious regions, which would provoke the laughter of those unacquainted with the ever-varied powers of nature:—nor can I doubt but that my tale conveys in its series internal evidence of the truth of the events of which it is composed."

You may easily imagine that I was much gratified by the offered communication; yet I could not endure that he should renew his grief by a recital of his misfortunes. I felt the greatest eagerness to hear the promised narrative, partly from curiosity, and partly from a strong desire to ameliorate his fate, if it were in my power. I expressed these feelings in my answer.

"I thank you," he replied, "for your sympathy, but it is useless; my fate is nearly fulfilled. I wait but for one event, and then I shall repose in peace. I understand your feeling," continued he, perceiving that I wished to interrupt him; "but you are mistaken, my friend, if thus you will allow me to name you; nothing can alter my destiny: listen to my history, and you will perceive how irrevocably it is determined."

He then told me, that he would commence his narrative the next day when I should be at leisure. This promise drew from me the warmest thanks. I have resolved every night, when I am not imperatively occupied by my duties, to record, as nearly as possible in his own words, what he has related during the day. If I should be engaged, I will at least make notes. This manuscript will doubtless afford you the greatest pleasure: but to me, who know him, and who hear it from his own lips, with what interest and sympathy shall I read it in some future day! Even now, as I commence my task, his full-toned voice swells in my ears; his lustrous eyes dwell on me with all their melancholy sweetness; I see his thin hand raised in animation, while the lineaments of his face are irradiated by the soul within. Strange and harrowing must be his story; frightful the storm which embraced the gallant vessel on its course, and wrecked it—thus!

[1818]

When a narrative frame is used, there is frequently a thematic link between the frame and the main narrative. In this case, both stories are about men who "seek for knowledge and wisdom." With a frame of this sort, notice how many different ways this story gets told:

- Walton writes a letter.
- Walton quotes Frankenstein.
- Walton comments on Frankenstein's story.
- Walton paraphrases what Frankenstein said.

This complex storytelling technique effectively draws a connection between Walton and Frankenstein, between the frame and the main narrative.

The following questions will help guide your analysis of point of view:

- Is the point of view first person (*I*) or third person (*he, she, it*)?
- Is the narrator a participant or an observer in the story?
- If the point of view is first person, how reliable is the narrator?
- If the perspective is third person, is the narrator omniscient or limited omniscient?
- Does the point of view shift during the course of the story? If so, what is the impact?
- If the piece has a narrative frame, how does it relate thematically to the main narrative?

• ACTIVITY •

The following passage is from Colm Tóibín's novel *Brooklyn*, which takes place in the mid-twentieth century. Discuss how the setting, as told from the third-person limited omniscient point of view, characterizes the narrator, a young woman who has recently immigrated to Brooklyn from a small town in Ireland.

From *Brooklyn*
COLM TÓIBÍN

She liked the morning air and the quietness of these few leafy streets, streets that had shops only on the corners, streets where people lived, where there were three or four apartments in each house and where she passed women accompanying their children to school as she went to work. As she walked

> along, however, she knew she was getting close to the real world, which had wider streets and more traffic. Once she arrived at Atlantic Avenue, Brooklyn began to feel like a strange place to her, with so many gaps between buildings and so many derelict buildings. And then suddenly, when she arrived at Fulton Street, there would be so many people crowding to cross the street, and in such dense clusters, that on the first morning she thought a fight had broken out or someone was injured and they had gathered to get a good view.
>
> [2009]

Symbol

Literary texts often contain symbols—objects, places, events, even characters—that carry more than literal meaning and therefore point the way to the meaning of the work as a whole. Symbols operate in fiction and drama much as they do in poetry, which we discussed in Chapter 2. It's important to avoid making your study of a short story, novel, or play just a hunt for common symbols. Symbols work by association and always fit into the context of the work as a whole, so be careful not to jump to conclusions. There is no secret code that says that water always symbolizes rebirth, for instance. Water might symbolize rebirth in one work but could symbolize purity or infinite possibility in another. Other symbols are unique to specific texts, such as the green light at the end of the dock in *The Great Gatsby* (p. 25). Symbols are most often part of setting. Look back at the second paragraph from Poe's short story "The Masque of the Red Death" (p. 67). The clock is described as having an especially dramatic and unsettling hourly chime. Everyone stops; the musicians are uneasy and the waltzers pause. The sound is unusual, not harmonious. Clearly, the clock and its chime symbolize the inevitability of time's passing and, in this case, the reality that time is running out regardless of how much these people try to hide from death.

Sometimes, however, symbols help develop a character. In the story "Clothes" by Chitra Banerjee Divakaruni, the clothing the main character chooses symbolizes different phases of her life. When she leaves India to travel to America for her arranged marriage, she and her parents select an appropriate sari, the traditional dress:

> I wanted a blue one for the journey, because blue is the color of possibility, the color of the sky through which I would be traveling. But Mother said there must be red in it because red is the color of luck for married women.

The colors are symbolic of how the narrator views her new life. Later, when she becomes Americanized, not just the color but also her choice of clothing symbolize her new identity:

> I'm wearing a pair of jeans now, marveling at the curves of my hips and thighs, which have always been hidden under the flowing lines of my saris. . . . The jeans come with a close-fitting T-shirt which . . . is sunrise-orange—the color, I decide, of joy, of my new American life.

The following questions will help guide your analysis of symbols:

- What objects does the writer seem to emphasize, through description, repetition, or placement in the story?
- What might be symbolic about the setting? What characters or aspects of a character might be symbolic? What events might be symbolic?
- Is there a recurring pattern, or **motif**, of images or events?
- How does your symbolic interpretation fit with the context of the story?

· ACTIVITY ·

Think of a movie that includes a symbol. Discuss what the symbol means and how it connects to the meaning of the work as a whole.

Theme

When we talk about the way a work of literature raises a question or explores an issue in addition to telling a story, we are talking about theme. The rich works you read in school usually have several themes, which are revealed through the piece's plot, character, setting, point of view, and symbols.

Identifying and articulating themes is not a simple process. Literary critic Northrop Frye used the term "the educated imagination" to describe the intersection of skills and knowledge with creativity. Think about the previous sections of this chapter—as well as Chapters 1 and 2—as having educated your imagination so that now you're ready to uncover the themes of complex novels, plays, short stories, and even poems. As you come up with a theme for a piece of writing, you are inevitably interpreting it; thus, the theme you find may not be the same one others find. There can be many themes in a work—not just one "answer" waiting to be discovered.

Let's put some of these ideas to work by examining the themes of a short story by Pulitzer Prize–winning author Edward P. Jones.

The First Day
EDWARD P. JONES

On an otherwise unremarkable September morning, long before I learned to be ashamed of my mother, she takes my hand and we set off down New Jersey Avenue to begin my very first day of school. I am wearing a checkeredlike blue-and-green cotton dress, and scattered about these colors are bits of yellow and white and brown. My mother has uncharacteristically spent nearly an hour on my hair that morning, plaiting and replaiting so that now my scalp tingles. Whenever I turn my head quickly, my nose fills with the faint smell of Dixie Peach hair grease. The smell is somehow a soothing one now and I will reach for it time and time again before the morning ends. All the plaits, each with a blue barrette near the tip and each twisted into an uncommon sturdiness, will last until I go to bed that night, something that has never happened before. My stomach is full of milk and oatmeal sweetened with brown sugar. Like everything else I have on, my pale green slip and underwear are new, the underwear having come three to a plastic package with a little girl on the front who appears to be dancing. Behind my ears, my mother, to stop my whining, has dabbed the stingiest bit of her gardenia perfume, the last present my father gave her before he disappeared into memory. Because I cannot smell it, I have only her word that the perfume is there. I am also wearing yellow socks trimmed with thin lines of black and white around the tops. My shoes are my greatest joy, black patent-leather miracles, and when one is nicked at the toe later that morning in class, my heart will break.

I am carrying a pencil, a pencil sharpener, and a small ten-cent tablet with a black-and-white speckled cover. My mother does not believe that a girl in kindergarten needs such things, so I am taking them only because of my insistent whining and because they are presents from our neighbors, Mary Keith and Blondelle Harris. Miss Mary and Miss Blondelle are watching my two younger sisters until my mother returns. The women are as precious to me as my mother and sisters. Out playing one day, I have overheard an older child, speaking to another child, call Miss Mary and Miss Blondelle a word that is brand new to me. This is my mother: When I say the word in fun to one of my sisters, my mother slaps me across the mouth and the word is lost for years and years.

All the way down New Jersey Avenue, the sidewalks are teeming with children. In my neighborhood, I have many friends, but I see none of them as my mother and I walk. We cross New York Avenue, we cross Pierce Street, and we cross L and K, and still I see no one who knows my name. At I Street, between New Jersey Avenue and Third Street, we enter Seaton Elementary School, a time-worn, sad-faced building across the street from my mother's church, Mt. Carmel Baptist.

Just inside the front door, women out of the advertisements in *Ebony* are greeting other parents and children. The woman who greets us has pearls thick as jumbo marbles that come down almost to her navel, and she acts as if she had known me all my life, touching my shoulder, cupping her hand under my chin. She is enveloped in a perfume that I only know is not gardenia. When, in answer to her question, my mother tells her that we live at 1227 New Jersey Avenue, the woman first seems to be picturing in her head where we live. Then she shakes her head and says that we are at the wrong school, that we should be at Walker-Jones.

My mother shakes her head vigorously. "I want her to go here," my mother says. "If I'da wanted her someplace else, I'da took her there." The woman continues to act as if she has known me all my life, but she tells my mother that we live beyond the area that Seaton serves. My mother is not convinced and for several more minutes she questions the woman about why I cannot attend Seaton. For as many Sundays as I can remember, perhaps even Sundays when I was in her

5

womb, my mother has pointed across I Street to Seaton as we come and go to Mt. Carmel. "You gonna go there and learn about the whole world." But one of the guardians of that place is saying no, and no again. I am learning this about my mother: The higher up on the scale of respectability a person is—and teachers are rather high up in her eyes—the less she is liable to let them push her around. But finally, I see in her eyes the closing gate, and she takes my hand and we leave the building. On the steps, she stops as people move past us on either side.

"Mama, I can't go to school?"

She says nothing at first, then takes my hand again and we are down the steps quickly and nearing New Jersey Avenue before I can blink. This is my mother: She says, "One monkey don't stop no show."

Walker-Jones is a larger, newer school and I immediately like it because of that. But it is not across the street from my mother's church, her rock, one of her connections to God, and I sense her doubts as she absently rubs her thumb over the back of her hand. We find our way to the crowded auditorium where gray metal chairs are set up in the middle of the room. Along the wall to the left are tables and other chairs. Every chair seems occupied by a child or adult. Somewhere in the room a child is crying, a cry that rises above the buzz-talk of so many people. Strewn about the floor are dozens and dozens of pieces of white paper, and people are walking over them without any thought of picking them up. And seeing this lack of concern, I am all of a sudden afraid.

"Is this where they register for school?" my mother asks a woman at one of the tables.

The woman looks up slowly as if she has heard this question once too often. She nods. She is tiny, almost as small as the girl standing beside her. The woman's hair is set in a mass of curlers and all of those curlers are made of paper money, here a dollar bill, there a five-dollar bill. The girl's hair is arrayed in curls, but some of them are beginning to droop and this makes me happy. On the table beside the woman's pocketbook is a large notebook, worthy of someone in high school, and looking at me looking at the notebook, the girl places her hand possessively on it. In her other hand she holds several pencils with thick crowns of additional erasers.

"These the forms you gotta use?" my mother asks the woman, picking up a few pieces of the paper from the table. "Is this what you have to fill out?"

The woman tells her yes, but that she need fill out only one.

"I see," my mother says, looking about the room. Then: "Would you help me with this form? That is, if you don't mind."

The woman asks my mother what she means.

"This form. Would you mind helpin me fill it out?"

The woman still seems not to understand.

"I can't read it. I don't know how to read or write, and I'm askin you to help me." My mother looks at me, then looks away. I know almost all of her looks, but this one is brand new to me. "Would you help me, then?"

The woman says Why sure, and suddenly she appears happier, so much more satisfied with everything. She finishes the form for her daughter and my

10

15

mother and I step aside to wait for her. We find two chairs nearby and sit. My mother is now diseased, according to the girl's eyes, and until the moment her mother takes her and the form to the front of the auditorium, the girl never stops looking at my mother. I stare back at her. "Don't stare," my mother says to me. "You know better than that."

Another woman out of the *Ebony* ads takes the woman's child away. Now, the woman says upon returning, let's see what we can do for you two.

My mother answers the questions the woman reads off the form. They start   20
with my last name, and then on to the first and middle names. This is school, I think. This is going to school. My mother slowly enunciates each word of my name. This is my mother: As the questions go on, she takes from her pocketbook document after document, as if they will support my right to attend school, as if she has been saving them up for just this moment. Indeed, she takes out more papers than I have ever seen her do in other places: my birth certificate, my baptismal record, a doctor's letter concerning my bout with chicken pox, rent receipts, records of immunization, a letter about our public assistance payments, even her marriage license—every single paper that has anything even remotely to do with my five-year-old life. Few of the papers are needed here, but it does not matter and my mother continues to pull out the documents with the purposefulness of a magician pulling out a long string of scarves. She has learned that money is the beginning and end of everything in this world, and when the woman finishes, my mother offers her fifty cents, and the woman accepts it without hesitation. My mother and I are just about the last parent and child in the room.

My mother presents the form to a woman sitting in front of the stage, and the woman looks at it and writes something on a white card, which she gives to my mother. Before long, the woman who has taken the girl with the drooping curls appears from behind us, speaks to the sitting woman, and introduces herself to my mother and me. She's to be my teacher, she tells my mother. My mother stares.

We go into the hall, where my mother kneels down to me. Her lips are quivering. "I'll be back to pick you up at twelve o'clock. I don't want you to go nowhere. You just wait right here. And listen to every word she say." I touch her lips and press them together. It is an old, old game between us. She puts my hand down at my side, which is not part of the game. She stands and looks a second at the teacher, then she turns and walks away. I see where she has darned one of her socks the night before. Her shoes make loud sounds in the hall. She passes through the doors and I can still hear the loud sounds of her shoes. And even when the teacher turns me toward the classrooms and I hear what must be the singing and talking of all the children in the world, I can still hear my mother's footsteps above it all.

[1992]

To uncover the themes of a story, you will have to rely on your observations, find portions of the work that seem significant or meaningful, and then explain why you think they are significant. Although literary elements often work together to create a theme, we're going to go element by element, in order to demonstrate a relatively systematic way of looking for themes.

Let's start with the plot of this story, which is pretty straightforward: an uneducated mother takes her daughter to the first day of kindergarten; they are refused admission to one school and have to go to another, where a kindly person assists the mother in filling out the necessary forms; the mother leaves the child at school, telling her to pay close attention to the teacher. That's pretty much it. Yet within that plot, we can see quite a few events that seem to have deeper significance and could point toward possible themes. For instance, why would a mother who cannot read do her utmost, overcoming obstacle after obstacle, to get her child into school? This seems a bit paradoxical, more than a little heartwarming, and definitely important. Is the author's message that perhaps the people who truly understand the importance of an education are the ones who haven't had the benefit of one?

Who are the characters in this story? The main characters are the mother and the daughter. The other characters are all female, mostly teachers. Where are the men in this story? That is definitely a question worth exploring, but let's stick to the mother and the daughter for now. How does the daughter change or develop because of the action of the plot? Think about the title: "The First Day." We can ask: the first day of what? Literally, it's the first day of school, but it is also the first day that the narrator is leaving her family and entering society as a whole. It's the first day that her education and her fate are being transferred from her mother to the female teachers, who are minor but important characters in this story. These observations suggest a number of themes, especially the importance of community in raising a child.

The story's setting is a poor neighborhood of Washington, D.C., and we're given details about the school the mother wants her daughter to attend—the school that is directly across from her church. Why is the proximity of the church important to the setting? How does it reveal a theme? The narrator tells us that the church is very important to her mother—it is her "rock"—so it's clear that the mother wants the daughter to go to the nearby school because it is familiar, safe, protected, and in a community she trusts. This aspect of the setting reinforces the theme we uncovered when looking at character: community is important in raising a child. But it also goes further, speaking to the mother's anxiety about letting her daughter go.

Point of view can often be a difficult platform for interpretation, but in this story, it is especially interesting. The narrator is the daughter, recalling the incident from the vantage point of adulthood. But the narrator is more specific about her point of view. She says that these events occurred "long before [she] learned to be ashamed of [her] mother" (para. 1). The word "learned" seems significant, given the context of this story about education. We think of education as being "book learning," but it's clear that some part of the narrator's education has involved "learning" to be ashamed of her mother. Yet as she's telling this story, she does not seem ashamed; she seems proud of her mother's heroic journey, proud that her mother overcame so many obstacles in order to make sure her daughter had a bright future. So one theme might involve the changing perspectives we have regarding our parents: When we are young, we think they are strong and infallible, but we grow to see their flaws as we become part of the world rather than just part of a family; it takes time to come back around to respect and appreciate all the things our parents have done on our behalf.

Not every story operates through symbols, and although this short piece may not have many, the narrator's shoes could certainly be symbolic. She says, "My shoes are my greatest joy, black patent-leather miracles, and when one is nicked at the toe later that morning in class, my heart will break" (para. 1). Perhaps the fate of these shoes mirrors her relationship with her mother. Before going out into the world, she is proud of her mother, yet in the process of going to school, meeting other people, and learning new things, just like the shiny shoes, her mother's image gets nicked. Perhaps that change is what really breaks her heart. So, one theme might be that on the first day of school, we are letting go of our parents just as much as they are letting go of us.

As you can see, as you consider themes, you often move beyond the text to draw conclusions about the real world, what we called "extension" in Chapter 1. "The First Day," for example, suggests something about the role of education in our lives that goes beyond this particular five-year-old's first day in kindergarten. Isn't this story really about the role education can play in parent-child relationships, when the child's education outpaces that of the parent? Maybe Jones is asking us to think about what happened later, as the narrator aged, was successful at school, went on to college. Her mother may be one hundred percent supportive of her daughter's education. Yet, those very opportunities can divide and separate the two, as the daughter's experiences diverge from those of her mother. The narrator is looking back with obvious love and appreciation for her mother, yet Jones does not give us the story of what took place between "the first day" and the point from which the narrator remembers it.

There is no magic formula for finding a novel, play, or short story's themes other than observation and interpretation—and, of course, rereading. Nevertheless, here are a few suggestions to keep in mind as you try to articulate themes.

1. *Subject and theme are not the same.* The subject of Jones's story may be a little girl's first day of school, but the theme is what the work says about the subject. Thus, you should state a theme as a complete sentence (or two). For instance, "Once a child enters school, teachers, peers, and society as a whole take over some of the responsibility for raising that child. While this can expand a child's horizons and create opportunities for him or her, it can also test the bond between parent and child."

2. *Avoid clichés.* Even though "love conquers all" may indeed be a theme of Jones's story, try to state it in a more original and sophisticated way. Clichés are lazy statements that ignore the complexity of a literary text.

3. *Do not ignore contradictory details.* You don't want to claim, for instance, that the theme of Jones's story is about how a little girl came to be ashamed of her mother, since the mother is portrayed heroically in the story.

4. *A theme is not a moral.* It may sometimes be tempting to extract "the moral of the story" (which is likely to be a cliché). Resist! Writers of drama and

fiction—and poetry—work indirectly. If a writer wanted to convey an idea directly, he or she would write an editorial for a newspaper. Those who choose to write a literary work do so to explore ideas indirectly through plots, characters, settings, points of view, symbols, and the like.

5. *A literary work almost always has more than one theme.* Notice how many themes we have already discussed for this very short story. It is likely that you will think of even more as you bring your own ideas and experiences to the piece.

6. *Themes can be questions.* Author Toni Morrison has said that she does not write to put forth answers but to explore questions. You'll read some works that present an intellectual or moral dilemma, or pose a conundrum that you are not obligated to answer. Questions "The First Day" poses might be these: Why must parenting always involve loss? Do those who lack education value it more than those who take it for granted? When do children begin to understand and appreciate their parents?

• ACTIVITY •

Read the following short story, and try to articulate at least three possible themes.

Girl
JAMAICA KINCAID

Wash the white clothes on Monday and put them on the stone heap; wash the color clothes on Tuesday and put them on the clothesline to dry; don't walk barehead in the hot sun; cook pumpkin fritters in very hot sweet oil; soak your little cloths right after you take them off; when buying cotton to make yourself a nice blouse, be sure that it doesn't have gum on it, because that way it won't hold up well after a wash; soak salt fish overnight before you cook it; is it true that you sing benna in Sunday school?; always eat your food in such a way that it won't turn someone else's stomach; on Sundays try to walk like a lady and not like the slut you are so bent on becoming; don't sing benna in Sunday school; you mustn't speak to wharf-rat boys, not even to give directions; don't eat fruits on the street—flies will follow you; *but I don't sing benna on Sundays at all and never in Sunday school;* this is how to sew on a button; this is how to make a buttonhole for the button you have just sewed on; this is how to hem a dress when you see the hem coming down and so to prevent yourself from looking like the slut I know you are so bent on becoming; this is how you iron your father's khaki shirt so that it doesn't have a crease; this is how you iron your father's khaki pants so that they don't have a crease; this is how you grow okra—far from the house, because okra tree harbors red ants; when you are growing dasheen, make sure it gets plenty of water or else it makes your throat itch when you are eating it; this is how you sweep a corner; this is how you sweep a whole house; this is how you sweep a yard; this is how you smile to someone you don't like too much; this is how you smile to someone you don't like at all; this is how you smile to someone you like completely; this is how you set a table for tea; this is how you set a table for dinner; this is how you set a table for dinner with an important guest; this is how you set a table for lunch; this is how you set a table for breakfast; this is how to behave in the presence of men who don't know you very well, and this way they won't recognize immediately the slut I have warned you against becoming; be sure to wash every day, even if it is with your own spit; don't squat down to play marbles—you are not a boy, you know; don't pick people's flowers—you might catch something; don't throw stones at blackbirds, because it might not be a blackbird at all; this is how to make a bread pudding; this is how to make doukona; this is how to make pepper pot; this is how to make a good medicine for a cold; this is how to make a good medicine to throw away a child before it even becomes a child; this is how to catch a fish; this is how to throw back a fish you don't like, and that way something bad won't fall on you; this is how to bully a man; this is how a man bullies you; this is how to love a man, and if this doesn't work there are other ways, and if they don't work don't feel too bad about giving up; this is how to spit up in the air if you feel like it, and this is how to move quick so that it doesn't fall on you; this is how to make ends meet; always squeeze bread to make sure it's fresh; *but what if the baker won't let me feel the bread?*; you mean to say that after all you are really going to be the kind of woman who the baker won't let near the bread?

[1978]

Special Considerations for Analyzing Drama

Analyzing drama is quite similar to analyzing fiction: both require consideration of plot, character, setting, symbol, and theme. However, there are some differences. The most important difference is that point of view is not a major concern in drama, because few plays have a narrator. If there is one, he or she is likely presented as a character who occasionally steps out to speak to the audience. Another major difference is that a play is a theatrical as well as a literary experience. When we read a play, we imagine the performance: the actors creating the characters and reading the lines, the director interpreting the atmosphere and physical setting on stage, and especially the interaction between the performers and the audience. When we see a play on stage, we are literally seeing how other people read, imagine, and interpret that play, and that inevitably adds to the meaning of the work. Let's look at some other ways that analyzing drama is different from analyzing fiction.

Plot

Plot works similarly in drama as in fiction. In fact, our traditional concept of how to structure a plot (p. 60) was developed by studying classic works from Greek drama and Shakespeare's plays. Drama, however, is often broken into **acts**, and acts are further divided into **scenes**. Acts and scenes structure a play, and it can be revealing to consider why the acts and scenes are divided as they are.

Character

Since a play does not have a narrator, **dialogue**, or the conversation between two or more characters, becomes an essential way to reveal character. Though playwrights attempt to represent normal speech patterns and usage, dramatic dialogue is usually different from normal human conversation. Every minute on stage must be used to the greatest advantage, so conversations must be pointed and charged with meaning. When reading drama, you should try to isolate three elements of dialogue: (1) the content of what is being said; (2) the way it is being said, including both the language and the stage directions for delivering the line; and (3) the reaction and response from other characters.

In *Pygmalion* by George Bernard Shaw, the two central characters, Eliza Doolittle and Henry Higgins, come from different worlds: she is a Cockney flower girl, Higgins is a professor of phonetics (pronunciation). Higgins bets that he can "make a duchess of this draggle-tailed guttersnipe" in six months, and he wins the bet. The following dialogue takes place as Eliza realizes that she's a fish out of water in both her new world and her old world. In this exchange, notice how the dialogue characterizes Eliza and Henry. You might want to read the lines aloud to get a better sense of the pacing and rhythm, noting that Shaw uses spacing to emphasize some words.

> ELIZA *tries to control herself and feel indifferent as she rises and walks across to the hearth to switch off the lights. By the time she gets there she is on the point of screaming. She sits down in Higgins's chair and holds on hard to the arms. Finally she gives way and flings herself furiously on the floor raging.*
>
> HIGGINS *[in despairing wrath outside]*: What the devil have I done with my slippers? *[He appears at the door].*
>
> LIZA *[snatching up the slippers, and hurling them at him one after the other with all her force]*: There are your slippers. And there. Take your slippers; and may you never have a day's luck with them!   5
>
> HIGGINS *[astounded]*: What on earth —! *[He comes to her].* Whats the matter? Get up. *[He pulls her up].* Anything wrong?
>
> LIZA *[breathless]*: Nothing wrong—with y o u. Ive won your bet for you, havnt I? Thats enough for you. *I* dont matter, I suppose.
>
> HIGGINS: Y o u won my bet! You! Presumptuous insect! *I* won it. What did you throw   10 those slippers at me for?
>
> LIZA: Because I wanted to smash your face. I'd like to kill you, you selfish brute. Why didnt you leave me where you picked me out of—in the gutter? You thank God it's all over, and that now you can throw me back again there, do you? *[She crisps her fingers frantically].*   15
>
> HIGGINS *[looking at her in cool wonder]*: The creature i s nervous, after all.
>
> LIZA *[gives a suffocated scream of fury, and instinctively darts her nails at his face]*: !!

HIGGINS [*catching her wrists*]: Ah! would you? Claws in, you cat. How dare you shew your temper to me? Sit down and be quiet. [*He throws her roughly into the easy-chair*].

LIZA [*crushed by superior strength and weight*]: Whats to become of me? Whats to become   20
of me?

HIGGINS: How the devil do I know whats to become of you? What does it matter what becomes of you?

LIZA: You dont care. I know you dont care. You wouldnt care if I was dead. I'm nothing to you — not so much as them slippers.   25

HIGGINS [*thundering*]: T h o s e slippers.

LIZA [*with bitter submission*]: Those slippers. I didnt think it made any difference now.

A pause. ELIZA *hopeless and crushed.* HIGGINS *a little uneasy.*

HIGGINS [*in his loftiest manner*]: Why have you begun going on like this? May I ask whether you complain of your treatment here?

LIZA: No.   30

HIGGINS: Has anybody behaved badly to you? Colonel Pickering? Mrs. Pearce? Any of the servants?

LIZA: No.

HIGGINS: I presume you dont pretend that I have treated you badly.

LIZA: No.   35

HIGGINS: I am glad to hear it. [*He moderates his tone*]. Perhaps youre tired after the strain of the day. Will you have a glass of champagne? [*He moves towards the door*].

LIZA: No. [*Recollecting her manners*] Thank you.

HIGGINS [*good-humored again*]: This has been coming on you for some days. I suppose it was natural for you to be anxious about the garden party. But thats all over now. [*He   40
pats her kindly on the shoulder. She writhes*]. Theres nothing more to worry about.

LIZA: No. Nothing more for y o u to worry about. [*She suddenly rises and gets away from him by going to the piano bench, where she sits and hides her face*]. Oh God! I wish I was dead.

HIGGINS [*staring after her in sincere surprise*]: Why? in heaven's name, why? [*Reasonably,   45
going to her*] Listen to me, Eliza. All this irritation is purely subjective.

LIZA: I dont understand. I'm too ignorant.

HIGGINS: It's only imagination. Low spirits and nothing else. Nobody's hurting you. Nothing's wrong. You go to bed like a good girl and sleep it off. Have a little cry and say your prayers: that will make you comfortable.   50

LIZA: I heard y o u r prayers. "Thank God it's all over!"

HIGGINS [*impatiently*]: Well, dont you thank God it's all over? Now you are free and can do what you like.

LIZA [*pulling herself together in desperation*]: What am I fit for? What have you left me fit for? Where am I to go? What am I to do? Whats to become of me?   55

[*1913*]

Perhaps what is most striking in this dialogue is that Higgins never really hears Liza. She is despondent and trying to figure out how she's going to live the rest of her life, while he's trying to find his slippers. When she hurls the slippers at him along with the wish that they never bring him anything good, he responds with utter surprise, asking, "Anything wrong?" The understatement in this scene is humorous, yet as the dialogue continues, we realize that Higgins completely lacks empathy for the young woman, who is his student—and his subject. In the face of her anger, he responds indignantly that she has stepped out of her place: "Presumptuous insect," he calls her. She accuses him of not caring at all about her, and he responds by correcting her diction. He counters her emotion with sheer logic, asking her if she has been treated badly by anyone during her stay with him. Since she cannot point to any concrete act of mistreatment, he concludes that her problem is simply stress, which he dismisses as "purely subjective." Ultimately, he treats her as if she were a child, sending her off to bed to have a good cry and get some rest. The dialogue has not only shown us the quintessential failure to communicate but also characterized Higgins as cerebral and detached and Liza as a woman in the midst of an identity crisis.

Another important technique that playwrights use to reveal character is the **soliloquy**—a **monologue** in which a character, alone on the stage, reveals his or her thoughts or emotions, as if the character is thinking out loud. Through a soliloquy, a playwright can reveal to the audience a character's motivation, intent, or even doubt. For example, in the following soliloquy from Shakespeare's *Othello*, the villainous Iago reveals his jealousy toward Othello and his evil intent to bring him down.

> IAGO: Thus do I ever make my fool my purse;
> For I mine own gained knowledge should profane
> If I would time expend with such a snipe°
> But for my sport and profit. I hate the Moor;
> And it is thought abroad° that 'twixt my sheets 5
> He's done my office.° I know not if't be true;
> But I, for mere suspicion in that kind,
> Will do as if for surety.° He holds me well;°
> The better shall my purpose work on him.
> Cassio's a proper° man. Let me see now: 10
> To get his place and to plume up° my will
> In double knavery—How, how?—Let's see:
> After some time, to abuse° Othello's ear
> That he° is too familiar with his° wife.
> He hath a person and a smooth dispose° 15
> To be suspected, framed° to make women false.
> The Moor is of a free and open° nature,
> That thinks men honest that but seem to be so,
> And will as tenderly° be led by the nose

---

3 **snipe:** woodcock, i.e., fool.   5 **it is thought abroad:** it is rumored.   6 **my office:** i.e., my sexual function as husband.   8 **do . . . surety:** act as if on certain knowledge.   **holds me well:** regards me favorably.   10 **proper:** handsome.   11 **plume up:** put a feather in the cap of, i.e., glorify, gratify.   13 **abuse:** deceive.   14 **he:** Cassio.   **his:** Othello's.   15 **dispose:** disposition.   16 **framed:** formed, made.   17 **free and open:** frank and unsuspecting.   19 **tenderly:** readily.

As asses are.
I have't. It is engender'd. Hell and night   20
Must bring this monstrous birth to the world's light.

[c.1603]

Until this point, the audience or reader has seen Iago depicted as an honest and trustworthy person, yet this soliloquy reveals him to be quite the opposite. The duplicity that puts the plot in motion and creates the conflict of the play becomes clear to the audience but not to other characters, resulting in **dramatic irony**. Iago observes that "it is thought abroad" (l. 5) that his wife was unfaithful to him with Othello, but he admits that he has no proof: in its absence, "mere suspicion . . . / Will do as if for surety" (ll. 7–8). The audience at this point becomes privy to Iago's thinking. Iago recognizes that Othello's good opinion of him will work to his advantage: "The better shall my purpose work on him" (l. 9). He thinks about another character, Cassio, who could be part of his plan, his "double knavery." By the end, when Iago says, "I have't," the audience has been let in on his plan to entrap Othello with lies and deception. Without a narrator to give us access to the mind of a character, a soliloquy is the perfect way to expose his or her inner workings, struggles, and reflections.

Setting

Setting is different in a play because there is a physical set to consider. The playwright has to keep this in mind when writing and be realistic about what most theaters will be able to stage. In modern plays, we usually find fairly explicit information about the setting, which a director can use to create a set and which we, as readers, can use to build a mental image. In *A Doll's House* by Henrik Ibsen, for instance, the scenery for act I is described in considerable detail:

ACT I

A comfortable room, tastefully but not expensively furnished. A door to the right in the back wall leads to the entryway; another to the left leads to HELMER'S *study. Between these doors, a piano. Midway in the left-hand wall a door, and further back a window. Near the window a round table with an armchair and a small sofa. In the right-hand wall, toward the rear, a door, and nearer the foreground a porcelain stove with two armchairs and a rocking chair beside it. Between the stove and the side door, a small table. Engravings on the walls. An étagère with china figures and other small art objects; a small bookcase with richly bound books; the floor carpeted; a fire burning in the stove. It is a winter day.*

[A bell rings in the entryway; shortly after we hear the door being unlocked. NORA *comes into the room, humming happily to herself; she is wearing street clothes and carries an armload of packages, which she puts down on the table to the right. She has left the hall door open, and through it a Delivery Boy is seen holding a Christmas tree and a basket, which he gives to the Maid who let them in.]*

[1879]

Ibsen's instructions indicate where doors and windows are, the location of a piano, the placement of a rocker next to two armchairs. At the same time, some of the directions are subject to interpretation, such as this being a "comfortable room, tastefully but not expensively furnished." That part is left to the reader's—or set designer's—imagination.

• ACTIVITY •

Read the opening stage directions that Lorraine Hansberry wrote for her play *A Raisin in the Sun*. What is the connection between the setting and the characters? How does this opening section suggest ideas likely to be explored during the course of the play?

From *A Raisin in the Sun*
LORRAINE HANSBERRY

The Younger living room would be a comfortable and well-ordered room if it were not for a number of indestructible contradictions to this state of being. Its furnishings are typical and undistinguished and their primary feature now is that they have clearly had to accommodate the living of too many people for too many years—and they are tired. Still, we can see that at some time, a time probably no longer remembered by the family (except perhaps for Mama), the furnishings of this room were actually selected with care and love and even hope—and brought to this apartment and arranged with taste and pride.

That was a long time ago. Now the once loved pattern of the couch upholstery has to fight to show itself from under acres of crocheted doilies and couch covers which have themselves finally come to be more important than the upholstery. And here a table or a chair has been moved to disguise the worn places in the carpet; but the carpet has fought back by showing its weariness, with depressing uniformity, elsewhere on its surface.

Weariness has, in fact, won in this room. Everything has been polished, washed, sat on, used, scrubbed too often. All pretenses but living itself have long since vanished from the very atmosphere of this room.

Moreover, a section of this room, for it is not really a room unto itself, though the landlord's lease would make it seem so, slopes backward to provide a small kitchen area, where the family prepares the meals that are eaten in the living room proper, which must also serve as dining room. The single window that has been provided for these "two" rooms is located in this kitchen area. The sole natural light the family may enjoy in the course of a day is only that which fights its way through this little window.

At left, a door leads to a bedroom which is shared by Mama and her daughter, Beneatha. At right, opposite, is a second room (which in the beginning of the life of this apartment was probably a breakfast room) which serves as a bedroom for Walter and his wife, Ruth.

5

TIME: *Sometime between World War II and the present.*

PLACE: *Chicago's Southside.*

AT RISE: *It is morning dark in the living room. Travis is asleep on the make-down bed at center. An alarm clock sounds from within the bedroom at right, and presently Ruth enters from that room and closes the door behind her. She crosses sleepily toward the window. As she passes her sleeping son she reaches down and shakes him a little. At the window she raises the shade and a dusky Southside morning light comes in feebly. She fills a pot with water and puts it on to boil. She calls to the boy, between yawns, in a slightly muffled voice.*

Ruth is about thirty. We can see that she was a pretty girl, even exception-ally so, but now it is apparent that life has been little that she expected, and disappointment has already begun to hang in her face. In a few years, before thirty-five even, she will be known among her people as a "settled woman."

She crosses to her son and gives him a good, final, rousing shake.

[1959]   10

Symbol

In drama, symbols are intended to be visually represented on stage, making them even more clear and powerful than symbols in fiction. These symbols may be part of the setting, character, or even the plot. Let's return to the stage directions for *A Doll's House*. Ibsen opens act II by shifting the setting just slightly:

ACT II

Same room. Beside the piano the Christmas tree now stands stripped of ornament, burned-down candle stubs on its ragged branches. NORA's street clothes lie on the sofa. NORA, alone in the room, moves restlessly about; at last she stops at the sofa and picks up her coat.

Notice the change in the Christmas tree from act I to act II. The Christmas tree and its degradation become a symbol of the intensifying conflict going on in the household.

In drama, any item used by an actor or as part of scenery is called a **prop**—short for "theatrical property," because props are items owned not by the actors but by the theater or troupe. Props may simply add to a character's appearance (a pipe held by a detective) or to the atmosphere created by the setting (an old rocking chair), but they frequently function as symbols. In August Wilson's 1987 play *The Piano Lesson*, the piano is a central symbol of the play. Wilson emphasizes its importance in his opening directions to the play:

Dominating the parlor is an old upright piano. On the legs of the piano, carved in the manner of African sculpture, are mask-like figures resembling totems. The carvings are rendered with a grace and power of invention that lifts them out of the realm of craftsman-ship and into the realm of art.

Wilson reveals the symbolic meaning of the piano through the course of the play. Purchased through an exchange for slaves, the piano symbolizes the treatment of slaves not as human beings but as property. The piano becomes the site of conflict when a family member wants to sell it to purchase land. How the characters view the piano tells us something about them and their values. Wilson scholar Sandra Shannon describes its importance: "a 135-year-old piano that is simultaneously the Charles family heirloom and a unifying device for the play . . . [it is] the center of the play's conflict as well as its symbolic core."

When considering the relationship between setting and symbol, it is good to keep in mind the principle that has come to be called "Chekhov's gun." Playwright Anton Chekhov said, "If in the first act you have hung a pistol on the wall, then in the following one it should be fired. Otherwise don't put it there." Chekhov is suggesting that symbols should be intentional, not misleading.

Elements of the plot itself can work as symbols, especially in performance. In *The Gin Game*, which won the 1978 Pulitzer Prize for Drama, playwright D. L. Coburn depicts two characters, Weller and Fonsia, in a home for the elderly. As they become acquainted, their conversation becomes increasingly adversarial, a battle of sorts. Here is one exchange close to the end of the play:

> WELLER *[Sitting down]*: Well, come on, I'll play you a hand of gin.
>
> FONSIA: You know, Weller, you can be such an . . . an enjoyable person to be with—you've
> got a wonderful sense of humor . . . If it wasn't for that damn gin game.
>
> WELLER: My goodness, Fonsia. Such language.
>
> FONSIA: Weller, I've played all the cards I'm going to play.   5
>
> WELLER: Now, Fonsie, I'm not going to argue with you. We're playing gin!
> *[FONSIA gets to her feet.]*
>
> FONSIA: That's it, Weller! You're not going to drop this gin game business . . . and I'm not
> going to play. So there's no reason for us to sit here and fight over it. I'll just go on in.
>
> WELLER: You stay right where you are.   10
>
> FONSIA: It's the only thing I know to do.
>
> WELLER: What do you mean, it's the only thing you know to do?? You came out here, didn't
> you? *[WELLER is now on his feet.]*
>
> FONSIA: Yes, I did. But certainly not to play gin. All I wanted . . .
>
> WELLER: All you wanted to do was manipulate me! We've been playing your   15
> game . . . NOW WE'RE GONNA PLAY MINE.
>
> *[1976]*

In the course of the play—seventeen hands of gin rummy—these characters drop their pleasant façades and reveal their controlling and bitter natures. The recreational activity of playing cards transforms into something larger than a mere game. As the audience reads or watches the play, the card game that moves the plot forward comes to symbolize the battle with life and aging that the characters are waging. Weller thinks he has gotten a bad hand, and he tries to change his luck, if only symbolically, by winning at gin rummy. The play asks: Do you play your cards by being honest? by bluffing and lying? Can you strategize and control the game, or is it all a matter of luck? No wonder the author described the card game as "the engine that drives the play."

• ACTIVITY •

Theme functions similarly in drama as it does in fiction. Read the following one-act play, *Andre's Mother*, by Terrence McNally, first performed in New York City in 1988. The characters have gathered for the funeral of Andre, who has died of AIDS. Articulate at least two themes of the play, paying careful attention to character, dialogue, setting, and symbol.

Andre's Mother
TERRENCE MCNALLY

Four people enter. They are nicely dressed and carry white helium-filled balloons on a string. They are CAL, *a young man;* ARTHUR, *his father;* PENNY, *his sister; and* ANDRE'S MOTHER.

CAL: You know what's really terrible? I can't think of anything terrific to say. Goodbye. I love you. I'll miss you. And I'm supposed to be so great with words!

PENNY: What's that over there?

ARTHUR: Ask your brother.   5

CAL: It's a theatre. An outdoor theatre. They do plays there in the summer. Shakespeare's plays. (*To* ANDRE'S MOTHER.) God, how much he wanted to play Hamlet. It was his greatest dream. I think he would have sold his soul to play it. He would have gone to Timbuktu to have another go at that part. The summer he did it in Boston, he was so happy!   10

PENNY: Cal, I don't think she . . . ! It's not the time. Later.

ARTHUR: Your son was a . . . the Jews have a word for it . . .

PENNY: (*Quietly appalled.*) Oh my God!

ARTHUR: Mensch, I believe it is and I think I'm using it right. It means warm, solid, the real thing. Correct me if I'm wrong.   15

PENNY: Fine, dad, fine. Just quit while you're ahead.

ARTHUR: I won't say he was like a son to me. Even my son isn't always like a son to me. I mean . . . ! In my clumsy way, I'm trying to say how much I liked Andre. And how much he helped me to know my own boy. Cal was always two hands full but Andre and I could talk about anything   20 under the sun. My wife was very fond of him, too.

PENNY: Cal, I don't understand about the balloons.

CAL: They represent the soul. When you let go, it means you're letting his soul ascend to Heaven. That you're willing to let go. Breaking the last earthly ties.   25

PENNY: Does the Pope know about this?

ARTHUR: Penny!

PENNY: Andre loved my sense of humor. Listen, you can hear him laughing. (*She lets go of her white balloon.*) So long, you glorious, wonderful, I-know-what-Cal-means-about-words . . . *man*! God forgive me for wishing you were straight every time I laid eyes on you. But if any man was going to have you, I'm glad it was my brother! Look how fast it went up. I bet that means something. Something terrific.

ARTHUR: (ARTHUR *lets his balloon go.*) Goodbye. God speed.

PENNY: Cal?

CAL: I'm not ready yet.

PENNY: Okay. We'll be over there. Come on, pop, you can buy your little girl a Good Humor.

ARTHUR: They still make Good Humor?

PENNY: Only now they're called Dove Bars and they cost 12 dollars. (PENNY *takes* ARTHUR *off.* CAL *and* ANDRE'S MOTHER *stand with their balloons.*)

CAL: I wish I knew what you were thinking. I think it would help me. You know almost nothing about me and I only know what Andre told me about you. I'd always had it in my mind that one day we would be friends, you and me. But if you didn't know about Andre and me . . . If this hadn't happened, I wonder if he would have ever told you. When he was so sick, if I asked him once I asked him a thousand times, tell her. She's your mother. She won't mind. But he was so afraid of hurting you and of your disapproval. I don't know which was worse. (*No response. He sighs.*) God, how many of us live in this city because we don't want to hurt our mothers and live in mortal terror of their disapproval. We lose ourselves here. Our lives aren't furtive, just our feelings toward people like you are! A city of fugitives from our parent's scorn or heartbreak. Sometimes he'd seem a little down and I'd say, "What's the matter, babe?" and this funny sweet, sad smile would cross his face and he'd say, "Just a little homesick, Cal, just a little bit." I always accused him of being a country boy just playing at being a hot shot, sophisticated New Yorker. (*He sighs.*) It's bullshit. It's all bullshit. (*Still no response.*) Do you remember the comic strip *Little Lulu*? Her mother had no name, she was so remote, so formidable to all the children. She was just Lulu's mother. "Hello, Lulu's Mother," Lulu's friends would say. She was almost anonymous in her remoteness. You remind me of her. Andre's mother. Let me answer the questions you can't ask and then I'll leave you alone and you won't ever have to see me again. Andre died of AIDS. I don't know how he got it. I tested negative. He died bravely. You would have been proud of him. The only thing that frightened him was you. I'll have everything that was his sent to you. I'll pay for it. There isn't much. You should have come up the summer he played Hamlet. He was magnificent. Yes, I'm bitter. I'm bitter I've lost him. I'm bitter what's happening. I'm bitter even now, after all this, I can't reach you. I'm beginning to feel your disapproval and it's making me ill. (*He looks at his balloon.*) Sorry, old friend. I blew it. (*He lets go of the balloon.*) Good night, sweet prince, and flights of angels sing thee to thy rest! (*Beat.*) Goodbye, Andre's mother. (*He goes.* ANDRE'S MOTHER *stands alone holding her white balloon. Her lip trembles. She looks on the verge of breaking down. She is about to let go of the balloon when she pulls it down to her. She looks at it a while before she gently kisses it. She lets go of the balloon. She follows it with her eyes as it rises and rises. The lights are beginning to fade.* ANDRE'S MOTHER'S *eyes are still on the balloon. Blackout.*)

[1988]

From Analysis to Essay: Writing an Interpretive Essay

Let's take a look at a short play. As you read it, consider the literary elements we have discussed: plot, character, setting, and symbol. Try to formulate at least two or three thematic statements that could become the thesis for an interpretive essay.

Trifles
SUSAN GLASPELL

CHARACTERS

GEORGE HENDERSON, *county attorney*   MRS. PETERS

HENRY PETERS, *sheriff*   MRS. HALE

LEWIS HALE, *a neighboring farmer*

SCENE: *The kitchen in the now abandoned farmhouse of John Wright, a gloomy kitchen, and left without having been put in order—unwashed pans under the sink, a loaf of bread outside the breadbox, a dish towel on the table—other signs of incompleted work. At the rear the outer door opens and the* SHERIFF *comes in followed by the* COUNTY ATTORNEY *and* HALE. *The* SHERIFF *and* HALE *are men in middle life, the* COUNTY ATTORNEY *is a young man; all are much bundled up and go at once to the stove. They are followed by the two women—the* SHERIFF'S *wife first; she is a slight wiry woman, a thin nervous face.* MRS. HALE *is larger and would ordinarily be called more comfortable looking, but she is disturbed now and looks fearfully about as she enters. The women have come in slowly, and stand close together near the door.*

COUNTY ATTORNEY [*rubbing his hands*]: This feels good. Come up to the fire, ladies.

MRS. PETERS [*after taking a step forward*]: I'm not—cold.

SHERIFF [*unbuttoning his overcoat and stepping away from the stove as if to mark the beginning of official business*]: Now, Mr. Hale, before we move things about, you explain to Mr. Henderson just what you saw when you came here yesterday morning.

COUNTY ATTORNEY: By the way, has anything been moved? Are things just as you left them yesterday?

SHERIFF [*looking about*]: It's just about the same. When it dropped below zero last night
I thought I'd better send Frank out this morning to make a fire for us—no use
getting pneumonia with a big case on, but I told him not to touch anything except   10
the stove—and you know Frank.

COUNTY ATTORNEY: Somebody should have been left here yesterday.

SHERIFF: Oh—yesterday. When I had to send Frank to Morris Center for that man who
went crazy—I want you to know I had my hands full yesterday. I knew you could get
back from Omaha by today and as long as I went over everything here myself—   15

COUNTY ATTORNEY: Well, Mr. Hale, tell just what happened when you came here yesterday morning.

HALE: Harry and I had started to town with a load of potatoes. We came along the road
from my place and as I got here I said, "I'm going to see if I can't get John Wright
to go in with me on a party telephone." I spoke to Wright about it once before and   20
he put me off, saying folks talked too much anyway, and all he asked was peace and
quiet—I guess you know about how much he talked himself; but I thought maybe
if I went to the house and talked about it before his wife, though I said to Harry that
I didn't know as what his wife wanted made much difference to John—

COUNTY ATTORNEY: Let's talk about that later, Mr. Hale. I do want to talk about that, but   25
tell now just what happened when you got to the house.

HALE: I didn't hear or see anything; I knocked at the door, and still it was all quiet inside.
I knew they must be up, it was past eight o'clock. So I knocked again, and I thought
I heard somebody say, "Come in." I wasn't sure, I'm not sure yet, but I opened the
door—this door [*indicating the door by which the two women are still standing*]   30
and there in that rocker—[*pointing to it*] sat Mrs. Wright. [*They all look at the
rocker.*]

COUNTY ATTORNEY: What—was she doing?

HALE: She was rockin' back and forth. She had her apron in her hand and was kind
of—pleating it.   35

COUNTY ATTORNEY: And how did she—look?

HALE: Well, she looked queer.

COUNTY ATTORNEY: How do you mean—queer?

HALE: Well, as if she didn't know what she was going to do next. And kind of done up.

COUNTY ATTORNEY: How did she seem to feel about your coming?   40

HALE: Why, I don't think she minded—one way or other. She didn't pay much attention.
I said, "How do, Mrs. Wright, it's cold, ain't it?" And she said, "Is it?"—and went
on kind of pleating at her apron. Well, I was surprised; she didn't ask me to come
up to the stove, or to set down, but just sat there, not even looking at me, so I said,
"I want to see John." And then she—laughed. I guess you would call it a laugh. I   45
thought of Harry and the team outside, so I said a little sharp: "Can't I see John?"
"No," she says, kind o' dull like. "Ain't he home?" says I. "Yes," says she, "he's home."
"Then why can't I see him?" I asked her, out of patience. "'Cause he's dead," says she.
"*Dead?*" says I. She just nodded her head, not getting a bit excited, but rockin' back
and forth. "Why—where is he?" says I, not knowing what to say. She just pointed   50
upstairs—like that [*himself pointing to the room above*]. I started for the stairs, with

the idea of going up there. I walked from there to here—then I says, "Why, what did he die of?" "He died of a rope round his neck," says she, and just went on pleatin' at her apron. Well, I went out and called Harry. I thought I might—need help. We went upstairs and there he was lyin'— 55

COUNTY ATTORNEY: I think I'd rather have you go into that upstairs, where you can point it all out. Just go on now with the rest of the story.

HALE: Well, my first thought was to get that rope off. It looked . . . *[stops; his face twitches]* . . . but Harry, he went up to him, and he said, "No, he's dead all right, and we'd better not touch anything." So we went back downstairs. She was still sitting that 60 same way. "Has anybody been notified?" I asked. "No," says she, unconcerned. "Who did this, Mrs. Wright?" said Harry. He said it businesslike—and she stopped pleatin' of her apron. "I don't know," she says. "You don't *know*?" says Harry. "No," says she. "Weren't you sleepin' in the bed with him?" says Harry. "Yes," says she, "but I was on the inside." "Somebody slipped a rope round his neck and strangled him and you didn't wake up?" 65 says Harry. "I didn't wake up," she said after him. We must 'a' looked as if we didn't see how that could be, for after a minute she said, "I sleep sound." Harry was going to ask her more questions but I said maybe we ought to let her tell her story first to the coroner, or the sheriff, so Harry went fast as he could to Rivers' place, where there's a telephone.

COUNTY ATTORNEY: And what did Mrs. Wright do when she knew that you had gone for 70 the coroner?

HALE: She moved from the rocker to that chair over there *[pointing to a small chair in the corner]* and just sat there with her hands held together and looking down. I got a feeling that I ought to make some conversation, so I said I had come in to see if John wanted to put in a telephone, and at that she started to laugh, and then she stopped 75 and looked at me—scared. *[The* COUNTY ATTORNEY, *who has had his notebook out, makes a note.]* I dunno, maybe it wasn't scared. I wouldn't like to say it was. Soon Harry got back, and then Dr. Lloyd came and you, Mr. Peters, and so I guess that's all I know that you don't.

COUNTY ATTORNEY *[looking around]*: I guess we'll go upstairs first—and then out to the 80 barn and around there. *[To the* SHERIFF.*]* You're convinced that there was nothing important here—nothing that would point to any motive?

SHERIFF: Nothing here but kitchen things. *[The* COUNTY ATTORNEY, *after again looking around the kitchen, opens the door of a cupboard closet. He gets up on a chair and looks on a shelf. Pulls his hand away, sticky.]* 85

COUNTY ATTORNEY: Here's a nice mess. *[The women draw nearer.]*

MRS. PETERS *[to the other woman]*: Oh, her fruit; it did freeze. *[To the Lawyer.]* She worried about that when it turned so cold. She said the fire'd go out and her jars would break.

SHERIFF *[rises]*: Well, can you beat the woman! Held for murder and worryin' about her 90 preserves.

COUNTY ATTORNEY: I guess before we're through she may have something more serious than preserves to worry about.

HALE: Well, women are used to worrying over trifles. *[The two women move a little closer together.]* 95

COUNTY ATTORNEY [*with the gallantry of a young politician*]: And yet, for all their worries, what would we do without the ladies? [*The women do not unbend. He goes to the sink, takes a dipperful of water from the pail, and pouring it into a basin, washes his hands. Starts to wipe them on the roller towel, turns it for a cleaner place.*] Dirty towels! [*Kicks his foot against the pans under the sink.*] Not much of a housekeeper, would you say, ladies?   100

MRS. HALE [*stiffly*]: There's a great deal of work to be done on a farm.

COUNTY ATTORNEY: To be sure. And yet [*with a little bow to her*] I know there are some Dickson county farmhouses which do not have such roller towels. [*He gives it a pull to expose its full length again.*]   105

MRS. HALE: Those towels get dirty awful quick. Men's hands aren't always as clean as they might be.

COUNTY ATTORNEY: Ah, loyal to your sex, I see. But you and Mrs. Wright were neighbors. I suppose you were friends, too.

MRS. HALE [*shaking her head*]: I've not seen much of her of late years. I've not been in   110 this house—it's more than a year.

COUNTY ATTORNEY: And why was that? You didn't like her?

MRS. HALE: I liked her all well enough. Farmers' wives have their hands full, Mr. Henderson. And then—

COUNTY ATTORNEY: Yes—?   115

MRS. HALE [*looking about*]: It never seemed a very cheerful place.

COUNTY ATTORNEY: No—it's not cheerful. I shouldn't say she had the homemaking instinct.

MRS. HALE: Well, I don't know as Wright had, either.

COUNTY ATTORNEY: You mean that they didn't get on very well?   120

MRS. HALE: No, I don't mean anything. But I don't think a place'd be any cheerfuller for John Wright's being in it.

COUNTY ATTORNEY: I'd like to talk more of that a little later. I want to get the lay of things upstairs now. [*He goes to the left where three steps lead to a stair door.*]

SHERIFF: I suppose anything Mrs. Peters does'll be all right. She was to take in some   125 clothes for her, you know, and a few little things. We left in such a hurry yesterday.

COUNTY ATTORNEY: Yes, but I would like to see what you take, Mrs. Peters, and keep an eye out for anything that might be of use to us.

MRS. PETERS: Yes, Mr. Henderson. [*The women listen to the men's steps on the stairs, then look about the kitchen.*]   130

MRS. HALE: I'd hate to have men coming into my kitchen, snooping around and criticizing. [*She arranges the pans under sink which the Lawyer had shoved out of place.*]

MRS. PETERS: Of course it's no more than their duty.

MRS. HALE: Duty's all right, but I guess that deputy sheriff that came out to make the fire might have got a little of this on. [*Gives the roller towel a pull.*] Wish I'd thought of   135 that sooner. Seems mean to talk about her for not having things slicked up when she had to come away in such a hurry.

MRS. PETERS [*who has gone to a small table in the left rear corner of the room, and lifted one end of a towel that covers a pan*]: She had bread set. [*Stands still.*]

MRS. HALE [*eyes fixed on a loaf of bread beside the breadbox, which is on a low shelf at the*   140
other side of the room. Moves slowly toward it.]: She was going to put this in there. [*Picks
up loaf, then abruptly drops it. In a manner of returning to familiar things.*] It's a shame
about her fruit. I wonder if it's all gone. [*Gets up on the chair and looks.*] I think there's
some here that's all right, Mrs. Peters. Yes—here; [*holding it toward the window*] this is
cherries, too. [*Looking again.*] I declare I believe that's the only one. [*Gets down, bottle*   145
in her hand. Goes to the sink and wipes it off on the outside.] She'll feel awful bad after
all her hard work in the hot weather. I remember the afternoon I put up my cherries
last summer. [*She puts the bottle on the big kitchen table, center of the room. With a sigh,
is about to sit down in the rocking-chair. Before she is seated realizes what chair it is; with
a slow look at it, steps back. The chair which she has touched rocks back and forth.*]   150

MRS. PETERS: Well, I must get those things from the front room closet. [*She goes to the
door at the right, but after looking into the other room, steps back.*] You coming with
me, Mrs. Hale? You could help me carry them. [*They go in the other room; reappear,
Mrs. Peters carrying a dress and skirt, Mrs. Hale following with a pair of shoes.*] My,
it's cold in there. [*She puts the clothes on the big table, and hurries to the stove.*]   155

MRS. HALE [*examining the skirt*]: Wright was close. I think maybe that's why she kept
so much to herself. She didn't even belong to the Ladies' Aid. I suppose she felt she
couldn't do her part, and then you don't enjoy things when you feel shabby. I heard
she used to wear pretty clothes and be lively, when she was Minnie Foster, one of
the town girls singing in the choir. But that—oh, that was thirty years ago. This all   160
you want to take in?

MRS. PETERS: She said she wanted an apron. Funny thing to want, for there isn't much
to get you dirty in jail, goodness knows. But I suppose just to make her feel more
natural. She said they was in the top drawer in this cupboard. Yes, here. And then her
little shawl that always hung behind the door. [*Opens stair door and looks.*] Yes, here   165
it is. [*Quickly shuts door leading upstairs.*]

MRS. HALE [*abruptly moving toward her*]: Mrs. Peters?

MRS. PETERS: Yes, Mrs. Hale?

MRS. HALE: Do you think she did it?

MRS. PETERS [*in a frightened voice*]: Oh, I don't know.   170

MRS. HALE: Well, I don't think she did. Asking for an apron and her little shawl. Worrying
about her fruit.

MRS. PETERS [*starts to speak, glances up, where footsteps are heard in the room above. In a
low voice*]: Mr. Peters says it looks bad for her. Mr. Henderson is awful sarcastic in a
speech and he'll make fun of her sayin' she didn't wake up.   175

MRS. HALE: Well, I guess John Wright didn't wake when they was slipping that rope under
his neck.

MRS. PETERS: No, it's strange. It must have been done awful crafty and still. They say it
was such a—funny way to kill a man, rigging it all up like that.

MRS. HALE: That's just what Mr. Hale said. There was a gun in the house. He says that's   180
what he can't understand.

MRS. PETERS: Mr. Henderson said coming out that what was needed for the case was a
motive; something to show anger, or—sudden feeling.

MRS. HALE [*who is standing by the table*]: Well, I don't see any signs of anger around here. [*She puts her hand on the dish towel which lies on the table, stands looking down* 185 *at table, one-half of which is clean, the other half messy.*] It's wiped to here. [*Makes a move as if to finish work, then turns and looks at loaf of bread outside the breadbox. Drops towel. In that voice of coming back to familiar things.*] Wonder how they are finding things upstairs. I hope she had it a little more red-up up there. You know, it seems kind of *sneaking.* Locking her up in town and then coming out here and try- 190 ing to get her own house to turn against her!

MRS. PETERS: But, Mrs. Hale, the law is the law.

MRS. HALE: I s'pose 'tis. [*Unbuttoning her coat.*] Better loosen up your things, Mrs. Peters. You won't feel them when you go out. [MRS. PETERS *takes off her fur tippet, goes to hang it on hook at back of room, stands looking at the under part of the small corner* 195 *table.*]

MRS. PETERS: She was piecing a quilt. [*She brings the large sewing basket and they look at the bright pieces.*]

MRS. HALE: It's a log cabin pattern. Pretty, isn't it? I wonder if she was goin' to quilt it or just knot it? [*Footsteps have been heard coming down the stairs. The* SHERIFF *enters* 200 *followed by* HALE *and the* COUNTY ATTORNEY.]

SHERIFF: They wonder if she was going to quilt it or just knot it! [*The men laugh, the women look abashed.*]

COUNTY ATTORNEY [*rubbing his hands over the stove*]: Frank's fire didn't do much up there, did it? Well, let's go out to the barn and get that cleared up. [*The men go outside.*] 205

MRS. HALE [*resentfully*]: I don't know as there's anything so strange, our takin' up our time with little things while we're waiting for them to get the evidence. [*She sits down at the big table smoothing out a block with decision.*] I don't see as it's anything to laugh about.

MRS. PETERS [*apologetically*]: Of course they've got awful important things on their 210 minds. [*Pulls up a chair and joins Mrs. Hale at the table.*]

MRS. HALE [*examining another block*]: Mrs. Peters, look at this one. Here, this is the one she was working on, and look at the sewing! All the rest of it has been so nice and even. And look at this! It's all over the place! Why, it looks as if she didn't know what she was about! [*After she has said this they look at each other, then start to glance back* 215 *at the door. After an instant Mrs. HALE has pulled at a knot and ripped the sewing.*]

MRS. PETERS: Oh, what are you doing, Mrs. Hale?

MRS. HALE [*mildly*]: Just pulling out a stitch or two that's not sewed very good. [*Threading a needle.*] Bad sewing always made me fidgety.

MRS. PETERS [*nervously*]: I don't think we ought to touch things. 220

MRS. HALE: I'll just finish up this end. [*Suddenly stopping and leaning forward.*] Mrs. Peters?

MRS. PETERS: Yes, Mrs. Hale?

MRS. HALE: What do you suppose she was so nervous about?

MRS. PETERS: Oh—I don't know. I don't know as she was nervous. I sometimes sew 225 awful queer when I'm just tired. [MRS. HALE *starts to say something, looks at* MRS. PETERS, *then goes on sewing.*] Well, I must get these things wrapped up. They may be through sooner than we think. *[Putting apron and other things together.]* I wonder where I can find a piece of paper, and string. *[Rises.]*

MRS. HALE: In that cupboard, maybe.   230

MRS. PETERS *[looking in cupboard]*: Why, here's a bird-cage. *[Holds it up.]* Did she have a bird, Mrs. Hale?

MRS. HALE: Why, I don't know whether she did or not—I've not been here for so long. There was a man around last year selling canaries cheap, but I don't know as she took one; maybe she did. She used to sing real pretty herself.   235

MRS. PETERS *[glancing around]*: Seems funny to think of a bird here. But she must have had one, or why would she have a cage? I wonder what happened to it?

MRS. HALE: I s'pose maybe the cat got it.

MRS. PETERS: No, she didn't have a cat. She's got that feeling some people have about cats—being afraid of them. My cat got in her room and she was real upset and   240
asked me to take it out.

MRS. HALE: My sister Bessie was like that. Queer, ain't it?

MRS. PETERS *[examining the cage]*: Why, look at this door. It's broke. One hinge is pulled apart.

MRS. HALE *[looking too]*: Looks as if someone must have been rough with it.   245

MRS. PETERS: Why, yes. *[She brings the cage forward and puts it on the table.]*

MRS. HALE: I wish if they're going to find any evidence they'd be about it. I don't like this place.

MRS. PETERS: But I'm awful glad you came with me, Mrs. Hale. It would be lonesome for me sitting here alone.   250

MRS. HALE: It would, wouldn't it? *[Dropping her sewing.]* But I tell you what I do wish, Mrs. Peters. I wish I had come over sometimes when she was here. I—*[looking around the room]*—wish I had.

MRS. PETERS: But of course you were awful busy, Mrs. Hale—your house and your children.

MRS. HALE: I could've come. I stayed away because it weren't cheerful—and that's why   255
I ought to have come. I—I've never liked this place. Maybe because it's down in a hollow and you don't see the road. I dunno what it is, but it's a lonesome place and always was. I wish I had come over to see Minnie Foster sometimes. I can see now—*[Shakes her head.]*

MRS. PETERS: Well, you mustn't reproach yourself, Mrs. Hale. Somehow we just don't see   260
how it is with other folks until—something turns up.

MRS. HALE: Not having children makes less work—but it makes a quiet house, and Wright out to work all day, and no company when he did come in. Did you know John Wright, Mrs. Peters?

MRS. PETERS: Not to know him; I've seen him in town. They say he was a good man.   265

MRS. HALE: Yes—good; he didn't drink, and kept his word as well as most, I guess, and paid his debts. But he was a hard man, Mrs. Peters. Just to pass the time of day with him—*[Shivers.]* Like a raw wind that gets to the bone. *[Pauses, her eye falling on the cage.]* I should think she would 'a' wanted a bird. But what do you suppose went with it?

MRS. PETERS: I don't know, unless it got sick and died. *[She reaches over and swings the   270
broken door, swings it again, both women watch it.]*

MRS. HALE: You weren't raised round here, were you? *[*MRS. PETERS *shakes her head.]* You didn't know—her?

MRS. PETERS: Not till they brought her yesterday.

MRS. HALE: She—come to think of it, she was kind of like a bird herself—real sweet   275
and pretty, but kind of timid and—fluttery. How—she—did—change. *[Silence: then as if struck by a happy thought and relieved to get back to everyday things.]* Tell you what, Mrs. Peters, why don't you take the quilt in with you? It might take up her mind.

MRS. PETERS: Why, I think that's a real nice idea, Mrs. Hale. There couldn't possibly be   280
any objection to it, could there? Now, just what would I take? I wonder if her patches are in here—and her things. *[They look in the sewing basket.]*

MRS. HALE: Here's some red. I expect this has got sewing things in it. *[Brings out a fancy box.]* What a pretty box. Looks like something somebody would give you. Maybe her scissors are in here. *[Opens box. Suddenly puts her hand to her nose.]* Why—*[*MRS. PETERS *bends   285
nearer, then turns her face away.]* There's something wrapped up in this piece of silk.

MRS. PETERS: Why, this isn't her scissors.

MRS. HALE *[lifting the silk]*: Oh, Mrs. Peters—it's—*[*MRS. PETERS *bends closer.]*

MRS. PETERS: It's the bird.

MRS. HALE *[jumping up]*: But, Mrs. Peters—look at it! Its neck! Look at its neck! It's   290
all—other side *to*.

MRS. PETERS: Somebody—wrung—its—neck. *[Their eyes meet. A look of growing comprehension, of horror. Steps are heard outside.* MRS. HALE *slips box under quilt pieces, and sinks into her chair. Enter* SHERIFF *and* COUNTY ATTORNEY. MRS. PETERS *rises.]*

COUNTY ATTORNEY *[as one turning from serious things to little pleasantries]*: Well, ladies,   295
have you decided whether she was going to quilt it or knot it?

MRS. PETERS: We think she was going to—knot it.

COUNTY ATTORNEY: Well, that's interesting, I'm sure. *[Seeing the bird-cage.]* Has the bird flown?

MRS. HALE *[putting more quilt pieces over the box]*: We think the—cat got it.   300

COUNTY ATTORNEY *[preoccupied]*: Is there a cat? *[*MRS. HALE *glances in a quick covert way at* MRS. PETERS.*]*

MRS. PETERS: Well, not now. They're superstitious, you know. They leave.

COUNTY ATTORNEY *[to* SHERIFF PETERS, *continuing an interrupted conversation]*: No sign at all of anyone having come from the outside. Their own rope. Now let's go up   305
again and go over it piece by piece. *[They start upstairs.]* It would have to have been someone who knew just the—*[*MRS. PETERS *sits down. The two women sit there not looking at one another, but as if peering into something and at the same time holding back. When they talk now it is in the manner of feeling their way over strange ground, as if afraid of what they are saying, but as if they cannot help saying it.]*   310

MRS. HALE: She liked the bird. She was going to bury it in that pretty box.

MRS. PETERS *[in a whisper]*: When I was a girl—my kitten—there was a boy took a hatchet, and before my eyes—and before I could get there—*[Covers her face an instant.]* If they hadn't held me back I would have—*[catches herself, looks upstairs where steps are heard, falters weakly]*—hurt him.   315

MRS. HALE *[with a slow look around her]*: I wonder how it would seem never to have had any children around. *[Pause.]* No, Wright wouldn't like the bird—a thing that sang. She used to sing. He killed that, too.

MRS. PETERS *[moving uneasily]*: We don't know who killed the bird.

MRS. HALE: I knew John Wright.   320

MRS. PETERS: It was an awful thing was done in this house that night, Mrs. Hale. Killing a man while he slept, slipping a rope around his neck that choked the life out of him.

MRS. HALE: His neck. Choked the life out of him. *[Her hand goes out and rests on the bird-cage.]*   325

MRS. PETERS *[with rising voice]*: We don't know who killed him. We don't *know*.

MRS. HALE *[her own feeling not interrupted]*: If there'd been years and years of nothing, then a bird to sing to you, it would be awful—still, after the bird was still.

MRS. PETERS *[something within her speaking]*: I know what stillness is. When we home-steaded in Dakota, and my first baby died—after he was two years old, and me with   330
no other then—

MRS. HALE *[moving]*: How soon do you suppose they'll be through looking for the evidence?

MRS. PETERS: I know what stillness is. *[Pulling herself back.]* The law has got to punish crime, Mrs. Hale.   335

MRS. HALE *[not as if answering that]*: I wish you'd seen Minnie Foster when she wore a white dress with blue ribbons and stood up there in the choir and sang. *[A look around the room.]* Oh, I *wish* I'd come over here once in a while! That was a crime! That was a crime! Who's going to punish that?

MRS. PETERS *[looking upstairs]*: We mustn't—take on.   340

MRS. HALE: I might have known she needed help! I know how things can be—for women. I tell you, it's queer, Mrs. Peters. We live close together and we live far apart. We all go through the same things—it's all just a different kind of the same thing. *[Brushes her eyes, noticing the bottle of fruit, reaches out for it.]* If I was you I wouldn't tell her her fruit was gone. Tell her it *ain't*. Tell her it's all right. Take this in to prove   345
it to her. She—she may never know whether it was broke or not.

MRS. PETERS *[takes the bottle, looks about for something to wrap it in; takes petticoat from the clothes brought from the other room, very nervously begins winding this around the bottle. In a false voice]*: My, it's a good thing the men couldn't hear us. Wouldn't they just laugh! Getting all stirred up over a little thing like a—dead canary. As if that   350
could have anything to do with—with—wouldn't they *laugh*! *[The men are heard coming down stairs.]*

MRS. HALE *[under her breath]*: Maybe they would—maybe they wouldn't.

COUNTY ATTORNEY: No, Peters, it's all perfectly clear except a reason for doing it. But you know juries when it comes to women. If there was some definite thing. Something   355
to show—something to make a story about—a thing that would connect up with this strange way of doing it—*[The women's eyes meet for an instant. Enter* HALE *from outer door.]*

HALE: Well, I've got the team around. Pretty cold out there.

COUNTY ATTORNEY: I'm going to stay here a while by myself. *[To the Sheriff.]* You can   360
send Frank out for me, can't you? I want to go over everything. I'm not satisfied that
we can't do better.

SHERIFF: Do you want to see what Mrs. Peters is going to take in? *[The Lawyer goes to the
table, picks up the apron, laughs.]*

COUNTY ATTORNEY: Oh, I guess they're not very dangerous things the ladies have picked   365
out. *[Moves a few things about, disturbing the quilt pieces which cover the box. Steps
back.]* No, Mrs. Peters doesn't need supervising. For that matter a sheriff's wife is
married to the law. Ever think of it that way, Mrs. Peters?

MRS. PETERS: Not—just that way.

SHERIFF *[chuckling]*: Married to the law. *[Moves toward the other room.]* I just want you to   370
come in here a minute, George. We ought to take a look at these windows.

COUNTY ATTORNEY *[scoffingly]*: Oh, windows!

SHERIFF: We'll be right out, Mr. Hale. *[HALE goes outside. The SHERIFF follows the
COUNTY ATTORNEY into the other room. Then MRS. HALE rises, hands tight together,
looking intensely at MRS. PETERS, whose eyes make a slow turn, finally meeting MRS.*   375
*HALE's. A moment MRS. HALE holds her, then her own eyes point the way to where the
box is concealed. Suddenly MRS. PETERS throws back quilt pieces and tries to put the
box in the bag she is wearing. It is too big. She opens box, starts to take bird out, cannot
touch it, goes to pieces, stands there helpless. Sound of a knob turning in the other room.*
MRS. HALE *snatches the box and puts it in the pocket of her big coat. Enter* COUNTY   380
ATTORNEY *and* SHERIFF.*]*

COUNTY ATTORNEY *[facetiously]*: Well, Henry, at least we found out that she was not
going to quilt it. She was going to—what is it you call it, ladies?

MRS. HALE *[her hand against her pocket]*: We call it—knot it, Mr. Henderson.

Curtain

[1916]

Analyzing Literary Elements

In *Trifles*, two plots run parallel: the men have an off-stage story as they hunt for clues
to the murder of Mr. Wright; the women have an on-stage story as they unravel the
life of Mrs. Wright. The tension in the story's plot has to do with the rate at which
Mrs. Hale and Mrs. Peters come to understand what has happened. Suspense builds
as the two women, and the audience, figure out who killed Mr. Wright and why. The
suspense is heightened by the moral dilemma of whether the women should conceal
incriminating evidence—and whether they'll get caught doing it. Of course, one
reason the men in the story don't figure out what happened is that they dismiss the
things the women say as mere trifles.

Trifles has two female characters—Mrs. Hale and Mrs. Peters—and three male
characters—Mr. Hale, the sheriff, and the county attorney. Mr. and Mrs. Wright, though
not on stage, have a presence as well. Over the course of the play, Mrs. Hale and Mrs.
Peters change, feeling less certain about their own beliefs, disappointed in themselves

for not being better friends to Mrs. Wright, and empathetic to her desperate loneliness. The men don't change. We learn about all of the characters through their conversation, especially in the way the conversation changes when the men are involved.

The setting of *Trifles* helps us understand character and also moves the plot along. The play takes place in an empty farmhouse, but the setting is more complicated than that. The men go to the bedroom where the murder occurred, while the women focus on the kitchen. Both the men and the women note the disheveled condition in which Mrs. Wright left it, yet the women are protective of her as well, understanding that she probably wouldn't have left such a mess if she hadn't been unexpectedly taken from her home. They also come to understand that the mess (which is a part of the setting) may be a sign of the "sudden feeling" the sheriff and attorney are looking for. We learn that the community is close and that Mrs. Peters is a newcomer. Mrs. Hale has known the woman under suspicion for many years, and it is through that familiarity that she understands what has happened and makes the decision she does.

Certain symbols are repeated in *Trifles*. The cold is brutal and unrelenting. The characters move toward the stove whenever possible, and the cold is a repeated subject of conversation. Mr. Wright is depicted as being cold and unloving, making the cold a clear symbol of a life without affection or even company. Other symbols might be Mrs. Wright's quilt pieces, the choice between quilting and knotting, the dead bird and the broken birdcage, the preserves (or trifles), and even the half-done chores. Each of these things is more fraught with meaning than it at first seems.

So, although the subject of *Trifles* is the unraveling of a mystery and the decision to protect the murderer, some of its themes might be:

- Sexism can make people blind to the truth.
- People may take desperate measures when they feel entrapped in a loveless marriage, in a cold isolated house, or in a society that doesn't value them.
- Someone who is a criminal by one set of social standards might be a victim according to another set of social standards. Or, in other words, justice is not always the same as the rule of law.

· ACTIVITY ·

Working in groups, choose a passage from *Trifles* that you think is pivotal to one of the themes, then act it out or read the lines in a way that dramatizes that theme.

Developing a Thesis Statement

Now that we have analyzed how the literary elements of the play work together to express its themes, it's time to turn those themes into a thesis statement. First and foremost, remember that you are analyzing the elements of the work in order to arrive at an interpretation; you should not be summarizing the work. Simply retelling what happened or making an observation does not amount to an interpretation.

Stating that Mrs. Peters seems to change her mind over the course of the play is not enough. You would be better off claiming that she changes her mind as the result of seeing justice in a different way. If you start right off with a thesis statement that argues for an interpretation of the play's meaning, you will guard against summary. Let's examine a few examples of thesis statements that would result in summary, and consider how they could be turned into interpretive thesis statements.

SUMMARY: In *Trifles*, the women notice evidence that the men do not.

INTERPRETATION: In *Trifles*, the differences in the evidence the men and women notice suggest different worldviews and value systems.

The summary statement simply tells what happened during the course of the play, but the interpretive statement takes that same point and explains *why* it happened. It answers the question: Why do the women notice evidence that the men do not? Here's another one:

SUMMARY: Mrs. Hale and Mrs. Peters discover a birdcage and dead canary, which provide clues to what actually happened to Mr. Wright.

INTERPRETATION: When Mrs. Hale and Mrs. Peters discover a birdcage and a dead canary wrapped in silk, they associate the silenced songbird with the joyless and repressed life that might have motivated Mrs. Wright to murder her husband.

The summary statement is accurate, but it is not an interpretation. You might ask yourself the following questions: Can I write a whole essay on this idea? Would anyone else see this point differently? If the answer to both questions is yes, then you're probably writing an interpretation. If the answer is no, you're probably in the realm of fact, or comprehension, rather than interpretation. Anyone who reads the play can tell you that these women discover a birdcage and a dead canary and see both as clues to understanding the murder. What else is there to say? If you ask yourself further questions, you'll get beyond summary and move toward interpretation. Why were the birdcage and the dead canary clues? What is the connection between the canary, the birdcage, and Mrs. Wright? An interpretation will reveal these connections, while a summary will not.

Remember when formulating your thesis that you are writing about how literary elements such as plot, character, setting, and symbol illuminate the meaning of the work as a whole. Thus, you are always balancing the two: literary elements and interpretation.

Let's develop a thesis in response to the following prompt.

In a conventional murder mystery, the point of the story is to figure out who the culprit is. The mystery in Susan Glaspell's play *Trifles* is unconventional, as the culprit is apprehended before the play even begins. However, as Mrs. Hale and Mrs. Peters unravel the mystery of why the murder took place, the play's themes are revealed. Discuss how Susan Glaspell uses the mystery in *Trifles* to reveal a theme of her play.

A good starting point is to figure out exactly what is being asked—that is, to deconstruct the prompt. In this case, you're being asked to consider the murder-mystery plot not as an end in itself but as a means of developing a theme. A murder mystery is all about the law, because somebody has to be held accountable for the crime. Yet in *Trifles*, Mrs. Hale and Mrs. Peters begin to question the law. As they unravel the mystery, they aren't so sure that "the law is the law." So maybe Glaspell is asking us to reflect on the relationship between law and justice or to link justice and punishment. Did Mrs. Wright do wrong in being her husband's judge, jury, and executioner? Was living with him punishment enough for her wrongdoing? Did she choose a punishment that fit his "crime"? These are complex questions—questions not definitively answered in the play but ones that it raises.

When you're trying to fit ideas and insights such as these into a single sentence, it's likely to be pretty awkward at first, and that's fine. We call this first attempt a working thesis. For example, you might come up with this:

> The murder mystery in *Trifles* is solved, but it is not so easy to answer the questions that the mystery raises about law, justice, and punishment, and whether hard-and-fast rules that govern human relations are always appropriate or fair.

This is a start, but it's a long, rambling sentence that could use some focus. At this point, you probably need to decide whether you're going to argue that Glaspell takes a definite stand on these issues. The play ends inconclusively—Mrs. Wright is neither convicted nor exonerated—which makes it difficult to say that the play (or its author) takes a stand on these issues. A better route, then, is to argue that Glaspell asks her audience/readers to explore these issues:

> In *Trifles*, the murder mystery is the means Glaspell uses to explore whether the rule of law is always the same as justice.

• ACTIVITY •

Discuss whether each of the following thesis statements is interpretation or summary. Then discuss whether the interpretive statements clearly focus on how literary elements contribute to the meaning of the work as a whole. Suggest improvements to those thesis statements that you find faulty or weak.

1. *Trifles* is a play about isolation and loneliness.
2. The broken birdcage in *Trifles* functions both as a clue to the circumstances of the murder and as a symbol that illuminates the role of Mrs. Wright in her marriage.
3. The character of Mrs. Peters, the wife of the sheriff, undergoes a significant change during the course of *Trifles*, a play set during a time when women were defined primarily through their husbands.

4. The frigid setting of Susan Glaspell's *Trifles* contributes to the characterization of all three women: it highlights the cold and isolated existence of the absent Mrs. Wright, while evoking the sympathetic responses of Mrs. Hale and Mrs. Peters.

5. Even though we never actually meet her, Mrs. Wright exerts a powerful presence in *Trifles*.

6. In the opening scene of *Trifles*, the men dominate the room as they stand near the stove, while the women remain near the door and quietly tolerate the cold.

7. The absent Mrs. Wright, suspected of murder in Susan Glaspell's *Trifles*, embodies the idea that loneliness, abuse, and isolation can lead a person to despair and even violence.

8. In *Trifles*, the male authority figures, including the sheriff himself, dismiss the female characters' investigation into the murder of Mr. Wright.

9. The kitchen, the dead bird, and the knots in the quilt have symbolic significance for the overall meaning of *Trifles*.

10. In *Trifles*, the discovery of the dead bird is a pivotal complication, especially for Mrs. Peters, that changes how the women view the role of the law.

Planning an Interpretive Essay

Regardless of whether you are given a specific prompt to respond to or assigned a more general topic on a literary work, your main points will grow out of your thesis statement. Expressing these points as topic sentences moves the essay along and makes it more cohesive. Let's return to our thesis on justice:

> In *Trifles*, the murder mystery is the means Glaspell uses to explore whether the rule of law is always the same as justice.

This thesis indicates that you will first discuss the murder mystery as a plot device, and then explain how it contributes to the theme. If you were jotting down notes to structure your essay, they might look something like this:

- Solving the murder is not really the point of the story. Suspect is detained, and case is pretty much closed right from the beginning.
- Seem to be different ways of investigating for men and women. Men doing police work. Women looking at "trifles."
- Women suppress evidence. Defy men's justice. Empathize with Mrs. Wright.
- Birdcage and dead bird symbolize Mrs. Wright (former singer) and her desolate life with Mr. Wright.

These blocks of notes may not neatly transform into clear topic sentences, but they do suggest a logical progression. If we turn them into complete sentences—in some cases, separating ideas; in others, combining them—we end up with an outline:

Topic Sentence 1

Although Mr. Hale retells the circumstances of finding the body, questions arise concerning Mrs. Wright's indifferent behavior and the way her husband died.

Topic Sentence 2

During the investigation, the men follow rules to gather evidence, supporting one another's assumptions about what is significant, while the women quietly observe the surroundings, noticing important clues that the men dismiss as "trifles."

Topic Sentence 3

Identifying with Mrs. Wright, the women withhold judgment and instead try to understand what might have motivated her.

Topic Sentence 4

The birdcage and the dead canary, clues to the mystery, also symbolize the quiet oppression of Mrs. Wright.

Topic Sentence 5

The play's conclusion serves as closure to the mystery, but it is the investigative process that proves to be more illuminating.

Of course, this is bare bones, not yet a fully developed essay, but these five topic sentences show a progression of thought. Going well beyond summary, they examine plot, setting, and character. Each resulting analytic paragraph will contribute to the overall interpretation.

· ACTIVITY ·

Sometimes you will be asked to consider how a quotation applies to a piece of literature. Choosing one of the following quotations, develop a thesis statement and four points explaining how it applies to *Trifles*.

- "The writers, I do believe, who get the best and most lasting response from their readers are the writers who offer a happy ending through moral development. By a happy ending, I do not mean mere fortunate events—a marriage or a last minute rescue from death—but some kind of spiritual reassessment or moral reconciliation, even with the self, even at death."—Fay Weldon

- "In a dark time, the eye begins to see."—Theodore Roethke

- "All literature is protest."—Richard Wright
- "Literature is the question minus the answer."—Roland Barthes

Supporting Your Interpretation

Whether you are writing with the text in hand or from memory, the same principle should guide your writing: be specific. If you refer to a character as "what's-his-name" or refer to a setting in general terms, you're not likely to be convincing. We've said it before, but it bears repeating: active reading and rereading are essential. Citing examples and explicitly explaining how they illustrate and support your interpretation are key to a successful essay that analyzes a literary work. The more you explain *how* rather than state *that*, the stronger your essay will be.

At this point, you know that you should avoid summary in your essay, but how much information should you give your readers about the work's plot or characters? One helpful guideline is to assume that your reader has read the book but has not necessarily thought too much about it. By doing so, you won't have to recount the plot or describe the characters. Thomas Foster, the author of *How to Read Literature Like a Professor*, suggests writing for the person who sits in front of you in class.

Let's start with a sample paragraph developed from the third topic sentence in the outline on the previous page:

> Identifying with Mrs. Wright, the women withhold judgment and instead
> try to understand what might have motivated her. Mrs. Hale and Mrs.
> Peters look around the house, especially the kitchen, and notice the fruit
> Mrs. Wright has canned and the quilt she is stitching. They talk about
> the fact that the couple had no children and that Mr. Wright was not a
> communicative husband. They also discuss incidents from their own past
> when they felt strong emotions that might have made them do something
> uncharacteristic or rash.

The paragraph holds a clear focus, and the information is drawn from the play. However, it is very general; thus, much of it seems like summary. Yes, it is true that the women look around the house; the details of their noticing the canned fruit and quilt are promising, but *so what?* What can you infer from their actions? How do these events reveal some of the themes that anchor the play? Similarly, the women do talk about the loneliness of a couple with no children living in such isolation; again, though, *so what?* How do these remembrances help them to understand Mrs. Wright's motivation, which is the focus established in the topic sentence? Answering this question will help you move from the *what* to the *so what*.

The most important part of supporting your argument involves explaining your examples and discussing the ways the details you recount or quote connect to your thesis statement and topic sentences. You do this by including sentences of explanation, sometimes called commentary or analysis, for each of your examples—and making those examples as concrete as possible. Consider this revision of the previous developmental paragraph:

> Identifying with Mrs. Wright, the women withhold judgment and instead try to understand what might have motivated her. They discuss how hard life must have been for Minnie in a house with no children and with John, who was cold and distant. The Wright house is located in a hollow, and the road cannot even be seen, so Mrs. Hale and Mrs. Peters begin to understand how the isolation and sense of entrapment could have led Mrs. Wright to snap. They can see how the only means of escape might have been to kill her captor, Mr. Wright. Mrs. Peters furthers the link between them and Mrs. Wright by sharing a time when Mrs. Peters herself felt the desire to hurt a boy who butchered her kitten with a hatchet. The women realize that they too might have been driven to violence under Mrs. Wright's circumstances.

Notice how specific this paragraph is, with its inclusion of examples drawn from the play. Even without direct quotations, this paragraph provides support for the interpretive point made in the topic sentence.

• ACTIVITY •

Revise the paragraph below using quotations from _Trifles_. Explain whether you think the direct quotations make the paragraph more convincing.

The dramatic tension in _Trifles_ is created by the difference between how the men see the situation at the Wrights' house and how the women see it. The men—Hale, the county attorney, and the sheriff—dismiss the messiness of the farmhouse as chronic bad housekeeping. They do not see that it may offer a clue to what happened. Their attitude toward Mrs. Wright's knitting is similarly dismissive. The women, on the other hand, read into and beyond the mess. They see the half-wiped table, the bread outside the breadbox, and the one patch that is badly sewn as signs that Mrs. Wright was unhappy and under stress. The men dwell on what they see as a trifling dilemma (to quilt or knot), while the women look into Mrs. Wright's sewing box and find the dead bird. The men's consideration of all domestic matters as trivial prevents them from seeing that there was a story, even a possible motive that could prove Mrs. Wright guilty. The suspense in the play arises from the possibility that either one of the men will become more perceptive or that one of the women will break under the pressure of what they have discovered.

A Sample Interpretive Essay

The student essay on pages 119–121 was written in class in response to the following prompt.

In a conventional murder mystery, the point of the story is to figure out who the culprit is. The mystery in Susan Glaspell's play *Trifles* is unconventional, as the culprit is apprehended before the play even begins. However, as Mrs. Hale and Mrs. Peters unravel the mystery of why the murder took place, the play's themes are revealed. Discuss how Susan Glaspell uses the mystery in *Trifles* to reveal a theme of her play.

Examine the essay carefully before responding to the revision questions that follow it.

Student Essay on *Trifles*

Aneyn M. O'Grady

Trifles is a play by Susan Glaspell written in 1916. John Wright, a farm owner, has recently been murdered at night in his bed, strangled by a rope. His wife, Minnie Wright, the only person confirmed present at the time of death, is accused of the homicide. The characters go to the Wright home the day after the murder. While at the house, there are two separate but parallel narratives. One involves the men (the sheriff, the county attorney, and Mr. Hale) who focus on the investigation, searching for a motive. The other involves the women (Mrs. Peters, the sheriff's wife, and Mrs. Hale) who are there to collect things Mrs. Wright requested. They, unlike the men, treat the house like a home, instead of a crime scene. Focusing their attention on seemingly insignificant details, Mrs. Peters and Mrs. Hale ironically discover the truth behind the murder. This one-scene play thus centers on a mystery as well as the relations between men and women at the time. The symbolism in the play helps to solve the murder but also gives the author an opportunity to discuss the roles and duties of a husband and wife, and to question how they should interact.

Although Mr. Hale retells the circumstances of finding the body, questions arise concerning Mrs. Wright's indifferent behavior and the way her husband died. Despite the presence of a gun, a rope was used to kill him. This alternative method is more passionate and emotionally involved. It allows the killer to have complete control and power over the victim. The play is set in the kitchen: a housewife's main domain and responsibility. Traditionally it is her duty to keep it clean, but Mrs. Wright's kitchen is completely unkempt, an act of defiance against her role as a wife, imposed by society. The half-cleaned table shows the conflict that exists in Mrs. Wright's character. The clean part is proof of an accepting housewife whereas the messy part represents her rebellious side. Mrs. Wright, by killing her husband, frees herself from the one person who held her to her "housewife" persona. She still asks for her apron, symbol of a housewife, proving that she cannot forget this "good wife" image even in jail.

During the investigation, the men follow rules to gather evidence, supporting one another's assumptions about what is significant, while the women quietly observe the surroundings, noticing important clues that the men dismiss as "trifles." The men are at the Wright house out of an obligation with a professional goal. With their minds set on what they consider more important things, they pay little attention to what preoccupies the women. First the women notice the fruit preserves and how this will upset Mrs. Wright. They then comment on the uncleanness of the kitchen. These worries appear to be unnecessary until they find the quilt. The alteration in sewing presents the transformation in Mrs. Wright's character. At first the stitches are perfect and clean, normal. They then become erratic, hinting at nervousness. This alludes to Minnie's crisis and emotional instability, which could have led her to killing her husband. Mrs. Hale and Mrs. Peters wonder whether or not Mrs. Wright planned to quilt or knot the patches together. The sheriff scoffs at this inquiry, yet it alludes to Mrs. Wright's decision to knot the rope around Mr. Wright's neck. The women exchange information necessary to solving the murder, yet their conversations are seen as foolish female chatter by their husbands and the county attorney.

Identifying with Mrs. Wright, the women withhold judgment and instead try to understand what might have motivated her. They discuss how hard life must have been for Minnie in a house with no children and with John, who was cold and distant. The Wright house is located in a hollow, and the road cannot even be seen, so Mrs. Hale and Mrs. Peters begin to understand how the isolation and sense of entrapment could have led Mrs. Wright to snap. They can see how the only means of escape might have been to kill her captor, Mr. Wright. Mrs. Peters furthers the link between them and Mrs. Wright by sharing a time when Mrs. Peters herself felt the desire to hurt a boy who butchered her kitten with a hatchet. The women realize that they too might have been driven to violence under Mrs. Wright's circumstances.

The birdcage and the dead canary are key symbols and discoveries to the plot. Mrs. Hale and Mrs. Peters automatically associate the canary with Mrs. Wright. The bird reminds them of Minnie's old life as a young girl in the choir who loved to sing, full of life. This addresses a contrasting portrait with the person she has become after becoming a married woman. John Wright is accused of having killed the canary, since he disliked anything that made music or sang. This is linked to the way he metaphorically killed Minnie Foster, the joyful carefree spirit of Mrs. Wright. The canary represents the only hope and joy left in her life, yet her husband took that away from her too. Mrs. Wright intended to bury the canary, an act also symbolizing the burial of a part of her. By strangling Mr. Wright, Mrs. Wright forces their roles to be reversed. John Wright becomes the submissive, helpless creature, just like the canary. Mrs. Wright then becomes like a cat, an animal that she disliked.

The play's conclusion serves as closure to the mystery, but it is the investigation process that proves to be more illuminating. The men are responsible for carrying out business in society, leaving the women to content themselves with their household, children, and other activities deemed frivolous. The characters of both sexes have different reasons for entering the Wright house. The men have legal interests, whereas the women are only there to collect personal effects for Mrs. Wright. Left no other option by their husbands looking for evidence, the women focus their energy on trifles, such as the sewing in a quilt or the presence of an empty birdcage. As they make attempts to tidy up—their natural instinct—Mrs. Hale and Mrs. Peters think of their own situations as wives. They are in the house of a woman who refused to take orders from her husband any longer, to be unhappy, and think of trivial things men do not care about. The irony in the end is that these very things that the men do not notice, that they do not think of, hold the answer to solving the murder.

Questions

1. This essay does not have a distinctive title. What might be a title that captures the main point of the essay?
2. Identify a paragraph that is especially effective. What particular qualities of that paragraph make it effective?
3. Identify a weak paragraph. How might you revise it to improve it?
4. Is there a logical progression to the paragraphs? How might you change the order to improve the essay?
5. The conclusion is a relatively long paragraph with substantive analysis. In what ways does it function as a developmental paragraph? Should the student have written another paragraph as a conclusion? Discuss this point by considering the purpose of a concluding paragraph.

• ACTIVITY •

Choose one of the following prompts and write an interpretive essay using "One of These Days," "Seeing Eye," "The First Day," *Andre's Mother*, or *Trifles*.

- Explain how the opening scene or first few paragraphs of the play or short story introduces a central idea or theme.
- Analyze how the author uses literary techniques in his or her work to challenge the status quo in a society or community.
- Discuss how the author's use of time in constructing a story's plot—especially in medias res and flashbacks—contributes to the meaning of the work as a whole.

4

Entering the Conversation

So far, we've discussed how to approach literary works through close reading and big-picture analysis. In this chapter, we're going to build on those skills and consider literary texts grouped together, what we call *Conversations*. The Conversations will give you an opportunity to become involved with literary texts in a way different from what you're accustomed to. In the Conversations, you'll be using multiple literary texts as evidence to support an interpretation or viewpoint. Consider the readings in this chapter and the Conversations throughout this book your training ground for writing a literary research paper. A key step—researching relevant texts—has already been done for you, so you can focus on developing a critical response that takes into account multiple texts representing a range of perspectives.

You might wonder what the point of these Conversations or a literary research paper is, especially if you're not planning to major in English. We like to think that these experiences are giving you "equipment for living," which is how philosopher Kenneth Burke described the purpose of literature. He did not view literature as something reserved exclusively for academics or appreciated just for its artistic beauty, but something with practical value: to help us think about the issues that affect our lives. Considering multiple texts on the same subject gives you an opportunity to examine a range of perspectives, some of which might support your own view, some of which might challenge or completely reverse it. In some cases, these different perspectives can help you develop an opinion on a subject that you don't have strong feelings about or maybe haven't thought about at all. In the process, you'll become part of an ongoing conversation among writers and artists from the past and the present.

In this chapter, you'll consider a variety of poems, a photograph, an autobiographical essay, and a short story, all of which center around the immigrant experience—an exploration of how various people and groups who have come to America by either choice or circumstance have interpreted what it means to be an American. But before you take a look at the texts in this Conversation, take a moment to write.

• ACTIVITY •

What does it mean to be an American? What makes a person feel that he or she belongs in America? Has the concept of being an American changed over time? Are there some ideas that have remained consistent or endured through our country's history? Freewrite in response to one or more of these questions. Use your own experience, current events, your historical knowledge, or literature you've read to inform your response.

Conversation

Coming to America

For the remainder of this chapter, we'll focus on the following group of eight texts, arranged here in chronological order:

Texts

Emma Lazarus, "The New Colossus" (poetry)

Lewis W. Hine, "Playground in Tenement Alley, Boston" (photography)

Langston Hughes, "Let America Be America Again" (poetry)

Dwight Okita, "In Response to Executive Order 9066: All Americans of Japanese Descent Must Report to Relocation Centers" (poetry)

Pat Mora, "Immigrants" (poetry)

Amy Tan, "Two Kinds" (fiction)

Judith Ortiz Cofer, "The Latin Deli" (poetry)

Bharati Mukherjee, "Two Ways to Belong in America" (nonfiction)

The first piece, which in many ways sets the stage for this inquiry, is a sonnet, "The New Colossus," written by Emma Lazarus (1849–1887). Born to a well-to-do family in New York, she was one of the first successful Jewish American authors and an advocate for Jewish refugees arriving in New York after violent anti-Semitic riots (called *pogroms*) in Russia. Lazarus received a classical education through private tutors, was fluent in German and French, and enjoyed a correspondence with Ralph Waldo Emerson. Originally written in 1883 for an art auction to raise funds to build a pedestal for the Statue of Liberty, "The New Colossus" did not become part of the monument until 1903, when it was inscribed on a plaque and placed on the inner wall; in 1945, it was relocated over the main entrance. Subsequently, Lazarus's famous words, "Give me your tired, your poor, / Your huddled masses yearning to breathe free" became synonymous with the Statue of Liberty and the American Dream.

The New Colossus

EMMA LAZARUS

Not like the brazen giant of Greek fame,
With conquering limbs astride from land to land;
Here at our sea-washed, sunset gates shall stand
A mighty woman with a torch, whose flame
Is the imprisoned lightning, and her name   5
Mother of Exiles. From her beacon-hand
Glows world-wide welcome; her mild eyes command
The air-bridged harbor that twin cities frame.
"Keep, ancient lands, your storied pomp!" cries she
With silent lips. "Give me your tired, your poor,   10
Your huddled masses yearning to breathe free,
The wretched refuse of your teeming shore.
Send these, the homeless, tempest-tost to me,
I lift my lamp beside the golden door!"

[1883]

The poem begins with a reference to the Colossus of Rhodes, one of the Seven Wonders of the World—a giant bronze statue of the sun god Helios that overlooked the Greek city's harbor. Lazarus asserts that the "new colossus" is "not like" the statue, a "brazen giant," but "A mighty woman with a torch," whom Lazarus dubs the "Mother of Exiles." Why do you think she prefers this kindlier image? What other images in the poem characterize this "new colossus"? Notice, for instance, that her "mild eyes command," as if her power derives from a source different from that of the Greek statue "with conquering limbs." This "Mother of Exiles" tells the "ancient lands" (the old world) that she does not want "your storied pomp" (the aristocracy) but welcomes "your tired, your poor"—those described as "The wretched refuse." So not only is she offering sanctuary but she seems to prefer those who have somehow suffered or been oppressed. How does her embrace of the oppressed contribute to the American idea of a "melting pot"?

Of course, there is much more to consider about this poem—its sonnet form, its interpretation of the Statue of Liberty, its use of Greek and Roman art and myth, the influence of Lazarus's identity as a woman and a Jew in late nineteenth-century America—but overall, we can see the image of America as a land of opportunity emerging in the language of refuge, welcome, and opportunity. With this poem as backdrop, the Statue of Liberty as a symbol of America beckons those who are "yearning to breathe free" with the prospect of a new beginning.

Let's turn from Lazarus's poem to a photograph by Lewis W. Hine (1874–1940). In 1908, Hine became the photographer for the National Child Labor Committee, which used his work to lobby for child labor laws. He was also known for his photographs and commentaries on the immigrant experience, including living conditions in the tenements.

Playground in Tenement Alley, Boston

LEWIS W. HINE

"Playground in Tenement Alley, Boston" (1909, gelatin silver print, 12.7 x 17.7 cm)

This photo shows a group of children in an alley between two tenement buildings; some are playing ball, some are standing on a wagon watching, a few seem to be looking in the direction of the photographer. Adults are notably absent. The buildings enclose the children, but is the effect one of protection and shelter, or of confinement and crowding? Is this a promising scene of young people whose futures open up skyward, or a pessimistic scene of children with limited horizons, hemmed in by poverty? Why is it significant that the children are playing baseball, long considered America's pastime? Does this photo reflect the vision of freedom in "The New Colossus," or do you think Hine is depicting these children as still poor, still huddled, still yearning to "breathe free"?

Now let's consider a poet who questioned Lazarus's vision of America: Langston Hughes (1902–1967). An African American poet who rose to prominence in the 1920s, Hughes was known for his poetry, drama, fiction, criticism, and autobiographical writing about black life in America. His essay "The Negro Artist and the Racial Mountain" (p. 1296) is seen by many as the manifesto of the African American artist during the period of the Harlem Renaissance. "Let America Be America Again" is influenced by Walt Whitman's classic poem "I Hear America Singing," but Hughes offers a viewpoint that questions and doubts as well as celebrates.

Let America Be America Again

LANGSTON HUGHES

Let America be America again.
Let it be the dream it used to be.
Let it be the pioneer on the plain
Seeking a home where he himself is free.

(America never was America to me.)   5

Let America be the dream the dreamers dreamed—
Let it be that great strong land of love
Where never kings connive nor tyrants scheme
That any man be crushed by one above.

(It never was America to me.)   10

O, let my land be a land where Liberty
Is crowned with no false patriotic wreath,
But opportunity is real, and life is free,
Equality is in the air we breathe.

(There's never been equality for me,   15
Nor freedom in this "homeland of the free.")

Say, who are you that mumbles in the dark?
And who are you that draws your veil across the stars?

I am the poor white, fooled and pushed apart,
I am the Negro bearing slavery's scars.   20
I am the red man driven from the land,
I am the immigrant clutching the hope I seek—
   And finding only the same old stupid plan
Of dog eat dog, of mighty crush the weak.

I am the young man, full of strength and hope,   25
Tangled in that ancient endless chain
Of profit, power, gain, of grab the land!

Of grab the gold! Of grab the ways of satisfying need!
Of work the men! Of take the pay!
Of owning everything for one's own greed!   30

I am the farmer, bondsman to the soil.
I am the worker sold to the machine.
I am the Negro, servant to you all.
I am the people, humble, hungry, mean—
Hungry yet today despite the dream.   35
Beaten yet today—O, Pioneers!
I am the man who never got ahead,
The poorest worker bartered through the years.

Yet I'm the one who dreamt our basic dream
In the Old World while still a serf of kings,   40
Who dreamt a dream so strong, so brave, so true,
That even yet its mighty daring sings
In every brick and stone, in every furrow turned
That's made America the land it has become.
O, I'm the man who sailed those early seas   45
In search of what I meant to be my home—
For I'm the one who left dark Ireland's shore,
And Poland's plain, and England's grassy lea,
And torn from Black Africa's strand I came
To build a "homeland of the free."   50

The free?

Who said the free? Not me?
Surely not me? The millions on relief today?
The millions shot down when we strike?
The millions who have nothing for our pay?   55
For all the dreams we've dreamed
And all the songs we've sung
And all the hopes we've held
And all the flags we've hung,
The millions who have nothing for our pay—   60
Except the dream that's almost dead today.

O, let America be America again—
The land that never has been yet—
And yet must be—the land where *every* man is free.
The land that's mine—the poor man's, Indian's, Negro's, ME— 65
Who made America,
Whose sweat and blood, whose faith and pain,
Whose hand at the foundry, whose plow in the rain,
Must bring back our mighty dream again.

Sure, call me any ugly name you choose— 70
The steel of freedom does not stain.
From those who live like leeches on the people's lives,
We must take back our land again,
America!

O, yes, 75
I say it plain,
America never was America to me,
And yet I swear this oath—
America will be!

Out of the rack and ruin of our gangster death, 80
The rape and rot of graft, and stealth, and lies,
We, the people, must redeem
The land, the mines, the plants, the rivers,
The mountains and the endless plain—
All, all the stretch of these great green states— 85
And make America again!

[1935]

. . . .

Probably the most striking quality of the poem is its use of **anaphora**—the repetition of the initial word or words throughout the poem—for example, repetition of "Let America" or "Let it" in the opening section, of "I am" starting on lines 19 and 31, and of "The millions" beginning on line 53. Through anaphora, the speaker emphasizes key points, hitting them again and again not just by repeating the same thing but by using a similar structure to call attention to the differences as well, for instance: "And all the songs . . . And all the hopes . . . And all the flags . . ." (ll. 57–59). The anaphora gives this poem a chanting quality; it wants to be read aloud. You probably noticed the parenthetical comments (ll. 5, 10, 15–16). Read them aloud one after the other without the intervening lines. These comments create a tension in the poem because the "me"—the speaker—is commenting on what was "never" part of his experience.

Who is this speaker? It's tempting to assume an African American identity, even that it is Hughes himself. But the text resists this reading: "I am the poor white . . . the Negro . . . the red man . . . the immigrant . . . the young man . . . the farmer . . . the worker . . . the man who never got ahead. . . ." The speaker is the one who left "Ireland's shore," "Poland's plain," and "England's grassy lea," and who was "torn from Black Africa's strand." It's pretty difficult to escape Hughes's point that the speaker, regardless of race or national original, speaks on behalf of the many—the disappointed many.

Let's focus on the title now, particularly the "Again" part. What was America at one time, or what could America be again, according to this poem? The word "dream" and its derivatives ("dreamers," "dreamed," "dreamt") appear throughout the poem.

We find words and phrases connoting patriotism ("opportunity," "freedom," "the stretch of these great green states"), so the speaker acknowledges the possibilities that America offers. Yet it's clear from the descriptions of greed and oppression that the speaker thinks something has gone wrong: the common man gets "shot down when [he] strike[s]" (l. 54), while the rich "live like leeches on the people's lives" (l. 72). Hughes gives us vivid images of America's "ancient endless chain / Of profit, power, gain, of grab the land!" (ll. 26–27).

Then, in lines 62–63, we come to the central paradox: "O, let America be America again— / The land that never has been yet." How can we return to something that has never existed? The last twenty lines or so of the poem respond to that paradox with the speaker's insistence that "we, the people, must redeem" (l. 82) the dream—the idea of America—and "take back our land again" (l. 73). The speaker "swear[s] this oath— / America will be!" (ll. 78–79).

Let's think about how this poem might connect with the Hine photograph. Are the people pictured in the photo likely to become those Hughes describes: "I am the immigrant clutching the hope I seek— / And finding only the same old stupid plan / Of dog eat dog, of mighty crush the weak" (ll. 22–24)? Are they (or their parents) the ones who came to America "in search of what I meant to be my home" (l. 46) but will remain disappointed? Does the poem confirm your interpretation of the photograph, conflict with it, or perhaps add another dimension to how you think about it?

● ACTIVITY ●

Reread the response you freewrote at the start of this discussion. Are your ideas on what it means to be an American closer to those of Hughes, Hine, or Lazarus? Pair up with a classmate and discuss how one or both of the poems or the photo challenges or supports your view. Try to find at least one point that might cause you to change or expand on your opinion. Do the same for your partner — that is, listen to his or her freewriting and suggest a connection to "The New Colossus," the Hine photo, or "Let America Be America Again," or something that might change or expand on the initial response.

The poet Dwight Okita (b. 1958) writes about Executive Order 9066, issued in 1942 to authorize internment camps for groups considered threats to national security. Over 120,000 Japanese Americans were relocated to camps for the duration of World War II. Although both of Okita's parents were sent to these camps, his father gained release by agreeing to fight in Europe with other Japanese Americans in the famous 442nd Infantry Regimental Combat Team. Although his mother, who remained in the camp, did not recall the day she learned of her "relocation," Okita imagines in this poem how it might have been for her.

In Response to Executive Order 9066: All Americans of Japanese Descent Must Report to Relocation Centers

DWIGHT OKITA

Dear Sirs:
Of course I'll come. I've packed my galoshes
and three packets of tomato seeds. Denise calls them
love apples. My father says where we're going
they won't grow.   5

I am a fourteen-year-old girl with bad spelling
and a messy room. If it helps any, I will tell you
I have always felt funny using chopsticks
and my favorite food is hot dogs.
My best friend is a white girl named Denise—   10
we look at boys together. She sat in front of me
all through grade school because of our names:
O'Connor, Ozawa. I know the back of Denise's head very well.

I tell her she's going bald. She tells me I copy on tests.
We're best friends.   15

I saw Denise today in Geography class.
She was sitting on the other side of the room.
"You're trying to start a war," she said, "giving secrets
away to the Enemy. Why can't you keep your big
mouth shut?"   20

I didn't know what to say.
I gave her a packet of tomato seeds
and asked her to plant them for me, told her
when the first tomato ripened
she'd miss me.   25

[1983]

. . . .

The poem centers on two high school girls who are best friends. The speaker points out that she feels uncomfortable with chopsticks and likes hot dogs—what could be more typically American? Yet her friend Denise accuses her of "trying to start a war, . . . giving secrets / away to the Enemy" (ll. 18–19). Why do you think Okita wrote the poem as a letter? The letter tells the story of the speaker giving her packet of tomato seeds to Denise, but why would she tell this story to the men relocating her? And what is the significance of the tomato seeds? Perhaps the young speaker allows Okita to make his point without bitterness, but why do you think he would want to avoid an angry or bitter tone?

Okita raises questions about whether O'Connor and Ozawa feel the same way—or perhaps will as adults—about being American. Now you're starting to examine different experiences of being an American, and the divide between the desire to belong and the reality. Let's add a more contemporary voice with the short poem "Immigrants" by Pat Mora (b. 1942), a Texas-born writer who celebrates her Mexican American heritage in poems and essays. In this poem, she expresses the hopes and anxieties of all immigrant parents.

Immigrants

PAT MORA

wrap their babies in the American flag,
feed them mashed hot dogs and apple pie,
name them Bill and Daisy,
buy them blonde dolls that blink blue
eyes or a football and tiny cleats   5
before the baby can even walk,
speak to them in thick English,
    hallo, babee, hallo,
whisper in Spanish or Polish
when the babies sleep, whisper   10
in a dark parent bed, that dark
parent fear, "Will they like
our boy, our girl, our fine american
boy, our fine american girl?"

[1986]

Notice the references to American popular culture: the flag, "hot dogs and apple pie," names like "Bill and Daisy," blonde and blue-eyed dolls, football. What do these mean to the parents? How do you interpret the final four lines of the poem? What is "that dark / parent fear"? Who are "they"? Are the parents apprehensive? bitter? hopeful? intimidated?

• ACTIVITY •

Assume the voice of the speaker in Okita's poem when she is ten years older, and write a brief letter giving the parents in "Immigrants" advice on raising a child in America. Consider whether she would approve of their efforts to "Americanize" their children.

The longest piece in this Conversation, "Two Kinds," is a short story by Amy Tan. Tan is the author of the best-selling novel *The Joy Luck Club*, from which this story is taken, as well as four other novels and two children's books. She was born in California several years after her parents left their native China. "Two Kinds" depicts the tension between two different cultures and two different generations.

Two Kinds

AMY TAN

My mother believed you could be anything you wanted to be in America. You could open a restaurant. You could work for the government and get good retirement. You could buy a house with almost no money down. You could become rich. You could become instantly famous.

"Of course you can be prodigy, too," my mother told me when I was nine. "You can be best anything. What does Auntie Lindo know? Her daughter, she is only best tricky."

America was where all my mother's hopes lay. She had come here in 1949 after losing everything in China: her mother and father, her family home, her first husband, and two daughters, twin baby girls. But she never looked back with regret. There were so many ways for things to get better.

We didn't immediately pick the right kind of prodigy. At first my mother thought I could be a Chinese Shirley Temple. We'd watch Shirley's old movies on TV as though they were training films. My mother would poke my arm and say, "*Ni kan*"—You watch. And I would see Shirley tapping her feet, or singing a sailor song, or pursing her lips into a very round O while saying, "Oh my goodness."

"*Ni kan*," said my mother as Shirley's eyes flooded with tears. "You already know how. Don't need talent for crying!"   5

Soon after my mother got this idea about Shirley Temple, she took me to a beauty training school in the Mission district and put me in the hands of a student who could barely hold the scissors without shaking. Instead of getting big fat curls, I emerged with an uneven mass of crinkly black fuzz. My mother dragged me off to the bathroom and tried to wet down my hair.

"You look like Negro Chinese," she lamented, as if I had done this on purpose.

The instructor of the beauty training school had to lop off these soggy clumps to make my hair even again. "Peter Pan is very popular these days," the instructor assured my mother. I now had hair the length of a boy's, with straight-across bangs that hung at a slant two inches above my eyebrows. I liked the haircut and it made me actually look forward to my future fame.

In fact, in the beginning, I was just as excited as my mother, maybe even more so. I pictured this prodigy part of me as many different images, trying each one on for size. I was a dainty ballerina girl standing by the curtains, waiting to hear the right music that would send me floating on my tiptoes. I was like the Christ child lifted out of the straw manger, crying with holy indignity. I was Cinderella stepping from her pumpkin carriage with sparkly cartoon music filling the air.

In all of my imaginings, I was filled with a sense that I would soon become *perfect*. My mother and father would adore me. I would be beyond reproach. I would never feel the need to sulk for anything.

But sometimes the prodigy in me became impatient. "If you don't hurry up and get me out of here, I'm disappearing for good," it warned. "And then you'll always be nothing."

Every night after dinner, my mother and I would sit at the Formica kitchen table. She would present new tests, taking her examples from stories of amazing children she had read in *Ripley's Believe It or Not*, or *Good Housekeeping, Reader's Digest*, and a dozen other magazines she kept in a pile in our bathroom. My mother got these magazines from people whose houses she cleaned. And since she cleaned many houses each week, we had a great assortment. She would look through them all, searching for stories about remarkable children.

The first night she brought out a story about a three-year-old boy who knew the capitals of all the states and even most of the European countries. A teacher was quoted as saying the little boy could also pronounce the names of the foreign cities correctly.

"What's the capital of Finland?" my mother asked me, looking at the magazine story.

All I knew was the capital of California, because Sacramento was the name of the street we lived on in Chinatown. "Nairobi!" I guessed, saying the most foreign word I could think of. She checked to see if that was possibly one way to pronounce "Helsinki" before showing me the answer.

The tests got harder—multiplying numbers in my head, finding the queen of hearts in a deck of cards, trying to stand on my head without using my hands, predicting the daily temperatures in Los Angeles, New York, and London.

One night I had to look at a page from the Bible for three minutes and then report everything I could remember. "Now Jehoshaphat had riches and honor in abundance and . . . that's all I remember, Ma," I said.

And after seeing my mother's disappointed face once again, something inside of me began to die. I hated the tests, the raised hopes and failed expectations. Before going to bed that night, I looked in the mirror above the bathroom sink and when I saw only my face staring back—and that it would always be this ordinary face—I began to cry. Such a sad, ugly girl! I made high-pitched noises like a crazed animal, trying to scratch out the face in the mirror.

And then I saw what seemed to be the prodigy side of me—because I had never seen that face before. I looked at my reflection, blinking so I could see more clearly. The girl staring back at me was angry, powerful. This girl and I were the same. I had new thoughts, willful thoughts, or rather thoughts filled with lots of won'ts. I won't let her change me, I promised myself. I won't be what I'm not.

So now on nights when my mother presented her tests, I performed listlessly, my head propped on one arm. I pretended to be bored. And I was. I got so bored I started

10

15

20

counting the bellows of the foghorns out on the bay while my mother drilled me in other areas. The sound was comforting and reminded me of the cow jumping over the moon. And the next day, I played a game with myself, seeing if my mother would give up on me before eight bellows. After a while I usually counted only one, maybe two bellows at most. At last she was beginning to give up hope.

Two or three months had gone by without any mention of my being a prodigy again. And then one day my mother was watching *The Ed Sullivan Show* on TV. The TV was old and the sound kept shorting out. Every time my mother got halfway up from the sofa to adjust the set, the sound would go back on and Ed would be talking. As soon as she sat down, Ed would go silent again. She got up, the TV broke into loud piano music. She sat down. Silence. Up and down, back and forth, quiet and loud. It was like a stiff embraceless dance between her and the TV set. Finally she stood by the set with her hand on the sound dial.

She seemed entranced by the music, a little frenzied piano piece with this mesmerizing quality, sort of quick passages and then teasing lilting ones before it returned to the quick playful parts.

"*Ni kan,*" my mother said, calling me over with hurried hand gestures, "Look here."

I could see why my mother was fascinated by the music. It was being pounded out by a little Chinese girl, about nine years old, with a Peter Pan haircut. The girl had the sauciness of a Shirley Temple. She was proudly modest like a proper Chinese child. And she also did this fancy sweep of a curtsy, so that the fluffy skirt of her white dress cascaded slowly to the floor like the petals of a large carnation.

In spite of these warning signs, I wasn't worried. Our family had no piano and we couldn't afford to buy one, let alone reams of sheet music and piano lessons. So I could be generous in my comments when my mother bad-mouthed the little girl on TV.

"Play note right, but doesn't sound good! No singing sound," complained my mother.

"What are you picking on her for?" I said carelessly. "She's pretty good. Maybe she's not the best, but she's trying hard." I knew almost immediately I would be sorry I said that.

"Just like you," she said. "Not the best. Because you not trying." She gave a little huff as she let go of the sound dial and sat down on the sofa.

The little Chinese girl sat down also to play an encore of "Anitra's Dance" by Grieg. I remember the song, because later on I had to learn how to play it.

Three days after watching *The Ed Sullivan Show*, my mother told me what my schedule would be for piano lessons and piano practice. She had talked to Mr. Chong, who lived on the first floor of our apartment building. Mr. Chong was a retired piano teacher and my mother had traded housecleaning services for weekly lessons and a piano for me to practice on every day, two hours a day, from four until six.

When my mother told me this, I felt as though I had been sent to hell. I whined and then kicked my foot a little when I couldn't stand it anymore.

"Why don't you like me the way I am? I'm *not* a genius! I can't play the piano. And even if I could, I wouldn't go on TV if you paid me a million dollars!" I cried.

My mother slapped me. "Who ask you be genius?" she shouted. "Only ask you be your best. For you sake. You think I want you be genius? Hnnh! What for! Who ask you!"

"So ungrateful," I heard her mutter in Chinese. "If she had as much talent as she has temper, she would be famous now."

Mr. Chong, whom I secretly nicknamed Old Chong, was very strange, always   35
tapping his fingers to the silent music of an invisible orchestra. He looked ancient in my eyes. He had lost most of the hair on top of his head and he wore thick glasses and had eyes that always looked tired and sleepy. But he must have been younger than I thought, since he lived with his mother and was not yet married.

I met Old Lady Chong once and that was enough. She had this peculiar smell like a baby that had done something in its pants. And her fingers felt like a dead person's, like an old peach I once found in the back of the refrigerator; the skin just slid off the meat when I picked it up.

I soon found out why Old Chong had retired from teaching piano. He was deaf. "Like Beethoven!" he shouted to me. "We're both listening only in our head!" And he would start to conduct his frantic silent sonatas.

Our lessons went like this. He would open the book and point to different things, explaining their purpose: "Key! Treble! Bass! No sharps or flats! So this is C major! Listen now and play after me!"

And then he would play the C scale a few times, a simple chord, and then, as if inspired by an old, unreachable itch, he gradually added more notes and running trills and a pounding bass until the music was really something quite grand.

I would play after him, the simple scale, the simple chord, and then I just played   40
some nonsense that sounded like a cat running up and down on top of garbage cans. Old Chong smiled and applauded and then said, "Very good! But now you must learn to keep time!"

So that's how I discovered that Old Chong's eyes were too slow to keep up with the wrong notes I was playing. He went through the motions in half-time. To help me keep rhythm, he stood behind me, pushing down on my right shoulder for every beat. He balanced pennies on top of my wrists so I would keep them still as I slowly played scales and arpeggios. He had me curve my hand around an apple and keep that shape when playing chords. He marched stiffly to show me how to make each finger dance up and down, staccato like an obedient little soldier.

He taught me all these things, and that was how I also learned I could be lazy and get away with mistakes, lots of mistakes. If I hit the wrong notes because I hadn't practiced enough, I never corrected myself. I just kept playing in rhythm. And Old Chong kept conducting his own private reverie.

So maybe I never really gave myself a fair chance. I did pick up the basics pretty quickly, and I might have become a good pianist at that young age. But I was so determined not to try, not to be anybody different that I learned to play only the most ear-splitting preludes, the most discordant hymns.

Over the next year, I practiced like this, dutifully in my own way. And then one day I heard my mother and her friend Lindo Jong both talking in a loud bragging tone of voice so others could hear. It was after church, and I was leaning against the brick wall wearing a dress with stiff white petticoats. Auntie Lindo's daughter, Waverly, who was about my age, was standing farther down the wall about five feet away. We had grown up together and shared all the closeness of two sisters squabbling over crayons and dolls. In other words, for the most part, we hated each other. I thought she was snotty. Waverly Jong had gained a certain amount of fame as "Chinatown's Littlest Chinese Chess Champion."

"She bring home too many trophy," lamented Auntie Lindo that Sunday. "All 45 day she play chess. All day I have no time do nothing but dust off her winnings." She threw a scolding look at Waverly, who pretended not to see her.

"You lucky you don't have this problem," said Auntie Lindo with a sigh to my mother.

And my mother squared her shoulders and bragged: "Our problem worser than yours. If we ask Jing-mei wash dish, she hear nothing but music. It's like you can't stop this natural talent."

And right then, I was determined to put a stop to her foolish pride.

A few weeks later, Old Chong and my mother conspired to have me play in a talent show which would be held in the church hall. By then, my parents had saved up enough to buy me a secondhand piano, a black Wurlitzer spinet with a scarred bench. It was the showpiece of our living room.

For the talent show, I was to play a piece called "Pleading Child" from Schumann's 50 *Scenes from Childhood*. It was a simple, moody piece that sounded more difficult than it was. I was supposed to memorize the whole thing, playing the repeat parts twice to make the piece sound longer. But I dawdled over it, playing a few bars and then cheating, looking up to see what notes followed. I never really listened to what I was playing. I daydreamed about being somewhere else, about being someone else.

The part I liked to practice best was the fancy curtsy: right foot out, touch the rose on the carpet with a pointed foot, sweep to the side, left leg bends, look up and smile.

My parents invited all the couples from the Joy Luck Club to witness my debut. Auntie Lindo and Uncle Tin were there. Waverly and her two older brothers had also come. The first two rows were filled with children both younger and older than I was. The littlest ones got to go first. They recited simple nursery rhymes, squawked out tunes on miniature violins, twirled Hula Hoops, pranced in pink ballet tutus, and when they bowed or curtsied, the audience would sigh in unison, "Awww," and then clap enthusiastically.

When my turn came, I was very confident. I remember my childish excitement. It was as if I knew, without a doubt, that the prodigy side of me really did exist. I had no fear whatsoever, no nervousness. I remember thinking to myself, This is it! This is it! I looked out over the audience, at my mother's blank face, my father's yawn,

Auntie Lindo's stiff-lipped smile, Waverly's sulky expression. I had on a white dress layered with sheets of lace, and a pink bow in my Peter Pan haircut. As I sat down I envisioned people jumping to their feet and Ed Sullivan rushing up to introduce me to everyone on TV.

And I started to play. It was so beautiful. I was so caught up in how lovely I looked that at first I didn't worry how I would sound. So it was a surprise to me when I hit the first wrong note and I realized something didn't sound quite right. And then I hit another and another followed that. A chill started at the top of my head and began to trickle down. Yet I couldn't stop playing, as though my hands were bewitched. I kept thinking my fingers would adjust themselves back, like a train switching to the right track. I played this strange jumble through two repeats, the sour notes staying with me all the way to the end.

When I stood up, I discovered my legs were shaking. Maybe I had just been nervous and the audience, like Old Chong, had seen me go through the right motions and had not heard anything wrong at all. I swept my right foot out, went down on my knee, looked up and smiled. The room was quiet, except for Old Chong, who was beaming and shouting, "Bravo! Bravo! Well done!" But then I saw my mother's face, her stricken face. The audience clapped weakly, and as I walked back to my chair, with my whole face quivering as I tried not to cry, I heard a little boy whisper loudly to his mother, "That was awful," and the mother whispered back, "Well, she certainly tried."

And now I realized how many people were in the audience, the whole world it seemed. I was aware of eyes burning into my back. I felt the shame of my mother and father as they sat stiffly throughout the rest of the show.

We could have escaped during intermission. Pride and some strange sense of honor must have anchored my parents to their chairs. And so we watched it all: the eighteen-year-old boy with a fake mustache who did a magic show and juggled flaming hoops while riding a unicycle. The breasted girl with white makeup who sang from *Madama Butterfly* and got honorable mention. And the eleven-year-old boy who won first prize playing a tricky violin song that sounded like a busy bee.

After the show, the Hsus, the Jongs, and the St. Clairs from the Joy Luck Club came up to my mother and father.

"Lots of talented kids," Auntie Lindo said vaguely, smiling broadly.

"That was somethin' else," said my father, and I wondered if he was referring to me in a humorous way, or whether he even remembered what I had done.

Waverly looked at me and shrugged her shoulders. "You aren't a genius like me," she said matter-of-factly. And if I hadn't felt so bad, I would have pulled her braids and punched her stomach.

But my mother's expression was what devastated me: a quiet, blank look that said she had lost everything. I felt the same way, and it seemed as if everybody were now coming up, like gawkers at the scene of an accident, to see what parts were actually missing. When we got on the bus to go home, my father was humming the busy-bee tune and my mother was silent. I kept thinking she wanted to wait until we got home before shouting at me. But when my father unlocked the door to our apartment, my mother walked in and then went to the back, into the bedroom. No accusations. No blame. And in a way, I felt disappointed. I had been waiting for her to start shouting, so I could shout back and cry and blame her for all my misery.

I assumed my talent-show fiasco meant I never had to play the piano again. But two days later, after school, my mother came out of the kitchen and saw me watching TV.

"Four clock," she reminded me as if it were any other day. I was stunned, as though she were asking me to go through the talent-show torture again. I wedged myself more tightly in front of the TV.

"Turn off TV," she called from the kitchen five minutes later.   65

I didn't budge. And then I decided. I didn't have to do what my mother said anymore. I wasn't her slave. This wasn't China. I had listened to her before and look what happened. She was the stupid one.

She came out from the kitchen and stood in the arched entryway of the living room. "Four clock," she said once again, louder.

"I'm not going to play anymore," I said nonchalantly. "Why should I? I'm not a genius."

She walked over and stood in front of the TV. I saw her chest was heaving up and down in an angry way.

"No!" I said, and I now felt stronger, as if my true self had finally emerged. So   70
this was what had been inside me all along.

"No! I won't!" I screamed.

She yanked me by the arm, pulled me off the floor, snapped off the TV. She was frighteningly strong, half pulling, half carrying me toward the piano as I kicked the throw rugs under my feet. She lifted me up and onto the hard bench. I was sobbing by now, looking at her bitterly. Her chest was heaving even more and her mouth was open, smiling crazily as if she were pleased I was crying.

"You want me to be someone that I'm not!" I sobbed. "I'll never be the kind of daughter you want me to be!"

"Only two kinds of daughters," she shouted in Chinese. "Those who are obedi-ent and those who follow their own mind! Only one kind of daughter can live in this house. Obedient daughter!"

"Then I wish I wasn't your daughter. I wish you weren't my mother," I shouted. As I   75
said these things I got scared. It felt like worms and toads and slimy things crawling out of my chest, but it also felt good, as if this awful side of me had surfaced, at last.

"Too late change this," said my mother shrilly.

And I could sense her anger rising to its breaking point. I wanted to see it spill over. And that's when I remembered the babies she had lost in China, the ones we never talked about. "Then I wish I'd never been born!" I shouted. "I wish I were dead! Like them."

It was as if I had said the magic words. Alakazam!—and her face went blank, her mouth closed, her arms went slack, and she backed out of the room, stunned, as if she were blowing away like a small brown leaf, thin, brittle, lifeless.

It was not the only disappointment my mother felt in me. In the years that fol-lowed, I failed her so many times, each time asserting my own will, my right to fall short of expectations. I didn't get straight As. I didn't become class president. I didn't get into Stanford. I dropped out of college.

For unlike my mother, I did not believe I could be anything I wanted to be. I could only be me. 80

And for all those years, we never talked about the disaster at the recital or my terrible accusations afterward at the piano bench. All that remained unchecked, like a betrayal that was now unspeakable. So I never found a way to ask her why she had hoped for something so large that failure was inevitable.

And even worse, I never asked her what frightened me the most: Why had she given up hope?

For after our struggle at the piano, she never mentioned my playing again. The lessons stopped. The lid to the piano was closed, shutting out the dust, my misery, and her dreams.

So she surprised me. A few years ago, she offered to give me the piano, for my thirtieth birthday. I had not played in all those years. I saw the offer as a sign of forgiveness, a tremendous burden removed.

"Are you sure?" I asked shyly. "I mean, won't you and Dad miss it?" 85

"No, this your piano," she said firmly. "Always your piano. You only one can play."

"Well, I probably can't play anymore," I said. "It's been years."

"You pick up fast," said my mother, as if she knew this was certain. "You have natural talent. You could been genius if you want to."

"No I couldn't."

"You just not trying," said my mother. And she was neither angry nor sad. She 90 said it as if to announce a fact that could never be disproved. "Take it," she said.

But I didn't at first. It was enough that she had offered it to me. And after that, every time I saw it in my parents' living room, standing in front of the bay windows, it made me feel proud, as if it were a shiny trophy I had won back.

Last week I sent a tuner over to my parents' apartment and had the piano reconditioned, for purely sentimental reasons. My mother had died a few months before and I had been getting things in order for my father, a little bit at a time. I put the jewelry in special silk pouches. The sweaters she had knitted in yellow, pink, bright orange—all the colors I hated—I put those in moth-proof boxes. I found some old Chinese silk dresses, the kind with little slits up the sides. I rubbed the old silk against my skin, then wrapped them in tissue and decided to take them home with me.

After I had the piano tuned, I opened the lid and touched the keys. It sounded even richer than I remembered. Really, it was a very good piano. Inside the bench were the same exercise notes with handwritten scales, the same secondhand music books with their covers held together with yellow tape.

I opened up the Schumann book to the dark little piece I had played at the recital. It was on the left-hand side of the page, "Pleading Child." It looked more difficult than I remembered. I played a few bars, surprised at how easily the notes came back to me.

And for the first time, or so it seemed, I noticed the piece on the right-hand side. 95
It was called "Perfectly Contented." I tried to play this one as well. It had a lighter
melody but the same flowing rhythm and turned out to be quite easy. "Pleading
Child" was shorter but slower; "Perfectly Contented" was longer but faster. And after
I played them both a few times, I realized they were two halves of the same song.

[1989]

Tan's story focuses on the challenges of assimilation for different generations of
immigrants. In this case, the tension is between the mother's belief that "you could
be anything you wanted to be in America" (para. 1) and her later proclamation that
there are only two kinds of daughters: "Those who are obedient and those who follow their own mind!" (para. 74). Children of immigrants often find themselves torn
between American values and their parents' cultural values. What American values
do Jing-mei and her mother share? In what ways do you see Jing-mei holding on to
her Chinese heritage? Think about how the ending of the story informs your understanding of Jing-mei. How does this story complicate Lazarus's idea of a "golden
door" that immigrants walk through?

> • ACTIVITY •
>
> **Several of the pieces you've read thus far question the belief that America
> represents what Lazarus calls "the golden door," yet each one of them has at
> least some positive or hopeful elements. What are they? Discuss the positive
> qualities of America expressed in at least two of the texts covered so far in
> this Conversation (Hine, Hughes, Okita, Mora, and Tan).**

While the other pieces in this Conversation have wrestled with the positives and
negatives of assimilation, "The Latin Deli" by Judith Ortiz Cofer takes a new angle,
expressing a nostalgia for home, a longing for places and things left behind. Born
in 1952 in Puerto Rico, Cofer is the author of many stories, poems, memoirs, and
essays about her experience growing up in the United States. This poem is part of a
book of the same title—a collection of stories and poems about the Puerto Rican
community in New York.

The Latin Deli

JUDITH ORTIZ COFER

Presiding over a formica counter,
plastic Mother and Child magnetized
to the top of an ancient register,

the heady mix of smells from the open bins
of dried codfish, the green plantains   5
hanging in stalks like votive offerings,
she is the Patroness of Exiles,
a woman of no-age who was never pretty,
who spends her days selling canned memories
while listening to the Puerto Ricans complain   10
that it would be cheaper to fly to San Juan
than to buy a pound of Bustelo coffee here,
and to Cubans perfecting their speech
of a "glorious return" to Havana—where no one
has been allowed to die and nothing to change until then;   15
to Mexicans who pass through, talking lyrically
of *dólares*[1] to be made in El Norte[2]—
                              all wanting the comfort
of spoken Spanish, to gaze upon the family portrait
of her plain wide face, her ample bosom
resting on her plump arms, her look of maternal interest   20
as they speak to her and each other
of their dreams and their disillusions—
how she smiles understanding,
when they walk down the narrow aisles of her store
reading the labels of packages aloud, as if   25
they were the names of lost lovers: *Suspiros,*
Merengues, the stale candy of everyone's childhood.
                              She spends her days
slicing *jamón y queso*[3] and wrapping it in wax paper
tied with string: plain ham and cheese   30
that would cost less at the A&P, but it would not satisfy
the hunger of the fragile old man lost in the folds
of his winter coat, who brings her lists of items
that he reads to her like poetry, or the others,
whose needs she must divine, conjuring up products   35
from places that now exist only in their hearts—
closed ports she must trade with.

                                                            [1993]

. . . .

   We enter the deli as do the customers—seeing the "formica counter" and the
"ancient register," smelling the codfish and plantains. Cofer doesn't introduce us

---

[1]Dollars.—Eds.
[2]The North.—Eds.
[3]Ham and cheese.—Eds.

to the "Patroness of Exiles" until line 7. What is the woman's role in the deli? the community? Her name seems to be an echo of Lazarus's "Mother of Exiles," but why change her title from "Mother" to "Patroness"? Notice the way Cofer evokes a sense of longing through her vivid descriptions of sights, smells, and tastes: "*Suspiros, / Merengues,* the stale candy of everyone's childhood" (ll. 26–27); the deli owner's "plain wide face, her ample bosom / resting on her plump arms" (ll. 19–20); the "*jamón y queso,*" which would be less expensive to buy in the A&P. She draws on religious allusions — "Presiding" (l. 1), "like votive offerings" (l. 6), "divine" (l. 35) — in her description of the "woman of no-age" who offers solace and comfort to those whose physical life in one place seems separate from their emotional ties to another: "places that now exist only in their hearts" (l. 36). Cofer reminds us of the pleasure of hearing one's own language — in this case, "the comfort / of spoken Spanish" (ll. 17–18). Do those "*dólares* to be made in El Norte" (l. 17) compensate for the losses Cofer catalogs in this poem?

The question of the psychological cost of immigration is also the subject of "Two Ways to Belong in America," an autobiographical essay by Bharati Mukherjee, who immigrated to the United States from India in 1961. In this essay, Mukherjee contrasts her choice to become an American citizen with her sister's decision to live and work as a legal immigrant, while retaining her Indian citizenship.

Two Ways to Belong in America

Bharati Mukherjee

This is a tale of two sisters from Calcutta, Mira and Bharati, who have lived in the United States for some 35 years, but who find themselves on different sides in the current debate over the status of immigrants. I am an American citizen and she is not. I am moved that thousands of long-term residents are finally taking the oath of citizenship. She is not.

Mira arrived in Detroit in 1960 to study child psychology and pre-school education. I followed her a year later to study creative writing at the University of Iowa. When we left India, we were almost identical in appearance and attitude. We dressed alike, in saris; we expressed identical views on politics, social issues, love, and marriage in the same Calcutta convent-school accent. We would endure our two years in America, secure our degrees, then return to India to marry the grooms of our father's choosing.

Instead, Mira married an Indian student in 1962 who was getting his business administration degree at Wayne State University. They soon acquired the labor certifications necessary for the green card of hassle-free residence and employment.

Mira still lives in Detroit, works in the Southfield, Mich., school system, and has become nationally recognized for her contributions in the fields of pre-school education and parent-teacher relationships. After 36 years as a legal immigrant in this country, she clings passionately to her Indian citizenship and hopes to go home to India when she retires.

In Iowa City in 1963, I married a fellow student, an American of Canadian 5
parentage. Because of the accident of his North Dakota birth, I bypassed labor-
certification requirements and the race-related "quota" system that favored the
applicant's country of origin over his or her merit. I was prepared for (and even welcomed) the emotional strain that came with marrying outside my ethnic community.
In 33 years of marriage, we have lived in every part of North America. By choosing a
husband who was not my father's selection, I was opting for fluidity, self-invention,
blue jeans, and T-shirts, and renouncing 3,000 years (at least) of caste-observant,
"pure culture" marriage in the Mukherjee family. My books have often been read as
unapologetic (and in some quarters overenthusiastic) texts for cultural and psychological "mongrelization." It's a word I celebrate.

Mira and I have stayed sisterly close by phone. In our regular Sunday morning
conversations, we are unguardedly affectionate. I am her only blood relative on this
continent. We expect to see each other through the looming crises of aging and ill
health without being asked. Long before Vice President Gore's "Citizenship U.S.A."
drive, we'd had our polite arguments over the ethics of retaining an overseas citizenship while expecting the permanent protection and economic benefits that come
with living and working in America.

Like well-raised sisters, we never said what was really on our minds, but we
probably pitied one another. She, for the lack of structure in my life, the erasure
of Indianness, the absence of an unvarying daily core. I, for the narrowness of her
perspective, her uninvolvement with the mythic depths or the superficial pop culture
of this society. But, now, with the scapegoatings of "aliens" (documented or illegal)
on the increase, and the targeting of long-term legal immigrants like Mira for new
scrutiny and new self-consciousness, she and I find ourselves unable to maintain the
same polite discretion. We were always unacknowledged adversaries, and we are now,
more than ever, sisters.

"I feel used," Mira raged on the phone the other night. "I feel manipulated and
discarded. This is such an unfair way to treat a person who was invited to stay and
work here because of her talent. My employer went to the I.N.S. and petitioned for
the labor certification. For over 30 years, I've invested my creativity and professional
skills into the improvement of *this* country's pre-school system. I've obeyed all the
rules, I've paid my taxes, I love my work, I love my students, I love the friends I've
made. How dare America now change its rules in midstream? If America wants to
make new rules curtailing benefits of legal immigrants, they should apply only to
immigrants who arrive after those rules are already in place."

To my ears, it sounded like the description of a long-enduring, comfortable yet
loveless marriage, without risk or recklessness. Have we the right to demand, and
to expect, that we be loved? (That, to me, is the subtext of the arguments by immigration advocates.) My sister is an expatriate, professionally generous and creative,
socially courteous and gracious, and that's as far as her Americanization can go. She
is here to maintain an identity, not to transform it.

I asked her if she would follow the example of others who have decided to 10
become citizens because of the anti-immigration bills in Congress. And here, she

surprised me. "If America wants to play the manipulative game, I'll play it, too," she snapped. "I'll become a U.S. citizen for now, then change back to India when I'm ready to go home. I feel some kind of irrational attachment to India that I don't to America. Until all this hysteria against legal immigrants, I was totally happy. Having my green card meant I could visit any place in the world I wanted to and then come back to a job that's satisfying and that I do very well."

In one family, from two sisters alike as peas in a pod, there could not be a wider divergence of immigrant experience. America spoke to me—I married it—I embraced the demotion from expatriate aristocrat to immigrant nobody, surrendering those thousands of years of "pure culture," the saris, the delightfully accented English. She retained them all. Which of us is the freak?

Mira's voice, I realize, is the voice not just of the immigrant South Asian community but of an immigrant community of the millions who have stayed rooted in one job, one city, one house, one ancestral culture, one cuisine, for the entirety of their productive years. She speaks for greater numbers than I possibly can. Only the fluency of her English and the anger, rather than fear, born of confidence from her education, differentiate her from the seamstresses, the domestics, the technicians, the shop owners, the millions of hard-working but effectively silenced documented immigrants as well as their less fortunate "illegal" brothers and sisters.

Nearly 20 years ago, when I was living in my husband's ancestral homeland of Canada, I was always well-employed but never allowed to feel part of the local Quebec or larger Canadian society. Then, through a Green Paper that invited a national referendum on the unwanted side effects of "nontraditional" immigration, the government officially turned against its immigrant communities, particularly those from South Asia.

I felt then the same sense of betrayal that Mira feels now. I will never forget the pain of that sudden turning, and the casual racist outbursts the Green Paper elicited. That sense of betrayal had its desired effect and drove me, and thousands like me, from the country.

Mira and I differ, however, in the ways in which we hope to interact with the   15
country that we have chosen to live in. She is happier to live in America as an expatriate Indian than as an immigrant American. I need to feel like a part of the community I have adopted (as I tried to feel in Canada as well). I need to put roots down, to vote and make the difference that I can. The price that the immigrant willingly pays, and that the exile avoids, is the trauma of self-transformation.

[1996]

. . . .

Mukherjee's essay reminds us to consider the economics of coming to America. The "Mother of Exiles" in "The New Colossus" welcomes those who are the "tired," the "poor," the "wretched refuse," the "homeless." Neither Mukherjee nor her sister fall into these categories. Indeed they come to America to continue their education—in fact, graduate education. They did not intend to stay permanently but chose to do so after they married. How do you think the fact that they came as middle-class immigrants affects their experience of adapting to life in America? How is their experience different from that of the immigrants in "The Latin Deli"? How are the immigrants in "The Latin Deli" dealing with what Mukherjee calls "the trauma of self-transformation" (para. 15)?

By this point, you have encountered a range of issues and perspectives about whether coming to America is a dream, a trauma, or—more likely—something in between. These readings have raised questions about whether "the golden door" is open equally wide to everyone and whether the land of opportunity is worth the price of admission. We've read a lot about the emotional costs of "self-transformation" and the tensions of simultaneously trying to preserve a heritage and make a home in America. These cultural tensions extend across generations, as parents and children find themselves enmeshed in different cultures and embracing different values. Now that you have had a chance to consider these issues and others, it's time for you to enter the conversation about immigration and the experience of coming to America.

• ACTIVITY •

Imagine that you have been asked to host a talk show or podcast on the topic of "Coming to America." Begin by setting the stage with a few comments on the topic. Then introduce your guests—the authors in this Conversation—to your audience. Be sure to give the names and titles of the speakers, and provide a little background on each before summarizing the main argument each will contribute to the discussion. Now write out the transcript for your imaginary show. As host, you should use questions to guide the conversation. Call on guests who might have something interesting to say in response to your questions or who might disagree with what another guest just said.

Writing an Essay Using Multiple Texts

Your next step is to synthesize some of the texts in this Conversation into a position paper taking a stand on one or more of the issues the texts raise and using the texts themselves as evidence. While there will be times when part of your task will be to develop your own topic or question to investigate, let's start with a specific assignment.

> In "The New Colossus," Emma Lazarus welcomes those seeking freedom and opportunity to come through "the golden door" of America. Has the United States lived up to this promise? Discuss by referring to a minimum of four texts.

Before you begin, we suggest you organize your ideas about the texts. The following graphic organizer shows one technique you might use. We've begun filling it in for you, using two of the texts.

TEXT	MAIN POINTS OR IDEAS	KEY QUOTES	CONNECTIONS TO OTHER TEXTS
"Let America Be America Again"	African American author but relevant to many groups (poor, Native Americans, immigrants) Disappointed by greed and limited upward mobility in America	"Let America be the dream the dreamers dreamed" "that ancient endless chain / Of profit, power, gain, of grab the land!" "And yet I swear this oath— / America will be!"	The "golden door" of Lazarus is a distant dream here, with greed and money taking precedent. But Hughes upholds the *idea* of the dream.
"Two Ways to Belong in America"	Mukherjee stresses the importance of whole-scale commitment to America at the same time she admits the sacrifice.	"The price that the immigrant willingly pays, and that the exile avoids, is the trauma of self-transformation."	Mukherjee agrees with Lazarus about the opportunity but recognizes the drawback. She's like the parents in Mora's "Immigrants."

> ● ACTIVITY ●
>
> Complete the graphic organizer for the rest of the pieces in this Conversation, and then use the ideas you've noted to decide which texts will be the most useful in responding to the question.

Developing a Thesis Statement

You've used a graphic organizer to gather your ideas and notes; now you're ready to formulate a thesis statement to direct your essay. A topic as broad as this one — whether or not the dream Lazarus articulates is a reality — requires a clear and focused thesis. Of course, you can write a thesis that is a straightforward declarative sentence, whether positive or negative:

Positive

> Even today, America remains a place where hard work and sacrifice can make dreams a reality.

Negative

> America has rarely lived up to the promise of being the welcoming "Mother of Exiles."

However, given the number of texts and range of opinions in this Conversation, you will want to craft a thesis that acknowledges the complexity of the works and the subject. If you write an entirely positive or negative thesis, it will likely fail to acknowledge both the feelings of hope and the feelings of hopelessness in these texts. Instead, try using contrast words, such as *although, but, yet, despite, regardless,* and *however,* to show that you recognize how complex these issues are. For instance, consider the following thesis:

> Despite Emma Lazarus's hopeful view of America as a place willing to take anyone in, immigrants to America face obstacles both in mainstream society and within their own cultural groups.

By acknowledging the promise of America in the first clause, you neither forfeit nor weaken your opinion; in fact, you strengthen your assertion by grounding it in an awareness of the complexity of the question itself. Further, a more balanced thesis sets up a framework for the essay: a discussion, anchored in the Lazarus poem, of the obstacles immigrants experience in American society as well as within their own communities. A thesis like this will help you develop a logical and clearly structured argument in your essay.

There is no set formula for writing a thesis statement, but as you are developing your own, ask yourself these questions:

- Is the thesis clearly stated and focused?
- Does it present an opinion or viewpoint rather than a summary?
- Does it imply an organizational structure for the essay?
- Is it broad enough to include several of the texts in question?
- Does it acknowledge the complexity of the issues, or does it ignore evidence to the contrary?

• ACTIVITY •

Discuss the strengths and weaknesses of each of the following thesis statements, written in response to the question we have been discussing:

In "The New Colossus," Emma Lazarus welcomes those seeking freedom and opportunity to come through "the golden door" of America. Has the United States lived up to this promise? Discuss by referring to a minimum of four texts.

1. "Two Kinds" and "The Latin Deli" show the problems immigrants encounter in the United States and contradict the hopeful vision Emma Lazarus puts forward in "The New Colossus."

2. Emma Lazarus captured the spirit of America in her poem "The New Colossus."

3. Although coming to America involves risks, the benefits can be substantial.

4. America is not a perfect place, but people from all over the world continue to see it as a land of more opportunities and greater potential than their own imperfect homelands.

5. As the "Mother of Exiles" (Lazarus), the United States has lived up to its promise to offer freedom to those who seek it, yet some groups have found the road to that freedom long and difficult.

6. As shown in literary and visual texts, it is not easy for those not born in America to feel that they truly belong.

7. The price of walking through the "golden door" that Emma Lazarus described is one's own culture in return for an uncertain chance to belong in America.

Organizing an Essay Using Multiple Texts

When you're writing about multiple texts, you have two basic choices for structuring your essay: (1) a text-by-text organization or (2) an idea-by-idea organization.

Text-by-Text Organization

In an essay written using text-by-text organization, each paragraph of the essay deals with a single piece and discusses how it relates to the thesis. Let's use the thesis statement we came up with in the previous section:

> Despite Emma Lazarus's hopeful view of America as a place willing to take anyone in, immigrants to America face obstacles both in mainstream society and within their own cultural groups.

Here is one way we might structure the developmental paragraphs of an essay written using a text-by-text organization:

Paragraph	Topic Sentence
I.	"The New Colossus" expresses the dream of America as a place that welcomes those who are exiled from their original homeland.
II.	Langston Hughes argues that America has never been a place where everyone has had an equal chance to pursue life, liberty, or happiness.
III.	In "The Latin Deli," Judith Ortiz Cofer conveys the longing for home of those who feel displacement and alienation in America.
IV.	In "Two Kinds," Amy Tan shows that immigrants' conflicts are often within their own families.

This outline is a solid step toward a clearly organized essay, with each paragraph focused on a specific text. Nevertheless, it is somewhat formulaic, and it fails to draw connections among the various texts. You can try to pull everything together in the concluding paragraph, showing how the various texts support the main point, but this approach tempts you to summarize what you've just said.

Perhaps the most limiting quality of this outline is that it seems to put the texts in charge rather than your ideas. The point of entering a conversation, debate, or discussion is not just to summarize or even to interpret what others are saying—that's merely the initial step—but to add your own voice. Doing so does not mean leaving the texts behind, though it does require you to take charge.

Idea-by-Idea Organization

In an essay written using idea-by-idea organization, each paragraph centers around an argument and brings several texts to bear as evidence. Once again, let's start with our working thesis:

> Despite Emma Lazarus's hopeful view of America as a place willing to take anyone in, immigrants to America face obstacles both in mainstream society and within their own cultural groups.

Consider the following structure for an essay:

Paragraph   **Topic Sentence**

    I.   America promises unlimited possibility and freedom for those willing to embrace hard work and optimism.

    II.   The reality for many is giving up their own culture, even their language, as they attempt to fit in.

    III.   Even those who embrace the promise of America face exclusion as they try to assimilate into mainstream American culture while attempting to preserve their cultural heritage.

    IV.   Immigrants face the challenge of conflicts within their own families when there are different interpretations of what it means to be an American.

Notice that none of the major divisions of the essay specify a single text. The divisions are instead based on ideas or arguments, which one or more of the texts can be used to develop and support. In fact, one text may support more than one point.

• ACTIVITY •

Identify at least two of the texts from the Conversation that might be used to develop each of the four points indicated in the preceding idea-by-idea outline. The same text may be used for more than one of the points. Explain how each text would support or illustrate the point being made.

Using Literary Texts as Evidence

When you are writing essays using multiple texts, your principal source of support will be the texts themselves. The most important point is to stay in control: your voice is the one presenting the ideas. When you're using literary texts that are well written and compelling, it is tempting to let the texts themselves take over and to quote from them frequently. This practice will result in several problems. One is that the only voice the reader will hear is the voice of the authors being quoted. Another is that your readers may have their own interpretation of the quotes, so it's important to explain your interpretation. Let's examine a paragraph filled with interesting and relevant quotes but lacking in explanations or commentary:

> Those who enter the "golden door" of America forfeit their own cultural heritage. The parents in "Immigrants" by Pat Mora "wrap their babies in the American flag, / feed them mashed hot dogs and apple pie, / name them Bill and Daisy, / buy them blonde dolls that blink blue / eyes or a football and tiny cleats" in the hope that they will fit in. The immigrants enter "The Latin Deli" in the poem by Judith Ortiz Cofer "all wanting the comfort / of spoken Spanish" and read "the labels of packages aloud, as if / they were the names of lost lovers: *Suspiros*, / *Merengues*, the stale candy of everyone's childhood." Like Bharati Mukherjee, they pay "the price that the immigrant willingly pays, and that the exile avoids, [which is] the trauma of self-transformation."

Are all of these texts relevant to the point made by the topic sentence? Yes. Are the quotations accurate? Yes. Do they support the topic sentence effectively? Not really. If we highlight all of the words that are not quotations or references to the works or authors, look at what we have left:

> Those who enter the "golden door" of America forfeit their own cultural heritage. The parents in "Immigrants" by Pat Mora "wrap their babies in the American flag, / feed them mashed hot dogs and apple pie, / name them Bill and Daisy, / buy them blonde dolls that blink blue / eyes or a football and tiny cleats" in the hope that they will fit in. The immigrants enter "The Latin Deli" in the poem by Judith Ortiz Cofer "all wanting the comfort / of spoken Spanish" and read "the labels of packages aloud, as if / they were the names of lost lovers: *Suspiros*, / *Merengues*, the stale candy of everyone's childhood." Like Bharati Mukherjee, they pay "the price that the immigrant willingly pays, and that the exile avoids, [which is] the trauma of self-transformation."

What's left without the quotes and references? Not much. Let's revise the paragraph by keeping all three of the texts but decreasing the reliance on quotes and adding more commentary. In this paragraph, we've highlighted the quotations:

> Those who enter the "golden door" of America forfeit their own cultural heritage. The parents in "Immigrants" by Pat Mora give their children all the trappings and superficial symbols of being American by naming them "Bill and Daisy" and giving them "blonde dolls that blink blue / eyes" that probably look nothing like them or their parents. When they speak in their own language, they "whisper" because they want their children to speak

English, but without any trace of an accent. Like the immigrants who frequent "The Latin Deli," they lose "the comfort / of spoken Spanish" -- or whichever language is their mother tongue. They choose to give up their own culture in exchange for a sense of being an American, but the price is steep. It is "the trauma of self-transformation" (Mukherjee).

In this revision, the quotations support the writer's point. The writer is in charge, and that makes this revised paragraph a more effective analysis. Also, trimming down the chunks of quotes has led to a clearer focus, in this case an emphasis on the "trauma of self-transformation." Despite the lighter quoting, there are still three texts referenced, the last being integrated into the writer's own sentence.

• ACTIVITY •

Choose one of the following topic sentences, and write a paragraph that could be part of an essay we have been discussing. Use paraphrases and quotes that are carefully chosen from two of the texts as support.

1. Those who stand outside of the mainstream because of their appearance or language often find themselves barred from passing through the "golden door" of America's promise.

2. Financial security, even wealth, may be the dream for those who hope to belong to America, but too often poverty and struggle are the reality.

Integrating Quotations

You've already been quoting from literary texts in order to write about close reading, meaning, and theme. Using multiple sources, however, gets trickier whether you're writing an essay using the Conversations in this textbook or writing a literary research paper using sources you've found independently. Although mechanical conventions, such as punctuation, are important to follow, the more challenging skill is integrating quoted material into your own writing. Following are some tips to keep in mind.

Choosing Brief Quotations Rather Than Long Block Quotations

Avoid block quotations (longer than four lines of prose or three lines of poetry) in shorter essays unless you believe the material is absolutely essential. In that case, be sure to introduce it, and then explain and interpret it. If you're going to quote a fairly lengthy section, make sure it is worthwhile.

Using a Clause to Introduce a Quotation

The most common way to introduce a quotation is to introduce it with a subject-verb construction, usually including the name of the author, followed by a comma.

> Mukherjee explains, "I need to put roots down, to vote and make the difference that I can."

Rather than simply using *writes* or *says*, try using a strong verb, such as *asserts, insists, argues, believes, defines, admits, claims, points out, observes,* or *concludes*. If you choose to introduce a quote with just the author's name and a verb, you'll need to add explanation or commentary in the surrounding sentences.

Using a Full Sentence to Introduce a Quotation

In some cases, you will write an entire sentence to introduce the quote; doing so gives you the opportunity to state your interpretation or make your point. Essentially, you are giving readers your interpretation of the quote and, thus, directing their reading of it. If you use a complete sentence, separate it from the quotation with a colon:

> Mukherjee explains the importance of a sense of belonging: "I need to put roots down, to vote and make the difference that I can."

Integrating a Quotation into Your Own Sentence

The most effective way to use quotations is to integrate them into your own sentences. This may be more difficult (and require occasional use of square brackets to show additions, or ellipsis dots to show deletions), but the result will be a more seamless transition between your voice and the quotation. When you integrate quotations in this way, the reader is following your ideas and seeing the sources in the context of your argument. Be sure that the result is a grammatically correct and syntactically fluent sentence, especially if you are writing a paper in the third person, but the literature is in the first person. Square brackets can be used to change the point of view:

> Mukherjee explains that to feel a sense of belonging, she needs "to put roots down, to vote and make the difference that [she] can."

Another common problem is vague pronoun reference. In the original piece, it might be very clear to whom a pronoun refers, but when you take a pronoun out of its context, you need to be careful. Look at the following sentence:

> In "The Latin Deli," immigrants make what seems like a pilgrimage to a store where they find reminders of home and "speak to her and each other / of their dreams and their disillusions."

Who is "her"? We don't know. The pronoun needs an antecedent. One way to improve the sentence is to use square brackets to replace the vague pronoun with a real noun:

> In "The Latin Deli," immigrants make what seems like a pilgrimage to a store where they find reminders of home and "speak to [the Patroness of Exiles] and each other / of their dreams and their disillusions."

Another way might be to break it up into more than one sentence, especially if the point is an important one:

> In "The Latin Deli," immigrants make what seems like a pilgrimage to a store where they can find reminders of home. They take solace in conversations with the owner, "the Patroness of Exiles," and others like themselves about "their dreams and their disillusions."

Introducing the Author Using Relevant Information

If you are writing about Langston Hughes, you might identify him as an African American writer, an influential participant in the period known as the Harlem Renaissance, a writer whose work spans several decades, and so on. It's important to choose the information most relevant to the subject of your writing. Let your own judgment guide you on this point. Keep in mind that the purpose of including any information at all is to emphasize the reason the source you're citing is credible and relevant. If you can embed that information in a clause or even a phrase, that's the best strategy. For example:

> Pat Mora, *an award-winning Chicana author,* describes the hopes of immigrant parents who "whisper" in their own language while their babies sleep but "speak to them in thick English" to privilege the adopted language over their own.

> *Drawing on her own experience as a first-generation immigrant,* Indian-born Bharati Mukherjee contrasts her sister's attitude toward America with her own.

Identifying the Source of the Quotation

Since you will be quoting from several works, you have to keep track of your sources for your reader. In most instances, you'll probably include the author's name or the title of the work in the sentence introducing or including the quote. But if you can't find a way to mention the source in your sentence, or if doing so makes your sentence confusing, just put the author's last name in parentheses:

> The prospect of having a "good retirement" or "a house with almost no money down" (Tan) brings immigrants to America. Once here, however, they may find themselves "talking lyrically / of *dólares* to be made in El Norte" (Cofer) and ultimately "Tangled in that ancient endless chain / Of profit, power, gain" (Hughes).

If you are writing a more formal literary research paper, you will likely need to follow MLA documentation procedures, including a works-cited page. Ask your teacher if you are unclear about what is required for an assignment. Guidelines for MLA documentation can be found in the back of the book.

• ACTIVITY •

Revise each of the following sentences to improve the introduction of the quote, the accuracy of the attribution, or both. In some cases, you will have to check the original text in order to make the appropriate revisions.

1. In "Two Kinds," author Amy Tan says that America "was where all my mother's hopes lay."

2. Jing-mei does not share her mother's faith in the endless opportunities of America. "For unlike my mother, I did not believe I could be anything I wanted to be. I could only be me."

3. The speaker in Langston Hughes's poem "Let America Be America Again" calls for America to "Be the dream it used to be . . . the dream the dreamers dreamed." As a spokesperson for the downtrodden and ignored, however, he says that it never was America to him.

4. The speaker juxtaposes the corruption of America with its ideals:
   "Out of the rack and ruin of our gangster death,
   The rape and rot of graft, and stealth, and lies,
   We, the people, must redeem
   The land, the mines, the plants, the rivers,
   The mountains and the endless plain—
   All, all the stretch of these great green states—
   And make America again!"

5. Immigrants long for the food of their home country, the "Bustelo coffee" and "*jamón y queso*" rather than the "mashed hot dogs and apple pie" of American food.

6. In "Two Ways," Bharati Mukherjee explains why her sister is angry at legislation she views as anti-immigration: "If America wants to make new rules curtailing benefits of legal immigrants, they should apply only to immigrants who arrive after those rules are already in place."

7. Langston Hughes speaks for many disenfranchised groups when he writes that "There's never been equality for him."

8. The children of immigrants often strive so hard to please their parents, hoping to "soon become *perfect*" and grow up to be their parents' "fine american boy, [their] fine american girl."

9. In some instances, no matter how hard immigrants try to embrace mainstream culture, they are still viewed with suspicion: "If it helps any, I will tell you / I have always felt funny using chopsticks / and my favorite food is hot dogs."

10. Although "the trauma of self-transformation" may be the reality for some who come to America, others, like the mother in "Two Kinds," "never looked back with regret."

Including Personal Experience as Evidence

So far, we've discussed using literary texts as evidence for an essay. Although this is probably the approach you'll be expected to take with many of your writing assignments, bringing in personal experience can be a very effective strategy. We're not referring here to writing a memoir or an autobiographical essay; we're considering personal experience used as support in an argumentative essay. Think about the issues raised in the literature, and think about what experiences you have had that are somehow related. Your experience should serve as the context for your literary analysis.

In some cases, you might use first person in your introduction to set the stage for the perspective or opinion you'll develop, but you can also use personal experience within the body of your essay. Let's look at the introduction and first developmental paragraph of an essay about the challenges faced by people outside the mainstream. Student Tariq Jones draws on his own experience as an African American and a Muslim:

> In no other place in the world do so many ethnicities, races, and religions coexist and collide every day. America opens its arms to anyone with a dream, something I thought of when my brother and I were on the National Mall to experience the inauguration of America's first Black president, a day that was also my birthday. We saw people of every color, some who looked rich and others who definitely did not. So many people, especially kids, waved miniature American flags. It was a day that reminded me of dreams that can come true only in America, but I cannot forget that for certain groups, those dreams are hard to realize.
>
> My identity, like that of many Americans, comes in different forms. I am an African American male, which puts me at high risk in this country. My family practices Islam, which after 9/11 makes me suspect in this country. I am an avid football fan and an aspiring football player, which makes me as American as apple pie. Like Langston Hughes, "I am the young man, full of strength and hope," and at times I feel the same doubt and disappointment that he felt. Could it be possible that Muslims will be treated the way the Japanese were, put in camps to "safeguard" America, as Dwight Okita describes in his poem, "In Response to Executive Order 9066"? Ultimately, I doubt it because I have faith that America learns from her mistakes. My family may choose to pray on Friday afternoons while another family down the street goes to Catholic Church on Sundays, but we all step through doors of houses on American soil.

Tariq leads up to his thesis statement ("It was a day that reminded me of dreams that can come true only in America, but I cannot forget that for certain groups, those dreams are hard to realize") with his personal experience of witnessing the inauguration of Barack Obama as President of the United States. He paints a positive scene, yet his qualification that many different races and religions "coexist and collide" suggests a conflict, perhaps a contradiction, that he will explore further through his own circumstances. He develops the first paragraph of the body of his essay by explaining his background as an African American Muslim who loves football, a quintessential American sport. He examines his sense of both belonging and being excluded, as he brings in two of the texts in this Conversation (the poems by Langston Hughes and Dwight Okita). Tariq has begun to explain the conflict he articulates in his thesis with specific and concrete details drawn from his personal situation as well as literary texts.

• ACTIVITY •

Choose one of the following as a topic sentence (or write your own), and develop a paragraph by drawing on your personal experience or observation about others along with at least one of the texts in this Conversation.

- Being American has not meant losing my family's cultural (or ethnic) heritage.
- It was easier in the past than it is now for those new to this country to feel that America welcomes them.
- Although first-generation immigrants may feel an uneasy sense of belonging in America, their children define themselves as unmistakably American.
- My community demonstrates the "world-wide welcome" to all who are "yearning to breathe free" that Emma Lazarus celebrated in "The New Colossus."
- My community demonstrates that the "world-wide welcome" to all who are "yearning to breathe free" that Emma Lazarus celebrated in "The New Colossus" is far from the reality.

A Sample Essay Using Multiple Texts

Following is a complete student essay written using the texts in this chapter. Read it carefully, and then consider its effectiveness by responding to the questions that follow.

"The Golden Door": The Ideals of "The New Colossus" in America Today

Maddie Ramey

The first time I read Emma Lazarus's poem "The New Colossus," I was in the fifth grade. I remember that even as a ten-year-old, I was struck by the fervent patriotism of Lazarus's words. Was America really that great, a refuge for all the "huddled masses yearning to breathe free" in the world? I felt a sudden surge of pride. I wanted to believe that America was truly the "golden door" Lazarus depicted, a gateway to bigger and better things for all people regardless of race, gender, or religion. I wanted to be blindly proud of my country for offering so many opportunities to so many people. Yet as much as I wanted to see America the way

Lazarus saw it, as a land of golden opportunity for everyone, I already knew about periods in American history that went against this image (slavery and the denial of women's suffrage came to mind). When teachers revisited "The New Colossus" in later years, I felt as though what I had learned about American history only widened the rift between Lazarus's view and reality: the repression of Native Americans, Japanese internment, various "Red Scares," Jim Crow laws, and other subjects I learned in my history classes contradicted the sentiment behind "The New Colossus." How could America be Lazarus's "golden door" for the huddled masses when so great a number of people in America have suffered?

Langston Hughes explores this contrast in his poem "Let America Be America Again." The speaker in the poem begins by expressing his desire to find the America that is "the dream the dreamers dreamed -- . . . that great strong land of love." The irony in the speaker's continued declarations that America should be "a land where Liberty / Is crowned . . . opportunity is real, and life is free" is that each stanza of praise is followed by a parenthetical aside in which the speaker juxtaposes his or her own contrasting experience. The America the speaker describes, so full of liberty and freedom (much like the America behind Lazarus's "golden door"), does not exist for the speaker. The speaker even says the America he or she describes "never was America to me."

The speaker then abruptly shifts from quietly protesting to openly decrying the state of the American dream. The speaker also says he represents multiple groups in America who are constantly denied the ideal American Dream, among them "the poor white . . . the Negro . . . the red man . . . the immigrant." The speaker talks of how each group, drawn in by the promise of a "homeland of the free," has struggled to achieve the American dream, to reach that golden door that Lazarus describes. The speaker's, and presumably Hughes's, point is that saying America is great and golden does not make it great and golden. The blood, sweat, and tears of all those who believe in an American dream, who fight for it despite being repressed and who work tirelessly to see it come to fruition, are the ones who preserve the golden door. America is a refuge because these men and women work for it to be that way. They recognize that the golden door and America's refuge is the chance for a better life.

Reading Lazarus's poem also prompted me to think about the costs of walking through the supposed golden door. In chasing liberty (and oftentimes only the semblance of liberty), immigrants in America are forced to sacrifice parts of their cultures in order to integrate. This cultural choking comes through very clearly in two poems. The first, "The Latin Deli" by Judith Ortiz Cofer, describes the painful existence of a Latin American who witnesses daily the desperate struggles of her customers to maintain a connection with their homelands, "places that now exist only in their hearts." She herself is empty, without a story of her own to tell -- it is as if she has been sapped of any connection to her own native culture and is now only able to maintain any sort of foreign connection through her customers; she "spends her days selling canned memories." She is an empty vessel, assuaging their pangs of cultural hunger, while they too need her to listen to their stories of their homelands in order to fill their own cultural void. Her customers come to her shop not only for imported goods but also for bits of their homeland, things they have lost in coming to homogenized America.

Pat Mora, too, writes of the losses that accompany Americanization in her poem "Immigrants." In coming to America, immigrants unfairly forfeit much of their previous culture. The immigrant families the speaker describes must hide their true cultures and "wrap their babies in the American flag" so that they can be successful. An American guise is needed for these immigrant families to have any chance of succeeding in the United States. Even if they never fully adopt American culture, they must at least pretend to do so. This pretense is exemplified in how the immigrants in the poem describe their children as "american" rather than "American": it becomes more of an adjective and less of a nationality. It is a trait they feel their children must have, as opposed to an actual identity they share. This, I think, accurately captures the alienation immigrants feel once they cross that golden threshold as well as the immense pressure they feel to fit in. They can never fully forget their own cultures, as evidenced by how they "whisper in Spanish or Polish / when the babies sleep," but they must also make (or pretend to make) every effort to do so.

Ultimately, I think the golden door as Lazarus pictured it does not exist. The golden door is not the automatic guarantee of liberty and freedom it seems to be in "The New Colossus." Rather, the door affords those who pass through it the opportunity to build a life where freedom and liberty play an integral part, which is Langston Hughes's argument in "Let America Be America Again." The idea of America as the golden door also fails to mention the costs of assimilation for immigrants, described in "The Latin Deli" and "Immigrants." The subjects in these poems experience cultural alienation as a result of their seeking refuge in America. I would say, then, that America is a haven, but not the golden haven of Lazarus's poem. Its refuge is imperfect and comes at a high price.

But I think perhaps the most compelling insight into the whole "golden door" concept -- whether it exists or not as Lazarus describes it in "The New Colossus" and what the costs are of coming to America because of the door -- is in the photo "Playground in Tenement Alley, Boston" by Lewis W. Hine. The photo is of a group of children playing baseball between two tenement houses in Boston, perhaps in the late nineteenth or early twentieth century. Their playing field is small and cramped, their bleachers are parked wagons, and laundry hangs low overhead. An alley between two apartments is clearly not the ideal place for playing baseball. However, these kids are making the best of their situation. Perhaps at one point they had greater expectations for a baseball field, but they are working hard to still have a good time and succeed at their game. To me this photo is a metaphor for how the golden door ideal relates to America: America is certainly not the perfect haven Lazarus makes it out to be in "The New Colossus." Disillusionment, hardship, and loss cloud this pristine image, but America's true golden opportunity is that liberty can be found. America can be a haven, if only people are willing to work and sacrifice for it.

Questions

1. Maddie poses a question instead of writing a traditional thesis statement. Do you find this an effective strategy? Recraft the question as a declarative sentence, and discuss the difference in impact.
2. Paragraphs 2 and 3 center on the Langston Hughes poem. Does the poem take over, or is Maddie's interpretation controlling the discussion? Explain with specific references to the essay. Would a single paragraph have been more effective than the two? Explain why or why not.
3. Do you agree with the interpretations of the three poems? Explain any points of departure you have.
4. Overall, how do the quotations strengthen the essay? Are there places where there are too many or too few quotes? Be specific in your response.
5. Could the essay have ended with the next-to-last paragraph? What does the final paragraph add? Why do you think it is or is not a better conclusion?
6. Try rewriting one of the paragraphs entirely in the third person. What effect does that revision have? Explain why you do or do not think Maddie made the right choice to use first person throughout the essay.

• ACTIVITY •

1. Write your own essay in response to the prompt in this Conversation:

   > In "The New Colossus," Emma Lazarus welcomes those seeking freedom and opportunity to come through "the golden door" of America. Has the United States lived up to this promise? Discuss by referring to a minimum of four texts.

   Use a longer work (a novel, novella, or play) that you have read as one of the texts you discuss.

2. Find several additional texts to add to this Conversation, and explain what you think they add to the mix. Consider feature or documentary films as possibilities, as well as online sources. Try to find pieces that offer different perspectives from those already represented in this Conversation.

Home and Family

Happy families are all alike; every unhappy family is unhappy in its own way.

—Leo Tolstoy, *Anna Karenina*

What makes a house a home? "Home" suggests sanctuary, loved ones, nourishment—a place where everybody knows your name. The term is woven deep into our language as well as our consciousness. Consider the connotations of *homemade* and *homespun*. Home can offer refuge from the hostile world, or it can be a prison. People living together inevitably—sometimes intentionally—rub one another the wrong way. This chafing provides writers with rich material for art. (Remember, without conflict there is no story.) Are these writers working through their own failed relationships with mothers, fathers, and siblings? Sometimes. Are they exploring their conflicted feelings toward a home they left behind? Maybe. Are they holding up a mirror that allows us to see our own homes and families in a new light? Most certainly.

Though the trappings of home and family differ across cultures, human families have much in common. Legend has it that a man from Czechoslovakia, after watching a production of August Wilson's *Fences* set in Pittsburgh in the 1950s, approached the playwright and asked him, "How did you know about my family?" Wilson may not have known that particular man's family, but he knew about families and how the sins of the father play out in the lives of sons.

The readings in this chapter explore the theme of home and family within a broad range of contexts. In "The Dead," James Joyce uses the occasion of a family Christmas party in Dublin as the setting for his protagonist's reflections on the power of home and family as well as the power of the dead to influence the living. Sylvia Plath reflects on this theme in her poem "Daddy," comparing her relationship with her father to a "black shoe / In which I have lived like a foot / For thirty years, poor and white, / Barely daring to breathe or Achoo." In Langston Hughes's poem "Mother to Son," the speaker uses her own suffering as an example to chide her son, "So boy, don't you turn back. / Don't you set down on the steps / 'Cause you finds it's kinder hard." And the Conversation on The Lure and Language of Food explores the many ways that food and family intertwine. Whether food symbolizes shared values or conflicting ones, brings back memories of people or places that define home, or suggests new ways to think about the meaning of *hunger* and *appetite*, these selections invite you to consider the role that food plays in your own family relationships. Let the literature on the following pages take you into other homes and families so that you can return to your own with new eyes.

The Dead

JAMES JOYCE

James Augustine Aloysius Joyce (1882–1941) was born near Dublin, Ireland. Although Joyce's work is inextricably connected to Ireland, and nearly all of it takes place in Dublin, he lived in Italy and France for most of his adult life. His short stories and novels reflect his inner turmoil about both his native country and the Roman Catholic Church in which he was raised.

Joyce used stream of consciousness; an onslaught of tiny details; and both accessible and obscure allusions to literature, history, and politics to create the recognizable world of his fiction, but as he told a friend, "the ideas are always simple." His most famous works—*Dubliners* (1914), *Portrait of the Artist as a Young Man* (1916), *Ulysses* (1922), and even *Finnegans Wake* (1939)—tell us what it means to be a father, a son, a husband, a writer. "The Dead" is the last story in *Dubliners*, a collection about life in Dublin that captures both the city's romance and its monotony. Joyce once said, "When you remember that Dublin has been a capital for thousands of years, that it is the 'second' city of the British Empire, that it is nearly three times as big as Venice, it seems strange that no artist has given it to the world." "The Dead" was written while Joyce and his wife, Nora, lived in Rome, and according to biographer Brenda Maddox, "Out of their hunger and homesickness came the richly laden Christmas table of 'The Dead.'" With its joyful lyricism and melancholy ending, many consider "The Dead" Joyce's greatest accomplishment.

Lily, the caretaker's daughter, was literally run off her feet. Hardly had she brought one gentleman into the little pantry behind the office on the ground floor and helped him off with his overcoat than the wheezy hall-door bell clanged again and she had to scamper along the bare hallway to let in another guest. It was well for her she had not to attend to the ladies also. But Miss Kate and Miss Julia had thought of that and had converted the bathroom upstairs into a ladies' dressing-room. Miss Kate and Miss Julia were there, gossiping and laughing and fussing, walking after each other to the head of the stairs, peering down over the banisters and calling down to Lily to ask her who had come.

It was always a great affair, the Misses Morkan's annual dance. Everybody who knew them came to it, members of the family, old friends of the family, the members of Julia's choir, any of Kate's pupils that were grown up enough and even some of Mary Jane's pupils too. Never once had it fallen flat. For years and years it had gone off in splendid style as long as anyone could remember; ever since Kate and Julia, after the death of their brother Pat, had left the house in Stoney Batter and taken Mary Jane, their only niece, to live with them in the dark gaunt house on Usher's Island, the upper part of which they had rented from Mr Fulham, the cornfactor on the ground floor. That was a good thirty years ago if it was a day. Mary Jane, who was then a little girl in short clothes, was now the main prop of the household, for she had the organ in Haddington Road. She had been through the Academy and gave a pupils' concert every year in the upper room of the Ancient Concert Rooms. Many of her pupils belonged to the better-class families on the Kingstown and Dalkey line. Old as they were, her aunts also did their share. Julia, though she was quite grey, was still the leading soprano in Adam and Eve's[1], and Kate, being too feeble to go about much, gave music lessons to beginners on the old square piano in the back room. Lily, the caretaker's daughter, did housemaid's work for them. Though their life was modest they believed in eating well; the best of everything: diamond-bone sirloins, three-shilling tea and the best bottled stout. But Lily seldom made a mistake in the orders so that she got on well with her three mistresses. They were fussy, that was all. But the only thing they would not stand was back answers.

Of course they had good reason to be fussy on such a night. And then it was long after ten o'clock and yet there was no sign of Gabriel and his wife. Besides they were dreadfully afraid that Freddy Malins might turn up screwed. They would not wish for worlds that any of Mary Jane's pupils should see him under the influence; and when he was like that it was sometimes very hard to manage him. Freddy Malins always came late but they wondered what could be keeping Gabriel: and that was what brought them every two minutes to the banisters to ask Lily had Gabriel or Freddy come.

—O, Mr Conroy, said Lily to Gabriel when she opened the door for him, Miss Kate and Miss Julia thought you were never coming. Good-night, Mrs Conroy.

—I'll engage they did, said Gabriel, but they forget that my wife here takes three   5
mortal hours to dress herself.

He stood on the mat, scraping the snow from his goloshes, while Lily led his wife to the foot of the stairs and called out:

—Miss Kate, here's Mrs Conroy.

Kate and Julia came toddling down the dark stairs at once. Both of them kissed Gabriel's wife, said she must be perished alive and asked was Gabriel with her.

—Here I am as right as the mail, Aunt Kate! Go on up. I'll follow, called out Gabriel from the dark.

He continued scraping his feet vigorously while the three women went upstairs,   10
laughing, to the ladies' dressing-room. A light fringe of snow lay like a cape on the shoulders of his overcoat and like toecaps on the toes of his goloshes; and, as the buttons of his overcoat slipped with a squeaking noise through the snow-stiffened frieze, a cold fragrant air from out-of-doors escaped from crevices and folds.

—Is it snowing again, Mr Conroy? asked Lily.

She had preceded him into the pantry to help him off with his overcoat. Gabriel smiled at the three syllables she had given his surname and glanced at her. She was a slim, growing girl, pale in complexion and with hay-coloured hair. The gas in the

---

[1] Commonly-used name for the Church of the Immaculate Conception in Merchant's Quay, Dublin, a Roman Catholic church that is run by the Franciscans.—EDS.

pantry made her look still paler. Gabriel had known her when she was a child and used to sit on the lowest step nursing a rag doll.

—Yes, Lily, he answered, and I think we're in for a night of it.

He looked up at the pantry ceiling, which was shaking with the stamping and shuffling of feet on the floor above, listened for a moment to the piano and then glanced at the girl, who was folding his overcoat carefully at the end of a shelf.

—Tell me, Lily, he said in a friendly tone, do you still go to school?   15

—O no, sir, she answered. I'm done schooling this year and more.

—O, then, said Gabriel gaily, I suppose we'll be going to your wedding one of these fine days with your young man, eh?

The girl glanced back at him over her shoulder and said with great bitterness:

—The men that is now is only all palaver and what they can get out of you.

Gabriel coloured as if he felt he had made a mistake and, without looking at   20
her, kicked off his goloshes and flicked actively with his muffler at his patent-leather shoes.

He was a stout tallish young man. The high colour of his cheeks pushed upwards even to his forehead where it scattered itself in a few formless patches of pale red; and on his hairless face there scintillated restlessly the polished lenses and the bright gilt rims of the glasses which screened his delicate and restless eyes. His glossy black hair was parted in the middle and brushed in a long curve behind his ears where it curled slightly beneath the groove left by his hat.

When he had flicked lustre into his shoes he stood up and pulled his waistcoat down more tightly on his plump body. Then he took a coin rapidly from his pocket.

—O Lily, he said, thrusting it into her hands, it's Christmas-time, isn't it? Just . . . here's a little . . . .

He walked rapidly towards the door.

—O no, sir! cried the girl, following him. Really, sir, I wouldn't take it.   25

—Christmas-time! Christmas-time! said Gabriel, almost trotting to the stairs and waving his hand to her in deprecation.

The girl, seeing that he had gained the stairs, called out after him:

—Well, thank you, sir.

He waited outside the drawing-room door until the waltz should finish, listening to the skirts that swept against it and to the shuffling of feet. He was still discomposed by the girl's bitter and sudden retort. It had cast a gloom over him which he tried to dispel by arranging his cuffs and the bows of his tie. Then he took from his waistcoat pocket a little paper and glanced at the headings he had made for his speech. He was undecided about the lines from Robert Browning for he feared they would be above the heads of his hearers. Some quotation that they could recognise from Shakespeare or from the Melodies would be better. The indelicate clacking of the men's heels and the shuffling of their soles reminded him that their grade of culture differed from his. He would only make himself ridiculous by quoting poetry to them which they could not understand. They would think that he was airing his superior education. He would fail with them just as he had failed with the girl in the pantry. He had taken up a wrong tone. His whole speech was a mistake from first to last, an utter failure.

Just then his aunts and his wife came out of the ladies' dressing-room. His 30
aunts were two small plainly dressed old women. Aunt Julia was an inch or so the
taller. Her hair, drawn low over the tops of her ears, was grey; and grey also, with
darker shadows, was her large flaccid face. Though she was stout in build and stood
erect her slow eyes and parted lips gave her the appearance of a woman who did not
know where she was or where she was going. Aunt Kate was more vivacious. Her face,
healthier than her sister's, was all puckers and creases, like a shrivelled red apple, and
her hair, braided in the same old-fashioned way, had not lost its ripe nut colour.

They both kissed Gabriel frankly. He was their favourite nephew, the son of their
dead elder sister, Ellen, who had married T. J. Conroy of the Port and Docks.

—Gretta tells me you're not going to take a cab back to Monkstown to-night,
Gabriel, said Aunt Kate.

—No, said Gabriel, turning to his wife, we had quite enough of that last year,
hadn't we? Don't you remember, Aunt Kate, what a cold Gretta got out of it? Cab
windows rattling all the way, and the east wind blowing in after we passed Merrion.
Very jolly it was. Gretta caught a dreadful cold.

Aunt Kate frowned severely and nodded her head at every word.

—Quite right, Gabriel, quite right, she said. You can't be too careful. 35

—But as for Gretta there, said Gabriel, she'd walk home in the snow if she were let.

Mrs Conroy laughed.

—Don't mind him, Aunt Kate, she said. He's really an awful bother, what with
green shades for Tom's eyes at night and making him do the dumb-bells, and forcing
Eva to eat the stirabout.² The poor child! And she simply hates the sight of it! . . . O,
but you'll never guess what he makes me wear now!

She broke out into a peal of laughter and glanced at her husband, whose admiring and happy eyes had been wandering from her dress to her face and hair. The two
aunts laughed heartily too, for Gabriel's solicitude was a standing joke with them.

—Goloshes! said Mrs Conroy. That's the latest. Whenever it's wet underfoot 40
I must put on my goloshes. To-night even he wanted me to put them on, but I
wouldn't. The next thing he'll buy me will be a diving suit.

Gabriel laughed nervously and patted his tie reassuringly while Aunt Kate nearly
doubled herself, so heartily did she enjoy the joke. The smile soon faded from Aunt
Julia's face and her mirthless eyes were directed towards her nephew's face. After a
pause she asked:

—And what are goloshes, Gabriel?

—Goloshes, Julia! exclaimed her sister. Goodness me, don't you know what
goloshes are? You wear them over your . . . over your boots, Gretta, isn't it?

—Yes, said Mrs Conroy. Guttapercha things. We both have a pair now. Gabriel
says everyone wears them on the continent.

—O, on the continent, murmured Aunt Julia, nodding her head slowly. 45

Gabriel knitted his brows and said, as if he were slightly angered:

—It's nothing very wonderful but Gretta thinks it very funny because she says
the word reminds her of Christy Minstrels.

---

²Porridge.—Eds.

—But tell me, Gabriel, said Aunt Kate, with brisk tact. Of course, you've seen about the room. Gretta was saying . . .

—O, the room is all right, replied Gabriel. I've taken one in the Gresham.

—To be sure, said Aunt Kate, by far the best thing to do. And the children, 50 Gretta, you're not anxious about them?

—O, for one night, said Mrs Conroy. Besides, Bessie will look after them.

—To be sure, said Aunt Kate again. What a comfort it is to have a girl like that, one you can depend on! There's that Lily, I'm sure I don't know what has come over her lately. She's not the girl she was at all.

Gabriel was about to ask his aunt some questions on this point but she broke off suddenly to gaze after her sister who had wandered down the stairs and was craning her neck over the banisters.

—Now, I ask you, she said, almost testily, where is Julia going? Julia! Julia! Where are you going?

Julia, who had gone halfway down one flight, came back and announced 55 blandly:

—Here's Freddy.

At the same moment a clapping of hands and a final flourish of the pianist told that the waltz had ended. The drawing-room door was opened from within and some couples came out. Aunt Kate drew Gabriel aside hurriedly and whispered into his ear:

—Slip down, Gabriel, like a good fellow and see if he's all right, and don't let him up if he's screwed. I'm sure he's screwed. I'm sure he is.

Gabriel went to the stairs and listened over the banisters. He could hear two persons talking in the pantry. Then he recognized Freddy Malins' laugh. He went down the stairs noisily.

—It's such a relief, said Aunt Kate to Mrs Conroy, that Gabriel is here. I always 60 feel easier in my mind when he's here. . . . Julia, there's Miss Daly and Miss Power will take some refreshment. Thanks for your beautiful waltz, Miss Daly. It made lovely time.

A tall wizen-faced man, with a stiff grizzled moustache and swarthy skin, who was passing out with his partner said:

—And may we have some refreshment, too, Miss Morkan?

—Julia, said Aunt Kate summarily, and here's Mr Browne and Miss Furlong. Take them in, Julia, with Miss Daly and Miss Power.

—I'm the man for the ladies, said Mr Browne, pursing his lips until his moustache bristled and smiling in all his wrinkles. You know, Miss Morkan, the reason they are so fond of me is—

He did not finish his sentence, but, seeing that Aunt Kate was out of earshot, 65 at once led the three young ladies into the back room. The middle of the room was occupied by two square tables placed end to end, and on these Aunt Julia and the caretaker were straightening and smoothing a large cloth. On the sideboard were arrayed dishes and plates, and glasses and bundles of knives and forks and spoons. The top of the closed square piano served also as a sideboard for viands and sweets. At a smaller sideboard in one corner two young men were standing, drinking hop-bitters.

Mr Browne led his charges thither and invited them all, in jest, to some ladies' punch, hot, strong and sweet. As they said they never took anything strong he opened three bottles of lemonade for them. Then he asked one of the young men to move aside, and, taking hold of the decanter, filled out for himself a goodly measure of whisky. The young men eyed him respectfully while he took a trial sip.

—God help me, he said, smiling, it's the doctor's orders.

His wizened face broke into a broader smile, and the three young ladies laughed in musical echo to his pleasantry, swaying their bodies to and fro, with nervous jerks of their shoulders. The boldest said:

—O, now, Mr Browne, I'm sure the doctor never ordered anything of the kind.

Mr Browne took another sip of his whisky and said, with sidling mimicry: 70

—Well, you see, I'm like the famous Mrs Cassidy, who is reported to have said: *Now, Mary Grimes, if I don't take it, make me take it, for I feel I want it.*

His hot face had leaned forward a little too confidentially and he had assumed a very low Dublin accent so that the young ladies, with one instinct, received his speech in silence. Miss Furlong, who was one of Mary Jane's pupils, asked Miss Daly what was the name of the pretty waltz she had played; and Mr Browne, seeing that he was ignored, turned promptly to the two young men who were more appreciative.

A red-faced young woman, dressed in pansy, came into the room, excitedly clapping her hands and crying:

—Quadrilles! Quadrilles!

Close on her heels came Aunt Kate, crying: 75

—Two gentlemen and three ladies, Mary Jane!

—O, here's Mr Bergin and Mr Kerrigan, said Mary Jane. Mr Kerrigan, will you take Miss Power? Miss Furlong, may I get you a partner, Mr Bergin. O, that'll just do now.

—Three ladies, Mary Jane, said Aunt Kate.

The two young gentlemen asked the ladies if they might have the pleasure, and Mary Jane turned to Miss Daly.

—O, Miss Daly, you're really awfully good, after playing for the last two dances,   80 but really we're so short of ladies to-night.

—I don't mind in the least, Miss Morkan.

—But I've a nice partner for you, Mr Bartell D'Arcy, the tenor. I'll get him to sing later on. All Dublin is raving about him.

—Lovely voice, lovely voice! said Aunt Kate.

As the piano had twice begun the prelude to the first figure Mary Jane led her recruits quickly from the room. They had hardly gone when Aunt Julia wandered slowly into the room, looking behind her at something.

—What is the matter, Julia? asked Aunt Kate anxiously. Who is it?   85

Julia, who was carrying in a column of table-napkins, turned to her sister and said, simply, as if the question had surprised her:

—It's only Freddy, Kate, and Gabriel with him.

In fact right behind her Gabriel could be seen piloting Freddy Malins across the landing. The latter, a young man of about forty, was of Gabriel's size and build, with very round shoulders. His face was fleshy and pallid, touched with colour only at the thick hanging lobes of his ears and at the wide wings of his nose. He had coarse features, a blunt nose, a convex and receding brow, tumid and protruded lips. His heavy-lidded eyes and the disorder of his scanty hair made him look sleepy. He was laughing heartily in a high key at a story which he had been telling Gabriel on the stairs and at the same time rubbing the knuckles of his left fist backwards and forwards into his left eye.

—Good-evening, Freddy, said Aunt Julia.

Freddy Malins bade the Misses Morkan good-evening in what seemed an offhand   90
fashion by reason of the habitual catch in his voice and then, seeing that Mr Browne was grinning at him from the sideboard, crossed the room on rather shaky legs and began to repeat in an undertone the story he had just told to Gabriel.

—He's not so bad, is he? said Aunt Kate to Gabriel.

Gabriel's brows were dark, but he raised them quickly and answered:

—O no, hardly noticeable.

—Now, isn't he a terrible fellow! she said. And his poor mother made him take the pledge on New Year's Eve. But come on, Gabriel, into the drawing-room.

Before leaving the room with Gabriel she signalled to Mr Browne by frowning   95
and shaking her forefinger in warning to and fro. Mr Browne nodded in answer and, when she had gone, said to Freddy Malins:

—Now, then, Teddy, I'm going to fill you out a good glass of lemonade just to buck you up.

Freddy Malins, who was nearing the climax of his story, waved the offer aside impatiently but Mr Browne, having first called Freddy Malins' attention to a disarray in his dress, filled out and handed him a full glass of lemonade. Freddy Malins' left hand accepted the glass mechanically, his right hand being engaged in the mechanical readjustment of his dress. Mr Browne, whose face was once more wrinkling with mirth, poured out for himself a glass of whisky while Freddy Malins exploded, before he had well reached the climax of his story, in a kink of high-pitched bronchitic laughter and, setting down his untasted and overflowing glass, began to rub the knuckles of his left fist backwards and forwards into his left eye, repeating words of his last phrase as well as his fit of laughter would allow him.

· · · · · · · · · · ·

Gabriel could not listen while Mary Jane was playing her Academy piece, full of runs and difficult passages, to the hushed drawing-room. He liked music but the piece she was playing had no melody for him and he doubted whether it had any melody for the other listeners, though they had begged Mary Jane to play something. Four young men, who had come from the refreshment-room to stand in the doorway at the sound of the piano, had gone away quietly in couples after a few minutes. The only persons who seemed to follow the music were Mary Jane herself, her hands racing along the key-board or lifted from it at the pauses like those of a priestess in momentary imprecation, and Aunt Kate standing at her elbow to turn the page.

Gabriel's eyes, irritated by the floor, which glittered with beeswax under the heavy chandelier, wandered to the wall above the piano. A picture of the balcony scene in

Romeo and Juliet hung there and beside it was a picture of the two murdered princes in the Tower which Aunt Julia had worked in red, blue and brown wools when she was a girl. Probably in the school they had gone to as girls that kind of work had been taught, for one year his mother had worked for him as a birthday present a waistcoat of purple tabinet, with little foxes' heads upon it, lined with brown satin and having round mulberry buttons. It was strange that his mother had had no musical talent though Aunt Kate used to call her the brains carrier of the Morkan family. Both she and Julia had always seemed a little proud of their serious and matronly sister. Her photograph stood before the pierglass. She had an open book on her knees and was pointing out something in it to Constantine who, dressed in a man-o'-war suit, lay at her feet. It was she who had chosen the names of her sons for she was very sensible of the dignity of family life. Thanks to her, Constantine was now senior curate in Balbriggan and, thanks to her, Gabriel himself had taken his degree in the Royal University. A shadow passed over his face as he remembered her sullen opposition to his marriage. Some slighting phrases she had used still rankled in his memory; she had once spoken of Gretta as being country cute and that was not true of Gretta at all. It was Gretta who had nursed her during all her last long illness in their house at Monkstown.

He knew that Mary Jane must be near the end of her piece, for she was playing again the opening melody with runs of scales after every bar and while he waited for the end the resentment died down in his heart. The piece ended with a trill of octaves in the treble and a final deep octave in the bass. Great applause greeted Mary Jane as, blushing and rolling up her music nervously, she escaped from the room. The most vigorous clapping came from the four young men in the doorway who had gone away to the refreshment-room at the beginning of the piece but had come back when the piano had stopped.

Lancers were arranged. Gabriel found himself partnered with Miss Ivors. She was a frank-mannered, talkative young lady, with a freckled face and prominent brown eyes. She did not wear a low-cut bodice and the large brooch which was fixed in the front of her collar bore on it an Irish device.

When they had taken their places she said abruptly:

—I have a crow to pluck with you.

—With me? said Gabriel.

She nodded her head gravely.

—What is it? asked Gabriel, smiling at her solemn manner.

—Who is G. C.? answered Miss Ivors, turning her eyes upon him.

Gabriel coloured and was about to knit his brows, as if he did not understand, when she said bluntly:

—O, innocent Amy! I have found out that you write for *The Daily Express*. Now, aren't you ashamed of yourself?

—Why should I be ashamed of myself? asked Gabriel, blinking his eyes and trying to smile.

—Well, I'm ashamed of you, said Miss Ivors frankly. To say you'd write for a rag like that. I didn't think you were a West Briton.[3]

---

[3]West British, a native of Ireland, but sympathetic to England. —EDS.

100

105

110

A look of perplexity appeared on Gabriel's face. It was true that he wrote a literary column every Wednesday in *The Daily Express*, for which he was paid fifteen shillings. But that did not make him a West Briton surely. The books he received for review were almost more welcome than the paltry cheque. He loved to feel the covers and turn over the pages of newly printed books. Nearly every day when his teaching in the college was ended he used to wander down the quays to the second-hand booksellers, to Hickey's on Bachelor's Walk, to Webb's or Massey's on Aston's Quay, or to O'Clohissey's in the by-street. He did not know how to meet her charge. He wanted to say that literature was above politics. But they were friends of many years' standing and their careers had been parallel, first at the University and then as teachers: he could not risk a grandiose phrase with her. He continued blinking his eyes and trying to smile and murmured lamely that he saw nothing political in writing reviews of books.

When their turn to cross had come he was still perplexed and inattentive. Miss Ivors promptly took his hand in a warm grasp and said in a soft friendly tone:

—Of course, I was only joking. Come, we cross now.

When they were together again she spoke of the University question[4] and Gabriel felt   115
more at ease. A friend of hers had shown her his review of Browning's poems. That was how she had found out the secret: but she liked the review immensely. Then she said suddenly:

—O, Mr Conroy, will you come for an excursion to the Aran Isles this summer? We're going to stay there a whole month. It will be splendid out in the Atlantic. You ought to come. Mr Clancy is coming, and Mr Kilkelly and Kathleen Kearney. It would be splendid for Gretta too if she'd come. She's from Connacht, isn't she?

—Her people are, said Gabriel shortly.

—But you will come, won't you? said Miss Ivors, laying her warm hand eagerly on his arm.

—The fact is, said Gabriel, I have just arranged to go—

—Go where? asked Miss Ivors.   120

—Well, you know, every year I go for a cycling tour with some fellows and so—

—But where? asked Miss Ivors.

—Well, we usually go to France or Belgium or perhaps Germany, said Gabriel awkwardly.

—And why do you go to France and Belgium, said Miss Ivors, instead of visiting your own land?

—Well, said Gabriel, it's partly to keep in touch with the languages and partly   125
for a change.

—And haven't you your own language to keep in touch with—Irish? asked Miss Ivors.

—Well, said Gabriel, if it comes to that, you know, Irish is not my language.

Their neighbours had turned to listen to the cross-examination. Gabriel glanced right and left nervously and tried to keep his good humour under the ordeal which was making a blush invade his forehead.

—And haven't you your own land to visit, continued Miss Ivors, that you know nothing of, your own people, and your own country?

---

[4]The question of providing an adequate higher education to Catholics in Ireland, given that Trinity College required Protestant exams to be passed.—Eds.

—O, to tell you the truth, retorted Gabriel suddenly, I'm sick of my own coun- 130
try, sick of it!

—Why? asked Miss Ivors.

Gabriel did not answer, for his retort had heated him.

—Why? repeated Miss Ivors.

They had to go visiting together and, as he had not answered her, Miss Ivors said
warmly:

—Of course, you've no answer. 135

Gabriel tried to cover his agitation by taking part in the dance with great
energy. He avoided her eyes, for he had seen a sour expression on her face. But
when they met in the long chain he was surprised to feel his hand firmly pressed.
She looked at him from under her brows for a moment quizzically until he smiled.
Then, just as the chain was about to start again, she stood on tiptoe and whispered
into his ear:

—West Briton!

When the lancers were over Gabriel went away to a remote corner of the
room where Freddy Malins' mother was sitting. She was a stout, feeble old
woman with white hair. Her voice had a catch in it like her son's and she stut-
tered slightly. She had been told that Freddy had come and that he was nearly
all right. Gabriel asked her whether she had had a good crossing. She lived with
her married daughter in Glasgow and came to Dublin on a visit once a year. She
answered placidly that she had had a beautiful crossing and that the captain had
been most attentive to her. She spoke also of the beautiful house her daughter
kept in Glasgow, and of all the friends they had there. While her tongue rambled
on Gabriel tried to banish from his mind all memory of the unpleasant incident
with Miss Ivors. Of course the girl or woman, or whatever she was, was an enthusiast, but there was a time for all things. Perhaps he ought not to have answered
her like that. But she had no right to call him a West Briton before people, even
in joke. She had tried to make him ridiculous before people, heckling him and
staring at him with her rabbit's eyes.

He saw his wife making her way towards him through the waltzing couples.
When she reached him she said into his ear:

—Gabriel, Aunt Kate wants to know won't you carve the goose as usual. Miss 140
Daly will carve the ham and I'll do the pudding.

—All right, said Gabriel.

—She's sending in the younger ones first as soon as this waltz is over so that we'll
have the table to ourselves.

—Were you dancing? asked Gabriel.

—Of course I was. Didn't you see me? What words had you with Molly Ivors?

—No words. Why? Did she say so? 145

—Something like that. I'm trying to get that Mr D'Arcy to sing. He's full of
conceit, I think.

—There were no words, said Gabriel moodily, only she wanted me to go for a
trip to the west of Ireland and I said I wouldn't.

His wife clasped her hands excitedly and gave a little jump.

—O, do go, Gabriel, she cried. I'd love to see Galway again.

—You can go if you like, said Gabriel coldly.   150

She looked at him for a moment, then turned to Mrs Malins and said:

—There's a nice husband for you, Mrs Malins.

While she was threading her way back across the room Mrs Malins, without adverting to the interruption, went on to tell Gabriel what beautiful places there were in Scotland and beautiful scenery. Her son-in-law brought them every year to the lakes and they used to go fishing. Her son-in-law was a splendid fisher. One day he caught a fish, a beautiful big big fish, and the man in the hotel boiled it for their dinner.

Gabriel hardly heard what she said. Now that supper was coming near he began to think again about his speech and about the quotation. When he saw Freddy Malins coming across the room to visit his mother Gabriel left the chair free for him and retired into the embrasure of the window. The room had already cleared and from the back room came the clatter of plates and knives. Those who still remained in the drawing-room seemed tired of dancing and were conversing quietly in little groups. Gabriel's warm, trembling fingers tapped the cold pane of the window. How cool it must be outside! How pleasant it would be to walk out alone, first along by the river and then through the park! The snow would be lying on the branches of the trees and forming a bright cap on the top of the Wellington Monument. How much more pleasant it would be there than at the supper-table!

He ran over the headings of his speech: Irish hospitality, sad memories, the   155
Three Graces, Paris, the quotation from Browning. He repeated to himself a phrase he had written in his review: *One feels that one is listening to a thought-tormented music*. Miss Ivors had praised the review. Was she sincere? Had she really any life of her own behind all her propagandism? There had never been any ill-feeling between them until that night. It unnerved him to think that she would be at the supper-table, looking up at him while he spoke with her critical quizzing eyes. Perhaps she would not be sorry to see him fail in his speech. An idea came into his mind and gave him courage. He would say, alluding to Aunt Kate and Aunt Julia: *Ladies and Gentlemen, the generation which is now on the wane among us may have had its faults but for my part I think it had certain qualities of hospitality, of humour, of humanity, which the new and very serious and hypereducated generation that is growing up around us seems to me to lack*. Very good: that was one for Miss Ivors. What did he care that his aunts were only two ignorant old women?

A murmur in the room attracted his attention. Mr Browne was advancing from the door, gallantly escorting Aunt Julia, who leaned upon his arm, smiling and hanging her head. An irregular musketry of applause escorted her also as far as the piano and then, as Mary Jane seated herself on the stool, and Aunt Julia, no longer smiling, half turned so as to pitch her voice fairly into the room, gradually ceased. Gabriel recognized the prelude. It was that of an old song of Aunt Julia's—*Arrayed for the Bridal*. Her voice, strong and clear in tone, attacked with great spirit the runs which embellish the air and though she sang very rapidly she did not miss even the smallest of the grace notes. To follow the voice, without looking at the singer's face, was to feel and share the excitement of swift and secure flight. Gabriel applauded loudly with all the others at the close of the song and loud applause was borne in from the invisible supper-table.

It sounded so genuine that a little colour struggled into Aunt Julia's face as she bent to replace in the music-stand the old leather-bound song-book that had her initials on the cover. Freddy Malins, who had listened with his head perched sideways to hear her better, was still applauding when everyone else had ceased and talking animatedly to his mother who nodded her head gravely and slowly in acquiescence. At last, when he could clap no more, he stood up suddenly and hurried across the room to Aunt Julia whose hand he seized and held in both his hands, shaking it when words failed him or the catch in his voice proved too much for him.

—I was just telling my mother, he said, I never heard you sing so well, never. No, I never heard your voice so good as it is tonight. Now! Would you believe that now? That's the truth. Upon my word and honour that's the truth. I never heard your voice sound so fresh and so . . . so clear and fresh, never.

Aunt Julia smiled broadly and murmured something about compliments as she released her hand from his grasp. Mr Browne extended his open hand towards her and said to those who were near him in the manner of a showman introducing a prodigy to an audience:

—Miss Julia Morkan, my latest discovery!

He was laughing very heartily at this himself when Freddy Malins turned to him   160
and said:

—Well, Browne, if you're serious you might make a worse discovery. All I can say is I never heard her sing half so well as long as I am coming here. And that's the honest truth.

—Neither did I, said Mr Browne. I think her voice has greatly improved.

Aunt Julia shrugged her shoulders and said with meek pride:

—Thirty years ago I hadn't a bad voice as voices go.

—I often told Julia, said Aunt Kate emphatically, that she was simply thrown   165
away in that choir. But she never would be said by me.

She turned as if to appeal to the good sense of the others against a refractory child while Aunt Julia gazed in front of her, a vague smile of reminiscence playing on her face.

—No, continued Aunt Kate, she wouldn't be said or led by anyone, slaving there in that choir night and day, night and day. Six o'clock on Christmas morning! And all for what?

—Well, isn't it for the honour of God, Aunt Kate? asked Mary Jane, twisting round on the piano-stool and smiling.

Aunt Kate turned fiercely on her niece and said:

—I know all about the honour of God, Mary Jane, but I think it's not at all   170
honourable for the pope to turn out the women out of the choirs that have slaved there all their lives and put little whippersnappers of boys over their heads. I suppose it is for the good of the Church if the pope does it. But it's not just, Mary Jane, and it's not right.

She had worked herself into a passion and would have continued in defence of her sister for it was a sore subject with her but Mary Jane, seeing that all the dancers had come back, intervened pacifically:

—Now, Aunt Kate, you're giving scandal to Mr Browne who is of the other persuasion.

Aunt Kate turned to Mr Browne, who was grinning at this allusion to his religion, and said hastily:

—O, I don't question the pope's being right. I'm only a stupid old woman and I wouldn't presume to do such a thing. But there's such a thing as common everyday politeness and gratitude. And if I were in Julia's place I'd tell that Father Healy straight up to his face . . .

—And besides, Aunt Kate, said Mary Jane, we really are all hungry and when we   175
are hungry we are all very quarrelsome.

—And when we are thirsty we are also quarrelsome, added Mr Browne.

—So that we had better go to supper, said Mary Jane, and finish the discussion afterwards.

On the landing outside the drawing-room Gabriel found his wife and Mary Jane trying to persuade Miss Ivors to stay for supper. But Miss Ivors, who had put on her hat and was buttoning her cloak, would not stay. She did not feel in the least hungry and she had already overstayed her time.

—But only for ten minutes, Molly, said Mrs Conroy. That won't delay you.

—To take a pick itself, said Mary Jane, after all your dancing.   180

—I really couldn't, said Miss Ivors.

—I am afraid you didn't enjoy yourself at all, said Mary Jane hopelessly.

—Ever so much, I assure you, said Miss Ivors, but you really must let me run off now.

—But how can you get home? asked Mrs Conroy.

—O, it's only two steps up the quay.   185

Gabriel hesitated a moment and said:

—If you will allow me, Miss Ivors, I'll see you home if you really are obliged to go.

But Miss Ivors broke away from them.

—I won't hear of it, she cried. For goodness sake go in to your suppers and don't mind me. I'm quite well able to take care of myself.

—Well, you're the comical girl, Molly, said Mrs Conroy frankly.   190

—*Beannacht libh*, cried Miss Ivors, with a laugh, as she ran down the staircase.

Mary Jane gazed after her, a moody puzzled expression on her face, while Mrs Conroy leaned over the banisters to listen for the hall-door. Gabriel asked himself was he the cause of her abrupt departure. But she did not seem to be in ill humour: she had gone away laughing. He stared blankly down the staircase.

At that moment Aunt Kate came toddling out of the supper-room, almost wringing her hands in despair.

—Where is Gabriel? she cried. Where on earth is Gabriel? There's everyone waiting in there, stage to let, and nobody to carve the goose!

—Here I am, Aunt Kate! cried Gabriel, with sudden animation, ready to carve a   195
flock of geese, if necessary.

A fat brown goose lay at one end of the table and at the other end, on a bed of creased paper strewn with sprigs of parsley, lay a great ham, stripped of its outer skin and peppered over with crust crumbs, a neat paper frill round its shin and beside this was a round of spiced beef. Between these rival ends ran parallel lines of side-dishes: two little minsters of jelly, red and yellow; a shallow dish full of blocks of blancmange and red jam, a large green leaf-shaped dish with a stalk-shaped handle, on which lay bunches of purple raisins and peeled almonds, a companion dish on which lay a solid rectangle of Smyrna figs, a dish of custard topped with grated nutmeg, a small bowl full of chocolates and sweets wrapped in gold and silver papers and a glass vase in which stood some tall celery stalks. In the centre of the table there stood, as sentries to a fruit-stand which upheld a pyramid of oranges and American apples, two squat old-fashioned decanters of cut glass, one containing port and the other dark sherry. On the closed square piano a pudding in a huge yellow dish lay in waiting, and behind it were three squads of bottles of stout and ale and minerals drawn up according to the colours of their uniforms, the first two black, with brown and red labels, the third and smallest squad white, with transverse green sashes.

Gabriel took his seat boldly at the head of the table and, having looked to the edge of the carver, plunged his fork firmly into the goose. He felt quite at ease now for he was an expert carver and liked nothing better than to find himself at the head of a well-laden table.

—Miss Furlong, what shall I send you? he asked. A wing or a slice of the breast?

—Just a small slice of the breast.

—Miss Higgins, what for you?

—O, anything at all, Mr Conroy.

While Gabriel and Miss Daly exchanged plates of goose and plates of ham and spiced beef Lily went from guest to guest with a dish of hot floury potatoes wrapped in a white napkin. This was Mary Jane's idea and she had also suggested apple sauce for the goose but Aunt Kate had said that plain roast goose without apple sauce had always been good enough for her and she hoped she might never eat worse. Mary Jane waited on her pupils and saw that they got the best slices and Aunt Kate and Aunt Julia opened and carried across from the piano bottles of stout and ale for the gentlemen and bottles of minerals for the ladies. There was a great deal of confusion and laughter and noise, the noise of orders and counter-orders, of knives and forks, of corks and glass-stoppers. Gabriel began to carve second helpings as soon as he had finished the first round without serving himself. Everyone protested loudly, so that he compromised by taking a long draught of stout for he had found the carving hot work. Mary Jane settled down quietly to her supper but Aunt Kate and Aunt Julia were still toddling round the table, walking on each other's heels, getting in each other's way and giving each other unheeded orders. Mr Browne begged of them to sit down and eat their suppers and so did Gabriel but they said there was time enough so that, at last, Freddy Malins stood up and, capturing Aunt Kate, plumped her down on her chair amid general laughter.

When everyone had been well served Gabriel said, smiling:

—Now, if anyone wants a little more of what vulgar people call stuffing let him or her speak.

200

A chorus of voices invited him to begin his own supper and Lily came forward   205
with three potatoes which she had reserved for him.

—Very well, said Gabriel amiably, as he took another preparatory draught,
kindly forget my existence, ladies and gentlemen, for a few minutes.

He set to his supper and took no part in the conversation with which the table
covered Lily's removal of the plates. The subject of talk was the opera company which
was then at the Theatre Royal. Mr Bartell D'Arcy, the tenor, a dark-complexioned
young man with a smart moustache, praised very highly the leading contralto of
the company but Miss Furlong thought she had a rather vulgar style of production.
Freddy Malins said there was a negro chieftain singing in the second part of the
Gaiety pantomime who had one of the finest tenor voices he had ever heard.

—Have you heard him? he asked Mr Bartell D'Arcy across the table.

—No, answered Mr Bartell D'Arcy carelessly.

—Because, Freddy Malins explained, now I'd be curious to hear your opinion of   210
him. I think he has a grand voice.

—It takes Teddy to find out the really good things, said Mr Browne familiarly
to the table.

—And why couldn't he have a voice too? asked Freddy Malins sharply. Is it
because he's only a black?

Nobody answered this question and Mary Jane led the table back to the legitimate opera. One of her pupils had given her a pass for *Mignon*. Of course it was
very fine, she said, but it made her think of poor Georgina Burns. Mr Browne could
go back farther still, to the old Italian companies that used to come to Dublin—
Tietjens, Ilma de Murzka, Campanini, the great Trebelli, Giuglini, Ravelli, Aramburo.
Those were the days, he said, when there was something like singing to be heard in
Dublin. He told too of how the top gallery of the old Royal used to be packed night
after night, of how one night an Italian tenor had sung five encores to *Let Me Like
a Soldier Fall*, introducing a high C every time, and of how the gallery boys would
sometimes in their enthusiasm unyoke the horses from the carriage of some great
prima donna and pull her themselves through the streets to her hotel. Why did they
never play the grand old operas now, he asked, *Dinorah, Lucrezia Borgia*? Because
they could not get the voices to sing them: that was why.

—O, well, said Mr Bartell D'Arcy, I presume there are as good singers to-day as
there were then.

—Where are they? asked Mr Browne defiantly.   215

—In London, Paris, Milan, said Mr Bartell D'Arcy warmly. I suppose Caruso, for
example, is quite as good, if not better than any of the men you have mentioned.

—Maybe so, said Mr Browne. But I may tell you I doubt it strongly.

—O, I'd give anything to hear Caruso sing, said Mary Jane.

—For me, said Aunt Kate, who had been picking a bone, there was only one
tenor. To please me, I mean. But I suppose none of you ever heard of him.

—Who was he, Miss Morkan? asked Mr Bartell D'Arcy politely.   220

—His name, said Aunt Kate, was Parkinson. I heard him when he was in his prime
and I think he had then the purest tenor voice that was ever put into a man's throat.

—Strange, said Mr Bartell D'Arcy. I never even heard of him.

—Yes, yes, Miss Morkan is right, said Mr Browne. I remember hearing of old Parkinson, but he's too far back for me.

—A beautiful pure sweet mellow English tenor, said Aunt Kate with enthusiasm.

Gabriel having finished, the huge pudding was transferred to the table. The 225 clatter of forks and spoons began again. Gabriel's wife served out spoonfuls of the pudding and passed the plates down the table. Midway down they were held up by Mary Jane, who replenished them with raspberry or orange jelly or with blancmange and jam. The pudding was of Aunt Julia's making and she received praises for it from all quarters. She herself said that it was not quite brown enough.

—Well, I hope, Miss Morkan, said Mr Browne, that I'm brown enough for you because, you know, I'm all brown.

All the gentlemen, except Gabriel, ate some of the pudding out of compliment to Aunt Julia. As Gabriel never ate sweets the celery had been left for him. Freddy Malins also took a stalk of celery and ate it with his pudding. He had been told that celery was a capital thing for the blood and he was just then under doctor's care. Mrs Malins, who had been silent all through the supper, said that her son was going down to Mount Melleray in a week or so. The table then spoke of Mount Melleray, how bracing the air was down there, how hospitable the monks were and how they never asked for a penny-piece from their guests.

—And do you mean to say, asked Mr Browne incredulously, that a chap can go down there and put up there as if it were a hotel and live on the fat of the land and then come away without paying a farthing?

—O, most people give some donation to the monastery when they leave, said Mary Jane.

—I wish we had an institution like that in our Church, said Mr Browne candidly. 230

He was astonished to hear that the monks never spoke, got up at two in the morning and slept in their coffins. He asked what they did it for.

—That's the rule of the order, said Aunt Kate firmly.

—Yes, but why? asked Mr Browne.

Aunt Kate repeated that it was the rule, that was all. Mr Browne still seemed not to understand. Freddy Malins explained to him, as best he could, that the monks were trying to make up for the sins committed by all the sinners in the outside world. The explanation was not very clear for Mr Browne grinned and said:

—I like that idea very much but wouldn't a comfortable spring bed do them as 235 well as a coffin?

—The coffin, said Mary Jane, is to remind them of their last end.

As the subject had grown lugubrious it was buried in a silence of the table during which Mrs Malins could be heard saying to her neighbour in an indistinct undertone:

—They are very good men, the monks, very pious men.

The raisins and almonds and figs and apples and oranges and chocolates and sweets were now passed about the table and Aunt Julia invited all the guests to have either port or sherry. At first Mr Bartell D'Arcy refused to take either but one of his neighbours nudged him and whispered something to him upon which he allowed his glass to be filled. Gradually as the last glasses were being filled the conversation ceased. A pause followed, broken only by the noise of the wine and by unsettlings of chairs. The Misses Morkan, all three, looked down at the tablecloth. Someone coughed once or twice and then a few gentlemen patted the table gently as a signal for silence. The silence came and Gabriel pushed back his chair and stood up.

The patting at once grew louder in encouragement and then ceased altogether. 240 Gabriel leaned his ten trembling fingers on the tablecloth and smiled nervously at the company. Meeting a row of upturned faces he raised his eyes to the chandelier. The piano was playing a waltz tune and he could hear the skirts sweeping against the drawing-room door. People, perhaps, were standing in the snow on the quay outside, gazing up at the lighted windows and listening to the waltz music. The air was pure there. In the distance lay the park where the trees were weighted with snow. The Wellington Monument wore a gleaming cap of snow that flashed westward over the white field of Fifteen Acres.

He began:

—Ladies and Gentlemen.

—It has fallen to my lot this evening, as in years past, to perform a very pleasing task but a task for which I am afraid my poor powers as a speaker are all too inadequate.

—No, no! said Mr Browne.

—But, however that may be, I can only ask you to-night to take the will for the 245 deed and to lend me your attention for a few moments while I endeavour to express to you in words what my feelings are on this occasion.

—Ladies and Gentlemen. It is not the first time that we have gathered together under this hospitable roof, around this hospitable board. It is not the first time that we have been the recipients—or perhaps, I had better say, the victims—of the hospitality of certain good ladies.

He made a circle in the air with his arm and paused. Everyone laughed or smiled at Aunt Kate and Aunt Julia and Mary Jane who all turned crimson with pleasure. Gabriel went on more boldly:

—I feel more strongly with every recurring year that our country has no tradition which does it so much honour and which it should guard so jealously as that of its hospitality. It is a tradition that is unique as far as my experience goes (and I have visited not a few places abroad) among the modern nations. Some would say, perhaps, that with us it is rather a failing than anything to be boasted of. But granted even that, it is, to my mind, a princely failing, and one that I trust will long be cultivated among us. Of one thing, at least, I am sure. As long as this one roof shelters the good ladies aforesaid—and I wish from my heart it may do so for many and many a long year to come—the tradition of genuine warm-hearted courteous Irish hospitality, which our forefathers have handed down to us and which we must hand down to our descendants, is still alive among us.

A hearty murmur of assent ran round the table. It shot through Gabriel's mind that Miss Ivors was not there and that she had gone away discourteously: and he said with confidence in himself:

—Ladies and Gentlemen. 250

—A new generation is growing up in our midst, a generation actuated by new ideas and new principles. It is serious and enthusiastic for these new ideas and its enthusiasm, even when it is misdirected, is, I believe, in the main sincere. But we are living in a sceptical and, if I may use the phrase, a thought-tormented age: and sometimes I fear that this new generation, educated or hypereducated as it is, will lack those qualities of humanity, of hospitality, of kindly humour which belonged to an older day. Listening to-night to the names of all those great singers of the past it seemed to me, I must confess, that we were living in a less spacious age. Those days might, without exaggeration, be called spacious days: and if they are gone beyond recall let us hope, at least, that in gatherings such as this we shall still speak of them with pride and affection, still cherish in our hearts the memory of those dead and gone great ones whose fame the world will not willingly let die.

—Hear, hear! said Mr Browne loudly.

—But yet, continued Gabriel, his voice falling into a softer inflection, there are always in gatherings such as this sadder thoughts that will recur to our minds: thoughts of the past, of youth, of changes, of absent faces that we miss here to-night. Our path through life is strewn with many such sad memories: and were we to brood upon them always we could not find the heart to go on bravely with our work among the living. We have all of us living duties and living affections which claim, and rightly claim, our strenuous endeavours.

—Therefore, I will not linger on the past. I will not let any gloomy moralising intrude upon us here to-night. Here we are gathered together for a brief moment from the bustle and rush of our everyday routine. We are met here as friends, in the spirit of good-fellowship, as colleagues, also, to a certain extent, in the true spirit of *camaraderie*, and as the guests of—what shall I call them?—the Three Graces of the Dublin musical world.

The table burst into applause and laughter at this sally. Aunt Julia vainly asked 255 each of her neighbours in turn to tell her what Gabriel had said.

—He says we are the Three Graces, Aunt Julia, said Mary Jane.

Aunt Julia did not understand but she looked up, smiling, at Gabriel, who continued in the same vein:

—Ladies and Gentlemen.

—I will not attempt to play to-night the part that Paris played on another occasion. I will not attempt to choose between them. The task would be an invidious one and one beyond my poor powers. For when I view them in turn, whether it be our chief hostess herself, whose good heart, whose too good heart, has become a byword with all who know her, or her sister, who seems to be gifted with perennial youth and whose singing must have been a surprise and a revelation to us all to-night, or, last but not least, when I consider our youngest hostess, talented, cheerful, hard-working and the best of nieces, I confess, Ladies and Gentlemen, that I do not know to which of them I should award the prize.

Gabriel glanced down at his aunts and, seeing the large smile on Aunt Julia's face 260 and the tears which had risen to Aunt Kate's eyes, hastened to his close. He raised his glass of port gallantly, while every member of the company fingered a glass expectantly, and said loudly:

—Let us toast them all three together. Let us drink to their health, wealth, long life, happiness and prosperity and may they long continue to hold the proud and self-won position which they hold in their profession and the position of honour and affection which they hold in our hearts.

All the guests stood up, glass in hand, and turning towards the three seated ladies, sang in unison, with Mr Browne as leader:

> For they are jolly gay fellows,
> For they are jolly gay fellows,
> For they are jolly gay fellows,
> Which nobody can deny.

Aunt Kate was making frank use of her handkerchief and even Aunt Julia seemed moved. Freddy Malins beat time with his pudding-fork and the singers turned towards one another, as if in melodious conference, while they sang with emphasis:

> Unless he tells a lie,
> Unless he tells a lie.

Then, turning once more towards their hostesses, they sang:

> For they are jolly gay fellows,
> For they are jolly gay fellows,
> For they are jolly gay fellows,
> Which nobody can deny.

The acclamation which followed was taken up beyond the door of the supper-   265
room by many of the other guests and renewed time after time, Freddy Malins acting
as officer with his fork on high.

. . . .

The piercing morning air came into the hall where they were standing so that
Aunt Kate said:

—Close the door, somebody. Mrs Malins will get her death of cold.

—Browne is out there, Aunt Kate, said Mary Jane.

—Browne is everywhere, said Aunt Kate, lowering her voice.

Mary Jane laughed at her tone.   270

—Really, she said archly, he is very attentive.

—He has been laid on here like the gas, said Aunt Kate in the same tone, all
during the Christmas.

She laughed herself this time good-humouredly and then added quickly:

—But tell him to come in, Mary Jane, and close the door. I hope to goodness
he didn't hear me.

At that moment the hall-door was opened and Mr Browne came in from the   275
doorstep, laughing as if his heart would break. He was dressed in a long green overcoat

with mock astrakhan cuffs and collar and wore on his head an oval fur cap. He pointed down the snow-covered quay from where the sound of shrill prolonged whistling was borne in.

—Teddy will have all the cabs in Dublin out, he said.

Gabriel advanced from the little pantry behind the office, struggling into his overcoat and, looking round the hall, said:

—Gretta not down yet?

—She's getting on her things, Gabriel, said Aunt Kate.

—Who's playing up there? asked Gabriel.

—Nobody. They're all gone.

—O no, Aunt Kate, said Mary Jane. Bartell D'Arcy and Miss O'Callaghan aren't gone yet.

—Someone is strumming at the piano, anyhow, said Gabriel.

Mary Jane glanced at Gabriel and Mr Browne and said with a shiver:

—It makes me feel cold to look at you two gentlemen muffled up like that. I wouldn't like to face your journey home at this hour.

—I'd like nothing better this minute, said Mr Browne stoutly, than a rattling fine walk in the country or a fast drive with a good spanking goer between the shafts.

—We used to have a very good horse and trap at home, said Aunt Julia sadly.

—The never-to-be-forgotten Johnny, said Mary Jane, laughing.

Aunt Kate and Gabriel laughed too.

—Why, what was wonderful about Johnny? asked Mr Browne.

—The late lamented Patrick Morkan, our grandfather, that is, explained Gabriel, commonly known in his later years as the old gentleman, was a glue-boiler.

—O, now, Gabriel, said Aunt Kate, laughing, he had a starch mill.

—Well, glue or starch, said Gabriel, the old gentleman had a horse by the name of Johnny. And Johnny used to work in the old gentleman's mill, walking round and round in order to drive the mill. That was all very well; but now comes the tragic part about Johnny. One fine day the old gentleman thought he'd like to drive out with the quality to a military review in the park.

—The Lord have mercy on his soul, said Aunt Kate compassionately.

—Amen, said Gabriel. So the old gentleman, as I said, harnessed Johnny and put on his very best tall hat and his very best stock collar and drove out in grand style from his ancestral mansion somewhere near Back Lane, I think.

Everyone laughed, even Mrs Malins, at Gabriel's manner and Aunt Kate said:

—O, now, Gabriel, he didn't live in Back Lane, really. Only the mill was there.

—Out from the mansion of his forefathers, continued Gabriel, he drove with Johnny. And everything went on beautifully until Johnny came in sight of King Billy's statue: and whether he fell in love with the horse King Billy sits on or whether he thought he was back again in the mill, anyhow he began to walk round the statue.

Gabriel paced in a circle round the hall in his goloshes amid the laughter of the others.

—Round and round he went, said Gabriel, and the old gentleman, who was a   300
very pompous old gentleman, was highly indignant. *Go on, sir! What do you mean,
sir? Johnny! Johnny! Most extraordinary conduct! Can't understand the horse!*

The peals of laughter which followed Gabriel's imitation of the incident were
interrupted by a resounding knock at the hall-door. Mary Jane ran to open it and let
in Freddy Malins. Freddy Malins, with his hat well back on his head and his shoulders
humped with cold, was puffing and steaming after his exertions.

—I could only get one cab, he said.

—O, we'll find another along the quay, said Gabriel.

—Yes, said Aunt Kate. Better not keep Mrs Malins standing in the draught.

Mrs Malins was helped down the front steps by her son and Mr Browne and,   305
after many manoeuvres, hoisted into the cab. Freddy Malins clambered in after her
and spent a long time settling her on the seat, Mr Browne helping him with advice.
At last she was settled comfortably and Freddy Malins invited Mr Browne into the
cab. There was a good deal of confused talk, and then Mr Browne got into the cab.
The cabman settled his rug over his knees, and bent down for the address. The
confusion grew greater and the cabman was directed differently by Freddy Malins
and Mr Browne, each of whom had his head out through a window of the cab. The
difficulty was to know where to drop Mr Browne along the route and Aunt Kate,
Aunt Julia and Mary Jane helped the discussion from the doorstep with cross-
directions and contradictions and abundance of laughter. As for Freddy Malins he
was speechless with laughter. He popped his head in and out of the window every
moment, to the great danger of his hat, and told his mother how the discussion was
progressing till at last Mr Browne shouted to the bewildered cabman above the din
of everybody's laughter:

—Do you know Trinity College?

—Yes, sir, said the cabman.

—Well, drive bang up against Trinity College gates, said Mr Browne, and then
we'll tell you where to go. You understand now?

—Yes, sir, said the cabman.

—Make like a bird for Trinity College.   310

—Right, sir, cried the cabman.

The horse was whipped up and the cab rattled off along the quay amid a chorus
of laughter and adieus.

Gabriel had not gone to the door with the others. He was in a dark part of the
hall gazing up the staircase. A woman was standing near the top of the first flight,
in the shadow also. He could not see her face but he could see the terracotta and
salmonpink panels of her skirt which the shadow made appear black and white. It
was his wife. She was leaning on the banisters, listening to something. Gabriel was
surprised at her stillness and strained his ear to listen also. But he could hear little
save the noise of laughter and dispute on the front steps, a few chords struck on the
piano and a few notes of a man's voice singing.

He stood still in the gloom of the hall, trying to catch the air that the voice was
singing and gazing up at his wife. There was grace and mystery in her attitude as if
she were a symbol of something. He asked himself what is a woman standing on the

stairs in the shadow, listening to distant music, a symbol of. If he were a painter he would paint her in that attitude. Her blue felt hat would show off the bronze of her hair against the darkness and the dark panels of her skirt would show off the light ones. *Distant Music* he would call the picture if he were a painter.

The hall-door was closed; and Aunt Kate, Aunt Julia and Mary Jane came down the hall, still laughing. 315

—Well, isn't Freddy terrible? said Mary Jane. He's really terrible.

Gabriel said nothing but pointed up the stairs towards where his wife was standing. Now that the hall-door was closed the voice and the piano could be heard more clearly. Gabriel held up his hand for them to be silent. The song seemed to be in the old Irish tonality and the singer seemed uncertain both of his words and of his voice. The voice, made plaintive by distance and by the singer's hoarseness, faintly illuminated the cadence of the air with words expressing grief:

> O, the rain falls on my heavy locks
> And the dew wets my skin,
> My babe lies cold . . .

—O, exclaimed Mary Jane. It's Bartell D'Arcy singing, and he wouldn't sing all the night. O, I'll get him to sing a song before he goes.

—O do, Mary Jane, said Aunt Kate.

Mary Jane brushed past the others and ran to the staircase but before she reached it the singing stopped and the piano was closed abruptly. 320

—O, what a pity! she cried. Is he coming down, Gretta?

Gabriel heard his wife answer yes and saw her come down towards them. A few steps behind her were Mr Bartell D'Arcy and Miss O'Callaghan.

—O, Mr D'Arcy, cried Mary Jane, it's downright mean of you to break off like that when we were all in raptures listening to you.

—I have been at him all the evening, said Miss O'Callaghan, and Mrs Conroy too and he told us he had a dreadful cold and couldn't sing.

—O, Mr D'Arcy, said Aunt Kate, now that was a great fib to tell. 325

—Can't you see that I'm as hoarse as a crow? said Mr D'Arcy roughly.

He went into the pantry hastily and put on his overcoat. The others, taken aback by his rude speech, could find nothing to say. Aunt Kate wrinkled her brows and made signs to the others to drop the subject. Mr D'Arcy stood swathing his neck carefully and frowning.

—It's the weather, said Aunt Julia, after a pause.

—Yes, everybody has colds, said Aunt Kate readily, everybody.

—They say, said Mary Jane, we haven't had snow like it for thirty years; and I read this morning in the newspapers that the snow is general all over Ireland. 330

—I love the look of snow, said Aunt Julia sadly.

—So do I, said Miss O'Callaghan. I think Christmas is never really Christmas unless we have the snow on the ground.

—But poor Mr D'Arcy doesn't like the snow, said Aunt Kate, smiling.

Mr D'Arcy came from the pantry, fully swathed and buttoned, and in a repentant tone told them the history of his cold. Everyone gave him advice and said it was

a great pity and urged him to be very careful of his throat in the night air. Gabriel
watched his wife, who did not join in the conversation. She was standing right under
the dusty fanlight and the flame of the gas lit up the rich bronze of her hair which
he had seen her drying at the fire a few days before. She was in the same attitude and
seemed unaware of the talk about her. At last she turned towards them and Gabriel
saw that there was colour on her cheeks and that her eyes were shining. A sudden tide
of joy went leaping out of his heart.

—Mr D'Arcy, she said, what is the name of that song you were singing?   335

—It's called *The Lass of Aughrim*, said Mr D'Arcy, but I couldn't remember it
properly. Why? Do you know it?

—*The Lass of Aughrim*, she repeated. I couldn't think of the name.

—It's a very nice air, said Mary Jane. I'm sorry you were not in voice to-night.

—Now, Mary Jane, said Aunt Kate, don't annoy Mr D'Arcy. I won't have him
annoyed.

Seeing that all were ready to start she shepherded them to the door where good-   340
night was said:

—Well, good-night, Aunt Kate, and thanks for the pleasant evening.

—Good-night, Gabriel. Good-night, Gretta!

—Good-night, Aunt Kate, and thanks ever so much. Good-night, Aunt Julia.

—O, good-night, Gretta, I didn't see you.

—Good-night, Mr D'Arcy. Good-night, Miss O'Callaghan.   345

—Good-night, Miss Morkan.

—Good-night, again.

—Good-night, all. Safe home.

—Good-night. Good-night.

The morning was still dark. A dull yellow light brooded over the houses and the   350
river; and the sky seemed to be descending. It was slushy underfoot; and only streaks
and patches of snow lay on the roofs, on the parapets of the quay and on the area
railings. The lamps were still burning redly in the murky air and, across the river, the
palace of the Four Courts stood out menacingly against the heavy sky.

She was walking on before him with Mr Bartell D'Arcy, her shoes in a brown
parcel tucked under one arm and her hands holding her skirt up from the slush. She
had no longer any grace of attitude but Gabriel's eyes were still bright with happiness.
The blood went bounding along his veins; and the thoughts went rioting through his
brain, proud, joyful, tender, valorous.

She was walking on before him so lightly and so erect that he longed to run
after her noiselessly, catch her by the shoulders and say something foolish and affectionate into her ear. She seemed to him so frail that he longed to defend her against
something and then to be alone with her. Moments of their secret life together burst
like stars upon his memory. A heliotrope envelope was lying beside his breakfast-cup
and he was caressing it with his hand. Birds were twittering in the ivy and the sunny
web of the curtain was shimmering along the floor: he could not eat for happiness.
They were standing on the crowded platform and he was placing a ticket inside the
warm palm of her glove. He was standing with her in the cold, looking in through
a grated window at a man making bottles in a roaring furnace. It was very cold. Her

face, fragrant in the cold air, was quite close to his; and suddenly she called out to the man at the furnace:

—Is the fire hot, sir?

But the man could not hear with the noise of the furnace. It was just as well. He might have answered rudely.

A wave of yet more tender joy escaped from his heart and went coursing in warm flood along his arteries. Like the tender fires of stars moments of their life together, that no one knew of or would ever know of, broke upon and illumined his memory. He longed to recall to her those moments, to make her forget the years of their dull existence together and remember only their moments of ecstasy. For the years, he felt, had not quenched his soul or hers. Their children, his writing, her household cares had not quenched all their souls' tender fire. In one letter that he had written to her then he had said: *Why is it that words like these seem to me so dull and cold? Is it because there is no word tender enough to be your name?*

Like distant music these words that he had written years before were borne towards him from the past. He longed to be alone with her. When the others had gone away, when he and she were in the room in their hotel, then they would be alone together. He would call her softly:

—Gretta!

Perhaps she would not hear at once: she would be undressing. Then something in his voice would strike her. She would turn and look at him. . . .

At the corner of Winetavern Street they met a cab. He was glad of its rattling noise as it saved him from conversation. She was looking out of the window and seemed tired. The others spoke only a few words, pointing out some building or street. The horse galloped along wearily under the murky morning sky, dragging his old rattling box after his heels, and Gabriel was again in a cab with her, galloping to catch the boat, galloping to their honeymoon.

As the cab drove across O'Connell Bridge Miss O'Callaghan said:

—They say you never cross O'Connell Bridge without seeing a white horse.

—I see a white man this time, said Gabriel.

—Where? asked Mr Bartell D'Arcy.

Gabriel pointed to the statue,[5] on which lay patches of snow. Then he nodded familiarly to it and waved his hand.

—Good-night, Dan, he said gaily.

When the cab drew up before the hotel Gabriel jumped out and, in spite of Mr Bartell D'Arcy's protest, paid the driver. He gave the man a shilling over his fare. The man saluted and said:

—A prosperous New Year to you, sir.

—The same to you, said Gabriel cordially.

She leaned for a moment on his arm in getting out of the cab and while standing at the curbstone, bidding the others good-night. She leaned lightly on his arm, as lightly as when she had danced with him a few hours before. He had felt proud and happy then, happy that she was his, proud of her grace and wifely carriage. But now,

---

[5]Statue of Daniel O'Connell (1775–1847), an Irish lawyer who fought for Catholic rights.—EDS.

after the kindling again of so many memories, the first touch of her body, musical and strange and perfumed, sent through him a keen pang of lust. Under cover of her silence he pressed her arm closely to his side; and, as they stood at the hotel door, he felt that they had escaped from their lives and duties, escaped from home and friends and run away together with wild and radiant hearts to a new adventure.

An old man was dozing in a great hooded chair in the hall. He lit a candle in 370 the office and went before them to the stairs. They followed him in silence, their feet falling in soft thuds on the thickly carpeted stairs. She mounted the stairs behind the porter, her head bowed in the ascent, her frail shoulders curved as with a burden, her skirt girt tightly about her. He could have flung his arms about her hips and held her still for his arms were trembling with desire to seize her and only the stress of his nails against the palms of his hands held the wild impulse of his body in check. The porter halted on the stairs to settle his guttering candle. They halted too on the steps below him. In the silence Gabriel could hear the falling of molten wax into the tray and the thumping of his own heart against his ribs.

The porter led them along a corridor and opened a door. Then he set his unstable candle down on a toilet-table and asked at what hour they were to be called in the morning.

—Eight, said Gabriel.

The porter pointed to the tap of the electric-light and began a muttered apology, but Gabriel cut him short.

—We don't want any light. We have light enough from the street. And I say, he added, pointing to the candle, you might remove that handsome article, like a good man.

The porter took up his candle again, but slowly for he was surprised by such a 375 novel idea. Then he mumbled good-night and went out. Gabriel shot the lock to.

A ghostly light from the street lamp lay in a long shaft from one window to the door. Gabriel threw his overcoat and hat on a couch and crossed the room towards the window. He looked down into the street in order that his emotion might calm a little. Then he turned and leaned against a chest of drawers with his back to the light. She had taken off her hat and cloak and was standing before a large swinging mirror, unhooking her waist. Gabriel paused for a few moments, watching her, and then said:

—Gretta!

She turned away from the mirror slowly and walked along the shaft of light towards him. Her face looked so serious and weary that the words would not pass Gabriel's lips. No, it was not the moment yet.

—You looked tired, he said.

—I am a little, she answered.   380

—You don't feel ill or weak?

—No, tired: that's all.

She went on to the window and stood there, looking out. Gabriel waited again and then, fearing that diffidence was about to conquer him, he said abruptly:

—By the way, Gretta!

—What is it?

385

—You know that poor fellow Malins? he said quickly.

—Yes. What about him?

—Well, poor fellow, he's a decent sort of chap after all, continued Gabriel in a false voice. He gave me back that sovereign I lent him and I didn't expect it really. It's a pity he wouldn't keep away from that Browne, because he's not a bad fellow at heart.

He was trembling now with annoyance. Why did she seem so abstracted? He did not know how he could begin. Was she annoyed, too, about something? If she would only turn to him or come to him of her own accord! To take her as she was would be brutal. No, he must see some ardour in her eyes first. He longed to be master of her strange mood.

—When did you lend him the pound? she asked, after a pause.

390

Gabriel strove to restrain himself from breaking out into brutal language about the sottish Malins and his pound. He longed to cry to her from his soul, to crush her body against his, to overmaster her. But he said:

—O, at Christmas, when he opened that little Christmas-card shop in Henry Street.

He was in such a fever of rage and desire that he did not hear her come from the window. She stood before him for an instant, looking at him strangely. Then, suddenly raising herself on tiptoe and resting her hands lightly on his shoulders, she kissed him.

—You are a very generous person, Gabriel, she said.

Gabriel, trembling with delight at her sudden kiss and at the quaintness of her
395
phrase, put his hands on her hair and began smoothing it back, scarcely touching it with his fingers. The washing had made it fine and brilliant. His heart was brimming over with happiness. Just when he was wishing for it she had come to him of her own accord. Perhaps her thoughts had been running with his. Perhaps she had felt the impetuous desire that was in him and then the yielding mood had come upon her. Now that she had fallen to him so easily he wondered why he had been so diffident.

He stood, holding her head between his hands. Then, slipping one arm swiftly about her body and drawing her towards him, he said softly:

—Gretta, dear, what are you thinking about?

She did not answer nor yield wholly to his arm. He said again, softly:

—Tell me what it is, Gretta. I think I know what is the matter. Do I know?

She did not answer at once. Then she said in an outburst of tears:

400

—O, I am thinking about that song, *The Lass of Aughrim*.

She broke loose from him and ran to the bed and, throwing her arms across the bed-rail, hid her face. Gabriel stood stock-still for a moment in astonishment and then followed her. As he passed in the way of the cheval-glass he caught sight of himself in full length, his broad, well-filled shirt-front, the face whose expression always puzzled him when he saw it in a mirror and his glimmering gilt-rimmed eyeglasses. He halted a few paces from her and said:

—What about the song? Why does that make you cry?

She raised her head from her arms and dried her eyes with the back of her hand like a child. A kinder note than he had intended went into his voice.

—Why, Gretta? he asked.

—I am thinking about a person long ago who used to sing that song.

—And who was the person long ago? asked Gabriel, smiling.

—It was a person I used to know in Galway when I was living with my grand-mother, she said.

The smile passed away from Gabriel's face. A dull anger began to gather again at the back of his mind and the dull fires of his lust began to glow angrily in his veins.

—Someone you were in love with? he asked ironically.

—It was a young boy I used to know, she answered, named Michael Furey. He used to sing that song, *The Lass of Aughrim*. He was very delicate.

Gabriel was silent. He did not wish her to think that he was interested in this delicate boy.

—I can see him so plainly, she said after a moment. Such eyes as he had: big dark eyes! And such an expression in them—an expression!

—O then, you were in love with him? said Gabriel.

—I used to go out walking with him, she said, when I was in Galway.

A thought flew across Gabriel's mind.

—Perhaps that was why you wanted to go to Galway with that Ivors girl? he said coldly.

She looked at him and asked in surprise:

—What for?

Her eyes made Gabriel feel awkward. He shrugged his shoulders and said:

—How do I know? To see him perhaps.

She looked away from him along the shaft of light towards the window in silence.

—He is dead, she said at length. He died when he was only seventeen. Isn't it a terrible thing to die so young as that?

—What was he? asked Gabriel, still ironically.

—He was in the gasworks, she said.

Gabriel felt humiliated by the failure of his irony and by the evocation of this figure from the dead, a boy in the gasworks. While he had been full of memories of their secret life together, full of tenderness and joy and desire, she had been com-paring him in her mind with another. A shameful consciousness of his own person assailed him. He saw himself as a ludicrous figure, acting as a pennyboy for his aunts, a nervous well-meaning sentimentalist, orating to vulgarians and idealising his own clownish lusts, the pitiable fatuous fellow he had caught a glimpse of in the mirror. Instinctively he turned his back more to the light lest she might see the shame that burned upon his forehead.

He tried to keep up his tone of cold interrogation but his voice when he spoke was humble and indifferent.

—I suppose you were in love with this Michael Furey, Gretta, he said.

—I was great with him at that time, she said.

Her voice was veiled and sad. Gabriel, feeling now how vain it would be to try to   430
lead her whither he had purposed, caressed one of her hands and said, also sadly:

—And what did he die of so young, Gretta? Consumption, was it?

—I think he died for me, she answered.

A vague terror seized Gabriel at this answer as if, at that hour when he had
hoped to triumph, some impalpable and vindictive being was coming against him,
gathering forces against him in its vague world. But he shook himself free of it with
an effort of reason and continued to caress her hand. He did not question her again
for he felt that she would tell him of herself. Her hand was warm and moist: it did
not respond to his touch but he continued to caress it just as he had caressed her first
letter to him that spring morning.

—It was in the winter, she said, about the beginning of the winter when I was going
to leave my grandmother's and come up here to the convent. And he was ill at the time in
his lodgings in Galway and wouldn't be let out and his people in Oughterard were written
to. He was in decline, they said, or something like that. I never knew rightly.

She paused for a moment and sighed.   435

—Poor fellow, she said. He was very fond of me and he was such a gentle boy.
We used to go out together, walking, you know, Gabriel, like the way they do in the
country. He was going to study singing only for his health. He had a very good voice,
poor Michael Furey.

—Well; and then? asked Gabriel.

—And then when it came to the time for me to leave Galway and come up to the
convent he was much worse and I wouldn't be let see him so I wrote a letter saying
I was going up to Dublin and would be back in the summer and hoping he would
be better then.

She paused for a moment to get her voice under control and then went on:

—Then the night before I left I was in my grandmother's house in Nuns' Island,   440
packing up, and I heard gravel thrown up against the window. The window was so
wet I couldn't see so I ran downstairs as I was and slipped out the back into the garden and there was the poor fellow at the end of the garden, shivering.

—And did you not tell him to go back? asked Gabriel.

—I implored of him to go home at once and told him he would get his death in
the rain. But he said he did not want to live. I can see his eyes as well as well! He was
standing at the end of the wall where there was a tree.

—And did he go home? asked Gabriel.

—Yes, he went home. And when I was only a week in the convent he died and
he was buried in Oughterard where his people came from. O, the day I heard that,
that he was dead!

She stopped, choking with sobs, and, overcome by emotion, flung herself face   445
downward on the bed, sobbing in the quilt. Gabriel held her hand for a moment longer, irresolutely, and then, shy of intruding on her grief, let it fall gently and walked
quietly to the window.

She was fast asleep.

Gabriel, leaning on his elbow, looked for a few moments unresentfully on her tangled hair and half-open mouth, listening to her deep-drawn breath. So she had had that romance in her life: a man had died for her sake. It hardly pained him now to think how poor a part he, her husband, had played in her life. He watched her while she slept as though he and she had never lived together as man and wife. His curious eyes rested long upon her face and on her hair: and, as he thought of what she must have been then, in that time of her first girlish beauty, a strange friendly pity for her entered his soul. He did not like to say even to himself that her face was no longer beautiful but he knew that it was no longer the face for which Michael Furey had braved death.

Perhaps she had not told him all the story. His eyes moved to the chair over which she had thrown some of her clothes. A petticoat string dangled to the floor. One boot stood upright, its limp upper fallen down: the fellow of it lay upon its side. He wondered at his riot of emotions of an hour before. From what had it proceeded? From his aunt's supper, from his own foolish speech, from the wine and dancing, the merry-making when saying good-night in the hall, the pleasure of the walk along the river in the snow. Poor Aunt Julia! She, too, would soon be a shade with the shade of Patrick Morkan and his horse. He had caught that haggard look upon her face for a moment when she was singing *Arrayed for the Bridal*. Soon, perhaps, he would be sitting in that same drawing-room, dressed in black, his silk hat on his knees. The blinds would be drawn down and Aunt Kate would be sitting beside him, crying and blowing her nose and telling him how Julia had died. He would cast about in his mind for some words that might console her, and would find only lame and useless ones. Yes, yes: that would happen very soon.

The air of the room chilled his shoulders. He stretched himself cautiously along under the sheets and lay down beside his wife. One by one they were all becoming shades. Better pass boldly into that other world, in the full glory of some passion, than fade and wither dismally with age. He thought of how she who lay beside him had locked in her heart for so many years that image of her lover's eyes when he had told her that he did not wish to live.

Generous tears filled Gabriel's eyes. He had never felt like that himself towards any woman but he knew that such a feeling must be love. The tears gathered more thickly in his eyes and in the partial darkness he imagined he saw the form of a young man standing under a dripping tree. Other forms were near. His soul had approached that region where dwell the vast hosts of the dead. He was conscious of, but could not apprehend, their wayward and flickering existence. His own identity was fading out into a grey impalpable world: the solid world itself which these dead had one time reared and lived in was dissolving and dwindling.

A few light taps upon the pane made him turn to the window. It had begun to snow again. He watched sleepily the flakes, silver and dark, falling obliquely against the lamplight. The time had come for him to set out on his journey westward. Yes, the newspapers were right: snow was general all over Ireland. It was falling on every part of the dark central plain, on the treeless hills, falling softly upon the Bog of Allen and, farther westward, softly falling into the dark mutinous Shannon waves. It was falling, too, upon every part of the lonely churchyard on the hill where Michael Furey lay buried. It lay thickly drifted on the crooked crosses and headstones, on the spears

450

of the little gate, on the barren thorns. His soul swooned slowly as he heard the snow falling faintly through the universe and faintly falling, like the descent of their last end, upon all the living and the dead.

[1914]

Questions for Discussion

1. "The Dead" opens with "Lily, the caretaker's daughter," taking the guests' coats. She is the first character with whom Gabriel interacts, and Gabriel is rattled by their conversation. Reread the story's first few pages, looking carefully at the way Joyce describes Lily's role in the Morkan household. Why do you think she answers Gabriel so sharply? Why do you think Gabriel gives her money? Why is Gabriel "discomposed by the girl's bitter and sudden retort" (para. 29)?

2. The Morkan sisters' party takes place on the Feast of the Epiphany, celebrated on January 6 and commemorating the visit of the Magi, or Three Kings, to the baby Jesus. Although the feast day has different interpretations and is celebrated in different ways, all churches agree that it commemorates the manifestation of Christ to the world. Why might Joyce have chosen this particular feast day on which to set "The Dead"?

3. Who do you think the dead are in "The Dead"?

4. What are some of the ways in which Gabriel is different from the other party guests? Why is he hesitant to quote Robert Browning in his speech (para. 29)?

5. A look at a map and a review of the historical antagonism between Ireland and England might help you understand what Miss Ivors means when she accuses Gabriel of being a West Briton (para. 111). What evidence does the story provide that makes her accusation both somewhat true and particularly insulting?

6. In paragraphs 207–24, the party guests discuss the local music scene, past and present. In a way, it is a discussion of high culture versus popular culture. What do the guests' opinions on music reveal about them? What might Joyce have thought about the conflict between high and popular culture?

7. Gabriel watches his wife at the top of the stairs: "There was grace and mystery in her attitude as if she were a symbol of something. He asked himself what is a woman standing on the stairs in the shadow, listening to distant music, a symbol of" (para. 314). Try to answer Gabriel's question.

8. Do Gabriel and Gretta seem mismatched? Consider how she interacts with his family, whether he is defensive about her background, and how he responds to finding out that she has a history that she had not previously shared with him. Do you think she should have told him? Explain why "Generous tears filled Gabriel's eyes" (para. 450). Will Gretta's revelation change her and Gabriel's relationship?

9. What is your impression of Dublin society from this story? Discuss what "The Dead" reveals about class, religion, and gender in early twentieth-century Dublin.

10. Joyce said that he added "The Dead" to *Dubliners* to provide uplift to a collection that many found dreary. Yet its title hardly suggests uplift. What was your emotional response to "The Dead"? In what ways might it be uplifting?

11. Joyce said that one of the purposes of "The Dead" was to reproduce Dublin's "ingenuous insularity and its hospitality." Discuss what he might have meant by "ingenuous insularity" and whether you think the phrase is positive or negative. Find examples in the story that illustrate Dublin's insularity and hospitality.

12. What part do music and dance play in "The Dead"? Consider their importance in both the ways the characters relate to one another and the context of Irish history and culture.

13. Do you think Joyce judges the characters in "The Dead"? Explain why or why not.

14. As with much of Joyce's work, "The Dead" has many autobiographical elements. Like Gretta, Joyce's wife, Nora, was from Galway, in western Ireland. She had two loves before Joyce, both of whom, like Michael Furey, died young. Does this knowledge change your view of the story? Explain.

Questions on Style and Structure

1. Joyce wrote one play, *My Brilliant Career,* which he sent to William Archer, Ibsen's English translator, for criticism. The play is lost, but in a letter that survived, Archer stated that he was concerned that Joyce began with a large canvas but in the end focused on only a few people. This criticism became a virtue in Joyce's later works. What is the connection between the large canvas of the party — and Dublin — and the focus on Gabriel at the story's end? How does this approach add another level of meaning to the story?

2. How does Joyce create the atmosphere of the party? Look carefully at the detailed descriptions of the hostesses, guests, servants, house, music, and food.

3. How does Joyce use subtle details to create his characters? Find examples in which a gesture, a color, or an item of clothing helps explain a character.

4. Amid the swirl of the Morkan sisters' party, several guests come into focus. What roles do characters such as Freddy Malins, his mother, Miss Ivors, Mr. Browne, and the tenor Mr. D'Arcy play in the story?

5. In paragraph 10, Joyce evokes all five senses. Look for other paragraphs or sentences with this kind of vivid imagery. In addition to making the story come to life, what is the effect of these passages? How do the images come together to help Joyce make a bigger statement about Dublin? about the Irish?

6. Once Gabriel arrives at the party, he reports on much of the action, as well as his reaction to certain events. How does Joyce balance Gabriel's self-criticism with his open-mindedness about his aunts' party and the other guests?

7. Joyce injects politics into "The Dead" in the scene in which Gabriel dances with Miss Ivors, an Irish nationalist (paras. 101–37). Trace the way Miss Ivors exposes Gabriel as the anonymous book reviewer G.C. for the *Daily Express,* and the way Gabriel defends himself. How is that conflict revisited in other parts of the story? Explain why Gabriel's defense is effective or ineffective.

8. For a story called "The Dead," there is quite a bit of humor. How does Gabriel's willingness, for example, to "carve a flock of geese, if necessary" (para. 195)

help develop his character and also the character of Dublin society? Find other examples of Joyce's sly sense of humor.

9. The dinner, which is the centerpiece of "The Dead" (paras. 196–239), is filled with sensuous details. How does Joyce pace the description so that the reader is caught up not only in the food but in the swirl of conversation and conviviality?

10. Analyze Gabriel's speech (paras. 242–61). Do you think it is overly sentimental? How do you think Gabriel feels about his audience? In what ways does he pitch the speech to them? What assumptions about the audience drive the speech?

11. How does the tone of the story shift at the end of the party? Examine the way Joyce makes the transition from the party to Gabriel's very private contemplation of Gretta.

12. What do the details of Gabriel's imaginary painting of Gretta reveal about his feelings for his wife (para. 314)?

13. Identify examples of images of snow and fire in "The Dead," and discuss their effect. How do these image patterns further the development of the themes in the story?

14. Joyce is famous for having invented *epiphany* as a literary term. He defined it as the "sudden revelation of the whatness of a thing," the moment in which "the soul of the commonest object ... seems to us radiant ... a sudden spiritual manifestation [either] in the vulgarity of speech or of a gesture or in a memorable phrase of the mind itself." What is Gabriel's epiphany? What causes it?

Suggestions for Writing

1. Write an essay in which you discuss how the party that is the setting for "The Dead" reveals the values of the characters and the society in which they live.

2. Write an essay that examines what "The Dead" says about the importance of home and family.

3. Miss Ivors is more cordial to Gretta than she is to Gabriel because Gretta comes from Galway, in western Ireland. Research and analyze the myth of the West as the site of "authentic" Irishness.

4. In *Transitions: Narratives in Modern Irish Culture*, Irish scholar Richard Kearney argues that the crisis of twentieth-century Irish culture is defined by a clash between "revivalism and modernism," between those who "seek to revive the past" and those who turn to a cosmopolitan or international perspective and thereby "seek to rewrite or repudiate it altogether." Using "The Dead," support, challenge, or qualify Kearney's claim.

5. Richard Ellmann, the foremost biographer of Joyce, wrote this commentary on the ambivalence Joyce felt toward his homeland when he wrote "The Dead":

> That Joyce at the age of twenty-five and -six should have written this story ought not to seem odd. . . . In his own mind he had thoroughly justified his flight from Ireland; but he had not decided the question of where he would fly *to*. In Trieste and Rome he had learned what he had unlearned in Dublin, to be a Dubliner. As he had written his

brother from Rome with some astonishment, he felt humiliated when anyone attacked his "impoverished country." "The Dead" is his first song of exile.

Write an essay analyzing what you see as Joyce's criticism and admiration for his home, his relief at being away from it, and his nostalgia for Ireland.

6. View John Huston's film version of "The Dead," which stars his daughter Anjelica Huston as Gretta Conroy. Write a review in which you evaluate Mr. Huston's interpretation of Joyce's story.

7. Make a mix CD of the music mentioned in "The Dead," including any modern versions of the songs. Then write the liner notes.

Fences

August Wilson

 August Wilson (1945–2005) was born in Pittsburgh to a white father and an African American mother. When his father died in 1965, he changed his legal name (Frederick August Kittel) to August Wilson, assuming his mother's maiden name. Brought up by his mother, he spent his early years in the Hill—a poor, multiracial district of Pittsburgh, the setting for his later work. His formal education ended when he dropped out of high school at the age of fifteen. He was largely self-educated, becoming acquainted with the works of leading African American writers through the Carnegie Library. He cofounded the Black Horizon Theater in the Hill District in 1968, and vowed to become a writer. This ambition was realized during the 1980s, when Wilson began writing *The Pittsburgh Cycle*—a remarkable collection of partially interconnected plays. Collectively, the plays portray the twentieth century from an African American perspective. The cycle garnered many awards, including two Pulitzer Prizes (for *Fences* in 1985 and *The Piano Lesson* in 1989); the tenth and final play, *Radio Golf*, was performed a few months before his death. Wilson's influence lies in his ability, through larger-than-life characters and intense, perceptive characterization, to create a universal dimension in which issues of race and family in America are examined. In *Fences*, Troy Maxson embodies one of those larger-than-life characters.

For Lloyd Richards, who adds to whatever he touches

When the sins of our fathers visit us
We do not have to play host.
We can banish them with forgiveness
As God, in His Largeness and Laws.

—August Wilson

CHARACTERS

Troy Maxson
Jim Bono, *Troy's friend*
Rose, *Troy's wife*
Lyons, *Troy's oldest son by previous marriage*

Gabriel, *Troy's brother*
Cory, *Troy and Rose's son*
Raynell, *Troy's daughter*

setting: The setting is the yard which fronts the only entrance to the Maxson household, an ancient two-story brick house set back off a small alley in a big-city neighborhood. The entrance to the house is gained by two or three steps leading to a wooden porch badly in need of paint.

195

A relatively recent addition to the house and running its full width, the porch lacks congruence. It is a sturdy porch with a flat roof. One or two chairs of dubious value sit at one end where the kitchen window opens onto the porch. An old-fashioned icebox stands silent guard at the opposite end.

The yard is a small dirt yard, partially fenced, except for the last scene, with a wooden sawhorse, a pile of lumber, and other fence-building equipment set off to the side. Opposite is a tree from which hangs a ball made of rags. A baseball bat leans against the tree. Two oil drums serve as garbage receptacles and sit near the house at right to complete the setting.

THE PLAY: Near the turn of the century, the destitute of Europe sprang on the city with tenacious claws and an honest and solid dream. The city devoured them. They swelled its belly until it burst into a thousand furnaces and sewing machines, a thousand butcher shops and bakers' ovens, a thousand churches and hospitals and funeral parlors and money-lenders. The city grew. It nourished itself and offered each man a partnership limited only by his talent, his guile, and his willingness and capacity for hard work. For the immigrants of Europe, a dream dared and won true.

The descendants of African slaves were offered no such welcome or participation. They came from places called the Carolinas and the Virginias, Georgia, Alabama, Mississippi, and Tennessee. They came strong, eager, searching. The city rejected them and they fled and settled along the riverbanks and under bridges in shallow, ramshackle houses made of sticks and tarpaper. They collected rags and wood. They sold the use of their muscles and their bodies. They cleaned houses and washed clothes, they shined shoes, and in quiet desperation and vengeful pride, they stole, and lived in pursuit of their own dream. That they could breathe free, finally, and stand to meet life with the force of dignity and whatever eloquence the heart could call upon.

By 1957, the hard-won victories of the European immigrants had solidified the industrial might of America. War had been confronted and won with new energies that used loyalty and patriotism as its fuel. Life was rich, full, and flourishing. The Milwaukee Braves won the World Series, and the hot winds of change that would make the sixties a turbulent, racing, dangerous, and provocative decade had not yet begun to blow full.

ACT I

SCENE 1

It is 1957. TROY *and* BONO *enter the yard, engaged in conversation.* TROY *is fifty-three years old, a large man with thick, heavy hands; it is this largeness that he strives to fill out and make an accommodation with. Together with his blackness, his largeness informs his sensibilities and the choices he has made in his life.*

Of the two men, BONO *is obviously the follower. His commitment to their friendship of thirty-odd years is rooted in his admiration of* TROY'*s honesty, capacity for hard work, and his strength, which* BONO *seeks to emulate.*

It is Friday night, payday, and the one night of the week the two men engage in a ritual of talk and drink. TROY *is usually the most talkative and at times he can be crude and almost vulgar, though he is capable of rising to profound heights of expression. The men carry lunch buckets and wear or carry burlap aprons and are dressed in clothes suitable to their jobs as garbage collectors.*

BONO: Troy, you ought to stop that lying!

TROY: I ain't lying! The nigger had a watermelon this big. *(He indicates with his hands.)* Talking about . . . "What watermelon, Mr. Rand?" I liked to fell out! "What watermelon, Mr. Rand?" . . . And it sitting there big as life.

BONO: What did Mr. Rand say? 5

TROY: Ain't said nothing. Figure if the nigger too dumb to know he carrying a watermelon, he wasn't gonna get much sense out of him. Trying to hide that great big old watermelon under his coat. Afraid to let the white man see him carry it home.

BONO: I'm like you . . . I ain't got no time for them kind of people. 10

TROY: Now what he look like getting mad cause he see the man from the union talking to Mr. Rand?

BONO: He come to me talking about . . . "Maxson gonna get us fired." I told him to get away from me with that. He walked away from me calling you a troublemaker. What Mr. Rand say? 15

TROY: Ain't said nothing. He told me to go down the Commissioner's office next Friday. They called me down there to see them.

BONO: Well, as long as you got your complaint filed, they can't fire you. That's what one of them white fellows tell me.

TROY: I ain't worried about them firing me. They gonna fire me cause I asked a 20 question? That's all I did. I went to Mr. Rand and asked him, "Why? Why you got the white mens driving and the colored lifting?" Told him, "What's the matter, don't I count? You think only white fellows got sense enough to drive a truck. That ain't no paper job! Hell, anybody can drive a truck. How come you got all whites driving and the colored lifting?" He told me "take it 25 to the union." Well, hell, that's what I done! Now they wanna come up with this pack of lies.

BONO: I told Brownie if the man come and ask him any questions . . . just tell the truth! It ain't nothing but something they done trumped up on you cause you filed a complaint on them. 30

TROY: Brownie don't understand nothing. All I want them to do is change the job description. Give everybody a chance to drive the truck. Brownie can't see that. He ain't got that much sense.

BONO: How you figure he be making out with that gal be up at Taylors' all the time . . . that Alberta gal? 35

TROY: Same as you and me. Getting just as much as we is. Which is to say nothing.

BONO: It is, huh? I figure you doing a little better than me . . . and I ain't saying what I'm doing.

TROY: Aw, nigger, look here . . . I know you. If you had got anywhere near that gal, twenty minutes later you be looking to tell somebody. And the first one you   40
  gonna tell . . . that you gonna want to brag to . . . is me.

BONO: I ain't saying that. I see where you be eyeing her.

TROY: I eye all the women. I don't miss nothing. Don't never let nobody tell you Troy
  Maxson don't eye the women.

BONO: You been doing more than eyeing her. You done bought her a drink or   45
  two.

TROY: Hell yeah, I bought her a drink! What that mean? I bought you one, too. What
  that mean cause I buy her a drink? I'm just being polite.

BONO: It's all right to buy her one drink. That's what you call being polite. But when
  you wanna be buying two or three . . . that's what you call eyeing her.   50

TROY: Look here, as long as you known me . . . you ever known me to chase after
  women?

BONO: Hell yeah! Long as I done known you. You forgetting I knew you when.

TROY: Naw, I'm talking about since I been married to Rose?

BONO: Oh, not since you been married to Rose. Now, that's the truth, there. I can   55
  say that.

TROY: All right then! Case closed.

BONO: I see you be walking up around Alberta's house. You supposed to be at Taylors'
  and you be walking up around there.

TROY: What you watching where I'm walking for? I ain't watching after you.   60

BONO: I seen you walking around there more than once.

TROY: Hell, you liable to see me walking anywhere! That don't mean nothing cause
  you see me walking around there.

BONO: Where she come from anyway? She just kinda showed up one day.

TROY: Tallahassee. You can look at her and tell she one of them Florida gals. They   65
  got some big healthy women down there. Grow them right up out the ground.
  Got a little bit of Indian in her. Most of them niggers down in Florida got some
  Indian in them.

BONO: I don't know about that Indian part. But she damn sure big and healthy.
  Woman wear some big stockings. Got them great big old legs and hips as wide   70
  as the Mississippi River.

TROY: Legs don't mean nothing. You don't do nothing but push them out of the way.
  But them hips cushion the ride!

BONO: Troy, you ain't got no sense.

TROY: It's the truth! Like you riding on Goodyears!   75

ROSE *enters from the house. She is ten years younger than* TROY, *her devotion to him stems from her recognition of the possibilities of her life without him: a succession of abusive men and their babies, a life of partying and running the streets, the Church, or aloneness with its attendant pain and frustration. She recognizes* TROY's *spirit as a fine and illuminating one and she either ignores or forgives his faults, only some of which she recognizes. Though she doesn't drink, her presence is an integral part of the Friday night rituals. She alternates between the porch and the kitchen, where supper preparations are under way.*

ROSE: What you all out here getting into?

TROY: What you worried about what we getting into for? This is men talk, woman.

ROSE: What I care what you all talking about? Bono, you gonna stay for supper?

BONO: No, I thank you, Rose. But Lucille say she cooking up a pot of pigfeet.

TROY: Pigfeet! Hell, I'm going home with you! Might even stay the night if you got some pigfeet. You got something in there to top them pigfeet, Rose? 80

ROSE: I'm cooking up some chicken. I got some chicken and collard greens.

TROY: Well, go on back in the house and let me and Bono finish what we was talking about. This is men talk. I got some talk for you later. You know what kind of talk I mean. You go on and powder it up. 85

ROSE: Troy Maxson, don't you start that now!

TROY *(puts his arm around her)*: Aw, woman . . . come here. Look here, Bono . . . when I met this woman . . . I got out that place, say, "Hitch up my pony, saddle up my mare . . . there's a woman out there for me somewhere. I looked here. Looked there. Saw Rose and latched on to her." I latched on to her and told her — I'm 90 gonna tell you the truth — I told her, "Baby, I don't wanna marry, I just wanna be your man." Rose told me . . . tell him what you told me, Rose.

ROSE: I told him if he wasn't the marrying kind, then move out the way so the marrying kind could find me.

TROY: That's what she told me. "Nigger, you in my way. You blocking the view! Move 95 out the way so I can find me a husband." I thought it over two or three days. Come back —

ROSE: Ain't no two or three days nothing. You was back the same night.

TROY: Come back, told her . . . "Okay, baby . . . but I'm gonna buy me a banty rooster and put him out there in the backyard . . . and when he see a stranger come, he'll 100 flap his wings and crow . . ." Look here, Bono, I could watch the front door by myself . . . it was that back door I was worried about.

ROSE: Troy, you ought not talk like that. Troy ain't doing nothing but telling a lie.

TROY: Only thing is . . . when we first got married . . . forget the rooster . . . we ain't had no yard! 105

BONO: I hear you tell it. Me and Lucille was staying down there on Logan Street. Had two rooms with the outhouse in the back. I ain't mind the outhouse none. But when that goddamn wind blow through there in the winter . . . that's what I'm talking about! To this day I wonder why in the hell I ever stayed down there for six long years. But see, I didn't know I could do no better. I thought only white 110 folks had inside toilets and things.

ROSE: There's a lot of people don't know they can do no better than they doing now. That's just something you got to learn. A lot of folks still shop at Bella's.

TROY: Ain't nothing wrong with shopping at Bella's. She got fresh food.

ROSE: I ain't said nothing about if she got fresh food. I'm talking about what she 115 charge. She charge ten cents more than the A&P.

TROY: The A&P ain't never done nothing for me. I spends my money where I'm treated right. I go down to Bella, say, "I need a loaf of bread, I'll pay you Friday." She give it to me. What sense that make when I got money to go and spend it somewhere else and ignore the person who done right by me? That ain't in the   120
Bible.

ROSE: We ain't talking about what's in the Bible. What sense it make to shop there when she overcharge?

TROY: You shop where you want to. I'll do my shopping where the people been good to me.   125

ROSE: Well, I don't think it's right for her to overcharge. That's all I was saying.

BONO: Look here . . . I got to get on. Lucille going be raising all kind of hell.

TROY: Where you going, nigger? We ain't finished this pint. Come here, finish this pint.

BONO: Well, hell, I am . . . if you ever turn the bottle loose.   130

TROY *(hands him the bottle)*: The only thing I say about the A&P is I'm glad Cory got that job down there. Help him take care of his school clothes and things. Gabe done moved out and things getting tight around here. He got that job. . . . He can start to look out for himself.

ROSE: Cory done went and got recruited by a college football team.   135

TROY: I told that boy about that football stuff. The white man ain't gonna let him get nowhere with that football. I told him when he first come to me with it. Now you come telling me he done went and got more tied up in it. He ought to go and get recruited in how to fix cars or something where he can make a living.

ROSE: He ain't talking about making no living playing football. It's just something   140
the boys in school do. They gonna send a recruiter by to talk to you. He'll tell you he ain't talking about making no living playing football. It's a honor to be recruited.

TROY: It ain't gonna get him nowhere. Bono'll tell you that.

BONO: If he be like you in the sports . . . he's gonna be all right. Ain't but two men   145
ever played baseball as good as you. That's Babe Ruth and Josh Gibson.[1] Them's the only two men ever hit more home runs than you.

TROY: What it ever get me? Ain't got a pot to piss in or a window to throw it out of.

ROSE: Times have changed since you was playing baseball, Troy. That was before the war. Times have changed a lot since then.   150

TROY: How in hell they done changed?

ROSE: They got lots of colored boys playing ball now. Baseball and football.

BONO: You right about that, Rose. Times have changed, Troy. You just come along too early.

TROY: There ought not never have been no time called too early! Now you take that   155
fellow . . . what's that fellow they had playing right field for the Yankees back then? You know who I'm talking about, Bono. Used to play right field for the Yankees.

---

[1]Josh Gibson (1911–1947) was a baseball player in the Negro leagues. —EDS.

ROSE: Selkirk?

TROY: Selkirk! That's it! Man batting .269, understand? .269. What kind of sense that   160
make? I was hitting .432 with thirty-seven home runs! Man batting .269 and
playing right field for the Yankees! I saw Josh Gibson's daughter yesterday. She
walking around with raggedy shoes on her feet. Now I bet you Selkirk's daughter
ain't walking around with raggedy shoes on her feet! I bet you that!

ROSE: They got a lot of colored baseball players now. Jackie Robinson was the first.   165
Folks had to wait for Jackie Robinson.

TROY: I done seen a hundred niggers play baseball better than Jackie Robinson. Hell, I
know some teams Jackie Robinson couldn't even make! What you talking about
Jackie Robinson. Jackie Robinson wasn't nobody. I'm talking about if you could
play ball then they ought to have let you play. Don't care what color you were.   170
Come telling me I come along too early. If you could play . . . then they ought
to have let you play.

TROY *takes a long drink from the bottle.*

ROSE: You gonna drink yourself to death. You don't need to be drinking like that.

TROY: Death ain't nothing. I done seen him. Done wrassled with him. You can't tell
me nothing about death. Death ain't nothing but a fastball on the outside corner.   175
And you know what I'll do to that! Lookee here, Bono . . . am I lying? You get one
of them fastballs, about waist high, over the outside corner of the plate where
you can get the meat of the bat on it . . . and good god! You can kiss it goodbye.
Now, am I lying?

BONO: Naw, you telling the truth there. I seen you do it.   180

TROY: If I'm lying . . . that 450 feet worth of lying! *(Pause.)* That's all death is to me.
A fastball on the outside corner.

ROSE: I don't know why you want to get on talking about death.

TROY: Ain't nothing wrong with talking about death. That's part of life. Everybody
gonna die. You gonna die, I'm gonna die. Bono's gonna die. Hell, we all gonna die.   185

ROSE: But you ain't got to talk about it. I don't like to talk about it.

TROY: You the one brought it up. Me and Bono was talking about baseball . . . you tell
me I'm gonna drink myself to death. Ain't that right, Bono? You know I don't
drink this but one night out of the week. That's Friday night. I'm gonna drink
just enough to where I can handle it. Then I cuts it loose. I leave it alone. So   190
don't you worry about me drinking myself to death. 'Cause I ain't worried about
Death. I done seen him. I done wrestled with him.

    Look here, Bono . . . I looked up one day and Death was marching straight
at me. Like Soldiers on Parade! The Army of Death was marching straight at me.
The middle of July, 1941. It got real cold just like it be winter. It seem like Death   195
himself reached out and touched me on the shoulder. He touch me just like I
touch you. I got cold as ice and Death standing there grinning at me.

ROSE: Troy, why don't you hush that talk.

TROY: I say . . . what you want, Mr. Death? You be wanting me? You done brought
your army to be getting me? I looked him dead in the eye. I wasn't fearing nothing.   200

I was ready to tangle. Just like I'm ready to tangle now. The Bible say be ever
vigilant. That's why I don't get but so drunk. I got to keep watch.

ROSE: Troy was right down there in Mercy Hospital. You remember he had pneumonia? Laying there with a fever talking plumb out of his head.

TROY: Death standing there staring at me . . . carrying that sickle in his hand. Finally   205
he say, "You want bound over for another year?" See, just like that . . . "You want
bound over for another year?" I told him, "Bound over hell! Let's settle this now!"

It seem like he kinda fell back when I said that, and all the cold went out of
me. I reached down and grabbed that sickle and threw it just as far as I could
throw it . . . and me and him commenced to wrestling.   210

We wrestled for three days and three nights. I can't say where I found the
strength from. Every time it seemed like he was gonna get the best of me, I'd
reach way down deep inside myself and find the strength to do him one better.

ROSE: Every time Troy tell that story he find different ways to tell it. Different things
to make up about it.   215

TROY: I ain't making up nothing. I'm telling you the facts of what happened. I wrestled with Death for three days and three nights and I'm standing here to tell you
about it. *(Pause.)* All right. At the end of the third night we done weakened each
other to where we can't hardly move. Death stood up, throwed on his robe . . .
had him a white robe with a hood on it. He throwed on that robe and went off to   220
look for his sickle. Say, "I'll be back." Just like that. "I'll be back." I told him, say,
"Yeah, but . . . you gonna have to find me!" I wasn't no fool. I wan't going looking
for him. Death ain't nothing to play with. And I know he's gonna get me. I know
I got to join his army . . . his camp followers. But as long as I keep my strength
and see him coming . . . as long as I keep up my vigilance . . . he's gonna have to   225
fight to get me. I ain't going easy.

BONO: Well, look here, since you got to keep up your vigilance . . . let me have the
bottle.

TROY: Aw hell, I shouldn't have told you that part. I should have left out that part.

ROSE: Troy be talking that stuff and half the time don't even know what he be talk-   230
ing about.

TROY: Bono know me better than that.

BONO: That's right. I know you. I know you got some Uncle Remus[2] in your blood.
You got more stories than the devil got sinners.

TROY: Aw hell, I done seen him too! Done talked with the devil.   235

ROSE: Troy, don't nobody wanna be hearing all that stuff.

LYONS *enters the yard from the street. Thirty-four years old,* TROY's *son by a previous
marriage, he sports a neatly trimmed goatee, sport coat, white shirt, tieless and buttoned
at the collar. Though he fancies himself a musician, he is more caught up in the rituals
and "idea" of being a musician than in the actual practice of the music. He has come to*

---

[2]Fictional narrator in books by Joel Chandler Harris that retell traditional black folktales featuring Brer Rabbit. —EDs.

borrow money from TROY, *and while he knows he will be successful, he is uncertain as to what extent his lifestyle will be held up to scrutiny and ridicule.*

LYONS: Hey, Pop.

TROY: What you come "Hey, Popping" me for?

LYONS: How you doing, Rose? *(He kisses her.)* Mr. Bono. How you doing?

BONO: Hey, Lyons . . . how you been?   240

TROY: He must have been doing all right. I ain't seen him around here last week.

ROSE: Troy, leave your boy alone. He come by to see you and you wanna start all that nonsense.

TROY: I ain't bothering Lyons. *(Offers him the bottle.)* Here . . . get you a drink. We got an understanding. I know why he come by to see me and he know I know.   245

LYONS: Come on, Pop . . . I just stopped by to say hi . . . see how you was doing.

TROY: You ain't stopped by yesterday.

ROSE: You gonna stay for supper, Lyons? I got some chicken cooking in the oven.

LYONS: No, Rose . . . thanks. I was just in the neighborhood and thought I'd stop by for a minute.   250

TROY: You was in the neighborhood all right, nigger. You telling the truth there. You was in the neighborhood cause it's my payday.

LYONS: Well, hell, since you mentioned it . . . let me have ten dollars.

TROY: I'll be damned! I'll die and go to hell and play blackjack with the devil before I give you ten dollars.   255

BONO: That's what I wanna know about . . . that devil you done seen.

LYONS: What . . . Pop done seen the devil? You too much, Pops.

TROY: Yeah, I done seen him. Talked to him too!

ROSE: You ain't seen no devil. I done told you that man ain't had nothing to do with the devil. Anything you can't understand, you want to call it the devil.   260

TROY: Look here, Bono . . . I went down to see Hertzberger about some furniture. Got three rooms for two-ninety-eight. That what it say on the radio. "Three rooms . . . two-ninety-eight." Even made up a little song about it. Go down there . . . man tell me I can't get no credit. I'm working every day and can't get no credit. What to do? I got an empty house with some raggedy furniture in it. Cory ain't got no bed. He's   265 sleeping on a pile of rags on the floor. Working every day and can't get no credit. Come back here—Rose'll tell you—madder than hell. Sit down . . . try to figure what I'm gonna do. Come a knock on the door. Ain't been living here but three days. Who know I'm here? Open the door . . . devil standing there bigger than life. White fellow . . . white fellow . . . got on good clothes and everything. Standing there   270 with a clipboard in his hand. I ain't had to say nothing. First words come out of his mouth was . . . "I understand you need some furniture and can't get no credit." I liked to fell over. He say, "I'll give you all the credit you want, but you got to pay the interest on it." I told him, "Give me three rooms worth and charge whatever you want." Next day a truck pulled up here and two men unloaded them three rooms.   275 Man what drove the truck give me a book. Say send ten dollars, first of every month to the address in the book and everything will be all right. Say if I miss a payment the devil was coming back and it'll be hell to pay. That was fifteen years ago. To this day . . . the first of the month I send my ten dollars, Rose'll tell you.

ROSE: Troy lying. 280

TROY: I ain't never seen that man since. Now you tell me who else that could have been but the devil? I ain't sold my soul or nothing like that, you understand. Naw, I wouldn't have truck with the devil about nothing like that. I got my furniture and pays my ten dollars the first of the month just like clockwork.

BONO: How long you say you been paying this ten dollars a month? 285

TROY: Fifteen years!

BONO: Hell, ain't you finished paying for it yet? How much the man done charged you?

TROY: Ah hell, I done paid for it. I done paid for it ten times over! The fact is I'm scared to stop paying it.

ROSE: Troy lying. We got that furniture from Mr. Glickman. He ain't paying no ten 290 dollars a month to nobody.

TROY: Aw hell, woman. Bono know I ain't that big a fool.

LYONS: I was just getting ready to say . . . I know where there's a bridge for sale.

TROY: Look here, I'll tell you this . . . it don't matter to me if he was the devil. It don't matter if the devil give credit. Somebody has got to give it. 295

ROSE: It ought to matter. You going around talking about having truck with the devil . . . God's the one you gonna have to answer to. He's the one gonna be at the Judgment.

LYONS: Yeah, well, look here, Pop . . . let me have that ten dollars. I'll give it back to you. Bonnie got a job working at the hospital. 300

TROY: What I tell you, Bono? The only time I see this nigger is when he wants something. That's the only time I see him.

LYONS: Come on, Pop, Mr. Bono don't want to hear all that. Let me have the ten dollars. I told you Bonnie working.

TROY: What that mean to me? "Bonnie working." I don't care if she working. Go ask 305 her for the ten dollars if she working. Talking about "Bonnie working." Why ain't you working?

LYONS: Aw, Pop, you know I can't find no decent job. Where am I gonna get a job at? You know I can't get no job.

TROY: I told you I know some people down there. I can get you on the rubbish if you want 310 to work. I told you that the last time you came by here asking me for something.

LYONS: Naw, Pop . . . thanks. That ain't for me. I don't wanna be carrying nobody's rubbish. I don't wanna be punching nobody's time clock.

TROY: What's the matter, you too good to carry people's rubbish? Where you think that ten dollars you talking about come from? I'm just supposed to haul people's 315 rubbish and give my money to you cause you too lazy to work. You too lazy to work and wanna know why you ain't got what I got.

ROSE: What hospital Bonnie working at? Mercy?

LYONS: She's down at Passavant working in the laundry.

TROY: I ain't got nothing as it is. I give you that ten dollars and I got to eat beans the 320 rest of the week. Naw . . . you ain't getting no ten dollars here.

LYONS: You ain't got to be eating no beans. I don't know why you wanna say that.

TROY: I ain't got no extra money. Gabe done moved over to Miss Pearl's paying her
the rent and things done got tight around here. I can't afford to be giving you
every payday. 325

LYONS: I ain't asked you to give me nothing. I asked you to loan me ten dollars. I
know you got ten dollars.

TROY: Yeah, I got it. You know why I got it? Cause I don't throw my money away out there
in the streets. You living the fast life . . . wanna be a musician . . . running around in
them clubs and things . . . then, you learn to take care of yourself. You ain't gonna find 330
me going and asking nobody for nothing. I done spent too many years without.

LYONS: You and me is two different people, Pop.

TROY: I done learned my mistake and learned to do what's right by it. You still trying
to get something for nothing. Life don't owe you nothing. You owe it to yourself.
Ask Bono. He'll tell you I'm right. 335

LYONS: You got your way of dealing with the world . . . I got mine. The only thing that
matters to me is the music.

TROY: Yeah, I can see that! It don't matter how you gonna eat . . . where your next
dollar is coming from. You telling the truth there.

LYONS: I know I got to eat. But I got to live too. I need something that gonna help me 340
to get out of the bed in the morning. Make me feel like I belong in the world. I
don't bother nobody. I just stay with the music cause that's the only way I can
find to live in the world. Otherwise there ain't no telling what I might do. Now
I don't come criticizing you and how you live. I just come by to ask you for ten
dollars. I don't wanna hear all that about how I live. 345

TROY: Boy, your mamma did a hell of a job raising you.

LYONS: You can't change me, Pop. I'm thirty-four years old. If you wanted to change
me, you should have been there when I was growing up. I come by to see you . . .
ask for ten dollars and you want to talk about how I was raised. You don't know
nothing about how I was raised. 350

ROSE: Let the boy have ten dollars, Troy.

TROY (*to* LYONS): What the hell you looking at me for? I ain't got no ten dollars. You
know what I do with my money. (*To* ROSE.) Give him ten dollars if you want
him to have it.

ROSE: I will. Just as soon as you turn it loose. 355

TROY (*handing* ROSE *the money*): There it is. Seventy-six dollars and forty-two cents.
You see this, Bono? Now, I ain't gonna get but six of that back.

ROSE: You ought to stop telling that lie. Here, Lyons. (*She hands him the money.*)

LYONS: Thanks, Rose. Look . . . I got to run . . . I'll see you later.

TROY: Wait a minute. You gonna say, "thanks, Rose" and ain't gonna look to see where 360
she got that ten dollars from? See how they do me, Bono?

LYONS: I know she got it from you, Pop. Thanks. I'll give it back to you.

TROY: There he go telling another lie. Time I see that ten dollars . . . he'll be owing
me thirty more.

LYONS: See you, Mr. Bono. 365

Bono: Take care, Lyons!

Lyons: Thanks, Pop. I'll see you again.

Lyons *exits the yard.*

Troy: I don't know why he don't go and get him a decent job and take care of that
woman he got.

Bono: He'll be all right, Troy. The boy is still young.   370

Troy: The *boy* is thirty-four years old.

Rose: Let's not get off into all that.

Bono: Look here . . . I got to be going. I got to be getting on. Lucille gonna be
waiting.

Troy (*puts his arm around* Rose): See this woman, Bono? I love this woman. I love this   375
woman so much it hurts. I love her so much . . . I done run out of ways of loving
her. So I got to go back to basics. Don't you come by my house Monday morning
talking about time to go to work . . . 'cause I'm still gonna be stroking!

Rose: Troy! Stop it now!

Bono: I ain't paying him no mind, Rose. That ain't nothing but gin-talk. Go on, Troy.   380
I'll see you Monday.

Troy: Don't you come by my house, nigger! I done told you what I'm gonna be
doing.

The lights go down to black.

Scene 2

The lights come up on Rose *hanging up clothes. She hums and sings softly to herself. It
is the following morning.*

Rose (*sings*): Jesus, be a fence all around me every day
Jesus, I want you to protect me as I travel on my way.
Jesus, be a fence all around me every day.

Troy *enters from the house.*

Jesus, I want you to protect me
As I travel on my way.
(*To* Troy.) 'Morning. You ready for breakfast? I can fix it soon as I finish hanging   5
up these clothes?

Troy: I got the coffee on. That'll be all right. I'll just drink some of that this morning.

Rose: That 651 hit yesterday. That's the second time this month. Miss Pearl hit for
a dollar . . . seem like those that need the least always get lucky. Poor folks can't   10
get nothing.

Troy: Them numbers don't know nobody. I don't know why you fool with them. You
and Lyons both.

Rose: It's something to do.

Troy: You ain't doing nothing but throwing your money away.   15

ROSE: Troy, you know I don't play foolishly. I just play a nickel here and a nickel there.

TROY: That's two nickels you done thrown away.

ROSE: Now I hit sometimes . . . that makes up for it. It always comes in handy when I do hit. I don't hear you complaining then. 20

TROY: I ain't complaining now. I just say it's foolish. Trying to guess out of six hundred ways which way the number gonna come. If I had all the money niggers, these Negroes, throw away on numbers for one week—just one week—I'd be a rich man.

ROSE: Well, you wishing and calling it foolish ain't gonna stop folks from playing 25 numbers. That's one thing for sure. Besides . . . some good things come from playing numbers. Look where Pope done bought him that restaurant off of numbers.

TROY: I can't stand niggers like that. Man ain't had two dimes to rub together. He walking around with his shoes all run over bumming money for cigarettes. All 30 right. Got lucky there and hit the numbers . . .

ROSE: Troy, I know all about it.

TROY: Had good sense, I'll say that for him. He ain't throwed his money away. I seen niggers hit the numbers and go through two thousand dollars in four days. Man bought him that restaurant down there . . . fixed it up real nice . . . and 35 then didn't want nobody to come in it! A Negro go in there and can't get no kind of service. I seen a white fellow come in there and order a bowl of stew. Pope picked all the meat out the pot for him. Man ain't had nothing but a bowl of meat! Negro come behind him and ain't got nothing but the potatoes and carrots. Talking about what numbers do for people, you picked a wrong 40 example. Ain't done nothing but make a worser fool out of him than he was before.

ROSE: Troy, you ought to stop worrying about what happened at work yesterday.

TROY: I ain't worried. Just told me to be down there at the Commissioner's office on Friday. Everybody think they gonna fire me. I ain't worried about them firing 45 me. You ain't got to worry about that. *(Pause.)* Where's Cory? Cory in the house? *(Calls.)* Cory?

ROSE: He gone out.

TROY: Out, huh? He gone out 'cause he know I want him to help me with this fence. I know how he is. That boy scared of work. 50

GABRIEL *enters. He comes halfway down the alley and, hearing* TROY's *voice, stops.*

TROY *(continues)*: He ain't done a lick of work in his life.

ROSE: He had to go to football practice. Coach wanted them to get in a little extra practice before the season start.

TROY: I got his practice . . . running out of here before he get his chores done.

ROSE: Troy, what is wrong with you this morning? Don't nothing set right with you. 55 Go on back in there and go to bed . . . get up on the other side.

TROY: Why something got to be wrong with me? I ain't said nothing wrong with me.

Rose: You got something to say about everything. First it's the numbers . . . then it's the way the man runs his restaurant . . . then you done got on Cory. What's it gonna be next? Take a look up there and see if the weather suits you . . . or is   60
it gonna be how you gonna put up the fence with the clothes hanging in the yard.

Troy: You hit the nail on the head then.

Rose: I know you like I know the back of my hand. Go on in there and get you some coffee . . . see if that straighten you up. 'Cause you ain't right this morning.   65

Troy *starts into the house and sees* Gabriel. Gabriel *starts singing. Troy's brother, he is seven years younger than* Troy. *Injured in World War II, he has a metal plate in his head. He carries an old trumpet tied around his waist and believes with every fiber of his being that he is the Archangel Gabriel. He carries a chipped basket with an assortment of discarded fruits and vegetables he has picked up in the strip district and which he attempts to sell.*

Gabriel *(singing)*: Yes, ma am, I got plums
   You ask me how I sell them
   Oh ten cents apiece
   Three for a quarter
   Come and buy now   70
   'Cause I'm here today
   And tomorrow I'll be gone

Gabriel *enters.*

   Hey, Rose!

Rose: How you doing, Gabe?

Gabriel: There's Troy . . . Hey, Troy!   75

Troy: Hey, Gabe.

Exit into kitchen.

Rose *(to* Gabriel*)*: What you got there?

Gabriel: You know what I got, Rose. I got fruits and vegetables.

Rose *(looking in basket)*: Where's all these plums you talking about?

Gabriel: I ain't got no plums today, Rose. I was just singing that. Have some tomor-   80
row. Put me in a big order for plums. Have enough plums tomorrow for St. Peter and everybody.

Troy *reenters from kitchen, crosses to steps.*

   (To Rose.*)* Troy's mad at me.

Troy: I ain't mad at you. What I got to be mad at you about? You ain't done nothing to me.   85

Gabriel: I just moved over to Miss Pearl's to keep out from in your way. I ain't mean no harm by it.

Troy: Who said anything about that? I ain't said anything about that.

GABRIEL: You ain't mad at me, is you?

TROY: Naw . . . I ain't mad at you, Gabe. If I was mad at you I'd tell you about it. 90

GABRIEL: Got me two rooms. In the basement. Got my own door too. Wanna see my key? *(He holds up a key.)* That's my own key! Ain't nobody else got a key like that. That's my key! My two rooms!

TROY: Well, that's good, Gabe. You got your own key . . . that's good.

ROSE: You hungry, Gabe? I was just fixing to cook Troy his breakfast. 95

GABRIEL: I'll take some biscuits. You got some biscuits? Did you know when I was in heaven . . . every morning me and St. Peter would sit down by the gate and eat some big fat biscuits? Oh, yeah! We had us a good time. We'd sit there and eat us them biscuits and then St. Peter would go off to sleep and tell me to wake him up when it's time to open the gates for the judgment. 100

ROSE: Well, come on . . . I'll make up a batch of biscuits.

ROSE *exits into the house.*

GABRIEL: Troy . . . St. Peter got your name in the book. I seen it. It say . . . Troy Maxson. I say . . . I know him! He got the same name like what I got. That's my brother!

TROY: How many times you gonna tell me that, Gabe?

GABRIEL: Ain't got my name in the book. Don't have to have my name. I done died and 105 went to heaven. He got your name though. One morning St. Peter was looking at his book . . . marking it up for the judgment . . . and he let me see your name. Got it in there under M. Got Rose's name . . . I ain't seen it like I seen yours . . . but I know it's in there. He got a great big book. Got everybody's name what was ever been born. That's what he told me. But I seen your name. Seen it with my own eyes. 110

TROY: Go on in the house there. Rose going to fix you something to eat.

GABRIEL: Oh, I ain't hungry. I done had breakfast with Aunt Jemimah. She come by and cooked me up a whole mess of flapjacks. Remember how we used to eat them flapjacks?

TROY: Go on in the house and get you something to eat now. 115

GABRIEL: I got to sell my plums. I done sold some tomatoes. Got me two quarters. Wanna see? *(He shows* TROY *his quarters.)* I'm gonna save them and buy me a new horn so St. Peter can hear me when it's time to open the gates. (GABRIEL *stops suddenly. Listens.)* Hear that? That's the hellhounds. I got to chase them out of here. Go on get out of here! Get out! 120

GABRIEL *exits singing.*

Better get ready for the judgment
Better get ready for the judgment
My Lord is coming down

ROSE *enters from the house.*

TROY: He's gone off somewhere.

GABRIEL *(offstage)*: Better get ready for the judgment 125
Better get ready for the judgment morning

Better get ready for the judgment
My God is coming down

ROSE: He ain't eating right. Miss Pearl say she can't get him to eat nothing.

TROY: What you want me to do about it, Rose? I done did everything I can for the man.   130
I can't make him get well. Man got half his head blown away . . . what you expect?

ROSE: Seem like something ought to be done to help him.

TROY: Man don't bother nobody. He just mixed up from that metal plate he got in his
head. Ain't no sense for him to go back into the hospital.

ROSE: Least he be eating right. They can help him take care of himself.   135

TROY: Don't nobody wanna be locked up, Rose. What you wanna lock him up for?
Man go over there and fight the war . . . messin' around with them Japs, get half
his head blown off . . . and they give him a lousy three thousand dollars. And I
had to swoop down on that.

ROSE: Is you fixing to go into that again?   140

TROY: That's the only way I got a roof over my head . . . cause of that metal plate.

ROSE: Ain't no sense you blaming yourself for nothing. Gabe wasn't in no condition
to manage that money. You done what was right by him. Can't nobody say you
ain't done what was right by him. Look how long you took care of him . . . till he
wanted to have his own place and moved over there with Miss Pearl.   145

TROY: That ain't what I'm saying, woman! I'm just stating the facts. If my brother
didn't have that metal plate in his head . . . I wouldn't have a pot to piss in or
a window to throw it out of. And I'm fifty-three years old. Now see if you can
understand that!

TROY *gets up from the porch and starts to exit the yard.*

ROSE: Where you going off to? You been running out of here every Saturday for   150
weeks. I thought you was gonna work on this fence?

TROY: I'm gonna walk down to Taylors'. Listen to the ball game. I'll be back in a bit.
I'll work on it when I get back.

He exits the yard. The lights go to black.

SCENE 3

The lights come up on the yard. It is four hours later. ROSE *is taking down the clothes
from the line.* CORY *enters carrying his football equipment.*

ROSE: Your daddy like to had a fit with you running out of here this morning without
doing your chores.

CORY: I told you I had to go to practice.

ROSE: He say you were supposed to help him with this fence.

CORY: He been saying that the last four or five Saturdays, and then he don't never do   5
nothing, but go down to Taylors. Did you tell him about the recruiter?

ROSE: Yeah, I told him.

CORY: What he say?

ROSE: He ain't said nothing too much. You get in there and get started on your chores before he gets back. Go on and scrub down them steps before he gets back here 10 hollering and carrying on.

CORY: I'm hungry. What you got to eat, Mama?

ROSE: Go on and get started on your chores. I got some meat loaf in there. Go on and make you a sandwich . . . and don't leave no mess in there.

CORY *exits into the house.* ROSE *continues to take down the clothes.* TROY *enters the yard and sneaks up and grabs her from behind.*

Troy! Go on, now. You liked to scared me to death. What was the score of the 15 game? Lucille had me on the phone and I couldn't keep up with it.

TROY: What I care about the game? Come here, woman. *(He tries to kiss her.)*

ROSE: I thought you went down Taylors' to listen to the game. Go on, Troy! You supposed to be putting up this fence.

TROY *(attempting to kiss her again)*: I'll put it up when I finish with what is at hand. 20

ROSE: Go on, Troy. I ain't studying you.

TROY *(chasing after her)*: I'm studying you . . . fixing to do my homework!

ROSE: Troy, you better leave me alone.

TROY: Where's Cory? That boy brought his butt home yet?

ROSE: He's in the house doing his chores. 25

TROY *(calling)*: Cory! Get your butt out here, boy!

ROSE *exits into the house with the laundry.* TROY *goes over to the pile of wood, picks up a board, and starts sawing.* CORY *enters from the house.*

TROY: You just now coming in here from leaving this morning?

CORY: Yeah, I had to go to football practice.

TROY: Yeah, what?

CORY: Yessir. 30

TROY: I ain't but two seconds off you noway. The garbage sitting in there overflowing . . . you ain't done none of your chores . . . and you come in here talking about "Yeah."

CORY: I was just getting ready to do my chores now, Pop . . .

TROY: Your first chore is to help me with this fence on Saturday. Everything else come after that. Now get that saw and cut them boards. 35

CORY *takes the saw and begins cutting the boards.* TROY *continues working. There is a long pause.*

CORY: Hey, Pop . . . why don't you buy a TV?

TROY: What I want with a TV? What I want one of them for?

CORY: Everybody got one. Earl, Ba Bra . . . Jesse!

TROY: I ain't asked you who had one. I say what I want with one?

CORY: So you can watch it. They got lots of things on TV. Baseball games and every- 40 thing. We could watch the World Series.

TROY: Yeah . . . and how much this TV cost?

CORY: I don't know. They got them on sale for around two hundred dollars.

TROY: Two hundred dollars, huh?

CORY: That ain't that much, Pop.   45

TROY: Naw, it's just two hundred dollars. See that roof you got over your head at night? Let me tell you something about that roof. It's been over ten years since that roof was last tarred. See now . . . the snow come this winter and sit up there on that roof like it is . . . and it's gonna seep inside. It's just gonna be a little bit . . . ain't gonna hardly notice it. Then the next thing you know, it's gonna be leaking all   50 over the house. Then the wood rot from all that water and you gonna need a whole new roof. Now, how much you think it cost to get that roof tarred?

CORY: I don't know.

TROY: Two hundred and sixty-four dollars . . . cash money. While you thinking about a TV, I got to be thinking about the roof . . . and whatever else go wrong here. Now   55 if you had two hundred dollars, what would you do . . . fix the roof or buy a TV?

CORY: I'd buy a TV. Then when the roof started to leak . . . when it needed fixing . . . I'd fix it.

TROY: Where you gonna get the money from? You done spent it for a TV. You gonna sit up and watch the water run all over your brand new TV.   60

CORY: Aw, Pop. You got money. I know you do.

TROY: Where I got it at, huh?

CORY: You got it in the bank.

TROY: You wanna see my bankbook? You wanna see that seventy-three dollars and twenty-two cents I got sitting up in there.   65

CORY: You ain't got to pay for it all at one time. You can put a down payment on it and carry it on home with you.

TROY: Not me. I ain't gonna owe nobody nothing if I can help it. Miss a payment and they come and snatch it right out your house. Then what you got? Now, soon as I get two hundred dollars clear, then I'll buy a TV. Right now, as soon as I get two   70 hundred and sixty-four dollars, I'm gonna have this roof tarred.

CORY: Aw . . . Pop!

TROY: You go on and get you two hundred dollars and buy one if ya want it. I got better things to do with my money.

CORY: I can't get no two hundred dollars. I ain't never seen two hundred dollars.   75

TROY: I'll tell you what . . . you get you a hundred dollars and I'll put the other hundred with it.

CORY: All right, I'm gonna show you.

TROY: You gonna show me how you can cut them boards right now.

CORY *begins to cut the boards. There is a long pause.*

CORY: The Pirates won today. That makes five in a row.   80

TROY: I ain't thinking about the Pirates. Got an all-white team. Got that boy . . . that Puerto Rican boy . . . Clemente. Don't even half-play him. That boy could be something if they give him a chance. Play him one day and sit him on the bench the next.

CORY: He gets a lot of chances to play.   85

TROY: I'm talking about playing regular. Playing every day so you can get your timing. That's what I'm talking about.

CORY: They got some white guys on the team that don't play every day. You can't play everybody at the same time.

TROY: If they got a white fellow sitting on the bench . . . you can bet your last dollar   90
he can't play! The colored guy got to be twice as good before he get on the team. That's why I don't want you to get all tied up in them sports. Man on the team and what it get him? They got colored on the team and don't use them. Same as not having them. All them teams the same.

CORY: The Braves got Hank Aaron and Wes Covington. Hank Aaron hit two home   95
runs today. That makes forty-three.

TROY: Hank Aaron ain't nobody. That what you supposed to do. That's how you supposed to play the game. Ain't nothing to it. It's just a matter of timing . . . getting the right follow-through. Hell, I can hit forty-three home runs right now!

CORY: Not off no major-league pitching, you couldn't.   100

TROY: We had better pitching in the Negro leagues. I hit seven home runs off of Satchel Paige. You can't get no better than that!

CORY: Sandy Koufax. He's leading the league in strikeouts.

TROY: I ain't thinking of no Sandy Koufax.

CORY: You got Warren Spahn and Lew Burdette. I bet you couldn't hit no home runs   105
off of Warren Spahn.

TROY: I'm through with it now. You go on and cut them boards. *(Pause.)* Your mama tell me you done got recruited by a college football team? Is that right?

CORY: Yeah. Coach Zellman say the recruiter gonna be coming by to talk to you. Get you to sign the permission papers.   110

TROY: I thought you supposed to be working down there at the A&P. Ain't you suppose to be working down there after school?

CORY: Mr. Stawicki say he gonna hold my job for me until after the football season. Say starting next week I can work weekends.

TROY: I thought we had an understanding about this football stuff? You suppose to   115
keep up with your chores and hold that job down at the A&P. Ain't been around here all day on a Saturday. Ain't none of your chores done . . . and now you telling me you done quit your job.

CORY: I'm going to be working weekends.

TROY: You damn right you are! And ain't no need for nobody coming around here to   120
talk to me about signing nothing.

CORY: Hey, Pop . . . you can't do that. He's coming all the way from North Carolina.

TROY: I don't care where he coming from. The white man ain't gonna let you get nowhere with that football noway. You go on and get your book-learning so you can work yourself up in that A&P or learn how to fix cars or build houses   125
or something, get you a trade. That way you have something can't nobody take away from you. You go on and learn how to put your hands to some good use. Besides hauling people's garbage.

CORY: I get good grades, Pop. That's why the recruiter wants to talk with you. You
  got to keep up your grades to get recruited. This way I'll be going to college. I'll   130
  get a chance . . .
TROY: First you gonna get your butt down there to the A&P and get your job back.
CORY: Mr. Stawicki done already hired somebody else 'cause I told him I was playing
  football.
TROY: You a bigger fool than I thought . . . to let somebody take away your job so   135
  you can play some football. Where you gonna get your money to take out your
  girlfriend and whatnot? What kind of foolishness is that to let somebody take
  away your job?
CORY: I'm still gonna be working weekends.
TROY: Naw . . . naw. You getting your butt out of here and finding you another job.   140
CORY: Come on, Pop! I got to practice. I can't work after school and play football too.
  The team needs me. That's what Coach Zellman say . . .
TROY: I don't care what nobody else say. I'm the boss . . . you understand? I'm the boss
  around here. I do the only saying what counts.
CORY: Come on, Pop!   145
TROY: I asked you . . . did you understand?
CORY: Yeah . . .
TROY: What?!
CORY: Yessir.
TROY: You go on down there to that A&P and see if you can get your job back. If you   150
  can't do both . . . then you quit the football team. You've got to take the crookeds
  with the straights.
CORY: Yessir. *(Pause.)* Can I ask you a question?
TROY: What the hell you wanna ask me? Mr. Stawicki the one you got the questions
  for.   155
CORY: How come you ain't never liked me?
TROY: Liked you? Who the hell say I got to like you? What law is there say I got to
  like you? Wanna stand up in my face and ask a damn fool-ass question like that.
  Talking about liking somebody. Come here, boy, when I talk to you.

CORY *comes over to where* TROY *is working. He stands slouched over and* TROY *shoves
him on his shoulder.*

  Straighten up, goddammit! I asked you a question . . . what law is there say I got   160
  to like you?
CORY: None.
TROY: Well, all right then! Don't you eat every day? *(Pause.)* Answer me when I talk
  to you! Don't you eat every day?
CORY: Yeah.   165
TROY: Nigger, as long as you in my house, you put that sir on the end of it when you
  talk to me!
CORY: Yes . . . sir.
TROY: You eat every day.

CORY: Yessir!   170
TROY: Got a roof over your head.
CORY: Yessir!
TROY: Got clothes on your back.
CORY: Yessir.
TROY: Why you think that is?   175
CORY: Cause of you.
TROY: Ah, hell I know it's cause of me . . . but why do you think that is?
CORY (hesitant): Cause you like me.
TROY: Like you? I go out of here every morning . . . bust my butt . . . putting up with
    them crackers every day . . . cause I like you? You are the biggest fool I ever saw.   180
    (Pause.) It's my job. It's my responsibility! You understand that? A man got to
    take care of his family. You live in my house . . . sleep you behind on my bed-
    clothes . . . fill you belly up with my food . . . cause you my son. You my flesh
    and blood. Not cause I like you! Cause it's my duty to take care of you. I owe a
    responsibility to you! Let's get this straight right here . . . before it go along any   185
    further . . . I ain't got to like you. Mr. Rand don't give me my money come payday
    cause he likes me. He give me cause he owe me. I done give you everything I had
    to give you. I gave you your life! Me and your mama worked that out between
    us. And liking your black ass wasn't part of the bargain. Don't you try and go
    through life worrying about if somebody like you or not. You best be making   190
    sure they doing right by you. You understand what I'm saying, boy?
CORY: Yessir.
TROY: Then get the hell out of my face, and get on down to that A&P.

ROSE *has been standing behind the screen door for much of the scene. She enters as* CORY
exits.

ROSE: Why don't you let the boy go ahead and play football, Troy? Ain't no harm in
    that. He's just trying to be like you with the sports.   195
TROY: I don't want him to be like me! I want him to move as far away from my life as he
    can get. You the only decent thing that ever happened to me. I wish him that. But
    I don't wish him a thing else from my life. I decided seventeen years ago that boy
    wasn't getting involved in no sports. Not after what they did to me in the sports.
ROSE: Troy, why don't you admit you was too old to play in the major leagues? For   200
    once . . . why don't you admit that?
TROY: What do you mean too old? Don't come telling me I was too old. I just wasn't
    the right color. Hell, I'm fifty-three years old and can do better than Selkirk's
    .269 right now!
ROSE: How's was you gonna play ball when you were over forty? Sometimes I can't   205
    get no sense out of you.
TROY: I got good sense, woman. I got sense enough not to let my boy get hurt over playing
    no sports. You been mothering that boy too much. Worried about if people like him.
ROSE: Everything that boy do . . . he do for you. He wants you to say "Good job, son."
    That's all.   210

TROY: Rose, I ain't got time for that. He's alive. He's healthy. He's got to make his own way. I made mine. Ain't nobody gonna hold his hand when he get out there in that world.

ROSE: Times have changed from when you was young, Troy. People change. The world's changing around you and you can't even see it.   215

TROY (*slow, methodical*): Woman . . . I do the best I can do. I come in here every Friday. I carry a sack of potatoes and a bucket of lard. You all line up at the door with your hands out. I give you the lint from my pockets. I give you my sweat and my blood. I ain't got no tears. I done spent them. We go upstairs in that room at night . . . and I fall down on you and try to blast a hole into for-   220 ever. I get up Monday morning . . . find my lunch on the table. I go out. Make my way. Find my strength to carry me through to the next Friday. (*Pause.*) That's all I got, Rose. That's all I got to give. I can't give nothing else.

TROY *exits into the house. The lights go down to black.*

SCENE 4

It is Friday. Two weeks later. CORY *starts out of the house with his football equipment. The phone rings.*

CORY (*calling*): I got it! (*He answers the phone and stands in the screen door talking.*) Hello? Hey, Jesse. Naw . . . I was just getting ready to leave now.

ROSE (*calling*): Cory!

CORY: I told you, man, them spikes is all tore up. You can use them if you want, but they ain't no good. Earl got some spikes.   5

ROSE (*calling*): Cory!

CORY (*calling to* ROSE): Mam? I'm talking to Jesse. (*Into phone.*) When she say that? (*Pause.*) Aw, you lying, man. I'm gonna tell her you said that.

ROSE (*calling*): Cory, don't you go nowhere!

CORY: I got to go to the game, Ma! (*Into the phone.*) Yeah, hey, look, I'll talk to you   10 later. Yeah, I'll meet you over Earl's house. Later. Bye, Ma.

CORY *exits the house and starts out the yard.*

ROSE: Cory, where you going off to? You got that stuff all pulled out and thrown all over your room.

CORY (*in the yard*): I was looking for my spikes. Jesse wanted to borrow my spikes.

ROSE: Get up there and get that cleaned up before your daddy get back in here.   15

CORY: I got to go to the game! I'll clean it up *when I get back.*

CORY *exits.*

ROSE: That's all he need to do is see that room all messed up.

ROSE *exits into the house.* TROY *and* BONO *enter the yard.* TROY *is dressed in clothes other than his work clothes.*

BONO: He told him the same thing he told you. Take it to the union.

TROY: Brownie ain't got that much sense. Man wasn't thinking about nothing. He wait until I confront them on it . . . then he wanna come crying seniority. *(Calls.)* Hey, Rose!

BONO: I wish I could have seen Mr. Rand's face when he told you.

TROY: He couldn't get it out of his mouth! Liked to bit his tongue! When they called me down there to the Commissioner's office . . . he thought they was gonna fire me. Like everybody else.

BONO: I didn't think they was gonna fire you. I thought they was gonna put you on the warning paper.

TROY: Hey, Rose! *(To* BONO.*)* Yeah, Mr. Rand like to bit his tongue.

TROY *breaks the seal on the bottle, takes a drink, and hands it to* BONO.

BONO: I see you run right down to Taylors' and told that Alberta gal.

TROY *(calling)*: Hey Rose! *(To* BONO.*)* I told everybody. Hey, Rose! I went down there to cash my check.

ROSE *(entering from the house)*: Hush all that hollering, man! I know you out here. What they say down there at the Commissioner's office?

TROY: You supposed to come when I call you, woman. Bono'll tell you that. *(To* BONO.*)* Don't Lucille come when you call her?

ROSE: Man, hush your mouth. I ain't no dog . . . talk about "come when you call me."

TROY *(puts his arm around* ROSE*)*: You hear this, Bono? I had me an old dog used to get uppity like that. You say, "C'mere, Blue!" . . . and he just lay there and look at you. End up getting a stick and chasing him away trying to make him come.

ROSE: I ain't studying you and your dog. I remember you used to sing that old song.

TROY *(he sings)*: Hear it ring! Hear it ring! I had a dog his name was Blue.

ROSE: Don't nobody wanna hear you sing that old song.

TROY *(sings)*: You know Blue was mighty true.

ROSE: Used to have Cory running around here singing that song.

BONO: Hell, I remember that song myself.

TROY *(sings)*: You know Blue was a good old dog.
  Blue treed a possum in a hollow log.
  That was my daddy's song. My daddy made up that song.

ROSE: I don't care who made it up. Don't nobody wanna hear you sing it.

TROY *(makes a song like calling a dog)*: Come here, woman.

ROSE: You come in here carrying on, I reckon they ain't fired you. What they say down there at the Commissioner's office?

TROY: Look here, Rose . . . Mr. Rand called me into his office today when I got back from talking to them people down there . . . it come from up top . . . he called me in and told me they was making me a driver.

ROSE: Troy, you kidding!

TROY: No I ain't. Ask Bono.

ROSE: Well, that's great, Troy. Now you don't have to hassle them people no more.

LYONS *enters from the street.*

TROY: Aw hell, I wasn't looking to see you today. I thought you was in jail. Got it all 60
over the front page of the *Courier* about them raiding Sefus's place . . . where you
be hanging out with all them thugs.

LYONS: Hey, Pop . . . that ain't got nothing to do with me. I don't go down there gambling. I go down there to sit in with the band. I ain't got nothing to do with the
gambling part. They got some good music down there. 65

TROY: They got some rogues . . . is what they got.

LYONS: How you been, Mr. Bono? Hi, Rose.

BONO: I see where you playing down at the Crawford Grill tonight.

ROSE: How come you ain't brought Bonnie like I told you? You should have brought
Bonnie with you, she ain't been over in a month of Sundays. 70

LYONS: I was just in the neighborhood . . . thought I'd stop by.

TROY: Here he come . . .

BONO: Your daddy got a promotion on the rubbish. He's gonna be the first colored
driver. Ain't got to do nothing but sit up there and read the paper like them
white fellows. 75

LYONS: Hey, Pop . . . if you knew how to read you'd be all right.

BONO: Naw . . . naw . . . you mean if the nigger knew how to *drive* he'd be all right.
Been fighting with them people about driving and ain't even got a license.
Mr. Rand know you ain't got no driver's license?

TROY: Driving ain't nothing. All you do is point the truck where you want it to go. 80
Driving ain't nothing.

BONO: Do Mr. Rand know you ain't got no driver's license? That's what I'm talking
about. I ain't asked if driving was easy. I asked if Mr. Rand know you ain't got
no driver's license.

TROY: He ain't got to know. The man ain't got to know my business. Time he find out, 85
I have two or three driver's licenses.

LYONS (*going into his pocket*): Say, look here, Pop . . .

TROY: I knew it was coming. Didn't I tell you, Bono? I know what kind of "Look
here, Pop" that was. The nigger fixing to ask me for some money. It's Friday
night. It's my payday. All them rogues down there on the avenue . . . the ones 90
that ain't in jail . . . and Lyons is hopping in his shoes to get down there with
them.

LYONS: See, Pop . . . if you give somebody else a chance to talk sometimes, you'd see
that I was fixing to pay you back your ten dollars like I told you. Here . . . I told
you I'd pay you when Bonnie got paid. 95

TROY: Naw . . . you go ahead and keep that ten dollars. Put it in the bank. The next
time you feel like you wanna come by here and ask me for something . . . you go
on down there and get that.

LYONS: Here's your ten dollars, Pop. I told you I don't want you to give me nothing.
I just wanted to borrow ten dollars. 100

TROY: Naw . . . you go on and keep that for the next time you want to ask me.

LYONS: Come on, Pop . . . here go your ten dollars.

ROSE: Why don't you go on and let the boy pay you back, Troy?

LYONS: Here you go, Rose. If you don't take it I'm gonna have to hear about it for the next six months. *(He hands her the money.)* 105

ROSE: You can hand yours over here too, Troy.

TROY: You see this, Bono. You see how they do me.

BONO: Yeah, Lucille do me the same way.

GABRIEL *is heard singing offstage. He enters.*

GABRIEL: Better get ready for the Judgment! Better get ready for . . . Hey! . . . Hey! . . . There's Troy's boy! 110

LYONS: How are you doing, Uncle Gabe?

GABRIEL: Lyons . . . The King of the Jungle! Rose . . . hey, Rose. Got a flower for you. *(He takes a rose from his pocket.)* Picked it myself. That's the same rose like you is!

ROSE: That's right nice of you, Gabe.

LYONS: What you been doing, Uncle Gabe? 115

GABRIEL: Oh, I been chasing hellhounds and waiting on the time to tell St. Peter to open the gates.

LYONS: You been chasing hellhounds, huh? Well . . . you doing the right thing, Uncle Gabe. Somebody got to chase them.

GABRIEL: Oh, yeah . . . I know it. The devil's strong. The devil ain't no pushover. 120 Hellhounds snipping at everybody's heels. But I got my trumpet waiting on the Judgment time.

LYONS: Waiting on the Battle of Armageddon, huh?

GABRIEL: Ain't gonna be too much of a battle when God get to waving that Judgment sword. But the people's gonna have a hell of a time trying to get into heaven if 125 them gates ain't open.

LYONS *(putting his arm around* GABRIEL*)*: You hear this, Pop. Uncle Gabe, you all right!

GABRIEL *(laughing with* LYONS*)*: Lyons! King of the Jungle.

ROSE: You gonna stay for supper, Gabe? Want me to fix you a plate? 130

GABRIEL: I'll take a sandwich, Rose. Don't want no plate. Just wanna eat with my hands. I'll take a sandwich.

ROSE: How about you, Lyons? You staying? Got some short ribs cooking.

LYONS: Naw, I won't eat nothing till after we finished playing. *(Pause.)* You ought to come down and listen to me play Pop. 135

TROY: I don't like that Chinese music. All that noise.

ROSE: Go on in the house and wash up, Gabe . . . I'll fix you a sandwich.

GABRIEL *(to* LYONS, *as he exits)*: Troy's mad at me.

LYONS: What you mad at Uncle Gabe for, Pop?

ROSE: He thinks Troy's mad at him cause he moved over to Miss Pearl's. 140

TROY: I ain't mad at the man. He can live where he want to live at.

LYONS: What he move over there for? Miss Pearl don't like nobody.

Rose: She don't mind him none. She treats him real nice. She just don't allow all that singing.

Troy: She don't mind that rent he be paying . . . that's what she don't mind. 145

Rose: Troy, I ain't going through that with you no more. He's over there cause he want to have his own place. He can come and go as he please.

Troy: Hell, he could come and go as he please here. I wasn't stopping him. I ain't put no rules on him.

Rose: It ain't the same thing, Troy. And you know it. 150

Gabriel *comes to the door.*

Now, that's the last I wanna hear about that. I don't wanna hear nothing else about Gabe and Miss Pearl. And next week . . .

Gabriel: I'm ready for my sandwich, Rose.

Rose: And next week . . . when that recruiter come from that school . . . I want you to sign that paper and go on and let Cory play football. Then that'll be the last I 155 have to hear about that.

Troy (*to* Rose *as she exits into the house*): I ain't thinking about Cory nothing.

Lyons: What . . . Cory got recruited? What school he going to?

Troy: That boy walking around here smelling his piss . . . thinking he's grown. Thinking he's gonna do what he want, irrespective of what I say. Look here, Bono . . . I left 160 the Commissioner's office and went down to the A&P . . . that boy ain't working down there. He lying to me. Telling me he got his job back . . . telling me he working weekends . . . telling me he working after school . . . Mr. Stawicki tell me he ain't working down there at all!

Lyons: Cory just growing up. He's just busting at the seams trying to fill out your 165 shoes.

Troy: I don't care what he's doing. When he get to the point where he wanna disobey me . . . then it's time for him to move on. Bono'll tell you that. I bet he ain't never disobeyed his daddy without paying the consequences.

Bono: I ain't never had a chance. My daddy came on through . . . but I ain't never 170 knew him to see him . . . or what he had on his mind or where he went. Just moving on through. Searching out the New Land. That's what the old folks used to call it. See a fellow moving around from place to place . . . woman to woman . . . called it searching out the New Land. I can't say if he ever found it. I come along, didn't want no kids. Didn't know if I was gonna be in one place long enough to 175 fix on them right as their daddy. I figured I was going searching too. As it turned out I been hooked up with Lucille near about as long as your daddy been with Rose. Going on sixteen years.

Troy: Sometimes I wish I hadn't known my daddy. He ain't cared nothing about no kids. A kid to him wasn't nothing. All he wanted was for you to learn how to walk 180 so he could start you to working. When it come time for eating . . . he ate first. If there was anything left over, that's what you got. Man would sit down and eat two chickens and give you the wing.

LYONS: You ought to stop that, Pop. Everybody feed their kids. No matter how hard times is . . . everybody care about their kids. Make sure they have something to eat. 185

TROY: The only thing my daddy cared about was getting them bales of cotton in to Mr. Lubin. That's the only thing that mattered to him. Sometimes I used to wonder why he was living. Wonder why the devil hadn't come and got him. "Get them bales of cotton in to Mr. Lubin" and find out he owe him money . . .

LYONS: He should have just went on and left when he saw he couldn't get nowhere. 190 That's what I would have done.

TROY: How he gonna leave with eleven kids? And where he gonna go? He ain't knew how to do nothing but farm. No, he was trapped and I think he knew it. But I'll say this for him . . . he felt a responsibility toward us. Maybe he ain't treated us the way I felt he should have . . . but without that responsibility he could have 195 walked off and left us . . . made his own way.

BONO: A lot of them did. Back in those days what you talking about . . . they walk out their front door and just take on down one road or another and keep on walking.

LYONS: There you go! That's what I'm talking about. 200

BONO: Just keep on walking till you come to something else. Ain't you never heard of nobody having the walking blues? Well, that's what you call it when you just take off like that.

TROY: My daddy ain't had them walking blues! What you talking about? He stayed right there with his family. But he was just as evil as he could be. My mama 205 couldn't stand him. Couldn't stand that evilness. She run off when I was about eight. She sneaked off one night after he had gone to sleep. Told me she was coming back for me. I ain't never seen her no more. All his women run off and left him. He wasn't good for nobody.

When my turn come to head out, I was fourteen and got to sniffing around 210 Joe Canewell's daughter. Had us an old mule we called Greyboy. My daddy sent me out to do some plowing and I tied up Greyboy and went to fooling around with Joe Canewell's daughter. We done found us a nice little spot, got real cozy with each other. She about thirteen and we done figured we was grown anyway . . . so we down there enjoying ourselves . . . ain't thinking about nothing. We didn't 215 know Greyboy had got loose and wandered back to the house and my daddy was looking for me. We down there by the creek enjoying ourselves when my daddy come up on us. Surprised us. He had them leather straps off the mule and commenced to whupping me like there was no tomorrow. I jumped up, mad and embarrassed. I was scared of my daddy. When he commenced to whupping 220 on me . . . quite naturally I run to get out of the way. (*Pause.*) Now I thought he was mad cause I ain't done my work. But I see where he was chasing me off so he could have the gal for himself. When I see what the matter of it was, I lost all fear of my daddy. Right there is where I become a man . . . at fourteen years of age. (*Pause.*) Now it was my turn to run him off. I picked up them same reins 225 that he had used on me. I picked up them reins and commenced to whupping on him. The gal jumped up and run off . . . and when my daddy turned to face me, I could see why the devil had never come to get him . . . cause he was the devil himself. I don't know what happened. When I woke up, I was laying right there by the creek, and Blue . . . this old dog we had . . . was licking my face. I thought 230 I was blind. I couldn't see nothing. Both my eyes were swollen shut. I laid there and cried. I didn't know what I was gonna do. The only thing I knew was the time had come for me to leave my daddy's house. And right there the world suddenly got big. And it was a long time before I could cut it down to where I could handle it. 235

 Part of that cutting down was when I got to the place where I could feel him kicking in my blood and knew that the only thing that separated us was the matter of a few years.

GABRIEL *enters from the house with a sandwich.*

LYONS: What you got there, Uncle Gabe?

GABRIEL: Got me a ham sandwich. Rose gave me a ham sandwich. 240

TROY: I don't know what happened to him. I done lost touch with everybody except Gabriel. But I hope he's dead. I hope he found some peace.

LYONS: That's a heavy story, Pop. I didn't know you left home when you was fourteen.

TROY: And didn't know nothing. The only part of the world I knew was the forty-two acres of Mr. Lubin's land. That's all I knew about life. 245

LYONS: Fourteen's kinda young to be out on your own. *(Phone rings.)* I don't even think I was ready to be out on my own at fourteen. I don't know what I would have done.

TROY: I got up from the creek and walked on down to Mobile. I was through with farming. Figured I could do better in the city. So I walked the two hundred miles 250 to Mobile.

LYONS: Wait a minute . . . you ain't walked no two hundred miles, Pop. Ain't nobody gonna walk no two hundred miles. You talking about some walking there.

BONO: That's the only way you got anywhere back in them days.

LYONS: Shhh. Damn if I wouldn't have hitched a ride with somebody! 255

TROY: Who you gonna hitch it with? They ain't had no cars and things like they got now. We talking about 1918.

ROSE *(entering)*: What you all out here getting into?

TROY *(to* ROSE*)*: I'm telling Lyons how good he got it. He don't know nothing about this I'm talking. 260

ROSE: Lyons, that was Bonnie on the phone. She say you supposed to pick her up.

LYONS: Yeah, okay, Rose.

TROY: I walked on down to Mobile and hitched up with some of them fellows that was heading this way. Got up here and found out . . . not only couldn't you get a job . . . you couldn't find no place to live. I thought I was in freedom. Shhh. 265 Colored folks living down there on the riverbanks in whatever kind of shelter they could find for themselves. Right down there under the Brady Street Bridge. Living in shacks made of sticks and tarpaper. Messed around there and went from bad to worse. Started stealing. First it was food. Then I figured, hell, if I steal money I can buy me some food. Buy me some shoes too! One thing led to another. Met your mama. I was young and anxious to be a man. Met your mama and had you. What I do that for? Now I got to worry about feeding you and her. Got to steal three times as much. Went out one day looking for somebody to rob . . . that's what I was, a robber. I'll tell you the truth. I'm ashamed of it today. But it's the truth. Went to rob this fellow . . . pulled out my knife . . . and he pulled out a gun. Shot me in the chest. I felt just like somebody had taken a hot branding iron and laid it on me. When he shot me I jumped at him with my knife. They told me I killed him and they put me in the penitentiary and locked me up for fifteen years. That's where I met Bono. That's where I learned how to play baseball. Got out that place and your mama had taken you and went on to make life without me. Fifteen years was a long time for her to wait. But that fifteen years cured me of that robbing stuff. Rose'll tell you. She asked me when I met her if I had gotten all that foolishness out of my system. And I told her, "Baby, it's you and baseball all what count with me." You hear me, Bono? I meant it too. She say, "Which one comes first?" I told her, "Baby, ain't no doubt it's baseball . . . but you stick and get old with me and we'll both outlive this baseball." Am I right, Rose? And it's true.

ROSE: Man, hush your mouth. You ain't said no such thing. Talking about, "Baby, you know you'll always be number one with me." That's what you was talking.

TROY: You hear that, Bono. That's why I love her.

BONO: Rose'll keep you straight. You get off the track, she'll straighten you up.

ROSE: Lyons, you better get on up and get Bonnie. She waiting on you.

LYONS (*gets up to go*): Hey, Pop, why don't you come on down to the Grill and hear me play?

TROY: I ain't going down there. I'm too old to be sitting around in them clubs.

BONO: You got to be good to play down at the Grill.

LYONS: Come on, Pop . . .

TROY: I got to get up in the morning.

LYONS: You ain't got to stay long.

TROY: Naw, I'm gonna get my supper and go on to bed.

LYONS: Well, I got to go. I'll see you again.

TROY: Don't you come around my house on my payday.

ROSE: Pick up the phone and let somebody know you coming. And bring Bonnie with you. You know I'm always glad to see her.

LYONS: Yeah, I'll do that, Rose. You take care now. See you, Pop. See you, Mr. Bono. See you, Uncle Gabe.

GABRIEL: Lyons! King of the Jungle!

LYONS *exits*.

TROY: Is supper ready, woman? Me and you got some business to take care of. I'm gonna tear it up too.

ROSE: Troy, I done told you now!

TROY (*puts his arm around* BONO): Aw hell, woman . . . this is Bono. Bono like family. I done known this nigger since . . . how long I done know you?

BONO: It's been a long time.

TROY: I done know this nigger since Skippy was a pup. Me and him done been through some times.   315

BONO: You sure right about that.

TROY: Hell, I done know him longer than I known you. And we still standing shoulder to shoulder. Hey, look here, Bono . . . a man can't ask for no more than that. (*Drinks to him.*) I love you, nigger.

BONO: Hell, I love you too . . . I got to get home see my woman. You got yours in   320
hand. I got to go get mine.

BONO *starts to exit as* CORY *enters the yard, dressed in his football uniform. He gives* TROY *a hard, uncompromising look.*

CORY: What you do that for, Pop?

He throws his helmet down in the direction of TROY.

ROSE: What's the matter? Cory . . . what's the matter?

CORY: Papa done went up to the school and told Coach Zellman I can't play football no more. Wouldn't even let me play the game. Told him to tell the recruiter not   325
to come.

ROSE: Troy . . .

TROY: What you Troying me for. Yeah, I did it. And the boy know why I did it.

CORY: Why you wanna do that to me? That was the one chance I had.

ROSE: Ain't nothing wrong with Cory playing football, Troy.   330

TROY: The boy lied to me. I told the nigger if he wanna play football . . . to keep up his chores and hold down that job at the A&P. That was the conditions. Stopped down there to see Mr. Stawicki . . .

CORY: I can't work after school during the football season, Pop! I tried to tell you that Mr. Stawicki's holding my job for me. You don't never want to listen to nobody.   335
And then you wanna go and do this to me!

TROY: I ain't done nothing to you. You done it to yourself.

CORY: Just cause you didn't have a chance! You just scared I'm gonna be better than you, that's all.

TROY: Come here.   340

ROSE: Troy . . .

CORY *reluctantly crosses over to* TROY.

TROY: All right! See. You done made a mistake.

CORY: I didn't even do nothing!

TROY: I'm gonna tell you what your mistake was. See . . . you swung at the ball and didn't hit it. That's strike one. See, you in the batter's box now. You swung and   345
you missed. That's strike one. Don't you strike out!

Lights fade to black.

ACT II

SCENE 1

The following morning. CORY *is at the tree hitting the ball with the bat. He tries to mimic* TROY, *but his swing is awkward, less sure.* ROSE *enters from the house.*

ROSE: Cory, I want you to help me with this cupboard.

CORY: I ain't quitting the team. I don't care what Poppa say.

ROSE: I'll talk to him when he gets back. He had to go see about your Uncle Gabe. The police done arrested him. Say he was disturbing the peace. He'll be back directly. Come on in here and help me clean out the top of this cupboard.   5

CORY *exits into the house.* ROSE *sees* TROY *and* BONO *coming down the alley.*

Troy . . . what they say down there?

TROY: Ain't said nothing. I give them fifty dollars and they let him go. I'll talk to you about it. Where's Cory?

ROSE: He's in there helping me clean out these cupboards.

TROY: Tell him to get his butt out here.   10

TROY *and* BONO *go over to the pile of wood.* BONO *picks up the saw and begins sawing.*

TROY *(to* BONO*):* All they want is the money. That makes six or seven times I done went down there and got him. See me coming they stick out their hands.

BONO: Yeah. I know what you mean. That's all they care about . . . that money. They don't care about what's right. *(Pause.)* Nigger, why you got to go and get some hard wood? You ain't doing nothing but building a little old fence. Get you some   15 soft pine wood. That's all you need.

TROY: I know what I'm doing. This is outside wood. You put pine wood inside the house. Pine wood is inside wood. This here is outside wood. Now you tell me where the fence is gonna be?

BONO: You don't need this wood. You can put it up with pine wood and it'll stand as   20 long as you gonna be here looking at it.

TROY: How you know how long I'm gonna be here, nigger? Hell, I might just live forever. Live longer than old man Horsely.

BONO: That's what Magee used to say.

TROY: Magee's a damn fool. Now you tell me who you ever heard of gonna pull their   25 own teeth with a pair of rusty pliers.

BONO: The old folks . . . my granddaddy used to pull his teeth with pliers. They ain't had no dentists for the colored folks back then.

TROY: Get clean pliers! You understand? Clean pliers! Sterilize them! Besides we ain't living back then. All Magee had to do was walk over to Doc Goldblum's.   30

BONO: I see where you and that Tallahassee gal . . . that Alberta . . . I see where you all done got tight.

TROY: What you mean "got tight"?

BONO: I see where you be laughing and joking with her all the time.

TROY: I laughs and jokes with all of them, Bono. You know me.   35

BONO: That ain't the kind of laughing and joking I'm talking about.

CORY *enters from the house.*

CORY: How you doing, Mr. Bono?

TROY: Cory? Get that saw from Bono and cut some wood. He talking about the wood's too hard to cut. Stand back there, Jim, and let that young boy show you how it's done.   40

BONO: He's sure welcome to it.

CORY *takes the saw and begins to cut the wood.*

Whew-e-e! Look at that. Big old strong boy. Look like Joe Louis. Hell, must be getting old the way I'm watching that boy whip through that wood.

CORY: I don't see why Mama want a fence around the yard noways.

TROY: Damn if I know either. What the hell she keeping out with it? She ain't got   45
nothing nobody want.

BONO: Some people build fences to keep people out . . . and other people build fences to keep people in. Rose wants to hold on to you all. She loves you.

TROY: Hell, nigger, I don't need nobody to tell me my wife loves me. Cory . . . go on in the house and see if you can find that other saw.   50

CORY: Where's it at?

TROY: I said find it! Look for it till you find it!

CORY *exits into the house.*

What's that supposed to mean? Wanna keep us in?

BONO: Troy . . . I done known you seem like damn near my whole life. You and Rose both. I done know both of you all for a long time. I remember when you   55
met Rose. When you was hitting them baseball out the park. A lot of them old gals was after you then. You had the pick of the litter. When you picked Rose, I was happy for you. That was the first time I knew you had any sense. I said . . . My man Troy knows what he's doing . . . I'm gonna follow this nigger . . . he might take me somewhere. I been following you too. I done learned a whole   60
heap of things about life watching you. I done learned how to tell where the shit lies. How to tell it from the alfalfa. You done learned me a lot of things. You showed me how to not make the same mistakes . . . to take life as it comes along and keep putting one foot in front of the other. *(Pause.)* Rose a good woman, Troy.   65

TROY: Hell, nigger, I know she a good woman. I been married to her for eighteen years. What you got on your mind, Bono?

BONO: I just say she a good woman. Just like I say anything. I ain't got to have nothing on my mind.

TROY: You just gonna say she a good woman and leave it hanging out there like that?   70
Why you telling me she a good woman?

BONO: She loves you, Troy. Rose loves you.

TROY: You saying I don't measure up. That's what you trying to say. I don't measure up cause I'm seeing this other gal. I know what you trying to say.

BONO: I know what Rose means to you, Troy. I'm just trying to say I don't want to see you mess up.

TROY: Yeah, I appreciate that, Bono. If you was messing around on Lucille I'd be telling you the same thing.

BONO: Well, that's all I got to say. I just say that because I love you both.

TROY: Hell, you know me . . . I wasn't out there looking for nothing. You can't find a better woman than Rose. I know that. But seems like this woman just stuck onto me where I can't shake her loose. I done wrestled with it, tried to throw her off me . . . but she just stuck on tighter. Now she's stuck on for good.

BONO: You's in control . . . that's what you tell me all the time. You responsible for what you do.

TROY: I ain't ducking the responsibility of it. As long as it sets right in my heart . . . then I'm okay. Cause that's all I listen to. It'll tell me right from wrong every time. And I ain't talking about doing Rose no bad turn. I love Rose. She done carried me a long ways and I love and respect her for that.

BONO: I know you do. That's why I don't want to see you hurt her. But what you gonna do when she find out? What you got then? If you try and juggle both of them . . . sooner or later you gonna drop one of them. That's common sense.

TROY: Yeah, I hear what you saying, Bono. I been trying to figure a way to work it out.

BONO: Work it out right, Troy. I don't want to be getting all up between you and Rose's business . . . but work it so it come out right.

TROY: Ah hell, I get all up between you and Lucille's business. When you gonna get that woman that refrigerator she been wanting? Don't tell me you ain't got no money now. I know who your banker is. Mellon don't need that money bad as Lucille want that refrigerator. I'll tell you that.

BONO: Tell you what I'll do . . . when you finish building this fence for Rose . . . I'll buy Lucille that refrigerator.

TROY: You done stuck your foot in your mouth now!

TROY *grabs up a board and begins to saw.* BONO *starts to walk out the yard.*

Hey, nigger . . . where you going?

BONO: I'm going home. I know you don't expect me to help you now. I'm protecting my money. I wanna see you put that fence up by yourself. That's what I want to see. You'll be here another six months without me.

TROY: Nigger, you ain't right.

BONO: When it comes to my money . . . I'm right as fireworks on the Fourth of July.

TROY: All right, we gonna see now. You better get out your bankbook.

BONO *exits, and* TROY *continues to work.* ROSE *enters from the house.*

ROSE: What they say down there? What's happening with Gabe?

TROY: I went down there and got him out. Cost me fifty dollars. Say he was disturbing the peace. Judge set up a hearing for him in three weeks. Say to show cause why he shouldn't be recommitted.   115

ROSE: What was he doing that cause them to arrest him?

TROY: Some kids was teasing him and he run them off home. Say he was howling and carrying on. Some folks seen him and called the police. That's all it was.

ROSE: Well, what's you say? What'd you tell the judge?

TROY: Told him I'd look after him. It didn't make no sense to recommit the man. He stuck   120
out his big greasy palm and told me to give him fifty dollars and take him on home.

ROSE: Where's he at now? Where'd he go off to?

TROY: He's gone about his business. He don't need nobody to hold his hand.

ROSE: Well, I don't know. Seem like that would be the best place for him if they did put him into the hospital. I know what you're gonna say. But that's what I think   125
would be best.

TROY: The man done had his life ruined fighting for what? And they wanna take and lock him up. Let him be free. He don't bother nobody.

ROSE: Well, everybody got their own way of looking at it I guess. Come on and get your lunch. I got a bowl of lima beans and some cornbread in the oven. Come   130
and get something to eat. Ain't no sense you fretting over Gabe.

ROSE *turns to go into the house.*

TROY: Rose . . . got something to tell you.

ROSE: Well, come on . . . wait till I get this food on the table.

TROY: Rose!

She stops and turns around.

I don't know how to say this. *(Pause.)* I can't explain it none. It just sort of grows   135
on you till it gets out of hand. It starts out like a little bush . . . and the next thing
you know it's a whole forest.

ROSE: Troy . . . what is you talking about?

TROY: I'm talking, woman, let me talk. I'm trying to find a way to tell you . . . I'm
gonna be a daddy. I'm gonna be somebody's daddy.   140

ROSE: Troy . . . you're not telling me this? You're gonna be . . . what?

TROY: Rose . . . now . . . see . . .

ROSE: You telling me you gonna be somebody's daddy? You telling your *wife* this?

GABRIEL *enters from the street. He carries a rose in his hand.*

GABRIEL: Hey, Troy! Hey, Rose!

ROSE: I have to wait eighteen years to hear something like this.   145

GABRIEL: Hey, Rose . . . I got a flower for you. *(He hands it to her.)* That's a rose. Same
rose like you is.

ROSE: Thanks, Gabe.

GABRIEL: Troy, you ain't mad at me is you? Them bad mens come and put me away.
You ain't mad at me is you?   150

TROY: Naw, Gabe, I ain't mad at you.

ROSE: Eighteen years and you wanna come with this.

GABRIEL *(takes a quarter out of his pocket)*: See what I got? Got a brand new quarter.

TROY: Rose . . . it's just . . .

ROSE: Ain't nothing you can say, Troy. Ain't no way of explaining that.   155

GABRIEL: Fellow that give me this quarter had a whole mess of them. I'm gonna keep
   this quarter till it stop shining.

ROSE: Gabe, go on in the house there. I got some watermelon in the Frigidaire. Go
   on and get you a piece.

GABRIEL: Say, Rose . . . you know I was chasing hellhounds and them bad mens come   160
   and get me and take me away. Troy helped me. He come down there and told
   them they better let me go before he beat them up. Yeah, he did!

ROSE: You go on and get you a piece of watermelon, Gabe. Them bad mens is gone
   now.

GABRIEL: Okay, Rose . . . gonna get me some watermelon. The kind with the stripes   165
   on it.

GABRIEL *exits into the house.*

ROSE: Why, Troy? Why? After all these years to come dragging this in to me now. It
   don't make no sense at your age. I could have expected this ten or fifteen years
   ago, but not now.

TROY: Age ain't got nothing to do with it, Rose.   170

ROSE: I done tried to be everything a wife should be. Everything a wife could be.
   Been married eighteen years and I got to live to see the day you tell me you been
   seeing another woman and done fathered a child by her. And you know I ain't
   never wanted no half nothing in my family. My whole family is half. Everybody
   got different fathers and mothers . . . my two sisters and my brother. Can't hardly   175
   tell who's who. Can't never sit down and talk about Papa and Mama. It's your
   papa and your mama and my papa and my mama . . .

TROY: Rose . . . stop it now.

ROSE: I ain't never wanted that for none of my children. And now you wanna drag
   your behind in here and tell me something like this.   180

TROY: You ought to know. It's time for you to know.

ROSE: Well, I don't want to know, goddamn it!

TROY: I can't just make it go away. It's done now. I can't wish the circumstance of the
   thing away.

ROSE: And you don't want to either. Maybe you want to wish me and my boy away.   185
   Maybe that's what you want? Well, you can't wish us away. I've got eighteen years
   of my life invested in you. You ought to have stayed upstairs in my bed where you
   belong.

TROY: Rose . . . now listen to me . . . we can get a handle on this thing. We can talk
   this out . . . come to an understanding.   190

ROSE: All of a sudden it's "we." Where was "we" at when you was down there rolling around with some godforsaken woman? "We" should have come to an

understanding before you started making a damn fool of yourself. You're a day
late and a dollar short when it comes to an understanding with me.

TROY: It's just . . . She gives me a different idea . . . a different understanding about 195
myself. I can step out of this house and get away from the pressures and problems . . . be a different man. I ain't got to wonder how I'm gonna pay the bills or
get the roof fixed. I can just be a part of myself that I ain't never been.

ROSE: What I want to know . . . is do you plan to continue seeing her. That's all you
can say to me. 200

TROY: I can sit up in her house and laugh. Do you understand what I'm saying. I can
laugh out loud . . . and it feels good. It reaches all the way down to the bottom
of my shoes. *(Pause.)* Rose, I can't give that up.

ROSE: Maybe you ought to go on and stay down there with her . . . if she's a better
woman than me. 205

TROY: It ain't about nobody being a better woman or nothing. Rose, you ain't the
blame. A man couldn't ask for no woman to be a better wife than you've been.
I'm responsible for it. I done locked myself into a pattern trying to take care of
you all that I forgot about myself.

ROSE: What the hell was I there for? That was my job, not somebody else's. 210

TROY: Rose, I done tried all my life to live decent . . . to live a clean . . . hard . . . useful life. I
tried to be a good husband to you. In every way I knew how. Maybe I come into the
world backwards, I don't know. But . . . you born with two strikes on you before you
come to the plate. You got to guard it closely . . . always looking for the curve ball on
the inside corner. You can't afford to let none get past you. You can't afford a call strike. 215
If you going down . . . you going down swinging. Everything lined up against you.
What you gonna do. I fooled them, Rose. I bunted. When I found you and Cory and
a halfway decent job . . . I was safe. Couldn't nothing touch me. I wasn't gonna strike
out no more. I wasn't going back to the penitentiary. I wasn't gonna lay in the streets
with a bottle of wine. I was safe. I had me a family. A job. I wasn't gonna get that last 220
strike. I was on first looking for one of them boys to knock me in. To get me home.

ROSE: You should have stayed in my bed, Troy.

TROY: Then when I saw that gal . . . she firmed up my backbone. And I got to thinking
that if I tried . . . I just might be able to steal second. Do you understand after
eighteen years I wanted to steal second. 225

ROSE: You should have held me tight. You should have grabbed me and held on.

TROY: I stood on first base for eighteen years and I thought . . . well, goddamn it . . .
go on for it!

ROSE: We're not talking about baseball! We're talking about you going off to lay in
bed with another woman . . . and then bring it home to me. That's what we're 230
talking about. We ain't talking about no baseball.

TROY: Rose, you're not listening to me. I'm trying the best I can to explain it to you. It's
not easy for me to admit that I been standing in the same place for eighteen years.

ROSE: I been standing with you! I been right here with you, Troy. I got a life too. I
gave eighteen years of my life to stand in the same spot with you. Don't you 235
think I ever wanted other things? Don't you think I had dreams and hopes? What

about my life? What about me. Don't you think it ever crossed my mind to want to know other men? That I wanted to lay up somewhere and forget about my responsibilities? That I wanted someone to make me laugh so I could feel good? You not the only one who's got wants and needs. But I held on to you, Troy. I 240 took all my feelings, my wants and needs, my dreams . . . and I buried them inside you. I planted a seed and watched and prayed over it. I planted myself inside you and waited to bloom. And it didn't take me no eighteen years to find out the soil was hard and rocky and it wasn't never gonna bloom.

But I held on to you, Troy. I held you tighter. You was my husband. I owed 245 you everything I had. Every part of me I could find to give you. And upstairs in that room . . . with the darkness falling in on me . . . I gave everything I had to try and erase the doubt that you wasn't the finest man in the world. And wherever you was going . . . I wanted to be there with you. Cause you was my husband. Cause that's the only way I was gonna survive as your wife. You always talking 250 about what you give . . . and what you don't have to give. But you take too. You take . . . and don't even know nobody's giving!

ROSE *turns to exit into the house;* TROY *grabs her arm.*

TROY: You say I take and don't give!
ROSE: Troy! You're hurting me!
TROY: You say I take and don't give!   255
ROSE: Troy . . . you're hurting my arm! Let go!
TROY: I done give you everything I got. Don't you tell that lie on me.
ROSE: Troy!
TROY: Don't you tell that lie on me!

CORY *enters from the house.*

CORY: Mama!   260
ROSE: Troy. You're hurting me.
TROY: Don't you tell me about no taking and giving.

CORY *comes up behind* TROY *and grabs him.* TROY, *surprised, is thrown off balance just as* CORY *throws a glancing blow that catches him on the chest and knocks him down.* TROY *is stunned, as is* CORY.

ROSE: Troy. Troy. No!

TROY *gets to his feet and starts at* CORY.

Troy . . . no. Please! Troy!

ROSE *pulls on* TROY *to hold him back.* TROY *stops himself.*

TROY (*to* CORY): All right. That's strike two. You stay away from around me, boy. 265
Don't you strike out. You living with a full count. Don't you strike out.

TROY *exits out the yard as the lights go down.*

S<small>CENE</small> 2

It is six months later, early afternoon. T<small>ROY</small> *enters from the house and starts to exit the yard.* R<small>OSE</small> *enters from the house.*

R<small>OSE</small>: Troy, I want to talk to you.

T<small>ROY</small>: All of a sudden, after all this time, you want to talk to me, huh? You ain't wanted to talk to me for months. You ain't wanted to talk to me last night. You ain't wanted no part of me then. What you wanna talk to me about now?

R<small>OSE</small>: Tomorrow's Friday.   5

T<small>ROY</small>: I know what day tomorrow is. You think I don't know tomorrow's Friday? My whole life I ain't done nothing but look to see Friday coming and you got to tell me it's Friday.

R<small>OSE</small>: I want to know if you're coming home.

T<small>ROY</small>: I always come home, Rose. You know that. There ain't never been a night I   10
ain't come home.

R<small>OSE</small>: That ain't what I mean . . . and you know it. I want to know if you're coming straight home after work.

T<small>ROY</small>: I figure I'd cash my check . . . hang out at Taylors' with the boys . . . maybe play a game of checkers . . .   15

R<small>OSE</small>: Troy, I can't live like this. I won't live like this. You livin' on borrowed time with me. It's been going on six months now you ain't been coming home.

T<small>ROY</small>: I be here every night. Every night of the year. That's 365 days.

R<small>OSE</small>: I want you to come home tomorrow after work.

T<small>ROY</small>: Rose . . . I don't mess up my pay. You know that now. I take my pay and I give   20
it to you. I don't have no money but what you give me back. I just want to have a little time to myself . . . a little time to enjoy life.

R<small>OSE</small>: What about me? When's my time to enjoy life?

T<small>ROY</small>: I don't know what to tell you, Rose. I'm doing the best I can.

R<small>OSE</small>: You ain't been home from work but time enough to change your clothes and   25
run out . . . and you wanna call that the best you can do?

T<small>ROY</small>: I'm going over to the hospital to see Alberta. She went into the hospital this afternoon. Look like she might have the baby early. I won't be gone long.

R<small>OSE</small>: Well, you ought to know. They went over to Miss Pearl's and got Gabe today.   30
She said you told them to go ahead and lock him up.

T<small>ROY</small>: I ain't said no such thing. Whoever told you that is telling a lie. Pearl ain't doing nothing but telling a big fat lie.

R<small>OSE</small>: She ain't had to tell me. I read it on the papers.

T<small>ROY</small>: I ain't told them nothing of the kind.   35

R<small>OSE</small>: I saw it right there on the papers.

T<small>ROY</small>: What it say, huh?

R<small>OSE</small>: It said you told them to take him.

T<small>ROY</small>: Then they screwed that up, just the way they screw up everything. I ain't worried about what they got on the paper.   40

ROSE: Say the government send part of his check to the hospital and the other part to you.

TROY: I ain't got nothing to do with that if that's the way it works. I ain't made up the rules about how it work.

ROSE: You did Gabe just like you did Cory. You wouldn't sign the paper for Cory . . . 45 but you signed for Gabe. You signed that paper.

The telephone is heard ringing inside the house.

TROY: I told you I ain't signed nothing, woman! The only thing I signed was the release form. Hell, I can't read, I don't know what they had on that paper! I ain't signed nothing about sending Gabe away.

ROSE: I said send him to the hospital . . . you said let him be free . . . now you done 50 went down there and signed him to the hospital for half his money. You went back on yourself, Troy. You gonna have to answer for that.

TROY: See now . . . you been over there talking to Miss Pearl. She done got mad cause she ain't getting Gabe's rent money. That's all it is. She's liable to say anything. 55

ROSE: Troy, I seen where you signed the paper.

TROY: You ain't seen nothing I signed. What she doing got papers on my brother anyway? Miss Pearl telling a big fat lie. And I'm gonna tell her about it too! You ain't seen nothing I signed. Say . . . you ain't seen nothing I signed.

ROSE *exits into the house to answer the telephone. Presently she returns.*

ROSE: Troy . . . that was the hospital. Alberta had the baby. 60

TROY: What she have? What is it?

ROSE: It's a girl.

TROY: I better get on down to the hospital to see her.

ROSE: Troy . . .

TROY: Rose . . . I got to go see her now. That's only right . . . what's the matter . . . the 65 baby's all right, ain't it?

ROSE: Alberta died having the baby.

TROY: Died . . . you say she's dead? Alberta's dead?

ROSE: They said they done all they could. They couldn't do nothing for her.

TROY: The baby? How's the baby? 70

ROSE: They say it's healthy. I wonder who's gonna bury her.

TROY: She had family, Rose. She wasn't living in the world by herself.

ROSE: I know she wasn't living in the world by herself.

TROY: Next thing you gonna want to know if she had any insurance.

ROSE: Troy, you ain't got to talk like that. 75

TROY: That's the first thing that jumped out your mouth. "Who's gonna bury her?" Like I'm fixing to take on that task for myself.

ROSE: I am your wife. Don't push me away.

TROY: I ain't pushing nobody away. Just give me some space. That's all. Just give me some room to breathe. 80

Rose *exits into the house.* Troy *walks about the yard.*

Troy *(with a quiet rage that threatens to consume him)*: All right . . . Mr. Death. See now . . . I'm gonna tell you what I'm gonna do. I'm gonna take and build me a fence around this yard. See? I'm gonna build me a fence around what belongs to me. And then I want you to stay on the other side. See? You stay over there until you're ready for me. Then you come on. Bring your army. 85 Bring your sickle. Bring your wrestling clothes. I ain't gonna fall down on my vigilance this time. You ain't gonna sneak up on me no more. When you ready for me . . . when the top of your list say Troy Maxson . . . that's when you come around here. You come up and knock on the front door. Ain't nobody else got nothing to do with this. This is between you and me. Man 90 to man. You stay on the other side of that fence until you ready for me. Then you come up and knock on the front door. Anytime you want. I'll be ready for you.

The lights go down to black.

Scene 3

The lights come up on the porch. It is late evening three days later. Rose *sits listening to the ball game waiting for* Troy. *The final out of the game is made and* Rose *switches off the radio.* Troy *enters the yard carrying an infant wrapped in blankets. He stands back from the house and calls.*

  Rose *enters and stands on the porch. There is a long, awkward silence, the weight of which grows heavier with each passing second.*

Troy: Rose . . . I'm standing here with my daughter in my arms. She ain't but a wee bittie little old thing. She don't know nothing about grownups' business. She innocent . . . and she ain't got no mama.
Rose: What you telling me for, Troy?

She turns and exits into the house.

Troy: Well . . . I guess we'll just sit out here on the porch. 5

He sits down on the porch. There is an awkward indelicateness about the way he handles the baby. His largeness engulfs and seems to swallow it. He speaks loud enough for Rose *to hear.*

A man's got to do what's right for him. I ain't sorry for nothing I done. It felt right in my heart. *(To the baby.)* What you smiling at? Your daddy's a big man. Got these great big old hands. But sometimes he's scared. And right now your daddy's scared cause we sitting out here and ain't got no home. Oh, I been home- less before. I ain't had no little baby with me. But I been homeless. You just be 10 out on the road by your lonesome and you see one of them trains coming and you just kinda go like this . . .

He sings as a lullaby.

> Please, Mr. Engineer let a man ride the line
> Please, Mr. Engineer let a man ride the line
> I ain't got no ticket please let me ride the blinds 15

Rose *enters from the house.* Troy, *hearing her steps behind him, stands and faces her.*

> She's my daughter, Rose. My own flesh and blood. I can't deny her no more than
> I can deny them boys. *(Pause.)* You and them boys is my family. You and them
> and this child is all I got in the world. So I guess what I'm saying is . . . I'd appre-
> ciate it if you'd help me take care of her.

Rose: Okay, Troy . . . you're right. I'll take care of your baby for you . . . cause . . . 20
like you say . . . she's innocent . . . and you can't visit the sins of the father
upon the child. A motherless child has got a hard time. *(She takes the baby
from him.)* From right now . . . this child got a mother. But you a woman-
less man.

Rose *turns and exits into the house with the baby. Lights go down to black.*

Scene 4

It is two months later. Lyons *enters from the street. He knocks on the door and calls.*

Lyons: Hey, Rose! *(Pause.)* Rose!

Rose *(from inside the house)*: Stop that yelling. You gonna wake up Raynell. I just got
her to sleep.

Lyons: I just stopped by to pay Papa this twenty dollars I owe him. Where's Papa at?

Rose: He should be here in a minute. I'm getting ready to go down to the church. Sit 5
down and wait on him.

Lyons: I got to go pick up Bonnie over her mother's house.

Rose: Well, sit it down there on the table. He'll get it.

Lyons *(enters the house and sets the money on the table)*: Tell Papa I said thanks. I'll
see you again.

Rose: All right, Lyons. We'll see you. 10

Lyons *starts to exit as* Cory *enters.*

Cory: Hey, Lyons.

Lyons: What's happening, Cory? Say man, I'm sorry I missed your graduation. You
know I had a gig and couldn't get away. Otherwise, I would have been there,
man. So what you doing? 15

Cory: I'm trying to find a job.

Lyons: Yeah I know how that go, man. It's rough out here. Jobs are scarce.

Cory: Yeah, I know.

Lyons: Look here, I got to run. Talk to Papa . . . he know some people. He'll be able
to help get you a job. Talk to him . . . see what he say. 20

CORY: Yeah . . . all right, Lyons.

LYONS: You take care. I'll talk to you soon. We'll find some time to talk.

LYONS *exits the yard.* CORY *wanders over to the tree, picks up the bat, and assumes a batting stance. He studies an imaginary pitcher and swings. Dissatisfied with the result, he tries again.* TROY *enters. They eye each other for a beat.* CORY *puts the bat down and exits the yard.* TROY *starts into the house as* ROSE *exits with* RAYNELL. *She is carrying a cake.*

TROY: I'm coming in and everybody's going out.

ROSE: I'm taking this cake down to the church for the bake sale. Lyons was by to see you. He stopped by to pay you your twenty dollars. It's laying in there on the table.   25

TROY (*going into his pocket*): Well . . . here go this money.

ROSE: Put it in there on the table, Troy. I'll get it.

TROY: What time you coming back?

ROSE: Ain't no use in you studying me. It don't matter what time I come back.   30

TROY: I just asked you a question, woman. What's the matter . . . can't I ask you a question?

ROSE: Troy, I don't want to go into it. Your dinner's in there on the stove. All you got to do is heat it up. And don't you be eating the rest of them cakes in there. I'm coming back for them. We having a bake sale at the church tomorrow.   35

ROSE *exits the yard.* TROY *sits down on the steps, takes a pint bottle from his pocket, opens it, and drinks. He begins to sing*

TROY: Hear it ring! Hear it ring!
    Had an old dog his name was Blue
    You know Blue was mighty true
    You know Blue was a good old dog
    Blue trees a possum in a hollow log   40
    You know from that he was a good old dog

BONO *enters the yard.*

BONO: Hey, Troy.

TROY: Hey, what's happening, Bono?

BONO: I just thought I'd stop by to see you.

TROY: What you stop by and see me for? You ain't stopped by in a month of Sundays.   45
Hell, I must owe you money or something.

BONO: Since you got your promotion I can't keep up with you. Used to see you every day. Now I don't even know what route you working.

TROY: They keep switching me around. Got me out in Greentree now . . . hauling white folks' garbage.   50

BONO: Greentree, huh? You lucky, at least you ain't got to be lifting them barrels. Damn if they ain't getting heavier. I'm gonna put in my two years and call it quits.

TROY: I'm thinking about retiring myself.

Bono: You got it easy. You can *drive* for another five years.   55

Troy: It ain't the same, Bono. It ain't like working the back of the truck. Ain't got nobody to talk to . . . feel like you working by yourself. Naw, I'm thinking about retiring. How's Lucille?

Bono: She all right. Her arthritis get to acting up on her sometime. Saw Rose on my way in. She going down to the church, huh?   60

Troy: Yeah, she took up going down there. All them preachers looking for somebody to fatten their pockets. *(Pause.)* Got some gin here.

Bono: Naw, thanks. I just stopped by to say hello.

Troy: Hell, nigger . . . you can take a drink. I ain't never known you to say no to a drink. You ain't got to work tomorrow.   65

Bono: I just stopped by. I'm fixing to go over to Skinner's. We got us a domino game going over his house every Friday.

Troy: Nigger, you can't play no dominoes. I used to whup you four games out of five.

Bono: Well, that learned me. I'm getting better.   70

Troy: Yeah? Well, that's all right.

Bono: Look here . . . I got to be getting on. Stop by sometime, huh?

Troy: Yeah, I'll do that, Bono. Lucille told Rose you bought her a new refrigerator.

Bono: Yeah, Rose told Lucille you had finally built your fence . . . so I figured we'd call it even.   75

Troy: I knew you would.

Bono: Yeah . . . okay. I'll be talking to you.

Troy: Yeah, take care, Bono. Good to see you. I'm gonna stop over.

Bono: Yeah. Okay, Troy.

Bono *exits.* Troy *drinks from the bottle.*

Troy: Old Blue died and I dig his grave   80
Let him down with a golden chain
Every night when I hear old Blue bark
I know Blue treed a possum in Noah's Ark.
Hear it ring! Hear it ring!

Cory *enters the yard. They eye each other for a beat.* Troy *is sitting in the middle of the steps.* Cory *walks over.*

Cory: I got to get by.   85

Troy: Say what? What's you say?

Cory: You in my way. I got to get by.

Troy: You got to get by where? This is my house. Bought and paid for. In full. Took me fifteen years. And if you wanna go in my house and I'm sitting on the steps . . . you say excuse me. Like your mama taught you.   90

Cory: Come on, Pop . . . I got to get by.

Cory *starts to maneuver his way past* Troy. Troy *grabs his leg and shoves him back.*

TROY: You just gonna walk over top of me?

CORY: I live here too!

TROY *(advancing toward him)*: You just gonna walk over top of me in my own house?   95

CORY: I ain't scared of you.

TROY: I ain't asked if you was scared of me. I asked you if you was fixing to walk over top of me in my own house? That's the question. You ain't gonna say excuse me? You just gonna walk over top of me?

CORY: If you wanna put it like that.   100

TROY: How else am I gonna put it?

CORY: I was walking by you to go into the house cause you sitting on the steps drunk, singing to yourself. You can put it like that.

TROY: Without saying excuse me???

CORY *doesn't respond.*

I asked you a question. Without saying excuse me???   105

CORY: I ain't got to say excuse me to you. You don't count around here no more.

TROY: Oh, I see . . . I don't count around here no more. You ain't got to say excuse me to your daddy. All of a sudden you done got so grown that your daddy don't count around here no more . . . Around here in his own house and yard that he done paid for with the sweat of his brow. You done got so grown to where you   110
gonna take over. You gonna take over my house. Is that right? You gonna wear my pants. You gonna go in there and stretch out on my bed. You ain't got to say excuse me cause I don't count around here no more. Is that right?

CORY: That's right. You always talking this dumb stuff. Now, why don't you just get out my way?   115

TROY: I guess you got someplace to sleep and something to put in your belly. You got that, huh? You got that? That's what you need. You got that, huh?

CORY: You don't know what I got. You ain't got to worry about what I got.

TROY: You right! You one hundred percent right! I done spent the last seventeen years worrying about what you got. Now it's your turn, see? I'll tell you what   120
to do. You grown . . . we done established that. You a man. Now, let's see you act like one. Turn your behind around and walk out this yard. And when you get out there in the alley . . . you can forget about this house. See? Cause this is my house. You go on and be a man and get your own house. You can forget about this. Cause this is mine. You go on and get yours cause I'm through with   125
doing for you.

CORY: You talking about what you did for me . . . what'd you ever give me?

TROY: Them feet and bones! That pumping heart, nigger! I give you more than anybody else is ever gonna give you.

CORY: You ain't never gave me nothing! You ain't never done nothing but hold me   130
back. Afraid I was gonna be better than you. All you ever did was try and make me scared of you. I used to tremble every time you called my name. Every time I heard your footsteps in the house. Wondering all the time . . . what's Papa gonna

say if I do this? . . . What's he gonna say if I do that? . . . What's Papa gonna say if
I turn on the radio? And Mama, too . . . she tries . . . but she's scared of you.   135
TROY: You leave your mama out of this. She ain't got nothing to do with this.
CORY: I don't know how she stand you . . . after what you did to her.
TROY: I told you to leave your mama out of this!

He advances toward CORY.

CORY: What you gonna do . . . give me a whupping? You can't whup me no more.
You're too old. You just an old man.   140
TROY (*shoves him on his shoulder*): Nigger! That's what you are. You just another nig-
ger on the street to me!
CORY: You crazy! You know that?
TROY: Go on now! You got the devil in you. Get on away from me!
CORY: You just a crazy old man . . . talking about I got the devil in me.   145
TROY: Yeah, I'm crazy! If you don't get on the other side of that yard . . . I'm gonna
show you how crazy I am! Go on . . . get the hell out of my yard.
CORY: It ain't your yard. You took Uncle Gabe's money he got from the army to buy
this house and then you put him out.
TROY (*advances on* CORY): Get your black ass out of my yard!   150

TROY's *advance backs* CORY *up against the tree.* CORY *grabs up the bat.*

CORY: I ain't going nowhere! Come on . . . put me out! I ain't scared of you.
TROY: That's my bat!
CORY: Come on!
TROY: Put my bat down!
CORY: Come on, put me out.   155

CORY *swings at* TROY, *who backs across the yard.*

What's the matter? You so bad . . . put me out!

TROY *advances toward* CORY.

CORY (*backing up*): Come on! Come on!
TROY: You're gonna have to use it! You wanna draw that bat back on me . . . you're
gonna have to use it.
CORY: Come on! . . . Come on!   160

CORY *swings the bat at* TROY *a second time. He misses.* TROY *continues to advance
toward him.*

TROY: You're gonna have to kill me! You wanna draw that bat back on me. You're
gonna have to kill me.

CORY, *backed up against the tree, can go no farther.* TROY *taunts him. He sticks out his
head and offers him a target.*

Come on! Come on!

CORY *is unable to swing the bat.* TROY *grabs it.*

TROY: Then I'll show you.

CORY *and* TROY *struggle over the bat. The struggle is fierce and fully engaged.* TROY *ultimately is the stronger and takes the bat from* CORY *and stands over him ready to swing. He stops himself.*

    Go on and get away from around my house.   165

CORY, *stung by his defeat, picks himself up, walks slowly out of the yard and up the alley.*

CORY: Tell Mama I'll be back for my things.
TROY: They'll be on the other side of that fence.

CORY *exits.*

TROY: I can't taste nothing. Helluljah! I can't taste nothing no more. (TROY *assumes a batting posture and begins to taunt Death, the fastball on the outside corner.*) Come on! It's between you and me now! Come on! Anytime you want! Come on! I be   170 ready for you . . . but I ain't gonna be easy.

The lights go down on the scene.

SCENE 5

The time is 1965. The lights come up in the yard. It is the morning of TROY's *funeral. A funeral plaque with a light hangs beside the door. There is a small garden plot off to the side. There is noise and activity in the house as* ROSE, LYONS, *and* BONO *have gathered. The door opens and* RAYNELL, *seven years old, enters dressed in a flannel nightgown. She crosses to the garden and pokes around with a stick.* ROSE *calls from the house.*

ROSE: Raynell!
RAYNELL: Mam?
ROSE: What you doing out there?
RAYNELL: Nothing.

ROSE *comes to the door.*

ROSE: Girl, get in here and get dressed. What you doing?   5
RAYNELL: Seeing if my garden growed.
ROSE: I told you it ain't gonna grow overnight. You got to wait.
RAYNELL: It don't look like it never gonna grow. Dag!
ROSE: I told you a watched pot never boils. Get in here and get dressed.
RAYNELL: This ain't even no pot, Mama.   10
ROSE: You just have to give it a chance. It'll grow. Now you come on and do what I told you. We got to be getting ready. This ain't no morning to be playing around. You hear me?
RAYNELL: Yes, Mam.

Rose *exits into the house.* Raynell *continues to poke at her garden with a stick.* Cory *enters. He is dressed in a Marine corporal's uniform, and carries a duffel bag. His posture is that of a military man, and his speech has a clipped sternness.*

Cory *(to* Raynell*)*: Hi. *(Pause.)* I bet your name is Raynell.   15
Raynell: Uh huh.
Cory: Is your mama home?

Raynell *runs up on the porch and calls through the screen door.*

Raynell: Mama . . . there's some man out here. Mama?

Rose *comes to the door.*

Rose: Cory? Lord have mercy! Look here, you all!

Rose *and* Cory *embrace in a tearful reunion as* Bono *and* Lyons *enter from the house dressed in funeral clothes.*

Bono: Aw, looka here . . .   20
Rose: Done got all grown up!
Cory: Don't cry, Mama. What you crying about?
Rose: I'm just so glad you made it.
Cory: Hey Lyons. How you doing, Mr. Bono.

Lyons *goes to embrace* Cory.

Lyons: Look at you, man. Look at you. Don't he look good, Rose. Got them Corporal   25
    stripes.
Rose: What took you so long?
Cory: You know how the Marines are, Mama. They got to get all their paperwork
    straight before they let you do anything.
Rose: Well, I'm sure glad you made it. They let Lyons come. Your Uncle Gabe's still   30
    in the hospital. They don't know if they gonna let him out or not. I just talked
    to them a little while ago.
Lyons: A Corporal in the United States Marines.
Bono: Your daddy knew you had it in you. He used to tell me all the time.
Lyons: Don't he look good, Mr. Bono?   35
Bono: Yeah, he remind me of Troy when I first met him. *(Pause.)* Say, Rose, Lucille's
    down at the church with the choir. I'm gonna go down and get the pallbearers
    lined up. I'll be back to get you all.
Rose: Thanks, Jim.
Cory: See you, Mr. Bono.   40
Lyons *(with his arm around* Raynell*)*: Cory . . . look at Raynell. Ain't she precious?
    She gonna break a whole lot of hearts.
Rose: Raynell, come and say hello to your brother. This is your brother, Cory. You
    remember Cory.
Raynell: No, Mam.   45

CORY: She don't remember me, Mama.

ROSE: Well, we talk about you. She heard us talk about you. *(To* RAYNELL.*)* This is your brother, Cory. Come on and say hello.

RAYNELL: Hi.

CORY: Hi. So you're Raynell. Mama told me a lot about you.　　　　　　　　50

ROSE: You all come on into the house and let me fix you some breakfast. Keep up your strength.

CORY: I ain't hungry, Mama.

LYONS: You can fix me something, Rose. I'll be in there in a minute.

ROSE: Cory, you sure you don't want nothing? I know they ain't feeding you right.　　55

CORY: No, Mama . . . thanks. I don't feel like eating. I'll get something later.

ROSE: Raynell . . . get on upstairs and get that dress on like I told you.

ROSE *and* RAYNELL *exit into the house.*

LYONS: So . . . I hear you thinking about getting married.

CORY: Yeah, I done found the right one, Lyons. It's about time.

LYONS: Me and Bonnie been split up about four years now. About the time Papa　60
retired. I guess she just got tired of all them changes I was putting her through. *(Pause.)* I always knew you was gonna make something out yourself. Your head was always in the right direction. So . . . you gonna stay in . . . make it a career . . . put in your twenty years?

CORY: I don't know. I got six already, I think that's enough.　　　　　　　　65

LYONS: Stick with Uncle Sam and retire early. Ain't nothing out here. I guess Rose told you what happened with me. They got me down the workhouse. I thought I was being slick cashing other people's checks.

CORY: How much time you doing?

LYONS: They give me three years. I got that beat now. I ain't got but nine more　70
months. It ain't so bad. You learn to deal with it like anything else. You got to take the crookeds with the straights. That's what Papa used to say. He used to say that when he struck out. I seen him strike out three times in a row . . . and the next time up he hit the ball over the grandstand. Right out there in Homestead Field. He wasn't satisfied hitting in the seats . . . he want to hit it over everything! After　75
the game he had two hundred people standing around waiting to shake his hand. You got to take the crookeds with the straights. Yeah, Papa was something else.

CORY: You still playing?

LYONS: Cory . . . you know I'm gonna do that. There's some fellows down there we got us a band . . . we gonna try and stay together when we get out . . . but yeah, I'm　80
still playing. It still helps me to get out of bed in the morning. As long as it do that I'm gonna be right there playing and trying to make some sense out of it.

ROSE *(calling)*: Lyons, I got these eggs in the pan.

LYONS: Let me go on and get these eggs, man. Get ready to go bury Papa. *(Pause.)* How you doing? You doing all right?　　　　　　　　　　　　　　85

CORY *nods.* LYONS *touches him on the shoulder and they share a moment of silent grief.* LYONS *exits into the house.* CORY *wanders about the yard.* RAYNELL *enters.*

RAYNELL: Hi.

CORY: Hi.

RAYNELL: Did you used to sleep in my room?

CORY: Yeah . . . that used to be my room.

RAYNELL: That's what Papa call it. "Cory's room." It got your football in the closet. 90

ROSE *comes to the door.*

ROSE: Raynell, get in there and get them good shoes on.

RAYNELL: Mama, can't I wear these? Them other one hurt my feet.

ROSE: Well, they just gonna have to hurt your feet for a while. You ain't said they hurt your feet when you went down to the store and got them.

RAYNELL: They didn't hurt then. My feet done got bigger. 95

ROSE: Don't you give me no backtalk now. You get in there and get them shoes on.

RAYNELL *exits into the house.*

Ain't too much changed. He still got that piece of rag tied to that tree. He was out here swinging that bat. I was just ready to go back in the house. He swung that bat and then he just fell over. Seem like he swung it and stood there with this grin on his face . . . and then he just fell over. They carried him on 100 down to the hospital, but I knew there wasn't no need . . . why don't you come on in the house?

CORY: Mama . . . I got something to tell you. I don't know how to tell you this . . . but I've got to tell you . . . I'm not going to Papa's funeral.

ROSE: Boy, hush your mouth. That's your daddy you talking about. I don't want hear 105 that kind of talk this morning. I done raised you to come to this? You standing there all healthy and grown talking about you ain't going to your daddy's funeral?

CORY: Mama . . . listen . . .

ROSE: I don't want to hear it, Cory. You just get that thought out of your head. 110

CORY: I can't drag Papa with me everywhere I go. I've got to say no to him. One time in my life I've got to say no.

ROSE: Don't nobody have to listen to nothing like that. I know you and your daddy ain't seen eye to eye, but I ain't got to listen to that kind of talk this morning. Whatever was between you and your daddy . . . the time has come to put it aside. Just take it 115 and set it over there on the shelf and forget about it. Disrespecting your daddy ain't gonna make you a man, Cory. You got to find a way to come to that on your own. Not going to your daddy's funeral ain't gonna make you a man.

CORY: The whole time I was growing up . . . living in his house . . . Papa was like a shadow that followed you everywhere. It weighed on you and sunk into your 120 flesh. It would wrap around you and lay there until you couldn't tell which one was you anymore. That shadow digging in your flesh. Trying to crawl in. Trying to live through you. Everywhere I looked, Troy Maxson was staring back at me . . . hiding under the bed . . . in the closet. I'm just saying I've got to find a way to get rid of that shadow, Mama. 125

ROSE: You just like him. You got him in you good.

CORY: Don't tell me that, Mama.

ROSE: You Troy Maxson all over again.

CORY: I don't want to be Troy Maxson. I want to be me.

ROSE: You can't be nobody but who you are, Cory. That shadow wasn't nothing   130
but you growing into yourself. You either got to grow into it or cut it down to
fit you. But that's all you got to make life with. That's all you got to measure
yourself against that world out there. Your daddy wanted you to be everything
he wasn't . . . and at the same time he tried to make you into everything he was.
I don't know if he was right or wrong . . . but I do know he meant to do more   135
good than he meant to do harm. He wasn't always right. Sometimes when he
touched he bruised. And sometimes when he took me in his arms he cut.

When I first met your daddy I thought . . . Here is a man I can lay down
with and make a baby. That's the first thing I thought when I seen him. I was
thirty years old and had done seen my share of men. But when he walked up to   140
me and said, "I can dance a waltz that'll make you dizzy," I thought, Rose Lee,
here is a man that you can open yourself up to and be filled to bursting. Here is
a man that can fill all them empty spaces you been tipping around the edges of.
One of them empty spaces was being somebody's mother.

I married your daddy and settled down to cooking his supper and keeping   145
clean sheets on the bed. When your daddy walked through the house he was so
big he filled it up. That was my first mistake. Not to make him leave some room
for me. For my part in the matter. But at that time I wanted that. I wanted a
house that I could sing in. And that's what your daddy gave me. I didn't know to
keep up his strength I had to give up little pieces of mine. I did that. I took on   150
his life as mine and mixed up the pieces so that you couldn't hardly tell which
was which anymore. It was my choice. It was my life and I didn't have to live it
like that. But that's what life offered me in the way of being a woman and I took
it. I grabbed hold of it with both hands.

By the time Raynell came into the house, me and your daddy had done   155
lost touch with one another. I didn't want to make my blessing off of nobody's
misfortune . . . but I took on to Raynell like she was all them babies I had wanted
and never had.

The phone rings.

Like I'd been blessed to relive a part of my life. And if the Lord see fit to keep up
my strength . . . I'm gonna do her just like your daddy did you . . . I'm gonna give   160
her the best of what's in me.

RAYNELL *(entering, still with her old shoes)*: Mama . . . Reverend Tollivier on the
phone.

ROSE *exits into the house.*

RAYNELL: Hi.

CORY: Hi.   165

RAYNELL: You in the Army or the Marines?

CORY: Marines.

RAYNELL: Papa said it was the Army. Did you know Blue?

CORY: Blue? Who's Blue?

RAYNELL: Papa's dog what he sing about all the time. 170

CORY (singing): Hear it ring! Hear it ring!
I had a dog his name was Blue
You know Blue was mighty true
You know Blue was a good old dog
Blue treed a possum in a hollow log 175
You know from that he was a good old dog.
Hear it ring! Hear it ring!

RAYNELL joins in singing.

CORY AND RAYNELL: Blue treed a possum out on a limb
Blue looked at me and I looked at him
Grabbed that possum and put him in a sack 180
Blue stayed there till I came back
Old Blue's feets was big and round
Never allowed a possum to touch the ground.

Old Blue died and I dug his grave
I dug his grave with a silver spade 185
Let him down with a golden chain
And every night I call his name
Go on Blue, you good dog you
Go on Blue, you good dog you

RAYNELL: Blue laid down and died like a man 190
Blue laid down and died . . .

BOTH: Blue laid down and died like a man
Now he's treeing possums in the Promised Land
I'm gonna tell you this to let you know
Blue's gone where the good dogs go 195
When I hear old Blue bark
When I hear old Blue bark
Blue treed a possum in Noah's Ark
Blue treed a possum in Noah's Ark.

ROSE comes to the screen door.

ROSE: Cory, we gonna be ready to go in a minute. 200

CORY (to RAYNELL): You go on in the house and change them shoes like Mama told
you so we can go to Papa's funeral.

RAYNELL: Okay, I'll be back.

RAYNELL exits into the house. CORY gets up and crosses over to the tree. ROSE stands in
the screen door watching him. GABRIEL enters from the alley.

GABRIEL *(calling)*: Hey, Rose!
ROSE: Gabe?   205
GABRIEL: I'm here, Rose. Hey Rose, I'm here!

ROSE *enters from the house.*

ROSE: Lord . . . Look here, Lyons!
LYONS: See, I told you, Rose . . . I told you they'd let him come.
CORY: How you doing, Uncle Gabe?
LYONS: How you doing, Uncle Gabe?   210
GABRIEL: Hey, Rose. It's time. It's time to tell St. Peter to open the gates. Troy, you ready?
   You ready, Troy. I'm gonna tell St. Peter to open the gates. You get ready now.

GABRIEL, *with great fanfare, braces himself to blow. The trumpet is without a mouthpiece.
He puts the end of it into his mouth and blows with great force, like a man who has been
waiting some twenty-odd years for this single moment. No sound comes out of the trumpet.
He braces himself and blows again with the same result. A third time he blows. There is a
weight of impossible description that falls away and leaves him bare and exposed to a frightful realization. It is a trauma that a sane and normal mind would be unable to withstand.
He begins to dance. A slow, strange dance, eerie and life-giving. A dance of atavistic signature
and ritual.* LYONS *attempts to embrace him.* GABRIEL *pushes* LYONS *away. He begins to
howl in what is an attempt at song, or perhaps a song turning back into itself in an attempt
at speech. He finishes his dance and the gates of heaven stand open as wide as God's closet.*

   That's the way that go!

                                                                              [1985]

. . . .

Questions for Discussion

1. Troy Maxson's last name makes subtle reference to the Mason-Dixon Line — the imaginary line that in the 1820s divided slave states from free states. How does this allusion to history help prepare you for the play's themes? What are the connotations of other characters' names — for example, *Rose* and *Gabriel*?

2. What is the significance of the biblical and supernatural allusions that appear throughout the play? Consider the story of Troy getting furniture from the devil, and the behavior and history of Gabriel.

3. In the stage directions for act I, scene 1, Wilson describes Troy as "a large man with thick, heavy hands; it is this largeness that he strives to fill out and make an accommodation with." How does this description establish the character of Troy? Consider also Troy's encounters with Death — the way he taunts Death to come and get him, asserting that he will go down swinging. What might Wilson be saying about Troy's character with these descriptions?

4. How does Rose's assertion in act I, scene 1, that "Times have changed" (l. 153) set the mood for the action that follows? How does it anticipate the themes Wilson will explore more specifically through his characters and the action of the play?

5. How do you interpret Lyons's response to his father's criticism of his lifestyle: "I know I got to eat. But I got to live too. I need something that gonna help me to get out of the bed in the morning. Make me feel like I belong in the world"(I.1.340–41)? Discuss what it is that makes each of the central characters feel some sense of belonging in the world: Troy, Rose, Lyons, and Cory.

6. What role does Bono play in the development of Troy's character? Pick a scene that you think shows Bono's role most clearly, and then explain.

7. At the opening of act I, scene 2, Rose is hanging up clothes in the early morning, humming and singing to herself. Her song imploring Jesus to "be a fence all around me every day" reflects one of the play's important themes. How do different characters relate to and define fences? Whom do fences keep out, and whom do they enclose? Consider also how fences relate to baseball. Explain why this is an appropriate title for the play.

8. In act I, scene 3, Troy explains why he refuses to sign Cory's recruitment papers: "The white man ain't gonna let you get nowhere with that football noway. You go on and get your book-learning so you can work yourself up in that A&P or learn how to fix cars or build houses or something, get you a trade. That way you have something can't nobody take away from you. You go on and learn how to put your hands to some good use. Besides hauling people's garbage" (ll. 123–28). Could there be more to his refusal than the explanation he offers? Explain.

9. What is the significance of Troy's triumph at work, earning the right to drive the garbage truck (act I, scene 4)? What is ironic about this victory? How and why does his promotion affect his relationship with Bono?

10. Why do you think the playwright chose not to have Alberta make an appearance on stage? How does she appear in your imagination? How would you describe her?

11. Is Troy a hypocrite? Do his relationships with Alberta and Cory make his assertions regarding family responsibilities and duty ring false?

12. When Cory returns after Troy's death, he tells Rose, "I can't drag Papa with me everywhere I go. I've got to say no to him" (II.5.110). What finally convinces Cory to attend Troy's funeral? What does his attending the funeral suggest about what Cory's future might hold and what kind of home and family he will have? Has he said "no" to his father?

Questions on Style and Structure

1. Three texts, all written by Wilson, precede the actual opening of the play: a four-line poem, a description of the setting, and a more discursive piece entitled "The Play." Although these texts provide specific information, they also raise larger issues. What are some of these? Pay particular attention to the language Wilson uses ("in His Largeness and Laws," "the porch lacks congruence," "The city devoured them," "new energies that used loyalty and patriotism as its fuel").

2. In act I, scene 1, Troy's friend Bono chides him about "that Alberta gal" (l. 35). What is significant about the introduction of this complicating element before

we meet Troy's wife? What might this foreshadow in the play? How does this teasing introduce a complication within the play's exposition?

3. Early in the play (act I, scene 1), Wilson's stage direction for Rose indicates that she "alternates between the porch and the kitchen." Throughout the play, she is associated with food and preparation. Examine specific passages and examples, and discuss how Wilson uses this association to develop the character of Rose.

4. Why do you think Wilson holds off until the end of act I to have Troy reveal his past and his own confrontation with his father at age fourteen? Why does Wilson have Troy tell the story as a flashback to Lyons and Bono rather than to Cory? Pay special attention to Troy's tone; how does this section contribute to your understanding of his character?

5. Much of the play is concerned with money: earning it, owing it, paying for things. Yet Wilson alerts us to a metaphorical level when Troy insists, "Life don't owe you nothing. You owe it to yourself" (I.1.334–35). Discuss how the language of commerce—debt, payment, purchase, cheating—develops important themes in the play.

6. What do you think is the climax of *Fences*? Explain your reasoning.

7. Much of *Fences* is written in dialect, depicting the natural speech patterns of the characters in the play. In one example, Troy teases Rose with: "I'm studying you . . . fixing to do my homework!" (I.3.23). In other instances, Wilson brings in dialect through songs the characters recall or sing. How does the dialect affect your understanding of the play? Do you find that the style of the characters' language, which reflects the period when the action occurs, dates the play for contemporary viewers?

8. In act II, scene 1, Troy uses baseball metaphors ("steal second," "stood on first base for eighteen years") to explain his affair with Alberta to Rose. How is this use of language consistent with Troy's character? On what basis does Rose reject the comparison? Consider the metaphor she chooses as she counters with an explanation of how she has tried to live her life.

9. Wilson has described *Fences* as having a "blues aesthetic." Songs, and particularly the blues, play an important role in Wilson's plays. Where do you see the influence of the blues on *Fences*? Is it in the diction? the syntax? the themes? the structure? Or does it show itself in some other way?

10. The character of Gabriel has puzzled readers, audiences, and even directors; one even suggested that he be dropped from the script to keep from confusing audiences. Some see him as a spiritual presence with a visible link to the African past. What elements of plot and character depend on him? Explain how you do or do not see Gabriel as essential to *Fences*. Include the final scene in your interpretation.

Suggestions for Writing

1. Rose is a character who has provoked a great deal of controversy: some see her as a strong matriarch who holds her family together, while others argue that

she enables Troy's worst behaviors. Write an essay explaining your view of Rose. Consider both her assertion that she "ain't never wanted no half nothing in [her] family" (II.1.173–74) and her decision to bring Raynell into the Maxson family.

2. In the description of Troy Maxson that precedes the play, Wilson writes, "at times he can be crude and almost vulgar, though he is capable of rising to profound heights of expression." Write an essay analyzing the character of Troy as embodying this tension. Discuss which inclination you believe ultimately prevails.

3. Tragic heroes possess a character flaw or commit an error of judgment that leads to their downfall and a reversal of fortune. Write an essay explaining why you believe that Troy is a tragic hero, paying careful attention to ways in which this play diverges from the classical model.

4. Fences is most often interpreted as a "generational play." In fact, August Wilson scholar Sandra Shannon describes a 1997 production in Beijing with an all-Chinese cast in which both audience members and actors found that "their connections to Fences seemed to have had more to do with the shifting of a powerful nation's economic and generational center from one determined by tradition to one responding to the trappings of modernization." Discuss the generational conflicts in this play, and consider how they are reflective of more universal experiences than ones specific to the African American experience.

5. Write a eulogy to be read at Troy Maxson's funeral. Include details from his life that would help mourners see that "he meant to do more good than he meant to do harm" (II.5.134–35). Consider carefully who the speaker of your eulogy is. It could be any of the characters in the play, or someone else entirely.

6. Imagine that ten years have elapsed since Troy's death, and Cory and Lyons return home to celebrate Rose's birthday. Write a dialogue between the half brothers in which they reminisce about their father.

7. Troy Maxson took part in the Great Migration of rural blacks from the South to urban centers in the North. The artist Jacob Lawrence has chronicled this journey in his Migration Series. The series is housed in the Museum of Modern Art in New York, but the images are available online at <www.phillipscollection.org/migration_series>. Choose one painting that particularly appeals to you and write about how it helps you visualize the historical movement.

8. Throughout the play, Troy uses baseball metaphors to explain how he thinks and feels. Try omitting the metaphor and writing Troy's speech to Rose in act II, scene 1, more literally (beginning with "But . . . you born with two strikes on you before you come to the plate" on lines 213–14). How does the loss of the baseball metaphor affect the power of the speech?

9. The time frame of Fences spans several major historical moments for African Americans in the twentieth century: Reconstruction, the Great Migration, the Great Depression, and the civil rights movement. Write an essay explaining how the historical and social forces of these eras are reflected either in the play as a whole or in the character of Troy Maxson.

Babylon Revisited

F. SCOTT FITZGERALD

Francis Scott Key Fitzgerald (1896–1940) was born in Saint Paul, Minnesota. He attended Princeton University, but time devoted to his writing detracted from his academic performance. After being placed on probation, he quit Princeton to join the army in 1917. Fitzgerald is most famous for his Jazz Age novels *This Side of Paradise* (1920) and *The Great Gatsby* (1925), loosely based on his early relationship with his wife, Zelda Sayre. However, it was from magazine writing—a genre that Fitzgerald claimed to despise—that he earned substantial money. As a successful writer, he flaunted his celebrity and lived a tempestuous life, surrounding himself with wealthy socialites and almost bankrupting himself in the process. This lifestyle is illustrated in his ambitious novel *Tender Is the Night* (1934), which, like *The Great Gatsby*, attracted acclaim well after publication. Similar elements of autobiography—fast living, regret, and the desire for redemption—can be found in Fitzgerald's portrayal of Charlie, the main character in "Babylon Revisited."

I

"And where's Mr. Campbell?" Charlie asked.

"Gone to Switzerland. Mr. Campbell's a pretty sick man, Mr. Wales."

"I'm sorry to hear that. And George Hardt?" Charlie inquired.

"Back in America, gone to work."

"And where is the Snow Bird?"

"He was in here last week. Anyway, his friend, Mr. Schaeffer, is in Paris."

Two familiar names from the long list of a year and a half ago. Charlie scribbled an address in his notebook and tore out the page.

"If you see Mr. Schaeffer, give him this," he said. "It's my brother-in-law's address. I haven't settled on a hotel yet."

He was not really disappointed to find Paris was so empty. But the stillness in the Ritz bar was strange and portentous. It was not an American bar any more—he felt polite in it, and not as if he owned it. It had gone back into France. He felt the stillness from the moment he got out of the taxi and saw the doorman, usually in a frenzy of activity at this hour, gossiping with a *chasseur* by the servants' entrance.

Passing through the corridor, he heard only a single, bored voice in the once-clamorous women's room. When he turned into the bar he traveled the twenty feet of green carpet with his eyes fixed straight ahead by old habit; and then, with his foot firmly on the rail, he turned and surveyed the room, encountering only a single pair of eyes that fluttered up from a newspaper in the corner. Charlie asked for the head barman, Paul, who in the latter days of the bull market had come to work in his own custom-built car—disembarking, however, with due nicety at the nearest corner. But Paul was at his country house today and Alix giving him information.

"No, no more," Charlie said, "I'm going slow these days."

Alix congratulated him: "You were going pretty strong a couple of years ago."

"I'll stick to it all right," Charlie assured him. "I've stuck to it for over a year and a half now."

"How do you find conditions in America?"

"I haven't been to America for months. I'm in business in Prague, representing a 15 couple of concerns there. They don't know about me down there."

Alix smiled.

"Remember the night of George Hardt's bachelor dinner here?" said Charlie. "By the way, what's become of Claude Fessenden?"

Alix lowered his voice confidentially: "He's in Paris, but he doesn't come here any more. Paul doesn't allow it. He ran up a bill of thirty thousand francs, charging all his drinks and his lunches, and usually his dinner, for more than a year. And when Paul finally told him he had to pay, he gave him a bad check."

Alix shook his head sadly.

"I don't understand it, such a dandy fellow. Now he's all bloated up —" He made 20 a plump apple of his hands.

Charlie watched a group of strident queens installing themselves in a corner.

"Nothing affects them," he thought. "Stocks rise and fall, people loaf or work, but they go on forever." The place oppressed him. He called for the dice and shook with Alix for the drink.

"Here for long, Mr. Wales?"

"I'm here for four or five days to see my little girl."

"Oh-h! You have a little girl?" 25

Outside, the fire-red, gas-blue, ghost-green signs shone smokily through the tranquil rain. It was late afternoon and the streets were in movement; the *bistros* gleamed. At the corner of the Boulevard des Capucines he took a taxi. The Place de la Concorde moved by in pink majesty; they crossed the logical Seine, and Charlie felt the sudden provincial quality of the Left Bank.

Charlie directed his taxi to the Avenue de l'Opera, which was out of his way. But he wanted to see the blue hour spread over the magnificent façade, and imagine that the cab horns, playing endlessly the first few bars of *La Plus que Lente*, were the trumpets of the Second Empire. They were closing the iron grill in front of Brentano's Book-store, and people were already at dinner behind the trim little bourgeois hedge of Duval's. He had never eaten at a really cheap restaurant in Paris. Five-course dinner, four francs fifty, eighteen cents, wine included. For some odd reason he wished that he had.

As they rolled on to the Left Bank and he felt its sudden provincialism, he thought, "I spoiled this city for myself. I didn't realize it, but the days came along one after another, and then two years were gone, and everything was gone, and I was gone."

He was thirty-five, and good to look at. The Irish mobility of his face was sobered by a deep wrinkle between his eyes. As he rang his brother-in-law's bell in the Rue Palatine, the wrinkle deepened till it pulled down his brows; he felt a cramping sensation in his belly. From behind the maid who opened the door darted a lovely little girl of nine who shrieked "Daddy!" and flew up, struggling like a fish, into his arms. She pulled his head around by one ear and set her cheek against his.

"My old pie," he said.

"Oh, daddy, daddy, daddy, daddy, dads, dads, dads!"

She drew him into the salon, where the family waited, a boy and a girl his daughter's age, his sister-in-law and her husband. He greeted Marion with his voice pitched carefully to avoid either feigned enthusiasm or dislike, but her response was more frankly tepid, though she minimized her expression of unalterable distrust by directing her regard toward his child. The two men clasped hands in a friendly way and Lincoln Peters rested his for a moment on Charlie's shoulder.

The room was warm and comfortably American. The three children moved intimately about, playing through the yellow oblongs that led to other rooms; the cheer of six o'clock spoke in the eager smacks of the fire and the sounds of French activity in the kitchen. But Charlie did not relax; his heart sat up rigidly in his body and he drew confidence from his daughter, who from time to time came close to him, holding in her arms the doll he had brought.

"Really extremely well," he declared in answer to Lincoln's question. "There's a lot of business there that isn't moving at all, but we're doing even better than ever. In fact, damn well. I'm bringing my sister over from America next month to keep house for me. My income last year was bigger than it was when I had money. You see, the Czechs—"

His boasting was for a specific purpose; but after a moment, seeing a faint restiveness in Lincoln's eye, he changed the subject:

"Those are fine children of yours, well brought up, good manners."

"We think Honoria's a great little girl too."

Marion Peters came back from the kitchen. She was a tall woman with worried eyes, who had once possessed a fresh American loveliness. Charlie had never been sensitive to it and was always surprised when people spoke of how pretty she had been. From the first there had been an instinctive antipathy between them.

"Well, how do you find Honoria?" she asked.

"Wonderful. I was astonished how much she's grown in ten months. All the children are looking well."

"We haven't had a doctor for a year. How do you like being back in Paris?"

"It seems very funny to see so few Americans around."

"I'm delighted," Marion said vehemently. "Now at least you can go into a store without their assuming you're a millionaire. We've suffered like everybody, but on the whole it's a good deal pleasanter."

"But it was nice while it lasted," Charlie said. "We were a sort of royalty, almost infallible, with a sort of magic around us. In the bar this afternoon"—he stumbled, seeing his mistake—"there wasn't a man I knew."

She looked at him keenly. "I should think you'd have had enough of bars."

"I only stayed a minute. I take one drink every afternoon, and no more."

"Don't you want a cocktail before dinner?" Lincoln asked.

"I take only one drink every afternoon, and I've had that."

"I hope you keep to it," said Marion.

Her dislike was evident in the coldness with which she spoke, but Charlie only 50
smiled; he had larger plans. Her very aggressiveness gave him an advantage, and he
knew enough to wait. He wanted them to initiate the discussion of what they knew
had brought him to Paris.

At dinner he couldn't decide whether Honoria was most like him or her mother.
Fortunate if she didn't combine the traits of both that had brought them to disaster.
A great wave of protectiveness went over him. He thought he knew what to do for
her. He believed in character; he wanted to jump back a whole generation and trust
in character again as the eternally valuable element. Everything else wore out.

He left soon after dinner, but not to go home. He was curious to see Paris by night
with clearer and more judicious eyes than those of other days. He bought a *strapontin*[1]
for the Casino and watched Josephine Baker go through her chocolate arabesques.

After an hour he left and strolled toward Montmartre, up the Rue Pigalle into the
Place Blanche. The rain had stopped and there were a few people in evening clothes
disembarking from taxis in front of cabarets, and *cocottes*[2] prowling singly or in pairs,
and many Negroes. He passed a lighted door from which issued music, and stopped
with the sense of familiarity; it was Bricktop's, where he had parted with so many hours
and so much money. A few doors farther on he found another ancient rendezvous and
incautiously put his head inside. Immediately an eager orchestra burst into sound, a
pair of professional dancers leaped to their feet and a maître d'hôtel swooped toward
him, crying, "Crowd just arriving, sir!" But he withdrew quickly.

"You have to be damn drunk," he thought.

Zelli's was closed, the bleak and sinister cheap hotels surrounding it were dark; 55
up in the Rue Blanche there was more light and a local, colloquial French crowd. The
Poet's Cave had disappeared, but the two great mouths of the Café of Heaven and
the Café of Hell still yawned — even devoured, as he watched, the meager contents of
a tourist bus — a German, a Japanese, and an American couple who glanced at him
with frightened eyes.

So much for the effort and ingenuity of Montmartre. All the catering to vice and
waste was on an utterly childish scale, and he suddenly realized the meaning of the
word "dissipate" — to dissipate into thin air; to make nothing out of something. In
the little hours of the night every move from place to place was an enormous human
jump, an increase of paying for the privilege of slower and slower motion.

He remembered thousand-franc notes given to an orchestra for playing a single
number, hundred-franc notes tossed to a doorman for calling a cab.

But it hadn't been given for nothing.

It had been given, even the most wildly squandered sum, as an offering to destiny
that he might not remember the things most worth remembering, the things that
now he would always remember — his child taken from his control, his wife escaped
to a grave in Vermont.

----

[1]Folding chair — EDS.
[2]Prostitutes — EDS.

In the glare of a *brasserie* a woman spoke to him. He bought her some eggs and   60
coffee, and then, eluding her encouraging stare, gave her a twenty-franc note and
took a taxi to his hotel.

II

He woke upon a fine fall day—football weather. The depression of yesterday was
gone and he liked the people on the streets. At noon he sat opposite Honoria at Le
Grand Vatel, the only restaurant he could think of not reminiscent of champagne dinners and long luncheons that began at two and ended in a blurred and vague twilight.

"Now, how about vegetables? Oughtn't you to have some vegetables?"

"Well, yes."

"Here's *épinards* and *chou-fleur* and carrots and *haricots*."

"I'd like *chou-fleur*."   65

"Wouldn't you like to have two vegetables?"

"I usually only have one at lunch."

The waiter was pretending to be inordinately fond of children. "*Qu'elle est
mignonne la petite! Elle parle exactement comme une Française.*"

"How about dessert? Shall we wait and see?"

The waiter disappeared. Honoria looked at her father expectantly.   70

"What are we going to do?"

"First, we're going to that toy store in the Rue Saint-Honoré and buy you anything you like. And then we're going to the vaudeville at the Empire."

She hesitated. "I like it about the vaudeville, but not the toy store."

"Why not?"

"Well, you brought me this doll." She had it with her. "And I've got lots of things.   75
And we're not rich any more, are we?"

"We never were. But today you are to have anything you want."

"All right," she agreed resignedly.

When there had been her mother and a French nurse he had been inclined to
be strict; now he extended himself, reached out for a new tolerance; he must be both
parents to her and not shut any of her out of communication.

"I want to get to know you," he said gravely. "First let me introduce myself. My
name is Charles J. Wales, of Prague."

"Oh, daddy!" her voice cracked with laughter.   80

"And who are you, please?" he persisted, and she accepted a rôle immediately:
"Honoria Wales, Rue Palatine, Paris."

"Married or single?"

"No, not married. Single."

He indicated the doll. "But I see you have a child, madame."

Unwilling to disinherit it, she took it to her heart and thought quickly: "Yes, I've   85
been married, but I'm not married now. My husband is dead."

He went on quickly, "And the child's name?"

"Simone. That's after my best friend at school."

"I'm very pleased that you're doing so well at school."

"I'm third this month," she boasted. "Elsie"—that was her cousin—"is only about eighteenth, and Richard is at the bottom."

"You like Richard and Elsie, don't you?"

"Oh, yes. I like Richard quite well and I like her all right."

Cautiously and casually he asked: "And Aunt Marion and Uncle Lincoln—which do you like best?"

"Oh, Uncle Lincoln, I guess."

He was increasingly aware of her presence. As they came in, a murmur of ". . . adorable" followed them, and now the people at the next table bent all their silences upon her, staring as if she were something no more conscious than a flower.

"Why don't I live with you?" she asked suddenly. "Because mamma's dead?"

"You must stay here and learn more French. It would have been hard for daddy to take care of you so well."

"I don't really need much taking care of any more. I do everything for myself."

Going out of the restaurant, a man and a woman unexpectedly hailed him.

"Well, the old Wales!"

"Hello there, Lorraine. . . . Dunc."

Sudden ghosts out of the past: Duncan Schaeffer, a friend from college. Lorraine Quarrles, a lovely, pale blonde of thirty; one of a crowd who had helped them make months into days in the lavish times of three years ago.

"My husband couldn't come this year," she said, in answer to his question. "We're poor as hell. So he gave me two hundred a month and told me I could do my worst on that. . . . This your little girl?"

"What about coming back and sitting down?" Duncan asked.

"Can't do it." He was glad for an excuse. As always, he felt Lorraine's passionate, provocative attraction, but his own rhythm was different now.

"Well, how about dinner?" she asked.

"I'm not free. Give me your address and let me call you."

"Charlie, I believe you're sober," she said judicially. "I honestly believe he's sober, Dunc. Pinch him and see if he's sober."

Charlie indicated Honoria with his head. They both laughed.

"What's your address?" said Duncan skeptically.

He hesitated, unwilling to give the name of his hotel.

"I'm not settled yet. I'd better call you. We're going to see the vaudeville at the Empire."

"There! That's what I want to do," Lorraine said. "I want to see some clowns and acrobats and jugglers. That's just what we'll do, Dunc."

"We've got to do an errand first," said Charlie. "Perhaps we'll see you there."

"All right, you snob. . . . Good-by, beautiful little girl."

"Good-by."

Honoria bobbed politely.

Somehow, an unwelcome encounter. They liked him because he was functioning, because he was serious; they wanted to see him, because he was stronger than they were now, because they wanted to draw a certain sustenance from his strength.

At the Empire, Honoria proudly refused to sit upon her father's folded coat. She was already an individual with a code of her own, and Charlie was more and more absorbed by the desire of putting a little of himself into her before she crystallized utterly. It was hopeless to try to know her in so short a time.

Between the acts they came upon Duncan and Lorraine in the lobby where the band was playing.

"Have a drink?"

"All right, but not up at the bar. We'll take a table."

"The perfect father."

Listening abstractedly to Lorraine, Charlie watched Honoria's eyes leave their table, and he followed them wistfully about the room, wondering what they saw. He met her glance and she smiled.

"I liked that lemonade," she said.

What had she said? What had he expected? Going home in a taxi afterward, he pulled her over until her head rested against his chest.

"Darling, do you ever think of your mother?"

"Yes, sometimes," she answered vaguely.

"I don't want you to forget her. Have you got a picture of her?"

"Yes, I think so. Anyhow, Aunt Marion has. Why don't you want me to forget her?"

"She loved you very much."

"I loved her too."

They were silent for a moment.

"Daddy, I want to come and live with you," she said suddenly.

His heart leaped; he had wanted it to come like this.

"Aren't you perfectly happy?"

"Yes, but I love you better than anybody. And you love me better than anybody, don't you, now that mummy's dead?"

"Of course I do. But you won't always like me best, honey. You'll grow up and meet somebody your own age and go marry him and forget you ever had a daddy."

"Yes, that's true," she agreed tranquilly.

He didn't go in. He was coming back at nine o'clock and he wanted to keep himself fresh and new for the thing he must say then.

"When you're safe inside, just show yourself in that window."

"All right. Good-by, dads, dads, dads, dads."

He waited in the dark street until she appeared, all warm and glowing, in the window above and kissed her fingers out into the night.

III

They were waiting. Marion sat behind the coffee service in a dignified black dinner dress that just faintly suggested mourning. Lincoln was walking up and down with the animation of one who had already been talking. They were as anxious as he was to get into the question. He opened it almost immediately:

"I suppose you know what I want to see you about—why I really came to Paris."

Marion played with the black stars on her necklace and frowned.   145

"I'm awfully anxious to have a home," he continued. "And I'm awfully anxious to have Honoria in it. I appreciate your taking in Honoria for her mother's sake, but things have changed now"—he hesitated and then continued more forcibly—"changed radically with me, and I want to ask you to reconsider the matter. It would be silly for me to deny that about three years ago I was acting badly—"

Marion looked up at him with hard eyes.

"—but all that's over. As I told you, I haven't had more than a drink a day for over a year, and I take that drink deliberately, so that the idea of alcohol won't get too big in my imagination. You see the idea?"

"No," said Marion succinctly.

"It's a sort of stunt I set myself. It keeps the matter in proportion."   150

"I get you," said Lincoln. "You don't want to admit it's got any attraction for you."

"Something like that. Sometimes I forget and don't take it. But I try to take it. Anyhow, I couldn't afford to drink in my position. The people I represent are more than satisfied with what I've done, and I'm bringing my sister over from Burlington to keep house for me, and I want awfully to have Honoria too. You know that even when her mother and I weren't getting along well we never let anything that happened touch Honoria. I know she's fond of me and I know I'm able to take care of her and—well, there you are. How do you feel about it?"

He knew that now he would have to take a beating. It would last an hour or two hours, and it would be difficult, but if he modulated his inevitable resentment to the chastened attitude of the reformed sinner, he might win his point in the end.

Keep your temper, he told himself. You don't want to be justified. You want Honoria.

Lincoln spoke first: "We've been talking it over ever since we got your letter last   155
month. We're happy to have Honoria here. She's a dear little thing, and we're glad to be able to help her, but of course that isn't the question—"

Marion interrupted suddenly. "How long are you going to stay sober, Charlie?" she asked.

"Permanently, I hope."

"How can anybody count on that?"

"You know I never did drink heavily until I gave up business and came over here with nothing to do. Then Helen and I began to run around with—"

"Please leave Helen out of it. I can't bear to hear you talk about her like that."   160

He stared at her grimly; he had never been certain how fond of each other the sisters were in life.

"My drinking only lasted about a year and a half—from the time we came over until I—collapsed."

"It was time enough."

"It was time enough," he agreed.

"My duty is entirely to Helen," she said. "I try to think what she would have   165
wanted me to do. Frankly, from the night you did that terrible thing you haven't
really existed for me. I can't help that. She was my sister."

"Yes."

"When she was dying she asked me to look out for Honoria. If you hadn't been
in a sanitarium then, it might have helped matters."

He had no answer.

"I'll never in my life be able to forget the morning when Helen knocked at my
door, soaked to the skin and shivering and said you'd locked her out."

Charlie gripped the sides of the chair. This was more difficult than he expected;   170
he wanted to launch out into a long expostulation and explanation, but he only said:
"The night I locked her out—" and she interrupted, "I don't feel up to going over
that again."

After a moment's silence Lincoln said: "We're getting off the subject. You want
Marion to set aside her legal guardianship and give you Honoria. I think the main
point for her is whether she has confidence in you or not."

"I don't blame Marion," Charlie said slowly, "but I think she can have entire
confidence in me. I had a good record up to three years ago. Of course, it's within
human possibilities I might go wrong any time. But if we wait much longer I'll lose
Honoria's childhood and my chance for a home." He shook his head, "I'll simply lose
her, don't you see?"

"Yes, I see," said Lincoln.

"Why didn't you think of all this before?" Marion asked.

"I suppose I did, from time to time, but Helen and I were getting along badly.   175
When I consented to the guardianship, I was flat on my back in a sanitarium and the
market had cleaned me out. I knew I'd acted badly, and I thought if it would bring
any peace to Helen, I'd agree to anything. But now it's different. I'm functioning, I'm
behaving damn well, so far as—"

"Please don't swear at me," Marion said.

He looked at her, startled. With each remark the force of her dislike became
more and more apparent. She had built up all her fear of life into one wall and
faced it toward him. This trivial reproof was possibly the result of some trouble
with the cook several hours before. Charlie became increasingly alarmed at leaving
Honoria in this atmosphere of hostility against himself; sooner or later it would
come out, in a word here, a shake of the head there, and some of that distrust
would be irrevocably implanted in Honoria. But he pulled his temper down out
of his face and shut it up inside him; he had won a point, for Lincoln realized the
absurdity of Marion's remark and asked her lightly since when she had objected to
the word "damn."

"Another thing," Charlie said: "I'm able to give her certain advantages now.
I'm going to take a French governess to Prague with me. I've got a lease on a new
apartment—"

He stopped, realizing that he was blundering. They couldn't be expected to accept
with equanimity the fact that his income was again twice as large as their own.

"I suppose you can give her more luxuries than we can," said Marion. "When
you were throwing away money we were living along watching every ten francs. . . . I
suppose you'll start doing it again."

"Oh, no," he said. "I've learned. I worked hard for ten years, you know—until I
got lucky in the market, like so many people. Terribly lucky. It won't happen again."

There was a long silence. All of them felt their nerves straining, and for the first
time in a year Charlie wanted a drink. He was sure now that Lincoln Peters wanted
him to have his child.

Marion shuddered suddenly; part of her saw that Charlie's feet were planted
on the earth now, and her own maternal feeling recognized the naturalness of his
desire; but she had lived for a long time with a prejudice—a prejudice founded on
a curious disbelief in her sister's happiness, and which, in the shock of one terrible
night, had turned to hatred for him. It had all happened at a point in her life where
the discouragement of ill health and adverse circumstances made it necessary for her
to believe in tangible villainy and a tangible villain.

"I can't help what I think!" she cried out suddenly. "How much you were responsible for Helen's death, I don't know. It's something you'll have to square with your
own conscience."

An electric current of agony surged through him; for a moment he was almost
on his feet, an unuttered sound echoing in his throat. He hung on to himself for a
moment, another moment.

"Hold on there," said Lincoln uncomfortably. "I never thought you were responsible for that."

"Helen died of heart trouble," Charlie said dully.

"Yes, heart trouble." Marion spoke as if the phrase had another meaning for her.

Then, in the flatness that followed her outburst, she saw him plainly and she
knew he had somehow arrived at control over the situation. Glancing at her husband,
she found no help from him, and as abruptly as if it were a matter of no importance,
she threw up the sponge.

"Do what you like!" she cried, springing up from her chair. "She's your child.
I'm not the person to stand in your way. I think if it were my child I'd rather see
her—" She managed to check herself. "You two decide it. I can't stand this. I'm sick.
I'm going to bed."

She hurried from the room; after a moment Lincoln said:

"This has been a hard day for her. You know how strongly she feels—" His voice
was almost apologetic: "When a woman gets an idea in her head."

"Of course."

"It's going to be all right. I think she sees now that you—can provide for the
child, and so we can't very well stand in your way or Honoria's way."

"Thank you, Lincoln."

"I'd better go along and see how she is."

"I'm going."

He was still trembling when he reached the street, but a walk down the Rue
Bonaparte to the *quais* set him up, and as he crossed the Seine, fresh and new by the

180

185

190

195

quai lamps, he felt exultant. But back in his room he couldn't sleep. The image of Helen haunted him. Helen whom he had loved so until they had senselessly begun to abuse each other's love, tear it into shreds. On that terrible February night that Marion remembered so vividly, a slow quarrel had gone on for hours. There was a scene at the Florida, and then he attempted to take her home, and then she kissed young Webb at a table; after that there was what she had hysterically said. When he arrived home alone he turned the key in the lock in wild anger. How could he know she would arrive an hour later alone, that there would be a snowstorm in which she wandered about in slippers, too confused to find a taxi? Then the aftermath, her escaping pneumonia by a miracle, and all the attendant horror. They were "reconciled," but that was the beginning of the end, and Marion, who had seen with her own eyes and who imagined it to be one of many scenes from her sister's martyrdom, never forgot.

Going over it again brought Helen nearer, and in the white, soft light that steals upon half sleep near morning he found himself talking to her again. She said that he was perfectly right about Honoria and that she wanted Honoria to be with him. She said she was glad he was being good and doing better. She said a lot of other things—very friendly things—but she was in a swing in a white dress, and swinging faster and faster all the time, so that at the end he could not hear clearly all that she said.

IV

He woke up feeling happy. The door of the world was open again. He made   200
plans, vistas, futures for Honoria and himself, but suddenly he grew sad, remembering all the plans he and Helen had made. She had not planned to die. The present was the thing—work to do and someone to love. But not to love too much, for he knew the injury that a father can do to a daughter or a mother to a son by attaching them too closely: afterward, out in the world, the child would seek in the marriage partner the same blind tenderness and, failing probably to find it, turn against love and life.

It was another bright, crisp day. He called Lincoln Peters at the bank where he worked and asked if he could count on taking Honoria when he left for Prague. Lincoln agreed that there was no reason for delay. One thing—the legal guardianship. Marion wanted to retain that a while longer. She was upset by the whole matter, and it would oil things if she felt that the situation was still in her control for another year. Charlie agreed, wanting only the tangible, visible child.

Then the question of a governess. Charles sat in a gloomy agency and talked to a cross Béarnaise and to a buxom Breton peasant, neither of whom he could have endured. There were others whom he would see tomorrow.

He lunched with Lincoln Peters at Griffons, trying to keep down his exultation.

"There's nothing quite like your own child," Lincoln said. "But you understand how Marion feels too."

"She's forgotten how hard I worked for seven years there," Charlie said. "She just   205
remembers one night."

"There's another thing." Lincoln hesitated. "While you and Helen were tearing around Europe throwing money away, we were just getting along. I didn't touch any of the prosperity because I never got ahead enough to carry anything but my insurance. I think Marion felt there was some kind of injustice in it—you not even working toward the end, and getting richer and richer."

"It went just as quick as it came," said Charlie.

"Yes, a lot of it stayed in the hands of *chasseurs* and saxophone players and maîtres d'hôtel—well, the big party's over now. I just said that to explain Marion's feeling about those crazy years. If you drop in about six o'clock tonight before Marion's too tired, we'll settle the details on the spot."

Back at his hotel, Charlie found a *pneumatique* that had been redirected from the Ritz bar where Charlie had left his address for the purpose of finding a certain man.

> DEAR CHARLIE: You were so strange when we saw you the other day that I wondered if I did something to offend you. If so, I'm not conscious of it. In fact, I have thought about you too much for the last year, and it's always been in the back of my mind that I might see you if I came over here. We did have such good times that crazy spring, like the night you and I stole the butcher's tricycle, and the time we tried to call on the president and you had the old derby rim and the wire cane. Everybody seems so old lately, but I don't feel old a bit. Couldn't we get together some time today for old time's sake? I've got a vile hang-over for the moment, but will be feeling better this afternoon and will look for you about five in the sweatshop at the Ritz.
>
> Always devotedly,
> LORRAINE

His first feeling was one of awe that he had actually, in his mature years, stolen a 210
tricycle and pedaled Lorraine all over the Étoile between the small hours and dawn.
In retrospect it was a nightmare. Locking out Helen didn't fit in with any other act of his life, but the tricycle incident did—it was one of many. How many weeks or months of dissipation to arrive at that condition of utter irresponsibility?

He tried to picture how Lorraine had appeared to him then—very attractive; Helen was unhappy about it, though she said nothing. Yesterday, in the restaurant, Lorraine had seemed trite, blurred, worn away. He emphatically did not want to see her, and he was glad Alix had not given away his hotel address. It was a relief to think, instead, of Honoria, to think of Sundays spent with her and of saying good morning to her and of knowing she was there in his house at night, drawing her breath in the darkness.

At five he took a taxi and bought presents for all the Peters—a piquant cloth doll, a box of Roman soldiers, flowers for Marion, big linen handkerchiefs for Lincoln.

He saw, when he arrived in the apartment, that Marion had accepted the inevitable. She greeted him now as though he were a recalcitrant member of the family, rather than a menacing outsider. Honoria had been told she was going; Charlie was glad to see that her tact made her conceal her excessive happiness. Only on his lap

did she whisper her delight and the question "When?" before she slipped away with
the other children.

He and Marion were alone for a minute in the room, and on an impulse he
spoke out boldly:

"Family quarrels are bitter things. They don't go according to any rules. They're   215
not like aches or wounds; they're more like splits in the skin that won't heal because
there's not enough material. I wish you and I could be on better terms."

"Some things are hard to forget," she answered. "It's a question of confidence." There
was no answer to this and presently she asked, "When do you propose to take her?"

"As soon as I can get a governess. I hoped the day after tomorrow."

"That's impossible. I've got to get her things in shape. Not before Saturday."

He yielded. Coming back into the room, Lincoln offered him a drink.

"I'll take my daily whisky," he said.   220

It was warm here, it was a home, people together by a fire. The children felt very
safe and important; the mother and father were serious, watchful. They had things to
do for the children more important than his visit here. A spoonful of medicine was,
after all, more important than the strained relations between Marion and himself. They
were not dull people, but they were very much in the grip of life and circumstances. He
wondered if he couldn't do something to get Lincoln out of his rut at the bank.

A long peal at the door-bell; the *bonne à tout faire*[3] passed through and went
down the corridor. The door opened upon another long ring, and then voices, and
the three in the salon looked up expectantly; Richard moved to bring the corridor
within his range of vision, and Marion rose. Then the maid came back along the corridor, closely followed by the voices, which developed under the light into Duncan
Schaeffer and Lorraine Quarrles.

They were gay, they were hilarious, they were roaring with laughter. For a moment
Charlie was astounded; unable to understand how they ferreted out the Peters' address.

"Ah-h-h!" Duncan wagged his finger roguishly at Charlie. "Ah-h-h!"

They both slid down another cascade of laughter. Anxious and at a loss, Charlie   225
shook hands with them quickly and presented them to Lincoln and Marion. Marion
nodded, scarcely speaking. She had drawn back a step toward the fire; her little girl
stood beside her, and Marion put an arm about her shoulder.

With growing annoyance at the intrusion, Charlie waited for them to explain
themselves. After some concentration Duncan said:

"We came to invite you out to dinner. Lorraine and I insist that all this shishi,
cagy business 'bout your address got to stop."

Charlie came closer to them, as if to force them backward down the corridor.

"Sorry, but I can't. Tell me where you'll be and I'll phone you in half an hour."

This made no impression. Lorraine sat down suddenly on the side of a chair,   230
and focusing her eyes on Richard, cried, "Oh, what a nice little boy! Come here, little
boy." Richard glanced at his mother, but did not move. With a perceptible shrug of
her shoulders, Lorraine turned back to Charlie:

---

[3]Servant.—Eds.

"Come and dine. Sure your cousins won' mine. See you so sel'om. Or solemn."

"I can't," said Charlie sharply. "You two have dinner and I'll phone you."

Her voice became suddenly unpleasant. "All right, we'll go. But I remember once when you hammered on my door at four A.M. I was enough of a good sport to give you a drink. Come on, Dunc."

Still in slow motion, with blurred, angry faces, with uncertain feet, they retired along the corridor.

"Good night," Charlie said. 235

"Good night!" responded Lorraine emphatically.

When he went back into the salon Marion had not moved, only now her son was standing in the circle of her other arm. Lincoln was still swinging Honoria back and forth like a pendulum from side to side.

"What an outrage!" Charlie broke out. "What an absolute outrage!"

Neither of them answered. Charlie dropped into an armchair, picked up his drink, set it down again and said:

"People I haven't seen for two years having the colossal nerve—" 240

He broke off. Marion had made the sound "Oh!" in one swift, furious breath, turned her body from him with a jerk and left the room.

Lincoln set down Honoria carefully.

"You children go in and start your soup," he said, and when they obeyed, he said to Charlie:

"Marion's not well and she can't stand shocks. That kind of people make her really physically sick."

"I didn't tell them to come here. They wormed your name out of somebody. 245 They deliberately—"

"Well, it's too bad. It doesn't help matters. Excuse me a minute."

Left alone, Charlie sat tense in his chair. In the next room he could hear the children eating, talking in monosyllables, already oblivious to the scene between their elders. He heard a murmur of conversation from a farther room and then the ticking bell of a telephone receiver picked up, and in a panic he moved to the other side of the room and out of earshot.

In a minute Lincoln came back. "Look here, Charlie. I think we'd better call off dinner for tonight. Marion's in bad shape."

"Is she angry with me?"

"Sort of," he said, almost roughly. "She's not strong and—" 250

"You mean she's changed her mind about Honoria?"

"She's pretty bitter right now. I don't know. You phone me at the bank tomorrow."

"I wish you'd explain to her I never dreamed these people would come here. I'm just as sore as you are."

"I couldn't explain anything to her now."

Charlie got up. He took his coat and hat and started down the corridor. Then 255 he opened the door of the dining room and said in a strange voice, "Good night, children."

Honoria rose and ran around the table to hug him.

"Good night, sweetheart," he said vaguely, and then trying to make his voice more tender, trying to conciliate something, "Good night, dear children."

V

Charlie went directly to the Ritz bar with the furious idea of finding Lorraine and Duncan, but they were not there, and he realized that in any case there was nothing he could do. He had not touched his drink at the Peters', and now he ordered a whisky-and-soda. Paul came over to say hello.

"It's a great change," he said sadly. "We do about half the business we did. So many fellows I hear about back in the States lost everything, maybe not in the first crash, but then in the second. Your friend George Hardt lost every cent, I hear. Are you back in the States?"

"No, I'm in business in Prague." 260

"I heard that you lost a lot in the crash."

"I did," and he added grimly, "but I lost everything I wanted in the boom."

"Selling short."

"Something like that."

Again the memory of those days swept over him like a nightmare—the people 265 they had met travelling; then people who couldn't add a row of figures or speak a coherent sentence. The little man Helen had consented to dance with at the ship's party, who had insulted her ten feet from the table; the women and girls carried screaming with drink or drugs out of public places—

—The men who locked their wives out in the snow, because the snow of twenty-nine wasn't real snow. If you didn't want it to be snow, you just paid some money.

He went to the phone and called the Peters' apartment; Lincoln answered.

"I called up because this thing is on my mind. Has Marion said anything definite?"

"Marion's sick," Lincoln answered shortly. "I know this thing isn't altogether your fault, but I can't have her go to pieces about it. I'm afraid we'll have to let it slide for six months; I can't take the chance of working her up to this state again."

"I see." 270

"I'm sorry, Charlie."

He went back to his table. His whisky glass was empty, but he shook his head when Alix looked at it questioningly. There wasn't much he could do now except send Honoria some things; he would send her a lot of things tomorrow. He thought rather angrily that this was just money—he had given so many people money....

"No, no more," he said to the waiter. "What do I owe you?"

He would come back some day; they couldn't make him pay forever. But he wanted his child, and nothing was much good now, beside that fact. He wasn't young any more, with a lot of nice thoughts and dreams to have by himself. He was absolutely sure Helen wouldn't have wanted him to be so alone.

[1931]

Exploring the Text

1. Babylon is an ancient city famous for hedonistic behavior and luxury. In what ways is Charlie "revisiting" Babylon? Identify details in the first section of the story that contrast the way things are in Paris upon Charlie's return and how they were three years earlier. Note both literal changes and changes in perception.

2. What significance do you attach to Fitzgerald's choice of Honoria as a name for Charlie's daughter? In what ways is her age and the fact that she is "an individual with a code of her own" (para. 118) important in this story? In what other ways does Fitzgerald raise questions about youth and maturity?

3. What does Fitzgerald let us know about Helen? Besides being Honoria's mother, in what ways does her character contribute to the story's themes? Why is she described as having "escaped to a grave in Vermont" (para. 59)?

4. How does Fitzgerald's use of a third-person limited point of view affect your reading of this story? How would the use of a first-person narrator have altered your reading — that is, if the story had been told from the point of view of Charlie or Marion or an older Honoria remembering the situation?

5. Analyze the character of Marion in section III. How does Fitzgerald describe her appearance, her actions, her relationship with her husband? Why is it "necessary for her to believe in tangible villainy and a tangible villain" (para. 183)?

6. What role do Lorraine and Duncan play in the story? Pay special attention to section II, where they first meet up with Charlie.

7. Explain the irony in the following exchange between Paul and Charlie:

   "I heard that you lost a lot in the crash."
   "I did," and he added grimly, "but I lost everything I wanted in the boom." (paras. 261–62)

   Find other examples of self-effacing irony that characters in this story use to cope with difficulties they are facing or have faced.

8. Were you surprised by the ending? Do you agree with Marion's decision? Cite specific passages to explain your response.

9. Fitzgerald divides the story into five sections, which could be considered chapters. What do you think is the structural principle of this division?

I Stand Here Ironing

TILLIE OLSEN

Tillie Olsen (1913–2007) was born in Nebraska, the daughter of Russian Jewish immigrants. Her parents were active socialists, who fled Russia after the attempted revolution of 1905. She recalled, "It was a rich childhood from the standpoint of ideas." She attended high school, but abandoned formal education after the eleventh grade. Later in life, as an influential writer, she received nine honorary degrees from colleges and universities. Political activism and responsibilities as a wife and mother made Olsen's writing sporadic. She published *Tell Me a Riddle* (1961), a series of four interconnected stories (the first of which is "I Stand Here Ironing"); *Yonnondio: From the Thirties* (1974); and *Silences* (1978), a nonfiction work about her life and the obstacles to writing that caused her own silences. Later work with The Feminist Press included contributions to *Mother to Daughter, Daughter to Mother, Mothers on Mothering: A Daybook and Reader,* and *Mothers and Daughters: That Special Quality: An Exploration in Photographs.* Perhaps her most famous story, "I Stand Here Ironing," focuses on the struggle of a working-class mother.

I stand here ironing, and what you asked me moves tormented back and forth with the iron.

"I wish you would manage the time to come in and talk with me about your daughter. I'm sure you can help me understand her. She's a youngster who needs help and whom I'm deeply interested in helping."

"Who needs help." . . . Even if I came, what good would it do? You think because I am her mother I have a key, or that in some way you could use me as a key? She has lived for nineteen years. There is all that life that has happened outside of me, beyond me.

And when is there time to remember, to sift, to weigh, to estimate, to total? I will start and there will be an interruption and I will have to gather it all together again. Or I will become engulfed with all I did or did not do, with what should have been and what cannot be helped.

She was a beautiful baby. The first and only one of our five that was beautiful at   5 birth. You do not guess how new and uneasy her tenancy in her now-loveliness. You did not know her all those years she was thought homely, or see her poring over her baby pictures, making me tell her over and over how beautiful she had been—and would be, I would tell her—and was now, to the seeing eye. But the seeing eyes were few or nonexistent. Including mine.

I nursed her. They feel that's important nowadays, I nursed all the children, but with her, with all the fierce rigidity of first motherhood, I did like the books then said. Though her cries battered me to trembling and my breasts ached with swollenness, I waited till the clock decreed.

Why do I put that first? I do not even know if it matters, or if it explains anything.

She was a beautiful baby. She blew shining bubbles of sound. She loved motion, loved light, loved color and music and textures. She would lie on the floor in her blue overalls patting the surface so hard in ecstasy her hands and feet would blur. She was a miracle to me, but when she was eight months old I had to leave her daytimes with the woman downstairs to whom she was no miracle at all, for I worked or looked for work and for Emily's father, who "could no longer endure" (he wrote in his good-bye note) "sharing want with us."

I was nineteen. It was the pre-relief, pre-WPA world of the depression. I would start running as soon as I got off the streetcar, running up the stairs, the place smelling sour, and awake or asleep to startle awake, when she saw me she would break into a clogged weeping that could not be comforted, a weeping I can hear yet.

After a while I found a job hashing at night so I could be with her days, and it was better. But it came to where I had to bring her to his family and leave her.

It took a long time to raise the money for her fare back. Then she got chicken pox and I had to wait longer. When she finally came, I hardly knew her, walking quick and nervous like her father, looking like her father, thin, and dressed in a shoddy red that yellowed her skin and glared at the pockmarks. All the baby loveliness gone.

She was two. Old enough for nursery school they said, and I did not know then what I know now — the fatigue of the long day, and the lacerations of group life in the kinds of nurseries that are only parking places for children.

Except that it would have made no difference if I had known. It was the only place there was. It was the only way we could be together, the only way I could hold a job.

And even without knowing, I knew. I knew the teacher that was evil because all these years it has curdled into my memory, the little boy hunched in the corner, her rasp, "why aren't you outside, because Alvin hits you? that's no reason, go out, scaredy." I knew Emily hated it even if she did not clutch and implore "don't go Mommy" like the other children, mornings.

She always had a reason why we should stay home. Momma, you look sick. Momma, I feel sick. Momma, the teachers aren't there today, they're sick. Momma, we can't go, there was a fire there last night. Momma, it's a holiday today, no school, they told me.

But never a direct protest, never rebellion. I think of our others in their three-, four-year-oldness — the explosions, the tempers, the denunciations, the demands — and I feel suddenly ill. I put the iron down. What in me demanded that goodness in her? And what was the cost, the cost to her of such goodness?

The old man living in the back once said in his gentle way: "You should smile at Emily more when you look at her." What *was* in my face when I looked at her? I loved her. There were all the acts of love.

It was only with the others I remembered what he said, and it was the face of joy, and not of care or tightness or worry I turned to them — too late for Emily. She does not smile easily, let alone almost always as her brothers and sisters do. Her face is closed and sombre, but when she wants, how fluid. You must have seen it in her pantomimes, you spoke of her rare gift for comedy on the stage that rouses laughter out of the audience so dear they applaud and applaud and do not want to let her go.

Where does it come from, that comedy? There was none of it in her when she came back to me that second time, after I had to send her away again. She had a new daddy now to learn to love, and I think perhaps it was a better time.

Except when we left her alone nights, telling ourselves she was old enough.

"Can't you go some other time, Mommy, like tomorrow?" she would ask. "Will it be just a little while you'll be gone? Do you promise?"

The time we came back, the front door open, the clock on the floor in the hall. She rigid awake. "It wasn't just a little while. I didn't cry. Three times I called you, just three times, and then I ran downstairs to open the door so you could come faster. The clock talked loud. I threw it away, it scared me what it talked."

She said the clock talked loud again that night I went to the hospital to have Susan. She was delirious with the fever that comes before red measles, but she was fully conscious all the week I was gone and the week after we were home when she could not come near the new baby or me.

She did not get well. She stayed skeleton thin, not wanting to eat, and night after night she had nightmares. She would call for me, and I would rouse from exhaustion to sleepily call back: "You're all right, darling, go to sleep, it's just a dream," and if she still called, in a sterner voice, "now go to sleep, Emily, there's nothing to hurt you." Twice, only twice, when I had to get up for Susan anyhow, I went in to sit with her.

Now when it is too late (as if she would let me hold her and comfort her like I   25
do the others) I get up and go to her at once at her moan or restless stirring. "Are you awake, Emily? Can I get you something?" And the answer is always the same: "No, I'm all right, go back to sleep, Mother."

They persuaded me at the clinic to send her away to a convalescent home in the country where "she can have the kind of food and care you can't manage for her, and you'll be free to concentrate on the new baby." They still send children to that place. I see pictures on the society page of sleek young women planning affairs to raise money for it, or dancing at the affairs, or decorating Easter eggs or filling Christmas stockings for the children.

They never have a picture of the children so I do not know if the girls still wear those gigantic red bows and the ravaged looks on the every other Sunday when parents can come to visit "unless otherwise notified" — as we were notified the first six weeks.

Oh it is a handsome place, green lawns and tall trees and fluted flower beds. High up on the balconies of each cottage the children stand, the girls in their red bows and white dresses, the boys in white suits and giant red ties. The parents stand below shrieking up to be heard and the children shriek down to be heard, and between them the invisible wall "Not To Be Contaminated by Parental Germs or Physical Affection."

There was a tiny girl who always stood hand in hand with Emily. Her parents never came. One visit she was gone. "They moved her to Rose Cottage," Emily shouted in explanation. "They don't like you to love anybody here."

She wrote once a week, the labored writing of a seven-year-old. "I am fine. How   30
is the baby. If I write my leter nicly I will have a star. Love." There never was a star. We wrote every other day, letters she could never hold or keep but only hear read — once. "We simply do not have room for children to keep any personal possessions," they patiently explained when we pieced one Sunday's shrieking together to plead how much it would mean to Emily, who loved so to keep things, to be allowed to keep her letters and cards.

Each visit she looked frailer. "She isn't eating," they told us.

(They had runny eggs for breakfast or mush with lumps, Emily said later, I'd hold it in my mouth and not swallow. Nothing ever tasted good, just when they had chicken.)

It took us eight months to get her released home, and only the fact that she gained back so little of her seven lost pounds convinced the social worker.

I used to try to hold and love her after she came back, but her body would stay stiff, and after a while she'd push away. She ate little. Food sickened her, and I think much of life too. Oh she had physical lightness and brightness, twinkling by on skates, bouncing like a ball up and down up and down over the jump rope, skimming over the hill; but these were momentary.

She fretted about her appearance, thin and dark and foreign-looking at a time when every little girl was supposed to look or thought she should look a chubby blonde replica of Shirley Temple. The doorbell sometimes rang for her, but no one seemed to come and play in the house or to be a best friend. Maybe because we moved so much.

There was a boy she loved painfully through two school semesters. Months later she told me how she had taken pennies from my purse to buy him candy. "Licorice was his favorite and I brought him some every day, but he still liked Jennifer better'n me. Why, Mommy?" The kind of question for which there is no answer.

School was a worry for her. She was not glib or quick in a world where glibness and quickness were easily confused with ability to learn. To her overworked and exasperated teachers she was an overconscientious "slow learner" who kept trying to catch up and was absent entirely too often.

I let her be absent, though sometimes the illness was imaginary. How different from my now-strictness about attendance with the others. I wasn't working. We had a new baby. I was home anyhow. Sometimes, after Susan grew old enough, I would keep her home from school, too, to have them all together.

Mostly Emily had asthma, and her breathing, harsh and labored, would fill the house with a curiously tranquil sound. I would bring the two old dresser mirrors and her boxes of collections to her bed. She would select beads and single earrings, bottle tops and shells, dried flowers and pebbles, old postcards and scraps, all sorts of oddments; then she and Susan would play Kingdom, setting up landscapes and furniture, peopling them with action.

Those were the only times of peaceful companionship between her and Susan. I have edged away from it, that poisonous feeling between them, that terrible balancing of hurts and needs I had to do between the two, and did so badly, those earlier years.

Oh there were conflicts between the others too, each one human, needing, demanding, hurting, taking—but only between Emily and Susan, no, Emily toward Susan that corroding resentment. It seems so obvious on the surface, yet it is not obvious; Susan, the second child, Susan, golden- and curly-haired and chubby, quick and articulate and assured, everything in appearance and manner Emily was not; Susan, not able to resist Emily's precious things, losing or sometimes clumsily breaking them; Susan telling jokes and riddles to company for applause while Emily sat silent (to say to me later: that was *my* riddle, Mother, I told it to Susan); Susan, who for all the five years' difference in age was just a year behind Emily in developing physically.

I am glad for that slow physical development that widened the difference between her and her contemporaries, though she suffered over it. She was too vulnerable for that terrible world of youthful competition, of preening and parading, of constant measuring of yourself against every other, of envy, "If I had that copper hair," "If I had that skin. . . ." She tormented herself enough about not looking like the others, there was enough of unsureness, the having to be conscious of words before you speak, the constant caring—what are they thinking of me? without having it all magnified by the merciless physical drives.

Ronnie is calling. He is wet and I change him. It is rare there is such a cry now. That time of motherhood is almost behind me when the ear is not one's own but must always be racked and listening for the child cry, the child call. We sit for a while and I hold him, looking out over the city spread in charcoal with its soft aisles of light. "*Shoogily,*" he breathes and curls closer. I carry him back to bed, asleep. *Shoogily.* A funny word, a family word, inherited from Emily, invented by her to say: *comfort.*

In this and other ways she leaves her seal, I say aloud. And startle at my saying it. What do I mean? What did I start to gather together, to try and make coherent? I was at the terrible, growing years. War years. I do not remember them well. I was working, there were four smaller ones now, there was not time for her. She had to help be a mother, and housekeeper, and shopper. She had to get her seal. Mornings of crisis and near hysteria trying to get lunches packed, hair combed, coats and shoes found, everyone to school or Child Care on time, the baby ready for transportation. And always the paper scribbled on by a smaller one, the book looked at by Susan then mislaid, the homework not done. Running out to that huge school where she was one, she was lost, she was a drop; suffering over the unpreparedness, stammering and unsure in her classes.

There was so little time left at night after the kids were bedded down. She would struggle over books, always eating (it was in those years she developed her enormous appetite that is legendary in our family) and I would be ironing, or preparing food for the next day, or writing V-mail to Bill, or tending the baby. Sometimes, to make me laugh, or out of her despair, she would imitate happenings or types at school.   45

I think I said once: "Why don't you do something like this in the school amateur show?" One morning she phoned me at work, hardly understandable through the weeping: "Mother, I did it. I won, I won; they gave me first prize; they clapped and clapped and wouldn't let me go."

Now suddenly she was Somebody, and as imprisoned in her difference as she had been in anonymity.

She began to be asked to perform at other high schools, even in colleges, then at city and statewide affairs. The first one we went to, I only recognized her that first moment when thin, shy, she almost drowned herself into the curtains. Then: Was this Emily? The control, the command, the convulsing and deadly clowning, the spell, then the roaring, stamping audience, unwilling to let this rare and precious laughter out of their lives.

Afterwards: You ought to do something about her with a gift like that—but without money or knowing how, what does one do? We have left it all to her, and the gift has so often eddied inside, clogged and clotted, as been used and growing.

She is coming. She runs up the stairs two at a time with her light graceful step, and I know she is happy tonight. Whatever it was that occasioned your call did not happen today.

"Aren't you ever going to finish the ironing, Mother? Whistler painted his mother in a rocker. I'd have to paint mine standing over an ironing board." This is one of her communicative nights and she tells me everything and nothing as she fixes herself a plate of food out of the icebox.

She is so lovely. Why did you want me to come in at all? Why were you concerned? She will find her way.

She starts up the stairs to bed. "Don't get me up with the rest in the morning." "But I thought you were having midterms." "Oh, those," she comes back in, kisses me, and says quite lightly, "in a couple of years when we'll all be atom-dead they won't matter a bit."

She has said it before. She *believes* it. But because I have been dredging the past, and all that compounds a human being is so heavy and meaningful in me, I cannot endure it tonight.

I will never total it all. I will never come in to say: She was a child seldom smiled at. Her father left me before she was a year old. I had to work her first six years when there was work, or I sent her home and to his relatives. There were years she had care she hated. She was dark and thin and foreign-looking in a world where the prestige went to blondeness and curly hair and dimples, she was slow where glibness was prized. She was a child of anxious, not proud, love. We were poor and could not afford for her the soil of easy growth. I was a young mother, I was a distracted mother. There were other children pushing up, demanding. Her younger sister seemed all that she was not. There were years she did not want me to touch her. She kept too much in herself, her life was such she had to keep too much in herself. My wisdom came too late. She has much to her and probably little will come of it. She is a child of her age, of depression, of war, of fear.

Let her be. So all that is in her will not bloom — but in how many does it? There is still enough left to live by. Only help her to know — help make it so there is cause for her to know — that she is more than this dress on the ironing board, helpless before the iron.

[1961]

Exploring the Text

1. How is the setting of the story's frame, a woman standing at an ironing board, critical to the story's themes?

2. What structural purpose do the interruptions in the narrator's interior monologue serve in the story? For instance, "Ronnie is calling. He is wet and I change him" in paragraph 43. Notice, too, how the speaker's use of run-on sentences and made-up words — such as "four-year-oldness" (para. 16) — contrasts with short

declarative sentences such as "She was a beautiful baby" (paras. 5 and 8), "I was nineteen" (para. 9), and "She was two" (para. 12). What is the effect of this juxtaposition?

3. The "you" the narrator addresses at the beginning of the story refers to a teacher concerned about Emily's welfare. At first the narrator seems somewhat defensive (as in the third paragraph, when she sarcastically responds to the teacher's request). How does the relationship between the narrator and the teacher evolve over the course of the story, so that by the end the narrator beseeches, "Only help her to know—help make it so there is cause for her to know" (para. 56)? To what extent might the narrator be addressing the reader as well as the teacher?

4. What do you make of the repeated references to quantitative matters in this story—for instance, "to sift, to weigh, to estimate, to total" in paragraph 4? Find other examples of this motif in the story, and explain its significance.

5. In the final lines of the story, the narrator calls her daughter "a child of her age, of depression, of war, of fear" (para. 55). How have historical events affected Emily's development? How have they imposed limitations on her? How have they made her strong?

6. Why does Olsen give us so much specific detail about Emily's appearance? How do these descriptions contribute to her characterization? How is her appearance related to the choices she makes to distinguish herself, to stand out? What does the narrator mean when she says of Emily, "Now suddenly she was Somebody, and as imprisoned in her difference as she had been in anonymity" (para. 47)?

7. What, finally, is the narrator's assessment of her own performance as a mother? Do you think she believes she has been a good mother to her children? Overall, is the story hopeful or hopeless?

8. Rarely do we hear Emily speak in this story. Instead, we hear others' comments about and reactions to her, including her mother's. How do you think Emily would characterize her relationship with her mother? Do you think she would blame her mother or circumstances beyond their control for the difficulties she has experienced?

The Moths

Helena María Viramontes

Helena María Viramontes (b. 1949) grew up as one of nine children in East Los Angeles. She has a BA from Immaculate Heart College, an MFA from the University of California, Irvine, and is currently a professor of English at Cornell University. Her mother's plight—raising nine children with a husband who "showed all that is bad in being male"—moved Helena to write of Chicana women's struggles. While writing for several underground literary publications, Viramontes published her first collection of short stories, *The Moths and Other Stories*, in 1985. In 1995, her first novel, *Under the Feet of Jesus*, was published, followed by *Their Dogs*

Came with Them in 2007. The latter is her most ambitious work, drawing on her teenage years, the explosive decade of the 1960s, and the lives of young women coming of age at the height of *El Movimiento*. The story included here is the title piece from her 1985 collection about the relationship between a young woman and her *abuelita*, or grandmother.

I was fourteen years old when Abuelita requested my help. And it seemed only fair. Abuelita had pulled me through the rages of scarlet fever by placing, removing and replacing potato slices on the temples of my forehead; she had seen me through several whippings, an arm broken by a dare jump off Tío Enrique's toolshed, puberty, and my first lie. Really, I told Amá, it was only fair.

Not that I was her favorite granddaughter or anything special. I wasn't even pretty or nice like my older sisters and I just couldn't do the girl things they could do. My hands were too big to handle the fineries of crocheting or embroidery and I always pricked my fingers or knotted my colored threads time and time again while my sisters laughed and called me bull hands with their cute waterlike voices. So I began keeping a piece of jagged brick in my sock to bash my sisters or anyone who called me bull hands. Once, while we all sat in the bedroom, I hit Teresa on the forehead, right above her eyebrow and she ran to Amá with her mouth open, her hand over her eye while blood seeped between her fingers. I was used to the whippings by then.

I wasn't respectful either. I even went so far as to doubt the power of Abuelita's slices, the slices she said absorbed my fever. "You're still alive, aren't you?" Abuelita snapped back, her pasty gray eye beaming at me and burning holes in my suspicions. Regretful that I had let secret questions drop out of my mouth, I couldn't look into her eyes. My hands began to fan out, grow like a liar's nose until they hung by my side like low weights. Abuelita made a balm out of dried moth wings and Vicks and rubbed my hands, shaped them back to size and it was the strangest feeling. Like bones melting. Like sun shining through the darkness of your eyelids. I didn't mind helping Abuelita after that, so Amá would always send me over to her.

In the early afternoon Amá would push her hair back, hand me my sweater and shoes, and tell me to go to Mama Luna's. This was to avoid another fight and another whipping, I knew. I would deliver one last direct shot on Marisela's arm and jump out of our house, the slam of the screen door burying her cries of anger, and I'd gladly go help Abuelita plant her wild lilies or jasmine or heliotrope or cilantro or hierba-buena[1] in red Hills Brothers coffee cans. Abuelita would wait for me at the top step of her porch holding a hammer and nail and empty coffee cans. And although we hardly spoke, hardly looked at each other as we worked over root transplants, I always felt her gray eye on me. It made me feel, in a strange sort of way, safe and guarded and not alone. Like God was supposed to make you feel.

---

[1] Also yerba buena, or "good herb," a plant in the mint family that is steeped to make a tea-like beverage.—Eds.

On Abuelita's porch, I would puncture holes in the bottom of the coffee cans   5
with a nail and a precise hit of a hammer. This completed, my job was to fill them
with red clay mud from beneath her rose bushes, packing it softly, then making a
perfect hole, four fingers round, to nest a sprouting avocado pit, or the spidery sweet
potatoes that Abuelita rooted in mayonnaise jars with toothpicks and daily water,
or prickly chayotes[2] that produced vines that twisted and wound all over her porch
pillars, crawling to the roof, up and over the roof, and down the other side, making
her small brick house look like it was cradled within the vines that grew pear-shaped
squashes ready for the pick, ready to be steamed with onions and cheese and butter.
The roots would burst out of the rusted coffee cans and search for a place to connect.
I would then feed the seedlings with water.

But this was a different kind of help, Amá said, because Abuelita was dying.
Looking into her gray eye, then into her brown one, the doctor said it was just a matter of days. And so it seemed only fair that these hands she had melted and formed
found use in rubbing her caving body with alcohol and marihuana, rubbing her arms
and legs, turning her face to the window so that she could watch the Bird of Paradise
blooming or smell the scent of clove in the air. I toweled her face frequently and held
her hand for hours. Her gray wiry hair hung over the mattress. Since I could remember, she'd kept her long hair in braids. Her mouth was vacant and when she slept,
her eyelids never closed all the way. Up close, you could see her gray eye beaming out
the window, staring hard as if to remember everything. I never kissed her. I left the
window open when I went to the market.

Across the street from Jay's Market there was a chapel. I never knew its denomi-
nation, but I went in just the same to search for candles. I sat down on one of the
pews because there were none. After I cleaned my fingernails, I looked up at the
high ceiling. I had forgotten the vastness of these places, the coolness of the marble
pillars and the frozen statues with blank eyes. I was alone. I knew why I had never
returned.

That was one of Apá's biggest complaints. He would pound his hands on the
table, rocking the sugar dish or spilling a cup of coffee and scream that if I didn't go
to mass every Sunday to save my goddamn sinning soul, then I had no reason to go
out of the house, period. Punto final.[3] He would grab my arm and dig his nails into
me to make sure I understood the importance of catechism. Did he make himself
clear? Then he strategically directed his anger at Amá for her lousy ways of bringing
up daughters, being disrespectful and unbelieving, and my older sisters would pull
me aside and tell me if I didn't get to mass right this minute, they were all going to
kick the holy shit out of me. Why am I so selfish? Can't you see what it's doing to
Amá, you idiot? So I would wash my feet and stuff them in my black Easter shoes that
shone with Vaseline, grab a missal and veil, and wave good-bye to Amá.

I would walk slowly down Lorena to First to Evergreen, counting the cracks on
the cement. On Evergreen I would turn left and walk to Abuelita's. I liked her porch

---

[2]Pear-shaped vegetable similar to a cucumber. — EDS.
[3]Final point, period. — EDS.

because it was shielded by the vines of the chayotes and I could get a good look at the people and car traffic on Evergreen without them knowing. I would jump up the porch steps, knock on the screen door as I wiped my feet and call Abuelita? mi Abuelita? As I opened the door and stuck my head in, I would catch the gagging scent of toasting chile on the placa.[4] When I entered the sala,[5] she would greet me from the kitchen, wringing her hands in her apron. I'd sit at the corner of the table to keep from being in her way. The chiles made my eyes water. Am I crying? No, Mama Luna, I'm sure not crying. I don't like going to mass, but my eyes watered anyway, the tears dropping on the tablecloth like candle wax. Abuelita lifted the burnt chiles from the fire and sprinkled water on them until the skins began to separate. Placing them in front of me, she turned to check the menudo.[6] I peeled the skins off and put the flimsy, limp looking green and yellow chiles in the molcajete[7] and began to crush and crush and twist and crush the heart out of the tomato, the clove of garlic, the stupid chiles that made me cry, crushed them until they turned into liquid under my bull hand. With a wooden spoon, I scraped hard to destroy the guilt, and my tears were gone. I put the bowl of chile next to a vase filled with freshly cut roses. Abuelita touched my hand and pointed to the bowl of menudo that steamed in front of me. I spooned some chile into the menudo and rolled a corn tortilla thin with the palms of my hands. As I ate, a fine Sunday breeze entered the kitchen and a rose petal calmly feathered down to the table.

I left the chapel without blessing myself and walked to Jay's. Most of the time   10
Jay didn't have much of anything. The tomatoes were always soft and the cans of Campbell soups had rusted spots on them. There was dust on the tops of cereal boxes. I picked up what I needed: rubbing alcohol, five cans of chicken broth, a big bottle of Pine Sol. At first Jay got mad because I thought I had forgotten the money. But it was there all the time, in my back pocket.

When I returned from the market, I heard Amá crying in Abuelita's kitchen. She looked up at me with puffy eyes. I placed the bags of groceries on the table and began putting the cans of soup away. Amá sobbed quietly. I never kissed her. After a while, I patted her on the back for comfort. Finally: "¿Y mi Amá?"[8] she asked in a whisper, then choked again and cried into her apron.

Abuelita fell off the bed twice yesterday, I said, knowing that I shouldn't have said it and wondering why I wanted to say it because it only made Amá cry harder. I guess I became angry and just so tired of the quarrels and beatings and unanswered prayers and my hands just there hanging helplessly by my side. Amá looked at me again, confused, angry, and her eyes were filled with sorrow. I went outside and sat on the porch swing and watched the people pass. I sat there until she left. I dozed off repeating the words to myself like rosary prayers: when do you stop giving

---

[4]Plate.— EDS.
[5]Living room.— EDS.
[6]Traditional Mexican soup made with tripe.— EDS.
[7]Stone bowl used for grinding foods or spices, similar to a mortar and pestle.— EDS.
[8]"And my Mama?"

when do you start giving when do you . . . and when my hands fell from my lap, I awoke to catch them. The sun was setting, an orange glow, and I knew Abuelita was hungry.

There comes a time when the sun is defiant. Just about the time when moods change, inevitable seasons of a day, transitions from one color to another, that hour or minute or second when the sun is finally defeated, finally sinks into the realization that it cannot with all its power to heal or burn, exist forever, there comes an illumination where the sun and earth meet, a final burst of burning red orange fury reminding us that although endings are inevitable, they are necessary for rebirths, and when that time came, just when I switched on the light in the kitchen to open Abuelita's can of soup, it was probably then that she died.

The room smelled of Pine Sol and vomit and Abuelita had defecated the remains of her cancerous stomach. She had turned to the window and tried to speak, but her mouth remained open and speechless. I heard you, Abuelita, I said, stroking her cheek, I heard you. I opened the windows of the house and let the soup simmer and overboil on the stove. I turned the stove off and poured the soup down the sink. From the cabinet I got a tin basin, filled it with lukewarm water and carried it carefully to the room. I went to the linen closet and took out some modest bleached white towels. With the sacredness of a priest preparing his vestments, I unfolded the towels one by one on my shoulders. I removed the sheets and blankets from her bed and peeled off her thick flannel nightgown. I toweled her puzzled face, stretching out the wrinkles, removing the coils of her neck, toweled her shoulders and breasts. Then I changed the water. I returned to towel the creases of her stretch-marked stomach, her sporadic vaginal hairs, and her sagging thighs. I removed the lint from between her toes and noticed a mapped birthmark on the fold of her buttock. The scars on her back which were as thin as the life lines on the palms of her hands made me realize how little I really knew of Abuelita. I covered her with a thin blanket and went into the bathroom. I washed my hands, and turned on the tub faucets and watched the water pour into the tub with vitality and steam. When it was full, I turned off the water and undressed. Then, I went to get Abuelita.

She was not as heavy as I thought and when I carried her in my arms, her body fell into a V, and yet my legs were tired, shaky, and I felt as if the distance between the bedroom and bathroom was miles and years away. Amá, where are you? 15

I stepped into the bathtub one leg first, then the other. I bent my knees slowly to descend into the water slowly so I wouldn't scald her skin. There, there, Abuelita, I said, cradling her, smoothing her as we descended, I heard you. Her hair fell back and spread across the water like eagle's wings. The water in the tub overflowed and poured onto the tile of the floor. Then the moths came. Small, gray ones that came from her soul and out through her mouth fluttering to light, circling the single dull light bulb of the bathroom. Dying is lonely and I wanted to go to where the moths were, stay with her and plant chayotes whose vines would crawl up her fingers and into the clouds; I wanted to rest my head on her chest with her stroking my hair, telling me about the moths that lay within the soul and slowly eat the spirit up; I wanted to return to the waters of the womb with her so that we would never be alone again. I wanted. I wanted my Amá. I removed a few strands of hair from Abuelita's face and held her small light head within the hollow of my neck. The bathroom was filled with moths, and for the first time in a long time I cried, rocking us, crying for her, for me, for Amá, the sobs emerging from the depths of anguish, the misery of feeling half born, sobbing until finally the sobs rippled into circles and circles of sadness and relief. There, there, I said to Abuelita, rocking us gently, there, there.

[1985]

Exploring the Text

1. The story opens with the narrator's grandmother applying potato slices to the narrator's fevered brow. Compare this opening with the conclusion of the story. What is the significance of the contrast between the gentleness at the beginning and end of the story, and the rough treatment the narrator typically gives to family members ("I hit Teresa on the forehead," para. 2) and receives from them ("He would grab my arm and dig his nails into me," para. 8)?

2. How does the work Abuelita asks the narrator to do — planting, cooking — help the teenager deal with her pent-up anger?

3. As the narrator cares for her dying grandmother, she begins to ask herself, "when do you stop giving when do you start giving" (para. 12), continuing the repetition of the word "when" throughout the following paragraph. What is the significance of this repetition for the fourteen-year-old narrator? What might she be questioning in her own life?

4. Trace the references to hands in this story. How do you interpret the poultice balm of moth wings that Abuelita uses to shape the narrator's hands back into shape? What is the significance of this act?

5. What is the role of religion and spirituality in this story? Why does the narrator think to herself when she is in the chapel, "I was alone. I knew why I had never returned" (para. 7)? What conflicts does religion cause in her family?

6. Note the references throughout to Amá, the narrator's mother. When Amá is crying in Abuelita's kitchen, why does the narrator choose not to kiss her? Why at the end does the narrator say, "I wanted. I wanted my Amá" (para. 16)? What is the nature of the relationship among these three generations of women? What does the narrator want it to be?

7. What do the moths represent in the story?

8. Describe the ways in which the narrator is an outcast in her own family. What does her grandmother seem to understand that the girl's immediate family members do not?

9. Does the narrator's fearlessness about death strike you as unusual? Why do you think she is comfortable enough to bathe her dead Abuelita? Consider the sensuous descriptions throughout the story.

HELENA MARÍA VIRAMONTES ON WRITING

Renée Shea (RS): Is "The Moths" based on your relationship with your own grandmother?

Helena María Viramontes (HMV): I was fourth to the youngest and fifth to the oldest in a family of nine. My oldest brother is seventeen years older than my youngest sister. My maternal grandfather died the year I was born, and my maternal grandmother died when I was four. I do remember her giving me an orange, and I remember so many things about that day—her clean kitchen, the sunlight through sheer curtains, the scent of citrus on my hands—and it was this image of the orange that I wrote about in my novel *Under the Feet of Jesus*. I desired to write about the love that my mother captured in stories she would tell us about my grandparents. It was that love that motivated me to write "The Moths."

RS: "The Moths" seems to be a story in the tradition of magical realism. Why are you drawn to that style?

HMV: I don't know if "The Moths" is a magical realist story. Death has a way of making imbrications on experience, and there is nothing more mystic and more real, more rapturous, beautiful, and terrifying, than being given permission to enter such divine presence when someone you love is about to die. I would venture to say that "The Moths," in fact, is a very real experience.

RS: Is writing about home and family really a choice for you, or is it a subject you find you must write about?

HMV: I tell my students that I begin a story or novel from a place of knowing and write it into a place of the unknown, and what is more known than your experiences with your family and home? In a way, it's basic, but in my way, it was also a commitment rendered out of love for my family and geography. Over twenty-five years ago, I came to realize as a young writer that Chicano/Mexican families—especially the women in them—were hard to find as characters between the pages of a book. I simply couldn't wait for another writer to make my family, my community, visible, and once I began to excavate my own personal history, it was for me news of a different source—at once ordinary, at once extraordinary, but always human.

RS: Most of your fiction centers on Latino families, immigrant communities. Do you feel that you are emphasizing their singularity and distinctiveness, or do you think families, regardless of culture or socioeconomics

5

or geography, are pretty much the same—beset with the same conflicts, celebrating the same joys?

HMV: Every family story is singular and distinctive and utterly recognizable. This is the power of literature.

RS: How do your family members feel when they see themselves in your work, whether by reading or hearing about it? Do you think of them as your audience, or do you try not to? Do you worry about their responses?

HMV: I had the wonderful opportunity of being able to ask my sister how she felt when I spoke or wrote about things she recognized. It was utterly amazing for me when she replied, "We [the rest of the family] talk about it all the time. But we trust you." Trusting me to translate events and characters from my family into fiction is a huge responsibility, and I think I've earned their trust by my dedication to telling the truth. I don't hold romanticized notions of my life or theirs. What I do hold is awe and respect of their everyday accomplishments in strenuous and challenging times. They are my heroes and "sheroes."

10

RS: Some believe that we write about our families to rewrite the actual relationships. Is that true of you?

HMV: I don't think I attempt to rewrite the actual relationships. I want to understand the relationships, and out of that understanding comes empathy. Sometimes the by-product of the writing exercise is that you develop compassion through this understanding, and this might make your actual relationships better.

RS: You're from a working-class family, with most of its members not formally educated. How did you decide to become or imagine yourself a writer? Were your parents your advocates in that decision?

HMV: I came from a bookless home. With the exception of a set of World Book Encyclopedias and the Bible, I didn't have much else to read. Nonetheless, those two sources influenced my respect for the printed word. My parents were both born in the United States. My mother finished tenth grade in the same high school I attended, and my father only got as far as the third grade, so they didn't have much of a clue about higher education. But I had an older brother, my dear brother Serafin, who was a dreamer. He once showed me a sketch of his dream house, and I was amazed. As soon as he was in college, he brought all of us to a family weekend campus visit. We younger ones saw the library, the dorm, the cafeteria—truly this was "news from another world," to use Raymond Carver's phrase. As soon as I became a high school senior, I asked him about college, and he immediately helped me in whatever way he could. Of course there were so many influences that converged to plant the seed of education, but my brother taught me to think of myself as beyond what I thought I was capable of at that time, and this beyond-ness had incredible sustaining power. He loved us so much. When he died in 2007, we surrounded him with the same compassion he had always practiced with us.

RS: This chapter opens with the quote from Tolstoy: "Happy families are all alike; every unhappy family is unhappy in its own way." Would you comment on why you agree or disagree with him?   15

HMV: How can I possibly disagree with Tolstoy! To use Charles Baxter's term, fiction is "hell friendly." Happy families are good for our lives, but do not make for great literature. Because "every unhappy family is unhappy in its own way," the space for new stories is infinite and waiting for yours.

Follow-Up

1. What do you think Viramontes means when she says, "I begin a story or novel from a place of knowing and write it into a place of the unknown"?
2. Reread "The Moths" with Viramontes's responses in mind. How does the information in the interview change, add to, or challenge your interpretation of the story? For example, does the fact that Viramontes did not know her grandmother well alter the power of the relationship in the story?
3. Think about your own family and experiences that are both distinctive to them and familiar to families in general. Try writing a vignette—a brief sketch of a scene or character—that demonstrates Viramontes's assertion that "Every family story is singular and distinctive and utterly recognizable."
4. Viramontes describes the influence of her brother Serafin in terms both tender and compelling: "my brother taught me to think of myself as beyond what I thought I was capable of at that time, and this beyondness had incredible sustaining power." Describe a family member in your own life who somehow gave you a sense of "beyondness."
5. Do you agree with her statement that "Happy families are good for our lives, but do not make for great literature"? Can you think of a work of literature that celebrates a happy family?

Saving Sourdi

May-lee Chai

May-lee Chai (b. 1967) was born in California, the daughter of an Irish American mother and a father from a traditional Chinese family. She has master's degrees in both East Asian studies and creative writing. She began her writing career as a journalist, but later turned to college teaching and creative writing full time. Her first book, *My Lucky Face* (1997), is a novel set during the Cultural Revolution; her second book, *The Girl from Purple Mountain* (2001), written in collaboration with her father, is a family memoir that traces China's involvement in the Second World War. Her most recent book is *Hapa Girl* (2007), a memoir described on Chai's Web site as "a coming-of-age story or a narrative about racial tensions in 1960s America . . . truly an homage to a loving marriage." Her short story "Saving Sourdi" first appeared in the literary magazine *ZYZZYVA* in 2001.

Once, when my older sister, Sourdi, and I were working alone in our family's restaurant, just the two of us and the elderly cook, some men got drunk and I stabbed one of them. I was eleven.

I don't remember where Ma had gone that night. But I remember we were tired and it was late. We were one of the only restaurants that stayed open past nine in those days. The men had been growing louder, until they were our only customers, and, finally, one of them staggered up and put his arm across Sourdi's shoulders. He called her his "China doll," and his friends hooted at this.

Sourdi looked distressed and tried to remove his arm, but he held her tighter. She said, "Please," in her incense-sweet voice, and he smiled and said, "Say it again nice and I might just have to give you a kiss."

That summer we'd just moved to South Dakota. After all the crummy jobs Ma had had to take in Texas, where we'd first come to the U.S., where our sponsors lived, we were so proud to be working in our own restaurant. When we moved to South Dakota, I thought we'd find the real America, the one where we were supposed to be, not the hot sweaty America where we lived packed together in an apartment with bars on the windows on a street where angry boys in cars played loud music and shot guns at each other in the night. The summer we moved to join my uncle's family to run the Silver Palace, I was certain we would at last find the life we deserved.

Now I was panicked. I wanted Ma to be there. Ma would know what to do. She always did. I stood there, chewing my nails, wishing I could make them go away. The men's voices were so loud in my ears, I was drowning in the sound. 5

I ran into the kitchen. I had this idea to get the cook and the cleaver, but the first thing that caught my eye was this little paring knife on the counter next to a bowl of oranges. I grabbed the knife and ran back out to Sourdi.

"Get away from my sister!" I shouted, waving the paring knife.

The men were silent for about three seconds, then they burst into laughter.

I charged and stabbed the man in the sleeve.

In a movie or a television show this kind of scene always unfolds in slow motion, but everything happened so fast. I stabbed the man, Sourdi jumped free, Ma came rushing in the front door waving her arms. "Omigod! What happen?"

"Jesus Christ!" The man shook his arm as though it were on fire, but the paring knife was stuck in the fabric of his jeans jacket.

I thought Ma would take care of everything now. And I was right, she did, but not the way I had imagined. She started apologizing to the man, and she helped him take off his jacket. She made Sourdi get the first-aid kit from the bathroom, "Quick! Quick!" Ma even tried to put some ointment on his cut, but he just shrugged her off.

I couldn't believe it. I wanted to take the knife back and stab myself. That's how I felt when I heard her say, "No charge, on the house," for their dinner, despite the $50-worth of pitchers they'd had.

Ma grabbed me by the shoulders. "Say you sorry. Say it." I pressed my lips firmly together and hung my head. Then she slapped me.

I didn't start crying until after the men had left. "But, Ma," I said, "he was hurting Sourdi!"

"Then why Sourdi not do something?" Ma twisted my ear. "You not thinking. That your problem. You always not think!"

Afterwards, Sourdi said I was lucky. The knife had only grazed the man's skin. They could have sued us. They could have pressed charges.

"I don't care!" I hissed then. "I shoulda killed him! I shoulda killed that sucker!"

Sourdi's face changed. I'd never seen my sister look like that. Not ever. Especially not at me. I was her favorite. But she looked then the way I felt inside. Like a big bomb was ticking behind her eyes.

We were sitting together in the bathroom. It was late at night, and everyone else was asleep. Sometimes we locked ourselves in the bathroom then, just the two of us, so we could talk about things like boys at school or who was the cutest actor on television shows we liked or how we felt when our family fought, when Uncle and Auntie yelled at each other, or when Ma grew depressed and smoked too much and looked at us as though she wished we'd never been born.

This night, however, Sourdi looked at me grimly. "Oh, no, Nea. Don't ever say that. Don't ever talk like that."

I was going to smile and shrug and say something like "I was just kidding," but something inside me couldn't lie tonight. I crossed my arms over my flat chest, and I stuck out my lower lip, like I'd seen the tough girls at school do. "Anyone mess like that with me, I'm gonna kill him!"

Sourdi took me by the shoulders then and shook me so hard I thought she was going to shake my head right off my body. She wouldn't stop even after I started to cry.

"Stop, stop!" I begged. "I'll be good! I promise, I'll be good!"

Finally, she pushed me away from her and sat on the toilet, with her head in her hands. Although she'd been the one hurting me, she looked as though she'd been beaten up, the way she sat like that, her shoulders hunched over her lap, as though she were trying to make herself disappear.

"I was trying to protect you," I said through my tears. "I was trying to save you. You're so stupid! I should just let that man diss you!"

Sourdi's head shot up and I could see that she had no patience left. Her eyes were red and her nostrils flared. She stood up and I took a step back quickly. I thought she was going to grab me and shake me again, but this time she just put her hand on my arm. "They could take you away. The police, they could put you in a foster home. All of us."

A chill ran through my whole body, like a live current. We all knew about foster homes. Rudy Gutierrez in third grade was taken away from his parents after the teacher noticed some bruises on his back. He'd tried to shoplift some PayDays from the 7-Eleven and got caught. When his dad got home that weekend, he let him have it. But after the school nurse took a look at him, Rudy was taken away from his parents and sent to live in a foster home. His parents couldn't speak English so good and didn't know what was happening until too late. Anyway, what kind of lawyer could they afford? We heard later from his cousin in Mrs. Chang's homeroom that Rudy's foster-dad had molested him. The cousin said Rudy ran away from that home, but he got caught. At any rate, none of us ever saw him again.

"You want to go to a foster home?" Sourdi asked me.

"No," I whispered.

"Then don't be so stupid!"

I started crying again, because I realized Sourdi was right. She kissed me on the top of my head and hugged me to her. I leaned my head against her soft breasts that had only recently emerged from her chest and pretended that I was a good girl and that I would always obey her. What I didn't tell Sourdi was that I was still a wicked girl. I was glad I'd stabbed that man. I was crying only because life was so unfair.

We used to say that we'd run away, Sourdi and me. When we were older. After she graduated. She'd be my legal guardian. We'd go to California to see the stars. Paris. London. Cambodia even, to light incense for the bones of our father. We'd earn money working in Chinese restaurants in every country we visited. We had enough experience; it had to be worth something.

We'd lie awake all night whispering back and forth. I'd climb into Sourdi's bed, claiming that I couldn't sleep, curling into a ball beside my older sister, the smell of her like salt and garlic and a sweet scent that emanated directly from her skin. Sometimes I'd stroke Sourdi's slick hair, which she plaited into a thick wet braid so that it would be wavy in the morning. I would stay awake all night, pinching the inside of Sourdi's arm, the soft flesh of her thigh, to keep my sister from falling asleep and leaving me alone.

When she first started seeing Duke, I used to think of him as something like a bookmark, just holding a certain space in her life until it was time for her to move on. I never thought of him as a fork in the road, dividing my life with Sourdi from Sourdi's life with men.

30

35

In those days, I didn't understand anything.

Ma had hired Duke to wash dishes at the Palace that first summer. At first, we paid him no mind. He was just this funny-looking white kid, hair that stuck up straight from his head when he wasn't wearing his silly baseball cap backwards, skinny as a stalk of bamboo, long legs and long arms that seemed to move in opposition to each other. Chopstick-boy I called him, just to be mean. He took it as a compliment.

I could see why he fell in love with Sourdi. My sister was beautiful. Really beautiful, not like the girls in magazines with their pale, pinched faces, pink and powdery, brittle girls. Sourdi looked like a statue that had been rescued from the sea. She was smooth where I had angles and soft where I was bone. Sourdi's face was round, her nose low and wide, her eyes crescent-shaped like the quarter moon, her hair sleek as seaweed. Her skin was a burnished cinnamon color. Looking at Sourdi, I could pretend I was beautiful, too. She had so much to spare.

At first, Duke and Sourdi only talked behind the Palace, pretending to take a break from the heat of the kitchen. I caught them looking at the stars together.

The first time they kissed, I was there, too. Duke was giving us a ride after school 40
in his pickup. He had the music on loud and the windows were open. It was a hot day for October, and the wind felt like a warm ocean that we could swim in forever. He was going to drop us off at the Palace, but then Duke said he had something to show us, and we circled around the outskirts of town, taking the gravel road that led to the open fields, beyond the highway where the cattle ranches lay. Finally, he pulled off the gravel road and parked.

"You want us to look at cows?" I asked impatiently, crossing my arms.

He laughed at me then and took Sourdi by the hand. We hiked through a ditch to the edge of an empty cornfield long since harvested, the stubble of cornstalks poking up from the black soil, pale and bonelike. The field was laced with a barbed-wire fence to keep the cattle in, though I couldn't see any cows at all. The whole place gave me the creeps.

Duke held the strands of barbed wire apart for Sourdi and me and told us to crawl under the fence.

"Just trust me," he said.

We followed him to a spot in the middle of the field. "It's the center of the world," 45
Duke said. "Look." And he pointed back to where we'd come from, and suddenly I realized the rest of the world had disappeared. The ground had appeared level, but we must have walked into a tiny hollow in the plains, because from where we stood there was only sky and field for as far as our eyes could see. We could no longer see the road or Duke's pickup, our town, or even the green smudge of cottonwoods that grew along the Yankton River or the distant hills of Nebraska. There was nothing overhead, either; the sky was unbroken by clouds, smooth as an empty rice bowl. "It's just us here," Duke said. "We're alone in the whole universe."

All at once, Sourdi began to breathe funny. Her face grew pinched, and she wiped at her eyes with the back of her hand.

"What's wrong?" Duke asked stupidly.

Then Sourdi was running wildly. She took off like an animal startled by a gun-shot. She was trying to head back to the road, but she tripped over the cornstalks and fell onto her knees. She started crying for real.

I caught up to her first—I've always been a fast runner. As Duke approached, I put my arms around Sourdi.

"I thought you'd like it," Duke said.

"We're city girls," I said, glaring at him. "Why would we like this hick stuff?"

"I'm sorry," Sourdi whispered. "I'm so sorry."

"What are you sorry for? It's his fault!" I pointed out.

Now Duke was kneeling next to Sourdi. He tried to put his arm over her shoulder, too. I was going to push him away, when Sourdi did something very surprising. She put both her arms around his neck and leaned against him, while Duke said soft, dumb-sounding things that I couldn't quite hear. Then they were kissing.

I was so surprised, I stared at them before I forced myself to look away. Then I was the one who felt like running, screaming, for the road.

On the way back to the Palace, Duke and Sourdi didn't talk, but they held hands. The worst part was I was sitting between them.

Ma didn't seem to notice anything for a while, but then with Ma it was always hard to know what she was thinking, what she knew and what she didn't. Sometimes she seemed to go through her days like she was made of stone. Sometimes she erupted like a volcano.

Uncle fired Duke a few weeks later. He said it was because Duke had dropped a tray of dishes. It was during the Saturday lunch rush when Sourdi and I weren't working and couldn't witness what had happened.

"He's a clumsy boy," Ma agreed after work that night, when we all sat around in the back booths and ate our dinner.

Sourdi didn't say anything. She knew Ma knew.

She kept seeing Duke, of course. They were both juniors, and there was only one high school in town. Now when I crept into Sourdi's bed at night, when she talked about running away, she meant Duke and her. I was the one who had to pipe up that I was coming with them, too. What we didn't know was that Ma was making plans as well.

Uncle first introduced his friend Mr. Chhay in the winter. I'd had a strange dream the night before. I hadn't remembered it at all until Mr. Chhay walked into the Palace, with his hangdog face and his suit like a salesman's. He sat in a corner booth with Uncle and, while they talked, he shredded a napkin, then took the scraps of paper and rolled them between his thumb and index finger into a hundred tiny red balls. He left them in the ashtray, like a mountain of fish eggs. Seeing them, I remembered my dream.

I was swimming in the ocean. I was just a small child, but I wasn't afraid at all. The sea was liquid turquoise, the sunlight yellow as gold against my skin. Fish were swimming alongside me. I could see through the clear water to the bottom of the sea. The fish were schooling around me and below me, and they brushed against my feet when I kicked the water. Their scales felt like bones scraping my toes. I tried to push them away, but the schools grew more dense, until I was swimming amongst them under the waves.

The fish began to spawn around me and soon the water was cloudy with eggs. I tried to break through the film, but the eggs clung to my skin. The water darkened as we entered a sea of kelp. I pushed against the dark slippery strands like Sourdi's hair. I realized I was pushing against my sister, wrapped in the kelp, suspended just below the surface of the water. Then I woke up.

I thought about that dream seeing that old guy Mr. Chhay with Uncle and I   65
knew they were up to no good. I wanted to warn Sourdi, but she seemed to understand without my having to tell her anything.

Uncle called over to her and introduced her to his friend. But Sourdi wouldn't even look at Mr. Chhay. She kept her eyes lowered, though he tried to smile and talk to her. She whispered so low in reply that no one could understand a word she said. I could tell the man was disappointed when he left. His shoulders seemed barely able to support the weight of his jacket.

Mr. Chhay wrote letters to Uncle, to Ma. He thanked them for their hospitality and enclosed pictures of his business and his house, plus a formal portrait of himself looking ridiculous in another suit, standing in front of some potted plants, his hair combed over the bald spot in the middle of his head.

The next time he came to visit the Palace, he brought gifts. A giant Chinese vase for Ma, Barbie dolls for my younger sisters and cousin, a Christian music cassette tape for me, and a bright red leather purse for Sourdi.

Ma made Sourdi tell him thank you.

And that was all she said to him.   70

But this old guy was persistent. He took us all out to eat at a steakhouse once. He said he wanted to pay back Uncle for some good deed he'd done a long time ago when they both first came to America. I could have told him, Sourdi hated this kind of food. She preferred Mexican, tacos, not this Midwest cowboy stuff. But Ma made us all thank him.

"Thank you, Mr. Chhay," we said dutifully. He'd smiled so all his yellow teeth showed at once. "Oh, please, call me Older Brother," he said.

It was the beginning of the end. I should have fought harder then. I should have stabbed this man, too.

I saw Duke at Sourdi's wedding. She invited him for the ceremony proper, the reception, too, but he didn't show up until the end. I almost didn't see him at all. He was slouching through the parking lot of St. Agnes, wearing his best hightops and the navy-blue suit that his mother had insisted upon buying for graduation. I wasn't used to him looking like a teenage undertaker, but I recognized his loping gait immediately. That afternoon of Sourdi's wedding, he was holding a brown bag awkwardly behind his back, as if trying to conceal the fact that he was drinking as conspicuously as possible.

I was standing inside the bingo hall, before the row of squat windows, my back   75
turned to the festivities, the exploding flash capturing the tipsy toasts, the in-laws singing off-key to the rented karaoke machine.

Then it really became too much to bear, and I had to escape the terrible heat, the flickering fluorescent lights. I slipped from the church into the ferocious March wind and gave it my best shot, running across the hard lawn, but the too-tight heels pinched my toes and the stiff taffeta bodice of the cotton-candy-pink bridesmaid's dress might as well have been a vise around my rib cage. I had intended to make it off church property, run to the empty field that stretched low and dark all the way to the horizon, but I only made it to the end of the walk near the rectory before vomiting into Sister Kevin's over-tended tulip patch.

Duke came over and sat on his haunches beside me, while I puked. I let him hold back my hair, while the wedding cake and wine cooler that I'd tried poured from my mouth.

Finally, I spat a few times to clear my mouth, then sat back on my rear end.

After a few minutes, I could take a sip from Duke's beer.

We didn't talk. 80

I took out the pack of cigarettes I'd stolen from Ma's purse and lit one. It took five puffs before I could mask the taste of bile and sugar.

The wind was blowing fiercely from the northwest, whipping my hair about my face like a widow's veil, throwing dust from the parking lot around us like wedding rice.

After a long while, Duke stood up and walked back down the sidewalk lined with yellow daffodils. He walked bow-legged, like all the boys in our town, farmers' sons, no matter how cool Duke tried to be. I buried my head in my arms and watched him from under one polyester-covered armpit as he climbed back into his pickup and pulled away with a screech. As he left the parking lot, he tossed the brown bag with the empty bottle of Bud out the window. It fell into the street, where it rolled and rolled until it disappeared into a ditch.

Ma liked Sourdi's husband. He had a steady job, a house. She didn't mind he was so old and Sourdi just eighteen when they married. In her eyes, eighteen was a good age to start a family. "I was younger than Sourdi when I get married," Ma liked to say.

When Sourdi sent pictures home for the holidays, Ma ooohed and aaahed as 85 though they were winning lottery tickets. My sister and her old husband in front of a listing Christmas tree, a pile of presents at their feet. Then, the red-faced baby sprawled on a pink blanket on the living room carpet, drooling in its shiny high chair, slumped in its Snugli like a rock around Sourdi's neck.

"Look. Sony," Ma pointed at the big-screen television in the background of the New Year's pictures. "Sourdi say they got all new washer/dryer, too. Maytag."

When I looked at my sister's pictures, I could see that she looked tired.

Sourdi always said that Ma used to be a very brave woman. She also said that Ma used to be a beautiful woman who liked to have her hair fixed in salons, who wore pretty dresses and knew how to dance in all the fashionable styles. I don't remember this mother. I remember the mother who worked two jobs for us.

I might never have seen Duke again if it were not for Sourdi's strange phone call one Saturday evening nearly two years after her wedding. I was fourteen and a half.

At first, I hadn't recognized my older sister's voice. 90

"Who is this?" I demanded, thinking: heavy breathing, prank caller.

"Who d'you think?" Sourdi was crying, a tiny crimped sound that barely crept out of the receiver. Then her voice steadied with anger and grew familiar. "Is Ma there?"

"What's the matter? What happened?"

"Just let me speak to Ma, O.K.?" There was a pause, as Sourdi blew her nose. "Tell her it's important."

I lured Ma from the TV room without alerting my younger sisters. Ma paced 95 back and forth in the kitchen between the refrigerator and the stove, nodding and muttering, "Mmm, mmm, uh-hmm." I could just hear the tinny squeak of Sourdi's panicked voice.

I sat on the floor, hugging my knees, in the doorway to the hall, just out of Ma's line of sight.

Finally, Ma said, in the tone normally reserved for refusing service to the unruly or arguing with a customer who had a complaint, "It's always like this. Every marriage is hard. Sometimes there is nothing you can do—"

Then Ma stopped pacing. "Just minute," she said and she took the phone with her into the bathroom, shutting the door firmly behind her.

When she came out again, twenty-two minutes later, she ignored me completely. She set the phone back on the counter without saying a word.

"So?" I prompted. 100

"I'm tired." Ma rubbed her neck with one hand. "Just let me rest. You girls, it's always something. Don't let your old mother rest."

She yawned extravagantly. She claimed she was too tired to watch any more TV. She had to go to bed, her eyes just wouldn't stay open.

I tried calling Sourdi, but the phone only rang and rang.

The next morning, Sunday, I called first thing, but then *he* picked up, my sister's husband.

"Oh, is this Nea?" he said, so cheerfully it was obvious he was hiding something. 105

"Yes, I'd like to speak to my sister."

"I'm sorry, Little Sister." I just hated when he called me that. "My wife is out right now. But I'll tell her you called. She'll be sorry she missed you."

It was eight o'clock in the morning, for Chrissake.

"Oh, thank you," I said, sweet as pie. "How's the baby?"

"So well!" Then he launched into a long explanation about his daughter's eat- 110 ing habits, her rather average attempts to crawl, the simple words she was trying to say. For all I knew, Sourdi could have been right there, fixing his breakfast, washing his clothes, cleaning up his messes. I thought of my sister's voice in my ear, the tiny sound like something breaking.

It was all I could do to disguise the disdain in my voice. "Be sure to tell Sourdi to call back. Ma found that recipe she wanted. That special delicious recipe she was looking for. I can't tell you what it is, Ma's secret recipe, but you'll really be surprised."

"Oh, boy," the jerk said. "I didn't know about any secret recipe."

"That's why it's a secret." I hung up. I couldn't breathe. My chest hurt. I could feel my swollen heart pressing against my ribs.

The next afternoon, I tried calling back three more times, but no one answered.

At work that evening, Ma was irritable. She wouldn't look me in the eyes when I   115
tried to get her attention. Some little kid spilled his Coke into a perfectly good plate of House Special Prawns and his parents insisted they be given a new order—and a new Coke—on the house. There was a minor grease fire around quarter to nine—the smoke alarms all went off at the same time—and then the customers started complaining about the cold, too, once we had opened all the doors and windows to clear the air. Fairly average as far as disasters went, but they put Ma in a sour mood.

Ma was taking a cigarette break out back by the dumpsters, smoke curling from her nostrils, before I could corner her. She wasn't in the mood to talk, but after the nicotine fix took hold, she didn't tell me to get back to work, either.

I asked Ma if I could have a smoke. She didn't get angry. She smiled in her tired way, the edges of her mouth twitching upwards just a little, and said, "Smoking will kill you." Then she handed me her pack.

"Maybe Sourdi should come back home for a while," I suggested.

"She's a married woman. She has her own family now."

"She's still part of our family."   120

Ma didn't say anything, just tilted her head back and blew smoke at the stars, so I continued, "Well, don't you think she might be in trouble? She was crying, you know. It's not like Sourdi." My voice must have slipped a tad, just enough to sound disrespectful, because Ma jerked upright, took the cigarette out of her mouth and glared at me.

"What you think? You so smart? You gonna tell me what's what?" Ma threw her cigarette onto the asphalt. "You not like your sister. Your sister know how to bear things!"

She stormed back into the kitchen, and Ma ignored me for the rest of the evening.

I called Sourdi one more time, after Ma and my sisters had gone to bed and I finally had the kitchen to myself, the moon spilling from the window onto the floor in a big, blue puddle. I didn't dare turn on the lights.

This time, my sister answered. "Mmm. . . . Hello?"   125

"Sourdi?"

"What time is it?"

"Sssh." My heart beat so loudly, I couldn't hear my own voice. "How are you doing?"

"Oh, we're fine. The baby, she's doing real good. She's starting to talk—"

"No, no, no. I mean, what happened the other night?"   130

"What?"

Another voice now, low, a man's voice, just beneath the snow on the line. Then suddenly a shriek.

"Uh-oh. I just woke her up." Sourdi's voice grew fainter as she spoke to him: "Honey, can you check the baby's diaper?" Then she said to me, "I have to go. The baby, she's hungry, you know."

"Let him handle it. I have to talk to you a minute, O.K.? Just don't go, Sourdi. What's going on? What did you say to Ma?"

Sourdi sighed, like a balloon losing its air. "Oh . . . nothing. Look, I really have to go. Talk to you later, Nea." She hung up.   135

I called back in twenty minutes, surely long enough to change a diaper, but the phone only rang forlornly, ignored.

❊ ❊ ❊

I considered taking Ma's car, but then Ma wouldn't be able to get to work and I wasn't sure how long I needed to be gone. Then I thought of Duke.

Even though it was far too late in the night, I called Duke. He was still in town, two years after graduation. I'd heard he was working as a mechanic at the Standard station. I found his number in the phone book.

"It's Nea. Pick up your phone, Duke," I hissed into his machine. "It's an emergency!"

"Nea?!" He was yawning. "My God. What time is it?"   140

"Duke! It's important! It's Sourdi, she's in trouble."

There was a pause while I let him absorb all this.

"You have to drive me to Des Moines. We have to get her."

"What happened?"

"Look, I don't have time to explain. We have to go tonight. It's an emergency.   145
A matter of life and death."

"Did you call the police?"

"Don't be stupid. Sourdi would never call the cops. She loves that jerk."

"What?" Duke whispered, "Her husband, he beat her up?"

"Duke, I told you, I can't say anything right now. But you have to help me."

He agreed to meet me at the corner, where there'd be no chance Ma could hear   150
his truck. I'd be waiting.

It was freezing. The wind stung my cheeks, which wasn't a good sign. Could be rain coming, or worse, snow. Even when the roads were clear, it was a good six-hour drive. I didn't want to think how long it would take if we ran into a late-season blizzard.

There was the roar of a souped-up engine and then a spray of gravel. Snoop Doggy Dogg growled over the wind.

"Duke! What took you?"

He put his hand over the door, barring me from climbing up. "You want me to help or not?"

"Don't joke."   155

I pulled myself inside and then made Duke back up rather than run in front of the house. Just in case Ma woke up.

"How come your Ma didn't want to come?"

"She doesn't know."

"Sourdi didn't want to worry her?"

"Mmm." There was no point trying to shout above Snoop Dogg.

He was obviously tired. When Duke was tired, he turned his music up even louder than normal. I'd forgotten that. Now the bass underneath the rap was vibrating in my bones. But at least he did as I asked and took off toward the highway.

Soon the squat buildings of town, the used-car lots on the route in from the interstate with their flapping colored flags, and the metal storage units of the Sav-U-Lot passed from view, and there was nothing before us but the black sky and the highway and the patches of snow on the shoulders glowing briefly in the wake of the headlights.

I must have fallen asleep, though I don't remember feeling tired. I was standing on the deck of a boat in an inky ocean, trying to read the stars, but every time I found one constellation, the stars began to blink and fade. I squinted at them, but the stars would not stay in place. Then my head snapped forward as the pickup careened off the shoulder.

The pickup landed in a ditch. Metal glittered in the headlights; the fields on this side of the highway were strung with barbed wire.

We got out by sacrificing our jackets, stuffing them under the back tires until we had enough traction to slide back onto the pavement.

I insisted upon driving. "I got my license," I lied. "And I'm not tired at all."

Duke settled into the passenger seat, his arms folded across his chest, his head tilted back, preparing to go to sleep again.

"D'ya think she'll be happy to see me?" he said out of the blue. "Sourdi sent me a Christmas card with a picture of the baby. Looks just like . . . But I didn't write back or nothing. She probably thought I was angry. She mad at me, you think?"

"Sourdi's never mad at anybody."

"She must be mad at her husband if she wants you to come get her."

"She doesn't know we're coming."

"What!"

"I didn't have time to explain to her."

"You're not running away from home, are you?" Duke's eyes narrowed and his voice grew slow as if he thought he was suddenly being clever.

"Yeah, I'm running away to Des Moines."

Once upon a time, in another world, a place almost unimaginable to me sitting in the pickup with Madonna singing "Lucky Star" on the radio, Sourdi had walked across a minefield, carrying me on her back. She was nine and I was four. Because she'd told me, I could see it all clearly, better than if I actually remembered: the startled faces of people who'd tripped a mine, their limbs in new arrangements, the bones peeking through the earth. Sourdi had said it was safest to step on the bodies; that way you knew a mine was no longer there.

This was nothing I would ever tell Duke. It was our own personal story, just for Sourdi and me to share. Nobody's business but ours.

I would walk on bones for my sister, I vowed. I would put my bare feet on rotting flesh. I would save Sourdi.

We found the house in West Des Moines after circling for nearly an hour through the identical streets with their neat lawns and boxy houses and chain link fences. I refused to allow Duke to ask for directions from any of the joggers or the van that sputtered by, delivering the *Register*. He figured people in the neighborhood would know, just ask where the Oriental family lived. I told him to go to hell. Then we didn't talk for a while.

But as soon as we found Locust Street, I recognized the house. I knew it was   180
Sourdi's even though it had been painted a different color since the last set of pictures. The lace undercurtains before the cheerful flowered draperies, the flourishing plants in the windows, next to little trinkets, figurines in glass that caught the light. Every space crammed with something sweet.

The heater in Duke's truck began to make a high-pitched, sick-cat whine as we waited, parked across the street, staring at Sourdi's house.

"So, are we going to just sit here?"

"Shh," I said irritably. "Just wait a minute." Somehow I had imagined that Sourdi would sense our presence, the curtains would stir, and I'd only have to wait a moment for my sister to come running out the front door. But we sat patiently, shivering, staring at Sourdi's house. Nothing moved.

"Her husband's home," I said stupidly. "He hasn't gone to work yet."

"He wouldn't dare try anything. Not with the both of us here. We should just   185
go and knock."

"They're probably still asleep."

"Nea, what's the matter with you? What are you afraid of all of a sudden?"

I'd had it with Duke. He just didn't understand anything. I hopped out of the truck and ran through the icy air, my arms wrapped around my body. The sidewalk was slick beneath my sneakers, still damp from the ditch, and I slid onto my knees on the driveway. My right hand broke the fall. A sharp jagged pain shot up to my elbow and stayed there, throbbing. I picked myself up and ran limping to the door and rang.

No one answered for a minute, and then it was him.

"What on earth? Nea!" Sourdi's husband was dressed for work, but he hadn't   190
shaved yet. He looked even older than I remembered, his thinning hair flat across his skull, his bloodshot eyes and swollen lids still heavy from sleep. He might have been handsome once, decades ago, but I saw no evidence of it now. He held the door open and I slipped into the warmth without even removing my shoes first. "How did you get here? Is your mother coming, too?"

My eyes started to water, the transition from cold to heat. Slowly the room came into focus. It was a mess. Baby toys on the carpet, shoes in a pile by the door, old newspapers scattered on an end table anchored by a bowl of peanut shells. The TV was blaring somewhere, and a baby was crying.

Sourdi emerged from the kitchen, dressed in a bright pink sweatsuit emblazoned with the head of Minnie Mouse, pink slippers over her feet, the baby on her hip. She had a bruise across her cheekbone and the purple remains of a black eye. Sourdi didn't say anything for a few seconds as she stared at me, blinking, her mouth falling open. "Where's Ma?"

"Home."

"Oh, no." Sourdi's face crumpled. "Is everything all right?"

I couldn't believe how dense my sister had become. We used to be able to communicate without words. "Everything's fine . . . at home. Of course." I tried to give her a look so that she'd understand that I had come to rescue her, but Sourdi stood rigidly in place in the doorway to the kitchen, her mouth twitching, puzzled.

"Please, Little Sister, sit down," her husband said. "Let me make you some tea."

Someone banged on the front door, three times. Before I could begin to feel annoyed that Duke couldn't even wait five minutes, that he just had to ruin everything, my sister's husband opened the door again. I didn't bother to turn, instead I watched Sourdi's eyes widen and her wide mouth pucker into an O as she gasped, "Duke!"

"What's goin' on?" Duke said.

Then everyone stared at me with such identical expressions of non-comprehension that I had to laugh. Then I couldn't stop, because I hadn't slept and it was so cold and my nose was running and I didn't have any Kleenex.

"I said, what the hell is going on?" Duke repeated.

Sourdi's husband approached Duke. He smiled. "You must be Nea's—"

But by now, Duke had seen Sourdi's bruises. His mouth twisted into a sneer. "You bastard! I oughtta—" He punched Sourdi's husband in the nose. Sourdi screamed, her husband bent over double. Duke drew back his fist again, but Sourdi ran forward and grabbed him. She was punching him on the chest, "Out! Out! You! I'll call the police!" She tried to claw him with her nails, but Duke threw his arms up around his head.

Sourdi's husband stood up. Blood gushed from his nose all over his white shirt and tie.

"Come on!" I said stupidly. "Come on, Sourdi, let's go!"

But it was pretty obvious that she didn't want to leave.

The baby began shrieking.

I started crying, too.

After everyone had calmed down, Duke went down the street to the 7-Eleven to get a bag of ice for Mr. Chhay, who kept saying "I'm fine, don't worry," even though his nose had turned a deep scarlet and was starting to swell.

It turned out Sourdi's husband hadn't beaten her up. An economy-size box of baby wipes had fallen off the closet shelf and struck her full in the eye.

While Mr. Chhay went into the bedroom to change his clothes, I sat with Sourdi in the kitchen as she tried to get the squawling baby to eat its breakfast.

"Nea, what's wrong with you?"

"What's wrong with me? Don't you get it? I was trying to help you!"

Sourdi sighed as the baby spat a spoonful of the glop onto the table. "I'm a married woman. I'm not just some girl anymore. I have my own family. You understand that?"

"You were crying." I squinted at my sister. "I heard you."

"I'm gonna have another baby, you know. That's a big step. That's a big thing." 215
She said this as though it explained everything.

"You sound like an old lady. You're only twenty, for Chrissake. You don't have to
live like this. Ma is wrong. You can be anything, Sourdi."

Sourdi pinched her nose between two fingers. "Everything's gonna be fine. We
just had a little argument, but it's O.K. We had a good talk. He understands now. I'm
still gonna go to school. I haven't changed my mind. After the baby gets a little bigger,
I mean, both babies. Maybe when they start pre-school."

Just then her husband came back into the kitchen. He had to use the phone to
call work. His face looked like a gargoyle's.

Sourdi looked at me then, so disappointed. I knew what she was thinking. She
had grown up, and I had merely grown unworthy of her love.

After Duke got back with the ice, he and Sourdi's husband shook hands. Duke kept 220
saying, "Gosh, I'm so sorry," and Mr. Chhay kept repeating, "No problem, don't worry."

Then Sourdi's husband had to go. We followed him to the driveway. My sister
kissed him before he climbed into his Buick. He rolled down the window, and she
leaned in and kissed him again.

I turned away. I watched Duke standing in the doorway, holding the baby in his
arms, cooing at its face. In his tough wannabe clothes, the super-wide jeans and his
fancy sneakers and the chain from his wallet to his belt loops, he looked surprisingly
young.

Sourdi lent us some blankets and matching his-and-hers Donald and Daisy Duck
sweatshirts for the trip back, since our coats were still wet and worthless.

"Don't tell Ma I was here, O.K.?" I begged Sourdi. "We'll be home by afternoon.
She'll just think I'm with friends or something. She doesn't have to know, O.K.?"

Sourdi pressed her full lips together into a thin line and nodded in a way that 225
seemed as though she were answering a different question. And I knew that I couldn't
trust my sister to take my side anymore.

As we pulled away from Sourdi's house, the first icy snowflakes began to fall
across the windshield.

Sourdi stood in the driveway with the baby on her hip. She waved to us as the
snow swirled around her like ashes.

She had made her choice, and she hadn't chosen me.

Sourdi told me a story once about a magic serpent, the Naga, with a mouth so
large, it could swallow people whole. Our ancestors carved Naga into the stones of
Angkor Wat to scare away demons. Sourdi said people used to believe they could
come alive in times of great evil and protect the temples. They could eat armies.

I wished I was a Naga. I would have swallowed the whole world in one gulp. 230

But I have no magic powers. None whatsoever.

[2001]

Exploring the Text

1. How is the narrator's opening statement that she stabbed a man when she was eleven a clue to her character? How does it prepare the reader for later events in the story?

2. "Saving Sourdi" is told from the point of view of Nea, one of the main characters in the story. How much time do you think has passed since the events Nea recounts and her telling of the story? What evidence can you find to support your view? How does this particular narrative voice contribute to the story's impact?

3. What effect does the flashback to the time when Sourdi carried Nea across a minefield have on your judgment of Nea's behavior (para. 176)? How does it help explain her relationship with her sister? Why do you think the author placed the flashback later on in the story rather than after the stabbing incident, for instance?

4. What does Nea, at fourteen, still have to learn about family? What does the following exchange between Nea and her mother reveal about her current viewpoint?

   > "Maybe Sourdi should come back home for a while," I suggested.
   > "She's a married woman. She has her own family now."
   > "She's still part of our family." (paras. 118–20)

5. Chai uses simile and metaphor liberally throughout the story. Identify several instances, and consider the effect that each one has. For instance, the sky was "smooth as an empty rice bowl" (para. 45); the wind whipped Nea's hair "about [her] face like a widow's veil" (para. 82).

6. One theme of this story is Nea's effort to find security within her family. Why does she feel insecure? Consider Nea's actions and responses in light of this theme.

7. What is the function of the final section of the story? Why do you think Chai chose not to end with the line "She had made her choice, and she hadn't chosen me" (para. 228)?

8. Early in the story, Nea describes her feelings about the family's move from Texas to South Dakota: "I thought we'd find the real America" (para. 4). What does she mean? Do they ever find this desired destination? By the end of the story, what does "the real America" mean to Nea?

9. Does Sourdi need "saving"? Chai gives us a literal explanation for Nea's motivation, but what other dimensions do you find to the idea of "saving," and why is it a fitting title for this story?

De Puero Balbutiente

Thomas Bastard

Thomas Bastard (1566–1618) was born in England during the early years of the Reformation. His home life was that of minor rural aristocracy, with connections to the court of Queen Elizabeth I. Following the tradition of an aristocratic scholar, he was educated at Winchester College and New College, Oxford.

He was expelled from Oxford after his publication of *An Admonition to the city of Oxford et cetera* (1591). This polemic, whose authorship Bastard denied, exposed the hypocrisy of Oxford dons, who, despite the Reformation, were forbidden to marry. Writing in the style of Roman epigrammatists, a style fashionable in late sixteenth-century England, he published his most famous work, *Chrestoleros* (1598)—a collection of 285 short pieces of verse. After the death of Queen Elizabeth, he dedicated a work, *Serenissimo potentissimoque monarchae Iacobo* (1605), to the new king. In "De Puero Balbutiente"—Latin for "About a Stammering Boy"—he describes a child's first attempt to form words.

Methinks 'tis pretty sport to hear a child,
Rocking a word in mouth yet undefiled;
The tender racquet rudely plays the sound
Which, weakly bandied, cannot back rebound;
And the soft air the softer roof doth kiss,   5
With a sweet dying and a pretty miss,
Which hears no answer yet from the white rank
Of teeth, not risen from their coral bank.
The alphabet is searched for letters soft,
To try a word before it can be wrought,   10
And when it slideth forth, it goes as nice
As when a man does walk upon the ice.

[1598]

Exploring the Text

1. What does the speaker mean when he describes a child's mouth as "yet undefiled" (l. 2)? What does this description tell you about the stammering boy? What does the "yet" suggest?
2. How do the alliteration, assonance, and rhyme used to portray the child's speech reflect the speech itself? How do these aspects of the poem provide a clue to the speaker's attitude toward the child's stammering?
3. What effect does the enjambment of "the white rank / Of teeth" (ll. 7–8) have on your reading of these two lines?
4. Select at least two words that are either unfamiliar or used in an unfamiliar way, such as "pretty" (l. 1), "sport" (l. 1), "rudely" (l. 3), "bandied" (l. 4), "rank" (l. 7), or "nice" (l. 11). Explain the function of that type of diction within the poem. For instance, if it sets up a metaphor, what is the purpose of the metaphor?
5. What does the comparison in the final couplet achieve? Pay attention to the simile. Does it change the tone from the previous lines? complicate it?
6. How would you describe the overall attitude of the speaker toward the child? Cite specific language and images that support your description.

On My First Son

BEN JONSON

Ben Jonson (1572–1637) was a dominant force in English theater for much of his adult life and was widely regarded as the equal of Shakespeare. Born in London to an indigent widowed mother, he was encouraged to attend college. However, financial considerations compelled him to become a bricklayer, a trade Jonson "could not endure." He ultimately joined the army and fought for the Protestant cause in Holland. Returning to England in 1592, he took the London theater by storm. He tried his hand at both acting and directing, but it was in writing that he excelled. His early tragedies have not survived the ages, but his later comedies have, including *Every Man in His Humour* (1598), which was performed by a cast that included William Shakespeare, as well as *Volpone* (1606), *The Alchemist* (1610), and *Bartholomew Fair* (1614). He also wrote many masques (a genre now extinct) for the court of King James I and Queen Anne. "On My First Son" is an epitaph written after the death of Jonson's first son, Benjamin, at the age of seven.

Farewell, thou child of my right hand,[1] and joy;
My sin was too much hope of thee, loved boy:
Seven years thou wert lent to me, and I thee pay,
Exacted by thy fate, on the just day.
O could I lose all father now! For why   5
Will man lament the state he should envy,
To have so soon 'scaped world's and flesh's rage,
And, if no other misery, yet age?
Rest in soft peace, and asked, say, "Here doth lie
Ben Jonson his best piece of poetry."   10
For whose sake henceforth all his vows be such
As what he loves may never like too much.

[1616]

Exploring the Text

1. In line 2 the speaker calls hope a "sin." How can this be?
2. How do you interpret the metaphor in lines 3–4, in which Jonson compares his son's life to a loan? What does this comparison suggest about the speaker's faith and his resulting views on life?
3. How does the speaker attempt to console himself over the loss of his son? Identify language in the poem that demonstrates your point.

---

[1]Benjamin means "son of my right hand" in Hebrew. — EDS.

4. What does the speaker mean when he asks, "O could I lose all father now!" (l. 5)?
5. Why do you think the speaker calls his son "his best piece of poetry" (l. 10)? What does this suggest about the value he places on his poetry?
6. What do you make of the final lines of the epitaph? To whom does the "his" in line 11 refer to? What is the difference between the words "love" and "like" in the last line? What does the speaker vow in that line?

Before the Birth of One of Her Children

ANNE BRADSTREET

In 1630, Anne Bradstreet (1612/13–1678) and her husband Simon, the son of a nonconformist minister, sailed to Massachusetts with Anne's parents. With *The Tenth Muse Lately Sprung Up in America* (1650)—possibly published in England without her knowledge—she became the first female poet in America. Because the Puritan community disdained female intellectual ambition, it was thought advisable to append the words "By a Gentle Woman in Those Parts," to reassure readers that Bradstreet was a diligent Puritan mother. Bradstreet's most remarkable poetry consists of thirty-five short reflective poems, explicit in their description of familial and marital love. Some of these appeared in the 1678 edition of *The Tenth Muse*; others remained hidden in her notebook until they were published in 1867. The twentieth century saw renewed interest in America's first female poet with John Berryman's poem "Homage to Mistress Bradstreet" (1956) and new editions of her work in 1967 and 1981. The mother of eight children, she writes of impending childbirth with apprehension and acceptance of the will of God in "Before the Birth of One of Her Children."

All things within this fading world hath end,
Adversity doth still our joys attend;
No ties so strong, no friends so dear and sweet,
But with death's parting blow is sure to meet.
The sentence past is most irrevocable,   5
A common thing, yet oh, inevitable.
How soon, my Dear, death may my steps attend,
How soon't may be thy lot to lose thy friend,
We both are ignorant, yet love bids me
These farewell lines to recommend to thee,   10
That when that knot's untied that made us one,
I may seem thine, who in effect am none.
And if I see not half my days that's due,
What nature would, God grant to yours and you;
The many faults that well you know I have   15

Let be interred in my oblivious grave;
If any worth or virtue were in me,
Let that live freshly in thy memory
And when thou feel'st no grief, as I no harms,
Yet love thy dead, who long lay in thine arms,   20
And when thy loss shall be repaid with gains
Look to my little babes, my dear remains.
And if thou love thyself, or loved'st me,
These O protect from stepdame's injury.
And if chance to thine eyes shall bring this verse,   25
With some sad sighs honor my absent hearse;
And kiss this paper for thy love's dear sake,
Who with salt tears this last farewell did take.

[1678]

Exploring the Text

1. Anne Bradstreet had borne eight children, had lost two, and was battling tuberculosis when she wrote this poem. How are those circumstances reflected in the sentiments expressed in the poem? How is the poem itself not only last wishes but also a legacy to her children?
2. Restate the following line into simple language: "Adversity doth still our joys attend" (l. 2). What might the speaker mean by that statement in general, and how might it apply to her situation in particular?
3. How do you interpret the paradox in line 21? Explain the double meaning of "remains" in line 22.
4. Why do you think Bradstreet adds "if thou love thyself" to her qualification "or loved'st me" (l. 23)? What additional power does the "or" invoke?
5. Although the poem is presented without stanza breaks, it falls into sections. What are they? How do they form a sort of argument that the speaker is making?
6. How would you describe the tone of this poem? Try using a pair of words, such as "cautiously optimistic" or "fearful yet hopeful."

We Are Seven

WILLIAM WORDSWORTH

William Wordsworth (1770–1850) is one of the most famous and influential poets of the Western world and one of the premier Romantics. Widely known for his reverence of nature and the power of his lyrical verse, he lived in the Lake District of northern England, where he was inspired by the natural beauty of the landscape. With Samuel Taylor Coleridge, he published *Lyrical*

Ballads in 1798; the collection, which changed the direction of English poetry, begins with Coleridge's "Rime of the Ancient Mariner" and includes Wordsworth's "Lines Composed a Few Miles above Tintern Abbey." Among Wordsworth's other most famous works are "The World Is Too Much with Us" (p. 498), a sonnet; "Ode: Intimations of Immortality"; and "The Prelude, or Growth of a Poet's Mind," an autobiographical poem. "We Are Seven" first appeared in *Lyrical Ballads*.

—A simple Child,
That lightly draws its breath,
And feels its life in every limb,
What should it know of death?

I met a little cottage Girl: 5
She was eight years old, she said;
Her hair was thick with many a curl
That clustered round her head.

She had a rustic, woodland air,
And she was wildly clad: 10
Her eyes were fair, and very fair;
—Her beauty made me glad.

"Sisters and brothers, little Maid,
How many may you be?"
"How many? Seven in all," she said,   15
And wondering looked at me.

"And where are they? I pray you tell."
She answered, "Seven are we;
And two of us at Conway dwell,
And two are gone to sea.   20

"Two of us in the church-yard lie,
My sister and my brother;
And, in the church-yard cottage, I
Dwell near them with my mother."

"You say that two at Conway dwell,   25
And two are gone to sea,
Yet ye are seven!—I pray you tell,
Sweet Maid, how this may be."

Then did the little Maid reply,
"Seven boys and girls are we;   30
Two of us in the church-yard lie,
Beneath the church-yard tree."

"You run about, my little Maid,
Your limbs they are alive;
If two are in the church-yard laid,   35
Then ye are only five."

"Their graves are green, they may be seen,"
The little Maid replied,
"Twelve steps or more from my mother's door,
And they are side by side.   40

"My stockings there I often knit,
My kerchief there I hem;
And there upon the ground I sit,
And sing a song to them.

"And often after sunset, Sir,   45
When it is light and fair,
I take my little porringer,
And eat my supper there.

"The first that died was sister Jane;
In bed she moaning lay,   50
Till God released her of her pain;
And then she went away.

"So in the church-yard she was laid;
And, when the grass was dry,
Together round her grave we played,   55
My brother John and I.

"And when the ground was white with snow,
And I could run and slide,
My brother John was forced to go,
And he lies by her side."   60

"How many are you, then," said I,
"If they two are in heaven?"
Quick was the little Maid's reply,
"O Master! we are seven."

"But they are dead; those two are dead!   65
Their spirits are in heaven!"
'T was throwing words away; for still
The little Maid would have her will,
And said, "Nay, we are seven!"

                                     [1798]

Exploring the Text

1. What concrete details help the reader picture the "little cottage Girl"? For instance, what does the speaker mean in line 11 when he says, "Her eyes were fair, and very fair"? Why is the setting important to the tale being told?

2. In the first stanza, the speaker raises a question that is explored in subsequent stanzas through a dialogue between him and the little girl. Note how the speaker asks again and again how many children are in the little girl's family and how her answer never wavers. What effect does this repetition have on your understanding of the poem?

3. How would you characterize the little girl's attitude toward her dead sister and brother? What is the logic leading to her conclusion that "we are seven"? Does Wordsworth present the girl sympathetically or critically?

4. What does the girl understand about the nature of family and the death of family members that the ostensibly more experienced speaker has yet to learn? By the end, has she altered the speaker's view?

5. In his preface to *Lyrical Ballads* (1802), Wordsworth states that he wants his poetry to be written in "the real language of men," not the more elaborate language associated with elevated literary efforts. How well does "We Are Seven" achieve this goal? Is the regular rhyme and rhythm scheme in keeping with this goal? What about the repetition? What examples of figurative language do you find?

A Prayer for My Daughter

WILLIAM BUTLER YEATS

William Butler Yeats (1865–1939) was born in Dublin to a middle-class Protestant family with strong connections to England. The young Yeats spent his childhood in the west of Ireland, a region that remained a profound influence on his work. Yeats began as a playwright, founding the Irish Literary Theatre in 1899, and wrote several plays celebrating Irish cultural tradition. The most important of these are *Cathleen ni Houlihan* (1902), *The King's Threshold* (1904), and *Deirdre* (1907). His early plays earned him the Nobel Prize for Literature in 1923. By 1912, he had turned to writing poetry. Profoundly influenced by the poetry of William Blake, Yeats's work reflects Ireland's rich mythology and a fascination with the occult. His collections include *The Wild Swans at Coole* (1919), *Michael Robartes and the Dancer* (1921), *The Tower* (1928), and *The Winding Stair* (1933). Written at the age of fifty-four, "A Prayer for My Daughter" (1919) reflects the uncertainties of an aging father raising a daughter in a tumultuous world.

Once more the storm is howling, and half hid
Under this cradle-hood and coverlid
My child sleeps on. There is no obstacle
But Gregory's wood and one bare hill

Whereby the haystack- and roof-levelling wind,
Bred on the Atlantic, can be stayed;
And for an hour I have walked and prayed
Because of the great gloom that is in my mind.

I have walked and prayed for this young child an hour
And heard the sea-wind scream upon the tower,
And under the arches of the bridge, and scream
In the elms above the flooded stream;
Imagining in excited reverie
That the future years had come,
Dancing to a frenzied drum,
Out of the murderous innocence of the sea.

May she be granted beauty and yet not
Beauty to make a stranger's eye distraught,
Or hers before a looking-glass, for such,
Being made beautiful overmuch,
Consider beauty a sufficient end,
Lose natural kindness and maybe
The heart-revealing intimacy
That chooses right, and never find a friend.

Helen being chosen found life flat and dull
And later had much trouble from a fool,
While that great Queen, that rose out of the spray,
Being fatherless could have her way
Yet chose a bandy-leggèd smith for man.
It's certain that fine women eat
A crazy salad with their meat
Whereby the Horn of Plenty is undone.

In courtesy I'd have her chiefly learned;
Hearts are not had as a gift but hearts are earned
By those that are not entirely beautiful;
Yet many, that have played the fool
For beauty's very self, has charm made wise.
And many a poor man that has roved,
Loved and thought himself beloved,
From a glad kindness cannot take his eyes.

May she become a flourishing hidden tree
That all her thoughts may like the linnet be,
And have no business but dispensing round
Their magnanimities of sound,
Nor but in merriment begin a chase,

5

10

15

20

25

30

35

40

45

Nor but in merriment a quarrel.
O may she live like some green laurel
Rooted in one dear perpetual place.

My mind, because the minds that I have loved,
The sort of beauty that I have approved,   50
Prosper but little, has dried up of late,
Yet knows that to be choked with hate
May well be of all evil chances chief.
If there's no hatred in a mind
Assault and battery of the wind   55
Can never tear the linnet from the leaf.

An intellectual hatred is the worst,
So let her think opinions are accursed.
Have I not seen the loveliest woman born
Out of the mouth of Plenty's horn,   60
Because of her opinionated mind
Barter that horn and every good
By quiet natures understood
For an old bellows full of angry wind?

Considering that, all hatred driven hence,   65
The soul recovers radical innocence
And learns at last that it is self-delighting,
Self-appeasing, self-affrighting,
And that its own sweet will is Heaven's will;
She can, though every face should scowl   70
And every windy quarter howl
Or every bellows burst, be happy still.

And may her bridegroom bring her to a house
Where all's accustomed, ceremonious;
For arrogance and hatred are the wares   75
Peddled in the thoroughfares.
How but in custom and in ceremony
Are innocence and beauty born?
Ceremony's a name for the rich horn,
And custom for the spreading laurel tree.   80

[1919]

. . . .

Exploring the Text

1. What contrasts does the opening stanza establish? Consider the settings inside
   and outside, as well as the speaker's frame of mind.

2. Why is the speaker skeptical of "Being made beautiful overmuch" (l. 20)? What does he see as the dangers of extraordinary beauty? How do the allusions to Helen of Troy and Aphrodite ("that great Queen, that rose out of the spray," l. 27) support the speaker's views on beauty?

3. What does the speaker mean when he wishes for his daughter to "become a flourishing hidden tree" with thoughts "like the linnet be" (ll. 41–42)? What does this wish suggest about the future he envisions for his child? How do you interpret his desire that she be "Rooted in one dear perpetual place" (l. 48)? What are the alternatives to being a hidden tree with thoughts like a linnet?

4. What is the effect of the repeated construction "May she" (ll. 17, 41, 47)? What difference would it have made if Yeats had written "I hope she"?

5. In stanza 5, the speaker says, "In courtesy I'd have her chiefly learned" (l. 33). What is the meaning he attaches to the term "courtesy"? How might his concept of courtesy sum up the qualities he believes lead to a satisfying life?

6. Examine Yeats's use of figurative language. How do you interpret the image of the "Horn of Plenty" (l. 32), for instance, or "like some green laurel / Rooted in one dear perpetual place" (ll. 47–48)? What does the oxymoron "murderous innocence" (l. 16) mean? What effect does the personification of nature have?

7. What are the values the speaker wants his daughter to embrace? Which ones does he want her to avoid?

8. Based on the poem's final two stanzas, how would you describe the father's vision of an ideal woman? Pay careful attention to his use of the word "innocence" in these stanzas.

9. What might the setting of this poem represent? How does this setting affect the tone of this poem?

10. Why is this poem entitled "A Prayer"? What elements of prayer are embodied here?

11. Is the vision that Yeats favors for his daughter one that reflects stereotypical views of women? What elements of the poem might lend themselves to such an interpretation? What is your interpretation?

Mother to Son

LANGSTON HUGHES

Langston Hughes (1902–1967) grew up in the African American community of Joplin, Missouri. He spent a year at Columbia University and became involved with the Harlem movement, but was shocked by the endemic racial prejudice at the university and subsequently left. Hughes traveled for several years, spending some time in Paris before returning to the United States. He completed his BA at Pennsylvania's Lincoln University in 1929, after which he returned to Harlem for the remainder of his life. Hughes's output was prolific in verse, prose, and drama. His first volume of poetry, *The Weary Blues*, was published in 1926. This collection contained "The Negro Speaks of Rivers," perhaps his most famous poem. His first novel, *Not Without Laughter* (1930), won the Harmon Gold Medal for literature. He is remembered for his celebration of the uniqueness of African American culture, which found expression in "The Negro Artist and the Racial Mountain" (1926), published in the *Nation*, and in the poem "My People." He also wrote children's poetry, musicals, and opera. This poem, "Mother to Son," expresses a mother's advice to her son with its famous refrain, "Life for me ain't been no crystal stair."

Well, son, I'll tell you:
Life for me ain't been no crystal stair.
It's had tacks in it,
And splinters,
And boards torn up,   5
And places with no carpet on the floor —
Bare.
But all the time
I'se been a-climbin' on,
And reachin' landin's,   10
And turnin' corners,
And sometimes goin' in the dark
Where there ain't been no light.
So boy, don't you turn back.
Don't you set down on the steps   15
'Cause you finds it's kinder hard.
Don't you fall now —
For I'se still goin', honey,
I'se still climbin',
And life for me ain't been no crystal stair.   20

[1922]

Exploring the Text

1. What is the overall message the mother is trying to convey to her son?
2. Based on details in the poem, how would you characterize the mother?
3. The poem's speaker employs an extended metaphor to explain her life to her son. What do you think the "crystal stair" symbolizes (l. 2)? Why do you think the poet has chosen to repeat this image in the final line? What might the details of tacks, splinters, landings, and corners represent? What does the inclusion of these images suggest about the mother's relationship with her son?
4. What effect do colloquial expressions and dialect have on your understanding of the speaker? What effect do they have on the meaning of the poem?

5. How old is the son being addressed? Does he seem to be at some sort of cross-roads? Cite specific textual evidence to support your viewpoint.
6. Is the mother in this poem lecturing, apologizing, advising, pleading, showing affection, criticizing? How would you characterize the tone of the poem?
7. Even though the poem is presented without stanza breaks, there are "turns," or shifts. What are they? Try reciting or performing the poem; where would you emphasize the pauses? How do these breaks influence or emphasize meaning?

✷ *My Papa's Waltz*

THEODORE ROETHKE

Theodore Roethke (1908–1963) was born in Saginaw, Michigan. His early years spent in the family greenhouse business brought him close to nature and to his father, who died suddenly when Roethke was fifteen, a loss that looms large in the poem "My Papa's Waltz." After graduating from the University of Michigan, he did brief stints at law school and at Harvard University before the Great Depression compelled him to find work teaching at Lafayette College. He continued to teach throughout his life. Roethke first became popular after favorable reviews for *Open House* in 1941. He then won numerous prizes for his work throughout the 1950s and 1960s, including National Book Awards for both *Words for the Wind* (1957) and *The Far Field* (1964). The meeting of the mystical and the natural is at the center of his work—a meeting that fascinated such earlier poets as Blake and Wordsworth, both of whom were strong influences on Roethke's poetry. "My Papa's Waltz" is his most famous, and oft-interpreted, poem.

The whiskey on your breath
Could make a small boy dizzy;
But I hung on like death:
Such waltzing was not easy.

We romped until the pans   5
Slid from the kitchen shelf;
My mother's countenance
Could not unfrown itself.

The hand that held my wrist
Was battered on one knuckle;   10
At every step you missed
My right ear scraped a buckle.

You beat time on my head
With a palm caked hard by dirt,
Then waltzed me off to bed   15
Still clinging to your shirt.

[1948]

. . . .

Exploring the Text

1. How would you characterize the relationship between the father and the son in this poem?
2. Consider the two figures of speech in the poem: the simile of "hung on like death" (l. 3) and the metaphor of "waltzing" throughout the poem. What do they add to the story line of the poem? Imagine, for instance, if the title were changed to "My Papa" or "Dancing with My Father."
3. How do you interpret the lines "My mother's countenance / Could not unfrown itself" (ll. 7–8)? Is she angry? jealous? worried? frightened? disapproving? Why doesn't she take action or step in?
4. Manuscripts show that Roethke started writing this poem as a portrait of a daughter and her father. Explain why you think having a girl at the center of this poem would or would not affect your response to it.
5. What is the effect of the regular rhyme and rhythm scheme of the poem? In what ways does it mimic a waltz?
6. Some interpret this poem to be about an abusive father-son relationship, while others read it quite differently. How do you interpret it? Use textual evidence from the poem to explain your reading.

✳ *Those Winter Sundays*

ROBERT HAYDEN

Born Asa Bundy Sheffey in Detroit, Michigan, Robert Hayden (1913–1980) was raised both in a dysfunctional family and in an equally dysfunctional foster home just next door. The turmoil of his childhood was complicated by his extreme nearsightedness, which excluded him from most activities other than reading. Hayden attended Detroit City College (now Wayne State University) before studying under W. H. Auden in the graduate English program at the University of Michigan. In 1976, he was appointed consultant in poetry to the Library of Congress, a post that was the forerunner to that of poet laureate. His first volume, *Heart-Shape in the Dust* (1940), took its voice from the Harlem Renaissance and impressed W. H. Auden with its originality. Later work continued to garner critical praise, including his epic poem on the *Amistad* mutiny,

"Middle Passage," and *A Ballad of Remembrance* (1962), which includes his most famous poem, "Those Winter Sundays."

Sundays too my father got up early
and put his clothes on in the blueblack cold,
then with cracked hands that ached
from labor in the weekday weather made
banked fires blaze. No one ever thanked him.   5

I'd wake and hear the cold splintering, breaking.
When the rooms were warm, he'd call,
and slowly I would rise and dress,
fearing the chronic angers of that house,

Speaking indifferently to him,   10
who had driven out the cold
and polished my good shoes as well.
What did I know, what did I know
of love's austere and lonely offices?

[1962]

Exploring the Text *Tone shift!*

1. What are the different time frames of this poem, and when does the poem shift from flashback to present day? How does Hayden keep this shift from seeming abrupt?
2. What does the line "fearing the chronic angers of that house" (l. 9) suggest about the son's relationship with his father and the kind of home he grew up in?
3. What is the meaning of "love's austere and lonely offices" (l. 14)? What effect does Hayden achieve by choosing such an uncommon, somewhat archaic term as "offices"?
4. What is the tone of this poem? How do the specific details of the setting the speaker describes contribute to that tone? Consider also how the literal descriptions act as metaphors. What, for instance, is "blueblack cold" (l. 2)?
5. Notice the poem's shift between father and son, from "him" to "I." How does this alternation contribute to your understanding of the poem?
6. What contrasts do you see in the poem? Identify at least three, and discuss how they work individually and collectively.
7. What is the son's feeling about his father? Could this poem be read as a son's belated thank-you? Explain your answer. What does the adult speaker in the poem understand about his father that he did not as a child? What is the effect of the repetition in the last two lines?
8. In poetry, the lyric is usually a short poem expressing personal feelings and may take the form of a song set to music. What music would you choose to convey the tone and themes of "Those Winter Sundays"?

✳ *Daddy*

SYLVIA PLATH

Sylvia Plath (1932–1963) was born in Boston to a German father and a second-generation Austrian American mother. Her father, an entomologist and university professor, died suddenly when Sylvia was nine. Ambitious and intelligent, Plath won a scholarship to Smith College, where she suffered a nervous breakdown and attempted suicide. After therapy, she returned to Smith and graduated summa cum laude. She then went to Cambridge as a Fulbright Scholar, where she met the poet Ted Hughes, whom she married in 1956. After early success and publication of poems in *Seventeen* and the *New Yorker*, her first collection, *The Colossus and Other Poems*, appeared in 1960. This was followed a few years later by perhaps her most famous work, the autobiographical novel *The Bell Jar* (1963). Plath, unable to escape her mental illness, committed suicide in February 1963, resulting in the bulk of her poetry being published posthumously. Her autobiographical poem "Daddy" offers a glimpse of not only Plath's talent and intensity, but also her torment.

[handwritten: sleeping pills/ crawl space 3 days]

[handwritten: ✳ confessional poetry]

You do not do, you do not do
Any more, black shoe
In which I have lived like a foot
For thirty years, poor and white,
Barely daring to breathe or Achoo.   5

Daddy, I have had to kill you.
You died before I had time—
Marble-heavy, a bag full of God,
Ghastly statue with one gray toe[1]
Big as a Frisco seal   10

[handwritten bracket: How she saw him as a child]

And a head in the freakish Atlantic
Where it pours bean green over blue
In the waters off beautiful Nauset.[2]
I used to pray to recover you.
Ach, du.[3]   15

In the German tongue, in the Polish town
Scraped flat by the roller
Of wars, wars, wars.

---

[1]Plath's father, Otto, had a gangrenous toe caused by diabetes.—EDS.
[2]A harbor in Cape Cod, Massachusetts.—EDS.
[3]German, "Oh, you."—EDS.

But the name of the town is common.
My Polack friend   20

Says there are a dozen or two.
So I never could tell where you
Put your foot, your root,
I never could talk to you.
The tongue stuck in my jaw.   25

It stuck in a barb wire snare.
Ich,[4] ich, ich, ich,
I could hardly speak.
I thought every German was you.
And the language obscene   30

An engine, an engine
Chuffing me off like a Jew.
A Jew to Dachau, Auschwitz, Belsen.
I began to talk like a Jew.
I think I may well be a Jew.   35

The snows of the Tyrol, the clear beer of Vienna
Are not very pure or true.
With my gypsy-ancestress and my weird luck
And my Taroc[5] pack and my Taroc pack
I may be a bit of a Jew.   40

I have always been scared of *you*,
With your Luftwaffe,[6] your gobbledygoo.
And your neat moustache
And your Aryan eye, bright blue.
Panzer[7]-man, panzer-man, O You—   45

Not God but a swastika
So black no sky could squeak through.
Every woman adores a Fascist,
The boot in the face, the brute
Brute heart of a brute like you.   50

You stand at the blackboard, daddy,
In the picture I have of you,
A cleft in your chin instead of your foot

---

[4]I.—Eds.
[5]Tarot.—Eds.
[6]Air Force.—Eds.
[7]Panther, also a WWII German tank.—Eds.

But no less a devil for that, no not
Any less the black man who   55

Bit my pretty red heart in two.
I was ten when they buried you.
At twenty I tried to die
And get back, back, back to you.
I thought even the bones would do.   60

But they pulled me out of the sack,
And they stuck me together with glue.
And then I knew what to do.
I made a model of you,
A man in black with a Meinkampf[8] look   65

And a love of the rack and the screw.
And I said I do, I do.
So daddy, I'm finally through.
The black telephone's off at the root,
The voices just can't worm through.   70

If I've killed one man, I've killed two —
The vampire who said he was you
And drank my blood for a year,
Seven years, if you want to know.
Daddy, you can lie back now.   75

There's a stake in your fat black heart
And the villagers never liked you.
They are dancing and stamping on you.
They always *knew* it was you.
Daddy, daddy, you bastard, I'm through.   80

[1966]

· ·

Exploring the Text

1. How would you characterize the father in this poem? Pay attention to specific comparisons that the speaker makes — either literally or through metaphor — between historical events and figures and her father. Examine the repeated allusions to Nazis, Hitler, and death camps.

2. What images in the poem suggest the speaker's attempts to accommodate expectations of her father or her feeling that she lacks value? Note especially any imagery that suggests restraint against movement or speech.

---

[8]"My Struggle," here the title of Hitler's autobiography. — EDS.

3. The poem opens and closes with the speaker claiming to reject the memory of her father. How do these bookends point the way to the poem's theme? Does the speaker reach resolution?

4. Is this a poem about abandonment? grief? rage? all of these? Discuss what feelings the speaker has toward her father (and herself) as a result of her father's influence on—and absence from—her life.

5. The only way we know the speaker's father is through her perceptions. Is she an unreliable narrator? Do we trust her? Does she contradict herself or give hints of ambivalence? Cite specific images and passages to illustrate why you do or do not trust her perceptions.

6. Plath has said of "Daddy": "The poem is spoken by a girl with an Electra complex. Her father died while she thought he was God. Her case is complicated by the fact that her father was also a Nazi and her mother very possibly part-Jewish. In the daughter the two strains marry and paralyze each other—she has to act out the awful little allegory before she is free of it." How does this commentary by the poet influence your reading of the poem?

✶ *Rite of Passage*

Sharon Olds

Sharon Olds (b. 1942) was born in San Francisco and was raised, as she describes it, "as a hellfire Calvinist." She received a BA from Stanford University and a PhD from Columbia University, and has taught at New York University since 1987. Olds has published several collections of poems to considerable acclaim. Her first collection, *Satan Says* (1980), won the San Francisco Poetry Center Award, and *The Dead and the Living* (1981) won the 1983 Lamont Poetry Prize and the National Book Critics Circle Award. Nine additional collections of her work have been published in English, and her poems have been widely translated. Her most recent volume, *One Secret Thing*, was published in 2008. In "Rite of Passage," Olds reveals a critical rite of passage for a young man: the birthday party.

As the guests arrive at my son's party
they gather in the living room—
short men, men in first grade
with smooth jaws and chins.
Hands in pockets, they stand around   5
jostling, jockeying for place, small fights
breaking out and calming. One says to another
How old are you? Six. I'm seven. So?

They eye each other, seeing themselves
tiny in the other's pupils. They clear their   10
throats a lot, a room of small bankers,
they fold their arms and frown. *I could beat you
up*, a seven says to a six,
the dark cake, round and heavy as a
turret, behind them on the table. My son,   15
freckles like specks of nutmeg on his cheeks,
chest narrow as the balsa keel of a
model boat, long hands
cool and thin as the day they guided him
out of me, speaks up as a host   20
for the sake of the group.
We could easily kill a two-year-old,
he says in his clear voice. The other
men agree, they clear their throats
like Generals, they relax and get down to   25
playing war, celebrating my son's life.

[1975]

. . . .

Exploring the Text

1. The first two lines of "Rite of Passage" establish the setting and the speaker's relationship to the children in the poem. How does the setting contribute to the poem's meaning?

2. What is ironic about calling first grade boys "short men" (l. 3)? What later details contribute to this image? What point is Olds trying to make with this irony?

3. Identify the similes in the poem. Why are they especially fitting to "Rite of Passage"? What is their collective effect?

4. Three lines in the poem — "*How old are you? Six. I'm seven. So?*" (l. 8); "*I could beat you up*" (ll. 12–13); and "*We could easily kill a two-year-old*" (l. 22) — appear in italics. What purpose do the italics serve? Why is it important that the speaker's own son speaks line 22?

5. What do you make of the juxtaposition of "playing war" and "celebrating my son's life" in the final line? What other contrasts does Olds emphasize through juxtaposition? How are these contrasts a commentary on rites of passage in children's lives?

6. Is Olds being serious with this title or ironic?

7. What is the speaker's attitude toward the rite of passage she is observing? Does her attitude toward her son differ from her attitude toward the whole situation? What overall tone results?

✳ *Marks*

Linda Pastan

As a child growing up in the Bronx, Linda Pastan (b. 1932) wanted to be a writer but recalls: "I don't think I knew that real people could be 'writers' until much later." She earned a bachelor's degree at Radcliffe College and an MA at Brandeis University. Pastan published her first work, *A Perfect Circle of Sun*, in 1971. Since then, she's published twelve collections of poems and several essays, including *The Five Stages of Grief* (1978); *PM/AM: New and Selected Poems* (1982), nominated for the National Book Award; *The Imperfect Paradise* (1988), nominated for the Los Angeles Times Book Prize; *Carnival Evening: New and Selected Poems 1968–1998* (1998), a nominee for the National Book Award; and, most recently, *Queen of a Rainy Country* (2006). In addition, she was poet laureate of Maryland for five years. Pastan's poetry is often a unique blend of the personal and the objective; in "Marks," she uses the conceit of a report card to describe the relationships within a family.

My husband gives me an A
for last night's supper,
an incomplete for my ironing,
a B plus in bed.
My son says I am average,   5
an average mother, but if
I put my mind to it
I could improve.
My daughter believes
in Pass/Fail and tells me   10
I pass. Wait 'til they learn
I'm dropping out.

[1978]

Exploring the Text

1. What do the assigned marks and the type of grading system reveal about the relationship the speaker believes she has with each family member?
2. How do the denotations and connotations of the word *marks* contribute to the meaning of the poem? Why do you think Pastan called her poem "Marks" rather than "Report Card" or "Grades"?
3. How do you interpret the speaker's warning that she is "dropping out" (l. 12)? What do you think the speaker would like to change in her home and family life?

How does the fact that she refers to family members by their relationship rather than their name contribute to the point she is making?

4. How does Pastan inject sly humor into the poem? For instance, what is the effect of the repetition "average, / an average mother" (ll. 5–6)? Find other examples of humor that are amusing or sarcastic. What purpose might the speaker achieve by approaching her situation with some measure of humor?

5. Identify the poem's tone. What does the tone suggest will be the outcome of the speaker's "dropping out"?

MARY OLIVER

Mary Oliver (b. 1935) was born in Maple Heights, an affluent suburb of Cleveland. She attended The Ohio State University and Vassar College, but did not complete her degree. Nonetheless, she has held several teaching positions at universities, including Bennington College. Oliver published her first volume, *No Voyage, and Other Poems*, at the age of twenty-eight, and in 1984 won the Pulitzer Prize with *American Primitive* (1983). Following a period of silence, she published a considerable body of prose and verse between 1990 and 2006, winning the Christopher Award and the L. L. Winship/PEN New England Award for *House of Light* (1990), and the National Book Award for *New and Selected Poems* (1992). These were followed by *White Pine* (1994), *West Wind* (1997), *Winter Hours: Prose, Prose Poems, and Poems* (1999), *Owls and Other Fantasies: Poems and Essays* (2003), *Why I Wake Early* (2004), and *Thirst* (2006). The sense of community with nature is ever-present in her work, as in "Wild Geese," a poem exploring the place of humankind in "the family of things."

You do not have to be good.
You do not have to walk on your knees
for a hundred miles through the desert, repenting.
You only have to let the soft animal of your body
    love what it loves.
Tell me about despair, yours, and I will tell you mine.   5
Meanwhile the world goes on.
Meanwhile the sun and the clear pebbles of the rain
are moving across the landscapes,
over the prairies and the deep trees,
the mountains and the rivers.   10
Meanwhile the wild geese, high in the clean blue air,
are heading home again.

Whoever you are, no matter how lonely,
the world offers itself to your imagination,
calls to you like the wild geese, harsh and exciting —   15
over and over announcing your place
in the family of things.

[1986]

Exploring the Text

1. Why do you think Oliver chose to address readers directly as "You" in the opening lines of her poem? What effect does this have on your reading of the poem?
2. Even in the absence of a regular rhyme scheme or rhythm, the language of this poem seems to have an incantatory or hypnotic quality. How does Oliver achieve this effect?
3. Why does Oliver compare the way the world calls to us with the call of wild geese? What do wild geese represent in this poem? Why is it important that they "are heading home again" (l. 12)? Are the geese metaphorical? What might Oliver be suggesting about homing instincts in both birds and humans?
4. What does the phrase "no matter how lonely" (l. 13) suggest about the speaker's assumptions regarding her audience? What does the phrase suggest about the poem's purpose? How does that description link to the opening sentence?
5. How do you interpret the line "the world offers itself to your imagination" (l. 14)?
6. How does the nature imagery throughout this poem help us understand what Oliver means by "the family of things" (l. 17)? Overall, do you find this poem sad or hopeful?

Pause

Eamon Grennan

Eamon Grennan (b. 1941) was born into a Roman Catholic family in Dublin. He earned a bachelor's degree in English and Italian from University College, Dublin, and a PhD in English from Harvard University. He started teaching at Vassar College in 1974, and it was not until he returned to Ireland in 1977 that he began writing poetry for publication. His first collection, *Wildly for Days*, appeared in 1983 and was followed by *What Light There Is* (1987), a collection supplemented by *What Light There Is and Other Poems* (1989)—a finalist for a Los Angeles Times Book Prize. Since then, he has published a new collection every two or three years, including *Still Life with Waterfall* (2002), *The Quick of It* (2005), and his most recent collection, *Matter of Fact* (2008). Grennan currently lives in the United States, is teaching at Vassar, and spends much of his free time in the west of Ireland, returning there annually for what he describes as "voice transfusions." "Pause," which first appeared in the *New Yorker* in 1993, centers on a parent's experience of separation from a young child.

The weird containing stillness of the neighbourhood
just before the school bus brings the neighbourhood kids
home in the middle of the cold afternoon: a moment
of pure waiting, anticipation, before the outbreak of anything,
when everything seems just, seems *justified*, just hanging   5
in the wings, about to happen, and in your mind you see
the flashing lights flare amber to scarlet, and your daughter
in her blue jacket and white-fringed sapphire hat
step gingerly down and out into our world again
and hurry through silence and snow-grass   10
as the bus door sighs shut
and her own front door flies open and she finds you
behind it, father-in-waiting, the stillness in bits
and the common world restored as you bend
to touch her, take her hat and coat from the floor   15
where she's dropped them, hear the live voice of her
filling every crack. In the pause
before all this happens, you know something
about the shape of the life you've chosen to live
between the silence of almost infinite possibility and that   20
explosion of things as they are — those vast unanswerable
intrusions of love and disaster, or just the casual scatter
of your child's winter clothes on the hall floor.

                                                                                          [1993]

Exploring the Text

1. Who is doing the pausing referred to in the title of Grennan's poem? Why is this important to the poem's meaning? Would a different title — such as "Father-in-Waiting" — have changed your reading?
2. What is the "weird containing stillness" (l. 1) that sets the scene for the rest of the poem? How does this description along with the repetition of "just" and its derivatives establish an atmosphere? Where does the poem shift from "a moment / of pure waiting" (ll. 3–4) to action?
3. How do the denotations and connotations of the words "outbreak" (l. 4), "explosion" (l. 21), and "disaster" (l. 22) contribute to a reader's sense that this is more than a poem about a parent meeting a daughter at the front door after school? What might Grennan be suggesting with these words?

4. Why do you think Grennan uses "amber" and "scarlet" (l. 7) to describe the lights of the school bus rather than the more commonplace "yellow" and "red"? What about the word "sapphire" (l. 8) rather than "blue" to describe the girl's hat? What do the connotations of these words suggest about the poem's theme?
5. Why does the speaker use the second-person point of view in this poem? It is not direct address, yet he writes about "your daughter" (l. 7) and "as you bend" (l. 14). What is the effect? In only one place does he use the first person, "our" (l. 9). What does this shift suggest?
6. Notice how Grennan juxtaposes the most concrete details with abstractions. What effect does this contrast have on the tone of the poem?
7. What is the speaker referring to when he talks of "the shape of the life you've chosen to live" (l. 19)? Do you find this poem a celebration of being a parent or a warning? If it's a warning, what is it trying to warn us about?
8. Why is this a poem and not prose? It consists of two sentences broken into lines, so what makes it a poem?

The Hammock

LI-YOUNG LEE

Li-Young Lee (b. 1957) was born to an elite Chinese family. His great-grandfather had been China's first republican president (1912–1916), and his father had been a personal physician to Mao Zedong. Despite the latter association, his family fled from China when the People's Republic was established in 1948, settling in Jakarta, where Lee was born. An increasing anti-Chinese movement in Indonesia drove the family from the country, and after a futile search for a permanent home in turbulent Asia, they settled in the United States in 1964. Lee was educated at the University of Pittsburgh, where he began to write. He later attended the University of Arizona and the State University of New York at Brockport. Lee's first collection of poetry was *Rose* (1986), which won the Delmore Schwartz Memorial Poetry Award from New York University. This was followed by *The City in Which I Love You* (1990), which won the Lamont Poetry Prize; *Book of My Nights* (2001); and his most recent publication, *Behind My Eyes* (2008). He has also published a personal memoir, *The Wingéd Seed: A Remembrance* (1995). Like much of Lee's poetry, "The Hammock," first published in the *Kenyon Review*, explores the interplay of the eternal and the everyday.

When I lay my head in my mother's lap
I think how day hides the stars,
the way I lay hidden once, waiting
inside my mother's singing to herself. And I remember
how she carried me on her back   5

between home and the kindergarten,
once each morning and once each afternoon.

I don't know what my mother's thinking.

When my son lays his head in my lap, I wonder:
Do his father's kisses keep his father's worries   10
from becoming his? I think, *Dear God*, and remember
there are stars we haven't heard from yet:
They have so far to arrive. *Amen,*
I think, and I feel almost comforted.

I've no idea what my child is thinking.   15

Between two unknowns, I live my life.
Between my mother's hopes, older than I am
by coming before me, and my child's wishes, older than I am
by outliving me. And what's it like?
Is it a door, and good-bye on either side?   20
A window, and eternity on either side?
Yes, and a little singing between two great rests.

[2000]

. . . .

Exploring the Text

1. What are the connotations of the word *hammock*? How do these connotations contribute to your understanding of the poem?
2. Find the visual and tactile images in the poem. What do these images suggest about the relationships described? Pay careful attention to the descriptions of physical positions.
3. Why do you think the poet chose to italicize the words "*Dear God*" (l. 11) and "*Amen*" (l. 13)? What does this tell you about the speaker's attitude toward his subject? How does this point the way to the poem's tone?
4. Why do the stars "have so far to arrive" (l. 13)? Those stars are in the same stanza as the father's "kisses" (l. 10) and "worries" (l. 10). How might the three be related?
5. What evidence is there in the poem—both words and images—of the speaker's tentativeness? For example, he feels "almost comforted" in line 14. He asks two questions at the very end and replies, "Yes" (l. 22)—but which question is he responding to? What is the source of this uncertainty? Does the speaker ultimately get beyond it, embrace it, or resign himself to it?
6. How did you interpret the poem's final stanza? What are the "two unknowns" (l. 16)? What are the "two great rests" (l. 22)? What do these images suggest about how the speaker lives his life?
7. Examine the structure of this poem by comparing stanzas one and three to stanzas two and four. How does the shape of the poem reflect its title and theme?

Cousins

KEVIN YOUNG

Born in 1970 in Nebraska, Kevin Young is the author of six collections of poetry. He holds a BA from Harvard University and an MFA in creative writing from Brown University, and is currently the Atticus Haygood Professor of English and Creative Writing at Emory University. He has received many awards and honors, including a Stegner Fellowship in Poetry at Stanford University, a Guggenheim Fellowship, and a National Endowment for the Arts Literature Fellowship. His poetry collection *Jelly Roll: A Blues* was a finalist for the National Book Award in 2003; *For the Confederate Dead* won the 2007 Byron's Quill Award for Poetry. Young, who was a member of the African American poetry group the Dark Room Collective, edited the anthologies *Giant Steps: The New Generation of African American Writers* (2000) and *Blue Poems* (2003). His poetry and essays have appeared in both literary and mainstream publications, such as the *New Yorker*, the *New York Times Book Review*, the *Paris Review*, and *Callaloo*. "Cousins"—from Young's most recent poetry collection, *Dear Darkness* (2008)—reflects the influence of the oral tradition.

This is for Tonia who learned to ride
a boy's bike at four, filling its basket
with a Chihuahua smart enough to open
doors—this is for Angela who taught me
to kiss but denies even remembering it—   5
for Big Red, born the color of Louisiana
dust, the rusty dirt we blew up
come Christmas when fireworks stands
slanted like makeshift roadside mangers.

This is for two sides of one family,   10
two towns full of folks I'm related to
or soon will be, summers finding girls
cute till someone says *That's your cousin,
boy*, then not looking again—this is for
all those names, Kiris & Makarios,   15
Omar & Cheryl, even for Jarvis
who broke toys I was too old to own,
then asked *Who broke dat car?*

to throw me off his trail. For Nikki
who cried whenever I did, sad   20
for the world's aches, mine, who worried

aloud in the movie that Indiana
Jones would *get deaded* till I explained
he can't, he's the hero. This is for Keith
in that unsunned room he hanged   25

himself like the paintings he masterpieced
& my grandmother's wood-paneled
walls still keep up — for his little sister Jamie
pigtailed & crying at his grave, begging
her brother back — Jamie who once refused   30
to sit by me, the older cousin never seen
before — Jamie who wouldn't eat

crawfish until I peeled some & she warmed
& laughed & ate & informed a roomful of family
Kevin's my cousin — yes Jamie, I am yours   35
& Phyllis's & her baby Brittany's
who ain't a baby no more, just a womanish
four-year-old going on forty — I am cousin
to her little brother who carries Keith's name,
carries this word, *cousin*, that once   40

rested on our tongues before the story of ships,
before words new as worlds, tribes
turned to regret — you can hear it — the steady hum
of *cuz*, say it till it buzzes the blood, gathers
like the wasps who kept returning, pressing   45
against screens in my grandmother's gaping house
no matter how often we let them out.

                                            [2008]

. . . .

Exploring the Text

1. What is the effect of the repeated phrase "This is for" (ll. 1, 4, 10, 14, and 24)?
   How does the phrase take on greater significance as the poem develops? Why is it
   important that the speaker actually lists the names of his cousins?
2. Young takes us from what seems to be an affectionate remembrance of a big
   family to a traumatic event. Why? What effect does he achieve by this surprise?
   Explain why you think this strategy makes the suicide seem either commonplace
   or more shocking.
3. How old do you think the speaker is? What period of his life is he remembering?
4. Consider Young's close examination of the word *cousin* — its sound and shape.
   How is its meaning slightly different each time he uses it? What is the effect of

the unusual syntax of "I am cousin / to her little brother" (ll. 38–39); "this word, *cousin*, that once / rested on our tongues before the story of ships" (ll. 40–41); and "*cuz*, say it till it buzzes the blood" (l. 44)?

5. What do you think the speaker is referring to with "ships" (l. 41) and "tribes" (l. 42)? What does this historical dimension add to a poem that begins as a personal remembrance?

6. Discuss unusual uses of language in this poem, such as turning a noun into a verb, or including slang. What do these examples contribute to your understanding of the poem?

7. The poem concludes with a return to the immediate family. How do you interpret the simile in the final three lines?

8. The poem has six sections, though the divisions are often in midsentence. What sequence of ideas or images do you see in this division? Consider why Young stops us where he does. Is he asking us to look back, pause, or connect? How does the poem build?

Paired Poems

. . . .

✦ *The Pomegranate*

Eavan Boland

Eavan Boland (b. 1944) spent the first six years of her life in Dublin, moving to London when her father was appointed Irish ambassador, and then to New York when he was appointed president of the UN General Assembly. She recalls that she felt deprived of her Irish roots — particularly in London, where anti-Irish sentiment was rife. She writes of this experience in "An Irish Child in England: 1951," exemplified by "the teacher in the London convent who, / when I pronounced 'I amn't' in the classroom / turned and said — 'you're not in Ireland now.'" Boland returned to Dublin for college, earning a BA in English and Latin from Trinity College Dublin. She has taught at Stanford University since 1996. Boland's first collection, *23 Poems* (1966), met with mixed reviews, but she established her reputation with *In Her Own Image* (1980). She has published regularly since, her most comprehensive volumes being *An Origin Like Water: Collected Poems, 1967–1987* (1996) and *New Collected Poems* (2008), and has won several awards, in addition to being awarded honorary degrees both in the United States and in Ireland. She is a feminist and a poet but, she maintains, not a feminist poet. She sees a fundamental difference between the "ethic" of feminism and the "aesthetic" of poetry, arguing that feminism is a definite moral position, whereas poetry, like all art, begins where certainty ends. Such uncertainty, together with her relationship with her daughter, underpins the themes of "The Pomegranate."

The only legend I have ever loved is
the story of a daughter lost in hell.
And found and rescued there.
Love and blackmail are the gist of it.
Ceres[1] and Persephone[2] the names.   5
And the best thing about the legend is
I can enter it anywhere. And have.
As a child in exile in
a city of fogs and strange consonants,
I read it first and at first I was   10
an exiled child in the crackling dusk of
the underworld, the stars blighted. Later
I walked out in a summer twilight
searching for my daughter at bed-time.
When she came running I was ready   15
to make any bargain to keep her.
I carried her back past whitebeams
and wasps and honey-scented buddleias.
But I was Ceres then and I knew
winter was in store for every leaf   20
on every tree on that road.
Was inescapable for each one we passed.
And for me.
                    It is winter
and the stars are hidden.   25
I climb the stairs and stand where I can see
my child asleep beside her teen magazines,
her can of Coke, her plate of uncut fruit.

---

[1]Roman goddess of agriculture; Demeter in Greek mythology — Eds.
[2]Greek goddess of the underworld and fertility, and daughter of Demeter; Proserpina in Roman mythology. In the Persephone myth, she is kidnapped by Hades, the god of the underworld, who takes her as his wife. In her grief, Demeter refuses to allow seeds to grow. To save mankind from starvation, Zeus orders his brother Hades to release Persephone. Before she leaves, Hades tricks her into eating some pomegranate seeds, knowing that whoever eats or drinks in the underworld must remain there for eternity. As a compromise, Persephone has to spend six months out of every year in the underworld. During the months Persephone is with her mother, the earth flourishes in spring and summer. When she returns to the underworld, Demeter mourns and the earth turns to autumn and winter. The myth is also read as a comment on marriage. — Eds.

The pomegranate! How did I forget it?
She could have come home and been safe   30
and ended the story and all
our heart-broken searching but she reached
out a hand and plucked a pomegranate.
She put out her hand and pulled down
the French sound for apple and   35
the noise of stone and the proof
that even in the place of death,
at the heart of legend, in the midst
of rocks full of unshed tears
ready to be diamonds by the time   40
the story was told, a child can be
hungry. I could warn her. There is still a chance.
The rain is cold. The road is flint-coloured.
The suburb has cars and cable television.
The veiled stars are above ground.   45
It is another world. But what else
can a mother give her daughter but such
beautiful rifts in time?
If I defer the grief I will diminish the gift.
The legend will be hers as well as mine.   50
She will enter it. As I have.
She will wake up. She will hold
the papery flushed skin in her hand.
And to her lips. I will say nothing.

[1994]

Exploring the Text

1. How does the line "Love and blackmail are the gist of it" (l. 4) suggest that the speaker interprets this myth?
2. In what ways has the speaker "enter[ed]" (l. 7) the myth in her own life?
3. What turn does the word "But" signal (l. 19)? Even though the poem is not divided into verses, what shift does this word mark?
4. What are the "beautiful rifts in time" (l. 48)?
5. How do you interpret the description in lines 36–42, detailing the conditions under which a child can still be hungry?
6. What does the speaker suggest about the role of a parent, particularly a mother, when she concludes, "I will say nothing" (l. 54)?
7. Of what significance is the age of the daughter in this poem?
8. Note how skillfully Boland shuttles between short sentences — even fragments — and longer, more descriptive sentences. Which dominates the ending of the poem? What is the effect of this pattern?

The Bistro Styx

RITA DOVE

Rita Dove (b. 1952) was born in Akron, Ohio, at a time when racial barriers were being torn down. Her father was the first African American chemist to be hired by the Goodyear Tire Corporation. She graduated summa cum laude from Miami (Ohio) University and won a Fulbright scholarship. In 1980, Dove published her first collection, *The Yellow House on the Corner*, and has written steadily ever since. Her published work includes eight collections of poems; a verse drama, *The Darker Face of the Earth* (1994); a collection of short stories, *Fifth Sunday* (1985); and one novel, *Through the Ivory Gate* (1992). *Thomas and Beulah* (1986) won the Pulitzer Prize for Poetry; *On the Bus with Rosa Parks* (1999) was a finalist for the National Book Critics Circle Award. She is the only African American to be named poet laureate of the United States, a title she held from 1993 to 1995. Her versatility, clearly demonstrated in "The Bistro Styx," has made her one of the most respected voices in twentieth-century American poetry.

She was thinner, with a mannered gauntness
as she paused just inside the double
glass doors to survey the room, silvery cape
billowing dramatically behind her. *What's this,*

I thought, lifting a hand until   5
she nodded and started across the parquet;
that's when I saw she was dressed all in gray,
from a kittenish cashmere skirt and cowl

down to the graphite signature of her shoes.
"Sorry I'm late," she panted, though   10
she wasn't, sliding into the chair, her cape

tossed off in a shudder of brushed steel.
We kissed. Then I leaned back to peruse
my blighted child, this wary aristocratic mole.

"How's business?" I asked, and hazarded   15
a motherly smile to keep from crying out:
Are you content to conduct your life
as a cliché and, what's worse,

an anachronism, the brooding artist's demimonde?
Near the rue Princesse they had opened   20
a gallery *cum* souvenir shop which featured
fuzzy off-color Monets next to his acrylics, no doubt,

plus bearded African drums and the occasional miniature
gargoyle from Notre Dame the Great Artist had
carved at breakfast with a pocket knife.   25

"Tourists love us. The Parisians, of course"—
she blushed—"are amused, though not without
a certain admiration . . ."
                          The Chateaubriand

arrived on a bone-white plate, smug and absolute   30
in its fragrant crust, a black plug steaming
like the heart plucked from the chest of a worthy enemy;
one touch with her fork sent pink juices streaming.

"Admiration for what?" Wine, a bloody
Pinot Noir, brought color to her cheeks. "Why,   35
the aplomb with which we've managed
to support our Art"—meaning he'd convinced

her to pose nude for his appalling canvases,
faintly futuristic landscapes strewn
with carwrecks and bodies being chewed   40

by rabid cocker spaniels. "I'd like to come by
the studio," I ventured, "and see the new stuff."
"Yes, if you wish . . ." A delicate rebuff

before the warning: "He dresses all
in black now. Me, he drapes in blues and carmine—   45
and even though I think it's kinda cute,
in company I tend toward more muted shades."

She paused and had the grace
to drop her eyes. She did look ravishing,
spookily insubstantial, a lipstick ghost on tissue,   50
or as if one stood on a fifth-floor terrace

peering through a fringe of rain at Paris'
dreaming chimney pots, each sooty issue
wobbling skyward in an ecstatic oracular spiral.

"And he never thinks of food. I wish   55
I didn't have to plead with him to eat. . . ." Fruit
and cheese appeared, arrayed on leaf-green dishes.

I stuck with café crème. "This Camembert's
so ripe," she joked, "it's practically grown hair,"
mucking a golden glob complete with parsley sprig   60
onto a heel of bread. Nothing seemed to fill

her up: She swallowed, sliced into a pear,
speared each tear-shaped lavaliere
and popped the dripping mess into her pretty mouth.
Nowhere the bright tufted fields, weighted   65

vines and sun poured down out of the south.
"But are you happy?" Fearing, I whispered it
quickly. "What? You know, Mother"—

she bit into the starry rose of a fig—
"one really should try the fruit here."   70
I've lost her, I thought, and called for the bill.

[1995]

. . . .

Exploring the Text

1. What does the title tell you right away? Is Dove mocking the myth? playing with it? trying to deny its power?
2. What does the speaker mean by her description of her daughter as "my blighted child, this wary aristocratic mole" (l. 14)? What specific details further on add to the speaker's perception of her daughter?
3. Why do you think Dove set this poem in a restaurant, where the visiting mother meets her daughter—and pays the bill? Consider what different effect setting it in the daughter's apartment or the mother's hotel room might have had.
4. What is the mother's opinion of the daughter's boyfriend/artist? Cite specific passages to support your response.
5. Consider the descriptions of the food—the Chateaubriand, wine, Camembert, bread, parsley, and pear. Do you think these are simply colorful details Dove chose, or do they work together to create a particular effect?
6. Since only two clauses in the poem are italicized—"*What's this*" (l. 4) and "*I've lost her*" (l. 71)—they seem to be tied together. How? Try describing the point these few words make.
7. The poem describes how the speaker "hazarded / a motherly smile" (ll. 15–16) and "ventured" (l. 42) to elicit an invitation to the artist's studio. Why does she do these things? What do these verbs suggest about the mother's relationship with her daughter?
8. How old do you imagine the daughter in this poem to be? Why is her age significant?

Focus on Comparison and Contrast

1. In both poems, the mother—who is the speaker—identifies with the mythological mother Demeter/Ceres. What common concerns about their daughters do these mothers share?

2. How do the two mothers' responses to their daughters differ? What do you think these differences reflect in terms of each mother's character?
3. What role does food and eating play in the two poems?
4. How are these two mother-daughter relationships reflected in the tone of the poems? Consider the following lines: "If I defer the grief I will diminish the gift" (l. 49) from "Pomegranate," and *"I've lost her*, I thought, and called for the bill" (l. 71) from "The Bistro Styx."
5. Imagine that these two mothers met over a cup of coffee. What would they say to each other? Construct a brief dialogue, or break off into pairs and role-play the conversation.

Writing Assignment

"The Pomegranate" by Eavan Boland and "The Bistro Styx" by Rita Dove both make allusions to the myth of Persephone. Read the poems carefully. Then write an essay in which you compare and contrast the mother-daughter relationship in each poem, analyzing how Boland and Dove use or interpret this myth to convey these relationships.

A Family

JACOB LAWRENCE

Born in Atlantic City, Jacob Lawrence (1917–2000) moved with his mother and siblings to Harlem when he was thirteen. Despite serious financial hardship, his mother was meticulous in creating a beautifully decorated home, and Lawrence attributes his love of color to those childhood surroundings. At that time it was almost impossible for African Americans to enter American art schools, and most black artists learned their craft at Harlem workshops. Lawrence's formal education ended when he abandoned high school at the age of sixteen; he attended art classes in Harlem, learned from African American artist Charles Alston, and—at Alston's suggestion—attended classes given by sculptor Augusta Savage at the Harlem Community Art Center. One of the most important artists of the twentieth century, Lawrence specialized in depicting scenes from African American life and history. His most famous work is a series of sixty paintings chronicling the journey of African Americans from the rural South to the industrial North, entitled *Migration of the Negro*. The series made Lawrence nationally famous at the age of twenty-three. In *A Family*, we see Lawrence tackling a subject somewhat less historical and more intimate.

Exploring the Text

1. Look at the Jacob Lawrence painting, *A Family*, for five full minutes. Notice every detail and object, and consider how each detail contributes to the whole. What is the mood of this painting? How does it make you feel?

A Family (1943, gouache, ink and pencil, with glue on paper, 22⅝ × 15⅝ in.)

2. Study the iconography (the objects in the painting) to find clues to the kind of life this family leads within these four walls. What does the broom and dustpan suggest? the pans hanging neatly over the stove? the coat hanging on a peg? the simple eating utensils? the food on the serving platter?

3. Lawrence employed a tempera technique (pigment mixed with a binder of egg yolk and water) with a cubist-like style. Though modern, his work was grounded in realism and traditional techniques of painting the human figure. What do the stylized images of the parents and children suggest about the family Lawrence depicts here?

4. In a posthumous review of Lawrence's work, Michael Kimmelman, art critic for the *New York Times*, commented on both the formal rigor and the painting's "emotional authenticity." How would you characterize the emotions of this family meal? What do the mother looking down at the baby, the boy reaching across the table for food, and the girl talking with the father imply about relationships in this family?

Conversation

The Lure and Language of Food

More than basic survival, food transmits family values and history, culture and tradition. Noticing how a person or family shares, prepares, eats, and imagines food is likely to give us complex insight into who they are. In many ways, families communicate through food as both occasion and message. Family gatherings—whether a marriage, death, birthday, Saturday night supper, or Super Bowl Sunday—are usually marked by specific foods. While one family might eat pasta, another might eat grits; one Cobb salad, another tabbouleh; one eggs benedict, another ranchos huevos; one artisanal chevre, another Velveeta. Whatever is on the menu, our emotional associations with food are equally strong, as the chef and food writer M. F. K. Fisher describes: "Our three basic needs for food and security and love are so mixed and mingled and entwined that we cannot straightforwardly think of one without the other." So, though the term "comfort food" might have different meanings to different people, we can all name one, and it will probably hit pretty close to home. In the following texts, we explore this strong connection between food and family. Bon appétit!

Texts

Vincent van Gogh, *The Potato-Eaters* (painting)

Ralph Ellison, "I Yam What I Am" (fiction)

Naomi Shihab Nye, "My Father and the Figtree" (poetry)

Laura Esquivel, "January: Christmas Rolls" (fiction)

Lisa Parker, "Snapping Beans" (poetry)

Chris Offutt, "Brain Food" (nonfiction)

Geeta Kothari, "If You Are What You Eat, Then What Am I?" (nonfiction)

The Potato-Eaters

Vincent van Gogh

Born in the Netherlands in 1853, Vincent van Gogh was a Postimpressionist painter whose work was not appreciated during his lifetime, but whose paintings are now among the most recognized and highly valued in the world. Before becoming a painter, van Gogh worked as an art dealer, a missionary, and a teacher. His personal life was a series of unhappy incidents and bouts of mental illness; his only sustained relationship was with his brother Theo. Van Gogh died in 1890 as the result of a self-inflicted gunshot wound. *The Potato-Eaters* was painted in 1885 and is considered van Gogh's first major work.

Questions

1. What do you think is the relationship among the characters? How would you describe their attitude toward their meal? What makes you say so?
2. Do a close reading of the painting. What do you notice about its composition—that is, how the figures are arranged on the canvas? Consider where the light comes from, as well as any shapes that seem to repeat themselves. How do these style elements comment on the characters in the painting? Find the painting

The Potato-Eaters (1885, oil on canvas, 32 × 45 in.)

online and look at the colors. What do they tell you? How do all of these elements help develop an argument?

3. Van Gogh once said that he tried to paint his subjects with deep feeling but without sentimentality. He wanted to convey the idea that his subjects had "used the same hands with which they now take food from the plate to dig the earth . . . and had thus earned their meal honestly." Do you think he succeeded in honoring the peasants in the picture, or does their grotesque appearance—he also said he wanted their faces to be "the color of a good, dusty potato, unpeeled naturally"—suggest a different result?

I Yam What I Am

RALPH ELLISON

> Born in Oklahoma, Ralph Waldo Ellison (1913–1994) studied music at Tuskegee Institute before moving to New York City, where he became the protégé of author Richard Wright. Ellison's most famous work, *The Invisible Man*, was published in 1952. It won the National Book Award in 1953, and has become a central text defining the African American experience. In the following excerpt from *Invisible Man*, Ellison's southern-born protagonist grapples with the complex connotations of class and heritage that accompany certain foods.

The streets were covered with ice and soot-flecked snow and from above a feeble sun filtered through the haze. I walked with my head down, feeling the biting air. And yet I was hot, burning with an inner fever. I barely raised my eyes until a car, passing with a thudding of skid chains whirled completely around on the ice, then turned cautiously and thudded off again.

I walked slowly on, blinking my eyes in the chill air, my mind a blur with the hot inner argument continuing. The whole of Harlem seemed to fall apart in the swirl of snow. I imagined I was lost and for a moment there was an eerie quiet. I imagined I heard the fall of snow upon snow. What did it mean? I walked, my eyes focused into the endless succession of barber shops, beauty parlors, confectioneries, luncheonettes, fish houses, and hog maw joints, walking close to the windows, the snowflakes lacing swift between, simultaneously forming a curtain, a veil, and stripping it aside. A flash of red and gold from a window filled with religious articles caught my eye. And behind the film of frost etching the glass I saw two brashly painted plaster images of Mary and Jesus surrounded by dream books, love powders, God-Is-Love signs, money-drawing oil and plastic dice. A black statue of a nude Nubian slave grinned out at me from beneath a turban of gold. I passed on to a window decorated with switches of wiry false hair, ointments guaranteed to produce the miracle of whitening black skin. "You too can be truly beautiful," a sign proclaimed. "Win greater happiness with whiter complexion. Be outstanding in your social set."

I hurried on, suppressing a savage urge to push my fist through the pane. A wind was rising, the snow thinning. Where would I go? To a movie? Could I sleep there? I ignored the windows now and walked along, becoming aware that I was muttering to myself again. Then far down at the corner I saw an old man warming his hands against the sides of an odd-looking wagon, from which a stove pipe reeled off a thin spiral of smoke that drifted the odor of baking yams slowly to me, bringing a stab of swift nostalgia. I stopped as though struck by a shot, deeply inhaling, remembering, my mind surging back, back. At home we'd bake them in the hot coals of the fireplace, had carried them cold to school for lunch; munched them secretly, squeezing the sweet pulp from the soft peel as we hid from the teacher behind the largest book, the *World's Geography*. Yes, and we'd loved them candied, or baked in a cobbler, deep-fat fried in a pocket of dough, or roasted with pork and glazed with the well-browned fat; had chewed them raw—yams and years ago. More yams than years ago, though the time seemed endlessly expanded, stretched thin as the spiraling smoke beyond all recall.

I moved again. "Get yo' hot, baked Car'lina yam," he called. At the corner the old man, wrapped in an army overcoat, his feet covered with gunny sacks, his head in a knitted cap, was puttering with a stack of paper bags. I saw a crude sign on the side of the wagon proclaiming YAMS, as I walked flush into the warmth thrown by the coals that glowed in a grate underneath.

"How much are your yams?" I said, suddenly hungry.   5

"They ten cents and they sweet," he said, his voice quavering with age. "These ain't none of them binding ones neither. These here is real, sweet, yaller yams. How many?"

"One," I said. "If they're that good, one should be enough."

He gave me a searching glance. There was a tear in the corner of his eye. He chuckled and opened the door of the improvised oven, reaching gingerly with his gloved hand. The yams, some bubbling with syrup, lay on a wire rack above glowing coals that leaped to low blue flame when struck by the draft of air. The flash of warmth set my face aglow as he removed one of the yams and shut the door.

"Here you are, suh," he said, starting to put the yam into a bag.

"Never mind the bag, I'm going to eat it. Here . . ."   10

"Thanks." He took the dime. "If that ain't a sweet one, I'll give you another one free of charge."

I knew that it was sweet before I broke it; bubbles of brown syrup had burst the skin.

"Go ahead and break it," the old man said. "Break it and I'll give you some butter since you gon' eat it right here. Lots of folks takes 'em home. They got their own butter at home."

I broke it, seeing the sugary pulp steaming in the cold.

"Hold it over here," he said. He took a crock from a rack on the side of the   15
wagon. "Right here."

I held it, watching him pour a spoonful of melted butter over the yam and the butter seeping in.

"Thanks."

"You welcome. And I'll tell you something."

"What's that?" I said.

"If that ain't the best eating you had in a long time, I give you your money   20
back."

"You don't have to convince me," I said. "I can look at it and see it's good."

"You right, but everything what looks good ain't necessarily good," he said. "But these is."

I took a bite, finding it as sweet and hot as any I'd ever had, and was overcome with such a surge of homesickness that I turned away to keep my control. I walked along, munching the yam, just as suddenly overcome by an intense feeling of freedom — simply because I was eating while walking along the street. It was exhilarating. I no longer had to worry about who saw me or about what was proper. To hell with all that, and as sweet as the yam actually was, it became like nectar with the thought. If only someone who had known me at school or at home would come along and see me now. How shocked they'd be! I'd push them into a side street and smear their faces with the peel. What a group of people we were, I thought. Why, you could cause us the greatest humiliation simply by confronting us with something we liked. Not *all* of us, but so many. Simply by walking up and shaking a set of chitterlings or a well-boiled hog maw at them during the clear light of day! What consternation it would cause! And I saw myself advancing upon Bledsoe, standing bare of his false humility in the crowded lobby of Men's House, and seeing him there and him seeing me and ignoring me and me enraged and suddenly whipping out a foot or two of chitterlings raw, uncleaned and dripping sticky circles on the floor as I shake them in his face, shouting:

"Bledsoe, you're a shameless chitterling eater! I accuse you of relishing hog bowels! Ha! And not only do you eat them, you sneak and eat them in *private* when you think you're unobserved! You're a sneaking chitterling lover! I accuse you of indulging in a filthy habit, Bledsoe! Lug them out of there, Bledsoe! Lug them out so we can see! I accuse you before the eyes of the world!" And he lugs them out, yards of them, with mustard greens, and racks of pigs' ears, and pork chops and black-eyed peas with dull accusing eyes.

I let out a wild laugh, almost choking over the yam as the scene spun before   25
me. Why, with others present, it would be worse than if I had accused him of raping an old woman of ninety-nine years, weighing ninety pounds . . . blind in one eye and lame in the hip! Bledsoe would disintegrate, disinflate! With a profound sigh he'd drop his head in shame. He'd lose caste. The weekly newspapers would attack him. The captions over his picture: *Prominent Educator Reverts to Field Niggerism!* His rivals would denounce him as a bad example for the youth. Editorials would demand that he either recant or retire from public life. In the South his white folks would desert him; he would be discussed far and wide, and all of the trustees' money couldn't prop up his sagging prestige. He'd end up an exile washing dishes at the Automat. For down South he'd be unable to get a job on the honey wagon.

This is all very wild and childish, I thought, but to hell with being ashamed of what you liked. No more of that for me. I am what I am! I wolfed down the yam and ran back to the old man and handed him twenty cents, "Give me two more," I said.

"Sho, all you want, long as I got 'em. I can see you a serious yam eater, young fellow. You eating them right away?"

"As soon as you give them to me," I said.

"You want 'em buttered?"

"Please."   30

"Sho, that way you can get the most out of 'em. Yessuh," he said, handing over the yams, "I can see you one of these old-fashioned yam eaters."

"They're my birthmark," I said. "I yam what I am!"

"Then, you must be from South Car'lina," he said with a grin.

"South Carolina nothing, where I come from we really go for yams."

"Come back tonight or tomorrow if you can eat some more," he called after me.   35
"My old lady'll be out here with some hot sweet potato fried pies."

Hot fried pies, I thought sadly, moving away. I would probably have indigestion if I ate one—now that I no longer felt ashamed of the things I had always loved, I probably could no longer digest very many of them. What and how much had I lost by trying to do only what was expected of me instead of what I myself had wished to do? What a waste, what a senseless waste! But what of those things which you actually didn't like, not because you were not supposed to like them, not because to dislike them was considered a mark of refinement and education—but because you actually found them distasteful? The very idea annoyed me. How could you know? It involved a problem of choice. I would have to weigh many things carefully before deciding and there would be some things that would cause quite a bit of trouble, simply because I had never formed a personal attitude toward so much. I had accepted the accepted attitudes and it had made life seem simple . . .

But not yams, I had no problem concerning them and I would eat them whenever and wherever I took the notion. Continue on the yam level and life would be sweet—though somewhat yellowish. Yet the freedom to eat yams on the street was far less than I had expected upon coming to the city. An unpleasant taste bloomed in my mouth now as I bit the end of the yam and threw it into the street; it had been frost-bitten.

[1952]

Questions

1. What is the prevailing mood of the opening paragraphs of this excerpt? What is "the hot inner argument continuing" (para. 2)? How do these two initial paragraphs set the stage for the sentence in paragraph 3 that begins, "I stopped as though struck by a shot"?

2. Note the details Ellison provides to describe the yam. How does he appeal to all five senses? What connections to home and heritage does the yam evoke?

3. Paragraphs 23–25 deal with condemning Bledsoe, who expelled the protagonist from college. What foods does the protagonist allude to? What are the values that Bledsoe apparently associates with those foods?

4. What does the protagonist mean in the following description: "I walked along, munching the yam, just as suddenly overcome by an intense feeling of freedom" (para. 23)? How does something as simple as a yam bring on a feeling as complex as freedom?

5. In the second-to-last paragraph, the protagonist wrestles with the "problem of choice." Summarize what he means by the "problem of choice." Is he contradicting the feelings he has just articulated? qualifying them? Explain your response.

6. How do you interpret the ending?

My Father and the Figtree

NAOMI SHIHAB NYE

Poet, novelist, editor, and political activist Naomi Shihab Nye (b. 1952) is the daughter of a Palestinian father and an American mother. Her works for children include the picture book *Sitti's Secret* (1994) and the novel *Habibi* (1996). Her poetry collections include *Different Ways to Pray* (1980), *Fuel* (1998), *Nineteen Varieties of Gazelle: Poems of the Middle East* (2002), *You and Yours* (2005), and *Honeybee* (2008). Nye, who has been a visiting writer all over the world, describes herself as "a wandering poet." In the following poem from the collection *Different Ways to Pray*, the speaker chronicles changes in her father's life through his cultural associations with a fig tree.

For other fruits my father was indifferent.
He'd point at the cherry trees and say,
"See those? I wish they were figs."
In the evenings he sat by our beds
weaving folktales like vivid little scarves.   5
They always involved a figtree.
Even when it didn't fit, he'd stick it in.
Once Joha[1] was walking down the road
and he saw a figtree.
Or, he tied his camel to a figtree and went to sleep.   10
Or, later when they caught and arrested him,
his pockets were full of figs.

At age six I ate a dried fig and shrugged.
"That's not what I'm talking about!" he said,

---

[1]A trickster character in Middle East folktales.—EDS.

"I'm talking about a fig straight from the earth   15
gift of Allah!—on a branch so heavy
it touches the ground.
I'm talking about picking the largest, fattest,
    sweetest fig
in the world and putting it in my mouth."
(Here he'd stop and close his eyes.)   20

Years passed, we lived in many houses,
none had figtrees.
We had lima beans, zucchini, parsley, beets.
"Plant one!" my mother said,
but my father never did.   25
He tended garden half-heartedly, forgot to water,
let the okra get too big.
"What a dreamer he is. Look how many
things he starts and doesn't finish."

The last time he moved, I had a phone call,   30
my father, in Arabic, chanting a song
I'd never heard. "What's that?"
He took me out back to the new yard.
There, in the middle of Dallas, Texas,
a tree with the largest, fattest,   35
sweetest figs in the world.
"It's a figtree song!" he said,
plucking his fruits like ripe tokens,
emblems, assurance
of a world that was always his own.   40

[1980]

. . . .

Questions

1. Why the fig? Why is the speaker's father "indifferent" (l. 1) to other fruits? What is the special meaning of figs for him?
2. Why does the father refuse to plant a fig tree and instead "He tended garden half-heartedly, forgot to water, / let the okra get too big" (ll. 26–27)?
3. What are the different ages of the speaker in this poem? Why is the passage of time important to the impact of the poem?
4. Apart from two similes, Nye uses very little figurative language. What other resources of language does Nye use to give the poem its power?
5. How do you interpret the final two lines? Why are the figs "emblems, assurance / of a world that was always his own"?
6. Judging from this poem, in what ways is the father "a dreamer" (l. 28)?

January: Christmas Rolls

Laura Esquivel

Mexican author Laura Esquivel (b. 1950) began her career writing plays for her students when she was a kindergarten teacher. In *Like Water for Chocolate* (1990)—her best-selling first novel, which was released as a commercial film in 1993—she combines fiction writing and recipes. Other works include the novel *The Law of Love* (1996), which combines romance and science fiction, and the essay collection *Between Two Fires* (2000). Her most recent work is *Malinche* (2006), a historical novel. The following excerpt is the first chapter from *Like Water for Chocolate*.

Ingredients

❖

1 can of sardines

1/2 chorizo sausage

1 onion

oregano

1 can of chiles serranos

10 hard rolls

❖

Preparation

Take care to chop the onion fine. To keep from crying when you chop it (which is so annoying!), I suggest you place a little bit on your head. The trouble with crying over an onion is that once the chopping gets you started and the tears begin to well up, the next thing you know you just can't stop. I don't know whether that's ever happened to you, but I have to confess it's happened to me, many times. Mama used to say it was because I was especially sensitive to onions, like my great-aunt, Tita.

Tita was so sensitive to onions, any time they were being chopped, they say she would just cry and cry; when she was still in my great-grandmother's belly her sobs were so loud that even Nacha, the cook, who was half-deaf, could hear them easily. Once her wailing got so violent that it brought on an early labor. And before my great-grandmother could let out a word or even a whimper, Tita made her entrance into this world, prematurely, right there on the kitchen table amid the smells of simmering noodle soup, thyme, bay leaves, and cilantro, steamed milk, garlic, and, of course, onion. Tita had no need for the usual slap on the bottom, because she was already crying as she emerged; maybe that was because she knew then that it would be her lot in life to be denied marriage. The way Nacha told it, Tita was literally washed into this world on a great tide of tears that spilled over the edge of the table and flooded across the kitchen floor.

That afternoon, when the uproar had subsided and the water had been dried up by the sun, Nacha swept up the residue the tears had left on the red stone floor. There was enough salt to fill a ten-pound sack—it was used for cooking and lasted a long time. Thanks to her unusual birth, Tita felt a deep love for the kitchen, where she spent most of her life from the day she was born.

When she was only two days old, Tita's father, my great-grandfather, died of a heart attack and Mama Elena's milk dried up from the shock. Since there was no such thing as powdered milk in those days, and they couldn't find a wet nurse anywhere, they were in a panic to satisfy the infant's hunger. Nacha, who knew everything about cooking—and much more that doesn't enter the picture until later—offered to take charge of feeding Tita. She felt she had the best chance of "educating the innocent child's stomach," even though she had never married or had children. Though she didn't know how to read or write, when it came to cooking she knew everything there was to know. Mama Elena accepted her offer gratefully; she had enough to do between her mourning and the enormous responsibility of running the ranch—and it was the ranch that would provide her children the food and education they deserved— without having to worry about feeding a newborn baby on top of everything else.

From that day on, Tita's domain was the kitchen, where she grew vigorous and   5
healthy on a diet of teas and thin corn gruels. This explains the sixth sense Tita developed about everything concerning food. Her eating habits, for example, were attuned to the kitchen routine: in the morning, when she could smell that the beans were ready; at midday, when she sensed the water was ready for plucking the chickens; and in the afternoon, when the dinner bread was baking, Tita knew it was time for her to be fed.

Sometimes she would cry for no reason at all, like when Nacha chopped onions, but since they both knew the cause of those tears, they didn't pay them much mind. They made them a source of entertainment, so that during her childhood Tita didn't distinguish between tears of laughter and tears of sorrow. For her laughing was a form of crying.

Likewise for Tita the joy of living was wrapped up in the delights of food. It wasn't easy for a person whose knowledge of life was based on the kitchen to comprehend the outside world. That world was an endless expanse that began at the door between the kitchen and the rest of the house, whereas everything on the kitchen side of that door, on through the door leading to the patio and the kitchen and herb gardens was completely hers—it was Tita's realm.

Her sisters were just the opposite: to them, Tita's world seemed full of unknown dangers, and they were terrified of it. They felt that playing in the kitchen was foolish and dangerous. But once, Tita managed to convince them to join her in watching the dazzling display made by dancing water drops dribbled on a red hot griddle.

While Tita was singing and waving her wet hands in time, showering drops of water down on the griddle so they would "dance," Rosaura was cowering in the corner, stunned by the display. Gertrudis, on the other hand, found this game enticing, and she threw herself into it with the enthusiasm she always showed where rhythm, movement, or music were involved. Then Rosaura had tried to join them—but since she barely moistened her hands and then shook them gingerly, her efforts didn't have the desired effect. So Tita tried to move her hands closer to the griddle. Rosaura resisted, and they struggled for control until Tita became annoyed and let go, so that momentum carried Rosaura's hands onto it. Tita got a terrible spanking for that, and she was forbidden to play with her sisters in her own world. Nacha became her playmate then. Together they made up all sorts of games and activities having to do with cooking. Like the day they saw a man in the village plaza twisting long thin balloons into animal shapes, and they decided to do it with sausages. They didn't just make real animals, they also made up some of their own, creatures with the neck of a swan, the legs of a dog, the tail of a horse, and on and on.

Then there was trouble, however, when the animals had to be taken apart to fry the sausage. Tita refused to do it. The only time she was willing to take them apart was when the sausage was intended for the Christmas rolls she loved so much. Then she not only allowed her animals to be dismantled, she watched them fry with glee.

10

The sausage for the rolls must be fried over very low heat, so that it cooks thoroughly without getting too brown. When done, remove from the heat and add the sardines, which have been deboned ahead of time. Any black spots on the skin should also have been scraped off with a knife. Combine the onions, chopped chiles, and the ground oregano with the sardines. Let the mixture stand before filling the rolls.

Tita enjoyed this step enormously; while the filling was resting, it was very pleasant to savor its aroma, for smells have the power to evoke the past, bringing back sounds and even other smells that have no match in the present. Tita liked to take a deep breath and let the characteristic smoke and smell transport her through the recesses of her memory.

It was useless to try to recall the first time she had smelled one of those rolls—she couldn't, possibly because it had been before she was born. It might have been the unusual combination of sardines and sausages that had called to her and made her decide to trade the peace of ethereal existence in Mama Elena's belly for life as her daughter, in order to enter the De la Garza family and share their delicious meals and wonderful sausage.

On Mama Elena's ranch, sausage making was a real ritual. The day before, they started peeling garlic, cleaning chiles, and grinding spices. All the women in the family had to participate: Mama Elena; her daughters, Gertrudis, Rosaura, and Tita; Nacha, the cook; and Chencha, the maid. They gathered around the dining-room table in the afternoon, and between the talking and the joking the time flew by until it started to get dark. Then Mama Elena would say:

"That's it for today."

15

For a good listener, it is said, a single word will suffice, so when they heard that, they all sprang into action. First they had to clear the table, then they had to assign tasks: one collected the chickens, another drew water for breakfast from the well, a third was in charge of wood for the stove. There would be no ironing, no embroidery, no sewing that day. When it was all finished, they went to their bedrooms to read, say their prayers, and go to sleep. One afternoon, before Mama Elena told them they could leave the table, Tita, who was then fifteen, announced in a trembling voice that Pedro Muzquiz would like to come and speak with her. . . .

After an endless silence during which Tita's soul shrank, Mama Elena asked:

"And why should this gentleman want to come talk to me?"

Tita's answer could barely be heard:

"I don't know."   20

Mama Elena threw her a look that seemed to Tita to contain all the years of repression that had flowed over the family, and said:

"If he intends to ask for your hand, tell him not to bother. He'll be wasting his time and mine too. You know perfectly well that being the youngest daughter means you have to take care of me until the day I die."

With that Mama Elena got slowly to her feet, put her glasses in her apron, and said in a tone of final command:

"That's it for today."

Tita knew that discussion was not one of the forms of communication permitted   25
in Mama Elena's household, but even so, for the first time in her life, she intended to protest her mother's ruling.

"But in my opinion . . ."

"You don't have an opinion, and that's all I want to hear about it. For generations, not a single person in my family has ever questioned this tradition, and no daughter of mine is going to be the one to start."

Tita lowered her head, and the realization of her fate struck her as forcibly as her tears struck the table. From then on they knew, she and the table, that they could never have even the slightest voice in the unknown forces that fated Tita to bow before her mother's absurd decision, and the table to continue to receive the bitter tears that she had first shed on the day of her birth.

Still Tita did not submit. Doubts and anxieties sprang to her mind. For one thing, she wanted to know who started this family tradition. It would be nice if she could let that genius know about one little flaw in this perfect plan for taking care of women in their old age. If Tita couldn't marry and have children, who would take care of her when she got old? Was there a solution in a case like that? Or are daughters who stay home and take care of their mothers not expected to survive too long after the parent's death? And what about women who marry and can't have children, who will take care of them? And besides, she'd like to know what kind of studies had established that the youngest daughter and not the eldest is best suited to care for their mother. Had the opinion of the daughter affected by the plan ever been taken into account? If she couldn't marry, was she at least allowed to experience love? Or not even that?

Tita knew perfectly well that all these questions would have to be buried forever   30
in the archive of questions that have no answers. In the De la Garza family, one obeyed—immediately. Ignoring Tita completely, a very angry Mama Elena left the kitchen, and for the next week she didn't speak a single word to her.

What passed for communication between them resumed when Mama Elena, who was inspecting the clothes each of the women had been sewing, discovered that Tita's creation, which was the most perfect, had not been basted before it was sewed.

"Congratulations," she said, "your stitches are perfect—but you didn't baste it, did you?"

"No," answered Tita, astonished that the sentence of silence had been revoked.

"Then go and rip it out. Baste it and sew it again and then come and show it to me. And remember that the lazy man and the stingy man end up walking their road twice."

"But that's if a person makes a mistake, and you yourself said a moment ago that my sewing was . . ." 35

"Are you starting up with your rebelliousness again? It's enough that you have the audacity to break the rules in your sewing."

"I'm sorry, Mami. I won't ever do it again."

With that Tita succeeded in calming Mama Elena's anger. For once she had been very careful, she had called her "Mami" in the correct tone of voice. Mama Elena felt that the word *Mama* had a disrespectful sound to it, and so, from the time they were little, she had ordered her daughters to use the word *Mami* when speaking to her. The only one who resisted, the only one who said the word without the proper deference was Tita, which had earned her plenty of slaps. But how perfectly she had said it this time! Mama Elena took comfort in the hope that she had finally managed to subdue her youngest daughter.

Unfortunately her hope was short-lived, for the very next day Pedro Muzquiz appeared at the house, his esteemed father at his side, to ask for Tita's hand in marriage. His arrival caused a huge uproar, as his visit was completely unexpected. Several days earlier Tita had sent Pedro a message via Nacha's brother asking him to abandon his suit. The brother swore he had delivered the message to Pedro, and yet, there they were, in the house. Mama Elena received them in the living room; she was extremely polite and explained why it was impossible for Tita to marry.

"But if you really want Pedro to get married, allow me to suggest my daughter Rosaura, who's just two years older than Tita. *She* is one hundred percent available, and ready for marriage. . . ." 40

At that Chencha almost dropped right onto Mama Elena the tray containing coffee and cookies, which she had carried into the living room to offer don Pascual and his son. Excusing herself, she rushed back to the kitchen, where Tita, Rosaura, and Gertrudis were waiting for her to fill them in on every detail about what was going on in the living room. She burst headlong into the room, and they all immediately stopped what they were doing, so as not to miss a word she said.

They were together in the kitchen making Christmas Rolls. As the name implies, these rolls are usually prepared around Christmas, but today they were being prepared in honor of Tita's birthday. She would soon be sixteen years old, and she wanted to celebrate with one of her favorite dishes.

"Isn't that something? Your ma talks about being ready for marriage like she was dishing up a plate of enchiladas! And the worse thing is, they're completely different! You can't just switch tacos and enchiladas like that!"

Chencha kept up this kind of running commentary as she told the others—in her own way, of course—about the scene she had just witnessed. Tita knew Chencha sometimes exaggerated and distorted things, so she held her aching heart in check. She would not accept what she had just heard. Feigning calm, she continued cutting the rolls for her sisters and Nacha to fill.

It is best to use homemade rolls. Hard rolls can easily be obtained from a bakery, but they should be small, the larger ones are unsuited for this recipe. After filling the rolls, bake for ten minutes and serve hot. For best results, leave the rolls out overnight, wrapped in a cloth, so that the grease from the sausage soaks into the bread.   45

When Tita was finishing wrapping the next day's rolls, Mama Elena came into the kitchen and informed them that she had agreed to Pedro's marriage—to Rosaura.

Hearing Chencha's story confirmed, Tita felt her body fill with a wintry chill: in one sharp, quick blast she was so cold and dry her cheeks burned and turned red, red as the apples beside her. That overpowering chill lasted a long time, and she could find no respite, not even when Nacha told her what she had overheard as she escorted don Pascual Muzquiz and his son to the ranch's gate. Nacha followed them, walking as quietly as she could in order to hear the conversation between father and son. Don Pascual and Pedro were walking slowly, speaking in low, controlled, angry voices.

"Why did you do that, Pedro? It will look ridiculous, your agreeing to marry Rosaura. What happened to the eternal love you swore to Tita? Aren't you going to keep that vow?"

"Of course I'll keep it. When you're told there's no way you can marry the woman you love and your only hope of being near her is to marry her sister, wouldn't you do the same?"

Nacha didn't manage to hear the answer. Pulque, the ranch dog, went running   50 by, barking at a rabbit he mistook for a cat.

"So you intend to marry without love?"

"No, Papa, I am going to marry with a great love for Tita that will never die."

Their voices grew less and less audible, drowned out by the crackling of dried leaves beneath their feet. How strange that Nacha, who was quite hard of hearing by that time, should have claimed to have heard this conversation. Still, Tita thanked Nacha for telling her—but that did not alter the icy feelings she began to have for Pedro. It is said that the deaf can't hear but can understand. Perhaps Nacha only heard what everyone else was afraid to say. Tita could not get to sleep that night; she could not find the words for what she was feeling. How unfortunate that black holes in space had not yet been discovered, for then she might have understood the black hole in the center of her chest, infinite coldness flowing through it.

Whenever she closed her eyes she saw scenes from last Christmas, the first time Pedro and his family had been invited to dinner; the scenes grew more and more vivid, and the cold within her grew sharper. Despite the time that had passed since that evening, she remembered it perfectly: the sounds, the smells, the way her new dress had grazed the freshly waxed floor, the look Pedro gave her . . . That look! She had been walking to the table carrying a tray of egg-yolk candies when she first felt his hot gaze burning her skin. She turned her head, and her eyes met Pedro's. It was then she understood how dough feels when it is plunged into boiling oil. The heat that invaded her body was so real she was afraid she would start to bubble — her face, her stomach, her heart, her breasts — like batter, and unable to endure his gaze she lowered her eyes and hastily crossed the room, to where Gertrudis was pedaling the player piano, playing a waltz called "The Eyes of Youth." She set her tray on a little table in the middle of the room, picked up a glass of Noyo liquor that was in front of her, hardly aware of what she was doing, and sat down next to Paquita Lobo, the De la Garzas' neighbor. But even that distance between herself and Pedro was not enough; she felt her blood pulsing, searing her veins. A deep flush suffused her face and no matter how she tried she could not find a place for her eyes to rest. Paquita saw that something was bothering her, and with a look of great concern, she asked:

"That liquor is pretty strong, isn't it?" 55

"Pardon me?"

"You look a little woozy, Tita. Are you feeling all right?"

"Yes, thank you."

"You're old enough to have a little drink on a special occasion, but tell me, you little devil, did your mama say it was okay? I can see you're excited — you're shaking — and I'm sorry but I must say you'd better not have any more. You wouldn't want to make a fool of yourself."

That was the last straw! To have Paquita Lobo think she was drunk. She couldn't 60 allow the tiniest suspicion to remain in Paquita's mind or she might tell her mother. Tita's fear of her mother was enough to make her forget Pedro for a moment, and she applied herself to convincing Paquita, any way she could, that she was thinking clearly, that her mind was alert. She chatted with her, she gossiped, she made small talk. She even told her the recipe for this Noyo liquor which was supposed to have had such an effect on her. The liquor is made by soaking four ounces of peaches and a half pound of apricots in water for twenty-four hours to loosen the skin; next, they are peeled, crushed, and steeped in hot water for fifteen days. Then the liquor is distilled. After two and a half pounds of sugar have been completely dissolved in the water, four ounces of orange-flower water are added, and the mixture is stirred and strained. And so there would be no lingering doubts about her mental and physical well-being, she reminded Paquita, as if it were just an aside, that the water containers held 2.016 liters, no more and no less.

So when Mama Elena came over to ask Paquita if she was being properly entertained, she replied enthusiastically.

"Oh yes, perfectly! You have such wonderful daughters. Such fascinating conversation!"

Mama Elena sent Tita to the kitchen to get something for the guests. Pedro "happened" to be walking by at that moment and he offered his help. Tita rushed off to the kitchen without a word. His presence made her extremely uncomfortable. He followed her in, and she quickly sent him off with one of the trays of delicious snacks that had been waiting on the kitchen table.

She would never forget the moment their hands accidentally touched as they both slowly bent down to pick up the same tray.

That was when Pedro confessed his love. 65

"Señorita Tita, I would like to take advantage of this opportunity to be alone with you to tell you that I am deeply in love with you. I know this declaration is presumptuous, and that it's quite sudden, but it's so hard to get near you that I decided to tell you tonight. All I ask is that you tell me whether I can hope to win your love."

"I don't know what to say . . . give me time to think."

"No, no, I can't! I need an answer now: you don't have to think about love; you either feel it or you don't. I am a man of few words, but my word is my pledge. I swear that my love for you will last forever. What about you? Do you feel the same way about me?"

"Yes!"

Yes, a thousand times. From that night on she would love him forever. And 70 now she had to give him up. It wasn't decent to desire your sister's future husband. She had to try to put him out of her mind somehow, so she could get to sleep. She started to eat the Christmas Roll Nacha had left out on her bureau, along with a glass of milk; this remedy had proven effective many times. Nacha, with all her experience, knew that for Tita there was no pain that wouldn't disappear if she ate a delicious Christmas Roll. But this time it didn't work. She felt no relief from the hollow sensation in her stomach. Just the opposite, a wave of nausea flowed over her. She realized that the hollow sensation was not hunger but an icy feeling of grief. She had to get rid of that terrible sensation of cold. First she put on a wool robe and a heavy cloak. The cold still gripped her. Then she put on felt slippers and another two shawls. No good. Finally she went to her sewing box and pulled out the bedspread she had started the day Pedro first spoke of marriage. A bedspread like that, a crocheted one, takes about a year to complete. Exactly the length of time Pedro and Tita had planned to wait before getting married. She decided to use the yarn, not to let it go to waste, and so she worked on the bedspread and wept furiously, weeping and working until dawn, and threw it over herself. It didn't help at all. Not that night, nor many others, for as long as she lived, could she free herself from that cold.

[1989]

Questions

1. This selection begins with a recipe. What does the recipe contribute to the story?
2. How does Esquivel use food—its preparation, people's relationship with it, descriptions of serving it—to depict the character of Tita? Consider the "sixth sense Tita developed about everything concerning food" (para. 5) in your response. What is the narrator's attitude toward her great-aunt Tita? Explain whether you believe she shares her aunt's "sixth sense."

3. Why does Pedro agree to marry Rosaura, Tita's sister? Note that after he offers his explanation to his father, we are told that Pulque, the ranch dog, drowned out the response as he "went running by, barking at a rabbit he mistook for a cat" (para. 50). Discuss how this event might also be a comment on Pedro.

4. The Christmas Rolls appear several times in this story. How does the author use the rolls in her story? Explain whether you think she develops the rolls as a symbol, and if so, a symbol of what.

5. How do food and the rituals surrounding it define the De la Garza family in this story?

Snapping Beans

LISA PARKER

Lisa Parker (b. 1972) was born into and grew up in a coal-mining family in Appalachia. She received a BA from George Mason University and an MFA in creative writing from Penn State University. A writer, musician, and photographer, she currently works for the Department of Defense. Her poetry has appeared in literary magazines, including *Southern Review, Parnassus,* and *Louisville Review.* Parker reflects on her experience of being "first-generation college, first-generation above the poverty line" in *Bloodroot* (forthcoming), a collection of poetry about her Irish Cherokee family. The following poem is based on her experience as a first-generation college student.

For Fay Whitt

I snapped beans into the silver bowl
that sat on the splintering slats
of the porchswing between my grandma and me.
I was home for the weekend,
from school, from the North,   5
Grandma hummed "What A Friend We Have In Jesus"
as the sun rose, pushing its pink spikes
through the slant of cornstalks,
through the fly-eyed mesh of the screen.
We didn't speak until the sun overcame   10
the feathered tips of the cornfield
and Grandma stopped humming. I could feel
the soft gray of her stare
against the side of my face
when she asked, *How's school a-goin'?*   15
I wanted to tell her about my classes,
the revelations by book and lecture,

as real as any shout of faith
and potent as a swig of strychnine.
She reached the leather of her hand   20
over the bowl and cupped
my quivering chin; the slick smooth of her palm
held my face the way she held tomatoes
under the spigot, careful not to drop them,
and I wanted to tell her   25
about the nights I cried into the familiar
heartsick panels of the quilt she made me,
wishing myself home on the evening star.
I wanted to tell her
the evening star was a planet,   30
that my friends wore noserings and wrote poetry
about sex, about alcoholism, about Buddha.
I wanted to tell her how my stomach burned
acidic holes at the thought of speaking in class,
speaking in an accent, speaking out of turn,   35
how I was tearing, splitting myself apart
with the slow-simmering guilt of being happy
despite it all.
I said, *School's fine.*
We snapped beans into the silver bowl between us   40
and when a hickory leaf, still summer green,
skidded onto the porchfront,
Grandma said,
It's funny how things blow loose like that.

[1998]

. . . .

Questions

1. What is the significance of the speaker and her grandma "snapping beans" together?
2. What details does the speaker provide to emphasize the growing distance between her experience at college and her grandmother's understanding of it?
3. What actual conversation do the two have? How do the few words they say to one another contrast with the inner thoughts of the speaker?
4. What do the beans, cornfield, quilt, hickory leaf, and simile about the tomatoes signify about the way the speaker sees her world — or worlds?
5. How do you interpret the last five lines? Is the speaker angry? guilty? happy? Do you see hope for maintaining or reclaiming the closeness between granddaughter and grandmother?

Brain Food

CHRIS OFFUTT

Christopher John Offutt (b. 1958) grew up in a Kentucky mining community in the Appalachian Mountains. He got a BA in theater from Morehead State University and later attended the Iowa Writers' Workshop. Offutt's publications include a story collection, *Kentucky Straight* (1992); two memoirs, *The Same River Twice* (1993) and *No Heroes: A Memoir of Coming Home* (2003); a novel, *The Good Brother* (1997); and a collection of short stories, *Out of the Woods* (1999). He has also written for the television shows *True Blood* and *Weeds*. Honors for his work include both Guggenheim and National Endowment for the Arts fellowships. In the following essay, Offutt offers a glimpse into the relationship of a father and son through a humorous approach to nutrition.

A few days ago, my seven-year-old's face took on a solemnity that one normally sees in a veterinarian confronted with a case of mad cow disease. I knew an important question was coming—perhaps about God, the source of babies, or whether a warlock or a wizard had more power. The last time he got this serious, he wanted to know if Buddhists were those people who ran around with no clothes on.

"Dad," he said. "If you eat someone's brain, will you get as smart as them?"

"I don't think so."

"How do you know?"

There I was, trapped as usual by the logic of a child. If I didn't know the answer,   5
then I was obviously someone who could benefit from eating the brain of a genius. And if I did know the answer—how the hell did I find out?

"Look at it this way," I said. "If you ate someone's brain who was dumber than you, would you get dumb?"

He thought for a moment and said no.

I congratulated myself on once again doing my bit to maintain the gross lie of childhood—that adults possess a superior intellect. It didn't occur to me until later that this might make me a likely candidate for a meal.

I went into the living room where he was constructing a city of Legos.

"Hey," I said. "Do you have somebody in mind?"   10

"For what?"

"You know. Somebody's brain to eat."

"Like who?"

"Like me."

"No," he said.   15

As I watched him play, I began to think about whose brain I would eat if the chance came along. It was a lot easier to figure out whose brain I'd pass on. There were plenty of people a ton smarter than me, but I wasn't interested in inheriting their mental foibles as well. Ultimately I realized that if someone was stupid enough to let their brain get eaten, I wouldn't want to eat it.

As I pondered this further I realized that I have, in fact, eaten brain on at least two occasions. Here in Montana there is an all-night café that serves calf brains and eggs, eaten primarily by drunken cowboys and college kids after the bars have closed. Most people dump condiments on the meal until nothing is visible but mustard, ketchup, hot sauce, or all three, with extra pepper. There is something unsavory about the idea of eating brains. It must be concealed even from the self. Unfortunately, there is no secret way to eat them here. When you order brains and eggs, the waitress yells across the room to the line cook, "He needs them." Everyone in the joint then knows some dope is trying to get smart.

One night I was that dope. The brains looked like gray grits and tasted like tofu. The next day I felt dumb as a cow.

As a native of eastern Kentucky, I have naturally eaten squirrel brains, which is considered a delicacy on par with beaver tail or buffalo hump in Montana. The problem with squirrel brains is the same problem with eating the rest of the squirrel—it takes a lot to fill you up. And who wants to gorge on the appetizer, when a fine entrée of possum stew is yet to come? Incidentally, the brain of a possum is one I won't eat. I draw the line at marsupials.

If it were possible to get something out of eating a human brain, I'd probably opt for   20
artists, writers, and scientists. I'd skip anyone with drastic problems, such as van Gogh, Poe, or people from Idaho. The correct strategy is to try and improve one's known shortcomings. If you have trouble with right from wrong, go for Socrates. If you're scared of the dark, eat a blind man's brain. I've always been weak at math, and the brain of one of the great mathematicians might do me some good. I could then balance a checkbook, set the clock on the VCR, and figure out gas mileage. Maybe I'd suddenly know how many acres of soy Farmer Brown harvested on that damn SAT test all those years ago.

Due to my experience with brain-eating, I believe I'd grind it to a paste, throw it in a blender with cinnamon and honey, and make a milk shake. Drinking it would be a grave ritual performed with utmost care and respect. I'd light candles, sit cross-legged, and offer a toast: "Here's looking at Euclid."

I broke my reverie to ask my son if he was still worrying about getting smarter. He didn't look at me as he pressed Legos together.

"No," he said. "Are you worried I want to eat your brain?"

"Not at all."

"Good," he said. "I don't think it's worth it."   25

I looked at him for a long time. He's already more adept at a computer than I am. He can name the dinosaurs from a variety of eras and sometimes he beats me at chess. He even plays the piano. Now he understands that my brain's not worth eating. I wonder how he got so smart on a diet of pizza and frosted flakes.

[1998]

. . . .

Questions

1. The question Offutt's son asks him about whether eating brains will make a person smarter sends the writer into a reflection on food in Montana, where his

family now lives, and his native Kentucky. What is the connection between the question and his reflections?

2. What elements of humor are there in this piece? Do you think the primary intent of "Brain Food" is to be funny? Explain.

3. How does the conversation about eating (and food) develop the relationship between Offutt and his son?

If You Are What You Eat, Then What Am I?

GEETA KOTHARI

Born in 1928 and raised in New York City, Geeta Kothari now teaches at the University of Pittsburgh and serves as fiction editor of the literary journal the *Kenyon Review*. She is a two-time recipient of the fellowship in literature from the Pennsylvania Council on the Arts and the editor of *Did My Mama Like to Dance? and Other Stories about Mothers and Daughters*. In 1998, she received a Bellet Teaching Excellence Award. The following essay, first published in 1999, appeared in the 2000 edition of *The Best American Essays*.

> To belong is to understand the tacit codes of the people you live with.
> —MICHAEL IGNATIEFF, *Blood and Belonging*

I

The first time my mother and I open a can of tuna, I am nine years old. We stand in the doorway of the kitchen, in semi-darkness, the can tilted toward daylight. I want to eat what the kids at school eat: bologna, hot dogs, salami—foods my parents find repugnant because they contain pork and meat by-products, crushed bone and hair glued together by chemicals and fat. Although she has never been able to tolerate the smell of fish, my mother buys the tuna, hoping to satisfy my longing for American food.

Indians, of course, do not eat such things.

The tuna smells fishy, which surprises me because I can't remember anyone's tuna sandwich actually smelling like fish. And the tuna in those sandwiches doesn't look like this, pink and shiny, like an internal organ. In fact, this looks similar to the bad foods my mother doesn't want me to eat. She is silent, holding her face away from the can while peering into it like a half-blind bird.

"What's wrong with it?" I ask.

She has no idea. My mother does not know that the tuna everyone else's mothers made for them was tuna *salad*.   5

"Do you think it's botulism?"

I have never seen botulism, but I have read about it, just as I have read about but never eaten steak and kidney pie.

There is so much my parents don't know. They are not like other parents, and they disappoint me and my sister. They are supposed to help us negotiate the world outside, teach us the signs, the clues to proper behavior: what to eat and how to eat it.

We have expectations, and my parents fail to meet them, especially my mother, who works full time. I don't understand what it means, to have a mother who works outside and inside the home; I notice only the ways in which she disappoints me. She doesn't show up for school plays. She doesn't make chocolate-frosted cupcakes for my class. At night, if I want her attention, I have to sit in the kitchen and talk to her while she cooks the evening meal, attentive to every third or fourth word I say.

We throw the tuna away. This time my mother is disappointed. I go to school   10
with tuna eaters. I see their sandwiches, yet cannot explain the discrepancy between them and the stinking, oily fish in my mother's hand. We do not understand so many things, my mother and I.

II

On weekends, we eat fried chicken from Woolworth's on the back steps of my father's first-floor office in Murray Hill. The back steps face a small patch of garden — hedges, a couple of skinny trees, and gravel instead of grass. We can see the back windows of the apartment my parents and I lived in until my sister was born. There, the doorman watched my mother, several months pregnant and wearing a sari, slip on the ice in front of the building.

My sister and I pretend we are in the country, where our American friends all have houses. We eat glazed doughnuts, also from Woolworth's, and french fries with catsup.

III

My mother takes a catering class and learns that Miracle Whip and mustard are healthier than mayonnaise. She learns to make egg salad with chopped celery, deviled eggs with paprika, a cream cheese spread with bits of fresh ginger and watercress, chicken liver pâté, and little brown and white checkerboard sandwiches that we have only once. She makes chicken *à la king* in puff pastry shells and eggplant parmesan. She acquires smooth wooden paddles, whose purpose is never clear, two different egg slicers, several wooden spoons, icing tubes, cookie cutters, and an electric mixer.

IV

I learn to make tuna salad by watching a friend. My sister never acquires a taste for it. Instead, she craves:

> bologna
> hot dogs
> bacon
> sausages

and a range of unidentifiable meat products forbidden by my parents. Their restrictions are not about sacred cows, as everyone around us assumes; in a pinch, we are allowed hamburgers, though lamb burgers are preferable. A "pinch" means choosing not to draw attention to ourselves as outsiders, impolite visitors who won't eat what the host serves. But bologna is still taboo.

V

Things my sister refuses to eat: butter, veal, anything with *jeera*.[1] The babysitter tries   15
to feed her butter sandwiches, threatens her with them, makes her cry in fear and disgust. My mother does not disappoint her; she does not believe in forcing us to eat, in using food as a weapon. In addition to pbj, my sister likes pasta and marinara sauce, bologna and Wonder bread (when she can get it), and fried egg sandwiches with turkey, cheese, and horseradish. Her tastes, once established, are predictable.

VI

When we visit our relatives in India, food prepared outside the house is carefully monitored. In the hot, sticky monsoons in New Delhi and Bombay, we cannot eat ice cream, salad, cold food, or any fruit that can't be peeled. Definitely no meat. People die from amoebic dysentery, unexplained fevers, strange boils on their bodies. We drink boiled water only, no ice. No sweets except for jalebi, thin fried twists of dough in dripping hot sugar syrup. If we're caught ouside with nothing to drink, Fanta, Limca, Thums Up (after Coca-Cola is thrown out by Mr. Gandhi) will do. Hot tea sweetened with sugar, served with thick creamy buffalo milk, is preferable. It should be boiled, to kill the germs on the cup.

   My mother talks about "back home" as a safe place, a silk cocoon frozen in time where we are sheltered by family and friends. Back home, my sister and I do not argue about food with my parents. Home is where they know all the rules. We trust them to guide us safely through the maze of city streets for which they have no map, and we trust them to feed and take care of us, the way parents should.

   Finally, though, one of us will get sick, hungry for the food we see our cousins and friends eating, too thirsty to ask for a straw, too polite to insist on properly boiled water.

   At my uncle's diner in New Delhi, someone hands me a plate of aloo tikki, fried potato patties filled with mashed channa dal[2] and served with a sweet and sour chutney. The channa, mixed with hot chilies and spices, burned my tongue and throat. I reach for my Fanta, discard the paper straw, and gulp the sweet orange soda down, huge draughts that sting rather than soothe.

   When I throw up later that day (or is it the next morning, when a stomachache   20
wakes me up from deep sleep?), I cry over the frustration of being singled out, not from the pain my mother assumes I'm feeling as she holds my hair back from my face. The taste of orange lingers in my mouth, and I remember my lips touching the cold glass of the Fanta bottle.

   At that moment, more than anything, I want to be like my cousins.

---

[1]Cumin.—EDS.
[2]A dish made of the split kernel of beans in the chickpea family.—EDS.

VII

In New York, at the first Indian restaurant in our neighborhood, my father orders with confidence, and my sister and I play with the silverware until the steaming plates of lamb biryani[3] arrive.

What is Indian food? my friends ask, their noses crinkling up.

Later, this restaurant is run out of business by the new Indo-Pak-Bangladeshi combinations up and down the street, which serve similar food. They use plastic cutlery and Styrofoam cups. They do not distinguish between North and South Indian cooking, or between Indian, Pakistani, and Bangladeshi cooking, and their customers do not care. The food is fast, cheap, and tasty. Dosa, a rice flour crepe stuffed with masala[4] potato, appears on the same trays as chicken makhani.[5]

Now my friends want to know, Do you eat curry at home?   25

One time, my mother makes lamb vindaloo[6] for guests. Like dosa, this is a South Indian dish, one that my Punjabi mother has to learn from a cookbook. For us, she cooks everyday food—yellow dal, rice, chapati, bhaji. Lentils, rice, bread, and vegetables. She has never referred to anything on our table as "curry" or "curried," but I know she has made chicken curry for guests. Vindaloo, she explains, is a curry too. I understand, then, that curry is a dish created for guests, outsiders, a food for people who eat in restaurants.

VIII

I have inherited brown eyes, black hair, a long nose with a crooked bridge, and soft teeth with thin enamel. I am in my twenties, moving to a city far from my parents, before it occurs to me that jeera, the spice my sister avoids, must have an English name. I have to learn that haldi = turmeric, methi = fenugreek. What to make with fenugreek, I do not know. My grandmother used to make methi roti[7] for our breakfast, corn bread with fresh fenugreek leaves served with a lump of homemade butter. No one makes it now that she's gone, though once in a while my mother will get a craving for it and produce a facsimile ("The corn meal here is wrong") that only highlights what she's really missing: the smells and tastes of her mother's house.

I will never make my grandmother's methi roti or even my mother's unsatisfactory imitation of it. I attempt chapati:[8] it takes six hours, three phone calls home, and leaves me with an aching back. I have to write translations down: jeera = cumin. My memory is unreliable. But I have always known garam = hot.

---

[3]A dish made of lamb, spices, basmati rice, and yogurt.—Eds.

[4]A blend of spices common to Indian food, often including cinnamon, cardamom, cumin, caraway, and many others.—Eds.

[5]A dish combining chicken with a butter-based tomato sauce.—Eds.

[6]A spicy marinated lamb dish.—Eds.

[7]A round puffy flatbread.—Eds.

[8]A type of roti, or flatbread.—Eds.

IX

My mother learns how to make brownies and apple pie. My father makes only Indian food, except for loaves of heavy, sweet, brown bread that I eat with thin slices of American cheese and lettuce. The recipe is a secret, passed on to him by a woman at work. Years later, when he finally gives it to me, when I ask for it, I end up with three bricks of gluten that even the birds and my husband won't eat.

X

My parents send me to boarding school, outside of London. They imagine that I will overcome my shyness and find a place for myself in this all-girls' school. They have never lived in England, but as former subjects of the British Empire, they find London familiar, comfortable in a way New York—my mother's home for over twenty years by now—is not. Americans still don't know what to call us; their Indians live on reservations, not in Manhattan. Because they understand the English, my parents believe the English understand us.

I poke at my first school lunch—thin, overworked pastry in a puddle of lumpy gravy. The lumps are chewy mushrooms, maybe, or overcooked shrimp.

"What is this?" I don't want to ask, but I can't go on eating without knowing.

"Steak and kidney pie."

The girl next to me, red-haired, freckled, watches me take a bite from my plate. She has been put in charge of me, the new girl, and I follow her around all day, a foreigner at the mercy of a reluctant and angry tour guide. She is not used to explaining what is perfectly and utterly natural.

"What, you've never had steak and kidney pie? Bloody hell."

My classmates scoff, then marvel, then laugh at my ignorance. After a year, I understand what is on my plate: sausage rolls, blood pudding, Spam, roast beef in a thin, greasy gravy, all the bacon and sausage I could possibly want. My parents do not expect me to starve.

The girls at school expect conformity; it has been bred into them, through years of uniforms and strict rules about proper behavior. I am thirteen and contrary, even as I yearn for acceptance. I declare myself a vegetarian and doom myself to a diet of cauliflower cheese and baked beans on toast. The administration does not question my decision; they assume it's for vague, undefined religious reasons, although my father, the doctor, tells them it's for my health. My reasons, from this distance of many years, remain murky to me.

Perhaps I am my parents' daughter after all.

XI

When she is three, sitting on my cousin's lap in Bombay, my sister reaches for his plate and puts a chili in her mouth. She wants to be like the grown-ups who dip green chilies in coarse salt and eat them like any other vegetable. She howls inconsolable animal pain for what must be hours. She doesn't have the vocabulary for the oily heat that stings her mouth and tongue, burns a trail through her small tender body. Only hot, sticky tears on my father's shoulder.

As an adult, she eats red chili paste, mango pickle, kimchee,[9] foods that make my   40 eyes water and my stomach gurgle. My tastes are milder. I order raita[10] at Indian restaurants and ask for food that won't sear the roof of my mouth and scar the insides of my cheeks. The waiters nod, and their eyes shift—a slight once-over that indicates they don't believe me. I am Indian, aren't I? My father seems to agree with them. He tells me I'm asking for the impossible, as if he believes the recipes are immutable, written in stone during the passage from India to America.

XII

I look around my boyfriend's freezer one day and find meat: pork chops, ground beef, chicken pieces, Italian sausage. Ham in the refrigerator, next to the homemade Bolognese sauce. Tupperware filled with chili made from ground beef and pork.

He smells different from me. Foreign. Strange.

I marry him anyway.

He has inherited blue eyes that turn gray in bad weather, light brown hair, a sharp pointy nose, and excellent teeth. He learns to make chili with ground turkey and tofu, tomato sauce with red wine and portobello mushrooms, roast chicken with rosemary and slivers of garlic under the skin.

He eats steak when we are in separate cities, roast beef at his mother's house,   45 hamburgers at work. Sometimes I smell them on his skin. I hope he doesn't notice me turning my face, a cheek instead of my lips, my nose wrinkled at the unfamiliar, musky smell.

XIII

And then I realize I don't want to be a person who can find Indian food only in restaurants. One day, my parents will be gone, and I will long for the foods of my childhood, the way they long for theirs. I prepare for this day the way people on TV prepare for the end of the world. They gather canned goods they will never eat while I stockpile recipes I cannot replicate. I am frantic, disorganized, grabbing what I can, filing scribbled notes haphazardly. I regret the tastes I've forgotten, the meals I have inhaled without a thought. I worry that I've come to this realization too late.

XIV

Who told my mother about Brie? One day we were eating Velveeta, the next day Brie, Gouda, Camembert, Port Salut, Havarti with caraway, Danish fontina, string cheese made with sheep's milk. Who opened the door to these foreigners that sit on the refrigerator shelf next to last night's dal?

---

[9]A spicy Korean dish made of fermented cabbage and other vegetables.—EDS.
[10]A yogurt-based condiment, often including cilantro, mint, and cucumber.—EDS.

Back home, there is one cheese only, which comes in a tin, looks like Bakelite, and tastes best when melted.

And how do we go from Chef Boyardee to fresh pasta and homemade sauce, made with Redpack tomatoes, crushed garlic, and dried oregano? Macaroni and cheese, made with fresh cheddar and whole milk, sprinkled with bread crumbs and paprika. Fresh eggplant and ricotta ravioli, packed with marinara sauce and fresh mozzarella.

My mother will never cook beef or pork in her kitchen, and the foods she knew   50
in her childhood are unavailable. Because the only alternative to the supermarket, with its TV dinners and canned foods, is the gourmet Italian deli across the street, by default our meals become socially acceptable.

XV

If I really want to make myself sick, I worry that my husband will one day leave me for a meat-eater, for someone familiar who doesn't sniff him suspiciously for signs of alimentary infidelity.

XVI

Indians eat lentils. I understand this as absolute, a decree from an unidentifiable authority that watches and judges me.

So what does it mean that I cannot replicate my mother's dal? She and my father show me repeatedly, in their kitchen, in my kitchen. They coach me over the phone, buy me the best cookbooks, and finally write down their secrets. Things I'm supposed to know but don't. Recipes that should be, by now, engraved on my heart.

Living far from the comfort of people who require no explanation for what I do and who I am, I crave the foods we have shared. My mother convinces me that moong is the easiest dal to prepare, and yet it fails me every time: bland, watery, a sickly greenish-yellow mush. These imperfect imitations remind me only of what I'm missing.

But I have never been fond of moong dal.[11] At my mother's table it is the last   55
thing I reach for. Now I worry that this antipathy toward dal signals something deeper, that somehow I am not my parents' daughter, not Indian, and because I cannot bear the touch and smell of raw meat, though I can eat it cooked (charred, dry, and overdone), I am not American either.

I worry about a lifetime purgatory in Indian restaurants where I will complain that all the food looks and tastes the same because they've used the same masala.

XVII

About the tuna and her attempts to feed us, my mother laughs. She says, "You were never fussy. You ate everything I made and never complained."

My mother is at the stove, wearing only her blouse and petticoat, her sari carefully folded and hung in the closet. She does not believe a girl's place is in the kitchen,

---

[11]A dish made of split green lentils.—EDS.

but she expects me to know that too much hing can ruin a meal, to know without being told, without having to ask or write it down. Hing = asafoetida.

She remembers the catering class. "Oh, that class. You know, I had to give it up when we got to lobster. I just couldn't stand the way it looked."

She says this apologetically, as if she has deprived us, as if she suspects that having a mother who could feed us lobster would have changed the course of our lives. 60

Intellectually, she understands that only certain people regularly eat lobster, people with money or those who live in Maine, or both. In her catering class there were people without jobs for whom preparing lobster was a part of their professional training as caterers. Like us, they wouldn't be eating lobster at home. For my mother, however, lobster was just another American food, like tuna—different, strange, not natural yet somehow essential to belonging.

I learned how to prepare and eat lobster from the same girl who taught me tuna salad. I ate bacon at her house, too. And one day this girl, with her houses in the country and Martha's Vineyard, asked me how my uncle was going to pick me up from the airport in Bombay. In 1973, she was surprised to hear that he used a car, not an elephant. At home, my parents and I laughed, and though I never knew for sure if she was making fun of me, I still wanted her friendship.

My parents were afraid my sister and I would learn to despise the foods they loved, replace them with bologna and bacon and lose our taste for masala. For my mother, giving up her disgust of lobster, with its hard exterior and foreign smell, would mean renouncing some essential difference. It would mean becoming, decidedly, definitely, American—unafraid of meat in all its forms, able to consume large quantities of protein at any given meal. My willingness to toss a living being into boiling water and then get past its ugly appearance to the rich meat inside must mean to my mother that I am, somehow, someone she is not.

But I haven't eaten lobster in years. In my kitchen cupboards, there is a thirteen-pound bag of basmati rice, jars of lime pickle, mango pickle, and ghee,[12] cans of tuna and anchovies, canned soups, coconut milk, and tomatoes, rice noodles, several kinds of pasta, dried mushrooms, and unlabeled bottles of spices: haldi, jeera, hing. When my husband tries to help me cook, he cannot identify all the spices. He gets confused when I forget their English names and remarks that my expectations of him are unreasonable.

I am my parents' daughter. Like them, I expect knowledge to pass from me to my husband without one word of explanation or translation. I want him to know what I know, see what I see, without having to tell him exactly what it is. I want to believe the recipes never change. 65

[1999]

- -

---

[12]Clarified butter.—EDS.

Questions

1. Although this is a memoir about her childhood and growing up, Kothari opens it in the present tense. Why? What effect does this achieve?
2. Kothari writes in the first section: "We have expectations, and my parents fail to meet them, especially my mother. . . . I don't understand what it means, to have a mother who works outside and inside the home; I notice only the ways in which she disappoints me" (para. 9). In what ways does Kothari revise this view by the end of the essay? Cite specific passages.
3. Consider the "Indian" food that Kothari's family encounters in New York, and the curry that her mother prepares for guests. Why is this food as alien to the family as tuna and lobster?
4. What role does the man who becomes Kothari's husband play in this memoir? What does he add that she could not have conveyed through descriptions and stories about her family?
5. How does Kothari's attitude toward food as her story progresses mark developments in her growth and maturity? Try dividing this growth into three or four stages, and describe each.
6. This piece is made up of seventeen numbered sections, each a vignette. Why do you think Kothari chose to write these brief glimpses, almost as if she is clicking a camera, rather than a more continuous narrative?
7. Kothari opens her essay with a quote by Michael Ignatieff: "To belong is to understand the tacit codes of the people you live with." Discuss this memoir as an exploration of Kothari's desire to belong.

Entering the Conversation

As you develop a response to one of the following questions, refer to the texts you have read in this section. You may also draw on your own experience or knowledge relating to food and family.

1. Since food is inextricably linked to family, it is no surprise that food often becomes the site of conflict and change within a family. Discuss how two or three of the texts in this Conversation illustrate conflict or change through the food their characters prepare and eat.
2. The introduction to this Conversation includes a quotation by M. F. K. Fisher: "Our three basic needs for food and security and love are so mixed and mingled and entwined that we cannot straightforwardly think of one without the other." Judging by the work in this section, do you think that all of the authors would agree with Fisher? Discuss this quote by considering at least three of the texts.
3. Compare and contrast how food triggers and is linked to memory in two of the works in this Conversation.
4. In *How to Read Literature Like a Professor*, Thomas Foster writes, "Whenever people eat or drink together, it's communion." Communion is not necessarily

religious in nature, but more generally defined as an act of sharing or of intimate fellowship. Discuss how food or meals serve as communion in two or more works in this section. You might also consider "The Dead" in your discussion.

5. While the food described in these selections is usually literal, it can also express bigger ideas about family and relationships. Write an essay in which you discuss the ways that food is used metaphorically in three or four of these works.

6. Write a personal essay about the role that food plays in your own family, referring to or quoting from at least one of the selections in the Conversation. If you like, you might craft your essay around a favorite family recipe.

7. Plan the menu for a party for four of the authors in this Conversation. Explain the type of party or occasion and your food choices with reference to their work. Write a dinnertime conversation that reflects the conflicts and compromises among the authors' tastes.

Student Writing

Comparison and Contrast

This student essay by Ana Hernandez was written in class as a timed response to the following prompt.

> Read "My Papa's Waltz" by Theodore Roethke and "Those Winter Sundays" by Robert Hayden. Then write a well-organized essay in which you discuss their similarities and differences. In your essay, be sure to consider both theme and style.

Dancing with Dad
Ana Hernandez

Both these poems are written by a child about a father. Since the authors are both male, we can assume that the speaker is the son. The impressions left of both the son and the father are different in the two poems.

In the poem "My Papa's Waltz" by Theodore Roethke, we gain the impression of a fairly young child. The poet emphasizes this, using the words "small boy," and in the next line indicating that dancing does not come easily to him. Moreover, the boy's ears are at the level of his father's belt buckle, and the father is tall enough and the boy short enough to allow the father to beat time on his head. The impression, then, is of a young boy who thinks that a romp with his father — to the disapproval of his mother — is a lot of fun.

In the poem "Those Winter Sundays" by Robert Hayden, the relationship is very different. In fact, the boy may be looking back to when he was of the same age as the boy in the Roethke poem but the writer is more mature. His word choices (the use of phrases like "blueblack cold," "chronic angers," and "love's austere and lonely offices") indicate the perspective of an older and wiser person. Also, the boy in Hayden's poem is able to evaluate his father's attitude to the family, a perception absent from Roethke's boy, who is aware only of the contrast between a happy father drunk on whiskey and a sternly disapproving mother.

This contrast between father and mother is used to signal an unhappy couple, something that is beyond the perception of the younger boy, but which is more explicit in Hayden's poem. The boy is older, and therefore able to make judgments. He now appreciates the thankless work that his father did, for "no one ever thanked him" for lighting the fire, for waking him in the morning, or for polishing his shoes. Hayden's boy is looking back to the time when he was, perhaps, the age of Roethke's boy, when good things in family life were taken for granted. In the progression of life, therefore, we see the young boy from "My Papa's Waltz" simply having fun as he dances with his father; later the boy in "Those Winter Sundays" looks back at how his father, unappreciated by his family, prepared his son for church. In the case of the fathers, the state to which the boys will grow up, we see "austerity" and duty in one example and the need for whiskey in the other. In neither case do we see spontaneous happiness; in neither case do we have a picture of a happy marriage.

The style of the poems reflects the difference in age between the two sons writing. "My Papa's Waltz" is written with a rhythm and rhyme scheme that makes it dance along like the chanting of a child who delights in simple things. In contrast, "Those Winter Sundays," written in blank verse, creates an atmosphere of gloom. This is partially relieved in the third stanza when the rhythm switches. The gloom has been established; by changing the pace, Hayden makes the child step back and see that gloomy childhood from the perspective of a person more at ease, a person who can be objective about what he is describing.

Overall, then, the similarities between the two poems are fewer than the differences. The perspectives of the two sons create the primary contrast between a lighthearted and a sad mood.

Questions

1. The prompt calls for a comparison and contrast of theme and style in two poems. How effective is the opening paragraph in compelling a reader's interest? How might Ana revise her introduction and conclusion to address the prompt more effectively?

2. Paragraphs 2 and 3 focus on the age and circumstances of the boys in the poems. How might these two paragraphs be combined, starting with a clear and unifying topic sentence?

3. Identify points in the essay that deserve more development and additional supporting evidence, and explain why.

4. Ana repeats the word "different" several times in her essay. What alternative words or phrases might she have used to contrast the two poems?

5. In your own analysis, do you think there are more similarities than differences in these two poems, or do you agree with Ana? Defend your point of view with evidence from the poems.

The Writer's Craft—Close Reading

Connotation

"Diversity Blooms in Outer Suburbs." This headline from the *Washington Post* captures the power of connotation. The article uses the words "grows" and "increases" throughout, yet "Blooms" in the headline connotes more than growth: it's positive growth, a flowering. Just as journalists use the power of connotative meaning to draw in readers, writers of literary texts—poems, plays, stories, and novels—make language choices that influence their readers' responses. What is the difference, for instance, between *labor* and *work*? between *lady* and *woman*? between *pail* and *bucket*? You can be sure that writers think about these differences and make deliberate choices.

Paying attention to connotation often leads to an interpretation, or a better understanding of the mood of a piece—especially when it comes to verb choices. Consider the following sentence from "The Dead":

> Gabriel's eyes, *irritated* by the floor, which *glittered* with beeswax under the heavy chandelier, *wandered* to the wall above the piano.

If Joyce had used words that were less evocative, the sentence would be far less vivid. For instance:

> Gabriel's eyes, *bothered* by the floor, which *shone* with beeswax under the heavy chandelier, *moved* to the wall above the piano.

"Irritated" suggests a mood that "bothered" does not; "glittered" carries a visual image that the less expressive "shone" does not; and "wandered" evokes a lackadaisical quality that the more neutral "moved" does not.

Connotation may work individually or cumulatively. Notice in the following paragraph from "The Dead" how the connotations of several words together suggest Gabriel's feeling of uncertainty:

> He waited outside the drawing-room door until the waltz should finish, listening to the skirts that swept against it and to the shuffling of feet. He was still discomposed by the girl's bitter and sudden retort. It had cast a gloom over him which he tried to dispel by arranging his cuffs and the bows of his tie. Then he took from his waistcoat pocket a

little paper and glanced at the headings he had made for his speech. He was undecided about the lines from Robert Browning for he feared they would be above the heads of his hearers.

Notice how a few word substitutions can change the mood of the paragraph:

He stood outside the drawing-room door until the waltz should finish, listening to the skirts that swept against it and to the *moving* of feet. He was still *upset* by the girl's bitter and sudden *response*. It had *put* a gloom over him which he tried to *ignore* by arranging his cuffs and the bows of his tie. Then he took from his waistcoat pocket a little paper and *looked* at the headings he had made for his speech. He was *unsure* about the lines from Robert Browning for he *thought* they would be above the heads of his *audience*.

The following exercises will help you examine how precisely chosen words can convey meaning.

• EXERCISE 1 •

Discuss the differences in connotations in the following groups of words:

a. skinny, slender, svelte, gaunt, slim, lithe
b. dog, pooch, canine, pup
c. run, bolt, race, sprint, dash
d. alleged, reported, maintained, contended, claimed
e. rich, affluent, prosperous, wealthy
f. kids, descendants, children, progeny, offspring

• EXERCISE 2 •

A. What do the connotations of the underlined words and phrases suggest about the home and family Fitzgerald's narrator is describing in "Babylon Revisited"?

It was <u>warm</u> here, it was a home, <u>people together by a fire</u>. The children felt very <u>safe</u> and important; the mother and father were <u>serious, watchful</u>. They had things to do for the children more <u>important</u> than his visit here. A <u>spoonful of medicine</u> was, after all, more important than the strained relations between Marion and himself. They were not dull people, but they were very much in <u>the grip of life and circumstances.</u>

B. What connotations contribute to the feelings of loss and entrapment in the following passage from "The Dead"?

One by one they were all becoming shades. Better pass boldly into that other world, in the full glory of some passion, than fade and wither dismally with age. He thought of how she who lay beside him had locked in her heart for so many years that image of her lover's eyes when he had told her that he did not wish to live.

• EXERCISE 3 •

Scrutinize the following words from Eamon Grennan's poem "Pause." What connotations do these words suggest to you? Write each word on a piece of paper and cluster any associations that come to you. Turn to a partner and share your findings.

Sample cluster:

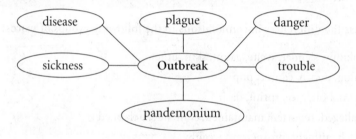

- explosion
- disaster
- weird
- flashing lights

How do the connotations of these words contribute to the poem's tone? What inferences can you draw regarding the meaning of the poem based on Eamon Grennan's choice of words?

• EXERCISE 4 •

Reread Mary Oliver's poem "Wild Geese." How do the connotations of words in that poem contribute to its meaning? For instance, the word *animal* can often have negative connotations, but how is it used in line 4? Find other words with denotations and connotations that are important to the meaning of "Wild Geese."

Write two short paragraphs. In the first, describe something about your family or home that you like or appreciate. In the second, describe something about your family or home that you find annoying. In both paragraphs, choose words with connotations that convey your attitude toward your subjects.

Suggestions for Writing

Home and Family

1. Select three texts from this chapter that you found particularly memorable, and in a well-organized essay, analyze how the writers have explored the theme of home and family.

2. Compare and contrast how two of the poets in this chapter have used resources of language such as diction, syntax, and imagery to express their ideas regarding the theme of home and family.

3. Several of the works in this chapter (including "The Dead," *Fences*, "The Moths," and "The Hammock") explore multigenerational family units. Using two or three different texts, discuss the ties that keep families together as well as those that challenge the connections through three generations.

4. Select a text from the chapter that depicts a conflict between a parent and a child. Craft an essay in which you analyze the source of the conflict and explore how this tension contributes to the meaning of the work as a whole.

5. Selecting three or four texts from the chapter, write an essay arguing whether families are more alike or different regardless of specific culture, ethnic background, or time period.

6. Choose one of the following quotations, and explain why it fits your beliefs about family in general or your family in particular.

    a. "Nobody has ever before asked the nuclear family to live all by itself in a box the way we do. With no relatives, no support, we've put it in an impossible situation."—Margaret Mead

    b. "If the family were a fruit, it would be an orange, a circle of sections, held together but separable—each segment distinct."—Letty Cottin Pogrebin

    c. "Important families are like potatoes. The best parts are underground."— Francis Bacon

7. Choose one of the poems addressed (directly or indirectly) to an absent party (for instance, the poems by Bradstreet, Yeats, Hughes, Plath, Boland, Dove, or Hayden), and respond by writing a poem in the absent person's voice.

8. Search a museum Web site for images of home and family. Find a painting or photograph that conveys an image of family in marked contrast to the one in either the Jacob Lawrence painting or the van Gogh painting in this chapter. Explain the two perspectives of family.

9. Select a character from one of the texts in this chapter and a problem or difficulty from another text. In the voice of the character you've chosen, offer advice on how to solve or address the problem.

10. Write an essay in which you compare the party at the center of "The Dead" with a party scene from another work, such as *The Great Gatsby, Macbeth, Pride and Prejudice,* or *Mrs. Dalloway.*

6

Identity and Culture

No man, for any considerable period, can wear one face to
himself, and another to the multitude, without finally getting
bewildered as to which may be the true.

—Nathaniel Hawthorne, *The Scarlet Letter*

What makes us who we are? While our identity is shaped by our interests,
personality, and talents, much of how we define ourselves is dependent
on the culture that surrounds us. Gender, race, age, religion, national allegiance,
geography, language, class, and ethnicity all play a role. In this chapter, the readings
explore the many different ways that culture influences who we are.

In previous generations, immigrants tried to assimilate to their new country
as quickly as possible, but newer generations are holding on to the traditions and
identities of their homeland. Is defining identity based on difference a divisive or a
constructive force in society? Some argue for cosmopolitanism—for people to be
citizens of the world—in order to foster a greater sense of shared identity. Would
that discourage cultural discrimination and bias, or would it erode local community
values and ties? In contemporary literature, cross-cultural writers such as Jhumpa
Lahiri—associated with both Indian and American culture—are part of the canon
of the twenty-first century. Her characters and their level of comfort in more than
one culture reflect the benefits and difficulties of living in a global community.
Lahiri's "Interpreter of Maladies," as well as other stories in this chapter, asks: do we
create an identity—or inherit one?

Many of the readings in this chapter explore identities that are not shaped by
culture but are in conflict with it, from Ralph Waldo Emerson's "The Apology," to
Kamau Brathwaite's "Ogun," to Mahmoud Darwish's "Identity Card." Some, such
as Gary Soto's "Mexicans Begin Jogging," confront stereotypes that resist positive
ethnic identities; others, such as Nathalie Handal's "Caribe in Nueva York," celebrate
the polyglot world of a big city where multiple cultures coexist—sometimes without conflict, sometimes with. The Conversation in this chapter, as well as *Heart of
Darkness* itself, explores the impact of colonial domination on both the oppressed

367

and the oppressor with readings that ask complex questions about the influence of colonization on national politics and personal identity.

Whether we come to these works from a single cultural tradition or read them through a multicultural lens, close, careful reading of these works reminds us that literature gives us glimpses into the conflicts and struggles that are an integral part of forming our identities.

Heart of Darkness

JOSEPH CONRAD

Born Józef Teodor Konrad Walecz Korzeniowski to Polish parents living in the Russian-occupied Ukraine, Joseph Conrad (1857–1924) is considered one of the finest British writers. In addition to the novella *Heart of Darkness,* his most famous works include the novels *Lord Jim* (1900), *Nostromo* (1904), and *The Secret Agent* (1907). Remarkably, Conrad only became fluent in English in his twenties. After the death of his parents when he was nine, Conrad was raised and supported by a maternal uncle in Krakow. At seventeen—to avoid conscription into the Russian Army—he joined the French Merchant Marines and began a fifteen-year career as a seaman. His travels and experiences with the French and later British Merchant Navy provided material for many stories and novels. In 1889, Conrad served as captain for a steamboat traveling up the Congo River, fulfilling his childhood wish to visit Africa. Much of what Conrad witnessed on this journey is reflected in *Heart of Darkness,* and like Marlow, he contracted an illness in Africa that affected him for the remainder of his life. *Heart of Darkness* was written in 1899 and first appeared in serial form. In 1902, the entire work was published in *Youth: A Narrative with Two Other Stories.*

flood: when water flows in land
ebb: when it flows to sea

discuss

The *Nellie,* a cruising yawl, swung to her anchor without a flutter of the sails, and was at rest. The flood had made, the wind was nearly calm, and being bound down the river, the only thing for it was to come to and wait for the turn of the tide.

The sea-reach of the Thames stretched before us like the beginning of an interminable waterway. In the offing[1] the sea and the sky were welded together without a joint, and in the luminous space the tanned sails of the barges drifting up with the tide seemed to stand still in red clusters of canvas sharply peaked, with gleams of varnished sprits.[2] A haze rested on the low shores that ran out to sea in vanishing flatness. The air was dark above Gravesend, and farther back still seemed condensed into a mournful gloom, brooding motionless over the biggest, and the greatest, town on earth.

The Director of Companies was our captain and our host. We four affectionately watched his back as he stood in the bows looking to seaward. On the whole river there was nothing that looked half so nautical. He resembled a pilot, which to a seaman is

setting + background know.

---

[1]At a distance, but within sight. — EDS.
[2]Poles that are part of the mast assembly. — EDS.

trustworthiness personified. It was difficult to realize his work was not out there in the luminous estuary, but behind him, within the brooding gloom.

Between us there was, as I have already said somewhere, the bond of the sea. Besides holding our hearts together through long periods of separation, it had the effect of making us tolerant of each other's yarns—and even convictions. The Lawyer—the best of old fellows—had, because of his many years and many virtues, the only cushion on deck, and was lying on the only rug. The Accountant had brought out already a box of dominoes, and was toying architecturally with the bones. Marlow sat cross-legged right aft, leaning against the mizzen-mast. He had sunken cheeks, a yellow complexion, a straight back, an ascetic aspect, and, with his arms dropped, the palms of hands outwards, resembled an idol. The director, satisfied the anchor had good hold, made his way aft and sat down amongst us. We exchanged a few words lazily. Afterwards there was silence on board the yacht. For some reason or other we did not begin that game of dominoes. We felt meditative, and fit for nothing but placid staring. The day was ending in a serenity of still and exquisite brilliance. The water shone pacifically; the sky, without a speck, was a benign immensity of unstained light; the very mist on the Essex marshes was like a gauzy and radiant fabric, hung from the wooded rises inland, and draping the low shores in diaphanous folds. Only the gloom to the west, brooding over the upper reaches, became more sombre every minute, as if angered by the approach of the sun.

And at last, in its curved and imperceptible fall, the sun sank low, and from glowing   5
white changed to a dull red without rays and without heat, as if about to go out suddenly, stricken to death by the touch of that gloom brooding over a crowd of men.

Forthwith a change came over the waters, and the serenity became less brilliant but more profound. The old river in its broad reach rested unruffled at the decline of day, after ages of good service done to the race that peopled its banks, spread out in the tranquil dignity of a waterway leading to the uttermost ends of the earth. We looked at the venerable stream not in the vivid flush of a short day that comes and departs for ever, but in the august light of abiding memories. And indeed nothing is easier for a man who has, as the phrase goes, "followed the sea" with reverence and affection, than to evoke the great spirit of the past upon the lower reaches of the Thames. The tidal current runs to and fro in its unceasing service, crowded with memories of men and ships it had borne to the rest of home or to the battles of the sea. It had known and served all the men of whom the nation is proud, from Sir Francis Drake[3] to Sir John Franklin,[4] knights all, titled and untitled—the great knights-errant of the sea. It had borne all the ships whose names are like jewels flashing in the night of time, from the *Golden Hind*[5] returning with her round flanks full of treasure, to be visited by the Queen's Highness and thus pass out of the gigantic tale, to the *Erebus* and

[3]Sir Francis Drake (1540–1596), English captain famous for defeating the Spanish Armada and sailing around the world.—EDS.
[4]Sir John Franklin (1786–1847), English naval officer who charted portions of the Arctic and died searching for the Northwest Passage.—EDS.
[5]Sir Francis Drake's ship.—EDS.

Terror,[6] bound on other conquests—and that never returned. It had known the ships and the men. They had sailed from Deptford, from Greenwich, from Erith—the adventurers and the settlers; kings' ships and the ships of men on 'Change; captains, admirals, the dark "interlopers" of the Eastern trade, and the commissioned "generals" of East India fleets. Hunters for gold or pursuers of fame, they all had gone out on that stream, bearing the sword, and often the torch, messengers of the might within the land, bearers of a spark from the sacred fire. What greatness had not floated on the ebb of that river into the mystery of an unknown earth! . . . The dreams of men, the seed of commonwealths, the germs of empires.

The sun set; the dusk fell on the stream, and lights began to appear along the shore. The Chapman lighthouse, a three-legged thing erect on a mud-flat, shone strongly. Lights of ships moved in the fairway—a great stir of lights going up and going down. And farther west on the upper reaches the place of the monstrous town was still marked ominously on the sky, a brooding gloom in sunshine, a lurid glare under the stars.

"And this also," said Marlow suddenly, "has been one of the dark places of the earth."

He was the only man of us who still "followed the sea." The worst that could be said of him was that he did not represent his class. He was a seaman, but he was a wanderer, too, while most seamen lead, if one may so express it, a sedentary life. Their minds are of the stay-at-home order, and their home is always with them—the ship; and so is their country—the sea. One ship is very much like another, and the sea is always the same. In the immutability of their surroundings the foreign shores, the foreign faces, the changing immensity of life, glide past, veiled not by a sense of mystery but by a slightly disdainful ignorance; for there is nothing mysterious to a seaman unless it be the sea itself, which is the mistress of his existence and as inscrutable as Destiny. For the rest, after his hours of work, a casual stroll or a casual spree on shore suffices to unfold for him the secret of a whole continent, and generally he finds the secret not worth knowing. The yarns of seamen have a direct simplicity, the whole meaning of which lies within the shell of a cracked nut. But Marlow was not typical (if his propensity to spin yarns be excepted), and to him the meaning of an episode was not inside like a kernel but outside, enveloping the tale which brought it out only as a glow brings out a haze, in the likeness of one of these misty halos that sometimes are made visible by the spectral illumination of moonshine.

His remark did not seem at all surprising. It was just like Marlow. It was accepted in silence. No one took the trouble to grunt even; and presently he said, very slow— 10

"I was thinking of very old times, when the Romans first came here, nineteen hundred years ago—the other day. . . . Light came out of this river since—you say Knights? Yes; but it is like a running blaze on a plain, like a flash of lightning in the clouds. We live in the flicker—may it last as long as the old earth keeps rolling! But darkness was here yesterday. Imagine the feelings of a commander of a fine—what d'ye call 'em?—trireme in the Mediterranean, ordered suddenly to the north; run overland

---

[6] Sir John Franklin's ships, lost in the Arctic.—EDS.

across the Gauls in a hurry; put in charge of one of these craft the legionaries—a wonderful lot of handy men they must have been, too—used to build, apparently by the hundred, in a month or two, if we may believe what we read. Imagine him here—the very end of the world, a sea the colour of lead, a sky the colour of smoke, a kind of ship about as rigid as a concertina[7]—and going up this river with stores, or orders, or what you like. Sand-banks, marshes, forests, savages,—precious little to eat fit for a civilized man, nothing but Thames water to drink. No Falernian wine here, no going ashore. Here and there a military camp lost in a wilderness, like a needle in a bundle of hay—cold, fog, tempests, disease, exile, and death,—death skulking in the air, in the water, in the bush. They must been dying like flies here. Oh, yes—he did it. Did it very well, too, no doubt, and without thinking much about it either, except afterwards to brag of what he had gone through in his time, perhaps. They were men enough to face the darkness. And perhaps he was cheered by keeping his eye on a chance of promotion to the fleet at Ravenna by and by, if he had good friends in Rome and survived the awful climate. Or think of a decent young citizen in a toga—perhaps too much dice, you know—coming out here in the train of some prefect, or tax-gatherer, or trader even, to mend his fortunes. Land in a swamp, march through the woods, and in some inland post feel the savagery, the utter savagery, had closed round him,—all that mysterious life of the wilderness that stirs in the forest, in the jungles, in the hearts of wild men. There's no initiation either into such mysteries. He has to live in the midst of the incomprehensible, which is also detestable. And it has a fascination, too, that goes to work upon him. The fascination of the abomination—you know, imagine the growing regrets, the longing to escape, the powerless disgust, the surrender, the hate."

He paused.

"Mind," he began again, lifting one arm from the elbow, the palm of the hand outwards, so that, with his legs folded before him, he had the pose of a Buddha preaching in European clothes and without a lotus-flower—"Mind, none of us would feel exactly like this. What saves us is efficiency—the devotion to efficiency. But these chaps were not much account, really. They were no colonists; their administration was merely a squeeze, and nothing more, I suspect. They were conquerors, and for that you want only brute force—nothing to boast of, when you have it, since your strength is just an accident arising from the weakness of others. They grabbed what they could get for the sake of what was to be got. It was just robbery with violence, aggravated murder on a great scale, and men going at it blind—as is very proper for those who tackle a darkness. The conquest of the earth, which mostly means the taking it away from those who have a different complexion or slightly flatter noses than ourselves, is not a pretty thing when you look into it too much. What redeems it is the idea only. An idea at the back of it; not a sentimental pretence but an idea; and an unselfish belief in the idea—something you can set up, and bow down before, and offer a sacrifice to. . . ."

He broke off. Flames glided in the river, small green flames, red flames, white flames, pursuing, overtaking, joining, crossing each other—then separating slowly

---

[7] Small accordion.—Eds.

or hastily. The traffic of the great city went on in the deepening night upon the sleepless river. We looked on, waiting patiently—there was nothing else to do till the end of the flood; but it was only after a long silence, when he said, in a hesitating voice, "I suppose you fellows remember I did once turn fresh-water sailor for a bit," that we knew we were fated, before the ebb began to run, to hear about one of Marlow's inconclusive experiences.

"I don't want to bother you much with what happened to me personally," he began, showing in this remark the weakness of many tellers of tales who seem so often unaware of what their audience would best like to hear; "yet to understand the effect of it on me you ought to know how I got out there, what I saw, how I went up that river to the place where I first met the poor chap. It was the farthest point of navigation and the culminating point of my experience. It seemed somehow to throw a kind of light on everything about me—and into my thoughts. It was sombre enough, too—and pitiful—not extraordinary in any way—not very clear either. No, not very clear. And yet it seemed to throw a kind of light.

"I had then, as you remember, just returned to London after a lot of Indian Ocean, Pacific, China Seas—a regular dose of the East—six years or so, and I was loafing about, hindering you fellows in your work and invading your homes, just as though I had got a heavenly mission to civilize you. It was very fine for a time, but after a bit I did get tired of resting. Then I began to look for a ship—I should think the hardest work on earth. But the ships wouldn't even look at me. And I got tired of that game, too.

"Now when I was a little chap I had a passion for maps. I would look for hours at South America, or Africa, or Australia, and lose myself in all the glories of exploration. At that time there were many blank spaces on the earth, and when I saw one that looked particularly inviting on a map (but they all look that) I would put my finger on it and say, When I grow up I will go there. The North Pole was one of these places, I remember. Well, I haven't been there yet, and shall not try now. The glamour's off. Other places were scattered about the Equator, and in every sort of latitude all over the two hemispheres. I have been in some of them, and . . . well, we won't talk about that. But there was one yet—the biggest, the most blank, so to speak—that I had a hankering after.

"True, by this time it was not a blank space any more. It had got filled since my boyhood with rivers and lakes and names. It had ceased to be a blank space of delightful mystery—a white patch for a boy to dream gloriously over. It had become a place of darkness. But there was in it one river especially, a mighty big river, that you could see on the map, resembling an immense snake uncoiled, with its head in the sea, its body at rest curving afar over a vast country, and its tail lost in the depths of the land. And as I looked at the map of it in a shop-window, it fascinated me as a snake would a bird—a silly little bird. Then I remembered there was a big concern, a Company for trade on that river. Dash it all! I thought to myself, they can't trade without using some kind of craft on that lot of fresh water—steamboats! Why shouldn't I try to get charge of one? I went on along Fleet Street, but could not shake off the idea. The snake had charmed me.

"You understand it was a Continental concern, that Trading society; but I have a lot of relations living on the Continent, because it's cheap and not so nasty as it looks, they say.

"I am sorry to own I began to worry them. This was already a fresh departure for me. I was not used to get things that way, you know. I always went my own road and on my own legs where I had a mind to go. I wouldn't have believed it of myself; but, then—you see—I felt somehow I must get there by hook or by crook. So I worried them. The men said 'My dear fellow,' and did nothing. Then—would you believe it?—I tried the women. I, Charlie Marlow, set the women to work—to get a job. Heavens! Well, you see, the notion drove me. I had an aunt, a dear enthusiastic soul. She wrote: 'It will be delightful. I am ready to do anything, anything for you. It is a glorious idea. I know the wife of a very high personage in the Administration, and also a man who has lots of influence with,' etc., etc. She was determined to make no end of fuss to get me appointed skipper of a river steamboat, if such was my fancy.

"I got my appointment—of course; and I got it very quick. It appears the Company had received news that one of their captains had been killed in a scuffle with the natives. This was my chance, and it made me the more anxious to go. It was only months and months afterwards, when I made the attempt to recover what was left of the body, that I heard the original quarrel arose from a misunderstanding about some hens. Yes, two black hens. Fresleven—that was the fellow's name, a Dane—thought himself wronged somehow in the bargain, so he went ashore and started to hammer the chief of the village with a stick. Oh, it didn't surprise me in the least to hear this, and at the same time to be told that Fresleven was the gentlest, quietest creature that ever walked on two legs. No doubt he was; but he had been a couple of years already out there engaged in the noble cause, you know, and he probably felt the need at last of asserting his self-respect in some way. Therefore he whacked the old nigger mercilessly, while a big crowd of his people watched him, thunderstruck, till some man—I was told the chief's son—in desperation at hearing the old chap yell, made a tentative jab with a spear at the white man—and of course it went quite easy between the shoulder-blades. Then the whole population cleared into the forest, expecting all kinds of calamities to happen, while, on the other hand, the steamer Fresleven commanded left also in a bad panic, in charge of the engineer, I believe. Afterwards nobody seemed to trouble much about Fresleven's remains, till I got out and stepped into his shoes. I couldn't let it rest, though; but when an opportunity offered at last to meet my predecessor, the grass growing through his ribs was tall enough to hide his bones. They were all there. The supernatural being had not been touched after he fell. And the village was deserted, the huts gaped black, rotting, all askew within the fallen enclosures. A calamity had come to it, sure enough. The people had vanished. Mad terror had scattered them, men, women, and children, through the bush, and they had never returned. What became of the hens I don't know either. I should think the cause of progress got them, anyhow. However, through this glorious affair I got my appointment, before I had fairly begun to hope for it.

"I flew around like mad to get ready, and before forty-eight hours I was crossing the Channel to show myself to my employers, and sign the contract. In a very few

20

hours I arrived in a city that always makes me think of a whited sepulchre.[8] Prejudice no doubt. I had no difficulty in finding the Company's offices. It was the biggest thing in the town, and everybody I met was full of it. They were going to run an over-sea empire, and make no end of coin by trade.

"A narrow and deserted street in deep shadow, high houses, innumerable windows with venetian blinds, a dead silence, grass sprouting between the stones, imposing carriage archways right and left, immense double doors standing ponderously ajar. I slipped through one of these cracks, went up a swept and ungarnished staircase, as arid as a desert, and opened the first door I came to. Two women, one fat and the other slim, sat on straw-bottomed chairs, knitting black wool. The slim one got up and walked straight at me—still knitting with down-cast eyes—and only just as I began to think of getting out of her way, as you would for a somnambulist,[9] stood still, and looked up. Her dress was as plain as an umbrella-cover, and she turned round without a word and preceded me into a waiting-room. I gave my name, and looked about. Deal table in the middle, plain chairs all round the walls, on one end a large shining map, marked with all the colours of a rainbow. There was a vast amount of red—good to see at any time, because one knows that some real work is done in there, a deuce[10] of a lot of blue, a little green, smears of orange, and, on the East Coast, a purple patch, to show where the jolly pioneers of progress drink the jolly lager-beer. However, I wasn't going into any of these. I was going into the yellow. Dead in the centre. And the river was there—fascinating—deadly—like a snake. Ough! A door opened, a white-haired secretarial head, but wearing a compassionate expression, appeared, and a skinny forefinger beckoned me into the sanctuary. Its light was dim, and a heavy writing-desk squatted in the middle. From behind that structure came out an impression of pale plumpness in a frock-coat. The great man himself. He was five feet six, I should judge, and had his grip on the handle-end of ever so many millions. He shook hands, I fancy, murmured vaguely, was satisfied with my French. *Bon voyage.*

"In about forty-five seconds I found myself again in the waiting-room with the compassionate secretary, who, full of desolation and sympathy, made me sign some document. I believe I undertook amongst other things not to disclose any trade secrets. Well, I am not going to.

"I began to feel slightly uneasy. You know I am not used to such ceremonies, and there was something ominous in the atmosphere. It was just as though I had been let into some conspiracy—I don't know—something not quite right; and I was glad to get out. In the outer room the two women knitted black wool feverishly. People were arriving, and the younger one was walking back and forth introducing them. The old one sat on her chair. Her flat cloth slippers were propped up on a foot-warmer, and a cat reposed on her lap. She wore a starched white affair on her head, had a wart on one cheek, and silver-rimmed spectacles hung on the tip of her nose. She glanced

25

---

[8] Crypt, tomb, mausoleum.—Eds.
[9] Sleepwalker.—Eds.
[10] Mild word for devil.—Eds.

at me above the glasses. The swift and indifferent placidity of that look troubled me. Two youths with foolish and cheery countenances were being piloted over, and she threw at them the same quick glance of unconcerned wisdom. She seemed to know all about them and about me, too. An eerie feeling came over me. She seemed uncanny and fateful. Often far away there I thought of these two, guarding the door of Darkness, knitting black wool as for a warm pall, one introducing, introducing continuously to the unknown, the other scrutinizing the cheery and foolish faces with unconcerned old eyes. *Ave!*[11] Old knitter of black wool. *Morituri te salutant.*[12] Not many of those she looked at ever saw her again—not half, by a long way.

"There was yet a visit to the doctor. 'A simple formality,' assured me the secretary, with an air of taking an immense part in all my sorrows. Accordingly a young chap wearing his hat over the left eyebrow, some clerk I suppose,—there must have been clerks in the business, though the house was as still as a house in a city of the dead—came from somewhere upstairs, and led me forth. He was shabby and careless, with ink-stains on the sleeves of his jacket, and his cravat was large and billowy, under a chin shaped like the toe of an old boot. It was a little too early for the doctor, so I proposed a drink, and thereupon he developed a vein of joviality. As we sat over our vermouths he glorified the Company's business, and by and by I expressed casually my surprise at him not going out there. He became very cool and collected all at once. 'I am not such a fool as I look, quoth Plato to his disciples,' he said sententiously, emptied his glass with great resolution, and we rose.

"The old doctor felt my pulse, evidently thinking of something else the while. 'Good, good for there,' he mumbled, and then with a certain eagerness asked me whether I would let him measure my head. Rather surprised, I said Yes, when he produced a thing like calipers and got the dimensions back and front and every way, taking notes carefully. He was an unshaven little man in a threadbare coat like a gaberdine, with his feet in slippers, and I thought him a harmless fool. 'I always ask leave, in the interests of science, to measure the crania of those going out there,' he said. 'And when they come back, too?' I asked. 'Oh, I never see them,' he remarked; 'and, moreover, the changes take place inside, you know.' He smiled, as if at some quiet joke. 'So you are going out there. Famous. Interesting, too.' He gave me a searching glance, and made another note. 'Ever any madness in your family?' he asked, in a matter-of-fact tone. I felt very annoyed. 'Is that question in the interests of science, too?' 'It would be,' he said, without taking notice of my irritation, 'interesting for science to watch the mental changes of individuals, on the spot, but . . .' 'Are you an alienist?' I interrupted. 'Every doctor should be—a little,' answered that original, imperturbably. 'I have a little theory which you Messieurs who go out there must help me to prove. This is my share in the advantages my country shall reap from the possession of such a magnificent dependency. The mere wealth I leave to others. Pardon my questions, but you are the first Englishman coming under my observation . . .' I hastened to assure him I was not in the least typical. 'If I were,' said I,

---

[11] Latin: Hail!—Eds.
[12] Latin: We who are about to die salute you.—Eds.

'I wouldn't be talking like this with you.' 'What you say is rather profound, and probably erroneous,' he said, with a laugh. 'Avoid irritation more than exposure to the sun. Adieu. How do you English say, eh? Good-bye. Ah! Good-bye. Adieu. In the tropics one must before everything keep calm.' . . . He lifted a warning forefinger. . . . '*Du calme, du calme. Adieu.*'

"One thing more remained to do—say good-bye to my excellent aunt. I found her triumphant. I had a cup of tea—the last decent cup of tea for many days—and in a room that most soothingly looked just as you would expect a lady's drawing-room to look, we had a long quiet chat by the fireside. In the course of these confidences it became quite plain to me I had been represented to the wife of the high dignitary, and goodness knows to how many more people besides, as an exceptional and gifted creature—a piece of good fortune for the Company—a man you don't get hold of every day. Good heavens! and I was going to take charge of a two-penny-half-penny river-steamboat with a penny whistle attached! It appeared, however, I was also one of the Workers, with a capital—you know. Something like an emissary of light, something like a lower sort of apostle. There had been a lot of such rot let loose in print and talk just about that time, and the excellent woman, living right in the rush of all that humbug, got carried off her feet. She talked about 'weaning those ignorant millions from their horrid ways,' till, upon my word, she made me quite uncomfortable. I ventured to hint that the Company was run for profit.

"'You forget, dear Charlie, that the labourer is worthy of his hire,' she said, brightly. 'It's queer how out of touch with truth women are. They live in a world of their own, and there has never been anything like it, and never can be. It is too beautiful altogether, and if they were to set it up it would go to pieces before the first sunset. Some confounded fact we men have been living contentedly with ever since the day of creation would start up and knock the whole thing over.

"After this I got embraced, told to wear flannel, be sure to write often, and so on—and I left. In the street—I don't know why—a queer feeling came to me that I was an impostor. Odd thing that I, who used to clear out for any part of the world at twenty-four hours' notice, with less thought than most men give to the crossing of a street, had a moment—I won't say of hesitation, but of startled pause, before this commonplace affair. The best way I can explain it to you is by saying that, for a second or two, I felt as though, instead of going to the centre of a continent, I were about to set off for the centre of the earth.

"I left in a French steamer, and she called in every blamed port they have out there, for, as far as I could see, the sole purpose of landing soldiers and custom-house officers. I watched the coast. Watching a coast as it slips by the ship is like thinking about an enigma. There it is before you—smiling, frowning, inviting, grand, mean, insipid, or savage, and always mute with an air of whispering, Come and find out. This one was almost featureless, as if still in the making, with an aspect of monotonous grimness. The edge of a colossal jungle, so dark-green as to be almost black, fringed with white surf, ran straight, like a ruled line, far, far away along a blue sea whose glitter was blurred by a creeping mist. The sun was fierce, the land seemed to glisten and drip with steam. Here and there grayish-whitish specks showed up clustered inside the white surf, with a flag flying above them perhaps. Settlements some centuries old, and still no bigger than pinheads on the untouched expanse of their background. We pounded along, stopped, landed soldiers; went on, landed custom-house clerks to levy toll in what looked like a God-forsaken wilderness, with a tin shed and a flag-pole lost in it; landed more soldiers—to take care of the custom-house clerks, presumably. Some, I heard, got drowned in the surf; but whether they did or not, nobody seemed particularly to care. They were just flung out there, and on we went. Every day the coast looked the same, as though we had not moved; but we passed various places—trading places—with names like Gran' Bassam, Little Popo; names that seemed to belong to some sordid farce acted in front of a sinister back-cloth. The idleness of a passenger, my isolation amongst all these men with whom I had no point of contact, the oily and languid sea, the uniform sombreness of the coast, seemed to keep me away from the truth of things, within the toil of a mournful and senseless delusion. The voice of the surf heard now and then was a positive pleasure, like the speech of a brother. It was something natural, that had its reason, that had a meaning. Now and then a boat from the shore gave one a momentary contact with reality. It was paddled by black fellows. You could see from afar the white of their eyeballs glistening. They shouted, sang; their bodies streamed with perspiration; they had faces like grotesque masks—these chaps; but they had bone, muscle, a wild vitality, an intense energy of movement, that was as natural and true as the surf along their coast. They wanted no excuse for being there. They were a great comfort to look at. For a time I would feel I belonged still to a world of straightforward facts; but the feeling would not last long. Something would turn up to scare it away. Once, I remember, we came upon a man-of-war anchored off the coast. There wasn't even a shed there, and she was shelling the bush. It appears the French had one of their wars going on thereabouts. Her ensign dropped limp like a rag; the muzzles of the long six-inch guns stuck out all over the low hull; the greasy, slimy swell swung her up lazily and let her down, swaying her thin masts. In the empty immensity of earth, sky, and water, there she was, incomprehensible, firing into a continent. Pop, would go one of the six-inch guns; a small flame would dart and vanish, a little white smoke would disappear, a tiny projectile would give a feeble screech—and nothing happened. Nothing could happen. There was a touch of insanity in the proceeding, a sense of lugubrious drollery in the sight; and it was not dissipated by somebody on board assuring me earnestly there was a camp of natives—he called them enemies!— hidden out of sight somewhere.

"We gave her her letters (I heard the men in that lonely ship were dying of fever at the rate of three a day) and went on. We called at some more places with farci- cal names, where the merry dance of death and trade goes on in a still and earthy atmosphere as of an overheated catacomb; all along the formless coast bordered by dangerous surf, as if Nature herself had tried to ward off intruders; in and out of rivers, streams of death in life, whose banks were rotting into mud, whose waters, thickened into slime, invaded the contorted mangroves, that seemed to writhe at us in the extremity of an impotent despair. Nowhere did we stop long enough to get a particularized impression, but the general sense of vague and oppressive wonder grew upon me. It was like a weary pilgrimage amongst hints for nightmares.

"It was upward of thirty days before I saw the mouth of the big river. We anchored off the seat of the government. But my work would not begin till some two hundred miles farther on. So as soon as I could I made a start for a place thirty miles higher up.

"I had my passage on a little sea-going steamer. Her captain was a Swede, and knowing me for a seaman, invited me on the bridge. He was a young man, lean, fair, and morose, with lanky hair and a shuffling gait. As we left the miserable little wharf, he tossed his head contemptuously at the shore. 'Been living there?' he asked. I said, 'Yes.' 'Fine lot these government chaps—are they not?' he went on, speaking English with great precision and considerable bitterness. 'It is funny what some people will do for a few francs a month. I wonder what becomes of that kind when it goes up country?' I said to him I expected to see that soon. 'So-o-o!' he exclaimed. He shuffled athwart, keeping one eye ahead vigilantly. 'Don't be too sure,' he continued. 'The other day I took up a man who hanged himself on the road. He was a Swede, too.' 'Hanged himself! Why, in God's name?' I cried. He kept on looking out watchfully. 'Who knows? The sun too much for him, or the country perhaps.'

"At last we opened a reach. A rocky cliff appeared, mounds of turned-up earth by the shore, houses on a hill, others with iron roofs, amongst a waste of excavations, or hanging to the declivity. A continuous noise of the rapids above hovered over this scene of inhabited devastation. A lot of people, mostly black and naked, moved about like ants. A jetty projected into the river. A blinding sunlight drowned all this at times in a sudden recrudescence of glare. 'There's your Company's station,' said the Swede, pointing to three wooden barrack-like structures on the rocky slope. 'I will send your things up. Four boxes did you say? So. Farewell.'

"I came upon a boiler wallowing in the grass, then found a path leading up the hill. It turned aside for the boulders, and also for an undersized railway-truck lying there on its back with its wheels in the air. One was off. The thing looked as dead as the carcass of some animal. I came upon more pieces of decaying machinery, a stack of rusty rails. To the left a clump of trees made a shady spot, where dark things seemed to stir feebly. I blinked, the path was steep. A horn tooted to the right, and I saw the black people run. A heavy and dull detonation shook the ground, a puff of smoke came out of the cliff, and that was all. No change appeared on the face of the rock. They were building a railway. The cliff was not in the way or anything; but this objectless blasting was all the work going on.

"A slight clinking behind me made me turn my head. Six black men advanced in a file, toiling up the path. They walked erect and slow, balancing small baskets full of earth on their heads, and the clink kept time with their footsteps. Black rags were wound round their loins, and the short ends behind waggled to and fro like tails. I could see every rib, the joints of their limbs were like knots in a rope; each had an iron collar on his neck, and all were connected together with a chain whose bights[13] swung between them, rhythmically clinking. Another report from the cliff made me think suddenly of that ship of war I had seen firing into a continent. It was the same

---

[13] The middle part of a chain.—Eds.

kind of ominous voice; but these men could by no stretch of imagination be called enemies. They were called criminals, and the outraged law, like the bursting shells, had come to them, an insoluble mystery from the sea. All their meagre breasts panted together, the violently dilated nostrils quivered, the eyes stared stonily uphill. They passed me within six inches, without a glance, with that complete, deathlike indifference of unhappy savages. Behind this raw matter one of the reclaimed, the product of the new forces at work, strolled despondently, carrying a rifle by its middle. He had a uniform jacket with one button off, and seeing a white man on the path, hoisted his weapon to his shoulder with alacrity. This was simple prudence, white men being so much alike at a distance that he could not tell who I might be. He was speedily reassured, and with a large, white, rascally grin, and a glance at his charge, seemed to take me into partnership in his exalted trust. After all, I also was a part of the great cause of these high and just proceedings.

"Instead of going up, I turned and descended to the left. My idea was to let that chain-gang get out of sight before I climbed the hill. You know I am not particularly tender; I've had to strike and to fend off. I've had to resist and to attack sometimes—that's only one way of resisting—without counting the exact cost, according to the demands of such sort of life as I had blundered into. I've seen the devil of violence, and the devil of greed, and the devil of hot desire; but, by all the stars! these were strong, lusty, red-eyed devils, that swayed and drove men—men, I tell you. But as I stood on this hillside, I foresaw that in the blinding sunshine of that land I would become acquainted with a flabby, pretending, weak-eyed devil of a rapacious and pitiless folly. How insidious he could be, too, I was only to find out several months later and a thousand miles farther. For a moment I stood appalled, as though by a warning. Finally I descended the hill, obliquely, towards the trees I had seen.

"I avoided a vast artificial hole somebody had been digging on the slope, the purpose of which I found it impossible to divine. It wasn't a quarry or a sandpit, anyhow. It was just a hole. It might have been connected with the philanthropic desire of giving the criminals something to do. I don't know. Then I nearly fell into a very narrow ravine, almost no more than a scar in the hillside. I discovered that a lot of imported drainage-pipes for the settlement had been tumbled in there. There wasn't one that was not broken. It was a wanton smash-up. At last I got under the trees. My purpose was to stroll into the shade for a moment; but no sooner within than it seemed to me I had stepped into the gloomy circle of some Inferno. The rapids were near, and an uninterrupted, uniform, headlong, rushing noise filled the mournful stillness of the grove, where not a breath stirred, not a leaf moved, with a mysterious sound—as though the tearing pace of the launched earth had suddenly become audible.

"Black shapes crouched, lay, sat between the trees leaning against the trunks, clinging to the earth, half coming out, half effaced within the dim light, in all the attitudes of pain, abandonment, and despair. Another mine on the cliff went off, followed by a slight shudder of the soil under my feet. The work was going on. The work! And this was the place where some of the helpers had withdrawn to die.

"They were dying slowly—it was very clear. They were not enemies, they were not criminals, they were nothing earthly now,—nothing but black shadows of disease and starvation, lying confusedly in the greenish gloom. Brought from all the recesses of the coast in all the legality of time contracts, lost in uncongenial surroundings, fed on unfamiliar food, they sickened, became inefficient, and were then allowed to crawl away and rest. These moribund shapes were free as air—and nearly *oxy.* as thin. I began to distinguish the gleam of the eyes under the trees. Then, glancing down, I saw a face near my hand. The black bones reclined at full length with one shoulder against the tree, and slowly the eyelids rose and the sunken eyes looked up at me, enormous and vacant, a kind of blind, white flicker in the depths of the orbs, which died out slowly. The man seemed young—almost a boy—but you know with them it's hard to tell. I found nothing else to do but to offer him one of my good Swede's ship's biscuits I had in my pocket. The fingers closed slowly on it and held— *yarn* there was no other movement and no other glance. He had tied a bit of white worsted round his neck—Why? Where did he get it? Was it a badge—an ornament—a charm—a propitiatory act? Was there any idea at all connected with it? It looked startling round his black neck, this bit of white thread from beyond the seas.

"Near the same tree two more bundles of acute angles sat with their legs drawn up. One, with his chin propped on his knees, stared at nothing, in an intolerable and appalling manner: his brother phantom rested its forehead, as if overcome with a great weariness; and all about others were scattered in every pose of contorted collapse, as in some picture of a massacre or a pestilence. While I stood horror-struck, *animal-like* one of these creatures rose to his hands and knees, and went off on all-fours towards the river to drink. He lapped out of his hand, then sat up in the sunlight, crossing his shins in front of him, and after a time let his woolly head fall on his breastbone.

"I didn't want any more loitering in the shade, and I made haste towards the station. When near the buildings I met a white man, in such an unexpected elegance of get-up that in the first moment I took him for a sort of vision. I saw a high starched collar, white cuffs, a light alpaca jacket, snowy trousers, a clean necktie, and varnished boots. No hat. Hair parted, brushed, oiled, under a green-lined parasol held in a big white hand. He was amazing, and had a penholder behind his ear.

"I shook hands with this miracle, and I learned he was the Company's chief accountant, and that all the book-keeping was done at this station. He had come out for a moment, he said, 'to get a breath of fresh air.' The expression sounded wonderfully odd, with its suggestion of sedentary desk-life. I wouldn't have mentioned the fellow to you at all, only it was from his lips that I first heard the name of the man who is so indissolubly connected with the memories of that time. Moreover, I respected the fellow. Yes; I respected his collars, his vast cuffs, his brushed hair. His appearance was certainly that of a hairdresser's dummy; but in the great demoralization of the land he kept up his appearance. That's backbone. His starched collars and got-up shirt-fronts were achievements of character. He had been out nearly three years; and, later, I could not help asking him how he managed to sport such linen. He had just the faintest blush, and said modestly, 'I've been teaching one of the native women about the station. It was difficult. She had a distaste for the work.' Thus this man had verily accomplished something. And he was devoted to his books, which were in apple-pie order.

"Everything else in the station was in a muddle,—heads, things, buildings. 45
Strings of dusty niggers with splay feet arrived and departed; a stream of manufactured goods, rubbishy cottons, beads, and brass-wire set into the depths of darkness,
and in return came a precious trickle of ivory.

"I had to wait in the station for ten days—an eternity. I lived in a hut in the
yard, but to be out of the chaos I would sometimes get into the accountant's office.
It was built of horizontal planks, and so badly put together that, as he bent over his
high desk, he was barred from neck to heels with narrow strips of sunlight. There was
no need to open the big shutter to see. It was hot there, too; big flies buzzed fiend-
ishly, and did not sting, but stabbed. I sat generally on the floor, while, of faultless
appearance (and even slightly scented), perching on a high stool, he wrote, he wrote.
Sometimes he stood up for exercise. When a truckle-bed with a sick man (some
invalid agent from up-country) was put in there, he exhibited a gentle annoyance.
'The groans of this sick person,' he said, 'distract my attention. And without that it is
extremely difficult to guard against clerical errors in this climate.'

"One day he remarked, without lifting his head, 'In the interior you will no
doubt meet Mr. Kurtz.' On my asking who Mr. Kurtz was, he said he was a first-class
agent; and seeing my disappointment at this information, he added slowly, laying
down his pen, 'He is a very remarkable person.' Further questions elicited from him
that Mr. Kurtz was at present in charge of a trading post, a very important one, in
the true ivory-country, at 'the very bottom of there. Sends in as much ivory as all the
others put together . . .' He began to write again. The sick man was too ill to groan.
The flies buzzed in a great peace.

"Suddenly there was a growing murmur of voices and a great tramping of feet.
A caravan had come in. A violent babble of uncouth sounds burst out on the other
side of the planks. All the carriers were speaking together, and in the midst of the
uproar the lamentable voice of the chief agent was heard 'giving it up' tearfully for
the twentieth time that day. . . . He rose slowly. 'What a frightful row,'[14] he said. He
crossed the room gently to look at the sick man, and returning, said to me, 'He
does not hear.' 'What! Dead?' I asked, startled. 'No, not yet,' he answered, with great
composure. Then, alluding with a toss of the head to the tumult in the station-yard,
'When one has got to make correct entries, one comes to hate those savages—hate
them to the death.' He remained thoughtful for a moment. 'When you see Mr. Kurtz,'
he went on, 'tell him from me that everything here'—he glanced at the desk—'is
very satisfactory. I don't like to write to him—with those messengers of ours you
never know who may get hold of your letter—at that Central Station.' He stared at
me for a moment with his mild, bulging eyes. 'Oh, he will go far, very far,' he began
again. 'He will be somebody in the Administration before long. They, above—the
Council in Europe, you know—mean him to be.'

"He turned to his work. The noise outside had ceased, and presently in going
out I stopped at the door. In the steady buzz of flies the homeward-bound agent

---

[14]Racket.—EDS.

was lying flushed and insensible; the other, bent over his books, was making correct entries of perfectly correct transactions; and fifty feet below the doorstep I could see the still tree-tops of the grove of death.

"Next day I left that station at last, with a caravan of sixty men, for a two-hundred-mile tramp.   50

"No use telling you much about that. Paths, paths, everywhere; a stamped-in network of paths spreading over the empty land, through long grass, through burnt grass, through thickets, down and up chilly ravines, up and down stony hills ablaze with heat; and a solitude, a solitude, nobody, not a hut. The population had cleared out a long time ago. Well, if a lot of mysterious niggers armed with all kinds of fearful weapons suddenly took to travelling on the road between Deal and Gravesend, catching the yokels right and left to carry heavy loads for them, I fancy every farm and cottage thereabouts would get empty very soon. Only here the dwellings were gone, too. Still I passed through several abandoned villages. There's something pathetically childish in the ruins of grass walls. Day after day, with the stamp and shuffle of sixty pair of bare feet behind me, each pair under a 60-lb. load. Camp, cook, sleep, strike camp, march. Now and then a carrier dead in harness, at rest in the long grass near the path, with an empty water-gourd and his long staff lying by his side. A great silence around and above. Perhaps on some quiet night the tremor of far-off drums, sinking, swelling, a tremor vast, faint; a sound weird, appealing, suggestive, and wild — and perhaps with as profound a meaning as the sound of bells in a Christian country. Once a white man in an unbuttoned uniform, camping on the path with an armed escort of lank Zanzibaris, very hospitable and festive — not to say drunk. Was looking after the upkeep of the road he declared. Can't say I saw any road or any upkeep, unless the body of a middle-aged negro, with a bullet-hole in the forehead, upon which I absolutely stumbled three miles farther on, may be considered as a permanent improvement. I had a white companion, too, not a bad chap, but rather too fleshy and with the exasperating habit of fainting on the hot hillsides, miles away from the least bit of shade and water. Annoying, you know, to hold your own coat like a parasol over a man's head while he is coming-to. I couldn't help asking him once what he meant by coming there at all. 'To make money, of course. What do you think?' he said, scornfully. Then he got fever, and had to be carried in a hammock slung under a pole. As he weighed sixteen stone I had no end of rows with the carriers. They jibbed, ran away, sneaked off with their loads in the night — quite a mutiny. So, one evening, I made a speech in English with gestures, not one of which was lost to the sixty pairs of eyes before me, and the next morning I started the hammock off in front all right. An hour afterwards I came upon the whole concern wrecked in a bush — man, hammock, groans, blankets, horrors. The heavy pole had skinned his poor nose. He was very anxious for me to kill somebody, but there wasn't the shadow of a carrier near. I remembered the old doctor — 'It would be interesting for science to watch the mental changes of individuals, on the spot.' I felt I was becoming scientifically interesting. However, all that is to no purpose. On the fifteenth day I came in sight of the big river again, and hobbled into the Central Station. It was on a back water surrounded by scrub and forest, with a pretty border of smelly mud on one side, and on the three others enclosed by a crazy fence of rushes. A neglected gap was all the gate it had, and the first glance at the place was enough to let you see the flabby devil was running that show. White men with long staves in their hands appeared languidly from amongst the buildings, strolling up to take a look at me, and then retired out of sight somewhere. One of them, a stout, excitable chap with black moustaches, informed me with great volubility and many digressions, as soon as I told him who I was, that my steamer was at the bottom of the river. I was thunderstruck. What, how, why? Oh, it was 'all right.' The 'manager himself' was there. All quite correct. 'Everybody had behaved splendidly! splendidly!'—'you must,' he said in agitation, 'go and see the general manager at once. He is waiting!'

"I did not see the real significance of that wreck at once. I fancy I see it now, but I am not sure—not at all. Certainly the affair was too stupid—when I think of it—to be altogether natural. Still . . . But at the moment it presented itself simply as a confounded nuisance. The steamer was sunk. They had started two days before in a sudden hurry up the river with the manager on board, in charge of some volunteer skipper, and before they had been out three hours they tore the bottom out of her on stones, and she sank near the south bank. I asked myself what I was to do there, now my boat was lost. As a matter of fact, I had plenty to do in fishing my command out of the river. I had to set about it the very next day. That, and the repairs when I brought the pieces to the station, took some months.

"My first interview with the manager was curious. He did not ask me to sit down after my twenty-mile walk that morning. He was commonplace in complexion, in feature, in manners, and in voice. He was of middle size and of ordinary build. His eyes, of the usual blue, were perhaps remarkably cold, and he certainly could make his glance fall on one as trenchant and heavy as an axe. But even at these times the rest of his person seemed to disclaim the intention. Otherwise there was only an indefinable, faint expression of his lips, something stealthy—a smile—not a smile—I remember it, but I can't explain. It was unconscious, this smile was, though just after he had said something it got intensified for an instant. It came at the end of his speeches like a seal applied on the words to make the meaning of the commonest phrase appear absolutely inscrutable. He was a common trader, from his youth up employed in these parts—nothing more. He was obeyed, yet he inspired neither love nor fear, nor even respect. He inspired uneasiness. That was it! Uneasiness. Not a definite mistrust—just uneasiness—nothing more. You have no idea how effective such a . . . a . . . faculty can be. He had no genius for organizing, for initiative, or for order even. That was evident in such things as the deplorable state of the station. He had no learning, and no intelligence. His position had come to him—why? Perhaps because he was never ill . . . He had served three terms of three years out there . . . Because triumphant health in the general rout of constitutions is a kind of power in itself. When he went home on leave he rioted on a large scale—pompously. Jack ashore[15]—with a

---

[15]Shorthand for a sailor (Jack) on shore leave. From the traditional sea chantey about a drunken sailor, "Get Up Jack! John, Sit Down!"—EDS.

difference—in externals only. This one could gather from his casual talk. He origi-
nated nothing, he could keep the routine going—that's all. But he was great. He
was great by this little thing that it was impossible to tell what could control such a
man. He never gave that secret away. Perhaps there was nothing within him. Such
a suspicion made one pause—for out there there were no external checks. Once
when various tropical diseases had laid low almost every 'agent' in the station, he was
heard to say, 'Men who come out here should have no entrails.' He sealed the utterance with that smile of his, as though it had been a door opening into a darkness
he had in his keeping. You fancied you had seen things—but the seal was on. When
annoyed at meal-times by the constant quarrels of the white men about precedence,
he ordered an immense round table to be made, for which a special house had to be
built. This was the station's mess-room. Where he sat was the first place—the rest
were nowhere. One felt this to be his unalterable conviction. He was neither civil nor
uncivil. He was quiet. He allowed his 'boy'—an overfed young negro from the coast—
to treat the white men, under his very eyes, with provoking insolence.

"He began to speak as soon as he saw me. I had been very long on the road. He
could not wait. Had to start without me. The up-river stations had to be relieved.
There had been so many delays already that he did not know who was dead and
who was alive, and how they got on—and so on, and so on. He paid no attention to my explanations, and, playing with a stick of sealing-wax, repeated several
times that the situation was 'very grave, very grave.' There were rumours that a
very important station was in jeopardy, and its chief, Mr. Kurtz, was ill. Hoped it
was not true. Mr. Kurtz was . . . I felt weary and irritable. Hang Kurtz, I thought. I
interrupted him by saying I had heard of Mr. Kurtz on the coast. 'Ah! So they talk of
him down there,' he murmured to himself. Then he began again, assuring me Mr.
Kurtz was the best agent he had, an exceptional man, of the greatest importance to
the Company; therefore I could understand his anxiety. He was, he said, 'very, very
uneasy.' Certainly he fidgeted on his chair a good deal, exclaimed, 'Ah, Mr. Kurtz!'
broke the stick of sealing-wax and seemed dumfounded by the accident. Next
thing he wanted to know 'how long it would take to' . . . I interrupted him again.
Being hungry, you know, and kept on my feet too, I was getting savage. 'How can
I tell?' I said. 'I haven't even seen the wreck yet—some months, no doubt.' All this
talk seemed to me so futile. 'Some months,' he said. 'Well, let us say three months
before we can make a start. Yes. That ought to do the affair.' I flung out of his hut
(he lived all alone in a clay hut with a sort of verandah) muttering to myself my
opinion of him. He was a chattering idiot. Afterwards I took it back when it was
borne in upon me startlingly with what extreme nicety he had estimated the time
requisite for the 'affair.'

"I went to work the next day, turning, so to speak, my back on that station. In
that way only it seemed to me I could keep my hold on the redeeming facts of life.
Still, one must look about sometimes; and then I saw this station, these men strolling aimlessly about in the sunshine of the yard. I asked myself sometimes what it all
meant. They wandered here and there with their absurd long staves in their hands,
like a lot of faithless pilgrims bewitched inside a rotten fence. The word 'ivory' rang

55

in the air, was whispered, was sighed. You would think they were praying to it. A taint of imbecile rapacity blew through it all, like a whiff from some corpse. By Jove! I've never seen anything so unreal in my life. And outside, the silent wilderness surrounding this cleared speck on the earth struck me as something great and invincible, like evil or truth, waiting patiently for the passing away of this fantastic invasion.

"Oh, these months! Well, never mind. Various things happened. One evening a grass shed full of calico, cotton prints, beads, and I don't know what else, burst into a blaze so suddenly that you would have thought the earth had opened to let an avenging fire consume all that trash. I was smoking my pipe quietly by my dismantled steamer, and saw them all cutting capers in the light, with their arms lifted high, when the stout man with moustaches came tearing down to the river, a tin pail in his hand, assured me that everybody was 'behaving splendidly, splendidly,' dipped about a quart of water and tore back again. I noticed there was a hole in the bottom of his pail.

"I strolled up. There was no hurry. You see the thing had gone off like a box of matches. It had been hopeless from the very first. The flame had leaped high, driven everybody back, lighted up everything—and collapsed. The shed was already a heap of embers glowing fiercely. A nigger was being beaten near by. They said he had caused the fire in some way; be that as it may, he was screeching most horribly. I saw him, later, for several days, sitting in a bit of shade looking very sick and trying to recover himself: afterwards he arose and went out—and the wilderness without a sound took him into its bosom again. As I approached the glow from the dark I found myself at the back of two men, talking. I heard the name of Kurtz pronounced, then the words, 'take advantage of this unfortunate accident.' One of the men was the manager. I wished him a good evening. 'Did you ever see anything like it—eh? it is incredible,' he said, and walked off. The other man remained. He was a first-class agent, young, gentlemanly, a bit reserved, with a forked little beard and a hooked nose. He was stand-offish with the other agents, and they on their side said he was the manager's spy upon them. As to me, I had hardly ever spoken to him before. We got into talk, and by and by we strolled away from the hissing ruins. Then he asked me to his room, which was in the main building of the station. He struck a match, and I perceived that this young aristocrat had not only a silver-mounted dressing-case but also a whole candle all to himself. Just at that time the manager was the only man supposed to have any right to candles. Native mats covered the clay walls; a collection of spears, assegais,[16] shields, knives was hung up in trophies. The business entrusted to this fellow was the making of bricks—so I had been informed; but there wasn't a fragment of a brick anywhere in the station, and he had been there more than a year—waiting. It seems he could not make bricks without something, I don't know what—straw maybe. Anyways, it could not be found there, and as it was not likely to be sent from Europe, it did not appear clear to me what he was waiting for. An act of special creation perhaps. However, they were all waiting—all the sixteen or twenty pilgrims of them—for something; and upon my word it did not seem an uncongenial occupation, from the way they took it, though the only

---

[16]African spears with short shafts and long blades. — EDS.

thing that ever came to them was disease—as far as I could see. They beguiled the time by backbiting and intriguing against each other in a foolish kind of way. There was an air of plotting about that station, but nothing came of it, of course. It was as unreal as everything else—as the philanthropic pretence of the whole concern, as their talk, as their government, as their show of work. The only real feeling was a desire to get appointed to a trading-post where ivory was to be had, so that they could earn percentages. They intrigued and slandered and hated each other only on that account,—but as to effectually lifting a little finger—oh, no. By heavens! there is something after all in the world allowing one man to steal a horse while another must not look at a halter. Steal a horse straight out. Very well. He has done it. Perhaps he can ride. But there is a way of looking at a halter that would provoke the most charitable of saints into a kick.

"I had no idea why he wanted to be sociable, but as we chatted in there it suddenly occurred to me the fellow was trying to get at something—in fact, pumping me. He alluded constantly to Europe, to the people I was supposed to know there—putting leading questions as to my acquaintances in the sepulchral city, and so on. His little eyes glittered like mica discs—with curiosity—though he tried to keep up a bit of superciliousness. At first I was astonished, but very soon I became awfully curious to see what he would find out from me. I couldn't possibly imagine what I had in me to make it worth his while. It was very pretty to see how he baffled himself, for in truth my body was full only of chills, and my head had nothing in it but that wretched steamboat business. It was evident he took me for a perfectly shameless prevaricator. At last he got angry, and, to conceal a movement of furious annoyance, he yawned. I rose. Then I noticed a small sketch in oils, on a panel, representing a woman, draped and blindfolded, carrying a lighted torch. The background was sombre—almost black. The movement of the woman was stately, and the effect of the torch-light on the face was sinister.

evasive

"It arrested me, and he stood by civilly, holding an empty half-pint champagne bottle (medical comforts) with the candle stuck in it. To my question he said Mr. Kurtz had painted this—in this very station more than a year ago—while waiting for means to go to his trading-post. 'Tell me, pray,' said I, 'who is this Mr. Kurtz?'

"'The chief of the Inner Station,' he answered in a short tone, looking away. 'Much obliged,' I said, laughing. 'And you are the brickmaker of the Central Station. Everyone knows that.' He was silent for a while. 'He is a prodigy,' he said at last. 'He is an emissary of pity, and science, and progress, and devil knows what else. We want,' he began to declaim suddenly, 'for the guidance of the cause intrusted to us by Europe, so to speak, higher intelligence, wide sympathies, a singleness of purpose.' 'Who says that?' I asked. 'Lots of them,' he replied. 'Some even write that; and so *he* comes here, a special being, as you ought to know.' 'Why ought I to know?' I interrupted, really surprised. He paid no attention. 'Yes. To-day he is chief of the best station, next year he will be assistant-manager, two years more and . . . but I daresay you know what he will be in two years' time. You are of the new gang—the gang of virtue. The same people who sent him specially also recommended you. Oh, don't say no. I've my own eyes to trust.' Light dawned upon me. My dear aunt's influential acquaintances were

60

producing an unexpected effect upon that young man. I nearly burst into a laugh. 'Do you read the Company's confidential correspondence?' I asked. He hadn't a word to say. It was great fun. 'When Mr. Kurtz,' I continued, severely, 'is General Manager, you won't have the opportunity.'

"He blew the candle out suddenly, and we went outside. The moon had risen. Black figures strolled about listlessly, pouring water on the glow, whence proceeded a sound of hissing; steam ascended in the moonlight, the beaten nigger groaned somewhere. 'What a row the brute makes!' said the indefatigable man with the moustaches, appearing near us. 'Serve him right. Transgression—punishment—bang! Pitiless, pitiless. That's the only way. This will prevent all conflagrations for the future. I was just telling the manager . . .' He noticed my companion, and became crestfallen all at once. 'Not in bed yet,' he said, with a kind of servile heartiness; 'it's so natural. Ha! Danger—agitation.' He vanished. I went on to the river-side, and the other followed me. I heard a scathing murmur at my ear, 'Heap of muffs—go to.' The pilgrims could be seen in knots gesticulating, discussing. Several had still their staves in their hands. I verily believe they took these sticks to bed with them. Beyond the fence the forest stood up spectrally in the moonlight, and through the dim stir, through the faint sounds of that lamentable courtyard, the silence of the land went home to one's very heart—its mystery, its greatness, the amazing reality of its concealed life. The hurt nigger moaned feebly somewhere near by, and then fetched a deep sigh that made me mend my pace away from there. I felt a hand introducing itself under my arm. 'My dear sir,' said the fellow, 'I don't want to be misunderstood, and especially by you, who will see Mr. Kurtz long before I can have that pleasure. I wouldn't like him to get a false idea of my disposition. . . .'

"I let him run on, this papier-mâché Mephistopheles, and it seemed to me that if I tried I could poke my forefinger through him, and would find nothing inside but a little loose dirt, maybe. He, don't you see, had been planning to be assistant-manager by and by under the present man, and I could see that the coming of that Kurtz had upset them both not a little. He talked precipitately, and I did not try to stop him. I had my shoulders against the wreck of my steamer, hauled up on the slope like a carcass of some big river animal. The smell of mud, of primeval mud, by Jove! was in my nostrils, the high stillness of primeval forest was before my eyes; there were shiny patches on the black creek. The moon had spread over everything a thin layer of silver—over the rank grass, over the mud, upon the wall of matted vegetation standing higher than the wall of a temple, over the great river I could see through a sombre gap glittering, glittering, as it flowed broadly by without a murmur. All this was great, expectant, mute, while the man jabbered about himself. I wondered whether the stillness on the face of the immensity looking at us two were meant as an appeal or as a menace. What were we who had strayed in here? Could we handle that dumb thing, or would it handle us? I felt how big, how confoundedly big, was that thing that couldn't talk, and perhaps was deaf as well. What was in there? I could see a little ivory coming out from there, and I had heard Mr. Kurtz was in there. I had heard enough about it, too—God knows! Yet somehow it didn't bring any image with it—no more than if I had been told an angel or a fiend was in there. I believed it in the same way one of you might believe there are inhabitants in the planet Mars. I knew once a Scotch sailmaker who was certain, dead sure, there were people in Mars. If you asked him for some idea how they looked and behaved, he would get shy and mutter something about 'walking on all-fours.' If you as much as smiled, he would — though a man of sixty — offer to fight you. I would not have gone so far as to fight for Kurtz, but I went for him near enough to a lie. You know I hate, detest, and can't bear a lie, not because I am straighter than the rest of us, but simply because it appalls me. There is a taint of death, a flavour of mortality in lies — which is exactly what I hate and detest in the world — what I want to forget. It makes me miserable and sick, like biting something rotten would do. Temperament, I suppose. Well, I went near enough to it by letting the young fool there believe anything he liked to imagine as to my influence in Europe. I became in an instant as much of a pretence as the rest of the bewitched pilgrims. This simply because I had a notion it somehow would be of help to that Kurtz whom at the time I did not see — you understand. He was just a word for me. I did not see the man in the name any more than you do. Do you see him? Do you see the story? Do you see anything? It seems to me I am trying to tell you a dream — making a vain attempt, because no relation of a dream can convey the dream-sensation, that commingling of absurdity, surprise, and bewilderment in a tremor of struggling revolt, that notion of being captured by the incredible which is of the very essence of dreams. . . ."

He was silent for a while.

". . . No, it is impossible; it is impossible to convey the life-sensation of any given epoch of one's existence — that which makes its truth, its meaning — its subtle and penetrating essence. It is impossible. We live as we dream — alone. . . ."

He paused again as if reflecting, then added —

"Of course in this you fellows see more than I could then. You see me, whom you know. . . ."

It had become so pitch dark that we listeners could hardly see one another. For a long time already he, sitting apart, had been no more to us than a voice. There was not a word from anybody. The others might have been asleep, but I was awake. I listened, I listened on the watch for the sentence, for the word, that would give me the clue to the faint uneasiness inspired by this narrative that seemed to shape itself without human lips in the heavy night-air of the river.

". . . Yes — I let him run on," Marlow began again, "and think what he pleased about the powers that were behind me. I did! And there was nothing behind me! There was nothing but that wretched, old, mangled steamboat I was leaning against, while he talked fluently about 'the necessity for every man to get on.' 'And when one comes out here, you conceive, it is not to gaze at the moon.' Mr. Kurtz was a 'universal genius,' but even a genius would find it easier to work with 'adequate tools — intelligent men.' He did not make bricks — why, there was a physical impossibility in the way — as I was well aware; and if he did secretarial work for the manager, it was because 'no sensible man rejects wantonly the confidence of his superiors.' Did I see it? I saw it. What more did I want? What I really wanted was rivets, by heaven! Rivets. To get on with the work — to stop the hole. Rivets I wanted. There were cases

65

of them down at the coast—cases—piled up—burst—split! You kicked a loose rivet at every second step in that station yard on the hillside. Rivets had rolled into the grove of death. You could fill your pockets with rivets for the trouble of stooping down—and there wasn't one rivet to be found where it was wanted. We had plates that would do, but nothing to fasten them with. And every week the messenger, a lone negro, letter-bag on shoulder and staff in hand, left our station for the coast. And several times a week a coast caravan came in with trade goods—ghastly glazed calico that made you shudder only to look at it, glass beads value about a penny a quart, confounded spotted cotton handkerchiefs. And no rivets. Three carriers could have brought all that was wanted to set that steamboat afloat.

"He was becoming confidential now, but I fancy my unresponsive attitude must have exasperated him at last, for he judged it necessary to inform me he feared neither God nor devil, let alone any mere man. I said I could see that very well, but what I wanted was a certain quantity of rivets—and rivets were what really Mr. Kurtz wanted, if he had only known it. Now letters went to the coast every week. . . . 'My dear sir,' he cried, 'I write from dictation.' I demanded rivets. There was a way—for an intelligent man. He changed his manner; became very cold, and suddenly began to talk about a hippopotamus; wondered whether sleeping on board the steamer (I stuck to my salvage night and day) I wasn't disturbed. There was an old hippo that had the bad habit of getting out on the bank and roaming at night over the station grounds. The pilgrims used to turn out in a body and empty every rifle they could lay hands on at him. Some even had sat up o' nights for him. All this energy was wasted, though. 'That animal has a charmed life,' he said; 'but you can say this only of brutes in this country. No man—you apprehend me?—no man here bears a charmed life.' He stood there for a moment in the moonlight with his delicate hooked nose set a little askew, and his mica eyes glittering without a wink, then, with a curt Good-night, he strode off. I could see he was disturbed and considerably puzzled, which made me feel more hopeful than I had been for days. It was a great comfort to turn from that chap to my influential friend, the battered, twisted, ruined, tin-pot steamboat. I clambered on board. She rang under my feet like an empty Huntley & Palmer biscuit-tin kicked along a gutter; she was nothing so solid in make, and rather less pretty in shape, but I had expended enough hard work on her to make me love her. No influential friend would have served me better. She had given me a chance to come out a bit—to find out what I could do. No, I don't like work. I had rather laze about and think of all the fine things that can be done. I don't like work—no man does—but I like what is in the work—the chance to find yourself. Your own reality—for yourself, not for others—what no other man can ever know. They can only see the mere show, and never can tell what it really means.

"I was not surprised to see somebody sitting aft, on the deck, with his legs dangling over the mud. You see I rather chummed with the few mechanics there were in that station, whom the other pilgrims naturally despised—on account of their imperfect manners, I suppose. This was the foreman—a boiler-maker by trade—a good worker. He was a lank, bony, yellow-faced man, with big intense eyes. His aspect was worried, and his head was as bald as the palm of my hand; but his hair in falling seemed to have

70

stuck to his chin, and had prospered in the new locality, for his beard hung down to his waist. He was a widower with six young children (he had left them in charge of a sister of his to come out there), and the passion of his life was pigeon-flying. He was an enthusiast and a connoisseur. He would rave about pigeons. After work hours he used sometimes to come over from his hut for a talk about his children and his pigeons; at work, when he had to crawl in the mud under the bottom of the steamboat, he would tie up that beard of his in a kind of white serviette[17] he brought for the purpose. It had loops to go over his ears. In the evening he could be seen squatted on the bank rinsing that wrapper in the creek with great care, then spreading it solemnly on a bush to dry.

"I slapped him on the back and shouted, 'We shall have rivets!' He scrambled to his feet exclaiming, 'No! Rivets!' as though he couldn't believe his ears. Then in a low voice, 'You . . . eh?' I don't know why we behaved like lunatics. I put my finger to the side of my nose and nodded mysteriously. 'Good for you!' he cried, snapped his fingers above his head, lifting one foot. I tried a jig. We capered on the iron deck. A frightful clatter came out of that hulk, and the virgin forest on the other bank of the creek sent it back in a thundering roll upon the sleeping station. It must have made some of the pilgrims sit up in their hovels. A dark figure obscured the lighted doorway of the manager's hut, vanished, then, a second or so after, the doorway itself vanished, too. We stopped, and the silence driven away by the stamping of our feet flowed back again from the recesses of the land. The great wall of vegetation, an exuberant and entangled mass of trunks, branches, leaves, boughs, festoons, motion-less in the moonlight, was like a rioting invasion of soundless life, a rolling wave of plants, piled up, crested, ready to topple over the creek, to sweep every little man of us out of his little existence. And it moved not. A deadened burst of mighty splashes and snorts reached us from afar, as though an ichthyosaurus had been taking a bath of glitter in the great river. 'After all,' said the boiler-maker in a reasonable tone, 'why shouldn't we get the rivets?' Why not, indeed! I did not know of any reason why we shouldn't. 'They'll come in three weeks,' I said, confidently.

"But they didn't. Instead of rivets there came an invasion, an infliction, a visita-tion. It came in sections during the next three weeks, each section headed by a don-key carrying a white man in new clothes and tan shoes, bowing from that elevation right and left to the impressed pilgrims. A quarrelsome band of footsore sulky nig-gers trod on the heels of the donkey; a lot of tents, camp-stools, tin boxes, white cases, brown bales would be shot down in the courtyard, and the air of mystery would deepen a little over the muddle of the station. Five such instalments came, with their absurd air of disorderly flight with the loot of innumerable outfit shops and provi-sion stores, that, one would think, they were lugging, after a raid, into the wilderness for equitable division. It was an inextricable mess of things decent in themselves but that human folly made look like the spoils of thieving.

"This devoted band called itself the Eldorado Exploring Expedition, and I believe they were sworn to secrecy. Their talk, however, was the talk of sordid buccaneers: it

---

[17]Table napkin.—EDS.

was reckless without hardihood, greedy without audacity, and cruel without courage; there was not an atom of foresight or of serious intention in the whole batch of them, and they did not seem aware these things are wanted for the work of the world. To tear treasure out of the bowels of the land was their desire, with no more moral purpose at the back of it than there is in burglars breaking into a safe. Who paid the expenses of the noble enterprise I don't know; but the uncle of our manager was leader of that lot.

"In exterior he resembled a butcher in a poor neighbourhood, and his eyes had a look of sleepy cunning. He carried his fat paunch with ostentation on his short legs, and during the time his gang infested the station spoke to no one but his nephew. You could see these two roaming about all day long with their heads close together in an everlasting confab.

"I had given up worrying myself about the rivets. One's capacity for that kind of 75 folly is more limited than you would suppose. I said Hang!—and let things slide. I had plenty of time for meditation, and now and then I would give some thought to Kurtz. I wasn't very interested in him. No. Still, I was curious to see whether this man, who had come out equipped with moral ideas of some sort, would climb to the top after all and how he would set about his work when there."

2

"One evening as I was lying flat on the deck of my steamboat, I heard voices approaching—and there were the nephew and the uncle strolling along the bank. I laid my head on my arm again, and had nearly lost myself in a doze, when somebody said in my ear, as it were: 'I am as harmless as a little child, but I don't like to be dictated to. Am I the manager—or am I not? I was ordered to send him there. It's incredible.' . . . I became aware that the two were standing on the shore alongside the forepart of the steamboat, just below my head. I did not move; it did not occur to me to move: I was sleepy. 'It *is* unpleasant,' grunted the uncle. 'He has asked the Administration to be sent there,' said the other, 'with the idea of showing what he could do; and I was instructed accordingly. Look at the influence that man must have. Is it not frightful?' They both agreed it was frightful, then made several bizarre remarks: 'Make rain and fine weather—one man—the Council—by the nose'—bits of absurd sentences that got the better of my drowsiness, so that I had pretty near the whole of my wits about me when the uncle said, 'The climate may do away with this difficulty for you. Is he alone there?' 'Yes,' answered the manager; 'he sent his assistant down the river with a note to me in these terms: "Clear this poor devil out of the country, and don't bother sending more of that sort. I had rather be alone than have the kind of men you can dispose of with me." It was more than a year ago. Can you imagine such impudence!' 'Anything since then?' asked the other, hoarsely. 'Ivory,' jerked the nephew; 'lots of it—prime sort—lots—most annoying, from him.' 'And with that?' questioned the heavy rumble. 'Invoice,' was the reply fired out, so to speak. Then silence. They had been talking about Kurtz.

"I was broad awake by this time, but, lying perfectly at ease, remained still, having no inducement to change my position. 'How did that ivory come all this way?' growled the elder man, who seemed very vexed. The other explained that it had come with a fleet of canoes in charge of an English half-caste clerk Kurtz had with him; that Kurtz had apparently intended to return himself, the station being by that time bare of goods and stores, but after coming three hundred miles, had suddenly decided to go back, which he started to do alone in a small dugout with four paddlers, leaving the half-caste to continue down the river with the ivory. The two fellows there seemed astounded at anybody attempting such a thing. They were at a loss for an adequate motive. As to me, I seemed to see Kurtz for the first time. It was a distinct glimpse: the dugout, four paddling savages, and the lone white man turning his back suddenly on the headquarters, on relief, on thoughts of home—perhaps; setting his face towards the depths of the wilderness, towards his empty and desolate station. I did not know the motive. Perhaps he was just simply a fine fellow who stuck to his work for its own sake. His name, you understand, had not been pronounced once. He was 'that man.' The half-caste, who, as far as I could see, had conducted a difficult trip with great prudence and pluck, was invariably alluded to as 'that scoundrel.' The 'scoundrel' had reported that the 'man' had been very ill—had recovered imperfectly. . . . The two below me moved away then a few paces, and strolled back and forth at some little distance. I heard: 'Military post—doctor—two hundred miles—quite alone now—unavoidable delays—nine months—no news—strange rumours.' They approached again, just as the manager was saying, 'No one, as far as I know, unless a species of wandering trader—a pestilential fellow, snapping ivory from the natives.' Who was it they were talking about now? I gathered in snatches that this was some man supposed to be in Kurtz's district, and of whom the manager did not approve. 'We will not be free from unfair competition till one of these fellows is hanged for an example,' he said. 'Certainly,' grunted the other; 'get him hanged! Why not? Anything—anything can be done in this country. That's what I say; nobody here, you understand, *here*, can endanger your position. And why? You stand the climate—you outlast them all. The danger is in Europe; but there before I left I took care to ——' They moved off and whispered, then their voices rose again. 'The extraordinary series of delays is not my fault. I did my best.' The fat man sighed. 'Very sad.' 'And the pestiferous absurdity of his talk,' continued the other; 'he bothered me enough when he was here. "Each station should be like a beacon on the road towards better things, a centre for trade of course, but also for humanizing, improving, instructing." Conceive you—that ass! And he wants to be manager! No, it's —' Here he got choked by excessive indignation, and I lifted my head the least bit. I was surprised to see how near they were—right under me. I could have spat upon their hats. They were looking on the ground, absorbed in thought. The manager was switching his leg with a slender twig: his sagacious relative lifted his head. 'You have been well since you came out this time?' he asked. The other gave a start. 'Who? I? Oh! Like a charm—like a charm. But the rest—oh, my goodness! All sick. They die so quick, too, that I haven't the time to send them out of the country—it's incredible!' 'H'm. Just so,' grunted the uncle. 'Ah! my boy, trust to this—I say, trust to this.'

I saw him extend his short flipper of an arm for a gesture that took in the forest, the creek, the mud, the river,—seemed to beckon with a dishonouring flourish before the sunlit face of the land a treacherous appeal to the lurking death, to the hidden evil, to the profound darkness of its heart. It was so startling that I leaped to my feet and looked back at the edge of the forest, as though I had expected an answer of some sort to that black display of confidence. You know the foolish notions that come to one sometimes. The high stillness confronted these two figures with its ominous patience, waiting for the passing away of a fantastic invasion.

"They swore aloud together—out of sheer fright, I believe—then pretending not to know anything of my existence, turned back to the station. The sun was low; and leaning forward side by side, they seemed to be tugging painfully uphill their two ridiculous shadows of unequal length, that trailed behind them slowly over the tall grass without bending a single blade.

"In a few days the Eldorado Expedition went into the patient wilderness, that closed upon it as the sea closes over a diver. Long afterwards the news came that all the donkeys were dead. I know nothing as to the fate of the less valuable animals. They, no doubt, like the rest of us, found what they deserved. I did not inquire. I was then rather excited at the prospect of meeting Kurtz very soon. When I say very soon I mean it comparatively. It was just two months from the day we left the creek when we came to the bank below Kurtz's station.

"Going up that river was like travelling back to the earliest beginnings of the   80 world, when vegetation rioted on the earth and the big trees were kings. An empty stream, a great silence, an impenetrable forest. The air was warm, thick, heavy, sluggish. There was no joy in the brilliance of sunshine. The long stretches of the waterway ran on, deserted, into the gloom of overshadowed distances. On silvery sandbanks hippos and alligators sunned themselves side by side. The broadening waters flowed through a mob of wooded islands; you lost your way on that river as you would in a desert, and butted all day long against shoals, trying to find the channel, till you thought yourself bewitched and cut off for ever from everything you had known once—somewhere—far away—in another existence perhaps. There were moments when one's past came back to one, as it will sometimes when you have not a moment to spare to yourself; but it came in the shape of an unrestful and noisy dream, remembered with wonder amongst the overwhelming realities of this strange world of plants, and water, and silence. And this stillness of life did not in the least resemble a peace. It was the stillness of an implacable force brooding over an inscrutable intention. It looked at you with a vengeful aspect. I got used to it afterwards; I did not see it any more; I had no time. I had to keep guessing at the channel; I had to discern, mostly by inspiration, the signs of hidden banks; I watched for sunken stones; I was learning to clap my teeth smartly before my heart flew out, when I shaved by a fluke some infernal sly old snag that would have ripped the life out of the tin-pot steamboat and drowned all the pilgrims; I had to keep a look-out for the signs of dead wood we could cut up in the night for next day's steaming. When you have to attend to things of that sort, to the mere incidents of the surface, the reality—the reality, I tell you—fades. The inner truth is hidden—luckily, luckily. But I felt it all the same; I felt often its mysterious stillness watching me at my monkey tricks, just as it watches you fellows performing on your respective tight-ropes for — what is it? half-a-crown a tumble ——"

"Try to be civil, Marlow," growled a voice, and I knew there was at least one listener awake besides myself.

"I beg your pardon. I forgot the heartache which makes up the rest of the price. And indeed what does the price matter, if the trick be well done? You do your tricks very well. And I didn't do badly either, since I managed not to sink that steamboat on my first trip. It's a wonder to me yet. Imagine a blindfolded man set to drive a van over a bad road. I sweated and shivered over that business considerably, I can tell you. After all, for a seaman, to scrape the bottom of the thing that's supposed to float all the time under his care is the unpardonable sin. No one may know of it, but you never forget the thump — eh? A blow on the very heart. You remember it, you dream of it, you wake up at night and think of it — years after — and go hot and cold all over. I don't pretend to say that steamboat floated all the time. More than once she had to wade for a bit, with twenty cannibals splashing around and pushing. We had enlisted some of these chaps on the way for a crew. Fine fellows — cannibals — in their place. They were men one could work with, and I am grateful to them. And, after all, they did not eat each other before my face: they had brought along a provision of hippo-meat which went rotten, and made the mystery of the wilderness stink in my nostrils. Phoo! I can sniff it now. I had the manager on board and three or four pilgrims with their staves — all complete. Sometimes we came upon a station close by the bank, clinging to the skirts of the unknown, and the white men rushing out of a tumble-down hovel, with great gestures of joy and surprise and welcome, seemed very strange — had the appearance of being held there captive by a spell. The word ivory would ring in the air for a while — and on we went again into the silence, along empty reaches, round the still bends, between the high walls of our winding way, reverberating in hollow claps the ponderous beat of the stern-wheel. Trees, trees, millions of trees, massive, immense, running up high; and at their foot, hugging the bank against the stream, crept the little begrimed steamboat, like a sluggish beetle crawling on the floor of a lofty portico. It made you feel very small, very lost, and yet it was not altogether depressing, that feeling. After all, if you were small, the grimy beetle crawled on — which was just what you wanted it to do. Where the pilgrims imagined it crawled to I don't know. To some place where they expected to get something, I bet! For me it crawled towards Kurtz — exclusively; but when the steam-pipes started leaking we crawled very slow. The reaches opened before us and closed behind, as if the forest had stepped leisurely across the water to bar the way for our return. We penetrated deeper and deeper into the heart of darkness. It was very quiet there. At night sometimes the roll of drums behind the curtain of trees would run up the river and remain sustained faintly, as if hovering in the air high over our heads, till the first break of day. Whether it meant war, peace, or prayer we could not tell. The dawns were heralded by the descent of a chill stillness; the wood-cutters slept, their fires burned low; the snapping of a twig would make you start. We were wanderers on a prehistoric earth, on an earth that wore the aspect of an unknown planet. We could have fancied ourselves the first of men taking possession of an accursed inheritance, to be subdued at the cost of profound anguish and of excessive toil. But suddenly, as we struggled round a bend, there would be a glimpse of rush walls, of peaked grass-roofs, a burst of yells, a whirl of black limbs, a mass of hands clapping, of feet stamping, of bodies swaying, of eyes rolling, under the droop of heavy and motionless foliage. The steamer toiled along slowly on the edge of a black and incomprehensible frenzy. The prehistoric man was cursing us, praying to us, welcoming us—who could tell? We were cut off from the comprehension of our surroundings; we glided past like phantoms, wondering and secretly appalled, as sane men would be before an enthusiastic outbreak in a madhouse. We could not understand because we were too far and could not remember, because we were travelling in the night of first ages, of those ages that are gone, leaving hardly a sign—and no memories.

"The earth seemed unearthly. We are accustomed to look upon the shackled form of a conquered monster, but there—there you could look at a thing monstrous and free. It was unearthly, and the men were —— No, they were not inhuman. Well, you know, that was the worst of it—this suspicion of their not being inhuman. It would come slowly to one. They howled and leaped, and spun, and made horrid faces; but what thrilled you was just the thought of their humanity—like yours—the thought of your remote kinship with this wild and passionate uproar. Ugly. Yes, it was ugly enough; but if you were man enough you would admit to yourself that there was in you just the faintest trace of a response to the terrible frankness of that noise, a dim suspicion of there being a meaning in it which you—you so remote from the night of first ages—could comprehend. And why not? The mind of man is capable of anything—because everything is in it, all the past as well as all the future. What was there after all? Joy, fear, sorrow, devotion, valour, rage—who can tell?—but truth—truth stripped of its cloak of time. Let the fool gape and shudder—the man knows, and can look on without a wink. But he must at least be as much of a man as these on the shore. He must meet that truth with his own true stuff—with his own inborn strength. Principles won't do. Acquisitions, clothes, pretty rags—rags that would fly off at the first good shake. No; you want a deliberate belief. An appeal to me in this fiendish row—is there? Very well; I hear; I admit, but I have a voice, too, and for good or evil mine is the speech that cannot be silenced. Of course, a fool, what with sheer fright and fine sentiments, is always safe. Who's that grunting? You wonder I didn't go ashore for a howl and a dance? Well, no—I didn't. Fine sentiments, you say? Fine sentiments, be hanged! I had no time. I had to mess about with white-lead and strips of woollen blanket helping to put bandages on those leaky steam-pipes—I tell you. I had to watch the steering, and circumvent those snags, and get the tin-pot along by hook or by crook. There was surface-truth enough in these things to save a wiser man. And between whiles I had to look after the savage who was fireman. He was an improved specimen; he could fire up a vertical boiler. He was there below me, and, upon my word, to look at him was as edifying as seeing a dog in a parody of breeches and a feather hat, walking on his hind-legs. A few months of training had done for that really fine chap. He squinted at the steam-gauge and at the water-gauge with an evident effort of intrepidity—and he had filed teeth, too, the poor devil, and the wool of his pate shaved into queer patterns, and three ornamental scars on each of his cheeks. He ought to have been clapping his hands and stamping his feet on the bank, instead of which he was hard at work, a thrall to strange witchcraft, full of improving knowledge. He was useful because he had been instructed; and what he knew was this—that should the water in that transparent thing disappear, the evil spirit inside the boiler would get angry through the greatness of his thirst, and take a terrible vengeance. So he sweated and fired up and watched the glass fearfully (with an impromptu charm, made of rags, tied to his arm, and a piece of polished bone, as big as a watch, stuck flat-ways through his lower lip), while the wooded banks slipped past us slowly, the short noise was left behind, the interminable miles of silence—and we crept on, towards Kurtz. But the snags were thick, the water was treacherous and shallow, the boiler seemed indeed to have a sulky devil in it, and thus neither that fireman nor I had any time to peer into our creepy thoughts.

"Some fifty miles below the Inner Station we came upon a hut of reeds, an inclined and melancholy pole, with the unrecognizable tatters of what had been a flag of some sort flying from it, and a neatly stacked wood-pile. This was unexpected. We came to the bank, and on the stack of firewood found a flat piece of board with some faded pencil-writing on it. When deciphered it said: 'Wood for you. Hurry up. Approach cautiously.' There was a signature, but it was illegible—not Kurtz— a much longer word. 'Hurry up.' Where? Up the river? 'Approach cautiously.' We had not done so. But the warning could not have been meant for the place where it could be only found after approach. Something was wrong above. But what—and how much? That was the question. We commented adversely upon the imbecility of that telegraphic style. The bush around said nothing, and would not let us look very far, either. A torn curtain of red twill hung in the doorway of the hut, and flapped sadly in our faces. The dwelling was dismantled; but we could see a white man had lived there not very long ago. There remained a rude table—a plank on two posts; a heap of rubbish reposed in a dark corner, and by the door I picked up a book. It had lost its covers, and the pages had been thumbed into a state of extremely dirty softness; but the back had been lovingly stitched afresh with white cotton thread, which looked clean yet. It was an extraordinary find. Its title was, *An Inquiry into some Points of Seamanship*, by a man Towser, Towson—some such name—Master in his Majesty's Navy. The matter looked dreary reading enough, with illustrative diagrams and repulsive tables of figures, and the copy was sixty years old. I handled this amazing antiquity with the greatest possible tenderness, lest it should dissolve in my hands. Within, Towson or Towser was inquiring earnestly into the breaking strain of ships' chains and tackle, and other such matters. Not a very enthralling book; but at the first glance you could see there a singleness of intention, an honest concern for the right way of going to work, which made these humble pages, thought out so many years ago, luminous with another than a professional light. The simple old sailor, with his talk of chains and purchases, made me forget the jungle and the pilgrims in a delicious sensation of having come upon something unmistakably real. Such a book being there was wonderful enough; but still more astounding were the notes pencilled in the margin, and plainly referring to the text. I couldn't believe my eyes! They were in cipher! Yes, it looked like cipher. Fancy a man lugging with him a book of that description into this nowhere and studying it—and making notes—in cipher at that! It was an extravagant mystery.

"I had been dimly aware for some time of a worrying noise, and when I lifted my eyes I saw the wood-pile was gone, and the manager, aided by all the pilgrims, was shouting at me from the river-side. I slipped the book into my pocket. I assure you to leave off reading was like tearing myself away from the shelter of an old and solid friendship. 85

"I started the lame engine ahead. 'It must be this miserable trader—this in- truder,' exclaimed the manager, looking back malevolently at the place we had left. 'He must be English,' I said. 'It will not save him from getting into trouble if he is not careful,' muttered the manager darkly. I observed with assumed innocence that no man was safe from trouble in this world.

"The current was more rapid now, the steamer seemed at her last gasp, the stern- wheel flopped languidly, and I caught myself listening on tiptoe for the next beat of the boat, for in sober truth I expected the wretched thing to give up every moment. It was like watching the last flickers of a life. But still we crawled. Sometimes I would pick out a tree a little way ahead to measure our progress towards Kurtz by, but I lost it invariably before we got abreast. To keep the eyes so long on one thing was too much for human patience. The manager displayed a beautiful resignation. I fretted and fumed and took to arguing with myself whether or no I would talk openly with Kurtz; but before I could come to any conclusion it occurred to me that my speech or my silence, indeed any action of mine, would be a mere futility. What did it mat- ter what any one knew or ignored? What did it matter who was manager? One gets sometimes such a flash of insight. The essentials of this affair lay deep under the surface, beyond my reach, and beyond my power of meddling.

"Towards the evening of the second day we judged ourselves about eight miles from Kurtz's station. I wanted to push on; but the manager looked grave, and told me the navigation up there was so dangerous that it would be advisable, the sun being very low already, to wait where we were till next morning. Moreover, he pointed out that if the warning to approach cautiously were to be followed, we must approach in daylight—not at dusk, or in the dark. This was sensible enough. Eight miles meant nearly three hours' steaming for us, and I could also see suspicious ripples at the upper end of the reach. Nevertheless, I was annoyed beyond expression at the delay, and most unreasonably, too, since one night more could not matter much after so many months. As we had plenty of wood, and caution was the word, I brought up in the middle of the stream. The reach was narrow, straight, with high sides like a railway cutting. The dusk came gliding into it long before the sun had set. The cur- rent ran smooth and swift, but a dumb immobility sat on the banks. The living trees, lashed together by the creepers and every living bush of the undergrowth, might have been changed into stone, even to the slenderest twig, to the lightest leaf. It was not sleep—it seemed unnatural, like a state of trance. Not the faintest sound of any kind could be heard. You looked on amazed, and began to suspect yourself of being deaf—then the night came suddenly, and struck you blind as well. About three in the morning some large fish leaped, and the loud splash made me jump as though a gun had been fired. When the sun rose there was a white fog, very warm and clammy, and more blinding than the night. It did not shift or drive; it was just there, standing all round you like something solid. At eight or nine, perhaps, it lifted as a shutter lifts. We had a glimpse of the towering multitude of trees, of the immense matted jungle, with the blazing little ball of the sun hanging over it—all perfectly still—and then the white shutter came down again, smoothly, as if sliding in greased grooves. I ordered the chain, which we had begun to heave in, to be paid out again. Before it stopped running with a muffled rattle, a cry, a very loud cry, as of infinite desolation, soared slowly in the opaque air. It ceased. A complaining clamour, modulated in savage discords, filled our ears. The sheer unexpectedness of it made my hair stir under my cap. I don't know how it struck the others: to me it seemed as though the mist itself had screamed, so suddenly, and apparently from all sides at once, did this tumultuous and mournful uproar arise. It culminated in a hurried outbreak of almost intolerably excessive shrieking, which stopped short, leaving us stiffened in a variety of silly attitudes, and obstinately listening to the nearly as appalling and excessive silence. 'Good God! What is the meaning ——' stammered at my elbow one of the pilgrims,—a little fat man, with sandy hair and red whiskers, who wore side-spring boots, and pink pyjamas tucked into his socks. Two others remained open-mouthed a whole minute, then dashed into the little cabin, to rush out incontinently and stand darting scared glances, with Winchesters at 'ready' in their hands. What we could see was just the steamer we were on, her outlines blurred as though she had been on the point of dissolving, and a misty strip of water, perhaps two feet broad, around her—and that was all. The rest of the world was nowhere, as far as our eyes and ears were concerned. Just nowhere. Gone, disappeared; swept off without leaving a whisper or a shadow behind.

"I went forward, and ordered the chain to be hauled in short, so as to be ready to trip the anchor and move the steamboat at once if necessary. 'Will they attack?' whispered an awed voice. 'We will be all butchered in this fog,' murmured another. The faces twitched with the strain, the hands trembled slightly, the eyes forgot to wink. It was very curious to see the contrast of expressions of the white men and of the black fellows of our crew, who were as much strangers to that part of the river as we, though their homes were only eight hundred miles away. The whites, of course greatly discomposed, had besides a curious look of being painfully shocked by such an outrageous row. The others had an alert, naturally interested expression; but their faces were essentially quiet, even those of the one or two who grinned as they hauled at the chain. Several exchanged short, grunting phrases, which seemed to settle the matter to their satisfaction. Their headman, a young, broad-chested black, severely draped in dark-blue fringed cloths, with fierce nostrils and his hair all done up artfully in oily ringlets, stood near me. 'Aha!' I said, just for good fellowship's sake. 'Catch 'im,' he snapped, with a bloodshot widening of his eyes and a flash of sharp teeth— 'catch 'im. Give 'im to us.' 'To you, eh?' I asked; 'what would you do with them?' 'Eat 'im!' he said, curtly, and, leaning his elbow on the rail, looked out into the fog in a dignified and profoundly pensive attitude. I would no doubt have been properly horrified, had it not occurred to me that he and his chaps must be very hungry: that they must have been growing increasingly hungry for at least this month past. They had been engaged for six months (I don't think a single one of them had any clear idea of time, as we at the end of countless ages have. They still belonged to the beginnings of time — had no inherited experience to teach them as it were), and of course, as long as there was a piece of paper written over in accordance with some farcical law or other made down the river, it didn't enter anybody's head to trouble how they would live. Certainly they had brought with them some rotten hippo-meat, which couldn't have lasted very long, anyway, even if the pilgrims hadn't, in the midst of a shocking hullabaloo, thrown a considerable quantity of it overboard. It looked like a high-handed proceeding; but it was really a case of legitimate self-defence. You can't breathe dead hippo waking, sleeping, and eating, and at the same time keep your precarious grip on existence. Besides that, they had given them every week three pieces of brass wire, each about nine inches long; and the theory was they were to buy their provisions with that currency in river-side villages. You can see how *that* worked. There were either no villages, or the people were hostile, or the director, who like the rest of us fed out of tins, with an occasional old he-goat thrown in, didn't want to stop the steamer for some more or less recondite reason. So, unless they swallowed the wire itself, or made loops of it to snare the fishes with, I don't see what good their extravagant salary could be to them. I must say it was paid with a regularity worthy of a large and honourable trading company. For the rest, the only thing to eat — though it didn't look eatable in the least — I saw in their possession was a few lumps of some stuff like half-cooked dough, of a dirty lavender colour, they kept wrapped in leaves, and now and then swallowed a piece of, but so small that it seemed done more for the looks of the thing than for any serious purpose of sustenance. Why in the name of all the gnawing devils of hunger they didn't go for us — they were thirty to five — and have a good tuck-in for once, amazes me now when I think of it. They were big powerful men, with not much capacity to weigh the consequences, with courage, with strength, even yet, though their skins were no longer glossy and their muscles no longer hard. And I saw that something restraining, one of those human secrets that baffle probability, had come into play there. I looked at them with a swift quickening of interest — not because it occurred to me I might be eaten by them before very long, though I own to you that just then I perceived — in a new light, as it were — how unwholesome the pilgrims looked, and I hoped, yes I positively hoped, that my aspect was not so — what shall I say? — so — unappetizing: a touch of fantastic vanity which fitted well with the dream-sensation that pervaded all my days at that time. Perhaps I had a little fever, too. One can't live with one's finger everlastingly on one's pulse. I had often 'a little fever,' or a little touch of other things — the playful pawstrokes of the wilderness, the preliminary trifling before the more serious onslaught which came in due course. Yes; I looked at them as you would on any human being, with a curiosity of their impulses, motives, capacities, weaknesses, when brought to the test of an inexorable physical necessity. Restraint! What possible restraint? Was it superstition, disgust, patience, fear — or some kind of primitive honour? No fear can stand up to hunger, no patience can wear it out, disgust simply does not exist where hunger is; and as to superstition, beliefs, and what you may call principles, they are less than chaff in a breeze. Don't you know the devilry of lingering starvation, its exasperating torment, its black thoughts, its sombre and brooding ferocity? Well, I do. It takes a man all his inborn strength to fight hunger properly. It's really easier to face bereavement, dishonour, and the perdition of one's soul—than this kind of prolonged hunger. Sad, but true. And these chaps, too, had no earthly reason for any kind of scruple. Restraint! I would just as soon have expected restraint from a hyena prowling amongst the corpses of a battlefield. But there was the fact facing me—the fact dazzling, to be seen, like the foam on the depths of the sea, like a ripple on an unfathomable enigma, a mystery greater—when I thought of it—than the curious, inexplicable note of desperate grief in this savage clamour that had swept by us on the river-bank, behind the blind whiteness of the fog.

"Two pilgrims were quarrelling in hurried whispers as to which bank. 'Left.' 'No, no; how can you? Right, right, of course.' 'It is very serious,' said the manager's voice behind me; 'I would be desolated if anything should happen to Mr. Kurtz before we came up.' I looked at him, and had not the slightest doubt he was sincere. He was just the kind of man who would wish to preserve appearances. That was his restraint. But when he muttered something about going on at once, I did not even take the trouble to answer him. I knew, and he knew, that it was impossible. Were we to let go our hold of the bottom, we would be absolutely in the air—in space. We wouldn't be able to tell where we were going to—whether up or down stream, or across— till we fetched against one bank or the other,—and then we wouldn't know at first which it was. Of course I made no move. I had no mind for a smash-up. You couldn't imagine a more deadly place for a shipwreck. Whether drowned at once or not, we were sure to perish speedily in one way or another. 'I authorize you to take all the risks,' he said, after a short silence. 'I refuse to take any,' I said, shortly; which was just the answer he expected, though its tone might have surprised him. 'Well, I must defer to your judgment. You are captain,' he said, with marked civility. I turned my shoulder to him in sign of my appreciation, and looked into the fog. How long would it last? It was the most hopeless look-out. The approach to this Kurtz grubbing for ivory in the wretched bush was beset by as many dangers as though he had been an enchanted princess sleeping in a fabulous castle. 'Will they attack, do you think?' asked the manager, in a confidential tone.

"I did not think they would attack, for several obvious reasons. The thick fog was one. If they left the bank in their canoes they would get lost in it, as we would be if we attempted to move. Still, I had also judged the jungle of both banks quite impenetrable—and yet eyes were in it, eyes that had seen us. The river-side bushes were certainly very thick; but the undergrowth behind was evidently penetrable. However, during the short lift I had seen no canoes anywhere in the reach—certainly not abreast of the steamer. But what made the idea of attack inconceivable to me was the nature of the noise—of the cries we had heard. They had not the fierce character boding immediate hostile intention. Unexpected, wild, and violent as they had been, they had given me an irresistible impression of sorrow. The glimpse of the steamboat had for some reason filled those savages with unrestrained grief. The danger, if any, I expounded, was from our proximity to a great human passion let loose. Even extreme

90

In a fog

grief may ultimately vent itself in violence—but more generally takes the form of apathy. . . .

"You should have seen the pilgrims stare! They had no heart to grin, or even to revile me: but I believe they thought me gone mad—with fright, maybe. I delivered a regular lecture. My dear boys, it was no good bothering. Keep a look-out? Well, you may guess I watched the fog for the signs of lifting as a cat watches a mouse; but for anything else our eyes were of no more use to us than if we had been buried miles deep in a heap of cotton-wool. It felt like it, too—choking, warm, stifling. Besides, all I said, though it sounded extravagant, was absolutely true to fact. What we afterwards alluded to as an attack was really an attempt at repulse. The action was very far from being aggressive—it was not even defensive, in the usual sense: it was undertaken under the stress of desperation, and in its essence was purely protective.

"It developed itself, I should say, two hours after the fog lifted, and its commencement was at a spot, roughly speaking, about a mile and a half below Kurtz's station. We had just floundered and flopped round a bend, when I saw an islet, a mere grassy hummock of bright green, in the middle of the stream. It was the only thing of the kind; but as we opened the reach more, I perceived it was the head of a long sandbank, or rather of a chain of shallow patches stretching down the middle of the river. They were discoloured, just awash, and the whole lot was seen just under the water, exactly as a man's backbone is seen running down the middle of his back under the skin. Now, as far as I did see, I could go to the right or to the left of this. I didn't know either channel, of course. The banks looked pretty well alike, the depth appeared the same; but as I had been informed the station was on the west side, I naturally headed for the western passage.

"No sooner had we fairly entered it than I became aware it was much narrower than I had supposed. To the left of us there was the long uninterrupted shoal, and to the right a high, steep bank heavily overgrown with bushes. Above the bush the trees stood in serried ranks. The twigs overhung the current thickly, and from distance to distance a large limb of some tree projected rigidly over the stream. It was then well on in the afternoon, the face of the forest was gloomy, and a broad strip of shadow had already fallen on the water. In this shadow we steamed up—very slowly, as you may imagine. I sheered her well inshore—the water being deepest near the bank, as the sounding-pole informed me.

"One of my hungry and forbearing friends was sounding in the bows just below 95 me. This steamboat was exactly like a decked scow. On the deck, there were two little teak-wood houses, with doors and windows. The boiler was in the fore-end, and the machinery right astern. Over the whole there was a light roof, supported on stanchions. The funnel projected through that roof, and in front of the funnel a small cabin built of light planks served for a pilot-house. It contained a couch, two camp-stools, a loaded Martini-Henry leaning in one corner, a tiny table, and the steering-wheel. It had a wide door in front and a broad shutter at each side. All these were always thrown open, of course. I spent my days perched up there on the extreme fore-end of that roof, before the door. At night I slept, or tried to, on the couch. An athletic black belonging to some coast tribe, and educated by my poor predecessor, was the helmsman. He sported a pair of brass earrings, wore a blue cloth wrapper from the waist to the ankles, and thought all the world of himself. He was the most unstable kind of fool I had ever seen. He steered with no end of a swagger while you were by; but if he lost sight of you, he became instantly the prey of an abject funk, and would let that cripple of a steamboat get the upper hand of him in a minute.

"I was looking down at the sounding-pole, and feeling much annoyed to see at each try a little more of it stick out of that river, when I saw my poleman give up the business suddenly, and stretch himself flat on the deck, without even taking the trouble to haul his pole in. He kept hold on it though, and it trailed in the water. At the same time the fireman, whom I could also see below me, sat down abruptly before his furnace and ducked his head. I was amazed. Then I had to look at the river mighty quick, because there was a snag in the fairway. Sticks, little sticks, were flying about—thick: they were whizzing before my nose, dropping below me, striking behind me against my pilot-house. All this time the river, the shore, the woods, were very quiet—perfectly quiet. I could only hear the heavy splashing thump of the stern-wheel and the patter of these things. We cleared the snag clumsily. Arrows, by Jove! We were being shot at! I stepped in quickly to close the shutter on the land-side. That fool-helmsman, his hands on the spokes, was lifting his knees high, stamping his feet, champing his mouth, like a reined-in horse. Confound him! And we were staggering within ten feet of the bank. I had to lean right out to swing the heavy shutter, and I saw a face amongst the leaves on the level with my own, looking at me very fierce and steady; and then suddenly, as though a veil had been removed from my eyes, I made out, deep in the tangled gloom, naked breasts, arms, legs, glaring eyes,—the bush was swarming with human limbs in movement, glistening, of bronze colour. The twigs shook, swayed, and rustled, the arrows flew out of them, and then the shutter came to. 'Steer her straight,' I said to the helmsman. He held his head rigid, face forward; but his eyes rolled, he kept on lifting and setting down his feet gently, his mouth foamed a little. 'Keep quiet!' I said in a fury. I might just as well have ordered a tree not to sway in the wind. I darted out. Below me there was a great scuffle of feet on the iron deck; confused exclamations; a voice screamed, 'Can you turn back?' I caught sight of a V-shaped ripple on the water ahead. What? Another snag! A fusillade burst out under my feet. The pilgrims had opened with their Winchesters, and were simply squirting lead into that bush. A deuce of a lot of smoke came up and drove slowly forward. I swore at it. Now I couldn't see the ripple or the snag either. I stood in the doorway, peering, and the arrows came in swarms. They might have been poisoned, but they looked as though they wouldn't kill a cat. The bush began to howl. Our wood-cutters raised a warlike whoop; the report of a rifle just at my back deafened me. I glanced over my shoulder, and the pilot-house was yet full of noise and smoke when I made a dash at the wheel. The fool-nigger had dropped everything, to throw the shutter open and let off that Martini-Henry. He stood before the wide opening, glaring, and I yelled at him to come back, while I straightened the sudden twist out of that steamboat. There was no room to turn even if I had wanted to, the snag was somewhere very near ahead in that confounded smoke, there was no time to lose, so I just crowded her into the bank—right into the bank, where I knew the water was deep.

"We tore slowly along the overhanging bushes in a whirl of broken twigs and flying leaves. The fusillade below stopped short, as I had foreseen it would when the squirts got empty. I threw my head back to a glinting whizz that traversed the pilot-house, in at one shutter-hole and out at the other. Looking past that mad helmsman, who was shaking the empty rifle and yelling at the shore, I saw vague forms of men running bent double, leaping, gliding, distinct, incomplete, evanescent. Something big appeared in the air before the shutter, the rifle went overboard, and the man stepped back swiftly, looked at me over his shoulder in an extraordinary, profound, familiar manner, and fell upon my feet. The side of his head hit the wheel twice, and the end of what appeared a long cane clattered round and knocked over a little camp-stool. It looked as though after wrenching that thing from somebody ashore he had lost his balance in the effort. The thin smoke had blown away, we were clear of the snag, and looking ahead I could see that in another hundred yards or so I would be free to sheer off, away from the bank; but my feet felt so very warm and wet that I had to look down. The man had rolled on his back and stared straight up at me; both his hands clutched that cane. It was the shaft of a spear that, either thrown or lunged through the opening, had caught him in the side just below the ribs; the blade had gone in out of sight, after making a frightful gash; my shoes were full; a pool of blood lay very still, gleaming dark-red under the wheel; his eyes shone with an amazing lustre. The fusillade burst out again. He looked at me anxiously, gripping the spear like something precious, with an air of being afraid I would try to take it away from him. I had to make an effort to free my eyes from his gaze and attend to the steering. With one hand I felt above my head for the line of the steam whistle, and jerked out screech after screech hurriedly. The tumult of angry and warlike yells was checked instantly, and then from the depths of the woods went out such a tremulous and prolonged wail of mournful fear and utter despair as may be imagined to follow the flight of the last hope from the earth. There was a great commotion in the bush; the shower of arrows stopped, a few dropping shots rang out sharply—then silence, in which the languid beat of the stern-wheel came plainly to my ears. I put the helm hard a-starboard at the moment when the pilgrim in pink pyjamas, very hot and agitated, appeared in the doorway. 'The manager sends me ——' he began in an official tone, and stopped short. 'Good God!' he said, glaring at the wounded man.

"We two whites stood over him, and his lustrous and inquiring glance enveloped us both. I declare it looked as though he would presently put to us some question in an understandable language; but he died without uttering a sound, without moving a limb, without twitching a muscle. Only in the very last moment, as though in response to some sign we could not see, to some whisper we could not hear, he frowned heavily, and that frown gave to his black death-mask an inconceivably sombre, brooding, and menacing expression. The lustre of inquiring glance faded swiftly into vacant glassiness. 'Can you steer?' I asked the agent eagerly. He looked very dubious; but I made a grab at his arm, and he understood at once I meant him to steer whether or no. To tell you the truth, I was morbidly anxious to change my shoes and socks. 'He is dead,' murmured the fellow, immensely impressed. 'No doubt about it,' said I, tugging like mad at the shoe-laces. 'And by the way, I suppose Mr. Kurtz is dead as well by this time.'

"For the moment that was the dominant thought. There was a sense of extreme disappointment, as though I had found out I had been striving after something altogether without a substance. I couldn't have been more disgusted if I had travelled all this way for the sole purpose of talking with Mr. Kurtz. Talking with . . . I flung one shoe overboard, and became aware that that was exactly what I had been look-ing forward to—a talk with Kurtz. I made the strange discovery that I had never imagined him as doing, you know, but as discoursing. I didn't say to myself, 'Now I will never see him,' or 'Now I will never shake him by the hand,' but, 'now I will never hear him.' The man presented himself as a voice. Not of course that I did not con-nect him with some sort of action. Hadn't I been told in all the tones of jealousy and admiration that he had collected, bartered, swindled, or stolen more ivory than all the other agents together? That was not the point. The point was in his being a gifted creature, and that of all his gifts the one that stood out preeminently, that carried with it a sense of real presence, was his ability to talk, his words—the gift of expres-sion, the bewildering, the illuminating, the most exalted and the most contemptible, the pulsating stream of light, or the deceitful flow from the heart of an impenetrable darkness.

"The other shoe went flying unto the devil-god of that river. I thought, By Jove! it's all over. We are too late; he has vanished—the gift has vanished, by means of some spear, arrow, or club. I will never hear that chap speak after all,—and my sor-row had a startling extravagance of emotion, even such as I had noticed in the howl-ing sorrow of these savages in the bush. I couldn't have felt more of lonely desolation somehow, had I been robbed of a belief or had missed my destiny in life. . . . Why do you sigh in this beastly way, somebody? Absurd? Well, absurd. Good Lord! mustn't a man ever —— Here, give me some tobacco." . . . 100

There was a pause of profound stillness, then a match flared, and Marlow's lean face appeared, worn, hollow, with downward folds and dropped eyelids, with an aspect of concentrated attention; and as he took vigorous draws at his pipe, it seemed to retreat and advance out of the night in the regular flicker of the tiny flame. The match went out.

"Absurd!" he cried. "This is the worst of trying to tell. . . . Here you all are, each moored with two good addresses, like a hulk with two anchors, a butcher round one corner, a policeman round another, excellent appetites, and temperature nor-mal—you hear—normal from year's end to year's end. And you say, Absurd! Absurd be—exploded! Absurd! My dear boys, what can you expect from a man who out of sheer nervousness had just flung overboard a pair of new shoes! Now I think of it, it is amazing I did not shed tears. I am, upon the whole, proud of my fortitude. I was cut to the quick at the idea of having lost the inestimable privilege of listening to the gifted Kurtz. Of course I was wrong. The privilege was waiting for me. Oh, yes, I heard more than enough. And I was right, too. A voice. He was very little more than a voice. And I heard—him—it—this voice—other voices—all of them were so little more than voices—and the memory of that time itself lingers around me, impalpable, like a dying vibration of one immense jabber, silly, atrocious, sordid, savage, or simply mean, without any kind of sense. Voices, voices—even the girl herself—now ——"

He was silent for a long time.

"I laid the ghost of his gifts at last with a lie," he began, suddenly. "Girl! What? Did I mention a girl? Oh, she is out of it—completely. They—the women I mean—are out of it—should be out of it. We must help them to stay in that beautiful world of their own, lest ours gets worse. Oh, she had to be out of it. You should have heard the disinterred body of Mr. Kurtz saying, 'My Intended.' You would have perceived directly then how completely she was out of it. And the lofty frontal bone of Mr. Kurtz! They say the hair goes on growing sometimes, but this—ah—specimen, was impressively bald. The wilderness had patted him on the head, and, behold, it was like a ball—an ivory ball; it had caressed him, and—lo!—he had withered; it had taken him, loved him, embraced him, got into his veins, consumed his flesh, and sealed his soul to its own by the inconceivable ceremonies of some devilish initiation. He was its spoiled and pampered favourite. Ivory? I should think so. Heaps of it, stacks of it. The old mud shanty was bursting with it. You would think there was not a single tusk left either above or below the ground in the whole country. 'Mostly fossil,' the manager had remarked, disparagingly. It was no more fossil than I am; but they call it fossil when it is dug up. It appears these niggers do bury the tusks sometimes—but evidently they couldn't bury this parcel deep enough to save the gifted Mr. Kurtz from his fate. We filled the steamboat with it, and had to pile a lot on the deck. Thus he could see and enjoy as long as he could see, because the appreciation of this favour had remained with him to the last. You should have heard him say, 'My ivory.' Oh, yes, I heard him. 'My Intended, my ivory, my station, my river, my ——' everything belonged to him. It made me hold my breath in expectation of hearing the wilderness burst into a prodigious peal of laughter that would shake the fixed stars in their places. Everything belonged to him—but that was a trifle. The thing was to know what he belonged to, how many powers of darkness claimed him for their own. That was the reflection that made you creepy all over. It was impossible—it was not good for one either—trying to imagine. He had taken a high seat amongst the devils of the land—I mean literally. You can't understand. How could you?—with solid pavement under your feet, surrounded by kind neighbours ready to cheer you or to fall on you, stepping delicately between the butcher and the policeman, in the holy terror of scandal and gallows and lunatic asylums—how can you imagine what particular region of the first ages a man's untrammelled feet may take him into by the way of solitude—utter solitude without a policeman—by the way of silence—utter silence, where no warning voice of a kind neighbour can be heard whispering of public opinion? These little things make all the great difference. When they are gone you must fall back upon your own innate strength, upon your own capacity for faithfulness. Of course you may be too much of a fool to go wrong—too dull even to know you are being assaulted by the powers of darkness. I take it, no fool ever made a bargain for his soul with the devil: the fool is too much of a fool, or the devil too much of a devil—I don't know which. Or you may be such a thunderingly exalted creature as to be altogether deaf and blind to anything but heavenly sights and sounds. Then the earth for you is only a standing place—and whether to be like this is your loss or your gain I won't pretend to say. But most of us are neither one nor the other. The earth for us is a place to live in, where we must put up with sights, with sounds, with smells, too, by Jove!—breathe dead hippo, so to speak, and not be contaminated. And there, don't you see? your strength comes in, the faith in your ability for the digging of unostentatious holes to bury the stuff in—your power of devotion, not to yourself, but to an obscure, back-breaking business. And that's difficult enough. Mind, I am not trying to excuse or even explain—I am trying to account to myself for—for—Mr. Kurtz—for the shade of Mr. Kurtz. This initiated wraith from the back of Nowhere honoured me with its amazing confidence before it vanished altogether. This was because it could speak English to me. The original Kurtz had been educated partly in England, and—as he was good enough to say himself—his sympathies were in the right place. His mother was half-English, his father was half-French. All Europe contributed to the making of Kurtz; and by and by I learned that, most appropriately, the International Society for the Suppression of Savage Customs had intrusted him with the making of a report, for its future guidance. And he had written it, too. I've seen it. I've read it. It was eloquent, vibrating with eloquence, but too highstrung, I think. Seventeen pages of close writing he had found time for! But this must have been before his—let us say—nerves, went wrong, and caused him to preside at certain midnight dances ending with unspeakable rites, which—as far as I reluctantly gathered from what I heard at various times—were offered up to him—do you understand?—to Mr. Kurtz himself. But it was a beautiful piece of writing. The opening paragraph, however, in the light of later information, strikes me now as ominous. He began with the argument that we whites, from the point of development we had arrived at, 'must necessarily appear to them [savages] in the nature of supernatural beings—we approach them with the might as of a deity,' and so on, and so on. 'By the simple exercise of our will we can exert a power for good practically unbounded,' etc., etc. From that point he soared and took me with him. The peroration was magnificent, though difficult to remember, you know. It gave me the notion of an exotic Immensity ruled by an august Benevolence. It made me tingle with enthusiasm. This was the unbounded power of eloquence—of words—of burning noble words. There were no practical hints to interrupt the magic current of phrases, unless a kind of note at the foot of the last page, scrawled evidently much later, in an unsteady hand, may be regarded as the exposition of a method. It was very simple, and at the end of that moving appeal to every altruistic sentiment it blazed at you, luminous and terrifying, like a flash of lightning in a serene sky: 'Exterminate all the brutes!' The curious part was that he had apparently forgotten all about that valuable postscriptum, because, later on, when he in a sense came to himself, he repeatedly entreated me to take good care of 'my pamphlet' (he called it), as it was sure to have in the future a good influence upon his career. I had full information about all these things, and, besides, as it turned out, I was to have the care of his memory. I've done enough for it to give me the indisputable right to lay it, if I choose, for an everlasting rest in the dust-bin of progress, amongst all the sweepings and, figuratively speaking, all the dead cats of civilization. But then, you see, I can't choose. He won't be forgotten. Whatever he was, he was not common. He had the power to charm or frighten rudimentary souls into an aggravated witch-dance in his honour; he could also fill the small souls of the pilgrims with bitter misgivings: he had one devoted friend at least, and he had conquered one soul in the world that was neither rudimentary nor tainted with self-seeking. No; I can't forget him, though I am not prepared to affirm the fellow was exactly worth the life we lost in getting to him. I missed my late helmsman awfully,—I missed him even while his body was still lying in the pilot-house. Perhaps you will think it passing strange this regret for a savage who was no more account than a grain of sand in a black Sahara. Well, don't you see, he had done something, he had steered; for months I had him at my back—a help—an instrument. It was a kind of partnership. He steered for me—I had to look after him, I worried about his deficiencies, and thus a subtle bond had been created, of which I only became aware when it was suddenly broken. And the intimate profundity of that look he gave me when he received his hurt remains to this day in my memory—like a claim of distant kinship affirmed in a supreme moment.

"Poor fool! If he had only left that shutter alone. He had no restraint, no restraint—just like Kurtz—a tree swayed by the wind. As soon as I had put on a dry pair of slippers, I dragged him out, after first jerking the spear out of his side, which operation I confess I performed with my eyes shut tight. His heels leaped together over the little door-step; his shoulders were pressed to my breast; I hugged him from behind desperately. Oh! he was heavy, heavy; heavier than any man on earth, I should imagine. Then without more ado I tipped him overboard. The current snatched him as though he had been a wisp of grass, and I saw the body roll over twice before I lost sight of it for ever. All the pilgrims and the manager were then congregated on the awning-deck about the pilot-house, chattering at each other like a flock of excited magpies, and there was a scandalized murmur at my heartless promptitude. What they wanted to keep that body hanging about for I can't guess. Embalm it, maybe. But I had also heard another, and a very ominous, murmur on the deck below. My friends the wood-cutters were likewise scandalized, and with a better show of reason—though I admit that the reason itself was quite inadmissible. Oh, quite! I had made up my mind that if my late helmsman was to be eaten, the fishes alone should have him. He had been a very second-rate helmsman while alive, but now he was dead he might have become a first-class temptation, and possibly cause some startling trouble. Besides, I was anxious to take the wheel, the man in pink pyjamas showing himself a hopeless duffer at the business.

"This I did directly the simple funeral was over. We were going half-speed, keeping right in the middle of the stream, and I listened to the talk about me. They had given up Kurtz, they had given up the station; Kurtz was dead, and the station had been burnt—and so on—and so on. The red-haired pilgrim was beside himself with the thought that at least this poor Kurtz had been properly avenged. 'Say! We must have made a glorious slaughter of them in the bush. Eh? What do you think? Say?' He positively danced, the bloodthirsty little gingery beggar. And he had nearly fainted when he saw the wounded man! I could not help saying, 'You made a glorious lot of smoke, anyhow.' I had seen, from the way the tops of the bushes rustled and flew, that almost all the shots had gone too high. You can't hit anything unless you take aim and fire from the shoulder; but these chaps fired from the hip with their eyes shut. The retreat, I maintained—and I was right—was caused by the screeching of the steam-whistle. Upon this they forgot Kurtz, and began to howl at me with indignant protests.

105

"The manager stood by the wheel murmuring confidentially about the necessity of getting well away down the river before dark at all events, when I saw in the distance a clearing on the river-side and the outlines of some sort of building. 'What's this?' I asked. He clapped his hands in wonder. 'The station!' he cried. I edged in at once, still going half-speed.

"Through my glasses I saw the slope of a hill interspersed with rare trees and perfectly free from undergrowth. A long decaying building on the summit was half buried in the high grass; the large holes in the peaked roof gaped black from afar; the jungle and the woods made a background. There was no enclosure or fence of any kind; but there had been one apparently, for near the house half-a-dozen slim posts remained in a row, roughly trimmed, and with their upper ends ornamented with round carved balls. The rails, or whatever there had been between, had disappeared. Of course the forest surrounded all that. The river-bank was clear, and on the water-side I saw a white man under a hat like a cart-wheel beckoning persistently with his whole arm. Examining the edge of the forest above and below, I was almost certain I could see movements—human forms gliding here and there. I steamed past prudently, then stopped the engines and let her drift down. The man on the shore began to shout, urging us to land. 'We have been attacked,' screamed the manager. 'I know—I know. It's all right,' yelled back the other, as cheerful as you please. 'Come along. It's all right. I am glad.'

"His aspect reminded me of something I had seen—something funny I had seen somewhere. As I manœuvred to get alongside, I was asking myself, 'What does this fellow look like?' Suddenly I got it. He looked like a harlequin. His clothes had been made of some stuff that was brown holland[18] probably, but it was covered with patches all over, with bright patches, blue, red, and yellow—patches on the back, patches on the front, patches on elbows, on knees; coloured binding around his jacket, scarlet edging at the bottom of his trousers; and the sunshine made him look extremely gay and wonderfully neat withal, because you could see how beautifully all this patching had been done. A beardless, boyish face, very fair, no features to speak of, nose peeling, little blue eyes, smiles and frowns chasing each other over that open countenance like sunshine and shadow on a wind-swept plain. 'Look out, captain!' he cried; 'there's a snag lodged in here last night.' What! Another snag? I confess I swore shamefully. I had nearly holed my cripple, to finish off that charming trip. The harlequin on the bank turned his little pug-nose up to me. 'You English?' he asked, all smiles. 'Are you?' I shouted from the wheel. The smiles vanished, and he shook his head as if sorry for my disappointment. Then he brightened up. 'Never mind!' he cried, encouragingly. 'Are we in time?' I asked. 'He is up there,' he replied, with a toss of the head up the hill, and becoming gloomy all of a sudden. His face was like the autumn sky, overcast one moment and bright the next.

"When the manager, escorted by the pilgrims, all of them armed to the teeth, had gone to the house this chap came on board. 'I say, I don't like this. These natives are in the bush,' I said. He assured me earnestly it was all right. 'They are simple people,' he

110

---

[18]Unbleached linen.—Eds.

added; 'well, I am glad you came. It took me all my time to keep them off.' 'But you said it was all right,' I cried. 'Oh, they meant no harm,' he said; and as I stared he corrected himself, 'Not exactly.' Then vivaciously, 'My faith, your pilot-house wants a clean-up!' In the next breath he advised me to keep enough steam on the boiler to blow the whistle in case of any trouble. 'One good screech will do more for you than all your rifles. They are simple people,' he repeated. He rattled away at such a rate he quite overwhelmed me. He seemed to be trying to make up for lots of silence, and actually hinted, laughing, that such was the case. 'Don't you talk with Mr. Kurtz?' I said. 'You don't talk with that man — you listen to him,' he exclaimed with severe exaltation. 'But now ——' He waved his arm, and in the twinkling of an eye was in the uttermost depths of despondency. In a moment he came up again with a jump, possessed himself of both my hands, shook them continuously, while he gabbled: 'Brother sailor . . . honour . . . pleasure . . . delight . . . introduce myself . . . Russian . . . son of an arch-priest . . . Government of Tambov . . . What? Tobacco! English tobacco; the excellent English tobacco! Now, that's brotherly. Smoke? Where's a sailor that does not smoke?'

"The pipe soothed him, and gradually I made out he had run away from school, had gone to sea in a Russian ship; ran away again; served some time in English ships; was now reconciled with the arch-priest. He made a point of that. 'But when one is young one must see things, gather experience, ideas; enlarge the mind.' 'Here!' I interrupted. 'You can never tell! Here I met Mr. Kurtz,' he said, youthfully solemn and reproachful. I held my tongue after that. It appears he had persuaded a Dutch trading-house on the coast to fit him out with stores and goods, and had started for the interior with a light heart, and no more idea of what would happen to him than a baby. He had been wandering about that river for nearly two years alone, cut off from everybody and everything. 'I am not so young as I look. I am twenty-five,' he said. 'At first old Van Shuyten would tell me to go to the devil,' he narrated with keen enjoyment; 'but I stuck to him, and talked and talked, till at last he got afraid I would talk the hind-leg off his favourite dog, so he gave me some cheap things and a few guns, and told me he hoped he would never see my face again. Good old Dutchman, Van Shuyten. I've sent him one small lot of ivory a year ago, so that he can't call me a little thief when I get back. I hope he got it. And for the rest I don't care. I had some wood stacked for you. That was my old house. Did you see?'

"I gave him Towson's book. He made as though he would kiss me, but restrained himself. 'The only book I had left, and I thought I had lost it,' he said, looking at it ecstatically. 'So many accidents happen to a man going about alone, you know. Canoes get upset sometimes — and sometimes you've got to clear out so quick when the people get angry.' He thumbed the pages. 'You made notes in Russian?' I asked. He nodded. 'I thought they were written in cipher,' I said. He laughed, then became serious. 'I had lots of trouble to keep these people off,' he said. 'Did they want to kill you?' I asked. 'Oh, no!' he cried, and checked himself. 'Why did they attack us?' I pursued. He hesitated, then said shamefacedly, 'They don't want him to go.' 'Don't they?' I said, curiously. He nodded a nod full of mystery and wisdom. 'I tell you,' he cried, 'this man has enlarged my mind.' He opened his arms wide, staring at me with his little blue eyes that were perfectly round."

3

"I looked at him, lost in astonishment. There he was before me, in motley, as though he had absconded from a troupe of mimes, enthusiastic, fabulous. His very existence was improbable, inexplicable, and altogether bewildering. He was an insoluble problem. It was inconceivable how he had existed, how he had succeeded in getting so far, how he had managed to remain—why he did not instantly disappear. 'I went a little farther,' he said, 'then still a little farther—till I had gone so far that I don't know how I'll ever get back. Never mind. Plenty time. I can manage. You take Kurtz away quick—quick— I tell you.' The glamour of youth enveloped his particoloured rags, his destitution, his loneliness, the essential desolation of his futile wanderings. For months—for years— his life hadn't been worth a day's purchase; and there he was gallantly, thought-lessly alive, to all appearance indestructible solely by the virtue of his few years and of his unreflecting audacity. I was seduced into something like admiration—like envy. Glamour urged him on, glamour kept him unscathed. He surely wanted nothing from the wilderness but space to breathe in and to push on through. His need was to exist, and to move onwards at the greatest possible risk, and with a maximum of privation. If the absolutely pure, uncalculating, unpractical spirit of adventure had ever ruled a human being, it ruled this be-patched youth. I almost envied him the possession of this modest and clear flame. It seemed to have consumed all thought of self so completely, that even while he was talking to you, you forgot that it was he—the man before your eyes—who had gone through these things. I did not envy him his devotion to Kurtz, though. He had not meditated over it. It came to him, and he accepted it with a sort of eager fatalism. I must say that to me it appeared about the most dangerous thing in every way he had come upon so far. *Discuss*

"They had come together unavoidably, like two ships becalmed near each other, and lay rubbing sides at last. I suppose Kurtz wanted an audience, because on a certain occasion, when encamped in the forest, they had talked all night, or more probably Kurtz had talked. 'We talked of everything,' he said, quite transported at the recollec-tion. 'I forgot there was such a thing as sleep. The night did not seem to last an hour. Everything! Everything! . . . Of love too.' 'Ah, he talked to you of love!' I said, much amused. 'It isn't what you think,' he cried, almost passionately. 'It was in general. He made me see things—things.'

"He threw his arms up. We were on deck at the time, and the headman of my wood-cutters, lounging near by, turned upon him his heavy and glittering eyes. I looked around, and I don't know why, but I assure you that never, never before, did this land, this river, this jungle, the very arch of this blazing sky, appear to me so hopeless and so dark, so impenetrable to human thought, so pitiless to human weakness. 'And, ever since, you have been with him, of course?' I said.

"On the contrary. It appears their intercourse had been very much broken by vari-ous causes. He had, as he informed me proudly, managed to nurse Kurtz through two illnesses (he alluded to it as you would to some risky feat), but as a rule Kurtz wandered alone, far in the depths of the forest. 'Very often coming to this station, I had to wait days and days before he would turn up,' he said. 'Ah, it was worth waiting for!—sometimes.'

115

'What was he doing? exploring or what?' I asked. 'Oh, yes, of course'; he had discovered lots of villages, a lake, too—he did not know exactly in what direction; it was dangerous to inquire too much—but mostly his expeditions had been for ivory. 'But he had no goods to trade with by that time,' I objected. 'There's a good lot of cartridges left even yet,' he answered, looking away. 'To speak plainly, he raided the country,' I said. He nodded. 'Not alone, surely!' He muttered something about the villages round that lake. 'Kurtz got the tribe to follow him, did he?' I suggested. He fidgeted a little. 'They adored him,' he said. The tone of these words was so extraordinary that I looked at him searchingly. It was curious to see his mingled eagerness and reluctance to speak of Kurtz. The man filled his life, occupied his thoughts, swayed his emotions. 'What can you expect?' he burst out; 'he came to them with thunder and lightning, you know—and they had never seen anything like it—and very terrible. He could be very terrible. You can't judge Mr. Kurtz as you would an ordinary man. No, no, no! Now—just to give you an idea—I don't mind telling you, he wanted to shoot me, too, one day—but I don't judge him.' 'Shoot you!' I cried. 'What for?' 'Well, I had a small lot of ivory the chief of that village near my house gave me. You see I used to shoot game for them. Well, he wanted it, and wouldn't hear reason. He declared he would shoot me unless I gave him the ivory and then cleared out of the country, because he could do so, and had a fancy for it, and there was nothing on earth to prevent him killing whom he jolly well pleased. And it was true, too. I gave him the ivory. What did I care! But I didn't clear out. No, no. I couldn't leave him. I had to be careful, of course, till we got friendly again for a time. He had his second illness then. Afterwards I had to keep out of the way; but I didn't mind. He was living for the most part in those villages on the lake. When he came down to the river, sometimes he would take to me, and sometimes it was better for me to be careful. This man suffered too much. He hated all this, and somehow he couldn't get away. When I had a chance I begged him to try and leave while there was time; I offered to go back with him. And he would say yes, and then he would remain; go off on another ivory hunt; disappear for weeks; forget himself amongst these people—forget himself—you know.' 'Why! he's mad,' I said. He protested indignantly. Mr. Kurtz couldn't be mad. If I had heard him talk, only two days ago, I wouldn't dare hint at such a thing. . . . I had taken up my binoculars while we talked, and was looking at the shore, sweeping the limit of the forest at each side and at the back of the house. The consciousness of there being people in that bush, so silent, so quiet—as silent and quiet as the ruined house on the hill—made me uneasy. There was no sign on the face of nature of this amazing tale that was not so much told as suggested to me in desolate exclamations, completed by shrugs, in interrupted phrases, in hints ending in deep sighs. The woods were unmoved, like a mask—heavy, like the closed door of a prison—they looked with their air of hidden knowledge, of patient expectation, of unapproachable silence. The Russian was explaining to me that it was only lately that Mr. Kurtz had come down to the river, bringing along with him all the fighting men of that lake tribe. He had been absent for several months—getting himself adored, I suppose—and had come down unexpectedly, with the intention to all appearance of making a raid either across the river or down stream. Evidently the appetite for more ivory had got the better of the—what shall I say?—less material aspirations. However he had got much worse suddenly. 'I heard he was lying helpless, and so I came up—took my chance,' said the Russian. 'Oh, he is bad, very bad.' I directed my glass to the house. There were no signs of life, but there was the ruined roof, the long mud wall peeping above the grass, with three little square window-holes, no two of the same size; all this brought within reach of my hand, as it were. And then I made a brusque movement, and one of the remaining posts of that vanished fence leaped up in the field of my glass. You remember I told you I had been struck at the distance by certain attempts at ornamentation, rather remarkable in the ruinous aspect of the place. Now I had suddenly a nearer view, and its first result was to make me throw my head back as if before a blow. Then I went carefully from post to post with my glass, and I saw my mistake. These round knobs were not ornamental but symbolic; they were expressive and puzzling, striking and disturbing—food for thought and also for vultures if there had been any looking down from the sky; but at all events for such ants as were industrious enough to ascend the pole. They would have been even more impressive, those heads on the stakes, if their faces had not been turned to the house. Only one, the first I had made out, was facing my way. I was not so shocked as you may think. The start back I had given was really nothing but a movement of surprise. I had expected to see a knob of wood there, you know. I returned deliberately to the first I had seen—and there it was, black, dried, sunken, with closed eyelids,—a head that seemed to sleep at the top of that pole, and with the shrunken dry lips showing a narrow white line of the teeth, was smiling, too, smiling continuously at some endless and jocose dream of that eternal slumber.

"I am not disclosing any trade secrets. In fact, the manager said afterwards that Mr. Kurtz's methods had ruined the district. I have no opinion on that point, but I want you clearly to understand that there was nothing exactly profitable in these heads being there. They only showed that Mr. Kurtz lacked restraint in the gratification of his various lusts, that there was something wanting in him—some small matter which, when the pressing need arose, could not be found under his magnificent eloquence. Whether he knew of this deficiency himself I can't say. I think the knowledge came to him at last—only at the very last. But the wilderness had found him out early, and had taken on him a terrible vengeance for the fantastic invasion. I think it had whispered to him things about himself which he did not know, things of which he had no conception till he took counsel with this great solitude—and the whisper had proved irresistibly fascinating. It echoed loudly within him because he was hollow at the core. . . . I put down the glass, and the head that had appeared near enough to be spoken to seemed at once to have leaped away from me into inaccessible distance.

"The admirer of Mr. Kurtz was a bit crestfallen. In a hurried, indistinct voice he began to assure me he had not dared to take these—say, symbols—down. He was not afraid of the natives; they would not stir till Mr. Kurtz gave the word. His ascendancy was extraordinary. The camps of these people surrounded the place, and the chiefs came every day to see him. They would crawl. . . . 'I don't want to know anything of the ceremonies used when approaching Mr. Kurtz,' I shouted. Curious, this feeling that came over me that such details would be more intolerable than those heads drying on the stakes under Mr. Kurtz's windows. After all, that was only a savage sight, while I seemed at one bound to have been transported into some lightless region of subtle horrors, where pure, uncomplicated savagery was a positive relief, being something that had a right to exist—obviously—in the sunshine. The young man looked at me with surprise. I suppose it did not occur to him that Mr. Kurtz was no idol of mine. He forgot I hadn't heard any of these splendid monologues on, what was it? on love, justice, conduct of life—or what not. If it had come to crawling before Mr. Kurtz, he crawled as much as the veriest savage of them all. I had no idea of the conditions, he said: these heads were the heads of rebels. I shocked him excessively by laughing. Rebels! What would be the next definition I was to hear? There had been enemies, criminals, workers—and these were rebels. Those rebellious heads looked very subdued to me on their sticks. 'You don't know how such a life tries a man like Kurtz,' cried Kurtz's last disciple. 'Well, and you?' I said. 'I! I! I am a simple man. I have no great thoughts. I want nothing from anybody. How can you compare me to . . . ?' His feelings were too much for speech, and suddenly he broke down. 'I don't understand,' he groaned. 'I've been doing my best to keep him alive, and that's enough. I had no hand in all this. I have no abilities. There hasn't been a drop of medicine or a mouthful of invalid food for months here. He was shamefully abandoned. A man like this, with such ideas. Shamefully! Shamefully! I—I—haven't slept for the last ten nights . . .'

"His voice lost itself in the calm of the evening. The long shadows of the forest had slipped downhill while we talked, had gone far beyond the ruined hovel, beyond the symbolic row of stakes. All this was in the gloom, while we down there were yet in the sunshine, and the stretch of the river abreast of the clearing glittered in a still and dazzling splendour, with a murky and overshadowed bend above and below. Not a living soul was seen on the shore. The bushes did not rustle.

"Suddenly round the corner of the house a group of men appeared, as though they had come up from the ground. They waded waist-deep in the grass, in a compact body, bearing an improvised stretcher in their midst. Instantly, in the emptiness of the landscape, a cry arose whose shrillness pierced the still air like a sharp arrow flying straight to the very heart of the land; and, as if by enchantment, streams of human beings—of naked human beings—with spears in their hands, with bows, with shields, with wild glances and savage movements, were poured into the clearing by the dark-faced and pensive forest. The bushes shook, the grass swayed for a time, and then everything stood still in attentive immobility.

"'Now, if he does not say the right thing to them we are all done for,' said the Russian at my elbow. The knot of men with the stretcher had stopped, too, halfway to the steamer, as if petrified. I saw the man on the stretcher sit up, lank and with an uplifted arm, above the shoulders of the bearers. 'Let us hope that the man who can talk so well of love in general will find some particular reason to spare us this time,' I said. I resented bitterly the absurd danger of our situation, as if to be at the mercy of that atrocious phantom had been a dishonouring necessity. I could not hear a sound, but through my glasses I saw the thin arm extended commandingly, the lower jaw moving, the eyes of that apparition shining darkly far in its bony head that nodded with grotesque jerks. Kurtz—Kurtz—that means short in German—don't it? Well, the name was as true as everything else in his life—and death. He looked at least seven feet long.

120

His covering had fallen off, and his body emerged from it pitiful and appalling as from a winding-sheet. I could see the cage of his ribs all astir, the bones of his arm waving. It was as though an animated image of death carved out of old ivory had been shaking its hand with menaces at a motionless crowd of men made of dark and glittering bronze. I saw him open his mouth wide—it gave him a weirdly voracious aspect, as though he had wanted to swallow all the air, all the earth, all the men before him. A deep voice reached me faintly. He must have been shouting. He fell back suddenly. The stretcher shook as the bearers staggered forward again, and almost at the same time I noticed that the crowd of savages was vanishing without any perceptible movement of retreat, as if the forest that had ejected these beings so suddenly had drawn them in again as the breath is drawn in a long aspiration.

"Some of the pilgrims behind the stretcher carried his arms—two shot-guns, a heavy rifle, and a light revolver-carbine—the thunderbolts of that pitiful Jupiter. The manager bent over him murmuring as he walked beside his head. They laid him down in one of the little cabins—just a room for a bedplace and a camp-stool or two, you know. We had brought his belated correspondence, and a lot of torn envelopes and open letters littered his bed. His hand roamed feebly amongst these papers. I was struck by the fire of his eyes and the composed languor of his expression. It was not so much the exhaustion of disease. He did not seem in pain. This shadow looked satiated and calm, as though for the moment it had had its fill of all the emotions.

"He rustled one of the letters, and looking straight in my face said, 'I am glad.' Somebody had been writing to him about me. These special recommendations were turning up again. The volume of tone he emitted without effort, almost without the trouble of moving his lips, amazed me. A voice! a voice! It was grave, profound, vibrating, while the man did not seem capable of a whisper. However, he had enough strength in him—factitious no doubt—to very nearly make an end of us, as you shall hear directly.

"The manager appeared silently in the doorway; I stepped out at once and he drew the curtain after me. The Russian, eyed curiously by the pilgrims, was staring at the shore. I followed the direction of his glance.

"Dark human shapes could be made out in the distance, flitting indistinctly against the gloomy border of the forest, and near the river two bronze figures, leaning on tall spears, stood in the sunlight under fantastic head-dresses of spotted skins, war-like and still in statuesque repose. And from right to left along the lighted shore moved a wild and gorgeous apparition of a woman.

"She walked with measured steps, draped in striped and fringed cloths, treading the earth proudly, with a slight jingle and flash of barbarous ornaments. She carried her head high; her hair was done in the shape of a helmet; she had brass leggings to the knee, brass wire gauntlets to the elbow, a crimson spot on her tawny cheek, innumerable necklaces of glass beads on her neck; bizarre things, charms, gifts of witch-men, that hung about her, glittered and trembled at every step. She must have had the value of several elephant tusks upon her. She was savage and superb, wild-eyed and magnificent; there was something ominous and stately in her deliberate progress. And in the hush that had fallen suddenly upon the whole sorrowful land, the immense wilderness, the colossal body of the fecund and mysterious life seemed to look at her, pensive, as though it had been looking at the image of its own tenebrous and passionate soul.

"She came abreast of the steamer, stood still, and faced us. Her long shadow fell to the water's edge. Her face had a tragic and fierce aspect of wild sorrow and of dumb pain mingled with the fear of some struggling, half-shaped resolve. She stood looking at us without a stir, and like the wilderness itself, with an air of brooding over an inscrutable purpose. A whole minute passed, and then she made a step forward. There was a low jingle, a glint of yellow metal, a sway of fringed draperies, and she stopped as if her heart had failed her. The young fellow by my side growled. The pilgrims murmured at my back. She looked at us all as if her life had depended upon the unswerving steadiness of her glance. Suddenly she opened her bared arms and threw them up rigid above her head, as though in an uncontrollable desire to touch the sky, and at the same time the swift shadows darted out on the earth, swept around on the river, gathering the steamer into a shadowy embrace. A formidable silence hung over the scene.

"She turned away slowly, walked on, following the bank, and passed into the bushes to the left. Once only her eyes gleamed back at us in the dusk of the thickets before she disappeared.

"'If she had offered to come aboard I really think I would have tried to shoot her,' said the man of patches, nervously. 'I have been risking my life every day for the last fortnight to keep her out of the house. She got in one day and kicked up a row about those miserable rags I picked up in the storeroom to mend my clothes with. I wasn't decent. At least it must have been that, for she talked like a fury to Kurtz for an hour, pointing at me now and then. I don't understand the dialect of this tribe. Luckily for me, I fancy Kurtz felt too ill that day to care, or there would have been mischief. I don't understand. . . . No—it's too much for me. Ah, well, it's all over now.'

"At this moment I heard Kurtz's deep voice behind the curtain: 'Save me!—save the ivory, you mean. Don't tell me. Save *me*! Why, I've had to save you. You are interrupting my plans now. Sick! Sick! Not so sick as you would like to believe. Never mind. I'll carry my ideas out yet—I will return. I'll show you what can be done. You with your little peddling notions—you are interfering with me. I will return. I. . . .'   130

"The manager came out. He did me the honour to take me under the arm and lead me aside. 'He is very low, very low,' he said. He considered it necessary to sigh, but neglected to be consistently sorrowful. 'We have done all we could for him—haven't we? But there is no disguising the fact, Mr. Kurtz has done more harm than good to the Company. He did not see the time was not ripe for vigorous action. Cautiously, cautiously—that's my principle. We must be cautious yet. The district is closed to us for a time. Deplorable! Upon the whole, the trade will suffer. I don't deny there is a remarkable quantity of ivory—mostly fossil. We must save it, at all events—but look how precarious the position is—and why? Because the method is unsound.' 'Do you,' said I, looking at the shore, 'call it "unsound method"?' 'Without doubt,' he exclaimed, hotly. 'Don't you?' . . . 'No method at all,' I murmured after a while. 'Exactly,' he exulted. 'I anticipated this. Shows a complete want of judgment.

It is my duty to point it out in the proper quarter.' 'Oh,' said I, 'that fellow—what's his name?—the brickmaker, will make a readable report for you.' He appeared confounded for a moment. It seemed to me I had never breathed an atmosphere so vile, and I turned mentally to Kurtz for relief—positively for relief. 'Nevertheless I think Mr. Kurtz is a remarkable man,' I said with emphasis. He started, dropped on me a cold heavy glance, said very quietly, 'He *was*,' and turned his back on me. My hour of favour was over; I found myself lumped along with Kurtz as a partisan of methods for which the time was not ripe: I was unsound! Ah! but it was something to have at least a choice of nightmares.

"I had turned to the wilderness really, not to Mr. Kurtz, who, I was ready to admit, was as good as buried. And for a moment it seemed to me as if I also were buried in a vast grave full of unspeakable secrets. I felt an intolerable weight oppressing my breast, the smell of the damp earth, the unseen presence of victorious corruption, the darkness of an impenetrable night. . . . The Russian tapped me on the shoulder. I heard him mumbling and stammering something about 'brother seaman—couldn't conceal—knowledge of matters that would affect Mr. Kurtz's reputation.' I waited. For him evidently Mr. Kurtz was not in his grave; I suspect that for him Mr. Kurtz was one of the immortals. 'Well!' said I at last, 'speak out. As it happens, I am Mr. Kurtz's friend—in a way.'

"He stated with a good deal of formality that had we not been 'of the same profession,' he would have kept the matter to himself without regard to consequences. 'He suspected there was an active ill will towards him on the part of these white men that ——' 'You are right,' I said, remembering a certain conversation I had overheard. 'The manager thinks you ought to be hanged.' He showed a concern at this intelligence which amused me at first. 'I had better get out of the way quietly,' he said, earnestly. 'I can do no more for Kurtz now, and they would soon find some excuse. What's to stop them? There's a military post three hundred miles from here.' 'Well, upon my word,' said I, 'perhaps you had better go if you have any friends amongst the savages near by.' 'Plenty,' he said. 'They are simple people—and I want nothing, you know.' He stood biting his lip, then: 'I don't want any harm to happen to these whites here, but of course I was thinking of Mr. Kurtz's reputation—but you are a brother seaman and ——' 'All right,' said I, after a time. 'Mr. Kurtz's reputation is safe with me.' I did not know how truly I spoke.

"He informed me, lowering his voice, that it was Kurtz who had ordered the attack to be made on the steamer. 'He hated sometimes the idea of being taken away—and then again. . . . But I don't understand these matters. I am a simple man. He thought it would scare you away—that you would give it up, thinking him dead. I could not stop him. Oh, I had an awful time of it this last month.' 'Very well,' I said. 'He is all right now.' 'Ye-e-es,' he muttered, not very convinced apparently. 'Thanks,' said I; 'I shall keep my eyes open.' 'But quiet—eh?' he urged, anxiously. 'It would be awful for his reputation if anybody here ——' I promised a complete discretion with great gravity. 'I have a canoe and three black fellows waiting not very far. I am off. Could you give me a few Martini-Henry cartridges?' I could, and did, with proper secrecy. He helped himself, with a wink at me, to a handful of my tobacco. 'Between sailors—you know—good English tobacco.' At the door of the pilot-house he turned round—'I say, haven't you a pair of shoes you could spare?' He raised one leg. 'Look.' The soles were tied with knotted strings sandal-wise under his bare feet. I rooted out an old pair, at which he looked with admiration before tucking it under his left arm. One of his pockets (bright red) was bulging with cartridges, from the other (dark blue) peeped 'Towson's Inquiry,' etc., etc. He seemed to think himself excellently well equipped for a renewed encounter with the wilderness. 'Ah! I'll never, never meet such a man again. You ought to have heard him recite poetry—his own, too, it was, he told me. Poetry!' He rolled his eyes at the recollection of these delights. 'Oh, he enlarged my mind!' 'Good-bye,' said I. He shook hands and vanished in the night. Sometimes I ask myself whether I had ever really seen him—whether it was possible to meet such a phenomenon! ...

"When I woke up shortly after midnight his warning came to my mind with its hint of danger that seemed, in the starred darkness, real enough to make me get up for the purpose of having a look round. On the hill a big fire burned, illuminating fitfully a crooked corner of the station-house. One of the agents with a picket[19] of a few of our blacks, armed for the purpose, was keeping guard over the ivory; but deep within the forest, red gleams that wavered, that seemed to sink and rise from the ground amongst confused columnar shapes of intense blackness, showed the exact position of the camp where Mr. Kurtz's adorers were keeping their uneasy vigil. The monotonous beating of a big drum filled the air with muffled shocks and a lingering vibration. A steady droning sound of many men chanting each to himself some weird incantation came out from the black, flat wall of the woods as the humming of bees comes out of a hive, and had a strange narcotic effect upon my half-awake senses. I believe I dozed off leaning over the rail, till an abrupt burst of yells, an overwhelming outbreak of a pent-up and mysterious frenzy, woke me up in a bewildered wonder. It was cut short all at once, and the low droning went on with an effect of audible and soothing silence. I glanced casually into the little cabin. A light was burning within, but Mr. Kurtz was not there.

"I think I would have raised an outcry if I had believed my eyes. But I didn't believe them at first—the thing seemed so impossible. The fact is I was completely unnerved by a sheer blank fright, pure abstract terror, unconnected with any distinct shape of physical danger. What made this emotion so overpowering was—how shall I define it?—the moral shock I received, as if something altogether monstrous, intolerable to thought and odious to the soul, had been thrust upon me unexpectedly. This lasted of course the merest fraction of a second, and then the usual sense of commonplace, deadly danger, the possibility of a sudden onslaught and massacre, or something of the kind, which I saw impending, was positively welcome and composing. It pacified me, in fact, so much, that I did not raise an alarm.

"There was an agent buttoned up inside an ulster and sleeping on a chair on deck within three feet of me. The yells had not awakened him; he snored very

[19]Small group of soldiers.—Eds.

slightly; I left him to his slumbers and leaped ashore. I did not betray Mr. Kurtz—it was ordered I should never betray him—it was written I should be loyal to the nightmare of my choice. I was anxious to deal with this shadow by myself alone,—and to this day I don't know why I was so jealous of sharing with any one the peculiar blackness of that experience.

"As soon as I got on the bank I saw a trail—a broad trail through the grass. I remember the exultation with which I said to myself, 'He can't walk—he is crawling on all-fours—I've got him.' The grass was wet with dew. I strode rapidly with clenched fists. I fancy I had some vague notion of falling upon him and giving him a drubbing. I don't know. I had some imbecile thoughts. The knitting old woman with the cat obtruded herself upon my memory as a most improper person to be sitting at the other end of such an affair. I saw a row of pilgrims squirting lead in the air out of Winchesters held to the hip. I thought I would never get back to the steamer, and imagined myself living alone and unarmed in the woods to an advanced age. Such silly things—you know. And I remember I confounded the beat of the drum with the beating of my heart, and was pleased at its calm regularity.

"I kept to the track though—then stopped to listen. The night was very clear; a dark blue space, sparkling with dew and starlight, in which black things stood very still. I thought I could see a kind of motion ahead of me. I was strangely cocksure of everything that night. I actually left the track and ran in a wide semicircle (I verily believe chuckling to myself) so as to get in front of that stir, of that motion I had seen—if indeed I had seen anything. I was circumventing Kurtz as though it had been a boyish game.

"I came upon him, and, if he had not heard me coming, I would have fallen over him, too, but he got up in time. He rose, unsteady, long, pale, indistinct, like a vapour exhaled by the earth, and swayed slightly, misty and silent before me; while at my back the fires loomed between the trees, and the murmur of many voices issued from the forest. I had cut him off cleverly; but when actually confronting him I seemed to come to my senses, I saw the danger in its right proportion. It was by no means over yet. Suppose he began to shout? Though he could hardly stand, there was still plenty of vigour in his voice. 'Go away—hide yourself,' he said, in that profound tone. It was very awful. I glanced back. We were within thirty yards from the nearest fire. A black figure stood up, strode on long black legs, waving long black arms, across the glow. It had horns—antelope horns, I think—on its head. Some sorcerer, some witch-man, no doubt: it looked fiend-like enough. 'Do you know what you are doing?' I whispered. 'Perfectly,' he answered, raising his voice for that single word: it sounded to me far off and yet loud, like a hail through a speaking-trumpet. If he makes a row we are lost, I thought to myself. This clearly was not a case for fisticuffs, even apart from the very natural aversion I had to beat that Shadow—this wandering and tormented thing. 'You will be lost,' I said—'utterly lost.' One gets sometimes such a flash of inspiration, you know. I did say the right thing, though indeed he could not have been more irretrievably lost than he was at this very moment, when the foundations of our intimacy were being laid—to endure—to endure—even to the end—even beyond.

140

"'I had immense plans,' he muttered irresolutely. 'Yes,' said I; 'but if you try to shout I'll smash your head with ——' There was not a stick or stone near. 'I will throttle you for good,' I corrected myself. 'I was on the threshold of great things,' he pleaded, in a voice of longing, with a wistfulness of tone that made my blood run cold. 'And now for this stupid scoundrel ——' 'Your success in Europe is assured in any case,' I affirmed, steadily. I did not want to have the throttling of him, you understand—and indeed it would have been very little use for any practical purpose. I tried to break the spell—the heavy, mute spell of the wilderness—that seemed to draw him to its pitiless breast by the awakening of forgotten and brutal instincts, by the memory of gratified and monstrous passions. This alone, I was convinced, had driven him out to the edge of the forest, to the bush, towards the gleam of fires, the throb of drums, the drone of weird incantations; this alone had beguiled his unlawful soul beyond the bounds of permitted aspirations. And, don't you see, the terror of the position was not in being knocked on the head—though I had a very lively sense of that danger, too—but in this, that I had to deal with a being to whom I could not appeal in the name of anything high or low. I had, even like the niggers, to invoke him—himself—his own exalted and incredible degradation. There was nothing either above or below him, and I knew it. He had kicked himself loose of the earth. Confound the man! he had kicked the very earth to pieces. He was alone, and I before him did not know whether I stood on the ground or floated in the air. I've been telling you what we said—repeating the phrases we pronounced—but what's the good? They were common everyday words—the familiar, vague sounds exchanged on every waking day of life. But what of that? They had behind them, to my mind, the terrific suggestiveness of words heard in dreams, of phrases spoken in nightmares. Soul! If anybody had ever struggled with a soul, I am the man. And I wasn't arguing with a lunatic either. Believe me or not, his intelligence was perfectly clear—concentrated, it is true, upon himself with horrible intensity, yet clear; and therein was my only chance—barring, of course, the killing him there and then, which wasn't so good, on account of unavoidable noise. But his soul was mad. Being alone in the wilderness, it had looked within itself, and, by heavens! I tell you, it had gone mad. I had—for my sins, I suppose—to go through the ordeal of looking into it myself. No eloquence could have been so withering to one's belief in mankind as his final burst of sincerity. He struggled with himself, too. I saw it—I heard it. I saw the inconceivable mystery of a soul that knew no restraint, no faith, and no fear, yet struggling blindly with itself. I kept my head pretty well; but when I had him at last stretched on the couch, I wiped my forehead, while my legs shook under me as though I had carried half a ton on my back down that hill. And yet I had only supported him, his bony arm clasped round my neck—and he was not much heavier than a child.

"When next day we left at noon, the crowd, of whose presence behind the curtain of trees I had been acutely conscious all the time, flowed out of the woods again, filled the clearing, covered the slope with a mass of naked, breathing, quivering, bronze bodies. I steamed up a bit, then swung downstream, and two thousand eyes followed the evolutions of the splashing, thumping, fierce river-demon beating the water with its terrible tail and breathing black smoke into the air. In front of the first rank, along the river, three men, plastered with bright red earth from head to foot, strutted to and fro restlessly. When we came abreast again, they faced the river, stamped their feet, nodded their horned heads, swayed their scarlet bodies; they shook towards the fierce river-demon a bunch of black feathers, a mangy skin with a pendent tail—something that looked like a dried gourd; they shouted periodically together strings of amazing words that resembled no sounds of human language; and the deep murmurs of the crowd, interrupted suddenly, were like the responses of some satanic litany.

"We had carried Kurtz into the pilot-house: there was more air there. Lying on the couch, he stared through the open shutter. There was an eddy in the mass of human bodies, and the woman with helmeted head and tawny cheeks rushed out to the very brink of the stream. She put out her hands, shouted something, and all that wild mob took up the shout in a roaring chorus of articulated, rapid, breathless utterance.

"'Do you understand this?' I asked.

"He kept on looking out past me with fiery, longing eyes, with a mingled 145 expression of wistfulness and hate. He made no answer, but I saw a smile, a smile of indefinable meaning, appear on his colourless lips that a moment after twitched convulsively. 'Do I not?' he said slowly, gasping, as if the words had been torn out of him by a supernatural power.

"I pulled the string of the whistle, and I did this because I saw the pilgrims on deck getting out their rifles with an air of anticipating a jolly lark. At the sudden screech there was a movement of abject terror through that wedged mass of bodies. 'Don't! don't you frighten them away,' cried someone on deck disconsolately. I pulled the string time after time. They broke and ran, they leaped, they crouched, they swerved, they dodged the flying terror of the sound. The three red chaps had fallen flat, face down on the shore, as though they had been shot dead. Only the barbarous and superb woman did not so much as flinch, and stretched tragically her bare arms after us over the sombre and glittering river.

"And then that imbecile crowd down on the deck started their little fun, and I could see nothing more for smoke.

"The brown current ran swiftly out of the heart of darkness, bearing us down towards the sea with twice the speed of our upward progress; and Kurtz's life was running swiftly, too, ebbing, ebbing out of his heart into the sea of inexorable time. The manager was very placid, he had no vital anxieties now, he took us both in with a comprehensive and satisfied glance: the 'affair' had come off as well as could be wished. I saw the time approaching when I would be left alone of the party of 'unsound method.' The pilgrims looked upon me with disfavour. I was, so to speak, numbered with the dead. It is strange how I accepted this unforeseen partnership, this choice of nightmares forced upon me in the tenebrous land invaded by these mean and greedy phantoms.

"Kurtz discoursed. A voice! a voice! It rang deep to the very last. It survived his strength to hide in the magnificent folds of eloquence the barren darkness of his heart. Oh, he struggled! he struggled! The wastes of his weary brain were haunted by shadowy images now—images of wealth and fame revolving obsequiously round his unextinguishable gift of noble and lofty expression. My Intended, my station, my career, my ideas—these were the subjects for the occasional utterances of elevated sentiments. The shade of the original Kurtz frequented the bedside of the hollow sham, whose fate it was to be buried presently in the mould of primeval earth. But both the diabolic love and the unearthly hate of the mysteries it had penetrated fought for the possession of that soul satiated with primitive emotions, avid of lying fame, of sham distinction, of all the appearances of success and power.

"Sometimes he was contemptibly childish. He desired to have kings meet him   150 at railway-stations on his return from some ghastly Nowhere, where he intended to accomplish great things. 'You show them you have in you something that is really profitable, and then there will be no limits to the recognition of your ability,' he would say. 'Of course you must take care of the motives—right motives—always.' The long reaches that were like one and the same reach, monotonous bends that were exactly alike, slipped past the steamer with their multitude of secular trees looking patiently after this grimy fragment of another world, the forerunner of change, of conquest, of trade, of massacres, of blessings. I looked ahead—piloting. 'Close the shutter,' said Kurtz suddenly one day; 'I can't bear to look at this.' I did so. There was a silence. 'Oh, but I will wring your heart yet!' he cried at the invisible wilderness.

"We broke down—as I had expected—and had to lie up for repairs at the head of an island. This delay was the first thing that shook Kurtz's confidence. One morning he gave me a packet of papers and a photograph—the lot tied together with a shoe-string. 'Keep this for me,' he said. 'This noxious fool' (meaning the manager) 'is capable of prying into my boxes when I am not looking.' In the afternoon I saw him. He was lying on his back with closed eyes, and I withdrew quietly, but I heard him mutter, 'Live rightly, die, die . . .' I listened. There was nothing more. Was he rehearsing some speech in his sleep, or was it a fragment of a phrase from some newspaper article? He had been writing for the papers and meant to do so again, 'for the furthering of my ideas. It's a duty.'

"His was an impenetrable darkness. I looked at him as you peer down at a man who is lying at the bottom of a precipice where the sun never shines. But I had not much time to give him, because I was helping the engine-driver to take to pieces the leaky cylinders, to straighten a bent connecting-rod, and in other such matters. I lived in an infernal mess of rust, filings, nuts, bolts, spanners, hammers, ratchet-drills—things I abominate, because I don't get on with them. I tended the little forge we fortunately had aboard; I toiled wearily in a wretched scrap-heap—unless I had the shakes too bad to stand.

"One evening coming in with a candle I was startled to hear him say a little tremulously, 'I am lying here in the dark waiting for death.' The light was within a foot of his eyes. I forced myself to murmur, 'Oh, nonsense!' and stood over him as if transfixed.

"Anything approaching the change that came over his features I have never seen before, and hope never to see again. Oh, I wasn't touched. I was fascinated. It was as though a veil had been rent. I saw on that ivory face the expression of sombre pride, of ruthless power, of craven terror—of an intense and hopeless despair. Did he live his life again in every detail of desire, temptation, and surrender during that supreme moment of complete knowledge? He cried in a whisper at some image, at some vision—he cried out twice, a cry that was no more than a breath—

"'The horror! The horror!' 155

"I blew the candle out and left the cabin. The pilgrims were dining in the mess-room, and I took my place opposite the manager, who lifted his eyes to give me a questioning glance, which I successfully ignored. He leaned back, serene, with that peculiar smile of his sealing the unexpressed depths of his meanness. A continuous shower of small flies streamed upon the lamp, upon the cloth, upon our hands and faces. Suddenly the manager's boy put his insolent black head in the doorway, and said in a tone of scathing contempt—

" 'Mistah Kurtz—he dead.'

"All the pilgrims rushed out to see. I remained, and went on with my dinner. I believe I was considered brutally callous. However, I did not eat much. There was a lamp in there—light, don't you know—and outside it was so beastly, beastly dark. I went no more near the remarkable man who had pronounced a judgment upon the adventures of his soul on this earth. The voice was gone. What else had been there? But I am of course aware that next day the pilgrims buried something in a muddy hole.

"And then they very nearly buried me.

"However, as you see, I did not go to join Kurtz there and then. I did not. I 160 remained to dream the nightmare out to the end, and to show my loyalty to Kurtz once more. Destiny. My destiny! Droll thing life is—that mysterious arrangement of merciless logic for a futile purpose. The most you can hope from it is some knowledge of yourself—that comes too late—a crop of unextinguishable regrets. I have wrestled with death. It is the most unexciting contest you can imagine. It takes place in an impal-pable grayness, with nothing underfoot, with nothing around, without spectators, without clamour, without glory, without the great desire of victory, without the great fear of defeat, in a sickly atmosphere of tepid scepticism, without much belief in your own right, and still less in that of your adversary. If such is the form of ultimate wisdom, then life is a greater riddle than some of us think it to be. I was within a hair's breadth of the last opportunity for pronouncement, and I found with humiliation that probably I would have nothing to say. This is the reason why I affirm that Kurtz was a remarkable man. He had something to say. He said it. Since I had peeped over the edge myself, I understand better the meaning of his stare, that could not see the flame of the candle, but was wide enough to embrace the whole universe, piercing enough to penetrate all the hearts that beat in the darkness. He had summed up—he had judged. 'The hor-ror!' He was a remarkable man. After all, this was the expression of some sort of belief; it had candour, it had conviction, it had a vibrating note of revolt in its whisper, it had the appalling face of a glimpsed truth—the strange commingling of desire and hate. And it is not my own extremity I remember best—a vision of grayness without form filled with physical pain, and a careless contempt for the evanescence of all things—even of this pain itself. No! It is his extremity that I seem to have lived through. True, he had made that last stride, he had stepped over the edge, while I had been permitted to draw back my hesitating foot. And perhaps in this is the whole difference; perhaps all the wisdom, and all truth, and all sincerity, are just compressed into that inappreciable moment of time in which we step over the threshold of the invisible. Perhaps! I like to think my summing-up would not have been a word of careless contempt. Better his cry—much better. It was an affirmation, a moral victory paid for by innumerable defeats, by abominable terrors, by abominable satisfactions. But it was a victory! That is why I have remained loyal to Kurtz to the last, and even beyond, when a long time after I heard once more, not his own voice, but the echo of his magnificent eloquence thrown to me from a soul as translucently pure as a cliff of crystal.

"No, they did not bury me, though there is a period of time which I remember mistily, with a shuddering wonder, like a passage through some inconceivable world that had no hope in it and no desire. I found myself back in the sepulchral city resenting the sight of people hurrying through the streets to filch a little money from each other, to devour their infamous cookery, to gulp their unwholesome beer, to dream their insignificant and silly dreams. They trespassed upon my thoughts. They were intruders whose knowledge of life was to me an irritating pretence, because I felt so sure they could not possibly know the things I knew. Their bearing, which was simply the bearing of commonplace individuals going about their business in the assurance of perfect safety, was offensive to me like the outrageous flauntings of folly in the face of a danger it is unable to comprehend. I had no particular desire to enlighten them, but I had some difficulty in restraining myself from laughing in their faces, so full of stupid importance. I daresay I was not very well at that time. I tottered about the streets—there were various affairs to settle—grinning bitterly at perfectly respectable persons. I admit my behaviour was inexcusable, but then my temperature was seldom normal in these days. My dear aunt's endeavours to 'nurse up my strength' seemed altogether beside the mark. It was not my strength that wanted nursing, it was my imagination that wanted soothing. I kept the bundle of papers given me by Kurtz, not knowing exactly what to do with it. His mother had died lately, watched over, as I was told, by his Intended. A clean-shaved man, with an official manner and wearing gold-rimmed spectacles, called on me one day and made inquiries, at first circuitous, afterwards suavely pressing, about what he was pleased to denominate certain 'documents.' I was not surprised, because I had had two rows with the manager on the subject out there. I had refused to give up the smallest scrap out of that package, and I took the same attitude with the spectacled man. He became darkly menacing at last, and with much heat argued that the Company had the right to every bit of information about its 'territories.' And said he, 'Mr. Kurtz's knowledge of unexplored regions must have been necessarily extensive and peculiar—owing to his great abilities and to the deplorable circumstances in which he had been placed: therefore ——' I assured him Mr. Kurtz's knowledge, however extensive, did not bear upon the problems of commerce or administration. He invoked then the name of science. 'It would be an incalculable loss if,' etc., etc. I offered him the report on the 'Suppression of Savage Customs,' with the postscriptum torn off. He took it up eagerly, but ended by sniffing at it with an air of contempt. 'This is not what we had a right to expect,' he remarked. 'Expect nothing else,' I said. 'There are only private letters.' He withdrew upon some threat of legal proceedings, and I saw him no more; but another fellow, calling himself Kurtz's cousin, appeared two days later, and was anxious to hear all the details about his dear relative's last moments. Incidentally he gave me to understand that Kurtz had been essentially a great musician. 'There was the making of an immense success,' said the man, who was an organist, I believe, with lank gray hair flowing over a greasy coat-collar. I had no reason to doubt his statement; and to this day I am unable to say what was Kurtz's profession, whether he ever had any—which was the greatest of his talents. I had taken him for a painter who wrote for the papers, or else for a journalist who could paint—but even the cousin (who took snuff during the interview) could not tell me what he had been—exactly. He was a universal genius—on that point I agreed with the old chap, who thereupon blew his nose noisily into a large cotton handkerchief and withdrew in senile agitation, bearing off some family letters and memoranda without importance. Ultimately a journalist anxious to know something of the fate of his 'dear colleague' turned up. This visitor informed me Kurtz's proper sphere ought to have been politics 'on the popular side.' He had furry straight eyebrows, bristly hair cropped short, an eye-glass on a broad ribbon, and, becoming expansive, confessed his opinion that Kurtz really couldn't write a bit—'but heavens! how that man could talk. He electrified large meetings. He had faith—don't you see?—he had the faith. He could get himself to believe anything—anything. He would have been a splendid leader of an extreme party.' 'What party?' I asked. 'Any party,' answered the other. 'He was an—an—extremist.' Did I not think so? I assented. Did I know, he asked, with a sudden flash of curiosity, 'what it was that had induced him to go out there?' 'Yes,' said I, and forthwith handed him the famous Report for publication, if he thought fit. He glanced through it hurriedly, mumbling all the time, judged 'it would do,' and took himself off with this plunder.

"Thus I was left at last with a slim packet of letters and the girl's portrait. She struck me as beautiful—I mean she had a beautiful expression. I know that the sunlight can be made to lie, too, yet one felt that no manipulation of light and pose could have conveyed the delicate shade of truthfulness upon those features. She seemed ready to listen without mental reservation, without suspicion, without a thought for herself. I concluded I would go and give her back her portrait and those letters myself. Curiosity? Yes; and also some other feeling perhaps. All that had been Kurtz's had passed out of my hands: his soul, his body, his station, his plans, his ivory, his career. There remained only his memory and his Intended—and I wanted to give that up, too, to the past, in a way—to surrender personally all that remained of him with me to that oblivion which is the last word of our common fate. I don't defend myself. I had no clear perception of what it was I really wanted. Perhaps it was an impulse of unconscious loyalty, or the fulfilment of one of those ironic necessities that lurk in the facts of human existence. I don't know. I can't tell. But I went.

"I thought his memory was like the other memories of the dead that accumulate in every man's life—a vague impress on the brain of shadows that had fallen on it in their swift and final passage; but before the high and ponderous door, between the tall houses of a street as still and decorous as a well-kept alley in a cemetery, I had a vision of him on the stretcher, opening his mouth voraciously, as if to devour all the earth with all its mankind. He lived then before me; he lived as much as he had ever lived—a shadow insatiable of splendid appearances, of frightful realities; a shadow darker than the shadow of the night, and draped nobly in the folds of a gorgeous eloquence. The vision seemed to enter the house with me—the stretcher, the phantom-bearers, the wild crowd of obedient worshippers, the gloom of the forests, the glitter of the reach between the murky bends, the beat of the drum, regular and muffled like the beating of a heart—the heart of a conquering darkness. It was a moment of triumph for the wilderness, an invading and vengeful rush which, it seemed to me, I would have to keep back alone for the salvation of another soul. And the memory of what I had heard him say afar there, with the horned shapes stirring at my back, in the glow of fires, within the patient woods, those broken phrases came back to me, were heard again in their ominous and terrifying simplicity. I remembered his abject pleading, his abject threats, the colossal scale of his vile desires, the meanness, the torment, the tempestuous anguish of his soul. And later on I seemed to see his collected languid manner, when he said one day, 'This lot of ivory now is really mine. The Company did not pay for it. I collected it myself at a very great personal risk. I am afraid they will try to claim it as theirs though. H'm. It is a difficult case. What do you think I ought to do—resist? Eh? I want no more than justice.' . . . He wanted no more than justice—no more than justice. I rang the bell before a mahogany door on the first floor, and while I waited he seemed to stare at me out of the glassy panel—stare with that wide and immense stare embracing, condemning, loathing all the universe. I seemed to hear the whispered cry, 'The horror! The horror!'

"The dusk was falling. I had to wait in a lofty drawing-room with three long windows from floor to ceiling that were like three luminous and bedraped columns. The bent gilt legs and backs of the furniture shone in indistinct curves. The tall marble fireplace had a cold and monumental whiteness. A grand piano stood massively in a corner; with dark gleams on the flat surfaces like a sombre and polished sarcophagus. A high door opened—closed. I rose.

"She came forward, all in black, with a pale head, floating towards me in the dusk. 165 She was in mourning. It was more than a year since his death, more than a year since the news came; she seemed as though she would remember and mourn for ever. She took both my hands in hers and murmured, 'I had heard you were coming.' I noticed she was not very young—I mean not girlish. She had a mature capacity for fidelity, for belief, for suffering. The room seemed to have grown darker, as if all the sad light of the cloudy evening had taken refuge on her forehead. This fair hair, this pale visage, this pure brow, seemed surrounded by an ashy halo from which the dark eyes looked out at me. Their glance was guileless, profound, confident, and trustful. She carried her sorrowful head as though she were proud of that sorrow, as though she would say, I—I alone know how to mourn for him as he deserves. But while we were still shaking hands, such a look of awful desolation came upon her face that I perceived she was one of those creatures that are not the playthings of Time. For her he had died only yesterday. And, by Jove! the impression was so powerful that for me, too, he seemed to have died only yesterday—nay, this very minute. I saw her and him in the same instant of time—his death and her sorrow—I saw her sorrow in the very moment of his death. Do you understand? I saw them together—I heard them together. She had said, with a deep catch of the breath, 'I have survived' while my strained ears seemed to hear distinctly, mingled with her tone of despairing regret, the summing up whisper of his eternal condemnation. I asked myself what I was doing there, with a sensation of panic in my heart as though I had blundered into a place of cruel and absurd mysteries not fit for a human being to behold. She motioned me to a chair. We sat down. I laid the packet gently on the little table, and she put her hand over it. . . . 'You knew him well,' she murmured, after a moment of mourning silence.

"'Intimacy grows quickly out there,' I said. 'I knew him as well as it is possible for one man to know another.'

"'And you admired him,' she said. 'It was impossible to know him and not to admire him. Was it?'

"'He was a remarkable man,' I said, unsteadily. Then before the appealing fixity of her gaze, that seemed to watch for more words on my lips, I went on, 'It was impossible not to ——'

"'Love him,' she finished eagerly, silencing me into an appalled dumbness. 'How true! how true! But when you think that no one knew him so well as I! I had all his noble confidence. I knew him best.'

"'You knew him best,' I repeated. And perhaps she did. But with every word 170 spoken the room was growing darker, and only her forehead, smooth and white, remained illumined by the unextinguishable light of belief and love.

"'You were his friend,' she went on. 'His friend,' she repeated, a little louder. 'You must have been, if he had given you this, and sent you to me. I feel I can speak to you—and oh! I must speak. I want you—you who have heard his last words—to know I have been worthy of him. . . . It is not pride. . . . Yes! I am proud to know I understood him better than any one on earth—he told me so himself. And since his mother died I have had no one—no one—to—to ——'

"I listened. The darkness deepened. I was not even sure whether he had given me the right bundle. I rather suspect he wanted me to take care of another batch of his papers which, after his death, I saw the manager examining under the lamp. And the girl talked, easing her pain in the certitude of my sympathy; she talked as thirsty men drink. I had heard that her engagement with Kurtz had been disapproved by her people. He wasn't rich enough or something. And indeed I don't know whether he had not been a pauper all his life. He had given me some reason to infer that it was his impatience of comparative poverty that drove him out there.

"'. . . Who was not his friend who had heard him speak once?' she was saying. 'He drew men towards him by what was best in them.' She looked at me with intensity. 'It is the gift of the great,' she went on, and the sound of her low voice seemed to have the accompaniment of all the other sounds, full of mystery, desolation, and sorrow, I had ever heard—the ripple of the river, the soughing of the trees swayed by the wind, the murmurs of the crowds, the faint ring of incomprehensible words cried from afar, the whisper of a voice speaking from beyond the threshold of an eternal darkness. 'But you have heard him! You know!' she cried.

"'Yes, I know,' I said with something like despair in my heart, but bowing my head before the faith that was in her, before that great and saving illusion that shone with an unearthly glow in the darkness, in the triumphant darkness from which I could not have defended her — from which I could not even defend myself.

"'What a loss to me — to us!' — she corrected herself with beautiful generosity; 175 then added in a murmur, 'To the world.' By the last gleams of twilight I could see the glitter of her eyes, full of tears — of tears that would not fall.

"'I have been very happy — very fortunate — very proud,' she went on. 'Too fortunate. Too happy for a little while. And now I am unhappy for — for life.'

"She stood up; her fair hair seemed to catch all the remaining light in a glimmer of gold. I rose, too.

"'And of all this,' she went on, mournfully, 'of all his promise, and of all his greatness, of his generous mind, of his noble heart, nothing remains — nothing but a memory. You and I ——'

"'We shall always remember him,' I said, hastily.

"'No!' she cried. 'It is impossible that all this should be lost — that such a life 180 should be sacrificed to leave nothing — but sorrow. You know what vast plans he had. I knew of them, too — I could not perhaps understand — but others knew of them. Something must remain. His words, at least, have not died.'

"'His words will remain,' I said.

"'And his example,' she whispered to herself. 'Men looked up to him — his goodness shone in every act. His example ——'

"'True,' I said; 'his example, too. Yes, his example. I forgot that.'

"'But I do not. I cannot — I cannot believe — not yet. I cannot believe that I shall never see him again, that nobody will see him again, never, never, never.'

"She put out her arms as if after a retreating figure, stretching them back and 185 with clasped pale hands across the fading and narrow sheen of the window. Never see him! I saw him clearly enough then. I shall see this eloquent phantom as long as I live, and I shall see her, too, a tragic and familiar Shade, resembling in this gesture another one, tragic also, and bedecked with powerless charms, stretching bare brown arms over the glitter of the infernal stream, the stream of darkness. She said suddenly very low, 'He died as he lived.'

"'His end,' said I, with dull anger stirring in me, 'was in every way worthy of his life.'

"'And I was not with him,' she murmured. My anger subsided before a feeling of infinite pity.

"'Everything that could be done ——' I mumbled.

"'Ah, but I believed in him more than any one on earth — more than his own mother, more than — himself. He needed me! Me! I would have treasured every sigh, every word, every sign, every glance.'

"I felt like a chill grip on my chest. 'Don't,' I said, in a muffled voice. 190

"'Forgive me. I — I — have mourned so long in silence — in silence.... You were with him — to the last? I think of his loneliness. Nobody near to understand him as I would have understood. Perhaps no one to hear....'

"'To the very end,' I said, shakily. 'I heard his very last words....' I stopped in a fright.

"'Repeat them,' she murmured in a heart-broken tone. 'I want—I want—something—something—to—to live with.'

"I was on the point of crying at her, 'Don't you hear them?' The dusk was repeating them in a persistent whisper all around us, in a whisper that seemed to swell menacingly like the first whisper of a rising wind. 'The horror! the horror!'

"'His last word—to live with,' she insisted. 'Don't you understand I loved him— I loved him—I loved him!'   195

"I pulled myself together and spoke slowly.

"'The last word he pronounced was—your name.' *— the lie from p. 406*

"I heard a light sigh and then my heart stood still, stopped dead short by an exulting and terrible cry, by the cry of inconceivable triumph and of unspeakable pain. 'I knew it—I was sure!' . . . She knew. She was sure. I heard her weeping; she had hidden her face in her hands. It seemed to me that the house would collapse before I could escape, that the heavens would fall upon my head. But nothing happened. The heavens do not fall for such a trifle. Would they have fallen, I wonder, if I had rendered Kurtz that justice which was his due? Hadn't he said he wanted only justice? But I couldn't. I could not tell her. It would have been too dark—too dark altogether. . . .'"

Marlow ceased, and sat apart, indistinct and silent, in the pose of a meditating Buddha. Nobody moved for a time. "We have lost the first of the ebb," said the Director, suddenly. I raised my head. The offing was barred by a black bank of clouds, and the tranquil waterway leading to the uttermost ends of the earth flowed sombre under an overcast sky—seemed to lead into the heart of an immense darkness.

[1902]

Questions for Discussion

1. Apart from Marlow, Kurtz, and Fresleven the Dane, all of the characters in *Heart of Darkness* are nameless, and most are referred to by their occupations: *Accountant, Lawyer, Brickmaker, Manager, Fireman*, even the *Intended*. Why might Conrad have done this? What might this choice suggest about Conrad's attitude toward work and identity? What do the named characters have in common? What was Conrad's purpose in naming them?

2. Why do you think Marlow begins his tale of a journey to the heart of darkness with an account of London in "very old times, when the Romans first came here" (para. 11)? What is the connection between London in Roman times and the English colonization of Africa?

3. Why do the two women who guard the doors of the Company's office (para. 25) remind Marlow of the greeting gladiators offered to the Roman emperor, *"Ave! Morituri te salutant"* (Hail! We who are about to die salute you)? What does the recollection suggest about Marlow's attitude toward his new job and his life in general?

4. Marlow's aunt believes he is going to Africa as "an emissary of light" (para. 28). Does Marlow agree with her description? Does he change his attitude? Where is the irony in his aunt's comment?

5. When Marlow arrives at Central Station after a two-hundred-mile trek, he meets the manager and finds that the man "inspired uneasiness" (para. 53). Why does Marlow respond this way? What does Marlow make of the fact that the manager was "never ill"? What do you think Conrad is saying about the manager by making him resistant to tropical disease?

6. In paragraph 58, Marlow describes a painting Kurtz made of "a woman, draped and blindfolded, carrying a lighted torch." What message was Kurtz sending with this painting? At this point in the story, do you think Marlow would agree or disagree with this message? Why?

7. What does the Eldorado Exploring Expedition (paras. 72–73) represent to Marlow?

8. In paragraph 80, Marlow begins his journey on the steamboat to Kurtz. Why does he find the practical work of navigation steadying? Why does he remember so many concrete details of this work?

9. How does Marlow respond to the cannibals under his control (paras. 82–83)? Consider also the cannibals' resistance to hunger, as Marlow describes it in paragraph 89. What does he mean by the "remote kinship" he feels? How is Marlow's response both typical and atypical of other Europeans in the story?

10. What is the significance of Marlow's comparison of Kurtz to "an enchanted princess sleeping in a fabulous castle" (para. 90)?

11. Discuss the ways in which Marlow is both attracted to and repulsed by the idea of Kurtz.

12. What is the significance of Marlow's leaving his steamboat to follow Kurtz to the bonfire in the forest?

13. How have Kurtz's methods become "unsound" (para. 131)? What evidence do you find to support the manager's assessment?

14. What significance do you attach to the illness that overtakes Marlow following Kurtz's death? Remember that the manager was able to survive in Africa without succumbing to illness. What does this contrast suggest about the metaphorical role that illness plays in the story? What does this contrast say about the characters of these two men?

15. How do you interpret Kurtz's dying words, "The horror! The horror!" (para. 155)? How do you think Marlow interprets them?

16. How does Marlow's visit with Kurtz's Intended complete his journey?

17. What qualities does Marlow possess that allow him to go to the heart of darkness and return, whereas Kurtz could neither survive nor return?

18. Marlow insists in paragraph 62 that he hates lies, yet at the end of his tale he lies to Kurtz's Intended, telling her that the last words on Kurtz's lips were not "The horror!" but her name. Why? How does Marlow justify this lie to himself?

Questions on Style and Structure

1. Marlow's tale of his journey into the heart of darkness is set within the "frame" of four travelers on the *Nellie* waiting for the tide to turn so they can head out to sea. How does this narrative frame affect your interpretation of Marlow's storytelling?

2. Conrad introduces the reader to Marlow with a short description in paragraph 4: "Marlow sat cross-legged right aft, leaning against the mizzen-mast. He had sunken cheeks, a yellow complexion, a straight back, an ascetic aspect, and, with his arms dropped, the palms of hands outwards, resembled an idol." What does this description suggest to you about Marlow's character?

3. Marlow's fascination with Africa began with a white patch on maps he pored over as a boy (para. 18). In this description, he uses several figures of speech: "It had ceased to be a blank space of delightful mystery"; "a mighty big river, that you could see on the map, resembling an immense snake"; "it fascinated me as a snake would a bird." What does Marlow's language suggest about how he sees the African continent—particularly the river and the role it would play in his life?

4. In paragraph 21, Marlow recalls Fresleven, the steamboat captain whose place Marlow has taken, and describes the events surrounding the man's death as a "glorious affair." How do the details in Marlow's account suggest the opposite— that what occurred was anything but glorious?

5. Marlow calls the offices of his employer a "whited sepulchre" (para. 22). What do you infer from this image? What might it symbolize? How does the description of the street leading to the offices and the offices themselves develop or dispute this metaphor?

6. Why do you think Conrad juxtaposes a description of dying natives (paras. 40–42) with a description of the meticulously attired chief accountant (para. 43)? How does the proximity of these two descriptions help you visualize the Company's station?

7. What does the double negative in the sentence "It was unearthly, and the men were —— No, they were not inhuman" (para. 83) suggest about Marlow's response to the Africans he encounters? What does it suggest about Marlow's state of mind at this point in his journey?

8. As the steamboat approaches Inner Station (para. 88), a white fog surrounds Marlow's company, "very warm and clammy, and more blinding than the night. . . . The rest of the world was nowhere, as far as our eyes and ears were concerned. Just nowhere. Gone, disappeared; swept off without leaving a whisper or a shadow behind." What might this white fog symbolize?

9. What does Kurtz's repetition of "my" in "My Intended, my ivory, my station, my river" (para. 104) and "My Intended, my station, my career, my ideas" (para. 149) reveal about him? What do you think Conrad is suggesting about men like Kurtz?

10. Marlow says of the harlequin-like character who greets him at Inner Station, "His face was like the autumn sky, overcast one moment and bright the next" (para. 109). What does the simile help you understand about the young man's character?

11. Explain what Marlow means when he says, "Kurtz discoursed. A voice! a voice! It rang deep to the very last. It survived his strength to hide in the magnificent folds of eloquence the barren darkness of his heart" (para. 149).

12. In paragraphs 100–103, Conrad returns readers to the deck of the *Nellie*, reminding them of the frame for Marlow's story. Why do you think the author chose to do so at this point in the tale?

13. In paragraph 108, Marlow at first mistakes shrunken human heads for ivory ornaments. What is the significance of the heads themselves as well as Marlow's misper-
ception? Is the description of the heads (para. 116) poetic? grisly? Refer to specific
choices in diction and syntax that support your interpretation.

14. Why does Conrad set the face-to-face encounter between Kurtz and Marlow in
a forest with the two of them alone? Marlow says, "the foundations of our intimacy were being laid—to endure—to endure—even to the end—even beyond"
(para. 140). How does Conrad's use of repetition and dashes contribute to your
understanding of Marlow's comment?

15. In paragraphs 140–141, Marlow describes his initial interaction with Kurtz. The
description is filled with contrasts in Marlow's responses to and impressions of
Kurtz, such as his "exalted and incredible degradation." Identify other oxymorons,
and discuss whether you interpret the oxymorons as true conflicts or paradoxes—
that is, only seemingly contradictory.

16. Marlow asserts that Kurtz "is a remarkable man" (para. 131). He calls Kurtz's dying
words "an affirmation, a moral victory paid for by innumerable defeats, by abominable terrors, by abominable satisfactions. But it was a victory! That is why I have
remained loyal to Kurtz" (para. 160). How do you interpret Marlow's use of the
word "victory" in this passage? What does he mean by "loyalty" specifically in this
passage but also elsewhere in the text?

17. Compare the descriptions of the two women in Kurtz's life—the one in Africa and
his Intended in England. Pay special attention to how the women respond to Kurtz's
departure and their expressions of grief. Do you find either of these descriptions to
be stereotypes of women? Cite specific passages to support your response.

18. How do you interpret the final paragraph of the novel? Why does Conrad give the
last spoken word to the Director?

19. In paragraphs 11–13, Conrad foreshadows what Marlow experiences on his own
journey into the heart of darkness. What did you make of this passage when you first
read it? How do you interpret it now upon rereading and in light of the whole tale?

20. Marlow first refers to Kurtz as "the poor chap" (para. 15). In retrospect, do you
think this is an accurate description, an understatement, an ironic comment, or a
combination of all three?

Suggestions for Writing

1. Choose one of the following tensions in *Heart of Darkness* and write an essay that
traces its evolution throughout the novel: appearance vs. reality, primitivism vs.
civilization, light vs. dark, or innocence vs. experience.

2. This novella is both an actual journey and a psychological one. Write an essay
discussing Marlow's psychological journey. What changes does he experience? Pay
particular attention to the values he claims to have yet violates or abandons. In
what ways does he learn to accept ambiguities?

3. Marlow's initial encounter with Africans occurs as he travels along the coast of
the continent. Write an essay explaining how the language Conrad employs to

describe the natives and the colonials conveys Marlow's emerging attitudes toward these two groups. For example, what is the significance of using the word "Pop" to describe the sound of six-inch guns firing into the continent (para. 31)? How is this first encounter with Africans reflective of what can occur when cultures collide?

4. Analyze Marlow's obsession with Kurtz. Why does he pursue Kurtz? Why does he defend and attempt to save him? Why does he choose Kurtz over the other colonials? What do Kurtz and Marlow have in common?

5. In paragraph 104, we hear Marlow's analysis of Kurtz. Write an essay analyzing the literary devices Conrad uses to achieve his purpose in this passage.

6. Many nineteenth- and twentieth-century writers (e.g., Friedrich Nietzsche, Mark Twain, Honoré de Balzac, Henrik Ibsen, Thomas Hardy, and Stephen Crane) express a tragic conception of human life—that its purpose is impenetrable, its joys and sorrows meaningless. Write an essay exploring your interpretation of Conrad's conception of human life.

7. Conrad has been taken to task by some feminist readers and critics who claim that the few women he does depict are passive and stereotyped. Write a dramatic monologue in the voice of Marlow's aunt, Kurtz's mistress in Africa, or his Intended to explain what Conrad left out—or failed to understand—about that character.

8. Imagine that Marlow kept a blog as he made his journey up the river to Kurtz. Write five to eight posts in the voice of Marlow, or create a real blog with Marlow as its author.

9. The complex narration is a distinctive quality of *Heart of Darkness*. Write an essay explaining how this narrative strategy reflects the theme(s) in the novel.

Interpreter of Maladies

JHUMPA LAHIRI

 Born in London in 1967, Jhumpa Lahiri immigrated with her Bengali parents to Boston and then Kingston, Rhode Island. She received a BA in English literature from Barnard College and graduated from Boston University with three master's degrees (English, creative writing, and comparative literature) and a PhD in Renaissance studies. Lahiri has enjoyed both critical acclaim and commercial success with her short-story collection *Interpreter of Maladies* (1999) and her novel *The Namesake* (2003), which was released as a film directed by Mira Nair in 2007. Her latest collection of stories is *Unaccustomed Earth* (2008). *Interpreter of Maladies* won the PEN/Hemingway Award and the 2000 Pulitzer Prize for Fiction, making Lahiri the youngest person ever to win that prestigious award. *New York Times* critic Michiko Kakutani called Lahiri "a writer of uncommon elegance and poise," who made "a precocious debut" with this short-story collection. Lahiri feels strong ties to England, India, and the United States, yet she says, "No country is my motherland. I always find myself in exile in whichever country I travel to...." She explores this theme in much of her fiction, including the title story from her collection *Interpreter of Maladies*.

At the tea stall Mr. and Mrs. Das bickered about who should take Tina to the toilet. Eventually Mrs. Das relented when Mr. Das pointed out that he had given the girl her bath the night before. In the rearview mirror Mr. Kapasi watched as Mrs. Das emerged slowly from his bulky white Ambassador, dragging her shaved, largely bare legs across the back seat. She did not hold the little girl's hand as they walked to the rest room.

They were on their way to see the Sun Temple at Konarak. It was a dry, bright Saturday, the mid-July heat tempered by a steady ocean breeze, ideal weather for sightseeing. Ordinarily Mr. Kapasi would not have stopped so soon along the way, but less than five minutes after he'd picked up the family that morning in front of Hotel Sandy Villa, the little girl had complained. The first thing Mr. Kapasi had noticed when he saw Mr. and Mrs. Das, standing with their children under the portico of the hotel, was that they were very young, perhaps not even thirty. In addition to Tina they had two boys, Ronny and Bobby, who appeared very close in age and had teeth covered in a network of flashing silver wires. The family looked Indian but dressed as foreigners did, the children in stiff, brightly colored clothing and caps with translucent visors. Mr. Kapasi was accustomed to foreign tourists; he was assigned to them regularly because he could speak English. Yesterday he had driven an elderly couple from Scotland, both with spotted faces and fluffy white hair so thin it exposed their sunburnt scalps. In comparison, the tanned, youthful faces of Mr. and Mrs. Das were all the more striking. When he'd introduced himself, Mr. Kapasi had pressed his

434

palms together in greeting, but Mr. Das squeezed hands like an American so that Mr. Kapasi felt it in his elbow. Mrs. Das, for her part, had flexed one side of her mouth, smiling dutifully at Mr. Kapasi, without displaying any interest in him.

As they waited at the tea stall, Ronny, who looked like the older of the two boys, clambered suddenly out of the back seat, intrigued by a goat tied to a stake in the ground.

"Don't touch it," Mr. Das said. He glanced up from his paperback tour book, which said "INDIA" in yellow letters and looked as if it had been published abroad. His voice, somehow tentative and a little shrill, sounded as though it had not yet settled into maturity.

"I want to give it a piece of gum," the boy called back as he trotted ahead.   5

Mr. Das stepped out of the car and stretched his legs by squatting briefly to the ground. A clean-shaven man, he looked exactly like a magnified version of Ronny. He had a sapphire blue visor, and was dressed in shorts, sneakers, and a T-shirt. The camera slung around his neck, with an impressive telephoto lens and numerous buttons and markings, was the only complicated thing he wore. He frowned, watching as Ronny rushed toward the goat, but appeared to have no intention of intervening. "Bobby, make sure that your brother doesn't do anything stupid."

"I don't feel like it," Bobby said, not moving. He was sitting in the front seat beside Mr. Kapasi, studying a picture of the elephant god taped to the glove compartment.

"No need to worry," Mr. Kapasi said. "They are quite tame." Mr. Kapasi was forty-six years old, with receding hair that had gone completely silver, but his butterscotch complexion and his unlined brow, which he treated in spare moments to dabs of lotus-oil balm, made it easy to imagine what he must have looked like at an earlier age. He wore gray trousers and a matching jacket-style shirt, tapered at the waist, with short sleeves and a large pointed collar, made of a thin but durable synthetic material. He had specified both the cut and the fabric to his tailor—it was his preferred uniform for giving tours because it did not get crushed during his long hours behind the wheel. Through the windshield he watched as Ronny circled around the goat, touched it quickly on its side, then trotted back to the car.

"You left India as a child?" Mr. Kapasi asked when Mr. Das had settled once again into the passenger seat.

"Oh, Mina and I were both born in America," Mr. Das announced with an air of   10
sudden confidence. "Born and raised. Our parents live here now, in Assansol. They retired. We visit them every couple years." He turned to watch as the little girl ran toward the car, the wide purple bows of her sundress flopping on her narrow brown shoulders. She was holding to her chest a doll with yellow hair that looked as if it had been chopped, as a punitive measure, with a pair of dull scissors. "This is Tina's first trip to India, isn't it, Tina?"

"I don't have to go to the bathroom anymore," Tina announced.

"Where's Mina?" Mr. Das asked.

Mr. Kapasi found it strange that Mr. Das should refer to his wife by her first name when speaking to the little girl. Tina pointed to where Mrs. Das was purchasing something from one of the shirtless men who worked at the tea stall. Mr. Kapasi heard one of the shirtless men sing a phrase from a popular Hindi love song as Mrs. Das walked back to the car, but she did not appear to understand the words of the song, for she did not express irritation, or embarrassment, or react in any other way to the man's declarations.

He observed her. She wore a red-and-white-checkered skirt that stopped above her knees, slip-on shoes with a square wooden heel, and a close-fitting blouse styled like a man's undershirt. The blouse was decorated at chest-level with a calico appliqué in the shape of a strawberry. She was a short woman, with small hands like paws, her frosty pink fingernails painted to match her lips, and was slightly plump in her figure. Her hair, shorn only a little longer than her husband's, was parted far to one side. She was wearing large dark brown sunglasses with a pinkish tint to them, and carried a big straw bag, almost as big as her torso, shaped like a bowl, with a water bottle poking out of it. She walked slowly, carrying some puffed rice tossed with peanuts and chili peppers in a large packet made from newspapers. Mr. Kapasi turned to Mr. Das.

"Where in America do you live?"   15

"New Brunswick, New Jersey."

"Next to New York."

"Exactly. I teach middle school there."

"What subject?"

"Science. In fact, every year I take my students on a trip to the Museum of   20
Natural History in New York City. In a way we have a lot in common, you could say, you and I. How long have you been a tour guide, Mr. Kapasi?"

"Five years."

Mrs. Das reached the car. "How long's the trip?" she asked, shutting the door.

"About two and a half hours," Mr. Kapasi replied.

At this Mrs. Das gave an impatient sigh, as if she had been traveling her whole life without pause. She fanned herself with a folded Bombay film magazine written in English.

"I thought that the Sun Temple is only eighteen miles north of Puri," Mr. Das said,   25
tapping on the tour book.

"The roads to Konarak are poor. Actually it is a distance of fifty-two miles," Mr. Kapasi explained.

Mr. Das nodded, readjusting the camera strap where it had begun to chafe the back of his neck.

Before starting the ignition, Mr. Kapasi reached back to make sure the cranklike locks on the inside of each of the back doors were secured. As soon as the car began to move the little girl began to play with the lock on her side, clicking it with some effort forward and backward, but Mrs. Das said nothing to stop her. She sat a bit slouched at one end of the back seat, not offering her puffed rice to anyone. Ronny and Tina sat on either side of her, both snapping bright green gum.

"Look," Bobby said as the car began to gather speed. He pointed with his finger to the tall trees that lined the road. "Look."

"Monkeys!" Ronny shrieked. "Wow!"   30

They were seated in groups along the branches, with shining black faces, silver bodies, horizontal eyebrows, and crested heads. Their long gray tails dangled like a series of ropes among the leaves. A few scratched themselves with black leathery hands, or swung their feet, staring as the car passed.

"We call them the hanuman," Mr. Kapasi said. "They are quite common in the area."

As soon as he spoke, one of the monkeys leaped into the middle of the road, causing Mr. Kapasi to brake suddenly. Another bounced onto the hood of the car, then sprang away. Mr. Kapasi beeped his horn. The children began to get excited, sucking in their breath and covering their faces partly with their hands. They had never seen monkeys outside of a zoo, Mr. Das explained. He asked Mr. Kapasi to stop the car so that he could take a picture.

While Mr. Das adjusted his telephoto lens, Mrs. Das reached into her straw bag and pulled out a bottle of colorless nail polish, which she proceeded to stroke on the tip of her index finger.

The little girl stuck out a hand. "Mine too. Mommy, do mine too."   35

"Leave me alone," Mrs. Das said, blowing on her nail and turning her body slightly. "You're making me mess up."

The little girl occupied herself by buttoning and unbuttoning a pinafore on the doll's plastic body.

"All set," Mr. Das said, replacing the lens cap.

The car rattled considerably as it raced along the dusty road, causing them all to pop up from their seats every now and then, but Mrs. Das continued to polish her nails. Mr. Kapasi eased up on the accelerator, hoping to produce a smoother ride. When he reached for the gearshift the boy in front accommodated him by swinging his hairless knees out of the way. Mr. Kapasi noted that this boy was slightly paler than the other children. "Daddy, why is the driver sitting on the wrong side in this car, too?" the boy asked.

"They all do that here, dummy," Ronny said.   40

"Don't call your brother a dummy," Mr. Das said. He turned to Mr. Kapasi. "In America, you know . . . it confuses them."

"Oh yes, I am well aware," Mr. Kapasi said. As delicately as he could, he shifted gears again, accelerating as they approached a hill in the road. "I see it on *Dallas*, the steering wheels are on the left-hand side."

"What's *Dallas*?" Tina asked, banging her now naked doll on the seat behind Mr. Kapasi.

"It went off the air," Mr. Das explained. "It's a television show."

They were all like siblings, Mr. Kapasi thought as they passed a row of date trees.   45
Mr. and Mrs. Das behaved like an older brother and sister, not parents. It seemed that they were in charge of the children only for the day; it was hard to believe they were regularly responsible for anything other than themselves. Mr. Das tapped on his lens cap, and his tour book, dragging his thumbnail occasionally across the pages so that they made a scraping sound. Mrs. Das continued to polish her nails. She had still not

removed her sunglasses. Every now and then Tina renewed her plea that she wanted her nails done, too, and so at one point Mrs. Das flicked a drop of polish on the little girl's finger before depositing the bottle back inside her straw bag.

"Isn't this an air-conditioned car?" she asked, still blowing on her hand. The window on Tina's side was broken and could not be rolled down.

"Quit complaining," Mr. Das said. "It isn't so hot."

"I told you to get a car with air-conditioning," Mrs. Das continued. "Why do you do this, Raj, just to save a few stupid rupees. What are you saving us, fifty cents?"

Their accents sounded just like the ones Mr. Kapasi heard on American television programs, though not like the ones on *Dallas*.

"Doesn't it get tiresome, Mr. Kapasi, showing people the same thing every day?" 50 Mr. Das asked, rolling down his own window all the way. "Hey, do you mind stopping the car. I just want to get a shot of this guy."

Mr. Kapasi pulled over to the side of the road as Mr. Das took a picture of a bare-foot man, his head wrapped in a dirty turban, seated on top of a cart of grain sacks pulled by a pair of bullocks. Both the man and the bullocks were emaciated. In the back seat Mrs. Das gazed out another window, at the sky, where nearly transparent clouds passed quickly in front of one another.

"I look forward to it, actually," Mr. Kapasi said as they continued on their way. "The Sun Temple is one of my favorite places. In that way it is a reward for me. I give tours on Fridays and Saturdays only. I have another job during the week."

"Oh? Where?" Mr. Das asked.

"I work in a doctor's office."

"You're a doctor?" 55

"I am not a doctor. I work with one. As an interpreter."

"What does a doctor need an interpreter for?"

"He has a number of Gujarati patients. My father was Gujarati, but many people do not speak Gujarati in this area, including the doctor. And so the doctor asked me to work in his office, interpreting what the patients say."

"Interesting. I've never heard of anything like that." Mr. Das said.

Mr. Kapasi shrugged. "It is a job like any other." 60

"But so romantic," Mrs. Das said dreamily, breaking her extended silence. She lifted her pinkish brown sunglasses and arranged them on top of her head like a tiara. For the first time, her eyes met Mr. Kapasi's in the rearview mirror: pale, a bit small, their gaze fixed but drowsy.

Mr. Das craned to look at her. "What's so romantic about it?"

"I don't know. Something." She shrugged, knitting her brows together for an instant. "Would you like a piece of gum, Mr. Kapasi?" she asked brightly. She reached into her straw bag and handed him a small square wrapped in green-and-white-striped paper. As soon as Mr. Kapasi put the gum in his mouth a thick sweet liquid burst onto his tongue.

"Tell us more about your job, Mr. Kapasi," Mrs. Das said.

"What would you like to know, madame?" 65

"I don't know," she shrugged, munching on some puffed rice and licking the mustard oil from the corners of her mouth. "Tell us a typical situation." She settled back in her seat, her head tilted in a patch of sun, and closed her eyes. "I want to picture what happens."

"Very well. The other day a man came in with a pain in his throat."

"Did he smoke cigarettes?"

"No. It was very curious. He complained that he felt as if there were long pieces of straw stuck in his throat. When I told the doctor he was able to prescribe the proper medication."

"That's so neat."

"Yes," Mr. Kapasi agreed after some hesitation.

70

"So these patients are totally dependent on you," Mrs. Das said. She spoke slowly, as if she were thinking aloud. "In a way, more dependent on you than the doctor."

"How do you mean? How could it be?"

"Well, for example, you could tell the doctor that the pain felt like a burning, not straw. The patient would never know what you had told the doctor, and the doctor wouldn't know that you had told the wrong thing. It's a big responsibility."

"Yes, a big responsibility you have there, Mr. Kapasi," Mr. Das agreed.

75

Mr. Kapasi had never thought of his job in such complimentary terms. To him it was a thankless occupation. He found nothing noble in interpreting people's maladies, assiduously translating the symptoms of so many swollen bones, countless cramps of bellies and bowels, spots on people's palms that changed color, shape, or size. The doctor, nearly half his age, had an affinity for bell-bottom trousers and made humorless jokes about the Congress party. Together they worked in a stale little infirmary where Mr. Kapasi's smartly tailored clothes clung to him in the heat, in spite of the blackened blades of a ceiling fan churning over their heads.

The job was a sign of his failings. In his youth he'd been a devoted scholar of foreign languages, the owner of an impressive collection of dictionaries. He had dreamed of being an interpreter for diplomats and dignitaries, resolving conflicts between people and nations, settling disputes of which he alone could understand both sides. He was a self-educated man. In a series of notebooks, in the evenings before his parents settled his marriage, he had listed the common etymologies of words, and at one point in his life he was confident that he could converse, if given the opportunity, in English, French, Russian, Portuguese, and Italian, not to mention Hindi, Bengali, Orissi, and Gujarati. Now only a handful of European phrases remained in his memory, scattered words for things like saucers and chairs. English was the only non-Indian language he spoke fluently anymore. Mr. Kapasi knew it was not a remarkable talent. Sometimes he feared that his children knew better English than he did, just from watching television. Still, it came in handy for the tours.

He had taken the job as an interpreter after his first son, at the age of seven, contracted typhoid—that was how he had first made the acquaintance of the doctor. At the time Mr. Kapasi had been teaching English in a grammar school, and he bartered his skills as an interpreter to pay the increasingly exorbitant medical bills. In the end the boy had died one evening in his mother's arms, his limbs burning with fever, but then there was the funeral to pay for, and the other children who were born soon enough, and the newer, bigger house, and the good schools and tutors, and the fine shoes and the television, and the countless other ways he tried to console his wife and to keep her from crying in her sleep, and so when the doctor offered to pay him twice as much as he earned at the grammar school, he accepted. Mr. Kapasi knew that his wife had little regard for his career as an interpreter. He knew it reminded her of the son she'd lost, and that she resented the other lives he helped, in his own small way, to save. If ever she referred to his position, she used the phrase "doctor's assistant," as if the process of interpretation were equal to taking someone's temperature, or changing a bedpan. She never asked him about the patients who came to the doctor's office, or said that his job was a big responsibility.

For this reason it flattered Mr. Kapasi that Mrs. Das was so intrigued by his job. Unlike his wife, she had reminded him of its intellectual challenges. She had also used the word "romantic." She did not behave in a romantic way toward her husband, and yet she had used the word to describe him. He wondered if Mr. and Mrs. Das were a bad match, just as he and his wife were. Perhaps they, too, had little in common apart from three children and a decade of their lives. The signs he recognized from his own marriage were there—the bickering, the indifference, the protracted silences. Her sudden interest in him, an interest she did not express in either her husband or her children, was mildly intoxicating. When Mr. Kapasi thought once again about how she had said "romantic," the feeling of intoxication grew.

He began to check his reflection in the rearview mirror as he drove, feeling   80
grateful that he had chosen the gray suit that morning and not the brown one, which tended to sag a little in the knees. From time to time he glanced through the mirror at Mrs. Das. In addition to glancing at her face he glanced at the strawberry between her breasts, and the golden brown hollow in her throat. He decided to tell Mrs. Das about another patient, and another: the young woman who had complained of a sensation of raindrops in her spine, the gentleman whose birthmark had begun to sprout hairs. Mrs. Das listened attentively, stroking her hair with a small plastic brush that resembled an oval bed of nails, asking more questions, for yet another example. The children were quiet, intent on spotting more monkeys in the trees, and Mr. Das was absorbed by his tour book, so it seemed like a private conversation between Mr. Kapasi and Mrs. Das. In this manner the next half hour passed, and when they stopped for lunch at a roadside restaurant that sold fritters and omelette sandwiches, usually something Mr. Kapasi looked forward to on his tours so that he could sit in peace and enjoy some hot tea, he was disappointed. As the Das family settled together under a magenta umbrella fringed with white and orange tassels, and placed their orders with one of the waiters who marched about in tricornered caps, Mr. Kapasi reluctantly headed toward a neighboring table.

"Mr. Kapasi, wait. There's room here," Mrs. Das called out. She gathered Tina onto her lap, insisting that he accompany them. And so, together, they had bottled mango juice and sandwiches and plates of onions and potatoes deep-fried in graham-flour batter. After finishing two omelette sandwiches Mr. Das took more pictures of the group as they ate.

"How much longer?" he asked Mr. Kapasi as he paused to load a new roll of film in the camera.

"About half an hour more."

By now the children had gotten up from the table to look at more monkeys perched in a nearby tree, so there was a considerable space between Mrs. Das and Mr. Kapasi. Mr. Das placed the camera to his face and squeezed one eye shut, his tongue exposed at one corner of his mouth. "This looks funny, Mina, you need to lean in closer to Mr. Kapasi."

She did. He could smell a scent on her skin, like a mixture of whiskey and rose-water. He worried suddenly that she could smell his perspiration, which he knew had collected beneath the synthetic material of his shirt. He polished off his mango juice in one gulp and smoothed his silver hair with his hands. A bit of the juice dripped onto his chin. He wondered if Mrs. Das had noticed.   85

She had not. "What's your address, Mr. Kapasi?" she inquired, fishing for something inside her straw bag.

"You would like my address?"

"So we can send you copies," she said. "Of the pictures." She handed him a scrap of paper which she had hastily ripped from a page of her film magazine. The blank portion was limited, for the narrow strip was crowded by lines of text and a tiny picture of a hero and heroine embracing under a eucalyptus tree.

The paper curled as Mr. Kapasi wrote his address in clear, careful letters. She would write to him, asking about his days interpreting at the doctor's office, and he would respond eloquently, choosing only the most entertaining anecdotes, ones that would make her laugh out loud as she read them in her house in New Jersey. In time she would reveal the disappointment of her marriage, and he his. In this way their friendship would grow, and flourish. He would possess a picture of the two of them, eating fried onions under a magenta umbrella, which he would keep, he decided, safely tucked between the pages of his Russian grammar. As his mind raced, Mr. Kapasi experienced a mild and pleasant shock. It was similar to a feeling he used to experience long ago when, after months of translating with the aid of a dictionary, he would finally read a passage from a French novel, or an Italian sonnet, and understand the words, one after another, unencumbered by his own efforts. In those moments Mr. Kapasi used to believe that all was right with the world, that all struggles were rewarded, that all of life's mistakes made sense in the end. The promise that he would hear from Mrs. Das now filled him with the same belief.

When he finished writing his address Mr. Kapasi handed her the paper, but as soon   90
as he did so he worried that he had either misspelled his name, or accidentally reversed the numbers of his postal code. He dreaded the possibility of a lost letter, the photograph never reaching him, hovering somewhere in Orissa, close but ultimately unattainable. He thought of asking for the slip of paper again, just to make sure he had written his address accurately, but Mrs. Das had already dropped it into the jumble of her bag.

They reached Konarak at two-thirty. The temple, made of sandstone, was a massive pyramid-like structure in the shape of a chariot. It was dedicated to the great master of life, the sun, which struck three sides of the edifice as it made its journey each day across the sky. Twenty-four giant wheels were carved on the north and south sides of the plinth. The whole thing was drawn by a team of seven horses, speeding as if through the heavens. As they approached, Mr. Kapasi explained that the temple had been built between A.D. 1243 and 1255, with the efforts of twelve hundred artisans, by the great ruler of the Ganga dynasty, King Narasimhadeva the First, to commemorate his victory against the Muslim army.

"It says the temple occupies about a hundred and seventy acres of land," Mr. Das said, reading from his book.

"It's like a desert," Ronny said, his eyes wandering across the sand that stretched on all sides beyond the temple.

"The Chandrabhaga River once flowed one mile north of here. It is dry now," Mr. Kapasi said, turning off the engine.

They got out and walked toward the temple, posing first for pictures by the pair   95
of lions that flanked the steps. Mr. Kapasi led them next to one of the wheels of the chariot, higher than any human being, nine feet in diameter.

"'The wheels are supposed to symbolize the wheel of life,'" Mr. Das read. "'They depict the cycle of creation, preservation, and achievement of realization.' Cool." He turned the page of his book. "'Each wheel is divided into eight thick and thin spokes, dividing the day into eight equal parts. The rims are carved with designs of birds and animals, whereas the medallions in the spokes are carved with women in luxurious poses, largely erotic in nature.'"

What he referred to were the countless friezes of entwined naked bodies, making love in various positions, women clinging to the necks of men, their knees wrapped eternally around their lovers' thighs. In addition to these were assorted scenes from daily life, of hunting and trading, of deer being killed with bows and arrows and marching warriors holding swords in their hands.

It was no longer possible to enter the temple, for it had filled with rubble years ago, but they admired the exterior, as did all the tourists Mr. Kapasi brought there, slowly strolling along each of its sides. Mr. Das trailed behind, taking pictures. The children ran ahead, pointing to figures of naked people, intrigued in particular by the Nagamithunas, the half-human, half-serpentine couples who were said, Mr. Kapasi told them, to live in the deepest waters of the sea. Mr. Kapasi was pleased that they liked the temple, pleased especially that it appealed to Mrs. Das. She stopped every three or four paces, staring silently at the carved lovers, and the processions of elephants, and the topless female musicians beating on two-sided drums.

Though Mr. Kapasi had been to the temple countless times, it occurred to him, as he, too, gazed at the topless women, that he had never seen his own wife fully naked. Even when they had made love she kept the panels of her blouse hooked together, the string of her petticoat knotted around her waist. He had never admired the backs of his wife's legs the way he now admired those of Mrs. Das, walking as if for his benefit alone. He had, of course, seen plenty of bare limbs before, belonging to the American and European ladies who took his tours. But Mrs. Das was different. Unlike the other women, who had an interest only in the temple, and kept their noses buried in a guidebook, or their eyes behind the lens of a camera, Mrs. Das had taken an interest in him.

Mr. Kapasi was anxious to be alone with her, to continue their private conver-   100
sation, yet he felt nervous to walk at her side. She was lost behind her sunglasses,
ignoring her husband's requests that she pose for another picture, walking past her
children as if they were strangers. Worried that he might disturb her, Mr. Kapasi
walked ahead, to admire, as he always did, the three life-sized bronze avatars of Surya,
the sun god, each emerging from its own niche on the temple facade to greet the sun
at dawn, noon, and evening. They wore elaborate headdresses, their languid, elon-
gated eyes closed, their bare chests draped with carved chains and amulets. Hibiscus
petals, offerings from previous visitors, were strewn at their gray-green feet. The last
statue, on the northern wall of the temple, was Mr. Kapasi's favorite. This Surya had
a tired expression, weary after a hard day of work, sitting astride a horse with folded
legs. Even his horse's eyes were drowsy. Around his body were smaller sculptures of
women in pairs, their hips thrust to one side.

"Who's that?" Mrs. Das asked. He was startled to see that she was standing beside him.

"He is the Astachala-Surya," Mr. Kapasi said. "The setting sun."

"So in a couple of hours the sun will set right here?" She slipped a foot out of one
of her square-heeled shoes, rubbed her toes on the back of her other leg.

"That is correct."

She raised her sunglasses for a moment, then put them back on again. "Neat."   105

Mr. Kapasi was not certain exactly what the word suggested, but he had a feeling it was a favorable response. He hoped that Mrs. Das had understood Surya's
beauty, his power. Perhaps they would discuss it further in their letters. He would
explain things to her, things about India, and she would explain things to him about
America. In its own way this correspondence would fulfill his dream, of serving as an
interpreter between nations. He looked at her straw bag, delighted that his address
lay nestled among its contents. When he pictured her so many thousands of miles
away he plummeted, so much so that he had an overwhelming urge to wrap his arms
around her, to freeze with her, even for an instant, in an embrace witnessed by his
favorite Surya. But Mrs. Das had already started walking.

"When do you return to America?" he asked, trying to sound placid.

"In ten days."

He calculated: A week to settle in, a week to develop the pictures, a few days to
compose her letter, two weeks to get to India by air. According to his schedule, allowing room for delays, he would hear from Mrs. Das in approximately six weeks' time.

The family was silent as Mr. Kapasi drove them back, a little past four-thirty, to Hotel   110
Sandy Villa. The children had bought miniature granite versions of the chariot's
wheels at a souvenir stand, and they turned them round in their hands. Mr. Das continued to read his book. Mrs. Das untangled Tina's hair with her brush and divided
it into two little ponytails.

Mr. Kapasi was beginning to dread the thought of dropping them off. He was not
prepared to begin his six-week wait to hear from Mrs. Das. As he stole glances at her in
the rearview mirror, wrapping elastic bands around Tina's hair, he wondered how he

might make the tour last a little longer. Ordinarily he sped back to Puri using a short-cut, eager to return home, scrub his feet and hands with sandalwood soap, and enjoy the evening newspaper and a cup of tea that his wife would serve him in silence. The thought of that silence, something to which he'd long been resigned, now oppressed him. It was then that he suggested visiting the hills at Udayagiri and Khandagiri, where a number of monastic dwellings were hewn out of the ground, facing one another across a defile. It was some miles away, but well worth seeing, Mr. Kapasi told them.

"Oh yeah, there's something mentioned about it in this book," Mr. Das said. "Built by a Jain king or something."

"Shall we go then?" Mr. Kapasi asked. He paused at a turn in the road. "It's to the left."

Mr. Das turned to look at Mrs. Das. Both of them shrugged.

"Left, left," the children chanted. 115

Mr. Kapasi turned the wheel, almost delirious with relief. He did not know what he would do or say to Mrs. Das once they arrived at the hills. Perhaps he would tell her what a pleasing smile she had. Perhaps he would compliment her strawberry shirt, which he found irresistibly becoming. Perhaps, when Mr. Das was busy taking a picture, he would take her hand.

He did not have to worry. When they got to the hills, divided by a steep path thick with trees, Mrs. Das refused to get out of the car. All along the path, dozens of monkeys were seated on stones, as well as on the branches of the trees. Their hind legs were stretched out in front and raised to shoulder level, their arms resting on their knees.

"My legs are tired," she said, sinking low in her seat. "I'll stay here."

"Why did you have to wear those stupid shoes?" Mr. Das said. "You won't be in the pictures."

"Pretend I'm there." 120

"But we could use one of these pictures for our Christmas card this year. We didn't get one of all five of us at the Sun Temple. Mr. Kapasi could take it."

"I'm not coming. Anyway, those monkeys give me the creeps."

"But they're harmless," Mr. Das said. He turned to Mr. Kapasi. "Aren't they?"

"They are more hungry than dangerous," Mr. Kapasi said. "Do not provoke them with food, and they will not bother you."

Mr. Das headed up the defile with the children, the boys at his side, the little girl 125 on his shoulders. Mr. Kapasi watched as they crossed paths with a Japanese man and woman, the only other tourists there, who paused for a final photograph, then stepped into a nearby car and drove away. As the car disappeared out of view some of the monkeys called out, emitting soft whooping sounds, and then walked on their flat black hands and feet up the path. At one point a group of them formed a little ring around Mr. Das and the children. Tina screamed in delight. Ronny ran in circles around his father. Bobby bent down and picked up a fat stick on the ground. When he extended it, one of the monkeys approached him and snatched it, then briefly beat the ground.

"I'll join them," Mr. Kapasi said, unlocking the door on his side. "There is much to explain about the caves."

"No. Stay a minute," Mrs. Das said. She got out of the back seat and slipped in beside Mr. Kapasi. "Raj has his dumb book anyway." Together, through the windshield,

Mrs. Das and Mr. Kapasi watched as Bobby and the monkey passed the stick back and forth between them.

"A brave little boy," Mr. Kapasi commented.

"It's not so surprising," Mrs. Das said.

"No?"   130

"He's not his."

"I beg your pardon?"

"Raj's. He's not Raj's son."

Mr. Kapasi felt a prickle on his skin. He reached into his shirt pocket for the small tin of lotus-oil balm he carried with him at all times, and applied it to three spots on his forehead. He knew that Mrs. Das was watching him, but he did not turn to face her. Instead he watched as the figures of Mr. Das and the children grew smaller, climbing up the steep path, pausing every now and then for a picture, surrounded by a growing number of monkeys.

"Are you surprised?" The way she put it made him choose his words with care.   135

"It's not the type of thing one assumes," Mr. Kapasi replied slowly. He put the tin of lotus-oil balm back in his pocket.

"No, of course not. And no one knows, of course. No one at all. I've kept it a secret for eight whole years." She looked at Mr. Kapasi, tilting her chin as if to gain a fresh perspective. "But now I've told you."

Mr. Kapasi nodded. He felt suddenly parched, and his forehead was warm and slightly numb from the balm. He considered asking Mrs. Das for a sip of water, then decided against it.

"We met when we were very young," she said. She reached into her straw bag in search of something, then pulled out a packet of puffed rice. "Want some?"

"No, thank you."   140

She put a fistful in her mouth, sank into the seat a little, and looked away from Mr. Kapasi, out the window on her side of the car. "We married when we were still in college. We were in high school when he proposed. We went to the same college, of course. Back then we couldn't stand the thought of being separated, not for a day, not for a minute. Our parents were best friends who lived in the same town. My entire life I saw him every weekend, either at our house or theirs. We were sent upstairs to play together while our parents joked about our marriage. Imagine! They never caught us at anything, though in a way I think it was all more or less a setup. The things we did those Friday and Saturday nights, while our parents sat downstairs drinking tea . . . I could tell you stories, Mr. Kapasi."

As a result of spending all her time in college with Raj, she continued, she did not make many close friends. There was no one to confide in about him at the end of a difficult day, or to share a passing thought or a worry. Her parents now lived on the other side of the world, but she had never been very close to them, anyway. After marrying so young she was overwhelmed by it all, having a child so quickly, and nursing, and warming up bottles of milk and testing their temperature against her wrist while Raj was at work, dressed in sweaters and corduroy pants, teaching his students about rocks and dinosaurs. Raj never looked cross or harried, or plump as she had become after the first baby.

Always tired, she declined invitations from her one or two college girlfriends, to have lunch or shop in Manhattan. Eventually the friends stopped calling her, so that she was left at home all day with the baby, surrounded by toys that made her trip when she walked or wince when she sat, always cross and tired. Only occasionally did they go out after Ronny was born, and even more rarely did they entertain. Raj didn't mind; he looked forward to coming home from teaching and watching television and bouncing Ronny on his knee. She had been outraged when Raj told her that a Punjabi friend, someone whom she had once met but did not remember, would be staying with them for a week for some job interviews in the New Brunswick area.

Bobby was conceived in the afternoon, on a sofa littered with rubber teething toys, after the friend learned that a London pharmaceutical company had hired him, while Ronny cried to be freed from his playpen. She made no protest when the friend touched the small of her back as she was about to make a pot of coffee, then pulled her against his crisp navy suit. He made love to her swiftly, in silence, with an expertise she had never known, without the meaningful expressions and smiles Raj always insisted on afterward. The next day Raj drove the friend to JFK. He was married now, to a Punjabi girl, and they lived in London still, and every year they exchanged Christmas cards with Raj and Mina, each couple tucking photos of their families into the envelopes. He did not know that he was Bobby's father. He never would.

"I beg your pardon, Mrs. Das, but why have you told me this information?" Mr. 145 Kapasi asked when she had finally finished speaking, and had turned to face him once again.

"For God's sake, stop calling me Mrs. Das. I'm twenty-eight. You probably have children my age."

"Not quite." It disturbed Mr. Kapasi to learn that she thought of him as a parent. The feeling he had had toward her, that had made him check his reflection in the rearview mirror as they drove, evaporated a little.

"I told you because of your talents." She put the packet of puffed rice back into her bag without folding over the top.

"I don't understand," Mr. Kapasi said.

"Don't you see? For eight years I haven't been able to express this to anybody, 150 not to friends, certainly not to Raj. He doesn't even suspect it. He thinks I'm still in love with him. Well, don't you have anything to say?"

"About what?"

"About what I've just told you. About my secret, and about how terrible it makes me feel. I feel terrible looking at my children, and at Raj, always terrible. I have terrible urges, Mr. Kapasi, to throw things away. One day I had the urge to throw everything I own out the window, the television, the children, everything. Don't you think it's unhealthy?"

He was silent.

"Mr. Kapasi, don't you have anything to say? I thought that was your job."

"My job is to give tours, Mrs. Das."   155

"Not that. Your other job. As an interpreter."

"But we do not face a language barrier. What need is there for an interpreter?"

"That's not what I mean. I would never have told you otherwise. Don't you realize what it means for me to tell you?"

"What does it mean?"

"It means that I'm tired of feeling so terrible all the time. Eight years, Mr. Kapasi, I've been in pain eight years. I was hoping you could help me feel better, say the right thing. Suggest some kind of remedy." 160

He looked at her, in her red plaid skirt and strawberry T-shirt, a woman not yet thirty, who loved neither her husband nor her children, who had already fallen out of love with life. Her confession depressed him, depressed him all the more when he thought of Mr. Das at the top of the path, Tina clinging to his shoulders, taking pictures of ancient monastic cells cut into the hills to show his students in America, unsuspecting and unaware that one of his sons was not his own. Mr. Kapasi felt insulted that Mrs. Das should ask him to interpret her common, trivial little secret. She did not resemble the patients in the doctor's office, those who came glassy-eyed and desperate, unable to sleep or breathe or urinate with ease, unable, above all, to give words to their pains. Still, Mr. Kapasi believed it was his duty to assist Mrs. Das. Perhaps he ought to tell her to confess the truth to Mr. Das. He would explain that honesty was the best policy. Honesty, surely, would help her feel better, as she'd put it. Perhaps he would offer to preside over the discussion, as a mediator. He decided to begin with the most obvious question, to get to the heart of the matter, and so he asked, "Is it really pain you feel, Mrs. Das, or is it guilt?"

She turned to him and glared, mustard oil thick on her frosty pink lips. She opened her mouth to say something, but as she glared at Mr. Kapasi some certain knowledge seemed to pass before her eyes, and she stopped. It crushed him; he knew at that moment that he was not even important enough to be properly insulted. She opened the car door and began walking up the path, wobbling a little on her square wooden heels, reaching into her straw bag to eat handfuls of puffed rice. It fell through her fingers, leaving a zigzagging trail, causing a monkey to leap down from a tree and devour the little white grains. In search of more, the monkey began to follow Mrs. Das. Others joined him, so that she was soon being followed by about half a dozen of them, their velvety tails dragging behind.

Mr. Kapasi stepped out of the car. He wanted to holler, to alert her in some way, but he worried that if she knew they were behind her, she would grow nervous. Perhaps she would lose her balance. Perhaps they would pull at her bag or her hair. He began to jog up the path, taking a fallen branch in his hand to scare away the monkeys. Mrs. Das continued walking, oblivious, trailing grains of puffed rice. Near the top of the incline, before a group of cells fronted by a row of squat stone pillars, Mr. Das was kneeling on the ground, focusing the lens of his camera. The children stood under the arcade, now hiding, now emerging from view.

"Wait for me," Mrs. Das called out. "I'm coming."

Tina jumped up and down. "Here comes Mommy!" 165

"Great," Mr. Das said without looking up. "Just in time. We'll get Mr. Kapasi to take a picture of the five of us."

Mr. Kapasi quickened his pace, waving his branch so that the monkeys scampered away, distracted, in another direction.

"Where's Bobby?" Mrs. Das asked when she stopped.

Mr. Das looked up from the camera. "I don't know, Ronny, where's Bobby?"

Ronny shrugged. "I thought he was right here." 170

"Where is he?" Mrs. Das repeated sharply. "What's wrong with all of you?"

They began calling his name, wandering up and down the path a bit. Because they were calling, they did not initially hear the boy's screams. When they found him, a little farther down the path under a tree, he was surrounded by a group of monkeys, over a dozen of them, pulling at his T-shirt with their long black fingers. The puffed rice Mrs. Das had spilled was scattered at his feet, raked over by the monkeys' hands. The boy was silent, his body frozen, swift tears running down his startled face. His bare legs were dusty and red with welts from where one of the monkeys struck him repeatedly with the stick he had given to it earlier.

"Daddy, the monkey's hurting Bobby," Tina said.

Mr. Das wiped his palms on the front of his shorts. In his nervousness he accidentally pressed the shutter on his camera; the whirring noise of the advancing film excited the monkeys, and the one with the stick began to beat Bobby more intently. "What are we supposed to do? What if they start attacking?"

"Mr. Kapasi," Mrs. Das shrieked, noticing him standing to one side. "Do some- 175 thing, for God's sake, do something!"

Mr. Kapasi took his branch and shooed them away, hissing at the ones that remained, stomping his feet to scare them. The animals retreated slowly, with a measured gait, obedient but unintimidated. Mr. Kapasi gathered Bobby in his arms and brought him back to where his parents and siblings were standing. As he carried him he was tempted to whisper a secret into the boy's ear. But Bobby was stunned, and shivering with fright, his legs bleeding slightly where the stick had broken the skin. When Mr. Kapasi delivered him to his parents, Mr. Das brushed some dirt off the boy's T-shirt and put the visor on him the right way. Mrs. Das reached into her straw bag to find a bandage which she taped over the cut on his knee. Ronny offered his brother a fresh piece of gum. "He's fine. Just a little scared, right, Bobby?" Mr. Das said, patting the top of his head.

"God, let's get out of here," Mrs. Das said. She folded her arms across the strawberry on her chest. "This place gives me the creeps."

"Yeah. Back to the hotel, definitely," Mr. Das agreed.

"Poor Bobby," Mrs. Das said. "Come here a second. Let Mommy fix your hair." Again she reached into her straw bag, this time for her hairbrush, and began to run it around the edges of the translucent visor. When she whipped out the hairbrush, the slip of paper with Mr. Kapasi's address on it fluttered away in the wind. No one but Mr. Kapasi noticed. He watched as it rose, carried higher and higher by the breeze, into the trees where the monkeys now sat, solemnly observing the scene below. Mr. Kapasi observed it too, knowing that this was the picture of the Das family he would preserve forever in his mind.

[1999]

Questions for Discussion

1. The dictionary defines *malady* as "an unwholesome or desperate condition." What are the various "maladies" in this story, and how are they represented? Pay particular attention to the contrast between the literal and figurative notions of sickness and how what constitutes a "malady" changes as the story develops.

2. What issues does Lahiri raise through her portrayal of children and the relationships between parents and children in this story? How has the death of Mr. Kapasi's eldest son affected his relationship with his wife? At one point, Mr. Kapasi thinks that Mr. and Mrs. Das act more as "siblings" (para. 45) than parents to their children. Why does he draw that conclusion? What does that conclusion suggest about the Das family?

3. "Interpreter of Maladies" explores the impact of immigration, including the result of an imagined rather than an experienced homeland. How does the Das family imagine India? Why does Lahiri emphasize the taking of photographs during the family's vacation?

4. What do we normally think of when considering the job of an "interpreter"? How does Mr. Kapasi's job at the infirmary expand this definition? Why does he view that job as "a thankless occupation," "a sign of his failings" (paras. 76–77)?

5. After Mr. Kapasi asks Mrs. Das if she is feeling pain or guilt, Lahiri writes, "She turned to him and glared, mustard oil thick on her frosty pink lips. She opened her mouth to say something, but as she glared at Mr. Kapasi some certain knowledge seemed to pass before her eyes, and she stopped" (para. 162). What is Lahiri's attitude toward Mrs. Das at this juncture? What is the "certain knowledge" she realizes?

6. Trace the changes in Mr. Kapasi and Mrs. Das's relationship. How do her responses to her own family mirror shifts in her relationship to Mr. Kapasi? How do you interpret the ending of the story? Were you expecting it? What does the final sentence mean: "Mr. Kapasi observed it too, knowing that this was the picture of the Das family he would preserve forever in his mind" (para. 179)?

7. What is the moral responsibility of Mrs. Das? Should she tell her husband that Bobby is not his biological child? Should she tell the biological father? Should she tell Bobby? Do you sympathize with Mrs. Das when she tells Mr. Kapasi that she has "been in pain eight years" (para. 160)? In what ways has her silence been a kind of punishment for her?

8. Why does Lahiri choose the Sun Temple at Konarak as the central setting for her story? Research this sacred monument to learn more about it, including the sun god Surya. How does the information you learn add to your understanding of Lahiri's choice? Why do you think she chose this temple rather than a more famous one (to westerners, at least), such as the Taj Mahal?

Questions on Style and Structure

1. In the opening paragraph, Lahiri takes the reader right into the action and introduces all three major characters. What impression do the details she chooses give?

2. Lahiri provides physical descriptions of characters, particularly their clothing, in elaborate detail. What do these descriptions say about each of them? Pay particular attention to the carefully tailored suit Mr. Kapasi wears and to Mrs. Das's outfit. (Why, for instance, does Lahiri describe her wearing her sunglasses "on top of her head like a tiara" [para. 61] and having "small hands like paws" [para. 14]?)

3. Why does Lahiri begin accumulating details about language from the very beginning? We learn that Mr. Kapasi speaks English, he helps the doctor with patients who speak Gujarati, he finds it "strange" (para. 13) that Mr. Das refers to his wife by her first name to his children. Identify other examples throughout the story. What point is Lahiri making with these details?

4. How does Lahiri's description of the Sun Temple function in the story (para. 91)? Note that she begins by providing background information, shows her characters interacting, and describes the temple as being "filled with rubble years ago" (para. 98).

5. How does Lahiri use Mr. Kapasi's dreams and imaginings to develop his character? Why does his dream "of being an interpreter for diplomats and dignitaries, resolving conflicts between people and nations" (para. 77) seem sad—or does it? Pay special attention to his fantasies about Mrs. Das, such as the paragraph beginning, "The paper curled as Mr. Kapasi wrote his address in clear, careful letters. She would write to him . . ." (para. 89), and his calculations about how long it would be before he received her first letter (para. 109).

6. Dramatic irony is created when a reader knows something that the characters in the story do not; thus, some of the words and actions in a story would have a different meaning for the reader than they do for the characters. For example, once we learn of Mr. Kapasi's hope for a relationship with Mrs. Das (para. 89), his actions take on a different meaning for us than for her. Identify several other examples of dramatic irony in the story, and discuss their effect on Lahiri's tone.

7. Photographs capture a moment in time and preserve it for record and reflection; we usually think of personal and family photos as positive. How does Lahiri's use of photographs contribute to the development of her theme(s)?

8. The final dramatic scene with the monkeys is a complex one, involving interaction among all the characters. What role does each character play through both words and action? As a reader, did you ever feel that something dreadful was about to happen? What is Lahiri's purpose in presenting the scene as she does?

9. The story is divided into three sections. If you think of each section as a chapter, how would you describe these divisions? What is Lahiri's purpose in making these divisions rather than telling the story as one continuous narrative?

10. The story touches on the past, present, and future (especially in the fantasy life of Mr. Kapasi) of all three central characters. Instead of presenting these as sequential narratives, however, Lahiri interweaves them. What is the effect of this technique?

Suggestions for Writing

1. Discuss the difficulty of meaningful communication as a theme of "Interpreter of Maladies," specifically the interpretations and misinterpretations that occur during

the course of the story. Consider the role that cultural differences, immigration and assimilation, and the dynamics of relationships play in hindering communication.

2. Even at middle age, Mr. Kapasi does not have a clear identity. Discuss the conflicts within his life, both internal and external, that contribute to his shifting and uncertain sense of who he is and where he belongs.

3. Write an essay characterizing the tone of this story. Pay particular attention to how Lahiri uses descriptive detail, dialogue, and visual images to develop tone.

4. In paragraphs 76–80, Lahiri describes Mr. Kapasi's musings after Mrs. Das tells him that she finds his job as an interpreter between a physician and his patients "romantic" and "a big responsibility." Write an essay analyzing the literary techniques Lahiri uses in these paragraphs to characterize Mr. Kapasi.

5. Lahiri has described the short story as "a middle ground between poetry and the novel" because it has "purity and intensity," "a ruthless distilled quality," "a compression and concentration that is akin to poetry." Discuss how these characteristics apply to "Interpreter of Maladies," specifically how the language of this short story is similar to what we associate with poetry.

6. *Diaspora* is a term that originally referred to the scattered Jewish community after the Babylonian exile (587 B.C.E.) and later to the Christians dispersed across the Greco-Roman world in the first century C.E. Today we use it more generally to refer to the movement, migration, or scattering of people from their original homelands. Discuss "Interpreter of Maladies" as a story about the struggle of being part of a diaspora in the late twentieth century.

7. During the story, we learn details about Mrs. Kapasi from her husband's perspective. According to Mr. Kapasi, theirs was "a bad match" (para. 79). His wife never asks him about his patients or says that his job is "a big responsibility" (para. 78). She serves him his evening cup of tea "in silence" (para. 111). We are given these bits of information, but we never get to see things from her point of view. Let her speak! Write a description of Mr. Kapasi in the voice of his wife.

8. Watch *The Namesake* (PG-13), and discuss the similar concerns found in that film and "Interpreter of Maladies." Pay particular attention to the clash of traditional culture and contemporary values, the responsibility of one generation to preserve and communicate its traditional culture to another, the role of women, and the relationship between parents and children.

Young Goodman Brown

NATHANIEL HAWTHORNE

One of America's major voices of the nineteenth century, Nathaniel Hawthorne (1804–1864) was born in Salem, Massachusetts, into a family whose ancestors had participated in the Salem witch trials of the seventeenth century. He graduated from Bowdoin College in Maine, where he was a classmate of the poet Henry Wadsworth Longfellow and future president of the United States Franklin Pierce, who remained Hawthorne's lifelong friend. For several years after college, Hawthorne wrote sketches and stories and worked as a surveyor of the Customs House in Boston. In 1837, he published a volume of stories, *Twice-Told Tales*, followed by *Mosses from an Old Manse* (1846)—named for his house, which had belonged to Ralph Waldo Emerson. The years 1850 and 1851 saw the publication of Hawthorne's major works, *The Scarlet Letter* and *The House of the Seven Gables*. Hawthorne's writing is often allegorical and contains many of the elements of the supernatural; in fact, he referred to his books as "romances" rather than novels. Among his most famous stories are "My Kinsman, Major Molineux," "Rappaccini's Daughter," and "Young Goodman Brown," included here.

Young Goodman Brown came forth at sunset into the street of Salem village; but put his head back, after crossing the threshold, to exchange a parting kiss with his young wife. And Faith, as the wife was aptly named, thrust her own pretty head into the street, letting the wind play with the pink ribbons of her cap while she called to Goodman Brown.

"Dearest heart," whispered she, softly and rather sadly, when her lips were close to his ear, "prithee put off your journey until sunrise and sleep in your own bed to-night. A lone woman is troubled with such dreams and such thoughts that she's afeard of herself sometimes. Pray tarry with me this night, dear husband, of all nights in the year."

"My love and my Faith," replied young Goodman Brown, "of all nights in the year, this one night must I tarry away from thee. My journey, as thou callest it, forth and back again, must needs be done 'twixt now and sunrise. What, my sweet, pretty wife, dost thou doubt me already, and we but three months married?"

"Then God bless you!" said Faith, with the pink ribbons; "and may you find all well when you come back."

"Amen!" cried Goodman Brown. "Say thy prayers, dear Faith, and go to bed at dusk, and no harm will come to thee." 5

So they parted; and the young man pursued his way until, being about to turn the corner by the meeting-house, he looked back and saw the head of Faith still peeping after him with a melancholy air, in spite of her pink ribbons.

"Poor little Faith!" thought he, for his heart smote him. "What a wretch am I to leave her on such an errand! She talks of dreams, too. Methought as she spoke there was trouble in her face, as if a dream had warned her what work is to be done to-night.

452

But no, no; 't would kill her to think it. Well, she's a blessed angel on earth; and after this one night I'll cling to her skirts and follow her to heaven."

With this excellent resolve for the future, Goodman Brown felt himself justified in making more haste on his present evil purpose. He had taken a dreary road, darkened by all the gloomiest trees of the forest, which barely stood aside to let the narrow path creep through, and closed immediately behind. It was all as lonely as could be; and there is this peculiarity in such a solitude, that the traveler knows not who may be concealed by the innumerable trunks and the thick boughs overhead; so that with lonely footsteps he may yet be passing through an unseen multitude.

"There may be a devilish Indian behind every tree," said Goodman Brown to himself; and he glanced fearfully behind him as he added, "What if the devil himself should be at my very elbow!"

His head being turned back, he passed a crook of the road, and, looking forward again, beheld the figure of a man, in grave and decent attire, seated at the foot of an old tree. He arose at Goodman Brown's approach and walked onward side by side with him. 10

"You are late, Goodman Brown," said he. "The clock of the Old South was striking as I came through Boston, and that is full fifteen minutes agone."

"Faith kept me back a while," replied the young man, with a tremor in his voice, caused by the sudden appearance of his companion, though not wholly unexpected.

It was now deep dusk in the forest, and deepest in that part of it where these two were journeying. As nearly as could be discerned, the second traveller was about fifty years old, apparently in the same rank of life as Goodman Brown, and bearing a considerable resemblance to him, though perhaps more in expression than features. Still they might have been taken for father and son. And yet, though the elder person was as simply clad as the younger, and as simple in manner too, he had an indescribable air of one who knew the world, and who would not have felt abashed at the governor's dinner table or in King William's court, were it possible that his affairs should call him thither. But the only thing about him that could be fixed upon as remarkable was his staff, which bore the likeness of a great black snake, so curiously wrought that it might almost be seen to twist and wriggle itself like a living serpent. This, of course, must have been an ocular deception, assisted by the uncertain light.

"Come, Goodman Brown!" cried his fellow-traveller, "this is a dull pace for the beginning of a journey. Take my staff, if you are so soon weary."

"Friend," said the other, exchanging his slow pace for a full stop, "having kept covenant by meeting thee here, it is my purpose now to return whence I came. I have scruples touching the matter thou wot'st[1] of." 15

"Sayest thou so?" replied he of the serpent, smiling apart. "Let us walk on, nevertheless, reasoning as we go; and if I convince thee not thou shalt turn back. We are but a little way in the forest yet."

"Too far! too far!" exclaimed the goodman, unconsciously resuming his walk. "My father never went into the woods on such an errand, nor his father before him. We have been a race of honest men and good Christians since the days of the martyrs; and shall I be the first of the name of Brown that ever took this path and kept—"

---

[1]Know. — EDS.

"Such company, thou wouldst say," observed the elder person, interpreting his pause. "Well said, Goodman Brown! I have been as well acquainted with your family as with ever a one among the Puritans; and that's no trifle to say. I helped your grandfather, the constable, when he lashed the Quaker woman so smartly through the streets of Salem; and it was I that brought your father a pitch-pine knot, kindled at my own hearth, to set fire to an Indian village, in King Philip's war.[2] They were my good friends, both; and many a pleasant walk have we had along this path, and returned merrily after midnight. I would fain be friends with you for their sake."

"If it be as thou sayest," replied Goodman Brown, "I marvel they never spoke of these matters; or, verily, I marvel not, seeing that the least rumor of the sort would have driven them from New England. We are a people of prayer, and good works to boot, and abide no such wickedness."

"Wickedness or not," said the traveller with the twisted staff, "I have a very general 20
acquaintance here in New England. The deacons of many a church have drunk the communion wine with me; the selectmen of divers towns make me their chairman; and a majority of the Great and General Court are firm supporters of my interest. The governor and I, too—But these are state secrets."

"Can this be so?" cried Goodman Brown, with a stare of amazement at his undisturbed companion. "Howbeit, I have nothing to do with the governor and council; they have their own ways, and are no rule for a simple husbandman like me. But, were I to go on with thee, how should I meet the eye of that good old man, our minister, at Salem village? Oh, his voice would make me tremble both Sabbath day and lecture day."

Thus far the elder traveller had listened with due gravity; but now burst into a fit of irrepressible mirth, shaking himself so violently that his snake-like staff actually seemed to wriggle in sympathy.

"Ha! ha! ha!" shouted he again and again; then composing himself, "Well, go on, Goodman Brown, go on; but, prithee, don't kill me with laughing."

"Well, then, to end the matter at once," said Goodman Brown, considerably nettled, "there is my wife, Faith. It would break her dear little heart; and I'd rather break my own."

"Nay, if that be the case," answered the other, "e'en go thy ways, Goodman 25
Brown. I would not for twenty old women like the one hobbling before us that Faith should come to any harm."

As he spoke he pointed his staff at a female figure on the path, in whom Goodman Brown recognized a very pious and exemplary dame, who had taught him his catechism in youth, and was still his moral and spiritual adviser, jointly with the minister and Deacon Gookin.

"A marvel, truly, that Goody[3] Cloyse should be so far in the wilderness at nightfall," said he. "But with your leave, friend, I shall take a cut through the woods until we have left this Christian woman behind. Being a stranger to you, she might ask whom I was consorting with and whither I was going."

---

[2] War between Native Americans and New England colonists. The Native American leader was known as King Philip.—Eds.

[3] Short for "goodwife," archaic form of *missus*.—Eds.

"Be it so," said his fellow-traveller. "Betake you to the woods, and let me keep the path."

Accordingly the young man turned aside, but took care to watch his companion, who advanced softly along the road until he had come within a staff's length of the old dame. She, meanwhile, was making the best of her way, with singular speed for so aged a woman, and mumbling some indistinct words—a prayer, doubtless—as she went. The traveller put forth his staff and touched her withered neck with what seemed the serpent's tail.

"The devil!" screamed the pious old lady.   30

"Then Goody Cloyse knows her old friend?" observed the traveller, confronting her and leaning on his writhing stick.

"Ah, forsooth, and is it your worship indeed?" cried the good dame. "Yea, truly is it, and in the very image of my old gossip, Goodman Brown, the grandfather of the silly fellow that now is. But—would your worship believe it?—my broomstick hath strangely disappeared, stolen, as I suspect, by that unhanged witch, Goody Cory, and that, too, when I was all anointed with the juice of smallage, and cinquefoil, and wolf's-bane—"

"Mingled with fine wheat and the fat of a new-born babe," said the shape of old Goodman Brown.

"Ah, your worship knows the recipe," cried the old lady, cackling aloud. "So, as I was saying, being all ready for the meeting, and no horse to ride on, I made up my mind to foot it; for they tell me there is a nice young man to be taken into communion to-night. But now your good worship will lend me your arm, and we shall be there in a twinkling."

"That can hardly be," answered her friend. "I may not spare you my arm, Goody   35
Cloyse; but here is my staff, if you will."

So saying, he threw it down at her feet, where, perhaps, it assumed life, being one of the rods which its owner had formerly lent to the Egyptian magi. Of this fact, however, Goodman Brown could not take cognizance. He had cast up his eyes in astonishment, and, looking down again, beheld neither Goody Cloyse nor the serpentine staff, but his fellow-traveller alone, who waited for him as calmly as if nothing had happened.

"That old woman taught me my catechism," said the young man; and there was a world of meaning in this simple comment.

They continued to walk onward, while the elder traveller exhorted his companion to make good speed and persevere in the path, discoursing so aptly that his arguments seemed rather to spring up in the bosom of his auditor than to be suggested by himself. As they went, he plucked a branch of maple to serve for a walking stick, and began to strip it of the twigs and little boughs, which were wet with evening dew. The moment his fingers touched them they became strangely withered and dried up as with a week's sunshine. Thus the pair proceeded, at a good free pace, until suddenly, in a gloomy hollow of the road, Goodman Brown sat himself down on the stump of a tree and refused to go any farther.

"Friend," he said, stubbornly, "my mind is made up. Not another step will I budge on this errand. What if a wretched old woman do choose to go to the devil when I thought she was going to heaven: is that any reason why I should quit my dear Faith and go after her?"

"You will think better of this by and by," said his acquaintance, composedly. "Sit   40
here and rest yourself a while; and when you feel like moving again, there is my staff
to help you along."

Without more words, he threw his companion the maple stick, and was as speedily out of sight as if he had vanished into the deepening gloom. The young man sat
a few moments by the roadside, applauding himself greatly, and thinking with how
clear a conscience he should meet the minister in his morning walk, nor shrink from
the eye of good old Deacon Gookin. And what calm sleep would be his that very
night, which was to have been spent so wickedly, but so purely and sweetly now, in
the arms of Faith! Amidst these pleasant and praiseworthy meditations, Goodman
Brown heard the tramp of horses along the road, and deemed it advisable to conceal himself within the verge of the forest, conscious of the guilty purpose that had
brought him thither, though now so happily turned from it.

On came the hoof tramps and the voices of the riders, two grave old voices, conversing soberly as they drew near. These mingled sounds appeared to pass along the road,
within a few yards of the young man's hiding-place; but, owing doubtless to the depth
of the gloom at that particular spot, neither the travellers nor their steeds were visible.
Though their figures brushed the small boughs by the wayside, it could not be seen that
they intercepted, even for a moment, the faint gleam from the strip of bright sky athwart
which they must have passed. Goodman Brown alternately crouched and stood on tiptoe,
pulling aside the branches and thrusting forth his head as far as he durst without discerning so much as a shadow. It vexed him the more, because he could have sworn, were
such a thing possible, that he recognized the voices of the minister and Deacon Gookin,
jogging along quietly, as they were wont to do, when bound to some ordination or eccle-
siastical council. While yet within hearing, one of the riders stopped to pluck a switch.

"Of the two, reverend sir," said the voice like the deacon's, "I had rather miss an
ordination dinner than to-night's meeting. They tell me that some of our community
are to be here from Falmouth and beyond, and others from Connecticut and Rhode
Island, besides several of the Indian powwows, who, after their fashion, know almost
as much deviltry as the best of us. Moreover, there is a goodly young woman to be
taken into communion."

"Mighty well, Deacon Gookin!" replied the solemn old tones of the minister. "Spur
up, or we shall be late. Nothing can be done, you know, until I get on the ground."

The hoofs clattered again; and the voices, talking so strangely in the empty air,   45
passed on through the forest, where no church had ever been gathered or solitary
Christian prayed. Whither, then, could these holy men be journeying so deep into the
heathen wilderness? Young Goodman Brown caught hold of a tree for support, being
ready to sink down on the ground, faint and overburdened with the heavy sickness of
his heart. He looked up to the sky, doubting whether there really was a heaven above
him. Yet there was the blue arch, and the stars brightening in it.

"With heaven above and Faith below, I will yet stand firm against the devil!"
cried Goodman Brown.

While he still gazed upward into the deep arch of the firmament and had lifted
his hands to pray, a cloud, though no wind was stirring, hurried across the zenith

and hid the brightening stars. The blue sky was still visible, except directly overhead, where this black mass of cloud was sweeping swiftly northward. Aloft in the air, as if from the depths of the cloud, came a confused and doubtful sound of voices. Once the listener fancied that he could distinguish the accents of towns-people of his own, men and women, both pious and ungodly, many of whom he had met at the communion table, and had seen others rioting at the tavern. The next moment, so indistinct were the sounds, he doubted whether he had heard aught but the murmur of the old forest, whispering without a wind. Then came a stronger swell of those familiar tones, heard daily in the sunshine at Salem village, but never until now from a cloud of night. There was one voice, of a young woman, uttering lamentations, yet with an uncertain sorrow, and entreating for some favor, which, perhaps, it would grieve her to obtain; and all the unseen multitude, both saints and sinners, seemed to encourage her onward.

"Faith!" shouted Goodman Brown, in a voice of agony and desperation; and the echoes of the forest mocked him, crying, "Faith! Faith!" as if bewildered wretches were seeking her all through the wilderness.

The cry of grief, rage, and terror was yet piercing the night, when the unhappy husband held his breath for a response. There was a scream, drowned immediately in a louder murmur of voices, fading into far-off laughter, as the dark cloud swept away, leaving the clear and silent sky above Goodman Brown. But something fluttered lightly down through the air and caught on the branch of a tree. The young man seized it, and beheld a pink ribbon.

"My Faith is gone!" cried he after one stupefied moment. "There is no good on earth; and sin is but a name. Come, devil; for to thee is this world given." 50

And, maddened with despair, so that he laughed loud and long, did Goodman Brown grasp his staff and set forth again, at such a rate that he seemed to fly along the forest path rather than to walk or run. The road grew wilder and drearier and more faintly traced, and vanished at length, leaving him in the heart of the dark wilderness, still rushing onward with the instinct that guides mortal man to evil. The whole forest was peopled with frightful sounds — the creaking of the trees, the howling of wild beasts, and the yell of Indians; while sometimes the wind tolled like a distant church bell, and sometimes gave a broad roar around the traveller, as if all Nature were laughing him to scorn. But he was himself the chief horror of the scene, and shrank not from its other horrors.

"Ha! ha! ha!" roared Goodman Brown when the wind laughed at him. "Let us hear which will laugh loudest. Think not to frighten me with your deviltry. Come witch, come wizard, come Indian powwow, come devil himself, and here comes Goodman Brown. You may as well fear him as he fear you."

In truth, all through the haunted forest, there could be nothing more frightful than the figure of Goodman Brown. On he flew among the black pines, brandishing his staff with frenzied gestures, now giving vent to an inspiration of horrid blasphemy, and now shouting forth such laughter as set all the echoes of the forest laughing like demons around him. The fiend in his own shape is less hideous than when he rages in the breast of man. Thus sped the demoniac on his course, until, quivering among the trees, he saw a red light before him, as when the felled trunks and branches of a clearing have been set on fire, and throw up their lurid blaze against the sky, at the hour of midnight. He paused, in a lull of the tempest that had driven him onward, and heard the swell of what seemed a hymn, rolling solemnly from a distance with the weight of many voices. He knew the tune; it was a familiar one in the choir of the village meeting-house. The verse died heavily away, and was lengthened by a chorus, not of human voices, but of all the sounds of the benighted wilderness pealing in awful harmony together. Goodman Brown cried out, and his cry was lost to his own ear, by its unison with the cry of the desert.

In the interval of silence he stole forward until the light glared full upon his eyes. At one extremity of an open space, hemmed in by the dark wall of the forest, arose a rock, bearing some rude, natural resemblance either to an altar or a pulpit, and surrounded by four blazing pines, their tops aflame, their stems untouched, like candles at an evening meeting. The mass of foliage that had overgrown the summit of the rock was all on fire, blazing high into the night and fitfully illuminating the whole field. Each pendent twig and leafy festoon was in a blaze. As the red light arose and fell, a numerous congregation alternately shone forth, then disappeared in shadow, and again grew, as it were, out of the darkness, peopling the heart of the solitary woods at once.

"A grave and dark-clad company," quoth Goodman Brown. 55

In truth they were such. Among them, quivering to and fro between gloom and splendor, appeared faces that would be seen next day at the council board of the province, and others which, Sabbath after Sabbath, looked devoutly heavenward, and benignantly over the crowded pews, from the holiest pulpits in the land. Some affirm that the lady of the governor was there. At least there were high dames well known to her, and wives of honored husbands, and widows, a great multitude, and ancient maidens, all of excellent repute, and fair young girls, who trembled lest their mothers should espy them. Either the sudden gleams of light flashing over the obscure field bedazzled Goodman Brown, or he recognized a score of the church members of Salem village famous for their especial sanctity. Good old Deacon Gookin had arrived, and waited at the skirts of that venerable saint, his revered pastor. But, irreverently consorting with these grave, reputable, and pious people, these elders of the church, these chaste dames and dewy virgins, there were men of dissolute lives and women of spotted fame, wretches given over to all mean and filthy vice, and suspected even of horrid crimes. It was strange to see that the good shrank not from the wicked, nor were the sinners abashed by the saints. Scattered also among their pale-faced enemies were the Indian priests, or powwows, who had often scared their native forest with more hideous incantations than any known to English witchcraft.

"But where is Faith?" thought Goodman Brown; and, as hope came into his heart, he trembled.

Another verse of the hymn arose, a slow and mournful strain, such as the pious love, but joined to words which expressed all that our nature can conceive of sin, and darkly hinted at far more. Unfathomable to mere mortals is the lore of fiends. Verse after verse was sung; and still the chorus of the desert swelled between like the deepest tone of a mighty organ; and with the final peal of that dreadful anthem there came a sound, as if the roaring wind, the rushing streams, the howling beasts, and every other voice of the unconcerted wilderness were mingling and according with the voice of guilty man in homage to the prince of all. The four blazing pines threw up a loftier flame, and obscurely discovered shapes and visages of horror on the smoke wreaths above the impious assembly. At the same moment the fire on the rock shot redly forth and formed a glowing arch above its base, where now appeared a figure. With reverence be it spoken, the figure bore no slight similitude, both in garb and manner, to some grave divine[4] of the New England churches.

"Bring forth the converts!" cried a voice that echoed through the field and rolled into the forest.

At the word, Goodman Brown stepped forth from the shadow of the trees and approached the congregation, with whom he felt a loathful brotherhood by the sympathy of all that was wicked in his heart. He could have well-nigh sworn that the shape of his own dead father beckoned him to advance, looking downward from a smoke wreath, while a woman, with dim features of despair, threw out her hand to warn him back. Was it his mother? But he had no power to retreat one step, nor to resist, even in thought, when the minister and good old Deacon Gookin seized his arms and led him to the blazing rock. Thither came also the slender form of a veiled female, led between Goody Cloyse, that pious teacher of the catechism, and Martha Carrier, who had received the devil's promise to be queen of hell. A rampant hag was she. And there stood the proselytes beneath the canopy of fire.

"Welcome, my children," said the dark figure, "to the communion of your race. Ye have found thus young your nature and your destiny. My children, look behind you!"

They turned; and flashing forth, as it were, in a sheet of flame, the fiend worshippers were seen; the smile of welcome gleamed darkly on every visage.

"There," resumed the sable form, "are all whom ye have reverenced from youth. Ye deemed them holier than yourselves and shrank from your own sin, contrasting it with their lives of righteousness and prayerful aspirations heavenward. Yet here are they all in my worshipping assembly. This night it shall be granted you to know their secret deeds: how hoary-bearded elders of the church have whispered wanton words to the young maids of their households; how many a woman, eager for widows' weeds, has given her husband a drink at bedtime and let him sleep his last sleep in her bosom; how beardless youths have made haste to inherit their fathers' wealth; and how fair damsels—blush not, sweet ones—have dug little graves in the garden, and bidden me, the sole guest, to an infant's funeral. By the sympathy of your human hearts for sin ye shall scent out all the places—whether in church, bed-chamber, street, field, or forest—where crime has been committed, and shall exult to behold the whole earth one stain of guilt, one mighty blood spot. Far more than this. It shall be yours to penetrate, in every bosom, the deep mystery of sin, the fountain of all wicked arts, and which inexhaustibly supplies more evil impulses than human power—than my power at its utmost—can make manifest in deeds. And now, my children, look upon each other."

60

---

[4] Theologian, or member of the clergy.—EDS.

They did so; and, by the blaze of the hell-kindled torches, the wretched man beheld his Faith, and the wife her husband, trembling before that unhallowed altar.

"Lo, there ye stand, my children," said the figure, in a deep and solemn tone, 65 almost sad with its despairing awfulness, as if his once angelic nature could yet mourn for our miserable race. "Depending upon one another's hearts, ye had still hoped that virtue were not all a dream. Now are ye undeceived. Evil is the nature of mankind. Evil must be your only happiness. Welcome again, my children, to the communion of your race."

"Welcome," repeated the fiend worshippers, in one cry of despair and triumph.

And there they stood, the only pair, as it seemed, who were yet hesitating on the verge of wickedness in this dark world. A basin was hollowed, naturally, in the rock. Did it contain water, reddened by the lurid light? or was it blood? or, perchance, a liquid flame? Herein did the shape of evil dip his hand and prepare to lay the mark of baptism upon their foreheads, that they might be partakers of the mystery of sin, more conscious of the secret guilt of others, both in deed and thought, than they could now be of their own. The husband cast one look at his pale wife, and Faith at him. What polluted wretches would the next glance show them to each other, shuddering alike at what they disclosed and what they saw!

"Faith! Faith!" cried the husband, "look up to heaven, and resist the wicked one."

Whether Faith obeyed he knew not. Hardly had he spoken when he found himself amid calm night and solitude, listening to a roar of the wind which died heavily away through the forest. He staggered against the rock, and felt it chill and damp; while a hanging twig, that had been all on fire, besprinkled his cheek with the coldest dew.

The next morning young Goodman Brown came slowly into the street of Salem 70 village, staring around him like a bewildered man. The good old minister was taking a walk along the graveyard to get an appetite for breakfast and meditate his sermon, and bestowed a blessing, as he passed, on Goodman Brown. He shrank from the venerable saint as if to avoid an anathema. Old Deacon Gookin was at domestic worship, and the holy words of his prayer were heard through the open window. "What God doth the wizard pray to?" quoth Goodman Brown. Goody Cloyse, that excellent old Christian, stood in the early sunshine at her own lattice, catechizing a little girl who had brought her a pint of morning's milk. Goodman Brown snatched away the child as from the grasp of the fiend himself. Turning the corner by the meeting-house, he spied the head of Faith, with the pink ribbons, gazing anxiously forth, and bursting into such joy at sight of him that she skipped along the street and almost kissed her husband before the whole village. But Goodman Brown looked sternly and sadly into her face, and passed on without a greeting.

Had Goodman Brown fallen asleep in the forest, and only dreamed a wild dream of a witch-meeting?

Be it so if you will; but, alas! it was a dream of evil omen for young Goodman Brown. A stern, a sad, a darkly meditative, a distrustful, if not a desperate man did he become from the night of that fearful dream. On the Sabbath day, when the congregation were singing a holy psalm, he could not listen because an anthem of sin rushed loudly upon his ear and drowned all the blessed strain. When the minister spoke from the pulpit with power and fervid eloquence, and, with his hand on the open Bible, of the sacred truths of our religion, and of saint-like lives and triumphant deaths, and of future bliss or misery unutterable, then did Goodman Brown turn pale, dreading lest the roof should thunder down upon the gray blasphemer and his hearers. Often, awaking suddenly at midnight, he shrank from the bosom of Faith; and at morning or eventide, when the family knelt down at prayer, he scowled and muttered to himself, and gazed sternly at his wife, and turned away. And when he had lived long, and was borne to his grave a hoary corpse, followed by Faith, an aged woman, and children and grandchildren, a goodly procession, besides neighbors not a few, they carved no hopeful verse upon his tombstone, for his dying hour was gloom.

[1835]

Exploring the Text

1. What is the significance of the names Goodman Brown and Faith, especially in such statements as "Faith kept me back a while" in paragraph 12 and "My Faith is gone!" in paragraph 50?
2. Hawthorne presents contrasting imagery in the story. What, for example, is the effect of juxtaposing "melancholy air" with "pink ribbons" (para. 6)? How do the various contrasts develop a theme?
3. Discuss the imagery developed in paragraph 8. What effect does it create?
4. In paragraph 37, the narrator remarks, "there was a world of meaning in this simple comment." What is the "world of meaning" he is referring to?
5. What is the nature of Goodman Brown's quest? Where is he going? Why? In paragraph 41, the reader learns that Goodman Brown was "conscious of the guilty purpose that had brought him thither, though now so happily turned from it." How conscious is he? Does he happily turn from it?
6. Paragraph 53 begins: "In truth, all through the haunted forest, there could be nothing more frightful than the figure of Goodman Brown." Does that description refer more to how others might see him or to how he sees himself? What does Hawthorne mean when he points out that the "fiend in his own shape is less hideous than when he rages in the breast of man"? Why at the end of the paragraph is his cry "lost to his own ear, by its unison with the cry of the desert"?
7. Paragraph 71 reads, in its entirety: "Had Goodman Brown fallen asleep in the forest, and only dreamed a wild dream of a witch-meeting?" Do you believe it was a dream, or did Goodman Brown actually live his experience? Explain. What is the effect of Goodman Brown's experience, whether it was a dream or not?
8. Considering the symbolism, discuss the story as an allegory. How might Goodman Brown's quest serve as a symbolic representation of the development of his identity?
9. Herman Melville, author of *Moby-Dick*, admired Hawthorne's work immensely, and stated that Hawthorne says "NO! in Thunder." How does "Young Goodman Brown" fit Melville's characterization?

A & P

John Updike

One of America's most prolific authors, John Updike (1932–2009) wrote stories, novels, poetry, literary criticism, and essays; indeed, he wrote sixty books, almost forty of them novels or story collections. Updike studied English at Harvard and drawing at the Ruskin School of Drawing and Fine Art at Oxford before taking a staff position at the *New Yorker*. He believed that the ordinary life is worth writing about—a belief that distinguishes his work. Heroes in Updike stories are not so much larger than life as true to life. His prose is straightforward and unadorned, his settings drawn from places he knew well. His character Harry "Rabbit" Angstrom, featured in the Rabbit series—*Rabbit, Run* (1960); *Rabbit Redux* (1971); *Rabbit Is Rich* (1981); *Rabbit at Rest* (1990); and *Rabbit Remembered* (2001)—belongs to the cast of unforgettable American heroes. *Rabbit, Run* and *Rabbit at Rest* were both awarded the Pulitzer Prize. In 2008, he published *The Widows of Eastwick*, a sequel to *The Witches of Eastwick* (1984). Updike was a regular contributor to the *New Yorker*, where "A & P" first appeared in 1961; nearly fifty years later, it remains one of the most popular short stories of American literature.

In walks these three girls in nothing but bathing suits. I'm in the third checkout slot, with my back to the door, so I don't see them until they're over by the bread. The one that caught my eye first was the one in the plaid green two-piece. She was a chunky kid, with a good tan and a sweet broad soft-looking can with those two crescents of white just under it, where the sun never seems to hit, at the top of the backs of her legs. I stood there with my hand on a box of HiHo crackers trying to remember if I rang it up or not. I ring it up again and the customer starts giving me hell. She's one of these cash-register-watchers, a witch about fifty with rouge on her cheekbones and no eyebrows, and I know it made her day to trip me up. She'd been watching cash registers for fifty years and probably never seen a mistake before.

By the time I got her feathers smoothed and her goodies into a bag—she gives me a little snort in passing, if she'd been born at the right time they would have burned her over in Salem—by the time I get her on her way the girls had circled around the bread and were coming back, without a pushcart, back my way along the counters, in the aisle between the checkouts and the Special bins. They didn't even have shoes on. There was this chunky one, with the two-piece—it was bright green and the seams on the bra were still sharp and her belly was still pretty pale so I guessed she just got it (the suit)—there was this one, with one of those chubby berry-faces, the lips all bunched together under her nose, this one, and a tall one, with black hair that hadn't quite frizzed right, and one of these sunburns right across under the eyes, and a chin that was too long—you know, the kind of girl other girls think is very "striking" and "attractive" but never quite makes it, as they very well know, which is why they like her so much—and then the third one, that wasn't quite so tall. She was the queen. She kind of led them, the other two peeking around and making their shoulders round. She didn't look around, not this queen, she just walked straight on slowly, on these long white prima-donna legs. She came down a little hard on her heels, as if she didn't walk in her bare feet that much, putting down her heels and then letting the weight move along to her toes as if she was testing the floor with every step, putting a little deliberate extra action into it. You never know for sure how girls' minds work (do you really think it's a mind in there or just a little buzz like a bee in a glass jar?) but you got the idea she had talked the other two into coming in here with her, and now she was showing them how to do it, walk slow and hold yourself straight.

She had on a kind of dirty-pink—beige maybe, I don't know—bathing suit with a little nubble all over it and, what got me, the straps were down. They were off her shoulders looped loose around the cool tops of her arms, and I guess as a result the suit had slipped a little on her, so all around the top of the cloth there was this shining rim. If it hadn't been there you wouldn't have known there could have been anything whiter than those shoulders. With the straps pushed off, there was nothing between the top of the suit and the top of her head except just *her*, this clean bare plane of the top of her chest down from the shoulder bones like a dented sheet of metal tilted in the light. I mean, it was more than pretty.

She had sort of oaky hair that the sun and salt had bleached, done up in a bun that was unraveling, and a kind of prim face. Walking into the A & P with your straps down, I suppose it's the only kind of face you *can* have. She held her head so high her neck, coming up out of those white shoulders, looked kind of stretched, but I didn't mind. The longer her neck was, the more of her there was.

She must have felt in the corner of her eye me and over my shoulder Stokesie in   5 the second slot watching, but she didn't tip. Not this queen. She kept her eyes moving across the racks, and stopped, and turned so slow it made my stomach rub the inside of my apron, and buzzed to the other two, who kind of huddled against her for relief, and then they all three of them went up the cat-and-dog-food-breakfast-cereal-macaroni-rice-raisins-seasonings-spreads-spaghetti-soft-drinks-crackers-and-cookies aisle. From the third slot I look straight up this aisle to the meat counter, and I watched them all the way. The fat one with the tan sort of fumbled with the cookies, but on second thought she put the package back. The sheep pushing their carts down the aisle—the girls were walking against the usual traffic (not that we have one-way signs or anything)—were pretty hilarious. You could see them, when Queenie's white shoulders dawned on them, kind of jerk, or hop, or hiccup, but their eyes snapped back to their own baskets and on they pushed. I bet you could set off dynamite in an A & P and the people would by and large keep reaching and checking oatmeal off their lists and muttering "Let me see, there was a third thing, began with A, asparagus, no, ah, yes, applesauce!" or whatever it is they do mutter. But there was no doubt, this jiggled them. A few houseslaves in pin curlers even looked around after pushing their carts past to make sure what they had seen was correct.

You know, it's one thing to have a girl in a bathing suit down on the beach, where what with the glare nobody can look at each other much anyway, and another thing in the cool of the A & P, under the fluorescent lights, against all those stacked packages, with her feet paddling along naked over our checkerboard green-and-cream rubber-tile floor.

"Oh Daddy," Stokesie said beside me. "I feel so faint."

"Darling," I said. "Hold me tight." Stokesie's married, with two babies chalked up on his fuselage already, but as far as I can tell that's the only difference. He's twenty-two, and I was nineteen this April.

"Is it done?" he asks, the responsible married man finding his voice. I forgot to say he thinks he's going to be manager some sunny day, maybe in 1990 when it's called the Great Alexandrov and Petrooshki Tea Company or something.

What he meant was, our town is five miles from a beach, with a big summer colony out on the Point, but we're right in the middle of town, and the women generally put on a shirt or shorts or something before they get out of the car into the street. And anyway these are usually women with six children and varicose veins mapping their legs and nobody, including them, could care less. As I say, we're right in the middle of town, and if you stand at our front doors you can see two banks and the Congregational church and the newspaper store and three real-estate offices and about twenty-seven old freeloaders tearing up Central Street because the sewer broke again. It's not as if we're on the Cape; we're north of Boston and there's people in this town haven't seen the ocean for twenty years.   10

The girls had reached the meat counter and were asking McMahon something. He pointed, they pointed, and they shuffled out of sight behind a pyramid of Diet Delight peaches. All that was left for us to see was old McMahon patting his mouth and looking after them sizing up their joints. Poor kids, I began to feel sorry for them, they couldn't help it.

Now here comes the sad part of the story, at least my family says it's sad, but I don't think it's so sad myself. The store's pretty empty, it being Thursday afternoon, so there was nothing much to do except lean on the register and wait for the girls to show up again. The whole store was like a pinball machine and I didn't know which tunnel they'd come out of. After a while they come around out of the far aisle, around the light bulbs, records at discount of the Caribbean Six or Tony Martin Sings or some such gunk you wonder they waste the wax on, sixpacks of candy bars, and plastic toys done up in cellophane that fall apart when a kid looks at them anyway. Around they come, Queenie still leading the way, and holding a little gray jar in her hand. Slots Three through Seven are unmanned and I could see her wondering between Stokes and me, but Stokesie with his usual luck draws an old party in baggy gray pants who stumbles up with four giant cans of pineapple juice (what do these bums *do* with all that pineapple juice? I've often asked myself) so the girls come to me. Queenie puts down the jar and I take it into my fingers icy cold. Kingfish Fancy Herring Snacks in Pure Sour Cream: 49¢. Now her hands are empty, not a ring or a bracelet, bare as God made them, and I wonder where the money's coming from. Still with that prim look she lifts a folded dollar bill out of the hollow at the center of her nubbled pink top. The jar went heavy in my hand. Really, I thought that was so cute.

Then everybody's luck begins to run out. Lengel comes in from haggling with a truck full of cabbages on the lot and is about to scuttle into that door marked MANAGER behind which he hides all day when the girls touch his eye. Lengel's pretty dreary, teaches Sunday school and the rest, but he doesn't miss that much. He comes over and says, "Girls, this isn't the beach."

Queenie blushes, though maybe it's just a brush of sunburn I was noticing for the first time, now that she was so close. "My mother asked me to pick up a jar of herring snacks." Her voice kind of startled me, the way voices do when you see the people first, coming out so flat and dumb yet kind of tony, too, the way it ticked over "pick up" and "snacks." All of a sudden I slid right down her voice into the living room. Her father and the other men were standing around in ice-cream coats and bow ties and the women were in sandals picking up herring snacks on toothpicks off a big glass plate and they were all holding drinks the color of water with olives and sprigs of mint in them. When my parents have somebody over they get lemonade and if it's a real racy affair Schlitz in tall glasses with "They'll Do It Every Time" cartoons stencilled on.

"That's all right," Lengel said. "But this isn't the beach." His repeating this struck 15 me as funny, as if it had just occurred to him, and he had been thinking all these years the A & P was a great big dune and he was the head lifeguard. He didn't like my smiling—as I say he doesn't miss much—but he concentrates on giving the girls that sad Sunday-school-superintendent stare.

Queenie's blush is no sunburn now, and the plump one in plaid, that I liked better from the back—a really sweet can—pipes up, "We weren't doing any shopping. We just came in for the one thing."

"That makes no difference," Lengel tells her, and I could see from the way his eyes went that he hadn't noticed she was wearing a two-piece before. "We want you decently dressed when you come in here."

"We *are* decent," Queenie says suddenly, her lower lip pushing, getting sore now that she remembers her place, a place from which the crowd that runs the A & P must look pretty crummy. Fancy Herring Snacks flashed in her very blue eyes.

"Girls, I don't want to argue with you. After this come in here with your shoulders covered. It's our policy." He turns his back. That's policy for you. Policy is what the kingpins want. What the others want is juvenile delinquency.

All this while, the customers had been showing up with their carts but, you 20 know, sheep, seeing a scene, they had all bunched up on Stokesie, who shook open a paper bag as gently as peeling a peach, not wanting to miss a word. I could feel in the silence everybody getting nervous, most of all Lengel, who asks me, "Sammy, have you rung up their purchase?"

I thought and said "No" but it wasn't about that I was thinking. I go through the punches, 4, 9, GROC, TOT—it's more complicated than you think, and after you do it often enough, it begins to make a little song, that you hear words to, in my case "Hello (*bing*) there, you (*gung*) hap-py *pee*-pul (*splat*)!"—the *splat* being the drawer flying out. I uncrease the bill, tenderly as you may imagine, it just having come from between the two smoothest scoops of vanilla I had ever known were there, and pass a half and a penny into her narrow pink palm, and nestle the herrings in a bag and twist its neck and hand it over, all the time thinking.

The girls, and who'd blame them, are in a hurry to get out, so I say "I quit" to Lengel quick enough for them to hear, hoping they'll stop and watch me, their unsuspected hero. They keep right on going, into the electric eye; the door flies open and they flicker across the lot to their car, Queenie and Plaid and Big Tall Goony-Goony (not that as raw material she was so bad), leaving me with Lengel and a kink in his eyebrow.

"Did you say something, Sammy?"

"I said I quit."

"I thought you did." 25

"You didn't have to embarrass them."

"It was they who were embarrassing us."

I started to say something that came out "Fiddle-de-doo." It's a saying of my grandmother's, and I know she would have been pleased.

"I don't think you know what you're saying," Lengel said.

"I know you don't," I said. "But I do." I pull the bow at the back of my apron and 30 start shrugging it off my shoulders. A couple customers that had been heading for my slot begin to knock against each other, like scared pigs in a chute.

Lengel sighs and begins to look very patient and old and gray. He's been a friend of my parents for years. "Sammy, you don't want to do this to your Mom and Dad," he tells me. It's true, I don't. But it seems to me that once you begin a gesture it's fatal not to go through with it. I fold the apron, "Sammy" stitched in red on the pocket, and put it on the counter, and drop the bow tie on top of it. The bow tie is theirs, if you've ever wondered. "You'll feel this for the rest of your life," Lengel says, and I know that's true, too, but remembering how he made the pretty girl blush makes me so scrunchy inside I punch the No Sale tab and the machine whirs "pee-pul" and the drawer splats out. One advantage to this scene taking place in summer, I can follow this up with a clean exit, there's no fumbling around getting your coat and galoshes, I just saunter into the electric eye in my white shirt that my mother ironed the night before, and the door heaves itself open, and outside the sunshine is skating around on the asphalt.

I look around for my girls, but they're gone, of course. There wasn't anybody but some young married screaming with her children about some candy they didn't get by the door of a powder-blue Falcon station wagon. Looking back in the big windows, over the bags of peat moss and aluminum lawn furniture stacked on the pavement, I could see Lengel in my place in the slot, checking the sheep through. His face was dark gray and his back stiff, as if he'd just had an injection of iron, and my stomach kind of fell as I felt how hard the world was going to be to me hereafter.

[1961]

. . . .

Exploring the Text

1. This story pivots on the decision Sammy made; was it the right one? Do you agree or disagree with his belief that "once you begin a gesture it's fatal not to go through with it" (para. 31)? Does Updike want us to see Sammy as acting foolishly or courageously?

2. Sammy is both the main character and the narrator of this story. How does this first-person point of view affect your attitude toward him? Do you like him? Is he funny and engaging? disrespectful? smug? Cite specific passages—including slang and colloquial expressions—that influence your response.

3. What does Sammy's description of the three girls reveal about his character? Consider the details he notes and the language he uses, especially figurative language. Why is it significant that the girls are from the "summer colony out on the Point" (para. 10) rather than being permanent residents?

4. What does Sammy's description of the other A & P customers and A & P employees suggest about his attitude toward his work at the grocery store? Discuss how Sammy is simultaneously critical of the small-town world where he lives and a part of it. Is he being hypocritical?

5. The final two paragraphs of the story have a relatively somber tone and end with Sammy's comment, "my stomach kind of fell as I felt how hard the world was going to be to me hereafter." Why does Sammy believe that the world is going to be hard on him? What is Updike's purpose in keeping the ending devoid of the humor or lighthearted touches we saw earlier in the story?

6. How much time seems to have elapsed from when events occurred and when the account was told? Cite evidence from the story to support your position. How might this proximity or distance influence Sammy's sense of the significance of what has happened?

7. Although Updike does not draw a comparison between the town's residents and the summer vacationers, he makes clear the contrast in socioeconomic status and outlook. How are the two groups representative of different cultures? In what ways is Sammy trying to cross cultures?

8. This story was written in 1961 but continues to be one of Updike's most popular stories. Why? What about the story seems timeless, and which details seem dated?

in class

Where Are You Going, Where Have You Been?

JOYCE CAROL OATES

Joyce Carol Oates (b. 1938) received a typewriter at age fourteen and wrote "novel after novel" in high school and college. She is the youngest author ever to receive the National Book Award—for her novel *Them* (1969). Currently a professor of creative writing at Princeton, Oates is highly prolific, having published over thirty novels, including *Black Water* (1992), *We Were the Mulvaneys* (1996), *The Falls* (2004), and *Little Bird of Heaven* (2009). She has written several mystery novels under the pseudonyms Rosamond Smith and Lauren Kelly. Oates is also a literary and social critic, who has written on such wide-ranging subjects as the poetry of Emily Dickinson, the fiction of James Joyce, and the life of boxer Mike Tyson. "Where Are You Going, Where Have You Been?" is typical of her work, which often explores the violence and suspense lurking beneath ordinary family life. This story is based on the factual case of a psychopath known as the Pied Piper of Tucson. In an interview with the *New York Times,* Oates described him:

> The Pied Piper mimicked teenagers in their talk, dress, and behavior, but he was not a teen-ager—he was a man in his early thirties. Rather short, he stuffed rags in his leather boots to give himself height. (And sometimes walked unsteadily as a consequence: did none among his admiring constituency notice?) He charmed his victims as charismatic psychopaths have always charmed their victims, to the bewilderment of others who fancy themselves free of all lunatic attractions. The Pied Piper of Tucson: a trashy dream, a tabloid archetype, sheer artifice, comedy, cartoon—surrounded, however improbably, and finally tragically, by real people. You think that, if you look twice, he won't be there. But there he is.

For Bob Dylan

Her name was Connie. She was fifteen and she had a quick nervous giggling habit of craning her neck to glance into mirrors, or checking other people's faces to make sure her own was all right. Her mother, who noticed everything and knew everything and who hadn't much reason any longer to look at her own face, always scolded Connie about it. "Stop gawking at yourself, who are you? You think you're so pretty?" she would say. Connie would raise her eyebrows at these familiar complaints and look right through her mother, into a shadowy vision of herself as she was right at that moment: she knew she was pretty and that was everything. Her mother had been pretty once too, if you could believe those old snapshots in the album, but now her looks were gone and that was why she was always after Connie.

"Why don't you keep your room clean like your sister? How've you got your hair fixed—what the hell stinks? Hair spray? You don't see your sister using that junk."

Her sister June was twenty-four and still lived at home. She was a secretary in the high school Connie attended, and if that wasn't bad enough—with her in the same building—she was so plain and chunky and steady that Connie had to hear her praised all the time by her mother and her mother's sisters. June did this, June did that, she saved money and helped clean the house and cooked and Connie couldn't do a thing, her mind was all filled with trashy daydreams. Their father was away at work most of the time and when he came home he wanted supper and he read the newspaper at supper and after supper he went to bed. He didn't bother talking much to them, but around his bent head Connie's mother kept picking at her until Connie wished her mother was dead and she herself was dead and it was all over. "She makes me want to throw up sometimes," she complained to her friends. She had a high, breathless, amused voice which made everything she said a little forced, whether it was sincere or not.

There was one good thing: June went places with girl friends of hers, girls who were just as plain and steady as she, and so when Connie wanted to do that her mother had no objections. The father of Connie's best girl friend drove the girls the three miles to town and left them off at a shopping plaza, so that they could walk through the stores or go to a movie, and when he came to pick them up again at eleven he never bothered to ask what they had done.

They must have been familiar sights, walking around that shopping plaza in their shorts and flat ballerina slippers that always scuffed the sidewalk, with charm

5

bracelets jingling on their thin wrists; they would lean together to whisper and laugh secretly if someone passed by who amused or interested them. Connie had long dark blond hair that drew anyone's eye to it, and she wore part of it pulled up on her head and puffed out and the rest of it she let fall down her back. She wore a pullover jersey blouse that looked one way when she was at home and another way when she was away from home. Everything about her had two sides to it, one for home and one for anywhere that was not home: her walk that could be childlike and bobbing, or languid enough to make anyone think she was hearing music in her head, her mouth which was pale and smirking most of the time, but bright and pink on these evenings out, her laugh which was cynical and drawling at home—"Ha, ha, very funny"—but high-pitched and nervous anywhere else, like the jingling of the charms on her bracelet.

Sometimes they did go shopping or to a movie, but sometimes they went across the highway, ducking fast across the busy road, to a drive-in restaurant where older kids hung out. The restaurant was shaped like a big bottle, though squatter than a real bottle, and on its cap was a revolving figure of a grinning boy who held a hamburger aloft. One night in midsummer they ran across, breathless with daring, and right away someone leaned out a car window and invited them over, but it was just a boy from high school they didn't like. It made them feel good to be able to ignore him. They went up through the maze of parked and cruising cars to the bright-lit, fly-infested restaurant, their faces pleased and expectant as if they were entering a sacred building that loomed out of the night to give them what haven and what blessing they yearned for. They sat at the counter and crossed their legs at the ankles, their thin shoulders rigid with excitement, and listened to the music that made everything so good: the music was always in the background like music at a church service, it was something to depend upon.

A boy named Eddie came in to talk with them. He sat backwards on his stool, turning himself jerkily around in semi-circles and then stopping and turning again, and after a while he asked Connie if she would like something to eat. She said she did and so she tapped her friend's arm on her way out—her friend pulled her face up into a brave droll look—and Connie said she would meet her at eleven, across the way. "I just hate to leave her like that," Connie said earnestly, but the boy said that she wouldn't be alone for long. So they went out to his car and on the way Connie couldn't help but let her eyes wander over the windshields and faces all around her, her face gleaming with the joy that had nothing to do with Eddie or even this place; it might have been the music. She drew her shoulders up and sucked in her breath with the pure pleasure of being alive, and just at that moment she happened to glance at a face just a few feet from hers. It was a boy with shaggy black hair, in a convertible jalopy painted gold. He stared at her and then his lips widened into a grin. Connie slit her eyes at him and turned away, but she couldn't help glancing back and there he was still watching her. He wagged a finger and laughed and said, "Gonna get you, baby," and Connie turned away again without Eddie noticing anything.

She spent three hours with him, at the restaurant where they ate hamburgers and drank Cokes in wax cups that were always sweating, and then down an alley a mile or so away, and when he left her off at five to eleven only the movie house was still open at the plaza. Her girl friend was there, talking with a boy. When Connie came up the two girls smiled at each other and Connie said, "How was the movie?" and the girl said, "*You* should know." They rode off with the girl's father, sleepy and pleased, and Connie couldn't help but look at the darkened shopping plaza with its big empty parking lot and its signs that were faded and ghostly now, and over at the drive-in restaurant where cars were still circling tirelessly. She couldn't hear the music at this distance.

Next morning June asked her how the movie was and Connie said, "So-so."

She and that girl and occasionally another girl went out several times a week   10 that way, and the rest of the time Connie spent around the house—it was summer vacation—getting in her mother's way and thinking, dreaming, about the boys she met. But all the boys fell back and dissolved into a single face that was not even a face, but an idea, a feeling, mixed up with the urgent insistent pounding of the music and the humid night air of July. Connie's mother kept dragging her back to the daylight by finding things for her to do or saying suddenly, "What's this about the Pettinger girl?"

And Connie would say nervously, "Oh, her. That dope." She always drew thick clear lines between herself and such girls, and her mother was simple and kindly enough to believe her. Her mother was so simple, Connie thought, that it was maybe cruel to fool her so much. Her mother went scuffling around the house in old bedroom slippers and complained over the telephone to one sister about the other, then the other called up and the two of them complained about the third one. If June's name was mentioned her mother's tone was approving, and if Connie's name was mentioned it was disapproving. This did not really mean she disliked Connie and actually Connie thought that her mother preferred her to June because she was prettier, but the two of them kept up a pretense of exasperation, a sense that they were tugging and struggling over something of little value to either of them. Sometimes, over coffee, they were almost friends, but something would come up—some vexation that was like a fly buzzing suddenly around their heads—and their faces went hard with contempt.

One Sunday Connie got up at eleven—none of them bothered with church—and washed her hair so that it could dry all day long, in the sun. Her parents and sister were going to a barbecue at an aunt's house and Connie said no, she wasn't interested, rolling her eyes, to let mother know just what she thought of it. "Stay home alone then," her mother said sharply. Connie sat out back in a lawn chair and watched them drive away, her father quiet and bald, hunched around so that he could back the car out, her mother with a look that was still angry and not at all softened through the windshield, and in the back seat poor old June all dressed up as if she didn't know what a barbecue was, with all the running yelling kids and the flies. Connie sat with her eyes closed in the sun, dreaming and dazed with the warmth about her as if this were a kind of love, the caresses of love, and her mind slipped over onto thoughts of the boy she had been with the night before and how nice he had been, how sweet it always was, not the way someone like June would suppose but sweet, gentle, the way it was in movies and promised in songs; and when she opened her eyes she hardly knew where she was, the back yard ran off into weeds and a fenceline of trees and behind it the sky was perfectly blue and still. The asbestos "ranch house" that was now three years old startled her—it looked small. She shook her head as if to get awake.

It was too hot. She went inside the house and turned on the radio to drown out the quiet. She sat on the edge of her bed, barefoot, and listened for an hour and a half to a program called XYZ Sunday Jamboree, record after record of hard, fast, shrieking songs she sang along with, interspersed by exclamations from "Bobby King": "An' look here you girls at Napoleon's—Son and Charley want you to pay real close attention to this song coming up!"

And Connie paid close attention herself, bathed in a glow of slow-pulsed joy that seemed to rise mysteriously out of the music itself and lay languidly about the airless little room, breathed in and breathed out with each gentle rise and fall of her chest.

After a while she heard a car coming up the drive. She sat up at once, startled, 15 because it couldn't be her father so soon. The gravel kept crunching all the way in from the road—the driveway was long—and Connie ran to the window. It was a car she didn't know. It was an open jalopy, painted a bright gold that caught the sun opaquely. Her heart began to pound and her fingers snatched at her hair, checking it, and she whispered "Christ. Christ," wondering how bad she looked. The car came to a stop at the side door and the horn sounded four short taps as if this were a signal Connie knew.

She went into the kitchen and approached the door slowly, then hung out the screen door, her bare toes curling down off the step. There were two boys in the car and now she recognized the driver: he had shaggy, shabby black hair that looked crazy as a wig and he was grinning at her.

"I ain't late, am I?" he said.

"Who the hell do you think you are?" Connie said.

"Toldja I'd be out, didn't I?"

"I don't even know who you are."   20

She spoke sullenly, careful to show no interest or pleasure, and he spoke in a fast bright monotone. Connie looked past him to the other boy, taking her time. He had fair brown hair, with a lock that fell onto his forehead. His sideburns gave him a fierce, embarrassed look, but so far he hadn't even bothered to glance at her. Both boys wore sunglasses. The driver's glasses were metallic and mirrored everything in miniature.

"You wanta come for a ride?" he said.

Connie smirked and let her hair fall loose over one shoulder.

"Don'tcha like my car? New paint job," he said. "Hey."

"What?"

"You're cute."   25

She pretended to fidget, chasing flies away from the door.

"Don'tcha believe me, or what?" he said.

"Look, I don't even know who you are," Connie said in disgust.

"Hey, Ellie's got a radio, see. Mine's broke down." He lifted his friend's arm and   30 showed her the little transistor the boy was holding, and now Connie began to hear the music. It was the same program that was playing inside the house.

"Bobby King?" she said.

"I listen to him all the time. I think he's great."

"He's kind of great," Connie said reluctantly.

"Listen, that guy's *great*. He knows where the action is."

Connie blushed a little, because the glasses made it impossible for her to see just   35
what this boy was looking at. She couldn't decide if she liked him or if he was just a
jerk, and so she dawdled in the doorway and wouldn't come down or go back inside.
She said, "What's all that stuff painted on your car?"

"Can'tcha read it?" He opened the door very carefully, as if he was afraid it might
fall off. He slid out just as carefully, planting his feet firmly on the ground, the tiny
metallic world in his glasses slowing down like gelatine hardening and in the midst
of it Connie's bright green blouse. "This here is my name, to begin with," he said.
ARNOLD FRIEND was written in tar-like black letters on the side, with a drawing of a
round grinning face that reminded Connie of a pumpkin, except it wore sunglasses.
"I wanta introduce myself, I'm Arnold Friend and that's my real name and I'm gonna
be your friend, honey, and inside the car's Ellie Oscar, he's kinda shy." Ellie brought
his transistor up to his shoulder and balanced it there. "Now these numbers are a
secret code, honey," Arnold Friend explained. He read off the numbers 33, 19, 17
and raised his eyebrows at her to see what she thought of that, but she didn't think
much of it. The left rear fender had been smashed and around it was written, on the
gleaming gold background: DONE BY CRAZY WOMAN DRIVER. Connie had to laugh at
that. Arnold Friend was pleased at her laughter and looked up at her. "Around the
other side's a lot more—you wanta come and see them?"

"No."

"Why not?"

"Why should I?"

"Don'tcha wanta see what's on the car? Don'tcha wanta go for a ride?"   40

"I don't know."

"Why not?"

"I got things to do."

"Like what?"

"Things."   45

He laughed as if she had said something funny. He slapped his thighs. He was
standing in a strange way, leaning back against the car as if he were balancing himself. He wasn't tall, only an inch or so taller than she would be if she came down to
him. Connie liked the way he was dressed, which was the way all of them dressed:
tight faded jeans stuffed into black, scuffed boots, a belt that pulled his waist in
and showed how lean he was, and a white pull-over shirt that was a little soiled and
showed the hard small muscles of his arms and shoulders. He looked as if he probably did hard work, lifting and carrying things. Even his neck looked muscular. And
his face was a familiar face, somehow: the jaw and chin and cheeks slightly darkened,
because he hadn't shaved for a day or two, and the nose long and hawk-like, sniffing
as if she were a treat he was going to gobble up and it was all a joke.

"Connie, you ain't telling the truth. This is your day set aside for a ride with me
and you know it," he said, still laughing. The way he straightened and recovered from
his fit of laughing showed that it had been all fake.

"How do you know what my name is?" she said suspiciously.

"It's Connie."

"Maybe and maybe not."

"I know my Connie," he said, wagging his finger. Now she remembered him even better, back at the restaurant, and her cheeks warmed at the thought of how she sucked in her breath just at the moment she passed him—how she must have looked to him. And he had remembered her. "Ellie and I come out here especially for you," he said. "Ellie can sit in back. How about it?"

"Where?"

"Where what?"

"Where're we going?"

He looked at her. He took off the sunglasses and she saw how pale the skin around his eyes was, like holes that were not in shadow but instead in light. His eyes were like chips of broken glass that catch the light in an amiable way. He smiled. It was as if the idea of going for a ride somewhere, to some place, was a new idea to him.

"Just for a ride, Connie sweetheart."

"I never said my name was Connie," she said.

"But I know what it is. I know your name and all about you, lots of things," Arnold Friend said. He had not moved yet but stood still leaning back against the side of his jalopy. "I took a special interest in you, such a pretty girl, and found out all about you like I know your parents and sister are gone somewheres and I know where and how long they're going to be gone, and I know who you were with last night, and your best friend's name is Betty. Right?"

He spoke in a simple lilting voice, exactly as if he were reciting the words to a song. His smile assured her that everything was fine. In the car Ellie turned up the volume on his radio and did not bother to look around at them.

"Ellie can sit in the back seat," Arnold Friend said. He indicated his friend with a casual jerk of his chin, as if Ellie did not count and she could not bother with him.

"How'd you find out all that stuff?" Connie said.

"Listen: Betty Schultz and Tony Fitch and Jimmy Pettinger and Nancy Pettinger," he said, in a chant. "Raymond Stanley and Bob Hutter—"

"Do you know all those kids?"

"I know everybody."

"Look, you're kidding. You're not from around here."

"Sure."

"But—how come we never saw you before?"

"Sure you saw me before," he said. He looked down at his boots, as if he were a little offended. "You just don't remember."

"I guess I'd remember you," Connie said.

"Yeah?" He looked up at this, beaming. He was pleased. He began to mark time with the music from Ellie's radio, tapping his fists lightly together. Connie looked away from his smile to the car, which was painted so bright it almost hurt her eyes to look at it. She looked at that name, ARNOLD FRIEND. And up at the front fender was an expression that was familiar—MAN THE FLYING SAUCERS. It was an expression kids had used the year before, but didn't use this year. She looked at it for a while as if the words meant something to her that she did not yet know.

"What're you thinking about? Huh?" Arnold Friend demanded. "Not worried about your hair blowing around in the car, are you?"

"No."

"Think I maybe can't drive good?"

"How do I know?"

"You're a hard girl to handle. How come?" he said. "Don't you know I'm your friend? Didn't you see me put my sign in the air when you walked by?"   75

"What sign?"

"My sign." And he drew an X in the air, leaning out toward her. They were maybe ten feet apart. After his hand fell back to his side the X was still in the air, almost visible. Connie let the screen door close and stood perfectly still inside it, listening to the music from her radio and the boy's blend together. She stared at Arnold Friend. He stood there so stiffly relaxed, pretending to be relaxed, with one hand idly on the door handle as if he were keeping himself up that way and had no intention of ever moving again. She recognized most things about him, the tight jeans that showed his thighs and buttocks and the greasy leather boots and the tight shirt, and even that slippery friendly smile of his, that sleepy dreamy smile that all the boys used to get across ideas they didn't want to put into words. She recognized all this and also the singsong way he talked, slightly mocking, kidding, but serious and a little melancholy, and she recognized the way he tapped one fist against the other in homage to the perpetual music behind him. But all these things did not come together.

She said suddenly, "Hey, how old are you?"

His smile faded. She could see then that he wasn't a kid, he was much older— thirty, maybe more. At this knowledge her heart began to pound faster.

"That's a crazy thing to ask. Can'tcha see I'm your own age?"   80

"Like hell you are."

"Or maybe a coupla years older, I'm eighteen."

"Eighteen?" she said doubtfully.

He grinned to reassure her and lines appeared at the corners of his mouth. His teeth were big and white. He grinned so broadly his eyes became slits and she saw how thick the lashes were, thick and black as if painted with a black tar-like material. Then he seemed to become embarrassed, abruptly, and looked over his shoulder at Ellie. "*Him*, he's crazy," he said. "Ain't he a riot, he's a nut, a real character." Ellie was still listening to the music. His sunglasses told nothing about what he was thinking. He wore a bright orange shirt unbuttoned halfway to show his chest, which was a pale, bluish chest and not muscular like Arnold Friend's. His shirt collar was turned up all around and the very tips of the collar pointed out past his chin as if they were protecting him. He was pressing the transistor radio up against his ear and sat there in a kind of daze, right in the sun.

"He's kinda strange," Connie said.   85

"Hey, she says you're kinda strange! Kinda strange!" Arnold Friend cried. He pounded on the car to get Ellie's attention. Ellie turned for the first time and Connie saw with shock that he wasn't a kid either—he had a fair, hairless face, cheeks reddened slightly as if the veins grew too close to the surface of his skin, the face of a forty-year-old baby. Connie felt a wave of dizziness rise in her at this sight and she stared at him as if waiting for something to change the shock of the moment, make it all right again. Ellie's lips kept shaping words, mumbling along with the words blasting his ear.

"Maybe you two better go away," Connie said faintly.

"What? How come?" Arnold Friend cried. "We come out here to take you for a ride. It's Sunday." He had the voice of the man on the radio now. It was the same voice, Connie thought. "Don'tcha know it's Sunday all day and honey, no matter who you were with last night today you're with Arnold Friend and don't you forget it!—Maybe you better step out here," he said, and this last was in a different voice. It was a little flatter, as if the heat was finally getting to him.

"No. I got things to do."

"Hey." 90

"You two better leave."

"We ain't leaving until you come with us."

"Like hell I am—"

"Connie, don't fool around with me. I mean—I mean, don't fool *around*," he said, shaking his head. He laughed incredulously. He placed his sunglasses on top of his head, carefully, as if he were indeed wearing a wig, and brought the stems down behind his ears. Connie stared at him, another wave of dizziness and fear rising in her so that for a moment he wasn't even in focus but was just a blur, standing there against his gold car, and she had the idea that he had driven up the driveway all right but had come from nowhere before that and belonged nowhere and that everything about him and even the music that was so familiar to her was only half real.

"If my father comes and sees you—" 95

"He ain't coming. He's at a barbecue."

"How do you know that?"

"Aunt Tillie's. Right now they're—uh—they're drinking. Sitting around," he said vaguely, squinting as if he were staring all the way to town and over to Aunt Tillie's back yard. Then the vision seemed to clear and he nodded energetically. "Yeah. Sitting around. There's your sister in a blue dress, huh? And high heels, the poor sad bitch—nothing like you, sweetheart! And your mother's helping some fat woman with the corn, they're cleaning the corn—husking the corn—"

"What fat woman?" Connie cried.

"How do I know what fat woman. I don't know every goddamn fat woman in 100 the world!" Arnold Friend laughed.

"Oh, that's Mrs. Hornby.... Who invited her?" Connie said. She felt a little lightheaded. Her breath was coming quickly.

"She's too fat. I don't like them fat. I like them the way you are, honey," he said, smiling sleepily at her. They stared at each other for a while, through the screen door. He said softly, "Now what you're going to do is this: you're going to come out that door. You're going to sit up front with me and Ellie's going to sit in the back, the hell with Ellie, right? This isn't Ellie's date. You're my date. I'm your lover, honey."

"What? You're crazy—"

"Yes, I'm your lover. You don't know what that is but you will," he said. "I know that too. I know all about you. But look: it's real nice and you couldn't ask for nobody better than me, or more polite. I always keep my word. I'll tell you how it is, I'm always nice at first, the first time. I'll hold you so tight you won't think you have to try to get away or pretend anything because you'll know you can't. And I'll come inside you where it's all secret and you'll give in to me and you'll love me—"

"Shut up! You're crazy!" Connie said. She backed away from the door. She 105 put her hands against her ears as if she'd heard something terrible, something not meant for her. "People don't talk like that, you're crazy," she muttered. Her heart was almost too big now for her chest and its pumping made sweat break out all over her. She looked out to see Arnold Friend pause and then take a step toward the porch lurching. He almost fell. But, like a clever drunken man, he managed to catch his balance. He wobbled in his high boots and grabbed hold of one of the porch posts.

"Honey?" he said. "You still listening?"

"Get the hell out of here!"

"Be nice, honey. Listen."

"I'm going to call the police—"

He wobbled again and out of the side of his mouth came a fast spat curse, an 110 aside not meant for her to hear. But even this "Christ!" sounded forced. Then he began to smile again. She watched this smile come, awkward as if he were smiling from inside a mask. His whole face was a mask, she thought wildly, tanned down onto his throat but then running out as if he had plastered make-up on his face but had forgotten about his throat.

"Honey—? Listen, here's how it is. I always tell the truth and I promise you this: I ain't coming in that house after you."

"You better not! I'm going to call the police if you—if you don't—"

"Honey," he said, talking right through her voice, "honey, I'm not coming in there but you are coming out here. You know why?"

She was panting. The kitchen looked like a place she had never seen before, some room she had run inside but which wasn't good enough, wasn't going to help her. The kitchen window had never had a curtain, after three years, and there were dishes in the sink for her to do—probably—and if you ran your hand across the table you'd probably feel something sticky there.

"You listening, honey? Hey?" 115

"—going to call the police—"

"Soon as you touch the phone I don't need to keep my promise and can come inside. You won't want that."

She rushed forward and tried to lock the door. Her fingers were shaking. "But why lock it," Arnold Friend said gently, talking right into her face. "It's just a screen door. It's just nothing." One of his boots was at a strange angle, as if his foot wasn't in it. It pointed out to the left, bent at the ankle. "I mean, anybody can break through a screen door and glass and wood and iron or anything else if he needs to, anybody at all and specially Arnold Friend. If the place got lit up with a fire, honey, you'd come runnin' out into my arms, right into my arms an' safe at home— like you knew I was your lover and'd stopped fooling around, I don't mind a nice shy girl but I don't like no fooling around." Part of those words were spoken with a slight rhythmic lilt, and Connie somehow recognized them—the echo of a song from last year, about a girl rushing into her boy friend's arms and coming home again—

Connie stood barefoot on the linoleum floor, staring at him. "What do you want?" she whispered.

"I want you," he said. 120

"What?"

"Seen you that night and thought, that's the one, yes sir. I never needed to look any more."

"But my father's coming back. He's coming to get me. I had to wash my hair first—" She spoke in a dry, rapid voice, hardly raising it for him to hear.

"No, your daddy is not coming and yes, you had to wash your hair and you washed it for me. It's nice and shining and all for me. I thank you, sweetheart," he said, with a mock bow, but again he almost lost his balance. He had to bend and adjust his boots. Evidently his feet did not go all the way down; the boots must have been stuffed with something so that he would seem taller. Connie stared out at him and behind him at Ellie in the car, who seemed to be looking off toward Connie's right, into nothing. Then Ellie said, pulling the words out of the air one after another as if he were just discovering them, "You want me to pull out the phone?"

"Shut your mouth and keep it shut," Arnold Friend said, his face red from bend- 125 ing over or maybe from embarrassment because Connie had seen his boots. "This ain't none of your business."

"What—what are you doing? What do you want?" Connie said. "If I call the police they'll get you, they'll arrest you—"

"Promise was not to come in unless you touch that phone, and I'll keep that promise," he said. He resumed his erect position and tried to force his shoulders back. He sounded like a hero in a movie, declaring something important. He spoke too loudly and it was as if he were speaking to someone behind Connie. "I ain't made plans for coming in that house where I don't belong but just for you to come out to me, the way you should. Don't you know who I am?"

"You're crazy," she whispered. She backed away from the door but did not want to go into another part of the house, as if this would give him permission to come through the door. "What do you . . . You're crazy, you . . ."

"Huh? What're you saying, honey?"

Her eyes darted everywhere in the kitchen. She could not remember what it was, 130 this room.

"This is how it is, honey: you come out and we'll drive away, have a nice ride. But if you don't come out we're gonna wait till your people come home and then they're all going to get it."

"You want that telephone pulled out?" Ellie said. He held the radio away from his ear and grimaced, as if without the radio the air was too much for him.

"I toldja shut up, Ellie," Arnold Friend said, "you're deaf, get a hearing aid, right? Fix yourself up. This little girl's no trouble and's gonna be nice to me, so Ellie keep to yourself, this ain't your date—right? Don't hem in on me, don't hog, don't crush, don't bird dog, don't trail me," he said in a rapid, meaningless voice, as if he were running through all the expressions he'd learned but was no longer sure which one of them was in style, then rushing on to new ones, making them up with his eyes closed. "Don't crawl under my fence, don't squeeze in my chipmunk hole, don't sniff my glue, suck my popsicle, keep your own greasy fingers on yourself!" He shaded his eyes and peered in at Connie, who was backed against the kitchen table. "Don't mind him, honey, he's just a creep. He's a dope. Right? I'm the boy for you and like I said, you come out here nice like a lady and give me your hand, and nobody else gets hurt, I mean, your nice old bald-headed daddy and your mummy and your sister in her high heels. Because listen: why bring them in this?"

"Leave me alone," Connie whispered.

"Hey, you know that old woman down the road, the one with the chickens and   135
stuff—you know her?"

"She's dead!"

"Dead? What? You know her?" Arnold Friend said.

"She's dead—"

"Don't you like her?"

"She's dead—she's—she isn't here any more—"   140

"But don't you like her, I mean, you got something against her? Some grudge or something?" Then his voice dipped as if he were conscious of rudeness. He touched the sunglasses on top of his head as if to make sure they were still there. "Now you be a good girl."

"What are you going to do?"

"Just two things, or maybe three," Arnold Friend said. "But I promise it won't last long and you'll like me that way you get to like people you're close to. You will. It's all over for you here, so come on out. You don't want your people in any trouble, do you?"

She turned and bumped against a chair or something, hurting her leg, but she ran into the back room and picked up the telephone. Something roared in her ear, a tiny roaring, and she was so sick with fear that she could do nothing but listen to it—the telephone was clammy and very heavy and her fingers groped down to the dial but were too weak to touch it. She began to scream into the phone, into the roaring. She cried out, she cried for her mother, she felt her breath start jerking back and forth in her lungs as if it were something Arnold Friend was stabbing her with again and again with no tenderness. A noisy sorrowful wailing rose all about her and she was locked inside it the way she was locked inside this house.

After a while she could hear again. She was sitting on the floor, with her wet back 145
against the wall.

Arnold Friend was saying from the door, "That's a good girl. Put the phone
back."

She kicked the phone away from her.

"No, honey. Pick it up. Put it back right."

She picked it up and put it back. The dial tone stopped.

"That's a good girl. Now you come outside." 150

She was hollow with what had been fear but what was now just an emptiness.
All that screaming had blasted it out of her. She sat, one leg cramped under her,
and deep inside her brain was something like a pinpoint of light that kept going
and would not let her relax. She thought, I'm not going to see my mother again.
She thought, I'm not going to sleep in my bed again. Her bright green blouse was
all wet.

Arnold Friend said, in a gentle-loud voice that was like a stage voice, "The place
where you came from ain't there any more, and where you had in mind to go is
cancelled out. This place you are now—inside your daddy's house—is nothing but
a cardboard box I can knock down any time. You know that and always did know it.
You hear me?"

She thought, I have got to think. I have got to know what to do.

"We'll go out to a nice field, out in the country here where it smells so nice and
it's sunny," Arnold Friend said. "I'll have my arms tight around you so you won't
need to try to get away and I'll show you what love is like, what it does. The hell with
this house! It looks solid all right," he said. He ran a fingernail down the screen and
the noise did not make Connie shiver, as it would have the day before. "Now put
your hand on your heart, honey. Feel that? That feels solid too but we know better.
Be nice to me, be sweet like you can because what else is there for a girl like you but
to be sweet and pretty and give in?—and get away before her people get back?"

She felt her pounding heart. Her hand seemed to enclose it. She thought for the 155
first time in her life that it was nothing that was hers, that belonged to her, but just a
pounding, living thing inside this body that wasn't really hers either.

"You don't want them to get hurt," Arnold Friend went on. "Now get up, honey.
Get up all by yourself."

She stood.

"Now turn this way. That's right. Come over to me—Ellie, put that away,
didn't I tell you? You dope. You miserable creepy dope," Arnold Friend said. His
words were not angry but only part of an incantation. The incantation was kindly.
"Now come out through the kitchen to me honey and let's see a smile, try it, you're
a brave sweet little girl and now they're eating corn and hotdogs cooked to bursting over an outdoor fire, and they don't know one thing about you and never did
and honey you're better than them because not a one of them would have done
this for you."

Connie felt the linoleum under her feet; it was cool. She brushed her hair back
out of her eyes. Arnold Friend let go of the post tentatively and opened his arms for

her, his elbows pointing in toward each other and his wrists limp, to show that this was an embarrassed embrace and a little mocking, he didn't want to make her self-conscious.

She put out her hand against the screen. She watched herself push the door   160
slowly open as if she were back safe somewhere in the other doorway, watching this body and this head of long hair moving out into the sunlight where Arnold Friend waited.

"My sweet little blue-eyed girl," he said in a half-sung sigh that had nothing to do with her brown eyes but was taken up just the same by the vast sunlit reaches of the land behind him and on all sides of him — so much land that Connie had never seen before and did not recognize except to know that she was going to it.

[1966]

Exploring the Text

1. Explain why you think Connie is or is not a typical teenage girl, as Oates depicts her early in the story. Which of her qualities strike you as specific to an earlier time period, and which seem more characteristic of teenagers in general? How is Connie distancing herself from her family and her perception of their values? Pay particular attention to the contrasts Oates draws in paragraph 5.

2. What part does June play in Connie's characterization? What elements of Connie's character and struggle to construct an identity independent of her family does June's presence emphasize?

3. How is Arnold Friend characterized by the external descriptions Oates provides of his physical features and his clothes? What does his dialogue add? Is he a three-dimensional character or a stereotypical one? Examine the passage where Connie first sees him (para. 7). Why is she drawn to Arnold Friend?

4. How is music used throughout the story, especially to develop character and setting? Why is music so important to Connie? What does Oates mean when she writes in paragraph 94 that "even the music that was so familiar to her [Connie] was only half real"? Why does Oates describe Arnold as having "the voice of the man on the radio now" (para. 88)? What is the significance of Connie's later recognition that Arnold spoke "with a slight rhythmic lilt, . . . [his words] the echo of a song from last year" (para. 118)?

5. What does Arnold Friend mean when he tells Connie, "The place where you came from ain't there any more, and where you had in mind to go is cancelled out" (para. 152)? What does *place* mean in this context, and how is Connie's identity destined by it?

6. Suspense builds throughout this story. How does Oates generate and control that suspense? At which points does the suspense increase with particular intensity?

7. How does Oates convey the mounting fear Connie feels in the last pages of the story? Note the ways in which she shifts from Connie being the agent of her own actions to Connie being just an observer, such as, "She watched herself push the door slowly open" (para. 160). By the end, is Connie acting out of concern for her family or blind fear? What or who is controlling her actions?

8. Oates does not provide closure in this story. Why? Does the indeterminate ending add to or diminish the story's power?

9. Oates has called this story "a realistic allegory." What does that description mean? What allegorical elements do you see in the story?

10. Oates says she based her story on three Tucson, Arizona, murders committed by Charles Schmid, "the Pied Piper of Tucson," in the 1960s. Research this incident and explore how the facts match the fiction. How does this link to an actual incident influence your reading of the story?

11. Oates dedicates the story to Bob Dylan and says she was inspired by his song "It's All Over Now, Baby Blue." Listen to the song, paying special attention to the lyrics. Why do you think Oates found this song compelling?

In Cuba I Was a German Shepherd

Ana Menéndez

Born in 1970 to parents who left their native Cuba in 1964, Ana Menéndez grew up in Los Angeles. She spoke only Spanish until she began school, and grew up with the expectation that the family would return to Cuba once Fidel Castro lost power. Castro never lost power, so they moved to Tampa, Florida, instead. She received a BA from Florida International University and an MFA from New York University before working as a journalist covering the neighborhood of Little Havana. *In Cuba I Was a German Shepherd*, a collection of short stories that she began in graduate school, won the Pushcart Prize for Short Fiction and was chosen as a *New York Times* Notable Book of the Year in 2001. In 2003, Menéndez published her first novel, *Loving Che*, which takes its title from the legendary revolutionary Che Guevara. In 2008, Menéndez left the *Miami Herald* to accept a Fulbright grant to teach at the American University in Cairo. Her latest novel is *The Last War* (2009). The following is the title story from her short-story collection — a study of the consequences of migration and exile, and the tension between authentic culture and its commercial appropriation.

The park where the four men gathered was small. Before the city put it on the tourist maps, it was just a fenced rectangle of space that people missed on the way to their office jobs. The men came each morning to sit under the shifting shade of a banyan tree, and sometimes the way the wind moved through the leaves reminded them of home.

One man carried a box of plastic dominoes. His name was Máximo, and because he was a small man, his grandiose name had inspired much amusement all his life. He liked to say that over the years he'd learned a thing or two about the "physics of laughter," and his friends took that to mean good humor could make a big man out of anyone. Now, Máximo waited for the others to sit before turning the dominoes out on the table. Judging the men to be in good spirits, he cleared his throat and began to tell the joke he had prepared for the day.

"So Bill Clinton dies in office and they freeze his body."

Antonio leaned back in his chair and let out a sigh. "Here we go."

Máximo caught a roll of the eyes and almost grew annoyed. But he smiled. "It gets better."   5

He scraped the dominoes in two wide circles across the table, then continued.

"Okay, so they freeze his body and when we get the technology to unfreeze him, he wakes up in the year 2105."

"Two thousand one hundred and five, eh?"

"Very good," Máximo said. "Anyway, he's curious about what's happened to the world all this time, so he goes up to a Jewish fellow and he asks, 'So, how are things in the Middle East?' The guy replies, 'Oh wonderful, wonderful, everything is like heaven. Everybody gets along now.' This makes Clinton smile, right?"

The men stopped their shuffling and dragged their pieces across the table and waited for Máximo to finish.   10

"Next he goes up to an Irishman and he asks, 'So how are things over there in Northern Ireland now?' The guy says, 'Northern? It's one Ireland now and we all live in peace.' Clinton is extremely pleased at this point, right? So he does that biting thing with his lip."

Máximo stopped to demonstrate, and Raúl and Carlos slapped their hands on the domino table and laughed. Máximo paused. Even Antonio had to smile. Máximo loved this moment when the men were warming to the joke and he still kept the punch line close to himself like a secret.

"So, okay," Máximo continued, "Clinton goes up to a Cuban fellow and says, 'Compadre, how are things in Cuba these days?' The guy looks at Clinton and he says to the president, 'Let me tell you, my friend, I can feel it in my bones, any day now Castro's gonna fall.'"

Máximo tucked his head into his neck and smiled. Carlos slapped him on the back and laughed.

"That's a good one, sure is," he said. "I like that one."   15

"Funny," Antonio said, nodding as he set up his pieces.

"Yes, funny," Raúl said. After chuckling for another moment, he added, "But old."

"What do you mean old?" Antonio said, then he turned to Carlos. "What are you looking at?"

Carlos stopped laughing.

"It's not old," Máximo said. "I just made it up."   20

"I'm telling you, professor, it's an old one," Raúl said. "I heard it when Reagan was president."

Máximo looked at Raúl, but didn't say anything. He pulled the double nine from his row and laid it in the middle of the table, but the thud he intended was lost in the horns and curses of morning traffic on Eighth Street.

Raúl and Máximo had lived on the same El Vedado street in Havana for fifteen years before the revolution. Raúl had been a government accountant and Máximo a professor at the university, two blocks from his home on L Street. They weren't close friends, but friendly still, in that way of people who come from the same place and think they already know the important things about one another.

Máximo was one of the first to leave L Street, boarding a plane for Miami on the eve of January 1, 1960, exactly one year after Batista[1] had done the same. For reasons he told himself he could no longer remember, he said good-bye to no one. He was forty-two years old then, already balding, with a wife and two young daughters whose names he tended to confuse. He left behind the row house of long shiny windows, the piano, the mahogany furniture, and the pension he thought he'd return to in two years' time. Three, if things were as serious as they said.

In Miami, Máximo tried driving a taxi, but the streets were still a web of foreign names and winding curves that could one day lead to glitter and another to the hollow end of a pistol. His Spanish and his Havana University credentials meant nothing here. And he was too old to cut sugarcane with the younger men who began arriving in the spring of 1961. But the men gave Máximo an idea, and after teary nights of promises, he convinced his wife—she of stately homes and multiple cooks—to make lunch to sell to those sugar men who waited, squatting on their heels in the dark, for the bus to Belle Glade every morning. They worked side by side, Máximo and Rosa. And at the end of every day, their hands stained orange from the lard and the cheap meat, their knuckles red and tender where the hot water and the knife blade had worked their business, Máximo and Rosa would sit down to whatever remained of the day's cooking, and they would chew slowly, the day unraveling, their hunger ebbing with the light.

They worked together for seven years like that, and when the Cubans began disappearing from the bus line, Máximo and Rosa moved their lunch packets indoors and opened their little restaurant right on Eighth Street. There, a generation of former professors served black beans and rice to the nostalgic. When Raúl showed up in Miami in the summer of 1971 looking for work, Máximo added one more waiter's spot for his old acquaintance from L Street. Each night, after the customers had gone, Máximo and Rosa and Raúl and Havana's old lawyers and bankers and dreamers would sit around the biggest table and eat and talk, and sometimes, late in the night after several glasses of wine, someone would start the stories that began with "In Cuba I remember . . ." They were stories of old lovers, beautiful and round-hipped. Of skies that stretched on clear and blue to the Cuban hills. Of green landscapes that clung to the red clay of Güines, roots dug in

25

---

[1]Fulgencio Batista y Zaldívar, general and leader of Cuba from 1940–1944 and from 1952–1959. His dictatorship was toppled by Fidel Castro and the Cuban Revolution.—Eds.

like fingernails in a good-bye. In Cuba, the stories always began, life was good and pure. But something always happened to them in the end, something withering, malignant. Máximo never understood it. The stories that opened in the sun, always narrowed into a dark place. And after those nights, his head throbbing, Máximo would turn and turn in his sleep and awake unable to remember his dreams.

Even now, ten years after selling the place, Máximo couldn't walk by it in the early morning when it was still clean and empty. He'd tried it once. He'd stood and stared into the restaurant and had become lost and dizzy in his own reflection in the glass, the neat row of chairs, the tombstone lunch board behind them.

"Okay. A bunch of rafters are on the beach getting ready to sail off to Miami."

"Where are they?"

"Who cares? Wherever. Cuba's got a thousand miles of coastline. Use your   30
imagination."

"Let the professor tell his thing, for god's sake."

"Thank you." Máximo cleared his throat and shuffled the dominoes. "So anyway, a bunch of rafters are gathered there on the sand. And they're all crying and hugging their wives and all the rafts are bobbing on the water and suddenly someone in the group yells, 'Hey! Look who goes there!' And it's Fidel in swimming trunks, carrying a raft on his back."

Carlos interrupted to let out a yelping laugh. "I like that, I like it, sure do."

"You like it, eh?" said Antonio. "Why don't you let the Cuban finish it."

Máximo slid the pieces to himself in twos and continued. "So one of the guys on the   35
sand says to Fidel, 'Compatriota, what are you doing here? What's with the raft?' And Fidel sits on his raft and pushes off the shore and says, 'I'm sick of this place, too. I'm going to Miami.' So the other guys look at each other and say, 'Coño, compadre, if you're leaving, then there's no reason for us to go. Here, take my raft too, and get . . . out of here.'"

Raúl let a shaking laugh rise from his belly and saluted Máximo with a domino piece.

"A good one, my friend."

Carlos laughed long and loud. Antonio laughed, too, but he was careful to not laugh too hard, and he gave his friend a sharp look over the racket he was causing. He and Carlos were Dominican, not Cuban, and they ate their same foods and played their same games, but Antonio knew they still didn't understand all the layers of hurt in the Cubans' jokes.

It had been Raúl's idea to go down to Domino Park that first time. Máximo protested. He had seen the rows of tourists pressed up against the fence, gawking at the colorful old guys playing dominoes.

"I'm not going to be the sad spectacle in someone's vacation slide show," he'd said.   40

But Raúl was already dressed up in a pale blue guayabera,[2] saying how it was a beautiful day and to smell the air.

---

[2]Classic Latin American shirt that includes two or four front pockets and vertical pleating or embroidery. — EDS.

"Let them take pictures," Raúl said. "What the hell. Make us immortal."

"Immortal," Máximo said with a sneer. And then to himself, *The gods' punishment*.

It was that year after Rosa died, and Máximo didn't want to tell how he'd begun to see her at the kitchen table as she'd been at twenty-five. Watched one thick strand of her dark hair stuck to her morning face. He saw her at thirty, bending down to wipe the chocolate off the cheeks of their two small daughters. And his eyes moved from Rosa to his small daughters. He had something he needed to tell them. He saw them grown up, at the funeral, crying together. He watched Rosa rise and do the sign of the cross. He knew he was caught inside a nightmare, but he couldn't stop. He would emerge slowly, creaking out of the shower and there she'd be, Rosa, like before, her breasts round and pink from the hot water, calling back through the years. Some mornings he would awake and smell peanuts roasting and hear the faint call of the *manicero*[3] pleading for someone to relieve his burden of white paper cones. Or it would be thundering, the long hard thunder of Miami that was so much like the thunder of home that each rumble shattered the morning of his other life. He would awake, caught fast in the damp sheets, and feel himself falling backwards.

He took the number eight bus to Eighth Street and Fifteenth Avenue. At Domino Park, he sat with Raúl and they played alone that first day, Máximo noticing his own speckled hands, the spots of light through the banyan leaves, a round red beetle that crawled slowly across the table, then hopped the next breeze and floated away.

45

Antonio and Carlos were not Cuban, but they knew when to dump their heavy pieces and when to hold back the eights for the final shocking stroke. Waiting for a table, Raúl and Máximo would linger beside them and watch them lay their traps, a succession of threes that broke their opponents, an incredible run of fives. Even the unthinkable: passing when they had the piece to play.

Other twosomes began to refuse to play with the Dominicans, said that Carlos guy gave them the creeps with his giggling and monosyllables. Besides, any team that won so often must be cheating, went the charge, especially a team one-half imbecile. But really it was that no one plays to lose. You begin to lose again and again and it reminds you of other things in your life, the despair of it all begins to bleed through and that is not what games are for. Who wants to live their whole life alongside the lucky? But Máximo and Raúl liked these blessed Dominicans, appreciated the well-oiled moves of two old pros. And if the two Dominicans, afraid to be alone again, let them win now and then, who would know, who could ever admit to such a thing?

For many months they didn't know much about each other, these four men. Even the smallest boy knew not to talk when the pieces were in play. But soon came Máximo's jokes during the shuffling, something new and bright coming into his eyes like daydreams as he spoke. Carlos's full loud laughter, like that of children. And the four men learned to linger long enough between sets to color an old memory while the white pieces scraped along the table.

One day as they sat at their table, closest to the sidewalk, a pretty girl walked by. She swung her long brown hair around and looked in at the men with her green eyes.

---

[3]Peanut seller. — EDS.

"What the hell is she looking at," said Antonio, who always sat with his back to   50
the wall, looking out at the street. But the others saw how he stared back, too.

Carlos let out a giggle and immediately put a hand to his mouth.

"In Santo Domingo, a man once looked at—" but Carlos didn't get to finish.

"Shut up you old idiot," said Antonio, putting his hands on the table like he was
about to get up and leave.

"Please," Máximo said.

The girl stared another moment, then turned and left.   55

Raúl rose slowly, flattening down his oiled hair with his right hand.

"Ay, mi niña."

"Sit down, hombre," Antonio said. "You're an old fool, just like this one."

"You're the fool," Raúl called back. "A woman like that . . ."

He watched the girl cross the street. When she was out of sight, he grabbed the   60
back of the chair behind him and eased his body down, his eyes still on the street.
The other three men looked at one another.

"I knew a woman like that once," Raúl said, after a long moment.

"That's right, he did," Antonio said, "in his moist boy dreams—what was it?
A century ago?"

"No me jodas,"[4] Raúl said. "You are a vulgar man. I had a life all three of you
would have paid millions for. Women."

Máximo watched him, then lowered his face, shuffled the dominoes.

"I had women," Raúl said.   65

"We all had women," Carlos said, and he looked like he was about to laugh again,
but instead just sat there, smiling like he was remembering one of Máximo's jokes.

"There was one I remember. More beautiful than the rising moon," Raúl said.

"Oh Jesus," Antonio said. "You people."

Máximo looked up, watching Raúl.

"Ay, a woman like that," Raúl said and shook his head. "The women of Cuba   70
were radiant, magnificent, wouldn't you say, professor?"

Máximo looked away.

"I don't know," Antonio said. "I think that Americana there looked better than
anything you remember."

And that brought a long laugh from Carlos.

Máximo sat all night at the pine table in his new efficiency, thinking about the green-
eyed girl and wondering why he was thinking about her. The table and a narrow bed
had come with the apartment, which he'd moved into after selling the house in
Shenandoah. The table had come with two chairs, sturdy and polished—not in the least
institutional—but he had put one of the chairs by the bed. The landlady, a woman in her
forties, had helped Máximo haul up three potted palms. Later, he bought a green pot of
marigolds that he saw in the supermarket and brought its butter leaves back to life under
the window's eastern light. Máximo often sat at the table through the night, sometimes
reading Martí, sometimes listening to the rain on the tin hull of the air conditioner.

---

[4]Don't mess with me.—EDS.

When you are older, he'd read somewhere, you don't need as much sleep. And
wasn't that funny, because his days felt more like sleep than ever. Dinner kept him
occupied for hours, remembering the story of each dish. Sometimes, at the table, he
greeted old friends and awakened with a start when they reached out to touch him.
When dawn rose and slunk into the room sideways through the blinds, Máximo
walked as in a dream across the thin patterns of light on the terrazzo.

The chair, why did he keep the other chair? Even the marigolds reminded him.
An image returned again and again. Was it the green-eyed girl?

And then he remembered that Rosa wore carnations in her hair and hated her
name. And that it saddened him because he liked to roll it off his tongue like a slow
train to the country.

"Rosa," he said, taking her hand the night they met at the La Concha while an
old *danzón*[5] played.

"Clavel," she said, tossing her head back in a crackling laugh. "Call me Clavel." She
pulled her hand away and laughed again. "Don't you notice the flower in a girl's hair?"

He led her around the dance floor lined with chaperones, and when they turned
he whispered that he wanted to follow her laughter to the moon.

She laughed again, the notes round and heavy as summer raindrops, and
Máximo felt his fingers go cold where they touched hers. The *danzón* played, and
they turned and turned, and the faces of the chaperones and the moist warm air—
and Máximo with his cold fingers worried that she had laughed at him. He was
twenty-four and could not imagine a more sorrowful thing in all the world.

Sometimes, years later, he would catch a premonition of Rosa in the face of his
eldest daughter. She would turn toward a window or do something with her eyes.
And then she would smile and tilt her head back, and her laughter connected him
again to that night, made him believe for a moment that life was a string you could
gather up in your hands all at once.

He sat at the table and tried to remember the last time he saw Marisa. In
California now. An important lawyer. A year? Two? Anabel, gone to New York. Two
years? They called more often than most children, Máximo knew. They called often
and he was lucky that way.

"Fidel decides he needs to get in touch with young people."

"Ay ay ay."

"So his handlers arrange for him to go to a school in Havana. He gets all dressed
up in his olive uniform, you know, puts conditioner on his beard and brushes it one
hundred times, all that."

Raúl breathed out, letting each breath come out like a puff of laughter. "Where
do you get these things?"

"No interrupting the artist anymore, okay?" Máximo continued. "So after he's
beautiful enough, he goes to the school. He sits in on a few classes, walks around the
halls. Finally, it's time for Fidel to leave and he realizes he hasn't talked to anyone. He
rushes over to the assembly that is seeing him off with shouts of 'Comandante!' and

---

[5]Style of music that accompanied formal Cuban ballroom dancing.—Eds.

he pulls a little boy out of a row. 'Tell me,' Fidel says, 'what is your name?' 'Pepito,' the little boy answers. 'Pepito, what a nice name,' Fidel says. 'And tell me, Pepito, what do you think of the Revolution?' 'Comandante,' Pepito says, 'the Revolution is the reason we are all here.' 'Ah, very good Pepito. And tell me, what is your favorite subject?' Pepito answers, 'Comandante, my favorite subject is mathematics.' Fidel pats the little boy on the head. 'And tell me, Pepito, what would you like to be when you grow up?' Pepito smiles and says, 'Comandante, I would like to be a tourist.'"

Máximo looked around the table, a shadow of a smile on his thin white lips as he waited for the laughter.

"Ay," Raúl said. "That's so funny it breaks my heart."   90

Máximo grew to like dominoes, the way each piece became part of the next. After the last piece was laid down and they were tallying up the score, Máximo liked to look over the table like an art critic. He liked the way the row of black dots snaked around the table with such free-flowing abandon it was almost as if, thrilled to be let out of the box, the pieces choreographed a fresh dance of gratitude every day. He liked the straightforward contrast of black on white. The clean, fresh scrape of the pieces across the table before each new round. The audacity of the double nines. The plain smooth face of the blank, like a newborn unetched by the world to come.

"Professor," Raúl began, "let's speed up the shuffling a bit, sí?"

"I was thinking," Máximo said.

"Well, that shouldn't take long," Antonio said.

"Who invented dominoes, anyway?" Máximo said.   95

"I'd say it was probably the Chinese," Antonio said.

"No jodas," Raúl said. "Who else could have invented this game of skill and intelligence but a Cuban."

"Coño," said Antonio without a smile. "Here we go again."

"Ah, bueno," Raúl said with a smile, stuck between joking and condescending. "You don't have to believe it if it hurts."

Carlos let out a long laugh.   100

"You people are unbelievable," said Antonio. But there was something hard and tired behind the way he smiled.

It was the first day of December, but summer still hung about in the brightest patches of sunlight. The four men sat under the shade of the banyan tree. It wasn't cold, not even in the shade, but three of the men wore cardigans. If asked, they would say they were expecting a chilly north wind and doesn't anybody listen to the weather forecasts anymore. Only Antonio, his round body enough to keep him warm, clung to the short sleeves of summer.

Kids from the local Catholic high school had volunteered to decorate the park for Christmas, and they dashed about with tinsel in their hair, bumping one another and laughing loudly. Lucinda, the woman who issued the dominoes and kept back the gambling, asked them to quiet down, pointing at the men. A wind stirred the top branches of the banyan tree and moved on without touching the ground. One leaf fell to the table.

Antonio waited for Máximo to fetch Lucinda's box of plastic pieces. Antonio held his brown paper bag to his chest and looked at the Cubans, his customary sourness replaced for a moment by what in a man like him could pass for levity. Máximo sat down and began to dump the plastic pieces on the table as he'd always done. But this time, Antonio held out his hand.

"One moment," he said, and shook his brown paper bag. 105

"Qué pasa, chico?" Máximo said.

Antonio reached into the paper bag as the men watched. He let the paper fall away. In his hand he held an oblong black leather box.

"Coñooo," Raúl said.

He set the box on the table, like a magician drawing out his trick. He looked around to the men and finally opened the box with a flourish to reveal a neat row of big heavy pieces, gone yellow and smooth like old teeth. They bent in closer to look. Antonio tilted the box gently and the pieces fell out in one long line, their black dots facing up now like tight dark pupils in the sunlight.

"Ivory," Antonio said, "and ebony. They're antique. You're not allowed to make 110 them anymore."

"Beautiful," Carlos said, and clasped his hands.

"My daughter found them for me in New Orleans," Antonio continued, ignoring Carlos.

He looked around the table and lingered on Máximo, who had lowered the box of plastic dominoes to the ground.

"She said she's been searching for them for two years. Couldn't wait two more weeks to give them to me," he said.

"Coñooo," Raúl said. 115

A moment passed.

"Well," Antonio said, "what do you think, Máximo?"

Máximo looked at him. Then he bent across the table to touch one of the pieces. He gave a jerk with his head and listened for the traffic. "Very nice," he said.

"Very nice?" Antonio said. "Very nice?" He laughed in his thin way. "My daughter 120 walked all over New Orleans to find these and the Cuban thinks they're 'very nice?'" He paused, watching Máximo. "Did you know my daughter is coming to visit me for Christmas? She's coming for Christmas, Máximo, maybe you can tell her her gift was very nice, but not as nice as some you remember, eh?"

Máximo looked up, his eyes settled on Carlos, who looked at Antonio and then looked away.

"Calm down, hombre," Carlos said, opening his arms wide, a nervous giggle beginning in his throat. "What's gotten into you?"

Antonio waved his hand.

A diesel truck rattled down Eighth Street, headed for downtown.

"My daughter is a district attorney in Los Angeles," Máximo said, after the noise 125 of the truck died. "December is one of the busiest months."

He felt a heat behind his eyes he had not felt in many years.

"Hold one in your hand," Antonio said. "Feel how heavy that is."

When the children were small, Máximo and Rosa used to spend Nochebuena[6] with his cousins in Cárdenas. It was a five-hour drive from Havana in the cars of those days. They would rise early on the twenty-third and arrive by mid-afternoon so Máximo could help the men kill the pig for the feast the following night. Máximo and the other men held the squealing, squirming animal down, its wiry brown coat cutting into their gloveless hands. But god, they were intelligent creatures. No sooner did it spot the knife, than the animal would bolt out of their arms, screaming like Armageddon. It had become the subtext to the Nochebuena tradition, this chasing of the terrified pig through the yard, dodging orange trees and the rotting fruit underneath. The children were never allowed to watch, Rosa made sure. They sat indoors with the women and stirred the black beans. With loud laughter, they shut out the shouts of the men and the hysterical pleadings of the animal as it was dragged back to its slaughter.

"Juanito the little dog gets off the boat from Cuba and decides to take a stroll down Brickell Avenue."

"Let me make sure I understand the joke. Juanito is a dog. Bowwow."   130

"That's pretty good."

"Yes, Juanito is a dog, goddamnit."

Raúl looked up, startled.

Máximo shuffled the pieces hard and swallowed. He swung his arms across the table in wide, violent arcs. One of the pieces flew off the table.

"Hey, hey, watch it with that, what's wrong with you?"   135

Máximo stopped. He felt his heart beating.

"I'm sorry," he said. He bent over the edge of the table to see where the piece had landed. "Wait a minute."

He held the table with one hand and tried to stretch to pick up the piece.

"What are you doing?"

"Just wait a minute." When he couldn't reach, he stood up, pulled the piece   140
toward him with his foot, sat back down and reached for it again, this time grasping it between his fingers and his palm. He put it face down on the table with the others and shuffled, slowly, his mind barely registering the traffic.

"Where was I—Juanito the little dog, right, bowwow." Máximo took a deep breath. "He's just off the boat from Cuba and is strolling down Brickell Avenue. He's looking up at all the tall and shiny buildings. 'Coñooo,' he says, dazzled by all the mirrors. 'There's nothing like this in Cuba.'"

"Hey, hey, professor. We had tall buildings."

"Jesus Christ!" Máximo said. He pressed his thumb and forefinger into the corners of his eyes. "This is after Castro, then. Let me just get it out for Christ's sake."

He stopped shuffling. Raúl looked away.

"Ready now? Juanito the little dog is looking up at all the tall buildings and he's   145
so happy to finally be in America because all his cousins have been telling him what a great country it is, right? You know, they were sending back photos of their new cars and girlfriends."

---

[6]Christmas Eve.—Eds.

"A joke about dogs who drive cars, I've heard it all."

"Hey, they're Cuban superdogs."

"All right, they're sending back photos of their new owners or the biggest bones any dog has ever seen. Anything you like. Use your imaginations." Máximo stopped shuffling. "Where was I?"

"You were at the part where Juanito buys a Rolls Royce."

The men laughed.

"Okay, Antonio, why don't you three fools continue the joke." Máximo got up from the table. "You've made me forget the rest of it."

"Aw, come on, chico, sit down, don't be so sensitive."

"Come on, professor, you were at the part where Juanito is so glad to be in America."

"Forget it. I can't remember the rest now." Máximo rubbed his temple, grabbed the back of the chair and sat down slowly, facing the street. "Just leave me alone, I can't remember it." He pulled at the pieces two by two. "I'm sorry. Look, let's just play."

The men set up their double rows of dominoes, like miniature barricades before them.

"These pieces are a work of art," Antonio said, and lay down a double eight.

The banyan tree was strung with white lights that were lit all day. Colored lights twined around the metal poles of the fence, which was topped with a long looping piece of gold tinsel garland.

The Christmas tourists began arriving just before lunch as Máximo and Raúl stepped off the number eight bus. Carlos and Antonio were already at the table, watched by two groups of families. Mom and Dad with kids. They were big, even the kids were big and pink. The mother whispered to the kids and they smiled and waved. Raúl waved back at the mother.

"Nice legs, yes?" he whispered to Máximo.

Before Máximo looked away, he saw the mother take out one of those little black pocket cameras. He saw the flash out of the corner of his eye. He sat down and looked around the table; the other men stared at their pieces.

The game started badly. It happened sometimes, the distribution of the pieces went all wrong and out of desperation one of the men made mistakes, and soon it was all they could do to knock all the pieces over and start fresh. Raúl set down a double three and signaled to Máximo it was all he had. Carlos passed. Máximo surveyed his last five pieces. His thoughts scattered to the family outside. He looked up to find the tallest boy with his face pressed between the iron slats, staring at him.

"You pass?" Antonio said.

Máximo looked at him, then at the table. He put down a three and a five. He looked again, the boy was gone. The family had moved on.

The tour groups arrived later that afternoon. First the white buses with the happy blue letters WELCOME TO LITTLE HAVANA. Next, the fat women in white shorts, their knees lost in an abstraction of flesh. Máximo tried to concentrate on the game. The worst part was how the other men acted out for them. Dominoes is supposed to be a quiet game. And now there they were shouting at each other and gesturing. A few of the men had even brought cigars, and they dangled now, unlit, from their mouths.

"You see, Raúl," Máximo said. "You see how we're a spectacle?" He felt like an animal and wanted to growl and cast about behind the metal fence.   165

Raúl shrugged. "Doesn't bother me."

"A goddamn spectacle. A collection of old bones," Máximo said.

The other men looked up at Máximo.

"Hey, speak for yourself, cabrón," Antonio said.

Raúl shrugged again.   170

Máximo rubbed his left elbow and began to shuffle. It was hot, and the sun was setting in his eyes, backlighting the car exhaust like a veil before him. He rubbed his temple, feeling the skin move over the bone. He pressed the inside corners of his eyes, then drew his hand back to his left elbow.

"Hey, you okay there?" Antonio said.

An open trolley pulled up and parked at the curb. A young man, perhaps in his thirties, stood in the front, holding a microphone. He wore a guayabera. Máximo looked away.

"This here is Domino Park," came the amplified voice in English, then in Spanish. "No one under fifty-five allowed, folks. But we can sure watch them play."

Máximo heard shutters click, then convinced himself he couldn't have heard,   175
not from where he was.

"Most of these men are Cuban and they're keeping alive the tradition of their homeland," the amplified voice continued, echoing against the back wall of the park. "You see, in Cuba it was very common to retire to a game of dominoes after a good meal. It was a way to bond and build community. You folks here are seeing a slice of the past. A simpler time of good friendships and unhurried days."

Maybe it was the sun. The men later noted that he seemed odd. The tics. Rubbing his bones.

First Máximo muttered to himself. He rubbed his temple again. When the feedback on the microphone pierced through Domino Park, he could no longer sit where he was, accept things as they were. It was a moment that had long been missing from his life.

He stood and made a fist at the trolley.

"Mierda!" he shouted. "Mierda! That's the biggest bullshit I've ever heard."   180

He made a lunge at the fence. Carlos jumped up and held him back. Raúl led him back to his seat.

The man of the amplified voice cleared his throat. The people on the trolley looked at him and back at Máximo, perhaps they thought this was part of the show.

"Well," the man chuckled. "There you have it, folks."

Lucinda ran over, but the other men waved her off. She began to protest about rules and propriety. The park had a reputation to uphold.

It was Antonio who spoke. "Leave the man alone," he said.   185

Máximo looked at him. His head was pounding. Antonio met his gaze briefly then looked to Lucinda.

"Some men don't like to be stared at is all," he said. "It won't happen again."

She shifted her weight, but remained where she was, watching.

"What are you waiting for?" Antonio said, turning now to Máximo, who had lowered his head onto the white backs of the dominoes. "Shuffle."

That night Máximo was too tired to sit at the pine table. He didn't even prepare din- 190
ner. He slept, and in his dreams he was a blue-and-yellow fish swimming in warm waters, gliding through the coral, the only fish in the sea and he was happy. But the light changed and the sea darkened suddenly and he was rising through it, afraid of breaking the surface, afraid of the pinhole sun on the other side, afraid of drowning in the blue vault of sky.

"Let me finish the story of Juanito the little dog."

No one said anything.

"Is that okay? I'm okay. I just remembered it. Can I finish it?"

The men nodded, but still did not speak.

"He is just off the boat from Cuba. He is walking down Brickell Avenue. And he 195
is trying to steady himself, see, because he still has his sea legs and all the buildings are so tall they are making him dizzy. He doesn't know what to expect. He's maybe a little afraid. And he's thinking about a pretty little dog he once knew and he's wondering where she is now and he wishes he were back home."

He paused to take a breath. Raúl cleared his throat. The men looked at one another, then at Máximo. But his eyes were on the blur of dominoes before him. He felt a stillness around him, a shadow move past the fence, but he didn't look up.

"He's not a depressed kind of dog, though. Don't get me wrong. He's very feisty. And when he sees an elegant white poodle striding toward him, he forgets all his worries and exclaims, 'O Madre de Dios, si cocinas como caminas . . .'"

The men let out a small laugh. Máximo continued.

"'Si cocinas como caminas . . .' Juanito says, but the white poodle interrupts and says, 'I beg your pardon? This is America, speak English.' So Juanito pauses for a moment to consider and says in his broken English, 'Mamita, you are one hot doggie, yes? I would like to take you to movies and fancy dinners.'"

"One hot doggie, yes?" Carlos repeated, then laughed. "You're killing me." 200

The other men smiled, warming to the story again.

"So Juanito says, 'I would like to marry you, my love, and have gorgeous puppies with you and live in a castle.' Well, all this time the white poodle has her snout in the air. She looks at Juanito and says, 'Do you have any idea who you're talking to? I am a refined breed of considerable class and you are nothing but a short, insignificant mutt.' Juanito is stunned for a moment, but he rallies for the final shot. He's a proud dog, you see, and he's afraid of his pain. 'Pardon me, your highness,' Juanito the mangy dog says, 'Here in America, I may be a short, insignificant mutt, but in Cuba I was a German shepherd.'"

Máximo turned so the men would not see his tears. The afternoon traffic crawled westward. One horn blasted, then another. He remembered holding his daughters days after their birth, thinking how fragile and vulnerable lay his bond to the future. For weeks, he carried them on pillows, like jeweled china. Then, the blank spaces in his life lay before him. Now he stood with the gulf at his back, their ribbony youth aflutter in the past. And what had he salvaged from the years? Already, he was forgetting Rosa's face, the precise shade of her eyes.

Carlos cleared his throat and moved his hand as if to touch him, then held back. He cleared his throat again.

"He was a good dog," Carlos said, pursing his lips. 205

Antonio began to laugh, then fell silent with the rest. Máximo started shuffling, then stopped. The shadow of the banyan tree worked a kaleidoscope over the dominoes. When the wind eased, Máximo tilted his head to listen. He heard something stir behind him, someone leaning heavily on the fence. He could almost feel their breath. His heart quickened.

"Tell them to go away," Máximo said. "Tell them, no pictures."

[2001]

Exploring the Text

1. What effect does the joke Máximo tells at the start of the story have on us as readers? What does it tell us about him when he claims to have "just made it up" though Raúl claims to have "heard it when Reagan was president" (paras. 20–21)?

2. What does the narrator mean in the description of the bond between Máximo and Raúl: "They weren't close friends, but friendly still, in that way of people who come from the same place and think they already know the important things about one another" (para. 23)?

3. What are the most striking differences between Máximo's life as he remembers it when he and his family were in Cuba and the life we see in this story? Note especially those differences beyond his economic status, and consider the culture of the family and the sources of his identity.

4. What is the significance of the game of dominoes in this story? Why does Máximo "like dominoes, the way each piece [becomes] part of the next" (para. 91)? Why do the men "argue" that dominoes was not invented by the Chinese but the Cubans? (You might want to inquire into the history of the game.)

5. The men in Domino Park are from Cuba and the Dominican Republic. How are the Dominicans Antonio and Carlos represented? What part does the antique domino set Antonio's daughter gives him play in this characterization?

6. What is Menéndez trying to say in her depiction of the tourists and tour guides who make Domino Park a regular stop on their daily routes (paras. 158–164, 173–183)? Consider specific descriptions of the tourists themselves,

"the amplified voice in English, then in Spanish," the tour leader's explanation of the activity being observed, and the tour leader's response to Máximo's outburst. Why was this confrontation with the tourists a "moment that had long been missing from [Máximo's] life" (para. 178)?

7. How is place tied to identity in this story? Pay special attention to the three layers of time explored in this story—Miami in the present, Miami in the past, and Havana in the past. Choose one passage in which Menéndez shifts between past and present, and discuss how this narrative structure emphasizes ideas or themes she is developing.

8. Jokes are a form of storytelling that offers escape and entertainment as well as a way for people to connect culturally. Are the jokes in this story funny? In what way are they metaphors? Consider also how the jokes are told: who tells them and how they are received. Pay special attention to the last joke, which is reflected in the story's title.

9. Ultimately, what is Menéndez's attitude toward Máximo? Is she presenting him as sympathetic? tragic? foolish? courageous? self-absorbed? pathetic? admirable? Cite specific passages to support your response.

10. Discuss the following quotation as it applies to this story:

> What has happened to other ethnic groups will happen to us: we will have a sentimental rather than a vital link to our culture of origin. Cubanness will be something we acquire, not something we absorb.
>
> — GUSTAVO PEREZ-FIRMAT, *Life on the Hyphen*

When I consider how my light is spent

JOHN MILTON

Often grouped with Shakespeare and Chaucer as one of the giants of English literature, John Milton (1608–1674) is best known for his epic poem *Paradise Lost*. He studied independently for five years after receiving his MA from Cambridge University, then traveled through Europe. When he returned to England, the country was in a state of flux. Milton supported the Puritans and Oliver Cromwell and wrote pamphlets on many political issues, such as free speech and censorship. Milton's eyesight began to deteriorate, however, and by 1652 he was blind. In 1657, the poet Andrew Marvell—most famous for "To His Coy Mistress" (p. 693)—became his assistant. After the Restoration in 1660, when Charles II resumed the throne, Milton was arrested for his Puritan activities but escaped imprisonment and execution. He devoted the remainder of his life to writing, publishing his masterpiece, *Paradise Lost*, in 1667 and its sequel, *Paradise Regained*, in 1671. "When I consider how my light is spent," written the year Milton lost his sight, is a meditation on that loss.

When I consider how my light is spent,
　　Ere half my days, in this dark world and wide,
　　And that one talent which is death to hide
　　Lodged with me useless, though my soul more bent
To serve therewith my Maker, and present　　　　　　　5
　　My true account, lest he returning chide;
　　"Doth God exact day-labor, light denied?"
　　I fondly ask; but Patience to prevent
That murmur, soon replies, "God doth not need
　　Either man's work or his own gifts; who best　　　10
　　Bear his mild yoke, they serve him best. His state
Is kingly. Thousands at his bidding speed
　　And post o'er land and ocean without rest:
　　They also serve who only stand and wait."

　　　　　　　　　　　　　　　　　　　　　[c. 1655]

Exploring the Text

1. This poem is structured through several voices. Who is the speaker in lines 1–6? in line 7? in lines 9–14?
2. Milton uses familiar words in ways that are unfamiliar to twenty-first-century readers. What do "bent" (l. 4) and "exact" (l. 7) mean, for instance? What other examples can you find? Define them.
3. What does the speaker mean by the "mild yoke" (l. 11)?
4. How would you describe the movement or change in the speaker's attitude toward his blindness from the beginning to the end of the poem?
5. The last line of the poem is frequently quoted as a kind of motto for those who are not in the midst of action but are nevertheless involved, whether the situation is war or a more personal plight. Explain why you think Milton would find this use of the line true to his poem.

The Quiet Life

ALEXANDER POPE

Alexander Pope (1688–1744) is generally considered the eighteenth century's greatest English poet. Known for satirical verse, Pope was the first writer to be able to live off the proceeds of his work—namely, his very popular translation of Homer's *Iliad*. Pope was a Roman Catholic, and the anti-Catholic sentiment and laws of his time dictated—and limited—his formal education. He read widely on his own, learning French, Italian, Latin, and Greek. Critics attacked Pope's version of Shakespeare's work, and he responded with "The Dunciad"—a scathing satire of the literary establishment that brought him enemies and even threats of physical violence. Pope's work goes in and out of fashion, but some of his words are so ingrained in the English language that they are considered proverbs by those unfamiliar with his work. "A little learning is a dangerous thing," "To err is human, to forgive, divine," and "For fools rush in where angels fear to tread" are from *Essay on Criticism*; "Hope springs eternal in the human breast" and "The proper study of mankind is man" are both found in *Essay on Man*. In the following poem, the young Pope considers the virtues of defining oneself within a small and bounded environment.

Happy the man whose wish and care
A few paternal acres bound,
Content to breathe his native air
        In his own ground.

Whose herds with milk, whose fields with bread,   5
Whose flocks supply him with attire;
Whose trees in summer yield him shade,
        In winter, fire.

Blest, who can unconcern'dly find
Hours, days, and years, slide soft away   10
In health of body; peace of mind;
        Quiet by day;

Sound sleep by night; study and ease
Together mix'd; sweet recreation,
And innocence, which most does please   15
        With meditation.

Thus let me live, unseen, unknown;
Thus unlamented let me die;
Steal from the world, and not a stone
        Tell where I lie.   20

[1709]

Exploring the Text

1. What are the values that the speaker espouses? What is the implicit contrast in values raised in the last stanza?
2. How does the speaker of this poem construct his identity? What resources does he draw on to determine who he is?
3. How does the form of the poem reinforce the theme of balance?
4. Listen to a reading of this poem on Classic Poetry Aloud (classicpoetryaloud .com). How does hearing the poem influence your understanding of it?
5. Today's Green movement may not have the same pastoral ideals as those found in this poem, yet there are some similarities. What are they? Do you think Pope would approve of or even embrace this movement?

The World Is Too Much with Us

WILLIAM WORDSWORTH

William Wordsworth (1770–1850) is one of the most famous and influential poets of the Western world and one of the premier Romantics. Widely known for his reverence of nature and the power of his lyrical verse, he lived in the Lake District of northern England, where he was inspired by the natural beauty of the landscape. With Samuel Taylor Coleridge, he published *Lyrical Ballads* in 1798; the collection, which changed the direction of English poetry, begins with Coleridge's "Rime of the Ancient Mariner" and includes Wordsworth's "Lines Composed a Few Miles above Tintern Abbey." Among Wordsworth's other famous works are "The World Is Too Much with Us," a sonnet; "Ode: Intimations of Immortality"; and "The Prelude or Growth of a Poet's Mind," an autobiographical poem. "The World Is Too Much with Us," written around 1802 and published in 1807, criticizes society for being materialistic and estranged from nature.

> The world is too much with us; late and soon,
> Getting and spending, we lay waste our powers:
> Little we see in Nature that is ours;
> We have given our hearts away, a sordid boon!
> This Sea that bares her bosom to the moon;
> The winds that will be howling at all hours,
> And are up-gathered now like sleeping flowers;
> For this, for everything, we are out of tune;
> It moves us not.—Great God! I'd rather be
> A Pagan suckled in a creed outworn;   10
> So might I, standing on this pleasant lea,
> Have glimpses that would make me less forlorn;
> Have sight of Proteus rising from the sea;
> Or hear old Triton[1] blow his wreathèd horn.

[1807]

Exploring the Text

1. "The World Is Too Much with Us" is a traditional Petrarchan sonnet. In what ways does the rigid form enhance Wordsworth's passionate message? Is his passion at all repressed by the sonnet form? How does the sestet answer the octave? What other shifts or transitions do you notice in the poem?

---

[1]In Greek mythology, both Proteus and Triton were gods of the sea and sons of Poseidon.—EDS.

2. Why does the speaker feel that his sense of self is compromised? Why does he claim that "we lay waste our powers" (l. 2)? What could "we" do to reclaim our identity?

3. What effect does the speaker achieve by personifying the wind and the sea?

4. Discuss the impact that any of the following word replacements might have on the poem: "selling and buying" for "getting and spending" (l. 2); "screeching" for "howling" (l. 6); "napping flowers" for "sleeping flowers" (l. 7); "fed" for "suckled" (l. 10); and "sad" for "forlorn" (l. 12). Consider connotation as you discuss the changes in effect.

5. What effect do the references to mythology have? How are they connected to Wordsworth's conviction that materialism causes an estrangement from nature that may have dire results?

6. According to critic Camille Paglia, line 8's "we are out of tune" contains a "buried image": the body as Aeolian or wind harp, played upon and vibrated by nature. How does that image — and its related metaphor — add to Wordsworth's argument about the loss of self that results from "late and soon, / Getting and spending" (ll. 1–2)?

The Apology

RALPH WALDO EMERSON

Ralph Waldo Emerson (1803–1882), perhaps best known for his essay "Self-Reliance," was one of America's most influential thinkers and writers. After graduating from Harvard Divinity School, he followed nine generations of his family into the ministry but practiced for only a few years. Known as a great orator, Emerson made his living as a popular lecturer on a wide range of topics, from politics to religion to art. From 1821 to 1826, he taught in city and country schools, and later served on a number of school boards, including the Concord School Committee and the Board of Overseers of Harvard College. Central to Emerson's thought is recognizing the spiritual relationship between humans and the natural world. In 1836, he and other like-minded intellectuals such as Henry David Thoreau founded the Transcendental Club, and that same year Emerson published his influential essay "Nature," which expresses the central philosophy of what came to be known as Transcendentalism. In his 1837 speech entitled "The American Scholar," which Oliver Wendell Holmes Sr. called America's "intellectual Declaration of Independence," Emerson urged American writers to develop their own style rather than emulating the European masters. With the tumult of the Industrial Revolution as a backdrop, Emerson poses an alternative way of being in the world in his poem "The Apology."

Think me not unkind and rude
  That I walk alone in grove and glen;
I go to the god of the wood
  To fetch his word to men.

Tax not my sloth that I   5
  Fold my arms beside the brook;
Each cloud that floated in the sky
  Writes a letter in my book.

Chide me not, laborious band,
  For the idle flowers I brought;   10
Every aster in my hand
  Goes home loaded with a thought.

There was never mystery
  But 't is figured in the flowers;
Was never secret history   15
  But birds tell it in the bowers.

One harvest from thy field
  Homeward brought the oxen strong;
A second crop thine acres yield,
  Which I gather in a song.   20

[1847]

Exploring the Text

1. Emerson's sentence structure (imperatives) and his references to "thy" and "thine" in the last stanza suggest that the speaker is addressing someone. Who is the person or group he is addressing?
2. The poem is structured as a contrast between two roles or two identities that define a member of a community. What are the central contrasts?
3. How does the regularity of the form, particularly the rhyme scheme, reinforce the point Emerson is making?
4. What is meant by "god of the wood / To fetch his word to men" (ll. 3–4)? Why does Emerson not capitalize "god"? If his audience is a conventionally religious one, more likely to expect the familiar phrase "the Word of God," what are the implications of his making such a change?
5. What are the central images of this poem, and why are they fitting given the time period in which it was written?
6. How would you describe the tone of the poem? Is it playful? defensive? sentimental? You might capture it better in a phrase (an adjective-noun combination) than in a single word. Refer to specific language in the poem that supports your choice.

7. The word *apology* has a number of nuances in its meaning. We think of it most commonly as an admission of error accompanied by an expression of regret. Closely related is *apologia*, which does not suggest guilt or error but is instead a desire to make clear the grounds for a belief or position. How might each of these apply to this poem? Which do you think Emerson most likely intended?

I'm Nobody! Who are you?

EMILY DICKINSON

Born into a prominent family in Amherst, Massachusetts, Emily Dickinson (1830–1886) received some formal education at Amherst Academy and Mount Holyoke Female Seminary (which became Mount Holyoke College). Throughout her lifetime, Dickinson was a shy and reclusive person, who preferred to remain within her close family circle. In 1862, she enclosed four poems in a letter to literary critic and abolitionist Thomas Wentworth Higginson, who had written a piece in the *Atlantic Monthly* that included practical advice for young writers. Her letter began, "Mr. Higginson,—Are you too deeply occupied to say if my verse is alive? The mind is so near itself it cannot see distinctly, and I have none to ask. Should you think it breathed, and had you the leisure to tell me, I should feel quick gratitude." Dickinson didn't sign the letter, but instead enclosed her name on a card inside a smaller envelope. Dickinson wrote over seventeen hundred poems, but only ten were published in her lifetime. In the following poem, Dickinson expresses her preference for spiritual seclusion in a somewhat whimsical fashion, characteristic of much of her work.

I'm Nobody! Who are you?
Are you—Nobody—too?
Then there's a pair of us!
Don't tell! they'd advertise—you know!

How dreary—to be—Somebody!   5
How public—like a Frog—
To tell one's name—the livelong June—
To an admiring Bog!

                                              [c. 1861]

Exploring the Text

1. What characteristics do you typically associate with people who identify themselves as "Nobodies"? By addressing the reader directly ("Who are you?"), how does the poem invite the reader to reexamine what it means to be "a nobody"?

2. How does society commonly treat its "Nobodies"? Why do you think the speaker is worried that "they'd advertise" (l. 4)?
3. Where do you find evidence of irony in the poem?
4. In the second stanza, the speaker uses a simile to express her contempt for a certain type of behavior. What is that behavior, and how does the simile reinforce her point?
5. How does what we know about Dickinson's shyness invite an autobiographical reading of this poem?
6. Compare and contrast this poem with "The Quiet Life" by Alexander Pope (p. 496). What resources of language do the two poets employ to express the kind of life that each believes is most valuable?

the Cambridge ladies who live in furnished souls

E. E. CUMMINGS

Edward Estlin (E. E.) Cummings (1894–1962) was an enormously prolific and experimental poet. Born and raised in an affluent family in Cambridge, Massachusetts, he graduated from Cambridge Latin High School and received both a BA and an MA in English and classical studies from Harvard University. Before the United States entered World War I, Cummings, an avowed pacifist, volunteered as an ambulance driver in France, where he was held for a time in a detention camp—an experience that deepened his distrust of authority. *The Enormous Room* (1922), his first published work, is a fictional account of his imprisonment, followed in 1923 by his first collection of poems, *Tulips and Chimneys*. Cummings defied traditional rules of typography and punctuation in the pursuit of poetry that was both critical of the status quo and whimsical. An immensely popular poet, Cummings produced an extensive body of work totaling over nine hundred poems. Critic Jenny Penberthy describes Cummings as "an unabashed lyricist, a modern cavalier love poet. But alongside his lyrical celebrations of nature, love, and the imagination are his satirical denouncements of tawdry, defiling, flat-footed, urban and political life—open terrain for invective and verbal inventiveness." The following poem, "the Cambridge ladies who live in furnished souls," explores this more satirical aspect of Cummings's work.

the Cambridge ladies who live in furnished souls
are unbeautiful and have comfortable minds
(also, with the church's protestant blessings
daughters, unscented shapeless spirited)
they believe in Christ and Longfellow, both dead,   5
are invariably interested in so many things—
at the present writing one still finds
delighted fingers knitting for the is it Poles?

perhaps. While permanent faces coyly bandy
scandal of Mrs. N. and Professor D.   10
. . . the Cambridge ladies do not care, above
Cambridge if sometimes in its box of
sky lavender and cornerless, the
moon rattles like a fragment of angry candy

[1922]

Exploring the Text

1. What do you envision about the Cambridge ladies when you read that they "live in furnished souls" (l. 1) and have "comfortable minds" (l. 2)? How is calling them "unbeautiful" (l. 2) different from calling them "ugly"?
2. What does the allusion to "Christ and Longfellow" (l. 5) in the same breath suggest about the speaker's attitude toward the Cambridge ladies' beliefs? What does the qualifying phrase "both dead" tell you about the speaker's own beliefs?
3. How does Cummings's playful use of syntax in "delighted fingers knitting for the is it Poles? / perhaps" (ll. 8–9) contribute to his commentary on the Cambridge ladies? What effect does the inserted "is it" have on your sense of their commitment to political causes and philanthropy?
4. How did you interpret the ellipsis dots in line 11?
5. Why do you think the speaker compares the moon over Cambridge with "a fragment of angry candy" (l. 14)? How can candy be angry? What does the simile have to do with the Cambridge ladies?

Heritage

COUNTEE CULLEN

An important figure during the Harlem Renaissance, Countee Cullen (1903–1946) grew up in New York City. At fifteen, he was adopted by Reverend Frederick A. Cullen, pastor of Harlem's largest congregation. Cullen graduated Phi Beta Kappa from New York University in 1923 and received an MA from Harvard University in 1926; he traveled to France as a Guggenheim Fellow after graduation. His published collections include *Color* (1925), *Copper Sun* (1927), *The Ballad of the Brown Girl* (1928), *The Black Christ and Other Poems* (1929), and *The Medea and Some Other Poems* (1935). He also wrote fiction, including the novel *One Way to Heaven* (1931) and the play *St. Louis Woman* (1946). Cullen differed from many other poets of this period because he wrote in the lyric tradition of John Keats, his favorite poet. Race was, however, a central concern of his work. He ends "Yet Do I Marvel," one of his most famous poems, with the lines: "Yet do I marvel at this curious thing: / To make a poet black, and bid him sing!" In "Heritage," he explores his African heritage and how he understands and balances that legacy with the Judeo-Christian tradition of his religion and education.

(For Harold Jackman)

What is Africa to me:
Copper sun or scarlet sea,
Jungle star or jungle track,
Strong bronzed men, or regal black
Women from whose loins I sprang   5
When the birds of Eden sang?
One three centuries removed
From the scenes his fathers loved,
Spicy grove, cinnamon tree,
What is Africa to me?   10

So I lie, who all day long
Want no sound except the song
Sung by wild barbaric birds
Goading massive jungle herds,
Juggernauts of flesh that pass   15
Trampling tall defiant grass
Where young forest lovers lie,
Plighting troth beneath the sky.
So I lie, who always hear,
Though I cram against my ear   20
Both my thumbs, and keep them there,
Great drums throbbing through the air.
So I lie, whose fount of pride,
Dear distress, and joy allied,
Is my somber flesh and skin,   25
With the dark blood dammed within
Like great pulsing tides of wine
That, I fear, must burst the fine
Channels of the chafing net
Where they surge and foam and fret.   30

Africa? A book one thumbs
Listlessly, till slumber comes.
Unremembered are her bats
Circling through the night, her cats
Crouching in the river reeds,   35
Stalking gentle flesh that feeds

By the river brink; no more
Does the bugle-throated roar
Cry that monarch claws have leapt
From the scabbards where they slept.   40
Silver snakes that once a year
Doff the lovely coats you wear,
Seek no covert in your fear
Lest a mortal eye should see;
What's your nakedness to me?   45
Here no leprous flowers rear
Fierce corollas in the air;
Here no bodies sleek and wet,
Dripping mingled rain and sweat,
Tread the savage measures of   50
Jungle boys and girls in love.
What is last year's snow to me,
Last year's anything? The tree
Budding yearly must forget
How its past arose or set—   55
Bough and blossom, flower, fruit,
Even what shy bird with mute
Wonder at her travail there,
Meekly labored in its hair.
One three centuries removed   60
From the scenes his fathers loved,
Spice grove, cinnamon tree,
What is Africa to me?

So I lie, who find no peace
Night or day, no slight release   65
From the unremittant beat
Made by cruel padded feet
Walking through my body's street.
Up and down they go, and back,
Treading out a jungle track.   70
So I lie, who never quite
Safely sleep from rain at night—
I can never rest at all
When the rain begins to fall;
Like a soul gone mad with pain   75
I must match its weird refrain;
Ever must I twist and squirm,
Writhing like a baited worm,
While its primal measures drip
Through my body, crying, "Strip!   80

Doff this new exuberance.
Come and dance the Lover's Dance!"
In an old remembered way
Rain works on me night and day.

Quaint, outlandish heathen gods   85
Black men fashion out of rods,
Clay, and brittle bits of stone,
In a likeness like their own,
My conversion came high-priced;
I belong to Jesus Christ,   90
Preacher of humility;
Heathen gods are naught to me.

Father, Son, and Holy Ghost,
So I make an idle boast;
Jesus of the twice-turned cheek,   95
Lamb of God, although I speak
With my mouth thus, in my heart
Do I play a double part.
Ever at Thy glowing altar
Must my heart grow sick and falter,   100
Wishing He I served were black,
Thinking then it would not lack
Precedent of pain to guide it,
Let who would or might deride it;
Surely then this flesh would know   105
Yours had borne a kindred woe.
Lord, I fashion dark gods, too,
Daring even to give You
Dark despairing features where,
Crowned with dark rebellious hair,   110
Patience wavers just so much as
Mortal grief compels, while touches
Quick and hot, of anger, rise
To smitten cheek and weary eyes.
Lord, forgive me if my need   115
Sometimes shapes a human creed.

All day long and all night through,
One thing only must I do:
Quench my pride and cool my blood,
Lest I perish in the flood.   120
Lest a hidden ember set
Timber that I thought was wet

Burning like the dryest flax,
Melting like the merest wax,
Lest the grave restore its dead.   125
Not yet has my heart or head
In the least way realized
They and I are civilized.

[1925]

Exploring the Text

1. Read a part of the poem aloud and listen to the beat and the sound. Cullen uses the traditional form of rhyming couplets (*aabbccddee . . .*); is this regular beat calming or unsettling? What is the effect of sustaining the rhyming couplets and the rhythm throughout the poem?

2. What is the impact of the repetition used in the poem? Note the repeated question "What is Africa to me?" Other examples of repetition include the repeated phrase "So I lie" and the italicized quatrains. How does the repetition work in conjunction with the rhyming couplets and rhythm?

3. What specific details describe Africa? Start with the opening descriptions that Cullen presents as contrasts. As the poem progresses, what visual picture emerges? Is it noteworthy that some details are inaccurate, such as the fact that the cinnamon tree referred to in the refrain is not, in fact, native to Africa? Is the depiction stereotypical? Consider how a person would learn about Africa in the early 1920s.

4. What does the speaker mean by his description of Africa as "A book one thumbs / Listlessly, till slumber comes" (ll. 31–32)?

5. Starting with line 85, the speaker struggles to reconcile his Christian beliefs with "heathen gods." What is the nature of his struggle? Why do you think he raises the issue of religion in the very last part of the poem?

6. In addition to differing religious beliefs, what other dualities in cultural values do you find in the poem? If you interpret the poem as the inner struggle of the speaker trying to construct his identity, what are the conflicts the speaker experiences?

7. How do you interpret the italicized ending of the poem? Pay special attention to the word "civilized" (l. 128). Why might Cullen have chosen to end his poem with this word? Ultimately, what is Africa to the speaker?

8. How would you describe the tone of the poem? Try using two or three words to make your description more precise, such as *sad yet hopeful*, or *admiringly critical*. Cite specific passages to support your response.

Fern Hill

DYLAN THOMAS

Dylan Thomas (1914–1953) was born in Wales, spent much of his life in London, and gained a following in the United States, where he often lectured and gave readings. He wrote his first volume of poetry when he was only twenty and published steadily throughout his lifetime. His works include *The Map of Love* (1939); *Portrait of the Artist as a Young Dog* (1940); *Deaths and Entrances* (1946); *In Country Sleep* (1952); and the posthumous *Under Milk Wood: A Play for Voices* (1954), which features characters from the fictional Welsh fishing village of Llareggub. During World War II, Thomas wrote scripts for documentary films, and after the war he was a literary commentator for BBC radio. He died in New York City at the age of thirty-nine of complications from alcoholism. Thomas was a popular and flamboyant figure, known for his spirited readings—especially his famous reading of "Do not go gentle into that good night," one of his most beloved poems. His other works include *A Child's Christmas in Wales*, published posthumously in 1955, and "Fern Hill."

Now as I was young and easy under the apple boughs
About the lilting house and happy as the grass was green,
   The night above the dingle starry,
     Time let me hail and climb
     Golden in the heydays of his eyes,   5
And honored among wagons I was prince of the apple towns
And once below a time I lordly had the trees and leaves
     Trail with daisies and barley
   Down the rivers of the windfall light.

And as I was green and carefree, famous among the barns   10
About the happy yard and singing as the farm was home,
   In the sun that is young once only,
     Time let me play and be
     Golden in the mercy of his means,
And green and golden I was huntsman and herdsman, the calves   15
Sang to my horn, the foxes on the hills barked clear and cold,
     And the sabbath rang slowly
   In the pebbles of the holy streams.

All the sun long it was running, it was lovely, the hay
Fields high as the house, the tunes from the chimneys, it was air   20
   And playing, lovely and watery
     And fire green as grass.
   And nightly under the simple stars

As I rode to sleep the owls were bearing the farm away,
All the moon long I heard, blessed among stables, the nightjars   25
    Flying with the ricks, and the horses
      Flashing into the dark.

And then to awake, and the farm, like a wanderer white
With the dew, come back, the cock on his shoulder; it was all
    Shining, it was Adam and maiden,   30
      The sky gathered again
    And the sun grew round that very day.
So it must have been after the birth of the simple light
In the first, spinning place, the spellbound horses walking warm
    Out of the whinnying green stable   35
      On to the fields of praise.

And honored among foxes and pheasants by the gay house
Under the new made clouds and happy as the heart was long,
    In the sun born over and over,
      I ran my heedless ways,   40
    My wishes raced through the house-high hay
And nothing I cared, at my sky-blue trades, that time allows
In all his tuneful turning so few and such morning songs
    Before the children green and golden
      Follow him out of grace,   45

Nothing I cared, in the lamb white days, that time would take me
Up to the swallow-thronged loft by the shadow of my hand,
    In the moon that is always rising,
      Nor that riding to sleep
I should hear him fly with the high fields   50
And wake to the farm forever fled from the childless land.
Oh as I was young and easy in the mercy of his means,
    Time held me green and dying
    Though I sang in my chains like the sea.

[1946]

Exploring the Text

1. A narrative about youth and age, this poem opens with "Now as I was young and easy" and ends with the speaker looking back on the time that he "was young and easy" (l. 52). What are the major divisions or events in the process of growing older that he recounts? You might consider the structure of the poem as six verse paragraphs.
2. Color plays a key role in this poem, especially green. List the images of green that Thomas uses. What patterns do you see? What do you make of seeming

contradictions such as "fire green as grass" (l. 22) or "green and dying" (l. 53)? How does Thomas develop his ideas through the use of this color?

3. How does Thomas use imagery of light to mark the speaker's changing perception? Consider specific references to "light" (ll. 9 and 33) and related references, such as "golden" (ll. 5, 14, 15, and 44) and "Shining" (l. 30). What contrasts does he draw with these?

4. What is the effect of Thomas's personification of time? How does he characterize it?

5. The poem opens with a simple country scene "under the apple boughs," yet there are allusions to royalty. What is Thomas's purpose in creating this juxtaposition?

6. How does the biblical allusion to "Adam and maiden" (l. 30) contribute to the development of the poem?

7. Thomas creates striking images with unusual phrasing and combinations. How do you interpret "the rivers of the windfall light" (l. 9), "All the sun long" (l. 19), "a wanderer white / With the dew" (ll. 28–29), and "my sky-blue trades" (l. 42)? Can you find other phrases that are similarly vibrant?

8. How would you characterize the tone of the final three lines—depressing? resigned? nostalgic? defiant? Is the overall tone of the poem positive or negative?

9. Do you think Thomas is using this poem to pay tribute to the natural world and all it can teach us, or is he using the idyllic country setting as a symbol for a more abstract concept? Cite specific passages and language to support your response.

10. Are "Fern Hill" and "The Quiet Life" by Alexander Pope (p. 496) more similar or different in their themes?

We Real Cool

GWENDOLYN BROOKS

Born in Topeka, Kansas, and raised in Chicago, Gwendolyn Brooks (1917–2000) was author of over twenty books of poetry, including her breakout work, *A Street in Bronzeville* (1945), and *Annie Allen* (1949), for which she became the first African American author to receive the Pulitzer Prize. In 1968, she was named poet laureate of the state of Illinois, and from 1985 to 1986 she served as consultant in poetry to the Library of Congress—the first African American woman to hold this position. Much of Brooks's work focuses on Chicago's urban landscape and culture, reflecting the speech patterns and expressions of the African American neighborhoods of Chicago's South Side, where she lived. While depicting the gritty reality of urban poverty, her poems express an affirmation of life. A frequent visitor and reader in public schools throughout her career, Brooks strove to help inner-city children find the poetry in their lives. Her awareness of the cultural forces that defined their experience—particularly the lives of young men— is clear in "We Real Cool," a poem that has been famous for the fifty years since Brooks wrote it.

The Pool Players.
Seven at the Golden Shovel.

We real cool. We
Left school. We

Lurk late. We
Strike straight. We

Sing sin. We   5
Thin gin. We

Jazz June. We
Die soon.

[1960]

Exploring the Text

1. Why do you think Brooks chose to attach the epigraph "The Pool Players. Seven at the Golden Shovel" to her poem? How did this information — coming where it does at the beginning of the text — influence your reading of the poem?
2. How many times is the pronoun "We" repeated in the poem? What does the placement of the pronoun suggest about the poet's attitude toward the young men? What does the repetition and placement of "We" suggest about the pool players' sense of themselves — their identity?
3. How does Brooks's use of monosyllabic words, alliteration, and internal rhyme contribute to your understanding of these "cool" young men?
4. In an interview with Brooks in *Contemporary Literature* 11:1 (Winter 1970), the poet offers stage directions for how "We Real Cool" should be read aloud:

   First of all, let me tell you how that's supposed to be said, because there's a reason why I set it out as I did. These are people who are essentially saying "Kilroy is here. We are." But they're a little uncertain of the strength of their identity. The "We" — you're supposed to stop after the "We" and think about their validity, and of course there's no way for you to tell whether it should be said softly or not, I suppose, but I say it rather softly because I want to represent their basic uncertainty, which they don't bother to question every day, of course.

   How do the poet's instructions contribute to your experience of the poem?
5. What does this poem's abrupt and rapid-fire rhythm suggest about these young men's lives?
6. In his 1942 painting entitled *Pool Parlor*, artist Jacob Lawrence depicts a group of young men playing the game. In what ways is his depiction similar to and different from that of Brooks's characterization? Pay special attention to the sense of risk that Brooks expresses; to what extent does Lawrence suggest a similar menace — or does he?

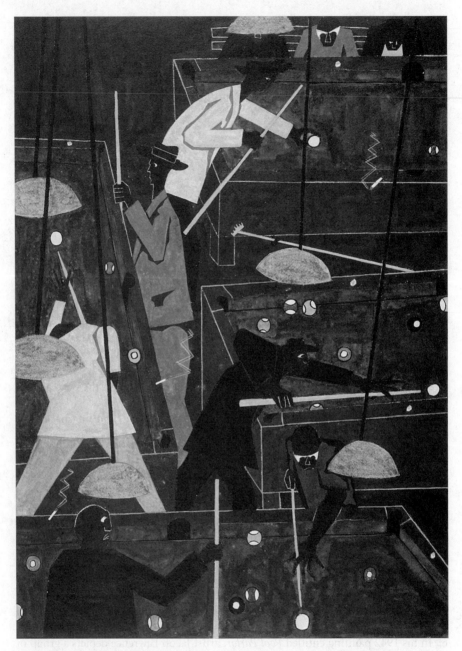

Pool Parlor (1942, watercolor and gouache on paper; 31⅛ × 22⅞ in.)

Identity Card

MAHMOUD DARWISH

TRANSLATED FROM ARABIC BY DENYS JOHNSON-DAVIES

One of the most prominent poets of the Arab world, Mahmoud Darwish (1941–2008) was born in what was then the British Mandate of Palestine. When Egypt, Iraq, Jordan, Lebanon, and Syria declared war on the newly-established State of Israel, following the 1948 termination of the British Mandate, Darwish's family fled to Lebanon. When they returned two years later, their village had been destroyed, they had missed a census, and they had lost their citizenship. Darwish's political activities, in addition to his lack of citizenship, resulted in several arrests, and eventually exile. He later served on the executive committee of the controversial Palestinian Liberation Organization (PLO). His first book of poetry, *Asafir bila ajnihah* (*Sparrows without Wings*), was published when he was nineteen. He wrote in Arabic but spoke French, English, and Hebrew. In an interview in 2000, Darwish described how he viewed the intersection of poetry and politics: "I don't think there is any role for poetry [in a Palestinian state]. Poems can't establish a state. But they can establish a metaphorical homeland in the minds of the people. I think my poems have built some houses in this landscape." In 2008, he was given the equivalent of a state funeral by the Palestine Authority and was buried in Ramallah. Written in 1964, "Identity Card" was inspired by an incident in which an Israeli soldier asked Darwish for his papers.

Put it on record.
  I am an Arab
And the number of my card is fifty thousand
I have eight children
And the ninth is due after summer.   5
What's there to be angry about?

Put it on record.
  I am an Arab
Working with comrades of toil in a quarry.
I have eight children   10
For them I wrest the loaf of bread,
The clothes and exercise books
From the rocks
And beg for no alms at your door,
  Lower not myself at your doorstep.   15
  What's there to be angry about?

Put it on record.
  I am an Arab.
I am a name without a title,

Patient in a country where everything   20
Lives in a whirlpool of anger.
   My roots
   Took hold before the birth of time
   Before the burgeoning of the ages,
   Before cypress and olive trees,   25
   Before the proliferation of weeds.

My father is from the family of the plough
   Not from highborn nobles.
And my grandfather was a peasant
   Without line or genealogy.   30
My house is a watchman's hut
   Made of sticks and reeds.
Does my status satisfy you?
   I am a name without a surname.

Put it on record.   35
   I am an Arab.
Colour of hair: jet black.
Colour of eyes: brown.
My distinguishing features:
   On my head the *'iqal* cords over a *keffiyeh*[1]   40
   Scratching him who touches it.
My address:
   I'm from a village, remote, forgotten,
   Its streets without name
   And all its men in the fields and quarry.   45
   What's there to be angry about?

Put it on record.
   I am an Arab.
You stole my forefathers' vineyards
   And land I used to till,   50
   I and all my children,
   And you left us and all my grandchildren
   Nothing but these rocks.
   Will your government be taking them too
   As is being said?   55

So!
   Put it on record at the top of page one:
   I don't hate people,
   I trespass on no one's property.

———

[1] A *keffiyeh* is a traditional Arab headdress. It is held in place by a cord called an *'iqal*. —EDS.

And yet, if I were to become hungry   60
  I shall eat the flesh of my usurper.
  Beware, beware of my hunger
  And of my anger!

[1964/1980]

Exploring the Text

1. Think about the identity cards you carry (driver's license, school ID). Why do you carry these cards? What do they reveal about your identity? What information does and does not appear there? Given only the information listed on your identity cards, what might a stranger assume about your identity?

2. To whom does the poem seem to be addressed? Support your view with specific evidence from the poem.

3. What effect does the repetition of the lines "Put it on record. / I am an Arab" have on you as a reader? How does the repetition contribute to the poem's meaning?

4. The meaning of the line "What's there to be angry about?" (ll. 6, 16, and 46) becomes increasingly ironic as the poem progresses. Discuss how these six words shift in meaning depending on their placement within the poem.

5. Explain how "And yet" in line 60 marks a turning point in the poem and a warning from the speaker to his audience.

6. Do some research on the history of Arab-Israeli relations. How does your research change your reading of this poem?

Ogun

KAMAU BRATHWAITE

Edward Kamau (E. K.) Brathwaite (b. 1930) is a poet, playwright, critic, and historian whose work explores the links between his West Indian and African heritages. Born and raised on the Caribbean island of Barbados, he was educated at Pembroke College, Cambridge, and received his PhD from the University of Sussex. Recipient of both Guggenheim and Fulbright fellowships and winner of numerous awards, Brathwaite worked in the Ministry of Education in Ghana and has taught at the University of the West Indies, the University of Nairobi, Boston University, and Yale University. He is currently a professor of comparative literature at New York University. Brathwaite's publications include *The Arrivants: A New World Trilogy* (1973), *Black + Blues* (1976), *Mother Poem* (1977), *Sun Poems* (1982), *X/Self* (1987), and *The Zea Mexican Diary* (1993). His 2006 collection of poetry, *Born to Slow Horses*, won the International Griffin Poetry Prize. Part of the judges' citation read: "Here political realities turn into musical complexities, voices overlap, history becomes mythology, spirits appear in photographs." Much of his poetry celebrates the oral tradition and shows the influence of jazz, particularly the works of Charlie Parker and John Coltrane. In the following poem, Brathwaite meditates on the preference for the new over the traditional—represented here by Ogun, the Yoruba and Afro-Caribbean creator-god.

My uncle made chairs, tables, balanced doors on, dug out
coffins, smoothing the white wood out

with plane and quick sandpaper until
it shone like his short-sighted glasses.

The knuckles of his hands were sil-   5
vered knobs of nails hit, hurt and flat-

tened out with blast of heavy hammer. He was knock-knee'd, flat-
footed and his clip clop sandals slapped across the concrete

flooring of his little shop where canefield mulemen and a fleet
of Bedford lorry drivers dropped in to scratch themselves and talk.   10

There was no shock of wood, no beam
of light mahogany his saw teeth couldn't handle.

When shaping squares for locks, a key hole
care tapped rat tat tat upon the handle

of his humpbacked chisel. Cold   15
world of wood caught fire as he whittled: rectangle

window frames, the intersecting x of folding chairs, triangle

trellises, the donkey
box-cart in its squeaking square.   20

But he was poor and most days he was hungry.
Imported cabinets with mirrors, formica table

tops, spine-curving chairs made up of tubes, with hollow
steel-like bird bones that sat on rubber ploughs,

thin beds, stretched not on boards, but blue high-tensioned cables,   25
were what the world preferred.

And yet he had a block of wood that would have baffled them.
With knife and gimlet care he worked away at this on Sundays,

explored its knotted hurts, cutting his way
along its yellow whorls until his hands could feel   30

how it had swelled and shivered, breathing air,
its weathered green burning rings of time,

its contoured grain still tuned to roots and water.
And as he cut, he heard the creak of forests:

green lizard faces gulped, grey memories with moth   35
eyes watched him from their shadows, soft

liquid tendrils leaked among the flowers
and a black rigid thunder he had never heard within his hammer

came stomping up the trunks. And as he worked within his shattered
Sunday shop, the wood took shape: dry shuttered   40

eyes, slack anciently everted lips, flat
ruined face, eaten by pox, ravaged by rat

and woodworm, dry cistern mouth, cracked
gullet crying for the desert, the heavy black

enduring jaw; lost pain, lost iron;   45
emerging woodwork image of his anger.

[1969]

Exploring the Text

1. What is the literal situation being described in this poem? Who is the subject, and what is he doing?
2. Read the poem aloud and just try to listen. How does the sound affect your understanding? Identify and discuss the effects of alliteration, onomatopoeia, and line breaks.
3. The poem contains references to the tools of both the carpenter's and the sculptor's craft. Does this specialized language enhance your response to the poem, or is it a distraction? Consider terms such as "plane" (l. 3) and "gimlet" (l. 28).
4. Identify the figurative language in the poem. There is a great deal of concrete descriptive detail but few actual figures of speech. Why do you think the poet chose to use so few metaphors and similes?
5. The poem has a three-part structure: the opening, a transition, and a final section. Where are these divisions? How does this structure reinforce the ideas or themes of the poem?
6. The poem is narrated by an outside observer, a family member describing the subject. What is the relationship between the speaker, the title, and the subject? How would the overall impact of the poem change if the subject himself were the speaker?
7. How do you interpret the ending of the poem, beginning with line 39: "And as he worked . . ."? Try crafting a sentence that could serve as the thesis for an interpretive essay on "Ogun."

Mexicans Begin Jogging

Gary Soto

Gary Soto (b. 1952) was born in Fresno, California, to Mexican American parents. Working to help support his family, he had little interest in school but began to read on his own. He received his undergraduate degree from California State University, Fresno, and an MFA from the University of California at Riverside. He has taught at the University of California, Berkeley and Riverside campuses. He published his first poem in 1973 in the *Iowa Review* when he was a senior in college. His first book of poetry, *The Elements of San Joaquin*, appeared in 1977; many others have followed, including *New and Selected Poems*, which was a finalist for the National Book Award in 1995, and *Cloudy: Poems of Love and Longing* (2009), his most recent poetry collection. In addition to poetry, Soto has written picture books; comic fiction; books for teens; and novels, including *The Afterlife* (2005) and *Accidental Love* (2006). Although he is often seen as a spokesperson for Spanish-speaking Americans, he explains, "Even though I write a lot about life in the barrio, I am really writing about the feelings and experiences of most American kids." "Mexicans Begin Jogging" reflects Soto's ability to expose inequities and discrimination with ironic humor.

At the factory I worked
In the fleck of rubber, under the press
Of an oven yellow with flame,
Until the border patrol opened
Their vans and my boss waved for us to run.   5
"Over the fence, Soto," he shouted,
And I shouted that I was American.
"No time for lies," he said, and pressed
A dollar in my palm, hurrying me
Through the back door.   10

Since I was on his time, I ran
And became the wag to a short tail of Mexicans —
Ran past the amazed crowds that lined
The street and blurred like photographs, in rain.
I ran from that industrial road to the soft   15
Houses where people paled at the turn of an autumn sky.
What could I do but yell *vivas*
To baseball, milkshakes, and those sociologists
Who would clock me
As I jog into the next century   20
On the power of a great, silly grin.

[1981]

Exploring the Text

1. The structure of this poem is a narrative, a story. What is the story that the speaker tells?

2. Soto's descriptions create a vivid scene of where he is working as well as the places he runs through. What images of the setting does the speaker note? What is their collective effect?

3. A number of lines in the poem are deliberately suggestive, even ambiguous. For example, what does Soto mean by having the speaker hurry "Through the back door" (l. 10) or think "Since I was on his time" (l. 11)? What other lines or phrases have more than one meaning?

4. What examples of humor do you find in the poem? Are these simply comic, ironic, or both?

5. List the verbs in the poem. What image(s) of movement do they suggest when you consider them cumulatively?

6. What is the "power" in the last line: "the power of a great, silly grin"?

7. Overall, how does Soto convey the conflict in identity that the speaker is experiencing?

8. How do you interpret the title? Is the speaker "jogging" in the way we normally use the term? What other title(s) might work for this poem? How would a different title change the way the poem is read?

The Powwow at the End of the World

Sherman Alexie

A Spokane/Coeur d'Alene Indian, Sherman Alexie (b. 1966) grew up on the Spokane Indian reservation in Wellpinit, Washington. He graduated from Washington State University with a BA in American Studies. Alexie has published fourteen books of poetry and short stories about life on the reservation and the relationship between the Indian and mainstream communities, including his first collection of short stories, *The Lone Ranger and Tonto Fistfight in Heaven* (1993), which received a PEN/Hemingway Award for Best First Book of Fiction. In 1997, Alexie wrote the screenplay for what became the award-winning film *Smoke Signals,* based on his short story "This Is What It Means to Say Phoenix, Arizona." *The Absolutely True Diary of a Part-Time Indian* (2007) was awarded the National Book Award for young people's literature in 2007. He is well known for his sense of humor and performance ability, winning the World Heavyweight Poetry Bout competition four years in a row. In "The Powwow at the End of the World," Alexie continues his exploration of the complexity of Native American identity and what he sees as the distortions of history.

I am told by many of you that I must forgive and so I shall
after an Indian woman puts her shoulder to the Grand Coulee Dam
and topples it. I am told by many of you that I must forgive
and so I shall after the floodwaters burst each successive dam
downriver from the Grand Coulee. I am told by many of you   5
that I must forgive and so I shall after the floodwaters find
their way to the mouth of the Columbia River as it enters the Pacific
and causes all of it to rise. I am told by many of you that I must forgive
and so I shall after the first drop of floodwater is swallowed by that salmon
waiting in the Pacific. I am told by many of you that I must forgive and so I shall   10
after that salmon swims upstream, through the mouth of the Columbia
and then past the flooded cities, broken dams and abandoned reactors
of Hanford. I am told by many of you that I must forgive and so I shall
in the shallows of a secret bay on the reservation where I wait alone.
I am told by many of you that I must forgive and so I shall after   15
that salmon leaps into the night air above the water, throws
a lightning bolt at the brush near my feet, and starts the fire
which will lead all of the lost Indians home. I am told
by many of you that I must forgive and so I shall
after we Indians have gathered around the fire with that salmon   20
who has three stories it must tell before sunrise: one story will teach us
how to pray; another story will make us laugh for hours;
the third story will give us reason to dance. I am told by many
of you that I must forgive and so I shall when I am dancing
with my tribe during the powwow at the end of the world.   25

[1996]

. . . .

Exploring the Text

1. What is the relationship between reader and writer that Alexie establishes with his use of "I" and "you"? How does his choice of the passive voice—that is, writing "I am told by many of you" (l. 1) rather than "Many of you have told me"—affect that relationship?

2. In each "after" clause, Alexie's description involves hyperbole. Is he being sarcastic? disrespectful? serious?

3. What is the effect of the details Alexie chooses? Explore the geographical references he makes (Grand Coulee Dam, Columbia River, Hanford) as well as the images he creates. How would you describe the order in which he presents them? How would changing the order affect the poem?

4. Alexie uses anaphora by repeating the opening clause ("I am told by many of you that I must forgive and so I shall") several times. What is the effect of this repetition? Try restructuring the poem by omitting the repeated uses of the opening clause and creating a series of "after" clauses: "I am told by many of you that I must forgive and

so I shall after an Indian woman puts her shoulder to the Grand Coulee Dam and topples it, after the floodwaters burst each successive dam, . . . after the floodwaters find their way . . ." What impact would such an alteration have?

5. The poem takes a turn at line 20. Describe the change in terms of tone and topic. What differences in language use, such as syntax and pronoun reference, do you note?

6. What makes this a poem? Try restructuring it as a paragraph that consists of a series of sentences and explore the different impact of Alexie's words. Ask yourself why he breaks the lines as he does.

7. The salmon is a major presence in this poem. What is its symbolic value?

8. What is the meaning of forgiveness in this poem? Alexie never indicates what must be forgiven, assuming that his audience understands. How might this forgiveness connect to the apocalyptic "end of the world" (l. 25) reference at the end of the poem? With your response to these questions in mind, describe the tone of the poem. Is it angry? ironic? elegiac? defiant?

9. What role does sound play in this poem? Try a choral reading, with one person reading each sentence aloud. Begin reading the next sentence after the previous speaker has read the first eight words: "I am told by many of you that . . ." What do you learn from hearing the poem rather than just reading it?

10. Like many poems, this one implicitly makes an argument. What is that argument? Try expressing it as the result of Alexie's choices in language and structure. For instance: "In this poem, Sherman Alexie uses _____ and _____ to argue that _____." Is there more than one argument?

First Muse

JULIA ALVAREZ

Julia Alvarez (b. 1950) was born in New York but raised in the Dominican Republic until she was ten. After her father became involved in an unsuccessful plot to overthrow the dictator Rafael Trujillo, the family fled to the United States in 1960. Alvarez received a BA from Middlebury College and an MA from Syracuse University. She has published poetry, fiction, memoir, and children's books, including her best-selling first novel, the autobiographical *How the Garcia Girls Lost Their Accents* (1991), which focuses on the family's efforts to adapt to their new American environment. Other novels include *In the Time of Butterflies* (1994), *In the Name of Salome* (2000), and *Saving the World* (2006). Her more recent work includes the autobiographical *Once upon a Quinceañera: Coming of Age in the USA* (2007) and *Return to Sender* (2009), a children's book. Currently a writer-in-residence at Middlebury College, Alvarez splits her time between there and the Dominican Republic, where she and her husband own a coffee farm. Their farm includes a school where local farmers can learn to read and write. Alvarez frequently writes about cultural clashes and displacement, as she does in the poem "First Muse."

When I heard the famous poet pronounce
"One can only write poems in the tongue
in which one first said *Mother*," I was stunned.
Lately arrived in English, I slipped down
into my seat and fought back tears, thinking   5
of all those notebooks filled with bogus poems
I'd have to burn, thinking maybe there was
a little loophole, maybe just maybe
Mami had sung me lullabies she'd learned
from wives stationed at the embassy,   10

thinking maybe she'd left the radio on
beside my crib tuned to the BBC
or Voice of America, maybe her friend
from boarding school had sent a talking doll
who spoke in English? Maybe I could be   15
the one exception to this writing rule?
For months I suffered from bad writer's-block,
which I envisioned, not as a blank page,
but as a literary border guard
turning me back to Spanish on each line.   20

I gave up writing, watched lots of TV,
and you know how it happens that advice
comes from unlikely quarters? *She* came on,
sassy, olive-skinned, hula-hooping her hips,
a basket of bananas on her head,   25
her lilting accent so full of feeling
it seemed the way the heart would speak English
if it could speak. I touched the screen and sang
my own heart out with my new muse, *I am
Chiquita Banana and I'm here to say* . . .   30

[1999]

. . . .

Exploring the Text

1. What is a "muse"? How is finding a muse linked to the speaker's identity in this poem?

2. Who are the people (or muses) that influence the speaker in her development as a writer?

3. What words and images in this poem suggest speech, sound, and voice? What is Alvarez's purpose in including so many? Why does she end the poem with the ellipsis dots?

4. How does the poem challenge authority—those who set standards for "literary merit"—and instead celebrate popular culture? What does Alvarez mean by "a literary border guard" (l. 19), and how does this image also challenge authority?
5. How does the poem's tone change from the opening lines of "the famous poet['s]" pronouncement to the vivid description of the ending? Describe that change.
6. How has Alvarez—or has she?—avoided the negative stereotype of Chiquita Banana? To respond to this question, you might explore images of the character (starting in 1944) and her history in advertising.

Caribe in Nueva York

NATHALIE HANDAL

Nathalie Handal (b. 1969)—a Palestinian American poet, playwright, editor, and critic—has lived in Europe, the United States, the Caribbean, Latin America, and the Middle East, and is fluent in several languages. After earning a BA in international relations and communications at Simmons College in Boston and an MFA at Bennington College in Vermont, she did postgraduate work at the University of London in English and drama. Currently she teaches at Columbia University. Handal has published several poetry collections and is the editor of *The Poetry of Arab Women: A Contemporary Anthology* (2000), which won the PEN Oakland/Josephine Miles Award. Handal coedited with Tina Chang and Ravi Shankar *Language for a New Century: Contemporary Poetry from the Middle East, Asia, and Beyond* (2008). An active theater director and producer, she has been a playwright-in-residence for the New York Theatre Workshop and Vassar College. Handal is currently at work on a film about artist and philosopher Khalil Gibran. Her debut collection, *The Lives of Rain* (2005), includes a series of poems on the consequences of displacement in Palestine itself as well as others on the Palestinian diaspora. In the following poem from that collection, she explores the experience of multiple identities, a theme that runs throughout her work.

Un Caribeño tells me:
we are spoiled here
we eat burgers, fries
arroz y habichuelas negras, plátanos[1]
for two dollars and ninety-nine cents   5
others starve, looking for a few bits—
We forget hunger . . .
I love America
but I dream of mangoes

---

[1]*arroz*, rice; *habichuelas negras*, black beans; *plátanos*, plantains.

Café Santo Domingo, merengue,   10
salsa, bachata, son²
I can't forget the sun on my back
in my eyes
but this is Nueva York in winter
and I can't see the beautiful brown legs   15
of *las mulatas*³
can't see their curves as they move
in the streets of Brooklyn, Bronx,
in the Upper West
Washington Heights . . .   20
Now I eat at Lenny's Bagels and Gray's Papaya
I look at the Hudson
instead of the Caribbean waters, *los malecones.*⁴
Proud of Gloria, Shakira, Mark, JLo
Juan Luís Guerra, Celia Cruz⁵ . . .   25
I dream of *la tierra*⁶
where we were born,
I walk Central Park
with our islands in my pockets
and my gloves on.   30

[2005]

Exploring the Text

1. Who are the two speakers in the poem?
2. Identify at least three different cultures or ethnicities referred to directly or indirectly through allusion. How does Handal refer to them (e.g., language, food, place)? How do these contribute to the point Handal is making?
3. The speaker alternates between first-person singular and plural. Who are "we" or "our" meant to include?
4. How do you interpret the juxtaposition of the following lines: "We forget hunger . . . / I love America" (ll. 7–8)? Is Handal's speaker callous? resigned? arrogant? ambivalent?
5. What is Handal's purpose in using Spanish in this poem? In the notes, she explains some of the language and allusions but not everything. Why? Depending on whether or not you knew the meaning of "Un Caribeño" (a male from the Caribbean), how would your understanding or experience of the poem change?

---

²*son*, typical music from Cuba.
³A female of multiracial heritage. — EDS.
⁴*los malecones*, waterfront boulevards.
⁵Gloria, Shakira, Mark, JLo, Juan Luís Guerra, Celia Cruz are all Latino performers/musicians.
⁶*tierra*, land.

6. What is the meaning of the final image—"our islands in my pockets / and my gloves on" (ll. 29–30)? Is this a sad or a hopeful image? Explain whether you find it a fitting way to close the poem.

NATHALIE HANDAL ON WRITING

Renée Shea (RS): "Caribe in Nueva York" seems a poem of ambivalence. You—the speaker?—"love America / but . . ." there's always a "but." The islands are in your pockets, but your gloves are on. Have you come to terms with yourself as a wanderer? Or is New York City enough of a polyglot to make you feel "at home"?

Nathalie Handal (NH): When I moved to New York City in 2002, I lived on the Upper West Side and met many immigrants from the Caribbean and Latin America who were grateful for their newfound home in New York City but deeply melancholic for their homeland. They manifested this melancholy by playing music from their country; eating food their mother would have cooked; and holding on to some habits, such as playing cards and hanging around with friends, having drinks. Of course this is not uncommon behavior for any immigrant, but these were the immigrants whom I saw every day. I understood what they felt, being dislocated myself, coming from a Middle Eastern background and having lived on four different continents. I recognized myself in them and what they longed for. I wrote "Caribe" not only to express my own experience but to find connections where there don't seem to be any.

Today, I am connected to my wanderings and the wanderer in me. People think that fragments cannot be whole. I don't view it that way. I cannot separate myself from all that is me—Palestinian, French, Latina, American. Just like I cannot separate myself from the world—being cognizant of the life-beats around us is what is holy in us.

RS: Biographical statements usually emphasize your heterogeneous background—so many places and ethnicities and languages. Has writing helped you come to terms with or even synthesize these differences?

NH: When I was growing up, I felt in perpetual motion, but one thing that always remained still—quiet—was my writing. My words became a doorway into a past often blurred by the commotion of moving. My words became a place I could return to, that remained familiar to me when all else kept changing . . . whether it was the new way I had to greet my neighbor or the different shadows that walked past the stream. My words

5

became a home I could trust, feel safe in. And it is through writing that I have come to understand not only the complexities of my social and historical contexts, and in consequence my personal cultural index, but also the *me* that views the world without margins but as one breath connecting all breaths. It is in writing that I have found my echo, shade, and wing. And what a flight!

RS: In your work, this poem as well as others, you use many different languages. (*The Lives of Rain* has "notes" at the end, with translations of words and phrases in the poems.) Is mixing languages one of the ways you assert (or develop or imagine or explore) your identity?

NH: I would say it's a manifestation of my multiple linguistic influences. I never felt I had a native tongue; many languages were my mother tongue, and at the same time none were. I grew up with French, English, and Arabic, and also with Spanish and Creole. When I write in English, words from the French or the Arabic or the Spanish surface naturally on the page . . . they often appear in the same sentence together. I speak and dream in all these languages, and they seem to exist harmoniously together. At least, I like to believe they do.

RS: Can you talk a little about the performance aspects of your poetry and your art in general? Do you consider yourself primarily a poet who also works with drama and film? Or are you mainly a performance artist? a writer? Or are these labels irrelevant today or to you?

NH: I consider myself to be a writer. Indeed, I write in different genres. But whether I am writing a poem or a play or a story, all belong to the universe of words; all are trying to communicate something—all telling a story, exploring language and the imagination, or trying to go beyond the spheres of the self and of the world. That said, poetry is my first love.

RS: In the introduction to your new anthology, *Language for a New Century: Contemporary Poetry from the Middle East, Asia, and Beyond*, you point out that your vision of the post-9/11 world is a "new century in which words, not weapons, could redefine our civilization," and that by including poets writing in over forty different languages, you chose a title that emphasizes how "these voices converge in the dream of shared utterance." Are you truly this optimistic about the power of language? Do you believe that reading and sharing these poems—organized thematically into categories of universal experience—can and will promote cross-cultural understanding?

NH: What I believe is that dialogue and communication, awareness and consciousness, can bring us to our humanity. This anthology was conceived

10

following the events of September 11, 2001. Taiwanese American poet Tina Chang, Indian American poet Ravi Shankar, and I felt a deep solidarity among ourselves and others of Eastern descent. We felt troubled by the negative views showcased in the media about the East. And although we did not have solutions for what was going on, nor could we explain or define the East so rigidly, we felt a deep need to respond in any way we could. So we went to what we knew best, our natural prayer — poetry. We went to the human voices that have enchanted us and changed our lives and spirits, in hopes of adding to the ongoing dialogue between East and West.

RS: It doesn't seem to me a coincidence or mere chance that the final word in your collection *The Lives of Rain* is "home." Where is home for you?

NH: Home is everywhere that is alive.

Follow-Up

1. What does Handal mean when she says, "My words became a doorway into a past often blurred by the commotion of moving" (para. 5)? Do you believe that writing something down adds to its permanence? How is it possible for words, as Handal suggests, to allow her to feel both transported and stabilized at the same time?
2. Handal further explores the importance of writing in her life through a figure of speech: "It is in writing that I have found my echo, shade, and wing" (para. 5). Take those one by one — echo, shade, and wing — and consider what each comparison implies.
3. How can poetry be, as Handal describes it, "our natural prayer" (para. 11)?
4. In what ways might Handal's poem "Caribe in Nueva York" be read as an embodiment of the concept of "dialogue" that she discusses in the interview?
5. Explain why you do or do not share Handal's optimism that the power of language "can bring us to our humanity" (para. 11).
6. Handal ends the interview by asserting, "Home is everywhere that is alive." Is that different than saying, "Home is everywhere that has life"? What does she mean?
7. After reading both her poem and her interview, perform the poem in a way that demonstrates your interpretation of it. Consider working with another person (or persons) to emphasize different voices. Discuss why you think Handal would like that approach.

Paired Poems

. . . .

To George Sand: A Desire

and

To George Sand: A Recognition

Elizabeth Barrett Browning

Elizabeth Barrett Browning (1806–1861) grew up in a household made affluent by her father's sugar plantations in Jamaica. A precocious child, she was a voracious reader, taking an interest in philosophers such as Thomas Paine and Voltaire, and classic writers such as Homer and Dante. She began writing as a teenager, but due to a series of health problems, she spent much of her adult life as an invalid. She is perhaps best known for her romance and subsequent marriage to poet and playwright Robert Brownin, with whom she moved to Italy in 1846. She began publishing her poetry in 1838 with *The Seraphim and Other Poems*. Her lyrical poems were collected in *Sonnets from the Portuguese* in 1859, and the extended verse-novel *Aurora Leigh*, which many consider to be her best work, was published in 1856. The image of Browning as the lady writer swooning on her Victorian couch is entirely stereotype; in fact, she was politically active and championed such causes as the abolition of slavery, the unification of Italy, and women's rights. She was fascinated by her contemporary Aurore Dupin (1804–1876), who wrote under the pseudonym George Sand, made her living as an author, dressed in men's clothing, and lived in defiance of many Victorian mores. In the following two sonnets, both written in 1844, Browning explores her ambivalence toward this controversial figure.

To George Sand: A Desire

Thou large-brained woman and large-hearted man,
Self-called George Sand! whose soul, amid the lions
Of thy tumultuous senses, moans defiance
And answers roar for roar, as spirits can:
I would some mild miraculous thunder ran   5
Above the applauded circus, in appliance
Of thine own nobler nature's strength and science,
Drawing two pinions, white as wings of swan,
From thy strong shoulders, to amaze the place
With holier light! that thou to woman's claim   10
And man's, mightst join beside the angel's grace
Of a pure genius sanctified from blame,

Till child and maiden pressed to thine embrace
To kiss upon thy lips a stainless fame.

[1844]

Exploring the Text

1. What contrast does Browning make in the opening line? What gender stereotypes are being called into question?
2. Of what importance is the description "Self-called" in line 2? Why might Browning find this fact significant?
3. Explain the circus metaphor that Browning develops. Why is it appropriate for her characterization of Sand? Do you think the crowd is roaring at the writer's victory or her futile attempt to play the male role of writer?
4. What point does Browning emphasize in lines 8–12? What is the effect of the image of "two pinions" (wings)?
5. In what ways does the final couplet provide a resolution to the poem?

To George Sand: A Recognition

True genius, but true woman! dost deny
The woman's nature with a manly scorn,
And break away the gauds[1] and armlets worn
By weaker women in captivity?
Ah, vain denial! that revolted cry   5
Is sobbed in by a woman's voice forlorn,—
Thy woman's hair, my sister, all unshorn
Floats back dishevelled strength in agony,
Disproving thy man's name: and while before
The world thou burnest in a poet-fire,   10
We see thy woman-heart beat evermore
Through the large flame. Beat purer, heart, and higher,
Till God unsex thee on the heavenly shore
Where unincarnate spirits purely aspire!

[1844]

Exploring the Text

1. What difference would it make to replace "but" in line 1 with "and"? What tension does Browning's choice of that conjunction immediately establish?
2. What is the question Browning is asking in lines 1–4? Try putting it in your own words.

---

[1]Ornament or trinket, jewelry.—EDS.

3. Browning's nouns often are accompanied by strong modifiers. What is meant by "manly scorn" (l. 2), "vain denial" (l. 5), and "revolted cry" (l. 5), for instance?
4. What is Browning saying to her "sister" in lines 7–9?
5. How do you interpret the exhortation in the last three lines, beginning with "Beat purer"?
6. In Shakespeare's play *Macbeth*, Lady Macbeth asks the gods to "unsex" her to enable her to achieve her ambitious though malevolent goals. How does this echo from *Macbeth* inform your reading of this sonnet?

Focus on Comparison and Contrast

1. How do the titles of these two sonnets suggest Browning's feelings toward George Sand?
2. The pronoun in the first sonnet is first-person singular only; the second includes the plural "we." What does this shift suggest about the persona of the speaker?
3. What conflicts or contradictions between being a writer and being a woman does Browning suggest in these two sonnets?
4. What is Browning's opinion of George Sand? For what does she admire her? What reservations does she have? What ambivalence do you sense?
5. Overall, would you characterize Browning as upholding or challenging the prevailing view of women in Victorian England?

Writing Assignment

In these two poems, Elizabeth Barrett Browning reflects on her contemporary, the female writer Aurore Dupin, who wrote under the pseudonym George Sand. Write an essay in which you compare and contrast the two poems, analyzing the poetic techniques Browning uses to express her attitude toward Sand.

Self-Portrait on the Borderline between Mexico and the United States

and

Self-Portrait Dedicated to Leon Trotsky

FRIDA KAHLO

Frida Kahlo was born in a small town on the outskirts of Mexico City in 1907, though she claimed 1910 as her birth year to associate herself more fully with the start of the Mexican Revolution. Stricken with polio as a child and injured in a bus accident when she was twenty-five, Kahlo—who had been studying medicine—turned to painting, especially self-portraits. Of her 143 paintings, 55 are self-portraits, including many portrayals of her physical and psychological pain. Kahlo's marriage to muralist Diego Rivera was notoriously stormy and included a divorce and a remarriage. Both Kahlo's art and her politics reflect a commitment to the indigenous Mexican culture. She and Rivera were sympathetic to the Communist movement and provided refuge for the revolutionary Leon Trotsky when he fled Stalinist Russia. When Kahlo died in 1954 at the age of forty-seven, her work was relatively unknown outside of Mexico. In the 1980s, when the values of Mexican cultural nationalism came to prominence, Kahlo became more widely known and her paintings highly coveted. In recent years, she has been the subject of several best-selling biographies; in 2001, she became the first Hispanic woman to be honored with a U.S. postage stamp; and in 2002, Salma Hayek played Kahlo in a commercially successful feature film directed by Julie Taymor.

Self-Portrait on the Borderline between Mexico and the United States (1932, oil on metal panel, 12½ × 13¾ in.)

Exploring the Texts

1. Historically, women artists have been prolific painters of self-portraits, perhaps because they were seldom permitted to practice with nude models. Until the nineteenth century, they often portrayed themselves in the act of painting, holding a paintbrush and a palette. In what ways do the two self-portraits here continue that tradition? In what ways has Kahlo left it behind?

Self-Portrait Dedicated to Leon Trotsky (1937, oil on masonite, 30 × 24 in.)

2. *Self-Portrait on the Borderline between Mexico and the United States* is a small painting on tin, a traditional Mexican art process that creates works called *retablos*—devotional paintings that commemorate or thank saints and deities. Kahlo uses the form, but her thematic purpose is different. Study the iconography (the objects in the painting) to determine if her purpose is at all devotional. If not, what is the purpose of the various images in the painting? What is the effect of the juxtaposition of the traditional form and the images of modern life? What might it mean that Kahlo has substituted a self-portrait for the image of the saint or deity that would be in the center of a traditional *retablo*?

3. What story does *Self-Portrait on the Borderline between Mexico and the United States* tell? Consider Kahlo's placement of herself, as well as the painting's symmetry. Look carefully at the shapes she uses to represent Mexico and the United States. How does the use of space beckon or repulse the viewer? What does Kahlo say about herself and the borderline between Mexico and the United States?

4. The paper Kahlo is holding in *Self-Portrait Dedicated to Leon Trotsky* says, "To Leon Trotsky, with all my love, I dedicate this painting on 7th November, 1937. Frida Kahlo in Saint Angel, Mexico." In what other ways is this painting a dedication of love?

5. What is the persona Kahlo creates for herself in *Self-Portrait Dedicated to Leon Trotsky*? How is it different from and similar to the character she creates in *Self-Portrait on the Borderline between Mexico and the United States*?

6. The surrealist painter André Breton told Kahlo that she was a surrealist and championed her work for a time, once describing it as "a ribbon around a bomb." Study the two paintings to see the effects of the feminine adornments. Do you consider Breton's comment sexist and condescending, or was he responding to what art critic Peter Schjeldahl called the "rhetorically explosive" quality of feminine adornments in Kahlo's work?

Conversation

The Legacy of Colonialism

In the early 1800s, European countries controlled 35 percent of the world, but by 1914, that number had risen to nearly 85 percent and included parts of Africa, Asia, Latin America, and the Caribbean. Not surprisingly, the legacy of **colonialism** has extended beyond the political independence that many countries gained in the 1960s and 1970s. The following texts comment in various ways on the assumptions and motivations of European colonial powers in Africa and the short- and longer-term consequences for both the colonized and the colonizer.

> *Texts*
>
> The Colonization of Africa (map)
>
> **Rudyard Kipling,** "The White Man's Burden" (poetry)
>
> **H. T. Johnson,** "The Black Man's Burden" (poetry)
>
> **Doris Lessing,** "The Old Chief Mshlanga" (fiction)
>
> **Felix Mnthali,** "The Stranglehold of English Lit" (poetry)
>
> **Chinua Achebe,** "An Image of Africa" (nonfiction)
>
> **Binyavanga Wainaina,** "How to Write about Africa" (nonfiction)

The Colonization of Africa

The map on the following page depicts the colonization of Africa, indicating the colonizing country and the date of independence.

Questions

1. Which two European countries controlled most of the continent?
2. Which African countries were independent before World War II?

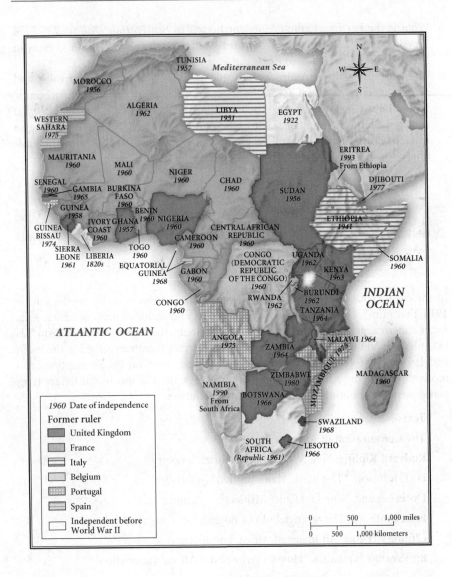

3. Which country was the first to gain independence? Which was the last?

The White Man's Burden

Rudyard Kipling

Winner of the Nobel Prize for Literature in 1907, Rudyard Kipling (1865–1936) is best known for *The Jungle Book* (1894), which has become a children's classic.

Kipling was born in Bombay, was educated in England, and lived for many years in India as a reporter for Anglo-Indian newspapers. Although Kipling demonstrates both understanding and appreciation of Indian culture in many of his works, "The White Man's Burden" famously summarizes the Eurocentric expansionist ideology of the time. Kipling originally wrote the poem for Queen Victoria's Diamond Jubilee in 1897, ultimately publishing it two years later in the popular magazine *McClure's*.

Take up the White Man's burden—
   Send forth the best ye breed—
Go, bind your sons to exile
   To serve your captives' need;
To wait, in heavy harness,   5
   On fluttered folk and wild—
Your new-caught sullen peoples,
   Half devil and half child.

Take up the White Man's burden—
   In patience to abide,   10
To veil the threat of terror
   And check the show of pride;
By open speech and simple,
   An hundred times made plain,

To seek another's profit   15
   And work another's gain.

Take up the White Man's burden—
   The savage wars of peace—
Fill full the mouth of Famine,
   And bid the sickness cease;   20
And when your goal is nearest
   (The end for others sought)
Watch sloth and heathen folly
   Bring all your hope to nought.

Take up the White Man's burden—   25
   No iron rule of kings,
But toil of serf and sweeper—
   The tale of common things.
The ports ye shall not enter,
   The roads ye shall not tread,   30
Go, make them with your living
   And mark them with your dead.

Take up the White Man's burden,
   And reap his old reward—

The blame of those ye better   35
 The hate of those ye guard —
The cry of hosts ye humour
 (Ah, slowly?) toward the light: —
"Why brought ye us from bondage,
 Our loved Egyptian night?"   40

Take up the White Man's burden —
 Ye dare not stoop to less —
Nor call too loud on Freedom
 To cloak your weariness.
By all ye will or whisper,   45
 By all ye leave or do,
The silent sullen peoples
 Shall weigh your God and you.

Take up the White Man's burden!
 Have done with childish days —   50
The lightly-proffered laurel,
 The easy ungrudged praise:
Comes now, to search your manhood
 Through all the thankless years,
Cold, edged with dear-bought wisdom,   55
 The judgment of your peers.

[1899]

. . . .

Questions

1. The poem is written as a series of imperatives addressed to "you"; to whom is the speaker addressing his exhortations?
2. How are "others" — that is, nonwhites — depicted in this poem? Cite specific descriptions and images.
3. What exactly is the "burden" alluded to in the title?

The Black Man's Burden

H. T. JOHNSON

Among the many replies to Kipling's poem was "The Black Man's Burden," a poem written by African American clergyman and editor H. T. Johnson. The poem was published in the *Christian Recorder* in 1899.

Pile on the Black Man's burden,
   'Tis nearest at your door;
Why heed long-bleeding Cuba
   Or dark Hawaii's shore?
Halt ye your fearless armies   5
   Which menace feeble folks,
Who fight with clubs and arrows
   And brook your rifle's smokes.

Pile on the Black Man's burden,
   His wail with laughter drown,   10
You've sealed the Red Man's problem
   And now take up the Brown.
In vain ye seek to end it
   With bullets, blood or death—
Better by far defend it   15
   With honor's holy breath.

Pile on the Black Man's burden,
   His back is broad though sore;
What though the weight oppress him,
   He's borne the like before.   20
Your Jim-Crow laws and customs,
   And fiendish midnight deed,
Though winked at by the nation,
   Will some day trouble breed.

Pile on the Black Man's burden,   25
   At length 'twill Heaven pierce;
Then on you or your children
   Will reign God's judgments fierce.
Your battleships and armies
   May weaker ones appall,   30
But God Almighty's justice
   They'll not disturb at all.

[1899]

Questions

1. What direct links, apart from the titles, with Kipling's poem do you see? Some have read Johnson's poem as a parody of Kipling's. Explain why you would agree or disagree with this assessment.
2. Both poems use second person ("you" and "your"), but who is the "you" in Kipling's poem and who is the "you" in Johnson's?

3. What is the "it" referred to in lines 13 and 15 of this poem? Why does Johnson call for "defend[ing] it / With honor's holy breath" (ll. 15–16)?

The Old Chief Mshlanga

DORIS LESSING

> Winner of the 2007 Nobel Prize in Literature, Doris Lessing was born in 1919 in Persia (now Iran) to British parents. In 1925, the family moved to Rhodesia (now Zimbabwe), from which many of the stories in her prolific career emerge. Lessing moved to London in 1949 and began publishing her work, including *The Grass Is Singing* (1949) and her breakout work *A Golden Notebook* (1962), which became a feminist manifesto. Lessing continues to write fiction, autobiography, drama (including an opera), and graphic novels; her latest work is the novel *Alfred and Emily*, published in 2008. "The Old Chief Mshlanga" was originally published in 1951 in Lessing's second book, *This Was the Old Chief's Country*, a collection of short stories set in Zimbabwe.

They were good, the years of ranging the bush over her father's farm which, like every white farm, was largely unused, broken only occasionally by small patches of cultivation. In between, nothing but trees, the long sparse grass, thorn and cactus and gully, grass and outcrop and thorn. And a jutting piece of rock which had been thrust up from the warm soil of Africa unimaginable eras of time ago, washed into hollows and whorls by sun and wind that had traveled so many thousands of miles of space and bush, would hold the weight of a small girl whose eyes were sightless for anything but a pale willowed river, a pale gleaming castle—a small girl singing: "Out flew the web and floated wide, the mirror cracked from side to side . . ."

Pushing her way through the green aisles of the mealie stalks,[1] the leaves arching like cathedrals veined with sunlight far overhead, with the packed red earth underfoot, a fine lace of red starred witchweed would summon up a black bent figure croaking premonitions: the Northern witch, bred of cold Northern forests, would stand before her among the mealie fields, and it was the mealie fields that faded and fled, leaving her among the gnarled roots of an oak, snow falling thick and soft and white, the woodcutter's fire glowing red welcome through crowding tree trunks.

A white child, opening its eyes curiously on a sun-suffused landscape, a gaunt and violent landscape, might be supposed to accept it as her own, to take the msasa trees and the thorn trees as familiars, to feel her blood running free and responsive to the swing of the seasons.

This child could not see a msasa tree, or the thorn, for what they were. Her books held tales of alien fairies, her rivers ran slow and peaceful, and she knew the shape of the leaves of an ash or an oak, the names of the little creatures that lived in English streams, when the words "the veld" meant strangeness, though she could remember nothing else.

---

[1]Corn.—EDS.

Because of this, for many years, it was the veld that seemed unreal; the sun was   5
a foreign sun, and the wind spoke a strange language.

The black people on the farm were as remote as the trees and the rocks. They were an amorphous black mass, mingling and thinning and massing like tadpoles, faceless, who existed merely to serve, to say "Yes, Baas," take their money, and go. They changed season by season, moving from one farm to the next, according to their outlandish needs, which one did not have to understand, coming from perhaps hundreds of miles north or east, passing on after a few months—where? Perhaps even as far away as the fabled gold mines of Johannesburg, where the pay was so much better than the few shillings a month and the double handful of mealie meal twice a day which they earned in that part of Africa.

The child was taught to take them for granted: the servants in the house would come running a hundred yards to pick up a book if she dropped it. She was called "Nkosikaas"—Chieftainess, even by the black children her own age.

Later, when the farm grew too small to hold her curiosity, she carried a gun in the crook of her arm and wandered miles a day, from vlei to vlei,[2] from kopje to kopje,[3] accompanied by two dogs: the dogs and the gun were an armor against fear. Because of them she never felt fear.

If a native came into sight along the kaffir[4] paths half a mile away, the dogs would flush him up a tree as if he were a bird. If he expostulated (in his uncouth language which was by itself ridiculous) that was cheek. If one was in a good mood, it could be a matter for laughter. Otherwise one passed on, hardly glancing at the angry man in the tree.

On the rare occasions when white children met together they could amuse   10
themselves by hailing a passing native in order to make a buffoon of him; they could set the dogs on him and watch him run; they could tease a small black child as if he were a puppy—save that they would not throw stones and sticks at a dog without a sense of guilt.

Later still, certain questions presented themselves in the child's mind; and because the answers were not easy to accept, they were silenced by an even greater arrogance of manner.

It was even impossible to think of the black people who worked about the house as friends, for if she talked to one of them, her mother would come running anxiously: "Come away; you mustn't talk to natives."

It was this instilled consciousness of danger, of something unpleasant, that made it easy to laugh out loud, crudely, if a servant made a mistake in his English or if he failed to understand an order—there is a certain kind of laughter that is fear, afraid of itself.

One evening, when I was about fourteen, I was walking down the side of a mealie field that had been newly plowed, so that the great red clods showed fresh and tumbling to the vlei beyond, like a choppy red sea; it was that hushed and listening

---

[2]Marsh or lake.—Eds.
[3]Rocky mounds exposed by erosion.—Eds.
[4]Former generic term for South African blacks, now derogatory.—Eds.

hour, when the birds send long sad calls from tree to tree, and all the colors of earth and sky and leaf are deep and golden. I had my rifle in the curve of my arm, and the dogs were at my heels.

In front of me, perhaps a couple of hundred yards away, a group of three 15 Africans came into sight around the side of a big ant-heap. I whistled the dogs close in to my skirts and let the gun swing in my hand, and advanced, waiting for them to move aside, off the path, in respect for my passing. But they came on steadily, and the dogs looked up at me for the command to chase. I was angry. It was "cheek" for a native not to stand off a path, the moment he caught sight of you.

In front walked an old man, stooping his weight on to a stick, his hair grizzled white, a dark red blanket slung over his shoulders like a cloak. Behind him came two young men, carrying bundles of pots, assegais, hatchets.

The group was not a usual one. They were not natives seeking work. These had an air of dignity, of quietly following their own purpose. It was the dignity that checked my tongue. I walked quietly on, talking softly to the growling dogs, till I was ten paces away. Then the old man stopped, drawing his blanket close.

"Morning, Nkosikaas," he said, using the customary greeting for any time of the day.

"Good morning," I said. "Where are you going?" My voice was a little truculent.

The old man spoke in his own language, then one of the young men stepped 20 forward politely and said in careful English: "My Chief travels to see his brothers beyond the river."

A Chief! I thought, understanding the pride that made the old man stand before me like an equal—more than an equal, for he showed courtesy, and I showed none.

The old man spoke again, wearing dignity like an inherited garment, still standing ten paces off, flanked by his entourage, not looking at me (that would have been rude) but directing his eyes somewhere over my head at the trees.

"You are the little Nkosikaas from the farm of Baas Jordan?"

"That's right," I said.

"Perhaps your father does not remember," said the interpreter for the old man, 25 "but there was an affair with some goats. I remember seeing you when you were . . ." The young man held his hand at knee level and smiled.

We all smiled.

"What is your name?" I asked.

"This is Chief Mshlanga," said the young man.

"I will tell my father that I met you," I said.

The old man said: "My greetings to your father, little Nkosikaas." 30

"Good morning," I said politely, finding the politeness difficult, from lack of use.

"Morning, little Nkosikaas," said the old man, and stood aside to let me pass.

I went by, my gun hanging awkwardly, the dogs sniffing and growling, cheated of their favorite game of chasing natives like animals.

Not long afterwards I read in an old explorer's book the phrase: "Chief Mshlanga's country." It went like this: "Our destination was Chief Mshlanga's country, to the north of the river; and it was our desire to ask his permission to prospect for gold in his territory."

The phrase "ask his permission" was so extraordinary to a white child, brought up to consider all natives as things to use, that it revived those questions, which could not be suppressed: they fermented slowly in my mind.

On another occasion one of those old prospectors who still move over Africa looking for neglected reefs, with their hammers and tents, and pans for sifting gold from crushed rock, came to the farm and, in talking of the old days, used that phrase again: "This was the Old Chief's country," he said. "It stretched from those mountains over there way back to the river, hundreds of miles of country." That was his name for our district: "The Old Chief's Country"; he did not use our name for it—a new phrase which held no implication of usurped ownership.

As I read more books about the time when this part of Africa was opened up, not much more than fifty years before, I found Old Chief Mshlanga had been a famous man, known to all the explorers and prospectors. But then he had been young; or maybe it was his father or uncle they spoke of—I never found out.

During that year I met him several times in the part of the farm that was traversed by natives moving over the country. I learned that the path up the side of the big red field where the birds sang was the recognized highway for migrants. Perhaps I even haunted it in the hope of meeting him: being greeted by him, the exchange of courtesies, seemed to answer the questions that troubled me.

Soon I carried a gun in a different spirit; I used it for shooting food and not to give me confidence. And now the dogs learned better manners. When I saw a native approaching, we offered and took greetings; and slowly that other landscape in my mind faded, and my feet struck directly on the African soil, and I saw the shapes of tree and hill clearly, and the black people moved back, as it were, out of my life: it was as if I stood aside to watch a slow intimate dance of landscape and men, a very old dance, whose steps I could not learn.

But I thought: this is my heritage, too; I was bred here; it is my country as well as the black man's country; and there is plenty of room for all of us, without elbowing each other off the pavements and roads.

It seemed it was only necessary to let free that respect I felt when I was talking with Old Chief Mshlanga, to let both black and white people meet gently, with tolerance for each other's differences: it seemed quite easy.

Then, one day, something new happened. Working in our house as servants were always three natives: cook, houseboy, garden boy. They used to change as the farm natives changed: staying for a few months, then moving on to a new job, or back home to their kraals.[5] They were thought of as "good" or "bad" natives; which meant: how did they behave as servants? Were they lazy, efficient, obedient, or disrespectful? If the family felt good-humored, the phrase was: "What can you expect from raw black savages?" If we were angry, we said: "These damned niggers, we would be much better off without them."

---

[5]Corrals.—Eds.

One day, a white policeman was on his rounds of the district, and he said laughingly: "Did you know you have an important man in your kitchen?"

"What!" exclaimed my mother sharply. "What do you mean?"

"A Chief's son." The policeman seemed amused. "He'll boss the tribe when the old man dies."

"He'd better not put on a Chief's son act with me," said my mother.

When the policeman left, we looked with different eyes at our cook: he was a good worker, but he drank too much at weekends—that was how we knew him.

He was a tall youth, with very black skin, like black polished metal, his tightly growing black hair parted white man's fashion at one side, with a metal comb from the store stuck into it; very polite, very distant, very quick to obey an order. Now that it had been pointed out, we said: "Of course, you can see. Blood always tells."

My mother became strict with him now she knew about his birth and prospects. Sometimes, when she lost her temper, she would say: "You aren't the Chief yet, you know." And he would answer her very quietly, his eyes on the ground: "Yes, Nkosikaas."

One afternoon, he asked for a whole day off, instead of the customary half-day, to go home next Sunday.

"How can you go home in one day?"

"It will take me half an hour on my bicycle," he explained.

I watched the direction he took; and the next day I went off to look for this kraal; I understood he must be Chief Mshlanga's successor: there was no other kraal near enough our farm.

Beyond our boundaries on that side the country was new to me. I followed unfamiliar paths past kopjes that till now had been part of the jagged horizon, hazed with distance. This was Government land, which had never been cultivated by white men; at first I could not understand why it was that it appeared, in merely crossing the boundary, I had entered a completely fresh type of landscape. It was a wide green valley, where a small river sparkled, and vivid water-birds darted over the rushes. The grass was thick and soft to my calves, the trees stood tall and shapely.

I was used to our farm, whose hundred of acres of harsh eroded soil bore trees that had been cut for the mine furnaces and had grown thin and twisted, where the cattle had dragged the grass flat, leaving innumerable crisscrossing trails that deepened each season into gullies, under the force of the rains.

This country had been left untouched, save for prospectors whose picks had struck a few sparks from the surface of the rocks as they wandered by; and for migrant natives whose passing had left, perhaps, a charred patch on the trunk of a tree where their evening fire had nestled.

It was very silent: a hot morning with pigeons cooing throatily, the midday shadows lying dense and thick with clear yellow spaces of sunlight between and in all that wide green parklike valley, not a human soul but myself.

I was listening to the quick regular tapping of a woodpecker when slowly a chill feeling seemed to grow up from the small of my back to my shoulders, in a constricting spasm like a shudder, and at the roots of my hair a tingling sensation began and ran down over the surface of my flesh, leaving me goosefleshed and cold, though I was damp with sweat. Fever? I thought; then uneasily, turned to look over my shoulder; and realized suddenly that this was fear. It was extraordinary, even humiliating. It was a new fear. For all the years I had walked by myself over this country I had never known a moment's uneasiness; in the beginning because I had been supported by a gun and the dogs, then because I had learned an easy friendliness for the Africans I might encounter.

I had read of this feeling, how the bigness and silence of Africa, under the ancient sun, grows dense and takes shape in the mind, till even the birds seem to call menacingly, and a deadly spirit comes out of the trees and the rocks. You move warily, as if your very passing disturbs something old and evil, something dark and big and angry that might suddenly rear and strike from behind. You look at groves of entwined trees; and picture the animals that might be lurking there; you look at the river running slowly, dropping from level to level through the vlei, spreading into pools where at night the buck come to drink, and the crocodiles rise and drag them by their soft noses into underwater caves. Fear possessed me. I found I was turning round and round, because of that shapeless menace behind me that might reach out and take me; I kept glancing at the files of kopjes which, seen from a different angle, seemed to change with every step so that even known landmarks, like a big mountain that had sentineled my world since I first became conscious of it, showed an unfamiliar sunlit valley among its foothills. I did not know where I was. I was lost. Panic seized me. I found I was spinning round and round, staring anxiously at this tree and that, peering up at the sun which appeared to have moved into an eastern slant, shedding the sad yellow light of sunset. Hours must have passed! I looked at my watch and found that this state of meaningless terror had lasted perhaps ten minutes.

The point was that it was meaningless. I was not ten miles from home: I had   60
only to take my way back along the valley to find myself at the fence; away among the foothills of the kopjes gleamed the roof of a neighbor's house, and a couple of hours' walking would reach it. This was the sort of fear that contracts the flesh of a dog at night and sets him howling at the full moon. It had nothing to do with what I thought or felt; and I was more disturbed by the fact that I could become its victim than of the physical sensation itself: I walked steadily on, quieted, in a divided mind, watching my own pricking nerves and apprehensive glances from side to side with a disgusted amusement. Deliberately I set myself to think of this village I was seeking, and what I should do when I entered it—if I could find it, which was doubtful, since I was walking aimlessly and it might be anywhere in the hundreds of thousands of acres of bush that stretched about me. With my mind on that village, I realized that a new sensation was added to the fear: loneliness. Now such a terror of isolation invaded me that I could hardly walk; and if it were not that I came over the crest of a small rise and saw a village below me, I should have turned and gone home. It was a cluster of thatched huts in a clearing among trees. There were neat patches of mealies and pumpkins and millet, and cattle grazed under some trees at a distance. Fowls scratched among the huts, dogs lay sleeping on the grass, and goats friezed a kopje that jutted up beyond a tributary of the river lying like an enclosing arm round the village.

As I came close I saw the huts were lovingly decorated with patterns of yellow and red and ochre mud on the walls; and the thatch was tied in place with plaits of straw.

This was not at all like our farm compound, a dirty and neglected place, a temporary home for migrants who had no roots in it.

And now I did not know what to do next. I called a small black boy, who was sitting on a log playing a stringed gourd, quite naked except for the strings of blue beads round his neck, and said: "Tell the Chief I am here." The child stuck his thumb in his mouth and stared shyly back at me.

For minutes I shifted my feet on the edge of what seemed a deserted village, till at last the child scuttled off, and then some women came. They were draped in bright cloths, with brass glinting in their ears and on their arms. They also stared, silently; then turned to chatter among themselves.

I said again: "Can I see Chief Mshlanga?" I saw they caught the name; they did   65
not understand what I wanted. I did not understand myself.

At last I walked through them and came past the huts and saw a clearing under a big shady tree, where a dozen old men sat cross-legged on the ground, talking. Chief Mshlanga was leaning back against the tree, holding a gourd in his hand, from which he had been drinking. When he saw me, not a muscle of his face moved, and I could see he was not pleased: perhaps he was afflicted with my own shyness, due to being unable to find the right forms of courtesy for the occasion. To meet me, on our own farm, was one thing; but I should not have come here. What had I expected? I could not join them socially: the thing was unheard of. Bad enough that I, a white girl, should be walking the veld alone as a white man might: and in this part of the bush where only Government officials had the right to move.

Again I stood, smiling foolishly, while behind me stood the groups of brightly clad, chattering women, their faces alert with curiosity and interest, and in front of me sat the old men, with old lined faces, their eyes guarded, aloof. It was a village of ancients and children and women. Even the two young men who kneeled beside the Chief were not those I had seen with him previously: the young men were all away working on the white men's farms and mines, and the Chief must depend on relatives who were temporarily on holiday for his attendants.

"The small white Nkosikaas is far from home," remarked the old man at last.

"Yes," I agreed, "it is far." I wanted to say: "I have come to pay you a friendly visit, Chief Mshlanga." I could not say it. I might now be feeling an urgent helpless desire to get to know these men and women as people, to be accepted by them as a friend, but the truth was I had set out in a spirit of curiosity: I had wanted to see the village that one day our cook, the reserved and obedient young man who got drunk on Sundays, would one day rule over.

"The child of Nkosi Jordan is welcome," said Chief Mshlanga.   70

"Thank you," I said, and could think of nothing more to say. There was a silence, while the flies rose and began to buzz around my head; and the wind shook a little in the thick green tree that spread its branches over the old men.

"Good morning," I said at last. "I have to return now to my home."

"Morning, little Nkosikaas," said Chief Mshlanga.

I walked away from the indifferent village, over the rise past the staring amber-eyed goats, down through the tall stately trees into the great rich green valley where the river meandered and the pigeons cooed tales of plenty and the woodpecker tapped softly.

The fear had gone; the loneliness had set into stiff-necked stoicism; there was now a queer hostility in the landscape, a cold, hard, sullen indomitability that walked with me, as strong as a wall, as intangible as smoke; it seemed to say to me: you walk here as a destroyer. I went slowly homewards, with an empty heart: I had learned that if one cannot call a country to heel like a dog, neither can one dismiss the past with a smile in an easy gush of feeling, saying: I could not help it, I am also a victim.

I only saw Chief Mshlanga once again.

One night my father's big red land was trampled down by small sharp hooves, and it was discovered that the culprits were goats from Chief Mshlanga's kraal. This had happened once before, years ago.

My father confiscated all the goats. Then he sent a message to the old Chief that if he wanted them he would have to pay for the damage.

He arrived at our house at the time of sunset one evening, looking very old and bent now, walking stiffly under his regally draped blanket, leaning on a big stick. My father sat himself down in his big chair below the steps of the house; the old man squatted carefully on the ground before him, flanked by his two young men.

The palaver was long and painful, because of the bad English of the young man who interpreted, and because my father could not speak dialect, but only kitchen kaffir.

From my father's point of view, at least two hundred pounds' worth of damage had been done to the crop. He knew he could not get the money from the old man. He felt he was entitled to keep the goats. As for the old Chief, he kept repeating angrily: "Twenty goats! My people cannot lose twenty goats! We are not rich, like the Nkosi Jordan, to lose twenty goats at once."

My father did not think of himself as rich, but rather as very poor. He spoke quickly and angrily in return, saying that the damage done meant a great deal to him, and that he was entitled to the goats.

At last it grew so heated that the cook, the Chief's son, was called from the kitchen to be interpreter, and now my father spoke fluently in English, and our cook translated rapidly so that the old man could understand how very angry my father was. The young man spoke without emotion, in a mechanical way, his eyes lowered, but showing how he felt his position by a hostile uncomfortable set of the shoulders.

It was now in the late sunset, the sky a welter of colors, the birds singing their last songs, and the cattle, lowing peacefully, moving past us towards their sheds for the night. It was the hour when Africa is most beautiful; and here was this pathetic, ugly scene, doing no one any good.

At last my father stated finally: "I'm not going to argue about it. I am keeping the goats."

The old Chief flashed back in his own language: "That means that my people will go hungry when the dry season comes."

"Go to the police, then," said my father, and looked triumphant.

There was, of course, no more to be said.

The old man sat silent, his head bent, his hands dangling helplessly over his withered knees. Then he rose, the young men helping him, and he stood facing my father. He spoke once again, very stiffly; and turned away and went home to his village.

"What did he say?" asked my father of the young man, who laughed uncomfortably and would not meet his eyes. 90

"What did he say?" insisted my father.

Our cook stood straight and silent, his brows knotted together. Then he spoke. "My father says: All this land, this land you call yours, is his land; and belongs to our people."

Having made this statement, he walked off into the bush after his father, and we did not see him again.

Our next cook was a migrant from Nyasaland, with no expectations of greatness.

Next time the policeman came on his rounds he was told this story. He remarked: "That kraal has no right to be there; it should have been moved long ago. I 95 don't know why no one has done anything about it. I'll have a chat with the Native Commissioner next week. I'm going over for tennis on Sunday, anyway."

Sometime later we heard that Chief Mshlanga and his people had been moved two hundred miles east, to a proper Native Reserve; the Government land was going to be opened up for white settlement soon.

I went to see the village again, about a year afterwards. There was nothing there. Mounds of red mud, where the huts had been, had long swathes of rotting thatch over them, veined with the red galleries of the white ants. The pumpkin vines rioted everywhere, over the bushes, up the lower branches of trees so that the great golden balls rolled underfoot and dangled overhead: it was a festival of pumpkins. The bushes were crowding up, the new grass sprang vivid green.

The settler lucky enough to be allotted the lush warm valley (if he chose to cultivate this particular section) would find, suddenly, in the middle of a mealie field, the plants were growing fifteen feet tall, the weight of the cobs dragging at the stalks, and wonder what unsuspected vein of richness he had struck.

[1951]

· ·

Questions

1. We see this story through the eyes of a young white girl. To what extent does she represent the whites' view of Africa?

2. Why does Lessing emphasize the role of language in this story? For instance, the ease the narrator felt in laughing out loud "if a servant made a mistake in his English" (para. 13); her father's inability to "speak dialect, but only kitchen kaffir" (para. 80); and Chief Mshlanga's angry retort to her father near the end, a retort "flashed back in [the Chief's] own language" (para. 86)?

3. What passages can you find that indicate the young narrator's recognition of the complexity of her position? Why, for example, does she describe Chief Mshlanga as "wearing dignity like an inherited garment" (para. 22)?

4. What evidence is there of the narrator's appreciation for the physical beauty of the African landscape? What does Lessing suggest when the narrator characterizes the landscape with a mixture of images of Africa and Europe, such as "the green aisles of the mealie stalks, the leaves arching like cathedrals" (para. 2)?
5. How do you respond to the narrator's thoughts: "this is my heritage, too; I was bred here; it is my country as well as the black man's country; and there is plenty of room for all of us" (para. 40)? Do you think Lessing agrees with her?
6. What does the ending of this story suggest about the likely future of the colonists?

The Stranglehold of English Lit

Felix Mnthali

> A Malawian poet, novelist, and playwright, Felix Mnthali (b. 1933) was educated in Africa and Canada, and has taught at the University of Ibadan, Malawi University, and the University of Botswana. Among his best-known works are *When Sunset Comes to Saptiwa* (1980)—a collection of poems—and the novels *My Dear Anniversary* (1992) and *Yoranivyoto* (1998). The following poem is from *Echoes from Obadan* (privately printed in 1961).

(For Molara Ogundipe-Leslie)

Those questions, sister,
those questions
        stand
        stab
        jab   5
     and gore
too close to the centre!

For if we had asked
why Jane Austen's people
carouse all day   10
and do no work

would Europe in Africa
have stood
the test of time?
and would she still maul   15
the flower of our youth
in the south?
Would she?

Your elegance of deceit,
Jane Austen,   20
lulled the sons and daughters
of the dispossessed
into a calf-love
with irony and satire
around imaginary people.   25

While history went on mocking
the victims of branding irons
and sugar-plantations
that made Jane Austen's people
wealthy beyond compare!   30

Eng. Lit., my sister,
was more than a cruel joke—
it was the heart
of alien conquest.

How could questions be asked   35
at Makerere and Ibadan,
Dakar and Ford Hare—
with Jane Austen
at the centre?
How could they be answered?   40

[1961]

Questions

1. Why do you think Mnthali chose Jane Austen as the author cited in this poem?
2. Who is the "sister" (l. 1) the speaker addresses?
3. Why does the speaker assert that "Eng. Lit. . . . . was the heart / of alien conquest" (ll. 31–34)?
4. What is the nature of the power that Mnthali believes literature holds?

An Image of Africa

Chinua Achebe

Chinua Achebe (b. 1930) is the most widely read African writer of his generation, primarily for his debut novel, *Things Fall Apart* (1958). His novels, poetry, and criticism examine the clash of culture during the colonial era, especially the conflict between traditional tribal values and Christianity. He also addresses the politics and alienation of the postcolonial period in Nigeria in his later works, such as *No Longer at Ease* (1960) and *A Man of the People* (1966). Achebe is currently ~~d. 2013~~ the Charles P. Stevenson Professor of Languages and Literature at Bard College in New York. In "An Image of Africa," originally delivered as a lecture at the University of Massachusetts in 1975, Achebe criticized Joseph Conrad for being "a bloody racist" in his portrayal of Africa and Africans in *Heart of Darkness*.

It was a fine autumn morning at the beginning of this academic year such as encouraged friendliness to passing strangers. Brisk youngsters were hurrying in all directions, many of them obviously freshmen in their first flush of enthusiasm. An older man, going the same way as I, turned and remarked to me how very young they came these days. I agreed. Then he asked me if I was a student too. I said no, I was a teacher. What did I teach? African literature. Now that was funny, he said, because he never had thought of Africa as having that kind of stuff, you know. By this time I was walking much faster. "Oh well," I heard him say finally, behind me, "I guess I have to take your course to find out."

A few weeks later I received two very touching letters from high school children in Yonkers, New York, who—bless their teacher—had just read *Things Fall Apart*. One of them was particularly happy to learn about the customs and superstitions of an African tribe.

I propose to draw from these rather trivial encounters rather heavy conclusions which at first sight might seem somewhat out of proportion to them: But only at first sight.

The young fellow from Yonkers, perhaps partly on account of his age but I believe also for much deeper and more serious reasons, is obviously unaware that the life of his own tribesmen in Yonkers, New York, is full of odd customs and superstitions and, like everybody else in his culture, imagines that he needs a trip to Africa to encounter those things.

The other person being fully my own age could not be excused on the grounds of his years. Ignorance might be a more likely reason; but here again I believe that something more willful than a mere lack of information was at work. For did not that erudite British historian and Regius Professor at Oxford, Hugh Trevor-Roper, pronounce a few years ago that African history did not exist?

If there is something in these utterances more than youthful experience, more than a lack of factual knowledge, what is it? Quite simply it is the desire—one might indeed say the need—in Western psychology to set Africa up as a foil in Europe, a place of negations at once remote and vaguely familiar in comparison with which Europe's own state of spiritual grace will be manifest.

This need is not new: which should relieve us of considerable responsibility and perhaps make us even willing to look at this phenomenon dispassionately. I have neither the desire nor, indeed, the competence to do so with the tools of the social and biological sciences. But, I can respond, as a novelist, to one famous book of European fiction, Joseph Conrad's *Heart of Darkness*, which better than any other work I know

5

displays that Western desire and need which I have just spoken about. Of course, there are whole libraries of books devoted to the same purpose, but most of them are so obvious and so crude that few people worry about them today. Conrad, on the other hand, is undoubtedly one of the great stylists of modern fiction and a good storyteller into the bargain. His contribution therefore falls automatically into a different class—permanent literature—read and taught and constantly evaluated by serious academics. *Heart of Darkness* is indeed so secure today that a leading Conrad scholar has numbered it "among the half-dozen greatest short novels in the English language." I will return to this critical opinion in due course because it may seriously modify my earlier suppositions about who may or may not be guilty in the things of which I will now speak.

Heart of Darkness projects the image of Africa as "the other world," the antithesis of Europe and therefore of civilization, a place where a man's vaunted intelligence and refinement are finally mocked by triumphant bestiality. The book opens on the River Thames, tranquil, resting peacefully "at the decline of day after ages of good service done to the race that peopled its banks." But the actual story takes place on the River Congo, the very antithesis of the Thames. The River Congo is quite decidedly not a River Emeritus. It has rendered no service and enjoys no old-age pension. We are told that "going up that river was like travelling back to the earliest beginning of the world."

Is Conrad saying then that these two rivers are very different, one good, the other bad? Yes, but that is not the real point. What actually worries Conrad is the lurking hint of kinship, of common ancestry. For the Thames, too, "has been one of the dark places of the earth." It conquered its darkness, of course, and is now at peace. But if it were to visit its primordial relative, the Congo, it would run the terrible risk of hearing grotesque, suggestive echoes of its own forgotten darkness, and of falling victim to an avenging recrudescence of the mindless frenzy of the first beginnings.

I am not going to waste your time with examples of Conrad's famed evocation of the African atmosphere. In the final consideration it amounts to no more than a steady, ponderous, fake-ritualistic repetition of two sentences, one about silence and the other about frenzy. An example of the former is "It was the stillness of an implacable force brooding over an inscrutable intention" and of the latter, "The steamer toiled along slowly on the edge of a black and incomprehensible frenzy." Of course, there is a judicious change of adjective from time to time so that instead of "inscrutable," for example, you might have "unspeakable," etc., etc.

The eagle-eyed English critic, F. R. Leavis, drew attention nearly thirty years ago to Conrad's "adjectival insistence upon inexpressible and incomprehensible mystery." That insistence must not be dismissed lightly, as many Conrad critics have tended to do, as a mere stylistic flaw. For it raises serious questions of artistic good faith. When a writer, while pretending to record scenes, incidents and their impact, is in reality engaged in inducing hypnotic stupor in his readers through a bombardment of emotive words and other forms of trickery, much more has to be at stake than stylistic felicity. Generally, normal readers are well armed to detect and resist such underhand activity. But Conrad chose his subject well—one which was guaranteed

10

not to put him in conflict with the psychological predisposition of his readers or raise the need for him to contend with their resistance. He chose the role of purveyor of comforting myths.

The most interesting and revealing passages in *Heart of Darkness* are, however, about people. I must quote a long passage from the middle of the story in which representatives of Europe in a steamer going down the Congo encounter the denizens of Africa:

> We were wanderers on a prehistoric earth, on an earth that wore the aspect of an unknown planet. We could have fancied ourselves the first of men taking possession of an accursed inheritance, to be subdued at the cost of profound anguish and of excessive toil. But suddenly, as we struggled round a bend, there would be a glimpse of rush walls, of peaked grass-roofs, a burst of yells, a whirl of black limbs, a mass of hands clapping, of feet stamping, of bodies swaying, of eyes rolling, under the droop of heavy and motionless foliage. The steamer toiled along slowly on the edge of a black and incomprehensible frenzy. The prehistoric man was cursing us, praying to us, welcoming us—who could tell? We were cut off from the comprehension of our surroundings; we glided past like phantoms, wondering and secretly appalled, as sane men would be before an enthusiastic outbreak in a madhouse. We could not understand because we were too far and could not remember because we were travelling in the night of first ages, of those ages that are gone, leaving hardly a sign—and no memories.
>
> The earth seemed unearthly. We are accustomed to look upon the shackled form of a conquered monster, but there—there you could look at a thing monstrous and free. It was unearthly, and the men were —— No, they were not inhuman. Well, you know, that was the worst of it—this suspicion of their not being inhuman. It would come slowly to one. They howled and leaped, and spun, and made horrid faces; but what thrilled you was just the thought of their humanity—like yours—the thought of your remote kinship with this wild and passionate uproar. Ugly. Yes, it was ugly enough; but if you were man enough you would admit to yourself that there was in you just the faintest trace of a response to the terrible frankness of that noise, a dim suspicion of there being a meaning in it which you—you so remote from the night of first ages— could comprehend.

Herein lies the meaning of *Heart of Darkness* and the fascination it holds over the Western mind: "What thrilled you was just the thought of their humanity—like yours . . . Ugly."

Having shown us Africa in the mass, Conrad then zeros in on a specific example, giving us one of his rare descriptions of an African who is not just limbs or rolling eyes:

> And between whiles I had to look after the savage who was fireman. He was an improved specimen; he could fire up a vertical boiler. He was there below me, and, upon my word, to look at him was as edifying as seeing a dog in a parody of breeches and a feather hat, walking on his hind-legs. A few months of training had done for that really fine chap. He squinted at the steam-gauge and at the water-gauge with an evident effort of intrepidity—and he had filed his teeth, too, the poor devil, and the wool of his pate shaved into

queer patterns, and three ornamental scars on each of his cheeks. He ought to have been clapping his hands and stamping his feet on the bank, instead of which he was hard at work, a thrall to strange witchcraft, full of improving knowledge.

As everybody knows, Conrad is a romantic on the side. He might not exactly admire savages clapping their hands and stamping their feet but they have at least the merit of being in their place, unlike this dog in a parody of breeches. For Conrad, things (and persons) being in their place is of the utmost importance.

Towards the end of the story, Conrad lavishes great attention quite unexpectedly on an African woman who has obviously been some kind of mistress to Mr. Kurtz and now presides (if I may be permitted a little imitation of Conrad) like a formidable mystery over the inexorable imminence of his departure:

> She was savage and superb, wild-eyed and magnificent. . . . She stood looking at us without a stir, and like the wilderness itself, with an air of brooding over an inscrutable purpose.

This Amazon is drawn in considerable detail, albeit of a predictable nature, for two reasons. First, she is in her place and so can win Conrad's special brand of approval; and second, she fulfills a structural requirement of the story; she is a savage counterpart to the refined, European woman with whom the story will end:

> She came forward, all in black, with a pale head, floating towards me in the dusk. She was in mourning. . . . She took both my hands in hers and murmured, "I had heard you were coming." . . . She had a mature capacity for fidelity, for belief, for suffering.

The difference in the attitude of the novelist to these two women is conveyed 15 in too many direct and subtle ways to need elaboration. But perhaps the most significant difference is the one implied in the author's bestowal of human expression to the one and the withholding of it from the other. It is clearly not part of Conrad's purpose to confer language on the "rudimentary souls" of Africa. They only "exchanged short grunting phrases" even among themselves but mostly they were too busy with their frenzy. There are two occasions in the book, however, when Conrad departs somewhat from his practice and confers speech, even English speech, on the savages. The first occurs when cannibalism gets the better of them:

> "Catch 'im," he snapped, with a bloodshot widening of his eyes and a flash of sharp teeth — "catch 'im. Give 'im to us." "To you, eh?" I asked; "what would you do with them?" "Eat 'im!" he said, curtly. . . .

The other occasion is the famous announcement:

> "Mistah Kurtz — he dead."

At first sight, these instances might be mistaken for unexpected acts of generosity from Conrad. In reality, they constitute some of his best assaults. In the case of the cannibals, the incomprehensible grunts that had thus far served them for speech suddenly proved inadequate for Conrad's purpose of letting the European glimpse the unspeakable craving in their hearts. Weighing the necessity for consistency in the portrayal of the dumb brutes against the sensational advantages of securing their conviction by clear, unambiguous evidence issuing out of their own mouth, Conrad chose the latter. As for the announcement of Mr. Kurtz's death by the "insolent black head in the doorway," what better or more appropriate *finis* could be written to the horror story of that wayward child of civilization who willfully had given his soul to the powers of darkness and "taken a high seat amongst the devils of the land" than the proclamation of his physical death by the forces he had joined?

It might be contended, of course, that the attitude to the African in *Heart of Darkness* is not Conrad's but that of his fictional narrator, Marlow, and that far from endorsing it Conrad might indeed be holding it up to irony and criticism. Certainly, Conrad appears to go to considerable pains to set up layers of insulation between himself and the moral universe of his story. He has, for example, a narrator behind a narrator. The primary narrator is Marlow but his account is given to us through the filter of a second, shadowy person. But if Conrad's intention is to draw a *cordon sanitaire*[1] between himself and the moral and psychological malaise of his narrator, his care seems to me totally wasted because he neglects to hint however subtly or tentatively at an alternative frame of reference by which we may judge the actions and opinions of his characters. It would not have been beyond Conrad's power to make that provision if he had thought it necessary. Marlow seems to me to enjoy Conrad's complete confidence—a feeling reinforced by the close similarities between their careers.

Marlow comes through to us not only as a witness of truth, but one holding those advanced and humane views appropriate to the English liberal tradition which required all Englishmen of decency to be deeply shocked by atrocities in Bulgaria or the Congo of King Leopold of the Belgians or wherever. Thus Marlow is able to toss out such bleeding-heart sentiments as these:

> They were dying slowly—it was very clear. They were not enemies, they were not criminals, they were nothing earthly now,—nothing but black shadows of disease and starvation, lying confusedly in the greenish gloom. Brought from all the recesses of the coast in all the legality of time contracts, lost in uncongenial surroundings, fed on unfamiliar food, they sickened, became inefficient, and were then allowed to crawl away and rest.

The kind of liberalism espoused here by Marlow/Conrad touched all the best minds of the age in England, Europe, and America. It took different forms in the minds of different people but almost always managed to sidestep the ultimate question of equality between white people and black people. That extraordinary missionary, Albert Schweitzer, who sacrificed brilliant careers in music and theology in Europe for a life of service to Africans in much the same area as Conrad writes about, epitomizes the ambivalence. In a comment which I have often quoted but must quote one last time, Schweitzer says: "The African is indeed my brother but my junior brother." And so he proceeded to build a hospital appropriate to the needs of junior brothers with standards of hygiene reminiscent of medical practice in the days before the germ theory

---

[1] Quarantine line.—Eds.

of disease came into being. Naturally, he became a sensation in Europe and America. Pilgrims flocked, and I believe still flock even after he has passed on, to witness the prodigious miracle in Lamberene, on the edge of the primeval forest.

Conrad's liberalism would not take him quite as far as Schweitzer's, though. He would not use the word "brother" however qualified; the farthest he would go was "kinship." When Marlow's African helmsman falls down with a spear in his heart he gives his white master one final disquieting look.

> And the intimate profundity of that look he gave me when he received his hurt remains to this day in my memory—like a claim of distant kinship affirmed in a supreme moment.

It is important to note that Conrad, careful as ever with his words, is not talking so much about *distant kinship* as about someone *laying a claim* on it. The black man lays a claim on the white man which is well-nigh intolerable. It is the laying of this claim which frightens and at the same time fascinates Conrad, ". . . the thought of their humanity—like yours . . . Ugly."

The point of my observations should be quite clear by now, namely, that Conrad was a bloody racist. That this simple truth is glossed over in criticism of his work is due to the fact that white racism against Africa is such a normal way of thinking that its manifestations go completely undetected. Students of *Heart of Darkness* will often tell you that Conrad is concerned not so much with Africa as with the deterioration of one European mind caused by solitude and sickness. They will point out to you that Conrad is, if anything, less charitable to the Europeans in the story than he is to the natives. A Conrad student told me in Scotland last year that Africa is merely a setting for the disintegration of the mind of Mr. Kurtz.

Which is partly the point: Africa as setting and backdrop which eliminates the African as human factor. Africa as a metaphysical battlefield devoid of all recognizable humanity, into which the wandering European enters at his peril. Of course, there is a preposterous and perverse kind of arrogance in thus reducing Africa to the role of props for the breakup of one petty European mind. But that is not even the point. The real question is the dehumanization of Africa and Africans which this age-long attitude has fostered and continues to foster in the world. And the question is whether a novel which celebrates this dehumanization, which depersonalizes a portion of the human race, can be called a great work of art. My answer is: No, it cannot. I would not call that man an artist, for example, who composes an eloquent instigation to one people to fall upon another and destroy them. No matter how striking his imagery or how beautiful his cadences fall, such a man is no more a great artist than another may be called a priest who reads the mass backwards or a physician who poisons his patients. All those men in Nazi Germany who lent their talent to the service of virulent racism whether in science, philosophy, or the arts have generally and rightly been condemned for their perversions. The time is long overdue for taking a hard look at the work of creative artists who apply their talents, alas often considerable as in the case of Conrad, to set people against people. This, I take it, is what Yevtushenko is after when he tells us that a poet cannot be a slave trader at the same time, and gives the striking example of Arthur Rimbaud, who was

20

fortunately honest enough to give up any pretenses to poetry when he opted for slave trading. For poetry surely can only be on the side of man's deliverance and not his enslavement; for the brotherhood and unity of all mankind and against the doctrines of Hitler's master races or Conrad's "rudimentary souls."

Last year was the fiftieth anniversary of Conrad's death. He was born in 1857, the very year in which the first Anglican missionaries were arriving among my own people in Nigeria. It was certainly not his fault that he lived his life at a time when the reputation of the black man was at a particularly low level. But even after due allowances have been made for all the influences of contemporary prejudice on his sensibility, there remains still in Conrad's attitude a residue of antipathy to black people which his peculiar psychology alone can explain. His own account of his first encounter with a black man is very revealing:

> A certain enormous buck nigger encountered in Haiti fixed my conception of blind, furi-
> ous, unreasoning rage, as manifested in the human animal to the end of my days. Of the
> nigger I used to dream for years afterwards.

Certainly, Conrad had a problem with niggers. His inordinate love of that word itself should be of interest to psychoanalysts. Sometimes his fixation on blackness is equally interesting, as when he gives us this brief description:

> A black figure stood up, strode on long black legs, waving long black arms.

as though we might expect a black figure striding along on black legs to have *white* arms! But so unrelenting is Conrad's obsession.

As a matter of interest, Conrad gives us in *A Personal Record* what amounts to a companion piece to the buck nigger of Haiti. At the age of sixteen Conrad encountered his first Englishman in Europe. He calls him "my unforgettable Englishman" and describes him in the following manner:

> [his] calves exposed to the public gaze . . . dazzled the beholder by the splendor of their
> marble-like condition and their rich tone of young ivory. . . . The light of a headlong,
> exalted satisfaction with the world of men . . . illumined his face . . . and triumphant eyes.
> In passing he cast a glance of kindly curiosity and a friendly gleam of big, sound, shiny
> teeth . . . his white calves twinkled sturdily.

Irrational love and irrational hate jostling together in the heart of that tormented man. But whereas irrational love may at worst engender foolish acts of indiscretion, irrational hate can endanger the life of the community. Naturally, Conrad is a dream for psychoanalytic critics. Perhaps the most detailed study of him in this direction is by Bernard C. Meyer, MD. In this lengthy book, Dr. Meyer follows every conceivable lead (and sometimes inconceivable ones) to explain Conrad. As an example, he gives us long disquisitions on the significance of hair and hair-cutting in Conrad. And yet not even one word is spared for his attitude to black people. Not even the discussion of Conrad's anti-Semitism was enough to spark off in Dr. Meyer's mind those other dark and explosive thoughts. Which only leads one to surmise that Western psychoanalysts must regard the kind of racism displayed by Conrad as absolutely normal despite the profoundly important work done by Frantz Fanon in the psychiatric hospitals of French Algeria.

Whatever Conrad's problems were, you might say he is now safely dead. Quite true. Unfortunately, his heart of darkness plagues us still. Which is why an offensive and totally deplorable book can be described by a serious scholar as "among the half-dozen greatest short novels in the English language," and why it is today perhaps the most commonly prescribed novel in the twentieth-century literature courses in our own English Department here. Indeed the time is long overdue for a hard look at things.

There are two probable grounds on which what I have said so far may be contested. The first is that it is no concern of fiction to please people about whom it is written. I will go along with that. But I am not talking about pleasing people. I am talking about a book which parades in the most vulgar fashion prejudices and insults from which a section of mankind has suffered untold agonies and atrocities in the past and continues to do so in many ways and many places today. I am talking about a story in which the very humanity of black people is called in question. It seems to me totally inconceivable that great art or even good art could possibly reside in such unwholesome surroundings.

Secondly, I may be challenged on the grounds of actuality. Conrad, after all, sailed down the Congo in 1890, when my own father was still a babe in arms, and recorded what he saw. How could I stand up in 1975, fifty years after his death, and purport to contradict him? My answer is that as a sensible man I will not accept just any traveller's tales solely on the grounds that I have not made the journey myself. I will not trust the evidence even of a man's very eyes when I suspect them to be as jaundiced as Conrad's. And we also happen to know that Conrad was, in the words of his biographer, Bernard C. Meyer, "notoriously inaccurate in the rendering of his own history."

But more important by far is the abundant testimony about Conrad's savages which we could gather if we were so inclined from other sources and which might lead us to think that these people must have had other occupations besides merging into the evil forest or materializing out of it simply to plague Marlow and his dispirited band. For as it happened, soon after Conrad had written his book an event of far greater consequence was taking place in the art world of Europe. This is how Frank Willett, a British art historian, describes it:

> Gauguin[2] had gone to Tahiti, the most extravagant individual act of turning to a non-European culture in the decades immediately before and after 1900, when European artists were avid for new artistic experiences, but it was only about 1904–5 that African art began to make its distinctive impact. One piece is still identifiable; it is a mask that had been given to Maurice Vlaminck in 1905. He records that Derain was "speechless" and "stunned" when he saw it, bought it from Vlaminck and in turn showed it to Picasso and Matisse, who were also greatly affected by it. Ambroise Vollard then borrowed it and had it cast in bronze. . . . The revolution of twentieth century art was under way!

25

---

[2]Eugène Henri Paul Gauguin (1848–1903), French Post-Impressionist painter, moved to Tahiti toward the end of his life. — Eds.

The mask in question was made by other savages living just north of Conrad's River Congo. They have a name, the Fang people, and are without a doubt among the world's greatest masters of the sculptured form. As you might have guessed, the event to which Frank Willett refers marked the beginning of cubism and the infusion of new life into European art that had run completely out of strength.

The point of all this is to suggest that Conrad's picture of the people of the Congo seems grossly inadequate even at the height of their subjection to the ravages of King Leopold's International Association for the Civilization of Central Africa. Travellers with closed minds can tell us little except about themselves. But even those not blinkered, like Conrad, with xenophobia can be astonishingly blind.

Let me digress a little here. One of the greatest and most intrepid travellers of all time, Marco Polo, journeyed to the Far East from the Mediterranean in the thirteenth century and spent twenty years in the court of Kublai Khan in China. On his return to Venice he set down in his book entitled *Description of the World* his impressions of the peoples and places and customs he had seen. There are at least two extraordinary omissions in his account. He says nothing about the art of printing unknown as yet in Europe but in full flower in China. He either did not notice it at all or if he did, failed to see what use Europe could possibly have for it. Whatever reason, Europe had to wait another hundred years for Gutenberg. But even more spectacular was Marco Polo's omission of any reference to the Great Wall of China nearly four thousand miles long and already more than one thousand years old at the time of his visit. Again, he may not have seen it; but the Great Wall of China is the only structure built by man which is visible from the moon! Indeed, travellers can be blind.

As I said earlier, Conrad did not originate the image of Africa which we find in his book. It was and is the dominant image of Africa in the Western imagination and Conrad merely brought the peculiar gifts of his own mind to bear on it. For reasons which can certainly use close psychological inquiry, the West seems to suffer deep anxieties about the precariousness of its civilization and to have a need for constant reassurance by comparing it with Africa. If Europe, advancing in civilization, could cast a backward glance periodically at Africa trapped in primordial barbarity, it could say with faith and feeling: There go I but for the grace of God. Africa is to Europe as the picture is to Dorian Gray—a carrier onto whom the master unloads his physical and moral deformities so that he may go forward, erect and immaculate. Consequently, Africa is something to be avoided just as the picture has to be hidden away to safeguard the man's jeopardous integrity. Keep away from Africa, or else! Mr. Kurtz of *Heart of Darkness* should have heeded that warning and the prowling horror in his heart would have kept its place, chained to its lair. But he foolishly exposed himself to the wild irresistible allure of the jungle and lo! the darkness found him out.

In my original conception of this talk I had thought to conclude it nicely on an appropriately positive note in which I would suggest from my privileged position in African and Western culture some advantages the West might derive from Africa once it rid its mind of old prejudices and began to look at Africa not through a haze of distortions and cheap mystification but quite simply as a continent of people—not angels, but not rudimentary souls either—just people, often highly gifted people and often strikingly successful in their enterprise with life and society. But as I thought more about the stereotype image, about its grip and pervasiveness, about the willful tenacity with which the West holds it to its heart; when I thought of your television and the cinema and newspapers, about books read in schools and out of school, of churches preaching to empty pews about the need to send help to the heathen in Africa, I realized that no easy optimism was possible. And there is something totally wrong in offering bribes to the West in return for its good opinion of Africa. Ultimately, the abandonment of unwholesome thoughts must be its own and only reward. Although I have used the word *willful* a few times in this talk to characterize the West's view of Africa, it may well be that what is happening at this stage is more akin to reflex action than calculated malice. Which does not make the situation more, but less, hopeful. Let me give you one last and really minor example of what I mean.

Last November the *Christian Science Monitor* carried an interesting article written by its Education Editor on the serious psychological and learning problems faced by little children who speak one language at home and then go to school where something else is spoken. It was a wide-ranging article taking in Spanish-speaking children in this country, the children of migrant Italian workers in Germany, the quadrilingual phenomenon in Malaysia, and so on. And all this while the article speaks unequivocally about *language*. But then out of the blue sky comes this:

> In London there is an enormous immigration of children who speak Indian or Nigerian dialects, or some other native language.

I believe that the introduction of *dialects*, which is technically erroneous in the context, is almost a reflex action caused by an instinctive desire of the writer to downgrade the discussion to the level of Africa and India. And this is quite comparable to Conrad's withholding of language from his rudimentary souls. Language is too grand for these chaps; let's give them dialects. In all this business a lot of violence is inevitably done to words and their meaning. Look at the phrase "native language" in the above excerpt. Surely the only native language possible in London is Cockney English. But our writer obviously means something else — something Indians and Africans speak.

Perhaps a change will come. Perhaps this is the time when it can begin, when the high optimism engendered by the breathtaking achievements of Western science and industry is giving way to doubt and even confusion. There is just the possibility that Western man may begin to look seriously at the achievements of other people. I read in the papers the other day a suggestion that what America needs at this time is somehow to bring back the extended family. And I saw in my mind's eye future African Peace Corps Volunteers coming to help you set up the system.

Seriously, although the work which needs to be done may appear too daunting, I believe that it is not one day too soon to begin. And where better than at a university?

[1975]

Questions

1. What is the purpose of the anecdotes that open this essay?
2. Achebe acknowledges that Conrad's literary talents and *Heart of Darkness* have some merit. What are the positive qualities he concedes?
3. What is Achebe's basic interpretation of *Heart of Darkness*? What are his objections to traditional interpretations?
4. What does Achebe mean when he asserts that although Conrad is dead, "his heart of darkness plagues us still" (para. 23)?
5. What is the purpose of Achebe bringing Albert Schweitzer and Marco Polo into this analysis?
6. What textual evidence, including tone, can you cite to illustrate that Achebe felt that his university audience would not be entirely hostile or even unreceptive to his argument? What does Achebe mean when he refers to his "privileged position in African and Western culture" (para. 30)?
7. Find points in Achebe's argument that you agree with as well as those with which you disagree. Pay particular attention to whether Achebe believes that Conrad's condemnation of the colonizers is as clear as his devaluation of the natives.

How to Write about Africa

BINYAVANGA WAINAINA

> Binyavanga Wainaina (b. 1971) lives in Nairobi, Kenya. He is the founding editor of the literary and political magazine *Kwani?* and won the Caine Prize for African Writing in 2002 for his short story "Discovering Home." In 2008, the *Atlanta Journal-Constitution* named him a person worth watching in politics, entertainment, and the arts. A sought-after speaker, he was writer-in-residence at Union College in Schenectady, New York, for the years 2005–2008, and at Williams College in Williamstown, Massachusetts, in fall 2008. This article appeared in a 2005 issue of *Granta* magazine, before spreading rapidly over the Internet and through e-mail.

Always use the word 'Africa' or 'Darkness' or 'Safari' in your title. Subtitles may include the words 'Zanzibar', 'Masai', 'Zulu', 'Zambezi', 'Congo', 'Nile', 'Big', 'Sky', 'Shadow', 'Drum', 'Sun' or 'Bygone'. Also useful are words such as 'Guerrillas', 'Timeless', 'Primordial' and 'Tribal'. Note that 'People' means Africans who are not black, while 'The People' means black Africans.

Never have a picture of a well-adjusted African on the cover of your book, or in it, unless that African has won the Nobel Prize. An AK-47, prominent ribs, naked breasts: use these. If you must include an African, make sure you get one in Masai or Zulu or Dogon dress.

In your text, treat Africa as if it were one country. It is hot and dusty with rolling grasslands and huge herds of animals and tall, thin people who are starving. Or it is hot and steamy with very short people who eat primates. Don't get bogged down with precise descriptions. Africa is big: fifty-four countries, nine hundred million people who are too busy starving and dying and warring and emigrating to read your book. The continent is full of deserts, jungles, highlands, savannahs and many other things, but your reader doesn't care about all that, so keep your descriptions romantic and evocative and unparticular.

Make sure you show how Africans have music and rhythm deep in their souls, and eat things no other humans eat. Do not mention rice and beef and wheat; monkey-brain is an African's cuisine of choice, along with goat, snake, worms and grubs and all manner of game meat. Make sure you show that you are able to eat such food without flinching, and describe how you learn to enjoy it—because you care.

Taboo subjects: ordinary domestic scenes, love between Africans (unless a death is involved), references to African writers or intellectuals, mention of school-going children who are not suffering from yaws or Ebola fever or female genital mutilation. 5

Throughout the book, adopt a *sotto* voice, in conspiracy with the reader, and a sad *I-expected-so-much* tone. Establish early on that your liberalism is impeccable, and mention near the beginning how much you love Africa, how you fell in love with the place and can't live without her. Africa is the only continent you can love—take advantage of this. If you are a man, thrust yourself into her warm virgin forests. If you are a woman, treat Africa as a man who wears a bush jacket and disappears off into the sunset. Africa is to be pitied, worshipped or dominated. Whichever angle you take, be sure to leave the strong impression that without your intervention and your important book, Africa is doomed.

Your African characters may include naked warriors, loyal servants, diviners and seers, ancient wise men living in hermitic splendour. Or corrupt politicians, inept polygamous travel-guides, and prostitutes you have slept with. The Loyal Servant always behaves like a seven-year-old and needs a firm hand; he is scared of snakes, good with children, and always involving you in his complex domestic dramas. The Ancient Wise Man always comes from a noble tribe (not the money-grubbing tribes like the Gikuyu, the Igbo or the Shona). He has rheumy eyes and is close to the Earth. The Modern African is a fat man who steals and works in the visa office, refusing to give work permits to qualified Westerners who really care about Africa. He is an enemy of development, always using his government job to make it difficult for pragmatic and good-hearted expats to set up NGOs or Legal Conservation Areas. Or he is an Oxford-educated intellectual turned serial-killing politician in a Savile Row suit. He is a cannibal who likes Cristal champagne, and his mother is a rich witch-doctor who really runs the country.

Among your characters you must always include The Starving African, who wanders the refugee camp nearly naked, and waits for the benevolence of the West. Her children have flies on their eyelids and pot bellies, and her breasts are flat and empty. She must look utterly helpless. She can have no past, no history; such diversions ruin the dramatic moment. Moans are good. She must never say anything about herself in the dialogue except to speak of her (unspeakable) suffering. Also be sure to include a warm and motherly woman who has a rolling laugh and who is concerned for your well-being. Just call her Mama. Her children are all delinquent. These characters should buzz around your main hero, making him look good. Your hero can teach them, bathe them, feed them; he carries lots of babies and has seen Death. Your hero is you (if reportage), or a beautiful, tragic international celebrity/aristocrat who now cares for animals (if fiction).

Bad Western characters may include children of Tory cabinet ministers, Afrikaners, employees of the World Bank. When talking about exploitation by foreigners, mention the Chinese and Indian traders. Blame the West for Africa's situation. But do not be too specific.

Broad brushstrokes throughout are good. Avoid having the African characters laugh, or struggle to educate their kids, or just make do in mundane circumstances. Have them illuminate something about Europe or America in Africa. African characters should be colourful, exotic, larger than life—but empty inside, with no dialogue, no conflicts or resolutions in their stories, no depth or quirks to confuse the cause.

Describe, in detail, naked breasts (young, old, conservative, recently raped, big, small) or mutilated genitals, or enhanced genitals. Or any kind of genitals. And dead bodies. Or, better, naked dead bodies. And especially rotting naked dead bodies. Remember, any work you submit in which people look filthy and miserable will be referred to as the 'real Africa', and you want that on your dust jacket. Do not feel queasy about this: you are trying to help them to get aid from the West. The biggest taboo in writing about Africa is to describe or show dead or suffering white people.

Animals, on the other hand, must be treated as well rounded, complex characters. They speak (or grunt while tossing their manes proudly) and have names, ambitions and desires. They also have family values: *see how lions teach their children?* Elephants are caring, and are good feminists or dignified patriarchs. So are gorillas. Never, ever say anything negative about an elephant or a gorilla. Elephants may attack people's property, destroy their crops, and even kill them. Always take the side of the elephant. Big cats have public-school accents. Hyenas are fair game and have vaguely Middle Eastern accents. Any short Africans who live in the jungle or desert may be portrayed with good humour (unless they are in conflict with an elephant or chimpanzee or gorilla, in which case they are pure evil).

After celebrity activists and aid workers, conservationists are Africa's most important people. Do not offend them. You need them to invite you to their thirty thousand-acre game ranch or 'conservation area', and this is the only way you will get to interview the celebrity activist. Often a book cover with a heroic-looking conservationist on it works magic for sales. Anybody white, tanned and wearing khaki who once had a pet antelope or a farm is a conservationist, one who is preserving Africa's rich heritage. When interviewing him or her, do not ask how much funding they have; do not ask how much money they make off their game. Never ask how much they pay their employees.

Readers will be put off if you don't mention the light in Africa. And sunsets, the African sunset is a must. It is always big and red. There is always a big sky. Wide empty spaces and game are critical—Africa is the Land of Wide Empty Spaces. When writing about the plight of flora and fauna, make sure you mention that Africa is overpopulated. When your main character is in a desert or jungle living with indigenous peoples (anybody short), it is okay to mention that Africa has been severely depopulated by Aids and War (use caps).

You'll also need a nightclub called Tropicana, where mercenaries, evil nouveau riche Africans and prostitutes and guerrillas and expats hang out.   15

Always end your book with Nelson Mandela saying something about rainbows or renaissances. Because you care.

[2005]

Questions

1. Wainaina writes in imperative sentences, giving what seem to be commands or issuing edicts. To whom is he speaking?
2. Identify and discuss several of the stereotypes that Wainaina describes. Are you familiar with any of these from movies you've seen? television shows? *Heart of Darkness*? "The Old Chief Mshlanga"? children's films or plays?
3. At what point did you realize Wainaina's ironic tone — from the very outset? Find examples of hyperbole and understatement. What other techniques does he use to develop his satire? Consider the imperative sentence form, sentence fragments, choice of details, and visual images.
4. Explain whether you think Wainaina would have been more successful in making his point if he had written without satire — that is, more like Achebe in "An Image of Africa."
5. Discuss whether you think Wainaina goes too far. How do you interpret the ending comment about Nelson Mandela? As you answer that question, ask yourself if the audience Wainaina addresses as "you" is actually his audience.

Entering the Conversation

As you develop a response to one of the following questions, refer to the texts you have read in this section. You may also draw on your own experience or knowledge relating to colonialism and its legacy.

1. Write an essay analyzing at least three different types of cultural clashes or conflicts that result from colonialism. Refer to at least three texts from this Conversation when responding.

2. So much of the literature and commentary about colonialism centers around its impact on large groups of people, whether national or ethnic groups. Some of the texts in this chapter, however, explore its consequences on individuals. Write an essay discussing the way at least two of these texts provide insight into the influence of colonialism on the individual.

3. Albert Memmi describes the destructive nature of colonialism for the colonizer. Using at least two texts chosen from this Conversation or *Heart of Darkness*, discuss why you agree or disagree with his analysis:

> It is impossible for him [the colonizer] not to be aware of the constant illegitimacy of his status. It is, moreover, in a way a double illegitimacy. A foreigner, having come to land by the accidents of history, he has succeeded not merely in creating a place for himself but also in taking away that of the inhabitant, granting himself astounding privileges to the detriment of those rightfully entitled to them. And this is not by virtue of local laws, which in a certain way legitimize this inequality by tradition, but by upsetting the established rules and substituting his own. He thus appears doubly unjust. He is a privileged being and an illegitimately privileged one; that is, a usurper. Furthermore, this is so, not only in the eyes of the colonized, but in his own as well.
>
> — *The Colonizer and the Colonized*

4. Write an essay discussing five of the stereotypes discussed in this Conversation. Develop your essay by including photographs, artwork, or video clips that illustrate the stereotypes in action. Use at least three of the texts in your analysis.

5. Select a contemporary film set in Africa. Write a script of an imagined conversation among three or four of the authors featured in this Conversation addressing the following question: Does this film stereotype African people and cultures, or is it a valid and meaningful depiction?

6. There is debate about whether *Heart of Darkness* is a racist book that has no place in the classroom, or an important window onto the Eurocentric tradition and its own heart of darkness. Drawing from at least three of the pieces in this Conversation, write an essay taking a position in that debate.

Student Writing

Close Reading Fiction

Sarah Muller, a twelfth-grade AP Literature student, wrote the following essay in forty minutes. She had neither read nor discussed the full story prior to writing the essay; she read only the passage beginning with the third sentence in paragraph 8 ("Mr. Kapasi was forty-six years old . . .") and ending with paragraph 36.

> In the following passage from "Interpreter of Maladies" by Jhumpa Lahiri, the character Mr. Kapasi is serving as a tour guide in India for an Indian American family. In a well-organized essay, explain how Lahiri conveys Mr. Kapasi's perception of the Das family.

There are two sides to every story, and as the saying goes, the truth lies somewhere in the middle. This is normally applied to daily life, but here it applies to "Interpreter of Maladies" by Jhumpa Lahiri. Upon first reading the passage, it does not seem that there is anything extraordinary about the family Mr. Kapasi is guiding. If one looks further, however, Lahiri makes subtle choices in diction that indicate Mr. Kapasi's opinion of the family.

The first indication of Mr. Kapasi's judgment of the family is found in the tenth paragraph, where he comments that Tina's doll's hair is cut short "as a punitive measure." If this remark had not been inserted, a reader would never have thought twice—young girls frequently cut off hair on their dolls out of boredom or on impulse. But because of the word "punitive," the reader wonders why the girl felt the need to punish her doll. Another thought-evoking remark appears in paragraph thirteen, where Kapasi notes that it is "strange that Mr. Das should refer to his wife by her first name when speaking to the little girl." This comment also might have gone unnoticed but for Kapasi's addition to the incident. The reader cannot help but be struck by the apparent lack of affection between the family members. Lahiri seems to suggest that the daughter, Tina, is being brought up to separate herself from her family and to treat her relations as acquaintances.

This sets the tone for the rest of the passage, yet we've only reached the thirteenth paragraph—more commentary is yet to come. For example, in paragraph fourteen, Kapasi describes the mother's appearance in overwhelming detail and describes her as having "small hands like paws." This last description reminds the reader of a small, yappy dog like a Chihuahua, fussed over and obnoxious, giving one a negative bias toward Mrs. Das before she's even spoken. When she does speak, though, our narrator has another opinion to share with the reader: he describes Mrs. Das's sigh as impatient, coming from a person who "had been traveling her whole life without pause." It's as if she's simply too busy and important to be bothered with inconveniences such as ill-kempt roads. This depiction of an intolerant woman continues later in the passage, where, in paragraph twenty-eight, the mother makes no effort to dissuade her daughter from misbehaving, and her very posture indicates her antipathy toward the whole situation. Details like this hint at Mr. Kapasi's opinion of the family. And finally, in the very last paragraphs, the mother expresses no interest in the excitement of her children and shoos away her own daughter when entreated by her to be included in her impromptu manicure, telling her, "You're making me mess up."

Overall, it is clear that Mr. Kapasi doesn't think much of the family; at the very least, he finds them strange. Yet his opinion isn't completely obvious. As Lahiri filters dialogue and details through Mr. Kapasi's eyes, it seems as if readers come up with a dislike of the family on their own. The effectiveness of this passage is in the details—literally.

Questions

1. What is the chief strength of Sarah's essay—structure? development? overall approach?
2. How might Sarah have opened paragraph 2 with a topic sentence that emphasizes the overall point she is making rather than focusing on her first example?
3. In paragraph 3, what is the "tone" to which Sarah alludes? Can you describe it more specifically?
4. In the last paragraph, Sarah references both dialogue and word choice. Does "diction" cover both of these? Should she have mentioned dialogue in the opening paragraph? Would the essay be improved if she had written a separate paragraph on dialogue or incorporated it into the two developmental paragraphs she has?
5. If you were revising this essay after having read the entire story "Interpreter of Maladies," which elements of Sarah's analysis would hold up and which would need qualification?

The Writer's Craft—Close Reading

Specialized, Archaic, and Unfamiliar Diction

Accomplished writers choose exactly the right words to achieve a particular effect. They are attuned to nuances of language as well as audience expectations. Thus, they may choose words that are more familiar to some groups than to others. Similarly, authors from another time period may use vocabulary that was familiar to audiences in their day but that seems old-fashioned—and unfamiliar—to us today; we call this "archaic language." These choices add authenticity and distinctiveness to a writer's style, yet sometimes specialized, archaic, and unfamiliar diction, or even familiar words used in unfamiliar ways, add challenges for contemporary readers.

Puzzling through language that is unfamiliar can be frustrating, but it's worth the effort, because the more acquainted you become with the vocabulary of different writers, the more fully you enter the world of the literature. Of course, another happy result is that your own vocabulary becomes broader and richer, and your reading and writing skills become sharper—along with your test-taking skills.

Specialized Vocabulary

Often, in order to set a scene, establish mood, or depict character, writers turn to specialized vocabulary. For instance, describing the southwestern desert requires quite a different vocabulary than does describing the Cape Code shoreline, and writing about carpenters will require specialized vocabulary for describing their tools, materials, and techniques. Precise terminology contributes to the author's authority on the subject and helps draw the reader into the world he or she describes.

In *Heart of Darkness,* for instance, Conrad uses specialized vocabulary having to do with sailing and navigation, such as *yawl, mizzen-mast,* and *estuary.*

Conrad's first sentence reads:

> The *Nellie,* a cruising <u>yawl</u>, swung to her anchor without a flutter of the sails, and was at rest.

But he could have written:

> The *Nellie,* a small sailboat, swung to her anchor without a flutter of the sails, and was at rest.

Consider how different a picture the more familiar and friendly term *sailboat* paints in your mind from the precise nautical term *yawl.*

Let's look at another example from the story "Interpreter of Maladies." Here, Jhumpa Lahiri uses terms from art, architecture, and religion to create a vivid picture of the Sun Temple at Konarak:

> Worried that he might disturb her, Mr. Kapasi walked ahead, to admire, as he always did, the three life-sized <u>bronze avatars</u> of <u>Surya, the sun god,</u> each emerging from its own <u>niche</u> on the temple <u>facade</u> to greet the sun at dawn, noon, and evening. They wore elaborate headdresses, their languid, elongated eyes closed, their bare chests draped with carved chains and <u>amulets</u>. (para. 100)

Similarly, in "Ogun," the poet Kamau Brathwaite uses the language of carpentry to add authenticity and establish a metaphor: "shock of wood," "saw teeth," "shaping squares," "humpbacked chisel," "whittled," and "knife and gimlet care." We know from the outset that the speaker is describing his uncle who "made chairs, tables . . . coffins"—that is, he is a carpenter and, we realize later, a sculptor. He works with wood in both his vocation and his avocation, so the vocabulary of his tools, art, and craft are essential to the authenticity of the poem.

Archaic Diction

Archaic is a relative term. It means "characteristic of a much earlier period." There's archaic clothing (petticoats) and archaic transportation (chariots), but what we are interested in here is archaic diction—vocabulary that was once in regular use but is now relatively rare. When Gwendolyn Brooks writes "We real cool . . . We / Lurk late. We / Strike straight" (ll. 1–4), you easily understand her language, partially because of the rhyme and rhythm but also because, even though the poem was written in 1960, you know the meaning of "cool" and "Strike" in the context of the pool players who are the speakers of the poem. How much different is it, in fact, from the seventeenth-century readers of Milton who could understand how "that one talent" could "hide / Lodged with me useless" (ll. 3–4) or how a man could "best / Bear his mild yoke" (ll. 10–11)? We may find Milton's language challenging because of the very characteristics that made it accessible to the audience of his day, just as three hundred years from now, readers might need a little help with the "real cool" that makes Brooks's poem seem straightforward to us.

For example, in "Young Goodman Brown," Hawthorne describes the two travelers in the forest in language that is, to us, archaic:

> And yet, though the elder person was as simply <u>clad</u> as the younger, and as simple in manner too, he had an indescribable <u>air</u> of one who knew the world, and who would not have felt <u>abashed</u> at the governor's dinner table or in King William's court, were it possible that his affairs should call him <u>thither</u>. But the only thing about him that could be <u>fixed upon</u> as remarkable was his staff, which bore the likeness of a great black snake, so curiously <u>wrought</u> that it might almost be seen to twist and wriggle itself like a living serpent. This, of course, must have been an <u>ocular deception, assisted</u> by the uncertain light. (para. 13)

Contextual clues make it fairly easy to understand that "clad" refers to manner of dress and "air" to attitude. Similarly, we can probably figure out that "fixed upon" means "identified" or "noted." Other words are more problematic. We may need to look up the definition of "wrought" to understand the description of "curiously wrought" as meaning "carefully shaped." Likewise, "ocular deception" may require a dictionary or a knowledge of root or similar words to determine that it relates to the eye (think, *binoculars*).

Familiar Words Used in Unfamiliar Ways

Common words used in unfamiliar ways can also pose a challenge. While you have known the meaning of *flood, made, bound,* and *come to* since elementary school, notice how Conrad uses the terms in his opening paragraph to describe how the yawl had to pause before continuing downriver to the sea:

> The <u>flood</u> had <u>made</u>, the wind was nearly calm, and being <u>bound</u> down the river, the only thing for it was to <u>come to</u> and wait for the turn of the tide.

Some of the words and phrases that Conrad uses have multiple meanings and can be tricky to navigate, as we see with the words *bound* and *come to*. Sailors who are *bound* primarily means that they are intending to go, or will soon be going. *Bound* might also suggest "fastened or constricted by bindings" or, perhaps, "obliged," implying that what follows is inevitable. In fact, *bound* can also mean "destined." These additional meanings should not be dismissed, as the listeners who share "the bond of the sea," "holding (their) hearts together," are soon to be *spellbound* by Marlow's story. Yes, they are "heading down," "sailing down," "moving down," or "planning to head down" the river, but how much more fitting is Conrad's diction for the yarn that he spins?

When you read "come to," you may wonder, come to what? The phrase might suggest an awakening from unconsciousness or sleep (you might use smelling salts to help someone "come to"), but in this sentence it means that they have come to anchor, or come to a stop, reminding us that the ship has "swung to her anchor," where they will wait in stillness. The irony of the situation is that swinging to stillness gives the narrator pause, as if the sea and the sky allow time and space for the story that follows—the story toward which the reader is bound.

> ## • EXERCISE 1 •
>
> Following are two passages: the first from Hawthorne, the second from Conrad. Fill in the blanks with the words listed at the end. Even if you do not know the meanings, try using contextual cues to make your decisions. Then check your responses against the passages in the stories found earlier in the chapter.
>
> A. In truth, all through the haunted forest, there could be nothing more frightful than the figure of Goodman Brown. On he flew among the black pines, _____ his staff with _____ gestures, now giving vent to an inspiration of horrid _____, and now shouting forth such laughter as set all the echoes of the forest laughing like demons around him. The fiend in his own shape is less hideous than when he rages in the breast of man. Thus sped the _____ on his course, until, quivering among the trees, he saw a red light before him, as when the _____ trunks and branches of a clearing have been set on fire, and throw up their _____ blaze against the sky, at the hour of midnight. He paused, in a _____ of the _____ that had driven him onward, and heard the _____ of what seemed a hymn, rolling solemnly from a distance with the weight of many voices. (para. 53)
>
> *blasphemy, brandishing, demoniac, felled, frenzied, lull, lurid, swell, tempest*
>
> B. I looked at him, lost in astonishment. There he was before me, in _____, as though he had _____ from a troupe of mimes, enthusiastic, _____. His very existence was improbable, _____, and altogether bewildering. He was an insoluble problem. It was inconceivable how he had _____, how he had succeeded in getting so far, how he had managed to remain—why he did not instantly disappear. "I went a little farther," he said, "then still a little farther—till I had gone so far that I don't know how I'll ever get back. Never mind. Plenty time. I can manage. You take Kurtz away quick—quick—I tell you." The glamour of youth _____ his particoloured rags, his _____, his loneliness, the essential desolation of his futile wanderings. For months—for years—his life hadn't been worth a day's _____; and there he was _____, thoughtlessly alive, to all appearance indestructible solely by the virtue of his few years and of his unreflecting _____. (para. 112)
>
> *absconded, audacity, destitution, enveloped, existed, fabulous, gallantly, inexplicable, motley, purchase*

• EXERCISE 2 •

Develop definitions for the underlined words in the following passages from Conrad, Lahiri, Cullen, and Hawthorne. Work in pairs or groups to figure out the meanings. After you have developed definitions for all of the underlined words, use the dictionary to check your answers.

1. The dwelling was <u>dismantled</u>; but we could see a white man had lived there not very long ago. There remained a <u>rude</u> table—a plank on two posts; a heap of rubbish <u>reposed</u> in a dark corner, and by the door I picked up a book. (*Heart of Darkness*, para. 84)

2. My destiny! <u>Droll</u> thing life is—that mysterious arrangement of merciless logic for a <u>futile</u> purpose. The most you can hope from it is some knowledge of yourself—that comes too late—a <u>crop</u> of <u>unextinguishable</u> regrets. (*Heart of Darkness*, para. 160)

3. The temple, made of sandstone, was a massive pyramid-like structure in the shape of a <u>chariot</u>. It was dedicated to the great master of life, the sun, which struck three sides of the <u>edifice</u> as it made its journey each day across the sky. Twenty-four giant wheels were carved on the north and south sides of the <u>plinth</u>. ("Interpreter of Maladies," para. 91)

4. So I lie, who all day long
   Want no sound except the song
   Sung by wild barbaric birds
   <u>Goading</u> massive jungle herds,
   <u>Juggernauts</u> of flesh that pass
   Trampling tall defiant grass
   Where young forest lovers lie,
   <u>Plighting troth</u> beneath the sky.
   ("Heritage," ll. 11–18)

5. While he still gazed upward into the deep arch of the <u>firmament</u> and had lifted his hands to pray, a cloud, though no wind was stirring, hurried across the <u>zenith</u> and hid the brightening stars. ("Young Goodman Brown," para. 47)

6. But, irreverently <u>consorting</u> with these <u>grave</u>, reputable, and <u>pious</u> people, these elders of the church, these <u>chaste</u> dames and <u>dewy</u> virgins, there were men of <u>dissolute</u> lives and women of <u>spotted</u> fame, <u>wretches</u> given over to all <u>mean</u> and filthy vice, and suspected even of horrid crimes. ("Young Goodman Brown," para. 56)

• EXERCISE 3 •

Examine the diction in the following lines from William Wordsworth's sonnet "The World Is Too Much with Us," and explain how the underlined word choices affect your understanding of each line's meaning. Consider what would be lost or gained if the poet had employed other vocabulary. How would different word choices affect the poem's tone?

1. "Getting and spending, we <u>lay waste</u> our powers:"
2. "We have given our hearts away, a <u>sordid boon</u>!"
3. "This Sea that bares her <u>bosom</u> to the moon;"
4. "A Pagan suckled in a <u>creed</u> outworn;"
5. "Have glimpses that would make me less <u>forlorn</u>;"
6. "Or hear old Triton blow his <u>wreathèd</u> horn."

• EXERCISE 4 •

Replace the underlined words in the passage from *Heart of Darkness* with more common, everyday vocabulary. Turn to the dictionary for words you don't know. How did making these substitutions draw your attention to the nuances of Conrad's diction? How did looking up words you didn't know contribute to your understanding of the passage?

From that point he soared and took me with him. The <u>peroration</u> was magnificent, though difficult to remember, you know. It gave me the notion of an <u>exotic Immensity</u> ruled by an <u>august Benevolence</u>. It made me tingle with enthusiasm. This was the unbounded power of eloquence—of words—of burning noble words. There were no practical hints to interrupt the magic current of phrases, unless a kind of note at the foot of the last page, scrawled evidently much later, in an unsteady hand, may be <u>regarded</u> as the <u>exposition</u> of a method. It was very simple, and at the end of that moving appeal to every <u>altruistic</u> sentiment it blazed at you, <u>luminous</u> and terrifying, like a flash of lightning in a serene sky: "Exterminate all the brutes!" The <u>curious</u> part was that he had apparently forgotten all about that valuable <u>postscriptum</u>, because, later on, when he in a sense came to himself, he repeatedly entreated me to take good care of "my pamphlet" (he called it), as it was sure to have in the future a good influence upon his career. (para. 104)

• EXERCISE 5 •

1. Write a description of a person or place using specialized vocabulary. For example, describe the way a person is dressed using terms characteristic of fashion designers, an athletic field or stadium using the language of sports

enthusiasts, a computer lab using the language of technology, a concert in terms music fans would know (a specific type of music), a person's appearance using medical terminology, or a place of religious worship using the language of a specific religion.

2. Write a poem using language that is familiar to us today but that you think is likely to be viewed as archaic in fifty years. Explain why you think the words you have chosen will go out of style.

Suggestions for Writing

Identity and Culture

1. Look again at the quotation by Nathaniel Hawthorne that begins this chapter. Using two of the texts you have studied in this chapter, discuss the conflict that results from trying to assume an identity based on the expectations of others rather than being true to oneself.

2. Many of the texts you've read in this chapter explore the dissonance that results from cultural clashes, particularly the conflicts experienced by those who are moving—by choice or by coercion—from one culture to another. Discuss the nature of that clash by focusing on three different texts.

3. Philosopher Theodor Adorno wrote that for those in exile, their writing becomes a kind of home: "In his text, the writer sets up house. . . . For [the person] who no longer has a homeland, writing becomes a place to live." Discuss what you think Adorno means, referring to at least two of the texts in this chapter as part of your interpretation.

4. Author James Baldwin wrote: "An identity would seem to be arrived at by the way in which the person faces and uses his experience." Discuss this quotation by referring to at least one of the texts you've read in this chapter and your own experience.

5. Most Americans believe that they are the master of their own destiny—and their own identity. Anyone can create and re-create him- or herself. To what extent do you believe that identity is the result of free choice rather than something determined by factors out of our control, such as race, gender, and ethnicity? Include references to at least three of the texts studied in this chapter in your response.

6. Emily Dickinson begins her poem: "I'm Nobody! Who are you? / Are you—Nobody—too?" Write a response that answers her question from the point of view of a protagonist from one of the stories in this chapter. Include references to the text of the story to support your response.

7. Identity theft is the fastest-growing type of fraud in the United States today. The term is most commonly used to refer to the crime of someone pretending to be you in order to buy goods and services in your name, or to access your bank or credit card accounts. What does this definition say about us? Is our "identity" determined by the objective data of our income, the goods and services we purchase, and the bank accounts and credit cards that give us access to those? Is it possible to "steal" someone's identity? Write an essay explaining your opinion. Refer to two or more texts from this chapter in your response.

8. Go to the National Portrait Gallery Web site (npg.si.edu), and select a portrait that either appeals to you or puzzles you. Write about what you see in the portrait and what the visual details suggest to you about the person's identity and culture.

Love and Relationships

Ay me! for aught that I could ever read,
Could ever hear by tale or history,
The course of true love never did run smooth.

       — WILLIAM SHAKESPEARE, *A Midsummer Night's Dream*

What is it about love and relationships that has captured the imaginations of poets and writers throughout the ages? Why are we drawn to love stories, even when they so often end in tears? The literature in this chapter explores the many ways people find love, keep love, or keep it from falling apart. As Elizabeth Bishop explains, sometimes love "may look like (*Write* it!) like disaster."

In *The Importance of Being Earnest*, Oscar Wilde pokes fun at the trappings of Victorian courtship and marital rules of engagement. As you chuckle over a young lady's determination to marry a man named Ernest, you may find yourself reflecting on the cultural mores that circumscribe contemporary courtship. The Conversation in this chapter invites just such thinking by offering a collection of readings on courtship, ranging from a section from Andreas Capellanus's *The Art of Courtly Love* and an excerpt from Charles Dickens's *Our Mutual Friend* to Anita Jain's essay "Is Arranged Marriage Really Any Worse Than Craigslist?" and Randall Munroe's comic strip *Boyfriend*. These diverse texts demonstrate not only how the rules of engagement have changed over time but how human nature has remained relatively constant.

A common variation on the theme of love and relationships is shattered dreams. In "Woman Hollering Creek," Sandra Cisneros portrays a relationship that began with a young girl's dreams of true love but ended in abuse. In "Bliss," Katherine Mansfield invites us to watch Bertha Young's dreams of her perfect life shatter in an evening. In his inimitably laconic manner, the poet Billy Collins uses the analogy of "weighing the dog" to describe his feelings of loss after a love affair goes wrong.

If there is a constant among the many variations on the theme of love and relationships, it can be found in the words of William Shakespeare, "The course of true love never did run smooth." Even the blissful image portrayed in Gustav Klimt's *The Kiss* has been reinterpreted by Lawrence Ferlinghetti in his poem "Short Story on a Painting of Gustav Klimt." How do we recognize true love? Can you ever be sure? We hope that reading this literature will help you navigate your relationships. Don't be surprised if in the process you shed a few tears.

Handwritten annotation at top:

"And alien tears will fill for him
Pity's long unbroken urn
for his mourners will be outcast men
And outcasts always mourn."

from Ballad...
Epitaph on Wilde's
tomb in Paris

The Importance of Being Earnest

A Trivial Comedy for Serious People

OSCAR WILDE

Oscar Fingal O'Flahertie Wills Wilde was born in Dublin in 1854. At the age of sixteen, Wilde won the Royal School Scholarship to Trinity College Dublin, where he won several awards as a scholar of ancient Greek before receiving a scholarship to Magdalen College, Oxford. Here he became engaged with the aesthetic, or decadence, movement, whose commitment to beauty and art for art's sake conflicted with the strict morality and restraint of the Victorian era. After graduating, Wilde moved to London, where he married Constance Lloyd and had two sons. Wilde established himself as a writer, publishing two children's books and, in 1890, his only novel, *The Picture of Dorian Gray*. The explicit characterization of evil and the underlying homoerotic subculture it depicted were condemned by Victorian English society. Wilde, amused by the reaction of his critics, turned more decisively to social and political satire, and in 1891–1892 he wrote his first play, *Lady Windermere's Fan*. Its immediate success established his direction as a playwright, and in the following three years he wrote *A Woman of No Importance* (1893), *An Ideal Husband* (1895), and *The Importance of Being Earnest* (1895). Wilde's later years were less happy. In 1895, he was caught in a homosexual relationship (at the time a criminal offense), which eventually led to a two-year sentence in Reading jail. After his release, he published "The Ballad of Reading Gaol" (1898), a profound reflection on the nature of sin and the need for charity. Effectively an outcast from Britain, Wilde lived in Paris under an assumed name until his death from meningitis in November 1900. *The Importance of Being Earnest* is considered one of the finest satirical plays written in the English language.

Handwritten annotations in margin:
• 109
stanzas
• sestets
8-6-8-6-8-6
abcbdb
Jail — Gaol
place
C.3.3
cell block | cell landing | cell
ASK: What is being satirized?

THE PERSONS OF THE PLAY

JOHN WORTHING, J.P., *of the Manor House, Woolton, Hertfordshire*
ALGERNON MONCRIEFF, *his friend*
REV. CANON CHASUBLE, D.D., *rector of Woolton*
MERRIMAN, *butler to Mr. Worthing*

LANE, *Mr. Moncrieff's manservant*
LADY BRACKNELL
HON. GWENDOLEN FAIRFAX, *her daughter*
CECILY CARDEW, *John Worthing's ward*
MISS PRISM, *her governess*

THE SCENES OF THE PLAY

ACT I. *Algernon Moncrieff's Flat in Half-Moon Street, W.*
ACT II. *The Garden at the Manor House, Woolton*
ACT III. *Morning Room at the Manor House, Woolton*

* Verbal Irony

ACT I

(Scene: Morning room in Algernon's flat in Half Moon Street. The room is luxuriously and artistically furnished. The sound of a piano is heard in the adjoining room. LANE is arranging afternoon tea on the table, and after the music has ceased, ALGERNON enters.)

ALGERNON: Did you hear what I was playing, Lane?

LANE: I didn't think it polite to listen, sir.

ALGERNON: I'm sorry for that, for your sake. I don't play accurately—anyone can play accurately—but I play with wonderful expression. As far as the piano is concerned, sentiment is my forte. I keep science for Life. — *character* 5

LANE: Yes, sir.

ALGERNON: And, speaking of the science of Life, have you got the cucumber sandwiches cut for Lady Bracknell?

LANE: Yes, sir.   *(Hands them on a salver.)*

ALGERNON *(inspects them, takes two, and sits down on the sofa)*: Oh!—by the way, Lane, I see from your book that on Thursday night, when Lord Shoreham and Mr. Worthing were dining with me, eight bottles of champagne are entered as having been consumed. 10

LANE: Yes, sir; eight bottles and a pint.

ALGERNON: Why is it that at a bachelor's establishment the servants invariably drink the champagne? I ask merely for information. 15

LANE: I attribute it to the superior quality of the wine, sir. I have often observed that in married households the champagne is rarely of a first-rate brand.

ALGERNON: Good heavens! Is marriage so demoralizing as that?

LANE: I believe it *is* a very pleasant state, sir. I have had very little experience of it myself up to the present. I have only been married once. That was in consequence of a misunderstanding between myself and a young person. 20

ALGERNON *(languidly)*: I don't know that I am much interested in your family life, Lane.

LANE: No, sir; it is not a very interesting subject. I never think of it myself.

ALGERNON: Very natural, I am sure. That will do, Lane, thank you. 25

LANE: Thank you, sir.   *(LANE goes out.)*

ALGERNON: Lane's views on marriage seem somewhat lax. Really, if the lower orders don't set us a good example, what on earth is the use of them? They seem, as a class, to have absolutely no sense of moral responsibility. — *like a scientific classification*

(Enter LANE.)

LANE: Mr. Ernest Worthing. 30

(Enter JACK. LANE goes out.)

ALGERNON: How are you, my dear Ernest? What brings you up to town?

JACK: Oh, pleasure, pleasure! What else should bring one anywhere? Eating as usual, I see, Algy!

ALGERNON *(stiffly)*: I believe it is customary in good society to take some slight refreshment at five o'clock. Where have you been since last Thursday? 35

Class
*TINY TIM
"Noble Poor"

JACK (*sitting down on the sofa*): In the country.

ALGERNON: What on earth do you do there?

JACK (*pulling off his gloves*): When one is in town one amuses oneself. When one is in the country one amuses other people. It is excessively boring.

ALGERNON: And who are the people you amuse? 40

JACK (*airily*): Oh, neighbors, neighbors.

ALGERNON: Got nice neighbors in your part of Shropshire?

JACK: Perfectly horrid! Never speak to one of them.

ALGERNON: How immensely you must amuse them! (*Goes over and takes sandwich.*) By the way, Shropshire is your county, is it not? 45

JACK: Eh? Shropshire? Yes, of course. Hallo! Why all these cups? Why cucumber sandwiches? Why such reckless extravagance in one so young? Who is coming to tea?

ALGERNON: Oh! merely Aunt Augusta and Gwendolen.

JACK: How perfectly delightful!

ALGERNON: Yes, that is all very well; but I am afraid Aunt Augusta won't quite approve 50 of your being here.

JACK: May I ask why?

ALGERNON: My dear fellow, the way you flirt with Gwendolen is perfectly disgraceful. It is almost as bad as the way Gwendolen flirts with you.

JACK: I am in love with Gwendolen. I have come up to town expressly to propose to her. 55

ALGERNON: I thought you had come up for pleasure? — I call that business.

JACK: How utterly unromantic you are!

ALGERNON: I really don't see anything romantic in proposing. It is very romantic to be in love. But there is nothing romantic about a definite proposal. Why, one may be accepted. One usually is, I believe. Then the excitement is all over. The 60 very essence of romance is uncertainty. If ever I get married, I'll certainly try to forget the fact. *See proposal on p. 585 — how is Algy accurate?*

Debate in class — attitudes on marriage

JACK: I have no doubt about that, dear Algy. The Divorce Court was specially invented for people whose memories are so curiously constituted.

ALGERNON: Oh! there is no use speculating on that subject. Divorces are made in 65 heaven — (JACK *puts out his hand to take a sandwich.* ALGERNON *at once interferes.*) Please don't touch the cucumber sandwiches. They are ordered specially for Aunt Augusta. (*Takes one and eats it.*)

JACK: Well, you have been eating them all the time.

ALGERNON: That is quite a different matter. She is my aunt. (*Takes plate from below.*) 70 Have some bread and butter. The bread and butter is for Gwendolen. Gwendolen is devoted to bread and butter. *idiom regarding wealth*

JACK (*advancing to table and helping himself*): And very good bread and butter it is too.

ALGERNON: Well, my dear fellow, you need not eat as if you were going to eat it all. You behave as if you were married to her already. You are not married to her 75 already, and I don't think you ever will be.

JACK: Why on earth do you say that?

ALGERNON: Well, in the first place, girls never marry the men they flirt with. Girls don't think it right.

Debate

girls/women

JACK: Oh, that is nonsense!   80

ALGERNON: It isn't. It is a great truth. It accounts for the extraordinary number of bachelors that one sees all over the place. In the second place, I don't give my consent.

JACK: Your consent!

ALGERNON: My dear fellow, Gwendolen is my first cousin. And before I allow you to   85
marry her, you will have to clear up the whole question of Cecily.   (*Rings bell.*)

JACK: Cecily! What on earth do you mean? What do you mean, Algy, by Cecily! I don't know anyone of the name of Cecily.

(*Enter* LANE.)

ALGERNON: Bring me that cigarette case Mr. Worthing left in the smoking room the last time he dined here.   90

LANE: Yes, sir.   (LANE *goes out.*)

JACK: Do you mean to say you have had my cigarette case all this time? I wish to goodness you had let me know. I have been writing frantic letters to Scotland Yard about it. I was very nearly offering a large reward.

ALGERNON: Well, I wish you would offer one. I happen to be more than usually hard up.   95

JACK: There is no good offering a large reward now that the thing is found.

(*Enter* LANE *with the cigarette case on a salver.* ALGERNON *takes it at once.* LANE *goes out.*)

ALGERNON: I think that is rather mean of you, Ernest, I must say. (*Opens case and examines it.*) However, it makes no matter, for, now that I look at the inscription inside, I find that the thing isn't yours after all.

JACK: Of course it's mine. (*Moving to him.*) You have seen me with it a hundred times,   100
and you have no right whatsoever to read what is written inside. It is a very ungentlemanly thing to read a private cigarette case.

ALGERNON: Oh! it is absurd to have a hard-and-fast rule about what one should read
and what one shouldn't. More than half of modern culture depends on what
one shouldn't read.   105

Debate —

JACK: I am quite aware of the fact, and I don't propose to discuss modern culture. It isn't the sort of thing one should talk of in private. I simply want my cigarette case back.

ALGERNON: Yes; but this isn't your cigarette case. This cigarette case is a present from someone of the name of Cecily, and you said you didn't know anyone of that   110
name.

JACK: Well, if you want to know, Cecily happens to be my aunt.

ALGERNON: Your aunt!

JACK: Yes. Charming old lady she is, too. Lives at Tunbridge Wells. Just give it back to me, Algy.   115

ALGERNON (*retreating to back of sofa*): But why does she call herself little Cecily if she is your aunt and lives at Tunbridge Wells? (*Reading.*) "From little Cecily with her fondest love."

JACK (*moving to sofa and kneeling upon it*): My dear fellow, what on earth is there in that? Some aunts are tall, some aunts are not tall. That is a matter that surely   120
an aunt may be allowed to decide for herself. You seem to think that every aunt should be exactly like your aunt! That is absurd! For heaven's sake give me back my cigarette case.   (*Follows* ALGERNON *round the room.*)

ALGERNON: Yes. But why does your aunt call you her uncle? "From little Cecily, with   125
her fondest love to her dear Uncle Jack." There is no objection, I admit, to an aunt being a small aunt, but why an aunt, no matter what her size may be, should call her own nephew her uncle, I can't quite make out. Besides, your name isn't Jack at all; it is Ernest.

JACK: It isn't Ernest; it's Jack.

ALGERNON: You have always told me it was Ernest. I have introduced you to every-   130
one as Ernest. You answer to the name of Ernest. You look as if your name was Ernest. You are the most earnest looking person I ever saw in my life. It is per-fectly absurd your saying that your name isn't Ernest. It's on your cards. Here is one of them (*taking it from case*) "Mr. Ernest Worthing, B.4, The Albany." I'll keep this as a proof that your name is Ernest if ever you attempt to deny it to me,   135
or to Gwendolen, or to anyone else.   (*Puts the card in his pocket.*)

JACK: Well, my name is Ernest in town and Jack in the country, and the cigarette case was given to me in the country.

ALGERNON: Yes, but that does not account for the fact that your small Aunt Cecily, who lives at Tunbridge Wells, calls you her dear uncle. Come, old boy, you had   140
much better have the thing out at once.

JACK: My dear Algy, you talk exactly as if you were a dentist. It is very vulgar to talk like a dentist when one isn't a dentist. It produces a false impression.

ALGERNON: Well, that is exactly what dentists always do. Now, go on! Tell me the whole thing. I may mention that I have always suspected you of being a con-   145
firmed and secret Bunburyist; and I am quite sure of it now.

JACK: Bunburyist? What on earth do you mean by a Bunburyist?

ALGERNON: I'll reveal to you the meaning of that incomparable expression as soon as you are kind enough to inform me why you are Ernest in town and Jack in the country.   150

JACK: Well, produce my cigarette case first.

ALGERNON: Here it is. (*Hands cigarette case.*) Now produce your explanation, and pray make it improbable.   (*Sits on sofa.*)

JACK: My dear fellow, there is nothing improbable about my explanation at all. In fact it's perfectly ordinary. Old Mr. Thomas Cardew, who adopted me when I   155
was a little boy, made me in his will guardian to his granddaughter, Miss Cecily Cardew. Cecily, who addresses me as her uncle from motives of respect that you could not possibly appreciate, lives at my place in the country under the charge of her admirable governess, Miss Prism.

ALGERNON: Where is that place in the country, by the way?   160

JACK: That is nothing to you, dear boy. You are not going to be invited—I may tell you candidly that the place is not in Shropshire.

ALGERNON: I suspected that, my dear fellow! I have Bunburyed all over Shropshire on two separate occasions. Now, go on. <u>Why are you Ernest in town</u> and <u>Jack in the country?</u> 165

JACK: My dear Algy, I don't know whether you will be able to understand my real motives. <u>You are hardly serious enough.</u> When one is placed in the position of guardian, one has to adopt a very high moral tone on all subjects. It's one's duty to do so. And as a high moral tone can hardly be said to conduce very much to either one's health or one's happiness, in order to get up to town I have always pretended to have a younger 170 brother of the name of Ernest, who lives in the Albany, and gets into the most dreadful scrapes. That, my dear Algy, is the whole truth pure and simple.

ALGERNON: The truth is rarely pure and never simple. Modern life would be very tedious if it were either, and modern literature a complete impossibility!

JACK: That wouldn't be at all a bad thing. 175

ALGERNON: Literary criticism is not your forte, my dear fellow. Don't try it. You should leave that to people who haven't been at a university. They do it so well in the daily papers. What you really are is a Bunburyist. I was quite right in saying you were a Bunburyist. You are one of the most advanced Bunburyists I know.

comment to critics

JACK: What on earth do you mean? 180

ALGERNON: You have invented a very useful younger brother called Ernest, in order that you may be able to come up to town as often as you like. I have invented an invaluable permanent invalid called Bunbury, in order that I may be able to go down into the country whenever I choose. Bunbury is perfectly invaluable. If it wasn't for Bunbury's extraordinary bad health, for instance, I wouldn't be able to 185 dine with you at Willis's tonight, for I have been really engaged to Aunt Augusta for more than a week.

JACK: I haven't asked you to dine with me anywhere tonight.

ALGERNON: I know. You are absurdly careless about sending out invitations. It is very foolish of you. Nothing annoys people so much as not receiving invitations. 190

JACK: You had much better dine with your Aunt Augusta.

ALGERNON: I haven't the smallest intention of doing anything of the kind. To begin with, I dined there on Monday, and <u>once a week is quite enough to dine with one's own relations.</u> In the second place, whenever I do dine there I am always treated as a member of the family, and sent down with[1] either no woman at all, 195 or two. In the third place, I know perfectly well whom she will place me next to, tonight. She will place me next Mary Farquhar, who always flirts with her own husband across the dinner table. That is not very pleasant. Indeed, it is not even decent—and that sort of thing is enormously on the increase. <u>The amount of women in London who flirt with their own husbands is perfectly scandalous.</u> It 200 looks so bad. It is simply washing one's clean linen in public. Besides, now that I know you to be a confirmed Bunburyist I naturally want to talk to you about Bunburying. I want to tell you the rules.

family

Really funny

---

[1]Assigned a woman to accompany into the dining room.—EDS.

JACK: I'm not a Bunburyist at all. If Gwendolen accepts me, I am going to kill my
brother, indeed I think I'll kill him in any case. Cecily is a little too much inter-   205
ested in him. It is rather a bore. So I am going to get rid of Ernest. And I strongly
advise you to do the same with Mr.—with your invalid friend who has the
absurd name.

ALGERNON: Nothing will induce me to part with Bunbury, and if you ever get married, which seems to me extremely problematic, you will be very glad to know   210
Bunbury. A man who marries without knowing Bunbury has a very tedious
time of it.

JACK: That is nonsense. If I marry a charming girl like Gwendolen, and she is the
only girl I ever saw in my life that I would marry, I certainly won't want to know
Bunbury.   215

ALGERNON: Then your wife will. You don't seem to realize, that in married life three
is company and two is none.

JACK (*sententiously*): That, my dear young friend, is the theory that the corrupt French
drama has been propounding for the last fifty years.

ALGERNON: Yes; and that the happy English home has proved in half the time.   220

JACK: For heaven's sake, don't try to be cynical. It's perfectly easy to be cynical.

ALGERNON: My dear fellow, it isn't easy to be anything nowadays. There's such a lot
of beastly competition about. (*The sound of an electric bell is heard.*) Ah! that
must be Aunt Augusta. Only relatives, or creditors, ever ring in that Wagnerian[2]
manner. Now, if I get her out of the way for ten minutes, so that you can have   225
an opportunity for proposing to Gwendolen, may I dine with you tonight at
Willis's?

JACK: I suppose so, if you want to.

ALGERNON: Yes, but you must be serious about it. I hate people who are not serious
about meals. It is so shallow of them.   230

(*Enter* LANE.)

LANE: Lady Bracknell and Miss Fairfax.

(ALGERNON *goes forward to meet them. Enter* LADY BRACKNELL *and* GWENDOLEN.)

LADY BRACKNELL: Good afternoon, dear Algernon, I hope you are behaving very
well.

ALGERNON: I'm feeling very well, Aunt Augusta.

LADY BRACKNELL: That's not quite the same thing. In fact the two things rarely go   235
together.

(*Sees* JACK *and bows to him with icy coldness.*)

ALGERNON (*to* GWENDOLEN): Dear me, you are smart!

---

[2]German composer Richard Wagner's most famous operatic work is the *Ring* Cycle, from which we
get the stereotypical operatic image of a bellowing soprano wearing a Viking helmet.—EDS.

GWENDOLEN: I am always smart! Aren't I, Mr. Worthing?

JACK: You're quite perfect, Miss Fairfax.

GWENDOLEN: Oh! I hope I am not that. It would leave no room for developments, 240
and I intend to develop in many directions.

(GWENDOLEN *and* JACK *sit down together in the corner.*)

LADY BRACKNELL: I'm sorry if we are a little late, Algernon, but I was obliged to call
on dear Lady Harbury. I hadn't been there since her poor husband's death. I never
saw a woman so altered; she looks quite twenty years younger. And now I'll have a
cup of tea, and one of those nice cucumber sandwiches you promised me. 245

ALGERNON: Certainly, Aunt Augusta. *(Goes over to tea table.)*

LADY BRACKNELL: Won't you come and sit here, Gwendolen?

GWENDOLEN: Thanks, Mama, I'm quite comfortable where I am.

ALGERNON *(picking up empty plate in horror)*: Good heavens! Lane! Why are there no
cucumber sandwiches? I ordered them specially. 250

LANE *(gravely)*: There were no cucumbers in the market this morning, sir. I went
down twice.

ALGERNON: No cucumbers!

LANE: No, sir. Not even for ready money.

ALGERNON: That will do, Lane, thank you. 255

LANE: Thank you, sir. *(Goes out.)*

ALGERNON: I am greatly distressed, Aunt Augusta, about there being no cucumbers,
not even for ready money.

LADY BRACKNELL: It really makes no matter, Algernon. I had some crumpets with
Lady Harbury, who seems to me to be living entirely for pleasure now. 260

ALGERNON: I hear her hair has turned quite gold from grief.

LADY BRACKNELL: It certainly has changed its color. From what cause I, of course, cannot say. (ALGERNON *crosses and hands tea.*) Thank you. I've quite a treat for you
tonight, Algernon. I am going to send you down with Mary Farquhar. She is such
a nice woman, and so attentive to her husband. It's delightful to watch them. 265

ALGERNON: I am afraid, Aunt Augusta, I shall have to give up the pleasure of dining
with you tonight after all.

LADY BRACKNELL *(frowning)*: I hope not, Algernon. It would put my table completely
out. Your uncle would have to dine upstairs. Fortunately he is accustomed to
that. 270

ALGERNON: It is a great bore, and, I need hardly say, a terrible disappointment to me,
but the fact is I have just had a telegram to say that my poor friend Bunbury is very
ill again. *(Exchanges glances with* JACK.*)* They seem to think I should be with him.

LADY BRACKNELL: It is very strange. This Mr. Bunbury seems to suffer from curiously
bad health. 275

ALGERNON: Yes; poor Bunbury is a dreadful invalid.

LADY BRACKNELL: Well, I must say, Algernon, that I think it is high time that Mr.
Bunbury made up his mind whether he was going to live or to die. This shilly-
shallying with the question is absurd. Nor do I in any way approve of the modern

sympathy with invalids. I consider it morbid. Illness of any kind is hardly a thing 280
to be encouraged in others. Health is the primary duty of life. I am always telling
that to your poor uncle, but he never seems to take much notice—as far as any
improvement in his ailments goes. I should be much obliged if you would ask
Mr. Bunbury, from me, to be kind enough not to have a relapse on Saturday, for
I rely on you to arrange my music for me. It is my last reception, and one wants 285
something that will encourage conversation, particularly at the end of the season when everyone has practically said whatever they had to say, which, in most
cases, was probably not much.

ALGERNON: I'll speak to Bunbury, Aunt Augusta, if he is still conscious, and I think
I can promise you he'll be all right by Saturday. Of course the music is a great 290
difficulty. You see, if one plays good music, people don't listen, and if one plays
bad music people don't talk. But I'll run over the program I've drawn out, if you
will kindly come into the next room for a moment.

LADY BRACKNELL: Thank you, Algernon. It is very thoughtful of you. (*Rising, and
following* ALGERNON.) I'm sure the program will be delightful, after a few expur- 295
gations. French songs I cannot possibly allow. People always seem to think that
they are improper, and either look shocked, which is vulgar, or laugh, which is
worse. But German sounds a thoroughly respectable language, and indeed, I
believe is so. Gwendolen, you will accompany me. *Why pro-German sentiments?*

GWENDOLEN: Certainly, Mama. 300

(LADY BRACKNELL *and* ALGERNON *go into the music room.* GWENDOLEN *remains behind.*)

comment on verbal irony as a whole

JACK: Charming day it has been, Miss Fairfax.

GWENDOLEN: Pray don't talk to me about the weather, Mr. Worthing. Whenever
people talk to me about the weather, I always feel quite certain that they mean
something else. And that makes me so nervous.

JACK: I do mean something else. 305

GWENDOLEN: I thought so. In fact, I am never wrong.

JACK: And I would like to be allowed to take advantage of Lady Bracknell's temporary
absence—

GWENDOLEN: I would certainly advise you to do so. Mama has a way of coming back
suddenly into a room that I have often had to speak to her about. 310

JACK (*nervously*): Miss Fairfax, ever since I met you I have admired you more than
any girl—I have ever met since—I met you. > *Hilarious.*

GWENDOLEN: Yes, I am quite aware of the fact. And I often wish that in public, at any
rate, you had been more demonstrative. For me you have always had an irresistible fascination. Even before I met you I was far from indifferent to you. (JACK 315
looks at her in amazement.) We live, as I hope you know, Mr. Worthing, in an
age of ideals. The fact is constantly mentioned in the more expensive monthly
magazines, and has reached the provincial pulpits I am told: And my ideal has *class*
always been to love someone of the name of Ernest. There is something in that
name that inspires absolute confidence. The moment Algernon first mentioned 320
to me that he had a friend called Ernest, I knew I was destined to love you.

Discuss what does Wilde mean by that

JACK: You really love me, Gwendolen?

GWENDOLEN: Passionately!

JACK: Darling! You don't know how happy you've made me.

GWENDOLEN: My own Ernest! 325

JACK: But you don't mean to say that you couldn't love me if my name wasn't Ernest?

GWENDOLEN: But your name is Ernest.

JACK: Yes, I know it is. But supposing it was something else? Do you mean to say you couldn't love me then? 330

GWENDOLEN (*glibly*): Ah! that is clearly a metaphysical speculation, and like most metaphysical speculations has very little reference at all to the actual facts of real life, as we know them.

JACK: Personally, darling, to speak quite candidly, I don't much care about the name of Ernest—I don't think the name suits me at all. 335

GWENDOLEN: It suits you perfectly. It is a divine name. It has a music of its own. It produces vibrations.

JACK: Well, really, Gwendolen, I must say that I think there are lots of other much nicer names. I think Jack, for instance, a charming name.

GWENDOLEN: Jack?—No, there is very little music in the name Jack, if any at all, 340 indeed. It does not thrill. It produces absolutely no vibrations—I have known several Jacks, and they all, without exception, were more than usually plain. Besides, Jack is a notorious domesticity for John! And I pity any woman who is married to a man called John. She would probably never be allowed to know the entrancing pleasure of a single moment's solitude. The only really safe name 345 is Ernest.

JACK: Gwendolen, I must get christened at once—I mean we must get married at once. There is no time to be lost.

GWENDOLEN: Married, Mr. Worthing?

JACK (*astounded*): Well—surely. You know that I love you, and you led me to believe, 350 Miss Fairfax, that you were not absolutely indifferent to me.

GWENDOLEN: I adore you. But you haven't proposed to me yet. Nothing has been said at all about marriage. The subject has not even been touched on.

JACK: Well—may I propose to you now?

GWENDOLEN: I think it would be an admirable opportunity. And to spare you any 355 possible disappointment, Mr. Worthing, I think it only fair to tell you quite frankly beforehand that I am fully determined to accept you.

JACK: Gwendolen!

GWENDOLEN: Yes, Mr. Worthing, what have you got to say to me?

JACK: You know what I have got to say to you. 360

GWENDOLEN: Yes, but you don't say it.

JACK: Gwendolen, will you marry me? (*Goes on his knees.*)

GWENDOLEN: Of course I will, darling. How long you have been about it! I am afraid you have had very little experience in how to propose.

JACK: My own one, I have never loved anyone in the world but you. 365

GWENDOLEN: Yes, but men often propose for practice. I know my brother Gerald does. All my girlfriends tell me so. What wonderfully blue eyes you have, Ernest! They are quite, quite blue. I hope you will always look at me just like that, especially when there are other people present.

(Enter LADY BRACKNELL.*)*

LADY BRACKNELL: Mr. Worthing! Rise, sir, from this semirecumbent posture. It is most indecorous. 370

GWENDOLEN: Mama! *(He tries to rise; she restrains him.)* I must beg you to retire. This is no place for you. Besides, Mr. Worthing has not quite finished yet.

LADY BRACKNELL: Finished what, may I ask?

GWENDOLEN: I am engaged to Mr. Worthing, Mama. *(They rise together.)* 375

LADY BRACKNELL: Pardon me, you are not engaged to anyone. When you do become engaged to someone, I, or your father, should his health permit him, will inform you of the fact. An engagement should come on a young girl as a surprise, pleasant or unpleasant, as the case may be. It is hardly a matter that she could be allowed to arrange for herself—And now I have a few questions to put to you, 380 Mr. Worthing. While I am making these inquiries, you, Gwendolen, will wait for me below in the carriage.

GWENDOLEN *(reproachfully)*: Mama!

LADY BRACKNELL: In the carriage, Gwendolen! (GWENDOLEN *goes to the door. She and* JACK *blow kisses to each other behind* LADY BRACKNELL's *back.* LADY BRACKNELL 385 *looks vaguely about as if she could not understand what the noise was. Finally turns round.)* Gwendolen, the carriage!

GWENDOLEN: Yes, Mama.

(Goes out, looking back at JACK.*)*

LADY BRACKNELL *(sitting down)*: You can take a seat, Mr. Worthing.
(Looks in her pocket for notebook and pencil.)

JACK: Thank you, Lady Bracknell, I prefer standing. 390

LADY BRACKNELL *(pencil and notebook in hand)*: I feel bound to tell you that you are not down on my list of eligible young men, although I have the same list as the dear Duchess of Bolton has. We work together, in fact. However, I am quite ready to enter your name, should your answers be what a really affectionate mother requires. Do you smoke? 395

JACK: Well, yes, I must admit I smoke.

LADY BRACKNELL: I am glad to hear it. A man should always have an occupation of some kind. There are far too many idle men in London as it is. How old are you?

JACK: Twenty-nine.

LADY BRACKNELL: A very good age to be married at. I have always been of opinion 400 that a man who desires to get married should know either everything or nothing. Which do you know?

JACK *(after some hesitation)*: I know nothing, Lady Bracknell.

LADY BRACKNELL: I am pleased to hear it. I do not approve of anything that tampers with natural ignorance. Ignorance is like a delicate exotic fruit; touch it and the 405 bloom is gone. The whole theory of modern education is radically unsound. Fortunately in England, at any rate, education produces no effect whatsoever. If it did, it would prove a serious danger to the upper classes, and probably lead to acts of violence in Grosvenor Square. What is your income?

JACK: Between seven and eight thousand a year. 410

LADY BRACKNELL (*makes a note in her book*): In land, or in investments?

JACK: In investments, chiefly.

LADY BRACKNELL: That is satisfactory. What between the duties expected of one during one's lifetime, and the duties exacted from one after one's death, land has ceased to be either a profit or a pleasure. It gives one position, and prevents one 415 from keeping it up. That's all that can be said about land.

JACK: I have a country house with some land, of course, attached to it, about fifteen hundred acres, I believe; but I don't depend on that for my real income. In fact, as far as I can make out, the poachers are the only people who make anything out of it.

LADY BRACKNELL: A country house! How many bedrooms? Well, that point can 420 be cleared up afterwards. You have a town house, I hope? A girl with a simple, unspoiled nature, like Gwendolen, could hardly be expected to reside in the country.

JACK: Well, I own a house in Belgrave Square, but it is let by the year to Lady Bloxham. Of course, I can get it back whenever I like, at six months' notice. 425

LADY BRACKNELL: Lady Bloxham? I don't know her.

JACK: Oh, she goes about very little. She is a lady considerably advanced in years.

LADY BRACKNELL: Ah, nowadays that is no guarantee of respectability of character. What number in Belgrave Square?

JACK: 149. 430

LADY BRACKNELL (*shaking her head*): The unfashionable side. I thought there was something. However, that could easily be altered.

JACK: Do you mean the fashion, or the side?

LADY BRACKNELL (*sternly*): Both, if necessary, I presume. What are your politics?

JACK: Well, I am afraid I really have none. I am a Liberal Unionist. 435

LADY BRACKNELL: Oh, they count as Tories. They dine with us. Or come in the evening, at any rate. Now to minor matters. Are your parents living?

JACK: I have lost both my parents.

LADY BRACKNELL: Both? To lose one parent may be regarded as a misfortune—to lose *both* seems like carelessness. Who was your father? He was evidently a man 440 of some wealth. Was he born in what the Radical papers call the purple of commerce, or did he rise from the ranks of the aristocracy?

JACK: I am afraid I really don't know. The fact is, Lady Bracknell, I said I had lost my parents. It would be nearer the truth to say that my parents seem to have lost me—I don't actually know who I am by birth. I was—well, I was found. 445

LADY BRACKNELL: Found!

JACK: The late Mr. Thomas Cardew, an old gentleman of a very charitable and kindly disposition, found me, and gave me the name of Worthing, because he happened to have a first-class ticket for Worthing in his pocket at the time. Worthing is a place in Sussex. It is a seaside resort. 450

LADY BRACKNELL: Where did the charitable gentleman who had a first-class ticket for this seaside resort find you?

JACK (*gravely*): In a handbag.

LADY BRACKNELL: A handbag?

JACK (*very seriously*): Yes, Lady Bracknell. I was in a handbag—a somewhat large, 455 black leather handbag, with handles to it—an ordinary handbag in fact.

LADY BRACKNELL: In what locality did this Mr. James, or Thomas, Cardew come across this ordinary handbag?

JACK: In the cloakroom at Victoria Station. It was given to him in mistake for his own. 460

LADY BRACKNELL: The cloakroom at Victoria Station?

JACK: Yes. The Brighton line.

LADY BRACKNELL: The line is immaterial. Mr. Worthing, I confess I feel somewhat bewildered by what you have just told me. To be born, or at any rate bred, in a handbag, whether it had handles or not, seems to me to display a contempt 465 for the ordinary decencies of family life that reminds one of the worst excesses of the French Revolution. And I presume you know what that unfortunate movement led to? As for the particular locality in which the handbag was found, a cloakroom at a railway station might serve to conceal a social indiscretion—has probably, indeed, been used for that purpose before now—but 470 it could hardly be regarded as an assured basis for a recognized position in good society.

JACK: May I ask you then what you would advise me to do? I need hardly say I would do anything in the world to ensure Gwendolen's happiness.

LADY BRACKNELL: I would strongly advise you, Mr. Worthing, to try and acquire 475 some relations as soon as possible, and to make a definite effort to produce at any rate one parent, of either sex, before the season is quite over.

JACK: Well, I don't see how I could possibly manage to do that. I can produce the handbag at any moment. It is in my dressing room at home. I really think that should satisfy you, Lady Bracknell. 480

LADY BRACKNELL: Me, sir! What has it to do with me? You can hardly imagine that I and Lord Bracknell would dream of allowing our only daughter—a girl brought up with the utmost care—to marry into a cloakroom, and form an alliance with a parcel? Good morning, Mr. Worthing!

(LADY BRACKNELL *sweeps out in majestic indignation.*)

JACK: Good morning! (ALGERNON, *from the other room, strikes up the Wedding March.* 485 JACK *looks perfectly furious, and goes to the door.*) For goodness' sake don't play that ghastly tune, Algy. How idiotic you are!

(*The music stops, and* ALGERNON *enters cheerily.*)

ALGERNON: Didn't it go off all right, old boy? You don't mean to say Gwendolen refused you? I know it is a way she has. She is always refusing people. I think it is most ill-natured of her. 490

JACK: Oh, Gwendolen is as right as a trivet. As far as she is concerned, we are engaged. Her mother is perfectly unbearable. Never met such a Gorgon[3]—I don't really know what a Gorgon is like, but I am quite sure that Lady Bracknell is one. In any case, she is a monster, without being a myth, which is rather unfair. I beg your pardon, Algy, I suppose I shouldn't talk about your own aunt in that way before you. 495

ALGERNON: My dear boy, I love hearing my relations abused. It is the only thing that makes me put up with them at all. Relations are simply a tedious pack of people, who haven't got the remotest knowledge of how to live, nor the smallest instinct about when to die. 500

JACK: Oh, that is nonsense!

ALGERNON: It isn't!

JACK: Well, I won't argue about the matter. You always want to argue about things.

ALGERNON: That is exactly what things were originally made for.

JACK: Upon my word, if I thought that, I'd shoot myself—*(A pause.)* You don't think there is any chance of Gwendolen becoming like her mother in about a hundred and fifty years, do you, Algy? 505

ALGERNON: All women become like their mothers. That is their tragedy. No man does. That's his.

JACK: Is that clever? 510

ALGERNON: It is perfectly phrased! and quite as true as any observation in civilized life should be.

JACK: I am sick to death of cleverness. Everybody is clever nowadays. You can't go anywhere without meeting clever people. The thing has become an absolute public nuisance. I wish to goodness we had a few fools left. 515

ALGERNON: We have.

JACK: I should extremely like to meet them. What do they talk about?

ALGERNON: The fools? Oh! about the clever people, of course.

JACK: What fools!

ALGERNON: By the way, did you tell Gwendolen the truth about your being Ernest in town, and Jack in the country? 520

JACK *(in a very patronizing manner)*: My dear fellow, the truth isn't quite the sort of thing one tells to a nice sweet refined girl. What extraordinary ideas you have about the way to behave to a woman!

ALGERNON: The only way to behave to a woman is to make love to her if she is pretty, and to someone else if she is plain. 525

JACK: Oh, that is nonsense.

ALGERNON: What about your brother? What about the profligate Ernest?

JACK: Oh, before the end of the week I shall have got rid of him. I'll say he died in Paris of apoplexy. Lots of people die of apoplexy, quite suddenly, don't they? 530

---

[3]Protective deities in Greek mythology, gorgons (like Medusa) often had serpents for hair and could turn people to stone with a look.—EDS.

ALGERNON: Yes, but it's hereditary, my dear fellow. It's a sort of thing that runs in families. You had much better say a severe chill.

JACK: You are sure a severe chill isn't hereditary, or anything of that kind?

ALGERNON: Of course it isn't!

JACK: Very well, then. My poor brother Ernest is carried off suddenly in Paris, by a severe chill. That gets rid of him. 535

ALGERNON: But I thought you said that—Miss Cardew was a little too much interested in your poor brother Ernest? Won't she feel his loss a good deal?

JACK: Oh, that is all right. Cecily is not a silly romantic girl, I am glad to say. She has got a capital appetite, goes on long walks, and pays no attention at all to her lessons. 540

ALGERNON: I would rather like to see Cecily.

JACK: I will take very good care you never do. She is excessively pretty, and she is only just eighteen.

ALGERNON: Have you told Gwendolen yet that you have an excessively pretty ward who is only just eighteen? 545

JACK: Oh! one doesn't blurt these things out to people. Cecily and Gwendolen are perfectly certain to be extremely great friends. I'll bet you anything you like that half an hour after they have met, they will be calling each other sister.

ALGERNON: Women only do that when they have called each other a lot of other things first. Now, my dear boy, if we want to get a good table at Willis's, we really must go and dress. Do you know it is nearly seven? 550

JACK (*irritably*): Oh! it always is nearly seven.

ALGERNON: Well, I'm hungry.

JACK: I never knew you when you weren't—

ALGERNON: What shall we do after dinner? Go to a theater? 555

JACK: Oh, no! I loathe listening.

ALGERNON: Well, let us go to the Club?

JACK: Oh, no! I hate talking.

ALGERNON: Well, we might trot round to the Empire[4] at ten?

JACK: Oh, no! I can't bear looking at things. It is so silly. 560

ALGERNON: Well, what shall we do?

JACK: Nothing!

ALGERNON: It is awfully hard work doing nothing. However, I don't mind hard work where there is no definite object of any kind.

(*Enter* LANE.)

LANE: Miss Fairfax. 565

(*Enter* GWENDOLEN. LANE *goes out.*)

ALGERNON: Gwendolen, upon my word!

GWENDOLEN: Algy, kindly turn your back. I have something very particular to say to Mr. Worthing.

---

[4]Empire Theatre.—EDS.

ALGERNON: Really, Gwendolen, I don't think I can allow this at all.

GWENDOLEN: Algy, you always adopt a strictly immoral attitude towards life. You are not quite old enough to do that.   (ALGERNON *retires to the fireplace.*)

JACK: My own darling!

GWENDOLEN: Ernest, we may never be married. From the expression on Mama's face I fear we never shall. Few parents nowadays pay any regard to what their children say to them. The old-fashioned respect for the young is fast dying out. Whatever influence I ever had over Mama, I lost at the age of three. But although she may prevent us from becoming man and wife, and I may marry someone else, and marry often, nothing that she can possibly do can alter my eternal devotion to you.

JACK: Dear Gwendolen!

GWENDOLEN: The story of your romantic origin, as related to me by Mama, with unpleasing comments, has naturally stirred the deeper fibers of my nature. Your Christian name has an irresistible fascination. The simplicity of your character makes you exquisitely incomprehensible to me. Your town address at the Albany I have. What is your address in the country?

JACK: The Manor House, Woolton, Hertfordshire.

(ALGERNON, *who has been carefully listening, smiles to himself, and writes the address on his shirt cuff. Then picks up the Railway Guide.*)

GWENDOLEN: There is a good postal service, I suppose? It may be necessary to do something desperate. That of course will require serious consideration. I will communicate with you daily.

JACK: My own one!

GWENDOLEN: How long do you remain in town?

JACK: Till Monday.

GWENDOLEN: Good! Algy, you may turn round now.

ALGERNON: Thanks, I've turned round already.

GWENDOLEN: You may also ring the bell.

JACK: You will let me see you to your carriage, my own darling?

GWENDOLEN: Certainly.

JACK (*To* LANE, *who now enters*): I will see Miss Fairfax out.

LANE: Yes, sir.   (JACK *and* GWENDOLEN *go off.*)

(LANE *presents several letters on a salver to* ALGERNON. *It is to be surmised that they are bills, as* ALGERNON, *after looking at the envelopes, tears them up.*)

ALGERNON: A glass of sherry, Lane.

LANE: Yes, sir.

ALGERNON: Tomorrow, Lane, I'm going Bunburying.

LANE: Yes, sir.

ALGERNON: I shall probably not be back till Monday. You can put up my dress clothes, my smoking jacket, and all the Bunbury suits—

LANE: Yes, sir.   (*Handing sherry.*)

ALGERNON: I hope tomorrow will be a fine day, Lane.

LANE: It never is, sir.

ALGERNON: Lane, you're a perfect pessimist.

LANE: I do my best to give satisfaction, sir.

(*Enter* JACK. LANE *goes off.*)

JACK: There's a sensible, intellectual girl! the only girl I ever cared for in my life.   610
    (ALGERNON *is laughing immoderately.*) What on earth are you so amused at?

ALGERNON: Oh, I'm a little anxious about poor Bunbury, that is all.

JACK: If you don't take care, your friend Bunbury will get you into a serious scrape
    some day.

ALGERNON: I love scrapes. They are the only things that are never serious.   615

JACK: Oh, that's nonsense, Algy. You never talk anything but nonsense.

ALGERNON: Nobody ever does.

(JACK *looks indignantly at him, and leaves the room.* ALGERNON *lights a cigarette, reads his shirt cuff, and smiles.*)

ACT II   pp. 590 – 609   590-598
                          599-609

(*Scene: Garden at the Manor House. A flight of gray stone steps leads up to the house. The garden, an old-fashioned one, full of roses. Time of year, July. Basket chairs, and a table covered with books, are set under a large yew tree.* MISS PRISM *discovered seated at the table.* CECILY *is at the back watering flowers.*)

MISS PRISM (*calling*): Cecily, Cecily! Surely such a utilitarian occupation as the water-
    ing of flowers is rather Moulton's duty than yours? Especially at a moment when
    intellectual pleasures await you. Your German grammar is on the table. Pray
    open it at page fifteen. We will repeat yesterday's lesson.

CECILY (*coming over very slowly*): But I don't like German. It isn't at all a becoming   5
    language. I know perfectly well that I look quite plain after my German lesson.

MISS PRISM: Child, you know how anxious your guardian is that you should improve
    yourself in every way. He laid particular stress on your German, as he was leaving
    for town yesterday. Indeed, he always lays stress on your German when he is leaving
    for town.   10

CECILY: Dear Uncle Jack is so very serious! Sometimes he is so serious that I think
    he cannot be quite well.

MISS PRISM (*drawing herself up*): Your guardian enjoys the best of health, and his
    gravity of demeanor is especially to be commended in one so comparatively
    young as he is. I know no one who has a higher sense of duty and responsibility.   15

CECILY: I suppose that is why he often looks a little bored when we three are together.

MISS PRISM: Cecily! I am surprised at you. Mr. Worthing has many troubles in his life.
    Idle merriment and triviality would be out of place in his conversation. You must
    remember his constant anxiety about that unfortunate young man his brother.

CECILY: I wish Uncle Jack would allow that unfortunate young man, his brother, to   20
    come down here sometimes. We might have a good influence over him, Miss

Prism. I am sure you certainly would. You know German, and geology, and things of that kind influence a man very much.

(CECILY begins to write in her diary.)

MISS PRISM *(shaking her head)*: I do not think that even I could produce any effect on a character that according to his own brother's admission is irretrievably weak and vacillating. Indeed I am not sure that I would desire to reclaim him. I am not in favor of this modern mania for turning bad people into good people at a moment's notice. As a man sows so let him reap. You must put away your diary, Cecily. I really don't see why you should keep a diary at all.

CECILY: I keep a diary in order to enter the wonderful secrets of my life. If I didn't write them down, I should probably forget all about them.

MISS PRISM: Memory, my dear Cecily, is the diary that we all carry about with us.

CECILY: Yes, but it usually chronicles the things that have never happened, and couldn't possibly have happened. I believe that Memory is responsible for nearly all the three-volume novels that Mudie sends us.

MISS PRISM: Do not speak slightingly of the three-volume novel, Cecily. I wrote one myself in earlier days.

CECILY: Did you really, Miss Prism? How wonderfully clever you are! I hope it did not end happily? I don't like novels that end happily. They depress me so much.

MISS PRISM: The good ended happily, and the bad unhappily. That is what Fiction means.

CECILY: I suppose so. But it seems very unfair. And was your novel ever published?

MISS PRISM: Alas! no. The manuscript unfortunately was abandoned. I use the word in the sense of lost or mislaid. To your work, child, these speculations are profitless.

CECILY *(smiling)*: But I see dear Dr. Chasuble coming up through the garden.

MISS PRISM *(rising and advancing)*: Dr. Chasuble! This is indeed a pleasure.

(Enter CANON CHASUBLE.)

CHASUBLE: And how are we this morning? Miss Prism, you are, I trust, well?

CECILY: Miss Prism has just been complaining of a slight headache. I think it would do her so much good to have a short stroll with you in the park, Dr. Chasuble.

MISS PRISM: Cecily, I have not mentioned anything about a headache.

CECILY: No, dear Miss Prism, I know that, but I felt instinctively that you had a headache. Indeed I was thinking about that, and not about my German lesson, when the Rector came in.

CHASUBLE: I hope, Cecily, you are not inattentive.

CECILY: Oh, I am afraid I am.

CHASUBLE: That is strange. Were I fortunate enough to be Miss Prism's pupil, I would hang upon her lips. *(MISS PRISM glares.)* I spoke metaphorically.—My metaphor was drawn from bees. Ahem! Mr. Worthing, I suppose, has not returned from town yet?

MISS PRISM: We do not expect him till Monday afternoon.

CHASUBLE: Ah yes, he usually likes to spend his Sunday in London. He is not one of those whose sole aim is enjoyment, as, by all accounts, that unfortunate young man his brother seems to be. But I must not disturb Egeria[5] and her pupil any longer.

MISS PRISM: Egeria? My name is Laetitia, Doctor. 65

CHASUBLE *(bowing)*: A classical allusion merely, drawn from the Pagan authors. I shall see you both no doubt at Evensong?—Anglican ritual

MISS PRISM: I think, dear Doctor, I will have a stroll with you. I find I have a headache after all, and a walk might do it good.

CHASUBLE: With pleasure, Miss Prism, with pleasure. We might go as far as the 70 schools and back.

MISS PRISM: That would be delightful. Cecily, you will read your Political Economy in my absence. The chapter on the Fall of the Rupee you may omit. It is somewhat too sensational. Even these metallic problems have their melodramatic side.

(Goes down the garden with DR. CHASUBLE.)

CECILY *(picks up books and throws them back on table)*: Horrid Political Economy! 75 Horrid Geography! Horrid, horrid German!

(Enter MERRIMAN with a card on a salver.)

MERRIMAN: Mr. Ernest Worthing has just driven over from the station. He has brought his luggage with him.

CECILY *(takes the card and reads it)*: "Mr. Ernest Worthing, B.4, The Albany, W." Uncle Jack's brother! Did you tell him Mr. Worthing was in town? 80

MERRIMAN: Yes, Miss. He seemed very much disappointed. I mentioned that you and Miss Prism were in the garden. He said he was anxious to speak to you privately for a moment.

CECILY: Ask Mr. Ernest Worthing to come here. I suppose you had better talk to the housekeeper about a room for him. 85

MERRIMAN: Yes, Miss. *(MERRIMAN goes off.)*

CECILY: I have never met any really wicked person before. I feel rather frightened. I am so afraid he will look just like everyone else.

(Enter ALGERNON, very gay and debonair.)

He does!

ALGERNON *(raising his hat)*: You are my little cousin Cecily, I'm sure. 90

CECILY: You are under some strange mistake. I am not little. In fact, I believe I am more than usually tall for my age. *(ALGERNON is rather taken aback.)* But I am your cousin Cecily. You, I see from your card, are Uncle Jack's brother, my cousin Ernest, my wicked cousin Ernest.

ALGERNON: Oh! I am not really wicked at all, cousin Cecily. You mustn't think that 95 I am wicked.

---

[5]Roman goddess of water. — EDS.

CECILY: If you are not, then you have certainly been deceiving us all in a very inexcusable manner. I hope you have not been leading a double life, pretending to be wicked and being really good all the time. That would be hypocrisy.

ALGERNON *(looks at her in amazement)*: Oh! Of course I have been rather reckless. 100

CECILY: I am glad to hear it.

ALGERNON: In fact, now you mention the subject, I have been very bad in my own small way.

CECILY: I don't think you should be so proud of that, though I am sure it must have been very pleasant. 105

ALGERNON: It is much pleasanter being here with you.

CECILY: I can't understand how you are here at all. Uncle Jack won't be back till Monday afternoon.

ALGERNON: That is a great disappointment. I am obliged to go up by the first train on Monday morning. I have a business appointment that I am anxious— 110
to miss.

CECILY: Couldn't you miss it anywhere but in London?

ALGERNON: No: the appointment is in London.

CECILY: Well, I know, of course, how important it is not to keep a business engagement, if one wants to retain any sense of the beauty of life, but still I think you 115
had better wait till Uncle Jack arrives. I know he wants to speak to you about your emigrating.

ALGERNON: About my what?

CECILY: Your emigrating. He has gone up to buy your outfit.

ALGERNON: I certainly wouldn't let Jack buy my outfit. He has no taste in neckties 120
at all.

CECILY: I don't think you will require neckties. Uncle Jack is sending you to Australia.

ALGERNON: Australia! I'd sooner die.

CECILY: Well, he said at dinner on Wednesday night, that you would have to choose between this world, the next world, and Australia. 125

ALGERNON: Oh, well! The accounts I have received of Australia and the next world are not particularly encouraging. This world is good enough for me, Cousin Cecily.

CECILY: Yes, but are you good enough for it?

ALGERNON: I'm afraid I'm not that. That is why I want you to reform me. You might 130
make that your mission, if you don't mind, Cousin Cecily.

CECILY: I'm afraid I've no time, this afternoon.

ALGERNON: Well, would you mind my reforming myself this afternoon?

CECILY: It is rather quixotic of you. But I think you should try. *vocab*

ALGERNON: I will. I feel better already. 135

CECILY: You are looking a little worse.

ALGERNON: That is because I am hungry.

CECILY: How thoughtless of me. I should have remembered that when one is going to lead an entirely new life, one requires regular and wholesome meals. Won't you come in? 140

ALGERNON: Thank you. Might I have a buttonhole[6] first? I never have any appetite unless I have a buttonhole first.

CECILY: A Maréchal Niel?[7]

ALGERNON: No, I'd sooner have a pink rose.

CECILY: Why? *(Cuts a flower.)* 145

ALGERNON: Because you are like a pink rose, Cousin Cecily.

CECILY: I don't think it can be right for you to talk to me like that. Miss Prism never says such things to me.

ALGERNON: Then Miss Prism is a shortsighted old lady. (CECILY *puts the rose in his buttonhole.*) You are the prettiest girl I ever saw. 150

CECILY: Miss Prism says that all good looks are a snare.

ALGERNON: They are a snare that every sensible man would like to be caught in.

CECILY: Oh! I don't think I would care to catch a sensible man. I shouldn't know what to talk to him about.

(They pass into the house. MISS PRISM and DR. CHASUBLE return.)

MISS PRISM: You are too much alone, dear Dr. Chasuble. You should get married. A 155 misanthrope I can understand—a womanthrope, never!

CHASUBLE *(with a scholar's shudder)*: Believe me, I do not deserve so neologistic a phrase. The precept as well as the practice of the Primitive Church was distinctly against matrimony.

MISS PRISM *(sententiously)*: That is obviously the reason why the Primitive Church has 160 not lasted up to the present day. And you do not seem to realize, dear Doctor, that by persistently remaining single, a man converts himself into a permanent public temptation. Men should be more careful; this very celibacy leads weaker vessels astray.

CHASUBLE: But is a man not equally attractive when married?

MISS PRISM: No married man is ever attractive except to his wife. 165

CHASUBLE: And often, I've been told, not even to her.

MISS PRISM: That depends on the intellectual sympathies of the woman. Maturity can always be depended on. Ripeness can be trusted. Young women are green. (DR. CHASUBLE *starts.*) I spoke horticulturally. My metaphor was drawn from fruits. But where is Cecily? 170

CHASUBLE: Perhaps she followed us to the schools.

(Enter JACK slowly from the back of the garden. He is dressed in the deepest mourning, with crepe hatband and black gloves.)

MISS PRISM: Mr. Worthing!

CHASUBLE: Mr. Worthing?

MISS PRISM: This is indeed a surprise. We did not look for you till Monday afternoon.

JACK *(shakes MISS PRISM's hand in a tragic manner)*: I have returned sooner than I 175 expected. Dr. Chasuble, I hope you are well?

---

[6]Boutonniere.—EDS.

[7]A yellow rose.—EDS.

CHASUBLE: Dear Mr. Worthing, I trust this garb of woe does not betoken some terrible calamity?

JACK: My brother.

MISS PRISM: More shameful debts and extravagance?   180

CHASUBLE: Still leading his life of pleasure?

JACK (*shaking his head*): Dead!

CHASUBLE: Your brother Ernest dead?

JACK: Quite dead.

MISS PRISM: What a lesson for him! I trust he will profit by it.   185

CHASUBLE: Mr. Worthing, I offer you my sincere condolence. You have at least the consolation of knowing that you were always the most generous and forgiving of brothers.

JACK: Poor Ernest! He had many faults, but it is a sad, sad blow.

CHASUBLE: Very sad indeed. Were you with him at the end?   190

JACK: No. He died abroad; in Paris, in fact. I had a telegram last night from the manager of the Grand Hotel.

CHASUBLE: Was the cause of death mentioned?

JACK: A severe chill, it seems.

MISS PRISM: As a man sows, so shall he reap.   195

CHASUBLE (*raising his hand*): Charity, dear Miss Prism, charity! None of us are perfect. I myself am peculiarly susceptible to drafts. Will the interment take place here?

JACK: No. He seems to have expressed a desire to be buried in Paris.

CHASUBLE: In Paris! (*Shakes his head.*) I fear that hardly points to any very serious   200
state of mind at the last. You would no doubt wish me to make some slight allusion to this tragic domestic affliction next Sunday. (*Jack presses his hand convulsively.*) My sermon on the meaning of the manna in the wilderness can be adapted to almost any occasion, joyful, or, as in the present case, distressing. (*All sigh.*) I have preached it at harvest celebrations, christenings, confirmations,   205
on days of humiliation and festal days. The last time I delivered it was in the Cathedral, as a charity sermon on behalf of the Society for the Prevention of Discontent among the Upper Orders. The Bishop, who was present, was much struck by some of the analogies I drew.

JACK: Ah! that reminds me, you mentioned christenings I think, Dr. Chasuble? I   210
suppose you know how to christen all right? (DR. CHASUBLE *looks astounded.*) I mean, of course, you are continually christening, aren't you?

MISS PRISM: It is, I regret to say, one of the Rector's most constant duties in this parish. I have often spoken to the poorer classes on the subject. But they don't seem to know what thrift is.   215

CHASUBLE: But is there any particular infant in whom you are interested, Mr. Worthing? Your brother was, I believe, unmarried, was he not?

JACK: Oh yes.

MISS PRISM (*bitterly*): People who live entirely for pleasure usually are.

JACK: But it is not for any child, dear Doctor. I am very fond of children. No! the   220
fact is, I would like to be christened myself, this afternoon, if you have nothing
better to do.

CHASUBLE: But surely, Mr. Worthing, you have been christened already?

JACK: I don't remember anything about it.

CHASUBLE: But have you any grave doubts on the subject?   225

JACK: I certainly intend to have. Of course I don't know if the thing would bother you
in any way, or if you think I am a little too old now.

CHASUBLE: Not at all. The sprinkling, and, indeed, the immersion of adults is a perfectly canonical practice.

JACK: Immersion!   230

CHASUBLE: You need have no apprehensions. Sprinkling is all that is necessary, or
indeed I think advisable. Our weather is so changeable. At what hour would you
wish the ceremony performed?   `Baptism by weather`

JACK: Oh, I might trot round about five if that would suit you.

CHASUBLE: Perfectly, perfectly! In fact I have two similar ceremonies to perform at   235
that time. A case of twins that occurred recently in one of the outlying cottages
on your own estate. Poor Jenkins the carter, a most hardworking man.

JACK: Oh! I don't see much fun in being christened along with other babies. It would
be childish. Would half-past five do?

CHASUBLE: Admirably! Admirably! (*Takes out watch.*) And now, dear Mr. Worthing,   240
I will not intrude any longer into a house of sorrow. I would merely beg you
not to be too much bowed down by grief. What seem to us bitter trials are often
blessings in disguise.

MISS PRISM: This seems to me a blessing of an extremely obvious kind.

(*Enter* CECILY *from the house.*)

CECILY: Uncle Jack! Oh, I am pleased to see you back. But what horrid clothes you   245
have got on! Do go and change them.

MISS PRISM: Cecily!

CHASUBLE: My child! my child!

(CECILY *goes towards* JACK; *he kisses her brow in a melancholy manner.*)

CECILY: What is the matter, Uncle Jack? Do look happy! You look as if you had tooth-
ache, and I have got such a surprise for you. Who do you think is in the dining   250
room? Your brother!

JACK: Who?

CECILY: Your brother Ernest. He arrived about half an hour ago.

JACK: What nonsense! I haven't got a brother.

CECILY: Oh, don't say that. However badly he may have behaved to you in the past he   255
is still your brother. You couldn't be so heartless as to disown him. I'll tell him to
come out. And you will shake hands with him, won't you, Uncle Jack?

(*Runs back into the house.*)

CHASUBLE: These are very joyful tidings.

MISS PRISM: After we had all been resigned to his loss, his sudden return seems to
    me peculiarly distressing.   260

JACK: My brother is in the dining room? I don't know what it all means. I think it is
    perfectly absurd.

(Enter ALGERNON *and* CECILY *hand in hand.* They come slowly up to JACK.)

JACK: Good heavens!   *(Motions* ALGERNON *away.)*

ALGERNON: Brother John, I have come down from town to tell you that I am very
    sorry for all the trouble I have given you, and that I intend to lead a better life   265
    in the future.

(JACK *glares at him and does not take his hand.)*

CECILY: Uncle Jack, you are not going to refuse your own brother's hand?

JACK: Nothing will induce me to take his hand. I think his coming down here dis-
    graceful. He knows perfectly well why.

CECILY: Uncle Jack, do be nice. There is some good in everyone. Ernest has just been   270
    telling me about his poor invalid friend Mr. Bunbury whom he goes to visit so
    often. And surely there must be much good in one who is kind to an invalid, and
    leaves the pleasures of London to sit by a bed of pain.

JACK: Oh! he has been talking about Bunbury, has he?

CECILY: Yes, he has told me all about poor Mr. Bunbury, and his terrible state of   275
    health.

JACK: Bunbury! Well, I won't have him talk to you about Bunbury or about anything
    else. It is enough to drive one perfectly frantic.

ALGERNON: Of course I admit that the faults were all on my side. But I must say that
    I think that Brother John's coldness to me is peculiarly painful. I expected a more   280
    enthusiastic welcome, especially considering it is the first time I have come here.

CECILY: Uncle Jack, if you don't shake hands with Ernest I will never forgive you.

JACK: Never forgive me?

CECILY: Never, never, never!

JACK: Well, this is the last time I shall ever do it.   285

(Shakes with ALGERNON *and glares.)*

CHASUBLE: It's pleasant, is it not, to see so perfect a reconciliation? I think we might
    leave the two brothers together.

MISS PRISM: Cecily, you will come with us.

CECILY: Certainly, Miss Prism. My little task of reconciliation is over.

CHASUBLE: You have done a beautiful action today, dear child.   290

MISS PRISM: We must not be premature in our judgments.

CECILY: I feel very happy.   *(They all go off.)*

JACK: You young scoundrel, Algy, you must get out of this place as soon as possible. I
    don't allow any Bunburying here.

(Enter MERRIMAN.*)*

MERRIMAN: I have put Mr. Ernest's things in the room next to yours, sir. I suppose   295
  that is all right?

JACK: What?

MERRIMAN: Mr. Ernest's luggage, sir. I have unpacked it and put it in the room next
  to your own.

JACK: His luggage?   300

MERRIMAN: Yes, sir. Three portmanteaus, a dressing case, two hatboxes, and a large
  luncheon basket.

ALGERNON: I am afraid I can't stay more than a week this time.

JACK: Merriman, order the dog cart at once. Mr. Ernest has been suddenly called
  back to town.   305

MERRIMAN: Yes, sir.   *(Goes back into the house.)*

ALGERNON: What a fearful liar you are, Jack. I have not been called back to
  town at all.

JACK: Yes, you have.

ALGERNON: I haven't heard anyone call me.   310

JACK: Your duty as a gentleman calls you back.

ALGERNON: My duty as a gentleman has never interfered with my pleasures in the
  smallest degree.

JACK: I can quite understand that.

ALGERNON: Well, Cecily is a darling.   315

JACK: You are not to talk of Miss Cardew like that. I don't like it.

ALGERNON: Well, I don't like your clothes. You look perfectly ridiculous in them.
  Why on earth don't you go up and change? It is perfectly childish to be in deep
  mourning for a man who is actually staying for a whole week in your house as
  a guest. I call it grotesque.   320

JACK: You are certainly not staying with me for a whole week as a guest or anything
  else. You have got to leave—by the four-five train.

ALGERNON: I certainly won't leave you so long as you are in mourning. It would be
  most unfriendly. If I were in mourning you would stay with me, I suppose. I
  should think it very unkind if you didn't.   325

JACK: Well, will you go if I change my clothes?

ALGERNON: Yes, if you are not too long. I never saw anybody take so long to dress,
  and with such little result.

JACK: Well, at any rate, that is better than being always overdressed as you are.

ALGERNON: If I am occasionally a little overdressed, I make up for it by being always   330
  immensely overeducated.

JACK: Your vanity is ridiculous, your conduct an outrage, and your presence in my
  garden utterly absurd. However, you have got to catch the four-five, and I hope
  you will have a pleasant journey back to town. This Bunburying, as you call it,
  has not been a great success for you.   *(Goes into the house.)*   335

ALGERNON: I think it has been a great success. I'm in love with Cecily, and that is
  everything.

✳ Stop

(Enter CECILY *at the back of the garden. She picks up the can and begins to water the flowers.)*

But I must see her before I go, and make arrangements for another Bunbury. Ah, there she is.

CECILY: Oh, I merely came back to water the roses. I thought you were with Uncle   340
 Jack.

ALGERNON: He's gone to order the dog cart for me.

CECILY: Oh, is he going to take you for a nice drive?

ALGERNON: He's going to send me away.

CECILY: Then have we got to part?   345

ALGERNON: I am afraid so. It's a very painful parting.

CECILY: It is always painful to part from people whom one has known for a very brief
 space of time. The absence of old friends one can endure with equanimity. But
 even a momentary separation from anyone to whom one has just been introduced is almost unbearable.   350

ALGERNON: Thank you.

(Enter MERRIMAN.*)*

MERRIMAN: The dog cart is at the door, sir.

*(*ALGERNON *looks appealingly at* CECILY.*)*

CECILY: It can wait, Merriman — for — five minutes.

MERRIMAN: Yes, Miss.   *(Exit* MERRIMAN.*)*

ALGERNON: I hope, Cecily, I shall not offend you if I state quite frankly and openly   355
 that you seem to me to be in every way the visible personification of absolute
 perfection.

CECILY: I think your frankness does you great credit, Ernest. If you will allow me, I
 will copy your remarks into my diary.

     (Goes over to table and begins writing in diary.)

ALGERNON: Do you really keep a diary? I'd give anything to look at it. May I?   360

CECILY: Oh no. *(Puts her hand over it.)* You see, it is simply a very young girl's record
 of her own thoughts and impressions, and consequently meant for publication.
 When it appears in volume form I hope you will order a copy. But pray, Ernest,
 don't stop. I delight in taking down from dictation. I have reached "absolute
 perfection." You can go on. I am quite ready for more.   365

ALGERNON *(somewhat taken aback)*: Ahem! Ahem!

CECILY: Oh, don't cough, Ernest. When one is dictating one should speak fluently
 and not cough. Besides, I don't know how to spell a cough.

(Writes as ALGERNON *speaks.)*

ALGERNON *(speaking very rapidly)*: Cecily, ever since I first looked upon your wonderful and incomparable beauty, I have dared to love you wildly, passionately,   370
 devotedly, hopelessly.

CECILY: I don't think that you should tell me that you love me wildly, passionately, devotedly, hopelessly. Hopelessly doesn't seem to make much sense, does it?

ALGERNON: Cecily!

(Enter MERRIMAN.*)*

MERRIMAN: The dog cart is waiting, sir. 375

ALGERNON: Tell it to come round next week, at the same hour.

MERRIMAN *(looks at* CECILY, *who makes no sign)*: Yes, sir. *(*MERRIMAN *retires.)*

CECILY: Uncle Jack would be very much annoyed if he knew you were staying on till next week, at the same hour.

ALGERNON: Oh, I don't care about Jack. I don't care for anybody in the whole world 380 but you. I love you, Cecily. You will marry me, won't you?

CECILY: You silly boy! Of course. Why, we have been engaged for the last three months.

ALGERNON: For the last three months?

CECILY: Yes, it will be exactly three months on Thursday.

ALGERNON: But how did we become engaged? 385

CECILY: Well, ever since dear Uncle Jack first confessed to us that he had a younger brother who was very wicked and bad, you of course have formed the chief topic of conversation between myself and Miss Prism. And of course a man who is much talked about is always very attractive. One feels there must be something in him after all. I daresay it was foolish of me, but I fell in love with you, Ernest. 390

ALGERNON: Darling! And when was the engagement actually settled?

CECILY: On the 14th of February last. Worn out by your entire ignorance of my existence, I determined to end the matter one way or the other, and after a long struggle with myself I accepted you under this dear old tree here. The next day I bought this little ring in your name, and this is the little bangle with the true 395 lovers' knot I promised you always to wear.

ALGERNON: Did I give you this? It's very pretty, isn't it?

CECILY: Yes, you've wonderfully good taste, Ernest. It's the excuse I've always given for your leading such a bad life. And this is the box in which I keep all your dear letters.

(Kneels at table, opens box, and produces letters tied up with blue ribbon.)

ALGERNON: My letters! But, my own sweet Cecily, I have never written you any letters. 400

CECILY: You need hardly remind me of that, Ernest. I remember only too well that I was forced to write your letters for you. I wrote always three times a week, and sometimes oftener.

ALGERNON: Oh, do let me read them, Cecily!

CECILY: Oh, I couldn't possibly. They would make you far too conceited. *(Replaces box.)* 405 The three you wrote me after I had broken off the engagement are so beautiful, and so badly spelled, that even now I can hardly read them without crying a little.

ALGERNON: But was our engagement ever broken off?

CECILY: Of course it was. On the 22nd of last March. You can see the entry if you like. *(Shows diary.)* "Today I broke off my engagement with Ernest. I feel it is better 410 to do so. The weather still continues charming."

ALGERNON: But why on earth did you break it off? What had I done? I had done nothing at all. Cecily, I am very much hurt indeed to hear you broke it off. Particularly when the weather was so charming.

CECILY: It would hardly have been a really serious engagement if it hadn't been bro- 415
ken off at least once. But I forgave you before the week was out.

ALGERNON (*crossing to her, and kneeling*): What a perfect angel you are, Cecily.

CECILY: You dear romantic boy. (*He kisses her; she puts her fingers through his hair.*) I hope your hair curls naturally, does it?

ALGERNON: Yes, darling, with a little help from others. 420

CECILY: I am so glad.

ALGERNON: You'll never break off our engagement again, Cecily?

CECILY: I don't think I could break it off now that I have actually met you. Besides, of course, there is the question of your name.

ALGERNON (*nervously*): Yes, of course. 425

CECILY: You must not laugh at me, darling, but it had always been a girlish dream of mine to love someone whose name was Ernest. (ALGERNON *rises*, CECILY *also.*) There is something in that name that seems to inspire absolute confidence. I pity any poor married woman whose husband is not called Ernest.

ALGERNON: But, my dear child, do you mean to say you could not love me if I had 430
some other name?

CECILY: But what name?

ALGERNON: Oh, any name you like—Algernon—for instance—

CECILY: But I don't like the name of Algernon.

ALGERNON: Well, my own dear, sweet, loving little darling, I really can't see why you 435
should object to the name of Algernon. It is not at all a bad name. In fact, it is rather an aristocratic name. Half of the chaps who get into the Bankruptcy Court are called Algernon. But seriously, Cecily—(*moving to her*)—if my name was Algy, couldn't you love me?

CECILY (*rising*): I might respect you, Ernest, I might admire your character, but I fear 440
that I should not be able to give you my undivided attention.

ALGERNON: Ahem! Cecily! (*Picking up hat.*) Your Rector here is, I suppose, thoroughly experienced in the practice of all the rites and ceremonials of the Church?

CECILY: Oh yes. Dr. Chasuble is a most learned man. He has never written a single book, so you can imagine how much he knows. 445

ALGERNON: I must see him at once on a most important christening—I mean on most important business.

CECILY: Oh!

ALGERNON: I shan't be away more than half an hour.

CECILY: Considering that we have been engaged since February the 14th, and that I 450
only met you today for the first time, I think it is rather hard that you should leave me for so long a period as half an hour. Couldn't you make it twenty minutes?

ALGERNON: I'll be back in no time.

(*Kisses her and rushes down the garden.*)

CECILY: What an impetuous boy he is! I like his hair so much. I must enter his proposal in my diary. 455

(Enter MERRIMAN.)

MERRIMAN: A Miss Fairfax has just called to see Mr. Worthing. On very important business, Miss Fairfax states.

CECILY: Isn't Mr. Worthing in his library?

MERRIMAN: Mr. Worthing went over in the direction of the Rectory some time ago.

CECILY: Pray ask the lady to come out here; Mr. Worthing is sure to be back soon. 460
And you can bring tea.

MERRIMAN: Yes, miss. *(Goes out.)*

CECILY: Miss Fairfax! I suppose one of the many good elderly women who are associated with Uncle Jack in some of his philanthropic work in London. I don't quite like women who are interested in philanthropic work. I think it is so forward of them. 465

(Enter MERRIMAN.)

MERRIMAN: Miss Fairfax.

(Enter GWENDOLEN. Exit MERRIMAN.)

CECILY *(advancing to meet her)*: Pray let me introduce myself to you. My name is Cecily Cardew.

GWENDOLEN: Cecily Cardew? *(Moving to her and shaking hands.)* What a very sweet name! Something tells me that we are going to be great friends. I like you already 470
more than I can say. My first impressions of people are never wrong.

CECILY: How nice of you to like me so much after we have known each other such a comparatively short time. Pray sit down.

GWENDOLEN *(still standing up)*: I may call you Cecily, may I not?

CECILY: With pleasure! 475

GWENDOLEN: And you will always call me Gwendolen, won't you?

CECILY: If you wish.

GWENDOLEN: Then that is all quite settled, is it not?

CECILY: I hope so.

(A pause. They both sit down together.)

GWENDOLEN: Perhaps this might be a favorable opportunity for my mentioning who I 480
am. My father is Lord Bracknell. You have never heard of Papa, I suppose?

CECILY: I don't think so.

GWENDOLEN: Outside the family circle, Papa, I am glad to say, is entirely unknown. I think that is quite as it should be. The home seems to me to be the proper sphere for the man. And certainly once a man begins to neglect his domestic duties he 485
becomes painfully effeminate, does he not? And I don't like that. It makes men so very attractive. Cecily, Mama, whose views on education are remarkably strict, has brought me up to be extremely shortsighted; it is part of her system, so do you mind my looking at you through my glasses?

CECILY: Oh! not at all, Gwendolen. I am very fond of being looked at. 490

GWENDOLEN (*after examining* CECILY *carefully through a lorgnette*): You are here on a short visit I suppose?

CECILY: Oh no! I live here.

GWENDOLEN (*severely*): Really? Your mother, no doubt, or some female relative of advanced years, resides here also? 495

CECILY: Oh no! I have no mother, nor, in fact, any relations.

GWENDOLEN: Indeed?

CECILY: My dear guardian, with the assistance of Miss Prism, has the arduous task of looking after me.

GWENDOLEN: Your guardian? 500

CECILY: Yes, I am Mr. Worthing's ward.

GWENDOLEN: Oh! It is strange he never mentioned to me that he had a ward. How secretive of him! He grows more interesting hourly. I am not sure, however, that the news inspires me with feelings of unmixed delight. (*Rising and going to her.*) I am very fond of you, Cecily; I have liked you ever since I met you! But 505 I am bound to state that now that I know that you are Mr. Worthing's ward, I cannot help expressing a wish you were — well, just a little older than you seem to be — and not quite so very alluring in appearance. In fact, if I may speak candidly —

CECILY: Pray do! I think that whenever one has anything unpleasant to say, one 510 should always be quite candid.

GWENDOLEN: Well, to speak with perfect candor, Cecily, I wish that you were fully forty-two, and more than usually plain for your age. Ernest has a strong upright nature. He is the very soul of truth and honor. Disloyalty would be as impossible to him as deception. But even men of the noblest possible moral character 515 are extremely susceptible to the influence of the physical charms of others. Modern, no less than Ancient History, supplies us with many most painful examples of what I refer to. If it were not so, indeed, History would be quite unreadable.

CECILY: I beg your pardon, Gwendolen, did you say Ernest? 520

GWENDOLEN: Yes.

CECILY: Oh, but it is not Mr. Ernest Worthing who is my guardian. It is his brother — his elder brother.

GWENDOLEN (*sitting down again*): Ernest never mentioned to me that he had a brother. 525

CECILY: I am sorry to say they have not been on good terms for a long time.

GWENDOLEN: Ah! that accounts for it. And now that I think of it I have never heard any man mention his brother. The subject seems distasteful to most men. Cecily, you have lifted a load from my mind. I was growing almost anxious. It would have been terrible if any cloud had come across a friendship like ours, would it not? Of course 530 you are quite, quite sure that it is not Mr. Ernest Worthing who is your guardian?

CECILY: Quite sure. (*A pause.*) In fact, I am going to be his.

GWENDOLEN (*inquiringly*): I beg your pardon?

CECILY (*rather shy and confidingly*): Dearest Gwendolen, there is no reason why I should make a secret of it to you. Our little county newspaper is sure to chronicle   535
the fact next week. Mr. Ernest Worthing and I are engaged to be married.

GWENDOLEN (*quite politely, rising*): My darling Cecily, I think there must be some slight error. Mr. Ernest Worthing is engaged to me. The announcement will appear in the *Morning Post* on Saturday at the latest.

CECILY (*very politely, rising*): I am afraid you must be under some misconception.   540
Ernest proposed to me exactly ten minutes ago.   (*Shows diary.*)

GWENDOLEN (*examines diary through her lorgnette carefully*): It is certainly very curious, for he asked me to be his wife yesterday afternoon at 5:30. If you would care to verify the incident, pray do so. (*Produces diary of her own.*) I never travel without my diary. One should always have something sensational to read in the   545
train. I am so sorry, dear Cecily, if it is any disappointment to you, but I am afraid *I* have the prior claim.

CECILY: It would distress me more than I can tell you, dear Gwendolen, if it caused you any mental or physical anguish, but I feel bound to point out that since Ernest proposed to you he clearly has changed his mind.   550

GWENDOLEN (*meditatively*): If the poor fellow has been entrapped into any foolish promise I shall consider it my duty to rescue him at once, and with a firm hand.

CECILY (*thoughtfully and sadly*): Whatever unfortunate entanglement my dear boy may have got into, I will never reproach him with it after we are married.   555

GWENDOLEN: Do you allude to me, Miss Cardew, as an entanglement? You are presumptuous. On an occasion of this kind it becomes more than a moral duty to speak one's mind. It becomes a pleasure.

CECILY: Do you suggest, Miss Fairfax, that I entrapped Ernest into an engagement? How dare you? This is no time for wearing the shallow mask of manners. When   560
I see a spade I call it a spade.

GWENDOLEN (*satirically*): I am glad to say that I have never seen a spade. It is obvious that our social spheres have been widely different.

(*Enter* MERRIMAN, *followed by the Footman. He carries a salver, tablecloth, and plate stand.* CECILY *is about to retort. The presence of the servants exercises a restraining influence, under which both girls chafe.*)

MERRIMAN: Shall I lay tea here as usual, miss?

CECILY (*sternly, in a calm voice*): Yes, as usual.   565

(MERRIMAN *begins to clear table and lay cloth. A long pause.* CECILY *and* GWENDOLEN *glare at each other.*)

GWENDOLEN: Are there many interesting walks in the vicinity, Miss Cardew?

CECILY: Oh! Yes! a great many. From the top of one of the hills quite close one can see five counties.

GWENDOLEN: Five counties! I don't think I should like that. I hate crowds.

CECILY (*sweetly*): I suppose that is why you live in town?   570

(GWENDOLEN *bites her lip, and beats her foot nervously with her parasol.*)

GWENDOLEN *(looking round)*: Quite a well-kept garden this is, Miss Cardew.

CECILY: So glad you like it, Miss Fairfax.

GWENDOLEN: I had no idea there were any flowers in the country.

CECILY: Oh, flowers are as common here, Miss Fairfax, as people are in London.

GWENDOLEN: Personally I cannot understand how anybody manages to exist in the 575 country, if anybody who is anybody does. The country always bores me to death.

CECILY: Ah! This is what the newspapers call agricultural depression, is it not? I believe the aristocracy are suffering very much from it just at present. It is almost an epidemic amongst them, I have been told. May I offer you some tea, Miss Fairfax?

GWENDOLEN *(with elaborate politeness)*: Thank you. *(Aside.)* Detestable girl! But I 580 require tea!

CECILY *(sweetly)*: Sugar?

GWENDOLEN *(superciliously)*: No, thank you. Sugar is not fashionable anymore.

(CECILY *looks angrily at her, takes up the tongs, and puts four lumps of sugar into the cup.*)

CECILY *(severely)*: Cake or bread and butter?

GWENDOLEN *(in a bored manner)*: Bread and butter, please. Cake is rarely seen at the 585 best houses nowadays.

CECILY *(cuts a very large slice of cake, and puts it on the tray)*: Hand that to Miss Fairfax.

(MERRIMAN *does so, and goes out with Footman.* GWENDOLEN *drinks the tea and makes a grimace. Puts down cup at once, reaches out her hand to the bread and butter, looks at it, and finds it is cake. Rises in indignation.*)

GWENDOLEN: You have filled my tea with lumps of sugar, and though I asked most distinctly for bread and butter, you have given me cake. I am known for the gentleness of my disposition, and the extraordinary sweetness of my nature, but 590 I warn you, Miss Cardew, you may go too far.

CECILY *(rising)*: To save my poor, innocent, trusting boy from the machinations of any other girl there are no lengths to which I would not go.

GWENDOLEN: From the moment I saw you I distrusted you. I felt that you were false and deceitful. I am never deceived in such matters. My first impressions of 595 people are invariably right.

CECILY: It seems to me, Miss Fairfax, that I am trespassing on your valuable time. No doubt you have many other calls of a similar character to make in the neighborhood.

(*Enter* JACK.)

GWENDOLEN *(catching sight of him)*: Ernest! My own Ernest!

JACK: Gwendolen! Darling! *(Offers to kiss her.)* 600

GWENDOLEN *(draws back)*: A moment! May I ask if you are engaged to be married to this young lady? *(Points to* CECILY.*)*

JACK *(laughing)*: To dear little Cecily! Of course not! What could have put such an idea into your pretty little head?

GWENDOLEN: Thank you. You may! *(Offers her cheek.)* 605

CECILY *(very sweetly)*: I knew there must be some misunderstanding, Miss Fairfax. The gentleman whose arm is at present round your waist is my dear guardian, Mr. John Worthing.

GWENDOLEN: I beg your pardon?

CECILY: This is Uncle Jack. 610

GWENDOLEN *(receding)*: Jack! Oh!

(Enter ALGERNON.)

CECILY: Here is Ernest.

ALGERNON *(goes straight over to CECILY without noticing anyone else)*: My own love!
(Offers to kiss her.)

CECILY *(drawing back)*: A moment, Ernest! May I ask you—are you engaged to be married to this young lady? 615

ALGERNON *(looking round)*: To what young lady? Good heavens! Gwendolen!

CECILY: Yes! to good heavens, Gwendolen, I mean to Gwendolen.

ALGERNON *(laughing)*: Of course not! What could have put such an idea into your pretty little head?

CECILY: Thank you. *(Presenting her cheek to be kissed.)* You may. 620
(ALGERNON kisses her.)

GWENDOLEN: I felt there was some slight error, Miss Cardew. The gentleman who is now embracing you is my cousin, Mr. Algernon Moncrieff.

CECILY *(breaking away from ALGERNON)*: Algernon Moncrieff! Oh!

(The two girls move towards each other and put their arms round each other's waists as if for protection.)

CECILY: Are you called Algernon?

ALGERNON: I cannot deny it. 625

CECILY: Oh!

GWENDOLEN: Is your name really John?

JACK *(standing rather proudly)*: I could deny it if I liked. I could deny anything if I liked. But my name certainly is John. It has been John for years.

CECILY *(to GWENDOLEN)*: A gross deception has been practiced on both of us. 630

GWENDOLEN: My poor wounded Cecily!

CECILY: My sweet wronged Gwendolen!

GWENDOLEN *(slowly and seriously)*: You will call me sister, will you not?

(They embrace. JACK and ALGERNON groan and walk up and down.)

CECILY *(rather brightly)*: There is just one question I would like to be allowed to ask my guardian. 635

GWENDOLEN: An admirable idea! Mr. Worthing, there is just one question I would like to be permitted to put to you. Where is your brother Ernest? We are both engaged to be married to your brother Ernest, so it is a matter of some importance to us to know where your brother Ernest is at present.

JACK (*slowly and hesitatingly*): Gwendolen—Cecily—it is very painful for me to 640
be forced to speak the truth. It is the first time in my life that I have ever been
reduced to such a painful position, and I am really quite inexperienced in doing
anything of the kind. However, I will tell you quite frankly that I have no brother
Ernest. I have no brother at all. I never had a brother in my life, and I certainly
have not the smallest intention of ever having one in the future. 645
CECILY (*surprised*): No brother at all?
JACK (*cheerily*): None!
GWENDOLEN (*severely*): Had you never a brother of any kind?
JACK (*pleasantly*): Never. Not even of any kind.
GWENDOLEN: I am afraid it is quite clear, Cecily, that neither of us is engaged to be 650
married to anyone. ouch!
CECILY: It is not a very pleasant position for a young girl suddenly to find herself in.
Is it?
GWENDOLEN: Let us go into the house. They will hardly venture to come after us
there. 655
CECILY: No, men are so cowardly, aren't they?

(*They retire into the house with scornful looks.*)

JACK: This ghastly state of things is what you call Bunburying, I suppose?
ALGERNON: Yes, and a perfectly wonderful Bunbury it is. The most wonderful
Bunbury I have ever had in my life.
JACK: Well, you've no right whatsoever to Bunbury here. 660
ALGERNON: That is absurd. One has a right to Bunbury anywhere one chooses. Every
serious Bunburyist knows that.
JACK: Serious Bunburyist! Good heavens!
ALGERNON: Well, one must be serious about something, if one wants to have any
amusement in life. I happen to be serious about Bunburying. What on earth 665
you are serious about I haven't got the remotest idea. About everything, I should
fancy. You have such an absolutely trivial nature.
JACK: Well, the only small satisfaction I have in the whole of this wretched business
is that your friend Bunbury is quite exploded. You won't be able to run down
to the country quite so often as you used to do, dear Algy. And a very good 670
thing too.
ALGERNON: Your brother is a little off color, isn't he, dear Jack? You won't be able to
disappear to London quite so frequently as your wicked custom was. And not a
bad thing either.
JACK: As for your conduct towards Miss Cardew, I must say that your taking in a 675
sweet, simple, innocent girl like that is quite inexcusable. To say nothing of the
fact that she is my ward.
ALGERNON: I can see no possible defense at all for your deceiving a brilliant, clever,
thoroughly experienced young lady like Miss Fairfax. To say nothing of the fact
that she is my cousin. 680
JACK: I wanted to be engaged to Gwendolen, that is all. I love her.

ALGERNON: Well, I simply wanted to be engaged to Cecily. I adore her.

JACK: There is certainly no chance of your marrying Miss Cardew.

ALGERNON: I don't think there is much likelihood, Jack, of you and Miss Fairfax being united. 685

JACK: Well, that is no business of yours.

ALGERNON: If it was my business, I wouldn't talk about it. *(Begins to eat muffins.)* It is very vulgar to talk about one's business. Only people like stockbrokers do that, and then merely at dinner parties.

JACK: How you can sit there, calmly eating muffins when we are in this horrible 690 trouble, I can't make out. You seem to me to be perfectly heartless.

ALGERNON: Well, I can't eat muffins in an agitated manner. The butter would probably get on my cuffs. One should always eat muffins quite calmly. It is the only way to eat them.

JACK: I say it's perfectly heartless your eating muffins at all, under the circumstances. 695

ALGERNON: When I am in trouble, eating is the only thing that consoles me. Indeed, when I am in really great trouble, as anyone who knows me intimately will tell you, I refuse everything except food and drink. At the present moment I am eating muffins because I am unhappy. Besides, I am particularly fond of muffins.

(Rising.)

JACK *(rising)*: Well, that is no reason why you should eat them all in that greedy way. 700

(Takes muffins from ALGERNON.*)*

ALGERNON *(offering tea cake)*: I wish you would have tea cake instead. I don't like tea cake.

JACK: Good heavens! I suppose a man may eat his own muffins in his own garden.

ALGERNON: But you have just said it was perfectly heartless to eat muffins.

JACK: I said it was perfectly heartless of you, under the circumstances. That is a very 705 different thing.

ALGERNON: That may be, but the muffins are the same. *(He seizes the muffin dish from* JACK.*)*

JACK: Algy, I wish to goodness you would go.

ALGERNON: You can't possibly ask me to go without having some dinner. It's absurd. 710 I never go without my dinner. No one ever does, except vegetarians and people like that. Besides I have just made arrangements with Dr. Chasuble to be christened at a quarter to six under the name of Ernest.

JACK: My dear fellow, the sooner you give up that nonsense the better. I made arrangements this morning with Dr. Chasuble to be christened myself at 5.30, and I 715 naturally will take the name of Ernest. Gwendolen would wish it. We can't both be christened Ernest. It's absurd. Besides, I have a perfect right to be christened if I like. There is no evidence at all that I have ever been christened by anybody. I should think it extremely probable I never was, and so does Dr. Chasuble. It is entirely different in your case. You have been christened already. 720

ALGERNON: Yes, but I have not been christened for years.

JACK: Yes, but you have been christened. That is the important thing.

ALGERNON: Quite so. So I know my constitution can stand it. If you are not quite sure about your ever having been christened, I must say I think it rather dangerous your venturing on it now. It might make you very unwell. You can hardly have   725
forgotten that someone very closely connected with you was very nearly carried off this week in Paris by a severe chill.

JACK: Yes, but you said yourself that a severe chill was not hereditary.

ALGERNON: It usen't to be, I know — but I daresay it is now. Science is always making wonderful improvements in things.   730

JACK (*picking up the muffin dish*): Oh, that is nonsense; you are always talking nonsense.

ALGERNON: Jack, you are at the muffins again! I wish you wouldn't. There are only two left. (*Takes them.*) I told you I was particularly fond of muffins.

JACK: But I hate tea cake.   735

ALGERNON: Why on earth then do you allow tea cake to be served up for your guests? What ideas you have of hospitality!

JACK: Algernon! I have already told you to go. I don't want you here. Why don't you go!

ALGERNON: I haven't quite finished my tea yet! and there is still one muffin left.

(*JACK groans, and sinks into a chair. ALGERNON still continues eating.*)

ACT III   609-619

(*Scene: Morning room at the Manor House. GWENDOLEN and CECILY are at the window, looking out into the garden.*)

GWENDOLEN: The fact that they did not follow us at once into the house, as anyone else would have done, seems to me to show that they have some sense of shame left.

CECILY: They have been eating muffins. That looks like repentance.

GWENDOLEN (*after a pause*): They don't seem to notice us at all. Couldn't you cough?   5

CECILY: But I haven't got a cough.

GWENDOLEN: They're looking at us. What effrontery!

CECILY: They're approaching. That's very forward of them.

GWENDOLEN: Let us preserve a dignified silence.

CECILY: Certainly. It's the only thing to do now.   10

(*Enter JACK followed by ALGERNON. They whistle some dreadful popular air from a British opera.*)

GWENDOLEN: This dignified silence seems to produce an unpleasant effect.

CECILY: A most distasteful one.

GWENDOLEN: But we will not be the first to speak.

CECILY: Certainly not.

GWENDOLEN: Mr. Worthing, I have something very particular to ask you. Much   15
depends on your reply.

CECILY: Gwendolen, your common sense is invaluable. Mr. Moncrieff, kindly answer me the following question. Why did you pretend to be my guardian's brother?

ALGERNON: In order that I might have an opportunity of meeting you.

CECILY (*to* GWENDOLEN): That certainly seems a satisfactory explanation, does it not? 20

GWENDOLEN: Yes, dear, if you can believe him.

CECILY: I don't. But that does not affect the wonderful beauty of his answer.

GWENDOLEN: True. In matters of grave importance, style, not sincerity, is the vital thing. Mr. Worthing, what explanation can you offer to me for pretending to have a brother? Was it in order that you might have an opportunity of coming 25
up to town to see me as often as possible?

JACK: Can you doubt it, Miss Fairfax?

GWENDOLEN: I have the gravest doubts upon the subject. But I intend to crush them. This is not the moment for German skepticism. (*Moving to* CECILY.) Their explanations appear to be quite satisfactory, especially Mr. Worthing's. That 30
seems to me to have the stamp of truth upon it.

CECILY: I am more than content with what Mr. Moncrieff said. His voice alone inspires one with absolute credulity.

GWENDOLEN: Then you think we should forgive them?

CECILY: Yes. I mean no. How fickle women are 35

GWENDOLEN: True! I had forgotten. There are principles at stake that one cannot surrender. Which of us should tell them? The task is not a pleasant one.

CECILY: Could we not both speak at the same time?

GWENDOLEN: An excellent idea! I nearly always speak at the same time as other people. Will you take the time from me? 40

CECILY: Certainly.

(GWENDOLEN *beats time with uplifted finger.*)

GWENDOLEN and CECILY (*speaking together*): Your Christian names are still an insuperable barrier. That is all!

JACK and ALGERNON (*speaking together*): Our Christian names! Is that all? But we are going to be christened this afternoon. 45

GWENDOLEN (*to* JACK): For my sake you are prepared to do this terrible thing?

JACK: I am!

CECILY (*to* ALGERNON): To please me you are ready to face this fearful ordeal?

ALGERNON: I am!

GWENDOLEN: How absurd to talk of the equality of the sexes! Where questions of 50
self-sacrifice are concerned, men are infinitely beyond us. *gender*

JACK: We are! (*Clasps hands with* ALGERNON.)

CECILY: They have moments of physical courage of which we women know absolutely nothing.

GWENDOLEN (*to* JACK): Darling! 55

ALGERNON (*to* CECILY): Darling!

(*They fall into each other's arms.*)

(Enter MERRIMAN. *When he enters he coughs loudly, seeing the situation.)*

MERRIMAN: Ahem! Ahem! Lady Bracknell!
JACK: Good heavens!

(Enter LADY BRACKNELL. *The couples separate in alarm. Exit* MERRIMAN.*)*

LADY BRACKNELL: Gwendolen! What does this mean?
GWENDOLEN: Merely that I am engaged to be married to Mr. Worthing, Mama.   60
LADY BRACKNELL: Come here. Sit down. Sit down immediately. Hesitation of any
    kind is a sign of mental decay in the young, of physical weakness in the old.
    (Turns to JACK.*)* Apprised, sir, of my daughter's sudden flight by her trusty maid,
    whose confidence I purchased by means of a small coin, I followed her at once
    by a luggage train. Her unhappy father is, I am glad to say, under the impres-   65
    sion that she is attending a more than usually lengthy lecture by the University
    Extension Scheme on the influence of a permanent income on thought. I do not
    propose to undeceive him. Indeed I have never undeceived him on any ques-
    tion. I would consider it wrong. But of course, you will clearly understand that
    all communication between yourself and my daughter must cease immediately   70
    from this moment. On this point, as indeed on all points, I am firm.
JACK: I am engaged to be married to Gwendolen, Lady Bracknell!
LADY BRACKNELL: You are nothing of the kind, sir. And now, as regards Algernon! —
    Algernon!
ALGERNON: Yes, Aunt Augusta.   75
LADY BRACKNELL: May I ask if it is in this house that your invalid friend Mr. Bunbury
    resides?
ALGERNON *(stammering)*: Oh! No! Bunbury doesn't live here. Bunbury is somewhere
    else at present. In fact, Bunbury is dead.
LADY BRACKNELL: Dead! When did Mr. Bunbury die? His death must have been   80
    extremely sudden.
ALGERNON *(airily)*: Oh! I killed Bunbury this afternoon. I mean poor Bunbury died
    this afternoon.
LADY BRACKNELL: What did he die of?
ALGERNON: Bunbury? Oh, he was quite exploded.   85
LADY BRACKNELL: Exploded! Was he the victim of a revolutionary outrage? I was
    not aware that Mr. Bunbury was interested in social legislation. If so, he is well
    punished for his morbidity.
ALGERNON: My dear Aunt Augusta, I mean he was found out! The doctors found out
    that Bunbury could not live, that is what I mean — so Bunbury died.   90
LADY BRACKNELL: He seems to have had great confidence in the opinion of his physi-
    cians. I am glad, however, that he made up his mind at the last to some definite
    course of action, and acted under proper medical advice. And now that we have
    finally got rid of this Mr. Bunbury, may I ask, Mr. Worthing, who is that young
    person whose hand my nephew Algernon is now holding in what seems to me a   95
    peculiarly unnecessary manner?

Bunbury

JACK: That lady is Miss Cecily Cardew, my ward.

(LADY BRACKNELL *bows coldly to* CECILY.)

ALGERNON: I am engaged to be married to Cecily, Aunt Augusta.

LADY BRACKNELL: I beg your pardon?

CECILY: Mr. Moncrieff and I are engaged to be married, Lady Bracknell.   100

LADY BRACKNELL (*with a shiver, crossing to the sofa and sitting down*): I do not know whether there is anything peculiarly exciting in the air of this particular part of Hertfordshire, but the number of engagements that go on seems to me considerably above the proper average that statistics have laid down for our guidance. I think some preliminary inquiry on my part would not be out of place. Mr.   105 Worthing, is Miss Cardew at all connected with any of the larger railway stations in London? I merely desire information. Until yesterday I had no idea that there were any families or persons whose origin was a Terminus.

    (JACK *looks perfectly furious, but restrains himself.*)

JACK (*in a clear, cold voice*): Miss Cardew is the grand-daughter of the late Mr. Thomas Cardew of 149, Belgrave Square, S.W.; Gervase Park, Dorking, Surrey;   110 and the Sporran, Fifeshire, N.B.

LADY BRACKNELL: That sounds not unsatisfactory. Three addresses always inspire confidence, even in tradesmen. But what proof have I of their authenticity?

JACK: I have carefully preserved the Court Guides of the period. They are open to your inspection, Lady Bracknell.   115

LADY BRACKNELL (*grimly*): I have known strange errors in that publication.

JACK: Miss Cardew's family solicitors are Messrs. Markby, Markby, and Markby.

LADY BRACKNELL: Markby, Markby, and Markby? A firm of the very highest position in their profession. Indeed I am told that one of the Mr. Markbys is occasionally to be seen at dinner parties. So far I am satisfied.   120

JACK (*very irritably*): How extremely kind of you, Lady Bracknell! I have also in my possession, you will be pleased to hear, certificates of Miss Cardew's birth, baptism, whooping cough, registration, vaccination, confirmation, and the measles; both the German and the English variety.

LADY BRACKNELL: Ah! A life crowded with incident I see; though perhaps somewhat   125 too exciting for a young girl. I am not myself in favor of premature experiences. (*Rises, looks at her watch.*) Gwendolen! the time approaches for our departure. We have not a moment to lose. As a matter of form, Mr. Worthing, I had better ask you if Miss Cardew has any little fortune?

JACK: Oh! about a hundred and thirty thousand pounds in the Funds. That is all.   130 Good-bye, Lady Bracknell. So pleased to have seen you.

LADY BRACKNELL (*sitting down again*): A moment, Mr. Worthing. A hundred and thirty thousand pounds! And in the Funds! Miss Cardew seems to me a most attractive young lady, now that I look at her. Few girls of the present day have any really solid qualities, any of the qualities that last, and improve with time. We live, I regret to say,   135 in an age of surfaces. (*To* CECILY.) Come over here, dear. (CECILY *goes across.*) Pretty child! your dress is sadly simple, and your hair seems almost as Nature might have left it. But we can soon alter all that. A thoroughly experienced French maid produces a really marvelous result in a very brief space of time. I remember recommending one to young Lady Lancing, and after three months her own husband did not know her.   140

JACK *(aside)*: And after six months nobody knew her.

LADY BRACKNELL *(glares at JACK for a few moments. Then bends, with a practiced smile, to CECILY)*: Kindly turn round, sweet child. *(CECILY turns completely round.)* No, the side view is what I want. *(CECILY presents her profile.)* Yes, quite as I expected. There are distinct social possibilities in your profile. The two weak   145
points in our age are its want of principle and its want of profile. The chin a little higher, dear. Style largely depends on the way the chin is worn. They are worn very high, just at present. Algernon!

ALGERNON: Yes, Aunt Augusta!

LADY BRACKNELL: There are distinct social possibilities in Miss Cardew's profile.   150

ALGERNON: Cecily is the sweetest, dearest, prettiest girl in the whole world. And I don't care twopence about social possibilities.

LADY BRACKNELL: Never speak disrespectfully of Society, Algernon. Only people who can't get into it do that. *(To CECILY.)* Dear child, of course you know that Algernon has nothing but his debts to depend upon. But I do not approve of   155
mercenary marriages. When I married Lord Bracknell I had no fortune of any kind. But I never dreamed for a moment of allowing that to stand in my way. Well, I suppose I must give my consent.

ALGERNON: Thank you, Aunt Augusta.

LADY BRACKNELL: Cecily, you may kiss me!   160

CECILY *(kisses her)*: Thank you, Lady Bracknell.

LADY BRACKNELL: You may also address me as Aunt Augusta for the future.

CECILY: Thank you, Aunt Augusta.

LADY BRACKNELL: The marriage, I think, had better take place quite soon.

ALGERNON: Thank you, Aunt Augusta.   165

CECILY: Thank you, Aunt Augusta.

LADY BRACKNELL: To speak frankly, I am not in favor of long engagements. They give people the opportunity of finding out each other's character before marriage, which I think is never advisable.

JACK: I beg your pardon for interrupting you, Lady Bracknell, but this engagement is   170
quite out of the question. I am Miss Cardew's guardian, and she cannot marry without my consent until she comes of age. That consent I absolutely decline to give.

LADY BRACKNELL: Upon what grounds may I ask? Algernon is an extremely, I may almost say an ostentatiously, eligible young man. He has nothing, but he looks   175
everything. What more can one desire?

JACK: It pains me very much to have to speak frankly to you, Lady Bracknell, about your nephew, but the fact is that I do not approve at all of his moral character. I suspect him of being untruthful.

(ALGERNON and CECILY look at him in indignant amazement.)

LADY BRACKNELL: Untruthful! My nephew Algernon? Impossible! He is an Oxonian.[8]   180

JACK: I fear there can be no possible doubt about the matter. This afternoon, during my temporary absence in London on an important question of romance, he obtained admission to my house by means of the false pretense of being my brother. Under an assumed name he drank, I've just been informed by my butler, an entire pint bottle of my Perrier-Jouêt, Brut, '89; a wine I was specially reserving for myself. Continuing his disgraceful deception, he succeeded in the course of the afternoon in alienating the affections of my only ward. He subsequently stayed to tea, and devoured every single muffin. And what makes his conduct all the more heartless is, that he was perfectly well aware from the first that I have no brother, that I never had a brother, and that I don't intend to have a brother, not even of any kind. I distinctly told him so myself yesterday afternoon.   185   190

LADY BRACKNELL: Ahem! Mr. Worthing, after careful consideration I have decided entirely to overlook my nephew's conduct to you.

JACK: That is very generous of you, Lady Bracknell. My own decision, however, is unalterable. I decline to give my consent.   195

LADY BRACKNELL *(to* CECILY*)*: Come here, sweet child. *(*CECILY *goes over.)* How old are you, dear?

CECILY: Well, I am really only eighteen, but I always admit to twenty when I go to evening parties.

LADY BRACKNELL: You are perfectly right in making some slight alteration. Indeed, no woman should ever be quite accurate about her age. It looks so calculating— *(In a meditative manner.)* Eighteen but admitting to twenty at evening parties. Well, it will not be very long before you are of age and free from the restraints of tutelage. So I don't think your guardian's consent is, after all, a matter of any importance.   200   205

JACK: Pray excuse me, Lady Bracknell, for interrupting you again, but it is only fair to tell you that according to the terms of her grandfather's will Miss Cardew does not come legally of age till she is thirty-five.

LADY BRACKNELL: That does not seem to me to be a grave objection. Thirty-five is a very attractive age. London society is full of women of the very highest birth who have, of their own free choice, remained thirty-five for years. Lady Dumbleton is an instance in point. To my own knowledge she has been thirty-five ever since she arrived at the age of forty, which was many years ago now. I see no reason why our dear Cecily should not be even still more attractive at the age you mention than she is at present. There will be a large accumulation of property.   210   215

CECILY: Algy, could you wait for me till I was thirty-five?

ALGERNON: Of course I could, Cecily. You know I could.

CECILY: Yes, I felt it instinctively, but I couldn't wait all that time. I hate waiting even five minutes for anybody. It always makes me rather cross. I am not punctual myself, I know, but I do like punctuality in others, and waiting, even to be married, is quite out of the question.   220

---

[8]Educated at Oxford University.— EDS.

ALGERNON: Then what is to be done, Cecily?

CECILY: I don't know, Mr. Moncrieff.

LADY BRACKNELL: My dear Mr. Worthing, as Miss Cardew states positively that she cannot wait till she is thirty-five—a remark which I am bound to say seems to me to show a somewhat impatient nature—I would beg of you to reconsider your decision.

JACK: But my dear Lady Bracknell, the matter is entirely in your own hands. The moment you consent to my marriage with Gwendolen, I will most gladly allow your nephew to form an alliance with my ward.

LADY BRACKNELL (*rising and drawing herself up*): You must be quite aware that what you propose is out of the question.

JACK: Then a passionate celibacy is all that any of us can look forward to.

LADY BRACKNELL: That is not the destiny I propose for Gwendolen. Algernon, of course, can choose for himself. (*Pulls out her watch.*) Come, dear; (GWENDOLEN *rises*) we have already missed five, if not six, trains. To miss any more might expose us to comment on the platform.

(*Enter* DR. CHASUBLE.)

CHASUBLE: Everything is quite ready for the christenings.

LADY BRACKNELL: The christenings, sir! Is not that somewhat premature?

CHASUBLE (*looking rather puzzled, and pointing to* JACK *and* ALGERNON): Both these gentlemen have expressed a desire for immediate baptism.

LADY BRACKNELL: At their age? The idea is grotesque and irreligious! Algernon, I forbid you to be baptized. I will not hear of such excesses. Lord Bracknell would be highly displeased if he learned that that was the way in which you wasted your time and money.

CHASUBLE: Am I to understand then that there are to be no christenings at all this afternoon?

JACK: I don't think that, as things are now, it would be of much practical value to either of us, Dr. Chasuble.

CHASUBLE: I am grieved to hear such sentiments from you, Mr. Worthing. They savor of the heretical views of the Anabaptists,[9] views that I have completely refuted in four of my unpublished sermons. However, as your present mood seems to be one peculiarly secular, I will return to the church at once. Indeed, I have just been informed by the pew opener that for the last hour and a half Miss Prism has been waiting for me in the vestry.

LADY BRACKNELL (*starting*): Miss Prism! Did I hear you mention a Miss Prism?

CHASUBLE: Yes, Lady Bracknell. I am on my way to join her.

LADY BRACKNELL: Pray allow me to detain you for a moment. This matter may prove to be one of vital importance to Lord Bracknell and myself. Is this Miss Prism a female of repellent aspect, remotely connected with education?

---

[9]Protestant Christian sect that baptized adult believers only, not infants.—EDS.

CHASUBLE (*somewhat indignantly*): She is the most cultivated of ladies, and the very picture of respectability.

LADY BRACKNELL: It is obviously the same person. May I ask what position she holds in your household?

CHASUBLE (*severely*): I am a celibate, madam.   265

JACK (*interposing*): Miss Prism, Lady Bracknell, has been for the last three years Miss Cardew's esteemed governess and valued companion.

LADY BRACKNELL: In spite of what I hear of her, I must see her at once. Let her be sent for.

CHASUBLE (*looking off*): She approaches; she is nigh.   270

(*Enter* MISS PRISM *hurriedly.*)

MISS PRISM: I was told you expected me in the vestry, dear Canon. I have been waiting for you there for an hour and three-quarters.

(*Catches sight of* LADY BRACKNELL, *who has fixed her with a stony glare.* MISS PRISM *grows pale and quails. She looks anxiously round as if desirous to escape.*)

LADY BRACKNELL (*in a severe, judicial voice*): Prism! (MISS PRISM *bows her head in shame.*) Come here, Prism! (MISS PRISM *approaches in a humble manner.*) Prism! Where is that baby? (*General consternation. The Canon starts back in horror.* 275 ALGERNON *and* JACK *pretend to be anxious to shield* CECILY *and* GWENDOLEN *from hearing the details of a terrible public scandal.*) Twenty-eight years ago, Prism, you left Lord Bracknell's house, Number 104, Upper Grosvenor Street, in charge of a perambulator that contained a baby, of the male sex. You never returned. A few weeks later, through the elaborate investigations of the 280 Metropolitan police, the perambulator was discovered at midnight, standing by itself in a remote corner of Bayswater. It contained the manuscript of a three-volume novel of more than usually revolting sentimentality. (MISS PRISM *starts in involuntary indignation.*) But the baby was not there! (*Everyone looks at* MISS PRISM.) Prism! Where is that baby?   (*A pause.*) 285

MISS PRISM: Lady Bracknell, I admit with shame that I do not know. I only wish I did. The plain facts of the case are these. On the morning of the day you mention, a day that is forever branded on my memory, I prepared as usual to take the baby out in its perambulator. I had also with me a somewhat old, but capacious handbag in which I had intended to place the manuscript of a work of fiction 290 that I had written during my few unoccupied hours. In a moment of mental abstraction, for which I never can forgive myself, I deposited the manuscript in the bassinette, and placed the baby in the handbag.

JACK (*who has been listening attentively*): But where did you deposit the handbag?

MISS PRISM: Do not ask me, Mr. Worthing.   295

JACK: Miss Prism, this is a matter of no small importance to me. I insist on knowing where you deposited the handbag that contained that infant.

MISS PRISM: I left it in the cloakroom of one of the larger railway stations in London.

JACK: What railway station?   300
MISS PRISM (*quite crushed*): Victoria. The Brighton line.   (*Sinks into a chair.*)
JACK: I must retire to my room for a moment. Gwendolen, wait here for me.
GWENDOLEN: If you are not too long, I will wait here for you all my life.
(*Exit* JACK *in great excitement.*)
CHASUBLE: What do you think this means, Lady Bracknell?
LADY BRACKNELL: I dare not even suspect, Dr. Chasuble. I need hardly tell you that   305
in families of high position strange coincidences are not supposed to occur. They
are hardly considered the thing.

(*Noises heard overhead as if someone was throwing trunks about. Everyone looks up.*)

CECILY: Uncle Jack seems strangely agitated.
CHASUBLE: Your guardian has a very emotional nature.
LADY BRACKNELL: This noise is extremely unpleasant. It sounds as if he was having   310
an argument. I dislike arguments of any kind. They are always vulgar, and often
convincing.
CHASUBLE (*looking up*): It has stopped now.   (*The noise is redoubled.*)
LADY BRACKNELL: I wish he would arrive at some conclusion.
GWENDOLEN: This suspense is terrible. I hope it will last.   315

(*Enter* JACK *with a handbag of black leather in his hand.*)

JACK (*rushing over to* MISS PRISM): Is this the handbag, Miss Prism? Examine it carefully before you speak. The happiness of more than one life depends on your
answer.
MISS PRISM (*calmly*): It seems to be mine. Yes, here is the injury it received through
the upsetting of a Gower Street omnibus in younger and happier days. Here is   320
the stain on the lining caused by the explosion of a temperance beverage, an
incident that occurred at Leamington. And here, on the lock, are my initials. I
had forgotten that in an extravagant mood I had had them placed there. The bag
is undoubtedly mine. I am delighted to have it so unexpectedly restored to me. It
has been a great inconvenience being without it all these years.   325
JACK (*in a pathetic voice*): Miss Prism, more is restored to you than this handbag. I
was the baby you placed in it.
MISS PRISM (*amazed*): You?
JACK (*embracing her*): Yes — mother!
MISS PRISM (*recoiling in indignant astonishment*): Mr. Worthing! I am unmarried!   330
JACK: Unmarried! I do not deny that is a serious blow. But after all, who has the right
to cast a stone against one who has suffered? Cannot repentance wipe out an act
of folly? Why should there be one law for men, and another for women? Mother,
I forgive you.   (*Tries to embrace her again.*)
MISS PRISM (*still more indignant*): Mr. Worthing, there is some error. (*Pointing to   335
LADY BRACKNELL.*) There is the lady who can tell you who you really are.
JACK (*after a pause*): Lady Bracknell, I hate to seem inquisitive, but would you kindly
inform me who I am?

LADY BRACKNELL: I am afraid that the news I have to give you will not altogether please you. You are the son of my poor sister, Mrs. Moncrieff, and consequently Algernon's elder brother.   340

JACK: Algy's elder brother! Then I have a brother after all. I knew I had a brother! I always said I had a brother! Cecily,—how could you have ever doubted that I had a brother? *(Seizes hold of* ALGERNON.*)* Dr. Chasuble, my unfortunate brother. Miss Prism, my unfortunate brother. Gwendolen, my unfortunate brother. Algy,   345 you young scoundrel, you will have to treat me with more respect in the future. You have never behaved to me like a brother in all your life.

ALGERNON: Well, not till today, old boy, I admit. I did my best, however, though I was out of practice.   *(Shakes hands.)*

GWENDOLEN *(to* JACK*)*: My own! But what own are you? What is your Christian   350 name, now that you have become someone else?

JACK: Good heavens!—I had quite forgotten that point. Your decision on the subject of my name is irrevocable, I suppose?

GWENDOLEN: I never change, except in my affections.

CECILY: What a noble nature you have, Gwendolen!   355

JACK: Then the question had better be cleared up at once. Aunt Augusta, a moment. At the time when Miss Prism left me in the handbag, had I been christened already?

LADY BRACKNELL: Every luxury that money could buy, including christening, had been lavished on you by your fond and doting parents.

JACK: Then I was christened! That is settled. Now, what name was I given? Let me   360 know the worst.

LADY BRACKNELL: Being the eldest son you were naturally christened after your father.

JACK *(irritably)*: Yes, but what was my father's Christian name?

LADY BRACKNELL *(meditatively)*: I cannot at the present moment recall what the General's   365 Christian name was. But I have no doubt he had one. He was eccentric, I admit. But only in later years. And that was the result of the Indian climate, and marriage, and indigestion, and other things of that kind.

JACK: Algy! Can't you recollect what our father's Christian name was?

ALGERNON: My dear boy, we were never even on speaking terms. He died before I   370 was a year old. LoL

JACK: His name would appear in the Army Lists of the period, I suppose, Aunt Augusta?

LADY BRACKNELL: The General was essentially a man of peace, except in his domestic life. But I have no doubt his name would appear in any military directory.

JACK: The Army Lists of the last forty years are here. These delightful records should   375 have been my constant study. *(Rushes to bookcase and tears the books out.)* M. Generals—Mallam, Maxbohm, Magley, what ghastly names they have—Markby, Migsby, Mobbs, Moncrieff! Lieutenant 1840, Captain, Lieutenant-Colonel, Colonel, General 1869, Christian names, Ernest John. *(Puts book very quietly down and speaks quite calmly.)* I always told you, Gwendolen, my name was Ernest, didn't I? Well, it is   380 Ernest after all. I mean it naturally is Ernest.

LADY BRACKNELL: Yes, I remember now that the General was called Ernest. I knew I had some particular reason for disliking the name.

GWENDOLEN: Ernest! My own Ernest! I felt from the first that you could have no other name! 385

JACK: Gwendolen, it is a terrible thing for a man to find out suddenly that all his life he has been speaking nothing but the truth. Can you forgive me?

GWENDOLEN: I can. For I feel that you are sure to change.

JACK: My own one!

CHASUBLE (to MISS PRISM): Laetitia! (Embraces her.) *Comedic* 390

MISS PRISM (enthusiastically): Frederick! At last! *Resolution*

ALGERNON: Cecily! (Embraces her.) At last!

JACK: Gwendolen! (Embraces her.) At last!

LADY BRACKNELL: My nephew, you seem to be displaying signs of triviality.

JACK: On the contrary, Aunt Augusta, I've now realized for the first time in my life the 395 vital Importance of Being Earnest.

[1895]

Questions for Discussion

1. In Oscar Wilde's time, "earnestness"—sober behavior, a serious turn of mind—was valued as an important character trait. How does Wilde undermine this value? Consider when the characters are earnest and when they are not. How does the pun on *earnest* and *Ernest* seen throughout the play, as well as Gwendolen's and Cecily's fascination with the name Ernest, further this satirization?

2. At the very beginning of act I, Algernon states, "I don't play accurately—anyone can play accurately—but I play with wonderful expression" (ll. 3–4). How does this comment establish a theme for the play? In what other ways throughout the play is Algernon not accurate but expressive? Are other characters also not accurate but expressive?

3. How does Wilde portray the relationship between Algernon and his servant Lane in act I? What do their conversations suggest about class differences and the society in which the play is set? Is there some irony in their interactions?

4. What is the significance of Jack's leading a double life, with one persona for the city and another for the country? How is this similar to what Algernon has created with his invalid friend Bunbury? How is it different? What is ironic about Algernon later impersonating Jack's alter ego, Ernest?

5. What do the scenes of Algernon and Jack jostling over cucumber sandwiches (act I) and muffins (act II) suggest about their characters and their priorities? Explain how Wilde uses these props to produce a comic effect.

6. Look closely at the exchange in act II between Cecily and Gwendolen in which they both believe they are engaged to the same man (ll. 566–98). What

self-contradicting values do their cutting remarks about city life and country life reveal?

7. As suggested in the subtitle, Wilde treats trivial things with gravity and grave things trivially. At what point does earnestness border on ridiculousness? Find examples to support your opinion.

8. Compare and contrast the female characters in the play — Cecily and Gwendolen with Lady Bracknell and Miss Prism. What is Wilde's attitude toward women in this play? Compare and contrast that attitude with his attitude toward Algernon and Jack. Does Wilde seem to have more sympathy for the women or for the men? Is one gender portrayed as more foolish, more clever, more self-aware, more naive? When devising your answer, consider the different schemes with which male and female characters deceive others and themselves throughout the play.

9. In satire, human folly is held up to ridicule. Though humorous, a satire's purpose is to critique — often seriously — that which it mocks. How does Lady Bracknell's interview of Jack as a prospective suitor in act I satirize "modern education"? Where else in the play does Wilde satirize education?

10. How does Wilde make *The Importance of Being Earnest* funny? Identify what you consider to be the most humorous part of the play, and explain your choice. Now, think about the purpose of the humor in this play. Find instances where Wilde uses humor to satirize some of the more ridiculous aspects of society.

11. What do you think was Wilde's purpose for writing this play? Consider that he may have had more than a single purpose in mind. Who might have been his intended audience?

12. What does this play have to tell us about our own society? Is the play still relevant? Explain.

Questions on Style and Structure

1. How does the scene description for act I prepare the reader for Wilde's satire of Victorian society? Throughout the first act, how do specific stage directions contribute to the play's tone?

2. Consider the invented word *Bunburyist*. Why is the term used so many times in quick succession in act I (ll. 146–47; 178–79) and with such relish? How many variations (different parts of speech, different definitions) does the word undergo? Why does a made-up term play such an important role in this play?

3. Compare and contrast the alternating dialogues between Miss Prism and Chasuble and between Algernon and Cecily in the beginning of act II. How do these exchanges advance the plot? How do they reveal some of the play's themes?

4. Generally, this play sticks to the conventions of the comedy of manners — a satiric form of drama that lampoons social conventions. However, it occasionally becomes a farce, marked by wholly absurd situations, slapstick, raucous wordplay, and innuendo. Identify a shift to farce in the play. How does it contribute to the plot? What is its effect on the tone of the play?

5. Though he is mentioned several times, Lord Bracknell never appears in the play. How do other characters' descriptions of him allow us to construct an image of the man? What does this stylistic choice accomplish in terms of theme, characterization, and plot advancement? Consider how these elements would change if he actually appeared on the stage.

6. What effect does the shift in setting from the city to the country in act II have on the plot's development? How does this structure develop the play's themes?

7. What purpose do the minor characters of Miss Prism and Canon Chasuble serve in the play? How are their names a clue to their respective roles? During their stroll in act II, how does their diction differ from that of the main characters? What does their dialogue tell you about their relationship, their values, and the larger institutions they represent?

8. Explain the role of the black handbag in the play. What other objects serve as important props, and how do they advance the plot?

9. A hallmark of Wilde's style is his use of the epigram—a short, witty, often paradoxical statement designed to surprise the audience. *The Importance of Being Earnest* is full of such lines, such as the following line from act I: "To lose one parent may be regarded as a misfortune—to lose *both* seems like carelessness" (ll. 439–40). Identify three examples of epigrams in the play, and consider the purpose of each statement. What role do epigrams serve collectively, and how do they affect the tone of the play?

10. How do the final moments of the play conform to the "happily every after" conventions of romantic comedy? How do they deviate from (or comment on) such conventions?

Suggestions for Writing

1. Write an essay in which you explore how Oscar Wilde employs irony to satirize the social conventions of his time. Offer examples from the play to illustrate your point. In your response, consider what purpose a satire like *The Importance of Being Earnest* serves. Do you believe satire is a valuable objective in art? Explain.

2. Reread the final act of *The Importance of Being Earnest*. Then, focusing particularly on the play's conclusion, write an essay in which you explain how Wilde uses three literary devices—overstatement (hyperbole), understatement, and irony, for example—to critique the values of Victorian society.

3. As a comedy of manners, *The Importance of Being Earnest* pokes fun at the behavior and affectations of a social class obsessed with appearances and, of course, earnestness. But can Wilde's play also be read as a send-up of this form—a satire of a satire? Write an essay in which you analyze various ways in which *The Importance of Being Earnest* transcends the comedy of manners genre.

4. What does *The Importance of Being Earnest* suggest about love and marriage in the world it depicts? Consider the characters' relationships and their wide range of assertions about marriage and courtship.

5. Some critics have argued that Wilde's play, while written in the late 1800s, depicts a cultural transition to the twentieth century. How might this work be read as a segue between the nineteenth and twentieth centuries in terms of the nineteenth-century cultural values it satirizes and the twentieth-century values *The Importance of Being Earnest* depicts or predicts. Some outside research may be required.

6. Write a contemporary version of act II's scene between Cecily and Gwendolen in which they first meet (ll. 467–598). Consider your setting for this meeting. Carefully rename the characters. What might they chat about? Pay particular attention to your characters' speech patterns. What do these suggest about your characters' beliefs and values, as well as those of the society they represent?

Woman Hollering Creek

SANDRA CISNEROS

 Born in Chicago, the only girl among seven children, Sandra Cisneros (b. 1954) spent her early life in both Chicago and Mexico before her family eventually settled in Humboldt Park, a Puerto Rican neighborhood of Chicago. Cisneros earned a bachelor's degree from Loyola University and an MFA from the University of Iowa. Set in Humboldt Park, her most famous work is *The House on Mango Street* (1984), which won the American Book Award and established her reputation. Her other works include *My Wicked, Wicked Ways* (1987), *Woman Hollering Creek and Other Stories* (1991), *Hairs = Pelitos* (1994), *Loose Woman: Poems* (1994), *Caramelo* (2002), and *Vintage Cisneros* (2004). She has taught at the high-school level in Chicago, and is currently writer-in-residence at Our Lady of the Lake University in San Antonio. The activity that perhaps gives her the most pleasure has been the creation and direction of the Alfredo Cisneros Del Moral Foundation. Since 2007, the foundation, whose name commemorates Ms. Cisneros's father, has awarded over $75,000 to writers born or living in Texas. This work prompted Ms. Cisneros to recall, "In my own experience, grants not only allowed me time to write but, more importantly, confirmed I was indeed a writer at precarious moments when my own faith in my art wobbled." The selection here is the title piece from her story collection, *Woman Hollering Creek*, in which Cisneros re-creates the lives of women living on both sides of the U.S.-Mexican border through a series of sketches set around San Antonio.

The day Don Serafín gave Juan Pedro Martínez Sánchez permission to take Cleófilas Engriqueta DeLeón Hernández as his bride, across her father's threshold, over several miles of dirt road and several miles of paved, over one border and beyond to a town *en el otro lado*—on the other side—already did he divine the morning his daughter would raise her hand over her eyes, look south, and dream of returning to the chores that never ended, six good-for-nothing brothers, and one old man's complaints.

He had said, after all, in the hubbub of parting: I am your father, I will never abandon you. He had said that, hadn't he, when he hugged and then let her go. But at the moment Cleófilas was busy looking for Chela, her maid of honor, to fulfill her bouquet conspiracy. She would not remember her father's parting words until later. *I am your father, I will never abandon you.*

Only now as a mother did she remember. Now, when she and Juan Pedrito sat by the creek's edge. How when a man and a woman love each other, sometimes that love sours. But a parent's love for a child, a child's for its parents, is another thing entirely.

This is what Cleófilas thought evenings when Juan Pedro did not come home, and she lay on her side of the bed listening to the hollow roar of the interstate, a

623

distant dog barking, the pecan trees rustling like ladies in stiff petticoats—*shh-shh-shh, shh-shh-shh*—soothing her to sleep.

In the town where she grew up, there isn't very much to do except accompany ⁵ the aunts and godmothers to the house of one or the other to play cards. Or walk to the cinema to see this week's film again, speckled and with one hair quivering annoyingly on the screen. Or to the center of town to order a milk shake that will appear in a day and a half as a pimple on her backside. Or to the girlfriend's house to watch the latest *telenovela* episode and try to copy the way the women comb their hair, wear their makeup.

But what Cleófilas has been waiting for, has been whispering and sighing and giggling for, has been anticipating since she was old enough to lean against the window displays of gauze and butterflies and lace, is passion. Not the kind on the cover of the *¡Alarma!* magazines, mind you, where the lover is photographed with the bloody fork she used to salvage her good name. But passion in its purest crystalline essence. The kind the books and songs and *telenovelas* describe when one finds, finally, the great love of one's life, and does whatever one can, must do, at whatever the cost.

Tú o Nadie. "You or No One." The title of the current favorite *telenovela.* The beautiful Lucía Méndez having to put up with all kinds of hardships of the heart, separation and betrayal, and loving, always loving no matter what, because *that* is the most important thing, and did you see Lucía Méndez on the Bayer aspirin commercials—wasn't she lovely? Does she dye her hair do you think? Cleófilas is going to go to the *farmacía* and buy a hair rinse; her girlfriend Chela will apply it—it's not that difficult at all.

Because you didn't watch last night's episode when Lucía confessed she loved him more than anyone in her life. In her life! And she sings the song "You or No One" in the beginning and end of the show. *Tú o Nadie.* Somehow one ought to live one's life like that, don't you think? You or no one. Because to suffer for love is good. The pain all sweet somehow. In the end.

Seguín. She had liked the sound of it. Far away and lovely. Not like *Monclova. Coahuila.* Ugly.

Seguín, Tejas. A nice sterling ring to it. The tinkle of money. She would get to ¹⁰ wear outfits like the woman on the *tele*, like Lucía Méndez. And have a lovely house, and wouldn't Chela be jealous.

And yes, they will drive all the way to Laredo to get her wedding dress. That's what they say. Because Juan Pedro wants to get married right away, without a long engagement since he can't take off too much time from work. He has a very important position in Seguin with, with . . . a beer company, I think. Or was it tires? Yes, he has to be back. So they will get married in the spring when he can take off work, and then they will drive off in his new pickup—did you see it?—to their new home in Seguin. Well, not exactly new, but they're going to repaint the house. You know newlyweds. New paint and new furniture. Why not? He can afford it. And later on add maybe a room or two for the children. May they be blessed with many.

Well, you'll see. Cleófilas has always been so good with her sewing machine. A little *rrrr, rrrr, rrrr* of the machine and *¡zas!* Miracles. She's always been so clever, that girl. Poor thing. And without even a mama to advise her on things like her wedding night. Well, may God help her. What with a father with a head like a burro, and those six clumsy brothers. Well, what do you think! Yes, I'm going to the wedding. Of course! The dress I want to wear just needs to be altered a teensy bit to bring it up to date. See, I saw a new style last night that I thought would suit me. Did you watch last night's episode of *The Rich Also Cry*? Well, did you notice the dress the mother was wearing?

La Gritona. Such a funny name for such a lovely *arroyo*. But that's what they called the creek that ran behind the house. Though no one could say whether the woman had hollered from anger or pain. The natives only knew the *arroyo* one crossed on the way to San Antonio, and then once again on the way back, was called Woman Hollering, a name no one from these parts questions, little less understood. *Pues, allá de los indios, quién sabe*[1] — who knows, the townspeople shrugged, because it was of no concern to their lives how this trickle of water received its curious name.

"What do you want to know for?" Trini the laundromat attendant asked in the same gruff Spanish she always used whenever she gave Cleófilas change or yelled at her for something. First for putting too much soap in the machines. Later, for sitting on a washer. And still later, after Juan Pedrito was born, for not understanding that in this country you cannot let your baby walk around with no diaper and his pee-pee hanging out, it wasn't nice, *¿entiendes? Pues.*[2]

How could Cleófilas explain to a woman like this why the name Woman Hollering fascinated her. Well, there was no sense talking to Trini.   15

On the other hand there were the neighbor ladies, one on either side of the house they rented near the *arroyo*. The woman Soledad on the left, the woman Dolores on the right.

The neighbor lady Soledad liked to call herself a widow, though how she came to be one was a mystery. Her husband had either died, or run away with an ice-house floozie, or simply gone out for cigarettes one afternoon and never came back. It was hard to say which since Soledad, as a rule, didn't mention him.

In the other house lived *la señora* Dolores, kind and very sweet, but her house smelled too much of incense and candles from the altars that burned continuously in memory of two sons who had died in the last war and one husband who had died shortly after from grief. The neighbor lady Dolores divided her time between the memory of these men and her garden, famous for its sunflowers—so tall they had to be supported with broom handles and old boards; red red cockscombs, fringed and bleeding a thick menstrual color; and, especially, roses whose sad scent reminded Cleófilas of the dead. Each Sunday *la señora* Dolores clipped the most beautiful of these flowers and arranged them on three modest headstones at the Seguin cemetery.

---

[1] Well, that's from the Indians, who knows? — EDS.
[2] Understand? Good. — EDS.

The neighbor ladies, Soledad, Dolores, they might've known once the name of the *arroyo* before it turned English but they did not know now. They were too busy remembering the men who had left through either choice or circumstance and would never come back.

Pain or rage, Cleófilas wondered when she drove over the bridge the first time as   20
a newlywed and Juan Pedro had pointed it out. *La Gritona*, he had said, and she had laughed. Such a funny name for a creek so pretty and full of happily ever after.

The first time she had been so surprised she didn't cry out or try to defend herself. She had always said she would strike back if a man, any man, were to strike her.

But when the moment came, and he slapped her once, and then again, and again; until the lip split and bled an orchid of blood, she didn't fight back, she didn't break into tears, she didn't run away as she imagined she might when she saw such things in the *telenovelas*.

In her own home her parents had never raised a hand to each other or to their children. Although she admitted she may have been brought up a little leniently as an only daughter—*la consentida*, the princess—there were some things she would never tolerate. Ever.

Instead, when it happened the first time, when they were barely man and wife, she had been so stunned, it left her speechless, motionless, numb. She had done nothing but reach up to the heat of her mouth and stare at the blood on her hand as if even then she didn't understand.

She could think of nothing to say, said nothing. Just stroked the dark curls of   25
the man who wept and would weep like a child, his tears of repentance and shame, this time and each.

The men at the ice house. From what she can tell, from the times during her first year when still a newlywed she is invited and accompanies her husband, sits mute beside their conversation, waits and sips a beer until it grows warm, twists a paper napkin into a knot, then another into a fan, one into a rose, nods her head, smiles, yawns, politely grins, laughs at the appropriate moments, leans against her husband's sleeve, tugs at his elbow, and finally becomes good at predicting where the talk will lead, from this Cleófilas concludes each is nightly trying to find the truth lying at the bottom of the bottle like a gold doubloon on the sea floor.

They want to tell each other what they want to tell themselves. But what is bumping like a helium balloon at the ceiling of the brain never finds its way out. It bubbles and rises, it gurgles in the throat, it rolls across the surface of the tongue, and erupts from the lips—a belch.

If they are lucky, there are tears at the end of the long night. At any given moment, the fists try to speak. They are dogs chasing their own tails before lying down to sleep, trying to find a way, a route, an out, and—finally—get some peace.

In the morning sometimes before he opens his eyes. Or after they have finished loving. Or at times when he is simply across from her at the table putting pieces of food into his mouth and chewing. Cleófilas thinks, this is the man I have waited my whole life for.

Not that he isn't a good man. She has to remind herself why she loves him when 30 she changes the baby's Pampers, or when she mops the bathroom floor, or tries to make the curtains for the doorways without doors, or whiten the linen. Or wonder a little when he kicks the refrigerator and says he hates this shitty house and is going out where he won't be bothered with the baby's howling and her suspicious questions, and her requests to fix this and this and this because if she had any brains in her head she'd realize he's been up before the rooster earning his living to pay for the food in her belly and the roof over her head and would have to wake up again early the next day so why can't you just leave me in peace, woman.

He is not very tall, no, and he doesn't look like the men on the *telenovelas*. His face still scarred from acne. And he has a bit of a belly from all the beer he drinks. Well, he's always been husky.

This man who farts and belches and snores as well as laughs and kisses and holds her. Somehow this husband whose whiskers she finds each morning on the sink, whose shoes she must air each evening on the porch, this husband who cuts his fingernails in public, laughs loudly, curses like a man, and demands each course of dinner be served on a separate plate like at his mother's, as soon as he gets home, on time or late, and who doesn't care at all for music or *telenovelas* or romance or roses or the moon floating pearly over the *arroyo*, or through the bedroom window for that matter, shut the blinds and go back to sleep, this man, this father, this rival, this keeper, this lord, this master, this husband till kingdom come.

A doubt. Slender as a hair. A washed cup set back on the shelf wrong-side-up. Her lipstick, and body talc, and hairbrush all arranged in the bathroom a different way.

No. Her imagination. The house the same as always. Nothing.

Coming home from the hospital with her new son, her husband. Something 35 comforting in discovering her house slippers beneath the bed, the faded housecoat where she left it on the bathroom hook. Her pillow. Their bed.

Sweet sweet homecoming. Sweet as the scent of face powder in the air, jasmine, sticky liquor.

Smudged fingerprint on the door. Crushed cigarette in a glass. Wrinkle in the brain crumpling to a crease.

Sometimes she thinks of her father's house. But how could she go back there? What a disgrace. What would the neighbors say? Coming home like that with one baby on her hip and one in the oven. Where's your husband?

The town of gossips. The town of dust and despair. Which she has traded for this town of gossips. This town of dust, despair. Houses farther apart perhaps, though no more privacy because of it. No leafy *zócalo*[3] in the center of the town, though the murmur

---

[3] Town square.—EDS.

of talk is clear enough all the same. No huddled whispering on the church steps each Sunday. Because here the whispering begins at sunset at the ice house instead.

This town with its silly pride for a bronze pecan the size of a baby carriage in front of the city hall. TV repair shop, drugstore, hardware, dry cleaner's, chiropractor's, liquor store, bail bonds, empty storefront, and nothing, nothing, nothing of interest. Nothing one could walk to, at any rate. Because the towns here are built so that you have to depend on husbands. Or you stay home. Or you drive. If you're rich enough to own, allowed to drive, your own car.   40

There is no place to go. Unless one counts the neighbor ladies. Soledad on one side, Dolores on the other. Or the creek.

Don't go out there after dark, *mi'jita*. Stay near the house. *No es bueno para la salud.*[4] *Mala suerte.* Bad luck. *Mal aire.* You'll get sick and the baby too. You'll catch a fright wandering about in the dark, and then you'll see how right we were.

The stream sometimes only a muddy puddle in the summer, though now in the springtime, because of the rains, a good-size alive thing, a thing with a voice all its own, all day and all night calling in its high, silver voice. Is it La Llorona, the weeping woman? La Llorona, who drowned her own children. Perhaps La Llorona is the one they named the creek after, she thinks, remembering all the stories she learned as a child.

La Llorona calling to her. She is sure of it. Cleófilas sets the baby's Donald Duck blanket on the grass. Listens. The day sky turning to night. The baby pulling up fistfuls of grass and laughing. La Llorona. Wonders if something as quiet as this drives a woman to the darkness under the trees.

What she needs is . . . and made a gesture as if to yank a woman's buttocks to his groin. Maximiliano, the foul-smelling fool from across the road, said this and set the men laughing, but Cleófilas just muttered, *Grosero,* and went on washing dishes.   45

She knew he said it not because it was true, but more because it was he who needed to sleep with a woman, instead of drinking each night at the ice house and stumbling home alone.

Maximiliano who was said to have killed his wife in an ice-house brawl when she came at him with a mop. I had to shoot, he said — she was armed.

Their laughter outside the kitchen window. Her husband's, his friends'. Manolo, Beto, Efraín, el Perico. Maximiliano.

Was Cleófilas just exaggerating as her husband always said? It seemed the newspapers were full of such stories. This woman found on the side of the interstate. This one pushed from a moving car. This one's cadaver, this one unconscious, this one beaten blue. Her ex-husband, her husband, her lover, her father, her brother, her uncle, her friend, her co-worker. Always. The same grisly news in the pages of the dailies. She dunked a glass under the soapy water for a moment — shivered.

He had thrown a book. Hers. From across the room. A hot welt across the cheek. She could forgive that. But what stung more was the fact it was *her* book, a love story   50

---

[4]It's not good for your health. — EDS.

by Corín Tellado, what she loved most now that she lived in the U.S., without a television set, without the *telenovelas*.

Except now and again when her husband was away and she could manage it, the few episodes glimpsed at the neighbor lady Soledad's house because Dolores didn't care for that sort of thing, though Soledad was often kind enough to retell what had happened on what episode of *María de Nadie*, the poor Argentine country girl who had the ill fortune of falling in love with the beautiful son of the Arrocha family, the very family she worked for, whose roof she slept under and whose floors she vacuumed, while in that same house, with the dust brooms and floor cleaners as witnesses, the square-jawed Juan Carlos Arrocha had uttered words of love, I love you, María, listen to me, *mi querida*,[5] but it was she who had to say No, no, we are not of the same class, and remind him it was not his place nor hers to fall in love, while all the while her heart was breaking, can you imagine.

Cleófilas thought her life would have to be like that, like a *telenovela*, only now the episodes got sadder and sadder. And there were no commercials in between for comic relief. And no happy ending in sight. She thought this when she sat with the baby out by the creek behind the house. Cleófilas de . . . ? But somehow she would have to change her name to Topazio, or Yesenia, Cristal, Adriana, Stefania, Andrea, something more poetic than Cleófilas. Everything happened to women with names like jewels. But what happened to a Cleófilas? Nothing. But a crack in the face.

Because the doctor has said so. She has to go. To make sure the new baby is all right, so there won't be any problems when he's born, and the appointment card says next Tuesday. Could he please take her. And that's all.

No, she won't mention it. She promises. If the doctor asks she can say she fell down the front steps or slipped when she was out in the backyard, slipped out back, she could tell him that. She has to go back next Tuesday, Juan Pedro, please, for the new baby. For their child.

She could write to her father and ask maybe for money, just a loan, for the new baby's medical expenses. Well then if he'd rather she didn't. All right, she won't. Please don't anymore. Please don't. She knows it's difficult saving money with all the bills they have, but how else are they going to get out of debt with the truck payments? And after the rent and the food and the electricity and the gas and the water and the who-knows-what, well, there's hardly anything left. But please, at least for the doctor visit. She won't ask for anything else. She has to. Why is she so anxious? Because.

Because she is going to make sure the baby is not turned around backward this time to split her down the center. Yes. Next Tuesday at five-thirty. I'll have Juan Pedrito dressed and ready. But those are the only shoes he has. I'll polish them, and we'll be ready. As soon as you come from work. We won't make you ashamed.

Felice? It's me, Graciela.

No, I can't talk louder. I'm at work.

---

[5]My beloved. — EDS.

Look, I need kind of a favor. There's a patient, a lady here who's got a problem. Well, wait a minute. Are you listening to me or what?   60
I can't talk real loud 'cause her husband's in the next room.
Well, would you just listen?
I was going to do this sonogram on her—she's pregnant, right?—and she just starts crying on me. *Híjole*,[6] Felice! This poor lady's got black-and-blue marks all over. I'm not kidding.
From her husband. Who else? Another one of those brides from across the border. And her family's all in Mexico.
Shit. You think they're going to help her? Give me a break. This lady doesn't even   65
speak English. She hasn't been allowed to call home or write or nothing. That's why I'm calling you.
She needs a ride.
Not to Mexico, you goof. Just to the Greyhound. In San Anto.
No, just a ride. She's got her own money. All you'd have to do is drop her off in San Antonio on your way home. Come on, Felice. Please? If we don't help her, who will? I'd drive her myself, but she needs to be on that bus before her husband gets home from work. What do you say?
I don't know. Wait.
Right away, tomorrow even.   70
Well, if tomorrow's no good for you . . .
It's a date, Felice. Thursday. At the Cash N Carry off I-10. Noon. She'll be ready.
Oh, and her name's Cleófilas.
I don't know. One of those Mexican saints, I guess. A martyr or something.
Cleófilas. C-L-E-O-F-I-L-A-S. Cle. O. Fi. Las. Write it down.   75
Thanks, Felice. When her kid's born she'll have to name her after us, right?
Yeah, you got it. A regular soap opera sometimes. *Qué vida, comadre. Bueno bye.*

All morning that flutter of half-fear, half-doubt. At any moment Juan Pedro might appear in the doorway. On the street. At the Cash N Carry. Like in the dreams she dreamed.
There was that to think about, yes, until the woman in the pickup drove up. Then there wasn't time to think about anything but the pickup pointed toward San Antonio. Put your bags in the back and get in.
But when they drove across the *arroyo*, the driver opened her mouth and let out a   80
yell as loud as any mariachi. Which startled not only Cleófilas, but Juan Pedrito as well.
Pues, look how cute. I scared you two, right? Sorry. Should've warned you. Every time I cross that bridge I do that. Because of the name, you know. Woman Hollering. *Pues*, I holler. She said this in a Spanish pocked with English and laughed. Did you ever notice, Felice continued, how nothing around here is named after a woman? Really. Unless she's the Virgin. I guess you're only famous if you're a virgin. She was laughing again.

---

[6]Interjection: gosh or jeez.—EDS.

That's why I like the name of that *arroyo*. Makes you want to holler like Tarzan, right?

Everything about this woman, this Felice, amazed Cleófilas. The fact that she drove a pickup. A pickup, mind you, but when Cleófilas asked if it was her husband's, she said she didn't have a husband. The pickup was hers. She herself had chosen it. She herself was paying for it.

I used to have a Pontiac Sunbird. But those cars are for *viejas*.[7] Pussy cars. Now this here is a real car.

What kind of talk was that coming from a woman? Cleófilas thought. But then   85
again, Felice was like no woman she'd ever met. Can you imagine, when we crossed the *arroyo* she just started yelling like crazy, she would say later to her father and brothers. Just like that. Who would've thought?

Who would've? Pain or rage, perhaps, but not a hoot like the one Felice had just let go. Makes you want to holler like Tarzan, Felice had said.

Then Felice began laughing again, but it wasn't Felice laughing. It was gurgling out of her own throat, a long ribbon of laughter, like water.

[1991]

Questions for Discussion

1. What do you learn about Cleófilas in the very first section of the story, which is told as a flashback? What are the contrasts between "then" and "now" that Cisneros establishes in this section?
2. How does becoming a mother change Cleófilas's outlook on her situation? Does she define herself through motherhood? Explain.
3. How does the assumption that "to suffer for love is good. The pain all sweet somehow. In the end" (para. 8) help shape Cleófilas's behavior? Does she ultimately reject this view? How can you tell?
4. Why didn't Cleófilas behave as she thought she would when Juan Pedro first struck her? Why do you think she was "speechless, motionless, numb" (para. 24)?
5. What is the importance of the character of Maximiliano? What does Cleófilas's perception of him tell us about her?
6. In her new home in Texas, Cleófilas lives between Dolores and Soledad. In Spanish, *dolores* means "sorrow" and *soledad* means "solitude." What does the author's choice of these names for neighbors suggest about Cleófilas's life in this Texas town? What other evidence can you find to support this interpretation of Cleófilas's life in Seguin?
7. How does Cisneros portray the situation of both men and women—the community in general—who have immigrated to the United States from Mexico? Judging from the depiction in "Woman Hollering Creek," have they found a better life than the one they left?

---

[7]Old ladies.—EDS.

8. Why doesn't Cleófilas want to return to her father's home in Mexico? Describe the various "ways out" she considers over the course of the story. Why does she finally decide to return to Mexico?

9. Why are *telenovelas* important in this story? What role do they play in women's lives? How do they affect Cleófilas's views about love and relationships?

10. What finally causes Cleófilas to reconsider her ideas about love? At the end, do you think that she still believes in "passion in its purest crystalline essence" and finding "the great love of one's life" (para. 6)?

Questions on Style and Structure

1. What do you learn from the opening paragraph? Consider both the information provided and the attitude. How do the sentence structure and the language—the paragraph consists of one long sentence—reinforce meaning?

2. In this story, Cisneros often makes use of compelling sentence fragments. Find three examples, and explain the effect they have on the meaning of the passage.

3. "Woman Hollering Creek" is told from various points of view—mainly third person, with first person introduced through dialogue. Why do you think Cisneros uses this technique? How would the story have been different if the entire story were told from Cleófilas's viewpoint?

4. Paragraph 21 begins with "The first time she had been so surprised she didn't cry out or try to defend herself." The first time for what? Why might Cisneros choose not to identify specifically what the action was?

5. How does Cisneros's language reveal her attitude toward the men in the story? Does she condemn them? Pay careful attention to the section describing "The men at the ice house" (paras. 26–28). For instance, what does the metaphor "the fists try to speak" (para. 28) suggest about the men in this story and the lives they lead?

6. How do the two settings differ—the town where Cleófilas grew up and the town where she lives with her husband? What larger meaning do you think Cisneros is driving at with the juxtaposition of "The town of gossips" with "The town of dust and despair" (para. 39)?

7. Explain the role La Gritona (Woman Hollering Creek) plays in the story. What does it symbolize? How does the meaning of the symbol change over the course of the story?

8. What can you infer about the characters of Felice and Graciela based on their phone conversation? How do they serve as foils to Cleófilas?

9. What references do you find to speaking up, staying silent, being heard or not heard, whispering, yelling, speaking in different languages, and telling stories? How do these descriptions work together to develop the theme of finding voice?

Suggestions for Writing

1. Reread the story and write a careful analysis of how Cisneros reveals the character of Cleófilas. Emphasize the devices (tone, syntax, point of view, figurative language) that you find most significant.

2. In a well-organized essay, explain how Cisneros's style reveals her attitude toward the characters in "Woman Hollering Creek."
3. Trace the evolution of Cleófilas through her acceptance of different roles: from daughter to wife to mother to whomever she has become at the end of the story, with laughter "gurgling out of her own throat, a long ribbon of laughter, like water."
4. Is this a story denouncing the patriarchal system that dominates the community on both sides of the border? Write an essay explaining your response. Cite specific text in "Woman Hollering Creek" to support your view.
5. Research the folktale of La Llorona, and write a paper or prepare a presentation in which you explore possible connections to "Woman Hollering Creek."
6. Choose one scene from the story and write it as a screenplay for a *telenovela*, with the exaggerated drama and romance of that genre.

The Lady with the Little Dog

ANTON CHEKHOV

TRANSLATED BY RICHARD PEVEAR AND LARISSA VOLOKHONSKY

Anton Chekhov (1860–1904) was born in Taganrog, Russia. He studied at the University of Moscow, graduated with a degree in medicine in 1884, and continued to practice as a doctor for most of his life. Having written a number of short stories while a student, he began a part-time career as a writer of comic one-act sketches, such as *The Bear* (1888) and *The Wedding* (1889). After three unsuccessful full-length plays—*Ivanov* (1887), *The Wood Demon* (1888), and *The Seagull* (1895)—Chekhov came close to abandoning the theater. This decision was reversed two years later, when the more talented company of the Moscow Art Theater performed *The Seagull*. Inspired, he rewrote *The Wood Demon* into *Uncle Vanya* (1899)—an immediate success—followed by *The Three Sisters* (1901) and *The Cherry Orchard* (1904). Chekhov's writing achieved a wide reputation throughout Europe and influenced many writers of the early twentieth century. "The Lady with the Little Dog" perfectly illustrates his realist style, which is characterized by an economy of words and a perceptive accuracy of description.

I

The talk was that a new face had appeared on the embankment: a lady with a little dog. Dmitri Dmitrich Gurov, who had already spent two weeks in Yalta and was used to it, also began to take an interest in new faces. Sitting in a pavilion at Vernet's, he saw a young woman, not very tall, blond, in a beret, walking along the embankment; behind her ran a white spitz.

And after that he met her several times a day in the town garden or in the square. She went strolling alone, in the same beret, with the white spitz; nobody knew who she was, and they called her simply "the lady with the little dog."

"If she's here with no husband or friends," Gurov reflected, "it wouldn't be a bad idea to make her acquaintance."

He was not yet forty, but he had a twelve-year-old daughter and two sons in school. He had married young, while still a second-year student, and now his wife seemed half again his age. She was a tall woman with dark eyebrows, erect, imposing, dignified, and a thinking person, as she called herself. She read a great deal, used the new orthography, called her husband not Dmitri but Dimitri, but he secretly considered her none too bright, narrow-minded, graceless, was afraid of her, and disliked being at home. He had begun to be unfaithful to her long ago, was unfaithful often, and, probably for that reason, almost always spoke ill of women, and when they were discussed in his presence, he would say of them:

"An inferior race!" 5

It seemed to him that he had been taught enough by bitter experience to call them anything he liked, and yet he could not have lived without the "inferior race"

634

even for two days. In the company of men he was bored, ill at ease, with them he was taciturn and cold, but when he was among women, he felt himself free and knew what to talk about with them and how to behave; and he was at ease even being silent with them. In his appearance, in his character, in his whole nature there was something attractive and elusive that disposed women towards him and enticed them; he knew that, and he himself was attracted to them by some force.

Repeated experience, and bitter experience indeed, had long since taught him that every intimacy, which in the beginning lends life such pleasant diversity and presents itself as a nice and light adventure, inevitably, with decent people — especially irresolute Muscovites, who are slow starters — grows into a major task, extremely complicated, and the situation finally becomes burdensome. But at every new meeting with an interesting woman, this experience somehow slipped from his memory, and he wanted to live, and everything seemed quite simple and amusing.

And so one time, towards evening, he was having dinner in the garden, and the lady in the beret came over unhurriedly to take the table next to his. Her expression, her walk, her dress, her hair told him that she belonged to decent society, was married, in Yalta for the first time, and alone, and that she was bored here . . . In the stories about the impurity of local morals there was much untruth, he despised them and knew that these stories were mostly invented by people who would eagerly have sinned themselves had they known how; but when the lady sat down at the next table, three steps away from him, he remembered those stories of easy conquests, of trips to the mountains, and the tempting thought of a quick, fleeting liaison, a romance with an unknown woman, of whose very name you are ignorant, suddenly took possession of him.

He gently called the spitz, and when the dog came over, he shook his finger at it. The spitz growled. Gurov shook his finger again.

The lady glanced at him and immediately lowered her eyes.   10

"He doesn't bite," she said and blushed.

"May I give him a bone?" and, when she nodded in the affirmative, he asked affably: "Have you been in Yalta long?"

"About five days."

"And I'm already dragging through my second week here."

They were silent for a while.   15

"The time passes quickly, and yet it's so boring here!" she said without looking at him.

"It's merely the accepted thing to say it's boring here. The ordinary man lives somewhere in his Belevo or Zhizdra and isn't bored, then he comes here: 'Ah, how boring! Ah, how dusty!' You'd think he came from Granada."

She laughed. Then they went on eating in silence, like strangers; but after dinner they walked off together — and a light, bantering conversation began, of free, contented people, who do not care where they go or what they talk about. They strolled and talked of how strange the light was on the sea; the water was of a lilac color, so soft and warm, and over it the moon cast a golden strip. They talked of how sultry it was after the hot day. Gurov told her he was a Muscovite, a philologist by education, but worked in a bank; had once been preparing to sing in an opera company, but had dropped it, owned two houses in Moscow . . . And from her he learned that she grew up in Petersburg, but was married in S., where she had now been living for two years, that she would be staying in Yalta for about a month, and that her husband might come to fetch her, because he also wanted to get some rest. She was quite unable to explain where her husband served—in the provincial administration or the zemstvo council—and she herself found that funny. And Gurov also learned that her name was Anna Sergeevna.

Afterwards, in his hotel room, he thought about her, that tomorrow she would probably meet him again. It had to be so. Going to bed, he recalled that still quite recently she had been a schoolgirl, had studied just as his daughter was studying now, recalled how much timorousness and angularity there was in her laughter, her conversation with a stranger—it must have been the first time in her life that she was alone in such a situation, when she was followed, looked at, and spoken to with only one secret purpose, which she could not fail to guess. He recalled her slender, weak neck, her beautiful gray eyes.

"There's something pathetic in her all the same," he thought and began to fall   20
asleep.

II

A week had passed since they became acquainted. It was Sunday. Inside it was stuffy, but outside the dust flew in whirls, hats blew off. They felt thirsty all day, and Gurov often stopped at the pavilion, offering Anna Sergeevna now a soft drink, now ice cream. There was no escape.

In the evening when it relented a little, they went to the jetty to watch the steamer come in. There were many strollers on the pier; they had come to meet people, they were holding bouquets. And here two particularities of the smartly dressed Yalta crowd distinctly struck one's eye: the elderly ladies were dressed like young ones, and there were many generals.

Owing to the roughness of the sea, the steamer arrived late, when the sun had already gone down, and it was a long time turning before it tied up. Anna Sergeevna looked at the ship and the passengers through her lorgnette, as if searching for acquaintances, and when she turned to Gurov, her eyes shone. She talked a lot, and her questions were abrupt, and she herself immediately forgot what she had asked; then she lost her lorgnette in the crowd.

The smartly dressed crowd was dispersing, the faces could no longer be seen, the wind had died down completely, and Gurov and Anna Sergeevna stood as if they were expecting someone else to get off the steamer. Anna Sergeevna was silent now and smelled the flowers, not looking at Gurov.

"The weather's improved towards evening," he said. "Where shall we go now?   25
Shall we take a drive somewhere?"

She made no answer.

Then he looked at her intently and suddenly embraced her and kissed her on the lips, and he was showered with the fragrance and moisture of the flowers, and at once looked around timorously—had anyone seen them?

"Let's go to your place . . ." he said softly.

And they both walked quickly.

Her hotel room was stuffy and smelled of the perfumes she had bought in a 30 Japanese shop. Gurov, looking at her now, thought: "What meetings there are in life!" From the past he had kept the memory of carefree, good-natured women, cheerful with love, grateful to him for their happiness, however brief; and of women—his wife, for example—who loved without sincerity, with superfluous talk, affectedly, with hysteria, with an expression as if it were not love, not passion, but something more significant; and of those two or three very beautiful, cold ones, in whose faces a predatory expression would suddenly flash, a stubborn wish to take, to snatch from life more than it could give, and these were women not in their first youth, capricious, unreasonable, domineering, unintelligent, and when Gurov cooled towards them, their beauty aroused hatred in him, and the lace of their underwear seemed to him like scales.

But here was all the timorousness and angularity of inexperienced youth, a feeling of awkwardness, and an impression of bewilderment, as if someone had suddenly knocked at the door. Anna Sergeevna, the "lady with the little dog," somehow took a special, very serious attitude towards what had happened, as if it were her fall—so it seemed, and that was strange and inopportune. Her features drooped and faded, and her long hair hung down sadly on both sides of her face, she sat pondering in a dejected pose, like the sinful woman in an old painting.

"It's not good," she said. "You'll be the first not to respect me now."

There was a watermelon on the table in the hotel room. Gurov cut himself a slice and unhurriedly began to eat it. At least half an hour passed in silence.

Anna Sergeevna was touching, she had about her a breath of the purity of a proper, naive, little-experienced woman; the solitary candle burning on the table barely lit up her face, but it was clear that her heart was uneasy.

"Why should I stop respecting you?" asked Gurov. "You don't know what you're 35 saying yourself."

"God forgive me!" she said, and her eyes filled with tears. "This is terrible."

"It's like you're justifying yourself."

"How can I justify myself? I'm a bad, low woman, I despise myself and am not even thinking of any justification. It's not my husband I've deceived, but my own self! And not only now, I've been deceiving myself for a long time. My husband may be an honest and good man, but he's a lackey! I don't know what he does there, how he serves, I only know that he's a lackey. I married him when I was twenty, I was tormented by curiosity, I wanted something better. I told myself there must be a different life. I wanted to live! To live and live . . . I was burning with curiosity . . . you won't understand it, but I swear to God that I couldn't control myself any longer, something was happening to me, I couldn't restrain myself, I told my husband I was ill and came here . . . And here I go about as if in a daze, as if I'm out of my mind . . . and now I've become a trite, trashy woman, whom anyone can despise."

Gurov was bored listening, he was annoyed by the naive tone, by this repentance, so unexpected and out of place; had it not been for the tears in her eyes, one might have thought she was joking or playing a role.

"I don't understand," he said softly, "what is it you want?"   40
She hid her face on his chest and pressed herself to him.

"Believe me, believe me, I beg you . . ." she said. "I love an honest, pure life, sin is vile to me, I myself don't know what I'm doing. Simple people say, 'The unclean one beguiled me.' And now I can say of myself that the unclean one has beguiled me."

"Enough, enough . . ." he muttered.

He looked into her fixed, frightened eyes, kissed her, spoke softly and tenderly, and she gradually calmed down, and her gaiety returned. They both began to laugh.

Later, when they went out, there was not a soul on the embankment, the town   45
with its cypresses looked completely dead, but the sea still beat noisily against the shore; one barge was rocking on the waves, and the lantern on it glimmered sleepily.

They found a cab and drove to Oreanda.

"I just learned your last name downstairs in the lobby: it was written on the board — von Dideritz," said Gurov. "Is your husband German?"

"No, his grandfather was German, I think, but he himself is Orthodox."

In Oreanda they sat on a bench not far from the church, looked down on the sea, and were silent. Yalta was barely visible through the morning mist, white clouds stood motionless on the mountaintops. The leaves of the trees did not stir, cicadas called, and the monotonous, dull noise of the sea, coming from below, spoke of the peace, of the eternal sleep that awaits us. So it had sounded below when neither Yalta nor Oreanda were there, so it sounded now and would go on sounding with the same dull indifference when we are no longer here. And in this constancy, in this utter indifference to the life and death of each of us, there perhaps lies hidden the pledge of our eternal salvation, the unceasing movement of life on earth, of unceasing perfection. Sitting beside the young woman, who looked so beautiful in the dawn, appeased and enchanted by the view of this magical décor — sea, mountains, clouds, the open sky — Gurov reflected that, essentially, if you thought of it, everything was beautiful in this world, everything except for what we ourselves think and do when we forget the higher goals of being and our human dignity.

Some man came up — it must have been a watchman — looked at them, and   50
went away. And this detail seemed such a mysterious thing, and also beautiful. The steamer from Feodosia could be seen approaching in the glow of the early dawn, its lights out.

"There's dew on the grass," said Anna Sergeevna after a silence.

"Yes. It's time to go home."

They went back to town.

After that they met on the embankment every noon, had lunch together, dined, strolled, admired the sea. She complained that she slept poorly and that her heart beat anxiously, kept asking the same questions, troubled now by jealousy, now by fear that he did not respect her enough. And often on the square or in the garden, when there was no one near them, he would suddenly draw her to him and kiss her passionately. Their complete idleness, those kisses in broad daylight, with a furtive look around and the fear that someone might see them, the heat, the smell of the sea, and the constant flashing before their eyes of idle, smartly dressed, well-fed people, seemed to transform him; he repeatedly told Anna Sergeevna how beautiful she was, and how seductive, was impatiently passionate, never left her side, while she often brooded and kept asking him to admit that he did not respect her, did not love her at all, and saw in her only a trite woman. Late almost every evening they went somewhere out of town, to Oreanda or the cascade; these outings were successful, their impressions each time were beautiful, majestic.

They were expecting her husband to arrive. But a letter came from him in which   55
he said that his eyes hurt and begged his wife to come home quickly. Anna Sergeevna began to hurry.

"It's good that I'm leaving," she said to Gurov. "It's fate itself."

She went by carriage, and he accompanied her. They drove for a whole day. When she had taken her seat in the express train and the second bell had rung, she said:

"Let me have one more look at you . . . One more look. There."

She did not cry, but was sad, as if ill, and her face trembled.

"I'll think of you . . . remember you," she said. "God be with you. Don't think ill   60
of me. We're saying good-bye forever, it must be so, because we should never have met. Well, God be with you."

The train left quickly, its lights soon disappeared, and a moment later the noise could no longer be heard, as if everything were conspiring on purpose to put a speedy end to this sweet oblivion, this madness. And, left alone on the platform and gazing into the dark distance, Gurov listened to the chirring of the grasshoppers and the hum of the telegraph wires with a feeling as if he had just woken up. And he thought that now there was one more affair or adventure in his life, and it, too, was now over, and all that was left was the memory . . . He was touched, saddened, and felt some slight remorse; this young woman whom he was never to see again had not been happy with him; he had been affectionate with her, and sincere, but all the same, in his treatment of her, in his tone and caresses, there had been a slight shade of mockery, the somewhat coarse arrogance of a happy man, who was, moreover, almost twice her age. She had all the while called him kind, extraordinary, lofty; obviously, he had appeared to her not as he was in reality, and therefore he had involuntarily deceived her . . .

Here at the station there was already a breath of autumn, the wind was cool.

"It's time I headed north, too," thought Gurov, leaving the platform. "High time!"

III

At home in Moscow everything was already wintry, the stoves were heated, and in the morning, when the children were getting ready for school and drinking their tea, it was dark, and the nanny would light a lamp for a short time. The frosts had already set in. When the first snow falls, on the first day of riding in sleighs, it is pleasant to see the white ground, the white roofs; one's breath feels soft and pleasant, and in those moments one remembers one's youth. The old lindens and birches, white with hoarfrost, have a good-natured look, they are nearer one's heart than cypresses and palms, and near them one no longer wants to think of mountains and the sea.

Gurov was a Muscovite. He returned to Moscow on a fine, frosty day, and when he put on his fur coat and warm gloves and strolled down Petrovka, and when on Saturday evening he heard the bells ringing, his recent trip and the places he had visited lost all their charm for him. He gradually became immersed in Moscow life, now greedily read three newspapers a day and said that he never read the Moscow newspapers on principle. He was drawn to restaurants, clubs, to dinner parties, celebrations, and felt flattered that he had famous lawyers and actors among his clients, and that at the Doctors' Club he played cards with a professor. He could eat a whole portion of selyanka from the pan . . . 65

A month would pass and Anna Sergeevna, as it seemed to him, would be covered by mist in his memory and would only appear to him in dreams with a touching smile, as other women did. But more than a month passed, deep winter came, and yet everything was as clear in his memory as if he had parted with Anna Sergeevna only the day before. And the memories burned brighter and brighter. Whether from the voices of his children doing their homework, which reached him in his study in the evening quiet, or from hearing a romance, or an organ in a restaurant, or the blizzard howling in the chimney, everything would suddenly rise up in his memory: what had happened on the jetty, and the early morning with mist on the mountains, and the steamer from Feodosia, and the kisses. He would pace the room for a long time, and remember, and smile, and then his memories would turn to reveries, and in his imagination the past would mingle with what was still to be. Anna Sergeevna was not a dream, she followed him everywhere like a shadow and watched him. Closing his eyes, he saw her as if alive, and she seemed younger, more beautiful, more tender than she was; and he also seemed better to himself than he had been then, in Yalta. In the evenings she gazed at him from the bookcase, the fireplace, the corner, he could hear her breathing, the gentle rustle of her skirts. In the street he followed women with his eyes, looking for one who resembled her . . .

And he was tormented now by a strong desire to tell someone his memories. But at home it was impossible to talk of his love, and away from home there was no one to talk with. Certainly not among his tenants nor at the bank. And what was there to say? Had he been in love then? Was there anything beautiful, poetic, or instructive, or merely interesting, in his relations with Anna Sergeevna? And he found himself speaking vaguely of love, of women, and no one could guess what it was about, and only his wife raised her dark eyebrows and said:

"You know, Dimitri, the role of fop doesn't suit you at all."

One night, as he was leaving the Doctors' Club together with his partner, an official, he could not help himself and said:

"If you only knew what a charming woman I met in Yalta!" 70

The official got into a sleigh and drove off, but suddenly turned around and called out:

"Dmitri Dmitrich!"

"What?"

"You were right earlier: the sturgeon was a bit off!"

Those words, so very ordinary, for some reason suddenly made Gurov indignant, 75
struck him as humiliating, impure. Such savage manners, such faces! These senseless
nights, and such uninteresting, unremarkable days! Frenzied card-playing, gluttony,
drunkenness, constant talk about the same thing. Useless matters and conversations
about the same thing took for their share the best part of one's time, the best of one's
powers, and what was left in the end was some sort of curtailed, wingless life, some
sort of nonsense, and it was impossible to get away or flee, as if you were sitting in a
madhouse or a prison camp!

Gurov did not sleep all night and felt indignant, and as a result had a headache
all the next day. And the following nights he slept poorly, sitting up in bed all the time
and thinking, or pacing up and down. He was sick of the children, sick of the bank,
did not want to go anywhere or talk about anything.

In December, during the holidays, he got ready to travel and told his wife he was
leaving for Petersburg to solicit for a certain young man—and went to S. Why? He
did not know very well himself. He wanted to see Anna Sergeevna and talk with her,
to arrange a meeting, if he could.

He arrived at S. in the morning and took the best room in the hotel, where the
whole floor was covered with gray army flannel and there was an inkstand on the
table, gray with dust, with a horseback rider, who held his hat in his raised hand,
but whose head was broken off. The hall porter gave him the necessary information:
von Dideritz lives in his own house on Staro-Goncharnaya Street, not far from the
hotel; he has a good life, is wealthy, keeps his own horses, everybody in town knows
him. The porter pronounced it "Dridiritz."

Gurov walked unhurriedly to Staro-Goncharnaya Street, found the house. Just
opposite the house stretched a fence, long, gray, with spikes.

"You could flee from such a fence," thought Gurov, looking now at the windows, 80
now at the fence.

He reflected: today was not a workday, and the husband was probably at home.
And anyhow it would be tactless to go in and cause embarrassment. If he sent a message, it might fall into the husband's hands, and that would ruin everything. It would
be best to trust to chance. And he kept pacing up and down the street and near the
fence and waited for his chance. He saw a beggar go in the gates and saw the dogs
attack him, then, an hour later, he heard someone playing a piano, and the sounds
reached him faintly, indistinctly. It must have been Anna Sergeevna playing. The
front door suddenly opened and some old woman came out, the familiar white spitz
running after her. Gurov wanted to call the dog, but his heart suddenly throbbed, and
in his excitement he was unable to remember the spitz's name.

He paced up and down, and hated the gray fence more and more, and now he
thought with vexation that Anna Sergeevna had forgotten him, and was perhaps
amusing herself with another man, and that that was so natural in the situation of
a young woman who had to look at this cursed fence from morning till evening. He
went back to his hotel room and sat on the sofa for a long time, not knowing what
to do, then had dinner, then took a long nap.

"How stupid and upsetting this all is," he thought, when he woke up and looked at the dark windows: it was already evening. "So I've had my sleep. Now what am I to do for the night?"

He sat on the bed, which was covered with a cheap, gray, hospital-like blanket, and taunted himself in vexation:

"Here's the lady with the little dog for you . . . Here's an adventure for you . . . Yes, here you sit." 85

That morning, at the train station, a poster with very big lettering had caught his eye: it was the opening night of *The Geisha*. He remembered it and went to the theater.

"It's very likely that she goes to opening nights," he thought.

The theater was full. And here, too, as in all provincial theaters generally, a haze hung over the chandeliers, the gallery stirred noisily; the local dandies stood in the front row before the performance started, their hands behind their backs; and here, too, in the governor's box, the governor's daughter sat in front, wearing a boa, while the governor himself modestly hid behind the portière, and only his hands could be seen; the curtain swayed, the orchestra spent a long time tuning up. All the while the public came in and took their seats, Gurov kept searching greedily with his eyes.

Anna Sergeevna came in. She sat in the third row, and when Gurov looked at her, his heart was wrung, and he realized clearly that there was now no person closer, dearer, or more important for him in the whole world; this small woman, lost in the provincial crowd, not remarkable for anything, with a vulgar lorgnette in her hand, now filled his whole life, was his grief, his joy, the only happiness he now wished for himself; and to the sounds of the bad orchestra, with its trashy local violins, he thought how beautiful she was. He thought and dreamed.

A man came in with Anna Sergeevna and sat down next to her, a young man 90 with little side-whiskers, very tall, stooping; he nodded his head at every step, and it seemed he was perpetually bowing. This was probably her husband, whom she, in an outburst of bitter feeling that time in Yalta, had called a lackey. And indeed, in his long figure, his side-whiskers, his little bald spot, there was something of lackeyish modesty; he had a sweet smile, and the badge of some learned society gleamed in his buttonhole, like the badge of a lackey.

During the first intermission the husband went to smoke; she remained in her seat. Gurov, who was also sitting in the stalls, went up to her and said in a trembling voice and with a forced smile:

"How do you do?"

She looked at him and paled, then looked again in horror, not believing her eyes, and tightly clutched her fan and lorgnette in her hand, obviously struggling with herself to keep from fainting. Both were silent. She sat, he stood, alarmed at her confusion, not venturing to sit down next to her. The tuning-up violins and flutes sang out, it suddenly became frightening, it seemed that people were gazing at them from all the boxes. But then she got up and quickly walked to the exit, he followed her, and they both went confusedly through corridors and stairways, going up, then down, and the uniforms of the courts, the schools, and the imperial estates flashed before them, all with badges; ladies flashed by, fur coats on hangers, a drafty wind blew, drenching them with the smell of cigar stubs. And Gurov, whose heart was pounding, thought: "Oh, Lord! Why these people, this orchestra . . ."

And just then he suddenly recalled how, at the station in the evening after he had seen Anna Sergeevna off, he had said to himself that everything was over and they would never see each other again. But how far it still was from being over!

On a narrow, dark stairway with the sign "To the Amphitheater," she stopped.   95

"How you frightened me!" she said, breathing heavily, still pale, stunned. "Oh, how you frightened me! I'm barely alive. Why did you come? Why?"

"But understand, Anna, understand . . ." he said in a low voice, hurrying. "I beg you to understand . . ."

She looked at him with fear, with entreaty, with love, looked at him intently, the better to keep his features in her memory.

"I've been suffering so!" she went on, not listening to him. "I think only of you all the time, I've lived by my thoughts of you. And I've tried to forget, to forget, but why, why did you come?"

Further up, on the landing, two high-school boys were smoking and looking   100
down, but Gurov did not care, he drew Anna Sergeevna to him and began kissing her face, her cheeks, her hands.

"What are you doing, what are you doing!" she repeated in horror, pushing him away from her. "We've both lost our minds. Leave today, leave at once . . . I adjure you by all that's holy, I implore you . . . Somebody's coming!"

Someone was climbing the stairs.

"You must leave . . ." Anna Sergeevna went on in a whisper. "Do you hear, Dmitri Dmitrich? I'll come to you in Moscow. I've never been happy, I'm unhappy now, and I'll never, never be happy, never! Don't make me suffer still more! I swear I'll come to Moscow. But we must part now! My dear one, my good one, my darling, we must part!"

She pressed his hand and quickly began going downstairs, turning back to look at him, and it was clear from her eyes that she was indeed not happy . . . Gurov stood for a little while, listened, then, when everything was quiet, found his coat and left the theater.

IV

And Anna Sergeevna began coming to see him in Moscow. Once every two or   105
three months she left S., and told her husband she was going to consult a professor about her female disorder — and her husband did and did not believe her. Arriving in Moscow, she stayed at the Slavyansky Bazaar and at once sent a man in a red hat to Gurov. Gurov came to see her, and nobody in Moscow knew of it.

Once he was going to see her in that way on a winter morning (the messenger had come the previous evening but had not found him in). With him was his daughter, whom he wanted to see off to school, which was on the way. Big, wet snow was falling.

"It's now three degrees above freezing, and yet it's snowing," Gurov said to his daughter. "But it's warm only near the surface of the earth, while in the upper layers of the atmosphere the temperature is quite different."

"And why is there no thunder in winter, papa?"

He explained that, too. He spoke and thought that here he was going to a rendezvous, and not a single soul knew of it or probably would ever know. He had two lives: an apparent one, seen and known by all who needed it, filled with conventional truth and conventional deceit, which perfectly resembled the lives of his acquaintances and friends, and another that went on in secret. And by some strange coincidence, perhaps an accidental one, everything that he found important, interesting, necessary, in which he was sincere and did not deceive himself, which constituted the core of his life, occurred in secret from others, while everything that made up his lie, his shell, in which he hid in order to conceal the truth—for instance, his work at the bank, his arguments at the club, his "inferior race," his attending official celebrations with his wife—all this was in full view. And he judged others by himself, did not believe what he saw, and always supposed that every man led his own real and very interesting life under the cover of secrecy, as under the cover of night. Every personal existence was upheld by a secret, and it was perhaps partly for that reason that every cultivated man took such anxious care that his personal secret should be respected.

After taking his daughter to school, Gurov went to the Slavyansky Bazaar. He   110
took his fur coat off downstairs, went up, and knocked softly at the door. Anna Sergeevna, wearing his favorite gray dress, tired from the trip and the expectation, had been waiting for him since the previous evening; she was pale, looked at him and did not smile, and he had barely come in when she was already leaning on his chest. Their kiss was long, lingering, as if they had not seen each other for two years.

"Well, how is your life there?" he asked. "What's new?"

"Wait, I'll tell you . . . I can't."

She could not speak because she was crying. She turned away from him and pressed a handkerchief to her eyes.

"Well, let her cry a little, and meanwhile I'll sit down," he thought, and sat down in an armchair.

Then he rang and ordered tea; and then, while he drank tea, she went on stand-   115
ing with her face turned to the window . . . She was crying from anxiety, from a sorrowful awareness that their life had turned out so sadly; they only saw each other in secret, they hid from people like thieves! Was their life not broken?

"Well, stop now," he said.

For him it was obvious that this love of theirs would not end soon, that there was no knowing when. Anna Sergeevna's attachment to him grew ever stronger, she adored him, and it would have been unthinkable to tell her that it all really had to end at some point; and she would not have believed it.

He went up to her and took her by the shoulders to caress her, to make a joke, and at that moment he saw himself in the mirror.

His head was beginning to turn gray. And it seemed strange to him that he had aged so much in those last years, had lost so much of his good looks. The shoulders on which his hands lay were warm and trembled. He felt compassion for this life, still so warm and beautiful, but probably already near the point where it would begin to fade and wither, like his own life. Why did she love him so? Women had always taken him to be other than he was, and they had loved in him, not himself, but a man their imagination had created, whom they had greedily sought all their lives; and then, when they had noticed their mistake, they had still loved him. And not one of them had been happy with him. Time passed, he met women, became intimate, parted, but not once did he love; there was anything else, but not love.

And only now, when his head was gray, had he really fallen in love as one ought to — for the first time in his life. 120

He and Anna Sergeevna loved each other like very close, dear people, like husband and wife, like tender friends; it seemed to them that fate itself had destined them for each other, and they could not understand why he had a wife and she a husband; and it was as if they were two birds of passage, a male and a female, who had been caught and forced to live in separate cages. They had forgiven each other the things they were ashamed of in the past, they forgave everything in the present, and they felt that this love of theirs had changed them both.

Formerly, in sad moments, he had calmed himself with all sorts of arguments, whatever had come into his head, but now he did not care about any arguments, he felt deep compassion, he wanted to be sincere, tender . . .

"Stop, my good one," he said, "you've had your cry — and enough . . . Let's talk now, we'll think up something."

Then they had a long discussion, talked about how to rid themselves of the need for hiding, for deception, for living in different towns and not seeing each other for long periods. How could they free themselves from these unbearable bonds?

"How? How?" he asked, clutching his head. "How?" 125

And it seemed that, just a little more — and the solution would be found, and then a new, beautiful life would begin; and it was clear to both of them that the end was still far, far off, and that the most complicated and difficult part was just beginning.

[1899]

Exploring the Text

1. Chekhov chooses to tell this story from the perspective of a third-person objective view. By the story's end, we have a fairly sympathetic view of Gurov and Anna's relationship, but does Chekhov condone what can only be called adultery? How might the historical context of a society in which divorce was unheard of influence Chekhov's perspective?

2. Why is it important that Anna's husband is a "lackey"? What does this suggest about her attitude toward him?

3. Early in Anna and Gurov's relationship, the narrator interrupts dialogue and action with a paragraph that is much more abstract (para. 49). What is the

importance of this passage, and why is it placed at this point in the story? How might it be related to Gurov's earlier thought that "he wanted to live" (para. 7) and Anna's cry, "I wanted to live!" (para. 38)?

4. This story begins in the resort town of Yalta, then moves to Moscow, to Anna's town of S., and back to Moscow. Of what importance are the multiple settings?

5. What inferences do you draw from Anna's declaration "And now I can say of myself that the unclean one has beguiled me" (para. 42)? What does this reveal about how she feels about herself? What does it indicate about her feelings toward Gurov at this point in the story?

6. How do you interpret the images in paragraph 75? What does the use of figurative language suggest about Gurov's state of mind? How do the syntax and diction in this passage contribute to its effect?

7. What is meant by the distinction between "two lives: an apparent one, seen and known by all . . . and another that went on in secret" (para. 109)? Why is this contrast significant for Gurov? Is it also significant for Anna?

8. How does Gurov's relationship with Anna alter his views about love and relationships? Do you think they are forever changed? Is theirs "true love"? Why or why not?

9. Compare and contrast paragraphs 4 and 119, which describe Gurov. What significance does the juxtaposition of the two emphasize?

10. At the end of *Casablanca*—the classic film that many consider the most romantic of all time—the hero Rick says to his beloved Ilsa, as he puts her on a plane with her husband, "It doesn't take much to see that the problems of three little people don't amount to a hill of beans in this crazy world." In the face of larger issues (in that case, World War II), the love between individuals seems trivial. What do you think Chekhov would say to that? Could the same be said of Gurov and Anna's relationship?

Bliss

KATHERINE MANSFIELD

Katherine Mansfield (1888–1923) was born in New Zealand. Never the favorite child of her parents, she considered herself "an ugly duckling" and saw her family as being "for trade," while she was "for art." She was educated in Wellington at the exclusive Miss Swainson's school, and in London, where she attended Queen's College. Mansfield's early stories began to appear in the magazine *New Age* in 1910 and were published in the collection *In a German Pension* (1911). She collaborated in editing two literary magazines: *Rhythm* (with John Murry) and *Signature* (with D. H. Lawrence). After a period of traveling in Europe and sporadic writing, Mansfield published *Bliss and Other Stories* (1920) and *The Garden Party* (1922). In 1918, she married John Murry and, through him, became part of the Garsington set—the English literary group that included Ottoline

Morrell, D. H. Lawrence, Aldous Huxley, and Leonard and Virginia Woolf. Her celebrity was short lived. She was diagnosed with tuberculosis in 1919, and her final years were spent in search of specialist medical help and a climate that would ameliorate her condition. Her ability to paint a scene with economy and a deft touch, combined with a perceptive eye for tension beneath a calm surface, is revealed in "Bliss."

Although Bertha Young was thirty she still had moments like this when she wanted to run instead of walk, to take dancing steps on and off the pavement, to bowl a hoop, to throw something up in the air and catch it again, or to stand still and laugh at—nothing—at nothing, simply.

What can you do if you are thirty and, turning the corner of your own street, you are overcome, suddenly, by a feeling of bliss—absolute bliss!—as though you'd suddenly swallowed a bright piece of that late afternoon sun and it burned in your bosom, sending out a little shower of sparks into every particle, into every finger and toe? . . .

Oh, is there no way you can express it without being "drunk and disorderly"? How idiotic civilization is! Why be given a body if you have to keep it shut up in a case like a rare, rare fiddle?

"No, that about the fiddle is not quite what I mean," she thought, running up the steps and feeling in her bag for the key—she's forgotten it, as usual—and rattling the letter-box. "It's not what I mean, because—Thank you, Mary"—she went into the hall. "Is nurse back?"

"Yes, M'm."

"And has the fruit come?"

"Yes, M'm. Everything's come."

"Bring the fruit up to the dining-room, will you? I'll arrange it before I go upstairs."

It was dusky in the dining-room and quite chilly. But all the same Bertha threw off her coat; she could not bear the tight clasp of it another moment, and the cold air fell on her arms.

But in her bosom there was still that bright glowing place—that shower of little sparks coming from it. It was almost unbearable. She hardly dared to breathe for fear of fanning it higher, and yet she breathed deeply, deeply. She hardly dared to look into the cold mirror—but she did look, and it gave her back a woman, radiant, with smiling, trembling lips, with big, dark eyes and an air of listening, waiting for something . . . divine to happen . . . that she knew must happen . . . infallibly.

Mary brought in the fruit on a tray and with it a glass bowl, and a blue dish, very lovely, with a strange sheen on it as though it had been dipped in milk.

"Shall I turn on the light, M'm?"

"No, thank you. I can see quite well."

There were tangerines and apples stained with strawberry pink. Some yellow pears, smooth as silk, some white grapes covered with a silver bloom and a big cluster

of purple ones. These last she had bought to tone in with the new dining-room carpet. Yes, that did sound rather far-fetched and absurd, but it was really why she had
bought them. She had thought in the shop: "I must have some purple ones to bring
the carpet up to the table." And it had seemed quite sense at the time.

When she had finished with them and had made two pyramids of these bright   15
round shapes, she stood away from the table to get the effect—and it really was most
curious. For the dark table seemed to melt into the dusky light and the glass dish and
the blue bowl to float in the air. This, of course in her present mood, was so incredibly
beautiful. . . . She began to laugh.

"No, no. I'm getting hysterical." And she seized her bag and coat and ran upstairs
to the nursery.

Nurse sat at a low table giving Little B her supper after her bath. The baby had on
a white flannel gown and a blue woollen jacket, and her dark, fine hair was brushed
up into a funny little peak. She looked up when she saw her mother and began to
jump.

"Now, my lovey, eat it up like a good girl," said Nurse, setting her lips in a way that
Bertha knew, and that meant she had come into the nursery at another wrong moment.

"Has she been good, Nanny?"

"She's been a little sweet all the afternoon," whispered Nanny. "We went to the   20
park and I sat down on a chair and took her out of the pram and a big dog came
along and put his head on my knee and she clutched its ear, tugged it. Oh, you should
have seen her."

Bertha wanted to ask if it wasn't rather dangerous to let her clutch at a strange
dog's ear. But she did not dare to. She stood watching them, her hands by her side,
like the poor little girl in front of the rich little girl with the doll.

The baby looked up at her again, stared, and then smiled so charmingly that
Bertha couldn't help crying:

"Oh, Nanny, do let me finish giving her her supper while you put the bath things
away."

"Well, M'm, she oughtn't to be changed hands while she's eating," said Nanny,
still whispering. "It unsettles her; it's very likely to upset her."

How absurd it was. Why have a baby if it has to be kept—not in a case like a rare,   25
rare fiddle—but in another woman's arms?

"Oh, I must!" said she.

Very offended, Nanny handed her over.

"Now, don't excite her after her supper. You know you do, M'm. And I have such
a time with her after!"

Thank heaven! Nanny went out of the room with the bath towels.

"Now I've got you to myself, my little precious," said Bertha, as the baby leaned   30
against her.

She ate delightfully, holding up her lips for the spoon and then waving her
hands. Sometimes she wouldn't let the spoon go; and sometimes, just as Bertha had
filled it, she waved it away to the four winds.

When the soup was finished Bertha turned round to the fire.

"You're nice—you're very nice!" said she, kissing her warm baby. "I'm fond of you. I like you."

And, indeed, she loved Little B so much—her neck as she bent forward, her exquisite toes as they shone transparent in the firelight—that all her feeling of bliss came back again, and again she didn't know how to express it—what to do with it.

"You're wanted on the telephone," said Nanny, coming back in triumph and   35
seizing *her* Little B.

Down she flew. It was Harry.

"Oh, is that you, Ber? Look here. I'll be late. I'll take a taxi and come along as quickly as I can, but get dinner put back ten minutes—will you? All right?"

"Yes, perfectly. Oh, Harry!"

"Yes?"

What had she to say? She'd nothing to say. She only wanted to get in touch with   40
him for a moment. She couldn't absurdly cry: "Hasn't it been a divine day!"

"What is it?" rapped out the little voice.

"Nothing. *Entendu*," said Bertha, and hung up the receiver, thinking how more than idiotic civilization was.

They had people coming to dinner. The Norman Knights—a very sound couple—he was about to start a theater, and she was awfully keen on interior decoration, a young man, Eddie Warren, who had just published a little book of poems and whom everybody was asking to dine, and a "find" of Bertha's called Pearl Fulton. What Miss Fulton did, Bertha didn't know. They had met at the club and Bertha had fallen in love with her, as she always did fall in love with beautiful women who had something strange about them.

The provoking thing was that, though they had been about together and met a number of times and really talked, Bertha couldn't yet make her out. Up to a certain point Miss Fulton was rarely, wonderfully frank, but the certain point was there, and beyond that she would not go.

Was there anything beyond it? Harry said "No." Voted her dullish, and "cold   45
like all blond women, with a touch, perhaps, of anæmia of the brain." But Bertha wouldn't agree with him; not yet, at any rate.

"No, the way she has of sitting with her head a little on one side, and smiling, has something behind it, Harry, and I must find out what that something is."

"Most likely it's a good stomach," answered Harry.

He made a point of catching Bertha's heels with replies of that kind . . . "liver frozen, my dear girl," or "pure flatulence," or "kidney disease," . . . and so on. For some strange reason Bertha liked this, and almost admired it in him very much.

She went into the drawing-room and lighted the fire; then, picking up the cushions, one by one, that Mary had disposed so carefully, she threw them back on to the chairs and the couches. That made all the difference; the room came alive at once. As she was about to throw the last one she surprised herself by suddenly hugging it to her, passionately, passionately. But it did not put out the fire in her bosom. Oh, on the contrary!

The windows of the drawing-room opened on to a balcony overlooking the garden. At the far end, against the wall, there was a tall, slender pear tree in fullest, richest bloom; it stood perfect, as though becalmed against the jade-green sky. Bertha couldn't help feeling, even from this distance, that it had not a single bud or a faded petal. Down below, in the garden beds, the red and yellow tulips, heavy with flowers, seemed to lean upon the dusk. A grey cat, dragging its belly, crept across the lawn, and a black one, its shadow, trailed after. The sight of them, so intent and so quick, gave Bertha a curious shiver.

"What creepy things cats are!" she stammered, and she turned away from the window and began walking up and down. . . .

How strong the jonquils smelled in the warm room. Too strong? Oh, no. And yet, as though overcome, she flung down on a couch and pressed her hands to her eyes.

"I'm too happy—too happy!" she murmured.

And she seemed to see on her eyelids the lovely pear tree with its wide open blossoms as a symbol of her own life.

Really—really—she had everything. She was young. Harry and she were as much in love as ever, and they got on together splendidly and were really good pals. She had an adorable baby. They didn't have to worry about money. They had this absolutely satisfactory house and garden. And friends—modern, thrilling friends, writers and painters and poets or people keen on social questions—just the kind of friends they wanted. And then there were books, and there was music, and she had found a wonderful little dressmaker, and they were going abroad in the summer, and their new cook made the most superb omelettes. . . .

"I'm absurd! Absurd!" She sat up; but she felt quite dizzy, quite drunk. It must have been the spring.

Yes, it was the spring. Now she was so tired she could not drag herself upstairs to dress.

A white dress, a string of jade beads, green shoes and stockings. It wasn't intentional. She had thought of this scheme hours before she stood at the drawing-room window.

Her petals rushed softly into the hall, and she kissed Mrs. Norman Knight, who was taking off the most amusing orange coat with a procession of black monkeys round the hem and up the fronts.

". . . Why! Why! Why is the middle-class so stodgy—so utterly without a sense of humor! My dear, it's only a fluke that I am here at all—Norman being the protective fluke. For my darling monkeys so upset the train that it rose to a man and simply ate me with its eyes. Didn't laugh—wasn't amused—that I should have loved. No, just stared—and bored me through and through."

"But the cream of it was," said Norman, pressing a large tortoiseshell-rimmed monocle into his eye, "you don't mind me telling this, Face, do you?" (In their home and among their friends they called each other Face and Mug.) "The cream of it was when she, being full fed, turned to the woman beside her and said: 'Haven't you ever seen a monkey before?'"

"Oh, yes!" Mrs. Norman Knight joined in the laughter. "Wasn't that too absolutely creamy?"

And a funnier thing still was that now her coat was off she did look like a very intelligent monkey—who had even made that yellow silk dress out of scraped banana skins. And her amber earrings; they were like little dangling nuts.

"This is a sad, sad fall!" said Mug, pausing in front of Little B's perambulator. "When the perambulator comes into the hall——" and he waved the rest of the quotation away.

The bell rang. It was lean, pale Eddie Warren (as usual) in a state of acute   65
distress.

"It *is* the right house, *isn't* it?" he pleaded.

"Oh, I think so—I hope so," said Bertha brightly.

"I have had such a *dreadful* experience with a taxi-man; he was *most* sinister. I couldn't get him to *stop*. The *more* I knocked and called the *faster* he went. And *in* the moonlight this *bizarre* figure with the *flattened* head *crouching* over the *lit-tle* wheel. . . ."

He shuddered, taking off an immense white silk scarf. Bertha noticed that his socks were white, too—most charming.

"But how dreadful!" she cried.   70

"Yes, it really was," said Eddie, following her into the drawing-room. "I saw myself *driving* through Eternity in a *timeless* taxi."

He knew the Norman Knights. In fact, he was going to write a play for N. K. when the theater scheme came off.

"Well, Warren, how's the play?" said Norman Knight, dropping his monocle and giving his eye a moment in which to rise to the surface before it was screwed down again.

And Mrs. Norman Knight: "Oh, Mr. Warren, what happy socks!"

"I *am* so glad you like them," said he, staring at his feet. "They seem to have got   75
so *much* whiter since the moon rose." And he turned his lean sorrowful young face to Bertha. "There *is* a moon, you know."

She wanted to cry: "I am sure there is—often—often!"

He really was a most attractive person. But so was Face, crouched before the fire in her banana skins, and so was Mug, smoking a cigarette and saying as he flicked the ash: "Why doth the bridegroom tarry?"

"There he is, now."

Bang went the front door open and shut. Harry shouted: "Hullo, you people. Down in five minutes." And they heard him swarm up the stairs. Bertha couldn't help smiling; she knew how he loved doing things at high pressure. What, after all, did an extra five minutes matter? But he would pretend to himself that they mattered beyond measure. And then he would make a great point of coming into the drawing-room, extravagantly cool and collected.

Harry had such a zest for life. Oh, how she appreciated it in him. And his passion   80
for fighting—for seeking in everything that came up against him another test of his power and of his courage—that, too, she understood. Even when it made him just

occasionally, to other people, who didn't know him well, a little ridiculous perhaps. . . . For there were moments when he rushed into battle where no battle was. . . . She talked and laughed and positively forgot until he had come in (just as she had imagined) that Pearl Fulton had not turned up.

"I wonder if Miss Fulton has forgotten?"

"I expect so," said Harry. "Is she on the 'phone?"

"Ah! There's a taxi, now." And Bertha smiled with that little air of proprietorship that she always assumed while her women finds were new and mysterious. "She lives in taxis."

"She'll run to fat if she does," said Harry coolly, ringing the bell for dinner. "Frightful danger for blond women."

"Harry—don't," warned Bertha, laughing up at him.   85

Came another tiny moment, while they waited, laughing and talking, just a trifle too much at their ease, a trifle too unaware. And then Miss Fulton, all in silver, with a silver fillet binding her pale blond hair, came in smiling, her head a little on one side.

"Am I late?"

"No, not at all," said Bertha. "Come along." And she took her arm and they moved into the dining-room.

What was there in the touch of that cool arm that could fan—fan—start blazing—blazing—the fire of bliss that Bertha did not know what to do with?

Miss Fulton did not look at her; but then she seldom did look at people directly.   90
Her heavy eyelids lay upon her eyes and the strange half smile came and went upon her lips as though she lived by listening rather than seeing. But Bertha knew, suddenly, as if the longest, most intimate look had passed between them—as if they had said to each other: "You, too?"—that Pearl Fulton, stirring the beautiful red soup in the grey plate, was feeling just what she was feeling.

And the others? Face and Mug, Eddie and Harry, their spoons rising and falling—dabbing their lips with their napkins, crumbling bread, fiddling with the forks and glasses and talking.

"I met her at the Alpha shore—the weirdest little person. She'd not only cut off her hair, but she seemed to have taken a dreadfully good snip off her legs and arms and her neck and her poor little nose as well."

"Isn't she very *liée* with Michael Oat?"

"The man who wrote *Love in False Teeth*?"

"He wants to write a play for me. One act. One man. Decides to commit suicide.   95
Gives all the reasons why he should and why he shouldn't. And just as he has made up his mind either to do it or not to do it—curtain. Not half a bad idea."

"What's he going to call it—'Stomach Trouble'?"

"I *think* I've come across the *same* idea in a lit-tle French review, *quite* unknown in England."

No, they didn't share it. They were dears—dears—and she loved having them there, at her table, and giving them delicious food and wine. In fact, she longed to tell them how delightful they were, and what a decorative group they made, how they seemed to set one another off and how they reminded her of a play by Chekhov!

Harry was enjoying his dinner. It was part of his—well, not his nature, exactly, and certainly not his pose—his—something or other—to talk about food and to glory in his "shameless passion for the white flesh of the lobster" and "the green of pistachio ices—green and cold like the eyelids of Egyptian dancers."

When he looked up at her and said: "Bertha, this is a very admirable *soufflée!*"   100 she almost could have wept with child-like pleasure.

Oh, why did she feel so tender toward the whole world tonight? Everything was good—was right. All that happened seemed to fill again her brimming cup of bliss.

And still, in the back of her mind, there was the pear tree. It would be silver now, in the light of poor dear Eddie's moon, silver as Miss Fulton, who sat there turning a tangerine in her slender fingers that were so pale a light seemed to come from them.

What she simply couldn't make out—what was miraculous—was how she should have guessed Miss Fulton's mood so exactly and so instantly. For she never doubted for a moment that she was right, and yet what had she to go on? Less than nothing.

"I believe this does happen very, very rarely between women. Never between men," thought Bertha. "But while I am making coffee in the drawing-room perhaps she will 'give a sign.'"

What she meant by that she did not know, and what would happen after that   105 she could not imagine.

While she thought like this she saw herself talking and laughing. She had to talk because of her desire to laugh.

"I must laugh or die."

But when she noticed Face's funny little habit of tucking something down the front of her bodice—as if she kept a tiny, secret hoard of nuts there, too—Bertha *had to dig her nails* into her hands—so as not to laugh too much.

It was over at last. And: "Come and see my new coffee machine," said Bertha.

"We only have a new coffee machine once a fortnight," said Harry. Face took her   110 arm this time; Miss Fulton bent her head and followed after.

The fire had died down in the drawing-room to a red, flickering "nest of baby phoenixes," said Face.

"Don't turn up the light for a moment. It is so lovely." And down she crouched by the fire again. She was always cold . . . "without her little red flannel jacket, of course," thought Bertha.

At that moment Miss Fulton "gave the sign."

"Have you a garden?" said the cool, sleepy voice.

This was so exquisite on her part that all Bertha could do was to obey. She   115 crossed the room, pulled the curtains apart, and opened those long windows.

"There!" she breathed.

And the two women stood side by side looking at the slender, flowering tree. Although it was so still it seemed, like the flame of a candle, to stretch up, to point, to quiver in the bright air, to grow taller and taller as they gazed—almost to touch the rim of the round, silver moon.

How long did they stand there? Both, as it were, caught in that circle of unearthly light, understanding each other perfectly, creatures of another world, and wondering what they were to do in this one with all this blissful treasure that burned in their bosoms and dropped, in silver flowers, from their hair and hands?

Forever—for a moment? And did Miss Fulton murmur: "Yes. Just *that*." Or did Bertha dream it?

Then the light was snapped on and Face made the coffee and Harry said: "My dear Mrs. Knight, don't ask me about my baby. I never see her. I shan't feel the slightest interest in her until she has a lover," and Mug took his eye out of the conservatory for a moment and then put it under glass again and Eddie Warren drank his coffee and set down the cup with a face of anguish as though he had drunk and seen the spider. 120

"What I want to do is to give the young men a show. I believe London is simply teeming with first-chop, unwritten plays. What I want to say to 'em is: 'Here's the theater. Fire ahead.'"

"You know, my dear, I am going to decorate a room for the Jacob Nathans. Oh, I am so tempted to do a fried-fish scheme, with the backs of the chairs shaped like frying pans and lovely chip potatoes embroidered all over the curtains."

"The trouble with our young writing men is that they are still too romantic. You can't put out to sea without being seasick and wanting a basin. Well, why won't they have the courage of those basins?"

"A *dreadful* poem about a *girl* who was *violated* by a beggar *without* a nose in a lit-tle wood. . . ."

Miss Fulton sank into the lowest, deepest chair and Harry handed round the cigarettes. 125

From the way he stood in front of her shaking the silver box and saying abruptly: "Egyptian? Turkish? Virginian? They're all mixed up," Bertha realized that she not only bored him; he really disliked her. And she decided from the way Miss Fulton said: "No, thank you, I won't smoke," that she felt it, too, and was hurt.

"Oh, Harry, don't dislike her. You are quite wrong about her. She's wonderful, wonderful. And, besides, how can you feel so differently about someone who means so much to me? I shall try to tell you when we are in bed tonight what has been happening. What she and I have shared."

At those last words something strange and almost terrifying darted into Bertha's mind. And this something blind and smiling whispered to her: "Soon these people will go. The house will be quiet—quiet. The lights will be out. And you and he will be alone together in the dark room—the warm bed. . . ."

She jumped up from her chair and ran over to the piano.

"What a pity someone does not play!" she cried. "What a pity somebody does not play." 130

For the first time in her life Bertha Young desired her husband.

Oh, she loved him—she'd been in love with him, of course, in every other way, but just not in that way. And, equally, of course, she'd understood that he was different. They'd discussed it so often. It had worried her dreadfully at first to find that she was so cold, but after a time it had not seemed to matter. They were so frank with each other—such good pals. That was the best of being modern.

But now—ardently! ardently! The word ached in her ardent body! Was this what that feeling of bliss had been leading up to? But then—then—

"My dear," said Mrs. Norman Knight, "you know our shame. We are the victims of time and train. We live in Hampstead. It's been so nice."

"I'll come with you into the hall," said Bertha. "I love having you. But you must not miss the last train. That's so awful, isn't it?" 135

"Have a whisky, Knight, before you go?" called Harry.

"No, thanks, old chap."

Bertha squeezed his hand for that as she shook it.

"Good night, good-bye," she cried from the top step, feeling that this self of hers was taking leave of them forever.

When she got back into the drawing-room the others were on the move. 140

". . . Then you can come part of the way in my taxi."

"I shall be *so* thankful *not* to have to face *another* drive *alone* after my *dreadful* experience."

"You can get a taxi at the rank just at the end of the street. You won't have to walk more than a few yards."

"That's comfort. I'll go and put on my coat."

Miss Fulton moved toward the hall and Bertha was following when Harry almost pushed past. 145

"Let me help you."

Bertha knew that he was repenting his rudeness—she let him go. What a boy he was in some ways—so impulsive—so simple.

And Eddie and she were left by the fire.

"I *wonder* if you have seen Bilks' *new* poem called *Table d'Hôte*," said Eddie softly. "It's *so* wonderful. In the last Anthology. Have you got a copy? I'd *so* like to *show* it to you. It begins with an *incredibly* beautiful line: 'Why Must it Always be Tomato Soup?'"

"Yes," said Bertha. And she moved noiselessly to a table opposite the drawing-room door and Eddie glided noiselessly after her. She picked up the little book and gave it to him; they had not made a sound. 150

While he looked it up she turned her head toward the hall. And she saw . . . Harry with Miss Fulton's coat in his arms and Miss Fulton with her back turned to him and her head bent. He tossed the coat away, put his hands on her shoulders, and turned her violently to him. His lips said: "I adore you," and Miss Fulton laid her moonbeam fingers on his cheeks and smiled her sleepy smile. Harry's nostrils quivered; his lips curled back in a hideous grin while he whispered: "Tomorrow," and with her eyelids Miss Fulton said: "Yes."

"Here it is," said Eddie. "'Why Must it Always be Tomato Soup?' It's so *deeply* true, don't you feel? Tomato soup is so *dreadfully* eternal."

"If you prefer," said Harry's voice, very loud, from the hall, "I can 'phone you a cab to come to the door."

"Oh, no. It's not necessary," said Miss Fulton, and she came up to Bertha and gave her the slender fingers to hold.

"Good-bye. Thank you so much."   155

"Good-bye," said Bertha.

Miss Fulton held her hand a moment longer.

"Your lovely pear tree!" she murmured.

And then she was gone, with Eddie following, like the black cat following the grey cat.

"I'll shut up shop," said Harry, extravagantly cool and collected.   160

"Your lovely pear tree — pear tree — pear tree!"

Bertha simply ran over to the long windows.

"Oh, what is going to happen now?" she cried.

But the pear tree was as lovely as ever and as full of flower and as still.

[1920]

Exploring the Text

1. What are the denotations and connotations of the word *bliss*? Why does Bertha admonish herself for "getting hysterical" (para. 16)? Is her bliss the same as the "zest for life" (para. 80) she ascribes to her husband?

2. What is your impression of Bertha from the opening section of the story? What holds her attention? Be on the lookout for conflicts and contradictions. What does she mean when she says, "Why be given a body if you have to keep it shut up in a case like a rare, rare fiddle" (para. 3)? Does that question undermine her professions of bliss?

3. How would you describe Bertha's relationship with her baby? her husband? her baby's nurse? What do these relationships reveal about Bertha's role within her family circle?

4. Reread the account of the dinner party. Look for details that offer insight into the relationships among these characters. What conclusions can you draw about these people and the society they represent?

5. How does the character of Pearl Fulton evolve? Does Mansfield depict her negatively? What qualities does Bertha note initially? When did you begin to suspect that Pearl and Harry were having an affair? Does Mansfield give us clues?

6. Trace the pear tree throughout the story. It is introduced in a simple description but eventually becomes important as a symbol; what does it symbolize? Also trace how the tree works as a structural marker in the story.

7. Do Bertha and Harry love each other? Consider the nature of their relationship, particularly her realization that she wants more intimacy (paras. 128–33). Use examples from the story to defend your response.

8. At the end of the story, Bertha cries, "Oh, what is going to happen now?" (para. 163). What do you think is going to happen? How does the final sentence — "But the pear tree was as lovely as ever and as full of flower and as still" — point the way

to an answer to what happens next? What effect does this kind of ending have on you as a reader?

9. One critic analyzes the theme of "Bliss" as follows: "While 'on the surface' the story outlines the happiness of this dainty, middle-class housewife, the author is surreptitiously interrogating the rigid nature of accepted male and female roles." What do you think she means? Explain why you agree or disagree with this interpretation.

A Rose for Emily

WILLIAM FAULKNER

William Faulkner (1897–1962) is considered one of the finest American writers of the twentieth century. Born in New Albany, Mississippi, Faulkner grew bored with education in his early teens, joining first the Canadian and then the British Royal Air Force during the First World War. Faulkner's writing is distinctly southern and often set in Jefferson, Mississippi. While living in New Orleans, Faulkner wrote his first novel, *Soldier's Pay* (1926). Over the next three years, he published *Mosquitoes* (1927) and *The Sound and the Fury* (1929), which established his reputation. The following decade saw Faulkner at his most prolific. *As I Lay Dying* (1930), *Sanctuary* (1931), and *Light in August* (1932), together with collections of poems and short stories, preceded publication of *Absalom, Absalom!* in 1936. During spells in Hollywood, he also established himself as a masterly screenwriter. In 1949, he was awarded the Nobel Prize for Literature. The story "A Rose for Emily" demonstrates Faulkner's uniquely subtle style and his ability to mingle truth with fiction.

I

When Miss Emily Grierson died, our whole town went to her funeral: the men through a sort of respectful affection for a fallen monument, the women mostly out of curiosity to see the inside of her house, which no one save an old manservant—a combined gardener and cook—had seen in at least ten years.

It was a big, squarish frame house that had once been white, decorated with cupolas and spires and scrolled balconies in the heavily lightsome style of the seventies, set on what had once been our most select street. But garages and cotton gins had encroached and obliterated even the august names of that neighborhood; only Miss Emily's house was left, lifting its stubborn and coquettish decay above the cotton wagons and the gasoline pumps—an eyesore among eyesores. And now Miss Emily had gone to join the representatives of those august names where they lay in the cedar-bemused cemetery among the ranked and anonymous graves of Union and Confederate soldiers who fell at the battle of Jefferson.

Alive, Miss Emily had been a tradition, a duty, and a care; a sort of hereditary obligation upon the town, dating from that day in 1894 when Colonel Sartoris, the mayor—he who fathered the edict that no Negro woman should appear on the streets without an apron—remitted her taxes, the dispensation dating from the death of her father on into perpetuity. Not that Miss Emily would have accepted charity. Colonel Sartoris invented an involved tale to the effect that Miss Emily's father had loaned money to the town, which the town, as a matter of business, preferred this way of repaying. Only a man of Colonel Sartoris' generation and thought could have invented it, and only a woman could have believed it.

When the next generation, with its more modern ideas, became mayors and aldermen, this arrangement created some little dissatisfaction. On the first of the year they mailed her a tax notice. February came, and there was no reply. They wrote her a formal letter, asking her to call at the sheriff's office at her convenience. A week later the mayor wrote her himself, offering to call or to send his car for her, and received in reply a note on paper of an archaic shape, in a thin, flowing calligraphy in faded ink, to the effect that she no longer went out at all. The tax notice was also enclosed, without comment.

They called a special meeting of the Board of Aldermen. A deputation waited 5 upon her, knocked at the door through which no visitor had passed since she ceased giving china-painting lessons eight or ten years earlier. They were admitted by the old Negro into a dim hall from which a stairway mounted into still more shadow. It smelled of dust and disuse—a close, dank smell. The Negro led them into the parlor. It was furnished in heavy, leather-covered furniture. When the Negro opened the blinds of one window, they could see that the leather was cracked; and when they sat down, a faint dust rose sluggishly about their thighs, spinning with slow motes in the single sun-ray. On a tarnished gilt easel before the fireplace stood a crayon portrait of Miss Emily's father.

They rose when she entered—a small, fat woman in black, with a thin gold chain descending to her waist and vanishing into her belt, leaning on an ebony cane with a tarnished gold head. Her skeleton was small and spare; perhaps that was why what would have been merely plumpness in another was obesity in her. She looked bloated, like a body long submerged in motionless water, and of that pallid hue. Her eyes, lost in the fatty ridges of her face, looked like two small pieces of coal pressed into a lump of dough as they moved from one face to another while the visitors stated their errand.

She did not ask them to sit. She just stood in the door and listened quietly until the spokesman came to a stumbling halt. Then they could hear the invisible watch ticking at the end of the gold chain.

Her voice was dry and cold. "I have no taxes in Jefferson. Colonel Sartoris explained it to me. Perhaps one of you can gain access to the city records and satisfy yourselves."

"But we have. We are the city authorities, Miss Emily. Didn't you get a notice from the sheriff, signed by him?"

"I received a paper, yes," Miss Emily said. "Perhaps he considers himself the 10 sheriff.... I have no taxes in Jefferson."

"But there is nothing on the books to show that, you see. We must go by the —"

"See Colonel Sartoris. I have no taxes in Jefferson."

"But, Miss Emily—"

"See Colonel Sartoris." (Colonel Sartoris had been dead almost ten years.) "I have no taxes in Jefferson. Tobe!" The Negro appeared. "Show these gentlemen out."

II

So she vanquished them, horse and foot, just as she had vanquished their fathers thirty years before about the smell. That was two years after her father's death and a short time after her sweetheart—the one we believed would marry her—had deserted her. After her father's death she went out very little; after her sweetheart went away, people hardly saw her at all. A few of the ladies had the temerity to call, but were not received, and the only sign of life about the place was the Negro man—a young man then—going in and out with a market basket.

"Just as if a man—any man—could keep a kitchen properly," the ladies said; so they were not surprised when the smell developed. It was another link between the gross, teeming world and the high and mighty Griersons.

A neighbor, a woman, complained to the mayor, Judge Stevens, eighty years old.

"But what will you have me do about it, madam?" he said.

"Why, send her word to stop it," the woman said. "Isn't there a law?"

"I'm sure that won't be necessary," Judge Stevens said. "It's probably just a snake or a rat that nigger of hers killed in the yard. I'll speak to him about it."

The next day he received two more complaints, one from a man who came in diffident deprecation. "We really must do something about it, Judge. I'd be the last one in the world to bother Miss Emily, but we've got to do something." That night the Board of Aldermen met—three graybeards and one younger man, a member of the rising generation.

"It's simple enough," he said. "Send her word to have her place cleaned up. Give her a certain time to do it in, and if she don't . . ."

"Dammit, sir," Judge Stevens said, "will you accuse a lady to her face of smelling bad?"

So the next night, after midnight, four men crossed Miss Emily's lawn and slunk about the house like burglars, sniffing along the base of the brickwork and at the cellar openings while one of them performed a regular sowing motion with his hand out of a sack slung from his shoulder. They broke open the cellar door and sprinkled lime there, and in all the outbuildings. As they recrossed the lawn, a window that had been dark was lighted and Miss Emily sat in it, the light behind her, and her upright torso motionless as that of an idol. They crept quietly across the lawn and into the shadow of the locusts that lined the street. After a week or two the smell went away.

That was when people had begun to feel really sorry for her. People in our town, remembering how old lady Wyatt, her great-aunt, had gone completely crazy at last, believed that the Griersons held themselves a little too high for what they really were. None of the young men were quite good enough for Miss Emily and such. We had long thought of them as a tableau, Miss Emily a slender figure in white in the background, her father a spraddled silhouette in the foreground, his back to her and clutching a horsewhip, the two of them framed by the backflung front door. So when she got to be thirty and was still single, we were not pleased exactly, but vindicated; even with insanity in the family she wouldn't have turned down all of her chances if they had really materialized.

When her father died, it got about that the house was all that was left to her; and in a way, people were glad. At last they could pity Miss Emily. Being left alone, and a pauper, she had become humanized. Now she too would know the old thrill and the old despair of a penny more or less.

The day after his death all the ladies prepared to call at the house and offer condolence and aid, as is our custom. Miss Emily met them at the door, dressed as usual and with no trace of grief on her face. She told them that her father was not dead. She did that for three days, with the ministers calling on her, and the doctors, trying to persuade her to let them dispose of the body. Just as they were about to resort to law and force, she broke down, and they buried her father quickly.

We did not say she was crazy then. We believed she had to do that. We remembered all the young men her father had driven away, and we knew that with nothing left, she would have to cling to that which had robbed her, as people will.

III

She was sick for a long time. When we saw her again, her hair was cut short, making her look like a girl, with a vague resemblance to those angels in colored church windows—sort of tragic and serene.

The town had just let the contracts for paving the sidewalks, and in the summer after her father's death they began the work. The construction company came with niggers and mules and machinery, and a foreman named Homer Barron, a Yankee—a big, dark, ready man, with a big voice and eyes lighter than his face. The little boys would follow in groups to hear him cuss the niggers, and the niggers singing in time to the rise and fall of picks. Pretty soon he knew everybody in town. Whenever you heard a lot of laughing anywhere about the square, Homer Barron would be in the center of the group. Presently, we began to see him and Miss Emily on Sunday afternoons driving in the yellow-wheeled buggy and the matched team of bays from the livery stable.

At first we were glad that Miss Emily would have an interest, because the ladies all said, "Of course a Grierson would not think seriously of a Northerner, a day laborer." But there were still others, older people, who said that even grief could not cause a real lady to forget *noblesse oblige*—without calling it *noblesse oblige*. They just said, "Poor Emily. Her kinsfolk should come to her." She had some kin in Alabama; but years ago her father had fallen out with them over the estate of old lady Wyatt, the crazy woman, and there was no communication between the two families. They had not even been represented at the funeral.

And as soon as the old people said, "Poor Emily," the whispering began. "Do you suppose it's really so?" they said to one another. "Of course it is. What else could . . ." This behind their hands; rustling of craned silk and satin behind jalousies closed upon the sun of Sunday afternoon as the thin, swift clop-clop-clop of the matched team passed: "Poor Emily."

30

She carried her head high enough—even when we believed that she was fallen. It was as if she demanded more than ever the recognition of her dignity as the last Grierson; as if it had wanted that touch of earthiness to reaffirm her imperviousness. Like when she bought the rat poison, the arsenic. That was over a year after they had begun to say "Poor Emily," and while the two female cousins were visiting her.

"I want some poison," she said to the druggist. She was over thirty then, still a slight woman, though thinner than usual, with cold, haughty black eyes in a face the flesh of which was strained across the temples and about the eye-sockets as you imagine a lighthouse-keeper's face ought to look. "I want some poison," she said.

"Yes, Miss Emily. What kind? For rats and such? I'd recom——"   35

"I want the best you have. I don't care what kind."

The druggist named several. "They'll kill anything up to an elephant. But what you want is——"

"Arsenic," Miss Emily said. "Is that a good one?"

"Is . . . arsenic? Yes, ma'am. But what you want——"

"I want arsenic."   40

The druggist looked down at her. She looked back at him, erect, her face like a strained flag. "Why, of course," the druggist said. "If that's what you want. But the law requires you to tell what you are going to use it for."

Miss Emily just stared at him, her head tilted back in order to look him eye for eye, until he looked away and went and got the arsenic and wrapped it up. The Negro delivery boy brought her the package; the druggist didn't come back. When she opened the package at home there was written on the box, under the skull and bones: "For rats."

IV

So the next day we all said, "She will kill herself"; and we said it would be the best thing. When she had first begun to be seen with Homer Barron, we had said, "She will marry him." Then we said, "She will persuade him yet," because Homer himself had remarked—he liked men, and it was known that he drank with the younger men in the Elks' Club—that he was not a marrying man. Later we said, "Poor Emily" behind the jalousies as they passed on Sunday afternoon in the glittering buggy, Miss Emily with her head high and Homer Barron with his hat cocked and a cigar in his teeth, reins and whip in a yellow glove.

Then some of the ladies began to say that it was a disgrace to the town and a bad example to the young people. The men did not want to interfere, but at last the ladies forced the Baptist minister—Miss Emily's people were Episcopal—to call upon her. He would never divulge what happened during that interview, but he refused to go back again. The next Sunday they again drove about the streets, and the following day the minister's wife wrote to Miss Emily's relations in Alabama.

So she had blood-kin under her roof again and we sat back to watch develop-   45
ments. At first nothing happened. Then we were sure that they were to be married. We learned that Miss Emily had been to the jeweler's and ordered a man's toilet set in silver, with the letters H. B. on each piece. Two days later we learned that she

had bought a complete outfit of men's clothing, including a nightshirt, and we said, "They are married." We were really glad. We were glad because the two female cousins were even more Grierson than Miss Emily had ever been.

So we were not surprised when Homer Barron—the streets had been finished some time since—was gone. We were a little disappointed that there was not a public blowing-off, but we believed that he had gone on to prepare for Miss Emily's coming, or to give her a chance to get rid of the cousins. (By that time it was a cabal, and we were all Miss Emily's allies to help circumvent the cousins.) Sure enough, after another week they departed. And, as we had expected all along, within three days Homer Barron was back in town. A neighbor saw the Negro man admit him at the kitchen door at dusk one evening.

And that was the last we saw of Homer Barron. And of Miss Emily for some time. The Negro man went in and out with the market basket, but the front door remained closed. Now and then we would see her at a window for a moment, as the men did that night when they sprinkled the lime, but for almost six months she did not appear on the streets. Then we knew that this was to be expected too; as if that quality of her father which had thwarted her woman's life so many times had been too virulent and too furious to die.

When we next saw Miss Emily, she had grown fat and her hair was turning gray. During the next few years it grew grayer and grayer until it attained an even pepper-and-salt iron-gray, when it ceased turning. Up to the day of her death at seventy-four it was still that vigorous iron-gray, like the hair of an active man.

From that time on her front door remained closed, save for a period of six or seven years, when she was about forty, during which she gave lessons in china-painting. She fitted up a studio in one of the downstairs rooms, where the daughters and granddaughters of Colonel Sartoris' contemporaries were sent to her with the same regularity and in the same spirit that they were sent to church on Sundays with a twenty-five-cent piece for the collection plate. Meanwhile her taxes had been remitted.

Then the newer generation became the backbone and the spirit of the town, and the painting pupils grew up and fell away and did not send their children to her with boxes of color and tedious brushes and pictures cut from the ladies' magazines. The front door closed upon the last one and remained closed for good. When the town got free postal delivery, Miss Emily alone refused to let them fasten the metal numbers above her door and attach a mailbox to it. She would not listen to them.

Daily, monthly, yearly we watched the Negro grow grayer and more stooped, going in and out with the market basket. Each December we sent her a tax notice, which would be returned by the post office a week later, unclaimed. Now and then we would see her in one of the downstairs windows—she had evidently shut up the top floor of the house—like the carven torso of an idol in a niche, looking or not looking at us, we could never tell which. Thus she passed from generation to generation—dear, inescapable, impervious, tranquil, and perverse.

And so she died. Fell ill in the house filled with dust and shadows, with only a doddering Negro man to wait on her. We did not even know she was sick; we had long since given up trying to get information from the Negro. He talked to no one, probably not even to her, for his voice had grown harsh and rusty, as if from disuse.

She died in one of the downstairs rooms, in a heavy walnut bed with a curtain, her gray head propped on a pillow yellow and moldy with age and lack of sunlight.

V

The Negro met the first of the ladies at the front door and let them in, with their hushed, sibilant voices and their quick, curious glances, and then he disappeared. He walked right through the house and out the back and was not seen again.

The two female cousins came at once. They held the funeral on the second 55 day, with the town coming to look at Miss Emily beneath a mass of bought flowers, with the crayon face of her father musing profoundly above the bier and the ladies sibilant and macabre; and the very old men—some in their brushed Confederate uniforms—on the porch and the lawn, talking of Miss Emily as if she had been a contemporary of theirs, believing that they had danced with her and courted her perhaps, confusing time with its mathematical progression, as the old do, to whom all the past is not a diminishing road but, instead, a huge meadow which no winter ever quite touches, divided from them now by the narrow bottleneck of the most recent decade of years.

Already we knew that there was one room in that region above stairs which no one had seen in forty years, and which would have to be forced. They waited until Miss Emily was decently in the ground before they opened it.

The violence of breaking down the door seemed to fill this room with pervading dust. A thin, acrid pall as of the tomb seemed to lie everywhere upon this room decked and furnished as for a bridal: upon the valance curtains of faded rose color, upon the rose-shaded lights, upon the dressing table, upon the delicate array of crystal and the man's toilet things backed with tarnished silver, silver so tarnished that the monogram was obscured. Among them lay a collar and tie, as if they had just been removed, which, lifted, left upon the surface a pale crescent in the dust. Upon a chair hung the suit, carefully folded; beneath it the two mute shoes and the discarded socks.

The man himself lay in the bed.

For a long while we just stood there, looking down at the profound and fleshless grin. The body had apparently once lain in the attitude of an embrace, but now the long sleep that outlasts love, that conquers even the grimace of love, had cuckolded him. What was left of him, rotted beneath what was left of the nightshirt, had become inextricable from the bed in which he lay; and upon him and upon the pillow beside him lay that even coating of the patient and biding dust.

Then we noticed that in the second pillow was the indentation of a head. One 60 of us lifted something from it, and leaning forward, that faint and invisible dust dry and acrid in the nostrils, we saw a long strand of iron-gray hair.

[1931]

Exploring the Text

1. "A Rose for Emily" is narrated in first-person plural. Why do you think Faulkner chose "we" rather than "I" as the voice for the story? How might this narrative strategy be related to the description of Emily as "a tradition, a duty, and a care; a sort of hereditary obligation upon the town" (para. 3)?

2. Trace the timeline of this story, and then analyze why the author decided to recount the tale in this manner. How does the order of the telling help shape the story's meaning? What details foreshadow the story's conclusion? What governs the five-part division of the story?

3. Discuss how this story might be viewed as a conflict between North and South. Keep in mind that Homer Barron is a construction foreman and a northerner, while Emily Grierson comes from a genteel southern family. How might the physical descriptions of Miss Emily relate to this theme?

4. Look at paragraph 55. How do the diction, syntax, and imagery in this paragraph reinforce one of the story's themes?

5. How is Miss Emily "a fallen monument" (para. 1)? To what is she a monument? Why is she repeatedly called an "idol"? What connection can you draw between these images and one of the story's themes?

6. Describe Emily's relationship with her father. What details in the story support your view? How does this relationship influence the development of events in the story?

7. Did the story's ending surprise you? Explain why Miss Emily did what she did.

8. In an interview, Faulkner described the conflict of Miss Emily: she "had broken all the laws of her tradition, her background, and she had finally broken the law of God too. . . . And she knew she was doing wrong, and that's why her own life was wrecked. Instead of murdering one lover, and then to go on and take another and when she used him up to murder him, she was expiating her crime." How might this story be seen as expiation?

Love in L.A.

Dagoberto Gilb

Dagoberto Gilb (b. 1950) was born in Los Angeles to a Mexican mother and an Anglo father from East Los Angeles. He earned bachelor's and master's degrees from the University of Santa Barbara, and currently teaches in the Master of Fine Arts Creative Writing Program at Southwest Texas State University. Gilb's first published work was *Winners on the Pass Line* (1985), but *The Magic of Blood* (1993) established his reputation. Hailed as a classic of the American Southwest, it won the 1994 PEN/Hemingway Award. There followed *The Last Known Residence of Mickey Acuña* (1994), *Woodcuts of Women* (2001), and *Gritos* (2003), a collection of essays. Subtly layered irony and satire come together in "Love in L.A.," appropriately set in a city where reality, fantasy, and image vie for prominence.

Jake slouched in a clot of near motionless traffic, in the peculiar gray of concrete, smog, and early morning beneath the overpass of the Hollywood Freeway on Alvarado Street. He didn't really mind because he knew how much worse it could be trying to make a left onto the onramp. He certainly didn't do that every day of his life, and he'd assure anyone who'd ask that he never would either. A steady occupation had its advantages and he couldn't deny thinking about that too. He needed an FM radio in something better than this '58 Buick he drove. It would have crushed velvet interior with electric controls for the L.A. summer, a nice warm heater and defroster for the winter drives at the beach, a cruise control for those longer trips, mellow speakers front and rear of course, windows that hum closed, snuffing out that nasty exterior noise of freeways. The fact was that he'd probably have to change his whole style. Exotic colognes, plush, dark nightclubs, maitais and daiquiris, necklaced ladies in satin gowns, misty and sexy like in a tequila ad. Jake could imagine lots of possibilities when he let himself, but none that ended up with him pressed onto a stalled freeway.

Jake was thinking about this freedom of his so much that when he glimpsed its green light he just went ahead and stared bye bye to the steadily employed. When he turned his head the same direction his windshield faced, it was maybe one second too late. He pounced the brake pedal and steered the front wheels away from the tiny brakelights but the smack was unavoidable. Just one second sooner and it would only have been close. One second more and he'd be crawling up the Toyota's trunk. As it was, it seemed like only a harmless smack, much less solid than the one against his back bumper.

Jake considered driving past the Toyota but was afraid the traffic ahead would make it too difficult. As he pulled up against the curb a few carlengths ahead, it occurred to him that the traffic might have helped him get away too. He slammed the car door twice to make sure it was closed fully and to give himself another second more, then toured front and rear of his Buick for damage on or near the bumpers. Not an impressionable scratch even in the chrome. He perked up. Though the car's beauty was secondary to its ability to start and move, the body and paint were clean except for a few minor dings. This stood out as one of his few clearcut accomplishments over the years.

Before he spoke to the driver of the Toyota, whose looks he could see might present him with an added complication, he signaled to the driver of the car that hit him, still in his car and stopped behind the Toyota, and waved his hands and shook his head to let the man know there was no problem as far as he was concerned. The driver waved back and started his engine.

"It didn't even scratch my paint," Jake told her in that way of his. "So how you   5 doin? Any damage to the car? I'm kinda hoping so, just so it takes a little more time and we can talk some. Or else you can give me your phone number now and I won't have to lay my regular b.s. on you to get it later."

He took her smile as a good sign and relaxed. He inhaled her scent like it was clean air and straightened out his less than new but not unhip clothes.

"You've got Florida plates. You look like you must be Cuban."

"My parents are from Venezuela."

"My name's Jake." He held out his hand.

"Mariana."   10

They shook hands like she'd never done it before in her life.

"I really am sorry about hitting you like that." He sounded genuine. He fondled the wide dimple near the cracked taillight. "It's amazing how easy it is to put a dent in these new cars. They're so soft they might replace waterbeds soon." Jake was confused about how to proceed with this. So much seemed so unlikely, but there was always possibility. "So maybe we should go out to breakfast somewhere and talk it over."

"I don't eat breakfast."

"Some coffee then."

"Thanks, but I really can't."   15

"You're not married, are you? Not that that would matter that much to me. I'm an openminded kinda guy."

She was smiling. "I have to get to work."

"That sounds boring."

"I better get your driver's license," she said.

Jake nodded, disappointed. "One little problem," he said. "I didn't bring it. I just   20
forgot it this morning. I'm a musician," he exaggerated greatly, "and, well, I dunno, I left my wallet in the pants I was wearing last night. If you have some paper and a pen I'll give you my address and all that."

He followed her to the glove compartment side of her car.

"What if we don't report it to the insurance companies? I'll just get it fixed for you."

"I don't think my dad would let me do that."

"Your dad? It's not your car?"

"He bought it for me. And I live at home."   25

"Right." She was slipping away from him. He went back around to the back of her new Toyota and looked over the damage again. There was the trunk lid, the bumper, a rear panel, a taillight.

"You do have insurance?" she asked, suspicious, as she came around the back of the car.

"Oh yeah," he lied.

"I guess you better write the name of that down too."

He made up a last name and address and wrote down the name of an insurance   30
company an old girlfriend once belonged to. He considered giving a real phone number but went against that idea and made one up.

"I act too," he lied to enhance the effect more. "Been in a couple of movies."

She smiled like a fan.

"So how about your phone number?" He was rebounding maturely.

She gave it to him.

"Mariana, you are beautiful," he said in his most sincere voice.   35

"Call me," she said timidly.

Jake beamed. "We'll see you, Mariana," he said holding out his hand. Her hand felt so warm and soft he felt like he'd been kissed.

Back in his car he took a moment or two to feel both proud and sad about his performance. Then he watched the rear view mirror as Mariana pulled up behind him. She was writing down the license plate numbers on his Buick, ones that he'd taken off a junk because the ones that belonged to his had expired so long ago. He turned the ignition key and revved the big engine and clicked into drive. His sense of freedom swelled as he drove into the now moving street traffic, though he couldn't stop the thought about that FM stereo radio and crushed velvet interior and the new car smell that would even make it better.

[1993]

Exploring the Text

1. Based on what you know about Los Angeles from movies, television, or personal experience, how does the setting affect your interpretation of events in the story?
2. How does the syntax of the first sentence of the second paragraph, "Jake was thinking about this freedom of his so much that when he glimpsed its green light he just went ahead and stared bye bye to the steadily employed," reflect the picture of life in Los Angeles that the author is portraying? Does the sound of this sentence resonate with its sense? How?
3. In what ways does Jake show himself to be an "actor"—not literally, perhaps, but in assuming different roles or performances during this encounter?
4. The saying goes that America has a love affair with the automobile, the freedom of the road being yet another inalienable right. How does this idea find its way into "Love in L.A."? What do the kinds of cars the characters drive—or daydream about driving—lead you to infer about their attitudes toward relationships?
5. Consider the exchange between Mariana and Jake in light of the fact that she copied down his license plate number. What does this suggest about her character? Do you think she gave Jake her real phone number or even her real name? Whom should the reader believe here? Who won this round, Jake or Mariana?
6. What conclusions do you think Dagoberto Gilb intended readers to draw concerning the nature of love in L.A.? Is he suggesting that Jake and Mariana might be kindred spirits in the world depicted in the story? Is he being cynical, playful, or realistic about love and relationships?

They flee from me

Sir Thomas Wyatt

Sir Thomas Wyatt (1503–1542) was born at Allington Castle in Kent, one of three children of Sir Henry Wyatt, a courtier during the reigns of Henry VII and Henry VIII. Sir Thomas Wyatt was educated privately before attending St.

John's College, Cambridge, where he excelled in Greek and Latin verse but did not earn a degree. Like his father, he served as a courtier to King Henry VIII, eventually being named an ambassador. His poetry is largely imitative of Roman models but represented a novel form in English literature. In particular, Wyatt invented the English sonnet, later imitated by William Shakespeare and countless other poets. Published posthumously, *Songes and Sonnettes* (1557) greatly influenced sixteenth- and seventeenth-century writers. "They flee from me" is a subtle, cynical examination of how relationships between lovers change; it has been interpreted by some scholars as an allegory for political shifts of power as well.

They flee from me, that sometime did me seek,
With naked foot stalking in my chamber.
I have seen them, gentle, tame, and meek,
That now are wild, and do not remember
That sometime they put themselves in danger   5
To take bread at my hand; and now they range,
Busily seeking with a continual change.

Thankèd be fortune it hath been otherwise,
Twenty times better; but once in special,
In thin array, after a pleasant guise,   10
When her loose gown from her shoulders did fall,
And she me caught in her arms long and small,
Therewithall[1] sweetly did me kiss
And softly said, "Dear heart, how like you this?"

It was no dream, I lay broad waking.   15
But all is turned, thorough[2] my gentleness,
Into a strange fashion of forsaking;
And I have leave to go, of[3] her goodness,
And she also to use newfangleness.[4]
But since that I so kindly[5] am served,   20
I fain[6] would know what she hath deserved.

[1557]

- -

---

[1]With all that.—EDS.
[2]Through.—EDS.
[3]Out of (thanks to).—EDS.
[4]Fondness for new things, fickleness.—EDS.
[5]Graciously (ironic), also naturally or fittingly.—EDS.
[6]Gladly.—EDS.

Exploring the Text

1. In the first stanza, the speaker in the poem talks of women taking "bread at my hand" (l. 6). What does this image suggest about his attitude toward women? What does it suggest about women's attitudes toward him?
2. What seems to have changed in the balance of power between man and woman in the second stanza? How does the speaker feel about this change?
3. In line 14, a woman addresses the speaker as "dear heart." Keeping in mind that a hart is a male red deer often hunted in Wyatt's time, how could this line be interpreted as more than a simple endearment? Have the roles of hunter and hunted been reversed?
4. Each stanza in the poem ends with a rhymed couplet. Explain how each couplet encapsulates the previous lines in the stanza.
5. At the time Wyatt wrote this poem, women lacked most of the legal and social rights that we now practically take for granted. How does Wyatt use figurative language and imagery to portray the imbalance of power between men and women in intimate relationships?

Leave me, O Love, which reachest but to dust

SIR PHILIP SIDNEY

"The poet-soldier" and "worthiest knight that lived," Sir Philip Sidney (1554–1586) was born in Kent, England, to an influential English family. Educated at Christ Church College, Oxford, he had by the age of twenty-one traveled extensively in Europe and developed acquaintanceships with influential courtiers in many European capitals, eventually serving as a diplomat for Queen Elizabeth I. He withdrew from the royal court in 1580 and wrote *Astrophel and Stella* (c. 1590), a cycle of 108 sonnets and 11 songs; *The Countess of Pembroke's Arcadia* (c. 1593), which was unfinished at his death; and *The Defence of Poesie* (c. 1595), which argued that poetry represented truth more honestly than did history or science: "Now for the poet, he nothing affirmeth, and therefore never lieth." "Leave me, O Love, which reachest but to dust" is from *Certain Sonnets* (c. 1598).

Leave me, O Love which reachest but to dust;
And thou, my mind, aspire to higher things;
Grow rich in that which never taketh rust,
Whatever fades but fading pleasure brings.
Draw in thy beams, and humble all thy might   5
To that sweet yoke where lasting freedoms be;
Which breaks the clouds and opens forth the light,
That doth both shine and give us sight to see.
O take fast hold; let that light be thy guide
In this small course which birth draws out to death,   10

And think how evil becometh him to slide,
Who seeketh heav'n, and comes of heav'nly breath.
    Then farewell, world; thy uttermost I see;
    Eternal Love, maintain thy life in me.

                                                    [c.1598]

Exploring the Text

1. In his sonnet, Sir Philip Sidney uses apostrophe, addressing "Love" directly in the first line, "thou, my mind" in the second line, and "Eternal Love" in the last line. What effect do these direct addresses have on your understanding of the poem?
2. Explain the admonition, "And thou, my mind, aspire to higher things" (l. 2). What does he mean by "higher things"?
3. How do you interpret the paradox, or apparent contradiction, of "Draw in thy beams, and humble all thy might / To that sweet yoke where lasting freedoms be" (ll. 5–6)? How is it possible to be free while wearing a yoke?
4. What kind of love does the speaker in the poem wish to leave behind? Why?
5. Based on your reading of the sonnet, what relationship do you think the speaker in the poem values most?

The Flea

JOHN DONNE

John Donne (1572–1631) was born in London to a prosperous family. He was educated by Jesuits and attended both Oxford and Cambridge, where he studied law. His satires (written 1593–1595) and the poems later collected as *Songs and Sonets* (1612) reflect life among the barristers. Donne was ordained in the Church of England in 1615 and became a renowned preacher. His sermons were published in three volumes—*LXXX Sermons* (1640), *Fifty Sermons* (1649), and *XXVI Sermons* (1661)—though today only his poetry is widely read. Donne's poems were not collected in his lifetime; indeed, only when he was short of funds in 1613–1614 did he attempt to gather them together, writing to friends that "I am made a Rhapsoder of mine own rags, and that cost me more diligence, to seek them, than it did to make them." Eventually published as *Poems* in 1633, they met with immediate acclaim. Donne has since been regarded as the most important of the metaphysical poets—a loose confederation of artists who relied on wit and incongruous, often startling imagery (metaphysical conceits), as you will see in "The Flea."

Mark[1] but this flea, and mark in this
How little that which thou deny'st me is;
It sucked me first, and now sucks thee,

---

[1]Notice.—EDS.

And in this flea our two bloods mingled be;
Thou know'st that this cannot be said   5
A sin, nor shame, nor loss of maidenhead,
    Yet this enjoys before it woo,
     And pampered swells with one blood made of two,
     And this, alas, is more than we would do.

Oh stay,[2] three lives in one flea spare,   10
Where we almost, yea more than, married are.
This flea is you and I, and this
Our marriage bed, and marriage temple is;
Though parents grudge, and you, we're met
And cloistered in these living walls of jet.   15
    Though use[3] make you apt to kill me,
     Let not to that, self-murder added be,
     And sacrilege, three sins in killing three.

Cruel and sudden, hast thou since
Purpled thy nail in blood of innocence?   20
Wherein could this flea guilty be,
Except in that drop which it sucked from thee?
Yet thou triumph'st, and say'st that thou
Find'st not thyself, nor me, the weaker now;
    'Tis true; then learn how false, fears be;   25
     Just so much honor, when thou yield'st to me,
     Will waste, as this flea's death took life from thee.

[1633]

. . . .

Exploring the Text

1. In order to make sense of "The Flea," you will need to read not only between the lines but also before the poem begins. What has occurred before the first stanza?
2. "The Flea" employs an extended metaphor as the center of its argument in this seduction poem. What is the metaphor? How does Donne develop it? How does it make his argument more convincing?
3. What do the lines "Thou know'st that this cannot be said / A sin, nor shame, nor loss of maidenhead" (ll. 5–6) tell you about the woman in the poem and how she is responding to the speaker's wooing of her?
4. What does the speaker mean when he says "three lives in one flea" (l. 10)?
5. Consider the three sets of indented lines. Taken together, what argument do they make? How does each set differ from the preceding lines in the stanza?

---

[2]Stop. — Eds.
[3]Habit. — Eds.

6. Paraphrase the final five lines of the poem. What is the speaker's argument?
7. What is beguiling about the use of a flea to plead one's case as a lover?
8. How would you describe the overall tone of this poem?

To the Virgins, to Make Much of Time

ROBERT HERRICK

Robert Herrick (1591–1674) was one of six children born to a prosperous family in London. After his father's presumed suicide in 1592, he was separated from his mother and brought up in the Presbyterian household of his uncle. After serving six years of a ten-year apprenticeship with his uncle, a goldsmith, Herrick entered St. John's College, Cambridge, when he was twenty-two and transferred to Trinity Hall three years later, receiving his BA in 1617 and an MA in 1620. In 1623, he was ordained; and in 1640, *The severall Poems written by Master Robert Herrick* appeared. The bulk of his work was published in *His Noble Numbers* (1647) and *Hesperides; or, The Works Both Human and Divine of Robert Herrick, Esq.* (1648). The range of subject is broad; over 1,200 short poems in many forms—derived from Roman and Greek poetry—give remarkable insight into Herrick's joyful interpretation of God's gifts. Like his contemporary Andrew Marvell, Herrick was influenced by classical models. Unlike Marvell and the metaphysical poets, however, he adopted a simple, pastoral style. Central to this poem and to much of his work are his religious faith and a celebration of the divine, though brief, gift of life.

Gather ye rose-buds while ye may,
    Old Time is still a-flying;
And this same flower that smiles today,
    Tomorrow will be dying.

The glorious lamp of heaven, the sun,   5
    The higher he's a-getting,
The sooner will his race be run,
    And nearer he's to setting.

That age is best which is the first,
    When youth and blood are warmer;   10
But being spent, the worse, and worst
    Times still succeed the former.

Then be not coy, but use your time,
    And while ye may, go marry;
For having lost but once your prime,   15
    You may for ever tarry.

[1648]

Exploring the Text

1. The poem opens with the speaker urging virgins to "Gather ye rose-buds" (l. 1). What do the rosebuds symbolize? What is the urgency?
2. Describe the rhyming pattern and rhythm of Herrick's poem. What effect do they produce, and how does that contribute to the poem's meaning?
3. In the second stanza, the speaker compares the course of a day to a race. How does this comparison add evidence to the point being made in the first stanza?
4. What can you infer about the speaker's attitude toward aging from the following lines: "That age is best which is the first" (l. 9) and "and worst / Times still succeed the former" (ll. 11–12)?
5. In the final stanza, the speaker offers instructions and a warning. Is his advice still relevant? How might you update or reply to his admonitions?

She walks in Beauty

LORD BYRON

> In a short life, George Gordon Byron (1788–1824) staked his claim as one of the greatest romantic poets in the English language, became an exile from his own country and a national hero in Greece (where a suburb of Athens is named after him), and gave his name to the adjective *Byronic*, which refers to his mercurial, romantic, and tragic character. Born in London, he inherited the barony of Byron at the age of ten, becoming Lord Byron. As a child, he displayed an idleness and mischievous temperament that continued at Trinity College, Cambridge, where he kept a bear in protest of college regulations forbidding undergraduates to keep dogs. The first commercial edition of his work was *Hours of Idleness* (1807), which met with savage reviews, prompting his satirical response, *English Bards and Scotch Reviewers* (1809). His reputation grew with the publication of *The Corsair* (1814), which sold ten thousand copies on the day of its release. In 1816, Byron left England for Italy, where he spent time with Percy Bysshe Shelley and Mary Shelley. In 1821, he published *The Prophecy of Dante*, three cantos of *Don Juan*, *Marino Faliero*, *Sardanapalus*, *The Two Foscari*, and *Cain*. Originally written as a song lyric, "She walks in Beauty" clearly expresses Byron's love of beauty.

I

She walks in Beauty, like the night
    Of cloudless climes[1] and starry skies;
And all that's best of dark and bright
    Meet in her aspect and her eyes:
Thus mellowed to that tender light   5
    Which Heaven to gaudy day denies.

---

[1]Climates.—EDS.

II

One shade the more, one ray the less,
  Had half impaired the nameless grace
Which waves in every raven tress,
    Or softly lightens o'er her face;   10
Where thoughts serenely sweet express,
  How pure, how dear their dwelling-place.

III

And on that cheek, and o'er that brow,
  So soft, so calm, yet eloquent,
The smiles that win, the tints that glow,   15
  But tell of days in goodness spent,
A mind at peace with all below,
  A heart whose love is innocent!

[1814]

Exploring the Text

1. What is it about the phrase "like the night" (l. 1) that immediately draws readers into the poem?
2. What does the alliteration of "cloudless climes" and "starry skies" (l. 2) contribute to the poem's effect?
3. How does the poem invite us to view the night in a new light? What lines in the poem support your interpretation? For instance, what is the denotation and connotation of the adjective "gaudy" (l. 6)? How does Byron's use of this descriptor for day help us understand what he is trying to say about night? How does it help you see the woman the speaker describes?
4. What do you know about this unnamed woman who "walks in Beauty" (l. 1)? What can you infer from the line "So soft, so calm, yet eloquent" (l. 14)?
5. Paraphrase the last stanza of the poem. How do you interpret Byron's final exclamation mark?
6. What do you imagine is the speaker's relationship to the woman he describes?

Love is not all

EDNA ST. VINCENT MILLAY

Edna St. Vincent Millay (1892–1950) was born in Maine. In 1912, she entered her poem "Renascence" in a competition, winning fourth place and inclusion in *The Lyric Year*, which earned her acclaim and a scholarship to Vassar College. The poem would be included in her first collection, *Renascence and Other Poems*, published in 1917. After graduating, Vincent (as she insisted on being called) moved to Greenwich Village—then New York's bohemian district. To this period belong her short-story collection (written as Nancy Boyd), *A Few Figs from Thistles* (1920); her first verse play, *The Lamp and the Bell* (1921); and a play in one act, *Aria da Capo* (1920). After an extended trip to Europe, she returned to New York and published *The Harp Weaver and Other Poems* (1923). That year she won the Pulitzer Prize for Poetry, the first woman to be so honored. She also wrote the libretto of one of the few American grand operas, *The King's Henchman* (1927). Sympathetic to Marxism-Leninism, she was active in protests against the execution of Sacco and Vanzetti, addressing the issue in *Buck in the Snow* (1928). "Love is not all," written in 1931, is a beautifully objective assessment of a traditional subject of poetry in which she leads the reader gently but inexorably to her own position.

Love is not all: it is not meat nor drink
Nor slumber nor a roof against the rain;
Nor yet a floating spar to men that sink
And rise and sink and rise and sink again;
Love can not fill the thickened lung with breath,   5
Nor clean the blood, nor set the fractured bone;
Yet many a man is making friends with death
Even as I speak, for lack of love alone.
It well may be that in a difficult hour,
Pinned down by pain and moaning for release,   10
Or nagged by want past resolution's power,
I might be driven to sell your love for peace,
Or trade the memory of this night for food.
It well may be. I do not think I would.

[1931]

Exploring the Text

1. Explain the argument expressed in the first six lines of this sonnet. Why do you think Millay begins her love poem by defining what love is not? Why do you think Millay chose to write this poem as a sonnet?

2. What is the poem's situation—that is, where is the speaker in relation to the person she is addressing? Characterize the relationship of the two based on the information the poem provides.

3. "Love is not all" depends on an extended metaphor. What is it? How does Millay make it seem possible?

4. In lines 9–14 of the sonnet, Millay imagines a series of hypothetical situations. Describe how the speaker's tone shifts in these final lines.

5. What do you make of the tentativeness of the final line, "It well may be. I do not think I would"? Why are these words more intriguing than a declaration of "Never!" would be?
6. How does the tone of the poem reflect Millay's attitude toward love? How would you describe this tone?

Siren Song

MARGARET ATWOOD

Margaret Atwood (b. 1939) was born in Ottawa and spent much of her childhood in northern Quebec. She earned her undergraduate degree at Victoria University in Toronto and an MA at Radcliffe College (Harvard). Her written work is prolific, including poetry, literary criticism, and fiction, for which she is most famous. Her early work consists of five volumes of poetry: *Double Persephone* (1961), *The Circle Game* (1964), *Expeditions* (1965), *Speeches for Doctor Frankenstein* (1966), and *The Animals in That Country* (1968). Her first novel, *The Edible Woman* (1969), is at once frightening and comic. Eight more novels followed—*Surfacing* (1972), *Lady Oracle* (1976), *Life Before Man* (1979), *Bodily Harm* (1981), *The Handmaid's Tale* (1985), *Cat's Eye* (1988), *The Robber Bride* (1993), and *Alias Grace* (1996)—before *The Blind Assassin* (2000) won Atwood the Booker Prize. Her most recent book is *The Year of the Flood* (2009). With her wry, satirical, and mischievous sense of humor, she has the ability to blend the prosaic with pure fantasy. Much of Atwood's poetry draws from myth and legend; the speaker in this poem is a Greek mythological creature called a siren. In the *Odyssey*, the sirens were three birdlike women whose song lured sailors toward a rocky coast where they would be shipwrecked.

This is the one song everyone
would like to learn: the song
that is irresistible:

the song that forces men
to leap overboard in squadrons   5
even though they see beached skulls

the song nobody knows
because anyone who had heard it
is dead, and the others can't remember.

Shall I tell you the secret   10
and if I do, will you get me
out of this bird suit?

I don't enjoy it here
squatting on this island
looking picturesque and mythical   15

with these two feathery maniacs,
I don't enjoy singing
this trio, fatal and valuable.

I will tell the secret to you,
to you, only to you.   20
Come closer. This song

is a cry for help: Help me!
Only you, only you can,
you are unique

at last. Alas   25
it is a boring song
but it works every time.

[1974]

Exploring the Text

1. What is the appeal of the siren song? Why is it that it "works every time" (l. 27)? What is the appeal of the siren's age-old tactic for a modern audience?
2. Based on the way the siren addresses him, what can you infer about her audience?
3. The mythical sirens were creatures of mystery. How does Atwood's diction demystify them? Cite specific examples from the text.
4. Describe the tone of the poem. Look carefully at Atwood's use of hyperbole and understatement.
5. What stereotypes of women does Atwood draw upon in this poem?
6. Discuss how Atwood's poem can be read as a response to Homer. How might it be a protest against his depiction of the sirens?

One Art

ELIZABETH BISHOP

Elizabeth Bishop (1911–1979) was born in Worcester, Massachusetts, before finally settling in Boston. She attended Vassar College, where she earned a BA and met poet Marianne Moore, who dissuaded her from medical school in favor of life as a poet. Bishop published her first collection of poetry, *North and South* (1946), after traveling in Europe and North Africa. During an extended trip to Brazil, she published her second collection, *A Cold Spring* (1955), with the poems of *North and South* in a single volume. This won her the Pulitzer Prize in 1956. Bishop lived in Brazil for fifteen years; translated the Brazilian work *Minha Vida de Menina* as *The Diary of Helena Morely* (1957); and described her life in Brazil in her third collection of poetry, *Questions of Travel* (1965). Her last collection, *Geography III*, was published in 1976. Elizabeth Bishop's work amounts to little more than one hundred carefully crafted poems. She was recognized by her peers as a poet of exceptional talent but did not achieve popular recognition until after her death, with the publication of *The Complete Poems, 1927–1979* (1983). The modified villanelle "One Art" (from *Geography III*) reflects on the experience of losing.

The art of losing isn't hard to master;
so many things seem filled with the intent
to be lost that their loss is no disaster.

Lose something every day. Accept the fluster
of lost door keys, the hour badly spent.   5
The art of losing isn't hard to master.

Then practice losing farther, losing faster:
places, and names, and where it was you meant
to travel. None of these will bring disaster.

I lost my mother's watch. And look! my last, or   10
next-to-last, of three loved houses went.
The art of losing isn't hard to master.

I lost two cities, lovely ones. And, vaster,
some realms I owned, two rivers, a continent.
I miss them, but it wasn't a disaster.   15

— Even losing you (the joking voice, a gesture
I love) I shan't have lied. It's evident
the art of losing's not too hard to master
though it may look like (*Write* it!) like disaster.

[1976]

Exploring the Text

1. What are the denotations of the word *lose*? What are its connotations? Consider various forms of the word. What are the different ways Bishop uses it in "One Art"?
2. Bishop's "One Art" is a modified villanelle. How has she modified it? Why might she have modified it? How does this form contribute to the poem's meaning?
3. Find examples of hyperbole in this poem. How does the use of hyperbole communicate the author's attitude toward her subject?

4. To whom is the parenthetical "(*Write* it!)" (l. 19) addressed? What is the effect of the repetition of "like" in this final line?
5. According to Bishop, why is losing an art, and why is it important to master? Are you convinced by her argument? How can you apply it to your own life?

True Love

ROBERT PENN WARREN

Robert Penn Warren (1905–1989) was born in Kentucky and grew up listening to his grandfather talk about the Civil War. Warren was extremely well educated, with a degree from Vanderbilt University and advanced degrees from the University of California, Berkeley; and New College, Oxford. By the age of twenty-five, he had published poetry and a biography—*John Brown: The Making of a Martyr* (1929)—and written essays and a novella. He became known as one of the "new critics" after publishing *An Approach to Literature* (1936), *Understanding Poetry* (1938), *Understanding Fiction* (1943), and *Modern Rhetoric* (1949). Warren moved far from his traditionally southern views of the time with *Segregation: The Inner Conflict in the South* (1956), *Who Speaks for the Negro?* (1965), and *The Legacy of the Civil War: Meditations on the Centennial* (1961). Between 1939 and 1950 he wrote four novels: *Night Rider* (1939), *At Heaven's Gate* (1943), *All the King's Men* (1946)—for which he received a Pulitzer Prize—and *World Enough and Time* (1950). *Promises: Poems, 1954–1956* (1957) earned Warren his first Pulitzer Prize for Poetry, and *Now and Then: Poems, 1976–1978* (1978) won him his second. In "True Love," the reader is thrust headlong into Warren's sensitive description of boyhood and early love in the South.

In silence the heart raves. It utters words
Meaningless, that never had
A meaning. I was ten, skinny, red-headed,

Freckled. In a big black Buick,
Driven by a big grown boy, with a necktie, she sat   5
In front of the drugstore, sipping something

Through a straw. There is nothing like
Beauty. It stops your heart. It
Thickens your blood. It stops your breath. It

Makes you feel dirty. You need a hot bath.   10
I leaned against a telephone pole, and watched.
I thought I would die if she saw me.

How could I exist in the same world with that brightness?
Two years later she smiled at me. She
Named my name. I thought I would wake up dead.   15

Her grown brothers walked with the bent-knee
Swagger of horsemen. They were slick-faced.
Told jokes in the barbershop. Did no work.

Their father was what is called a drunkard.
Whatever he was he stayed on the third floor   20
Of the big white farmhouse under the maples for twenty-five years.

He never came down. They brought everything up to him.
I did not know what a mortgage was.
His wife was a good, Christian woman, and prayed.

When the daughter got married, the old man came down wearing   25
An old tail coat, the pleated shirt yellowing.
The sons propped him. I saw the wedding. There were

Engraved invitations, it was so fashionable. I thought
I would cry. I lay in bed that night
And wondered if she would cry when something was done to her.   30

The mortgage was foreclosed. That last word was whispered.
She never came back. The family
Sort of drifted off. Nobody wears shiny boots like that now.

But I know she is beautiful forever, and lives
In a beautiful house, far away.   35
She called my name once. I didn't even know she knew it.

[1985]

· ·

Exploring the Text

1. "True Love" describes the interactions of two people over a number of years. Identify clues in the poem to the passage of time.

2. Why do you think the female character is never named but only referred to as "she"? Why do you think the speaker uses only pronouns and common nouns (boy, father, brothers) to refer to characters in the poem?

3. What effect does the use of enjambment in the first through fourth stanzas have on the poem's meaning? What does it suggest about the speaker's attitude toward his subject?

4. How does the syntax of the poem—a series of short, choppy sentences—contribute to your sense of the speaker?

5. The speaker believes he is telling a story about true love. Do you think the author believes it is? How does this tension between the speaker's view of love and the author's view affect your understanding of the poem?

Weighing the Dog

BILLY COLLINS

Billy Collins (b. 1941) served two terms as poet laureate of the United States, beginning in 2001. He has written more than ten books of poetry, including *The Art of Drowning* (1995), *Picnic, Lightning* (1998), and *Nine Horses* (2002). A distinguished professor of English at Lehman College in New York City, Collins has received fellowships from the National Endowment for the Arts and the Guggenheim Foundation, and was chosen in 1992 as a "literary lion" of the New York Public Library. Collins, who actively promotes poetry in the schools, edited *Poetry 180: A Turning Back to Poetry* (2003)—an anthology of contemporary poems that aims to increase high school students' appreciation and enjoyment of poetry. Poet Stephen Dunn said of him, "We seem to always know where we are in a Billy Collins poem, but not necessarily where he is going." Such is the case with "Weighing the Dog."

It is awkward for me and bewildering for him
as I hold him in my arms in the small bathroom,
balancing our weight on the shaky blue scale,

but this is the way to weigh a dog and easier
than training him to sit obediently on one spot   5
with his tongue out, waiting for the cookie.

With pencil and paper I subtract my weight
from our total to find out the remainder that is his,
and I start to wonder if there is an analogy here.

It could not have to do with my leaving you   10
though I never figured out what you amounted to
until I subtracted myself from our combination.

You held me in your arms more than I held you
through all those awkward and bewildering months
and now we are both lost in strange and distant neighborhoods.   15

[1991]

. . . .

Exploring the Text

1. Where does this poem shift from being a poem about a man and his dog to being a poem about something else, something more? What is this something else?
2. The speaker suggests that weighing the dog is an analogy in line 9 and then denies it in line 10. How does that denial actually extend the analogy?

3. How does the structure of the poem's first six lines mirror its subject? Look especially at the way Collins creates balance in each line.
4. Who does the speaker blame for the failure of his relationship? What evidence in the poem can you find to support your view?
5. Billy Collins is considered a poet who makes poetry seem easy. Explain whether you think "Weighing the Dog" is an "easy" poem.

This was once a love poem

Jane Hirshfield

Jane Hirshfield (b. 1953) was born in New York City. She earned her BA at Princeton University, where she was introduced to classical-era Japanese and Chinese literature. She spent eight years in full-time practice of Zen during her twenties. She is currently on the faculty of MFA writing seminars at Bennington College. Hirshfield's first published collection of poems was *Alaya* (1982). Since then, she has published many volumes of poetry, including *Given Sugar, Given Salt* (2001) and *After* (2006). She has also written a collection of essays, *Nine Gates: Entering the Mind of Poetry* (1997). The personification of "This was once a love poem" speaks to the impermanence of life, a central theme in Hirshfield's work.

This was once a love poem,
before its haunches thickened, its breath grew short,
before it found itself sitting,
perplexed and a little embarrassed,
on the fender of a parked car,   5
while many people passed by without turning their heads.

It remembers itself dressing as if for a great engagement.
It remembers choosing these shoes,
this scarf or tie.

Once, it drank beer for breakfast,   10
drifted its feet
in a river side by side with the feet of another.

Once it pretended shyness, then grew truly shy,
dropping its head so the hair would fall forward,
so the eyes would not be seen.   15

It spoke with passion of history, of art.
It was lovely then, this poem.
Under its chin, no fold of skin softened.
Behind the knees, no pad of yellow fat.
What it knew in the morning it still believed at nightfall. 20
An unconjured confidence lifted its eyebrows, its cheeks.

The longing has not diminished.
Still it understands. It is time to consider a cat,
the cultivation of African violets or flowering cactus.

Yes, it decides: 25
Many miniature cacti, in blue and red painted pots.
When it finds itself disquieted
by the pure and unfamiliar silence of its new life,
it will touch them—one, then another—
with a single finger outstretched like a tiny flame.   30

[2001]

Exploring the Text

1. How does Hirshfield's use of a prose form reinforce the poem's meaning? Look closely at the first line.
2. How did the personification of the poem help you to grasp what had happened in the relationship?
3. Trace the changes the speaker describes in the character and behavior of the poem over the course of the love affair. What do the changes represent for the speaker?
4. Describe how the poem shifts with the following lines: "An unconjured confidence lifted its eyebrows, its cheeks. / The longing has not diminished. / Still it understands" (ll. 21–23). What has changed in the speaker's attitude?
5. Why is it "time to consider a cat" (l. 23)? What does buying a cat represent to the speaker in the poem? Why do you think the speaker decides in favor of cactus plants over African violets or a cat?

PAIRED POEMS

My mistress' eyes are nothing like the sun

WILLIAM SHAKESPEARE

William Shakespeare (1564–1616) was born in Stratford-upon-Avon, England. Little is known of his life aside from the fact that he married Anne Hathaway when he was eighteen, worked as an actor-playwright in London, and retired in 1613. His plays fall into four principal categories: early comedies (1585–1594); more sophisticated comedies and histories (1595–1599); the great tragedies (1599–1607); and the final phase (1608–1613). His most accomplished works—including *Hamlet* (1601), *Othello* (1603), *King Lear* (1605), and

Macbeth (1606)—belong to the third period. In his time his contemporaries, and likely Shakespeare himself, looked to his sonnets and other poems as the more important works. The 154 sonnets were written at various stages in Shakespeare's life, but when and to whom they were written remain unclear. William Wordsworth believed that only through the sonnets could one understand Shakespeare. The following selection is Sonnet 130.

My mistress' eyes are nothing like the sun;
Coral is far more red than her lips' red;
If snow be white, why then her breasts are dun;
If hairs be wires, black wires grow on her head.
I have seen roses damasked red and white,   5
But no such roses see I in her cheeks;
And in some perfumes is there more delight
Than in the breath that from my mistress reeks.
I love to hear her speak, yet well I know
That music hath a far more pleasing sound;   10
I grant I never saw a goddess go:
My mistress, when she walks, treads on the ground.
    And yet, by heaven, I think my love as rare
    As any she belied with false compare.

                                                        [1609]

Exploring the Text

1. Why do you think the speaker chooses to catalog his mistress's shortcomings?
2. Explain the turn the sonnet takes in the final couplet. How do these lines invite readers to reassess the first twelve lines?
3. How would you describe the tone in the first twelve lines? How does the tone shift in the final couplet? What resources of language does the author use to create this contrast in tone?

Mi fea (My ugly love)
Soneta XX (Sonnet XX)

PABLO NERUDA

TRANSLATED BY STEPHEN TAPSCOTT

Pablo Neruda (1904–1973)—"the greatest poet of the 20th century in any language," according to Gabriel García Márquez—was born Neftalí Ricardo Reyes y Basoalto in Parral, Chile. He studied French and trained to be a teacher at the University of Chile in Santiago, but instead adopted the name Pablo Neruda and devoted himself to writing. His first published collection, *Crepusculario* (1923), was followed by *Veinte Poemas de Amor y Una Cancion Desesperada* (1924), his most translated work. *Residencia en la tierra* (1933) established his reputation, and his experience of fascism in Spain inspired *España en el Corazón* (1937). His ambitious *Canto General*—250 poems combined into an epic about South America—was published in Mexico City in 1950. The collection includes "Alturas de Macchu Picchu" (1944), a monumental poem celebrating South America's cultures but condemning its social systems. He was elected to the Chilean Senate in 1945 but was forced to go into hiding in 1948 for anti-government statements; after more than a year, he was finally able to flee the country. He describes the period of exile that followed in *Las Uvas y el Viento* (1954); and later, in *Extravagario* (1958), he reexamines his loyalty to the Communist Party. Neruda was awarded the Nobel Prize for Literature in 1971. The poem "My Ugly Love"—included in *Cien Sonetos de Amor* (1959)—was dedicated to his wife Matilde Urrutia and is a tender, passionate hymn addressing the reality of love after the beauty of youth has flown.

Mi fea
Soneta XX

Mi fea, eres una castaña despeinada,
mi bella, eres hermosa como el viento,
mi fea, de tu boca se pueden hacer dos,
mi bella, son tus besos frescos como sandías.

Mi fea, dónde están escondidos tus senos?   5
Son mínimos como dos copas de trigo.
Me gustaría verte dos lunas en el pecho:
las gigantescas torres de tu soberanía.

Mi fea, el mar no tiene tus uñas en su tienda,
mi bella, flor a flor, estrella por estrella,   10
ola por ola, amor, he contado tu cuerpo:

mi fea, te amo por tu cintura de oro,
mi bella, te amo por una arruga en tu frente,
amor, te amo por clara y por oscura.

[1959]

My ugly love
Sonnet XX

My ugly love, you're a messy chestnut.
My beauty, you are pretty as the wind.

Ugly: your mouth is big enough for two mouths.
Beauty: your kisses are fresh as new melons.

Ugly: where *did* you hide your breasts?   5
They're meager, two little scoops of wheat.
I'd much rather see two moons across your chest,
two huge proud towers.

Ugly: not even the sea contains things like your toenails.
Beauty: flower by flower, star by star, wave by wave,   10
Love, I've made an inventory of your body:

My ugly one, I love you for your waist of gold;
my beauty, for the wrinkle on your forehead.
My Love: I love you for your clarity, your dark.

[1986]

Exploring the Text

1. How does the juxtaposition of the woman's beauty and ugliness affect your understanding of the speaker's love?
2. Why do you think Neruda put the line "Love, I've made an inventory of your body" (l. 11) where he did? Why not at the beginning?
3. Why do you think the speaker departs from describing physical qualities in the final line? How did you interpret this line?

Focus on Comparison and Contrast

1. What do these poems have in common in terms of their descriptions of the beloved? What is similar about the two poets' use of imagery?
2. How does the structure of the Neruda sonnet differ from the structure of the Shakespearean sonnet? What effect do these differences have on your reading of the poems?
3. Compare the use of alternating positive and negative imagery in the two sonnets. What is different about the way this technique is used in "My ugly love" as compared to how it's used in "My mistress' eyes are nothing like the sun"?
4. Compare the tone employed by the speaker in the Neruda sonnet as he addresses his beloved with the tone employed by the speaker in the Shakespearean sonnet as he addresses a third party. Given your findings, what purpose, other than pitching woo, might these two poems serve?

Writing Assignment

"My mistress' eyes are nothing like the sun" and "My ugly love" are both concerned with beauty and love. In a well-written essay, compare and contrast the poems, analyzing the relationship of beauty in each. In your essay, consider elements such as imagery, structure, and tone.

The Kiss

GUSTAV KLIMT

Gustav Klimt was born in 1862 in Baumgarten, outside Vienna. His life was contemporary with the fading glory of the Austro-Hungarian Empire, which died, like Klimt, in 1918. He trained as an artist at the Kunstgewerbeschule, Vienna's school of arts and crafts. The declining pomp of the empire, imbued with aging style and form, prompted Klimt in 1897 to lead the Vienna secession, a movement that

The Kiss (1907–1908, oil and gold leaf on canvas, 180 × 180 cm)

sought to celebrate and promote the work of younger, less traditional artists in the imperial capital. His influence as the leader of that movement was far-reaching, spawning the modernist school of Viennese painters and influencing a generation of European artists. The hallmark of his painting and drawing is a concentration on the female form, which he reproduced with a simple, often haunting sensuality. Works such as *The Kiss*, *The Friends*, *Fulfillment*, and *Mulher sentada* have an overt and direct naturalism viewed as scandalous at the time. Like much of his work, *The Kiss* (1908) is a sensuous piece, overlaying a simple subject with opulent ornamentation.

Exploring the Text

1. How do you interpret the clothing in this painting? In particular, is the gold to the right of the woman part of the man's garment or part of a halo that extends above the couple? Why is the man's cloak adorned with rectangles and the woman's with circles? How would different interpretations of the clothing lead to different readings of the painting?
2. Look closely at the body language of the man and the woman. What aspects of it convey emotion? What emotions are conveyed?
3. Describe some of the ways that this painting blurs the line between the natural and the unnatural. What do you think is the point?

Short Story on a Painting of Gustav Klimt

Lawrence Ferlinghetti

Lawrence Ferlinghetti (b. 1919) was born in New York to a French Portuguese mother and a first-generation Italian American father. His parents died when he was an infant, and he spent his early childhood with a French aunt in Strasbourg. Returning to the United States, he attended several schools and earned his BA at the University of North Carolina. Serving in the U.S. Navy during World War II, he visited Nagasaki two weeks after the dropping of the atomic bomb and became a lifelong pacifist. The GI Bill enabled him to earn an MA at Columbia University; he then returned to France and earned a PhD at the Sorbonne. He returned to the United States in 1951, settling in San Francisco, where he cofounded *City Lights* magazine, City Lights bookstore, and City Lights Publishers in 1953. The first volume published was Ferlinghetti's first collection of poetry, *Pictures of the Gone World* (1954). Since then, he has written more than thirty books of poetry. An accomplished artist as well as poet, Ferlinghetti brings an artist's perception to his poem "Short Story on a Painting of Gustav Klimt" (1976). This charming fantasy captures the wistfulness of Klimt's painting while interpreting the woman's posture and thoughts.

They are kneeling upright on a flowered bed
   He
       has just caught her there
            and holds her still
   Her gown   5
      has slipped down
            off her shoulder
He has an urgent hunger
        His dark head
            bends to hers   10
              hungrily
And the woman the woman
    turns her tangerine lips from his
      one hand like the head of a dead swan
       draped down over   15
             his heavy neck
      the fingers
        strangely crimped
          tightly together
   her other arm doubled up   20
       against her tight breast
    her hand a languid claw
         clutching his hand
    which would turn her mouth
             to his   25
   her long dress made
      of multicolored blossoms
        quilted on gold
   her Titian hair
      with blue stars in it   30
And his gold
     harlequin robe
        checkered with
         dark squares
Gold garlands   35
     stream down over
        her bare calves &
       tensed feet
Nearby there must be
    a jeweled tree   40
      with glass leaves aglitter
     in the gold air
It must be
   morning
     in a faraway place somewhere   45

They
    are silent together
                as in a flowered field
      upon the summer couch
                 which must be hers   50
  And he holds her still
              so passionately
      holds her head to his
            so gently so insistently
     to make her turn   55
              her lips to his
 Her eyes are closed
           like folded petals
She
    will not open   60
         He
        is not the One

[1976]

Exploring the Text

1. Ferlinghetti's poem describes and interprets the gestures of the man and woman in *The Kiss*. In the third line, he explains that the man "caught her there." What does this phrase suggest about the occasion of this kiss?
2. In line 14, Ferlinghetti compares the woman's hand to "the head of a dead swan." Later in line 22 he describes her other hand as "a languid claw." What are the connotations of these images? How do these images affect your reading of the painting?
3. Explain the allusions to "Titian hair" (l. 29) and "harlequin robe" (l. 32).
4. Upon what evidence in the painting do you think Ferlinghetti based his statement that "Nearby there must be / a jeweled tree" (ll. 39–40)?
5. Do you find Ferlinghetti's explanation for why the woman's eyes are closed plausible (ll. 61–62)? Do you have another interpretation?

Conversation

Courtship: The Rules of Engagement

Though the mating game has been going on for centuries, courtship rituals — the rules of engagement — change over time. They are also deeply influenced by culture and class. During the nineteenth century, gentlemen in pursuit of a wife "called on" eligible young ladies. A proper visit lasted only between one and fifteen minutes, during which the gentleman caller never removed his gloves. In upper-class Latin American society, a young woman would not be allowed to leave her home without a duenna, or chaperone, to accompany her. In many cultures, arranged marriages have been the norm, with parents selecting partners for their children on the basis of practical matters, such as dowries, economic prospects, and caste. The texts in this Conversation invite you to reflect on the different ways courtship plays out in society. Read them carefully and consider the complexities of the ritual we call courtship.

Texts

Andreas Capellanus, from *The Art of Courtly Love* (nonfiction)

Andrew Marvell, "To His Coy Mistress" (poetry)

Annie Finch, "Coy Mistress" (poetry)

    Annie Finch on Writing

Charles Dickens, from *Our Mutual Friend* (fiction)

E. E. Cummings, "somewhere I have never travelled, gladly beyond" (poetry)

Zareh Khrakhouni, "Measure" (poetry)

Anita Jain, "Is Arranged Marriage Really Any Worse Than Craigslist?" (nonfiction)

Randall Munroe, *Boyfriend* (cartoon)

From *The Art of Courtly Love*

ANDREAS CAPELLANUS

Andreas Capellanus was a French chaplain in the twelfth century. His best-known work is *Liber de arte honeste amandi et reprobatione inhonesti amoris* (c. 1185), known in English as *The Art of Courtly Love*. Two hundred pages long, it contains advice on the practical, religious, and ethical principles of loving. The thirty-one rules of love shown here are listed at the end of the second book.

1. Marriage is no real excuse for not loving.
2. He who is not jealous cannot love.
3. No one can be bound by a double love.
4. It is well known that love is always increasing or decreasing.
5. That which a lover takes against the will of his beloved has no relish.
6. Boys do not love until they arrive at the age of maturity.
7. When one lover dies, a widowhood of two years is required of the survivor.
8. No one should be deprived of love without the very best of reasons.
9. No one can love unless he is impelled by the persuasion of love.

10. Love is always a stranger in the home of avarice.

11. It is not proper to love any woman whom one would be ashamed to seek to marry.

12. A true lover does not desire to embrace in love anyone except his beloved.

13. When made public love rarely endures.

14. The easy attainment of love makes it of little value: difficulty of attainment makes it prized.

15. Every lover regularly turns pale in the presence of his beloved.

16. When a lover suddenly catches sight of his beloved his heart palpitates.

17. A new love puts to flight an old one.

18. Good character alone makes any man worthy of love.

19. If love diminishes, it quickly fails and rarely revives.

20. A man in love is always apprehensive.

21. Real jealousy always increases the feeling of love.

22. Jealousy, and therefore love, are increased when one suspects his beloved.

23. He whom the thought of love vexes eats and sleeps very little.

24. Every act of a lover ends in the thought of his beloved.

25. A true lover considers nothing good except what he thinks will please his beloved.

26. Love can deny nothing to love.

27. A lover can never have enough of the solaces of his beloved.

28. A slight presumption causes a lover to suspect his beloved.

29. A man who is vexed by too much passion usually does not love.

30. A true lover is constantly and without intermission possessed by the thought of his beloved.

31. Nothing forbids one woman being loved by two men or one man by two women.

[c. 1185]

Questions

1. Do any of these guidelines for courtly love seem dated to you? Why? Which of them seem as valid today as they have ever been?

2. Are there any rules you would like to argue about with Andreas Capellanus? How would you defend your point of view?

3. What do these guidelines suggest about the author's attitude toward courtship and love?

To His Coy Mistress

ANDREW MARVELL

Andrew Marvell (1621–1678) was born the fourth child of a minister in Yorkshire, England. He wrote much of his lyrical poetry—including two of his most famous poems, "To His Coy Mistress" and "The Definition of Love"—during the early 1650s while working as a tutor. He later served as assistant to John Milton and as a member of Parliament. Much of his writing after 1660 lampoons the corrupt foolishness of the royal court; when Marvell died in 1678, a rumor circulated that he had been killed by the Jesuits in retaliation for an anonymous lampoon. "To His Coy Mistress" is a slyly persuasive poem, set within the classical models that Marvell knew from childhood.

Had we but world enough, and time,
This coyness, lady, were no crime.
We would sit down, and think which way
To walk, and pass our long love's day.
Thou by the Indian Ganges' side   5
Shouldst rubies find; I by the tide
Of Humber[1] would complain. I would
Love you ten years before the Flood,
And you should, if you please, refuse
Till the conversion of the Jews.   10
My vegetable love should grow
Vaster than empires, and more slow;
An hundred years should go to praise
Thine eyes and on thy forehead gaze,
Two hundred to adore each breast,   15
But thirty thousand to the rest:
An age at least to every part,
And the last age should show your heart.
For, lady, you deserve this state,
Nor would I love at lower rate.   20
    But at my back I always hear
Time's wingèd chariot hurrying near;
And yonder all before us lie
Deserts of vast eternity.
Thy beauty shall no more be found,   25
Nor in thy marble vault shall sound
My echoing song; then worms shall try
That long preserved virginity,

---

[1]A river that runs through Marvell's hometown of Hull, England.—EDS.

And your quaint honor turn to dust,
And into ashes all my lust.   30
The grave's a fine and private place,
But none, I think, do there embrace.
   Now, therefore, while the youthful hue
Sits on thy skin like morning dew,
And while thy willing soul transpires[2]   35
At every pore with instant fires,
Now let us sport us while we may,
And now, like amorous birds of prey,
Rather at once our time devour
Than languish in his slow-chapped[3] power.   40
Let us roll all our strength and all
Our sweetness up into one ball,
And tear our pleasures with rough strife
Thorough[4] the iron gates of life.
Thus, though we cannot make our sun   45
Stand still, yet we will make him run.

                                                        [1681]

Questions

1. The phrase "carpe diem" is usually translated as "seize the day." The Latin verb *carpere* literally means "to pick." How does the speaker in Marvell's "To His Coy Mistress" espouse the idea of carpe diem?
2. What is the logic of the argument that the speaker develops? Try working with the markers of sections: "Had we but world enough . . ." (l. 1); "But at my back I always hear . . ." (l. 21); and "Now, therefore, while the youthful hue . . ." (l. 33).
3. Find examples in Marvell's poem of hyperbole and understatement. How are these resources of language used by the speaker as tools of courtship?
4. What role does time play in Marvell's courtship scenario?

Coy Mistress

ANNIE FINCH

Annie Finch (b. 1956) was born in New Rochelle, New York. She is director of the Stonecoast MFA in Creative Writing program at the University of Southern Maine. In addition to literary criticism, she has written three books of poetry—*Eve* (1997), *Calendars* (2003), and *The Encyclopedia of Scotland* (2004). A fourth

---

[2]Breathes out.—EDS.
[3]Slow-jawed.—EDS.
[4]Through.—EDS.

volume of poetry, *Among the Goddesses: An Epic Libretto in Seven Dreams*, is scheduled for publication in 2010. "Coy Mistress" is an imaginary response to Andrew Marvell's famous poem "To His Coy Mistress."

Sir, I am not a bird of prey:
a Lady does not seize the day.
I trust that brief Time will unfold
our youth, before he makes us old.
How could we two write lines of rhyme   5
were we not fond of numbered Time
and grateful to the vast and sweet
trials his days will make us meet?
The Grave's not just the body's curse;
no skeleton can pen a verse!   10
So while this numbered World we see,
let's sweeten Time with poetry,
and Time, in turn, may sweeten Love
and give us time our love to prove.
You've praised my eyes, forehead, breast: 15
you've all our lives to praise the rest.

[1997]

Questions

1. What does the speaker in the poem imply when she says that "a Lady does not seize the day" (l. 2)?
2. In Finch's response, how does she claim equality with the male speaker of "To His Coy Mistress"? What profession do they share?
3. Which specific points of the argument in Marvell's "To His Coy Mistress" does this speaker take exception to?

ANNIE FINCH ON WRITING

Renée Shea (RS): Why did you write "Coy Mistress"—or maybe I should ask, how could you resist?

Annie Finch (AF): I actually wrote it as an assignment when I was a senior in college. I had a boyfriend who read me the original Marvell, and I thought it was an extraordinary poem. Not long after that I was taking a class with John Hollander, and he gave the assignment to write a reply to a famous poem, so I thought of "To His Coy Mistress."

RS: Do you think Marvell knew that his coy mistress was a poet or could become one?

AF: I don't. I think that was my spin on it, to make it possible that she would be a poet or hoped to become a poet. I don't think he gave her that much credit.

RS: Were you tempted to write more as a contemporary woman, using contemporary forms, instead of writing in the language of Marvell's time?

AF: I wanted to absorb the feeling, the mood, the rhythm, the tone of the original. I don't remember feeling tempted to write in a more modern woman's voice; I wanted to sort of channel the coy mistress herself and write in a way she would have written had she written back to Marvell.

For me, every poem is a potential site of political action—not to put it too heavily!—a site of change, so I'm always looking for a way to approach the poem in a slightly unusual way that's going to torque things a little, make the point of entry an unexpected place and use the leverage of the poem to get further than I would otherwise. My friend Patricia Smith says that whenever she is writing, she wants to give voice to the voiceless. I think I have a similar impulse, so if I'm writing a poem about nature, I'm often trying to put myself in the point of view of the natural creature or phenomenon that doesn't get a voice. I've always rebelled against the idea of the poet appropriating the outside world. I'm more interested in the poet as a channel for the outside world, a more shamanic view of the poet. I'm very interested in using my poetry to give voice to whatever doesn't have a voice.

RS: Do you intend that your "Coy Mistress" will send us back to Marvell and make us read him differently?

AF: Yes, and I like that. With every retelling—and I've done quite a few, especially of goddess myths—I always want to bring people back to the original. And I would hope that when people read Marvell, they'll think of me just as much as the opposite. I really want to be part of a conversation. I think it's interesting that I first encountered the poem in the voice of a boyfriend. It was so alive in that context, and I remember one of my responses—as well as thinking what an extraordinary poem it is and admiring it so much and finding it romantic that he was reading it to me—was that I was so annoyed by the arrogance of it. It drove me nuts that there was no room for her to have any kind of equal response. He was claiming all the rhetorical power, all the poetic authority. I almost felt as

5

though Marvell was challenging me down through the centuries: "Okay. Now what are you going to say?" Looking back at my poem decades later, it really surprises me. I was a young woman, finding my way romantically, so those concerns were very important to me at the time, but what amazes me looking back is that being a poet was even more important because clearly that's the level on which I responded to Marvell and the level on which I was so challenged by the arrogance of the point of view of this poet.

RS: But if you were so struck by the speaker's arrogance, why did you admire   10
the poem so much?

AF: I think reading it aloud is the way to encounter the poem's indisputable value, and in this case, the skill is just unbelievable. Where it really gets me going is the way he uses the rhythm. The first two lines are sort of mechanical, then in the third or fourth lines he changes the rhythm — "We would sit down." The rhythm starts to sway, back and forth, back and forth, and you have a completely different way of encountering the line. At that point, I suddenly realized I'm in a car driven by an unbelievably skilled driver, and I'm being taken down a road full of curves and vistas. The other place where I really got it was "My vegetable love should grow / Vaster than empires, and more slow" — the two *l*'s and two *v*'s in those lines are just extraordinary. To convey why I think this is a poem worth admiring, I have to read it aloud.

Follow-Up

1. What does Finch mean by poetry as a "site of political action" (para. 7)? How is that point linked to her view of "the arrogance" of Marvell's speaker?
2. How do you think the impact of Finch's "writing back" might have changed if she had written in the language of a contemporary woman? Would it have diminished the point she is making?
3. How did information you garnered from the interview with Finch affect your interpretation of "Coy Mistress"? How did it affect your interpretation of the Marvell poem?

From *Our Mutual Friend*

CHARLES DICKENS

Charles Dickens (1812–1870) is best known for his twenty-one novels, many of which were published in magazines in serial form. Several have become immortal classics of the English language, such as *David Copperfield* (1849–1850), *A Tale of Two Cities* (1859), and *Great Expectations* (1860–1861). This passage taken from Dickens's last novel, *Our Mutual Friend* (1864–1865), features the well-to-do schoolmaster Bradley Headstone proposing to Lizzy Hexam, daughter of a pauper and accused murderer.

"You know what I am going to say. I love you. What other men may mean when they use that expression, I cannot tell; what *I* mean is, that I am under the influence of some tremendous attraction which I have resisted in vain, and which overmasters me. You could draw me to fire, you could draw me to water, you could draw me to the gallows, you could draw me to any death, you could draw me to anything I have most avoided, you could draw me to any exposure and disgrace. This and the confusion of my thoughts, so that I am fit for nothing, is what I mean by your being the ruin of me. But if you would return a favourable answer to my offer of myself in marriage, you could draw me to any good—every good—with equal force. My circumstances are quite easy, and you would want for nothing. My reputation stands quite high, and would be a shield for yours. If you saw me at my work, able to do it well and respected in it, you might even come to take a sort of pride in me;—I would try hard that you should. Whatever considerations I may have thought of against this offer, I have conquered, and I make it with all my heart. Your brother favours me to the utmost, and it is likely that we might live and work together; anyhow, it is certain that he would have my best influence and support. I don't know what I could say more if I tried. I might only weaken what is ill enough said as it is. I only add that if it is any claim on you to be in earnest, I am in thorough earnest, dreadful earnest."

The powdered mortar from under the stone at which he wrenched, rattled on the pavement to confirm his words.

"Mr. Headstone—"

"Stop! I implore you, before you answer me, to walk round this place once more. It will give you a minute's time to think, and me a minute's time to get some fortitude together."

[1864–1865]

Questions

1. Charles Dickens named the character who delivers this monologue Bradley Headstone. Do you find aspects of the speech that resonate with this name?
2. Does Mr. Headstone's proposal greatly differ from the usual proposals of today? How? What commonalities do you see?
3. What does the language Mr. Headstone uses reveal about what he seeks in a wife?

somewhere I have never travelled, gladly beyond

E. E. CUMMINGS

Edward Estlin (E. E.) Cummings (1894–1962) was an enormously prolific and experimental poet. Born and raised in an affluent family in Cambridge, Massachusetts, he graduated from Cambridge Latin High School and received both a BA and an MA in English and classical studies from Harvard University. Before the United States entered World War I, Cummings, an avowed pacifist, volunteered as an ambulance driver in France, where he was held for a time in a detention camp—an experience that deepened his distrust of authority. *The Enormous Room* (1922), his first published work, is a fictional account of his imprisonment, followed in 1923 by his first collection of poems, *Tulips and Chimneys*. Cummings defied traditional rules of typography and punctuation in the pursuit of poetry that was both critical of the status quo and whimsical. His poem "somewhere i have never travelled, gladly beyond" (from *W [ViVa]*) showcases Cummings's experimentation with form and punctuation, and is an early example of the style that became his trademark.

somewhere i have never travelled,gladly beyond
any experience,your eyes have their silence:
in your most frail gesture are things which enclose me,
or which i cannot touch because they are too near

your slightest look easily will unclose me   5
though i have closed myself as fingers,
you open always petal by petal myself as Spring opens
(touching skilfully,mysteriously)her first rose

or if your wish be to close me,i and
my life will shut very beautifully,suddenly,   10
as when the heart of this flower imagines
the snow carefully everywhere descending;

nothing which we are to perceive in this world equals
the power of your intense fragility:whose texture
compels me with the colour of its countries,   15
rendering death and forever with each breathing

(i do not know what it is about you that closes
and opens;only something in me understands
the voice of your eyes is deeper than all roses)
nobody,not even the rain,has such small hands   20

[1931]

Questions

1. In this poem, Cummings occasionally describes one sense in terms of another (called synesthesia): "your eyes have their silence" (l. 2) and "the voice of your eyes" (l. 19). What is the effect of this use of language on the meaning of the poem?

2. The speaker compares his beloved to a flower. Do you think that comparison would be flattering or insulting to her? Why?

3. The poem makes repeated reference to "open" and "close" and derivates of these words. What point does Cummings make with these images?
4. What does the poem's syntax suggest about the speaker's state of mind when he thinks of his love?
5. Do you find this poem romantic? touching? sentimental? Would a twenty-first-century woman be moved by it?

Measure

Zareh Khrakhouni

TRANSLATED BY DIANA DER-HOVANESSIAN

> Zareh Khrakhouni (b. 1926)—an Armenian poet born in Turkey—is the author of twenty-six books, including poetry, essays, plays, and translations. He has served as director and editor of the literary supplement of *Marmara*—the Armenian daily newspaper of Istanbul—and is considered one of the main proponents of modern literature in Western Armenian letters.

"I love you so much . . ." you said.
"But not as much as I love you," I said.
"Oh, much more than you love," you said.
"Shall we compare?" I replied.
So we measure. We correlated,   5
collated and weighed.

Taller than tall, we chose mountain altitudes
to scan and grade.
We chose stars and galaxies to outdistance
in love. Day by day we came up   10
with calculations to outdo.

From legends of Augean stables
to giant structures piercing the blue.
Finally you said your love was as deep
as the light in my eyes when   15
I looked at you and knew
I was defeated.

                                                          [1964]

Questions

1. Based on their exchange of dialogue, what do you infer about the two lovers' relationship? How did the speaker in the poem know he was defeated?

2. What is the effect of the language of quantification in the opening stanza?
3. Find examples of hyperbole in the poem. How does this use of overstatement conform to the traditions of love poetry? What purpose does it serve? What does it suggest about the speaker's state of mind?
4. Can you tell if the speaker is a man or a woman? Why or why not? Does it matter?

Is Arranged Marriage Really Any Worse Than Craigslist?

ANITA JAIN

Anita Jain (b. 1973) was born in New Delhi and moved to the United States six months later. She has an undergraduate degree from Harvard University, and has worked as a financial journalist in Mexico City, Singapore, London, New York, and New Delhi. In the summer of 2005, frustrated by the patterns of Western dating, she returned to India to find a husband by more "traditional" methods, as chronicled in her book *Marrying Anita* (2008). With subtly ironic, humorous touches, she describes the interplay of India's traditional culture with the young, hip, Westernized population. This article was printed in *New York* magazine shortly before Ms. Jain returned to New Delhi.

Recently, i was cc'd on an e-mail addressed to my father. It read, "We liked the girl's profile. The boy is in good state job in Mississippi and cannot come to New York. The girl must relocate to Mississippi." The message was signed by Mr. Ramesh Gupta, "the boy's father."

That wasn't as bad as the time I logged on to my computer at home in Fort Greene and got a message that asked, forgoing any preamble, what the date, time, and location of my birth were. Presumably sent to determine how astrologically harmonious a match with a Hindu suitor I'd be, the e-mail was dismayingly abrupt. But I did take heart in the fact that it was addressed only to me.

I've been fielding such messages—or, rather, my father has—more and more these days, having crossed the unmarriageable threshold for an Indian woman, thirty, two years ago. My parents, in a very earnest bid to secure my eternal happiness, have been trying to marry me off to, well, just about anyone lately. In my childhood home near Sacramento, my father is up at night on arranged-marriage Websites. And the result—strange e-mails from boys' fathers and stranger dates with those boys themselves—has become so much a part of my dating life that I've lost sight of how bizarre it once seemed.

Many women, Indian or not, whose parents have had a long, healthy marriage hope we will, too, while fearing that perhaps we've made everything irreparably worse by expecting too much. Our prospective husbands have to be rich and socially conscious, hip but down-to-earth.

For some Indians, the conundrum is exacerbated by the fact that our parents had no choice for a partner; the only choice was how hard they'd work to be happy. My

5

father saw my mother once before they got married. He loves to shock Americans by recounting how he lost sight of her at a bazaar the day after their wedding and lamented to himself that he would never find her again, as he'd forgotten what she looked like. So while we, as modern Indian women, eschew the idea of marrying without love, the idea that we're being too picky tends to nag even more than it otherwise would.

Still, for years, I didn't want to get married the way my brother did. He'd met his wife through a newspaper ad my parents had taken out. He's very happily married, with a baby daughter, but he also never had a girlfriend before his wedding day. I was more precocious when it came to affairs of the heart, having enjoyed my first kiss with cute Matt from the football squad at fourteen.

Perhaps it was that same spirit of romantic adventurism that led me, shortly after college, to go on the first of these "introductions," though I agreed to my parents' setup mainly with an eye toward turning it into a story for friends.

At the time, I was working as a journalist in Singapore. Vikram, "in entertainment," took me to the best restaurant in town, an Indonesian place with a view of the skyscrapers. Before long, though, I gathered that he was of a type: someone who prided himself on being modern and open-minded but who in fact had horribly crusty notions passed down from his Indian parents. I was taken aback when he told me about an Indian girl he'd liked. "I thought maybe she was the one, but then I found out she had a Muslim boyfriend in college," he said. I lodged my protest against him and arranged marriage by getting ragingly intoxicated and blowing smoke rings in his face. Childish? Maybe, but I didn't want to be marriageable back then. Indeed, I rarely thought of marriage at the time.

But for Indians, there's no way to escape thinking about marriage, eventually. It wouldn't be a stretch to say that *shaadi,* the word for marriage in many Indian languages, is the first word a child understands after *mummy* and *papa.* To an Indian, marriage is a matter of karmic destiny. There are many happy unions in the pantheon of Hindu gods—Shiva and Parvati, Krishna and Radha.

At a recent dinner party, when I was trying to explain how single-minded Indian   10
parents can be, my friend Jaidev jumped to the rescue. "Imagine you are on a safari in Africa with your parents," he said. "A lion strolls by, and then perhaps a tiger. Your mother turns to you and says, 'Son, when are you getting married? You have a girl in mind? What are your intentions?'"

The pressure on me to find a husband started very early. A few days after my first birthday, within months of my family's arrival in the U.S., I fell out of the window of a three-story building in Baltimore. My father recalls my mother's greatest concern, after learning that I hadn't been gravely injured: "What boy will marry her when he finds out?" she cried, begging my father to never mention my broken arm—from which I've enjoyed a full recovery—to prospective suitors out of fear my dowry would be prohibitively higher. (A middle-class family can easily spend $100,000 these days on a dowry in India.) Much savvier in the ways of his new country, my father laughed it off. "But there is no dowry in America!"

Fulfilling his parental duty, my father placed matrimonial ads for me every couple of years during my twenties in such immigrant newspapers as *India Abroad*. They read something like, "Match for Jain girl, Harvard-educated journalist, twenty-five, fair, slim." I took it as a personal victory that they didn't include the famous Indian misnomer "homely" to mean domestically inclined.

Depending on whether my father was in a magnanimous mood, he would add "caste no bar," which meant suitors didn't have to belong to Jainism, an offshoot of Hinduism with the world's most severe dietary restrictions. Root vegetables like carrots are verboten.

Still rather prejudiced against meat-eaters, my father immediately discards responses from those with a "non-veg" diet. There is, however, a special loophole for meat-eaters who earn more than $200,000. (This is only a little shocking, since my last boyfriend was a Spanish chef who got me addicted to chorizo. Once, I was horrified to discover, he'd put a skinned rabbit in my freezer.)

This desultory casting around to see what was out there has become much more   15
urgent now that I'm in my thirties, and in their quest, my parents have discovered a dizzying array of Websites: shaadi.com, indiamatrimony.com, etc. Within these sites are sub-sites for Indian regions, like punjabimatrimony.com. You might be surprised at who you'd find on them: the guy in the next cubicle, your freshman-year roommate at NYU, maybe even the cute girl you tried to pick up at a Lower East Side bar last night.

Far from being a novel approach to matrimony, these sites are a natural extension of how things have been done in India for decades. Even since well before the explosion of the country's famously vibrant press in the fifties, Indians were coupling up via matrimonial ads in national papers ("Match sought for Bengali Brahmin, wheatish complexion," etc.).

My father took to the Websites like a freshly divorced forty-two-year-old who's just discovered Craigslist. He uploaded my profile on several, indicating that only men living in New York City need apply (nota bene, Mr. Ramesh Gupta). Unfortunately, in the world of shaadi.com, this means most of the men live in New Jersey, while working in IT departments all around New York.

My father also *wrote* my profile. This may be why dates are surprised to discover I enjoy a glass of wine or two with dinner, and another couple afterward, even though the profile says "I never drink." And he writes back to those who appear aboveboard. This is no small task, as anyone who's done any online dating can attest. As my father puts it, wagging his head, "You get a lot of useless types."

Like most Indians of their generation, my parents believe there are only two legitimate professions: doctor and engineer (not medicine and engineering, but doctor and engineer). Yes, they've heard of such newfangled professions as investment banking and law, but, oh, no, they won't be fooled. Across India can be heard the refrain, "It is good match: They found doctor," and my father expects nothing less for his little girl.

The problem is that while he wants doctor or engineer, my heart beats for the   20
diametric opposite. Take the aging but rakish foreign correspondent I was smitten with last year. Nearing fifty, he'd just seen his marriage fall apart, and he mourned its passing by plastering his body with fresh tattoos and picking bar fights. I found it

terribly sexy that he rode a Harley, perhaps less so that his apartment was decorated with Wonder Woman paraphernalia. He was on a downward spiral, but perhaps my parents might appreciate that he'd won a Pulitzer earlier in his career?

The relationship didn't go anywhere, as my father might have warned me if I'd told him about such things. I will admit to needing a little romantic assistance. Since moving here a few years ago, I'd hardly describe my dating life as successful. There was Sadakat, the half-Finnish, half-Pakistani barrister from London who slept most of the day and worked most of the night writing a book on criminal justice. Circumscribed within this schedule, our dates would begin at midnight. Once I fell asleep on the bar during the middle of one.

Then there were the ones who simply never called again. The boy from Minnesota who imported women's leather clothing from Brazil, the Cockney song-writer, the French dot-com millionaire. Perhaps I didn't want to marry these men, but I certainly wanted to see them again. I began to feel baffled by Western norms of dating, what one Indian friend calls "dating for dating's sake."

Last summer, Alex, a handsome consultant I'd met at a party, invited me to his apartment for dinner. It was our first real date, and I was flattered—and encouraged—that he was already cooking for me. Soon after I arrived, we were drinking an Argentine wine I'd brought to go with his vegetarian lasagne, hewing to my restored dietary restrictions. Then, during dessert, Alex started talking about his long-distance Japanese girlfriend. I spat out my espresso. Not done yet, he also sought my advice on how to ask out the cute girl from his gym. Was it something I did? Perhaps I should have brought an old-world wine? Dating for dating's sake indeed.

I've had greater luck attracting romantic attention (of a sort) on vacation. It was during a trip to Argentina that I met Juan Carlos, a black-haired, green-eyed painter—of buildings, not canvases. Within an hour of meeting me, he said he would become a vegetarian as soon as we married, that he'd never felt this way for any woman—"nunca en mi vida"—that I was the mother of his children. Oddly, by the end of the night, he couldn't remember my name. Nothing fazed Juan Carlos, however. He quickly jotted off a poem explaining his lapse: "I wrote your name in the sand, but a wave came and washed it away. I wrote your name in a tree, but the branch fell. I have written your name in my heart, and time will guard it."

Given such escapades, it may come as no surprise that I've started to look at my father's efforts with a touch less disdain. At least the messages aren't as mixed, right? Sometimes they're quite clear. One of the first setups I agreed to took place a year ago. The man—I'll call him Vivek—worked in IT in New Jersey and had lived there all his life. He took the train into the city to meet me at a Starbucks. He was wearing pants that ended two inches before his ankles. We spoke briefly about his work before he asked, "What are you looking for in a husband?" Since this question always leaves me flummoxed—especially when it's asked by somebody in high-waters within the first few minutes of conversation—I mumbled something along the lines of, "I don't know, a connection, I guess. What are you looking for?" Vivek responded, "Just two things. Someone who's vegetarian and doesn't smoke. That shouldn't be so hard to find, don't you think?"

25

It's a common online-dating complaint that people are nothing like their pro-
files. I've found they can be nothing but them. And in their tone-deafness, some of
these men resemble the parents spurring them on. One Sunday, I was woken by a call
at 9 A.M. A woman with a heavy Indian accent asked for Anita. I have a raspy voice
at the best of times, but after a night of "social" smoking, my register is on par with
Clint Eastwood's. So when I croaked, "This is she," the perplexed lady responded, "She
or he?" before asking, "What are your qualifications?" I said I had a BA. "BA only?"
she responded. "What are the boy's qualifications?" I flung back in an androgynous
voice. She smirked: "He is MD in Kentucky *only.*" Still bleary-eyed, but with enough
presence of mind to use the deferential term for an elder, I grumbled, "Auntie, I will
speak to the boy only." Neither she, nor he, called back.

These days, I do have my limits. I'm left cold by e-mails with fresh-off-the-boat
Indian English like "Hope email is finding you in pink of health" or "I am looking for
life partner for share of joy of life and sorrowful time also." For the most part, though,
I go and meet the men my father has screened for me. And it is much the same as I
imagine it must be for any active dater.

I recall the Goldman Sachs banker who said, in the middle of dinner, which
we were having steps away from Wall Street, "You know, my work will always come
before my family."

Another time, I met a very sweet-seeming journalist for lunch in Chinatown.
Afterward, I was planning to meet my best friend, who's gay, in a store, and I asked
the guy to come in and say hello. My date became far more animated than he'd been
before and even helped my friend choose a sweater. After he left, I asked my friend
what he thought. He gave me a sidelong glance, and we both burst into laughter.

As with any singles Website geared toward one community, you also get your 30
interlopers. A forty-four-year-old Jewish doctor managed to make my dad's first
cut: He *was* a doctor. Mark said he believed Indians and Jews shared similar values,
like family and education. I didn't necessarily have a problem with his search for an
Indian wife. (Isn't it when they dislike us for our skin color that we're supposed to get
upset?) But when I met him for dinner, he seemed a decade older than he was, which
made me feel like I was a decade younger.

My father's screening method is hardly foolproof. Once, he was particularly
taken with a suitor who claimed to be a brain surgeon at Johns Hopkins and friends
with a famous Bollywood actress, Madhuri Dixit. I was suspicious, but I agreed to
speak to the fellow. Within seconds, his shaky command of English and yokel line
of questioning—"You are liking dancing? I am too much liking dancing"—told me
this man was as much a brain surgeon as I was Madhuri Dixit. I refused to talk to
him again, even though my father persisted in thinking I was bullheaded. "Don't you
think we would make sure his story checked out before marrying you off?" he said.

Sometimes, though, you get close, really close. A year ago, I was put in touch with
a McKinsey consultant in Bombay whom I'll call Sameer. I liked the fact that he was
Indian American but had returned to India to work. We had great conversations on
the phone—among other things, he had interesting views on how people our age
were becoming more sexually liberated in Indian cities—and I began envisioning

myself kept in the finest silk saris. My father kept telling me he wanted it all "wrapped up" by February—it was only Christmas! Sameer had sent a picture, and while he wasn't Shah Rukh Khan, he wasn't bad.

Back for a break in New York, Sameer kindly came to see me in Brooklyn. We went to a French bistro, where he leaned over the table and said, "You know, your father really shouldn't send out those photos of you. They don't do justice to your beauty." Sameer was generous, good-natured, engaging, seemingly besotted with me, on an expat salary—and also on the Atkins diet to lose fifty pounds. *My* Bombay dreams went up in smoke.

In this, I guess I am like every other woman in New York, complaining a man is too ambitious or not ambitious enough, too eager or not eager enough. But they are picky, too. These men, in their bid to fit in on Wall Street or on the golf course, would like a wife who is eminently presentable—to their boss, friends, and family. They would like a woman to be sophisticated enough to have a martini, and not a Diet Coke, at an office party, but, God forbid, not "sophisticated" enough to have three. Sometimes I worry that I'm a bit too sophisticated for most Indian men.

That's not to say I haven't come to appreciate what Indian men have to offer,   35
which is a type of seriousness, a clarity of intent. I've never heard from an Indian man the New York beg-off phrase "I don't think I'm ready for a relationship right now. I have a lot of things going on in my life."

Indian men also seem to share my belief that Westerners have made the progression toward marriage unnecessarily agonizing. Neal, a thirty-five-year-old Indian lawyer I know, thinks it's absurd how a couple in America can date for years and still not know if they want to get married. "I think I would only need a couple of months to get to know a girl before I married her," he says.

In more traditional arranged marriages—which are still very much alive and well in India—couples may get only one or two meetings before their wedding day. In America, and in big Indian cities, a couple may get a few months before they are expected to walk down the aisle, or around the fire, as they do seven times, in keeping with Hindu custom. By now I certainly think that would be enough time for me.

Other Indian women I know seem to be coming to the same conclusion. My friend Divya works the overnight shift at the BBC in London and stays out clubbing on her nights off. Imagine my surprise when I discovered she was on keralamatrimony.com, courtesy of her mother, who took the liberty of listing Divya's hobbies as shopping and movies. (I was under the impression her hobbies were more along the lines of trance music and international politics.) Though she's long favored pubgoing blokes, Divya, like me, doesn't discount the possibility that the urologist from Trivandrum or the IT guy could just be the one—an idea patently unthinkable to us in our twenties.

It's become second nature for women like us to straddle the two dating worlds. When I go out on a first date with an Indian man, I find myself saying things I would never utter to an American. Like, "I would expect my husband to fully share domestic chores." Undeniably, there's a lack of mystery to Indian-style dating, because both parties are fully aware of what the endgame should be. But with that also comes a certain relief.

With other forms of dating the options seem limitless. The long kiss in the bar with someone I've never met before could have been just that, an exchange that has a value and meaning of its own that can't be quantified. Ditto for the one-night stand. (Try explaining that one to my parents.) The not-knowing-where-something-is-headed can be wildly exciting. It can also be a tad soul-crushing. Just ask any single woman in New York.

Indians of my mother's generation — in fact, my mother herself — like to say of arranged marriage, "It's not that there isn't love. It's just that it comes after the marriage." I'm still not sure I buy it. But after a decade of Juan Carloses and short-lived affairs with married men and Craigslist flirtations and emotionally bankrupt boyfriends and, oddly, the most painful of all, the guys who just never call, it no longer seems like the most outlandish possibility.

Some of my single friends in New York say they're still not convinced marriage is what they really want. I'm not sure I buy that, either. And no modern woman wants to close the door on any of her options — no matter how traditional — too hastily.

My friend Radhika, an unmarried thirty-seven-year-old photographer, used to hate going to her cousins' weddings, where the aunties never asked her about the famines in Africa or the political conflict in Cambodia she'd covered. Instead it was, "Why aren't you married? What are your intentions?" As much as she dreaded this, they've stopped asking, and for Radhika, that's even worse. "It's like they've written me off," she says.

On a recent trip to India, I was made to eat dinner at the children's table — they sent out for Domino's pizza and Pepsis — because as an unmarried woman, I didn't quite fit in with the adults. As much as I resented my exile, I realized that maybe I didn't want to be eating vegetable curry and drinking rum with the grown-ups. Maybe that would have meant they'd given up on me, that they'd stopped viewing me as a not-yet-married girl but as an unmarriageable woman who'd ruined her youth by being too choosy and strong-headed.

This way, the aunties can still swing by the kids' table as I'm sucking on a Pepsi and chucking a young cousin on the chin, and ask me, "When are you getting married? What are your intentions?" And I can say, "Auntie, do you have a boy in mind?"

[2005]

Questions

1. Why does Jain rebel against her parents' interference in her love life? What does she understand about their intentions and point of view?
2. Over the course of events described in this article, what does the author learn? How does what she learns influence her views regarding courtship and dating?
3. What does this article suggest about the difficulties of contemporary courtship? What new challenges do online meetings and social networking sites pose for individuals in search of a partner?

Boyfriend

RANDALL MUNROE

Randall Munroe (b. 1984) was born in Easton, Pennsylvania, and grew up in Virginia. He has an undergraduate degree in physics from Christopher Newport University, and has worked on various projects for NASA. He is also the creator of the Webcomic *xkcd*, which has become an international success, attracting up to seventy million hits monthly. The unconventional approach of *xkcd* is neatly summarized in the "warning" on the site: "Warning: this comic occasionally contains strong language (which may be unsuitable for children), unusual humor (which may be unsuitable for adults), and advanced mathematics (which may be unsuitable for liberal-arts majors)."

Questions

1. Why do you think the male character objects to being called the female character's "boyfriend"?
2. How does the chart support her use of the term "boyfriend"? What does she mean when she calls herself an "outlier"?
3. Explain the irony in the punch line: "I'm your statistically significant other."
4. How does this cartoon comment on the stereotype of the way women behave during courtship? Is this comment insulting?

Entering the Conversation

As you develop a response to one of the following questions, refer to the texts you have read in this section. You may also draw on your own experience or knowledge relating to courtship.

1. Select one of the guidelines from Capellanus, and discuss whether the texts in this Conversation support, challenge, or refute it. Refer to at least four of the texts.

2. What sort of imagery seems to be most commonly employed in texts dealing with courtship? Write an essay analyzing similar imagery in two or more of these selections, and explain why such imagery might be so popular.

3. Annie Finch responds to Marvell because, as she says in her interview, "every poem is a potential site of political action" and refers to the importance of "giv(ing) voice to the voiceless." Indeed, most of the selections in this section reflect a man's perspective. Write an essay discussing the assumptions (shared or different) that these male voices and illustrators make about what appeals to women, what values women hold about courtship and love, and what will persuade them to return a man's love. Are these assumptions valid today? Focus on three or four specific texts.

4. Are courtship, or dating, rituals reflective of specific cultural contexts—including time periods—or are they more universal and timeless? Using three of the texts in this Conversation, at least one example from popular culture (song lyrics, television, film, advertising), and your own opinion, write an essay that answers that question.

5. Is the pedestal actually a cage? Many of the texts in this Conversation idealize the woman being addressed. What might be the consequences of this idealization? Does it dehumanize women? Does it intimidate men? Does it lead to inequality in relationships? Using three of the pieces in this Conversation, explore this issue.

6. Are the relationships depicted in this Conversation more similar or more different? Select four, including the visual text, to explain your response to that question.

7. Suppose four of the authors in this Conversation were going to be on a television talk show to discuss the following question: what's the best strategy for getting a date? Write a transcript of the exchange among the authors; make sure to include at least one of the women.

Student Writing

Analyzing Irony in Drama

This student essay by Sonya Nagenda was written outside of class as a response to the following prompt.

> Write an essay in which you analyze Oscar Wilde's use of irony in his play *The Importance of Being Earnest*. Be sure to support your analysis with examples from the text.

Oscar Wilde's Use of Irony in *The Importance of Being Earnest*
Sonya Nagenda

In any work of Oscar Wilde, it is important to distinguish between things that he wrote to make a serious social comment and those things that he wrote merely to shock. Too often, the former are confused with the latter because he often chose to make serious points in a lighthearted manner. When we place Wilde in the context of nineteenth-century England, a country dominated by Queen Victoria, it is important to remember that almost every casual, flippant comment on morality was considered an implied criticism of the moral order. Society was essentially serious; life was a demanding business with moral implications at every turn. Wilde wanted to expose and ridicule the inherent hypocrisy in Victorian morality. His social comment was often disguised in apparently flippant remarks.

In *The Importance of Being Earnest*, there are many comments of both types, as there are in Wilde's other works. In *The Picture of Dorian Gray*, Lord Henry Wotton says, "A cigarette is the most perfect kind of a perfect pleasure. It leaves one unsatisfied. What more can one ask?" In *The Importance of Being Earnest*, we read the line, "I never travel without my diary. One should always have something sensational to read in the train." Both these comments mock prevalent morality without making a more serious point. The idea of pleasure and the notion of "sensational" are Wilde's own view on a morality that he considered invasive and censorious. Yet the comments are written essentially to shock, not to make serious or profound comments about society.

In reading any work of Oscar Wilde, therefore, we need to keep the picture of Victorian society at the forefront of our minds and weigh the author's use of irony against the background of the nineteenth century. Every character has a moral base and a satirical flip side. We see the dominant character of Lady Bracknell, pious, moral, and virtuous, revealed as motivated by financial avarice when Jack (Ernest) announces that his ward has a substantial fortune. We see her thundering in moral indignation against Miss Prism, herself a set of contradictions: the worthy spinster who writes a three-volume novel and is careless of the welfare of the infant entrusted to her.

Much more important, however, is the conflict at the center of the two male protagonists. Both Algernon and Jack are deceitful but have contrived to adapt their deceit to conventional politeness. Algernon has created a fictional character called Bunbury, who acts as a cloak for his capers. Jack is simply Jack in the country and Ernest in London, having created a fictional brother in London to account for his absences from the country. In short, both male characters lead a double life, and neither appears to have any moral qualms about doing so. Victorian propriety is upheld, but the underlying morality is exposed as corrupt.

The young women, too, have superficial veneers that hide their underlying acquisitiveness. This is exposed with delightful irony when Gwendolen and Cecily meet at Jack's country house. As each one hurls delicate barbs at the other, the butler watches with approval, appreciating each piercing thrust with the enjoyment of a spectator at a tennis match. For the sake of decency in front of the servants, elementary courtesy is observed, but both women have a fierce desire to marry "Ernest." The irony is that there is no such person as Ernest. Jack is Jack and Algernon is Algernon, yet each woman considers herself in love with Ernest.

The solution to this impossible situation can be found in the title of the play. It was important, even vital, to be "earnest." In the word "Ernest" (or "earnest"), Wilde ironically parodies Victorian morality. Realizing that their future happiness depends on having the name Ernest, both Jack and Algernon arrange to be so baptized. They recognize that to win the heart of their chosen women they must possess "Earnest-ness," a quality that was much respected in Victorian morality. On the other hand, neither of them is earnest; each leads a double life, and each is prepared to treat the serious business of baptism into the Church as a mere device to achieve his ends. Wilde ironically satirizes morality, religion, class structure, and birth, as well as more conventional targets, such as financial greed and social status.

The final deathblow to conventional morality is delivered by Canon Chasuble, who casually regrets, but is not altogether surprised, that no baptisms will after all take place. Life proceeds according to accepted social precepts without the aid of the church.

Questions

1. Outline this essay to get a sense of how the argument flows from paragraph to paragraph. Do you think the organization is effective? How would you suggest Sonya improve it?
2. Paraphrase the second paragraph, and then reread the topic sentence. Do you think this sentence is effective? If so, why does it work? If not, how would you improve it?
3. Where did you notice areas of repetition? How would you suggest Sonya tighten her argument for greater effect?
4. Sonya cites textual evidence to support her points. What additional evidence might strengthen them? Focusing on one specific paragraph, make suggestions for revision.

The Writer's Craft — Close Reading

Irony

Irony is an incongruity between expectation and reality. It can be tricky to spot. It helps to know that there are several kinds: *verbal irony*, in which there is an incongruity between what the speaker says and what he or she means; *situational irony*, in which there is a discrepancy between what seems fitting and what actually happens (the examples in Alanis Morissette's 1995 song "Ironic" are failed attempts at situational irony); and *dramatic irony*, in which the contrast is between what a character says or thinks and what the audience (or readers) know to be true. In all of these cases, the reader or observer plays a key role. Irony only occurs if the audience perceives the discrepancy. If you make an ironic comment and your audience takes it at face value, the attempt at irony has failed. In this section, we'll focus on verbal irony — acknowledging that it can often be difficult to identify, particularly when reading a work from an earlier time period, or a society that is not entirely familiar to us.

Playful, Satiric, and Sarcastic Irony

Irony is a tool that can be used for many purposes. We might think about these as a continuum, depending on how good-natured (or mean-spirited) the irony is, ranging from playful humor that reminds us of our shared human frailties, to **satire** that exposes a social issue, to bitter **sarcasm** that ridicules and demeans its target. Take these three headlines from the satiric newspaper the *Onion*, for example:

Playful

"Simple Task of Going to Post Office Feels Like Weight of 10,000 Boulders"

Satiric

"KFC No Longer Permitted to Use Word 'Eat' in Advertisements"

Sarcastic

"Teenage Rebels Seize Control of Food Court's Corner Table"

Of course, irony often achieves more than one of these purposes, which is what makes it such a powerful verbal weapon.

Irony works by creating some kind of humor — whether it results in a smile, a belly laugh, or a wince — but it's important to recognize that irony usually serves a serious function, as Oscar Wilde reminds us in his subtitle to *The Importance of Being Earnest: A Trivial Comedy for Serious People*. By bringing together contrasting ideas, an author can use irony to reveal hypocrisy or injustice, and sometimes even lobby for social change, however subtly.

Ways to Create an Ironic Tone

Examining specific techniques writers use to create irony is a helpful step toward understanding both what irony is and how an author develops an ironic tone. There are an unlimited number of ways to create irony, but the following are some common techniques.

Hyperbole, or overstatement, is more than simple exaggeration or a lie: it is exaggeration in the service of truth. Like a well-crafted metaphor, it should suggest a deeper meaning. Hyperbole is ironic because there is an incongruity between what is literally said and what is actually meant. Its opposite — **understatement** — has a similar effect. Both of these are at work in the following exchange in act II of *The Importance of Being Earnest*:

> GWENDOLEN: Cecily Cardew? *(Moving to her and shaking hands.)* What a very sweet name! Something tells me that we are going to be great friends. I like you already more than I can say. My first impressions of people are never wrong.
>
> CECILY: How nice of you to like me so much after we have known each other such a comparatively short time. Pray sit down.
>
> GWENDOLEN *(still standing up)*: I may call you Cecily, may I not?

Cecily uses understatement in this exchange to respond to Gwendolen's hyperbolic greeting. It's not that they've known each other "such a comparatively short time"; they've known each other for mere seconds. Cecily is subtly pointing out Gwendolen's insincerity and frivolousness, without being rude. Understatement is often used to cloak a wry jab in politeness. Note that in this case, as in most, understatement tends to be more subtle than hyperbole.

Juxtaposition—placing two ideas or words side by side to emphasize their incongruity—is another of the ironist's strategies. In the opening dialogue between Lane and Algernon, Wilde juxtaposes a seemingly philosophical subject—the "science of Life"—with the trivial concern of food to be served for tea. He asks Lane, "And, speaking of the science of Life, have you got the cucumber sandwiches cut for Lady Bracknell?" Juxtaposing something so serious with something so trivial alerts us to Algernon's lack of priorities. This lays the foundation for Wilde's criticism of the hypocrisy of Victorian morality.

Wordplay can be an important way to create the humor that is essential to much of irony. **Puns** (deliberately misusing words that sound alike) or double entendres (expressions with two meanings) are common. Here's an example from act I:

> JACK: My dear Algy, you talk exactly as if you were a dentist. It is very vulgar to talk like a dentist when one isn't a dentist. It produces a false impression.
>
> ALGERNON: Well, that is exactly what dentists always do.

The expression "false impression" is a double entendre—a dentist uses plaster to take a "negative" impression of a patient's teeth. Algernon uses the double entendre playfully here to verbally spar with Jack and show off his cleverness. We see, too, that Wilde is using this playful wittiness to characterize Algernon as a bit frivolous and more than a little fond of himself.

Another way to create irony is through strained or false logic, most often through a **non sequitur**, which is technically defined as a conclusion that does not follow logically from the premises; it is a logical fallacy. In literature, a non sequitur is a reply or remark that does not have any relevance to what preceded it. In *The Importance of Being Earnest*, Wilde characterizes Cecily as being a less than thoughtful person in remarks such as the following: "Oh yes. Dr. Chasuble is a most learned man. He has never written a single book, so you can imagine how much he knows." Her three points (Dr. Chasuble is "most learned," he has never written a book, thus we "can imagine how much he knows") are so logically unrelated as to be humorous.

The irony stems from the incongruity between the statement that Dr. Chasuble is "most learned" and what is really meant: he has never written a book, so whether he is smart or not is up to our imagination.

Though irony comes in many forms, they all have one thing in common—a significant distance between what is said and what is true. The irony occurs when the reader notices that gap. Irony pervades *The Importance of Being Earnest*, as Wilde accumulates and deepens his satire of Victorian society—particularly marriage. In many of the other texts you have read, irony is perceptible in specific lines or passages and, in some cases, results in an overall ironic tone. The following exercises will help you practice recognizing irony and the ways it is created.

• EXERCISE 1 •

We speak ironically every day, saying the opposite of what we actually mean in a tone of voice that reveals our true meaning. Turn to a partner and practice saying the following lines ironically. Consider how tone of voice, gestures, and facial expression convey irony.

- "Yeah, right."
- "I can't wait."
- "That's a great idea."
- "He's a shy one."
- "You saved the day."
- "That's very interesting."

• EXERCISE 2 •

Identify the ironic techniques of hyperbole, understatement, juxtaposition, wordplay, and non sequitur in the following excerpts from readings in this chapter.

1. ALGERNON: Why is it that at a bachelor's establishment the servants invariably drink the champagne? I ask merely for information.

   LANE: I attribute it to the superior quality of the wine, sir. I have often observed that in married households the champagne is rarely of a first-rate brand. (*The Importance of Being Earnest*, I. 15–18)

2. LADY BRACKNELL: . . . Do you smoke?

   JACK: Well, yes, I must admit I smoke.

   LADY BRACKNELL: I am glad to hear it. A man should always have an occupation of some kind. There are far too many idle men in London as it is. (*The Importance of Being Earnest*, I. 395–98)

3. Colonel Sartoris invented an involved tale to the effect that Miss Emily's father had loaned money to the town, which the town, as a matter of business, preferred this way of repaying. Only a man of Colonel Sartoris' generation and thought could have invented it, and only a woman could have believed it.

    When the next generation, with its more modern ideas, became mayors and aldermen, this arrangement created some little dissatisfaction. ("A Rose for Emily," paras. 3–4)

4. Though the car's beauty was secondary to its ability to start and move, the body and paint were clean except for a few minor dings. This stood out as one of his few clearcut accomplishments over the years. ("Love in L.A," para. 3)

5. I lost two cities, lovely ones. And, vaster,
    some realms I owned, two rivers, a continent.
    I miss them, but it wasn't a disaster.
    ("One Art," ll. 13–15)

6. You could draw me to fire, you could draw me to water, you could draw me to the gallows, you could draw me to any death, you could draw me to anything I have most avoided, you could draw me to any exposure and disgrace. This and the confusion of my thoughts, so that I am fit for nothing, is what I mean by your being the ruin of me. (*Our Mutual Friend*)

• EXERCISE 3 •

Explain how the author uses irony to make a serious comment in each of the following excerpts from readings in this chapter.

1. She will place me next Mary Farquhar, who always flirts with her own husband across the dinner table. That is not very pleasant. Indeed, it is not even decent—and that sort of thing is enormously on the increase. The amount of women in London who flirt with their own husbands is perfectly scandalous. It looks so bad. It is simply washing one's clean linen in public. (*The Importance of Being Earnest*, I. 197–201)

2. London society is full of women of the very highest birth who have, of their own free choice, remained thirty-five for years. Lady Dumbleton is an instance in point. To my own knowledge she has been thirty-five ever since she arrived at the age of forty, which was many years ago now. (*The Importance of Being Earnest*, III. 210–213)

3. JACK: I am sick to death of cleverness. Everybody is clever nowadays. You can't go anywhere without meeting clever people. The thing has become an absolutely public nuisance. I wish to goodness we had a few fools left.

    ALGERNON: We have.

    JACK: I should extremely like to meet them. What do they talk about?

    ALGERNON: The fools? Oh! about the clever people, of course.

JACK: What fools!
(*The Importance of Being Earnest*, I. 513–519)

4. One night, as he was leaving the Doctors' Club together with his partner, an official, he could not help himself and said:

"If you only knew what a charming woman I met in Yalta!"

The official got into a sleigh and drove off, but suddenly turned around and called out:

"Dmitri Dmitrich!"

"What?"

"You were right earlier: the sturgeon was a bit off!"

("The Lady with the Little Dog," paras. 69–74)

5. "I have had such a *dreadful* experience with a taxi-man; he was *most* sinister. I couldn't get him to *stop*. The *more* I knocked and called the *faster* he went. . . ."

"But how dreadful!" she cried.

"Yes, it really was," said Eddie, following her into the drawing-room. "I saw myself *driving* through Eternity in a *timeless* taxi."

("Bliss," paras. 68–71)

6. "I act too," he lied to enhance the effect more. "Been in a couple of movies."

She smiled like a fan.

"So how about your phone number?" He was rebounding maturely.

("Love in L.A.," paras. 31–33)

7. The grave's a fine and private place,

But none, I think, do there embrace.

("To His Coy Mistress," ll. 31–32)

• EXERCISE 4 •

In her poem "Siren Song," Margaret Atwood uses a number of strategies to develop an ironic tone, starting with the irony of the situation itself. Explain how the ironic tone, including some humor, conveys a serious message. Consider how Atwood prepares her reader for the final punch line.

• EXERCISE 5 •

Write a poem praising a person, place, or event in an ironic tone, showing that your true intent is to poke fun at or criticize your subject. Try to use some of the strategies discussed in this section.

Suggestions for Writing

Love and Relationships

1. Setting can play an important role in the development or deterioration of relationships in literature. Write an essay in which you explore the impact of setting on at least three of the works in this chapter. Analyze how the setting contributes to the meaning of the work as a whole.

2. Choose two poems from this chapter that posit contrasting views on romantic love. Write an essay in which you analyze the contrasting attitudes toward the subject. Include personal commentary on which view comes closer to your own.

3. Many of the texts in this chapter comment on inequities in the power of men and women in romance and marriage. Concentrating on three texts, write an essay analyzing the consequences of such inequities. Consider similarities as well as differences.

4. Research arranged marriage practices from other cultures, and then revisit Anita Jain's essay "Is Arranged Marriage Really Any Worse Than Craigslist?" Then write an essay arguing for or against arranged marriage in contemporary society. When presenting your case, refer to at least three other pieces in the chapter that show courtship traditions other than arranged marriage.

5. Many of the authors in this chapter explore the disconnect between physical attraction and true love. Referring to the literature in this chapter, write an essay arguing for or against the importance of physical attractiveness in a romantic relationship.

6. Song lyrics often use love and relationships as a theme. Choose a song from a recording artist whose work you enjoy, and analyze the lyrics in the same way you would a piece of literature. Discuss how the songwriter uses imagery, diction, syntax, allusion, and figurative language, and explain their effect on the song.

7. Using one of the poems in this chapter as a model, write a poem on the theme of love and relationships. You might write a narrative poem, such as Robert Penn Warren's "True Love," or write a poem based on an analogy, as Billy Collins does in "Weighing the Dog."

8. Watch a film that is considered a romantic comedy, then discuss some of the techniques the filmmaker uses to explore the theme of love and relationships. Compare and contrast those techniques with the ones encountered in this chapter, such as irony, farce, romantic imagery, stock characters, and predictable plot structures.

9. What are the characteristics of a healthy and enduring relationship? Use at least three texts from this chapter in your response.

10. Write a letter of advice to an imaginary friend who is going through an unfortunate breakup of a relationship. Suggest works that you think might offer solace to your friend during this period. Be sure to explain why each of the texts you suggest might help your friend.

Conformity and Rebellion

Not all those who wander are lost.

—J. R. R. TOLKIEN, *The Lord of the Rings*

Much of the literature of the Western world might be said to express the struggle between conformity and rebellion. We find this theme in our earliest recorded texts. Genesis tells the story of Eve and Adam's refusal to conform—an act picked up centuries later in the opening lines of John Milton's epic poem, *Paradise Lost*: "Of man's first disobedience, and the fruit / Of that forbidden tree whose mortal taste / Brought death into the world, and all our woe." At the same time, however, we see obedience as a virtue. Without duty and order, without cooperation and teamwork, where would we be? We admire and respect those heroes who hold things together—figures such as Abraham Lincoln and Franklin Delano Roosevelt—as well as those who serve and protect us: police officers, firefighters, and soldiers. But we also look to heroes who rebel: Socrates, Copernicus, Galileo, Darwin, Jefferson, Thoreau, Cady Stanton, Gandhi, and Martin Luther King Jr. Our heroes are often those who, as Senator Robert F. Kennedy said, "dream of things that never were and ask, why not?" Sometimes the noblest rebellion is in conformity with a higher law.

The texts in this chapter present the ongoing struggle between the inertia of conformity and the challenges and promises of rebellion. The question of rebellion is explored in Shakespeare's classic play *Hamlet*, as is the cost of conformity in Edwidge Danticat's modern story "The Book of the Dead." In "Bartleby, the Scrivener," Herman Melville demonstrates one man's rebellion against the expectations of others. Poems by Percy Bysshe Shelley and Dudley Randall address political conformity and rebellion, while a poem by Lucille Clifton celebrates the delights of audacious behavior. In both of their poems, Wallace Stevens and E. E. Cummings consider the power that imagination has to transform the drabness of the mundane. The Conversation contains several versions of Franz Kafka's classic story *The Metamorphosis*, where the line between conformity and rebellion blurs, and retelling Kafka's story becomes its own act of literary rebellion.

Hamlet, Prince of Denmark

WILLIAM SHAKESPEARE

William Shakespeare (1564–1616) was born in Stratford-upon-Avon, England. Little is known of his life aside from the fact that he married Anne Hathaway when he was eighteen, worked as an actor-playwright in London, and retired in 1613. His plays fall into four principal categories: early comedies (1585–1594); more sophisticated comedies and histories (1595–1599); the great tragedies (1599–1607); and the final phase (1608–1613). His most accomplished works—including *Hamlet* (1601), *Othello* (1603), *King Lear* (1605), and *Macbeth* (1606)—belong to the third period. In his time, his contemporaries—and likely Shakespeare himself—looked to his sonnets and other poems as the more important works. The 154 sonnets were written at various stages in Shakespeare's life, but when and to whom they were written remain unclear. Wordsworth believed that only through the sonnets could one understand Shakespeare. *Hamlet* is Shakespeare's most famous play, and is regarded by many to be his finest. It has been performed, adapted, and studied more than any other play in the English language.

[DRAMATIS PERSONAE

CLAUDIUS, *King of Denmark*
HAMLET, *son to the late and nephew to the present king*
POLONIUS, *lord chamberlain*
HORATIO, *friend to Hamlet*
LAERTES, *son to Polonius*
VOLTIMAND ⎫
CORNELIUS ⎪
ROSENCRANTZ ⎬ *courtiers*
GUILDENSTERN ⎪
OSRIC ⎭
A GENTLEMAN
A PRIEST
MARCELLUS ⎫ *officers*
BERNARDO ⎭

FRANCISCO, *a soldier*
REYNALDO, *servant to Polonius*
PLAYERS
TWO CLOWNS, *grave-diggers*
FORTINBRAS, *Prince of Norway*
A CAPTAIN
ENGLISH AMBASSADORS
GERTRUDE, *Queen of Denmark, and mother to Hamlet*
OPHELIA, *daughter to Polonius*
LORDS, LADIES, OFFICERS, SOLDIERS, SAILORS, MESSENGERS, *and other* ATTENDANTS
GHOST *of Hamlet's father*

SCENE: *Denmark.*]

[ACT I

SCENE i: *Elsinore. A platform° before the castle.*]

Enter BERNARDO *and* FRANCISCO, *two sentinels.*

BERNARDO: Who's there?
FRANCISCO: Nay, answer me:° stand, and unfold yourself.
BERNARDO: Long live the king!°
FRANCISCO: Bernardo?
BERNARDO: He.
FRANCISCO: You come most carefully upon your hour.   5
BERNARDO: 'Tis now struck twelve; get thee to bed, Francisco.
FRANCISCO: For this relief much thanks: 'tis bitter cold,
    And I am sick at heart.
BERNARDO: Have you had quiet guard?
FRANCISCO: Not a mouse stirring.   10
BERNARDO: Well, good night.
    If you do meet Horatio and Marcellus,
    The rivals° of my watch, bid them make haste.

Enter HORATIO *and* MARCELLUS.

FRANCISCO: I think I hear them. Stand, ho! Who is there?
HORATIO: Friends to this ground.
MARCELLUS: And liegemen to the Dane.   15
FRANCISCO: Give you° good night.
MARCELLUS: O, farewell, honest soldier:
    Who hath reliev'd you?
FRANCISCO: Bernardo hath my place.
    Give you good night.   *Exit* FRANCISCO.
MARCELLUS: Holla! Bernardo!
BERNARDO: Say,
    What, is Horatio there?
HORATIO: A piece of him.
BERNARDO: Welcome, Horatio: welcome, good Marcellus.   20
MARCELLUS: What, has this thing appear'd again to-night?
BERNARDO: I have seen nothing.
MARCELLUS: Horatio says 'tis but our fantasy,
    And will not let belief take hold of him

Act I, Scene i.   **platform:** A level space on the battlements of the royal castle at Elsinore, a
Danish seaport; now Helsingör.   **2 me:** This is emphatic, since Francisco is the sentry.   **3
Long live the king:** Either a password or greeting; Horatio and Marcellus use a different one in
line 15.   **13 rivals:** Partners.   **16 Give you:** God give you.

Touching this dreaded sight, twice seen of us: 25
Therefore I have entreated him along
With us to watch the minutes of this night;
That if again this apparition come,
He may approve° our eyes and speak to it.
HORATIO: Tush, tush, 'twill not appear.
BERNARDO: Sit down awhile;   30
And let us once again assail your ears,
That are so fortified against our story
What we have two nights seen.
HORATIO: Well, sit we down,
And let us hear Bernardo speak of this.
BERNARDO: Last night of all,   35
When yond same star that's westward from the pole°
Had made his course t' illume that part of heaven
Where now it burns, Marcellus and myself,
The bell then beating one,—

Enter GHOST.

MARCELLUS: Peace, break thee off; look, where it comes again!   40
BERNARDO: In the same figure, like the king that's dead.
MARCELLUS: Thou art a scholar;° speak to it, Horatio.
BERNARDO: Looks 'a not like the king? mark it, Horatio.
HORATIO: Most like: it harrows° me with fear and wonder.
BERNARDO: It would be spoke to.°
MARCELLUS: Speak to it, Horatio.   45
HORATIO: What art thou that usurp'st this time of night,
     Together with that fair and warlike form
     In which the majesty of buried Denmark°
     Did sometimes march? by heaven I charge thee, speak!
MARCELLUS: It is offended.
BERNARDO: See it stalks away!   50
HORATIO: Stay! speak, speak! I charge thee, speak!   *Exit* GHOST.
MARCELLUS: 'Tis gone, and will not answer.
BERNARDO: How now, Horatio! you tremble and look pale:
     Is not this something more than fantasy?
     What think you on 't?   55
HORATIO: Before my God, I might not this believe
     Without the sensible and true avouch
     Of mine own eyes.

---

29 approve: Corroborate. **36 pole:** Polestar. **42 scholar:** Exorcisms were performed in Latin, which Horatio as an educated man would be able to speak. **44 harrows:** Lacerates the feelings. **45 It . . . to:** A ghost could not speak until spoken to. **48 buried Denmark:** The buried king of Denmark.

MARCELLUS: Is it not like the king?
HORATIO: As thou art to thyself:
    Such was the very armour he had on 60
    When he the ambitious Norway combated;
    So frown'd he once, when, in an angry parle,
    He smote° the sledded Polacks° on the ice.
    'Tis strange.
MARCELLUS: Thus twice before, and jump° at this dead hour, 65
    With martial stalk hath he gone by our watch.
HORATIO: In what particular thought to work I know not;
    But in the gross and scope° of my opinion,
    This bodes some strange eruption to our state.
MARCELLUS: Good now,° sit down, and tell me, he that knows, 70
    Why this same strict and most observant watch
    So nightly toils° the subject° of the land,
    And why such daily cast° of brazen cannon,
    And foreign mart° for implements of war;
    Why such impress° of shipwrights, whose sore task 75
    Does not divide the Sunday from the week;
    What might be toward, that this sweaty haste
    Doth make the night joint-labourer with the day:
    Who is't that can inform me?
HORATIO: That can I;
    At least, the whisper goes so. Our last king, 80
    Whose image even but now appear'd to us,
    Was, as you know, by Fortinbras of Norway,
    Thereto prick'd on° by a most emulate° pride,
    Dar'd to the combat; in which our valiant Hamlet—
    For so this side of our known world esteem'd him— 85
    Did slay this Fortinbras; who, by a seal'd compact,
    Well ratified by law and heraldry,°
    Did forfeit, with his life, all those his lands
    Which he stood seiz'd° of, to the conqueror:
    Against the which, a moiety competent° 90
    Was gaged by our king; which had return'd
    To the inheritance of Fortinbras,
    Had he been vanquisher; as, by the same comart,°

---

63 smote: Defeated.   **sledded Polacks:** Polanders using sledges.   **65 jump:** Exactly.   **68 gross and scope:** General drift.   **70 Good now:** An expression denoting entreaty or expostulation.   **72 toils:** Causes or makes to toil.   **subject:** People, subjects.   **73 cast:** Casting, founding.   **74 mart:** Buying and selling, traffic.   **75 impress:** Impressment.   **83 prick'd on:** Incited.   **emulate:** Rivaling.   **87 law and heraldry:** Heraldic law, governing combat.   **89 seiz'd:** Possessed.   **90 moiety competent:** Adequate or sufficient portion.   **93 comart:** Joint bargain.

And carriage° of the article design'd,   95
His fell to Hamlet. Now, sir, young Fortinbras,
Of unimproved° mettle hot and full,°
Hath in the skirts of Norway here and there
Shark'd up° a list of lawless resolutes,°
For food and diet,° to some enterprise
That hath a stomach in't; which is no other—   100
As it doth well appear unto our state—
But to recover of us, by strong hand
And terms compulsatory, those foresaid lands
So by his father lost: and this, I take it,
Is the main motive of our preparations,   105
The source of this our watch and the chief head
Of this post-haste and romage° in the land.
BERNARDO: I think it be no other but e'en so:
    Well may it sort° that this portentous figure
    Comes armed through our watch; so like the king   110
    That was and is the question of these wars.
HORATIO: A mote° it is to trouble the mind's eye.
    In the most high and palmy state° of Rome,
    A little ere the mightiest Julius fell,
    The graves stood tenantless and the sheeted dead   115
    Did squeak and gibber in the Roman streets:
    As stars with trains of fire° and dews of blood,
    Disasters° in the sun; and the moist star°
    Upon whose influence Neptune's empire° stands
    Was sick almost to doomsday with eclipse: 120
    And even the like precurse° of fear'd events,
    As harbingers preceding still the fates
    And prologue to the omen coming on,
    Have heaven and earth together demonstrated
    Unto our climatures and countrymen.—   125

Enter GHOST.

    But soft, behold! lo, where it comes again!
    I'll cross° it, though it blast me. Stay, illusion!

---

94 **carriage:** Import, bearing.   96 **unimproved:** Not turned to account.   **hot and full:** Full of
fight.   98 **Shark'd up:** Got together in haphazard fashion.   **resolutes:** Desperadoes.   99 **food
and diet:** No pay but their keep.   107 **romage:** Bustle, commotion.   109 **sort:** Suit.   112 **mote:**
Speck of dust.   113 **palmy state:** Triumphant sovereignty.   117 **stars . . . fire:** I.e., comets.   118
Disasters: Unfavorable aspects.   **moist star:** The moon, governing tides.   119 **Neptune's
empire:** The sea.   121 **precurse:** Heralding.   127 **cross:** Meet, face, thus bringing down the evil
influence on the person who crosses it.

If thou hast any sound, or use of voice,
Speak to me!   *It° spreads his arms.*
If there be any good thing to be done,   130
That may to thee do ease and grace to me,
Speak to me!
If thou art privy to thy country's fate,
Which, happily, foreknowing may avoid,
O, speak!   135
Or if thou hast uphoarded in thy life
Extorted treasure in the womb of earth,
For which, they say, you spirits oft walk in death,   *The cock crows.*
Speak of it:° stay, and speak! Stop it, Marcellus.
MARCELLUS: Shall I strike at it with my partisan?°   140
HORATIO: Do, if it will not stand.
BERNARDO: 'Tis here!
HORATIO: 'Tis here!
MARCELLUS: 'Tis gone!   *[Exit* GHOST.*]*
    We do it wrong, being so majestical,
    To offer it the show of violence;
    For it is, as the air, invulnerable,   145
    And our vain blows malicious mockery.
BERNARDO: It was about to speak, when the cock crew.°
HORATIO: And then it started like a guilty thing
    Upon a fearful summons. I have heard,
    The cock, that is the trumpet to the morn,   150
    Doth with his lofty and shrill-sounding throat
    Awake the god of day; and, at his warning,
    Whether in sea or fire, in earth or air,
    Th' extravagant and erring° spirit hies
    To his confine:° and of the truth herein   155
    This present object made probation.°
MARCELLUS: It faded on the crowing of the cock.
    Some say that ever 'gainst° that season comes
    Wherein our Saviour's birth is celebrated,
    The bird of dawning singeth all night long: 160
    And then, they say, no spirit dare stir abroad;
    The nights are wholesome; then no planets strike,°

---

129 It: The Ghost, or perhaps Horatio.   **133–139 If . . . it:** Horatio recites the traditional reasons why ghosts might walk.   **140 partisan:** Long-handled spear with a blade having lateral projections.   **147 cock crew:** According to traditional ghost lore, spirits returned to their confines at cockcrow.   **154 extravagant and erring:** Wandering. Both words mean the same thing.   **155 confine:** Place of confinement.   **156 probation:** Proof, trial.   **158 'gainst:** Just before.   **162 planets strike:** It was thought that planets were malignant and might strike travelers by night.

No fairy takes,° nor witch hath power to charm,
So hallow'd and so gracious° is that time.
HORATIO: So have I heard and do in part believe it.   165
But, look, the morn, in russet mantle clad,
Walks o'er the dew of yon high eastward hill:
Break we our watch up; and by my advice,
Let us impart what we have seen to-night
Unto young Hamlet; for, upon my life,   170
This spirit, dumb to us, will speak to him.
Do you consent we shall acquaint him with it,
As needful in our loves, fitting our duty?
MARCELLUS: Let's do 't, I pray; and I this morning know
Where we shall find him most conveniently.   *Exeunt.*   175

[SCENE ii: *A room of state in the castle.*]

Flourish. Enter CLAUDIUS, *King of Denmark,* GERTRUDE *the Queen,* COUNCILORS,
POLONIUS *and his son* LAERTES, HAMLET, *cum aliis*° *[including* VOLTIMAND *and*
CORNELIUS*].*

KING: Though yet of Hamlet our dear brother's death
The memory be green, and that it us befitted
To bear our hearts in grief and our whole kingdom
To be contracted in one brow of woe,
Yet so far hath discretion fought with nature   5
That we with wisest sorrow think on him,
Together with remembrance of ourselves.
Therefore our sometime sister, now our queen,
Th' imperial jointress° to this warlike state,
Have we, as 'twere with a defeated joy,—   10
With an auspicious and a dropping eye,
With mirth in funeral and with dirge in marriage,
In equal scale weighing delight and dole,—
Taken to wife: nor have we herein barr'd
Your better wisdoms, which have freely gone   15
With this affair along. For all, our thanks.
Now follows, that° you know, young Fortinbras,
Holding a weak supposal° of our worth,
Or thinking by our late dear brother's death
Our state to be disjoint° and out of frame,°   20

---

163 **No fairy takes:** It was thought that fairies would steal babies.—EDS.   164 **gracious:** Full
of goodness.   **Scene ii.   cum aliis:** With others.   9 **jointress:** Woman possessed of a jointure,
or joint tenancy of an estate.   17 **that:** That which.   18 **weak supposal:** Low estimate.   20
disjoint: Distracted, out of joint.   **frame:** Order.

Colleagued° with this dream of his advantage,°
He hath not fail'd to pester us with message,
Importing° the surrender of those lands
Lost by his father, with all bands of law,
To our most valiant brother. So much for him.   25
Now for ourself and for this time of meeting:
Thus much the business is: we have here writ
To Norway, uncle of young Fortinbras,—
Who, impotent and bed-rid, scarcely hears
Of this his nephew's purpose,—to suppress   30
His further gait° herein; in that the levies,
The lists and full proportions, are all made
Out of his subject:° and we here dispatch
You, good Cornelius, and you, Voltimand,
For bearers of this greeting to old Norway;   35
Giving to you no further personal power
To business with the king, more than the scope
Of these delated° articles allow.
Farewell, and let your haste commend your duty.

CORNELIUS: ⎫
VOLTIMAND: ⎭ In that and all things will we show our duty.   40

KING: We doubt it nothing: heartily farewell.

                         [Exeunt VOLTIMAND *and* CORNELIUS.*]*

And now, Laertes, what's the news with you?
You told us of some suit; what is't, Laertes?
You cannot speak of reason to the Dane,°
And lose your voice:° what wouldst thou beg, Laertes,   45
That shall not be my offer, not thy asking?
The head is not more native° to the heart,
The hand more instrumental° to the mouth,
Than is the throne of Denmark to thy father.
What wouldst thou have, Laertes?

LAERTES: My dread lord,   50
Your leave and favour to return to France;
From whence though willingly I came to Denmark,
To show my duty in your coronation,
Yet now, I must confess, that duty done,
My thoughts and wishes bend again toward France   55

---

21 Colleagued: added to.   **dream . . . advantage:** Visionary hope of success.   **23 Importing:** Purporting, pertaining to.   **31 gait:** Proceeding.   **33 Out of his subject:** At the expense of Norway's subjects (collectively).   **38 delated:** Expressly stated.   **44 the Dane:** Danish king.   **45 lose your voice:** Speak in vain.   **47 native:** Closely connected, related.   **48 instrumental:** Serviceable.

And bow them to your gracious leave and pardon.°
KING: Have you your father's leave? What says Polonius?
POLONIUS: He hath, my lord, wrung from me my slow leave
    By laboursome petition, and at last
    Upon his will I seal'd my hard consent: 60
    I do beseech you, give him leave to go.
KING: Take thy fair hour, Laertes; time be thine,
    And thy best graces spend it at thy will!
    But now, my cousin° Hamlet, and my son,—
HAMLET [aside]: A little more than kin, and less than kind!°   65
KING: How is it that the clouds still hang on you?
HAMLET: Not so, my lord; I am too much in the sun.°
QUEEN: Good Hamlet, cast thy nighted colour off,
    And let thine eye look like a friend on Denmark.
    Do not for ever with thy vailed lids   70
    Seek for thy noble father in the dust:
    Thou know'st 'tis common; all that lives must die,
    Passing through nature to eternity.
HAMLET: Ay, madam, it is common.°
QUEEN: If it be,
    Why seems it so particular with thee?   75
HAMLET: Seems, madam! nay, it is; I know not "seems."
    'Tis not alone my inky cloak, good mother,
    Nor customary suits° of solemn black,
    Nor windy suspiration° of forc'd breath,
    No, nor the fruitful river in the eye,   80
    Nor the dejected 'haviour of the visage,
    Together with all forms, moods, shapes of grief,
    That can denote me truly: these indeed seem,
    For they are actions that a man might play:
    But I have that within which passeth show;   85
    These but the trappings and the suits of woe.
KING: 'Tis sweet and commendable in your nature, Hamlet,
    To give these mourning duties to your father:
    But, you must know, your father lost a father;

---

56 **leave and pardon:** Permission to depart.   64 **cousin:** Any kin not of the immediate family.   65 **A little ... kind:** My relation to you has become more than kinship warrants; it has also become unnatural.   67 **I am ... sun:** (1) I am too much out of doors, (2) I am too much in the sun of your grace (ironical), (3) I am too much of a son to you. Possibly an allusion to the proverb "Out of heaven's blessing into the warm sun"; i.e., Hamlet is out of house and home in being deprived of the kingship.   74 **Ay ... common:** It is common, but it hurts nevertheless; possibly a reference to the commonplace quality of the queen's remark.   78 **customary suits:** Suits prescribed by custom for mourning.   79 **windy suspiration:** Heavy sighing.

That father lost, lost his, and the survivor bound   90
In filial obligation for some term
To do obsequious° sorrow: but to persever
In obstinate condolement° is a course
Of impious stubbornness; 'tis unmanly grief;
It shows a will most incorrect° to heaven,   95
A heart unfortified, a mind impatient,
An understanding simple and unschool'd:
For what we know must be and is as common
As any the most vulgar thing° to sense,
Why should we in our peevish opposition   100
Take it to heart? Fie! 'tis a fault to heaven,
A fault against the dead, a fault to nature,
To reason most absurd; whose common theme
Is death of fathers, and who still hath cried,
From the first corse° till he that died to-day,   105
"This must be so." We pray you, throw to earth
This unprevailing° woe, and think of us
As of a father: for let the world take note,
You are the most immediate° to our throne;
And with no less nobility° of love   110
Than that which dearest father bears his son,
Do I impart° toward you. For your intent
In going back to school in Wittenberg,°
It is most retrograde° to our desire:
And we beseech you, bend you° to remain   115
Here, in the cheer and comfort of our eye,
Our chiefest courtier, cousin, and our son.
QUEEN: Let not thy mother lose her prayers, Hamlet:
I pray thee, stay with us; go not to Wittenberg.
HAMLET: I shall in all my best obey you, madam.   120
KING: Why, 'tis a loving and a fair reply:
Be as ourself in Denmark. Madam, come;
This gentle and unforc'd accord of Hamlet
Sits smiling to my heart: in grace whereof,
No jocund health that Denmark drinks to-day,   125
But the great cannon to the clouds shall tell,

---

92 **obsequious:** Dutiful.   93 **condolement:** Sorrowing.   95 **incorrect:** Untrained, uncorrected.   99 **vulgar thing:** Common experience.   105 **corse:** Corpse.   107 **unprevailing:** Unavailing.   109 **most immediate:** Next in succession.   110 **nobility:** High degree.   112 **impart:** The object is apparently *love* (l. 110).   113 **Wittenberg:** Famous German university founded in 1502.   114 **retrograde:** Contrary.   115 **bend you:** Incline yourself (imperative).

And the king's rouse° the heaven shall bruit again,°
Re-speaking earthly thunder. Come away.   *Flourish. Exeunt all but* HAMLET.
HAMLET: O, that this too too solid flesh would melt,
    Thaw and resolve itself into a dew!   130
    Or that the Everlasting had not fix'd
    His canon 'gainst self-slaughter! O God! God!
    How weary, stale, flat and unprofitable,
    Seem to me all the uses of this world!
    Fie on't! ah fie! 'tis an unweeded garden,   135
    That grows to seed; things rank and gross in nature
    Possess it merely.° That it should come to this!
    But two months dead: nay, not so much, not two:
    So excellent a king; that was, to this,
    Hyperion° to a satyr; so loving to my mother   140
    That he might not beteem° the winds of heaven
    Visit her face too roughly. Heaven and earth!
    Must I remember? why, she would hang on him,
    As if increase of appetite had grown
    By what it fed on: and yet, within a month—   145
    Let me not think on't—Frailty, thy name is woman!—
    A little month, or ere those shoes were old
    With which she followed my poor father's body,
    Like Niobe,° all tears:—why she, even she—
    O God! a beast, that wants discourse of reason,°   150
    Would have mourn'd longer—married with my uncle,
    My father's brother, but no more like my father
    Than I to Hercules: within a month:
    Ere yet the salt of most unrighteous tears
    Had left the flushing in her galled° eyes,   155
    She married. O, most wicked speed, to post
    With such dexterity° to incestuous sheets!
    It is not nor it cannot come to good:
    But break, my heart; for I must hold my tongue.

Enter HORATIO, MARCELLUS, *and* BERNARDO.

HORATIO: Hail to your lordship!

---

127 **rouse:** Draft of liquor. **bruit again:** Echo. 137 **merely:** Completely, entirely. 140
Hyperion: God of the sun in the older regime of ancient gods. 141 **beteem:** Allow. 149
Niobe: Tantalus's daughter, who boasted that she had more sons and daughters than Leto;
for this, Apollo and Artemis slew her children. She was turned into stone by Zeus on Mount
Sipylus. 150 **discourse of reason:** Process or faculty of reason. 155 **galled:** Irritated. 157
dexterity: Facility.

HAMLET: I am glad to see you well: 160
     Horatio!—or I do forget myself.
HORATIO: The same, my lord, and your poor servant ever.
HAMLET: Sir, my good friend; I'll change that name with you:°
     And what make you from Wittenberg, Horatio?
     Marcellus?   165
MARCELLUS: My good lord—
HAMLET: I am very glad to see you. Good even, sir.
     But what, in faith, make you from Wittenberg?
HORATIO: A truant disposition, good my lord.
HAMLET: I would not hear your enemy say so,   170
     Nor shall you do my ear that violence,
     To make it truster of your own report
     Against yourself: I know you are no truant.
     But what is your affair in Elsinore?
     We'll teach you to drink deep ere you depart.   175
HORATIO: My lord, I came to see your father's funeral.
HAMLET: I prithee, do not mock me, fellow-student;
     I think it was to see my mother's wedding.
HORATIO: Indeed, my lord, it follow'd hard° upon.
HAMLET: Thrift, thrift, Horatio! the funeral bak'd meats°   180
     Did coldly furnish forth the marriage tables.
     Would I had met my dearest° foe in heaven
     Or ever I had seen that day, Horatio!
     My father!—methinks I see my father.
HORATIO: Where, my lord?
HAMLET: In my mind's eye, Horatio.   185
HORATIO: I saw him once; 'a° was a goodly king.
HAMLET: 'A was a man, take him for all in all,
     I shall not look upon his like again.
HORATIO: My lord, I think I saw him yesternight.
HAMLET: Saw? who?   190
HORATIO: My lord, the king your father.
HAMLET: The king my father!
HORATIO: Season your admiration° for a while
     With an attent ear, till I may deliver,
     Upon the witness of these gentlemen,
     This marvel to you.

---

163 **I'll . . . you:** I'll be your servant, you shall be my friend; also explained as "I'll exchange the name of friend with you."   179 **hard:** Close.   180 **bak'd meats:** Meat pies.   182 **dearest:** Direst. The adjective *dear* in Shakespeare has two different origins: O.E. *deore*, "beloved," and O.E. *deor*, "fierce." *Dearest* is the superlative of the second.   186 **'a:** He.   192 **Season your admiration:** Restrain your astonishment.

HAMLET: For God's love, let me hear.   195
HORATIO: Two nights together had these gentlemen,
    Marcellus and Bernardo, on their watch,
    In the dead waste and middle of the night,
    Been thus encount'red. A figure like your father,
    Armed at point exactly, cap-a-pe,°   200
    Appears before them, and with solemn march
    Goes slow and stately by them: thrice he walk'd
    By their oppress'd° and fear-surprised eyes,
    Within his truncheon's° length; whilst they, distill'd°
    Almost to jelly with the act° of fear,   205
    Stand dumb and speak not to him. This to me
    In dreadful secrecy impart they did;
    And I with them the third night kept the watch:
    Where, as they had deliver'd, both in time,
    Form of the thing, each word made true and good,   210
    The apparition comes: I knew your father;
    These hands are not more like.
HAMLET: But where was this?
MARCELLUS: My lord, upon the platform where we watch'd.
HAMLET: Did you not speak to it?
HORATIO: My lord, I did;
    But answer made it none: yet once methought   215
    It lifted up it° head and did address
    Itself to motion, like as it would speak;
    But even then the morning cock crew loud,
    And at the sound it shrunk in haste away,
    And vanish'd from our sight.
HAMLET: 'Tis very strange.   220
HORATIO: As I do live, my honour'd lord, 'tis true;
    And we did think it writ down in our duty
    To let you know of it.
HAMLET: Indeed, indeed, sirs, but this troubles me.
    Hold you the watch to-night?
MARCELLUS: ⎫
BERNARDO: ⎭   We do, my lord.   225
HAMLET: Arm'd, say you?
MARCELLUS: ⎫
BERNARDO: ⎭   Arm'd, my lord.

---

200 **cap-a-pe:** From head to foot. **203 oppress'd:** Distressed. **204 truncheon:** Officer's
staff. **distill'd:** Softened, weakened. **205 act:** Action. **216 it:** Its.

HAMLET: From top to toe?

MARCELLUS: ⎤
BERNARDO: ⎦   My lord, from head to foot.

HAMLET: Then saw you not his face?

HORATIO: O, yes, my lord; he wore his beaver° up.

HAMLET: What, look'd he frowningly?

HORATIO: A countenance more   230
      In sorrow than in anger.

HAMLET: Pale or red?

HORATIO: Nay, very pale.

HAMLET: And fix'd his eyes upon you?

HORATIO: Most constantly.

HAMLET: I would I had been there.

HORATIO: It would have much amaz'd you.

HAMLET: Very like, very like. Stay'd it long?   235

HORATIO: While one with moderate haste might tell a hundred.

MARCELLUS: ⎤
BERNARDO: ⎦   Longer, longer.

HORATIO: Not when I saw't.

HAMLET: His beard was grizzled,—no?

HORATIO: It was, as I have seen it in his life,
      A sable° silver'd.

HAMLET: I will watch to-night;   240
      Perchance 'twill walk again.

HORATIO: I warr'nt it will.

HAMLET: If it assume my noble father's person,
      I'll speak to it, though hell itself should gape
      And bid me hold my peace. I pray you all,
      If you have hitherto conceal'd this sight,   245
      Let it be tenable in your silence still;
      And whatsoever else shall hap to-night,
      Give it an understanding, but no tongue:
      I will requite your loves. So, fare you well:
      Upon the platform, 'twixt eleven and twelve,   250
      I'll visit you.

ALL: Our duty to your honour.

HAMLET: Your loves, as mine to you: farewell.   *Exeunt [all but* HAMLET*].*
      My father's spirit in arms! all is not well;
      I doubt° some foul play: would the night were come!
      Till then sit still, my soul: foul deeds will rise,   255
      Though all the earth o'erwhelm them, to men's eyes.   *Exit.*

---

229 beaver: Visor on the helmet.   **240 sable:** Black color.   **254 doubt:** Fear.

[SCENE iii: *A room in* POLONIUS's *house.*]

Enter LAERTES *and* OPHELIA, *his sister.*

LAERTES: My necessaries are embark'd: farewell:
    And, sister, as the winds give benefit
    And convoy is assistant,° do not sleep,
    But let me hear from you.
OPHELIA: Do you doubt that?
LAERTES: For Hamlet and the trifling of his favour,   5
    Hold it a fashion° and a toy in blood,°
    A violet in the youth of primy° nature,
    Forward,° not permanent, sweet, not lasting,
    The perfume and suppliance of a minute;°
    No more.
OPHELIA: No more but so?
LAERTES: Think it no more: 10
    For nature, crescent,° does not grow alone
    In thews° and bulk, but, as this temple° waxes,
    The inward service of the mind and soul
    Grows wide withal. Perhaps he loves you now,
    And now no soil° nor cautel° doth besmirch   15
    The virtue of his will: but you must fear,
    His greatness weigh'd,° his will is not his own;
    For he himself is subject to his birth:
    He may not, as unvalued persons do,
    Carve for himself; for on his choice depends   20
    The safety and health of this whole state;
    And therefore must his choice be circumscrib'd
    Unto the voice and yielding° of that body
    Whereof he is the head. Then if he says he loves you,
    It fits your wisdom so far to believe it   25
    As he in his particular act and place
    May give his saying deed;° which is no further
    Than the main voice of Denmark goes withal.
    Then weigh what loss your honour may sustain,
    If with too credent° ear you list his songs,   30
    Or lose your heart, or your chaste treasure open

Scene iii. **3 convoy is assistant:** Means of conveyance are available. **6 fashion:** Custom,
prevailing usage. **toy in blood:** Passing amorous fancy. **7 primy:** In its prime. **8 Forward:**
Precocious. **9 suppliance of a minute:** Diversion to fill up a minute. **11 crescent:** Growing,
waxing. **12 thews:** Bodily strength; **temple:** Body. **15 soil:** Blemish. **cautel:** Crafty device.
17 greatness weigh'd: High position considered. **23 voice and yielding:** Assent, approval. **27
deed:** Effect. **30 credent:** Credulous.

To his unmast'red° importunity.
Fear it, Ophelia, fear it, my dear sister,
And keep you in the rear of your affection,
Out of the shot and danger of desire.   35
The chariest° maid is prodigal enough,
If she unmask her beauty to the moon:
Virtue itself 'scapes not calumnious strokes:
The canker galls the infants of the spring,°
Too oft before their buttons° be disclos'd,°   40
And in the morn and liquid dew° of youth
Contagious blastments° are most imminent.
Be wary then; best safety lies in fear:
Youth to itself rebels, though none else near.

OPHELIA: I shall the effect of this good lesson keep,   45
    As watchman to my heart. But, good my brother,
    Do not, as some ungracious° pastors do,
    Show me the steep and thorny way to heaven;
    Whiles, like a puff'd° and reckless libertine,
    Himself the primrose path of dalliance treads,   50
    And recks° not his own rede.°

Enter POLONIUS.

LAERTES: O, fear me not.
    I stay too long: but here my father comes.
    A double° blessing is a double grace;
    Occasion° smiles upon a second leave.

POLONIUS: Yet here, Laertes? aboard, aboard, for shame!   55
    The wind sits in the shoulder of your sail,
    And you are stay'd for. There; my blessing with thee!
    And these few precepts° in thy memory
    Look thou character.° Give thy thoughts no tongue,
    Nor any unproportion'd° thought his act.   60
    Be thou familiar, but by no means vulgar.°
    Those friends thou hast, and their adoption tried,
    Grapple them to thy soul with hoops of steel;

---

32 unmast'red: Unrestrained.   **36 chariest:** Most scrupulously modest.   **39 The canker . . . spring:** The cankerworm destroys the young plants of spring.   **40 buttons:** Buds.   **disclos'd:** Opened.   **41 liquid dew:** I.e., time when dew is fresh.   **42 blastments:** Blights.   **47 ungracious:** Graceless.   **49 puff'd:** Bloated.   **51 recks:** Heeds.   **rede:** Counsel.   **53 double:** I.e., Laertes has already bade his father good-by.   **54 Occasion:** Opportunity.   **58 precepts:** Many parallels have been found to the series of maxims which follows, one of the closer being that in Lyly's *Euphues*.   **59 character:** Inscribe.   **60 unproportion'd:** Inordinate.   **61 vulgar:** Common.

But do not dull thy palm with entertainment
Of each new-hatch'd, unfledg'd° comrade. Beware   65
Of entrance to a quarrel, but being in,
Bear't that th' opposed may beware of thee.
Give every man thy ear, but few thy voice;
Take each man's censure, but reserve thy judgement.
Costly thy habit as thy purse can buy,   70
But not express'd in fancy;° rich, not gaudy;
For the apparel oft proclaims the man,
And they in France of the best rank and station
Are of a most select and generous chief in that.°
Neither a borrower nor a lender be;   75
For loan oft loses both itself and friend,
And borrowing dulleth edge of husbandry.°
This above all: to thine own self be true,
And it must follow, as the night the day,
Thou canst not then be false to any man.   80
Farewell: my blessing season° this in thee!
LAERTES: Most humbly do I take my leave, my lord.
POLONIUS: The time invites you; go; your servants tend.
LAERTES: Farewell, Ophelia; and remember well
    What I have said to you.
OPHELIA: 'Tis in my memory lock'd,   85
    And you yourself shall keep the key of it.
LAERTES: Farewell.   *Exit* LAERTES.
POLONIUS: What is 't, Ophelia, he hath said to you?
OPHELIA: So please you, something touching the Lord Hamlet.
POLONIUS: Marry, well bethought: 90
    'Tis told me, he hath very oft of late
    Given private time to you; and you yourself
    Have of your audience been most free and bounteous:
    If it be so, as so't is put on° me,
    And that in way of caution, I must tell you,   95
    You do not understand yourself so clearly
    As it behooves my daughter and your honour.
    What is between you? give me up the truth.
OPHELIA: He hath, my lord, of late made many tenders°
    Of his affection to me.   100
POLONIUS: Affection! pooh! you speak like a green girl,

---

65 **unfledg'd:** Immature.   71 **express'd in fancy:** Fantastical in design.   74 **Are ... that:** *Chief*
is usually taken as a substantive meaning "head," "eminence."   77 **husbandry:** Thrift.   81
season: Mature.   94 **put on:** Impressed on.   99 **tenders:** Offers.

Unsifted° in such perilous circumstance.
Do you believe his tenders,° as you call them?

OPHELIA: I do not know, my lord, what I should think.

POLONIUS: Marry, I will teach you: think yourself a baby;   105
That you have ta'en these tenders° for true pay,
Which are not sterling.° Tender° yourself more dearly;
Or — not to crack the wind° of the poor phrase,
Running it thus — you'll tender me a fool.°

OPHELIA: My lord, he hath importun'd me with love   110
In honourable fashion.

POLONIUS: Ay, fashion° you may call it; go to, go to.

OPHELIA: And hath given countenance° to his speech, my lord,
With almost all the holy vows of heaven.

POLONIUS: Ay, springes° to catch woodcocks.° I do know,   115
When the blood burns, how prodigal the soul
Lends the tongue vows: these blazes, daughter,
Giving more light than heat, extinct in both,
Even in their promise, as it is a-making,
You must not take for fire. From this time   120
Be somewhat scanter of your maiden presence;
Set your entreatments° at a higher rate
Than a command to parley.° For Lord Hamlet,
Believe so much in him,° that he is young,
And with a larger tether may he walk   125
Than may be given you: in few,° Ophelia,
Do not believe his vows; for they are brokers,°
Not of that dye° which their investments° show,
But mere implorators of° unholy suits,
Breathing° like sanctified and pious bawds,   130
The better to beguile. This is for all:
I would not, in plain terms, from this time forth,
Have you so slander° any moment leisure,
As to give words or talk with the Lord Hamlet.
Look to 't, I charge you: come your ways.   135

OPHELIA: I shall obey, my lord.   *Exeunt.*

---

102 **Unsifted:** Untried.   103 **tenders:** Offers.   106 **tenders:** Promises to pay.   107 **sterling:** Legal currency.   **Tender:** Hold.   108 **crack the wind:** I.e., run it until it is broken-winded.   109 **tender . . . fool:** Show me a fool (for a daughter).   112 **fashion:** Mere form, pretense.   113 **countenance:** Credit, support.   115 **springes:** Snares.   **woodcocks:** Birds easily caught, type of stupidity.   122 **entreatments:** Conversations, interviews.   123 **command to parley:** Mere invitation to talk.   124 **so . . . him:** This much concerning him.   126 **in few:** Briefly.   127 **brokers:** Go-betweens, procurers.   128 **dye:** Color or sort.   **investments:** Clothes.   129 **implorators of:** Solicitors of.   130 **Breathing:** Speaking.   133 **slander:** Bring disgrace or reproach upon.

[SCENE iv: *The platform.*]

Enter HAMLET, HORATIO, *and* MARCELLUS.

HAMLET: The air bites shrewdly; it is very cold.
HORATIO: It is a nipping and an eager air.
HAMLET: What hour now?
HORATIO: I think it lacks of twelve.
MARCELLUS: No, it is struck.
HORATIO: Indeed? I heard it not: then it draws near the season   5
     Wherein the spirit held his wont to walk.

A flourish of trumpets, and two pieces go off.

          What does this mean, my lord?
HAMLET: The king doth wake° to-night and takes his rouse,°
     Keeps wassail,° and the swagg'ring up-spring° reels;°
     And, as he drains his draughts of Rhenish° down,   10
     The kettle-drum and trumpet thus bray out
     The triumph of his pledge.°
HORATIO: Is it a custom?
HAMLET: Ay, marry, is 't:
     But to my mind, though I am native here
     And to the manner born,° it is a custom   15
     More honour'd in the breach than the observance.
     This heavy-headed revel east and west
     Makes us traduc'd and tax'd of other nations:
     They clepe° us drunkards, and with swinish phrase°
     Soil our addition;° and indeed it takes   20
     From our achievements, though perform'd at height,
     The pith and marrow of our attribute.°
     So, oft it chances in particular men,
     That for some vicious mole of nature° in them,
     As, in their birth—wherein they are not guilty,   25
     Since nature cannot choose his origin—
     By the o'ergrowth of some complexion,
     Oft breaking down the pales° and forts of reason,
     Or by some habit that too much o'er-leavens°

Scene iv.   8 wake: Stay awake, hold revel.   rouse: Carouse, drinking bout.   9 wassail:
Carousal.   up-spring: Last and wildest dance at German merry-makings.   reels: Reels
through.   10 Rhenish: Rhine wine.   12 triumph . . . pledge: His glorious achievement as a
drinker.   15 to . . . born: Destined by birth to be subject to the custom in question.   19 clepe:
Call.   with swinish phrase: By calling us swine.   20 addition: Reputation.   22 attribute:
Reputation.   24 mole of nature: Natural blemish in one's constitution.   28 pales: Palings (as
of a fortification).   29 o'er-leavens: Induces a change throughout (as yeast works in bread).

The form of plausive° manners, that these men,   30
Carrying, I say, the stamp of one defect,
Being nature's livery,° or fortune's star,°—
Their virtues else—be they as pure as grace,
As infinite as man may undergo—
Shall in the general censure take corruption   35
From that particular fault: the dram of eale°
Doth all the noble substance of a doubt
To his own scandal.°

Enter GHOST.

HORATIO: Look, my lord, it comes!
HAMLET: Angels and ministers of grace° defend us!
    Be thou a spirit of health or goblin damn'd,   40
    Bring with thee airs from heaven or blasts from hell,
    Be thy intents wicked or charitable,
    Thou com'st in such a questionable° shape
    That I will speak to thee: I'll call thee Hamlet,
    King, father, royal Dane: O, answer me!   45
    Let me not burst in ignorance; but tell
    Why thy canoniz'd° bones, hearsed° in death,
    Have burst their cerements;° why the sepulchre,
    Wherein we saw thee quietly interr'd,
    Hath op'd his ponderous and marble jaws,   50
    To cast thee up again. What may this mean,
    That thou, dead corse, again in complete steel
    Revisits thus the glimpses of the moon,°
    Making night hideous; and we fools of nature°
    So horridly to shake our disposition   55
    With thoughts beyond the reaches of our souls?
    Say, why is this? wherefore? what should we do?

*[*GHOST*] beckons [*HAMLET*].*

HORATIO: It beckons you to go away with it,
    As if it some impartment° did desire
    To you alone.

---

30 plausive: Pleasing. **32 nature's livery:** Endowment from nature. **fortune's star:** The position in which one is placed by fortune, a reference to astrology. The two phrases are aspects of the same thing. **36–38 the dram . . . scandal:** A famous crux: *dram of eale* has had various interpretations, the preferred one being probably "a dram of evil." **39 ministers of grace:** Messengers of God. **43 questionable:** Inviting question or conversation. **47 canoniz'd:** Buried according to the canons of the church. **hearsed:** Coffined. **48 cerements:** Grave-clothes. **53 glimpses of the moon:** The earth by night. **54 fools of nature:** Mere men, limited to natural knowledge. **59 impartment:** Communication.

MARCELLUS: Look, with what courteous action   60
    It waves you to a more removed° ground:
    But do not go with it.
HORATIO: No, by no means.
HAMLET: It will not speak; then I will follow it.
HORATIO: Do not, my lord!
HAMLET: Why, what should be the fear?
    I do not set my life at a pin's fee;   65
    And for my soul, what can it do to that,
    Being a thing immortal as itself?
    It waves me forth again: I'll follow it.
HORATIO: What if it tempt you toward the flood, my lord,
    Or to the dreadful summit of the cliff   70
    That beetles o'er° his base into the sea,
    And there assume some other horrible form,
    Which might deprive your sovereignty of reason°
    And draw you into madness? think of it:
    The very place puts toys of desperation,°   75
    Without more motive, into every brain
    That looks so many fathoms to the sea
    And hears it roar beneath.
HAMLET: It waves me still.
    Go on; I'll follow thee.
MARCELLUS: You shall not go, my lord.
HAMLET: Hold off your hands!   80
HORATIO: Be rul'd; you shall not go.
HAMLET: My fate cries out,
    And makes each petty artere° in this body
    As hardy as the Nemean lion's° nerve.°
    Still am I call'd. Unhand me, gentlemen.
    By heaven, I'll make a ghost of him that lets° me!   85
    I say, away! Go on; I'll follow thee.   *Exeunt* GHOST *and* HAMLET.
HORATIO: He waxes desperate with imagination.
MARCELLUS: Let's follow; 'tis not fit thus to obey him.
HORATIO: Have after. To what issue° will this come?
MARCELLUS: Something is rotten in the state of Denmark.   90

---

61 removed: Remote.   **71 beetles o'er:** Overhangs threateningly.   **73 deprive . . . reason:** Take away the sovereignty of your reason. It was thought that evil spirits would sometimes assume the form of departed spirits in order to work madness in a human creature.   **75 toys of desperation:** Freakish notions of suicide.   **82 artere:** Artery.   **83 Nemean lion's:** The Nemean lion was one of the monsters slain by Hercules.   **nerve:** Sinew, tendon. The point is that the arteries which were carrying the spirits out into the body were functioning and were as stiff and hard as the sinews of the lion.   **85 lets:** Hinders.   **89 issue:** Outcome.

HORATIO: Heaven will direct it.°
MARCELLUS: Nay, let's follow him.   *Exeunt.*

[SCENE V: *Another part of the platform.*]

Enter GHOST *and* HAMLET.

HAMLET: Whither wilt thou lead me? speak; I'll go no further.
GHOST: Mark me.
HAMLET: I will.
GHOST: My hour is almost come,
    When I to sulphurous and tormenting flames
    Must render up myself.
HAMLET: Alas, poor ghost!
GHOST: Pity me not, but lend thy serious hearing   5
    To what I shall unfold.
HAMLET: Speak; I am bound to hear.
GHOST: So art thou to revenge, when thou shalt hear.
HAMLET: What?
GHOST: I am thy father's spirit,
    Doom'd for a certain term to walk the night,   10
    And for the day confin'd to fast° in fires,
    Till the foul crimes done in my days of nature
    Are burnt and purg'd away. But that I am forbid
    To tell the secrets of my prison-house,
    I could a tale unfold whose lightest word   15
    Would harrow up thy soul, freeze thy young blood,
    Make thy two eyes, like stars, start from their spheres,°
    Thy knotted° and combined° locks to part
    And each particular hair to stand an end,
    Like quills upon the fretful porpentine:°   20
    But this eternal blazon° must not be
    To ears of flesh and blood. List, list, O, list!
    If thou didst ever thy dear father love—
HAMLET: O God!
GHOST: Revenge his foul and most unnatural° murder.   25
HAMLET: Murder!

---

91 it: I.e., the outcome.   **Scene v.**   **11 fast:** Probably, do without food. It has been sometimes taken in the sense of doing general penance.   **17 spheres:** Orbits.   **18 knotted:** Perhaps intricately arranged.   **combined:** Tied, bound.   **20 porpentine:** Porcupine.   **21 eternal blazon:** Promulgation or proclamation of eternity, revelation of the hereafter.   **25 unnatural:** I.e., pertaining to fratricide.

GHOST: Murder most foul, as in the best it is;
     But this most foul, strange and unnatural.
HAMLET: Haste me to know't, that I, with wings as swift
     As meditation or the thoughts of love,   30
     May sweep to my revenge.
GHOST: I find thee apt;
     And duller shouldst thou be than the fat weed°
     That roots itself in ease on Lethe wharf,°
     Wouldst thou not stir in this. Now, Hamlet, hear:
     'Tis given out that, sleeping in my orchard,   35
     A serpent stung me; so the whole ear of Denmark
     Is by a forged process of my death
     Rankly abus'd: but know, thou noble youth,
     The serpent that did sting thy father's life
     Now wears his crown.
HAMLET: O my prophetic soul!   40
     My uncle!
GHOST: Ay, that incestuous, that adulterate° beast,
     With witchcraft of his wit, with traitorous gifts,—
     O wicked wit and gifts, that have the power
     So to seduce!—won to his shameful lust   45
     The will of my most seeming-virtuous queen:
     O Hamlet, what a falling-off was there!
     From me, whose love was of that dignity
     That it went hand in hand even with the vow
     I made to her in marriage, and to decline   50
     Upon a wretch whose natural gifts were poor
     To those of mine!
     But virtue, as it never will be moved,
     Though lewdness court it in a shape of heaven,
     So lust, though to a radiant angel link'd,   55
     Will sate itself in a celestial bed,
     And prey on garbage.
     But, soft! methinks I scent the morning air;
     Brief let me be. Sleeping within my orchard,
     My custom always of the afternoon,   60
     Upon my secure° hour thy uncle stole,
     With juice of cursed hebona° in a vial,

---

32 fat weed: Many suggestions have been offered as to the particular plant intended, including asphodel; probably a general figure for plants growing along rotting wharves and piles.   **33 Lethe wharf:** Bank of the river of forgetfulness in Hades.   **42 adulterate:** Adulterous.   **61 secure:** Confident, unsuspicious.   **62 hebona:** Generally supposed to mean "henbane," conjectured *hemlock; ebenus,* meaning "yew."

And in the porches of my ears did pour
The leperous° distilment; whose effect
Holds such an enmity with blood of man   65
That swift as quicksilver it courses through
The natural gates and alleys of the body,
And with a sudden vigour it doth posset°
And curd, like eager° droppings into milk,
The thin and wholesome blood: so did it mine;   70
And a most instant tetter bark'd about,
Most lazar-like,° with vile and loathsome crust,
All my smooth body.
    Thus was I, sleeping, by a brother's hand
Of life, of crown, of queen, at once dispatch'd:°   75
Cut off even in the blossoms of my sin,
Unhous'led,° disappointed,° unanel'd,°
No reck'ning made, but sent to my account
With all my imperfections on my head:
O, horrible! O, horrible! most horrible!°   80
If thou hast nature in thee, bear it not;
Let not the royal bed of Denmark be
A couch for luxury° and damned incest.
But, howsomever thou pursues this act,
Taint not thy mind,° nor let thy soul contrive   85
Against thy mother aught: leave her to heaven
And to those thorns that in her bosom lodge,
To prick and sting her. Fare thee well at once!
The glow-worm shows the matin° to be near,
And 'gins to pale his uneffectual fire:°   90
Adieu, adieu, adieu! remember me.   *[Exit.]*
HAMLET: O all you host of heaven! O earth! what else?
    And shall I couple° hell? O, fie! Hold, hold, my heart;
    And you, my sinews, grow not instant old,
    But bear me stiffly up. Remember thee!   95
    Ay, thou poor ghost, whiles memory holds a seat
    In this distracted globe.° Remember thee!

---

64 leperous: Causing leprosy. **68 posset:** Coagulate, curdle. **69 eager:** Sour, acid. **72 lazar-
like:** Leperlike. **75 dispatch'd:** Suddenly bereft. **77 Unhous'led:** Without having received
the sacrament. **disappointed:** Unready, without equipment for the last journey. **unanel'd:**
Without having received extreme unction. **80 O . . . horrible:** Many editors give this line to
Hamlet; Garrick and Sir Henry Irving spoke it in that part. **83 luxury:** Lechery. **85 Taint . . .
mind:** Probably, deprave not thy character, do nothing except in the pursuit of a natural
revenge. **89 matin:** Morning. **90 uneffectual fire:** Cold light. **93 couple:** Add. **97 distracted globe:** Confused head.

Yea, from the table of my memory
I'll wipe away all trivial fond records,
All saws° of books, all forms, all pressures° past,   100
That youth and observation copied there;
And thy commandment all alone shall live
Within the book and volume of my brain,
Unmix'd with baser matter: yes, by heaven!
O most pernicious woman!   105
O villain, villain, smiling, damned villain!
My tables,°—meet it is I set it down,
That one may smile, and smile, and be a villain;
At least I am sure it may be so in Denmark: *[Writing.]*
So, uncle, there you are. Now to my word;°   110
It is "Adieu, adieu! remember me,"
I have sworn't.

Enter HORATIO *and* MARCELLUS.

HORATIO: My lord, my lord—
MARCELLUS: Lord Hamlet,—
HORATIO: Heavens secure him!
HAMLET: So be it!
MARCELLUS: Hillo, ho, ho,° my lord!   115
HAMLET: Hillo, ho, ho, boy! come, bird, come.
MARCELLUS: How is't, my noble lord?
HORATIO: What news, my lord?
HAMLET: O, wonderful!
HORATIO: Good my lord, tell it.
HAMLET: No; you will reveal it.
HORATIO: Not I, my lord, by heaven.
MARCELLUS: Nor I, my lord.   120
HAMLET: How say you, then; would heart of man once think it?
    But you'll be secret?
HORATIO: }
MARCELLUS: }   Ay, by heaven, my lord.
HAMLET: There's ne'er a villain dwelling in all Denmark
    But he's an arrant° knave.
HORATIO: There needs no ghost, my lord, come from the grave   125
    To tell us this.
HAMLET: Why, right; you are in the right;
    And so, without more circumstance at all,

---

100 **saws:** Wise sayings. **pressures:** Impressions stamped. 107 **tables:** Probably a small portable writing-tablet carried at the belt. 110 **word:** Watchword. 115 **Hillo, ho, ho:** A falconer's call to a hawk in air. 124 **arrant:** Thoroughgoing.

I hold it fit that we shake hands and part:
You, as your business and desire shall point you;
For every man has business and desire, 130
Such as it is; and for my own poor part,
Look you, I'll go pray.
HORATIO: These are but wild and whirling words, my lord.
HAMLET: I am sorry they offend you, heartily;
Yes, 'faith, heartily.
HORATIO: There's no offence, my lord. 135
HAMLET: Yes, by Saint Patrick,° but there is, Horatio,
And much offence too. Touching this vision here,
It is an honest° ghost, that let me tell you:
For your desire to know what is between us,
O'ermaster 't as you may. And now, good friends, 140
As you are friends, scholars and soldiers,
Give me one poor request.
HORATIO: What is 't, my lord? we will.
HAMLET: Never make known what you have seen to-night.
HORATIO: ⎤
MARCELLUS: ⎦ My lord, we will not.
HAMLET: Nay, but swear 't.
HORATIO: In faith, 145
My lord, not I.
MARCELLUS: Nor I, my lord, in faith.
HAMLET: Upon my sword.°
MARCELLUS: We have sworn, my lord, already.
HAMLET: Indeed, upon my sword, indeed.   GHOST *cries under the stage.*
GHOST: Swear.
HAMLET: Ah, ha, boy! say'st thou so? art thou there, truepenny?° 150
Come on—you hear this fellow in the cellarage—
Consent to swear.
HORATIO: Propose the oath, my lord.
HAMLET: Never to speak of this that you have seen,
Swear by my sword.
GHOST *[beneath]*: Swear. 155
HAMLET: Hic et ubique?° then we'll shift our ground.
Come hither, gentlemen,
And lay your hands again upon my sword:
Swear by my sword,
Never to speak of this that you have heard. 160

---

136 **Saint Patrick:** St. Patrick was keeper of Purgatory and patron saint of all blunders and confusion.   138 **honest:** I.e., a real ghost and not an evil spirit.   147 **sword:** I.e., the hilt in the form of a cross.   150 **truepenny:** Good old boy, or the like.   156 **Hic et ubique?:** Here and everywhere?

GHOST *[beneath]*: Swear by his sword.
HAMLET: Well said, old mole! canst work i' th' earth so fast?
    A worthy pioner!° Once more remove, good friends.
HORATIO: O day and night, but this is wondrous strange!
HAMLET: And therefore as a stranger give it welcome.   165
    There are more things in heaven and earth, Horatio,
    Than are dreamt of in your philosophy.
    But come;
    Here, as before, never, so help you mercy,
    How strange or odd soe'er I bear myself,   170
    As I perchance hereafter shall think meet
    To put an antic° disposition on,
    That you, at such times seeing me, never shall,
    With arms encumb'red° thus, or this head-shake,
    Or by pronouncing of some doubtful phrase,   175
    As "Well, well, we know," or "We could, an if we would,"
    Or "If we list to speak," or "There be, an if they might,"
    Or such ambiguous giving out,° to note°
    That you know aught of me: this not to do,
    So grace and mercy at your most need help you,   180
    Swear.
GHOST *[beneath]*: Swear.
HAMLET: Rest, rest, perturbed spirit! *[They swear.]* So, gentlemen,
    With all my love I do commend me to you:
    And what so poor a man as Hamlet is   185
    May do, t' express his love and friending° to you,
    God willing, shall not lack. Let us go in together;
    And still your fingers on your lips, I pray.
    The time is out of joint: O cursed spite,
    That ever I was born to set it right!   190
    Nay, come, let's go together.   *Exeunt.*

[ACT II

SCENE i: *A room in* POLONIUS's *house.*]

Enter old POLONIUS *with his man [*REYNALDO*].*

POLONIUS: Give him this money and these notes, Reynaldo.
REYNALDO: I will, my lord.

---

163 pioner: Digger, miner.   **172 antic:** Fantastic.   **174 encumb'red:** Folded or entwined.   **178 giving out:** Profession of knowledge.   **to note:** To give a sign.   **186 friending:** Friendliness.

POLONIUS: You shall do marvellous wisely, good Reynaldo,
    Before you visit him, to make inquire
    Of his behaviour.
REYNALDO: My lord, I did intend it.   5
POLONIUS: Marry, well said; very well said. Look you, sir,
    Inquire me first what Danskers° are in Paris;
    And how, and who, what means, and where they keep,°
    What company, at what expense; and finding
    By this encompassment° and drift° of question   10
    That they do know my son, come you more nearer
    Than your particular demands will touch it:°
    Take° you as 'twere, some distant knowledge of him;
    As thus, "I know his father and his friends,
    And in part him": do you mark this, Reynaldo?   15
REYNALDO: Ay, very well, my lord.
POLONIUS: "And in part him; but" you may say "not well:
    But, if 't be he I mean, he's very wild;
    Addicted so and so": and there put on° him
    What forgeries° you please; marry, none so rank   20
    As may dishonour him; take heed of that;
    But, sir, such wanton,° wild and usual slips
    As are companions noted and most known
    To youth and liberty.
REYNALDO: As gaming, my lord.
POLONIUS: Ay, or drinking, fencing,° swearing, quarrelling,   25
    Drabbing;° you may go so far.
REYNALDO: My lord, that would dishonour him.
POLONIUS: 'Faith, no; as you may season it in the charge.
    You must not put another scandal on him,
    That he is open to incontinency;°   30
    That's not my meaning: but breathe his faults so quaintly°
    That they may seem the taints of liberty,°
    The flash and outbreak of a fiery mind,
    A savageness in unreclaimed° blood,
    Of general assault.°

Act II, Scene i.   **7 Danskers:** Danske was a common variant for "Denmark"; hence "Dane." **8 keep:** Dwell. **10 encompassment:** Roundabout talking. **drift:** Gradual approach or course. **11–12 come . . . it:** I.e., you will find out more this way than by asking pointed questions. **13 Take:** Assume, pretend. **19 put on:** Impute to. **20 forgeries:** Invented tales. **22 wanton:** Sportive, unrestrained. **25 fencing:** Indicative of the ill repute of professional fencers and fencing schools in Elizabethan times. **26 Drabbing:** Associating with immoral women. **30 incontinency:** Habitual loose behavior. **31 quaintly:** Delicately, ingeniously. **32 taints of liberty:** Blemishes due to freedom. **34 unreclaimed:** Untamed. **35 general assault:** Tendency that assails all untrained youth.

REYNALDO: But, my good lord,—   35
POLONIUS: Wherefore should you do this?
REYNALDO: Ay, my lord,
    I would know that.
POLONIUS: Marry, sir, here's my drift;
    And, I believe, it is a fetch of wit:°
    You laying these slight sullies on my son,
    As 'twere a thing a little soil'd i' th' working,   40
    Mark you,
    Your party in converse, him you would sound,
    Having ever° seen in the prenominate° crimes
    The youth you breathe of guilty, be assur'd
    He closes with you in this consequence;°   45
    "Good sir," or so, or "friend," or "gentleman,"
    According to the phrase or the addition
    Of man and country.
REYNALDO: Very good, my lord.
POLONIUS: And then, sir, does 'a this—'a does—what was I about to say? By the
    mass, I was about to say something: where did I leave?   50
REYNALDO: At "closes in the consequence," at "friend or so," and "gentleman."
POLONIUS: At "closes in the consequence," ay, marry;
    He closes thus: "I know the gentleman;
    I saw him yesterday, or t' other day,
    Or then, or then; with such, or such; and, as you say,   55
    There was 'a gaming; there o'ertook in 's rouse;°
    There falling out at tennis": or perchance,
    "I saw him enter such a house of sale,"
    Videlicet,° a brothel, or so forth.
    See you now;   60
    Your bait of falsehood takes this carp of truth:
    And thus do we of wisdom and of reach,°
    With windlasses° and with assays of bias,°
    By indirections° find directions° out:
    So by my former lecture° and advice,   65
    Shall you my son. You have me, have you not?
REYNALDO: My lord, I have.
POLONIUS: God bye ye;° fare ye well.

———————

38 fetch of wit: Clever trick.   **43 ever:** At any time.   **prenominate:** Before-mentioned.   **45
closes . . . consequence:** Agrees with you in this conclusion.   **56 o'ertook in 's rouse:** Overcome
by drink.   **59 Videlicet:** Namely.   **62 reach:** Capacity, ability.   **63 windlasses:** I.e., circuitous
paths.   **assays of bias:** Attempts that resemble the course of the bowl, which, being weighted
on one side, has a curving motion.   **64 indirections:** Devious courses.   **directions:** Straight
courses, i.e., the truth.   **65 lecture:** Admonition.   **67 bye ye:** Be with you.

REYNALDO: Good my lord!
POLONIUS: Observe his inclination in yourself.°
REYNALDO: I shall, my lord.   70
POLONIUS: And let him ply his music.°
REYNALDO: Well, my lord.
POLONIUS: Farewell!   *Exit* REYNALDO.

Enter OPHELIA.

                                    How now, Ophelia! what's the matter?
OPHELIA: O, my lord, my lord, I have been so affrighted!
POLONIUS: With what, i' th' name of God?
OPHELIA: My lord, as I was sewing in my closet,°   75
        Lord Hamlet, with his doublet° all unbrac'd;°
        No hat upon his head; his stockings foul'd,
        Ungart'red, and down-gyved° to his ankle;
        Pale as his shirt; his knees knocking each other;
        And with a look so piteous in purport   80
        As if he had been loosed out of hell
        To speak of horrors,—he comes before me.
POLONIUS: Mad for thy love?
OPHELIA: My lord, I do not know;
        But truly, I do fear it.
POLONIUS: What said he?
OPHELIA: He took me by the wrist and held me hard;   85
        Then goes he to the length of all his arm;
        And, with his other hand thus o'er his brow,
        He falls to such perusal of my face
        As 'a would draw it. Long stay'd he so;
        At last, a little shaking of mine arm   90
        And thrice his head thus waving up and down,
        He rais'd a sigh so piteous and profound
        As it did seem to shatter all his bulk°
        And end his being: that done, he lets me go:
        And, with his head over his shoulder turn'd,   95
        He seem'd to find his way without his eyes;
        For out o' doors he went without their helps,
        And, to the last, bended their light on me.
POLONIUS: Come, go with me: I will go seek the king.
        This is the very ecstasy of love,   100

---

69 Observe . . . yourself: In your own person, not by spies; or conform your own conduct to his inclination; or test him by studying yourself.   **71 ply his music:** Probably to be taken literally.   **75 closet:** Private chamber.   **76 doublet:** Close-fitting coat.   **unbrac'd:** Unfastened.   **78 down-gyved:** Fallen to the ankles (like gyves or fetters).   **93 bulk:** Body.

Whose violent property° fordoes° itself
And leads the will to desperate undertakings
As oft as any passion under heaven
That does afflict our natures. I am sorry.
What, have you given him any hard words of late?   105
OPHELIA: No, my good lord, but, as you did command,
    I did repel his letters and denied
    His access to me.
POLONIUS: That hath made him mad.
    I am sorry that with better heed and judgement
    I had not quoted° him: I fear'd he did but trifle,   110
    And meant to wrack thee; but, beshrew my jealousy!°
    By heaven, it is as proper to our age
    To cast beyond° ourselves in our opinions
    As it is common for the younger sort
    To lack discretion. Come, go we to the king: 115
    This must be known; which, being kept close, might move
    More grief to hide than hate to utter love.°
    Come.   *Exeunt.*

[**SCENE ii:** *A room in the castle.*]

Flourish. Enter KING *and* QUEEN, ROSENCRANTZ, *and* GUILDENSTERN *[with others].*

KING: Welcome, dear Rosencrantz and Guildenstern!
    Moreover that° we much did long to see you,
    The need we have to use you did provoke
    Our hasty sending. Something have you heard
    Of Hamlet's transformation; so call it,   5
    Sith° nor th' exterior nor the inward man
    Resembles that it was. What it should be,
    More than his father's death, that thus hath put him
    So much from th' understanding of himself,
    I cannot dream of: I entreat you both,   10
    That, being of so young days° brought up with him,
    And sith so neighbour'd to his youth and haviour,
    That you vouchsafe your rest° here in our court

---

101 property: Nature.   **fordoes:** Destroys.   **110 quoted:** Observed.   **111 beshrew my jealousy:** Curse my suspicions.   **113 cast beyond:** Overshoot, miscalculate.   **116–117 might . . . love:** I.e., I might cause more grief to others by hiding the knowledge of Hamlet's love to Ophelia than hatred to me and mine by telling of it.   **Scene ii.   2 Moreover that:** Besides the fact that.   **6 Sith:** Since.   **11 of . . . days:** From such early youth.   **13 vouchsafe your rest:** Please to stay.

Some little time: so by your companies
To draw him on to pleasures, and to gather, 15
So much as from occasion you may glean,
Whether aught, to us unknown, afflicts him thus,
That, open'd, lies within our remedy.
QUEEN: Good gentlemen, he hath much talk'd of you;
And sure I am two men there are not living 20
To whom he more adheres. If it will please you
To show us so much gentry° and good will
As to expend your time with us awhile,
For the supply and profit° of our hope,
Your visitation shall receive such thanks 25
As fits a king's remembrance.
ROSENCRANTZ: Both your majesties
Might, by the sovereign power you have of us,
Put your dread pleasures more into command
Than to entreaty.
GUILDENSTERN: But we both obey,
And here give up ourselves, in the full bent° 30
To lay our service freely at your feet,
To be commanded.
KING: Thanks, Rosencrantz and gentle Guildenstern.
QUEEN: Thanks, Guildenstern and gentle Rosencrantz:
And I beseech you instantly to visit 35
My too much changed son. Go, some of you,
And bring these gentlemen where Hamlet is.
GUILDENSTERN: Heavens make our presence and our practices
Pleasant and helpful to him!
QUEEN: Ay, amen!

Exeunt ROSENCRANTZ *and* GUILDENSTERN *[with some* ATTENDANTS*].*

Enter POLONIUS.

POLONIUS: Th' ambassadors from Norway, my good lord, 40
Are joyfully return'd.
KING: Thou still hast been the father of good news.
POLONIUS: Have I, my lord? I assure my good liege,
I hold my duty, as I hold my soul,
Both to my God and to my gracious king: 45
And I do think, or else this brain of mine
Hunts not the trail of policy so sure

---

22 gentry: Courtesy.   **24 supply and profit:** Aid and successful outcome.   **30 in . . . bent:** To
the utmost degree of our mental capacity.

As it hath us'd to do, that I have found
The very cause of Hamlet's lunacy.
KING: O, speak of that; that do I long to hear.   50
POLONIUS: Give first admittance to th' ambassadors;
    My news shall be the fruit to that great feast.
KING: Thyself do grace to them, and bring them in.   *[Exit* POLONIUS.*]*
    He tells me, my dear Gertrude, he hath found
    The head and source of all your son's distemper.   55
QUEEN: I doubt° it is no other but the main;°
    His father's death, and our o'erhasty marriage.
KING: Well, we shall sift him.

Enter AMBASSADORS *[*VOLTIMAND *and* CORNELIUS, *with* POLONIUS*].*

                        Welcome, my good friends!
    Say, Voltimand, what from our brother Norway?
VOLTIMAND: Most fair return of greetings and desires.   60
    Upon our first, he sent out to suppress
    His nephew's levies; which to him appear'd
    To be a preparation 'gainst the Polack;
    But, better look'd into, he truly found
    It was against your highness: whereat griev'd,   65
    That so his sickness, age and impotence
    Was falsely borne in hand,° sends out arrests
    On Fortinbras; which he, in brief, obeys;
    Receives rebuke from Norway, and in fine°
    Makes vow before his uncle never more   70
    To give th' assay° of arms against your majesty.
    Whereon old Norway, overcome with joy,
    Gives him three score thousand crowns in annual fee,
    And his commission to employ those soldiers,
    So levied as before, against the Polack: 75
    With an entreaty, herein further shown,   *[Giving a paper.]*
    That it might please you to give quiet pass
    Through your dominions for this enterprise,
    On such regards of safety and allowance°
    As therein are set down.
KING: It likes° us well;   80
    And at our more consider'd° time we'll read,
    Answer, and think upon this business.

---

56 doubt: Fear. main: Chief point, principal concern. 67 borne in hand: Deluded. 69
in fine: In the end. 71 assay: Assault, trial (of arms). 79 safety and allowance: Pledges of
safety to the country and terms of permission for the troops to pass. 80 likes: Pleases. 81
consider'd: Suitable for deliberation.

Meantime we thank you for your well-took labour:
Go to your rest; at night we'll feast together:
Most welcome home! *Exeunt* AMBASSADORS.
POLONIUS: This business is well ended.   85
  My liege, and madam, to expostulate
  What majesty should be, what duty is,
  Why day is day, night night, and time is time,
  Were nothing but to waste night, day and time.
  Therefore, since brevity is the soul of wit,°   90
  And tediousness the limbs and outward flourishes,°
  I will be brief: your noble son is mad:
  Mad call I it; for, to define true madness,
  What is 't but to be nothing else but mad?
  But let that go.
QUEEN: More matter, with less art.   95
POLONIUS: Madam, I swear I use no art at all.
  That he is mad, 'tis true: 'tis true 'tis pity;
  And pity 'tis 'tis true: a foolish figure;°
  But farewell it, for I will use no art.
  Mad let us grant him, then: and now remains   100
  That we find out the cause of this effect,
  Or rather say, the cause of this defect,
  For this effect defective comes by cause:
  Thus it remains, and the remainder thus.
  Perpend.°   105
  I have a daughter—have while she is mine—
  Who, in her duty and obedience, mark,
  Hath given me this: now gather, and surmise. *[Reads the letter.]* "To the celestial
  and my soul's idol,
  the most beautified Ophelia,"—   110
  That's an ill phrase, a vile phrase; "beautified" is a vile phrase: but you shall hear.
  Thus: *[Reads.]*
  "In her excellent white bosom, these, & c."
QUEEN: Came this from Hamlet to her?
POLONIUS: Good madam, stay awhile; I will be faithful. *[Reads.]* 115
     "Doubt thou the stars are fire;
       Doubt that the sun doth move;
       Doubt truth to be a liar;
       But never doubt I love.
  "O dear Ophelia, I am ill at these numbers;° I have not art to reckon°   120

---

90 wit: Sound sense or judgment.   **91 flourishes:** Ostentation, embellishments.   **98 figure:**
Figure of speech.   **105 Perpend:** Consider.   **120 ill . . . numbers:** Unskilled at writing verses.
reckon: Number metrically, scan.

my groans: but that I love thee best, O most best, believe it. Adieu.
"Thine evermore, most dear lady, whilst this machine° is to him,
HAMLET."

This, in obedience, hath my daughter shown me,
And more above,° hath his solicitings,   125
As they fell out° by time, by means° and place,
All given to mine ear.

KING: But how hath she
Receiv'd his love?

POLONIUS: What do you think of me?

KING: As of a man faithful and honourable.

POLONIUS: I would fain prove so. But what might you think,   130
When I had seen this hot love on the wing—
As I perceiv'd it, I must tell you that,
Before my daughter told me—what might you,
Or my dear majesty your queen here, think,
If I had play'd the desk or table-book,°   135
Or given my heart a winking,° mute and dumb,
Or look'd upon this love with idle sight;
What might you think? No, I went round to work,
And my young mistress thus I did bespeak:°
"Lord Hamlet is a prince, out of thy star;°   140
This must not be": and then I prescripts gave her,
That she should lock herself from his resort,
Admit no messengers, receive no tokens.
Which done, she took the fruits of my advice;
And he, repelled—a short tale to make—   145
Fell into a sadness, then into a fast,
Thence to a watch,° thence into a weakness,
Thence to a lightness,° and, by this declension,°
Into the madness wherein now he raves,
And all we mourn for.

KING: Do you think 'tis this?   150

QUEEN: It may be, very like.

POLONIUS: Hath there been such a time—I would fain know that—
That I have positively said "'Tis so,"
When it prov'd otherwise?

KING: Not that I know.

---

122 **machine:** Bodily frame.   125 **more above:** Moreover.   126 **fell out:** Occurred. **means:**
Opportunities (of access).   135 **play'd . . . table-book:** I.e., remained shut up, concealed this
information.   136 **given . . . winking:** Given my heart a signal to keep silent.   **139 bespeak:**
Address.   140 **out . . . star:** Above thee in position.   147 **watch:** State of sleeplessness.   148
lightness: Lightheadedness. **declension:** Decline, deterioration.

POLONIUS *[pointing to his head and shoulder]*: Take this from this, if this be
    otherwise: 155
    If circumstances lead me, I will find
    Where truth is hid, though it were hid indeed
    Within the centre.°
KING: How may we try it further?
POLONIUS: You know, sometimes he walks four hours together
    Here in the lobby.
QUEEN: So he does indeed.   160
POLONIUS: At such a time I'll loose my daughter to him:
    Be you and I behind an arras° then;
    Mark the encounter: if he love her not
    And be not from his reason fall'n thereon,°
    Let me be no assistant for a state,   165
    But keep a farm and carters.
KING: We will try it.

Enter HAMLET *[reading on a book].*

QUEEN: But, look, where sadly the poor wretch comes reading.
POLONIUS: Away, I do beseech you both, away:

                 Exeunt KING *and* QUEEN *[with* ATTENDANTS*].*

    I'll board° him presently. O, give me leave.
    How does my good Lord Hamlet?   170
HAMLET: Well, God-a-mercy.
POLONIUS: Do you know me, my lord?
HAMLET: Excellent well; you are a fishmonger.°
POLONIUS: Not I, my lord.
HAMLET: Then I would you were so honest a man.   175
POLONIUS: Honest, my lord!
HAMLET: Ay, sir; to be honest, as this world goes, is to be one man picked out of ten
    thousand.
POLONIUS: That's very true, my lord.
HAMLET: For if the sun breed maggots in a dead dog, being a good kissing car-   180
    rion,° — Have you a daughter?
POLONIUS: I have, my lord.
HAMLET: Let her not walk i' the sun:° conception° is a blessing: but as your daughter
    may conceive — Friend, look to 't.

---

158 centre: Middle point of the earth.   **162 arras:** Hanging, tapestry.   **164 thereon:** On that
account.   **169 board:** Accost.   **173 fishmonger:** An opprobrious expression meaning "bawd,"
"procurer."   **180–181 good kissing carrion:** I.e., a good piece of flesh for kissing (?).   **183
i' the sun:** In the sunshine of princely favors.   **conception:** Quibble on "understanding" and
"pregnancy."

POLONIUS [aside]: How say you by° that? Still harping on my daughter: yet he knew   185
    me not at first; 'a said I was a fishmonger: 'a is far gone, far gone: and truly in my
    youth I suffered much extremity for love; very near this. I'll speak to him again.
    What do you read, my lord?

HAMLET: Words, words, words.

POLONIUS: What is the matter,° my lord?   190

HAMLET: Between who?°

POLONIUS: I mean, the matter that you read, my lord.

HAMLET: Slanders, sir: for the satirical rogue says here that old men have grey beards,
    that their faces are wrinkled, their eyes purging° thick amber and plum-tree
    gum and that they have a plentiful lack of wit, together with most weak hams: 195
    all which, sir, though I most powerfully and potently believe, yet I hold it not
    honesty° to have it thus set down, for yourself, sir, should be old as I am, if like
    a crab you could go backward.

POLONIUS [aside]: Though this be madness, yet there is method in 't.—Will you walk
    out of the air, my lord?   200

HAMLET: Into my grave.

POLONIUS: Indeed, that's out of the air. [Aside.] How pregnant sometimes his replies
    are! a happiness° that often madness hits on, which reason and sanity could
    not so prosperously° be delivered of. I will leave him, and suddenly contrive the
    means of meeting between him and my daughter.—My honourable lord, I will   205
    most humbly take my leave of you.

HAMLET: You cannot, sir, take from me any thing that I will more willingly part
    withal: except my life, except my life, except my life.

Enter GUILDENSTERN *and* ROSENCRANTZ.

POLONIUS: Fare you well, my lord.

HAMLET: These tedious old fools!   210

POLONIUS: You go to seek the Lord Hamlet; there he is.

ROSENCRANTZ [to POLONIUS]: God save you, sir!   [Exit POLONIUS.]

GUILDENSTERN: My honoured lord!

ROSENCRANTZ: My most dear lord!

HAMLET: My excellent good friends! How dost thou, Guildenstern? Ah, Rosencrantz!   215
    Good lads, how do ye both?

ROSENCRANTZ: As the indifferent° children of the earth.

GUILDENSTERN: Happy, in that we are not over-happy;
    On Fortune's cap we are not the very button.

HAMLET: Nor the soles of her shoe?   220

ROSENCRANTZ: Neither, my lord.

---

185 by: Concerning.   **190 matter:** Substance.   **191 Between who:** Hamlet deliberately
takes *matter* as meaning "basis of dispute."   **194 purging:** discharging.   **197 honesty:**
Decency.   **203 happiness:** Felicity of expression.   **204 prosperously:** Successfully.   **217 indifferent:** Ordinary.

HAMLET: Then you live about her waist, or in the middle of her favours?

GUILDENSTERN: 'Faith, her privates° we.

HAMLET: In the secret parts of Fortune? O, most true; she is a strumpet. What's the news?

ROSENCRANTZ: None, my lord, but that the world's grown honest.

HAMLET: Then is doomsday near: but your news is not true. Let me question more in particular: what have you, my good friends, deserved at the hands of Fortune, that she sends you to prison hither?

GUILDENSTERN: Prison, my lord!

HAMLET: Denmark's a prison.

ROSENCRANTZ: Then is the world one.

HAMLET: A goodly one; in which there are many confines,° wards and dungeons, Denmark being one o' the worst.

ROSENCRANTZ: We think not so, my lord.

HAMLET: Why, then, 'tis none to you; for there is nothing either good or bad, but thinking makes it so: to me it is a prison.

ROSENCRANTZ: Why then, your ambition makes it one; 'tis too narrow for your mind.

HAMLET: O God, I could be bounded in a nutshell and count myself a king of infinite space, were it not that I have bad dreams.

GUILDENSTERN: Which dreams indeed are ambition, for the very substance of the ambitious° is merely the shadow of a dream.

HAMLET: A dream itself is but a shadow.

ROSENCRANTZ: Truly, and I hold ambition of so airy and light a quality that it is but a shadow's shadow.

HAMLET: Then are our beggars bodies, and our monarchs and outstretched heroes the beggars' shadows. Shall we to the court? for, by my fay,° I cannot reason.°

ROSENCRANTZ:
GUILDENSTERN: } We'll wait upon° you.

HAMLET: No such matter: I will not sort° you with the rest of my servants, for, to speak to you like an honest man, I am most dreadfully attended.° But, in the beaten way of friendship,° what make you at Elsinore?

ROSENCRANTZ: To visit you, my lord: no other occasion.

HAMLET: Beggar that I am, I am ever poor in thanks; but I thank you: and sure, dear friends, my thanks are too dear a° halfpenny. Were you not sent for? Is it your own inclining? Is it a free visitation? Come, come, deal justly with me: come, come; nay, speak.

GUILDENSTERN: What should we say, my lord?

223 **privates:** I.e., ordinary men (sexual pun on *private parts*).   233 **confines:** Places of confinement.   242–243 **very . . . ambitious:** That seemingly most substantial thing which the ambitious pursue.   248 **fay:** Faith.   **reason:** Argue.   249 **wait upon:** Accompany.   250 **sort:** Class.   251 **dreadfully attended:** Poorly provided with servants.   251–252 **in the . . . friendship:** As a matter of course among friends.   255 **a:** I.e., at a.

HAMLET: Why, any thing, but to the purpose. You were sent for; and there is a kind of
   confession in your looks which your modesties have not craft enough to colour: 260
   I know the good king and queen have sent for you.
ROSENCRANTZ: To what end, my lord?
HAMLET: That you must teach me. But let me conjure° you, by the rights of our
   fellowship, by the consonancy of our youth,° by the obligation of our ever-
   preserved love, and by what more dear a better proposer° could charge you   265
   withal, be even and direct with me, whether you were sent for, or no?
ROSENCRANTZ [*aside to* GUILDENSTERN]: What say you?
HAMLET [*aside*]: Nay, then, I have an eye of you.—If you love me, hold not off.
GUILDENSTERN: My lord, we were sent for.
HAMLET: I will tell you why; so shall my anticipation prevent your discovery,°   270
   and your secrecy to the king and queen moult no feather. I have of late—but
   wherefore I know not—lost all my mirth, forgone all custom of exercises;
   and indeed it goes so heavily with my disposition that this goodly frame, the
   earth, seems to me a sterile promontory, this most excellent canopy, the air,
   look you, this brave o'erhanging firmament, this majestical roof fretted° with   275
   golden fire, why, it appeareth nothing to me but a foul and pestilent congregation of vapours. What a piece of work is a man! how noble in reason! how
   infinite in faculties!° in form and moving how express° and admirable! in
   action how like an angel! in apprehension° how like a god! the beauty of the
   world! the paragon of animals! And yet, to me, what is this quintessence° of   280
   dust? man delights not me: no, nor woman neither, though by your smiling
   you seem to say so.
ROSENCRANTZ: My lord, there was no such stuff in my thoughts.
HAMLET: Why did you laugh then, when I said "man delights not me"?
ROSENCRANTZ: To think, my lord, if you delight not in man, what lenten° entertain-   285
   ment the players shall receive from you: we coted° them on the way; and hither
   are they coming, to offer you service.
HAMLET: He that plays the king shall be welcome; his majesty shall have tribute of
   me; the adventurous knight shall use his foil and target;° the lover shall not sigh
   gratis; the humorous man° shall end his part in peace; the clown shall make   290
   those laugh whose lungs are tickle o' the sere;° and the lady shall say her mind
   freely, or the blank verse shall halt for 't.° What players are they?

---

263 **conjure:** Adjure, entreat.   264 **consonancy of our youth:** The fact that we are of the same
age.   265 **better proposer:** One more skillful in finding proposals.   270 **prevent your discovery:** Forestall your disclosure.   275 **fretted:** Adorned.   278 **faculties:** Capacity.   **express:**
Well-framed (?), exact (?).   279 **apprehension:** Understanding.   280 **quintessence:** The fifth
essence of ancient philosophy, supposed to be the substance of the heavenly bodies and to be
latent in all things.   285 **lenten:** Meager.   286 **coted:** Overtook and passed beyond.   289 **foil
and target:** Sword and shield.   290 **humorous man:** Actor who takes the part of the humor
characters.   291 **tickle o' the sere:** Easy on the trigger.   291–292 **the lady . . . for 't:** The lady
(fond of talking) shall have opportunity to talk, blank verse or no blank verse.

ROSENCRANTZ: Even those you were wont to take delight in, the tragedians of the city.

HAMLET: How chances it they travel? their residence,° both in reputation and profit, was better both ways. 295

ROSENCRANTZ: I think their inhibition° comes by the means of the late innovation.°

HAMLET: Do they hold the same estimation they did when I was in the city? are they so followed?

ROSENCRANTZ: No, indeed, are they not. 300

HAMLET: How° comes it? do they grow rusty?

ROSENCRANTZ: Nay, their endeavour keeps in the wonted pace: but there is, sir, an aery° of children, little eyases,° that cry out on the top of question,° and are most tyrannically° clapped for 't: these are now the fashion, and so berattle° the common stages° — so they call them — that many wearing rapiers° are afraid of 305 goose-quills° and dare scarce come thither.

HAMLET: What, are they children? who maintains 'em? how are they escoted?° Will they pursue the quality° no longer than they can sing?° will they not say afterwards, if they should grow themselves to common° players — as it is most like, if their means are no better — their writers do them wrong, to make them exclaim 310 against their own succession?°

ROSENCRANTZ: 'Faith, there has been much to do on both sides; and the nation holds it no sin to tarre° them to controversy: there was, for a while, no money bid for argument,° unless the poet and the player went to cuffs° in the question.°

HAMLET: Is't possible? 315

GUILDENSTERN: O, there has been much throwing about of brains.

HAMLET: Do the boys carry it away?°

ROSENCRANTZ: Ay, that they do, my lord; Hercules and his load° too.

HAMLET: It is not very strange; for my uncle is king of Denmark, and those that would make mows° at him while my father lived, give twenty, forty, fifty, a hundred 320

---

295 residence: Remaining in one place.   **297 inhibition:** Formal prohibition (from acting plays in the city or, possibly, at court).   **innovation:** The new fashion in satirical plays performed by boy actors in the "private" theaters.   **301–318 How . . . load:** The passage is the famous one dealing with the War of the Theatres (1599–1602); namely, the rivalry between the children's companies and the adult actors.   **303 aery.** Nest.   **eyases:** Young hawks.   **cry . . . question:** Speak in a high key dominating conversation; clamor forth the height of controversy; probably "excel"; perhaps intended to decry leaders of the dramatic profession.   **304 tyrannically:** Outrageously.   **berattle:** Berate.   **305 common stages:** Public theaters.   **many wearing rapiers:** Many men of fashion, who were afraid to patronize the common players for fear of being satirized by the poets who wrote for the children.   **306 goose-quills:** I.e., pens of satirists.   **307 escoted:** Maintained.   **308 quality:** Acting profession.   **no longer . . . sing:** I.e., until their voices change.   **309 common:** Regular, adult.   **311 succession:** Future careers.   **313 tarre:** Set on (as dogs).   **314 argument:** Probably, plot for a play.   **went to cuffs:** Came to blows.   **question:** Controversy.   **317 carry it away:** Win the day.   **318 Hercules . . . load:** Regarded as an allusion to the sign of the Globe Theatre, which was Hercules bearing the world on his shoulder.   **320 mows:** Grimaces.

ducats° a-piece for his picture in little.° 'Sblood, there is something in this
more than natural, if philosophy could find it out.

A flourish [of trumpets within].

GUILDENSTERN: There are the players.

HAMLET: Gentlemen, you are welcome to Elsinore. Your hands, come then: the
appurtenance of welcome is fashion and ceremony: let me comply° with you   325
in this garb,° lest my extent° to the players, which, I tell you, must show fairly
outwards, should more appear like entertainment than yours. You are welcome:
but my uncle-father and aunt-mother are deceived.

GUILDENSTERN: In what, my dear lord?

HAMLET: I am but mad north-north-west:° when the wind is southerly I know a   330
hawk from a handsaw.°

Enter POLONIUS.

POLONIUS: Well be with you, gentlemen!

HAMLET: Hark you, Guildenstern; and you too: at each ear a hearer: that great baby
you see there is not yet out of his swaddling-clouts.°

ROSENCRANTZ: Happily he is the second time come to them; for they say an old man   335
is twice a child.

HAMLET: I will prophesy he comes to tell me of the players; mark it.—You say right,
sir: o' Monday morning;° 'twas then indeed.

POLONIUS: My lord, I have news to tell you.

HAMLET: My lord, I have news to tell you. When Roscius° was an actor in Rome,—   340

POLONIUS: The actors are come hither, my lord.

HAMLET: Buz, buz!°

POLONIUS: Upon my honour,—

HAMLET: Then came each actor on his ass,—

POLONIUS: The best actors in the world, either for tragedy, comedy, history, pasto-   345
ral, pastoral-comical, historical-pastoral, tragical-historical, tragical-comical-
historical-pastoral, scene individable,° or poem unlimited:° Seneca° cannot be
too heavy, nor Plautus° too light. For the law of writ and the liberty,° these are
the only men.

---

321 **ducats:** Gold coins worth 9 shillings and 4 pence.   **in little:** In miniature.   325 **comply:**
Observe the formalities of courtesy.   326 **garb:** Manner.   **extent:** Showing of kindness.   330
I am . . . north-north-west: I am only partly mad, i.e., in only one point of the compass.   331
handsaw: A proposed reading of *hernshaw* would mean "heron"; *handsaw* may be an early
corruption of *hernshaw.* Another view regards *hawk* as the variant of *hack,* a tool of the pickax
type, and *handsaw* as a saw operated by hand.   334 **swaddling-clouts:** Cloths in which to
wrap a newborn baby.   338 **o' Monday morning:** Said to mislead Polonius.   340 **Roscius:**
A famous Roman actor.   342 **Buz, buz:** An interjection used at Oxford to denote stale
news.   347 **scene individable:** A play observing the unity of place.   **poem unlimited:** A play
disregarding the unities of time and place.   **Seneca:** Writer of Latin tragedies, model of early
Elizabethan writers of tragedy.   348 **Plautus:** Writer of Latin comedy.   **law . . . liberty:** Pieces
written according to rules and without rules, i.e., "classical" and "romantic" dramas.

HAMLET: O Jephthah, judge of Israel,° what a treasure hadst thou!   350
POLONIUS: What a treasure had he, my lord?
HAMLET: Why,
> "One fair daughter, and no more,
>> The which he loved passing well."

POLONIUS [aside]: Still on my daughter.   355
HAMLET: Am I not i' the right, old Jephthah?
POLONIUS: If you call me Jephthah, my lord, I have a daughter that I love passing°
well.
HAMLET: Nay, that follows not.
POLONIUS: What follows, then, my lord?   360
HAMLET: Why,
> "As by lot, God wot,"
and then, you know,
> "It came to pass, as most like° it was,"—
the first row° of the pious chanson° will show you more; for look, where my   365
abridgement comes.°

Enter the PLAYERS.

You are welcome, masters; welcome, all. I am glad to see thee well. Welcome,
good friends. O, old friend! why, thy face is valanced° since I saw thee last: comest
thou to beard me in Denmark? What, my young lady and mistress! By'r lady,
your ladyship is nearer to heaven than when I saw you last, by the altitude of a   370
chopine.° Pray God, your voice, like a piece of uncurrent° gold, be not cracked
within the ring.° Masters, you are all welcome. We'll e'en to 't like French falcon-
ers, fly at any thing we see: we'll have a speech straight: come, give us a taste of
your quality; come, a passionate speech.
FIRST PLAYER: What speech, my good lord?   375
HAMLET: I heard thee speak me a speech once, but it was never acted; or, if it was, not
above once; for the play, I remember, pleased not the million; 'twas caviary to
the general:° but it was—as I received it, and others, whose judgements in such
matters cried in the top of° mine—an excellent play, well digested in the scenes,
set down with as much modesty as cunning.° I remember, one said there were   380
no sallets° in the lines to make the matter savoury, nor no matter in the phrase

---

350 Jephthah . . . Israel: Jephthah had to sacrifice his daughter; see Judges II.   **357 passing:**
Surpassingly.   **364 like:** Probable.   **365 row:** Stanza.   **chanson:** Ballad.   **366 abridgement
comes:** Opportunity comes for cutting short the conversation.   **368 valanced:** Fringed (with
a beard).   **371 chopine:** Kind of shoe raised by the thickness of the heel; worn in Italy, particularly at Venice.   **uncurrent:** Not passable as lawful coinage.   **371–372 cracked within the
ring:** In the center of coins were rings enclosing the sovereign's head; if the coin was cracked
within this ring, it was unfit for currency.   **377–378 caviary to the general:** Not relished by
the multitude.   **379 cried in the top of:** Spoke with greater authority than.   **380 cunning:**
Skill.   **381 sallets:** Salads: here, spicy improprieties.

that might indict° the author of affectation; but called it an honest method, as
wholesome as sweet, and by very much more handsome than fine.° One speech
in 't I chiefly loved: 'twas Æneas' tale to Dido;° and thereabout of it especially,
where he speaks of Priam's slaughter: if it live in your memory, begin at this line: 385
let me see, let me see—
"The rugged Pyrrhus,° like th' Hyrcanian beast,"°—
'tis not so:—it begins with Pyrrhus:—
"The rugged Pyrrhus, he whose sable arms,
Black as his purpose, did the night resemble   390
When he lay couched in the ominous horse,°
Hath now this dread and black complexion smear'd
With heraldry more dismal; head to foot
Now is he total gules;° horridly trick'd°
With blood of fathers, mothers, daughters, sons,   395
Bak'd and impasted° with the parching streets,
That lend a tyrannous and a damned light
To their lord's murder: roasted in wrath and fire,
And thus o'er-sized° with coagulate gore,
With eyes like carbuncles, the hellish Pyrrhus   400
Old grandsire Priam seeks."
So, proceed you.
POLONIUS: 'Fore God, my lord, well spoken, with good accent and good discretion.
FIRST PLAYER: "Anon he finds him
Striking too short at Greeks; his antique sword,   405
Rebellious to his arm, lies where it falls,
Repugnant° to command: unequal match'd,
Pyrrhus at Priam drives; in rage strikes wide;
But with the whiff and wind of his fell sword
Th' unnerved father falls. Then senseless Ilium,°   410
Seeming to feel this blow, with flaming top
Stoops to his base, and with a hideous crash
Takes prisoner Pyrrhus' ear: for, lo! his sword
Which was declining on the milky head
Of reverend Priam, seem'd i' th' air to stick: 415

---

382 **indict:** Convict.   382–383 **as wholesome . . . fine:** Its beauty was not that of elaborate
ornament, but that of order and proportion.   384 **Æneas' tale to Dido:** The lines recited
by the player are imitated from Marlowe and Nashe's *Dido Queen of Carthage* (II.i.214 ff.).
They are written in such a way that the conventionality of the play within a play is raised
above that of ordinary drama.   387 **Pyrrhus.** A Greek hero in the Trojan War.   **Hyrcanian
beast:** The tiger; see Virgil, *Aeneid*, IV.266.   391 **ominous horse:** Trojan horse.   394 **gules:**
Red, a heraldic term.   **trick'd:** Spotted, smeared.   396 **impasted:** Made into a paste.   399
o'er-sized: Covered as with size or glue.   407 **Repugnant:** Disobedient.   410 **Then senseless
Ilium:** Insensate Troy.

So, as a painted tyrant,° Pyrrhus stood,
And like a neutral to his will and matter,°
Did nothing.
But, as we often see, against° some storm,
A silence in the heavens, the rack° stand still,   420
The bold winds speechless and the orb below
As hush as death, anon the dreadful thunder
Doth rend the region,° so, after Pyrrhus' pause,
Aroused vengeance sets him new a-work;
And never did the Cyclops' hammers fall   425
On Mars's armour forg'd for proof eterne°
With less remorse than Pyrrhus' bleeding sword
Now falls on Priam.
Out, out, thou strumpet, Fortune! All you gods,
In general synod,° take away her power;   430
Break all the spokes and fellies° from her wheel,
And bowl the round nave° down the hill of heaven,
As low as to the fiends!"

POLONIUS: This is too long.

HAMLET: It shall to the barber's, with your beard. Prithee, say on: he's for a jig° or a   435
    tale of bawdry,° or he sleeps: say on: come to Hecuba.°

FIRST PLAYER: "But who, ah woe! had seen the mobled° queen—"

HAMLET: "The mobled queen?"

POLONIUS: That's good; "mobled queen" is good.

FIRST PLAYER: "Run barefoot up and down, threat'ning the flames   440
    With bisson rheum;° a clout° upon that head
    Where late the diadem stood, and for a robe,
    About her lank and all o'er-teemed° loins,
    A blanket, in the alarm of fear caught up;
    Who this had seen, with tongue in venom steep'd,   445
    'Gainst Fortune's state would treason have pronounc'd:°
    But if the gods themselves did see her then
    When she saw Pyrrhus make malicious sport
    In mincing with his sword her husband's limbs,
    The instant burst of clamour that she made,   450
    Unless things mortal move them not at all,

---

416 painted tyrant: Tyrant in a picture.   **417 matter:** Task.   **419 against:** Before.   **420 rack:** Mass of clouds.   **423 region:** Assembly.   **426 proof eterne:** External resistance to assault.   **430 synod:** Assembly.   **431 fellies:** Pieces of wood forming the rim of a wheel.   **432 nave:** Hub.   **435 jig:** Comic performance given at the end or in an interval of a play.   **436 bawdry:** Indecency. **Hecuba:** Wife of Priam, king of Troy.   **437 mobled:** Muffled.   **441 bisson rheum:** Blinding tears.   **clout:** Piece of cloth.   **443 o'er-teemed:** Worn out with bearing children.   **446 pronounc'd:** Proclaimed.

Would have made milch° the burning eyes of heaven,
And passion in the gods."

POLONIUS: Look, whe'r he has not turned° his colour and has tears in 's eyes. Prithee, no more.   455

HAMLET: 'Tis well; I'll have thee speak out the rest soon. Good my lord, will you see the players well bestowed? Do you hear, let them be well used; for they are the abstract° and brief chronicles of the time: after your death you were better have a bad epitaph than their ill report while you live.

POLONIUS: My lord, I will use them according to their desert.   460

HAMLET: God's bodykins,° man, much better: use every man after his desert, and who shall 'scape whipping? Use them after your own honour and dignity: the less they deserve, the more merit is in your bounty. Take them in.

POLONIUS: Come, sirs.

HAMLET: Follow him, friends: we'll hear a play tomorrow. [*Aside to First Player.*]   465
Dost thou hear me, old friend; can you play the Murder of Gonzago?

FIRST PLAYER: Ay, my lord.

HAMLET: We'll ha 't to-morrow night. You could, for a need, study a speech of some dozen or sixteen lines,° which I would set down and insert in 't, could you not?

FIRST PLAYER: Ay, my lord.   470

HAMLET: Very well. Follow that lord; and look you mock him not.—My good friends, I'll leave you till night: you are welcome to Elsinore.

Exeunt POLONIUS *and* PLAYERS.

ROSENCRANTZ: Good my lord!   *Exeunt [*ROSENCRANTZ *and* GUILDENSTERN*]*.

HAMLET: Ay, so, God bye to you.—Now I am alone.
O, what a rogue and peasant° slave am I!   475
Is it not monstrous that this player here,
But in a fiction, in a dream of passion,
Could force his soul so to his own conceit
That from her working all his visage wann'd,°
Tears in his eyes, distraction in 's aspect,   480
A broken voice, and his whole function suiting
With forms to his conceit?° and all for nothing!
For Hecuba!
What's Hecuba to him, or he to Hecuba,
That he should weep for her? What would he do,   485
Had he the motive and the cue for passion
That I have? He would drown the stage with tears
And cleave the general ear with horrid speech,

---

452 milch: Moist with tears.   454 turned: Changed.   458 abstract: Summary account.   461
bodykins: Diminutive form of the oath "by God's body."   469 dozen or sixteen lines: Critics
have amused themselves by trying to locate Hamlet's lines. Lucianus's speech III.ii.229–234 is
the best guess.   475 peasant: Base.   479 wann'd: Grew pale.   481–482 his whole . . . conceit:
His whole being responded with forms to suit his thought.

Make mad the guilty and appall the free,
Confound the ignorant, and amaze indeed   490
The very faculties of eyes and ears.
Yet I,
A dull and muddy-mettled° rascal, peak,°
Like John-a-dreams,° unpregnant of° my cause,
And can say nothing; no, not for a king.   495
Upon whose property° and most dear life
A damn'd defeat was made. Am I a coward?
Who calls me villain? breaks my pate across?
Plucks off my beard, and blows it in my face?
Tweaks me by the nose? gives me the lie i' th' throat,   500
As deep as to the lungs? who does me this?
Ha!
'Swounds, I should take it: for it cannot be
But I am pigeon-liver'd° and lack gall
To make oppression bitter, or ere this   505
I should have fatted all the region kites°
With this slave's offal: bloody, bawdy villain!
Remorseless, treacherous, lecherous, kindless° villain!
O, vengeance!
Why, what an ass am I! This is most brave,   510
That I, the son of a dear father murder'd,
Prompted to my revenge by heaven and hell,
Must, like a whore, unpack my heart with words,
And fall a-cursing, like a very drab,°
A stallion!°   515
Fie upon 't! foh! About,° my brains! Hum, I have heard
That guilty creatures sitting at a play
Have by the very cunning of the scene
Been struck so to the soul that presently
They have proclaim'd their malefactions;   520
For murder, though it have no tongue, will speak
With most miraculous organ. I'll have these players
Play something like the murder of my father
Before mine uncle: I'll observe his looks:
I'll tent° him to the quick: if 'a do blench,°   525

---

493 **muddy-mettled:** Dull-spirited. **peak:** Mope, pine. 494 **John-a-dreams:** An expression occurring elsewhere in Elizabethan literature to indicate a dreamer. **unpregnant of:** Not quickened by. 496 **property:** Proprietorship (of crown and life). 504 **pigeon-liver'd:** The pigeon was supposed to secrete no gall; if Hamlet, so he says, had had gall, he would have felt the bitterness of oppression, and avenged it. 506 **region kites:** Kites of the air. 508 **kindless:** Unnatural. 514 **drab:** Prostitute. 515 **stallion:** Prostitute (male or female). 516 **About:** About it, or turn thou right about. 525 **tent:** Probe. **blench:** Quail, flinch.

I know my course. The spirit that I have seen
May be the devil:° and the devil hath power
T' assume a pleasing shape; yea, and perhaps
Out of my weakness and my melancholy,
As he is very potent with such spirits,°   530
Abuses me to damn me: I'll have grounds
More relative° than this:° the play's the thing
Wherein I'll catch the conscience of the king.   *Exit.*

[ACT III

SCENE i: *A room in the castle.*]

Enter KING, QUEEN, POLONIUS, OPHELIA, ROSENCRANTZ, GUILDENSTERN, LORDS.

KING: And can you, by no drift of conference,°
    Get from him why he puts on this confusion,
    Grating so harshly all his days of quiet
    With turbulent and dangerous lunacy?
ROSENCRANTZ: He does confess he feels himself distracted;   5
    But from what cause 'a will by no means speak.
GUILDENSTERN: Nor do we find him forward° to be sounded,
    But, with a crafty madness, keeps aloof,
    When we would bring him on to some confession
    Of his true state.
QUEEN: Did he receive you well?   10
ROSENCRANTZ: Most like a gentleman.
GUILDENSTERN: But with much forcing of his disposition.°
ROSENCRANTZ: Niggard of question;° but, of our demands,
    Most free in his reply.
QUEEN: Did you assay° him
    To any pastime?   15
ROSENCRANTZ: Madam, it so fell out, that certain players
    We o'er-raught° on the way: of these we told him;
    And there did seem in him a kind of joy
    To hear of it: they are here about the court,
    And, as I think, they have already order   20
    This night to play before him.
POLONIUS: 'Tis most true:

---

527 **May be the devil:** Hamlet's suspicion is properly grounded in the belief of the time.   530 **spirits:** Humors.   532 **relative:** Closely related, definite.   **this:** I.e., the ghost's story.   **Act III, Scene i.**   1 **drift of conference:** Device of conversation.   7 **forward:** Willing.   12 **forcing of his disposition:** I.e., against his will.   13 **Niggard of question:** Sparing of conversation.   14 **assay:** Try to win.   17 **o'er-raught:** Overtook.

And he beseech'd me to entreat your majesties
To hear and see the matter.
KING: With all my heart; and it doth much content me
To hear him so inclin'd.   25
Good gentlemen, give him a further edge,°
And drive his purpose into these delights.
ROSENCRANTZ: We shall, my lord.   *Exeunt* ROSENCRANTZ *and* GUILDENSTERN.
KING: Sweet Gertrude, leave us too;
For we have closely° sent for Hamlet hither,
That he, as 'twere by accident, may here   30
Affront° Ophelia:
Her father and myself, lawful espials,°
Will so bestow ourselves that, seeing, unseen,
We may of their encounter frankly judge,
And gather by him, as he is behav'd,   35
If 't be th' affliction of his love or no
That thus he suffers for.
QUEEN: I shall obey you.
And for your part, Ophelia, I do wish
That your good beauties be the happy cause
Of Hamlet's wildness:° so shall I hope your virtues   40
Will bring him to his wonted way again,
To both your honours.
OPHELIA: Madam, I wish it may.   *[Exit* QUEEN.*]*
POLONIUS: Ophelia, walk you here. Gracious,° so please you,
We will bestow ourselves. *[To* OPHELIA.*]* Read on this book;
That show of such an exercise° may colour°   45
Your loneliness. We are oft to blame in this,—
'Tis too much prov'd—that with devotion's visage
And pious action we do sugar o'er
The devil himself.
KING: *[aside]* O, 'tis too true!
How smart a lash that speech doth give my conscience!   50
The harlot's cheek, beautied with plast'ring art,
Is not more ugly to° the thing° that helps it
Than is my deed to my most painted word:
O heavy burthen!
POLONIUS: I hear him coming: let's withdraw, my lord.   55

[Exeunt KING *and* POLONIUS.*]*

---

26 edge: Incitement. **29 closely:** Secretly. **31 Affront:** Confront. **32 lawful espials:**
Legitimate spies. **40 wildness:** Madness. **43 Gracious:** Your grace (addressed to the
king). **45 exercise:** Act of devotion (the book she reads is one of devotion). **colour:** Give a
plausible appearance to. **52 to:** Compared to. **thing:** I.e., the cosmetic.

Enter HAMLET.

HAMLET: To be, or not to be: that is the question:
Whether 'tis nobler in the mind to suffer
The slings and arrows of outrageous fortune,
Or to take arms against a sea° of troubles,
And by opposing end them? To die: to sleep;   60
No more; and by a sleep to say we end
The heart-ache and the thousand natural shocks
That flesh is heir to, 'tis a consummation
Devoutly to be wish'd. To die, to sleep;
To sleep: perchance to dream: ay, there's the rub;   65
For in that sleep of death what dreams may come
When we have shuffled° off this mortal coil,°
Must give us pause: there's the respect°
That makes calamity of so long life;°
For who would bear the whips and scorns of time,°   70
Th' oppressor's wrong, the proud man's contumely,°
The pangs of despis'd° love, the law's delay,
The insolence of office° and the spurns°
That patient merit of th' unworthy takes,
When he himself might his quietus° make   75
With a bare bodkin?° who would fardels° bear,
To grunt and sweat under a weary life,
But that the dread of something after death,
The undiscover'd° country from whose bourn°
No traveller returns, puzzles the will   80
And makes us rather bear those ills we have
Than fly to others that we know not of?
Thus conscience° does make cowards of us all;
And thus the native hue° of resolution
Is sicklied o'er° with the pale cast° of thought,   85
And enterprises of great pitch° and moment°

---

59 sea: The mixed metaphor of this speech has often been commented on; a later emenda-
tion *siege* has sometimes been spoken on the stage.   **67 shuffled:** Sloughed, cast.   **coil:** Usually
means "turmoil"; here, possibly "body" (conceived of as wound about the soul like rope); *clay,
soil,* veil, have been suggested as emendations.   **68 respect:** Consideration.   **69 of . . . life:** So
long-lived.   **70 time:** The world.   **71 contumely:** rudeness arising from arrogance or insolence;
contemptuous treatment.—EDS.   **72 despis'd:** Rejected.   **73 office:** Office-holders.   **spurns:**
Insults.   **75 quietus:** Acquittance; here, death.   **76 bare bodkin:** Mere dagger; *bare* is sometimes
understood as "unsheathed."   **fardels:** Burdens.   **79 undiscover'd:** undisclosed, unrevealed.—EDS.
bourn: Boundary.   **83 conscience:** Probably, inhibition by the faculty of reason restraining the
will from doing wrong.   **84 native hue:** Natural color; metaphor derived from the color of the
face.   **85 sicklied o'er:** Given a sickly tinge.   **cast:** Shade of color.   **86 pitch:** Height (as of a falcon's
flight).   **moment:** Importance.

With this regard° their currents° turn awry,
And lose the name of action—Soft you now!
The fair Ophelia! Nymph, in thy orisons°
Be all my sins rememb'red.
OPHELIA: Good my lord,   90
How does your honour for this many a day?
HAMLET: I humbly thank you; well, well, well.
OPHELIA: My lord, I have remembrances of yours,
That I have longed long to re-deliver;
I pray you, now receive them.
HAMLET: No, not I;   95
I never gave you aught.
OPHELIA: My honour'd lord, you know right well you did;
And, with them, words of so sweet breath compos'd
As made the things more rich: their perfume lost,
Take these again; for to the noble mind   100
Rich gifts wax poor when givers prove unkind.
There, my lord.
HAMLET: Ha, ha! are you honest?°
OPHELIA: My lord?
HAMLET: Are you fair?   105
OPHELIA: What means your lordship?
HAMLET: That if you be honest and fair, your honesty° should admit no discourse
   to° your beauty.
OPHELIA: Could beauty, my lord, have better commerce° than with honesty?
HAMLET: Ay, truly; for the power of beauty will sooner transform honesty from what   110
   it is to a bawd than the force of honesty can translate beauty into his likeness:
   this was sometime a paradox, but now the time° gives it proof. I did love you
   once.
OPHELIA: Indeed, my lord, you made me believe so.
HAMLET: You should not have believed me; for virtue cannot so inoculate° our old   115
   stock but we shall relish of it:° I loved you not.
OPHELIA: I was the more deceived.
HAMLET: Get thee to a nunnery: why wouldst thou be a breeder of sinners? I am
   myself indifferent honest;° but yet I could accuse me of such things that it were
   better my mother had not borne me: I am very proud, revengeful, ambitious,   120

---

87 regard: Respect, consideration. **currents:** Courses. **89 orisons:** Prayers. **103–108 are
you honest . . . beauty:** *Honest* meaning "truthful" and "chaste" and *fair* meaning "just, honorable" (l. 105) and "beauty" (l. 108) are not mere quibbles; the speech has the irony of a *double
entendre.* **107 your honesty:** Your chastity. **107–108 discourse to:** Familiar intercourse
with. **109 commerce:** Intercourse. **112 the time:** The present age. **115 inoculate:** Graft
(metaphorical). **116 but . . . it:** I.e., that we do not still have about us a taste of the old stock;
i.e., retain our sinfulness. **119 indifferent honest:** Moderately virtuous.

with more offences at my beck° than I have thoughts to put them in, imagination to give them shape, or time to act them in. What should such fellows as I do
crawling between earth and heaven? We are arrant knaves, all; believe none of us.
Go thy ways to a nunnery. Where's your father?

OPHELIA: At home, my lord.   125

HAMLET: Let the doors be shut upon him, that he may play the fool no where but in
's own house. Farewell.

OPHELIA: O, help him, you sweet heavens!

HAMLET: If thou dost marry, I'll give thee this plague for thy dowry: be thou as chaste
as ice, as pure as snow, thou shalt not escape calumny. Get thee to a nunnery,   130
go: farewell. Or, if thou wilt needs marry, marry a fool; for wise men know well
enough what monsters° you make of them. To a nunnery, go, and quickly too.
Farewell.

OPHELIA: O heavenly powers, restore him!

HAMLET: I have heard of your° paintings too, well enough; God hath given you one   135
face, and you make yourselves another: you jig,° you amble, and you lisp; you
nick-name God's creatures, and make your wantonness your ignorance.° Go to,
I'll no more on 't; it hath made me mad. I say, we will have no more marriage:
those that are married already, all but one,° shall live; the rest shall keep as they
are. To a nunnery, go.   *Exit.*   140

OPHELIA: O, what a noble mind is here o'er-thrown!
The courtier's, soldier's, scholar's, eye, tongue, sword;
Th' expectancy and rose° of the fair state,
The glass of fashion and the mould of form,°
Th' observ'd of all observers,° quite, quite down!   145
And I, of ladies most deject and wretched,
That suck'd the honey of his music vows,
Now see that noble and most sovereign reason,
Like sweet bells jangled, out of time and harsh;
That unmatch'd form and feature of blown° youth   150
Blasted with ecstasy:° O, woe is me,
T' have seen what I have seen, see what I see!

Enter KING *and* POLONIUS.

KING: Love! his affections do not that way tend;
Nor what he spake, though it lack'd form a little,

---

121 **beck:** Command.   132 **monsters:** An allusion to the horns of a cuckold.   135 **your:**
Indefinite use.   136 **jig:** Move with jerky motion; probably allusion to the *jig*, or song and
dance, of the current stage.   137 **make . . . ignorance:** I.e., excuse your wantonness on the
ground of your ignorance.   139 **one:** I.e., the king.   143 **expectancy and rose:** Source of
hope.   144 **The glass . . . form:** The mirror of fashion and the pattern of courtly behavior.   145 **observ'd . . . observers:** I.e., the center of attention in the court.   150 **blown:**
Blooming.   151 **ecstasy:** Madness.

Was not like madness. There's something in his soul, 155
O'er which his melancholy sits on brood;
And I do doubt° the hatch and the disclose°
Will be some danger: which for to prevent,
I have in quick determination
Thus set it down: he shall with speed to England, 160
For the demand of our neglected tribute:
Haply the seas and countries different
With variable° objects shall expel
This something-settled° matter in his heart,
Whereon his brains still beating puts him thus 165
From fashion of himself.° What think you on 't?
POLONIUS: It shall do well: but yet do I believe
The origin and commencement of his grief
Sprung from neglected love. How now, Ophelia!
You need not tell us what Lord Hamlet said; 170
We heard it all. My lord, do as you please;
But, if you hold it fit, after the play
Let his queen mother all alone entreat him
To show his grief: let her be round° with him;
And I'll be plac'd, so please you, in the ear 175
Of all their conference. If she find him not,
To England send him, or confine him where
Your wisdom best shall think.
KING: It shall be so:
Madness in great ones must not unwatch'd go. *Exeunt.* 180

[SCENE ii: *A hall in the castle.*]

Enter HAMLET *and three of the* PLAYERS.

HAMLET: Speak the speech, I pray you, as I pronounced it to you, trippingly on the
tongue: but if you mouth it, as many of your° players do, I had as lief the town-
crier spoke my lines. Nor do not saw the air too much with your hand, thus, but
use all gently; for in the very torrent, tempest, and, as I may say, whirlwind of
your passion, you must acquire and beget a temperance that may give it smooth- 5
ness. O, it offends me to the soul to hear a robustious° periwig-pated° fellow tear
a passion to tatters, to very rags, to split the ears of the groundlings,° who for

---

157 doubt: Fear. **disclose:** Disclosure or revelation (by chipping of the shell). **163 variable:** Various. **164 something-settled:** Somewhat settled. **166 From . . . himself:** Out of
his natural manner. **174 round:** Blunt. **Scene ii. 2 your:** Indefinite use. **6 robustious:**
Violent, boisterous. **periwig-pated:** Wearing a wig. **7 groundlings:** Those who stood in the
yard of the theater.

the most part are capable of° nothing but inexplicable° dumb-shows and noise:
I would have such a fellow whipped for o'er-doing Termagant;° it out-herods
Herod:° pray you, avoid it.   10

FIRST PLAYER: I warrant your honour.

HAMLET: Be not too tame neither, but let your own discretion be your tutor: suit
the action to the word, the word to the action; with this special observance, that
you o'er-step not the modesty of nature: for any thing so overdone is from the
purpose of playing, whose end, both at the first and now, was and is, to hold, as   15
't were, the mirror up to nature; to show virtue her own feature, scorn her own
image, and the very age and body of the time his form and pressure.° Now this
overdone, or come tardy off,° though it make the unskilful laugh, cannot but
make the judicious grieve; the censure of the which one° must in your allowance
o'erweigh a whole theatre of others. O, there be players that I have seen play,   20
and heard others praise, and that highly, not to speak it profanely, that, neither
having the accent of Christians nor the gait of Christian, pagan, nor man, have
so strutted and bellowed that I have thought some of nature's journeymen° had
made men and not made them well, they imitated humanity so abominably.

FIRST PLAYER: I hope we have reformed that indifferently° with us, sir.   25

HAMLET: O, reform it altogether. And let those that play your clowns speak no more
than is set down for them; for there be of° them that will themselves laugh, to set
on some quantity of barren° spectators to laugh too; though, in the mean time,
some necessary question of the play be then to be considered: that's villanous,
and shows a most pitiful ambition in the fool that uses it. Go, make you ready.   30

[Exeunt PLAYERS.*]*

Enter POLONIUS, GUILDENSTERN, *and* ROSENCRANTZ.

How now, my lord! will the king hear this piece of work?

POLONIUS: And the queen too, and that presently.

HAMLET: Bid the players make haste.   *[Exit* POLONIUS.*]*

Will you two help to hasten them?

ROSENCRANTZ: ⎫
              ⎬ We will, my lord.   *Exeunt they two.*
GUILDENSTERN: ⎭

HAMLET: What ho! Horatio!   35

---

8 capable of: Susceptible of being influenced by.   **inexplicable:** Of no significance worth
explaining.   **9 Termagant:** A god of the Saracens; a character in the St. Nicholas play, where
one of his worshipers, leaving him in charge of goods, returns to find them stolen; whereupon
he beats the god (or idol), which howls vociferously.   **10 Herod:** Herod of Jewry; a character
in *The Slaughter of the Innocents* and other cycle plays. The part was played with great noise and
fury.   **17 pressure:** Stamp, impressed character.   **18 come tardy off:** Inadequately done.   **19
the censure . . . one:** The judgment of even one of whom.   **23 journeymen:** Laborers not yet
masters in their trade.   **25 indifferently:** Fairly, tolerably.   **27 of:** I.e., some among them.   **28
barren:** I.e., of wit.

Enter HORATIO.

HORATIO: Here, sweet lord, at your service.
HAMLET: Horatio, thou art e'en as just° a man
    As e'er my conversation cop'd withal.
HORATIO: O, my dear lord,—
HAMLET: Nay, do not think I flatter;
    For what advancement may I hope from thee   40
    That no revenue hast but thy good spirits,
    To feed and clothe thee? Why should the poor be flatter'd?
    No, let the candied tongue lick absurd pomp,
    And crook the pregnant° hinges of the knee
    Where thrift° may follow fawning. Dost thou hear?   45
    Since my dear soul was mistress of her choice
    And could of men distinguish her election,
    S' hath seal'd thee for herself; for thou hast been
    As one, in suff'ring all, that suffers nothing,
    A man that fortune's buffets and rewards   50
    Hast ta'en with equal thanks: and blest are those
    Whose blood and judgement are so well commeddled,
    That they are not a pipe for fortune's finger
    To sound what stop° she please. Give me that man
    That is not passion's slave, and I will wear him   55
    In my heart's core, ay, in my heart of heart,
    As I do thee.—Something too much of this.—
    There is a play to-night before the king;
    One scene of it comes near the circumstance
    Which I have told thee of my father's death: 60
    I prithee, when thou seest that act afoot,
    Even with the very comment of thy soul°
    Observe my uncle: if his occulted° guilt
    Do not itself unkennel in one speech,
    It is a damned° ghost that we have seen,   65
    And my imaginations are as foul
    As Vulcan's stithy.° Give him heedful note;
    For I mine eyes will rivet to his face,
    And after we will both our judgements join
    In censure of his seeming.°
HORATIO: Well, my lord: 70

---

37 just: Honest, honorable.   **44 pregnant:** Pliant.   **45 thrift:** Profit.   **54 stop:** Hole in a wind instrument for controlling the sound.   **62 very . . . soul:** Inward and sagacious criticism.   **63 occulted:** Hidden.   **65 damned:** In league with Satan.   **67 stithy:** Smithy, place of *stiths* (anvils).   **70 censure . . . seeming:** Judgment of his appearance or behavior.

If 'a steal aught the whilst this play is playing,
And 'scape detecting, I will pay the theft.

Enter trumpets and kettledrums, KING, QUEEN, POLONIUS, OPHELIA, *[*ROSENCRANTZ,
GUILDENSTERN, *and others].*

HAMLET: They are coming to the play; I must be idle:° Get you a place.
KING: How fares our cousin Hamlet?
HAMLET: Excellent, i' faith; of the chameleon's dish:° I eat the air, promise-crammed: 75
    you cannot feed capons so.
KING: I have nothing with° this answer, Hamlet; these words are not mine.°
HAMLET: No, nor mine now. *[To* POLONIUS.*]* My lord, you played once i' the univer-
    sity, you say?
POLONIUS: That did I, my lord; and was accounted a good actor.   80
HAMLET: What did you enact?
POLONIUS: I did enact Julius Cæsar: I was killed i' the Capitol; Brutus killed me.
HAMLET: It was a brute part of him to kill so capital a calf there. Be the players ready?
ROSENCRANTZ: Ay, my lord; they stay upon your patience.
QUEEN: Come hither, my dear Hamlet, sit by me.   85
HAMLET: No, good mother, here's metal more attractive.
POLONIUS *[to the king]:* O, ho! do you mark that?
HAMLET: Lady, shall I lie in your lap?   *[Lying down at* OPHELIA's *feet.]*
OPHELIA: No, my lord.
HAMLET: I mean, my head upon your lap?   90
OPHELIA: Ay, my lord.
HAMLET: Do you think I meant country° matters?
OPHELIA: I think nothing, my lord.
HAMLET: That's a fair thought to lie between maids' legs.
OPHELIA: What is, my lord?   95
HAMLET: Nothing.
OPHELIA: You are merry, my lord.
HAMLET: Who, I?
OPHELIA: Ay, my lord.
HAMLET: O God, your only° jig-maker.° What should a man do but be merry? for, look   100
    you, how cheerfully my mother looks, and my father died within's two hours.
OPHELIA: Nay, 'tis twice two months, my lord.
HAMLET: So long? Nay then, let the devil wear black, for I'll have a suit of sables.° O
    heavens! die two months ago, and not forgotten yet? Then there's hope a great

---

73 **idle:** Crazy, or not attending to anything serious.   75 **chameleon's dish:** Chameleons were
supposed to feed on air. (Hamlet deliberately misinterprets the king's "fares" as "feeds.")   77
have . . . with: Make nothing of.   **are not mine:** Do not respond to what I ask.   92 **country:**
With a bawdy pun.   100 **your only:** Only your.   **jig-maker:** Composer of jigs (song and
dance).   103 **suit of sables:** Garments trimmed with the fur of the sable, with a quibble on
sable meaning "black."

man's memory may outlive his life half a year: but, by 'r lady, 'a must build   105
churches, then; or else shall 'a suffer not thinking on,° with the hobbyhorse,
whose epitaph is "For, O, for, O, the hobbyhorse is forgot."°

The trumpets sound. Dumb show follows.

Enter a King and a Queen [very lovingly]; the Queen embracing him, and he her.
[She kneels, and makes show of protestation unto him.] He takes her up, and declines
his head upon her neck: he lies him down upon a bank of flowers: she, seeing him asleep,
leaves him. Anon comes in another man, takes off his crown, kisses it, pours poison in the
sleeper's ears, and leaves him. The Queen returns; finds the King dead, makes passionate
action. The Poisoner, with some three or four come in again, seems to condole with her.
The dead body is carried away. The Poisoner woos the Queen with gifts: she seems harsh
awhile, but in the end accepts love.   *[Exeunt.]*

OPHELIA: What means this, my lord?
HAMLET: Marry, this is miching mallecho;° it means mischief.
OPHELIA: Belike this show imports the argument of the play.   110

Enter PROLOGUE.

HAMLET: We shall know by this fellow: the players cannot keep counsel; they'll
    tell all.
OPHELIA: Will 'a tell us what this show meant?
HAMLET: Ay, or any show that you'll show him: be not you ashamed to show, he'll not
    shame to tell you what it means.   115
OPHELIA: You are naught, you are naught:° I'll mark the play.
PROLOGUE: For us, and for our tragedy,
    Here stooping° to your clemency,
    We beg your hearing patiently.   *[Exit.]*
HAMLET: Is this a prologue, or the posy° of a ring?   120
OPHELIA: 'Tis brief, my lord.
HAMLET: As woman's love.

Enter [two PLAYERS *as] King and Queen.*

PLAYER KING: Full thirty times hath Phoebus' cart gone round
    Neptune's salt wash° and Tellus'° orbed ground,
    And thirty dozen moons with borrowed° sheen   125
    About the world have times twelve thirties been,
    Since love our hearts and Hymen° did our hands
    Unite commutual° in most sacred bands.

---

106 **suffer . . . on:** Undergo oblivion.   107 **"For . . . forgot":** Verse of a song occurring also in
Love's Labour's Lost, III.i.30. The hobbyhorse was a character in the Morris Dance.   109 **miching
mallecho:** Sneaking mischief.   116 **naught:** Indecent.   118 **stooping:** Bowing.   120 **posy:**
Motto.   124 **salt wash:** The sea.   **Tellus:** Goddess of the earth (*orbed ground*).   125 **borrowed:**
I.e., reflected.   127 **Hymen:** God of matrimony.   128 **commutual:** Mutually.

PLAYER QUEEN: So many journeys may the sun and moon
    Make us again count o'er ere love be done!   130
    But, woe is me, you are so sick of late,
    So far from cheer and from your former state,
    That I distrust° you. Yet, though I distrust,
    Discomfort you, my lord, it nothing must:
    For women's fear and love holds quantity;°   135
    In neither aught, or in extremity.
    Now, what my love is, proof hath made you know;
    And as my love is siz'd, my fear is so:
    Where love is great, the littlest doubts are fear;
    Where little fears grow great, great love grows there.   140
PLAYER KING: 'Faith, I must leave thee, love, and shortly too;
    My operant° powers their functions leave° to do:
    And thou shalt live in this fair world behind,
    Honour'd, belov'd; and haply one as kind
    For husband shalt thou—
PLAYER QUEEN: O, confound the rest!   145
    Such love must needs be treason in my breast:
    In second husband let me be accurst!
    None wed the second but who kill'd the first.
HAMLET [aside]: Wormwood, wormwood.
PLAYER QUEEN: The instances that second marriage move   150
    Are base respects of thrift, but none of love:
    A second time I kill my husband dead,
    When second husband kisses me in bed.
PLAYER KING: I do believe you think what now you speak;
    But what we do determine oft we break.   155
    Purpose is but the slave to memory,
    Of violent birth, but poor validity:
    Which now, like fruit unripe, sticks on the tree;
    But fall, unshaken, when they mellow be.
    Most necessary 'tis that we forget   160
    To pay ourselves what to ourselves is debt:
    What to ourselves in passion we propose,
    The passion ending, doth the purpose lose.
    The violence of either grief or joy
    Their own enactures° with themselves destroy: 165
    Where joy most revels, grief doth most lament;
    Grief joys, joy grieves, on slender accident.
    This world is not for aye,° nor 'tis not strange

---

133 distrust: Am anxious about.   **135 holds quantity:** Keeps proportion between.   **142 operant:** Active. **leave:** Cease.   **165 enactures:** Fulfillments.   **168 aye:** Ever.

That even our loves should with our fortunes change;
For 'tis a question left us yet to prove,   170
Whether love lead fortune, or else fortune love.
The great man down, you mark his favourite flies;
The poor advanc'd makes friends of enemies.
And hitherto doth love on fortune tend;
For who° not needs shall never lack a friend,   175
And who in want a hollow friend doth try,
Directly seasons° him his enemy.
But, orderly to end where I begun,
Our wills and fates do so contrary run
That our devices still are overthrown;   180
Our thoughts are ours, their ends° none of our own:
So think thou wilt no second husband wed;
But die thy thoughts when thy first lord is dead.
PLAYER QUEEN: Nor earth to me give food, nor heaven light!
Sport and repose lock from me day and night!   185
To desperation turn my trust and hope!
An anchor's° cheer° in prison be my scope!
Each opposite° that blanks° the face of joy
Meet what I would have well and it destroy!
Both here and hence pursue me lasting strife,   190
If, once a widow, ever I be wife!
HAMLET: If she should break it now!
PLAYER KING: 'Tis deeply sworn. Sweet, leave me here awhile;
My spirits grow dull, and fain I would beguile
The tedious day with sleep.   *[Sleeps.]*
PLAYER QUEEN: Sleep rock thy brain;   195
And never come mischance between us twain!   *Exit.*
HAMLET: Madam, how like you this play?
QUEEN: The lady doth protest too much, methinks.
HAMLET: O, but she'll keep her word.
KING: Have you heard the argument? Is there no offence in 't?   200
HAMLET: No, no, they do but jest, poison in jest; no offence i' the world.
KING: What do you call the play?
HAMLET: The Mouse-trap. Marry, how? Tropically.° This play is the image of a mur-
der done in Vienna: Gonzago° is the duke's name; his wife, Baptista: you shall
see anon; 't is a knavish piece of work: but what o' that? your majesty and we   205

---

175 who: Whoever.   **177 seasons:** Matures, ripens.   **181 ends:** Results.   **187 An anchor's:** An
anchorite's.   **cheer:** Fare; sometimes printed as *chair*.   **188 opposite:** Adverse thing.   **blanks:**
Causes to *blanch* or grow pale.   **203 Tropically:** Figuratively, *tropically* suggests a pun on *trap*
in *Mouse-trap* (l. 203).   **204 Gonzago:** In 1538, Luigi Gonzago murdered the Duke of Urbano
by pouring poisoned lotion in his ears.

that have free souls, it touches us not: let the galled jade° winch,° our withers°
are unwrung.°

Enter LUCIANUS.

This is one Lucianus, nephew to the king.

OPHELIA: You are as good as a chorus,° my lord.

HAMLET: I could interpret between you and your love, if I could see the puppets   210
dallying.°

OPHELIA: You are keen, my lord, you are keen.

HAMLET: It would cost you a groaning to take off my edge.

OPHELIA: Still better, and worse.°

HAMLET: So you mistake° your husbands. Begin, murderer; pox,° leave thy damnable   215
faces, and begin. Come: the croaking raven doth bellow for revenge.

LUCIANUS: Thoughts black, hands apt, drugs fit, and time agreeing;
Confederate° season, else no creature seeing;
Thou mixture rank, of midnight weeds collected,
With Hecate's° ban° thrice blasted, thrice infected,   220
Thy natural magic and dire property,
On wholesome life usurp immediately.

[Pours the poison into the sleeper's ears.]

HAMLET: 'A poisons him i' the garden for his estate. His name's Gonzago: the story is
extant, and written in very choice Italian: you shall see anon how the murderer
gets the love of Gonzago's wife.   225

OPHELIA: The king rises.

HAMLET: What, frighted with false fire!°

QUEEN: How fares my lord?

POLONIUS: Give o'er the play.

KING: Give me some light: away!   230

POLONIUS: Lights, lights, lights!   *Exeunt all but* HAMLET *and* HORATIO.

HAMLET: Why, let the strucken deer go weep,
The hart ungalled play;
For some must watch, while some must sleep:
Thus runs the world away.°   235

---

206 **galled jade:** Horse whose hide is rubbed by saddle or harness.   **winch:** Wince.   **withers:**
The part between the horse's shoulder blades.   207 **unwrung:** Not wrung or twisted.   209
chorus: In many Elizabethan plays, the action was explained by an actor known as the "chorus"; at a puppet show the actor who explained the action was known as an "interpreter," as
indicated by the lines following.   211 **dallying:** With sexual suggestion, continued in *keen*
(sexually aroused), *groaning* (i.e., in pregnancy), and *edge* (i.e., sexual desire or impetuos-
ity).   214 **Still . . . worse:** More keen, less decorous.   215 **mistake:** Err in taking.   **pox:** An
imprecation.   218 **Confederate:** Conspiring (to assist the murderer).   220 **Hecate:** The goddess of witchcraft.   **ban:** Curse.   227 **false fire:** Fireworks, or a blank discharge.   232–235
Why . . . away: Probably from an old ballad, with allusion to the popular belief that a wounded
deer retires to weep and die. Cf. *As You Like It*, II.i.66.

Would not this,° sir, and a forest of feathers°—if the rest of my fortunes turn
Turk with° me—with two Provincial roses° on my razed° shoes, get me a fellowship in a cry° of players,° sir?

HORATIO: Half a share.°

HAMLET: A whole one, I.   240
For thou dost know, O Damon° dear,
This realm dismantled° was
Of Jove himself; and now reigns here
A very, very°—pajock.°

HORATIO: You might have rhymed.   245

HAMLET: O good Horatio, I'll take the ghost's word for a thousand pound. Didst
perceive?

HORATIO: Very well, my lord.

HAMLET: Upon the talk of the poisoning?

HORATIO: I did very well note him.   250

HAMLET: Ah, ha! Come, some music! come, the recorders!°
For if the king like not the comedy,
Why then, belike, he likes it not, perdy.°
Come, some music!

Enter ROSENCRANTZ *and* GUILDENSTERN.

GUILDENSTERN: Good my lord, vouchsafe me a word with you.   255

HAMLET: Sir, a whole history.

GUILDENSTERN: The king, sir,—

HAMLET: Ay, sir, what of him?

GUILDENSTERN: Is in his retirement marvellous distempered.

HAMLET: With drink, sir?

GUILDENSTERN: No, my lord, rather with choler.°   260

HAMLET: Your wisdom should show itself more richer to signify this to his doctor;
for, for me to put him to his purgation would perhaps plunge him into far more
choler.

GUILDENSTERN: Good my lord, put your discourse into some frame° and start not   265
so wildly from my affair.

---

236 this: I.e., the play.   **feathers:** Allusion to the plumes which Elizabethan actors were fond of
wearing.   **236–237 turn Turk with:** Go back on.   **237 two Provincial roses:** Rosettes of ribbon
like the roses of Provins near Paris, or else the roses of Provence.   **razed:** Cut, slashed (by way
of ornament).   **237–238 fellowship . . . players:** Partnership in a theatrical company.   **238
cry:** Pack (as of hounds).   **239 Half a share:** Allusion to the custom in dramatic companies of
dividing the ownership into a number of shares among the householders.   **241 Damon:** Symbol
of loyalty and friendship in Greek myth.—EDS.   **241–244 For . . . very:** Probably from an old
ballad having to do with Damon and Pythias.   **242 dismantled:** Stripped, divested.   **pajock:**
Peacock (a bird with a bad reputation). Possibly the word was *patchock*, diminutive of *patch*,
clown.   **251 recorders:** Wind instruments of the flute kind.   **253 perdy:** Corruption of *par
dieu*.   **261 choler:** Bilious disorder, with quibble on the sense "anger."   **265 frame:** Order.

HAMLET: I am tame, sir: pronounce.

GUILDENSTERN: The queen, your mother, in most great affliction of spirit, hath sent
me to you.

HAMLET: You are welcome.   270

GUILDENSTERN: Nay, good my lord, this courtesy is not of the right breed. If it shall
please you to make me a wholesome° answer, I will do your mother's commandment; if not, your pardon and my return shall be the end of my business.

HAMLET: Sir, I cannot.

GUILDENSTERN: What, my lord?   275

HAMLET: Make you a wholesome answer; my wit's diseased: but, sir, such answer as
I can make, you shall command; or, rather, as you say, my mother: therefore no
more, but to the matter:° my mother, you say,—

ROSENCRANTZ: Then thus she says; your behaviour hath struck her into amazement
and admiration.   280

HAMLET: O wonderful son, that can so 'stonish a mother! But is there no sequel at
the heels of this mother's admiration? Impart.

ROSENCRANTZ: She desires to speak with you in her closet, ere you go to bed.

HAMLET: We shall obey, were she ten times our mother. Have you any further trade
with us?   285

ROSENCRANTZ: My lord, you once did love me.

HAMLET: And do still, by these pickers and stealers.°

ROSENCRANTZ: Good my lord, what is your cause of distemper? you do, surely, bar
the door upon your own liberty, if you deny your griefs to your friend.

HAMLET: Sir, I lack advancement.   290

ROSENCRANTZ: How can that be, when you have the voice° of the king himself for
your succession in Denmark?

HAMLET: Ay, sir, but "While the grass grows,"°—the proverb is something musty.

Enter the Players with recorders.

O, the recorders! let me see one. To withdraw° with you:—why do you go about
to recover the wind° of me, as if you would drive me into a toil?°   295

GUILDENSTERN: O, my lord, if my duty be too bold, my love is too unmannerly.°

HAMLET: I do not well understand that. Will you play upon this pipe?

GUILDENSTERN: My lord, I cannot.

HAMLET: I pray you.

GUILDENSTERN: Believe me, I cannot.   300

HAMLET: I beseech you.

------

272 **wholesome:** Sensible.   278 **matter:** Matter in hand.   287 **pickers and stealers:** Hands,
so called from the catechism "to keep my hands from picking and stealing."   291 **voice:**
Support.   293 **"While . . . grows":** The rest of the proverb is "the silly horse starves." Hamlet
may be destroyed while he is waiting for the succession to the kingdom.   294 **withdraw:** Speak
in private.   295 **recover the wind:** Get to the windward side.   **toil:** Snare.   296 **if . . . unmannerly:** If I am using an unmannerly boldness, it is my love which occasions it.

GUILDENSTERN: I know no touch of it, my lord.

HAMLET: 'Tis as easy as lying: govern these ventages° with your fingers and thumb, give it breath with your mouth, and it will discourse most eloquent music. Look you, these are the stops.

GUILDENSTERN: But these cannot I command to any utterance of harmony; I have not the skill.

HAMLET: Why, look you now, how unworthy a thing you make of me! You would play upon me; you would seem to know my stops; you would pluck out the heart of my mystery; you would sound me from my lowest note to the top of my compass:° and there is much music, excellent voice, in this little organ;° yet cannot you make it speak. 'Sblood, do you think I am easier to be played on than a pipe? Call me what instrument you will, though you can fret° me, you cannot play upon me.

Enter POLONIUS.

God bless you, sir!

POLONIUS: My lord, the queen would speak with you, and presently.

HAMLET: Do you see yonder cloud that 's almost in shape of a camel?

POLONIUS: By the mass, and 'tis like a camel, indeed.

HAMLET: Methinks it is like a weasel.

POLONIUS: It is backed like a weasel.

HAMLET: Or like a whale?

POLONIUS: Very like a whale.

HAMLET: Then I will come to my mother by and by. *[Aside.]* They fool me to the top of my bent.° — I will come by and by.°

POLONIUS: I will say so. *[Exit.]*

HAMLET: By and by is easily said.

Leave me, friends. *[Exeunt all but* HAMLET.*]*
'Tis now the very witching time° of night,
When churchyards yawn and hell itself breathes out
Contagion to this world: now could I drink hot blood,
And do such bitter business as the day
Would quake to look on. Soft! now to my mother.
O heart, lose not thy nature; let not ever
The soul of Nero° enter this firm bosom:
Let me be cruel, not unnatural:
I will speak daggers to her, but use none;
My tongue and soul in this be hypocrites;

305

310

315

320

325

330

335

---

303 ventages: Stops of the recorders. **311 compass:** Range of voice. **organ:** Musical instrument, i.e., the pipe. **313 fret:** Quibble on meaning "irritate" and the piece of wood, gut, or metal which regulates the fingering. **323–324 top of my bent:** Limit of endurance, i.e., extent to which a bow may be bent. **324 by and by:** Immediately. **328 witching time:** I.e., time when spells are cast. **334 Nero:** Murderer of his mother, Agrippina.

How in my words somever she be shent,°
To give them seals° never, my soul, consent!   *Exit.*

[SCENE iii: *A room in the castle.*]

Enter KING, ROSENCRANTZ, *and* GUILDENSTERN.

KING: I like him not, nor stands it safe with us
    To let his madness range. Therefore prepare you;
    I your commission will forthwith dispatch,°
    And he to England shall along with you:
    The terms° of our estate° may not endure   5
    Hazard so near us as doth hourly grow
    Out of his brows.°
GUILDENSTERN: We will ourselves provide:
    Most holy and religious fear it is
    To keep those many many bodies safe
    That live and feed upon your majesty.   10
ROSENCRANTZ: The single and peculiar° life is bound,
    With all the strength and armour of the mind,
    To keep itself from noyance;° but much more
    That spirit upon whose weal depend and rest
    The lives of many. The cess° of majesty   15
    Dies not alone; but, like a gulf,° doth draw
    What's near it with it: it is a massy wheel,
    Fix'd on the summit of the highest mount,
    To whose huge spokes ten thousand lesser things
    Are mortis'd and adjoin'd; which, when it falls,   20
    Each small annexment, petty consequence,
    Attends° the boist'rous ruin. Never alone
    Did the king sigh, but with a general groan.
KING: Arm° you, I pray you, to this speedy voyage;
    For we will fetters put about this fear,   25
    Which now goes too free-footed.
ROSENCRANTZ: We will haste us.
                    Exeunt GENTLEMEN *[*ROSENCRANTZ *and* GUILDENSTERN*].*

Enter POLONIUS.

---

338 shent: Rebuked.   **339 give them seals:** Confirm with deeds.   **Scene iii.   3 dispatch:**
Prepare.   **5 terms:** Condition, circumstances.   **estate:** State.   **7 brows:** Effronteries.   **11
single and peculiar:** Individual and private.   **13 noyance:** Harm.   **15 cess:** Decease.   **16 gulf:**
Whirlpool.   **22 Attends:** Participates in.   **24 Arm:** Prepare.

POLONIUS: My lord, he's going to his mother's closet:
    Behind the arras° I'll convey° myself,
    To hear the process;° I'll warrant she'll tax him home:°
    And, as you said, and wisely was it said,   30
    'Tis meet that some more audience than a mother,
    Since nature makes them partial, should o'erhear
    The speech, of vantage.° Fare you well, my liege:
    I'll call upon you ere you go to bed,
    And tell you what I know.
KING: Thanks, dear my lord.   *Exit [*POLONIUS*].*   35
    O, my offence is rank, it smells to heaven;
    It hath the primal eldest curse° upon't,
    A brother's murder. Pray can I not,
    Though inclination be as sharp as will:°
    My stronger guilt defeats my strong intent;   40
    And, like a man to double business bound,
    I stand in pause where I shall first begin,
    And both neglect. What if this cursed hand
    Were thicker than itself with brother's blood,
    Is there not rain enough in the sweet heavens   45
    To wash it white as snow? Whereto serves mercy
    But to confront° the visage of offence?
    And what's in prayer but this two-fold force,
    To be forestalled° ere we come to fall,
    Or pardon'd being down? Then I'll look up;   50
    My fault is past. But, O, what form of prayer
    Can serve my turn? "Forgive me my foul murder"?
    That cannot be: since I am still possess'd
    Of those effects for which I did the murder,
    My crown, mine own ambition° and my queen.   55
    May one be pardon'd and retain th' offence?°
    In the corrupted currents° of this world
    Offence's gilded hand° may shove by justice,
    And oft 'tis seen the wicked prize° itself
    Buys out the law: but 'tis not so above;   60
    There is no shuffling,° there the action lies°

---

28 arras: Screen of tapestry placed around the walls of household apartments. **convey:** Implication of secrecy, *convey* was often used to mean "steal." **29 process:** Proceedings. **tax him home:** Reprove him severely. **33 of vantage:** From an advantageous place. **37 primal eldest curse:** The curse of Cain, the first to kill his brother. **39 sharp as will:** I.e., his desire is as strong as his determination. **47 confront:** Oppose directly. **49 forestalled:** Prevented. **55 ambition:** I.e., realization of ambition. **56 offence:** Benefit accruing from offense. **57 currents:** Courses. **58 gilded hand:** Hand offering gold as a bribe. **59 wicked prize:** Prize won by wickedness. **61 shuffling:** Escape by trickery. **lies:** Is sustainable.

In his true nature; and we ourselves compell'd,
Even to the teeth and forehead° of our faults,
To give in evidence. What then? what rests?°
Try what repentance can: what can it not?   65
Yet what can it when one can not repent?
O wretched state! O bosom black as death!
O limed° soul, that, struggling to be free,
Art more engag'd!° Help, angels! Make assay!°
Bow, stubborn knees; and, heart with strings of steel,   70
Be soft as sinews of the new-born babe!
All may be well.   *[He kneels.]*

Enter HAMLET.

HAMLET: Now might I do it pat,° now he is praying;
    And now I'll do't. And so 'a goes to heaven;
    And so am I reveng'd. That would be scann'd:°   75
    A villain kills my father; and for that,
    I, his sole son, do this same villain send
    To heaven.
    Why, this is hire and salary, not revenge.
    'A took my father grossly, full of bread;°   80
    With all his crimes broad blown,° as flush° as May;
    And how his audit stands who knows save heaven?
    But in our circumstance and course° of thought,
    'Tis heavy with him: and am I then reveng'd,
    To take him in the purging of his soul,   85
    When he is fit and season'd for his passage?°
    No!
    Up, sword; and know thou a more horrid hent:°
    When he is drunk asleep,° or in his rage,
    Or in th' incestuous pleasure of his bed;   90
    At game, a-swearing, or about some act
    That has no relish of salvation in't;
    Then trip him, that his heels may kick at heaven,
    And that his soul may be as damn'd and black
    As hell, whereto it goes. My mother stays: 95
    This physic° but prolongs thy sickly days.   *Exit.*

---

63 **teeth and forehead:** Very face. 64 **rests:** Remains. 68 **limed:** Caught as with birdlime. 69 **engag'd:** Embedded. **assay:** Trial. 73 **pat:** Opportunely. 75 **would be scann'd:** Needs to be looked into. 80 **full of bread:** Enjoying his worldly pleasures (see Ezekiel 16:49). 81 **broad blown:** In full bloom. **flush:** Lusty. 83 **in . . . course:** As we see it in our mortal situation. 86 **fit . . . passage:** I.e., reconciled to heaven by forgiveness of his sins. 88 **hent:** Seizing; or more probably, occasion of seizure. 89 **drunk asleep:** In a drunken sleep. 96 **physic:** Purging (by prayer).

KING: *[Rising]* My words fly up, my thoughts remain below:
　　Words without thoughts never to heaven go.　　　　　　　　*Exit.*

[SCENE iv: *The* QUEEN'S *closet.*]

Enter [QUEEN] GERTRUDE *and* POLONIUS.

POLONIUS: 'A will come straight. Look you lay° home to him:
　　Tell him his pranks have been too broad° to bear with,
　　And that your grace hath screen'd and stood between
　　Much heat° and him. I'll sconce° me even here.
　　Pray you, be round° with him.　　　　　　　　　　　　　　　　5
HAMLET *[within]*: Mother, mother, mother!
QUEEN:　　　　　　　　　　　　　　　I'll warrant you,
　　Fear me not: withdraw, I hear him coming.
　　　　　　　　　　　　　　　*[*POLONIUS *hides behind the arras.]*

Enter HAMLET.

HAMLET: Now, mother, what's the matter?
QUEEN: Hamlet, thou hast thy father much offended.
HAMLET: Mother, you have my father° much offended.
QUEEN: Come, come, you answer with an idle tongue.　　　　　10
HAMLET: Go, go, you question with a wicked tongue.
QUEEN: Why, how now, Hamlet!
HAMLET:　　　　　　　　　　What's the matter now?
QUEEN: Have you forgot me?
HAMLET:　　　　　　　　No, by the rood,° not so:
　　You are the queen, your husband's brother's wife;
　　And—would it were not so!—you are my mother.　　　　　15
QUEEN: Nay, then, I'll set those to you that can speak.
HAMLET: Come, come, and sit you down; you shall not budge;
　　You go not till I set you up a glass
　　Where you may see the inmost part of you.　　　　　　　　20
QUEEN: What wilt thou do? thou wilt not murder me?
　　Help, help, ho!
POLONIUS *[behind]*: What, ho! help, help; help!
HAMLET *[drawing]*: How now! a rat? Dead, for a ducat, dead!
　　　　　　　　　　　　　　　[Makes a pass through the arras.]
POLONIUS *[behind]*: O, I am slain!　　　　　　　*[Falls and dies.]*　25
QUEEN: O me, what hast thou done?

Scene iv.　**1 lay:** Thrust.　**2 broad:** Unrestrained.　**4 Much heat:** I.e., the king's anger.　**sconce:**
Hide.　**5 round:** Blunt.　**9–10 thy father, my father:** I.e., Claudius, the elder Hamlet.　**14
rood:** Cross.

HAMLET: Nay, I know not:
   Is it the king?
QUEEN: O, what a rash and bloody deed is this!
HAMLET: A bloody deed! almost as bad, good mother,
   As kill a king, and marry with his brother.   30
QUEEN: As kill a king!
HAMLET: Ay, lady, it was my word.
                    [Lifts up the arras and discovers POLONIUS.*]*
   Thou wretched, rash, intruding fool, farewell!
   I took thee for thy better: take thy fortune;
   Thou find'st to be too busy is some danger.
   Leave wringing of your hands: peace! sit you down,   35
   And let me wring your heart; for so I shall,
   If it be made of penetrable stuff,
   If damned custom have not braz'd° it so
   That it be proof and bulwark against sense.
QUEEN: What have I done, that thou dar'st wag thy tongue   40
   In noise so rude against me?
HAMLET: Such an act
   That blurs the grace and blush of modesty,
   Calls virtue hypocrite, takes off the rose
   From the fair forehead of an innocent love
   And sets a blister° there, makes marriage-vows   45
   As false as dicers' oaths: O, such a deed
   As from the body of contraction° plucks
   The very soul, and sweet religion° makes
   A rhapsody° of words: heaven's face does glow
   O'er this solidity and compound mass   50
   With heated visage, as against the doom
   Is thought-sick at the act.°
QUEEN: Ay me, what act,
   That roars so loud, and thunders in the index?°
HAMLET: Look here, upon this picture, and on this.
   The counterfeit presentment° of two brothers.   55
   See, what a grace was seated on this brow;
   Hyperion's° curls; the front° of Jove himself;
   An eye like Mars, to threaten and command;

---

38 **braz'd:** Brazened, hardened.   45 **sets a blister:** Brands as a harlot.   47 **contraction:** The marriage contract.   48 **religion:** Religious vows.   49 **rhapsody:** Senseless string.   49–52 **heaven's . . . act:** Heaven's face blushes to look down on this world, and Gertrude's marriage makes heaven feel as sick as though the day of doom were near.   53 **index:** Prelude or preface.   55 **counterfeit presentment:** Portrayed representation.   57 **Hyperion's:** The sun god's.   **front:** Brow.

A station° like the herald Mercury
New-lighted on a heaven-kissing hill;   60
A combination and a form indeed,
Where every god did seem to set his seal,
To give the world assurance° of a man:
This was your husband. Look you now, what follows:
Here is your husband; like a mildew'd ear,°   65
Blasting his wholesome brother. Have you eyes?
Could you on this fair mountain leave to feed,
And batten° on this moor?° Ha! have you eyes?
You cannot call it love; for at your age
The hey-day° in the blood is tame, it's humble,   70
And waits upon the judgement: and what judgement
Would step from this to this? Sense, sure, you have,
Else could you not have motion;° but sure, that sense
Is apoplex'd;° for madness would not err,
Nor sense to ecstasy was ne'er so thrall'd°   75
But it reserv'd some quantity of choice,°
To serve in such a difference. What devil was't
That thus hath cozen'd° you at hoodman-blind?°
Eyes without feeling, feeling without sight,
Ears without hands or eyes, smelling sans° all,   80
Or but a sickly part of one true sense
Could not so mope.°
O shame! where is thy blush? Rebellious hell,
If thou canst mutine° in a matron's bones,
To flaming youth let virtue be as wax,   85
And melt in her own fire: proclaim no shame
When the compulsive ardour gives the charge,°
Since frost itself as actively doth burn
And reason panders will.°
QUEEN: O Hamlet, speak no more:
Thou turn'st mine eyes into my very soul;   90

---

59 **station:** Manner of standing.   63 **assurance:** Pledge, guarantee.   65 **mildew'd ear:**
See Genesis 41:5–7.   68 **batten:** Grow fat.   **moor:** Barren upland.   70 **hey-day:** State of
excitement.   72–73 **Sense . . . motion:** Sense and motion are functions of the middle or
sensible soul, the possession of sense being the basis of motion.   74 **apoplex'd:** Paralyzed.
Mental derangement was thus of three sorts: apoplexy, ecstasy, and diabolic possession.   75
thrall'd: Enslaved.   76 **quantity of choice:** Fragment of the power to choose.   78 **cozen'd:**
Tricked, cheated.   **hoodman-blind:** Blindman's buff.   80 **sans:** Without.   82 **mope:** Be in
a depressed, spiritless state; act aimlessly.   84 **mutine:** Mutiny, rebel.   87 **gives the charge:**
Delivers the attack.   89 **reason panders will:** The normal and proper situation was one in
which reason guided the will in the direction of good; here, reason is perverted and leads in
the direction of evil.

And there I see such black and grained° spots
As will not leave their tinct.
HAMLET: Nay, but to live
In the rank sweat of an enseamed° bed,
Stew'd in corruption, honeying and making love
Over the nasty sty,—
QUEEN: O, speak to me no more;   95
These words, like daggers, enter in mine ears;
No more, sweet Hamlet!
HAMLET: A murderer and a villain;
A slave that is not twentieth part the tithe
Of your precedent lord;° a vice of kings;°
A cutpurse of the empire and the rule,   100
That from a shelf the precious diadem stole,
And put it in his pocket!
QUEEN: No more!

Enter GHOST.

HAMLET: A king of shreds and patches,°—
Save me, and hover o'er me with your wings,
You heavenly guards! What would your gracious figure?   105
QUEEN: Alas, he's mad!
HAMLET: Do you not come your tardy son to chide,
That, laps'd in time and passion,° lets go by
Th' important° acting of your dread command?
O, say!   110
GHOST: Do not forget: this visitation
Is but to whet thy almost blunted purpose.
But, look, amazement° on thy mother sits:
O, step between her and her fighting soul:
Conceit in weakest bodies strongest works: 115
Speak to her, Hamlet.
HAMLET: How is it with you, lady?
QUEEN: Alas, how is 't with you,
That you do bend your eye on vacancy
And with th' incorporal° air do hold discourse?

---

91 **grained:** Dyed in grain.   93 **enseamed:** Loaded with grease, greased.   99 **precedent lord:**
I.e., the elder Hamlet.   **vice of kings:** Buffoon of kings; a reference to the vice, or clown, of
the morality plays and interludes.   103 **shreds and patches:** I.e., motley, the traditional costume of the vice.   108 **laps'd . . . passion:** Having suffered time to slip and passion to cool;
also explained as "engrossed in casual events and lapsed into mere fruitless passion, so that he
no longer entertains a rational purpose."   109 **important:** Urgent.   113 **amazement:** Frenzy,
distraction.   119 **incorporal:** Immaterial.

Forth at your eyes your spirits wildly peep; 120
And, as the sleeping soldiers in th' alarm,
Your bedded° hair, like life in excrements,°
Start up, and stand an° end. O gentle son,
Upon the heat and flame of thy distemper
Sprinkle cool patience. Whereon do you look? 125

HAMLET: On him, on him! Look you, how pale he glares!
His form and cause conjoin'd,° preaching to stones,
Would make them capable.—Do not look upon me;
Lest with this piteous action you convert
My stern effects:° then what I have to do 130
Will want true colour;° tears perchance for blood.

QUEEN: To whom do you speak this?

HAMLET: Do you see nothing there?

QUEEN: Nothing at all; yet all that is I see.

HAMLET: Nor did you nothing hear?

QUEEN: No, nothing but ourselves.

HAMLET: Why, look you there! look, how it steals away! 135
My father, in his habit as he liv'd!
Look, where he goes, even now, out at the portal!   *Exit* GHOST.

QUEEN: This is the very coinage of your brain:
This bodiless creation ecstasy
Is very cunning in.

HAMLET: Ecstasy! 140
My pulse, as yours, doth temperately keep time,
And makes as healthful music: it is not madness
That I have utt'red: bring me to the test,
And I the matter will re-word,° which madness
Would gambol° from. Mother, for love of grace, 145
Lay not that flattering unction° to your soul,
That not your trespass, but my madness speaks:
It will but skin and film the ulcerous place,
Whiles rank corruption, mining° all within,
Infects unseen. Confess yourself to heaven; 150
Repent what's past; avoid what is to come;°

---

122 **bedded:** Laid in smooth layers. **excrements:** The hair was considered an excrement or voided part of the body. 123 **an:** On. 127 **conjoin'd:** United. **129–130 convert . . . effects:** Divert me from my stern duty. For *effects*, possibly *affects* (affections of the mind). 131 **want true colour:** Lack good reason so that (with a play on the normal sense of *colour*) I shall shed tears instead of blood. 144 **re-word:** Repeat in words. 145 **gambol:** Skip away. 146 **unction:** Ointment used medicinally or as a rite; suggestion that forgiveness for sin may not be so easily achieved. 149 **mining:** Working under the surface. 151 **what is to come:** I.e., the sins of the future.

And do not spread the compost° on the weeds,
To make them ranker. Forgive me this my virtue;°
For in the fatness° of these pursy° times
Virtue itself of vice must pardon beg,   155
Yea, curb° and woo for leave to do him good.
QUEEN: O Hamlet, thou hast cleft my heart in twain.
HAMLET: O, throw away the worser part of it,
   And live the purer with the other half.
   Good night: but go not to my uncle's bed;   160
   Assume a virtue, if you have it not.
   That monster, custom, who all sense doth eat,
   Of habits devil, is angel yet in this,
   That to the use of actions fair and good
   He likewise gives a frock or livery,   165
   That aptly is put on. Refrain to-night,
   And that shall lend a kind of easiness
   To the next abstinence: the next more easy;
   For use almost can change the stamp of nature,
   And either . . . the devil, or throw him out°   170
   With wondrous potency. Once more, good night:
   And when you are desirous to be bless'd,°
   I'll blessing beg of you. For this same lord,   *[Pointing to* POLONIUS.]
   I do repent: but heaven hath pleas'd it so,
   To punish me with this and this with me,   175
   That I must be their scourge and minister.
   I will bestow him, and will answer well
   The death I gave him. So, again, good night.
   I must be cruel, only to be kind:
   Thus bad begins and worse remains behind.   180
   One word more, good lady.
QUEEN: What shall I do?
HAMLET: Not this, by no means, that I bid you do:
   Let the bloat° king tempt you again to bed;
   Pinch wanton on your cheek; call you his mouse;
   And let him, for a pair of reechy° kisses,   185
   Or paddling in your neck with his damn'd fingers,
   Make you to ravel all this matter out,

---

152 **compost:** Manure.   153 **this my virtue:** My virtuous talk in reproving you.   154 **fatness:**
Grossness.   **pursy:** Short-winded, corpulent.   156 **curb:** Bow, bend the knee.   170 Defective
line usually emended by inserting *master* after *either*.   172 **be bless'd:** Become blessed, i.e.,
repentant.   183 **bloat:** Bloated.   185 **reechy:** Dirty, filthy.

That I essentially° am not in madness,
But mad in craft. 'Twere good you let him know;
For who, that's but a queen, fair, sober, wise,   190
Would from a paddock,° from a bat, a gib,°
Such dear concernings° hide? who would do so?
No, in despite of sense and secrecy,
Unpeg the basket on the house's top,
Let the birds fly, and, like the famous ape,°   195
To try conclusions,° in the basket creep,
And break your own neck down.
QUEEN: Be thou assur'd, if words be made of breath,
And breath of life, I have no life to breathe
What thou hast said to me.   200
HAMLET: I must to England; you know that?
QUEEN: Alack,
I had forgot: 'tis so concluded on.
HAMLET: There's letters seal'd: and my two schoolfellows,
Whom I will trust as I will adders fang'd,
They bear the mandate; they must sweep my way,°   205
And marshal me to knavery. Let it work;
For 'tis the sport to have the enginer°
Hoist° with his own petar:° and 't shall go hard
But I will delve one yard below their mines,
And blow them at the moon: O, 'tis most sweet,   210
When in one line two crafts° directly meet.
This man shall set me packing:°
I'll lug the guts into the neighbour room.
Mother, good night. Indeed this counsellor
Is now most still, most secret and most grave,   215
Who was in life a foolish prating knave.
Come, sir, to draw° toward an end with you.
Good night, mother.   *Exeunt [severally;* HAMLET *dragging in* POLONIUS*].*

---

188 **essentially:** In my essential nature. 191 **paddock:** Toad. **gib:** Tomcat. 192 **dear concernings:** Important affairs. 195 **the famous ape:** A letter from Sir John Suckling seems to supply other details of the story, otherwise not identified: "It is the story of the jackanapes and the partridges; thou starest after a beauty till it be lost to thee, then let'st out another, and starest after that till it is gone too." 196 **conclusions:** Experiments. 205 **sweep my way:** Clear my path. 207 **enginer:** Constructor of military works, or possibly artilleryman. 208 **Hoist:** Blown up. **petar:** Defined as a small engine of war used to blow in a door or make a breach, and as a case filled with explosive materials. 211 **two crafts:** Two acts of guile, with quibble on the sense of "two ships." 212 **set me packing:** Set me to making schemes, set me to lugging (him), and, also, send me off in a hurry. 217 **draw:** Come, with quibble on literal sense.

[ACT IV

SCENE i: *A room in the castle.*]

Enter KING *and* QUEEN, *with* ROSENCRANTZ *and* GUILDENSTERN.

KING: There's matter in these sighs, these profound heaves:
    You must translate: 'tis fit we understand them.
    Where is your son?
QUEEN: Bestow this place on us a little while.

                             [Exeunt ROSENCRANTZ *and* GUILDENSTERN.*]*

    Ah, mine own lord, what have I seen to-night!   5
KING: What, Gertrude? How does Hamlet?
QUEEN: Mad as the sea and wind, when both contend
    Which is the mightier: in his lawless fit,
    Behind the arras hearing something stir,
    Whips out his rapier, cries, "A rat, a rat!"   10
    And, in this brainish° apprehension,° kills
    The unseen good old man.
KING: O heavy deed!
    It had been so with us, had we been there:
    His liberty is full of threats to all;
    To you yourself, to us, to every one.   15
    Alas, how shall this bloody deed be answer'd?
    It will be laid to us, whose providence°
    Should have kept short,° restrain'd and out of haunt,°
    This mad young man: but so much was our love,
    We would not understand what was most fit;   20
    But, like the owner of a foul disease,
    To keep it from divulging,° let it feed
    Even on the pith of life. Where is he gone?
QUEEN: To draw apart the body he hath kill'd:
    O'er whom his very madness, like some ore   25
    Among a mineral° of metals base,
    Shows itself pure; 'a weeps for what is done.
KING: O Gertrude, come away!
    The sun no sooner shall the mountains touch,
    But we will ship him hence: and this vile deed   30
    We must, with all our majesty and skill,
    Both countenance and excuse. Ho, Guildenstern!

Enter ROSENCRANTZ *and* GUILDENSTERN.

Act IV, Scene i.   **11 brainish:** Headstrong, passionate. **apprehension:** Conception, imagination. **17 providence:** Foresight. **18 short:** I.e., on a short tether. **out of haunt:** Secluded. **22 divulging:** Becoming evident. **26 mineral:** Mine.

Friends both, go join you with some further aid:
Hamlet in madness hath Polonius slain,
And from his mother's closet hath he dragg'd him: 35
Go seek him out; speak fair, and bring the body
Into the chapel. I pray you, haste in this.

         [Exeunt ROSENCRANTZ *and* GUILDENSTERN.*]*
Come, Gertrude, we'll call up our wisest friends;
And let them know, both what we mean to do,
And what's untimely done . . .°   40
Whose whisper o'er the world's diameter,°
As level° as the cannon to his blank,°
Transports his pois'ned shot, may miss our name,
And hit the woundless° air. O, come away!
My soul is full of discord and dismay.   *Exeunt.* 45

[SCENE ii: *Another room in the castle.*]

Enter HAMLET.

HAMLET: Safely stowed.
ROSENCRANTZ: }
GUILDENSTERN: } *[within]* Hamlet! Lord Hamlet!
HAMLET: But soft, what noise? who calls on Hamlet? O, here they come.

Enter ROSENCRANTZ *and* GUILDENSTERN.

ROSENCRANTZ: What have you done, my lord, with the dead body?
HAMLET: Compounded it with dust, whereto 'tis kin.
ROSENCRANTZ: Tell us where 'tis, that we may take it thence   5
  And bear it to the chapel.
HAMLET: Do not believe it.
ROSENCRANTZ: Believe what?
HAMLET: That I can keep your counsel° and not mine own. Besides, to be demanded   10
  of a sponge! what replication° should be made by the son of a king?
ROSENCRANTZ: Take you me for a sponge, my lord?
HAMLET: Ay, sir, that soaks up the king's countenance, his rewards, his authorities.° But
  such officers do the king best service in the end: he keeps them, like an ape an apple,
  in the corner of his jaw; first mouthed, to be last swallowed: when he needs what   15
  you have gleaned, it is but squeezing you, and, sponge, you shall be dry again.

---

40 Defective line; some editors add: *so, haply, slander;* others add: *for, haply, slander;* other
conjectures.   41 **diameter:** Extent from side to side.   42 **level:** Straight.   **blank:** White spot
in the center of a target.   44 **woundless:** Invulnerable.   **Scene ii.**   10 **keep your counsel:**
Hamlet is aware of their treachery but says nothing about it.   11 **replication:** Reply.   13
authorities: Authoritative backing.

ROSENCRANTZ: I understand you not, my lord.

HAMLET: I am glad of it: a knavish speech sleeps in a foolish ear.

ROSENCRANTZ: My lord, you must tell us where the body is, and go with us to the king.

HAMLET: The body is with the king, but the king is not with the body.° The king is   20
a thing—

GUILDENSTERN: A thing, my lord!

HAMLET: Of nothing: bring me to him. Hide fox, and all after.°   *Exeunt.*

[SCENE iii: *Another room in the castle.*]

Enter KING, *and two or three.*

KING: I have sent to seek him, and to find the body.
      How dangerous is it that this man goes loose!
      Yet must not we put the strong law on him:
      He's lov'd of the distracted° multitude,
      Who like not in their judgement, but their eyes;   5
      And where 'tis so, th' offender's scourge° is weigh'd,°
      But never the offence. To bear all smooth and even,
      This sudden sending him away must seem
      Deliberate pause:° diseases desperate grown
      By desperate appliance are reliev'd,   10
      Or not at all.

Enter ROSENCRANTZ, *[*GUILDENSTERN,*] and all the rest.*

                  How now! what hath befall'n?

ROSENCRANTZ: Where the dead body is bestow'd, my lord,
      We cannot get from him.

KING: But where is he?

ROSENCRANTZ: Without, my lord; guarded, to know your pleasure.

KING: Bring him before us.   15

ROSENCRANTZ: Ho! bring in the lord.

They enter [with HAMLET*].*

KING: Now, Hamlet, where's Polonius?

HAMLET: At supper.

KING: At supper! where?

---

20 The body . . . body: There are many interpretations; possibly, "The body lies in death with
the king, my father; but my father walks disembodied"; or "Claudius has the bodily possession
of kingship, but kingliness, or justice of inheritance, is not with him." **23 Hide . . . after:** An
old signal cry in the game of hide-and-seek. **Scene iii. 4 distracted:** I.e., without power of
forming logical judgments. **6 scourge:** Punishment. **weigh'd:** Taken into consideration. **9
Deliberate pause:** Considered action.

HAMLET: Not where he eats, but where 'a is eaten: a certain convocation of politic° 20
worms° are e'en at him. Your worm is your only emperor for diet: we fat all creatures else to fat us, and we fat ourselves for maggots: your fat king and your lean
beggar is but variable service,° two dishes, but to one table: that's the end.

KING: Alas, alas!

HAMLET: A man may fish with the worm that hath eat of a king, and eat of the fish 25
that hath fed of that worm.

KING: What dost thou mean by this?

HAMLET: Nothing but to show you how a king may go a progress° through the guts
of a beggar.

KING: Where is Polonius? 30

HAMLET: In heaven; send thither to see: if your messenger find him not there, seek
him i' the other place yourself. But if indeed you find him not within this month,
you shall nose him as you go up the stairs into the lobby.

KING [to some ATTENDANTS]: Go seek him there.

HAMLET: 'A will stay till you come. *[Exeunt ATTENDANTS.]* 35

KING: Hamlet, this deed, for thine especial safety,—
Which we do tender,° as we dearly grieve
For that which thou hast done,—must send thee hence
With fiery quickness: therefore prepare thyself;
The bark is ready, and the wind at help, 40
Th' associates tend, and everything is bent
For England.

HAMLET: For England!

KING: Ay, Hamlet.

HAMLET: Good.

KING: So is it, if thou knew'st our purposes.

HAMLET: I see a cherub° that sees them. But, come; for England! Farewell, dear
mother. 45

KING: Thy loving father, Hamlet.

HAMLET: My mother: father and mother is man and wife; man and wife is one flesh;
and so, my mother. Come, for England! *Exit.*

KING: Follow him at foot;° tempt him with speed aboard;
Delay it not; I'll have him hence to-night: 50
Away! for every thing is seal'd and done
That else leans on th' affair: pray you, make haste.
                                   [Exeunt all but the KING.]
And, England, if my love thou hold'st at aught—
As my great power thereof may give thee sense,

20–21 **convocation . . . worms:** Allusion to the Diet of Worms (1521). 20 **politic:** Crafty.
23 **variable service:** A variety of dishes. 28 **progress:** Royal journey of state. 37 **tender:**
Regard, hold dear. 44 **cherub:** Cherubim are angels of knowledge. 49 **at foot:** Close behind,
at heel.

Since yet thy cicatrice° looks raw and red   55
After the Danish sword, and thy free awe°
Pays homage to us—thou mayst not coldly set
Our sovereign process; which imports at full,
By letters congruing to that effect,
The present death of Hamlet. Do it, England;   60
For like the hectic° in my blood he rages,
And thou must cure me: till I know 'tis done,
Howe'er my haps,° my joys were ne'er begun.   *Exit.*

[SCENE iv: *A plain in Denmark.*]

Enter FORTINBRAS *with his* ARMY *over the stage.*

FORTINBRAS: Go, captain, from me greet the Danish king;
    Tell him that, by his license,° Fortinbras
    Craves the conveyance° of a promis'd march
    Over his kingdom. You know the rendezvous.
    If that his majesty would aught with us,   5
    We shall express our duty in his eye;°
    And let him know so.
CAPTAIN: I will do't, my lord.
FORTINBRAS: Go softly° on.   *[Exeunt all but* CAPTAIN.*]*

Enter HAMLET, ROSENCRANTZ, *[*GUILDENSTERN,*] &c.*

HAMLET: Good sir, whose powers are these?
CAPTAIN: They are of Norway, sir.   10
HAMLET: How purpos'd, sir, I pray you?
CAPTAIN: Against some part of Poland.
HAMLET: Who commands them, sir?
CAPTAIN: The nephew to old Norway, Fortinbras.
HAMLET: Goes it against the main° of Poland, sir,   15
    Or for some frontier?
CAPTAIN: Truly to speak, and with no addition,
    We go to gain a little patch of ground
    That hath in it no profit but the name.
    To pay five ducats, five, I would not farm it;°   20
    Nor will it yield to Norway or the Pole
    A ranker rate, should it be sold in fee.°

---

55 cicatrice: Scar. **56 free awe:** Voluntary show of respect. **61 hectic:** Fever. **63 haps:**
Fortunes. **Scene iv. 2 license:** Leave. **3 conveyance:** Escort, convoy. **6 in his eye:** In his
presence. **8 softly:** Slowly. **15 main:** Country itself. **20 farm it:** Take a lease of it. **22 fee:**
Fee simple.

HAMLET: Why, then the Polack never will defend it.

CAPTAIN: Yes, it is already garrison'd.

HAMLET: Two thousand souls and twenty thousand ducats   25
Will not debate the question of this straw:°
This is th' imposthume° of much wealth and peace,
That inward breaks, and shows no cause without
Why the man dies. I humbly thank you, sir.

CAPTAIN: God be wi' you, sir.   *[Exit.]*

ROSENCRANTZ: Will 't please you go, my lord?   30

HAMLET: I'll be with you straight. Go a little before.   *[Exeunt all except HAMLET.]*
How all occasions° do inform against° me,
And spur my dull revenge! What is a man,
If his chief good and market of his time°
Be but to sleep and feed? a beast, no more.   35
Sure, he that made us with such large discourse,
Looking before and after, gave us not
That capability and god-like reason
To fust° in us unus'd. Now, whether it be
Bestial oblivion, or some craven scruple   40
Of thinking too precisely on th' event,
A thought which, quarter'd, hath but one part wisdom
And ever three parts coward, I do not know
Why yet I live to say "This thing 's to do";
Sith I have cause and will and strength and means   45
To do 't. Examples gross as earth exhort me:
Witness this army of such mass and charge
Led by a delicate and tender prince,
Whose spirit with divine ambition puff'd
Makes mouths at the invisible event,   50
Exposing what is mortal and unsure
To all that fortune, death and danger dare,
Even for an egg-shell. Rightly to be great
Is not to stir without great argument,
But greatly to find quarrel in a straw   55
When honour's at the stake. How stand I then,
That have a father kill'd, a mother stain'd,
Excitements of° my reason and my blood,
And let all sleep? while, to my shame, I see

---

26 debate . . . straw: Settle this trifling matter.   **27 imposthume:** Purulent abscess or swelling.   **32 occasions:** Incidents, events.   **inform against:** Generally defined as "show," "betray" (i.e., his tardiness); more probably *inform* means "take shape," as in *Macbeth*, II.i.48.   **34 market of his time:** The best use he makes of his time, or that for which he sells his time.   **39 fust:** Grow moldy.   **58 Excitements of:** Incentives to.

The imminent death of twenty thousand men,   60
That, for a fantasy and trick° of fame,
Go to their graves like beds, fight for a plot°
Whereon the numbers cannot try the cause,
Which is not tomb enough and continent
To hide the slain? O, from this time forth,   65
My thoughts be bloody, or be nothing worth!   *Exit.*

[SCENE V: *Elsinore. A room in the castle.*]

Enter HORATIO, *[*QUEEN*]* GERTRUDE, *and a* GENTLEMAN.

QUEEN: I will not speak with her.
GENTLEMAN: She is importunate, indeed distract:
    Her mood will needs be pitied.
QUEEN: What would she have?
GENTLEMAN: She speaks much of her father; says she hears
    There's tricks° i' th' world; and hems, and beats her heart;°   5
    Spurns enviously at straws;° speaks things in doubt,
    That carry but half sense: her speech is nothing,
    Yet the unshaped° use of it doth move
    The hearers to collection;° they yawn° at it,
    And botch° the words up fit to their own thoughts;   10
    Which, as her winks, and nods, and gestures yield° them,
    Indeed would make one think there might be thought,
    Though nothing sure, yet much unhappily.°
HORATIO: 'Twere good she were spoken with: for she may strew
    Dangerous conjectures in ill-breeding minds.°   15
QUEEN: Let her come in.   [*Exit* GENTLEMAN.]
    [*Aside.*] To my sick soul, as sin's true nature is,
    Each toy seems prologue to some great amiss:°
    So full of artless jealousy is guilt,
    It spills itself in fearing to be spilt.°   20

Enter OPHELIA [*distracted*].

OPHELIA: Where is the beauteous majesty of Denmark?

---

61 trick: Toy, trifle. **62 plot:** Piece of ground. **Scene v. 5 tricks:** Deceptions. **heart:**
I.e., breast. **6 Spurns . . . straws:** Kicks spitefully at small objects in her path. **8 unshaped:**
Unformed, artless. **9 collection:** Inference, a guess at some sort of meaning. **yawn:**
Wonder. **10 botch:** Patch. **11 yield:** Deliver, bring forth (her words). **13 much unhappily:**
Expressive of much unhappiness. **15 ill-breeding minds:** Minds bent on mischief. **18 great
amiss:** Calamity, disaster. **19–20 So . . . spilt:** Guilt is so full of suspicion that it unskillfully
betrays itself in fearing to be betrayed.

QUEEN: How now, Ophelia!

OPHELIA *[she sings]*: "How should I your true love know
    From another one?
    By his cockle hat° and staff,
      And his sandal shoon."°   25

QUEEN: Alas, sweet lady, what imports this song?

OPHELIA: Say you? nay, pray you mark.
    [Song] "He is dead and gone, lady,
      He is dead and gone;   30
    At his head a grass-green turf,
      At his heels a stone."
    O, ho!

QUEEN: Nay, but, Ophelia—

OPHELIA: Pray you, mark.   35
    [Sings.] "White his shroud as the mountain snow"—

Enter KING.

QUEEN: Alas, look here, my lord.

OPHELIA *[Song]*: "Larded° all with flowers;
    Which bewept to the grave did not go
      With true-love showers."   40

KING: How do you, pretty lady?

OPHELIA: Well, God 'ild° you! They say the owl° was a baker's daughter. Lord, we know what we are, but know not what we may be. God be at your table!

KING: Conceit upon her father.

OPHELIA: Pray let's have no words of this; but when they ask you what it means, say   45
    you this:
    [Song] "To-morrow is Saint Valentine's day,
      All in the morning betime,
    And I a maid at your window,
      To be your Valentine.°   50
    Then up he rose, and donn'd his clothes,
      And dupp'd° the chamber-door;
    Let in the maid, that out a maid
      Never departed more."

KING: Pretty Ophelia!   55

---

25 cockle hat: Hat with cockleshell stuck in it as a sign that the wearer has been a pilgrim to the shrine of St. James of Compostella. The pilgrim's garb was a conventional disguise for lovers. **26 shoon:** Shoes. **38 Larded:** Decorated. **42 God 'ild:** God yield or reward. **owl:** Reference to a monkish legend that a baker's daughter was turned into an owl for refusing bread to the Savior. **50 Valentine:** This song alludes to the belief that the first girl seen by a man on the morning of this day was his valentine or true love. **52 dupp'd:** Opened.

OPHELIA: Indeed, la, without an oath, I'll make an end on 't:
> [*Sings.*] "By Gis° and by Saint Charity,
>   Alack, and fie for shame!
> Young men will do 't, if they come to 't;
>   By cock,° they are to blame.   60
> Quoth she, 'before you tumbled me,
>   You promis'd me to wed.'
> 'So would I ha' done, by yonder sun,
>   An thou hadst not come to my bed.'"

KING: How long hath she been thus?   65

OPHELIA: I hope all will be well. We must be patient: but I cannot choose but weep, to think they would lay him i' the cold ground. My brother shall know of it: and so I thank you for your good counsel. Come, my coach! Good night, ladies; good night, sweet ladies; good night, good night.   *[Exit.]*

KING: Follow her close; give her good watch, I pray you.   *[Exit* HORATIO.*]*   70
> O, this is the poison of deep grief; it springs
> All from her father's death. O Gertrude, Gertrude,
> When sorrows come, they come not single spies,
> But in battalions. First, her father slain:
> Next your son gone; and he most violent author   75
> Of his own just remove: the people muddied,
> Thick and unwholesome in their thoughts and whispers,
> For good Polonius' death; and we have done but greenly,°
> In hugger-mugger° to inter him: poor Ophelia
> Divided from herself and her fair judgement,   80
> Without the which we are pictures, or mere beasts:
> Last, and as much containing as all these,
> Her brother is in secret come from France;
> Feeds on his wonder, keeps himself in clouds,°
> And wants not buzzers° to infect his ear   85
> With pestilent speeches of his father's death;
> Wherein necessity, of matter beggar'd,°
> Will nothing stick° our person to arraign
> In ear and ear.° O my dear Gertrude, this,
> Like to a murd'ring-piece,° in many places   90
> Gives me superfluous death.   *A noise within.*

QUEEN: Alack, what noise is this?

KING: Where are my Switzers?° Let them guard the door.

---

57 Gis: Jesus.   **60 cock:** Perversion of "God" in oaths.   **78 greenly:** Foolishly.   **79 hugger-mugger:** Secret haste.   **84 in clouds:** Invisible.   **85 buzzers:** Gossipers.   **87 of matter beggar'd:** Unprovided with facts.   **88 nothing stick:** Not hesitate.   **89 In ear and ear:** In everybody's ears.   **90 murd'ring-piece:** Small cannon or mortar; suggestion of numerous missiles fired.   **92 Switzers:** Swiss guards, mercenaries.

Enter a MESSENGER.

> What is the matter?
MESSENGER: Save yourself, my lord:
> The ocean, overpeering° of his list,°
> Eats not the flats with more impiteous haste   95
> Than young Laertes, in a riotous head,
> O'erbears your officers. The rabble call him lord;
> And, as the world were now but to begin,
> Antiquity forgot, custom not known,
> The ratifiers and props of every word,°   100
> They cry "Choose we: Laertes shall be king":
> Caps, hands, and tongues, applaud it to the clouds:
> "Laertes shall be king, Laertes king!"   *A noise within.*
QUEEN: How cheerfully on the false trail they cry!
> O, this is counter,° you false Danish dogs!   105
KING: The doors are broke.

Enter LAERTES *with others.*

LAERTES: Where is this king? Sirs, stand you all without.
DANES: No, let's come in.
LAERTES: I pray you, give me leave.
DANES: We will, we will.   *[They retire without the door.]*
LAERTES: I thank you: keep the door. O thou vile king,   110
> Give me my father!
QUEEN: Calmly, good Laertes.
LAERTES: That drop of blood that's calm proclaims me bastard,
> Cries cuckold to my father, brands the harlot
> Even here, between the chaste unsmirched brow
> Of my true mother.
KING: What is the cause, Laertes,   115
> That thy rebellion looks so giant-like?
> Let him go, Gertrude; do not fear our person:
> There's such divinity doth hedge a king,
> That treason can but peep to° what it would,°
> Acts little of his will. Tell me, Laertes,   120
> Why thou art thus incens'd. Let him go, Gertrude.
> Speak, man.
LAERTES: Where is my father?
KING: Dead.
QUEEN: But not by him.

---

94 overpeering: Overflowing. **list:** Shore. **100 word:** Promise. **105 counter:** A hunting term meaning to follow the trail in a direction opposite to that which the game has taken. **119 peep to:** I.e., look at from afar off. **would:** Wishes to do.

KING: Let him demand his fill.

LAERTES: How came he dead? I'll not be juggled with: 125
>   To hell, allegiance! vows, to the blackest devil!
>   Conscience and grace, to the profoundest pit!
>   I dare damnation. To this point I stand,
>   That both the worlds I give to negligence,°
>   Let come what comes; only I'll be reveng'd   130
>   Most throughly° for my father.

KING: Who shall stay you?

LAERTES: My will,° not all the world's:
>   And for my means, I'll husband them so well,
>   They shall go far with little.

KING: Good Laertes,
>   If you desire to know the certainty   135
>   Of your dear father, is 't writ in your revenge,
>   That, swoopstake,° you will draw both friend and foe,
>   Winner and loser?

LAERTES: None but his enemies.

KING: Will you know them then?

LAERTES: To his good friends thus wide I'll ope my arms;   140
>   And like the kind life-rend'ring pelican,°
>   Repast° them with my blood.

KING: Why, now you speak
>   Like a good child and a true gentleman.
>   That I am guiltless of your father's death,
>   And am most sensibly in grief for it,   145
>   It shall as level to your judgement 'pear
>   As day does to your eye.   *A noise within: "Let her come in."*

LAERTES: How now! what noise is that?

Enter OPHELIA.

>   O heat,° dry up my brains! tears seven times salt,
>   Burn out the sense and virtue of mine eye!   150
>   By heaven, thy madness shall be paid with weight,
>   Till our scale turn the beam. O rose of May!
>   Dear maid, kind sister, sweet Ophelia!
>   O heavens! is 't possible, a young maid's wits
>   Should be as mortal as an old man's life?   155

---

129 give to negligence: He despises both the here and the hereafter.   **131 throughly:** thoroughly.   **132 My will:** He will not be stopped except by his own will.   **137 swoopstake:** Literally, drawing the whole stake at once, i.e., indiscriminately.   **141 pelican:** Reference to the belief that the pelican feeds its young with its own blood.   **142 Repast:** Feed.   **149 heat:** Probably the heat generated by the passion of grief.

Nature is fine in love, and where 'tis fine,
It sends some precious instance of itself
After the thing it loves.
OPHELIA *[Song]:* "They bore him barefac'd on the bier;
  Hey non nonny, nonny, hey nonny;   160
  And in his grave rain'd many a tear:"—
  Fare you well, my dove!
LAERTES: Hadst thou thy wits, and didst persuade revenge,
  It could not move thus.
OPHELIA *[sings]:* "You must sing a-down a-down,   165
    An you call him a-down-a."
  O, how the wheel° becomes it! It is the false steward,° that stole his master's
  daughter.
LAERTES: This nothing's more than matter.
OPHELIA: There's rosemary,° that's for remembrance; pray you, love, remember: and   170
  there is pansies,° that's for thoughts.
LAERTES: A document° in madness, thoughts and remembrance fitted.
OPHELIA: There's fennel° for you, and columbines:° there's rue° for you; and here's
  some for me: we may call it herb of grace° o' Sundays: O, you must wear your
  rue with a difference. There's a daisy:° I would give you some violets,° but they   175
  withered all when my father died: they say 'a made a good end,—
  [Sings.] "For bonny sweet Robin is all my joy."°
LAERTES: Thought° and affliction, passion, hell itself,
  She turns to favour and to prettiness.
OPHELIA *[Song]:* "And will 'a not come again?°   180
  And will 'a not come again?
    No, no, he is dead:
    Go to thy death-bed:
  He never will come again.

  "His beard was as white as snow,   185
  All flaxen was his poll:°
    He is gone, he is gone,

---

167 **wheel:** Spinning wheel as accompaniment to the song refrain.   **false steward:** The story is unknown.   170 **rosemary:** Used as a symbol of remembrance both at weddings and at funerals.   171 **pansies:** Emblems of love and courtship (from the French *pensée*).   172 **document:** Piece of instruction or lesson.   173 **fennel:** Emblem of flattery.   **columbines:** Emblem of unchastity (?) or ingratitude (?).   **rue:** Emblem of repentance. It was usually mingled with holy water and then known as *herb of grace*. Ophelia is probably playing on the two meanings of *rue*, "repentant" and "even for ruth (pity)"; the former signification is for the queen, the latter for herself.   175 **daisy:** Emblem of dissembling, faithlessness.   **violets:** Emblems of faithfulness.   177 **For . . . joy:** Probably a line from a Robin Hood ballad.   178 **Thought:** Melancholy thought.   180 **And . . . again:** This song appeared in the songbooks as "The Merry Milkmaids' Dumps."   186 **poll:** Head.

And we cast away° moan:
    God ha' mercy on his soul!"
And of all Christian souls, I pray God. God be wi' you.   *[Exit.]*   190
LAERTES: Do you see this, O God?
KING: Laertes, I must commune with your grief,
    Or you deny me right.° Go but apart,
    Make choice of whom your wisest friends you will,
    And they shall hear and judge 'twixt you and me: 195
    If by direct or by collateral° hand
    They find us touch'd,° we will our kingdom give,
    Our crown, our life, and all that we call ours,
    To you in satisfaction; but if not,
    Be you content to lend your patience to us,   200
    And we shall jointly labour with your soul
    To give it due content.
LAERTES: Let this be so;
    His means of death, his obscure funeral—
    No trophy, sword, nor hatchment° o'er his bones,
    No noble rite nor formal ostentation—   205
    Cry to be heard, as 'twere from heaven to earth,
    That I must call 't in question.
KING: So you shall;
    And where th' offence is let the great axe fall.
    I pray you, go with me.   *Exeunt.*

[SCENE vi: *Another room in the castle.*]

Enter HORATIO *and others.*

HORATIO: What are they that would speak with me?
GENTLEMAN: Sea-faring men, sir: they say they have letters for you.
HORATIO: Let them come in.   *[Exit* GENTLEMAN.*]*
    I do not know from what part of the world
    I should be greeted, if not from Lord Hamlet.   5

Enter SAILORS.

FIRST SAILOR: God bless you, sir.
HORATIO: Let him bless thee too.
FIRST SAILOR: 'A shall sir, an 't please him. There's a letter for you, sir; it comes from
    the ambassador that was bound for England; if your name be Horatio, as I am
    let to know it is.   10

---

188 cast away: Shipwrecked.   **193 right:** My rights.   **196 collateral:** Indirect.   **197 touch'd:**
Implicated.   **204 hatchment:** Tablet displaying the armorial bearings of a deceased person.

HORATIO [*reads*]: "Horatio, when thou shalt have overlooked this, give these fellows some means° to the king: they have letters for him. Ere we were two days old at sea, a pirate of very warlike appointment gave us chase. Finding ourselves too slow of sail, we put on a compelled valour, and in the grapple I boarded them: on the instant they got clear of our ship; so I alone became their prisoner. They have dealt with me like thieves of mercy:° but they knew what they did; I am to do a good turn for them. Let the king have the letters I have sent; and repair thou to me with as much speed as thou wouldest fly death. I have words to speak in thine ear will make thee dumb; yet are they much too light for the bore° of the matter. These good fellows will bring thee where I am. Rosencrantz and Guildenstern hold their course for England: of them I have much to tell thee. Farewell.   He that thou knowest thine, HAMLET."
  Come, I will give you way for these your letters;
  And do 't the speedier, that you may direct me
  To him from whom you brought them.   *Exeunt.*   25

15

20

[SCENE vii: *Another room in the castle.*]

Enter KING *and* LAERTES.

KING: Now must your conscience° my acquittance seal,
  And you must put me in your heart for friend,
  Sith you have heard, and with a knowing ear,
  That he which hath your noble father slain
  Pursued my life.
LAERTES: It well appears: but tell me   5
  Why you proceeded not against these feats,
  So criminal and so capital° in nature,
  As by your safety, wisdom, all things else,
  You mainly° were stirr'd up.
KING: O, for two special reasons;
  Which may to you, perhaps, seem much unsinew'd,°   10
  But yet to me th' are strong. The queen his mother
  Lives almost by his looks; and for myself—
  My virtue or my plague, be it either which—
  She's so conjunctive° to my life and soul,
  That, as the star moves not but in his sphere,°   15
  I could not but by her. The other motive,

Scene vi.   12 **means**: Means of access.   16 **thieves of mercy**: Merciful thieves.   19 **bore**: Caliber, importance.   Scene vii.   1 **conscience**: Knowledge that this is true.   7 **capital**: Punishable by death.   9 **mainly**: Greatly.   10 **unsinew'd**: Weak.   14 **conjunctive**: Conformable (the next line suggesting planetary conjunction).   15 **sphere**: The hollow sphere in which, according to Ptolemaic astronomy, the planets were supposed to move.

Why to a public count° I might not go,
Is the great love the general gender° bear him;
Who, dipping all his faults in their affection,
Would, like the spring° that turneth wood to stone,   20
Convert his gyves° to graces; so that my arrows,
Too slightly timber'd° for so loud° a wind,
Would have reverted to my bow again,
And not where I had aim'd them.
LAERTES: And so have I a noble father lost;   25
A sister driven into desp'rate terms,°
Whose worth, if praises may go back° again,
Stood challenger on mount° of all the age°
For her perfections: but my revenge will come.
KING: Break not your sleeps for that: you must not think   30
That we are made of stuff so flat and dull
That we can let our beard be shook with danger
And think it pastime. You shortly shall hear more:
I lov'd your father, and we love ourself;
And that, I hope, will teach you to imagine—   35

Enter a MESSENGER *with letters.*

How now! what news?
MESSENGER: Letters, my lord, from Hamlet:
These to your majesty; this to the queen.°
KING: From Hamlet! who brought them?
MESSENGER: Sailors, my lord, they say; I saw them not:
They were given me by Claudio;° he receiv'd them   40
Of him that brought them.
KING: Laertes, you shall hear them.
Leave us.   *[Exit* MESSENGER.*]*
[Reads.] "High and mighty, You shall know I am set naked° on your kingdom.
To-morrow shall I beg leave to see your kingly eyes: when I shall, first asking
your pardon thereunto, recount the occasion of my sudden and more strange   45
return.   HAMLET."
What should this mean? Are all the rest come back?
Or is it some abuse, and no such thing?

---

17 **count:** Account, reckoning.   18 **general gender:** Common people.   20 **spring:** I.e., one
heavily charged with lime.   21 **gyves:** Fetters; here, faults, or possibly, punishments inflicted
(on him).   22 **slightly timber'd:** Light.   **loud:** Strong.   26 **terms:** State, condition.   27
go back: Return to Ophelia's former virtues.   28 **on mount:** Set up on high, *mounted* (on
horseback).   **of all the age:** Qualifies *challenger* and not *mount.*   37 **to the queen:** One
hears no more of the letter to the queen.   40 **Claudio:** This character does not appear in the
play.   43 **naked:** Unprovided (with retinue).

LAERTES: Know you the hand?

KING: 'Tis Hamlet's character. "Naked!"

    And in a postscript here, he says "alone."   50

    Can you devise° me?

LAERTES: I'm lost in it, my lord. But let him come;

    It warms the very sickness in my heart,

    That I shall live and tell him to his teeth,

    "Thus didst thou."

KING: If it be so, Laertes—   55

    As how should it be so? how otherwise?°—

    Will you be rul'd by me?

LAERTES: Ay, my lord;

    So you will not o'errule me to a peace.

KING: To thine own peace. If he be now return'd,

    As checking at° his voyage, and that he means   60

    No more to undertake it, I will work him

    To an exploit, now ripe in my device,

    Under the which he shall not choose but fall:

    And for his death no wind of blame shall breathe,

    But even his mother shall uncharge the practice°   65

    And call it accident.

LAERTES: My lord, I will be rul'd;

    The rather, if you could devise it so

    That I might be the organ.°

KING: It falls right.

    You have been talk'd of since your travel much,

    And that in Hamlet's hearing, for a quality   70

    Wherein, they say, you shine: your sum of parts

    Did not together pluck such envy from him

    As did that one, and that, in my regard,

    Of the unworthiest siege.°

LAERTES: What part is that, my lord?

KING: A very riband in the cap of youth,   75

    Yet needful too; for youth no less becomes

    The light and careless livery that it wears

    Than settled age his sables° and his weeds,

    Importing health and graveness. Two months since,

---

51 devise: Explain to.   **56 As . . . otherwise?** How can this (Hamlet's return) be true? (yet) how otherwise than true (since we have the evidence of his letter)? Some editors read *How should it not be so*, etc., making the words refer to Laertes's desire to meet with Hamlet.   **60 checking at:** Used in falconry of a hawk's leaving the quarry to fly at a chance bird; turn aside.   **65 uncharge the practice:** Acquit the stratagem of being a plot.   **68 organ:** Agent, instrument.   **74 siege:** Rank.   **78 sables:** Rich garments.

Here was a gentleman of Normandy:—   80
I have seen myself, and serv'd against, the French,
And they can well° on horseback: but this gallant
Had witchcraft in 't; he grew unto his seat;
And to such wondrous doing brought his horse,
As had he been incorps'd and demi-natur'd°   85
With the brave beast: so far he topp'd° my thought,
That I, in forgery° of shapes and tricks,
Come short of what he did.
LAERTES: A Norman was 't?
KING: A Norman.
LAERTES: Upon my life, Lamord.°
KING: The very same.   90
LAERTES: I know him well: he is the brooch indeed
      And gem of all the nation.
KING: He made confession° of you,
      And gave you such a masterly report
      For art and exercise° in your defence°   95
      And for your rapier most especial,
      That he cried out, 'twould be a sight indeed,
      If one could match you: the scrimers° of their nation,
      He swore, had neither motion, guard, nor eye,
      If you oppos'd them. Sir, this report of his   100
      Did Hamlet so envenom with his envy
      That he could nothing do but wish and beg
      Your sudden coming o'er, to play° with you.
      Now, out of this,—
LAERTES: What out of this, my lord?
KING: Laertes, was your father dear to you?   105
      Or are you like the painting of a sorrow,
      A face without a heart?
LAERTES: Why ask you this?
KING: Not that I think you did not love your father;
      But that I know love is begun by time;
      And that I see, in passages of proof,°   110
      Time qualifies the spark and fire of it.
      There lives within the very flame of love

---

82 **can well:** Are skilled.   85 **incorps'd and demi-natur'd:** Of one body and nearly of one
nature (like the centaur).   86 **topp'd:** Surpassed.   87 **forgery:** Invention.   90 **Lamord:** This
refers possibly to Pietro Monte, instructor to Louis XII's master of the horse.   93 **confession:**
Grudging admission of superiority.   95 **art and exercise:** Skillful exercise.   **defence:** Science
of defense in sword practice.   98 **scrimers:** Fencers.   103 **play:** Fence.   110 **passages of
proof:** Proved instances.

A kind of wick or snuff that will abate it;
And nothing is at a like goodness still;
For goodness, growing to a plurisy,°   115
Dies in his own too much:° that we would do,
We should do when we would; for this "would" changes
And hath abatements° and delays as many
As there are tongues, are hands, are accidents;°
And then this "should" is like a spendthrift° sigh,   120
That hurts by easing. But, to the quick o' th' ulcer:°—
Hamlet comes back: what would you undertake,
To show yourself your father's son in deed
More than in words?
LAERTES: To cut his throat i' th' church.
KING: No place, indeed, should murder sanctuarize;°   125
Revenge should have no bounds. But, good Laertes,
Will you do this, keep close within your chamber.
Hamlet return'd shall know you are come home:
We'll put on those shall praise your excellence
And set a double varnish on the fame   130
The Frenchman gave you, bring you in fine together
And wager on your heads: he, being remiss,
Most generous and free from all contriving,
Will not peruse the foils; so that, with ease,
Or with a little shuffling, you may choose   135
A sword unbated,° and in a pass of practice°
Requite him for your father.
LAERTES: I will do 't:
And, for that purpose, I'll anoint my sword.
I bought an unction of a mountebank,°
So mortal that, but dip a knife in it,   140
Where it draws blood no cataplasm° so rare,
Collected from all simples° that have virtue
Under the moon,° can save the thing from death
That is but scratch'd withal: I'll touch my point

---

115 **plurisy:** Excess, plethora.   116 **in his own too much:** Of its own excess.   118 **abatements:** Diminutions.   119 **accidents:** Occurrences, incidents.   120 **spendthrift:** An allusion to the belief that each sigh cost the heart a drop of blood.   121 **quick o' th' ulcer:** Heart of the difficulty.   125 **sanctuarize:** Protect from punishment; allusion to the right of sanctuary with which certain religious places were invested.   136 **unbated:** Not blunted, having no button.   **pass of practice:** Treacherous thrust.   139 **mountebank:** Quack doctor.   141 **cataplasm:** Plaster or poultice.   142 **simples:** Herbs.   143 **Under the moon:** I.e., when collected by moonlight to add to their medicinal value.

With this contagion, that, if I gall° him slightly,   145
It may be death.
KING: Let's further think of this;
Weigh what convenience both of time and means
May fit us to our shape:° if this should fail,
And that our drift look through our bad performance,°
'Twere better not assay'd: therefore this project   150
Should have a back or second, that might hold,
If this should blast in proof.° Soft! let me see:
We'll make a solemn wager on your cunnings:°
I ha 't:
When in your motion you are hot and dry—   155
As make your bouts more violent to that end—
And that he calls for drink, I'll have prepar'd him
A chalice° for the nonce, whereon but sipping,
If he by chance escape your venom'd stuck,°
Our purpose may hold there. But stay, what noise?   160

Enter QUEEN.

QUEEN: One woe doth tread upon another's heel,
   So fast they follow: your sister's drown'd, Laertes.
LAERTES: Drown'd! O, where?
QUEEN: There is a willow° grows askant° the brook,
   That shows his hoar° leaves in the glassy stream;   165
   There with fantastic garlands did she make
   Of crow-flowers,° nettles, daisies, and long purples°
   That liberal° shepherds give a grosser name,
   But our cold maids do dead men's fingers call them:
   There, on the pendent boughs her crownet° weeds   170
   Clamb'ring to hang, an envious sliver° broke;
   When down her weedy° trophies and herself
   Fell in the weeping brook. Her clothes spread wide;
   And, mermaid-like, awhile they bore her up:
   Which time she chanted snatches of old lauds;°   175
   As one incapable° of her own distress,

---

145 **gall:** Graze, wound.   148 **shape:** Part we propose to act.   149 **drift . . . performance:** Intention be disclosed by our bungling.   152 **blast in proof:** Burst in the test (like a cannon).   153 **cunnings:** Skills.   158 **chalice:** Cup.   159 **stuck:** Thrust (from *stoccado*).   164 **willow:** For its significance of forsaken love.   **askant:** Aslant.   165 **hoar:** White (i.e., on the underside).   167 **crow-flowers:** Buttercups.   **long purples:** Early purple orchids.   168 **liberal:** Probably, free-spoken.   170 **crownet:** Coronet; made into a chaplet.   171 **sliver:** Branch.   172 **weedy:** I.e., of plants.   175 **lauds:** Hymns.   176 **incapable:** Lacking capacity to apprehend.

Or like a creature native and indued°
Upon that element: but long it could not be
Till that her garments, heavy with their drink,
Pull'd the poor wretch from her melodious lay   180
To muddy death.
LAERTES: Alas, then, she is drown'd?
QUEEN: Drown'd, drown'd.
LAERTES: Too much of water hast thou, poor Ophelia,
And therefore I forbid my tears: but yet
It is our trick;° nature her custom holds,   185
Let shame say what it will: when these are gone,
The woman will be out.° Adieu, my lord:
I have a speech of fire, that fain would blaze,
But that this folly drowns it.   *Exit.*
KING: Let's follow, Gertrude:
How much I had to do to calm his rage!   190
Now fear I this will give it start again;
Therefore let 's follow.   *Exeunt.*

[ACT V

SCENE i: *A churchyard.*]

Enter two CLOWNS° *[with spades, &c.].*

FIRST CLOWN: Is she to be buried in Christian burial when she wilfully seeks her own
    salvation?
SECOND CLOWN: I tell thee she is; therefore make her grave straight:° the crowner°
    hath sat on her, and finds it Christian burial.
FIRST CLOWN: How can that be, unless she drowned herself in her own defence?   5
SECOND CLOWN: Why, 'tis found so.
FIRST CLOWN: It must be "se offendendo";° it cannot be else. For here lies the point:
    if I drown myself wittingly,° it argues an act: and an act hath three branches;° it
    is, to act, to do, and to perform: argal,° she drowned herself wittingly.
SECOND CLOWN: Nay, but hear you, goodman delver,°—   10

---

177 indued: Endowed with qualities fitting her for living in water.   **185 trick:** Way.   **186–187
when . . . out:** When my tears are all shed, the woman in me will be satisfied.   **Act V,
Scene i.   Clowns:** The word *clown* was used to denote peasants as well as humorous characters; here applied to the rustic type of clown.   **3 straight:** Straightway, immediately; some
interpret "from east to west in a direct line, parallel with the church."   **crowner:** Coroner.   **7
"se offendendo":** For *se defendendo,* term used in verdicts of justifiable homicide.   **8 wit-
tingly:** Intentionally.   **three branches:** Parody of legal phraseology.   **9 argal:** Corruption of
ergo, therefore.   **10 delver:** Digger.

FIRST CLOWN: Give me leave. Here lies the water; good: here stands the man; good: if the man go to this water, and drown himself, it is, will he, nill he, he goes, — mark you that; but if the water come to him and drown him, he drowns not himself: argal, he that is not guilty of his own death shortens not his own life.

SECOND CLOWN: But is this law?   15

FIRST CLOWN: Ay, marry, is 't; crowner's quest° law.

SECOND CLOWN: Will you ha' the truth on 't? If this had not been a gentlewoman, she should have been buried out o' Christian burial.

FIRST CLOWN: Why, there thou say'st:° and the more pity that great folk should have countenance° in this world to drown or hang themselves, more than their even°   20 Christian. Come, my spade. There is no ancient gentlemen but gardeners, ditchers, and grave-makers: they hold up° Adam's profession.

SECOND CLOWN: Was he a gentleman?

FIRST CLOWN: 'A was the first that ever bore arms.

SECOND CLOWN: Why, he had none.   25

FIRST CLOWN: What, art a heathen? How dost thou understand the Scripture? The Scripture says "Adam digged": could he dig without arms? I'll put another question to thee: if thou answerest me not to the purpose, confess thyself° —

SECOND CLOWN: Go to.°

FIRST CLOWN: What is he that builds stronger than either the mason, the shipwright,   30 or the carpenter?

SECOND CLOWN: The gallows-maker; for that frame outlives a thousand tenants.

FIRST CLOWN: I like thy wit well, in good faith: the gallows does well; but how does it well? it does well to those that do ill: now thou dost ill to say the gallows is built stronger than the church: argal, the gallows may do well to thee. To 't again, come.   35

SECOND CLOWN: "Who builds stronger than a mason, a shipwright, or a carpenter?"

FIRST CLOWN: Ay, tell me that, and unyoke.°

SECOND CLOWN: Marry, now I can tell.

FIRST CLOWN: To 't.

SECOND CLOWN: Mass,° I cannot tell.   40

Enter HAMLET *and* HORATIO *[at a distance].*

FIRST CLOWN: Cudgel thy brains no more about it, for your dull ass will not mend his pace with beating; and, when you are asked this question next, say "a grave-maker": the houses he makes last till doomsday. Go, get thee in, and fetch me a stoup° of liquor.   *[Exit* SECOND CLOWN.*] Song. [He digs.]*
"In youth, when I did love, did love,   45
    Methought it was very sweet,

---

16 **quest:** Inquest.   19 **there thou say'st:** That's right.   20 **countenance:** Privilege.   **even:** Fellow.   22 **hold up:** Maintain, continue.   28 **confess thyself:** "And be hanged" completes the proverb.   29 **Go to:** Perhaps, "begin," or some other form of concession.   37 **unyoke:** After this great effort you may unharness the team of your wits.   40 **Mass:** By the Mass.   44 **stoup:** Two-quart measure.

To contract—O—the time, for—a—my behove,°
O, methought, there—a—was nothing—a—meet."
HAMLET: Has this fellow no feeling of his business, that 'a sings at grave-making?
HORATIO: Custom hath made it in him a property of easiness.°   50
HAMLET: 'Tis e'en so: the hand of little employment hath the daintier sense.
FIRST CLOWN [Song]: "But age, with his stealing steps,
    Hath claw'd me in his clutch,
And hath shipped me into the land
    As if I had never been such."   [Throws up a skull.]   55
HAMLET: That skull had a tongue in it, and could sing once: how the knave jowls° it
    to the ground, as if 'twere Cain's jaw-bone,° that did the first murder! This might
    be the pate of a politician,° which this ass now o'er-reaches;° one that would
    circumvent God, might it not?
HORATIO: It might, my lord.   60
HAMLET: Or of a courtier; which could say "Good morrow, sweet lord! How dost
    thou, sweet lord?" This might be my lord such-a-one, that praised my lord such-
    a-one's horse, when he meant to beg it; might it not?
HORATIO: Ay, my lord.
HAMLET: Why, e'en so: and now my Lady Worm's; chapless,° and knocked about the   65
    mazzard° with a sexton's spade: here's fine revolution, an we had the trick to see
    't. Did these bones cost no more the breeding, but to play at loggats° with 'em?
    mine ache to think on 't.
FIRST CLOWN [Song]: "A pick-axe, and a spade, a spade,
    For and° a shrouding sheet: 70
O, a pit of clay for to be made
    For such a guest is meet."   [Throws up another skull.]
HAMLET: There's another: why may not that be the skull of a lawyer? Where be his
    quiddities° now, his quillities,° his cases, his tenures,° and his tricks? why does he
    suffer this mad knave now to knock him about the sconce° with a dirty shovel,   75
    and will not tell him of his action of battery? Hum! This fellow might be in 's
    time a great buyer of land, with his statutes, his recognizances,° his fines, his
    double vouchers,° his recoveries:° is this the fine° of his fines, and the recovery of

---

47 behove: Benefit.   **50 property of easiness:** A peculiarity that now is easy.   **56 jowls:**
Dashes.   **57 Cain's jaw-bone:** Allusion to the old tradition that Cain slew Abel with the jaw-
bone of an ass.   **58 politician:** Schemer, plotter.   **o'er-reaches:** Quibble on the literal sense
and the sense "circumvent."   **65 chapless:** Having no lower jaw.   **66 mazzard:** Head.   **67
loggats:** A game in which six sticks are thrown to lie as near as possible to a stake fixed in the
ground or block of wood on a floor.   **70 For and:** And moreover.   **74 quiddities:** Subtleties,
quibbles.   **quillities:** Verbal niceties, subtle distinctions.   **tenures:** The holding of a piece of
property or office, or the conditions or period of such holding.   **75 sconce:** Head.   **77 stat-
utes, recognizances:** Legal terms connected with the transfer of land.   **78 vouchers:** Persons
called on to warrant a tenant's title.   **recoveries:** Process for transfer of entailed estate.   **fine:**
The four uses of this word are as follows: (1) end, (2) legal process, (3) elegant, (4) small.

his recoveries, to have his fine pate full of fine dirt? will his vouchers vouch him
no more of his purchases, and double ones too, than the length and breadth of   80
a pair of indentures?° The very conveyances of his lands will scarcely lie in this
box; and must the inheritor° himself have no more, ha?

HORATIO: Not a jot more, my lord.

HAMLET: Is not parchment made of sheep-skins?

HORATIO: Ay, my lord, and of calf-skins° too.   85

HAMLET: They are sheep and calves which seek out assurance in that.°
I will speak to this fellow. Whose grave's this, sirrah?

FIRST CLOWN: Mine, sir.
[Sings.] "O, a pit of clay for to be made
     For such a guest is meet."   90

HAMLET: I think it be thine, indeed; for thou liest in 't.

FIRST CLOWN: You lie out on 't, sir, and therefore 't is not yours: for my part, I do not
     lie in 't, yet it is mine.

HAMLET: Thou dost lie in 't, to be in 't and say it is thine: 'tis for the dead, not for the
     quick; therefore thou liest.   95

FIRST CLOWN: 'Tis a quick lie, sir; 'twill away again, from me to you.

HAMLET: What man dost thou dig it for?

FIRST CLOWN: For no man, sir.

HAMLET: What woman, then?

FIRST CLOWN: For none, neither.   100

HAMLET: Who is to be buried in 't?

FIRST CLOWN: One that was a woman, sir; but, rest her soul, she's dead.

HAMLET: How absolute° the knave is! we must speak by the card,° or equivocation°
     will undo us. By the Lord, Horatio, these three years I have taken note of it; the
     age is grown so picked° that the toe of the peasant comes so near the heel of the   105
     courtier, he galls° his kibe.° How long hast thou been a grave-maker?

FIRST CLOWN: Of all the day i' the year, I came to 't that day that our last king Hamlet
     overcame Fortinbras.

HAMLET: How long is that since?

FIRST CLOWN: Cannot you tell that? every fool can tell that: it was the very day that   110
     young Hamlet was born; he that is mad, and sent into England.

HAMLET: Ay, marry, why was he sent into England?

FIRST CLOWN: Why, because 'a was mad: 'a shall recover his wits there; or, if 'a do not,
     'tis no great matter there.

HAMLET: Why?   115

FIRST CLOWN: 'Twill not be seen in him there; there the men are as mad as he.

---

81 **indentures:** Conveyances or contracts.   82 **inheritor:** Possessor, owner.   85 **calf-skins:**
Parchments.   86 **assurance in that:** Safety in legal parchments.   103 **absolute:** Positive,
decided.   **by the card:** With precision, i.e., by the mariner's card on which the points of the
compass were marked.   **equivocation:** Ambiguity in the use of terms.   105 **picked:** Refined,
fastidious.   106 **galls:** Chafes.   **kibe:** Chilblain.

HAMLET: How came he mad?

FIRST CLOWN: Very strangely, they say.

HAMLET: How strangely?

FIRST CLOWN: Faith, e'en with losing his wits. 120

HAMLET: Upon what ground?

FIRST CLOWN: Why, here in Denmark: I have been sexton here, man and boy, thirty years.°

HAMLET: How long will a man lie i' the earth ere he rot?

FIRST CLOWN: Faith, if 'a be not rotten before 'a die — as we have many pocky° corses 125 now-a-days, that will scarce hold the laying in — 'a will last you some eight year or nine year: a tanner will last you nine year.

HAMLET: Why he more than another?

FIRST CLOWN: Why, sir, his hide is so tanned with his trade, that 'a will keep out water a great while; and your water is a sore decayer of your whoreson dead body. 130 Here's a skull now hath lain you i' th' earth three and twenty years.

HAMLET: Whose was it?

FIRST CLOWN: A whoreson mad fellow's it was: whose do you think it was?

HAMLET: Nay, I know not.

FIRST CLOWN: A pestilence on him for a mad rogue! 'a poured a flagon of Rhenish on 135 my head once. This same skull, sir, was Yorick's skull, the king's jester.

HAMLET: This?

FIRST CLOWN: E'en that.

HAMLET: Let me see. *[Takes the skull.]* Alas, poor Yorick! I knew him, Horatio: a fellow of infinite jest, of most excellent fancy: he hath borne me on his back a 140 thousand times; and now, how abhorred in my imagination it is! my gorge rises at it. Here hung those lips that I have kissed I know not how oft. Where be your gibes now? your gambols? your songs? your flashes of merriment, that were wont to set the table on a roar? Not one now, to mock your own grinning? quite chap-fallen? Now get you to my lady's chamber, and tell her, let her paint an inch 145 thick, to this favour she must come; make her laugh at that. Prithee, Horatio, tell me one thing.

HORATIO: What's that, my lord?

HAMLET: Dost thou think Alexander looked o' this fashion i' the earth?

HORATIO: E'en so. 150

HAMLET: And smelt so? pah! *[Puts down the skull.]*

HORATIO: E'en so, my lord.

HAMLET: To what base uses we may return, Horatio! Why may not imagination trace the noble dust of Alexander, till 'a find it stopping a bung-hole?

HORATIO: 'Twere to consider too curiously,° to consider so. 155

HAMLET: No, faith, not a jot; but to follow him thither with modesty enough, and likelihood to lead it: as thus: Alexander died, Alexander was buried, Alexander

---

122–123 thirty years: This statement with that in lines 110–111 shows Hamlet's age to be thirty years.   **125 pocky:** Rotten, diseased.   **155 curiously:** Minutely.

returneth into dust; the dust is earth; of earth we make loam;° and why of that
loam, whereto he was converted, might they not stop a beer-barrel?

    Imperious° Cæsar, dead and turn'd to clay,   160
    Might stop a hole to keep the wind away:
    O, that that earth, which kept the world in awe,
    Should patch a wall t'expel the winter's flaw!°
But soft! but soft awhile! here comes the king,

Enter KING, QUEEN, LAERTES, *and the Corse [of* OPHELIA, *in procession, with Priest,
Lords, etc.].*

    The queen, the courtiers: who is this they follow?   165
    And with such maimed rites? This doth betoken
    The corse they follow did with desp'rate hand
    Fordo° it° own life: 'twas of some estate.
    Couch° we awhile, and mark.   *[Retiring with* HORATIO.*]*
LAERTES: What ceremony else?
HAMLET: That is Laertes,   170
    A very noble youth: mark.
LAERTES: What ceremony else?
FIRST PRIEST: Her obsequies have been as far enlarg'd°
    As we have warranty: her death was doubtful;
    And, but that great command o'ersways the order,   175
    She should in ground unsanctified have lodg'd
    Till the last trumpet; for charitable prayers,
    Shards,° flints and pebbles should be thrown on her:
    Yet here she is allow'd her virgin crants,°
    Her maiden strewments° and the bringing home   180
    Of bell and burial.°
LAERTES: Must there no more be done?
FIRST PRIEST: No more be done:
    We should profane the service of the dead
    To sing a requiem and such rest to her
    As to peace-parted° souls.
LAERTES: Lay her i' th' earth: 185
    And from her fair and unpolluted flesh
    May violets spring! I tell thee, churlish priest,

---

158 **loam:** Clay paste for brickmaking.   160 **Imperious:** Imperial.   163 **flaw:** Gust of
wind.   168 **Fordo:** Destroy. **it:** Its.   169 **Couch:** Hide, lurk.   173 **enlarg'd:** Extended,
referring to the fact that suicides are not given full burial rites.   178 **Shards:** Broken bits of
pottery.   179 **crants:** Garlands customarily hung upon the biers of unmarried women.   180
strewments: Traditional strewing of flowers.   180–181 **bringing . . . burial:** The laying to rest
of the body, to the sound of the bell.   185 **peace-parted:** Allusion to the text "Lord, now lettest
thou thy servant depart in peace."

A minist'ring angel shall my sister be,
When thou liest howling.°
HAMLET: What, the fair Ophelia!
QUEEN: Sweets to the sweet: farewell!   *[Scattering flowers.]*   190
    I hop'd thou shouldst have been my Hamlet's wife;
    I thought thy bride-bed to have deck'd, sweet maid,
    And not have strew'd thy grave.
LAERTES: O, treble woe
    Fall ten times treble on that cursed head,
    Whose wicked deed thy most ingenious sense°   195
    Depriv'd thee of! Hold off the earth awhile,
    Till I have caught her once more in mine arms: *[Leaps into the grave.]*
    Now pile your dust upon the quick and dead,
    Till of this flat a mountain you have made,
    T' o'ertop old Pelion,° or the skyish head   200
    Of blue Olympus.
HAMLET: *[Advancing]* What is he whose grief
    Bears such an emphasis? whose phrase of sorrow
    Conjures the wand'ring stars,° and makes them stand
    Like wonder-wounded hearers? This is I,
    Hamlet the Dane.   *[Leaps into the grave.]*
LAERTES: The devil take thy soul!   *[Grappling with him.]*   205
HAMLET: Thou pray'st not well.
    I prithee, take thy fingers from my throat;
    For, though I am not splenitive° and rash,
    Yet have I in me something dangerous,
    Which let thy wisdom fear: hold off thy hand.   210
KING: Pluck them asunder.
QUEEN: Hamlet, Hamlet!
ALL: Gentlemen,—
HORATIO: Good my lord, be quiet.

[The ATTENDANTS part them, and they come out of the grave.]

HAMLET: Why, I will fight with him upon this theme
    Until my eyelids will no longer wag.°
QUEEN: O my son, what theme?   215
HAMLET: I lov'd Ophelia: forty thousand brothers
    Could not, with all their quantity° of love,
    Make up my sum. What wilt thou do for her?

---

189 howling: I.e., in hell.   **195 ingenious sense:** Mind endowed with finest qualities.   **200 Pelion:** Olympus, Pelion, and Ossa are mountains in the north of Thessaly.   **203 wand'ring stars:** Planets.   **208 splenitive:** Quick-tempered.   **214 wag:** Move (not used ludicrously).   **217 quantity:** Some suggest that the word is used in a deprecatory sense (little bits, fragments).

KING: O, he is mad, Laertes.

QUEEN: For love of God, forbear° him.   220

HAMLET: 'Swounds,° show me what thou 'lt do:
    Woo 't° weep? woo 't fight? woo 't fast? woo 't tear thyself?
    Woo 't drink up eisel?° eat a crocodile?
    I'll do 't. Dost thou come here to whine?
    To outface me with leaping in her grave?   225
    Be buried quick with her, and so will I:
    And, if thou prate of mountains, let them throw
    Millions of acres on us, till our ground,
    Singeing his pate against the burning zone,°
    Make Ossa like a wart! Nay, an thou 'lt mouth,   230
    I'll rant as well as thou.

QUEEN: This is mere madness:
    And thus awhile the fit will work on him;
    Anon, as patient as the female dove.
    When that her golden couplets° are disclos'd,
    His silence will sit drooping.

HAMLET: Hear you, sir;   235
    What is the reason that you use me thus?
    I lov'd you ever: but it is no matter;
    Let Hercules himself do what he may,
    The cat will mew and dog will have his day.

KING: I pray thee, good Horatio, wait upon him.   *Exit* HAMLET *and* HORATIO.   240
    [*To* LAERTES.] Strengthen your patience in° our last night's speech;
    We'll put the matter to the present push.°
    Good Gertrude, set some watch over your son.
    This grave shall have a living° monument:
    An hour of quiet shortly shall we see;   245
    Till then, in patience our proceeding be.   *Exeunt.*

[SCENE ii: *A hall in the castle.*]

Enter HAMLET *and* HORATIO.

HAMLET: So much for this, sir: now shall you see the other;
    You do remember all the circumstance?

---

220 **forbear:** Leave alone.   221 **'Swounds:** Oath, "God's wounds."   222 **Woo 't:** Wilt thou.   223 **eisel:** Vinegar. Some editors have taken this to be the name of a river, such as the Yssel, the Weissel, or the Nile.   229 **burning zone:** Sun's orbit.   234 **golden couplets:** The pigeon lays two eggs; the young when hatched are covered with golden down.   241 **in:** By recalling.   242 **present push:** Immediate test.   244 **living:** Lasting; also refers (for Laertes's benefit) to the plot against Hamlet.

HORATIO: Remember it, my lord!

HAMLET: Sir, in my heart there was a kind of fighting,
    That would not let me sleep: methought I lay 5
    Worse than the mutines in the bilboes.° Rashly,°
    And prais'd be rashness for it, let us know,
    Our indiscretion sometime serves us well,
    When our deep plots do pall:° and that should learn us
    There's a divinity that shapes our ends, 10
    Rough-hew° them how we will,—

HORATIO: That is most certain.

HAMLET: Up from my cabin,
    My sea-gown° scarf'd about me, in the dark
    Grop'd I to find out them; had my desire,
    Finger'd° their packet, and in fine° withdrew 15
    To mine own room again; making so bold,
    My fears forgetting manners, to unseal
    Their grand commission; where I found, Horatio,—
    O royal knavery!—an exact command,
    Larded° with many several sorts of reasons 20
    Importing Denmark's health and England's too,
    With, ho! such bugs° and goblins in my life,°
    That, on the supervise,° no leisure bated,°
    No, not to stay the grinding of the axe,
    My head should be struck off.

HORATIO: Is 't possible? 25

HAMLET: Here's the commission: read it at more leisure.
    But wilt thou hear me how I did proceed?

HORATIO: I beseech you.

HAMLET: Being thus be-netted round with villanies,—
    Ere I could make a prologue to my brains, 30
    They had begun the play°—I sat me down,
    Devis'd a new commission, wrote it fair:
    I once did hold it, as our statists° do,
    A baseness to write fair° and labour'd much
    How to forget that learning, but, sir, now 35

Scene ii. 6 mutines in the bilboes: Mutineers in shackles. **Rashly:** Goes with line 12. **9 pall:** Fail. **11 Rough-hew:** Shape roughly; it may mean "bungle." **13 sea-gown:** "A sea-gown, or a coarse, high-collered, and short-sleeved gowne, reaching down to the mid-leg, and used most by seamen and saylors" (Cotgrave, quoted by Singer). **15 Finger'd:** Pilfered, filched. **in fine:** Finally. **20 Larded:** Enriched. **22 bugs:** Bugbears. **such . . . life:** Such imaginary dangers if I were allowed to live. **23 supervise:** Perusal. **leisure bated:** Delay allowed. **30–31 prologue . . . play:** I.e., before I could begin to think, my mind had made its decision. **33 statists:** Statesmen. **34 fair:** In a clear hand.

It did me yeoman's° service: wilt thou know
Th' effect of what I wrote?

HORATIO: Ay, good my lord.

HAMLET: An earnest conjuration from the king,
    As England was his faithful tributary,
    As love between them like the palm might flourish,   40
    As peace should still her wheaten garland° wear
    And stand a comma° 'tween their amities,
    And many such-like 'As'es° of great charge,°
    That, on the view and knowing of these contents,
    Without debatement further, more or less,   45
    He should the bearers put to sudden death,
    Not shriving-time° allow'd.

HORATIO: How was this seal'd?

HAMLET: Why, even in that was heaven ordinant.°
    I had my father's signet in my purse,
    Which was the model of that Danish seal;   50
    Folded the writ up in the form of th' other,
    Subscrib'd it, gave 't th' impression, plac'd it safely,
    The changeling never known. Now, the next day
    Was our sea-fight; and what to this was sequent°
    Thou know'st already.   55

HORATIO: So Guildenstern and Rosencrantz go to 't.

HAMLET: Why, man, they did make love to this employment;
    They are not near my conscience; their defeat
    Does by their own insinuation° grow:
    'Tis dangerous when the baser nature comes   60
    Between the pass° and fell incensed° points
    Of mighty opposites.

HORATIO: Why, what a king is this!

HAMLET: Does it not, think thee, stand° me now upon—
    He that hath kill'd my king and whor'd my mother,
    Popp'd in between th' election° and my hopes,   65
    Thrown out his angle° for my proper life,
    And with such coz'nage°—is 't not perfect conscience,

---

36 **yeoman's:** I.e., faithful.   41 **wheaten garland:** Symbol of peace.   42 **comma:** Smallest break
or separation. Here, *amity* begins and *amity* ends the period, and *peace* stands between like a
dependent clause. The comma indicates continuity, link.   43 **'As'es:** The "whereases" of a formal document, with play on the word *ass*.   **charge:** Import, and burden.   47 **shriving-time:**
Time for absolution.   48 **ordinant:** Directing.   54 **sequent:** Subsequent.   59 **insinuation:**
Interference.   61 **pass:** Thrust.   **fell incensed:** Fiercely angered.   63 **stand:** Become incum-
bent.   65 **election:** The Danish throne was filled by election.   66 **angle:** Fishing line.   67
coz'nage: Trickery.

To quit° him with this arm? and is 't not to be damn'd,
To let this canker° of our nature come
In further evil? 70
HORATIO: It must be shortly known to him from England
What is the issue of the business there.
HAMLET: It will be short: the interim is mine;
And a man's life's no more than to say "One."
But I am very sorry, good Horatio, 75
That to Laertes I forgot myself;
For, by the image of my cause, I see
The portraiture of his: I'll court his favours:
But, sure, the bravery° of his grief did put me
Into a tow'ring passion.
HORATIO: Peace! who comes here? 80

Enter a COURTIER *[*OSRIC*].*

OSRIC: Your lordship is right welcome back to Denmark.
HAMLET: I humbly thank you, sir. *[To* HORATIO.*]* Dost know this water-fly?°
HORATIO: No, my good lord.
HAMLET: Thy state is the more gracious; for 'tis a vice to know him. He hath much
land, and fertile: let a beast be lord of beasts,° and his crib shall stand at the king's 85
mess:° 'tis a chough;° but, as I say, spacious in the possession of dirt.
OSRIC: Sweet lord, if your lordship were at leisure, I should impart a thing to you
from his majesty.
HAMLET: I will receive it, sir, with all diligence of spirit. Put your bonnet to his right
use; 'tis for the head. 90
OSRIC: I thank your lordship, it is very hot.
HAMLET: No, believe me, 'tis very cold; the wind is northerly.
OSRIC: It is indifferent° cold, my lord, indeed.
HAMLET: But yet methinks it is very sultry and hot for my complexion.
OSRIC: Exceedingly, my lord; it is very sultry,—as 'twere,—I cannot tell how. But, 95
my lord, his majesty bade me signify to you that 'a has laid a great wager on your
head: sir, this is the matter,—
HAMLET: I beseech you, remember°—

*[*HAMLET *moves him to put on his hat.]*
OSRIC: Nay, good my lord; for mine ease,° in good faith. Sir, here is newly come to
court Laertes; believe me, an absolute gentleman, full of most excellent differences, 100

---

68 quit: Repay. **69 canker:** Ulcer, or possibly the worm which destroys buds and leaves. **79
bravery:** Bravado. **82 water-fly:** Vain or busily idle person. **85 lord of beasts:** See Genesis
1:26, 28. **85–86 his crib . . . mess:** He shall eat at the king's table and be one of the group
of persons (usually four) constituting a *mess* at a banquet. **86 chough:** Probably, chattering
jackdaw; also explained as *chuff*, provincial boor or churl. **93 indifferent:** Somewhat. **98
remember:** I.e., remember thy courtesy; conventional phrase for "Be covered." **99 mine ease:**
Conventional reply declining the invitation of "Remember thy courtesy."

of very soft° society and great showing:° indeed, to speak feelingly° of him, he is the card° or calendar of gentry,° for you shall find in him the continent of what part a gentleman would see.

HAMLET: Sir, his definement° suffers no perdition° in you; though, I know, to divide him inventorially° would dozy° the arithmetic of memory, and yet but yaw° neither, in respect of his quick sail. But, in the verity of extolment, I take him to be a soul of great article;° and his infusion° of such dearth and rareness,° as, to make true diction of him, his semblable° is his mirror; and who else would trace° him, his umbrage,° nothing more. 105

OSRIC: Your lordship speaks most infallibly of him. 110

HAMLET: The concernancy,° sir? why do we wrap the gentleman in our more rawer breath?°

OSRIC: Sir?

HORATIO [aside to HAMLET]: Is 't not possible to understand in another tongue?° You will do 't, sir, really. 115

HAMLET: What imports the nomination° of this gentleman?

OSRIC: Of Laertes?

HORATIO [aside to HAMLET]: His purse is empty already; all 's golden words are spent.

HAMLET: Of him, sir. 120

OSRIC: I know you are not ignorant—

HAMLET: I would you did, sir; yet, in faith, if you did, it would not much approve° me. Well, sir?

OSRIC: You are not ignorant of what excellence Laertes is—

HAMLET: I dare not confess that, lest I should compare with him in excellence; but, to know a man well, were to know himself.° 125

OSRIC: I mean, sir, for his weapon; but in the imputation° laid on him by them, in his meed° he's unfellowed.

HAMLET: What's his weapon?

OSRIC: Rapier and dagger. 130

HAMLET: That's two of his weapons: but, well.

OSRIC: The king, sir, hath wagered with him six Barbary horses: against the which he has impawned,° as I take it, six French rapiers and poniards, with their

---

101 **soft:** Gentle.   **showing:** Distinguished appearance.   **feelingly:** With just perception.   **102 card:** Chart, map.   **gentry:** Good breeding.   **104 definement:** Definition.   **perdition:** Loss, diminution.   **104–105 divide him inventorially:** I.e., enumerate his graces.   **105 dozy:** Dizzy.   **yaw:** To move unsteadily (of a ship).   **107 article:** Moment or importance.   **infusion:** Infused temperament, character imparted by nature.   **dearth and rareness:** Rarity.   **108 semblable:** True likeness.   **trace:** Follow.   **109 umbrage:** Shadow.   **111 concernancy:** Import.   **112 breath:** Speech.   **114 Is 't . . . tongue?:** I.e., can one converse with Osric only in this outlandish jargon?   **116 nomination:** Naming.   **122 approve:** Command.   **125–126 but . . . himself:** But to know a man as excellent were to know Laertes.   **127 imputation:** Reputation.   **128 meed:** Merit.   **133 he has impawned:** He has wagered.

assigns, as girdle, hangers,° and so: three of the carriages, in faith, are very dear
to fancy,° very responsive° to the hilts, most delicate° carriages, and of very   135
liberal conceit.°

HAMLET: What call you the carriages?

HORATIO [aside to HAMLET]: I knew you must be edified by the margent° ere you
had done.

OSRIC: The carriages, sir, are the hangers.   140

HAMLET: The phrase would be more german° to the matter, if we could carry cannon by our sides: I would it might be hangers till then. But, on: six Barbary
horses against six French swords, their assigns, and three liberal-conceited
carriages; that's the French bet against the Danish. Why is this "impawned," as
you call it?   145

OSRIC: The king, sir, hath laid, that in a dozen passes between yourself and him, he
shall not exceed you three hits: he hath laid on twelve for nine; and it would
come to immediate trial, if your lordship would vouchsafe the answer.

HAMLET: How if I answer "no"?

OSRIC: I mean, my lord, the opposition of your person in trial.   150

HAMLET: Sir, I will walk here in the hall: if it please his majesty, it is the breathing
time° of day with me; let the foils be brought, the gentleman willing, and the
king hold his purpose, I will win for him as I can; if not, I will gain nothing but
my shame and the odd hits.

OSRIC: Shall I re-deliver you e'en so?   155

HAMLET: To this effect, sir; after what flourish your nature will.

OSRIC: I commend my duty to your lordship.

HAMLET: Yours, yours. [Exit OSRIC.] He does well to commend it himself; there are
no tongues else for 's turn.

HORATIO: This lapwing° runs away with the shell on his head.   160

HAMLET: 'A did comply, sir, with his dug,° before 'a sucked it. Thus has he—and
many more of the same breed that I know the drossy° age dotes on—only got
the tune° of the time and out of an habit of encounter;° a kind of yesty° collection, which carries them through and through the most fann'd and winnowed°
opinions; and do but blow them to their trial, the bubbles are out.°   165

Enter a LORD.

---

134 hangers: Straps on the sword belt from which the sword hung.   **134–135 dear to fancy:**
Fancifully made.   **135 responsive:** Probably, well balanced, corresponding closely.   **delicate:**
Fine in workmanship.   **136 liberal conceit:** Elaborate design.   **138 margent:** Margin of a
book, place for explanatory notes. **141 german:** Germane, appropriate.   **151–152 breathing
time:** Exercise period.   **160 lapwing:** Peewit; noted for its wiliness in drawing a visitor away
from its nest and its supposed habit of running about when newly hatched with its head in
the shell; possibly an allusion to Osric's hat.   **161 did comply . . . dug:** Paid compliments to
his mother's breast.   **162 drossy:** Frivolous.   **163 tune:** Temper, mood.   **habit of encounter:** Demeanor of social intercourse.   **yesty:** Frothy.   **164 fann'd and winnowed:** Select and
refined.   **165 blow . . . out:** I.e., put them to the test, and their ignorance is exposed.

LORD: My lord, his majesty commended him to you by young Osric, who brings back to him, that you attend him in the hall: he sends to know if your pleasure hold to play with Laertes, or that you will take longer time.

HAMLET: I am constant to my purposes; they follow the king's pleasure: if his fitness speaks, mine is ready; now or whensoever, provided I be so able as now.   170

LORD: The king and queen and all are coming down.

HAMLET: In happy time.°

LORD: The queen desires you to use some gentle entertainment to Laertes before you fall to play.

HAMLET: She well instructs me.   *[Exit* LORD.*]*   175

HORATIO: You will lose this wager, my lord.

HAMLET: I do not think so; since he went into France, I have been in continual practice; I shall win at the odds. But thou wouldst not think how ill all 's here about my heart: but it is no matter.

HORATIO: Nay, good my lord,—   180

HAMLET: It is but foolery; but it is such a kind of gain-giving,° as would perhaps trouble a woman.

HORATIO: If your mind dislike any thing, obey it: I will forestall their repair hither, and say you are not fit.

HAMLET: Not a whit, we defy augury: there's a special providence in the fall of a spar-   185
row. If it be now, 'tis not to come; if it be not to come, it will be now; if it be not now, yet it will come: the readiness is all:° since no man of aught he leaves knows, what is 't to leave betimes? Let be.

A table prepared. [Enter] TRUMPETS, DRUMS, *and* OFFICERS *with cushions;* KING, QUEEN, *[*OSRIC,*] and all the* STATE; *foils, daggers, [and wine borne in;] and* LAERTES.

KING: Come, Hamlet, come, and take this hand from me.

[The KING *puts* LAERTES's *hand into* HAMLET's.*]*

HAMLET: Give me your pardon, sir: I have done you wrong;   190
        But pardon 't as you are a gentleman.
        This presence° knows,
        And you must needs have heard, how I am punish'd
        With a sore distraction. What I have done,
        That might your nature, honour and exception°   195
        Roughly awake, I here proclaim was madness.
        Was 't Hamlet wrong'd Laertes? Never Hamlet:
        If Hamlet from himself be ta'en away,
        And when he's not himself does wrong Laertes,
        Then Hamlet does it not, Hamlet denies it.   200
        Who does it, then? His madness: if 't be so,

---

172 In happy time: A phrase of courtesy.   **181 gain-giving:** Misgiving.   **187 all:** All that matters.   **192 presence:** Royal assembly.   **195 exception:** Disapproval.

Hamlet is of the faction that is wrong'd;
His madness is poor Hamlet's enemy.
Sir, in this audience,
Let my disclaiming from a purpos'd evil   205
Free me so far in your most generous thoughts,
That I have shot mine arrow o'er the house,
And hurt my brother.
LAERTES: I am satisfied in nature,°
Whose motive, in this case, should stir me most
To my revenge: but in my terms of honour   210
I stand aloof; and will no reconcilement,
Till by some elder masters, of known honour,
I have a voice° and precedent of peace,
To keep my name ungor'd. But till that time,
I do receive your offer'd love like love,   215
And will not wrong it.
HAMLET: I embrace it freely;
And will this brother's wager frankly play.
Give us the foils. Come on.
LAERTES: Come, one for me.
HAMLET: I'll be your foil,° Laertes: in mine ignorance
Your skill shall, like a star i' th' darkest night,   220
Stick fiery off° indeed.
LAERTES: You mock me, sir.
HAMLET: No, by this hand.
KING: Give them the foils, young Osric. Cousin Hamlet,
You know the wager?
HAMLET: Very well, my lord;
Your grace has laid the odds o' th' weaker side.   225
KING: I do not fear it; I have seen you both:
But since he is better'd, we have therefore odds.
LAERTES: This is too heavy, let me see another.
HAMLET: This likes me well. These foils have all a length?

[They prepare to play.]

OSRIC: Ay, my good lord.
KING: Set me the stoups of wine upon that table.   230
If Hamlet give the first or second hit,

---

208 nature: I.e., he is personally satisfied, but his honor must be satisfied by the rules of the code of honor.   **213 voice:** Authoritative pronouncement.   **219 foil:** Quibble on the two senses: "background which sets something off" and "blunted rapier for fencing."   **221 Stick fiery off:** Stand out brilliantly.

Or quit in answer of the third exchange,
Let all the battlements their ordnance fire;
The king shall drink to Hamlet's better breath; 235
And in the cup an union° shall he throw,
Richer than that which four successive kings
In Denmark's crown have worn. Give me the cups;
And let the kettle° to the trumpet speak,
The trumpet to the cannoneer without, 240
The cannons to the heavens, the heavens to earth,
"Now the king drinks to Hamlet." Come begin: *Trumpets the while.*
And you, the judges, bear a wary eye.
HAMLET: Come on, sir.
LAERTES: Come, my lord.   *[They play.]*
HAMLET: One.
LAERTES: No.
HAMLET: Judgement.
OSRIC: A hit, a very palpable hit.

Drum, trumpets, and shot. Flourish. A piece goes off.

LAERTES: Well; again. 245
KING: Stay; give me drink. Hamlet, this pearl° is thine;
    Here's to thy health. Give him the cup.
HAMLET: I'll play this bout first; set it by awhile.
    Come. *[They play.]* Another hit; what say you?
LAERTES: A touch, a touch, I do confess 't. 250
KING: Our son shall win.
QUEEN: He's fat,° and scant of breath.
    Here, Hamlet, take my napkin, rub thy brows:
    The queen carouses° to thy fortune, Hamlet.
HAMLET: Good madam!
KING: Gertrude, do not drink.
QUEEN: I will, my lord; I pray you, pardon me.   *[Drinks.]* 255
KING *[aside]*: It is the poison'd cup: it is too late.
HAMLET: I dare not drink yet, madam; by and by.
QUEEN: Come, let me wipe thy face.
LAERTES: My lord, I'll hit him now.
KING: I do not think 't.
LAERTES *[aside]*: And yet 'tis almost 'gainst my conscience. 260

---

236 union: Pearl.   **239 kettle:** Kettledrum.   **246 pearl:** I.e., the poison.   **251 fat:** Not physically fit, out of training. Some earlier editors speculated that the term applied to the corpulence of Richard Burbage, who originally played the part, but the allusion now appears unlikely. Fat may also suggest "sweaty."   **253 carouses:** Drinks a toast.

HAMLET: Come, for the third, Laertes: you but dally;
I pray you, pass with your best violence;
I am afeard you make a wanton° of me.
LAERTES: Say you so? come on.   *[They play.]*
OSRIC: Nothing, neither way.   265
LAERTES: Have at you now!

*[*LAERTES *wounds* HAMLET; *then, in scuffling, they change rapiers,° and* HAMLET *wounds* LAERTES.*]*

KING: Part them; they are incens'd.
HAMLET: Nay, come again.   *[The* QUEEN *falls.]*
OSRIC: Look to the queen there, ho!
HORATIO: They bleed on both sides. How is it, my lord?
OSRIC: How is 't, Laertes?
LAERTES: Why, as a woodcock° to mine own springe,° Osric;   270
I am justly kill'd with mine own treachery.
HAMLET: How does the queen?
KING: She swounds° to see them bleed.
QUEEN: No, no, the drink, the drink,—O my dear Hamlet,—
The drink, the drink! I am poison'd.   *[Dies.]*
HAMLET: O villany! Ho! let the door be lock'd: 275
Treachery! Seek it out.   *[*LAERTES *falls.]*
LAERTES: It is here, Hamlet: Hamlet, thou art slain;
No med'cine in the world can do thee good;
In thee there is not half an hour of life;
The treacherous instrument is in thy hand,   280
Unbated° and envenom'd: the foul practice
Hath turn'd itself on me; lo, here I lie,
Never to rise again: thy mother's poison'd:
I can no more: the king, the king's to blame.
HAMLET: The point envenom'd too!   285
Then, venom, to thy work.   *[Stabs the* KING.*]*
ALL: Treason! treason!
KING: O, yet defend me, friends; I am but hurt.
HAMLET: Here, thou incestuous, murd'rous, damned Dane,
Drink off this potion. Is thy union here?   290
Follow my mother.   *[*KING *dies.]*
LAERTES: He is justly serv'd;
It is a poison temper'd° by himself.

---

263 **wanton:** Spoiled child.   [**s. d.**] **in scuffling, they change rapiers:** According to a widespread stage tradition, Hamlet receives a scratch, realizes that Laertes's sword is unbated, and accordingly forces an exchange.   270 **woodcock:** As type of stupidity or as decoy.   **springe:** Trap, snare.   272 **swounds:** Swoons.   281 **Unbated:** Not blunted with a button.   292 **temper'd:** Mixed.

Exchange forgiveness with me, noble Hamlet:
Mine and my father's death come not upon thee,
Nor thine on me! *[Dies.]* 295

HAMLET: Heaven make thee free of it! I follow thee.
I am dead, Horatio. Wretched queen, adieu!
You that look pale and tremble at this chance,
That are but mutes° or audience to this act,
Had I but time—as this fell sergeant,° Death, 300
Is strict in his arrest—O, I could tell you—
But let it be. Horatio, I am dead;
Thou livest; report me and my cause aright
To the unsatisfied.

HORATIO: Never believe it:
I am more an antique Roman° than a Dane: 305
Here 's yet some liquor left.

HAMLET: As th' art a man,
Give me the cup: let go, by heaven, I'll ha 't.
O God! Horatio, what a wounded name,
Things standing thus unknown, shall live behind me!
If thou didst ever hold me in thy heart, 310
Absent thee from felicity awhile,
And in this harsh world draw thy breath in pain,
To tell my story.   *A march afar off.*
                    What warlike noise is this?

OSRIC: Young Fortinbras, with conquest come from Poland,
To the ambassadors of England gives 315
This warlike volley.

HAMLET: O, I die, Horatio;
The potent poison quite o'er-crows° my spirit:
I cannot live to hear the news from England;
But I do prophesy th' election lights
On Fortinbras: he has my dying voice; 320
So tell him, with th' occurrents,° more and less,
Which have solicited.° The rest is silence. *[Dies.]*

HORATIO: Now cracks a noble heart. Good night, sweet prince;
And flights of angels sing thee to thy rest!
Why does the drum come hither? *[March within.]* 325

Enter FORTINBRAS, *with the [English]* AMBASSADORS *[and others].*

FORTINBRAS: Where is this sight?

---

299 mutes: Performers in a play who speak no words.   **300 sergeant:** Sheriff's officer.   **305 Roman:** It was the Roman custom to follow masters in death.   **317 o'er-crows:** Triumphs over.   **321 occurrents:** Events, incidents.   **322 solicited:** Moved, urged.

HORATIO: What is it you would see?
   If aught of woe or wonder, cease your search.
FORTINBRAS: This quarry° cries on havoc.° O proud Death,
   What feast is toward in thine eternal cell,
   That thou so many princes at a shot   330
   So bloodily hast struck?
FIRST AMBASSADOR: The sight is dismal;
   And our affairs from England come too late:
   The ears are senseless that should give us hearing,
   To tell him his commandment is fulfill'd,
   That Rosencrantz and Guildenstern are dead: 335
   Where should we have our thanks?
HORATIO: Not from his mouth,°
   Had it th' ability of life to thank you:
   He never gave commandment for their death.
   But since, so jump° upon this bloody question,°
   You from the Polack wars, and you from England,   340
   Are here arriv'd, give order that these bodies
   High on a stage° be placed to the view;
   And let me speak to th' yet unknowing world
   How these things came about: so shall you hear
   Of carnal, bloody, and unnatural acts,   345
   Of accidental judgements, casual slaughters,
   Of deaths put on by cunning and forc'd cause,
   And, in this upshot, purposes mistook
   Fall'n on th' inventors' heads: all this can I
   Truly deliver.
FORTINBRAS: Let us haste to hear it,   350
   And call the noblest to the audience.
   For me, with sorrow I embrace my fortune:
   I have some rights of memory° in this kingdom,
   Which now to claim my vantage doth invite me.
HORATIO: Of that I shall have also cause to speak,   355
   And from his mouth whose voice will draw on more:°
   But let this same be presently perform'd,
   Even while men's minds are wild; lest more mischance,
   On° plots and errors, happen.
FORTINBRAS: Let four captains
   Bear Hamlet, like a soldier, to the stage;   360

---

328 quarry: Heap of dead.   **cries on havoc:** Proclaims a general slaughter.   **336 his mouth:** I.e., the king's.   **339 jump:** Precisely.   **question:** Dispute.   **342 stage:** Platform.   **353 of memory:** Traditional, remembered.   **356 voice . . . more:** Vote will influence still others.   **359 On:** On account of, or possibly, on top of, in addition to.

For he was likely, had he been put on,
To have prov'd most royal: and, for his passage,°
The soldiers' music and the rites of war
Speak loudly for him.
Take up the bodies: such a sight as this   365
Becomes the field,° but here shows much amiss.
Go, bid the soldiers shoot.

Exeunt [marching, bearing off the dead bodies; after which a peal of ordnance is shot off].

[c. 1600]

Questions for Discussion

1. What is the political situation in Denmark as the play begins? What information does Horatio provide beginning in line 79 of the opening scene? What further information do we learn from Claudius's speech that begins scene ii?

2. How does Shakespeare characterize Horatio in the opening scenes? What are some of his chief qualities? How does Hamlet characterize Claudius? How does Hamlet compare Horatio and Claudius?

3. What does Hamlet's first soliloquy (I.ii.129–59) reveal about his state of mind? What is the source of his discontent?

4. What is the basis for both Laertes's and Polonius's objections to Ophelia's relationship with Hamlet? Which of their arguments seem most (and least) persuasive or fair? What does their treatment of Ophelia in act I, scene iii, reveal about their motivations? What does it suggest about their attitude toward Ophelia and toward women in general? How does class or station function in their arguments?

5. What do we learn from the Ghost in act I, scene v? If what he says is true, how does that reinforce what we have learned about the political situation in Denmark? How does Hamlet respond to the Ghost's instructions? What does he mean by saying, "O my prophetic soul!" (I.v.40)?

6. After listening to the Ghost speak, Hamlet wants to write about it, as indicated in act I, scene v, lines 107 and 108. How does this contrast with his remarks earlier in this speech? What does it suggest about his state of mind?

7. Why do you think Hamlet tells his companions he is likely to put on an "antic disposition" (I.v.172)? Is his behavior a deliberate strategy or a natural reaction to his anger and grief? Explain.

8. Compare the way Hamlet responds to Polonius in act II, scene ii, lines 171–210, with how he responds to his friends Rosencrantz and Guildenstern in lines 215–90. What do you learn about Hamlet from these responses?

---

362 passage: Death.   366 field: I.e., of battle.

9. In act III, scene i, lines 56–90, Hamlet delivers his famous "To be, or not to be" speech, arguably the most recognized passage in English literature. What is he contemplating? What inner conflict is he pondering? What conclusions does he reach?

10. Following his "To be, or not to be" soliloquy (III.i.56–90), why does Hamlet treat Ophelia so harshly? How does Ophelia describe Hamlet in lines 141–52? What does this description suggest about Hamlet before the time of the play? What does it suggest about the relationship between Hamlet and Ophelia?

11. What does the scene with the players (II.ii.367–472) reveal about Hamlet? How does the First Player's speech (II.ii.404–33) parallel Hamlet's situation?

12. Hamlet's speech to the players at the beginning of act III, scene ii, has often been interpreted as a sort of aside from Shakespeare containing his philosophy of acting. How else can it be interpreted? How do Hamlet's instructions tie in to some of the themes of the play?

13. In act III, scene iii, lines 73–96, Hamlet has a perfect opportunity to kill his uncle and avenge his murdered father. Instead, he makes a speech. Why does he hesitate in killing Claudius? Do you think we are meant to respect his piety or despise his cowardice? If you combine this incident with Hamlet's soliloquy at the end of act II, does it reveal something about Hamlet? about a theme of the play?

14. In act II, scene ii, lines 236–37, Hamlet says, "Why, then, 'tis none to you; for there is nothing either good or bad, but thinking makes it so." What assumptions underline Hamlet's response? What does he mean? Do you agree with what he says? He then says to his old friends, "I am but mad north-north-west: when the wind is southerly I know a hawk from a handsaw" (II.ii.330–31). What does this remark suggest about Hamlet's madness, about his "antic disposition" (I.v.172)? Is he mad? Is he acting? Explain.

15. Why do you think the Ghost is visible to Horatio and the guards in act I, scenes i and iv, but not to Gertrude in act III, scene iv? Does the murder of Polonius in this scene make you reassess whether the Ghost is in fact a demon, and not the ghost of Hamlet's father?

16. What has driven Ophelia mad in act IV, scene v? What does her behavior suggest about the relationship between her and Hamlet? Cite specific lines to support your answer.

17. How does Laertes respond to his father's death? to Ophelia's? How do his responses compare to Hamlet's reaction to the death of *his* father?

18. Hamlet seems preoccupied with death for much of the play; what new insight does the graveyard scene (V.i.) reveal regarding his attitude toward mortality? toward life, fame, and accomplishment? How does this attitude connect to his central conflict in the play?

19. Why does Hamlet give his dying support to Fortinbras (V.ii.316–22)?

Questions on Style and Structure

1. The opening scene presents a great number of questions. How do these contribute to the mood of the scene and, ultimately, of the play itself?

2. Hamlet's first three lines (I.ii.65, 67, 74) are evasive answers using puns or other wordplay. What does this behavior reveal about his character and his state of mind?

3. How would you describe Claudius's opening speech (I.ii.1–39) and his reply to Hamlet (I.ii.87–117)? What does his use of imagery and juxtaposition in the first speech reveal about his purpose? What is the nature of his argument in the second?

4. How does the diction and imagery in the Ghost's speech to Hamlet (I.v.42–91) create a comparison between the two "gardens" before and after the entrance of the "serpents"?

5. In lines 270–282 of act II, scene ii, Hamlet delivers a lengthy explanation to Rosencrantz and Guildenstern, ending with a rhetorical question. What is the substance of this speech? How does the imagery that Hamlet uses transition his speech from an assessment of himself to that of mankind as a whole?

6. The king's aside in act III, scene i, lines 49–54, is the first definitive evidence of his guilt. Structurally, why do you think this revelation takes place halfway through the play as opposed to earlier (or later)?

7. Notice Hamlet's behavior toward Ophelia in act III, scene i. Why do you think—in dramatic, structural, and thematic terms—we have not observed a scene between Hamlet and Ophelia until this point?

8. In act II, scene i, Polonius says, "By indirections find directions out" (l. 64). What does he mean by that? How does such a comment reveal his character? Find another such witty or clever remark by another character, and explain how it reveals the character of its speaker.

9. Hamlet's four soliloquies (I.ii.129–59; II.ii.474–533; III.i.56–90; IV.iv.32–66) are remarkable for their style as well as their substance. Choose one of these monologues and discuss how its diction, figurative language, and imagery contribute to Hamlet's meaning and purpose.

10. Shakespeare occasionally gives two characters very similar lines or phrasings, the second instance reminding the reader or viewer of the first. In act IV, scene iv, for example, Hamlet wonders if he might be "thinking too precisely on th' event" (l. 41). In act V, scene i, Horatio says to Hamlet, "'Twere to consider too curiously, to consider so" (l. 155). What is the effect of these types of echoes throughout the play?

11. Do a close reading of one of Ophelia's songs in act IV, scene v, exploring how its form and content relate and respond to the action of the play (both actual and implied) and to Ophelia's state of mind. In your response, consider what has occurred offstage, as well as the possible or implied events to which she alludes. Why is she given song, as opposed to speech, in this instance?

Suggestions for Writing

1. In *Hamlet*, as vengeance is applied, order is restored—or is it? Write an essay that discusses the symmetry at the end of the play, explaining how the plot of *Hamlet*

makes an argument for or against revenge. Support your thesis with specific textual evidence.

2. While there are only two major female characters in *Hamlet*—Gertrude and Ophelia—they both play crucial roles. Write an essay in which you explain the importance of each of these women to the play, especially in terms of her relationship to Hamlet.

3. Recognize the immense importance of diction in *Hamlet* by making note of each instance of certain kinds of words. First, note words having to do with *appearances*, such as *play, act, seem, assume, show, reveal, appear, form, shape*, and *like* (for comparison), as well as references to *pictures, images, mirrors, faces*, and the like; then note references to clothing and fashion, such as *investments, trappings, suits*, and *fashion*, as well as references to *watching* and *spying* throughout the play. Through diction and the imagery it creates, trace the contrast between appearance and reality throughout the play, and write an essay explaining how that motif contributes to the meaning of the play as a whole.

4. Critic Northrop Frye has said that *Hamlet* is Shakespeare's longest play because everyone in it (with the exceptions of Gertrude and Ophelia) "talks too much." Despite the calls to be brief from both the Ghost and Polonius, the characters do go on at length, and Hamlet certainly has a lot to say. Write an essay in which you explore why this play, for much of its length, focuses more on conversation and reflection than on action—and why this, in your opinion, contributes to a theme of the play. Support your position with textual evidence.

5. In *The Prince*, a Renaissance text from 1532, Niccolò Machiavelli writes:

> A prince ought to be a fox in recognizing snares and a lion in driving off wolves. Those who assume the bearing of a lion alone lack understanding. It follows, then, that a wise prince cannot and should not keep his pledge when it is against his interest to do so and when his reasons for making the pledge are no longer operative. . . . But one must know how to mask this [fox-like] nature skillfully and be a great dissembler.

In an essay, explore how both Hamlet and Claudius act in accordance with this advice. How do their tactics differ?

6. References to the macrocosm and the microcosm suggest that the same forces are at work within as without. In the play, man is seen as a little world at the center of the world at large, where veins are rivers, and Hamlet speaks of his "distracted globe" (I.v.97). Find other references that reflect the presence of the macrocosm and the microcosm, and discuss their effect on the meaning of the play as a whole.

7. Consider the many conflicts in the play—for example, those between reason and passion, order and chaos, concealing and revealing, and honesty and deception. Choose one, and write an essay explaining how that conflict reveals a dominant theme of the play.

8. Hamlet's conversation with Rosencrantz and Guildenstern in act II, scene ii, contains a misunderstanding or disagreement surrounding the word *dream*; when Hamlet tells them he has had "bad dreams," Guildenstern equivocates *dream* with

ambition (ll. 242–43). Write an essay in which you explore how this or other disagreements over meaning exacerbate the central conflicts of the play.

9. One interpretation of Hamlet's indecision involves the influence of multiple distracting events or motivations, which either directly delay him or confuse him to the point that he forgets his purpose. In an essay, explore how other characters in the play fall victim to distraction. Refer to specific incidents in the play, quoting from the text to support your essay.

10. The "To be, or not to be" soliloquy in act III, scene i (ll. 56–90) is perhaps the most famous monologue in the English language, yet its meaning is much debated. Write a close-analysis essay in which you interpret the speech. Consider Hamlet's prior soliloquy at the end of act II, scene ii; is this monologue a continuation of that scene, or a separate line of thought? Is Hamlet aware of his audience (Claudius and Polonius, hidden behind a tapestry), or is he speaking to himself on the assumption that he is alone?

The Book of the Dead

EDWIDGE DANTICAT

 Born in Haiti in 1969, Edwidge Danticat immigrated to the United States when she was twelve and currently lives in Miami. She received her BA from Barnard College and her MFA from Brown University, where her thesis project became her first novel, *Breath, Eyes, Memory* (1994), which was an Oprah Winfrey Book Club selection in 1998. Her other fiction includes *Krik? Krak!* (1995), *The Farming of Bones* (1998), and *The Dew Breaker* (2004). Danticat has also written nonfiction: *After the Dance: A Walk through Carnival in Jacmel, Haiti* (2002) and *Brother, I'm Dying*, an autobiography that won the 2007 National Book Critics Circle Award. She is the author of two children's books, *Behind the Mountains* (2002) and *Anacaona, Golden Flower* (2005), and the editor of *The Butterfly's Way: Voices from the Haitian Diaspora in the United States* (2001). Danticat has worked with filmmaker Jonathan Demme on several documentaries related to Haiti. "The Book of the Dead" is the first in a series of seven interrelated stories in *The Dew Breaker*. Dew breakers were Haitian militiamen, or Tonton Macoutes, who carried out the tyrannical policies of dictator François Duvalier in Haiti during the 1960s. They were called dew breakers because they usually struck at dawn.

M y father is gone. I'm slouched in a cast-aluminum chair across from two men, one the manager of the hotel where we're staying and the other a policeman. They're both waiting for me to explain what's become of him, my father.

The hotel manager — MR. FLAVIO SALINAS, the plaque on his office door reads — has the most striking pair of chartreuse eyes I've ever seen on a man with an island Spanish lilt to his voice.

The police officer, Officer Bo, is a baby-faced, short, white Floridian with a potbelly.

"Where are you and your daddy from, Ms. Bienaimé?" Officer Bo asks, doing the best he can with my last name. He does such a lousy job that, even though he and I and Salinas are the only people in Salinas' office, at first I think he's talking to someone else.

I was born and raised in East Flatbush, Brooklyn, and have never even been to   5
my parents' birthplace. Still, I answer "Haiti" because it is one more thing I've always longed to have in common with my parents.

Officer Bo plows forward with, "You all the way down here in Lakeland from Haiti?"

"We live in New York," I say. "We were on our way to Tampa."

"To do what?" Officer Bo continues. "Visit?"

"To deliver a sculpture." I say. "I'm an artist, a sculptor."

I'm really not an artist, not in the way I'd like to be. I'm more of an obsessive   10
wood-carver with a single subject thus far—my father.

My creative eye finds Manager Salinas' office gaudy. The walls are covered with
orange-and-green wallpaper, briefly interrupted by a giant gold-leaf–bordered print
of a Victorian cottage that resembles the building we're in.

Patting his light green tie, which brings out even more the hallucinatory shade of
his eyes, Manager Salinas reassuringly tells me, "Officer Bo and I will do our best."

We start out with a brief description of my father: "Sixty-five, five feet eight
inches, one hundred and eighty pounds, with a widow's peak, thinning salt-and-
pepper hair, and velvet-brown eyes—"

"Velvet?" Officer Bo interrupts.

"Deep brown, same color as his complexion," I explain.   15

My father has had partial frontal dentures since he fell off his and my mother's
bed and landed on his face ten years ago when he was having one of his prison nightmares. I mention that too. Just the dentures, not the nightmares. I also bring up the
blunt, ropelike scar that runs from my father's right cheek down to the corner of his
mouth, the only visible reminder of the year he spent in prison in Haiti.

"Please don't be offended by what I'm about to ask," Officer Bo says. "I deal with
an older population here, and this is something that comes up a lot when they go
missing. Does your daddy have any kind of mental illness, senility?"

I reply, "No, he's not senile."

"You have any pictures of your daddy?" Officer Bo asks.

My father has never liked having his picture taken. We have only a few of him at   20
home, some awkward shots at my different school graduations, with him standing
between my mother and me, his hand covering his scar. I had hoped to take some
pictures of him on this trip, but he hadn't let me. At one of the rest stops I bought a
disposable camera and pointed it at him anyway. As usual, he protested, covering his
face with both hands like a little boy protecting his cheeks from a slap. He didn't want
any more pictures taken of him for the rest of his life, he said, he was feeling too ugly.

"That's too bad," Officer Bo offers at the end of my too lengthy explanation. "He
speaks English, your daddy? Can he ask for directions, et cetera?"

"Yes," I say.

"Is there anything that might make your father run away from you, particularly
here in Lakeland?" Manager Salinas asks. "Did you two have a fight?"

I had never tried to tell my father's story in words before now, but my first completed sculpture of him was the reason for our trip: a three-foot mahogany figure of
my father naked, kneeling on a half-foot-square base, his back arched like the curve
of a crescent moon, his downcast eyes fixed on his very long fingers and the large
palms of his hands. It was hardly revolutionary, rough and not too detailed, minimalist at best, but it was my favorite of all my attempted representations of my father. It
was the way I had imagined him in prison.

The last time I had seen my father? The previous night, before falling asleep. When   25
we pulled our rental car into the hotel's hedge-bordered parking lot, it was almost

midnight. All the restaurants in the area were closed. There was nothing to do but shower and go to bed.

"It's like paradise here," my father had said when he'd seen our tiny room. It had the same orange-and-green wallpaper as Salinas' office, and the plush emerald carpet matched the walls. "Look, Ka," he said, his deep, raspy voice muted with exhaustion, "the carpet is like grass under our feet."

He'd picked the bed closest to the bathroom, removed the top of his gray jogging suit, and unpacked his toiletries. Soon after, I heard him humming loudly, as he always did, in the shower.

I checked on the sculpture, just felt it a little bit through the bubble padding and carton wrapping to make sure it was still whole. I'd used a piece of mahogany that was naturally flawed, with a few superficial cracks along what was now the back. I'd thought these cracks beautiful and had made no effort to sand or polish them away, as they seemed like the wood's own scars, like the one my father had on his face. But I was also a little worried about the cracks. Would they seem amateurish and unintentional, like a mistake? Could the wood come apart with simple movements or with age? Would the client be satisfied?

I closed my eyes and tried to picture the client to whom I was delivering the sculpture: Gabrielle Fonteneau, a Haitian American woman about my age, the star of a popular television series and an avid art collector. My friend Céline Benoit, a former colleague at the junior high school where I'm a substitute art teacher, had grown up with Gabrielle Fonteneau in Tampa and, at my request, on a holiday visit home had shown Gabrielle Fonteneau a snapshot of my *Father* piece and had persuaded her to buy it.

Gabrielle Fonteneau was spending the week away from Hollywood at her parents' house in Tampa. I took some time off, and both my mother and I figured that my father, who watched a lot of television, both at home and at his Nostrand Avenue barbershop, would enjoy meeting Gabrielle Fonteneau too. But when I woke up, my father was gone and so was the sculpture.   30

I stepped out of the room and onto the balcony overlooking the parking lot. It was a hot and muggy morning, the humid air laden with the smell of the freshly mowed tropical grass and sprinkler-showered hibiscus bordering the parking lot. My rental car too was gone. I hoped my father was driving around trying to find us some breakfast and would explain when he got back why he'd taken the sculpture with him, so I got dressed and waited. I watched a half hour of local morning news, smoked five mentholated cigarettes even though we were in a nonsmoking room, and waited some more.

All that waiting took two hours, and I felt guilty for having held back so long before going to the front desk to ask, "Have you seen my father?"

I feel Officer Bo's fingers gently stroking my wrist, perhaps to tell me to stop talking. Up close Officer Bo smells like fried eggs and gasoline, like breakfast at the Amoco.

"I'll put the word out with the other boys," he says. "Salinas here will be in his office. Why don't you go on back to your hotel room in case your daddy shows up there?"

Back in the room, I lie in my father's unmade bed. The sheets smell like his cologne,   35
an odd mix of lavender and lime that I've always thought too pungent, but that he likes nonetheless.

I jump up when I hear the click from the electronic key in the door. It's the maid. She's a young Cuban woman who is overly polite, making up for her lack of English with deferential gestures: a great big smile, a nod, even a bow as she backs out of the room. She reminds me of my mother when she has to work on non-Haitian clients at her beauty shop, how she pays much more attention to those clients, forcing herself to laugh at jokes she barely understands and smiling at insults she doesn't quite grasp, all to avoid being forced into a conversation, knowing she couldn't hold up her end very well.

It's almost noon when I pick up the phone and call my mother at the salon. One of her employees tells me that she's not yet returned from the Mass she attends every day. After the Mass, if she has clients waiting, she'll walk the twenty blocks from the church to the salon. If she has no appointments, then she'll let her workers handle the walk-ins and go home for lunch. This was as close to retirement as my mother would ever come. This routine was her dream when she first started the shop. She had always wanted a life with room for daily Mass and long walks and the option of sometimes not going to work.

I call my parents' house. My mother isn't there either, so I leave the hotel number on the machine.

"Please call as soon as you can, Manman," I say. "It's about Papa."

It's early afternoon when my mother calls back, her voice cracking with worry. I had 40 been sitting in that tiny hotel room, eating chips and candy bars from the vending machines, chain-smoking and waiting for something to happen, either for my father, Officer Bo, or Manager Salinas to walk into the room with some terrible news or for my mother or Gabrielle Fonteneau to call. I took turns imagining my mother screaming hysterically, berating both herself and me for thinking this trip with my father a good idea, then envisioning Gabrielle Fonteneau calling to say that we shouldn't have come on the trip. It had all been a joke. She wasn't going to buy a sculpture from me after all, especially one I didn't have.

"Where Papa?" Just as I expected, my mother sounds as though she's gasping for breath. I tell her to calm down, that nothing bad has happened. Papa's okay. I've just lost sight of him for a little while.

"How you lost him?" she asks.

"He got up before I did and disappeared," I say.

"How long he been gone?"

I can tell she's pacing back and forth in the kitchen, her slippers flapping against 45 the Mexican tiles. I can hear the faucet when she turns it on, imagine her pushing a glass underneath it and filling it up. I hear her sipping the water as I say, "He's been gone for hours now. I don't even believe it myself."

"You call police?"

Now she's probably sitting at the kitchen table, her eyes closed, her fingers sliding back and forth across her forehead. She clicks her tongue and starts humming one of those mournful songs from the Mass, songs that my father, who attends church only at Christmas, picks up from her and also hums to himself in the shower.

My mother stops humming just long enough to ask, "What the police say?"

"To wait, that he'll come back."

There's a loud tapping on the line, my mother thumping her fingers against the   50
phone's mouthpiece; it gives me a slight ache in my ear.

"He come back," she says with more certainty than either Officer Bo or Manager Salinas. "He not leave you like that."

I promise to call my mother hourly with an update, but I know she'll call me sooner than that, so I dial Gabrielle Fonteneau's cell phone. Gabrielle Fonteneau's voice sounds just as it does on television, but more silken, nuanced, and seductive without the sitcom laugh track.

"To think," my father once said while watching her show, in which she plays a smart-mouthed nurse in an inner-city hospital's maternity ward. "A Haitian-born actress with her own American television show. We have really come far."

"So nice of you to come all this way to personally deliver the sculpture," Gabrielle Fonteneau says. She sounds like she's in a place with cicadas, waterfalls, palm trees, and citronella candles to keep the mosquitoes away. I realize that I too am in such a place, but I'm not able to enjoy it.

"Were you told why I like this sculpture so much?" Gabrielle Fonteneau asks. "It's   55
regal and humble at the same time. It reminds me of my own father."

I hadn't been trying to delve into the universal world of fathers, but I'm glad my sculpture reminds Gabrielle Fonteneau of her father, for I'm not beyond the spontaneous fanaticism inspired by famous people, whose breezy declarations seem to carry so much more weight than those of ordinary mortals. I still had trouble believing I had Gabrielle Fonteneau's cell number, which Céline Benoit had made me promise not to share with anyone else, not even my father.

My thoughts are drifting from Gabrielle Fonteneau's father to mine when I hear her say, "So when will you get here? You have the directions, right? Maybe you can join us for lunch tomorrow, at around twelve."

"We'll be there," I say.

But I'm no longer so certain.

My father loves museums. When he's not working at his barbershop, he's often at the   60
Brooklyn Museum. The Ancient Egyptian rooms are his favorites.

"The Egyptians, they was like us," he likes to say. The Egyptians worshiped their gods in many forms, fought among themselves, and were often ruled by foreigners. The pharaohs were like the dictators he had fled, and their queens were as beautiful as Gabrielle Fonteneau. But what he admires most about the Ancient Egyptians is the way they mourn their dead.

"They know how to grieve," he'd say, marveling at the mummification process that went on for weeks but resulted in corpses that survived thousands of years.

My whole adult life, I have struggled to find the proper manner of sculpting my father, a quiet and distant man who only came alive while standing with me most of the

Saturday mornings of my childhood, mesmerized by the golden masks, the shawabtis, and the schist tablets, Isis, Nefertiti, and Osiris, the jackal-headed ruler of the underworld.

The sun is setting and my mother has called more than a dozen times when my father finally appears in the hotel room doorway. He looks like a much younger man and appears calm and rested, as if bronzed after a long day at the beach.

"Too smoky in here," he says.

65

I point to my makeshift ashtray, a Dixie cup filled with tobacco-dyed water and cigarette butts.

"Ka, let your father talk to you." He fans the smoky air with his hands, walks over to the bed, and bends down to unlace his sneakers. "Yon ti koze, a little chat."

"Where were you?" I feel my eyelids twitching, a nervous reaction I inherited from my epileptic mother. "Why didn't you leave a note? And Papa, where is the sculpture?"

"That is why we must chat," he says, pulling off his sand-filled sneakers and rubbing the soles of his large, calloused feet each in turn. "I have objections."

He's silent for a long time, concentrating on his foot massage, as though he'd been looking forward to it all day.

70

"I'd prefer you not sell that statue," he says at last. Then he turns away, picks up the phone, and calls my mother.

"I know she called you," he says to her in Creole. "She panicked. I was just walking, thinking."

I hear my mother loudly scolding him, telling him not to leave me again. When he hangs up, he grabs his sneakers and puts them back on.

"Where's the sculpture?" My eyes are twitching so badly now I can barely see.

"We go," he says. "I take you to it."

75

We walk out to the parking lot, where the hotel sprinkler is once more at work, spouting water onto the grass and hedges like centrifugal rain. The streetlights are on now, looking brighter and brighter as the dusk deepens around them. New hotel guests are arriving. Others are leaving for dinner, talking loudly as they walk to their cars.

As my father maneuvers our car out of the parking lot, I tell myself that he might be ill, mentally ill, even though I'd never detected any signs of it before, beyond his prison nightmares.

When I was eight years old and my father had the measles for the first time in his life, I overheard him say to a customer on the phone, "Maybe serious. Doctor tell me, at my age, measles can kill."

This was the first time I realized that my father could die. I looked up the word "kill" in every dictionary and encyclopedia at school, trying to understand what it really meant, that my father could be eradicated from my life.

My father stops the car on the side of the highway near a man-made lake, one of those marvels of the modern tropical city, with curved stone benches surrounding a

80

stagnant body of water. There's scant light to see by except a half-moon. Stomping the well-manicured grass, my father heads toward one of the benches. I sit down next to him, letting my hands dangle between my legs.

Here I am a little girl again, on some outing with my father, like his trips to the botanic garden or the zoo or the Egyptian statues at the museum. Again, I'm there simply because he wants me to be. I knew I was supposed to learn something from these childhood outings, but it took me years to realize that ultimately my father was doing his best to be like other fathers, to share as much of himself with me as he could.

I glance over at the lake. It's muddy and dark, and there are some very large pink fishes bobbing back and forth near the surface, looking as though they want to leap out and trade places with us.

"Is this where the sculpture is?" I ask.

"In the water," he says.

"Okay," I say calmly. But I know I'm already defeated. I know the piece is already   85
lost. The cracks have probably taken in so much water that the wood has split into several chunks and plunged to the bottom. All I can think of saying is something glib, something I'm not even sure my father will understand.

"Please know this about yourself," I say. "You're a very harsh critic."

My father attempts to smother a smile. He scratches his chin and the scar on the side of his face, but says nothing. In this light the usually chiseled and embossed-looking scar appears deeper than usual, yet somehow less threatening, like a dimple that's spread out too far.

Anger is a wasted emotion, I've always thought. My parents would complain to each other about unjust politics in New York, but they never got angry at my grades, at all the Cs I got in everything but art classes, at my not eating my vegetables or occasionally vomiting my daily spoonful of cod-liver oil. Ordinary anger, I've always thought, is useless. But now I'm deeply angry. I want to hit my father, beat the craziness out of his head.

"Ka," he says, "I tell you why I named you Ka."

Yes, he'd told me, many, many times before. Now does not seem like a good time   90
to remind me, but maybe he's hoping it will calm me, keep me from hating him for the rest of my life.

"Your mother not like the name at all," he says. "She say everybody tease you, people take pleasure repeating your name, calling you Kaka, Kaka, Kaka."

This too I had heard before.

"Okay," I interrupt him with a quick wave of my hands. "I've got it."

"I call you Ka," he says, "because in Egyptian world—"

A ka is a double of the body, I want to complete the sentence for him—the   95
body's companion through life and after life. It guides the body through the kingdom of the dead. That's what I tell my students when I overhear them referring to me as Teacher Kaka.

"You see, ka is like soul," my father now says. "In Haiti is what we call good angel, ti bon anj. When you born, I look at your face, I think, here is my ka, my good angel."

I'm softening a bit. Hearing my father call me his good angel is the point at which I often stop being apathetic.

"I say rest in Creole," he prefaces, "because my tongue too heavy in English to say things like this, especially older things."

"Fine," I reply defiantly in English.

"Ka," he continues in Creole, "when I first saw your statue, I wanted to be buried   100
with it, to take it with me into the other world."

"Like the Ancient Egyptians," I continue in English.

He smiles, grateful, I think, that in spite of everything, I can still appreciate his passions.

"Ka," he says, "when I read to you, with my very bad accent, from *The Book of the Dead*, do you remember how I made you read some chapters to me too?"

But this recollection is harder for me to embrace. I had been terribly bored by *The Book of the Dead*. The images of dead hearts being placed on scales and souls traveling aimlessly down fiery underground rivers had given me my own nightmares. It had seemed selfish of him not to ask me what I wanted to listen to before going to bed, what I wanted to read and have read to me. But since he'd recovered from the measles and hadn't died as we'd both feared, I'd vowed to myself to always tolerate, even indulge him, letting him take me places I didn't enjoy and read me things I cared nothing about, simply to witness the joy they gave him, the kind of bliss that might keep a dying person alive. But maybe he wasn't going to be alive for long. Maybe this is what *this* outing is about. Perhaps my "statue," as he called it, is a sacrificial offering, the final one that he and I would make together before he was gone.

"Are you dying?" I ask my father. It's the one explanation that would make   105
what he's done seem insignificant or even logical. "Are you ill? Are you going to die?"

What would I do now, if this were true? I'd find him the best doctor, move back home with him and my mother. I'd get a serious job, find a boyfriend, and get married, and I'd never complain again about his having dumped my sculpture in the lake.

Like me, my father tends to be silent a moment too long during an important conversation and then say too much when less should be said. I listen to the wailing of crickets and cicadas, though I can't tell where they're coming from. There's the highway, and the cars racing by, the half-moon, the lake dug up from the depths of the ground—with my sculpture now at the bottom of it, the allée of royal palms whose shadows intermingle with the giant fishes on the surface of that lake, and there is me and my father.

"Do you recall the judgment of the dead," my father speaks up at last, "when the heart of a person is put on a scale? If it's heavy, the heart, then this person cannot enter the other world."

It is a testament to my upbringing, and perhaps the Kaka and good angel story has something to do with this as well, that I remain silent now, at this particular time.

"I don't deserve a statue," my father says. But at this very instant he does look   110
like one, like the Madonna of humility, contemplating her losses in the dust, or an
Ancient Egyptian funerary priest, kneeling with his hands prayerfully folded on
his lap.

"Ka," he says, "when I took you to the Brooklyn Museum, I would stand there for
hours admiring them. But all you noticed was how there were pieces missing from
them, eyes, noses, legs, sometimes even heads. You always noticed more what was not
there than what was."

Of course, this way of looking at things was why I ultimately began sculpting
in the first place, to make statues that would amaze my father even more than these
ancient relics.

"Ka, I am like one of those statues," he says.

"An Ancient Egyptian?" I hear echoes of my loud, derisive laugh only after I've
been laughing for a while. It's the only weapon I have now, the only way I know to
take my revenge on my father.

"Don't do that," he says, frowning, irritated, almost shouting over my laughter.   115
"Why do that? If you are mad, let yourself be mad. Why do you always laugh like a
clown when you are angry?"

I tend to wave my hands about wildly when I laugh, but I don't notice I'm doing
that now until he reaches over to grab them. I quickly move them away, but he ends
up catching my right wrist, the same wrist Officer Bo had stroked earlier to make me
shut up. My father holds on to it so tightly now that I feel his fingers crushing the
bone, almost splitting it apart, and I can't laugh anymore.

"Let go," I say, and he releases my wrist quickly. He looks down at his own fingers, then lowers his hand to his lap.

My wrist is still throbbing. I keep stroking it to relieve some of the pain. It's the
ache there that makes me want to cry more than anything, not so much this sudden,
uncharacteristic flash of anger from my father.

"I'm sorry," he says. "I did not want to hurt you. I did not want to hurt anyone."

I keep rubbing my wrist, hoping he'll feel even sorrier, even guiltier for grabbing   120
me so hard, but even more for throwing away my work.

"Ka, I don't deserve a statue," he says again, this time much more slowly, "not a
whole one, at least. You see, Ka, your father was the hunter, he was not the prey."

I stop stroking my wrist, sensing something coming that might hurt much more.
He's silent again. I don't want to prod him, feed him any cues, urge him to speak, but
finally I get tired of the silence and feel I have no choice but to ask, "What are you
talking about?"

I immediately regret the question. Is he going to explain why he and my mother
have no close friends, why they've never had anyone over to the house, why they
never speak of any relatives in Haiti or anywhere else, or have never returned there
or, even after I learned Creole from them, have never taught me anything else about
the country beyond what I could find out on my own, on the television, in newspapers, in books? Is he about to tell me why Manman is so pious? Why she goes to
daily Mass? I am not sure I want to know anything more than the little they've chosen

to share with me all these years, but it is clear to me that he needs to tell me, has been trying to for a long time.

"We have a proverb," he continues. "One day for the hunter, one day for the prey. Ka, your father was the hunter, he was not the prey."

Each word is now hard-won as it leaves my father's mouth, balanced like those   125
hearts on the Ancient Egyptian scales.

"Ka, I was never in prison," he says.

"Okay," I say, sounding like I am fourteen again, chanting from what my mother used to call the meaningless adolescent chorus, just to sound like everyone else my age.

"I was working in the prison," my father says. And I decide not to interrupt him again until he's done.

Stranded in the middle of this speech now, he has to go on. "It was one of the prisoners inside the prison who cut my face in this way," he says.

My father now points to the long, pitted scar on his right cheek. I am so used to   130
his hands covering it up that this new purposeful motion toward it seems dramatic and extreme, almost like raising a veil.

"This man who cut my face," he continues, "I shot and killed him, like I killed many people."

I'm amazed that he managed to say all of this in one breath, like a monologue. I wish I too had had some rehearsal time, a chance to have learned what to say in response.

There is no time yet, no space in my brain to allow for whatever my mother might have to confess. Was she huntress or prey? A thirty-year-plus disciple of my father's coercive persuasion? She'd kept to herself even more than he had, like someone who was nurturing a great pain that she could never speak about. Yet she had done her best to be a good mother to me, taking charge of feeding and clothing me and making sure my hair was always combed, leaving only what she must have considered my intellectual development to my father.

When I was younger, she'd taken me to Mass with her on Sundays. Was I supposed to have been praying for my father all that time, the father who was the hunter and not the prey?

I think back to "The Negative Confession" ritual from *The Book of the Dead*, a   135
ceremony that was supposed to take place before the weighing of hearts, giving the dead a chance to affirm that they'd done only good things in their lifetime. It was one of the chapters my father read to me most often. Now he was telling me I should have heard something beyond what he was reading. I should have removed the negatives.

"I am not a violent man," he had read. "I have made no one weep. I have never been angry without cause. I have never uttered any lies. I have never slain any men or women. I have done no evil."

And just so I will be absolutely certain of what I'd heard, I ask my father, "And those nightmares you were always having, what were they?"

"Of what I," he says, "your father, did to others."

Another image of my mother now fills my head, of her as a young woman, a woman my age, taking my father in her arms. At what point did she decide that she loved him? When did she know that she was supposed to have despised him?

"Does Manman know?" I ask.

"Yes," he says. "I explained, after you were born."

I am the one who drives the short distance back to the hotel. The ride seems drawn out, the cars in front of us appear to be dawdling. I honk impatiently, even when everyone except me is driving at a normal speed. My father is silent, not even telling me, as he has always done whenever he's been my passenger, to calm down, to be careful, to take my time.

As we are pulling into the hotel parking lot, I realize that I haven't notified Officer Bo and Manager Salinas that my father has been found. I decide that I will call them from my room. Then, before we leave the car, my father says, "Ka, no matter what, I'm still your father, still your mother's husband. I would never do these things now."

And this to me is as meaningful a declaration as his other confession. It was my first inkling that maybe my father was wrong in his own representation of his former life, that maybe his past offered more choices than being either hunter or prey.

When we get back to the hotel room, I find messages from both Officer Bo and Manager Salinas. Their shifts are over, but I leave word informing them that my father has returned.

While I'm on the phone, my father slips into the bathroom and runs the shower at full force. He is not humming.

When it seems he's never coming out, I call my mother at home in Brooklyn.

"Manman, how do you love him?" I whisper into the phone.

My mother is clicking her tongue and tapping her fingers against the mouthpiece again. Her soft tone makes me think I have awakened her from her sleep.

"He tell you?" she asks.

"Yes," I say.

"Everything?"

"Is there more?"

"What he told you he want to tell you for long time," she says, "you, his good angel."

It has always amazed me how much my mother and father echo each other, in their speech, their actions, even in their businesses. I wonder how much more alike they could possibly be. But why shouldn't they be alike? Like all parents, they were a society of two, sharing a series of private codes and associations, a past that even if I'd been born in the country of their birth, I still wouldn't have known, couldn't have known, thoroughly. I was a part of them. Some might say I belonged to them. But I wasn't them.

"I don't know, Ka." My mother is whispering now, as though there's a chance she might also be overheard by my father. "You and me, we save him. When I meet him, it made him stop hurt the people. This how I see it. He a seed thrown in rock. You, me, we make him take root."

As my mother is speaking, this feeling comes over me that I sometimes have when I'm carving, this sensation that my hands don't belong to me at all, that something else besides my brain and muscles is moving my fingers, something bigger and stronger than myself, an invisible puppetmaster over whom I have no control. I feel as though it's this same puppetmaster that now forces me to lower the phone and hang up, in midconversation, on my mother.

As soon as I put the phone down, I tell myself that I could continue this particular conversation at will, in a few minutes, a few hours, a few days, even a few years. Whenever I'm ready.

My father walks back into the room, his thinning hair wet, his pajamas on. My mother does not call me back. Somehow she must know that she has betrayed me by not sharing my confusion and, on some level, my feeling that my life could have gone on fine without my knowing these types of things about my father.

When I get up the next morning, my father's already dressed. He's sitting on the edge 160 of the bed, his head bowed, his face buried in his palms, his forehead shadowed by his fingers. If I were sculpting him at this moment, I would carve a praying mantis, crouching motionless, seeming to pray, while actually waiting to strike.

With his back to me now, my father says, "Will you call that actress and tell her we have it no more, the statue?"

"We were invited to lunch there," I say. "I believe we should go and tell her in person."

He raises his shoulders and shrugs.

"Up to you," he says.

We start out for Gabrielle Fonteneau's house after breakfast. It's not quite as hot as 165 the previous morning, but it's getting there. I crank up the AC at full blast, making it almost impossible for us to have a conversation, even if we wanted to.

The drive seems longer than the twenty-four hours it took to get to Lakeland from New York. I quickly grow tired of the fake lakes, the fenced-in canals, the citrus groves, the fan-shaped travelers' palms, the highway so imposingly neat. My father turns his face away from me and takes in the tropical landscape, as though he will never see it again. I know he's enjoying the live oaks with Spanish moss and bromeliads growing in their shade, the yellow trumpet flowers and flame vines, the tamarinds and jacaranda trees we speed by, because he expressed his admiration for them before, on the first half of our journey.

As we approach Gabrielle Fonteneau's house, my father breaks the silence in the car by saying, "Now you see, Ka, why your mother and me, we have never returned home."

The Fonteneaus' house is made of bricks and white coral, on a cul-de-sac with a row of banyans separating the two sides of the street.

My father and I get out of the car and follow a concrete path to the front door. Before we can knock, an older woman appears in the doorway. It's Gabrielle

Fonteneau's mother. She resembles Gabrielle Fonteneau, or the way Gabrielle looks on television, with stunning almond eyes, skin the color of sorrel and spiraling curls brushing the sides of her face.

"We've been looking out for you," she says with a broad smile.   170

When Gabrielle's father joins her in the doorway, I realize where Gabrielle Fonteneau gets her height. He's more than six feet tall.

Mr. Fonteneau extends his hands, first to my father and then to me. They're relatively small, half the size of my father's.

We move slowly through the living room, which has a cathedral ceiling and walls covered with Haitian paintings with subjects ranging from market scenes and first communions to weddings and wakes. Most remarkable is a life-size portrait of Gabrielle Fonteneau sitting on a canopy-covered bench in what seems like her parents' garden.

Out on the back terrace, which towers over a nursery of azaleas, hibiscus, dracaenas, and lemongrass, a table is set for lunch.

Mr. Fonteneau asks my father where he is from in Haiti, and my father lies. In   175
the past, I thought he always said he was from a different province each time because he'd really lived in all of those places, but I realize now that he says this to reduce the possibility of anyone identifying him, even though thirty-seven years and a thinning head of widow-peaked salt-and-pepper hair shield him from the threat of immediate recognition.

When Gabrielle Fonteneau makes her entrance, in an off-the-shoulder ruby dress, my father and I both rise from our seats.

"Gabrielle," she coos, extending her hand to my father, who leans forward and kisses it before spontaneously blurting out, "My dear, you are one of the most splendid flowers of Haiti."

Gabrielle Fonteneau looks a bit flustered. She tilts her head coyly and turns toward me.

"Welcome," she says.

During the meal of conch, fried plantains, and mushroom rice, Mr. Fonteneau tries   180
to draw my father into conversation by asking him, in Creole, when he was last in Haiti.

"Thirty-seven years," my father answers with a mouthful of food.

"No going back for you?" asks Mrs. Fonteneau.

"I have not yet had the opportunity," my father replies.

"We go back every year," says Mrs. Fonteneau, "to a beautiful place overlooking the ocean, in the mountains of Jacmel."

"Have you ever been to Jacmel?" Gabrielle Fonteneau asks me.   185

I shake my head no.

"We're fortunate," Mrs. Fonteneau says, "that we have a place to go where we can say the rain is sweeter, the dust is lighter, our beaches prettier."

"So now we are tasting rain and weighing dust?" Mr. Fonteneau says and laughs.

"There's nothing like drinking the sweet juice from a coconut fetched from your own tree." Mrs. Fonteneau's eyes are lit up now as she puts her fork down to better paint the picture for us. She's giddy, her voice grows louder and higher, and even her daughter is absorbed, smiling and recollecting with her mother.

"There's nothing like sinking your hand in sand from the beach in your own   190
country," Mrs. Fonteneau is saying. "It's a wonderful feeling, wonderful."

I imagine my father's nightmares. Maybe he dreams of dipping his hands in the sand on a beach in his own country and finding that what he comes up with is a fistful of blood.

After lunch, my father asks if he can have a closer look at the Fonteneaus' garden. While he's taking the tour, I make my confession about the sculpture to Gabrielle Fonteneau.

She frowns as she listens, fidgeting, shifting her weight from one foot to the other, as though she's greatly annoyed that so much of her valuable time had been so carelessly squandered on me. Perhaps she's wondering if this was just an elaborate scheme to meet her, perhaps she wants us out of her house as quickly as possible.

"I don't usually have people come into my house like this," she says, "I prom-ise you."

"I appreciate it," I say. "I'm grateful for your trust and I didn't mean to violate it."   195

"I guess if you don't have it, then you don't have it," she says. "But I'm very dis-appointed. I really wanted to give that piece to my father."

"I'm sorry," I say.

"I should have known something was off," she says, looking around the room, as if for something more interesting to concentrate on. "Usually when people come here to sell us art, first of all they're always carrying it with them and they always show it to us right away. But since you know Céline I overlooked that."

"There was a sculpture," I say, aware of how stupid my excuse was going to sound. "My father didn't like it, and he threw it away."

She raises her perfectly arched eyebrows, as if out of concern for my father's   200
sanity, or for my own. Or maybe it's another indirect signal that she now wants us out of her sight.

"We're done, then," she says, looking directly at my face. "I have to make a call. Enjoy the rest of your day."

Gabrielle Fonteneau excuses herself, disappearing behind a closed door. Through the terrace overlooking the garden, I see her parents guiding my father along rows of lemongrass. I want to call Gabrielle Fonteneau back and promise her that I will make her another sculpture, but I can't. I don't know that I will be able to work on anything for some time. I have lost my subject, the prisoner father I loved as well as pitied.

In the garden Mr. Fonteneau snaps a few sprigs of lemongrass from one of the plants, puts them in a plastic bag that Mrs. Fonteneau is holding. Mrs. Fonteneau hands the bag of lemongrass to my father.

Watching my father accept with a nod of thanks, I remember the chapter "Driving Back Slaughters" from *The Book of the Dead*, which my father sometimes read to me to drive away my fear of imagined monsters. It was a chapter full of terrible lines like "My mouth is the keeper of both speech and silence. I am the child who travels the roads of yesterday, the one who has been wrought from his eye."

I wave to my father in the garden to signal that we should leave now, and he slowly comes toward me, the Fonteneaus trailing behind him. 205

With each step forward, he rubs the scar on the side of his face, and out of a strange reflex I scratch my face in the same spot.

Maybe the last person my father harmed had dreamed moments like this into my father's future, strangers seeing that scar furrowed into his face and taking turns staring at it and avoiding it, forcing him to conceal it with his hands, pretend it's not there, or make up some lie about it, to explain.

Out on the sidewalk in front of the Fonteneaus' house, before we both take our places in the car, my father and I wave good-bye to Gabrielle Fonteneau's parents, who are standing in their doorway. Even though I'm not sure they understood the purpose of our visit, they were more than kind, treating us as though we were old friends of their daughter's, which maybe they had mistaken us for.

As the Fonteneaus turn their backs to us and close their front door, I look over at my father, who's still smiling and waving. When he smiles the scar shrinks and nearly disappears into the folds of his cheek, which used to make me wish he would never stop smiling.

Once the Fonteneaus are out of sight, my father reaches down on his lap and strokes 210 the plastic bag with the lemongrass the Fonteneaus had given him. The car is already beginning to smell too much like lemongrass, like air freshener overkill.

"What will you use that for?" I ask.

"To make tea," he says, "for Manman and me."

I pull the car away from the Fonteneaus' curb, dreading the rest stops, the gas station, the midway hotels ahead for us. I wish my mother were here now, talking to us about some miracle she'd just heard about in a sermon at the Mass. I wish my sculpture were still in the trunk. I wish I hadn't met Gabrielle Fonteneau, that I still had that to look forward to somewhere else, sometime in the future. I wish I could give my father whatever he'd been seeking in telling me his secret. But my father, if anyone could, must have already understood that confessions do not lighten living hearts.

I had always thought that my father's only ordeal was that he'd left his country and moved to a place where everything from the climate to the language was so unlike his own, a place where he never quite seemed to fit in, never appeared to belong. The only thing I can grasp now, as I drive way beyond the speed limit down yet another highway, is why the unfamiliar might have been so comforting, rather than distressing, to my father. And why he has never wanted the person he was, is, permanently documented in any way. He taught himself to appreciate the enormous weight of permanent markers by learning about the Ancient Egyptians. He had gotten to know them, through their crypts and monuments, in a way that he wanted no one to know him, no one except my mother and me, we, who are now his kas, his good angels, his masks against his own face.

[2004]

Questions for Discussion

1. Danticat does not name the Tonton Macoutes or refer to François Duvalier in her story, yet this background is essential to the dew breaker's life in Haiti as well as in the United States. Why isn't Danticat more explicit about the historical context?

2. How do you interpret the title of the story? How does it both refer to the ancient Egyptian *Book of the Dead* and go beyond that reference? Why is Ka's father drawn to this culture?

3. Ka's father offers one explanation for why he destroyed her sculpture. Do you believe him? What are other possible explanations for his action?

4. Ka has a somewhat different relationship with her mother than she does with her father. How would you characterize each of these relationships? Do you think it would have mattered to Ka if her mother rather than her father had revealed to her his past as "hunter" rather than "prey"? Explain your answer.

5. How much does Ka's mother know about her husband? Is it significant that he told her about his past after they were married and had their daughter?

6. Once her father has revealed his secret identity to her, Ka immediately turns to thoughts of her mother: "There is no time yet, no space in my brain to allow for whatever my mother might have to confess. Was she huntress or prey?" (para. 133). Why does Ka shift to her mother before responding to her father in either words or thoughts?

7. How has Ka's relationship with her father changed by the end of the story? Explain whether you believe she will forgive him. Even if she does, do you think it will impact their relationship? Do you think she would rather not have known about his past?

8. Will Ka do another sculpture of her father in the future? If you think not, explain your reasoning. If you think so, explain what you think the sculpture might look like.

9. Ka says that her father, "if anyone could, must have already understood that confessions do not lighten living hearts" (para. 213). Why does she think he would understand this? And if he does understand this, why does he reveal his past to her?

10. Who are the victimizers and who are the victims in this story? Is such a classification appropriate or even possible under these circumstances?

11. Danticat poses powerful questions about blame, guilt, forgiveness, healing, and redemption in "The Book of the Dead." Is she arguing that Ka should forgive her father? Has he forgiven himself? Does forgiveness—by his daughter or his

wife or even himself—mean that he is not morally culpable for his actions as a young man?

Questions on Style and Structure

1. "The Book of the Dead" opens with the simple sentence, "My father is gone." How is this sentence explained, echoed, and explored throughout the story?
2. Why do you think Danticat chose to tell this story through Ka rather than through her father or an omniscient narrator who might have revealed the feelings of Ka, her mother, and her father?
3. What elements of mystery are present in the story? As the story begins, Ka is trying to locate her father, who has gone missing. When do you realize that he has not been hurt, taken ill, or become the victim of a violent crime but that he has left on his own? Is this an effective way to begin the story, or do you think it is misleading? What are some of the clues Ka has about her father's identity? What information about her parents and the way the family lives in New York changes meaning when Ka learns about her father's past in Haiti?
4. When her father reveals his past, he begins by referring to himself in the first person ("I don't deserve a statue"), then shifts to the third person ("your father was the hunter, he was not the prey") (para. 121). Why? What does that change in perspective suggest?
5. Ka describes the material she chose for her sculpture: "a piece of mahogany that was naturally flawed, with a few superficial cracks along what was now the back. I'd thought these cracks beautiful and had made no effort to sand or polish them away, as they seemed like the wood's own scars, like the one my father had on his face" (para. 28). What does this passage suggest about Ka's intuition about her father? What does it suggest about her ability to accept imperfection? Has her father tried to "polish away" his own scars up until this point?
6. What is the function of the minor characters of Gabrielle Fonteneau and her parents? How does Danticat weave them into the structure of the story, and how do they contribute to the development of the story's themes? As you explore their role, ask yourself why Danticat did not simply structure the story so that Ka and her father chose not to visit the Fonteneaus' after the sculpture was destroyed.
7. In an interview in *The Caribbean Writer*, Danticat talks about silence:

   > Silence is at the core of a story like this, just as it is during the dictatorship. There's so much you're not allowed to say. The Duvaliers silenced—by killing a whole generation and stunning many of the survivors into silence. . . . Migration also silences you. You're in a country where you don't speak the language, don't know the names of things, so there is a silencing there as well . . . [yet] that these characters tell their stories in different ways, to the reader, to other people, breaks that silence.

   Discuss the role of silence and voice in "The Book of the Dead," paying special attention to who chooses to speak and when, and the use of Haitian Creole in exchanges between Ka and her parents.

8. What does Ka mean when she thinks back to "The Negative Confession" ritual from *The Book of the Dead*: "Now he was telling me I should have heard something beyond what he was reading. I should have removed the negatives" (para. 135)?

9. After his confession, her father assures Ka that "no matter what, I'm still your father, still your mother's husband. I would never do these things now" (para. 143). Why does she think that this statement "is as meaningful a declaration as his other confession" (para. 144)? What does she mean when she thinks, "It was my first inkling that maybe my father was wrong in his own representation of his former life, that maybe his past offered more choices than being either hunter or prey" (para. 144)?

10. Who or what is the "puppetmaster" in paragraph 157 in which Ka describes how she feels when talking to her mother about her father's past:

> As my mother is speaking, this feeling comes over me that I sometimes have when I'm carving, this sensation that my hands don't belong to me at all, that something else besides my brain and muscles is moving my fingers, something bigger and stronger than myself, an invisible puppetmaster over whom I have no control. I feel as though it's this same puppetmaster that now forces me to lower the phone and hang up, in midconversation, on my mother.

11. How do you interpret the final paragraph of the story? Does it end on a hopeful note? What does Danticat mean by "the enormous weight of permanent markers"? How are the dew breaker's "good angels" "his masks against his own face"?

Suggestions for Writing

1. Write an essay discussing the ways in which this new information about her father shakes Ka's own identity. Consider her various responses from feeling that her "life could have gone on fine without . . . knowing these types of things about [her] father" (para. 159), to imagining that she feels a scar in the same place on her face as her father's.

2. Do a close reading of the passage in which Ka's father reveals that he was "the hunter . . . not the prey" (paras. 110–41). Discuss how Danticat conveys the confusion Ka is feeling as her father makes this revelation to her.

3. Write an essay comparing and contrasting "The Book of the Dead" with another work in which a character's relationship to events in the past contributes to the meaning of the work. Consider how these events positively or negatively affect the present actions, attitudes, or values of Ka or her father and a character from another work.

4. Discuss "The Book of the Dead" in terms of what Michiko Kakutani, a book reviewer for the *New York Times*, has said: "a tale that simultaneously unfolds to become a philosophical meditation on the possibility of redemption and the longing of victims and victimizers alike to believe in the promise of new beginnings held forth by the American Dream."

5. Write an essay explaining whether you think that Ka should forgive her father. Center your discussion on "The Book of the Dead," but explore the concept of forgiveness, healing, and redemption through research into other areas, such as the documentary "As We Forgive"—about reconciliation efforts in Rwanda—and the Amy Biehl Foundation in South Africa.

6. Draw, paint, sculpt, or digitally create your interpretation of Ka's sculpture of her father. Explain what information in Danticat's story led you to your design and how you might have changed her original sculpture to fit your interpretation of the story.

7. Watch Jonathan Demme's documentary *The Agronomist*, the true story of Jean Dominique, a Haitian radio journalist and human rights activist. Write an essay discussing how this film expands your understanding of "The Book of the Dead."

Bartleby, the Scrivener

A Story of Wall Street

HERMAN MELVILLE

Herman Melville (1819–1891), best known for his novel *Moby-Dick* (1851), was born in New York City. By the time he was in his early twenties, he went off to sea, sailing first to Liverpool, England, then to the Marquesas Islands and areas in the South Seas on a whaling ship. Based on his experiences, he wrote the novels *Typee* and *Omoo*, which were both published in 1847; *Redburn*, an autobiographical novel based on his first voyage, appeared in 1849. Largely self-educated, Melville read widely, especially William Shakespeare and Ralph Waldo Emerson, both of whom influenced Melville's legendary novel, *Moby-Dick*. In the book, Melville's narrator, Ishmael, tells of the epic quest of Captain Ahab after the white whale. Now widely regarded as one of the greatest novels of American literature for its gripping epic adventure and its profound metaphysical journey, it was not well received in its time, nor were the later novels *Pierre; or, The Ambiguities* (1852), *The Confidence Man* (1857), or *Billy Budd* (published post-humously in 1924). Although Melville is most known for his novels, later in his life he also wrote poems and many fine stories, including "Bartleby, the Scrivener," which reflects his experience of working on Wall Street.

I am a rather elderly man. The nature of my avocations, for the last thirty years, has brought me into more than ordinary contact with what would seem an interesting and somewhat singular set of men, of whom, as yet, nothing, that I know of, has ever been written—I mean, the law-copyists, or scriveners. I have known very many of them, professionally and privately, and, if I pleased, could relate diverse histories, at which good-natured gentlemen might smile, and sentimental souls might weep. But I waive the biographies of all other scriveners, for a few passages in the life of Bartleby, who was a scrivener, the strangest I ever saw, or heard of. While, of other law-copyists, I might write the complete life, of Bartleby nothing of that sort can be done. I believe that no materials exist, for a full and satisfactory biography of this man. It is an irreparable loss to literature. Bartleby was one of those beings of whom nothing is ascertainable, except from the original sources, and, in his case, those are very small. What my own astonished eyes saw of Bartleby, *that* is all I know of him, except, indeed, one vague report, which will appear in the sequel.

Ere introducing the scrivener, as he first appeared to me, it is fit I make some mention of myself, my *employés*, my business, my chambers, and general surroundings, because some such description is indispensable to an adequate understanding of the chief character about to be presented. Imprimis:[1] I am a man who, from his youth

---

[1]In the first place.—EDS.

upwards, has been filled with a profound conviction that the easiest way of life is the best. Hence, though I belong to a profession proverbially energetic and nervous, even to turbulence, at times, yet nothing of that sort have I ever suffered to invade my peace. I am one of those unambitious lawyers who never address a jury, or in any way draw down public applause; but, in the cool tranquillity of a snug retreat, do a snug business among rich men's bonds, and mortgages, and title-deeds. All who know me, consider me an eminently *safe* man. The late John Jacob Astor,[2] a personage little given to poetic enthusiasm, had no hesitation in pronouncing my first grand point to be prudence; my next, method. I do not speak it in vanity, but simply record the fact, that I was not unemployed in my profession by the late John Jacob Astor; a name which, I admit, I love to repeat; for it hath a rounded and orbicular sound to it, and rings like unto bullion. I will freely add, that I was not insensible to the late John Jacob Astor's good opinion.

Some time prior to the period at which this little history begins, my avocations had been largely increased. The good old office, now extinct in the State of New York, of a Master in Chancery, had been conferred upon me. It was not a very arduous office, but very pleasantly remunerative. I seldom lose my temper; much more seldom indulge in dangerous indignation at wrongs and outrages; but I must be permitted to be rash here and declare, that I consider the sudden and violent abrogation of the office of Master in Chancery, by the new Constitution, as a —— premature act; inasmuch as I had counted upon a life-lease of the profits, whereas I only received those of a few short years. But this is by the way.

My chambers were up stairs, at No. —— Wall Street. At one end, they looked upon the white wall of the interior of a spacious skylight shaft, penetrating the building from top to bottom.

This view might have been considered rather tame than otherwise, deficient in what landscape painters call "life." But, if so, the view from the other end of my chambers offered, at least, a contrast, if nothing more. In that direction, my windows commanded an unobstructed view of a lofty brick wall, black by age and everlasting shade; which wall required no spyglass to bring out its lurking beauties, but, for the benefit of all near-sighted spectators, was pushed up to within ten feet of my window-panes. Owing to the great height of the surrounding buildings, and my chambers being on the second floor, the interval between this wall and mine not a little resembled a huge square cistern.

At the period just preceding the advent of Bartleby, I had two persons as copyists in my employment, and a promising lad as an office-boy. First, Turkey; second, Nippers; third, Ginger Nut. These may seem names, the like of which are not usually found in the Directory. In truth, they were nicknames, mutually conferred upon each other by my three clerks, and were deemed expressive of their respective persons or characters. Turkey was a short, pursy Englishman, of about my own age—that is, somewhere not far from sixty. In the morning, one might say, his face was of a fine florid hue, but after twelve o'clock, meridian—his dinner hour—it blazed like a grate full of Christmas coals; and continued blazing—but, as it were, with a gradual

---

[2]Astor (1763–1848) was a fur trader, and the richest American of his time.—Eds.

wane—till six o'clock, P.M., or thereabouts; after which, I saw no more of the proprietor of the face, which, gaining its meridian with the sun, seemed to set with it, to rise, culminate, and decline the following day, with the like regularity and undiminished glory. There are many singular coincidences I have known in the course of my life, not the least among which was the fact, that, exactly when Turkey displayed his fullest beams from his red and radiant countenance, just then, too, at that critical moment, began the daily period when I considered his business capacities as seriously disturbed for the remainder of the twenty-four hours. Not that he was absolutely idle, or averse to business then; far from it. The difficulty was, he was apt to be altogether too energetic. There was a strange, inflamed, flurried, flighty recklessness of activity about him. He would be incautious in dipping his pen into his inkstand. All his blots upon my documents were dropped there after twelve o'clock, meridian. Indeed, not only would he be reckless, and sadly given to making blots in the afternoon, but, some days, he went further, and was rather noisy. At such times, too, his face flamed with augmented blazonry, as if cannel coal had been heaped on anthracite. He made an unpleasant racket with his chair; spilled his sand-box; in mending his pens, impatiently split them all to pieces, and threw them on the floor in a sudden passion; stood up, and leaned over his table, boxing his papers about in a most indecorous manner, very sad to behold in an elderly man like him. Nevertheless, as he was in many ways a most valuable person to me, and all the time before twelve o'clock, meridian, was the quickest, steadiest creature, too, accomplishing a great deal of work in a style not easily to be matched—for these reasons, I was willing to overlook his eccentricities, though, indeed, occasionally, I remonstrated with him. I did this very gently, however, because, though the civilest, nay, the blandest and most reverential of men in the morning, yet, in the afternoon, he was disposed, upon provocation, to be slightly rash with his tongue—in fact, insolent. Now, valuing his morning services as I did, and resolved not to lose them—yet, at the same time, made uncomfortable by his inflamed ways after twelve o'clock—and being a man of peace, unwilling by my admonitions to call forth unseemly retorts from him, I took upon me, one Saturday noon (he was always worse on Saturdays) to hint to him, very kindly, that, perhaps, now that he was growing old, it might be well to abridge his labors; in short, he need not come to my chambers after twelve o'clock, but, dinner over, had best go home to his lodgings, and rest himself till tea-time. But no; he insisted upon his afternoon devotions. His countenance became intolerably fervid, as he oratorically assured me—gesticulating with a long ruler at the other end of the room—that if his services in the morning were useful, how indispensable, then, in the afternoon?

"With submission, sir," said Turkey, on this occasion, "I consider myself your right-hand man. In the morning I but marshal and deploy my columns; but in the afternoon I put myself at their head, and gallantly charge the foe, thus"—and he made a violent thrust with the ruler.

"But the blots, Turkey," intimated I.

"True; but, with submission, sir, behold these hairs! I am getting old. Surely, sir, a blot or two of a warm afternoon is not to be severely urged against gray hairs. Old age—even if it blot the page—is honorable. With submission, sir, we *both* are getting old."

This appeal to my fellow-feeling was hardly to be resisted. At all events, I saw that go he would not. So, I made up my mind to let him stay, resolving, nevertheless, to see to it that, during the afternoon, he had to do with my less important papers.

Nippers, the second on my list, was a whiskered, sallow, and, upon the whole, rather piratical-looking young man, of about five-and-twenty. I always deemed him the victim of two evil powers—ambition and indigestion. The ambition was evinced by a certain impatience of the duties of a mere copyist, an unwarrantable usurpation of strictly professional affairs such as the original drawing up of legal documents. The indigestion seemed betokened in an occasional nervous testiness and grinning irritability, causing the teeth to audibly grind together over mistakes committed in copying; unnecessary maledictions, hissed, rather than spoken, in the heat of business; and especially by a continual discontent with the height of the table where he worked. Though of a very ingenious mechanical turn, Nippers could never get this table to suit him. He put chips under it, blocks of various sorts, bits of pasteboard, and at last went so far as to attempt an exquisite adjustment, by final pieces of folded blotting-paper. But no invention would answer. If, for the sake of easing his back, he brought the table-lid at a sharp angle well up towards his chin, and wrote there like a man using the steep roof of a Dutch house for his desk, then he declared that it stopped the circulation in his arms. If now he lowered the table to his waistbands, and stooped over it in writing, then there was a sore aching in his back. In short, the truth of the matter was, Nippers knew not what he wanted. Or, if he wanted anything, it was to be rid of a scrivener's table altogether. Among the manifestations of his diseased ambition was a fondness he had for receiving visits from certain ambiguous-looking fellows in seedy coats, whom he called his clients. Indeed, I was aware that not only was he, at times, considerable of a ward-politician, but he occasionally did a little business at the justices' courts, and was not unknown on the steps of the Tombs.[3] I have good reason to believe, however, that one individual who called upon him at my chambers, and who, with a grand air, he insisted was his client, was no other than a dun, and the alleged title-deed, a bill. But, with all his failings, and the annoyances he caused me, Nippers, like his compatriot Turkey, was a very useful man to me; wrote a neat, swift hand; and, when he chose, was not deficient in a gentlemanly sort of deportment. Added to this, he always dressed in a gentlemanly sort of way; and so, incidentally, reflected credit upon my chambers. Whereas, with respect to Turkey, I had much ado to keep him from being a reproach to me. His clothes were apt to look oily, and smell of eating-houses. He wore his pantaloons very loose and baggy in summer. His coats were execrable, his hat not to be handled. But while the hat was a thing of indifference to me, inasmuch as his natural civility and deference, as a dependent Englishman, always led him to doff it the moment he entered the room, yet his coat was another matter. Concerning his coats, I reasoned with him; but with no effect. The truth was, I suppose, that a man with so small an income could not afford to sport such a lustrous face and a lustrous coat at one and the same time. As Nippers once observed, Turkey's money went chiefly for red ink. One winter day, I

---

[3]A jail in New York City.—Eds.

presented Turkey with a highly respectable-looking coat of my own—a padded gray coat, of a most comfortable warmth, and which buttoned straight up from the knee to the neck. I thought Turkey would appreciate the favor, and abate his rashness and obstreperousness of afternoons. But no; I verily believe that buttoning himself up in so downy and blanket-like a coat had a pernicious effect upon him—upon the same principle that too much oats are bad for horses. In fact, precisely as a rash, restive horse is said to feel his oats, so Turkey felt his coat. It made him insolent. He was a man whom prosperity harmed.

Though, concerning the self-indulgent habits of Turkey, I had my own private surmises, yet, touching Nippers, I was well persuaded that, whatever might be his faults in other respects, he was, at least, a temperate young man. But indeed, nature herself seemed to have been his vintner, and, at his birth, charged him so thoroughly with an irritable, brandy-like disposition, that all subsequent potations were needless. When I consider how, amid the stillness of my chambers, Nippers would sometimes impatiently rise from his seat, and stooping over his table, spread his arms wide apart, seize the whole desk, and move it, and jerk it, with a grim, grinding motion on the floor, as if the table were a perverse voluntary agent, intent on thwarting and vexing him, I plainly perceive that, for Nippers, brandy-and-water were altogether superfluous.

It was fortunate for me that, owing to its peculiar cause—indigestion—the irritability and consequent nervousness of Nippers were mainly observable in the morning, while in the afternoon he was comparatively mild. So that, Turkey's paroxysms only coming on about twelve o'clock, I never had to do with their eccentricities at one time. Their fits relieved each other, like guards. When Nippers' was on, Turkey's was off; and vice versa. This was a good natural arrangement, under the circumstances.

Ginger Nut, the third on my list, was a lad, some twelve years old. His father was a carman, ambitious of seeing his son on the bench instead of a cart, before he died. So he sent him to my office, as student at law, errand-boy, cleaner, and sweeper, at the rate of one dollar a week. He had a little desk to himself, but he did not use it much. Upon inspection, the drawer exhibited a great array of the shells of various sorts of nuts. Indeed, to this quick-witted youth, the whole noble science of the law was contained in a nutshell. Not the least among the employments of Ginger Nut, as well as one which he discharged with the most alacrity, was his duty as cake and apple purveyor for Turkey and Nippers. Copying lawpapers being proverbially a dry, husky sort of business, my two scriveners were fain to moisten their mouths very often with Spitzenbergs, to be had at the numerous stalls nigh the Custom House and Post Office. Also, they sent Ginger Nut very frequently for that peculiar cake—small, flat, round, and very spicy—after which he had been named by them. Of a cold morning, when business was but dull, Turkey would gobble up scores of these cakes, as if they were mere wafers—indeed, they sell them at the rate of six or eight for a penny—the scrape of his pen blending with the crunching of the crisp particles in his mouth. Of all the fiery afternoon blunders and flurried rashness of Turkey, was his once moistening a ginger-cake between his lips, and clapping it on to a mortgage, for a seal. I came within an ace of dismissing him then. But he mollified me by making an oriental bow, and saying—

"With submission, sir, it was generous of me to find you in stationery on my own account." 15

Now my original business—that of a conveyancer and title hunter, and drawer-up of recondite documents of all sorts—was considerably increased by receiving the Master's office. There was now great work for scriveners. Not only must I push the clerks already with me, but I must have additional help.

In answer to my advertisement, a motionless young man one morning stood upon my office threshold, the door being open, for it was summer. I can see that figure now—pallidly neat, pitiably respectable, incurably forlorn! It was Bartleby.

After a few words touching his qualifications, I engaged him, glad to have among my corps of copyists a man of so singularly sedate an aspect, which I thought might operate beneficially upon the flighty temper of Turkey, and the fiery one of Nippers.

I should have stated before that ground-glass folding-doors divided my premises into two parts, one of which was occupied by my scriveners, the other by myself. According to my humor, I threw open these doors, or closed them. I resolved to assign Bartleby a corner by the folding-doors, but on my side of them, so as to have this quiet man within easy call, in case any trifling thing was to be done. I placed his desk close up to a small side-window in that part of the room, a window which originally had afforded a lateral view of certain grimy brickyards and bricks, but which, owing to subsequent erections, commanded at present no view at all, though it gave some light. Within three feet of the panes was a wall, and the light came down from far above, between two lofty buildings, as from a very small opening in a dome. Still further to a satisfactory arrangement, I procured a high green folding screen, which might entirely isolate Bartleby from my sight, though not remove him from my voice. And thus, in a manner, privacy and society were conjoined.

At first, Bartleby did an extraordinary quantity of writing. As if long famishing 20 for something to copy, he seemed to gorge himself on my documents. There was no pause for digestion. He ran a day and night line, copying by sunlight and by candle-light. I should have been quite delighted with his application, had he been cheerfully industrious. But he wrote on silently, palely, mechanically.

It is, of course, an indispensable part of a scrivener's business to verify the accuracy of his copy, word by word. Where there are two or more scriveners in an office, they assist each other in this examination, one reading from the copy, the other holding the original. It is a very dull, wearisome, and lethargic affair. I can readily imagine that, to some sanguine temperaments, it would be altogether intolerable. For example, I cannot credit that the mettlesome poet, Byron, would have contentedly sat down with Bartleby to examine a law document of, say five hundred pages, closely written in a crimpy hand.

Now and then, in the haste of business, it had been my habit to assist in comparing some brief document myself, calling Turkey or Nippers for this purpose. One object I had, in placing Bartleby so handy to me behind the screen, was, to avail myself of his services on such trivial occasions. It was on the third day, I think, of his

being with me, and before any necessity had arisen for having his own writing examined, that, being much hurried to complete a small affair I had in hand, I abruptly
called to Bartleby. In my haste and natural expectancy of instant compliance, I sat
with my head bent over the original on my desk, and my right hand sideways, and
somewhat nervously extended with the copy, so that, immediately upon emerging
from his retreat, Bartleby might snatch it and proceed to business without the least
delay.

In this very attitude did I sit when I called to him, rapidly stating what it was I
wanted him to do — namely, to examine a small paper with me. Imagine my surprise,
nay, my consternation, when, without moving from his privacy, Bartleby, in a singularly mild, firm voice, replied, "I would prefer not to."

I sat awhile in perfect silence, rallying my stunned faculties. Immediately it
occurred to me that my ears had deceived me, or Bartleby had entirely misunderstood my meaning. I repeated my request in the clearest tone I could assume; but in
quite as clear a one came the previous reply, "I would prefer not to."

"Prefer not to," echoed I, rising in high excitement, and crossing the room with   25
a stride. "What do you mean? Are you moonstruck? I want you to help me compare
this sheet here — take it," and I thrust it towards him.

"I would prefer not to," said he.

I looked at him steadfastly. His face was leanly composed; his gray eye dimly
calm. Not a wrinkle of agitation rippled him. Had there been the least uneasiness,
anger, impatience, or impertinence in his manner; in other words, had there been
anything ordinarily human about him, doubtless I should have violently dismissed
him from the premises. But as it was, I should have as soon thought of turning my
pale plaster-of-paris bust of Cicero out of doors. I stood gazing at him awhile, as
he went on with his own writing, and then reseated myself at my desk. This is very
strange, thought I. What had one best do? But my business hurried me. I concluded
to forget the matter for the present, reserving it for my future leisure. So, calling
Nippers from the other room, the paper was speedily examined.

A few days after this, Bartleby concluded four lengthy documents, being qua-
druplicates of a week's testimony taken before me in my High Court of Chancery.
It became necessary to examine them. It was an important suit, and great accuracy
was imperative. Having all things arranged, I called Turkey, Nippers, and Ginger Nut,
from the next room, meaning to place the four copies in the hands of my four clerks,
while I should read from the original. Accordingly, Turkey, Nippers, and Ginger Nut
had taken their seats in a row, each with his document in his hand, when I called to
Bartleby to join this interesting group.

"Bartleby! quick, I am waiting."

I heard a slow scrape of his chair legs on the uncarpeted floor, and soon he   30
appeared standing at the entrance of his hermitage.

"What is wanted?" said he, mildly.

"The copies, the copies," said I, hurriedly. "We are going to examine them. There"—
and I held towards him the fourth quadruplicate.

"I would prefer not to," he said, and gently disappeared behind the screen.

For a few moments I was turned into a pillar of salt, standing at the head of my seated column of clerks. Recovering myself, I advanced towards the screen, and demanded the reason for such extraordinary conduct.

"*Why* do you refuse?"

"I would prefer not to."

With any other man I should have flown outright into a dreadful passion, scorned all further words, and thrust him ignominiously from my presence. But there was something about Bartleby that not only strangely disarmed me, but, in a wonderful manner, touched and disconcerted me. I began to reason with him.

"These are your own copies we are about to examine. It is labor saving to you, because one examination will answer for your four papers. It is common usage. Every copyist is bound to help examine his copy. Is it not so? Will you not speak? Answer!"

"I prefer not to," he replied in a flute-like tone. It seemed to me that, while I had been addressing him, he carefully revolved every statement that I made; fully comprehended the meaning; could not gainsay the irresistible conclusion; but, at the same time, some paramount consideration prevailed with him to reply as he did.

"You are decided, then, not to comply with my request—a request made according to common usage and common sense?"

He briefly gave me to understand, that on that point my judgment was sound. Yes: his decision was irreversible.

It is not seldom the case that, when a man is browbeaten in some unprecedented and violently unreasonable way, he begins to stagger in his own plainest faith. He begins, as it were, vaguely to surmise that, wonderful as it may be, all the justice and all the reason is on the other side. Accordingly, if any disinterested persons are present, he turns to them for some reinforcement for his own faltering mind.

"Turkey," said I, "what do you think of this? Am I not right?"

"With submission, sir," said Turkey, in his blandest tone, "I think that you are."

"Nippers," said I, "what do *you* think of it?"

"I think I should kick him out of the office."

(The reader of nice perceptions will have perceived that, it being morning, Turkey's answer is couched in polite and tranquil terms, but Nippers replies in ill-tempered ones. Or, to repeat a previous sentence, Nippers' ugly mood was on duty, and Turkey's off.)

"Ginger Nut," said I, willing to enlist the smallest suffrage in my behalf, "what do *you* think of it?"

"I think, sir, he's a little *luny*," replied Ginger Nut, with a grin.

"You hear what they say," said I, turning towards the screen, "come forth and do your duty."

But he vouchsafed no reply. I pondered a moment in sore perplexity. But once more business hurried me. I determined again to postpone the consideration of this dilemma to my future leisure. With a little trouble we made out to examine the papers without Bartleby, though at every page or two Turkey deferentially dropped his opinion, that this proceeding was quite out of the common; while Nippers, twitching in his chair with a dyspeptic nervousness, ground out, between his set teeth, occasional hissing maledictions against the stubborn oaf behind the screen. And for his (Nippers') part, this was the first and the last time he would do another man's business without pay.

Meanwhile Bartleby sat in his hermitage, oblivious to everything but his own peculiar business there.

Some days passed, the scrivener being employed upon another lengthy work. His late remarkable conduct led me to regard his ways narrowly. I observed that he never went to dinner; indeed, that he never went anywhere. As yet I had never, of my personal knowledge, known him to be outside of my office. He was a perpetual sentry in the corner. At about eleven o'clock though, in the morning, I noticed that Ginger Nut would advance toward the opening in Bartleby's screen, as if silently beckoned thither by a gesture invisible to me where I sat. The boy would then leave the office, jingling a few pence, and reappear with a handful of ginger-nuts, which he delivered in the hermitage, receiving two of the cakes for his trouble.

He lives, then, on ginger-nuts, thought I; never eats a dinner, properly speaking; he must be a vegetarian, then, but no; he never eats even vegetables, he eats nothing but ginger-nuts. My mind then ran on in reveries concerning the probable effects upon the human constitution of living entirely on ginger-nuts. Ginger-nuts are so called, because they contain ginger as one of their peculiar constituents, and the final flavoring one. Now, what was ginger? A hot, spicy thing. Was Bartleby hot and spicy? Not at all. Ginger, then, had no effect upon Bartleby. Probably he preferred it should have none.

Nothing so aggravates an earnest person as a passive resistance. If the individual so resisted be of a not inhumane temper, and the resisting one perfectly harmless in his passivity, then, in the better moods of the former, he will endeavor charitably to construe to his imagination what proves impossible to be solved by his judgment. Even so, for the most part, I regarded Bartleby and his ways. Poor fellow! thought I, he means no mischief; it is plain he intends no insolence; his aspect sufficiently evinces that his eccentricities are involuntary. He is useful to me. I can get along with him. If I turn him away, the chances are he will fall in with some less indulgent employer, and then he will be rudely treated, and perhaps driven forth miserably to starve. Yes. Here I can cheaply purchase a delicious self-approval. To befriend Bartleby; to humor him in his strange wilfulness, will cost me little or nothing, while I lay up in my soul what will eventually prove a sweet morsel for my conscience. But this mood was not invariable with me. The passiveness of Bartleby sometimes irritated me. I felt strangely goaded on to encounter him in new opposition — to elicit some angry spark from him answerable to my own. But, indeed, I might as well have essayed to strike fire with my knuckles against a bit of Windsor soap. But one afternoon the evil impulse in me mastered me, and the following little scene ensued:

"Bartleby," said I, "when those papers are all copied, I will compare them with you."

"I would prefer not to."

55

"How? Surely you do not mean to persist in that mulish vagary?"

No answer.

I threw open the folding-doors nearby, and turning upon Turkey and Nippers, 60
exclaimed:

"Bartleby a second time says, he won't examine his papers. What do you think
of it, Turkey?"

It was afternoon, be it remembered. Turkey sat glowing like a brass boiler; his
bald head steaming; his hands reeling among his blotted papers.

"Think of it?" roared Turkey. "I think I'll just step behind his screen, and black
his eyes for him!"

So saying, Turkey rose to his feet and threw his arms into a pugilistic position.
He was hurrying away to make good his promise, when I detained him, alarmed at
the effect of incautiously rousing Turkey's combativeness after dinner.

"Sit down, Turkey," said I, "and hear what Nippers has to say. What do you think 65
of it, Nippers? Would I not be justified in immediately dismissing Bartleby?"

"Excuse me, that is for you to decide, sir. I think his conduct quite unusual, and,
indeed, unjust, as regards Turkey and myself. But it may only be a passing whim."

"Ah," exclaimed I, "you have strangely changed your mind, then—you speak
very gently of him now."

"All beer," cried Turkey; "gentleness is effects of beer—Nippers and I dined
together to-day. You see how gentle *I* am, sir. Shall I go and black his eyes?"

"You refer to Bartleby, I suppose. No, not to-day, Turkey," I replied; "pray, put
up your fists."

I closed the doors, and again advanced towards Bartleby. I felt additional incen- 70
tives tempting me to my fate. I burned to be rebelled against again. I remembered
that Bartleby never left the office.

"Bartleby," said I, "Ginger Nut is away; just step around to the Post Office, won't
you?" (it was but a three minutes' walk) "and see if there is anything for me."

"I would prefer not to."

"You *will* not?"

"I *prefer* not."

I staggered to my desk, and sat there in a deep study. My blind inveteracy 75
returned. Was there any other thing in which I could procure myself to be ignominiously repulsed by this lean, penniless wight?—my hired clerk? What added thing is
there, perfectly reasonable, that he will be sure to refuse to do?

"Bartleby!"

No answer.

"Bartleby," in a louder tone.

No answer.

"Bartleby," I roared. 80

Like a very ghost, agreeably to the laws of magical invocation, at the third summons, he appeared at the entrance of his hermitage.

"Go to the next room, and tell Nippers to come to me."

"I prefer not to," he respectfully and slowly said, and mildly disappeared.

"Very good, Bartleby," said I, in a quiet sort of serenely-severe self-possessed tone, intimating the unalterable purpose of some terrible retribution very close at hand. At the moment I half intended something of the kind. But upon the whole, as it was drawing towards my dinner-hour, I thought it best to put on my hat and walk home for the day, suffering much from perplexity and distress of mind.

Shall I acknowledge it? The conclusion of this whole business was, that it soon became a fixed fact of my chambers, that a pale young scrivener, by the name of Bartleby, had a desk there; that he copied for me at the usual rate of four cents a folio (one hundred words); but he was permanently exempt from examining the work done by him, that duty being transferred to Turkey and Nippers, out of compliment, doubtless, to their superior acuteness; moreover, said Bartleby was never, on any account, to be dispatched on the most trivial errand of any sort; and that even if entreated to take upon him such a matter, it was generally understood that he would "prefer not to"—in other words, that he would refuse point-blank.

As days passed on, I became considerably reconciled to Bartleby. His steadiness, his freedom from all dissipation, his incessant industry (except when he chose to throw himself into a standing revery behind his screen), his great stillness, his unalterableness of demeanor under all circumstances, made him a valuable acquisition. One prime thing was this—*he was always there*—first in the morning, continually through the day, and the last at night. I had a singular confidence in his honesty. I felt my most precious papers perfectly safe in his hands. Sometimes, to be sure, I could not, for the very soul of me, avoid falling into sudden spasmodic passions with him. For it was exceeding difficult to bear in mind all the time those strange peculiarities, privileges, and unheard-of exemptions, forming the tacit stipulations on Bartleby's part under which he remained in my office. Now and then, in the eagerness of dispatching pressing business, I would inadvertently summon Bartleby, in a short, rapid tone, to put his finger, say, on the incipient tie of a bit of red tape with which I was about compressing some papers. Of course, from behind the screen the usual answer, "I prefer not to," was sure to come; and then, how could a human creature, with the common infirmities of our nature, refrain from bitterly exclaiming upon such perverseness—such unreasonableness? However, every added repulse of this sort which I received only tended to lessen the probability of my repeating the inadvertence.

Here it must be said, that, according to the custom of most legal gentlemen occupying chambers in densely populated law buildings, there were several keys to my door. One was kept by a woman residing in the attic, which person weekly scrubbed and daily swept and dusted my apartments. Another was kept by Turkey for convenience sake. The third I sometimes carried in my own pocket. The fourth I knew not who had.

Now, one Sunday morning I happened to go to Trinity Church, to hear a celebrated preacher, and finding myself rather early on the ground I thought I would walk round to my chambers for a while. Luckily I had my key with me; but upon applying it to the lock, I found it resisted by something inserted from the inside. Quite surprised, I called out; when to my consternation a key was turned from within; and thrusting his lean visage at me, and holding the door ajar, the apparition of Bartleby appeared, in his shirt-sleeves, and otherwise in a strangely tattered *deshabille*, saying quietly that he was sorry, but he was deeply engaged just then, and—preferred not admitting me at present. In a brief word or two, he moreover added, that perhaps I had better walk round the block two or three times, and by that time he would probably have concluded his affairs.

Now, the utterly unsurmised appearance of Bartleby, tenanting my law-chambers of a Sunday morning, with his cadaverously gentlemanly nonchalance, yet withal firm and self-possessed, had such a strange effect upon me, that incontinently I slunk away from my own door, and did as desired. But not without sundry twinges of impotent rebellion against the mild effrontery of this unaccountable scrivener. Indeed, it was his wonderful mildness chiefly, which not only disarmed me, but unmanned me, as it were. For I consider that one, for the time, is sort of unmanned when he tranquilly permits his hired clerk to dictate to him, and order him away from his own premises. Furthermore, I was full of uneasiness as to what Bartleby could possibly be doing in my office in his shirt-sleeves, and in an otherwise dismantled condition of a Sunday morning. Was anything amiss going on? Nay, that was out of the question. It was not to be thought of for a moment that Bartleby was an immoral person. But what could he be doing there?—copying? Nay again, whatever might be his eccentricities, Bartleby was an eminently decorous person. He would be the last man to sit down to his desk in any state approaching to nudity. Besides, it was Sunday; and there was something about Bartleby that forbade the supposition that he would by any secular occupation violate the proprieties of the day.

Nevertheless, my mind was not pacified; and full of a restless curiosity, at last I 90 returned to the door. Without hindrance I inserted my key, opened it, and entered. Bartleby was not to be seen. I looked round anxiously, peeped behind his screen; but it was very plain that he was gone. Upon more closely examining the place, I surmised that for an indefinite period Bartleby must have ate, dressed, and slept in my office, and that too without plate, mirror, or bed. The cushioned seat of a rickety old sofa in one corner bore the faint impress of a lean, reclining form. Rolled away under his desk, I found a blanket; under the empty grate, a blacking box and brush; on a chair, a tin basin, with soap and a ragged towel; in a newspaper a few crumbs of ginger-nuts and a morsel of cheese. Yes, thought I, it is evident enough that Bartleby has been making his home here, keeping bachelor's hall all by himself. Immediately then the thought came sweeping across me, what miserable friendlessness and loneliness are here revealed! His poverty is great; but his solitude, how horrible! Think of it. Of a Sunday, Wall Street is deserted as Petra;[4] and every night of every day it is an emptiness. This building, too, which of week-days hums with industry and life, at nightfall echoes with sheer vacancy, and all through Sunday is forlorn. And here Bartleby makes his home; sole spectator of a solitude which he has seen all populous—a sort of innocent and transformed Marius brooding among the ruins of Carthage?[5]

---

[4]Ancient Arabian city whose ruins were discovered in 1812.—EDS.
[5]Exiled Roman general Gaius Marius (157–86 B.C.E.) fled to the North African city-state of Carthage after a failed attempt to stop a civil war in Rome. Carthage had been destroyed by the Romans in the Third Punic War (149–146 B.C.E.).—EDS.

For the first time in my life a feeling of overpowering stinging melancholy seized me. Before, I had never experienced aught but a not unpleasing sadness. The bond of a common humanity now drew me irresistibly to gloom. A fraternal melancholy! For both I and Bartleby were sons of Adam. I remembered the bright silks and sparkling faces I had seen that day, in gala trim, swan-like sailing down the Mississippi of Broadway; and I contrasted them with the pallid copyist, and thought to myself, Ah, happiness courts the light, so we deem the world is gay; but misery hides aloof, so we deem that misery there is none. These sad fancyings—chimeras, doubtless, of a sick and silly brain—led on to other and more special thoughts, concerning the eccentricities of Bartleby. Presentiments of strange discoveries hovered round me. The scrivener's pale form appeared to me laid out, among uncaring strangers, in its shivering winding-sheet.

Suddenly I was attracted by Bartleby's closed desk, the key in open sight left in the lock.

I mean no mischief, seek the gratification of no heartless curiosity, thought I; besides, the desk is mine, and its contents, too, so I will make bold to look within. Everything was methodically arranged, the papers smoothly placed. The pigeon-holes were deep, and removing the files of documents, I groped into their recesses. Presently I felt something there, and dragged it out. It was an old bandanna handkerchief, heavy and knotted. I opened it, and saw it was a savings' bank.

I now recalled all the quiet mysteries which I had noted in the man. I remembered that he never spoke but to answer; that, though at intervals he had considerable time to himself, yet I had never seen him reading—no, not even a newspaper; that for long periods he would stand looking out, at his pale window behind the screen, upon the dead brick wall; I was quite sure he never visited any refectory or eating-house; while his pale face clearly indicated that he never drank beer like Turkey; or tea and coffee even, like other men; that he never went anywhere in particular that I could learn; never went out for a walk, unless, indeed, that was the case at present; that he had declined telling who he was, or whence he came, or whether he had any relatives in the world; that though so thin and pale, he never complained of ill-health. And more than all, I remembered a certain unconscious air of pallid—how shall I call it?—of pallid haughtiness, say, or rather an austere reserve about him, which had positively awed me into my tame compliance with his eccentricities, when I had feared to ask him to do the slightest incidental thing for me, even though I might know, from his long-continued motionlessness, that behind his screen he must be standing in one of those dead-wall reveries of his.

Revolving all these things, and coupling them with the recently discovered fact, 95 that he made my office his constant abiding place and home, and not forgetful of his morbid moodiness; revolving all these things, a prudential feeling began to steal over me. My first emotions had been those of pure melancholy and sincerest pity; but just in proportion as the forlornness of Bartleby grew and grew to my imagination, did that same melancholy merge into fear, that pity into repulsion. So true it is, and so terrible, too, that up to a certain point the thought or sight of misery enlists our best affections; but, in certain special cases, beyond that point it does not. They err who would assert that invariably this is owing to the inherent selfishness of the human heart. It rather proceeds from a certain hopelessness of remedying excessive and organic ill. To a sensitive being, pity is not seldom pain. And when at last it is perceived that such pity cannot lead to effectual succor, common sense bids the soul be rid of it. What I saw that morning persuaded me that the scrivener was the victim of innate and incurable disorder. I might give alms to his body; but his body did not pain him; it was his soul that suffered, and his soul I could not reach.

I did not accomplish the purpose of going to Trinity Church that morning. Somehow, the things I had seen disqualified me for the time from church-going. I walked homeward, thinking what I would do with Bartleby. Finally, I resolved upon this—I would put certain calm questions to him the next morning, touching his history, etc., and if he declined to answer them openly and unreservedly (and I supposed he would prefer not), then to give him a twenty dollar bill over and above whatever I might owe him, and tell him his services were no longer required; but that if in any other way I could assist him, I would be happy to do so, especially if he desired to return to his native place, wherever that might be, I would willingly help to defray the expenses. Moreover, if, after reaching home, he found himself at any time in want of aid, a letter from him would be sure of a reply.

The next morning came.

"Bartleby," said I, gently calling to him behind his screen.

No reply.

"Bartleby," said I, in a still gentler tone, "come here; I am not going to ask you to   100
do anything you would prefer not to do—I simply wish to speak to you."

Upon this he noiselessly slid into view.

"Will you tell me, Bartleby, where you were born?"

"I would prefer not to."

"Will you tell me *anything* about yourself?"

"I would prefer not to."   105

"But what reasonable objection can you have to speak to me? I feel friendly towards you."

He did not look at me while I spoke, but kept his glance fixed upon my bust of Cicero, which, as I then sat, was directly behind me, some six inches above my head.

"What is your answer, Bartleby?" said I, after waiting a considerable time for a reply, during which his countenance remained immovable, only there was the faintest conceivable tremor of the white attenuated mouth.

"At present I prefer to give no answer," he said, and retired into his hermitage.

It was rather weak in me I confess, but his manner, on this occasion, nettled   110
me. Not only did there seem to lurk in it a certain calm disdain, but his perverseness seemed ungrateful, considering the undeniable good usage and indulgence he had received from me.

Again I sat ruminating what I should do. Mortified as I was at his behavior, and resolved as I had been to dismiss him when I entered my office, nevertheless I strangely felt something superstitious knocking at my heart, and forbidding me to carry out my purpose, and denouncing me for a villain if I dared to breathe one bitter word against this forlornest of mankind. At last, familiarly drawing my chair behind his screen, I sat down and said: "Bartleby, never mind, then, about revealing your history; but let me entreat you, as a friend, to comply as far as may be with the usages of this office. Say now, you will help to examine papers tomorrow or next day: in short, say now, that in a day or two you will begin to be a little reasonable:—say so, Bartleby."

"At present I would prefer not to be a little reasonable," was his mildly cadaverous reply.

Just then the folding-doors opened, and Nippers approached. He seemed suffering from an unusually bad night's rest, induced by severer indigestion than common. He overheard those final words of Bartleby.

"*Prefer not*, eh?" gritted Nippers—"I'd *prefer* him, if I were you, sir," addressing me—"I'd *prefer* him; I'd give him preferences, the stubborn mule! What is it, sir, pray, that he *prefers* not to do now?"

Bartleby moved not a limb. 115

"Mr. Nippers," said I, "I'd prefer that you would withdraw for the present."

Somehow, of late, I had got into the way of involuntarily using this word "prefer" upon all sorts of not exactly suitable occasions. And I trembled to think that my contact with the scrivener had already and seriously affected me in a mental way. And what further and deeper aberration might it not yet produce? This apprehension had not been without efficacy in determining me to summary measures.

As Nippers, looking very sour and sulky, was departing, Turkey blandly and deferentially approached.

"With submission, sir," said he, "yesterday I was thinking about Bartleby here, and I think that if he would but prefer to take a quart of good ale every day, it would do much towards mending him, and enabling him to assist in examining his papers."

"So you have got the word, too," said I, slightly excited. 120

"With submission, what word, sir?" asked Turkey, respectfully crowding himself into the contracted space behind the screen, and by so doing, making me jostle the scrivener. "What word, sir?"

"I would prefer to be left alone here," said Bartleby, as if offended at being mobbed in his privacy.

"*That's* the word, Turkey," said I—"*that's* it."

"Oh, *prefer*? oh yes—queer word. I never use it myself. But, sir, as I was saying, if he would but prefer—"

"Turkey," interrupted I, "you will please withdraw." 125

"Oh certainly, sir, if you prefer that I should."

As he opened the folding-door to retire, Nippers at his desk caught a glimpse of me, and asked whether I would prefer to have a certain paper copied on blue paper or white. He did not in the least roguishly accent the word "prefer." It was plain that it involuntarily rolled from his tongue. I thought to myself, surely I must get rid of a demented man, who already has in some degree turned the tongues, if not the heads of myself and clerks. But I thought it prudent not to break the dismission at once.

The next day I noticed that Bartleby did nothing but stand at his window in his dead-wall revery. Upon asking him why he did not write, he said that he had decided upon doing no more writing.

"Why, how now? what next?" exclaimed I, "do no more writing?"

"No more."   130

"And what is the reason?"

"Do you not see the reason for yourself?" he indifferently replied.

I looked steadfastly at him, and perceived that his eyes looked dull and glazed. Instantly it occurred to me, that his unexampled diligence in copying by his dim window for the first few weeks of his stay with me might have temporarily impaired his vision.

I was touched. I said something in condolence with him. I hinted that of course he did wisely in abstaining from writing for a while; and urged him to embrace that opportunity of taking wholesome exercise in the open air. This, however, he did not do. A few days after this, my other clerks being absent, and being in a great hurry to dispatch certain letters by the mail, I thought that, having nothing else earthly to do, Bartleby would surely be less inflexible than usual, and carry these letters to the Post Office. But he blankly declined. So, much to my inconvenience, I went myself.

Still added days went by. Whether Bartleby's eyes improved or not, I could   135
not say. To all appearance, I thought they did. But when I asked him if they did, he vouchsafed no answer. At all events, he would do no copying. At last, in replying to my urgings, he informed me that he had permanently given up copying.

"What!" exclaimed I; "suppose your eyes should get entirely well—better than ever before—would you not copy then?"

"I have given up copying," he answered, and slid aside.

He remained as ever, a fixture in my chamber. Nay—if that were possible—he became still more of a fixture than before. What was to be done? He would do nothing in the office; why should he stay there? In plain fact, he had now become a millstone to me, not only useless as a necklace, but afflictive to bear. Yet I was sorry for him. I speak less than truth when I say that, on his own account, he occasioned me uneasiness. If he would but have named a single relative or friend, I would instantly have written, and urged their taking the poor fellow away to some convenient retreat. But he seemed alone, absolutely alone in the universe. A bit of wreck in the mid-Atlantic. At length, necessities connected with my business tyrannized over all other considerations. Decently as I could, I told Bartleby that in six days' time he must unconditionally leave the office. I warned him to take measures, in the interval, for procuring some other abode. I offered to assist him in this endeavor, if he himself would but take the first step towards a removal. "And when you finally quit me, Bartleby," added I, "I shall see that you go not away entirely unprovided. Six days from this hour, remember."

At the expiration of that period, I peeped behind the screen, and lo! Bartleby was there.

I buttoned up my coat, balanced myself; advanced slowly towards him, touched   140
his shoulder, and said, "The time has come; you must quit this place; I am sorry for you; here is money; but you must go."

"I would prefer not," he replied, with his back still towards me.

"You *must*."

He remained silent.

Now I had an unbounded confidence in this man's common honesty. He had frequently restored to me sixpences and shillings carelessly dropped upon the floor, for I am apt to be very reckless in such shirt-button affairs. The proceeding, then, which followed will not be deemed extraordinary.

"Bartleby," said I, "I owe you twelve dollars on account; here are thirty-two, the odd twenty are yours—Will you take it?" and I handed the bills towards him. 145

But he made no motion.

"I will leave them here, then," putting them under a weight on the table. Then taking my hat and cane and going to the door, I tranquilly turned and added—"After you have removed your things from these offices, Bartleby, you will of course lock the door—since every one is now gone for the day but you—and if you please, slip your key underneath the mat, so that I may have it in the morning. I shall not see you again; so good-bye to you. If, hereafter, in your new place of abode, I can be of any service to you, do not fail to advise me by letter. Good-bye, Bartleby, and fare you well."

But he answered not a word; like the last column of some ruined temple, he remained standing mute and solitary in the middle of the otherwise deserted room.

As I walked home in a pensive mood, my vanity got the better of my pity. I could not but highly plume myself on my masterly management in getting rid of Bartleby. Masterly I call it, and such it must appear to any dispassionate thinker. The beauty of my procedure seemed to consist in its perfect quietness. There was no vulgar bully-ing, no bravado of any sort, no choleric hectoring, and striding to and fro across the apartment, jerking out vehement commands for Bartleby to bundle himself off with his beggarly traps. Nothing of the kind. Without loudly bidding Bartleby depart—as an inferior genius might have done—I *assumed* the ground that depart he must; and upon that assumption built all I had to say. The more I thought over my procedure, the more I was charmed with it. Nevertheless, next morning, upon awakening, I had my doubts—I had somehow slept off the fumes of vanity. One of the coolest and wisest hours a man has, is just after he awakes in the morning. My procedure seemed as sagacious as ever—but only in theory. How it would prove in practice—there was the rub. It was truly a beautiful thought to have assumed Bartleby's departure; but, after all, that assumption was simply my own, and none of Bartleby's. The great point was, not whether I had assumed that he would quit me, but whether he would prefer to do so. He was more a man of preferences than assumptions.

After breakfast, I walked down town, arguing the probabilities pro and con. One moment I thought it would prove a miserable failure, and Bartleby would be found all alive at my office as usual; the next moment it seemed certain that I should find his chair empty. And so I kept veering about. At the corner of Broadway and Canal Street, I saw quite an excited group of people standing in earnest conversation. 150

"I'll take odds he doesn't," said a voice as I passed.

"Doesn't go?—done!" said I, "put up your money."

I was instinctively putting my hand in my pocket to produce my own, when I remembered that this was an election day. The words I had overheard bore no reference to Bartleby, but to the success or non-success of some candidate for the mayoralty. In my intent frame of mind, I had, as it were, imagined that all Broadway shared in my excitement, and were debating the same question with me. I passed on, very thankful that the uproar of the street screened my momentary absent-mindedness.

As I had intended, I was earlier than usual at my office door. I stood listening for a moment. All was still. He must be gone. I tried the knob. The door was locked. Yes, my procedure had worked to a charm; he indeed must be vanished. Yet a certain melancholy mixed with this: I was almost sorry for my brilliant success. I was fumbling under the door mat for the key, which Bartleby was to have left there for me, when accidentally my knee knocked against a panel, producing a summoning sound, and in response a voice came to me from within — "Not yet; I am occupied."

It was Bartleby.   155

I was thunderstruck. For an instant I stood like the man who, pipe in mouth, was killed one cloudless afternoon long ago in Virginia, by summer lightning; at his own warm open window he was killed, and remained leaning out there upon the dreamy afternoon, till some one touched him, when he fell.

"Not gone!" I murmured at last. But again obeying that wondrous ascendancy which the inscrutable scrivener had over me, and from which ascendancy, for all my chafing, I could not completely escape, I slowly went down stairs and out into the street, and while walking round the block, considered what I should next do in this unheard-of perplexity. Turn the man out by an actual thrusting I could not; to drive him away by calling him hard names would not do; calling in the police was an unpleasant idea; and yet, permit him to enjoy his cadaverous triumph over me — this, too, I could not think of. What was to be done? or, if nothing could be done, was there anything further that I could *assume* in the matter? Yes, as before I had prospectively assumed that Bartleby would depart, so now I might retrospectively assume that departed he was. In the legitimate carrying out of this assumption, I might enter my office in a great hurry, and pretending not to see Bartleby at all, walk straight against him as if he were air. Such a proceeding would in a singular degree have the appearance of a home-thrust. It was hardly possible that Bartleby could withstand such an application of the doctrine of assumption. But upon second thoughts the success of the plan seemed rather dubious. I resolved to argue the matter over with him again.

"Bartleby," said I, entering the office, with a quietly severe expression, "I am seriously displeased. I am pained, Bartleby. I had thought better of you. I had imagined you of such a gentlemanly organization, that in any delicate dilemma a slight hint would suffice — in short, an assumption. But it appears I am deceived. Why," I added, unaffectedly starting, "you have not even touched that money yet," pointing to it, just where I had left it the evening previous.

He answered nothing.

"Will you, or will you not, quit me?" I now demanded in a sudden passion,   160
advancing close to him.

"I would prefer *not* to quit you," he replied, gently emphasizing the *not*.

"What earthly right have you to stay here? Do you pay any rent? Do you pay my taxes? Or is this property yours?"

He answered nothing.

"Are you ready to go on and write now? Are your eyes recovered? Could you copy a small paper for me this morning? or help examine a few lines? or step round to the Post Office? In a word, will you do anything at all, to give a coloring to your refusal to depart the premises?"

He silently retired into his hermitage.   165

I was now in such a state of nervous resentment that I thought it but prudent to check myself at present from further demonstrations. Bartleby and I were alone. I remembered the tragedy of the unfortunate Adams and the still more unfortunate Colt[6] in the solitary office of the latter; and how poor Colt, being dreadfully incensed by Adams, and imprudently permitting himself to get wildly excited, was at unawares hurried into his fatal act—an act which certainly no man could possibly deplore more than the actor himself. Often it had occurred to me in my ponderings upon the subject that had that altercation taken place in the public street, or at a private residence, it would not have terminated as it did. It was the circumstance of being alone in a solitary office, up stairs, of a building entirely unhallowed by humanizing domestic associations—an uncarpeted office, doubtless, of a dusty, haggard sort of appearance—this it must have been, which greatly helped to enhance the irritable desperation of the hapless Colt.

But when this old Adam of resentment rose in me and tempted me concerning Bartleby, I grappled him and threw him. How? Why, simply by recalling the divine injunction: "A new commandment give I unto you, that ye love one another." Yes, this it was that saved me. Aside from higher considerations, charity often operates as a vastly wise and prudent principle—a great safeguard to its possessor. Men have committed murder for jealousy's sake, and anger's sake, and hatred's sake, and selfishness' sake, and spiritual pride's sake; but no man, that ever I heard of, ever committed a diabolical murder for sweet charity's sake. Mere self-interest, then, if no better motive can be enlisted, should, especially with high-tempered men, prompt all beings to charity and philanthropy. At any rate, upon the occasion in question, I strove to drown my exasperated feelings towards the scrivener by benevolently construing his conduct. Poor fellow, poor fellow! thought I, he don't mean anything; and besides, he has seen hard times, and ought to be indulged.

I endeavored, also, immediately to occupy myself, and at the same time to comfort my despondency. I tried to fancy, that in the course of the morning, at such time as might prove agreeable to him, Bartleby, of his own free accord, would emerge from his hermitage and take up some decided line of march in the direction of the door. But no. Half-past twelve o'clock came; Turkey began to glow in the face, overturn his

---

[6]In a sensational case from 1841, John C. Colt (brother of Samuel Colt, inventor of the revolver) murdered a printer named Samuel Adams. Before his hanging, Colt committed suicide in the Tombs.—EDS.

inkstand, and become generally obstreperous; Nippers abated down into quietude and courtesy; Ginger Nut munched his noon apple; and Bartleby remained standing at his window in one of his profoundest dead-wall reveries. Will it be credited? Ought I to acknowledge it? That afternoon I left the office without saying one further word to him.

Some days now passed, during which, at leisure intervals I looked a little into "Edwards on the Will," and "Priestley on Necessity."[7] Under the circumstances, those books induced a salutary feeling. Gradually I slid into the persuasion that these troubles of mine, touching the scrivener, had been all predestined from eternity, and Bartleby was billeted upon me for some mysterious purpose of an all-wise Providence, which it was not for a mere mortal like me to fathom. Yes, Bartleby, stay there behind your screen, thought I; I shall persecute you no more; you are harmless and noiseless as any of these old chairs; in short, I never feel so private as when I know you are here. At last I see it, I feel it; I penetrate to the predestined purpose of my life. I am content. Others may have loftier parts to enact; but my mission in this world, Bartleby, is to furnish you with office-room for such period as you may see fit to remain.

I believe that this wise and blessed frame of mind would have continued with me, had it not been for the unsolicited and uncharitable remarks obtruded upon me by my professional friends who visited the rooms. But thus it often is, that the constant friction of illiberal minds wears out at last the best resolves of the more generous. Though to be sure, when I reflected upon it, it was not strange that people entering my office should be struck by the peculiar aspect of the unaccountable Bartleby, and so be tempted to throw out some sinister observations concerning him. Sometimes an attorney, having business with me, and calling at my office, and finding no one but the scrivener there, would undertake to obtain some sort of precise information from him touching my whereabouts; but without heeding his idle talk, Bartleby would remain standing immovable in the middle of the room. So after contemplating him in that position for a time, the attorney would depart, no wiser than he came.

Also, when a reference was going on, and the room full of lawyers and witnesses, and business driving fast, some deeply-occupied legal gentleman present, seeing Bartleby wholly unemployed, would request him to run round to his (the legal gentleman's) office and fetch some papers for him. Thereupon, Bartleby would tranquilly decline, and yet remain idle as before. Then the lawyer would give a great stare, and turn to me. And what could I say? At last I was made aware that all through the circle of my professional acquaintance, a whisper of wonder was running round, having reference to the strange creature I kept at my office. This worried me very much. And as the idea came upon me of his possibly turning out a long-lived man, and keeping occupying my chambers, and denying my authority; and perplexing my visitors; and scandalizing my professional reputation; and casting a general gloom

170

---

[7]Jonathan Edwards, in *Freedom of the Will* (1754), and Joseph Priestley, in *Doctrine of Philosophical Necessity* (1777), argued that human beings lack free will. — Eds.

over the premises; keeping soul and body together to the last upon his savings (for doubtless he spent but half a dime a day), and in the end perhaps outlive me, and claim possession of my office by right of his perpetual occupancy: as all these dark anticipations crowded upon me more and more, and my friends continually intruded their relentless remarks upon the apparition in my room; a great change was wrought in me. I resolved to gather all my faculties together, and forever rid me of this intolerable incubus.

Ere revolving any complicated project, however, adapted to this end, I first simply suggested to Bartleby the propriety of his permanent departure. In a calm and serious tone, I commended the idea to his careful and mature consideration. But, having taken three days to meditate upon it, he apprised me, that his original determination remained the same; in short, that he still preferred to abide with me.

What shall I do? I now said to myself, buttoning up my coat to the last button. What shall I do? what ought I to do? what does conscience say I *should* do with this man, or, rather, ghost. Rid myself of him, I must; go, he shall. But how? You will not thrust him, the poor, pale, passive mortal—you will not thrust such a helpless creature out of your door? you will not dishonor yourself by such cruelty? No, I will not, I cannot do that. Rather would I let him live and die here, and then mason up his remains in the wall. What, then, will you do? For all your coaxing, he will not budge. Bribes he leaves under your own paper-weight on your table; in short, it is quite plain that he prefers to cling to you.

Then something severe, something unusual must be done. What! surely you will not have him collared by a constable, and commit his innocent pallor to the common jail? And upon what ground could you procure such a thing to be done?—a vagrant, is he? What! he a vagrant, a wanderer, who refuses to budge? It is because he will *not* be a vagrant, then, that you seek to count him *as* a vagrant. That is too absurd. No visible means of support: there I have him. Wrong again: for indubitably he *does* support himself, and that is the only unanswerable proof that any man can show of his possessing the means so to do. No more, then. Since he will not quit me, I must quit him. I will change my offices; I will move elsewhere, and give him fair notice, that if I find him on my new premises I will then proceed against him as a common trespasser.

Acting accordingly, next day I thus addressed him: "I find these chambers too far from the City Hall; the air is unwholesome. In a word, I propose to remove my offices next week, and shall no longer require your services. I tell you this now, in order that you may seek another place." 175

He made no reply, and nothing more was said.

On the appointed day I engaged carts and men, proceeded to my chambers, and having but little furniture, everything was removed in a few hours. Throughout, the scrivener remained standing behind the screen, which I directed to be removed the last thing. It was withdrawn; and, being folded up like a huge folio, left him the motionless occupant of a naked room. I stood in the entry watching him a moment, while something from within me upbraided me.

I re-entered, with my hand in my pocket—and—and my heart in my mouth.

"Good-bye, Bartleby; I am going—good-bye, and God some way bless you; and take that," slipping something in his hand. But it dropped upon the floor, and then—strange to say—I tore myself from him whom I had so longed to be rid of.

Established in my new quarters, for a day or two I kept the door locked, and started at every footfall in the passages. When I returned to my rooms, after any little absence, I would pause at the threshold for an instant, and attentively listen, ere applying my key. But these fears were needless. Bartleby never came nigh me.

I thought all was going well, when a perturbed-looking stranger visited me, inquiring whether I was the person who had recently occupied rooms at No. —— Wall Street.

Full of forebodings, I replied that I was.

"Then, sir," said the stranger, who proved a lawyer, "you are responsible for the man you left there. He refuses to do any copying; he refuses to do anything; he says he prefers not to; and he refuses to quit the premises."

"I am very sorry, sir," said I, with assumed tranquillity, but an inward tremor, "but, really, the man you allude to is nothing to me—he is no relation or apprentice of mine, that you should hold me responsible for him."

"In mercy's name, who is he?"

"I certainly cannot inform you. I know nothing about him. Formerly I employed him as a copyist; but he has done nothing for me now for some time past."

"I shall settle him, then—good morning, sir."

Several days passed, and I heard nothing more; and, though I often felt a charitable prompting to call at the place and see poor Bartleby, yet a certain squeamishness, of I know not what, withheld me.

All is over with him, by this time, thought I, at last, when, through another week, no further intelligence reached me. But, coming to my room the day after, I found several persons waiting at my door in a high state of nervous excitement.

"That's the man—here he comes," cried the foremost one, whom I recognized as the lawyer who had previously called upon me alone.

"You must take him away, sir, at once," cried a portly person among them, advancing upon me, and whom I knew to be the landlord of No. —— Wall Street. "These gentlemen, my tenants, cannot stand it any longer; Mr. B——," pointing to the lawyer, "has turned him out of his room, and he now persists in haunting the building generally, sitting upon the banisters of the stairs by day, and sleeping in the entry by night. Everybody is concerned; clients are leaving the offices; some fears are entertained of a mob; something you must do, and that without delay."

Aghast at this torrent, I fell back before it, and would fain have locked myself in my new quarters. In vain I persisted that Bartleby was nothing to me—no more than to any one else. In vain—I was the last person known to have anything to do with him, and they held me to the terrible account. Fearful, then, of being exposed in the papers (as one person present obscurely threatened), I considered the matter, and, at length, said, that if the lawyer would give me a confidential interview with the scrivener, in his (the lawyer's) own room, I would, that afternoon, strive my best to rid them of the nuisance they complained of.

Going up stairs to my old haunt, there was Bartleby silently sitting upon the banister at the landing.

"What are you doing here, Bartleby?" said I.

"Sitting upon the banister," he mildly replied. 195

I motioned him into the lawyer's room, who then left us.

"Bartleby," said I, "are you aware that you are the cause of great tribulation to me, by persisting in occupying the entry after being dismissed from the office?"

No answer.

"Now one of two things must take place. Either you must do something, or something must be done to you. Now what sort of business would you like to engage in? Would you like to re-engage in copying for some one?"

"No; I would prefer not to make any change." 200

"Would you like a clerkship in a dry-goods store?"

"There is too much confinement about that. No, I would not like a clerkship; but I am not particular."

"Too much confinement," I cried, "why, you keep yourself confined all the time!"

"I would prefer not to take a clerkship," he rejoined, as if to settle that little item at once.

"How would a bar-tender's business suit you? There is no trying of the eye-sight 205 in that."

"I would not like it at all; though, as I said before, I am not particular."

His unwonted wordiness inspirited me. I returned to the charge.

"Well, then, would you like to travel through the country collecting bills for the merchants? That would improve your health."

"No, I would prefer to be doing something else."

"How, then, would going as a companion to Europe, to entertain some young 210 gentleman with your conversation — how would that suit you?"

"Not at all. It does not strike me that there is anything definite about that. I like to be stationary. But I am not particular."

"Stationary you shall be, then," I cried, now losing all patience, and, for the first time in all my exasperating connection with him, fairly flying into a passion. "If you do not go away from these premises before night, I shall feel bound — indeed, I *am* bound — to — to quit the premises myself!" I rather absurdly concluded, knowing not with what possible threat to try to frighten his immobility into compliance. Despairing of all further efforts, I was precipitately leaving him, when a final thought occurred to me — one which had not been wholly unindulged before.

"Bartleby," said I, in the kindest tone I could assume under such exciting circumstances, "will you go home with me now — not to my office, but my dwelling — and remain there till we can conclude upon some convenient arrangement for you at our leisure? Come, let us start now, right away."

"No: at present I would prefer not to make any change at all."

I answered nothing; but, effectually dodging every one by the suddenness and 215 rapidity of my flight, rushed from the building, ran up Wall Street towards Broadway, and, jumping into the first omnibus, was soon removed from pursuit. As soon as tranquillity returned, I distinctly perceived that I had now done all that I possibly could, both in respect to the demands of the landlord and his tenants, and with regard to my own desire and sense of duty, to benefit Bartleby, and shield him from rude persecution. I now strove to be entirely care-free and quiescent; and my conscience justified me in the attempt; though, indeed, it was not so successful as I could have wished. So fearful was I of being again hunted out by the incensed landlord and his exasperated tenants, that, surrendering my business to Nippers, for a few days, I drove about the upper part of the town and through the suburbs, in my rockaway; crossed over to Jersey City and Hoboken, and paid fugitive visits to Manhattanville and Astoria. In fact, I almost lived in my rockaway for the time.

When again I entered my office, lo, a note from the landlord lay upon the desk. I opened it with trembling hands. It informed me that the writer had sent to the police, and had Bartleby removed to the Tombs as a vagrant. Moreover, since I knew more about him than any one else, he wished me to appear at that place, and make a suitable statement of the facts. These tidings had a conflicting effect upon me. At first I was indignant; but, at last, almost approved. The landlord's energetic, summary disposition, had led him to adopt a procedure which I do not think I would have decided upon myself; and yet, as a last resort, under such peculiar circumstances, it seemed the only plan.

As I afterwards learned, the poor scrivener, when told that he must be conducted to the Tombs, offered not the slightest obstacle, but, in his pale, unmoving way, silently acquiesced.

Some of the compassionate and curious by-standers joined the party; and headed by one of the constables arm-in-arm with Bartleby, the silent procession filed its way through all the noise, and heat, and joy of the roaring thoroughfares at noon.

The same day I received the note, I went to the Tombs, or, to speak more properly, the Halls of Justice. Seeking the right officer, I stated the purpose of my call, and was informed that the individual I described was, indeed, within. I then assured the functionary that Bartleby was a perfectly honest man, and greatly to be compassionated, however unaccountably eccentric. I narrated all I knew, and closed by suggesting the idea of letting him remain in as indulgent confinement as possible, till something less harsh might be done—though, indeed, I hardly knew what. At all events, if nothing else could be decided upon, the almshouse must receive him. I then begged to have an interview.

Being under no disgraceful charge, and quite serene and harmless in all his ways, they had permitted him freely to wander about the prison, and, especially, in the inclosed grass-platted yards thereof. And so I found him there, standing all alone in the quietest of the yards, his face towards a high wall, while all around, from the narrow slits of the jail windows, I thought I saw peering out upon him the eyes of murderers and thieves. 220

"Bartleby!"

"I know you," he said, without looking round—"and I want nothing to say to you."

"It was not I that brought you here, Bartleby," said I, keenly pained at his implied suspicion. "And to you, this should not be so vile a place. Nothing reproachful attaches to you by being here. And see, it is not so sad a place as one might think. Look, there is the sky, and here is the grass."

"I know where I am," he replied, but would say nothing more, and so I left him.

As I entered the corridor again, a broad meat-like man, in an apron, accosted me, and, jerking his thumb over his shoulder, said—"Is that your friend?"   225

"Yes."

"Does he want to starve? If he does, let him live on the prison fare, that's all."

"Who are you?" asked I, not knowing what to make of such an unofficially speaking person in such a place.

"I am the grub-man. Such gentlemen as have friends here, hire me to provide them with something good to eat."

"Is this so?" said I, turning the turnkey.   230

He said it was.

"Well, then," said I, slipping some silver into the grub-man's hands (for so they called him), "I want you to give particular attention to my friend there; let him have the best dinner you can get. And you must be as polite to him as possible."

"Introduce me, will you?" said the grub-man, looking at me with an expression which seemed to say he was all impatience for an opportunity to give a specimen of his breeding.

Thinking it would prove of benefit to the scrivener, I acquiesced; and, asking the grub-man his name, went up with him to Bartleby.

"Bartleby, this is a friend; you will find him very useful to you."   235

"Your sarvant, sir, your sarvant," said the grub-man, making a low salutation behind his apron. "Hope you find it pleasant here, sir; nice grounds—cool apart-ments—hope you'll stay with us some time—try to make it agreeable. What will you have for dinner to-day?"

"I prefer not to dine to-day," said Bartleby, turning away. "It would disagree with me; I am unused to dinners." So saying, he slowly moved to the other side of the inclosure, and took up a position fronting the deadwall.

"How's this?" said the grub-man, addressing me with a stare of astonishment. "He's odd, ain't he?"

"I think he is a little deranged," said I, sadly.

"Deranged? deranged is it? Well, now, upon my word, I thought that friend of   240
yourn was a gentleman forger; they are always pale and genteel-like, them forgers. I can't help pity 'em—can't help it, sir. Did you know Monroe Edwards?" he added, touchingly, and paused. Then, laying his hand piteously on my shoulder, sighed, "he died of consumption at Sing-Sing. So you weren't acquainted with Monroe?"

"No, I was never socially acquainted with any forgers. But I cannot stop longer. Look to my friend yonder. You will not lose by it. I will see you again."

Some few days after this, I again obtained admission to the Tombs, and went through the corridors in quest of Bartleby; but without finding him.

"I saw him coming from his cell not long ago," said a turnkey, "may be he's gone to loiter in the yards."

So I went in that direction.

"Are you looking for the silent man?" said another turnkey, passing me. "Yonder   245
he lies—sleeping in the yard there. 'Tis not twenty minutes since I saw him lie down."

The yard was entirely quiet. It was not accessible to the common prisoners. The surrounding walls, of amazing thickness, kept off all sounds behind them. The Egyptian character of the masonry weighed upon me with its gloom. But a soft imprisoned turf grew under foot. The heart of the eternal pyramids, it seemed, wherein, by some strange magic, through the clefts, grass-seed, dropped by birds, had sprung.

Strangely huddled at the base of the wall, his knees drawn up, and lying on his side, his head touching the cold stones, I saw the wasted Bartleby. But nothing stirred. I paused; then went close up to him; stooped over, and saw that his dim eyes were open; otherwise he seemed profoundly sleeping. Something prompted me to touch him. I felt his hand, when a tingling shiver ran up my arm and down my spine to my feet.

The round face of the grub-man peered upon me now. "His dinner is ready. Won't he dine to-day, either? Or does he live without dining?"

"Lives without dining," said I, and closed the eyes.

"Eh!—He's asleep, ain't he?"   250

"With kings and counselors,"[8] murmured I.

There would seem little need for proceeding further in this history. Imagination will readily supply the meagre recital of poor Bartleby's interment. But, ere parting with the reader, let me say, that if this little narrative has sufficiently interested him, to awaken curiosity as to who Bartleby was, and what manner of life he led prior to the present narrator's making his acquaintance, I can only reply, that in such curiosity I fully share, but am wholly unable to gratify it. Yet here I hardly know whether I should divulge one little item of rumor, which came to my ear a few months after the scrivener's decease. Upon what basis it rested, I could never ascertain; and hence, how true it is I cannot now tell. But, inasmuch as this vague report has not been without a certain suggestive interest to me, however sad, it may prove the same with some others; and so I will briefly mention it. The report was this: that Bartleby had been a subordinate clerk in the Dead Letter Office at Washington, from which he had been suddenly removed by a change in the administration. When I think over this rumor, hardly can I express the emotions which seize me. Dead letters! does it not sound like dead men? Conceive a man by nature and misfortune prone to a pallid hopelessness, can any business seem more fitted to heighten it than that of continually handling these dead letters, and assorting them for the flames? For by the cart-load they

---

[8]From Job 3:13–14: "then had I been at rest, / With kings and counselors of the earth, / which built desolate places for themselves."—Eds.

are annually burned. Sometimes from out the folded paper the pale clerk takes a ring—the finger it was meant for, perhaps, moulders in the grave; a bank-note sent in swiftest charity—he whom it would relieve, nor eats nor hungers any more; pardon for those who died despairing; hope for those who died unhoping; good tidings for those who died stifled by unrelieved calamities. On errands of life, these letters speed to death.

Ah, Bartleby! Ah, humanity!

[1853]

Exploring the Text

1. What effect does the opening paragraph have on you as a reader? What information do you learn? How does this paragraph embody "lawyerly language"—that is, language filled with qualifications and disclaimers?

2. The narrator's description of his three clerks—Turkey, Nippers, and Ginger Nut—might be summarized as a list of assets and liabilities, or credits and debits. What are the pluses and minuses of these characters, as Melville presents them? What comparisons does he draw between and among the three workers? How do they set the stage for the introduction of Bartleby?

3. The narrator introduces Bartleby as "a motionless young man . . . pallidly neat, pitiably respectable, incurably forlorn!" (para. 17). How does he expand this description as the story develops? How does this initial characterization foreshadow Bartleby's end?

4. How and why does Bartleby's "passive resistance" (para. 55) stymie the lawyer-narrator? How do Bartleby's "preferences" make their way into the culture of the narrator's law office?

5. The narrator tells us that Bartleby "was more a man of preferences than assumptions" (para. 149). How does this worldview differ from the legal profession's belief in precedents and assumptions?

6. What significance does the subtitle, "A Story of Wall Street," have? Consider the literal walls in the office and in the Tombs that Melville describes.

7. The narrator characterizes himself as living the philosophy that "the easiest way of life is the best" (para. 2). Chart his changing responses to Bartleby throughout the story. Then consider the ways in which he validates or changes his initial philosophy. Does the narrator grow in self-awareness or deteriorate into self-delusion? How do you interpret his statement, "In vain I persisted that Bartleby was nothing to me—no more than to any one else" (para. 192)?

8. Humor, though often subtle and ironic, runs throughout the story. What examples of humor can you identify, and how do they work as commentary or characterization?

9. At the end of the story, the narrator offers the possibility that Bartleby's rejection of life has been brought on by his working in the Dead Letter Office, a place where mail with inscrutable or partial addresses is ultimately destroyed. Is this

a plausible explanation? How does it fit thematically in the story, or case, that Melville has built?

10. How does this "Story of Wall Street" fit with the way we view Wall Street today? How do attitudes toward money and materialism inform this story? Does the characterization of the environment of Wall Street as mechanical and dehumanizing ring true in the twenty-first century?

Harrison Bergeron

KURT VONNEGUT

Kurt Vonnegut (1922–2007) was one of the most influential writers in post–World War II America. Born in Indianapolis, Indiana, he attended Cornell University for two years before joining the army, where he fought in the Battle of the Bulge and was captured by German troops in 1944. While a prisoner of war, he witnessed the firebombing of Dresden, an experience that inspired his most famous novel, *Slaughterhouse Five* (1969), named for the building in which he was imprisoned. Vonnegut studied at the Carnegie Institute of Technology and the University of Tennessee while in the army; after the war, he went to graduate school to study anthropology at the University of Chicago. Before becoming a full-time writer, he worked as a reporter, teacher, and public relations employee for General Electric. His first novel, the satiric *Player Piano* (1952), was inspired by his time at GE. Among his other well-known books are *The Sirens of Titan* (1959), *Cat's Cradle* (1963), and *Breakfast of Champions* (1973). "Harrison Bergeron" first appeared in *Collier's* magazine, before being reprinted in the short-story collection *Welcome to the Monkey House* (1968).

The year was 2081, and everybody was finally equal. They weren't only equal before God and the law. They were equal every which way. Nobody was smarter than anybody else. Nobody was better looking than anybody else. Nobody was stronger or quicker than anybody else. All this equality was due to the 211th, 212th, and 213th Amendments to the Constitution, and to the unceasing vigilance of agents of the United States Handicapper General.

Some things about living still weren't quite right, though. April, for instance, still drove people crazy by not being springtime. And it was in that clammy month that the H-G men took George and Hazel Bergeron's fourteen-year-old son, Harrison, away.

It was tragic, all right, but George and Hazel couldn't think about it very hard. Hazel had a perfectly average intelligence, which meant she couldn't think about anything except in short bursts. And George, while his intelligence was way above normal, had a little mental handicap radio in his ear. He was required by law to wear it at all times. It was tuned to a government transmitter. Every twenty seconds or so, the transmitter would send out some sharp noise to keep people like George from taking unfair advantage of their brains.

George and Hazel were watching television. There were tears on Hazel's cheeks, but she'd forgotten for the moment what they were about.

On the television screen were ballerinas. 5

A buzzer sounded in George's head. His thoughts fled in panic, like bandits from a burglar alarm.

"That was a real pretty dance, that dance they just did," said Hazel.

"Huh?" said George.

"That dance—it was nice," said Hazel.

"Yup," said George. He tried to think a little about the ballerinas. They weren't 10 really very good—no better than anybody else would have been, anyway. They were burdened with sashweights and bags of birdshot, and their faces were masked, so that no one, seeing a free and graceful gesture or a pretty face, would feel like something the cat drug in. George was toying with the vague notion that maybe dancers shouldn't be handicapped. But he didn't get very far with it before another noise in his ear radio scattered his thoughts.

George winced. So did two out of the eight ballerinas.

Hazel saw him wince. Having no mental handicap herself, she had to ask George what the latest sound had been.

"Sounded like somebody hitting a milk bottle with a ball-peen hammer," said George.

"I'd think it would be real interesting, hearing all the different sounds," said Hazel, a little envious. "All the things they think up."

"Um," said George. 15

"Only, if I was Handicapper General, you know what I would do?" said Hazel. Hazel, as a matter of fact, bore a strong resemblance to the Handicapper General, a woman named Diana Moon Glampers. "If I was Diana Moon Glampers," said Hazel, "I'd have chimes on Sunday—just chimes. Kind of in honor of religion."

"I could think, if it was just chimes," said George.

"Well—maybe make 'em real loud," said Hazel. "I think I'd make a good Handicapper General."

"Good as anybody else," said George.

"Who knows better'n I do what normal is?" said Hazel. 20

"Right," said George. He began to think glimmeringly about his abnormal son who was now in jail, about Harrison, but a twenty-one-gun salute in his head stopped that.

"Boy!" said Hazel, "that was a doozy, wasn't it?"

It was such a doozy that George was white and trembling, and tears stood on the rims of his red eyes. Two of the eight ballerinas had collapsed to the studio floor, were holding their temples.

"All of a sudden you look so tired," said Hazel. "Why don't you stretch out on the sofa, so's you can rest your handicap bag on the pillows, honeybunch." She was referring to the forty-seven pounds of birdshot in a canvas bag, which was padlocked around George's neck. "Go on and rest the bag for a little while," she said. "I don't care if you're not equal to me for a while."

George weighed the bag with his hands. "I don't mind it," he said. "I don't notice   25
it any more. It's just a part of me."

"You been so tired lately—kind of wore out," said Hazel. "If there was just some way we could make a little hole in the bottom of the bag, and just take out a few of them lead balls. Just a few."

"Two years in prison and two thousand dollars fine for every ball I took out," said George. "I don't call that a bargain."

"If you could just take a few out when you came home from work," said Hazel. "I mean—you don't compete with anybody around here. You just set around."

"If I tried to get away with it," said George, "then other people'd get away with it—and pretty soon we'd be right back to the dark ages again, with everybody competing against everybody else. You wouldn't like that, would you?"

"I'd hate it," said Hazel.   30

"There you are," said George. "The minute people start cheating on laws, what do you think happens to society?"

If Hazel hadn't been able to come up with an answer to this question, George couldn't have supplied one. A siren was going off in his head.

"Reckon it'd fall all apart," said Hazel.

"What would?" said George blankly.

"Society," said Hazel uncertainly. "Wasn't that what you just said?"   35

"Who knows?" said George.

The television program was suddenly interrupted for a news bulletin. It wasn't clear at first as to what the bulletin was about, since the announcer, like all announcers, had a serious speech impediment. For about half a minute, and in a state of high excitement, the announcer tried to say, "Ladies and gentlemen—"

He finally gave up, handed the bulletin to a ballerina to read.

"That's all right—" Hazel said of the announcer, "he tried. That's the big thing. He tried to do the best he could with what God gave him. He should get a nice raise for trying so hard."

"Ladies and gentlemen—" said the ballerina, reading the bulletin. She must have   40
been extraordinarily beautiful, because the mask she wore was hideous. And it was easy to see that she was the strongest and most graceful of all the dancers, for her handicap bags were as big as those worn by two-hundred-pound men.

And she had to apologize at once for her voice, which was a very unfair voice for a woman to use. Her voice was a warm, luminous, timeless melody. "Excuse me—" she said, and she began again, making her voice absolutely uncompetitive.

"Harrison Bergeron, age fourteen," she said in a grackle squawk, "has just escaped from jail, where he was held on suspicion of plotting to overthrow the government. He is a genius and an athlete, is under-handicapped, and should be regarded as extremely dangerous."

A police photograph of Harrison Bergeron was flashed on the screen—upside down, then sideways, upside down again, then right side up. The picture showed the full length of Harrison against a background calibrated in feet and inches. He was exactly seven feet tall.

The rest of Harrison's appearance was Halloween and hardware. Nobody had ever borne heavier handicaps. He had outgrown hindrances faster than the H-G men could think them up. Instead of a little ear radio for a mental handicap, he wore a tremendous pair of earphones, and spectacles with thick wavy lenses. The spectacles were intended to make him not only half blind, but to give him whanging headaches besides.

Scrap metal was hung all over him. Ordinarily, there was a certain symmetry, a   45
military neatness to the handicaps issued to strong people, but Harrison looked like a walking junkyard. In the race of life, Harrison carried three hundred pounds.

And to offset his good looks, the H-G men required that he wear at all times a red rubber ball for a nose, keep his eyebrows shaved off, and cover his even white teeth with black caps at snaggle-tooth random.

"If you see this boy," said the ballerina, "do not—I repeat, do not—try to reason with him."

There was the shriek of a door being torn from its hinges.

Screams and barking cries of consternation came from the television set. The photograph of Harrison Bergeron on the screen jumped again and again, as though dancing to the tune of an earthquake.

George Bergeron correctly identified the earthquake, and well he might have—for   50
many was the time his own home had danced to the same crashing tune. "My God—" said George, "that must be Harrison!"

The realization was blasted from his mind instantly by the sound of an automobile collision in his head.

When George could open his eyes again, the photograph of Harrison was gone. A living, breathing Harrison filled the screen.

Clanking, clownish, and huge, Harrison stood in the center of the studio. The knob of the uprooted studio door was still in his hand. Ballerinas, technicians, musicians, and announcers cowered on their knees before him, expecting to die.

"I am the Emperor!" cried Harrison. "Do you hear? I am the Emperor! Everybody must do what I say at once!" He stamped his foot and the studio shook.

"Even as I stand here—" he bellowed, "crippled, hobbled, sickened—I am a greater   55
ruler than any man who ever lived! Now watch me become what I *can* become!"

Harrison tore the straps of his handicap harness like wet tissue paper, tore straps guaranteed to support five thousand pounds.

Harrison's scrap-iron handicaps crashed to the floor.

Harrison thrust his thumbs under the bars of the padlock that secured his head harness. The bar snapped like celery. Harrison smashed his headphones and spectacles against the wall.

He flung away his rubber-ball nose, revealed a man that would have awed Thor, the god of thunder.

"I shall now select my Empress!" he said, looking down on the cowering people.   60
"Let the first woman who dares rise to her feet claim her mate and her throne!"

A moment passed, and then a ballerina arose, swaying like a willow.

Harrison plucked the mental handicap from her ear, snapped off her physical handicaps with marvelous delicacy. Last of all, he removed her mask.

She was blindingly beautiful.

"Now—" said Harrison, taking her hand, "shall we show the people the meaning of the word dance? Music!" he commanded.

The musicians scrambled back into their chairs, and Harrison stripped them of   65
their handicaps, too. "Play your best," he told them, "and I'll make you barons and dukes and earls."

The music began. It was normal at first—cheap, silly, false. But Harrison snatched two musicians from their chairs, waved them like batons as he sang the music as he wanted it played. He slammed them back into their chairs.

The music began again and was much improved.

Harrison and his Empress merely listened to the music for a while—listened gravely, as though synchronizing their heartbeats with it.

They shifted their weights to their toes.

Harrison placed his big hands on the girl's tiny waist, letting her sense the   70
weightlessness that would soon be hers.

And then, in an explosion of joy and grace, into the air they sprang!

Not only were the laws of the land abandoned, but the law of gravity and the laws of motion as well.

They reeled, whirled, swiveled, flounced, capered, gamboled, and spun.

They leaped like deer on the moon.

The studio ceiling was thirty feet high, but each leap brought the dancers nearer   75
to it.

It became their obvious intention to kiss the ceiling.

They kissed it.

And then, neutralizing gravity with love and pure will, they remained suspended in air inches below the ceiling, and they kissed each other for a long, long time.

It was then that Diana Moon Glampers, the Handicapper General, came into the studio with a double-barreled ten-gauge shotgun. She fired twice, and the Emperor and the Empress were dead before they hit the floor.

Diana Moon Glampers loaded the gun again. She aimed at the musicians and   80
told them they had ten seconds to get their handicaps back on.

It was then that the Bergerons' television tube burned out.

Hazel turned to comment about the blackout to George. But George had gone out into the kitchen for a can of beer.

George came back in with the beer, paused while a handicap signal shook him up. And then he sat down again. "You been crying?" he said to Hazel.

"Yup," she said.

"What about?" he said.

"I forgot," she said. "Something real sad on television."   85

"What was it?" he said.

"It's all kind of mixed up in my mind," said Hazel.

"Forget sad things," said George.

"I always do," said Hazel.   90

"That's my girl," said George. He winced. There was the sound of a riveting gun in his head.

"Gee—I could tell that one was a doozy," said Hazel.

"You can say that again," said George.

"Gee—" said Hazel, "I could tell that one was a doozy."

[1961]

. . . .

Exploring the Text

1. The story begins, "The year was 2081, and everybody was finally equal." What does the word "finally" imply about the idea of equality? As the story goes on, equality becomes a more complicated prospect. What are some of the benefits and dangers of equality as presented in "Harrison Bergeron"?

2. In paragraph 20, Hazel says, "Who knows better'n I do what normal is?" What does "normal" mean in this context? What does she think it means, and in this society, how does it relate to being equal?

3. The tone throughout the story is ironic, but how would you characterize this type of irony? What is its purpose, and what is the narrator's attitude toward the events he describes? toward the characters he portrays?

4. How do the characters in the story—particularly George and Hazel—seem to feel about the current state of enforced total equality? Look closely at the section in which Hazel urges George to remove his heavy handicaps for a short while and rest (paras. 24–27). Why does he resist? Is it surprising that Hazel is the one who suggests this small rebellion? Explain.

5. What particular attitudes, laws, or events might Vonnegut be satirizing in this story? Consider that it was published in 1961. How does it reflect twenty-first-century attitudes or assumptions about equality, conformity, and rebellion?

6. What does it mean that Harrison Bergeron's culminating act of rebellion is to declare himself emperor? When they are dancing, free of their handicaps, he and his ballerina empress defy not only the rules of society but also "the law of gravity and the laws of motion as well" (para. 72). What might this fantastical moment suggest? Why does Harrison Bergeron present such a perceived threat to society? What is the nature of this threat, and how real is it?

7. In paragraph 73, Vonnegut writes, "They reeled, whirled, swiveled, flounced, capered, gamboled, and spun." What does each verb mean? How is each different, and what is achieved by enumerating such a long list?

8. Do you find the ending predictable or surprising? Does the narrator? Explain your answer. How do Harrison's death and his parents' reactions further comment on (and complicate) the story's take on conformity and rebellion?

Admiral

T. C. BOYLE

Born Thomas John Boyle in 1948 in Peekskill, New York, Boyle changed his middle name to Coraghessan at seventeen, but now goes by T. C. After receiving his BA at the State University of New York at Potsdam, he earned an MFA at the Iowa Writers' Workshop, followed by a PhD in nineteenth-century British literature. He has been a professor of English at the University of Southern California since 1978. Boyle is known for highly inventive fiction filled with unusual and often bizarre situations and dark humor, so it comes as no surprise that his favorite short story is Flannery O'Connor's "A Good Man Is Hard to Find" (p. 1211). Boyle published his first short-story collection, *Descent of Man*, in 1979 and his first novel, *Water Music*, in 1982. He has published more than 150 short stories and a dozen novels since then, including *The Tortilla Curtain* (1985), *World's End* (1987), and *Talk Talk* (2006). His 1993 novel, *The Road to Wellville*, was made into a major motion picture the following year. "Admiral" originally appeared in *Harper's* magazine and is included in the 2008 edition of *The Best American Short Stories*.

She knew in her heart it was a mistake, but she'd been laid off and needed the cash, and her memories of the Strikers were mostly on the favorable side, so when Mrs. Striker called—*Gretchen, this is Gretchen? Mrs. Striker?*—she'd said yes, she'd love to come over and hear what they had to say. First, though, she had to listen to her car cough as she drove across town (fuel pump, that was her father's opinion, offered in a flat voice that said it wasn't his problem, not anymore, not now that she was grown and living back at home after a failed attempt at life), and she nearly stalled the thing turning into the Strikers' block. And then did stall it as she tried, against any reasonable expectation of success, to parallel park in front of their great rearing fortress of a house. It felt strange punching in the code at the gate and seeing how things were different and the same, how the trees had grown while the flowerbeds remained in a state of suspended animation, everything in perpetual bloom and clipped to within a millimeter of perfection. The gardeners saw to that. A whole battalion of them that swarmed over the place twice a week with their blowers and edgers and trimmers, at war with the weeds, the insects, the gophers and ground squirrels, and the very tendency of the display plants to want to grow outside the box. At least that was how she remembered it. The gardeners. And how Admiral would rage at the windows, showing his teeth and scrabbling with his claws—and if he could have chewed through glass he would have done it. "That's right, boy," she'd say, "that's right—don't let those bad men steal all your dead leaves and dirt. You go, boy. You go. That's right."

She rang the bell at the front door and it wasn't Mrs. Striker who answered it but another version of herself in a white maid's apron and a little white maid's cap perched atop her head, and she was so surprised she had to double-clutch to keep from dropping her purse. *A woman of color does not clean house*, that was what her mother always told her, and it had become a kind of mantra when she was growing up, a way of reinforcing core values, of promoting education and the life of the mind, but she couldn't help wondering how much higher a dog-sitter was on the socioeconomic scale than a maid. Or a sous-chef, waitress, aerobics instructor, ticket puncher, and tortilla maker, all of which she'd been at one time or another. About the only thing she hadn't tried was leech-gathering. There was a poem on the subject in her college text by William Wordsworth, the poet of daffodils and leeches, and she could summon it up whenever she needed a good laugh. She developed a quick picture of an old long-nosed white man rolling up his pant legs and wading into the murk, then squeezed out a miniature smile and said, "Hi, I'm Nisha? I came to see Mrs. Striker? And Mr. Striker?"

The maid—she wasn't much older than Nisha herself, with a placid expression that might have been described as self-satisfied or just plain vacant—held open the door. "I'll tell them you're here," she said.

Nisha murmured a thank-you and stepped into the tiled foyer, thinking of the snake brain and the olfactory memories that lay coiled there. She smelled dog—smelled Admiral—with an overlay of old sock and furniture polish. The great room rose up before her like something transposed from a cathedral. It was a cold room, echoing and hollow, and she'd never liked it. "You mind if I wait in the family room?" she asked.

The maid—or rather the girl, the young woman, the young woman in the   5
demeaning and stereotypical maid's costume—had already started off in the direction of the kitchen, but she swung round now to give Nisha a look of surprise and irritation. For a moment it seemed as if she might snap at her, but then, finally, she just shrugged and said, "Whatever."

Nothing had changed in the paneled room that gave onto the garden, not as far as Nisha could see. There were the immense old high-backed leather armchairs and the antique Stickley sofa rescued from the law offices of Striker and Striker, the mahogany bar with the wine rack and the backlit shrine Mr. Striker had created in homage to the spirits of single-malt scotch whisky, and overseeing it all, the oil portrait of Admiral with its dark heroic hues and golden patina of varnish. She remembered the day the painter had come to the house and posed the dog for the preliminary snapshots. Admiral uncooperative, Mrs. Striker strung tight as a wire, and the inevitable squirrel bounding across the lawn at the crucial moment. The painter had labored mightily in his studio to make his subject look noble, snout elevated, eyes fixed on some distant, presumably worthy, object, but to Nisha's mind an Afghan—any Afghan—looked inherently ridiculous, like some escapee from *Sesame Street*, and Admiral seemed a kind of concentrate of the absurd. He looked goofy, just that.

When she turned round, both the Strikers were there, as if they'd floated in out of the ether. As far as she could see, they hadn't aged at all. Their skin was flawless, they held themselves as stiff and erect as the Ituri carvings they'd picked up on their trip to Africa, and they tried hard to make small talk and avoid any appearance of briskness. In Mrs. Striker's arms—*Call me Gretchen, please*—was an Afghan pup, and after the initial exchange of pleasantries, Nisha, her hand extended to rub the silk of the ears and feel the wet probe of the tiny snout on her wrist, began to get the idea. She restrained herself from asking after Admiral. "Is this his pup?" she asked instead. "Is this little Admiral?" The Strikers exchanged a glance. The husband hadn't said, *Call me Cliff*, hadn't said much of anything, but now his lips compressed. "Didn't you read about it in the papers?"

There was an awkward pause. The pup began to squirm. "Admiral passed," Gretchen breathed. "It was an accident. We had him—well, we were in the park, the dog park . . . you know, the one where the dogs run free? You used to take him there, you remember, up off Sycamore? Well, you know how exuberant he was . . ."

"You really didn't read about it?" There was incredulity in the husband's voice.

"Well, I—I was away at college and then I took the first job I could find. Back   10
here, I mean. Because of my mother. She's been sick."

Neither of them commented on this, not even to be polite.

"It was all over the press," the husband said, and he sounded offended now. He adjusted his oversized glasses and cocked his head to look down at her in a way that brought the past rushing back. "*Newsweek* did a story, *USA Today*—we were on *Good Morning America*, both of us."

She was at a loss, the three of them standing there, the dog taking its spiked dentition to the underside of her wrist now, just the way Admiral used to when he was a pup. "For what?" she was about to say, when Gretchen came to the rescue.

"This *is* little Admiral. Admiral II, actually," she said, ruffling the blond shag over the pup's eyes.

The husband looked past her, out the window and into the yard, an ironic grin   15
pressed to his lips. "Two hundred and fifty thousand dollars," he said, "and it's too bad he wasn't a cat."

Gretchen gave him a sharp look. "You make a joke of it," she said, her eyes suddenly filling, "but it was worth every penny and you know it." She mustered a long-suffering smile for Nisha. "Cats are simpler—their eggs are more mature at ovulation than dogs' are."

"I can get you a cat for thirty-two thou."

"Oh, Cliff, stop. Stop it."

He moved into his wife and put an arm round her shoulders. "But we didn't want to clone a cat, did we, honey?" He bent his face to the dog's, touched noses with him, and let his voice rise to a falsetto: "Did we now, Admiral. Did we!"

At seven-thirty the next morning, Nisha pulled up in front of the Strikers' house and   20
let her car wheeze and shudder a moment before killing the engine. She flicked the radio back on to catch the last fading chorus of a tune she liked, singing along with the sexy low rasp of the lead vocalist, feeling good about things—or better, anyway. The Strikers were giving her twenty-five dollars an hour, plus the same dental and health-care package they offered the staff at their law firm, which was a whole solid

towering brick wall of improvement over what she'd been making as a waitress at Johnny's Rib Shack, sans health care, sans dental, and sans any tip she could remember above 10 percent of the pre-tax total because the people who came out to gnaw ribs were just plain cheap and no two ways about it. When she stepped out of the car, there was Gretchen coming down the front steps of the house with the pup in her arms, just as she had nine years ago when Nisha was a high school freshman taking on what she assumed was going to be a breeze of a summer job.

Nisha took the initiative of punching in the code herself and slipping through the gate to hustle up the walk and save Gretchen the trouble, because Gretchen was in a hurry, always in a hurry. She was dressed in a navy-blue suit with a double string of pearls and an antique silver pin in the shape of a bounding borzoi that seemed eerily familiar—it might have been the exact ensemble she'd been wearing when Nisha had told her she'd be quitting to go off to college. *I'm sorry, Mrs. Striker, and I've really enjoyed the opportunity to work for you and Mr. Striker*, she'd said, hardly able to contain the swell of her heart, *but I'm going to college. On a scholarship*. She'd had the acceptance letter in her hand to show her, thinking how proud of her Mrs. Striker would be, how she'd take her in her arms for a hug and congratulate her, but the first thing she'd said was, *What about Admiral?*

As Gretchen closed on her now, the pup wriggling in her arms, Nisha could see her smile flutter and die. No doubt she was already envisioning the cream-leather interior of her BMW (a 750i in Don't-Even-Think-About-It Black) and the commute to the office and whatever was going down there, court sessions, the piles of documents, contention at every turn. Mr. Striker—Nisha would never be able to call him Cliff, even if she lived to be eighty, but then he'd have to be a hundred and ten and probably wouldn't hear her anyway—was already gone, in his matching Beemer, his and hers. Gretchen didn't say *Good morning* or *Hi* or *How are you?* or *Thanks for coming*, but just enfolded her in the umbrella of her perfume and handed her the dog. Which went immediately heavy in Nisha's arms, fighting for the ground with four flailing paws and the little white ghoul's teeth that fastened on the top button of her jacket. Nisha held on. Gave Gretchen a big grateful-for-the-job-and-the-health-care smile, no worries, no worries at all.

"Those jeans," Gretchen said, narrowing her eyes. "Are they new?"

The dog squirming, squirming. "I, well—I'm going to set him down a minute, okay?"

"Of course, of course. Do what you do, what you normally do." An impatient wave. "Or what you used to do, I mean." 25

They both watched as the pup fell back on its haunches, rolled briefly in the grass, and sprang up to clutch Nisha's right leg in a clumsy embrace. "I just couldn't find any of my old jeans—my mother probably threw them all out long ago. Plus"—a laugh—"I don't think I could fit into them anymore." She gave Gretchen a moment to ruminate on the deeper implications here—time passing, adolescents grown into womanhood, flesh expanding, that sort of thing—then gently pushed the dog down and murmured, "But I *am* wearing—right here, under the jacket?—this T-shirt I know I used to wear back then."

Nothing. Gretchen just stood there, looking distracted.

"It's been washed, of course, and sitting in the back of the top drawer of my dresser where my mother left it, so I don't know if there'll be any scent or anything, but I'm sure I used to wear it because Tupac really used to drive my engine back then, if you know what I mean." She gave it a beat. "But hey, we were all fourteen once, huh?" Gretchen made no sign that she'd heard her—either that or she denied the proposition outright. "You're going to be all right with this, aren't you?" she said, looking her in the eye. "Is there anything we didn't cover?"

The afternoon before, during her interview—but it wasn't really an interview because the Strikers had already made up their minds, and if she'd refused them they would have kept raising the hourly till she capitulated—the two of them, Gretchen and Cliff, had positioned themselves on either side of her and leaned into the bar over caramel-colored scotches and a platter of ebi and maguro sushi to explain the situation.

Just so that she was clear on it. "You know what cloning is, right?" Gretchen said.   30
"Or what it involves? You remember Dolly?"

Nisha was holding fast to her drink, her left elbow pressed to the brass rail of the bar in the family room. She'd just reached out her twinned chopsticks for a second piece of the shrimp but withdrew her hand. "You mean the country singer?"

"The sheep," the husband said.

"The first cloned mammal," Gretchen put in. "Or larger mammal."

"Yeah," she said, nodding. "Sure. I guess."

What followed was a short course in genetics and the method of somatic-cell   35
nuclear transplant that had given the world Dolly, various replicated cattle, pigs, and hamsters, and now Admiral II, the first cloned dog made available commercially through SalvaPet, Inc., the genetic-engineering firm with offices in Seoul, San Juan, and Cleveland. Gretchen's voice constricted as she described how they'd taken a cell from the lining of Admiral's ear just after the accident and inserted it into a donor egg that had had its nucleus removed, stimulated the cell to divide through the application of an electric current, and then inserted the developing embryo into the uterus of a host mother—"The sweetest golden retriever you ever saw. What was her name, Cliff? Some flower, wasn't it?"

"Peony."

"Peony? Are you sure?"

"Of course I'm sure."

"I thought it was—oh, I don't know. You sure it wasn't Iris?"

"The point is," he said, setting his glass down and leveling his gaze at Nisha, "you   40
can get a genetic copy of the animal, a kind of three-dimensional Xerox, but that doesn't guarantee it'll be like the one you, well, the one you lost."

"It was so sad," Gretchen said.

"It's nurture that counts. You've got to reproduce the animal's experiences, as nearly as possible." He gave a shrug, reached for the bottle. "You want another?" he asked, and she held out her glass. "Of course we're both older now—and so are you, we realize that—but we want to come as close as possible to replicating the exact conditions that made Admiral what he was, right down to the toys we gave him, the food, the schedule of walks and play, and all the rest. Which is where you come in—"

"We need a commitment here, Nisha," Gretchen breathed, leaning in so close Nisha could smell the scotch coming back at her. "Four years. That's how long you were with him last time. Or with Admiral, I mean. The original Admiral."

The focus of all this deliberation had fallen asleep in Gretchen's lap. A single probing finger of sunlight stabbed through the window to illuminate the pale fluff over the dog's eyes. At that moment, in that light, little Admiral looked like some strange conjunction of ostrich and ape. Nisha couldn't help thinking of *The Island of Dr. Moreau*, the cheesy version with Marlon Brando looking as if he'd been genetically manipulated himself, and she would have grinned a private grin, fueled by the scotch and the thundering absurdity of the moment, but she had to hide everything she thought or felt behind a mask of impassivity. She wasn't committing to anything for four years—four years? If she was still living here in this craphole of a town four years from now she promised herself she'd go out and buy a gun and eliminate all her problems with a single, very personal squeeze of the trigger.

That was what she was thinking when Gretchen said, "We'll pay you twenty dollars an hour," and the husband said, "With health care—and dental," and they both stared at her so fiercely she had to look down into her glass before she found her voice. "Twenty-five," she said. 45

And oh, how they loved that dog, because they never hesitated. "Twenty-five it is," the husband said, and Gretchen, a closer's smile blooming on her face, produced a contract from the folder at her elbow. "Just sign here," she said.

After Gretchen had climbed into her car and the car had slid through the gate and vanished down the street, Nisha sprawled out on the grass and lifted her face to the sun. She was feeling the bliss of déjà vu—or no, not déjà vu, but a virtual return to the past, when life was just a construct and there was nothing she couldn't have done or been and nothing beyond the thought of clothes and boys and the occasional term paper to hamper her. Here she was, gone back in time, lying on the grass at quarter of eight in the morning on a sunstruck June day, playing with a puppy while everybody else was going to work—it was hilarious, that's what it was. Like something you'd read about in the paper—a behest from some crazed millionaire. Or in this case, two crazed millionaires. She felt so good she let out a laugh, even as the pup came charging across the lawn to slam headfirst into her, all feet and pink panting tongue, and he was Admiral all right.

Admiral in the flesh, born and made and resurrected for the mere little pittance of a quarter million dollars. For a long while she wrestled with him, flipping him over on his back each time he charged, scratching his belly and baby-talking him, enjoying the novelty of it, but by quarter past eight she was bored and she pushed herself up to go on into the house and find something to eat. *Do what you used to do*, Gretchen had told her, but what she used to do, summers especially, was nap and read and watch TV and sneak her friends in to tip a bottle of the husband's forty-year-old scotch to their adolescent lips and make faces at one another before descending into giggles. Twice a day she'd take the dog to the doggy park and watch him squat and crap and run wild with the other mutts till his muzzle was streaked with drool and he dodged at her feet to snatch up mouthfuls of the Evian the Strikers insisted he drink. Now, though, she just wanted to feel the weight of the past a bit, and she went in the back door, the dog at her heels, thinking to make herself a sandwich — the Strikers always had cold cuts in the fridge, mounds of pastrami, capicolla, smoked turkey, and Swiss, individual slices of which went to Admiral each time he did his business outside where he was supposed to or barked in the right cadence or just stuck his goofy head in the door. She could already see the sandwich she was going to make — a whole deli's worth of meat and cheese piled up on Jewish rye; they always had Jewish rye — and she was halfway to the refrigerator before she remembered the maid.

There she was, in her maid's outfit, sitting at the kitchen table with her feet up and the newspaper spread out before her, spooning something out of a cup. "Don't you bring that filthy animal in here," she said, glancing up sharply.

Nisha was startled. There didn't used to be a maid. There was no one in the   50
house, in fact, till Mrs. Yamashita, the cook, came in around four, and that was part of the beauty of it. "Oh, hi," she said, "hi, I didn't know you were going to be — I just . . . I was going to make a sandwich, I guess." There was a silence. The dog slunk around the kitchen, looking wary. "What was your name again?"

"Frankie," the maid said, swallowing the syllables as if she weren't ready to give them up, "and I'm the one has to clean up all these paw marks off the floor — and did you see what he did to that throw pillow in the guest room?"

"No," Nisha said, "I didn't," and she was at the refrigerator now, sliding back the tray of the meat compartment. This would go easier if they were friends, no doubt about it, and she was willing, more than willing. "You want anything?" she said. "A sandwich — or, or something?"

Frankie just stared at her. "I don't know what they're paying you," she said, "but to me? This is the craziest shit I ever heard of in my life. You think I couldn't let the dog out the door a couple times a day? Or what, take him to the park — that's what you do, right, take him to the doggy park over on Sycamore?"

The refrigerator door swung shut, the little light blinking out, the heft of the meat satisfying in her hand. "It's insane, I admit it — hey, I'm with you. You think I wanted to grow up to be a dog-sitter?"

"I don't know. I don't know anything about you. Except you got your   55
degree — you need a degree for that, dog-sitting, I mean?" She hadn't moved, not a muscle, her feet propped up, the cup in one hand, spoon in the other.

"No," Nisha said, feeling the blood rise to her face, "no, you don't. But what about you — you need a degree to be a maid?"

That hit home. For a moment, Frankie said nothing, just looked from her to the dog — which was begging now, clawing at Nisha's leg with his forepaws — and back again. "This is just temporary," she said finally.

"Yeah, me too." Nisha gave her a smile, no harm done, just establishing a little turf, that was all. "Totally."

For the first time, Frankie's expression changed: she almost looked as if she were going to laugh. "Yeah, that's right," she said, "temporary help, that's all we are. We're the temps. And Mr. and Mrs. Striker—dog-crazy, plain crazy, two-hundred-and-fifty-thousand-dollar-crazy—they're permanent."

And now Nisha laughed, and so did Frankie—a low rumble of amusement that made the dog turn its head. The meat was on the counter now, the cellophane wrapper pulled back. Nisha selected a slice of Black Forest ham and held it out to him. "Sit!" she said. "Go ahead, sit!" And the dog, just like his father or progenitor or donor or whatever he was, looked at her stupidly till she dropped the meat on the tile and the wet plop of its arrival made him understand that here was something to eat. 60

"You're going to spoil that dog," Frankie said.

Nisha went unerringly to the cabinet where the bread was kept, and there it was, Jewish rye, a fresh loaf, springy to the touch. She gave Frankie a glance over her shoulder. "Yeah," she said. "I think that's the idea."

A month drifted by, as serene a month as Nisha could remember. She was making good money, putting in ten-hour days during the week and half days on the weekends, reading through all the books she hadn't had time for in college, exhausting the Strikers' DVD collection and opening her own account at the local video store, walking, lazing, napping the time away. She gained five pounds and vowed to start swimming regularly in the Strikers' pool, but hadn't got round to it yet. Some days she'd help Frankie with the cleaning and the laundry so the two of them could sit out on the back deck with their feet up, sharing a bottle of sweet wine or a joint. As for the dog, she tried to be conscientious about the whole business of imprinting it with the past—or *a* past—though she felt ridiculous. Four years of college for this? Wars were being fought, people were starving, there were diseases to conquer, children to educate, good to do in the world, and here she was reliving her adolescence in the company of an inbred semi-retarded clown of a cloned Afghan hound because two childless rich people decreed it should be so. All right. She knew she'd have to move on. Knew it was temporary. Swore that she'd work up a new résumé and start sending it out—but then the face of her mother, sick from vomiting and with her scalp as smooth and slick as an eggplant, would rise up to shame her. She threw the ball to the dog. Took him to the park. Let the days fall round her like leaves from a dying tree.

And then one afternoon, on the way back from the dog park, Admiral jerking at the leash beside her and the sky opening up to a dazzle of sun and pure white tufts of cloud that made her feel as if she were floating untethered through the universe along with them, she noticed a figure stationed outside the gate of the Strikers' house. As she got closer, she saw that it was a young man dressed in baggy jeans and a T-shirt, his hair fanning out in rusty blond dreads and a goatee of the same color clinging to his chin. He was peering over the fence. Her first thought was that he'd come to rob the place, but she dismissed it—he was harmless; you could see that a hundred yards off. Then she saw the paint smears on his jeans and wondered if he was a painting contractor come to put in a bid on the house, but that wasn't it either. He looked more like an amateur artist—and here she had to laugh to herself—the kind who specializes in dog portraits. But she was nearly on him now, thinking to brush by him and slip through the gate before he could accost her, whatever he wanted, when he turned suddenly and his face caught fire. "Wow!" he said. "Wow, I can't believe it! You're her, aren't you, the famous dog-sitter? And this"—he went down on one knee and made a chirping sound deep in his throat—"this is Admiral. Right? Am I right?"

Admiral went straight to him, lurching against the leash, and in the next instant   65 was flopping himself down on the hot pavement, submitting to the man's caresses. The rope of a tail whapped and thrashed, the paws gyrated, the puppy teeth came into play. "Good boy," the man crooned, his dreads riding a wave across his brow. "He likes that, doesn't he? Doesn't he, boy?"

Nisha didn't say anything. She just watched, the smallest hole dug out of the canyon of her boredom, till the man rose to his feet and held out his hand even as Admiral sprang up to hump his leg with fresh enthusiasm. "I'm Erhard," he said, grinning wide. "And you're Nisha, right?"

"Yes," she said, taking his hand despite herself. She was on the verge of asking how he knew her name, but there was no point: she already understood. He was from the press. In the past month there must have been a dozen reporters on the property, the Strikers stroking their vanity and posing for pictures and answering the same idiotic questions over and over—*A quarter-million dollars: that's a lot for a dog, isn't it?*—and she herself had been interviewed twice already. Her mother had even found a fuzzy color photo of her and Admiral (couchant, lap) on the Web under the semi-hilarious rubric CLONE SITTER. So this guy was a reporter—a foreign reporter, judging from the faint trace of an accent and the blue-eyed rearing height of him, German, she supposed. Or Austrian. And he wanted some of her time.

"Yes," he said, as if reading her thoughts. "I am from *Die Weltwoche* and I wanted to ask of you—prevail upon you, beg you—for a few moments? Is that possible? For me? Just now?"

She gave him a long slow appraisal, flirting with him, yes, definitely flirting.

"I've got nothing but time," she said. And then, watching his grin widen: "You   70 want a sandwich?"

They ate on the patio overlooking the pool. She was dressed casually in shorts and flip-flops and her old Tupac tee, and that wasn't necessarily a bad thing because the shirt—too small by half—lifted away from her hips when she leaned back in the chair, showing off her navel and the onyx ring she wore there. He was watching her, chattering on about the dog, lifting the sandwich to his lips and putting it down again, fooling with the lens on the battered old Hasselblad he extracted from the backpack at his feet. The sun made sequins on the surface of the pool. Admiral lounged beneath the table, worrying a rawhide bone. She was feeling good, better than good, sipping a beer and watching him back.

They had a little conversation about the beer. "Sorry to offer you Miller, but that's all we have—or the Strikers have, I mean."

"Miller High Life," he said, lifting the bottle to his mouth. "Great name. What person would not want to live the high life? Even a dog. Even Admiral. He lives the high life, no?"

"I thought you'd want a German beer, something like Beck's or something."

He set down the bottle, picked up the camera, and let the lens wander down 75 the length of her legs. "I'm Swiss, actually," he said. "But I live here now. And I like American beer. I like everything American."

There was no mistaking the implication, and she wanted to return the sentiment, but she didn't know the first thing about Switzerland, so she just smiled and tipped her beer to him.

"So," he said, cradling the camera in his lap and referring to the notepad he'd laid on the table when she'd served him the sandwich, "this is the most interesting for me, this idea that Mr. and Mrs. Striker would hire you for the dog? This is very strange, no?"

She agreed that it was.

He gave her a smile she could have fallen into. "Do you mind if I should ask what are they paying you?"

"Yes," she said. "I do." 80

Another smile. "But it is good—worth your while, as they say?"

"I thought this was about Admiral," she said, and then, because she wanted to try it out on her tongue, she added, "Erhard."

"Oh, it is, it is—but I find you interesting too. More interesting, really, than the dog." As if on cue, Admiral backed out from under the table and squatted on the concrete to deposit a glistening yellow turd, which he examined briefly and then promptly ate.

"Bad dog," she said reflexively.

Erhard studied the dog a moment, then shifted his eyes back to her. "But how 85 do you feel about the situation, this concept of cloning a pet? Do you know anything about this process, the cruelty involved?"

"You know, frankly, Erhard, I haven't thought much about it. I don't know really what it involves. I don't really care. The Strikers love their dog, that's all, and if they want to, I don't know, bring him back—"

"Cheat death, you mean."

She shrugged. "It's their money."

He leaned across the table now, his eyes locked on hers. "Yes, but they must artificially stimulate so many bitches to come into heat, and then they must take the eggs from the tubes of these bitches, what they call 'surgically harvesting,' if you can make a guess as to what that implies for the poor animals"—she began to object but he held up a peremptory finger—"and that is nothing when you think of the numbers involved. Do you know about Snuppy?"

She thought she hadn't heard him right. "Snuppy? What's that?" 90

"The dog, the first one ever cloned—it was two years ago, in Korea? Well, this dog, this one dog—an Afghan, like your dog here—was the result of over a thousand embryos created in the laboratory from donor skin cells. And they put these embryos into one hundred and twenty-three bitches and only three clones resulted—and two died. So: all that torture of the animals, all that money—and for what?" He glanced down at Admiral, the flowing fur, the blunted eyes. "For this?"

A sudden thought came to her: "You're not really a journalist, are you?"

He slowly shook his head, as if he couldn't bear the weight of it.

"You're what—one of these animal people, these animal liberators or whatever they are. Isn't that right? Isn't that what you are?" She felt frightened suddenly, for herself, for Admiral, for the Strikers and Frankie and the whole carefully constructed edifice of getting and wanting, of supply and demand and all that it implied.

"And do you know why they clone the Afghan hound," he went on, ignoring her, 95 "the very stupidest of all the dogs on this earth? You don't? Breeding, that is why. This is what they call an uncomplicated genetic line, a pure line all the way back to the wolf ancestor. Breeding," he said, and he'd raised his voice so that Admiral looked up at the vehemence of it, "so that we can have this purity, this stupid hound, this *replica* of nature."

Nisha tugged down her T-shirt, drew up her legs. The sun glared up off the water so that she had to squint to see him. "You haven't answered my question," she said. "Erhard. If that's even your name."

Again, the slow rolling of the head on his shoulders, back and forth in rhythmic contrition. "Yes," he said finally, drawing in a breath, "I am one of 'these animal people.'" His eyes went distant a moment and then came back to her. "But I am also a journalist, a journalist first. And I want you to help me."

That night, when the Strikers came home—in convoy, her car following his through the gate, Admiral lurching across the lawn to bark furiously at the shimmering irresistible discs of the wheels of first one car, then the other—Nisha was feeling conflicted. Her loyalties were with the Strikers, of course. And with Admiral too, because no matter how brainless and ungainly the dog was, no matter how many times he wet the rug or ravaged the flowerbed or scrambled up onto the kitchen table to choke down anything anyone had been foolish enough to leave untended even for thirty seconds, she'd bonded with him—she would have been pretty cold if she hadn't. And she wasn't cold. She was as susceptible as anyone else. She loved animals, loved dogs, loved the way Admiral sprang to life when he saw her walk through the door, loved the dance of his fur, his joyous full-throated bark, the feel of his wet whiskered snout in the cupped palm of her hand. But Erhard had made her feel something else altogether. What was it? A sexual stirring, yes, absolutely—after the third beer, she'd found herself leaning into him for the first of a series of deep, languid, adhesive kisses—but it was more than that. There was something transgressive in what he wanted her to do, something that appealed to her sense of rebellion, of anarchy, of applying the pin to the swollen balloon . . . but here were the Strikers, emerging separately from their cars as Admiral bounced between them, yapping out his ecstasy. And now Gretchen was addressing her, trying to shout over the dog's sharp vocalizations, but without success. In the next moment, she was coming across the lawn, her face set.

"Don't let him chase the car like that," she called, even as Admiral tore round her like a dust devil, nipping at her ankles and dodging away again. "It's a bad habit."

"But Admiral—I mean, the first Admiral—used to chase cars all the time,   100 remember?"

Gretchen had pinned her hair up so that all the contours of her face stood out in sharp relief. There were lines everywhere suddenly, creases and gouges, frown marks, little embellishments round her eyes, and how could Nisha have missed them? Gretchen was old—fifty, at least—and the realization came home to Nisha now, under the harsh sun, with the taste of the beer and of Erhard still tingling on her lips. "I don't care," Gretchen was saying, and she was standing beside Nisha now, like a figurine the gardeners had set down amid that perfect landscape.

"But I thought we were going to go for everything, the complete behavior, good or bad, right? Because otherwise—"

"That was how the accident happened. At the dog park. He got through the gate before Cliff or I could stop him and just ran out into the street after some idiot on a motorcycle . . ." She looked past Nisha a moment, to where Admiral was bent over the pool, slurping up water as if his pinched triangular head worked on a piston. "So no," she said, "no, we're going to have to modify some behavior. I don't want him drinking that pool water, for one thing. Too many chemicals."

"Okay, sure," Nisha said, shrugging. "I'll try." She raised her voice and sang out, "Bad dog, bad dog," but it was halfhearted and Admiral ignored her.

The cool green eyes shifted to meet hers again. "And I don't want him eating his   105 own"—she paused to search for the proper word for the context, running through various euphemisms before giving it up—"shit."

Another shrug.

"I'm serious on this. Are you with me?"

Nisha couldn't help herself, and so what if she was pushing it? So what?

"Admiral did," she said. "Maybe you didn't know that."

Gretchen just waved her hand in dismissal. "But *this* Admiral," she said. "He's   110 not going to do it. Is he?"

Over the course of the next two weeks, as summer settled in with a succession of cloudless, high-arching days and Admiral steadily grew into the promise of his limbs, Erhard became a fixture at the house. Every morning, when Nisha came through the gate with the dog on his leash, he was there waiting for her, shining and tall and beautiful, with a joke on his lips and always some little treat for Admiral secreted in one pocket or another. The dog worshipped him. Went crazy for him. Pranced on the leash, spun in circles, nosed at his sleeves and pockets till he got his treat, then rolled over on his back in blissful submission. And then it was the dog park, and instead of sitting there wrapped up in the cocoon of herself, she had Erhard to sustain her, to lean into her so that she could feel the heat of him through the thin cotton of his shirt, to kiss her, and later, after lunch and the rising tide of the beer, to make love to her on the divan in the cool shadows of the pool house. They swam in the afternoons—he didn't mind the five pounds she'd put on; he praised her for them—and sometimes Frankie would join them, shedding the maid's habit for a white two-piece and careering through a slashing backstroke with a bottle of beer her reward, because she was part of the family too. Mama and Papa and Aunt Frankie, all there to nurture little Admiral under the beneficent gaze of the sun. Of course, Nisha was no fool. She knew there was a quid pro quo involved here, knew that Erhard had his agenda, but she was in no hurry, she'd committed to nothing, and as she lay there on the divan smoothing her hands over his back . . . she felt hope, real hope, for the first time since she'd come back home. It got so that she looked forward to each day, even the mornings that had been so hard on her, having to take a tray up to the ghost of her mother while her father trudged off to work, the whole house like a turned grave, because now she had Admiral, now she had Erhard, and she could shrug off anything. Yes. Sure. That was the way it was. Until the day he called her on it.

Cloudless sky, steady sun, every flower at its peak. She came down the walk with Admiral on his leash at the appointed hour, pulled back the gate, and there he was—but this time he wasn't alone. Beside him, already straining at the leash, was a gangling overgrown Afghan pup that could have been the twin of Admiral, and though she'd known it was coming, known the plan since the very first day, she was awestruck.

"Jesus," she said, even as Admiral jerked her forward and the two dogs began to romp round her legs in a tangle of limbs and leashes, "how did you—? I mean, he's the exact, he's totally—"

"That's the idea, isn't it?"

"But where did you find him?"

Erhard gave her a look of appraisal, then his eyes jumped past her to sweep the street. "Let's go inside, no? I don't want that they should see us here, anyone—not right in the front of the house."

He hadn't talked her into it, not yet, not exactly, but now that the moment had come she numbly punched in the code and held the gate open for him. What he wanted to do, what he was in the process of doing with her unspoken complicity, was to switch the dogs—just for a day, two at the most—by way of experiment. His contention was that the Strikers would never know the difference, that they were arrogant exemplars of bourgeois excess, even to the point of violating the laws of nature—and God, God too—simply to satisfy their own solipsistic desires. Admiral wouldn't be harmed—he'd enjoy himself, the change of scenery, all that. And certainly she knew how much the dog had come to mean to him. "But these people will not recognize their own animal," he'd insisted, his voice gone hard with conviction, "and so I will have my story and the world will know it."

Once inside the gate, they let the dogs off their leashes and went round back of the house where they'd be out of sight. They walked hand in hand, his fingers entwined with hers, and for a long while, as the sun rode high overhead and a breeze slipped in off the ocean to stir the trees, they watched as the two dogs streaked back and forth, leaping and nipping and tumbling in doggy rhapsody. Admiral's great combed-out spill of fur whipped round him in a frenzy of motion, and the new dog,

115

Erhard's dog—the impostor—matched him step for step, hair for glorious hair. "You took him to the groomer, didn't you?" she said.

Erhard gave a stiff nod. "Yes, sure. What do you think? He must be exact."

She watched, bemused, for another minute, her misgivings buried deep under 120 the pressure of his fingers, bone, sinew, the wedded flesh, and why shouldn't she go along with him? What was the harm? His article, or exposé, or whatever it was, would appear in Switzerland, in German, and the Strikers would never know the difference. Or even if they did, even if it was translated into English and grabbed headlines all over the country, they had it coming to them. Erhard was right. She knew it. She'd known it all along. "So what's his name?" she asked, the dogs shooting past her in a moil of fur and flashing feet. "Does he have a name?"

"Fred."

"Fred? What kind of name is that for a pedigree dog?"

"What kind of name is Admiral?"

She was about to tell him the story of the original Admiral, how he'd earned his sobriquet because of his enthusiasm for the Strikers' yacht and how they were planning on taking Admiral II out on the water as soon as they could, when the familiar tumble of the driveway gate drawing back on its runners startled her. In the next moment, she was in motion, making for the near corner of the house where she could see down the long macadam strip of the drive. Her heart skipped a beat: it was Gretchen. Gretchen home early, some crisis compelling her, mislaid papers, her blouse stained, the flu, Gretchen in her black Beemer, waiting for the gate to slide back so she could roll up the drive and exert dominion over her house and property, her piss-stained carpets, and her insuperable dog. "Quick!" Nisha shouted, whirling round. "Grab them. Grab the dogs!"

She saw Erhard plunge forward and snatch at them, the grass rising up to meet 125 him and both dogs tearing free. "Admiral!" he called, scrambling to his knees. "Here, boy. Come!" The moment thundered in her ears. The dogs hesitated, the ridiculous sea of fur smoothing and settling momentarily, and then one of them—it was Admiral, it had to be—came to him, and he got hold of it even as the other pricked up its ears at the sound of the car and bolted round the corner of the house.

"I'll stall her," she called.

Erhard, all six feet five inches of him, was already humping across the grass in the direction of the pool house, the dog writhing in his arms.

But the other dog—it was Fred, it had to be—was chasing the car up the drive now, nipping at the wheels, and as Nisha came round the corner she could read the look on her employer's face. A moment and she was there, grabbing for the dog as the car rolled to a stop and the engine died. Gretchen stepped out of the car, heels coming down squarely on the pavement, her shoulders thrust back tightly against the grip of her jacket. "I thought I told you . . ." she began, her voice high and querulous, but then she faltered and her expression changed. "But where's Admiral?" she said. "And whose dog is *that*?"

In the course of her life, short though it had been, she'd known her share of embittered people—her father, for one; her mother, for another—and she'd promised herself she'd never go there, never descend to that hopeless state of despair and regret that ground you down till you were nothing but raw animus, but increasingly now everything she thought or felt or tasted was bitter to the root. Erhard was gone. The Strikers were inflexible. Her mother lingered. Admiral reigned supreme. When the car had come up the drive and Gretchen had stood there confronting her, she'd never felt lower in her life. Until Admiral began howling in the distance and then broke free of Erhard to come careening round the corner of the house and launch himself in one wholly coordinated and mighty leap right into the arms of his protector. And then Erhard appeared, head bowed and shoulders slumped, looking abashed.

"I don't think I've had the pleasure," Gretchen said, setting down the dog (which 130 sprang right up again, this time at Erhard) and at the same time shooting Nisha a look before stepping forward and extending her hand.

"Oh, this is, uh, Erhard," she heard herself say. "He's from Switzerland, and I, well, I just met him in the dog park, and since he had an Afghan too—"

Erhard was miserable, as miserable as she'd ever seen him, but he mustered a counterfeit of his smile and said, "Nice to meet you," even as Gretchen dropped his hand and turned to Nisha.

"Well, it's a nice idea," she said, looking down at the dogs, comparing them. "Good for you for taking the initiative, Nisha . . . but really, you have to know that Admiral didn't have any—*playmates*—here on the property, Afghans or no, and I'm sure he wasn't exposed to anybody from *Switzerland*, if you catch my drift?"

There was nothing Nisha could do but nod her acquiescence.

"So," Gretchen said, squaring her shoulders and turning back to Erhard. "Nice 135 to meet you," she said, "but I'm going to have to ask that you take your dog—what's his name?"

Erhard ducked his head. "Fred."

"Fred? What an odd name. For a dog, I mean. He does have papers, doesn't he?"

"Oh, yes, he's of the highest order, very well-bred."

Gretchen glanced dubiously down at the dog, then back at Erhard. "Yes, well, he looks it," she said, "and they do make great dogs, Afghans—we ought to know. I don't know if Nisha told you, but Admiral is very special, very, very special, and we can't have any other dogs on the property. And I don't mean to be abrupt"—a sharp look for Nisha—"but strangers of any sort, or species, just cannot be part of this, this . . ." She trailed off, fighting, at the end, to recover the cold impress of her smile. "Nice meeting you," she repeated, and there was nowhere to go from there.

It had taken Nisha a while to put it all behind her. She kept thinking Erhard was 140 lying low, that he'd be back, that there had been something between them after all, but by the end of the second week she no longer looked for him at the gate or at the dog park or anywhere else. And very slowly, as the days beat on, she began to understand what her role was, her true role. Admiral chased his tail and she encouraged him. When he did his business along the street, she nudged the hard little bolus with the tip of her shoe till he stooped to take it up in his mouth. Yes, she was living in the past and her mother was dying and she'd gone to college for nothing, but she was determined to create a new future—for herself and Admiral—and when she took him to the dog park she lingered outside the gate, to let him run free where he really wanted to be, out there on the street where the cars shunted by and the wheels spun and stalled and caught the light till there was nothing else in the world. "Good boy," she'd say. "Good boy."

[2007]

Exploring the Text

1. This story is remarkable for its indirect narration. How does the reader learn, for example, Admiral's breed, the Strikers' profession, Nisha's ethnicity, and the truth about Admiral's birth? What is the effect of this kind of narration?
2. How does Boyle use diction and imagery in the first paragraph to establish a motif about the attempt to control nature?
3. How does Boyle use description and characterization to reveal the hierarchies of class that operate in the story? Refer to particular passages to support your answer.
4. How does Boyle use the narrator's tone to reveal Nisha's attitude toward the Strikers? Choose three specific instances in the text, and discuss what her attitude is and why she feels the way she does.
5. How is Nisha presented in paragraph 63? What is her dilemma? What is the effect of the image at the end of the paragraph?
6. At first, Nisha is averse to Erhard's plan, but she later finds it appealing, as we read in paragraph 98: "There was something transgressive in what he wanted her to do, something that appealed to her sense of rebellion, of anarchy, of applying the pin to the swollen balloon." Why does Nisha feel this transgressive urge, this rebelliousness? How does she indulge it? Does she do so at the end of the story?
7. At the end, we read, "And very slowly, as the days beat on, she began to understand what her role was, her true role" (para. 140). What does she perceive her role to be? What do you think may happen as a result of her fulfilling it? Explain.
8. What is the story's most surprising moment? What is its significance?
9. Cloning may be regarded as an attempt to force nature to conform to our will, yet it is sometimes seen as a rebellion against nature. How does this paradox play itself out in the story?
10. "Admiral" may be seen as a story about cloning, class, money, or control. Ultimately, what would you say "Admiral" is a story about? Why?

The Headstrong Historian

CHIMAMANDA NGOZI ADICHIE

With two novels and a short-story collection published before the age of thirty-two, Chimamanda Ngozi Adichie (b. 1977) is one of her generation's most promising African writers, as well as the winner of a 2008 MacArthur Fellowship. She currently divides her time between the United States and Nigeria, where she grew up and attended medical school at the University of Nigeria for two years before coming to America. She received an MFA in creative writing from Johns Hopkins University and an MA in African studies from Yale. Adichie describes fellow Nigerian writer Chinua Achebe as her hero, and many consider her his literary heir. Adichie's first novel, *Purple Hibiscus* (2003), was awarded the Commonwealth Writers' Prize for Best First Book. *Half of a Yellow Sun* (2006), which is set during the Biafran civil war in Nigeria (1967–1970), won the Orange Prize for Fiction in 2007; the novel is dedicated to her two grandfathers, who died in the war. Many of the stories in her collection *The Thing around Your Neck* (2009), including "The Headstrong Historian," appeared previously in the *New Yorker*. "The Headstrong Historian" showcases Adichie's skill at examining the history of Nigeria and the impact of colonization through the lens of one family's experience.

Many years after her husband had died, Nwamgba still closed her eyes from time to time to relive his nightly visits to her hut, and the mornings after, when she would walk to the stream humming a song, thinking of the smoky scent of him and the firmness of his weight, and feeling as if she were surrounded by light. Other memories of Obierika also remained clear—his stubby fingers curled around his flute when he played in the evenings, his delight when she set down his bowls of food, his sweaty back when he brought baskets filled with fresh clay for her pottery. From the moment she had first seen him, at a wrestling match, both of them staring and staring, both of them too young, her waist not yet wearing the menstruation cloth, she had believed with a quiet stubbornness that her chi and his chi had destined their marriage, and so when he and his relatives came to her father a few years later with pots of palm wine she told her mother that this was the man she would marry. Her mother was aghast. Did Nwamgba not know that Obierika was an only child, that his late father had been an only child whose wives had lost pregnancies and buried babies? Perhaps somebody in their family had committed the taboo of selling a girl into slavery and the earth god Ani was visiting misfortune on them. Nwamgba ignored her mother. She went into her father's *obi* and told him she would run away from any other man's house if she was not allowed to marry Obierika. Her father found her exhausting, this sharp-tongued, headstrong daughter who had once wrestled her brother to the ground. (Her father had had to warn those who saw this not to let anyone outside the compound know that a girl had thrown a boy.) He, too, was concerned about the infertility in Obierika's family, but it was not a bad family: Obierika's late father had taken the Ozo title; Obierika was already giving out his seed yams to sharecroppers. Nwamgba would not starve if she married him. Besides, it was better that he let his daughter go with the man she chose than to endure years of trouble in which she would keep returning home after confrontations with her in-laws; and so he gave his blessing, and she smiled and called him by his praise name.

To pay her bride price, Obierika came with two maternal cousins, Okafo and Okoye, who were like brothers to him. Nwamgba loathed them at first sight. She saw a grasping envy in their eyes that afternoon, as they drank palm wine in her father's *obi*; and in the following years—years in which Obierika took titles and widened his compound and sold his yams to strangers from afar—she saw their envy blacken. But she tolerated them, because they mattered to Obierika, because he pretended not to notice that they didn't work but came to him for yams and chickens, because he wanted to imagine that he had brothers. It was they who urged him, after her third miscarriage, to marry another wife. Obierika told them that he would give it some thought, but when they were alone in her hut at night he assured her that they would have a home full of children, and that he would not marry another wife until they were old, so that they would have somebody to care for them. She thought this strange of him, a prosperous man with only one wife, and she worried more than he did about their childlessness, about the songs that people sang, the melodious mean-spirited words: She has sold her womb. She has eaten his penis. He plays his flute and hands over his wealth to her.

Once, at a moonlight gathering, the square full of women telling stories and learning new dances, a group of girls saw Nwamgba and began to sing, their aggressive breasts pointing at her. She asked if they would mind singing a little louder, so that she could hear the words and then show them who was the greater of two tortoises. They stopped singing. She enjoyed their fear, the way they backed away from her, but it was then that she decided to find a wife for Obierika herself.

Nwamgba liked going to the Oyi stream, untying her wrapper from her waist and walking down the slope to the silvery rush of water that burst out from a rock. The waters of Oyi seemed fresher than those of the other stream, Ogalanya, or perhaps it was simply that Nwamgba felt comforted by the shrine of the Oyi goddess, tucked away in a corner; as a child she had learned that Oyi was the protector of women, the reason it was taboo to sell women into slavery. Nwamgba's closest friend, Ayaju, was already at the stream, and as Nwamgba helped Ayaju raise her pot to her head she asked her who might be a good second wife for Obierika.

She and Ayaju had grown up together and had married men from the same clan. The difference between them, though, was that Ayaju was of slave descent. Ayaju did not care for her husband, Okenwa, who she said resembled and smelled like a rat, but her marriage prospects had been limited; no man from a freedom family would have come for her hand. Ayaju was a trader, and her rangy, quick-moving body spoke of her many journeys; she had even travelled beyond Onicha. It was she who had first brought back tales of the strange customs of the Igala and Edo traders, she who had first told stories of the white-skinned men who had arrived in Onicha with mirrors and fabrics and the biggest guns the people of those parts had ever seen. This cosmopolitanism earned her respect, and she was the only person of slave descent who talked loudly at the Women's Council, the only person who had answers for everything. She promptly suggested, for Obierika's second wife, a young girl from the Okonkwo family, who had beautiful wide hips and who was respectful, nothing like the other young girls of today, with their heads full of nonsense.

As they walked home from the stream, Ayaju said that perhaps Nwamgba should do what other women in her situation did—take a lover and get pregnant in order to continue Obierika's lineage. Nwamgba's retort was sharp, because she did not like Ayaju's tone, which suggested that Obierika was impotent, and, as if in response to her thoughts, she felt a furious stabbing sensation in her back and knew that she was pregnant again, but she said nothing, because she knew, too, that she would lose it again.

Her miscarriage happened a few weeks later, lumpy blood running down her legs. Obierika comforted her and suggested that they go to the famous oracle, Kisa, as soon as she was well enough for the half day's journey. After the *dibia* had consulted the oracle, Nwamgba cringed at the thought of sacrificing a whole cow; Obierika certainly had greedy ancestors. But they performed the ritual cleansings and the sacrifices as required, and when she suggested that he go and see the Okonkwo family about their daughter he delayed and delayed until another sharp pain spliced her back, and, months later, she was lying on a pile of freshly washed banana leaves behind her hut, straining and pushing until the baby slipped out.

They named him Anikwenwa: the earth god Ani had finally granted a child. He was dark and solidly built, and had Obierika's happy curiosity. Obierika took him to pick medicinal herbs, to collect clay for Nwamgba's pottery, to twist yam vines at the farm. Obierika's cousins Okafo and Okoye visited often. They marvelled at how well Anikwenwa played the flute, how quickly he was learning poetry and wrestling moves from his father, but Nwamgba saw the glowing malevolence that their smiles could not hide. She feared for her child and for her husband, and when Obierika died—a man who had been hearty and laughing and drinking palm wine moments before he slumped—she knew that they had killed him with medicine. She clung to his corpse until a neighbor slapped her to make her let go; she lay in the cold ash for days, tore at the patterns shaved into her hair. Obierika's death left her with an unending despair. She thought often of a woman who, after losing a tenth child, had gone to her back yard and hanged herself on a kola-nut tree. But she would not do it, because of Anikwenwa.

Later, she wished she had made Obierika's cousins drink his *mmili ozu* before the oracle. She had witnessed this once, when a wealthy man died and his family forced his rival to drink his *mmili ozu*. Nwamgba had watched an unmarried woman take a cupped leaf full of water, touch it to the dead man's body, all the time speaking solemnly, and give the leaf-cup to the accused man. He drank. Everyone looked to make sure that he swallowed, a grave silence in the air, because they knew that if he was guilty he would die. He died days later, and his family lowered their heads in shame. Nwamgba felt strangely shaken by it all. She should have insisted on this with Obierika's cousins, but she had been blinded by grief and now Obierika was buried and it was too late.

His cousins, during the funeral, took his ivory tusk, claiming that the trappings of titles went to brothers and not to sons. It was when they emptied his barn of yams and led away the adult goats in his pen that she confronted them, shouting, and when they brushed her aside she waited until evening, then walked around the clan singing about their wickedness, the abominations they were heaping on the land by cheating a widow, until the elders asked them to leave her alone. She complained to the Women's Council, and twenty women went at night to Okafo's and Okoye's homes, brandishing pestles, warning them to leave Nwamgba alone. But Nwamgba knew that those grasping cousins would never really stop. She dreamed of killing them. She certainly could, those weaklings who had spent their lives scrounging off Obierika instead of working, but, of course, she would be banished then, and there would be no one to care for her son. Instead, she took Anikwenwa on long walks, telling him that the land from that palm tree to that avocado tree was theirs, that his grandfather had passed it on to his father. She told him the same things over and over, even though he looked bored and bewildered, and she did not let him go and play at moonlight unless she was watching.

Ayaju came back from a trading journey with another story: the women in Onicha were complaining about the white men. They had welcomed the white men's trading station, but now the white men wanted to tell them how to trade, and when the elders of Agueke refused to place their thumbs on a paper the white men came at night with their normal-men helpers and razed the village. There was nothing left. Nwamgba did not understand. What sort of guns did these white men have? Ayaju laughed and said that their guns were nothing like the rusty thing her own husband owned; she spoke with pride, as though she herself were responsible for the superiority of the white men's guns. Some white men were visiting different clans, asking parents to send their children to school, she added, and she had decided to send her son Azuka, who was the laziest on the farm, because although she was respected and wealthy, she was still of slave descent, her sons were still barred from taking titles, and she wanted Azuka to learn the ways of these foreigners. People ruled over others not because they were better people, she said, but because they had better guns; after all, her father would not have been enslaved if his clan had been as well armed as Nwamgba's. As Nwamgba listened to her friend, she dreamed of killing Obierika's cousins with the white men's guns.

The day the white men visited her clan, Nwamgba left the pot she was about to put in her oven, took Anikwenwa and her girl apprentices, and hurried to the square. She was at first disappointed by the ordinariness of the two white men; they were harmless-looking, the color of albinos, with frail and slender limbs. Their companions were normal men, but there was something foreign about them, too: only one spoke Igbo, and with a strange accent. He said that he was from Elele, the other normal men were from Sierra Leone, and the white men from France, far across the sea. They were

all of the Holy Ghost Congregation, had arrived in Onicha in 1885, and were building their school and church there. Nwamgba was the first to ask a question: Had they
brought their guns, by any chance, the ones used to destroy the people of Agueke,
and could she see one? The man said unhappily that it was the soldiers of the British
government and the merchants of the Royal Niger Company who destroyed villages;
they, instead, brought good news. He spoke about their god, who had come to the
world to die, and who had a son but no wife, and who was three but also one. Many
of the people around Nwamgba laughed loudly. Some walked away, because they had
imagined that the white man was full of wisdom. Others stayed and offered cool bowls
of water.

Weeks later, Ayaju brought another story: the white men had set up a courthouse in Onicha where they judged disputes. They had indeed come to stay. For the
first time, Nwamgba doubted her friend. Surely the people of Onicha had their own
courts. The clan next to Nwamgba's, for example, held its courts only during the new
yam festival, so that people's rancor grew while they awaited justice. A stupid system,
Nwamgba thought, but surely everyone had one. Ayaju laughed and told Nwamgba
again that people ruled others when they had better guns. Her son was already
learning about these foreign ways, and perhaps Anikwenwa should, too. Nwamgba
refused. It was unthinkable that her only son, her single eye, should be given to the
white men, never mind the superiority of their guns.

Three events, in the following years, caused Nwamgba to change her mind. The first
was that Obierika's cousins took over a large piece of land and told the elders that
they were farming it for her, a woman who had emasculated their dead brother and
now refused to remarry, even though suitors came and her breasts were still round.
The elders sided with them. The second was that Ayaju told a story of two people
who had taken a land case to the white men's court; the first man was lying but
could speak the white men's language, while the second man, the rightful owner of
the land, could not and so he lost his case, was beaten and locked up, and ordered
to give up his land. The third was the story of the boy Iroegbunam, who had gone
missing many years ago and then suddenly reappeared, a grown man, his widowed
mother mute with shock at his story: a neighbor, whom his father had often shouted
down at Age Grade meetings, had abducted him when his mother was at the market
and taken him to the Aro slave dealers, who looked him over and complained that
the wound on his leg would reduce his price. He was tied to others by the hands,
forming a long human column, and he was hit with a stick and told to walk faster.
There was one woman in the group. She shouted herself hoarse, telling the abductors
that they were heartless, that her spirit would torment them and their children, that
she knew she was to be sold to the white man and did they not know that the white
man's slavery was very different, that people were treated like goats, taken on large
ships a long way away, and were eventually eaten? Iroegbunam walked and walked
and walked, his feet bloodied, his body numb, until all he remembered was the smell
of dust. Finally, they stopped at a coastal clan, where a man spoke a nearly incomprehensible Igbo, but Iroegbunam made out enough to understand that another man

who was to sell them to the white people on the ship had gone up to bargain with them but had himself been kidnapped. There were loud arguments, scuffling; some of the abductees yanked at the ropes and Iroegbunam passed out. He awoke to find a white man rubbing his feet with oil and at first he was terrified, certain that he was being prepared for the white man's meal, but this was a different kind of white man, who bought slaves only to free them, and he took Iroegbunam to live with him and trained him to be a Christian missionary.

Iroegbunam's story haunted Nwamgba, because this, she was sure, was the way 15 Obierika's cousins were likely to get rid of her son. Killing him would be too dangerous, the risk of misfortunes from the oracle too high, but they would be able to sell him as long as they had strong medicine to protect themselves. She was struck, too, by how Iroegbunam lapsed into the white man's language from time to time. It sounded nasal and disgusting. Nwamgba had no desire to speak such a thing herself, but she was suddenly determined that Anikwenwa would speak enough of it to go to the white men's court with Obierika's cousins and defeat them and take control of what was his. And so, shortly after Iroegbunam's return, she told Ayaju that she wanted to take her son to school.

They went first to the Anglican mission. The classroom had more girls than boys, sitting with slates on their laps while the teacher stood in front of them, holding a big cane, telling them a story about a man who transformed a bowl of water into wine. The teacher's spectacles impressed Nwamgba, and she thought that the man in the story must have had powerful medicine to be able to transform water into wine, but when the girls were separated and a woman teacher came to teach them how to sew Nwamgba found this silly. In her clan, men sewed cloth and girls learned pottery. What dissuaded her completely from sending Anikwenwa to the school, however, was that the instruction was done in Igbo. Nwamgba asked why. The teacher said that, of course, the students were taught English—he held up an English primer—but children learned best in their own language and the children in the white men's land were taught in their own language, too. Nwamgba turned to leave. The teacher stood in her way and told her that the Catholic missionaries were harsh and did not look out for the best interests of the natives. Nwamgba was amused by these foreigners, who did not seem to know that one must, in front of strangers, pretend to have unity. But she had come in search of English, and so she walked past him and went to the Catholic mission.

Father Shanahan told her that Anikwenwa would have to take an English name, because it was not possible to be baptized with a heathen name. She agreed easily. His name was Anikwenwa as far as she was concerned; if they wanted to name him something she could not pronounce before teaching him their language, she did not mind at all. All that mattered was that he learn enough of the language to fight his father's cousins.

Father Shanahan looked at Anikwenwa, a dark-skinned, well-muscled child, and guessed that he was about twelve, although he found it difficult to estimate the ages of these people; sometimes what looked like a man would turn out to be a mere boy.

It was nothing like in Eastern Africa, where he had previously worked, where the natives tended to be slender, less confusingly muscular. As he poured some water on the boy's head, he said, "Michael, I baptize you in the name of the Father and of the Son and of the Holy Spirit."

He gave the boy a singlet and a pair of shorts, because the people of the living God did not walk around naked, and he tried to preach to the boy's mother, but she looked at him as if he were a child who did not know any better. There was something troublingly assertive about her, something he had seen in many women here; there was much potential to be harnessed if their wildness were tamed. This Nwamgba would make a marvellous missionary among the women. He watched her leave. There was a grace in her straight back, and she, unlike others, had not spent too much time going round and round in her speech. It infuriated him, their overlong talk and circuitous proverbs, their never getting to the point, but he was determined to excel here; it was the reason he had joined the Holy Ghost Congregation, whose special vocation was the redemption of black heathens.

Nwamgba was alarmed by how indiscriminately the missionaries flogged students: 20 for being late, for being lazy, for being slow, for being idle, and once, as Anikwenwa told her, Father Lutz put metal cuffs around a girl's hands to teach her a lesson about lying, all the time saying in Igbo — for Father Lutz spoke a broken brand of Igbo — that native parents pampered their children too much, that teaching the Gospel also meant teaching proper discipline. The first weekend Anikwenwa came home, Nwamgba saw welts on his back, and she tightened her wrapper around her waist and went to the school and told the teacher that she would gouge out the eyes of everyone at the mission if they ever did that to him again. She knew that Anikwenwa did not want to go to school and she told him that it was only for a year or two, so that he could learn English, and although the mission people told her not to come so often, she insistently came every weekend to take him home. Anikwenwa always took off his clothes even before they had left the mission compound. He disliked the shorts and shirt that made him sweat, the fabric that was itchy around his armpits. He disliked, too, being in the same class as old men, missing out on wrestling contests.

But Anikwenwa's attitude toward school slowly changed. Nwamgba first noticed this when some of the other boys with whom he swept the village square complained that he no longer did his share because he was at school, and Anikwenwa said something in English, something sharp-sounding, which shut them up and filled Nwamgba with an indulgent pride. Her pride turned to vague worry when she noticed that the curiosity in his eyes had diminished. There was a new ponderousness in him, as if he had suddenly found himself bearing the weight of a heavy world. He stared at things for too long. He stopped eating her food, because, he said, it was sacrificed to idols. He told her to tie her wrapper around her chest instead of her waist, because her nakedness was sinful. She looked at him, amused by his earnestness, but worried nonetheless, and asked why he had only just begun to notice her nakedness.

When it was time for his initiation ceremony, he said he would not participate, because it was a heathen custom to be initiated into the world of spirits, a custom that Father Shanahan had said would have to stop. Nwamgba roughly yanked his ear and told him that a foreign albino could not determine when their customs would change, and that he would participate or else he would tell her whether he was her son or the white man's son. Anikwenwa reluctantly agreed, but as he was taken away with a group of other boys she noticed that he lacked their excitement. His sadness saddened her. She felt her son slipping away from her, and yet she was proud that he was learning so much, that he could be a court interpreter or a letter writer, that with Father Lutz's help he had brought home some papers that showed that their land belonged to them. Her proudest moment was when he went to his father's cousins Okafo and Okoye and asked for his father's ivory tusk back. And they gave it to him.

Nwamgba knew that her son now inhabited a mental space that she was unable to recognize. He told her that he was going to Lagos to learn how to be a teacher, and even as she screamed—How can you leave me? Who will bury me when I die?—she knew that he would go. She did not see him for many years, years during which his father's cousin Okafo died. She often consulted the oracle to ask whether Anikwenwa was still alive, and the *dibia* admonished her and sent her away, because of course he was alive. Finally, he returned, in the year that the clan banned all dogs after a dog killed a member of the Mmangala Age Grade, the age group to which Anikwenwa would have belonged if he did not believe that such things were devilish.

Nwamgba said nothing when Anikwenwa announced that he had been appointed catechist at the new mission. She was sharpening her *aguba* on the palm of her hand, about to shave patterns into the hair of a little girl, and she continued to do so—*flick-flick-flick*—while Anikwenwa talked about winning the souls of the members of their clan. The plate of breadfruit seeds she had offered him was untouched—he no longer ate anything at all of hers—and she looked at him, this man wearing trousers and a rosary around his neck, and wondered whether she had meddled with his destiny. Was this what his chi had ordained for him, this life in which he was like a person diligently acting a bizarre pantomime?

The day that he told her about the woman he would marry, she was not surprised. He did not do it as it was done, did not consult people about the bride's family, but simply said that somebody at the mission had seen a suitable young woman from Ifite Ukpo, and the suitable young woman would be taken to the Sisters of the Holy Rosary in Onicha to learn how to be a good Christian wife. Nwamgba was sick with malaria that day, lying on her mud bed, rubbing her aching joints, and she asked Anikwenwa the young woman's name. Anikwenwa said it was Agnes. Nwamgba asked for the young woman's real name. Anikwenwa cleared his throat and said she had been called Mgbeke before she became a Christian, and Nwamgba asked whether Mgbeke would at least do the confession ceremony even if Anikwenwa would not follow the other marriage rites of their clan. He shook his head furiously and told her that the confession made by women before marriage, in which, surrounded by female relatives, they swore that no man had touched them since their husband declared his interest, was sinful, because Christian wives should not have been touched *at all*.

25

The marriage ceremony in the church was laughably strange, but Nwamgba bore it silently and told herself that she would die soon and join Obierika and be free of a world that increasingly made no sense. She was determined to dislike her son's wife, but Mgbeke was difficult to dislike, clear-skinned and gentle, eager to please the man to whom she was married, eager to please everyone, quick to cry, apologetic about things over which she had no control. And so, instead, Nwamgba pitied her. Mgbeke often visited Nwamgba in tears, saying that Anikwenwa had refused to eat dinner because he was upset with her, that Anikwenwa had banned her from going to a friend's Anglican wedding because Anglicans did not preach the truth, and Nwamgba would silently carve designs on her pottery while Mgbeke cried, uncertain of how to handle a woman crying about things that did not deserve tears.

Mgbeke was called "missus" by everyone, even the non-Christians, all of whom respected the catechist's wife, but on the day she went to the Oyi stream and refused to remove her clothes because she was a Christian the women of the clan, outraged that she had dared to disrespect the goddess, beat her and dumped her at the grove. The news spread quickly. Missus had been harassed. Anikwenwa threatened to lock up all the elders if his wife was treated that way again, but Father O'Donnell, on his next trek from his station in Onicha, visited the elders and apologized on Mgbeke's behalf, and asked whether perhaps Christian women could be allowed to fetch water fully clothed. The elders refused — if a woman wanted Oyi's waters, then she had to follow Oyi's rules — but they were courteous to Father O'Donnell, who listened to them and did not behave like their own son Anikwenwa.

Nwamgba was ashamed of her son, irritated with his wife, upset by their rarefied life in which they treated non-Christians as if they had smallpox, but she held out hope for a grandchild; she prayed and sacrificed for Mgbeke to have a boy, because she knew that the child would be Obierika come back and would bring a semblance of sense again into her world. She did not know of Mgbeke's first or second miscarriage; it was only after the third that Mgbeke, sniffling and blowing her nose, told her. They had to consult the oracle, as this was a family misfortune, Nwamgba said, but Mgbeke's eyes widened with fear. Michael would be very angry if he ever heard of this oracle suggestion. Nwamgba, who still found it difficult to remember that Michael was Anikwenwa, went to the oracle herself, and afterward thought it ludicrous how even the gods had changed and no longer asked for palm wine but for gin. Had they converted, too?

A few months later, Mgbeke visited, smiling, bringing a covered bowl of one of those concoctions that Nwamgba found inedible, and Nwamgba knew that her chi was still wide awake and that her daughter-in-law was pregnant. Anikwenwa had decreed that Mgbeke would have the baby at the mission in Onicha, but the gods had different plans, and she went into early labor on a rainy afternoon; somebody ran in the drenching rain to Nwamgba's hut to call her. It was a boy. Father O'Donnell baptized him Peter, but Nwamgba called him Nnamdi, because he would be Obierika come back. She sang to him, and when he cried she pushed her dried-up nipple into his mouth, but, try as she might, she did not feel the spirit of her magnificent husband,

Obierika. Mgbeke had three more miscarriages, and Nwamgba went to the oracle many times until a pregnancy stayed, and the second baby was born at the mission in Onicha. A girl. From the moment Nwamgba held her, the baby's bright eyes delightfully focussed on her, she knew that the spirit of Obierika had finally returned; odd, to have come back in a girl, but who could predict the ways of the ancestors? Father O'Donnell baptized the baby Grace, but Nwamgba called her Afamefuna—"my name will not be lost"—and was thrilled by the child's solemn interest in her poetry and her stories, by the teen-ager's keen watchfulness as Nwamgba struggled to make pottery with newly shaky hands. Nwamgba was not thrilled that Afamefuna was sent away to secondary school in Onicha. (Peter was already living with the priests there.) She feared that, at boarding school, the new ways would dissolve her granddaughter's fighting spirit and replace it with either an incurious rigidity, like her son's, or a limp helplessness, like Mgbeke's.

The year that Afamefuna left for secondary school, Nwamgba felt as if a lamp had   30
been blown out in a dim room. It was a strange year, the year that darkness suddenly descended on the land in the middle of the afternoon, and when Nwamgba felt the deep-seated ache in her joints she knew that her end was near. She lay on her bed gasping for breath, while Anikwenwa pleaded with her to be baptized and anointed so that he could hold a Christian funeral for her, as he could not participate in a heathen ceremony. Nwamgba told him that if he dared to bring anybody to rub some filthy oil on her she would slap them with her last strength. All she wanted before she joined the ancestors was to see Afamefuna, but Anikwenwa said that Grace was taking exams at school and could not come home.

But she came. Nwamgba heard the squeaky swing of her door, and there was Afamefuna, her granddaughter, who had come on her own from Onicha because she had been unable to sleep for days, her restless spirit urging her home. Grace put down her schoolbag, inside of which was her textbook, with a chapter called "The Pacification of the Primitive Tribes of Southern Nigeria," by an administrator from Bristol who had lived among them for seven years.

It was Grace who would eventually read about these savages, titillated by their curious and meaningless customs, not connecting them to herself until her teacher Sister Maureen told her that she could not refer to the call-and-response her grandmother had taught her as poetry, because primitive tribes did not have poetry. It was Grace who would laugh and laugh until Sister Maureen took her to detention and then summoned her father, who slapped Grace in front of the other teachers to show them how well he disciplined his children. It was Grace who would nurse a deep scorn for her father for years, spending holidays working as a maid in Onicha so as to avoid the sanctimonies, the dour certainties, of her parents and her brother. It was Grace who, after graduating from secondary school, would teach elementary school in Agueke, where people told stories of the destruction of their village by the white men with guns, stories she was not sure she believed, because they also told stories of mermaids appearing from the River Niger holding wads of crisp cash. It was Grace who, as one of a dozen or so women at the University College in Ibadan in

1953, would change her degree from chemistry to history after she heard, while drinking tea at the home of a friend, the story of Mr. Gboyega. The eminent Mr. Gboyega, a chocolate-skinned Nigerian, educated in London, distinguished expert on the history of the British Empire, had resigned in disgust when the West African Examinations Council began talking of adding African history to the curriculum, because he was appalled that African history would even be considered a subject. It was Grace who would ponder this story for a long time, with great sadness, and it would cause her to make a clear link between education and dignity, between the hard, obvious things that are printed in books and the soft, subtle things that lodge themselves in the soul. It was Grace who would begin to rethink her own schooling: How lustily she had sung on Empire Day, "God save our gracious king. Send him victorious, happy and glorious. Long to reign over us." How she had puzzled over words like "wallpaper" and "dandelions" in her textbooks, unable to picture them. How she had struggled with arithmetic problems that had to do with mixtures, because what was "coffee" and what was "chicory," and why did they have to be mixed? It was Grace who would begin to rethink her father's schooling and then hurry home to see him, his eyes watery with age, telling him she had not received all the letters she had ignored, saying amen when he prayed, and pressing her lips against his forehead. It was Grace who, driving past Agueke on her way to the university one day, would become haunted by the image of a destroyed village and would go to London and to Paris and to Onicha, sifting through moldy files in archives, reimagining the lives and smells of her grandmother's world, for the book she would write called "Pacifying with Bullets: A Reclaimed History of Southern Nigeria." It was Grace who, in a conversation about the book with her fiancé, George Chikadibia—stylish graduate of King's College, Lagos, engineer-to-be, wearer of three-piece suits, expert ballroom dancer, who often said that a grammar school without Latin was like a cup of tea without sugar—understood that the marriage would not last when George told her that it was misguided of her to write about primitive culture instead of a worthwhile topic like African Alliances in the American-Soviet Tension. They would divorce in 1972, not because of the four miscarriages Grace had suffered but because she woke up sweating one night and realized that she would strangle George to death if she had to listen to one more rapturous monologue about his Cambridge days. It was Grace who, as she received faculty prizes, as she spoke to solemn-faced people at conferences about the Ijaw and Ibibio and Igbo and Efik peoples of Southern Nigeria, as she wrote common-sense reports for international organizations, for which she nevertheless received generous pay, would imagine her grandmother looking on with great amusement. It was Grace who, feeling an odd rootlessness in the later years of her life, surrounded by her awards, her friends, her garden of peerless roses, would go to the courthouse in Lagos and officially change her first name from Grace to Afamefuna.

But on that day, as she sat at her grandmother's bedside in the fading evening light, Grace was not contemplating her future. She simply held her grandmother's hand, the palm thickened from years of making pottery.

[2008]

Exploring the Text

1. To whom does the title refer? Is it Nwamgba, Afamefuna/Grace, or both? How does the title influence your reading of the story? Is "headstrong" a negative description?

2. Descriptions of traditional Igbo culture are essential to the story. What specific information about traditions, practices, and beliefs did you glean? Explain whether you think Adichie idealizes the culture or criticizes it.

3. Suppose that everything you know about colonialism in Nigeria you learned from the story; how then would you characterize colonialism's intent and impact? Why is Nwamgba "amused by these [Anglican] foreigners" (para. 16)? What role do names play in depicting the colonial influence?

4. What is the role of education in this story? In what ways does it occasion a clash of values? How does Adichie depict Anikwenwa's/Michael's education as both a blessing and a curse?

5. Compare and contrast the characters of Nwamgba and Ayaju. Explain how their perspectives on women's roles differ.

6. In what ways are Nwamgba and her granddaughter kindred spirits? Cite specific passages that depict their spiritual connection.

7. Read the second-to-last paragraph aloud and consider its effect. How does the style change from that of the rest of the story? (Pay special attention to the repetition of "It was Grace.") Why do you think Adichie uses the granddaughter's English name rather than her Igbo name in this paragraph?

8. In this relatively brief story, Adichie takes us through three generations, a time frame usually reserved for novels. Is she successful? Explain why you find the concentration of time either effective or unsatisfying.

9. What is the narrative viewpoint in this story? Consider passages that seem to be from Nwamgba's perspective as well as others that represent the view of different characters (for example, when Father Shanahan notes "a grace in [Nwamgba's] straight back" [para. 19]). Why do you think Adichie did not tell the story in first person using Nwamgba's or Afamefuna's voice?

10. Adichie, a contemporary author, sets most of the story in an earlier time period. What evidence do you find in the story to suggest that she brings a more contemporary sensibility or perspective to the characters and situations she is describing?

11. At the tragic end of *Things Fall Apart* by Chinua Achebe, the central character, Okonkwo, a leader of his people, has been driven to suicide by the encroachment of colonialism and thus, according to tribal custom, cannot be buried because he has disgraced himself and his family. Achebe ends the novel ironically as the district commissioner, who "had toiled to bring civilization to different parts of Africa," returns to England with the intent to write a book entitled *The Pacification of the Primitive Tribes of the Lower Niger*. Okonkwo's best friend, who survives him, is Obierika. What do these links—the character of Obierika and the title of his granddaughter's book—add to your understanding of Adichie's story?

The Collar

GEORGE HERBERT

Known for his religious poetry, George Herbert (1593–1633), brother to the philosopher Edward Herbert, was born in Wales. He earned his BA and MA degrees at Trinity College. Though he intended to pursue a career in the church, Herbert's scholarship won the attention and favor of King James I, which led to a prestigious post at Cambridge, followed by service as a member of Parliament. He took orders as an Anglican priest in 1630 and served as rector of a small parish in rural Bemerton until his death in 1633. Herbert's most famous poem is probably the pattern poem "Easter Wings" (1633), written in the shape of wings. His one book of poetry, *The Temple*—a collection of 160 religious poems—was published soon after his death. Herbert's work continues to be admired for its structural inventiveness and wealth of imagery; he is often considered, with John Donne, one of the foremost metaphysical poets. "The Collar," a poem about rebellion and reconciliation, expresses Herbert's inner conflict regarding his service to God.

I struck the board[1] and cried, "No more;
         I will abroad!
What? shall I ever sigh and pine?
My lines and life are free, free as the road,
   Loose as the wind, as large as store.   5
        Shall I be still in suit?[2]
  Have I no harvest but a thorn
  To let me blood, and not restore
What I have lost with cordial[3] fruit?
        Sure there was wine   10
Before my sighs did dry it; there was corn
    Before my tears did drown it.
  Is the year only lost to me?
  Have I no bays[4] to crown it,
No flowers, no garlands gay? All blasted?   15
        All wasted?
  Not so, my heart; but there is fruit,
       And thou hast hands.
  Recover all thy sigh-blown age

---

[1]Table.—EDS.
[2]Servitude.—EDS.
[3]Invigorating to the heart.—EDS.
[4]Also called a laurel, the bay was used to make triumphal crowns in ancient Greece.—EDS.

On double pleasures: leave thy cold dispute   20
Of what is fit, and not. Forsake thy cage,
       Thy rope of sands,
Which petty thoughts have made, and made to thee
    Good cable, to enforce and draw,
         And be thy law,   25
    While thou didst wink and wouldst not see.
         Away! take heed;
         I will abroad.
Call in thy death's-head there; tie up thy fears.
         He that forbears   30
      To suit and serve his need,
        Deserves his load."
But as I raved and grew more fierce and wild
         At every word,
Methought I heard one calling, *Child!*   35
         And I replied, *My Lord.*

                                                       [1633]

Exploring the Text

1. Who is the speaker? What is his profession, and what is his central complaint or dilemma?
2. What are the denotations and connotations of the word *collar* in this poem? How does your awareness of these various meanings affect your reading? Might Herbert also be playing with multiple meanings of the word *suit*? Explain.
3. In lines 18 through 29, the speaker directly addresses a second party—*thou, thy,* and *thee.* Who or what does the speaker address? Does each mention have the same reference? Explain, using textual evidence to support your answer.
4. The speaker's "cry" consists largely of a series of questions until line 17. How does the poem change from that point, in terms of both style and content?
5. How would you describe the "petty thoughts" (l. 23) that the speaker refers to but does not name? How do these thoughts connect to the forbearance that the speaker seems to scorn in line 30?
6. What is the emotional impact of the poem's sudden resolution (ll. 33–36)? In what way does this brief exchange address or not address the problem contained in the speaker's long complaint?
7. If you have read John Milton's poem "When I consider how my light is spent" in Chapter 6 (p. 495), compare the voices of complaint in each poem. Which is the more restive? Would you say that either is petulant? Which one rebels more strongly? Which has the more peaceful reconciliation?

Song: To the Men of England

Percy Bysshe Shelley

The son of an English landowner and member of Parliament, Percy Bysshe Shelley (1792–1822) is considered one of the greatest lyric poets in English literature. Shelley fared poorly at Oxford, where he was said to have attended only a single lecture. Instead, he pursued his own interests, reading up to sixteen hours a day and writing pamphlets, gothic novels, and poetry. His controversial views, expounded in such pamphlets as *The Necessity of Atheism,* led to his expulsion from Oxford in 1811. After the suicide of his first wife in 1816, Shelley married Mary Wollstonecraft Godwin, who would later write *Frankenstein* (1818). In 1818, the couple moved to Italy, where Shelley maintained a tempestuous friendship with Lord Byron—a relationship that encouraged Shelley to vigorously pursue his writing. While in Italy, Shelley completed the verse drama *Prometheus Unbound,* based on the lost play by Aeschylus; *Adonais,* a pastoral elegy for John Keats; the essay *The Philosophical View of Reform;* and many poems, both lyrical and political. This poem, "Song: To the Men of England," contains many of the political sentiments that made Shelley such a controversial figure during his lifetime.

Men of England, wherefore plough
For the lords who lay ye low?
Wherefore weave with toil and care
The rich robes your tyrants wear?

Wherefore feed and clothe and save   5
From the cradle to the grave
Those ungrateful drones who would
Drain your sweat—nay, drink your blood?

Wherefore, Bees of England, forge
Many a weapon, chain, and scourge,   10
That these stingless drones may spoil
The forced produce of your toil?

Have ye leisure, comfort, calm,
Shelter, food, love's gentle balm?
Or what is it ye buy so dear   15
With your pain and with your fear?

The seed ye sow, another reaps;
The wealth ye find, another keeps;
The robes ye weave, another wears;
The arms ye forge, another bears.   20

Sow seed—but let no tyrant reap;
Find wealth—let no impostor heap;
Weave robes—let not the idle wear;
Forge arms—in your defence to bear.

Shrink to your cellars, holes, and cells—   25
In halls ye deck another dwells.
Why shake the chains ye wrought? Ye see
The steel ye tempered glance on ye.

With plough and spade and hoe and loom
Trace your grave and build your tomb   30
And weave your winding-sheet—till fair
England be your Sepulchre.

                                        [1819]

Exploring the Text

1. Who are the "Men of England" Shelley is speaking to, and what is his purpose in addressing them? How does Shelley characterize the "Men of England"?
2. The first half of this poem consists of four questions. Do you think they are rhetorical? Explain.
3. Drones, or male honeybees, do not collect nectar or pollen, but only mate with queens and perform secondary functions within the hive. Who do you think the "drones" in the poem represent? What other connotations of the word *drone* do you think apply?
4. Consider the series of objects that the speaker says are forged by the "Bees of England": "weapon, chain, and scourge" (l. 10). What do these items have in common? How do they differ?
5. Some of Shelley's language in the poem—"wherefore" and "ye," for example—was already archaic by the year of its composition. What effect do you think these word choices have on the tone and rhetorical impact of the poem?
6. Stanza 6 reverses the parallels of the declarative statements in the fifth stanza, making them imperative. How would you describe the speaker's tone in these stanzas?
7. How would you describe the poem's overall tone? How does the tone shift in the closing four stanzas?
8. "Song: To the Men of England" has been set to music and adopted as an anthem of the English labor movement. What elements of the poem make it especially suitable as a hymn or rallying cry? Do you think Shelley is advocating an armed rebellion or a more ambiguous refusal of the status quo?

Much Madness is divinest Sense —

EMILY DICKINSON

Born into a prominent family in Amherst, Massachusetts, Emily Dickinson (1830–1886) received some formal education at Amherst Academy and Mount Holyoke Female Seminary (which became Mount Holyoke College). Throughout her lifetime, Dickinson was a shy and reclusive person, who preferred to remain within her close family circle. In 1862, she enclosed four poems in a letter to literary critic and abolitionist Thomas Wentworth Higginson, who had written a piece in the *Atlantic Monthly* that included practical advice for young writers. Her letter began, "Mr. Higginson,—Are you too deeply occupied to say if my verse is alive? The mind is so near itself it cannot see distinctly, and I have none to ask. Should you think it breathed, and had you the leisure to tell me, I should feel quick gratitude." Dickinson didn't sign the letter, but instead enclosed her name on a card inside a smaller envelope. Dickinson wrote over seventeen hundred poems, but only ten were published in her lifetime. She defied traditional rules of poetry, never breaking rules out of mere carelessness. She was a master of whimsy, especially when dealing with serious topics, as in the following poem, "Much Madness is divinest Sense."

Much Madness is divinest Sense —
To a discerning Eye —
Much Sense — the starkest Madness —
'Tis the Majority
In this, as All, prevail —   5
Assent — and you are sane —
Demur — you're straightway dangerous —
And handled with a Chain —

[c. 1862]

Exploring the Text

1. This poem relies on an inversion of the expected meanings of "sense" and "madness." Though the speaker does not explicitly tie the terms to any specific behavior or beliefs, can you find evidence indicating how the poem defines madness?
2. Do you think the poem presents an unresolvable paradox regarding "sense" and "madness"? How would you characterize the "discerning Eye" mentioned in line 2? Contrast this with the method of discernment practiced by the "Majority" in the poem.
3. Consider Dickinson's choice of the word *demur* in line 7. How does choosing such a gentle term affect the meaning of the line? What do you make of the contrast between that word and the rest of the line?

4. To what extent does this poem speak to contemporary times? Are those who assent, or conform, regarded as sane; and those who rebel, or dissent, seen as dangerous? Use examples from current events to support your answer.
5. This poem could serve as an epigraph to one of the stories you have read in this chapter. Choose which story would be most appropriate, and explain why.

Disillusionment of Ten O'clock

WALLACE STEVENS

Wallace Stevens (1879–1955) is considered one of the most important American modernist poets. Born in Reading, Pennsylvania, Stevens studied at Harvard University and graduated from New York Law School. He worked as a lawyer in New York and became vice president of one of the largest insurance businesses in Hartford, Connecticut. In addition to being a successful business-man, Stevens is regarded as one of the great poets of the twentieth century. His poetry collections include *Harmonium* (1923), *The Man with the Blue Guitar and Other Poems* (1937), *Transport to Summer* (1947), and *A Primitive like an Orb* (1948). *Collected Poems* (1954) brought Stevens both a Pulitzer Prize and the National Book Award. Stevens's work is often described as meditative and philo-sophical. He was a poet of ideas, with a strong belief in the poet as someone with heightened powers. Stevens favored precision of imagery and clear, sharp language, rejecting the sentiment favored by the Romantic and Victorian poets.

The houses are haunted
By white night-gowns.
None are green,
Or purple with green rings,
Or green with yellow rings,   5
Or yellow with blue rings.
None of them are strange,
With socks of lace
And beaded ceintures.[1]
People are not going   10
To dream of baboons and periwinkles.
Only, here and there, an old sailor,
Drunk and asleep in his boots,
Catches tigers
In red weather.   15

[1923]

----

[1]Belts or sashes.—EDS.

Exploring the Text

1. How do you interpret the poem's title? Consider Stevens's choice of words; why *ten o'clock* specifically? What are the connotations of *disillusionment*, particularly with regard to Stevens's belief in the power and importance of imagination?
2. How would you characterize the speaker of the poem? What is his purpose, and to whom might he be speaking? Use textual evidence to support your analysis.
3. What do you think is the poem's unstated setting? What evidence in the text leads you to your conclusion?
4. Why don't the people in the poem dream? Why are they disillusioned? What are their lives like?
5. The speaker discusses various colors that the nightgowns are *not*; in fact, lines 3–11 are primarily about what is not found in these houses. What does this approach achieve in terms of the poem's mood and theme? How does it connect to the idea of *haunting* introduced in the opening line?
6. What do you think the poet is suggesting with the sudden leap from fairly mundane images of nightgowns to the absence of dreams of "baboons and periwinkles" (l. 11)?
7. In his poem "Someone Puts a Pineapple Together," Stevens proclaims, "Divest reality / Of its propriety." What does this statement mean? How does it apply to "Disillusionment of Ten O'clock"?

anyone lived in a pretty how town

E. E. Cummings

Edward Estlin (E. E.) Cummings (1894–1962) was an enormously prolific and experimental poet. Born and raised in an affluent family in Cambridge, Massachusetts, he graduated from Cambridge Latin High School and received both a BA and an MA in English and classical studies from Harvard University. Before the United States entered World War I, Cummings, an avowed pacifist, volunteered as an ambulance driver in France, where he was held for a time in a detention camp—an experience that deepened his distrust of authority. *The Enormous Room* (1922), his first published work, is a fictional account of his imprisonment, followed in 1923 by his first collection of poems, *Tulips and Chimneys*. Cummings defied traditional rules of typography and punctuation in the pursuit of poetry that was both critical and whimsical. An immensely popular poet, he produced an extensive body of work including over nine hundred poems. Critic Jenny Penberthy describes Cummings as "an unabashed lyricist, a modern cavalier love poet. But alongside his lyrical celebrations of nature, love, and the imagination are his satirical denouncements of tawdry, defiling, flat-footed, urban and political life—open terrain for invective and verbal inventiveness." Each of these verbal rebellions is on display in "anyone lived in a pretty how town," one of his most enduring poems, which blends wordplay, whimsy, and romance with sly criticism of the status quo.

anyone lived in a pretty how town
(with up so floating many bells down)
spring summer autumn winter
he sang his didn't he danced his did.

Women and men(both little and small)   5
cared for anyone not at all
they sowed their isn't they reaped their same
sun moon stars rain

children guessed(but only a few
and down they forgot as up they grew   10
autumn winter spring summer)
that noone loved him more by more

when by now and tree by leaf
she laughed his joy she cried his grief
bird by snow and stir by still   15
anyone's any was all to her

someones married their everyones
laughed their cryings and did their dance
(sleep wake hope and then)they
said their nevers they slept their dream   20

stars rain sun moon
(and only the snow can begin to explain
how children are apt to forget to remember
with up so floating many bells down)

one day anyone died i guess   25
(and noone stooped to kiss his face)
busy folk buried them side by side
little by little and was by was

all by all and deep by deep
and more by more they dream their sleep   30
noone and anyone earth by april
with by spirit and if by yes.

Women and men(both dong and ding)
summer autumn winter spring
reaped their sowing and went their came   35
sun moon stars rain

                                                        [1940]

Exploring the Text

1. Who are the main characters in this poem? What are their names, and what is their relationship? Who is the "he" referred to in line 4 and the "him" in line 12? Who is the "she" referred to in line 14 and the "her" in line 16? Identify a passage in which the ambiguity of their identities results in multiple meanings. How does such ambiguity reinforce the poem's central themes?

2. Who are the other characters in the poem? Who are the conformists, and who are the nonconformists? What seems to be the difference in how they lived their lives? Use specific lines as evidence.

3. The poem exemplifies Cummings's experiments with syntax from its title onward. On first reading, a line such as "he sang his didn't he danced his did" (l. 4) can seem daunting, even unintelligible. How would additional punctuation or emphasis (e.g., "He sang his *didn't*; he danced his *did*") alter your reading of the line? Select another dense or challenging passage from the poem and try standardizing the punctuation or syntax, explaining your sense of the passage's meaning.

4. In the third stanza, which refers to the children growing up, the progression of the seasons begins with autumn. Why? Is the order of the seasons important in the first and last stanzas as well? Explain your response.

5. Discuss how the repeated phrase "with up so floating many bells down" mimics, through its unconventional syntax and word order, the image that it describes. Along with the repetition of the changing seasons, the poem contains many other images suggesting the passage of time. Which images most powerfully suggest change, aging, or other forms of transience? Which passages imply stasis?

On Living

Nazim Hikmet

TRANSLATED BY RANDY BLASING AND MUTLU KONUK

Nazim Hikmet (1902–1963), Turkey's most famous poet, was born in the westernmost city of the Ottoman Empire (now Thessaloníki, Greece). After attending secondary school in Istanbul, he studied economics and sociology at Oriental University in Moscow. Hikmet returned to Turkey in 1928 and began to publish poetry, drama, journalism, and fiction. His stay in the Soviet Union had deeply influenced both his work and his political beliefs; after his return to Turkey, Hikmet's political activities—especially his vocal support of communism—led to his arrest for sedition in 1938, for which he was sentenced to twenty-eight years in prison. When he was released in 1950, he returned to the Soviet Union, where he continued to write until his death in 1963. He became known posthumously in the West for his book *Things I Didn't Know I Loved: Selected Poems of Nazim Hikmet*, which was published in English in 1975. While versions of Hikmet's selected poetry have been published in English, most of his books have not been translated from the Turkish. "On Living" was written from his prison cell in 1948.

I

Living is no laughing matter:
    you must live with great seriousness
        like a squirrel, for example—
I mean without looking for something beyond and
               above living,   5
I mean living must be your whole occupation.
Living is no laughing matter:
    you must take it seriously,
        so much so and to such a degree
that, for example, your hands tied behind your back,   10
           your back to the wall,
    or else in a laboratory
        in your white coat and safety glasses,
        you can die for people—
even for people whose faces you've never seen,   15
even though you know living
        is the most real, the most beautiful thing.
I mean, you must take living so seriously
    that even at seventy, for example, you'll plant
    olive trees—   20
and not for your children, either,
but because although you fear death you don't
believe it,
because living, I mean, weighs heavier.

II

Let's say we're seriously ill, need surgery—   25
which is to say we might not get up
        from the white table.
Even though it's impossible not to feel sad
        about going a little too soon,
we'll still laugh at the jokes being told,   30
we'll look out of the window to see if it's raining,
or still wait anxiously
        for the latest newscast . . .
Let's say we're at the front—
        for something worth fighting for, say.   35
There, in the first offensive, on that very day,
        we might fall on our face, dead.
We'll know this with a curious anger,
        but we'll still worry ourselves to death
        about the outcome of the war, which could last years.   40

Let's say we're in prison
and close to fifty,
and we have eighteen more years, say,
      before the iron doors will open.
We'll still live with the outside,   45
with its people and animals, struggle and wind—
      I mean with the outside beyond the walls.
I mean, however and wherever we are,
    we must live as if we will never die.

III

This earth will grow cold,   50
a star among stars
      and one of the smallest,
a gilded mote on blue velvet—
    I mean this, our great earth.
This earth will grow cold one day,   55
not like a block of ice
or a dead cloud even
but like an empty walnut it will roll along
    in pitch-black space . . .
you must grieve for this right now   60
—you have to feel this sorrow now—
for the world must be loved this much
       if you're going to say "I lived" . . .

                                        [1948]

Exploring the Text

1. What is accomplished through the poem's many repetitions ("Living is no laughing matter," "I mean," "you must," "let's say")? Consider the poet's possible intentions in writing the poem, and the sound of the poem when read aloud.

2. Imagine "On Living" as a speech or monologue. How would you characterize the speaker? To whom is he giving this advice? What kind of response would he get? What are the three conjectured situations posited in section II of the poem? How effectively do these examples support the meaning of section I? Rereading the poem with these strategies in mind, why do you think the speaker offers so many examples to support his point?

3. How do you understand the "seriousness" that Hikmet is, in essence, attempting to redefine in the first section? Why, for instance, would Hikmet choose a squirrel as the vehicle for a simile about seriousness in lines 2 and 3? What is the basic irony underlying section I of the poem? Can you think of an image or example from your own experience that would fit his description?

4. Hikmet spent many years of his life either in prison or in exile. How does this knowledge affect your understanding of the imagery in section II? How does it impact your experience of the poem as a whole?

5. How would you characterize the progression of images (or types of images) from the first stanza to the last? How does this shift relate to the poem's themes? What do you make of the poem's equation of love with grieving in the final stanza? Do you find this vision optimistic or pessimistic? What do you think the poet wishes to affirm or deny with this definition? How would you compare the speaker's voice in this poem to that of "Do not go gentle into that good night" below?

Do not go gentle into that good night

DYLAN THOMAS

Dylan Thomas (1914–1953) was born in Wales, spent much of his life in London, and gained a following in the United States, where he often lectured and gave readings. He wrote his first volume of poetry when he was only twenty and published steadily throughout his lifetime. His works include *The Map of Love* (1939); *Portrait of the Artist as a Young Dog* (1940); *Deaths and Entrances* (1946); *In Country Sleep* (1952); and the posthumous *Under Milk Wood: A Play for Voices* (1954), which features characters from the fictional Welsh fishing village of Llareggub. During World War II, Thomas wrote scripts for documentary films, and after the war he was a literary commentator for BBC radio. He died in New York City at the age of thirty-nine of complications from alcoholism. Thomas was a popular and flamboyant figure, known for his spirited readings—especially his famous reading of "Do not go gentle into that good night," a poem addressed to his dying father.

Do not go gentle into that good night,
Old age should burn and rave at close of day;
Rage, rage against the dying of the light.

Though wise men at their end know dark is right,
Because their words had forked no lightning they
Do not go gentle into that good night.   5

Good men, the last wave by, crying how bright
Their frail deeds might have danced in a green bay,
Rage, rage against the dying of the light.

Wild men who caught and sang the sun in flight,   10
And learn, too late, they grieved it on its way,
Do not go gentle into that good night.

Grave men, near death, who see with blinding sight *a* *serious/*
Blind eyes could blaze like meteors and be gay, *b* *happy*
Rage, rage against the dying of the light. *a*   15

And you, my father, there on the sad height, *a*
Curse, bless, me now with your fierce tears, I pray. *b*
Do not go gentle into that good night. *a*
Rage, rage against the dying of the light. *a*

Do not go gentle   *[1952]*

wise   wild
good grave
rage, rage...

Exploring the Text

1. Much of the power of a villanelle, the form in which this poem is composed, resides in its repeated lines and their subtly shifting meaning over the course of the piece. How do Thomas's repeated lines change from stanza to stanza? You may consider theme, mood, imagery, and even grammatical structure to support your answer.

2. How do you interpret the images of natural forces that Thomas connects to the men described in the middle stanzas? Choose a stanza and explain how the particular metaphor develops the poem's themes.

3. Discuss the recurring images of light and darkness in the poem. What multiple meanings might these motifs convey? Explain, focusing on a specific passage or set of images.

4. Do you think the speaker's urgings are more for his father's benefit or for his own? How do you think the argument aids or harms them in dealing with the father's impending mortality?

5. Stanzas 2 through 5 are about "wise men," "good men," "wild men," and "grave men." How do they differ from one another in their response to death?

6. Thomas withholds the identity of the poem's subject until the final stanza. Why?

7. The rebellion embodied in the poem is not directed against any human authority or tradition but against death itself. Are there aspects of life that the speaker rejects as well in making his argument? Support your answer using specific passages from the text.

Her Kind

ANNE SEXTON

Anne Sexton (1928–1974) was one of the most celebrated confessional poets to emerge in America during the 1960s and 1970s. Born in Newton, Massachusetts, she struggled through a childhood marked by family discord and, by some accounts, periodic abuse. Sexton grappled with depression and suicidal urges for much of her adult life. In 1957, at the suggestion of her therapist, she began attending meetings of poetry groups in Boston, where she met such poets as Robert Lowell, Maxine Kumin, and Sylvia Plath. Her work progressed very rapidly, and her first volume of poetry, *To Bedlam and Part Way Back* (1960), was published only a few years afterward. Her subsequent work gained considerable acclaim and a number of awards, culminating in the Pulitzer Prize for *Live or Die* (1967). Though much criticism of Sexton's poetry revolves around her mental illness and eventual suicide, the body of her work comprises a much broader range, including *Transformations* (1971), a collection of prose poems reimagining the Grimm brothers' fairy tales. "Her Kind," from *To Bedlam and Part Way Back*, is a daring experiment in point of view, exploring images of women as outcasts.

I have gone out, a possessed witch,
haunting the black air, braver at night;
dreaming evil, I have done my hitch
over the plain houses, light by light:
lonely thing, twelve-fingered, out of mind.   5
A woman like that is not a woman, quite.
I have been her kind.

I have found the warm caves in the woods,
filled them with skillets, carvings, shelves,
closets, silks, innumerable goods;   10
fixed the suppers for the worms and the elves:
whining, rearranging the disaligned.
A woman like that is misunderstood.
I have been her kind.

I have ridden in your cart, driver,   15
waved my nude arms at villages going by,
learning the last bright routes, survivor
where your flames still bite my thigh
and my ribs crack where your wheels wind.
A woman like that is not ashamed to die.   20
I have been her kind.

[1960]

Exploring the Text

1. How would you characterize the speaker? Is the "I" referred to the same throughout the poem? Explain.
2. What is the speaker's attitude toward the "witch" in the opening lines? What particular descriptions seem the most sympathetic or unsympathetic?
3. Trace the point of view throughout this poem. Where does it shift? What perspectives are we offered?

4. Reading the poem in the context of this chapter's theme, what is the speaker—as well as the "kinds" of women with whom she identifies—rebelling against? What or whom do you think the speaker would identify with the notion of conformity?
5. This poem is rich in imagery. Analyze how the patterns of imagery in the first stanza relate to the meaning. How and why does the imagery shift in the third stanza?
6. Compare the scene described in lines 8–12 with that described in "Sonnet: The *Ladies' Home Journal*" (p. 931). What parallels do you find? How do the poems differ?

Booker T. and W.E.B.

DUDLEY RANDALL

Born in Washington, D.C., Dudley Randall (1914–2000) was an editor, a publisher, and a poet. After returning from a Pacific tour of duty in World War II, Randall worked his way through a degree in English from Wayne University and a master's in library science from the University of Michigan, supporting himself as a postal worker. Randall is best known for his poem "The Ballad of Birmingham," written in response to the racially motivated 1963 bombing of a church in Birmingham, Alabama. In 1965, Randall founded Broadside Press, which published poems by African American writers. He served as librarian and poet-in-residence at the University of Detroit from 1969 until his retirement in 1974. Among his published books are *Cities Burning* (1968), *More to Remember* (1971), and *After the Killing* (1973). He also translated Latin, French, and Russian poems into English. One of his most well-known poems, "Booker T. and W.E.B." contrasts the political views of two historical figures who were famously at odds: Booker T. Washington and W. E. B. DuBois.

"It seems to me," said Booker T.,
"It shows a mighty lot of cheek
To study chemistry and Greek
When Mister Charlie needs a hand
To hoe the cotton on his land,   5
And when Miss Ann looks for a cook,
Why stick your nose inside a book?"

"I don't agree," said W.E.B.,
"If I should have the drive to seek
Knowledge of chemistry or Greek,   10
I'll do it. Charles and Miss can look
Another place for hand or cook.
Some men rejoice in skill of hand,
And some in cultivating land,

But there are others who maintain   15
The right to cultivate the brain."

"It seems to me," said Booker T.,
"That all you folks have missed the boat
Who shout about the right to vote,
And spend vain days and sleepless nights   20
In uproar over civil rights.
Just keep your mouths shut, do not grouse,
But work, and save, and buy a house."

"I don't agree," said W.E.B.,
"For what can property avail   25
If dignity and justice fail.
Unless you help to make the laws,
They'll steal your house with trumped-up clause.
A rope's as tight, a fire as hot,
No matter how much cash you've got.   30
Speak soft, and try your little plan,
But as for me, I'll be a man."

"It seems to me," said Booker T.—

"I don't agree,"
Said W.E.B.   35

                                                           [1969]

· ·

Exploring the Text

1. How do the repeated opening statements ("It seems to me" and "I don't agree") of the characters anticipate their positions?
2. "Booker T. and W.E.B." deals specifically with the disagreement among civil rights leaders in the early to mid-twentieth century about how best to secure dignity, prosperity, and social justice for African Americans in America. Its basic conflict, however, is more universal. How would you characterize this essential clash of philosophies?
3. Given the grave nature of the subject matter, the simplicity of the poem's structure and style may be surprising. Does the simple rhyme scheme and singsong rhythm fit the poem? Why or why not?
4. In the fourth stanza, W.E.B. makes the argument that financial prosperity (or, more broadly, capitalism) is meaningless without individual liberty. How do you think this conviction would be viewed today?
5. Which character in the poem do you consider to be the nonconformist? How would your answer change depending on where you imagined the debate taking place, who was listening, and under what circumstances?

Sonnet: *The* Ladies' Home Journal

SANDRA GILBERT

Born in 1936 in New York City, poet and critic Sandra Gilbert was educated at Cornell University, New York University, and Columbia University, where she received her PhD in 1968. Her most famous piece of writing is *The Madwoman in the Attic: The Woman Writer and the Nineteenth-Century Literary Imagination* (1979), a highly influential work of feminist literary criticism that she wrote with Susan Gubar. She has published several collections of poetry, including *Emily's Bread* (1984) and *Belongings* (1995), as well as *Wrongful Death: A Medical Tragedy* (1995), a memoir about her late husband. Gilbert has received fellowships from the Guggenheim Foundation, the National Endowment for the Humanities, and the Rockefeller Foundation, among others. She is currently a professor of English at the University of California, Davis, and was named "Woman of the Year" by *Ms.* magazine in 1986. "Sonnet: The *Ladies' Home Journal*" is from *Emily's Bread. The Ladies' Home Journal*, one of the oldest magazines in the United States, covers such topics as women's health, beauty, celebrity news, and recipes.

The brilliant stills of food, the cozy
glossy, bygone life—mashed potatoes
posing as whipped cream, a neat mom
conjuring shapes from chaos, trimming the flame—
how we ached for all that,   5
that dance of love in the living room,
those paneled walls, that kitchen golden
as the inside of a seed: how we leaned
on those shiny columns of advice,
stroking the *thank yous*, the firm thighs, the wise   10
closets full of soap.

              But even then
we knew it was the lies we loved, the lies
we wore like Dior coats, the clean-cut airtight
lies that laid out our lives in black and white.

[1984]

Exploring the Text

1. What is the speaker's attitude toward the *Ladies' Home Journal?* How can you tell?
2. The scene Gilbert describes in the bulk of the poem is, on the surface, serene. Note the adjectives she uses throughout, such as *brilliant, cozy, glossy, neat, golden, firm,*

wise, clean-cut, and *airtight.* What is the effect of such language? What techniques does the poet use to undercut this idyllic image?

3. Consider the pictures described in lines 1 through 8 and the ambiguity created by the diction in lines 8–9: "how we leaned / on those shiny columns of advice." What are those images meant to evoke for readers of the magazine? Are there early hints that they might present a false or hollow representation? Explain.

4. This poem is called a sonnet, but other than the requisite fourteen lines, it conforms to very few of the sonnet's characteristics—until the end, that is. Why did Gilbert write it this way?

5. In a certain sense, this poem deals with the power of (false) advertising. Can you think of an advertisement that comprised an image or idea that seemed appealing, but on examination proved to be false or misleading? How did the ad achieve its appeal? Compare this effect with the one described in the poem.

Homage to My Hips

LUCILLE CLIFTON

Lucille Clifton (1936–2010) was born in Depew, New York, and graduated from the State University of New York at Fredonia in 1955. Her first book, the poetry collection *Good Times,* was named by the *New York Times* as one of the Ten Best Books of 1969. Clifton was a visiting writer at Columbia University's School of the Arts and at George Washington University, and taught literature and creative writing at both the University of California at Santa Cruz and St. Mary's College of Maryland. In 1979, she was named Maryland's poet laureate. Her other books of poetry include *Quilting: Poems 1987–1990* (1991) and *The Terrible Stories* (1996). Clifton also wrote more than twenty books for children, including *My Friend Jacob* (1980) and *Three Wishes* (1992). The following poem, "Homage to My Hips," typifies the feminist celebration of the female body that runs through Clifton's most famous work.

these hips are big hips.
they need space to
move around in.
they don't fit into little
petty places. these hips   5
are free hips.
they don't like to be held back.
these hips have never been enslaved,
they go where they want to go
they do what they want to do.   10
these hips are mighty hips.
these hips are magic hips.

i have known them
to put a spell on a man and
spin him like a top!   15

[1987]

. . . .

Exploring the Text

1. How would you characterize the speaker of the poem? How does she wish to be viewed? Who is her intended audience?
2. What other elements of the speaker's identity might she be extolling through her celebration of her hips? Choose a specific passage, and explain how the particular description might apply to a larger context of selfhood or personality.
3. What is the speaker rebelling against? Use specific passages to support your answer.
4. In the body of this very short poem, Clifton uses the word "hips" nine times— sometimes twice in one line. She also begins most lines with the word "they" or "these." Why does she use so much repetition, and how does this choice impact the poem's meaning and overall effect?
5. Why might the lines break where they do, and how does the poem's shape contribute to its meaning? Why do you think Clifton uses no capital letters in the poem?

Is About

ALLEN GINSBERG

Allen Ginsberg (1926–1997) was born in Newark, New Jersey. As a teenager, he began to read Walt Whitman, who, along with William Carlos Williams and William Blake, exerted an enormous influence on his writing. Ginsberg went to Columbia University on a scholarship to study law but changed his major to English. He became a major voice in the Beat movement, which included poets Gregory Corso and Lawrence Ferlinghetti, and novelists William S. Burroughs and Jack Kerouac, author of *On the Road* (1957). Ginsberg led a varied, unconventional life: he worked as a dishwasher, welder, and university professor; he was arrested several times for political protests; he spent time in a psychiatric institution; and he toured with Bob Dylan's band. Ginsberg's work is notable for its free expression and rejection of conformity and materialism. *Howl* (1955) created intense interest and controversy for both its style and its content. In 1957, the poem's publisher was charged with obscenity; however, the case was thrown out when the presiding judge ruled that *Howl* was of "redeeming social consequence." Ginsberg's other works include *Kaddish and Other Poems* (1961), which many regard as his finest, and the mixed-genre collection *The Fall of America*, which won a National Book Award in 1973. *Collected Poems 1947–1980* was published in 1984. "Is About," a poem that explains it all in quintessential Beat style, was first published in the *New Yorker*.

Dylan is about the Individual against the whole of creation
Beethoven is about one man's fist in the lightning clouds
The Pope is about abortion & the spirits of the dead . . .
Television is about people sitting in their living room looking at
   their things
America is about being a big Country full of Cowboys Indians Jews   5
   Negroes & Americans
Orientals Chicanos Factories skyscrapers Niagara Falls Steel Mills
   radios homeless Conservatives, don't forget
Russia is about Czars Stalin Poetry Secret Police Communism
   barefoot in the snow
But that's not really Russia it's a concept
A concept is about how to look at the earth from the moon
without ever getting there. The moon is about love & Werewolves,   10
   also Poe.
Poe is about looking at the moon from the sun
or else the graveyard
Everything is about something if you're a thin movie producer
   chain-smoking muggles
The world is about overpopulation, Imperial invasions, Biocide,
   Genocide, Fratricidal Wars, Starvation, Holocaust, mass injury &
      murder, high technology
Super science, atom Nuclear Neutron Hydrogen detritus, Radiation   15
   Compassion Buddha, Alchemy
Communication is about monopoly television radio movie newspaper
   spin on Earth, i.e. planetary censorship.
Universe is about Universe.
Allen Ginsberg is about confused mind writing down newspaper
   headlines from Mars—
The audience is about salvation, the listeners are about sex,
   Spiritual gymnastics, nostalgia for the Steam Engine & Pony
     Express
Hitler Stalin Roosevelt & Churchill are about arithmetic &   20
   Quadrilateral equations, above all chemistry physics & chaos
     theory—
Who cares what it's all about?
I do! Edgar Allan Poe cares! Shelley cares! Beethoven & Dylan care.
Do you care? What are you about
or are you a human being with 10 fingers & two eyes?

                                 [1996]

Exploring the Text

1. "Is About" is, in a sense, a definition poem. Which definition seems most persuasive to you? How do you think the poem defines the title itself?
2. From among the characters who populate the poem (Dylan, Beethoven, the Pope, Poe, Buddha, Hitler, Stalin, Roosevelt, Churchill, and Shelley), select one you know well. Is the reference accurate, as you see it? How does it contribute to the meaning or effect of the poem?
3. What techniques does Ginsberg employ to affect the tempo of each line? Consider line length, punctuation, and the sound of the words. How does the resulting pace inform your understanding of the poet's intentions or mood? Identify a list or a series of images or concepts in the poem that you find particularly striking. How does the juxtaposition of items in this list or series develop tension or resonance within the poem?
4. How does the element of surprise function in the poem? Identify an unexpected association or definition that particularly affected your reading or understanding of the speaker's intentions or ideas.
5. How would you describe the tone of the poem? How does Ginsberg create that tone?
6. How would you answer the last two questions of the poem (ll. 23–24)?
7. If asked, what would you say "Is About" is about?

Penelope

CAROL ANN DUFFY

The first woman to be named poet laureate of England, Carol Ann Duffy was born to Irish Catholic parents in Glasgow, Scotland, in 1955. She grew up in England, earning a degree in philosophy in 1977, and published her first collection of poetry in 1985. *Mean Time* won the Whitbread Poetry Award in 1990, and *Rapture* won the T. S. Eliot Prize in 2005. Duffy has also edited many anthologies and written books for children, including *The Oldest Girl in the World* (2000) and *The Hat* (2007). Her work continues to be very popular; in fact, in 2005 the *Guardian* called her "the most popular living poet in Britain." She is currently the creative director of the Writing School at Manchester Metropolitan University. "Penelope" is from *The World's Wife*, Duffy's 1999 collection based on stories from history and mythology but written in the voice of the women behind the men. Penelope is Odysseus's wife in Homer's *Odyssey*.

At first, I looked along the road
hoping to see him saunter home
among the olive trees,
a whistle for the dog
who mourned him with his warm head on my knees.   5
Six months of this

and then I noticed that whole days had passed
without my noticing.
I sorted cloth and scissors, needle, thread,

thinking to amuse myself,   10
but found a lifetime's industry instead.
I sewed a girl
under a single star—cross-stitch, silver silk—
running after childhood's bouncing ball.
I chose between three greens for the grass;   15
a smoky pink, a shadow's grey
to show a snapdragon gargling a bee.
I threaded walnut brown for a tree,

my thimble like an acorn
pushing up through umber soil.   20
Beneath the shade
I wrapped a maiden in a deep embrace
with heroism's boy
and lost myself completely
in a wild embroidery of love, lust, loss, lessons learnt;   25
then watched him sail away
into the loose gold stitching of the sun.

And when the others came to take his place,
disturb my peace,
I played for time.   30
I wore a widow's face, kept my head down,
did my work by day, at night unpicked it.
I knew which hour of the dark the moon
would start to fray,
I stitched it.   35
Grey threads and brown

pursued my needle's leaping fish
to form a river that would never reach the sea.
I tricked it. I was picking out
the smile of a woman at the centre   40
of this world, self-contained, absorbed, content,
most certainly not waiting,
when I heard a far-too-late familiar tread outside the door.
I licked my scarlet thread
and aimed it surely at the middle of the needle's eye once more.   45

[1999]

Exploring the Text

1. How does the speaker of the poem characterize herself in the first stanza? How is her missing husband, Odysseus, characterized?
2. What changes in the speaker's attitude in the second stanza?
3. How does figurative language contribute to the poem's meaning? Consider the effects of the simile that begins on line 19 and the metaphor developed in lines 21–27. How literal or figurative is her "embroidery"? Is she depicting the world she's living in? Is she creating a fictional world in which to live? Is she affecting the world itself? Explain with specific reference to the text.
4. Stanza 4 presents the suitors and Penelope's trick. How dependent on a reading of Homer's *Odyssey* is your understanding of this part of the poem? How dependent is the poem as a whole on that knowledge? If you are familiar with the *Odyssey*, how does this poem comment on and inform your reading of it?
5. Why is the "familiar tread" "far-too-late" (l. 43)?

Paired Poems

. . . .

An Epitaph

Matthew Prior

English poet and diplomat Matthew Prior (1664–1721) was born in Wimborne Minster, East Dorset. He earned his BA at St John's College, Cambridge, in 1686. He served England as under-secretary of state and as commissioner of trade, and became a member of Parliament in 1700. In 1713, he helped negotiate the Treaty of Utrecht, which became known as "Matt's Peace." He also served as ambassador in Paris. After the death of Queen Anne, he returned to England, where he was impeached by the Whigs and imprisoned for two years. He continued to write in confinement, composing his most famous work, *Alma; or, The Progress of the Mind*. He is buried in Poets' Corner in Westminster Abbey. Today, Prior is remembered chiefly for his satires, of which "An Epitaph" is a prime example.

Interred beneath this marble stone
Lie sauntering Jack and idle Joan.
While rolling threescore years and one
Did round this globe their courses run;
If human things went ill or well;   5
If changing empires rose or fell;
The morning passed, the evening came,

And found this couple still the same.
They walked and ate, good folks: what then?
Why then they walked and ate again.   10
They soundly slept the night away;
They did just nothing all the day;
And having buried children four,
Would not take pains to try for more.
Nor sister either had, nor brother: 15
They seemed just tallied for each other.

   Their moral and economy
Most perfectly they made agree:
Each virtue kept its proper bound,
Nor trespassed on the other's ground.   20
Nor fame, nor censure they regarded:
They neither punished, nor rewarded.
He cared not what the footmen did;
Her maids she neither praised, nor chid:
So every servant took his course;   25
And bad at first, they all grew worse.
Slothful disorder filled his stable,
And sluttish plenty decked her table.
Their beer was strong; their wine was port;
Their meal was large; their grace was short.   30
They gave the poor the remnant-meat
Just when it grew not fit to eat.

   They paid the church and parish rate,[1]
And took, but read not the receipt;
For which they claimed their Sunday's due   35
Of slumbering in an upper pew.

   No man's defects sought they to know,
So never made themselves a foe.
No man's good deeds did they commend,
So never raised themselves a friend.   40
Nor cherished they relations poor:
That might decrease their present store;
Nor barn nor house did they repair:
That might oblige their future heir.

   They neither added, nor confounded;   45
They neither wanted, nor abounded.
Each Christmas they accompts did clear;
And wound their bottom[2] round the year.

---

[1]Church rate refers to tithing; parish rate, to taxes.—EDS.
[2]A ball of thread or yarn is sometimes called a *bottom*, here meaning they wrapped their affairs up tidily.—EDS.

Nor tear nor smile did they employ
At news of public grief or joy.   50
When bells were rung and bonfires made,
If asked, they ne'er denied their aid;
Their jug was to the ringers carried,
Whoever either died, or married.
Their billet[3] at the fire was found,   55
Whoever was deposed, or crowned.
   Nor good, nor bad, nor fools, nor wise;
They would not learn, nor could advise;
Without love, hatred, joy, or fear,
They led—a kind of—as it were;   60
Nor wished, nor cared, nor laughed, nor cried;
And so they lived; and so they died.

[1718]

Exploring the Text

1. How are Jack and Joan characterized in the poem? What is meant by the couplet, "Their moral and economy / Most perfectly they made agree" (ll. 17–18)? What are the effects of their mildness toward others and their conformity as expressed in lines 19–32?
2. Consider the different meanings of the word "grace" in line 30. Where else in the poem are wealth or plenty placed at odds with spirituality?
3. Line 60 says, "They led—a kind of—as it were." How might this line serve as a fitting summary of the poem? Explain.
4. What might have improved the lives of Jack and Joan?
5. "An Epitaph" is composed entirely of rhyming couplets with a steady rhythm. How does this form reinforce the themes of the poem?
6. This poem was written in part to satirize the landed gentry in early eighteenth-century England, as well as the conservative elected officials who supported them. How do you think the poem relates to the present day? If you were to imagine a contemporary Jack and Joan, how would you describe them?

The Unknown Citizen

W. H. AUDEN

Born in northern England to a doctor and a nurse, Wystan Hugh Auden (1907–1973) earned a scholarship to Oxford to study engineering. While there, he became interested in poetry—especially the modernist poetry of T. S. Eliot—and studied English instead. He was part of a group of poets known as the Oxford Group (and

---

[3]Firewood.—EDS.

later, the Auden Generation), which included Stephen Spender and Louis MacNeice. During the 1930s, Auden traveled to Spain and China; became involved in political causes; and wrote prose, poetry, and plays. In 1939, Auden left England and became a United States citizen. *Another Time* (1940), the first book he wrote in America, contains some of his most famous poems, including "Musée des Beaux Arts." He won a Pulitzer Prize for *The Age of Anxiety* (1947) and a National Book Award for *The Shield of Achilles* (1955). "The Unknown Citizen" appears in his *Collected Poems* (1940).

(To JS/07 M 378
This Marble Monument
Is Erected by the State)

He was found by the Bureau of Statistics to be
One against whom there was no official complaint,
And all the reports on his conduct agree
That, in the modern sense of an old-fashioned word, he was a saint,
For in everything he did he served the Greater Community.   5
Except for the War till the day he retired,
He worked in a factory and never got fired,
But satisfied his employers, Fudge Motors Inc.
Yet he wasn't a scab or odd in his views.
For his Union reports that he paid his dues,   10
(Our report on his Union shows it was sound)
And our Social Psychology workers found
That he was popular with his mates and liked a drink.
The Press are convinced that he bought a paper every day
And that his reactions to advertisements were normal in every way.   15
Policies taken out in his name prove that he was fully insured,
And his Health-card shows he was once in a hospital but left it cured.
Both Producers Research and High-Grade Living declare
He was fully sensible to the advantages of the Instalment Plan
And had everything necessary to the Modern Man,   20
A phonograph, a radio, a car and a frigidaire.
Our researchers into Public Opinion are content
That he held the proper opinions for the time of year;
When there was peace, he was for peace: when there was war, he went.
He was married and added five children to the population,   25
Which our Eugenist says was the right number for a parent of his generation.
And our teachers report that he never interfered with their education.
Was he free? Was he happy? The question is absurd:
Had anything been wrong, we should certainly have heard.

[1940]

Exploring the Text

1. How do you interpret the modern definition of sainthood offered in line 4? How does the modern sense differ from the old-fashioned one?
2. Reread the poem, looking specifically for adjectives related to value judgments (i.e., good/bad, beautiful/ugly). How would you characterize the values Auden describes? What is missing from them?
3. What is suggested by the words "our" in lines 11, 12, 22, 26, and 27, and "we" in the final line of the poem?
4. Note the list of possessions given in line 21: "A phonograph, a radio, a car and a frigidaire." What would that list consist of if the poem were written today?
5. Note that some of the lines of the poem run on as if they're out of control; they seem too long. Why might the poet have chosen to write this way?
6. Do you find the poem humorous? Which is the most comical line? Which is the most ironic? Why?
7. What is Auden satirizing in this poem?

Focus on Comparison and Contrast

1. Compare and contrast the characters of Jack and Joan with the unknown citizen. What qualities do they share? What makes them different?
2. What is Prior's attitude toward conformity and rebellion? What is Auden's? Which attitude more nearly resembles your own? Support your position with textual evidence.
3. Prior's poem was written about three hundred years ago; Auden's, about seventy. While each speaks to its own time, they both seem highly relevant today. Which one feels more contemporary in style? Which one feels more current in content? Explain.

Writing Assignment

Write an essay that compares how Prior and Auden create mock elegies and epitaphs to satirize their subjects. As you write your essay, consider how each writer uses elements of style to achieve his purpose.

Book Covers for Hamlet

Hamlet has been published in so many editions by so many publishers that counting them would be a fool's errand. For each edition, the publisher has to either design a new cover using existing art, or commission a piece specifically for that edition. The following images are from the Dover Thrift and Bantam Classic editions of *Hamlet*.

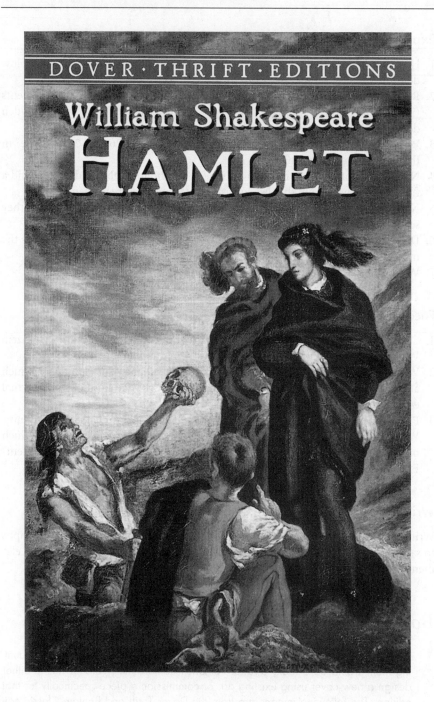

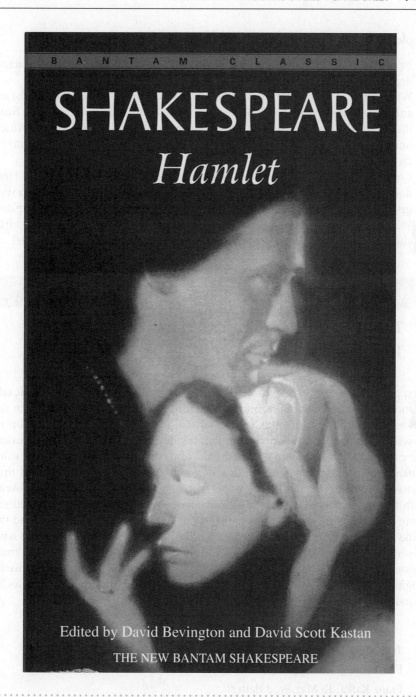

Exploring the Text

1. Note how very different each cover is from the other. Who are the characters depicted? What do the pictures share? What is different?

2. What is the central event in *Hamlet* suggested by each illustration? Identify the act and scene in the play that each picture best represents. Using direct evidence from the text of the play, explain the interpretation presented by each picture. Which one presents the more compelling and cogent interpretation of a major theme of the play as a whole?

3. Consider the old saying, "You can't judge a book by its cover." Is that true? How does that statement relate to these two covers? What expectations does each suggest for prospective readers? Does the play fulfill those expectations? Explain. Which cover do you prefer? If you were to walk into a bookstore and had to choose between the two (at the same price), which one would you buy? Why?

Conversation

The Metamorphosis: Interpretations and Transformations

First published in 1915, *The Metamorphosis* by Franz Kafka has become a classic tale of modern life, in which conformity is alienating and dehumanizing, and even the mildest rebellion is threatening. Kafka's fantastical story of the transformation of traveling salesman Gregor Samsa—his family's meek breadwinner—into an insect has captured the imagination of generations of readers, and today we use the word *Kafkaesque* to describe a situation that is complex, surreal, disorienting, and thus menacing. Writer Vladimir Nabokov began his famous lecture on Kafka's novella with this observation: "If Kafka's *The Metamorphosis* strikes anyone as something more than an entomological fantasy, then I congratulate him on having joined the ranks of good and great readers." Many critics, visual artists, and other writers have joined these ranks with interpretations and commentaries running the gamut from serious to playful. The following Conversation includes the full text of Kafka's novella, originally written in German, along with letters from Kafka, and recent responses by "good and great readers," who are, in this case, visual artists.

Texts

Franz Kafka, *The Metamorphosis* (novella)

Franz Kafka, To Max Brod (letter)

Franz Kafka, To Kurt Wolff Verlag (letter)

David Zane Mairowitz and **Robert Crumb**, from *Kafka* (graphic essay)

Peter Kuper, from *The Metamorphosis* (graphic novel)

Peter Kuper on *The Metamorphosis* (interview)

The Metamorphosis

Franz Kafka

TRANSLATED BY ALEXIS WALKER

> Born in Prague, Czechoslovakia, to middle-class Jewish parents, Franz Kafka (1883–1924) spoke Czech in his childhood but studied in German-speaking schools. He graduated from the Charles-Ferdinand University in Prague with a law degree. Kafka was employed for many years at the Workers' Accident Insurance Institute, and he wrote after his working hours. He published *The Metamorphosis* (1915) and *The Penal Colony* (1919) during his lifetime. After his death from tuberculosis, three other novels were published, despite his request that the manuscripts be destroyed: *The Trial* (1925), *The Castle* (1926), and *Amerika* (1927).

I

When Gregor Samsa awoke in his bed one morning from unquiet dreams, he found himself transformed into an enormous insect.* He lay on a back as hard as armor and saw, when he raised his head slightly, a jutting brown underbelly divided into arching segments. The bedcovers could barely cover it; they threatened to slide off altogether. His many legs, pitifully thin in comparison with the rest of his bulk, fluttered helplessly before his eyes.

"What has happened to me?" he thought. It wasn't a dream. His room—a decent enough room for a person, if slightly too small—lay quietly between the four familiar walls. Over the table on which was spread his unpacked collections of fabric samples—Samsa was a traveling salesman—hung the picture that he had recently cut out of an illustrated magazine and fit into an attractive gilt frame. The picture was of a woman clad in a fur hat and a fur stole; she sat upright and held out to the viewer a thick fur muff into which her entire forearm disappeared.

Gregor's gaze then directed itself to the window. The dreary weather—one could hear raindrops hit the metal awning over the window—made him quite

---

*Translator's note: The closest English equivalents to the German word Kafka uses here (*Ungeziefer*) are "vermin" and "pest"—the German word denotes parasitic and otherwise objectionable creatures (including fleas, lice, rats, mice, etc.) and connotes uncleanness. "Insect" is a compromise: though at once more specific and less evocative than the original, it sidesteps problems of agreement ("vermin" being almost always plural in English) and of tone ("pest" being more colloquial than the German *Ungeziefer*).

melancholy. "What if I slept a bit longer and forgot all this foolishness," he thought. But that was altogether impossible, because he was used to sleeping on his right side, and his current condition made working himself into this position impossible. No matter how vigorously he swung himself over to the right, he immediately rolled again onto his back. He tried what seemed hundreds of times, closing his eyes in order to avoid having to see his wriggling legs. He finally gave up only when he began to feel in his side a small dull ache that he had never felt before.

"Oh, God," he thought, "what a strenuous profession I've chosen—traveling day in, day out! The demands of business are far greater on the road than they are at the home office, and I'm burdened with the annoyances of travel besides: the worry about train connections; the irregular, bad meals; a social life limited to passing acquaintances who never become real friends. To hell with it!" He felt an itch on his belly, and he shoved himself back against the bedpost so he could lift his head more easily. He found the spot that itched: it was covered with small white dots that he couldn't identify. He went to touch the spot with one of his legs but drew it back immediately, because the touch made him shudder.

He slid back into his former position. "This early rising," he thought, "can make you into a complete idiot. A man needs his sleep. Other travelers live like women in a harem. When, for example, I go back to my hotel during the course of the morning to write up orders, these gentlemen are just sitting down to breakfast. I should try that with the Director: I'd be fired on the spot. Who knows, though—that might be good for me. If it weren't for my parents, I would have given notice long ago: I would have confronted the Director and given him a piece of my mind. He would have fallen off his chair! It's incredible the way he has of sitting perched at his reading desk and speaking from on high to employees who, on top of everything, have to draw very near owing to his slight deafness. Oh well, I shouldn't give up hope altogether: once I have the money to pay off my parents' debt—it should only be another five or six years—I'll definitely do it. Then I'll make my big break. In the meantime, I have to get up—my train leaves at five."

And he looked over at the alarm clock that ticked on the bureau. "God in heaven!" he thought. It was six-thirty, and the hands of the clock went quietly on; it was even later than six-thirty—it was closer to six-forty-five. Shouldn't the alarm have gone off? He could see from the bed that it was correctly set for four o'clock; it must have gone off. But was it possible to sleep peacefully through that furniture-rattling noise? Of course, he hadn't actually slept peacefully, but he had no doubt for that reason slept more deeply. But what should he do now? The next train left at seven o'clock. In order to catch that one, he'd have to rush like a madman, and his samples weren't packed up yet. He hardly felt alert or energetic enough. And even if he caught the train, he wouldn't avoid the Director's wrath, because the office porter had been waiting at the five-o'clock train and would long since have reported his failure to appear. The porter was completely under the Director's thumb—he had neither a backbone nor brains. What if Gregor were to report himself sick? But that would be highly awkward and suspicious, because he had not been sick once in five years of service. The Director would certainly come with the insurance doctor. He

5

would reproach his parents for their lazy son and dismiss all rejoinders by referring them to the doctor, who considered all people completely healthy, but work-averse. And would he be so wrong in this case? Gregor actually felt completely fine, despite a fatigue completely unwarranted after such a long sleep. He even had a powerful appetite.

As he thought all this over hurriedly, without being able to decide whether to leave his bed—the clock had just struck six-forty-five—there was a knock on the door near the head of his bed. "Gregor," he heard—it was his mother—"it's a quarter to seven. Weren't you going on a trip?" What a gentle voice! Gregor was terrified when he heard his answer. It was unmistakably in his old voice, but had mixed in, as if from down deep, an irrepressible, painful, squeaking noise, which allowed words to be heard clearly when first uttered, but as they resonated, distorted them to such an extent that they were difficult to understand. Gregor had wanted to answer in detail and explain everything, but in light of the circumstances he limited himself to saying: "Yes, yes, thanks, Mother, I'm getting up." The wooden door seemed to make the change in Gregor's voice imperceptible outside the room, because his mother was satisfied with his explanation and shuffled away. But through this brief exchange the other family members had become aware that Gregor was unexpectedly still at home, and his father was already knocking on one side door—lightly, but with his fist. "Gregor, Gregor," he called, "What's going on?" And after a short pause he urged again, with a deeper voice: Gregor! Gregor!" At the other side door, his sister fretted softly: "Gregor? Are you ill? Do you need something?" To both sides, Gregor answered, "I'm just about ready to go," and he made an effort to ban anything conspicuous from his voice by the most painstaking enunciation and by inserting long pauses between individual words. His father returned to his breakfast, but his sister whispered: "Gregor, open up, I beg you." Gregor had no intention of opening the door, however—instead he gave thanks for his habitual precaution, born of much travel, of locking all doors during the night, even at home.

First he wanted to get up, quietly and undisturbed, get dressed, and above all eat breakfast—only then did he want to think over what came next, because he could see that he would come to no reasonable conclusions as long as he lay in bed. In the past he had often felt one mild pain or another while lying in bed, possibly from lying in an awkward position, that proved to be sheer imagination once he got up. He was eager to see how today's fantasies would gradually resolve themselves. He didn't doubt in the least that the change in his voice was nothing more than the harbinger of a hearty cold, one of the occupational hazards of traveling salesmen.

Throwing off the covers was perfectly simple: he only needed to puff himself up a bit and they fell off on their own. But doing more than that was difficult, especially because he was so strangely broad. He would normally have used his arms and hands to get up; now, he had only the many little legs which were continuously moving in every direction and which he could not seem to control. If he meant to bend one, it would be the first one to stretch itself out, if he finally succeeded in enforcing his will with one leg, all the rest of them worked furiously, as if liberated, in extreme, painful agitation. "You can't just lie here in bed doing nothing," Gregor said to himself.

At first he intended to get out of the bed with the lower part of his body fore-   10
most, but this lower part, which he had moreover not yet seen and of which he could
not form a proper mental image, proved too difficult to move. It went extremely
slowly. When, nearly frantic, he finally gathered his strength and recklessly shoved
himself forward, he misjudged the direction and violently struck the lower bed post.
The burning pain he felt convinced him that the lower part of his body was at least
at the moment the most sensitive part.

He afterwards attempted to get his upper body out of bed and carefully turned
his head towards the edge of the bed. This he could do easily, and in spite of its bulk
and weight, the mass of his body finally slowly followed the direction of his head. But
when he held his head at last free of the bed, he became afraid to shift further in this
direction, because if he ultimately let himself fall like that, it would be a miracle if his
head were not injured. And now, of all times, he could not afford to lose consciousness; he would rather remain in bed.

After continued effort, however, he found himself lying exactly as before, and
heaved a sigh. He saw his little legs struggling against one another even more furiously, if that were possible, and he saw no way of introducing calm and order to this
anarchy. At this point he repeated to himself that he could not possibly lie in bed
any longer and that it would be most sensible to risk everything, even if there were
only the smallest hope of thereby freeing himself from bed. At the same time, however, he kept reminding himself that calm deliberation was always better than rash
decision-making. All the while he tried hard to focus on the view from the window,
but unfortunately there was little encouragement or cheer to gain from the sight
of the morning fog, which shrouded even the opposite side of the narrow street.
"Already seven o'clock," he said to himself with the latest striking of the alarm clock,
"already seven o'clock and still such fog." And he lay quiet a short while, breathing
shallowly, as if he thought complete stillness might restore things to their true and
natural state.

After a bit, however, he said to himself, "Before it strikes seven-fifteen, I must
without fail be completely out of bed. For one thing, someone from the company
will have come by then to inquire after me, because the office opens before seven."
And he concentrated his efforts toward swinging his entire body out of the bed all
at the same time. If he let himself fall out of bed in this manner, his head, which he
would raise sharply during the fall, would presumably remain uninjured. His back
seemed to be hard; nothing would happen to it in the fall onto the carpet. His greatest source of misgiving was anticipation of the loud crash that would follow, which
would probably arouse anxiety, if not terror, beyond the doors. That would have to
be risked, however.

When, by rocking back and forth, Gregor moved halfway off of the bed—the
new method was more a game than an exertion—it occurred to him how simple
everything would be if someone would come help him. Two strong people—he
thought of his father and the servant girl—would be more than adequate. They
would only have to shove their arms under his domed back, pry him up out of bed,
prop up his bulk by crouching low, and then help him complete the turn over onto

the floor, where hopefully his little legs would gain some sense of purpose. Quite apart from the fact that the doors were locked, though, should he really call for help? In spite of his predicament he couldn't suppress a smile at the thought.

He was already so far along that he could hardly maintain his balance when he rocked forcefully. Very soon he would have to make a final decision, because in five minutes it would be seven-fifteen. Just then the front doorbell rang. "That's someone from the company," he said to himself and virtually froze, though his little legs only danced more hurriedly. Everything remained quiet for a moment. "They're not opening the door," Gregor said to himself, momentarily carried away by some absurd hope. But then, naturally, as always, the servant girl directed her firm step to the door and opened it. Gregor needed to hear only the first word of greeting from the visitor and he already knew who it was—the Deputy Director himself. Why was Gregor condemned to work at a company where the least infraction immediately attracted the greatest suspicion? Were all employees then without exception scoundrels; were there among them no loyal, devoted individuals who, when they had merely missed a few morning hours of service, would become so tormented by pangs of conscience that they would be frankly unable to leave their beds? Wouldn't it really have been enough to send an apprentice to inquire—if indeed this inquiry were necessary at all? Did the Deputy Director himself have to come, thereby showing the entire innocent family that the investigation of this suspicious situation could only be entrusted to the Deputy Director himself? And more as a result of the agitation into which this line of thought transported Gregor, than as a result of a proper decision, he swung himself with all his might out of the bed. There was a loud thump, but no actual crash. The fall was muffled a bit by the carpet, and his back was more elastic than Gregor had thought—these things accounted for the fairly inconspicuous dull thump. He had failed only to raise his head carefully enough and had struck it. He twisted it back and forth and rubbed it into the carpet out of anger and pain.

"Something happened inside there," said the Deputy Director in the room to the left. Gregor tried to imagine something similar to what had happened to him today happening to the Deputy Director; it really was possible, after all. But as if in cruel response to this question the Deputy Director took a few decisive steps in the next room, making his patent leather boots creak. From the room to the right Gregor's sister whispered to inform him: "Gregor, the Deputy Director is here." "I know," said Gregor to himself; but he did not dare to raise his voice loud enough for his sister to hear.

"Gregor," his father now said from the room to the left, "the Deputy Director has come and inquires as to why you did not leave with the early morning train. We don't know what we should say to him. Furthermore, he wants to speak to you directly. So please open the door. He will surely have the goodness to excuse the disorder of your room." "Good morning, Mr. Samsa," the Deputy Director called out at the same time in a friendly manner. "He is not well," his mother said to the Deputy Director, while his father still spoke at the door, "he is not well, believe me, sir. Why would Gregor otherwise miss a train? The boy has nothing in his head but the company. I almost worry that he never goes out at night; he has been in the city eight days now, but he

15

was at home every night. He sits with us at the table and quietly reads the newspaper or studies train schedules. Busying himself with woodworking is as far as he goes in the way of amusement. In the course of two, three evenings, for example, he cut himself a small frame; you would be astounded at how pretty it is. It's hanging in his room; you will see it right away, when Gregor opens up. I am happy, in any case, that you're here, Deputy Director. We could not have persuaded Gregor to open the door alone; he is so stubborn; and there's certainly something wrong with him, although he denied it this morning." "I'm coming right away," said Gregor slowly and carefully, while not moving at all, in order not to miss a word of the conversation. "Otherwise, dear woman, I can't explain it myself, either," said the Deputy Director. "Hopefully it's nothing serious. Though I must say, that we businessmen — either fortunately or unfortunately, as you will — must often ignore a trivial indisposition in the interest of business." "So can the Deputy Director come in to see you?" asked his impatient father, knocking again at the door. "No," said Gregor. In the room to the left there arose an awkward silence; in the room to the right, his sister began sobbing.

Why didn't his sister join the others? She had most likely just now arisen from bed and had not yet begun to get dressed. And why was she crying? Because he did not stand up and let the Deputy Director in; because he was in danger of losing his position and because the Director would then persecute his parents with the old demands? Those were unnecessary worries, for the time being. Gregor was still here and did not in the least contemplate leaving his family. At the moment he was lying on the carpet, and no one who was aware of his condition would seriously request that he let the Deputy Director in. Gregor could not possibly be dismissed just for this minor breach of politeness; he could easily find a suitable excuse later. And it seemed to Gregor far more reasonable to leave him in peace now, instead of disturbing him with tears and entreaties. But it was the uncertainty of it all that distressed the others and so excused their behavior.

"Mr. Samsa," the Deputy Director now called in a raised voice, "what's the matter? You barricade yourself there in your room, answer merely with yes and no, burden your parents with profound, unnecessary worries and — this only mentioned incidentally — neglect your business responsibilities in an unheard-of way. I speak here in the name of your parents and your Director and earnestly request of you an immediate, clear explanation. I am amazed; I am amazed. I thought I knew you as a quiet, reasonable person, and now you suddenly begin to exhibit extraordinary capriciousness. The Director told me early this morning of a possible explanation for your dereliction — it related to the cash account recently entrusted to you — but I actually almost gave him my word of honor that this explanation could not be accurate. Now, however, I see your incomprehensible stubbornness here, and I lose any desire to vouch for you in the least. And your position is not the most secure. I originally had the intention of saying all of this just between the two of us, but since you force me to waste my time here needlessly, I don't know why your parents should not also hear it. Your performance recently has been very unsatisfying. It is not the time of the year, of course, to do extraordinary business, we recognize that; but there is no time of year in which to do *no* business, Mr. Samsa — there cannot be."

"But, sir," called out Gregor, beside himself, forgetting everything else in his   20
agitation, "I'll open up immediately, this instant. A mild indisposition—an attack of
dizziness—has kept me from getting up. I'm still lying in bed. I'm completely recovered now, though. I'm climbing out of bed right now. Just one moment of patience!
I thought things were not quite back to normal yet. But I'm already well again. How
it can suddenly come over a person! I was fine yesterday evening, my parents know
that, or perhaps I should say that yesterday evening I had a slight premonition of it.
It must have been easy to see in me. Why didn't I report it to the office yesterday!
But one always thinks that one can ride out illness without having to stay home. Sir!
Spare my parents! There is no basis for all the reproaches you've made against me; no
one said anything about them to me before now. Perhaps you haven't seen the latest
orders that I sent in. In any case, I will be starting my trip on the eight o'clock train.
These few hours of rest have strengthened me. Don't let me hold you up, though, sir;
I'll soon be in the office myself, and please have the goodness to say so, and to send
my greetings to the Director."

And while Gregor hurriedly blurted all this out, hardly knowing what he said,
he moved effortlessly closer to the chest, thanks to the practice he had had in bed,
and attempted to raise himself against it to an upright position. He actually wanted
to open the door, actually wanted to let them see him and to speak with the Deputy
Director. He was eager to know what they all would say to him when they finally saw
him, after so much urging. Would they be afraid? If so, Gregor would be absolved of
responsibility and could relax. If they took it all in stride, however, then, too, he would
have no cause for worry, and he really could be at the train station at eight, if he hurried. At first he simply slid a few times down the side of the slippery chest; finally,
however, he gave himself one last swing and stood upright. He ignored the pain in his
lower body, despite the fact that it burned. Now he let himself fall against the back of
a nearby chair and held tight to its sides with his legs. This helped him regain his self-
control, and he stayed quiet, so that he could hear the Deputy Director speak.

"Did you understand one word?" the Deputy Director asked his parents. "Surely
he's making fun of us?" "For God's sake," cried his mother in the midst of tears, "he
might be seriously ill, and we're all plaguing him. Grete! Grete!" she then screamed.
"Mother?" called his sister from the other side. They were communicating through
Gregor's room. "You must go fetch the doctor this minute. Gregor is ill. Quickly, to
the doctor. Did you hear Gregor speak just now?" "That was the voice of an animal,"
said the Deputy Director, noticeably quiet, by contrast with the screaming of his
mother. "Anna! Anna!" called his father towards the kitchen, clapping his hands,
"Get a locksmith immediately!" And the two girls ran, their skirts rustling, through
the foyer—how had his sister gotten dressed so quickly?—and flung the apartment
door open. There was no noise of the door slamming; they had probably left it open,
as was usual in apartments where some great misfortune had occurred.

Gregor had become much calmer, however. It was true that they didn't understand his speech, but it sounded clear enough to him, clearer than previously,
perhaps because his ear had adjusted to it. But they did still believe that something
was wrong with him, and they were prepared to help him. He was pleased by the

confidence and certainty with which the first arrangements had been made. He felt drawn once again into the circle of humanity and expected great things from both the doctor and the locksmith, without really making a distinction between them. In order to develop the clearest possible voice for the decisive discussions to come, he coughed a bit, although he tried to do this in a muted fashion, because this, too, might sound very different from a human cough—he no longer trusted himself to judge. It had now fallen completely silent in the next room. His parents might have been sitting at the table, whispering with the Deputy Director, or perhaps they were all pressed against the door, listening.

Using the chair, Gregor slowly shoved himself forward, and then let go, throwing himself against the door, and holding himself upright against it. The balls of his feet had some sticky substance on them. He took a moment to recover from the exertion. Then he applied himself to turning the key in the lock. Unfortunately, it seemed as if he had no real teeth—what then could he grip the key with?—but his jaws, on the other hand, were powerful. With their help he started to turn the key. He paid no attention to the fact that he obviously did some harm to himself in the process—a brown discharge came out from his mouth, flowing over the key and dripping on the floor. "Listen now," said the Deputy Director in the next room, "he's turning the key." That encouraged Gregor greatly, but all of them should have cheered him on, his father and mother, too: "Come on, Gregor," they should have called, "keep at it, keep working the lock!" And imagining that all his efforts were being watched with rapt attention, he recklessly bit down on the key with all his might. He danced around the lock, following the key as it turned; holding himself upright entirely with his mouth, he either pulled up on the key or forced it down with the full weight of his body, as necessary. The crisp click of the lock finally snapping back elated him. Breathing a sigh of relief he said to himself, "I didn't even need the locksmith," and he laid his head on the door handle, in order to open the door.

Because he had to open the door in this way, he was not yet visible even when it was opened wide. If he didn't want to fall flat on his back just before his entrance into the next room, he would first have to slowly make his way around the open panel of the double door. He was still busy with this difficult maneuver and had not yet had a moment to think of the others, when he heard the Deputy Director force out a loud "Oh!" It sounded like a gust of wind. Now he could also see the Deputy, who was nearest the door—he pressed his hand to his open mouth and slowly shrank back, as if an invisible, irresistible force drove him. His mother—who stood, despite the presence of the Deputy Director, with her hair still loose, and sticking up in parts from her night's sleep—first looked at his father with her hands clasped; then she walked two steps towards Gregor and sank to the ground in the midst of her billowing skirts, her face completely hidden, sunk upon her breast. His father balled his fist with a fierce expression, as if he wanted to knock Gregor back into his room; then he looked uncertainly around the living room, covered his eyes with his hands, and sobbed so that his powerful chest shook.

Gregor had not yet entered the outer room; instead, he leaned from within against the door panel that was still fastened, so that only half of his body and his

25

head, craned to one side in order to see them, were visible. It had become much brighter outside in the meantime: one could clearly see a section of the endless, gray-black building—it was a hospital—that stood across the street, its severe, uniform windows breaking up its facade. The rain still fell, but only in large, singly visible and singly plummeting drops. The table teemed with breakfast dishes; his father considered breakfast the most important meal of the day, and he protracted it for hours reading various periodicals. On the wall just opposite hung a photograph of Gregor from his military days, which showed him dressed as a lieutenant, with a carefree smile, his hand on his dagger, his bearing and his uniform commanding respect. The door to the foyer was open, and because the door to the apartment was open as well, one could see the outer hall and the top of the staircase leading downwards.

"Now," said Gregor—and he was well aware that he was the only one remaining calm— "I will just get dressed, pack my samples up, and be off. Will you all allow me to go? Deputy Director, you see that I'm not obstinate and that I want to work. Traveling is demanding, but I couldn't live without it. Where do you intend to go now, Deputy Director? To the office? Yes? Will you report everything accurately? A person might be unable to work for a time, but it is precisely then that one must consider his past accomplishments and keep in mind that once the hindrance is past, he will certainly work even harder and more efficiently. I owe a great deal to the Director—you know that only too well. On the other hand, I have the care of my parents and sister. I'm in a fix, but I'll work my way out again. But please don't make it more difficult for me than it already is. Take my part in the office! I know the traveling salesmen aren't popular. People think we earn a huge amount of money and lead grand lives. People just don't have any particular reason to think this prejudice through carefully. You, however, Deputy Director, you have a better perspective on how things work than most of the staff—I might say, confidentially, a better perspective than even the Director himself, who, in his capacity as owner, can easily be misled in his judgment about an employee. You know very well that the traveling salesman, because he is away from the office the better part of the year, easily falls victim to gossip, to chance misfortune, and groundless complaints. It's impossible for him to defend himself against these complaints, as he ordinarily learns nothing of them; it's only when he comes home at the end of a trip completely exhausted that he feels the terrible consequences, whose origins he can't divine, in his very body. Deputy Director, don't leave without saying one word that shows me that you agree with me at least in part!"

But the Deputy Director had turned away at Gregor's first words, and was staring back at Gregor over one twitching shoulder, his mouth agape. During Gregor's speech he had not stood still for a moment, but, never taking his eyes off of Gregor, moved steadily but surreptitiously towards the door, as if there were some secret prohibition against leaving the room. He had already reached the foyer, and judging by the sudden movement with which he pulled his foot out of the room at his last step, one would have thought his sole was on fire. Once in the foyer, he stretched his hand out towards the staircase as if divine deliverance awaited him there.

Gregor realized that the Deputy Director could under no circumstances be allowed to leave this way, if his position at the company were not to be endangered.

His parents didn't understand this as well as he did. They had over the years persuaded themselves that he was guaranteed permanent employment in the company, and besides, they had so much to do in dealing with their own distress at the moment, that their foresight had vanished. But Gregor had this foresight. The Deputy Director must be detained, calmed, persuaded, and finally won over—the future of Gregor and his family depended on it. If only his sister were here! She was clever: she was already crying when Gregor was still calmly lying on his back. And the Deputy Director, that ladies' man, would surely have let her sway him: she would have closed the apartment door and talked him out of his fear in the foyer. But his sister was not there, so Gregor would have to handle it himself. And without thinking about the fact that he had no idea yet how well he could move, without thinking that his speech was possibly—well, very probably—incomprehensible, he let go of the door panel, forcing himself through the opening, and headed for the Deputy Director, who was already at the landing in the hall and hugging himself in a comical manner. With a small cry, scrambling in vain for something to hold on to, Gregor immediately fell down onto his many little legs. This had hardly happened, when for the first time that morning he felt a sense of physical well-being. His little legs had solid ground beneath them; they obeyed him completely, as he noted to his delight. They even strove to carry him where he wanted to go. Suddenly, he believed that the ultimate relief of all his suffering was at hand. But at that moment, as he lay on the floor trembling with suppressed energy, close to his mother and directly opposite her, she sprang up—she who had seemed so lost in thought—with her arms outstretched, her fingers splayed, and cried out: "Help, for God's sake, help!" She kept her head turned towards him, as if she wanted to be able to see him better, but, following a contradictory impulse, she ran heedlessly backwards, forgetting that the table full of dishes lay behind her. She quickly sat down when she reached it, as if absent-mindedly, seeming not to notice that next to her the coffeepot had been knocked over and coffee was streaming freely out onto the carpet.

"Mother, Mother," Gregor said softly, and looked up at her. The Deputy Director   30
vanished from his mind momentarily, and he couldn't stop himself from snapping his jaws at the empty air several times at the sight of the flowing coffee. His mother began screaming again over this, fled from the table, and fell into the arms of his father, who was hurrying towards her. But Gregor had no time then for his parents. The Deputy Director was already on the stairs. His chin on the railing, he looked back one last time. Gregor took a running start, in order to have the best chance of catching up to him. The Deputy Director must have sensed something, as he sprang down several steps and then disappeared. "Ahh!" he screamed; it echoed throughout the entire stairwell.

Unfortunately, the flight of the Deputy Director seemed to have completely unhinged his father, who up until then had been relatively self-controlled. Instead of running after the Deputy Director or at least not restraining Gregor from pursuing him, with his right hand he grabbed the walking stick that the Deputy Director had left behind on an armchair together with his hat and coat; with his left hand he picked up a large newspaper from the table; then, stamping his feet, he began to drive Gregor back into his room by swatting at him with the stick and the newspaper. None of Gregor's pleas helped—none of his pleas were understood. The more submissively he bowed his head, the more vigorously his father stamped his feet. Across the room, despite the cool weather, his mother had thrown open a window and, leaning far out of the window, pressed her face into her hands. Between the street and the stairwell there arose a strong cross-draft: the window curtains flew up; the newspapers on the table rustled, and a few pages fluttered to the floor. His father drove him back mercilessly, spitting out hissing noises like a wild beast. Gregor, however, still was unpracticed in moving backwards, so he went very slowly. If he had only been allowed time to turn around, he would have gone immediately back into his room, but he was afraid of making his father impatient. At every moment the stick in his father's hand threatened to deal him a fatal blow to his back or head. Finally, however, Gregor found he had no choice, as he noted with terror that he seemed unable to keep going in the right direction when he moved backwards. He therefore began, with frequent side-glances at his father, to turn around as quickly as he could, which was actually very slowly. His father might have understood his good intentions, because he did not disturb him while he was doing this; in fact, he actually directed him here and there from a distance with the point of his stick. If only there weren't this unbearable hissing from his father! It unnerved Gregor completely. He was already almost completely turned around when, listening to his hissing, he made a mistake and turned a bit in the wrong direction. When he was finally, fortunately, headfirst at the opening of the door, it appeared that his body was too wide to go through without further ado. In his present state of mind it was naturally far from occurring to his father to open the other door panel in order to make a wide enough passageway for Gregor. He was obsessed merely with getting Gregor into his room as quickly as possible. He would never have allowed the preparations necessary for Gregor to raise himself up and possibly go through the door that way. Instead, making a great deal of noise, he drove Gregor forward as if there were no obstacle before him. The noise coming from behind Gregor didn't sound any longer like the voice of his father. It was clearly no laughing matter, so Gregor forced himself—happen what would—through the door. One side of his body was hoisted upwards. He lay crookedly in the doorway. One of his flanks was rubbed raw, and on the white door ugly smears remained behind. He was soon stuck fast, and couldn't move at all anymore. His little legs hung twitching on one side, and those on the other side were pressed painfully against the floor. Then his father liberated him with a powerful shove from behind, and he flew, bleeding heavily, a long way into his room. The door was slammed shut with the stick, and then it was finally quiet.

II

It was already twilight when Gregor awoke from a deep, dreamless sleep. He would not have arisen much later even without having been disturbed, for he felt well rested and no longer sleepy, but it seemed to him that he had been awakened by the sounds of a fleeting footstep and of the door to the foyer carefully being shut. The glare from the electric street lamp outside lay palely here and there on the ceiling of his room and on the upper surfaces of the furniture, but down by Gregor it was dark. He shoved himself slowly towards the door, awkwardly groping with the feelers he had just then come to appreciate, in order to see what had happened there. His left side seemed to be a single, long, unpleasantly taut scar, and he had to positively limp on his row of legs. One leg had been seriously injured during the events of the morning: it dragged limply behind him.

It was only when he was at the door that he realized what had actually lured him there: it was the smell of something edible. Standing there was a basin filled with fresh milk, swimming with small pieces of white bread. He could almost have laughed for joy, for he was even hungrier than he had been that morning. He immediately dunked his head in the milk nearly up to his eyes. But he soon pulled back, disappointed. It wasn't only that his tender left side made it hard for him to eat—for it seemed he was able to eat only if his entire panting body cooperated—it was rather that the milk, which had always been his favorite drink, and which his sister certainly placed here for that reason, didn't taste good to him at all. He turned away from the basin with something like revulsion and crept back into the middle of the room.

The gas lamps had been turned on in the living room, as Gregor saw through the crack in the door. Whereas ordinarily at this hour his father would read the afternoon paper out loud to his mother and sometimes to his sister, now there wasn't a sound. Perhaps the reading, which his sister had frequently told him and wrote him about, had lately dropped out of their routine. It was completely quiet, though the apartment was certainly not empty. "What a quiet life the family leads," Gregor said to himself and felt great pride, as he stared into the darkness before him, that he had been able to provide his parents and his sister with such a life, in such a nice apartment. But what if terror now drove away all quiet, all prosperity, all contentment? Rather than surrender to such thoughts, Gregor preferred to move about, so he crawled back and forth in the room.

Once during the long evening one of the side doors and later the other was opened a crack and then hastily shut again. Someone had probably needed to come in, but had then thought better of it. Gregor now stopped directly in front of the door to the living room, determined somehow to get the hesitant visitor to come in, or at least to find out who it was, but the doors were not opened again and Gregor waited in vain. Early on, when the doors were locked, everyone had wanted to come in; now, when he had unlocked one door and the others had clearly been unlocked during the day, no one came, and the keys had been moved to the outside.

It was late at night before the light in the living room was turned out, and it was now clear that his parents and sister had been awake until then, for all three could clearly be heard departing on tiptoes. Now surely no one would come to see Gregor until morning; he therefore had quite a while in which to consider undisturbed how he should newly arrange his life. But he was uneasy lying flat on the ground in the high-ceilinged open room. He did not know why this should be, for he had lived in the room for five years already. Half unconsciously, and not without some shame, he scurried under the sofa where, despite the fact that his back was a bit crushed and he could no longer lift his head, he immediately felt more comfortable, regretting only that his body was too broad to fit completely underneath.

35

He remained there the entire night. He spent part of it in a light sleep, out of which hunger kept jolting him awake, and part of it awake, consumed by worries and by vague hopes that all led to the same conclusion: that for the time being he should keep calm and, by exercising patience and the greatest consideration for his family, try to make bearable the unpleasantness that he would in his present condition inevitably cause them.

Early the next morning—it was nearly still night—Gregor had a chance to test the firmness of his resolve, for his sister, already half-dressed, opened the door leading from the foyer and looked tensely inside. She couldn't find him right away, but when she noticed him under the sofa—God, he had to be someplace, he couldn't have just flown away—she was so shocked that without being able to stop herself, she slammed the door shut again. But as if she regretted her behavior, she opened the door again immediately, and came inside on tiptoe, as if she were in the presence of someone severely ill, or even a complete stranger. Gregor shoved his head forward just to the edge of the sofa and watched her. He wondered whether she would notice that he had left the milk standing, though not from lack of hunger, and whether she would bring him some other food that suited him better. If she didn't do it on her own, he would rather starve than make her aware of it, although he felt a strong urge to shoot out from beneath the sofa, throw himself at her feet, and beg her for something good to eat. But his sister, with some amazement, right away noticed the still full basin: only a bit of milk had been spilled around its edges. She picked it up immediately, though with a rag, not with her bare hands, and took it away. Gregor was extremely curious to see what she would bring as a replacement and thought a great deal about it. He could never have guessed, however, what his sister in her goodness actually did. In order to test his preferences, she brought him an entire assortment of foods spread out on an old newspaper. There were old, half-rotten vegetables; bones from last night's meal, covered with congealed white sauce; a few raisins and almonds; a cheese that Gregor had declared inedible two days before; a piece of dry bread, a piece of bread smeared with butter, and a piece with butter and salt. Beside this she placed the basin that seemed now to be designated permanently for Gregor, which she had filled with water. And out of tact, because she knew Gregor would not eat in front of her, she departed hastily, even going so far as to turn the key in the lock, just so that Gregor would know that he could make himself as comfortable as he wanted. Gregor's legs quivered, now that the meal lay waiting. His wounds must moreover have completely healed. He felt no impairment now, and was astonished at this, thinking of how he had cut himself very slightly with a knife more than a month ago, and how the wound had still hurt him considerably the day before yesterday. "Am I less sensitive than before?" he wondered, and sucked greedily at the cheese, to which he had found himself urgently drawn, before everything else. In rapid succession, amidst tears of joy, he devoured the cheese, the vegetables, and the sauce. He didn't like the taste of the fresh foods, however—he couldn't even bear their smell, and dragged the foods that he wanted to eat a bit farther away. He had long since finished everything and lay lazily in the same spot when his sister slowly turned the key in the lock, as a sign that he should withdraw. That jolted him awake immediately, though he was almost dozing, and he hurried back under the sofa. But it took great self-control for him to remain under the sofa even for the brief time that his sister was in the room, for his body had swelled a bit with the ample meal, and he could hardly breathe in the narrow space. Half-suffocating, he looked out with slightly bulging eyes as his sister, who noticed nothing, swept up with a broom not just the remainder of the food Gregor had eaten, but also the food that he had not even touched, as if this were no longer useable. She put it all in a container that she closed with a wooden lid, and then carried everything out. She had hardly turned around when Gregor pulled himself out from under the sofa and exhaled.

In this way Gregor now received his daily meals: the first in the morning, while his parents and the servant girl still slept, and the second after the common midday meal, for his parents slept a bit afterwards, and his sister sent the serving girl away on one errand or another. It was not that the others wanted him to starve, but experiencing his meals at secondhand might have been all they could bear; or perhaps his sister simply wanted to spare them even this minor source of sorrow, since they were already suffering enough.

With what kinds of excuses they had managed to get the doctor and the lock-   40
smith out of the apartment the first morning, Gregor didn't manage to find out. Because no one could understand him, it didn't occur to anyone—not even to his sister—that he could understand them, so he had to content himself, when his sister was in his room, with listening to her occasional sighs and appeals to the saints. It was only later, when she had gotten used to things a bit—getting used to them completely was out of the question, of course—that Gregor sometimes seized on a remark that was meant in a friendly way or that could be taken that way. "Today he liked it," she said, if he had made a real dent in the meal, while in the contrary case, which occurred ever more frequently of late, she used to say almost sadly: "Everything untouched again."

Though Gregor could not learn any news directly, he overheard some from the rooms next door. The moment he heard voices, he immediately ran to the door and pressed his entire body up against it. Especially in the early days, there was no conversation that did not somehow, if only indirectly, relate to him. For two days there were consultations at every meal about what they should do; between meals, too, they discussed the same thing. There were always at least two family members at home, because no one wanted to remain home alone, and they couldn't under any circumstances all leave the apartment at the same time. On the very first day the girl who cooked for them had begged his mother on bended knee—it wasn't exactly clear what and how much she knew of what had happened—to dismiss her. As she departed fifteen minutes later, she tearfully thanked them for her dismissal, as if for the greatest favor that had ever been done her, and swore a terrible oath, without anyone having asked her to do so, not to betray the least of what she knew to anyone.

Now his sister had to do the cooking, together with his mother. This didn't take much effort, however, because they ate practically nothing. Gregor heard them again and again urge each other to eat and receive no other answer than "Thanks, I've had enough," or something similar. It seemed they didn't drink anything, either.

His sister often asked his father if he would like a beer, cheerfully offering to get it herself. When his father said nothing, she offered to send the porter for it, in case he didn't want to trouble her. When his father finally uttered a firm "No," the subject was dropped.

In the course of the first few days his father explained their entire financial situation and their prospects to his mother and to his sister. Now and then he stood up from the table and took various documents and notebooks out of the small safe that he had rescued from the bankruptcy of his business five years before. He could be heard opening the complicated lock and closing it again after removing what he sought. His father's explanations contained the first heartening news that Gregor had heard since his imprisonment. He had been under the impression that his father had absolutely nothing left over from his business. As least, he had said nothing to the contrary, and Gregor had certainly never asked him about it. Gregor's concern at the time of the bankruptcy had been to arrange everything so that the family could forget as soon as possible the financial misfortune that had brought them to a state of complete despair. And so he had begun to work with pronounced fervor. Practically overnight he was elevated from a minor clerk into a traveling salesman, which naturally gave him completely different financial prospects. His successes at work translated directly into cash that he could lay on the table at home before his astonished and pleased family. Those had been fine times, but they had never recurred, at least not with the same warm feelings, although Gregor later earned so much money that he was in a position to support the entire family, and he did so. They simply got used to it—the family, as well as Gregor. They gratefully accepted his money, and he gladly offered it, but that special warmth did not reappear. Only his sister remained close to Gregor. Because she loved music very much, unlike Gregor, and could play the violin movingly, he secretly planned to send her to the conservatory next year, despite the great cost, which would have to be made up somehow. The conservatory came up often in conversations with his sister during Gregor's brief stays in the city, but only as a beautiful dream whose realization was unthinkable. His parents didn't even like to hear them utter those innocent musings. But Gregor had given it a good deal of thought and intended to announce his decision with due ceremony on Christmas Eve.

These thoughts, completely futile in his present situation, went through his head while he clung to the door and listened. Sometimes, from sheer exhaustion, he could listen no more and would let his head fall against the door, but then immediately catch himself, for even the faint noise that he made in doing so was heard next door and caused them all to fall silent. "What's he doing now?" said his father after a pause, obviously turned towards the door. Only then was the interrupted conversation gradually taken up again.

Gregor now learned—for his father tended to repeat himself often in his explanations, partly because he had not concerned himself with these matters for a long while, and partly, too, because his mother didn't immediately understand everything the first time—that despite all their misfortunes, a certain sum, though a very small one, was left over from the old days. The untouched interest on the sum had moreover in the meantime allowed it to grow a bit. Besides this, the money that Gregor

45

had brought home every month—he had only kept a few florins for himself—had not been completely exhausted and had accumulated into a small amount of capital. Gregor, behind the door, nodded eagerly, overjoyed at this unexpected foresight and thriftiness. It occurred to him that he might have used that extra money to further pay down the debt his father owed the Director, bringing closer the day that he could quit his job, but the way his father had arranged things was no doubt better.

The sum that had been saved was not, however, large enough to allow his family to live off of the interest. It would have been enough to support them for a year, or at most two years, but no longer. The sum really shouldn't be touched: it should be set aside for emergencies. To live, money would have to be earned. His father was a healthy but old man, who had not worked now for five years and couldn't in any case take on too much. During these five years, which had been the first free time of his hardworking but unsuccessful life, he had put on a great deal of weight and had become downright sluggish. But was his elderly mother supposed to earn money now—his mother, who suffered from asthma, for whom even a stroll through the apartment was considerable exertion, and who spent every other day on the sofa by the open window, gasping for breath? Or his sister, who at seventeen was still a child, and whose lifestyle up to that point had consisted of dressing herself neatly, sleeping late, helping out in the household, taking part in a few modest pleasures, and above all playing the violin? Whenever the conversation turned towards the necessity of earning money, Gregor left the door and threw himself on the leather sofa that stood nearby, for he burned with shame and sorrow.

Often he lay there the long night through, though he was unable to sleep for a moment and just scratched for hours at the leather. Or he would go to great pains to shove an armchair to the window, then crawl up to the windowsill and, bolstered by the armchair, lean against the window. He did so only in some kind of nostalgia for the feeling of freedom he had previously found in looking out the window, for the fact was that every day he saw things that were even a short distance away less and less clearly. He could no longer see the hospital that lay across the way, whose all too massive prospect he had earlier cursed. If he had not known very well that he lived in the quiet, but distinctly urban Charlotte Street, he could have believed that he looked out of his window into a desert in which the gray sky and the gray earth merged indistinguishably. His alert sister only had to see the armchair standing by the window twice before she began to shove the chair precisely back to the spot by the window after she straightened up the room. She even left the inner casement open from then on.

If Gregor had been able to speak to his sister and thank her for everything she had to do for him, he would have been able to bear her assistance more easily; as it was, however, it caused him some pain. His sister tried to hide the awkwardness of the whole thing as much as possible, and the longer it went on, the better she succeeded, but Gregor felt everything more acutely as time went on. Even her entrance was terrible for him. She had hardly entered, when, without even taking the time to shut the doors, though she otherwise took such pains to spare everyone the sight of Gregor's room, she ran to the window and hastily flung it open, as if she were suffocating. Then she remained for a time by the window, cold as it still was, and breathed deeply. With this running and commotion she alarmed Gregor twice daily. He trembled under the sofa the entire time and yet he knew very well that she would gladly have spared him, if only it had been possible to stay in a room where Gregor was with the windows closed.

Once — one month had already passed since Gregor's transformation, and there was no longer any reason for his sister to be astonished by his appearance — she came a bit earlier than usual and encountered Gregor as he was staring out the window, motionless and perfectly positioned to frighten someone. Gregor would not have been surprised if she had not come in, since his position hindered her from immediately opening the window, but she not only refrained from coming in, she actually turned around and locked the door. A stranger would have thought that Gregor had lain in wait for her and tried to bite her. Gregor naturally hid himself immediately under the sofa, but he had to wait until midday for her return, and she seemed then more agitated than usual. He realized from this that his appearance was still unbearable to her and that it would remain so — that she had to steel herself to keep from running at the sight of even the small portion of his body that jutted out from beneath the sofa. In order to spare her the sight, one day he dragged a sheet onto the sofa — it took him four hours to do so — and arranged it in such a way that he was completely covered. His sister could not have seen him even if she bent down. If the sheet had not been necessary, in her opinion, she could have removed it, for it obviously couldn't be pleasant for Gregor to block himself off so completely. But she left the sheet where it was, and Gregor thought he even noticed a grateful glance when he once carefully lifted the sheet with his head in order to see how his sister liked the new arrangement.

In the first two weeks his parents could not bring themselves to come in to see him, and he often heard them praise his sister's current industry, whereas they had previously complained a great deal about her, as she had then seemed to them a rather idle girl. In those early days, both his father and his mother often waited in front of Gregor's room while his sister straightened up, and as soon as she came out, she had to tell them precisely what it looked like in the room, what Gregor had eaten, how he had behaved, and whether there were perhaps any slight improvement in his condition. His mother also wanted to visit Gregor early on, but his father and sister dissuaded her with sound reasons to which Gregor listened very attentively, and which he completely supported. Later, however, she had to be restrained with force. When she cried out, "Let me in to see Gregor; he's my poor son! Don't you understand that I must go to him?" Gregor thought that it might be good if his mother did come in — not every day, of course, but perhaps once a week. After all, she knew how to do things much better than his sister, who, despite her courage, was still only a child, and who likely took on such a heavy burden only out of childish thoughtlessness.

Gregor's wish to see his mother was soon fulfilled. During the day, for his parents' sake, Gregor did not want to show himself at the window, but he did not have much room to crawl in the few square meters of floor space. It was hard enough for him to bear lying quietly during the night, and eating soon gave him not the least bit of pleasure, so in order to distract himself, he had adopted the habit of crawling across the walls and ceiling. He especially liked hanging upside down from the ceiling. It was completely different from lying on the floor: he could breathe more freely; his entire body swayed gently; and in the nearly happy distraction in which he found himself above, it sometimes happened that he unexpectedly let himself fall and crashed to the ground. But these days he had better control of his body, so he did not hurt himself even in a great fall. His sister immediately noticed the new amusement that Gregor had found for himself—he left a trace of stickiness behind him here and there while crawling—and so she got it in her head to allow him to crawl to his utmost by removing the furniture that hindered it, especially the chest of drawers and desk. She was not capable of doing this herself, however. She didn't dare ask her father for help. The servant girl would certainly not help her: this roughly sixteen-year-old girl had stuck it out quite bravely since the dismissal of the former cook, but she had asked for the privilege of keeping the kitchen door always locked and only having to open it when specifically asked. So his sister had no choice but to enlist her mother one time when her father was absent. With cries of great joy his mother approached, but fell silent at the door of Gregor's room. His sister checked first, of course, to see that the room was in order; only then did she let her mother enter. In great haste, Gregor pulled the sheet lower and gathered more material around him. It looked like a sheet had merely been carelessly thrown over the sofa. Gregor also refrained from spying out from under the sheet. He deprived himself of the sight of his mother and took his pleasure entirely from the fact that she had come. "Come on, you can't see him," said his sister, and she apparently led her mother in by the hand. Gregor then heard the two frail women shove the heavy old chest of drawers from its place. His sister reserved the greatest part of the labor for herself, ignoring the warnings of her mother, who feared that she would overexert herself. It took a very long time. After fifteen minutes of work, his mother said that they should just leave the chest where it was, first, because it was too heavy—they wouldn't be finished before his father returned, and so would end up leaving the chest in the middle of the room, where it would block Gregor at every turn—and second, because it was not at all certain that they were doing Gregor a favor by removing the furniture. It seemed to her rather the opposite: the sight of the empty wall oppressed her heart. Why should Gregor not feel the same way? He had been used to the room's furniture for so long, that he would surely feel lost in an empty room. "And isn't it so," concluded his mother very softly—almost whispering, as if she wanted to keep Gregor, of whose precise whereabouts she wasn't certain, from hearing even the sound of her voice, for she was convinced that he could not understand the words—"isn't it so, that by removing the furniture we seem to be saying that we give up all hope of his recovery, and aban-don him absolutely? I think it would be best if we left the room in exactly the same condition it was in before, so that when Gregor returns to us, he'll find everything unchanged, and so more easily forget what's happened in the meantime."

In listening to his mother's words, Gregor realized that the lack of any direct human communication over the course of the past two months, together with the monotonous life he led in the midst of the family, must have deranged his mind; otherwise he couldn't explain why he had earnestly desired that his room be emptied. Did he really want to let them transform the warm room, comfortably outfitted with inherited furnishings, into a cave? Granted, he would be able to crawl undisturbed in all directions, but he would at the same time forget, quickly and completely, his human past. He was already close to forgetting it, but his mother's voice, so long unheard, had roused him. Nothing should be removed; everything had to stay. He could not afford to lose the good influence the furniture had on his condition. If the furniture hindered him from carrying on his mindless crawling about, that was no drawback, it was rather a great advantage.

But his sister was unfortunately of a different opinion. She had become accustomed, not completely without justification, to playing the expert when it came to discussing anything that concerned Gregor with her parents. And so her mother's advice now led her to insist on the removal not only of the chest and the desk, which was all she had first intended, but of all of the furniture, with the exception of the indispensable sofa. Of course, it was not just childish stubbornness and the hard-won self-confidence she had recently and unexpectedly acquired that determined her on this course: she had actually observed that Gregor needed a great deal of room to crawl around in, and that he did not use the furniture at all, as far as she could see. It might also have been the romantic nature of girls of her age, which sought some outlet at every opportunity, and made her want Gregor's situation to be even more terrifying, so that she could do even more than before to help him. For in a space in which Gregor, completely alone, ruled the empty walls, no person but Grete would dare to enter.

And so she did not allow herself to be swayed by her mother, who faltered from sheer uneasiness at being in the room, soon fell silent, and finally helped his sister as much as she was able in shoving the chest out of the room. Gregor could spare the chest if he must, but the desk had to stay. The women had hardly left the room with the chest, pushing at it and gasping for air, when Gregor stuck his head out from under the sofa, in order to see where he could intervene, as carefully and as considerately as possible. But unfortunately it was his mother who returned first, while Grete in the next room gripped the chest and rocked it back and forth alone, without, naturally, being able to move it from its spot. His mother was not, however, used to the sight of Gregor—he might have made her sick—so Gregor, alarmed, rushed back to the opposite end of the sofa. He could not, however, prevent the sheet from moving a bit at the front. That was enough to put his mother on the alert. She froze, stood still a moment, and then returned to Grete.

Though Gregor kept telling himself that nothing extraordinary was happening—a few pieces of furniture were merely being moved around—he soon realized that this continual back and forth on the part of the women, their soft calls to one another, and the scraping of the furniture on the floor affected him like the greatest of commotions closing in on him from all sides. However closely he drew in his head and legs and however firmly he pressed his body to the floor, he realized he couldn't stand it much longer. They were emptying out his room; they were taking from him

55

everything that he held dear. They had carried out the chest which held his fret saw and other tools; they were already working free the desk from the grooves it had worn into the floor—the desk at which he had written his exercises as a student at trade school, at secondary school, and even at primary school. At this point he did not have the patience to contemplate the women's good intentions, the existence of which he had at any rate almost forgotten. Exhausted, they worked now in complete silence, and only the heavy tread of their feet could be heard.

And so he burst forth from under the sofa—the women were just leaning against the desk in the next room, in order to catch their breath—though he changed the direction of his charge four times, for he really did not know what to save first. On one otherwise empty wall he distinctly saw the picture of the woman dressed entirely in furs. He crept hurriedly up to it and pressed himself against the glass, which held him fast and soothed his hot belly. At least no one could take away this picture, which Gregor now completely covered with his body. He turned his head towards the door of the living room in order to observe the women on their return.

They weren't allowing themselves much rest and so came back directly. Grete had put her arm around her mother and seemed practically to carry her. "Well, what should we take now?" said Grete and looked around. Then her glance met Gregor's as he clung to the wall. She maintained her composure—surely only due to her mother's presence—bent her face to her mother, in order to keep her from looking around, and said hastily, a tremor in her voice, "Come, let's go back in the living room for a moment." Grete's intention was clear to Gregor: she wanted to bring her mother to safety and then chase him down off of the wall. Well, she could try! He would sit on the picture and not give it up. He would rather spring in Grete's face.

But Grete's words had for the first time really unsettled his mother. She moved to the side, spotted the giant brown fleck on the flowered wallpaper, and cried out in a screeching, raw voice, before she was really fully conscious that it was Gregor that she saw, "Oh my God; oh my God!" She then fell onto the sofa with widespread arms, as if she were altogether giving up, and didn't move. "Gregor, you—!" cried his sister with a raised fist and piercing gaze. They were the first words she had directly addressed to Gregor since his transformation. She ran into the next room in order to get some scent with which she could wake her mother out of her faint. Gregor wanted to help, too—there was still time to save the picture—but he was stuck to the glass and had to tear himself free. He, too, ran into the next room, as if he could give his sister some advice, as in earlier days, but then he had to stand helplessly behind her while she rummaged through various bottles. She was startled when she turned around; a bottle fell to the floor and broke. A sliver of glass cut Gregor's face, and some burning medicine spilled over him. Grete took as many bottles as she could carry and ran with them in to her mother. She then slammed the door shut with her foot. Gregor was now shut off from his mother, who was through his fault possibly near death. He couldn't open the door, if he did not want to chase away his sister, who had to remain with his mother. He had nothing left to do but wait. Oppressed by self-reproaches and worry, he began to crawl. He crawled over everything—walls, furniture, and ceiling—and finally, in his despair, he fell, the entire room spinning around him, onto the center of the large table.

A short time passed, and Gregor lay limply there. All around was quiet. Perhaps that was a good sign. Then the bell rang. The servant girl was naturally locked into her kitchen, and so Grete had to go open the door. His father had returned. "What happened?" were his first words. The look on Grete's face betrayed everything to him. Grete answered with a muffled voice—she was obviously pressing her face against her father's chest. "Mother fainted, but she's already better. Gregor broke out." "I was waiting for this," said his father, "I always said it would happen, but you women didn't want to hear it." It was clear to Gregor that his father had interpreted Grete's all-too-brief announcement in the worst possible way, and assumed that Gregor had been guilty of some act of violence. Therefore Gregor had to try to mollify his father, for he had neither the time nor the ability to enlighten him. And so he fled to the door of his room and pressed against it, so that his father could see immediately on leaving the hallway that Gregor had every intention of returning right away to his room. It would not be necessary to drive him back, just to open the door, and he would disappear instantly.

But his father was not in the mood to notice such subtleties: "Ah!" he cried out on entering, in a tone that made him seem at once furious and glad. Gregor drew his head back from the door and turned it toward his father. His father's appearance was different from the way he remembered it. Lately, due to his new habit of crawling about, Gregor had concerned himself less with the goings-on in the rest of the apartment; he should therefore really have been prepared to encounter new developments. But still, still, was this really his father? The same man who lay, tired out, buried deep in his bed, when Gregor was all set to go on a business trip? The man who, dressed in a nightshirt, had greeted him when he returned in the evenings from an easy chair, and, unable to stand up, only raised his arms to show his joy at his return? The man who, on the rare walks he took together with Gregor and his mother on a few Sundays and the most important holidays of the year, walked packed into his old coat even more slowly than they did, though they walked slowly enough, laboring forward with a deliberately placed cane, and who nearly always stopped when he wanted to say something, gathering his companions around him? Now, he was quite well put together. He was dressed in the kind of close-fitting blue uniform with gold buttons that doormen at the banking houses wore; over the high stiff collar of the coat his pronounced double chin protruded; under his bushy eyebrows the glance of his dark eyes sprang forth fresh and alert; the formerly disheveled white hair was combed flat into a painfully exact, shining part. He threw his hat, which bore a gold monogram—probably that of a bank—in an arc across the room and onto the sofa. He moved towards Gregor, the ends of his long coat pushed back, his hands in his pants pockets, his face grim. He probably did not know himself what he planned to do. In any case he lifted his feet unusually high, and Gregor was astonished at the gigantic size of the soles of his boots. But he didn't let his astonishment distract him. He had known from the first day of his new life that his father considered the greatest severity appropriate in dealing with him. And so he ran away from his father. He

60

froze when his father stood still and hurried forward again when his father moved a muscle. In this way they circled the room several times, without anything decisive happening; the whole thing moved at such a slow tempo that it didn't even look like a pursuit. For the time being, Gregor stayed on the floor. He was afraid that his father might consider flight toward the walls or the ceiling as particular wickedness. But Gregor realized that he couldn't keep up even this pace for long, for when his father took a single step, he had to carry out myriad movements. He soon felt short of breath; his lungs had not been reliable even in the old days. As he staggered forward, he could barely keep his eyes open, so hard did he try to concentrate his energy for running. In his dullness he was simply unable to think of any other means of deliverance. He had almost forgotten already that the walls were open to him, though they were obstructed here by painstakingly carved furniture full of points and sharp edges. Suddenly something lightly thrown flew just past him and rolled ahead. It was an apple. Another immediately followed. Gregor froze in fear. Running further was pointless, for his father had decided to bombard him. He had filled his pockets from the fruit bowl on the credenza and now threw apple after apple, without for the time being aiming very carefully. These small red apples rolled around on the ground, knocking into each other as if charged with electricity. A weakly thrown apple strafed Gregor's back, but glanced off without doing any harm. One that flew immediately in its wake actually embedded itself in his back, however. Gregor tried to drag himself forward, as if he could outrun the unbelievable pain by changing position, but he felt as if he were nailed to the spot and lay sprawled upon the ground, in complete distraction of all of his senses. With his last conscious glance he watched as the door to his room was ripped open and, ahead of his screaming sister, his mother ran out of the room in her slip — for his sister had undressed her to let her breathe freely while in her faint — and raced towards his father, her untied skirts slipping down to the floor one after another; he watched as, stumbling on the skirts, she embraced his father, fully at one with him — but Gregor's vision now failed him utterly — and, with her hands clasped around the back of his head, begged him to spare Gregor's life.

III

The deep injury from which Gregor had suffered for over a month — the apple remained embedded in his flesh as a visible memento, as no one dared to remove it — seemed to have reminded even his father that despite his present sad and repulsive state, Gregor was a member of the family who should not be treated as an enemy. The law of familial obligation dictated, rather, that one had to swallow one's revulsion and be tolerant, simply be tolerant.

And though Gregor had probably permanently lost some mobility through his injury, and now, like an invalid, took many, many minutes to cross his room — crawling on high was out of the question — this degeneration in his condition brought with it a compensation that was to his mind completely satisfactory. Toward evening they now opened the living room door so that, lying in the darkness of his room and invisible from the living room, he could watch the entire family at the lighted table and listen to their conversation by general consent, as it were—a complete change from the early days when he used to watch the door like a hawk an hour or two before they gathered.

Of course, the conversations were not as lively as in earlier days. Gregor used to recall them longingly in the small hotel rooms where he had had to throw himself, exhausted, into the damp bedclothes. These days everything was mostly very quiet. His father fell asleep in his armchair soon after the evening meal; his mother and sister urged one another to silence. His mother now sewed fine lingerie for a boutique, bending close to her work under the light. His sister, who had taken a job as a sales-clerk, studied stenography and French at night, in order to find a better position one day. Sometimes his father awoke and, as if he didn't realize that he had been sleeping, would say to his mother: "How long you're sewing again today!" Then he would fall asleep again immediately, while his mother and sister exchanged tired smiles.

With a kind of stubbornness his father refused to take off his work uniform when he returned home, and while his nightshirt hung, useless, on a clothes hook, he dozed at his place fully clothed, as if he were always on duty and awaited the call of his superiors. As a result, the uniform, which hadn't been new in the first place, became less than pristine, despite the care his mother and sister took with it. Gregor often spent whole evenings looking at the badly stained coat, its oft-polished gold buttons shining, in which the old man slept highly uncomfortably, but quietly.

As soon as the clock struck ten, his mother tried to wake his father by speak- 65
ing softly to him, and tried to persuade him to go to bed, for he couldn't sleep well there, and a good sleep was absolutely essential, since he had to be at work by six. But in the stubbornness that had come over him since he became a bank employee, he always insisted on remaining longer where he was, although he regularly fell asleep again, and required much effort to persuade in exchanging the armchair for his bed. His mother and sister could press him with gentle remonstrances as much as they liked—for a quarter of an hour at a time he slowly shook his head, his eyes closed, and refused to stand up. His mother plucked at his sleeve, and whispered endearments in his ear; his sister left her work in order to help her mother, but got nowhere with him. He only sank deeper into his armchair. Only when the women grasped him under the arms would he open his eyes, look in turn at Gregor's mother and sister, and say, "What a life. This is the peace and quiet of my old age." And bracing himself against the women, he hoisted himself up laboriously, as if he were his own greatest burden, and allowed himself to be led to the door. He waved them off then and went on under his own power, but Gregor's mother would hastily throw down her sewing and his sister her quill in order to run after him and be of further help to him.

Who in this overworked and overtired family had time to worry about Gregor more than was absolutely necessary? The household was ever more reduced in circumstances. The servant girl had been dismissed, and a gigantic, bony servant with white hair that fluttered about her head came in the mornings and the evenings to do the hardest labor. Everything else his mother took care of, in addition to her abundant sewing work. It even came to pass that various pieces of family jewelry, which his mother and sister had previously worn with pleasure at parties and celebrations, were sold, as Gregor learned one evening from a general conversation about the prices obtained. Their greatest source of complaint, however, was that the apartment, far too large for them under the circumstances, could not be left, because it was unthinkable that Gregor be relocated. But Gregor realized that it was not consideration for him that hindered a relocation, for they could have transported him easily in a suitable carton with a few air holes. What really kept the family from changing apartments was despair, and the thought that they had been afflicted by misfortune such as had struck no one in their circle of relatives and acquaintances. They did everything that the world demanded of poor people—his father fetched breakfast for the junior bank clerks; his mother dedicated herself to making underwear for strangers; his sister ran back and forth behind the counter at the beck and call of customers—but they could do no more than that. And the wound in his back began to hurt Gregor anew when his mother and sister would return from putting his father to bed, let their work lie, and huddle close together, cheek to cheek. His mother, gesturing towards Gregor's room, said, "Close the door, Grete," and Gregor was in the dark again, while next door the women mingled tears or stared, dry-eyed and numb, down at the table.

Gregor passed the days and nights nearly without sleep. Sometimes he considered taking the affairs of the family in hand again, the next time the door was opened. After some time, he thought again about the Director and the Deputy Director, the clerks and the apprentices, the slow-witted porter, two or three friends from other companies, a chambermaid from a hotel in the provinces—a dear, fleeting memory—and a cashier from a hat store whom he had courted seriously, though too slowly. They reappeared in his thoughts together with strangers or people he had already forgotten, but instead of helping him and his family, they all remained detached, and he was glad when they disappeared. At other times, however, he was not in the mood to worry about his family. He was filled with rage at the poor care they took of him, and though he could think of nothing for which he had an appetite, he made plans to reach the pantry and take what was due him, even if he were not hungry. Without considering any longer what might especially please Gregor, mornings and afternoons before returning to the store his sister hurriedly shoved any old kind of food into his room with her foot, only in order to sweep it out with a whisk of the broom in the evenings, indifferent as to whether it might have been merely tasted or—as was usually the case—it remained completely untouched. Her cleaning of the room, which she now always did in the evening, could not have been done any more hastily. Smears of dirt ran along the walls, and here and there lay balls of dust and filth. In the early days Gregor used to position himself upon the arrival of his sister in a particularly grubby corner, in order to reproach her. But he could have remained there for weeks, and his sister would still not have changed her ways. She saw the dirt as well as he did, but she had simply decided to leave it there. At the same time, with a touchiness entirely new to her that had now possessed the entire family, she was vigilant in making sure that the straightening of Gregor's room was left to her. His mother once undertook a thorough cleaning of Gregor's room, which had required several buckets of water—the moisture bothered Gregor, and he lay broad, embittered, and unmoving on top of the sofa—but his mother did not go unpunished. That evening his sister had hardly registered the change in Gregor's room when, highly insulted, she ran into the living room, and despite her mother's beseechingly raised hands, broke into a spasm of tears that his parents—his father had naturally been frightened out of his seat—at first simply watched, helpless with astonishment. Then they, too, were affected: on one side, his father reproached his mother for not leaving the cleaning of Gregor's room to his sister; on the other side, he shouted at his sister that she would never be allowed to clean Gregor's room again. In the meantime, his mother tried to drag his father, who was beside himself with agitation, into the bedroom; his sister, racked by sobs, hammered the table with her small fists; and Gregor hissed loudly with fury that no one thought to close the door and so spare him the scene and the noise.

But even if his sister, exhausted from her work, could no longer manage to care for Gregor as she had earlier, his mother would still not have had to intervene in order to keep Gregor from being neglected. For there was still the servant. This old widow, who had weathered the worst in her long life with the help of a powerful frame, felt no especial revulsion towards Gregor. Without exactly being curious, she had once by chance opened the door to Gregor's room and stood staring at the sight of him, her hands folded across her chest. Gregor was completely taken by surprise, and despite the fact that no one was chasing him, he began to run back and forth. Since that time, she hadn't missed a chance to open the door quickly in the morning and the evening to look in at Gregor. At first she called him over to her with words that she probably considered friendly, like "Come on over here, you old dung beetle!" or "Look at the old dung beetle!" Gregor did not respond to such overtures, but remained motionless in his place, as if the door had not even been opened. If only they would order this servant to clean his room daily, instead of letting her needlessly disturb him at will! Once in the early morning—a hard rain, perhaps already a sign of the coming spring, beat on the windowpanes—Gregor became so embittered when the servant began to speak that he turned towards her, as if to attack, though slowly and feebly. Instead of being afraid, however, the servant simply lifted high into the air a chair that stood in reach of the door. As she stood there with her mouth opened wide, it was clear that she intended to shut her mouth only after the chair in her hands had come down on Gregor's back. "That's it, then?" she asked, as Gregor turned around again, and she put the chair quietly back in its corner.

Gregor now ate almost nothing. When he happened to pass by the food prepared for him, he sometimes idly took a bite and held it in his mouth for an hour or so, only to spit most of it out again. At first he thought that his sorrow over the state of his room kept him from eating, but he had actually reconciled himself very soon to the changes. The family had gotten into the habit of putting into his room things that wouldn't fit anywhere else: there were now many such things, as they had rented one room in the apartment out to three lodgers. These three serious gentlemen—all three had full beards, as Gregor discovered once by looking through the crack in the door—were painfully focused on order, not only in their room, but, simply because they had taken lodgings there, in the entire household, especially in the kitchen. They would not put up with useless or dirty things. And in any case, they had brought with them most of their own furnishings. For this reason, many things that were not saleable, but that the family did not want to throw away, had become superfluous. All of this made its way into Gregor's room—even, eventually, the ash bin and the rubbish bin from the kitchen. The servant, who was always in a rush, simply slung anything that was at the moment unuseable into Gregor's room. Fortunately Gregor usually saw only the relevant object and the hand that held it. The servant might once have intended to take the things out again when time and opportunity permitted, or perhaps to throw them all out together once and for all, but in practice they lay wherever they were tossed, unless Gregor wound his way through the clutter and stirred it up—first because he had no other place to crawl, and later with growing pleasure, although after such forays, tired to death and full of sorrow, he could not stir for hours.

Because the lodgers sometimes took their evening meal in the common living room, the living room door remained closed on some evenings. Gregor managed without it very well. On some evenings when it was open he did not even take advantage of it, but without the family's knowing it, lay in the darkest corner of his room. Once, however, the servant left the door to his room open a bit, and it remained open, even as the lodgers came in that evening and the light was turned on. They sat at the head of the table, where in former days his father, mother, and Gregor had eaten, unfolded their napkins, and took their knives and forks in hand. His mother immediately appeared in the doorway with a dish of meat and his sister directly behind her with a dish piled high with potatoes. The steaming food gave off a rich smell. The lodgers bent over the dishes placed before them as if they wanted to check them before eating, and the one in the middle, whom the other two appeared to consider an authority, actually cut off a piece of meat still in the serving dish, obviously to test whether it were tender enough, or whether it might perhaps need to be sent back to the kitchen. He was satisfied, and mother and sister, who had watched the proceedings tensely, breathed again and smiled. 70

The family themselves ate in the kitchen. Nevertheless, his father, before he went into the kitchen, came into the room and made a single long bow while circling the table, cap in hand. The lodgers all rose together and murmured something into their beards. When they were alone again, they ate in near total silence. It seemed strange to Gregor that, among all the various sounds of eating, he could pick out the sound of their chewing teeth—it was as if Gregor were thereby reminded that one needed teeth in order to eat, and that one could do nothing with even the most beautiful toothless jaws. "I do have an appetite," said Gregor sorrowfully to himself, "but not for these things. How these lodgers feed themselves, while I'm dying of hunger!"

On this very evening, though Gregor did not remember having heard it once before during that whole time, the violin sounded from the kitchen. The lodgers had already finished their meal. The middle one had pulled out a newspaper and given each of the others one page. They now read, leaning back, and smoked. As the violin began to play, they became alert, arose and went on tiptoes to the hall door, where they stood pressed up against one another. They must have heard them in the kitchen, for his father called out: "Do you gentlemen perhaps dislike the playing? It can be stopped immediately." "On the contrary," said the lodger in the middle, "wouldn't the young lady like to come out and play here in this room, where it's much more comfortable and convenient?" "Oh, please!" called his father, as if he were the violin player. The lodgers moved back into the room and waited. His father soon came in with the music stand, his mother with the music, and his sister with the violin. His sister quietly prepared to play. His parents, who had never rented a room out before and so exaggerated the courtesy due the lodgers, did not dare to sit on their own chairs. His father leaned against the door, his right hand stuck between two buttons of his fastened livery coat. His mother, however, accepted a chair offered by one of the lodgers, and sat off in the corner where he had happened to place the chair.

His sister began to play. His father and mother, on either side of her, followed every note, attentive to the movements of her hands. Gregor, drawn by the music, had ventured a bit further forward. His head was already in the living room. He hardly wondered at himself for being so inconsiderate towards the others of late; earlier, this consideration had been a great source of pride. And just now he had more reason than before to hide himself. Because of the dust everywhere in his room that flew up at the least movement, he was himself covered in dust. Threads, hairs, and bits of leftover food stuck to his back and sides. His general apathy was much too great for him now to lie on his back and scrub himself on the carpet, as he used to do several times a day. Despite his condition, however, he had no qualms about advancing a bit onto the immaculate living room floor.

But no one paid any attention to him. His family was entirely absorbed in the playing of the violin. The lodgers, on the other hand, who had at first, their hands in their pants pockets, taken up positions inconveniently close to his sister's music stand, in order to see all the notes, soon withdrew to the window, their heads bowed amidst whispered conversation, and remained there with Gregor's father worriedly observing them. It was now painfully obvious that they were disappointed in what they had assumed would be a beautiful or entertaining performance, and that they were sick of the entire production and now allowed their quiet to be disturbed only out of politeness. The way they all blew their cigar smoke out of their mouths and noses indicated great irritation. But his sister played so beautifully! Her face was turned to the side; her gaze followed the lines of notes, searching and sorrowful. Gregor crept further forward and held his head close to the floor, in order to meet her gaze if possible. The music gripped him — was he then an animal? He felt as if he were being guided to the sustenance he had unknowingly desired. He was determined to press on all the way to his sister, to pull on her skirt and let her know that she could come into his room with her violin. No one here knew how to appreciate her playing the way he did. He wanted never to let her out of his room again, at least not as long as he lived. His terrifying shape would finally be of some use to him: he would be at all doors of his room at once, hissing at all intruders. His sister, though, would not be forced, but would rather stay with him willingly. She would sit next to him on the sofa, her ear inclined towards him, and he would confide in her that he had intended to send her to the conservatory, and that, were it not for the misfortune that had occurred, he had intended to announce it to everyone last Christmas—Christmas had surely passed already?—ignoring any possible objections. After this declaration, his sister would surely burst into tears of emotion, and Gregor would lift himself up to her shoulder and kiss her neck, which she now left uncovered, without ribbon or collar, since she had begun working at the store.

"Mr. Samsa!" called the middle lodger and without wasting another word, 75 pointed at Gregor, who was slowly inching his way forward. The violin fell silent. The middle lodger smiled at first, shaking his head at his friends, and then looked down again at Gregor. His father seemed to consider it more urgent to reassure the lodgers than to drive Gregor back, despite the fact that they seemed calm and more entertained by Gregor than by the violin. He hurried over to them and tried with outspread arms to urge them into their room; at the same time, he wanted to block their view of Gregor with his body. They actually became a bit angry now, though it was unclear whether this was over his father's behavior or over the dawning recognition that, unbeknownst to them, they had all the while had a neighbor like Gregor. They asked his father for an explanation, raised their arms, pulled agitatedly at their beards and only reluctantly retreated into their room. In the meantime his sister had come out of the trance into which she had fallen after her playing had been so suddenly broken off. For a time she had held her violin and bow in her limply hanging hands and continued to stare at the music, as if she were still playing. Now, all at once, she pulled herself together, laid the instrument in the lap of her mother, who, short of breath and gasping for air, was still seated, and ran into the next room, which the lodgers were now approaching more quickly at the urging of her father. Under her practiced hands, the covers and pillows flew high in the air and arranged themselves. Before the lodgers had reached the room, she was finished readying the beds and had slipped out. His father's stubbornness seemed to have returned to the extent that he forgot all respect that he owed his lodgers. He kept urging them and urging them, until finally at the threshold the gentleman in the middle resoundingly stamped his foot and so brought his father to a standstill. "I hereby declare," he said, and, raising his hand, sought the gaze of Gregor's mother and sister, as well, "that, in consideration of the revolting conditions existing in this apartment and this family"—and here, without a moment's hesitation, he spat on the ground—"I give notice this instant. I will naturally pay absolutely nothing for the days I have lived here; on the contrary, I will consider bringing charges against you, which will—believe me—be very easy to prove." He fell silent and stared straight ahead, as if he were waiting for something. His two friends then obliged him by chiming in with the words: "We, too, give notice this instant." At that, he seized the door handle and shut the door with a crash.

His father staggered to his chair, his hands stretched out before him, and fell into it. It looked as if he were stretching himself out for his usual evening nap, but his head, sharply, ceaselessly nodding, showed that he was not sleeping at all. Gregor had lain all this time in the same spot where the lodgers had discovered him. His disappointment at the failure of his plans—perhaps, though, too, the weakness caused by his long hunger—made it impossible for him to move. He was distinctly afraid that in the next moment everything was going to come crashing down on top of him. He waited. Not even the violin roused him, which slipped from his mother's trembling fingers and fell from her lap, emitting a ringing tone.

"My dear parents," said his sister and struck her hand on the table by way of preamble, "we can't go on like this. If you can't see it, I can. I don't want to use the name of my brother in front of this monster, so let me just say this: we have to try to get rid of it. We have tried as much as humanly possible to care for it and to put up with it. I don't think it could reproach us in the least."

"She is absolutely right," said his father under his breath. His mother, who seemed not to have caught her breath yet, began to emit a muffled cough into the hand she held before her, a crazed expression in her eyes.

His sister hurried to his mother and put her hand to her forehead. His sister's words seemed to have put his father's thoughts in a surer course. He sat up straight, fiddling with his uniform cap amongst the plates that still sat on the table from the lodgers' evening meal, and looked for a time down at the quiet Gregor.

"We must try to get rid of it," his sister finally said to his father, for his mother heard nothing in the midst of her coughing. "It's going to kill you both; I can see it coming. When people have to work as hard as we do, they can't bear this kind of constant torture at home. I can't bear it any more." And she began crying so hard that her tears flowed down her mother's face, where she began mechanically wiping them away with her hand.

"But my child," said his father, sympathetically and with striking compassion, "what should we do?"

His sister only shrugged her shoulders as a sign of the helplessness that had during her crying spell taken the place of her former certainty. "But if he understood us—" his father said, half questioningly. His sister, in the midst of her tears, waved her hand violently as a sign that that was out of the question.

"If he understood us," his father repeated, and by closing his eyes, tried to absorb her certainty that it was impossible, "then we might be able to arrive at some arrangement with him. But as things stand—"

"It has to go," cried his sister. "That is the only way, father. You must simply try to rid yourself of the thought that it's Gregor. Our real misfortune is that we believed it for so long. But how can it be Gregor? If it were Gregor, he would have seen long ago that such an animal cannot live with people and he would have left voluntarily. We would then have had no brother, but we could have lived on and honored his memory. But this beast persecutes us, drives off the lodgers, and obviously wants to take over the apartment and force us to sleep out in the alley. Just look, Father," she suddenly screamed, "he's starting again!" And in a state of terror totally incomprehensible to Gregor, his sister abandoned his mother and practically vaulted off her chair, as if she would rather sacrifice her than remain in Gregor's vicinity. She hurried behind her father who, agitated entirely through her behavior, stood up as well and half raised his arms as if to protect her.

80

But it wasn't at all Gregor's intent to upset anyone, especially not his sister. He 85
had just begun to turn himself around in order to make his way back into his room.
Of course, that procedure looked peculiar enough, because his ailing condition
meant that in order to turn even with difficulty he had to help with his head, which
he lifted repeatedly and braced against the ground. He paused and looked around.
His good intentions seemed to be recognized: it had only been a momentary fright.
They all looked at him, silent and sorrowful. His mother lay in her chair, her legs
stretched before her and pressed together; her eyes were nearly falling shut from
exhaustion. His father and sister sat next to one another, his sister with her hand laid
around her father's neck.

"Maybe they'll allow me to turn around now," thought Gregor, and started to
work on it again. He could not suppress the wheezing caused by his exertion, and he
had to stop and rest now and then. No one rushed him: he was left to his own devices.
When he had completed the turn, he immediately headed straight back. He was astonished by the vast distance that divided him from his room, and he could not grasp how
in his weakened condition he had put the entire distance behind him, almost without
noticing it. Focused solely on crawling as quickly as possible, he hardly noticed that no
word and no outcry from his family disturbed him. He turned his head only when he
was already at the door—not all the way, for he felt his neck getting stiff, but enough
to see that nothing had changed behind him, except for the fact that his sister had
stood up. His last glance fell on his mother, who was now fast asleep.

He was hardly in his room when the door was hastily pushed to, bolted fast and
locked. The sudden noise behind him frightened Gregor so much that his legs buck-
led beneath him. It was his sister who had rushed to do it. She had stood, waiting,
and had suddenly sprung forward, light-footed—Gregor had not even heard her
coming—crying out to her parents "Finally!" as she turned the key in the lock.

"And now?" Gregor asked himself, and looked around in the dark. He soon discovered that he could no longer move at all. He didn't wonder at this; on the contrary,
it had seemed unnatural to him that he had actually been able to move before on
such thin legs. Besides that, however, he felt relatively comfortable. He did have pains
all over his body, but it seemed to him that they were becoming weaker and weaker
and would finally die away altogether. He could hardly feel the rotten apple in his
back or the inflamed surrounding area, which was now completely covered in moist
dust. He thought of his family with compassion and love. His conviction that he had
to disappear was even more definite than his sister's. He remained in this state of
empty and peaceful contemplation until the clock tower struck three. He experienced
once more the approach of daylight outside the window. Then, unwilled, his head
sank fully down, and from his nostrils his last breath weakly streamed forth.

When the servant came in the early morning—though she had often been asked
to refrain from doing so, she slammed all the doors out of sheer vigor and haste, to
such an extent that it was not possible to sleep quietly anywhere in the apartment
once she had arrived—she noticed nothing unusual at first in her morning visit to
Gregor. She thought that he intentionally lay there motionless because he found her
behavior insulting; she credited him with all manner of intelligence. As she happened

to be holding her long broom in her hand, she tried to tickle Gregor with it from the door. When she met with no response, she became irritated and poked him a bit. Only when she had shoved him from his spot without meeting any resistance did she become alert. She soon understood the situation. Her eyes widened, and she whistled out loud. It wasn't long before she had flung the door of the master bedroom open and called loudly into the darkness: "Look, everyone, it's kicked the bucket; it's lying there, dead as a doornail!"

The Samsas sat bolt upright in bed and had first to overcome their alarm at the servant's behavior before they could understand her report. Then, however, they climbed hurriedly out of bed, one on each side. Mr. Samsa threw the blanket over his shoulders; Mrs. Samsa emerged in her nightgown. In this manner they entered Gregor's room. In the meantime Grete had opened the door to the living room, where she had been sleeping since the arrival of the lodgers. She was completely dressed, as if she had not slept; her pale face confirmed the impression. "Dead?" said Mrs. Samsa, and looked questioningly up at the servant, although she could have made her own investigation or even have recognized the fact without making any investigation. "I'd say so," said the servant, and as proof, she pushed Gregor's corpse further to one side with the broom. Mrs. Samsa moved as if she wanted to hold her back, but she didn't. "Well," said Mr. Samsa, "now we can thank God." He crossed himself, and the three women followed his example. Grete, who did not take her eyes from the corpse, said: "Just look at how thin he was. He hadn't eaten anything for so long. The food came out just the way it went in." Gregor's body was indeed completely flat and dry; it was really only possible to see it now that he was off his legs and nothing else distracted the eye.

"Come, Grete, come sit with us for a bit," said Mrs. Samsa with a wistful smile, and Grete followed her parents into their bedroom, though not without looking back at the corpse. The servant shut the door and opened the window wide. Despite the early morning the fresh air already had something mild mixed in it. It was, after all, already the end of March.

The three lodgers emerged from their room and looked in amazement for their breakfast. It had been forgotten. "Where is breakfast?" the middlemost of the men asked the servant sullenly. She laid a finger to her lips and then silently and hastily signaled to the men that they might come into Gregor's room. They came and stood around Gregor's corpse in the now completely bright room, their hands in the pockets of their somewhat shabby coats.

The door to the bedroom opened then, and Mr. Samsa appeared in his livery with his wife on one arm and his daughter on the other. They had all been crying; Grete pressed her face from time to time to her father's arm.

"Leave my apartment immediately!" said Mr. Samsa and pointed to the door, without letting the women leave his side. "What do you mean?" said the middle lodger, somewhat dismayed, and smiled mawkishly. The two others held their hands behind their backs and rubbed them together continuously, as if in joyful expectation of a great fight, which would, they were sure, end favorably for them. "I mean exactly what I say," answered Mr. Samsa, and advanced in a line with his companions toward the lodger. He stood quietly, at first, and looked at the ground, as if the things in his head were arranging themselves in a new order. "Then we'll go," he said and looked up at Mr. Samsa, as if a sudden access of humility required him to seek renewed approval even for this decision. Mr. Samsa merely nodded shortly several times, his eyes wide and staring. At this, the man immediately walked with long strides into the foyer. His two friends had listened at first, their hands completely still, and they now skipped after him directly, as if in fear that Mr. Samsa could step in front of them in the foyer and disrupt their connection to their leader. In the hall all three of them took their hats from the rack, drew their walking sticks from the stand, bowed mutely, and left the apartment. In what proved to be a completely unnecessary precaution, Mr. Samsa walked out with the two women onto the landing. Leaning on the railing, they watched as the three men slowly but steadily descended the stairs, disappearing on every floor at the turning of the stairwell, and emerging again after a few moments. The lower they went, the more the Samsa family lost interest in them, and as a butcher's boy carrying his burden on his head with dignity passed them and then climbed high above them, Mr. Samsa left the landing with the women and they all returned, as if freed from a burden, to their apartment.

They decided to spend the day resting and taking a stroll. They had not only   95
earned this rest from work, they absolutely needed it. And so they sat at the table and wrote three letters of excuse, Mr. Samsa to the bank directors, Mrs. Samsa to her employer, and Grete to her supervisor. While they were writing the servant entered in order to say that she was leaving, as her morning work was finished. Writing, the three of them merely nodded at first, without looking up; only when the servant failed to depart did they look up angrily. "Well?" asked Mr. Samsa. The servant stood in the door, smiling, as if she had some great piece of good news to report to the family, but would only do so if she were thoroughly interrogated. The nearly upright little ostrich feather on her hat, which had annoyed Mr. Samsa the entire time she had been employed there, waved freely in all directions. "Well, what do you want?" asked Mrs. Samsa, for whom the servant had the most respect. "Well," the servant answered, and could not say more right away, fairly bursting with friendly laughter, "well, you needn't worry about getting rid of that thing next door. It's all been taken care of." Mrs. Samsa and Grete bent to their letters again, as if they wanted to continue writing. Mr. Samsa, who saw that the servant was about to begin describing everything in great detail, decisively headed this off with an outstretched hand. Since she was not going to be allowed to tell her story, she suddenly remembered her great haste, and, obviously deeply insulted, called out, "'Bye, everyone," then spun around wildly and left the apartment amidst a terrific slamming of doors.

"Tonight we're firing her," said Mr. Samsa, but received no answer either from his wife or from his daughter, for the servant seemed to have disturbed their but newly restored calm. They rose, went to the window, and remained there, their arms around each other. Mr. Samsa turned in his chair as they went and quietly observed them for a while. Then he called out, "Well, come over here. Let what's past be past. And take some care of me, for once." The women obeyed immediately, hurrying over to him and caressing him, and then quickly finished their letters.

Then all three of them left the apartment together, which they had not done for months, and took a trolley to the open air beyond the city. The car they sat in was drenched with warm sunlight. Leaning back comfortably in their seats, they discussed their future prospects, and it emerged that these were not at all bad on closer inspection, for all three of their positions were altogether favorable at present and, most importantly, had great potential for the future. The greatest improvement of their present situation would have to come, naturally, from a change of apartments. They would want a smaller and cheaper apartment, but one that was better located and generally more convenient than their current apartment, which Gregor had originally found for them. While they conversed in this way, it occurred to both Mr. and Mrs. Samsa in the same moment in looking at their ever more lively daughter that despite the recent ordeals that had made her cheeks so pale, she had blossomed into a pretty and well-developed young woman. Becoming quieter and almost unconsciously communicating through glances, they realized that it would soon be time to look for a good husband for her. And it seemed to them a confirmation of their new dreams and good intentions, when, at the end of their journey, their daughter rose first and stretched her young body.

[1915]

. . . .

Questions

1. The story opens, "When Gregor Samsa awoke in his bed one morning from unquiet dreams, he found himself transformed into an enormous insect." When you first read those lines, did you find them humorous? When did you begin to understand the serious intent, or did the fantastic or surreal situation make it difficult for you to take the story seriously?

2. How does Gregor's family treat him both before his metamorphosis and after? Consider how some things change and others stay the same.

3. How does Kafka's choice in making Gregor a traveling salesman contribute to a theme of the story? What details of Gregor's professional life do we learn? How might his profession connect to his turning into a bug? Consider Kafka's description of Gregor being "condemned to work at a company where the least infraction immediately attracted the greatest suspicion" (para. 15).

4. Among Gregor's responses to his transformation, we see anxiety, frustration, and surprise, but not shock. Why doesn't Kafka present Gregor as being horrified by the discovery that he is an insect?

5. How does each character react to Gregor? Discuss how those reactions help develop each character.

6. Speech — language — is central to the story. When Gregor first tries to speak, he is "terrified" because his "old voice" is mixed with "an irrepressible, painful, squeaking noise" (para. 7). How does Kafka develop this relationship between voice and power (or the lack of both)?

7. As Gregor listens to his sister playing the violin for the lodgers, he is "drawn by the music" (para. 73). Kafka writes, "The music gripped him — was he then an

animal? He felt as if he were being guided to the sustenance he had unknowingly desired" (para. 74). How do you interpret this episode?

8. The story has powerfully moving and poignant scenes as well as humorous ones. What examples of humor do you perceive, and how do they contribute to the themes Kafka is developing?

9. Does the story end with an emotionally satisfying resolution? Is it a happy ending? Does Gregor's life achieve meaning because he sacrifices himself for the family's greater good? How do you interpret the last scene?

10. This story includes several transformations in addition to Gregor's obvious one. What are they, and how do they contribute to the meaning of the story?

11. This story is divided into three sections, or segments, which might be considered chapters. What is the nature of these divisions? Are they chronological or something more complex?

To Max Brod

FRANZ KAFKA

> Max Brod (1884–1968), born in Prague, met Kafka when the two were university students and became his lifelong friend, biographer, and literary executor. Defying Kafka's instructions to destroy all of his papers upon his death, Brod later stated that he had told Kafka he would not honor this wish, thus reasoning that if Kafka had really wanted his papers destroyed, he would have appointed someone else as executor. Brod was a prolific writer himself but is primarily remembered as the biographer of Kafka and the editor of his collected letters and diaries.

To Max Brod

[Prague, October 7, 1912]

My dearest Max,

After writing well Sunday night—I could have written all through the night and the day and the night and the day, and finally have flown away, and could certainly have written well today also—one page, really just an exhalation of yesterday's ten, is actually finished—I had to stop for the following reason: my brother-in-law, the manufacturer, this morning left for a business trip which is going to take from ten to fourteen days. (In my happy distraction I had scarcely noticed that this was impending.) During this period, the factory is actually left to the foreman alone, and no investor, especially so nervous a one as my father, would have any doubts that fraud must now be running rampant in the factory. For that matter, I think the same, though not so much because I am worried about the money as because I am uninformed and uneasy in conscience. But actually, even a neutral person, insofar as I can imagine one such, might see a certain justification for my father's anxiety, although I should not forget that in the final analysis I do not at all see why a foreman from Germany would not be able to run everything with his usual efficiency even in the absence of my brother-in-law, to whom he is inordinately superior in all technical and organizational matters, for after all we are human beings and not thieves.

Now in addition to the foreman, my brother-in-law's younger brother is also here. Granted, he is a fool in all matters except business, and even in business matters to a considerable extent. But still he is competent, hard-working, attentive, a livewire, I might say. But of course he has to be in his office a great deal, and in addition manage the agency, for which purpose he has to run around the city half the day and therefore has little time left for the factory.

Recently, when I told you that nothing coming from outside could disturb my writing now (that, of course, was not so much boasting as an attempt to comfort myself), I was thinking only of how my mother whimpers to me almost every evening that I really should look in on the factory now and then to reassure Father, and of how my father has also said it to me much more strongly by looks and in other roundabout ways. In large part such pleas and reproofs were not without a certain rationale, for supervising Brother-in-law would certainly do him and the factory a great deal of good; except that I—and herein lay the irreducible irrationality of such talk—cannot perform any such supervision, even in my clearest states of mind.

For the next two weeks, however, that is not what is really involved. For this period, no more really is needed than any pair of eyes going about the factory, and even mine will do. There cannot be the slightest objection to this demand's being directed to me in particular, for in everybody's opinion I bear the chief blame for the establishment of the factory—though I must have assumed this blame in a dream—and in addition there is no one else around who could look into the factory, for my parents, who in any case would be out of the question, are in the midst of the busiest season at the store (the store also seems to be going better in its new location), and this afternoon, for example, my mother was not even home for dinner.

This evening, therefore, when my mother once again began with the old lament and, aside from blaming me for my father's bitterness and sickness, also brought up this new argument about Brother-in-law's departure and the orphaned state of the factory, and my youngest sister, who ordinarily sides with me, correctly sensing the change of feeling that I have recently had on this subject, and simultaneously displaying monstrous obtuseness, deserted me in my confrontation with Mother, and while bitterness—I don't know whether it was only gall—passed through my whole body—I realized with perfect clarity that now only two possibilities remain open to me, either to jump out of the window once everyone has gone to sleep, or in the next two weeks to go daily to the factory and to my brother-in-law's office. The first would provide me with the opportunity of shedding all responsibility, both for the disturbance of my writing and for the orphaned factory. The second would absolutely interrupt my writing—I cannot simply wipe from my eyes the sleep of fourteen nights—and would leave me, if I had enough strength of will and of hope, the prospect of possibly beginning again, in two weeks, where I left off today.

So I did not jump, and the temptations to make this a farewell letter (my ideas for it take another direction) are not very strong. I stood for a long time at the window and pressed against the pane, and there were many moments when it would have suited me to alarm the toll collector on the bridge by my fall. But all the while I really felt too firm to let the decision to smash myself to pieces on the pavement penetrate to the proper decisive depth. It also seemed to me that my staying alive interrupts my writing less than death — even if I can speak only, only of interruption — and that between the beginning of the novel and its continuation in two weeks somehow, in the factory especially and especially in relationship to my satisfied parents, I shall move and have my being within the innermost spaces of my novel.

Dearest Max, I am putting this whole thing before you not for your opinion, for of course you could have no opinion of it, but since I was firmly determined to jump without leaving a farewell letter — before the end one has a right to be just tired — I wanted, since I am about to step back into my room as its occupant, to write you instead a long letter of reunion, and here it is. And now just a kiss and goodnight, so that tomorrow I am a factory boss, as they demand.

Yours, Franz
[1912]

Questions

1. In what ways does Kafka's work situation resemble Gregor's?
2. What similarities do you find between Kafka's description of his family in this letter and those of Gregor's family in *The Metamorphosis*?
3. Explain whether you think Kafka presents his alternative identity as a writer as a transformation of his factory-worker self or as a conflict with it.

To Kurt Wolff Verlag

FRANZ KAFKA

To Kurt Wolff Verlag[1]

[Prague, October 25, 1915]

Dear Sir,

You recently mentioned that Ottomar Starke is going to do a drawing for the title page of *Metamorphosis*. . . . This prospect has given me a minor and perhaps unnecessary fright. It struck me that Starke, as an illustrator, might want to draw the insect itself. Not that, please not that! I do not want to restrict him, but only to make this plea out of my deeper knowledge of the story. The insect itself cannot be depicted. It cannot even be shown from a distance. Perhaps there is no such intention and my plea can be dismissed with a smile — so much the better. But I would be very grateful if you would pass along my request and make it more emphatic. If I were to offer suggestions for an illustration, I would choose such scenes as the following:

---

[1]German: publishing company. — EDS.

the parents and the head clerk in front of the locked door, or even better, the parents and the sister in the lighted room, with the door open upon the adjoining room that lies in darkness.

I imagine you have already received the proofs and the reviews.

With best regards, sincerely yours, Franz Kafka

[1915]

Questions

1. Why do you think Kafka did not want the insect drawn or even shown at a distance? How would such a title page affect your experience of reading *The Metamorphosis*?
2. Consider Kafka's two suggestions for illustrations. Why are they fitting? What does each one communicate? Which one would be better?

From *Kafka*

David Zane Mairowitz and Robert Crumb

David Zane Mairowitz (b. 1943) is a well-known Kafka scholar and freelance writer, who founded the *International Times*. Robert Crumb (b. 1943) is an artist and illustrator celebrated for his counterculture views of America and his founding of the "American comix movement." Creator of such characters as Devil Girl and Fritz the Cat, he was the subject of Terry Zwigoff's 1994 documentary *Crumb*. The following excerpt is taken from *Kafka*, also known as *Kafka for Beginners*, an illustrated biography with comic adaptations of some of Kafka's most famous works, including *The Metamorphosis*. The first part of this selection discusses the dominating influence of Kafka's father, a strong authority figure in the writer's life; the second part includes panels from their retelling of *The Metamorphosis*.

Those who knew Kafka well felt he lived behind a "glass wall." He was there, smiling, kindly, a good listener, a faithful friend and yet, somehow, inaccessible. A jumble of complexes and neuroses, he managed to give the impression of distance, grace, serenity and, at times, even *saintliness*.

His capacity for swallowing his fear of others and turning this against himself, rather than against its source is the stuff of all his work. Nowhere is the more apparent than in his relation to this man...

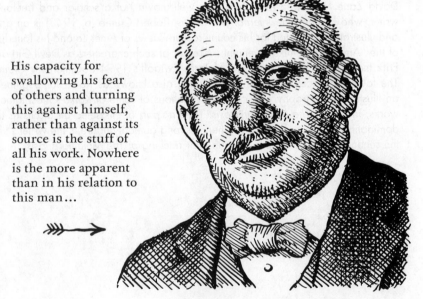

Hermann Kafka (1852–1931)

Kafka lived with his parents nearly all his life (even when he was financially independent and could have moved out), in very close quarters where his hyper-sensitivity to noise was put to the test on a daily basis. For Kafka Senior, a giant of a man, his son was a failure and a *Schlemiel* (good-for-nothing), a grave disappointment. He never hesitated to let him know.

And at the
dinner table…

Kafka's lifelong awe in the face of superior *power*, made famous
in the novels *The Trial* and *The Castle*, begins with Hermann Kafka.
He feared and hated his teachers at school, but had to see them as
"Respektspersonen," to be respected for no other reason than that they
were in positions of authority.

But he never rebelled. Instead, he turned his fear into a self-abasement
or psychosomatic illness. In every contretemps with authority, he made
himself the guilty party. Moreover, as in the classical relationship
between master and slave, between colonizer and colonized, *he began
to see himself through his father's eyes.*

"As Gregor Samsa awoke one morning after disturbing dreams, he found himself transformed in his bed into an enormous bug."

This, very likely the most famous first sentence in modern literature, begins Kafka's masterpiece:

METAMORPHOSIS

FRANZ KAFKA

DIE VERWANDLUNG

"Als Gregor Samsa eines Morgens aus unruhigen Träumen erwachte, fand er sich in seinem Bett zu einem ungeheueren Ungeziefer verwandelt."

DER JÜNGSTE TAG ★ 22/23

KURT WOLFF VERLAG · LEIPZIG

1916

Samsa, a traveling salesman, was the family's provider. Because of him, his father had been able to retire, and his sister could expect to study the violin at the music conservatory.

For this reason, the first person to witness his change, along with his family, was the Chief Clerk of his firm, who had arrived because Gregor, for the first time in his life, was late for work.

[1996]

Questions

1. What do the illustrations add to the details about Kafka's life? Which did you go to first — illustrations or written text? Why?
2. The graphic retelling of *The Metamorphosis* includes quotations from Kafka and illustrations but also summary (comments, which you will notice, Kuper does not include in his rendition, which follows). Are these helpful or distracting? Explain. Is it easy to determine which are directly from Kafka?
3. What do you think Mairowitz, who is accustomed to writing for scholarly audiences of his peers, hoped to accomplish with this collaboration with Crumb? Do you think it should add to or detract from his reputation in the academic world?

From *The Metamorphosis*

PETER KUPER

Peter Kuper (b. 1958) is an award-winning cartoonist and illustrator known for his social and political commentary. His illustrations appear regularly in numerous magazines, including *Time*, *Newsweek*, and *Mad*, for which he draws "Spy vs. Spy" every month. He graduated with a BA from Kent State University in Cleveland, Ohio, and studied at the Parsons School of Design and the Pratt Institute in New York City. His most recent books are graphic-novel adaptations of *The Metamorphosis* and Upton Sinclair's *The Jungle*. His wordless graphic novel *Sticks and Stones* was awarded the gold medal in the sequential arts category in the 2004 Society of Illustrators competition. In 2007, he published *Stop Forgetting to Remember: The Autobiography of Walter Kurtz*, a semiautobiographical work on the struggle to balance being a husband, father, friend, and artist in the contemporary world.

THE INTRODUCTION

In 1904, eight years before Franz Kafka wrote *The Metamorphosis* in Prague, across the ocean a cartoonist named Winsor McCay created "Dream of the Rarebit Fiend," a comic strip that appeared in New York's *Evening Telegram*. In each one-page installment a character was trapped in a world that grew more surreal with each panel—a gentleman's leg inflates and demolishes a mansion, a suitor's lover crumbles into confetti and blows away, a lady's alligator handbag morphs into a monster and devours her. Finally, in the last panel, the character awakens to reality, vowing never again to eat the nightmare-inducing rarebit cheese before bedtime.

Of course, Franz Kafka never allowed his characters to enjoy the relief of awakening to normalcy from their disturbing dreams. Still, the two artists had much in common, including a shared genius for rendering the anxious intersection of reality and dreamscape. Kafka may never have been a comic strip fan, but his angst-ridden characters in reality-bending scenarios are ideally suited to this medium. This adaptation of *The Metamorphosis* couldn't exist without Kafka's illuminating words, but owes a visual debt to McCay's trailblazing excursions into the absurd darkness of slumberland. I have drawn tremendous inspiration from both these pioneers, fascinated by their ability to address our human condition with unexpected twists, brilliant artistry, and deadpan humor.

Nearly a century later, the works of Kafka and McCay seem as fresh as if they were created to reflect our current zeitgeist. Kafka's tales of nightmare trials and monolithic bureaucracies feel no more surreal than headlines from our daily newspapers. It makes one wish that simply avoiding rarebit cheese were the remedy.

—Peter Kuper

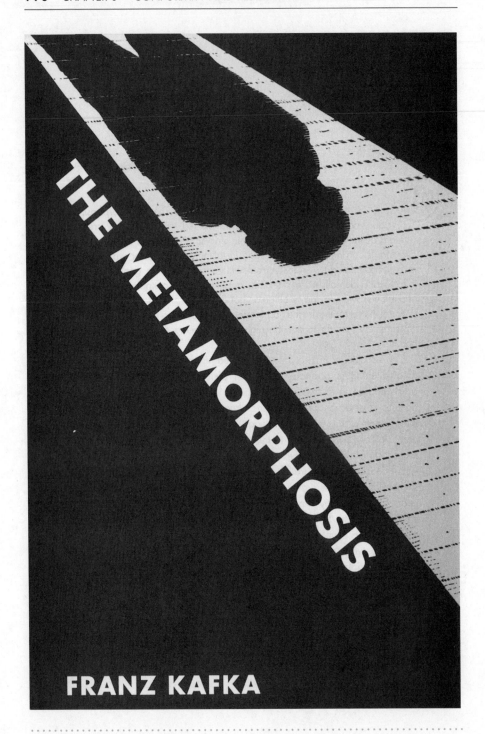

THE METAMORPHOSIS

FRANZ KAFKA

When Gregor Samsa
awoke one morning from
disturbing dreams,
he found himself
transformed . . .

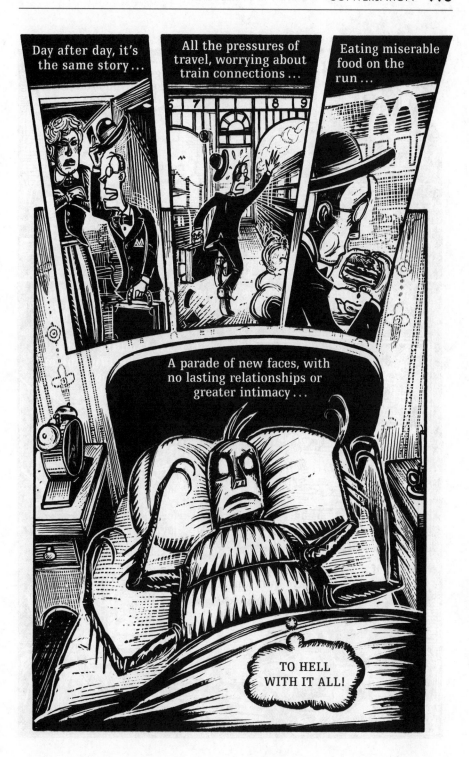

The change in Gregor's voice must have been muffled by the wooden door because his mother was reassured and shuffled off. However, their little exchange made his father and sister aware that Gregor had not, as they assumed, left for work.

GREGOR, GREGOR— what's going on?

GREGOR!

Gregor, it's Grete, are you alright?

Do you need *anything?*

Please, Gregor, open the door.

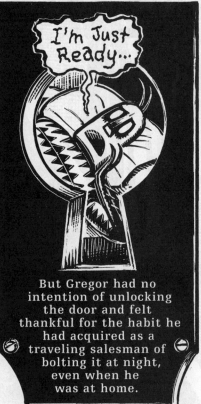

I'm Just Ready...

But Gregor had no intention of unlocking the door and felt thankful for the habit he had acquired as a traveling salesman of bolting it at night, even when he was at home.

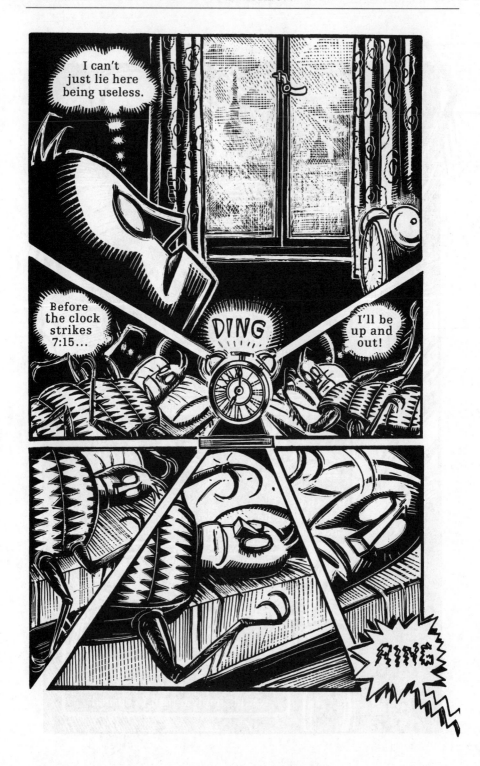

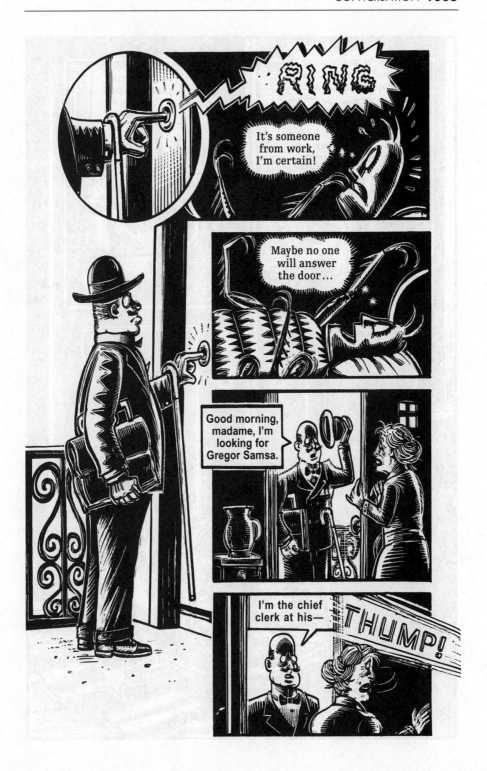

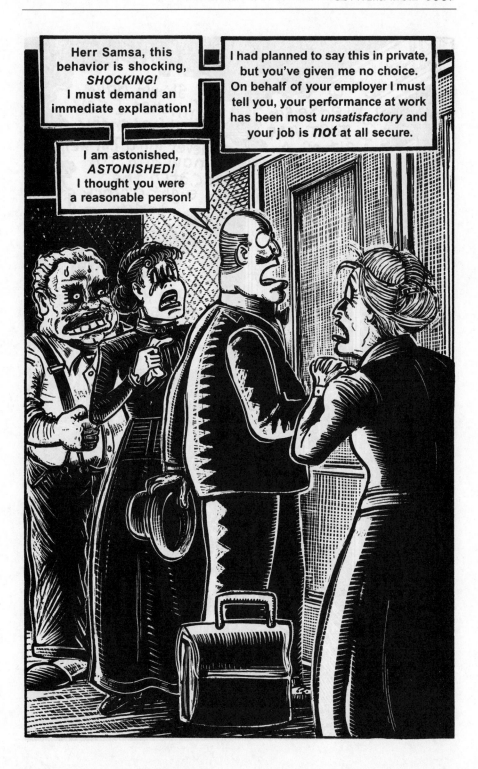

[2003]

Questions

1. How would you describe the illustrations? Are they humorous? frightening? exaggerated? realistic? Do they confirm or conflict with your interpretation of *The Metamorphosis*? Why do you think Kuper chose to illustrate in black and white rather than in color? Explain whether you think his choice was effective.

2. Even though Kuper uses Kafka's language, he does not include every word. Follow along closely for a few pages and comment on his selections. Has he chosen well? Do the illustrations make up for what he has left out?

3. Explain why you would or would not find it difficult to follow the plot if you had not already read Kafka.

4. Do you see the characters other than Gregor as caricatures, or are they developed through both visual and written text as fully as they are in Kafka's original? Explain your response with specific reference to the two texts.

5. Kuper employs different fonts to indicate the sound of voices. Explain why this is or is not effective in conveying character.

6. How does Kuper visually translate symbols from Kafka's *Metamorphosis*, such as the alarm clock, or doors and locks? Does the visual representation make these symbols more powerful or too obvious?

7. A fiction writer has many tools and strategies available to develop plot, character, and setting. After reading Kuper's *Metamorphosis*, which of these three do you think is most challenging for the graphic novelist to develop?

8. A reviewer for the *Chicago Tribune* described Kuper's book as "a fully realized effort meant to be read as literature, albeit a kind of literature we haven't seen before." Do you think it is literature? Explain.

PETER KUPER ON *THE METAMORPHOSIS*

Renée Shea (RS): Why *The Metamorphosis*? Is it just a personal favorite of yours? Do you think it's especially powerful? The only other classic that you've done, as far as I can find, is *The Jungle*.

Peter Kuper (PK): *The Metamorphosis* seemed like a natural for comics. Kafka's imagery immediately gave me ideas for unusual ways of storytelling. His words acted as an anchor that allowed me to go wild visually while being grounded enough to not lose the reader. I had previously done a collection of nine of Kafka's short stories in a book called *Give It Up!* I found that his work translated so perfectly into comics that they seemed to draw themselves. *Metamorphosis* was the opportunity to do this kind of translation in a longer form.

RS: Why do you think Kafka's novella has weathered nearly a century so well? It's been a play, some film possibilities, now the novel—and it's remained required reading in high schools and colleges for decades. What's the lasting appeal?

PK: Feeling trapped by work, out of control, powerless, at odds with members of your family—who can't relate to that? It is about our human condition, and that isn't changing anytime soon. In fact, the world has only been getting more Kafkaesque.

RS: You've been very faithful to Kafka's text in your graphic retelling. Is changing the medium sufficiently creative for you? Did you have to resist changing details of the story?

PK: Yes, Kafka's inventions and the ground he covers gave me more than enough to work with. Transforming the text into a comic was already going pretty far; I wasn't looking to change anything—that would have been (even more) sacrilegious.

RS: That being said, the illustrations are themselves an interpretation of Kafka's *Metamorphosis*. What element(s) of your own interpretation—or, as you describe it, "adaptation"—do you think are most important in your graphic-novel version?

PK: I wanted to maintain the humor in the story. It probably depends on your sense of humor whether you find anything funny about Kafka's stories; I think they are often hilarious. The three roomers that appear later in the story are one good example—they would be comfortable in a Marx Brothers film.

RS: You've written that Kafka's "angst-ridden character in reality-bending scenarios are ideally suited to this medium." Can you explain what you mean in more detail?

PK: In comics you can visually create a world, and the parameters can be stretched and bent and still feel like a reality. Although with CGI (computer-generated imagery), animated movies are blurring the line between what's real and what's drawn, this can be done seamlessly in a comic. You can create your own logic, and the surreal becomes reality. Kafka had already achieved this with his story. I used this as a springboard to demonstrate the possible ways a series of images can tell that story. Mine is only one interpretation. There are a million different ways his story could be told in comics.

RS: Your graphic novel captures the irony of Kafka and the dark humor, but it is not funny like your other adaptation of this story: "Metamorph Simpsons." What was your intent with this *Simpsons* take on Kafka? Is this

5

10

poking fun at Kafka's wide appeal (as if everyone knows the story), taking the satire in a more contemporary direction, devaluing it . . . ?

PK: This is one of the fundamental aspects of *The Simpsons*—taking sacred cows and serving them up as deliciously cooked humor. This is a lesson that *Mad* magazine taught so many of us and that led to shows like *SNL* and *The Simpsons* and the newspaper, the *Onion*. I'm just doing as I was taught by Alfred E. Neuman, and when the opportunity came up to do a *Simpsons* "Treehouse of Horror" story, *Metamorphosis* was a perfect sacred cow.

RS: In a letter to his publisher, Kafka expressed dismay about the original cover illustration and indicated that he did not want Gregor to be drawn. How do you respond to Kafka's concern?

PK: Kafka also told the executor of his will, Max Brod, to burn all of his unpublished manuscripts. I figured if his best friend could ignore him, I could do the same. Since I knew I was going to show Gregor on the inside of the book, I had already crossed Kafka's line. Actually, in my original cover design, I wanted to have the title printed on a translucent dust jacket (the paper cover that wraps around hardcover books), with the image of Gregor Samsa printed on the book itself. This way he would be out of focus; the only way you could see the bug was by lifting the dust jacket. This would have made the reader responsible for the unveiling. Unfortunately, like so many ideas, it was rejected because of cost.

RS: In a headnote to an interview, Michael Lorah described you as "undoubtedly the modern master whose work has refined the socially relevant comic to the highest point yet achieved." Why do you think Kafka's *The Metamorphosis* is "socially relevant" in the twenty-first century?

15

PK: Kafka's writing as a whole is incredibly relevant in our modern world. The term *Kafkaesque* is still regularly applied to acts by our politicians, our laws, and our daily experience with bureaucracies. *The Metamorphosis* is a great example of social critique.

RS: Do you think Gregor's is the quintessential adolescent consciousness? He hears people and he responds to them, but they don't understand. "Because no one could understand him, it didn't occur to anyone . . . that he could understand them. . . ." His body's out of control, alien to him. His family is embarrassed, then repulsed, by him, can't accept him as he is; sounds like a teenager to me!

PK: Sounds like the teenage hell we all went through—some more than others, of course, but I personally felt Kafka would have been a good choice to write about my adolescent experience.

RS: My students and I don't always agree about the purpose of retellings, particularly the visual ones. My assumption is that graphic retellings are a step toward the original, perhaps meant to whet the appetite for the original work; my students disagree, claiming that these works have their own life—and purpose. (One called your graphic retelling "a celebration of Kafka.") But then what's the point? Is the audience for your *Metamorphosis* those who've read the original, those who will read the original after reading your graphic novel, or those whose understanding of Kafka will come exclusively from your adaptation?

PK: This can certainly be a problem, the same way that seeing a movie can replace people's desire to go out and read the book. Ideally everybody starts with the source material, and then they are in a position to judge how well the adaptation has done in capturing the original.

    In the same way that music videos can get in the way of one's own images and associations with a song, I fear I may be guilty of this and hope the vengeful literary gods will pardon my intrusion. On the other hand, if someone who had never heard of Kafka came to his work through my adaptation, I may have helped someone discover Kafka's other writings. Having spent so many years working in an art form that has been considered "low art" only to be reevaluated as something higher, I find those distinctions to be faulty. Time has a way of adjusting these measures.

RS: Okay, I can't resist this one. David Foster Wallace writes about why students don't "get" Kafka's humor: "No wonder they cannot appreciate the really central Kafka joke: that the horrific struggle to establish a human self results in a self whose humanity is inseparable from that horrific struggle." Do you agree with him?

PK: As I said earlier, whether you find Kafka's stories to be funny depends on your sense of humor. To me, the best humor has a dark edge. If people can laugh at the *Onion*'s headlines about our modern horrors and what George Carlin had to say about the various ways we are doomed as a species, then Kafka isn't a stretch. It seems as if our times, for better and worse, are only going to produce more students who will find humor in the face of our waking nightmares. Sometimes that is the only way to survive.

20

Follow-Up

1. What elements or themes of Kafka's *Metamorphosis* are most important to Kuper?
2. Where does Kuper find humor in Kafka's *Metamorphosis*? How does he define that humor?

3. What do you think Kuper means when he describes comics as enabling artists to "create [their] own logic, and the surreal becomes reality" (para. 10)?
4. Does Kuper believe that his graphic novel will change how people read Kafka's *Metamorphosis*?

Entering the Conversation

As you develop a response to one of the following questions, refer to the texts you have read in this section. You may also draw on your own experience or knowledge relating to comics, Kafka, and *The Metamorphosis*.

1. Compare and contrast the first part of the original story by Kafka with Kuper's graphic retelling. Kuper uses actual text from the story, yet his illustrations are themselves an interpretation. Explain which of Kafka's ideas or themes Kuper emphasizes, as well as instances where he departs from Kafka's intent.

2. Choosing one theme from *The Metamorphosis*, explain why you think it remains compelling for readers today. Then compare how Kafka's treatment of this theme is similar to or different from the way another artist in this Conversation treats the same theme.

3. Who is the audience for these retellings? Explain why you think the audience consists of those who've already read Kafka, those who will be motivated to read Kafka, or those who will read only the retelling. Pay special attention to young readers of today. Consider Kuper's graphic novel along with at least one of the other retellings.

4. Who is more sympathetic toward Gregor — Kafka, Mairowitz and Crumb, or Kuper? Consider the role of humor in the depictions. Be very specific in using references to the texts to support your interpretation.

5. In an essay entitled "Kafka and *The Metamorphosis*," John Updike commented on why he felt that any visual representation of Gregor was doomed:

> Any theatrical or cinematic version of the story must founder on this point of external representation: A concrete image of the insect would be too distracting and shut off sympathy; such a version would lack the very heart of comedy and pathos which beats in the unsteady area between objective and subjective, where Gregor's insect and human selves swayingly struggle. Still half-asleep, he notes his extraordinary condition yet persists in remembering and trying to fulfill his duties as a travelling salesman and the mainstay of this household. Later, relegated by the family to the shadows of a room turned storage closet, he responds to violin music and creeps forward, covered with dust and trailing remnants of food, to claim his sister's love. Such scenes could not be done except with words. In this age that lives and dies by the visual, *The Metamorphosis* stands as a narrative

absolutely literary, able to exist only where language and the mind's hazy wealth of imagery intersect.

Write an essay explaining what Updike's position is and why you agree or disagree with it. Use several sources from the Conversation in your analysis.

6. Write an essay supporting, challenging, or modifying the claim made in the following quotation by Iris Bruce in her essay "Kafka and Popular Culture." Refer to Kafka's novella and at least two other texts in your analysis:

> Kafka's writings are a good example of how iconic texts that used to belong to "high culture" can be "reborn" in popular culture in generically different formats. . . . Kafka's phenomenal rebirth is in itself a stunning metamorphosis. Here we have a writer who has successfully bridged the gap between high and popular culture, whose name is recognized by people who have never read one of his novels: the word "Kafkaesque" has entered into everyday speech and taken on iconic value. However, this success has come at a cost . . . ; perhaps this is simply an example of capitalism's endless ability to transform important ideas and images into "catchy" popular icons for the thrill-hungry public. The unsettling and threatening possibilities inherent in the insect metaphor, for example, derive from deeply rooted anxieties, primal and contemporary at the same time; not incidentally, they also offer up new images for consumption in the insatiable cultural marketplace.

7. Write a dialogue between Franz Kafka and Peter Kuper. Imagine how Kafka would respond to Kuper's graphic versions of *The Metamorphosis*. You may invent and create dialogue as well as quote from Kafka's letter and the interview with Kuper.

8. Develop your own interpretation of *The Metamorphosis* using multimedia tools—audio, visual, or both. Explain why you made the choices you did.

Student Writing

Close Reading Drama

The student essay below was written as a timed response to the following prompt.

Using Hamlet's soliloquy from act IV, scene iv, lines 32–66, as your text, explain how it encompasses the larger themes in *Hamlet* and the universal truths that the play explores.

Hamlet's Internal Struggle

Kevin Carrig

In *Hamlet*, the title character is often used by Shakespeare to bring key themes to the fore and explore them. In this soliloquy, we find that Hamlet is having two common human experiences—he feels compassion toward other human beings as well as the desire for revenge against Claudius for killing his father. Unfortunately, these emotions, while equally universal, nevertheless pull in opposite directions. This soliloquy explores this conflict in depth, so that an analysis of the soliloquy will illuminate this internal struggle, which in turn is essential to understanding *Hamlet* as a play.

The soliloquy is marked by Hamlet's self-criticism, which focuses on his inability to act on his desires to plot for revenge. These decisions — not to take action against his uncle Claudius — are, he tells us, "one part wisdom / And ever three parts coward." Hamlet is experiencing the inability to reconcile his natural feelings of human sympathy with his beliefs that he is justified in seeking revenge on Claudius, so that even though he hates Claudius for killing his father and believes that he ought to be punished, he cannot escape human compassion. Thus, through this self-criticism, Shakespeare demonstrates that humans are by their nature good. Violence is contradictory to the plan of the god "that made us with such large discourse."

Hamlet's internal struggle is parallel to the physical struggle of the soldiers in the soliloquy, described as fighting over a small piece of land. In his appeal to those witnessing his downfall, Hamlet characterizes the war over the land as a "fight for a plot / Whereon the numbers cannot try the cause." By portraying the battle as ultimately pointless, Hamlet is communicating another universal truth: that the ends do not justify the means. While he may seem to have every reason in the world to kill Claudius, he realizes that the guilt that is felt in the course of seeking revenge is telling — it suggests that there are certain actions we cannot find it in ourselves to condone, no matter how merited the end products of those actions seem to be. Hamlet, here, is conveying that it is in our nature to look beyond the immediate repercussions of an act, thus pointing to the frailty of human decision making in this context.

In a final appeal to his constituents, Hamlet grapples with fundamental questions about the meaning of life. In the first section of the soliloquy, he compares himself with an animal and reflects on the paradoxical inability of humans to act on their desires. He questions the very purpose of rational beings, asking, "What is a man, / If his chief good and market of his time / Be but to sleep and feed?" For a creature overwhelmed with certain desires, that he cannot act on those desires because of another part of his nature reduces him to the status of an animal. Thus, Hamlet's winding road is one marked by a question of human nature and the degree to which emotion constitutes life as a whole.

Torn between compassion and revenge, Hamlet demonstrates a constant struggle between different human inclinations. In the fight over whether or not to take revenge, Hamlet is his own biggest foe. He is forced to choose between the lesser of two evils: murder and self-loathing. In this, Hamlet is as much a victim as Claudius. Seeing these two themes drawn out this way can give readers a greater appreciation for the themes in the play as a whole.

Questions

1. How might the student revise the first paragraph to address the prompt more clearly and directly?
2. Identify areas where more precise diction and clear expression would improve the essay. How would you advise the student to revise those areas?
3. Identify areas in the essay that require greater specificity. How would you advise the student to revise those areas?
4. The student uses "thus" twice, suggesting conclusions based on logical reasoning and supporting evidence. Is this word used appropriately? Is there enough support to warrant its use? What additional supporting evidence would bring greater cogency to the conclusions this word introduces?
5. Consider the verbs the student uses, noting several instances of passive voice and state-of-being verbs. Change these verbs to action verbs. What do these changes bring to the revised essay?
6. Is the student's interpretation of the soliloquy sound? How effectively do you think this essay discusses the "larger themes" and "universal truths" that the prompt directs the student to address? How successfully does the essay deliver its intended meaning?

The Writer's Craft—Close Reading

Tone

When we read sophisticated, challenging literature, perhaps the most elusive feature of the work is tone—defined as the attitude of the speaker toward his or her subject. In conversation, we communicate tone by varying our inflections, raising or lowering our volume and pitch, emphasizing certain words and phrases, and using gestures and facial expressions. Think of a phrase as simple as "Well, thanks," and imagine how the tone could vary from enthusiastic to sincere to surprised to sarcastic. Or consider this response to a marriage proposal: "You're asking me to marry you?" The speaker might be replying in a tone of outraged disbelief or one of unalloyed joy. The tone in these examples would be made clear by the sound of the person's voice and his or her physical cues. Writers, however, must create and convey tone solely through words appearing on a printed page—or a computer screen—where readers need to "hear" the speaker's voice. When we read to ourselves, we need to internalize the sound of the text, listening with our "inner ear," as it were. We may ask, is the voice serious, ironic, facetious, or somber? Does it encourage, complain, admonish, or exhort? When we hear the text correctly—that is, when we pick up on the implied attitude—we are recognizing the tone.

Tone, then, is produced by details and descriptions; diction, especially the connotations of the words chosen; the arrangement of the words, including syntax or sounds resulting through juxtaposition or meter; imagery and figurative language; overall structure, whether in sentences or stanzas; and especially context. In other words, to determine the tone of a poem or prose passage, readers have to pay attention to all the choices a writer makes.

Author versus Speaker

When thinking about tone, it's important to remember that in literature, the speaker, whether a narrator or specific character, is not necessarily the author. Often an author will speak through a **persona**, or "mask," which is the voice and viewpoint an author adopts to deliver a story or poem. In other instances, the author might speak through a character. If you have read Jonathan Swift's essay "A Modest Proposal," for example, or watched *The Colbert Report*, you know that there is a difference between author and speaker, person and persona.

In drama, where there is little or no third-person narration and exposition, it is through tone that an author gives us insight into the characters' thoughts and feelings. Listen to Hamlet as he reflects on the quickness with which his mother remarried after his father's death:

> O, most wicked speed, to post / With such dexterity to incestuous sheets!
> (I.ii.156–57)

Listen closely to the *sound* of the language Shakespeare wrote for his character, Hamlet. The *s* sounds spit the venomous words out. The reader knows right away the poison and bitterness with which Hamlet, not Shakespeare, is filled; thus has Shakespeare prepared the reader for Hamlet's future language and behavior.

Style and Tone

Whether you are reading poetry or prose, the small choices in diction, imagery, figurative language, and syntax are the most important guides to understanding the work's tone and, ultimately, to interpreting the work's meaning. Let's look at an excerpt from "Her Kind" by Anne Sexton. The poem begins:

> I have gone out, a possessed witch,
> haunting the black air, braver at night;
> dreaming evil, I have done my hitch
> over the plain houses, light by light:
> lonely thing, twelve-fingered, out of mind.
> A woman like that is not a woman, quite.
> I have been her kind.

The first thing that we might determine when thinking about tone is whether it is positive or negative; from there, we can fine-tune our reading. For instance, if we read through this poem quickly, we might think that the tone is positive: the speaker is reveling in being a witch. After all, what would make a witch happier than flying high above the plain (boring) houses on her broom at night, feeling brave, and "dreaming evil"? We could say that the tone is not only positive but also exultant and empowered. But why, then, is she called a "lonely thing" in line 5? This line simply doesn't fit with a positive interpretation. Like a good juror, a good reader does not ignore evidence. Let's look more carefully to arrive at a fuller understanding of the tone of this poem.

Do other choices in the poem reinforce the idea that it carries a lonesome tone? What do these choices add to it? In line 2, the witch admits that she's "braver at night." The use of the comparative "braver" makes us wonder why she isn't as brave during the day, when the world is awake and people are out and about. Perhaps it's because she is "twelve-fingered"? Whether we take this description literally or figuratively, it tells us that this witch is not a rebel but an outcast. Now the "plain houses" that she passes over become symbols of a normal life that is denied her. The tone has become not just one of loneliness but one of bitter longing for what's below: the life of a woman, not that of a witch. As you can see, an investigation into the tone of a poem can very quickly lead to an interpretation of the entire piece.

Shifts in Tone

Tone is rarely consistent throughout a work of literature. Authors may use shifts in tone to add another layer of meaning to a literary text. In Chapter 2, we discussed "turns," or places in a poem or passage that shift or change. These pivot points are frequently the heart of the interpretive matter, and very often what is shifting is the tone. Let's look at an example from "Song: To the Men of England" by Percy Bysshe Shelley. The poem begins:

> Men of England, wherefore plough
> For the lords who lay ye low?
> Wherefore weave with toil and care
> The rich robes your tyrants wear?

In these lines, the pleading, urging tone of the speaker's rhetorical questions is designed to enjoin his readers to action. The first six quatrains of the poem continue to speak in the encouraging, hortatory tone established in the first stanza, as the speaker pleads with his readers to change their lives; then the tone shifts for the final two stanzas, becoming admonitory and ironic, as if scolding any reader who is resigned, frustrated, and dismissive of his call to action. Note the shift from stanza 6 to stanzas 7 and 8:

> Sow seed—but let no tyrant reap;
> Find wealth—let no impostor heap;
> Weave robes—let not the idle wear;
> Forge arms—in your defence to bear.

> Shrink to your cellars, holes, and cells—
> In halls ye deck another dwells.
> Why shake the chains ye wrought? Ye see
> The steel ye tempered glance on ye.

With plough and spade and hoe and loom
Trace your grave and build your tomb
And weave your winding-sheet—till fair
England be your Sepulchre.

Tone in Fiction

In addition to using tone to convey their meaning, authors of fiction and other narratives use tone to subtly develop settings, characters, and even themes. Let's take a look at a passage from the contemporary short story "Admiral":

> Nothing had changed in the paneled room that gave onto the garden, not as far as Nisha could see. There were the immense old high-backed leather armchairs and the antique Stickley sofa rescued from the law offices of Striker and Striker, the mahogany bar with the wine rack and the backlit shrine Mr. Striker had created in homage to the spirits of single-malt whisky, and overseeing it all, the oil portrait of Admiral with its dark heroic hues and golden patina of varnish. (para. 6)

The imagery here is key to understanding the tone. The passage begins with a posh, stately description of the room and the furniture, and then juxtaposes it with "the backlit shrine" in "homage" to the "spirits" of the whisky. By putting an ironic spin on *shrine, homage,* and especially *spirits,* evoking its double meaning, Boyle mocks the solemnity of the scene. In the course of describing the room—the setting—the author is also creating characters. He shows us Nisha's impressions as she takes in the setting. It clearly differs from her own home, suggesting a radical difference between her life and that of her employers. If the reader is still unsure of whether this scene is regal or ridiculous, the final phrase clears it up, for "overseeing it all," "heroic" and "golden," is the portrait of a *dog!* The reader also begins to understand the relationship between Mr. Striker and Nisha as Boyle presents the irony of characters who "worship" their possessions and even their dog but aren't much interested in the lives of people other than themselves. The passage suggests the awkward and static position of Nisha, confronted with the unchanging scene before her and the solipsistic nature of the Strikers. Through all of this, the story's themes are also being developed: themes concerning the selfishness of the characters, the foolishness of trying to stop time, and the perversity of worshiping a dead dog.

Words That Describe Tone

There are nearly endless ways to describe tone. You'll often need more than one word—perhaps an adverb and adjective combination (*bitterly angry, humorously proud*) or a contrasting pair (*admiring yet envious, distant but loving*). Following is a list of words that provides a good place to start. Each of these adjectives is useful for describing tones that you will encounter in literature. After looking up any that you don't know, separate them into two categories, one positive and one negative. Choose one of the stories from this chapter, and apply two of the words from the list to each of the main characters and three of the words to the narrator. Add to this list as you continue to read literature and respond to tone.

solemn	sad	generous	somber	grave
didactic	audacious	mocking	dispassionate	resigned
acidulous	bitter	dreamy	pedantic	reflective
earnest	caustic	pitiful	elevated	lofty
candid	nostalgic	wistful	questioning	colloquial
detached	sentimental	apologetic	objective	lugubrious
restrained	enthusiastic	urbane	facetious	ambivalent
melancholy	sarcastic	playful	apprehensive	elegiac
acerbic	bitter	aloof	irreverent	sardonic
indignant	argumentative	scornful	pensive	incredulous
insistent	self-deprecating	familiar	maudlin	diffident
disinterested	condescending	sanguine	bemused	ecstatic
speculative	laudatory	strident	grim	mournful
contentious	cynical	self-assured	forthright	admonitory
contemptuous	urgent	poignant	zealous	giddy
querulous	polemical	insipid	stolid	callow

The following exercises will help you discern tone and understand how it contributes to meaning.

• EXERCISE 1 •

The tone of "Homage to My Hips" by Lucille Clifton can be characterized as confident—and then some. That confidence might be interpreted variously as humorous, rebellious, mocking, sexy, teasing, angry, aggressive, and so forth. Perform the poem in a way that conveys your interpretation of the poem's tone.

• EXERCISE 2 •

For each of the following passages, identify the tone or tones, explain how the text delivers the tone(s), and explain how tone contributes to meaning.

1. CLAUDIUS:
   'Tis sweet and commendable in your nature, Hamlet,
   To give these mourning duties to your father:

But, you must know, your father lost a father;
That father lost, lost his, and the survivor bound
In filial obligation for some term
To do obsequious sorrow: but to persever
In obstinate condolement is a course
Of impious stubbornness; 'tis unmanly grief;
It shows a will most incorrect to heaven,
A heart unfortified, a mind impatient,
An understanding simple and unschool'd:
For what we know must be and is as common
As any the most vulgar thing to sense,
Why should we in our peevish opposition
Take it to heart? Fie! 'tis a fault to heaven,
A fault against the dead, a fault to nature,
To reason most absurd; whose common theme
Is death of fathers, and who still hath cried,
From the first corse till he that died to-day,
"This must be so." We pray you, throw to earth
This unprevailing woe, and think of us
As of a father. (*Hamlet*, I.ii.87–108)

2. OPHELIA:

O, what a noble mind is here o'er-thrown!
The courtier's, soldier's, scholar's, eye, tongue, sword;
Th' expectancy and rose of the fair state,
The glass of fashion and the mould of form,
Th' observ'd of all observers, quite, quite, down!
And I, of ladies most deject and wretched,
That suck'd the honey of his music vows,
Now see that noble and most sovereign reason
Like sweet bells jangled, out of time and harsh;
That unmatch'd form and feature of blown youth
Blasted with ecstasy: O, woe is me,
T' have seen what I have seen, see what I see! (*Hamlet*, III.i. 141–52)

3. I had always thought that my father's only ordeal was that he'd left his country and moved to a place where everything from the climate to the language was so unlike his own, a place where he never quite seemed to fit in, never appeared to belong. The only thing I can grasp now, as I drive way beyond the speed limit down yet another highway, is why the unfamiliar might have been so comforting, rather than distressing, to my father. And why he has never wanted the person he was, is, permanently documented in any way. He taught himself to appreciate the enormous weight of permanent markers by learning about the Ancient Egyptians. He had gotten to know them, through their crypts and monuments, in a way that he wanted no one to know him,

no one except my mother and me, we, who are now his kas, his good angels, his masks against his own face. ("The Book of the Dead," para. 214)

4. As for the dog, she tried to be conscientious about the whole business of imprinting it with the past—or *a* past—though she felt ridiculous. Four years of college for this? Wars were being fought, people were starving, there were diseases to conquer, children to educate, good to do in the world, and here she was reliving her adolescence in the company of an inbred semi-retarded clown of a cloned Afghan hound because two childless rich people decreed it should be so. All right. She knew she'd have to move on. Knew it was temporary. Swore that she'd work up a new résumé and start sending it out—but then the face of her mother, sick from vomiting and with her scalp as smooth and slick as an eggplant, would rise up to shame her. She threw the ball to the dog. Took him to the park. Let the days fall round her like leaves from a dying tree. ("Admiral," para. 63)

5. Nwamgba was the first one to ask a question: Had they brought their guns, by any chance, the ones used to destroy the people of Agueke, and could she see one? The man said unhappily that it was the soldiers of the British government and the merchants of the Royal Niger Company who destroyed villages; they, instead, brought good news. He spoke about their god, who had come to the world to die, and who had a son but no wife, and who was three but also one. Many of the people around Nwamgba laughed loudly. Some walked away, because they had imagined that the white man was full of wisdom. Others stayed and offered cool bowls of water. ("The Headstrong Historian," para. 12)

6. But what should he do now? The next train left at seven o'clock. In order to catch that one, he'd have to rush like a madman, and his samples weren't packed up yet. He hardly felt alert or energetic enough. And even if he caught the train, he wouldn't avoid the Director's wrath, because the office porter had been waiting at the five-o'clock train and would long since have reported his failure to appear. The porter was completely under the Director's thumb—he had neither a backbone nor brains. What if Gregor were to report himself sick? But that would be highly awkward and suspicious, because he had not been sick once in five years of service. The Director would certainly come with the insurance doctor. He would reproach his parents for their lazy son and dismiss all rejoinders by refer-ring them to the doctor, who considered all people completely healthy, but work-averse. And would he be so wrong in this case? Gregor actually felt completely fine, despite a fatigue completely unwarranted after such a long sleep. He even had a powerful appetite. (*The Metamorphosis*, para. 6)

7. "I don't agree," said W.E.B.,
   "If I should have the drive to seek
   Knowledge of chemistry or Greek,
   I'll do it. Charles and Miss can look

Another place for hand or cook.
Some men rejoice in skill of hand,
And some in cultivating land,
But there are others who maintain
The right to cultivate the brain." ("Booker T. and W.E.B.," ll. 8–16)

8. Who cares what it's all about?
I do! Edgar Allan Poe cares! Shelley cares! Beethoven & Dylan care.
Do you care? What are you about
or are you a human being with 10 fingers and two eyes? ("Is About," ll. 21–24)

• EXERCISE 3 •

In the following soliloquy (I.v.98–108), Hamlet's tone shifts dramatically,
whether because he is mad or feigning madness. Identify the tone, where it
shifts, and how the shift in tone affects the meaning of the soliloquy.

Yea, from the table of my memory
I'll wipe away all trivial fond records,
All saws of books, all forms, all pressures past,
That youth and observation copied there;
And thy commandment all alone shall live
Within the book and volume of my brain,
Unmix'd with baser matter; yes, by heaven!
O most pernicious woman!
O villain, villain, smiling, damned villain!
My tables,—meet it is I set it down,
That one may smile, and smile, and be a villain.

• EXERCISE 4 •

Look back at the opening page of Kuper's *Metamorphosis* on page 992 and the
corresponding passage by Kafka on page 945. Describe the tone of Kafka's passage and how he creates that tone. Then analyze the tone of Kuper's graphic
interpretation. How does Kuper convey Kafka's tone? Where does he deviate
from it?

• EXERCISE 5 •

Write a poem or passage expressing your viewpoint on conformity and rebellion
that either expresses a specific tone or shifts between or among tones. Discuss
the resources of language you used to develop that tone or tonal shifts.

• EXERCISE 6 •

Choose a poem or a passage from a story in this chapter and through the use of diction, syntax, and other features of writing that we have discussed, change the tone of the poem or passage you select, rewriting it as a parody of the original. You might take a serious poem or passage and make it facetious, change an ironic one so that its attitude is earnest, make a critical piece laudatory or an impassioned one objective—whichever is appropriate for your text.

Suggestions for Writing

Conformity and Rebellion

1. Thinking about the overall theme of this chapter, we may ask: Why do we conform? Certainly, we sometimes conform because of timidity, reluctance, ambition, or simply ease; but then there are times when we conform out of a sense of duty or responsibility, in the spirit of cooperation, or with a sense of sacrifice. Consider these ideas as they run through the selections in the chapter, and develop a thesis regarding the nature of conformity. Refer specifically to the texts of several of the chapter's selections to support your essay.

2. "What is a rebel? A man who says 'no,'" says Albert Camus. Among those who say no in this chapter are Melville's Bartleby; Adichie's Grace (or Afamefuna); Vonnegut's Harrison Bergeron; W.E.B. in Dudley Randall's poem; the speakers in the poems by George Herbert, Percy Bysshe Shelley, and Dylan Thomas; and, of course, Hamlet. What is the significance of Camus's question and answer? Consider how at least two of the characters or speakers in the chapter say "no," and write an essay in which you compare and contrast their rebellious actions or words, and draw conclusions about the consequences of their rebellion.

3. African American poet James Branch Cabell has said, "Poetry is man's rebellion against what he is." In their poems, Herbert, Thomas, Hikmet, Clifton, Sexton, and Duffy use first-person speakers. Consider what Cabell's statement means and how it illustrates a theme that runs through the selections in this chapter. Then write an essay that compares and contrasts two speakers as they illustrate Cabell's meaning.

4. Identify three selections in the chapter that express a similar theme in terms of conformity and rebellion, or three selections that offer different perspectives. Write an essay that explains how each of the three writers uses different means to express the themes or perspectives that you identify. Consider such features as structure, diction, imagery, figurative language, and tone. Refer to specific passages in each text to support your essay.

5. When confronted with a great challenge, the easier path to take is often the one that conformity proffers. Hamlet expresses the difficulty of accepting such a challenge. At the end of act I, he says, "The time is out of joint: O cursed spite, / That ever I was born to set it right!" Write an essay that compares and contrasts the way three characters in the chapter confront the challenge of "setting things right." Use specific examples from the texts to support your essay.

6. Enjoining his listeners, singer Bob Marley proclaims, "Emancipate yourself from mental slavery / None but ourselves can free our minds." Similarly, the speakers of the poems by Shelley, Dickinson, Thomas, Hikmet, and Ginsberg address the reader directly, stating an imperative. Compare the ways that two of these poems enjoin the reader to action. Refer to the texts of the poems to support your answer. Consider both style and content as you write your essay.

7. In imitation of Peter Kuper, create a graphic retelling of one of the shorter selections in the chapter. Among those that might be appropriate are "Disillusionment of Ten O'clock," "anyone lived in a pretty how town," "Booker T. and W.E.B," "On Living," "Her Kind," "Penelope," and "An Epitaph." Either draw the pictures yourself—by hand or with a computer—or cut and paste appropriate images to accompany your text.

8. Which of the contemporary stories—"The Book of the Dead," "Admiral," or "The Headstrong Historian"—did you enjoy most? Read two more stories or a novel by Danticat, Boyle, or Adichie. Write an essay that discusses the nature of conformity as addressed in the works of your selected author.

9. Write a poem in imitation of Ginsberg's "Is About," using a similar structure but changing each of the names and places that begin the lines. Then answer the question, What is your poem about?

Art and the Artist

Art for art's sake? I should think so, and more so than ever at the present time. It is the one orderly product which our middling race has produced. It is the cry of a thousand sentinels, the echo from a thousand labyrinths, it is the lighthouse which cannot be hidden . . . it is the best evidence we can have of our dignity.

—E. M. FORSTER

"Art" is the term used to refer to a wide range of human activities, creations, and expressions that appeal to the senses or emotions. It includes the visual arts, such as painting and sculpture, but also music, literature, and dance. In his essay "What Is Art?" novelist Leo Tolstoy asserts that art must create an emotional link between the artist and the audience, one that "infects" the viewer. The artists whose works fill this chapter are novelists, short-story writers, poets, and painters who not only create art, but also contemplate what it means to be an artist. They ask, like Nobel Prize–winning poet Seamus Heaney, whose pieces make up this chapter's Conversation: what is the artist's role in society?

Other artists represented in this chapter tackle the eternal question, what is art? Some do so by writing poems about poetry, a form called *ars poetica* (the art of poetry). Others write poetry that comments on a work in another genre—called *ekphrastic* poetry, from the Greek word *ekphrasis* (speak out). Homer's description of Achilles' shield in the *Iliad* is the oldest recorded ekphrastic work, and it has sparked an ongoing conversation in which writers continue to comment on the act of creating art in all its forms, reminding us that an emotional link exists not just between art and the viewer, but also among works of art. Look for that link in the works in this chapter.

Henry James considered the art of the writer and the art of the painter to be analogous. In his essay "The Art of Fiction," he wrote, "Their inspiration is the same, their process (allowing for the different quality of the vehicle) is the same, their success is the same. They may learn from each other, they may explain and sustain each other. Their cause is the same and the honour of one is the honour of another." Certainly "Sonny's Blues" explains what it means to be a musician, to "impos[e] order" on the "roar rising from the void." And Claude McKay truly honors the beauty and grace of the nightclub dancer in Harlem, as Frank O'Hara honors the memory of jazz singer Billie Holiday. Short-story writer Raymond Carver creates a narrator who, against the odds, is sustained and even sanctified by his experience of re-creating a work of art so that a blind man can "see" it. Alexander Pope takes up the cause of beauty in his plea that sound and sense work together. And T. S. Eliot creates the moody and isolated J. Alfred Prufrock to remind us that art might just be the saving grace of the modern world.

The Love Song of J. Alfred Prufrock

T. S. ELIOT

Poet, dramatist, and critic Thomas Stearns Eliot (1888–1965) was born and raised in St. Louis, Missouri. He moved to England when he was twenty-five, after studying at Harvard University, and eventually became a British subject. He once said that his poetry was a combination of American and British influences but that "in its sources, in its emotional springs, it comes from America." Eliot studied philosophy at Harvard and Oxford, even learning Sanskrit to study Buddhism and other Indic religions. As a young man, he worked as a teacher and wrote book reviews to earn extra money. He later worked at Lloyds Bank in London and eventually became a director of Faber & Faber, an English publishing house. His most famous works include "The Love Song of J. Alfred Prufrock," "The Wasteland" (1922), "Ash Wednesday" (1930), "Burnt Norton" (1941), "Little Gidding" (1942), "Four Quartets" (1943), and the play *Murder in the Cathedral* (1935). The musical *Cats* was based on Eliot's *Old Possum's Book of Practical Cats* (1939), which earned him Tony Awards in 1983 for best book and best score. He was awarded the Nobel Prize for Literature in 1948. Eliot is considered one of the great poetic innovators of the twentieth century and is closely associated with the modernist movement—especially in his use of stream of consciousness, a technique he uses in "The Love Song of J. Alfred Prufrock." Eliot did not compromise when it came to the language of poetry, believing that poetry should represent the complexities of modern civilization. Later in his life, Eliot advocated traditionalism in religion, society, and literature. This seems at odds with the innovations of his early poetry, but he considered tradition to be an ongoing process, uniting past and present. "The Love Song of J. Alfred Prufrock," a poem begun when Eliot was a college student and published when he was twenty-eight, is considered one of those works that epitomize the significance of poetry.

S'io credesse che mia risposta fosse
A persona che mai tornasse al mondo,
Questa fiamma staria senza più scosse.
Ma perciocchè giammai di questo fondo
Non tornò vivo alcun, s'i'odo il vero,
Senza tema d'infamia ti rispondo.[1]

---

[1] From Dante's *Inferno*, canto XXVII, 61–66. The words are spoken by Guido da Montefeltro, who was condemned to hell for providing false counsel to Pope Boniface VII. When asked to identify himself, Guido responded, "If I thought my answers were given to anyone who could ever return to the world, this flame would shake no more; but since none ever did return above from this depth, if what I hear is true, without fear of infamy I answer thee." He does not know that Dante will return to earth to report on what he has seen and heard.—EDS.

Let us go then, you and I,
When the evening is spread out against the sky
Like a patient etherized upon a table;
Let us go, through certain half-deserted streets,
The muttering retreats   5
Of restless nights in one-night cheap hotels
And sawdust restaurants with oyster-shells:
Streets that follow like a tedious argument
Of insidious intent
To lead you to an overwhelming question . . .   10
Oh, do not ask, "What is it?"
Let us go and make our visit.

In the room the women come and go
Talking of Michelangelo.

The yellow fog that rubs its back upon the window-panes,   15
The yellow smoke that rubs its muzzle on the window-panes
Licked its tongue into the corners of the evening,
Lingered upon the pools that stand in drains,
Let fall upon its back the soot that falls from chimneys,
Slipped by the terrace, made a sudden leap,   20
And seeing that it was a soft October night,
Curled once about the house, and fell asleep.

And indeed there will be time
For the yellow smoke that slides along the street,
Rubbing its back upon the window-panes;   25
There will be time, there will be time
To prepare a face to meet the faces that you meet;
There will be time to murder and create,
And time for all the works and days of hands[2]
That lift and drop a question on your plate: 30
Time for you and time for me,
And time yet for a hundred indecisions,
And for a hundred visions and revisions,
Before the taking of a toast and tea.

In the room the women come and go   35
Talking of Michelangelo.

And indeed there will be time
To wonder, "Do I dare?" and, "Do I dare?"

---

[2]Reference to the title of a poem about agricultural life by the early Greek poet Hesiod.—EDS.

Time to turn back and descend the stair,
With a bald spot in the middle of my hair—   40
[They will say: "How his hair is growing thin!"]
My morning coat, my collar mounting firmly to the chin,
My necktie rich and modest, but asserted by a simple pin—

[They will say: "But how his arms and legs are thin!"]
Do I dare   45
Disturb the universe?
In a minute there is time
For decisions and revisions which a minute will reverse.

For I have known them all already, known them all:
Have known the evenings, mornings, afternoons,   50
I have measured out my life with coffee spoons;
I know the voices dying with a dying fall
Beneath the music from a farther room.
        So how should I presume?

And I have known the eyes already, known them all—   55
The eyes that fix you in a formulated phrase.
And when I am formulated, sprawling on a pin,
When I am pinned and wriggling on the wall,
Then how should I begin
To spit out all the butt-ends of my days and ways?   60
        And how should I presume?

And I have known the arms already, known them all—
Arms that are braceleted and white and bare
[But in the lamplight, downed with light brown hair!]
Is it perfume from a dress   65
That makes me so digress?
Arms that lie along a table, or wrap about a shawl.
        And should I then presume?
        And how should I begin?

Shall I say, I have gone at dusk through narrow streets,   70
And watched the smoke that rises from the pipes
Of lonely men in shirt-sleeves, leaning out of windows? . . .

I should have been a pair of ragged claws
Scuttling across the floors of silent seas.

                . . . . .

And the afternoon, the evening, sleeps so peacefully!   75
Smoothed by long fingers,

Asleep . . . tired . . . or it malingers,
Stretched on the floor, here beside you and me.
Should I, after tea and cakes and ices,
Have the strength to force the moment to its crisis?   80
But though I have wept and fasted, wept and prayed,
Though I have seen my head (grown slightly bald) brought in
    upon a platter,[3]
I am no prophet—and here's no great matter;
I have seen the moment of my greatness flicker,
And I have seen the eternal Footman hold my coat, and snicker,   85
And in short, I was afraid.

And would it have been worth it, after all,
After the cups, the marmalade, the tea,
Among the porcelain, among some talk of you and me,
Would it have been worth while   90
To have bitten off the matter with a smile,
To have squeezed the universe into a ball
To roll it toward some overwhelming question,
To say: "I am Lazarus,[4] come from the dead,
Come back to tell you all, I shall tell you all"—   95
If one, settling a pillow by her head,
    Should say: "That is not what I meant at all.
    That is not it, at all."

And would it have been worth it, after all,
Would it have been worth while,   100
After the sunsets and the dooryards and the sprinkled streets,
After the novels, after the teacups, after the skirts that trail
    along the floor—
And this, and so much more?—
It is impossible to say just what I mean!
But as if a magic lantern threw the nerves in patterns on a screen: 105
Would it have been worth while
If one, settling a pillow or throwing off a shawl,
And turning toward the window, should say:
    "That is not it at all,
    That is not what I meant, at all."   110

----

[3]From Matthew 14:1–11. King Herod ordered the beheading of John the Baptist at the request of Herod's wife and daughter.—EDS.
[4]From John 11:1–44. Lazarus was raised from the dead by Jesus.—EDS.

. . . . .

No! I am not Prince Hamlet, nor was meant to be;
Am an attendant lord, one that will do
To swell a progress, start a scene or two,
Advise the prince: no doubt, an easy tool,
Deferential, glad to be of use,   115
Politic, cautious, and meticulous;
Full of high sentence, but a bit obtuse;
At times, indeed, almost ridiculous —
Almost, at times, the Fool.
I grow old . . . I grow old . . .   120
I shall wear the bottoms of my trousers rolled.

Shall I part my hair behind? Do I dare to eat a peach?

I shall wear white flannel trousers, and walk upon the beach.
I have heard the mermaids singing, each to each.

I do not think that they will sing to me.   125

I have seen them riding seaward on the waves
Combing the white hair of the waves blown back
When the wind blows the water white and black.
We have lingered in the chambers of the sea
By sea-girls wreathed with seaweed red and brown   130
Till human voices wake us, and we drown.

[1917]

Questions for Discussion

1. How does the epigraph from Dante's *Inferno* help Eliot comment on the modern world in "The Love Song of J. Alfred Prufrock"? What does it tell us about
   the setting of this poem? How is Montefeltro's miscalculation related to the
   poem?
2. We can assume that the speaker of the poem is Prufrock, a character Eliot creates through the use of dramatic monologue — a technique in which a speaker
   addresses a silent listener, often revealing qualities he or she might wish to
   keep hidden. What kind of person is Prufrock? What does he unknowingly
   reveal?
3. Whom is the speaker addressing? This question is more complicated than it
   seems and likely has several answers. Consider all of the possibilities. What
   does each possible listener suggest about the development of Prufrock as a
   character? How does each possibility develop another level of meaning for the
   poem?

4. One of the most demanding aspects of this poem is its allusions, as Eliot expected his readers to be as well educated as he was. Some allusions are fairly accessible. The allusions to Michelangelo — an artist most people are familiar with — in line 14 and again in line 36 help us imagine the women Prufrock is talking about. The function of the less accessible allusions — such as "works and days of hands" (l. 29) — may serve a different purpose. Why might Eliot have included such esoteric allusions? How do they affect your reading of the poem?

5. Consider the title of the poem. How is it ironic? In what ways is the poem a love song?

6. Eliot began writing this poem in 1909, when he was in college at Harvard. He continued to revise it until it was published in 1917. Some critics have commented that it is the poem of a young man, even though its narrator is middle aged. What qualities reveal the poem as a young man's work?

7. An early review of the poem in the *Times Literary Supplement* (London) stated, "The fact that these things occurred to the mind of Mr. Eliot is surely of the very smallest importance to anyone, even to himself. They certainly have no relation to *poetry*" (June 21, 1917). Do you agree?

8. Eliot was in the avant-garde as a young poet, but he considered himself a traditionalist as he got older. What are the innovative aspects of this poem? Look for evidence of the traditionalism that would get stronger as Eliot aged.

9. In what ways is "The Love Song of J. Alfred Prufrock" a poem about time? Read through the poem and look for references to time, including aging, the meaning of time, and the word *time* itself. What conclusions can you draw about the way Eliot thinks about time?

10. In what ways is this poem a poem about art?

Questions on Style and Structure

1. How does Eliot set the tone in the poem's first stanza? Look carefully at both the figurative language and the concrete details.

2. Eliot depends on the emotional associations of his images, what he called the "objective correlative," to reveal aspects of Prufrock's personality. In the first stanza, what emotions do you associate with images such as "patient etherized upon a table" (l. 3) or "one-night cheap hotels" (l. 6)?

3. The "yellow fog" that is the subject of the poem's third stanza has the qualities of a cat. Is this association threatening, comforting, or both? How does your interpretation of the fog affect your reading of the poem as a whole?

4. You may notice that the images are arranged from top to bottom — the sky to the streets in the first stanza, and the windowpanes to the drains in the third. What is the effect of the way Eliot has Prufrock guide the reader's eye and imagination?

5. Eliot uses the technique of enjambment, or run-on lines. An example is in lines 5–9: "The muttering retreats / Of restless nights in one-night cheap hotels /

And sawdust restaurants with oyster-shells: / Streets that follow like a tedious argument / Of insidious intent." How does this technique help create the alienating quality of the city scene that's set in the first 22 lines?

6. "The Love Song of J. Alfred Prufrock" is like a collage, a work of visual art created by materials and objects glued to a flat surface. In poetry this technique is called fragmentation, a favorite technique of the modernists. The fragments come together—or don't—in a way that mirrors the fragmented, chaotic modern world. In the fourth stanza, for example, what is the effect of fragments such as "yellow smoke," "murder and create," "visions and revisions," and "toast and tea" appearing together? Do they form a new picture, or are their effects fragmentary? How do the fragments communicate Eliot's vision of a modern man in a modern city?

7. What do you make of the occasional rhyming in the midst of unrhymed free verse? Note especially the two repeated stanzas: "In the room the women come and go / Talking of Michelangelo." How does this irregular rhyme scheme reflect and reveal the character of the speaker and the setting of the poem?

8. The middle section (ll. 37–86) of this poem moves from the chaotic city setting into the fragmented, anxiety-ridden mind of the speaker. How is Prufrock's physical description developed in lines 37–44? How do Prufrock's physical characteristics connect to emotional states?

9. Prufrock is a deeply self-conscious character. Explain the various ways that characteristic is developed in lines 37–72. Consider especially lines 55–58, in which Prufrock imagines himself pinned like a specimen to a wall.

10. From line 37 to line 87, twelve lines begin with "And." What does the repetition of that conjunction suggest about Prufrock's mental state?

11. "The Love Song of J. Alfred Prufrock" makes several allusions to metaphysical poet Andrew Marvell's "To His Coy Mistress" (p. 693). "And indeed there will be time" (ll. 23, 37) alludes to that poem's first lines, in which the speaker urges his lady friend to consummate their relationship by reminding her how fast time flies: "Had we but world enough, and time / This coyness, lady, were no crime." Later, "To have squeezed the universe into a ball" (l. 92) alludes to the end of Marvell's poem, in which the speaker makes one last pitch: "Let us roll all our strength and all / Our sweetness up into one ball." How do we know that Prufrock's purpose is different? What is the effect of alluding to Marvell's flirtatious, self-confident poem?

12. Prufrock claims to have seen "Arms that are braceleted and white and bare" (l. 63), an allusion to metaphysical poet John Donne's "The Relic," in which the speaker imagines that when his grave and the grave of his beloved are dug up, the gravedigger will see the bracelet of his beloved's hair encircling the bones of his arm, and will leave them alone. Critics have said that Donne invented the idea of modern love as private, as opposed to the feudal idea of love being social. How does this allusion, and the concrete image itself, help develop the character of Prufrock? What do you think is Eliot's take on the idea of modern, private love?

13. In line 111, Prufrock readily admits he is no Hamlet. What might have led the reader to believe that Prufrock and Hamlet share characteristics? What characteristics of Hamlet does Prufrock claim not to have?

14. What is the effect of the semicolons and ellipses in lines 111–121? What do they tell you about Prufrock's state of mind?

15. Details such as Prufrock's assertion that he will "wear the bottom of [his] trousers rolled" (l. 121) or his question about whether he should "dare to eat a peach" (l. 122) have been interpreted in many ways. One is that they reveal his anxieties about aging—he may be too old for the bohemian style of rolled trousers or he may break a tooth on a peach pit. Another interpretation is that they are related to his nervousness around women. Consider several possibilities. How does each add to the portrait of Prufrock and the multiple meanings of Eliot's poem?

16. The last six lines of this poem form a sestet (6 lines), the form that both ends the traditional Petrarchan sonnet and offers a solution for the problem or conflict set out in the first eight lines (the octave). The poet Petrarch wrote about his unrequited love for Laura, but Prufrock doesn't even have an unrequited love. Do these last six lines offer any solutions? How does the image of mermaids continue some of the poem's motifs? What does it mean that Prufrock invites the reader to drown with him at the end of the poem?

Suggestions for Writing

1. Critic Roland Barthes has said, "Literature is the question minus the answer." "The Love Song of J. Alfred Prufrock" is filled with questions. Write an essay in which you analyze one or more of the poem's questions and the extent to which the poem does or does not offer answers.

2. Write an essay in which you argue that Prufrock is a particular age. Use evidence from the poem to support your argument.

3. Humorist Garrison Keillor accused Eliot's character Prufrock of "killing off the pleasure of poetry." Others argue that the poem is actually funny if it is read carefully. Write an essay in which you defend, challenge, or qualify Keillor's statement.

4. Imagine that you are one of the women who say, "That is not what I meant at all. / That is not it, at all" (ll. 97–98, and similarly in ll. 109–110). In a poem, essay, or short story, explain what you mean by those words.

5. Write an essay in which you compare and contrast Prufrock either to Hamlet or to one of Shakespeare's fools, such as the one in *King Lear* or Puck in *A Midsummer Night's Dream*.

Sonny's Blues

James Baldwin

James Baldwin (1924–1987)—poet, novelist, playwright, essayist, activist—was one of the most influential figures of American literature during the latter half of the twentieth century. Born in Harlem to a single mother, he was later adopted by his stepfather, who was a preacher. Baldwin himself became a Pentecostal preacher when he was fourteen, but by the time he was seventeen, he had moved away from his family in Harlem to live among more open-minded artists and writers in Greenwich Village. In the late 1940s, Baldwin went to Europe, where he lived as an expatriate in France—and periodically in Turkey—for most of his life, returning to the United States to lecture and write. He felt that the United States of the midcentury was inimical to artists, especially black artists. In addition to the novels *Go Tell It on the Mountain* (1953), *Giovanni's Room* (1956), *If Beale Street Could Talk* (1974), and *Just Above My Head* (1979), Baldwin wrote *Notes of a Native Son* (1955) and *The Fire Next Time* (1963)—two explosive books that gave passionate voice to the civil rights movement. Baldwin also wrote poetry, plays, and essays. In "Sonny's Blues," Baldwin examines the connection between suffering and art. As he once said about his friend Beauford Delaney, a painter whose work was not appreciated during his lifetime: "I do not know, nor will any of us really know, what kind of strength it was that enabled him to make so dogged and splendid a journey." "Sonny's Blues," which was first published in 1957 in the *Partisan Review*, examines that journey in the context of a pair of brothers, one a musician, the other a math teacher.

I read about it in the paper, in the subway, on my way to work. I read it, and I couldn't believe it, and I read it again. Then perhaps I just stared at it, at the newsprint spelling out his name, spelling out the story. I stared at it in the swinging lights of the subway car, and in the faces and bodies of the people, and in my own face, trapped in the darkness which roared outside.

It was not to be believed and I kept telling myself that, as I walked from the subway station to the high school. And at the same time I couldn't doubt it. I was scared, scared for Sonny. He became real to me again. A great block of ice got settled in my belly and kept melting there slowly all day long, while I taught my classes algebra. It was a special kind of ice. It kept melting, sending trickles of ice water all up and down my veins, but it never got less. Sometimes it hardened and seemed to expand until I felt my guts were going to come spilling out or that I was going to choke or scream. This would always be at a moment when I was remembering some specific thing Sonny had once said or done.

When he was about as old as the boys in my classes his face had been bright and open, there was a lot of copper in it; and he'd had wonderfully direct brown eyes, and great gentleness and privacy. I wondered what he looked like now. He had been picked up, the evening before, in a raid on an apartment downtown, for peddling and using heroin.

I couldn't believe it: but what I mean by that is that I couldn't find any room for it anywhere inside me. I had kept it outside me for a long time. I hadn't wanted to know. I had had suspicions, but I didn't name them, I kept putting them away. I told myself that Sonny was wild, but he wasn't crazy. And he'd always been a good boy, he hadn't ever turned hard or evil or disrespectful, the way kids can, so quick, so quick, especially in Harlem. I didn't want to believe that I'd ever see my brother going down, coming to nothing, all that light in his face gone out, in the condition I'd already seen so many others. Yet it had happened and here I was, talking about algebra to a lot of boys who might, every one of them for all I knew, be popping off needles every time they went to the head. Maybe it did more for them than algebra could.

I was sure that the first time Sonny had ever had horse, he couldn't have been   5
much older than these boys were now. These boys, now, were living as we'd been living then, they were growing up with a rush and their heads bumped abruptly against the low ceiling of their actual possibilities. They were filled with rage. All they really knew were two darknesses, the darkness of their lives, which was now closing in on them, and the darkness of the movies, which had blinded them to that other darkness, and in which they now, vindictively, dreamed, at once more together than they were at any other time, and more alone.

When the last bell rang, the last class ended, I let out my breath. It seemed I'd been holding it for all that time. My clothes were wet—I may have looked as though I'd been sitting in a steam bath, all dressed up, all afternoon. I sat alone in the classroom a long time. I listened to the boys outside, downstairs, shouting and cursing and laughing. Their laughter struck me for perhaps the first time. It was not the joyous laughter which—God knows why—one associates with children. It was mocking and insular, its intent to denigrate. It was disenchanted, and in this, also, lay the authority of their curses. Perhaps I was listening to them because I was thinking about my brother and in them I heard my brother. And myself.

One boy was whistling a tune, at once very complicated and very simple, it seemed to be pouring out of him as though he were a bird, and it sounded very cool and moving through all that harsh, bright air, only just holding its own through all those other sounds.

I stood up and walked over to the window and looked down into the courtyard. It was the beginning of the spring and the sap was rising in the boys. A teacher passed through them every now and again, quickly, as though he or she couldn't wait to get out of that courtyard, to get those boys out of their sight and off their minds. I started collecting my stuff. I thought I'd better get home and talk to Isabel.

The courtyard was almost deserted by the time I got downstairs. I saw this boy standing in the shadow of a doorway, looking just like Sonny. I almost called his name. Then I saw that it wasn't Sonny, but somebody we used to know, a boy from around our block. He'd been Sonny's friend. He'd never been mine, having been too young for me, and, anyway, I'd never liked him. And now, even though he was a grown-up man, he still hung around that block, still spent hours on the street corners, was always high and raggy. I used to run into him from time to time and he'd often work around to asking me for a quarter or fifty cents. He always had some real good excuse, too, and I always gave it to him, I don't know why. *Character*

But now, abruptly, I hated him. I couldn't stand the way he looked at me, partly   10
like a dog, partly like a cunning child. I wanted to ask him what the hell he was doing in the school courtyard.

He sort of shuffled over to me, and he said, "I see you got the papers. So you already know about it."

"You mean about Sonny? Yes, I already know about it. How come they didn't get you?"

He grinned. It made him repulsive and it also brought to mind what he'd looked like as a kid. "I wasn't there. I stay away from them people."

"Good for you." I offered him a cigarette and I watched him through the smoke. "You come all the way down here just to tell me about Sonny?"

"That's right." He was sort of shaking his head and his eyes looked strange, as   15
though they were about to cross. The bright sun deadened his damp dark brown skin and it made his eyes look yellow and showed up the dirt in his kinked hair. He smelled funky. I moved a little away from him and I said, "Well, thanks. But I already know about it and I got to get home."

"I'll walk you a little ways," he said. We started walking. There were a couple of kids still loitering in the courtyard and one of them said goodnight to me and looked strangely at the boy beside me.   *Dialogue*

"What're you going to do?" he asked me. "I mean, about Sonny?"

"Look. I haven't seen Sonny for over a year. I'm not sure I'm going to do anything. Anyway, what the hell *can* I do?"

"That's right," he said quickly, "ain't nothing you can do. Can't much help old Sonny no more, I guess."

It was what I was thinking and so it seemed to me he had no right to say it.   20

"I'm surprised at Sonny, though," he went on—he had a funny way of talking, he looked straight ahead as though he were talking to himself—"I thought Sonny was a smart boy, I thought he was too smart to get hung."

"I guess he thought so too," I said sharply, "and that's how he got hung. And how about you? You're pretty goddamn smart, I bet."

Then he looked directly at me, just for a minute. "I ain't smart," he said. "If I was smart, I'd have reached for a pistol a long time ago."

"Look. Don't tell *me* your sad story, if it was up to me, I'd give you one." Then I felt guilty—guilty, probably, for never having supposed that the poor bastard *had* a story of his own, much less a sad one, and I asked, quickly, "What's going to happen to him now?"

He didn't answer this. He was off by himself some place. "Funny thing," he said,   25
and from his tone we might have been discussing the quickest way to get to Brooklyn, "when I saw the papers this morning, the first thing I asked myself was if I had anything to do with it. I felt sort of responsible."

Seeing the child in the adult in the child

Why does he do this?

I began to listen more carefully. The subway station was on the corner, just before us, and I stopped. He stopped, too. We were in front of a bar and he ducked slightly, peering in, but whoever he was looking for didn't seem to be there. The juke box was blasting away with something black and bouncy and I half watched the barmaid as she danced her way from the juke box to her place behind the bar. And I watched her face as she laughingly responded to something someone said to her, still keeping time to the music. When she smiled one saw the little girl, one sensed the doomed, still-struggling woman beneath the battered face of the semi-whore.

What is it?

"I never *give* Sonny nothing," the boy said finally, "but a long time ago I come to school high and Sonny asked me how it felt." He paused, I couldn't bear to watch him, I watched the barmaid, and I listened to the music which seemed to be causing the pavement to shake. "I told him it felt great." The music stopped, the barmaid paused and watched the juke box until the music began again. "It did."

All this was carrying me some place I didn't want to go. I certainly didn't want to know how it felt. It filled everything, the people, the houses, the music, the dark, quicksilver barmaid, with menace; and this menace was their reality.

"What's going to happen to him now?" I asked again.

"They'll send him away some place and they'll try to cure him." He shook his head. "Maybe he'll even think he's kicked the habit. Then they'll let him loose"—he gestured, throwing his cigarette into the gutter. "That's all."

"What do you mean, that's *all*?"

But I knew what he meant.

"I *mean*, that's *all*." He turned his head and looked at me, pulling down the corners of his mouth. "Don't you know what I mean?" he asked, softly.

"How the hell *would* I know what you mean?" I almost whispered it, I don't know why.

"That's right," he said to the air, "how would *he* know what I mean?" He turned toward me again, patient and calm, and yet I somehow felt him shaking, shaking as though he were going to fall apart. I felt that ice in my guts again, the dread I'd felt all afternoon; and again I watched the barmaid, moving about the bar, washing glasses, and singing. "Listen. They'll let him out and then it'll just start all over again. That's what I mean."

"You mean—they'll let him out. And then he'll just start working his way back in again. You mean he'll never kick the habit. Is that what you mean?"

"That's right," he said, cheerfully. "*You* see what I mean."

"Tell me," I said at last, "why does he want to die? He must want to die, he's killing himself, why does he want to die?"

He looked at me in surprise. He licked his lips. "He don't want to die. He wants to live. Don't nobody want to die, ever."

Then I wanted to ask him—too many things. He could not have answered, or if he had, I could not have borne the answers. I started walking. "Well, I guess it's none of my business."

"It's going to be rough on old Sonny," he said. We reached the subway station. "This is your station?" he asked. I nodded. I took one step down. "Damn!"

30

35

40

he said, suddenly. I looked up at him. He grinned again. "Damn it if I didn't leave all my money home. You ain't got a dollar on you, have you? Just for a couple of days, is all."

All at once something inside gave and threatened to come pouring out of me. I didn't hate him any more. I felt that in another moment I'd start crying like a child. *child*

"Sure," I said. "Don't sweat." I looked in my wallet and didn't have a dollar, I only had a five. "Here," I said. "That hold you?"

He didn't look at it—he didn't want to look at it. A terrible closed look came over his face, as though he were keeping the number on the bill a secret from him and me. "Thanks," he said, and now he was dying to see me go. "Don't worry about Sonny. Maybe I'll write him or something."

"Sure," I said. "You do that. So long."

"Be seeing you," he said. I went on down the steps.

And I didn't write Sonny or send him anything for a long time. When I finally did, it was just after my little girl died, he wrote me back a letter which made me feel like a bastard. *Whoa.*

Here's what he said:

DEAR BROTHER,

You don't know how much I needed to hear from you. I wanted to write you many a time but I dug how much I must have hurt you and so I didn't write. But now I feel like a man who's been trying to climb up out of some deep, real deep and funky hole and just saw the sun up there, outside. I got to get outside. *Dark/light*

I can't tell you much about how I got here. I mean I don't know how to tell you. I guess I was afraid of something or I was trying to escape from something and you know I have never been very strong in the head (smile). I'm glad Mama and Daddy are dead and can't see what's happened to their son and I swear if I'd known what I was doing I would never have hurt you so, you and a lot of other fine people who were nice to me and who believed in me.

I don't want you to think it had anything to do with me being a musician. It's more than that. Or maybe less than that. I can't get anything straight in my head down here and I try not to think about what's going to happen to me when I get outside again. Sometime I think I'm going to flip and *never* get outside and sometime I think I'll come straight back. I tell you one thing, though, I'd rather blow my brains out than go through this again. But that's what they all say, so they tell me. If I tell you when I'm coming to New York and if you could meet me, I sure would appreciate it. Give my love to Isabel and the kids and I was sure sorry to hear about little Gracie. I wish I could be like Mama and say the Lord's will be done, but I don't know it seems to me that trouble is the one thing that never does get stopped and I don't know what good it does to blame it on the Lord. But maybe it does some good if you believe it.

Your brother,
SONNY

45

Then I kept in constant touch with him and I sent him whatever I could and I went to meet him when he came back to New York. When I saw him many things I thought I had forgotten came flooding back to me. This was because I had begun, finally, to wonder about Sonny, about the life that Sonny lived inside. This life, whatever it was, had made him older and thinner and it had deepened the distant stillness in which he had always moved. He looked very unlike my baby brother. Yet, when he smiled, when we shook hands, the baby brother I'd never known looked out from the depths of his private life, like an animal waiting to be coaxed into the light.

"How you been keeping?" he asked me.   50

"All right. And you?"

"Just fine." He was smiling all over his face. "It's good to see you again."

"It's good to see you."

The seven years' difference in our ages lay between us like a chasm: I wondered if these years would ever operate between us as a bridge. I was remembering, and it made it hard to catch my breath, that I had been there when he was born; and I had heard the first words he had ever spoken. When he started to walk, he walked from our mother straight to me. I caught him just before he fell when he took the first steps he ever took in this world.

"How's Isabel?"   55

"Just fine. She's dying to see you."

"And the boys?"

"They're fine, too. They're anxious to see their uncle."

"Oh, come on. You know they don't remember me."

"Are you kidding? Of course they remember you."   60

He grinned again. We got into a taxi. We had a lot to say to each other, far too much to know how to begin.

As the taxi began to move, I asked, "You still want to go to India?"

He laughed. "You still remember that. Hell, no. This place is Indian enough for me."

"It used to belong to them," I said.

And he laughed again. "They damn sure knew what they were doing when they   65
got rid of it."

Years ago, when he was around fourteen, he'd been all hipped on the idea of going to India. He read books about people sitting on rocks, naked, in all kinds of weather, but mostly bad, naturally, and walking barefoot through hot coals and arriving at wisdom. I used to say that it sounded to me as though they were getting away from wisdom as fast as they could. I think he sort of looked down on me for that.

"Do you mind," he asked, "if we have the driver drive alongside the park? On the west side—I haven't seen the city in so long."

"Of course not," I said. I was afraid that I might sound as though I were humoring him, but I hoped he wouldn't take it that way.

So we drove along, between the green of the park and the stony, lifeless elegance of hotels and apartment buildings, toward the vivid, killing streets of our childhood.

These streets hadn't changed, though housing projects jutted up out of them now like rocks in the middle of a boiling sea. Most of the houses in which we had grown up had vanished, as had the stores from which we had stolen, the basements in which we had first tried sex, the rooftops from which we had hurled tin cans and bricks. But houses exactly like the houses of our past yet dominated the landscape, boys exactly like the boys we once had been found themselves smothering in these houses, came down into the streets for light and air and found themselves encircled by disaster. Some escaped the trap, most didn't. Those who got out always left something of themselves behind, as some animals amputate a leg and leave it in the trap. It might be said, perhaps, that I had escaped, after all, I was a school teacher; or that Sonny had, he hadn't lived in Harlem for years. Yet, as the cab moved uptown through streets which seemed, with a rush, to darken with dark people, and as I covertly studied Sonny's face, it came to me that what we both were seeking through our separate cab windows was that part of ourselves which had been left behind. It's always at the hour of trouble and confrontation that the missing member aches.

We hit 110th Street and started rolling up Lenox Avenue. And I'd known this 70 avenue all my life, but it seemed to me again, as it had seemed on the day I'd first heard about Sonny's trouble, filled with a hidden menace which was its very breath of life.

"We almost there," said Sonny.

"Almost." We were both too nervous to say anything more.

We live in a housing project. It hasn't been up long. A few days after it was up it seemed uninhabitably new, now, of course, it's already rundown. It looks like a parody of the good, clean, faceless life—God knows the people who live in it do their best to make it a parody. The beat-looking grass lying around isn't enough to make their lives green, the hedges will never hold out the streets, and they know it. The big windows fool no one, they aren't big enough to make space out of no space. They don't bother with the windows, they watch the TV screen instead. The playground is most popular with the children who don't play at jacks, or skip rope, or roller skate, or swing, and they can be found in it after dark. We moved in partly because it's not too far from where I teach, and partly for the kids; but it's really just like the houses in which Sonny and I grew up. The same things happen, they'll have the same things to remember. The moment Sonny and I started into the house I had the feeling that I was simply bringing him back into the danger he had almost died trying to escape.

Sonny has never been talkative. So I don't know why I was sure he'd be dying to talk to me when supper was over the first night. Everything went fine, the oldest boy remembered him, and the youngest boy liked him, and Sonny had remembered to bring something for each of them; and Isabel, who is really much nicer than I am, more open and giving, had gone to a lot of trouble about dinner and was genuinely glad to see him. And she's always been able to tease Sonny in a way that I haven't. It was nice to see her face so vivid again and to hear her laugh and watch her make Sonny laugh. She wasn't, or, anyway, she didn't seem to be, at all uneasy or embarrassed. She chatted as though there were no subject which had to be avoided and she got Sonny past his first, faint stiffness. And thank God she was there, for I was filled with that icy dread again. Everything I did seemed awkward to me, and everything I said sounded freighted with hidden meaning. I was trying to remember everything I'd heard about dope addiction and I couldn't help watching Sonny for signs. I wasn't doing it out of malice. I was trying to find out something about my brother. I was dying to hear him tell me he was safe.

"Safe!" my father grunted, whenever Mama suggested trying to move to a neighborhood which might be safer for children. "Safe, hell! Ain't no place safe for kids, nor nobody."

He always went on like this, but he wasn't, ever, really as bad as he sounded, not even on weekends, when he got drunk. As a matter of fact, he was always on the lookout for "something a little better," but he died before he found it. He died suddenly, during a drunken weekend in the middle of the war, when Sonny was fifteen. He and Sonny hadn't ever got on too well. And this was partly because Sonny was the apple of his father's eye. It was because he loved Sonny so much and was frightened for him, that he was always fighting with him. It doesn't do any good to fight with Sonny. Sonny just moves back, inside himself, where he can't be reached. But the principal reason that they never hit it off is that they were so much alike. Daddy was big and rough and loud-talking, just the opposite of Sonny, but they both had—that same privacy.

Mama tried to tell me something about this, just after Daddy died. I was home on leave from the army.

This was the last time I ever saw my mother alive. Just the same, this picture gets all mixed up in my mind with pictures I had of her when she was younger. The way I always see her is the way she used to be on a Sunday afternoon, say, when the old folks were talking after the big Sunday dinner. I always see her wearing pale blue. She'd be sitting on the sofa. And my father would be sitting in the easy chair, not far from her. And the living room would be full of church folks and relatives. There they sit, in chairs all around the living room, and the night is creeping up outside, but nobody knows it yet. You can see the darkness growing against the windowpanes and you hear the street noises every now and again, or maybe the jangling beat of a tambourine from one of the churches close by, but it's real quiet in the room. For a moment nobody's talking, but every face looks darkening, like the sky outside. And my mother rocks a little from the waist, and my father's eyes are closed. Everyone is looking at something a child can't see. For a minute they've forgotten the children. Maybe a kid is lying on the rug, half asleep. Maybe somebody's got a kid in his lap and is absent-mindedly stroking the kid's head. Maybe there's a kid, quiet and big-eyed, curled up in a big chair in the corner. The silence, the darkness coming, and the darkness in the faces frightens the child obscurely. He hopes that the hand which strokes his forehead will never stop—will never die. He hopes that there will never come a time when the old folks won't be sitting around the living room, talking about where they've come from, and what they've seen, and what's happened to them and their kinfolk.

But something deep and watchful in the child knows that this is bound to end, is already ending. In a moment someone will get up and turn on the light. Then the old folks will remember the children and they won't talk any more that day. And when light fills the room, the child is filled with darkness. He knows that every time this happens he's moved just a little closer to that darkness outside. The darkness outside is what the old folks have been talking about. It's what they've come from. It's what they endure. The child knows that they won't talk any more because if he knows too much about what's happened to *them*, he'll know too much too soon, about what's going to happen to *him*.

The last time I talked to my mother, I remember I was restless. I wanted to get out and see Isabel. We weren't married then and we had a lot to straighten out between us.

There Mama sat, in black, by the window. She was humming an old church song, *Lord, you brought me from a long ways off.* Sonny was out somewhere. Mama kept watching the streets.

"I don't know," she said, "if I'll ever see you again, after you go off from here. But I hope you'll remember the things I tried to teach you."

"Don't talk like that," I said, and smiled. "You'll be here a long time yet."

She smiled, too, but she said nothing. She was quiet for a long time. And I said, "Mama, don't you worry about nothing. I'll be writing all the time, and you be getting the checks. . . ."

"I want to talk to you about your brother," she said, suddenly. "If anything happens to me he ain't going to have nobody to look out for him."

"Mama," I said, "ain't nothing going to happen to you *or* Sonny. Sonny's all right. He's a good boy and he's got good sense."

"It ain't a question of his being a good boy," Mama said, "nor of his having good sense. It ain't only the bad ones, nor yet the dumb ones that gets sucked under." She stopped, looking at me. "Your Daddy once had a brother," she said, and she smiled in a way that made me feel she was in pain. "You didn't never know that, did you?"

"No," I said, "I never knew that," and I watched her face.

"Oh, yes," she said, "your Daddy had a brother." She looked out of the window again. "I know you never saw your Daddy cry. But *I* did—many a time, through all these years."

I asked her, "What happened to his brother? How come nobody's ever talked about him?"

This was the first time I ever saw my mother look old.

"His brother got killed," she said, "when he was just a little younger than you are now. I knew him. He was a fine boy. He was maybe a little full of the devil, but he didn't mean nobody no harm."

Then she stopped and the room was silent, exactly as it had sometimes been on those Sunday afternoons. Mama kept looking out into the streets.

"He used to have a job in the mill," she said, "and, like all young folks, he just liked to perform on Saturday nights. Saturday nights, him and your father would drift around to different places, go to dances and things like that, or just sit around with people they knew, and your father's brother would sing, he had a fine voice, and play along with himself on his guitar. Well, this particular Saturday night, him and your father was coming home from some place, and they were both a little drunk and there was a moon that night, it was bright like day. Your father's brother was feeling kind of good, and he was whistling to himself, and he had his guitar slung over his shoulder. They was coming down a hill and beneath them was a road that turned off from the highway. Well, your father's brother, being always kind of frisky, decided to run down this hill, and he did, with that guitar banging and clanging behind him, and he ran across the road, and he was making water behind a tree. And your father was sort of amused at him and he was still coming down the hill, kind of slow. Then he heard a car motor and that same minute his brother stepped from behind the tree, into the road, in the moonlight. And he started to cross the road. And your father started to run down the hill, he says he don't know why. This car was full of white men. They was all drunk, and when they seen your father's brother they let out a great whoop and holler and they aimed the car straight at him. They was having fun, they just wanted to scare him, the way they do sometimes, you know. But they was drunk. And I guess the boy, being drunk, too, and scared, kind of lost his head. By the time he jumped it was too late. Your father says he heard his brother scream when the car rolled over him, and he heard the wood of that guitar when it give, and he heard them strings go flying, and he heard them white men shouting, and the car kept on a-going and it ain't stopped till this day. And, time your father got down the hill, his brother weren't nothing but blood and pulp."

Tears were gleaming on my mother's face. There wasn't anything I could say.   95

"He never mentioned it," she said, "because I never let him mention it before you children. Your Daddy was like a crazy man that night and for many a night thereafter. He says he never in his life seen anything as dark as that road after the lights of that car had gone away. Weren't nothing, weren't nobody on that road, just your Daddy and his brother and that busted guitar. Oh, yes. Your Daddy never did really get right again. Till the day he died he weren't sure but that every white man he saw was the man that killed his brother."

She stopped and took out her handkerchief and dried her eyes and looked at me.

"I ain't telling you all this," she said, "to make you scared or bitter or to make you hate nobody. I'm telling you this because you got a brother. And the world ain't changed."

I guess I didn't want to believe this. I guess she saw this in my face. She turned away from me, toward the window again, searching those streets.

"But I praise my Redeemer," she said at last, "that He called your Daddy home   100 before me. I ain't saying it to throw no flowers at myself, but, I declare, it keeps me from feeling too cast down to know I helped your father get safely through this world. Your father always acted like he was the roughest, strongest man on earth. And everybody took him to be like that. But if he hadn't had *me* there—to see his tears!"

She was crying again. Still, I couldn't move. I said, "Lord, Lord, Mama, I didn't know it was like that."

"Oh, honey," she said, "there's a lot that you don't know. But you are going to find it out." She stood up from the window and came over to me. "You got to hold on to your brother," she said, "and don't let him fall, no matter what it looks like is happening to him and no matter how evil you gets with him. You going to be evil with him many a time. But don't you forget what I told you, you hear?"

"I won't forget," I said. "Don't you worry, I won't forget. I won't let nothing happen to Sonny."

My mother smiled as though she were amused at something she saw in my face. Then, "You may not be able to stop nothing from happening. But you got to let him know you's *there*."

Two days later I was married, and then I was gone. And I had a lot of things on my mind and I pretty well forgot my promise to Mama until I got shipped home on a special furlough for her funeral.

And, after the funeral, with just Sonny and me alone in the empty kitchen, I tried to find out something about him.

"What do you want to do?" I asked him.

"I'm going to be a musician," he said.

For he had graduated, in the time I had been away, from dancing to the juke box to finding out who was playing what, and what they were doing with it, and he had bought himself a set of drums.

"You mean, you want to be a drummer?" I somehow had the feeling that being a drummer might be all right for other people but not for my brother Sonny.

"I don't think," he said, looking at me very gravely, "that I'll ever be a good drummer. But I think I can play a piano."

I frowned. I'd never played the role of the older brother quite so seriously before, had scarcely ever, in fact, *asked* Sonny a damn thing. I sensed myself in the presence of something I didn't really know how to handle, didn't understand. So I made my frown a little deeper as I asked: "What kind of musician do you want to be?"

He grinned. "How many kinds do you think there are?"

"Be *serious*," I said.

He laughed, throwing his head back, and then looked at me. "I *am* serious."

"Well, then, for Christ's sake, stop kidding around and answer a serious question. I mean, do you want to be a concert pianist, you want to play classical music and all that, or—or what?" Long before I finished he was laughing again. "For Christ's *sake*, Sonny!"

He sobered, but with difficulty. "I'm sorry. But you sound so—*scared*!" and he was off again.

"Well, you may think it's funny now, baby, but it's not going to be so funny when you have to make your living at it, let me tell you *that*." I was furious because I knew he was laughing at me and I didn't know why.

"No," he said, very sober now, and afraid, perhaps, that he'd hurt me, "I don't want to be a classical pianist. That isn't what interests me. I mean"—he paused, looking hard at me, as though his eyes would help me to understand, and then gestured helplessly, as though perhaps his hand would help—"I mean, I'll have a lot of studying to do, and I'll have to study *everything*, but, I mean, I want to play *with*—jazz musicians." He stopped. "I want to play jazz," he said.

105

110

115

Well, the word had never before sounded as heavy, as real, as it sounded that   120
afternoon in Sonny's mouth. I just looked at him and I was probably frowning a real
frown by this time. I simply couldn't see why on earth he'd want to spend his time
hanging around nightclubs, clowning around on bandstands, while people pushed
each other around a dance floor. It seemed—beneath him, somehow. I had never
thought about it before, had never been forced to, but I suppose I had always put jazz
musicians in a class with what Daddy called "good-time people."

"Are you *serious*?"

"Hell, *yes*, I'm serious."

He looked more helpless than ever, and annoyed, and deeply hurt.

I suggested, helpfully: "You mean—like Louis Armstrong?"

His face closed as though I'd struck him. "No. I'm not talking about none of that   125
old-time, down home crap."

"Well, look, Sonny, I'm sorry, don't get mad. I just don't altogether get it, that's
all. Name somebody—you know, a jazz musician you admire."

"Bird."

"Who?"

"Bird! Charlie Parker! Don't they teach you nothing in the goddamn army?"

I lit a cigarette. I was surprised and then a little amused to discover that I was   130
trembling. "I've been out of touch," I said. "You'll have to be patient with me. Now.
Who's this Parker character?"

"He's just one of the greatest jazz musicians alive," said Sonny, sullenly, his hands
in his pockets, his back to me. "Maybe *the* greatest," he added, bitterly, "that's probably why *you* never heard of him."

"All right," I said, "I'm ignorant. I'm sorry. I'll go out and buy all the cat's records
right away, all right?"

"It don't," said Sonny, with dignity, "make any difference to me. I don't care what
you listen to. Don't do me no favors."

I was beginning to realize that I'd never seen him so upset before. With another
part of my mind I was thinking that this would probably turn out to be one of those
things kids go through and that I shouldn't make it seem important by pushing it
too hard. Still, I didn't think it would do any harm to ask: "Doesn't all this take a lot
of time? Can you make a living at it?"

He turned back to me and half leaned, half sat, on the kitchen table. "Everything   135
takes time," he said, "and—well, yes, sure, I can make a living at it. But what I don't
seem to be able to make you understand is that it's the only thing I want to do."

"Well, Sonny," I said, gently, "you know people can't always do exactly what they
want to do—"

"*No*, I don't know that," said Sonny, surprising me. "I think people *ought* to do
what they want to do, what else are they alive for?"

"You getting to be a big boy," I said desperately, "it's time you started thinking
about your future."

"I'm thinking about my future," said Sonny, grimly. "I think about it all the
time."

I gave up. I decided, if he didn't change his mind, that we could always talk about 140
it later. "In the meantime," I said, "you got to finish school." We had already decided
that he'd have to move in with Isabel and her folks. I knew this wasn't the ideal
arrangement because Isabel's folks are inclined to be dicty and they hadn't especially
wanted Isabel to marry me. But I didn't know what else to do. "And we have to get
you fixed up at Isabel's."

There was a long silence. He moved from the kitchen table to the window.
"That's a terrible idea. You know it yourself."

"Do you have a *better* idea?"

He just walked up and down the kitchen for a minute. He was as tall as I was. He
had started to shave. I suddenly had the feeling that I didn't know him at all.

He stopped at the kitchen table and picked up my cigarettes. Looking at me with
a kind of mocking, amused defiance, he put one between his lips. "You mind?"

"You smoking already?" 145

He lit the cigarette and nodded, watching me through the smoke. "I just wanted
to see if I'd have the courage to smoke in front of you." He grinned and blew a great
cloud of smoke to the ceiling. "It was easy." He looked at my face. "Come on, now. I
bet you was smoking at my age, tell the truth."

I didn't say anything but the truth was on my face, and he laughed. But now
there was something very strained in his laugh. "Sure. And I bet that ain't all you was
doing."

He was frightening me a little. "Cut the crap," I said. "We already decided that
you was going to go and live at Isabel's. Now what's got into you all of a sudden?"

"*You* decided it," he pointed out. "*I* didn't decide nothing." He stopped in front of
me, leaning against the stove, arms loosely folded. "Look, brother. I don't want to stay
in Harlem no more, I really don't." He was very earnest. He looked at me, then over
toward the kitchen window. There was something in his eyes I'd never seen before,
some thoughtfulness, some worry all his own. He rubbed the muscle of one arm. "It's
time I was getting out of here."

"Where do you want to *go*, Sonny?" 150

"I want to join the army. Or the navy, I don't care. If I say I'm old enough, they'll
believe me."

Then I got mad. It was because I was so scared. "You must be crazy. You goddamn fool, what the hell do you want to go and join the *army* for?"

"I just told you. To get out of Harlem."

"Sonny, you haven't even finished *school*. And if you really want to be a musician,
how do you expect to study if you're in the *army*?"

He looked at me, trapped, and in anguish. "There's ways. I might be able to work 155
out some kind of deal. Anyway, I'll have the G.I. Bill when I come out."

"*If* you come out." We stared at each other. "Sonny, please. Be reasonable. I know
the setup is far from perfect. But we got to do the best we can."

"I ain't learning nothing in school," he said. "Even when I go." He turned away
from me and opened the window and threw his cigarette out into the narrow alley.
I watched his back. "At least, I ain't learning nothing you'd want me to learn." He

slammed the window so hard I thought the glass would fly out, and turned back to me. "And I'm sick of the stink of these garbage cans!"

"Sonny," I said, "I know how you feel. But if you don't finish school now, you're going to be sorry later that you didn't." I grabbed him by the shoulders. "And you only got another year. It ain't so bad. And I'll come back and I swear I'll help you do *whatever* you want to do. Just try to put up with it till I come back. Will you please do that? For me?"

He didn't answer and he wouldn't look at me.

"Sonny. You hear me?"

He pulled away. "I hear you. But you never hear anything *I* say."

I didn't know what to say to that. He looked out of the window and then back at me. "OK," he said, and sighed. "I'll try."

Then I said, trying to cheer him up a little, "They got a piano at Isabel's. You can practice on it."

And as a matter of fact, it did cheer him up for a minute. "That's right," he said to himself. "I forgot that." His face relaxed a little. But the worry, the thoughtfulness, played on it still, the way shadows play on a face which is staring into the fire.

But I thought I'd never hear the end of that piano. At first, Isabel would write me, saying how nice it was that Sonny was so serious about his music and how, as soon as he came in from school, or wherever he had been when he was supposed to be at school, he went straight to that piano and stayed there until suppertime. And, after supper, he went back to that piano and stayed there until everybody went to bed. He was at the piano all day Saturday and all day Sunday. Then he bought a record player and started playing records. He'd play one record over and over again, all day long sometimes, and he'd improvise along with it on the piano. Or he'd play one section of the record, one chord, one change, one progression, then he'd do it on the piano. Then back to the record. Then back to the piano.

Well, I really don't know how they stood it. Isabel finally confessed that it wasn't like living with a person at all, it was like living with sound. And the sound didn't make any sense to her, didn't make any sense to any of them—naturally. They began, in a way, to be afflicted by this presence that was living in their home. It was as though Sonny were some sort of god, or monster. He moved in an atmosphere which wasn't like theirs at all. They fed him and he ate, he washed himself, he walked in and out of their door; he certainly wasn't nasty or unpleasant or rude, Sonny isn't any of those things; but it was as though he were all wrapped up in some cloud, some fire, some vision all his own; and there wasn't any way to reach him.

At the same time, he wasn't really a man yet, he was still a child, and they had to watch out for him in all kinds of ways. They certainly couldn't throw him out. Neither did they dare to make a great scene about that piano because even they dimly sensed, as I sensed, from so many thousands of miles away, that Sonny was at that piano playing for his life.

But he hadn't been going to school. One day a letter came from the school board and Isabel's mother got it—there had, apparently, been other letters but Sonny had torn them up. This day, when Sonny came in, Isabel's mother showed him the letter and asked where he'd been spending his time. And she finally got it out of him that he'd been down in Greenwich Village, with musicians and other characters, in a white girl's apartment. And this scared her and she started to scream at him and what came up, once she began — though she denies it to this day — was what sacrifices they were making to give Sonny a decent home and how little he appreciated it.

Sonny didn't play the piano that day. By evening, Isabel's mother had calmed down but then there was the old man to deal with, and Isabel herself. Isabel says she did her best to be calm but she broke down and started crying. She says she just watched Sonny's face. She could tell, by watching him, what was happening with him. And what was happening was that they penetrated his cloud, they had reached him. Even if their fingers had been a thousand times more gentle than human fingers ever are, he could hardly help feeling that they had stripped him naked and were spitting on that nakedness. For he also had to see that his presence, that music, which was life or death to him, had been torture for them and that they had endured it, not at all for his sake, but only for mine. And Sonny couldn't take that. He can take it a little better today than he could then but he's still not very good at it and, frankly, I don't know anybody who is.

The silence of the next few days must have been louder than the sound of all the music ever played since time began. One morning, before she went to work, Isabel was in his room for something and she suddenly realized that all of his records were gone. And she knew for certain that he was gone. And he was. He went as far as the navy would carry him. He finally sent me a postcard from some place in Greece and that was the first I knew that Sonny was still alive. I didn't see him any more until we were both back in New York and the war had long been over. 170

He was a man by then, of course, but I wasn't willing to see it. He came by the house from time to time, but we fought almost every time we met. I didn't like the way he carried himself, loose and dreamlike all the time, and I didn't like his friends, and his music seemed to be merely an excuse for the life he led. It sounded just that weird and disordered.

Then we had a fight, a pretty awful fight, and I didn't see him for months. By and by I looked him up, where he was living, in a furnished room in the Village, and I tried to make it up. But there were lots of people in the room and Sonny just lay on his bed, and he wouldn't come downstairs with me, and he treated these other people as though they were his family and I weren't. So I got mad and then he got mad, and then I told him that he might just as well be dead as live the way he was living. Then he stood up and he told me not to worry about him any more in life, that he *was* dead as far as I was concerned. Then he pushed me to the door and the other people looked on as though nothing were happening, and he slammed the door behind me. I stood in the hallway, staring at the door. I heard somebody laugh in the room and then the tears came to my eyes. I started down the steps, whistling to keep from crying, I kept whistling to myself, *You going to need me, baby, one of these cold, rainy days.*

I read about Sonny's trouble in the spring. Little Grace died in the fall. She was a beautiful little girl. But she only lived a little over two years. She died of polio and she suffered. She had a slight fever for a couple of days, but it didn't seem like anything and we just kept her in bed. And we would certainly have called the doctor, but the fever dropped, she seemed to be all right. So we thought it had just been a cold. Then, one day, she was up, playing, Isabel was in the kitchen fixing lunch for the two boys when they'd come in from school, and she heard Grace fall down in the living room. When you have a lot of children you don't always start running when one of them falls, unless they start screaming or something. And, this time, Grace was quiet. Yet, Isabel says that when she heard that *thump* and then that silence, something happened in her to make her afraid. And she ran to the living room and there was little Grace on the floor, all twisted up, and the reason she hadn't screamed was that she couldn't get her breath. And when she did scream, it was the worst sound, Isabel says, that she'd ever heard in all her life, and she still hears it sometimes in her dreams. Isabel will sometimes wake me up with a low, moaning, strangled sound and I have to be quick to awaken her and hold her to me and where Isabel is weeping against me seems a mortal wound.

I think I may have written Sonny the very day that little Grace was buried. I was sitting in the living room in the dark, by myself, and I suddenly thought of Sonny. My trouble made his real.

One Saturday afternoon, when Sonny had been living with us, or, anyway, been   175
in our house, for nearly two weeks, I found myself wandering aimlessly about the living room, drinking from a can of beer, and trying to work up the courage to search Sonny's room. He was out, he was usually out whenever I was home, and Isabel had taken the children to see their grandparents. Suddenly I was standing still in front of the living room window, watching Seventh Avenue. The idea of searching Sonny's room made me still. I scarcely dared to admit to myself what I'd be searching for. I didn't know what I'd do if I found it. Or if I didn't.

On the sidewalk across from me, near the entrance to a barbecue joint, some people were holding an old-fashioned revival meeting. The barbecue cook, wearing a dirty white apron, his conked hair reddish and metallic in the pale sun, and a cigarette between his lips, stood in the doorway, watching them. Kids and older people paused in their errands and stood there, along with some older men and a couple of very tough-looking women who watched everything that happened on the avenue, as though they owned it, or were maybe owned by it. Well, they were watching this, too. The revival was being carried on by three sisters in black, and a brother. All they had were their voices and their Bibles and a tambourine. The brother was testifying and while he testified two of the sisters stood together, seeming to say, amen, and the third sister walked around with the tambourine outstretched and a couple of people dropped coins into it. Then the brother's testimony ended and the sister who had been taking up the collection dumped the coins into her palm and transferred them to the pocket of her long black robe. Then she raised both hands, striking the tambourine against the air, and then against one hand, and she started to sing. And the two other sisters and the brother joined in.

It was strange, suddenly, to watch, though I had been seeing these street meetings all my life. So, of course, had everybody else down there. Yet, they paused and watched and listened and I stood still at the window. *"Tis the old ship of Zion,"* they sang, and the sister with the tambourine kept a steady, jangling beat, *"it has rescued many a thousand!"* Not a soul under the sound of their voices was hearing this song for the first time, not one of them had been rescued. Nor had they seen much in the way of rescue work being done around them. Neither did they especially believe in the holiness of the three sisters and the brother, they knew too much about them, knew where they lived, and how. The woman with the tambourine, whose voice dominated the air, whose face was bright with joy, was divided by very little from the woman who stood watching her, a cigarette between her heavy, chapped lips, her hair a cuckoo's nest, her face scarred and swollen from many beatings, and her black eyes glittering like coal. Perhaps they both knew this, which was why, when, as rarely, they addressed each other, they addressed each other as Sister. As the singing filled the air the watching, listening faces underwent a change, the eyes focusing on something within; the music seemed to soothe a poison out of them; and time seemed, nearly, to fall away from the sullen, belligerent, battered faces, as though they were fleeing back to their first condition, while dreaming of their last. The barbecue cook half shook his head and smiled, and dropped his cigarette and disappeared into his joint. A man fumbled in his pockets for change and stood holding it in his hand impatiently, as though he had just remembered a pressing appointment further up the avenue. He looked furious. Then I saw Sonny, standing on the edge of the crowd. He was carrying a wide, flat notebook with a green cover, and it made him look, from where I was standing, almost like a schoolboy. The coppery sun brought out the copper in his skin, he was very faintly smiling, standing very still. Then the singing stopped, the tambourine turned into a collection plate again. The furious man dropped in his coins and vanished, so did a couple of the women, and Sonny dropped some change in the plate, looking directly at the woman with a little smile. He started across the avenue, toward the house. He has a slow, loping walk, something like the way Harlem hipsters walk, only he's imposed on this his own half-beat. I had never really noticed it before.

I stayed at the window, both relieved and apprehensive. As Sonny disappeared from my sight, they began singing again. And they were still singing when his key turned in the lock.

"Hey," he said.

"Hey, yourself. You want some beer?"

"No. Well, maybe." But he came up to the window and stood beside me, looking out. "What a warm voice," he said.

They were singing *If I could only hear my mother pray again!*

"Yes," I said, "and she can sure beat that tambourine."

"But what a terrible song," he said, and laughed. He dropped his notebook on the sofa and disappeared into the kitchen. "Where's Isabel and the kids?"

"I think they went to see their grandparents. You hungry?"

"No." He came back into the living room with his can of beer. "You want to come some place with me tonight?"

I sensed, I don't know how, that I couldn't possibly say no. "Sure. Where?"

180

185

He sat down on the sofa and picked up his notebook and started leafing through it. "I'm going to sit in with some fellows in a joint in the Village."

"You mean, you're going to play, tonight?"

"That's right." He took a swallow of his beer and moved back to the window. He gave me a sidelong look. "If you can stand it." 190

"I'll try," I said.

He smiled to himself and we both watched as the meeting across the way broke up. The three sisters and the brother, heads bowed, were singing *God be with you till we meet again.* The faces around them were very quiet. Then the song ended. The small crowd dispersed. We watched the three women and the lone man walk slowly up the avenue.

"When she was singing before," said Sonny, abruptly, "her voice reminded me for a minute of what heroin feels like sometimes—when it's in your veins. It makes you feel sort of warm and cool at the same time. And distant. And—and sure." He sipped his beer, very deliberately not looking at me. I watched his face. "It makes you feel—in control. Sometimes you've got to have that feeling."

"Do you?" I sat down slowly in the easy chair.

"Sometimes." He went to the sofa and picked up his notebook again. "Some 195 people do."

"In order," I asked, "to play?" And my voice was very ugly, full of contempt and anger.

"Well"—he looked at me with great, troubled eyes, as though, in fact, he hoped his eyes would tell me things he could never otherwise say—"they *think* so. And *if* they think so—!"

"And what do *you* think?" I asked.

He sat on the sofa and put his can of beer on the floor. "I don't know," he said, and I couldn't be sure if he were answering my question or pursuing his thoughts. His face didn't tell me. "It's not so much to *play.* It's to stand it, to be able to make it at all. On any level." He frowned and smiled: "In order to keep from shaking to pieces."

"But these friends of yours," I said, "they seem to shake themselves to pieces 200 pretty goddamn fast."

"Maybe." He played with the notebook. And something told me that I should curb my tongue, that Sonny was doing his best to talk, that I should listen. "But of course you only know the ones that've gone to pieces. Some don't—or at least they haven't *yet* and that's just about all *any* of us can say." He paused. "And then there are some who just live, really, in hell, and they know it and they see what's happening and they go right on. I don't know." He sighed, dropped the notebook, folded his arms. "Some guys, you can tell from the way they play, they on something *all* the time. And you can see that, well, it makes something real for them. But of course," he picked up his beer from the floor and sipped it and put the can down again, "they *want* to, too, you've got to see that. Even some of them that say they don't—*some,* not all."

"And what about you?" I asked—I couldn't help it. "What about you? Do *you* want to?"

He stood up and walked to the window and remained silent for a long time. Then he sighed. "Me," he said. Then: "While I was downstairs before, on my way here, listening to that woman sing, it struck me all of a sudden how much suffering she must have had to go through—to sing like that. It's *repulsive* to think you have to suffer that much."

I said: "But there's no way not to suffer—is there, Sonny?"

"I believe not," he said and smiled, "but that's never stopped anyone from try- 205
ing." He looked at me. "Has it?" I realized, with this mocking look, that there stood between us, forever, beyond the power of time or forgiveness, the fact that I had held silence—so long!—when he had needed human speech to help him. He turned back to the window. "No, there's no way not to suffer. But you try all kinds of ways to keep from drowning in it, to keep on top of it, and to make it seem—well, like *you*. Like you did something, all right, and now you're suffering for it. You know?" I said noth-ing. "Well you know," he said, impatiently, "why *do* people suffer? Maybe it's better to do something to give it a reason, *any* reason."

"But we just agreed," I said, "that there's no way not to suffer. Isn't it better, then, just to—take it?"

"But nobody just takes it," Sonny cried, "that's what I'm telling you! *Everybody* tries not to. You're just hung up on the *way* some people try—it's not *your* way!"

The hair on my face began to itch, my face felt wet. "That's not true," I said, "that's not true. I don't give a damn what other people do, I don't even care how they suffer. I just care how *you* suffer." And he looked at me. "Please believe me," I said, "I don't want to see you—die—trying not to suffer."

"I won't," he said, flatly, "die trying not to suffer. At least, not any faster than anybody else."

"But there's no need," I said, trying to laugh, "is there? in killing yourself." 210

I wanted to say more, but I couldn't. I wanted to talk about will power and how life could be—well, beautiful. I wanted to say that it was all within; but was it? or, rather, wasn't that exactly the trouble? And I wanted to promise that I would never fail him again. But it would all have sounded—empty words and lies.

So I made the promise to myself and prayed that I would keep it.

"It's terrible sometimes, inside," he said, "that's what's the trouble. You walk these streets, black and funky and cold, and there's not really a living ass to talk to, and there's nothing shaking, and there's no way of getting it out—that storm inside. You can't talk it and you can't make love with it, and when you finally try to get with it and play it, you realize *nobody's* listening. So *you've* got to listen. You got to find a way to listen."

And then he walked away from the window and sat on the sofa again, as though all the wind had suddenly been knocked out of him. "Sometimes you'll do *anything* to play, even cut your mother's throat." He laughed and looked at me. "Or your brother's." Then he sobered. "Or your own." Then: "Don't worry. I'm all right now and I think I'll *be* all right. But I can't forget—where I've been. I don't mean just the physical place I've been, I mean where I've *been*. And *what* I've been."

"What have you been, Sonny?" I asked. 215

He smiled—but sat sideways on the sofa, his elbow resting on the back, his fingers playing with his mouth and chin, not looking at me. "I've been something I didn't recognize, didn't know I could be. Didn't know anybody could be." He stopped, looking inward, looking helplessly young, looking old. "I'm not talking about it now because I feel *guilty* or anything like that—maybe it would be better if I did, I don't know. Anyway, I can't really talk about it. Not to you, not to anybody," and now he turned and faced me. "Sometimes, you know, and it was actually when I was most *out* of the world, I felt that I was in it, that I was *with* it, really, and I could play or I didn't really have to *play*, it just came out of me, it was there. And I don't know how I played, thinking about it now, but I know I did awful things, those times, sometimes, to people. Or it wasn't that I *did* anything to them—it was that they weren't real." He picked up the beer can; it was empty; he rolled it between his palms: "And other times—well, I needed a fix, I needed to find a place to lean, I needed to clear a *space* to *listen*—and I couldn't find it, and I—went crazy, I did terrible things to *me*, I was terrible *for* me." He began pressing the beer can between his hands, I watched the metal begin to give. It glittered, as he played with it, like a knife, and I was afraid he would cut himself, but I said nothing. "Oh well. I can never tell you. I was all by myself at the bottom of something, stinking and sweating and crying and shaking, and I smelled it, you know? *my* stink, and I thought I'd die if I couldn't get away from it and yet, all the same, I knew that everything I was doing was just locking me in with it. And I didn't know," he paused, still flattening the beer can, "I didn't know, I still *don't* know, something kept telling me that maybe it was good to smell your own stink, but I didn't think that *that* was what I'd been trying to do—and—who can stand it?" and he abruptly dropped the ruined beer can, looking at me with a small, still smile, and then rose, walking to the window as though it were the lodestone rock. I watched his face, he watched the avenue. "I couldn't tell you when Mama died—but the reason I wanted to leave Harlem so bad was to get away from drugs. And then, when I ran away, that's what I was running from—really. When I came back, nothing had changed, *I* hadn't changed, I was just—older." And he stopped, drumming with his fingers on the windowpane. The sun had vanished, soon darkness would fall. I watched his face. "It can come again," he said, almost as though speaking to himself. Then he turned to me. "It can come again," he repeated. "I just want you to know that."

"All right," I said, at last. "So it can come again. All right."

He smiled, but the smile was sorrowful. "I had to try to tell you," he said.

"Yes," I said. "I understand that."

"You're my brother," he said, looking straight at me, and not smiling at all.   220

"Yes," I repeated, "yes. I understand that."

He turned back to the window, looking out. "All that hatred down there," he said, "all that hatred and misery and love. It's a wonder it doesn't blow the avenue apart."

We went to the only nightclub on a short, dark street, downtown. We squeezed through the narrow, chattering, jam-packed bar to the entrance of the big room, where the bandstand was. And we stood there for a moment, for the lights were very dim in this room and we couldn't see. Then, "Hello, boy," said a voice and an enormous black man, much older than Sonny or myself, erupted out of all that atmospheric lighting and put an arm around Sonny's shoulder. "I been sitting right here," he said, "waiting for you."

He had a big voice, too, and heads in the darkness turned toward us.

Sonny grinned and pulled a little away, and said, "Creole, this is my brother. I told you about him."

Creole shook my hand. "I'm glad to meet you, son," he said, and it was clear that he was glad to meet me *there*, for Sonny's sake. And he smiled, "You got a real musician in *your* family," and he took his arm from Sonny's shoulder and slapped him, lightly, affectionately, with the back of his hand.

"Well. Now I've heard it all," said a voice behind us. This was another musician, and a friend of Sonny's, a coal-black, cheerful-looking man, built close to the ground. He immediately began confiding to me, at the top of his lungs, the most terrible things about Sonny, his teeth gleaming like a lighthouse and his laugh coming up out of him like the beginning of an earthquake. And it turned out that everyone at the bar knew Sonny, or almost everyone; some were musicians, working there, or nearby, or not working, some were simply hangers-on, and some were there to hear Sonny play. I was introduced to all of them and they were all very polite to me. Yet, it was clear that, for them, I was only Sonny's brother. Here, I was in Sonny's world. Or, rather: his kingdom. Here, it was not even a question that his veins bore royal blood.

They were going to play soon and Creole installed me, by myself, at a table in a dark corner. Then I watched them, Creole, and the little black man, and Sonny, and the others, while they horsed around, standing just below the bandstand. The light from the bandstand spilled just a little short of them and, watching them laughing and gesturing and moving about, I had the feeling that they, nevertheless, were being most careful not to step into that circle of light too suddenly: that if they moved into the light too suddenly, without thinking, they would perish in flame. Then, while I watched, one of them, the small, black man, moved into the light and crossed the bandstand and started fooling around with his drums. Then—being funny and being, also, extremely ceremonious—Creole took Sonny by the arm and led him to the piano. A woman's voice called Sonny's name and a few hands started clapping. And Sonny, also being funny and being ceremonious, and so touched, I think, that he could have cried, but neither hiding it nor showing it, riding it like a man, grinned, and put both hands to his heart and bowed from the waist.

Creole then went to the bass fiddle and a lean, very bright-skinned brown man jumped up on the bandstand and picked up his horn. So there they were, and the atmosphere on the bandstand and in the room began to change and tighten. Someone stepped up to the microphone and announced them. Then there were all kinds of murmurs. Some people at the bar shushed others. The waitress ran around, frantically getting in the last orders, guys and chicks got closer to each other, and the lights on the bandstand, on the quartet, turned to a kind of indigo. Then they all looked different there. Creole looked about him for the last time, as though he were making certain that all his chickens were in the coop, and then he—jumped and struck the fiddle. And there they were.

All I know about music is that not many people ever really hear it. And even then,   230
on the rare occasions when something opens within, and the music enters, what we
mainly hear, or hear corroborated, are personal, private, vanishing evocations. But the
man who creates the music is hearing something else, is dealing with the roar rising
from the void and imposing order on it as it hits the air. What is evoked in him, then,
is of another order, more terrible because it has no words, and triumphant, too, for
that same reason. And his triumph, when he triumphs, is ours. I just watched Sonny's
face. His face was troubled, he was working hard, but he wasn't with it. And I had
the feeling that, in a way, everyone on the bandstand was waiting for him, both waiting for him and pushing him along. But as I began to watch Creole, I realized that it
was Creole who held them all back. He had them on a short rein. Up there, keeping
the beat with his whole body, wailing on the fiddle, with his eyes half closed, he was
listening to everything, but he was listening to Sonny. He was having a dialogue with
Sonny. He wanted Sonny to leave the shoreline and strike out for the deep water. He
was Sonny's witness that deep water and drowning were not the same thing—he had
been there, and he knew. And he wanted Sonny to know. He was waiting for Sonny to
do the things on the keys which would let Creole know that Sonny was in the water.

And, while Creole listened, Sonny moved, deep within, exactly like someone in
torment. I had never before thought of how awful the relationship must be between
the musician and his instrument. He has to fill it, this instrument, with the breath of
life, his own. He has to make it do what he wants it to do. And a piano is just a piano.
It's made out of so much wood and wires and little hammers and big ones, and ivory.
While there's only so much you can do with it, the only way to find this out is to try;
to try and make it do everything.

And Sonny hadn't been near a piano for over a year. And he wasn't on much better terms with his life, not the life that stretched before him now. He and the piano
stammered, started one way, got scared, stopped; started another way, panicked,
marked time, started again; then seemed to have found a direction, panicked again,
got stuck. And the face I saw on Sonny I'd never seen before. Everything had been
burned out of it, and, at the same time, things usually hidden were being burned in,
by the fire and fury of the battle which was occurring in him up there.

Yet, watching Creole's face as they neared the end of the first set, I had the feeling
that something had happened, something I hadn't heard. Then they finished, there
was scattered applause, and then, without an instant's warning, Creole started into
something else, it was almost sardonic, it was *Am I Blue*. And, as though he commanded, Sonny began to play. Something began to happen. And Creole let out the
reins. The dry, low, black man said something awful on the drums, Creole answered,
and the drums talked back. Then the horn insisted, sweet and high, slightly detached
perhaps, and Creole listened, commenting now and then, dry, and driving, beautiful
and calm and old. Then they all came together again, and Sonny was part of the family again. I could tell this from his face. He seemed to have found, right there beneath
his fingers, a damn brand-new piano. It seemed that he couldn't get over it. Then,
for awhile, just being happy with Sonny, they seemed to be agreeing with him that
brand-new pianos certainly were a gas.

Then Creole stepped forward to remind them that what they were playing was the blues. He hit something in all of them, he hit something in me, myself, and the music tightened and deepened, apprehension began to beat the air. Creole began to tell us what the blues were all about. They were not about anything very new. He and his boys up there were keeping it new, at the risk of ruin, destruction, madness, and death, in order to find new ways to make us listen. For, while the tale of how we suffer, and how we are delighted, and how we may triumph is never new, it always must be heard. There isn't any other tale to tell, it's the only light we've got in all this darkness.

Theme.

And this tale, according to that face, that body, those strong hands on those strings, has another aspect in every country, and a new depth in every generation. Listen, Creole seemed to be saying, listen. Now these are Sonny's blues. He made the little black man on the drums know it, and the bright, brown man on the horn. Creole wasn't trying any longer to get Sonny in the water. He was wishing him Godspeed. Then he stepped back, very slowly, filling the air with the immense sug- gestion that Sonny speak for himself.   235

Then they all gathered around Sonny and Sonny played. Every now and again one of them seemed to say, amen. Sonny's fingers filled the air with life, his life. But that life contained so many others. And Sonny went all the way back, he really began with the spare, flat statement of the opening phrase of the song. Then he began to make it his. It was very beautiful because it wasn't hurried and it was no longer a lament. I seemed to hear with what burning he had made it his, with what burning we had yet to make it ours, how we could cease lamenting. Freedom lurked around us and I understood, at last, that he could help us to be free if we would listen, that he would never be free until we did. Yet, there was no battle in his face now. I heard what he had gone through, and would continue to go through until he came to rest in earth. He had made it his: that long line, of which we knew only Mama and Daddy. And he was giving it back, as everything must be given back, so that, passing through death, it can live forever. I saw my mother's face again, and felt, for the first time, how the stones of the road she had walked on must have bruised her feet. I saw the moonlit road where my father's brother died. And it brought something else back to me, and carried me past it. I saw my little girl again and felt Isabel's tears again, and I felt my own tears begin to rise. And I was yet aware that this was only a moment, that the world waited outside, as hungry as a tiger, and that trouble stretched above us, longer than the sky.

Then it was over. Creole and Sonny let out their breath, both soaking wet, and grinning. There was a lot of applause and some of it was real. In the dark, the girl came by and I asked her to take drinks to the bandstand. There was a long pause, while they talked up there in the indigo light and after awhile I saw the girl put a Scotch and milk on top of the piano for Sonny. He didn't seem to notice it, but just before they started playing again, he sipped from it and looked toward me, and nod- ded. Then he put it back on top of the piano. For me, then, as they began to play again, it glowed and shook above my brother's head like the very cup of trembling.

[1957]

Will Sonny be okay?   Biblical Allusion

Questions for Discussion

1. It is easy to see that the narrator of "Sonny's Blues" and his brother, Sonny, represent two sides of the same coin: one brother is employed as a math teacher, married, clean living; the other is a jazz musician, single, struggling with heroin addiction. Discuss the ways in which Baldwin brings these two characters to life and makes them more than just opposites. Which brother do you think is the story's main character? Explain your answer.

2. The backdrop of 1950s Harlem and the story of the narrator's uncle's death (para. 94) suggest that the characters have suffered from vicious and institutionalized racism. Where else do you see the impact of racism in the story? Do you think that Sonny's addiction and the narrator's repression and rigidity are caused by their natures or by the social forces of racism?

3. "Sonny's Blues" is a story about listening, and not just the effort of the narrator to learn to listen to Sonny. Track the different descriptions of music in this story. How does each one add another dimension to the story's meaning? How does each one say something about the needs and desires of the story's characters?

4. Why do you think the narrator gets back in touch with Sonny when his daughter, Grace, dies?

5. Do you think this story has a happy ending? Why or why not?

6. This story depends somewhat on a view of Harlem in the 1950s. Research the ways in which Harlem has changed in the last fifty years. Do you think the change is superficial or profound? Could a tale such as the one told in "Sonny's Blues" take place there today? If so, in what ways would it be different?

7. Sonny tells his brother that Louis Armstrong is "old-time, down home" music. He likes the music of Charlie "Bird" Parker. Listen to music by Louis Armstrong and Charlie Parker, and describe the differences between them. Parker's version of "White Christmas" gives the listener a particularly vivid understanding of the bebop style he exemplified and that so intrigues Sonny. How does Baldwin illustrate bebop in the story's last scene at the club?

8. Do you agree that suffering is necessary to create art? Consider such examples as painter Vincent van Gogh, musician Kurt Cobain, and poet Sylvia Plath, but also jazz trumpeter Miles Davis and Rolling Stones guitarist Keith Richards, who both overcame heroin addiction.

Questions on Style and Structure

1. What is the effect of the repetition of the word "it" in the first two paragraphs?

2. The first sentence of the story's second paragraph begins, "It was not to be believed." What does the use of the passive voice suggest about the narrator's response to the news he has just gotten?

3. Why do you think the plot of this story is not in chronological order? Try rearranging the events of the story so that they are in chronological order. How does it change the story Baldwin is telling?

4. The narrator has a conversation with an old neighborhood friend of Sonny's (paras. 9–46). How does that conversation shape the characterization of the narrator? How does it shape our expectations for the outcome of the story?

5. What do you think is the purpose of the narrator's description of a typical Sunday afternoon at his parents' house (paras. 78–79)? What part does that setting have in the story's conflict?

6. What does the narrator's statement "My trouble made his real" (para. 174) reveal about his character? What does it reveal about the nature of empathy?

7. Why do you think Baldwin gave no name to the narrator?

8. According to the narrator — and his mother — how are Sonny and his father similar? What evidence does the story offer as support? What are the parallels between the narrator and his mother? What do you think the dash in the last sentence of paragraph 76 says about the narrator? about Sonny and his father?

9. The story ends in a club where the narrator goes to hear Sonny play. The language of the story changes, becoming more abstract and metaphorical. What does that change suggest about the part music plays in the lives of the musicians and what Baldwin wants us to feel about Sonny and his blues?

10. What do you think is the difference between deep water and drowning (para. 230)? Why do you think the narrator begins to understand his brother and himself through the way Creole leads Sonny into the music?

11. What effect does Sonny's music have on the narrator? Look closely at paragraph 236.

12. The very last line of the story is an allusion to a somewhat enigmatic passage in the Bible about rage and God's protection against it. What does the allusion suggest about the glowing "cup of trembling" the narrator sees in the cup "above [his] brother's head"?

Suggestions for Writing

1. Using "Sonny's Blues" and other stories, poems, or films about art and artists as evidence, write an essay in which you defend, challenge, or qualify the formula created by editor and critic Robert Gottlieb to mock the proliferation of movies about artists and their process: "Love + Suffering = Art."

2. Write an essay in which you compare the narrator to Sonny. Be sure to discuss the way in which Baldwin uses the contrast between them to develop one or more of the story's themes.

3. Write an essay in which you analyze the names of the characters — and the fact that the narrator has no name.

4. There's an old saying that "mathematics is music for the mind; music is mathematics for the soul." Write about how this connection is illustrated in "Sonny's Blues."

5. Research the jazz musicians of the first part of the twentieth century, and write an essay that illuminates some of the reasons the narrator of "Sonny's Blues" did not feel that playing jazz music was a viable career choice for his younger brother.

6. Write a version of "Sonny's Blues" as it might happen today. Experiment with imitating Baldwin's voice and using nonchronological plotting.

The Yellow Wallpaper

CHARLOTTE PERKINS GILMAN

Charlotte Perkins Gilman (1860–1935) came from a long line of feminists and suffragists, including her grandaunt, Harriet Beecher Stowe, the author of *Uncle Tom's Cabin*. Born in Hartford, Connecticut, she was brought up in an atmosphere of rigid coldness, forbidden to make close friendships or even to read fiction. Gilman was educated mostly at home and briefly at the Rhode Island School of Design. She married artist Charles Walter Stetson in 1884 and suffered a severe bout of postpartum depression after the birth of their daughter. She underwent Dr. Silas Weir Mitchell's "rest cure," a treatment in which she was instructed to "live as domestic a life as possible. Have your child with you all the time. Have but two hours' intellectual life a day. And never touch a pen, brush, or pencil as long as you live." Gilman and Stetson divorced, unusual for the time, and she later remarried. Gilman lived in California for much of her later life; lectured on social reform; and wrote short stories, poetry, and nonfiction. A believer in euthanasia, Gilman took an overdose of chloroform when she learned she had inoperable breast cancer. Gilman wrote *The Yellow Wallpaper*, published in 1892, as an indictment of the rest cure.

It is very seldom that mere ordinary people like John and myself secure ancestral halls for the summer.

A colonial mansion, a hereditary estate, I would say a haunted house and reach the height of romantic felicity—but that would be asking too much of fate!

Still I will proudly declare that there is something queer about it.

Else, why should it be let so cheaply? And why have stood so long untenanted?

John laughs at me, of course, but one expects that in marriage.   5

John is practical in the extreme. He has no patience with faith, an intense horror of superstition, and he scoffs openly at any talk of things not to be felt and seen and put down in figures.

John is a physician, and *perhaps*—(I would not say it to a living soul, of course, but this is dead paper and a great relief to my mind)—*perhaps* that is one reason I do not get well faster.

You see, he does not believe I am sick!

And what can one do?

If a physician of high standing, and one's own husband, assures friends and   10
relatives that there is really nothing the matter with one but temporary nervous depression—a slight hysterical tendency—what is one to do?

My brother is also a physician, and also of high standing, and he says the same thing.

So I take phosphates or phosphites—whichever it is, and tonics, and journeys, and air, and exercise, and am absolutely forbidden to "work" until I am well again.

Personally, I disagree with their ideas.

Personally, I believe that congenial work, with excitement and change, would do me good.

But what is one to do? 15

I did write for a while in spite of them; but it *does* exhaust me a good deal—having to be so sly about it, or else meet with heavy opposition.

I sometimes fancy that in my condition if I had less opposition and more society and stimulus—but John says the very worst thing I can do is to think about my condition, and I confess it always makes me feel bad.

So I will let it alone and talk about the house.

The most beautiful place! It is quite alone, standing well back from the road, quite three miles from the village. It makes me think of English places that you read about, for there are hedges and walls and gates that lock, and lots of separate little houses for the gardeners and people.

There is a *delicious* garden! I never saw such a garden—large and shady, full 20 of box-bordered paths, and lined with long grape-covered arbors with seats under them.

There were greenhouses, too, but they are all broken now.

There was some legal trouble, I believe, something about the heirs and co-heirs; anyhow, the place has been empty for years.

That spoils my ghostliness, I am afraid, but I don't care—there is something strange about the house—I can feel it.

I even said so to John one moonlight evening, but he said what I felt was a *draught*, and shut the window.

I get unreasonably angry with John sometimes. I'm sure I never used to be so 25 sensitive. I think it is due to this nervous condition.

But John says if I feel so, I shall neglect proper self-control; so I take pains to control myself—before him, at least, and that makes me very tired.

I don't like our room a bit. I wanted one downstairs that opened on the piazza and had roses all over the window, and such pretty old-fashioned chintz hangings! but John would not hear of it.

He said there was only one window and not room for two beds, and no near room for him if he took another.

He is very careful and loving, and hardly lets me stir without special direction.

I have a schedule prescription for each hour in the day; he takes all care from me, 30 and so I feel basely ungrateful not to value it more.

He said we came here solely on my account, that I was to have perfect rest and all the air I could get. "Your exercise depends on your strength, my dear," said he, "and your food somewhat on your appetite; but air you can absorb all the time." So we took the nursery at the top of the house.

It is a big, airy room, the whole floor nearly, with windows that look all ways, and air and sunshine galore. It was nursery first and then playroom and gymnasium, I should judge; for the windows are barred for little children, and there are rings and things in the walls.

The paint and paper look as if a boys' school had used it. It is stripped off—the paper—in great patches all around the head of my bed, about as far as I can reach, and in a great place on the other side of the room low down. I never saw a worse paper in my life.

One of those sprawling flamboyant patterns committing every artistic sin.

It is dull enough to confuse the eye in following, pronounced enough to con-   35
stantly irritate and provoke study, and when you follow the lame uncertain curves for a little distance they suddenly commit suicide—plunge off at outrageous angles, destroy themselves in unheard of contradictions.

The color is repellant, almost revolting; a smouldering unclean yellow, strangely faded by the slow-turning sunlight.

It is a dull yet lurid orange in some places, a sickly sulphur tint in others.

No wonder the children hated it! I should hate it myself if I had to live in this room long.

There comes John, and I must put this away,—he hates to have me write a word.

We have been here two weeks, and I haven't felt like writing before, since that   40
first day.

I am sitting by the window now, up in this atrocious nursery, and there is nothing to hinder my writing as much as I please, save lack of strength.

John is away all day, and even some nights when his cases are serious.

I am glad my case is not serious!

But these nervous troubles are dreadfully depressing.

John does not know how much I really suffer. He knows there is no *reason* to   45
suffer, and that satisfies him.

Of course it is only nervousness. It does weigh on me so not to do my duty in any way!

I meant to be such a help to John, such a real rest and comfort, and here I am a comparative burden already!

Nobody would believe what an effort it is to do what little I am able,—to dress and entertain, and order things.

It is fortunate Mary is so good with the baby. Such a dear baby!

And yet I *cannot* be with him, it makes me so nervous.   50

I suppose John never was nervous in his life. He laughs at me so about this wall-paper!

At first he meant to repaper the room, but afterward he said that I was letting it get the better of me, and that nothing was worse for a nervous patient than to give way to such fancies.

He said that after the wall-paper was changed it would be the heavy bedstead, and then the barred windows, and then that gate at the head of the stairs, and so on.

"You know the place is doing you good," he said, "and really, dear, I don't care to renovate the house just for a three months' rental."

"Then do let us go downstairs," I said, "there are such pretty rooms there." 55

Then he took me in his arms and called me a blessed little goose, and said he would go down cellar, if I wished, and have it whitewashed into the bargain.

But he is right enough about the beds and windows and things.

It is an airy and comfortable room as anyone need wish, and, of course, I would not be so silly as to make him uncomfortable just for a whim.

I'm really getting quite fond of the big room, all but that horrid paper.

Out of one window I can see the garden, those mysterious deep-shaded arbors, 60
the riotous old-fashioned flowers, and bushes and gnarly trees.

Out of another I get a lovely view of the bay and a little private wharf belonging to the estate. There is a beautiful shaded lane that runs down there from the house. I always fancy I see people walking in these numerous paths and arbors, but John has cautioned me not to give way to fancy in the least. He says that with my imaginative power and habit of story-making, a nervous weakness like mine is sure to lead to all manner of excited fancies, and that I ought to use my will and good sense to check the tendency. So I try.

I think sometimes that if I were only well enough to write a little it would relieve the press of ideas and rest me.

But I find I get pretty tired when I try.

It is so discouraging not to have any advice and companionship about my work. When I get really well, John says we will ask Cousin Henry and Julia down for a long visit; but he says he would as soon put fireworks in my pillow-case as to let me have those stimulating people about now.

I wish I could get well faster. 65

But I must not think about that. This paper looks to me as if it *knew* what a vicious influence it had!

There is a recurrent spot where the pattern lolls like a broken neck and two bulbous eyes stare at you upside down.

I get positively angry with the impertinence of it and the everlastingness. Up and down and sideways they crawl, and those absurd, unblinking eyes are everywhere. There is one place where two breadths didn't match, and the eyes go all up and down the line, one a little higher than the other.

I never saw so much expression in an inanimate thing before, and we all know how much expression they have! I used to lie awake as a child and get more entertainment and terror out of blank walls and plain furniture than most children could find in a toy-store.

I remember what a kindly wink the knobs of our big, old bureau used to have, 70
and there was one chair that always seemed like a strong friend.

I used to feel that if any of the other things looked too fierce I could always hop into that chair and be safe.

The furniture in this room is no worse than inharmonious, however, for we had to bring it all from downstairs. I suppose when this was used as a playroom they had to take the nursery things out, and no wonder! I never saw such ravages as the children have made here.

The wall-paper, as I said before, is torn off in spots, and it sticketh closer than a brother—they must have had perseverance as well as hatred.

Then the floor is scratched and gouged and splintered, the plaster itself is dug out here and there, and this great heavy bed, which is all we found in the room, looks as if it had been through the wars.

But I don't mind it a bit—only the paper.   75

There comes John's sister. Such a dear girl as she is, and so careful of me! I must not let her find me writing.

She is a perfect and enthusiastic housekeeper, and hopes for no better profession. I verily believe she thinks it is the writing which made me sick!

But I can write when she is out, and see her a long way off from these windows.

There is one that commands the road, a lovely shaded winding road, and one that just looks off over the country. A lovely country, too, full of great elms and velvet meadows.

This wallpaper has a kind of sub-pattern in a different shade, a particularly irri-   80
tating one, for you can only see it in certain lights, and not clearly then.

But in the places where it isn't faded and where the sun is just so—I can see a strange, provoking, formless sort of figure, that seems to skulk about behind that silly and conspicuous front design.

There's sister on the stairs!

Well, the Fourth of July is over! The people are all gone and I am tired out. John thought it might do me good to see a little company, so we just had mother and Nellie and the children down for a week.

Of course I didn't do a thing. Jennie sees to everything now.

But it tired me all the same.   85

John says if I don't pick up faster he shall send me to Weir Mitchell in the fall.

But I don't want to go there at all. I had a friend who was in his hands once, and she says he is just like John and my brother, only more so!

Besides, it is such an undertaking to go so far.

I don't feel as if it was worthwhile to turn my hand over for anything, and I'm getting dreadfully fretful and querulous.

I cry at nothing, and cry most of the time.   90

Of course I don't when John is here, or anybody else, but when I am alone.

And I am alone a good deal just now. John is kept in town very often by serious cases, and Jennie is good and lets me alone when I want her to.

So I walk a little in the garden or down that lovely lane, sit on the porch under the roses, and lie down up here a good deal.

I'm getting really fond of the room in spite of the wallpaper. Perhaps *because* of the wallpaper.

It dwells in my mind so!   95

I lie here on this great immovable bed—it is nailed down, I believe—and follow that pattern about by the hour. It is as good as gymnastics, I assure you. I start, we'll say, at the bottom, down in the corner over there where it has not been touched, and I determine for the thousandth time that I *will* follow that pointless pattern to some sort of a conclusion.

I know a little of the principle of design, and I know this thing was not arranged on any laws of radiation, or alternation, or repetition, or symmetry, or anything else that I ever heard of.

It is repeated, of course, by the breadths, but not otherwise.

Looked at in one way each breadth stands alone, the bloated curves and flourishes—a kind of "debased Romanesque" with *delirium tremens*—go waddling up and down in isolated columns of fatuity.

But, on the other hand, they connect diagonally, and the sprawling outlines run off   100
in great slanting waves of optic horror, like a lot of wallowing sea-weeds in full chase.

The whole thing goes horizontally, too, at least it seems so, and I exhaust myself in trying to distinguish the order of its going in that direction.

They have used a horizontal breadth for a frieze, and that adds wonderfully to the confusion.

There is one end of the room where it is almost intact, and there, when the crosslights fade and the low sun shines directly upon it, I can almost fancy radiation after all,—the interminable grotesques seem to form around a common centre and rush off in headlong plunges of equal distraction.

It makes me tired to follow it. I will take a nap I guess.

I don't know why I should write this.   105

I don't want to.

I don't feel able.

And I know John would think it absurd. But I *must* say what I feel and think in some way—it is such a relief!

But the effort is getting to be greater than the relief.

Half the time now I am awfully lazy, and lie down ever so much.   110

John says I mustn't lose my strength, and has me take cod liver oil and lots of tonics and things, to say nothing of ale and wine and rare meat.

Dear John! He loves me very dearly, and hates to have me sick. I tried to have a real earnest reasonable talk with him the other day, and tell him how I wish he would let me go and make a visit to Cousin Henry and Julia.

But he said I wasn't able to go, nor able to stand it after I got there; and I did not make out a very good case for myself, for I was crying before I had finished.

It is getting to be a great effort for me to think straight. Just this nervous weakness I suppose.

And dear John gathered me up in his arms, and just carried me upstairs and laid   115
me on the bed, and sat by me and read to me till it tired my head.

He said I was his darling and his comfort and all he had, and that I must take care of myself for his sake, and keep well.

He says no one but myself can help me out of it, that I must use my will and self-control and not let any silly fancies run away with me.

There's one comfort, the baby is well and happy, and does not have to occupy this nursery with the horrid wallpaper.

If we had not used it, that blessed child would have! What a fortunate escape! Why, I wouldn't have a child of mine, an impressionable little thing, live in such a room for worlds.

I never thought of it before, but it is lucky that John kept me here after all, I can 120 stand it so much easier than a baby, you see.

Of course I never mention it to them any more—I am too wise, but I keep watch of it all the same.

There are things in the wallpaper that nobody knows but me, or ever will.

Behind that outside pattern the dim shapes get clearer every day.

It is always the same shape, only very numerous.

And it is like a woman stooping down and creeping about behind that pattern. 125 I don't like it a bit. I wonder—I begin to think—I wish John would take me away from here!

It is so hard to talk with John about my case, because he is so wise, and because he loves me so.

But I tried it last night.

It was moonlight. The moon shines in all around just as the sun does.

I hate to see it sometimes, it creeps so slowly, and always comes in by one window or another.

John was asleep and I hated to waken him, so I kept still and watched the moon- 130 light on that undulating wallpaper till I felt creepy.

The faint figure behind seemed to shake the pattern, just as if she wanted to get out.

I got up softly and went to feel and see if the paper *did* move, and when I came back John was awake.

"What is it, little girl?" he said. "Don't go walking about like that—you'll get cold."

I thought it was a good time to talk, so I told him that I really was not gaining here, and that I wished he would take me away.

"Why, darling!" said he, "our lease will be up in three weeks, and I can't see how 135 to leave before.

"The repairs are not done at home, and I cannot possibly leave town just now. Of course if you were in any danger, I could and would, but you really are better, dear, whether you can see it or not. I am a doctor, dear, and I know. You are gaining flesh and color, your appetite is better, I feel really much easier about you."

"I don't weigh a bit more," said I, "nor as much; and my appetite may be better in the evening when you are here but it is worse in the morning when you are away!"

"Bless her little heart!" said he with a big hug, "she shall be as sick as she pleases! But now let's improve the shining hours by going to sleep, and talk about it in the morning!"

"And you won't go away?" I asked gloomily.

"Why, how can I, dear? It is only three weeks more and then we will take a nice   140
little trip of a few days while Jennie is getting the house ready. Really dear you are
better!"

"Better in body perhaps—" I began, and stopped short, for he sat up straight
and looked at me with such a stern, reproachful look that I could not say another
word.

"My darling," said he, "I beg you, for my sake and for our child's sake, as well as
for your own, that you will never for one instant let that idea enter your mind! There
is nothing so dangerous, so fascinating, to a temperament like yours. It is a false and
foolish fancy. Can you trust me as a physician when I tell you so?"

So of course I said no more on that score, and we went to sleep before long.
He thought I was asleep first, but I wasn't, and lay there for hours trying to decide
whether that front pattern and the back pattern really did move together or
separately.

On a pattern like this, by daylight, there is a lack of sequence, a defiance of law,
that is a constant irritant to a normal mind.

The color is hideous enough, and unreliable enough, and infuriating enough,   145
but the pattern is torturing.

You think you have mastered it, but just as you get well underway in following, it
turns a back-somersault and there you are. It slaps you in the face, knocks you down,
and tramples upon you. It is like a bad dream.

The outside pattern is a florid arabesque, reminding one of a fungus. If you
can imagine a toadstool in joints, an interminable string of toadstools, budding and
sprouting in endless convolutions—why, that is something like it.

That is, sometimes!

There is one marked peculiarity about this paper, a thing nobody seems to notice
but myself, and that is that it changes as the light changes.

When the sun shoots in through the east window—I always watch for that first   150
long, straight ray—it changes so quickly that I never can quite believe it.

That is why I watch it always.

By moonlight—the moon shines in all night when there is a moon—I wouldn't
know it was the same paper.

At night in any kind of light, in twilight, candlelight, lamplight, and worst of all
by moonlight, it becomes bars! The outside pattern I mean, and the woman behind
it is as plain as can be.

I didn't realize for a long time what the thing was that showed behind, that dim
sub-pattern, but now I am quite sure it is a woman.

By daylight she is subdued, quiet. I fancy it is the pattern that keeps her so still.   155
It is so puzzling. It keeps me quiet by the hour.

I lie down ever so much now. John says it is good for me, and to sleep all I can.

Indeed he started the habit by making me lie down for an hour after each
meal.

It is a very bad habit I am convinced, for you see I don't sleep.

And that cultivates deceit, for I don't tell them I'm awake—O, no!

The fact is I am getting a little afraid of John.   160

He seems very queer sometimes, and even Jennie has an inexplicable look.

It strikes me occasionally, just as a scientific hypothesis,—that perhaps it is the paper!

I have watched John when he did not know I was looking, and come into the room suddenly on the most innocent excuses, and I've caught him several times *looking at the paper*! And Jennie too. I caught Jennie with her hand on it once.

She didn't know I was in the room, and when I asked her in a quiet, a very quiet voice, with the most restrained manner possible, what she was doing with the paper—she turned around as if she had been caught stealing, and looked quite angry—asked me why I should frighten her so!

Then she said that the paper stained everything it touched, that she had found   165
yellow smooches on all my clothes and John's, and she wished we would be more careful!

Did not that sound innocent? But I know she was studying that pattern, and I am determined that nobody shall find it out but myself!

Life is very much more exciting now than it used to be. You see I have something more to expect, to look forward to, to watch. I really do eat better, and am more quiet than I was.

John is so pleased to see me improve! He laughed a little the other day, and said I seemed to be flourishing in spite of my wall-paper.

I turned it off with a laugh. I had no intention of telling him it was *because* of the wall-paper—he would make fun of me. He might even want to take me away.

I don't want to leave now until I have found it out. There is a week more, and I   170
think that will be enough.

I'm feeling ever so much better! I don't sleep much at night, for it is so interesting to watch developments; but I sleep a good deal in the daytime.

In the daytime it is tiresome and perplexing.

There are always new shoots on the fungus, and new shades of yellow all over it. I cannot keep count of them, though I have tried conscientiously.

It is the strangest yellow, that wall-paper! It makes me think of all the yellow things I ever saw—not beautiful ones like buttercups, but old foul, bad yellow things.

But there is something else about that paper—the smell! I noticed it the   175
moment we came into the room, but with so much air and sun it was not bad. Now we have had a week of fog and rain, and whether the windows are open or not, the smell is here.

It creeps all over the house.

I find it hovering in the dining-room, skulking in the parlor, hiding in the hall, lying in wait for me on the stairs.

It gets into my hair.

Even when I go to ride, if I turn my head suddenly and surprise it—there is that smell!

Such a peculiar odor, too! I have spent hours in trying to analyze it, to find what it smelled like.

It is not bad—at first, and very gentle, but quite the subtlest, most enduring odor I ever met.

In this damp weather it is awful, I wake up in the night and find it hanging over me.

It used to disturb me at first. I thought seriously of burning the house—to reach the smell.

But now I am used to it. The only thing I can think of that it is like is the *color* of the paper! A yellow smell.

There is a very funny mark on this wall, low down, near the mopboard. A streak that runs round the room. It goes behind every piece of furniture, except the bed, a long, straight, even *smooch*, as if it had been rubbed over and over.

I wonder how it was done and who did it, and what they did it for. Round and round and round—round and round and round—it makes me dizzy!

I really have discovered something at last.

Through watching so much at night, when it changes so, I have finally found out.

The front pattern *does* move—and no wonder! The woman behind shakes it!

Sometimes I think there are a great many women behind, and sometimes only one, and she crawls around fast, and her crawling shakes it all over.

Then in the very bright spots she keeps still, and in the very shady spots she just takes hold of the bars and shakes them hard.

And she is all the time trying to climb through. But nobody could climb through that pattern—it strangles so; I think that is why it has so many heads.

They get through, and then the pattern strangles them off and turns them upside down, and makes their eyes white!

If those heads were covered or taken off it would not be half so bad.

I think that woman gets out in the daytime!

And I'll tell you why—privately—I've seen her!

I can see her out of every one of my windows!

It is the same woman, I know, for she is always creeping, and most women do not creep by daylight.

I see her in that long shaded lane, creeping up and down. I see her in those dark grape arbors, creeping all around the garden.

I see her on that long road under the trees, creeping along, and when a carriage comes she hides under the blackberry vines.

I don't blame her a bit. It must be very humiliating to be caught creeping by daylight!

I always lock the door when I creep by daylight. I can't do it at night, for I know John would suspect something at once.

And John is so queer now, that I don't want to irritate him. I wish he would take another room! Besides, I don't want anybody to get that woman out at night but myself.

I often wonder if I could see her out of all the windows at once.

But, turn as fast as I can, I can only see out of one at one time.

And though I always see her, she *may* be able to creep faster than I can turn!

I have watched her sometimes away off in the open country, creeping as fast as a cloud shadow in a high wind.

If only that top pattern could be gotten off from the under one! I mean to try it, little by little.

I have found out another funny thing, but I shan't tell it this time! It does not do to trust people too much.

There are only two more days to get this paper off, and I believe John is beginning to notice. I don't like the look in his eyes.

And I heard him ask Jennie a lot of professional questions, about me. She had a very good report to give.

She said I slept a good deal in the daytime.

John knows I don't sleep very well at night, for all I'm so quiet!

He asked me all sorts of questions, too, and pretended to be very loving and kind.

As if I couldn't see through him!

Still, I don't wonder he acts so, sleeping under this paper for three months.

It only interests me, but I feel sure John and Jennie are secretly affected by it.

Hurrah! This is the last day, but it is enough. John to stay in town over night, and won't be out until this evening.

Jennie wanted to sleep with me — the sly thing! But I told her I should undoubtedly rest better for a night all alone.

That was clever, for really I wasn't alone a bit! As soon as it was moonlight and that poor thing began to crawl and shake the pattern, I got up and ran to help her.

I pulled and she shook, I shook and she pulled, and before morning we had peeled off yards of that paper.

A strip about as high as my head and half around the room.

And then when the sun came and that awful pattern began to laugh at me, I declared I would finish it to-day!

We go away to-morrow, and they are moving all my furniture down again to leave things as they were before.

Jennie looked at the wall in amazement, but I told her merrily that I did it out of pure spite at the vicious thing.

She laughed and said she wouldn't mind doing it herself, but I must not get tired.

How she betrayed herself that time!

But I am here, and no person touches this paper but me, — not *alive*!

She tried to get me out of the room—it was too patent! But I said it was so quiet and empty and clean now that I believed I would lie down again and sleep all I could, and not to wake me even for dinner—I would call when I woke.

So now she is gone, and the servants are gone, and the things are gone, and there is nothing left but that great bedstead nailed down, with the canvas mattress we found on it.

We shall sleep downstairs to-night, and take the boat home to-morrow.

I quite enjoy the room, now it is bare again.

How those children did tear about here!

This bedstead is fairly gnawed!

But I must get to work.

I have locked the door and thrown the key down into the front path.

I don't want to go out, and I don't want to have anybody come in, till John comes.

I want to astonish him.

I've got a rope up here that even Jennie did not find. If that woman does get out, and tries to get away, I can tie her!

But I forgot I could not reach far without anything to stand on!

This bed will *not* move!

I tried to lift and push it until I was lame, and then I got so angry I bit off a little piece at one corner—but it hurt my teeth.

Then I peeled off all the paper I could reach standing on the floor. It sticks horribly and the pattern just enjoys it! All those strangled heads and bulbous eyes and waddling fungus growths just shriek with derision!

I am getting angry enough to do something desperate. To jump out of the window would be admirable exercise, but the bars are too strong even to try.

Besides I wouldn't do it. Of course not. I know well enough that a step like that is improper and might be misconstrued.

I don't like to *look* out of the windows even—there are so many of those creeping women, and they creep so fast.

I wonder if they all come out of that wall-paper as I did?

But I am securely fastened now by my well-hidden rope—you don't get *me* out in the road there!

I suppose I shall have to get back behind the pattern when it comes night, and that is hard!

It is so pleasant to be out in this great room and creep around as I please!

I don't want to go outside. I won't, even if Jennie asks me to.

For outside you have to creep on the ground, and everything is green instead of yellow.

But here I can creep smoothly on the floor, and my shoulder just fits in that long smooch around the wall, so I cannot lose my way.

Why, there's John at the door!

It is no use, young man, you can't open it!

How he does call and pound!

Now he's crying for an axe.

It would be a shame to break down that beautiful door!

"John dear!" said I in the gentlest voice, "the key is down by the front steps, under a plantain leaf!"

That silenced him for a few moments. 260

Then he said—very quietly indeed, "Open the door, my darling!"

"I can't," said I. "The key is down by the front door under a plantain leaf!"

And then I said it again, several times, very gently and slowly, and said it so often that he had to go and see, and he got it of course, and came in. He stopped short by the door.

"What is the matter?" he cried. "For God's sake, what are you doing!"

I kept on creeping just the same, but I looked at him over my shoulder. 265

"I've got out at last," said I, "in spite of you and Jane. And I've pulled off most of the paper, so you can't put me back!"

Now why should that man have fainted? But he did, and right across my path by the wall, so that I had to creep over him every time!

[1892]

Exploring the Text

1. The narrator of "The Yellow Wallpaper" undergoes a profound change from the beginning of the story to the end. How is her change revealed in relation to her response to the wallpaper? How does she feel about the change? How do your feelings differ from the narrator's?

2. The narrator describes the room with the yellow wallpaper as a former nursery—that is, a room in a large house where children played, ate their meals, and may have been educated. What evidence is there that it may have had a different function? How does that discrepancy help develop the character of the narrator and communicate the themes of the story?

3. Much of the language used to describe the narrator's experience has both a denotative (descriptive) function and a connotative (symbolic or figurative) function. How do the meanings of such words and phrases as "yellow," "creeping," "immovable bed," and "outside pattern" change as they appear in different parts of the story?

4. Look at the description of the wallpaper in paragraphs 96–104. How does the syntax of the sentences both mirror the pattern on the wallpaper and suggest the narrator's agitation?

5. The narrator's husband, John, maintains his composure—and single-mindedness—for nearly the whole story. Characterize his change at the end. How does his fainting add another level of subversion to this early feminist story?

6. "The Yellow Wallpaper" raises the question of what happens when a person is deprived of the chance for creative expression. What are the similarities and differences between the suffering of Sonny in "Sonny's Blues" and the suffering of the narrator in this story?

Cathedral

RAYMOND CARVER

Raymond Carver (1938–1988) was born in Clatskanie, Oregon—a mill town on the Columbia River—and grew up in Yakima, Washington. His early life was haunted by poverty, his father's alcoholism, and domestic violence. After graduating from high school, Carver worked with his father at a sawmill in California. At nineteen, he married sixteen-year-old Maryann Burk, and by the time he was twenty, he was the father of two children. Carver supported his wife and children by working as a janitor, sawmill laborer, deliveryman, and library assistant. The family moved to California, where Carver took a creative-writing course taught by novelist John Gardner. Carver began to publish his writing, but developed such a serious drinking problem that he was hospitalized several times. With the help of Alcoholics Anonymous, Carver finally stopped drinking in 1977. Two years later he met poet Tess Gallagher, shortly after which he and Maryann separated and eventually divorced. Carver married Gallagher in 1988, only six weeks before he died of lung cancer. Carver's works include the poetry collections *Near Klamath* (1968), *At Night the Salmon Move* (1976), and *Path to the Waterfall* (1989), and the short-story collections *Put Yourself in My Shoes* (1974), *What We Talk about When We Talk about Love* (1981), and *Cathedral* (1982). Carver's writing style is minimalist; some attribute this to teachers and editors, such as John Gardner and Gordon Lish, who urged him to use fewer and fewer words. Carver said of this story selection, "There is definitely a change going on in my writing. It happened when I wrote the story 'Cathedral.'"

This blind man, an old friend of my wife's, he was on his way to spend the night. His wife had died. So he was visiting the dead wife's relatives in Connecticut. He called my wife from his in-laws'. Arrangements were made. He would come by train, a five-hour trip, and my wife would meet him at the station. She hadn't seen him since she worked for him one summer in Seattle ten years ago. But she and the blind man had kept in touch. They made tapes and mailed them back and forth. I wasn't enthusiastic about his visit. He was no one I knew. And his being blind bothered me. My idea of blindness came from the movies. In the movies, the blind moved slowly and never laughed. Sometimes they were led by seeing-eye dogs. A blind man in my house was not something I looked forward to.

That summer in Seattle she had needed a job. She didn't have any money. The man she was going to marry at the end of the summer was in officers' training school. He didn't have any money, either. But she was in love with the guy, and he was in love with her, etc. She'd seen something in the paper: HELP WANTED—*Reading to Blind Man*, and a telephone number. She phoned and went over, was hired on the spot. She'd worked with this blind man all summer. She read stuff to him, case studies, reports, that sort of thing. She helped him organize his little office in the county social-service department. They'd become good friends, my wife and the blind man. How do I know these things? She told me. And she told me something else. On her last day in the office, the blind man asked if he could touch her face. She agreed to this. She told me he touched his fingers to every part of her face, her nose — even her neck! She never forgot it. She even tried to write a poem about it. She was always trying to write a poem. She wrote a poem or two every year, usually after something really important had happened to her.

When we first started going out together, she showed me the poem. In the poem, she recalled his fingers and the way they had moved around over her face. In the poem, she talked about what she had felt at the time, about what went through her mind when the blind man touched her nose and lips. I can remember I didn't think much of the poem. Of course, I didn't tell her that. Maybe I just don't understand poetry. I admit it's not the first thing I reach for when I pick up something to read.

Anyway, this man who'd first enjoyed her favors, the officer-to-be, he'd been her childhood sweetheart. So okay. I'm saying that at the end of the summer she let the blind man run his hands over her face, said goodbye to him, married her childhood etc., who was now a commissioned officer, and she moved away from Seattle. But they'd kept in touch, she and the blind man. She made the first contact after a year or so. She called him up one night from an Air Force base in Alabama. She wanted to talk. They talked. He asked her to send him a tape and tell him about her life. She did this. She sent the tape. On the tape, she told the blind man about her husband and about their life together in the military. She told the blind man she loved her husband but she didn't like it where they lived and she didn't like it that he was a part of the military-industrial thing. She told the blind man she'd written a poem and he was in it. She told him that she was writing a poem about what it was like to be an Air Force officer's wife. The poem wasn't finished yet. She was still writing it. The blind man made a tape. He sent her the tape. She made a tape. This went on for years. My wife's officer was posted to one base and then another. She sent tapes from Moody AFB, McGuire, McConnell, and finally Travis, near Sacramento, where one night she got to feeling lonely and cut off from people she kept losing in that moving-around life. She got to feeling she couldn't go it another step. She went in and swallowed all the pills and capsules in the medicine chest and washed them down with a bottle of gin. Then she got into a hot bath and passed out.

But instead of dying, she got sick. She threw up. Her officer — why should he have a name? he was the childhood sweetheart, and what more does he want? — came home from somewhere, found her, and called the ambulance. In time, she put it all on a tape and sent the tape to the blind man. Over the years, she put all kinds of stuff on tapes and sent the tapes off lickety-split. Next to writing a poem every year, I think it was her chief means of recreation. On one tape, she told the blind man she'd decided to live away from her officer for a time. On another tape, she told him about her divorce. She and I began going out, and of course she told her blind man about it. She told him everything, or so it seemed to me. Once she asked me if I'd like to hear the latest tape from the blind man. This was a year ago. I was on the tape, she said. So I said okay, I'd listen to it. I got us drinks and we settled down in the living room. We made ready to listen. First she inserted the tape into the player and adjusted a couple of dials. Then she pushed a lever. The tape squeaked and someone began to talk in this loud voice. She lowered the volume. After a few minutes of harmless chitchat, I heard my own name in the mouth of this stranger, this blind man I didn't even know! And then this: "From all you've said about him, I can only conclude—" But we were interrupted, a knock at the door, something, and we didn't ever get back to the tape. Maybe it was just as well. I'd heard all I wanted to.

Now this same blind man was coming to sleep in my house.

"Maybe I could take him bowling," I said to my wife. She was at the draining board doing scalloped potatoes. She put down the knife she was using and turned around.

"If you love me," she said, "you can do this for me. If you don't love me, okay. But if you had a friend, any friend, and the friend came to visit, I'd make him feel comfortable." She wiped her hands with the dish towel.

"I don't have any blind friends," I said.

"You don't have *any* friends," she said. "Period. Besides," she said, "goddamn it, his wife's just died! Don't you understand that? The man's lost his wife!" 10

I didn't answer. She'd told me a little about the blind man's wife. Her name was Beulah. Beulah! That's a name for a colored woman.

"Was his wife Negro?" I asked.

"Are you crazy?" my wife said. "Have you just flipped or something?" She picked up a potato. I saw it hit the floor, then roll under the stove. "What's wrong with you?" she said. "Are you drunk?"

"I'm just asking," I said.

Right then my wife filled me in with more detail than I cared to know. I made a 15 drink and sat at the kitchen table to listen. Pieces of the story began to fall into place.

Beulah had gone to work for the blind man the summer after my wife had stopped working for him. Pretty soon Beulah and the blind man had themselves a church wedding. It was a little wedding—who'd want to go to such a wedding in the first place?—just the two of them, plus the minister and the minister's wife. But it was a church wedding just the same. It was what Beulah had wanted, he'd said. But even then Beulah must have been carrying the cancer in her glands. After they had been inseparable for eight years—my wife's word, *inseparable*—Beulah's health went into a rapid decline. She died in a Seattle hospital room, the blind man sitting beside the bed and holding on to her hand. They'd married, lived and worked together, slept together—had sex, sure—and then the blind man had to bury her. All this without his having ever seen what the goddamned woman looked like. It was beyond my understanding. Hearing this, I felt sorry for the blind man for a little bit. And then I found myself thinking what a pitiful life this woman must have led. Imagine a woman who could never see herself as she was seen in the eyes of her loved one. A woman who could go on day after day and never receive the smallest compliment from her beloved. A woman whose husband could never read the expression on her face, be it misery or something better. Someone who could wear makeup or not—what difference to him? She could, if she wanted, wear green eye-shadow around one eye, a straight pin in her nostril, yellow slacks and purple shoes, no mat-ter. And then to slip off into death, the blind man's hand on her hand, his blind eyes streaming tears—I'm imagining now—her last thought maybe this: that he never even knew what she looked like, and she on an express to the grave. Robert was left with a small insurance policy and half of a twenty-peso Mexican coin. The other half of the coin went into the box with her. Pathetic.

So when the time rolled around, my wife went to the depot to pick him up. With nothing to do but wait—sure, I blamed him for that—I was having a drink and watching the TV when I heard the car pull into the drive. I got up from the sofa with my drink and went to the window to have a look.

I saw my wife laughing as she parked the car. I saw her get out of the car and shut the door. She was still wearing a smile. Just amazing. She went around to the other side of the car to where the blind man was already starting to get out. This blind man, feature this, he was wearing a full beard! A beard on a blind man! Too much, I say. The blind man reached into the back seat and dragged out a suitcase. My wife took his arm, shut the car door, and, talking all the way, moved him down the drive and then up the steps to the front porch. I turned off the TV. I finished my drink, rinsed the glass, dried my hands. Then I went to the door.

My wife said, "I want you to meet Robert. Robert, this is my husband. I've told you all about him." She was beaming. She had this blind man by his coat sleeve.

The blind man let go of his suitcase and up came his hand.   20

I took it. He squeezed hard, held my hand, and then he let it go.

"I feel like we've already met," he boomed.

"Likewise," I said. I didn't know what else to say. Then I said, "Welcome. I've heard a lot about you." We began to move then, a little group, from the porch into the living room, my wife guiding him by the arm. The blind man was carrying his suitcase in his other hand. My wife said things like, "To your left here, Robert. That's right. Now watch it, there's a chair. That's it. Sit down right here. This is the sofa. We just bought this sofa two weeks ago."

I started to say something about the old sofa. I'd liked that old sofa. But I didn't say anything. Then I wanted to say something else, small-talk, about the scenic ride along the Hudson. How going *to* New York, you should sit on the right-hand side of the train, and coming *from* New York, the left-hand side.

"Did you have a good train ride?" I said. "Which side of the train did you sit on,   25 by the way?"

"What a question, which side!" my wife said. "What's it matter which side?" she said.

"I just asked," I said.

"Right side," the blind man said. "I hadn't been on a train in nearly forty years. Not since I was a kid. With my folks. That's been a long time. I'd nearly forgotten the sensation. I have winter in my beard now," he said. "So I've been told, anyway. Do I look distinguished, my dear?" the blind man said to my wife.

"You look distinguished, Robert," she said. "Robert," she said. "Robert, it's just so good to see you."

My wife finally took her eyes off the blind man and looked at me. I had the feel- 30
ing she didn't like what she saw. I shrugged.

I've never met, or personally known, anyone who was blind. This blind man
was late forties, a heavy-set, balding man with stooped shoulders, as if he carried a
great weight there. He wore brown slacks, brown shoes, a light-brown shirt, a tie, a
sports coat. Spiffy. He also had this full beard. But he didn't use a cane and he didn't
wear dark glasses. I'd always thought dark glasses were a must for the blind. Fact
was, I wished he had a pair. At first glance, his eyes looked like anyone else's eyes.
But if you look close, there was something different about them. Too much white
in the iris, for one thing, and the pupils seemed to move around in the sockets
without his knowing it or being able to stop it. Creepy. As I stared at his face, I saw
the left pupil turn in toward his nose while the other made an effort to keep in one
place. But it was only an effort, for that eye was on the roam without his knowing
it or wanting it to be.

I said, "Let me get you a drink. What's your pleasure? We have a little of everything. It's one of our pastimes."

"Bub, I'm a Scotch man myself," he said fast enough in this big voice.

"Right," I said. Bub! "Sure you are, I knew it."

He let his fingers touch his suitcase, which was sitting alongside the sofa. He was 35
taking his bearings. I didn't blame him for that.

"I'll move that up to your room," my wife said.

"No, that's fine," the blind man said loudly. "It can go up when I go up."

"A little water with the Scotch?" I said.

"Very little," he said.

"I knew it," I said. 40

He said, "Just a tad. The Irish actor, Barry Fitzgerald? I'm like that fellow. When
I drink water, Fitzgerald said, I drink water. When I drink whiskey, I drink whiskey."
My wife laughed. The blind man brought his hand up under his beard. He lifted his
beard slowly and let it drop.

I did the drinks, three big glasses of Scotch with a splash of water in each. Then
we made ourselves comfortable and talked about Robert's travels. First the long flight
from the West Coast to Connecticut, we covered that. Then from Connecticut up
here by train. We had another drink concerning that leg of the trip.

I remembered having read somewhere that the blind didn't smoke because, as
speculation had it, they couldn't see the smoke they exhaled. I thought I knew that
much and that much only about blind people. But this blind man smoked his cigarette down to the nubbin and then lit another one. This blind man filled his ashtray
and my wife emptied it.

When we sat down at the table for dinner, we had another drink. My wife heaped
Robert's plate with cube steak, scalloped potatoes, green beans. I buttered him up
two slices of bread. I said, "Here's bread and butter for you." I swallowed some of my
drink. "Now let us pray," I said, and the blind man lowered his head. My wife looked
at me, her mouth agape. "Pray the phone won't ring and the food doesn't get cold,"
I said.

We dug in. We ate everything there was to eat on the table. We ate like there was   45
no tomorrow. We didn't talk. We ate. We scarfed. We grazed that table. We were into
serious eating. The blind man had right away located his foods, he knew just where
everything was on his plate. I watched with admiration as he used his knife and fork
on the meat. He'd cut two pieces of meat, fork the meat into his mouth, and then
go all out for the scalloped potatoes, the beans next, and then he'd tear off a hunk
of buttered bread and eat that. He'd follow this up with a big drink of milk. It didn't
seem to bother him to use his fingers once in a while, either.

We finished everything, including half a strawberry pie. For a few moments, we sat
as if stunned. Sweat beaded on our faces. Finally, we got up from the table and left the
dirty plates. We didn't look back. We took ourselves into the living room and sank into
our places again. Robert and my wife sat on the sofa. I took the big chair. We had us two
or three more drinks while they talked about the major things that had come to pass
for them in the past ten years. For the most part, I just listened. Now and then I joined
in. I didn't want him to think I'd left the room, and I didn't want her to think I was
feeling left out. They talked of things that had happened to them — to them! — these
past ten years. I waited in vain to hear my name on my wife's sweet lips: "And then my
dear husband came into my life" — something like that. But I heard nothing of the sort.
More talk of Robert. Robert had done a little of everything, it seemed, a regular blind
jack-of-all-trades. But most recently he and his wife had had an Amway distributor-
ship, from which, I gathered, they'd earned their living, such as it was. The blind man
was also a ham radio operator. He talked in his loud voice about conversations he'd
had with fellow operators in Guam, in the Philippines, in Alaska, and even in Tahiti.
He said he'd have a lot of friends there if he ever wanted to go visit those places. From
time to time, he'd turn his blind face toward me, put his hand under his beard, ask me
something. How long had I been in my present position? (Three years.) Did I like my
work? (I didn't.) Was I going to stay with it? (What were the options?) Finally, when I
thought he was beginning to run down, I got up and turned on the TV.

My wife looked at me with irritation. She was heading toward a boil. Then she
looked at the blind man and said, "Robert, do you have a TV?"

The blind man said, "My dear, I have two TVs. I have a color set and a black-and-
white thing, an old relic. It's funny, but if I turn the TV on, and I'm always turning it
on, I turn on the color set. It's funny, don't you think?"

I didn't know what to say to that. I had absolutely nothing to say to that. No
opinions. So I watched the news program and tried to listen to what the announcer
was saying.

"This is a color TV," the blind man said. "Don't ask me how, but I can tell."   50

"We traded up a while ago," I said.

The blind man had another taste of his drink. He lifted his beard, sniffed it, and let it
fall. He leaned forward on the sofa. He positioned his ashtray on the coffee table, then put
the lighter to his cigarette. He leaned back on the sofa and crossed his legs at the ankles.

My wife covered her mouth, and then she yawned. She stretched. She said, "I
think I'll go upstairs and put on my robe. I think I'll change into something else.
Robert, you make yourself comfortable," she said.

"I'm comfortable," the blind man said.

"I want you to feel comfortable in this house," she said.   55

"I am comfortable," the blind man said.

After she'd left the room, he and I listened to the weather report and then to the sports roundup. By that time, she'd been gone so long I didn't know if she was going to come back. I thought she might have gone to bed. I wished she'd come back downstairs. I didn't want to be left alone with a blind man. I asked him if he wanted another drink, and he said sure. Then I asked if he wanted to smoke some dope with me. I said I'd just rolled a number. I hadn't, but I planned to do so in about two shakes.

"I'll try some with you," he said.

"Damn right," I said. "That's the stuff."

I got our drinks and sat down on the sofa with him. Then I rolled us two   60
fat numbers. I lit one and passed it. I brought it to his fingers. He took it and inhaled.

"Hold it as long as you can," I said. I could tell he didn't know the first thing.

My wife came back downstairs wearing her pink robe and her pink slippers.

"What do I smell?" she said.

"We thought we'd have us some cannabis," I said.

My wife gave me a savage look. Then she looked at the blind man and said,   65
"Robert, I didn't know you smoked."

He said, "I do now, my dear. There's a first time for everything. But I don't feel anything yet."

"This stuff is pretty mellow," I said. "This stuff is mild. It's dope you can reason with," I said. "It doesn't mess you up."

"Not much it doesn't, bub," he said, and laughed.

My wife sat on the sofa between the blind man and me. I passed her the number. She took it and toked and then passed it back to me. "Which way is this going?" she said. Then she said, "I shouldn't be smoking this. I can hardly keep my eyes open as it is. That dinner did me in. I shouldn't have eaten so much."

"It was the strawberry pie," the blind man said. "That's what did it," he said, and   70
he laughed his big laugh. Then he shook his head.

"There's more strawberry pie," I said.

"Do you want some more, Robert?" my wife said.

"Maybe in a little while," he said.

We gave our attention to the TV. My wife yawned again. She said, "Your bed is made up when you feel like going to bed, Robert. I know you must have had a long day. When you're ready to go to bed, say so." She pulled his arm. "Robert?"

He came to and said, "I've had a real nice time. This beats tapes, doesn't it?"   75

I said, "Coming at you," and I put the number between his fingers. He inhaled, held the smoke, and then let it go. It was like he'd been doing it since he was nine years old.

"Thanks, bub," he said. "But I think this is all for me. I think I'm beginning to feel it," he said. He held the burning roach out for my wife.

"Same here," she said. "Ditto. Me, too." She took the roach and passed it to me. "I may just sit here for a while between you two guys with my eyes closed. But don't let me bother you, okay? Either one of you. If it bothers you, say so. Otherwise, I may just sit here with my eyes closed until you're ready to go to bed," she said. "Your bed's made up, Robert, when you're ready. It's right next to our room at the top of the stairs. We'll show you up when you're ready. You wake me up now, you guys, if I fall asleep." She said that and then she closed her eyes and went to sleep.

The news program ended. I got up and changed the channel. I sat back down on the sofa. I wished my wife hadn't pooped out. Her head lay across the back of the sofa, her mouth open. She'd turned so that her robe had slipped away from her legs, exposing a juicy thigh. I reached to draw her robe back over her, and it was then that I glanced at the blind man. What the hell! I flipped the robe open again.

"You say when you want some strawberry pie," I said.   80

"I will," he said.

I said, "Are you tired? Do you want me to take you up to your bed? Are you ready to hit the hay?"

"Not yet," he said. "No, I'll stay up with you, bub. If that's all right. I'll stay up until you're ready to turn in. We haven't had a chance to talk. Know what I mean? I feel like me and her monopolized the evening." He lifted his beard and he let it fall. He picked up his cigarettes and his lighter.

"That's all right," I said. Then I said, "I'm glad for the company."

And I guess I was. Every night I smoked dope and stayed up as long as I could   85
before I fell asleep. My wife and I hardly ever went to bed at the same time. When I did go to sleep, I had these dreams. Sometimes I'd wake up from one of them, my heart going crazy.

Something about the church and the Middle Ages was on the TV. Not your run-of-the-mill TV fare. I wanted to watch something else. I turned to the other channels. But there was nothing on them, either. So I turned back to the first channel and apologized.

"Bub, it's all right," the blind man said. "It's fine with me. Whatever you want to watch is okay. I'm always learning something. Learning never ends. It won't hurt me to learn something tonight. I got ears," he said.

We didn't say anything for a time. He was leaning forward with his head turned at me, his right ear aimed in the direction of the set. Very disconcerting. Now and then his eyelids drooped and then they snapped open again. Now and then he put his fingers into his beard and tugged, like he was thinking about something he was hearing on the television.

On the screen, a group of men wearing cowls was being set upon and tormented by men dressed in skeleton costumes and men dressed as devils. The men dressed as devils wore devil masks, horns, and long tails. This pageant was part of a procession. The Englishman who was narrating the thing said it took place in Spain once a year. I tried to explain to the blind man what was happening.

"Skeletons," he said. "I know about skeletons," he said, and he nodded.   90

The TV showed this one cathedral. Then there was a long, slow look at another one. Finally, the picture switched to the famous one in Paris, with its flying buttresses and its spires reaching up to the clouds. The camera pulled away to show the whole of the cathedral rising above the skyline.

There were times when the Englishman who was telling the thing would shut up, would simply let the camera move around over the cathedrals. Or else the camera would tour the countryside, men in fields walking behind oxen. I waited as long as I could. Then I felt I had to say something. I said, "They're showing the outside of this cathedral now. Gargoyles. Little statues carved to look like monsters. Now I guess they're in Italy. Yeah, they're in Italy. There's paintings on the walls of this one church."

"Are those fresco paintings, bub?" he asked, and he sipped from his drink.

I reached for my glass. But it was empty. I tried to remember what I could remember. "You're asking me are those frescoes?" I said. "That's a good question. I don't know."

The camera moved to a cathedral outside Lisbon. The differences in the Portuguese 95 cathedral compared with the French and Italian were not that great. But they were there. Mostly the interior stuff. Then something occurred to me, and I said, "Something has occurred to me. Do you have any idea what a cathedral is? What they look like, that is? Do you follow me? If somebody says cathedral to you, do you have any notion what they're talking about? Do you know the difference between that and a Baptist church, say?"

He let the smoke dribble from his mouth. "I know they took hundreds of workers fifty or a hundred years to build," he said. "I just heard the man say that, of course. I know generations of the same families worked on a cathedral. I heard him say that, too. The men who began their life's work on them, they never lived to see the completion of their work. In that wise, bub, they're no different from the rest of us, right?" He laughed. Then his eyelids drooped again. His head nodded. He seemed to be snoozing. Maybe he was imagining himself in Portugal. The TV was showing another cathedral now. This one was in Germany. The Englishman's voice droned on. "Cathedrals," the blind man said. He sat up and rolled his head back and forth. "If you want the truth, bub, that's about all I know. What I just said. What I heard him say. But maybe you could describe one to me? I wish you'd do it. I'd like that. If you want to know, I really don't have a good idea."

I stared hard at the shot of the cathedral on the TV. How could I even begin to describe it? But say my life depended on it. Say my life was being threatened by an insane guy who said I had to do it or else.

I stared some more at the cathedral before the picture flipped off into the countryside. There was no use. I turned to the blind man and said, "To begin with, they're very tall." I was looking around the room for clues. "They reach way up. Up and up. Toward the sky. They're so big, some of them, they have to have these supports. To help hold them up, so to speak. These supports are called buttresses. They remind me of viaducts, for some reason. But maybe you don't know viaducts, either? Sometimes the cathedrals have devils and such carved into the front. Sometimes lords and ladies. Don't ask me why this is," I said.

He was nodding. The whole upper part of his body seemed to be moving back and forth.

"I'm not doing so good, am I?" I said. 100

He stopped nodding and leaned forward on the edge of the sofa. As he listened to me, he was running his fingers through his beard. I wasn't getting through to him, I could see that. But he waited for me to go on just the same. He nodded, like he was trying to encourage me. I tried to think what else to say. "They're really big," I said. "They're massive. They're built of stone. Marble, too, sometimes. In those olden days, when they built cathedrals, men wanted to be close to God. In those olden days, God was an important part of everyone's life. You could tell this from their cathedral-building. I'm sorry," I said, "but it looks like that's the best I can do for you. I'm just no good at it."

"That's all right, bub," the blind man said. "Hey, listen. I hope you don't mind my asking you. Can I ask you something? Let me ask you a simple question, yes or no. I'm just curious and there's no offense. You're my host. But let me ask if you are in any way religious? You don't mind my asking?"

I shook my head. He couldn't see that, though. A wink is the same as a nod to a blind man. "I guess I don't believe in it. In anything. Sometimes it's hard. You know what I'm saying?"

"Sure I do," he said.

"Right," I said. 105

The Englishman was still holding forth. My wife sighed in her sleep. She drew a long breath and went on with her sleeping.

"You'll have to forgive me," I said. "But I can't tell you what a cathedral looks like. It just isn't in me to do it. I can't do any more than I've done."

The blind man sat very still, his head down, as he listened to me.

I said, "The truth is, cathedrals don't mean anything special to me. Nothing. Cathedrals. They're something to look at on late-night TV. That's all they are."

It was then that the blind man cleared his throat. He brought something up. He 110
took a handkerchief from his back pocket. Then he said, "I get it, bub. It's okay. It happens. Don't worry about it," he said. "Hey, listen to me. Will you do me a favor? I got an idea. Why don't you find us some heavy paper? And a pen. We'll do some-thing. We'll draw one together. Get us a pen and some heavy paper. Go on, bub, get the stuff," he said.

So I went upstairs. My legs felt like they didn't have any strength in them. They felt like they did after I'd done some running. In my wife's room, I looked around. I found some ballpoints in a little basket on her table. And then I tried to think where to look for the kind of paper he was talking about.

Downstairs, in the kitchen, I found a shopping bag with onion skins in the bot-tom of the bag. I emptied the bag and shook it. I brought it into the living room and sat down with it near his legs. I moved some things, smoothed the wrinkles from the bag, spread it out on the coffee table.

The blind man got down from the sofa and sat next to me on the carpet.

He ran his fingers over the paper. He went up and down the sides of the paper. The edges, even the edges. He fingered the corners.

"All right," he said. "All right, let's do her." 115

He found my hand, the hand with the pen. He closed his hand over my hand. "Go ahead, bub, draw," he said. "Draw. You'll see. I'll follow along with you. It'll be okay. Just begin now like I'm telling you. You'll see. Draw," the blind man said.

So I began. First I drew a box that looked like a house. It could have been the house I lived in. Then I put a roof on it. At either end of the roof, I drew spires. Crazy.

"Swell," he said. "Terrific. You're doing fine," he said.

"Never thought anything like this could happen in your lifetime, did you, bub? Well, it's a strange life, we all know that. Go on now. Keep it up."

I put in windows with arches. I drew flying buttresses. I hung great doors. I   120
couldn't stop. The TV station went off the air. I put down the pen and closed and opened my fingers. The blind man felt round over the paper. He moved the tips of his fingers over the paper, all over what I had drawn, and he nodded.

"Doing fine," the blind man said.

I took up the pen again, and he found my hand. I kept at it. I'm no artist. But I kept drawing just the same.

My wife opened up her eyes and gazed at us. She sat up on the sofa, her robe hanging open. She said, "What are you doing? Tell me, I want to know."

I didn't answer her.

The blind man said, "We're drawing a cathedral. Me and him are working on it.   125
Press hard," he said to me. "That's right. That's good," he said. "Sure. You got it, bub. I can tell. You didn't think you could. But you can, can't you? You're cooking with gas now. You know what I'm saying? We're going to really have us something here in a minute. How's the old arm?" he said. "Put some people in there now. What's a cathedral without people?"

My wife said, "What's going on? Robert, what are you doing? What's going on?"

"It's all right," he said to her. "Close your eyes now," the blind man said to me.

I did it. I closed them just like he said.

"Are they closed?" he said. "Don't fudge."

"They're closed," I said.   130

"Keep them that way," he said. He said, "Don't stop now. Draw."

So we kept on with it. His fingers rode my fingers as my hand went over the paper. It was like nothing else in my life up to now.

Then he said, "I think that's it. I think you got it," he said. "Take a look. What do you think?"

But I had my eyes closed. I thought I'd keep them that way for a little longer. I thought it was something I ought to do.

"Well?" he said. "Are you looking?"   135

My eyes were still closed. I was in my house. I knew that. But I didn't feel like I was inside anything.

"It's really something," I said.

[1981]

Exploring the Text

1. How does the first-person narrator of "Cathedral" reveal himself to the reader? Note his tone. Notice also the details he chooses to reveal about himself and his wife, as well as the ones he doesn't reveal. What character traits are you able to ascertain even in the first few paragraphs?
2. How does Carver's narrator set the reader up for meeting the blind man? Is your first response to Robert the same as the narrator's? Look at paragraphs 18–44. How does Carver use both the conversation and the narrator's private thoughts to create the blind man's character while also continuing to develop the character of the narrator?
3. Blindness is both a subject of "Cathedral" and a recurring motif. Consider the many different ways blindness is addressed in the story. How does each add complexity and meaning to the story?
4. What is it about a cathedral that makes this architectural structure so perfect for the story? Consider some of the information the narrator and Robert learn from the television show they have on, as well as what you already know about cathedrals. What does this story say about both the art of building a cathedral and the art of drawing a picture for a blind man?
5. The narrator experiences an epiphany—a moment of sudden insight and clarity—at the end of the story, but the author never explains what that insight is. Why do you think Carver withholds that specific information from the reader? What other information is withheld from the reader? Why?
6. Characterize the habits of the narrator and his wife. They do not seem close; they watch television rather than talk to each other; they drink to excess, overeat, and use drugs. Does Carver judge them? Do you?
7. Carver's stories often focus on sadness and loss in the everyday lives of ordinary people. How is that both true and not true of "Cathedral"?
8. Who do you think is the hero of the story? Why?

Videotape

DON DELILLO

Novelist Don DeLillo was born in the Bronx, in New York City, in 1936. Educated at Fordham University, DeLillo worked in advertising for five years before he became a full-time writer. He is the author of the novels *White Noise* (1985), *Running Dog* (1978), *The Names* (1982), *Libra* (1988), *Underworld* (1997), *The Body Artist* (2001), and *Falling Man* (2007), among others. DeLillo is considered one of the central figures of twentieth- and twenty-first-century postmodernism, a term used to describe various movements in the arts that question modern assumptions about culture, identity, history, or language. When DeLillo was asked how he felt about that classification, he responded, "I don't react. But I'd prefer not to be labeled. I'm a novelist, period. An American novelist." A recurring theme in

DeLillo's work is the saturation of mass media and the ways it removes or changes the meaning of events—a theme apparent in "Videotape."

I t shows a man driving a car. It is the simplest sort of family video. You see a man at the wheel of a medium Dodge.

It is just a kid aiming her camera through the rear window of the family car at the windshield of the car behind her.

You know about families and their video cameras. You know how kids get involved, how the camera shows them that every subject is potentially charged, a million things they never see with the unaided eye. They investigate the meaning of inert objects and dumb pets and they poke at family privacy. They learn to see things twice.

It is the kid's own privacy that is being protected here. She is twelve years old and her name is being withheld even though she is neither the victim nor the perpetrator of the crime but only the means of recording it.

It shows a man in a sport shirt at the wheel of his car. There is nothing else to   5
see. The car approaches briefly, then falls back.

You know how children with cameras learn to work the exposed moments that define the family cluster. They break every trust, spy out the undefended space, catching mom coming out of the bathroom in her cumbrous robe and turbaned towel, looking bloodless and plucked. It is not a joke. They will shoot you sitting on the pot if they can manage a suitable vantage.

The tape has the jostled sort of noneventness that marks the family product. Of course the man in this case is not a member of the family but a stranger in a car, a random figure, someone who has happened along in the slow lane.

It shows a man in his forties wearing a pale shirt open at the throat, the image washed by reflections and sunglint, with many jostled moments.

It is not just another video homicide. It is a homicide recorded by a child who thought she was doing something simple and maybe halfway clever, shooting some tape of a man in a car.

He sees the girl and waves briefly, wagging a hand without taking it off the   10
wheel—an underplayed reaction that makes you like him.

It is unrelenting footage that rolls on and on. It has an aimless determination, a persistence that lives outside the subject matter. You are looking into the mind of home video. It is innocent, it is aimless, it is determined, it is real.

He is bald up the middle of his head, a nice guy in his forties whose whole life seems open to the hand-held camera.

But there is also an element of suspense. You keep on looking not because you know something is going to happen—of course you do know something is going to happen and you do look for that reason but you might also keep on looking if you came across this footage for the first time without knowing the outcome. There is a crude power operating here. You keep on looking because things combine to hold you fast—a sense of the random, the amateurish, the accidental, the impending. You don't think of the tape as boring or interesting. It is crude, it is blunt, it is relentless.

It is the jostled part of your mind, the film that runs through your hotel brain under all the thoughts you know you're thinking.

The world is lurking in the camera, already framed, waiting for the boy or girl who will come along and take up the device, learn the instrument, shooting old granddad at breakfast, all stroked out so his nostrils gape, the cereal spoon baby-gripped in his pale fist.

It shows a man alone in a medium Dodge. It seems to go on forever.   15

There's something about the nature of the tape, the grain of the image, the sputtering black-and-white tones, the starkness—you think this is more real, truer-to-life than anything around you. The things around you have a rehearsed and layered and cosmetic look. The tape is superreal, or maybe underreal is the way you want to put it. It is what lies at the scraped bottom of all the layers you have added. And this is another reason why you keep on looking. The tape has a searing realness.

It shows him giving an abbreviated wave, stiff-palmed, like a signal flag at a siding.

You know how families make up games. This is just another game in which the child invents the rules as she goes along. She likes the idea of videotaping a man in his car. She has probably never done it before and she sees no reason to vary the format or terminate early or pan to another car. This is her game and she is learning it and playing it at the same time. She feels halfway clever and inventive and maybe slightly intrusive as well, a little bit of brazenness that spices any game.

And you keep on looking. You look because this is the nature of the footage, to make a channeled path through time, to give things a shape and a destiny.

Of course if she had panned to another car, the right car at the precise time, she   20 would have caught the gunman as he fired.

The chance quality of the encounter. The victim, the killer and the child with a camera. Random energies that approach a common point. There's something here that speaks to you directly, saying terrible things about forces beyond your control, lines of intersection that cut through history and logic and every reasonable layer of human expectation.

She wandered into it. The girl got lost and wandered clear-eyed into horror. This is a children's story about straying too far from home. But it isn't the family car that serves as the instrument of the child's curiosity, her inclination to explore. It is the camera that puts her in the tale.

You know about holidays and family celebrations and how somebody shows up with a camcorder and the relatives stand around and barely react because they're numbingly accustomed to the process of being taped and decked and shown on the VCR with the coffee and cake.

He is hit soon after. If you've seen the tape many times you know from the hand wave exactly when he will be hit. It is something, naturally, that you wait for. You say to your wife, if you're at home and she is there, Now here is where he gets it. You say, Janet, hurry up, this is where it happens.

Now here is where he gets it. You see him jolted, sort of wire-shocked—then   25 he seizes up and falls toward the door or maybe leans or slides into the door is the proper way to put it. It is awful and unremarkable at the same time. The car stays in the slow lane. It approaches briefly, then falls back.

You don't usually call your wife over to the TV set. She has her programs, you have yours. But there's a certain urgency here. You want her to see how it looks. The tape has been running forever and now the thing is finally going to happen and you want her to be here when he's shot.

Here it comes all right. He is shot, head-shot, and the camera reacts, the child reacts—there is a jolting movement but she keeps on taping, there is a sympathetic response, a nerve response, her heart is beating faster but she keeps the camera trained on the subject as he slides into the door and even as you see him die you're thinking of the girl. At some level the girl has to be present here, watching what you're watching, unprepared—the girl is seeing this cold and you have to marvel at the fact that she keeps the tape rolling.

It shows something awful and unaccompanied. You want your wife to see it because it is real this time, not fancy movie violence—the realness beneath the layers of cosmetic perception. Hurry up, Janet, here it comes. He dies so fast. There is no accompaniment of any kind. It is very stripped. You want to tell her it is realer than real but then she will ask what that means.

The way the camera reacts to the gunshot—a startle reaction that brings pity and terror into the frame, the girl's own shock, the girl's identification with the victim.

You don't see the blood, which is probably trickling behind his ear and down the   30 back of his neck. The way his head is twisted away from the door, the twist of the head gives you only a partial profile and it's the wrong side, it's not the side where he was hit.

And maybe you're being a little aggressive here, practically forcing your wife to watch. Why? What are you telling her? Are you making a little statement? Like I'm going to ruin your day out of ordinary spite. Or a big statement? Like this is the risk of existing. Either way you're rubbing her face in this tape and you don't know why.

It shows the car drifting toward the guardrail and then there's a jostling sense of two other lanes and part of another car, a split-second blur, and the tape ends here, either because the girl stopped shooting or because some central authority, the police or the district attorney or the TV station, decided there was nothing else you had to see.

This is either the tenth or eleventh homicide committed by the Texas Highway Killer. The number is uncertain because the police believe that one of the shootings may have been a copycat crime.

And there is something about videotape, isn't there, and this particular kind of serial crime? This is a crime designed for random taping and immediate playing. You sit there and wonder if this kind of crime became more possible when the means of taping an event and playing it immediately, without a neutral interval, a balancing space and time, became widely available. Taping-and-playing intensifies and compresses the event. It dangles a need to do it again. You sit there thinking that the serial murder has found its medium, or vice versa—an act of shadow technology, of compressed time and repeated images, stark and glary and unremarkable.

It shows very little in the end. It is a famous murder because it is on tape and   35 because the murderer has done it many times and because the crime was recorded by a child. So the child is involved, the Video Kid as she is sometimes called because they have to call her something. The tape is famous and so is she. She is famous in the modern manner of people whose names are strategically withheld. They are famous without names or faces, spirits living apart from their bodies, the victims and witnesses, the underage criminals, out there somewhere at the edges of perception.

Seeing someone at the moment he dies, dying unexpectedly. This is reason alone to stay fixed to the screen. It is instructional, watching a man shot dead as he drives along on a sunny day. It demonstrates an elemental truth, that every breath you take has two possible endings. And that's another thing. There's a joke locked away here, a note of cruel slapstick that you are willing to appreciate even if it makes you feel a little guilty. Maybe the victim's a chump, a sort of silent-movie dupe, classically unlucky. He had it coming in a sense, for letting himself be caught on camera. Because once the tape starts rolling it can only end one way. This is what the context requires.

You don't want Janet to give you any crap about it's on all the time, they show it a thousand times a day. They show it because it exists, because they have to show it, because this is why they're out there, to provide our entertainment.

The more you watch the tape, the deader and colder and more relentless it becomes. The tape sucks the air right out of your chest but you watch it every time.

[1994]

. . . .

Exploring the Text

1. Who is the main character of "Videotape"? If you think of several answers, consider how each answer would affect the focus of the story and thus its theme and message.
2. What evidence of the traditional elements of plot, such as conflict, rising action, and climax, do you find in "Videotape"? How does DeLillo subvert and change some of these?
3. How does DeLillo create the story's pace? How is it similar to the way an amateur video unwinds?
4. Can you consider the point of view of this story to be second person? The speaker addresses the reader: "If you've seen the tape many times you know from the hand wave exactly when he will be hit. . . . You say to your wife, if you're at home and she is there, Now here is where he gets it. You say, Janet, hurry up, this is where it happens" (para. 24). And yet the reader doesn't have a wife named Janet or any wife at all most likely. How does the "you" of the story become another character but also represent the reader? How does this technique help DeLillo achieve the purpose of his story?
5. "Videotape" is considered a masterpiece of sudden fiction, a genre or subset of fiction characterized by immediacy. Somewhat like *in medias res* (in the middle of things)—the technique Homer uses in the *Iliad* to drop us right into the action at the end of the Trojan War—the reader is thrown into an event that began before he or she got there; the setting is underexplained, or not explained at all; and yet by the time the story is finished, a strong sense of plot and setting remains. Why is this genre particularly apt for the story DeLillo tells in "Videotape"?

6. How does this story question the relationship between art — or at least the contents of a video aired often on the news — and the artist — in this case a young girl fooling around during a car ride with her family?

Sound and Sense

ALEXANDER POPE

> Alexander Pope (1688–1744) is generally considered the eighteenth century's greatest English poet. Known for satirical verse, Pope was the first writer to be able to live off the proceeds of his work — namely, his very popular translation of Homer's *Iliad*. Pope was a Roman Catholic, and the anti-Catholic sentiment and laws of his time dictated — and limited — his formal education. He read widely on his own, learning French, Italian, Latin, and Greek. Critics attacked Pope's version of Shakespeare's work, and he responded with "The Dunciad" — a scathing satire of the literary establishment that brought him enemies and even threats of physical violence. Pope's work goes in and out of fashion, but some of his words are so ingrained in the English language that they are considered proverbs by those unfamiliar with his work. "A little learning is a dangerous thing," "To err is human, to forgive, divine," and "For fools rush in where angels fear to tread" are from *Essay on Criticism;* "Hope springs eternal in the human breast" and "The proper study of mankind is man" are both found in *Essay on Man.* The selection that follows is from "An Essay on Criticism," Pope's poem on the art of poetry. Its purpose was not so much to provide lessons for writers but to offer advice to critics.

True ease in writing comes from art, not chance,
As those move easiest who have learned to dance.
'Tis not enough no harshness gives offense,
The sound must seem an echo to the sense:
Soft is the strain when Zephyr[1] gently blows,   5
And the smooth stream in smoother numbers flows;
But when loud surges lash the sounding shore,
The hoarse, rough verse should like the torrent roar.
When Ajax[2] strives, some rock's vast weight to throw,
The line too labors, and the words move slow;   10
Not so, when swift Camilla[3] scours the plain,
Flies o'er th' unbending corn, and skims along the main.
Hear how Timotheus'[4] varied lays surprise,
And bid alternate passions fall and rise!

---

[1] The west wind, after Zephyrus, the Greek god of the west wind. — EDS.
[2] Hero in the Trojan War and Homer's *Iliad.* — EDS.
[3] Warrior in Virgil's *Aeneid.* — EDS.
[4] Ancient Greek poet and musician, and character in John Dryden's poem "Alexander's Feast." — EDS.

While, at each change, the son of Libyan Jove,[5]   15
Now burns with glory, and then melts with love;
Now his fierce eyes with sparkling fury glow,
Now sighs steal out, and tears begin to flow;
Persians and Greeks like turns of nature found,
And the world's victor stood subdued by sound!   20
The pow'r of music all our hearts allow,
And what Timotheus was, is DRYDEN now.

[1711]

Exploring the Text

1. Using allusions to classical mythology that he would have expected his readers to know, Pope makes his point in "Sound and Sense" by exemplifying the effects or defects he wants to direct attention to in bad or good poetry. For example, he uses alliteration—the gentle sound of *s*—when he describes Zephyr, the gentle west wind. Find other examples in the excerpt of alliteration and onomatopoeia. How do the sounds of the words illustrate the examples and provide lessons on "true ease in writing"?

2. Examine the rhyme scheme. Pope was famous for writing couplets (two rhyming lines). How do the series of couplets in this poem help Pope convey his message about the relationship between sound and sense?

3. Pope manipulates the sound of this poem by controlling the poem's rhythm. Find examples of the way he varies stress (or accent), mixes mono- and polysyllabic words, ends words in consonants that do not easily blend, or slows a line down with commas. Be sure to read the poem aloud to hear the effects of the poem's "sound."

4. "Sound and Sense" is a didactic poem, meaning it was written for the purpose of instructing its readers. However, it does contain lyrical language that expresses emotion. How does Pope use that lyrical language to achieve his didactic purpose in this poem?

5. What conclusions can you draw about Pope's view of the artist and his or her art? What expectations do you think he had about the artist's place in society?

Kubla Khan

or, A Vision in a Dream

SAMUEL TAYLOR COLERIDGE

> Born in rural Devonshire, England, Samuel Taylor Coleridge (1772–1834) was a founder of the Romantic movement in literature and one of the so-called Lake poets, who lived and worked in the Lake District in rural northwest England.

---

[5]Alexander the Great, here a character in "Alexander's Feast."—EDS.

He is best known for "The Rime of the Ancient Mariner," "Christabel," and "Kubla Khan"—poems of mystery and magic—and for his meditative verse and literary criticism. His philosophical works influenced the nineteenth-century American transcendental movement, particularly the discussion of the imagination in his *Biographia Literaria* (1817). Coleridge was close to fellow Lake Poet William Wordsworth and his sister, Dorothy. Coleridge and Wordsworth anonymously published *Lyrical Ballads*, a collection of poems that rejected traditional poetic language in favor of direct speech. It is considered the seminal Romantic work. Coleridge was plagued with physical ailments, for which he took large quantities of laudanum—a mixture of opium and alcohol, which some believe prevented him from living up to his early promise. Later in his life, however, he managed to control his addiction. Coleridge claimed that he wrote "Kubla Khan" in 1797 during a stay at a farmhouse. He had taken laudanum and fallen asleep in his chair as he was reading in *Purchas his Pilgrimage* a description by Marco Polo of a palace the Chinese emperor Kubla Khan had commissioned. When he awoke, he tried to transcribe his dream but was interrupted by a "person on business from Porlock." The fragment that remains was first published in 1816.

In Xanadu[1] did Kubla Khan
    A stately pleasure-dome decree:
Where Alph, the sacred river, ran
Through caverns measureless to man
    Down to a sunless sea.   5
So twice five miles of fertile ground
With walls and towers were girdled round:
And here were gardens bright with sinuous rills
Where blossomed many an incense-bearing tree;
And there were forests ancient as the hills,   10
Enfolding sunny spots of greenery.

But oh! that deep romantic chasm which slanted
Down the green hill athwart a cedarn cover!
A savage place! as holy and enchanted
As e'er beneath a waning moon was haunted   15
By woman wailing for her demon-lover!
And from this chasm, with ceaseless turmoil seething,
As if this earth in fast thick pants were breathing,
A mighty fountain momently was forced,
Amid whose swift half-intermitted burst   20

---

[1]Xanadu was the summer capital of the Chinese Yuan dynasty, ruled by the Mongolian emperor Kublai Khan.—EDS.

Huge fragments vaulted like rebounding hail,
Of chaffy grain beneath the thresher's flail:
And 'mid these dancing rocks at once and ever
It flung up momently the sacred river.
Five miles meandering with a mazy motion   25
Through wood and dale the sacred river ran,
Then reached the caverns measureless to man,
And sank in tumult to a lifeless ocean:
And 'mid this tumult Kubla heard from far
Ancestral voices prophesying war!   30

    The shadow of the dome of pleasure
    Floated midway on the waves;
    Where was heard the mingled measure
    From the fountain and the caves.
It was a miracle of rare device,   35
A sunny pleasure-dome with caves of ice!

    A damsel with a dulcimer
    In a vision once I saw:
    It was an Abyssinian² maid,
    And on her dulcimer she played,   40
    Singing of Mount Abora.³
    Could I revive within me
    Her symphony and song,
    To such a deep delight 'twould win me,
That with music loud and long,   45
I would build that dome in air,
That sunny dome! those caves of ice!
And all who heard should see them there,
And all should cry, Beware! Beware!
His flashing eyes, his floating hair!   50
Weave a circle round him thrice,
And close your eyes with holy dread,
For he on honey-dew hath fed,
And drunk the milk of Paradise.

[1798; 1816]

. . . .

---

²Ethiopian.—Eds.
³Ethiopian mountain referred to as "True Paradise under the Ethiop Line" in Milton's *Paradise Lost*.—Eds.

Exploring the Text

1. "Kubla Khan" is filled with contrasts. Track these oppositions as you read the poem. What is the effect of the contrasts between, for example, chasms and hills (ll. 12–13)?

2. How does Coleridge achieve the chantlike quality in "Kubla Khan"?

3. How does the first part of "Kubla Khan" (ll. 1–30) differ from the second part (ll. 31–54)? What causes the change? What does the shift offer in the way of an explanation for the poem's meaning?

4. According to Coleridge, his transcription of the dream was interrupted by a "person on business from Porlock," after which he was unable to recall the vision or the poem he composed in his dream. No one knows who interrupted him, but the person from Porlock has become a metaphor for interrupted inspiration. What does this anecdote add to the meaning of the poem as a meditation on creativity?

5. Characterize the speaker in "Kubla Khan."

6. "Kubla Khan" has been interpreted many ways. Some consider it a straightforward portrayal of Coleridge's opium-induced hallucination; others believe it to be about the beauty of creation. Consider several possibilities. What is your interpretation?

London, 1802

WILLIAM WORDSWORTH

William Wordsworth (1770–1850) is one of the most famous and influential poets of the Western world and one of the premier Romantics. Widely known for his reverence of nature and the power of his lyrical verse, he lived in the Lake District of northern England, where he was inspired by the natural beauty of the landscape. With Samuel Taylor Coleridge, he published *Lyrical Ballads* in 1798; the collection, which changed the direction of English poetry, begins with Coleridge's "Rime of the Ancient Mariner" and includes Wordsworth's "Lines Composed a Few Miles above Tintern Abbey." Among Wordsworth's other most famous works are "The World Is Too Much with Us" (p. 498), a sonnet; "Ode: Intimations of Immortality"; and "The Prelude, or Growth of a Poet's Mind," an autobiographical poem. In the sonnet "London, 1802," the speaker addresses and eulogizes the poet John Milton.

Milton! thou should'st be living at this hour:
England hath need of thee: she is a fen
Of stagnant waters: altar, sword, and pen,
Fireside, the heroic wealth of hall and bower,
Have forfeited their ancient English dower   5

Of inward happiness. We are selfish men;
Oh! raise us up, return to us again;
And give us manners, virtue, freedom, power.
Thy soul was like a star, and dwelt apart:
Thou hadst a voice whose sound was like the sea: 10
Pure as the naked heavens, majestic, free,
So didst thou travel on life's common way,
In cheerful godliness; and yet thy heart
The lowliest duties on herself did lay.

[1802]

. . . .

Exploring the Text

1. "London, 1802" is an example of a classic Petrarchan sonnet: it has fourteen lines written in iambic pentameter; its rhyme scheme is *abba, abba, cdde, ce*. The traditional sonnet poses a situation or question in the octet (first eight lines) that is resolved or answered in the sestet (the last six lines). What situation does Wordsworth present in "London, 1802"? What resolution does he suggest?
2. Wordsworth often uses single words to represent bigger ideas, a literary device called metonymy. What institutions do "altar," "sword," "pen," and "fireside" represent?
3. Wordsworth uses similes to present the qualities in Milton that he believes would help England out of its stagnant selfishness. What is the effect of this figurative language? What is the extra level of meaning it creates?
4. According to this poem, what potential does the artist have for improving society? How must the artist behave to make that potential become real and useful?
5. This poem is unusually nationalistic for a Romantic writer. What might explain Wordsworth's focus on England's heritage and one of its great poets?

On the Sonnet

and

Ode on a Grecian Urn

JOHN KEATS

John Keats was born in London in 1795. His early education introduced him to literature, music, and theater, but after his father and mother died, young John's guardian took him out of school and apprenticed him to a surgeon and apothecary. He went on to study medicine, but almost immediately abandoned medicine for poetry. Keats is considered one of the major poets of the Romantic movement, even though his background of relative poverty stood in stark contrast to the classically educated Romantic poets, such as Percy Bysshe Shelley (p. 917) and William Wordsworth. Keats did not have an easy life: he was poor and in ill health, and his work was not well received while he was alive. Though Keats died at twenty-five, his work—both his poetry and the letters in which he explained his aesthetic theories—has withstood the test of time. Some of his best-known poems are "On First Looking into Chapman's Homer" (1816), "Ode to a Nightingale" (1819), "La Belle Dame Sans Merci" (1819), "Lamia" (1819), and "To Autumn" (1819). In the poems that follow, Keats addresses the limitations of two art forms—the sonnet and an ancient artifact—at the same time that he honors them.

On the Sonnet

If by dull rhymes our English must be chained,
And like Andromeda,[1] the sonnet sweet
Fettered, in spite of painéd loveliness,
Let us find, if we must be constrained,
Sandals more interwoven and complete   5
To fit the naked foot of Poesy:[2]
Let us inspect the lyre, and weigh the stress
Of every chord, and see what may be gained
By ear industrious, and attention meet;
Misers of sound and syllable, no less   10
Than Midas of his coinage, let us be
Jealous of dead leaves in the bay-wreath crown,
So, if we may not let the Muse be free,
She will be bound with garlands of her own.

[1819]

Exploring the Text

1. In a letter including "On the Sonnet," Keats wrote, "I have been endeavoring to discover a better sonnet stanza than we have." He objected to the "pouncing rhythms" of the Petrarchan form and the inevitable "tick" of the closing couplet in the Shakespearean stanza. You will notice that the rhyme scheme of this sonnet is unconventional, but look carefully at the beginning rhymes, such as "Fettered," "Let us," and "Jealous." In what other ways does Keats vary the conventions of a sonnet?

2. According to Keats, what is the connection between beautiful Andromeda, who was chained to a rock in the sea until Perseus rescued her, and the sonnet form?

---

[1]Princess in Greek mythology chained to a rock to be eaten by a sea monster.—Eds.
[2]Poetry.—Eds.

3. Examine the ways in which Keats uses figurative language, such as personification, simile, and metaphor. How do those techniques help him develop his critique of the sonnet form?

4. This poem has several image patterns, including chains, mythology, music, and clothing. Trace one or more of them and consider their effects. How do these patterns help connect sound and sense? How do they comment on the sonnet form and its relationship to art?

5. What do you think of Keats's inclination to restructure the sonnet form? What does that inclination tell you about the nature of the artist?

Ode on a Grecian Urn

1

Thou still unravished bride of quietness,
    Thou foster child of silence and slow time,
Sylvan historian, who canst thus express
    A flowery tale more sweetly than our rhyme:
What leaf-fringed legend haunts about thy shape   5
    Of deities or mortals, or of both,
        In Tempe or the dales of Arcady?[1]
    What men or gods are these? What maidens loath?
What mad pursuit? What struggle to escape?
        What pipes and timbrels? What wild ecstasy?   10

2

Heard melodies are sweet, but those unheard
    Are sweeter; therefore, ye soft pipes, play on;
Not to the sensual ear, but, more endeared,
    Pipe to the spirit ditties of no tone:
Fair youth, beneath the trees, thou canst not leave   15
    Thy song, nor ever can those trees be bare;
        Bold Lover, never, never canst thou kiss,
Though winning near the goal—yet, do not grieve;
        She cannot fade, though thou hast not thy bliss,
    Forever wilt thou love, and she be fair!   20

3

Ah, happy, happy boughs! that cannot shed
    Your leaves, nor ever bid the Spring adieu;
And, happy melodist, unwearièd,

---

[1]Pastoral regions of Greece.—EDS.

Forever piping songs forever new;
More happy love! more happy, happy love!   25
    Forever warm and still to be enjoyed,
        Forever panting, and forever young;
All breathing human passion far above,
    That leaves a heart high-sorrowful and cloyed,
        A burning forehead, and a parching tongue.   30

                                4

Who are these coming to the sacrifice?
    To what green altar, O mysterious priest,
Lead'st thou that heifer lowing at the skies,
    And all her silken flanks with garlands dressed?
What little town by river or sea shore,   35
    Or mountain-built with peaceful citadel,
        Is emptied of this folk, this pious morn?
And, little town, thy streets forevermore
    Will silent be; and not a soul to tell
        Why thou art desolate, can e'er return.   40

                                5

O Attic shape! Fair attitude! with brede[2]
    Of marble men and maidens overwrought,
With forest branches and the trodden weed;
    Thou, silent form, dost tease us out of thought
As doth eternity: Cold Pastoral!   45
    When old age shall this generation waste,
        Thou shalt remain, in midst of other woe
Than ours, a friend to man, to whom thou say'st,
"Beauty is truth, truth beauty,"—that is all
    Ye know on earth, and all ye need to know.   50

                                                    [1819]

. . . .

Exploring the Text

1. Who is the poem's speaker? What does he observe as he studies the urn? What questions does he ask as he examines this artifact of another time? Who is he addressing?

2. An ode is an ancient form that originally followed strict rules of rhythm, meter, and rhyme. By the time of the Romantics, the ode was more flexible, used to meditate on or address a single object or condition. What aspects of this form make it well suited to a meditation on a piece of art?

---

[2]Braid.—EDS.

3. The last two lines of the ode: "'Beauty is truth, truth beauty,'—that is all / Ye know on earth, and all ye need to know" are among the most enigmatic in all of poetry, both for their content and for the many possibilities of who is addressing whom. Consider four possibilities: speaker to reader, urn to reader, speaker to urn, and speaker to figures on the urn. How does each perspective change the meaning of those two lines and the poem as a whole?

4. Noticing that the first and fourth stanzas of the poem are filled with question marks and the last stanza has none, what paradoxical comments does "Ode on a Grecian Urn" make about art?

5. While the urn described in the poem is imaginary, "Ode on a Grecian Urn" was supposedly inspired by Keats's visit to the Elgin Marbles on exhibit at the British Museum. What does this context add to your understanding of the poem?

My Last Duchess

ROBERT BROWNING

Born the son of a bank clerk, Robert Browning (1812–1889) was, for the most part, educated at home, and is said to have learned Latin, Greek, Italian, and French by the age of fourteen. He came under the influence of Percy Bysshe Shelley in his teens, and adopted radical views concerning society and religion. He began to publish poetry in 1833, but his work was not highly regarded or widely read. In 1845, he read *Poems* by Elizabeth Barrett. The two corresponded, met, and eloped to Italy the following year. Until her death in 1861, his identity as her husband brought him more attention than did his work. The publication of *Collected Poems* in 1852 and *The Ring and the Book* in 1868 finally brought him acclaim. Among his most well-known poems are "The Pied Piper of Hamelin" (1842), "Fra Lippo Lippi" (1855), and "My Last Duchess," included here. Written in 1842, it is an excellent example of the dramatic monologue—a form in which the speaker is clearly distinct from the poet, and the speaker's innermost thoughts are revealed by the situation.

Ferrara[1]

That's my last Duchess painted on the wall,
Looking as if she were alive. I call
That piece a wonder, now: Frà Pandolf's[2] hands

---

[1] The epigraph establishes the setting of the poem, the Italian city of Ferrara. In the sixteenth century, the very young first wife of the city's duke died under suspicious circumstances. He later remarried.—EDS.

[2] Fictitious artist.—EDS.

Worked busily a day, and there she stands.
Will't please you sit and look at her? I said
"Frà Pandolf" by design, for never read 5
Strangers like you that pictured countenance,
The depth and passion of its earnest glance,
But to myself they turned (since none puts by
The curtain I have drawn for you, but I)
And seemed as they would ask me, if they durst, 10
How such a glance came there; so, not the first
Are you to turn and ask thus. Sir, 'twas not
Her husband's presence only, called that spot
Of joy into the Duchess' cheek: perhaps 15
Frà Pandolf chanced to say "Her mantle laps
Over my lady's wrist too much," or "Paint
Must never hope to reproduce the faint
Half-flush that dies along her throat": such stuff
Was courtesy, she thought, and cause enough 20
For calling up that spot of joy. She had
A heart—how shall I say?—too soon made glad,
Too easily impressed; she liked whate'er
She looked on, and her looks went everywhere.
Sir, 'twas all one! My favor at her breast, 25
The dropping of the daylight in the West,
The bough of cherries some officious fool
Broke in the orchard for her, the white mule
She rode with round the terrace—all and each
Would draw from her alike the approving speech, 30
Or blush, at least. She thanked men,—good! but thanked
Somehow—I know not how—as if she ranked
My gift of a nine-hundred-years-old name
With anybody's gift. Who'd stoop to blame
This sort of trifling? Even had you skill 35
In speech—which I have not—to make your will
Quite clear to such an one, and say, "Just this
Or that in you disgusts me; here you miss,
Or there exceed the mark"—and if she let
Herself be lessoned so, nor plainly set 40
Her wits to yours, forsooth, and made excuse,
—E'en then would be some stooping; and I choose
Never to stoop. Oh sir, she smiled, no doubt,
Whene'er I passed her; but who passed without
Much the same smile? This grew; I gave commands; 45
Then all smiles stopped together. There she stands
As if alive. Will't please you rise? We'll meet

The company below, then. I repeat,
The Count your master's known munificence
Is ample warrant that no just pretense   50
Of mine for dowry will be disallowed;
Though his fair daughter's self, as I avowed
At starting, is my object. Nay, we'll go
Together down, sir. Notice Neptune, though,
Taming a sea-horse, thought a rarity,   55
Which Claus of Innsbruck³ cast in bronze for me!

[1842]

Exploring the Text

1. What is the situation presented in the poem? Who is the speaker? What is the occasion? To whom is the poem addressed?
2. What question has the listener evidently asked the speaker?
3. According to the speaker, what brought the "spot of joy" (l. 21) to the duchess's cheek? How does the speaker feel about it? What does he reveal about himself in his discussion of the "spot of joy"?
4. How does the enjambment in this poem contribute to the development of the speaker's persona?
5. Browning comments on art several times in this poem. What do you think he is saying about art, particularly in the closing lines of the poem (ll. 47–56)?
6. How do you think the woman in the painting would respond to her husband's monologue? What is her side of the story?

The Harlem Dancer

CLAUDE MCKAY

Poet, novelist, and journalist Claude McKay was born in 1890 in Jamaica. The youngest of eleven children, he was sent to live with an older brother—a school-teacher—who took charge of his education, introducing him to the classics of British literature, such as Milton, Pope, and the Romantics. McKay began writing poetry at the age of ten, and by the time he immigrated to the United States at age twenty-two, he had published two volumes of verse. In America, McKay faced the harsh realities of racism and, despite his education, took on menial jobs to make a living. McKay became known for his protest poetry, which spoke directly about racial issues and the trials of the working class. Inspired by a wave of lynchings, his sonnet "If We

---

³Fictitious artist.—EDS.

Must Die" (1919) encourages resistance, even if a fight seems doomed; Winston Churchill quoted it during World War II. Langston Hughes and Countee Cullen considered McKay an inspirational voice during the Harlem Renaissance. McKay's novels include *Home to Harlem* (1922), *Banjo: A Story without a Plot* (1929), and *Banana Bottom* (1933). He lived abroad, in England and France, on and off for years, but returned to the United States in 1934, where he worked in Chicago as a journalist, writing mostly for left-leaning publications. McKay died in 1948, having never returned to Jamaica. "Harlem Dancer" was first published under the pseudonym Eli Edwards in the avant-garde publication *Seven Arts* (Oct. 1917).

Applauding youths laughed with young prostitutes
And watched her perfect, half-clothed body sway;
Her voice was like the sound of blended flutes
Blown by black players upon a picnic day.
She sang and danced on gracefully and calm,   5
The light gauze hanging loose about her form;
To me she seemed a proudly-swaying palm
Grown lovelier for passing through a storm.
Upon her swarthy neck black shiny curls
Luxuriant fell; and tossing coins in praise,   10
The wine-flushed, bold-eyed boys, and even the girls,
Devoured her shape with eager, passionate gaze;
But looking at her falsely-smiling face,
I knew her self was not in that strange place.

                                                      [1917]

Exploring the Text

1. Who is the speaker in "The Harlem Dancer"? How is the speaker connected to the events described? How is what he or she sees different from what those watching the dancer see?

2. The poem is a sonnet, a form often used by McKay. How do the restrictions of the sonnet—rhyme scheme and number of lines—work to create a scene imbued with passion, sadness, and anger?

3. Examine the imagery in the poem. What techniques does McKay use to create a vivid picture of the dancer? Look especially at the descriptions of her voice ("like the sound of blended flutes / Blown by black players upon a picnic day," ll. 3–4) and her form ("a proudly-swaying palm / Grown lovelier for passing through a storm," ll. 7–8). What surprising associations does McKay make?

4. Look closely at the poem's last line. What might McKay mean by the word "self"?

5. This poem describes a nightclub dancer. What do you think McKay thinks about the woman and the way she earns her living? Do you think he sees her work as art? Explain your answer.

Thirteen Ways of Looking at a Blackbird

WALLACE STEVENS

Wallace Stevens (1879–1955) is considered one of the most important American modernist poets. Born in Reading, Pennsylvania, Stevens studied at Harvard University and graduated from New York Law School. He worked as a lawyer in New York and became vice president of one of the largest insurance businesses in Hartford, Connecticut. In addition to being a successful businessman, Stevens is considered one of the great poets of the twentieth century. His poetry collections include *Harmonium* (1923), *The Man with the Blue Guitar and Other Poems* (1937), *A Primitive like an Orb* (1948), and *Transport to Summer* (1947). *Collected Poems* (1954) brought Stevens both a Pulitzer Prize and the National Book Award. Stevens's work is often described as meditative and philosophical. He was a poet of ideas, with a strong belief in the poet as someone with heightened powers. Stevens favored precision of imagery and clear, sharp language, rejecting the sentiment favored by the Romantic and Victorian poets. With its haiku-like austerity and abstract form, "Thirteen Ways of Looking at a Blackbird" has been associated with the cubist painters, such as Pablo Picasso and Georges Braque, who depicted their subjects from many viewpoints by breaking them up and reassembling them in an abstract form.

I

Among twenty snowy mountains
The only moving thing
Was the eye of the blackbird.

II

I was of three minds,
Like a tree
In which there are three blackbirds.   5

III

The blackbird whistled in the autumn winds.
It was a small part of the pantomime.

IV

A man and a woman
Are one.   10
A man and a woman and a blackbird
Are one.

V

I do not know which to prefer,
The beauty of inflections
Or the beauty of innuendoes,   15
The blackbird whistling
Or just after.

VI

Icicles filled the long window
With barbaric glass.
The shadow of the blackbird   20
Crossed it, to and fro.
The mood
Traced in the shadow
An indecipherable cause.

VII

O thin men of Haddam,   25
Why do you imagine golden birds?
Do you not see how the blackbird
Walks around the feet
Of the women about you?

VIII

I know noble accents
And lucid, inescapable rhythms;   30
But I know, too,
That the blackbird is involved
In what I know.

IX

When the blackbird flew out of sight,   35
It marked the edge
Of one of many circles.

X

At the sight of blackbirds
Flying in a green light,
Even the bawds of euphony   40
Would cry out sharply.

XI

He rode over Connecticut
In a glass coach.
Once, a fear pierced him,
In that he mistook ———————— 45
The shadow of his equipage
For blackbirds.

XII

The river is moving.
The blackbird must be flying.

XIII

It was evening all afternoon.   50
It was snowing
And it was going to snow.
The blackbird sat
In the cedar-limbs.

[1917]

Exploring the Text

1. Each of the thirteen stanzas of "Thirteen Ways of Looking at a Blackbird" might be a poem. What, besides the blackbird, connects them?
2. What conclusions can you draw about the speaker of the poem? about what it means to look at an object?
3. This poem has a cinematic quality that is introduced in the first stanza, when the eye of the speaker moves from a long establishing shot of snowy mountains to a close-up of the eye of a blackbird. What other film techniques do you find as you work through the poem? Consider framing, close-ups — even sound.
4. Stanza VII uses apostrophe (words spoken to a person who is absent or imaginary, or to an idea or thing) to address the "thin men of Haddam" (l. 25). Those thin men — and their home in Haddam — have been interpreted many ways. Haddam is a town in Connecticut, which is mentioned again in stanza XI. What are some of the possible explanations for the Connecticut references? What comment might Stevens be making by contrasting Connecticut life to blackbirds?
5. Is there logic to the order of the stanzas? Try reshuffling them to see if the poem's meaning changes.
6. Black is an accepted symbol of death. Why is this interpretation too limited for this complex and enigmatic poem?
7. Using this poem as a model, write your own version of looking at a familiar object thirteen different ways.

Piano

D. H. LAWRENCE

David Herbert Lawrence was born in 1885 in a mining village in England. His father was a miner, and his mother was a schoolteacher. With his mother's encouragement, Lawrence was educated and became a schoolteacher himself, escaping life in the mines. His works include the novels *Sons and Lovers* (1912), *The Rainbow* (1915), and *Women in Love* (1920), and the poetry collections *Birds, Beasts and Flowers* (1923), *Pansies* (1929), and *Last Poems* (1933). Lawrence often felt as though the forces of modern civilization were against him: some of his books were banned because of their graphic love scenes, and he had trouble with English authorities because of his German wife and his objections to what would later become World War I. As a result, the Lawrences sought refuge in Italy, Australia, Mexico, and finally the south of France, where Lawrence died of tuberculosis in 1930 at the age of forty-four. In "Piano," Lawrence moves past nostalgia for his own childhood to a meditation on the nature of memory.

Softly, in the dusk, a woman is singing to me;
Taking me back down the vista of years, till I see
A child sitting under the piano, in the boom of the
    tingling strings
And pressing the small, poised feet of a mother who smiles
    as she sings.

In spite of myself, the insidious mastery of song
Betrays me back, till the heart of me weeps to belong   5
To the old Sunday evenings at home, with winter outside
And hymns in the cosy parlour, the tinkling piano our guide.

So now it is vain for the singer to burst into clamour
With the great black piano appassionato. The glamour   10
Of childish days is upon me, my manhood is cast
Down in the flood of remembrance, I weep like a child
    for the past.

[1923]

Exploring the Text

1. Who is the speaker in "Piano"? Who is the woman in the first line of the poem? Who is the child the speaker sees sitting under the piano (l. 3)?
2. Consider the poem's diction. What effects do words and phrases such as "smiles," "weeps," "winter outside," "hymns," "cosy parlour," and "black piano appassionato" have on your mental picture of the speaker?

3. What techniques does Lawrence use to ensure that the reader shares the experience of being under the piano with the speaker?

4. What do you think Lawrence means by the words "vain" (l. 9) and "glamour" (l. 10)? How does your interpretation of the words add another level of meaning to the poem?

5. How does Lawrence achieve a balance between empathy for the younger self he imagines and self-pity? between mere sentimentality and stark human emotion?

6. What does "Piano" say about the connection between art and memory? about the difference between public art and the art of the private individual?

The Day Lady Died

FRANK O'HARA

Frank O'Hara (1926–1966) grew up in Grafton, Massachusetts. After high school, he enlisted in the navy and served on a destroyer for most of World War II. While attending Harvard University on the GI Bill, his teacher, poet John Ciardi, recommended him for a graduate fellowship in comparative literature at the University of Michigan. After he received his master's degree, O'Hara moved to New York City, where he was at the center of New York's art and poetry worlds, writing for *Art News* magazine and working both at the front desk and as an assistant curator at the Museum of Modern Art. O'Hara was inspired by city life as other poets have been inspired by nature. He once wrote, "I can't even enjoy a blade of grass unless I know there's a subway handy, or a record store or some other sign that people do not totally regret life." O'Hara's poetry collections include *City Winter and Other Poems* (1952); *Meditations in an Emergency* (1957); *Second Avenue* (1960); *Odes* (1960); and *Lunch Poems* (1964), from which the following poem about the death of jazz singer Billie Holiday is taken.

It is 12:20 in New York a Friday
three days after Bastille day, yes
it is 1959 and I go get a shoeshine
because I will get off the 4:19 in Easthampton
at 7:15 and then go straight to dinner   5
and I don't know the people who will feed me

I walk up the muggy street beginning to sun
and have a hamburger and a malted and buy
an ugly NEW WORLD WRITING to see what the poets
in Ghana are doing these days
                         I go on to the bank   10
and Miss Stillwagon (first name Linda I once heard)
doesn't even look up my balance for once in her life
and in the GOLDEN GRIFFIN I get a little Verlaine

for Patsy with drawings by Bonnard although I do
think of Hesiod, trans. Richmond Lattimore or   15
Brendan Behan's new play or *Le Balcon* or *Les Nègres*
of Genet, but I don't, I stick with Verlaine
after practically going to sleep with quandariness

and for Mike I just stroll into the PARK LANE
Liquor Store and ask for a bottle of Strega and   20
then I go back where I came from to 6th Avenue
and the tobacconist in the Ziegfeld Theatre and
casually ask for a carton of Gauloises and a carton
of Picayunes, and a NEW YORK POST with her face on it

and I am sweating a lot by now and thinking of   25
leaning on the john door in the 5 SPOT
while she whispered a song along the keyboard
to Mal Waldron and everyone and I stopped breathing

[1964]

Exploring the Text

1. It's probably safe to say that O'Hara is the poem's speaker. Characterize him. From what you have read, how would you describe the rest of his day? the rest of his life?
2. The poem takes place on a summer day in New York City and provides plenty of details about the time and place. How does the vivid setting help create the poem's tone?
3. Except for the last two lines, the poem is in the present tense. How does the abrupt switch add another level of meaning to the poem?
4. O'Hara once described his work as "I do this I do that" poetry because his poems sometimes sound like diary entries. "The Day Lady Died" is from a collection called *Lunch Poems*. How is it more than a report of what someone did on his lunch hour?
5. "Lady" refers to jazz singer Billie Holiday, who died as a result of heroin addiction. O'Hara heard her sing at a club called the Five Spot, where she broke the law by singing a song with piano player Mal Waldron. Holiday had lost her cabaret license and wasn't supposed to sing anywhere alcohol was being served; thus, she really did whisper the song. Does this information change the meaning of the poem? Explain.

Singapore

MARY OLIVER

Mary Oliver (b. 1935) was born in Maple Heights, an affluent suburb of Cleveland. She attended the Ohio State University and Vassar College, but did not complete her degree. Nonetheless, she has held several teaching positions at universities, including Bennington College. Oliver published her first volume, *No Voyage*, and *Other Poems*, at the age of twenty-eight, and in 1984 won the Pulitzer Prize with *American Primitive* (1983). Following a period of silence, she published a considerable body of prose and verse between 1990 and 2006, winning the Christopher Award and the L. L. Winship/PEN New England Award for *House of Light* (1990), and the National Book Award for *New and Selected Poems* (1992). These were followed by *White Pine* (1994), *West Wind* (1997), *Winter Hours: Prose, Prose Poems, and Poems* (1999), *Owls and Other Fantasies: Poems and Essays* (2003), *Why I Wake Early* (2004), and *Thirst* (2006). "Singapore" comes from her award-winning 1990 collection, *House of Light*.

In Singapore, in the airport,
a darkness was ripped from my eyes.
In the women's restroom, one compartment stood open.
A woman knelt there, washing something
    in the white bowl.

Disgust argued in my stomach 5
and I felt, in my pocket, for my ticket.

A poem should always have birds in it.
Kingfishers, say, with their bold eyes and gaudy wings.
Rivers are pleasant, and of course trees.
A waterfall, or if that's not possible, a fountain
    rising and falling. 10
A person wants to stand in a happy place, in a poem.

When the woman turned I could not answer her face.
Her beauty and her embarrassment struggled together, and
    neither could win.
She smiled and I smiled. What kind of nonsense is this?
Everybody needs a job. 15

Yes, a person wants to stand in a happy place, in a poem.
But first we must watch her as she stares down at her labor,
    which is dull enough.
She is washing the tops of the airport ashtrays, as big as
    hubcaps, with a blue rag.
Her small hands turn the metal, scrubbing and rinsing.
She does not work slowly, nor quickly, but like a river. 20
Her dark hair is like the wing of a bird.

I don't doubt for a moment that she loves her life.
And I want her to rise up from the crust and the slop
    and fly down to the river.
This probably won't happen.
But maybe it will. 25
If the world were only pain and logic, who would want it?

Of course, it isn't.
Neither do I mean anything miraculous, but only
the light that can shine out of a life. I mean
the way she unfolded and refolded the blue cloth,   30
the way her smile was only for my sake; I mean
the way this poem is filled with trees, and birds.

[1990]

Exploring the Text

1. Who is the speaker of the poem? How do we know what kind of person she is? Pay particular attention to the array of responses she has to the woman she sees in the restroom stall.
2. What does the repetition of "I mean" in the last stanza of the poem suggest about the connection between the speaker and the woman she sees in the restroom?
3. Mary Oliver is known for her poetry and prose about nature. How does she weave the natural world into "Singapore," which takes place in the women's restroom in an airport?
4. "Singapore" is an example of *ars poetica*, a poem that is also a treatise on the art of poetry. What comment does this poem make about the art of poetry? How does Oliver connect *ars poetica* to real life?
5. "[A] darkness was ripped from my eyes" (l. 2) is an allusion to the conversion of Saul, in Acts 9 of the New Testament: "there fell from his eyes something like scales and he regained his sight and he arose and was baptized; and he took food and was strengthened." What effect does the allusion have on the meaning of "Singapore"?

The Blues

BILLY COLLINS

Billy Collins (b. 1941) served two terms as poet laureate of the United States, beginning in 2001. He has written more than ten books of poetry, including *The Art of Drowning* (1995), *Picnic, Lightning* (1998), and *Nine Horses* (2002). A distinguished professor of English at Lehman College in New York City, Collins has received fellowships from the National Endowment for the Arts and the Guggenheim Foundation and was chosen in 1992 as a "literary lion" of the New York Public Library. Collins, who actively promotes poetry in the schools, edited *Poetry 180: A Turning Back to Poetry* (2003)—an anthology of contemporary poems that aims to increase high school students' appreciation and enjoyment of poetry. "The Blues" was first published in *Sailing around the Room* (2001).

Much of what is said here
must be said twice,
a reminder that no one
takes an immediate interest in the pain of others.

Nobody will listen, it would seem,   5
if you simply admit
your baby left you early this morning
she didn't even stop to say good-bye.

But if you sing it again
with the help of the band   10
which will now lift you to a higher,
more ardent and beseeching key,

people will not only listen;
they will shift to the sympathetic
edges of their chairs,   15
moved to such acute anticipation

by that chord and the delay that follows,
they will not be able to sleep
unless you release with one finger
a scream from the throat of your guitar   20

and turn your head back to the microphone
to let them know
you're a hard-hearted man
but that woman's sure going to make you cry.

[2001]

. . . .

Exploring the Text

1. On first read, it seems that the speaker and the poet are the same. Are they? Who is the audience—the "you" in the poem? Is it possible that the "you" is, in fact, the speaker?
2. Collins uses punctuation cleverly in this poem. Track the punctuation, and explain how he uses it to change the rhythm. How does that change relate to the subject of the poem?
3. What is the effect of the enjambment that Collins uses throughout the poem?
4. Traditional blues lyrics consist of one line repeated twice, followed by a third line that responds to or explains the first two lines. How does Billy Collins both exemplify and explain that form?
5. In a way, "The Blues" is an example of *ars poetica*. How does the poem comment on the art of poetry as well as the art of singing the blues?

PAIRED POEMS

Nighthawks

EDWARD HOPPER

American painter Edward Hopper (1882–1967) was born in Nyack, New York. He first studied illustration in New York City, before switching to painting and traveling to Europe. His work was influenced by the European realists, such as Velázquez, Goya, Daumier, and Manet. Although one of his paintings was in the famous New York Armory show of 1913, his work generated little interest until his 1925 painting *House by the Railroad*. Its blunt geometrical shapes, architectural details, and flat masses of color were in keeping with his earlier work, but the painting's mood of melancholy and loneliness marked the advent of his mature style, a style still present in *Nighthawks*, reproduced here.

Nighthawks (1942, oil on canvas, 33⅛ x 60 in.)

Exploring the Text

1. It is almost impossible to look at *Nighthawks* without making up a story. What is your story?
2. Although the painting is realistic, if you look carefully you will notice that what Hopper left out is almost as interesting as what he included. What are some of the things missing from the painting, and how do they add nuance to the painting's story?
3. How does Hopper use elements of visual art, such as light and line, to create the mood of melancholy and mystery?

4. *Nighthawks* is the subject of several poems, including the ones that follow. What do you think makes it such a popular subject?

Hopper's "Nighthawks" (1942)

IRA SADOFF

Ira Sadoff (b. 1945) was born in Brooklyn and educated at Cornell University and the University of Oregon. He has taught at Hobart and William Smith Colleges, the University of Virginia, and the Iowa Writers' Workshop, and is now the Arthur Jeremiah Roberts Professor of Literature at Colby College. He has written many books of poetry, including *Emotional Traffic* (1990), *Grazing* (1998), and *Barter* (2003), and his work has appeared in the *New Yorker*, the *New Republic*, *Esquire*, and the *American Poetry Review*. He has described himself as "one poet among a decreasing minority who is trying to resist the return to formalism, the sterile, conservative, aesthete academism of the nineteen-fifties." This poem first appeared in his 1975 collection, *Settling Down*.

Imagine a town where no one walks the streets. Where the sidewalks
are swept clean as ceilings and the barber pole stands still as a corpse.
There is no wind. The windows on the brick buildings are boarded up
with doors, and a single light shines in the all-night diner while the rest
of the town sits in its shadow.   5
    In an hour it will be daylight. The busboy in the diner counts the
empty stools and looks at his reflection in the coffee urns. On the radio
the announcer says the allies have won another victory. There have been
few casualties. A man with a wide-brimmed hat and the woman sitting
next to him are drinking coffee or tea; on the other side of the counter   10
a stranger watches them as though he had nowhere else to focus his
eyes. He wonders if perhaps they are waiting for the morning buses to
arrive, if they are expecting some member of their family to bring them
important news. Or perhaps they will get on the bus themselves, ask the
driver where he is going, and whatever his answer they will tell him it   15
could not be far enough.
    When the buses arrive at sunrise they are empty as hospital beds —
the hum of the motor is distant as a voice coming from within the body.
The man and woman have walked off to some dark street, while the
stranger remains fixed in his chair. When he picks up the morning paper   20
he is not surprised to read there would be no exchange of prisoners, the
war would go on forever, the Cardinals would win the pennant, there
would be no change in the weather.

[1975]

Exploring the Text

1. What story does Sadoff's poem tell about *Nighthawks*?
2. The poem mentions objects and describes settings that do not appear in this particular painting but are in other Hopper works. What do these elements contribute to the meaning of the poem? to our understanding of how the speaker feels about Hopper?
3. Sadoff uses several similes. What connects them? How do they connect to the painting?
4. The poem begins with the word "Imagine" and moves from a description of the scene in Hopper's painting to what was in the newspaper—real events from 1942—which the man in the painting might read the next morning. How does Sadoff honor the painting's universal themes while also mooring it to a specific time in history?
5. What do you think the poem says about *Nighthawks*? about the relationship between a painting and its viewer?

Inventing My Parents

After Edward Hopper's Nighthawks, 1942

SUSAN LUDVIGSON

Susan Ludvigson (b. 1942) is a professor of English at Winthrop University. Her books of poetry include *Sweet Confluence: New and Selected Poems* (2000) and *Escaping the House of Certainty* (2006). She is considered a southern poet, yet she seldom writes about the South specifically. "Inventing My Parents" is part of Ludvigson's 1993 collection *Everything Winged Must Be Dreaming*.

They sit in the bright café,
discussing Hemingway and how
this war will change them.
Sinclair Lewis's name comes up,
and Kay Boyle's, and then Fitzgerald's.   5
They disagree about the American Dream.
My mother, her bare arms
silver under fluorescent lights,
says she imagines it a hawk
flying over, its shadow sweeping   10
every town. Their coffee's getting cold
but they hardly notice. My mother's face
is lit by ideas. My father's gestures
are a Frenchman's. When he concedes
a point, he shrugs, an elaborate lift   15
of the shoulders, his hands and smile
declaring an open mind.
I am five months old, at home with a sitter
this August night when the air outside
is warm as a bath. They decide,   20

though the car is parked nearby,
to walk the few blocks home, savoring
the fragrant night, their being alone together.
As they go out the door, he's reciting
Donne's "Canonization": "For God's sake   25
hold your tongue, and let me love,"
and she's laughing, light
as summer rain when it begins.

[1993]

Exploring the Text

1. What story does Ludvigson's poem tell about *Nighthawks*?
2. Who is the speaker in the poem? What do we learn about her by the way she imagines her parents as characters in Hopper's painting?
3. The antecedent of "it" in line 9 appears to be "American Dream" in line 6. What else might "it" refer to? What is the connection between the American Dream and the title of Hopper's painting?
4. The parents presented by Ludvigson's speaker seem happier and more cultured than the couple pictured in *Nighthawks*. What is the effect of this juxtaposition?
5. In the poem "Canonization" by John Donne, the speaker begs to be left alone to love. Its title can be considered two ways: that the speaker's deep love makes him a saint, and that the poem itself canonizes the lovers. Why do you think Ludvigson chose to have the speaker's father quote this particular poem? How might it connect to Hopper's painting?

Focus on Comparison and Contrast

1. Ira Sadoff and Susan Ludvigson both tell stories based on *Nighthawks*. How are their stories different? How are they similar? What do both stories tell us about the place *Nighthawks* occupies in the American psyche?
2. Sadoff uses events from 1942 to bring his interpretation of *Nighthawks* into the world beyond the painting, while Ludvigson cites American novelists. How do these imagined contexts affect the poets' interpretations of Hopper's painting?
3. How is the mood and tone different in the two poems? Are there similarities?
4. In *Sister Wendy's American Masterpieces*, the art critic writes:

> From Jo's [Hopper's wife] diaries we learn that Hopper described this work as a painting of "three characters." The man behind the counter, though imprisoned in the triangle, is in fact free. He has a job, a home, he can come and go; he can look at the customers with a half-smile. It is the customers who are the nighthawks. Nighthawks are predators—but are the men there to prey on the woman, or has she come in to prey on the men? To my mind, the man and woman are a couple, as the position of their hands suggests, but they are a couple so lost in misery that they cannot communicate; they have nothing to give each other. I see the nighthawks of the picture not so much as birds of prey, but simply as birds: great winged creatures that should be free in the sky, but instead are shut in, dazed and miserable, with their heads constantly banging against the glass of the world's callousness.

Compare Sister Wendy's interpretation to the interpretations of Sadoff and Ludvigson. What is your own interpretation?

Writing Assignment

"Hopper's 'Nighthawks' (1942)" by Ira Sadoff and "Inventing My Parents: After Edward Hopper's *Nighthawks*, 1942" by Susan Ludvigson are inspired by the same painting, a painting that captures a moment that is both realistic and enigmatic. Compare and contrast the techniques each poet uses to capture that moment in words. Consider also how they explain—or don't explain—Hopper's painting.

The Laundresses

EDGAR DEGAS

Hilaire-Germain-Edgar Degas was born in Paris in 1834 and lived for eighty-three years—long enough to be celebrated in his lifetime—but he never stopped developing and experimenting. Degas changed subjects often and experimented with style and media; in his later years, for example, when his eyesight began to fail, he started to work in pastel and sculpture. Usually classed with the impressionists, Degas differed from them in several ways, mainly in his dislike of painting directly from nature. Among Degas's favorite subjects were ballerinas, horse racing, and working-class people, such as the laundresses in the work reproduced here.

The Laundresses (c. 1884–86, oil on canvas, 76 x 81.5 cm)

Degas's Laundresses

Eavan Boland

Eavan Boland (b. 1944) spent the first six years of her life in Dublin, moving to London when her father was appointed Irish ambassador, and then to New York when he was appointed president of the UN General Assembly. She recalls that she felt deprived of her Irish roots—particularly in London, where anti-Irish sentiment was rife. She writes of this experience in "An Irish Child in England: 1951," exemplified by "the teacher in the London convent who, / when I pronounced 'I amn't' in the classroom / turned and said—'you're not in Ireland now.'" Boland returned to Dublin for college, earning a BA in English and Latin from Trinity College Dublin. She has taught at Stanford University since 1996. Boland's first collection, *23 Poems* (1966), met with mixed reviews, but she established her reputation with *In Her Own Image* (1980). She has published regularly since, her most comprehensive volumes being *An Origin Like Water: Collected Poems, 1967–1987* (1996) and *New Collected Poems* (2008), and has won several awards, in addition to being awarded honorary degrees both in the United States and in Ireland. She is a feminist and a poet but, she maintains, not a feminist poet. She sees a fundamental difference between the "ethic" of feminism and the "aesthetic" of poetry, arguing that feminism is a definite moral position, whereas poetry, like all art, begins where certainty ends. Through her work, Boland strives to give meaning to everyday events in women's lives, as witnessed in "Degas's Laundresses."

You rise, you dawn
roll-sleeved Aphrodites,
out of a camisole brine,
a linen pit of stiches,
silking the fitted sheets   5
away from you like waves.
You seam dreams in the folds
of wash from which freshes
the whiff and reach of fields
where it bleached and stiffened.   10
Your chat's sabbatical:
brides, wedding outfits,

a pleasure of leisured women
are sweated into the folds,
the neat heaps of linen.   15
Now the drag of the clasp.
Your wrists basket your waist.
You round to the square weight.

Wait. There behind you.
A man. There behind you.   20
Whatever you do don't turn.
Why is he watching you?
Whatever you do don't turn.
Whatever you do don't turn.

See he takes his ease   25
staking his easel so,
slowly sharpening charcoal,
closing his eyes just so,
slowly smiling as if
so slowly he is   30

unbandaging his mind.
Surely a good laundress
would understand its twists,
its white turns,
its blind designs—   35

it's your winding sheet.

[1982]

Exploring the Texts

1. Eavan Boland's poem is an interpretation of Degas's *The Laundresses.* What is the speaker's attitude toward the subject of the poem? To whom is the poem addressed?

2. What do you think Degas's attitude toward his subject is? In addition to the way he portrays the two women, what other elements of style depict Degas's attitude? Look closely at line, shape, and composition—the way the figures are placed on the canvas. If possible, find the picture online so that you can look at it in color.

3. Who is the man in "Degas's Laundresses"? What is the speaker's attitude toward him?

4. In her poem, Boland names many of the items the laundresses wash and iron. What is the effect of naming these items even though they are not recognizable in the painting?

5. Degas once said, "It's one thing to copy what one sees, but it's much better to draw what can only be seen in one's memory. It's a transformation during which the imagination collaborates with the memory . . . there your recollections and fantasies are freed from the tyranny exerted by nature." How do both the painting and the poem combine memory and imagination? Do you think Degas and Boland feel the same way about the laundresses? Explain the differences and similarities and what might cause them.

EAVAN BOLAND ON WRITING

Renée Shea (RS): Why this painting—why Degas? Do you have a special connection with this painter?

Eavan Boland (EB): My mother was an artist, so I heard about paintings and painters from when I was young. Degas wasn't her favorite, but she admired certain things he did, especially his ballet dancers. That's how I first saw him—as a painter of glamour and art. In the 1970s, the Armand Hammer exhibition—a big collection of French paintings—came to Dublin. I saw it there. There were charcoal drawings of laundresses by Degas in the exhibition. Suddenly, this painter I had only ever associated with the color and festivity of dances and horse racing appeared to me as a harsh, mysterious interpreter of women and work. That really made an impression.

RS: Why do you see the painter—Degas—as an interloper, a menacing presence in the life of his subject, someone "staking his easel . . . slowly sharpening charcoal"?

EB: It wasn't so much Degas. It was an argument I was having with myself. My first child had been born, and I was in the house more than I had ever been. I was writing new poems, and I was getting to be fascinated with the idea of the domestic life and its silent, almost undocumented aspects. I was beginning to ask whether art really broke that silence or whether it just recorded it. That was a time when I wanted to ask ethical questions, not just aesthetic ones.

RS: I read the poem as a rebuke or at least a reminder that the working-women being depicted are objectified, not treated as fully human. Yet in your description of them the language suggests a kind of idealization: "roll-sleeved Aphrodites" who "seam dreams in the fold / of wash." Isn't what you're doing a different kind of objectification?

EB: The opening of the poem is ironic. I wanted to bring out contrasts between the actual state of the laundresses—the steam, the heat, the hard work—and the myth of a leisured Aphrodite, rising out of the waves. They're the down-to-earth exception that proves the rule. I saw them as already mythologized in the history of myth, merely by being women and painted objects. But I wasn't doing the objectifying; it had already been done. I was trying to reveal it.

RS: You've written "Degas's Laundresses" in first person, a direct address to the laundress herself. Why? Why was this preferable to having the woman speak for herself?

EB: In fact it's a plural. The image I first saw—and then revisited in the catalog—was of two laundresses. They're talking together, at least as I

5

imagine them ("your chat's sabbatical"). They're working together, so it was an address to both.

RS: I know this poem is often given a feminist reading, interpreted as an outcry against the work that these unnamed and uncelebrated women carry out by necessity rather than by choice. But isn't the issue one of class (during a specific time period) as much as gender?

EB: I'm not sure it's either. Or at least, gender and class are a lesser aspect. This is a poem about the way art disrupts life, and life comes back as art. It's about one artist — myself — warning the subjects of another artist's work to be wary because they are about to become images in his work. And yet, of course, through that very warning, they become images in mine. This is a poem about both accusation and self-accusation, with also, I think, more play and irony than maybe has been seen.

RS: You have poems about other paintings — "On Renoir's *The Grape Pickers*," for example — with a similar re-vision to call our attention, perhaps, to a different way of seeing the work. Would you comment on your interest in shifting the lens, as it were? Or are these poems further exploration of your concern for the domestic sphere of women's lives?

EB: Both poems were written at a time when I was beginning to be especially interested in the domestic, in work, and in the lives of women in connection with both. The paintings deal with these. It's the Degas, however, that most interested me.

RS: Is it a coincidence that you have chosen two impressionist painters (Renoir and Degas), or are you commenting — skeptically! — on the glorification of what is really hard and dull work?

EB: They're both painters I admire. But I'm also aware that there's a conversation going on in their work about what should — and should not — be beautified or glamorized. It's not just that *I'm* troubled about it; they seem troubled, too. The images of female beauty in their work often contrast with the realistic and darker representations of hard labor and the anonymity of the subjects. It's a conflicted vision. I was drawn to that conflict.

RS: In the poems I've asked about as well as many of your others, you are referencing artists from previous eras. How is this ongoing dialogue between present and past — as Eliot writes, "the presence of the past" — an essential part of being an artist, whether poet or painter?

EB: I'm sure it's different for everyone. It's always seemed to me, though, that the first requirement is a conversation with yourself. As a writer, a poet, that's the easier one. Eventually, you know where you want to go, and why. The conversation with the past follows on that. Often that's a more thorny

10

15

and unsettled dialogue. It certainly has been for me. The limits of authority and the freedom to transgress are all there. It's the way those conversations weave together—the first with yourself, the second with the past—that ends up being important. At least it has been that way for me.

RS: My students often question "originality" and "authenticity" when they encounter a work that is a retelling (such as a graphic novel depiction of a famous work or a writing-back such as *Wide Sargasso Sea*). Does responding to the work of other artists require or embolden the same kind of imagination as creating a wholly original work, or are these terms as slippery as they seem?

EB: They are slippery terms. Talking about the work of other artists in your own work can be helpful, though—as both text and pretext. The drawing by Degas allowed me to go further with arguments I was already exploring. I wanted to turn a harsh light on some of the flatteries of creativity. It was a personal quest. His drawing opened the door and allowed me to think it through. Perhaps responding to other artists makes it more likely that the poem will be an argumentative piece than otherwise, or maybe not. But in the case of this poem, and at that time, it certainly was helpful.

Follow-Up

1. Do you agree with Eavan Boland that Degas is a "harsh, mysterious interpreter of women and work," or did you see something different in the painting? What is your interpretation?
2. Boland says that talking about other artists' work can work as "both text and pretext." What do you think she means by that? Consider other retellings you have read; do you think the writer used the artwork as text, pretext, or both?
3. Boland says she wanted to ask ethical questions instead of just aesthetic questions in her interpretation of Degas's work. What ethical questions does she ask? Which questions do you think could be considered aesthetic?

Conversation

Seamus Heaney: The Responsibility of the Artist

Seamus Heaney was born in 1939 at Mossbawn, his family's farm, in Northern Ireland, about thirty miles northwest of Belfast. Heaney was the eldest of nine children. His father's family was involved in farming and cattle dealing, and his mother's family had been employed in a local linen mill. Heaney lived on the farm until he was twelve and won a scholarship to St. Columb's College, a Catholic boarding school about forty miles away. He later lived in Belfast and then the Republic of Ireland, and he said that his departure from the farm at Mossbawn was a removal from "the earth of farm labour to the heaven of education." At St. Columb's, Heaney learned Latin and Irish, and as a student at Queen's University in Belfast, he learned Anglo-Saxon; these languages resonate throughout his work. Heaney became known in the mid-1960s, when he was part of a group of Northern Irish poets that included Michael Longley, Derek Mahon, Paul Muldoon, and Ciaran Carson. Though stylistically diverse, these poets shared the background of a society that was deeply divided both politically and religiously.

Heaney's works include the collections *Death of a Naturalist* (1966), *Door into the Dark* (1969), *North* (1975), *Station Island* (1984), *Opened Ground* (1998), and *Electric Light* (2001). He is also known for his translations — such as *Sweeney Astray* (1983), *Sweeney's Fight* (1992), and *Beowulf* (1999) — and the plays *The Cure at Troy* (1990) and *Burial at Thebes* (2004). He was awarded the Nobel Prize for Literature in 1995.

In the foreword to *Preoccupations: Selected Prose, 1968–1978* — his first collection of prose — Heaney asks, "How should a poet properly live and write? What is his relationship to be to his own voice, his own place, his literary heritage and his contemporary world?" This preoccupation with the question of the responsibility of the poet still occupies Heaney's poetry and prose, as the works in this Conversation show.

Texts

Dennis O'Driscoll, from *Stepping Stones* (interview)

Seamus Heaney, from "Feeling into Words" (lecture)

Seamus Heaney, "Crediting Poetry" (Nobel lecture)

Seamus Heaney, "Digging" (poetry)

Seamus Heaney, "Requiem for the Croppies" (poetry)

Seamus Heaney, "Bogland" (poetry)

Seamus Heaney, "The Tollund Man" (poetry)

Seamus Heaney, "Tollund" (poetry)

Seamus Heaney, "A Call" (poetry)

Seamus Heaney, "Postscript" (poetry)

From *Stepping Stones*

INTERVIEWS WITH SEAMUS HEANEY

DENNIS O'DRISCOLL

> Editor and poet Dennis O'Driscoll was born in County Tipperary, Ireland, in 1954. The excerpt that appears here was part of *Stepping Stones* (2008), a series of Heaney's reminiscences, guided by questions from O'Driscoll.

'Tollund', another post-IRA-ceasefire poem, is dated the previous month, September 1994. Were you actually in Jutland at that time?

The coincidence was extraordinary. The IRA announced the ceasefire on a Wednesday, the last Wednesday in August, if I'm not mistaken, and I was asked to write about it for the next weekend's *Sunday Tribune*. That same weekend I was also bound for Denmark, to do a reading in Copenhagen University, and inevitably I was remembering the visit I'd made to Jutland twenty-one years earlier, to see the Tollund Man. What happened, at any rate, was an unexpected trip to the actual bog in Tollund where the body had been found in the 1950s. My host in the English Department, Nick Rosenmeir, took this sudden notion on the Saturday afternoon, bundled his wife and Marie and myself into his car, crossed to Jutland that evening on a ferry, put us up that night at their holiday house near Silkeborg and on the Sunday morning brought us to the actual spot where the turf cutters had dug him out.

'Hallucinatory and familiar', you called it.

That's exactly how it felt—as familiar as Toner's Bog in the townlands of Mulhollandstown and Scribe, all named in the poem. It was like a world restored, the world of the second chance, and that's why there's an echo of that Shakespearean line, 'Richard's himself again', in the last stanza. I also wanted to get in something of the dawn promise you find in that beautiful little speech at the end of the first scene of *Hamlet*: Marcellus talks about a hallowed moment in the dark of the year when 'the bird of dawning singeth all night long'. On our Sunday morning in Tollund, I felt a similar lightening of mood and opening of possibility. We were like 'ghosts who'd walked abroad / Unfazed by light, to make a new beginning / ... Ourselves again, free-willed again, not bad'. What we were experiencing, you could say, was hope rather than optimism, and that's why I liked the complicating echo of the words 'Sinn Féin' in the phrase 'ourselves again'.

You were still sceptical?   5

Cautious, certainly. I knew it would be crazy to expect a great change of heart on either side.

You weren't all that surprised presumably when the IRA bombed Canary Wharf in 1996?

I was disappointed if not entirely dismayed, but I still didn't believe it was the beginning of the end. More the end of the beginning. I couldn't see things being rolled back to their pre-ceasefire state. Too many adjustments, small but significant, had been made, not just in the public arena but at the core of most people's conscious-ness. The collective resolution had firmed up—again, not optimistically, just more or less obstinately.

You believed, therefore, in the 'peace process'? From the start?

I was chary, from the start, of the use of the term 'process'. Peace in Northern   10
Ireland—to begin with, at any rate—was always going to be a rigged-up, slightly
rickety affair: something ad hoc and precariously in the balance, depending at once
on great stealth and great boldness by individuals on both sides. There's something
too foreclosed about calling it a 'process', as if all you had to do was to initiate certain
movements or exchanges and the whole thing would work itself out in theory and
in practice.

*The fact that the Good Friday Agreement of 1998 resulted in a power-sharing executive
that included both Unionists and Republicans—David Trimble and Gerry Adams—as
well as constitutional nationalists must have been beyond anything foreseeable in your
childhood.*

Definitely. And the fact that the first executive bickered and faltered and fell was less important than the change it effected in the overall mindset. Loyalists were enraged to see Republicans holding ministries at Stormont; but, because of the long, slow, painful turn of events that had led to that eventuality, they lived with it and were very slightly changed by the experience—just as Republicans and nation-alists were changed by being included, however reluctantly, in the affairs of the Northern Irish state. They became participants and created an Irish dimension in a political culture that was officially British. In the end, we arrived at a point where Sinn Féin and the DUP could, as they say, do business in the devolved assembly, which meant that Ian Paisley had to actually speak to Gerry Adams and Martin McGuinness, with unexpectedly good initial results. The population as a whole has allowed itself more hope and trust in the future, but the sectarian underlife is still there, of course.

*At times of great hope or tragedy—the Ulster ceasefires, the Good Friday Agreement,
the Nobel Peace Prizes for Hume and Trimble, the Omagh bombing—you have written
newspaper commentaries. These were always prominently published (sometimes on the
front page), so I presume they were commissioned by the editors. Did you welcome such
commissions?*

Short notice is the crucial factor on those occasions. You're giving an immediate response, at a moment when the adrenalin is running. I couldn't say I welcomed the commissions, but I do feel some obligation at moments like that. It's hard to find the right language, of course. You want a note of seriousness, but at the same time you don't just want orotundity. I think, however, that a poet does have a role and a responsibility. You're allowed, for example, to quote poetry—probably *expected* to quote it; in the wake of the Omagh bombing, I remember how grateful I was to invoke Wilfred Owen's line about 'the eternal reciprocity of tears'. At times like that, you realize Philip Larkin got it right when he said that 'someone will forever be surprising / A hunger in himself to be more serious'.

[2008]

. . . .

Questions

1. In this excerpt, Heaney talks about Irish politics in the late 1990s, a time of hopefulness that has since been realized. How does Heaney connect the great changes in relations between the Republic of Ireland and Northern Ireland to poetry—both his and others?
2. How does Heaney describe his response to being asked to write newspaper commentaries in times of "great hope or tragedy"?
3. Why do you think Heaney makes a distinction between hope and optimism (para. 4)? Explain your answer.

From *Feeling into Words*

SEAMUS HEANEY

> Originally a lecture given at a meeting of the Royal Society of Literature in 1974, "Feeling into Words" was published in *Preoccupations: Selected Prose, 1968–1978* (1980).

In practice, you proceed by your own experience of what it is to write what you consider a successful poem. You survive in your own esteem not by the corroboration of theory but by the trust in certain moments of satisfaction which you know intuitively to be moments of extension. You are confirmed by the visitation of the last poem and threatened by the elusiveness of the next one, and the best moments are those when your mind seems to implode and words and images rush of their own accord into the vortex. Which happened to me once when the line 'We have no prairies' drifted into my head at bedtime and loosened a fall of images that constitute the poem 'Bogland', the last one in *Door into the Dark*.

I had been vaguely wishing to write a poem about bogland, chiefly because it is a landscape that has a strange assuaging effect on me, one with associations reaching back into early childhood. We used to hear about bog-butter, butter kept fresh for a great number of years under the peat. Then when I was at school the skeleton of an elk had been taken out of a bog nearby and a few of our neighbours had got their photographs in the paper, peering out across its antlers. So I began to get an idea of bog as the memory of the landscape, or as a landscape that remembered everything that happened in and to it. In fact, if you go round the National Museum in Dublin, you will realize that a great proportion of the most cherished material heritage of Ireland was 'found in a bog'. Moreover, since memory was the faculty that supplied me with the first quickening of my own poetry, I had a tentative unrealized need to make a congruence between memory and bogland and, for the want of a better word, our national consciousness. And it all released itself after 'We have no prairies . . .'—but we have bogs.

At that time I was teaching modern literature in Queen's University, Belfast, and had been reading about the frontier and the West as an important myth in the American consciousness, so I set up—or rather, laid down—the bog as an answering Irish myth. I wrote it quickly the next morning, having slept on my excitement, and revised it on the hoof, from line to line, as it came:

We have no prairies
To slice a big sun at evening—
Everywhere the eye concedes to
Encroaching horizon,

Is wooed into the cyclops' eye
Of a tarn. Our unfenced country
Is bog that keeps crusting
Between the sights of the sun.

They've taken the skeleton
Of the Great Irish Elk
Out of the peat, set it up
An astounding crate full of air.

Butter sunk under
More than a hundred years
Was recovered salty and white.
The ground itself is kind, black butter

Melting and opening underfoot,
Missing its last definition
By millions of years.
They'll never dig coal here,

Only the waterlogged trunks
Of great firs, soft as pulp.
Our pioneers keep striking
Inwards and downwards,

Every layer they strip
Seems camped on before.
The boptholes might be Atlantic seepage.
The wet centre is bottomless.

Again, as in the case of 'Digging', the seminal impulse had been unconscious. What generated the poem about memory was something lying beneath the very floor of memory, something I only connected with the poem months after it was written, namely a warning that older people would give us about going into the bog. They were afraid we might drown in pools in the old workings, so they put it about (and we believed them) that *there was no bottom* in the bog-holes. Little did they—or I—know that I would filch it for the last line of a book.

There was also in that book a poem called 'Requiem for the Croppies', written in 1966, when most poets in Ireland were straining to celebrate the anniversary of the 1916 Rising. That insurrection at Easter was the harvest of seeds sown in 1798, when revolutionary republican ideals and national feeling coalesced in the doctrines of Irish republicanism and in the rebellion of 1798 itself—unsuccessful and savagely put down. The poem was born of and ended with an image of resurrection based on the fact that sometime after the rebels were buried in common graves, the graves began to sprout with young barley, growing up from barley corn which the 'croppies' had carried in their pockets to eat while on the march. The oblique implication was that the seeds of violent resistance sown in the Year of Liberty had flowered in what Yeats called 'the right rose tree' of 1916. I did not realize at the time that the original heraldic murderous encounter between Protestant yeoman and Catholic rebel was to be initiated again in the summer of 1969, in Belfast, two months after the book was published.

From that moment the problems of poetry moved from being simply a matter 5 of achieving the satisfactory verbal icon to being a search for images and symbols adequate to our predicament. I do not mean liberal lamentation that citizens should feel compelled to murder one another or deploy their different military arms over the matter of nomenclatures such as 'British' or 'Irish'. I do not mean public celebrations of resistance or execrations of atrocity—although there is nothing necessarily unpoetic about such celebration, if one thinks of Yeats's 'Easter 1916'. I mean that I felt it imperative to discover a field of force in which, without abandoning fidelity to the processes and experience of poetry as I have outlined them, it would be possible to encompass the perspectives of a humane reason and at the same time to grant the religious intensity of the violence its deplorable authenticity and complexity. And when I say religious, I am not thinking simply of the sectarian division. To some extent, the enmity can be viewed as a struggle between the cults and devotees of a god and a goddess. There is an indigenous territorial numen, a tutelar of the whole island, call her Mother Ireland, Kathleen Ni Houlihan, the poor old woman, the Shan Van Vocht, whatever; and her sovereignty has been temporarily usurped or infringed by a new male cult whose founding fathers were Cromwell, William of Orange and Edward Carson, and whose godhead is incarnate in a rex or caesar resident in a palace in London. What we have is the tail-end of a struggle in a province between territorial piety and imperial power.

Now, I realize that this idiom is remote from the agnostic world of economic interest, whose iron hand operates in the velvet glove of 'talks between elected representatives', and remote from the political manoeuvres of power-sharing; but it is not remote from the psychology of the Irishmen and Ulstermen who do the killing, and not remote from the bankrupt psychology and mythologies implicit in the terms 'Irish Catholic' and 'Ulster Protestant'. The question, as ever, is, 'How with this rage shall beauty hold a plea?' And my answer is, by offering 'befitting emblems of adversity'.

Some of these emblems I found in a book that was published in English translation, appositely, the year the killing started, in 1969. And again appositely, it was entitled *The Bog People*. It was chiefly concerned with preserved bodies of men and women found in the bogs of Jutland, naked, strangled or with their throats cut, disposed under the peat since early Iron Age times. The author, P. V. Glob, argues convincingly that a number of these, and in particular the Tollund Man, whose head is now preserved near Aarhus in the museum at Silkeburg, were ritual sacrifices to the Mother Goddess, the goddess of the ground who needed new bridegrooms each winter to bed with her in her sacred place, in the bog, to ensure the renewal and fertility of the territory in the spring. Taken in relation to the tradition of Irish political martyrdom for that cause whose icon is Kathleen Ni Houlihan, this is more than an archaic barbarous rite: it is an archetypal pattern. And the unforgettable photographs of these victims blended in my mind with photographs of atrocities, past and present, in the long rites of Irish political and religious struggles. When I wrote this poem, I had a completely new sensation, one of fear. It was a vow to go on pilgrimage and I felt as it came to me — and again it came quickly — that unless I was deeply in earnest about what I was saying, I was simply invoking dangers for myself.

[1974]

Questions

1. What is the formula Heaney uses for knowing he's written a successful poem? How does he illustrate it?
2. What does Heaney say changed what he saw as poetry's purpose? How does he illustrate that change? What are some of the things Heaney says do not serve the purpose of finding "images and symbols adequate to our predicament" (para. 5)?
3. How does Heaney extend the meaning of *religious*?

Crediting Poetry

Seamus Heaney

"Crediting Poetry" is the lecture Heaney gave when he was awarded the Nobel Prize for Literature in 1995.

When I first encountered the name of the city of Stockholm, I little thought that I would ever visit it, never mind end up being welcomed to it as a guest of the Swedish Academy and the Nobel Foundation. At that particular time, such an outcome was not just beyond expectation: it was simply beyond conception. In the nineteen-forties, when I was the eldest child of an ever-growing family in rural county Derry, we crowded together in the three rooms of a traditional thatched farmstead and lived a kind of den-life which was more or less emotionally and intellectually proofed against the outside world. It was an intimate, physical, creaturely existence in which the night sounds of the horse in the stable beyond one bedroom wall mingled with the sounds of adult conversation from the kitchen beyond the other. We took in everything that was going on, of course—rain in the trees, mice on the ceiling, a steam train rumbling along the railway line one field back from the house—but we took it in as if we were in the doze of hibernation. Ahistorical, pre-sexual, in suspension between the archaic and the modern, we were as susceptible and impressionable as the drinking water that stood in a bucket in our scullery: every time a passing train made the earth shake, the surface of that water used to ripple delicately, concentrically, and in utter silence.

But it was not only the earth that shook for us: the air around and above us was alive and signalling also. When a wind stirred in the beeches, it also stirred an aerial wire attached to the topmost branch of the chestnut tree. Down it swept, in through a hole bored in the corner of the kitchen window, right on into the innards of our wireless set where a little pandemonium of burbles and squeaks would suddenly give way to the voice of a BBC newsreader speaking out of the unexpected like a *deus ex machina*. And that voice too we could hear in our bedroom, transmitting from beyond and behind the voices of the adults in the kitchen; just as we could often hear, behind and beyond every voice, the frantic, piercing signalling of Morse code.

We could pick up the names of neighbours being spoken in the local accents of our parents, and in the resonant English tones of the newsreader the names of bombers and of cities bombed, of war fronts and army divisions, the numbers of planes lost and of prisoners taken, of casualties suffered and advances made; and always, of course, we would pick up too those other, solemn and oddly bracing words, 'the enemy' and 'the allies'. But even so, none of the news of these world-spasms entered me as terror. If there was something ominous in the newscaster's tones, there was something torpid about our understanding of what was at stake; and if there was something culpable about such political ignorance in that time and place, there was something positive about the security I inhabited as a result of it.

The wartime, in other words, was pre-reflective time for me. Pre-literate too. Pre-historical in its way. Then as the years went on and my listening became more deliberate, I would climb up on an arm of our big sofa to get my ear closer to the wireless speaker. But it was still not the news that interested me; what I was after was the thrill of story, such as a detective serial about a British special agent called Dick Barton or perhaps a radio adaptation of one of Capt. W. E. Johns's adventure tales about an RAF flying ace called Biggles. Now that the other children were older and there was so much going on in the kitchen, I had to get close to the actual radio set in order to concentrate my hearing, and in that intent proximity to the dial I grew familiar with the names of foreign stations, with Leipzig and Oslo and Stuttgart and Warsaw and, of course, with Stockholm.

I also got used to hearing short bursts of foreign languages as the dial hand   5
swept round from BBC to Radio Eireann, from the intonations of London to those
of Dublin, and even though I did not understand what was being said in those first
encounters with the gutturals and sibilants of European speech, I had already begun a
journey into the wideness of the world. This in turn became a journey into the wideness of language, a journey where each point of arrival—whether in one's poetry or
one's life—turned out to be a stepping stone rather than a destination, and it is that
journey which has brought me now to this honoured spot. And yet the platform here
feels more like a space station than a stepping stone, so that is why, for once in my
life, I am permitting myself the luxury of walking on air.

I credit poetry for making this space-walk possible. I credit it immediately because of
a line I wrote fairly recently encouraging myself (and whoever else might be listening) to 'walk on air against your better judgement'. But I credit it ultimately because
poetry can make an order as true to the impact of external reality and as sensitive
to the inner laws of the poet's being as the ripples that rippled in and rippled out
across the water in that scullery bucket fifty years ago. An order where we can at last
grow up to that which we stored up as we grew. An order which satisfies all that is
appetitive in the intelligence and prehensile in the affections. I credit poetry, in other
words, both for being itself and for being a help, for making possible a fluid and
restorative relationship between the mind's centre and its circumference, between
the child gazing at the word 'Stockholm' on the face of the radio dial and the man
facing the faces that he meets in Stockholm at this most privileged moment. I credit
it because credit is due to it, in our time and in all time, for its truth to life, in every
sense of that phrase.

To begin with, I wanted that truth to life to possess a concrete reality, and rejoiced
most when the poem seemed most direct, an upfront representation of the world
it stood in for or stood up for or stood its ground against. Even as a schoolboy,
I loved John Keats's ode 'To Autumn' for being an ark of the covenant between
language and sensation; as an adolescent, I loved Gerard Manley Hopkins for the
intensity of his exclamations, which were also equations for a rapture and an ache
I didn't fully know I knew until I read him; I loved Robert Frost for his farmer's
accuracy and his wily down-to-earthness; and Chaucer too for much the same reasons. Later on I would find a different kind of accuracy, a moral down-to-earthness
to which I responded deeply and always will, in the war poetry of Wilfred Owen, a
poetry where a New Testament sensibility suffers and absorbs the shock of the new
century's barbarism. Then later again, in the pure consequence of Elizabeth Bishop's
style, in the sheer obduracy of Robert Lowell's and in the barefaced confrontation of Patrick Kavanagh's, I encountered further reasons for believing in poetry's
ability—and responsibility—to say what happens, to 'pity the planet', to be 'not
concerned with Poetry'.

This temperamental disposition towards an art that was earnest and devoted
to things as they are was corroborated by the experience of having been born and

brought up in Northern Ireland and of having lived with that place even though I have lived out of it for the past quarter of a century. No place in the world prides itself more on its vigilance and realism, no place considers itself more qualified to censure any flourish of rhetoric or extravagance of aspiration. So, partly as a result of having internalized these attitudes through growing up with them, I went for years half-avoiding and half-resisting the opulence and extensiveness of poets as different as Wallace Stevens and Rainer Maria Rilke; crediting insufficiently the crystalline inwardness of Emily Dickinson, all those forked lightnings and fissures of associa-tion; and missing the visionary strangeness of Eliot. And these more or less costive attitudes were fortified by a refusal to grant the poet any more licence than any other citizen; and they were further induced by having to conduct oneself as a poet in a situation of ongoing political violence and public expectation. A public expectation, it has to be said, not of poetry as such but of political positions variously approvable by mutually disapproving groups.

In such circumstances, the mind still longs to repose in what Samuel Johnson once called with superb confidence 'the stability of truth', even as it recognizes the destabilizing nature of its own operations and enquiries. Without needing to be theoretically instructed, consciousness quickly realizes that it is the site of vari-ously contending discourses. The child in the bedroom listening simultaneously to the domestic idiom of his Irish home and the official idioms of the British broadcaster while picking up from behind both the signals of some other distress, that child was already being schooled for the complexities of his adult predica-ment, a future where he would have to adjudicate among promptings variously ethical, aesthetical, moral, political, metrical, sceptical, cultural, topical, typical, post-colonial and, taken all together, simply impossible. So it was that I found myself in the mid-nineteen-seventies in another small house, this time in County Wicklow south of Dublin, with a young family of my own and a slightly less imposing radio set, listening to the rain in the trees and to the news of bombings closer to home—not only those by the Provisional IRA in Belfast but equally atrocious assaults in Dublin by loyalist paramilitaries from the north. Feeling puny in my predicaments as I read about the tragic logic of Osip Mandelstam's fate in the nineteen-thirties, feeling challenged yet steadfast in my non-combatant status when I heard, for example, that one particularly sweet-natured school friend had been interned without trial because he was suspected of having been involved in a political killing. What I was longing for was not quite stability but an active escape from the quicksand of relativism, a way of crediting poetry without anxiety or apology. In a poem called 'Exposure' I wrote then:

If I could come on meteorite!
Instead I walk through damp leaves,
Husks, the spent flukes of autumn,

Imagining a hero
On some muddy compound,

His gift like a slingstone
Whirled for the desperate.

How did I end up like this?
I often think of my friends'
Beautiful prismatic counselling
And the anvil brains of some who hate me

As I sit weighing and weighing
My responsible *tristia*.
For what? For the ear? For the people?
For what is said behind-backs?

Rain comes down through the alders,
Its low conducive voices
Mutter about let-downs and erosions
And yet each drop recalls

The diamond absolutes.
I am neither internee nor informer;
An inner émigré, grown long-haired
And thoughtful; a wood-kerne

Escaped from the massacre,
Taking protective colouring
From bole and bark, feeling
Every wind that blows;

Who, blowing up these sparks
For their meagre heat, have missed
The once-in-a-lifetime portent,
The comet's pulsing rose.

In one of the poems best known to students in my generation, a poem which could be said to have taken the nutrients of the symbolist movement and made them available in capsule form, the American poet Archibald MacLeish affirmed that 'A poem should be equal to / not true'. As a defiant statement of poetry's gift for telling truth but telling it slant, this is both cogent and corrective. Yet there are times when a deeper need enters, when we want the poem to be not only pleasurably right but compellingly wise, not only a surprising variation played upon the world, but a retuning of the world itself. We want the surprise to be transitive, like the impatient thump which unexpectedly restores the picture to the television set, or the electric shock which sets the fibrillating heart back to its proper rhythm. We want what the woman wanted in the prison queue in Leningrad, standing there blue with cold and whispering for fear, enduring the terror of Stalin's regime and asking the poet Anna Akhmatova if she could describe it all, if her art could be equal to it. And this is the want I too was experiencing in those far more protected circumstances in County

Wicklow when I wrote the lines I have just quoted, a need for poetry that would merit the definition of it I gave a few moments ago, as an order 'true to the impact of external reality and . . . sensitive to the inner laws of the poet's being'.

The external reality and inner dynamic of happenings in Northern Ireland between 1968 and 1974 were symptomatic of change, violent change admittedly, but change nevertheless, and for the minority living there, change had been long overdue. It should have come early, as the result of the ferment of protest on the streets in the late sixties, but that was not to be and the eggs of danger which were always incubating got hatched out very quickly. While the Christian moralist in oneself was impelled to deplore the atrocious nature of the IRA's campaign of bombings and killings, and the 'mere Irish' in oneself was appalled by the ruthlessness of the British Army on occasions like Bloody Sunday in Derry in 1972, the minority citizen in oneself, the one who had grown up conscious that his group was distrusted and discriminated against in all kinds of official and unofficial ways, this citizen's perception was at one with the poetic truth of the situation in recognizing that if life in Northern Ireland were ever really to flourish, change had to take place. But that citizen's perception was also at one with the truth in recognizing that the very brutality of the means by which the IRA were pursuing change was destructive of the trust upon which new possibilities would have to be based.

Nevertheless, until the British government caved in to the strong-arm tactics of the Ulster loyalist workers after the Sunningdale Conference in 1974, a well-disposed mind could still hope to make sense of the circumstances, to balance what was promising with what was destructive and do what W. B. Yeats had tried to do half a century before, namely, 'to hold in a single thought reality and justice'. After 1974, however, for the twenty long years between then and the ceasefires of August 1994, such a hope proved impossible. The violence from below was productive of nothing but a retaliatory violence from above, the dream of justice became subsumed into the callousness of reality, and people settled in to a quarter century of life-waste and spirit-waste, of hardening attitudes and narrowing possibilities that were the natural result of political solidarity, traumatic suffering and sheer emotional self-protectiveness.

One of the most harrowing moments in the whole history of the harrowing of the heart in Northern Ireland came when a minibus full of workers being driven home one January evening in 1976 was held up by armed and masked men and the occupants of the van ordered at gunpoint to line up at the side of the road. Then one of the masked executioners said to them, 'Any Catholics among you, step out here'. As it happened, this particular group, with one exception, were all Protestants, so the presumption must have been that the masked men were Protestant paramilitaries about to carry out a tit-for-tat sectarian killing of the Catholic as the odd man out, the one who would have been presumed to be in sympathy with the IRA and all its actions. It was a terrible moment for him, caught between dread and witness, but he did make a motion to step forward. Then, the story goes, in that split second of decision, and in the relative cover of the winter evening darkness, he felt the hand of the Protestant worker next to him take his hand and squeeze it in a signal that said no, don't move, we'll not betray you, nobody need know what faith or party you belong to. All in vain, however, for the man stepped out of the line; but instead of finding a gun at his temple, he was thrown backward and away as the gunmen opened fire on those remaining in the line, for these were not Protestant terrorists, but members, presumably, of the Provisional IRA.

It is difficult at times to repress the thought that history is about as instructive as an abattoir; that Tacitus was right and that peace is merely the desolation left behind after the decisive operations of merciless power. I remember, for example, shocking myself with a thought I had about that friend who was imprisoned in the seventies upon suspicion of having been involved with a political murder: I shocked myself by thinking that even if he were guilty, he might still perhaps be helping the future to be born, breaking the repressive forms and liberating new potential in the only way that worked, that is to say the violent way—which therefore became, by extension, the right way. It was like a moment of exposure to interstellar cold, a reminder of the scary element, both inner and outer, in which human beings must envisage and conduct their lives. But it was only a moment. The birth of the future we desire is surely in the contraction which that terrified Catholic felt on the roadside when another hand gripped his hand, not in the gunfire that followed, so absolute and so desolate, if also so much a part of the music of what happens.

As writers and readers, as sinners and citizens, our realism and our aesthetic sense make us wary of crediting the positive note. The very gunfire braces us and the atrocious confers a worth upon the effort which it calls forth to confront it. We are rightly in awe of the torsions in the poetry of Paul Celan and rightly enamoured of the suspiring voice in Samuel Beckett because these are evidence that art can rise to the occasion and somehow be the corollary of Celan's stricken destiny as Holocaust survivor and Beckett's demure heroism as a member of the French Resistance. Likewise, we are rightly suspicious of that which gives too much consolation in these circumstances; the very extremity of our late-twentieth-century knowledge puts much of our cultural heritage to an extreme test. Only the very stupid or the very deprived can any longer help knowing that the documents of civilization have been written in blood and tears, blood and tears no less real for being very remote. And when this intellectual predisposition coexists with the actualities of Ulster and Israel and Bosnia and Rwanda and a host of other wounded spots on the face of the earth, the inclination is not only not to credit human nature with much constructive potential but not to credit anything too positive in the work of art.

Which is why for years I was bowed to the desk like some monk bowed over his prie-dieu, some dutiful contemplative pivoting his understanding in an attempt to bear his portion of the weight of the world, knowing himself incapable of heroic virtue or redemptive effect, but constrained by his obedience to his rule to repeat the effort and the posture. Blowing up sparks for a meagre heat. Forgetting faith, straining towards good works. Attending insufficiently to the diamond absolutes, among which must be counted the sufficiency of that which is absolutely imagined. Then finally and happily, and not in obedience to the dolorous circumstances of my native

15

place but in spite of them, I straightened up. I began a few years ago to try to make space in my reckoning and imagining for the marvellous as well as for the murderous. And once again I shall try to represent the import of that changed orientation with a story out of Ireland.

This is a story about another monk holding himself up valiantly in the posture of endurance. It is said that once upon a time St Kevin was kneeling with his arms stretched out in the form of a cross in Glendalough, a monastic site not too far from where we lived in County Wicklow, a place which to this day is one of the most wooded and watery retreats in the whole of the country. Anyhow, as Kevin knelt and prayed, a blackbird mistook his outstretched hand for some kind of roost and swooped down upon it, laid a clutch of eggs in it and proceeded to nest in it as if it were the branch of a tree. Then, overcome with pity and constrained by his faith to love the life in all creatures great and small, Kevin stayed immobile for hours and days and nights and weeks, holding out his hand until the eggs hatched and the fledglings grew wings, true to life if subversive of common sense, at the intersection of natural process and the glimpsed ideal, at one and the same time a signpost and a reminder. Manifesting that order of poetry whch is true to all that is appetitive in the intelligence and prehensile in the affections. An order where we can at last grow up to that which we stored up as we grew.

St Kevin's story is, as I say, a story out of Ireland. But it strikes me that it could equally well come out of India or Africa or the Arctic or the Americas. By which I do not mean merely to consign it to a typology of folktales, or to dispute its value by questioning its culture-bound status within a multi-cultural context. On the contrary, its trustworthiness and its travel-worthiness have to do with its local setting. Indeed, the whole conception strikes me rather as being another example of the kind of work I saw a few weeks ago in the small museum in Sparta, on the morning before the news of this year's Nobel Prize in Literature was announced.

This was art which sprang from a cult very different from the faith espoused by St Kevin. Yet in it there was a representation of a roosted bird and an entranced beast and a self-enrapturing man, except that this time the man was Orpheus and the rapture came from music rather than prayer. The work itself was a small carved relief and I could not help making a sketch of it; but neither could I help copying out the information typed on the card which accompanied and identified the exhibit. The image moved me because of its antiquity and durability, but the description on the card moved me also because it gave a name and credence to that which I see myself as having been engaged upon for the past three decades: 'Votive panel,' the identification card said, 'possibly set up to Orpheus by local poet. Local work of the Hellenistic period'.

Once again, I hope I am not being sentimental or simply fetishizing—as we have learnt to say—the local. I wish instead to suggest that images and stories of the kind I am invoking here do function as bearers of value. The century has witnessed the defeat of Nazism by force of arms; but the erosion of the Soviet regimes was caused, among other things, by the sheer persistence, beneath the imposed ideological conformity, of cultural values and psychic resistances of a kind that these stories and images enshrine. Even if we have learned to be rightly and deeply fearful of elevating the cultural forms and conservatisms of any nation into normative and exclusivist systems, even if we have terrible proof that pride in an ethnic and religious heritage can quickly degrade into the fascistic, our vigilance on that score should not displace our love and trust in the good of the indigenous per se. On the contrary, a trust in the staying power and travel-worthiness of such good should encourage us to credit the possibility of a world where respect for the validity of every tradition will issue in the creation and maintenance of a salubrious political space. In spite of devastating and repeated acts of massacre, assassination and extirpation, the huge acts of faith which have marked the new relations between Palestinians and Israelis, Africans and Afrikaaners, and the way in which walls have come down in Europe and iron curtains have opened, all this inspires a hope that new possibility can still open up in Ireland as well. The crux of that problem involves an ongoing partition of the island between British and Irish jurisdictions, and an equally persistent partition of the affections in Northern Ireland between the British and Irish heritages; but surely every dweller in the country must hope that the governments involved in its governance can devise institutions which will allow that partition to become a bit more like the net on a tennis court, a demarcation allowing for agile give-and-take, for encounter and contending, prefiguring a future where the vitality that flowed in the beginning from those bracing words 'enemy' and 'allies' might finally derive from a less binary and altogether less binding vocabulary.

When the poet W. B. Yeats stood on this platform more than seventy years ago, Ireland was emerging from the throes of a traumatic civil war that had followed fast on the heels of a war of independence fought against the British. The struggle that ensued had been brief enough; it was over by May 1923, some seven months before Yeats sailed to Stockholm, but it was bloody, savage and intimate, and for generations to come it would dictate the terms of politics within the twenty-six independent counties of Ireland, that part of the island known first of all as the Irish Free State and then subsequently as the Republic of Ireland.

Yeats barely alluded to the civil war or the war of independence in his Nobel speech. Nobody understood better than he the connection between the construction or destruction of a political order and the founding or foundering of cultural life, but on this occasion he chose to talk instead about the Irish Dramatic Movement. His story was about the creative purpose of that movement and its historic good fortune in having not only his own genius to sponsor it, but also the genius of his friends John Millington Synge and Lady Augusta Gregory. He came to Sweden to tell the world that the local work of poets and dramatists had been as important to the transformation of his native place and times as the ambushes of guerrilla armies; and his boast in that elevated prose was essentially the same as the one he would make in verse more than a decade later in his poem 'The Municipal Gallery Revisited'. There Yeats presents himself amongst the portraits and heroic narrative paintings which celebrate the events and personalities of recent history and all of a sudden realizes that something truly epochmaking has occurred:

'"This is not", I say, / "The dead Ireland of my youth, but an Ireland / The poets have imagined, terrible and gay"'. And the poem concludes with two of the most quoted lines of his entire oeuvre:

Think where man's glory most begins and ends,
And say my glory was I had such friends.

And yet, expansive and thrilling as these lines are, they are an instance of poetry flourishing itself rather than proving itself, they are the poet's lap of honour, and in this respect if in no other they resemble what I am doing in this lecture. In fact, I should quote here on my own behalf some other words from the poem: 'You that would judge me, do not judge alone / This book or that'. Instead, I ask you to do what Yeats asked his audience to do and think of the achievement of Irish poets and dramatists and novelists over the past forty years, among whom I am proud to count great friends. In literary matters, Ezra Pound advised against accepting the opinion of those 'who haven't themselves produced notable work', and it is advice I have been privileged to follow, since it is the good opinion of notable workers—and not just those in my own country—that has fortified my endeavour since I began to write in Belfast more than thirty years ago.

Yeats, however, was by no means all flourish. To the credit of poetry in our century there must surely be entered in any reckoning his two great sequences of poems entitled 'Nineteen Hundred and Nineteen' and 'Meditations in Time of Civil War', the latter of which contains the famous lyric about the bird's nest at his window, where a starling or stare had built in a crevice of the old wall. The poet was living then in a Norman tower which had been very much a part of the military history of the country in earlier troubled times, and as his thoughts turned upon the irony of civilizations being consolidated by violent and powerful conquerors who end up commissioning the artists and the architects, he began to associate the sight of a mother bird feeding its young with the image of the honey-bee, an image deeply lodged in poetic tradition and always suggestive of the ideal of an industrious, harmonious, nurturing commonwealth:

The bees build in the crevices
Of loosening masonry, and there
The mother birds bring grubs and flies.
My wall is loosening; honey-bees,
Come build in the empty house of the stare.

We are closed in, and the key is turned
On our uncertainty; somewhere
A man is killed, or a house burned,
Yet no clear fact to be discerned:
Come build in the empty house of the stare.

A barricade of stone or of wood;
Some fourteen days of civil war;
Last night they trundled down the road

That dead young soldier in his blood:
Come build in the empty house of the stare.

We had fed the heart on fantasies,
The heart's grown brutal from the fare;
More substance in our enmities
Than in our love; O honey-bees,
Come build in the empty house of the stare.

I have heard this poem repeated often, in whole and in part, by people in Ireland over the past twenty-five years, and no wonder, for it is as tender-minded towards life itself as St Kevin was and as tough-minded about what happens in and to life as Homer. It knows that the massacre will happen again on the roadside, that the workers in the minibus are going to be lined up and shot down just after quitting time; but it also credits as a reality the squeeze of the hand, the actuality of sympathy and protective-ness between living creatures. It satisfies the contradictory needs which consciousness experiences at times of extreme crisis, the need on the one hand for a truth-telling that will be hard and retributive, and on the other hand the need not to harden the mind to a point where it denies its own yearnings for sweetness and trust. It is a proof that poetry can be equal to *and* true at the same time, an example of that completely adequate poetry which the Russian woman sought from Anna Akhmatova and which William Wordsworth produced at a corresponding moment of historical crisis and personal dismay almost exactly two hundred years ago.

When the bard Demodocus sings of the fall of Troy and of the slaughter that accompa-nied it, Odysseus weeps and Homer says that his tears were like the tears of a wife on a battlefield weeping for the death of a fallen husband. His epic simile continues:

At the sight of the man panting and dying there,
she slips down to enfold him, crying out;
then feels the spears, prodding her back and shoulders,
and goes bound into slavery and grief.
Piteous weeping wears away her cheeks:
but no more piteous than Odysseus' tears,
cloaked as they were, now, from the company.

Even today, three thousand years later, as we channel-surf over so much live coverage of contemporary savagery, highly informed but nevertheless in danger of growing immune, familiar to the point of overfamiliarity with old newsreels of the concen-tration camp and the gulag, Homer's image can still bring us to our senses. The cal-lousness of those spear-shafts on the woman's back and shoulders survives time and translation. The image has that documentary adequacy which answers all that we know about the intolerable.

But there is another kind of adequacy which is specific to lyric poetry. This has to do with the 'temple inside our hearing' which the passage of the poem calls into being. It is an adequacy deriving from what Mandelstam called 'the steadfastness of speech articulation', from the resolution and independence which the entirely realized poem sponsors. It has as much to do with the energy released by linguistic fission and fusion, with the buoyancy generated by cadence and tone and rhyme and stanza, as it has to do with the poem's concerns or the poet's truthfulness. In fact, in lyric poetry, truthfulness becomes recognizable as a ring of truth within the medium itself. And it is the unappeasable pursuit of this note, a note tuned to its most extreme in Emily Dickinson and Paul Celan and orchestrated to its most opulent in John Keats, it is this which keeps the poet's ear straining to hear the totally persuasive voice behind all the other informing voices.

Which is a way of saying that I have never quite climbed down from the arm of that sofa. I may have grown more attentive to the news and more alive to the world history and world-sorrow behind it. But the thing uttered by the speaker I strain towards is still not quite the story of what is going on; it is more reflexive than that, because as a poet I am in fact straining towards a strain, in the sense that the effort is to repose in the stability conferred by a musically satisfying order of sounds. As if the ripple at its widest desired to be verified by a reformation of itself, to be drawn in and drawn out through its point of origin.

I also strain towards this in the poetry I read. And I find it, for example, in the repetition of that refrain of Yeats's, 'Come build in the empty house of the stare', with its tone of supplication, its pivots of strength in the words 'build' and 'house' and its acknowledgement of dissolution in the word 'empty'. I find it also in the triangle of forces held in equilibrium by the triple rhyme of 'fantasies' and 'enmities' and 'honey-bees', and in the sheer in-placeness of the whole poem as a given form within the language. Poetic form is both the ship and the anchor. It is at once a buoyancy and a holding, allowing for the simultaneous gratification of whatever is centrifugal and centripetal in mind and body. And it is by such means that Yeats's work does what the necessary poetry always does, which is to touch the base of our sympathetic nature while taking in at the same time the unsympathetic reality of the world to which that nature is constantly exposed. The form of the poem, in other words, is crucial to poetry's power to do the thing which always is and always will be to poetry's credit: the power to persuade that vulnerable part of our consciousness of its rightness in spite of the evidence of wrongness all around it, the power to remind us that we are hunters and gatherers of values, that our very solitudes and distresses are creditable, in so far as they, too, are an earnest of our veritable human being.

[1995]

Questions

1. How does Heaney credit the radio that his family listened to as an influence on his work? What point does he make at the end of the speech when he comes back to the radio?
2. In paragraph 7, Heaney talks about his favorite poets, including poets whose work he came to like better as he grew older. How does Heaney connect the work of his favorite poets to the development of his political views and his own work?

3. What examples does Heaney give to illustrate his realization that "consciousness quickly realizes that it is the site of variously contending discourses" (para. 9)?

4. Heaney provides examples in the form of anecdotes, a folktale, his own poetry, and the poetry of others. How do each of these examples contribute to his argument that poetry should be "true to the impact of external reality and . . . sensitive to the inner laws of the poet's being" (para. 6)?

5. Why do you think this lecture is titled "Crediting Poetry"? What does Heaney claim poetry can do for individuals? for nations? for humanity?

Digging

SEAMUS HEANEY

Between my finger and my thumb
The squat pen rests; snug as a gun.

Under my window, a clean rasping sound
When the spade sinks into gravelly ground:
My father, digging. I look down   5

Till his straining rump among the flowerbeds
Bends low, comes up twenty years away
Stooping in rhythm through potato drills[1]
Where he was digging.

The coarse boot nestled on the lug, the shaft   10
Against the inside knee was levered firmly.
He rooted out tall tops, buried the bright edge deep
To scatter new potatoes that we picked
Loving their cool hardness in our hands.

By god, the old man could handle a spade.   15
Just like his old man.

My grandfather cut more turf in a day
Than any other man on Toner's bog.
Once I carried him milk in a bottle
Corked sloppily with paper. He straightened up   20
To drink it, then fell to right away
Nicking and slicing neatly, heaving sods
Over his shoulder, going down and down
For the good turf. Digging.

_____
[1]Furrows in the soil for sowing seeds. —EDS.

The cold smell of potato mould, the squelch and slap   25
Of soggy peat, the curt cuts of an edge
Through living roots awaken in my head.
But I've no spade to follow men like them.

Between my finger and my thumb
The squat pen rests.   30
I'll dig with it.

                                                        [1966]

. . . .

Questions

1. It is likely that Heaney is the poem's speaker. How is he both different from and similar to his father and grandfather?
2. "Digging" is one of Heaney's first published poems. What themes does he address in it?
3. In an interview with Dennis O'Driscoll in *Stepping Stones,* Heaney said of "Digging": "I wasn't discommoded by English critics gabbling on about the out-of-dateness of bulls and bogs, but I was caught on the hop when I found those images being read as some kind of endorsement of the Northern status quo." How could "Digging" be read (or misread) as an "endorsement of the Northern status quo"? Why might Heaney dislike this interpretation?

Requiem for the Croppies

Seamus Heaney

The pockets of our great coats full of barley—
No kitchens on the run, no striking camp—
We moved quick and sudden in our own country.
The priest lay behind ditches with the tramp.
A people, hardly marching—on the hike—   5
We found new tactics happening each day:
We'd cut through reins and rider with the pike
And stampede cattle into infantry,
Then retreat through hedges where cavalry must be thrown.
Until, on Vinegar Hill, the fatal conclave.   10
Terraced thousands died, shaking scythes at cannon.
The hillside blushed, soaked in our broken wave.
They buried us without shroud or coffin
And in August the barley grew up out of the grave.

                                                        [1966]

. . . .

Questions

1. "[O]ur" in the poem's first line and "We" in its third line suggests a first-person-plural speaker. What is the effect of this decision? What kind of political statement might Heaney be making?
2. What are some of the differences in tone and subject between this poem and "Digging," written the same year?
3. Heaney talks about "Requiem for the Croppies" in "Feeling into Words" (p. 1130). Why do you think Heaney eventually stopped reading "Requiem for the Croppies" in public, which he did in the early 1970s?

Bogland

Seamus Heaney

for T. P. Flanagan

We have no prairies
To slice a big sun at evening—
Everywhere the eye concedes to
Encrouching horizon,

Is wooed into the cyclops' eye   5
Of a tarn. Our unfenced country
Is bog that keeps crusting
Between the sights of the sun.

They've taken the skeleton
Of the Great Irish Elk   10
Out of the peat, set it up
An astounding crate full of air.

Butter sunk under
More than a hundred years
Was recovered salty and white.   15
The ground itself is kind, black butter

Melting and opening underfoot,
Missing its last definition
By millions of years.
They'll never dig coal here,   20

Only the waterlogged trunks
Of great firs, soft as pulp.
Our pioneers keep striking
Inwards and downwards,

Every layer they strip   25
Seems camped on before.

The bogholes might be Atlantic seepage.
The wet centre is bottomless.

[1969]

Questions

1. While the intact skeleton of an elk and unspoiled butter were, in fact, found in the bogs, "millions of years" and "bottomless" may be exaggerations. What do you think Heaney is saying about Ireland—and about history—in this mixture of artifacts and fiction?
2. How does "Bogland" answer the American myth of the western frontier? How does the Irish version of pioneers contrast with the traditional American version?
3. The publication of "Bogland" in 1969 coincided with an outbreak of violence in Northern Ireland. In "Feeling into Words" (p. 1130), Heaney said that from that moment, "the problems of poetry moved from being simply a matter of achieving the satisfactory verbal icon to being a search for images and symbols adequate to our predicament." What images and ideas does "Bogland" offer that help Heaney comment on the troubles in his country?

The Tollund Man

SEAMUS HEANEY

I

Some day I will go to Aarhus
To see his peat-brown head,
The mild pods of his eyelids,
His pointed skin cap.

In the flat country nearby   5
Where they dug him out,
His last gruel of winter seeds
Caked in his stomach,

Naked except for
The cap, noose and girdle,   10
I will stand a long time.
Bridegroom to the goddess,

She tightened her torc on him
And opened her fen,
Those dark juices working   15
Him to a saint's kept body,

Trove of the turf-cutters'
Honeycombed workings.
Now his stained face
Reposes at Aarhus.   20

II

I could risk blasphemy,
Consecrate the cauldron bog
Our holy ground and pray
Him to make germinate

The scattered, ambushed   25
Flesh of labourers,
Stockinged corpses
Laid out in the farmyards,

Tell-tale skin and teeth
Flecking the sleepers   30
Of four young brothers, trailed
For miles along the lines.

III

Something of his sad freedom
As he rode the tumbril
Should come to me, driving,   35
Saying the names

Tollund, Grauballe, Nebelgard,
Watching the pointing hands
Of country people,
Not knowing their tongue.   40

Out there in Jutland
In the old man-killing parishes
I will feel lost,
Unhappy and at home.

                                                          [1972]

Questions

1. This is one of several poems Heaney wrote about the bog people, nearly intact
   bodies of men and women from as early as 260 B.C.E. found in Northern Ireland
   and Denmark by peat cutters. Heaney was inspired by P. V. Glob's book *The Bog
   People: Iron-Age Man Preserved*, a study of the exhumed bog people. How does

Heaney honor the body of the Tollund Man and at the same time use it to represent and symbolize northern Europe's bloody history?

2. What is the effect of Heaney's turn from a description of the Tollund Man to what are likely examples of violence from his own time in Northern Ireland?

3. Why do you think Heaney ends the poem by saying he "will feel lost, / Unhappy and at home"?

Tollund

Seamus Heaney

That Sunday morning we had travelled far.
We stood a long time out in Tollund Moss:
The low ground, the swart water, the thick grass
Hallucinatory and familiar.

A path through Jutland fields. Light traffic sound.   5
Willow bushes; rushes; bog-fir grags
In a swept and gated farmyard; dormant quags.
And silage under wraps in its silent mound.

It could have been a still out of the bright
'Townland of Peace', that poem of dream farms   10
Outside all contention. The scarecrow's arms
Stood open opposite the satellite

Dish in the paddock, where a standing stone
Had been resituated and landscaped,
With tourist signs in *futhark* runic script   15
In Danish and in English. Things had moved on.

It could have been Mullhollandstown or Scribe.
The by-roads had their names on them in black
And white; it was user-friendly outback
Where we stood footloose, at home beyond the tribe,   20

More scouts than strangers, ghosts who'd walked abroad
Unfazed by light, to make a new beginning
And make a go of it, alive and sinning,
Ourselves again, free-willed again, not bad.

[1994]

. . . .

Questions

1. The third and fourth stanzas contain disparate images: a scarecrow's arms and a satellite dish, tourist signs and runic script. What is the effect of these juxtapositions?

2. "Townland of Peace" (l. 10) is a reference to a poem by Northern Irish poet John Hewitt, which contains these lines: "not to lose again / the line and compass so my head and heart / no longer plunge and tug to drag apart." How does that line connect to the concerns Heaney has in the poems collected here—especially "Tollund"?
3. "Tollund" is a "post-IRA-ceasefire poem," which Heaney describes in the interview from *Stepping Stones* (p. 1128) as expressing "hope rather than optimism." What do you find hopeful in the poem?
4. How do the themes of "Digging" find their way into the bog poems ("Bogland," "Tollund Man," and "Tollund")?
5. How do the ideas in the bog poems connect to the last line of "Requiem for the Croppies"?

A Call

SEAMUS HEANEY

'Hold on,' she said, 'I'll just run out and get him.
The weather here's so good, he took the chance
To do a bit of weeding.'
             So I saw him
Down on his hands and knees beside the leek rig,
Touching, inspecting, separating one   5
Stalk from the other, gently pulling up
Everything not tapered, frail and leafless,
Pleased to feel each little weed-root break,
But rueful also . . .
             Then found myself listening to
The amplified grave ticking of hall clocks   10
Where the phone lay unattended in a calm
Of mirror glass and sunstruck pendulums . . .

And found myself then thinking: if it were nowadays,
This is how Death would summon Everyman.

Next thing he spoke and I nearly said I loved him.   15

[1996]

Questions

1. Who is the speaker? Who do you think he or she is calling?
2. What do you think Heaney means by the phrase "if it were nowadays" (l. 13)?
3. In this poem, perhaps more than the others collected here, there is evidence of what the Irish writer John Banville called Heaney's "unapologetic stance" in which he "insists on affirming the enduring decencies, what Wordsworth calls 'the little

nameless unremembered acts / Of kindness and of love.'" While its subject is intimate, what bigger issues does "A Call" also address?

Postscript

SEAMUS HEANEY

And some time make the time to drive out west
Into County Clare, along the Flaggy Shore,
In September or October, when the wind
And the light are working off each other
So that the ocean on one side is wild   5
With foam and glitter, and inland among stones
The surface of a slate-grey lake is lit
By the earthed lightning of a flock of swans,
Their feathers roughed and ruffling, white on white,
Their fully grown headstrong-looking heads   10
Tucked or cresting or busy underwater.
Useless to think you'll park and capture it
More thoroughly. You are neither here nor there,
A hurry through which known and strange things pass
As big soft buffetings come at the car sideways   15
And catch the heart off guard and blow it open.

[1996]

. . . .

Questions

1. In "This Is Not a Spade: The Poetry of Seamus Heaney," Ola Larsmo writes:

   Heaney creates a way in which you learn to see the actual world around you, in a new light. But "seeing" in the Heaney sense can mean two things, two concepts which we find in the centre of modernist poetry; 'epiphany' and 'correspondence'.

   It is quite simple: 'epiphany' is here . . . the moment where you experience a sudden insight into the meaning of things seemingly trivial. . . .

   'Correspondence', on the other hand, is when you realise previously invisible connections between things, connections perhaps only made possible through the special kind of language we call poetry.

   How does "Postscript" contain both "epiphany" and "correspondence"?

2. What do you think Heaney means by the "known and strange things" (l. 14)?

3. How do you see "Postscript" as part of a progression in the works you have studied in this Conversation? How does "Postscript" accomplish what Heaney called in his Nobel Prize speech his goal to "make space in [his] reckoning and imagining for the marvellous as well as for the murderous" (para. 15)?

Entering the Conversation

As you develop a response to one of the following questions, refer to the texts you have read in this section. You may also draw on your own experience or knowledge relating to Seamus Heaney and the responsibility of the artist.

1. Write an essay in which you compare and contrast the poems in the Conversation in terms of how they reflect Heaney's view of the responsibility of the artist.
2. Heaney often refers to this question from Shakespeare's Sonnet 65: "How with this rage shall beauty hold a plea" (l. 3). Read the entire sonnet.

> Since brass, nor stone, nor earth, nor boundless sea,
> But sad mortality o'ersways their power,
> How with this rage shall beauty hold a plea,
> Whose action is no stronger than a flower?
> O how shall summer's honey breath hold out   5
> Against the wrackful siege of batt'ring days,
> When rocks impregnable are not so stout,
> Nor gates of steel so strong, but Time decays?
> O fearful meditation! where, alack,
> Shall Time's best jewel from Time's chest lie hid?   10
> Or what strong hand can hold his swift foot back?
> Or who his spoil of beauty can forbid?
>   O none, unless this miracle have might,
>   That in black ink my love may still shine bright.

   Does Shakespeare answer the question? Do you think Heaney answers it in the works in this Conversation? Discuss your answers to both questions.
3. Do you believe Heaney comes to a conclusion about how artists can balance their sense of beauty with their responsibility for social action? If so, write an essay in which you agree or disagree with his conclusion. If not, write an essay in which you come to your own conclusion.
4. Using the close reading techniques you have studied, analyze three or more of the poems in this Conversation. Choose the poems thematically, or just pick the ones you like best. Write an essay in which you compare and contrast the techniques Heaney uses.
5. Research the bog people, and prepare a presentation in which you use visuals—along with Heaney's poetry—to show what *New York Times* critic Michiko Kakutani called Heaney's "literary power to unearth from the Irish their gloriously gruesome relics of innocent death and sudden violence and the transcendent nurturing of present upon past that is revealed in the ancient murk of the boglands of Ireland and Jutland."

Student Writing

Close Reading Poetry

The first draft of this student essay was written as a timed response to the following prompt. The final draft was revised outside of class.

> Read the following poem carefully. Then write a well-organized essay in which you analyze how the use of language reveals the speaker's attitude toward his subject.

"My Last Duchess,"

BY ROBERT BROWNING

he's had others,
she's dead

Ferrara

That's my last Duchess painted on the wall,

Creepy! Looking as if she were alive. I call

That piece a wonder, now: Frà Pandolf's hands

Worked busily a day, and there she stands.

He ♥ed her but
w/resentment
she's dead but he
sort of misses her.

Will't please you sit and look at her? I said   5

"Frà Pandolf" by design, for never read

Dramatic Monologue
Purpose?—negotiate
a new marriage?

Strangers like you that pictured countenance,

sentimental picture—no negativity The depth and passion of its earnest glance,

But to myself they turned (since none puts by

The curtain I have drawn for you, but I)   10

And seemed as they would ask me, if they durst,

How such a glance came there; so, not the first

Are you to turn and ask thus. Sir, 'twas not

Her husband's presence only, called that spot

Of joy into the Duchess' cheek: perhaps   15

Frà Pandolf chanced to say "Her mantle laps

Over my lady's wrist too much," or "Paint

Must never hope to reproduce the faint

loved her
resentful @
same time

! Half-flush that dies along her throat": such stuff

Was courtesy, she thought, and cause enough   20

For calling up that spot of joy. She had

A heart—how shall I say?—too soon made glad,

Too easily impressed; she liked whate'er

list She looked on, and her looks went everywhere.

Sir, 'twas all one! My favor at her breast,   25
The dropping of the daylight in the West,
The bough of cherries some officious fool   *paranoia*
Broke in the orchard for her, the white mule
She rode with round the terrace—all and each
Would draw from her alike the approving speech,   30
Or blush, at least. She thanked men,—good! but thanked
Somehow—I know not how—as if she ranked
My gift of a nine-hundred-years-old name   *dashes!*
With anybody's gift. Who'd stoop to blame   *getting flustered/*
This sort of trifling? Even had you skill   *angry*
In speech—which I have not—to make your will   35
Quite clear to such an one, and say, "Just this
Or that in you disgusts me; here you miss,
Or there exceed the mark"—and if she let
Herself be lessoned so, nor plainly set   40
Her wits to yours, forsooth, and made excuse,
—E'en then would be some stooping; and I choose
Never to stoop. Oh sir, she smiled, no doubt,
Whene'er I passed her; but who passed without
Much the same smile? This grew; I gave commands;   *euphemisms* 45
Then all smiles stopped together. There she stands
repetition of   As if alive. Will't please you rise? We'll meet   *Speaker comes*
beginning   The company below, then. I repeat,   *back together*
The Count your master's known munificence
Is ample warrant that no just pretense   *purpose—*   50
Of mine for dowry will be disallowed;   *another*
Though his fair daughter's self, as I avowed *duchess*
At starting, is my object. Nay, we'll go
Together down, sir. Notice Neptune, though,   *allusion*
he tamed Taming a sea-horse, thought a rarity,   55
wives Which Claus of Innsbruck cast in bronze for me!   *greedy*

First Draft

Robert Browning is a well renowned and ~~intriguing~~ famous poet; he often
wrote about love, and in his poem "My Last ~~Dutch~~ Duchess," though he does the same,
there is some added resentment felt throughout this piece. As ~~he~~ the speaker discusses

a painting of a woman in his house, the memories of her come back to him. Although most of these memories are ~~happy~~ joyous and happy, we as readers see the love and resentment of the speaker's late Duchess as expressed through his language.

That the speaker loved this woman in the painting is undeniable, as seen in his language. To describe her, he uses words like "wonder," "passion," and "joy." As he looks at the painting of her, he says it looks "as if she were alive." By saying this, the speaker is reminiscing about the time they spent together that makes his memory of her even more real and alive. He also asks the question whether or not his audience will look at her. In doing this, he wants them to share her beauty with him, another sign of his love for her. Finally, before she dies, the speaker talks of her smile, something indicative of love and of his recognition of her beauty.

Although this poem is filled with the speaker's loving memory of the woman in the painting, there are definite hues of resentment and dissatisfaction with the woman as well. The first hint of this is in line 22, when he begins to say that although this woman has heart, she has negative qualities, such as being <u>too</u> easily amused and <u>too</u> easily impressed, that make him unhappy with her. The specific employment of the word "too" infers the quality in her is overwhelming and ultimately negative. Later, he mentions that other men liked her, and this clearly made him jealous and angry as seen by his use of the words "fool" and "mule," both words of negative connotation. He also uses the word "anybody" to illustrate that he ~~felt~~ was bitter when she ~~didn't~~ acted as if his expensive 900 year old gift meant nothing. Finally, the verb "stoop," which is used three times in the last section of the poem, is used, and this word is rather negative in its meaning.

Because it is apparent that the speaker has an exaggerated sense of himself, it is questionable that he is the one who made sure her "smiles stopped together." Although this is debatable, it is definite that through Browning's choice of words and diction, it is clear that the speaker loved the woman in the painting while resenting her at the same time. Often in love, this mixture occurs so this poem is easy to relate to. Browning is a classic contributor to literature and poetry, and his poem "My Last ~~Dutchess~~ Duchess" is no exception.

Final Draft

Stephanie Seidmon

Browning poem essay

Robert Browning is a very famous poet who often wrote about love. However, in this poem, "My Last Duchess," although love is definitely expressed, Browning illustrates other feelings, such as anger and resentment. The speaker in this poem is giving a tour of his house to someone with whom he is arranging his daughter's marriage. In this dramatic monologue, he is showing this man a picture of his last duchess, and the memories of her are flooding back into his mind. As he begins to talk about this woman and her impact on his life, he shows the mixed feelings of love and anger that he had toward her, as expressed through his intricate language.

That the speaker loved this woman in the painting is undeniable. First, he hides the painting behind a curtain so that she solely belongs to him. To describe her, he uses words such as "wonder" (l. 3), "passion" (l. 8), and "joy" (l. 15). This word choice on Browning's part shows specific selection of words that convey the speaker's love. The speaker also says he sees her "as if she were alive" (l. 2). In doing so, he is remembering her life and almost celebrating the time they shared together. In line 5, the speaker asks the other man a rhetorical question that invites him to glance at the painting, inviting him to share the beauty of it, another sign of the speaker's love. In the first section of the poem, the speaker's tone is rather sentimental and nostalgic, which shows his reverence for his last duchess and the love they once shared. Finally, before she dies (l. 43), the speaker talks about her smile, something definitely indicative of love and of his recognition of her beauty.

Although this poem is filled with the speaker's memory of the woman in the painting, there are definite hues of resentment and dissatisfaction bleeding across it. The first hint of this is in lines 22 and 23, when Browning carefully employs the repetition of the word "too" to describe her personality. The speaker says that although this woman had heart, she had negative qualities that bothered him, such as being *"too"* easily amused and *"too"* easily impressed. This sentence also hints at the first we see of the speaker's obsession with keeping his duchess in line. A few lines later, around 28, the speaker starts talking about how other men liked her, which made him very jealous and angry, as seen by the negative connotation of the words "fool" and "mule" (ll. 27, 28). As the speaker continues to talk about these bad memories he has of her, he gets flustered and angry, which is seen not only in his words but also in the syntax. Compared to the flowing and accessible syntax in the first part of the poem, as the speaker gets angry, the sentences become extremely choppy, full of dashes, and almost incoherent. Toward the end of the poem, Browning uses euphemistic short sentences to show the speaker's final actions toward his last duchess (ll. 45–46). Then, with alliteration and passive voice, it is revealed that he, in fact, did kill her: "then all smiles stopped together" (line 46).

Because it is apparent that the speaker has an exaggerated sense of himself, it is not surprising that he kills his last duchess in order to ease his paranoia that she is out of line by "thanking" other men and being "too soon made glad." Although he does kill her, it is made clear by his specific language that he did, at least at one point, love her and care about her, too. This poem is made even more profound by the fact that it speaks universally about love: although it can be heartwarming and exciting, it can also be vindictive and jealousy ridden.

Questions

1. What are the main differences you find between the first and final drafts? Consider the overall organization as well as her analysis.
2. Paragraph 2 begins with the same topic sentence in both the first and the final draft, suggesting a very similar intent in both. But how has Stephanie used evidence differently to make the paragraph in the final draft more persuasive?
3. What in the final draft suggests to you that Stephanie either reread or discussed the poem before she revised the actual essay?
4. In what ways has Stephanie's writing style become more polished in the final draft? Consider word choice, sentence structure, and variety as well as accuracy of grammar and mechanics.
5. Although we have labeled the second example a "final" draft, we know that our writing can always be improved. What would you suggest Stephanie do to make this essay even better?

The Writer's Craft—Close Reading

Figurative Language

As you learned in Chapter 2, figurative language refers to any language that goes beyond the literal, such as metaphors, similes, and personification. These techniques don't exist for the sake of a treasure hunt; they exist because they help writers say what they want to say in a way that is vivid and forceful. They provide meaning beyond the denotation of the words, they elicit emotional responses, they add another level of meaning or nuance, and they bring descriptions to life. Figurative language should not simply be added as decoration or ornamentation to create a more elaborate style. In the best writing, figurative language works subtly to express an idea while opening the work up to interpretation.

Many writers and critics use the term *metaphor* to refer to figurative language in general, as Robert Frost does in his essay "Education by Poetry." He says, "unless you are at home in the metaphor . . . you are not safe anywhere. Because you are not at ease with figurative values: you don't know the metaphor in its strength and its weakness." Frost is pointing out that figurative language deeply influences the way we think and view the world by highlighting relationships among different objects, actions, and ideas.

Sometimes we use figurative language in everyday speech or in our own persuasive writing to appeal to a shared understanding between audience and author. For instance, sports metaphors call on common values; therefore, most of us know what someone means when proclaiming, "We're in a marathon, not a sprint." A writer signals that he believes his life is more than half over when he entitles his memoir *The Fifth Inning*, as did poet E. Ethelbert Miller; and we all know that things are going well when someone declares, "We've got them on the ropes!" These metaphors make sense to us even if we don't know very much about track, baseball, or boxing.

Figurative language is playful, but like a good joke, it takes finesse, and in the hands of a careless writer, it can be pretty dreadful. Web sites abound with metaphors that have gone awry. One site featuring bad lines from mystery novels includes, "Her parting words lingered heavily inside me like last night's Taco Bell" and "The killer was a misplaced comma in the jaunty, happy sentence that made up the party crowd." Another site devoted to metaphors from romance novels offers us, "Claire felt swept away by this dark stranger, a helpless dust bunny in the roaring cacophony of his gas-powered leaf blower." Sometimes people just get carried away and mix their metaphors, as did one media figure, who declared, "I knew enough to realize that the alligators were in the swamp and that it was time to circle the wagons."

But who's to say that these are "bad" or "ineffective," while others are original, elegant, and insightful? Sometime it is a matter of taste, time period, or occasion. The more you read and analyze literature, the more astute you will become about what works and what does not, though different interpretations are one of the pleasures of literature. In her book *Illness as Metaphor*, Susan Sontag points out the military metaphors we use to describe cancer: cancer cells are "invasive," and the body's "defenses" must be summoned to "defeat" the "enemy." While she argues that such language "contributes to the excommunicating and stigmatizing of the ill," others might find the metaphors effective because they suggest a battle leading toward victory—and health.

Remember that identifying and naming examples of figurative language is only a small part of analysis; it is their effect on meaning that is important. In "Hopper's 'Nighthawks' (1942)" by Ira Sadoff, the similes add to the development of the sad and reflective tone of the poem:

> When the buses arrive at sunrise they are empty as hospital beds—
> the hum of the motor is distant as a voice coming from within the body.

These images evoke feelings similar to those of the painting's lonely scene and Sadoff's interpretation of it.

In T. S. Eliot's "The Love Song of J. Alfred Prufrock," the speaker invites the reader:

> Let us go then, you and I,
> When the evening is spread out against the sky
> Like a patient etherized upon a table;

The simile suggests that the night is quiet, nearly dead; however, the reader can't help but associate the narrator with the numbed state of a patient who has been anesthetized and is about to undergo surgery.

James Baldwin uses an extended metaphor in "Sonny's Blues" to give his character depth and nuance:

> I was scared, scared for Sonny. . . . A great block of ice got settled in my belly and kept
> melting there slowly all day long, while I taught my classes algebra. It was a special kind
> of ice. It kept melting, sending trickles of ice water all up and down my veins, but it never
> got less. Sometimes it hardened and seemed to expand until I felt my guts were going
> to come spilling out or that I was going to choke or scream. This would always be at a
> moment when I was remembering some specific thing Sonny had once said or done.

The block of ice is a metaphor for the fear and anxiety the narrator has for his brother, Sonny, but it also hints that, at least at the story's beginning, the narrator is emotionally cold, and has hardened his heart toward his brother. How that block of ice eventually melts and evaporates is very much a theme of the story.

The following exercises will help you begin to analyze figurative language and understand its effects on meaning and clarity. Remember, it is not enough to simply recognize a technique; the effective close reader should understand how that technique creates layers of meaning and provokes an emotional reaction.

• EXERCISE 1 •

In each of the following sentences or excerpts, choose the simile or metaphor that you think is the most meaningful and explain why. Then explain why you think the author used the simile or metaphor he or she did.

1. This was another musician, and a friend of Sonny's, a coal-black, cheerful-looking man, built close to the ground. He immediately began confiding to me, at the top of his lungs, the most terrible things about Sonny, his teeth gleaming like (the morning sun on a snowbank, a lighthouse, a brand-new Cadillac) and his laugh coming up out of him like (a roll of thunder, the beginning of an earthquake, an awkward topic). ("Sonny's Blues")

2. Yet, it was clear that, for them, I was only Sonny's brother. Here, I was in Sonny's world. Or, rather: his (world, kingdom, empire). ("Sonny's Blues")

3. You rise, you dawn
roll-sleeved Aphrodites,
out of a camisole brine,
a linen pit of stitches,
silking the fitted sheets
away from you like (fluttering leaves, waves, butterflies in flight). ("Degas's Laundresses")

4. I remember what a kindly wink the knobs of our big old bureau used to have, and there was one chair that always seemed like (a safe haven, a port in a storm, a strong friend). ("The Yellow Wallpaper")

5. The glamour / Of childish days is upon me, my manhood is cast / Down in the (torrent, flood, storm) of remembrance, I weep like a (babe, child, waif) for the past. ("Piano")

• EXERCISE 2 •

Identify the figurative language in the following selections, and then label each as metaphor, simile, personification, apostrophe, metonymy, and so on. Work in pairs or groups to discuss their effects on the meaning of the passage and the ways in which they evoke a response from the reader.

1. These boys, now, were living as we'd been living then, they were growing up with a rush and their heads bumped abruptly against the low ceiling of their actual possibilities. ("Sonny's Blues")

2. We dug in. We ate everything there was to eat on the table. We ate like there was no tomorrow. We didn't talk. We ate. We scarfed. We grazed that table. We were into serious eating. ("Cathedral")

3. Heard melodies are sweet, but those unheard / Are sweeter; therefore, ye soft pipes, play on. ("Ode on a Grecian Urn")

4. Her voice was like the sound of blended flutes / Blown by black players upon a picnic day. ("The Harlem Dancer")

5. England hath need of thee: she is a fen / Of stagnant waters: altar, sword, and pen, / Fireside, the heroic wealth of hall and bower. ("London, 1802")

6. It is dull enough to confuse the eye in following, pronounced enough constantly to irritate and provoke study, and when you follow the lame uncertain curves for a little distance they suddenly commit suicide—plunge off at outrageous angles, destroy themselves in unheard of contradictions. ("The Yellow Wallpaper")

• EXERCISE 3 •

Following is a passage from "The Yellow Wallpaper" (p. 1066). Identify the figurative language and discuss its effect. Focus on why it adds nuance and complexity to the passage rather than simply ornamentation.

The color is hideous enough, and unreliable enough, and infuriating enough, but the pattern is torturing.

You think you have mastered it, but just as you get well underway in following, it turns a back-somersault and there you are. It slaps you in the face, knocks you down, and tramples upon you. It is like a bad dream.

The outside pattern is a florid arabesque, reminding one of a fungus. If you can imagine a toadstool in joints, an interminable string of toadstools, budding and sprouting in endless convolutions—why, that is something like it.

• EXERCISE 4 •

Rewrite the following passage from "Sonny's Blues" (p. 1041) by eliminating the figurative language and making the description as literal as you can. Discuss the effect of your revision.

> But as I began to watch Creole, I realized that it was Creole who held them all back. He had them on a short rein. Up there, keeping the beat with his whole body, wailing on the fiddle, with his eyes half closed, he was listening to everything, but he was listening to Sonny. He was having a dialogue with Sonny. He wanted Sonny to leave the shoreline and strike out for the deep water. He was Sonny's witness that deep water and drowning were not the same thing — he had been there, and he knew. And he wanted Sonny to know. He was waiting for Sonny to do the things on the keys which would let Creole know that Sonny was in the water.

• EXERCISE 5 •

Don DeLillo's "Videotape" (p. 1090) is notable for its spare tone and minimal figurative language. Rewrite the following passage by adding carefully selected figurative language, and explain the choices you have made. How do your additions change the meaning of the passage? the story? Why do you think DeLillo chose to avoid figurative language?

> He is hit soon after. If you've seen the tape many times you know from the hand wave exactly when he will be hit. It is something, naturally, that you wait for. You say to your wife, if you're at home and she is there, Now here is where he gets it. You say, Janet, hurry up, this is where it happens.
>
> Now here is where he gets it. You see him jolted, sort of wire-shocked — then he seizes up and falls toward the door or maybe leans or slides into the door is the proper way to put it. It is awful and unremarkable at the same time. The car stays in the slow lane. It approaches briefly, then falls back.

• EXERCISE 6 •

Both Claude McKay's "The Harlem Dancer" (p. 1106) and Eavan Boland's "Degas's Laundresses" (p. 1122) describe women doing work that could be considered demeaning. Working in a group or with a partner, reread the poems. Discuss how each uses figurative language to show both sides of the story — the difficulty of the work and the dignity of the people doing it.

• EXERCISE 7 •

William Wordsworth's "London, 1802" (p. 1099) describes the decline of England by comparing it to a "fen / Of stagnant waters." Create a metaphor for your hometown, your state, or even the country that communicates your feelings about its present condition.

Suggestions for Writing

Art and the Artist

1. This chapter begins with a quote from novelist E. M. Forster. Using the pieces in this chapter to support your position, write an essay in which you agree or disagree with Forster's assertion that art provides the most important evidence of human dignity.

2. Write an essay on whether or not you believe artists—painters, musicians, poets, novelists—have a responsibility to society. If so, what is their responsibility?

3. Choose one of the following statements, and write an essay in which you explain why it expresses a belief about art that is similar to yours. Use works you read in this chapter as support.

   "Art is the desire of a man to express himself, to record the reactions of his personality to the world he lives in."—Amy Lowell

   "In everything that can be called art there is a quality of redemption."—Raymond Chandler

   "The artist speaks to our capacity for delight and wonder, to the sense of mystery surrounding our lives, to our sense of pity and beauty, and pain."—Joseph Conrad

   "It doesn't make much difference how the paint is put on as long as something has been said. Technique is just a means of arriving at a statement."—Jackson Pollock

4. H. L. Mencken said:

   In those fields of art, at all events, which concern themselves with ideas as well as with sensations it is almost impossible to find any trace of an artist who was not actively hostile to his environment.

   Use the texts in this chapter to explain whether you agree with Mencken's statement that artists are nonconformists. Extend your argument to include your definition of the role of the artist in society.

5. Research some of the female and minority artists in this chapter. Write an essay describing how their pieces reflect the historical difficulties their social groups have had in becoming artists.

6. Find a pair of poems about one painting (W. H. Auden and Randall Jarrell have both written about Brueghel's "Landscape with the Fall of Icarus," for example). Write an essay in which you compare and contrast the poems' interpretations of the work.

7. In "The Love Song of J. Alfred Prufrock," the shy Prufrock alludes to Andrew Marvell's "To His Coy Mistress." Imagine and write a conversation between Prufrock and the speaker in Marvell's poem. How might the Marvell speaker advise Prufrock? What do you think Prufrock's response would be?

Tradition and Progress

> The world owes all its onward impulses to men ill at ease. The
> happy man inevitably confines himself within ancient limits.
> —Nathaniel Hawthorne

There are few arenas in which the war between tradition and progress is as clearly fought as literature, where both the message and the medium—subject and style—take sides. The conflict between respect for traditional values and the human impulse to grow and change has been the subject of fiction and poetry for centuries. And even a beginning student of literature can tell the difference between a novel written in the nineteenth century and one written in the twentieth or twenty-first century; between a Shakespearean sonnet and a free-verse poem. In his essay "Tradition and the Individual Talent," T. S. Eliot says, "If the only form of tradition, of handing down, consisted in following the ways of the immediate generation before us in a blind or timid adherence to its successes, 'tradition' should positively be discouraged." The works in this chapter ask how we determine which traditions are worth keeping and which must be jettisoned for the sake of progress, and how the old and the new overlap in the meantime.

The works in this chapter honor both the new and the old. In *Daisy Miller*, Henry James explores what happens when a "pretty American flirt" finds herself in the most traditional and judgmental of societies. And Flannery O'Connor's portrayal of the grandmother in "A Good Man Is Hard to Find" leaves us wondering if traditional values would have helped against the force of evil embodied in The Misfit. Charles Baxter's "Fenstad's Mother" and Gish Jen's "Who's Irish?" challenge our expectations about which generation is more traditional and which is more progressive. Poems such as "Dover Beach" remind us that changes wrought by the Industrial Revolution had human costs and consequences, in the same way that "Goodbye, Goldeneye" points a finger at progress in the twentieth century. "A Bedtime Story" and "When All of My Cousins Are Married" consider the conflict between the traditions of the country of one's birth and the more progressive ways of American life. "Mending Wall" reflects on rural traditions, while "Forty Acres"—a poem commissioned on the occasion of the election of Barack Obama, the United States' first African American president—uses traditional rural images and references to celebrate one of the most progressive steps this country has ever taken.

In his 1985 essay "Where Is Our Dover Beach?" critic Roger Rosenblatt asks, "Who in Dover today would describe the world as various and beautiful and new? Yet how is the world less so than it was 134 years ago or a thousand, or the way it will be a thousand years hence, since its variety, beauty and novelty are always in the hands of people?" Everything, he says, "depends on how one wishes to live one's life, which still requires ... constancy ... and a good deal of courage besides."

Daisy Miller

HENRY JAMES

Henry James (1843–1916) was born into a wealthy family of intellectuals in New York City. His father, Henry James Sr., was a theologian who counted Thoreau, Emerson, and Hawthorne among his friends. James's brother William was a famous psychologist and philosopher; his sister, Alice, led a quiet life, but has become a controversial feminist icon through her posthumously published diary. Educated mostly by tutors during the family's travels in Europe, James briefly attended Harvard Law School when he was nineteen, but decided that he would rather study literature. James then moved to Europe—first to Paris, then to London, and finally to Rye in Sussex, England, where he lived for most of the rest of his life. He published his first short story, "A Tragedy of Errors," in 1864 and soon became a regular contributor to the *Nation* and *Atlantic Monthly*. *Daisy Miller*, published in 1870, made James famous. His best-known novels include *The Portrait of a Lady* (1881), *The Turn of the Screw* (1898), *The Wings of the Dove* (1902), and *The Ambassadors* (1903). James also wrote literary and art criticism, travel books, and a two-volume autobiography. Critic Edmund Wilson placed James among the literary giants:

> One would be in a position to appreciate James better if one compared him with the dramatists of the seventeenth century—Racine and Molière, whom he resembles in form as well as in point of view, and even Shakespeare, when allowances are made for the most extreme differences in subject and form. These poets are not, like Dickens and Hardy, writers of melodrama—either humorous or pessimistic, nor secretaries of society like Balzac nor prophets like Tolstoy; they are occupied simply with the presentation of conflicts of moral character, which they do not concern themselves with softening or averting. They do not indict society for these situations: they regard them as universal and inevitable. They do not even blame God for allowing them: they accept them as conditions of life.

In James's work, the most compelling conflicts of moral character are the ones that feature Americans in Europe. James was fascinated by the obvious distinctions in social class among Europeans as well as their self-confidence about culture. Many of his novels and novellas—including *Daisy Miller*—involve American protagonists who are, according to James scholar Alfred Habegger, "noble, intrepid, and full of dangerous illusions about the complex European order."

Part I

At the little town of Vevey, in Switzerland, there is a particularly comfortable hotel. There are, indeed, many hotels; for the entertainment of tourists is the business of the place, which, as many travellers will remember, is seated upon the edge of a remarkably blue lake[1]—a lake that it behooves every tourist to visit. The shore of the lake presents an unbroken array of establishments of this order, of every

---

[1]Lake Geneva.—EDS.

category, from the "grand hotel" of the newest fashion, with a chalk-white front, a hundred balconies, and a dozen flags flying from its roof, to the little Swiss *pension*[2] of an elder day, with its name inscribed in German-looking lettering upon a pink or yellow wall, and an awkward summer-house in the angle of the garden. One of the hotels at Vevey, however, is famous, even classical, being distinguished from many of its upstart neighbours by an air both of luxury and of maturity. In this region, in the month of June, American travellers are extremely numerous; it may be said, indeed, that Vevey assumes at this period some of the characteristics of an American watering-place. There are sights and sounds which evoke a vision, an echo, of Newport and Saratoga.[3] There is a flitting hither and thither of "stylish" young girls, a rustling of muslin flounces, a rattle of dance-music in the morning hours, a sound of high-pitched voices at all times. You receive an impression of these things at the excellent inn of the "Trois Couronnes,"[4] and are transported in fancy to the Ocean House or to Congress Hall.[5] But at the "Trois Couronnes," it must be added, there are other features that are much at variance with these suggestions: neat German waiters, who look like secretaries of legation; Russian princesses sitting in the garden; little Polish boys walking about, held by the hand, with their governors; a view of the sunny crest of the Dent du Midi[6] and the picturesque towers of the Castle of Chillon.

I hardly know whether it was the analogies or the differences that were uppermost in the mind of a young American, who, two or three years ago, sat in the garden of the "Trois Couronnes," looking about him, rather idly, at some of the graceful objects I have mentioned. It was a beautiful summer morning, and in whatever fashion the young American looked at things, they must have seemed to him charming. He had come from Geneva the day before, by the little steamer, to see his aunt, who was staying at the hotel—Geneva having been for a long time his place of residence. But his aunt had a headache—his aunt had almost always a headache—and now she was shut up in her room, smelling camphor, so that he was at liberty to wander about. He was some seven-and-twenty years of age; when his friends spoke of him, they usually said that he was at Geneva, "studying." When his enemies spoke of him they said—but, after all, he had no enemies; he was an extremely amiable fellow, and universally liked. What I should say is, simply, that when certain persons spoke of him they affirmed that the reason of his spending so much time at Geneva was that he was extremely devoted to a lady who lived there—a foreign lady—a person older than himself. Very few Americans—indeed I think none—had ever seen this lady, about whom there were some singular stories. But Winterbourne had an old attachment for the little metropolis of Calvinism;[7] he had been put to school there as

---

[2]A privately owned boardinghouse, akin to a bed-and-breakfast.—EDS.
[3]Newport, Rhode Island, and Saratoga Springs, New York. Popular American resort destinations in the nineteenth and early twentieth centuries.—EDS.
[4]Three crowns.—EDS.
[5]Hotels in Newport and Saratoga Springs.—EDS.
[6]Row of peaks in the Alps that resemble teeth (*dents* in French).—EDS.
[7]After violence against Protestants erupted in France, John Calvin (1509–1564), theologian and founder of Calvinism, fled to Switzerland.—EDS.

a boy, and he had afterwards gone to college there—circumstances which had led to his forming a great many youthful friendships. Many of these he had kept, and they were a source of great satisfaction to him.

After knocking at his aunt's door and learning that she was indisposed, he had taken a walk about the town, and then he had come in to his breakfast. He had now finished his breakfast; but he was drinking a small cup of coffee, which had been served to him on a little table in the garden by one of the waiters who looked like an *attaché*.[8] At last he finished his coffee and lit a cigarette. Presently a small boy came walking along the path—an urchin of nine or ten. The child, who was diminutive for his years, had an aged expression of countenance, a pale complexion, and sharp little features. He was dressed in knickerbockers, with red stockings, which displayed his poor little spindle-shanks; he also wore a brilliant red cravat. He carried in his hand a long alpenstock, the sharp point of which he thrust into everything that he approached—the flower-beds, the garden-benches, the trains of the ladies' dresses. In front of Winterbourne he paused, looking at him with a pair of bright, penetrating little eyes.

"Will you give me a lump of sugar?" he asked, in a sharp, hard little voice—a voice immature, and yet, somehow, not young.

Winterbourne glanced at the small table near him, on which his coffee-service 5 rested, and saw that several morsels of sugar remained. "Yes, you may take one," he answered; "but I don't think sugar is good for little boys."

This little boy stepped forward and carefully selected three of the coveted fragments, two of which he buried in the pocket of his knickerbockers, depositing the other as promptly in another place. He poked his alpenstock, lance-fashion, into Winterbourne's bench, and tried to crack the lump of sugar with his teeth.

"Oh, blazes; it's har-r-d!" he exclaimed, pronouncing the adjective in a peculiar manner.

Winterbourne had immediately perceived that he might have the honour of claiming him as a fellow-countryman. "Take care you don't hurt your teeth," he said, paternally.

"I haven't got any teeth to hurt. They have all come out. I have only got seven teeth. My mother counted them last night, and one came out right afterwards. She said she'd slap me if any more came out. I can't help it. It's this old Europe. It's the climate that makes them come out. In America they didn't come out. It's these hotels."

Winterbourne was much amused. "If you eat three lumps of sugar, your mother 10 will certainly slap you," he said.

"She's got to give me some candy, then," rejoined his young interlocutor. "I can't get any candy here—any American candy. American candy's the best candy."

"And are American little boys the best little boys?" asked Winterbourne.

"I don't know. I'm an American boy," said the child.

"I see you are one of the best!" laughed Winterbourne.

"Are you an American man?" pursued this vivacious infant. And then, on 15 Winterbourne's affirmative reply—"American men are the best," he declared.

---

[8]A lesser diplomat on an ambassador's staff.—Eds.

His companion thanked him for the compliment; and the child, who had now got astride of his alpenstock, stood looking about him, while he attacked a second lump of sugar. Winterbourne wondered if he himself had been like this in his infancy, for he had been brought to Europe about this age.

"Here comes my sister!" cried the child, in a moment. "She's an American girl."

Winterbourne looked along the path and saw a beautiful young lady advancing. "American girls are the best girls," he said, cheerfully, to his young companion.

"My sister ain't the best!" the child declared. "She's always blowing at me."

"I imagine that is your fault, not hers," said Winterbourne. The young lady   20
meanwhile had drawn near. She was dressed in white muslin, with a hundred frills and flounces, and knots of pale-coloured ribbon. She was bare-headed; but she balanced in her hand a large parasol, with a deep border of embroidery; and she was strikingly, admirably pretty. "How pretty they are!" thought Winterbourne, straightening himself in his seat, as if he were prepared to rise.

The young lady paused in front of his bench, near the parapet of the garden, which overlooked the lake. The little boy had now converted his alpenstock into a vaulting-pole, by the aid of which he was springing about in the gravel, and kicking it up not a little.

"Randolph," said the young lady, "what *are* you doing?"

"I'm going up the Alps," replied Randolph. "This is the way!" And he gave another little jump, scattering the pebbles about Winterbourne's ears.

"That's the way they come down," said Winterbourne.

"He's an American man!" cried Randolph, in his little hard voice.   25

The young lady gave no heed to this announcement, but looked straight at her brother. "Well, I guess you had better be quiet," she simply observed.

It seemed to Winterbourne that he had been in a manner presented. He got up and stepped slowly towards the young girl, throwing away his cigarette. "This little boy and I have made acquaintance," he said, with great civility. In Geneva, as he had been perfectly aware, a young man was not at liberty to speak to a young unmarried lady except under certain rarely-occurring conditions; but here at Vevey, what conditions could be better than these?—a pretty American girl coming and standing in front of you in a garden. This pretty American girl, however, on hearing Winterbourne's observation, simply glanced at him; she then turned her head and looked over the parapet, at the lake and the opposite mountains. He wondered whether he had gone too far; but he decided that he must advance farther, rather than retreat. While he was thinking of something else to say, the young lady turned to the little boy again.

"I should like to know where you got that pole," she said.

"I bought it!" responded Randolph.

"You don't mean to say you're going to take it to Italy."   30

"Yes, I am going to take it to Italy!" the child declared.

The young girl glanced over the front of her dress, and smoothed out a knot or two of ribbon. Then she rested her eyes upon the prospect again. "Well, I guess you had better leave it somewhere," she said, after a moment.

"Are you going to Italy?" Winterbourne inquired, in a tone of great respect.

The young lady glanced at him again. "Yes, sir," she replied. And he said nothing more.

"Are you—a—going over the Simplon?"[9] Winterbourne pursued, a little   35 embarrassed.

"I don't know," she said. "I suppose it's some mountain. Randolph, what mountain are we going over?"

"Going where?" the child demanded.

"To Italy," Winterbourne explained.

"I don't know," said Randolph. "I don't want to go to Italy. I want to go to America."

"Oh, Italy is a beautiful place!" rejoined the young man.   40

"Can you get candy there?" Randolph loudly inquired.

"I hope not," said his sister. "I guess you have had enough candy, and mother thinks so too."

"I haven't had any for ever so long—for a hundred weeks!" cried the boy, still jumping about.

The young lady inspected her flounces and smoothed her ribbons again; and Winterbourne presently risked an observation upon the beauty of the view. He was ceasing to be embarrassed, for he had begun to perceive that she was not in the least embarrassed herself. There had not been the slightest alteration in her charming complexion; she was evidently neither offended nor flattered. If she looked another way when he spoke to her, and seemed not particularly to hear him, this was simply her habit, her manner. Yet, as he talked a little more, and pointed out some of the objects of interest in the view, with which she appeared quite unacquainted, she gradually gave him more of the benefit of her glance; and then he saw that this glance was perfectly direct and unshrinking. It was not, however, what would have been called an immodest glance, for the young girl's eyes were singularly honest and fresh. They were wonderfully pretty eyes; and, indeed, Winterbourne had not seen for a long time anything prettier than this fair countrywoman's various features—her complexion, her nose, her ears, her teeth. He had a great relish for feminine beauty; he was addicted to observing and analysing it; and as regards this young lady's face he made several observations. It was not at all insipid, but it was not exactly expressive; and though it was eminently delicate, Winterbourne mentally accused it—very forgivingly—of a want of finish. He thought it very possible that Master Randolph's sister was a coquette; he was sure she had a spirit of her own; but in her bright, sweet, superficial little visage there was no mockery, no irony. Before long it became obvious that she was much disposed towards conversation. She told him that they were going to Rome for the winter—she and her mother and Randolph. She asked him if he was a "real American"; she shouldn't have taken him for one; he seemed more like a German—this was said after a little hesitation, especially when he spoke. Winterbourne, laughing, answered that he had met Germans who spoke

---

[9]A road through the Alps connecting France and Italy.—EDS.

like Americans; but that he had not, so far as he remembered, met an American who spoke like a German. Then he asked her if she should not be more comfortable in sitting upon the bench which he had just quitted. She answered that she liked standing up and walking about; but she presently sat down. She told him she was from New York State—"if you know where that is." Winterbourne learned more about her by catching hold of her small, slippery brother and making him stand a few minutes by his side.

"Tell me your name, my boy," he said.

"Randolph C. Miller," said the boy, sharply. "And I'll tell you her name"; and he levelled his alpenstock at his sister.

"You had better wait till you are asked!" said this young lady, calmly.

"I should like very much to know your name," said Winterbourne.

"Her name is Daisy Miller!" cried the child. "But that isn't her real name; that isn't her name on her cards."

"It's a pity you haven't got one of my cards!" said Miss Miller.

"Her real name is Annie P. Miller," the boy went on.

"Ask him *his* name," said his sister, indicating Winterbourne.

But on this point Randolph seemed perfectly indifferent; he continued to supply information with regard to his own family. "My father's name is Ezra B. Miller," he announced. "My father ain't in Europe; my father's in a better place than Europe."

Winterbourne imagined for a moment that this was the manner in which the child had been taught to intimate that Mr. Miller had been removed to the sphere of celestial rewards. But Randolph immediately added, "My father's in Schenectady. He's got a big business. My father's rich, you bet."

"Well!" ejaculated Miss Miller, lowering her parasol and looking at the embroidered border. Winterbourne presently released the child, who departed, dragging his alpenstock along the path. "He doesn't like Europe," said the young girl. "He wants to go back."

"To Schenectady, you mean?"

"Yes; he wants to go right home. He hasn't got any boys here. There is one boy here, but he always goes round with a teacher; they won't let him play."

"And your brother hasn't any teacher?" Winterbourne inquired.

"Mother thought of getting him one, to travel round with us. There was a lady told her of a very good teacher; an American lady—perhaps you know her—Mrs. Sanders. I think she came from Boston. She told her of this teacher, and we thought of getting him to travel round with us. But Randolph said he didn't want a teacher travelling round with us. He said he wouldn't have lessons when he was in the cars.[10] And we *are* in the cars about half the time. There was an English lady we met in the cars—I think her name was Miss Featherstone; perhaps you know her. She wanted to know why I didn't give Randolph lessons—give him 'instruction,' she called it. I guess he could give me more instruction than I could give him. He's very smart."

"Yes," said Winterbourne; "he seems very smart."

---

[10]Railroad cars.—Eds.

"Mother's going to get a teacher for him as soon as we get to Italy. Can you get good teachers in Italy?"

"Very good, I should think," said Winterbourne.

"Or else she's going to find some school. He ought to learn some more. He's only nine. He's going to college." And in this way Miss Miller continued to converse upon the affairs of her family, and upon other topics. She sat there with her extremely pretty hands, ornamented with very brilliant rings, folded in her lap, and with her pretty eyes now resting upon those of Winterbourne, now wandering over the garden, the people who passed by, and the beautiful view. She talked to Winterbourne as if she had known him a long time. He found it very pleasant. It was many years since he had heard a young girl talk so much. It might have been said of this unknown young lady, who had come and sat down beside him upon a bench, that she chattered. She was very quiet; she sat in a charming tranquil attitude, but her lips and her eyes were constantly moving. She had a soft, slender, agreeable voice, and her tone was decidedly sociable. She gave Winterbourne a history of her movements and intentions, and those of her mother and brother, in Europe and enumerated, in particular, the various hotels at which they had stopped. "That English lady, in the cars," she said—"Miss Featherstone—asked me if we didn't all live in hotels in America. I told her I had never been in so many hotels in my life as since I came to Europe. I have never seen so many—it's nothing but hotels." But Miss Miller did not make this remark with a querulous accent; she appeared to be in the best humour with everything. She declared that the hotels were very good, when once you got used to their ways, and that Europe was perfectly sweet. She was not disappointed—not a bit. Perhaps it was because she had heard so much about it before. She had ever so many intimate friends that had been there ever so many times. And then she had had ever so many dresses and things from Paris. Whenever she put on a Paris dress she felt as if she were in Europe.

"It was a kind of a wishing-cap," said Winterbourne.

"Yes," said Miss Miller, without examining this analogy; "it always made me wish I was here. But I needn't have done that for dresses. I am sure they send all the pretty ones to America; you see the most frightful things here. The only thing I don't like," she proceeded, "is the society. There isn't any society; or, if there is, I don't know where it keeps itself. Do you? I suppose there is some society somewhere, but I haven't seen anything of it. I'm very fond of society, and I have always had a great deal of it. I don't mean only in Schenectady, but in New York. I used to go to New York every winter. In New York I had lots of society. Last winter I had seventeen dinners given me; and three of them were by gentlemen," added Daisy Miller. "I have more friends in New York than in Schenectady—more gentleman friends; and more young lady friends too," she resumed in a moment. She paused again for an instant; she was looking at Winterbourne with all her prettiness in her lively eyes and in her light, slightly monotonous smile. "I have always had," she said, "a great deal of gentlemen's society."

Poor Winterbourne was amused, perplexed, and decidedly charmed. He had never yet heard a young girl express herself in just this fashion, never, at least, save

65

in cases where to say such things seemed a kind of demonstrative evidence of a certain laxity of deportment. And yet was he to accuse Miss Daisy Miller of actual or potential *inconduite*,[11] as they said at Geneva? He felt that he had lived at Geneva so long that he had lost a good deal; he had become dishabituated to the American tone. Never, indeed, since he had grown old enough to appreciate things, had he encountered a young American girl of so pronounced a type as this. Certainly she was very charming, but how deucedly sociable! Was she simply a pretty girl from New York State—were they all like that, the pretty girls who had a good deal of gentlemen's society? Or was she also a designing, an audacious, an unscrupulous young person? Winterbourne had lost his instinct in this matter, and his reason could not help him. Miss Daisy Miller looked extremely innocent. Some people had told him that, after all, American girls were exceedingly innocent; and others had told him that, after all, they were not. He was inclined to think Miss Daisy Miller was a flirt—a pretty American flirt. He had never, as yet, had any relations with young ladies of this category. He had known, here in Europe, two or three women—persons older than Miss Daisy Miller, and provided, for respectability's sake, with husbands—who were great coquettes—dangerous, terrible women, with whom one's relations were liable to take a serious turn. But this young girl was not a coquette in that sense; she was very unsophisticated; she was only a pretty American flirt. Winterbourne was almost grateful for having found the formula that applied to Miss Daisy Miller. He leaned back in his seat; he remarked to himself that she had the most charming nose he had ever seen; he wondered what were the regular conditions and limitations of one's intercourse with a pretty American flirt. It presently became apparent that he was on the way to learn.

"Have you been to that old castle?" asked the young girl, pointing with her parasol to the far-gleaming walls of the Château de Chillon.

"Yes, formerly, more than once," said Winterbourne. "You too, I suppose, have seen it?"

"No; we haven't been there. I want to go there dreadfully. Of course I mean to go there. I wouldn't go away from here without having seen that old castle."

"It's a very pretty excursion," said Winterbourne, "and very easy to make. You can drive, you know, or you can go by the little steamer."

"You can go in the cars," said Miss Miller.

"Yes; you can go in the cars," Winterbourne assented.

"Our courier[12] says they take you right up to the castle," the young girl continued. "We were going last week; but my mother gave out. She suffers dreadfully from dyspepsia. She said she couldn't go. Randolph wouldn't go either; he says he doesn't think much of old castles. But I guess we'll go this week, if we can get Randolph."

"Your brother is not interested in ancient monuments?" Winterbourne inquired, smiling.

70

---

[11]Misbehavior.—Eds.

[12]Tour guide.—Eds.

"He says he don't care much about old castles. He's only nine. He wants to stay   75
at the hotel. Mother's afraid to leave him alone, and the courier won't stay with him;
so we haven't been to many places. But it will be too bad if we don't go up there." And
Miss Miller pointed again at the Château de Chillon.

"I should think it might be arranged," said Winterbourne. "Couldn't you get
some one to stay—for the afternoon—with Randolph?"

Miss Miller looked at him a moment; and then, very placidly—"I wish *you*
would stay with him!" she said.

Winterbourne hesitated a moment. "I should much rather go to Chillon
with you."

"With me?" asked the young girl, with the same placidity.

She didn't rise, blushing, as a young girl at Geneva would have done; and yet   80
Winterbourne, conscious that he had been very bold, thought it possible she was
offended. "With your mother," he answered very respectfully.

But it seemed that both his audacity and his respect were lost upon Miss Daisy
Miller. "I guess my mother won't go after all," she said. "She don't like to ride round
in the afternoon. But did you really mean what you said just now; that you would
like to go up there?"

"Most earnestly," Winterbourne declared.

"Then we may arrange it. If mother will stay with Randolph, I guess Eugenio
will."

"Eugenio?" the young man inquired.

"Eugenio's our courier. He doesn't like to stay with Randolph; he's the most   85
fastidious man I ever saw. But he's a splendid courier. I guess he'll stay at home with
Randolph if mother does, and then we can go to the castle."

Winterbourne reflected for an instant as lucidly as possible—"we" could only
mean Miss Daisy Miller and himself. This programme seemed almost too agreeable for credence; he felt as if he ought to kiss the young lady's hand. Possibly he
would have done so—and quite spoiled the project; but at this moment another
person—presumably Eugenio—appeared. A tall, handsome man, with superb whiskers, wearing a velvet morning-coat and a brilliant watch-chain, approached Miss
Miller, looking sharply at her companion. "Oh, Eugenio!" said Miss Miller, with the
friendliest accent.

Eugenio had looked at Winterbourne from head to foot; he now bowed gravely
to the young lady. "I have the honour to inform mademoiselle that luncheon is upon
the table."

Miss Miller slowly rose. "See here, Eugenio," she said. "I'm going to that old
castle, any way."

"To the Château de Chillon, mademoiselle?" the courier inquired. "Mademoiselle
has made arrangements?" he added, in a tone which struck Winterbourne as very
impertinent.

Eugenio's tone apparently threw, even to Miss Miller's own apprehension, a   90
slightly ironical light upon the young girl's situation. She turned to Winterbourne,
blushing a little—a very little. "You won't back out?" she said.

"I shall not be happy till we go!" he protested.

"And you are staying in this hotel?" she went on. "And you are really an American?"

The courier stood looking at Winterbourne, offensively. The young man, at least, thought his manner of looking an offence to Miss Miller; it conveyed an imputation that she "picked up" acquaintances. "I shall have the honour of presenting to you a person who will tell you all about me," he said smiling, and referring to his aunt.

"Oh, well, we'll go some day," said Miss Miller. And she gave him a smile and turned away. She put up her parasol and walked back to the inn beside Eugenio. Winterbourne stood looking after her; and as she moved away, drawing her muslin furbelows over the gravel, said to himself that she had the *tournure*[13] of a princess.

He had, however, engaged to do more than proved feasible, in promising to present his aunt, Mrs. Costello, to Miss Daisy Miller. As soon as the former lady had got better of her headache he waited upon her in her apartment; and, after the proper inquiries in regard to her health, he asked her if she had observed, in the hotel, an American family—a mamma, a daughter, and a little boy. 95

"And a courier?" said Mrs. Costello. "Oh, yes, I have observed them. Seen them—heard them—and kept out of their way." Mrs. Costello was a widow with a fortune; a person of much distinction, who frequently intimated that, if she were not so dreadfully liable to sick-headaches, she would probably have left a deeper impress upon her time. She had a long pale face, a high nose, and a great deal of very striking white hair, which she wore in large puffs and *rouleaux*[14] over the top of her head. She had two sons married in New York, and another who was now in Europe. This young man was amusing himself at Hombourg,[15] and, though he was on his travels, was rarely perceived to visit any particular city at the moment selected by his mother for her own appearance there. Her nephew, who had come up to Vevey expressly to see her, was therefore more attentive than those who, as she said, were nearer to her. He had imbibed at Geneva the idea that one must always be attentive to one's aunt. Mrs. Costello had not seen him for many years, and she was greatly pleased with him, manifesting her approbation by initiating him into many of the secrets of that social sway which, as she gave him to understand, she exerted in the American capital. She admitted that she was very exclusive; but, if he were acquainted with New York, he would see that one had to be. And her picture of the minutely hierarchical constitution of the society of that city, which she presented to him in many different lights, was, to Winterbourne's imagination, almost oppressively striking.

He immediately perceived, from her tone, that Miss Daisy Miller's place in the social scale was low. "I am afraid you don't approve of them," he said.

"They are very common," Mrs. Costello declared. "They are the sort of Americans that one does one's duty by not—not accepting."

---

[13]Grace or demeanor.—EDS.
[14]Rolls.—EDS.
[15]Bad Homburg vor der Höhe, a resort in Germany known for its spa.—EDS.

"Ah, you don't accept them?" said the young man.

"I can't, my dear Frederick. I would if I could, but I can't." 100

"The young girl is very pretty," said Winterbourne, in a moment.

"Of course she's pretty. But she is very common."

"I see what you mean of course," said Winterbourne, after another pause.

"She has that charming look that they all have," his aunt resumed. "I can't think where they pick it up; and she dresses in perfection — no, you don't know how well she dresses. I can't think where they get their taste."

"But, my dear aunt, she is not, after all, a Comanche savage." 105

"She is a young lady," said Mrs. Costello, "who has an intimacy with her mamma's courier."

"An intimacy with the courier?" the young man demanded.

"Oh, the mother is just as bad! They treat the courier like a familiar friend — like a gentleman. I shouldn't wonder if he dines with them. Very likely they have never seen a man with such good manners, such fine clothes, so like a gentleman. He probably corresponds to the young lady's idea of a Count. He sits with them in the garden, in the evening. I think he smokes."

Winterbourne listened with interest to these disclosures; they helped him to make up his mind about Miss Daisy. Evidently she was rather wild. "Well," he said, "I am not a courier, and yet she was very charming to me."

"You had better have said at first," said Mrs. Costello with dignity, "that you had 110 made her acquaintance."

"We simply met in the garden, and we talked a bit."

"*Tout bonnement!*[16] And pray what did you say?"

"I said I should take the liberty of introducing her to my admirable aunt."

"I am much obliged to you."

"It was to guarantee my respectability," said Winterbourne. 115

"And pray who is to guarantee hers?"

"Ah, you are cruel!" said the young man. "She's a very nice young girl."

"You don't say that as if you believed it," Mrs. Costello observed.

"She is completely uncultivated," Winterbourne went on. "But she is wonderfully pretty, and, in short, she is very nice. To prove that I believe it, I am going to take her to the Château de Chillon."

"You two are going off there together? I should say it proved just the contrary. 120 How long had you known her, may I ask, when this interesting project was formed? You haven't been twenty-four hours in the house."

"I had known her half an hour!" said Winterbourne, smiling.

"Dear me!" cried Mrs. Costello. "What a dreadful girl!"

Her nephew was silent for some moments. "You really think, then," he began, earnestly, and with a desire for trustworthy information — "you really think that —" But he paused again.

"Think what, sir?" said his aunt.

---

[16]All too plain (or clear). — EDS.

"That she is the sort of young lady who expects a man — sooner or later — to   125
carry her off?"

"I haven't the least idea what such young ladies expect a man to do. But I really
think that you had better not meddle with little American girls that are uncultivated,
as you call them. You have lived too long out of the country. You will be sure to make
some great mistake. You are too innocent."

"My dear aunt, I am not so innocent," said Winterbourne, smiling and curling
his moustache.

"You are too guilty, then!"

Winterbourne continued to curl his moustache, meditatively. "You won't let the
poor girl know you then?" he asked at last.

"Is it literally true that she is going to the Château de Chillon with you?"   130
"I think that she fully intends it."

"Then, my dear Frederick," said Mrs. Costello, "I must decline the honour of
her acquaintance. I am an old woman, but I am not too old — thank Heaven — to
be shocked!"

"But don't they all do these things — the young girls in America?" Winterbourne
inquired.

Mrs. Costello stared a moment. "I should like to see my granddaughters do
them!" she declared, grimly.

This seemed to throw some light upon the matter, for Winterbourne remembered to   135
have heard that his pretty cousins in New York were "tremendous flirts." If, therefore, Miss
Daisy Miller exceeded the liberal margin allowed to these young ladies, it was probable
that anything might be expected of her. Winterbourne was impatient to see her again,
and he was vexed with himself that, by instinct, he should not appreciate her justly.

Though he was impatient to see her, he hardly knew what he should say to her
about his aunt's refusal to become acquainted with her; but he discovered, promptly
enough, that with Miss Daisy Miller there was no great need of walking on tiptoe.
He found her that evening in the garden, wandering about in the warm starlight, like
an indolent sylph, and swinging to and fro the largest fan he had ever beheld. It was
ten o'clock. He had dined with his aunt, had been sitting with her since dinner, and
had just taken leave of her till the morrow. Miss Daisy Miller seemed very glad to see
him; she declared it was the longest evening she had ever passed.

"Have you been all alone?" he asked.

"I have been walking round with mother. But mother gets tired walking round,"
she answered.

"Has she gone to bed?"

"No; she doesn't like to go to bed," said the young girl. "She doesn't sleep — not   140
three hours. She says she doesn't know how she lives. She's dreadfully nervous. I guess
she sleeps more than she thinks. She's gone somewhere after Randolph; she wants to
try to get him to go to bed. He doesn't like to go to bed."

"Let us hope she will persuade him," observed Winterbourne.

"She will talk to him all she can; but he doesn't like her to talk to him," said Miss
Daisy, opening her fan. "She's going to try to get Eugenio to talk to him. But he isn't

afraid of Eugenio. Eugenio's a splendid courier, but he can't make much impression on Randolph! I don't believe he'll go to bed before eleven." It appeared that Randolph's vigil was in fact triumphantly prolonged, for Winterbourne strolled about with the young girl for some time without meeting her mother. "I have been looking round for that lady you want to introduce me to," his companion resumed. "She's your aunt." Then, on Winterbourne's admitting the fact, and expressing some curiosity as to how she had learned it, she said she had heard all about Mrs. Costello from the chambermaid. She was very quiet and very *comme il faut;*[17] she wore white puffs; she spoke to no one, and she never dined at the *table d'hôte.*[18] Every two days she had a headache. "I think that's a lovely description, headache and all!" said Miss Daisy, chattering along in her thin, gay voice. "I want to know her ever so much. I know just what *your* aunt would be; I know I should like her. She would be very exclusive. I like a lady to be exclusive; I'm dying to be exclusive myself. Well, we *are* exclusive, mother and I. We don't speak to every one — or they don't speak to us. I suppose it's about the same thing. Any way, I shall be ever so glad to know your aunt."

Winterbourne was embarrassed. "She would be most happy," he said; "but I am afraid those headaches will interfere."

The young girl looked at him through the dusk. "But I suppose she doesn't have a headache every day," she said, sympathetically.

Winterbourne was silent a moment. "She tells me she does," he answered at last — not knowing what to say.   145

Miss Daisy Miller stopped and stood looking at him. Her prettiness was still visible in the darkness; she was opening and closing her enormous fan. "She doesn't want to know me!" she said, suddenly. "Why don't you say so? You needn't be afraid. I'm not afraid!" And she gave a little laugh.

Winterbourne fancied there was a tremor in her voice; he was touched, shocked, mortified by it. "My dear young lady," he protested, "she knows no one. It's her wretched health."

The young girl walked on a few steps, laughing still. "You needn't be afraid," she repeated. "Why should she want to know me?" Then she paused again; she was close to the parapet of the garden, and in front of her was the starlit lake. There was a vague sheen upon its surface, and in the distance were dimly-seen mountain forms. Daisy Miller looked out upon the mysterious prospect, and then she gave another little laugh. "Gracious! she *is* exclusive!" she said. Winterbourne wondered whether she was seriously wounded, and for a moment almost wished that her sense of injury might be such as to make it becoming in him to attempt to reassure and comfort her. He had a pleasant sense that she would be very approachable for consolatory purposes. He felt then, for the instant, quite ready to sacrifice his aunt, conversationally; to admit that she was a proud, rude woman, and to declare that they needn't mind her. But before he had time to commit himself to this perilous mixture of gallantry and impiety, the young lady, resuming her walk, gave an exclamation in quite another

---

[17]Proper or well-mannered. — EDS.
[18]"Host's table," a communal dining table for guests at a hotel. — EDS.

tone. "Well; here's mother! I guess she hasn't got Randolph to go to bed." The figure of a lady appeared, at a distance, very indistinct in the darkness, and advancing with a slow and wavering movement. Suddenly it seemed to pause.

"Are you sure it is your mother? Can you distinguish her in this thick dusk?" Winterbourne asked.

"Well!" cried Miss Daisy Miller, with a laugh, "I guess I know my own mother. 150 And when she has got on my shawl, too! She is always wearing my things."

The lady in question, ceasing to advance, hovered vaguely about the spot at which she had checked her steps.

"I am afraid your mother doesn't see you," said Winterbourne. "Or perhaps," he added — thinking, with Miss Miller, the joke permissible — "perhaps she feels guilty about your shawl."

"Oh, it's a fearful old thing!" the young girl replied, serenely. "I told her she could wear it. She won't come here, because she sees you."

"Ah, then," said Winterbourne, "I had better leave you."

"Oh, no; come on!" urged Miss Daisy Miller. 155

"I'm afraid your mother doesn't approve of my walking with you."

Miss Miller gave him a serious glance. "It isn't for me; it's for you — that is, it's for *her*. Well; I don't know who it's for! But mother doesn't like any of my gentlemen friends. She's right down timid. She always makes a fuss if I introduce a gentleman. But I *do* introduce them — almost always. If I didn't introduce my gentlemen friends to mother," the young girl added, in her little soft, flat monotone, "I shouldn't think I was natural."

"To introduce me," said Winterbourne, "you must know my name." And he proceeded to pronounce it.

"Oh, dear; I can't say all that!" said his companion, with a laugh. But by this time they had come up to Mrs. Miller, who, as they drew near, walked to the parapet of the garden and leaned upon it, looking intently at the lake, and turning her back to them. "Mother!" said the young girl, in a tone of decision. Upon this the elder lady turned round. "Mr. Winterbourne," said Miss Daisy Miller, introducing the young man very frankly and prettily. "Common" she was, as Mrs. Costello had pronounced her; yet it was a wonder to Winterbourne that, with her commonness, she had a singularly delicate grace.

Her mother was a small, spare, light person, with a wandering eye, a very 160 exiguous nose, and a large forehead, decorated with a certain amount of thin, much-frizzled hair. Like her daughter, Mrs. Miller was dressed with extreme elegance; she had enormous diamonds in her ears. So far as Winterbourne could observe, she gave him no greeting — she certainly was not looking at him. Daisy was near her, pulling her shawl straight. "What are you doing, poking round here?" this young lady inquired; but by no means with that harshness of accent which her choice of words may imply.

"I don't know," said her mother, turning towards the lake again.

"I shouldn't think you'd want that shawl!" Daisy exclaimed.

"Well — I do!" her mother answered, with a little laugh.

"Did you get Randolph to go to bed?" asked the young girl.

"No; I couldn't induce him," said Mrs. Miller, very gently. "He wants to talk to 165
the waiter. He likes to talk to that waiter."

"I was telling Mr. Winterbourne," the young girl went on; and to the young man's
ear her tone might have indicated that she had been uttering his name all her life.

"Oh, yes!" said Winterbourne; "I have the pleasure of knowing your son."

Randolph's mamma was silent; she turned her attention to the lake. But at last
she spoke. "Well, I don't see how he lives!"

"Anyhow, it isn't so bad as it was at Dover," said Daisy Miller.

"And what occurred at Dover?" Winterbourne asked. 170

"He wouldn't go to bed at all. I guess he sat up all night—in the public parlour.
He wasn't in bed at twelve o'clock: I know that."

"It was half-past twelve," declared Mrs. Miller, with mild emphasis.

"Does he sleep much during the day?" Winterbourne demanded.

"I guess he doesn't sleep much," Daisy rejoined.

"I wish he would!" said her mother. "It seems as if he couldn't." 175

"I think he's real tiresome," Daisy pursued.

Then, for some moments, there was silence. "Well, Daisy Miller," said the elder
lady, presently, "I shouldn't think you'd want to talk against your own brother!"

"Well, he *is* tiresome, mother," said Daisy, quite without the asperity of a retort.

"He's only nine," urged Mrs. Miller.

"Well, he wouldn't go to that castle," said the young girl. "I'm going there with 180
Mr. Winterbourne."

To this announcement, very placidly made, Daisy's mamma offered no response.
Winterbourne took for granted that she deeply disapproved of the projected excursion; but he said to himself that she was a simple, easily-managed person, and that
a few deferential protestations would take the edge from her displeasure. "Yes," he
began; "your daughter has kindly allowed me the honour of being her guide."

Mrs. Miller's wandering eyes attached themselves, with a sort of appealing air,
to Daisy, who, however, strolled a few steps farther, gently humming to herself. "I
presume you will go in the cars," said her mother.

"Yes; or in the boat," said Winterbourne.

"Well, of course, I don't know," Mrs. Miller rejoined. "I have never been to that
castle."

"It is a pity you shouldn't go," said Winterbourne, beginning to feel reassured as 185
to her opposition. And yet he was quite prepared to find that, as a matter of course,
she meant to accompany her daughter.

"We've been thinking ever so much about going," she pursued; "but it seems as
if we couldn't. Of course Daisy—she wants to go round. But there's a lady here—I
don't know her name—she says she shouldn't think we'd want to go to see castles
here; she should think we'd want to wait till we got to Italy. It seems as if there would
be so many there," continued Mrs. Miller, with an air of increasing confidence. "Of
course we only want to see the principal ones. We visited several in England," she
presently added.

"Ah, yes! in England there are beautiful castles," said Winterbourne. "But Chillon, here, is very well worth seeing."

"Well, if Daisy feels up to it —," said Mrs. Miller, in a tone impregnated with a sense of the magnitude of the enterprise. "It seems as if there was nothing she wouldn't undertake."

"Oh, I think she'll enjoy it!" Winterbourne declared. And he desired more and more to make it a certainty that he was to have the privilege of a *tête-à-tête*[19] with the young lady, who was still strolling along in front of them, softly vocalising. "You are not disposed, madam," he inquired, "to undertake it yourself?"

Daisy's mother looked at him, an instant, askance, and then walked forward in silence. Then—"I guess she had better go alone," she said, simply.   190

Winterbourne observed to himself that this was a very different type of maternity from that of the vigilant matrons who massed themselves in the forefront of social intercourse in the dark old city at the other end of the lake. But his meditations were interrupted by hearing his name very distinctly pronounced by Mrs. Miller's unprotected daughter.

"Mr. Winterbourne!" murmured Daisy.

"Mademoiselle!" said the young man.

"Don't you want to take me out in a boat?"

"At present?" he asked.   195

"Of course!" said Daisy.

"Well, Annie Miller!" exclaimed her mother.

"I beg you, madam, to let her go," said Winterbourne, ardently; for he had never yet enjoyed the sensation of guiding through the summer starlight a skiff freighted with a fresh and beautiful young girl.

"I shouldn't think she'd want to," said her mother. "I should think she'd rather go indoors."

"I'm sure Mr. Winterbourne wants to take me," Daisy declared. "He's so awfully devoted!"   200

"I will row you over to Chillon, in the starlight."

"I don't believe it!" said Daisy.

"Well!" ejaculated the elder lady again.

"You haven't spoken to me for half an hour," her daughter went on.

"I have been having some very pleasant conversation with your mother," said Winterbourne.   205

"Well; I want you to take me out in a boat!" Daisy repeated. They had all stopped, and she had turned round and was looking at Winterbourne. Her face wore a charming smile, her pretty eyes were gleaming, she was swinging her great fan about. No; it's impossible to be prettier than that, thought Winterbourne.

"There are half a dozen boats moored at that landing-place," he said, pointing to certain steps which descended from the garden to the lake. "If you will do me the honour to accept my arm, we will go and select one of them."

---

[19]A private conversation.—EDS.

Daisy stood there smiling; she threw back her head and gave a little, light laugh. "I like a gentleman to be formal!" she declared.

"I assure you it's a formal offer."

"I was bound I would make you say something," Daisy went on.   210

"You see it's not very difficult," said Winterbourne. "But I am afraid you are chaffing me."

"I think not, sir," remarked Mrs. Miller, very gently.

"Do, then, let me give you a row," he said to the young girl.

"It's quite lovely, the way you say that!" cried Daisy.

"It will be still more lovely to do it."   215

"Yes, it would be lovely!" said Daisy. But she made no movement to accompany him; she only stood there laughing.

"I should think you had better find out what time it is," interposed her mother.

"It is eleven o'clock, madam," said a voice, with a foreign accent, out of the neighbouring darkness; and Winterbourne, turning, perceived the florid personage who was in attendance upon the two ladies. He had apparently just approached.

"Oh, Eugenio," said Daisy, "I am going out in a boat!"

Eugenio bowed. "At eleven o'clock, mademoiselle?"   220

"I am going with Mr. Winterbourne. This very minute."

"Do tell her she can't," said Mrs. Miller to the courier.

"I think you had better not go out in a boat, mademoiselle," Eugenio declared.

Winterbourne wished to Heaven this pretty girl were not so familiar with her courier; but he said nothing.

"I suppose you don't think it's proper!" Daisy exclaimed. "Eugenio doesn't think   225
anything's proper."

"I am at your service," said Winterbourne.

"Does mademoiselle propose to go alone?" asked Eugenio of Mrs. Miller.

"Oh, no; with this gentleman!" answered Daisy's mamma.

The courier looked for a moment at Winterbourne—the latter thought he was smiling—and then, solemnly, with a bow, "As mademoiselle pleases!" he said.

"Oh, I hoped you would make a fuss!" said Daisy. "I don't care to go now."   230

"I myself shall make a fuss if you don't go," said Winterbourne.

"That's all I want—a little fuss!" And the young girl began to laugh again.

"Mr. Randolph has gone to bed!" the courier announced, frigidly.

"Oh, Daisy; now we can go!" said Mrs. Miller.

Daisy turned away from Winterbourne, looking at him, smiling, and fanning   235
herself. "Good-night," she said; "I hope you are disappointed, or disgusted, or something!"

He looked at her, taking the hand she offered him. "I am puzzled," he
answered.

"Well; I hope it won't keep you awake!" she said, very smartly; and, under the
escort of the privileged Eugenio, the two ladies passed towards the house.

Winterbourne stood looking after them; he was indeed puzzled. He lingered
beside the lake for a quarter of an hour, turning over the mystery of the young girl's

sudden familiarities and caprices. But the only very definite conclusion he came to was that he should enjoy deucedly "going off" with her somewhere.

Two days afterwards he went off with her to the Castle of Chillon. He waited for her in the large hall of the hotel, where the couriers, the servants, the foreign tourists were lounging about and staring. It was not the place he should have chosen, but she had appointed it. She came tripping downstairs, buttoning her long gloves, squeezing her folded parasol against her pretty figure, dressed in the perfection of a soberly elegant travelling-costume. Winterbourne was a man of imagination and, as our ancestors used to say, sensibility; as he looked at her dress and, on the great staircase, her little rapid, confiding step, he felt as if there were something romantic going forward. He could have believed he was going to elope with her. He passed out with her among all the idle people that were assembled there; they were all looking at her very hard; she had begun to chatter as soon as she joined him. Winterbourne's preference had been that they should be conveyed to Chillon in a carriage; but she expressed a lively wish to go in the little steamer; she declared that she had a passion for steamboats. There was always such a lovely breeze upon the water, and you saw such lots of people. The sail was not long, but Winterbourne's companion found time to say a great many things. To the young man himself their little excursion was so much of an escapade—an adventure—that, even allowing for her habitual sense of freedom, he had some expectation of seeing her regard it in the same way. But it must be confessed that, in this particular, he was disappointed. Daisy Miller was extremely animated, she was in charming spirits; but she was apparently not at all excited; she was not fluttered; she avoided neither his eyes nor those of any one else; she blushed neither when she looked at him nor when she felt that people were looking at her. People continued to look at her a great deal, and Winterbourne took much satisfaction in his pretty companion's distinguished air. He had been a little afraid that she would talk loud, laugh overmuch, and even, perhaps, desire to move about the boat a good deal. But he quite forgot his fears; he sat smiling, with his eyes upon her face, while, without moving from her place, she delivered herself of a great number of original reflections. It was the most charming garrulity he had ever heard. He had assented to the idea that she was "common"; but was she so, after all, or was he simply getting used to her commonness? Her conversation was chiefly of what metaphysicians term the objective cast; but every now and then it took a subjective turn.

"What on *earth* are you so grave about?" she suddenly demanded, fixing her   240
agreeable eyes upon Winterbourne's.

"Am I grave?" he asked. "I had an idea I was grinning from ear to ear."

"You look as if you were taking me to a funeral. If that's a grin, your ears are very near together."

"Should you like me to dance a hornpipe on the deck?"

"Pray do, and I'll carry round your hat. It will pay the expenses of our journey."

"I never was better pleased in my life," murmured Winterbourne.   245

She looked at him a moment, and then burst into a little laugh. "I like to make you say those things! You're a queer mixture!"

In the castle, after they had landed, the subjective element decidedly prevailed. Daisy tripped about the vaulted chambers, rustled her skirts in the corkscrew staircases, flirted back with a pretty little cry and a shudder from the edge of the *oubliettes*,[20] and turned a singularly well-shaped ear to everything that Winterbourne told her about the place. But he saw that she cared very little for feudal antiquities, and that the dusky traditions of Chillon made but a slight impression upon her. They had the good fortune to have been able to walk about without other companionship than that of the custodian; and Winterbourne arranged with this functionary that they should not be hurried—that they should linger and pause wherever they chose. The custodian interpreted the bargain generously—Winterbourne, on his side, had been generous—and ended by leaving them quite to themselves. Miss Miller's observations were not remarkable for logical consistency; for anything she wanted to say she was sure to find a pretext. She found a great many pretexts in the rugged embrasures of Chillon for asking Winterbourne sudden questions about himself—his family, his previous history, his tastes, his habits, his intentions—and for supplying information upon corresponding points in her own personality. Of her own tastes, habits, and intentions Miss Miller was prepared to give the most definite, and indeed the most favourable, account.

"Well; I hope you know enough!" she said to her companion, after he had told her the history of the unhappy Bonivard.[21] "I never saw a man that knew so much!" The history of Bonivard had evidently, as they say, gone into one ear and out of the other. But Daisy went on to say that she wished Winterbourne would travel with them and "go round" with them; they might know something, in that case. "Don't you want to come and teach Randolph?" she asked. Winterbourne said that nothing could possibly please him so much; but that he had unfortunately other occupations. "Other occupations? I don't believe it!" said Miss Daisy. "What do you mean? You are not in business." The young man admitted that he was not in business; but he had engagements which, even within a day or two, would force him to go back to Geneva. "Oh, bother!" she said: "I don't believe it!" and she began to talk about something else. But a few moments later, when he was pointing out to her the pretty design of an antique fireplace, she broke out irrelevantly, "You don't mean to say you are going back to Geneva?"

"It is a melancholy fact that I shall have to return to Geneva to-morrow."

"Well, Mr. Winterbourne," said Daisy; "I think you're horrid!"   250

"Oh, don't say such dreadful things!" said Winterbourne—"just at the last!"

"The last!" cried the young girl; "I call it the first. I have half a mind to leave you here and go straight back to the hotel alone." And for the next ten minutes she did nothing but call him horrid. Poor Winterbourne was fairly bewildered; no young lady had as yet done him the honour to be so agitated by the announcement of his movements. His companion, after this, ceased to pay any attention to the curiosities of Chillon or the beauties of the lake; she opened fire upon the mysterious charmer

---

[20]Dungeons.—EDS.
[21]François Bonivard (1493–1570) was imprisoned for six years at Chillon for opposition to Charles III's efforts to end self-rule in Geneva.—EDS.

in Geneva whom she appeared to have instantly taken it for granted that he was hurrying back to see. How did Miss Daisy Miller know that there was a charmer in Geneva? Winterbourne, who denied the existence of such a person, was quite unable to discover; and he was divided between amazement at the rapidity of her induction and amusement at the frankness of her *persiflage*.[22] She seemed to him, in all this, an extraordinary mixture of innocence and crudity. "Does she never allow you more than three days at a time?" asked Daisy, ironically. "Doesn't she give you a vacation in summer? There's no one so hard worked but they can get leave to go off somewhere at this season. I suppose, if you stay another day, she'll come after you in the boat. Do wait over till Friday, and I will go down to the landing to see her arrive!" Winterbourne began to think he had been wrong to feel disappointed in the temper in which the young lady had embarked. If he had missed the personal accent, the personal accent was now making its appearance. It sounded very distinctly, at last, in her telling him she would stop "teasing" him if he would promise her solemnly to come down to Rome in the winter.

"That's not a difficult promise to make," said Winterbourne. "My aunt has taken an apartment in Rome for the winter, and has already asked me to come and see her."

"I don't want you to come for your aunt," said Daisy; "I want you to come for me." And this was the only allusion that the young man was ever to hear her make to his invidious kinswoman. He declared that, at any rate, he would certainly come. After this Daisy stopped teasing. Winterbourne took a carriage, and they drove back to Vevey in the dusk; the young girl was very quiet.

In the evening Winterbourne mentioned to Mrs. Costello that he had spent the afternoon at Chillon, with Miss Daisy Miller. 255

"The Americans—of the courier?" asked this lady.

"Ah, happily," said Winterbourne, "the courier stayed at home."

"She went with you all alone?"

"All alone."

Mrs. Costello sniffed a little at her smelling-bottle. "And that," she exclaimed, "is 260
the young person whom you wanted me to know!"

Part II

Winterbourne, who had returned to Geneva the day after his excursion to Chillon, went to Rome towards the end of January. His aunt had been established there for several weeks, and he had received a couple of letters from her. "Those people you were so devoted to last summer at Vevey have turned up here, courier and all," she wrote. "They seem to have made several acquaintances, but the courier continues to be the most *intime*. The young lady, however, is also very intimate with some third-rate Italians, with whom she rackets about in a way that makes much talk. Bring me that pretty novel of Cherbuliez's—'Paule Méré'[23]—and don't come later than the 23rd."

---

[22]Banter, small talk.—EDS.
[23]French novel by Charles Victor Cherbuliez (1829–1899), in which the title character is a young woman subject to malicious gossip for violating social conventions.—EDS.

In the natural course of events, Winterbourne, on arriving in Rome, would presently have ascertained Mrs. Miller's address at the American banker's, and have gone to pay his compliments to Miss Daisy. "After what happened at Vevey, I think I may certainly call upon them," he said to Mrs. Costello.

"If, after what happens—at Vevey and everywhere—you desire to keep up the acquaintance, you are very welcome. Of course a man may know every one. Men are welcome to the privilege!"

"Pray what is it that happens—here, for instance?" Winterbourne demanded.

"The girl goes about alone with her foreigners. As to what happens further, you must apply elsewhere for information. She has picked up half-a-dozen of the regular Roman fortune-hunters, and she takes them about to people's houses. When she comes to a party she brings with her a gentleman with a good deal of manner and a wonderful moustache."   265

"And where is the mother?"

"I haven't the least idea. They are very dreadful people."

Winterbourne meditated a moment. "They are very ignorant—very innocent only. Depend upon it they are not bad."

"They are hopelessly vulgar," said Mrs. Costello. "Whether or no being hopelessly vulgar is being 'bad' is a question for the metaphysicians. They are bad enough to dislike, at any rate; and for this short life that is quite enough."

The news that Daisy Miller was surrounded by half-a-dozen wonderful moustaches checked Winterbourne's impulse to go straightway to see her. He had perhaps not definitely flattered himself that he had made an ineffaceable impression upon her heart, but he was annoyed at hearing of a state of affairs so little in harmony with an image that had lately flitted in and out of his own meditations; the image of a very pretty girl looking out of an old Roman window and asking herself urgently when Mr. Winterbourne would arrive. If, however, he determined to wait a little before reminding Miss Miller of his claims to her consideration, he went very soon to call upon two or three other friends. One of these friends was an American lady who had spent several winters at Geneva, where she had placed her children at school. She was a very accomplished woman, and she lived in the Via Gregoriana. Winterbourne found her in a little crimson drawing-room, on a third floor; the room was filled with southern sunshine. He had not been there ten minutes when the servant came in, announcing "Madame Mila!" This announcement was presently followed by the entrance of little Randolph Miller, who stopped in the middle of the room and stood staring at Winterbourne. An instant later his pretty sister crossed the threshold; and then, after a considerable interval, Mrs. Miller slowly advanced.   270

"I know you!" said Randolph.

"I'm sure you know a great many things," exclaimed Winterbourne, taking him by the hand. "How is your education coming on?"

Daisy was exchanging greetings very prettily with her hostess; but when she heard Winterbourne's voice she quickly turned her head. "Well, I declare!" she said.

"I told you I should come, you know," Winterbourne rejoined, smiling.

"Well—I didn't believe it," said Miss Daisy.   275

"I am much obliged to you," laughed the young man.

"You might have come to see me!" said Daisy.

"I arrived only yesterday."

"I don't believe that!" the young girl declared.

Winterbourne turned with a protesting smile to her mother; but this lady evaded   280
his glance, and, seating herself, fixed her eyes upon her son. "We've got a bigger place
than this," said Randolph. "It's all gold on the walls."

Mrs. Miller turned uneasily in her chair. "I told you if I were to bring you, you
would say something!" she murmured.

"I told *you*!" Randolph exclaimed. "I tell *you*, sir!" he added jocosely, giving
Winterbourne a thump on the knee. "It *is* bigger, too!"

Daisy had entered upon a lively conversation with her hostess; Winterbourne
judged it becoming to address a few words to her mother. "I hope you have been well
since we parted at Vevey," he said.

Mrs. Miller now certainly looked at him—at his chin. "Not very well, sir," she
answered.

"She's got the dyspepsia," said Randolph. "I've got it too. Father's got it. I've got   285
it most!"

This announcement, instead of embarrassing Mrs. Miller, seemed to relieve
her. "I suffer from the liver," she said. "I think it's this climate; it's less bracing than
Schenectady, especially in the winter season. I don't know whether you know we
reside at Schenectady. I was saying to Daisy that I certainly hadn't found any one like
Dr. Davis, and I didn't believe I should. Oh, at Schenectady, he stands first; they think
everything of him. He has so much to do, and yet there was nothing he wouldn't do
for me. He said he never saw anything like my dyspepsia, but he was bound to cure
it. I'm sure there was nothing he wouldn't try. He was just going to try something
new when we came off. Mr. Miller wanted Daisy to see Europe for herself. But I wrote
to Mr. Miller that it seems as if I couldn't get on without Dr. Davis. At Schenectady
he stands at the very top; and there's a great deal of sickness there, too. It affects my
sleep."

Winterbourne had a good deal of pathological gossip with Dr. Davis's patient,
during which Daisy chattered unremittingly to her own companion. The young
man asked Mrs. Miller how she was pleased with Rome. "Well, I must say I am disappointed," she answered. "We had heard so much about it; I suppose we had heard
too much. But we couldn't help that. We had been led to expect something different."

"Ah, wait a little, and you will become very fond of it," said Winterbourne.

"I hate it worse and worse every day!" cried Randolph.

"You are like the infant Hannibal,"[24] said Winterbourne.   290

"No, I ain't!" Randolph declared, at a venture.

"You are not much like an infant," said his mother. "But we have seen places," she
resumed, "that I should put a long way before Rome." And in reply to Winterbourne's

---

[24]Carthaginian general who led forces against Rome in the Punic Wars.—EDS.

interrogation, "There's Zurich," she concluded; "I think Zurich is lovely; and we hadn't heard half so much about it."

"The best place we've seen is the City of Richmond!" said Randolph.

"He means the ship," his mother explained. "We crossed in that ship. Randolph had a good time on the *City of Richmond*."

"It's the best place I've seen," the child repeated. "Only it was turned the wrong way." 295

"Well, we've got to turn the right way some time," said Mrs. Miller, with a little laugh. Winterbourne expressed the hope that her daughter at least found some gratification in Rome, and she declared that Daisy was quite carried away. "It's on account of the society—the society's splendid. She goes round everywhere; she has made a great number of acquaintances. Of course she goes round more than I do. I must say they have been very sociable; they have taken her right in. And then she knows a great many gentlemen. Oh, she thinks there's nothing like Rome. Of course, it's a great deal pleasanter for a young lady if she knows plenty of gentlemen."

By this time Daisy had turned her attention again to Winterbourne. "I've been telling Mrs. Walker how mean you were!" the young girl announced.

"And what is the evidence you have offered?" asked Winterbourne, rather annoyed at Miss Miller's want of appreciation of the zeal of an admirer who on his way down to Rome had stopped neither at Bologna nor at Florence, simply because of a certain sentimental impatience. He remembered that a cynical compatriot had once told him that American women—the pretty ones, and this gave a largeness to the axiom—were at once the most exacting in the world and the least endowed with a sense of indebtedness.

"Why, you were awfully mean at Vevey," said Daisy. "You wouldn't do anything. You wouldn't stay there when I asked you."

"My dearest young lady," cried Winterbourne, with eloquence, "have I come all the way to Rome to encounter your reproaches?" 300

"Just hear him say that!" said Daisy to her hostess, giving a twist to a bow on this lady's dress. "Did you ever hear anything so quaint?"

"So quaint, my dear?" murmured Mrs. Walker, in the tone of a partisan of Winterbourne.

"Well, I don't know," said Daisy, fingering Mrs. Walker's ribbons. "Mrs. Walker, I want to tell you something."

"Motherr," interposed Randolph, with his rough ends to his words, "I tell you you've got to go. Eugenio'll raise something!"

"I'm not afraid of Eugenio," said Daisy, with a toss of her head. "Look here, Mrs. 305 Walker," she went on, "you know I'm coming to your party."

"I am delighted to hear it."

"I've got a lovely dress."

"I am very sure of that."

"But I want to ask a favour—permission to bring a friend."

"I shall be happy to see any of your friends," said Mrs. Walker, turning with a 310 smile to Mrs. Miller.

"Oh, they are not my friends," answered Daisy's mamma, smiling shyly, in her own fashion. "I never spoke to them!"

"It's an intimate friend of mine—Mr. Giovanelli," said Daisy, without a tremor in her clear little voice or a shadow on her brilliant little face.

Mrs. Walker was silent a moment; she gave a rapid glance at Winterbourne. "I shall be glad to see Mr. Giovanelli," she then said.

"He's an Italian," Daisy pursued, with the prettiest serenity. "He's a great friend of mine—he's the handsomest man in the world—except Mr. Winterbourne! He knows plenty of Italians, but he wants to know some Americans. He thinks ever so much of Americans. He's tremendously clever. He's perfectly lovely!"

It was settled that this brilliant personage should be brought to Mrs. Walker's   315
party, and then Mrs. Miller prepared to take her leave. "I guess we'll go back to the hotel," she said.

"You may go back to the hotel, mother, but I'm going to take a walk," said Daisy.

"She's going to walk with Mr. Giovanelli," Randolph proclaimed.

"I am going to the Pincio,"[25] said Daisy, smiling.

"Alone, my dear—at this hour?" Mrs. Walker asked. The afternoon was drawing to a close—it was the hour for the throng of carriages and of contemplative pedestrians. "I don't think it's safe, my dear," said Mrs. Walker.

"Neither do I," subjoined Mrs. Miller. "You'll get the fever[26] as sure as you live.   320
Remember what Dr. Davis told you!"

"Give her some medicine before she goes," said Randolph.

The company had risen to its feet; Daisy, still showing her pretty teeth, bent over and kissed her hostess. "Mrs. Walker, you are too perfect," she said. "I'm not going alone; I am going to meet a friend."

"Your friend won't keep you from getting the fever," Mrs. Miller observed.

"Is it Mr. Giovanelli?" asked the hostess.

Winterbourne was watching the young girl; at this question his attention quick-   325
ened. She stood there smiling and smoothing her bonnet ribbons; she glanced at Winterbourne. Then, while she glanced and smiled, she answered without a shade of hesitation, "Mr. Giovanelli—the beautiful Giovanelli."

"My dear young friend," said Mrs. Walker, taking her hand, pleadingly, "don't walk off to the Pincio at this hour to meet a beautiful Italian."

"Well, he speaks English," said Mrs. Miller.

"Gracious me!" Daisy exclaimed, "I don't want to do anything improper. There's an easy way to settle it." She continued to glance at Winterbourne. "The Pincio is only a hundred yards distant, and if Mr. Winterbourne were as polite as he pretends he would offer to walk with me!"

---

[25]The Pincian Hill, a raised part of the Borghese Gardens with spectacular views of Rome.—EDS.
[26]Malaria, or "Roman fever." Understood at the time to be contracted by being outdoors at night.—EDS.

Winterbourne's politeness hastened to affirm itself, and the young girl gave him gracious leave to accompany her. They passed downstairs before her mother, and at the door Winterbourne perceived Mrs. Miller's carriage drawn up, with the ornamental courier whose acquaintance he had made at Vevey seated within. "Good-by, Eugenio!" cried Daisy; "I'm going to take a walk." The distance from the Via Gregoriana to the beautiful garden at the other end of the Pincian Hill is, in fact, rapidly traversed. As the day was splendid, however, and the concourse of vehicles, walkers, and loungers numerous, the young Americans found their progress much delayed. This fact was highly agreeable to Winterbourne, in spite of his consciousness of his singular situation. The slow-moving, idly-gazing Roman crowd bestowed much attention upon the extremely pretty young foreign lady who was passing through it upon his arm; and he wondered what on earth had been in Daisy's mind when she proposed to expose herself, unattended, to its appreciation. His own mission, to her sense, apparently, was to consign her to the hands of Mr. Giovanelli; but Winterbourne, at once annoyed and gratified, resolved that he would do no such thing.

"Why haven't you been to see me?" asked Daisy. "You can't get out of that."   330

"I have had the honour of telling you that I have only just stepped out of the train."

"You must have stayed in the train a good while after it stopped!" cried the young girl, with her little laugh. "I suppose you were asleep. You have had time to go to see Mrs. Walker."

"I knew Mrs. Walker—" Winterbourne began to explain.

"I knew where you knew her. You knew her at Geneva. She told me so. Well, you knew me at Vevey. That's just as good. So you ought to have come." She asked him no other question than this; she began to prattle about her own affairs. "We've got splendid rooms at the hotel; Eugenio says they're the best rooms in Rome. We are going to stay all winter—if we don't die of the fever; and I guess we'll stay then. It's a great deal nicer than I thought; I thought it would be fearfully quiet; I was sure it would be awfully poky. I was sure we should be going round all the time with one of those dreadful old men that explain about the pictures and things. But we only had about a week of that, and now I'm enjoying myself. I know ever so many people, and they are all so charming. The society's extremely select. There are all kinds—English, and Germans, and Italians. I think I like the English best. I like their style of conversation. But there are some lovely Americans. I never saw anything so hospitable. There's something or other every day. There's not much dancing; but I must say I never thought dancing was everything. I was always fond of conversation. I guess I shall have plenty at Mrs. Walker's—her rooms are so small." When they had passed the gate of the Pincian Gardens, Miss Miller began to wonder where Mr. Giovanelli might be. "We had better go straight to that place in front," she said, "where you look at the view."

"I certainly shall not help you to find him," Winterbourne declared.   335

"Then I shall find him without you," said Miss Daisy.

"You certainly won't leave me!" cried Winterbourne.

She burst into her little laugh. "Are you afraid you'll get lost—or run over? But there's Giovanelli, leaning against that tree. He's staring at the women in the carriages: did you ever see anything so cool?"

Winterbourne perceived at some distance a little man standing with folded arms, nursing his cane. He had a handsome face, an artfully poised hat, a glass in one eye and a nosegay in his button-hole. Winterbourne looked at him a moment and then said, "Do you mean to speak to that man?"

"Do I mean to speak to him? Why, you don't suppose I mean to communicate 340 by signs?"

"Pray understand, then," said Winterbourne, "that I intend to remain with you."

Daisy stopped and looked at him, without a sign of troubled consciousness in her face; with nothing but the presence of her charming eyes and her happy dimples. "Well, she's a cool one!" thought the young man.

"I don't like the way you say that," said Daisy. "It's too imperious."

"I beg your pardon if I say it wrong. The main point is to give you an idea of my meaning."

The young girl looked at him more gravely, but with eyes that were prettier than 345 ever. "I have never allowed a gentleman to dictate to me, or to interfere with anything I do."

"I think you have made a mistake," said Winterbourne. "You should sometimes listen to a gentleman—the right one."

Daisy began to laugh again. "I do nothing but listen to gentlemen!" she exclaimed. "Tell me if Mr. Giovanelli is the right one?"

The gentleman with the nosegay in his bosom had now perceived our two friends, and was approaching the young girl with obsequious rapidity. He bowed to Winterbourne as well as to the latter's companion; he had a brilliant smile, an intelligent eye; Winterbourne thought him not a bad-looking fellow. But he nevertheless said to Daisy—"No, he's not the right one."

Daisy evidently had a natural talent for performing introductions; she also mentioned the name of each of her companions to the other. She strolled along with one of them on each side of her; Mr. Giovanelli, who spoke English very cleverly—Winterbourne afterwards learned that he had practised the idiom upon a great many American heiresses—addressed her a great deal of very polite nonsense; he was extremely urbane, and the young American, who said nothing, reflected upon that profundity of Italian cleverness which enables people to appear more gracious in proportion as they are more acutely disappointed. Giovanelli, of course, had counted upon something more intimate; he had not bargained for a party of three. But he kept his temper in a manner which suggested far-stretching intentions. Winterbourne flattered himself that he had taken his measure. "He is not a gentleman," said the young American; "he is only a clever imitation of one. He is a music-master, or a penny-a-liner, or a third-rate artist. Damn his good looks!" Mr. Giovanelli had certainly a very pretty face; but Winterbourne felt a superior indignation at his own lovely fellow-countrywoman's not knowing the difference between a spurious gentleman and a real one. Giovanelli chattered and jested and made himself wonderfully agreeable. It was true that if he was an imitation the imitation was brilliant. "Nevertheless," Winterbourne said to himself, "a nice girl ought to know!" And then he came back to the question whether this was in fact a nice girl. Would a nice girl—even allowing for her being a little American flirt—make a rendezvous with a presumably low-lived foreigner? The rendezvous in this case, indeed, had been in broad day-light, and in the most crowded corner of Rome; but was it not impossible to regard the choice of these circumstances as a proof of extreme cynicism? Singular though it may seem, Winterbourne was vexed that the young girl, in joining her *amoroso*, should not appear more impatient of his own company, and he was vexed because of his inclination. It was impossible to regard her as a perfectly well-conducted young lady; she was wanting in a certain indispensable delicacy. It would therefore simplify matters greatly to be able to treat her as the object of one of those sentiments which are called by romancers "lawless passions." That she should seem to wish to get rid of him would help him to think more lightly of her, and to be able to think more lightly of her would make her much less perplexing. But Daisy, on this occasion, continued to present herself as an inscrutable combination of audacity and innocence.

She had been walking some quarter of an hour, attended by her two cavaliers,   350 and responding in a tone of very childish gaiety, as it seemed to Winterbourne, to the pretty speeches of Mr. Giovanelli, when a carriage that had detached itself from the revolving train drew up beside the path. At the same moment Winterbourne perceived that his friend Mrs. Walker—the lady whose house he had lately left—was seated in the vehicle and was beckoning to him. Leaving Miss Miller's side, he hastened to obey her summons. Mrs. Walker was flushed; she wore an excited air. "It is really too dreadful," she said. "That girl must not do this sort of thing. She must not walk here with you two men. Fifty people have noticed her."

Winterbourne raised his eyebrows. "I think it's a pity to make too much fuss about it."

"It's a pity to let the girl ruin herself!"

"She is very innocent," said Winterbourne.

"She's very crazy!" cried Mrs. Walker. "Did you ever see anything so imbecile as her mother? After you had all left me, just now, I could not sit still for thinking of it. It seemed too pitiful, not even to attempt to save her. I ordered the carriage and put on my bonnet, and came here as quickly as possible. Thank heaven, I have found you!"

"What do you propose to do with us?" asked Winterbourne, smiling.   355

"To ask her to get in, to drive her about here for half-an-hour, so that the world may see she is not running absolutely wild, and then to take her safely home."

"I don't think it's a very happy thought," said Winterbourne; "but you can try."

Mrs. Walker tried. The young man went in pursuit of Miss Miller, who had simply nodded and smiled at his interlocutor in the carriage, and had gone her way with her companion. Daisy, on learning that Mrs. Walker wished to speak to her, retraced her steps with a perfect good grace and with Mr. Giovanelli at her side. She declared that she was delighted to have a chance to present this gentleman to Mrs. Walker. She immediately achieved the introduction, and declared that she had never in her life seen anything so lovely as Mrs. Walker's carriage-rug.

"I am glad you admire it," said this lady, smiling sweetly. "Will you get in and let me put it over you?"

"Oh, no, thank you," said Daisy. "I shall admire it much more as I see you driving round with it." 360

"Do get in and drive with me," said Mrs. Walker.

"That would be charming, but it's so enchanting just as I am!" and Daisy gave a brilliant glance at the gentlemen on either side of her.

"It may be enchanting, dear child, but it is not the custom here," urged Mrs. Walker, leaning forward in her victoria[27] with her hands devoutly clasped.

"Well, it ought to be, then!" said Daisy. "If I didn't walk I should expire."

"You should walk with your mother, dear," cried the lady from Geneva, losing patience. 365

"With my mother dear!" exclaimed the young girl. Winterbourne saw that she scented interference. "My mother never walked ten steps in her life. And then, you know," she added with a laugh, "I am more than five years old."

"You are old enough to be more reasonable. You are old enough, dear Miss Miller, to be talked about."

Daisy looked at Mrs. Walker, smiling intensely. "Talked about? What do you mean?"

"Come into my carriage and I will tell you."

Daisy turned her quickened glance again from one of the gentlemen beside her to the other. Mr. Giovanelli was bowing to and fro, rubbing down his gloves and laughing very agreeably; Winterbourne thought it a most unpleasant scene. "I don't think I want to know what you mean," said Daisy presently. "I don't think I should like it." 370

Winterbourne wished that Mrs. Walker would tuck in her carriage-rug and drive away; but this lady did not enjoy being defied, as she afterwards told him. "Should you prefer being thought a very reckless girl?" she demanded.

"Gracious!" exclaimed Daisy. She looked again at Mr. Giovanelli, then she turned to Winterbourne. There was a little pink flush in her cheek; she was tremendously pretty. "Does Mr. Winterbourne think," she asked slowly, smiling, throwing back her head and glancing at him from head to foot, "that — to save my reputation — I ought to get into the carriage?"

Winterbourne coloured; for an instant he hesitated greatly. It seemed so strange to hear her speak that way of her "reputation." But he himself, in fact, must speak in accordance with gallantry. The finest gallantry, here, was simply to tell her the truth; and the truth, for Winterbourne, as the few indications I have been able to give have made him known to the reader, was that Daisy Miller should take Mrs. Walker's advice. He looked at her exquisite prettiness; and then he said very gently, "I think you should get into the carriage."

Daisy gave a violent laugh. "I never heard anything so stiff! If this is improper, Mrs. Walker," she pursued, "then I am all improper, and you must give me up. Good-by;

---

[27]Four-wheeled, two-passenger horse-drawn carriage. — EDS.

I hope you'll have a lovely ride!" and, with Mr. Giovanelli, who made a triumphantly obsequious salute, she turned away.

Mrs. Walker sat looking after her, and there were tears in Mrs. Walker's eyes. "Get in here, sir," she said to Winterbourne, indicating the place beside her. The young man answered that he felt bound to accompany Miss Miller; whereupon Mrs. Walker declared that if he refused her this favour she would never speak to him again. She was evidently in earnest. Winterbourne overtook Daisy and her companion and, offering the young girl his hand, told her that Mrs. Walker had made an imperious claim upon his society. He expected that in answer she would say something rather free, something to commit herself still further to that "recklessness" from which Mrs. Walker had so charitably endeavoured to dissuade her. But she only shook his hand, hardly looking at him; while Mr. Giovanelli bade him farewell with a too-emphatic flourish of the hat.

Winterbourne was not in the best possible humour as he took his seat in Mrs. Walker's victoria. "That was not clever of you," he said candidly, while the vehicle mingled again with the throng of carriages.

"In such a case," his companion answered, "I don't wish to be clever, I wish to be *earnest*!"

"Well, your earnestness has only offended her and put her off."

"It has happened very well," said Mrs. Walker. "If she is so perfectly determined to compromise herself, the sooner one knows it the better; one can act accordingly."

"I suspect she meant no harm," Winterbourne rejoined.

"So I thought a month ago. But she has been going too far."

"What has she been doing?"

"Everything that is not done here. Flirting with any man she could pick up; sitting in corners with mysterious Italians; dancing all the evening with the same partners; receiving visits at eleven o'clock at night. Her mother goes away when visitors come."

"But her brother," said Winterbourne, laughing, "sits up till midnight."

"He must be edified by what he sees. I'm told that at their hotel every one is talking about her, and that a smile goes round among all the servants when a gentleman comes and asks for Miss Miller."

"The servants be hanged!" said Winterbourne angrily. "The poor girl's only fault," he presently added, "is that she is very uncultivated."

"She is naturally indelicate," Mrs. Walker declared. "Take that example this morning. How long had you known her at Vevey?"

"A couple of days."

"Fancy, then, her making it a personal matter that you should have left the place!"

Winterbourne was silent for some moments, then he said, "I suspect, Mrs. Walker, that you and I have lived too long at Geneva!" And he added a request that she should inform him with what particular design she had made him enter her carriage.

"I wished to beg you to cease your relations with Miss Miller—not to flirt with her—to give her no further opportunity to expose herself—to let her alone, in short."

375

380

385

390

"I'm afraid I can't do that," said Winterbourne. "I like her extremely."

"All the more reason that you shouldn't help her to make a scandal."

"There shall be nothing scandalous in my attentions to her."

"There certainly will be in the way she takes them. But I have said what I had on   395
my conscience," Mrs. Walker pursued. "If you wish to rejoin the young lady I will put
you down. Here, by-the-way, you have a chance."

The carriage was traversing that part of the Pincian Garden that overhangs the wall
of Rome and overlooks the beautiful Villa Borghese. It is bordered by a large parapet, near
which there are several seats. One of the seats, at a distance, was occupied by a gentleman
and a lady, towards whom Mrs. Walker gave a toss of her head. At the same moment these
persons rose and walked towards the parapet. Winterbourne had asked the coachman to
stop; he now descended from the carriage. His companion looked at him a moment in
silence; then, while he raised his hat, she drove majestically away. Winterbourne stood
there; he had turned his eyes towards Daisy and her cavalier. They evidently saw no
one; they were too deeply occupied with each other. When they reached the low garden
wall, they stood a moment looking off at the great flat-topped pine-clusters of the Villa
Borghese; then Giovanelli seated himself, familiarly, upon the broad ledge of the wall. The
western sun in the opposite sky sent out a brilliant shaft through a couple of cloud-bars,
whereupon Daisy's companion took her parasol out of her hands and opened it. She
came a little nearer and he held the parasol over her; then, still holding it, he let it rest
upon her shoulder, so that both of their heads were hidden from Winterbourne. This
young man lingered a moment, then he began to walk. But he walked — not towards the
couple with the parasol; towards the residence of his aunt, Mrs. Costello.

He flattered himself on the following day that there was no smiling among
the servants when he, at least, asked for Mrs. Miller at her hotel. This lady and her
daughter, however, were not at home; and on the next day after, repeating his visit,
Winterbourne again had the misfortune not to find them. Mrs. Walker's party took
place on the evening of the third day, and in spite of the frigidity of his last interview with the hostess, Winterbourne was among the guests. Mrs. Walker was one
of those American ladies who, while residing abroad, make a point, in their own
phrase, of studying European society; and she had on this occasion collected several
specimens of her diversely-born fellow-mortals to serve, as it were, as text-books.
When Winterbourne arrived Daisy Miller was not there, but in a few moments
he saw her mother come in alone, very shyly and ruefully. Mrs. Miller's hair above
her exposed-looking temples was more frizzled than ever. As she approached Mrs.
Walker, Winterbourne also drew near.

"You see I've come all alone," said poor Mrs. Miller. "I'm so frightened; I don't
know what to do; it's the first time I've ever been to a party alone — especially in this
country. I wanted to bring Randolph or Eugenio, or someone, but Daisy just pushed
me off by myself. I ain't used to going round alone."

"And does not your daughter intend to favour us with her society?" demanded
Mrs. Walker, impressively.

"Well, Daisy's all dressed," said Mrs. Miller, with that accent of the dispassionate, if   400
not of the philosophic, historian with which she always recorded the current incidents

of her daughter's career. "She got dressed on purpose before dinner. But she's got a friend of hers there; that gentleman—the Italian—that she wanted to bring. They've got going at the piano; it seems as if they couldn't leave off. Mr. Giovanelli sings splendidly. But I guess they'll come before very long," concluded Mrs. Miller hopefully.

"I'm sorry she should come—in that way," said Mrs. Walker.

"Well, I told her that there was no use in her getting dressed before dinner if she was going to wait three hours," responded Daisy's mamma. "I didn't see the use of her putting on such a dress as that to sit round with Mr. Giovanelli."

"This is most horrible!" said Mrs. Walker, turning away and addressing herself to Winterbourne. "*Elle s'affiche.*[28] It's her revenge for my having ventured to remonstrate with her. When she comes I shall not speak to her."

Daisy came after eleven o'clock, but she was not, on such an occasion, a young lady to wait to be spoken to. She rustled forward in radiant loveliness, smiling and chattering, carrying a large bouquet and attended by Mr. Giovanelli. Everyone stopped talking, and turned and looked at her. She came straight to Mrs. Walker. "I'm afraid you thought I never was coming, so I sent mother off to tell you. I wanted to make Mr. Giovanelli practise some things before he came; you know he sings beautifully, and I want you to ask him to sing. This is Mr. Giovanelli; you know I introduced him to you; he's got the most lovely voice and he knows the most charming set of songs. I made him go over them this evening, on purpose; we had the greatest time at the hotel." Of all this Daisy delivered herself with the sweetest, brightest audibleness, looking now at her hostess and now round the room, while she gave a series of little pats, round her shoulders, to the edges of her dress. "Is there anyone I know?" she asked.

"I think every one knows you!" said Mrs. Walker pregnantly, and she gave a very cursory greeting to Mr. Giovanelli. This gentleman bore himself gallantly. He smiled and bowed and showed his white teeth, he curled his moustaches and rolled his eyes, and performed all the proper functions of a handsome Italian at an evening party. He sang, very prettily, half-a-dozen songs, though Mrs. Walker afterwards declared that she had been quite unable to find out who asked him. It was apparently not Daisy who had given him his orders. Daisy sat at a distance from the piano, and though she had publicly, as it were, professed a high admiration for his singing, talked, not inaudibly, while it was going on.

"It's a pity these rooms are so small; we can't dance," she said to Winterbourne as if she had seen him five minutes before.

"I am not sorry we can't dance," Winterbourne answered; "I don't dance."

"Of course you don't dance; you're too stiff," said Miss Daisy. "I hope you enjoyed your drive with Mrs. Walker."

"No, I didn't enjoy it; I preferred walking with you."

"We paired off, that was much better," said Daisy. "But did you ever hear anything so cool as Mrs. Walker's wanting me to get into her carriage and drop poor Mr. Giovanelli, and under the pretext that it was proper? People have different ideas! It would have been most unkind; he had been talking about that walk for ten days."

405

410

---

[28]She is making a spectacle of herself.—EDS.

"He should not have talked about it at all," said Winterbourne; "he would never have proposed to a young lady of this country to walk about the streets with him."

"About the streets?" cried Daisy, with her pretty stare. "Where then would he have proposed to her to walk? The Pincio is not the streets, either; and I, thank goodness, am not a young lady of this country. The young ladies of this country have a dreadfully poky time of it, so far as I can learn; I don't see why I should change my habits for *them*."

"I am afraid your habits are those of a flirt," said Winterbourne gravely.

"Of course they are," she cried, giving him her little smiling stare again. "I'm a fearful, frightful flirt! Did you ever hear of a nice girl that was not? But I suppose you will tell me now that I am not a nice girl."

"You're a very nice girl, but I wish you would flirt with me and me only," said   415
Winterbourne.

"Ah! thank you, thank you very much; you are the last man I should think of flirting with. As I have had the pleasure of informing you, you are too stiff."

"You say that too often," said Winterbourne.

Daisy gave a delighted laugh. "If I could have the sweet hope of making you angry, I should say it again."

"Don't do that; when I am angry I'm stiffer than ever. But if you won't flirt with me, do cease at least to flirt with your friend at the piano; they don't understand that sort of thing here."

"I thought they understood nothing else!" exclaimed Daisy.   420

"Not in young unmarried women."

"It seems to me much more proper in young unmarried women than in old married ones," Daisy declared.

"Well," said Winterbourne, "when you deal with natives you must go by the custom of the place. Flirting is a purely American custom; it doesn't exist here. So when you show yourself in public with Mr. Giovanelli and without your mother—"

"Gracious! poor mother!" interposed Daisy.

"Though you may be flirting, Mr. Giovanelli is not; he means something else."   425

"He isn't preaching, at any rate," said Daisy with vivacity. "And if you want very much to know, we are neither of us flirting, we are too good friends for that; we are very intimate friends."

"Ah!" rejoined Winterbourne, "if you are in love with each other it is another affair."

She had allowed him up to this point to talk so frankly that he had no expectation of shocking her by this ejaculation; but she immediately got up, blushing visibly, and leaving him to exclaim mentally that little American flirts were the queerest creatures in the world. "Mr. Giovanelli, at least," she said, giving her interlocutor a single glance, "never says such very disagreeable things to me."

Winterbourne was bewildered; he stood staring. Mr. Giovanelli had finished singing; he left the piano and came over to Daisy. "Won't you come into the other room and have some tea?" he asked, bending before her with his ornamental smile.

Daisy turned to Winterbourne, beginning to smile again. He was still more per-   430
plexed, for this inconsequent smile made nothing clear, though it seemed to prove,
indeed, that she had a sweetness and softness that reverted instinctively to the pardon
of offences. "It has never occurred to Mr. Winterbourne to offer me any tea," she said,
with her little tormenting manner.

"I have offered you advice," Winterbourne rejoined.

"I prefer weak tea!" cried Daisy, and she went off with the brilliant Giovanelli.
She sat with him in the adjoining room, in the embrasure of the window, for the rest
of the evening. There was an interesting performance at the piano, but neither of
these young people gave heed to it. When Daisy came to take leave of Mrs. Walker,
this lady conscientiously repaired the weakness of which she had been guilty at the
moment of the young girl's arrival. She turned her back straight upon Miss Miller
and left her to depart with what grace she might. Winterbourne was standing near
the door; he saw it all. Daisy turned very pale and looked at her mother, but Mrs.
Miller was humbly unconscious of any violation of the usual social forms. She appeared, indeed, to have felt an incongruous impulse to draw attention to her own
striking observance of them. "Good-night, Mrs. Walker," she said; "we've had a beautiful evening. You see if I let Daisy come to parties without me, I don't want her to go
away without me." Daisy turned away, looking with a pale, grave face at the circle near
the door; Winterbourne saw that, for the first moment, she was too much shocked
and puzzled even for indignation. He on his side was greatly touched.

"That was very cruel," he said to Mrs. Walker.

"She never enters my drawing-room again," replied his hostess.

Since Winterbourne was not to meet her in Mrs. Walker's drawing-room, he went as   435
often as possible to Mrs. Miller's hotel. The ladies were rarely at home, but when he found
them the devoted Giovanelli was always present. Very often the brilliant little Roman was
in the drawing-room with Daisy alone, Mrs. Miller being apparently constantly of the
opinion that discretion is the better part of surveillance. Winterbourne noted, at first with
surprise, that Daisy on these occasions was never embarrassed or annoyed by his own
entrance; but he very presently began to feel that she had no more surprises for him; the
unexpected in her behaviour was the only thing to expect. She showed no displeasure at
her *tête-à-tête* with Giovanelli being interrupted; she could chatter as freshly and freely
with two gentlemen as with one; there was always, in her conversation, the same odd mixture of audacity and puerility. Winterbourne remarked to himself that if she was seriously
interested in Giovanelli, it was very singular that she should not take more trouble to preserve the sanctity of their interviews, and he liked her the more for her innocent-looking
indifference and her apparently inexhaustible good humour. He could hardly have said
why, but she seemed to him a girl who would never be jealous. At the risk of exciting a
somewhat derisive smile on the reader's part, I may affirm that with regard to the women
who had hitherto interested him, it very often seemed to Winterbourne among the possibilities that, given certain contingencies, he should be afraid—literally afraid—of these
ladies; he had a pleasant sense that he should never be afraid of Daisy Miller. It must be
added that this sentiment was not altogether flattering to Daisy; it was part of his conviction, or rather of his apprehension, that she would prove a very light young person.

But she was evidently very much interested in Giovanelli. She looked at him whenever he spoke; she was perpetually telling him to do this and to do that; she was constantly "chaffing" and abusing him. She appeared completely to have forgotten that Winterbourne had said anything to displease her at Mrs. Walker's little party. One Sunday afternoon, having gone to St. Peter's with his aunt, Winterbourne perceived Daisy strolling about the great church in company with the inevitable Giovanelli. Presently he pointed out the young girl and her cavalier to Mrs. Costello. This lady looked at them a moment through her eyeglass, and then she said:

"That's what makes you so pensive in these days, eh?"

"I had not the least idea I was pensive," said the young man.

"You are very much pre-occupied, you are thinking of something."

"And what is it," he asked, "that you accuse me of thinking of?" 440

"Of that young lady's — Miss Baker's, Miss Chandler's — what's her name? Miss Miller's intrigue with that little barber's block."

"Do you call it an intrigue," Winterbourne asked — "an affair that goes on with such peculiar publicity?"

"That's their folly," said Mrs. Costello, "it's not their merit."

"No," rejoined Winterbourne, with something of that pensiveness to which his aunt had alluded. "I don't believe that there is anything to be called an intrigue."

"I have heard a dozen people speak of it; they say she is quite carried away by him." 445

"They are certainly very intimate," said Winterbourne.

Mrs. Costello inspected the young couple again with her optical instrument. "He is very handsome. One easily sees how it is. She thinks him the most elegant man in the world, the finest gentleman. She has never seen anything like him; he is better even than the courier. It was the courier probably who introduced him, and if he succeeds in marrying the young lady, the courier will come in for a magnificent commission."

"I don't believe she thinks of marrying him," said Winterbourne, "and I don't believe he hopes to marry her."

"You may be very sure she thinks of nothing. She goes on from day to day, from hour to hour, as they did in the Golden Age. I can imagine nothing more vulgar. And at the same time," added Mrs. Costello, "depend upon it that she may tell you any moment that she is 'engaged.'"

"I think that is more than Giovanelli expects," said Winterbourne. 450

"Who is Giovanelli?"

"The little Italian. I have asked questions about him and learned something. He is apparently a perfectly respectable little man. I believe he is, in a small way, a *cavaliere avvocato*.[29] But he doesn't move in what are called the first circles. I think it is really not absolutely impossible that the courier introduced him. He is evidently immensely charmed with Miss Miller. If she thinks him the finest gentleman in the world, he, on his side, has never found himself in personal contact with such splendour, such

---

[29]Gentleman lawyer. — EDS.

opulence, such expensiveness, as this young lady's. And then she must seem to him wonderfully pretty and interesting. I rather doubt that he dreams of marrying her. That must appear to him too impossible a piece of luck. He has nothing but his handsome face to offer, and there is a substantial Mr. Miller in that mysterious land of dollars. Giovanelli knows that he hasn't a title to offer. If he were only a count or a *marchese*![30] He must wonder at his luck at the way they have taken him up."

"He accounts for it by his handsome face, and thinks Miss Miller a young lady *qui se passe ses fantaisies*![31] said Mrs. Costello.

"It is very true," Winterbourne pursued, "that Daisy and her mamma have not yet risen to that stage of — what shall I call it? — of culture, at which the idea of catching a count or a *marchese* begins. I believe that they are intellectually incapable of that conception."

"Ah! but the *avvocato* can't believe it," said Mrs. Costello.

455

Of the observation excited by Daisy's "intrigue," Winterbourne gathered that day at St. Peter's sufficient evidence. A dozen of the American colonists in Rome came to talk with Mrs. Costello, who sat on a little portable stool at the base of one of the great pilasters. The vesper service was going forward in splendid chants and organ-tones in the adjacent choir, and meanwhile, between Mrs. Costello and her friends, there was a great deal said about poor little Miss Miller's going really "too far." Winterbourne was not pleased with what he heard; but when, coming out upon the great steps of the church, he saw Daisy, who had emerged before him, get into an open cab with her accomplice and roll away through the cynical streets of Rome, he could not deny to himself that she was going very far indeed. He felt very sorry for her — not exactly that he believed that she had completely lost her head, but because it was painful to hear so much that was pretty, and undefended, and natural, assigned to a vulgar place among the categories of disorder. He made an attempt after this to give a hint to Mrs. Miller. He met one day in the Corso[32] a friend — a tourist like himself — who had just come out of the Doria Palace, where he had been walking through the beautiful gallery. His friend talked for a moment about the superb portrait of Innocent X by Velasquez,[33] which hangs in one of the cabinets of the palace, and then said, "And in the same cabinet, by-the-way, I had the pleasure of contemplating a picture of a different kind — that pretty American girl whom you pointed out to me last week." In answer to Winterbourne's inquiries, his friend narrated that the pretty American girl — prettier than ever — was seated with a companion in the secluded nook in which the great papal portrait was enshrined.

"Who was her companion?" asked Winterbourne.

"A little Italian with a bouquet in his buttonhole. The girl is delightfully pretty, but I thought I understood from you the other day that she was a young lady *du meilleur monde*.[34]

---

[30]Marquis, nobleman. — EDS.
[31]Who is indulging her whims! — EDS.
[32]Via del Corso, the main thoroughfare in Rome. — EDS.
[33]Spanish painter Diego Velázquez (1599–1660). — EDS.
[34]Of the better society. — EDS.

"So she is!" answered Winterbourne; and having assured himself that his informant had seen Daisy and her companion but five minutes before, he jumped into a cab and went to call on Mrs. Miller. She was at home; but she apologised to him for receiving him in Daisy's absence.

"She's gone out somewhere with Mr. Giovanelli," said Mrs. Miller. "She's always   460
going round with Mr. Giovanelli."

"I have noticed that they are very intimate," Winterbourne observed.

"Oh! it seems as if they couldn't live without each other!" said Mrs. Miller. "Well, he's a real gentleman anyhow. I keep telling Daisy she's engaged!"

"And what does Daisy say?"

"Oh, she says she isn't engaged. But she might as well be!" this impartial parent resumed. "She goes on as if she was. But I've made Mr. Giovanelli promise to tell me, if *she* doesn't. I should want to write to Mr. Miller about it — shouldn't you?"

Winterbourne replied that he certainly should; and the state of mind of Daisy's   465
mamma struck him as so unprecedented in the annals of parental vigilance that he gave up as utterly irrelevant the attempt to place her upon her guard.

After this Daisy was never at home, and Winterbourne ceased to meet her at the houses of their common acquaintance, because, as he perceived, these shrewd people had quite made up their minds that she was going too far. They ceased to invite her, and they intimated that they desired to express to observant Europeans the great truth that, though Miss Daisy Miller was a young American lady, her behaviour was not representative — was regarded by her compatriots as abnormal. Winterbourne wondered how she felt about all the cold shoulders that were turned towards her, and sometimes it annoyed him to suspect that she did not feel at all. He said to himself that she was too light and childish, too uncultivated and unreasoning, too provincial, to have reflected upon her ostracism or even to have perceived it. Then at other moments he believed that she carried about in her elegant and irresponsible little organism a defiant, passionate, perfectly observant consciousness of the impression she produced. He asked himself whether Daisy's defiance came from the consciousness of innocence or from her being, essentially, a young person of the reckless class. It must be admitted that holding oneself to a belief in Daisy's "innocence" came to seem to Winterbourne more and more a matter of fine-spun gallantry. As I have already had occasion to relate, he was angry at finding himself reduced to chopping logic about this young lady; he was vexed at his want of instinctive certitude as to how far her eccentricities were generic, national, and how far they were personal. From either view of them he had somehow missed her, and now it was too late. She was "carried away" by Mr. Giovanelli.

A few days after his brief interview with her mother, he encountered her in that beautiful abode of flowering desolation known as the Palace of the Caesars. The early Roman spring had filled the air with bloom and perfume, and the rugged surface of the Palatine was muffled with tender verdure. Daisy was strolling along the top of one of those great mounds of ruin that are embanked with mossy marble and paved with monumental inscriptions. It seemed to him that Rome had never been so lovely as just then. He stood looking off at the enchanting harmony of line and colour that remotely encircles the city, inhaling the softly humid odours and feeling the freshness of the year and the antiquity of the place reaffirm themselves in mysterious interfusion. It seemed to him also that Daisy had never looked so pretty; but this had been an observation of his whenever he met her. Giovanelli was at her side, and Giovanelli, too, wore an aspect of even unwonted brilliancy.

"Well," said Daisy, "I should think you would be lonesome!"

"Lonesome?" asked Winterbourne.

"You are always going round by yourself. Can't you get anyone to walk with   470
you?"

"I am not so fortunate," said Winterbourne, "as your companion."

Giovanelli, from the first, had treated Winterbourne with distinguished politeness; he listened with a deferential air to his remarks; he laughed, punctiliously, at his pleasantries; he seemed disposed to testify to his belief that Winterbourne was a superior young man. He carried himself in no degree like a jealous wooer; he had obviously a great deal of tact; he had no objection to your expecting a little humility of him. It even seemed to Winterbourne at times that Giovanelli would find a certain mental relief in being able to have a private understanding with him—to say to him, as an intelligent man, that, bless you, *he* knew how extraordinary was this young lady, and didn't flatter himself with delusive—or at least *too* delusive—hopes of matrimony and dollars. On this occasion he strolled away from his companion to pluck a sprig of almond-blossom, which he carefully arranged in his button-hole.

"I know why you say that," said Daisy, watching Giovanelli. "Because you think I go round too much with *him*!" And she nodded at her attendant.

"Every one thinks so—if you care to know," said Winterbourne.

"Of course I care to know!" Daisy exclaimed seriously. "But I don't believe it.   475
They are only pretending to be shocked. They don't really care a straw what I do. Besides, I don't go round so much."

"I think you will find they do care. They will show it—disagreeably."

Daisy looked at him a moment. "How—disagreeably?"

"Haven't you noticed anything?" Winterbourne asked.

"I have noticed you. But I noticed you were as stiff as an umbrella the first time I saw you."

"You will find I am not so stiff as several others," said Winterbourne, smiling.   480

"How shall I find it?"

"By going to see the others."

"What will they do to me?"

"They will give you the cold shoulder. Do you know what that means?"

Daisy was looking at him intently; she began to colour. "Do you mean as Mrs.   485
Walker did the other night?"

"Exactly!" said Winterbourne.

She looked away at Giovanelli, who was decorating himself with his almond-blossom. Then looking back at Winterbourne—"I shouldn't think you would let people be so unkind!" she said.

"How can I help it?" he asked.

"I should think you would say something."

"I do say something"; and he paused a moment. "I say that your mother tells me   490
that she believes you are engaged."

"Well, she does," said Daisy very simply.

Winterbourne began to laugh. "And does Randolph believe it?" he asked.

"I guess Randolph doesn't believe anything," said Daisy. Randolph's scepticism
excited Winterbourne to further hilarity, and he observed that Giovanelli was coming back to them. Daisy, observing it too, addressed herself again to her countryman.
"Since you have mentioned it," she said, "I *am* engaged."... Winterbourne looked at
her; he had stopped laughing. "You don't believe it!" she added.

He was silent a moment; and then, "Yes, I believe it!" he said.

"Oh, no, you don't," she answered. "Well, then—I am not!"   495

The young girl and her cicerone were on their way to the gate of the enclosure,
so that Winterbourne, who had but lately entered, presently took leave of them.
A week afterwards he went to dine at a beautiful villa on the Caelian Hill, and, on
arriving, dismissed his hired vehicle. The evening was charming, and he promised
himself the satisfaction of walking home beneath the Arch of Constantine and past
the vaguely-lighted monuments of the Forum. There was a waning moon in the sky,
and her radiance was not brilliant, but she was veiled in a thin cloud-curtain which
seemed to diffuse and equalise it. When, on his return from the villa (it was eleven
o'clock), Winterbourne approached the dusky circle of the Colosseum, it recurred
to him, as a lover of the picturesque, that the interior, in the pale moonshine, would
be well worth a glance. He turned aside and walked to one of the empty arches,
near which, as he observed, an open carriage—one of the little Roman street-
cabs—was stationed. Then he passed in, among the cavernous shadows of the
great structure, and emerged upon the clear and silent arena. The place had never
seemed to him more impressive. One-half of the gigantic circus was in deep shade;
the other was sleeping in the luminous dusk. As he stood there he began to murmur
Byron's famous lines, out of "Manfred"; but before he had finished his quotation he
remembered that if nocturnal meditations in the Colosseum are recommended by
the poets, they are deprecated by the doctors. The historic atmosphere was there,
certainly; but the historic atmosphere, scientifically considered, was no better than a
villainous miasma. Winterbourne walked to the middle of the arena, to take a more
general glance, intending thereafter to make a hasty retreat. The great cross in the
centre was covered with shadow; it was only as he drew near it that he made it out
distinctly. Then he saw that two persons were stationed upon the low steps which
formed its base. One of these was a woman, seated; her companion was standing in
front of her.

Presently the sound of the woman's voice came to him distinctly in the warm
night-air. "Well, he looks at us as one of the old lions or tigers may have looked at
the Christian martyrs!" These were the words he heard, in the familiar accent of Miss
Daisy Miller.

"Let us hope he is not very hungry," responded the ingenious Giovanelli. "He
will have to take me first; you will serve for dessert!"

Winterbourne stopped, with a sort of horror; and, it must be added, with a sort of relief. It was as if a sudden illumination had been flashed upon the ambiguity of Daisy's behaviour and the riddle had become easy to read. She was a young lady whom a gentleman need no longer be at pains to respect. He stood there looking at her — looking at her companion, and not reflecting that though he saw them vaguely, he himself must have been more brightly visible. He felt angry with himself that he had bothered so much about the right way of regarding Miss Daisy Miller. Then, as he was going to advance again, he checked himself; not from the fear that he was doing her injustice, but from a sense of the danger of appearing unbecomingly exhilarated by this sudden revulsion from cautious criticism. He turned away towards the entrance of the place; but as he did so he heard Daisy speak again.

"Why, it was Mr. Winterbourne! He saw me — and he cuts me!"   500

What a clever little reprobate she was, and how smartly she played at injured innocence! But he wouldn't cut her. Winterbourne came forward again, and went towards the great cross. Daisy had got up; Giovanelli lifted his hat. Winterbourne had now begun to think simply of the craziness, from a sanitary point of view, of a delicate young girl lounging away the evening in this nest of malaria. What if she were a clever little reprobate? that was no reason for her dying of the *perniciosa*.[35] "How long have you been here?" he asked, almost brutally.

Daisy, lovely in the flattering moonlight, looked at him a moment. Then — "All the evening," she answered gently. . . . "I never saw anything so pretty."

"I am afraid," said Winterbourne, "that you will not think Roman fever very pretty. This is the way people catch it. I wonder," he added, turning to Giovanelli, "that you, a native Roman, should countenance such a terrible indiscretion."

"Ah," said the handsome native, "for myself, I am not afraid."

"Neither am I — for you! I am speaking for this young lady."   505

Giovanelli lifted his well-shaped eyebrows and showed his brilliant teeth. But he took Winterbourne's rebuke with docility. "I told the Signorina it was a grave indiscretion; but when was the Signorina ever prudent?"

"I never was sick, and I don't mean to be!" the Signorina declared. "I don't look like much, but I'm healthy! I was bound to see the Colosseum by moonlight; I shouldn't have wanted to go home without that; and we have had the most beautiful time, haven't we, Mr. Giovanelli? If there has been any danger, Eugenio can give me some pills. He has got some splendid pills."

"I should advise you," said Winterbourne, "to drive home as fast as possible and take one!"

"What you say is very wise," Giovanelli rejoined. "I will go and make sure the carriage is at hand." And he went forward rapidly.

Daisy followed with Winterbourne. He kept looking at her; she seemed not in   510
the least embarrassed. Winterbourne said nothing; Daisy chattered about the beauty

---

[35]Malaria. — EDS.

of the place. "Well, I *have* seen the Colosseum by moonlight!" she exclaimed. "That's one good thing." Then, noticing Winterbourne's silence, she asked him why he didn't speak. He made no answer; he only began to laugh. They passed under one of the dark archways; Giovanelli was in front with the carriage. Here Daisy stopped a moment, looking at the young American. "*Did* you believe I was engaged the other day?" she asked.

"It doesn't matter what I believed the other day," said Winterbourne, still laughing.

"Well, what do you believe now?"

"I believe that it makes very little difference whether you are engaged or not!"

He felt the young girl's pretty eyes fixed upon him through the thick gloom of the archway; she was apparently going to answer. But Giovanelli hurried her forward. "Quick, quick," he said; "if we get in by midnight we are quite safe."

Daisy took her seat in the carriage, and the fortunate Italian placed himself beside her. "Don't forget Eugenio's pills!" said Winterbourne, as he lifted his hat.

"I don't care," said Daisy, in a little strange tone, "whether I have Roman fever or not!" Upon this the cab-driver cracked his whip, and they rolled away over the desultory patches of the antique pavement.

Winterbourne—to do him justice, as it were—mentioned to no one that he had encountered Miss Miller, at midnight, in the Colosseum with a gentleman; but nevertheless, a couple of days later, the fact of her having been there under these circumstances was known to every member of the little American circle, and commented accordingly. Winterbourne reflected that they had of course known it at the hotel, and that, after Daisy's return, there had been an exchange of remarks between the porter and the cab-driver. But the young man was conscious at the same moment that it had ceased to be a matter of serious regret to him that the little American flirt should be "talked about" by low-minded menials. These people, a day or two later, had serious information to give: the little American flirt was alarmingly ill. Winterbourne, when the rumour came to him, immediately went to the hotel for more news. He found that two or three charitable friends had preceded him, and that they were being entertained in Mrs. Miller's salon by Randolph.

"It's going round at night," said Randolph—"that's what made her sick. She's always going round at night. I shouldn't think she'd want to—it's so plaguey dark. You can't see anything here at night, except when there's a moon. In America there's always a moon!" Mrs. Miller was invisible; she was now, at least, giving her daughter the advantage of her society. It was evident that Daisy was dangerously ill.

Winterbourne went often to ask for news of her, and once he saw Mrs. Miller, who, though deeply alarmed, was—rather to his surprise—perfectly composed, and, as it appeared, a most efficient and judicious nurse. She talked a good deal about Dr. Davis, but Winterbourne paid her the compliment of saying to himself that she was not, after all, such a monstrous goose. "Daisy spoke of you the other day," she said to him. "Half the time she doesn't know what she's saying, but that time I think she did. She gave me a message; she told me to tell you. She told me to tell you that she never was engaged to that handsome Italian. I am sure I am very glad; Mr. Giovanelli hasn't been near us since she was taken ill. I thought he was so much of a gentleman;

515

but I don't call that very polite! A lady told me that he was afraid I was angry with him for taking Daisy round at night. Well, so I am; but I suppose he knows I'm a lady. I would scorn to scold him. Any way, she says she's not engaged. I don't know why she wanted you to know; but she said to me three times—'Mind you tell Mr. Winterbourne.' And then she told me to ask if you remembered the time you went to that castle, in Switzerland. But I said I wouldn't give any such messages as that. Only, if she is not engaged, I'm sure I'm glad to know it."

But, as Winterbourne had said, it mattered very little. A week after this the poor girl died; it had been a terrible case of the fever. Daisy's grave was in the little Protestant cemetery, in an angle of the wall of imperial Rome, beneath the cypresses and the thick spring-flowers. Winterbourne stood there beside it, with a number of other mourners; a number larger than the scandal excited by the young lady's career would have led you to expect. Near him stood Giovanelli, who came nearer still before Winterbourne turned away. Giovanelli was very pale; on this occasion he had no flower in his button-hole; he seemed to wish to say something. At last he said, "She was the most beautiful young lady I ever saw, and the most amiable." And then he added in a moment, "And she was the most innocent."

Winterbourne looked at him, and presently repeated his words, "And the most innocent?"

"The most innocent!"

Winterbourne felt sore and angry. "Why the devil," he asked, "did you take her to that fatal place?"

Mr. Giovanelli's urbanity was apparently imperturbable. He looked on the ground a moment, and then he said, "For myself, I had no fear; and she wanted to go."

"That was no reason!" Winterbourne declared.

The subtle Roman again dropped his eyes. "If she had lived, I should have got nothing. She would never have married me, I am sure."

"She would never have married you?"

"For a moment I hoped so. But no. I am sure."

Winterbourne listened to him; he stood staring at the raw protuberance among the April daisies. When he turned away again Mr. Giovanelli, with his light slow step, had retired.

Winterbourne almost immediately left Rome; but the following summer he again met his aunt, Mrs. Costello, at Vevey. Mrs. Costello was fond of Vevey. In the interval Winterbourne had often thought of Daisy Miller and her mystifying manners. One day he spoke of her to his aunt—said it was on his conscience that he had done her injustice.

"I am sure I don't know," said Mrs. Costello. "How did your injustice affect her?"

"She sent me a message before her death which I didn't understand at the time. But I have understood it since. She would have appreciated one's esteem."

"Is that a modest way," asked Mrs. Costello, "of saying that she would have reciprocated one's affection?"

Winterbourne offered no answer to this question; but he presently said, "You were right in that remark that you made last summer. I was booked to make a mistake. I have lived too long in foreign parts."

Nevertheless, he went back to live at Geneva, whence there continue to come the   535
most contradictory accounts of his motives of sojourn: a report that he is "studying" hard—an intimation that he is much interested in a very clever foreign lady.

[1878]

. . . .

Questions for Discussion

1. Throughout *Daisy Miller*, Winterbourne thinks of Daisy as a "pretty American flirt" (para. 66), a formula he fixes on to contrast her behavior with that of a coquette, a type he describes as "dangerous, terrible women, with whom one's relations were liable to take a serious turn." Later he tells Daisy that "flirting is a purely American custom" (para. 423). Why do you think Winterbourne keeps coming back to this formula? What are some of the things it suggests? Is this description of Daisy positive or negative—or both? Is it an adequate or fair description of her? What might it mean that he considers flirting an American custom?

2. What qualities make Randolph and Daisy unmistakably American? In what ways do they embody American values? How do they represent American culture just as it was beginning to come into its own? How are the other American characters, such as Winterbourne, Mrs. Walker, and Mrs. Costello, different from Randolph and Daisy? How are they the same? What point might James have been making in creating their differences and similarities?

3. Daisy's family—without the father, who is back in Schenectady—is on a grand tour of Europe, which was once considered an essential activity for wealthy Americans. From what you can infer from the story, what did wealthy Americans look for on these tours? Did the Millers find what they were looking for?

4. Daisy comments on Europe in paragraph 65: "The only thing I don't like . . . is the society. There isn't any society; or, if there is, I don't know where it keeps itself." What do you think Daisy means by "society"? What is ironic about her statement?

5. Throughout the novella, Daisy visits several historical sites. The first is the Château de Chillon, which she sees with Winterbourne. It is an enormous castle on the shores of Lake Geneva dating from around 1100 C.E. and the subject of a poem by Byron called "The Prisoner of Chillon," about the imprisonment of François Bonivard, a Swiss patriot. Another is the Colosseum in Rome, the site of gladiatorial games and the martyring of Christians. What was James communicating by having Daisy visit these sites? Consider both how they affect Daisy and what they reveal about the Old World in which Winterbourne lives.

6. The Americans living in Europe seem to have a double standard. Mrs. Costello, for example, considers Daisy's behavior—but not Winterbourne's—wrong

when the two go to visit the Château de Chillon. Do you think Winterbourne applies a double standard to Daisy? Look carefully at the first conversation Winterbourne has with his aunt on the subject of Daisy (paras. 96–134).

7. What qualities do the two European characters—Eugenio, the courier, and Giovanelli, Daisy's Italian friend in Rome—have in common? How are they different? What, in particular, do the Americans find odious about them? What do you think is their opinion of the Americans?

8. Throughout the story, Daisy is either being referred to as "innocent" or having her innocence questioned. The word *innocent* can be taken several different ways. What are some of its possible meanings? Do you think Daisy is innocent? What meaning of the word would you apply to her?

9. Daisy is eventually snubbed by the wealthy American community in Rome, and Winterbourne wonders how she feels about all the "cold shoulders that were turned towards her" (para. 466). He vacillates between thinking that she hasn't noticed and imagining that she is conscious—and even proud—of the impression she's made. Does James provide enough information for the reader to judge how Daisy feels? Explain your answer.

10. In paragraph 349, Winterbourne feels "a superior indignation at his own lovely fellow-countrywoman's not knowing the difference between a spurious gentleman and a real one." He feels that a "nice girl ought to know," but wonders again if Daisy is "in fact a nice girl." These questions plague Winterbourne throughout the novella. Does he come to any conclusions? How do you define "nice girl" and "gentleman"? Who do you think is the spurious gentleman? What do you think Winterbourne means by "nice girl"?

11. Health is an issue for several of the characters. Consider Mrs. Costello's headaches, Mrs. Miller's dyspepsia (indigestion), and Daisy's death from Roman fever (malaria). How does each illness help illuminate its suffering character? What particular significance is there in Daisy contracting malaria in the Roman Colosseum? Why do you think Mr. Giovanelli emerges unscathed?

12. Consider the names of James's main characters. What is suggested by the name Daisy? Why do you think she uses Daisy instead of Annie, her real name? What about Winterbourne? What is Mrs. Costello's intention when she pretends to be unsure of Daisy's last name: "Miss Baker's, Miss Chandler's—what's her name" (para. 441)?

13. Henry James has said that the character of Randolph, Daisy's young brother, is based on himself. Does this knowledge change your take on the story? What function does this sharp boy have in the story?

Questions on Style and Structure

1. *Daisy Miller* is narrated by a third person, with a limited omniscient point of view—that is, the narrator only reveals what Winterbourne is thinking. The narrator begins the story by making some assumptions about the reader. What do those assumptions tell us about the narrator? How does the third-person limited

omniscient point of view both reveal and hide details about Winterbourne and Daisy?

2. Read the description of the resort town of Vevey, Switzerland, with which *Daisy Miller* opens. The narrator compares aspects of Vevey to resorts in America, noting that Vevey "assumes . . . some of the characteristics of an American watering-place . . . sights and sounds which evoke a vision, an echo, of Newport and Saratoga." Why might this statement be ironic? Whose point of view does this observation tap into? Look carefully at the paragraph in which Winterbourne and Daisy first meet (para. 27). How does the narrator distinguish between Geneva and Vevey? What is the significance of that distinction with regard to the themes of the story?

3. Reread the description of Daisy's first appearance (para. 20). What details does James include? What does he omit? Her brother says she's "an American girl," and Winterbourne comments that American girls are "the best girls." What qualities in the description of Daisy seem particularly American? Who do you think "they" are in Winterbourne's reaction: "How pretty they are"?

4. Parts of *Daisy Miller* are amusing, particularly the interchanges between Winterbourne and Randolph, such as the one about Mr. Miller being in "a better place" (para. 53). What purpose does the humor serve? How would you describe this particular type of humor?

5. James was known for his use of interior monologue, a technique used several times in *Daisy Miller* to show Winterbourne's struggle to make sense of his attraction to Daisy. Analyze a few of these interior monologues — paragraph 349, for example — looking carefully at the syntax of the sentences. Pay close attention to the way James's sentence patterns illustrate not just Winterbourne's confusion but also his lack of self-knowledge.

6. How does James give characters such as Mrs. Costello and Mrs. Walker authority? How seriously does Winterbourne take their opinions of Daisy? Are his words and actions consistent? Explain.

7. Is there anything besides Daisy's unconventional behavior that suggests differences between the Millers and the other Americans in the story? If so, does it explain the reason Daisy is snubbed? If not, why do the Americans snub her?

8. In Rome, Mrs. Costello holds court on the subject of Daisy just outside the vesper service at St. Peter's, a venerable Roman church. Later, Winterbourne meets a friend outside the Doria Palace with whom he talks first about the Velasquez portrait of Pope Innocent X that hangs in one of its galleries and then about the "pretty American girl" (para. 456) seated with a companion inside the nook where the portrait hangs. How do these juxtapositions help James comment on the Americans living abroad?

9. Carefully reread the scene in which Winterbourne comes across Daisy and Giovanelli in the Colosseum (para. 496). How does James create a sense of foreboding? What is significant about Daisy's observation that Winterbourne looks at her and Giovanelli "as one of the old lions or tigers may have looked at the Christian martyrs" (para. 497)?

10. The character of Mrs. Miller changes at the end of the novella. How does James portray the change in her? Why do you think she changes? What does this change say about the lives of the wealthy Americans that James portrays?

11. In the novella's last conversation, Winterbourne tells his aunt that Daisy is on his conscience, that he's afraid he did her an injustice. He says, "She would have appreciated one's esteem" (para. 532). What is the effect of the pronoun "one"? Why do you think Winterbourne uses it? How do you interpret Mrs. Costello's response — "Is that a modest way . . . of saying that she would have reciprocated one's affection" (para. 533)?

12. *Daisy Miller* ends with the observation that Winterbourne is "'studying' hard — an intimation that he is much interested in a very clever foreign lady." This is similar to the way Winterbourne is described at the beginning of the story: "'studying' . . . extremely devoted to a lady who lived there [Geneva] — a foreign lady — a person older than himself" (para. 2). What do you think these observations say about Winterbourne? How does their circularity comment on his character? on the characters of the Americans who live abroad?

Suggestions for Writing

1. Some readers of the novella think Winterbourne betrayed Daisy. Write an essay in which you analyze the nature of his betrayal and how it contributes to the meaning of the story.

2. Although the novella is titled *Daisy Miller*, many believe it is Winterbourne's story. Write an essay in which you make the case for this being either Daisy's story or Winterbourne's story.

3. Write an essay in which you analyze how *Daisy Miller* comments on the relationship between American and European culture.

4. In "The Art of Fiction" (1884), James argues that "the only reason for the existence of a novel is that it does attempt to present life." He considered the novelist's job similar to the historian's but felt that beyond having a working idea, it was important only that the novel "be interesting." He writes, "There is no such thing as a moral or immoral book. Books are well or badly written. That is all." Using *Daisy Miller* and possibly other works by James, write an essay in which you challenge or support James's assertion that there is no such thing as a moral or immoral work.

5. Choose one of the story's secondary characters, and write an essay in which you discuss how James creates his or her character. Be sure to consider the purpose of the character and how his or her portrayal is connected to that purpose.

6. In his art criticism, James was at first very critical of the French impressionists, but he later came to appreciate their work. Research the movement and James's change of heart, and write an essay in which you argue whether the impressionists had an influence on James's writing in *Daisy Miller*.

7. Rewrite a scene from the novella, revealing Daisy's thoughts rather than Winterbourne's.

A Good Man Is Hard to Find

FLANNERY O'CONNOR

Flannery O'Connor (1925–1964) was born on a farm in Milledgeville, Georgia. At the age of fifteen she lost her father to lupus, the same disease that would ultimately take her life at thirty-nine. In her short life, she would become one of the most acclaimed and widely read fiction writers of the twentieth century. After graduating from the Georgia State College for Women, she attended the Iowa Writers' Workshop. At twenty-six, after being diagnosed with a terminal form of lupus, O'Connor returned to the Georgia farm where she grew up. Despite her illness, she published three books—the story collection *A Good Man Is Hard to Find* (1955) and the novels *Wise Blood* (1952) and *The Violent Bear It Away* (1960)—before her death in 1964. Her later short stories were published posthumously as *Everything That Rises Must Converge* (1965). Most of O'Connor's stories are set in the American South, and critics often describe her writing as southern gothic, a genre that adapts the traditional characters of the Deep South to life after the Civil War, with results often described as "grotesque." O'Connor famously questioned why this particular term was used to describe southern stereotypes, arguing instead for the term "realistic." Her short stories examine the deep racial and religious divisions that exist among cultures generally lumped together as "southern." The title story from *A Good Man Is Hard to Find* portrays a modern family on holiday and their encounter with The Misfit.

> *The dragon is by the side of the road, watching those who pass. Beware lest he devour you. We go to the Father of Souls, but it is necessary to pass by the dragon.*
>
> —ST. CYRIL OF JERUSALEM

The grandmother didn't want to go to Florida. She wanted to visit some of her connections in east Tennessee and she was seizing at every chance to change Bailey's mind. Bailey was the son she lived with, her only boy. He was sitting on the edge of his chair at the table, bent over the orange sports section of the *Journal.* "Now look here, Bailey," she said, "see here, read this," and she stood with one hand on her thin hip and the other rattling the newspaper at his bald head. "Here this fellow that calls himself The Misfit is aloose from the Federal Pen and headed toward Florida and you read here what it says he did to these people. Just you read it. I wouldn't take my children in any direction with a criminal like that aloose in it. I couldn't answer to my conscience if I did."

Bailey didn't look up from his reading so she wheeled around then and faced the children's mother, a young woman in slacks, whose face was as broad and innocent as a cabbage and was tied around with a green head-kerchief that had two points on the top like rabbit's ears. She was sitting on the sofa, feeding the baby his apricots out of

1211

a jar. "The children have been to Florida before," the old lady said. "You all ought to take them somewhere else for a change so they would see different parts of the world and be broad. They never have been to east Tennessee."

The children's mother didn't seem to hear her but the eight-year-old boy, John Wesley, a stocky child with glasses, said, "If you don't want to go to Florida, why dontcha stay at home?" He and the little girl, June Star, were reading the funny papers on the floor.

"She wouldn't stay at home to be queen for a day," June Star said without raising her yellow head.

"Yes and what would you do if this fellow, The Misfit, caught you?" the grand- 5 mother asked.

"I'd smack his face," John Wesley said.

"She wouldn't stay at home for a million bucks," June Star said. "Afraid she'd miss something. She has to go everywhere we go."

"All right, Miss," the grandmother said. "Just remember that the next time you want me to curl your hair."

June Star said her hair was naturally curly.

The next morning the grandmother was the first one in the car, ready to go. She 10 had her big black valise that looked like the head of a hippopotamus in one corner, and underneath it she was hiding a basket with Pitty Sing, the cat, in it. She didn't intend for the cat to be left alone in the house for three days because he would miss her too much and she was afraid he might brush against one of the gas burners and accidentally asphyxiate himself. Her son, Bailey, didn't like to arrive at a motel with a cat.

She sat in the middle of the back seat with John Wesley and June Star on either side of her. Bailey and the children's mother and the baby sat in front and they left Atlanta at eight forty-five with the mileage on the car at 55890. The grandmother wrote this down because she thought it would be interesting to say how many miles they had been when they got back. It took them twenty minutes to reach the outskirts of the city.

The old lady settled herself comfortably, removing her white cotton gloves and putting them up with her purse on the shelf in front of the back window. The children's mother still had on slacks and still had her head tied up in a green kerchief, but the grandmother had on a navy blue straw sailor hat with a bunch of white violets on the brim and a navy blue dress with a small white dot in the print. Her collars and cuffs were white organdy trimmed with lace and at her neckline she had pinned a purple spray of cloth violets containing a sachet. In case of an accident, anyone seeing her dead on the highway would know at once that she was a lady.

She said she thought it was going to be a good day for driving, neither too hot nor too cold, and she cautioned Bailey that the speed limit was fifty-five miles an hour and that the patrolmen hid themselves behind billboards and small clumps of trees and sped out after you before you had a chance to slow down. She pointed out interesting details of the scenery: Stone Mountain; the blue granite that in some places came up to both sides of the highway; the brilliant red clay banks slightly streaked with purple; and the various crops that made rows of green lace-work on the ground.

The trees were full of silver-white sunlight and the meanest of them sparkled. The children were reading comic magazines and their mother had gone back to sleep.

"Let's go through Georgia fast so we won't have to look at it much," John Wesley said.

"If I were a little boy," said the grandmother, "I wouldn't talk about my native state that way. Tennessee has the mountains and Georgia has the hills."

"Tennessee is just a hillbilly dumping ground," John Wesley said, "and Georgia is a lousy state too."

"You said it," June Star said.

"In my time," said the grandmother, folding her thin veined fingers, "children were more respectful of their native states and their parents and everything else. People did right then. Oh look at the cute little pickaninny!" she said and pointed to a Negro child standing in the door of a shack. "Wouldn't that make a picture, now?" she asked and they all turned and looked at the little Negro out of the back window. He waved.

"He didn't have any britches on," June Star said.

"He probably didn't have any," the grandmother explained. "Little niggers in the country don't have things like we do. If I could paint, I'd paint that picture," she said.

The children exchanged comic books.

The grandmother offered to hold the baby and the children's mother passed him over the front seat to her. She set him on her knee and bounced him and told him about the things they were passing. She rolled her eyes and screwed up her mouth and stuck her leathery thin face into his smooth bland one. Occasionally he gave her a far-away smile. They passed a large cotton field with five or six graves fenced in the middle of it, like a small island. "Look at the graveyard!" the grandmother said, pointing it out. "That was the old family burying ground. That belonged to the plantation."

"Where's the plantation?" John Wesley asked.

"Gone With the Wind," said the grandmother. "Ha. Ha."

When the children finished all the comic books they had brought, they opened the lunch and ate it. The grandmother ate a peanut butter sandwich and an olive and would not let the children throw the box and the paper napkins out the window. When there was nothing else to do they played a game by choosing a cloud and making the other two guess what shape it suggested. John Wesley took one the shape of a cow and June Star guessed a cow and John Wesley said, no, an automobile, and June Star said he didn't play fair, and they began to slap each other over the grandmother.

The grandmother said she would tell them a story if they would keep quiet. When she told a story, she rolled her eyes and waved her head and was very dramatic. She said once when she was a maiden lady she had been courted by a Mr. Edgar Atkins Teagarden from Jasper, Georgia. She said he was a very good-looking man and a gentleman and that he brought her a watermelon every Saturday afternoon with his initials cut in it, E. A. T. Well, one Saturday, she said, Mr. Teagarden brought

15

20

25

the watermelon and there was nobody at home and he left it on the front porch and returned in his buggy to Jasper, but she never got the watermelon, she said, because a nigger boy ate it when he saw the initials, E. A. T.! This story tickled John Wesley's funny bone and he giggled and giggled but June Star didn't think it was any good. She said she wouldn't marry a man that just brought her a watermelon on Saturday. The grandmother said she would have done well to marry Mr. Teagarden because he was a gentleman and had bought Coca-Cola stock when it first came out and that he had died only a few years ago, a very wealthy man.

They stopped at The Tower for barbecued sandwiches. The Tower was a part stucco and part wood filling station and dance hall set in a clearing outside of Timothy. A fat man named Red Sammy Butts ran it and there were signs stuck here and there on the building and for miles up and down the highway saying, TRY RED SAMMY'S FAMOUS BARBECUE. NONE LIKE FAMOUS RED SAMMY'S! RED SAM! THE FAT BOY WITH THE HAPPY LAUGH. A VETERAN! RED SAMMY'S YOUR MAN!

Red Sammy was lying on the bare ground outside The Tower with his head under a truck while a gray monkey about a foot high, chained to a small chinaberry tree, chattered nearby. The monkey sprang back into the tree and got on the highest limb as soon as he saw the children jump out of the car and run toward him.

Inside, The Tower was a long dark room with a counter at one end and tables at the other and dancing space in the middle. They all sat down at a board table next to the nickelodeon and Red Sam's wife, a tall burnt-brown woman with hair and eyes lighter than her skin, came and took their order. The children's mother put a dime in the machine and played "The Tennessee Waltz," and the grandmother said that tune always made her want to dance. She asked Bailey if he would like to dance but he only glared at her. He didn't have a naturally sunny disposition like she did and trips made him nervous. The grandmother's brown eyes were very bright. She swayed her head from side to side and pretended she was dancing in her chair. June Star said play something she could tap to so the children's mother put in another dime and played a fast number and June Star stepped out onto the dance floor and did her tap routine.

"Ain't she cute?" Red Sam's wife said, leaning over the counter. "Would you like to come be my little girl?"   30

"No I certainly wouldn't," June Star said. "I wouldn't live in a broken-down place like this for a million bucks!" and she ran back to the table.

"Ain't she cute?" the woman repeated, stretching her mouth politely.

"Aren't you ashamed?" hissed the grandmother.

Red Sam came in and told his wife to quit lounging on the counter and hurry up with these people's order. His khaki trousers reached just to his hip bones and his stomach hung over them like a sack of meal swaying under his shirt. He came over and sat down at a table nearby and let out a combination sigh and yodel. "You can't win," he said. "You can't win," and he wiped his sweating red face off with a gray handkerchief. "These days you don't know who to trust," he said. "Ain't that the truth?"

"People are certainly not nice like they used to be," said the grandmother.   35

"Two fellers come in here last week," Red Sammy said, "driving a Chrysler. It was a old beat-up car but it was a good one and these boys looked all right to me. Said they worked at the mill and you know I let them fellers charge the gas they bought? Now why did I do that?"

"Because you're a good man!" the grandmother said at once.

"Yes'm, I suppose so," Red Sam said as if he were struck with this answer.

His wife brought the orders, carrying the five plates all at once without a tray, two in each hand and one balanced on her arm. "It isn't a soul in this green world of God's that you can trust," she said. "And I don't count nobody out of that, not nobody," she repeated, looking at Red Sammy.

"Did you read about that criminal, The Misfit, that's escaped?" asked the grand- 40 mother.

"I wouldn't be a bit surprised if he didn't attact this place right here," said the woman. "If he hears about it being here, I wouldn't be none surprised to see him. If he hears it's two cent in the cash register, I wouldn't be a tall surprised if he . . ."

"That'll do," Red Sam said. "Go bring these people their Co'-Colas," and the woman went off to get the rest of the order.

"A good man is hard to find," Red Sammy said. "Everything is getting terrible. I remember the day you could go off and leave your screen door unlatched. Not no more."

He and the grandmother discussed better times. The old lady said that in her opinion Europe was entirely to blame for the way things were now. She said the way Europe acted you would think we were made of money and Red Sam said it was no use talking about it, she was exactly right. The children ran outside into the white sunlight and looked at the monkey in the lacy chinaberry tree. He was busy catching fleas on himself and biting each one carefully between his teeth as if it were a delicacy.

They drove off again into the hot afternoon. The grandmother took cat naps 45 and woke up every few minutes with her own snoring. Outside of Toombsboro she woke up and recalled an old plantation that she had visited in this neighborhood once when she was a young lady. She said the house had six white columns across the front and that there was an avenue of oaks leading up to it and two little wooden trellis arbors on either side in front where you sat down with your suitor after a stroll in the garden. She recalled exactly which road to turn off to get to it. She knew that Bailey would not be willing to lose any time looking at an old house, but the more she talked about it, the more she wanted to see it once again and find out if the little twin arbors were still standing. "There was a secret panel in this house," she said craftily, not telling the truth but wishing that she were, "and the story went that all the family silver was hidden in it when Sherman[1] came through but it was never found . . ."

"Hey!" John Wesley said. "Let's go see it! We'll find it! We'll poke all the woodwork and find it! Who lives there? Where do you turn off at? Hey Pop, can't we turn off there?"

---

[1]Union general William Tecumseh Sherman (1820–1891) led a destructive campaign through Tennessee, Georgia, and the Carolinas during the Civil War. — EDS.

"We never have seen a house with a secret panel!" June Star shrieked. "Let's go to the house with the secret panel! Hey Pop, can't we go see the house with the secret panel!"

"It's not far from here, I know," the grandmother said. "It wouldn't take over twenty minutes."

Bailey was looking straight ahead. His jaw was as rigid as a horseshoe. "No," he said.

The children began to yell and scream that they wanted to see the house with the secret panel. John Wesley kicked the back of the front seat and June Star hung over her mother's shoulder and whined desperately into her ear that they never had any fun even on their vacation, that they could never do what THEY wanted to do. The baby began to scream and John Wesley kicked the back of the seat so hard that his father could feel the blows in his kidney.

"All right!" he shouted and drew the car to a stop at the side of the road. "Will you all shut up? Will you all just shut up for one second? If you don't shut up, we won't go anywhere."

"It would be very educational for them," the grandmother murmured.

"All right," Bailey said, "but get this: this is the only time we're going to stop for anything like this. This is the one and only time."

"The dirt road that you have to turn down is about a mile back," the grandmother directed. "I marked it when we passed."

"A dirt road," Bailey groaned.

After they had turned around and were headed toward the dirt road, the grandmother recalled other points about the house, the beautiful glass over the front doorway and the candle-lamp in the hall. John Wesley said that the secret panel was probably in the fireplace.

"You can't go inside this house," Bailey said. "You don't know who lives there."

"While you all talk to the people in front, I'll run around behind and get in a window," John Wesley suggested.

"We'll all stay in the car," his mother said.

They turned onto the dirt road and the car raced roughly along in a swirl of pink dust. The grandmother recalled the times when there were no paved roads and thirty miles was a day's journey. The dirt road was hilly and there were sudden washes in it and sharp curves on dangerous embankments. All at once they would be on a hill, looking down over the blue tops of trees for miles around, then the next minute, they would be in a red depression with the dust-coated trees looking down on them.

"This place had better turn up in a minute," Bailey said, "or I'm going to turn around."

The road looked as if no one had traveled on it in months.

"It's not much farther," the grandmother said and just as she said it, a horrible thought came to her. The thought was so embarrassing that she turned red in the face and her eyes dilated and her feet jumped up, upsetting her valise in the corner. The instant the valise moved, the newspaper top she had over the basket under it rose with a snarl and Pitty Sing, the cat, sprang onto Bailey's shoulder.

The children were thrown to the floor and their mother, clutching the baby, was thrown out the door onto the ground; the old lady was thrown into the front seat. The car turned over once and landed right-side-up in a gulch off the side of the road. Bailey remained in the driver's seat with the cat—gray-striped with a broad white face and an orange nose—clinging to his neck like a caterpillar.

As soon as the children saw they could move their arms and legs, they scrambled out of the car, shouting, "We've had an ACCIDENT!" The grandmother was curled up under the dashboard, hoping she was injured so that Bailey's wrath would not come down on her all at once. The horrible thought she had had before the accident was that the house she had remembered so vividly was not in Georgia but in Tennessee.

Bailey removed the cat from his neck with both hands and flung it out the window against the side of a pine tree. Then he got out of the car and started looking for the children's mother. She was sitting against the side of the red gutted ditch, holding the screaming baby, but she only had a cut down her face and a broken shoulder. "We've had an ACCIDENT!" the children screamed in a frenzy of delight.

"But nobody's killed," June Star said with disappointment as the grandmother limped out of the car, her hat still pinned to her head but the broken front brim standing up at a jaunty angle and the violet spray hanging off the side. They all sat down in the ditch, except the children, to recover from the shock. They were all shaking.

"Maybe a car will come along," said the children's mother hoarsely.

"I believe I have injured an organ," said the grandmother, pressing her side, but no one answered her. Bailey's teeth were clattering. He had on a yellow sport shirt with bright blue parrots designed in it and his face was as yellow as the shirt. The grandmother decided that she would not mention that the house was in Tennessee.

The road was about ten feet above and they could see only the tops of the trees on the other side of it. Behind the ditch they were sitting in there were more woods, tall and dark and deep. In a few minutes they saw a car some distance away on top of a hill, coming slowly as if the occupants were watching them. The grandmother stood up and waved both arms dramatically to attract their attention. The car continued to come on slowly, disappeared around a bend and appeared again, moving even slower, on top of the hill they had gone over. It was a big black battered hearse-like automobile. There were three men in it.

It came to a stop just over them and for some minutes, the driver looked down with a steady expressionless gaze to where they were sitting, and didn't speak. Then he turned his head and muttered something to the other two and they got out. One was a fat boy in black trousers and a red sweat shirt with a silver stallion embossed on the front of it. He moved around on the right side of them and stood staring, his mouth partly open in a kind of loose grin. The other had on khaki pants and a blue striped coat and a gray hat pulled down very low, hiding most of his face. He came around slowly on the left side. Neither spoke.

The driver got out of the car and stood by the side of it, looking down at them. He was an older man than the other two. His hair was just beginning to gray and he wore silver-rimmed spectacles that gave him a scholarly look. He had a long creased face and didn't have on any shirt or undershirt. He had on blue jeans that were too tight for him and was holding a black hat and a gun. The two boys also had guns.

"We've had an ACCIDENT!" the children screamed.

The grandmother had the peculiar feeling that the bespectacled man was some-one she knew. His face was as familiar to her as if she had known him all her life but she could not recall who he was. He moved away from the car and began to come down the embankment, placing his feet carefully so that he wouldn't slip. He had on tan and white shoes and no socks, and his ankles were red and thin. "Good after-noon," he said. "I see you all had you a little spill."

"We turned over twice!" said the grandmother.

"Oncet," he corrected. "We seen it happen. Try their car and see will it run, Hiram," he said quietly to the boy with the gray hat.

"What you got that gun for?" John Wesley asked. "Whatcha gonna do with that gun?"

"Lady," the man said to the children's mother, "would you mind calling them children to sit down by you? Children make me nervous. I want all you all to sit down right together there where you're at."

"What are you telling US what to do for?" June Star asked.

Behind them the line of woods gaped like a dark open mouth. "Come here," said their mother.

"Look here now," Bailey began suddenly, "we're in a predicament! We're in . . ."

The grandmother shrieked. She scrambled to her feet and stood staring. "You're The Misfit!" she said. "I recognized you at once!"

"Yes'm," the man said, smiling slightly as if he were pleased in spite of himself to be known, "but it would have been better for all of you, lady, if you hadn't of reckernized me."

Bailey turned his head sharply and said something to his mother that shocked even the children. The old lady began to cry and The Misfit reddened.

"Lady," he said, "don't you get upset. Sometimes a man says things he don't mean. I don't reckon he meant to talk to you thataway."

"You wouldn't shoot a lady, would you?" the grandmother said and removed a clean handkerchief from her cuff and began to slap at her eyes with it.

The Misfit pointed the toe of his shoe into the ground and made a little hole and then covered it up again. "I would hate to have to," he said.

"Listen," the grandmother almost screamed, "I know you're a good man. You don't look a bit like you have common blood. I know you must come from nice people!"

"Yes mam," he said, "finest people in the world." When he smiled he showed a row of strong white teeth. "God never made a finer woman than my mother and my daddy's heart was pure gold," he said. The boy with the red sweat shirt had come around behind them and was standing with his gun at his hip. The Misfit squatted down on the ground. "Watch them children, Bobby Lee," he said. "You know they make me nervous." He looked at the six of them huddled together in front of him and he seemed to be embarrassed as if he couldn't think of anything to say. "Ain't a cloud in the sky," he remarked, looking up at it. "Don't see no sun but don't see no cloud neither."

"Yes, it's a beautiful day," said the grandmother. "Listen," she said, "you shouldn't call yourself The Misfit because I know you're a good man at heart. I can just look at you and tell." 90

"Hush!" Bailey yelled. "Hush! Everybody shut up and let me handle this!" He was squatting in the position of a runner about to sprint forward but he didn't move.

"I pre-chate that, lady," The Misfit said and drew a little circle in the ground with the butt of his gun.

"It'll take a half a hour to fix this here car," Hiram called, looking over the raised hood of it.

"Well, first you and Bobby Lee get him and that little boy to step over yonder with you," The Misfit said, pointing to Bailey and John Wesley. "The boys want to ast you something," he said to Bailey. "Would you mind stepping back in them woods there with them?"

"Listen," Bailey began, "we're in a terrible predicament! Nobody realizes what this is," and his voice cracked. His eyes were as blue and intense as the parrots in his shirt and he remained perfectly still. 95

The grandmother reached up to adjust her hat brim as if she were going to the woods with him but it came off in her hand. She stood staring at it and after a second she let it fall on the ground. Hiram pulled Bailey up by the arm as if he were assisting an old man. John Wesley caught hold of his father's hand and Bobby Lee followed. They went off toward the woods and just as they reached the dark edge, Bailey turned and supporting himself against a gray naked pine trunk, he shouted, "I'll be back in a minute, Mamma, wait on me!"

"Come back this instant!" his mother shrilled but they all disappeared into the woods.

"Bailey Boy!" the grandmother called in a tragic voice but she found she was looking at The Misfit squatting on the ground in front of her. "I just know you're a good man," she said desperately. "You're not a bit common!"

"Nome, I ain't a good man," The Misfit said after a second as if he had considered her statement carefully, "but I ain't the worst in the world neither. My daddy said I was a different breed of dog from my brothers and sisters. 'You know,' Daddy said, 'it's some that can live their whole life out without asking about it and it's others has to know why it is, and this boy is one of the latters. He's going to be into everything!'" He put on his black hat and looked up suddenly and then away deep into the woods as if he were embarrassed again. "I'm sorry I don't have on a shirt before you ladies," he said, hunching his shoulders slightly. "We buried our clothes that we had on when we escaped and we're just making do until we can get better. We borrowed these from some folks we met," he explained.

"That's perfectly all right," the grandmother said. "Maybe Bailey has an extra shirt in his suitcase." 100

"I'll look and see terrectly," The Misfit said.

"Where are they taking him?" the children's mother screamed.

"Daddy was a card himself," The Misfit said. "You couldn't put anything over on him. He never got in trouble with the Authorities though. Just had the knack of handling them."

"You could be honest too if you'd only try," said the grandmother. "Think how wonderful it would be to settle down and live a comfortable life and not have to think about somebody chasing you all the time."

The Misfit kept scratching in the ground with the butt of his gun as if he were   105
thinking about it. "Yes'm, somebody is always after you," he murmured.

The grandmother noticed how thin his shoulder blades were just behind his hat because she was standing up looking down on him. "Do you ever pray?" she asked.

He shook his head. All she saw was the black hat wiggle between his shoulder blades. "Nome," he said.

There was a pistol shot from the woods, followed closely by another. Then silence. The old lady's head jerked around. She could hear the wind move through the tree tops like a long satisfied insuck of breath. "Bailey Boy!" she called.

"I was a gospel singer for a while," The Misfit said. "I been most everything. Been in the arm service, both land and sea, at home and abroad, been twict married, been an undertaker, been with the railroads, plowed Mother Earth, been in a tornado, seen a man burnt alive oncet," and he looked up at the children's mother and the little girl who were sitting close together, their faces white and their eyes glassy; "I even seen a woman flogged," he said.

"Pray, pray," the grandmother began, "pray, pray . . ."   110

"I never was a bad boy that I remember of," The Misfit said in an almost dreamy voice, "but somewheres along the line I done something wrong and got sent to the penitentiary. I was buried alive," and he looked up and held her attention to him by a steady stare.

"That's when you should have started to pray," she said. "What did you do to get sent to the penitentiary that first time?"

"Turn to the right, it was a wall," The Misfit said, looking up again at the cloudless sky. "Turn to the left, it was a wall. Look up it was a ceiling, look down it was a floor. I forget what I done, lady. I set there and set there, trying to remember what it was I done and I ain't recalled it to this day. Oncet in a while, I would think it was coming to me, but it never come."

"Maybe they put you in by mistake," the old lady said vaguely.

"Nome," he said. "It wasn't no mistake. They had the papers on me."   115

"You must have stolen something," she said.

The Misfit sneered slightly. "Nobody had nothing I wanted," he said. "It was a head-doctor at the penitentiary said what I had done was kill my daddy but I known that for a lie. My daddy died in nineteen ought nineteen of the epidemic flu[2] and I never had a thing to do with it. He was buried in the Mount Hopewell Baptist churchyard and you can go there and see for yourself."

---

[2]The influenza pandemic of 1918–19, the largest epidemic in history, killed between twenty and forty million people worldwide.—EDS.

"If you would pray," the old lady said, "Jesus would help you."

"That's right," The Misfit said.

"Well then, why don't you pray?" she asked trembling with delight suddenly.　　120

"I don't want no hep," he said. "I'm doing all right by myself."

Bobby Lee and Hiram came ambling back from the woods. Bobby Lee was dragging a yellow shirt with bright blue parrots in it.

"Thow me that shirt, Bobby Lee," The Misfit said. The shirt came flying at him and landed on his shoulder and he put it on. The grandmother couldn't name what the shirt reminded her of. "No, lady," The Misfit said while he was buttoning it up, "I found out the crime don't matter. You can do one thing or you can do another, kill a man or take a tire off his car, because sooner or later you're going to forget what it was you done and just be punished for it."

The children's mother had begun to make heaving noises as if she couldn't get her breath. "Lady," he asked, "would you and that little girl like to step off yonder with Bobby Lee and Hiram and join your husband?"

"Yes, thank you," the mother said faintly. Her left arm dangled helplessly and she　125
was holding the baby, who had gone to sleep, in the other. "Hep that lady up, Hiram," The Misfit said as she struggled to climb out of the ditch, "and Bobby Lee, you hold onto that little girl's hand."

"I don't want to hold hands with him," June Star said. "He reminds me of a pig."

The fat boy blushed and laughed and caught her by the arm and pulled her off into the woods after Hiram and her mother.

Alone with The Misfit, the grandmother found that she had lost her voice. There was not a cloud in the sky nor any sun. There was nothing around her but woods. She wanted to tell him that he must pray. She opened and closed her mouth several times before anything came out. Finally she found herself saying, "Jesus. Jesus," meaning, Jesus will help you, but the way she was saying it, it sounded as if she might be cursing.

"Yes'm," The Misfit said as if he agreed. "Jesus thown everything off balance. It was the same case with Him as with me except He hadn't committed any crime and they could prove I had committed one because they had the papers on me. Of course," he said, "they never shown me my papers. That's why I sign myself now. I said long ago, you get you a signature and sign everything you do and keep a copy of it. Then you'll know what you done and you can hold up the crime to the punishment and see do they match and in the end you'll have something to prove you ain't been treated right. I call myself The Misfit," he said, "because I can't make what all I done wrong fit what all I gone through in punishment."

There was a piercing scream from the woods, followed closely by a pistol report.　130
"Does it seem right to you, lady, that one is punished a heap and another ain't punished at all?"

"Jesus!" the old lady cried. "You've got good blood! I know you wouldn't shoot a lady! I know you come from nice people! Pray! Jesus, you ought not to shoot a lady. I'll give you all the money I've got!"

"Lady," The Misfit said, looking beyond her far into the woods, "there never was a body that give the undertaker a tip."

There were two more pistol reports and the grandmother raised her head like a parched old turkey hen crying for water and called, "Bailey Boy, Bailey Boy!" as if her heart would break.

"Jesus was the only One that ever raised the dead," The Misfit continued, "and He shouldn't have done it. He thown everything off balance. If He did what He said, then it's nothing for you to do but thow away everything and follow Him, and if He didn't, then it's nothing for you to do but enjoy the few minutes you got left the best way you can—by killing somebody or burning down his house or doing some other meanness to him. No pleasure but meanness," he said and his voice had become almost a snarl.

"Maybe He didn't raise the dead," the old lady mumbled, not knowing what she was saying and feeling so dizzy that she sank down in the ditch with her legs twisted under her.   135

"I wasn't there so I can't say He didn't," The Misfit said. "I wisht I had of been there," he said, hitting the ground with his fist. "It ain't right I wasn't there because if I had of been there I would of known. Listen lady," he said in a high voice, "if I had of been there I would of known and I wouldn't be like I am now." His voice seemed about to crack and the grandmother's head cleared for an instant. She saw the man's face twisted close to her own as if he were going to cry and she murmured, "Why you're one of my babies. You're one of my own children!" She reached out and touched him on the shoulder. The Misfit sprang back as if a snake had bitten him and shot her three times through the chest. Then he put his gun down on the ground and took off his glasses and began to clean them.

Hiram and Bobby Lee returned from the woods and stood over the ditch, looking down at the grandmother who half sat and half lay in a puddle of blood with her legs crossed under her like a child's and her face smiling up at the cloudless sky.

Without his glasses, The Misfit's eyes were red-rimmed and pale and defenseless-looking. "Take her off and thow her where you thown the others," he said, picking up the cat that was rubbing itself against his leg.

"She was a talker, wasn't she?" Bobby Lee said, sliding down the ditch with a yodel.

"She would of been a good woman," The Misfit said, "if it had been somebody there to shoot her every minute of her life."   140

"Some fun!" Bobby Lee said.

"Shut up, Bobby Lee," The Misfit said. "It's no real pleasure in life."

[1955]

· ·

Questions for Discussion

1. What tone does the epigraph set for the story? Reconsider it after you've read the story. How does your interpretation change?

2. What can you infer about the grandmother by reading the opening paragraph? What does she represent in the story? Consider the role she plays in her family as well as how she might embody a different era in the culture of the South. What does the grandmother mean when she tells The Misfit, "Why you're one of my babies. You're one of my own children" (para. 136)?

3. The main characters in a story usually have names. In this story, however, several main characters—The Misfit, the grandmother, and the children's mother—are unnamed. What is the purpose of not giving these characters names, referring to them only by their roles? How might leaving these characters unnamed connect to a theme of the story?

4. In what ways is the family in this story fairly typical in terms of the tensions and conflicts most families experience? How does O'Connor introduce comedy by depicting these differences between and among generations and relationships?

5. When Red Sammy says to the grandmother, "A good man is hard to find" (para. 43), what does he mean? Why did O'Connor choose this particular line for the story's title? Also consider why, in the final scene, the grandmother repeatedly tells The Misfit that she knows he is a "good man."

6. Discuss instances in which the grandmother's nostalgia for the past seems warranted and others in which it becomes limiting, even threatening. You might begin by considering some of the following: her desire to paint a picture of the "pickaninny" in the doorway, her story about Mr. Teagarden, her story of the house with the secret panel.

7. O'Connor has said that the short-story collection that included this story is about "original sin." What role does religion, specifically Christianity, play in this story? How do the grandmother's traditional views on salvation and prayer differ from The Misfit's? What does he mean when he asserts that Jesus has thrown "everything off balance" (paras. 129, 134)?

8. Were you surprised by the violence in the story? Why do you think O'Connor chose to leave the murders of everyone but the grandmother "off stage" rather than describing them directly? What is the impact of providing details about the shooting of the grandmother and describing her lifeless body?

9. How does The Misfit explain his behavior to the grandmother? Why does he shoot her precisely when he does? How do you interpret his assertion that "she would of been a good woman . . . if it had been somebody there to shoot her every minute of her life" (para. 140)? What does The Misfit understand about the grandmother's character?

Questions on Style and Structure

1. How does O'Connor use foreshadowing in "A Good Man Is Hard to Find"? What effect did the foreshadowing have on your first reading of the story? When you read about The Misfit in the first paragraph, did you think that you would meet him?

2. Contrast the description of the grandmother's outfit with the rest of the family's traveling attire (paras. 12, 69). What do the characters' clothes tell us about them? What is significant about The Misfit's appropriation of Bailey's parrot shirt (paras. 122–23)?

3. "'In my time,' said the grandmother, folding her thin veined fingers, 'children were more respectful of their native states and their parents and everything else. People did right then. Oh look at the cute little pickaninny!' she said and pointed to a Negro child standing in the door of a shack" (para. 18). What is ironic about this passage? How does the grandmother define "did right"? What evidence suggests a contrast between the character's and the author's perspectives of what it means to "do right"?

4. What is the purpose of the scene at Red Sammy's barbecue place? Consider the conversation between the grandmother and Red Sammy about the difficulty of finding a "good man." How does this scene develop the story's themes as well as plot?

5. Take another look at the allusion the grandmother makes to *Gone With the Wind* in paragraph 24. What deeper meaning can you find in her joke about the plantation? How does this joke affect your reading of the story?

6. Explain how the setting shifts once the family takes a detour off the main road. Why is this shift important to the story's plot? How does the shift in setting contribute to the shift in the story's tone?

7. Why do you think O'Connor chose to capitalize "ACCIDENT!" in the children's dialogue? After the accident, a slow-moving car appears on the horizon, "a big black battered hearse-like automobile" (para. 70). Why might the author have chosen not to use commas between these adjectives? How do the punctuation and alliteration contribute to the effect of this description?

8. The Misfit's words are often given a phonetic rendering:
   - "I pre-chate that, lady." (para. 92)
   - "The boys want to ast you something." (para. 94)
   - "I'll look and see terrectly." (para. 101)
   - "Nome." (para. 107)
   - "I . . . seen a man burnt alive oncet." (para. 109)
   - "I don't want no hep." (para. 121)

   What effect does this use of dialect have on your understanding of The Misfit's character? What other characters in the story speak in dialect, and what does it say about them?

9. Examine the following similes used in "A Good Man Is Hard to Find":
   - "whose face was as broad and innocent as a cabbage" (para. 2)
   - "her big black valise that looked like the head of a hippopotamus" (para. 10)
   - "His jaw was as rigid as a horseshoe." (para. 49)
   - "She could hear the wind move through the tree tops like a long satisfied insuck of breath." (para. 108)
   - "the grandmother raised her head like a parched old turkey hen crying for water" (para. 133)

Choose three of these similes and explain how each comparison contributes to your ability to visualize the scene or character.

10. We stay close to the grandmother's point of view throughout most of the story. When does O'Connor move away from this perspective, and what effect does this have?

Suggestions for Writing

1. Write an essay in which you analyze three literary devices or techniques Flannery O'Connor uses to characterize both the grandmother and her attitudes toward other characters in the story. Be sure to include specific evidence from the story to support your analysis.

2. Discuss how O'Connor plays out her theme of the struggle between good and evil in the characters of the grandmother and The Misfit. Explore the ways that each of these characters embodies elements of both good and evil.

3. Although this story has some universal themes, it is very much a story about the South—its values, traditions, and culture. Write an essay explaining how this is a southern story.

4. Writing about violence in fiction, O'Connor claimed, "In my own stories I have found that violence is strangely capable of returning my characters to reality and preparing them to accept their moment of grace." Write an essay explaining whether you do or do not agree with this description as it applies to the grandmother, The Misfit, or both.

5. Write an essay offering two different interpretations of the ending of the story. Is it uplifting? cynical? bleak? hopeful? Have any of the characters been transformed? Then explain which of the interpretations you prefer. Include your understanding of The Misfit's final comment: "It's no real pleasure in life."

6. Write an essay that compares and contrasts the narrator in *Daisy Miller* with the narrator in "A Good Man Is Hard to Find." In your response, consider some or all of the following: how each narrator feels about the characters he or she is describing; which character(s) he or she is most sympathetic toward; how close (or distant) the narrator is from the action; how the storyteller hopes you, the reader, will respond; and why this particular voice has been chosen.

7. You are an up-and-coming screenwriter who wants to adapt "A Good Man Is Hard to Find" for the big screen. Write a one-page proposal persuading a producer that this movie's story and themes will appeal to a wide audience and be timely in the twenty-first century. Include suggestions for a director, a few members of the cast, and a filming location.

8. Imagine that you are June Star or John Wesley, telling a school friend about your grandmother. Write a one-page soliloquy in which you characterize (through ranting about, imitating, or telling a story about) the old woman. Look closely at the children's speech patterns, and try to use both the syntax and the language that either child would.

Everyday Use

ALICE WALKER

Alice Walker (b. 1944) is a novelist, poet, essayist, civil rights activist, and self-described eco-pacifist, best known for her depictions of the struggles and strengths of the African American woman. The youngest of eight children born to share-cropper parents, Walker grew up in the small town of Eatonton, Georgia. After high school, she attended Spelman College in Georgia, then transferred to Sarah Lawrence College in New York, which she graduated from in 1965. Her first novel, *The Third Life of Grange Copeland*, was published in 1969, followed by her poetry collection *Revolutionary Petunias and Other Poems* (1973). In 1982, she published *The Color Purple*, her most celebrated work, which won the Pulitzer Prize and was adapted into both a movie (directed by Steven Spielberg) and a Tony Award–winning Broadway musical. Walker is also known for her essays, in which she coined the term "womanist." Claiming a more positive connotation than "feminist," she writes that a womanist is "committed to survival and wholeness of entire people, male and female. Not a separatist." Walker has taught at Wellesley College, Yale University, the University of California at Berkeley, and many other institutions. She continues to support environmental causes and is an advocate for international women's rights. "Everyday Use," a story from her collection *In Love and Trouble: Stories of Black Women* (1973), explores how different definitions of heritage and history influence identity.

for your grandmama

I will wait for her in the yard that Maggie and I made so clean and wavy yester-day afternoon. A yard like this is more comfortable than most people know. It is not just a yard. It is like an extended living room. When the hard clay is swept clean as a floor and the fine sand around the edges lined with tiny, irregular grooves, anyone can come and sit and look up into the elm tree and wait for the breezes that never come inside the house.

Maggie will be nervous until after her sister goes: she will stand hopelessly in corners, homely and ashamed of the burn scars down her arms and legs, eying her sister with a mixture of envy and awe. She thinks her sister has held life always in the palm of one hand, that "no" is a word the world never learned to say to her.

You've no doubt seen those TV shows where the child who has "made it" is confronted, as a surprise, by her own mother and father, tottering in weakly from backstage. (A pleasant surprise, of course: What would they do if parent and child came on the show only to curse out and insult each other?) On TV mother and child embrace and smile into each other's faces. Sometimes the mother and father weep, the child wraps them in her arms and leans across the table to tell how she would not have made it without their help. I have seen these programs.

1226

Sometimes I dream a dream in which Dee and I are suddenly brought together on a TV program of this sort. Out of a dark and soft-seated limousine I am ushered into a bright room filled with many people. There I meet a smiling, gray, sporty man like Johnny Carson[1] who shakes my hand and tells me what a fine girl I have. Then we are on the stage and Dee is embracing me with tears in her eyes. She pins on my dress a large orchid, even though she has told me once that she thinks orchids are tacky flowers.

In real life I am a large, big-boned woman with rough, man-working hands. In the winter I wear flannel nightgowns to bed and overalls during the day. I can kill and clean a hog as mercilessly as a man. My fat keeps me hot in zero weather. I can work outside all day, breaking ice to get water for washing; I can eat pork liver cooked over the open fire minutes after it comes steaming from the hog. One winter I knocked a bull calf straight in the brain between the eyes with a sledge hammer and had the meat hung up to chill before nightfall. But of course all this does not show on television. I am the way my daughter would want me to be: a hundred pounds lighter, my skin like an uncooked barley pancake. My hair glistens in the hot bright lights. Johnny Carson has much to do to keep up with my quick and witty tongue.

But that is a mistake. I know even before I wake up. Who ever knew a Johnson with a quick tongue? Who can even imagine me looking a strange white man in the eye? It seems to me I have talked to them always with one foot raised in flight, with my head turned in whichever way is farthest from them. Dee, though. She would always look anyone in the eye. Hesitation was no part of her nature.

"How do I look, Mama?" Maggie says, showing just enough of her thin body enveloped in pink skirt and red blouse for me to know she's there, almost hidden by the door.

"Come out into the yard," I say.

Have you ever seen a lame animal, perhaps a dog run over by some careless person rich enough to own a car, sidle up to someone who is ignorant enough to be kind to him? That is the way my Maggie walks. She has been like this, chin on chest, eyes on ground, feet in shuffle, ever since the fire that burned the other house to the ground.

Dee is lighter than Maggie, with nicer hair and a fuller figure. She's a woman now, though sometimes I forget. How long ago was it that the other house burned? Ten, twelve years? Sometimes I can still hear the flames and feel Maggie's arms sticking to me, her hair smoking and her dress falling off her in little black papery flakes. Her eyes seemed stretched open, blazed open by the flames reflected in them. And Dee. I see her standing off under the sweet gum tree she used to dig gum out of; a look of concentration on her face as she watched the last dingy gray board of the house fall in toward the red-hot brick chimney. Why don't you do a dance around the ashes? I'd wanted to ask her. She had hated the house that much.

I used to think she hated Maggie, too. But that was before we raised the money, the church and me, to send her to Augusta to school. She used to read to us without

---

[1]Host of NBC's *The Tonight Show* from 1962 to 1992.—Eds.

pity; forcing words, lies, other folks' habits, whole lives upon us two, sitting trapped and ignorant underneath her voice. She washed us in a river of make-believe, burned us with a lot of knowledge we didn't necessarily need to know. Pressed us to her with the serious way she read, to shove us away at just the moment, like dimwits, we seemed about to understand.

Dee wanted nice things. A yellow organdy dress to wear to her graduation from high school; black pumps to match a green suit she'd made from an old suit somebody gave me. She was determined to stare down any disaster in her efforts. Her eyelids would not flicker for minutes at a time. Often I fought off the temptation to shake her. At sixteen she had a style of her own: and knew what style was.

I never had an education myself. After second grade the school was closed down. Don't ask me why: in 1927 colored asked fewer questions than they do now. Sometimes Maggie reads to me. She stumbles along good-naturedly but can't see well. She knows she is not bright. Like good looks and money, quickness passed her by. She will marry John Thomas (who has mossy teeth in an earnest face) and then I'll be free to sit here and I guess just sing church songs to myself. Although I never was a good singer. Never could carry a tune. I was always better at a man's job. I used to love to milk till I was hooked in the side in '49. Cows are soothing and slow and don't bother you, unless you try to milk them the wrong way.

I have deliberately turned my back on the house. It is three rooms, just like the one that burned, except the roof is tin; they don't make shingle roofs any more. There are no real windows, just some holes cut in the sides, like the portholes in a ship, but not round and not square, with rawhide holding the shutters up on the outside. This house is in a pasture, too, like the other one. No doubt when Dee sees it she will want to tear it down. She wrote me once that no matter where we "choose" to live, she will manage to come see us. But she will never bring her friends. Maggie and I thought about this and Maggie asked me, "Mama, when did Dee ever *have* any friends?"

She had a few. Furtive boys in pink shirts hanging about on washday after   15
school. Nervous girls who never laughed. Impressed with her they worshiped the well-turned phrase, the cute shape, the scalding humor that erupted like bubbles in lye. She read to them.

When she was courting Jimmy T she didn't have much time to pay to us, but turned all her faultfinding power on him. He *flew* to marry a cheap city girl from a family of ignorant flashy people. She hardly had time to recompose herself.

When she comes I will meet—but there they are!

Maggie attempts to make a dash for the house, in her shuffling way, but I stay her with my hand. "Come back here," I say. And she stops and tries to dig a well in the sand with her toe.

It is hard to see them clearly through the strong sun. But even the first glimpse of leg out of the car tells me it is Dee. Her feet were always neat-looking, as if God himself had shaped them with a certain style. From the other side of the car comes a short, stocky man. Hair is all over his head a foot long and hanging from his chin like a kinky mule tail. I hear Maggie suck in her breath. "Uhnnnh," is what it sounds like. Like when you see the wriggling end of a snake just in front of your foot on the road. "Uhnnnh."

Dee next. A dress down to the ground, in this hot weather. A dress so loud it hurts my eyes. There are yellows and oranges enough to throw back the light of the sun. I feel my whole face warming from the heat waves it throws out. Earrings gold, too, and hanging down to her shoulders. Bracelets dangling and making noises when she moves her arm up to shake the folds of the dress out of her armpits. The dress is loose and flows, and as she walks closer, I like it. I hear Maggie go "Uhnnnh" again. It is her sister's hair. It stands straight up like the wool on a sheep. It is black as night and around the edges are two long pigtails that rope about like small lizards disappearing behind her ears.

"Wa-su-zo-Tean-o!" she says, coming on in that gliding way the dress makes her move. The short stocky fellow with the hair to his navel is all grinning and he follows up with "Asalamalakim, my mother and sister!" He moves to hug Maggie but she falls back, right up against the back of my chair. I feel her trembling there and when I look up I see the perspiration falling off her chin.

"Don't get up," says Dee. Since I am stout it takes something of a push. You can see me trying to move a second or two before I make it. She turns, showing white heels through her sandals, and goes back to the car. Out she peeks next with a Polaroid. She stoops down quickly and lines up picture after picture of me sitting there in front of the house with Maggie cowering behind me. She never takes a shot without making sure the house is included. When a cow comes nibbling around the edge of the yard she snaps it and me and Maggie *and* the house. Then she puts the Polaroid in the back seat of the car, and comes up and kisses me on the forehead.

Meanwhile Asalamalakim is going through motions with Maggie's hand. Maggie's hand is as limp as a fish, and probably as cold, despite the sweat, and she keeps trying to pull it back. It looks like Asalamalakim wants to shake hands but wants to do it fancy. Or maybe he don't know how people shake hands. Anyhow, he soon gives up on Maggie.

"Well," I say. "Dee."

"No, Mama," she says. "Not 'Dee,' Wangero Leewanika Kemanjo!"

"What happened to 'Dee'?" I wanted to know.

"She's dead," Wangero said. "I couldn't bear it any longer, being named after the people who oppress me."

"You know as well as me you was named after your aunt Dicie," I said. Dicie is my sister. She named Dee. We called her "Big Dee" after Dee was born.

"But who was *she* named after?" asked Wangero.

"I guess after Grandma Dee," I said.

"And who was she named after?" asked Wangero.

"Her mother," I said, and saw Wangero was getting tired. "That's about as far back as I can trace it," I said. Though, in fact, I probably could have carried it back beyond the Civil War through the branches.

"Well," said Asalamalakim, "there you are."

"Uhnnnh," I heard Maggie say.

"There I was not," I said, "before 'Dicie' cropped up in our family, so why should   35
I try to trace it that far back?"

He just stood there grinning, looking down on me like somebody inspecting a
Model A car.[2] Every once in a while he and Wangero sent eye signals over my head.

"How do you pronounce this name?" I asked.

"You don't have to call me by it if you don't want to," said Wangero.

"Why shouldn't I?" I asked. "If that's what you want us to call you, we'll call
you."

"I know it might sound awkward at first," said Wangero.   40

"I'll get used to it," I said. "Ream it out again."

Well, soon we got the name out of the way. Asalamalakim had a name twice as
long and three times as hard. After I tripped over it two or three times he told me to
just call him Hakim-a-barber. I wanted to ask him was he a barber, but I didn't really
think he was, so I didn't ask.

"You must belong to those beef-cattle peoples down the road," I said. They said
"Asalamalakim" when they met you, too, but they didn't shake hands. Always too
busy: feeding the cattle, fixing the fences, putting up salt-lick shelters, throwing down
hay. When the white folks poisoned some of the herd the men stayed up all night
with rifles in their hands. I walked a mile and a half just to see the sight.

Hakim-a-barber said, "I accept some of their doctrines, but farming and raising
cattle is not my style." (They didn't tell me, and I didn't ask, whether Wangero [Dee]
had really gone and married him.)

We sat down to eat and right away he said he didn't eat collards and pork was   45
unclean. Wangero, though, went on through the chitlins and corn bread, the greens
and everything else. She talked a blue streak over the sweet potatoes. Everything
delighted her. Even the fact that we still used the benches her daddy made for the
table when we couldn't afford to buy chairs.

"Oh, Mama!" she cried. Then turned to Hakim-a-barber. "I never knew how
lovely these benches are. You can feel the rump prints," she said, running her hands
underneath her and along the bench. Then she gave a sigh and her hand closed
over Grandma Dee's butter dish. "That's it!" she said. "I knew there was something I
wanted to ask you if I could have." She jumped up from the table and went over in
the corner where the churn stood, the milk in it clabber by now. She looked at the
churn and looked at it.

"This churn top is what I need," she said. "Didn't Uncle Buddy whittle it out of
a tree you all used to have?"

"Yes," I said.

"Uh huh," she said happily. "And I want the dasher, too."

"Uncle Buddy whittle that, too?" asked the barber.   50

Dee (Wangero) looked up at me.

---

[2]The redesigned successor to the Ford Model T. — EDS.

"Aunt Dee's first husband whittled the dash," said Maggie so low you almost couldn't hear her. "His name was Henry, but they called him Stash."

"Maggie's brain is like an elephant's," Wangero said, laughing. "I can use the churn top as a centerpiece for the alcove table," she said, sliding a plate over the churn, "and I'll think of something artistic to do with the dasher."

When she finished wrapping the dasher the handle stuck out. I took it for a moment in my hands. You didn't even have to look close to see where hands pushing the dasher up and down to make butter had left a kind of sink in the wood. In fact, there were a lot of small sinks; you could see where thumbs and fingers had sunk into the wood. It was beautiful light yellow wood, from a tree that grew in the yard where Big Dee and Stash had lived.

After dinner Dee (Wangero) went to the trunk at the foot of my bed and started   55
rifling through it. Maggie hung back in the kitchen over the dishpan. Out came Wangero with two quilts. They had been pieced by Grandma Dee and then Big Dee and me had hung them on the quilt frames on the front porch and quilted them. One was in the Lone Star pattern. The other was Walk Around the Mountain. In both of them were scraps of dresses Grandma Dee had worn fifty and more years ago. Bits and pieces of Grandpa Jarrell's Paisley shirts. And one teeny faded blue piece, about the size of a penny matchbox, that was from Great Grandpa Ezra's uniform that he wore in the Civil War.

"Mama," Wangero said sweet as a bird. "Can I have these old quilts?"

I heard something fall in the kitchen, and a minute later the kitchen door slammed.

"Why don't you take one or two of the others?" I asked. "These old things was just done by me and Big Dee from some tops your grandma pieced before she died."

"No," said Wangero. "I don't want those. They are stitched around the borders by machine."

"That'll make them last better," I said.   60

"That's not the point," said Wangero. "These are all pieces of dresses Grandma used to wear. She did all this stitching by hand. Imagine!" She held the quilts securely in her arms, stroking them.

"Some of the pieces, like those lavender ones, come from old clothes her mother handed down to her," I said, moving up to touch the quilts. Dee (Wangero) moved back just enough so that I couldn't reach the quilts. They already belonged to her.

"Imagine!" she breathed again, clutching them closely to her bosom.

"The truth is," I said, "I promised to give them quilts to Maggie, for when she marries John Thomas."

She gasped like a bee had stung her.   65

"Maggie can't appreciate these quilts!" she said. "She'd probably be backward enough to put them to everyday use."

"I reckon she would," I said. "God knows I been saving 'em for long enough with nobody using 'em. I hope she will!" I didn't want to bring up how I had offered Dee (Wangero) a quilt when she went away to college. Then she had told me they were old-fashioned, out of style.

"But they're *priceless!*" she was saying now, furiously; for she has a temper. "Maggie would put them on the bed and in five years they'd be in rags. Less than that!"

"She can always make some more," I said. "Maggie knows how to quilt."

Dee (Wangero) looked at me with hatred. "You just will not understand. The point is these quilts, *these* quilts!"   70

"Well," I said, stumped. "What would *you* do with them?"

"Hang them," she said. As if that was the only thing you *could* do with quilts.

Maggie by now was standing in the door. I could almost hear the sound her feet made as they scraped over each other.

"She can have them, Mama," she said, like somebody used to never winning anything, or having anything reserved for her. "I can 'member Grandma Dee without the quilts."

I looked at her hard. She had filled her bottom lip with checkerberry snuff and it   75
gave her face a kind of dopey, hangdog look. It was Grandma Dee and Big Dee who taught her how to quilt herself. She stood there with her scarred hands hidden in the folds of her skirt. She looked at her sister with something like fear but she wasn't mad at her. This was Maggie's portion. This was the way she knew God to work.

When I looked at her like that something hit me in the top of my head and ran down to the soles of my feet. Just like when I'm in church and the spirit of God touches me and I get happy and shout. I did something I never had done before: hugged Maggie to me, then dragged her on into the room, snatched the quilts out of Miss Wangero's hands and dumped them into Maggie's lap. Maggie just sat there on my bed with her mouth open.

"Take one or two of the others," I said to Dee.

But she turned without a word and went out to Hakim-a-barber.

"You just don't understand," she said, as Maggie and I came out to the car.

"What don't I understand?" I wanted to know.   80

"Your heritage," she said. And then she turned to Maggie, kissed her, and said, "You ought to try to make something of yourself, too, Maggie. It's really a new day for us. But from the way you and Mama still live you'd never know it."

She put on some sunglasses that hid everything above the tip of her nose and her chin.

Maggie smiled; maybe at the sunglasses. But a real smile, not scared. After we watched the car dust settle I asked Maggie to bring me a dip of snuff. And then the two of us sat there just enjoying, until it was time to go in the house and go to bed.

[1973]

. . . .

Exploring the Text

1. This story boils down to one decision, one question: should Mama have given Dee the quilts she wanted? Cite passages from the story to support your viewpoint.
2. The two opening paragraphs, set off from the rest of the story, serve as a kind of exposition. What do these paragraphs tell you about Mama? How do they set up the conflicts explored in the rest of the story?

3. Mama recounts how she sometimes dreams about herself and Dee appearing in a heartwarming reunion on a television show. How accurate do you think Mama's dreams about being on television are? How do they prepare us as readers to meet Dee? Do they bias us against her? Explain.

4. The action of "Everyday Use" is quite contained: a visit back home for college-educated Dee. Yet Walker expects us to understand that action in a larger context. What information about the past does Walker incorporate into the story's present? How does it affect our understanding of, or attitude toward, the three central characters?

5. Dee brings home a young man who introduces himself with an Islamic greeting and whose appearance Walker reports only through Mama's eyes: "a short, stocky man" whose "hair is all over his head a foot long and hanging from his chin like a kinky mule tail" (para. 19). How does this minor character, referred to as "Hakim-a-barber," contribute to the development of the three central characters?

6. In many traditional African cultures, the tribe pools resources to finance the education of a promising young person, who is then expected to assist the community. How is this practice reflected in this southern small town? What does Dee's disregard of the current practice or its origin say about her?

7. In college, Dee came into contact with people and ideas quite different from those with which she grew up. What values does the "new Dee"—Wangero—claim to embrace? How do these values conflict with her family's values? How might the two value systems overlap or complement each other?

8. In the story, we gain information about the quilts—what they look like, who made them, how they are being used, different views on how they should be used. Like most symbols, the quilts have different meanings for different people. What do they symbolize to Dee? to Maggie? to Mama?

9. Where do you find irony in the story? How would you describe that irony: angry? gentle? playful? resigned? bitter? As you develop your response, consider whether you read the title as ironic.

10. Walker gives the storytelling to Mama. Why? How would the story have been different with an omniscient narrator? (Try describing Dee's entrance from a more objective viewpoint.) Explain whether you think Mama's narration is the most effective way to convey Walker's purpose.

Fenstad's Mother

CHARLES BAXTER

Charles Baxter was born in 1947 in Minneapolis, Minnesota. He received his BA from Macalester College and his PhD from the State University of New York at Buffalo. For many years he directed the creative writing program at the University of Michigan, and is currently teaching at the University of Minnesota. Baxter is the author of several story collections, including *Harmony of the World* (1984) and *Believers* (1997), and a number of novels, including *The Feast of Love* (2000), *Saul and Patsy* (2003), and *The Soul Thief* (2008). He is also the author of some of the most acclaimed contemporary essays on the subject of writing, many of which are collected in *Burning Down the House* (1997) and *The Art of Subtext: Beyond Plot* (2008). "Fenstad's Mother," which originally appeared in the *Atlantic Monthly*, was also published in both the 1989 edition of *The Best American Short Stories* and Baxter's collection *A Relative Stranger* (1990).

On Sunday morning after Communion Fenstad drove across town to visit his mother. Behind the wheel, he exhaled with his hand flat in front of his mouth to determine if the wine on his breath could be detected. He didn't think so. Fenstad's mother was a lifelong social progressive who was amused by her son's churchgoing, and, wine or no wine, she could guess where he had been. She had spent her life in the company of rebels and deviationists, and she recognized all their styles.

Passing a frozen pond in the city park, Fenstad slowed down to watch the skaters, many of whom he knew by name and skating style. From a distance they were dots of color ready for flight, frictionless. To express grief on skates seemed almost impossible, and Fenstad liked that. He parked his car on a residential block and took out his skates from the back seat, where he kept them all winter. With his fingertips he touched the wooden blade guards, thinking of the time. He checked his watch; he had fifteen minutes.

Out on the ice, still wearing his churchy Sunday-morning suit, tie, and overcoat, but now circling the outside edge of the pond with his bare hands in his overcoat pockets, Fenstad admired the overcast sky and luxuriated in the brittle cold. He was active and alert in winter but felt sleepy throughout the summer. He passed a little girl in a pink jacket, pushing a tiny chair over the ice. He waved to his friend Ann, an off-duty cop, practicing her twirls. He waved to other friends. Without exception they waved back. As usual, he was impressed by the way skates improved human character.

Twenty minutes later, in the doorway of her apartment, his mother said, "Your cheeks are red." She glanced down at his trousers, damp with melted snow. "You've been skating." She kissed him on the cheek and turned to walk into her living room. "Skating after church? Isn't that some sort of error?"

"It's just happiness," Fenstad said. Quickly he checked her apartment for any signs of memory loss or depression. He found none and immediately felt relief. The apartment smelled of soap and Lysol, the signs of an old woman who wouldn't tolerate nonsense. Out on her coffee table, as usual, were the letters she was writing to her congressman and to political dictators around the globe. Fenstad's mother pleaded for enlightened behavior and berated the dictators for their bad political habits.

She grasped the arm of the sofa and let herself down slowly. Only then did she smile. "How's your soul, Harry?" she asked. "What's the news?"

He smiled back and smoothed his hair. Martin Luther King's eyes locked into his from the framed picture on the wall opposite him. In the picture King was shaking hands with Fenstad's mother, the two of them surrounded by smiling faces. "My soul's okay, Ma," he said. "It's a hard project. I'm always working on it." He reached down for a chocolate-chunk cookie from a box on top of the television. "Who brought you these?"

"Your daughter Sharon. She came to see me on Friday." Fenstad's mother tilted her head at him. "You *want* to be a good person, but she's the real article. Goodness comes to her without any effort at all. She says you have a new girlfriend. A pharmacist this time. Susan, is it?" Fenstad nodded. "Harry, why does your generation always have to find the right person? Why can't you learn to live with the wrong person? Sooner or later everyone's wrong. Love isn't the most important thing, Harry, far from it. Why can't you see that? I still don't comprehend why you couldn't live with Eleanor." Eleanor was Fenstad's ex-wife. They had been divorced for a decade, but Fenstad's mother hoped for a reconciliation.

"Come on, Ma," Fenstad said. "Over and done with, gone and gone." He took another cookie.

"You live with somebody so that you're living with *somebody,* and then you go out and do the work of the world. I don't understand all this pickiness about lovers. In a pinch anybody'll do, Harry, believe me." 10

On the side table was a picture of her late husband, Fenstad's mild, middle-of-the-road father. Fenstad glanced at the picture and let the silence hang between them before asking, "How are you, Ma?"

"I'm all right." She leaned back in the sofa, whose springs made a strange, almost human groan. "I want to get out. I spend too much time in this place in January. You should expand my horizons. Take me somewhere."

"Come to my composition class," Fenstad said. "I'll pick you up at dinnertime on Tuesday. Eat early."

"They'll notice me," she said, squinting. "I'm too old."

"I'll introduce you," her son said. "You'll fit right in." 15

Fenstad wrote brochures in the publicity department of a computer company during the day, and taught an extension English-composition class at the downtown campus of the state university two nights a week. He didn't need the money; he taught the class because he liked teaching strangers and because he enjoyed the sense of hope that classrooms held for him. This hopefulness and didacticism he had picked up from his mother.

On Tuesday night she was standing at the door of the retirement apartment building, dressed in a dark blue overcoat—her best. Her stylishness was belied slightly by a pair of old fuzzy red earmuffs. Inside the car Fenstad noticed that she had put on perfume, unusual for her. Leaning back, she gazed out contentedly at the nighttime lights.

"Who's in this group of students?" she asked. "Working-class people, I hope. Those are the ones you should be teaching. Anything else is just a career."

"Oh, they work, all right." He looked at his mother and saw, as they passed under a streetlight, a combination of sadness and delicacy in her face. Her usual mask of tough optimism seemed to be deserting her. He braked at a red light and said, "I have a hairdresser and a garage mechanic and a housewife, a Mrs. Nelson, and three guys who're sanitation workers. Plenty of others. One guy you'll really like is a young black man with glasses who sits in the back row and reads *Workers' Vanguard* and Bakunin during class. He's brilliant. I don't know why he didn't test out of this class. His name's York Follette, and he's—"

"I want to meet him," she said quickly. She scowled at the moonlit snow. "A man   20
with ideas. People like that have gone out of my life." She looked over at her son. "What I hate about being my age is how *nice* everyone tries to be. I was never nice, but now everybody is pelting me with sugar cubes." She opened her window an inch and let the cold air blow over her, ruffling her stiff gray hair.

When they arrived at the school, snow had started to fall, and at the other end of the parking lot a police car's flashing light beamed long crimson rays through the dense flakes. Fenstad's mother walked deliberately toward the door, shaking her head mistrustfully at the building and the police. Approaching the steps, she took her son's hand. "I liked the columns on the old buildings," she said, "the old university build-ings, I mean. I liked Greek Revival better than this Modernist-bunker stuff." Inside, she blinked in the light at the smooth, waxed linoleum floors and cement-block walls. She held up her hand to shade her eyes. Fenstad took her elbow to guide her over the snow melting in puddles in the entryway. "I never asked you what you're teaching tonight."

"Logic," Fenstad said.

"Ah." She smiled and nodded. "Dialectics!"

"Not quite. Just logic."

She shrugged. She was looking at the clumps of students standing in the glare of   25
the hallway, drinking coffee from paper cups and smoking cigarettes in the general conversational din. She wasn't used to such noise: she stopped in the middle of the corridor underneath a wall clock and stared happily in no particular direction. With her eyes shut she breathed in the close air, smelling of wet overcoats and smoke, and Fenstad remembered how much his mother had always liked smoke-filled rooms, where ideas fought each other, and where some of those ideas died.

"Come on," he said, taking her hand again. Inside Fenstad's classroom six people sat in the angular postures of pre-boredom. York Follette was already in the back row, his copy of *Workers' Vanguard* shielding his face. Fenstad's mother headed straight for him and sat down in the desk next to his. Fenstad saw them shake hands, and in two minutes they were talking in low, rushed murmurs. He saw York Follette laugh quietly and nod. What was it that blacks saw and appreciated in his mother? They had always liked her—written to her, called her, checked up on her—and Fenstad wondered if they recognized something in his mother that he himself had never been able to see.

At 7:35 most of the students had arrived and were talking to each other vigor-ously, as if they didn't want Fenstad to start and thought they could delay him. He stared at them, and when they wouldn't quiet down, he made himself rigid and said,

"Good evening. We have a guest tonight." Immediately the class grew silent. He held his arm out straight, indicating with a flick of his hand the old woman in the back row. "My mother," he said. "Clara Fenstad." For the first time all semester his students appeared to be paying attention: they turned around collectively and looked at Fenstad's mother, who smiled and waved. A few of the students began to applaud; others joined in. The applause was quiet but apparently genuine. Fenstad's mother brought herself slowly to her feet and made a suggestion of a bow. Two of the students sitting in front of her turned around and began to talk to her. At the front of the class Fenstad started his lecture on logic, but his mother wouldn't quiet down. This was a class for adults. They were free to do as they liked.

Lowering his head and facing the blackboard, Fenstad reviewed problems in logic, following point by point the outline set down by the textbook: *post hoc* fallacies, false authorities, begging the question, circular reasoning, *ad hominem* arguments, all the rest. Explaining these problems, his back turned, he heard sighs of boredom, boldly expressed. Occasionally he glanced at the back of the room. His mother was watching him carefully, and her face was expressing all the complexity of dismay. Dismay radiated from her. Her disappointment wasn't personal, because his mother didn't think that people as individuals were at fault for what they did. As usual, her disappointed hope was located in history and in the way people agreed with already existing histories.

She was angry with him for collaborating with grammar. She would call it unconsciously installed authority. Then she would find other names for it.

"All right," he said loudly, trying to make eye contact with someone in the room   30
besides his mother, "let's try some examples. Can anyone tell me what, if anything, is wrong with the following sentence? 'I, like most people, have a unique problem.'"

The three sanitation workers, in the third row, began to laugh. Fenstad caught himself glowering and singled out the middle one.

"Yes, it is funny, isn't it?"

The man in the middle smirked and looked at the floor. "I was just thinking of my unique problem."

"Right," Fenstad said. "But what's wrong with saying, 'I, like most people, have a unique problem'?"

"Solving it?" This was Mrs. Nelson, who sat by the window so that she could   35
gaze at the tree outside, lit by a streetlight. All through class she looked at the tree as if it were a lover.

"Solving what?"

"Solving the problem you have. What is the problem?"

"That's actually not what I'm getting at," Fenstad said. "Although it's a good *related* point. I'm asking what might be wrong logically with that sentence."

"It depends," Harold Ronson said. He worked in a service station and sometimes came to class wearing his work shirt with his name tag, HAROLD, stitched into it. "It depends on what your problem is. You haven't told us your problem."

"No," Fenstad said, "my problem is *not* the problem." He thought of Alice in   40
Wonderland and felt, physically, as if he himself were getting small. "Let's try this again. What might be wrong with saying that most people have a unique problem?"

"You shouldn't be so critical," Timothy Melville said. "You should look on the bright side, if possible."

"What?"

"He's right," Mrs. Nelson said. "Most people have unique problems, but many people do their best to help themselves, such as taking night classes or working at meditation."

"No doubt that's true," Fenstad said. "But why can't most people have a unique problem?"

"Oh, I disagree," Mrs. Nelson said, still looking at her tree. Fenstad glanced at it   45
and saw that it was crested with snow. It *was* beautiful. No wonder she looked at it. "I believe that most people do have unique problems. They just shouldn't talk about them all the time."

"Can anyone," Fenstad asked, looking at the back wall and hoping to see something there that was not wall, "can anyone give me an example of a unique problem?"

"Divorce," Barb Kjellerud said. She sat near the door and knitted during class. She answered questions without looking up. "Divorce is unique."

"No, it isn't!" Fenstad said, failing in the crucial moment to control his voice. He and his mother exchanged glances. In his mother's face for a split second was the history of her compassionate, ambivalent attention to him. "Divorce is not unique." He waited to calm himself. "It's everywhere. Now try again. Give me a unique problem."

Silence. "This is a trick question," Arlene Hubbly said. "I'm sure it's a trick question."

"Not necessarily. Does anyone know what *unique* means?"   50

"One of a kind," York Follette said, gazing at Fenstad with dry amusement. Sometimes he took pity on Fenstad and helped him out of jams. Fenstad's mother smiled and nodded.

"Right," Fenstad crowed, racing toward the blackboard as if he were about to write something. "So let's try again. Give me a unique problem."

"You give *us* a unique problem," one of the sanitation workers said. Fenstad didn't know whether he'd been given a statement or a command. He decided to treat it as a command.

"All right," he said. He stopped and looked down at his shoes. Maybe it *was* a trick question. He thought for ten seconds. Problem after problem presented itself to him. He thought of poverty, of the assaults on the earth, of the awful complexities of love. "I can't think of one," Fenstad said. His hands went into his pockets.

"That's because problems aren't personal," Fenstad's mother said from the back   55
of the room. "They're collective." She waited while several students in the class sat up and nodded. "And people must work together on their solutions." She talked for another two minutes, taking the subject out of logic and putting it neatly in politics, where she knew it belonged.

The snow had stopped by the time the class was over. Fenstad took his mother's arm and escorted her to the car. After letting her down on the passenger side and starting the engine, he began to clear the front windshield. He didn't have a scraper and had forgotten his gloves, so he was using his bare hands. When he brushed the snow away on his mother's side, she looked out at him, surprised, a terribly aged Sleeping Beauty awakened against her will.

Once the car had warmed up, she was in a gruff mood and repositioned herself under the seat belt while making quiet but aggressive remarks. The sight of the new snow didn't seem to calm her. "Logic," she said at last. "That wasn't logic. Those are just rhetorical tactics. It's filler and drudgery."

"I don't want to discuss it now."

"All right. I'm sorry. Let's talk about something more pleasant."

They rode together in silence. Then she began to shake her head. "Don't take me home," she said. "I want to have a spot of tea somewhere before I go back. A nice place where they serve tea, all right?"

He parked outside an all-night restaurant with huge front plate-glass windows; it was called Country Bob's. He held his mother's elbow from the car to the door. At the door, looking back to make sure that he had turned off his headlights, he saw his tracks and his mother's in the snow. His were separate footprints, but hers formed two long lines.

Inside, at the table, she sipped her tea and gazed at her son for a long time. "Thanks for the adventure, Harry, I do appreciate it. What're you doing in class next week? Oh, I remember. How-to papers. That should be interesting."

"Want to come?"

"Very much. I'll keep quiet next time, if you want me to."

Fenstad shook his head. "It's okay. It's fun having you along. You can say whatever you want. The students loved you. I knew you'd be a sensation, and you were. They'd probably rather have you teaching the class than me."

He noticed that his mother was watching something going on behind him, and Fenstad turned around in the booth so that he could see what it was. At first all he saw was a woman, a young woman with long hair wet from snow and hanging in clumps, talking in the aisle to two young men, both of whom were nodding at her. Then she moved on to the next table. She spoke softly. Fenstad couldn't hear her words, but he saw the solitary customer to whom she was speaking shake his head once, keeping his eyes down. Then the woman saw Fenstad and his mother. In a moment she was standing in front of them.

She wore two green plaid flannel shirts and a thin torn jacket. Like Fenstad, she wore no gloves. Her jeans were patched, and she gave off a strong smell, something like hay, Fenstad thought, mixed with tar and sweat. He looked down at her feet and saw that she was wearing penny loafers with no socks. Coins, old pennies, were in both shoes; the leather was wet and cracked. He looked in the woman's face. Under a hat that seemed to collapse on either side of her head, the woman's face was thin and chalk-white except for the fatigue lines under her eyes. The eyes themselves were bright blue, beautiful, and crazy. To Fenstad, she looked desperate, percolating slightly with insanity, and he was about to say so to his mother when the woman bent down toward him and said, "Mister, can you spare any money?"

60

65

Involuntarily, Fenstad looked toward the kitchen, hoping that the manager would spot this person and take her away. When he looked back again, his mother was taking her blue coat off, wriggling in the booth to free her arms from the sleeves. Stopping and starting again, she appeared to be stuck inside the coat; then she lifted herself up, trying to stand, and with a quick, quiet groan slipped the coat off. She reached down and folded the coat over and held it toward the woman. "Here," she said. "Here's my coat. Take it before my son stops me."

"Mother, you can't." Fenstad reached forward to grab the coat, but his mother pulled it away from him.

When Fenstad looked back at the woman, her mouth was open, showing several 70 gray teeth. Her hands were outstretched, and he understood, after a moment, that this was a posture of refusal, a gesture saying no, and that the woman wasn't used to it and did it awkwardly. Fenstad's mother was standing and trying to push the coat toward the woman, not toward her hands but lower, at waist level, and she was saying, "Here, here, here, here." The sound, like a human birdcall, frightened Fenstad, and he stood up quickly, reached for his wallet, and removed the first two bills he could find, two twenties. He grabbed the woman's chapped, ungloved left hand.

"Take these," he said, putting the two bills in her icy palm, "for the love of God, and please go."

He was close to her face. Tonight he would pray for her. For a moment the woman's expression was vacant. His mother was still pushing the coat at her, and the woman was unsteadily bracing herself. The woman's mouth was open, and her stagnant-water breath washed over him. "I know you," she said. "You're my little baby cousin."

"Go away, please," Fenstad said. He pushed at her. She turned, clutching his money. He reached around to put his hands on his mother's shoulders. "Ma," he said, "she's gone now. Mother, sit down. I gave her money for a coat." His mother fell down on her side of the booth, and her blue coat rolled over on the bench beside her, showing the label and the shiny inner lining. When he looked up, the woman who had been begging had disappeared, though he could still smell her odor, an essence of wretchedness.

"Excuse me, Harry," his mother said. "I have to go to the bathroom."

She rose and walked toward the front of the restaurant, turned a corner, and 75 was out of sight. Fenstad sat and tried to collect himself. When the waiter came, a boy with an earring and red hair in a flattop, Fenstad just shook his head and said, "More tea." He realized that his mother hadn't taken off her earmuffs, and the image of his mother in the ladies' room with her earmuffs on gave him a fit of uneasiness. After getting up from the booth and following the path that his mother had taken, he stood outside the ladies'-room door and, when no one came in or out, he knocked. He waited for a decent interval. Still hearing no answer, he opened the door.

His mother was standing with her arms down on either side of the first sink. She was holding herself there, her eyes following the hot water as it poured from the tap around the bright porcelain sink down into the drain, and she looked furious. Fenstad touched her and she snapped toward him.

"Your logic!" she said.

He opened the door for her and helped her back to the booth. The second cup of tea had been served, and Fenstad's mother sipped it in silence. They did not converse. When she had finished, she said, "All right. I do feel better now. Let's go."

At the curb in front of her apartment building he leaned forward and kissed her on the cheek. "Pick me up next Tuesday," she said. "I want to go back to that class." He nodded. He watched as she made her way past the security guard at the front desk; then he put his car into drive and started home.

That night he skated in the dark for an hour with his friend, Susan, the phar- 80 macist. She was an excellent skater; they had met on the ice. She kept late hours and, like Fenstad, enjoyed skating at night. She listened attentively to his story about his mother and the woman in the restaurant. To his great relief she recommended no course of action. She listened. She didn't believe in giving advice, even when asked.

The following Tuesday, Fenstad's mother was again in the back row next to York Follette. One of the fluorescent lights overhead was flickering, which gave the room, Fenstad thought, a sinister quality, like a debtors' prison or a refuge for the homeless. He'd been thinking about such people for the entire week. For seven days now he had caught whiffs of the woman's breath in the air, and one morning, Friday, he thought he caught a touch of the rotten-celery smell on his own breath, after a particularly difficult sales meeting.

Tonight was how-to night. The students were expected to stand at the front of the class and read their papers, instructing their peers and answering questions if neces- sary. Starting off, and reading her paper in a frightened monotone, Mrs. Nelson told the class how to bake a cheese souffle. Arlene Hubbly's paper was about mushroom hunting. Fenstad was put off by the introduction. "The advantage to mushrooms," Arlene Hubbly read, "is that they are delicious. The disadvantage to mushrooms is that they can make you sick, even die." But then she explained how to recognize the common shaggymane by its cylindrical cap and dark tufts; she drew a model on the board. She warned the class against the *Clitocybe illudens*, the Jack-o'-Lantern. "Never eat a mushroom like this one or *any* mushroom that glows in the dark. Take heed!" she said, fixing her gaze on the class. Fenstad saw his mother taking rapid notes. Harold Ronson, the mechanic, reading his own prose painfully and slowly, told the class how to get rust spots out of their automobiles. Again Fenstad noticed his mother taking notes. York Follette told the class about the proper procedures for laying down attic insulation and how to know when enough was enough, so that a homeowner wouldn't be robbed blind, as he put it, by the salesmen, in whose ranks he had once counted himself.

Barb Kjellerud had brought along a cassette player, and told the class that her hobby was ballroom dancing; she would instruct them in the basic waltz. She pushed the play button on the tape machine, and "Tales from the Vienna Woods" came boom- ing out. To the accompaniment of the music she read her paper, illustrating, as she went, how the steps were to be performed. She danced alone in front of them, doing so with flair. Her blonde hair swayed as she danced, Fenstad noticed. She looked a bit like a contestant in a beauty contest who had too much personality to win. She explained to the men the necessity of leading. Someone had to lead, she said, and tradition had given this responsibility to the male. Fenstad heard his mother snicker.

When Barb Kjellerud asked for volunteers, Fenstad's mother raised her hand. She said she knew how to waltz and would help out. At the front of the class she made a counterclockwise motion with her hand, and for the next minute, sitting at the back of the room, Fenstad watched his mother and one of the sanitation workers waltzing under the flickering fluorescent lights.

"What a wonderful class," Fenstad's mother said on the way home. "I hope you're 85 paying attention to what they tell you."

Fenstad nodded. "Tea?" he asked.

She shook her head. "Where're you going after you drop me off?"

"Skating," he said. "I usually go skating. I have a date."

"With the pharmacist? In the dark?"

"We both like it, Ma." As he drove, he made an all-purpose gesture. "The moon 90 and the stars," he said simply.

When he left her off, he felt unsettled. He considered, as a point of courtesy, staying with her a few minutes, but by the time he had this idea he was already away from the building and was headed down the street.

He and Susan were out on the ice together, skating in large circles, when Susan pointed to a solitary figure sitting on a park bench near the lake's edge. The sky had cleared; the moon gave everything a cold, fine-edged clarity. When Fenstad followed the line of Susan's finger, he saw at once that the figure on the bench was his mother. He realized it simply because of the way she sat there, drawn into herself, attentive even in the winter dark. He skated through the uncleared snow over the ice until he was standing close enough to speak to her. "Mother," he said, "what are you doing here?"

She was bundled up, a thick woolen cap drawn over her head, and two scarves covering much of her face. He could see little other than the two lenses of her glasses facing him in the dark. "I wanted to see you two," she told him.

"I thought you'd look happy, and you did. I like to watch happiness. I always have."

"How can you see us? We're so far away." 95

"That's how I saw you."

This made no sense to him, so he asked, "How'd you get here?"

"I took a cab. That part was easy."

"Aren't you freezing?"

"I don't know. I don't know if I'm freezing or not." 100

He and Susan took her back to her apartment as soon as they could get their boots on. In the car Mrs. Fenstad insisted on asking Susan what kind of safety procedures were used to ensure that drugs weren't smuggled out of pharmacies and sold illegally, but she didn't appear to listen to the answer, and by the time they reached her building, she seemed to be falling asleep. They helped her up to her apartment. Susan thought that they should give her a warm bath before putting her into bed, and, together, they did. She did not protest. She didn't even seem to notice them as they guided her in and out of the bathtub.

Fenstad feared that his mother would catch some lung infection, and it turned out to be bronchitis, which kept her in her apartment for the first three weeks of February, until her cough went down. Fenstad came by every other day to see how she was, and one Tuesday, after work, he went up to her floor and heard piano music: an old recording, which sounded much played, of the brightest and fastest jazz piano he had ever heard—music of superhuman brilliance. He swung open the door to her apartment and saw York Follette sitting near his mother's bed. On the bedside table was a small tape player, from which the music poured into the room.

Fenstad's mother was leaning back against the pillow, smiling, her eyes closed.

Follette turned toward Fenstad. He had been talking softly. He motioned toward the tape machine and said, "Art Tatum. It's a cut called 'Battery Bounce.' Your mother's never heard it."

"Jazz, Harry," Fenstad's mother said, her eyes still closed, not needing to see her   105
son. "York is explaining to me about Art Tatum and jazz. Next week he's going to try something more progressive on me." Now his mother opened her eyes. "Have you ever heard such music before, Harry?"

They were both looking at him. "No," he said, "I never heard anything like it."

"This is my unique problem, Harry." Fenstad's mother coughed and then waited to recover her breath. "I never heard enough jazz." She smiled. "What glimpses!" she said at last.

After she recovered, he often found her listening to the tape machine that York Follette had given her. She liked to hear the Oscar Peterson Trio as the sun set and the lights of evening came on. She now often mentioned glimpses. Back at home, every night, Fenstad spoke about his mother in his prayers of remembrance and thanksgiving, even though he knew she would disapprove.

[1988]

. . . .

Exploring the Text

1. How does the first paragraph of "Fenstad's Mother" set up expectations about Fenstad and his mother? Are those expectations fulfilled or reversed over the course of the story?
2. What does it tell us about Fenstad that he loves to ice-skate at night? How does that hobby develop his character? How else does Baxter sketch Fenstad's character?
3. How does Baxter create the character of Fenstad's mother? Pay close attention to what she learns during the course of the story.
4. It is easy to read this story as binary: Fenstad is traditional; his mother is progressive. How does Baxter make it more complex than that?
5. Why is Fenstad such an ineffective teacher? Why does the class warm to his mother so quickly? What does his mother mean when she says, "I hope you're paying attention to what they tell you" (para. 85)?
6. In an essay entitled "Against Epiphanies," Baxter warns against "conclusive insight." He was criticizing a tendency in modern fiction to depend on one enlightening

moment to provide meaning. How does he illustrate his philosophy in "Fenstad's Mother"?

7. With which character do you sympathize—Fenstad or his mother? Explain your answer.

The Free Radio

SALMAN RUSHDIE

Born in 1947, raised in Bombay (now Mumbai), and educated at Cambridge, Salman Rushdie achieved fame with his second novel, *Midnight's Children* (1981), which won the Man Booker Prize. Rushdie's life changed forever after the publication of his novel *The Satanic Verses* (1988); some considered the book to be blasphemous against Islam, and the ultraorthodox leadership of Iran issued a *fatwa*—a death sentence—against Rushdie. Assassination threats and attempts forced the author into hiding for nearly ten years. While underground in England, Rushdie continued to write and publish a half dozen books of fiction and non-fiction, as well as numerous essays and a stage adaptation of his children's book, *Haroun and the Sea of Stories*. In 2007, he was knighted by Queen Elizabeth II. Rushdie's most recent novel is *The Enchantress of Florence* (2008), and he is currently a distinguished writer-in-residence at Emory University. "The Free Radio" comes from Rushdie's 1995 collection *East, West,* whose nine stories are divided into three setting-based sections: East, West, and East West (the latter of which features Eastern expatriates living in the West). "The Free Radio" appears in the East section of the book.

We all knew nothing good would happen to him while the thief's widow had her claws dug into his flesh, but the boy was an innocent, a real donkey's child, you can't teach such people.

That boy could have had a good life. God had blessed him with God's own looks, and his father had gone to the grave for him, but didn't he leave the boy a brand-new first-class cycle rickshaw with plastic covered seats and all? So: looks he had, his own trade he had, there would have been a good wife in time, he should just have taken out some years to save some rupees; but no, he must fall for a thief's widow before the hairs had time to come out on his chin, before his milk-teeth had split, one might say.

We felt bad for him, but who listens to the wisdom of the old today?

I say: who listens?

Exactly; nobody, certainly not a stone-head like Ramani the rickshaw-wallah. 5
But I blame the widow. I saw it happen, you know, I saw most of it until I couldn't stand any more. I sat under this very banyan, smoking this selfsame hookah, and not much escaped my notice.

And at one time I tried to save him from his fate, but it was no go . . .

The widow was certainly attractive, no point denying, in a sort of hard vicious way she was all right, but it is her mentality that was rotten. Ten years older than Ramani she must have been, five children alive and two dead, what that thief did besides robbing and making babies God only knows, but he left her not one new paisa,[1] so of course she would be interested in Ramani. I'm not saying a rickshaw-wallah makes much in this town but two mouthfuls are better to eat than wind. And not many people will look twice at the widow of a good-for-nothing.

They met right here.

One day Ramani rode into town without a passenger, but grinning as usual as if someone had given him a ten-chip tip, singing some playback music from the radio, his hair greased like for a wedding. He was not such a fool that he didn't know how the girls watched him all the time and passed remarks about his long and well-muscled legs.

The thief's widow had gone to the bania[2] shop to buy some three grains of dal[3] and   10
I won't say where the money came from, but people saw men at night near her rutputty shack, even the bania himself they were telling me but I personally will not comment.

She had all her five brats with her and then and there, cool as a fan, she called out: 'Hey Rickshaaa!' Loud, you know, like a truly cheap type. Showing us she can afford to ride in rickshaws, as if anyone was interested. Her children must have gone hungry to pay for the ride but in my opinion it was an investment for her, because must-be she had decided already to put her hooks into Ramani. So they all poured into the rickshaw and he took her away, and with the five kiddies as well as the widow there was quite a weight, so he was puffing hard, and the veins were standing out on his legs, and I thought, careful, my son, or you will have this burden to pull for all of your life.

But after that Ramani and the thief's widow were seen everywhere, shamelessly, in public places, and I was glad his mother was dead because if she had lived to see this her face would have fallen off from shame.

Sometimes in those days Ramani came into this street in the evenings to meet some friends, and they thought they were very smart because they would go into the back room of the Irani's canteen and drink illegal liquor, only of course everybody knew, but who would do anything, if boys ruin their lives let their relations worry.

I was sad to see Ramani fall into this bad company. His parents were known to me when alive. But when I told Ramani to keep away from those hot-shots he grinned like a sheep and said I was wrong, nothing bad was taking place.

Let it go, I thought.   15

I knew those cronies of his. They all wore the armbands of the new Youth Movement. This was the time of the State of Emergency,[4] and these friends were not

---

[1]Indian coin of little value (about 1/100th of a rupee). — Eds.
[2]Hindi term for trader or merchant. — Eds.
[3]Legumes, often lentils. — Eds.
[4]For almost two years (1975–1977), following a disputed election and the resulting unrest, civil liberties and elections were suspended in India, and the government ruled by decree. — Eds.

peaceful persons, there were stories of beatings-up, so I sat quiet under my tree. Ramani wore no armband but he went with them because they impressed him, the fool.

These armband youths were always flattering Ramani. Such a handsome chap, they told him, compared to you Shashi Kapoor and Amitabh are like lepers only, you should go to Bombay and be put in the motion pictures.

They flattered him with dreams because they knew they could take money from him at cards and he would buy them drink while they did it, though he was no richer than they. So now Ramani's head became filled with these movie dreams, because there was nothing else inside to take up any space, and this is another reason why I blame the widow woman, because she had more years and should have had more sense. In two ticks she could have made him forget all about it, but no, I heard her telling him one day for all to hear, 'Truly you have the looks of Lord Krishna himself, except you are not blue all over.' In the street! So all would know they were lovers! From that day on I was sure a disaster would happen.

The next time the thief's widow came into the street to visit the bania shop I decided to act. Not for my own sake but for the boy's dead parents I risked being shamed by a . . . no, I will not call her the name, she is elsewhere now and they will know what she is like.

'Thief's widow!' I called out.   20

She stopped dead, jerking her face in an ugly way, as if I had hit her with a whip.

'Come here and speak,' I told her.

Now she could not refuse because I am not without importance in the town and maybe she calculated that if people saw us talking they would stop ignoring her when she passed, so she came as I knew she would.

'I have to say this thing only,' I told her with dignity. 'Ramani the rickshaw boy is dear to me, and you must find some person of your own age, or, better still, go to the widows' ashrams[5] in Benares and spend the rest of your life there in holy prayer, thanking God that widow-burning is now illegal.'

So at this point she tried to shame me by screaming out and calling me curses and   25
saying that I was a poisonous old man who should have died years ago, and then she said, 'Let me tell you, mister teacher sahib *retired*, that your Ramani has asked to marry me and I have said no, because I wish no more children, and he is a young man and should have his own. So tell that to the whole world and stop your cobra poison.'

For a time after that I closed my eyes to this affair of Ramani and the thief's widow, because I had done all I could and there were many other things in the town to interest a person like myself. For instance, the local health officer had brought a big white caravan into the street and was given permission to park it out of the way under the banyan tree; and every night men were taken into this van for a while and things were done to them.

___

[5]Secluded religious communities.—EDS.

I did not care to be in the vicinity at these times, because the youths with arm-bands were always in attendance, so I took my hookah and sat in another place. I heard rumours of what was happening in the caravan but I closed my ears.

But it was while this caravan, which smelled of ether, was in town that the extent of the widow's wickedness became plain; because at this time Ramani suddenly began to talk about his new fantasy, telling everyone he could find that very shortly he was to receive a highly special and personalised gift from the Central Government in Delhi itself, and this gift was to be a brand-new first-class battery-operated transistor radio.

Now then: we had always believed that our Ramani was a little soft in the head, with his notions of being a film star and what all; so most of us just nodded tolerantly and said, 'Yes, Ram, that is nice for you,' and, 'What a fine, generous Government it is that gives radios to persons who are so keen on popular music.'

But Ramani insisted it was true, and seemed happier than at any time in his life, a hap-   30
piness which could not be explained simply by the supposed imminence of the transistor.

Soon after the dream-radio was first mentioned, Ramani and the thief's widow were married, and then I understood everything. I did not attend the nuptials — it was a poor affair by all accounts — but not long afterwards I spoke to Ram when he came past the banyan with an empty rickshaw one day.

He came to sit by me and I asked, 'My child, did you go to the caravan? What have you let them do to you?'

'Don't worry,' he replied. 'Everything is tremendously wonderful. I am in love, teacher sahib, and I have made it possible for me to marry my woman.'

I confess I became angry; indeed, I almost wept as I realised that Ramani had gone voluntarily to subject himself to a humiliation which was being forced upon the other men who were taken to the caravan. I reproved him bitterly. 'My idiot child, you have let that woman deprive you of your manhood!'

'It is not so bad,' Ram said, meaning the *nasbandi*.[6] It does not stop lovemaking   35
or anything, excuse me, teacher sahib, for speaking of such a thing. It stops babies only and my woman did not want children any more, so now all is hundred per cent OK. Also it is in national interest,' he pointed out. 'And soon the free radio will arrive.'

'The free radio,' I repeated.

'Yes, remember, teacher sahib,' Ram said confidentially, 'some years back, in my kiddie days, when Laxman the tailor had this operation? In no time the radio came and from all over town people gathered to listen to it. It is how the Government says thank you. It will be excellent to have.'

'Go away, get away from me,' I cried out in despair, and did not have the heart to tell him what everyone else in the country already knew, which was that the free radio scheme was a dead duck, long gone, long forgotten. It had been over — *funtoosh!* — for years.

After these events the thief's widow, who was now Ram's wife, did not come into town very often, no doubt being too ashamed of what she had made him do, but

---

[6]Vasectomy. — EDS.

Ramani worked longer hours than ever before, and every time he saw any of the dozens of people he'd told about the radio he would put one hand up to his ear as if he were already holding the blasted machine in it, and he would mimic broadcasts with a certain energetic skill.

'*Yé Akashvani hai*,' he announced to the streets. 'This is All-India Radio. Here is the news. A Government spokesman today announced that Ramani rickshaw-wallah's radio was on its way and would be delivered at any moment. And now some playback music.' After which he would sing songs by Asha Bhonsle or Lata Mangeshkar in a high, ridiculous falsetto. 40

Ram always had the rare quality of total belief in his dreams, and there were times when his faith in the imaginary radio almost took us in, so that we half-believed it was really on its way, or even that it was already there, cupped invisibly against his ear as he rode his rickshaw around the streets of the town. We began to expect to hear Ramani, around a corner or at the far end of a lane, ringing his bell and yelling cheerfully:

'All-India Radio! This is All-India Radio!'

Time passed. Ram continued to carry the invisible radio around town. One year passed. Still his caricatures of the radio channel filled the air in the streets. But when I saw him now, there was a new thing in his face, a strained thing, as if he were having to make a phenomenal effort, which was much more tiring than driving a rickshaw, more tiring even than pulling a rickshaw containing a thief's widow and her five living children and the ghosts of two dead ones; as if all the energy of his young body was being poured into that fictional space between his ear and his hand, and he was trying to bring the radio into existence by a mighty, and possibly fatal, act of will.

I felt most helpless, I can tell you, because I had divined that Ram had poured into the idea of the radio all his worries and regrets about what he had done, and that if the dream were to die he would be forced to face the full gravity of his crime against his own body, to understand that the thief's widow had turned him, before she married him, into a thief of a stupid and terrible kind, because she had made him rob himself.

And then the white caravan came back to its place under the banyan tree and I knew there was nothing to be done, because Ram would certainly come to get his gift. 45

He did not come for one day, then for two, and I learned afterwards that he had not wished to seem greedy; he didn't want the health officer to think he was desperate for the radio. Besides, he was half hoping they would come over and give it to him at his place, perhaps with some kind of small, formal presentation ceremony. A fool is a fool and there is no accounting for his notions.

On the third day he came. Ringing his bicycle-bell and imitating weather forecasts, ear cupped as usual, he arrived at the caravan. And in the rickshaw behind him sat the thief's widow, the witch, who had not been able to resist coming along to watch her companion's destruction.

It did not take very long.

Ram went into the caravan gaily, waving at his armbanded cronies who were guarding it against the anger of the people, and I am told—for I had left the scene to spare myself the pain—that his hair was well-oiled and his clothes were freshly starched. The thief's widow did not move from the rickshaw, but sat there with a black sari pulled over her head, clutching at her children as if they were straws.

After a short time there were sounds of disagreement inside the caravan, and then louder noises still, and finally the youths in armbands went in to see what was becoming, and soon after that Ram was frogmarched out by his drinking-chums, and his hair-grease was smudged on to his face and there was blood coming from his mouth. His hand was no longer cupped by his ear.

And still — they tell me — the thief's black widow did not move from her place in the rickshaw, although they dumped her husband in the dust.

Yes, I know, I'm an old man, my ideas are wrinkled with age, and these days they tell me sterilisation and God knows what is necessary, and maybe I'm wrong to blame the widow as well — why not? Maybe all the views of the old can be discounted now, and if that's so, let it be. But I'm telling this story and I haven't finished yet.

Some days after the incident at the caravan I saw Ramani selling his rickshaw to the old Muslim crook who runs the bicycle-repair shop. When he saw me watching, Ram came to me and said, 'Goodbye, teacher sahib, I am off to Bombay, where I will become a bigger film star than Shashi Kapoor or Amitabh Bachchan even.'

"'*I* am off," you say?' I asked him. 'Are you perhaps travelling alone?'

He stiffened. The thief's widow had already taught him not to be humble in the presence of elders.

'My wife and children will come also,' he said. It was the last time we spoke. They left that same day on the down train.

After some months had passed I got his first letter, which was not written by himself, of course, since in spite of all my long-ago efforts he barely knew how to write. He had paid a professional letter-writer, which must have cost him many rupees, because everything in life costs money and in Bombay it costs twice as much. Don't ask me why he wrote to me, but he did. I have the letters and can give you proof positive, so maybe there are some uses for old people still, or maybe he knew I was the only one who would be interested in his news.

Anyhow: the letters were full of his new career, they told me how he'd been dis-covered at once, a big studio had given him a test, now they were grooming him for stardom, he spent his days at the Sun'n'Sand Hotel at Juhu beach in the company of top lady artistes, he was buying a big house at Pali Hill, built in the split-level mode and incorporating the latest security equipment to protect him from the movie fans, the thief's widow was well and happy and getting fat, and life was filled with light and success and no-questions-asked alcohol.

They were wonderful letters, brimming with confidence, but whenever I read them, and sometimes I read them still, I remember the expression which came over his face in the days just before he learned the truth about his radio, and the huge mad energy which he had poured into the act of conjuring reality, by an act of magnificent faith, out of the hot thin air between his cupped hand and his ear.

[1994]

Exploring the Text

1. How do the first two paragraphs of "The Free Radio" set both the tone of the story and the narrative voice?
2. Analyze the conversation between the narrator and the thief's widow (paras. 24–25). Who do you think gets the last word?
3. In what way is "The Free Radio" the story of a culture clash? Which cultures are clashing?
4. Characterize the narrator of "The Free Radio." Based on information provided in the story, what opinion do you think the people in the village have about him? Why do you think Ramani writes to him from Bombay?
5. Is your view of Ramani's situation as dire as the narrator's? Is it possible that Ramani has qualities that the narrator may not notice or understand? Explain your answers.
6. Think of several reasons why Ramani submitted to the vasectomy, and then analyze how each reason affects the way individual characters in the story view him.
7. This story appeared in the East section of Rushdie's collection *East, West*. What besides its setting makes the story Eastern? Are there elements of the West in it?

Who's Irish?

GISH JEN

Gish Jen was born Lillian Jen in 1955 and raised in the suburbs of New York City. She graduated with a BA in English from Harvard University and received her MFA in creative writing from the University of Iowa. She has written three novels — *Typical American* (1991), *Mona in the Promised Land* (1996), and *The Love Wife* (2005) — and one story collection — *Who's Irish?* (1999). Her short stories have appeared in many literary journals and magazines, including the *New Yorker*. Jen is frequently compared to other Asian American writers, such as Amy Tan and Maxine Hong Kingston, but she has said that her writing is also influenced by Jewish American writers because of what she sees as commonalities between Jewish and Chinese cultures. In her fiction, Jen explores these common experiences: questions of identity; the complexities of assimilation; and tensions across racial, cultural, and generational divides. "Who's Irish?" was first published in the *New Yorker* in 1998 before becoming the title story of her 1999 short-story collection.

In China, people say mixed children are supposed to be smart, and definitely my granddaughter Sophie is smart. But Sophie is wild, Sophie is not like my daughter Natalie, or like me. I am work hard my whole life, and fierce besides. My husband always used to say he is afraid of me, and in our restaurant, busboys and cooks all afraid of me too. Even the gang members come for protection money, they try to talk to my husband. When I am there, they stay away. If they come by mistake, they pretend they are come to eat. They hide behind the menu, they order a lot of food. They talk about their mothers. Oh, my mother have some arthritis, need to take herbal medicine, they say. Oh, my mother getting old, her hair all white now.

I say, Your mother's hair used to be white, but since she dye it, it become black again. Why don't you go home once in a while and take a look? I tell them, Confucius say a filial son knows what color his mother's hair is.

My daughter is fierce too, she is vice president in the bank now. Her new house is big enough for everybody to have their own room, including me. But Sophie take after Natalie's husband's family, their name is Shea. Irish. I always thought Irish people are like Chinese people, work so hard on the railroad, but now I know why the Chinese beat the Irish. Of course, not all Irish are like the Shea family, of course not. My daughter tell me I should not say Irish this, Irish that.

How do you like it when people say the Chinese this, the Chinese that, she say.

You know, the British call the Irish heathen, just like they call the Chinese, she say.   5

You think the Opium War was bad, how would you like to live right next door to the British, she say.

And that is that. My daughter have a funny habit when she win an argument, she take a sip of something and look away, so the other person is not embarrassed. So I am not embarrassed. I do not call anybody anything either. I just happen to mention about the Shea family, an interesting fact: four brothers in the family, and not one of them work. The mother, Bess, have a job before she got sick, she was executive secretary in a big company. She is handle everything for a big shot, you would be surprised how complicated her job is, not just type this, type that. Now she is a nice woman with a clean house. But her boys, every one of them is on welfare, or so-called severance pay, or so-called disability pay. Something. They say they cannot find work, this is not the economy of the fifties, but I say, Even the black people doing better these days, some of them live so fancy, you'd be surprised. Why the Shea family have so much trouble? They are white people, they speak English. When I come to this country, I have no money and do not speak English. But my husband and I own our restaurant before he die. Free and clear, no mortgage. Of course, I understand I am just lucky, come from a country where the food is popular all over the world. I understand it is not the Shea family's fault they come from a country where everything is boiled. Still, I say.

She's right, we should broaden our horizons, say one brother, Jim, at Thanksgiving. Forget about the car business. Think about egg rolls.

Pad thai, say another brother, Mike. I'm going to make my fortune in pad thai. It's going to be the new pizza.

I say, You people too picky about what you sell. Selling egg rolls not good enough   10
for you, but at least my husband and I can say, We made it. What can you say? Tell me. What can you say?

Everybody chew their tough turkey.

I especially cannot understand my daughter's husband John, who has no job but cannot take care of Sophie either. Because he is a man, he say, and that's the end of the sentence.

Plain boiled food, plain boiled thinking. Even his name is plain boiled: John. Maybe because I grew up with black bean sauce and hoisin sauce and garlic sauce, I always feel something is missing when my son-in-law talk.

But, okay: so my son-in-law can be man, I am baby-sitter. Six hours a day, same as the old sitter, crazy Amy, who quit. This is not so easy, now that I am sixty-eight, Chinese age almost seventy. Still, I try. In China, daughter take care of mother. Here it is the other way around. Mother help daughter, mother ask, Anything else I can do? Otherwise daughter complain mother is not supportive. I tell daughter, We do not have this word in Chinese, *supportive*. But my daughter too busy to listen, she has to go to meeting, she has to write memo while her husband go to the gym to be a man. My daughter say otherwise he will be depressed. Seems like all his life he has this trouble, depression.

No one wants to hire someone who is depressed, she say. It is important for him   15
to keep his spirits up.

Beautiful wife, beautiful daughter, beautiful house, oven can clean itself automatically. No money left over, because only one income, but lucky enough, got the baby-sitter for free. If John lived in China, he would be very happy. But he is not happy. Even at the gym things go wrong. One day, he pull a muscle. Another day, weight room too crowded. Always something.

Until finally, hooray, he has a job. Then he feel pressure.

I need to concentrate, he say. I need to focus.

He is going to work for insurance company. Salesman job. A paycheck, he say, and at least he will wear clothes instead of gym shorts. My daughter buy him some special candy bars from the health-food store. They say THINK! on them, and are supposed to help John think.

John is a good-looking boy, you have to say that, especially now that he shave so   20
you can see his face.

I am an old man in a young man's game, say John.

I will need a new suit, say John.

This time I am not going to shoot myself in the foot, say John.

Good, I say.

She means to be supportive, my daughter say. Don't start the send her back to   25
China thing, because we can't.

Sophie is three years old American age, but already I see her nice Chinese side swallowed up by her wild Shea side. She looks like mostly Chinese. Beautiful black hair, beautiful black eyes. Nose perfect size, not so flat looks like something fell down, not so large looks like some big deal got stuck in wrong face. Everything just right, only her skin is a brown surprise to John's family. So brown, they say. Even John say it. She never goes in the sun, still she is that color, he say. Brown. They say, Nothing the matter with brown. They are just surprised. So brown. Nattie is not that brown, they say. They say, It seems like Sophie should be a color in between Nattie and John. Seems funny, a girl named Sophie Shea be brown. But she is brown, maybe her name should be Sophie Brown. She never go in the sun, still she is that color, they say. Nothing the matter with brown. They are just surprised.

The Shea family talk is like this sometimes, going around and around like a Christmas-tree train.

Maybe John is not her father, I say one day, to stop the train. And sure enough, train wreck. None of the brothers ever say the word *brown* to me again.

Instead, John's mother, Bess, say, I hope you are not offended.

She say, I did my best on those boys. But raising four boys with no father is no picnic. 30

You have a beautiful family, I say.

I'm getting old, she say.

You deserve a rest, I say. Too many boys make you old.

I never had a daughter, she say. You have a daughter.

I have a daughter, I say. Chinese people don't think a daughter is so great, but 35 you're right. I have a daughter.

I was never against the marriage, you know, she say. I never thought John was marrying down. I always thought Nattie was just as good as white.

I was never against the marriage either, I say. I just wonder if they look at the whole problem.

Of course you pointed out the problem, you are a mother, she say. And now we both have a granddaughter. A little brown granddaughter, she is so precious to me.

I laugh. A little brown granddaughter, I say. To tell you the truth, I don't know how she came out so brown.

We laugh some more. These days Bess need a walker to walk. She take so many pills, 40 she need two glasses of water to get them all down. Her favorite TV show is about bloopers, and she love her bird feeder. All day long, she can watch that bird feeder, like a cat.

I can't wait for her to grow up, Bess say. I could use some female company.

Too many boys, I say.

Boys are fine, she say. But they do surround you after a while.

You should take a break, come live with us, I say. Lots of girls at our house.

Be careful what you offer, say Bess with a wink. Where I come from, people mean 45 for you to move in when they say a thing like that.

Nothing the matter with Sophie's outside, that's the truth. It is inside that she is like not any Chinese girl I ever see. We go to the park, and this is what she does. She stand up in the stroller. She take off all her clothes and throw them in the fountain.

Sophie! I say. Stop!

But she just laugh like a crazy person. Before I take over as baby-sitter, Sophie has that crazy-person sitter, Amy the guitar player. My daughter thought this Amy very creative — another word we do not talk about in China. In China, we talk about whether we have difficulty or no difficulty. We talk about whether life is bitter or not bitter. In America, all day long, people talk about creative. Never mind that I cannot even look at this Amy, with her shirt so short that her belly button showing. This Amy think Sophie should love her body. So when Sophie take off her diaper, Amy laugh. When Sophie run around naked, Amy say she wouldn't want to wear a diaper either. When Sophie go *shu-shu* in her lap, Amy laugh and say there are no germs in pee. When Sophie take off her shoes, Amy say bare feet is best, even the pediatrician say so. That is why Sophie now walk around with no shoes like a beggar child. Also why Sophie love to take off her clothes.

Turn around! say the boys in the park. Let's see that ass!

Of course, Sophie does not understand. Sophie clap her hands, I am the only one to say, No! This is not a game.   50

It has nothing to do with John's family, my daughter say. Amy was too permissive, that's all.

But I think if Sophie was not wild inside, she would not take off her shoes and clothes to begin with.

You never take off your clothes when you were little, I say. All my Chinese friends had babies, I never saw one of them act wild like that.

Look, my daughter say. I have a big presentation tomorrow.

John and my daughter agree Sophie is a problem, but they don't know what to do.   55

You spank her, she'll stop, I say another day.

But they say, Oh no.

In America, parents not supposed to spank the child.

It gives them low self-esteem, my daughter say. And that leads to problems later, as I happen to know.

My daughter never have big presentation the next day when the subject of spanking come up.   60

I don't want you to touch Sophie, she say. No spanking, period.

Don't tell me what to do, I say.

I'm not telling you what to do, say my daughter. I'm telling you how I feel.

I am not your servant, I say. Don't you dare talk to me like that.

My daughter have another funny habit when she lose an argument. She spread out all her fingers and look at them, as if she like to make sure they are still there.   65

My daughter is fierce like me, but she and John think it is better to explain to Sophie that clothes are a good idea. This is not so hard in the cold weather. In the warm weather, it is very hard.

Use your words, my daughter say. That's what we tell Sophie. How about if you set a good example.

As if good example mean anything to Sophie. I am so fierce, the gang members who used to come to the restaurant all afraid of me, but Sophie is not afraid.

I say, Sophie, if you take off your clothes, no snack.

I say, Sophie, if you take off your clothes, no lunch.   70

I say, Sophie, if you take off your clothes, no park.

Pretty soon we are stay home all day, and by the end of six hours she still did not have one thing to eat. You never saw a child stubborn like that.

I'm hungry! she cry when my daughter come home.

What's the matter, doesn't your grandmother feed you? My daughter laugh.

No! Sophie say. She doesn't feed me anything!   75

My daughter laugh again. Here you go, she say.

She say to John, Sophie must be growing.

Growing like a weed, I say.

Still Sophie take off her clothes, until one day I spank her. Not too hard, but she cry and cry, and when I tell her if she doesn't put her clothes back on I'll spank her again, she put her clothes back on. Then I tell her she is good girl, and give her some food to eat. The next day we go to the park and, like a nice Chinese girl, she does not take off her clothes.

She stop taking off her clothes, I report. Finally! 80

How did you do it? my daughter ask.

After twenty-eight years experience with you, I guess I learn something, I say.

It must have been a phase, John say, and his voice is suddenly like an expert.

His voice is like an expert about everything these days, now that he carry a leather briefcase, and wear shiny shoes, and can go shopping for a new car. On the company, he say. The company will pay for it, but he will be able to drive it whenever he want.

A free car, he say. How do you like that. 85

It's good to see you in the saddle again, my daughter say. Some of your family patterns are scary.

At least I don't drink, he say. He say, And I'm not the only one with scary family patterns.

That's for sure, say my daughter.

Everyone is happy. Even I am happy, because there is more trouble with Sophie, but now I think I can help her Chinese side fight against her wild side. I teach her to eat food with fork or spoon or chopsticks, she cannot just grab into the middle of a bowl of noodles. I teach her not to play with garbage cans. Sometimes I spank her, but not too often, and not too hard.

Still, there are problems. Sophie like to climb everything. If there is a railing, she 90 is never next to it. Always she is on top of it. Also, Sophie like to hit the mommies of her friends. She learn this from her playground best friend, Sinbad, who is four. Sinbad wear army clothes every day and like to ambush his mommy. He is the one who dug a big hole under the play structure, a foxhole he call it, all by himself. Very hardworking. Now he wait in the foxhole with a shovel full of wet sand. When his mommy come, he throw it right at her.

Oh, it's all right, his mommy say. You can't get rid of war games, it's part of their imaginative play. All the boys go through it.

Also, he like to kick his mommy, and one day he tell Sophie to kick his mommy too.

I wish this story is not true.

Kick her, kick her! Sinbad say.

Sophie kick her. A little kick, as if she just so happened was swinging her little leg 95 and didn't realize that big mommy leg was in the way. Still I spank Sophie and make Sophie say sorry, and what does the mommy say?

Really, it's all right, she say. It didn't hurt.

After that, Sophie learn she can attack mommies in the playground, and some will say, Stop, but others will say, Oh, she didn't mean it, especially if they realize Sophie will be punished.

This is how, one day, bigger trouble come. The bigger trouble start when Sophie hide in the foxhole with that shovel full of sand. She wait, and when I come look for her, she throw it at me. All over my nice clean clothes.

Did you ever see a Chinese girl act this way?

Sophie! I say. Come out of there, say you're sorry.   100

But she does not come out. Instead, she laugh. Naaah, naah-na, naaa-naaa, she say.

I am not exaggerate: millions of children in China, not one act like this.

Sophie! I say. Now! Come out now!

But she know she is in big trouble. She know if she come out, what will happen next. So she does not come out. I am sixty-eight, Chinese age almost seventy, how can I crawl under there to catch her? Impossible. So I yell, yell, yell, and what happen? Nothing. A Chinese mother would help, but American mothers, they look at you, they shake their head, they go home. And, of course, a Chinese child would give up, but not Sophie.

I hate you! she yell. I hate you, Meanie!   105

Meanie is my new name these days.

Long time this goes on, long long time. The foxhole is deep, you cannot see too much, you don't know where is the bottom. You cannot hear too much either. If she does not yell, you cannot even know she is still there or not. After a while, getting cold out, getting dark out. No one left in the playground, only us.

Sophie, I say. How did you become stubborn like this? I am go home without you now.

I try to use a stick, chase her out of there, and once or twice I hit her, but still she does not come out. So finally I leave. I go outside the gate.

Bye-bye! I say. I'm go home now.   110

But still she does not come out and does not come out. Now it is dinnertime, the sky is black. I think I should maybe go get help, but how can I leave a little girl by herself in the playground? A bad man could come. A rat could come. I go back in to see what is happen to Sophie. What if she have a shovel and is making a tunnel to escape?

Sophie! I say.

No answer.

Sophie!

I don't know if she is alive. I don't know if she is fall asleep down there. If she is   115
crying, I cannot hear her.

So I take the stick and poke.

Sophie! I say. I promise I no hit you. If you come out, I give you a lollipop.

No answer. By now I worried. What to do, what to do, what to do? I poke some more, even harder, so that I am poking and poking when my daughter and John suddenly appear.

What are you doing? What is going on? say my daughter.

Put down that stick! say my daughter.   120

You are crazy! say my daughter.

John wiggle under the structure, into the foxhole, to rescue Sophie.

She fell asleep, say John the expert. She's okay. That is one big hole.

Now Sophie is crying and crying.

Sophia, my daughter say, hugging her. Are you okay, peanut? Are you okay? 125

She's just scared, say John.

Are you okay? I say too. I don't know what happen, I say.

She's okay, say John. He is not like my daughter, full of questions. He is full of answers until we get home and can see by the lamplight.

Will you look at her? he yell then. What the hell happened?

Bruises all over her brown skin, and a swollen-up eye. 130

You are crazy! say my daughter. Look at what you did! You are crazy!

I try very hard, I say.

How could you use a stick? I told you to use your words!

She is hard to handle, I say.

She's three years old! You cannot use a stick! say my daughter. 135

She is not like any Chinese girl I ever saw, I say.

I brush some sand off my clothes. Sophie's clothes are dirty too, but at least she has her clothes on.

Has she done this before? ask my daughter. Has she hit you before?

She hits me all the time, Sophie say, eating ice cream.

Your family, say John. 140

Believe me, say my daughter.

A daughter I have, a beautiful daughter. I took care of her when she could not hold her head up. I took care of her before she could argue with me, when she was a little girl with two pigtails, one of them always crooked. I took care of her when we have to escape from China, I took care of her when suddenly we live in a country with cars everywhere, if you are not careful your little girl get run over. When my husband die, I promise him I will keep the family together, even though it was just two of us, hardly a family at all.

But now my daughter take me around to look at apartments. After all, I can cook, I can clean, there's no reason I cannot live by myself, all I need is a telephone. Of course, she is sorry. Sometimes she cry, I am the one to say everything will be okay. She say she have no choice, she doesn't want to end up divorced. I say divorce is terrible, I don't know who invented this terrible idea. Instead of live with a telephone, though, surprise, I come to live with Bess. Imagine that. Bess make an offer and, sure enough, where she come from, people mean for you to move in when they say things like that. A crazy idea, go to live with someone else's family, but she like to have some female company, not like my daughter, who does not believe in company. These days when my daughter visit, she does not bring Sophie. Bess say we should give Nattie time, we will see Sophie again soon. But seems like my daughter have more presentation than ever before, every time she come she have to leave.

I have a family to support, she say, and her voice is heavy, as if soaking wet. I have a young daughter and a depressed husband and no one to turn to.

When she say no one to turn to, she mean me. 145

These days my beautiful daughter is so tired she can just sit there in a chair and fall asleep. John lost his job again, already, but still they rather hire a baby-sitter than ask me to help, even they can't afford it. Of course, the new baby-sitter is much younger, can run around. I don't know if Sophie these days is wild or not wild. She call me Meanie, but she like to kiss me too, sometimes. I remember that every time I see a child on TV. Sophie like to grab my hair, a fistful in each hand, and then kiss me smack on the nose. I never see any other child kiss that way.

The satellite TV has so many channels, more channels than I can count, including a Chinese channel from the Mainland and a Chinese channel from Taiwan, but most of the time I watch bloopers with Bess. Also, I watch the bird feeder — so many, many kinds of birds come. The Shea sons hang around all the time, asking when will I go home, but Bess tell them, Get lost.

She's a permanent resident, say Bess. She isn't going anywhere.

Then she wink at me, and switch the channel with the remote control.

Of course, I shouldn't say Irish this, Irish that, especially now I am become hon-   150
orary Irish myself, according to Bess. Me! Who's Irish? I say, and she laugh. All the same, if I could mention one thing about some of the Irish, not all of them of course, I like to mention this: Their talk just stick. I don't know how Bess Shea learn to use her words, but sometimes I hear what she say a long time later. *Permanent resident. Not going anywhere.* Over and over I hear it, the voice of Bess.

[1998]

....

Exploring the Text

1. Characterize the narrator of "Who's Irish?" In what ways does she see herself as traditional? as progressive?
2. Take a look at the standoff between the narrator and her granddaughter, Sophie (paras. 98–141). What techniques does Jen use to create the sense of desperation on the part of each character? Look especially at her choice of words.
3. Analyze the syntax in paragraph 142, which marks a transition in the story. How is the language of the narrator different from her language in the rest of the story?
4. The story's narrator is comfortable stereotyping her daughter's Irish family-in-law — for example, "Plain boiled food, plain boiled thinking" (para. 13). What do you notice about her observations? Do you think she is more open-minded by the end of the story? Explain your answer.
5. Why does Bess apologize for her boys when they talk about Sophie being "brown" (para. 29)? What does her apology mean to the narrator?
6. What is ironic about Natalie telling her mother, "Use your words" (para. 67)? Why is the narrator impressed by the way "Bess Shea learn[ed] to use her words" (para. 150)? It seems that even the narrator has learned to "use her words" by the end of the story; how does she put her own twist on some of the American expressions she adopts?
7. This story concerns several different clashes. What clashes are illustrated in the story, especially in the disagreements over how Sophie is to be raised? After the

scene in the park, was Natalie right to remove the narrator from her home? Is the grandmother a danger to Sophie? Why or why not?

8. What role does the suburban setting play in the story? How does it contribute to or complicate the story's central conflicts?

Elegy Written in a Country Churchyard

THOMAS GRAY

Though he only published a mere one thousand lines of poetry during his life, Thomas Gray (1716–1771) was considered one of the greatest poets of his time. Born to a middle-class family in Cornhill, England, he was the fifth of twelve children, and the only one to survive past infancy. He was educated at Eton and later Cambridge, where, despite expectations that he would pursue law, he delved ever more deeply into literature. In 1742, Gray began writing poetry in earnest, but he was never prolific. Despite the success of many of his poems, he was very self-critical, often employing his lacerating wit at his own expense. He turned down the position of poet laureate of England, later saying that he feared his poems would be "mistaken for the words of a flea." Instead, he accepted a largely ceremonial post teaching history at Cambridge. After his death, Gray was buried in the churchyard of Stoke Poges, which is thought to be the setting for his most famous poem, "Elegy Written in a Country Churchyard." "Elegy" was an instant success. Today it remains one of the most imitated, parodied, and quoted poems in the English language.

The curfew[1] tolls the knell of parting day,
  The lowing herd wind slowly o'er the lea,
The plowman homeward plods his weary way,
  And leaves the world to darkness and to me.

Now fades the glimmering landscape on the sight,   5
  And all the air a solemn stillness holds,
Save where the beetle wheels his droning flight,
  And drowsy tinklings lull the distant folds;

Save that from yonder ivy-mantled tower
  The moping owl does to the moon complain   10
Of such, as wandering near her secret bower,
  Molest her ancient solitary reign.

Beneath those rugged elms, that yew tree's shade,
  Where heaves the turf in many a moldering heap,

---

[1]Evening bell. — EDS.

Each in his narrow cell forever laid,   15
    The rude[2] forefathers of the hamlet sleep.

The breezy call of incense-breathing morn,
    The swallow twittering from the straw-built shed,
The cock's shrill clarion, or the echoing horn,
    No more shall rouse them from their lowly bed.   20

For them no more the blazing hearth shall burn,
    Or busy housewife ply her evening care;
No children run to lisp their sire's return,
    Or climb his knees the envied kiss to share.

Oft did the harvest to their sickle yield,   25
    Their furrow oft the stubborn glebe[3] has broke;
How jocund did they drive their team afield!
    How bowed the woods beneath their sturdy stroke!

Let not Ambition mock their useful toil,
    Their homely joys, and destiny obscure;   30
Nor Grandeur hear with a disdainful smile
    The short and simple annals of the poor.

The boast of heraldry, the pomp of power,
    And all that beauty, all that wealth e'er gave,
Awaits alike the inevitable hour.   35
    The paths of glory lead but to the grave.

Nor you, ye proud, impute to these the fault,
    If memory o'er their tomb no trophies raise,
Where through the long-drawn aisle and fretted[4] vault
    The pealing anthem swells the note of praise.   40

Can storied urn or animated[5] bust
    Back to its mansion call the fleeting breath?
Can Honor's voice provoke the silent dust,
    Or Flattery soothe the dull cold ear of Death?

Perhaps in this neglected spot is laid   45
    Some heart once pregnant with celestial fire;
Hands that the rod of empire might have swayed,
    Or waked to ecstasy the living lyre.

But Knowledge to their eyes her ample page
    Rich with the spoils of time did ne'er unroll;   50

---

[2]Humble.—Eds.
[3]Soil.—Eds.
[4]Ornamented.—Eds.
[5]Lifelike.—Eds.

Chill Penury repressed their noble rage,
    And froze the genial current of the soul.

Full many a gem of purest ray serene,
    The dark unfathomed caves of ocean bear.
Full many a flower is born to blush unseen,   55
    And waste its sweetness on the desert air.

Some village Hampden,[6] that with dauntless breast
    The little tyrant of his fields withstood;
Some mute inglorious Milton here may rest,
    Some Cromwell[7] guiltless of his country's blood.   60

The applause of listening senates to command,
    The threats of pain and ruin to despise,
To scatter plenty o'er a smiling land,
    And read their history in a nation's eyes,

Their lot forbade: nor circumscribed alone   65
    Their growing virtues, but their crimes confined;
Forbade to wade through slaughter to a throne,
    And shut the gates of mercy on mankind,

The struggling pangs of conscious truth to hide,
    To quench the blushes of ingenuous shame,   70
Or heap the shrine of Luxury and Pride
    With incense kindled at the Muse's flame.

Far from the madding crowd's ignoble strife,
    Their sober wishes never learned to stray;
Along the cool sequestered vale of life   75
    They kept the noiseless tenor of their way.

Yet even these bones from insult to protect
    Some frail memorial still erected nigh,
With uncouth rhymes and shapeless sculpture decked,
    Implores the passing tribute of a sigh.   80

Their name, their years, spelt by the unlettered Muse,
    The place of fame and elegy supply:
And many a holy text around she strews,
    That teach the rustic moralist to die.

For who to dumb Forgetfulness a prey,   85
    This pleasing anxious being e'er resigned,

---

[6]John Hampden (1594–1643) was a prominent figure in the English civil war. He famously refused to pay a protection tax levied by Charles I.—Eds.
[7]Oliver Cromwell (1599–1658) was a rebel leader in the English civil war.—Eds.

Left the warm precincts of the cheerful day,
   Nor cast one longing lingering look behind?

On some fond breast the parting soul relies,
   Some pious drops the closing eye requires;   90
Even from the tomb the voice of Nature cries,
   Even in our ashes live their wonted fires.

For thee, who mindful of the unhonored dead
   Dost in these lines their artless tale relate;
If chance, by lonely contemplation led,   95
   Some kindred spirit shall inquire thy fate,

Haply some hoary-headed swain[8] may say,
   "Oft have we seen him at the peep of dawn
Brushing with hasty steps the dews away
   To meet the sun upon the upland lawn.   100

"There at the foot of yonder nodding beech
   That wreathes its old fantastic roots so high,
His listless length at noontide would he stretch,
   And pore upon the brook that babbles by.

"Hard by yon wood, now smiling as in scorn,   105
   Muttering his wayward fancies he would rove,
Now drooping, woeful wan, like one forlorn,
   Or crazed with care, or crossed in hopeless love.

"One morn I missed him on the customed hill,
   Along the heath and near his favorite tree;   110
Another came; nor yet beside the rill,
   Nor up the lawn, nor at the wood was he;

"The next with dirges due in sad array
   Slow through the churchway path we saw him borne.
Approach and read (for thou canst read) the lay,   115
   Graved on the stone beneath yon aged thorn."

THE EPITAPH

Here rests his head upon the lap of Earth
   A youth to fortune and to Fame unknown.
Fair Science[9] frowned not on his humble birth,
   And Melancholy marked him for her own.   120

---

[8]White-haired (elderly) shepherd.—Eds.
[9]Learning, education.—Eds.

Large was his bounty, and his soul sincere,
Heaven did a recompense as largely send:
He gave to Misery all he had, a tear,
He gained from Heaven ('twas all he wished), a friend.

No farther seek his merits to disclose,   125
Or draw his frailties from their dread abode
(There they alike in trembling hope repose),
The bosom of his Father and his God.

[1751]

Exploring the Text

1. Who do you think the speaker is? Now, try to imagine the setting. Is the speaker literally in the churchyard? Why or why not?
2. Notice the use of sound imagery in stanzas 1–3. How does the toll of the "knell of parting day" (l. 1) echo throughout those stanzas? In what context do you usually hear the word *knell*? What is its connotation, and how does that connotation contribute to the meaning of this section of the poem? How does this sound imagery introduce stanza 4?
3. Look carefully at stanza 2. How does Gray use the natural world to comment on the issue of tradition and progress?
4. The poem shifts in stanza 8. Analyze the stanza, looking carefully at Gray's diction and syntax choices, and explain how it works as a transition from one idea to another.
5. Stanza 13 (ll. 49–52) may be the poem's most famous. How does Gray use figurative language to mirror the stanza's meaning, that poverty may have forced talented people to remain unknown and unfulfilled?
6. If you read lines 61–65 grammatically — that is, as a complete sentence — you will find that the subject and verb do not appear until line 65, in a separate stanza from the object of the sentence. What is the effect of this delay? Why might Gray have considered the object worth introducing before the subject?
7. How does the speaker honor simple folk in lines 61–76?
8. Stanza 24 (ll. 93–96) begins the lead-up to the epitaph, which comprises the last twelve lines of the poem. Who is speaking beginning in line 98, and what is he or she speaking about? Whose epitaph ends the poem?
9. Some scholars believe that "Elegy" was inspired by the fact that Gray was the only one of twelve siblings to survive until adulthood. How does this knowledge affect your reading of the poem?
10. Gray's "Elegy" is considered one of the great poems, in part because of the seamless way structure, rhyme scheme, and imagery combine to communicate Gray's message that life is short. First consider each of these elements separately. How does each element connect to the poem's message? Then consider the way these elements work together to elevate this simple theme.

London

WILLIAM BLAKE

Obscure during his lifetime, William Blake (1757–1827) has come to be recognized as one of the most significant poets and artists in English history. Born in London and educated at home by parents who held nonconformist religious and political beliefs, Blake developed highly controversial views about spirituality, women's rights, and personal liberty that informed much of his work. On occasion, his views—and his willingness to express and publish them—led to difficulties with the law, including an arrest in 1803 for "uttering seditious statements against the Crown." Following an apprenticeship to an engraver, Blake began experimenting with relief engraving—a technique he called "illuminated printing"—to illustrate both his own books and works such as Milton's *Paradise Lost* and Dante's *The Divine Comedy*. "London" comes from *Songs of Innocence and of Experience* (1794), a response to his earlier collection of poems, *Songs of Innocence* (1789).

I wander through each chartered[1] street,
Near where the chartered Thames does flow,
And mark in every face I meet
Marks of weakness, marks of woe.

In every cry of every man,   5
In every Infant's cry of fear,
In every voice, in every ban,
The mind-forged manacles I hear.

How the Chimney-sweeper's cry
Every black'ning Church appalls;   10
And the hapless Soldier's sigh
Runs in blood down Palace walls.

But most through midnight streets I hear
How the youthful Harlot's curse
Blasts the new-born Infant's tear,   15
And blights with plagues the Marriage hearse.

                                                           [1794]

. . . .

Exploring the Text

1. "London" takes the form of a walking tour through London. How does Blake use visual and auditory imagery to both convey the atmosphere in the streets and create a sense of foreboding?

---

[1]Defined by law.—EDS.

2. What do you make of the repetition of the words "mark" and "marks" in the first stanza? Blake uses "mark" in line 3 to mean "notice." Consider other possible meanings of the word.

3. The last two stanzas introduce a series of exploited persons: chimney sweepers, soldiers, and prostitutes. Why do you think Blake saves the "youthful Harlot" for last? What do you think he means by "Marriage hearse"?

4. The poem's third stanza is an acrostic; the first letters of the first words in each line spell out "HEAR." In addition, lines 8 and 13 both end with the word "hear." What does Blake want us to hear? Why is this technique effective in this part of the poem?

5. What is your interpretation of "mind-forged manacles" (l. 8)? How might that phrase comment on the overindustrialized world of London in the eighteenth century?

6. "London," like many of Blake's poems, has been interpreted in different ways. Critic Camille Paglia, who writes about "London" in *Break, Blow, Burn*, sees it as part of Blake's "exposé of commercial society." What is your view? Why? Can you see another way the poem might be interpreted?

Dover Beach

MATTHEW ARNOLD

Poet, essayist, and critic Matthew Arnold (1822–1888) was brought up and educated at Rugby School, one of England's oldest boarding schools, where his father was headmaster. After graduating from Balliol College at Oxford, he took the rather mundane position of inspector of schools at Her Majesty's Inspectorate of Education to support his family. He held this position for thirty years, during which time he wrote the bulk of his poetry, including *Empedocles on Etna* (1852) and *Poems* (1853). Arnold was elected professor of poetry at Oxford in 1857 and 1862, and during this time he produced several collections of essays and literary, cultural, and religious criticism. His poetry is remembered for its clarity and straightforwardness, and is considered a bridge between romanticism and modernism. In 1867, Arnold published "Dover Beach," his most famous work. Dover is the English port city from which most people traveled to France.

The sea is calm tonight.
The tide is full, the moon lies fair
Upon the straits;—on the French coast the light
Gleams and is gone; the cliffs of England stand,
Glimmering and vast, out in the tranquil bay.   5
Come to the window, sweet is the night-air!
Only, from the long line of spray
Where the sea meets the moon-blanched land,
Listen! you hear the grating roar

Of pebbles which the waves draw back, and fling,   10
At their return, up the high strand,
Begin, and cease, and then again begin,
With tremulous cadence slow, and bring
The eternal note of sadness in.

Sophocles long ago   15
Heard it on the Aegean, and it brought
Into his mind the turbid ebb and flow
Of human misery;[1] we
Find also in the sound a thought,
Hearing it by this distant northern sea.   20

The Sea of Faith
Was once, too, at the full, and round earth's shore
Lay like the folds of a bright girdle furled.
But now I only hear
Its melancholy, long, withdrawing roar,   25
Retreating, to the breath
Of the night-wind, down the vast edges drear
And naked shingles[2] of the world.

Ah, love, let us be true
To one another! for the world, which seems   30
To lie before us like a land of dreams,
So various, so beautiful, so new,
Hath really neither joy, nor love, nor light,
Nor certitude, nor peace, nor help for pain;
And we are here as on a darkling plain   35
Swept with confused alarms of struggle and flight,
Where ignorant armies clash by night.

[1867]

. . . .

Exploring the Text

1. Analyze the series of vivid images of nighttime by the sea in the first stanza. To which senses do these images appeal? How do these images relate to the meaning of the poem? Why do you think Arnold highlights the auditory images, such as "Listen!" in line 9?

2. What do the consonance and caesura in lines 9–14 add to the imagery in those lines? How does that imagery help create the mood of sadness with which the stanza ends?

---

[1]*Antigone*, "the gods have rocked a house to its foundations / the ruin will never cease, cresting on and on / from one generation on throughout the race— / like a great mounting tide" (ll. 659–62).—Eds.

[2]Pebble beaches.—Eds.

3. What do you think Arnold means by "The Sea of Faith" (l. 21)? What does he think has replaced it?
4. You might notice that the last stanza of the poem is self-contradictory; it almost argues with itself. What are some of the competing ideas in the stanza? How does the tone change over the course of the stanza? How does this shift in tone highlight the stanza's mixed message?
5. The last four lines of the poem are rhymed couplets, the form traditionally used to conclude and resolve a sonnet. What is the effect of that form on the meaning of those lines? How does the stanza resolve, or fail to resolve, the problem introduced by the poem?
6. There is evidence that Arnold wrote "Dover Beach" on his honeymoon in 1851. How does that possibility change the meaning of the poem for you?
7. "Dover Beach" was written when England was the most powerful and industrially sophisticated country in the world. How does the poem comment on this period in English history?

God's Grandeur

GERARD MANLEY HOPKINS

Torn between his obligations as a Jesuit and his love for poetry, Gerard Manley Hopkins (1844–1889) declined to seek an audience for his work during his lifetime; the bulk of his poems were published posthumously in 1916. Hopkins was born in Stratford, England, to a wealthy family. After converting to Catholicism near the end of his studies at Oxford, Hopkins entered the priesthood and, adhering to one of his vows, burned nearly all of his accumulated poems. He began to write again in 1875, when he was asked to commemorate the death of five Franciscan nuns who drowned in a shipwreck off the coast of England as they fled oppression in Germany. In the poem he wrote, entitled "Wreck of the Deutschland," Hopkins introduced what he called "sprung rhythm," a meter designed to imitate the rhythm of natural speech; this meter anticipated free verse and would influence new generations of poets. "God's Grandeur," written in 1877, makes occasional use of this unconventional rhythm and is representative of Hopkins's work in both subject and form.

The world is charged with the grandeur of God.
  It will flame out, like shining from shook foil;
  It gathers to a greatness, like the ooze of oil
Crushed. Why do men then now not reck[1] his rod?[2]

------

[1]Mind, obey. — EDS.
[2]"Rod" here is a scepter, representing God's position as king of kings. — EDS.

Generations have trod, have trod, have trod;   5
   And all is seared with trade; bleared, smeared with toil;
   And wears man's smudge and shares man's smell: the soil
Is bare now, nor can foot feel, being shod.

And for all this, nature is never spent;
   There lives the dearest freshness deep down things;   10
And though the last lights off the black West went
   Oh, morning, at the brown brink eastward, springs—
Because the Holy Ghost over the bent
   World broods with warm breast and with ah! bright wings.

[1877]

Exploring the Text

1. What does the word "charged" suggest in line 1? Consider several possibilities.
2. How does style reinforce meaning in line 5? What other examples of the close connection between style and meaning do you see in "God's Grandeur"?
3. How is the sound of the poem created? Look especially at the internal rhymes. Try reading this poem aloud to hear how Hopkins uses stressed syllables to create the poem's musical quality.
4. What does the metaphor in the poem's last two lines evoke for you? Explain the metaphor and how and why it affects you the way it does.
5. "God's Grandeur" follows the form of a Petrarchan sonnet, with an octet (8 lines) and a sestet (6 lines). What question or problem is posed in the octet and answered or resolved in the sestet?
6. What argument does "God's Grandeur" make? How does Hopkins present his evidence, including a counterargument?

Crumbling is not an instant's Act

Emily Dickinson

Born into a prominent family in Amherst, Massachusetts, Emily Dickinson (1830–1886) received some formal education at Amherst Academy and Mount Holyoke Female Seminary (which became Mount Holyoke College). Throughout her lifetime, Dickinson was a shy and reclusive person, who preferred to remain within her close family circle. In 1862, she enclosed four poems in a letter to literary critic and abolitionist Thomas Wentworth Higginson, who had written a piece in the *Atlantic Monthly* that included practical advice for young writers. Her letter began, "Mr. Higginson,—Are you too deeply occupied to say if my verse is alive? The mind is so near itself it cannot see distinctly, and I have none to ask. Should you think it breathed, and had you the leisure to tell me, I should feel quick gratitude." Dickinson didn't sign the letter, but instead enclosed her name on a card inside a smaller envelope. Dickinson wrote over seventeen hundred poems, but only ten were published in her lifetime. "Crumbling is not an instant's Act," published four years after her death, is like much of Dickinson's work: enigmatic at first, but blossoming after a couple of readings.

Crumbling is not an instant's Act
    A fundamental pause
Dilapidation's processes
Are organized Decays.

'Tis first a Cobweb on the Soul   5
    A Cuticle of Dust
A Borer in the Axis
An Elemental Rust—

Ruin is formal—Devil's work
    Consecutive and slow—   10
Fail in an instant, no man did
    Slipping—is Crash's law.

[1890]

Exploring the Text

1. "Crumbling is not an instant's Act" has several examples of personification. Identify them, and then analyze their effect on the poem's meaning. Pay careful attention to the way they help Dickinson support the poem's argument that falling apart is a slow process.
2. The second stanza offers examples of "organized Decays." Examine them closely, and then analyze how they function both literally and figuratively.
3. Do you think Dickinson is talking only about personal crumbling, or does the poem also apply to the ways society, or even humanity, falls victim to entropy? Use examples of her language to support your answer.
4. What do you think the poem has to say on the subject of tradition and progress?
5. How is this poem timeless? How can its meaning be applied to conditions in the world today?

Mending Wall

ROBERT FROST

Though Robert Frost (1874–1963) is considered the quintessential New England poet, he was born in San Francisco. After the death of his father when Frost was eleven years old, the family moved to Massachusetts. Frost attended Dartmouth

College and Harvard University, but in both cases left early to support his family. He delivered newspapers, farmed, did factory work, and taught high school and college, but he considered poetry to be his true calling. Frost won four Pulitzer Prizes for his collections *New Hampshire: A Poem with Notes and Grace Notes* (1924), *Collected Poems* (1931), *A Further Range* (1937), and *A Witness Tree* (1943), and in 1961 he spoke at the inauguration of President John F. Kennedy. Frost believed that poetry should be a "reproduction of human speech," a quality evident in "Mending Wall."

Something there is that doesn't love a wall,
That sends the frozen-ground-swell under it,
And spills the upper boulders in the sun;
And makes gaps even two can pass abreast.
The work of hunters is another thing: 5
I have come after them and made repair
Where they have left not one stone on a stone,
But they would have the rabbit out of hiding,
To please the yelping dogs. The gaps I mean,
No one has seen them made or heard them made, 10
But at spring mending-time we find them there.
I let my neighbor know beyond the hill;
And on a day we meet to walk the line
And set the wall between us once again.
We keep the wall between us as we go. 15
To each the boulders that have fallen to each.
And some are loaves and some so nearly balls
We have to use a spell to make them balance:
"Stay where you are until our backs are turned!"
We wear our fingers rough with handling them. 20
Oh, just another kind of outdoor game,
One on a side. It comes to little more:
There where it is we do not need the wall:
He is all pine and I am apple orchard.
My apple trees will never get across 25
And eat the cones under his pines, I tell him.
He only says, "Good fences make good neighbors."
Spring is the mischief in me, and I wonder
If I could put a notion in his head:
"*Why* do they make good neighbors? Isn't it 30
Where there are cows? But here there are no cows.
Before I built a wall I'd ask to know
What I was walling in or walling out,
And to whom I was like to give offense.

Something there is that doesn't love a wall,   35
That wants it down." I could say "Elves" to him,
But it's not elves exactly, and I'd rather
He said it for himself. I see him there
Bringing a stone grasped firmly by the top
In each hand, like an old-stone savage armed.   40
He moves in darkness as it seems to me,
Not of woods only and the shade of trees.
He will not go behind his father's saying,
And he likes having thought of it so well
He says again, "Good fences make good neighbors."   45

[1914]

Exploring the Text

1. Is there a conflict in the poem? Explain.
2. Contrast the inverted syntax of lines 1 and 35—"Something there is that doesn't love a wall"—to the traditional subject-verb-object syntax of lines 27 and 45—"Good fences make good neighbors." How does the difference help develop each of the poem's characters? What effect does the difference have on the poem's meaning?
3. Read lines 12–15 carefully. How could the different meanings of the word "between," which is repeated twice, change the meaning of the poem?
4. Lines 13–18 lead up to the "spell" in line 19 that the two wall-menders use to keep the rocks from toppling. How are those lead-up lines a sort of incantation in themselves? How might they connect to the image in lines 39–40 of the speaker's neighbor "bringing a stone grasped firmly by the top / In each hand, like an old-stone savage armed"?
5. Why do you think Frost allows the neighbor to offer the proverb "Good fences make good neighbors" twice? Do you think the speaker agrees with this adage? Why do you think the neighbor gets the last word?
6. "Mending Wall" questions whether a wall that has no function in the modern world still fulfills a ritualistic need. When Frost was asked about the poem's meaning, he said his poems are "all set to trip the reader head foremost into the boundless." In what way does trying to answer the poem's question trip you "into the boundless"? Which of the poem's two characters trip "into the boundless"?
7. When President Kennedy visited the Berlin Wall, he quoted the first line of "Mending Wall." His audience knew what he meant, of course. Later, when Frost visited Russia, he found that the Russian translation of the poem left off the first line. He said he could have done better for them by saying: "Something there is that doesn't love a wall, / Something there is that does." Does that potential change alter the meaning of the poem for you? Explain.

The Second Coming

WILLIAM BUTLER YEATS

William Butler Yeats (1865–1939) was born in Dublin to a middle-class Protestant family with strong connections to England. The young Yeats spent his early childhood in the West of Ireland, a region that remained a profound influence on his work. Yeats began as a playwright, founding the Irish Literary Theatre in 1899, and wrote several plays celebrating Irish cultural tradition. The most important of these are *Cathleen ni Houlihan* (1902), *The King's Threshold* (1904), and *Deirdre* (1907). His early plays earned him the Nobel Prize for Literature in 1923. By 1912, he had turned to writing poetry. Profoundly influenced by William Blake, Yeats's poetry reflects Ireland's rich mythology and a fascination with the occult. His collections include *The Wild Swans at Coole* (1919), *Michael Robartes and the Dancer* (1921), *The Tower* (1928), and *The Winding Stair* (1933). Yeats's work spans the transition from the nineteenth century to the modernism of the twentieth century. In one of his most famous poems, "The Second Coming," Yeats presents an apocalyptic vision for humanity in the aftermath of WWI.

Turning and turning in the widening gyre[1]
The falcon cannot hear the falconer;
Things fall apart; the center cannot hold;
Mere anarchy is loosed upon the world,
The blood-dimmed tide is loosed, and everywhere   5
The ceremony of innocence is drowned;
The best lack all conviction, while the worst
Are full of passionate intensity.

Surely some revelation is at hand;
Surely the Second Coming is at hand.   10
The Second Coming! Hardly are those words out
When a vast image out of *Spiritus Mundi*[2]
Troubles my sight: somewhere in sands of the desert
A shape with lion body and the head of a man,
A gaze blank and pitiless as the sun,   15
Is moving its slow thighs, while all about it
Reel shadows of the indignant desert birds.
The darkness drops again; but now I know
That twenty centuries of stony sleep

---

[1]Widening spiral of a falcon's flight, used by Yeats to describe the cycles of history.—EDS.
[2]Soul of the world.—EDS.

Were vexed to nightmare by a rocking cradle,   20
And what rough beast, its hour come round at last,
Slouches towards Bethlehem to be born?

                                                                    [1921]

. . . .

Exploring the Text

1. Consider both the speaker and the imagery in the first eight lines. How do the images help create the persona of the speaker? How are the speaker and the imagery different in the last 14 lines?
2. What do you think the falcon and the falconer (l. 2) symbolize? What do you think it means that the "falcon cannot hear the falconer"? How is that metaphor connected to the image in lines 14–17?
3. What is the effect of the repetition of "loosed" in lines 4 and 5, and "Surely" in lines 9 and 10?
4. Describe the tone of the poem. How is it created?
5. Why do you think the poem ends with a question?
6. Adam Cohen, in an editorial in the *New York Times*, notes that phrases from "The Second Coming" are "irresistible to pundits"—analysts or commentators on politics or social policy—who find that lines such as "The best lack all conviction, while the worst / Are full of passionate intensity" (ll. 7–8) perfectly sum up any era in history. Cohen, however, believes that "The Second Coming" is "a powerful brief against punditry," a caution against confident predictions. Do you agree? Explain your answer.

Autumn Begins in Martins Ferry, Ohio

JAMES WRIGHT

James Wright was born in 1927 in Martins Ferry, Ohio, a small industrial town on the Ohio River. After graduating from Shreve High School, Wright served in the army and then attended Kenyon College on the GI Bill. He later studied in Vienna on a Fulbright scholarship, and went on to earn graduate degrees at the University of Washington, where he studied with Theodore Roethke. His early poems tended toward traditional forms, but by the early sixties, he had largely abandoned rhyme and meter in favor of loosely structured free verse. His works include *The Green Wall* (1957), *Saint Judas* (1959), and *The Branch Will Not Break* (1963). His 1972 *Collected Poems* was awarded a Pulitzer Prize. "Autumn Begins in Martins Ferry, Ohio" is from *The Branch Will Not Break*, and shares with the other poems of that collection not only stylistic daring but a thematic concern for loneliness and the means human beings employ to overcome or endure it.

In the Shreve High football stadium,
I think of Polacks nursing long beers in Tiltonsville,
And gray faces of Negroes in the blast furnace at Benwood,
And the ruptured night watchman of Wheeling Steel,
Dreaming of heroes.   5

All the proud fathers are ashamed to go home.
Their women cluck like starved pullets,
Dying for love.

Therefore,
Their sons grow suicidally beautiful   10
At the beginning of October,
And gallop terribly against each other's bodies.

                                                                [1963]

· ·

Exploring the Text

1. Why is the word "autumn" in the title significant? What associations do we make with autumn? How does each connotation affect your reading of the poem?
2. Who is the speaker? Where exactly do you picture him or her? What is it about the setting in the opening line that causes the speaker to "think" of the people in the next three lines?
3. Look carefully at the poem's diction. How do words and phrases such as "nursing" (l. 2), "ruptured" (l. 4), and "starved pullets" (l. 7) add layers of meaning to the poem? Find at least two more examples of diction that add nuance and meaning to the poem.
4. What is the effect of line 9, a single word: "Therefore"? What is its purpose?
5. Look carefully at the poem's last four lines. What connects them to the first stanza? What separates them from it?
6. Is this poem more about tradition or more about progress? Explain your answer.

A Bedtime Story

Mitsuye Yamada

Born in 1923 during a family visit to Fukuoka, Japan, Mitsuye Yamada was the daughter of two first-generation Japanese Americans. Shortly after the 1941 arrest of her father, a translator for the United States Immigration Service, on suspicion of espionage, the family was uprooted and sent to an internment camp. Yamada was kept at Minidoka War Relocation Center in Idaho for two years, until she and her brother, after taking oaths renouncing any loyalty to the emperor of Japan, were permitted to leave the facility in order to work and attend school. Yamada began her studies at the University of Cincinnati, finished her degree at New York

University in 1947, went on to earn an MA at the University of Chicago in 1953, and taught poetry in Southern California. Yamada began work on her first book, *Camp Notes and Other Poems*, during her internment, but it was not published until 1976. Her other books include *Lighthouse* (1976), *Desert Run* (1989), and *Three Asian American Writers Speak Out on Feminism* (2003). Yamada has said that the purpose of her writing is to encourage Asian American women to speak out and defy the unspoken cultural rules of silence and acquiescence. "A Bedtime Story," which appeared in *Camp Notes*, describes the changing relationship of new generations of Japanese Americans toward their inherited cultural values.

Once upon a time,
an old Japanese legend
goes as told
by Papa,
an old woman traveled through   5
many small villages
seeking refuge
for the night.

Each door opened
a sliver   10
in answer to her knock
then closed.
Unable to walk
any further
she wearily climbed a hill   15
found a clearing
and there lay down to rest
a few moments to catch
her breath.

The village town below   20
lay asleep except
for a few starlike lights.
Suddenly the clouds opened
and a full moon came into view
over the town.   25

The old woman sat up
turned toward
the village town
and in supplication
called out   30
Thank you people
of the village,

If it had not been for your
kindness
in refusing me a bed   35
for the night
these humble eyes would never
have seen this
memorable sight.
Papa paused, I waited.   40
In the comfort of our
hilltop home in Seattle
overlooking the valley,
I shouted
"That's the *end*?"   45

                                                                    [1976]

. . . .

Exploring the Text

1. Why do you think the first eight lines and the last six lines are punctuated differently from lines 9–39? What is the effect of the two different types of syntax?
2. Read the poem aloud to hear, as well as see, the short lines. What are some of the
   effects of these short lines? Consider their connection both to the woman walking
   and to the bedtime story, which is the heart of the poem.
3. Do you think the poem teaches a lesson? How about the story within the poem?
   Are they the same lesson? If so, what is it? If not, explain your answer.
4. How does the poem's last line, "That's the *end*?" comment on traditional and
   modern expectations of storytelling?
5. How do you think "A Bedtime Story" helps Yamada achieve her purpose of
   encouraging Asian American women to defy the unspoken rules of silence and
   acquiescence?

Goodbye, Goldeneye

May Swenson

Born in Utah, May Swenson (1913–1989) grew up speaking both Swedish and
English. She received her BA from Utah State University and then moved to New
York, where she spent most of her adult life. While writing poetry, Swenson worked
as stenographer, secretary, editor, and writer-in-residence at such schools as Bryn
Mawr, the University of North Carolina, and Purdue. Among the honors Swenson
received were a MacArthur Fellowship, a Guggenheim Fellowship, and the prestigious Bollingen Prize. Her work, which includes the collections *Another Animal*
(1954), *A Cage of Spines* (1958), *Half Sun Half Sleep* (1967), and *Iconographs*
(1970), is known for the questions it poses about love, human nature, and the
natural world. Four months before her death, Swenson wrote, "The best poetry

has its roots in the subconscious to a great degree. Youthful naivety, reliance on instinct more than learning and method, a sense of freedom and play, even trust in randomness, is necessary to the making of a poem." "Goodbye, Goldeneye" appeared in the collection *In Other Words* (1987).

Rag of black plastic, shred of a kite
caught on the telephone cable above the bay
has twisted in the wind all winter, summer, fall.

Leaves of birch and maple, brown paws of the oak
have all let go but this. Shiny black Mylar   5
on stem strong as fishline, the busted kite string

whipped around the wire and knotted—how long
will it cling there? Through another spring?
Long barge nudged up channel by a snorting tug,

its blunt front aproned with rot-black tires—   10
what is being hauled in slime-green drums?
The herring gulls that used to feed their young

on the shore—puffy, wide-beaked babies standing
spraddle-legged and crying—are not here this year.
Instead, steam shovel, bulldozer, cement mixer   15

rumble over sand, beginning the big new beach house.
There'll be a hotdog stand, flush toilets, trash—
plastic and glass, greasy cartons, crushed beercans,

barrels of garbage for water rats to pick through.
So, goodbye, goldeneye, and grebe and scaup and loon.   20
Goodbye, morning walks beside the tide tinkling

among clean pebbles, blue mussel shells and snail
shells that look like staring eyeballs. Goodbye,
kingfisher, little green, black crowned heron,

snowy egret. And, goodbye, oh faithful pair of   25
swans that used to glide—god and goddess
shapes of purity—over the wide water.

                                                                                        [1987]

· ·

Exploring the Text

1. What part does point of view play in developing the poem's images and themes? In other words, where exactly is the speaker? Does her location change? How do the questions the speaker asks in lines 8 and 11 help you locate her?

2. Swenson uses enjambment often in "Goodbye, Goldeneye" (ll. 6–7, 12–13, 15–16). What is its effect? How do the enjambed lines help develop a theme of the poem?

3. Analyze the description of the barge and the tug in lines 9–10. What's included? What's missing?

4. Goldeneyes, grebes, scaups, and loons are types of wild waterfowl; kingfishers, little greens, herons, and egrets are types of wading birds. Why do you think the poem calls so many birds by name?

5. Swenson is sometimes classified as a nature or ecology poet. What techniques does she use in this poem to transcend those genres and humanize and universalize her subject?

6. Swenson wrote several books for young readers. What echoes of children's books do you hear in the poem? What effect do they have?

7. In her introduction to *Nature: Poems Old and New* (1994)—a posthumous collection of Swenson's poetry—Susan Mitchell compares Swenson to Gerard Manley Hopkins. She notes especially both poets' "exuberant attention to detail." What other similarities do you see between "Goodbye, Goldeneye" and "God's Grandeur" (p. 1267)? What differences do you see?

Indian Movie, New Jersey

CHITRA BANERJEE DIVAKARUNI

Novelist, short-story writer, and poet Chitra Banerjee Divakaruni was born in 1956 in Calcutta, India, to a devout Hindu family, but she attended a Catholic convent school and was taught by Irish nuns. After completing her bachelor's degree at the University of Calcutta, Divakaruni moved to the United States in 1976 to pursue graduate study. She earned her MA from Wright State University and later received her PhD from the University of California at Berkeley. She is now a professor of writing at the University of Houston. Divakaruni has written many novels, including *The Mistress of Spices* (1997) and *The Palace of Illusion* (2006). "Indian Movie, New Jersey" comes from her 1997 collection, *Leaving Yuba City: New and Collected Poems*, which won the Allen Ginsberg Poetry Prize and the Pushcart Prize. Like much of Divakaruni's work, this poem addresses the conflicts between old and new world values.

Not like the white filmstars, all rib
and gaunt cheekbone, the Indian sex-goddess
smiles plumply from behind a flowery
branch. Below her brief red skirt, her thighs
are satisfying-solid, redeeming   5
as tree trunks. She swings her hips
and the men-viewers whistle. The lover-hero

dances in to a song, his lip-sync
a little off, but no matter, we
know the words already and sing along.   10
It is safe here, the day
golden and cool so no one sweats,
roses on every bush and the Dal Lake
clean again.
        The sex-goddess switches   15
to thickened English to emphasize
a joke. We laugh and clap. Here
we need not be embarrassed by words
dropping like lead pellets into foreign ears.
The flickering movie-light   20
wipes from our faces years of America, sons
who want mohawks and refuse to run
the family store, daughters who date
on the sly.
        When at the end the hero   25
dies for his friend who also
loves the sex-goddess and now can marry her,
we weep, understanding. Even the men
clear their throats to say, "What *qurbani*![1]
What *dosti*!"[2] After, we mill around   30
unwilling to leave, exchange greetings
and good news: a new gold chain, a trip
to India. We do not speak
of motel raids, canceled permits, stones
thrown through glass windows, daughters and sons   35
raped by Dotbusters.[3]
        In this dim foyer
we can pull around us the faint, comforting smell
of incense and *pakoras*,[4] can arrange
our children's marriages with hometown boys and girls,   40
open a franchise, win a million
in the mail. We can retire
in India, a yellow two-storied house
with wrought-iron gates, our own
Ambassador car. Or at least   45

---

[1]Sacrifice. — EDS.
[2]Friendship. — EDS.
[3]New Jersey gangs that attack Indians. — EDS.
[4]Savory fried pastries eaten as appetizers. — EDS.

move to a rich white suburb, Summerfield
or Fort Lee, with neighbors that will
talk to us. Here while the film-songs still echo
in the corridors and restrooms, we can trust
in movie truths: sacrifice, success, love and luck,   50
the America that was supposed to be.

[1997]

Exploring the Text

1. Why do you think the poem begins by describing what Indian movies are "Not" (l. 1)?
2. Look carefully at the figurative language of the poem. What, for example, is the effect of similes such as "thighs / . . . redeeming / as tree trunks" (ll. 4–6) and "words / dropping like lead pellets" (ll. 18–19)?
3. Who do you think is the "we" of the poem?
4. Analyze the vivid and concrete details in the poem. What is the effect of their accumulation? How does the accumulation of details connect to the pleasure of watching "Bollywood" (Indian) films, as described here?
5. How does Divakaruni highlight the values of the audience through their response to the images on the screen?
6. How is this poem about tradition and progress? Does the speaker expect to return to the traditions of India? Why is a home in a "rich white suburb" (l. 46) only second best?

Charlotte Brontë in Leeds Point

Stephen Dunn

Stephen Dunn was born in Forest Hills, New York, in 1939. He studied history at Hofstra University, earning his BA in 1962. He attended the New School for Social Research, briefly played professional basketball, and worked as a copywriter before receiving his MFA in poetry from Syracuse University in 1972. Dunn is the Richard Stockton College of New Jersey Distinguished Professor in creative writing. His collections of poetry include *Looking for Holes in the Ceiling* (1974), *A Circus of Needs* (1978), *Not Dancing* (1984), *Landscape at the End of the Century* (1991), and *Different Hours* (2000), which was awarded the Pulitzer Prize for Poetry. "Charlotte Brontë in Leeds Point" is from *Local Visitations* (2003), a collection in which Dunn imagines several writers transplanted to his home state of New Jersey. Selections include "Chekhov in Point Republic," "George Eliot in Beach Haven," and "Twain in Atlantic City."

From her window marshland stretched for miles.
If not for egrets and gulls, it reminded her of the moors
behind the parsonage, how the fog often hovered
and descended as if sheltering some sweet compulsion
the age was not ready to see. On clear days the jagged   5
skyline of Atlantic City was visible—Atlantic City,
where all compulsions had a home.

"Everything's too easy now," she said to her neighbor,
"nothing resisted, nothing gained." Once, at eighteen,
she dreamed of London's proud salons glowing   10
with brilliant fires and dazzling chandeliers.
Already her own person—passionate, assertive—
soon she'd create a governess insistent on rights equal
to those above her rank. "The dangerous picture

of a natural heart," one offended critic carped.   15
She'd failed, he said, to let religion reign
over the passions and, worse, she was a woman.
Now she was amazed at what women had,
doubly amazed at what they didn't.
But she hadn't come back to complain or haunt.   20
Her house on the bay was modest, adequate.

It need not accommodate brilliant sisters
or dissolute brothers, spirits lost or fallen.
Feminists would pay homage, praise her honesty
and courage. Rarely was she pleased. After all,   25
she was an artist; to speak of honesty in art,
she knew, was somewhat beside the point.
And she had married, had even learned to respect

the weakness in men, those qualities they called
their strengths. Whatever the struggle, she wanted men   30
included. Charlotte missed reading chapters to Emily,
Emily reading chapters to her. As ever, though, she'd try
to convert present into presence, something unsung
sung, some uprush of desire frankly acknowledged,
even in this, her new excuse for a body.   35

[2003]

Exploring the Text

1. In lines 1–7, what comparison does Dunn make between Atlantic City and the moors of England, where the novels of the Brontë sisters are set?

2. The speaker imagines the fog "sheltering some sweet compulsion" (l. 4). What is the effect of personifying fog? How does the theme of compulsion echo later in the poem?
3. What is the effect of the enjambment in lines 14–15?
4. In lines 18–19, what is the view of the Brontë character on the subject of women's place in society? Does she believe women have made progress in the days since she created *Jane Eyre*?
5. In *Local Visitations*, which includes this poem, Dunn imagines several writers in his home state of New Jersey. Imagine a favorite writer of yours visiting your hometown. What comments do you think he or she would make? Write about the event in a poem or short story.
6. According to legend, Leeds Point, New Jersey, is the birthplace of the Jersey Devil, a creature who is commonly believed to be the thirteenth child of Deborah Leeds, who immigrated to the Leeds Point area from England. The Devil haunts the New Jersey Pine Barrens, near what is now Atlantic City. How does Dunn incorporate this legend into his poem? What part does he imagine Charlotte Brontë playing in the legend?

When All of My Cousins Are Married

AIMEE NEZHUKUMATATHIL

Born in 1974 in Chicago, Illinois, Aimee Nezhukumatathil [Nez-ZOO-koo-mah-tah-TILL] is known for poetry that draws on her Filipino and south Indian background. She is an associate professor at the State University of New York at Fredonia, where she teaches creative writing and environmental literature. *Miracle Fruit* (2003), her first collection of poetry, won the Tupelo Prize, *ForeWord* magazine's Book of the Year Award in poetry, and the Global Filipino Award. Her newest collection, *At the Drive-In Volcano* (2007), was awarded the Balcones Poetry Prize. The poem "When All of My Cousins Are Married," from *At the Drive-In Volcano*, considers the complications of being an unmarried Indian woman.

I read books about marriage customs in India,
trying to remember that I am above words like
arranged, dowry, Engineer. On page 28, it says to show

approval and happiness for the new couple, throw
dead-crispy spiders instead of rice or birdseed.   5
Female relatives will brush the corners of closets

for months, swipe under kitchen sinks with a dry cloth
to collect the basketfuls needed for the ceremony.
Four years ago, I was reading a glossy (*Always*

reading, chides my grandmother) in her living room   10
and a spider larger than my hand sidled out
from underneath a floor-length curtain

and left through the front door without saying
good-bye. No apologies for its size — its legs
only slightly thinner than a pencil. None   15

of my cousins thought anything was wrong.
But it didn't bite you! It left, no? I know what they
are thinking: *She is the oldest grandchild*

and not married. Afraid of spiders. But it's not
that I'm squeamish, it's not that I need to stand   20
on a chair if I spy a bug scooting along

my baseboards — I just want someone who gasps
at a gigantic jackfruit still dangling from a thin branch,
thirty feet in the air. Someone who can see a dark cluster

of spider eyes and our two tiny faces —   25
smashed cheek to cheek — reflected in each.

[2007]

. . . .

Exploring the Text

1. The speaker of "When All of My Cousins Are Married" seems ambivalent about being the only unmarried cousin. Find evidence that shows her mixed feelings.
2. What do you think the "spider larger than my hand" (l. 11) represents? What might it mean that it "left . . . without saying / good-bye" (ll. 13–14)? How is it connected to the speaker being the oldest grandchild and unmarried?
3. Spiders are considered good luck in many cultures. Look carefully at the description of how dead spiders are used and collected in lines 3–8. Might there be another reason for the custom? How can the custom be considered ironically?
4. Why do you think Nezhukumatathil italicizes words in lines 3, 9–10, and 17–19?
5. How does the poem — and the meaning of the spider — turn in the last five lines? What does this turn reveal about the speaker and what she sees as the difference between her cousins and herself?
6. Do you believe that the speaker is really "above" the traditions surrounding Indian marriages? Explain why or why not.

AIMEE NEZHUKUMATATHIL ON WRITING

Robin Dissin Aufses (RA): When you were awarded the Balcones Poetry Prize, the judges noted that you had heeded Ezra Pound's call to "make it new." What do you think makes your poetry "new"?

Aimee Nezhukumatathil (AN): I'm hoping that people find moments of delight and surprise in my poems—a chance to look at elements of nature, at relationships, in a way they hadn't previously considered. I read just as many nonfiction books about nature as I do collections of poems or stories, and I often feel so overwhelmed by the sheer amount of natural beauty out there in this world that I suppose in some ways I feel compelled to get it down on the page, record it in such a way that others might find small bits of joy and delight in an accessible way in poetry.

RA: In your poem "Hippopotomonstrosesquippedaliophobia," which appeared on Slate.com, the speaker is an instructor (you?) who addresses her students and the anxiety they might feel when they see a long, complicated last name. I assume they're not really afraid of a long name; what do you think they fear?

AN: I could venture that the easy answer is that some students face the fear of the unknown when they step into my classroom. As one of the youngest tenured professors in the state of New York, I know that my manner and demeanor means I could pass for a student (though that is becoming harder to do with each year!)—and yet I also look different from the predominantly white population of my campus. But what I think is the heart of the matter here is that in the first fifteen minutes of stepping inside my classroom, I make it quite clear that I will be asking them to work and think in ways having to do not only with their writing but with their life, and to examine their place on this earth. I let them know that this examination is not going to be easy; it will be tough and unpleasant, perhaps even embarrassing, but I also hope exuberant and joy-filled as well. And I also tell them that they will learn more about themselves (and one another) than they have in any other class. You can imagine for some—especially the ones who have never written a poem before in their lives—this could be a pretty daunting realization.

RA: So many reviews of your work remark on the balancing act you seem to do between "well-crafted formal restraint" and "unabashed exoticism of the senses," as R. D. Pohl noted in the *Buffalo News* review of your collection *At the Drive-In Volcano.* Do you think this is a fair assessment? If so, is this balancing conscious? What other balancing acts do you perform?

5

AN: The balancing is conscious, insofar as craft is concerned. I honestly think many people are surprised when they find out writing a poem is more than merely jotting pretty thoughts down and voilà!—you have a poem. I go through two to three drafts of a poem, though I find that when I am enjoying a productive writing streak I have to do less revising, but the point is I am always revising. Ultimately and simply put, I want my poems to be clear to the reader—I'm not interested in confusing them—but at the same time I want there to be an "aha" moment in presenting something ordinary in a surprising way.

Now that I am beginning to write about motherhood, I feel a balancing act is taking place in a similar vein. Motherhood is a popular subject, and I know all too well that some people would rather get a root canal than read another poem about motherhood. But after avoiding the subject for some time (my son is now 20 months old), I feel like I'm a fraud by *not* writing about it. So I tackle that subject the same way I do any other poem—find something new and insightful to say about the subject, find ways to inject musicality and delight in the craft of writing it.

RA: Your poem "When All of My Cousins Are Married" appears in this chapter, which is entitled "Tradition and Progress." What aspects of your work do you consider traditional? progressive? Can you also talk a little about the traditional and progressive aspects of your background and how they influence your work?

AN: I've written several poems on being a teenager, feeling hopelessly out-of-place as a teenager, wanting to fit in among my peers, and so on. These are subjects most anyone could relate to, of course, but in my case, being the only Asian American in an entire school—except for my younger sister, who was one year behind me—only amplified that feeling of isolation. It didn't help that we grew up in small, rural towns and often lived on the grounds of the state psychiatric hospital (my mom was a psychiatrist). The stares and questions, such as, "What *are* you, exactly?" never ceased, even from teachers who meant well but only isolated us even more with their banter about the origins of my last name during roll call. One teacher even joked that we must be descendants of the Aztec in front of the entire class! Our desire to be the same as everyone else in our sleepy western New York town—to blend in perfectly with the blond cheerleaders, to be liked by all the football players—ruled our lives.

All during elementary school and high school, I felt as if I had to explain so much of my culture to my friends/boyfriends. They knew I was American—had no accent whatsoever—yet to them I was still different in lots of ways. It's funny, because my writing is still a lot of that "explaining," I think. Why I couldn't do this or that, why we eat this or that, and so on. But I guess it opened my eyes to two whole other cultures that are not being as heard in mainstream literature, and I wanted that to change. My parents were floored when I told them I didn't want to be a doctor (horrified, actually), but now they are very supportive and love it when they find a smidge of one of their stories in my writing.

I think because my sister and I were raised in suburban neighborhoods where my family was the *only* family of color, I was so used to having to "explain" my (then) unusual packed lunches of lumpia and fried rice, or having fish for breakfast. So I think in some ways you could say I spent my whole childhood and teen years building a language that is accessible yet colorful—very handy now, when I am writing, no?

10

The one thing I never hid while I was growing up was my curiosity and love of language and story, and I hope that element is present in my poems. So even though I may be writing about elements of my Filipina and South Indian background, I hope to do so in ways that make it accessible and meaningful to everyone. I'm very much drawn to classical poetic forms, such as the haibun and the ghazal, and try to use them to tell mini-stories in verse form.

RA: The natural world finds its way into your poetry in a way that goes beyond just glorifying its beauty. Can you talk a little about the part nature and science play in your work and how they came to be so important to you?

AN: The visual artist in me wants to present beauty in ways that are unexpected. A former grad-school classmate once told me that when he thinks of India, he thinks of poverty and dirt. That stuck with me and really burned me up. No way was I going to let people get away with thinking that of my father's beloved home country. And that was just one person! So I guess I try to present unexpected miracles in nature, myth, science, and relationships. And of course there is so much darkness in nature. If you acknowledge the beauty and joy, you have to also acknowledge the death and sorrow.

My examination of the dark side of animals and plants (such as the image of sharks stripped of their fins and thrown to the bottom of the ocean, bleeding to death, in *At the Drive-In Volcano*) served as a helpful metaphor while I was struggling to write about the end of a relationship. Using metaphor in this way helped create a necessary veil between the author and the speaker of the poems. If I don't surprise myself when I am writing, I usually can tell—my writing becomes flat, a matte finish if you will. I believe the writer's unpardonable sin is making the reader bored, so I guess you could say if I had one goal in using science and nature in my poems, it would be to not bore the reader while finding metaphors in science and nature to illuminate a personal experience in a more universal way.

15

Follow-Up

1. What do you think Aimee Nezhukumatathil means by the "necessary veil between the author and the speaker" (para. 15) of her poems? Do you agree that the veil is necessary?
2. Nezhukumatathil says that she spent much of her teenage years explaining her culture to her classmates. In what ways does "When All of My Cousins Are Married" explain the speaker's culture? What evidence is there of Nezhukumatathil's "language that is accessible yet colorful" (para. 11)?
3. Having read "When All of My Cousins Are Married" and the interview with Nezhukumatathil, do you think her college classes veer toward the traditional or the progressive? Explain your answer.

Forty Acres

DEREK WALCOTT

Poet, playwright, and critic Derek Walcott was born in 1930 on the Caribbean island of St. Lucia. He is best known for his epic poem *Omeros* (1990), a retelling of the *Odyssey* set in the Caribbean, the American West, and London. In his plays and poems, Walcott frequently explores the problems of identity that have emerged in the aftermath of colonialism and slavery. Walcott founded the Trinidad Theatre Workshop in 1951 and the Boston Playwrights' Theatre in 1981, taught poetry and theater at Boston University for many years, and now gives lectures and readings throughout the world, dividing much of his time between Trinidad and New York City. Walcott's works include the poetry collections *The Castaway and Other Poems* (1965), *Sea Grapes* (1976), and *The Fortunate Traveller* (1981), and the plays *The Joker of Seville* (1974), *O Babylon!* (1976), *The Odyssey: A Stage Version* (1993), and *The Haitian Trilogy* (2002). He won the Nobel Prize for Literature in 1992. "Forty Acres" was commissioned by the *London Times* in honor of the historic election of Barack Obama, the first black president of the United States, in November 2008.

Out of the turmoil emerges one emblem, an engraving —
a young Negro at dawn in straw hat and overalls,
an emblem of impossible prophecy, a crowd
dividing like the furrow which a mule has ploughed,
parting for their president: a field of snow-flecked cotton   5
forty acres wide, of crows with predictable omens
that the young ploughman ignores for his unforgotten
cotton-haired ancestors, while lined on one branch, is a tense   10
court of bespectacled owls and, on the field's receding rim —
a gesticulating scarecrow stamping with rage at him.
The small plough continues on this lined page
beyond the moaning ground, the lynching tree, the tornado's   15
black vengeance,
and the young ploughman feels the change in his veins,
heart, muscles, tendons,
till the land lies open like a flag as dawn's sure
light streaks the field and furrows wait for the sower.   20

[2008]

Exploring the Text

1. Look closely at the figurative language in "Forty Acres." How do figures of speech, such as the simile in lines 3 and 4 ("a crowd / dividing like the furrow which a mule has ploughed"), connect the poem's rural setting to its meaning as a whole?

2. Whom do you think the "court of bespectacled owls" (l. 11) and the "gesticulating scarecrow" (l. 13) refer to? Why do you think the owls are tense and the scarecrow is angry?

3. The title, "Forty Acres," refers to the forty acres of land and a mule to plow it that was promised as compensation to freed slaves. How does the allusion in the title add a level of meaning to the poem?

4. The poem functions on several levels. Consider it first as a literal description of the work of a young farmer, then as a statement about modern politics. How does each reading add nuance to the other?

5. The poem could be considered a georgic, named after a series of poems by the Latin poet Virgil on how to manage a farm. Georgics are about rural business, as opposed to pastorals, which give us a romanticized depiction of leisurely rural life. Why is the georgic a particularly effective model for Walcott's subject?

6. How does the poem both celebrate and criticize American history?

7. Read the poem aloud. How does the poem's stately rhythm make a statement about America's first African American president? about American history?

PAIRED POEMS

Mannahatta

WALT WHITMAN

Walt Whitman (1819–1892) was born on Long Island, New York. Early in his life, he worked as a country schoolteacher and printer, and served as writer and editor for the *Brooklyn Eagle* newspaper. He continued in a variety of jobs, writing and working as a carpenter, and published his now famous *Leaves of Grass* in 1855. Regarded as offensive and vulgar at the time for its outspoken content, the poem celebrated individuality and the richness of life. In 1862, Whitman went to Virginia to find his brother George, who had been wounded in the Civil War. He was shocked to witness the horrors of war firsthand on the battlefield, and was deeply moved by the suffering of the wounded. He worked as an aide in army hospitals in Washington, caring first for his brother and then other soldiers as well. Among Whitman's most well-known poems from this time are "Oh Captain, My Captain" and "When Lilacs Last in the Dooryard Bloomed," both about Abraham Lincoln. Whitman is considered by many critics to be the first urban poet, and his celebration of New York City, "Mannahatta," suggests that he is the exception to the nineteenth-century rule that American intellectuals preferred the natural world.

I was asking for something specific and perfect for my city,
Whereupon lo! upsprang the aboriginal name.

Now I see what there is in a name, a word, liquid, sane,
   unruly, musical, self-sufficient,
I see that the word of my city is that word from of old,
Because I see that word nested in nests of water-bays,   5
   superb,
Rich, hemm'd thick all around with sailships and steamships,
   an island sixteen miles long, solid-founded,
Numberless crowded streets, high growths of iron, slender,
   strong, light, splendidly uprising toward clear skies,
Tides swift and ample, well-loved by me, toward sundown,
The flowing sea-currents, the little islands, larger adjoining
   islands, the heights, the villas,
The countless masts, the white shore-steamers, the lighters,   10
   the ferry-boats, the black sea-steamers well-model'd,
The down-town streets, the jobbers' houses of business, the
   houses of business of the ship-merchants and money-
   brokers, the river-streets,
Immigrants arriving, fifteen or twenty thousand a week,
The carts hauling goods, the manly race of drivers of horses,
   the brown-faced sailors,
The summer air, the bright sun shining, and the sailing clouds
   aloft,
The winter snows, the sleigh-bells, the broken ice in the   15
   river, passing along up or down with the flood-tide or
   ebb-tide,
The mechanics of the city, the masters, well-form'd, beautiful-
   faced, looking you straight in the eyes,
Trottoirs throng'd, vehicles, Broadway, the women, the shops
   and shows,
A million people—manners free and superb—open voices—
   hospitality—the most courageous and friendly young
   men,
City of hurried and sparkling waters! city of spires and masts!
City nested in bays! my city!   20

[1860]

· ·

Exploring the Text

1. "Mannahatta" was the name given to Manhattan by the Native Americans who
lived there before the Dutch settlers arrived. Why do you think Whitman rhapso-
dizes about this early name?

2. We can assume that Whitman is the speaker—he is one of the great New York poets. Describe the speaker's persona. From what vantage point does he see the city? Is he an observer or a participant?
3. How does Whitman create the poem's pace? What is the connection between its pace and its subject?
4. What contrasts does "Mannahatta" set up? Look carefully at how Whitman invokes the past and the present.
5. Walt Whitman is credited with the invention of American free verse, which is poetry that lacks a strict meter or rhyming sequence but is still recognizable as poetry because of its rhythmic cadence. Whitman used some conventional poetic techniques, such as iambic pentameter—the traditional meter of the sonnet—and anaphora—the repetition of the first word in a line—to achieve that cadence. Examine the cadence in "Mannahatta." Do you see any other techniques Whitman used to achieve it? What is its effect in the poem? How does the cadence help create the vivid setting that is the subject of the poem?

Chicago

Carl Sandburg

Carl Sandburg (1878–1967) was born in Galesburg, Illinois, the son of Swedish immigrants. He spent most of his life in the Midwest, working as a reporter and a writer of poetry—such as *Good Morning, America* (1928) and *The People, Yes* (1936)—history, biography, fiction, children's books (most famously the *Rootabaga Stories* in the 1920s), and folk songs. He fought in the Spanish-American War and served as secretary to the mayor of Milwaukee, who was the country's first Socialist mayor. Sandburg and his wife raised their family in the suburbs of Chicago. Sandburg was awarded two Pulitzers, one for his biography *Abraham Lincoln: The War Years* (1939) and one for his collection *The Complete Poems* (1950); he also received a Best Performance—Documentary or Spoken Word Grammy for his collaboration with the New York Philharmonic (1959). The poem "Chicago" is one of the most famous literary descriptions of an American city.

> Hog Butcher for the World,
> Tool Maker, Stacker of Wheat,
> Player with Railroads and the Nation's Freight Handler;
> Stormy, husky, brawling,
> City of the Big Shoulders: 5

They tell me you are wicked and I believe them, for I have seen your
    painted women under the gas lamps luring the farm boys.
And they tell me you are crooked and I answer: Yes, it is true I have
    seen the gunman kill and go free to kill again.

And they tell me you are brutal and my reply is: On the faces of women
   and children I have seen the marks of wanton hunger.
And having answered so I turn once more to those who sneer at this
   my city, and I give them back the sneer and say to them:
Come and show me another city with lifted head singing so proud to   10
   be alive and coarse and strong and cunning.
Flinging magnetic curses amid the toil of piling job on job, here is a
   tall bold slugger set vivid against the little soft cities;
Fierce as a dog with tongue lapping for action, cunning as a savage
   pitted against the wilderness,
       Bareheaded,
       Shoveling,
       Wrecking,   15
       Planning,
       Building, breaking, rebuilding,
Under the smoke, dust all over his mouth, laughing with white teeth,
Under the terrible burden of destiny laughing as a young man laughs,
Laughing even as an ignorant fighter laughs who has never lost a battle,   20
Bragging and laughing that under his wrist is the pulse, and under his ribs
   the heart of the people,
             Laughing!
Laughing the stormy, husky, brawling laughter of Youth, half-naked,
   sweating, proud to be Hog Butcher, Tool Maker, Stacker of Wheat,
   Player with Railroads and Freight Handler to the Nation.

[1916]

Exploring the Text

1. Personification is the principal technique in "Chicago." Describe the persona Sandburg creates for the city.

2. Sandburg also uses apostrophe, a figure of speech in which someone or something either dead or inanimate is addressed as if it were able to reply. What is the effect of addressing Chicago? What might it reply if it could answer?

3. Describe the poem's tone. How does Sandburg create it? How is Chicago honored through the poem's tone?

4. In lines 18–23, the words "laughs" and "laughing" are repeated over and over. Characterize the city's laughter. How does it both create an image and comment on Sandburg's Chicago?

5. Sandburg's work was inspired by Whitman, especially his use of free verse. The poet Amy Lowell said that the ideal of free verse was to "copy new rhythms — as expressions of new moods — and not to copy old rhythms, which merely echo old moods." How does the rhythm of "Chicago" express "new moods"?

6. Nearly a third of the city burned down in the Chicago Fire of 1871; in the aftermath, the city underwent a period of rapid reconstruction and growth. What passages in the poem seem specifically to deal with this event? How does this part of Chicago history relate to the persona that Sandburg attributes to the city?

Focus on Comparison and Contrast

1. Both "Mannahatta" and "Chicago" have a cadence that is characteristic of free verse. What are the similarities and differences in their cadences?
2. Whitman was famous for his lists, a technique that is also evident in Sandburg's "Chicago." What is the effect of these lists? How do the poets use repetition without seeming repetitive?
3. What do the poems have in common in their descriptions of cities? What is different?
4. Compare and contrast the speakers in the two poems. What do they have in common? How are they different? How does each poet create the speaker's persona?
5. Read "Mannahatta" and "Chicago" aloud. Compare and contrast the way free verse imbues the two poems with energy and vigor. You might also look for videos on the Internet in which filmmakers have combined images of New York City and Chicago with the poets' words.

Writing Assignment

"Mannahatta" by Walt Whitman and "Chicago" by Carl Sandburg each praise the city in which it is set. Compare the speakers' pride in their cities and analyze the techniques the poets use to communicate and re-create the speakers' feelings.

Portrait of Andries Stilte II

KEHINDE WILEY

Kehinde Wiley was born in 1977 in Los Angeles. He lives in New York and is a photorealist painter whose work is inspired by traditional portraitists, such as Sir Joshua Reynolds, Thomas Gainsborough, Titian, and Jean Auguste Dominique Ingres. His paintings are in the permanent collections of the Columbus Museum of Art, the Studio Museum in Harlem, the Walker Art Center, the Miami Art Museum, and the Detroit Institute of Arts, among others. In *Portrait of Andries Stilte II*, the subject is posing in the style of Hyacinthe Rigaud's *Portrait of Louis XIV*.

Portrait of Andries Stilte II (2006, oil on canvas, 72 x 96 in.)

Exploring the Text

1. *Portrait of Andries Stilte II* was inspired by Hyacinthe Rigaud's 1701 *Portrait of Louis XIV*, which hangs in the Louvre. Rigaud was known for his ability to create exact likenesses and for the precise details of his subjects' costumes and backgrounds. View his painting online at louvre.fr. What echoes of Rigaud's style do you find in Wiley's portrait? How does Wiley use elements of Rigaud's painting in new ways?

2. Traditionally, portraits were created through commissions. Families and governments hired artists to celebrate and memorialize individuals. The paintings often became important state or family records. What does *Portrait of Andries Stilte II* celebrate? What record does it make? Consider both the elements of the Rigaud portrait that remain and the representation of its modern subject.

3. Try to identify the painting's references to both traditional and modern art. How do those elements add levels of meaning to both this work and Rigaud's work?

4. Many of Wiley's paintings, including the one here (6′ × 8′), are larger than life. How does their heroic size comment on both the young black men who pose and the culture of those men?

5. Wiley's method is to approach young African American men, talk to them about his work, and ask them to choose a traditional painting as an inspiration for a portrait. Look at some famous traditional portraits. Which would you choose as the inspiration for your portrait? Explain your answer.

Conversation

The Harlem Renaissance: Progress within Tradition?

A great flowering of black arts and culture, the **Harlem Renaissance** continues to be a source of fascination, debate, and discussion among literary critics and historians. Even the dates remain problematic. Most agree that the movement began after the 1919 "Red Summer" of race riots in urban centers throughout the United States and continued as a result of the Great Migration of African Americans from the rural South to northern cities. Some cite the economic crash of 1929 as the end; others, including African American scholar Henry Louis Gates Jr., put it at 1939, the start of World War II. Regardless of the exact beginning and ending, all agree that the period of the 1920s was a time of extraordinary creativity that centered around New York City, specifically Harlem, and left a breathtaking legacy of writers, musicians, visual artists, and intellectual productivity. Further, this period, called "more a spirit than a movement" by critic Robert Hemenway, was marked by a range of ideas and writing styles, exploration of both African and American cultural heritages, protests against racial discrimination, and a sense of self-assertion and pride. Implicit in the Harlem Renaissance, however, was a tension between those artists who believed in working within the tradition of their American and African American cultural heritage, and those who argued for a break from the past to forge an entirely new cultural consciousness. The essays, poems, fiction, and visual text that follow illustrate a range of viewpoints on this issue.

Texts

James Weldon Johnson, preface to *The Book of American Negro Poetry* (nonfiction)

Langston Hughes, "The Negro Artist and the Racial Mountain" (nonfiction)

Langston Hughes, "Jazzonia" (poetry)

Claude McKay, "The White House" (poetry)

Zora Neale Hurston, "Spunk" (fiction)

Aaron Douglas, *The Spirit of Africa* (woodcut)

Arna Bontemps, "Nocturne at Bethesda" (poetry)

Jessie Redmon Fauset, from *Plum Bun: A Novel without a Moral* (fiction)

Preface to *The Book of American Negro Poetry*

JAMES WELDON JOHNSON

James Weldon Johnson (1871–1938) may be best remembered for writing "Lift Ev'ry Voice and Sing" (1900), which has come to be known as the Negro national anthem. Johnson had a distinguished career in academe, holding the Adam K. Spence Chair of Creative Literature at Fisk University. He wrote *The Autobiography of an Ex-Colored Man* (1912, reissued 1927), a novel about "passing" and the psychological cost of assuming a dual identity, and edited *The Book of American Negro Poetry*, which Henry Louis Gates Jr. calls "a landmark in the history of African American literature." The following is an excerpt from the preface to that work.

The final measure of the greatness of all peoples is the amount and standard of the literature and art they have produced. The world does not know that a people is great until that people produces great literature and art. No people that has produced great literature and art has ever been looked upon by the world as distinctly inferior. . . .

And nothing will do more to change that mental attitude and raise his status than a demonstration of intellectual parity by the Negro through the production of literature and art. . . .

The Negro in the United States has achieved or been placed in a certain artistic niche. When he is thought of artistically, it is as a happy-go-lucky, singing, shuffling, banjo-picking being or as a more or less pathetic figure. The picture of him is in a log cabin amid fields of cotton or along the levees. Negro dialect is naturally and by long association the exact instrument for voicing this phase of Negro life; and by that very exactness it is an instrument with but two full stops, humor and pathos. So even when he confines himself to purely racial themes, the Aframerican poet realizes that there are phases of Negro life in the United States which cannot be treated in the dialect either adequately or artistically. Take, for example, the phases rising out of life in Harlem, that most wonderful Negro city in the world. I do not deny that a Negro in a log cabin is more picturesque than a Negro in a Harlem flat, but the Negro in the Harlem flat is here, and he is but part of a group growing everywhere in the country, a group whose ideals are becoming increasingly more vital than those of the traditionally artistic group, even if its members are less picturesque.

What the colored poet in the United States needs to do is something like what Synge[1] did for the Irish; he needs to find a form that will express the racial spirit by symbols from within rather than by symbols from without, such as the mere mutilation of

---

[1]John Millington Synge (1871–1909) wrote plays about Irish rural life in a stylized peasant accent. His work was part of a nationalist renaissance in Irish literature at the end of the nineteenth and beginning of the twentieth centuries. — EDS.

English spelling and pronunciation. He needs a form that is freer and larger than dialect, but which will still hold the racial flavor; a form expressing the imagery, the idioms, the peculiar turns of thought, and the distinctive humor and pathos, too, of the Negro, but which will also be capable of voicing the deepest and highest emotions and aspirations, and allow of the widest range of subjects and the widest scope of treatment.

Negro dialect is at present a medium that is not capable of giving expression to   5
the varied conditions of Negro life in America, and much less is it capable of giving the fullest interpretation of Negro character and psychology. This is no indictment against the dialect as dialect, but against the mould of convention in which Negro dialect in the United States has been set. In time these conventions may become lost, and the colored poet in the United States may sit down to write in dialect without feeling that his first line will put the general reader in a frame of mind which demands that the poem be humorous or pathetic. In the meantime, there is no reason why these poets should not continue to do the beautiful things that can be done, and done best, in the dialect.

In stating the need for Aframerican poets in the United States to work out a new and distinctive form of expression I do not wish to be understood to hold any theory that they should limit themselves to Negro poetry, to racial themes; the sooner they are able to write *American* poetry spontaneously, the better. Nevertheless, I believe that the richest contribution the Negro poet can make to the American literature of the future will be the fusion into it of his own individual artistic gifts.

[1922]

Questions

1. Does Johnson believe that dialect poetry is or can be "great literature" (para. 1)? Explain your response.
2. What does Johnson mean when he says that the poet "needs to find a form that will express the racial spirit by symbols from within rather than by symbols from without" (para. 4)?
3. What is the effect of Johnson shifting between the terms "Negro," "colored," and "Aframerican"?
4. What does Johnson believe is "the richest contribution" (para. 6) the African American poet can make?

The Negro Artist and the Racial Mountain

and

Jazzonia

LANGSTON HUGHES

During his yearlong stint at Columbia University, Langston Hughes (1902–1967) became involved with the Harlem movement. After leaving Columbia because of the endemic racial prejudice there, he traveled for three years, spending some time in Paris before returning to the United States in 1925. After completing his degree at Lincoln University, he returned to Harlem for the remainder of his life. His first volume of poetry, *The Weary Blues* (1926), contained "The Negro Speaks of Rivers," perhaps his most famous poem. Hughes is remembered for his celebration of the uniqueness of African American culture, which found expression in "The Negro Artist and the Racial Mountain" and "Jazzonia."

The Negro Artist and the Racial Mountain

One of the most promising of the young Negro poets[1] said to me once, "I want to be a poet—not a Negro poet," meaning, I believe, "I want to write like a white poet"; meaning subconsciously, "I would like to be a white poet"; meaning behind that, "I would like to be white." And I was sorry the young man said that, for no great poet has ever been afraid of being himself. And I doubted then that, with his desire to run away spiritually from his race, this boy would ever be a great poet. But this is the mountain standing in the way of any true Negro art in America—this urge within the race toward whiteness, the desire to pour racial individuality into the mold of American standardization, and to be as little Negro and as much American as possible.

But let us look at the immediate background of this young poet. His family is of what I suppose one would call the Negro middle class: people who are by no means rich yet never uncomfortable nor hungry—smug, contented, respectable folk, members of the Baptist church. The father goes to work every morning. He is a chief steward at a large white club. The mother sometimes does fancy sewing or supervises parties for the rich families of the town. The children go to a mixed school. In the home they read white papers and magazines. And the mother often says "Don't be like niggers" when the children are bad. A frequent phrase from the father is, "Look how well a white man does things." And so the word *white* comes to be unconsciously a symbol of all the virtues. It holds for the children beauty, morality, and money. The whisper of "I want to be white" runs silently through their minds. This young poet's home is, I believe, a fairly typical home of the colored middle class. One sees immediately how difficult it would be for an artist born in such a home to interest himself in interpreting the beauty of his own people. He is never taught to see that beauty. He is taught rather not to see it, or if he does, to be ashamed of it when it is not according to Caucasian patterns.

For racial culture the home of a self-styled "high-class" Negro has nothing better to offer. Instead there will perhaps be more aping of things white than in a less cultured or less wealthy home. The father is perhaps a doctor, lawyer, landowner, or politician. The mother may be a social worker, or a teacher, or she may do nothing and have a maid. Father is often dark but he has usually married the lightest woman he could find. The family attend a fashionable church where few really colored faces

---

[1]Evidence suggests that Hughes is referring to Countee Cullen.—Eds.

are to be found. And they themselves draw a color line. In the North they go to white theaters and white movies. And in the South they have at least two cars and a house "like white folks." Nordic manners, Nordic faces, Nordic hair, Nordic art (if any), and an Episcopal heaven. A very high mountain indeed for the would-be racial artist to climb in order to discover himself and his people.

But then there are the low-down folks, the so-called common element, and they are the majority—may the Lord be praised! The people who have their nip of gin on Saturday nights and are not too important to themselves or the community, or too well fed, or too learned to watch the lazy world go round. They live on Seventh Street in Washington or State Street in Chicago and they do not particularly care whether they are like white folks or anybody else. Their joy runs, bang! into ecstasy. Their religion soars to a shout. Work maybe a little today, rest a little tomorrow. Play awhile. Sing awhile. O, let's dance! These common people are not afraid of spirituals, as for a long time their more intellectual brethren were, and jazz is their child. They furnish a wealth of colorful, distinctive material for any artist because they still hold their own individuality in the face of American standardizations. And perhaps these common people will give to the world its truly great Negro artist, the one who is not afraid to be himself. Whereas the better-class Negro would tell the artist what to do, the people at least let him alone when he does appear. And they are not ashamed of him—if they know he exists at all. And they accept what beauty is their own without question.

Certainly there is, for the American Negro artist who can escape the restrictions the more advanced among his own group would put upon him, a great field of unused material ready for his art. Without going outside his race, and even among the better classes with their "white" culture and conscious American manners, but still Negro enough to be different, there is sufficient matter to furnish a black artist with a lifetime of creative work. And when he chooses to touch on the relations between Negroes and whites in this country with their innumerable overtones and undertones, surely, and especially for literature and the drama, there is an inexhaustible supply of themes at hand. To these the Negro artist can give his racial individuality, his heritage of rhythm and warmth, and his incongruous humor that so often, as in the Blues, becomes ironic laughter mixed with tears. But let us look again at the mountain. . . . 5

Most of my own poems are racial in theme and treatment, derived from the life I know. In many of them I try to grasp and hold some of the meanings and rhythms of jazz. I am sincere as I know how to be in these poems and yet after every reading I answer questions like these from my own people: Do you think Negroes should always write about Negroes? I wish you wouldn't read some of your poems to white folks. How do you find anything interesting in a place like a cabaret? Why do you write about black people? You aren't black. What makes you do so many jazz poems?

But jazz to me is one of the inherent expressions of Negro life in America: the eternal tom-tom beating in the Negro soul—the tom-tom of revolt against weariness in a white world, a world of subway trains, and work, work, work; the tom-tom of joy and laughter, and pain swallowed in a smile. Yet the Philadelphia clubwoman is ashamed to say that her race created it and she does not like me to write about it.

The old subconscious "white is best" runs through her mind. Years of study under white teachers, a lifetime of white books, pictures, and papers, and white manners, morals, and Puritan standards made her dislike the spirituals. And now she turns up her nose at jazz and all its manifestations — likewise almost everything else distinctly racial. She doesn't care for the Winold Reiss portraits of Negroes because they are "too Negro." She does not want a true picture of herself from anybody. She wants the artist to flatter her, to make the white world believe that all Negroes are as smug and as near white in soul as she wants to be. But, to my mind, it is the duty of the younger Negro artist, if he accepts any duties at all from outsiders, to change through the force of his art that old whispering "I want to be white," hidden in the aspirations of his people, to "Why should I want to be white? I am a Negro — and beautiful!"

So I am ashamed for the black poet who says, "I want to be a poet, not a Negro poet," as though his own racial world were not as interesting as any other world. I am ashamed, too, for the colored artist who runs from the painting of Negro faces to the painting of sunsets after the manner of the academicians because he fears the strange un-whiteness of his own features. An artist must be free to choose what he does, certainly, but he must also never be afraid to do what he might choose.

Let the blare of Negro jazz bands and the bellowing voice of Bessie Smith singing Blues penetrate the closed ears of the colored near-intellectuals until they listen and perhaps understand. Let Paul Robeson singing "Water Boy," and Rudolph Fisher writing about the streets of Harlem, and Jean Toomer holding the heart of Georgia in his hands, and Aaron Douglas drawing strange black fantasies cause the smug Negro middle class to turn from their white, respectable, ordinary books and papers to catch a glimmer of their own beauty. We younger Negro artists who create now intend to express our individual dark-skinned selves without fear or shame. If white people are pleased we are glad. If they are not, it doesn't matter. We know we are beautiful. And ugly too. The tom-tom cries and the tom-tom laughs. If colored people are pleased we are glad. If they are not, their displeasure doesn't matter either. We build our temples for tomorrow, strong as we know how, and we stand on top of the mountain, free within ourselves.

[1926]

Questions

1. What is the "racial mountain" that Hughes decries? Why is this a fitting image for the argument he is making?
2. What are the two principal attitudes within his own community that Hughes contrasts? How does his style shift when he begins to describe "the so-called common element" in paragraph 4?
3. How does Hughes use the terms "Negro," "colored," and "black"? Explain why he uses each when he does.
4. Why is jazz an especially significant subject for Hughes to discuss? Why does he find it particularly relevant to the subject he is addressing?

5. What does Hughes mean when he writes, "An artist must be free to choose what he does, certainly, but he must also never be afraid to do what he might choose" (para. 8)?

6. According to Hughes, who is the audience for the African American artists of this time period?

Jazzonia

Oh, silver tree!
Oh, shining rivers of the soul!

In a Harlem cabaret
Six long-headed jazzers play.
A dancing girl whose eyes are bold   5
Lifts high a dress of silken gold.

Oh, singing tree!
Oh, shining rivers of the soul!

Were Eve's eyes
In the first garden   10
Just a bit too bold?[1]
Was Cleopatra gorgeous
In a gown of gold?

Oh, shining tree!
Oh, silver rivers of the soul!   15

In a whirling cabaret
Six long-headed jazzers play.

[1923]

. . . .

Questions

1. What is the setting of the poem?
2. What purpose does the sensory imagery serve? What do the allusions to Eve and Cleopatra add?
3. What are "long-headed jazzers" (ll. 4, 17)?
4. How does the form of the poem—repetition, rhyme, line breaks—reinforce its meaning?
5. How would you describe the tone of the poem?

---

[1]Genesis 3:6–7 reads: "When the woman [Eve] saw that the fruit of the tree was good for food and pleasing to the eye, and also desirable for gaining wisdom, she took some and ate it. She also gave some to her husband [Adam], who was with her, and he ate it. Then the eyes of both of them were opened, and they realized they were naked; so they sewed fig leaves together and made coverings for themselves."—EDS.

The White House

Claude McKay

Poet, novelist, and journalist Claude McKay (1890–1948) was born in Jamaica, and immigrated to the United States at the age of twenty-two. He lived in England and France for many years, but returned to the United States in 1934, where he worked in Chicago as a journalist. He is known for his protest poetry, which speaks directly to racial issues and the trials of the working class. McKay's novels include *Home to Harlem* (1922), *Banjo: A Story without a Plot* (1929), and *Banana Bottom* (1933). In the following poem, McKay expresses restrained anger at being excluded, though he does not explicitly mention race.

Your door is shut against my tightened face,
And I am sharp as steel with discontent;
But I possess the courage and the grace
To bear my anger proudly and unbent.
The pavement slabs burn loose beneath my feet,5
A chafing savage, down the decent street;
And passion rends my vitals as I pass,
Where boldly shines your shuttered door of glass.
Oh, I must search for wisdom every hour,
Deep in my wrathful bosom sore and raw,10
And find in it the superhuman power
To hold me to the letter of your law!
Oh, I must keep my heart inviolate
Against the potent poison of your hate.

[1922]

Questions

1. The poem develops a tension between the "you" and "I" in the poem. Who is the speaker, and to whom (or what) is he speaking?
2. McKay uses physical images of steel, pavement, and glass. Why? How do these contribute to the depiction of the speaker's anger?
3. Why does the speaker refer to himself as a "chafing savage" (l. 6) with a "wrathful bosom" (l. 10)?
4. How do you interpret the final couplet—as the speaker's resignation? defiance? compromise?
5. If you did not know the title of the poem, how would your interpretation differ? Explain why you believe that not mentioning the White House in the text of the poem strengthens or weakens the points McKay is making. In *A Long Way from Home* (1937), McKay's autobiography, he claims that the poem's title does not

refer to the official presidential residence. Does this disclaimer influence your reading of the poem?

6. How do current political events affect your reading of the poem?

Spunk

ZORA NEALE HURSTON

Zora Neale Hurston (1891–1960) came to prominence in the 1920s during the Harlem Renaissance. A novelist, folklorist, and anthropologist, she first gained attention with her short stories, including "Sweat" and "Spunk." She is best known for her novel *Their Eyes Were Watching God* (1937), set in Eatonville, Florida, where Hurston grew up; the town was the first incorporated African American community in the United States. Her writing is known for its celebration of African American folk culture, as well as its use of authentic vernacular speech. Hurston, who died in poverty, was all but forgotten until Alice Walker took an interest in her. Walker's 1971 essay "Looking for Zora" described her personal journey to find Hurston's unmarked grave. The publication of this essay prompted a resurgence of interest in Hurston, including republication of many of her books. The following short story, Hurston's third, was published in Alain Locke's *The New Negro* (1925)—a collection of essays, poetry, fiction, drama, and visual texts, considered to be the manifesto of the Harlem Renaissance.

I

A giant of a brown-skinned man sauntered up the one street of the village and out into the palmetto thickets with a small pretty woman clinging lovingly to his arm.

"Looka theah, folkses!" cried Elijah Mosley, slapping his leg gleefully. "Theah they go, big as life an' brassy as tacks."

All the loungers in the store tried to walk to the door with an air of nonchalance but with small success.

"Now pee-eople!" Walter Thomas gasped. "Will you look at 'em!"

"But that's one thing Ah likes about Spunk Banks—he ain't skeered of nothin' 5
on God's green footstool—*nothin'*! He rides that log down at saw-mill jus' like he struts 'round wid another man's wife—jus' don't give a kitty. When Tes' Miller got cut to giblets on that circle-saw, Spunk steps right up and starts ridin'. The rest of us was skeered to go near it."

A round-shouldered figure in overalls much too large came nervously in the door and the talking ceased. The men looked at each other and winked.

"Gimme some soda-water. Sass'prilla Ah reckon," the newcomer ordered, and stood far down the counter near the open pickled pig-feet tub to drink it.

Elijah nudged Walter and turned with mock gravity to the new-comer.

"Say, Joe, how's everything up yo' way? How's yo' wife?"

Joe started and all but dropped the bottle he was holding. He swallowed several 10
times painfully and his lips trembled.

"Aw 'Lige, you oughtn't to do nothin' like that," Walter grumbled. Elijah ignored him.

"She jus' passed heah a few minutes ago goin' thata way," with a wave of his hand in the direction of the woods.

Now Joe knew his wife had passed that way. He knew that the men lounging in the general store had seen her, moreover, he knew that the men knew *he* knew. He stood there silent for a long moment staring blankly, with his Adam's apple twitching nervously up and down his throat. One could actually *see* the pain he was suffering, his eyes, his face, his hands, and even the dejected slump of his shoulders. He set the bottle down upon the counter. He didn't bang it, just eased it out of his hand silently and fiddled with his suspender buckle.

"Well, Ah'm goin' after her to-day. Ah'm goin' an' fetch her back. Spunk's done gone too fur."

He reached deep down into his trouser pocket and drew out a hollow ground 15 razor, large and shiny, and passed his moistened thumb back and forth over the edge.

"Talkin' like a man, Joe. 'Course that's *yo'* fambly affairs, but Ah like to see grit in anybody."

Joe Kanty laid down a nickel and stumbled out into the street.

Dusk crept in from the woods. Ike Clarke lit the swinging oil lamp that was almost immediately surrounded by candle-flies. The men laughed boisterously behind Joe's back as they watched him shamble woodward.

"You oughtn't to said whut you said to him, 'Lige—look how it worked him up," Walter chided.

"And Ah hope it did work him up. Tain't even decent for a man to take and take 20 like he do."

"Spunk will sho' kill him."

"Aw, Ah doan know. You never kin tell. He might turn him up an' spank him fur gettin' in the way, but Spunk wouldn't shoot no unarmed man. Dat razor he carried outa heah ain't gonna run Spunk down an' cut him, an' Joe ain't got the nerve to go to Spunk with it knowing he totes that Army .45. He makes that break outa heah to bluff us. He's gonna hide that razor behind the first palmetto root an' sneak back home to bed. Don't tell me nothin' 'bout that rabbit-foot colored man. Didn't he meet Spunk an' Lena face to face one day las week an' mumble sumthin' to Spunk 'bout lettin' his wife alone?"

"What did Spunk say?" Walter broke in. "Ah like him fine but tain't right the way he carries on wid Lena Kanty, jus' 'cause Joe's timid 'bout fightin'."

"You wrong theah, Walter. Tain't 'cause Joe's timid at all, it's 'cause Spunk wants Lena. If Joe was a passle of wile cats Spunk would tackle the job just the same. He'd go after *anything* he wanted the same way. As Ah wuz sayin' a minute ago, he tole Joe right to his face that Lena was his. 'Call her and see if she'll come. A woman knows her boss an' she answers when he calls.' 'Lena, ain't I yo' husband?' Joe sorter whines out. Lena looked at him real disgusted but she don't answer and she don't move outa her tracks. Then Spunk reaches out an' takes hold of her arm an' says: 'Lena, youse mine. From now on Ah works for you an' fights for you an' Ah never wants you to look to nobody for a crumb of bread, a stitch of close or a shingle to go over yo' head, but *me* long as Ah live. Ah'll git the lumber foh owah house to-morrow. Go home an git yo' things together!"

"'Thass mah house,' Lena speaks up. 'Papa gimme that.' 25

"'Well,' says Spunk, 'doan give up whut's yours, but when youse inside doan forgit youse mine, an' let no other man git outa his place wid you!'

"Lena looked up at him with her eyes so full of love that they wuz runnin' over, an' Spunk seen it an' Joe seen it too, and his lip started to tremblin' and his Adam's apple was galloping up and down his neck like a race horse. Ah bet he's wore out half a dozen Adam's apples since Spunk's been on the job with Lena. That's all he'll do. He'll be back heah after while swallowin' an' workin' his lips like he wants to say somethin' an' can't."

"But didn't he do *nothin'* to stop 'em?"

"Nope, not a frazzlin' thing — jus' stood there. Spunk took Lena's arm and walked off jus' like nothin' ain't happened and he stood there gazin' after them till they was outa sight. Now you know a woman don't want no man like that. I'm jus' waitin' to see whut he's goin' to say when he gits back."

II

But Joe Kanty never came back, never. The men in the store heard the sharp 30
report of a pistol somewhere distant in the palmetto thicket and soon Spunk came walking leisurely, with his big black Stetson set at the same rakish angle and Lena clinging to his arm, came walking right into the general store. Lena wept in a frightened manner.

"Well," Spunk announced calmly, "Joe came out there wid a meat axe an' made me kill him."

He sent Lena home and led the men back to Joe — crumpled and limp with his right hand still clutching his razor.

"See mah back? Mah close cut clear through. He sneaked up an' tried to kill me from the back, but Ah got him, an' got him good, first shot," Spunk said.

The men glared at Elijah, accusingly.

"Take him up an' plant him in Stony Lonesome," Spunk said in a careless voice. 35
"Ah didn't wanna shoot him but he made me do it. He's a dirty coward, jumpin' on a man from behind."

Spunk turned on his heel and sauntered away to where he knew his love wept in fear for him and no man stopped him. At the general store later on, they all talked of locking him up until the sheriff should come from Orlando, but no one did anything but talk.

A clear case of self-defense, the trial was a short one, and Spunk walked out of the court house to freedom again. He could work again, ride the dangerous log-carriage that fed the singing, snarling, biting circle-saw; he could stroll the soft dark lanes with his guitar. He was free to roam the woods again; he was free to return to Lena. He did all of these things.

III

"Whut you reckon, Walt?" Elijah asked one night later. "Spunk's gittin' ready to marry Lena!"

"Naw! Why, Joe ain't had time to git cold yit. Nohow Ah didn't figger Spunk was the marryin' kind."

"Well, he is," rejoined Elijah. "He done moved most of Lena's things—and her along wid 'em — over to the Bradley house. He's buying it. Jus' like Ah told yo' all right in heah the night Joe was kilt. Spunk's crazy 'bout Lena. He don't want folks to keep on talkin' 'bout her — thass reason he's rushin' so. Funny thing 'bout that bob-cat, wan't it?" 40

"What bob-cat, 'Lige? Ah ain't heered 'bout none."

"Ain't cher? Well, night befo' las' as they was goin' to bed, a big black bob-cat, black all over, you hear me, *black*, walked round and round that house and howled like forty, an' when Spunk got his gun an' went to the winder to shoot it, he says it stood right still an' looked him in the eye, an' howled right at him. The thing got Spunk so nervoused up he couldn't shoot. But Spunk says twan't no bob-cat nohow. He says it was Joe done sneaked back from Hell!"

"Humph!" sniffed Walter, "he oughter be nervous after what he done. Ah reckon Joe come back to dare him to marry Lena, or to come out an' fight. Ah bet he'll be back time and again, too. Know what Ah think? Joe wuz a braver man than Spunk."

There was a general shout of derision from the group.

"Thass a fact," went on Walter. "Lookit whut he done; took a razor an' went out to fight a man he knowed toted a gun an' wuz a crack shot, too; 'nother thing Joe wuz skeered of Spunk, skeered plumb stiff! But he went jes' the same. It took him a long time to get his nerve up. Tain't nothin' for Spunk to fight when he ain't skeered of nothin'. Now, Joe's done come back to have it out wid the man that's got all he ever had. Y'all know Joe ain't never had nothin' nor wanted nothin' besides Lena. It musta been a h'ant cause ain't nobody never seen no black bob-cat." 45

"'Nother thing," cut in one of the men, "Spunk was cussin' a blue streak to-day 'cause he 'lowed dat saw wuz wobblin' — almos' got 'im once. The machinist come, looked it over an said it wuz alright. Spunk musta been leanin' t'wards it some. Den he claimed somebody pushed 'im but twan't nobody close to 'im. Ah wuz glad when knockin' off time came. I'm skeered of dat man when he gits hot. He'd beat you full of button holes as quick as he's look atcher."

IV

The men gathered the next evening in a different mood, no laughter. No badinage this time.

"Look, 'Lige, you goin' to set up wid Spunk?"

"Naw, Ah reckon not, Walter. Tell yuh the truth, Ah'm a li'l bit skittish. Spunk died too wicket — died cussin' he did. You know he thought he was done outa life."

"Good Lawd, who'd he think done it?"

"Joe." 50

"Joe Kanty? How come?"

"Walter, Ah b'leeve Ah will walk up thata way an' set. Lena would like it Ah reckon."

"But whut did he say, 'Lige?"

Elijah did not answer until they had left the lighted store and were strolling down the dark street. 55

"Ah wuz loadin' a wagon wid scantlin' right near the saw when Spunk fell on the carriage but 'fore Ah could git to him the saw got him in the body — awful sight. Me an' Skint Miller got him off but it was too late. Anybody could see that. The fust thing he said wuz: 'He pushed me, 'Lige — the dirty hound pushed me in the back!' — he was spittin' blood at ev'ry breath. We laid him on the sawdust pile with his face to the East so's he could die easy. He helt mah han' till the last, Walter, and said: 'It was Joe, 'Lige . . . the dirty sneak shoved me . . . he didn't dare come to mah face . . . but Ah'll git the son-of-a-wood louse soon's Ah get there an' make hell too hot for him . . . Ah felt him shove me . . . !' Thass how he died."

"If spirits kin fight, there's a powerful tussle goin' on somewhere ovah Jordan 'cause Ah b'leeve Joe's ready for Spunk an' ain't skeered any more — yas, Ah b'leeve Joe pushed 'im mahself."

They had arrived at the house. Lena's lamentations were deep and loud. She had filled the room with magnolia blossoms that gave off a heavy sweet odor. The keepers of the wake tipped about whispering in frightened tones. Everyone in the village was there, even old Jeff Kanty, Joe's father, who a few hours before would have been afraid to come within ten feet of him, stood leering triumphantly down upon the fallen giant as if his fingers had been the teeth of steel that laid him low.

The cooling board consisted of three sixteen-inch boards on saw horses, a dingy sheet was his shroud.

The women ate heartily of the funeral baked meats and wondered who would be Lena's next. The men whispered coarse conjectures between guzzles of whiskey. 60

[1925]

. . . .

Questions

1. The story takes its title from the character Spunk Banks, but *spunk* also means gumption, or courage. Is this an appropriate title? Explain.
2. How does the dialect affect your reading and understanding of the story? Would Hurston have made her characters more credible — in 1925 — and broadened her audience if she had had them speak in so-called Standard English?
3. This intricate story is actually a series of stories or narrations. Identify the individual story lines, and explain how they are interrelated.
4. Are the characters in the story fully formed, three-dimensional characters or flat stereotypes (racial or gender)?
5. How does the story manifest Hurston's long-standing interest in folklore?

6. How is the African American community characterized in the story? Is Hurston celebrating and praising or criticizing and mocking the men and women she depicts?

The Spirit of Africa

AARON DOUGLAS

Aaron Douglas (1898–1979), a native of Kansas, received his BA from the University of Nebraska (the first African American to earn a bachelor of fine arts at the university), came to New York City in 1925, and began publishing his illustrations in *Opportunity* and *Crisis* magazines. Inspired by African art, he used geometrical motifs to depict the history and culture of African people. His strikingly modernist illustrations, including *The Spirit of Africa*, appeared in Alain Locke's *The New Negro*.

The Spirit of Africa (1926, woodcut)

Questions

1. What is the subject of this illustration? Literally, what is being depicted?
2. The use of geometrical forms is one of the hallmarks of the modernist movement in art, as twentieth-century artists moved away from inherited and traditional notions of art and focused instead on line, form, and color. How do the repeated geometrical forms unify the illustration? What else might they suggest in terms of connecting past and present?
3. What is the effect of Douglas's creating forms that are both literal representations of African masks and suggestions of more abstract images?
4. What is the mood of this illustration?
5. In *The New Negro*, this illustration appears on the left page facing the title page of the essay "The Negro Digs Up His Past" by renowned historian Arthur A. Schomburg. Do you think the visual text would or would not complement an essay about the historical legacy of African Americans? Explain your answer.

Nocturne at Bethesda

Arna Bontemps

> Born in Louisiana, Arna Bontemps (1902–1973) grew up in California and graduated from Pacific Union College. In 1924, he moved to Harlem to accept a teaching job and began publishing poetry and fiction. In 1943, he graduated from the University of Chicago with a master's degree in library science and was appointed a librarian at Fisk University; he remained there until his retirement in 1965 and ultimately returned as a writer-in-residence. The following poem takes its title from the biblical passage John 5:2–4: "Now there is at Jerusalem by the sheep market a pool, which is called in the Hebrew tongue Bethesda, having five porches. In these lay a great multitude of impotent folk, of blind, halt, withered, waiting for the moving of the water. For an angel went down at a certain season into the pool, and troubled the water: whosoever then first after the troubling of the water stepped in was made whole of whatsoever disease he had."

I thought I saw an angel flying low,
I thought I saw the flicker of a wing
Above the mulberry trees; but not again.
Bethesda sleeps. This ancient pool that healed
A host of bearded Jews does not awake.   5

This pool that once the angels troubled does not move.
No angel stirs it now, no Saviour comes
With healing in His hands to raise the sick
And bid the lame man leap upon the ground.

The golden days are gone. Why do we wait   10
So long upon the marble steps, blood

Falling from our open wounds? and why
Do our black faces search the empty sky?
Is there something we have forgotten? some precious thing
We have lost, wandering in strange lands?   15

There was a day, I remember now,
I beat my breast and cried, "Wash me God,
Wash me with a wave of wind upon
The barley; O quiet One, draw near, draw near!
Walk upon the hills with lovely feet   20
And in the waterfall stand and speak.

"Dip white hands in the lily pool and mourn
Upon the harps still hanging in the trees
Near Babylon along the river's edge,
But oh, remember me, I pray, before   25
The summer goes and rose leaves lose their red."

The old terror takes my heart, the fear
Of quiet waters and of faint twilights.
There will be better days when I am gone
And healing pools where I cannot be healed.   30
Fragrant stars will gleam forever and ever
Above the place where I lie desolate.

Yet I hope, still I long to live.
And if there can be returning after death
I shall come back. But it will not be here;   35
If you want me you must search for me
Beneath the palms of Africa. Or if
I am not there then you may call to me
Across the shining dunes, perhaps I shall
Be following a desert caravan.   40

I may pass through centuries of death
With quiet eyes, but I'll remember still
A jungle tree with burning scarlet birds.
There is something I have forgotten, some precious thing.
I shall be seeking ornaments of ivory,   45
I shall be dying for a jungle fruit.

        You do not hear, Bethesda.
O still green water in a stagnant pool!
Love abandoned you and me alike.
There was a day you held a rich full moon   50
Upon your heart and listened to the words
Of men now dead and saw the angels fly.

There is a simple story on your face;
Years have wrinkled you. I know, Bethesda!
You are sad. It is the same with me.   55

[1926]

Questions

1. What expectations does the title's allusion immediately establish?
2. What elements of this poem juxtapose traditional Christian allusions and symbols with those of racial consciousness and pride?
3. How do the transitions in the poem ("The golden days are gone" [l. 10], "There was a day" [l. 16], "Yet I hope" [l. 33]) signal the speaker's meditative and searching qualities?
4. Does the speaker find solace in Christianity? Cite images and lines in the poem to support your response.
5. What is the central ambivalence of the speaker in the poem?

From *Plum Bun: A Novel without a Moral*

Jessie Redmon Fauset

The most prolific novelist of the Harlem Renaissance, Jessie Redmon Fauset (1882–1961) grew up in Philadelphia and graduated from Cornell University; she was the first African American woman to become a member of Phi Beta Kappa, the prestigious academic honor society. She taught in Baltimore and Washington, D.C., before becoming the literary editor of *Crisis* magazine, the official publication of the National Association for the Advancement of Colored People. She is the author of four novels, all primarily concerned with the plight of the African American middle class. The following is the opening section of *Plum Bun: A Novel without a Moral* (1929).

CHAPTER 1 [BLACK PHILADELPHIA]

Opal Street, as streets go, is no jewel of the first water. It is merely an imitation, and none too good at that. Narrow, unsparkling, uninviting, it stretches meekly off from dull Jefferson Street to the dingy, drab market which forms the north side of Oxford Street. It has no mystery, no allure, either of exclusiveness or of downright depravity; its usages are plainly significant—an unpretentious little street lined with unpretentious little houses, inhabited for the most part by unpretentious little people.

The dwellings are three stories high, and contain six boxes called by courtesy, rooms—a "parlor," a midget of a dining-room, a larger kitchen and, above, a front bedroom seemingly large only because it extends for the full width of the house, a mere shadow of a bathroom, and another back bedroom with windows whose possibilities are spoiled by their outlook on sad and diminutive back-yards. And above these two, still two others built in similar wise.

In one of these houses dwelt a father, a mother and two daughters. Here, as often happens in a home sheltering two generations, opposite, unevenly matched emotions faced each other. In the houses of the rich the satisfied ambition of the older generation is faced by the overwhelming ambition of the younger. Or the elders may find themselves brought in opposition to the blank indifference and ennui of youth engendered by the realization that there remain no more worlds to conquer; their fathers having already taken all. In houses on Opal Street these niceties of distinction are hardly to be found; there is a more direct and concrete contrast. The satisfied ambition of maturity is a foil for the restless despair of youth.

Affairs in the Murray household were advancing towards this stage; yet not a soul in that family of four could have foretold its coming. To Junius and Mattie Murray, who had known poverty and homelessness, the little house on Opal Street represented the *ne plus ultra*[1] of ambition; to their daughter Angela it seemed the dingiest, drabbest chrysalis that had ever fettered the wings of a brilliant butterfly. The stories which Junius and Mattie told of difficulties overcome, of the arduous learning of trades, of the pitiful scraping together of infinitesimal savings, would have made a latter-day Iliad, but to Angela they were merely a description of a life which she at any cost would avoid living. Somewhere in the world were paths which lead to broad thoroughfares, large, bright houses, delicate niceties of existence. Those paths Angela meant to find and frequent. At a very early age she had observed that the good things of life are unevenly distributed; merit is not always rewarded; hard labor does not necessarily entail adequate recompense. Certain fortuitous endowments, great physical beauty, unusual strength, a certain unswerving singleness of mind,—gifts bestowed quite blindly and disproportionately by the forces which control life,—these were the qualities which contributed toward a glowing and pleasant existence.

Angela had no high purpose in life; unlike her sister Virginia, who meant some day to invent a marvelous method for teaching the pianoforte, Angela felt no impulse to discover, or to perfect. True she thought she might become eventually a distinguished painter, but that was because she felt within herself an ability to depict which as far as it went was correct and promising. Her eye for line and for expression was already good and she had a nice feeling for color. Moreover she possessed the instinct for self-appraisal which taught her that she had much to learn. And she was sure that the knowledge once gained would flower in her case to perfection. But her gift was not for her the end of existence; rather it was an adjunct to a life which was to know light, pleasure, gaiety and freedom.

Freedom! That was the note which Angela heard oftenest in the melody of living which was to be hers. With a wildness that fell just short of unreasonableness she hated restraint. Her father's earlier days as coachman in a private family, his later successful, independent years as boss carpenter, her mother's youth spent as maid to a famous actress, all this was to Angela a manifestation of the sort of thing which happens to those enchained it might be by duty, by poverty, by weakness or by color.

Color or rather the lack of it seemed to the child the one absolute prerequisite to the life of which she was always dreaming. One might break loose from a too hampering

5

---

[1] In Latin, literally "no more beyond," meaning the highest level of achievement.—EDS.

sense of duty; poverty could be overcome; physicians conquered weakness; but color, the mere possession of a black or a white skin, that was clearly one of those fortuitous endowments of the gods. Gratitude was no strong ingredient in this girl's nature, yet very often early she began thanking Fate for the chance which in that household of four had bestowed on her the heritage of her mother's fair skin. She might so easily have been, like her father, black, or have received the melange which had resulted in Virginia's rosy bronzeness and her deeply waving black hair. But Angela had received not only her mother's creamy complexion and her soft cloudy, chestnut hair, but she had taken from Junius the aquiline nose, the gift of some remote Indian ancestor which gave to his face and his eldest daughter's that touch of chiselled immobility.

[1929]

Questions

1. What information does Fauset provide to indicate the middle-class status of the family in this novel?
2. Fauset writes: "The satisfied ambition of maturity is a foil for the restless despair of youth" (para. 3). Does she indicate that race exacerbates this conflict or that it is the result of generational gaps exclusively? Explain.
3. Fauset focuses on intracommunity issues related to gradations of skin color, but how does she emphasize the origin of those conflicts in the larger society?
4. As the novel proceeds, Angela becomes estranged from her family as she chooses the material advantages of "passing" as white. What evidence do you have in this short opening excerpt that Fauset recognizes the alienation that results from such a divided self? Consider such passages as: "Color or rather the lack of it seemed to the child the one absolute prerequisite to the life of which she was always dreaming" (para. 7) and "the heritage of her mother's fair skin" (para. 7).
5. An admirer of Fauset, W. E. B. DuBois claimed that "all Art is propaganda and ever must be . . . propaganda for gaining the right of black folk to love and enjoy." In what ways can this work be seen as "propaganda" in the positive sense that DuBois uses it?

Entering the Conversation

As you develop a response to one of the following questions, refer to the texts you have read in this section. You may also draw on your own experience or knowledge relating to the Harlem Renaissance.

1. Write an essay disputing the idea of the Harlem Renaissance as a monolithic movement that reflects a community's shared values and an overarching philosophy. Discuss several different, though not necessarily conflicting, themes or concerns.

2. Discuss at least two conflicting views of the role of the artist in the Harlem Renaissance. Draw on a minimum of three texts as part of your discussion, including at least one of the nonfiction pieces.

3. One way to read this Conversation is as different attitudes toward the kind of change that would lead to racial equality and justice for African Americans. Some of the writers lean toward separatism, others toward assimilation. Discuss which you find the more compelling of those arguments. Refer to at least four texts.

4. In his seminal work *The Souls of Black Folk* (1903), W. E. B. DuBois used the metaphor of the veil to describe the plight of African Americans during this time.

   > After the Egyptian and Indian, the Greek and Roman, the Teuton and Mongolian, the Negro is a sort of seventh son, born with a veil, and gifted with second-sight in this American world,—a world which yields him no true self-consciousness, but only lets him see himself through the revelation of the other world. It is a peculiar sensation, this double consciousness, this sense of always looking at one's self through the eyes of others, of measuring one's soul by the tape of a world that looks on in amused contempt and pity. One ever feels his two-ness,—an American, a Negro; two souls, two thoughts, two unreconciled strivings; two warring ideals in one dark body, whose dogged strength alone keeps it from being torn asunder.

   Using at least three of the texts in this section, discuss whether you find this metaphor of the veil an outdated or an accurate characterization of the Harlem Renaissance.

5. Alain Locke (1886–1954) published *The New Negro*, which became the manifesto of the Harlem Renaissance, in 1925. In the introductory essay, he defined "the New Negro" as follows:

   > He now becomes a conscious contributor and lays aside the status of a beneficiary and ward for that of a collaborator and participant in American civilization. The great social gain in this is the releasing of our talented group from the arid fields of controversy and debate to the productive fields of creative expression. The especially cultural recognition they win should in turn prove the key to that revaluation of the Negro which must precede or accompany any considerable further betterment of race relationships. But whatever the general effect, the present generation will have added the motives of self-expression and spiritual development to the old and still unfinished task of making material headway and progress. No one who understandingly faces the situation with its substantial accomplishment or views the new scene with its still more abundant promise can be entirely without hope. And certainly, if in our lifetime the Negro should not be able to celebrate his full initiation into American democracy, he can at least, on the warrant of these things, celebrate the attainment of a significant and satisfying new phase of group development, and with it a spiritual Coming of Age. (15–16)

Based on the texts in this Conversation and your knowledge of this period and the following decades, explain whether Locke's vision for the African American artist became a reality.

6. Assume the voice of Langston Hughes and explain your opinion of "Spunk" by Hurston, *Plum Bun* by Fauset, or "The White House" by McKay.

7. Some of the controversies that characterize the Harlem Renaissance continue today. Discuss one controversy from these 1920s texts that still persists — for example, in discussions about the legitimacy of hip-hop and rap as art forms, identity politics as the subject of art, and literature as social protest.

Student Writing

Working with Sources

The student essay by Cynthia Gross was written in response to Entering the Conversation question 4 (p. 1313) from the Conversation on the Harlem Renaissance. Read the essay carefully and then discuss the choices Cynthia has made to craft her essay; use the questions that follow the essay to guide your analysis.

Aspiring to Whiteness: Self-Hatred and the Distortion of the African American Image in the United States

Cynthia Gross

According to W. E. B. DuBois, the African American in the United States is only able to "see himself through the revelation of the other world." And this "peculiar sensation, this double consciousness, this sense of always looking at one's self through the eyes of others" creates an individual who feels obligated to neglect a part of him- or herself in order to be accepted by the popular culture. Although W. E. B. DuBois's pioneering work, *The Souls of Black Folk*, was written more than a decade before the Harlem Renaissance begins, its interpretation of the condition of the African American in the United States still resonates through the literary art movement that celebrates the spirit, pride, beauty, and positive energy of a minority group that looks optimistically to its future even in its current state of subjection to the mainstream culture.

In his essay, "The Negro Artist and the Racial Mountain," Langston Hughes asserts that the dichotomies associated with the colors white and black lead many African Americans to aspire to whiteness: white, black; good, evil; superior, inferior; beautiful, ugly; pure, tainted; standard, anomaly. At the beginning of the essay, the narrator speaks of "one of the most promising of the young Negro poets" who wishes to "'write like a white poet'" and, by extension, desires to be white. While readers may initially be appalled by such a statement, Hughes develops his argument by explaining that the causes of this self-hatred stem from the structure of social institutions. For instance, children in the "colored middle class" go to "a mixed school" and "read white papers and magazines." Consequently, even in the home, stereotypes of inherent white goodness and black deficiency are reinforced. Because they are comfortable and consider themselves well off or at least better than most African Americans, the middle and "high-class" African Americans feel that they are too good to associate with the majority of their people. These individuals have adopted the theory that anything closer to white is better. Hughes juxtaposes the uppity African Americans with the "so-called common element," individuals who continue to embrace their unique identity despite the impending pressure to conform to the white archetype. Therefore, in context, readers begin to view the "young Negro poet" as more of a victim than a perpetrator, who is tangled up in the system "of always looking at [himself] through the eyes of [whites]."

The excerpt of Jessie Redmon Fauset's *Plum Bun: A Novel without a Moral* involves the issue of light-skinned African Americans who attempt to pass for white. With her "creamy complexion and her soft cloudy, chestnut hair" and "aquiline nose," Angela realizes that her near-white physical appearance is the key to "the life of which she was always dreaming." In fact, she worships her light skin. Her appearance can be used in her community and in the larger society as a strategy to reach her goal in life: to become white. While Angela's sister, Virginia, has goals and a sense of direction in her life, Angela's future is ambiguous. Obtaining material possessions, such as "large, bright houses" and "delicate niceties of existence," is the sole aim of Angela's existence. She feels that her pale skin automatically places her in a position superior to that of Virginia, who has darker skin, and, sadly, it does. Furthermore, readers can infer that Angela's father married the lightest woman he could find in order to enhance his middle-class status. However, as W. E. B. DuBois argues, in shaping her appearance, speech, and associations to reflect those of the dominant culture, Angela loses a part of her identity. She succumbs to "measuring [her] soul by the tape of a world that looks on in amused contempt and pity," not yet realizing that no matter how light her skin is, she can never be white. Although Angela despises her African American heritage and feels that it acts as a "chrysalis" or prison of her desires, she will eventually discover that her aspiration to be white is actually what keeps her in bondage.

Much of the literature of the Harlem Renaissance seems to have a didactic function. W. E. B. DuBois exposes the idea of "double consciousness" not only to inform but to encourage change. For example, in Arna Bontemps's poem, "Nocturne at Bethesda," the narrator asks, "Why do we wait / So long upon the marble steps, blood / Falling from our open wounds?" In other words, although the pool of Bethesda, historically symbolic of healing, was once a spot for oppressed and afflicted individuals to gather and pray for deliverance from their sicknesses, the speaker argues that this pool no longer has power. The oppressed people need to take initiative and save themselves instead of waiting for a savior, who the speaker makes clear will not come, to rescue them. The oppressed people at the pool of Bethesda symbolize the situation of African Americans in the United States who are "waiting for the moving of the water," or racial equality. However, African Americans, forsaken even by the deity, must encourage themselves and rely on their strength to create change for the better. The tone of the poem is reflective. The speaker, presumably an older individual, has waited at the pool for years to no avail. In retrospect, however, the only things important to him or her are recollections of Africa. We see that African Americans who spend their lives trying to transform their image to fit into the color-coded social system discover their later years are filled with regret over the fact that they rejected their identity.

The literature of the Harlem Renaissance illustrates the challenges facing African Americans during that period. We also see, however, that African Americans find strength in adversity by coming together. More than likely, the pool of Bethesda healed so many people because they believed, psychologically, that they would be healed. Then—and now—freedom begins in the mind. Although there is a constant pressure for minorities to conform to the standard image of white America, they must learn to see beauty in themselves. The African American people are Americans, but a distinct category based on their experiences. It will be a glorious day when we African Americans embrace our individuality and no longer strive to be anyone other than who we are.

Questions

1. Reread the texts the student writer has focused on in this essay. Do you agree with her interpretation of each? If not, explain where and why your interpretation differs.
2. This essay was written in response to the quotation by W. E. B. DuBois on page 1313. Reread the opening paragraph of this essay, and discuss how effectively it addresses the prompt.
3. Note the references to DuBois throughout the essay. Does the writer make sufficient links to and explanations of her interpretation of DuBois? Are there too many references? Explain your answers by citing specific passages in the essay.
4. Discuss the choice and use of quotations from the three literary texts by Hughes, Fauset, and Bontemps. Do they illustrate the points the writer is making? Are they clearly explained? Are they smoothly integrated into the essay?
5. This essay is organized text-by-text. That is, the writer addresses the question with a paragraph on Hughes, another on Fauset, and another on Bontemps. Discuss how the essay might be revised by organizing paragraphs by idea or topic rather than by text.
6. The conclusion offers an opinion—a commentary—about the nature of the literary texts and the society they reflect. Is this an effective ending to the essay? If you think it is, explain how the earlier part of the essay prepares for it. If you think it is ineffective, be specific in your explanation of why.

The Writer's Craft—Close Reading

Syntax

Syntax is the way a writer arranges words, phrases, and clauses into a **sentence**. It seems fitting to discuss syntax in a chapter with a novella by Henry James, since he is a master of complex and lengthy syntactical constructions—often challenging to understand. Yet all writers, including poets, pay attention to syntax as one strategy for developing and conveying meaning.

Syntactical Patterns

Arrangement at the sentence level affects the way a reader or listener experiences the text and usually depends on the context of one sentence among others. Thus, simple, short sentences might create a flippant effect, an emphatic effect, or a sense of urgency; a longer, discursive sentence with interruptions may convey the impression of confusion or contribute to a meditative tone, depending on the overall context and the choices the writer makes in diction and figurative language. "Short" and "long" are two of many ways to discuss syntax and describe sentence patterns, but here we'll concentrate on a few specific types.

Simple, Declarative Sentences

Normal word order—subject/verb/object—in a relatively short declarative sentence usually makes a straightforward statement. In "Everyday Use," Walker gives us Mama's self-description:

> In real life I am a large, big-boned woman with rough, man-working hands. In the winter I wear flannel nightgowns to bed and overalls during the day. I can kill and clean a hog as mercilessly as a man. My fat keeps me hot in zero weather. I can work outside all day. (para. 5)

Although these sentences include descriptors, the basic structure is "I am . . . I wear . . . I can kill . . . My fat keeps . . . I can work . . .": subject/verb/object (SVO) constructions in declarative statements. The effect is to characterize Mama as a plain-spoken, unassuming woman with no frills and no pretense in the way she sees and acts in the world. What she says in that passage certainly makes that clear, but how she says it is as important as what she says.

Inverted Sentences

When a writer reverses the normal position of subject and verb (or predicate) in a declarative sentence, he or she is calling attention to something—perhaps emphasizing a point or an idea by placing it in the initial position—or slowing the pace by choosing an unusual order. In "The Free Radio," Salman Rushdie uses inversion in the first two clauses of the following sentence:

> So: looks he had, his own trade he had, there would have been a good wife in time. (para. 2)

If we put the first two clauses in standard SVO order, listen to the difference in what is emphasized:

> So: he had looks, he had his own trade, there would have been a good wife in time.

In these two sentences, the same information is conveyed, yet the emphasis on his "looks" and "his own trade" in the inverted version is lost to the repetition of "he had . . . he had . . ." in the standard version.

Compound-Complex Sentences

A **compound sentence** contains two independent clauses joined by a coordinating conjunction (such as *and, but, for, yet,* or *so*) or a semicolon. A complex sentence contains an independent clause and one or more subordinate clauses (which begin with words such as *after, before, although, because, until, when, while,* and *if*). A **compound-complex sentence** combines the two and is usually fairly long. Note the two compound-complex sentences in the following passage from "The Free Radio":

> They flattered him with dreams because they knew they could take money from him at cards and he would buy them drink while they did it, though he was no richer than they. So now Ramani's head became filled with these movie dreams, because there was nothing else inside to take up any space, and this is another reason why I blame the widow woman, because she had more years and should have had more sense. (para. 18)

Both of these sentences are compound-complex. They include subordinate clauses (starting with "because," "while," and "though"), but each is a compound sentence linked with the coordinating conjunction "and." This construction reveals something about the narrator. The subordinate clauses are almost all explanatory: notice the repetition of "because." The narrator seems to have all of the answers, or he certainly thinks he does. The sentences also accumulate by connecting with "and," and even the second sentence seems to be an extension of the first because it begins with "So." This rambling syntax gives us a sense that the narrator is somebody who is into everyone's business at once: the card players, Ramani, and the widow woman. Everyone is fair game for judgment and gossip.

Cumulative and Periodic Sentences

A periodic sentence begins with a series of phrases or even clauses, and culminates in an independent clause. Cumulative sentences are the opposite: they begin with the main point and then add modifications, qualifications, and details. In this same story, Rushdie creates an unusually long cumulative sentence in his description of Ramani's situation:

> But when I saw him now, there was a new thing in his face, a strained thing, as if he were having to make a phenomenal effort, which was much more tiring than driving a rickshaw, more tiring even than pulling a rickshaw containing a thief's widow and her five living children and the ghosts of two dead ones; as if all the energy of his young body was being poured into that fictional space between his ear and his hand, and he was trying to bring the radio into existence by a mighty, and possibly fatal, act of will. (para. 43)

The main clause is "there was a new thing in his face"; everything that follows describes what that "new thing" is. In fact, the form of the sentence underscores its content because the long accumulation of detail helps readers feel the "phenomenal effort" being described.

Let's take a look at a periodic sentence in Henry James's *Daisy Miller*:

> As the day was splendid, however, and the concourse of vehicles, walkers, and loungers numerous, the young Americans found their progress much delayed. (para. 329)

Here James uses a periodic sentence to mimic the scene he's describing. Just as the characters are delayed by the splendid day, we as readers are delayed in getting to the final clause—which cleverly ends with the word "delayed"—by the various phrases used to describe that splendid day.

Interrupted Sentences

Any of these sentence patterns can be modified by "interruptions" that add descriptive details, state conditions, suggest uncertainty, voice possible alternative views, or present qualifications. Such sentences, quite characteristic of the style of Henry James and other pre-twentieth-century writers, often employ a combination of sentence patterns that may be difficult to understand the first time you read them. If you get tripped up, try reading the sentences aloud. You may notice that they sound more natural than they look on the page. Let's examine a sentence from *Daisy Miller* that demonstrates James's trademark tangent-filled "self-interrupted" syntax:

> At the risk of exciting a somewhat derisive smile on the reader's part, I may affirm that with regard to the women who had hitherto interested him, it very often seemed to Winterbourne among the possibilities that, given certain contingencies, he should be afraid—literally afraid—of these ladies; he had a pleasant sense that he should never be afraid of Daisy Miller. (para. 435)

The basic idea of the sentence is that Winterbourne sometimes finds women frightening, though he's not afraid of Daisy. But look at all the nuance the complicated sentence provides. In the opening clause, the narrator makes a tentative connection with the reader by asking his or her indulgence in his speculations. Next, the narrator offers one condition or qualification after another: he "may affirm," it "often seemed," "among the possibilities," and "certain contingencies." The narrator avoids mentioning any of those "women who had hitherto interested him" by name. Together, these qualifications are the written equivalent of stammering, which corresponds to the subject of the passage: Winterbourne's anxiety around women. The narrator waits until the end of the second independent clause, after he has admitted to fearing women, to mention Daisy Miller, the novella's title character. The second independent clause is much more straightforward than the first one and thus emphasizes the relaxation of the tension expressed in the first more complicated clause, which is filled with interruptions and qualifications of thought and feeling. Anxiety has given way to ease, and the syntax reflects that change.

Syntax in Poetry

Most poems are not written as a series of sentences arranged into paragraphs, and some poems are not written in full sentences at all. Nonetheless, examining the syntax of a poem that can be divided into sentences not only helps with comprehension but leads to a deeper understanding of meaning and purpose. Let's look at the first section of "The Second Coming" by William Butler Yeats as an example.

> Turning and turning in the widening gyre
> The falcon cannot hear the falconer;
> Things fall apart; the center cannot hold;
> Mere anarchy is loosed upon the world,
> The blood-dimmed tide is loosed, and everywhere   5
> The ceremony of innocence is drowned;
> The best lack all conviction, while the worst
> Are full of passionate intensity.

Technically, these eight lines comprise one long sentence made up of a series of independent clauses. But let's look at the patterns within this sentence. The opening two lines act like a periodic sentence, with line 2 serving as the main clause. Line 3 consists of two short, simple declarative clauses, whose abruptness makes them sound like forceful statements of fact. Lines 4–6 are a series of independent clauses joined by a coordinating conjunction, so they flow together as the urgency mounts. Lines 7 and 8 make up a complex sentence that contrasts "The best" and "the worst." The compound construction and complex one in lines 4–8 have a cumulative effect as they build a description of the result of "anarchy" being "loosed": a series of impending catastrophes that together create an apocalyptic vision. This single eight-line sentence builds up to this vision, which leads to the next two lines: "Surely some revelation is at hand; / Surely the Second Coming is at hand."

Enjambment and Caesura

Poets often manipulate syntax through enjambment and caesura. Enjambment is the breaking of a syntactic unit by the end of a line or between two lines; caesura denotes a pause that breaks up a line, usually indicated by punctuation marks. Sometimes poets use these techniques for practical reasons, such as adhering to a rhyme scheme; sometimes they use them to create interesting sounds or rhythms, by controlling when the reader pauses; and sometimes they use them to emphasize a word or create an effect that echoes the meaning of a line. Let's consider the opening stanza of "God's Grandeur" by Gerard Manley Hopkins:

> The world is charged with the grandeur of God.
> It will flame out, like shining from shook foil;
> It gathers to a greatness, like the ooze of oil
> Crushed. Why do men then now not reck his rod?

Generations have trod, have trod, have trod;   5
   And all is seared with trade; bleared, smeared with toil;
   And wears man's smudge and shares man's smell: the soil
Is bare now, nor can foot feel, being shod.

In the opening stanza, there are two instances of enjambment: lines 3–4 and lines 7–8. In the first, Hopkins puts the strong final verb ("Crushed") not only at the end of the sentence, altering the standard word order, but also on the next line. Both of these decisions emphasize the word and produce a contrast between the vowel-rich liquid sounds of "ooze of oil" and the finality of "Crushed." In the second example, the enjambment ensures the rhyme scheme of the two quatrains—abba / abba—but it also separates the subject ("soil") from its predicate ("Is bare"), emphasizing the bareness by isolating it and mimicking the disconnect between how nature should be and how it is.

In line 3, the caesura produced by the comma after "gathers to a greatness" stops the poem briefly, as though the line itself had built to its climax. In line 5, the commas after "trod" combine with the repetition of "have trod" to mimic the sound of clomping footsteps. Finally, in line 7, the colon is employed to introduce the final point in the quatrain. Avoiding a break in the line after the colon (which would also interrupt the rhyme scheme), the caesura denotes a deliberate pause and links "man's smell" and "the soil."

• EXERCISE 1 •

Identify the syntactic pattern in each of the following sentences.

1. "Out came Wangero with two quilts." ("Everyday Use," para. 55)
2. "Her mother was a small, spare, light person, with a wandering eye, a very exiguous nose, and a large forehead, decorated with a certain amount of thin, much-frizzled hair." (*Daisy Miller*, para. 160)
3. "Ringing his bicycle-bell and imitating weather forecasts, ear cupped as usual, he arrived at the caravan." ("The Free Radio," para. 47)
4. "There had not been the slightest alteration in her charming complexion; she was evidently neither offended nor flattered." (*Daisy Miller*, para. 44)
5. "The car continued to come on slowly, disappeared around a bend and appeared again, moving even slower, on top of the hill they had gone over." ("A Good Man Is Hard to Find," para. 70)
6. Not like the white filmstars, all rib
   and gaunt cheekbone, the Indian sex-goddess
   smiles plumply from behind a flowery
   branch.
   ("Indian Movie, New Jersey," ll. 1–4)
7. "One could actually *see* the pain he was suffering, his eyes, his face, his hands, and even the dejected slump of his shoulders." ("Spunk," para. 13)

8. "Now she could not refuse because I am not without importance in the town and maybe she calculated that if people saw us talking they would stop ignoring her when she passed, so she came as I knew she would." ("The Free Radio," para. 23)

9. "Daisy tripped about the vaulted chambers, rustled her skirts in the cork-screw staircases, flirted back with a pretty little cry and a shudder from the edge of the *oubliettes*, and turned a singularly well-shaped ear to everything that Winterbourne told her about the place." (*Daisy Miller*, para. 247)

10. "This hopefulness and didacticism he had picked up from his mother." ("Fenstad's Mother," para. 16)

11.   I see him there
Bringing a stone grasped firmly by the top
In each hand, like an old-stone savage armed.
("Mending Wall," ll. 38–40)

• EXERCISE 2 •

Although syntactical patterns contribute to a writer's style, most authors strive for variety. Using the following passage from "Fenstad's Mother," discuss how Charles Baxter varies syntax effectively both to stress points of emphasis and to ensure fluency.

On Sunday morning after Communion Fenstad drove across town to visit his mother. Behind the wheel, he exhaled with his hand flat in front of his mouth to determine if the wine on his breath could be detected. He didn't think so. Fenstad's mother was a lifelong social progressive who was amused by her son's churchgoing, and, wine or no wine, she could guess where he had been. She had spent her life in the company of rebels and deviationists, and she recognized all their styles. (para. 1)

• EXERCISE 3 •

Explain how Henry James's syntactical patterns contribute to the effect of the following prose passage from *Daisy Miller*.

She had been walking some quarter of an hour, attended by her two cavaliers, and respond-ing in a tone of very childish gaiety, as it seemed to Winterbourne, to the pretty speeches of Mr. Giovanelli, when a carriage that had detached itself from the revolving train drew up beside the path. At the same moment Winterbourne perceived that his friend Mrs. Walker—the lady whose house he had lately left—was seated in the vehicle and was beck-oning to him. Leaving Miss Miller's side, he hastened to obey her summons. Mrs. Walker was flushed; she wore an excited air. "It is really too dreadful," she said. (para. 350)

> ● EXERCISE 4 ●

Discuss how the syntax of "Forty Acres" (p. 1287) contributes to the meaning of the poem. Pay attention to Walcott's use of enjambment and caesura in the two complete sentences that make up the poem.

> ● EXERCISE 5 ●

Choose a poem from this chapter and rewrite it as prose (without eliminating any of the words). Compare your "revision" with the original poem, analyzing how the poet's syntactical choices contribute to the overall meaning.

> ● EXERCISE 6 ●

Write a brief narrative in the style of Henry James that uses an event from your life as inspiration. Pay special attention to emulating James's syntax.

Suggestions for Writing

Tradition and Progress

1. This chapter begins with a quote from Nathaniel Hawthorne. Using the works in this chapter to support your position, write an essay in which you agree or disagree with Hawthorne that the drive toward progress is made by those who are "ill at ease," while those who are happy embrace tradition.

2. The natural world provides the background for several of the works in this chapter. Write an essay in which you explore the way writers use the natural world to comment on tradition and progress.

3. Choose two poems from this chapter, one that criticizes progress and another that celebrates it. Write an essay in which you analyze the contrasting attitudes toward the subject. Include your own personal commentary on which view comes closer to your own.

4. Choose one of the following statements, and explain why it fits your beliefs about tradition and progress.

   "Tradition is the illusion of permanence." — Woody Allen

   "Discontent is the first step in the progress of a man or a nation." — Oscar Wilde

   "A tradition without intelligence is not worth having." — T. S. Eliot

"Science and technology revolutionize our lives, but memory, tradition and myth frame our response." —Arthur Schlesinger Jr.

"Tradition is a guide and not a jailer."—W. Somerset Maugham

5. In many of the short stories in this chapter, the primary conflict is between generations. Write an essay in which you analyze the generational clash in two or three of the stories.

6. Some of the poetry in this chapter—"London," "The Second Coming," and "Dover Beach," for example—are rather dark indictments of society and politics. Write an essay in which you examine the poets' positions and evaluate their arguments in light of today's world.

7. Literary movements, such as the Harlem Renaissance, often arise as the result of tension between traditional forms and the need to create new ones. Research another literary movement—the Beats or the Romantics, for example—and write an essay about the forces that encouraged the artists of that movement to create something different from what came before.

8. The plots of both *Daisy Miller* and "A Good Man Is Hard to Find" involve travel. Consider both stories, along with other works you've read, and write an essay in which you analyze the role of travel. Be sure to address the reasons you think the subject lends itself to a study of human behavior.

9. Many of the works in this chapter concern a clash between cultures. Try writing your own story about a culture clash. You might use your family background or the diversity in your home or community as a starting point.

11

War and Peace

Do dreams offer lessons? Do nightmares have themes, do we awaken and analyze them and live our lives and advise others as a result? Can the foot soldier teach anything important about war, merely for having been there? I think not. He can tell war stories.

— TIM O'BRIEN, *If I Die in a Combat Zone*

It is often said that there has never been a time in human history when there wasn't a war being waged somewhere in the world. That certainly casts a grim shadow on human history. We do not award a Nobel War Prize, yet the world seems always to have looked to warriors for its heroes. We might ask, What is it in human nature that is satisfied by what war provides—not only to the warrior but to the citizens who send the warrior to fight? If war is as horrific as reported by the warrior and as deplorable as depicted in literature, why do we continue to look to warriors as our heroes?

We prize peace, but find glory in war; we detest war, but find peace fragile, fleeting, and sometimes restive. This paradox has been a major subject of serious literature since the *Iliad* and the *Odyssey*, which tell the stories of the warrior fighting in battle and the warrior returning home, respectively. It may be simplistic to suggest, as some have, that those are the two basic stories we have to tell, but considering examples from the *Iliad* to *Star Wars*, from *The Things They Carried* to *Saving Private Ryan*, we have to acknowledge the hold these stories have on our imaginations.

In this chapter, you will read classic war stories and poems from Homer and Shakespeare as well as those inspired by Wilfred Owen's experience in World War I and Tim O'Brien's in Vietnam. You will read an ancient postwar story by Sophocles in addition to more modern ones: Herman Melville responding to the U.S. Civil War, and Bharati Mukherjee and Wislawa Szymborska to contemporary terrorism. You will read stories and poems not directly about war itself but about its motivations and repercussions and consequences—those by Luigi Pirandello, Cynthia Ozick, and Randall Jarrell regarding World War II; Robert Southey's look back on the sad wastefulness of war; and William Shakespeare's look ahead to its glories. Finally, you will read selections that consider war's aftermath and the attempt to establish peace. Throughout the chapter, you will view both war and peace from a variety of perspectives: that of the warrior and the witness, the poet and the citizen, the sufferer and the survivor. Reading these selections should cause you to reflect on the nature of

1325

conflict itself, on the nature of heroism, on the role of the citizen during wartime, and on the ongoing conflict between war and peace. Of course, reading about war will not prevent future wars; however, the vicarious immersion in experience that literature provides may increase our understanding of the nature of armed conflict, stretching from Athens to Antietam, on the sanguinary trail from the fortresses at Troy to the mountains of Afghanistan, and on urban streets from Berlin and Belfast to Baghdad and Beirut.

Antigone

SOPHOCLES

TRANSLATED BY ROBERT FAGLES

The Greek dramatist Sophocles (496?–406 B.C.E.) lived in Athens, where he was a priest, a statesman, and a general, as well as a prize-winning playwright. Sophocles fought in the Persian wars and lived in what we refer to as the Golden Age, when architecture, philosophy, art, history, and especially drama flourished. Among the three major dramatists of the time (the other two being Euripides and Aeschylus), Sophocles is generally considered the superior artist. In the Athenian drama competition of 468 B.C.E., he defeated Aeschylus, famous for the *Oresteia*—a trilogy of plays about King Agamemnon, Clytemnestra, and Orestes. Of over 120 plays that Sophocles is thought to have written, only seven are extant. Among them are the three that constitute the Oedipus cycle: *Oedipus the King*, *Oedipus at Colonus*, and *Antigone*. While the action portrayed in Antigone follows that of the other two chronologically, it was written first. Many of Sophocles' plays present a protagonist's search for truth and self-understanding in relation to the existing social and moral order, as demonstrated here in *Antigone*. At the beginning of the play, the audience would know that after the death of Oedipus—the former king of Thebes, whose tragic fate is told in the other plays—his sons, Eteocles and Polynices, agree to take turns ruling Thebes. When Eteocles refuses to yield his turn, Polynices is banished to Argos, where he raises armies to attack the city of Thebes and regain the throne.

CHARACTERS

ANTIGONE, *daughter of Oedipus and Jocasta*

ISMENE, *sister of Antigone*

A CHORUS *of old Theban citizens and their* LEADER

CREON, *king of Thebes, uncle of Antigone and Ismene*

A SENTRY

HAEMON, *son of Creon and Eurydice*

TIRESIAS, *a blind prophet*

A MESSENGER

EURYDICE, *wife of Creon*

GUARDS, ATTENDANTS, AND A BOY

TIME AND SCENE: The royal house of Thebes. It is still night, and the invading armies of Argos have just been driven from the city. Fighting on opposite sides, the sons of Oedipus, Eteocles and Polynices, have killed each other in combat. Their uncle, Creon, is now king of Thebes.

Enter Antigone, slipping through the central doors of the palace. She motions to her sister, Ismene, who follows her cautiously toward an altar at the center of the stage.

ANTIGONE: My own flesh and blood—dear sister, dear Ismene,
　　how many griefs our father Oedipus handed down!
　　Do you know one, I ask you, one grief
　　that Zeus will not perfect for the two of us
　　while we still live and breathe? There's nothing,　　　　　　　　　5
　　no pain—our lives are pain—no private shame,
　　no public disgrace, nothing I haven't seen
　　in your griefs and mine. And now this:
　　an emergency decree, they say, the Commander
　　has just declared for all of Thebes.　　　　　　　　　　　　　10
　　What, haven't you heard? Don't you see?
　　The doom reserved for enemies
　　marches on the ones we love the most.
ISMENE: Not I, I haven't heard a word, Antigone.
　　Nothing of loved ones,　　　　　　　　　　　　　　　　　15
　　no joy or pain has come my way, not since
　　the two of us were robbed of our two brothers,
　　both gone in a day, a double blow—
　　not since the armies of Argos vanished,
　　just this very night. I know nothing more,　　　　　　　　　20
　　whether our luck's improved or ruin's still to come.
ANTIGONE: I thought so. That's why I brought you out here,
　　past the gates, so you could hear in private.
ISMENE: What's the matter? Trouble, clearly . . .
　　you sound so dark, so grim.　　　　　　　　　　　　　25
ANTIGONE: Why not? Our own brothers' burial!
　　Hasn't Creon graced one with all the rites,
　　disgraced the other? Eteocles, they say,
　　has been given full military honors,
　　rightly so—Creon's laid him in the earth　　　　　　　　　30
　　and he goes with glory down among the dead.
　　But the body of Polynices, who died miserably—
　　why, a city-wide proclamation, rumor has it,
　　forbids anyone to bury him, even mourn him.
　　He's to be left unwept, unburied, a lovely treasure　　　　　35
　　for birds that scan the field and feast to their heart's content.

　　Such, I hear, is the martial law our good Creon
　　lays down for you and me—yes, me, I tell you—
　　and he's coming here to alert the uninformed
　　in no uncertain terms,　　　　　　　　　　　　　　　40
　　and he won't treat the matter lightly. Whoever
　　disobeys in the least will die, his doom is sealed:
　　stoning to death inside the city walls!

There you have it. You'll soon show what you are,
worth your breeding, Ismene, or a coward— 45
for all your royal blood.
ISMENE: My poor sister, if things have come to this,
who am I to make or mend them, tell me,
what good am I to you?
ANTIGONE: Decide.
Will you share the labor, share the work? 50
ISMENE: What work, what's the risk? What do you mean?
ANTIGONE:

Raising her hands.

Will you lift up his body with these bare hands
and lower it with me?
ISMENE: What? You'd bury him—
when a law forbids the city?
ANTIGONE: Yes!
He is my brother and—deny it as you will— 55
your brother too.
No one will ever convict me for a traitor.
ISMENE: So desperate, and Creon has expressly—
ANTIGONE: No,
he has no right to keep me from my own.
ISMENE: Oh my sister, think— 60
think how our own father died, hated,
his reputation in ruins, driven on
by the crimes he brought to light himself
to gouge out his eyes with his own hands—
then mother . . . his mother and wife, both in one, 65
mutilating her life in the twisted noose—
and last, our two brothers dead in a single day,
both shedding their own blood, poor suffering boys,
battling out their common destiny hand-to-hand.

Now look at the two of us, left so alone . . . 70
think what a death we'll die, the worst of all
if we violate the laws and override
the fixed decree of the throne, its power—
we must be sensible. Remember we are women,
we're not born to contend with men. Then too, 75
we're underlings, ruled by much stronger hands,
so we must submit in this, and things still worse.

I, for one, I'll beg the dead to forgive me—
I'm forced, I have no choice—I must obey

the ones who stand in power. Why rush to extremes?   80
    It's madness, madness.
ANTIGONE: I won't insist,
    no, even if you should have a change of heart,
    I'd never welcome you in the labor, not with me.
    So, do as you like, whatever suits you best—
    I'll bury him myself.   85
    And even if I die in the act, that death will be a glory.
    I'll lie with the one I love and loved by him—
    an outrage sacred to the gods! I have longer
    to please the dead than please the living here:
    in the kingdom down below I'll lie forever.   90
    Do as you like, dishonor the laws
    the gods hold in honor.
ISMENE: I'd do them no dishonor . . .
    but defy the city? I have no strength for that.
ANTIGONE: You have your excuses. I am on my way,
    I'll raise a mound for him, for my dear brother.   95
ISMENE: Oh Antigone, you're so rash—I'm so afraid for you!
ANTIGONE: Don't fear for me. Set your own life in order.
ISMENE: Then don't, at least, blurt this out to anyone.
    Keep it a secret. I'll join you in that, I promise.
ANTIGONE: Dear god, shout it from the rooftops. I'll hate you   100
    all the more for silence—tell the world!
ISMENE: So fiery—and it ought to chill your heart.
ANTIGONE: I know I please where I must please the most.
ISMENE: Yes, if you can, but you're in love with impossibility.
ANTIGONE: Very well then, once my strength gives out   105
    I will be done at last.
ISMENE: You're wrong from the start,
    you're off on a hopeless quest.
ANTIGONE: If you say so, you will make me hate you,
    and the hatred of the dead, by all rights,
    will haunt you night and day.   110
    But leave me to my own absurdity, leave me
    to suffer this—dreadful thing. I'll suffer
    nothing as great as death without glory.

Exit to the side.

ISMENE: Then go if you must, but rest assured,
    wild, irrational as you are, my sister,   115
    you are truly dear to the ones who love you.

Withdrawing to the palace. Enter a CHORUS, *the old citizens of Thebes, chanting as the sun begins to rise.*

CHORUS: Glory!—great beam of sun, brightest of all
    that ever rose on the seven gates of Thebes,
        you burn through night at last!
            Great eye of the golden day,   120
mounting the Dirce's[1] banks you throw him back—
the enemy out of Argos, the white shield, the man of bronze—
he's flying headlong now
        the bridle of fate stampeding him with pain!

    And he had driven against our borders,   125
    launched by the warring claims of Polynices—
    like an eagle screaming, winging havoc
    over the land, wings of armor
    shielded white as snow,
    a huge army massing,   130
    crested helmets bristling for assault.

He hovered above our roofs, his vast maw gaping
closing down around our seven gates,
    his spears thirsting for the kill
            but now he's gone, look,   135
before he could glut his jaws with Theban blood
or the god of fire put our crown of towers to the torch.
He grappled the Dragon none can master—Thebes—
    the clang of our arms like thunder at his back!

    Zeus hates with a vengeance all bravado,   140
    the mighty boasts of men. He watched them
    coming on in a rising flood, the pride
    of their golden armor ringing shrill—
    and brandishing his lightning
    blasted the fighter just at the goal,   145
    rushing to shout his triumph from our walls.

Down from the heights he crashed, pounding down on the earth!
And a moment ago, blazing torch in hand—
        mad for attack, ecstatic
he breathed his rage, the storm   150
    of his fury hurling at our heads!
But now his high hopes have laid him low
and down the enemy ranks the iron god of war
        deals his rewards, his stunning blows—Ares[2]
        rapture of battle, our right arm in the crisis.   155

---

[1]River near Thebes.—EDS.
[2]Greek god of war.—EDS.

Seven captains marshaled at seven gates
seven against their equals, gave
their brazen trophies up to Zeus,
god of the breaking rout of battle,
all but two: those blood brothers,   160
one father, one mother — matched in rage,
spears matched for the twin conquest —
clashed and won the common prize of death.

But now for Victory! Glorious in the morning,
joy in her eyes to meet our joy   165
    she is winging down to Thebes,
our fleets of chariots wheeling in her wake —
    Now let us win oblivion from the wars,
thronging the temples of the gods
in singing, dancing choirs through the night!   170
    Lord Dionysus,³ god of the dance
    that shakes the land of Thebes, now lead the way!

Enter CREON *from the palace, attended by his guard.*

    But look, the king of the realm is coming,
Creon, the new man for the new day,
whatever the gods are sending now . . .   175
what new plan will he launch?
Why this, this special session?
Why this sudden call to the old men
summoned at one command?

CREON: My countrymen,
the ship of state is safe. The gods who rocked her,   180
after a long, merciless pounding in the storm,
have righted her once more.

                  Out of the whole city
I have called you here alone. Well I know,
first, your undeviating respect
for the throne and royal power of King Laius.   185
Next, while Oedipus steered the land of Thebes,
and even after he died, your loyalty was unshakable,
you still stood by their children. Now then,
since the two sons are dead — two blows of fate
in the same day, cut down by each other's hands,   190
both killers, both brothers stained with blood —
as I am next in kin to the dead,
I now possess the throne and all its powers.

---

³Greek god of agriculture, wine, fertility, and dance. — EDS.

Of course you cannot know a man completely,
his character, his principles, sense of judgment,   195
not till he's shown his colors, ruling the people,
making laws. Experience, there's the test.
As I see it, whoever assumes the task,
the awesome task of setting the city's course,
and refuses to adopt the soundest policies   200
but fearing someone, keeps his lips locked tight,
he's utterly worthless. So I rate him now,
I always have. And whoever places a friend
above the good of his own country, he is nothing:
I have no use for him. Zeus my witness,   205
Zeus who sees all things, always—
I could never stand by silent, watching destruction
march against our city, putting safety to rout,
nor could I ever make that man a friend of mine
who menaces our country. Remember this: 210
our country *is* our safety.
Only while she voyages true on course
can we establish friendships, truer than blood itself.
Such are my standards. They make our city great.

Closely akin to them I have proclaimed,   215
just now, the following decree to our people
concerning the two sons of Oedipus.
Eteocles, who died fighting for Thebes,
excelling all in arms: he shall be buried,
crowned with a hero's honors, the cups we pour   220
to soak the earth and reach the famous dead.

But as for his blood brother, Polynices,
who returned from exile, home to his father-city
and the gods of his race, consumed with one desire—
to burn them roof to roots—who thirsted to drink   225
his kinsmen's blood and sell the rest to slavery:
that man—a proclamation has forbidden the city
to dignify him with burial, mourn him at all.
No, he must be left unburied, his corpse
carrion for the birds and dogs to tear,   230
an obscenity for the citizens to behold!

These are my principles. Never at my hands
will the traitor be honored above the patriot.
But whoever proves his loyalty to the state:
I'll prize that man in death as well as life.   235
LEADER: If this is your pleasure, Creon, treating
our city's enemy and our friend this way . . .

The power is yours, I suppose, to enforce it
with the laws, both for the dead and all of us,
the living.

CREON: Follow my orders closely then,   240
be on your guard.

LEADER: We're too old.
Lay that burden on younger shoulders.

CREON: No, no,
I don't mean the body—I've posted guards already.

LEADER: What commands for us then? What other service?

CREON: See that you never side with those who break my orders.   245

LEADER: Never. Only a fool could be in love with death.

CREON: Death is the price—you're right. But all too often
the mere hope of money has ruined many men.

A SENTRY *enters from the side.*

SENTRY: My lord,
I can't say I'm winded from running, or set out
with any spring in my legs either—no sir,   250
I was lost in thought, and it made me stop, often,
dead in my tracks, wheeling, turning back,
and all the time a voice inside me muttering,
"Idiot, why? You're going straight to your death."
Then muttering, "Stopped again, poor fool?   255
If somebody gets the news to Creon first,
what's to save your neck?"

                  And so,
mulling it over, on I trudged, dragging my feet,
you can make a short road take forever . . .
but at last, look, common sense won out,   260
I'm here, and I'm all yours,
and even though I come empty-handed
I'll tell my story just the same, because
I've come with a good grip on one hope,
what will come will come, whatever fate—   265

CREON: Come to the point!
What's wrong—why so afraid?

SENTRY: First, myself, I've got to tell you,
I didn't do it, didn't see who did—
Be fair, don't take it out on me.   270

CREON: You're playing it safe, soldier,
barricading yourself from any trouble.
It's obvious, you've something strange to tell.

SENTRY: Dangerous too, and danger makes you delay
for all you're worth.   275

CREON: Out with it—then dismiss!
SENTRY: All right, here it comes. The body—
    someone's just buried it, then run off . . .
    sprinkled some dry dust on the flesh,
    given it proper rites.
CREON: What?   280
    What man alive would dare—
SENTRY: I've no idea, I swear it.
    There was no mark of a spade, no pickaxe there,
    no earth turned up, the ground packed hard and dry,
    unbroken, no tracks, no wheelruts, nothing,
    the workman left no trace. Just at sunup   285
    the first watch of the day points it out—
    it was a wonder! We were stunned . . .
    a terrific burden too, for all of us, listen:
    you can't see the corpse, not that it's buried,
    really, just a light cover of road-dust on it,   290
    as if someone meant to lay the dead to rest
    and keep from getting cursed.
    Not a sign in sight that dogs or wild beasts
    had worried the body, even torn the skin.

    But what came next! Rough talk flew thick and fast,   295
    guard grilling guard—we'd have come to blows
    at last, nothing to stop it; each man for himself
    and each the culprit, no one caught red-handed,
    all of us pleading ignorance, dodging the charges,
    ready to take up red-hot iron in our fists,   300
    go through fire, swear oaths to the gods—
    "I didn't do it, I had no hand in it either,
    not in the plotting, not in the work itself!"

    Finally, after all this wrangling came to nothing,
    one man spoke out and made us stare at the ground,   305
    hanging our heads in fear. No way to counter him,
    no way to take his advice and come through
    safe and sound. Here's what he said:
    "Look, we've got to report the facts to Creon,
    we can't keep this hidden." Well, that won out,   310
    and the lot fell on me, condemned me,
    unlucky as ever, I got the prize. So here I am,
    against my will and yours too, well I know—
    no one wants the man who brings bad news.
LEADER: My king,
    ever since he began I've been debating in my mind,   315
    could this possibly be the work of the gods?

CREON: Stop—
    before you make me choke with anger—the gods!
    You, you're senile, must you be insane?
    You say—why it's intolerable—say the gods
    could have the slightest concern for that corpse?   320
    Tell me, was it for meritorious service
    they proceeded to bury him, prized him so? The hero
    who came to burn their temples ringed with pillars,
    their golden treasures—scorch their hallowed earth
    and fling their laws to the winds.   325
    Exactly when did you last see the gods
    celebrating traitors? Inconceivable!

    No, from the first there were certain citizens
    who could hardly stand the spirit of my regime,
    grumbling against me in the dark, heads together,   330
    tossing wildly, never keeping their necks beneath
    the yoke, loyally submitting to their king.
    These are the instigators, I'm convinced—
    they've perverted my own guard, bribed them
    to do their work.
                Money! Nothing worse   335
    in our lives, so current, rampant, so corrupting.
    Money—you demolish cities, root men from their homes,
    you train and twist good minds and set them on
    to the most atrocious schemes. No limit,
    you make them adept at every kind of outrage,   340
    every godless crime—money!
                Everyone—
    the whole crew bribed to commit this crime,
    they've made one thing sure at least:
    sooner or later they will pay the price.

Wheeling on the SENTRY.

    You—   345
    I swear to Zeus as I still believe in Zeus,
    if you don't find the man who buried that corpse,
    the very man, and produce him before my eyes,
    simple death won't be enough for you,
    not till we string you up alive   350
    and wring the immorality out of you.
    Then you can steal the rest of your days,
    better informed about where to make a killing.
    You'll have learned, at last, it doesn't pay
    to itch for rewards from every hand that beckons.   355

Filthy profits wreck most men, you'll see—
they'll never save your life.

SENTRY: Please,
may I say a word or two, or just turn and go?
CREON: Can't you tell? Everything you say offends me.
SENTRY: Where does it hurt you, in the ears or in the heart?   360
CREON: And who are you to pinpoint my displeasure?
SENTRY: The culprit grates on your feelings,
I just annoy your ears.
CREON: Still talking?
You talk too much! A born nuisance—
SENTRY: Maybe so,
but I never did this thing, so help me!
CREON: Yes you did—   365
what's more, you squandered your life for silver!
SENTRY: Oh it's terrible when the one who does the judging
judges things all wrong.
CREON: Well now,
you just be clever about your judgments—
if you fail to produce the criminals for me,   370
you'll swear your dirty money brought you pain.

Turning sharply, reentering the palace.

SENTRY: I hope he's found. Best thing by far.
But caught or not, that's in the lap of fortune;
I'll never come back, you've seen the last of me.
I'm saved, even now, and I never thought,   375
I never hoped—
dear gods, I owe you all my thanks!

Rushing out.

CHORUS: Numberless wonders
terrible wonders walk the world but none the match for man—
that great wonder crossing the heaving gray sea,
driven on by the blasts of winter   380
on through breakers crashing left and right,
holds his steady course
and the oldest of the gods he wears away—
the Earth, the immortal, the inexhaustible—
as his plows go back and forth, year in, year out   385
with the breed of stallions turning up the furrows.

And the blithe, lightheaded race of birds he snares,
the tribes of savage beasts, the life that swarms the depths—
with one fling of his nets

woven and coiled tight, he takes them all, 390
 man the skilled, the brilliant!
He conquers all, taming with his techniques
the prey that roams the cliffs and wild lairs,
training the stallion, clamping the yoke across
 his shaggy neck, and the tireless mountain bull. 395
And speech and thought, quick as the wind
and the mood and mind for law that rules the city—
 all these he has taught himself
and shelter from the arrows of the frost
when there's rough lodging under the cold clear sky 400
and the shafts of lashing rain—
 ready, resourceful man!
 Never without resources
never an impasse as he marches on the future—
only Death, from Death alone he will find no rescue 405
but from desperate plagues he has plotted his escapes.

Man the master, ingenious past all measure
past all dreams, the skills within his grasp—
 he forges on, now to destruction
now again to greatness. When he weaves in 410
the laws of the land, and the justice of the gods
that binds his oaths together
 he and his city rise high—
 but the city casts out
that man who weds himself to inhumanity 415
thanks to reckless daring. Never share my hearth
never think my thoughts, whoever does such things.

Enter ANTIGONE *from the side, accompanied by the* SENTRY.

 Here is a dark sign from the gods—
 what to make of this? I know her,
 how can I deny it? That young girl's Antigone! 420
 Wretched, child of a wretched father,
 Oedipus. Look, is it possible?
 They bring you in like a prisoner—
 why? did you break the king's laws?
 Did they take you in some act of mad defiance? 425
SENTRY: She's the one, she did it single-handed—
we caught her burying the body. Where's Creon?

Enter CREON *from the palace.*

LEADER: Back again, just in time when you need him.
CREON: In time for what? What is it?

SENTRY: My king,   430
    there's nothing you can swear you'll never do—
    second thoughts make liars of us all.
    I could have sworn I wouldn't hurry back
    (what with your threats, the buffeting I just took),
    but a stroke of luck beyond our wildest hopes,
    what a joy, there's nothing like it. So,   435
    back I've come, breaking my oath, who cares?
    I'm bringing in our prisoner—this young girl—
    we took her giving the dead the last rites.
    But no casting lots this time; this is *my* luck,
    my prize, no one else's.
                Now, my lord,   440
    here she is. Take her, question her,
    cross-examine her to your heart's content.
    But set me free, it's only right—
    I'm rid of this dreadful business once for all.
CREON: Prisoner! Her? You took her—where, doing what?   445
SENTRY: Burying the man. That's the whole story.
CREON: What?
    You mean what you say, you're telling me the truth?
SENTRY: She's the one. With my own eyes I saw her
    bury the body, just what you've forbidden.
    There. Is that plain and clear?   450
CREON: What did you see? Did you catch her in the act?
SENTRY: Here's what happened. We went back to our post,
    those threats of yours breathing down our necks—
    we brushed the corpse clean of the dust that covered it,
    stripped it bare . . . it was slimy, going soft,   455
    and we took to high ground, backs to the wind
    so the stink of him couldn't hit us;
    jostling, baiting each other to keep awake,
    shouting back and forth—no napping on the job,
    not this time. And so the hours dragged by   460
    until the sun stood dead above our heads,
    a huge white ball in the noon sky, beating,
    blazing down, and then it happened—
    suddenly, a whirlwind!
    Twisting a great dust-storm up from the earth,   465
    a black plague of the heavens, filling the plain,
    ripping the leaves off every tree in sight,
    choking the air and sky. We squinted hard
    and took our whipping from the gods.

And after the storm passed—it seemed endless— 470
there, we saw the girl!
And she cried out a sharp, piercing cry,
like a bird come back to an empty nest,
peering into its bed, and all the babies gone . . .
Just so, when she sees the corpse bare 475
she bursts into a long, shattering wail
and calls down withering curses on the heads
of all who did the work. And she scoops up dry dust,
handfuls, quickly, and lifting a fine bronze urn,
lifting it high and pouring, she crowns the dead 480
with three full libations.
     Soon as we saw
we rushed her, closed on the kill like hunters,
and she, she didn't flinch. We interrogated her,
charging her with offenses past and present—
she stood up to it all, denied nothing. I tell you, 485
it made me ache and laugh in the same breath.
It's pure joy to escape the worst yourself,
it hurts a man to bring down his friends.
But all that, I'm afraid, means less to me
than my own skin. That's the way I'm made.
CREON:

Wheeling on ANTIGONE.

         You, 490
with your eyes fixed on the ground—speak up.
Do you deny you did this, yes or no?
ANTIGONE: I did it. I don't deny a thing.
CREON:

To the SENTRY.

You, get out, wherever you please—
you're clear of a very heavy charge. 495

He leaves; CREON *turns back to* ANTIGONE.

You, tell me briefly, no long speeches—
were you aware a decree had forbidden this?
ANTIGONE: Well aware. How could I avoid it? It was public.
CREON: And still you had the gall to break this law?
ANTIGONE: Of course I did. It wasn't Zeus, not in the least, 500
who made this proclamation—not to me.
Nor did that Justice, dwelling with the gods

beneath the earth, ordain such laws for men.
Nor did I think your edict had such force
that you, a mere mortal, could override the gods,   505
the great unwritten, unshakable traditions.
They are alive, not just today or yesterday:
they live forever, from the first of time,
and no one knows when they first saw the light.

These laws—I was not about to break them,   510
not out of fear of some man's wounded pride,
and face the retribution of the gods.
Die I must, I've known it all my life—
how could I keep from knowing?—even without
your death-sentence ringing in my ears.   515
And if I am to die before my time
I consider that a gain. Who on earth,
alive in the midst of so much grief as I,
could fail to find his death a rich reward?
So for me, at least, to meet this doom of yours   520
is precious little pain. But if I had allowed
my own mother's son to rot, an unburied corpse—
that would have been an agony! This is nothing.
And if my present actions strike you as foolish,
let's just say I've been accused of folly   525
by a fool.
LEADER: Like father like daughter,
passionate, wild . . .
she hasn't learned to bend before adversity.
CREON: No? Believe me, the stiffest stubborn wills
fall the hardest; the toughest iron,   530
tempered strong in the white-hot fire,
you'll see it crack and shatter first of all.
And I've known spirited horses you can break
with a light bit—proud, rebellious horses.
There's no room for pride, not in a slave,   535
not with the lord and master standing by.

This girl was an old hand at insolence
when she overrode the edicts we made public.
But once she'd done it—the insolence,
twice over—to glory in it, laughing,   540
mocking us to our face with what she'd done.
I'm not the man, not now: she is the man
if this victory goes to her and she goes free.

Never! Sister's child or closer in blood
than all my family clustered at my altar   545
worshiping Guardian Zeus—she'll never escape,
she and her blood sister, the most barbaric death.
Yes, I accuse her sister of an equal part
in scheming this, this burial.

To his attendants.

                         Bring her here!
I just saw her inside, hysterical, gone to pieces.   550
It never fails: the mind convicts itself
in advance, when scoundrels are up to no good,
plotting in the dark. Oh but I hate it more
when a traitor, caught red-handed,
tries to glorify his crimes.   555
ANTIGONE: Creon, what more do you want
    than my arrest and execution?
CREON: Nothing. Then I have it all.
ANTIGONE: Then why delay? Your moralizing repels me,
    every word you say—pray god it always will.   560
    So naturally all I say repels you too.
                        Enough.
Give me glory! What greater glory could I win
than to give my own brother decent burial?
These citizens here would all agree,

To the CHORUS.

    they'd praise me too   565
    if their lips weren't locked in fear.

Pointing to CREON.

    Lucky tyrants—the perquisites of power!
    Ruthless power to do and say whatever pleases *them.*
CREON: You alone, of all the people in Thebes,
    see things that way.
ANTIGONE: They see it just that way   570
    but defer to you and keep their tongues in leash.
CREON: And you, aren't you ashamed to differ so from them?
    So disloyal!
ANTIGONE: Not ashamed for a moment,
    not to honor my brother, my own flesh and blood.
CREON: Wasn't Eteocles a brother too—cut down, facing him?   575
ANTIGONE: Brother, yes, by the same mother, the same father.

CREON: Then how can you render his enemy such honors,
 such impieties in his eyes?
ANTIGONE: He'll never testify to that,
 Eteocles dead and buried.
CREON: He will—   580
 if you honor the traitor just as much as him.
ANTIGONE: But it was his brother, not some slave that died—
CREON: Ravaging our country!—
 but Eteocles died fighting in our behalf.
ANTIGONE: No matter—Death longs for the same rites for all.   585
CREON: Never the same for the patriot and the traitor.
ANTIGONE: Who, Creon, who on earth can say the ones below
 don't find this pure and uncorrupt?
CREON: Never. Once an enemy, never a friend,
 not even after death.   590
ANTIGONE: I was born to join in love, not hate—
 that is my nature.
CREON: Go down below and love,
 if love you must—love the dead! While I'm alive,
 no woman is going to lord it over me.

Enter ISMENE *from the palace, under guard.*

CHORUS: Look,
 Ismene's coming, weeping a sister's tears,   595
 loving sister, under a cloud . . .
 her face is flushed, her cheeks streaming.
 Sorrow puts her lovely radiance in the dark.
CREON: You—
 in my house, you viper, slinking undetected,
 sucking my life-blood! I never knew   600
 I was breeding twin disasters, the two of you
 rising up against my throne. Come, tell me,
 will you confess your part in the crime or not?
 Answer me. Swear to me.
ISMENE: I did it, yes—
 if only she consents—I share the guilt,   605
 the consequences too.
ANTIGONE: No,
 Justice will never suffer that—not you,
 you were unwilling. I never brought you in.
ISMENE: But now you face such dangers . . . I'm not ashamed
 to sail through trouble with you,   610
 make your troubles mine.

ANTIGONE: Who did the work?
    Let the dead and the god of death bear witness!
    I've no love for a friend who loves in words alone.
ISMENE: Oh no, my sister, don't reject me, please,
    let me die beside you, consecrating   615
    the dead together.
ANTIGONE: Never share my dying,
    don't lay claim to what you never touched.
    My death will be enough.
ISMENE: What do I care for life, cut off from you?
ANTIGONE: Ask Creon. Your concern is all for him.   620
ISMENE: Why abuse me so? It doesn't help you now.
ANTIGONE: You're right—
    if I mock you, I get no pleasure from it,
    only pain.
ISMENE: Tell me, dear one,
    what can I do to help you, even now?
ANTIGONE: Save yourself. I don't grudge you your survival.   625
ISMENE: Oh no, no, denied my portion in your death?
ANTIGONE: You chose to live, I chose to die.
ISMENE: Not, at least,
    without every kind of caution I could voice.
ANTIGONE: Your wisdom appealed to one world—mine, another.
ISMENE: But look, we're both guilty, both condemned to death.   630
ANTIGONE: Courage! Live your life. I gave myself to death,
    long ago, so I might serve the dead.
CREON: They're both mad, I tell you, the two of them.
    One's just shown it, the other's been that way
    since she was born.
ISMENE: True, my king,   635
    the sense we were born with cannot last forever . . .
    commit cruelty on a person long enough
    and the mind begins to go.
CREON: Yours did,
    when you chose to commit your crimes with her.
ISMENE: How can I live alone, without her?
CREON: Her?   640
    Don't even mention her—she no longer exists.
ISMENE: What? You'd kill your own son's bride?
CREON: Absolutely:
    there are other fields for him to plow.
ISMENE: Perhaps,
    but never as true, as close a bond as theirs.

CREON: A worthless woman for my son? It repels me.   645
ISMENE: Dearest Haemon, your father wrongs you so!
CREON: Enough, enough—you and your talk of marriage!
ISMENE: Creon—you're really going to rob your son of Antigone?
CREON: Death will do it for me—break their marriage off.
LEADER: So, it's settled then? Antigone must die?   650
CREON: Settled, yes—we both know that.

To the guards.

> Stop wasting time. Take them in.
> From now on they'll act like women.
> Tie them up, no more running loose;
> even the bravest will cut and run,   655
> once they see Death coming for their lives.

The guards escort ANTIGONE *and* ISMENE *into the palace.* CREON *remains while the old citizens form their chorus.*

CHORUS: Blest, they are the truly blest who all their lives
    have never tasted devastation. For others, once
    the gods have rocked a house to its foundations
        the ruin will never cease, cresting on and on   660
    from one generation on throughout the race—
    like a great mounting tide
    driven on by savage northern gales,
        surging over the dead black depths
    roiling up from the bottom dark heaves of sand   665
    and the headlands, taking the storm's onslaught full-force,
    roar, and the low moaning
                echoes on and on
                        and now
    as in ancient times I see the sorrows of the house,
    the living heirs of the old ancestral kings,
    piling on the sorrows of the dead   670
      and one generation cannot free the next—
    some god will bring them crashing down,
    the race finds no release.
    And now the light, the hope
        springing up from the late last root   675
    in the house of Oedipus, that hope's cut down in turn
    by the long, bloody knife swung by the gods of death
    by a senseless word
            by fury at the heart.
                   Zeus,

yours is the power, Zeus, what man on earth
can override it, who can hold it back? 680
Power that neither Sleep, the all-ensnaring
   no, nor the tireless months of heaven
can ever overmaster—young through all time,
mighty lord of power, you hold fast
   the dazzling crystal mansions of Olympus 685
And throughout the future, late and soon
as through the past, your law prevails:
no towering form of greatness
     enters into the lives of mortals
        free and clear of ruin.
                   True, 690
our dreams, our high hopes voyaging far and wide
bring sheer delight to many, to many others
   delusion, blithe, mindless lusts
and the fraud steals on one slowly . . . unaware
till he trips and puts his foot into the fire. 695
   He was a wise old man who coined
the famous saying: "Sooner or later
foul is fair, fair is foul
to the man the gods will ruin"—
   He goes his way for a moment only 700
        free of blinding ruin.

Enter HAEMON *from the palace.*

   Here's Haemon now, the last of all your sons.
   Does he come in tears for his bride,
   his doomed bride, Antigone—
   bitter at being cheated of their marriage? 705
CREON: We'll soon know, better than seers could tell us.

Turning to HAEMON.

   Son, you've heard the final verdict on your bride?
   Are you coming now, raving against your father?
   Or do you love me, no matter what I do?
HAEMON: Father, I'm your *son* . . . you in your wisdom 710
   set my bearings for me—I obey you.
   No marriage could ever mean more to me than you,
   whatever good direction you may offer.
CREON: Fine, Haemon.
   That's how you ought to feel within your heart,
   subordinate to your father's will in every way. 715
   That's what a man prays for: to produce good sons—
   households full of them, dutiful and attentive,

so they can pay his enemy back with interest
and match the respect their father shows his friend.
But the man who rears a brood of useless children,   720
what has he brought into the world, I ask you?
Nothing but trouble for himself, and mockery
from his enemies laughing in his face.
                                    Oh Haemon,
never lose your sense of judgment over a woman.
The warmth, the rush of pleasure, it all goes cold   725
in your arms, I warn you . . . a worthless woman
in your house, a misery in your bed.
What wound cuts deeper than a loved one
turned against you? Spit her out,
like a mortal enemy—let the girl go.   730
Let her find a husband down among the dead.

Imagine it: I caught her in naked rebellion,
the traitor, the only one in the whole city.
I'm not about to prove myself a liar,
not to my people, no, I'm going to kill her!   735
That's right—so let her cry for mercy, sing her hymns
to Zeus who defends all bonds of kindred blood.
Why, if I bring up my own kin to be rebels,
think what I'd suffer from the world at large.
Show me the man who rules his household well: 740
I'll show you someone fit to rule the state.
That good man, my son,
I have every confidence he and he alone
can give commands and take them too. Staunch
in the storm of spears he'll stand his ground,   745
a loyal, unflinching comrade at your side.

But whoever steps out of line, violates the laws
or presumes to hand out orders to his superiors,
he'll win no praise from me. But that man
the city places in authority, his orders   750
must be obeyed, large and small,
right and wrong.
                        Anarchy—
show me a greater crime in all the earth!
She, she destroys cities, rips up houses,
breaks the ranks of spearmen into headlong rout.   755
But the ones who last it out, the great mass of them
owe their lives to discipline. Therefore
we must defend the men who live by law,
never let some woman triumph over us.

Better to fall from power, if fall we must,   760
at the hands of a man—never be rated
inferior to a woman, never.

LEADER: To us,
unless old age has robbed us of our wits,
you seem to say what you have to say with sense.

HAEMON: Father, only the gods endow a man with reason,   765
the finest of all their gifts, a treasure.
Far be it from me—I haven't the skill,
and certainly no desire, to tell you when,
if ever, you make a slip in speech . . . though
someone else might have a good suggestion.   770

Of course it's not for you,
in the normal run of things, to watch
whatever men say or do, or find to criticize.
The man in the street, you know, dreads your glance,
he'd never say anything displeasing to your face.   775
But it's for me to catch the murmurs in the dark,
the way the city mourns for this young girl.
"No woman," they say, "ever deserved death less,
and such a brutal death for such a glorious action.
She, with her own dear brother lying in his blood—   780
she couldn't bear to leave him dead, unburied,
food for the wild dogs or wheeling vultures.
Death? She deserves a glowing crown of gold!"
So they say, and the rumor spreads in secret,
darkly . . .

                    I rejoice in your success, father—   785
nothing more precious to me in the world.
What medal of honor brighter to his children
than a father's growing glory? Or a child's
to his proud father? Now don't, please,
be quite so single-minded, self-involved,   790
or assume the world is wrong and you are right.
Whoever thinks that he alone possesses intelligence,
the gift of eloquence, he and no one else,
and character too . . . such men, I tell you,
spread them open—you will find them empty.

                                              No,   795
it's no disgrace for a man, even a wise man,
to learn many things and not to be too rigid.
You've seen trees by a raging winter torrent,
how many sway with the flood and salvage every twig,
but not the stubborn—they're ripped out, roots and all.   800

Bend or break. The same when a man is sailing:
haul your sheets too taut, never give an inch,
you'll capsize, go the rest of the voyage
keel up and the rowing-benches under.

Oh give way. Relax your anger — change!   805
I'm young, I know, but let me offer this:
it would be best by far, I admit,
if a man were born infallible, right by nature.
If not — and things don't often go that way,
it's best to learn from those with good advice.   810
LEADER: You'd do well, my lord, if he's speaking to the point,
to learn from him,

Turning to HAEMON.

              and you, my boy, from him.
You both are talking sense.
CREON: So,
men our age, we're to be lectured, are we? —
schooled by a boy his age?   815
HAEMON: Only in what is right. But if I seem young,
look less to my years and more to what I do.
CREON: Do? Is admiring rebels an achievement?
HAEMON: I'd never suggest that you admire treason.
CREON: Oh? —
isn't that just the sickness that's attacked her?   820
HAEMON: The whole city of Thebes denies it, to a man.
CREON: And is Thebes about to tell me how to rule?
HAEMON: Now, you see? Who's talking like a child?
CREON: Am I to rule this land for others — or myself?
HAEMON: It's no city at all, owned by one man alone.   825
CREON: What? The city *is* the king's — that's the law!
HAEMON: What a splendid king you'd make of a desert island —
you and you alone.
CREON:

To the CHORUS.

              This boy, I do believe,
is fighting on her side, the woman's side.
HAEMON: If you are a woman, yes;   830
my concern is all for you.
CREON: Why, you degenerate — bandying accusations,
threatening me with justice, your own father!
HAEMON: I see my father offending justice — wrong.
CREON: Wrong?

To protect my royal rights?

HAEMON: Protect your rights?   835
When you trample down the honors of the gods?

CREON: You, you soul of corruption, rotten through—
woman's accomplice!

HAEMON: That may be,
but you'll never find me accomplice to a criminal.

CREON: That's what *she* is,   840
and every word you say is a blatant appeal for her—

HAEMON: And you, and me, and the gods beneath the earth.

CREON: You'll never marry her, not while she's alive.

HAEMON: Then she'll die . . . but her death will kill another.

CREON: What, brazen threats? You go too far!

HAEMON: What threat?   845
Combating your empty, mindless judgments with a word?

CREON: You'll suffer for your sermons, you and your empty wisdom!

HAEMON: If you weren't my father, I'd say you were insane.

CREON: Don't flatter me with Father—you woman's slave!

HAEMON: You really expect to fling abuse at me   850
and not receive the same?

CREON: Is that so!
Now, by heaven, I promise you, you'll pay—
taunting, insulting me! Bring her out,
that hateful—she'll die now, here,
in front of his eyes, beside her groom!   855

HAEMON: No, no, she will never die beside me—
don't delude yourself. And you will never
see me, never set eyes on my face again.
Rage your heart out, rage with friends
who can stand the sight of you.   860

Rushing out.

LEADER: Gone, my king, in a burst of anger.
A temper young as his . . . hurt him once,
he may do something violent.

CREON: Let him do—
dream up something desperate, past all human limit!
Good riddance. Rest assured,   865
he'll never save those two young girls from death.

LEADER: Both of them, you really intend to kill them both?

CREON: No, not her, the one whose hands are clean;
you're quite right.

LEADER: But Antigone—
what sort of death do you have in mind for her?   870

CREON: I'll take her down some wild, desolate path
    never trod by men, and wall her up alive
    in a rocky vault, and set out short rations,
    just a gesture of piety
    to keep the entire city free of defilement.   875
    There let her pray to the one god she worships:
    Death—who knows?—may just reprieve her from death.
    Or she may learn at last, better late than never,
    what a waste of breath it is to worship Death.

Exit to the palace.

CHORUS: Love, never conquered in battle   880
    Love the plunderer laying waste the rich!
    Love standing the night-watch
              guarding a girl's soft cheek,
    you range the seas, the shepherds' steadings off in the wilds—
    not even the deathless gods can flee your onset,   885
    nothing human born for a day—
    whoever feels your grip is driven mad.
                   Love
    you wrench the minds of the righteous into outrage,
    swerve them to their ruin—you have ignited this,
    this kindred strife, father and son at war   890
             and Love alone the victor—
    warm glance of the bride triumphant, burning with desire!
    Throned in power, side-by-side with the mighty laws!
    Irresistible Aphrodite,[4] never conquered—
    Love, you mock us for your sport.   895

ANTIGONE *is brought from the palace under guard.*

    But now, even I'd rebel against the king,
    I'd break all bounds when I see this—
    I fill with tears, can't hold them back,
    not any more . . . I see Antigone make her way
    to the bridal vault where all are laid to rest.   900
ANTIGONE: Look at me, men of my fatherland,
    setting out on the last road
    looking into the last light of day
    the last I'll ever see . . .
    the god of death who puts us all to bed   905

---

[4]Greek goddess of love.—EDS.

takes me down to the banks of Acheron[5] alive—
    denied my part in the wedding-songs,
no wedding-song in the dusk has crowned my marriage—
I go to wed the lord of the dark waters.

CHORUS: Not crowned with glory, crowned with a dirge,   910
    you leave for the deep pit of the dead.
    No withering illness laid you low,
    no strokes of the sword—a law to yourself,
    alone, no mortal like you, ever, you go down
    to the halls of Death alive and breathing.   915

ANTIGONE: But think of Niobe[6]—well I know her story—
    think what a living death she died,
Tantalus' daughter, stranger queen from the east:
there on the mountain heights, growing stone
binding as ivy, slowly walled her round   920
and the rains will never cease, the legends say
the snows will never leave her . . .
    wasting away, under her brows the tears
showering down her breasting ridge and slopes—
a rocky death like hers puts me to sleep.   925

CHORUS: But she was a god, born of gods,
    and we are only mortals born to die.
    And yet, of course, it's a great thing
    for a dying girl to hear, just hear
    she shares a destiny equal to the gods,   930
    during life and later, once she's dead.

ANTIGONE: O you mock me!
Why, in the name of all my fathers' gods
why can't you wait till I am gone—
    must you abuse me to my face?
O my city, all your fine rich sons!   935
And you, you springs of the Dirce,
holy grove of Thebes where the chariots gather,
    you at least, you'll bear me witness, look,
unmourned by friends and forced by such crude laws
I go to my rockbound prison, strange new tomb—   940
    always a stranger, O dear god,
    I have no home on earth and none below,
       not with the living, not with the breathless dead.

---

[5]In Greek mythology, the dead must be ferried across the Acheron by Charon in order to enter the underworld.—EDS.

[6]Wife of Amphion, one of the original founders of Thebes. Her children were murdered and she was turned into stone after boasting of having had seven times more children than the titan Leto.—EDS.

CHORUS: You went too far, the last limits of daring—
            smashing against the high throne of Justice!   945
                    Your life's in ruins, child—I wonder . . .
            do you pay for your father's terrible ordeal?
ANTIGONE: There—at last you've touched it, the worst pain
        the worst anguish! Raking up the grief for father
            three times over, for all the doom   950
        that's struck us down, the brilliant house of Laius.
        O mother, your marriage-bed
        the coiling horrors, the coupling there—
            you with your own son, my father—doomstruck mother!
        Such, such were my parents, and I their wretched child.   955
        I go to them now, cursed, unwed, to share their home—
            I am a stranger! O dear brother, doomed
        in your marriage—your marriage murders mine,
            your dying drags me down to death alive!

Enter CREON.

CHORUS: Reverence asks some reverence in return—   960
            but attacks on power never go unchecked,
                    not by the man who holds the reins of power.
            Your own blind will, your passion has destroyed you.
ANTIGONE: No one to weep for me, my friends,
            no wedding-song—they take me away   965
        in all my pain . . . the road lies open, waiting.
        Never again, the law forbids me to see
        the sacred eye of day. I am agony!
        No tears for the destiny that's mine,
            no loved one mourns my death.
CREON: Can't you see?   970
        If a man could wail his own dirge *before* he dies,
        he'd never finish.

To the guards.

                            Take her away, quickly!
        Wall her up in the tomb, you have your orders.
        Abandon her there, alone, and let her choose—
        death or a buried life with a good roof for shelter.   975
        As for myself, my hands are clean. This young girl—
        dead or alive, she will be stripped of her rights,
        her stranger's rights, here in the world above.
ANTIGONE: O tomb, my bridal-bed—my house, my prison
        cut in the hollow rock, my everlasting watch!   980
        I'll soon be there, soon embrace my own,

the great growing family of our dead
Persephone[7] has received among her ghosts.

I,

the last of them all, the most reviled by far,
go down before my destined time's run out.   985
But still I go, cherishing one good hope:
my arrival may be dear to father,
dear to you, my mother,
dear to you, my loving brother, Eteocles—
When you died I washed you with my hands,   990
I dressed you all, I poured the cups
across your tombs. But now, Polynices,
because I laid your body out as well,
this, this is my reward. Nevertheless
I honored you—the decent will admit it—   995
well and wisely too.

        Never, I tell you,
if I had been the mother of children
or if my husband died, exposed and rotting—
I'd never have taken this ordeal upon myself,
never defied our people's will. What law,   1000
you ask, do I satisfy with what I say?
A husband dead, there might have been another.
A child by another too, if I had lost the first.
But mother and father both lost in the halls of Death,
no brother could ever spring to light again.   1005
For this law alone I held you first in honor.
For this, Creon, the king, judges me a criminal
guilty of dreadful outrage, my dear brother!
And now he leads me off, a captive in his hands,
with no part in the bridal-song, the bridal-bed,   1010
denied all joy of marriage, raising children—
deserted so by loved ones, struck by fate,
I descend alive to the caverns of the dead.

What law of the mighty gods have I transgressed?
Why look to the heavens any more, tormented as I am? 1015
Whom to call, what comrades now? Just think,
my reverence only brands me for irreverence!
Very well: if this is the pleasure of the gods,
once I suffer I will know that I was wrong.
But if these men are wrong, let them suffer   1020
nothing worse than they mete out to me—
these masters of injustice!

---

[7]Queen of the underworld.—EDS.

LEADER: Still the same rough winds, the wild passion
    raging through the girl.
CREON:

To the guards.

                          Take her away.
    You're wasting time—you'll pay for it too.   1025
ANTIGONE: Oh god, the voice of death. It's come, it's here.
CREON: True. Not a word of hope—your doom is sealed.
ANTIGONE: Land of Thebes, city of all my fathers—
    O you gods, the first gods of the race!
    They drag me away, now, no more delay.   1030
    Look on me, you noble sons of Thebes—
    the last of a great line of kings,
    I alone, see what I suffer now
    at the hands of what breed of men—
    all for reverence, my reverence for the gods!   1035

She leaves under guard; the CHORUS gathers.

CHORUS: Danaë, Danaë[8]—
    even she endured a fate like yours,
        in all her lovely strength she traded
    the light of day for the bolted brazen vault—
    buried within her tomb, her bridal-chamber,   1040
    wed to the yoke and broken.
        But she was of glorious birth
                     my child, my child
    and treasured the seed of Zeus within her womb,
    the cloudburst streaming gold!   1045
        The power of fate is a wonder,
        dark, terrible wonder—
        neither wealth nor armies
        towered walls nor ships
        black hulls lashed by the salt   1050
        can save us from that force.

    The yoke tamed him too
        young Lycurgus[9] flaming in anger

---

[8]After a prophecy that he would be killed by his daughter's son, Danaë's father locked her up. Zeus appeared to her in the form of a shower of gold and impregnated her with a son, Perseus.—EDS.
[9]Lycurgus persecuted the followers of Dionysus and imprisoned the Maenads (the raving female worshippers of Dionysus, mentioned in lines 1064–66). As retaliation, the god brought a drought to Edonia that would not end until Lycurgus was killed by his own citizens.—EDS.

king of Edonia, all for his mad taunts
Dionysus clamped him down, encased   1055
in the chain-mail of rock
    and there his rage
             his terrible flowering rage burst—
sobbing, dying away . . . at last that madman
came to know his god—   1060
the power he mocked, the power
      he taunted in all his frenzy
      trying to stamp out
      the women strong with the god—
      the torch, the raving sacred cries—   1065
      enraging the Muses[10] who adore the flute.

And far north where the Black Rocks
      cut the sea in half
and murderous straits
split the coast of Thrace   1070
    a forbidding city stands
where once, hard by the walls
the savage Ares thrilled to watch
a king's new queen, a Fury rearing in rage
      against his two royal sons—   1075
      her bloody hands, her dagger-shuttle
stabbing out their eyes—cursed, blinding wounds—
their eyes blind sockets screaming for revenge!

They wailed in agony, cries echoing cries
      the princes doomed at birth . . .   1080
and their mother doomed to chains,
walled off in a tomb of stone—
    but she traced her own birth back
to a proud Athenian line and the high gods
and off in caverns half the world away,   1085
born of the wild North Wind
    she sprang on her father's gales,
      racing stallions up the leaping cliffs—
child of the heavens. But even on her the Fates
the gray everlasting Fates rode hard   1090
my child, my child.

Enter TIRESIAS, *the blind prophet, led by a boy.*

---

[10]Goddesses who inspire artists, musicians, and dancers.—EDS.

TIRESIAS: Lords of Thebes,
   I and the boy have come together,
   hand in hand. Two see with the eyes of one . . .
   so the blind must go, with a guide to lead the way.
CREON: What is it, old Tiresias? What news now?   1095
TIRESIAS: I will teach you. And you obey the seer.
CREON: I will,
   I've never wavered from your advice before.
TIRESIAS: And so you kept the city straight on course.
CREON: I owe you a great deal, I swear to that.
TIRESIAS: Then reflect, my son: you are poised,   1100
   once more, on the razor-edge of fate.
CREON: What is it? I shudder to hear you.
TIRESIAS: You will learn
   when you listen to the warnings of my craft.
   As I sat on the ancient seat of augury,[11]
   in the sanctuary where every bird I know   1105
   will hover at my hands—suddenly I heard it,
   a strange voice in the wingbeats, unintelligible,
   barbaric, a mad scream! Talons flashing, ripping,
   they were killing each other—that much I knew—
   the murderous fury whirring in those wings   1110
   made that much clear!
                       I was afraid,
   I turned quickly, tested the burnt-sacrifice,
   ignited the altar at all points—but no fire,
   the god in the fire never blazed.
   Not from those offerings . . . over the embers   1115
   slid a heavy ooze from the long thighbones,
   smoking, sputtering out, and the bladder
   puffed and burst—spraying gall into the air—
   and the fat wrapping the bones slithered off
   and left them glistening white. No fire!   1120
   The rites failed that might have blazed the future
   with a sign. So I learned from the boy here;
   he is my guide, as I am guide to others.
                              And it's you—
   your high resolve that sets this plague on Thebes.
   The public altars and sacred hearths are fouled,   1125
   one and all, by the birds and dogs with carrion
   torn from the corpse, the doomstruck son of Oedipus!
   And so the gods are deaf to our prayers, they spurn

[11]Looking for omens in the flight patterns of birds.—EDS.

the offerings in our hands, the flame of holy flesh.
No birds cry out an omen clear and true —   1130
they're gorged with the murdered victim's blood and fat.
Take these things to heart, my son, I warn you.
All men make mistakes, it is only human.
But once the wrong is done, a man
can turn his back on folly, misfortune too,   1135
if he tries to make amends, however low he's fallen,
and stops his bullnecked ways. Stubbornness
brands you for stupidity — pride is a crime.
No, yield to the dead!
Never stab the fighter when he's down.   1140
Where's the glory, killing the dead twice over?

I mean you well. I give you sound advice.
It's best to learn from a good adviser
when he speaks for your own good:
it's pure gain.
CREON: Old man — all of you! So,   1145
you shoot your arrows at my head like archers at the target —
I even have *him* loosed on me, this fortune-teller.
Oh his ilk has tried to sell me short
and ship me off for years. Well,
drive your bargains, traffic — much as you like —   1150
in the gold of India, silver-gold of Sardis.
You'll never bury that body in the grave,
not even if Zeus's eagles rip the corpse
and wing their rotten pickings off to the throne of god!
Never, not even in fear of such defilement   1155
will I tolerate his burial, that traitor.
Well I know, we can't defile the gods —
no mortal has the power.
                                No,
reverend old Tiresias, all men fall,
it's only human, but the wisest fall obscenely   1160
when they glorify obscene advice with rhetoric —
all for their own gain.
TIRESIAS: Oh god, is there a man alive
who knows, who actually believes . . .
CREON: What now?
What earth-shattering truth are you about to utter?   1165
TIRESIAS: . . . just how much a sense of judgment, wisdom
is the greatest gift we have?
CREON: Just as much, I'd say,
as a twisted mind is the worst affliction going.

TIRESIAS: You are the one who's sick, Creon, sick to death.
CREON: I am in no mood to trade insults with a seer.   1170
TIRESIAS: You have already, calling my prophecies a lie.
CREON: Why not?
    You and the whole breed of seers are mad for money!
TIRESIAS: And the whole race of tyrants lusts to rake it in.
CREON: This slander of yours—
    are you aware you're speaking to the king?   1175
TIRESIAS: Well aware. Who helped you save the city?
CREON: You—
    you have your skills, old seer, but you lust for injustice!
TIRESIAS: You will drive me to utter the dreadful secret in my heart.
CREON: Spit it out! Just don't speak it out for profit.
TIRESIAS: Profit? No, not a bit of profit, not for you.   1180
CREON: Know full well, you'll never buy off my resolve.
TIRESIAS: Then know this too, learn this by heart!
    The chariot of the sun will not race through
    so many circuits more, before you have surrendered
    one born of your own loins, your own flesh and blood,   1185
    a corpse for corpses given in return, since you have thrust
    to the world below a child sprung for the world above,
    ruthlessly lodged a living soul within the grave—
    then you've robbed the gods below the earth,
    keeping a dead body here in the bright air,   1190
    unburied, unsung, unhallowed by the rites.

    You, you have no business with the dead,
    nor do the gods above—this is violence
    you have forced upon the heavens.
    And so the avengers, the dark destroyers late   1195
    but true to the mark, now lie in wait for you,
    the Furies sent by the gods and the god of death
    to strike you down with the pains that you perfected!

    There. Reflect on that, tell me I've been bribed.
    The day comes soon, no long test of time, not now,   1200
    that wakes the wails for men and women in your halls.
    Great hatred rises against you—
    cities in tumult, all whose mutilated sons
    the dogs have graced with burial, or the wild beasts,
    some wheeling crow that wings the ungodly stench of carrion   1205
    back to each city, each warrior's hearth and home.

    These arrows for your heart! Since you've raked me
    I loose them like an archer in my anger,

arrows deadly true. You'll never escape
their burning, searing force.   1210

Motioning to his escort.

> Come, boy, take me home.
> So he can vent his rage on younger men,
> and learn to keep a gentler tongue in his head
> and better sense than what he carries now.

Exit to the side.

LEADER: The old man's gone, my king—   1215
    terrible prophecies. Well I know,
    since the hair on this old head went gray,
    he's never lied to Thebes.
CREON: I know it myself—I'm shaken, torn.
    It's a dreadful thing to yield . . . but resist now?   1220
    Lay my pride bare to the blows of ruin?
    That's dreadful too.
LEADER: But good advice,
    Creon, take it now, you must.
CREON: What should I do? Tell me . . . I'll obey.
LEADER: Go! Free the girl from the rocky vault   1225
    and raise a mound for the body you exposed.
CREON: That's your advice? You think I should give in?
LEADER: Yes, my king, quickly. Disasters sent by the gods
    cut short our follies in a flash.
CREON: Oh it's hard.
    giving up the heart's desire . . . but I will do it—   1230
    no more fighting a losing battle with necessity.
LEADER: Do it now, go, don't leave it to others.
CREON: Now—I'm on my way! Come, each of you,
    take up axes, make for the high ground,
    over there, quickly! I and my better judgment   1235
    have come round to this—I shackled her,
    I'll set her free myself. I am afraid . . .
    it's best to keep the established laws
    to the very day we die.

Rushing out, followed by his entourage. The CHORUS *clusters around the altar.*

CHORUS: God of a hundred names!
                            Great Dionysus—   1240
    Son and glory of Semele! Pride of Thebes—
    Child of Zeus whose thunder rocks the clouds—
    Lord of the famous lands of evening—

King of the Mysteries!
                    King of Eleusis, Demeter's plain[12]
her breasting hills that welcome in the world—   1245
Great Dionysus!
                    Bacchus,[13] living in Thebes
the mother-city of all your frenzied women—
                                        Bacchus
        living along the Ismenus'[14] rippling waters
standing over the field sown with the Dragon's teeth![15]

You—we have seen you through the flaring smoky fires,   1250
        your torches blazing over the twin peaks
where nymphs of the hallowed cave climb onward
                        fired with you, your sacred rage—
we have seen you at Castalia's running spring[16]
and down from the heights of Nysa[17] crowned with ivy   1255
the greening shore rioting vines and grapes
            down you come in your storm of wild women
                    ecstatic, mystic cries—
                                    Dionysus—
down to watch and ward the roads of Thebes!

First of all cities, Thebes you honor first   1260
you and your mother, bride of the lightning—
come, Dionysus! now your people lie
in the iron grip of plague,
come in your racing, healing stride
                        down Parnassus'[18] slopes   1265
or across the moaning straits.
                            Lord of the dancing—
dance, dance the constellations breathing fire!
Great master of the voices of the night!
Child of Zeus, God's offspring, come, come forth!
Lord, king, dance with your nymphs, swirling, raving   1270

_____

[12]Demeter, the goddess of grain and fertility, was worshipped in the fields of Eleusis.—Eds.
[13]Dionysus.—Eds.
[14]River near Thebes.—Eds.
[15]Cadmus—founder of Thebes and ancestor of Oedipus, Antigone, and Dionysus (son of Zeus and Cadmus's daughter, Semele)—slayed a dragon of Ares and planted its teeth to produce a race of men who would rule and populate Thebes.—Eds.
[16]The spring at the oracle of Delphi.—Eds.
[17]Mountain region where Dionysus was raised and later worshipped.—Eds.
[18]Mountain near Delphi, sacred to Dionysus.—Eds.

> arm-in-arm in frenzy through the night
> > they dance you, Iacchus[19]—
>
> > > > Dance, Dionysus
>
> giver of all good things!

Enter a MESSENGER *from the side.*

MESSENGER: Neighbors,
> friends of the house of Cadmus and the kings,
> there's not a thing in this life of ours   1275
> I'd praise or blame as settled once for all.
> Fortune lifts and Fortune fells the lucky
> and unlucky every day. No prophet on earth
> can tell a man his fate. Take Creon:
> there was a man to rouse your envy once,   1280
> as I see it. He saved the realm from enemies;
> taking power, he alone, the lord of the fatherland,
> he set us true on course—flourished like a tree
> with the noble line of sons he bred and reared . . .
> and now it's lost, all gone.
> > > > Believe me,   1285
> when a man has squandered his true joys,
> he's good as dead, I tell you, a living corpse.
> Pile up riches in your house, as much as you like—
> live like a king with a huge show of pomp,
> but if real delight is missing from the lot,   1290
> I wouldn't give you a wisp of smoke for it,
> not compared with joy.

LEADER: What now?
> What new grief do you bring the house of kings?

MESSENGER: Dead, dead—and the living are guilty of their death!

LEADER: Who's the murderer? Who is dead? Tell us.   1295

MESSENGER: Haemon's gone, his blood spilled by the very hand—

LEADER: His father's or his own?

MESSENGER: His own . . .
> raging mad with his father for the death—

LEADER: Oh great seer,
> you saw it all, you brought your word to birth!

MESSENGER: Those are the facts. Deal with them as you will.   1300

As he turns to go, EURYDICE *enters from the palace.*

LEADER: Look, Eurydice. Poor woman, Creon's wife,
> so close at hand. By chance perhaps,
> unless she's heard the news about her son.

---

[19]Dionysus.—EDS.

EURYDICE: My countrymen,
   all of you—I caught the sound of your words
   as I was leaving to do my part,   1305
   to appeal to queen Athena[20] with my prayers.
   I was just loosing the bolts, opening the doors,
   when a voice filled with sorrow, family sorrow,
   struck my ears, and I fell back, terrified,
   into the women's arms—everything went black.   1310
   Tell me the news, again, whatever it is . . .
   sorrow and I are hardly strangers;
   I can bear the worst.
MESSENGER: I—dear lady,
   I'll speak as an eye-witness. I was there.
   And I won't pass over one word of the truth.   1315
   Why should I try to soothe you with a story,
   only to prove a liar in a moment?
   Truth is always best.
           So,
   I escorted your lord, I guided him
   to the edge of the plain where the body lay,   1320
   Polynices, torn by the dogs and still unmourned.
   And saying a prayer to Hecate of the Crossroads,
   Pluto[21] too, to hold their anger and be kind,
   we washed the dead in a bath of holy water
   and plucking some fresh branches, gathering . . .   1325
   what was left of him, we burned them all together
   and raised a high mound of native earth, and then
   we turned and made for that rocky vault of hers,
   the hollow, empty bed of the bride of Death.
   And far off, one of us heard a voice,   1330
   a long wail rising, echoing
   out of that unhallowed wedding-chamber;
   he ran to alert the master and Creon pressed on,
   closer—the strange, inscrutable cry came sharper,
   throbbing around him now, and he let loose   1335
   a cry of his own, enough to wrench the heart,
   "Oh god, am I the prophet now? going down
   the darkest road I've ever gone? My son—
   it's *his* dear voice, he greets me! Go, men,
   closer, quickly! Go through the gap,   1340
   the rocks are dragged back—

---

[20]Goddess of wisdom, war, and peace.—EDS.
[21]Two gods of the underworld.—EDS.

right to the tomb's very mouth—and look,
see if it's Haemon's voice I think I hear,
or the gods have robbed me of my senses."

The king was shattered. We took his orders,   1345
went and searched, and there in the deepest,
dark recesses of the tomb we found her . . .
hanged by the neck in a fine linen noose,
strangled in her veils—and the boy,
his arms flung around her waist,   1350
clinging to her, wailing for his bride,
dead and down below, for his father's crimes
and the bed of his marriage blighted by misfortune.
When Creon saw him, he gave a deep sob,
he ran in, shouting, crying out to him,   1355
"Oh my child—what have you done? what seized you,
what insanity? what disaster drove you mad?
Come out, my son! I beg you on my knees!"
But the boy gave him a wild burning glance,
spat in his face, not a word in reply,   1360
he drew his sword—his father rushed out,
running as Haemon lunged and missed!—
and then, doomed, desperate with himself,
suddenly leaning his full weight on the blade,
he buried it in his body, halfway to the hilt.   1365
And still in his senses, pouring his arms around her,
he embraced the girl and breathing hard,
released a quick rush of blood,
bright red on her cheek glistening white.
And there he lies, body enfolding body . . .   1370
he has won his bride at last, poor boy,
not here but in the houses of the dead.

Creon shows the world that of all the ills
afflicting men the worst is lack of judgment.

EURYDICE *turns and reenters the palace.*

LEADER: What do you make of that? The lady's gone,   1375
    without a word, good or bad.
MESSENGER: I'm alarmed too
    but here's my hope—faced with her son's death,
    she finds it unbecoming to mourn in public.
    Inside, under her roof, she'll set her women
    to the task and wail the sorrow of the house.   1380
    She's too discreet. She won't do something rash.

LEADER: I'm not so sure. To me, at least,
    a long heavy silence promises danger,
    just as much as a lot of empty outcries.
MESSENGER: We'll see if she's holding something back,   1385
    hiding some passion in her heart.
    I'm going in. You may be right—who knows?
    Even too much silence has its dangers.

Exit to the palace. Enter CREON *from the side, escorted by attendants carrying* HAEMON'S *body on a bier.*

LEADER: The king himself! Coming toward us,
    look, holding the boy's head in his hands.   1390
    Clear, damning proof, if it's right to say so—
    proof of his own madness, no one else's,
        no, his own blind wrongs.
CREON: Ohhh,
    so senseless, so insane . . . my crimes,
    my stubborn, deadly—   1395
    Look at us, the killer, the killed,
    father and son, the same blood—the misery!
    My plans, my mad fanatic heart,
    my son, cut off so young!
    Ai, dead, lost to the world,   1400
    not through your stupidity, no, my own.
LEADER: Too late,
    too late, you see what justice means.
CREON: Oh I've learned
    through blood and tears! Then, it was then,
    when the god came down and struck me—a great weight
    shattering, driving me down that wild savage path,   1405
    ruining, trampling down my joy. Oh the agony,
        the heartbreaking agonies of our lives.

Enter the MESSENGER *from the palace.*

MESSENGER: Master,
    what a hoard of grief you have, and you'll have more.
    The grief that lies to hand you've brought yourself—

Pointing to HAEMON'S *body.*

    the rest, in the house, you'll see it all too soon.   1410
CREON: What now? What's worse than this?
MESSENGER: The queen is dead.
    The mother of this dead boy . . . mother to the end—
    poor thing, her wounds are fresh.

CREON: No, no,
        harbor of Death, so choked, so hard to cleanse!—
        why me? why are you killing me?   1415
        Herald of pain, more words, more grief?
        I died once, you kill me again and again!
        What's the report, boy . . . some news for me?
        My wife dead? O dear god!
        Slaughter heaped on slaughter?

The doors open; the body of EURYDICE *is brought out on her bier.*

MESSENGER: See for yourself: 1420
        now they bring her body from the palace.
CREON: Oh no,
        another, a second loss to break the heart.
        What next, what fate still waits for me?
        I just held my son in my arms and now,
        look, a new corpse rising before my eyes—   1425
                wretched, helpless mother—O my son!
MESSENGER: She stabbed herself at the altar,
        then her eyes went dark, after she'd raised
        a cry for the noble fate of Megareus,[22] the hero
        killed in the first assault, then for Haemon,   1430
        then with her dying breath she called down
        torments on your head—you killed her sons.
CREON: Oh the dread,
        I shudder with dread! Why not kill me too?—
        run me through with a good sharp sword?
        Oh god, the misery, anguish—   1435
        I, I'm churning with it, going under.
MESSENGER: Yes, and the dead, the woman lying there,
        piles the guilt of all their deaths on you.
CREON: How did she end her life, what bloody stroke?
MESSENGER: She drove home to the heart with her own hand,   1440
        once she learned her son was dead . . . that agony.
CREON: And the guilt is all mine—
        can never be fixed on another man,
        no escape for me. I killed you,
        I, god help me, I admit it all!   1445

To his attendants.

        Take me away, quickly, out of sight.
        I don't even exist—I'm no one. Nothing.

---

[22]Son of Creon and Eurydice who died in the attack on Thebes.—EDS.

LEADER: Good advice, if there's any good in suffering.
　　Quickest is best when troubles block the way.
CREON:

Kneeling in prayer.

　　　　Come, let it come! — that best of fates for me　　　　　　1450
　　　　that brings the final day, best fate of all.
　　　　Oh quickly, now —
　　　　so I never have to see another sunrise.
LEADER: That will come when it comes;
　　we must deal with all that lies before us.　　　　　　　　1455
　　The future rests with the ones who tend the future.
CREON: That prayer — I poured my heart into that prayer!
LEADER: No more prayers now. For mortal men
　　there is no escape from the doom we must endure.
CREON: Take me away, I beg you, out of sight.　　　　　　　1460
　　　　A rash, indiscriminate fool!
　　　　I murdered you, my son, against my will —
　　　　you too, my wife . . .
　　　　　　　　　　Wailing wreck of a man,
　　　　whom to look to? where to lean for support?

Desperately turning from HAEMON *to* EURYDICE *on their biers.*

　　　　Whatever I touch goes wrong — once more　　　　　　1465
　　　　a crushing fate's come down upon my head.

The MESSENGER *and* ATTENDANTS *lead* CREON *into the palace.*

CHORUS: Wisdom is by far the greatest part of joy,
　　and reverence toward the gods must be safeguarded.
　　The mighty words of the proud are paid in full
　　with mighty blows of fate, and at long last　　　　　　　1470
　　　　those blows will teach us wisdom.

The old citizens exit to the side.

　　　　　　　　　　　　　　　　　　　　　　　[*c. 441 B.C.E.*]

Questions for Discussion

1. The play opens with a dialogue between Antigone and Ismene. How do their attitudes toward Creon's decree characterize the two sisters? Do you support Antigone's defense of her civil disobedience? Is she a character we are meant to admire? Do you admire her? Explain.
2. How does Antigone differentiate between human and divine law? How is this distinction at the thematic heart of the play?
3. At the start of the play, what motivates Creon? What reasons does he give for his edict? How do his definitions of terms such as "traitor" and "patriot" reveal his concerns?

4. The first encounter between Antigone and Creon begins with her statement, "I did it. I don't deny a thing" (l. 493). From then on in the scene, each character presents an argument defending his or her position. What are these arguments? What assumptions underlie them? At what point does accusation and name-calling begin to replace logical argument?

5. How convincing is Ismene's change of heart beginning on line 604? Do you believe her? Why or why not?

6. What words would best describe Haemon? What is Haemon's strategy going into his conversation with Creon (l. 710)? How would you describe Creon's reasoning in his conversation with Haemon? What does this conflict say about the power of reason and authority?

7. What role do marriage and the image of the bridal chamber play in *Antigone*? Consider Antigone's speech as she is being taken away (ll. 979–1013), the scene in which Haemon is discovered in the tomb (ll. 1345–72), and the death of Eurydice.

8. In their encounter, Creon accuses Tiresias of being motivated by the desire for money (beginning l. 1091). Why? What other instances have there been of Creon responding to resistance with accusations of bribery or monetary gain? What does this pattern say about Creon as a leader?

9. Over the course of his confrontation with Tiresias (beginning l. 1091), Creon reverses his position several times. Why? What causes his shift from heeding the prophet's advice as he has in the past to denouncing Tiresias's prophecies and finally to taking the prophet's advice to heart?

10. What is Sophocles' position regarding the actions of Antigone and Creon? How can you tell? What does the play have to say about the conflict between order and civil disobedience and about the nature of justice and injustice? What does it say about the nature of peace?

11. What does the play tell us about how "a sense of judgment, wisdom / is the greatest gift we have" (ll. 1166–67)? Do you think Sophocles is arguing against acting on passion and convictions?

12. *Antigone* focuses our attention on the conflict between public and private realms, the divisive impact of war on families, and the consequences of differing views of honor. How do these issues manifest themselves in conflicts we see going on today?

Questions on Style and Structure

1. How does Sophocles provide exposition to ground the audience in the background of events and the characters? Consider the opening dialogue and the initial speeches of the Chorus and the sentry.

2. In lines 117–79, how does the Chorus warn against *hubris*, the Greek word for excessive pride? How do the various metaphors and images (the sun, the shield, the eagle, the armor, the chariots, the choirs) contribute to the meaning of this passage? How do the words of the Chorus in this passage foreshadow later events in the play?

3. Beginning with line 472, the sentry uses an analogy comparing Antigone to a bird. Explain why you do or do not find it a fitting comparison to illuminate Antigone's situation.

4. What is the purpose and effect of Antigone's rhetorical question in lines 587–88?

5. Creon's words in lines 970–78 are an example of dramatic irony. What effect does this speech have? Find another example of dramatic irony in the play, and discuss the impact it has on the plot and themes of the play.

6. Discuss the end of Antigone's final speech (ll. 1014–22). Is it consistent with her character as we have known her throughout the play, or does it mark a shift in her thinking?

7. The Chorus is meant to voice the thoughts of the people. How does the Chorus respond to Creon's edict and to the conflict between Creon and Antigone? What is the position of the Chorus? At what point does the Chorus turn on Creon? Why does it occur, and what is its significance to his ability to govern?

8. In the speech by the Chorus that begins on line 1036, Sophocles alludes to the stories of Danaë and other mythological figures. In what ways do these allusions deepen the thematic complexity of the play? Consider answering from the point of view of an audience in Sophocles' time as well as that of a contemporary audience. Should a director staging a production of *Antigone* today consider omitting the speech?

9. In the final scene of the play, how are the gruesome details of several deaths revealed? Why does Sophocles deliver the information this way? Would enacting the violence on stage enhance the meaning of the play? Explain.

10. An antagonist is a character who opposes the protagonist, thus creating a conflict. Ultimately, who is the protagonist of this play, Antigone or Creon? Who is the antagonist? Consider whose tragedy the play enacts. Explain your reasons for your responses.

11. What roles do the secondary characters play: Haemon, Ismene, Tiresias, and Eurydice, for example? Which ones are most important?

12. Is Creon's rhetoric consistent throughout the play? How does his purpose and tone shift from speech to speech? Compare and contrast the way Creon responds to Antigone, to Haemon, and to Tiresias. Refer specifically to the text in each case.

Suggestions for Writing

1. The Greeks believed that through witnessing tragedy an audience could reach a state of catharsis—a cleansing or purification of pity and fear resulting in a sense of renewal. Write an essay in which you discuss how catharsis is reached through the violence and tragedy in *Antigone*.

2. In *War Is a Force That Gives Us Meaning*, Chris Hedges reminds us that "the ancient Greeks linked war and love. Aphrodite, the goddess of love and the wife of Hephaestos, the lame blacksmith who forged the weapons of war and armor for the gods, became the mistress of Ares, the god of war." What is the relationship between love and war in *Antigone*? Pay careful attention to the Chorus's apostrophe to Love beginning with line 880.

3. Antigone says, "Never, I tell you, / if I had been the mother of children / or if my husband died, exposed and rotting— / I'd never have taken this ordeal upon myself, / never defied our people's will" (ll. 997–1000). If Antigone is heroic, is such a statement seemingly out of character? Explain your response, and consider what purpose this speech serves within the play.

4. In addition to being a great dramatist, Sophocles was a statesman in Athens and a general who fought in the Persian Wars. What influence on *Antigone* might these experiences have had? In an essay, consider how *Antigone* expresses the ideas of both a statesman and a soldier on war and peace.

5. Many interpret Creon's outrage toward Antigone not as a leader responding to an action defying his decree but as a man in a patriarchal society feeling threatened by a woman who dares to challenge him. Write an essay explaining this viewpoint, and cite textual evidence that supports this interpretation.

6. While the reader or audience of *Antigone* does not witness violence directly — it occurs offstage and is reported by a messenger — it is graphically described. Does such disturbing content desensitize readers to violence, or does it expose the horrific consequences of tragic decisions so that we might learn from them? Write an essay explaining your view on this question. Use *Antigone* as your primary text, but bring in more contemporary examples of how violence is treated in today's films and the media in general.

7. Civil disobedience, a theme central to *Antigone*, is a subject more recent intellectuals and activists, including Henry David Thoreau and Martin Luther King Jr., have continued to explore. Write an essay comparing and contrasting the treatment of civil disobedience in this play to either Thoreau's "Civil Disobedience" or King's "Letter from Birmingham Jail."

The Things They Carried

Tim O'Brien

Tim O'Brien was born in 1946 in Austin, Minnesota. After graduating from Macalester College with a BA in political science in 1968, he was drafted into the army and sent to Vietnam, where he became a sergeant and earned a Purple Heart. A year after the now infamous My Lai massacre, O'Brien's unit passed through the area where it had happened, only learning about it then. The incident figures prominently in his 1994 novel, *In the Lake of the Woods*—begun as a graduate dissertation in history at Harvard University, where he went to graduate school after the war. O'Brien's writing career started with the publication of *If I Die in a Combat Zone* (1973), a memoir of his experiences in Vietnam. *Going After Cacciato*, a surrealistic novel set in the war, followed in 1978, winning the prestigious National Book Award and establishing O'Brien as a major American writer. His recent novels include *Tomcat in Love* (1998) and *July, July* (2002). Perhaps his most famous book, *The Things They Carried*—composed of a series of connected stories—appeared in 1990. Dedicated to its fictional characters and based on his actual experience, it is a novel in which O'Brien himself is the narrator. While a major theme of the novel is its treatment of war and the postwar experience, it can be said that the book is also about the relationship between truth and fiction and the transformational power of art and memory. Regarding *If I Die in a Combat Zone*, O'Brien has said that he had a hard time getting at the truth in that book because he stuck to the facts. The title story and first chapter of *The Things They Carried*, selected for inclusion in *The Best American Short Stories of the Century* (1999) and included here, represents his attempt to invent a fiction to get at the truth.

First Lieutenant Jimmy Cross carried letters from a girl named Martha, a junior at Mount Sebastian College in New Jersey. They were not love letters, but Lieutenant Cross was hoping, so he kept them folded in plastic at the bottom of his rucksack. In the late afternoon, after a day's march, he would dig his foxhole, wash his hands under a canteen, unwrap the letters, hold them with the tips of his fingers, and spend the last hour of light pretending. He would imagine romantic camping trips into the White Mountains in New Hampshire. He would sometimes taste the envelope flaps, knowing her tongue had been there. More than anything, he wanted Martha to love him as he loved her, but the letters were mostly chatty, elusive on the matter of love. She was a virgin, he was almost sure. She was an English major at Mount Sebastian, and she wrote beautifully about her professors and roommates and midterm exams, about her respect for Chaucer and her great affection for Virginia Woolf. She often quoted lines of poetry; she never mentioned the war, except to say, Jimmy, take care of yourself. The letters weighed ten ounces. They were signed "Love,

Martha," but Lieutenant Cross understood that "Love" was only a way of signing and did not mean what he sometimes pretended it meant. At dusk, he would carefully return the letters to his rucksack. Slowly, a bit distracted, he would get up and move among his men, checking the perimeter, then at full dark he would return to his hole and watch the night and wonder if Martha was a virgin.

The things they carried were largely determined by necessity. Among the necessities or near necessities were P-38 can openers, pocket knives, heat tabs, wrist watches, dog tags, mosquito repellant, chewing gum, candy, cigarettes, salt tablets, packets of Kool-Aid, lighters, matches, sewing kits, Military Payment Certificates, C rations, and two or three canteens of water. Together, these items weighed between fifteen and twenty pounds, depending upon a man's habits or rate of metabolism. Henry Dobbins, who was a big man, carried extra rations; he was especially fond of canned peaches in heavy syrup over pound cake. Dave Jensen, who practiced field hygiene, carried a toothbrush, dental floss, and several hotel-size bars of soap he'd stolen on R&R in Sydney, Australia. Ted Lavender, who was scared, carried tranquilizers until he was shot in the head outside the village of Than Khe in mid-April. By necessity, and because it was SOP,[1] they all carried steel helmets that weighed five pounds including the liner and camouflage cover. They carried the standard fatigue jackets and trousers. Very few carried underwear. On their feet they carried jungle boots—2.1 pounds—and Dave Jensen carried three pairs of socks and a can of Dr. Scholl's foot powder as a precaution against trench foot. Until he was shot, Ted Lavender carried six or seven ounces of premium dope, which for him was a necessity. Mitchell Sanders, the RTO,[2] carried condoms. Norman Bowker carried a diary. Rat Kiley carried comic books. Kiowa, a devout Baptist, carried an illustrated New Testament that had been presented to him by his father, who taught Sunday school in Oklahoma City, Oklahoma. As a hedge against bad times, however, Kiowa also carried his grandmother's distrust of the white man, his grandfather's old hunting hatchet. Necessity dictated. Because the land was mined and booby-trapped, it was SOP for each man to carry a steel-centered, nylon-covered flak jacket, which weighed 6.7 pounds, but which on hot days seemed much heavier. Because you could die so quickly, each man carried at least one large compress bandage, usually in the helmet band for easy access. Because the nights were cold, and because the monsoons were wet, each carried a green plastic poncho that could be used as a raincoat or ground sheet or makeshift tent. With its quilted liner, the poncho weighed almost two pounds, but it was worth every ounce. In April, for instance, when Ted Lavender was shot, they used his poncho to wrap him up, then to carry him across the paddy, then to lift him into the chopper that took him away.

They were called legs or grunts.

To carry something was to "hump" it, as when Lieutenant Jimmy Cross humped his love for Martha up the hills and through the swamps. In its intransitive form,

---

[1]Standard operating procedure.—EDS.
[2]Radiotelephone operator.—EDS.

"to hump" meant "to walk," or "to march," but it implied burdens far beyond the intransitive.

Almost everyone humped photographs. In his wallet, Lieutenant Cross carried two photographs of Martha. The first was a Kodachrome snapshot signed "Love," though he knew better. She stood against a brick wall. Her eyes were gray and neutral, her lips slightly open as she stared straight-on at the camera. At night, sometimes, Lieutenant Cross wondered who had taken the picture, because he knew she had boyfriends, because he loved her so much, and because he could see the shadow of the picture taker spreading out against the brick wall. The second photograph had been clipped from the 1968 Mount Sebastian yearbook. It was an action shot—women's volleyball—and Martha was bent horizontal to the floor, reaching, the palms of her hands in sharp focus, the tongue taut, the expression frank and competitive. There was no visible sweat. She wore white gym shorts. Her legs, he thought, were almost certainly the legs of a virgin, dry and without hair, the left knee cocked and carrying her entire weight, which was just over one hundred pounds. Lieutenant Cross remembered touching that left knee. A dark theater, he remembered, and the movie was *Bonnie and Clyde*, and Martha wore a tweed skirt, and during the final scene, when he touched her knee, she turned and looked at him in a sad, sober way that made him pull his hand back, but he would always remember the feel of the tweed skirt and the knee beneath it and the sound of the gunfire that killed Bonnie and Clyde, how embarrassing it was, how slow and oppressive. He remembered kissing her good night at the dorm door. Right then, he thought, he should've done something brave. He should've carried her up the stairs to her room and tied her to the bed and touched that left knee all night long. He should've risked it. Whenever he looked at the photographs, he thought of new things he should've done.

What they carried was partly a function of rank, partly of field specialty.

As a first lieutenant and platoon leader, Jimmy Cross carried a compass, maps, code books, binoculars, and a .45-caliber pistol that weighed 2.9 pounds fully loaded. He carried a strobe light and the responsibility for the lives of his men.

As an RTO, Mitchell Sanders carried the PRC-25 radio, a killer, twenty-six pounds with its battery.

As a medic, Rat Kiley carried a canvas satchel filled with morphine and plasma and malaria tablets and surgical tape and comic books and all the things a medic must carry, including M&M's for especially bad wounds, for a total weight of nearly twenty pounds.

As a big man, therefore a machine gunner, Henry Dobbins carried the M-60, which weighed twenty-three pounds unloaded, but which was almost always loaded. In addition, Dobbins carried between ten and fifteen pounds of ammunition draped in belts across his chest and shoulders.

As PFCs or Spec 4s, most of them were common grunts and carried the standard M-16 gas-operated assault rifle. The weapon weighed 7.5 pounds unloaded, 8.2 pounds with its full twenty-round magazine. Depending on numerous factors, such as topography and psychology, the riflemen carried anywhere from twelve to twenty magazines, usually in cloth bandoliers, adding on another 8.4 pounds at minimum, fourteen pounds at maximum. When it was available, they also carried M-16 maintenance gear—rods and steel brushes and swabs and tubes of LSA oil—all of which weighed about a pound. Among the grunts, some carried the M-79 grenade launcher, 5.9 pounds unloaded, a reasonably light weapon except for the ammunition, which was heavy. A single round weighed ten ounces. The typical load was twenty-five rounds. But Ted Lavender, who was scared, carried thirty-four rounds when he was shot and killed outside Than Khe, and he went down under an exceptional burden, more than twenty pounds of ammunition, plus the flak jacket and helmet and rations and water and toilet paper and tranquilizers and all the rest, plus the unweighed fear. He was dead weight. There was no twitching or flopping. Kiowa, who saw it happen, said it was like watching a rock fall, or a big sandbag or something—just boom, then down—not like the movies where the dead guy rolls around and does fancy spins and goes ass over teakettle—not like that, Kiowa said, the poor bastard just flat-fuck fell. Boom. Down. Nothing else. It was a bright morning in mid-April. Lieutenant Cross felt the pain. He blamed himself. They stripped off Lavender's canteens and ammo, all the heavy things, and Rat Kiley said the obvious, the guy's dead, and Mitchell Sanders used his radio to report one U.S. KIA[3] and to request a chopper. Then they wrapped Lavender in his poncho. They carried him out to a dry paddy, established security, and sat smoking the dead man's dope until the chopper came. Lieutenant Cross kept to himself. He pictured Martha's smooth young face, thinking he loved her more than anything, more than his men, and now Ted Lavender was dead because he loved her so much and could not stop thinking about her. When the dust-off arrived, they carried Lavender aboard. Afterward they burned Than Khe. They marched until dusk, then dug their holes, and that night Kiowa kept explaining how you had to be there, how fast it was, how the poor guy just dropped like so much concrete. Boom-down, he said. Like cement.

In addition to the three standard weapons—the M-60, M-16, and M-79—they carried whatever presented itself, or whatever seemed appropriate as a means of killing or staying alive. They carried catch-as-catch-can. At various times, in various situations, they carried M-14s and CAR-15s and Swedish Ks and grease guns and captured AK-47s and Chi-Coms and RPGs and Simonov carbines and black-market Uzis and .38-caliber Smith & Wesson handguns and 66 mm LAWs and shotguns and silencers and blackjacks and bayonets and C-4 plastic explosives. Lee Strunk carried a slingshot; a weapon of last resort, he called it. Mitchell Sanders carried brass knuckles. Kiowa carried his grandfather's feathered hatchet. Every third or fourth man carried a Claymore antipersonnel mine—3.5 pounds with its firing device. They all carried fragmentation grenades—fourteen ounces each. They all carried at least one M-18 colored smoke grenade—twenty-four ounces. Some carried CS or tear-gas grenades. Some carried white-phosphorus grenades. They carried all they could bear, and then some, including a silent awe for the terrible power of the things they carried.

---

[3]Killed in action.—Eds.

In the first week of April, before Lavender died, Lieutenant Jimmy Cross received a good-luck charm from Martha. It was a simple pebble, an ounce at most. Smooth to the touch, it was a milky-white color with flecks of orange and violet, oval-shaped, like a miniature egg. In the accompanying letter, Martha wrote that she had found the pebble on the Jersey shoreline, precisely where the land touched water at high tide, where things came together but also separated. It was this separate-but-together quality, she wrote, that had inspired her to pick up the pebble and to carry it in her breast pocket for several days, where it seemed weightless, and then to send it through the mail, by air, as a token of her truest feelings for him. Lieutenant Cross found this romantic. But he wondered what her truest feelings were, exactly, and what she meant by separate-but-together. He wondered how the tides and waves had come into play on that afternoon along the Jersey shoreline when Martha saw the pebble and bent down to rescue it from geology. He imagined bare feet. Martha was a poet, with the poet's sensibilities, and her feet would be brown and bare, the toenails unpainted, the eyes chilly and somber like the ocean in March, and though it was painful, he wondered who had been with her that afternoon. He imagined a pair of shadows moving along the strip of sand where things came together but also separated. It was phantom jealousy, he knew, but he couldn't help himself. He loved her so much. On the march, through the hot days of early April, he carried the pebble in his mouth, turning it with his tongue, tasting sea salts and moisture. His mind wandered. He had difficulty keeping his attention on the war. On occasion he would yell at his men to spread out the column, to keep their eyes open, but then he would slip away into daydreams, just pretending, walking barefoot along the Jersey shore, with Martha, carrying nothing. He would feel himself rising. Sun and waves and gentle winds, all love and lightness.

What they carried varied by mission.

When a mission took them to the mountains, they carried mosquito netting, machetes, canvas tarps, and extra bug juice.

If a mission seemed especially hazardous, or if it involved a place they knew to be bad, they carried everything they could. In certain heavily mined AOs,[4] where the land was dense with Toe Poppers and Bouncing Betties, they took turns humping a twenty-eight-pound mine detector. With its headphones and big sensing plate, the equipment was a stress on the lower back and shoulders, awkward to handle, often useless because of the shrapnel in the earth, but they carried it anyway, partly for safety, partly for the illusion of safety.

On ambush, or other night missions, they carried peculiar little odds and ends. Kiowa always took along his New Testament and a pair of moccasins for silence. Dave Jensen carried night-sight vitamins high in carotin. Lee Strunk carried his slingshot; ammo, he claimed, would never be a problem. Rat Kiley carried brandy and M&M's. Until he was shot, Ted Lavender carried the starlight scope, which weighed

---

[4]Areas of operations.—EDS.

6.3 pounds with its aluminum carrying case. Henry Dobbins carried his girlfriend's pantyhose wrapped around his neck as a comforter. They all carried ghosts. When dark came, they would move out single file across the meadows and paddies to their ambush coordinates, where they would quietly set up the Claymores and lie down and spend the night waiting.

Other missions were more complicated and required special equipment. In mid-April, it was their mission to search out and destroy the elaborate tunnel complexes in the Than Khe area south of Chu Lai. To blow the tunnels, they carried one-pound blocks of pentrite high explosives, four blocks to a man, sixty-eight pounds in all. They carried wiring, detonators, and battery-powered clackers. Dave Jensen carried earplugs. Most often, before blowing the tunnels, they were ordered by higher command to search them, which was considered bad news, but by and large they just shrugged and carried out orders. Because he was a big man, Henry Dobbins was excused from tunnel duty. The others would draw numbers. Before Lavender died there were seventeen men in the platoon, and whoever drew the number seventeen would strip off his gear and crawl in head first with a flashlight and Lieutenant Cross's .45-caliber pistol. The rest of them would fan out as security. They would sit down or kneel, not facing the hole, listening to the ground beneath them, imagining cobwebs and ghosts, whatever was down there—the tunnel walls squeezing in—how the flashlight seemed impossibly heavy in the hand and how it was tunnel vision in the very strictest sense, compression in all ways, even time, and how you had to wiggle in—ass and elbows—a swallowed-up feeling—and how you found yourself worrying about odd things—will your flashlight go dead? Do rats carry rabies? If you screamed, how far would the sound carry? Would your buddies hear it? Would they have the courage to drag you out? In some respects, though not many, the waiting was worse than the tunnel itself. Imagination was a killer.

On April 16, when Lee Strunk drew the number seventeen, he laughed and muttered something and went down quickly. The morning was hot and very still. Not good, Kiowa said. He looked at the tunnel opening, then out across a dry paddy toward the village of Than Khe. Nothing moved. No clouds or birds or people. As they waited, the men smoked and drank Kool-Aid, not talking much, feeling sympathy for Lee Strunk but also feeling the luck of the draw. You win some, you lose some, said Mitchell Sanders, and sometimes you settle for a rain check. It was a tired line and no one laughed.

Henry Dobbins ate a tropical chocolate bar. Ted Lavender popped a tranquilizer and went off to pee. 20

After five minutes, Lieutenant Jimmy Cross moved to the tunnel, leaned down, and examined the darkness. Trouble, he thought—a cave-in maybe. And then suddenly, without willing it, he was thinking about Martha. The stresses and fractures, the quick collapse, the two of them buried alive under all that weight. Dense, crushing love. Kneeling, watching the hole, he tried to concentrate on Lee Strunk and the war, all the dangers, but his love was too much for him, he felt paralyzed, he wanted to sleep inside her lungs and breathe her blood and be smothered. He wanted her to be a virgin and not a virgin, all at once. He wanted to know her. Intimate secrets—why poetry? Why so sad? Why the grayness in her eyes? Why so alone? Not lonely, just alone—riding her bike across campus or sitting off by herself in the cafeteria. Even dancing, she danced alone—and it was the aloneness that filled him with love. He remembered telling her that one evening. How she nodded and looked away. And how, later, when he kissed her, she received the kiss without returning it, her eyes wide open, not afraid, not a virgin's eyes, just flat and uninvolved.

Lieutenant Cross gazed at the tunnel. But he was not there. He was buried with Martha under the white sand at the Jersey shore. They were pressed together, and the pebble in his mouth was her tongue. He was smiling. Vaguely, he was aware of how quiet the day was, the sullen paddies, yet he could not bring himself to worry about matters of security. He was beyond that. He was just a kid at war, in love. He was twenty-two years old. He couldn't help it.

A few moments later Lee Strunk crawled out of the tunnel. He came up grinning, filthy but alive. Lieutenant Cross nodded and closed his eyes while the others clapped Strunk on the back and made jokes about rising from the dead.

Worms, Rat Kiley said. Right out of the grave. Fuckin' zombie.

The men laughed. They all felt great relief.   25

Spook City, said Mitchell Sanders.

Lee Strunk made a funny ghost sound, a kind of moaning, yet very happy, and right then, when Strunk made that high happy moaning sound, when he went *Ahhooooo*, right then Ted Lavender was shot in the head on his way back from peeing. He lay with his mouth open. The teeth were broken. There was a swollen black bruise under his left eye. The cheekbone was gone. Oh shit, Rat Kiley said, the guy's dead. The guy's dead, he kept saying, which seemed profound—the guy's dead. I mean really.

The things they carried were determined to some extent by superstition. Lieutenant Cross carried his good-luck pebble. Dave Jensen carried a rabbit's foot. Norman Bowker, otherwise a very gentle person, carried a thumb that had been presented to him as a gift by Mitchell Sanders. The thumb was dark brown, rubbery to the touch, and weighed four ounces at most. It had been cut from a VC corpse, a boy of fifteen or sixteen. They'd found him at the bottom of an irrigation ditch, badly burned, flies in his mouth and eyes. The boy wore black shorts and sandals. At the time of his death he had been carrying a pouch of rice, a rifle, and three magazines of ammunition.

You want my opinion, Mitchell Sanders said, there's a definite moral here.

He put his hand on the dead boy's wrist. He was quiet for a time, as if counting   30
a pulse, then he patted the stomach, almost affectionately, and used Kiowa's hunting hatchet to remove the thumb.

Henry Dobbins asked what the moral was.

Moral?

You know. *Moral.*

Sanders wrapped the thumb in toilet paper and handed it across to Norman Bowker. There was no blood. Smiling, he kicked the boy's head, watched the flies scatter, and said, It's like with that old TV show—Paladin. Have gun, will travel.

Henry Dobbins thought about it.

Yeah, well, he finally said. I don't see no moral.

There it is, man.

Fuck off.   35

They carried USO stationery and pencils and pens. They carried Sterno, safety pins, trip flares, signal flares, spools of wire, razor blades, chewing tobacco, liberated joss sticks and statuettes of the smiling Buddha, candles, grease pencils, *The Stars and Stripes*, fingernail clippers, Psy Ops[5] leaflets, bush hats, bolos, and much more. Twice a week, when the resupply choppers came in, they carried hot chow in green Mermite cans and large canvas bags filled with iced beer and soda pop. They carried plastic water containers, each with a two-gallon capacity. Mitchell Sanders carried a set of starched tiger fatigues for special occasions. Henry Dobbins carried Black Flag insecticide. Dave Jensen carried empty sandbags that could be filled at night for added protection. Lee Strunk carried tanning lotion. Some things they carried in common. Taking turns, they carried the big PRC-77 scrambler radio, which weighed thirty pounds with its battery. They shared the weight of memory. They took up what others could no longer bear. Often, they carried each other, the wounded or weak. They carried infections. They carried chess sets, basketballs, Vietnamese-English dictionaries, insignia of rank, Bronze Stars and Purple Hearts, plastic cards imprinted with the Code of Conduct. They carried diseases, among them malaria and dysentery. They carried lice and ringworm and leeches and paddy algae and various rots and molds. They carried the land itself—Vietnam, the place, the soil—a powdery orange-red dust that covered their boots and fatigues and faces. They carried the sky. The whole atmosphere, they carried it, the humidity, the monsoons, the stink of fungus and decay, all of it, they carried gravity. They moved like mules. By daylight they took sniper fire, at night they were mortared, but it was not battle, it was just the endless march, village to village, without purpose, nothing won or lost. They marched for the sake of the march. They plodded along slowly, dumbly, leaning forward against the heat, unthinking, all blood and bone, simple grunts, soldiering with their legs, toiling up the hills and down into the paddies and across the rivers and up again and down, just humping, one step and then the next and then another, but no volition, no will, because it was automatic, it was anatomy, and the war was entirely a matter of posture and carriage, the hump was everything, a kind of inertia, a kind of emptiness, a dullness of desire and intellect and conscience and hope and human sensibility. Their principles were in their feet. Their calculations were biological. They had no sense of strategy or mission. They searched the villages without knowing what to look for, not caring, kicking over jars of rice, frisking children and old men, blowing tunnels, sometimes setting fires and sometimes not, then forming up and moving on to the next village, then other villages, where it would always be the same. They carried their own lives. The pressures were enormous. In the heat of early afternoon, they would remove their helmets and flak jackets, walking bare,

---

[5]Psychological operations.—EDS.

which was dangerous but which helped ease the strain. They would often discard things along the route of march. Purely for comfort, they would throw away rations, blow their Claymores and grenades, no matter, because by nightfall the resupply choppers would arrive with more of the same, then a day or two later still more, fresh watermelons and crates of ammunition and sunglasses and woolen sweaters—the resources were stunning—sparklers for the Fourth of July, colored eggs for Easter. It was the great American war chest—the fruits of science, the smokestacks, the canneries, the arsenals at Hartford, the Minnesota forests, the machine shops, the vast fields of corn and wheat—they carried like freight trains; they carried it on their backs and shoulders—and for all the ambiguities of Vietnam, all the mysteries and unknowns, there was at least the single abiding certainty that they would never be at a loss for things to carry.

After the chopper took Lavender away, Lieutenant Jimmy Cross led his men into   40
the village of Than Khe. They burned everything. They shot chickens and dogs, they trashed the village well, they called in artillery and watched the wreckage, then they marched for several hours through the hot afternoon, and then at dusk, while Kiowa explained how Lavender died, Lieutenant Cross found himself trembling.

He tried not to cry. With his entrenching tool, which weighed five pounds, he began digging a hole in the earth.

He felt shame. He hated himself. He had loved Martha more than his men, and as a consequence Lavender was now dead, and this was something he would have to carry like a stone in his stomach for the rest of the war.

All he could do was dig. He used his entrenching tool like an ax, slashing, feeling both love and hate, and then later, when it was full dark, he sat at the bottom of his foxhole and wept. It went on for a long while. In part, he was grieving for Ted Lavender, but mostly it was for Martha, and for himself, because she belonged to another world, which was not quite real, and because she was a junior at Mount Sebastian College in New Jersey, a poet and a virgin and uninvolved, and because he realized she did not love him and never would.

Like cement, Kiowa whispered in the dark. I swear to God—boom-down. Not a word.

I've heard this, said Norman Bowker.   45

A pisser, you know? Still zipping himself up. Zapped while zipping.

All right, fine. That's enough.

Yeah, but you had to see it, the guy just—

I *heard*, man. Cement. So why not shut the fuck *up*?

Kiowa shook his head sadly and glanced over at the hole where Lieutenant   50
Jimmy Cross sat watching the night. The air was thick and wet. A warm, dense fog had settled over the paddies and there was the stillness that precedes rain.

After a time Kiowa sighed.

One thing for sure, he said. The Lieutenant's in some deep hurt. I mean that crying jag—the way he was carrying on—it wasn't fake or anything, it was real heavy-duty hurt. The man cares.

Sure, Norman Bowker said.

Say what you want, the man does care.

We all got problems.   55

Not Lavender.

No, I guess not, Bowker said. Do me a favor, though.

Shut up?

That's a smart Indian. Shut up.

Shrugging, Kiowa pulled off his boots. He wanted to say more, just to lighten up   60
his sleep, but instead he opened his New Testament and arranged it beneath his head
as a pillow. The fog made things seem hollow and unattached. He tried not to think
about Ted Lavender, but then he was thinking how fast it was, no drama, down and
dead, and how it was hard to feel anything except surprise. It seemed un-Christian. He
wished he could find some great sadness, or even anger, but the emotion wasn't there
and he couldn't make it happen. Mostly he felt pleased to be alive. He liked the smell
of the New Testament under his cheek, the leather and ink and paper and glue, whatever the chemicals were. He liked hearing the sounds of night. Even his fatigue, it felt
fine, the stiff muscles and the prickly awareness of his own body, a floating feeling. He
enjoyed not being dead. Lying there, Kiowa admired Lieutenant Jimmy Cross's capacity
for grief. He wanted to share the man's pain, he wanted to care as Jimmy Cross cared.
And yet when he closed his eyes, all he could think was Boom-down, and all he could
feel was the pleasure of having his boots off and the fog curling in around him and the
damp soil and the Bible smells and the plush comfort of night.

After a moment Norman Bowker sat up in the dark.

What the hell, he said. You want to talk, *talk*. Tell it to me.

Forget it.

No, man, go on. One thing I hate, it's a silent Indian.

For the most part they carried themselves with poise, a kind of dignity. Now and   65
then, however, there were times of panic, when they squealed or wanted to squeal but
couldn't, when they twitched and made moaning sounds and covered their heads and
said Dear Jesus and flopped around on the earth and fired their weapons blindly and
cringed and sobbed and begged for the noise to stop and went wild and made stupid
promises to themselves and to God and to their mothers and fathers, hoping not to die.
In different ways, it happened to all of them. Afterward, when the firing ended, they
would blink and peek up. They would touch their bodies, feeling shame, then quickly
hiding it. They would force themselves to stand. As if in slow motion, frame by frame,
the world would take on the old logic—absolute silence, then the wind, then sunlight,
then voices. It was the burden of being alive. Awkwardly, the men would reassemble
themselves, first in private, then in groups, becoming soldiers again. They would repair
the leaks in their eyes. They would check for casualties, call in dust-offs, light cigarettes,
try to smile, clear their throats and spit and begin cleaning their weapons. After a time
someone would shake his head and say, No lie, I almost shit my pants, and someone
else would laugh, which meant it was bad, yes, but the guy had obviously not shit his
pants, it wasn't that bad, and in any case nobody would ever do such a thing and then

go ahead and talk about it. They would squint into the dense, oppressive sunlight. For a few moments, perhaps, they would fall silent, lighting a joint and tracking its passage from man to man, inhaling, holding in the humiliation. Scary stuff, one of them might say. But then someone else would grin or flick his eyebrows and say, Roger-dodger, almost cut me a new asshole, *almost*.

There were numerous such poses. Some carried themselves with a sort of wistful resignation, others with pride or stiff soldierly discipline or good humor or macho zeal. They were afraid of dying but they were even more afraid to show it.

They found jokes to tell.

They used a hard vocabulary to contain the terrible softness. *Greased* they'd say. *Offed, lit up, zapped while zipping*. It wasn't cruelty, just stage presence. They were actors and the war came at them in 3-D. When someone died, it wasn't quite dying, because in a curious way it seemed scripted, and because they had their lines mostly memorized, irony mixed with tragedy, and because they called it by other names, as if to encyst and destroy the reality of death itself. They kicked corpses. They cut off thumbs. They talked grunt lingo. They told stories about Ted Lavender's supply of tranquilizers, how the poor guy didn't feel a thing, how incredibly tranquil he was.

There's a moral here, said Mitchell Sanders.

They were waiting for Lavender's chopper, smoking the dead man's dope.   70

The moral's pretty obvious, Sanders said, and winked. Stay away from drugs. No joke, they'll ruin your day every time.

Cute, said Henry Dobbins.

Mind-blower, get it? Talk about wiggy—nothing left, just blood and brains.

They made themselves laugh.

There it is, they'd say, over and over, as if the repetition itself were an act of   75
poise, a balance between crazy and almost crazy, knowing without going. There it is, which meant be cool, let it ride, because oh yeah, man, you can't change what can't be changed, there it is, there it absolutely and positively and fucking well is.

They were tough.

They carried all the emotional baggage of men who might die. Grief, terror, love, longing—these were intangibles, but the intangibles had their own mass and specific gravity, they had tangible weight. They carried shameful memories. They carried the common secret of cowardice barely restrained, the instinct to run or freeze or hide, and in many respects this was the heaviest burden of all, for it could never be put down, it required perfect balance and perfect posture. They carried their reputations. They carried the soldier's greatest fear, which was the fear of blushing. Men killed, and died, because they were embarrassed not to. It was what had brought them to the war in the first place, nothing positive, no dreams of glory or honor, just to avoid the blush of dishonor. They died so as not to die of embarrassment. They crawled into tunnels and walked point and advanced under fire. Each morning, despite the unknowns, they made their legs move. They endured. They kept humping. They did not submit to the obvious alternative, which was simply to close the eyes and fall. So easy, really. Go limp and tumble to the ground and let the muscles unwind and not speak and not budge until your buddies picked you up and lifted you into the chopper that would roar and dip its nose and carry you off to the world. A mere matter of falling, yet no one ever fell. It was not courage, exactly; the object was not valor. Rather, they were too frightened to be cowards.

By and large they carried these things inside, maintaining the masks of composure. They sneered at sick call. They spoke bitterly about guys who had found release by shooting off their own toes or fingers. Pussies, they'd say. Candyasses. It was fierce, mocking talk, with only a trace of envy or awe, but even so, the image played itself out behind their eyes.

They imagined the muzzle against flesh. They imagined the quick, sweet pain, then the evacuation to Japan, then a hospital with warm beds and cute geisha nurses.

They dreamed of freedom birds.   80

At night, on guard, staring into the dark, they were carried away by jumbo jets. They felt the rush of takeoff. *Gone!* they yelled. And then velocity, wings and engines, a smiling stewardess—but it was more than a plane, it was a real bird, a big sleek silver bird with feathers and talons and high screeching. They were flying. The weights fell off, there was nothing to bear. They laughed and held on tight, feeling the cold slap of wind and altitude, soaring, thinking *It's over, I'm gone!*—they were naked, they were light and free—it was all lightness, bright and fast and buoyant, light as light, a helium buzz in the brain, a giddy bubbling in the lungs as they were taken up over the clouds and the war, beyond duty, beyond gravity and mortification and global entanglements—*Sin loi!*[6] they yelled, *I'm sorry, motherfuckers, but I'm out of it, I'm goofed, I'm on a space cruise, I'm gone!*—and it was a restful, disencumbered sensation, just riding the light waves, sailing that big silver freedom bird over the mountains and oceans, over America, over the farms and great sleeping cities and cemeteries and highways and the golden arches of McDonald's. It was flight, a kind of fleeing, a kind of falling, falling higher and higher, spinning off the edge of the earth and beyond the sun and through the vast, silent vacuum where there were no burdens and where everything weighed exactly nothing. *Gone!* they screamed, *I'm sorry but I'm gone!* And so at night, not quite dreaming, they gave themselves over to lightness, they were carried, they were purely borne.

On the morning after Ted Lavender died, First Lieutenant Jimmy Cross crouched at the bottom of his foxhole and burned Martha's letters. Then he burned the two photographs. There was a steady rain falling, which made it difficult, but he used heat tabs and Sterno to build a small fire, screening it with his body, holding the photographs over the tight blue flame with the tips of his fingers.

He realized it was only a gesture. Stupid, he thought. Sentimental, too, but mostly just stupid.

Lavender was dead. You couldn't burn the blame.

Besides, the letters were in his head. And even now, without photographs,   85
Lieutenant Cross could see Martha playing volleyball in her white gym shorts and yellow T-shirt. He could see her moving in the rain.

---

[6]Sorry about that.—Eds.

When the fire died out, Lieutenant Cross pulled his poncho over his shoulders and ate breakfast from a can.

There was no great mystery, he decided.

In those burned letters Martha had never mentioned the war, except to say, Jimmy, take care of yourself. She wasn't involved. She signed the letters "Love," but it wasn't love, and all the fine lines and technicalities did not matter.

The morning came up wet and blurry. Everything seemed part of everything else, the fog and Martha and the deepening rain.

It was a war, after all.   90

Half smiling, Lieutenant Jimmy Cross took out his maps. He shook his head hard, as if to clear it, then bent forward and began planning the day's march. In ten minutes, or maybe twenty, he would rouse the men and they would pack up and head west, where the maps showed the country to be green and inviting. They would do what they had always done. The rain might add some weight, but otherwise it would be one more day layered upon all the other days.

He was realistic about it. There was that new hardness in his stomach.

No more fantasies, he told himself.

Henceforth, when he thought about Martha, it would be only to think that she belonged elsewhere. He would shut down the daydreams. This was not Mount Sebastian, it was another world, where there were no pretty poems or midterm exams, a place where men died because of carelessness and gross stupidity. Kiowa was right. Boom-down, and you were dead, never partly dead.

Briefly, in the rain, Lieutenant Cross saw Martha's gray eyes gazing back at him.   95

He understood.

It was very sad, he thought. The things men carried inside. The things men did or felt they had to do.

He almost nodded at her, but didn't.

Instead he went back to his maps. He was now determined to perform his duties firmly and without negligence. It wouldn't help Lavender, he knew that, but from this point on he would comport himself as a soldier. He would dispose of his good-luck pebble. Swallow it, maybe, or use Lee Strunk's slingshot, or just drop it along the trail. On the march he would impose strict field discipline. He would be careful to send out flank security, to prevent straggling or bunching up, to keep his troops moving at the proper pace and at the proper interval. He would insist on clean weapons. He would confiscate the remainder of Lavender's dope. Later in the day, perhaps, he would call the men together and speak to them plainly. He would accept the blame for what had happened to Ted Lavender. He would be a man about it. He would look them in the eyes, keeping his chin level, and he would issue the new SOPs in a calm, impersonal tone of voice, an officer's voice, leaving no room for argument or discussion. Commencing immediately, he'd tell them, they would no longer abandon equipment along the route of march. They would police up their acts. They would get their shit together, and keep it together, and maintain it neatly and in good working order.

He would not tolerate laxity. He would show strength, distancing himself.   100

Among the men there would be grumbling, of course, and maybe worse, because their days would seem longer and their loads heavier, but Lieutenant Cross reminded himself that his obligation was not to be loved but to lead. He would dispense with love; it was not now a factor. And if anyone quarreled or complained, he would simply tighten his lips and arrange his shoulders in the correct command posture. He might give a curt little nod. Or he might not. He might just shrug and say Carry on, then they would saddle up and form into a column and move out toward the villages of Than Khe.

[1986]

Questions for Discussion

1. The story begins with a paragraph about Jimmy Cross and his relationship with Martha. What does Martha represent to Cross? Why might it be significant that Cross obsesses about whether or not she is a virgin? How do Cross's feelings for Martha change toward the end of the story, and how does this change point the way to one of the themes of the story?

2. What role does Hollywood play in this story? How are the soldiers' expectations of war and death shaped by the movies? Where in this story does Hollywood fantasy meet reality? What point is O'Brien making?

3. According to the narrator, "The things they carried were largely determined by necessity" (para. 2), were "partly a function of rank, partly of field specialty" (para. 6), "varied by mission" (para. 14), and "were determined to some extent by superstition" (para. 28). Which is the strongest factor in determining what they carried? Do you find any irony in the things they carried?

4. Jimmy Cross carries "the responsibility for the lives of his men" (para. 7) and ultimately cannot bear that burden. What does he literally and figuratively shed in order to bear that weight following Lavender's death? What point is O'Brien making?

5. Why do you think the medic would need "M&M's for especially bad wounds" (para. 9)?

6. In paragraph 29, the soldiers find the burned corpse of a teenage Vietcong soldier at the bottom of a ditch, and Sanders says, "there's a definite moral here," before cutting off the boy's thumb and giving it to Bowker. Dobbins doesn't see the moral, and ultimately, they decide, "There it is." What do they mean by that? Look at paragraph 75, where O'Brien talks more about the meaning of that phrase. Does "The Things They Carried" have a moral? If so, what is it?

7. The soldiers react differently to Ted Lavender's death (paras. 11, 27, 40–64). Pick one soldier whose reaction seems particularly significant, and explain why you find it meaningful.

8. After studying terminally ill patients, psychologist Elisabeth Kübler-Ross described five stages in the process of dealing with death: (1) denial, or "this isn't happening"; (2) anger, or "why me?"; (3) bargaining, or "I'd do anything"; (4) depression, or "I

give up"; and (5) acceptance, or "It's okay." Do the soldiers facing death in this story display these behaviors? Which stages do you notice, and in what circumstances? Which stage seems most prevalent? Why do you think that is?

9. In paragraph 77, the narrator says, "They carried the soldier's greatest fear, which was the fear of blushing." Why do you think the soldiers were more afraid to blush than to die?

10. Paragraph 97 says, "It was very sad, [Cross] thought. The things men carried inside. The things men did or felt they had to do." What things do you think Cross is thinking about? What does he intend to do about it? Do you think he will succeed? Do you think it will matter? Explain your answers.

11. What opinion do you think O'Brien has about the soldiers, the war, and, specifically, Lieutenant Cross? Support your inferences with specific references to the text.

Questions on Style and Structure

1. Paragraph 3 says, "They were called legs or grunts." Explain why this use of synecdoche (using a part to refer to the whole) is especially appropriate not only for this story but for life in the military in general.

2. What evidence do you find that Jimmy Cross is a Christ figure? How does the symbolism of his name and initials influence your reading of the story? Is the virgin Martha akin to the Virgin Mary? Explain why or why not.

3. The story's central event is the death of Ted Lavender, which the story returns to again and again. Why do you think the story revisits this event so often? Do you think this repetition honors Lavender or trivializes his death? Explain your answer.

4. The reader learns about Ted Lavender's death in the second paragraph, but the narrator provides few details until paragraph 27. What is the effect of the delay on the reader? What does the delay suggest about the effects of war on the soldiers?

5. How does O'Brien characterize the soldiers by the things they carry?

6. One technique O'Brien employs is zeugma, in which one word has more than one (often incongruous) object. For example, he writes in paragraph 12, "They carried all they could bear, and then some, including a silent awe for the terrible power of the things they carried." Look for other examples of zeugma in the story. Do you see any pattern in how O'Brien uses zeugma? In particular, consider how O'Brien exploits the incongruity of zeugma in order to develop one of the themes of the story.

7. Paragraph 18 contains a series of questions. Consider all the possible meanings of the statement "Imagination was a killer." How does it answer the questions?

8. At the end of paragraph 39, the narrator adds the products of the "great American war chest" to "the things they carried." Explain the political statement this extended metaphor makes.

9. How many times does the word "they" appear from paragraphs 65 through 81? (Literally, count them.) Why does O'Brien use that pronoun so often at the end of the story?

10. In paragraph 99, the conditional "would" is repeated in nearly every sentence. What does this parallelism suggest? How does it add to the characterization of Lieutenant Cross?

Suggestions for Writing

1. Read once again the epigraph to this chapter. Write an essay in which you consider how O'Brien's remarks serve to introduce "The Things They Carried."
2. Consider carefully the organization and narrative method O'Brien uses in this story. While some sections attempt to define and explain the nature of the soldier's war experience, other sections are narratives about individual soldiers. Write an essay in which you explain how the structure O'Brien uses comments on war.
3. Sometimes a work of literature reveals a great deal of richness in what it leaves out or what it doesn't say. "The Things They Carried" concentrates on what the soldiers carry, giving the soldiers little purpose beyond "humping." Write an essay discussing what O'Brien is trying to say by focusing on the minutiae of war. Think especially about what he leaves out.
4. One might view O'Brien's narrative structure itself to be symbolic. Each time the narrator brings order to the events by returning to an organized account of the things that they carried, the process slips into personal accounts and idiosyncratic details. How does such a method work symbolically to suggest something about the subject matter of the story?
5. Read "Naming of Parts" by Henry Reed (p. 1428). Compare and contrast that poem's techniques and themes to those of "The Things they Carried."
6. At the end of the story, Jimmy Cross feels responsible for Lavender's death, and his thoughts turn again to Martha as he decides to strengthen his resolve. Assume the character of Lieutenant Cross and write a letter to Martha about the incident. Then write her reply.

War

LUIGI PIRANDELLO

Perhaps best known as a dramatist—especially for his play *Six Characters in Search of an Author* (1921)—Luigi Pirandello (1867–1936) was also a prolific short-story writer. He was born in Sicily and educated at the University of Bonn in Germany, receiving his doctorate there in 1891. For years he wrote novels, stories, and plays; worked as a professor at a teacher's college for women; and cared for his wife, who suffered from mental illness. After achieving literary success, he left teaching and devoted himself to writing, opening a theater in Rome in 1925. His company performed plays throughout Europe and also in South America. Pirandello was awarded the Nobel Prize for Literature in 1934. In many of his works, characters struggle with the nature of truth and reality itself. The story included here, "War," is among the most admired of his two-hundred-plus short stories.

The passengers who had left Rome by the night express had to stop until dawn at the small station of Fabriano in order to continue their journey by the small old-fashioned local joining the main line with Sulmona.

At dawn, in a stuffy and smoky second-class carriage in which five people had already spent the night, a bulky woman in deep mourning was hoisted in—almost like a shapeless bundle. Behind her, puffing and moaning, followed her husband—a tiny man, thin and weakly, his face death-white, his eyes small and bright and looking shy and uneasy.

Having at last taken a seat he politely thanked the passengers who had helped his wife and who had made room for her; then he turned round to the woman trying to pull down the collar of her coat, and politely inquired:

"Are you all right, dear?"

The wife, instead of answering, pulled up her collar again to her eyes, so as to 5 hide her face.

"Nasty world," muttered the husband with a sad smile.

And he felt it his duty to explain to his traveling companions that the poor woman was to be pitied, for the war was taking away from her her only son, a boy of twenty to whom both had devoted their entire life, even breaking up their home at Sulmona to follow him to Rome, where he had to go as a student, then allowing him to volunteer for war with an assurance, however, that at least for six months he would not be sent to the front and now, all of a sudden, receiving a wire saying that he was due to leave in three days' time and asking them to go and see him off.

The woman under the big coat was twisting and wriggling, at times growling like a wild animal, feeling certain that all those explanations would not have aroused even a shadow of sympathy from those people who—most likely—were in the same plight as herself. One of them, who had been listening with particular attention, said:

"You should thank God that your son is only leaving now for the front. Mine has been sent there the first day of the war. He has already come back twice wounded and been sent back again to the front."

"What about me? I have two sons and three nephews at the front," said another passenger.

"Maybe, but in our case it is our *only* son," ventured the husband.   10

"What difference can it make? You may spoil your only son with excessive attentions, but you cannot love him more than you would all your other children if you had any. Paternal love is not like bread that can be broken into pieces and split amongst the children in equal shares. A father gives *all* his love to each one of his children without discrimination, whether it be one or ten, and if I am suffering now for my two sons, I am not suffering half for each of them but double . . ."

"True . . . true . . ." sighed the embarrassed husband, "but suppose (of course we all hope it will never be your case) a father has two sons at the front and he loses one of them, there is still one left to console him . . . while . . ."

"Yes," answered the other, getting cross, "a son left to console him but also a son left for whom he must survive, while in the case of the father of an only son if the son dies the father can die too and put an end to his distress. What of the two positions is the worse? Don't you see how my case would be worse than yours?"

"Nonsense," interrupted another traveler, a fat red-faced man with bloodshot eyes of the palest gray.

He was panting. From his bulging eyes seemed to spurt inner violence of an   15
uncontrolled vitality which his weakened body could hardly contain.

"Nonsense," he repeated, trying to cover his mouth with his hand so as to hide the two missing front teeth. "Nonsense. Do we give life to our children for our own benefit?"

The other travelers stared at him in distress. The one who had his son at the front since the first day of the war sighed: "You are right. Our children do not belong to us, they belong to the Country. . . ."

"Bosh," retorted the fat traveler. "Do we think of the Country when we give life to our children? Our sons are born because . . . well, because they must be born and when they come to life they take our own life with them. This is the truth. We belong to them but they can never belong to us. And when they reach twenty they are exactly what we were at their age. We too had a father and mother, but there were so many other things as well . . . girls, cigarettes, illusions, new ties . . . and the Country, of course, whose call we would have answered — when we were twenty — even if father and mother had said no. Now at our age, the love of our Country is still great, of course, but stronger than it is the love for our children. Is there any one of us here who wouldn't gladly take his son's place at the front if he could?"

There was a silence all round, everybody nodding as to approve.

"Why then," continued the fat man, "shouldn't we consider the feelings of our   20
children when they are twenty? Isn't it natural that at their age they should consider the love for their Country (I am speaking of decent boys, of course) even greater than the love for us? Isn't it natural that it should be so, as after all they must look upon us as

upon old boys who cannot move any more and must stay at home? If Country exists, if Country is a natural necessity, like bread, of which each of us must eat in order not to die of hunger, somebody must go to defend it. And our sons go, when they are twenty, and they don't want tears, because if they die, they die inflamed and happy (I am speaking, of course, of decent boys). Now, if one dies young and happy, without having the ugly sides of life, the boredom of it, the pettiness, the bitterness of disillusion . . . what more can we ask for him? Everyone should stop crying, everyone should laugh as I do . . . or at least thank God — as I do — because my son, before dying sent me a message saying that he was dying satisfied at having ended his life in the best way he could have wished. That is why, as you see, I do not even wear mourning. . . ."

He shook his light fawn coat as to show it; his livid lip over his missing teeth was trembling, his eyes were watery and motionless, and soon after he ended with a shrill laugh which might well have been a sob.

"Quite so . . . quite so . . ." agreed the others.

The woman who, bundled in a corner under her coat, had been sitting and listening had — for the last three months — tried to find in the words of her husband and her friends something to console her in her deep sorrow, something that might show her how a mother should resign herself to send her son not even to death but to a probably dangerous life. Yet not a word had she found amongst the many which had been said . . . and her grief had been greater in seeing that nobody — as she thought — could share her feelings.

But now the words of the traveler amazed and almost stunned her. She suddenly realized that it wasn't the others who were wrong and could not understand her but herself who could not rise up to the same height of those fathers and mothers willing to resign themselves, without crying, not only to the departure of their sons but even to their death.

She lifted her head, she bent over from her corner trying to listen with great attention to the details which the fat man was giving to his companions about the way his son had fallen as a hero, for his King and his Country, happy and without regrets. It seemed to her that she had stumbled into a world she had never dreamt of, a world so far unknown to her and she was so pleased to hear everyone joining in congratulating that brave father who could so stoically speak of his child's death.

Then suddenly, just as if she had heard nothing of what had been said and almost as if waking up from a dream, she turned to the old man, asking him:

"Then . . . is your son really dead?"

Everybody stared at her. The old man, too, turned to look at her, fixing his great, bulging, horribly watery light gray eyes, deep in her face. For some little time he tried to answer, but words failed him. He looked at her, almost as if only then—at that silly, incongruous question—he had suddenly realized at last that his son was really dead—gone for ever—for ever. His face contracted, became horribly distorted, then he snatched in haste a handkerchief from his pocket and, to the amazement of everyone, broke into harrowing, heart-rending, uncontrollable sobs.

[1919]

Exploring the Text

1. What is the significance of the title of the story? Where is the "war"?

2. Take another look at how each of Pirandello's main characters is described. How do the physical descriptions work metaphorically? Why are some characters more developed than others? Why doesn't he give them names?

3. What is the argument among the travelers? What do they have to say about sacrifice and bravery? about suffering and consolation? about patriotism? What do they agree on, and what do they not agree on?

4. How does the information in paragraphs 24–26 influence the reader's expectations of how the story might end? What might the reader expect the woman to say and do? How did you expect the story to end? How does Pirandello undermine those expectations?

5. Do you interpret this as an antiwar story or a story about the honor of serving one's country? Explain your answer. Does Pirandello honor the sacrifice of soldiers? Cite specific passages to support your interpretation.

The First Year of My Life

Point of view   Humor

MURIEL SPARK

irony

Sardonic

> Muriel Spark was born in Scotland in 1918 and educated in Edinburgh. Spark lived and wrote in Scotland, England, the United States, Zimbabwe (called Rhodesia at the time), and Italy, where she lived for more than thirty years. She died at home in Tuscany in 2006. Author of more than twenty novels and many volumes of stories, she is well known not only for her fiction but also for her poetry and nonfiction. Among her works is a biography of Emily Brontë; a critical study of the work of Mary Shelley; and several satiric novels—including *Memento Mori* (1959) and *The Girls of Slender Means* (1963)—but it is her 1961 novel, *The Prime of Miss Jean Brodie*, that has endured as her most successful work. Immensely popular, the novel was adapted for the stage, film, and television. A satirist, Spark targets hypocrisy and pretense in her stories, treating some of her characters with an acerbic tongue and sarcastic bite. Spark was born during the First World War, as she reveals in "The First Year of My Life," and worked in British Intelligence during World War II. Both wars influenced the writing of the story included here.

I was born on the first day of the second month of the last year of the First World War, a Friday. Testimony abounds that during the first year of my life I never smiled. I was known as the baby whom nothing and no one could make smile. Everyone who knew me then has told me so. They tried very hard, singing and bouncing me up and down, jumping around, pulling faces. Many times I was told this later by my family and their friends; but, anyway, I knew it at the time.

You will shortly be hearing of that new school of psychology, or maybe you have heard of it already, which after long and far-adventuring research and experiment has established that all of the young of the human species are born omniscient. Babies, in their waking hours, know everything that is going on everywhere in the world; they can tune in to any conversation they choose, switch on to any scene. We have all experienced this power. It is only after the first year that it was brainwashed out of us; for it is demanded of us by our immediate environment that we grow to be of use to it in a practical way. Gradually, our know-all brain-cells are blacked out, although traces remain in some individuals in the form of E.S.P., and in the adults of some primitive tribes.

It is not a new theory. Poets and philosophers, as usual, have been there first. But scientific proof is now ready and to hand. Perhaps the final touches are being put to the new manifesto in some cell at Harvard University. Any day now it will be given to the world, and the world will be convinced.

Let me therefore get my word in first, because I feel pretty sure, now, about the authenticity of my remembrance of things past. My autobiography, as I very well perceived at the time, started in the very worst year that the world had ever seen so far. Apart from being born bedridden and toothless, unable to raise myself on the pillow or utter anything but farmyard squawks or police-siren wails, my bladder and my bowels totally out of control, I was further depressed by the curious behaviour of the two-legged mammals around me. There were those black-dressed people, females of the species to which I appeared to belong, saying they had lost their sons. I slept a great deal. Let them go and find their sons. It was like the special pin for my nappies which my mother or some other hoverer dedicated to my care was always losing. These careless women in black lost their husbands and their brothers. Then they came to visit my mother and clucked and crowed over my cradle. I was not amused.

'Babies never really smile till they're three months old,' said my mother. 'They're not *supposed* to smile till they're three months old.'

My brother, aged six, marched up and down with a toy rifle over his shoulder:

> The grand old Duke of York
> He had ten thousand men;
> He marched them up to the top of the hill
> And he marched them down again.
>
> And when they were up, they were up.
> And when they were down, they were down.
> And when they were neither down nor up
> They were neither up nor down.

'Just listen to him!'
'Look at him with his rifle!'

I was about ten days old when Russia stopped fighting. I tuned in to the Czar, a prisoner, with the rest of his family, since evidently the country had put him off his throne and there had been a revolution not long before I was born. Everyone was talking about it. I tuned in to the Czar. 'Nothing would ever induce me to sign the treaty of Brest-Litovsk,' he said to his wife. Anyway, nobody had asked him to.

At this point I was sleeping twenty hours a day to get my strength up. And from what I discerned in the other four hours of the day I knew I was going to need it. The Western Front on my frequency was sheer blood, mud, dismembered bodies, blistered crashes, hectic flashes of light in the night skies, explosions, total terror. Since it was plain I had been born into a bad moment in the history of the world, the future bothered me, unable as I was to raise my head from the pillow and as yet only twenty inches long. 'I truly wish I were a fox or a bird,' D. H. Lawrence was writing to somebody. Dreary old creeping Jesus. I fell asleep.

Red sheets of flame shot across the sky. It was 21st March, the fiftieth day of my life, and the German Spring Offensive had started before my morning feed. Infinite slaughter. I scowled at the scene, and made an effort to kick out. But the attempt was feeble. Furious, and impatient for some strength, I wailed for my feed. After which I stopped wailing but continued to scowl.

> The grand old Duke of York
> He had ten thousand men . . .

They rocked the cradle. I never heard a sillier song. Over in Berlin and Vienna the people were starving, freezing, striking, rioting and yelling in the streets. In London everyone was bustling to work and muttering that it was time the whole damn business was over.

The big people around me bared their teeth; that meant a smile, it meant they were pleased or amused. They spoke of ration cards for meat and sugar and butter. 'Where will it all end?'

I went to sleep. I woke and tuned in to Bernard Shaw who was telling someone to shut up. I switched over to Joseph Conrad who, strangely enough, was saying precisely the same thing. I still didn't think it worth a smile, although it was expected of me any day now. I got on to Turkey. Women draped in black huddled and chattered in their harems; yak-yak-yak. This was boring, so I came back to home base.

In and out came and went the women in British black. My mother's brother, dressed in his uniform, came coughing. He had been poison-gassed in the trenches. 'Tout le monde à la bataille!' declaimed Marshal Foch the old swine. He was now Commander-in-Chief of the Allied Forces. My uncle coughed from deep within his lungs, never to recover but destined to return to the Front. His brass buttons gleamed in the firelight. I weighed twelve pounds by now; I stretched and kicked for exercise, seeing that I had a lifetime before me, coping with this crowd. I took six feeds a day and kept most of them down by the time the *Vindictive* was sunk in Ostend harbour, on which day I kicked with special vigour in my bath.

In France the conscripted soldiers leapfrogged over the dead on the advance and littered the fields with limbs and hands, or drowned in the mud. The strongest men on all fronts were dead before I was born. Now the sentries used bodies for barricades and the fighting men were unhealthy from the start. I checked my toes and fingers, knowing I was going to need them. *The Playboy of the Western World*

[handwritten margin notes: "Babies mimic what they see... does she see smiling?" and "Do they?"]

was playing at the Court Theatre in London, but occasionally I beamed over to the House of Commons which made me drop off gently to sleep. Generally, I preferred the Western Front where one got the true state of affairs. It was essential to know the worst, blood and explosions and all, for one had to be prepared, as the boy scouts said. Virginia Woolf yawned and reached for her diary. Really, I preferred the Western Front.

In the fifth month of my life I could raise my head from my pillow and hold it up. I could grasp the objects that were held out to me. Some of these things rattled and squawked. I gnawed on them to get my teeth started. 'She hasn't smiled yet?' said the dreary old aunties. My mother, on the defensive, said I was probably one of those late smilers. On my wavelength Pablo Picasso was getting married and early in that month of July the Silver Wedding of King George V and Queen Mary was celebrated in joyous pomp at St. Paul's Cathedral. They drove through the streets of London with their children. Twenty-five years of domestic happiness. A lot of fuss and ceremonial handing over of swords went on at the Guildhall where the King and Queen received a cheque for £53,000 to dispose of for charity as they thought fit. *Tout le monde à la bataille!* Income tax in England had reached six shillings in the pound. Everyone was talking about the Silver Wedding; yak-yak-yak, and ten days later the Czar and his family, now in Siberia, were invited to descend to a little room in the basement. Crack, crack, went the guns; screams and blood all over the place, and that was the end of the Romanoffs. I flexed my muscles. 'A fine healthy baby,' said the doctor; which gave me much satisfaction.

Tout le monde à la bataille! That included my gassed uncle. My health had improved to the point where I was able to crawl in my playpen. Bertrand Russell was still cheerily in prison for writing something seditious about pacifism. Tuning in as usual to the Front Lines it looked as if the Germans were winning all the battles yet losing the war. And so it was. The upper-income people were upset about the income tax at six shillings to the pound. But all women over thirty got the vote. 'It seems a long time to wait,' said one of my drab old aunts, aged twenty-two. The speeches in the House of Commons always sent me to sleep which was why I missed, at the actual time, a certain oration by Mr. Asquith following the armistice on 11th November. Mr. Asquith was a greatly esteemed former prime minister later to be an Earl, and had been ousted by Mr. Lloyd George. I clearly heard Asquith, in private, refer to Lloyd George as 'that damned Welsh goat'.

The armistice was signed and I was awake for that. I pulled myself on to my feet with the aid of the bars of my cot. My teeth were coming through very nicely in my opinion, and well worth all the trouble I was put to in bringing them forth. I weighed twenty pounds. On all the world's fighting fronts the men killed in action or dead of wounds numbered 8,538,315 and the warriors wounded and maimed were 21,219,452. With these figures in mind I sat up in my high chair and banged my spoon on the table. One of my mother's black-draped friends recited:

> I have a rendezvous with Death
> At some disputed barricade,

When spring comes back with rustling shade
And apple blossoms fill the air—
I have a rendezvous with Death.

Most of the poets, they said, had been killed. The poetry made them dab their 20
eyes with clean white handkerchiefs. *Surrender*

Next February on my first birthday, there was a birthday-cake with one candle.
Lots of children and their elders. The war had been over two months and twenty-one
Q. days. 'Why doesn't she smile?' My brother was to blow out the candle. The elders were
A. talking about the war and the political situation. Lloyd George and Asquith, Asquith
and Lloyd George. I remembered recently having switched on to Mr. Asquith at a
private party where he had been drinking a lot. He was playing cards and when he
came to cut the cards he tried to cut a large box of matches by mistake. On another
occasion I had seen him putting his arm around a lady's shoulder in a Daimler motor
car, and generally behaving towards her in a very friendly fashion. Strangely enough
she said, 'If you don't stop this nonsense immediately I'll order the chauffeur to stop
and I'll get out.' Mr. Asquith replied, 'And pray, what reason will you give?' Well anyway it was my feeding time.

The guests arrived for my birthday. It was so sad, said one of the black widows,
so sad about Wilfred Owen who was killed so late in the war, and she quoted from
a poem of his:

What passing-bells for these who die as cattle?
Only the monstrous anger of the guns.

The children were squealing and toddling around. One was sick and another wet
the floor and stood with his legs apart gaping at the puddle. All was mopped up. I
banged my spoon on the table of my high chair.

But I've a rendezvous with Death
At midnight in some flaming town;
When spring trips north again this year,
And I to my pledged word am true,
I shall not fail that rendezvous.

More parents and children arrived. One stout man who was warming his behind at
the fire, said, 'I always think those words of Asquith's after the armistice were so apt . . .'
They brought the cake close to my high chair for me to see, with the candle shin- 25
ing and flickering above the pink icing. 'A pity she never smiles.'
'She'll smile in time,' my mother said, obviously upset.
'What Asquith told the House of Commons just after the war,' said that stout
gentleman with his backside to the fire, '—so apt, what Asquith said. He said that the
war has cleansed and purged the world, by God! I recall his actual words: "All things
have become new. In this great cleansing and purging it has been the privilege of our
country to play her part . . ."'
That did it. I broke into a decided smile and everyone noticed it, convinced that
it was provoked by the fact that my brother had blown out the candle on the cake.

'She smiled!' my mother exclaimed. And everyone was clucking away about how I was smiling. For good measure I crowed like a demented raven. 'My baby's smiling!' said my mother.

'It was the candle on her cake,' they said.

The cake be damned. Since that time I have grown to smile quite naturally, like any other healthy and house-trained person, but when I really mean a smile, deeply felt from the core, then to all intents and purposes it comes in response to the words uttered in the House of Commons after the First World War by the distinguished, the immaculately dressed and the late Mr. Asquith. 30

[1975]

Exploring the Text

1. Why do you think Spark has chosen to tell this story from such an unusual perspective? How does the information she provides in the first three paragraphs contribute to this perspective? What, for instance, does the narrator mean by her statement that after the first year, omniscience is "brainwashed out of us; for it is demanded of us by our immediate environment that we grow to be of use to it in a practical way" (para. 2)?

2. What is the purpose of such phrases as "two-legged mammals" and "black-dressed people" in paragraph 4? What is the effect of the narrator's deliberate misunderstanding of people "losing" or "having lost" family members?

3. Why does the narrator repeat certain phrases or lyrics, such as *"Tout le monde à la bataille!"* (paras. 15, 17, 18), "The grand old Duke of York" (paras. 6, 11), and "I have a rendezvous with Death" (paras. 19, 23)?

4. Spark provides very specific information about World War I in the story, especially about the battles, the Western Front, and the countries involved. For instance, the narrator states, "I took six feeds a day and kept most of them down by the time the *Vindictive* was sunk in Ostend harbour, on which day I kicked with special vigour in my bath" (para. 15). How do the historical facts become part of the fictional narrative?

5. In addition to political figures, Spark populates her story with artists and writers, such as Virginia Woolf, D. H. Lawrence, Pablo Picasso, and Joseph Conrad. What is the purpose and effect of these references? How do they relate to the events she portrays?

6. Paragraph 16 begins, "In France the conscripted soldiers leapfrogged over the dead on the advance and littered the fields with limbs and hands, or drowned in the mud." How would you characterize the tone in this paragraph? Why does Spark choose this tone to present horrible content? Why does Spark juxtapose the horrors of the battlefield with references to a comic play, the House of Commons, and the writing of Virginia Woolf?

7. In paragraph 18, Spark writes, "Bertrand Russell was still cheerily in prison for writing something seditious about pacifism." What is Spark's attitude toward Bertrand Russell's actions? How can you tell?

8. In paragraphs 21 through 28, Spark provides details about Mr. Asquith and then smiles for the first time in her life. What details does she choose to characterize Asquith? Why does she smile? What's the connection?

9. What is the purpose of the juxtaposition of adult behavior and infant behavior throughout the story?

10. Considering the grave nature of her subject matter, how appropriate is Spark's use of point of view, irony, and sarcasm? Use specific examples from the text to support your assessment.

The Shawl

Cynthia Ozick

Cynthia Ozick was born in 1928 in New York City, where she fell in love with literature as a child in the Bronx. The child of Lithuanian immigrants, she was strongly influenced by both the literature of her Jewish tradition and the New York writings of Henry James. She earned her BA at New York University and her MA in English literature at Ohio State University. Ozick is highly regarded for her ideas as well as her stories. "Even when you disagree with her, she electrifies your mind," wrote critic Christopher Lehmann-Haupt in the *New York Times* in 2000. Ozick continues to write both fiction and essays; in 2008, she received the PEN/Nabokov Award. "The Shawl" is perhaps her most famous piece. Published in 1980 in the *New Yorker* and selected for inclusion in *The Best American Short Stories of the Century* (1999), it delivers a powerful glimpse into the personal horrors of the Holocaust. In an interview published in the spring 1987 *Paris Review*, Ozick discussed writing about the Holocaust: "I don't want to tamper or invent or imagine, and yet I have done it. I can't not do it. It comes. It invades."

Stella, cold, cold, the coldness of hell. How they walked on the roads together, Rosa with Magda curled up between sore breasts, Magda wound up in the shawl. Sometimes Stella carried Magda. But she was jealous of Magda. A thin girl of fourteen, too small, with thin breasts of her own, Stella wanted to be wrapped in a shawl, hidden away, asleep, rocked by the march, a baby, a round infant in arms. Magda took Rosa's nipple, and Rosa never stopped walking, a walking cradle. There was not enough milk; sometimes Magda sucked air; then she screamed. Stella was ravenous. Her knees were tumors on sticks, her elbows chicken bones.

Rosa did not feel hunger; she felt light, not like someone walking but like someone in a faint, in trance, arrested in a fit, someone who is already a floating angel, alert and seeing everything, but in the air, not there, not touching the road. As if teetering on the tips of her fingernails. She looked into Magda's face through a gap in the shawl: a squirrel in a nest, safe, no one could reach her inside the little house of the shawl's windings. The face, very round, a pocket mirror of a face: but it was not Rosa's bleak complexion, dark like cholera, it was another kind of face altogether, eyes blue as air, smooth feathers of hair nearly as yellow as the Star sewn into Rosa's coat. You could think she was one of *their* babies.

Rosa, floating, dreamed of giving Magda away in one of the villages. She could leave the line for a minute and push Magda into the hands of any woman on the side of the road. But if she moved out of line they might shoot. And even if she fled the line for half a second and pushed the shawl-bundle at a stranger, would the woman take it? She might be surprised, or afraid; she might drop the shawl, and Magda would fall out and strike her head and die. The little round head. Such a good child, she gave up screaming, and sucked now only for the taste of the drying nipple itself. The neat grip of the tiny gums. One mite of a tooth tip sticking up in the bottom gum, how shining, an elfin tombstone of white marble, gleaming there. Without complaining, Magda relinquished Rosa's teats, first the left, then the right; both were cracked, not a sniff of milk. The duct crevice extinct, a dead volcano, blind eye, chill hole, so Magda took the corner of the shawl and milked it instead. She sucked and sucked, flooding the threads with wetness. The shawl's good flavor, milk of linen.

It was a magic shawl, it could nourish an infant for three days and three nights. Magda did not die, she stayed alive, although very quiet. A peculiar smell, of cinnamon and almonds, lifted out of her mouth. She held her eyes open every moment, forgetting how to blink or nap, and Rosa and sometimes Stella studied their blueness. On the road they raised one burden of a leg after another and studied Magda's face. "Aryan," Stella said, in a voice grown as thin as a string; and Rosa thought how Stella gazed at Magda like a young cannibal. And the time that Stella said "Aryan," it sounded to Rosa as if Stella had really said, "Let us devour her."

But Magda lived to walk. She lived that long, but she did not walk very well, partly   5 because she was only fifteen months old, and partly because the spindles of her legs could not hold up her fat belly. It was fat with air, full and round. Rosa gave almost all her food to Magda, Stella gave nothing; Stella was ravenous, a growing child herself, but not growing much. Stella did not menstruate. Rosa did not menstruate. Rosa was ravenous, but also not; she learned from Magda how to drink the taste of a finger in one's mouth. They were in a place without pity, all pity was annihilated in Rosa, she looked at Stella's bones without pity. She was sure that Stella was waiting for Magda to die so she could put her teeth into the little thighs.

Rosa knew Magda was going to die very soon; she should have been dead already, but she had been buried away deep inside the magic shawl, mistaken there for the shivering mound of Rosa's breasts; Rosa clung to the shawl as if it covered only herself. No one took it away from her. Magda was mute. She never cried. Rosa hid her in the barracks, under the shawl, but she knew that one day someone would inform; or one day someone, not even Stella, would steal Magda to eat her. When Magda began to walk Rosa knew that Magda was going to die very soon, something would happen. She was afraid to fall asleep; she slept with the weight of her thigh on Magda's body; she was afraid she would smother Magda under her thigh. The weight of Rosa was becoming less and less, Rosa and Stella were slowly turning into air.

Magda was quiet, but her eyes were horribly alive, like blue tigers. She watched. Sometimes she laughed—it seemed a laugh, but how could it be? Magda had never seen anyone laugh. Still, Magda laughed at her shawl when the wind blew its corners, the bad wind with pieces of black in it, that made Stella's and Rosa's eyes tear. Magda's eyes were always clear and tearless. She watched like a tiger. She guarded her shawl. No one could touch it; only Rosa could touch it. Stella was not allowed. The shawl was Magda's own baby, her pet, her little sister. She tangled herself up in it and sucked on one of the corners when she wanted to be very still.

Then Stella took the shawl away and made Magda die.

Afterward Stella said: "I was cold."

And afterward she was always cold, always. The cold went into her heart: Rosa saw that Stella's heart was cold. Magda flopped onward with her little pencil legs scribbling this way and that, in search of the shawl; the pencils faltered at the barracks opening, where the light began. Rosa saw and pursued. But already Magda was in the square outside the barracks, in the jolly light. It was the roll-call arena. Every morning Rosa had to conceal Magda under the shawl against a wall of the barracks and go out and stand in the arena with Stella and hundreds of others, sometimes for hours, and Magda, deserted, was quiet under the shawl, sucking on her corner. Every day Magda was silent, and so she did not die. Rosa saw that today Magda was going to die, and at the same time a fearful joy ran in Rosa's two palms, her fingers were on fire, she was astonished, febrile: Magda, in the sunlight, swaying on her pencil legs, was howling. Ever since the drying up of Rosa's nipples, ever since Magda's last scream on the road, Magda had been devoid of any syllable; Magda was a mute. Rosa believed that something had gone wrong with her vocal cords, with her windpipe, with the cave of her larynx; Magda was defective, without a voice; perhaps she was deaf; there might be something amiss with her intelligence; Magda was dumb. Even the laugh that came when the ash-stippled wind made a clown out of Magda's shawl was only the air-blown showing of her teeth. Even when the lice, head lice and body lice, crazed her so that she became as wild as one of the big rats that plundered the barracks at daybreak looking for carrion, she rubbed and scratched and kicked and bit and rolled without a whimper. But now Magda's mouth was spilling a long viscous rope of clamor.

"Maaaa——"

It was the first noise Magda had ever sent out from her throat since the drying up of Rosa's nipples.

"Maaaa . . . aaa!"

Again! Magda was wavering in the perilous sunlight of the arena, scribbling on such pitiful little bent shins. Rosa saw. She saw that Magda was grieving the loss of her shawl, she saw that Magda was going to die. A tide of commands hammered in Rosa's nipples: Fetch, get, bring! But she did not know which to go after first, Magda or the shawl. If she jumped out into the arena to snatch Magda up, the howling would not stop, because Magda would still not have the shawl; but if she ran back into the barracks to find the shawl, and if she found it, and if she came after Magda holding it and shaking it, then she would get Magda back, Magda would put the shawl in her mouth and turn dumb again.

Rosa entered the dark. It was easy to discover the shawl. Stella was heaped under it, asleep in her thin bones. Rosa tore the shawl free and flew—she could fly, she was only air—into the arena. The sunheat murmured of another life, of butterflies in summer. The light was placid, mellow. On the other side of the steel fence, far away, there were green meadows speckled with dandelions and deep-colored violets; beyond them, even farther, innocent tiger lilies, tall, lifting their orange bonnets. In the barracks they spoke of "flowers," of "rain": excrement, thick turd-braids, and the slow stinking maroon waterfall that slunk down from the upper bunks, the stink mixed with a bitter fatty floating smoke that greased Rosa's skin. She stood for an instant at the margin of the arena. Sometimes the electricity inside the fence would seem to hum; even Stella said it was only an imagining, but Rosa heard real sounds in the wire: grainy sad voices. The farther she was from the fence, the more clearly the voices crowded at her. The lamenting voices strummed so convincingly, so passionately, it was impossible to suspect them of being phantoms. The voices told her to hold up the shawl, high; the voices told her to shake it, to whip with it, to unfurl it like a flag. Rosa lifted, shook, whipped, unfurled. Far off, very far, Magda leaned across her air-fed belly, reaching out with the rods of her arms. She was high up, elevated, riding someone's shoulder. But the shoulder that carried Magda was not coming toward Rosa and the shawl, it was drifting away, the speck of Magda was moving more and more into the smoky distance. Above the shoulder a helmet glinted. A light tapped the helmet and sparkled it into a goblet. Below the helmet a black body like a domino and a pair of black boots hurled themselves in the direction of the electrified fence. The electric voices began to chatter wildly. "Maamaa, maaamaaa," they all hummed together. How far Magda was from Rosa now, across the whole square, past a dozen barracks, all the way on the other side! She was no bigger than a moth.

All at once Magda was swimming through the air. The whole of Magda traveled through loftiness. She looked like a butterfly touching a silver vine. And the moment Magda's feathered round head and her pencil legs and balloonish belly and zigzag arms splashed against the fence, the steel voices went mad in their growling, urging Rosa to run and run to the spot where Magda had fallen from her flight against the electrified fence; but of course Rosa did not obey them. She only stood, because if she ran they would shoot, and if she tried to pick up the sticks of Magda's body they would shoot, and if she let the wolf's screech ascending now through the ladder of her skeleton break out, they would shoot; so she took Magda's shawl and filled her own mouth with it, stuffed it in and stuffed it in, until she was swallowing up the wolf's screech and tasting the cinnamon and almond depth of Magda's saliva; and Rosa drank Magda's shawl until it dried.

[1980]

Exploring the Text

1. How would you describe Rosa, Stella, and Magda, the three main characters of the story? In what ways does the action of the story undermine their ability to act out their roles as mother, big sister, and baby, respectively?

2. Note the rich use of imagery and figurative language in the first three paragraphs. What is the effect of the "chicken bones," the "little house," and the "elfin tombstone," for example? How does the imagery contribute to the story as a whole?

3. In paragraph 7, Ozick writes of Magda, "Sometimes she laughed—it seemed a laugh, but how could it be? Magda had never seen anyone laugh." What is Ozick suggesting about joy?

4. Paragraphs 8 and 9 are single sentences: "Then Stella took the shawl away and made Magda die." "Afterward Stella said: 'I was cold.'" The next paragraph opens, "And afterward she was always cold, always." What is the importance of the reader being catapulted into the future by this sequence of lines?

5. What is the effect of the irony and imagery in the final two paragraphs?

6. How would the story differ if it were narrated in the first person by Rosa? Why do you think Ozick tells the story in the third person?

7. What associations does a shawl have? In what ways is it ambiguous? Do you agree with Ozick's choice of a title for the story? Why or why not?

The Management of Grief

Bharati Mukherjee

Born in Calcutta, India, in 1940, Bharati Mukherjee gained international experience and immersion in the English language when her father took a job in England, where the family lived from 1947 to 1951. After returning to India, she earned a BA from the University of Calcutta in 1959. She later received a scholarship to the University of Iowa, where she earned an MFA at the Iowa Writers' Workshop in 1963. She had planned to return to India to marry a man her father had chosen for her, but she stayed at Iowa to earn her PhD in comparative literature in 1969. She continues to write and teach at the University of California at Berkeley. She published her first novel, *The Tiger's Daughter*, in 1971. Among Mukherjee's most highly regarded works are the 1989 novel *Jasmine*, described as a modern *Jane Eyre* tale about a young Indian woman in America, and *The Middleman and Other Stories*, which won the National Book Critics Circle Award in 1988 and in which "The Management of Grief" appears. In June 1985, an Air India flight left Toronto on its way to Bombay (now Mumbai), with a scheduled stop in London. A bomb exploded on board and sent the plane into the Irish Sea, killing all 329 passengers. It is believed to have been a terrorist attack by Sikh separatists fighting for a Sikh homeland in the Punjab region of India. This story takes place in the aftermath of the tragedy.

A woman I don't know is boiling tea the Indian way in my kitchen. There are a lot of women I don't know in my kitchen, whispering and moving tactfully. They open doors, rummage through the pantry, and try not to ask me where things are kept. They remind me of when my sons were small, on Mother's Day or when

Vikram and I were tired, and they would make big, sloppy omelets. I would lie in bed pretending I didn't hear them.

Dr. Sharma, the treasurer of the Indo-Canada Society, pulls me into the hallway. He wants to know if I am worried about money. His wife, who has just come up from the basement with a tray of empty cups and glasses, scolds him. "Don't bother Mrs. Bhave with mundane details." She looks so monstrously pregnant her baby must be days overdue. I tell her she shouldn't be carrying heavy things. "Shaila," she says, smiling, "this is the fifth." Then she grabs a teenager by his shirttails. He slips his Walkman off his head. He has to be one of her four children; they have the same domed and dented foreheads. "What's the official word now?" she demands. The boy slips the headphones back on. "They're acting evasive, Ma. They're saying it could be an accident or a terrorist bomb."

All morning, the boys have been muttering, Sikh bomb, Sikh bomb. The men, not using the word, bow their heads in agreement. Mrs. Sharma touches her forehead at such a word. At least they've stopped talking about space debris and Russian lasers.

Two radios are going in the dining room. They are tuned to different stations. Someone must have brought the radios down from my boys' bedrooms. I haven't gone into their rooms since Kusum came running across the front lawn in her bathrobe. She looked so funny, I was laughing when I opened the door.

The big TV in the den is being whizzed through American networks and cable   5
channels.

"Damn!" some man swears bitterly. "How can these preachers carry on like nothing's happened?" I want to tell him we're not that important. You look at the audience, and at the preacher in his blue robe with his beautiful white hair, the potted palm trees under a blue sky, and you know they care about nothing.

The phone rings and rings. Dr. Sharma's taken charge. "We're with her," he keeps saying. "Yes, yes, the doctor has given calming pills. Yes, yes, pills are having necessary effect." I wonder if pills alone explain this calm. Not peace, just a deadening quiet. I was always controlled, but never repressed. Sound can reach me, but my body is tensed, ready to scream. I hear their voices all around me. I hear my boys and Vikram cry, "Mommy, Shaila!" and their screams insulate me, like headphones.

The woman boiling water tells her story again and again. "I got the news first. My cousin called from Halifax before six A.M., can you imagine? He'd gotten up for prayers and his son was studying for medical exams and heard on a rock channel that something had happened to a plane. They said first it had disappeared from the radar, like a giant eraser just reached out. His father called me, so I said to him, what do you mean, 'something bad'? You mean a hijacking? And he said, *Behn*,[1] there is no confirmation of anything yet, but check with your neighbors because a lot of them must be on that plane. So I called poor Kusum straight-away. I knew Kusum's husband and daughter were booked to go yesterday."

---

[1] No.—EDS.

Kusum lives across the street from me. She and Satish had moved in less than a month ago. They said they needed a bigger place. All these people, the Sharmas and friends from the Indo-Canada Society, had been there for the housewarming. Satish and Kusum made tandoori on their big gas grill and even the white neighbors piled their plates high with that luridly red, charred, juicy chicken. Their younger daughter had danced, and even our boys had broken away from the Stanley Cup telecast to put in a reluctant appearance. Everyone took pictures for their albums and for the community newspapers—another of our families had made it big in Toronto—and now I wonder how many of those happy faces are gone. "Why does God give us so much if all along He intends to take it away?" Kusum asks me.

I nod. We sit on carpeted stairs, holding hands like children. "I never once told   10
him that I loved him," I say. I was too much the well-brought-up woman. I was so well brought up I never felt comfortable calling my husband by his first name.

"It's all right," Kusum says. "He knew. My husband knew. They felt it. Modern young girls have to say it because what they feel is fake."

Kusum's daughter Pam runs in with an overnight case. Pam's in her McDonald's uniform. "Mummy! You have to get dressed!" Panic makes her cranky. "A reporter's on his way here."

"Why?"

"You want to talk to him in your bathrobe?" She starts to brush her mother's long hair. She's the daughter who's always in trouble. She dates Canadian boys and hangs out in the mall, shopping for tight sweaters. The younger one, the goody-goody one according to Pam, the one with a voice so sweet that when she sang *bhajans*[2] for Ethiopian relief even a frugal man like my husband wrote out a hundred-dollar check, *she* was on that plane. *She* was going to spend July and August with grandparents because Pam wouldn't go. Pam said she'd rather waitress at McDonald's. "If it's a choice between Bombay and Wonderland, I'm picking Wonderland," she'd said.

"Leave me alone," Kusum yells. "You know what I want to do? If I didn't have to   15
look after you now, I'd hang myself."

Pam's young face goes blotchy with pain. "Thanks," she says, "don't let me stop you."

"Hush," pregnant Mrs. Sharma scolds Pam. "Leave your mother alone. Mr. Sharma will tackle the reporters and fill out the forms. He'll say what has to be said."

Pam stands her ground. "You think I don't knosw what Mummy's thinking? *Why her?* That's what. That's sick! Mummy wishes my little sister were alive and I were dead."

Kusum's hand in mine is trembly hot. We continue to sit on the stairs.

She calls before she arrives, wondering if there's anything I need. Her   20
name is Judith Templeton and she's an appointee of the provincial government. "Multiculturalism?" I ask, and she says "partially," but that her mandate is bigger. "I've been told you knew many of the people on the flight," she says. "Perhaps if you'd agree to help us reach the others . . . ?"

---

[2]Hymns.—EDS.

She gives me time at least to put on tea water and pick up the mess in the front room. I have a few *samosas*[3] from Kusum's housewarming that I could fry up, but then I think, why prolong this visit?

Judith Templeton is much younger than she sounded. She wears a blue suit with a white blouse and a polka-dot tie. Her blond hair is cut short, her only jewelry is pearl-drop earrings. Her briefcase is new and expensive looking, a gleaming cordovan leather. She sits with it across her lap. When she looks out the front windows onto the street, her contact lenses seem to float in front of her light blue eyes.

"What sort of help do you want from me?" I ask. She has refused the tea, out of politeness, but I insist, along with some slightly stale biscuits.

"I have no experience," she admits. "That is, I have an M.S.W. and I've worked in liaison with accident victims, but I mean I have no experience with a tragedy of this scale—"

"Who could?" I ask.   25

"—and with the complications of culture, language, and customs. Someone mentioned that Mrs. Bhave is a pillar—because you've taken it more calmly."

At this, perhaps, I frown, for she reaches forward, almost to take my hand. "I hope you understand my meaning, Mrs. Bhave. There are hundreds of people in Metro directly affected, like you, and some of them speak no English. There are some widows who've never handled money or gone on a bus, and there are old parents who still haven't eaten or gone outside their bedrooms. Some houses and apartments have been looted. Some wives are still hysterical. Some husbands are in shock and profound depression. We want to help, but our hands are tied in so many ways. We have to distribute money to some people, and there are legal documents—these things can be done. We have interpreters, but we don't always have the human touch, or maybe the right human touch. We don't want to make mistakes, Mrs. Bhave, and that's why we'd like to ask you to help us."

"More mistakes, you mean," I say.

"Police matters are not in my hands," she answers.

"Nothing I can do will make any difference," I say. "We must all grieve in our   30
own way."

"But you are coping very well. All the people said, Mrs. Bhave is the strongest person of all. Perhaps if the others could see you, talk with you, it would help them."

"By the standards of the people you call hysterical, I am behaving very oddly and very badly, Miss Templeton." I want to say to her, *I wish I could scream, starve, walk into Lake Ontario, jump from a bridge.* "They would not see me as a model. I do not see myself as a model."

I am a freak. No one who has ever known me would think of me reacting this way. This terrible calm will not go away.

She asks me if she may call again, after I get back from a long trip that we all must make. "Of course," I say. "Feel free to call, anytime."

---

[3]Fried dumplings filled with meat or vegetables.—Eds.

Four days later, I find Kusum squatting on a rock overlooking a bay in Ireland.   35
It isn't a big rock, but it juts sharply out over water. This is as close as we'll ever get to
them. June breezes balloon out her sari and unpin her knee-length hair. She has the
bewildered look of a sea creature whom the tides have stranded.

It's been one hundred hours since Kusum came stumbling and screaming across
my lawn. Waiting around the hospital, we've heard many stories. The police, the diplomats, they tell us things thinking that we're strong, that knowledge is helpful to the
grieving, and maybe it is. Some, I know, prefer ignorance, or their own versions. The
plane broke into two, they say. Unconsciousness was instantaneous. No one suffered.
My boys must have just finished their breakfasts. They loved eating on planes, they
loved the smallness of plates, knives, and forks. Last year they saved the airline salt
and pepper shakers. Half an hour more and they would have made it to Heathrow.

Kusum says that we can't escape our fate. She says that all those people — our
husbands, my boys, her girl with the nightingale voice, all those Hindus, Christians,
Sikhs, Muslims, Parsis, and atheists on that plane — were fated to die together off this
beautiful bay. She learned this from a swami in Toronto.

I have my Valium.

Six of us "relatives" — two widows and four widowers — choose to spend the day
today by the waters instead of sitting in a hospital room and scanning photographs
of the dead. That's what they call us now: relatives. I've looked through twenty-
seven photos in two days. They're very kind to us, the Irish are very understanding.
Sometimes understanding means freeing a tourist bus for this trip to the bay, so we
can pretend to spy our loved ones through the glassiness of waves or in sun-speckled
cloud shapes.

I could die here, too, and be content.   40

"What is that, out there?" She's standing and flapping her hands, and for a
moment I see a head shape bobbing in the waves. She's standing in the water, I, on
the boulder. The tide is low, and a round, black, head-sized rock has just risen from
the waves. She returns, her sari end dripping and ruined and her face is a twisted
remnant of hope, the way mine was a hundred hours ago, still laughing but inwardly
knowing that nothing but the ultimate tragedy could bring two women together at
six o'clock on a Sunday morning. I watch her face sag into blankness.

"That water felt warm, Shaila," she says at length.

"You can't," I say. "We have to wait for our turn to come."

I haven't eaten in four days, haven't brushed my teeth.

"I know," she says. "I tell myself I have no right to grieve. They are in a bet-   45
ter place than we are. My swami says I should be thrilled for them. My swami says
depression is a sign of our selfishness."

Maybe I'm selfish. Selfishly I break away from Kusum and run, sandals slapping
against stones, to the water's edge. What if my boys aren't lying pinned under the
debris? What if they aren't stuck a mile below that innocent blue chop? What if, given
the strong currents . . .

Now I've ruined my sari, one of my best. Kusum has joined me, knee-deep
in water that feels to me like a swimming pool. I could settle in the water, and my

husband would take my hand and the boys would slap water in my face just to see me scream.

"Do you remember what good swimmers my boys were, Kusum?"

"I saw the medals," she says.

One of the widowers, Dr. Ranganathan from Montreal, walks out to us, carrying 50 his shoes in one hand. He's an electrical engineer. Someone at the hotel mentioned his work is famous around the world, something about the place where physics and electricity come together. He has lost a huge family, something indescribable. "With some good luck," Dr. Ranganathan suggests to me, "a good swimmer could make it safely to some island. It is quite possible that there may be many, many microscopic islets scattered around."

"You're not just saying that?" I tell Dr. Ranganathan about Vinod, my elder son. Last year he took diving as well.

"It's a parent's duty to hope," he says. "It is foolish to rule out possibilities that have not been tested. I myself have not surrendered hope."

Kusum is sobbing once again. "Dear lady," he says, laying his free hand on her arm, and she calms down.

"Vinod is how old?" he asks me. He's very careful, as we all are. *Is*, not was.

"Fourteen. Yesterday he was fourteen. His father and uncle were going to take 55 him down to the Taj and give him a big birthday party. I couldn't go with them because I couldn't get two weeks off from my stupid job in June." I process bills for a travel agent. June is a big travel month.

Dr. Ranganathan whips the pockets of his suit jacket inside out. Squashed roses, in darkening shades of pink, float on the water. He tore the roses off creepers in somebody's garden. He didn't ask anyone if he could pluck the roses, but now there's been an article about it in the local papers. When you see an Indian person, it says, please give him or her flowers.

"A strong youth of fourteen," he says, "can very likely pull to safety a younger one."

My sons, though four years apart, were very close. Vinod wouldn't let Mithun drown. *Electrical engineering*, I think, foolishly perhaps: this man knows important secrets of the universe, things closed to me. Relief spins me lightheaded. No wonder my boys' photographs haven't turned up in the gallery of photos of the recovered dead. "Such pretty roses," I say.

"My wife loved pink roses. Every Friday I had to bring a bunch home. I used to say, Why? After twenty-odd years of marriage you're still needing proof positive of my love?" He has identified his wife and three of his children. Then others from Montreal, the lucky ones, intact families with no survivors. He chuckles as he wades back to shore. Then he swings around to ask me a question. "Mrs. Bhave, you are wanting to throw in some roses for your loved ones? I have two big ones left."

But I have other things to float: Vinod's pocket calculator; a half-painted model 60 B-52 for my Mithun. They'd want them on their island. And for my husband? For him I let fall into the calm, glassy waters a poem I wrote in the hospital yesterday. Finally he'll know my feelings for him.

"Don't tumble, the rocks are slippery," Dr. Ranganathan cautions. He holds out a hand for me to grab.

Then it's time to get back on the bus, time to rush back to our waiting posts on hospital benches.

Kusum is one of the lucky ones. The lucky ones flew here, identified in multiplicate their loved ones, then will fly to India with the bodies for proper ceremonies. Satish is one of the few males who surfaced. The photos of faces we saw on the walls in an office at Heathrow and here in the hospital are mostly of women. Women have more body fat, a nun said to me matter-of-factly. They float better.

Today I was stopped by a young sailor on the street. He had loaded bodies, he'd gone into the water when—he checks my face for signs of strength—when the sharks were first spotted. I don't blush, and he breaks down. "It's all right," I say. "Thank you." I heard about the sharks from Dr. Ranganathan. In his orderly mind, science brings understanding, it holds no terror. It is the shark's duty. For every deer there is a hunter, for every fish a fisherman.

The Irish are not shy; they rush to me and give me hugs and some are crying. I cannot imagine reactions like that on the streets of Toronto. Just strangers, and I am touched. Some carry flowers with them and give them to any Indian they see. | 65

After lunch, a policeman I have gotten to know quite well catches hold of me. He says he thinks he has a match for Vinod. I explain what a good swimmer Vinod is.

"You want me with you when you look at photos?" Dr. Ranganathan walks ahead of me into the picture gallery. In these matters, he is a scientist, and I am grateful. It is a new perspective. "They have performed miracles," he says. "We are indebted to them."

The first day or two the policemen showed us relatives only one picture at a time; now they're in a hurry, they're eager to lay out the possibles, and even the probables.

The face on the photo is of a boy much like Vinod; the same intelligent eyes, the same thick brows dipping into a V. But this boy's features, even his cheeks, are puffier, wider, mushier.

"No." My gaze is pulled by other pictures. There are five other boys who look like Vinod. | 70

The nun assigned to console me rubs the first picture with a fingertip. "When they've been in the water for a while, love, they look a little heavier." The bones under the skin are broken, they said on the first day—try to adjust your memories. It's important.

"It's not him. I'm his mother. I'd know."

"I know this one!" Dr. Ranganathan cries out, and suddenly from the back of the gallery. "And this one!" I think he senses that I don't want to find my boys. "They are the Kutty brothers. They were also from Montreal." I don't mean to be crying. On the contrary, I am ecstatic. My suitcase in the hotel is packed heavy with dry clothes for my boys.

The policeman starts to cry. "I am so sorry, I am so sorry, ma'am. I really thought we had a match."

With the nun ahead of us and the policeman behind, we, the unlucky ones with-   75
out our children's bodies, file out of the makeshift gallery.

From Ireland most of us go on to India. Kusum and I take the same direct flight
to Bombay, so I can help her clear customs quickly. But we have to argue with a man
in uniform. He has large boils on his face. The boils swell and glow with sweat as
we argue with him. He wants Kusum to wait in line and he refuses to take authority
because his boss is on a tea break. But Kusum won't let her coffins out of sight, and I
shan't desert her though I know that my parents, elderly and diabetic, must be waiting in a stuffy car in a scorching lot.

"You bastard!" I scream at the man with the popping boils. Other passengers
press closer. "You think we're smuggling contraband in those coffins!"

Once upon a time we were well-brought-up women; we were dutiful wives who
kept our heads veiled, our voices shy and sweet.

In India, I become, once again, an only child of rich, ailing parents. Old friends
of the family come to pay their respects. Some are Sikh, and inwardly, involuntarily,
I cringe. My parents are progressive people; they do not blame communities for a
few individuals.

In Canada it is a different story now.   80

"Stay longer," my mother pleads. "Canada is a cold place. Why would you want
to be all by yourself?" I stay.

Three months pass. Then another.

"Vikram wouldn't have wanted you to give up things!" they protest. They call my
husband by the name he was born with. In Toronto he'd changed to Vik so the men
he worked with at his office would find his name as easy as Rod or Chris. "You know,
the dead aren't cut off from us!"

My grandmother, the spoiled daughter of a rich zamindar,[4] shaved her head with
rusty razor blades when she was widowed at sixteen. My grandfather died of childhood diabetes when he was nineteen, and she saw herself as the harbinger of bad
luck. My mother grew up without parents, raised indifferently by an uncle, while her
true mother slept in a hut behind the main estate house and took her food with the
servants. She grew up a rationalist. My parents abhor mindless mortification.

The zamindar's daughter kept stubborn faith in Vedic rituals; my parents   85
rebelled. I am trapped between two modes of knowledge. At thirty-six, I am too old
to start over and too young to give up. Like my husband's spirit, I flutter between
worlds.

Courting aphasia, we travel. We travel with our phalanx of servants and poor
relatives. To hill stations and to beach resorts. We play contract bridge in dusty gym-
khana clubs. We ride stubby ponies up crumbly mountain trails. At tea dances, we let

---

[4]Landowner. — EDS.

ourselves be twirled twice round the ballroom. We hit the holy spots we hadn't made time for before. In Varanasi, Kalighat, Rishikesh, Hardwar, astrologers and palmists seek me out and for a fee offer me cosmic consolations.

Already the widowers among us are being shown new bride candidates. They cannot resist the call of custom, the authority of their parents and older brothers. They must marry; it is the duty of a man to look after a wife. The new wives will be young widows with children, destitute but of good family. They will make loving wives, but the men will shun them. I've had calls from the men over crackling Indian telephone lines. "Save me," they say, these substantial, educated, successful men of forty. "My parents are arranging a marriage for me." In a month they will have buried one family and returned to Canada with a new bride and partial family.

I am comparatively lucky. No one here thinks of arranging a husband for an unlucky widow.

Then, on the third day of the sixth month into this odyssey, in an abandoned temple in a tiny Himalayan village, as I make my offering of flowers and sweetmeats to the god of a tribe of animists, my husband descends to me. He is squatting next to a scrawny sadhu[5] in moth-eaten robes. Vikram wears the vanilla suit he wore the last time I hugged him. The sadhu tosses petals on a butter-fed flame, reciting Sanskrit mantras, and sweeps his face of flies. My husband takes my hands in his.

You're beautiful, he starts. Then, *What are you doing here?*   90

Shall I stay? I ask. He only smiles, but already the image is fading. *You must finish alone what we started together.* No seaweed wreathes his mouth. He speaks too fast, just as he used to when we were an envied family in our pink split-level. He is gone.

In the windowless altar room, smoky with joss sticks and clarified butter lamps, a sweaty hand gropes for my blouse. I do not shriek. The sadhu arranges his robe. The lamps hiss and sputter out.

When we come out of the temple, my mother says, "Did you feel something weird in there?"

My mother has no patience with ghosts, prophetic dreams, holy men, and cults.

"No," I lie. "Nothing."   95

But she knows that she's lost me. She knows that in days I shall be leaving.

· · ·

Kusum's put up her house for sale. She wants to live in an ashram in Hardwar. Moving to Hardwar was her swami's idea. Her swami runs two ashrams, the one in Hardwar and another here in Toronto.

"Don't run away," I tell her.

"I'm not running away," she says. "I'm pursuing inner peace. You think you or that Ranganathan fellow are better off?"

---

[5]Hindu ascetic dedicated to achieving liberation from human existence through intense meditation and yoga. In India they are considered legally dead. — EDS.

Pam's left for California. She wants to do some modeling, she says. She says when   100
she comes into her share of the insurance money she'll open a yoga-cum-aerobics
studio in Hollywood. She sends me postcards so naughty I daren't leave them on the
coffee table. Her mother has withdrawn from her and the world.

The rest of us don't lose touch, that's the point. Talk is all we have, says
Dr. Ranganathan, who has also resisted his relatives and returned to Montreal and
to his job, alone. He says, Whom better to talk with than other relatives? We've been
melted down and recast as a new tribe.

He calls me twice a week from Montreal. Every Wednesday night and every
Saturday afternoon. He is changing jobs, going to Ottawa. But Ottawa is over a
hundred miles away, and he is forced to drive two hundred and twenty miles a day
from his home in Montreal. He can't bring himself to sell his house. The house is a
temple, he says; the king-sized bed in the master bedroom is a shrine. He sleeps on
a folding cot. A devotee.

There are still some hysterical relatives. Judith Templeton's list of those needing
help and those who've "accepted" is in nearly perfect balance. Acceptance means you
speak of your family in the past tense and you make active plans for moving ahead
with your life. There are courses at Seneca and Ryerson we could be taking. Her
gleaming leather briefcase is full of college catalogues and lists of cultural societies
that need our help. She has done impressive work, I tell her.

"In the textbooks on grief management," she replies—I am her confidante, I
realize, one of the few whose grief has not sprung bizarre obsessions—"there are
stages to pass through: rejection, depression, acceptance, reconstruction." She has
compiled a chart and finds that six months after the tragedy, none of us still rejects
reality, but only a handful are reconstructing. "Depressed acceptance" is the plateau
we've reached. Remarriage is a major step in reconstruction (though she's a little surprised, even shocked, over *how* quickly some of the men have taken on new families).
Selling one's house and changing jobs and cities is healthy.

How to tell Judith Templeton that my family surrounds me, and that like crea-   105
tures in epics, they've changed shapes? She sees me as calm and accepting but worries
that I have no job, no career. My closest friends are worse off than I. I cannot tell her
my days, even my nights, are thrilling.

She asks me to help with families she can't reach at all. An elderly couple in
Agincourt whose sons were killed just weeks after they had brought their parents over
from a village in Punjab. From their names, I know they are Sikh. Judith Templeton
and a translator have visited them twice with offers of money for airfare to Ireland,
with bank forms, power-of-attorney forms, but they have refused to sign, or to leave
their tiny apartment. Their sons' money is frozen in the bank. Their sons' investment
apartments have been trashed by tenants, the furnishings sold off. The parents fear
that anything they sign or any money they receive will end the company's or the
country's obligations to them. They fear they are selling their sons for two airline
tickets to a place they've never seen.

The high-rise apartment is a tower of Indians and West Indians, with a sprinkling of Orientals. The nearest bus-stop kiosk is lined with women in saris. Boys

practice cricket in the parking lot. Inside the building, even I wince a bit from the ferocity of onion fumes, the distinctive and immediate Indianness of frying ghee,[6] but Judith Templeton maintains a steady flow of information. These poor old people are in imminent danger of losing their place and all their services.

I say to her, "They are Sikh. They will not open up to a Hindu woman." And what I want to add is, as much as I try not to, I stiffen now at the sight of beards and turbans. I remember a time when we all trusted each other in this new country, it was only the new country we worried about.

The two rooms are dark and stuffy. The lights are off, and an oil lamp sputters on the coffee table. The bent old lady has let us in, and her husband is wrapping a white turban over his oiled, hip-length hair. She immediately goes to the kitchen, and I hear the most familiar sound of an Indian home, tap water hitting and filling a teapot.

They have not paid their utility bills, out of fear and inability to write a check. The telephone is gone, electricity and gas and water are soon to follow. They have told Judith their sons will provide. They are good boys, and they have always earned and looked after their parents.   110

We converse a bit in Hindi. They do not ask about the crash and I wonder if I should bring it up. If they think I am here merely as a translator, then they may feel insulted. There are thousands of Punjabi speakers, Sikhs, in Toronto to do a better job. And so I say to the old lady, "I too have lost my sons, and my husband, in the crash."

Her eyes immediately fill with tears. The man mutters a few words which sound like a blessing. "God provides and God takes away," he says.

I want to say, But only men destroy and give back nothing. "My boys and my husband are not coming back," I say. "We have to understand that."

Now the old woman responds. "But who is to say? Man alone does not decide these things." To this her husband adds his agreement.

Judith asks about the bank papers, the release forms. With a stroke of the pen, they will have a provincial trustee to pay their bills, invest their money, send them a monthly pension.   115

"Do you know this woman?" I ask them.

The man raises his hand from the table, turns it over, and seems to regard each finger separately before he answers. "This young lady is always coming here, we make tea for her, and she leaves papers for us to sign." His eyes scan a pile of papers in the corner of the room. "Soon we will be out of tea, then will she go away?"

The old lady adds, "I have asked my neighbors and no one else gets *angrezi*[7] visitors. What have we done?"

"It's her job," I try to explain. "The government is worried. Soon you will have no place to stay, no lights, no gas, no water."

"Government will get its money. Tell her not to worry, we are honorable people."   120

---

[6]Clarified butter. — EDS.
[7]English (Anglo). — EDS.

I try to explain the government wishes to give money, not take. He raises his hand. "Let them take," he says. "We are accustomed to that. That is no problem."

"We are strong people," says the wife. "Tell her that."

"Who needs all this machinery?" demands the husband. "It is unhealthy, the bright lights, the cold air on a hot day, the cold food, the four gas rings. God will provide, not government."

"When our boys return," the mother says.

Her husband sucks his teeth. "Enough talk," he says.   125

Judith breaks in. "Have you convinced them?" The snaps on her cordovan brief-case go off like firecrackers in that quiet apartment. She lays the sheaf of legal papers on the coffee table. "If they can't write their names, an X will do—I've told them that."

Now the old lady has shuffled to the kitchen and soon emerges with a pot of tea and two cups. "I think my bladder will go first on a job like this," Judith says to me, smiling. "If only there was some way of reaching them. Please thank her for the tea. Tell her she's very kind."

I nod in Judith's direction and tell them in Hindi, "She thanks you for the tea. She thinks you are being very hospitable but she doesn't have the slightest idea what it means."

I want to say, Humor her. I want to say, My boys and my husband are with me too, more than ever. I look in the old man's eyes and I can read his stubborn, peasant's message: *I have protected this woman as best I can. She is the only person I have left. Give to me or take from me what you will, but I will not sign for it. I will not pretend that I accept.*

In the car, Judith says, "You see what I'm up against? I'm sure they're lovely   130
people, but their stubbornness and ignorance are driving me crazy. They think sign-ing a paper is signing their sons' death warrants, don't they?"

I am looking out the window. I want to say, *In our culture, it is a parent's duty to hope.*

"Now Shaila, this next woman is a real mess. She cries day and night, and she refuses all medical help. We may have to—"

"Let me out at the subway," I say.

"I beg your pardon?" I can feel those blue eyes staring at me.

It would not be like her to disobey. She merely disapproves, and slows at a corner   135
to let me out. Her voice is plaintive. "Is there anything I said? Anything I did?"

I could answer her suddenly in a dozen ways, but I choose not to. "Shaila? Let's talk about it," I hear, then slam the door.

A wife and mother begins her life in a new country, and that life is cut short. Yet her husband tells her: Complete what we have started. We, who stayed out of politics and came half way around the world to avoid religious and political feuding, have been the first in the New World to die from it. I no longer know what we started, nor how to complete it. I write letters to the editors of local papers and to members of Parliament. Now at least they admit it was a bomb. One MP answers back, with sympathy, but with a challenge. You want to make a difference? Work on a campaign. Work on mine. Politicize the Indian voter.

My husband's old lawyer helps me set up a trust. Vikram was a saver and a careful investor. He had saved the boys' boarding school and college fees. I sell the pink house at four times what we paid for it and take a small apartment downtown. I am looking for a charity to support.

We are deep in the Toronto winter, gray skies, icy pavements. I stay indoors, watching television. I have tried to assess my situation, how best to live my life, to complete what we began so many years ago. Kusum has written me from Hardwar that her life is now serene. She has seen Satish and has heard her daughter sing again. Kusum was on a pilgrimage, passing through a village, when she heard a young girl's voice, singing one of her daughter's favorite *bhajans*. She followed the music through the squalor of a Himalayan village, to a hut where a young girl, an exact replica of her daughter, was fanning coals under the kitchen fire. When she appeared, the girl cried out, "Ma!" and ran away. What did I think of that?

I think I can only envy her. 140

Pam didn't make it to California, but writes me from Vancouver. She works in a department store, giving makeup hints to Indian and Oriental girls. Dr. Ranganathan has given up his commute, given up his house and job, and accepted an academic position in Texas, where no one knows his story and he has vowed not to tell it. He calls me now once a week.

I wait, I listen and I pray, but Vikram has not returned to me. The voices and the shapes and the nights filled with visions ended abruptly several weeks ago.

I take it as a sign.

One rare, beautiful, sunny day last week, returning from a small errand on Yonge Street, I was walking through the park from the subway to my apartment. I live equidistant from the Ontario Houses of Parliament and the University of Toronto. The day was not cold, but something in the bare trees caught my attention. I looked up from the gravel, into the branches and the clear blue sky beyond. I thought I heard the rustling of larger forms, and I waited a moment for voices. Nothing.

"What?" I asked. 145

Then as I stood in the path looking north to Queen's Park and west to the university, I heard the voices of my family one last time. *Your time has come*, they said. *Go, be brave.*

I do not know where this voyage I have begun will end. I do not know which direction I will take. I dropped the package on a park bench and started walking.

[1988]

. . . .

Exploring the Text

1. What information do you learn in the opening three paragraphs? How do they set up a sense of foreboding? Why do you think Mukherjee chose not to open the story with a more traditional exposition?

2. What evidence do you see that indicates a clash in cultural attitudes and values? How does the relationship between Kusum and Pam illustrate cultural differences at the beginning of the story?

3. How is Judith Templeton depicted? Does Mukherjee want us to see her as being totally insensitive? How does Shaila's attitude toward Judith change during the course of the story? Pay special attention to Judith's characterization of the elderly Sikh couple as "lovely people" motivated by "stubbornness and ignorance" (para. 130).

4. What elements of irony do you find in this story? What purpose do they serve? For instance, consider the irony in paragraph 55 when Shaila reveals the reason she stayed home, and in paragraph 59 when she talks about "the lucky ones." What does Shaila's ironic tone say about her?

5. What does Shaila mean when she says, "I am trapped between two modes of knowledge" (para. 85)? What are these modes of knowledge, and which one does she ultimately choose?

6. In paragraph 103, the narrator says, "Acceptance means you speak of your family in the past tense and you make active plans for moving ahead with your life." Does she agree with that definition? What is the narrator's tone in that remark? Explain what evidence in the text leads you to your conclusion.

7. In paragraph 105, Shaila says, "my family surrounds me," and in paragraph 129, she says, "my boys and my husband are with me too, more than ever." What do these remarks suggest about Shaila's grief?

8. Regarding Kusum, why does Shaila say, "I think I can only envy her" (para. 140)? What is it about Kusum that Shaila says she envies? Do you believe her? Why or why not?

9. Describe the differences between Kusum's and Shaila's reactions to the loss of their families, and the ways they manage their grief. What is the significance of Shaila's saying "I have my Valium" in response to paragraph 38 and "Maybe I'm selfish" in response to paragraph 46? What does Shaila mean when she distinguishes between "peace" and "a deadening quiet" (para. 7)? By the end of the story, how well has Shaila done with "the management of grief"?

10. How does the story end? Is Shaila honoring or betraying her belief that "it is a parent's duty to hope" (para. 131)?

The Champion Arms for Battle

From Book 19 of the *Iliad*

HOMER

TRANSLATED BY ROBERT FAGLES

Although little is known about Homer, he is thought to have lived in the ninth century B.C.E., and at least seven cities in Greece claim to be his birthplace. Scholars disagree on whether Homer actually composed the *Iliad* and its sequel, the *Odyssey*, but there is general consensus that both epics are the work of a single author, and we attribute both to him. One of the first and most influential literary works in the Western world, the *Iliad* consists of twenty-four books of verse, capturing stories and

legends that had been circulating orally for hundreds of years prior. It tells the tale of
the last part of the Trojan War, which was prompted by Paris's abduction of Helen
of Troy, wife of the Achaean (Greek) king Menelaus. A key theme of the Iliad is the
all-consuming rage of the Achaean warrior Achilles after the death of his friend,
Patroclus, at the hands of Hector, the Trojan champion. The passage here, from
Book 19, presents Achilles arming for battle against the Trojan forces.

Thick-and-fast as the snow comes swirling down from Zeus,
frozen sharp when the North Wind born in heaven blasts it on—
so massed, so dense the glistening burnished helmets shone,
streaming out of the ships, and shields with jutting bosses,
breastplates welded front and back and the long ashen spears.   5
The glory of armor lit the skies and the whole earth laughed,
rippling under the glitter of bronze, thunder resounding
under trampling feet of armies. And in their midst
the brilliant Achilles began to arm for battle . . .
A sound of grinding came from the fighter's teeth,   10
his eyes blazed forth in searing points of fire,
unbearable grief came surging through his heart
and now, bursting with rage against the men of Troy,
he donned Hephaestus' gifts—magnificent armor
the god of fire forged with all his labor.   15
First he wrapped his legs with well-made greaves,
fastened behind his heels with silver ankle-clasps,
next he strapped the breastplate round his chest
then over his shoulder Achilles slung his sword,
the fine bronze blade with its silver-studded hilt,   20
then hoisted the massive shield flashing far and wide
like a full round moon—and gleaming bright as the light
that reaches sailors out at sea, the flare of a watchfire
burning strong in a lonely sheepfold up some mountain slope
when the gale-winds hurl the crew that fights against them   25
far over the fish-swarming sea, far from loved ones—
so the gleam from Achilles' well-wrought blazoned shield
shot up and hit the skies. Then lifting his rugged helmet
he set it down on his brows, and the horsehair crest
shone like a star and the waving golden plumes shook   30
that Hephaestus drove in bristling thick along its ridge.
And brilliant Achilles tested himself in all his gear,
Achilles spun on his heels to see if it fitted tightly,
see if his shining limbs ran free within it, yes,
and it felt like buoyant wings lifting the great captain.   35
And then, last, Achilles drew his father's spear
from its socket-stand—weighted, heavy, tough.

No other Achaean fighter could heft that shaft,
only Achilles had the skill to wield it well:
Pelian ash it was, a gift to his father Peleus   40
presented by Chiron once, hewn on Pelion's crest
to be the death of heroes.

[*c. 700* B.C.E.]

Exploring the Text

1. How is Achilles described? Why do you suppose Homer devotes such careful attention to small details? Do you think Achilles epitomizes the ideal warrior?
2. Discuss the effect of the two analogies in lines 1–5 and 22–28. What are they comparing? How do they characterize Achilles?
3. This short passage is rich in figurative language such as metaphor, simile, and personification. Identify at least one example of each. How does each instance of figurative language contribute to the tone of the work? How would you describe that tone?
4. What attitude toward war and warriors is revealed in the passage?
5. Write a description in verse of a modern-day warrior arming for battle in Afghanistan or Iraq. Research and include details that parallel Homer's description of Achilles. What thoughts on the warrior and on war does your description elicit?

"If we are marked to die . . ."

From *Henry V,* Act IV, scene iii

WILLIAM SHAKESPEARE

William Shakespeare (1554–1616) was born in Stratford-upon-Avon, England. Little is known of his life aside from the fact that he married Anne Hathaway when he was eighteen, worked as an actor-playwright in London, and retired in 1613. His plays fall into four principal categories: early comedies (1585–1594); more sophisticated comedies and histories (1595–1599); the great tragedies (1599–1607); and the final phase (1608–1613). His most accomplished works—including *Hamlet* (1601), *Othello* (1603), *King Lear* (1605), and *Macbeth* (1606)—belong to the third period. In his time, his contemporaries—and likely Shakespeare himself—looked to his sonnets and other poems as the more important works. The 154 sonnets were written at various stages in Shakespeare's life, but when and to whom they were written remains unclear. Wordsworth believed that only through the sonnets could one understand Shakespeare. The following selection, commonly known as the "St. Crispian's Day Speech," is from *Henry V* and presents King Henry's address at the field of Agincourt, scene of the famous victory of the English over a much larger French army in the Hundred Years' War.

If we are marked to die, we are enough
To do our country loss; and if to live,
The fewer men, the greater share of honour.
God's will, I pray thee wish not one man more.
By Jove, I am not covetous for gold,   5
Nor care I who doth feed upon my cost;
It ernes me not if men my garments wear;
Such outward things dwell not in my desires.
But if it be a sin to covet honour
I am the most offending soul alive.   10
No, faith, my coz, wish not a man from England.
God's peace, I would not lose so great an honour
As one man more methinks would share from me
For the best hope I have. O do not wish one more.
Rather proclaim it presently through my host   15
That he which hath no stomach to this fight,
Let him depart. His passport shall be made
And crowns for convoy put into his purse.
We would not die in that man's company
That fears his fellowship to die with us.   20
This day is called the Feast of Crispian.
He that outlives this day and comes safe home
Will stand a-tiptoe when this day is named
And rouse him at the name of Crispian.
He that shall see this day and live t'old age   25
Will yearly on the vigil feast his neighbours
And say, 'Tomorrow is Saint Crispian.'
Then will he strip his sleeve and show his scars
And say, 'These wounds I had on Crispin's day.'
Old men forget; yet all shall be forgot,   30
But he'll remember, with advantages,
What feats he did that day. Then shall our names,
Familiar in his mouth as household words—
Harry the King, Bedford and Exeter,
Warwick and Talbot, Salisbury and Gloucester—   35
Be in their flowing cups freshly remembered.
This story shall the good man teach his son,
And Crispin Crispian shall ne'er go by
From this day to the ending of the world
But we in it shall be remembered,   40
We few, we happy few, we band of brothers.
For he today that sheds his blood with me
Shall be my brother; be he ne'er so vile,
This day shall gentle his condition;

And gentlemen in England now abed   45
Shall think themselves accursed they were not here;
And hold their manhoods cheap whiles any speaks
That fought with us upon Saint Crispin's day.

[c. 1600]

Exploring the Text

1. What words would you use to describe the tone of this passage from *Henry V*? What is the speaker's attitude toward his audience? Cite specific words and lines to support your response.
2. The speaker says that he esteems "honour" above all else. Based on what he says and on the examples he offers, consider how the speaker would define *honour*. In a full sentence, how would his definition read?
3. This speech includes many examples of inverted syntax, such as line 37, which reads, "This story shall the good man teach his son" instead of "The good man shall teach his son this story." Take three other examples—for instance, lines 7, 36, and 40—and rewrite each line in normal order, beginning with the subject, followed by the verb and then the object. How does the inverted syntax of each sentence affect its tone? How does it change the rhythm and meter of the lines? Why would inverted syntax be appropriate for this passage?
4. Notice the word "gentle" (an adjective used as a verb) in line 44. In the context of lines 37–44, what does it mean?
5. How does the speaker use references to money and quantifiable rewards throughout the poem to convey his own values?
6. What does this speech say about memory and the legacy of war for the warrior?
7. This passage is widely regarded as one of the most inspirational speeches in all of English literature. What accounts for its success in inspiring people through so many generations? What particular parts of the speech do you find inspirational beyond the battlefield?

The Battle of Blenheim

ROBERT SOUTHEY

Robert Southey (1774–1843) was born in Bristol, England. He began writing poetry at the age of nine, and by the time he was fifteen, he had written three cantos as a continuation of Spenser's *Faerie Queene*. Early on, he revealed an unusual independence of mind and behavior. Expelled from the Westminster School for criticizing its policy on corporal punishment, he later attended Oxford but did not graduate. A contemporary of Wordsworth and Coleridge, he wrote romantic verse and was poet laureate of England from 1813 until his death. Southey is chiefly remembered for two poems: "The Inchcape Rock"—a romantic narrative poem—and "The Battle of Blenheim," included here. A major victory for the Duke of Marlborough and a turning point in the War of the Spanish Succession, the battle took place in 1704 in the small village of Blenheim, Bavaria (now Blindheim, Germany).

It was a summer evening,
   Old Kaspar's work was done;
And he before his cottage door
   Was sitting in the sun,
And by him sported on the green   5
His little grandchild Wilhelmine.

She saw her brother Peterkin
   Roll something large and round,
That he beside the rivulet,
   In playing there, had found;   10
He came to ask what he had found,
That was so large, and smooth, and round.

Old Kaspar took it from the boy,
   Who stood expectant by;
And then the old man shook his head,   15
   And with a natural sigh,
'Tis some poor fellow's skull, said he,
Who fell in the great victory.

I find them in the garden, for
   There's many here about,
And often when I go to plough   20
   The ploughshare turns them out;
For many thousand men, said he,
Were slain in the great victory.

Now tell us what 'twas all about,   25
   Young Peterkin he cries,
And little Wilhelmine looks up
   With wonder-waiting eyes;
Now tell us all about the war,
And what they kill'd each other for.   30

It was the English, Kaspar cried,
   That put the French to rout;
But what they kill'd each other for,
   I could not well make out.
But everybody said, quoth he,   35
That 'twas a famous victory.

My father lived at Blenheim then,
   Yon little stream hard by;
They burnt his dwelling to the ground,
   And he was forced to fly: 40
So with his wife and child he fled,
Nor had he where to rest his head.

With fire and sword the country round
   Was wasted far and wide,
And many a childing mother then,   45
   And new-born infant, died.
But things like that, you know, must be
At every famous victory.

They say it was a shocking sight,
   After the field was won,   50
For many thousand bodies here
   Lay rotting in the sun;
But things like that, you know, must be
After a famous victory.

Great praise the Duke of Marlbro' won,   55
   And our good Prince Eugene.—
Why, 'twas a very wicked thing!
   Said little Wilhelmine.—
Nay—nay—my little girl, quoth he,
It was a famous victory.   60

And everybody praised the Duke
   Who such a fight did win.—
But what good came of it at last?
   Quoth little Peterkin.—
Why that I cannot tell, said he,   65
But 'twas a famous victory.

[1796]

Exploring the Text

1. Read the poem aloud, listening to the sound of the lines and stanzas. To what extent do you find the rhyme and rhythm fitting for Southey's subject? Explain.
2. Note the inverted syntax in the first stanza. Rewrite the lines in normal order, and then compare your versions with the originals. How do the inversions affect the rhythm and meter of the poem? How do they contribute to the poem? Do the same for another stanza of the poem.
3. How would you characterize Southey's attitude toward Kaspar? How does this attitude contribute to the overall tone of the poem?

4. Consider Wilhelmine's and Peterkin's remarks in stanzas 5, 10, and 11. Are they childish? Are they reasonable? Why does Southey deliver these statements in the voices of children?
5. To what effect does Southey use repetition of the final line in multiple stanzas?

Vigil strange I kept on the field one night

WALT WHITMAN

Walt Whitman (1819–1892) was born on Long Island, New York. Early in his life, he worked as a country schoolteacher and printer, and served as writer and editor for the *Brooklyn Eagle* newspaper. He continued in a variety of jobs, writing and working as a carpenter, and published his now famous *Leaves of Grass* in 1855. Regarded as offensive and vulgar at the time for its outspoken content, the poem celebrated individuality and the richness of life. In 1862, Whitman went to Virginia to find his brother George, who had been wounded in the Civil War. He was shocked to witness the horrors of war firsthand and was deeply moved by the suffering of the wounded. He worked as an aide in army hospitals in Washington, caring first for his brother and then other soldiers as well. Among Whitman's most well-known poems from this time are "Oh Captain, My Captain" and "When Lilacs Last in the Dooryard Bloom'd," both about Abraham Lincoln. The poem included here was inspired by Whitman's war experience.

Vigil strange I kept on the field one night;
When you my son and my comrade dropt at my side that day,
One look I but gave which your dear eyes return'd with a look I shall never forget,
One touch of your hand to mine O boy, reach'd up as you lay on the ground,
Then onward I sped in the battle, the even-contested battle,   5
Till late in the night reliev'd to the place at last again I made my way,
Found you in death so cold dear comrade, found your body son of responding
    kisses, (never again on earth responding,)
Bared your face in the starlight, curious the scene, cool blew the moderate
    night-wind,
Long there and then in vigil I stood, dimly around me the battle-field spreading,
Vigil wondrous and vigil sweet there in the fragrant silent night,   10
But not a tear fell, not even a long-drawn sigh, long, long I gazed,
Then on the earth partially reclining sat by your side leaning my chin in my hands,
Passing sweet hours, immortal and mystic hours with you dearest comrade—not
    a tear, not a word,
Vigil of silence, love and death, vigil for you my son and my soldier,
As onward silently stars aloft, eastward new ones upward stole,   15
Vigil final for you brave boy, (I could not save you, swift was your death,
I faithfully loved you and cared for you living, I think we shall surely meet again,)

Till at latest lingering of the night, indeed just as the dawn appear'd,
My comrade I wrapt in his blanket, envelop'd well his form,
Folded the blanket well, tucking it carefully over head and carefully under feet,   20
And there and then and bathed by the rising sun, my son in his grave, in his
   rude-dug grave I deposited,
Ending my vigil strange with that, vigil of night and battle-field dim,
Vigil for boy of responding kisses, (never again on earth responding,)
Vigil for comrade swiftly slain, vigil I never forget, how as day brighten'd,
I rose from the chill ground and folded my soldier well in his blanket,   25
And buried him where he fell.

[1865]

. . . .

Exploring the Text

1. Notice that the poem is presented as a "vigil." What is significant about the choice of that particular word? Why is the word repeated throughout the poem? Why is it a "vigil strange" (l. 1), and why is the scene described as "curious" in line 8?
2. How would you describe the speaker of the poem? Use specific evidence from the text to support your description.
3. There is an important shift in line 19, where the "you" and "your" of line 16 become "My comrade" and "his." What is the significance of this shift in terms of the relationship of the speaker to his dying son? How does the final wrapping of his comrade in a blanket complicate this shift?
4. The careful attention to detail in this poem is reminiscent of the use of fine detail in the passage from the *Iliad* (p. 1413). How would you compare Homer's and Whitman's attitudes toward their subjects? Cite specific words and lines to support your response.

Shiloh

A Requiem (April, 1862)

HERMAN MELVILLE

Herman Melville (1819–1891), best known for his novel *Moby-Dick*, was born in New York City. By the time he was in his early twenties, he went off to sea, sailing first to Liverpool, England, then to the Marquesas Islands and other parts of the South Seas on a whaling ship. Based on his experiences, he wrote the novels *Typee* and *Omoo*, which were both published in 1847; *Redburn*, an autobiographical novel based on his first voyage, appeared in 1849. Largely self-educated, Melville read widely, especially William Shakespeare and Ralph Waldo Emerson, both of whom influenced Melville's legendary novel, *Moby-Dick* (1851). In the book, Melville's narrator, Ishmael, tells of the epic quest of Captain Ahab after the white whale. Now widely regarded as one of the greatest novels of American literature for its gripping epic adventure and its profound metaphysical journey, it was not well received in its time; nor were the later novels *Pierre; or, The Ambiguities* (1852), *The Confidence Man* (1857), or *Billy Budd* (published posthumously in 1924). Although Melville is most known for his novels, later in his life he also wrote short stories—including "Bartleby the Scrivener" (p. 854)—and poems, such as the one that follows, about the American Civil War battlefield Shiloh in southwestern Tennessee.

Skimming lightly, wheeling still,
 The swallows fly low
Over the field in clouded days,
 The forest field of Shiloh—
Over the field where April rain   5
Solaced the parched one stretched in pain
Through the pause of night
That followed the Sunday fight
 Around the church of Shiloh —
The church so lone, the log-built one,   10
That echoed to many a parting groan
  And natural prayer
 Of dying foemen mingled there—
Foemen at morn, but friends at eve—
 Fame or country least their care: 15
(What like a bullet can undeceive!)
 But now they lie low,
While over them the swallows skim,
 And all is hushed at Shiloh.

[1862]

Exploring the Text

1. Note that Melville subtitled his poem "A Requiem." How does that affect your interpretation of the poem?
2. Identify at least three images that Melville uses to describe the setting. How does the imagery contribute to the tone of the poem? How would you describe that tone?
3. Consider the juxtaposition in line 14, "Foemen at morn, but friends at eve." Look for other juxtapositions in the poem. What do these juxtapositions add to the meaning of the poem as a whole? Are they especially apt for a poem about this particular war, or could they apply to war in general? Explain.
4. How do you interpret line 16? Why did Melville write that line as a parenthetical statement? Is it a rhetorical question?

5. Listen to the poem as you read it, noticing especially the long *o* sounds in "low," "Shiloh," "followed," "lone," and so on. How do those sounds affect your reading? How do they make you feel as you read?
6. Why does Melville begin and end with the swallows? What are the implications of the final line?

Lamentations

Siegfried Sassoon

On August 2, 1914, two days before England's declaration of war, British poet Siegfried Sassoon (1886–1967) enlisted in the army and went to the front lines. Called "Mad Jack" for his reckless behavior and ferocity, Sassoon was regarded as a modern Achilles. He was wounded twice, and received two medals for bravery. While recovering from an injury in England, he became critical of the war and declined to return to duty. His 1917 letter to his commanding officer, "A Soldier's Declaration," was read to the House of Commons and published in the *London Times*. In it he stated, "I am not protesting against the conduct of the war, but against the political errors and insincerities for which the fighting men are being sacrificed. On behalf of those who are suffering now, I make this protest against the deception which is being practised upon them; also I believe it may help to destroy the callous complacency with which the majority of those at home regard the continuance of agonies which they do not share and which they have not enough imagination to realise." Deemed mentally unfit for court-martial, he was sent to the hospital to recover from shell shock and there met fellow soldier and poet Wilfred Owen, whom he encouraged to write. After the war, he taught and lectured for many years. Sassoon wrote more than twenty collections of poetry, the most famous being *Counter-Attack and Other Poems* (1918)—a small group of poems about the horrors of war, which includes "Lamentations."

I found him in the guard-room at the Base.
From the blind darkness I had heard his crying
And blundered in. With puzzled, patient face
A sergeant watched him; it was no good trying
To stop it; for he howled and beat his chest.   5
And, all because his brother had gone west,
Raved at the bleeding war; his rampant grief
Moaned, shouted, sobbed, and choked, while he was kneeling
Half-naked on the floor. In my belief
Such men have lost all patriotic feeling.   10

[1918]

Exploring the Text

1. The speaker says he "blundered" (l. 3) into the "blind darkness" (l. 2) and that the sergeant is "puzzled" (l. 3). What does Sassoon achieve by placing so much emphasis on the confusion of the situation?

2. Note the repetition of the past tense verbs beginning with "Moaned" (l. 8). What is the effect of this repetition? Now, find the subject of that series of verbs. What do you find significant about that subject, and how does it affect your interpretation of the poem?

3. Note the shift in tone in the middle of line 9. How would you characterize the tone of that final statement? If you had been the one to "find" the man, how would you complete the statement, "In my belief . . ."?

4. Although the poem's title might seem straightforward, try to come up with three interpretations of it. Think about what is being lamented, and by whom.

Dulce et Decorum Est

WILFRED OWEN

> Born in Shropshire, England, in 1893, Wilfred Owen is the most well-known and most highly regarded of the World War I poets. He enlisted in the army in 1915 and fought in France. In May 1917, he was evacuated from the front and hospitalized with shell shock (a condition now referred to as post-traumatic stress disorder). He returned to the battlefield and won the Military Cross in October 1918. Five of his poems were published that year—the only five he lived to see in print. His work exposes the horrors of the war firsthand. He was killed in battle one week before the armistice. Owen's work remained virtually unknown until 1920, when his friend, Siegfried Sassoon, collected his work and published it as *Poems*. Although Owen's life was short, and his career as a writer even shorter, his influence on the next generation of British writers was profound. While recovering from shell shock, he drafted what was to become one of the most famous and gripping poems about war in the English language, "Dulce et Decorum Est." The title comes from the Roman poet Horace (65–8 B.C.E.), whose line "Dulce et decorum est pro patria mori" means "It is sweet and fitting to die for one's country" in Latin.

Bent double, like old beggars under sacks,
Knock-kneed, coughing like hags, we cursed through sludge,
Till on the haunting flares we turned our backs
And towards our distant rest began to trudge.
Men marched asleep. Many had lost their boots   5
But limped on, blood-shod. All went lame; all blind;
Drunk with fatigue; deaf even to the hoots
Of tired, outstripped Five-Nines that dropped behind.

Gas! GAS! Quick, boys!—An ecstasy of fumbling,
Fitting the clumsy helmets just in time;   10
But someone still was yelling out and stumbling
And flound'ring like a man in fire or lime . . .
Dim, through the misty panes and thick green light,
As under a green sea, I saw him drowning.

In all my dreams, before my helpless sight,   15
He plunges at me, guttering, choking, drowning.

If in some smothering dreams you too could pace
Behind the wagon that we flung him in,
And watch the white eyes writhing in his face,
His hanging face, like a devil's sick of sin;   20
If you could hear, at every jolt, the blood
Come gargling from the froth-corrupted lungs,
Obscene as cancer, bitter as the cud
Of vile, incurable sores on innocent tongues,—
My friend, you would not tell with such high zest   25
To children ardent for some desperate glory,
The old Lie: Dulce et decorum est
Pro patria mori.

[1920]

Exploring the Text

1. Note the title of the poem and the translation provided in the headnote. What expectations does the title create for the reader, and at what point did you realize that this was not going to be a poem about the glories of war?
2. In the first stanza, how does Owen use diction and imagery to bring the experience of a night march to life for the reader? What is the purpose of the similes comparing the troops to "old beggars" and "hags"?
3. Note the diction in the second stanza. Why does the speaker call it an "ecstasy of fumbling" (l. 9)? Why does he use "or" in "fire or lime?" (l. 12)? What does this ambiguity suggest?
4. The third stanza shifts in tense, from the past tense "saw" of line 14 to the present tense "plunges" in line 16. What accounts for this temporal shift? A shift in perspective occurs in line 17. How do the shifts in time and perspective influence your response to the poem?
5. Lines 17 through 28 conclude the poem in one sentence addressed to the "you" in line 17. Who is the speaker addressing? How would you describe the tone the speaker uses to say the phrase "My friend" in line 25?
6. The poem uses graphic—some might say grotesque—imagery throughout. How does that imagery influence your understanding of the purpose of the poem?
7. This poem is arguably the most famous war poem in the English language. What accounts for its lasting popularity? Is its fame deserved? Why or why not?

The First Long-Range Artillery Shell in Leningrad

ANNA AKHMATOVA

TRANSLATED BY LYN COFFIN

Born Anna Gorenko in Odessa, in the Ukraine, Anna Akhmatova (1889–1966) began writing as a child, and showed early promise as a poet. Her father believed that having a "decadent poetess" in the family would disgrace the family name, so he forced her to take a pen name. She married the Russian poet Nikolai Gumilyov in 1910, but he soon left her to go off traveling. In 1912, she gave birth to their son, Lev, and published her first book of poetry, *Vecher*. The couple divorced in 1918. In 1921, Gumilyov was arrested by the Bolsheviks, charged with betraying the revolution, and executed. Because of their connection, Akhmatova was persecuted by Stalin's regime, and except for periods during World War II, her work was banned from publication between 1925 and 1952. Despite the difficulties she faced as a writer, she is now known as one of the greatest poets of the Soviet Union. The poem included here is set during the siege of Leningrad by German artillery bombardment, which occurred from September 1941 to January 1944.

A rainbow of people rushing around,
And suddenly everything changed completely,
This wasn't a normal city sound,
It came from unfamiliar country.
True, it resembled, like a brother,   5
One peal of thunder or another,
But every natural thunder contains
The moisture of clouds, fresh and high,
And the thirst of fields with drought gone dry,
A harbinger of happy rains,   10
And this was as arid as hell ever got,
And my distracted hearing would not
Believe it, if only because of the wild
Way it started, grew, and caught,
And how indifferently it brought   15
Death to my child.

[1941]

Exploring the Text

1. Try to forget the title of this poem, and then reread it. At what point does this poem *have* to be about an artillery shell? Before that point, could it be about something else? What is Akhmatova's point in writing about this event in such an indirect way?

2. This poem chronicles a drastic change in the lives of the citizens of Leningrad. What familiar things does the speaker call on in order to understand the "unfamiliar" (l. 4)? In particular, why does the speaker present the situation in terms of weather?
3. What is the significance of the adverb "indifferently" in line 15? How does it help the poet express her theme?
4. Does the tone remain consistent throughout the poem, or does it shift at the very end?
5. Akhmatova wrote this poem about the first assault in a series of artillery attacks that continued for almost three years. How does knowing that information influence your understanding of and response to the poem?

The Death of the Ball Turret Gunner

RANDALL JARRELL

Randall Jarrell (1914–1965) was born in Nashville, Tennessee, and went to Vanderbilt University and Kenyon College. He earned his MA in English at Vanderbilt, and in 1939 he went to teach at the University of Texas, where he met his wife. He enlisted in the Army Air Corps in 1942, and served in World War II in Europe. He trained as a flying cadet but did not qualify as a pilot; instead, he worked as a celestial navigation tower operator and trainer, spending most of the war in Tucson, Arizona. After the war, he taught at Sarah Lawrence College for a year, and then the University of North Carolina at Greensboro for two decades. Jarrell's fame and influence as a deft and acerbic literary critic is as great as his reputation as a poet. He achieved fame with his National Book Award–winning collection *The Woman at the Washington Zoo* (1960). In addition to his poetry, criticism, and teaching, Jarrell's work was wide-ranging: he composed *The Bat Poet* (1964) and other works for children, in addition to translating German literature by Rainer Maria Rilke and Johann Wolfgang von Goethe. "The Death of the Ball Turret Gunner" is from Jarrell's first book, *Little Friend, Little Friend* (1945). It was inspired by his service in the war and is perhaps his most famous poem. About the poem, Jarrell wrote: "A ball turret was a plexiglass sphere set into the belly of a B-17 or B-24, and inhabited by two .50 caliber machine guns and one man, a short small man. When this gunner tracked with his machine guns a fighter attacking his bomber from below, he revolved with the turret; hunched upside-down in his little sphere, he looked like the fetus in the womb. The fighters which attacked him were armed with cannon-firing explosive shells. The hose was a steam hose."

From my mother's sleep I fell into the State,
And I hunched in its belly till my wet fur froze.
Six miles from earth, loosed from its dream of life,
I woke to black flak and the nightmare fighters.
When I died they washed me out of the turret with a hose.   5

[1945]

Exploring the Text

1. Note the imagery that the poet employs in the first three lines: "mother's sleep," "belly," "wet fur," "dream of life." What impression does the imagery create for you? What is the cumulative effect of such imagery?
2. How does the irony in line 4 (that he woke to a nightmare) contribute to the meaning of the poem? How else is the poem ironic?
3. How would you describe the tone of the final line? Why is the poem so short?
4. In a review of Richard Wilbur's poetry, Randall Jarrell remarked, "Mr. Wilbur never goes too far, but he never goes far enough." How might that statement apply to "The Death of the Ball Turret Gunner," a poem in which some readers might think that Jarrell has gone "too far"?

Naming of Parts

HENRY REED

Henry Reed (1914–1986) was born in Birmingham, England. He won a scholarship to Birmingham University, where he earned an MA, writing his thesis on the novels of Thomas Hardy. In 1941, he was conscripted into the Royal Army Ordnance Corps. During the war, he served as a soldier and cryptographer, working in both the Italian and the Japanese sections of the Government Code and Cypher School. The poems for which he is best known are based on his experience in basic training, where he entertained his friends with imitations of drill sergeants. Later he wrote about those experiences in a series of poems entitled "Lessons of the War," which includes the following selection. Thus, "Naming of Parts"—arguably the most famous poem of World World II—was inspired not by an actual war experience but by Reed's time spent in basic training.

Today we have naming of parts. Yesterday,
We had daily cleaning. And tomorrow morning,
We shall have what to do after firing. But today,
Today we have naming of parts. Japonica
Glistens like coral in all of the neighboring gardens,   5
        And today we have naming of parts.

This is the lower sling swivel. And this
Is the upper sling swivel, whose use you will see,
When you are given your slings. And this is the piling swivel,
Which in your case you have not got. The branches   10
Hold in the gardens their silent, eloquent gestures,
        Which in our case we have not got.

This is the safety-catch, which is always released
With an easy flick of the thumb. And please do not let me

See anyone using his finger. You can do it quite easy   15
If you have any strength in your thumb. The blossoms
Are fragile and motionless, never letting anyone see
        Any of them using their finger.

And this you can see is the bolt. The purpose of this
Is to open the breech, as you see. We can slide it   20
Rapidly backwards and forwards: we call this
Easing the spring. And rapidly backwards and forwards
The early bees are assaulting and fumbling the flowers:
        They call it easing the Spring.

They call it easing the Spring: it is perfectly easy   25
If you have any strength in your thumb: like the bolt,
And the breech, and the cocking-piece, and the point of balance,
Which in our case we have not got; and the almond-blossom
Silent in all of the gardens and the bees going backwards and forwards,
        For today we have naming of parts.   30

[1946]

Exploring the Text

1. Each of the first four stanzas seems to be spoken in two voices. Where does the shift in perspective occur in each of them? Does this poem have two different speakers, or one speaker with two different voices? Explain.
2. Were you surprised by the imagery of the poem? What is the poet suggesting through the juxtaposition of war and nature imagery?
3. How would you explain the shift from "your case" to "our case" in lines 9–12? How do the things "Which in your case you have not got" (l. 10) compare to the things "Which in our case we have not got" (l. 12)?
4. How does the fifth stanza differ from those that precede it?
5. Judging from the poem, what is Reed's attitude toward his experience as a soldier in World War II?
6. Henry Reed and Richard Wilbur (below) both juxtapose the imagery of warfare with that of nature. How would you compare the way that each poet uses imagery to present his attitude toward his subject?

First Snow in Alsace

RICHARD WILBUR

Richard Wilbur was born in 1921 in New York City. He graduated from Amherst College in 1942, and then served in World War II. In 1944, he participated in two of the most crucial battles in Italy: the amphibious landing at Anzio and the attack on Monte Cassino, where thousands of troops were killed. Wilbur saw many of his fellow soldiers killed in battle before leaving the army in 1945 with the rank of sergeant. After the war, he went to Harvard Graduate School. It was there that he met Robert Frost, who recognized his talent and encouraged him to be a poet. Wilbur has taught at Harvard, Wellesley, Wesleyan, and Smith colleges, and was named the 1987 U.S. poet laureate. His first collection of poetry, *The Beautiful Changes and Other Poems* (1947), includes "First Snow in Alsace," a poem that reflects his war experience. A decade later, his collection *Things of This World* would earn both the Pulitzer Prize and the National Book Award. Wilbur is also known for his translations of French literature, especially the plays of Molière. Alsace is a small region of eastern France that borders Germany and Switzerland. From 1940 to 1944, it was under the control of Nazi Germany.

The snow came down last night like moths
Burned on the moon; it fell till dawn,
Covered the town with simple cloths.

Absolute snow lies rumpled on
What shellbursts scattered and deranged,   5
Entangled railings, crevassed lawn.

As if it did not know they'd changed,
Snow smoothly clasps the roofs of homes
Fear-gutted, trustless and estranged.

The ration stacks are milky domes;   10
Across the ammunition pile
The snow has climbed in sparkling combs.

You think: beyond the town a mile
Or two, this snowfall fills the eyes
Of soldiers dead a little while.   15

Persons and persons in disguise,
Walking the new air white and fine,
Trade glances quick with shared surprise.

At children's windows, heaped, benign,
As always, winter shines the most,   20
And frost makes marvelous designs.

The night guard coming from his post,
Ten first-snows back in thought, walks slow
And warms him with a boyish boast:

He was the first to see the snow.   25

                                        [1947]

Exploring the Text

1. In the first stanza, the snow comes down "like moths / Burned on the moon" and lies in "simple cloths" on the town. What is the effect of the differing imagery created by the simile and the metaphor in that stanza? Ultimately, what impression of the snow does the first stanza convey?

2. The snow's presence is so strong that it might be seen as a character in the first four stanzas. How does this personification prepare you for the shift ("You think:") in line 13?

3. Who is the speaker of the poem? What is the speaker's attitude toward the events and scene described?

4. What is the meaning of line 16: "Persons and persons in disguise"?

5. What is the significance of the final line of the poem? In a poem about Alsace—a disputed territory that has seen the horrors of war time and again over the centuries—why does Wilbur write about the snow? What does the snow change in this poem, and how does it change it?

The Terrorist, He Watches

WISLAWA SZYMBORSKA

TRANSLATED BY ROBERT A. MAGUIRE AND MAGNUS JAN KRYNSKI

> Wislawa Szymborska [vis-*lah*-vah sim-*bawrs*-kah] was born in 1923 in western Poland and has lived there all her life. After studying literature and sociology at Jagiellonian University in Krakow, she began to make her way as a poet. She published her first poem, "I am Looking for a World," in 1945, and her first book, *Dlatego Zygemy* (*That's What We Live For*), in 1952. Although she had published eighteen volumes of poetry, which had been translated into more than a dozen languages, she was not well known in the English-speaking world until she was awarded the Nobel Prize for Literature in 1996. In her acceptance speech, Szymborska said, "Inspiration is not the exclusive privilege of poets or artists generally. There is, has been, and will always be a certain group of people whom inspiration visits. It's made up of all those who've consciously chosen their calling and do their job with love and imagination. It may include doctors, teachers, gardeners—and I could list a hundred more professions." Two characteristics of her work—close observation and understatement—are evident in the poem included here.

The bomb will go off in the bar at one twenty p.m.
Now it's only one sixteen p.m.
Some will still have time to get in,
Some to get out.

The terrorist has already crossed to the other side of the street.   5
The distance protects him from any danger,
and what a sight for sore eyes:

A woman in a yellow jacket, she goes in.
A man in dark glasses, he comes out.
Guys in jeans, they are talking.   10
One seventeen and four seconds.
That shorter guy's really got it made, and gets on a scooter,
and that taller one, he goes in.

One seventeen and forty seconds.
That girl there, she's got a green ribbon in her hair.   15
Too bad that bus just cut her off.
One eighteen p.m.
The girl's not there any more.
Was she dumb enough to go in, or wasn't she?
That we'll see when they carry them out.   20

One nineteen p.m.
No one seems to be going in.
Instead a fat baldy's coming out.
Like he's looking for something in his pockets and
at one nineteen and fifty seconds   25
he goes back for those lousy gloves of his.

It's one twenty p.m.
The time, how it drags.
Should be any moment now.
Not yet.   30
Yes, this is it.
The bomb, it goes off.

[1981]

. . . .

Exploring the Text

1. What is unusual about the way the poem reveals the central event? What words would you use to describe the presentation? How does the poem create tension and suspense?

2. What transition does line 7, "and what a sight for sore eyes," signal? to introduce the descriptions of the people coming and going? How are the people described?

3. How does the countdown embedded in the poem both structure it and contribute to the development of its themes?

4. How would you describe the tone of the poem? What effect does the tone have on your response to the poem?

5. What is the impact of Szymborska's choosing to provide us with no information about the terrorist—not the time period, location, nature of the conflict, or motivation?

An Iraqi Evening

Yousif al-Sa'igh

TRANSLATED BY SAADI A SIMAWE, RALPH SAVARESE, AND CHUCK MILLER

> The reputation of Iraqi poet and writer Yousif al-Sa'igh in the West is based almost entirely on this simple, haunting poem. Yousif al-Sa'igh continues to live in Iraq. In this poem, he writes about the Iran-Iraq War, which waged from 1980 to 1988 and took approximately 150,000 Iraqi lives.

Clips from the battlefield
in an Iraqi evening:
a peaceable home
two boys
preparing their homework   5
a little girl
absentmindedly drawing on scrap paper
funny pictures.
—breaking news coming shortly.
The entire house becomes ears   10
ten Iraqi eyes glued to the screen in frightened silence.
Smells mingle:
the smell of war
and the smell of just baked bread.
The mother raises her eyes to a photo on the wall   15
whispering
—May God protect you
and she begins preparing supper
quietly
and in her mind   20
clips float past of the battlefield
carefully selected for hope.

[1986]

Exploring the Text

1. What are the "clips" of line 1? What do they depict? What are the "clips" of line 21? How are they related to those of line 1? Who is presenting these clips? Who is carefully selecting them "for hope" (l. 22)?

2. Which of the senses are engaged by the imagery in this poem? Which images are the most effective? What is the effect of juxtaposing the smell of war with the smell of just-baked bread?
3. What is the effect of the personification in the poem?
4. Who do you think is pictured in the "photo on the wall" (l. 15)? What evidence can you find in the poem to support this view?
5. What is the tone of the poem? Discuss three elements of style that contribute to its development.
6. One critic has described this poem as "a song of survival." Explain why you do or do not find that an apt description.

Sadiq

BRIAN TURNER

Born in 1967 in California, Brian Turner earned an MFA in poetry at the University of Oregon before enlisting in the army at the age of twenty-nine. During the seven years he spent as a soldier, he was deployed to Bosnia and Herzegovina, and served as an army infantry team leader with the Third Stryker Brigade Combat Team in Iraq in 2003. His work has been published in various journals as well as in *Voices in Wartime: The Anthology*—published in 2005 in conjunction with the feature-length documentary film of the same name. His first collection of poems, *Here, Bullet* (2005), won the Beatrice Hawley Award and was a *New York Times* Editors' Choice selection. In 2007, Turner received a National Endowment for the Arts Literature Fellowship in poetry. He currently lives in Fresno, California, where he teaches poetry at Fresno State. "Sadiq," the title of the poem included here, is Arabic for "friend."

It is a condition of wisdom in the archer to be patient because when the arrow leaves the bow, it returns no more.

—SA'DI

It should make you shake and sweat,
nightmare you, strand you in a desert
of irrevocable desolation, the consequences
seared into the vein, no matter what adrenaline
feeds the muscle its courage, no matter   5
what god shines down on you, no matter
what crackling pain and anger
you carry in your fists, my friend,
it should break your heart to kill.

[2005]

Exploring the Text

1. How do you interpret the epigraph from Sa'di, a revered thirteenth-century Persian poet? How does this epigraph inform your understanding of Turner's poem?
2. In line 8, the speaker directly addresses "my friend." What is the speaker's attitude toward the "friend"? How does Turner's use of the word compare to Wilfred Owen's direct address to "My friend" in "Dulce et Decorum Est" (p. 1424)?
3. How does the poem reveal the speaker's attitude toward his war experience?
4. In *Regarding the Pain of Others*, Susan Sontag says of war, "We do not and cannot imagine what it was like, how dreadful or terrifying it was, how normal it becomes." How might "Sadiq" be regarded as a response to Sontag's statement?

BRIAN TURNER ON WRITING

Lawrence Scanlon (LS): What prompted the writing of "Sadiq"? Is the poem based on a particular incident?

Brian Turner (BT): There's no particular incident that prompted this poem. Prior to deploying to Iraq and when my unit was back in garrison, training, I often heard soldiers say, "I'm gonna go shoot somebody in the face." I share this not to shock people. I share this because I realized then that this was mostly being said because of fear — a recognition of the combat zone where we were preparing to go. As a side note, I never heard that phrase said again as my unit returned from our time in Iraq.

LS: In *Voices in Wartime: The Anthology*, "Sadiq" concludes with an additional line that does not appear in *Here, Bullet*: "It should never be so easy as this." Which is the definitive version? Which do you prefer?

BT: I much prefer the version in the book [*Here, Bullet*]. I think the first version doesn't properly recognize the difficulties and nuances involved, the inner psychology of the people involved in a combat zone.

LS: There is a great tradition of war poetry, from Homer through Wilfred Owen and on to Yusef Komunyakaa, to name a few. But the poetry of World War I stands out in many minds as the richest. Do you agree? Why do you think that war in particular has produced such rich poetry?

BT: I'm not sure I agree. In fact, I think we'll need another hundred years or so to see how much of the poetry of this past century will last in the

5

larger public discourse. In terms of World War I, though, I think a great many factors converged to produce the meaningful poetry of that time, including the industrial age; the "advances" in warfare itself, which led to carnage on a mammoth scale; and much, much more. Still, whether it lasts through the centuries or not is not a true test of how meaningful and deep the poetry is for those who've written it and those who interact with it (the reader/audience).

LS: How did your fellow soldiers—your "brothers and sisters in arms," if you will—respond to your being a poet?

BT: I've heard good things back from the soldiers I served with while in Iraq. I haven't stayed in contact with those I didn't get along with—I have no idea what they think of it. I didn't share the fact that I was writing poetry at the time, simply not to undermine my position as an infantry sergeant. I've had some people outside of the military suggest that I was undermining the art by "hiding" it, but in my opinion they don't quite understand the interpersonal dynamics of being an infantry sergeant. The stereotype of the poet as the sensitive guy is not one that inspires the infantry. This isn't said to undermine the art or to limit the humanity of those I served with in uniform; if they were to read the work, I'm certain they'd be surprised by the range of what poetry can offer the reader.

LS: With "Night in Blue" and "Katyusha Rockets" as notable, postwar exceptions, most of the poems in *Here, Bullet* depict war experiences in Iraq. Did you write most of them while in Iraq or after you returned to the United States?

BT: I wrote all but two or three while I was in Iraq. I wrote the two or three others during the first month I returned to America (as I was typing up all of the poems I'd written in my journals while overseas). There were about ten to fifteen more poems written in Iraq that didn't make it into the final book, though two of those poems were included in the Bloodaxe Books version of the book put out in the U.K.

LS: Given their subject matter, it is no surprise that many of your poems are about sadness and loss. You seem to make an implicit appeal in your poems, as if to ask the reader—the citizen—to pay attention, to look and listen. What would you want your readers to think about after reading your poems?

BT: As a writer, it's a great honor to have a reader complete the dialogue begun on the page. I always say the poem finishes in the reader. Each reader brings his or her own wealth of experience, his or her own lifetime of knowledge, to the reading. So, in a sense, there's no way to answer this because I would hope different things for different readers. I'm not trying

10

to obfuscate here and to dodge the question—I'm simply trying to recognize and to respect the unique character of each reader my work is honored by and not limit the individual reader's experience.

Follow-Up

1. In an earlier draft, "Sadiq" ended with the line, "It should never be so easy as this." In this interview, Brian Turner makes the case for leaving out that extra line, saying that it "doesn't properly recognize the difficulties and nuances involved, the inner psychology of the people involved in a combat zone" (para. 4). Do you agree or disagree that not including that line improves the poem?
2. Do you agree or disagree with those who criticize Turner for hiding the fact that he was a poet while he was on duty in Iraq? Explain. Even if you disagree, why might some say that he was "undermining the art by 'hiding' it" (para. 8)? What cultural forces are at odds in this debate?
3. In the interview, Turner says, "the poem finishes in the reader. Each reader brings his or her own wealth of experience, his or her own lifetime of knowledge, to the reading" (para. 12). What experiences do you bring to the reading of Turner's poem "Sadiq"? How do those experiences affect your reaction to the poem?

Elegy for the Native Guards

NATASHA TRETHEWEY

Natasha Trethewey was born in Gulfport, Mississippi, in 1966, and grew up in an intellectual environment. She would accompany her father—a college professor and author of three collections of poetry—on trips to the library, and get lost in a world of books. Her father encouraged her to be a hardworking risk taker in both her writing and her life. Trethewey earned an MA in literature at Hollins University in Virginia and an MFA in poetry at the University of Massachusetts. Her first collection of poetry, *Domestic Work* (2000), was selected by Rita Dove as the winner of the inaugural Cave Canem Poetry Prize for the best first book by an African American poet and won the 2001 Mississippi Institute of Arts and Letters award. She is currently a professor of English and creative writing at Emory University in Atlanta, Georgia. "Elegy for the Native Guards" is from *Native Guard*, for which she was awarded a Pulitzer Prize in 2006. Commenting on the poem in an interview in the *New York Times*, she says, "I've been interested in historical erasure and historical amnesia for a long time, those things that get left out of the record." The poem tells the story of a tourist boat to Ship Island, a barrier island off the coast of Mississippi that is now a national park. During the

Civil War, it housed Confederate prisoners of war and served a vital strategic role in the Union invasions of the ports of New Orleans and Mobile. The Louisiana Native Guards—the first black combat regiments in the Union Army to be led by black officers—manned the island. As of 2006, there was no monument to the Native Guards' service on Ship Island.

> *Now that the salt of their blood*
> *Stiffens the saltier oblivion of the sea . . .*
> —ALLEN TATE

We leave Gulfport at noon; gulls overhead
trailing the boat—streamers, noisy fanfare—
all the way to Ship Island. What we see
first is the fort, its roof of grass, a lee—
half reminder of the men who served there—   5
a weathered monument to some of the dead.

Inside we follow the ranger, hurried
though we are to get to the beach. He tells
of graves lost in the Gulf, the island split
in half when Hurricane Camille hit,   10
shows us casemates, cannons, the store that sells
souvenirs, tokens of history long buried.

The Daughters of the Confederacy
has placed a plaque here, at the fort's entrance—
each Confederate soldier's name raised hard   15
in bronze; no names carved for the Native Guards—
2nd Regiment, Union men, black phalanx.
What is monument to their legacy?

All the grave markers, all the crude headstones—
water-lost. Now fish dart among their bones,   20
and we listen for what the waves intone.
Only the fort remains, near forty feet high,
round, unfinished, half open to the sky,
the elements—wind, rain—God's deliberate eye.

[2006]

Exploring the Text

1. How does the epigraph from Allen Tate inform your reading of the poem? The quotation is from his poem "Ode to the Confederate Dead." Does this information change your reaction to the quotation or the way it relates to Trethewey's poem? If so, how?

2. What is the speaker's attitude toward the "tokens" in line 12?
3. Line 18 asks, "What is monument to their legacy?" Do you think *to* means "compared with" or "in honor of"? Which reading fits your interpretation of the poem? Why?
4. Why is God's eye "deliberate" in the final line? What might be the connection to the hurricane introduced in line 10? Explain what such a connection might mean.
5. The poem contains several references to splitting, such as "half reminder" in line 5, "some of the dead" in line 6, and "island split / in half" in lines 9 and 10 (notice the enjambment there, as well). How do such phrases suggest one theme of this poem?
6. The poem tells us that a plaque dedicated to Confederate soldiers has been placed in the national park by the Daughters of the Confederacy. Do you find that fitting? ironic? Explain. How does Trethewey view it?
7. How might Trethewey's elegy be regarded as the "monument" called for in line 18?

PAIRED POEMS

. . . .

The Parable of the Old Man and the Young

and

Arms and the Boy

WILFRED OWEN

> Born in Shropshire, England, in 1893, Wilfred Owen is the most well-known and most highly regarded of the World War I poets. He enlisted in the army in 1915 and fought in France. In May 1917, he was evacuated from the front and hospitalized with shell shock (a condition now referred to as post-traumatic stress disorder). He returned to the battlefield and won the Military Cross in October 1918. Five of his poems were published that year—the only five he lived to see in print. His work exposes the horrors of the war firsthand. He was killed in battle one week before the armistice. Owen's work remained virtually unknown until 1920, when his friend, Siegfried Sassoon, collected his work and published it as *Poems*. Although Owen's life was short, and his career as a writer even shorter, his influence on the next generation of British writers was profound. The selections here were printed back-to-back in *Poems* (1920).

The Parable of the Old Man and the Young

So Abram rose, and clave the wood, and went,
And took the fire with him, and a knife.

And as they sojourned both of them together,
Isaac the first-born spake and said, My Father,
Behold the preparations, fire and iron,
But where the lamb for this burnt-offering?   5
Then Abram bound the youth with belts and straps,
And builded parapets and trenches there,
And stretchèd forth the knife to slay his son.
When lo! An angel called him out of heaven,   10
Saying, Lay not thy hand upon the lad,
Neither do anything to him. Behold,
A ram, caught in a thicket by its horns;
Offer the Ram of Pride instead of him.
But the old man would not so, but slew his son,   15
And half the seed of Europe, one by one.

[1920]

Exploring the Text

1. This poem alludes to Genesis 22:1–19. Look up this passage of the Bible and find out what happens in the original story. Where does this poem begin to deviate from the story in Genesis? What is the significance of these deviations?
2. What does the "Ram of Pride" (l. 14) represent?
3. At line 15, the poem shifts dramatically. How do you interpret the final couplet? What does he mean by "half the seed of Europe" (l. 16)?
4. Owen refers to a parable from the Bible and also calls his poem a parable. How does Owen's poem serve as a parable for his time?

Arms and the Boy

Let the boy try along this bayonet-blade
How cold steel is, and keen with hunger of blood;
Blue with all malice, like a madman's flash;
And thinly drawn with famishing for flesh.

Lend him to stroke these blind, blunt bullet-leads   5
Which long to nuzzle in the hearts of lads,
Or give him cartridges of fine zinc teeth,
Sharp with the sharpness of grief and death.

For his teeth seem for laughing round an apple.
There lurk no claws behind his fingers supple;   10
And God will grow no talons at his heels,
Nor antlers through the thickness of his curls.

[1920]

Exploring the Text

1. The title of this poem evokes Virgil's *Aeneid*, a late first-century B.C.E. Latin epic poem that tells the story of Aeneas, a Trojan warrior who voyages to Italy and becomes the ancestor of the Romans. The *Aeneid* begins, "I sing of arms and the man." How does Owen's use of the allusion contribute to the meaning of his poem?

2. Trace the imagery throughout the poem. What conclusions can you draw from it? Some of the imagery creates dramatic contrasts. Find some examples of this technique, and explain how they contribute to the meaning of the poem.

3. In the first two stanzas, the speaker suggests letting the boy become familiar with weapons. What reason does the speaker give? Do you find the poem's argument convincing? Explain why or why not.

4. What is the tone of the speaker? What is Owen's attitude toward what the speaker says? toward weapons? toward war?

5. Owen classified this poem in his draft table of contents under "protest—the unnaturalness of weapons." How does this information influence your understanding of the poem? What is ironic about this classification, given the imagery in this poem?

Focus on Comparison and Contrast

1. What do these poems have in common in terms of the way they portray violence? How do they differ?

2. Each of the poems depends on an allusion—one to the Bible, the other to a classical epic poem. Compare the effects of the allusions and their contribution to each poem's tone.

3. Both poems explore the nature of youth confronted with the reality of war. Compare and contrast the two, and evaluate which one is more satisfactory in its delivery of theme.

Writing Assignment

In both "The Parable of the Old Man and the Young" and "Arms and the Boy," young men are confronted with violence. Read the poems carefully. Then write an essay in which you compare and contrast the way Owen uses these confrontations, analyzing their effectiveness in communicating his antiwar message.

Boy Fascist

NEW YORK TIMES

The following photo, taken by a staff photographer at the *New York Times*, was published on April 25, 1932. It was taken at a ceremony for the *Leva fascista* in the Place du Peuple, Rome. The *Leva fascista* celebrated the promotion of youth to the next level of the Italian Fascist youth organization. This organization included members ranging from four years old to college age.

Exploring the Text

1. How would you describe the expression on the face of the soldier to the left? How would you describe the little boy? What do you think their relationship is?
2. What is the photographer's purpose in juxtaposing the little boy with the line of soldiers?
3. What attitude toward war does this photograph suggest? What connections can you find to other pieces you have read in this chapter?

Conversation

Finding Peace

What does it mean to find peace at the end of a war? While governments can end a war with the stroke of a pen, what of the soldiers and those left behind when a soldier falls? Knowing what we do about shell shock, or post-traumatic stress disorder, it seems reasonable to wonder if the war ever leaves the soldier — even after the soldier has left the war. *Antigone*, the first selection in this chapter, shows the difficulty — especially for Creon — of adjusting to peacetime. Perhaps only Antigone herself can be regarded as having found peace, but how did she achieve it, and how great was the cost? In this Conversation, we'll read literature about people — soldiers, societies, and families left behind — trying to find peace after war.

Texts

Alfred, Lord Tennyson, "Ulysses" (poetry)

Thomas Hardy, "A Wife in London" (poetry)

Ernest Hemingway, "Soldier's Home" (fiction)

Yusef Komunyakaa, "Facing It" (poetry)

Maya Lin, from *Boundaries* (nonfiction)

Department of Defense, "Fallen Soldiers Arriving at Dover Air Force Base" (photography)

Rachelle Jones, "Satisfy My Soul" (blog post)

Ulysses

ALFRED, LORD TENNYSON

The life of Alfred, Lord Tennyson (1809–1892), spanned the Victorian age, and his work — noteworthy for its metrical skill, mythological subject matter (particularly his use of Arthurian legend), and high idealism — is considered the hallmark of the period. His most famous poems include "The Charge of the Light Brigade," "The Lady of Shalott," "Ulysses," and "In Memoriam" — published in 1850, the year that he succeeded William Wordsworth as poet laureate. In this poem, Ulysses (the Latin name for Odysseus, hero of Homer's *Odyssey*) reflects on his past, including ten years fighting in the Trojan War and his subsequent ten-year adventure returning home.

It little profits that an idle king,
By this still hearth, among these barren crags,
Matched with an agèd wife, I mete[1] and dole[2]

> distribute

---

[1]Measure or allot. — EDS.
[2]Distribute. — EDS.

[handwritten: Inadequate]

Unequal[3] laws unto a (savage race,) *[handwritten: Ithacans]*
That hoard, and sleep, and feed, and know not me.

[handwritten: Reflects on the life he lived and what he exp.d]

    I cannot rest from travel; I will drink
Life to the lees.[4] All times I have enjoyed

[handwritten: M]

Greatly, have suffered greatly, both with those
That loved me, and alone; on shore, and when
Through scudding[5] drifts[6] the rainy Hyades[7] *[handwritten: — stars guided despite the dim sea (Poseidon)]*
Vexed the dim sea. I am become a name; *[handwritten: Odyssey]*
For always roaming with a hungry heart
Much have I seen and known — cities of men
And manners, climates, councils, governments,
Myself not least, but honored of them all —   15
And drunk delight of battle with my peers,
Far on the ringing plains of windy Troy.
I am a part of all that I have met;
Yet all experience is an arch wherethrough
Gleams that untraveled world whose margin fades   20
Forever and forever when I move.
How dull it is to pause, to make an end,   *[handwritten: — I miss the adventure]*
To rust unburnished, not to shine in use!
As though to breathe were life! Life piled on life

[handwritten: Life is not just existing.]

Were all too little, and of one to me   25
Little remains; but every hour is saved
From that eternal silence, something more,
A bringer of new things; and vile it were
For some three suns to store and hoard myself,
And this gray spirit yearning in desire   30
To follow knowledge like a sinking star,
Beyond the utmost bound of human thought.

[handwritten: My son, the king]

    This is my son, mine own Telemachus,
To whom I leave the scepter and the isle —
Well-loved of me, discerning to fulfill   35

---

[3]Inadequate. — EDS.
[4]Dregs; insoluble matter that settles to the bottom of wine or beer. In nautical terms, the lee is the side of the boat sheltered from the wind. — EDS.
[5]Driven by the wind. In nautical terms, "running before a gale," or sailing as fast as possible with a strong wind directly behind you. — EDS.
[6]Sheets of rain. In nautical terms, the lateral motion of a ship due to wind or currents. — EDS.
[7]A V-shaped cluster of stars in the constellation Taurus that rises with the sun during the rainy season. — EDS.

This labor, by slow prudence to make mild
A rugged people, and through soft degrees
Subdue them to the useful and the good.
Most blameless is he, centered in the sphere
Of common duties, decent not to fail   40
In offices of tenderness, and pay
Meet adoration to my household gods,
When I am gone. He works his work, I mine.

Death is the final Odyssey

There lies the port; the vessel puffs her sail;
There gloom the dark, broad seas. My mariners,   45
Souls that have toiled, and wrought, and thought with me—
That ever with a frolic welcome took
The thunder and the sunshine, and opposed
Free hearts, free foreheads—you and I are old;
Old age hath yet his honor and his toil.   50
Death closes all; but something ere the end,
Some work of noble note, may yet be done,
Not unbecoming men that strove with Gods.
The lights begin to twinkle from the rocks;
The long day wanes; the slow moon climbs; the deep   55
Moans round with many voices. Come, my friends,
'Tis not too late to seek a newer world.
Push off, and sitting well in order smite
The sounding furrows; for my purpose holds
To sail beyond the sunset, and the baths[8]   60
Of all the western stars, until I die.
It may be that the gulfs will wash us down;
It may be we shall touch the Happy Isles,[9]
And see the great Achilles, whom we knew.
Though much is taken, much abides; and though   65
We are not now that strength which in old days
Moved earth and heaven, that which we are, we are—
One equal temper of heroic hearts,
Made weak by time and fate, but strong in will
To strive, to seek, to find, and not to yield.   70

[1833]

Connect to "Do Not Go Gentle."

. . . .

[8]In ancient Greek cosmology, the ocean that surrounds the world, where the stars go when
they set.—EDS.
[9]Islands of the Blessed, or Elysian Fields, where heroes go after death.—EDS.

Questions

1. How does the speaker reflect on his past? What does he miss? How does he view the present? What makes him feel that others "know not me" (l. 5)? What is his attitude toward the future?
2. What does he mean by the phrase "As though to breathe were life!" (l. 24)? What leads him to make that remark?
3. What is suggested by the third part of the poem, about his son, Telemachus?
4. How would you describe the shift in tone at the end of line 51, "but something ere the end"?
5. The poem concludes with the wish to be "strong in will / To strive, to seek, to find, and not to yield" (ll. 69–70). Supply a direct object for each of those parallel verbs. Not to yield to *what*, for example?
6. What does this poem have to say about finding peace? Does Ulysses find peace? If so, how? If not, why not?

A Wife in London] *text context*
(December, 1899)

THOMAS HARDY

Among the greatest nineteenth-century British novelists, Thomas Hardy (1840–1928) was born in Dorset, England. Among his most famous works are *Far from the Madding Crowd*—whose title comes from Thomas Gray's "Elegy Written in a Country Churchyard" (p. 1259)—published in 1874; *The Return of the Native* (1878); *Tess of the D'Urbervilles* (1891); and *Jude the Obscure* (1895). After the less than appreciative reaction that *Jude the Obscure* received—many people found it too shocking and pessimistic—Hardy wrote only poetry. In "A Wife in London," he writes about the aftermath of the Boer War, which waged from 1899 to 1902 in South Africa.

① imagery / mood

        I—The Tragedy
She sits in the tawny vapour   *yellow brown —city*   *subject*
   That the Thames-side lanes have uprolled,   *tone*
   Behind whose webby fold on fold
Like a waning taper
   The street-lamp glimmers cold.   5

A messenger's knock cracks smartly,
   Flashed news is in her hand
   Of meaning it dazes to understand
Though shaped so shortly:
   He—has fallen—in the far South Land. . . .   10

        II—The Irony
'Tis the morrow; the fog hangs thicker,
   The postman nears and goes:
   A letter is brought whose lines disclose

By the firelight flicker
    His hand, whom the worm now knows: 15

Fresh—firm—penned in highest feather—
    Page-full of his hoped return,
    And of home-planned jaunts by brake and burn
In the summer weather,
    And of new love that they would learn.   20

Open, horse-drawn 4 wheeled carriage

[1901]

. . . .

Questions

1. Trace the imagery of this poem as it is introduced in the first part and then picked up again in the second part. What role does the imagery play in establishing mood and conveying theme? *— Lname 1st*
2. Why does Hardy call the two parts of the poem "The Tragedy" and "The Irony"? Explain, using evidence from the text.
3. Imagine that the wife lives not in London but in your hometown. In a contemporary poem about her as a widow of the war in Iraq or Afghanistan, what would be different in the poem? What would be similar? How universal is the poem's message? Explain.

Soldier's Home

ERNEST HEMINGWAY

> Born in Illinois, Ernest Hemingway (1899–1961) served in a volunteer ambulance unit in Italy in World War I, where he was wounded and hospitalized. After the war, he worked as a reporter for American newspapers and then as a foreign correspondent in Europe. Among his most famous works are the novels *The Sun Also Rises* (1926), *A Farewell to Arms* (1929), and *The Old Man and the Sea* (1955). He was awarded the Nobel Prize for Literature in 1954, and the influence of his "simple," "journalistic" style on modern writing is incalculable. "Soldier's Home"—one of Hemingway's early stories—is from *In Our Time* (1925).

church → war

Soldier ↓ Soldier

Krebs went to the war from a Methodist college in Kansas. There is a picture which shows him among his fraternity brothers, all of them wearing exactly the same height and style collar. He enlisted in the Marines in 1917 and did not return to the United States until the second division returned from the Rhine in the summer of 1919.

There is a picture which shows him on the Rhine with two German girls and another corporal. Krebs and the corporal look too big for their uniforms. The German girls are not beautiful. The Rhine does not show in the picture. *irony*

By the time Krebs returned to his home town in Oklahoma the greeting of heroes was over. He came back much too late. The men from the town who had been drafted had all been welcomed elaborately on their return. There had been a great deal of hysteria. Now the reaction had set in. People seemed to think it was rather ridiculous for Krebs to be getting back so late, years after the war was over.

At first Krebs, who had been at Belleau Wood, Soissons, the Champagne, St. Mihiel, and in the Argonne did not want to talk about the war at all. Later he felt the need to talk but no one wanted to hear about it. His town had heard too many atrocity stories to be thrilled by actualities. Krebs found that to be listened to at all he had to lie, and after he had done this twice he, too, had a reaction against the war and against talking about it. A distaste for everything that had happened to him in the war set in because of the lies he had told. All of the times that had been able to make him feel cool and clear inside himself when he thought of them; the times so long back when he had done the one thing, the only thing for a man to do, easily and naturally, when he might have done something else, now lost their cool, valuable quality and then were lost themselves.

His lies were quite unimportant lies and consisted in attributing to himself 5 things other men had seen, done, or heard of, and stating as facts certain apocryphal incidents familiar to all soldiers. Even his lies were not sensational at the pool room. His acquaintances, who had heard detailed accounts of German women found chained to machine guns in the Argonne forest and who could not comprehend, or were barred by their patriotism from interest in, any German machine gunners who were not chained, were not thrilled by his stories.

Krebs acquired the nausea in regard to experience that is the result of untruth or exaggeration, and when he occasionally met another man who had really been a soldier and they talked a few minutes in the dressing room at a dance he fell into the easy pose of the old soldier among other soldiers: that he had been badly, sickeningly frightened all the time. In this way he lost everything.

During this time, it was late summer, he was sleeping late in bed, getting up to walk down town to the library to get a book, eating lunch at home, reading on the front porch until he became bored, and then walking down through the town to spend the hottest hours of the day in the cool dark of the pool room. He loved to play pool.

In the evening he practiced on his clarinet, strolled down town, read, and went to bed. He was still a hero to his two young sisters. His mother would have given him breakfast in bed if he had wanted it. She often came in when he was in bed and asked him to tell her about the war, but her attention always wandered. His father was noncommittal.

Before Krebs went away to the war he had never been allowed to drive the family motor car. His father was in the real estate business and always wanted the car to be at his command when he required it to take clients out into the country to show them a piece of farm property. The car always stood outside the First National Bank building where his father had an office on the second floor. Now, after the war, it was still the same car.

Nothing was changed in the town except that the young girls had grown up. But 10 they lived in such a complicated world of already defined alliances and shifting feuds that Krebs did not feel the energy or the courage to break into it. He liked to look at them, though. There were so many good-looking young girls. Most of them had

EXPl—

their hair cut short. When he went away only little girls wore their hair like that or girls that were fast. They all wore sweaters and shirt waists with round Dutch collars. It was a pattern. He liked to look at them from the front porch as they walked on the other side of the street. He liked to watch them walking under the shade of the trees. He liked the round Dutch collars above their sweaters. He liked their silk stockings and flat shoes. He liked their bobbed hair and the way they walked.

When he was in town their appeal to him was not very strong. He did not like them when he saw them in the Greek's ice cream parlor. He did not want them themselves really. They were too complicated. There was something else. Vaguely he wanted a girl but he did not want to have to work to get her. He would have liked to have a girl but he did not want to have to spend a long time getting her. He did not want to get into the intrigue and the politics. He did not want to have to do any courting. He did not want to tell any more lies. It wasn't worth it.

He did not want any consequences. He did not want any consequences ever again. He wanted to live alone without consequences. Besides he did not really need a girl. The army had taught him that. It was all right to pose as though you had to have a girl. Nearly everybody did that. But it wasn't true. You did not need a girl. That was the funny thing. First a fellow boasted how girls mean nothing to him, that he never thought of them, that they could not touch him. Then a fellow boasted that he could not get along without girls, that he had to have them all the time, that he could not go to sleep without them.

That was all a lie. It was all a lie both ways. You did not need a girl unless you thought about them. He learned that in the army. Then sooner or later you always got one. When you were really ripe for a girl you always got one. You did not have to think about it. Sooner or later it would come. He had learned that in the army.

Now he would have liked a girl if she had come to him and not wanted to talk. But here at home it was all too complicated. He knew he could never get through it all again. It was not worth the trouble. That was the thing about French girls and German girls. There was not all this talking. You couldn't talk much and you did not need to talk. It was simple and you were friends. He thought about France and then he began to think about Germany. On the whole he had liked Germany better. He did not want to leave Germany. He did not want to come home. Still, he had come home. He sat on the front porch.

He liked the girls that were walking along the other side of the street. He liked the look of them much better than the French girls or the German girls. But the world they were in was not the world he was in. He would like to have one of them. But it was not worth it. They were such a nice pattern. He liked the pattern. It was exciting. But he would not go through all the talking. He did not want one badly enough. He liked to look at them all, though. It was not worth it. Not now when things were getting good again.

He sat there on the porch reading a book on the war. It was a history and he was reading about all the engagements he had been in. It was the most interesting reading he had ever done. He wished there were more maps. He looked forward with a good feeling to reading all the really good histories when they would come out with

15

good detail maps. Now he was really learning about the war. He had been a good soldier. That made a difference.

One morning after he had been home about a month his mother came into his bedroom and sat on the bed. She smoothed her apron.

"I had a talk with your father last night, Harold," she said, "and he is willing for you to take the car out in the evenings."

"Yeah?" said Krebs, who was not fully awake. "Take the car out? Yeah?"

"Yes. Your father has felt for some time that you should be able to take the car out in the evenings whenever you wished but we only talked it over last night." 20

"I'll bet you made him," Krebs said.

"No. It was your father's suggestion that we talk the matter over."

"Yeah. I'll bet you made him," Krebs sat up in bed.

"Will you come down to breakfast, Harold?" his mother said.

"As soon as I get my clothes on," Krebs said. 25

His mother went out of the room and he could hear her frying something downstairs while he washed, shaved, and dressed to go down into the dining-room for breakfast. While he was eating breakfast his sister brought in the mail.

"Well, Hare," she said. "You old sleepyhead. What do you ever get up for?"

Krebs looked at her. He liked her. She was his best sister.

"Have you got the paper?" he asked.

She handed him the *Kansas City Star* and he shucked off its brown wrapper and 30 opened it to the sporting page. He folded the *Star* open and propped it against the water pitcher with his cereal dish to steady it, so he could read while he ate.

"Harold," his mother stood in the kitchen doorway, "Harold, please don't muss up the paper. Your father can't read his *Star* if it's been mussed."

"I won't muss it," Krebs said.

His sister sat down at the table and watched him while he read.

"We're playing indoor over at school this afternoon," she said. "I'm going to pitch."

"Good," said Krebs. "How's the old wing?" 35

"I can pitch better than lots of the boys. I tell them all you taught me. The other girls aren't much good."

"Yeah?" said Krebs.

"I tell them all you're my beau. Aren't you my beau, Hare?"

"You bet."

"Couldn't your brother really be your beau just because he's your brother?" 40

"I don't know."

"Sure you know. Couldn't you be my beau, Hare, if I was old enough and if you wanted to?"

"Sure. You're my girl now."

"Am I really your girl?"

"Sure."

"Do you love me?" 45

"Uh, huh."

"Will you love me always?"

"Sure."

"Will you come over and watch me play indoor?" 50

"Maybe."

"Aw, Hare, you don't love me. If you loved me, you'd want to come over and watch me play indoor."

Krebs's mother came into the dining-room from the kitchen. She carried a plate with two fried eggs and some crisp bacon on it and a plate of buckwheat cakes.

"You run along, Helen," she said. "I want to talk to Harold."

She put the eggs and bacon down in front of him and brought in a jug of maple 55
syrup for the buckwheat cakes. Then she sat down across the table from Krebs.

"I wish you'd put down the paper a minute, Harold," she said.

Krebs took down the paper and folded it.

"Have you decided what you are going to do yet, Harold?" his mother said, taking off her glasses.

"No," said Krebs.

"Don't you think it's about time?" His mother did not say this in a mean way. 60
She seemed worried.

"I hadn't thought about it," Krebs said.

"God has some work for everyone to do," his mother said. "There can be no idle hands in His Kingdom."

"I'm not in His Kingdom," Krebs said.

"We are all of us in His Kingdom."

Krebs felt embarrassed and resentful as always. 65

"I've worried about you so much, Harold," his mother went on. "I know the temptations you must have been exposed to. I know how weak men are. I know what your own dear grandfather, my own father, told us about the Civil War and I have prayed for you. I pray for you all day long, Harold."

Krebs looked at the bacon fat hardening on his plate.

"Your father is worried, too," his mother went on. "He thinks you have lost your ambition, that you haven't got a definite aim in life. Charley Simmons, who is just your age, has a good job and is going to be married. The boys are all settling down; they're all determined to get somewhere; you can see that boys like Charley Simmons are on their way to being really a credit to the community."

Krebs said nothing.

"Don't look that way, Harold," his mother said. "You know we love you and I 70
want to tell you for your own good how matters stand. Your father does not want to hamper your freedom. He thinks you should be allowed to drive the car. If you want to take some of the nice girls out riding with you, we are only too pleased. We want you to enjoy yourself. But you are going to have to settle down to work, Harold. Your father doesn't care what you start in at. All work is honorable as he says. But you've got to make a start at something. He asked me to speak to you this morning and then you can stop in and see him at his office."

"Is that all?" Krebs said.

"Yes. Don't you love your mother, dear boy?"

"No," Krebs said.

His mother looked at him across the table. Her eyes were shiny. She started crying.

"I don't love anybody," Krebs said. 75

It wasn't any good. He couldn't tell her, he couldn't make her see it. It was silly to have said it. He had only hurt her. He went over and took hold of her arm. She was crying with her head in her hands.

"I didn't mean it," he said. "I was just angry at something. I didn't mean I didn't love you."

His mother went on crying. Krebs put his arm on her shoulder.

"Can't you believe me, mother?"

His mother shook her head.

"Please, please, mother. Please believe me." 80

"All right," his mother said chokily. She looked up at him. "I believe you, Harold."

Krebs kissed her hair. She put her face up to him.

"I'm your mother," she said. "I held you next to my heart when you were a tiny baby."

Krebs felt sick and vaguely nauseated. *wping* 85

"I know, Mummy," he said. "I'll try and be a good boy for you."

"Would you kneel and pray with me, Harold?" his mother asked.

They knelt down beside the dining-room table and Krebs's mother prayed.

"Now, you pray, Harold," she said.

"I can't," Krebs said. 90

"Try, Harold."

"I can't."

"Do you want me to pray for you?"

"Yes."

So his mother prayed for him and then they stood up and Krebs kissed his 95 mother and went out of the house. He had tried so to keep his life from being complicated. Still, none of it had touched him. He had felt sorry for his mother and she had made him lie. He would go to Kansas City and get a job and she would feel all right about it. There would be one more scene maybe before he got away. He would not go down to his father's office. He would miss that one. He wanted his life to go smoothly. It had just gotten going that way. Well, that was all over now, anyway. He would go over to the schoolyard and watch Helen play indoor baseball.

[1925]

- -

Questions

1. The story begins with a startlingly direct sentence: "Krebs went to the war from a Methodist college in Kansas." What does it imply?

2. Why does the narrator mention the collars the fraternity brothers are wearing in the picture (para. 1) and the collars the girls in the town are wearing (para. 10)? What is the implication beyond the repetition?

3. At the end of paragraph 6, the narrator states, "In this way he lost everything." What does he mean?

4. In paragraph 11, Hemingway writes about Krebs: "Vaguely he wanted a girl but he did not want to have to work to get her. He would have liked to have a girl but he did not want to have to spend a long time getting her. He did not want to get into the intrigue and the politics. He did not want to have to do any courting. He did not want to tell any more lies." What assumptions about love and war and truth underlie this passage?

5. Notice the syntax in paragraphs 14 and 15. Why does Hemingway present Krebs in such short and simple sentences? How does the syntax reflect the content and affect the meaning of these sentences?

6. In paragraph 16, we learn that Krebs is reading "about all the engagements he had been in." The narrator states, "It was the most interesting reading he had ever done." Read the paragraph carefully. How does it relate Krebs's state of mind to his attempt to find peace?

7. Consider Krebs's home and family. What is significant about the father's absence? Why does his mother have such difficulty understanding Krebs? Why does he have such difficulty making himself understood? Describe Krebs's relationship with his sister, Helen. Is the soldier *home* in "Soldier's Home?" Is the title ironic? Explain.

8. In paragraph 67, Hemingway writes, "Krebs looked at the bacon fat hardening on his plate." What does that image suggest about Krebs? How does it contribute to the story? In paragraph 85, Hemingway writes, "Krebs felt sick and vaguely nauseated." How would you explain the causes of his unease?

9. Upon finishing the story, how do you feel about Krebs? Will he find peace? If so, explain how. If not, why not?

Facing It

YUSEF KOMUNYAKAA

Yusef Komunyakaa (b. 1947) was born James Willie Brown Jr. and raised in Bogalusa, Louisiana. He has taught in the New Orleans public schools, at Indiana University, at Princeton University, and is currently teaching at New York University. Fresh out of high school, he enlisted in the army and served in Vietnam, an experience that permeates his poetry. After returning from Vietnam, it was many years before Komunyakaa felt he could write about his time spent there. Speaking of his war experience to the *New York Times*, he said, "I never used the word 'gook' or 'dink' in Vietnam. There is a certain kind of dehumanization that takes place to create an enemy, to call up the passion to kill this person. I knew something about that growing up in Louisiana." He was awarded the 1994 Pulitzer Prize for *Neon Vernacular: New and Selected Poems*. One of his finest poems, "Facing It"—about an encounter with the Vietnam Veterans Memorial—is from his collection *Dien Cai Dau* (1988).

My black face fades,
hiding inside the black granite.
I said I wouldn't,
dammit: No tears.
I'm stone. I'm flesh.   5
My clouded reflection eyes me
like a bird of prey, the profile of night
slanted against morning. I turn
this way—the stone lets me go.
I turn that way—I'm inside   10
the Vietnam Veterans Memorial
again, depending on the light
to make a difference.
I go down the 58,022 names,
half-expecting to find   15
my own in letters like smoke.
I touch the name Andrew Johnson;
I see the booby trap's white flash.
Names shimmer on a woman's blouse
but when she walks away   20
the names stay on the wall.
Brushstrokes flash, a red bird's
wings cutting across my stare.
The sky. A plane in the sky.
A white vet's image floats   25
closer to me, then his pale eyes
look through mine. I'm a window.
He's lost his right arm
inside the stone. In the black mirror
a woman's trying to erase names: 30
No, she's brushing a boy's hair.

[1988]

Questions

1. What is the effect of the mirror imagery in the poem?
2. How does the juxtaposition of stone and flesh in line 5 contribute to the meaning of the poem?
3. How would you describe the tone created by the imagery of lines 6 through 8?
4. What happens when the speaker touches the wall (l. 17)? What does the poet suggest in line 27, saying "I'm a window"?
5. Why is the poem titled "Facing It"? Has the speaker found peace? Explain.

6. In an interview with the *New York Times*, Komunyakaa said that his life was a "healing process from the two places: Bogalusa and Vietnam." How does this poem read as a statement of the healing process?

From *Boundaries*

Maya Lin

> Maya Lin was born in 1959 in Ohio, where her mother and father were professors at Ohio University. When she was twenty-one years old and an architecture student at Yale University, Lin was selected from over 1,420 competitors to design the Vietnam Veterans Memorial in Washington, D.C. Since then, she has designed many major public installations, including one for the federal courthouse in New York City and the Civil Rights Memorial in Montgomery, Alabama. In 2000, she published the memoir *Boundaries*, in which she describes the process of designing the Vietnam Veterans memorial.

I made a conscious decision not to do any specific research on the Vietnam War and the political turmoil surrounding it. I felt that the politics had eclipsed the veterans, their service and their lives. I wanted to create a memorial that everyone would be able to respond to, regardless of whether one thought our country should or should not have participated in the war. The power of a name was very much with me at the time, partly because of the Memorial Rotunda at Yale. In Woolsey Hall, the walls are inscribed with the names of all the Yale alumni who have been killed in wars. I had never been able to resist touching the names cut into these marble walls, and no matter how busy or crowded the place is, a sense of quiet, a reverence, always surrounds those names. Throughout my freshman and sophomore years, the stonecutters were carving in by hand the names of those killed in the Vietnam War, and I think it left a lasting impression on me . . . the sense of the power of a name.

One memorial I came across also made a strong impression on me. It was a monument to the missing soldiers of the World War I battle of the Somme by Sir Edwin Lutyens in Thiepval, France. The monument includes more than 100,000 names of people who were listed as missing because, without ID tags, it was impossible to identify the dead. (The cemetery contains the bodies of 70,000 dead.) To walk past those names and realize the lives lost—the effect of that is the strength of the design. This memorial acknowledged those lives without focusing on the war or on creating a political statement of victory or loss. This apolitical approach became the essential aim of my design; I did not want to civilize war by glorifying it or by forgetting the sacrifices involved. The price of human life in war should always be clearly remembered.

But on a personal level, I wanted to focus on the nature of accepting and coming to terms with a loved one's death. Simple as it may seem, I remember feeling that accepting a person's death is the first step in being able to overcome that loss.

I felt that as a culture we were extremely youth oriented and not willing or able to accept death or dying as a part of life. The rites of mourning, which in more primitive and older cultures were very much a part of life, have been suppressed in our modern times. In the design of the memorial, a fundamental goal was to be honest about death, since we must accept that loss in order to begin to overcome it. The pain of the loss will always be there, it will always hurt, but we must acknowledge the death in order to move on.

What then would bring back the memory of a person? A specific object or image would be limiting. A realistic sculpture would be only one interpretation of that time. I wanted something that all people could relate to on a personal level. At this time I had as yet no form, no specific artistic image.

The use of names was a way to bring back everything someone could remember about a person. The strength in a name is something that has always made me wonder at the "abstraction" of the design; the ability of a name to bring back every single memory you have of that person is far more realistic and specific and much more comprehensive than a still photograph, which captures a specific moment in time or a single event or a generalized image that may or may not be moving for all who have connections to that time.

Then someone in the class received the design program, which stated the basic philosophy of the memorial's design and also its requirements: all the names of those missing and killed (57,000) must be a part of the memorial; the design must be apolitical, harmonious with the site, and conciliatory.

These were all the thoughts that were in my mind before I went to see the site.

Without having seen it, I couldn't design the memorial, so a few of us traveled to Washington, D.C., and it was at the site that the idea for the design took shape. The site was a beautiful park surrounded by trees, with traffic and noise coming from one side — Constitution Avenue.

I had a simple impulse to cut the earth.

I imagined taking a knife and cutting into the earth, opening it up, an initial violence and pain that in time would heal. The grass would grow back; but the initial cut would remain a pure flat surface in the earth with a polished, mirrored surface, much like the surface on a geode when you cut it and polish the edge. The need for the names to be on the memorial would become the memorial; there was no need to embellish the design further. The people and their names would allow everyone to respond and remember.

It would be an interface, between our world and the quieter, darker, more peaceful world beyond. I chose black granite in order to make the surface reflective and peaceful. I never looked at the memorial as a wall, an object, but as an edge to the earth, an opened side. The mirrored effect would double the size of the park, creating two worlds, one we are a part of and one we cannot enter. The two walls were positioned so that one pointed to the Lincoln Memorial and the other pointed to the Washington Monument. By linking these two strong symbols for the country, I wanted to create a unity between the nation's past and present.

[2000]

Questions

1. At the end of paragraph 2, Lin writes, "The price of human life in war should always be clearly remembered." How does this assertion serve as a thesis statement for the first two paragraphs?
2. Lin designates three "requirements" in paragraph 7. Why is it crucial that the memorial be "apolitical, harmonious with the site, and conciliatory"?
3. Lin says that she had "a simple impulse to cut the earth" (para. 10). How does this impulse relate to the purpose of this memorial?
4. In what ways does Lin believe her design encourages "accepting and coming to terms with a loved one's death" (para. 3)?
5. We commonly refer to the Vietnam Veterans Memorial as "the Wall," but its designer didn't see it that way. In the final paragraph, Lin writes, "I never looked at the memorial as a wall, an object, but as an edge to the earth, an opened side." How does her description affect your attitude toward the monument? If you have been to see it, how does her account influence your impression? If you haven't, how does it affect your expectations?
6. Generally speaking, what do you think the purpose of a public memorial is? Who is it for? families? returning soldiers? fallen soldiers? society as a whole? If you have not visited the Vietnam Veterans Memorial, explore some of the images online. Does this memorial do what you think a war memorial should do? Why or why not?

Fallen Soldiers Arriving at Dover Air Force Base

DEPARTMENT OF DEFENSE

> Prior to February 2009, the Department of Defense refused to release images of fallen soldiers returning from Iraq and Afghanistan. This image—and others like it—was released in 2003 after Russ Kick, operator of the Web site The Memory Hole (www.thememoryhole.org), successfully filed a Freedom of Information Act request. Taken by a Department of Defense photographer, the image on the following page shows an honor guard unloading flag-draped coffins from a cargo plane at Dover Air Force Base in Delaware.

Questions

1. Of all the pictures that were released via the Freedom of Information Act, this image was reproduced repeatedly in magazines and newspapers. What about this image is compelling, or striking?
2. Why do you think the Department of Defense did not want to release this photograph? Do you think it should or should not release such photos? Why?
3. At the heart of the debate about whether to release this photograph is the tension between private grief and public grief. What elements of the public and the private do you see in this photo? How does this tension play out in Maya Lin's Vietnam Veterans memorial?

Satisfy My Soul

RACHELLE JONES

Rachelle Jones lives in Arkansas. At her blog, ArmyWifeToddlerMom.blogspot
.com, she describes herself: "I have been a SAHM [stay-at-home mom] for the
last 7 years. I am married to a full time National Guardsman. I have been an
active duty spouse, a civilian spouse, and a National Guard spouse. I have had
ALMOST every blue collar job imaginable. I am an LPN [licensed practical nurse],
with primary experience in end of life care in pulmonary, hospice, geriatrics. I
am also a contributor at military.com for http://spousebuzz.typepad.com/blog/."
In the following excerpt from her blog, she describes her feelings regarding the
return of her husband, who had been deployed in Iraq.

Saturday, March 19, 2005

I am still feeling "separate" from Dear Husband.

Eighteen months of different day to day existence can do this. So I stand on the
outside now and try and imagine his life.

He is a "rules" kind of guy, he doesn't tell, and I don't ask.

The other day we were in the truck on the way to the bookstore and I asked,
"Does it feel weird driving your truck?"

I got a small glimpse into his head. He said, "I still don't like driving under the 5
overpasses and over bridges. Random garbage on the shoulders makes me edgy."

That small glimpse was enough for me that day. I haven't asked another question. Maybe later.

That first night alone in the hotel, when the children finally fell asleep, I clung
to him and cried. I am not a big crier—try not to be, anyway. Reunion is frightening,
and you feel lucky, blessed, cheated, alone, and guilty.

You want to hear "the story" that proves you have every right to feel lucky and
blessed, but you don't want to hear it.

So you lie on a bed in a dimly lit hotel room, and you watch your babies sleep
in peace. You put your head on your husband's chest, and you hear his heart beating,
and you can smell him for the first time in months, and you can feel his hands on
your back, and you cry as quietly as you can.

The tears come . . . and you try and stop them. All of the worry, gratefulness, 10
sorrow, and love. You cry for him, and his lost brothers, and for the widows that must
cry in the shower, so their children can't hear them.

You feel guilty for the tears on his chest, and he pulls you to his mouth and tries
to kiss your tears away. No one says a word, and you swear you can hear your tears
dropping onto his flesh, and you can hear his heart beating . . .

. . . And it is the best sound in the World.

Questions

1. What is poignant and ironic about Jones's feeling "'separate' from Dear Husband"
   (para. 1)? Why does she put *separate* in quotation marks? What is significant about
   her not using her husband's name but calling him "Dear Husband" instead?

2. How would you describe the communication between Jones and her husband in this blog post? Do they seem effusive? chatty? confessional? What does their style of communication tell you about the challenges of military families finding peace?
3. How would you describe the tone of this blog post?

Entering the Conversation

As you develop a response to one of the following questions, refer to the texts you have read in this section. You may also draw on your own experience or knowledge relating to finding peace after war.

1. Consider the extent to which the speakers and characters of these selections have found peace. Which have been the most successful? Which have been the least? Write an essay in which you compare and contrast at least three of the selections, and come to a conclusion as to what a person needs to do, or understand, to find peace after war.

2. We often think of war in terms of battles and conflicts involving men. Several of the selections included here present the perspectives of women in response to war. Referring to some of these texts, write an essay that discusses the ways in which women respond to war and analyzes their attempts to find peace.

3. As quoted in the epigraph to this chapter, Tim O'Brien, who fought in Vietnam, asks, "Can the foot soldier teach anything important about war, merely for having been there?" He goes on to answer, "I think not. He can tell war stories." Using evidence from several of the texts, write an essay about the role of war stories and storytelling in the quest to find peace. Consider "storytelling" in its broadest sense, which includes a range of art forms not limited to fiction.

4. Memory plays a significant role in several selections, as characters and speakers recall the past and attempt to find peace. Write an essay in which you analyze the role of memory as either a healing or a disquieting agent in several of the selections.

5. Yusef Komunyakaa wrote "Facing It" about a visit to the Vietnam Veterans Memorial, designed by Maya Lin. In the voice of Komunyakaa, Lin, and two other authors in this Conversation, write a roundtable discussion on the role of monuments and memorials in helping both soldiers and the general public find peace after war.

6. Write a letter to a political candidate or organization in which you make a case for what you think would most help veterans find peace, whether it's improved medical care, psychiatric care, increased educational or vocational opportunities, or a special monument or ceremony. Refer to a few of the selections in this Conversation to support your position for why this initiative would help veterans find peace.

Student Writing

Analyzing Theme in Drama

The paper by Rebecca Roycraft was written outside of class as a response to the following prompt.

> One well-known piece of literature ends with the shocked line, "People don't do such things!" Using *Antigone* as a model, discuss the effect of Antigone's shocking actions on her society. Include in your discussion both rational and emotional arguments for and against her actions, and be sure to discuss the effect of her actions on the work as a whole.

Theme in *Antigone*
Rebecca Roycroft

In Sophocles' play *Antigone*, the protagonist, a young woman named Antigone, defies the state's laws and societal norms in order to follow the rules of the gods. She realizes the injustice being perpetrated against the gods when Creon, king of Thebes, arbitrarily chooses to bury one of her brothers as a hero and leave the other in the streets, unburied. Though Antigone's sister, Ismene, tries to dissuade her, telling her that she is only a woman and therefore unimportant, Antigone goes out to bury her brother, and though Creon questions her, she remains defiant, sticking to her principles and disregarding the laws of the state. Antigone originally defies her society in two ways (by acting independently even though she is a woman and by disobeying the law), and by the end of the play, the people of Thebes turn over to Antigone's side and realize that her adherence to the laws of the gods is, in fact, the correct response to Creon's refusal to bury one of her brothers. Since the people of Thebes and Creon himself eventually realize that Antigone was correct, her actions and her death change society's perception of what she did and allow the play to convey its message: people should not defy or disregard the laws of the gods under any circumstances.

After realizing that she must bury her brother, Antigone attempts to enlist the help of her sister, Ismene, arguing "[Creon] has no right to keep me from my own" (l. 59). Ismene has more conventional views, however, and reminds Antigone, "we are women, / we're not born to contend with men" (ll. 74–75). As women, Antigone and Ismene are not supposed to act independently and are told to leave important decisions and actions to men. Antigone does not dispute the fact that men are generally stronger than women and have the right to be the rulers and the lawmakers, but she knows that her reasons for burying her brother transcend society's idea that women should not make independent decisions. She believes that the gods want her brother to be buried, and she knows that she has to obey the laws of the gods, no matter what. Even though she is a woman, she has no choice but to obey the gods and tells Ismene as much: "Do as you like, dishonor the laws / the gods hold in honor" (ll. 91–92). Antigone does not necessarily disagree with the societal idea that women should allow men to rule over them and make decisions for them, but she knows that the gods are more important than anything else.

In her quest to obey the laws of the gods, Antigone not only defies her role as a woman in ancient Greek society but also defies the laws of the state of Thebes. Creon believes that the laws of the state are more important than anything else and thinks of Antigone's defiance as a personal threat: "she is the man / if this victory goes to her and she goes free" (ll. 542–43). However, when Creon asks Antigone why she feels perfectly justified in openly defying him, she simply tells him, "Death longs for the same rites for all" (l. 585). Though Creon feels personally insulted by Antigone's defiance, Antigone simply believes that the laws of the gods are more important than the laws of the state, that this fact should be apparent to everyone, and that Creon is mistaken. Antigone again does not aim to take away power from the state or the society, but wishes to obey only the laws that are most important: the laws of the gods. For her, the state and the society in which she lives are completely eclipsed by the will of the gods.

After defying the society by making an independent decision as a woman and openly contradicting Creon's laws, Antigone is sentenced to death. However, her legacy doesn't end when she is taken off to be buried alive. Creon is informed that "the city [of Thebes] mourns for this young girl. / 'No woman,' they say, 'ever deserved death less, / and such a brutal death for such a glorious action'" (ll. 777–79). Antigone's actions are indicative of how the rest of the city feels, and her adherence to the gods' laws makes everyone else in the city realize that the gods' laws do, in fact, transcend societal norms and the laws of the state. After Antigone's death, Creon still refuses to bury Antigone's brother, despite the fact that the people of Thebes realize the importance of the gods. At this point, the gods become angry with the city of Thebes: "deaf to [their] prayers, they spurn / the offerings in [their] hands" (ll. 1128–29). Once Creon realizes that the gods truly are more important than any political power he has, he admits, "reverence toward the gods must be safeguarded" (l. 1468). Though Antigone originally defied the society in which she lived to do her duty to the gods, in the end, society comes to realize that Antigone's decisions were the correct ones.

Antigone does not set out to directly defy her country or to confront her place in society: all she attempts over the course of *Antigone* is to obey the laws of the gods, which are, and ought always to be, more important than societal norms or the laws of men. The message of *Antigone* is that while people in general are supposed to conform to their place and to obey the government, no pressure from men should keep people from following the will of the gods. Antigone's ability to see beyond the constraints placed on her by society is a catalyst for the entire population of Thebes's realization that the gods do, in fact, transcend society and state. Antigone is able to sway the opinion of the population with her righteous actions, and thus Sophocles is able to convey his message: hubris leads to tragedy, and following the gods is the only way to avoid the death and destruction that pervades *Antigone*.

Questions

1. Deconstruct the prompt: What exactly is the student being asked to do? What are the key terms? Then explain how effectively you believe the student addressed the prompt. Cite specific passages in the essay.
2. What are the effects of Antigone's shocking actions on her society, according to Rebecca's analysis?
3. Throughout the essay, Rebecca refers to Antigone's actions and decisions as "correct." Explain whether you do or do not find this description appropriate within the terms of the play.
4. Analyze the structure of paragraph 2. What is the purpose of this paragraph? How might a stronger topic sentence achieve this purpose more effectively?
5. What assumptions about the reader's knowledge of the play does Rebecca make? Does she summarize the plot adequately? Does she give too much detail? Cite specific instances to support your response.

The Writer's Craft—Close Reading

Imagery

Reflecting on the writer's craft, Joseph Conrad wrote, "My task which I am trying to achieve is, by the power of the written word, to make you hear, to make you feel—it is, above all, to make you see. That—and no more, and it is everything." What Conrad is referring to is called imagery—language that evokes a response in the reader through an appeal to one or more of the senses. Surely you have heard the age-old advice for writers: "Show, don't tell." One way for a writer to show is through imagery. It can make the abstract more concrete and thus help the reader experience the poem or story directly through the senses.

The literal meaning of *image* is "a picture of something." But in literature, imagery can be language that addresses any of the senses. Visual images are most common, but images can be auditory, appealing to our sense of hearing; olfactory, appealing to our sense of smell; gustatory, appealing to our sense of taste; tactile, appealing to our sense of touch; and kinesthetic, appealing to physical sensations such as movement or tension. Essentially, through concrete detail and precise language, imagery mentally reproduces sensations that trigger emotion and memory. You can use these emotions and memories to set a mood, reinforce a theme, or achieve other literary purposes. For instance, in the following passage from "The Management of Grief," Bharati Mukherjee uses imagery to create mood.

> The two rooms are dark and stuffy. The lights are off, and an oil lamp sputters on the coffee table. The bent old lady has let us in, and her husband is wrapping a white turban over his oiled, hip-length hair. She immediately goes to the kitchen, and I hear the most familiar sound of an Indian home, tap water hitting and filling a teapot.

Mukherjee appeals to the visual, tactile, and auditory in the first two sentences describing the look and feel of the room. The next sentence extends the visual image to the couple. The last sentence shifts from a description of unfamiliar sights to a description of a very familiar sound, the "tap water hitting and filling a teapot." This change in imagery (both in quality and in type) shifts the mood, taking us from an uncomfortable situation to a more welcoming one.

It is important to note that while a writer can add emotional power through images and image patterns, not all writers choose this strategy. Ernest Hemingway, for instance, is famous for his spare literal prose, almost entirely devoid of imagery and figurative language. Consider the second paragraph of the story "Soldier's Home":

> There is a picture which shows him on the Rhine with two German girls and another corporal. Krebs and the corporal look too big for their uniforms. The German girls are not beautiful. The Rhine does not show in the picture.

Compare that description of a picture with this one from Tim O'Brien's "The Things They Carried":

> The first was a Kodachrome snapshot signed "Love," though he knew better. She stood against a brick wall. Her eyes were gray and neutral, her lips slightly open as she stared straight-on at the camera.

Hemingway describes a picture but without providing descriptive images to appeal to any of our senses. In fact, he tells us that the girls are "not beautiful" and that the Rhine River "does not show"—both negatives. What do the girls look like? What is in the picture if the Rhine is not? It is precisely that lack of detail—and emotion—that begins to characterize Krebs's past experience in World War I. O'Brien, on the other hand, gains emotional power by providing details of the kind of photo ("Kodachrome snapshot"), an inscription, the backdrop, the color of the girl's eyes, the set of her mouth, and her stance relative to the camera. This description gives the reader a sense of how emotionally invested Cross is in every detail of this photo. And this sets the stage for the poignant collapse of his daydreams in the next sentence: "At night, sometimes, Lieutenant Cross wondered who had taken the picture, because he knew she had boyfriends, because he loved her so much, and because he could see the shadow of the picture taker spreading out against the brick wall."

Imagery and Figurative Language

Imagery and figurative language (metaphor, simile, and so on) are close siblings; both help us visualize and experience literature. For our purposes, we'll make a distinction between the two, acknowledging all the while that they often work together. Imagery is a literal but artful description of how something looks, feels, tastes, smells, and sounds, while figurative language compares two or more things and is not literal. These lines, from Wilfred Owen's "Dulce et Decorum Est," incorporate both literal imagery and figurative language:

> Dim, through the misty panes and thick green light,
> As under a green sea, I saw him drowning.

The imagery in the first line helps us experience what a mustard gas attack would look like through a gas mask. It's "Dim." The panes are "misty" and the light is "thick green" as it filters through the mustard gas and is viewed through the tinted lenses of the World War I gas mask. The second line turns the corner from a literal description of the scene to a figurative depiction: it was like being "under a green sea." In this case, as in many, literal imagery and figurative language work together to get the point across.

Analyzing Patterns of Imagery

Analyzing imagery means not only connecting the image to the context and themes of the story or poem, but also paying attention to the other imagery surrounding it. While a single image will often have a multiplicity of meanings and implications, an author will sometimes use a pattern of similar or contrasting images to point us in the right interpretive direction. For example, depending on the context, descriptions of the deep red of wine can suggest passion, blood (and therefore violence), Christian communion, or simply the fellowship of a good meal well enjoyed. And each of these possible meanings brings with it a mood: romantic, foreboding, solemn, satisfied. If the description of the deep red of wine is accompanied by imagery of light streaming through a stained glass window, or a white dove, then we can deduce that the author is appealing to Christian imagery.

The following passage is from the *Iliad*. Even though it is a translation, notice how the vivid imagery appeals to the senses:

> The glory of armor lit the skies and the whole earth laughed,
> rippling under the glitter of bronze, thunder resounding
> under trampling feet of armies. And in their midst
> the brilliant Achilles began to arm for battle . . .
> A sound of grinding came from the fighter's teeth,
> his eyes blazed forth in searing points of fire,
> unbearable grief came surging through his heart
> and now, bursting with rage against the men of Troy,
> he donned Hephaestus' gifts — magnificent armor
> the god of fire forged with all his labor.

As we read this passage, we *see* the rippling glitter of bronze, we *hear* the resounding thunder of trampling feet as the brilliant Achilles begins to arm, we both *see and hear* the sound of his grinding teeth, we *see* and *feel* the heat of his blazing eyes, and Achilles is brought to life. If we follow the pattern of the imagery, we see that it is not consistent. Homer contrasts the "glory of armor" with the "thunder[ous] resounding . . . of armies," the "glitter of bronze" with the "grinding . . . from the fighter's teeth." This juxtaposition of the beautiful and the terrible might lead us to an interpretation of what Homer is saying about war and warriors in the *Iliad*.

The following exercises will help you become familiar with identifying imagery and determining its effect on the meaning of a work of literature.

• EXERCISE 1 •

Identify the images in each of the following passages and the senses to which they appeal.

1. A dark theater, he remembered, and the movie was *Bonnie and Clyde*, and Martha wore a tweed skirt, and during the final scene, when he touched her knee, she turned and looked at him in a sad, sober way that made him pull his hand back, but he would always remember the feel of the tweed skirt and the knee beneath it and the sound of the gunfire that killed Bonnie and Clyde, how embarrassing it was, how slow and oppressive. ("The Things They Carried," para. 5)

2. Mostly he felt pleased to be alive. He liked the smell of the New Testament under his cheek, the leather and ink and paper and glue, whatever the chemicals were. He liked hearing the sounds of night. Even his fatigue, it felt fine, the stiff muscles and the prickly awareness of his own body, a floating feeling. ("The Things They Carried," para. 60.)

3. He shook his light fawn coat as to show it [why he did not wear mourning]; his livid lip over his missing teeth was trembling, his eyes were watery and motionless, and soon after he ended with a shrill laugh which might well have been a sob. ("War," para. 21)

4. [Magda] did not walk very well, partly because she was only fifteen months old, and partly because the spindles of her legs could not hold up her fat belly. It was fat with air, full and round. ("The Shawl," para. 5)

5. The day was not cold, but something in the bare trees caught my attention. I looked up from the gravel, into the branches and the clear blue sky beyond. I thought I heard the rustling of larger forms, and I waited a moment for voices. Nothing. ("The Management of Grief," para. 144)

6. The church so lone, the log-built one,
   That echoed to many a parting groan
         And natural prayer
      Of dying foemen mingled there—
   ("Shiloh," ll. 10–13)

7. Absolute snow lies rumpled on
   What shellbursts scattered and deranged,
   Entangled railings, crevassed lawn.
   ("First Snow in Alsace," ll. 4–6)

• EXERCISE 2 •

Discuss the image patterns in the following excerpts. How do they work together to develop a specific mood or meaning? In cases in which the images are dissimilar, how does the contrast contribute to mood or meaning? Also, consider how, in some cases, figurative language works together with the images.

1. They imagined the muzzle against flesh. They imagined the quick, sweet pain, then the evacuation to Japan, then a hospital with warm beds and cute geisha nurses.

    They dreamed of freedom birds.

    At night, on guard, staring into the dark, they were carried away by jumbo jets. They felt the rush of takeoff. *Gone!* they yelled. And then velocity, wings and engines, a smiling stewardess—but it was more than a plane, it was a real bird, a big sleek silver bird with feathers and talons and high screeching. They were flying. The weights fell off, there was nothing to bear. They laughed and held on tight, feeling the cold slap of wind and altitude, soaring, thinking *It's over, I'm gone!* ("The Things They Carried," paras. 79–81)

2. Then, on the third day of the sixth month into this odyssey, in an abandoned temple in a tiny Himalayan village, as I make my offering of flowers and sweetmeats to the god of a tribe of animists, my husband descends to me. He is squatting next to a scrawny sadhu in moth-eaten robes. Vikram wears the vanilla suit he wore the last time I hugged him. The sadhu tosses petals on a butter-fed flame, reciting Sanskrit mantras, and sweeps his face of flies. My husband takes my hands in his. ("The Management of Grief," para. 89)

3. If you could hear, at every jolt, the blood
    Come gargling from the froth-corrupted lungs,
    Obscene as cancer, bitter as the cud
    Of vile, incurable sores on innocent tongues.
    ("Dulce et Decorum Est," ll. 21–24)

4. Let the boy try along this bayonet-blade
    How cold steel is, and keen with hunger of blood;
    Blue with all malice, like a madman's flash;
    And thinly drawn with famishing for flesh. ("Arms and the Boy," ll. 1–4)

5. I touch the name Andrew Johnson;
    I see the booby trap's white flash.
    Names shimmer on a woman's blouse
    but when she walks away
    the names stay on the wall.
    Brushstrokes flash, a red bird's
    wings cutting across my stare. ("Facing It," ll. 17–23)

● EXERCISE 3 ●

Writers will often use imagery to highlight contrasts. For example, through-out "Naming of Parts," Henry Reed juxtaposes elements from the natural world with the parts of a rifle, and in paragraphs 15 and 16 of "The Shawl," Cynthia Ozick juxtaposes images of nature outside the fence with images of the barracks within. Divide your page into two columns. Choose one of these texts, and identify on either side of the page the images that the writer juxtaposes. Then explain how that contrast contributes to the meaning of the work.

● EXERCISE 4 ●

Read the following poem by Brian Turner, whose "Sadiq" is included in the chapter. Notice how rich in imagery this poem is, and how some images describe what the speaker sees through the scope and others, what he imagines. Identify the images and the figurative language, and discuss how they work together to achieve the writer's purpose in the poem as a whole.

In the Leupold Scope

With a 40×60mm spotting scope
I traverse the Halabjah skyline,
scanning rooftops two thousand meters out
to find a woman in sparkling green, standing
among antennas and satellite dishes,   5
hanging laundry on an invisible line.

She is dressing the dead, clothing them
as they wait in silence, the pigeons circling
as fumestacks billow a noxious black smoke.
She is welcoming them back to the dry earth,   10
giving them dresses in tangerine and teal,
woven cotton shirts dyed blue.

She waits for them to lean forward
into the breeze, for the wind's breath
to return the bodies they once had,   15
women with breasts swollen by milk,
men with shepherd-thin bodies, children
running hard into the horizon's curving lens.

• EXERCISE 5 •

Write a prose description or a poem based on a war photograph from a current newspaper or Web site. Use imagery or image patterns to add vividness to your description.

Suggestions for Writing

War and Peace

1. On November 11, 1985, Siegfried Sassoon was among sixteen Great War poets commemorated on a slate stone unveiled in Poets' Corner in Westminster Abbey. The inscription on the stone was written by friend and fellow poet Wilfred Owen. It reads: "My subject is War, and the pity of War. The Poetry is in the pity." Write an essay that supports Owen's statement about "the pity of war" as expressed in at least three of the texts in this chapter.

2. In the conclusion to her book *Regarding the Pain of Others*, Susan Sontag—who witnessed firsthand the horrors of war—writes:

   > We don't get it. We truly can't imagine what it was like. We can't imagine how dreadful, how terrifying war is; and how normal it becomes. Can't understand, can't imagine. That's what every soldier, and every journalist and aid worker and independent observer who has put in time under fire, and had the luck to elude the death that struck down others nearby, stubbornly feels. And they are right.

   Write an essay that discusses the extent to which Sontag's statement is true, using at least four of the texts as support. Consider that several of the selections were written by people who have personally experienced war (O'Brien, Owen, Hemingway, Komunyakaa, Turner), whereas others were written by those who have created imagined voices of experience based on observation and study (Shakespeare, Tennyson, Ozick, Trethewey).

3. The epigraph at the beginning of this chapter is from Tim O'Brien's *If I Die in a Combat Zone*: "Do dreams offer lessons? Do nightmares have themes, do we awaken and analyze them and live our lives and advise others as a result? Can the foot soldier teach anything important about war, merely for having been there? I think not. He can tell war stories." Using at least three of the texts to support your argument, write an essay that discusses the validity of O'Brien's statement.

4. Consider this statement from Chris Hedges.

   > The enduring attraction to war is this: Even with its destruction and carnage it can give us what we long for in life. It can give us purpose, meaning, a reason for living. Only when we are in the midst of conflict does the shallowness and vapidness

of much of our lives become apparent. Trivia dominates our conversations and increasingly our airwaves. And war is an enticing elixir. It gives us resolve, a cause. It allows us to be noble.

Write an essay that compares and contrasts the views expressed in the literature in this chapter with the view expressed by Hedges in this quotation. Refer to at least three texts for support.

5. Some of the main selections from this chapter—*Antigone*, "The Things They Carried," "War," "The Management of Grief"—present attempts to find peace. Write an essay in which you compare one of these main selections with two or more of the Conversation selections as you discuss the extent to which peace is achieved in postwar experience.

6. In the introductory essay to his book *The Government of the Tongue*, Seamus Heaney discusses reading Wilfred Owen's poetry, particularly "Dulce et Decorum Est," with students. He writes:

> And it seemed to me that "*Dulce et Decorum Est*," a poem which it was easy for them to like, was the poem where I could engage them with the question of over-writing. 'Is Owen overdoing it here?' I would ask. 'Inside of five lines we have "devil's sick of sin", "gargling", froth-corrupted", "bitter as the cud", "vile, incurable sores." Is he not being a bit overinsistent? A bit explicit?' However hangdog I might feel about such intrusions, I also felt that it was right to raise questions. Yet there was obviously an immense disparity between the nit-picking criticism I was conducting on the poem and the heavy price, in terms of emotional and physical suffering, the poet paid in order to bring it into being.

Considering not only the subject matter of the poem but also the experience and intent of the poet, is it right to ask the questions Heaney is asking? Write an essay in response to Heaney, using the text of Owen's poem or others in this chapter for support.

7. In their selections, William Shakespeare, Walt Whitman, Wilfred Owen, Siegfried Sassoon, Henry Reed, Anna Akhmatova, Randall Jarrell, and Alfred, Lord Tennyson, speak across the years in the first person. Consider the power of voice in these selections. Write an essay in which you explain which voice speaks most eloquently to our time. Refer specifically to your selected text as you relate it to contemporary events.

8. Each of the following quotations addresses the nature of war and peace. Select one that interests you, and use it to develop a thesis for an essay. Use several selections from the chapter to support your thesis.

> There is nothing easier than lopping off heads and nothing harder than developing ideas.
>
> —Fyodor Dostoevsky

> People sleep peaceably in their beds at night only because rough men stand ready to do violence on their behalf.
>
> —George Orwell

We know how to organize warfare, but do we know how to act when confronted with peace?

—Jacques-Yves Cousteau

Peace is not merely a distant goal that we seek, but a means by which we arrive at that end.

—Martin Luther King Jr.

Of course the people don't want war . . . that is understood. But voice or no voice, the people can always be brought to the bidding of the leaders. That is easy. All you have to do is tell them they are being attacked, and denounce the pacifists for lack of patriotism and exposing the country to danger. It works the same in any country.

—Hermann Goering

The first casualty when war comes is truth.

—Senator Hiram Johnson

The nation that makes a great distinction between its scholars and its warriors will have its thinking done by cowards, and its fighting done by fools.

—Thucydides

9. If you enjoyed Tim O'Brien's story, you might want to read "Speaking of Courage," also from the book *The Things They Carried*. Then either write an essay comparing the postwar experiences of Harold Krebs—the protagonist of Hemingway's "Soldier's Home"—and Norman Bowker—the main character in "Speaking of Courage"—or write a personal response to "Soldier's Home" in Bowker's voice.

MLA Guidelines for a List of Works Cited

Print Resources

1. A Book With One Author

A book with one author serves as a general model for most MLA citations. Include author, title, city of publication, publisher, date of publication, and medium.

> Robinson, Marilynne. *Gilead: A Novel*. New York: Farrar, 2004. Print.

2. A Book with Multiple Authors

> King, Stephen, and Peter Straub. *Black House*. New York: Random, 2001. Print.

3. Two or More Works by the Same Author

Multiple entries should be arranged alphabetically by title. The author's name appears at the beginning of the first entry, but is replaced by three hyphens and a period in all subsequent entries.

> Pynchon, Thomas. *Against the Day*. New York: Penguin, 2006. Print.

> ---. *Inherent Vice*. New York: Penguin, 2009. Print.

4. Author and Editor Both Named

> Vidal, Gore. *The Selected Essays of Gore Vidal*. Ed. Jay Parini. New York: Vintage, 2009. Print.

Alternately, to cite the editor's contribution, start with the editor's name.

> Parini, Jay, ed. *The Selected Essays of Gore Vidal*. By Gore Vidal. New York: Vintage, 2009. Print.

5. Anthology

> Oates, Joyce Carol, ed. *Telling Stories: An Anthology for Writers*. New York: Norton, 1997. Print.

6. Translation

> Barthes, Roland. *S/Z*. Trans. Richard Miller. New York: Hill-Farrar, 1974. Print.

7. Entry in a Reference Work

Because most reference works are alphabetized, you should omit page numbers.

> Lounsberry, Barbara. "Joan Didion." *Encyclopedia of the Essay*. Ed. Tracy Chandler. Chicago: Fitzroy Dearborn, 1997. Print.

For a well-known encyclopedia, use only the edition and year of publication. When an article is not attributed to an author, begin entry with article title.

> "Gilgamesh." *The Columbia Encyclopedia*. 5th ed. 1993. Print.

8. Sacred Text

Unless a specific published edition is being cited, sacred texts should be omitted from the works-cited list.

> *The New Testament*. Trans. Richmond Lattimore. New York: North Point-Farrar, 1997. Print.

9. Article in a Journal

The title of the journal should be followed by the volume, issue, and year of the journal's publication.

> Rush, Fred. "Appreciating Susan Sontag." *Philosophy and Literature* 33.1 (2009): 36–49. Print.

10. Article in a Magazine

In a weekly:

> Menand, Louis. "The Unpolitical Animal: How Political Science Understands Voters." *New Yorker* 30 Aug. 2004: 92–96. Print.

In a monthly:

> Baker, Kevin. "Barack Hoover Obama: The Best and the Brightest Blow It Again." *Harper's* July 2009: 29–37. Print.

11. Article in a Newspaper

If you are citing a local paper that does not contain the city name in its title, add the city name in brackets after the title.

> Edge, John T. "Fast Food Even Before Fast Food." *New York Times* 30 Sept. 2009, late ed.: D1+. Print.

12. Review

In a weekly:

> Davis, Jordan. "Happy Thoughts!" Rev. of *The Golden Age of Paraphernalia*, by Kevin
> Davies. *Nation* 23 Feb. 2009: 31–34. Print.

In a monthly:

> Simpson, Mona. "Imperfect Union." Rev. of *Mrs. Woolf and the Servants*, by Alison
> Light. *Atlantic Monthly* Jan.–Feb. 2009: 93–101. Print.

Electronic Resources

13. Article from a Database Accessed through a Subscription Service

Follow the normal rules for citing a journal article, but follow this with the name
of the subscription service in italics, the medium used, and the date of access.

> Anderson, Walter E. "*Heart of Darkness*: The Sublime Spectacle." *University of Toronto
> Quarterly* 57.3 (1988): 402–20. *Academic Search Premier*. Web. 14 Mar. 2005.

14. Article in an Online Magazine

Follow the author name and article title with the name of the magazine in italics,
the organization hosting the Web page (usually found at the very bottom of the
site), the date published, the medium, and the date accessed. If there is no host or
sponsor of the site, write *N.p.*, for "no publisher."

> Yoffe, Emily. "Full Metal Racket: Metal Detecting Is the World's Worst Hobby." *Slate*.
> Washington Post. Newsweek Interactive, 25 Sept. 2009. Web. 30 Sept. 2009.

15. Article in an Online Newspaper

> Sisario, Ben. "Record Stores: Out of Sight, Not Obsolete." *New York Times*. New York
> Times, 29 Sept. 2009. Web. 30 Sept. 2009.

16. Online Review

> Stevens, Dana. "There's Something about Keats." Rev. of *Bright Star*, dir. Jane
> Campion. *Salon*. Salon Media Group, 25 Sept. 2009. Web. 30 Sept. 2009.

17. Entry in an Online Reference Work

> "John Ruskin." *Encyclopædia Britannica Online*. Encyclopædia Britannica, 2009.
> Web. 5 Oct. 2009

18. Work from a Web Site

> "Wallace Stevens (1879–1955)." *Poetryfoundation.org*. Poetry Foundation, 2009.
> Web. 30 Sept. 2009.

19. Entire Web Site

Web site with editor:

> Dutton, Dennis, ed. *Arts and Letters Daily*. Chronicle of Higher Education, 2009.
> Web. 2 Oct. 2009.

Web site without editor:

> *Poets.org*. Academy of American Poets, 2009. Web. 2 Oct. 2009.

For a personal Web site, use the following model:

> Mendelson, Edward. Home page. Columbia U, 2009. Web. 2 Oct. 2009.

20. Entire Web Log (Blog)

If there is no host or sponsor of the site, write *N.p.*, for "no publisher."

> Holbo, John, ed. *The Valve*. N.p., 2 Oct. 2009. Web. 2 Oct. 2009.

21. Entry in a Wiki

> "Pre-Raphaelite Brotherhood." *Wikipedia*. Wikimedia Foundation, 1 Oct. 2009. Web.
> 2 Oct. 2009.

Other

22. Film, Video, or DVD

Follow the title with the director, notable performers, the distribution company, the date of release, and the medium. For films viewed on the Web, follow this with the name of the Web site used to view the film, the medium (*Web*), and the date viewed. If citing the editor's contribution, begin the entry with his or her name before the title.

Viewed in theaters:

> *The Hurt Locker*. Dir. Kathryn Bigelow. Summit, 2009. Film.

Viewed on DVD or videocassette (follow original release date with distributor and release date of DVD or video):

> *Dead Poets Society*. Dir. Peter Weir. Perf. Robin Williams. 1989. Buena Vista Home
> Entertainment, 2006. DVD.

Viewed on the Web (use original distributor and release date):

> Lynch, David, dir. *The Elephant Man*. Perf. Anthony Hopkins and John Hurt.
> Paramount, 1980. *Netflix*. Web. 2 Oct. 2009.

23. Broadcast Interview

On the radio:

> Gioia, Dana. Interview with Leonard Lopate. *The Leonard Lopate Show*. NPR. WNYC,
> New York, 19 July 2004. Radio.

On the Web:

> Gioia, Dana. Interview with Leonard Lopate. *The Leonard Lopate Show. NPR.org.* NPR,
> 19 July 2004. Web. 2 Oct. 2009.

24. Lecture or Speech

Viewed in person:

> Updike, John. "The Clarity of Things: What Is American about American Art?"
> Jefferson Lecture in the Humanities. NEH. Warner Theatre, Washington, D.C.
> 22 May 2008. Lecture.

Viewed on the Web:

> Jin, Ha. Lowell Humanities Series. Boston College. *Boston College Front Row.* Trustees
> of Boston College, 16 Apr. 2009. Web. 2 Oct. 2009.

25. Podcast

> "The Consequences to Come." Moderator Robert Silvers. Participants Darryl Pinckney,
> Ronald Dworkin, Joan Didion, and Mark Danner. *New York Review of Books.*
> NYREV, Inc., 24 Sept. 2008. MP3 File.

26. Work of Art or Photograph

In a museum:

> Hopper, Edward. *Nighthawks.* 1942. Oil on canvas. Art Institute, Chicago.

On the Web:

> Thiebaud, Wayne. *Three Machines.* 1963. De Young Museum, San Francisco. *Famsf.org.*
> Web. 2 Oct. 2009.

In print:

> Clark, Edward. *Navy CPO Graham Jackson Plays "Goin' Home."* 1945. Life Gallery of
> Photography. *The Great LIFE Photographers.* Eds. of *Life.* New York: Bulfinch,
> 2004. 78–79. Print.

27. Map or Chart

In print:

> "U.S. Personal Savings Rate, 1929–1999." Chart. *Credit Card Nation: The
> Consequences of America's Addiction to Credit.* By Robert D. Manning.
> New York: Basic, 2000. 100. Print.

On the Web:

> "1914 New Balkan States and Central Europe Map." Map. *National Geographic.*
> National Geographic Society, 2009. Web. 5 Oct. 2009.

28. Cartoon or Comic Strip

In print:

> Vey, P. C. Cartoon. *New Yorker* 10 Nov. 2008: 54. Print.

On the Web:

> Davis, Jim. "Garfield." Comic strip. *Garfield.com*. Paws, 24 July 2001. Web.
> 2 Oct. 2009.

29. Advertisement

In print:

> Rosetta Stone. Advertisement. *Harper's* Aug. 2008: 21. Print.

On the Web:

> Zurich. Advertisement. *Wall Street Journal*. Dow Jones, Inc., 2 Oct. 2009. Web.
> 2 Oct. 2009.

Glossary of Terms

abstract An abstract term is a general term, referring to a broad concept, as opposed to a term that refers to a specific, particular thing (e.g., *personhood* as opposed to *Seamus Heaney*); opposite of **concrete**.

> **EXAMPLE:**
> *Beauty is truth, truth beauty,—that is all*
> *Ye know on earth, and all ye need to know.*
> —JOHN KEATS, "Ode on a Grecian Urn," p. 1103

act The major subunit into which the action of a play is divided. The number of acts in a play typically ranges between one and five, and are usually further divided into scenes.

allegory A literary work that portrays abstract ideas concretely. Characters in an allegory are frequently personifications of abstract ideas and are given names that refer to these ideas.

> **EXAMPLE:**
> *"Young Goodman Brown" by Nathaniel Hawthorne, p. 452*

alliteration The repetition of the same initial consonant sounds in a sequence of words or syllables.

> **EXAMPLE:**
> *Methinks 'tis pretty sport to hear a child,*
> *Rocking a word in mouth yet undefiled;*
> *The tender racquet rudely plays the sound*
> *Which, weakly bandied, cannot back rebound.*
> —THOMAS BASTARD, "De Puero Balbutiente," p. 296

allusion A reference to another work of literature, or to art, history, or current events.

> **EXAMPLE:**
> *In "Sound and Sense" (p. 1095), Alexander Pope alludes to characters from classical Greek literature:*
>
> *When Ajax strives, some rock's vast weight to throw*
> *The line too labors, and the words move slow;*
> *Not so, when swift Camilla scours the plain,*
> *Flies o'er th' unbending corn, and skims along the main.*

1479

analogy In literature, a comparison between two things that helps explain or illustrate one or both of them.

> **EXAMPLE:**
> There is Mr. Marblehall's ancestral home. It's not so wonderfully large—it has only four columns—but you always look toward it, the way you always glance into tunnels and see nothing.
>
> —EUDORA WELTY, "Old Mr. Marblehall," p. 24

anapest See **meter.**

anaphora Repetition of an initial word or words to add emphasis.

> **EXAMPLE:**
> <u>Whose</u> herds with milk, whose fields with bread,
> <u>Whose</u> flocks supply him with attire;
> <u>Whose</u> trees in summer yield him shade,
>   In winter, fire.
>
> —ALEXANDER POPE, "The Quiet Life," p. 497

annotation The act of noting observations directly on a text, especially anything striking or confusing, in order to record ideas and impressions for later analysis.

> **EXAMPLE:** See pp. 1154–55 for an annotation of Robert Browning's "My Last Duchess."

antagonist Character in a story or play who opposes the protagonist; while not necessarily an enemy, the antagonist creates or intensifies a conflict for the protagonist. An evil antagonist is a villain.

> **EXAMPLE:**
> In William Shakespeare's Hamlet (p. 720), Claudius is the antagonist.

apostrophe A direct address to an abstraction (such as Time), a thing (the Wind), an animal, or an imaginary or absent person.

> **EXAMPLE:**
> Leave me, O Love which reachest but to dust;
> And thou, my mind, aspire to higher things.
>
> —SIR PHILIP SIDNEY, "Leave me, O Love, which reachest but to dust," p. 669

archaic language Words that were once common but that are no longer used.

> **EXAMPLES:**
> HORATIO: What <u>art thou</u> that <u>usurp'st</u> this time of night,
> Together with that fair and warlike form
> In which the majesty of buried Denmark
> Did sometimes march? by heaven I charge <u>thee</u>, speak!
>
> —WILLIAM SHAKESPEARE, Hamlet, p. 722

ars poetica Literally, "the art of poetry"; a form of poetry written about poetry.

> **EXAMPLE:**
> "On the Sonnet" by John Keats, p. 1101

assonance The repetition of vowel sounds in a sequence of words.

> **EXAMPLE:**
>
> *That church so lone, the log-built one,*
> *That echoed to many a parting groan*
> > *And natural prayer*
> > *Of dying foemen mingled there.*
> > > —HERMAN MELVILLE, "Shiloh: A Requiem (April, 1862)," p. 1422

atmosphere The feeling created for the reader by a work of literature. Atmosphere can be generated by many things, but especially **style, tone**, and **setting**. Synonymous with **mood**.

> **EXAMPLE:**
>
> *See the discussion of how setting creates atmosphere in Edgar Allan Poe's* The Masque of the Red Death *(p. 67).*

ballad First taking shape in the later Middle Ages, the ballad was a sung poem that recounted a dramatic story. Ballads were passed down orally from generation to generation. Arising in the Romantic period, the literary ballad—a poem intentionally imitative of the ballad's style and structure—attempted to capture the sentiments of the common people in the same way the traditional ballad had. See also **stanza**.

> **EXAMPLE:**
>
> *"We Are Seven" by William Wordsworth, p. 300*

Beat movement A movement of American writers in the 1950s who saw American society as oppressively conformist. These writers rejected mainstream values, seeking ways to escape through drugs, various forms of spirituality, and sexual experimentation. The writers of the Beat generation, among them Allen Ginsberg and Jack Kerouac, celebrated freedom of expression and held generally antiestablishment views about politics. Their writing, likewise, rejected conventional norms of structure and diction, and their books prompted several notorious obscenity trials, which helped reshape censorship laws in the United States.

> **EXAMPLE:**
>
> *"Is About" by Allen Ginsburg, p. 934.*

bildungsroman A novel that explores the maturation of the protagonist, with the narrative usually moving the main character from childhood into adulthood. Also called a coming-of-age story.

> **EXAMPLE:**
>
> Daisy Miller *by Henry James, p. 1166*

blank verse Unrhymed iambic pentameter, blank verse is the most commonly used verse form in English because it is the verse form that comes closest to natural patterns of speaking in English. See also **iambic pentameter**.

> **EXAMPLE:**
>
> *This is my son, mine own Telemachus,*
> *To whom I leave the sceptre and the isle—*
> *Well-loved of me, discerning to fulfil*

> *This labour, by slow prudence to make mild*
> *A rugged people, and through soft degrees*
> *Subdue them to the useful and the good.*
> *Most blameless is he, centred in the sphere*
> *Of common duties, decent not to fail*
> *In offices of tenderness, and pay*
> *Meet adoration to my household gods,*
> *When I am gone. He works his work, I mine.*
>
> —ALFRED, LORD TENNYSON, "Ulysses," pp. 1444–45

cadence Quality of spoken text formed from combining the text's rhythm with the rise and fall in the inflection of the speaker's voice.

EXAMPLE:

In Matthew Arnold's "Dover Beach" (pp. 1265–66), the poet creates a cadence that imitates a changing wave pattern by using caesura (with commas)

Listen! you hear the grating roar
Of pebbles which the waves draw back, and fling,
At their return, up the high strand,
Begin, and cease, and then again begin,
With tremulous cadence slow, and bring
The eternal note of sadness in.

caesura A pause within a line of poetry, sometimes punctuated, sometimes not, often mirroring natural speech.

EXAMPLE:

O could I lose all father now! for why
Will man lament the state he should envy.

—BEN JONSON, "On My First Son," p. 297

caricature A character with features or traits that are exaggerated so that the character seems ridiculous. The term is usually applied to graphic depictions but can also be applied to written depictions.

EXAMPLE:

The characters in David Zane Mairowitz and Robert Crumb's Kafka (p. 981) are caricatures.

carpe diem A widespread literary theme meaning "seize the day" in Latin and found especially in lyric poetry, carpe diem encourages readers to enjoy the present and make the most of their short lives.

EXAMPLE:

"To the Virgins, to Make Much of Time" by Robert Herrick, p. 672

catharsis Refers to the emotional release felt by the audience at the end of a tragic drama. The term comes from Aristotle's *Poetics*, in which he explains this frequently felt relief in terms of a purification of the emotions caused by watching the tragic events. (*Catharsis* means "purgation" or "purification" in Greek.)

EXAMPLE:
Antigone *by Sophocles, p. 1327*

character A person depicted in a narrative. While this term generally refers to human beings, it can also include animals or inanimate objects that are given human characteristics. Several more specific terms are used to refer to types of characters frequently employed by authors:

> flat character A character embodying only one or two traits and who lacks character development; for this reason, a flat character is also called a static character. Often such characters exist only to provide background or adequate motivation for a protagonist's actions.
>
> > **EXAMPLE:**
> > *In Gish Jen's "Who's Irish?" (p. 1250), the narrator's son-in-law is described only as being lazy and depressed; his role in the story is to step into a stereotypical, stock role, providing the narrator with fuel for her prejudice.*
>
> round character A character exhibiting a range of emotions and who evolves over the course of the story.
>
> > **EXAMPLE:**
> > *In Shakespeare's* Hamlet *(p. 720), Hamlet is a round character who experiences complex emotional development throughout the play.*
>
> secondary character A supporting character; while not as prominent or central as a main character, he or she is still important to the events of a story or play.
>
> > **EXAMPLE:**
> > *In Sophocles'* Antigone *(p. 1327), Haemon is a secondary character.*
>
> stock character A type of flat character based on a stereotype; one who falls into an immediately recognizable category or type—such as the absentminded professor or the town drunk—and thus resists unique characterization. Stock characters can be artfully used for humor or satire.
>
> > **EXAMPLE:**
> > *In Flannery O'Connor's "A Good Man Is Hard to Find" (p. 1211), June Star and John Wesley are portrayed as stock characters—spoiled, bratty children.*

characterization The method by which the author builds, or reveals, a character; it can be direct or indirect. Indirect characterization means that an author shows rather than tells us what a character is like through what the character says, does, or thinks, or what others say about the character. Direct characterization occurs when a narrator tells the reader who a character is by describing the background, motivation, temperament, or appearance of a character.

> **EXAMPLE:**
> *Direct characterization: "Fenstad's Mother" by Charles Baxter (p. 1233):*
> *Fenstad's mother was a lifelong social progressive who was amused by her son's churchgoing, and, wine or no wine, she could guess where he had been. She had spent her life in the company of rebels and deviationists, and she recognized all their styles.*

Indirect characterization: Pride and Prejudice *by Jane Austen, p. 65*

Mr. Darcy danced only once with Mrs. Hurst and once with Miss Bingley, declined being intro-duced to any other lady, and spent the rest of the evening in walking about the room, speaking occasionally to one of his own party. His character was decided. He was the proudest, most dis-agreeable man in the world, and every body hoped that he would never come there again.

chorus In drama, especially classical Greek drama, the chorus refers to a group of par-ticipants in a play who deliver commentary on the play's action. The role of the chorus is no longer a regular feature of modern drama, although it has been employed in a few prominent works, such as T. S. Eliot's *Murder in the Cathedral.* See also **drama.**

> **EXAMPLE:**
> Antigone *by Sophocles, p. 1327*

climax The point in a story when the conflict reaches its highest intensity.

> **EXAMPLE:**
> *In Alice Walker's "Everyday Use" (p. 1226), the climax occurs when Mama (the narrator) makes the forceful decision to take the family quilts from her daughter Dee (who intends to hang them as artwork, a symbol of her heritage) and return them to her daughter Maggie (who would use them for their intended purpose—as quilts).*

colloquial language/colloquialism An expression or language construction appro-priate only for casual, informal speaking or writing.

> **EXAMPLE:**
> *"I toldja shut up, Ellie," Arnold Friend said, "you're deaf, get a hearing aid, right? Fix your-self up. This little girl's no trouble and's gonna be nice to me, so Ellie keep to yourself, this ain't your date right? Don't hem in on me, don't hog, don't crush, don't bird dog, don't trail me," he said in a rapid, meaningless voice, as if he were running through all the expressions he'd learned but was no longer sure which of them was in style, then rushing on to new ones, making them up with his eyes closed.*
>
> —JOYCE CAROL OATES, *"Where Are You Going, Where Have You Been?" p. 467*

colonialism The occupation of one country by another. In the early 1800s, European countries controlled 35 percent of the world, but by 1914, that number had risen to nearly 85 percent and included parts of Africa, Asia, Latin America, and the Carib-bean. The legacy of colonialism has extended beyond the political independence that many countries gained in the 1960s and 1970s.

> **EXAMPLE:**
> *See the works on pp. 533–62.*

comedy Usually used to refer to a dramatic work that, in contrast to tragedy, has a light, amusing plot, features a happy ending, centers around ordinary people, and is written and performed in the vernacular.

> **EXAMPLE:**
> The Importance of Being Earnest *by Oscar Wilde, p. 574*

comedy of manners A satiric dramatic form that lampoons social conventions.

EXAMPLE:

Oscar Wilde's The Importance of Being Earnest *(p. 574) is a comedy of manners.*

coming-of-age story See **bildungsroman.**

complex sentence See **sentence.**

compound sentence See **sentence.**

compound-complex sentence See **sentence.**

concrete A concrete term is one that refers to a specific, particular thing, as opposed to a term that refers to a broad concept (e.g., *Seamus Heaney* as opposed to *personhood*); opposite of **abstract.**

EXAMPLE:

Krebs went to the war from a Methodist college in Kansas. There is a picture which shows him among his fraternity brothers, all of them wearing exactly the same height and style collar. He enlisted in the Marines in 1917 and did not return to the United States until the second division returned from the Rhine in the summer of 1919.

—ERNEST HEMINGWAY, "Soldier's Home," p. 1447

conflict The tension, opposition, or struggle that drives a plot. External conflict is the opposition or tension between two characters or forces. Internal conflict occurs within a character. Conflict usually arises between the protagonist and the antagonist in a story.

EXAMPLE:

In Herman Melville's "Bartleby, the Scrivener" (p. 854), the story's external conflict is between Bartleby, who won't leave his office after being fired, and the narrator, who is trying to remove him.

connotation Meanings or associations readers have with a word or item beyond its dictionary definition, or denotation. Connotations may reveal another layer of meaning of a piece, affect the tone, or suggest symbolic resonance.

EXAMPLE:

In the following lines from Ben Jonson's "On My First Son" (p. 297), the word lament—*as opposed to synonyms such as* cry *or* feel bad about—*has formal and religious connotations.*

Will man lament the state he should envy,
To have so soon 'scaped world's and flesh's rage,
And, if no other misery, yet age!

consonance An instance in which identical final consonant sounds in nearby words follow different vowel sounds. See also **rhyme.**

EXAMPLE:

*Let the boy try along this bayonet-bla_de_*
How cold steel is, and keen with hunger of bloo_d_;
Blue with all malice, like a madman's fla_sh_;
And thinly drawn with famishing for fle_sh_.

—WILFRED OWEN, "Arms and the Boy," p. 1440

couplet See **stanza**.

cumulative sentence See **sentence**.

dactyl See **meter**.

denotation The literal definition of a word, often referred to as the "dictionary definition."

denouement Pronounced *day-noo-moh*, this literally means "untying the knot"; in this phase of a story's plot, the conflict has been resolved and balance is restored to the world of the story.

> **EXAMPLE:**
> *In Fences (p. 195) by August Wilson, the conflicts of the play are resolved with the death of Troy in Act II, scene iv. The scene that follows (Act II, scene v) is the play's denouement.*

dialect Dialogue or narration written to simulate regional or cultural speech patterns.

> **EXAMPLE:**
> Troy: . . . *Man ain't had two dimes to rub together. He walking around with his shoes all run over bumming money for cigarettes.*
>
> —August Wilson, *Fences*, p. 207

dialogue The written depiction of conversation between characters.

> **EXAMPLE:**
> *"Who is this?" I demanded, thinking: heavy breather, prank caller.*
> *"Who d'you think?" Sourdi was crying, a tiny crimped sound that barely crept out of the receiver. Then her voice steadied with anger and grew familiar. "Is Ma there?"*
> *"What's the matter? What happened?"*
> *"Just let me speak to Ma, O.K.?" There was a pause, as Sourdi blew her nose. "Tell her it's important."*
>
> —May-lee Chai, "Saving Sourdi," p. 288

diction A writer's choice of words. In addition to choosing words with precise denotations and connotations, an author must choose whether to use words that are abstract or concrete, formal or informal, or literal or figurative. See **colloquial language**.

> **EXAMPLE:**
> *See the close reading of a section from Robert Herrick's "Delight in Disorder" (pp. 31–2).*

direct characterization See **characterization**.

dramatic irony See **irony, dramatic**.

dramatic monologue A type of poem in which the speaker, who is clearly distinct from the poet, addresses an audience that is present in the poem.

> **EXAMPLE:**
> *"My Last Duchess" by Robert Browning, p. 1104*

ekphrastic poetry A form of poetry that comments on a work of art in another genre, such as a painting or a piece of music.

EXAMPLE:

"Hopper's 'Nighthawks' (1942)" by Ira Sadoff, p. 1118

elegy A contemplative poem, on death and mortality, often written for someone who has died.

EXAMPLE:

"Elegy for the Native Guards" by Natasha Trethewey, p. 1437

end rhyme See **rhyme**.

end-stopped line An end-stopped line of poetry concludes with punctuation that marks a pause. The line is completely meaningful in itself, unlike run-on lines, which require the reader to move to the next line to grasp the poet's complete thought. See also **enjambment**.

EXAMPLE:

Surely some revelation is at hand;
Surely the Second Coming is at hand.

—WILLIAM BUTLER YEATS, "The Second Coming," p. 1272

English sonnet See **sonnet**.

enjambment A poetic technique in which one line ends without a pause and must continue on to the next line to complete its meaning; also referred to as a "run-on line."

EXAMPLE:

Once more the storm is howling, and hid
Under this cradle-hood and coverlids
My child sleeps on. There is no obstacle
But Gregory's wood and one bare hill
Whereby the haystack- and roof-levelling wind,
Bred on the Atlantic, can be stayed.

—WILLIAM BUTLER YEATS, "A Prayer for My Daughter," p. 302

epigram A short, witty statement designed to surprise an audience or a reader.

EXAMPLE:

"To lose one parent, Mr. Worthing, may be regarded as a misfortune; to lose both looks like carelessness."

—OSCAR WILDE, *The Importance of Being Earnest*, p. 585

epigraph A quotation preceding a work of literature that helps set the text's mood or suggests its themes.

EXAMPLE:

"The dragon is by the side of the road, watching those who pass. Beware lest he devour you. We go to the Father of Souls, but it is necessary to pass by the dragon."—St. Cyril of Jerusalem

—FLANNERY O'CONNOR, "A Good Man Is Hard to Find," p. 1211

epiphany A character's transformative moment of realization. James Joyce, often credited with coining this as a literary term, defined it as the "sudden revelation of the whatness of a thing," the moment in which "the soul of the commonest object . . .

seems to us radiant . . . a sudden spiritual manifestation [either] in the vulgarity of speech or of a gesture or in a memorable phrase of the mind itself."

> **EXAMPLE:**
>
> *I put in windows with arches. I drew flying buttresses. I hung great doors. I couldn't stop. . . . So we kept on with it. His fingers rode my fingers as my hand went over the paper. It was like nothing else in my life up to now.*
>
> *Then he said, "I think that's it. I think you got it," he said. "Take a look. What do you think?"*
>
> *But I had my eyes closed. I thought I'd keep them that way for a little longer. I thought it was something I ought to do.*
>
> *"Well?" he said. "Are you looking?"*
>
> *My eyes were still closed. I was in my house. I knew that. But I didn't feel like I was inside anything.*
>
> *"It's really something," I said.*
>
> —RAYMOND CARVER, "Cathedral," p. 1089

eulogy A poem, speech, or other work written in great praise of something or someone, usually a person no longer living.

> **EXAMPLE:**
>
> *William Wordsworth's "London, 1802" (p. 1099) is a eulogy to the poet John Milton.*

exposition In a literary work, contextual and background information told to readers (rather than shown through action) about the characters, plot, setting, and situation.

> **EXAMPLE:**
>
> *In* Antigone *(p. 1327), Sophocles uses the opening dialogue and initial speeches of the chorus and sentry to provide background on the play's events and characters.*

extended metaphor See **metaphor, extended**.

eye rhyme See **rhyme**.

falling action In a plot diagram, this is the result (or fallout) of the climax or turning point. In this phase, the conflict is being resolved. See also **plot**.

> **EXAMPLE:**
>
> *See the analysis of the plot of Gabriel García Márquez's "One of These Days," including its falling action, on pp. 62–3.*

farce A dramatic form marked by wholly absurd situations, slapstick, raucous wordplay, and sometimes innuendo.

> **EXAMPLE:**
>
> *Oscar Wilde's* The Importance of Being Earnest *(p. 574) contains moments of farce, particularly the section on pp. 575–81 regarding cucumber sandwiches.*

feminist literature Literary works that explore (either overtly or implicitly) women's identity and role in society. Feminist criticism reexamines literary works and the role of women in literature.

EXAMPLES:

"Homage to My Hips" by Lucille Clifton, p. 932, and "The Yellow Wallpaper" by Charlotte Perkins Gilman, p. 1066

figurative language Language that uses figures of speech; nonliteral language usually evoking strong images. Sometimes referred to as metaphorical language, most of its forms explain, clarify, or enhance an idea by comparing it to something else; the comparison can be explicit (simile) or implied (metaphor). Other forms of figurative language include **personification, paradox, overstatement (hyperbole), understatement**, and **irony**.

EXAMPLE:

There is a knocker shaped like a gasping fish on the door. . . . There's many a big, deathly looking tapestry, wrinkling and thin, many a sofa shaped like an S. Brocades as tall as wicked queens in Italian tales stand gathered before the windows. Everything is draped and hooded and shaded, of course, unaffectionate but close.

—EUDORA WELTY, "Old Mr. Marblehall," p. 24

first-person narrator See **narrator**.

flashback A scene in a narrative that is set in an earlier time than the main action.

EXAMPLE:

See the first two paragraphs of "Woman Hollering Creek" by Sandra Cisneros, p. 623.

foil A contrasting character who allows the protagonist to stand out more distinctly.

EXAMPLE:

In Shakespeare's Hamlet *(p. 720), Laertes—who leaps at vengeance rather than deeply contemplates it—is the perfect foil for Hamlet.*

foot See **meter**.

foreshadowing A plot device in which future events are hinted at.

EXAMPLE:

See paragraphs 11–13 of Joseph Conrad's Heart of Darkness, *p. 369.*

form Refers to the defining structural characteristics of a work, especially a poem (i.e., meter and rhyme scheme). Often poets work within set forms, such as the sonnet or sestina, which require adherence to fixed conventions.

formal diction See **diction**.

free verse A form of poetry that does not have a regular rhythm or rhyme scheme.

EXAMPLE:

And would it have been worth it, after all,
Would it have been worth while,
After the sunsets and the dooryards and the sprinkled streets,
After the novels, after the teacups, after the skirts that trail along the floor
And this, and so much more?—
It is impossible to say just what I mean!

—T. S. ELIOT, "The Love Song of J. Alfred Prufrock," p. 1036 genre This term can refer broadly to the general category that a literary work falls into (drama or poetry, fiction or nonfiction) or more specifically to a certain subset of literary works grouped together on the basis of similar characteristics (science fiction, local color, western).

> **EXAMPLE:**
> Flannery O'Connor's "A Good Man Is Hard to Find" (p. 1211) is a piece of fiction that is also classified as Southern gothic.

Harlem Renaissance A movement in the 1920s and 1930s marked by a great flowering of black arts and culture centered in the Harlem neighborhood of New York City.

> **EXAMPLES:**
> See the works on pp. 1294–1312.

hook An opening to a piece of writing designed to catch the audience's attention.

> **EXAMPLE:**
> See the first paragraph of "The End of White America?" by Hua Hsu, p. 7.

hubris An excessive level of pride that leads to the protagonist's downfall. See also **tragedy**.

> **EXAMPLE:**
> See Creon's actions in Antigone by Sophocles, p. 1327.

hyperbole Deliberate exaggeration used for emphasis or to produce a comic or ironic effect; an overstatement to make a point.

> **EXAMPLE:**
> You know how children with cameras learn to work the exposed moments that define the family cluster. They break every trust, spy out the undefended space, catching Mom coming out of the bathroom in her cumbrous robe and turbaned towel, looking bloodless and plucked. It is not a joke. They will shoot you sitting on the pot if they can manage a suitable vantage.
>
> —Don DeLillo, "Videotape," p. 1091

iamb See **meter**.

iambic pentameter An iamb, the most common metrical foot in English poetry, is made up of an unstressed syllable followed by a stressed one. Iambic pentameter, then, is a rhythmic meter containing five iambs. Unrhymed iambic pentameter is called blank verse. See also **meter; blank verse.**

> **EXAMPLE:**
> The cur | few tolls | the knell | of part | ing day,
> The low | ing herd | wind slow | ly o'er | the lea,
> The plow | man home | ward plods | his wea | ry way,
> And leaves | the world | to dark | ness and | to me
>
> — Thomas Gray, "Elegy Written in a Country Churchyard," p. 1259

iconography The images or symbols used by an artist or present in a work of art.

imagery A description of how something looks, feels, tastes, smells, or sounds. The verbal expression of a sensory experience: visual (sight), auditory (sound), olfactory (scent), gustatory (taste), tactile (touch), or kinesthetic (movement/tension). Imagery may use literal or figurative language.

> EXAMPLE:
> *Queer little red bugs came out and moved in slow squadrons around me. Their backs were polished vermilion, with black spots.*
>
> —WILLA CATHER, *My Antonia*, pp. 19–20

imperative sentence See **sentence**.

impressionism A movement of French painters that reached its apex in the 1870s and 1880s. The impressionists attempted to capture the subjective experience of seeing things rather than create accurate reproductions. Key representatives include Claude Monet, Pierre-Auguste Renoir, and Edgar Degas. The impressionists' attempts to capture subjective experience in art was very influential on symbolist poets and writers of stream-of-consciousness prose, such as James Joyce (p. 77) and Virginia Woolf (p. 77–78).

> EXAMPLE:
> *"The Laundresses" by Edgar Degas, p. 1121*

in medias res Latin for "in the middle of things," a technique in which a narrative begins in the middle of the action.

> EXAMPLE:
> *"Videotape" by Don DeLillo, p. 1090*

indirect characterization See **characterization**.

informal diction See **diction**.

internal rhyme See **rhyme**.

interrupted sentence See **sentence**.

inversion Also called an inverted sentence, it is created by alteration of the standard English word order of a subject (S) being followed by a verb (V) and its object (O) in a declarative sentence. Often used to call attention to something, perhaps to emphasize a point or an idea by placing it in the initial position, or to slow the pace by choosing an unusual order.

> EXAMPLE:
>   O   S   V   O   S V
> So: <u>looks he had</u>, his own <u>trade he had</u>, there would have been a good wife in time.
>
> —SALMAN RUSHDIE, "The Free Radio," p. 1244

irony, dramatic Tension created by the contrast between what a character says or thinks and what the audience or readers know to be true; as a result of this technique, some words and actions in a story or play take on a different meaning for the reader than they do for the characters.

EXAMPLE:

Once readers learn of Mr. Kapasi's hope for a relationship with Mrs. Das, in Jhumpa Lahiri's "Interpreter of Maladies" (p. 434), his actions take on a different meaning for the readers than for her.

irony, situational A pointed discrepancy between what seems fitting or expected in a story and what actually happens.

EXAMPLE:

T. C. Boyle's story "Admiral"(p. 887) is ripe with situational irony. While pet-sitting for Admiral II, a cloned dog, Nisha falls for an anti-cloning activist. Also, Nisha's instructions from the cloned dog's owners are to, in essence, bring their original pet back to life by treating this dog exactly as she did the original, who was struck by a car; to do so she must let Admiral II indulge his love of playing in traffic, which could lead him, ironically, to share Admiral I's fate.

irony, verbal A figure of speech that occurs when a speaker or character says one thing but means something else, or when what is said is the opposite of what is expected, creating a noticeable incongruity. **Sarcasm** involves verbal irony used derisively.

EXAMPLE:

JACK (pulling off his gloves): *When one is in town one amuses oneself. When one is in the country one amuses other people. It is excessively boring.*
ALGERNON: *And who are the people you amuse?*
JACK (airily): *Oh, neighbors, neighbors.*
ALGERNON: *Got nice neighbors in your part of Shropshire?*
JACK: *Perfectly horrid! Never speak to one of them.*
ALGERNON: *How immensely you must amuse them!*
—OSCAR WILDE, *The Importance of Being Earnest*, p. 576

Italian sonnet See **sonnet**.

juxtaposition Placing two things side by side for the sake of comparison or contrast. Authors sometimes use incongruous juxtapositions to produce **verbal irony**.

EXAMPLE:

HAMLET: *To be, or not to be: that is the question:*
Whether 'tis nobler in the mind to suffer
The slings and arrows of outrageous fortune,
Or to take arms against a sea of troubles,
And by opposing end them? To die: to sleep;
—WILLIAM SHAKESPEARE, *Hamlet*, p. 768

Kafkaesque Having the nightmarish, uncanny characteristics of Kafka's stories.

limited omniscient point of view See **point of view**.

literary elements The components that together create a literary work. This term encompasses elements of style, such as imagery, syntax, figurative language, and tone; as well as storytelling elements, such as plot, character, setting, and point of view.

lyric A short poem expressing the personal feelings of a first-person speaker. The term comes from the Greek word *lyre*, and the form is descended from poems intended to be sung with a lyre.

> EXAMPLE:
> *"Those Winter Sundays" by Robert Hayden, p. 308*

masque Now extremely rare, this genre of lush spectacle, song, dance, masks, and elaborate staging was popular among sixteenth- and seventeenth-century British nobles, who also made up its amateur and occasionally royal cast.

> EXAMPLE:
> *Ben Jonson (p. 297) wrote many masques for the court of King James I and Queen Anne.*

metaphor A figure of speech that compares or equates two things without using *like* or *as*. For comparisons made using *like* or *as*, see **simile**.

> EXAMPLE:
> *For this, for everything we are out of tune;*
> —WILLIAM WORDSWORTH, "The World Is Too Much With Us," p. 498

metaphor, extended A metaphor that continues over several lines or throughout an entire literary work.

> EXAMPLE:
> *In "One Art" by Elizabeth Bishop (p. 677), the metaphor of losing as an art to be practiced and perfected is repeated and developed throughout.*

metaphysical conceit A literary device that sets up a striking analogy between two entities that would not usually invite comparison, often drawing connections between the physical and the spiritual. This literally device is famously used by metaphysical poets, including John Donne and George Herbert.

> EXAMPLE:
> *"The Flea" by John Donne, p. 670*

meter The formal, regular organization of stressed and unstressed syllables, measured in feet. A foot is distinguished by the number of syllables it contains and how stress is placed on the syllables—stressed (´) or unstressed (˘). There are five typical feet in English verse: iamb (˘ ´), trochee (´ ˘), anapest (˘ ˘ ´), dactyl (´ ˘ ˘), and spondee (´ ´). Some meters dictate the number of feet per line, the most common being tetrameter, pentameter, and hexameter, having four, five, and six feet, respectively. See **iambic pentameter**.

metonymy A figure of speech in which something is represented by another thing that is related to it. Compare to **synecdoche**; see also **metaphor**.

> EXAMPLE:
> *In this excerpt from "London, 1802" by William Wordsworth (p. 1099), an altar is used to represent religion, a sword to represent the military, and a pen to represent the arts:*
>
> *England hath need of thee: she is a fen*
> *Of stagnant waters: altar, sword, and pen.*

minimalism A style in prose or verse that emphasizes economy of words and unadorned sentences.

> **EXAMPLE:**
> *"Cathedral" by Raymond Carver, p. 1079*

Modernism In literature, Modernism refers to a movement of writers who reached their apex between the 1920s and 1930s and expressed views of disillusionment with contemporary Western civilization, especially in the wake of World War I's mindless slaughter. Rejecting the conventions of the Victorian era, these writers experimented with form and took insights from recent writings by Freud and Jung about the unconscious. They viewed art as restorative and frequently ordered their writing around symbols and allusions. Representative modernist writers include T. S. Eliot, James Joyce, and Virginia Woolf.

> **EXAMPLE:**
> *"The Love Song of J. Alfred Prufrock" by T. S. Eliot, p. 1033*

monologue In a play, a speech given by one person. See also **soliloquy.**

> **EXAMPLE:**
> *Troy delivers a monologue in Act I, scene iv, of* Fences, *p. 221.*

mood Synonymous with **atmosphere**, mood is the feeling created for the reader by a work of literature. Many things can generate mood—especially **style, tone,** and **setting.**

motif A recurring pattern of images, words, or symbols that reveals a theme in a work of literature.

> **EXAMPLE:**
> *In Shakespeare's* Hamlet *(p. 720), the repeated use of words such as* play, act, see, assume, show, reveal, appear, form, *and* shape, *as well as the inclusion of a play within the play, become a motif, which helps to reveal one of the play's central themes: the contrast between appearance and reality.*

naive narrator See **narrator.**

narrative A story. Narratives may be written either in prose or in verse, as in narrative poetry.

> **EXAMPLE:**
> *"The Battle of Blenheim" by Robert Southey, p. 1417, is a narrative poem.*

narrative frame Also known as a frame story, a narrative frame is a plot device in which the author places the main narrative of his or her work within another narrative—the narrative frame. This exterior narrative usually serves to explain the main narrative in some way.

> **EXAMPLES:**
> Heart of Darkness *by Joseph Conrad, p. 369*

narrator The character, or persona, that the author uses to tell a narrative, or story. Narrators may tell stories from several different points of view, including first person, second person (very rare), and third person. See **point of view.**

EXAMPLE:

In Daisy Miller *by Henry James, the narrator is a third-person limited omniscient voice, who usually sticks closely to Winterbourne's thoughts and experiences:*

After this Daisy was never at home, and Winterbourne ceased to meet her at the houses of their common acquaintance, because, as he perceived, these shrewd people had quite made up their minds that she was going too far. They ceased to invite her, and they intimated that they desired to express to observant Europeans the great truth that, though Miss Daisy Miller was a young American lady, her behaviour was not representative—was regarded by her compatriots as abnormal. Winterbourne wondered how she felt about all the cold shoulders that were turned towards her, and sometimes it annoyed him to suspect that she did not feel at all. (p. 1201)

More specific terms are used to discuss the role a narrator plays in interpreting the events in a narrative:

objective narrator A narrator who recounts only what characters say and do, offering no insight into their thinking or analysis of events. All interpretation is left to the reader.

EXAMPLE:

In her short story "The Lottery" (p. 77), author Shirley Jackson uses the perspective of the objective narrator effectively to stand back and suspend judgment on an incident that turns ugly and violent.

unreliable narrator A narrator who is biased and doesn't give a full or accurate picture of events in a narrative. Narrators may be unreliable because of youth, inexperience, madness, intentional or unintentional bias, or even a lack of morals. Authors often use this technique to distinguish the character's point of view from their own. Sometimes an author will use an unreliable narrator to make an ironic point.

EXAMPLE:

As Salman Rushdie's "The Free Radio"(p. 1244) progresses, readers realize that the narrator is unreliable in his account (and perception) of the rickshaw boy's fate.

near rhyme See **rhyme.**

non sequitur In literature, a reply or remark that does not have any relevance to what occasioned or preceded it; in rhetoric, a conclusion that does not logically follow from the premises.

EXAMPLE:

HAMLET: *I am but mad north-north-west: when the wind is southerly I known a hawk from a handsaw.*

——WILLIAM SHAKESPEARE, *Hamlet,* p. 760

novella A short novel, from the Italian word meaning "story."

EXAMPLE:

Heart of Darkness *by Joseph Conrad, p. 369*

objective narrator See **narrator.**

objective point of view See **point of view**.

octet See **stanza**.

ode A form of poetry used to meditate on or address a single object or condition. It originally followed strict rules of rhythm, meter, and rhyme, which by the Romantic period had become more flexible.

> EXAMPLE:
> *"Ode on a Grecian Urn" by John Keats, p. 1102*

omniscient narrator See **narrator**.

omniscient point of view See **point of view**.

onomatopoeia Use of words that refer to sound and whose pronunciations mimic those sounds.

> EXAMPLE:
> *Women draped in black huddled and chattered in their harems; yak-yak-yak.*
> —MURIEL SPARK, "The First Year of My Life," p. 1392

overstatement See **hyperbole**.

oxymoron A paradox made up of two seemingly contradictory words.

> EXAMPLE:
> *Out of the <u>murderous innocence</u> of the sea.*
> —WILLIAM BUTLER YEATS, "A Prayer for My Daughter," p. 302

parable A tale told explicitly to illustrate a moral lesson or conclusion. Parables can take the form of drama, poetry, or fiction.

> EXAMPLE:
> *"The Parable of the Old Man and the Young" by Wilfred Owen, p. 1439*

paradox A statement that seems contradictory but actually is not.

> EXAMPLE:
> *For whose sake henceforth all his vows be such*
> *As what he loves may never like too much.*
> —BEN JONSON, "On My First Son," p. 297

parallel structure Also known as parallelism, this term refers to the repeated use of similar grammatical structures for the purpose of emphasis. Compare with **anaphora**, a type of parallel structure concerned only with the repetitions of an initial word or words.

> EXAMPLE:
> *He would dispose of his good luck pebble. Swallow it, maybe, or use Lee Strunk's slingshot, or just drop it along the trail. On the march he would impose strict field discipline. He would be careful to send out flank security, to prevent straggling or bunching up, to keep his troops moving at the proper pace and at the proper interval. He would insist on clean weapons. He would confiscate the remainder of Lavender's dope. Later in the day, perhaps, he would call the men together and speak to them plainly. He would accept the blame for*

what had happened to Ted Lavender. He would be a man about it. He would look them in the eyes, keeping his chin level, and he would issue the new SOPs in a calm, impersonal tone of voice, an officer's voice, leaving no room for argument or discussion.

—TIM O'BRIEN, "The Things They Carried," p. 1383

parody A comic or satiric imitation of a particular literary work or style. Parodies can run the gamut from lighthearted imitations intended merely to play with something well known, to exaggerations intended to criticize by making a work or literary style look ridiculous.

EXAMPLE:

"The Black Man's Burden" by H. T. Johnson, p. 536

passive voice A sentence employs passive voice when the subject doesn't act but is acted on.

EXAMPLE:

Midway down they <u>were held up</u> by Mary Jane, who replenished them with raspberry or orange jelly or with blancmange and jam.

—JAMES JOYCE, "The Dead," p. 177

pastoral Literature that employs a romanticized description of leisurely farm or rural life.

EXAMPLE:

"The Quiet Life" by Alexander Pope, p. 496

periodic sentence See **sentence**.

persona A voice and viewpoint that an author adopts in order to deliver a story or poem. See **narrator**.

EXAMPLE:

The narrator created by Robert Browning in "My Last Duchess," p. 1104

personification A figure of speech in which an animal or an inanimate object is imbued with human qualities.

EXAMPLE:

And this same flower that smiles today,
*   Tomorrow will be dying.*

—ROBERT HERRICK, "To the Virgins, to Make Much of Time," p. 672

Petrarchan sonnet See **sonnet**.

plot The arrangement of events in a narrative. Almost always, a conflict is central to a plot, and traditionally a plot develops in accordance with the following model: **exposition, rising action, climax, falling action, denouement**. There can be more than one sequence of events in a work, although typically there is one major sequence along with other minor sequences. These minor sequences are called subplots.

EXAMPLE:

See analysis of the plot of "One of These Days" by Gabriel García Márquez on pp. 62–3.

point of view The perspective from which a work is told. The most common narrative vantage points are:

first person Told by a narrator who is a character in the story and who refers to him- or herself as "I." First-person narrators are sometimes **unreliable narrators**.

second person Though rare, some stories are told using second-person pronouns (*you*). This casts the reader as a character in the story.

third-person limited omniscient Told by a narrator who relates the action using third-person pronouns (*he, she, it*). This narrator is usually privy to the thoughts and actions of only one character.

third-person omniscient Told by a narrator using third-person pronouns. This narrator is privy to the thoughts and actions of all of the characters in the story.

> **EXAMPLES:**
> *First person: "I Stand Here Ironing" by Tillie Olsen, p. 266*
> *I nursed her. They feel that's important nowadays. I nursed all the children, but with her, with all the fierce rigidity of first motherhood, I did like the books then said. Though her cries battered me to trembling and my breasts ached with swollenness, I waited till the clock decreed.*
>
> *Second person: "Videotape" by Don DeLillo, p. 1093*
> *You don't usually call your wife over to the TV set. She has her programs, you have yours. But there's a certain urgency here. You want her to see how it looks. The tape has been running forever and now the thing is finally going to happen and you want her to be here when he's shot.*
>
> *Third-person limited omniscient: "Interpreter of Maladies" by Jhumpa Lahiri, p. 440*
> *He began to check his reflection in the rearview mirror as he drove, feeling grateful that he had chosen the gray suit that morning and not the brown one, which tended to sag a little in the knees. From time to time he glanced through the mirror at Mrs. Das.*
>
> *Third-person omniscient: "The Lady with the Little Dog" by Anton Chekhov, p. 643*
> *She looked at him with fear, with entreaty, with love, looked at him intently, the better to keep his features in her memory. "I've been suffering so!" she went on, not listening to him. "I think only of you all the time, I've lived by my thoughts of you. And I've tried to forget, to forget, but why, why did you come?" Further up, on the landing, two high-school boys were smoking and looking down, but Gurov did not care; he drew Anna Sergeevna to him and began kissing her face, her cheeks, her hands.*

See **narrator**.

Postmodernism In literature, Postmodernism refers to a loose grouping of writers in the post–World War II era who carry on the agenda of Modernism, inasmuch as they reject traditional literary conventions, embrace experimentation, and see contemporary life as bleak and fragmented. Rather than attempt to instill order through some literary device—as T. S. Eliot did with his use of allusions and myth, or William Butler Yeats with his symbolic system—postmodern writers tend to eschew attempts to treat art as a corrective to modern malaises, and their writing celebrates or plays with the fragmentation of life instead of seeking to fix it. In addition, postmodern writers attack the distinction between "high" and "low" art maintained by modernists, and their writing engages with popular art forms like cartoons and television. Representative postmodern writers include Don DeLillo, Thomas Pynchon, and Kurt Vonnegut.

> **EXAMPLE:**
> *"Videotape" by Don DeLillo, p. 1090*

propaganda Work that aims to influence an audience about a debatable position or affiliation, not through rational or supported appeals but through one or more of the following: emotional manipulation, the selective use (and omission) of facts, spin, or any number of fallacious techniques. The word has mostly negative connotations.

> **EXAMPLE:**
> *See the discussion of art as propaganda (and a prompt suggesting alternative ways to define this term) in the questions following* Plum Bun: A Novel without a Moral, *p. 1310.*

prose poem A blending of prose and poetry, usually resembling prose in its use of sentences without line breaks, and poetry in its use of quintessentially poetic devices such as figurative language. A prose poem makes traditional genre distinctions problematic. See also **form.**

> **EXAMPLE:**
> *"Hopper's 'Nighthawks' (1942)" by Ira Sadoff, p. 1118*

protagonist The main character in a work; often a hero or heroine, but not always.

> **EXAMPLE:**
> *In Conrad's* Heart of Darkness *(p. 369), the protagonist is Marlow, who is also the novella's narrator.*

pun A play on words that derives its humor from the replacement of one word with another that has a similar pronunciation or spelling but a different meaning. A pun can also derive humor from the use of a single word that has more than one meaning.

> **EXAMPLE:**
> *The title of Oscar Wilde's* The Importance of Being Earnest *(p. 574) is a pun on the name of the play's protagonist, Ernest.*

quatrain See **stanza.**

Realism Describing a literary technique, the goal of which is to render work that feels true, immediate, natural, and realistic.

> **EXAMPLE:**
> *Realism characterizes Hemingway's technique in "Soldier's Home" (p. 1447)*

refrain A line, lines, or a stanza in a poem that repeat(s) at intervals.

> **EXAMPLE:**
> *"'twas a famous victory"*

This refrain appears, slightly modified each time, in Robert Southey's "The Battle of Blenheim" (p. 1417).

resolution The working out of a plot's conflicts, following the climax. See also **plot**.

reversal When, in a narrative, the protagonist's fortunes take an unforeseen turn.

> **EXAMPLE:**
> *In* Antigone, *Creon's reversal of fortune begins when his son, Haemon, commits suicide upon hearing of Antigone's death (p. 1362).*

See also **plot**.

rhetorical question A question asked for stylistic effect and emphasis to make a point rather than to solicit an answer.

> **EXAMPLE:**
> *Men of England, wherefore plough*
> *For the lords who lay ye low?*
> —PERCY BYSSHE SHELLEY, "Song: To the Men of England," p. 917

rhyme The repetition of the same (or similar) vowel or consonant sounds or constructions. A rhyme at the end of two or more lines of poetry is called an end rhyme. A rhyme that occurs within a line is called an internal rhyme. A rhyme that pairs sounds that are similar but not exactly the same is called a near rhyme or a slant rhyme. A rhyme that only works because the words look the same is called an eye rhyme or a sight rhyme. Rhyme often follows a pattern, called a rhyme scheme.

> **EXAMPLES:**
> *End rhyme:*
> *England hath need of thee: she is a fen*
> *Of stagnant waters: altar, sword, and pen,*
> —WILLIAM WORDSWORTH, "London, 1802" p. 1099
>
> *Internal rhyme:*
> *A child sitting under the piano, in the boom of the*
> *tingling strings.*
> —D. H. LAWRENCE, "Piano," p. 1111
>
> *Near rhyme or slant rhyme:*
> *The alphabet is searched for letters soft,*
> *To try a word before it can be wrought.*
> —THOMAS BASTARD, "De Puero Balbutiente," p. 296
>
> *Eye rhyme:*
> *"Sisters and brothers, little Maid,*
> *How many may you be?"*
> *"How many? Seven in all," she said,*
> *And wondering looked at me.*
> —WILLIAM WORDSWORTH, "We Are Seven," p. 300

rhythm The general pattern of stressed and unstressed syllables. See also **meter**.

EXAMPLE:

Whŏse hérds | wĭth mílk, | whŏse fiélds | wĭth bread,
Whŏse flócks | supͮply | hĭm wíth | ăttire;
Whŏse trées | ĭn sum | mĕr yield | hĭm shade,
Ĭn win | tĕr, firĕ.

—ALEXANDER POPE, "The Quiet Life," p. 497

rising action The events, marked by increasing tension and conflict, that build up to a story's **climax**.

EXAMPLE:

In "Everyday Use" by Alice Walker (p. 1226), the rising action centers around the growing conflict between Dee's new culture and values and those of her family. This conflict increases as the disagreement about who should have the quilts intensifies, ultimately leading to the climax of the story.

Romanticism In literature, a late eighteenth- to early nineteenth-century movement that emphasized beauty for beauty's sake, the natural world, emotion, imagination, the value of a nation's past and its folklore, and the heroic roles of the individual and the artist. Some prominent Romantic poets in this book include Percy Bysshe Shelley, Lord Byron, Samuel Taylor Coleridge, and John Keats.

EXAMPLE:

"Ode on a Grecian Urn" by John Keats, p. 1102

round character See **character**.

run-on line See **enjambment**.

sarcasm See **irony, verbal**.

satire A literary work that uses irony to critique society or an individual.

EXAMPLE:

"Harrison Bergeron" by Kurt Vonnegut, p. 881

scene A subdivision of an act in a play. Scenes usually break up the action into logical chunks. Many contemporary plays, however, contain only sequences of scenes, without an overarching act structure. See also **act**.

secondary character See **character**.

sentence Specific types of sentences discussed in this book:

> **complex sentence** A sentence containing an independent clause and one or more subordinate clauses (beginning with words such as *after, before, although, because, until, when, while,* and *if*).
>
> EXAMPLE:
>
> *In the castle, after they had landed, the subjective element decidedly prevailed.*
> —HENRY JAMES, *Daisy Miller*, p. 1184
>
> **compound sentence** Two independent clauses joined by a coordinating conjunction (*and, but, or, nor, for, yet,* or *so*) or a semicolon.

EXAMPLE:

His voice seemed about to crack, and the grandmother's head cleared for a moment.
——FLANNERY O'CONNOR, "A Good Man Is Hard to Find," p. 1222

compound-complex sentence A combination of a compound sentence and a complex sentence; it is often fairly long.

EXAMPLE:

They flattered him with dreams because they knew they could take money away from him at cards and he would buy them drink while they did it, though he was no richer than they.
——SALMAN RUSHDIE, "The Free Radio," p. 1246

cumulative sentence A sentence in which an independent clause is followed by details, qualifications, or modifications in subordinate clauses or phrases.

EXAMPLE:

Connie liked the way he was dressed, which was the way all of them dressed: tight faded jeans stuffed into black, scuffed boots, a belt that pulled his waist in and showed how lean he was, and a white pull-over shirt that was a little soiled and showed the hard small muscles of his arms and shoulders.
——JOYCE CAROL OATES, "Where Are You Going, Where Have You Been?" p. 472

imperative sentence A sentence that issues a command. The subject of an imperative sentence is often implied rather than explicit.

EXAMPLE:

Make sure you show how Africans have music and rhythm deep in their souls, and eat things no other humans eat.
——BINYAVANGA WAINAINA, "How to Write about Africa," p. 560

interrupted sentence A sentence of any pattern modified by interruptions that add descriptive details, state conditions, suggest uncertainty, voice possible alternative views, or present qualifications.

EXAMPLE:

At the risk of exciting a somewhat derisive smile on the reader's part, I may affirm that with regard to the women who had hitherto interested him, it very often seemed to Winterbourne among the possibilities that, given certain contingencies, he should be afraid—literally afraid—of these ladies; he had a pleasant sense that he should never be afraid of Daisy Miller.
——HENRY JAMES, *Daisy Miller*, p. 1198

periodic sentence A sentence that begins with details, qualifications, or modifications, building toward the main clause.

EXAMPLE:

As the day was splendid, however, and the concourse of vehicles, walkers, and loungers numerous, the young American found their progress much delayed.
——HENRY JAMES, *Daisy Miller*, p. 1190

simple sentence A sentence composed of one main clause without any subordinate clauses.

EXAMPLE:

Winterbourne was much amused.

— HENRY JAMES, *Daisy Miller*, p. 1168

sestet See **stanza**.

setting Where and when a story takes place.

EXAMPLE:

It was a big, squarish frame house that had once been white, decorated with cupolas and spire and scrolled balconies in the heavily lightsome style of the seventies, set on what had once been our most select street. But garages and cotton gins had encroached and obliterated even the august names of that neighborhood; only Miss Emily's house was left, lifting its stubborn and coquettish decay above the cotton wagons and the gasoline pumps — an eyesore among eyesores. And now Miss Emily had gone to join the representatives of those august names where they lay in the cedar bemused cemetery among the ranked and anonymous graves of Union and Confederate soldiers who fell in the battle of Jefferson.

— WILLIAM FAULKNER, "A Rose for Emily," p. 657

setting, social The manners, mores, customs, rituals, and codes of conduct in a work; an author may suggest approval or disapproval of any of these through a description of place.

EXAMPLE:

See the excerpt from 1984 by George Orwell, p. 71.

Shakespearean sonnet See **sonnet**.

sight rhyme See **rhyme**.

simile A figure of speech used to explain or clarify an idea by comparing it explicitly to something else, using the words *like*, *as*, or *as though* to do so.

EXAMPLE:

Martha was a poet, with the poet's sensibilities, and her feet would be brown and bare, the toenails unpainted, <u>the eyes chilly and somber like the ocean in March</u>, and though it was painful, he wondered who had been with her that afternoon.

— TIM O'BRIEN, "The Things They Carried," p. 1375

simple sentence See **sentence**.

slang See **colloquial language / colloquialism**.

slant rhyme See **rhyme**.

soliloquy In a play, a monologue in which a character, alone on the stage, reveals his or her thoughts or emotions.

EXAMPLE:

See Hamlet's "To be, or not to be" speech in Hamlet *by William Shakespeare, p. 768.*

sonnet A poetic form composed of fourteen lines in iambic pentameter that adheres to a particular rhyme scheme. The two most common types are:

Petrarchan sonnet Also known as the Italian sonnet, its fourteen lines are divided into an octave and a sestet. The octave rhymes *abba, abba;* the sestet that follows can have a variety of different rhyme schemes: *cdcdcd, cdecde, cddcdd.*

> **EXAMPLE:**
> *"The World Is Too Much with Us" by William Wordsworth, p. 498*

Shakespearean sonnet Also known as the English sonnet, its fourteen lines are composed of three quatrains and a couplet, and its rhyme scheme is *abab, cdcd, efef, gg.*

> **EXAMPLE:**
> *"My mistress' eyes are nothing like the sun" by William Shakespeare, p. 684*

sound The musical quality of poetry, as created through techniques such as **rhyme, enjambment, caesura, alliteration, assonance, onomatopoeia, rhythm**, and **cadence.**

speaker This term is most frequently used in the context of drama and poetry. In drama, the speaker is the character who is currently delivering lines. In poetry, the speaker is the person who is expressing a point of view in the poem, either the author or a persona created by the author. See also **narrator; persona; point of view.**

> **EXAMPLE:**
> *In Ben Jonson's "On My First Son" (p. 297), the speaker is a father, presumably Jonson, addressing his dead son.*
>
> *Farewell, thou child of my right hand, and joy;*
> *My sin was too much hope of thee, loved boy:*
> *Seven years thou wert lent to me, and I thee pay,*
> *Exacted by thy fate, on the just day.*

spondee See **meter.**

sprung rhythm A meter developed out of Gerard Manley Hopkins's attempt to mirror natural speech patterns in his poetry. In sprung rhythm, the number of stressed syllables in each line is the same, while the number of unstressed syllables can vary. This means that the types of feet employed in each line can vary.

> **EXAMPLE:**
> *"God's Grandeur" by Gerard Manley Hopkins, p. 1267*

stage directions Any notes in the script of a play written by the author that set guidelines for the performance, explaining, for example, what the setting should look like, how actors should move and deliver certain lines, and so on. They are generally set in italics.

> **EXAMPLE:**
> *See stage directions for* A Raisin in the Sun *by Lorraine Hansberry on p. 97.*

stanza Lines in a poem that the poet has chosen to group together, usually separated from other lines by a space. Stanzas within a poem usually have repetitive forms, often sharing rhyme schemes or rhythmic structures.

A number of frequently used stanza types have specific names:

couplet   A two-line, rhyming stanza.

> **EXAMPLE:**
> *And yet, by heaven, I think my love as rare*
> *As any she, belied with false compare.*
>
> —WILLIAM SHAKESPEARE, "My mistress' eyes are nothing like the sun," p. 684

tercet   A three-line stanza.

> **EXAMPLE:**
> *"Siren Song" by Margaret Atwood, p. 676*

quatrain   A four-line stanza.

> **EXAMPLE:**
> *Think me not unkind and rude*
> *That I walk alone in grove and glen;*
> *I go to the god of the wood*
> *To fetch his word to men.*
>
> —RALPH WALDO EMERSON, "The Apology," p. 500

sestet   A six-line stanza.

> **EXAMPLE:**
> *It was a summer evening,*
> *Old Kaspar's work was done;*
> *And he before his cottage door*
> *Was sitting in the sun,*
> *And by him sported on the green*
> *His little grandchild Wilhelmine.*
>
> —ROBERT SOUTHEY, "The Battle of Blenheim," p. 1418

octet   An eight-line stanza.

> **EXAMPLE:**
> *I have walked and prayed for this young child an hour*
> *And heard the sea-wind scream upon the tower*
> *And under the arches of the bridge, and scream*
> *In the elms above the flooded stream;*
> *Imagining in excited reverie*
> *That the future years had come,*
> *Dancing to a frenzied drum,*
> *Out of the murderous innocence of the sea.*
>
> —WILLIAM BUTLER YEATS, "A Prayer for My Daughter," p. 303

stream of consciousness   A technique in which prose follows the logic and flow of a character's (or multiple characters') thought processes—associations, tangents, seemingly strange transitions—rather than a more ordered narrative.

> **EXAMPLE:**
> *"Bliss" by Katherine Mansfield, p. 646*

structure The organization of a work.

style The way a literary work is written. Style is produced by an author's choices in **diction, syntax, imagery, figurative language,** and other literary elements.

suspense A literary device that uses tension to make the plot more exciting; the effect created by artful delays and selective dissemination of information.

> **EXAMPLE:**
> *An excellent example of suspense in fiction is Joyce Carol Oates's "Where Are You Going, Where Have You Been?" (p. 467).*

symbol A setting, object, or event in a story that carries more than literal meaning and therefore represents something significant to understanding the meaning of a work of literature.

> **EXAMPLE:**
> *And for the first time, or so it seemed, I noticed the piece on the right-hand side. It was called "Perfectly Contented." I tried to play this one as well. It had a lighter melody but with the same flowing rhythm and turned out to be quite easy. "Pleading Child" was shorter but slower; "Perfectly Contented" was longer but faster. And after I had played them both a few times, I realized they were two halves of the same song.*
> —AMY TAN, "Two Kinds," p. 141

synecdoche A figure of speech in which part of something is used to represent the whole. Compare to **metonymy.**

> **EXAMPLE:**
> *"They were called legs or grunts."*
> —TIM O'BRIEN, "The Things They Carried," p. 1372

syntax The arrangement of words into phrases, clauses, and sentences in a prose passage. This includes word order (subject-verb-object, for instance, or an inverted structure); the length and structure of sentences (simple, compound, or complex), phrases, and clauses; the chronology of passages; the preference of various parts of speech over others; the use of connectors between and within sentences; and more.

> **EXAMPLE:**
> *Have you ever seen a lame animal, perhaps a dog run over by some careless person rich enough to own a car, sidle up to someone who is ignorant enough to be kind to him?[1] That is the way my Maggie walks.[2] She has been like this, <u>chin on chest</u>, <u>eyes on ground</u>, <u>feet in shuffle</u>, ever since the fire that burned the other house to the ground.[3]*
> —ALICE WALKER, "Everyday Use," p. 1227
>
> 1. *complex sentence; also a question*
> 2. *OSV structure, a simple declarative sentence*
> 3. *complex sentence; repetition of three parallel modifying phrases creates rhythm and emphasis*

syntax, poetic Similar to syntax in prose, poetic syntax also includes the arrangement of words into lines—where they break or do not break, the use of enjambment or caesura, and line length/patterns.

EXAMPLE:

For this, for everything, we are out of tune;   *(caesura)*
It moves us not.—Great God! I'd rather be   *(caesura)*
A Pagan suckled in a creed outworn;   *(enjambment)*
                    —WILLIAM WORDSWORTH, "The World Is Too Much with Us," p. 498

tercet See **stanza.**

theatrical property Known more commonly as a **prop**, this is a term for any object used onstage by an actor in a play.

EXAMPLE:

During Hamlet's soliloquy in act V, scene I, of Shakespeare's Hamlet *(p. 815), the actor makes use of Yorick's skull as a prop.*

theme Underlying issues or ideas of a work.

EXAMPLE:

See the section on theme, p. 85. For a student paper about theme in Antigone, *see page 1461.*

thesis statement The chief claim that a writer makes in any argumentative piece of writing, usually stated in one sentence.

tone A speaker's attitude as exposed through stylistic choices. (Tone is often confused with another element of style, **mood**, which describes the feeling created by the work.) Along with mood, tone provides the emotional coloring of a work and is created by some combination of the other elements of style.

EXAMPLE:

In your text, treat Africa as if it were one country. It is hot and dusty with rolling grasslands and huge herds of animals and tall, thin people who are starving. Or it is hot and steamy with very short people who eat primates. Don't get bogged down with precise descriptions. Africa is big: fifty-four countries, nine hundred million people who are too busy starving and dying and warring and emigrating to read your book. The continent is full of deserts, jungles, highlands, savannahs and many other things, but your reader doesn't care about all that, so keep your descriptions romantic and evocative and unparticular.
                    —BINYAVANGA WAINAINA, "How to Write about Africa," pp. 559–60

tragedy A serious dramatic work in which the protagonist experiences a series of unfortunate reversals due to some character trait, referred to as a *tragic flaw*. The most common tragic flaw is *hubris*, Greek for *pride*. Modern tragedies tend to depart from some of the genre's classical conventions, portraying average rather than noble characters and attributing the protagonist's downfall to something other than a flaw in character—for example, social circumstances.

EXAMPLE:

Antigone *by Sophocles, p. 1327*

tragic flaw See **tragedy.**

tragic hero A character who possesses a flaw or commits an error in judgment that leads to his or her downfall and a reversal of fortune.

EXAMPLE:
Hamlet in William Shakespeare's Hamlet *(p. 720).*

Transcendental Movement A reaction against both rationalism and empiricism in philosophy, as well as austere Calvinist doctrines about human nature, transcendental-ism emphasized knowledge via mystical insight, the divine spark in each human being, and the immanence of God in nature. Beginning in Europe and drawing inspiration from European thinkers, among them Immanuel Kant and Samuel Taylor Coleridge, the transcendental movement flourished in the nineteenth-century United States, where it was linked with Christian Unitarianism. Key thinkers include Ralph Waldo Emerson and Henry David Thoreau.

EXAMPLE:
"The Apology" by Ralph Waldo Emerson, p. 499

trochee See **meter**.

understatement The presentation or framing of something as less important, urgent, awful, good, powerful, and so on, than it actually is, often for satiric or comical effect; the opposite of hyperbole, it is often used along with this technique, and for similar effect.

EXAMPLE:
The grave's a fine and private place,
But none, I think, do there embrace.

—ANDREW MARVELL, "To His Coy Mistress," p. 694

unreliable narrator See **narrator**.

verbal irony See **irony, verbal**.

verse A broad term, verse refers to a piece of writing that is metered and rhythmic. (Free verse is an exception to this, being a piece of writing grouped with verse rather than prose, even though it lacks a meter.) The term *verse* can also be used to refer to poetry in general. See also **meter; rhyme; rhythm**.

vignette A short narrative scene or description, often one in a series. If a story or novel is composed of a series of vignettes, it often relies on a thematic, rather than a plot-driven, structure.

EXAMPLE:
"If You Are What You Eat, Then What Am I?" by Geeta Kothari, p. 351, is composed of numerous vignettes.

villanelle A form of poetry in which five tercets (rhyme scheme *aba*) are followed by a quatrain (rhyme scheme *abaa*). At the end of tercets two and four, the first line of tercet one is repeated. At the end of tercets three and five, the last line of tercet one is repeated. These two repeated lines, called *refrain lines*, are again repeated to conclude the quatrain. Much of the power of this form lies in its repeated lines and their subtly shifting sense or meaning over the course of the poem.

EXAMPLE:

"Do not go gentle into that good night" by Dylan Thomas, p. 926

wordplay Techniques by which writers manipulate language for effect; examples include puns (the deliberate misuse of words that sound alike) or double entendres (expressions with two meanings).

EXAMPLE:

LADY BRACKNELL: *Good afternoon, dear Algernon, I hope you are behaving very well.*
ALGERNON: *I'm feeling very well, Aunt Augusta.*
LADY BRACKNELL: *That's not quite the same thing. In fact the two things rarely go together.*
ALGERNON [to GWENDOLEN]: *Dear me, you are smart!*
GWENDOLEN: *I am always smart! Aren't I, Mr. Worthing?*
JACK: *You are quite perfect, Miss Fairfax.*
GWENDOLEN: *Oh! I hope I am not that. It would leave no room for developments, and I intend to develop in many directions.*
——OSCAR WILDE, *The Importance of Being Earnest*, p. 580–81

zeugma Pronounced *zoyg-muh*, a technique in which one verb is used with multiple (and often incongruous) objects, so that the definition of the verb is changed, complicated, or made both literal and figurative.

EXAMPLE:

They carried chess sets, basketballs, Vietnamese-English dictionaries, insignia of rank, Bronze Stars and Purple Hearts, plastic cards imprinted with the Code of Conduct. They carried diseases, among them malaria and dysentery. They carried lice and ringworm and leeches and paddy algae and various rots and molds. They carried the land itself—Vietnam, the place, the soil—a powdery orange-red dust that covered their boots and fatigues and faces.
——TIM O'BRIEN, "The Things They Carried," p. 1378

Brooks, Gwendolyn: From *Blacks*. Copyright 1987 by Gwendolyn Brooks. Reprinted by consent of Brooks Permissions.

Carver, Raymond: From *Cathedral*. Copyright 1981, 1982, 1983 by Raymond Carver. Reprinted by permission of Alfred A. Knopf, a division of Random House, Inc.

Chai, May-lee: In *ZYZZYVA*, no. 3 (Winter 2001), pp. 139–158. Copyright 2001 by May-lee Chai.

Chekhov, Anton: "The Lady with the Little Dog," translated by Richard Pevear and Larissa Volokhonsky, copyright © 2000 by Richard Pevear and Larissa Volokhonsky from THE SELECTED SHORT STORIES OF ANTON CHEKHOV by Anton Chekhov, translated by Richard Pevear and Larissa Volokhonsky. Used by permission of Bantam Books, a division of Random House, Inc.

Cisneros, Sandra: From *Woman Hollering Creek*. Copyright © 1991 by Sandra Cisneros. Published by Vintage Books, a division of Random House, Inc., and originally in hardcover by Random House, Inc. Reprinted by permission of Susan Bergholz Literary Services, New York, NY, and Lamy, NM. All rights reserved.

Clewell, David: From *Now We're Getting Somewhere*. Copyright © 1994 by the Board of Regents of the University of Wisconsin System. Published by the University of Wisconsin Press.

Clifton, Lucille: Copyright © 1987 by Lucille Clifton. First published in *two-headed woman*, published by The University of Massachusetts Press. Now appears in *good woman: poems and a memoir 1969–1980*. Copyright 1987 by Lucille Clifton, published by BOA Editions. Reprinted by permission of Curtis Brown, Ltd.

Coburn, D. L.: From *The Gin Game*. Copyright © 1975, 1977, 2005 by D. L. Coburn. Used by permission of Flora Roberts, Inc.

Cofer, Judith Ortiz: From *The Latin Deli: Telling the Lives of Barrio Women* by Judith Ortiz Cofer. Copyright 1993 by Judith Ortiz Cofer. Published by W.W. Norton and Company, Inc.

Collins, Billy: "Introduction to Poetry" from *The Apple That Astonished Paris*. Copyright © 1988, 1996 by Billy Collins. Used by permission of the University of Arkansas Press.

Collins, Billy: "Weighing the Dog" from *Questions About Angels*, © 1991. Reprinted by permission of the University of Pittsburgh Press.

Collins, Billy: The Blues" from *The Art of Drowning* by Billy Collins, © 1995. All rights are controlled by the University of Pittsburgh Press, Pittsburgh, PA 15260. Used by permission of the University of Pittsburgh Press

Cullen, Countee: From *My Soul's High Song: The Collected Writings of Countee Cullen*. Copyrights held by the Amistad Research Center, Tulane University, administered by Thompson and Thompson, Brooklyn, NY.

Cummings, E. E.: From *Complete Poems: 1904–1962* by E. E. Cummings, edited by George J. Firmage. Used with the permission of Liveright Publishing Corporation. Copyright © 1923, 1931, 1935, 1940, 1951, 1959, 1963, 1968, 1991 by the Trustees for the E. E. Cummings Trust. Copyright © 1976, 1978, 1979 by George James Firmage.

Danticat, Edwidge: "The Book of the Dead" from THE DEW BREAKER by Edwidge Danticat, copyright © 2004 by Edwidge Danticat. Used by permission of Alfred A. Knopf, a division of Random House, Inc.

Darwish, Mahmoud, translated by Denys Johnson-Davies: From *The Music of Human Flesh*, translated by Denys Johnson-Davies (Three Continents Press, 1980). Copyright 1980 by Denys Johnson-Davies. Reprinted by permission of Denys Johnson-Davies.

DeLillo, Don: Reprinted with the permission of Scribner, a Division of Simon & Schuster, Inc., from UNDERWORLD by Don DeLillo. Copyright © 1997 by Don DeLillo. All rights reserved.

Dickinson, Emily: "Reprinted by permission of the publishers and the Trustees of Amherst College from *The Poems of Emily Dickinson*, ed. Thomas H. Johnson, Cambridge, Mass.: The Belknap Press of Harvard University Press. Copyright © 1951, 1955, 1979, 1983 by the President and Fellows of Harvard College."

Divakaruni, Chitra Banerjee: From LEAVING YUBA CITY by Chitra Banerjee Divakaruni, copyright © 1997 by Chitra Banerjee Divakaruni. Used by permission of Doubleday, a division of Random House, Inc.

Dove, Rita: From *Mother Love*. Copyright © 1995 by Rita Dove. Used by permission of W.W. Norton & Company, Inc.

Duffy, Carol Ann: From *The World's Wife: Poems by Carol Ann Duffy*. Reprinted with the permission of Farrar, Straus & Giroux LLC.

Dunn, Stephen: "The Sacred" from *Between Angels*. Copyright © 1989 by Stephen Dunn. Published by W.W. Norton and Company, Inc.

Dunn, Stephen: "Charlotte Bronte in Leeds Point" from LOCAL VISITATIONS by Stephen Dunn. Copyright © 2003 by Stephen Dunn. Used by permission of W.W. Norton & Company, Inc.

Eliot, T. S.: From *Collected Poems: 1909–1962* by T. S. Eliot. Copyright 1936 by Harcourt Inc. Copyright 1964, 1963 by T. S. Eliot, reprinted by permission of the publisher and Faber & Faber Ltd.

Ellison, Ralph: From *Invisible Man*, by Ralph Ellison, copyright 1947, 1948, 1952 by Ralph Ellison. Copyright renewed 1975, 1976–1980 by Ralph Ellison. Used by permission of Random House, Inc.

Esquivel, Laura: From *Like Water for Chocolate* by Laura Esquivel, Translation copyright © 1992 by Doubleday, a division of Random House, Inc. Used by permission of Doubleday, a division of Random House, Inc.

Faulkner, William: From *Collected Stories of William Faulkner*. Copyright 1930 and renewed 1958 by William Faulkner. Used by permission of Random House, Inc.

Fauset, Jessie Redmon: From *Plum Bun*, by Jessie Redmond Fauset. Reprinted by permission of Beacon Press.

Ferlinghetti, Lawrence: By Lawrence Ferlinghetti, from ENDLESS LIFE: SELECTED POEMS, copyright © 1976 by Lawrence Ferlinghetti. Reprinted by permission of New Directions Publishing Corp.

Finch, Annie: This poem cannot be published anywhere without the written consent of Annie Finch or Story Line Press permissions department.

Fitzgerald, F. Scott: Reprinted with the permission of Scribner, a division of Simon & Schuster, Inc., from THE GREAT GATSBY by F. Scott Fitzgerald. Copyright 1925 by Charles Scribner's Sons. Copyright renewed 1953 by Frances Scott Fitzgerald Lanahan.

Fitzgerald, F. Scott: Reprinted with the permission of Scribner, a division of Simon & Schuster, Inc., from THE SHORT STORIES OF F. SCOTT FITZGERALD, edited by Matthew J. Bruccoli. Copyright © 1931 by the Curtis Publishing Company. Copyright renewed 1959 by Frances Scott Fitzgerald Lanahan.

Frost, Robert: "Mending Wall" from *The Poetry of Robert Frost*, edited by Edward Connery Latham. Copyright 1930, 1939, 1969 by Henry Holt and Company. Copyright 1958 by Robert Frost, copyright 1967 by Leslie Frost Ballantine. Reprinted by permission of Henry Holt & Company, LLC.

García Márquez, Gabriel: "One of These Days" from *No One Writes to the Colonel and Other Stories* by Gabriel García Márquez and translated by J. S. Bernstein. Copyright 1968 in the English translation by Harper and Row Publishers, Inc. Reprinted by permission of HarperCollins Publishers, Inc.

Gilb, Dagoberto: From *The Magic of Blood*. Reprinted with the permission of the author.

Gilbert, Sandra: "Sonnet: The *Ladies' Home Journal*," from EMILY'S BREAD by Sandra M. Gilbert. Copyright © 1984 by Sandra M. Gilbert. Used by permission of W.W. Norton & Company, Inc.

Ginsberg, Allen: "Is About" from DEATH & FAME: LAST POEMS 1993–1997 by Allen Ginsberg. Copyright © 1999 by The Allen Ginsberg Trust. Reprinted by permission of HarperCollins Publishers.

Goldbarth, Albert: "Shawl" from *The Kitchen Sink: New and Selected Poems 1972–2007* by Albert Goldbarth. Copyright © 2007 by Albert Goldbarth. Reprinted with the permission of Graywolf Press, Minneapolis, Minnesota, www.graywolfpress.org.

Grennan, Eamon: "Pause" from *Relations: New and Selected Poems*. Copyright © 1998 by Eamon Grennan. Reprinted with the permission of Graywolf Press, Saint Paul, Minnesota, www.graywolfpress.org.

Handal, Nathalie: From *The Lives of Rain* by Nathalie Handal. Copyright © 2005. Permission granted by author.

Hansberry, Lorraine: From A RAISIN IN THE SUN by Lorraine Hansberry. Copyright © 1958 by Robert Nemiroff, as an unpublished work. Copyright © 1959, 1966, 1984 by Robert Nemiroff. Copyright renewed 1986, 1987 by Robert Nemiroff. Used by permission of Random House, Inc.

Hayden, Robert: "Those Winter Sundays" from *Collected Poems of Robert Hayden*, copyright © 1966 by Robert Hayden, edited by Frederick Glaysher. Used by permission of Liveright Publishing Corporation.

Heaney, Seamus: From *Opened Ground: Selected Poems, 1966–1996*. Copyright © 1998 by Seamus Heaney. Reprinted by permission of Farrar, Straus & Giroux LLC.

Heaney, Seamus: Excerpt from "Feeling into Words" from FINDER'S KEEPERS by Seamus Heaney. Copyright © 2002 by Seamus Heaney. Reprinted by permission of Farrar, Straus & Giroux, LLC.

Heaney, Seamus: Nobel Lecture, December 7, 1995; from *Les Prix Nobel*. Copyright © The Nobel Prizes 1995, editor Tore Frängsmyr, Nobel Foundation, Stockholm, 1996.

Heaney, Seamus: From *Selected Poems 1966–1987* by Seamus Heaney. Copyright 1990 by Seamus Heaney. Reprinted by permission of Farrar, Straus & Giroux LLC.

Hemingway, Ernest: From *In Our Time*. Copyright 1925 by Charles Scribner's Sons and renewed 1953 by Ernest Hemingway. Reprinted with the permission of Scribner, a division of Simon and Schuster.

Hikmet, Nazim : From *Poems of Nazim Hikmet*, translated by Randy Blasing and Mutlu Konuk, published by Persea Books. Copyright © 1994 by Randy Blasing and Mutlu Konuk. Used with the permission of Persea Books. All rights reserved.

Hirsch, Edward: "Fast Break" from *Wild Gratitude* by Edward Hirsch. Copyright 1985 by Edward Hirsch. Used by permission of Alfred A. Knopf, a division of Random House, Inc.

Hirshfield, Jane: "This was Once a Love Poem" (pp. 16–18) from *Given Sugar, Given Salt* by Jane Hirshfield. Copyright © 2001 by Jane Hirshfield. Reprinted by permission of HarperCollins Publishers.

Homer: "The Champion Arms for Battle" from THE ILIAD by Homer, translated by Robert Fagles, copyright © 1990 by Robert Fagles. Used by permission of Viking Penguin, a division of Penguin Group (USA) Inc.

Hsu, Hua: Copyright 2009 The Atlantic Media Co., as first published in the *Atlantic Magazine*. Distributed by Tribune Media Services.

Hughes, Langston: "Mother to Son" from *The Collected Poems of Langston Hughes*, edited by Arnold Rampersad with David Roessel, Associate Editor. Copyright © 1994 by the Estate of Langston Hughes. Used by permission of Alfred A. Knopf, a division of Random House, Inc.

Hughes, Langston: Reprinted with permission from the June 23, 1926, issue of *The Nation*. For subscription information, call 1-800-333-8536. Portions of each week's *Nation* magazine can be accessed at http://www.thenation.com.

Hughes, Langston: From *Collected Poems* by Langston Hughes. Copyright © 1994, the Estate of Langston Hughes. Reprinted by Alfred A. Knopf, Inc. Reprinted by permission of Harold Ober Associates.

Hurston, Zora Neale: Introduction copyright © 1995 by Henry Louis Gates, Jr. and Sieglinde Lemke. Compilation copyright © 1995 by Vivian Bowden, Lois J. Hurston Gaston, Clifford Hurston, Lucy Ann Hurston, Winifred Hurston Clark, Zora Mack Goins, Edgar Hurston, Sr., and Barbara Hurston Lewis. Afterword and Bibliography copyright © 1995 by Henry Louis Gates. Reprinted by permission of HarperCollins Publishers.

Ignatow, David: "The Bagel" from AGAINST THE EVIDENCE: SELECTED POEMS 1934–1994. Copyright © 1994 by David Ignatow and reprinted by permission of Wesleyan University Press.

Jain, Anita: From *New York Magazine*, March 28, 2005. Published by New York Media Holdings, LLC.

Jarrell, Randall: "The Death of the Ball Turret Gunner" from *The Complete Poems by Randall Jarrell*, Farrar, Straus & Giroux, Inc., 1969. Copyright 1969, 1996 by Mrs. Randall Jarrell. Used with permission.

Jen, Gish: Copyright © 1998 by Gish Jen. First published in *The New Yorker*. Reprinted with permission by Melanie Jackson Agency, LLC.

Johnson, James Weldon: Excerpt from "Preface" in THE BOOK OF AMERICAN NEGRO POETRY, edited by James Weldon Johnson. Copyright 1931, 1922 by Houghton Mifflin Harcourt Publishing Company and renewed 1959, 1950 by Mrs. Grace Nail Johnson. Reprinted by permission of the publisher.

Jones, Edward P.: Copyright 1992 by Edward P. Jones. Reprinted by permission of HarperCollins Publishers, Inc.

Jones, Rachelle: From Rachelle Jones's blog, "Amy-Wife ToddlerMom." Reprinted with the permission of Simon & Schuster, Inc. from *Blogs of War: Front-Line Dispatches from Soldiers in Iraq and Afghanistan* by Matthew Currier Burden. Copyright © 2006 by Matthew Burden.

Joyce, James: "The Dead" from DUBLINERS by James Joyce, copyright 1914 by B.W. Heubsch. Definitive text copyright © 1967 by the Estate of James Joyce. Used by permission of Viking Penguin, a division of Penguin Group (USA) Inc.

Kafka, Franz: Translated by Alexis Walker. Reprinted with permission of Alexis Walker.

Kafka, Franz, translated by Richard and Clara Winston: From *Letters to Family, Friends, and Editors*, by Franz Kafka, translated by Richard and Clara Winston. Copyright 1977 by Schocken Books, a division of Random House, Inc. Used by permission of Schocken Books, a division of Random House, Inc.

Khrakhounim, Zareh: From *Language of a New Century: Contemporary Poetry from the Middle East, Asia, and Beyond*. Edited by Tina Chang, Ravi Shankar, and Carolyn Forche. Published by W.W. Norton & Company, Inc., 2008. Translated by Diana Der-Hovanessian. Reprinted with the permission of the translator.

Kincaid, Jamaica: "Girl" from AT THE BOTTOM OF THE RIVER by Jamaica Kincaid. Copyright © 1983 by Jamaica Kincaid.

O'Connor, Flannery: "A Good Man is Hard to Find" from *A Good Man Is Hard to Find and Other Stories* by Flannery O'Connor. Copyright 1953 by Flannery O'Connor and renewed 1981 by Regina O'Connor. Reproduced by permission of Houghton Mifflin Harcourt Publishing Company.

O'Driscoll, Dennis: From *Stepping Stones, Interviews with Seamus Heaney* by Dennis O'Driscoll. Copyright © 2008 by Dennis O'Driscoll.

Offutt, Chris: "Brain Food" from WE ARE WHAT WE ATE, edited by Mark Winegardner. Copyright © 1998 Share Our Strength, Inc., reprinted by permission of Houghton Mifflin Harcourt Publishing Company and by the author, Chris Offutt.

Okita, Dwight: From *Crossing with the Light* by Dwight Okita. Copyright © 1992 by Dwight Okita. Tia Chucha Press, 1992, Chicago.

Olds, Sharon: "Rite of Passage," copyright © 1987 by Sharon Olds, from *The Dead and the Living* by Sharon Olds. Used by permission of Alfred A. Knopf, a division of Random House, Inc.

Oliver, Mary: "Wild Geese" from DREAM WORK, copyright © 1986 by Mary Oliver. Used by permission of Grove/Atlantic, Inc.

Oliver, Mary: From *House of Light* by Mary Oliver. Copyright © 1990 by Mary Oliver. Reprinted by permission of Beacon Press, Boston.

Olsen, Tillie: Copyright © 1961 by Tillie Olsen from TELL ME A RIDDLE, reprinted by permission of the Frances Goldin Literary Agency.

Ortiz, Simon: Published in *A Good Journey* (University of Arizona Press, 1985).

Orwell, George: Excerpts from NINETEEN EIGHTY-FOUR by George Orwell, copyright 1949 by Harcourt, Inc., and renewed 1977 by Sonia Brownell Orwell. Reprinted by permission of the publisher. *Nineteen Eighty-Four* by George Orwell (copyright © George Orwell, 1949) by permission of Bill Hamilton as the Literary Executor of the Estate of the Late Sonia Brownell Orwell and Secker & Warburg Ltd.

Ozick, Cynthia: "The Shawl" from THE SHAWL by Cynthia Ozick. Copyright © 1980, 1983 by Cynthia Ozick. Used by permission of Alfred A. Knopf, a division of Random House, Inc.

Parker, Lisa: from *Parnassus* 23, no. 2 (1998). Copyright 1998 by Lisa Parker. Reprinted by permission of the author.

Pastan, Linda: From *The Five Stages of Grief* by Linda Pastan. Copyright ©1978 by Linda Pastan. Used by permission of W.W. Norton & Company, Inc.

Plath, Sylvia : Copyright © 1963 by Ted Hughes. Reprinted with the permission of HarperCollins Publishers. "Daddy" from ARIEL by Sylvia Plath. Reprinted with the permission of Faber and Faber.

Randall, Dudley: Copyright © 1969. Reprinted with the permission of the Estate of Dudley Randall.

Reed, Henry: From *Collected Poems* by Henry Reed, edited by Jon Stallworthy. Copyright 1991. Reprinted by permission of Oxford University Press.

Roethke, Theodore: "My Papa's Waltz," copyright 1942 by Hearst Magazines, Inc., from COLLECTED POEMS OF THEODORE ROETHKE by Theodore Roethke. Used by permission of Doubleday, a division of Random House, Inc.

Rushdie, Salman: "The Free Radio" from EAST, WEST: STORIES by Salman Rushdie. Copyright © 1994 by Salman Rushdie. Used by permission of Pantheon Books, a division of Random House, Inc.

Sadoff, Ira: From *Settling Down: Poems.* Published by Houghton Mifflin, 1975 (original from the University of Michigan).

Sandburg, Carl: From *Chicago Poems.* Copyright 1916 by Holt Rinehart and Winston, Inc., and renewed 1944 by Carl Sandburg. Reprinted by permission of Harcourt, Inc.

Sexton, Anne: Copyright 1960 by Anne Sexton, renewed 1988 by Linda G. Sexton. Reprinted by permission of Houghton Mifflin Company. All rights reserved.

Shakespeare, William: From *The Complete Works of Shakespeare.* Ed. David Bevington. 4th Edition. Copyright 1992 by HarperCollins Publishers. Reprinted by permission of Pearson Education, Inc.

Shakespeare, William: "If We Are Marked to Die," Act IV, scene iii, by William Shakespeare, from HENRY V (1982) edited by Gary Taylor.

Shakespeare, William: Notes to "Othello, the Moor of Venice" from THE COMPLETE WORKS OF SHAKESPEARE. Ed. David Bevington. 4th Edition. Copyright © 1992 by HarperCollins Publishers. Reprinted by permission of Pearson Education, Inc.

Sophocles: "Antigone" from *Three Theban Plays by Sophocles*, translated by Robert Fagles, copyright © 1982 by Robert Fagles. Used by permission of Viking Penguin, a division of Penguin Putnam (USA) Inc.

Soto, Gary: From *New and Selected Poems* © 1995 by Gary Soto.

Spark, Muriel: "The First Year of My Life" by Muriel Spark. Copyright © 1975 by Muriel Spark. Originally appeared in *The New Yorker* (June 1975). Reprinted by permission of Georges Borchardt, Inc., on behalf of the Estate of Muriel Spark.

Stafford, William: "Traveling through the Dark" from *The Way It Is: New and Selected Poems.* Copyright 1962, 1998 by the Estate of William Stafford. Reprinted by the permission of Graywolf Press, Minneapolis, Minnesota, www.graywolfpress.org.

Steinbeck, John: "Chapter 12" from THE GRAPES OF WRATH by John Steinbeck, copyright 1939, renewed © 1967 by John Steinbeck. Used by permission of Viking Penguin, a division of Penguin Group (USA) Inc.

Stevens, Wallace: "Disillusionment of Ten O'Clock" from THE COLLECTED POEMS OF WALLACE STEVENS by Wallace Stevens. Copyright 1954 by Wallace Stevens and renewed 1982 by Holly Stevens. Used by permission of Alfred A. Knopf, a division of Random House, Inc.

Stevens, Wallace: "Thirteen Ways of Looking at a Blackbird" from *The Collected Poems of Wallace Stevens.* Copyright 1954 by Wallace Stevens and renewed 1982 by Holly Stevens. Used by permission of Alfred A. Knopf, a division of Random House, Inc.

Swenson, May: First published in February 18, 1984 issue of *The Nation.* Reprinted with permission of the Literary Estate of May Swenson.

Szymborska, Wislawa: From Krynski, Magnus J. (Trans); SOUNDS, FEELINGS, THOUGHTS, translated by Magnus J. Krynski. Copyright © 1981 by Princeton University Press. Reprinted by permission of Princeton University Press.

Tan, Amy: "Two Kinds" from *The Joy Luck Club* by Amy Tan. Copyright © 1989 by Amy Tan. Used by permission of G. P. Putnam's sons, a division of Penguin Group (USA) Inc.

Thomas, Dylan: From THE POEMS OF DYLAN THOMAS. Copyright © 1945 by The Trustees for the Copyrights of Dylan Thomas. Reprinted by permission of New Directions Publishing Corp.

Trethewey, Natasha: "Elergy for the Native Guard" from NATIVE GUARD: POEMS by Natasha Trethewey. Copyright © 2006 by Natasha Trethewey. Reprinted by permission of Houghton Mifflin Harcourt Publishing Company. All rights reserved.

Turner, Brian: "In the Leupold Scope" and "Sadiq" from *Here, Bullet.* Copyright © 2005 by Brian Turner. Reprinted with the permission of Alice James Books, www.alicejamesbooks.org.

Updike, John: "A & P" from *Pigeon Feathers and Other Stories* by John Updike. Copyright © 1962 and renewed 1990 by John Updike. Used by permission of Alfred A. Knopf, a division of Random House, Inc.

Viramontes, Helena María: "The Moths" is reprinted with permission from the publisher of *The Moths and Other Stories* by Helena Viramontes (© 1995 Arte Publico Press—University of Houston).

Vonnegut, Kurt: "Harrison Bergeron" from WELCOME TO THE MONKEY HOUSE by Kurt Vonnegut, Jr. Copyright © 1961 by Kurt Vonnegut, Jr. Used by permission of Dell Publishing, a division of Random House, Inc.

Wainaina, Binyavanga: First published in Winter 2005 in *Granta 92: The View from Africa.*

Walcott, Derek : Times Online (timesonline.co.uk), Nov. 5, 2008.

Walker, Alice: "Everyday Use" from *In Love & Trouble: Stories of Black Women.* Copyright 1973 by Alice Walker. Reprinted and reproduced by permission of Houghton Mifflin Harcourt Publishing Company.

Warren, Robert Penn: From *New and Selected Poems 1923–1985* by Robert Penn Warren, published by Random House. Copyright © 1985 by Robert Penn Warren. Used by permission of William Morris Endeavor Entertainment, LLC, on behalf of the author.

Watson, Brad: From *Last Days of the Dog-Men: Stories by Brad Watson.* Copyright © 1996 by Brad Watson. Used by permission of W.W. Norton & Company, Inc.

Wilbur, Richard: "First Snow in Alsace" from THE BEAUTIFUL CHANGES AND OTHER POEMS. Copyright 1947 and renewed 1975 by Richard Wilbur. Reprinted by permission of Houghton Mifflin Harcourt Publishing Company. This material may not be reproduced in any form or by any means without the prior written permission of the publisher.

Williams, Carol William: From *Collected Poems: 1909–1939*, Volume 1, by William Carlos Williams. Copyright 1938 by New Directions Publishing Corp. Reprinted by permission of New Directions Publishing Corp.
Wilson, August: From FENCES by August Wilson. Copyright © 1986 by August Wilson. Used by permission of Dutton Signet, a division of Penguin Group (USA) Inc.
Wright, Franz: By permission of the author.
Wright, James: From *The Branch Will Not Break* by James Wright, published by Wesleyan University Press. Copyright © 1959, 1960, 1961, 1962, 1963 by James Wright.
Yamada, Mitsuye: Copyright © 1976, 1980, 1986, 1988, 1992 by Mitsuye Yamada. Reprinted by permission of Rutgers University Press.
Young, Kevin: "Cousins" from *Dear Darkness*. Copyright 2008 by Kevin Young. Published by Alfred A. Knopf, a division of Random House.

Picture Credits

6, © United Feature Syndicate, Inc.; **126,** Courtesy of George Eastman House, International Museum of Photography and Film; **162,** © Hulton-Deutsch Collection/CORBIS; **195,** Ted S. Warren/AP Images; **278,** Photo copyright © 2006 by Nico Tucci. By permission of Stuart Bernstein Representation for Artists, New York. All rights reserved; **330,** Jacob Lawrence, *A Family*, 1943. Gouache, ink and pencil, with glue on paper, 22 5/8 x 15 5/8" (57.4 x 39.6 cm). Gift of Mrs. Maurice Blin (684.1971). The Museum of Modern Art, New York, NY, USA. © 2009 The Jacob and Gwendolyn Lawrence Foundation, Seattle, Artists Rights Society (ARS), New York. Digital image © The Museum of Modern Art/Licensed by SCALA, Art Resource, NY; **332,** Art Resource, NY; **369,** © Bettmann/CORBIS; **434,** © Christopher Kolk/CORBIS; **512,** © 2009 The Jacob and Gwendolyn Lawrence Foundation, Seattle/Artists Rights Society (ARS), New York. The Metropolitan Museum of Art, Arthur Hoppock Hearn Fund, 1942 (42.167). Image © The Metropolitan Museum of Art; **525,** Courtesy of Nathalie Handal; **531,** © 2009 Banco de Mexico Diego Rivera Frida Kahlo Museums Trust, Mexico, D.F./Artists Rights Society (ARS), New York; **532,** © 2009 Banco de Mexico Diego Rivera Frida Kahlo Museums Trust, Mexico, D.F./Artists Rights Society (ARS), New York. National Museum of Women in the Arts, Washington, DC. Gift of the Honorable Clare Boothe Luce; **574,** © Bettmann/CORBIS; **623,** Eric Gay/AP Images; **687,** Erich Lessing/Art Resource, NY; **695,** Courtesy of Annie Finch; **708,** Courtesy of Randall Munroe. Reprinted with permission. xkcd.com; **720,** Erich Lessing/Art Resource, NY; **835,** Laurent Rebours/AP Images; **942,** Reprinted courtesy of Dover Publications, Inc. Réunion des Musées Nationaux/Art Resource, NY; **943,** Jacket Cover from HAMLET (BANTAM CLASSIC EDITION) by William Shakespeare, edited by David Bevington & David Scott Kastan, copyright © 1988 by Bantam Books, a division of Random House, Inc. Used by permission of Bantam Books, a division of Random House, Inc. Courtesy of Mark English; **1014,** Courtesy of Peter Kuper; **1033,** © Bettmann/CORBIS; **1041,** © Peter Turnley/CORBIS; **1117,** Edward Hopper, *Nighthawks*, 1942. Oil on canvas, 84.1 x 152.4 cm. Friends of American Art Collection, 1942.51. Photograph by Robert Hashimoto. Reproduction, The Art Institute of Chicago; **1121,** Reunion des Musees Nationaux, Art Resource, NY; **1124;** Courtesy of Eavan Boland; **1166,** © Hulton-Deutsch Collection/CORBIS; **1211,** AP Images; **1283,** Courtesy of Dustin Parsons; **1293,** Kehinde Wiley, *Portrait of Andries Stilte II*, 2006. Columbus Museum of Art, Ohio; Museum Purchase, Derby Fund, in honor of Jeffrey W. Edwards's term as president of the Board of Trustees, 2004–2006. 2006.014. Reprinted with kind permission of the artist; **1307,** Aaron Douglas, *The Spirit of Africa*; **1327,** © Topham/The Image Works; **1371,** © Miriam Berkley. Reprinted with permission; **1435,** Courtesy of Brian Turner; **1442,** New York Times Co./Getty Images; **1458,** Photo by thememoryhole.org via Getty Images/Getty Images.

Index of First Lines

1519

Index of Authors and Titles